Literature

Approaches to Fiction, Poetry, and Drama

Second Edition

Robert DiYanni
New York University

Boston Burr Ridge, IL Dubuque, IA Madison, WI New York
San Francisco St. Louis Bangkok Bogotá Caracas Kuala Lumpur
Lisbon London Madrid Mexico City Milan Montreal New Delhi
Santiago Seoul Singapore Sydney Taipei Toronto

The McGraw·Hill Companies

Mc Graw Hill **Higher Education**

LITERATURE: APPROACHES TO FICTION, POETRY, AND DRAMA
Published by McGraw-Hill, a business unit of The McGraw-Hill Companies, Inc. 1221 Avenue of the Americas, New York, NY, 10020.

This book is printed on acid-free paper.

11 DOC/DOC 1 0 9 8 7 6 5 4 3

ISBN: 978-0-07-312445-2
MHID: 0-07-312445-1

Vice President and Editor in Chief: *Emily Barrosse*
Publisher: *Lisa Moore*
Developmental Editor: *Bennett Morrison*
Editorial Assistant: *Melissa Currier*
Marketing Manager: *Sharon Loeb*
Managing Editor: *Jean Dal Porto*
Project Manager: *Ruth Smith*
Art Editor: *Katherine McNab*
Designer: *Marianna Kinigakis*
Cover Design: *Jenny El-Shamy*
Cover Credit: *'Gather Ye Rosebuds While Ye May,' 1908 (oil on canvas), John William Waterhouse, (1849–1917)/Private Collection/Bridgeman Art Library*
Photo Research Coordinator: *Natalia C. Peschiera*
Lead Media Project Manager: *Marc Mattson*
Media Producer: *Alexander Rohrs*
Production Supervisor: *Janean A. Utley*
Composition: *10.5/12 Bembo, Thompson Type*
Printing: *24# Vista Opaque Thin, R. R. Donnelley & Sons*

Credits: The Credits section for this book begins on page C-1 and AC-1 is considered an extension of the copyright page.

Library of Congress Cataloging-in-Publication Data
DiYanni, Robert.
Literature : approaches to fiction, poetry, and drama / Robert DiYanni.—2nd ed.
p. cm.
Includes bibliographical references and index.
ISBN-13: 978-0-07-312445-2 (alk. paper)
ISBN-10: 0-07-312445-1 (alk. paper)
1. Literature. 2. Literature—Collections. I. Title.
PN49.D52 2008
808—dc22 2006048176

www.mhhe.com

About the Author

Robert DiYanni, Director of K–12 International Services for the College Board, is Adjunct Professor of Humanities at New York University. Dr. DiYanni, who earned his A.B. from Rutgers and his Ph.D. from the City University of New York, taught for many years at Queens College (CUNY), Pace, and Harvard. He has published more than thirty-five books on writing, literature, and the humanities, mostly for university students. In addition to *Literature,* his books include *Modern American Poets, Modern American Prose, The McGraw-Hill Book of Poetry, The McGraw-Hill Book of Fiction, Encounters, The Scribner Handbook for Writers, Writing about the Humanities, Frames of Mind,* and *Arts and Culture: An Introduction to the Humanities.* Dr. DiYanni lectures and offers workshops on teaching worldwide and has also published books for students of English in China and Taiwan. He is currently working on a book for students in India and another, *An ABC of Chinese Culture,* for visitors to the Beijing 2008 Olympics.

For Diether Raff
Professor Dr. Dr. (h.c.)
Cherished Colleague and Friend

Brief Contents

Contents

*New selection for this edition

THINKING CRITICALLY ABOUT POETRY 594

PART THREE DRAMA 897

READING AND WRITING ABOUT DRAMA 899

Preface

Like its larger counterpart, *Literature: Approaches to Reading Fiction, Poetry, and Drama* has been unique in the way it encourages students to make the reading of literature an *active* enterprise that involves both thought and feeling. This approach to literature helps students understand and articulate their experience of literature and translate that experience into effective literary interpretations and evaluations. The second edition continues the tradition of helping students not only understand the traditional elements of literature but also provides students with a methodology to apply what they learn by making connections among texts, by thinking critically about what they read, and by writing about literature.

HALLMARK FEATURES OF *LITERATURE*

A number of enduring and distinct features of both the hardcover *Literature* and this shorter, softcover version have helped bring the joy of literature to countless students.

Three-Part Approach: Experience, Interpretation, and Evaluation

Literature is designed to involve students in the twin acts of reading and analysis. Each of the genres is introduced by a three-part approach to the reading process inspired by the approach to texts outlined by Robert Scholes's *Textual Power* (Yale University Press, 1985). The three aspects are these:

1. the **experience** of literature
2. the **interpretation** of literature
3. the **evaluation** of literature

The *experience* of literature concerns our individual impressions of a work, especially our subjective and emotional responses. The *Interpretation* of literature involves intellectual and analytical thinking. Finally, the *evaluation* of literature involves assessments and considerations of a work's social, moral, and cultural values. This three-part approach helps students understand how their own impressions inform effective analysis and criticism of literary works.

Comprehensive Introductions to Genres and Elements of Literature

In addition to emphasizing the subjective, analytical, and evaluative aspects of reading literature, *Literature* introduces traditional elements such as plot, character, imagery, and dialogue in such a way that students can relate these sometimes arcane fundamentals to their own experience of life and language. Throughout these discussions, students are asked to return to certain works and reconsider them from different perspectives. This repetition reinforces the *recursive* aspect of reading described in the opening chapters on each genre and demonstrates the need to reread literary works for the fullest possible intellectual, emotional, and aesthetic enjoyment.

For each genre introduction, *Literature* provides a separate illustration of the *act of reading*. These illustrations suggest specific strategies for critical reading that are reinforced in the chapters that follow.

Selections: Diversity and Balance

The guiding principle of choosing selections for *Literature* has always been to balance the classic with the contemporary and upcoming, the familiar with the new and surprising, the accessible with the complex and challenging. The selections for every edition of *Literature* have attempted to include the widest range of diversity in works by a spectrum of writers. Attention has been paid to female writers and writers of color who span a wide range of cultures and ethnicities. **Specific chapters on contemporary and world authors** call out the diversity of the selections, and **works in translation** introduce the richness of world literature to students.

Writers-in-Context Chapters

Long known for its in-depth coverage of selected writers and their works, *Literature* provides chapters that give in-depth coverage to two authors (**Edgar Allen Poe,** and **Flannery O'Connor,**), three poets (**Emily Dickinson, Robert Frost,** and **Langston Hughes**), and three playwrights (**Sophocles, William Shakespeare,** and **Henrik Ibsen**). This material helps students understand how historical and cultural context influence each writer by providing detailed biographies of the authors and discussions of their times and cultural influence. Critical casebooks for each author demonstrate how critics have responded to these significant writers. In addition, the fiction chapter also includes selections from Poe and O'Connor on the craft of fiction. The poetry chapter features poets who imitate, emulate, and respond to Dickinson, Frost, and Hughes.

Transformations

The poetry section of *Literature* broadens the study of the genre with a unique chapter on *poetic transformations:* examples of ways in which poets have modified their own and other artists' work by means of revision, parody, response, and adaptation. This examination of poetic transformations allows students to explore the richness of poetic language and forms.

Writing about Literature

Literature has long provided students detailed strategies and guidance for writing about literature. The introduction familiarizes students with the writing process, and each genre includes a comprehensive chapter for writing about that genre, with sample annotations, student papers, and general questions and suggestions for writing. In Part 4, Chapter 30 provides a detailed guide for writing with sources and writing a research paper that includes information on finding and evaluating sources, a guide for MLA documentation, and two sample research papers.

Additional Features to Help Students Relate to Literature

In addition to the primary features of the anthology, several ancillary features help students relate to literature, interpret texts, and place texts in historical and cultural context. An **extensive visual program** of author photos, manuscripts, adaptations, and other illustrations for each genre offer an added dimension to the experience of literature. **Connection questions** help students draw common themes and compare texts. **Timelines** in the Writers in Context chapters and in an appendix at the end of the book provide easily understandable historical and cultural information. Finally, the **glossary** and the **accessible introduction to critical theory** provide students with clear explanations of literary terms and theory.

NEW FEATURES FOR THE SECOND EDITION

Based on surveys of thoughtful instructors who teach literature and careful consideration of what has made each edition of *Literature* a more helpful anthology for teaching students how to read and write about literature, I have revised this edition to include expanded coverage of critical thinking and argument, new chapters on envisioning literature, and exciting new selections.

Expanded Coverage of Critical Thinking

Literature's purpose of making reading an active enterprise is developed further in this edition with an expanded emphasis on thinking critically about literature. The thoroughly revised introduction explains to students the importance of thinking critically and helps them develop strategies that will get them thinking critically about what they read. The critical thinking component is reinforced in Questions for Critical Thinking and Writing that appear throughout the text, for works in every genre.

Envisioning Literature Chapters

As one of the first literature anthologies to pair paintings and poetry, *Literature* has long been a book that demonstrates how visual texts and images enrich the act of reading literature. In the second edition, each genre features new visual chapters that show how artists visually interpret that genre: Chapter 28: Envisioning Drama shows students with reproductions and photographs how *Glass Menagerie* and *Death of a Salesman* went from sketches to staged performances; Chapter 15: Envisioning Poetry places poems and paintings side-by-side so students can compare how words interact with images; and Chapter 6: Envisioning Narrative shows students how graphic novelists use narration in illustrated stories.

New Selections: Canonical and Contemporary

With every edition, *Literature* has sought to feature the most popular and well taught selections alongside some of the newest and freshest voices. The second edition includes new selections that reflect both the canonical and the contemporary. The fifteen new stories include both essential works—such as "The Lady with the Little Dog" by Anton Chekov, "The Storm" by Kate Chopin, and "The Chrysanthemums" by John Steinbeck—and works by contemporary authors, like Gish Jen and Jhumpa Lahiri. The over eighty new poems include selections by such well-known poets as Randall Jarrell and Elizabeth Bishop, new selections for the casebooks on Emily Dickinson, Robert Frost, and James Baldwin, and selections by such contemporary poets as Billy Collins, Deborah Garrison, and Taylor Mali. The two new plays in the second edition include the important and popular *A Raisin in the Sun* by Lorraine Hansberry and the contemporary *The Cuban Swimmer* by Milcha Sanchez-Scott.

Expanded Coverage of Argument and Writing about Literature

Lastly, the coverage of writing has been expanded to include coverage of argument in the introduction that will help students craft sound arguments about literature and fresh student papers that demonstrate effective literary analysis and interpretation.

SUPPLEMENTS ACCOMPANYING LITERATURE

A full range of supplements are available with *Literature* to help teachers and students get the most from the study of literature.

ARIEL: A Readers Interactive Exploration of Literature

ARIEL is an exciting tool that introduces students to the pleasures of studying literature. The CD features nearly thirty author casebooks; authors featured on ARIEL are marked in the margin of this text with an ARIEL icon. Each casebook offers a rich array of resources, including hyperlinked texts; video and audio clips; critical essays; a biography, bibliography, and webliography; essay questions, quizzes, and photos. General resources include a contextual timeline and robust glossary.

WWW

Online Learning Center to Accompany Literature *www.mhhe.com/diyanni*

This rich Web site offers numerous author casebooks, indicated in the text with a WWW in the margin. In addition, the Online Learning Center features complete texts of selected classical works; links for additional literary resources; a complete glossary; and interactive quizzes, Web exercises, and writing prompts that offer students additional practice in literary response, interpretation, and evaluation.

Instructor's Manual

This popular resource, authored by Thomas M. Kitts of St. John's University, has been thoroughly updated and revised for this new edition. The Manual offers brief introductions, additional questions, and essay topics for major selections, a comprehensive list of videos and DVDs for suitable classroom use, and much more.

Novels and Other Books for Package Options

A number of modern and contemporary works of fiction and non-fiction are available as a package option with *Literature*. Contact your McGraw-Hill representative for all options and details. Available books include: Chinua Achebe, *Things Fall Apart*; Sherman Alexie, *The Lone Ranger and Tonto Fistfight in Heaven*; Maya Angelou, *I Know Why the Caged Bird Sings*; Sandra Cisneros, *The House on Mango Street*; Joseph Conrad, *Heart of Darkness*; Annie Dillard, *The Pilgrim at Tinker Creek*; Louis Erdrich, *Love Medicine*; Ha Jin, *Waiting*; Zora Neal Hurston, *Their Eyes Were Watching God*; Maxine Hong Kingston, *Woman Warrior*; Toni Morrison, *Beloved*; Art Spiegelman, *Maus, Vol. 1*; and Amy Tan, *Joy Luck Club*.

Blackboard, PageOut, and Other Online Resources

The online content of *Literature* is supported for WebCT, and Blackboard. Additionally, our PageOut service is available to get you and your course up and running online in a matter of hours—at no cost! To find out more, contact your local McGraw-Hill representative or visit http://www.pageout.net.

ACKNOWLEDGMENTS

Throughout its many editions, *Literature* has always reflected the cooperative efforts of many people, beginning with Steven Pessinger, legendary editor and publisher, whose vision inspired the book from the beginning. Steve's associates at Random House, where the book was initially published, and at McGraw-Hill, which afterward took over the revised editions of the book, always brought intelligence and enthusiasm to their collective work on the project. They continue to deserve my thanks for their help.

For this edition, I am indebted to the many valuable people at McGraw-Hill: Publisher Lisa Moore, Development Editor Bennett Morrison, Editorial Coordinator Betty Chen, Project Manager Ruth Smith, Designer Marianna Kinigakis, Production Supervisor Janean Utley, Photo Editor Natalia Peschiera, Permissions Manager Marty Granahan, and Permissions Freelancer Marcy Lunetta. Each one of these talented individuals contributed to the completion of this edition.

I have also benefited from the suggestions of many colleagues around the country who teach the introductory writing and literature course, many with earlier editions of this book. The following thoughtful instructors graciously responded to a survey that informed this edition: Martha Ambrose, Edison College; Paige Anderson, Pensacola Junior College; Rebecca Anderson, University of South Dakota; Patricia Atwood, Florida Community College at Jacksonville; Christopher Baker, Armstrong Atlantic State University; Craig Barrette, Brescia University; Courtney Beggs, Texas A&M University; Ferol Benavides, Anne Arundel Community College; Ethel Bonds, Virginia Western Community College; Barbara Brown, San Jacinto College Central; Laurie Brown-Pressly, Clemson University; Jeff Calkins, Tacoma Community College; Kristina Chew, Seton Hall University; Paul Connell, Quinsigamond Community College; Jim Dervin, Winston-Salem State University; Kay Dickson, Appalachian State; Cheryl Duffus, Normandale Community College; Rudra Dundzila, Harry S. Truman College; Taylor Emery, Austin Peay State University; Robert Foreman, Pasadena City College; Mary Lynn Gehrett, Indian Hills Community College; Donna Goldstone, Austin Peay State University; Joanne Grumet, Baruch College; John Hardecke, East Central College; Alexander Howe, University of the District of Columbia; Ron Hulewicz, Broward Community College; Rita Hulsey, Columbia State Community College; Laura Jeffries, Florida Community College at Jacksonville; J. Paul Johnson, Winona State University; Mary Johnston, Minnesota State University; Douglas Jole, Tacoma Community College; Kathryn Karczewska Ohren, Suffolk University; Andrea Kaston Tange, Eastern Michigan University; Gina Ladinsky, Santa Monica College and El Camino College; James Lake, Louisiana State University-Shreveport; Joseph Lehmann, Grace College; Nick Lilly, Tarleton State University; John Lore, Cumberland County College; Janna Lynn, FIU and MDC-Kendall; Tara Lyons, Illinois Valley Community College; Janis Marchant, Hawaii Pacific University; Alice Marciel, DeAnza College; Edith Miller, Angelina College; Raymond Mize, Southeastern Community College; Steve Moiles, Western Illinois University, Edwardsville; Cleatta Morris, Louisiana State University-Shreveport; Roxanne Munch, Joliet Junior College; Barbara Murray,

Dalton State College; Helen Oesterheld, California State University, Dominguez Hills; Daniel Olson, North Harris College; Catherine Olson, Tomball College; Janet Palmer, Caldwell Community College and Technical Institute; Joe Pellegrino, University of South Carolina Upstate; Tamara Ponzo Brattoli, Joliet Junior College; Gerald Poulin, Roane State Community College; Don Presnell, Caldwell Community College; Elizabeth Rambo, Campbell University; Courtney Ruffner, Manatee Community College; Arundhati Sanyal, Seton Hall University; Sharon Schakel, Mesa State College; Erika Solberg, Monmouth College; Joel Sperber, Seton Hall University; Christine Swiridoff, Cerro Coso Community College; Isera Tyson, Manatee Community College; Pamela Ubl, Florida Community College at Jacksonville; Bradley Waltman, Community College of Southern Nevada; Marian Wernicke, Pensacola Junior College; Jana Wesson-Martin, Western Texas College; Matthew Williams, Caldwell Community College & Technical Institute; Teresa Winterhalter, Armstrong Atlantic State University; Guangping Zeng, Pensacola Junior College; Michelle Zollars, Patrick Henry Community College.

Reviewers of previous editions of *Literature* gave me much good advice. For the fifth edition, thanks to the following: Michael Aaij, University of Alabama; Beverly Bailey, Seminole Community College; Rosemary Baker, State University of New York, Morrisville; Mary K. Bayer, Grand Rapids Community College; Mark Bernier, Blinn College; Aniko Costantine, State University of New York, Alfred; Jim Creel, Alvin Community College; Theresa M. Dickman, Cumberland College; Tina D. Eliopulos, Community College of Southern Nevada; Audley Hall, NorthWest Arkansas Community College; Diane Hyer, Truett-McConnell College; Mary D. Jamieson, Broward Community College; Carol Jamison, Armstrong Atlantic State University; Thomas M. Kitt, St. John's University; Andrea Krause, Hesston College; Carol Swain Lewis, Three Rivers Community College; Steven Lynn, University of South Carolina; Patricia Menhart, Broward Community College; Paul Resnick, Illinois Central College; Katherine M. Restino, Fairleigh Dickinson University; Demise Rogers, University of Louisiana; and Jeff Schonenberg, Angelo State University.

For the fourth edition, thanks to the following: Thomas Tuggle, Gainesville College; Richard La Manna, St. Petersburg Junior College; Gary Grassinger, Community College of Allegheny County; Hephzibah Roskelly, University of N. Carolina at Greensboro; Lawrence Milbourn, El Paso Community College; Barbara Thompson, Columbus State Community College; Irene Fairley, Northeastern University; W. David Winsper, Springfield Technical Community College; and William Provost, University of Georgia.

For their third edition suggestions thanks to the following: Stephen Behrendt, Barbara Belson, Jon Burton, Cornelius Cronin, Charles Crow, Lois Cuddy, Robert Dell, Alan Ehmann, Ruth Eisenberg, Peter Evarts, Chris Farris, Paula Feldman, Elizabeth Flynn, Robert Fraser, Susan Gannon, Frank Garratt, Harold Gleason, John Hanes, Jacqueline Hartwich, J. G. Janssen, Michael Johnson, Leonard Leff, Barry Maid, William McIntosh, George Miller, Hugh Ruppersburg, Robert Sayre, Thomas Watson, A. K. Weatherhead, Joseph Zavadil, and Karl Zender.

For the second edition I received lively and thoughtful advice from William McIntosh of the United States Military Academy, and also from: Bertha N. Booker, Virginia State University; Carl Brucker, Arkansas Tech University; Terre Burton, Laramie County Community College, Wyoming; James Bynum, Georgia Institute of

Technology; Charles Dean, Middle Tennessee State University; William J. Everts, Jr., St. Michael's College, Vermont; John Hoey, SUNY–Genesee; Ted Johnston, El Paso Community College; Larry G. Mapp, Middle Tennessee State University; Sara M. Putzell, Georgia Institute of Technology; and Sharon Sellers, Clayton State College, Georgia.

Four reviewers of the first edition deserve acknowledgment for their perceptive comments on the entire manuscript: Richard F. Dietrich, University of South Florida; Kelley Griffith, University of North Carolina; Frank Hodgins, University of Illinois; and Richard Larson, Lehman College of the City University of New York. In addition, I benefited enormously on that edition from the expert assistance of Donald McQuade, University of California at Berkeley, and Robert B. Lyons, Queens College, City University of New York, who served as consultants.

I have had the additional pleasure of working with Professor Tom Kitts of St. John's University. Professor Kitts has written a practical and graceful instructor's manual, which serves as a rich and rewarding source of practical and provocative classroom applications. Tom also provided the excellent questions for many of the stories in the anthology of fiction.

Finally, I want to thank my wife, Mary, whose loving and steadfast support enabled me to complete this revision on schedule. She is a treasure beyond compare.

ROBERT DIYANNI

INTRODUCTION

Literature: Reading, Writing, and Critical Thinking

Many people read literature for pleasure. Many others read literary works mainly to satisfy academic requirements. Duty and pleasure, however, are not mutually exclusive. And so, even though you may be reading the literature in this book to fulfill course assignments, you may find yourself enjoying at least some of the works you read here. One of the purposes of this chapter is to introduce you to some of the pleasures literature offers.

Another is to help you think critically about literature, to develop your ability to analyze and interpret literature in relation to your experience, your knowledge, your observations, and your values. You can learn to do this kind of critical thinking when you read literary works and also when you write about them. And so, this chapter also includes some introductory notes for writing about literature.

CRITICAL THINKING AND THE PLEASURES OF LITERATURE

Among the pleasures of literature is thinking critically about a work while you read it and again later as it lingers in your memory. But we need to be clear from the start about what we do and do not mean by "critical thinking" when applied to literature.

What we do *not* mean is being critical in a negative way, finding fault with the literature—with the characters in stories, the language of poems, the ideas and plots of literary works. Instead, you *are* encouraged to think critically about literature when you read it attentively and actively, when you think about not only what happens in a play or a story, but also about why things happen as they do, and what the significance of those events might be. In thinking critically about literature, you attend to details; you look for patterns and connections; you make inferences, or informed guesses based on those details and patterns; and you formulate tentative, provisional conclusions (your interpretations) of literary works. In thinking critically about literary works, you ask questions about them—questions about the motivation and values of characters, questions about the meaning of images and symbols, questions about the writer's attitude toward the characters, questions about the form of a poem, the structure of a story, the dialogue in a play.

Thinking critically is thinking that questions. It is also thinking that speculates and wonders and imagines. When you read literature as a critical thinker, you use your imagination to speculate about the future of characters beyond the conclusion of the stories in which they appear, you consider alternative outcomes and endings for literary works, and you consider different choices of language and structure authors could have used in their works.

We will discuss these aspects and other aspects of critical thinking throughout this book. The important thing is to use your reading of literature as an opportunity to develop your critical and imaginative thinking capacities. We begin by considering the pleasures of reading fiction.

The Pleasures of Fiction

We read stories largely for the emotional and intellectual pleasures they bring us—the pleasure of being surprised or disturbed by an unexpected turn of events or of being satisfied as our expectations are met. Well-told stories involve us emotionally in the lives of their characters. Such stories provide us with pleasures of recognition in the worlds they portray and in the characters who inhabit those fictional worlds.

Stories, however, do more than entertain. They provide us with something more than the pleasures of plot and recognizable characters, with whom we may sympathize or identify. Stories also instruct us by showing us things about our world we had not known before, or perhaps by enabling us to see things we do know about, but in another way. In reading fiction, we share the imaginative vision of another person, adopting, however briefly, his or her way of perceiving the world. Through reading a wide variety of stories, we can enter many different imaginative worlds. In the process we can enlarge our imaginative capacities and deepen our perception of the world.

Thinking Critically about a Story

As you read the following brief story, ask yourself why the characters attempt what they do and why they act as they do. In the discussion that follows the story, you will have a chance to develop your thinking about it, as you learn a few critical thinking strategies.

Learning to Be Silent

The pupils of the Tendai school used to study meditation before Zen entered Japan. Four of them who were intimate friends promised one another to observe seven days of silence.

On the first day all were silent. Their meditation had begun auspiciously, but when night came and the oil lamps were growing dim, one of the pupils could not help exclaiming to a servant: "Fix those lamps."

The second pupil was surprised to hear the first one talk: "We are not supposed to say a word," he remarked.

"You two are stupid. Why did you talk?" asked the third.

"I am the only one who has not talked," concluded the fourth pupil.

(13th century)

Although part of our pleasure in reading and hearing such a story comes from making sense of it, part derives from watching its unfolding action and display of character. In "Learning to Be Silent" we may enjoy the simplicity and clarity of the action. We may enjoy the crispness and directness of the dialogue. We may enjoy the slightly different ways each of the four friends violates the promise to keep silent. Each of them says something different, yet each winds up failing to keep silent. We can also take pleasure in the way the author paces the narrative, in how, as in a well-told joke, we sense a buildup toward a deftly delivered punch line.

As we think critically about "Learning to Be Silent," we need to ask ourselves what its point might be. And to do that, we need to decide what is central, what is essential, what truths the story conveys. Moreover, we also need to ask why such a story would be told in the first place—and by whom. Those last questions lead us to considerations of context.

But first, let's consider the story's focus and central concerns. What do you think? Is this story primarily about silence, perhaps about the difficulty of achieving a silent state for any length of time? Or do you think it is more concerned with the larger issue of self-control, the discipline of monitoring one's behavior, of gaining control of one's need to talk, but for some larger purpose? Perhaps you think the story is more about vanity and one-upmanship, about people's desire to outperform others, about their desire to succeed where others fail, and to enjoy their failure as well. Or perhaps you have another idea about what is most important in "Learning to Be Silent."

Considering Multiple Perspectives: Setting a Quota of Possibilities

In raising this series of possible ways to think about "Learning to Be Silent," we have been trying on different perspectives, as we consider different meanings that the story embodies. One strategy of critical thinking, then, is to consider multiple perspectives, different emphases and interpretations of a work. You might set yourself a quota of possibilities, three or four ways of interpreting the story, perhaps, as a way to stretch your thinking abilities. This, of course, is what you have been doing in thinking about each of the different story emphases mentioned earlier.

Now, you may decide that one of those possibilities is more important than the others and that it addresses the central issue of the story better than the others. And that, too, is a good thing. Once you make that decision, however, you need to use other critical thinking strategies to support your interpretation—providing details from the text, for example, that lead you to your conclusion. We will have much more to say about the process of analysis and interpretation in later chapters. For now, it is more important to think about how the story can be read in different ways—even though you may prefer one way of reading it to other alternatives.

Reversing Perspective: Seeing from Opposite Sides

Another critical thinking strategy to help you expand your ability to see the story in different ways is to consider not just different possible focuses and emphases but to look for opposite possibilities. In thinking critically about "Learning to Be Silent," for example, we may first focus on the failure of the four students to keep their vow of silence. And they do fail—miserably, in fact—since they do not make it through even one full day of the seven days of silence they promised one another to observe.

Yet, on the other hand, in seeing the story from an opposite standpoint, we might, for the sake of argument, consider the positive outcome of their effort. They did, after all, make it through part of the day—the daylight part—keeping silent. That's a start, isn't it? And by emphasizing for a moment what they accomplished rather than how they failed, we might realize that these are "students," not "masters," and that being a student involves a process of learning that includes failure. And so, we might think back to the story's title, with an emphasis on its first word rather than its last one—"*Learning* to Be Silent." If being silent is a worthwhile goal, and if it is difficult, then it will need to be learned and practiced. These four friends have embarked on a journey, and they have made some first halting steps. In speculating about their future, we might consider the possibility that their next try might be more successful, that they might get through a whole day or two of silence, although it might take them a long time, indeed, before they are able to maintain silence for a full week.

Shifting Attention among Details

Another helpful strategy of critical and imaginative thinking is to shift attention from one focus to something different. Sometimes, when we are trying to solve a problem, we get stuck because we keep looking in the same place, at the same details, and thinking along the same lines. In such situations, we need to head in a new direction, to look at something else, try something different.

In reading a very brief story like "Learning to Be Silent," we won't have as much use for this strategy as when reading longer, more intricate literary works. Nonetheless, we might ask ourselves even here about the keepers of the lamps, something we have not mentioned as of yet. Who are the servants in this story? What is their role? Are they novice monks? Are they local people who work at a monastery? Does it make a difference?

And this might lead us to ask some other questions not yet raised. Where, in fact, does the story's action take place? Is the setting a monastery? A hotel? What do we know about the location of the story's action and when it occurs? Is the setting contemporary? A hundred years ago? In a particular country? If we cannot answer these questions, we might ask why the story does not provide those details, and what the significance of their absence might be.

By considering all these types of questions and possibilities, you are thinking critically. And in raising objections to these possibilities, in questioning them, you are also thinking critically. That's the goal, whether you are reading a brief parable, like "Learning to Be Silent," or a long and complex play, such as Shakespeare's *Hamlet*.

Critical Thinking and Contexts: "Learning to Be Silent"

When we ask why a story is told or by whom, we are asking about context—conditions outside the text itself. In the case of "Learning to Be Silent," it is important to consider the context of its genre and also its religious context. The story is a religious parable, which, as parables typically do, teaches a lesson. What this lesson, or teaching is, we must determine for ourselves since it is not spelled out explicitly in the story. Instead, as is customary of parables, the details of the narrative embody the meaning and convey the lesson. In thinking more specifically about the religious tradition from which "Learning to Be Silent" derives—the Zen Buddhist tradition—we may know or come to learn the value of silence as a way to shut out the cares of the world and to focus on spiritual concerns, including achieving an inner stillness. As an offshoot of Buddhism, Zen puts great emphasis on meditation, on the need for the mind to control the body, to shut down and to shut out its insistent distractions so that inner peace can be found and enlightenment achieved.

These contextual aspects of "Learning to Be Silent"—knowing that it is a parable, and considering its particular tradition as a Zen parable—enrich our understanding of it. Without such contextual knowledge, we can still enjoy the parable, though in that case our emphasis on its central message is likely to be more secular than religious.

The accompanying box summarizes the critical and imaginative thinking strategies we have been applying to "Learning to Be Silent." You can use these strategies deliberately as ways to help prompt your thinking about any work of literature.

LITERATURE AND CRITICAL THINKING STRATEGIES

- Setting a quota of possibilities
- Seeing from opposite sides
- Shifting attention among details
- Considering contexts

The Pleasures of Poetry

We read poetry for the many pleasures it offers—pleasures of sound and speech, of symbol and image, of rhythm and rhyme, of feeling and thought. Some of poetry's pleasures are verbal, some are intellectual, and some are emotional. We respond to the words in poems, to the ideas they spark and to the feelings they generate—of sorrow or pity, fear or joy. And we respond to the sheer physical force of poems—to the way they make our skin tingle and our feet tap in time to a rhythmic beat.

Poetry sharpens our perception of the world around us since poems draw their energy from the fresh observation of life. Poems reveal to us things we didn't know we knew; they heighten our perception of things we knew only vaguely before reading them. Poems can make us feel more acutely and increase our receptiveness to beauty. Poems stimulate our imaginations. And, of course, reading poetry attentively improves our ability to understand and use language since poems are made of words—at their most successful, the best words in the best order.

Thinking Critically about a Poem

Consider the following short poem.

ROBERT FROST

(1874–1963)

Dust of Snow

The way a crow
Shook down on me
The dust of snow
From a hemlock tree

Has given my heart
A change of mood
And saved some part
Of a day I had rued.

(1923)

Part of our enjoyment of this poem may derive from its brevity. It offers a quick take on an experience, and it provides that swift glimpse in short fast lines of a few beats each. We may be struck by the poem's action—a crow jounces a tree limb, which unloads its burden of snow on a man beneath it. We may wonder to what extent this action may have been an accident and to what extent it could possibly have been intentional. Thinking critically about "Dust of Snow" leads us to questions like these and to others that derive from them, as, for example, whether crows are capable of performing such an act intentionally, and whether they could be said to "enjoy" the result. What we may decide about such questions is, finally, less important than that we consider them in the first place.

Consider Form and Structure

Thinking critically about Frost's poem also requires that we notice its form or structure—that it is split into two brief equal parts of four short lines each, and that together the two short stanzas form a single sentence. We might ask ourselves why, if the poem is only one sentence long, the poet casts it in two stanzas. Reading the lines attentively we notice that something happens in each stanza. In the first stanza the action is external—something happens outside, under the tree. The action of the second stanza, by contrast, we notice, is internal. Something happens within the speaker; he has what he calls a "change of mood." In thinking critically about the poem we should consider the nature of this change. The details of the poem suggest that it is a positive change—from something that was "rued" to something that is "saved." And so we need to consider how a day that was somehow lost can somehow be saved. Using the critical thinking strategy of seeing opposites, we ask how getting dusted with snow can lead to positive thoughts and feelings.

Thinking critically about "Dust of Snow" requires us also to attend carefully to its details, not just of action, but also of language. We may wonder why Frost includes "hemlock" trees, and we may consider how the poem would be different if we substituted a different tree—a maple, perhaps, for the hemlock. In the same way, we might wonder about the poet's choice of the word "rued" to end the poem. Why, we might ask ourselves, did he select that word? For the rhyme? For its old-fashioned feeling and tone? For its meaning? And just what does "rued" mean, anyway?

Make Connections

Critical thinking also prods us to ask about the relationship between the two stanzas. Just how are they related? As cause to effect? As an external action prompting an internal response? Employing the thinking strategy of setting a quota of alternatives, we can try to characterize the relationship of the stanzas in half a dozen ways: (1) as cause leading to effect; (2) as external event triggering internal response; (3) as the natural world influencing human feeling and response; (4) as an action triggering a reaction; (5) as a subject of a sentence followed by its predicate; or (6) as a movement from outdoors to indoors, from crow to person, from sorrow to joy.

In thinking critically about Frost's little poem, we may relate our sense of the change it records to our own experience. Surely we have experienced changes of mood. We must certainly have had "bad days" that were somehow "saved" or redeemed by some surprising change of luck, some incident that made us smile, that turned our day around.

Critical Thinking and Contexts: "Dust of Snow"

"Dust of Snow" can also be looked at in the context of its subject, most obviously, nature, and more specifically the relationship between the natural world and the human world. How can "Dust of Snow" be linked with other poems about "nature" or with other poems that describe a relationship between people and the natural world? We can put Frost's poem in the context of Romanticism—the literary and artistic movement that swept Europe in the early part of the nineteenth century in works by poets such as Wordsworth, Keats, and Blake and that appeared in America later in the century in the works of Emerson and Thoreau, Dickinson and Whitman, among others.

Another kind of context into which we can place "Dust of Snow" is that of poems (or indeed other literary works) that describe or record a "change of mood," a movement from negative to positive, from sadness to joy. This context includes poems like Shakespeare's sonnet 116 "When In Disgrace with Fortune and Men's Eyes" (page 848), which describes how a speaker near despair over his imperfections experiences a dramatic change of heart when he thinks about his beloved. And either or both of these poems can be placed in the context of our own actual experience. We can relate to Frost's "Dust of Snow" and to Shakespeare's sonnet 116 because we have ourselves undergone experiences similar to those the poets describe, because we have experienced the shifting emotions each of their poems charts.

The Pleasures of Drama

Unlike the other genres of fiction and poetry, drama is meant to be performed on a stage by actors rather than read off a page by readers. Much of drama's pleasure comes from the way the language of the play's script—its printed text—comes alive in the speech of living actors who play the roles of the characters the playwright invents. When we watch a play performed, we appreciate the way the actors walk and talk, the ways they interact with each other, as well as their facial expressions and bodily gestures. The smallest gesture, such as the lowering of a hand, and the slightest facial movement, such as the raising of an eyebrow, contribute to our sense of the play's human reality.

Drama and Imaginative Thinking

These brief remarks about drama highlight the necessity of reading drama imaginatively. To learn to read drama with some appreciation of what it offers, we need to read drama in the light of its theatricality. While we realize that reading a play differs from viewing the same play performed in a theater, our attempts to read it imaginatively, as if we were watching it, can enhance both our appreciation and our understanding.

But what does it mean to read a play imaginatively—with an awareness of its theatricality? How can we reconstruct a play imaginatively in our minds as we read its script? Essentially, by translating the script into a mental performance. By attending to the performative implications of the words on the page, we see, imaginatively, how they might be dramatized on stage. In reading drama imaginatively, we try to envision how the words of the script might be uttered—gently or threateningly, sweetly or sarcastically, slowly or swiftly, loudly or softly, and in what tone of voice.

We also imagine where a play's characters are positioned relative to one another, how close or far apart. We can imagine their ways of walking, the ways they gesture and gesticulate, the subtle ways they vary their voices and alter their facial expressions and body postures. These details, coupled with characters' costumes, the play's scenery, music, and sound effects all contribute to the richness of our imaginative reenactment of a play. The better we can imagine such elements, the better we will absorb the atmosphere and feeling of the play, and the more complete and theatrical will be our reading experience.

How do we learn to do this kind of imaginative theatrical reading? We do it by reading the play with care and attentiveness not only for the literal meaning of dialogue, but also for its sounds and accents, its rhythms and implications. We do it by reading aloud, by reading with others in small groups, and by talking with others about our mental reconstructions of scenes. In the process of learning to read plays imaginatively, we will also attend to the fullest expression of their literary meaning. For drama is literature as well as theater; and like fiction and poetry, drama is an art that provides an imaginative extension of life's possibilities.

Critical Thinking and Oprah's Book Club: An Exercise

As a different kind of exercise in thinking critically about literature, consider the issues at stake in the story of Oprah Winfrey's famous Book Club.

Oprah decided a few years ago to scale back her influential book club. She cut her regular monthly book selection and discussion to a much less regular and much more occasional status. For six years, Miss Winfrey's book club selections helped authors and their publishers sell hundreds of thousands of copies of each book selected, propelling most of her book picks to become instantaneous best sellers, with sales of some of her choices exceeding half a million copies.

Part of the reason for Oprah's decision to cut back dramatically on her book club is that, as she put it, "it has become harder and harder to find books" that she feels "absolutely compelled to share" with her audience. One incident that affected Ms. Winfrey's reconsideration was the criticism of her selecting Jonathan Franzen's novel *The Corrections* by no less than the author himself, who objected to his book being turned into a mass-market commodity. Franzen said that he wanted his book to be taken seriously as literature and that he did not want it being read by a lot of people who wouldn't understand or appreciate it.

One popular element of Oprah's book club was her televised interview of and segment on the author and his or her book. The lucky authors received national attention and were watched by millions of Oprah's television viewers, many of whom purchased or borrowed the books the host chose. Mr. Franzen's invitation to appear on the show was rescinded.

Oprah's book club continues but on a reduced scale and with considerably less fanfare and public attention than before. She has also switched from contemporary works to classics.

CRITICAL THINKING QUESTIONS

1. What do you think of Oprah Winfrey's idea to have such a book club in the first place? Do you see value in a national media celebrity promoting reading particular books? Why or why not? Explain.
2. What do you think of Jonathan Franzen's objections to having his novel chosen and promoted by Ms. Winfrey? Do you think Mr. Franzen would have objected had his book been not a novel, but say, a self-help book or a memoir?
3. Do you now belong to a book club, or have you ever joined a book club or reading group, where each person reads the same book and comes together at an agreed-upon time and place to discuss it together? What do you think are the reasons some people find value in such book clubs and reading groups?

APPROACHING LITERATURE WITH CRITICAL THINKING: EXPERIENCE, INTERPRETATION, EVALUATION

We can approach literary works by means of three interrelated perspectives: experience, interpretation, and evaluation. All three of these approaches demand different critical thinking strategies.

Experience

When we read a literary work, something happens to us. A poem, for example, may provoke our thinking, evoke a memory, or elicit an emotional response. A short story may arouse our curiosity, engage our feelings, or stimulate our thinking. A play may bring us to laughter or tears, and a piece of creative nonfiction may connect in some way with our experience.

In responding to literary works in these and other ways, we bring our personal and shared human experience to our reading. This kind of response—subjective, impressionistic, emotional—illustrates what we mean by the *experience* of literature. Our experience of literature, in this sense, however, is not enough for critical understanding. For that we must move beyond our subjective impressions and emotional responses to other types of comprehension. We might call these preliminary, subjective responses "precritical" in that they come before we engage in careful analysis of a literary work and before we consciously ask ourselves questions about its meaning.

If we want to think critically about our experience, we need to ask questions of ourselves. For example, we need to ask why we find something funny or sad, exciting or boring. As we think about those questions and our answers to them, we move beyond our personal subjective experience of literary works and toward interpretation and evaluation of them.

Interpretation

A second way to approach literature involves analysis and interpretation. Our understanding of literary works results from our effort to analyze and interpret them, to make sense of their implied meanings. Our *interpretation* of literature provides an intellectual counterpart to our emotional *experience* of literary works. When we interpret poems and plays, stories and essays, we concern ourselves less with how they affect us and more with what they mean. Interpretation, in short, aims at understanding.

How do we come to understand works of literature? How do we develop an ability to interpret literature with competence and with confidence? One way is to become familiar with its basic elements or characteristics—with plot, character, and setting in fiction, for example; with imagery, syntax, and sound effects in poetry; with dialogue, stage directions, and structure in plays. These and other literary elements are explained and illustrated in later chapters.

Along with learning to analyze the elements of literature, we also need to understand the basis of analysis more generally. All literary interpretation is grounded in observation—what we notice about the details of a work, including its language and form. We seek connections among the details we observe, looking for patterns such as contrast and repetition and variation. Based on our observations and connections we make inferences, or educated guesses or surmises. We check and test our inferences as we read and think critically about literary works and as we reread them and discuss them with others. Following upon our inferences (and revisions of our thinking) we formulate provisional interpretations of literary works. That is, we come to conclusions about their meaning and significance. We call these interpretations "provisional" because we can change our minds and revise our ways of understanding literary works based on further reading, talking, and thinking.

Evaluation

Complementing our personal and subjective responses to literary works and our analysis and interpretation of them is a consideration of their values—social, cultural, political, and moral. This third way of approaching literature, *evaluation,* is related to the other two, *experience* and *interpretation*. All three aspects of reading literature are interrelated.

Let's consider how values inhabit a literary work by reading a brief piece of fiction by the modern American writer, Ernest Hemingway. Hemingway's paragraph-long sketch was published in 1925 in his first book, *In Our Time.* It describes a scene of war, which was based on the author's experience in World War I.

> While the bombardment was knocking the trench to pieces at Fossalta, he lay very flat and sweated and prayed oh jesus christ get me out of here. Dear jesus please get me out. Christ please please please christ. If you'll only keep me from getting killed I'll do anything you say. I believe in you and I'll tell every one in the world that you are the only one that matters. Please please dear jesus. The shelling moved further up the line. We went to work on the trench and in the morning the sun came up and the day was hot and muggy, and cheerful and quiet. The next night back at Mestre he did not tell the girl he went upstairs with at the Villa Rossa about Jesus. And he never told anybody.

Hemingway's sketch says little directly. It's a very reticent piece of writing—close-mouthed and tight-lipped, somewhat like the soldier described in it who "never told anybody" about his experience. But the sketch makes a strong statement, nonetheless, by implication, in what it suggests obliquely about its three subjects: war, love, and religion. It does so largely by playing off conventional expectations about these three subjects.

In thinking critically about Hemingway's sketch, we would raise questions about the values it conveys regarding the subjects of war, love, and religion. We would examine the behavior of the character it describes and think about the values that underlie his behavior. Our evaluation of the soldier turns on whether he really believes in Jesus, for example, and on what such a belief may mean. It turns on whether we think the soldier's prayer is "answered" by God in a providential intervention to move the shelling "further up the line," or whether we see that as a coincidence, attributable purely to luck. And our evaluation is affected also by whether his visit to a house of prostitution is something we can understand, sympathize with, and approve—or not—and whether his not telling the girl or anybody else about Jesus is a perfectly understandable response to his circumstances or a serious violation of a solemn vow.

Besides evaluating the behavior of the soldier, we also make a judgment about the values we think the sketch espouses. Does Hemingway seem to display sympathy for the soldier? Does the narrator judge the soldier harshly? Is there, in fact, any judgment rendered of the soldier, or of the girl he sleeps with? Such are some of the kinds of critical thinking questions we ask ourselves in considering the values of Hemingway's little fictional sketch.

Critical Thinking and Context: Hemingway's Sketch

Although Hemingway's vignette is brief, it is rich in cultural implications. What are the contexts in which we read it? We read it in light of what we know about war and love and religion. We read it in the context of what is expected when a soldier goes to war, when a man makes love to a woman, when a man prays to God. Hemingway's sketch, thus, assumes a modest knowledge of war as it was fought in the early twentieth century. It assumes, for example, that readers know what "trenches" are and what "shelling" is. It also assumes some familiarity with a soldier going "upstairs" with a "girl" at a place like the "Villa Rossa" (the Red House).

Contrary to the conventional expectations of bravery and courage, the young soldier does not acquit himself heroically. Instead, he cringes in the trench to avoid being hit by enemy mortar fire. Nor does he adhere to the conventions of prayer, thanking God and praying for assistance. Instead, he bargains with God, saying, in effect, "if you do this for me, then I'll do that for you." He promises to be "good" if God lets him off the hook and saves him from death or disfigurement. Similarly, the young soldier's approach to love also reveals a sense of diminishment. For instead of love, there is only sex, a mere physical encounter, and one devoid of relationship or commitment.

Reading Hemingway's little piece in the context of conventional expectations about war, religion, and love enriches our understanding of what it says and suggests. Such reading in context helps us appreciate how authors rely on what their readers bring to the reading of literary works.

CRITICAL THINKING AND WRITING ABOUT LITERATURE

Critical thinking is not only an essential skill for reading literature but also a necessary one for writing about literature as well. Reading, writing, and thinking, in fact, are interrelated skills that need to be practiced and developed in concert rather than independently. Each of these skills is enhanced by being linked with the others. Reading is enriched by our deliberations of thinking. Writing is improved by our critical and imaginative thinking. Thinking is more complex and interesting when we stimulate our thinking through reading and writing.

Reasons for Writing about Literature

Why write about literature? First, writing about a literary work encourages us to read it attentively and notice things we might miss during a more casual reading. Second, writing stimulates thinking and enables us to discover what we think about literary works, how we feel about them, and why. Third, writing provides opportunities for us to state our views about the ideas and values expressed in literary works. Finally, through writing about literary works we enhance our enjoyment of the many pleasures they offer and deepen our appreciation of their artistic achievement.

A truly active engagement with literature intellectually and emotionally will broaden our understanding of life and language and will refine our aesthetic sensibilities. The literary works we read carefully will become a meaningful part of our lives, absorbed into our storehouse of knowledge and experience to become part of who we are, what we know, and how we feel.

Ways of Writing about Literature

Just as there are many reasons for writing about literature, there are many ways to write about it. In this section we will introduce a few common ways to write about literary works.

Explicating

A type of analysis frequently used to explain literary works is *explication,* a careful line-by-line or word-by-word examination of a passage in a poem, story, play, or essay. Explication involves a scrupulously close reading to unfold the layers of meaning in a text. It provides a close-up look at the language of a passage with a view to explaining its significance. Because explication involves such careful attention to detail, it is usually reserved for specific sections or parts of longer works, and sometimes even for parts of short works as well. As with any type of analysis, however, explication is most effective when it is used to illuminate the meaning of the work as a whole.

Explication is particularly useful for unraveling the meaning of a complex passage, something as long as a section, paragraph, stanza, or scene, or as brief as a bit of dialogue, a sentence, a line of poetry, or even a phrase. Our analysis of the ironic quality of the opening sentences of *Pride and Prejudice* is one example. Others include the analysis of the final paragraph of Joyce's "Araby" (page 86) and the final couplet of Hopkins's "Spring and Fall" (page 811). Beginnings and endings of literary works, whether they are as long as Jane Austen's novel or as short as a brief lyric poem, offer promising sections of text to explicate. These strategic locations afford opportunities for the writer to make a lasting impression on the reader.

Comparing and Contrasting

One of the most common approaches to writing interpretive papers is *comparison and contrast,* which can be applied in numerous ways. You might compare and contrast elements in a single work, or you might compare and contrast a particular aspect of two different works. You could compare and contrast, for example, the differing perspectives on knowledge and learning of the astronomer and the speaker in Whitman's "When I heard the learn'd astronomer." Or you might compare the uses of irony in Crane's "War Is Kind" (page 19) with Hardy's "Channel Firing" (page 804). You might compare and contrast the speech and actions of the two male characters in Boyle's "Astronomer's Wife" (page 62). Or you could compare the central character in Boyle's story with the protagonist of Gilman's "The Yellow Wallpaper" (page 379). Topics that reflect such a comparative approach would include these: "Active and Passive Learning in Whitman's 'When I heard the learn'd astronomer'"; "Two Uses of Irony: Satire and Humor in Poems by Stephen Crane and Thomas Hardy"; "Enchantment and Disenchantment: The Two Men in the Life of Kay Boyle's 'Astronomer's Wife'"; "Sanity or Madness: Women Protagonists in 'Astronomer's Wife' and 'The Yellow Wallpaper.'"

Such comparative analyses can sharpen your perception of the works under consideration. By looking at two works together or at two aspects of a single work, you see their differences more clearly. In comparing two poems, you might notice, for example, that one includes rhyme and the other does not; that the action is external in one poem or story and internal in the other; that one story includes much dialogue and the other little; that the settings, tone, or points of the works differ in significant and interesting ways. Such comparative observations will lead you to ask why those differences exist and why the writers developed their works as they did.

When you write comparative papers, keep the following guidelines in mind:

1. Compare two things that seem worth the trouble, that will reward your effort. By attending carefully to a work's details you will often find significant parallels and contrasts. Follow the leads the work provides.
2. Compare works that have a significant feature in common, such as authorship, style, genre, historical period, subject, situation, or an aspect of technique like meter or point of view.
3. Make a point. Use comparison and contrast in the service of an idea, an argument, an interpretation. Your comparative analysis should lead you to a conclusion, perhaps to an evaluation, not merely to a set of parallels.
4. Decide whether to organize your comparative discussion according to the "block" method in which you discuss each subject separately, or according to the "alternating" method in which you discuss the two central subjects in point-by-point comparisons of specific characteristics. If you are comparing two characters according to the block method, for example, you would devote the first half of your paper to one and the second half to the other character. If you followed the alternating structure, you would consider each side by side as you focused on such characteristics as their physical appearance, their interactions with other characters, their behavior at critical moments of the action, and so on.

Arguing about Literature

An *argument* in the context of writing about literature refers to making a case for an experience, interpretation, or evaluation of a work of literature. In developing an argument about a literary work, your goal is to persuade your readers that your ideas are viable and worth considering.

Argument or persuasive writing provides evidence to support a writer's claims. Depending on the type of paper you are writing, your evidence will come from personal experience (for a personal response paper); from the text (for an analysis or interpretive paper); or from comparisons with other works or from ideas about culture and values (for an evaluative paper). Depending on the nature of a reader's interpretation and a paper's focus, the emphasis on a work's literary elements can be supplemented by experiential, evaluative, and contextual matters.

In writing an argument about literature, you should strive to make your thesis and claims clear. What is it, exactly, that you are claiming about Frost's "Dust of Snow," for example? Do you want to argue that Frost's poem illustrates or demonstrates the benevolence of nature? Do you want to claim, on the other hand, that the poem depicts nature as oblivious to human need, that its view of nature is indifferent and not benevolent at all? The key is to be clear about your thesis or main idea.

Second, in developing an argument, you need to provide evidence to support the claim made in your thesis. What evidence can you find in the poem to support your viewpoint? What evidence can you bring from your knowledge and experience of the world? What evidence can you bring from external sources of information—from research you do on the author's life or on his works?

Third, your argument needs to be logically developed and organized. As in any paper you write, you need a clear and sensible plan for how to proceed—how to begin and end, and how to order your evidence in the middle of the paper. What reasons will you provide and in what order? What examples will you give and in what order? These are some logical and organizational considerations you need to wrestle with as you develop your argument about a work.

Fourth and finally, your argument requires consideration of opposing views. Once you develop an idea about a work that you want to develop and support with evidence, you also need to think about what someone who does not agree with your claim might say. What would someone skeptical of your view of the work say in response to your claim and your evidence? Think of a lawyer arguing both sides of a case. First the lawyer looks for evidence to support one view—the innocence of his client—in our case a particular way of understanding a literary work. Second, the lawyer makes a case about evidence against his client, in our case a contrary view. This is like the examples mentioned earlier about "Dust of Snow" as a poem presenting a positive and beneficial view of nature, on one hand, or, on the other, a negative and pessimistic view of the natural world. Both views need to be taken into account when you write an argument.

Argument and Experience For papers that focus primarily on your personal response to a literary work, your evidence begins with the text, but your discussion moves from there to your life experience, to your feelings, to your subjective impressions. An argument based on personal response tends to carry less weight than an argument based on close analysis of the literary elements of a work—its diction and imagery, its structure and dialogue, for example.

In basing or building an argument around personal experience, you need to be clear as to how your experience is related to the work. In arguing that Frost's "Dust of Snow," for example, is about nature's lack of concern for human beings, you might cite one or more of your own experiences with nature. You might remember a time when a bird dropped not snow on you, but something less pleasant. Or you might remember a time when you suffered frostbite or some other physical debility in the cold of winter. Arguments made about literature primarily from experience, though often interesting, are rarely convincing because the experience of each reader is partial. Other readers may have had very different experiences, which may lead them to very different experience-based interpretations. Thus, when you do write from experience or base a literary paper on personal response and experience, you need to remember the limitations of this approach and try to balance the argument from experience with references to other kinds of evidence, including the evidence provided in the text of the work itself.

Argument and Interpretation Most of the writing about literature that you will be required to do involves interpreting literary works. Although you may bring in your personal experience (or not, depending on your instructor's preference), your task most often will be to interpret the story or poem, play or novel your are reading.

Interpretive papers, like others that you write, need to possess a clear thesis or main idea, a logical organization, and a sense of plausibility. In developing a paper on "Learning to Be Silent," for example, you would need to decide on your thesis—perhaps the idea that although the four students fail in their attempt to observe seven days of silence, they succeed in making a start toward an important and worthy goal, and that their effort was not without merit and value. How you might develop and explain that idea could vary, but one way would be to first present a view that you want to reject—that the students failed abysmally and completely because they were either unprepared for the rigors of keeping silent or they were arrogant, with each thinking he was better at keeping silence than the others. You could present this idea first and then argue that while it is an interesting approach to the story and has some merit as an interpretation, there is an even more interesting and more persuasive way to interpret it, as indicated in the first thesis.

In addition to a clear thesis and a logical organization for developing and supporting that thesis, an interpretive paper also needs evidence, primarily evidence from the text of the work. In "Learning to Be Silent" the evidence appears in the descriptive details and in the dialogue of the parable; it also appears in the title. In fact, for a reader who wanted to argue the positive interpretation advanced in the previous paragraph, the title is extremely important because it suggests that the students are only novices beginning their learning about silence and not at the end of their efforts toward becoming masters of silence.

We have much more to say about interpretation in succeeding chapters, including the chapters on the elements of fiction, poetry, and drama, where you will also find guidance on interpretation.

Argument and Evaluation In making an argument that centers on evaluation you first need to be clear which type of evaluation you are making. Are you arguing about the quality, relevance, and value of a particular work—about the worth of "Learning to Be Silent" or "Dust of Snow" for living our lives, or the skill and artistry with which the parable and poem have been made? Or are you considering the social, cultural, and other values—the contexts of culture and value that the works reflect or embody?

In this book, you will find discussions of this second type of evaluation throughout the sections on fiction, poetry, and drama, including questions about values following many of the stories, poems, and plays. Arguments about relative value—whether one poem is better or worse than another, one play or story is greater than another—are generally matters of personal taste and are not considered. Our evaluation considerations will focus instead on the social and cultural contexts of the works and the ways our values as readers support or conflict with those reflected by and embodied in the stories, plays, and poems collected here.

Consider the little vignette from his book *In Our Time* by Ernest Hemingway printed on page 11. In reviewing the discussion of that short prose text on page 12, you will see how the emphasis falls on making an argument about the piece based on cultural expectations. The soldier "hero" of that little story is, of course, not a "hero" in the traditional sense at all. He is fearful and cowardly rather than heroic; his behavior from a moral and religious standpoint is worthy of condemnation. But in advancing those judgments, in making this particular argument about the work—that its protagonist is flawed and perhaps that he represents a loss of dignity, courage, and honor from a bygone day—we must refer to social, cultural, and historical contexts and the values those contexts reflect. An evaluation argument needs to use these contexts as evidence.

The Writing Process

The writing process generally consists of planning, drafting, revising, and editing. Planning involves the preliminary thinking you do before you actually write a draft of your paper. Planning can also involve writing *prewriting* mostly in the form of annotations, short notes, or an outline. Drafting is the first large-scale effort to record your ideas and begin supporting them with evidence. Revising occurs after you have written a draft and had a chance to review it after some time away from it, and sometimes after receiving feedback from others who have read and responded to it. Editing for grammar and spelling is the last part of the writing process.

Planning

In the planning phase of writing you begin thinking about what your focus will be. You make a decision about your topic and about how to approach it. Your decision will be influenced by your instructor's guidelines about the length of an assigned paper as well as other constraints, like whether it should include research in secondary sources or whether it should focus on one or another literary element—the setting of a story, for example, or the structure of a poem.

Prewriting planning strategies include taking notes on a work you will write about and making notes in the margins of the work. These annotations and notes provide the kernel of thought that you can develop into an outline of key points that you want to make in the paper. You can expand many of your notes and annotations by writing sentences and paragraphs that explain why you recorded them—what prompted you to record the notes and annotations in the first place. Your notes can help you decide on your topic and your approach to it.

Drafting

Once you have arrived at a tentative subject and an angle of approach, you are ready to write a rough draft of your paper. The purpose of this draft is simply to write down your ideas and to see how they can be developed and supported. Think of the rough draft as an opportunity to discover what you think about the subject and to test and refine your ideas. Don't worry about having a clearly defined thesis or main idea for your paper before beginning to write it. Instead, use your initial draft to discover an idea, to find a thesis and sharpen it so that your idea-thesis becomes clear, first to you and then to your readers.

In drafting your paper, consider your purpose. Are you writing to provide information and make observations about the work? Are you writing to argue for a particular way to interpret it? When you write about a literary work you will often attempt to convince others that what you see and say about it makes sense. In doing so, you will be arguing for the validity of your way of seeing, not necessarily to the exclusion of all other ways, but to demonstrate that your understanding of the work is reasonable and valuable. Since your readers will respond as much to how you support your arguments as to your ideas themselves, you will need to concentrate on providing evidence for your ideas. Most often this *evidence* will come in the form of textual support—details of action, dialogue, imagery, description, language, and structure. Additional evidence may come from secondary sources, from the comments of experienced readers whose observations and interpretations may influence and support your own thinking. In marshalling evidence for your ideas, keep the following guidelines in mind:

1. *Be fair-minded.* Avoid oversimplifying or distorting either the work or what others have written about it.
2. *Be cautious.* Qualify your claims. Limit your discussion to what you feel confident you can reasonably demonstrate.
3. *Be logical.* See that the various elements of your argument fit together and that one part of your approach doesn't contradict another.
4. *Be accurate.* If you present facts, details, or quotations, present them accurately.
5. *Be confident.* You should believe in your ideas and present them with conviction.

After writing the first draft, try to forget it for a while—for at least a day or two, longer if possible. When you return to it, read the draft critically: assess whether what you are saying *makes sense,* whether you have provided enough *examples* to clarify your ideas and presented sufficient evidence to make them persuasive. Consider whether the draft centers on a *single idea* and stays *on track.* If the first draft accomplishes these things, you can begin thinking about how to tighten the paper's organization and polish its style. If, on the other hand, the draft contains frequent changes of direction, then you will need to decide what to salvage and what to get rid of and how to focus the paper more sharply.

When you have written an acceptable draft (and this often requires that you write multiple drafts), you are ready to view its organization yet more critically. A general organizational framework should have an introductory section that clarifies your purpose and intention; a set of successive paragraphs that develop, explore, and explain your ideas; and a conclusion that rounds off the discussion. Within that framework, consider whether your ideas and examples have been arranged in a coherent and logical manner. Ask yourself whether your paper will be clear to readers. Consider whether sufficient space (or perhaps too much space) has been allotted to clarifying and supporting your views. Ask someone to read your paper with an eye to its organization and structure. Ask them—and yourself—if your beginning clearly sets up your discussion or argument and if your conclusion suitably finishes it off.

Sample Outline for Student Paper on a Poem

STEPHEN CRANE

[1871–1900]

War Is Kind

Do not weep, maiden, for war is kind.
Because your lover threw wild hands toward the sky
And the affrighted steed ran on alone,
Do not weep.
War is kind.

Hoarse, booming drums of the regiment,
Little souls who thirst for fight,
These men were born to drill and die.
The unexplained glory flies above them,
Great is the battle god, great, and his kingdom
A field where a thousand corpses lie.

Do not weep, babe, for war is kind.
Because your father tumbled in the yellow trenches,
Raged at his breast, gulped and died,
Do not weep.
War is kind.

Swift blazing flag of the regiment,
Eagle with crest of red and gold,
These men were born to drill and die.
Point for them the virtue of slaughter,
Make plain to them the excellence of killing
And a field where a thousand corpses lie.

Mother whose heart hung humble as a button
On the bright splendid shroud of your son,
Do not weep.
War is kind.

(1899)

In discussing the ironic tone of "War Is Kind" you might focus on three or four details. You might decide to discuss first the ironic quality of the title. The word *kind* is not usually associated with war; war is associated instead with suffering, waste, death, and destruction. The title, then, cannot be taken literally. Next you might decide to include the speaker's advice to the lover, child, and mother of a slain soldier not to cry, since war is "kind." (These examples too will have to be arranged in a sequence that makes sense to you.) You will probably want to comment on how details such as the "field where a thousand corpses lie" and the soldier who "tumbled in the yellow trenches" can stand alongside the more seemingly patriotic images of regimental flag and thundering drums.

Ask yourself how the ironic aspects of the poem can be related. Consider what these details contribute to the poem. Some details will seem more important than others; you may thus be able to subdivide and pair your examples, and perhaps contrast them. Or you may decide to consider them in order of increasing complexity, emotion, or importance. It is necessary, though, to devise an organizational plan that makes sense to you and that will seem sensible to your readers. If you write a comparative paper, your outline might look like this:

Ironic Contrasts in Crane's "War Is Kind"

```
  I. Advice to maiden
     A. Expectation: Sympathy for loss
     B. Reality: Command not to weep
        1. details horrible—not comforting
           a. "wild hands"
           b. "affrighted steed"
        2. repetition of "war is kind"
           a. emphasizes irony
           b. leads to stanza two, details of war
 II. Advice to babe
     A. Expectation: Commentary on sorrow
     B. Reality: Command not to weep
        1. details ugly—not noble
           a. "yellow trenches"
           b. "raged . . . gulped and died"
        2. repetition of "war is kind"
           a. emphasizes irony
           b. leads to stanza three, details of war
III. Advice to mother
     A. Expectation: Empathy with bereavement
     B. Reality: Command not to weep
        1. details highlight ironic contrast
           a. mother's love is "humble as a button"
           b. son's shroud (furnished by military) is
              "bright" and "splendid"
        2. repetition of "war is kind"
           a. emphasizes irony
           b. ties together the three civilians who have
              suffered deep losses from "kind" war
```

On the other hand, you might want to examine the relationship of stanzas 1, 3, and 5 to stanzas 2 and 4. In that case, your outline might look like this:

War at Home and on the Battlefield

```
 I. Repetition
    A. Stanzas 1, 3, 5 repeat "war is kind"
       1. represents the politic lies told to keep
          survivors quiet
       2. provides ironic contrast with details
    B. Stanzas 2, 4 repeat "A field where a thousand
       corpses lie"
       1. emphasizes the enormous losses of war
       2. contrasts with the "war is kind" lie told to
          those at home
       3. suggests that for everyone of the thousand
          corpses a "maiden," "babe," or "mother" mourns
II. Images: Effects of War
    A. Stanzas 1, 3, 5 show the sorrow of those left behind
       1. images suggest reality of death in war "threw
          wild hands"; "tumbled in the yellow trenches,"
          which those at home must picture
       2. images suggest all that is left to those at home
          are empty symbols: "bright splendid shroud"
    B. Stanzas 2, 4 images show how the propaganda of war
       contrasts with its reality
       1. propaganda: "unexplained glory flies above them";
          "Great is the battle god"; "Swift blazing flag of
          the regiment"
       2. reality: "drill and die"; "a thousand corpses lie"
```

Besides deciding on the order of ideas and examples in the paper and the amount of space allotted to each, you must consider how to move from one example to another. You will need to link the sections of your discussion so that the writing flows smoothly. Generally, you can create transitions with phrases and sentences at the beginnings of paragraphs. (Examples include such words and phrases as "first, . . . second, . . ."; "on the other hand, . . ."; "in addition to . . . "; "another way in which . . ."). Sometimes, however, such explicit marks of transition from one point to another will not be necessary: careful ordering of the details that support your argument will be evidence enough of how one paragraph follows from and is related to another.

Revising and Editing

Revision is your continual engagement with your project, not something that occurs only once, toward the end of the writing process. Redrafting your paper to consider the ordering of paragraphs and deleting something or adding to your examples are significant acts of revision. So too is just rereading the work and thinking about it a second or third time or more. Revision occurs throughout the entire span of writing and rereading and writing again. It requires you to reconsider your writing and your thinking not once, but many times. This reconsideration occurs on three levels: conceptual, organizational, and stylistic.

Conceptual revision involves reconsidering your ideas. As you write a first or second draft, your understanding of the work and what you plan to say about it may change. While accumulating textual evidence in support of one interpretation of the work, you may discover stronger evidence for a contrasting view. When this happens, you may need to go back to the note-taking stage to explore your revised vision of the work. You will then need to make major changes in the original draft. You may end up discarding much of it and beginning again with a stronger conviction about a different approach or a revised idea. In writing about Crane's "War Is Kind," for example, you may have started out with a literal interpretation, arguing that the poem is patriotic rather than ironic. Developing your idea, however, you may have become uneasy with certain details that run counter to your interpretation and that prompt you to change your mind about what the poem means. In that case, you revise your idea and begin again.

Organizational or *structural* revision involves asking yourself whether the arrangement best presents your line of thinking. Is the organizational framework readily discernible? Does it make sense? Have you written an introduction that clarifies your topic and intention? Have you organized your supporting details in a sensible and logical manner? Does your conclusion follow logically from your discussion and bring it to a satisfying close? Again, taking Crane's poem as an example, you might begin by identifying its general subject—war—and move toward suggesting that even though the poem contains some language that idealizes war, its details and its tone undermine a romanticized conception. From there you would move to the body of your argument, in which you would present details that appear supportive of war's glory and show how other details of incident and language contradict them. Capping your argument/interpretation would be a precise analysis of the poem's ironies. In your conclusion, you would repeat your main point, perhaps responding personally to the poem as you understand it. You could also relate the poem to some other work you've read (by Crane or by another writer), and perhaps include an apt quotation that sums up your sense of the work's significance.

However you choose to end your paper, remember that your conclusion should finally answer the question "So what?" for your reader. Even though you have presented details, reasons, and examples to support your views, your reader will still expect you to sum up or highlight their significance once more.

Stylistic revision concerns the details of **syntax** (word order), **diction** (word choice), **tone, imagery,** and **rhythm.** We will consider such matters in the "Writing" chapters of this book. Even though you should think about these things in early drafts, it is better to defer major critical attention to them until after writing a nearly final draft, because such stylistic considerations may undergo significant alteration as you rethink and reorganize your paper. Nevertheless, the details are crucial and errors in spelling or grammar may destroy your readers' confidence in you. A lapse in tone can distract your readers' attention as much as a lapse in logic can confuse them.

To help you focus on aspects of style that may require revision, and editing, use the following questions as a guide.

1. Are your *sentences concise* and clear?
2. Can you *eliminate words* that are not doing their job?
3. Are your tone and voice *consistent*? (For example, you should *eliminate shifts* from a formal to an informal, even colloquial, style.)
4. Is your level of *language appropriate for* the subject of your paper?
5. Do your words and sentences *say what you want them to*? Do they say anything you don't want them to?
6. Are there any *grammatical errors:* inconsistencies in verb tenses, problems with subject–verb agreement, run-on sentences, fragments, and the like?
7. Are there any errors in *spelling and punctuation*?

As a final step, always carefully proofread your paper, of course, and make sure it conforms to your instructor's guidelines on manuscript form.

PART ONE

Fiction

Irish author James Joyce on the street.

CHAPTER ONE

Reading Stories

We read stories for pleasure; they entertain us. And we read them for profit; they enlighten us. Stories draw us into their imaginative worlds and engage us with the power of their invention. They provide us with more than the immediate interest of narrative—of something happening—and more than the pleasures of imagination: they enlarge our understanding of ourselves and deepen our appreciation of life.

Consider this famous early story about a father and his two sons:

LUKE

[1st century]

The author known simply as Luke is recognized as having written the third gospel of the New Testament. He is thought to have been a physician and also the author of the New Testament Acts of the Apostles.

The Prodigal Son

A certain man had two sons: and the younger of them said to his father, "Father, give me the portion of goods that falleth to me." And he divided unto them his living. And not many days after, the younger son gathered all together, and took his journey into a far country, and there wasted his substance with riotous living. And when he had spent all, there arose a mighty famine in that land, and he began to be in want. And he went and joined himself to a citizen of that country, and he sent him into his fields to feed swine. And he would fain have filled his belly with the husks that the swine did eat: and no man gave unto him. And when he came to himself, he said, "How many hired servants of my father's have bread enough and to spare, and I perish with hunger? I will arise and go to my father, and will say unto him, 'Father, I have sinned against heaven, and before thee. And am no more worthy to be called thy son: make me as one of thy hired servants.' " And he arose, and came to his father. But when he was yet a great way off, his father saw him, and had compassion, and ran, and fell on his neck, and kissed him. And the son said unto him, "Father, I have sinned against heaven, and in thy sight, and am no more worthy to be called thy son." But the father said to his servants, "Bring forth the best robe, and put it on him, and put a ring on his hand, and shoes on his feet. And bring hither the fatted calf, and kill it, and let us eat, and be merry. For this my son was dead, and is alive again; he was lost, and is found." And they began to be merry. Now his elder son was in the field, and as he came and drew nigh to the house, he heard music and dancing. And he called one of the servants, and asked what these things meant. And he said unto him, "Thy brother is come, and thy father hath killed the fatted calf, because he hath received him safe and sound." And he was angry, and would not go in: therefore came his father out, and entreated him. And he answering said to his father, "Lo, these many years do I serve thee, neither transgressed I at any time thy commandment, and yet thou never gavest me a kid, that I might make merry with my friends: but as soon as this thy son was come, which hath devoured thy living with harlots, thou hast killed for him the fatted calf." And he said unto him, "Son, thou art ever with me, and all that I have is thine. It was meet that we should make merry, and be glad: for this thy brother was dead, and is alive again: and was lost, and is found."

When we read the story of "The Prodigal Son," we essentially do three things: (1) we take in its surface features, and form impressions of character and action; (2) we observe details, make connections among them, and draw inferences and conclusions from those connections; and (3) we evaluate the story, measuring its moral, political, and cultural values against our own. We can call these three aspects of the reading process "experience," "interpretation," and "evaluation."

THE EXPERIENCE OF FICTION

Our *experience* of fiction concerns our feelings about the characters, our sense of involvement in the story's developing action, our pleasure or confusion in its language, our joy or sorrow at its outcome. We are concerned, in short, with what the story does to us, how it affects us—and why.

How did you react to "The Prodigal Son"? What feelings did the story evoke? Did you feel sorry for the prodigal son? Did you feel anger or resentment at his behavior? At his father's or brother's behavior? Did your feelings about any of the characters change during the course of your reading or afterward? How does the story relate to your experiences as a member of a family? How does it reflect what you have observed of family relations generally?

It is important to remember that readers respond to stories in different ways. When you compare the reactions of your classmates and teacher to "The Prodigal Son," you will discover different perceptions, attitudes, and feelings about it. Why is this so? Essentially, it is because we bring to our reading a wide range of personal experience, social attitudes, religious beliefs, and cultural dispositions that influence our responses.

We do not read a story in a vacuum: Our reading is always affected by who we are, what we believe, and how we think; that is, by the context we bring to our reading. Christians, for example, may experience "The Prodigal Son" differently from how Muslims, Buddhists, or atheists experience it. Women experience the story differently from men. Practiced readers experience the story differently from inexperienced ones. Parents experience it differently from those who have no children. And as we change—as we become more practiced readers, or have children, for example–our ways of understanding life and literature change too.

In sorting out our thoughts and feelings about "The Prodigal Son," we have been emphasizing our subjective impressions of the story—how it affects us. We have been reading it in the context of our own experience. But while we experience a story subjectively, we are also interpreting and evaluating it. This is inevitable, since the three parts of reading are interrelated.

THE INTERPRETATION OF FICTION

When we interpret a story we explain it to ourselves and try to make sense of it. We form subjective impressions as we experience fiction, but we have relatively *objective* considerations in mind when we interpret it. We say "relatively" objective because no reading of a story is entirely objective: Every interpretation is one way of understanding the text among many; every interpretation is influenced by our particular language, culture, and experience. What then do we mean by *interpretation?* Understanding, essentially. An interpretation is an argument about a story's meaning as we understand it. It's our way of stating and supporting, with arguments based on analysis, what the story *means,* what it says or suggests, rather than how it affects us. Interpretation, in short, relies on our intellectual comprehension rather than on our emotional response to the literary work.

Interpretation involves four related intellectual acts: *observing, connecting, inferring,* and *concluding.* To understand a fictional work, we first observe its details. We notice, for example, descriptive details about the time and place of its action; we listen carefully to what the characters say and to their manner of saying it; we note how the characters interact. As we observe, we make connections among the details and begin to formulate a sense of the story's emphasis and point. On the basis of these connections we develop inferences or interpretive hypotheses about their significance. Finally, we come to some conclusion about the story's meaning based on our observations, connections, and inferences.

The four interpretive actions of observing, connecting, inferring, and concluding often occur simultaneously, and not in neatly segregated sequential stages. We don't delay making inferences, for example, until after we have registered and related all our observations. Instead, we develop tentative conclusions *as* we read and observe, *while* we relate our observations and develop our inferences. We may change and adjust our inferences and provisional conclusions both *during* our reading of a story and *afterward* as we think back over its details. This analytical process, however, is not something we keep separate from our subjective reactions and emotional responses as we read.

In "The Prodigal Son," for example, we notice that the father sees his younger son coming from far off, that he runs to him, falls on his neck, and kisses him. Such details imply that the father has been watching for his son and hoping for his return. The father's actions speak eloquently of his unreserved acceptance of his son and deep joy at his return. Reflecting on these actions, we may connect them with the father's behavior toward his elder son and wonder what is responsible for the difference. In the process of noticing and wondering, we may also respond emotionally, thinking perhaps of our own experience or of the situation of someone we know. And we may evaluate the father's behavior according to standards we adhere to either consciously or unconsciously. Even in performing the rational, analytical act of interpretation, we cannot entirely escape a tendency to respond emotionally or to evaluate.

Reading in Context

Our approach to interpreting stories involves something else as well: that we see a story as a story, and even more important as a particular *kind* of story. We know, for example, that "The Prodigal Son" is not a factual account of the actions of a particular father and son. A journalistic account would have included their names, perhaps their ages and address, and details about the son's behavior in the foreign land, which would have been identified. But the story gives none of this information. In fact, the details included are not those we would typically expect to find in a newspaper. It's not just that "The Prodigal Son" is short on information, but that it goes out of its way to include the kind of repetitions, for example, that would be considered unnecessary in a factual account.

It is helpful to know that "The Prodigal Son" is *fiction,* an imagined story that is not based on historical fact, and to know the conventions or implicit rules of fiction. Furthermore, this story is a particular kind of fiction—a *parable* or brief story that teaches a lesson, often religious or spiritual in nature. As someone once cleverly put it, a parable is "an earthly story with a heavenly meaning." Parables point toward spiritual beliefs or truths and should be read symbolically, with emphasis on their spiritual meaning.

But we must go further. "The Prodigal Son" is a Christian parable—not a Hebrew or Zen parable. It was spoken by Jesus roughly two thousand years ago and recorded by the evangelist Luke in his New Testament Gospel. Thus, we look to the parable for a religious idea consistent with Jesus's teaching. It has a religious meaning that may be paraphrased like this: God (the father) is willing to forgive man (the prodigal son) any sin man commits, no matter how grievous, if only he repents and asks God's forgiveness. Alternatively: God is eager to welcome the sinner back, and in fact is happier at his return than with the fidelity of those in no spiritual danger. We can read the parable, thus, as an example of God's love, as an illustration of man's need for repentance, as a description of the relationship between God and man—or as all three.

Whatever we decide about its religious meaning, we should realize that "The Prodigal Son" means more than any interpretive comments we can make about it. This is so because the full meaning of any literary work includes our experience in reading it as well as our understanding of it—our *emotional apprehension* as well as our *intellectual comprehension*. And it includes, further, our perceptions of what is valuable, important, significant about it, for these perceptions reflect our own social, political, moral, and cultural values.

THE EVALUATION OF FICTION

The third part of our approach to reading fiction is *evaluation*. When we evaluate a story we do two different things. First, we assess its literary quality; we make a judgment about how good it is, how successfully it realizes its intentions, how effectively it pleases us. Second, we consider the values the story endorses—or refutes.

An evaluation is essentially a judgment, an opinion about a work formulated as a conclusion. We may agree or disagree with the father's forgiveness or the elder brother's complaint in "The Prodigal Son." We may confirm or deny the models of behavior illustrated in this or any other story. However we evaluate them, though, we invariably measure the story's values against our own.

When we evaluate a story, we appraise it according to our own special combination of cultural, moral, and aesthetic values. Our cultural values derive from our lives as members of families and societies. These values are affected by our race and gender and by the language we speak. Our moral values reflect our ethical norms—what we consider to be good and evil, right and wrong. Our aesthetic values determine what we see as beautiful or ugly, well or ill made. Over time, with education and experience, our values often change. Through contact with other cultures, we may come to understand the limiting perspectives of our own. When we live with people other than our immediate families, we may be persuaded to different ways of seeing many things we previously took for granted. Some of our beliefs, assumptions, and attitudes about religion, family, marriage, sex, love, school, work, money, and other aspects of life are almost sure to change.

As our lives and outlooks change, we may change the way we view particular literary works. A story that we once admired for what it reveals about human behavior or one whose moral perspective impressed us may come to seem trivial or unimportant. Conversely, we may find that a work we once disliked later seems engaging. Just as individual tastes in literature change over time, so do collective literary tastes. Culture evolves; moral beliefs, aesthetic values, and social attitudes change. Literary works, like musical compositions and political ideas, go in and out of fashion.

Of the kinds of evaluations we make in reading fiction, those about a story's aesthetic qualities are hardest to discuss. Aesthetic responses are difficult to describe because they involve our memories and sensations, our feelings and perceptions, our subjective impressions. They also involve our expectations, which are further affected by our prior experience of reading fiction. And they are additionally complicated by our tendency to react quickly and decisively to what we like and dislike, often without knowing why. Consider the aesthetic value of "The Prodigal Son." Is it a "beautiful" story? Does it seem to be a good example of its kind—the religious parable that teaches lessons about divine forgiveness? (Or should we emphasize its human dimension, especially the relationships between people?) As we mentioned in the discussion of interpretation, understanding what kind of work we are reading affects how we interpret it. Similarly, our perception of its genre or kind also affects our evaluation. Our preference for one kind of fiction over another complicates matters still further. (We may dislike ironic stories, for example, or we may love melodrama and adventure.) When we evaluate a story, we should judge it against what it attempts to do, what it is, rather than against something it is not.

How we arrive at an aesthetic evaluation is no easy matter. We develop our aesthetic responses to fiction by letting the informed responses of other experienced readers enrich our own perceptions, by determining the criteria for what makes a story "good," and by gradually developing our sense of literary tact—the kind of balanced judgment that comes with experience in reading and living coupled with thoughtful reflection on both. There are no shortcuts or simple formulas for this development; it comes only with practice and patience.

Admittedly, without a good deal of experience in reading fiction, judgments about the values supported in a story and about its aesthetic worth need to be made cautiously. But we must begin somewhere, since evaluation is inevitable. We cannot really avoid judging the stories we read any more than we can avoid judging the people we meet. The process is natural. What we should strive for in evaluating fiction is to understand the different kinds of values it presents, and to clarify our own attitudes, dispositions, and values in responding to them.

Consider the values in John Updike's "A & P." Evaluate the behavior of each of the major characters, particularly Sammy and Lengel. Consider their attitudes toward the three girls in the story and what those attitudes reveal about each of the males. Try to assess what part your experiences and personal values play in your assessment of the story, both as an embodiment of cultural values and as an object of aesthetic value.

JOHN UPDIKE

[b. 1932]

John Updike, American novelist, short-story writer, and poet, was born and raised in Pennsylvania. Following his graduation from Harvard, Updike worked at The New Yorker *before devoting himself full time to writing. Updike has long been a versatile writer, publishing criticism, essays, poetry, novels, and short stories for more than forty years. He is best known for his portrayals of suburban life and for characters who experience the anxieties, tensions, and frustrations of middle-class existence.*

A & P

In walks these three girls in nothing but bathing suits. I'm in the third check-out slot, with my back to the door, so I don't see them until they're over by the bread. The one that caught my eye first was the one in the plaid green two-piece. She was a chunky kid, with a good tan and a sweet broad soft-looking can with those two crescents of white just under it, where the sun never seems to hit, at the top of the backs of her legs. I stood there with my hand on a box of HiHo crackers trying to remember if I rang it up or not. I ring it up again and the customer starts giving me hell. She's one of these cash-register-watchers, a witch about fifty with rouge on her cheekbones and no eyebrows, and I know it made her day to trip me up. She'd been watching cash registers for fifty years and probably never seen a mistake before.

By the time I got her feathers smoothed and her goodies into a bag—she gives me a little snort in passing, if she'd been born at the right time they would have burned her over in Salem—by the time I get her on her way the girls had circled around the bread and were coming back, without a pushcart, back my way along the counters, in the aisle between the check-outs and the Special bins. They didn't even have shoes on. There was this chunky one, with the two-piece—it was bright green and the seams on the bra were still sharp and her belly was still pretty pale so I guessed she just got it (the suit)—there was this one, with one of those chubby berry-faces, the lips all bunched together under her nose, this one, and a tall one, with black hair that hadn't quite frizzed right, and one of these sunburns right across under the eyes, and a chin that was too long—you know, the kind of girl other girls think is very "striking" and "attractive" but never quite makes it, as they very well know, which is why they like her so much—and then the third one, that wasn't quite so tall. She was the queen. She kind of led them, the other two peeking around and making their shoulders round. She didn't look around, not this queen, she just walked straight on slowly, on these long white prima donna legs. She came down a little hard on her heels, as if she didn't walk in her bare feet that much, putting down her heels and then letting the weight move along to her toes as if she was testing the floor with every step, putting a little deliberate extra action into it. You never know for sure how girls' minds work (do you really think it's a mind in there or just a little buzz like a bee in a glass jar?) but you got the idea she had talked the other two into coming in here with her, and now she was showing them how to do it, walk slow and hold yourself straight.

She had on a kind of dirty-pink—beige maybe, I don't know—bathing suit with a little nubble all over it and, what got me, the straps were down. They were off her shoulders looped loose around the cool tops of her arms, and I guess as a result the suit had slipped a little on her, so all around the top of the cloth there was this shining rim. If it hadn't been there you wouldn't have known there could have been anything whiter than those shoulders. With the straps pushed off, there was nothing between the top of the suit and the top of her head except just *her,* this clean bare plane of the top of her chest down from the shoulder bones like a dented sheet of metal tilted in the light. I mean, it was more than pretty.

She had sort of oaky hair that the sun and salt had bleached, done up in a bun that was unravelling, and a kind of prim face. Walking into the A & P with your straps down, I suppose it's the only kind of face you *can* have. She held her head so high her neck, coming up out of those white shoulders, looked kind of stretched, but I didn't mind. The longer her neck was, the more of her there was.

She must have felt in the corner of her eye me and over my shoulder Stokesie in the second slot watching, but she didn't tip. Not this queen. She kept her eyes moving across the racks, and stopped, and turned so slow it made my stomach rub the inside of my apron, and buzzed to the other two, who kind of huddled against her for relief, and they all three of them went up the cat-and-dog-food-breakfast-cereal-macaroni-rice-raisins-seasonings-spreads-spaghetti-soft-drinks-crackers-and-cookies aisle. From the third slot I look straight up this aisle to the meat counter, and I watched them all the way. The fat one with the tan sort of fumbled with the cookies, but on second thought she put the packages back. The sheep pushing their carts down the aisle—the girls were walking against the usual traffic (not that we have one-way signs or anything)—were pretty hilarious. You could see them, when Queenie's white shoulders dawned on them, kind of jerk, or hop, or hiccup, but their eyes snapped back to their own baskets and on they pushed. I bet you could set off dynamite in an A & P and the people would by and large keep reaching and checking oatmeal off their lists and muttering "Let me see, there was a third thing, began with A, asparagus, no, ah, yes, applesauce!" or whatever it is they do mutter. But there was no doubt, this jiggled them. A few houseslaves in pin curlers even looked around after pushing their carts past to make sure what they had seen was correct.

You know, it's one thing to have a girl in a bathing suit down on the beach, where what with the glare nobody can look at each other much anyway, and another thing in the cool of the A & P, under the fluorescent lights, against all those stacked packages, with her feet paddling along naked over our checkerboard green-and-cream rubber-tile floor.

"Oh Daddy," Stokesie said beside me. "I feel so faint."

"Darling," I said. "Hold me tight." Stokesie's married, with two babies chalked up on his fuselage already, but as far as I can tell that's the only difference. He's twenty-two, and I was nineteen this April.

"Is it done?" he asks, the responsible married man finding his voice. I forgot to say he thinks he's going to be manager some sunny day, maybe in 1990 when it's called the Great Alexandrov and Petrooshki Tea Company or something.

What he meant was, our town is five miles from a beach, with a big summer colony out on the Point, but we're right in the middle of town, and the women generally put on a shirt or shorts or something before they get out of the car into the street. And anyway these are usually women with six children and varicose veins mapping their legs and nobody, including them, could care less. As I say, we're right in the middle of town, and if you stand at our front doors you can see two banks and the Congregational church and the newspaper store and three real-estate offices and about twenty-seven old freeloaders tearing up Central Street because the sewer broke again. It's not as if we're on the Cape; we're north of Boston and there's people in this town haven't seen the ocean for twenty years.

The girls had reached the meat counter and were asking McMahon something. He pointed, they pointed, and they shuffled out of sight behind a pyramid of Diet Delight peaches. All that was left for us to see was old McMahon patting his mouth and looking after them sizing up their joints. Poor kids, I began to feel sorry for them, they couldn't help it.

Now here comes the sad part of the story, at least my family says it's sad but I don't think it's sad myself. The store's pretty empty, it being Thursday afternoon, so there was nothing much to do except lean on the register and wait for the girls to show up again. The whole store was like a pinball machine and I didn't know which tunnel they'd come out of. After a while they come around out of the far aisle, around the light bulbs, records at discount of the Caribbean Six or Tony Martin Sings or some such gunk you wonder they waste the wax on, sixpacks of candy bars, and plastic toys done up in cellophane that fall apart when a kid looks at them anyway. Around they come, Queenie still leading the way, and holding a little gray jar in her hand. Slots Three through Seven are unmanned and I could see her wondering between Stokes and me, but Stokesie with his usual luck draws an old party in baggy gray pants who stumbles up with four giant cans of pineapple juice (what do these bums *do* with all that pineapple juice? I've often asked myself) so the girls come to me. Queenie puts down the jar and I take it into my fingers icy cold. Kingfish Fancy Herring Snacks in Pure Sour Cream: 49¢. Now her hands are empty, not a ring or a bracelet, bare as God made them, and I wonder where the money's coming from. Still with that prim look she lifts a folded dollar bill out of the hollow at the center of her nubbled pink top. The jar went heavy in my hand. Really, I thought that was so cute.

Then everybody's luck begins to run out. Lengel comes in from haggling with a truck full of cabbages on the lot and is about to scuttle into that door marked MANAGER behind which he hides all day when the girls touch his eye. Lengel's pretty dreary, teaches Sunday school and the rest, but he doesn't miss that much. He comes over and says, "Girls, this isn't the beach."

Queenie blushes, though maybe it's just a brush of sunburn I was noticing for the first time, now that she was so close. "My mother asked me to pick up a jar of herring snacks." Her voice kind of startled me, the way voices do when you see the people first, coming out so flat and dumb yet kind of tony, too, the way it ticked over "pick up" and "snacks." All of a sudden I slid right down her voice into her living room. Her father and the other men were standing around in ice-cream coats and bow ties and the women were in sandals picking up herring snacks on toothpicks off a big plate and they were all holding drinks the color of water with olives and sprigs of mint in them. When my parents have somebody over they get lemonade and if it's a real racy affair Schlitz in tall glasses with "They'll Do It Every Time" cartoons stencilled on.

"That's all right," Lengel said. "But this isn't the beach." His repeating this struck me as funny, as if it had just occurred to him, and he had been thinking all these years the A & P was a great big dune and he was the head lifeguard. He didn't like my smiling—as I say he doesn't miss much—but he concentrates on giving the girls that sad Sunday-school-superintendent stare.

Queenie's blush is no sunburn now, and the plump one in plaid, that I liked better from the back—a really sweet can—pipes up, "We weren't doing any shopping. We just came in for the one thing."

"That makes no difference," Lengel tells her, and I could see from the way his eyes went that he hadn't noticed she was wearing a two-piece before. "We want you decently dressed when you come in here."

"We *are* decent," Queenie says suddenly, her lower lip pushing, getting sore now that she remembers her place, a place from which the crowd that runs the A & P must look pretty crummy. Fancy Herring Snacks flashed in her very blue eyes.

"Girls, I don't want to argue with you. After this come in here with your shoulders covered. It's our policy." He turns his back. That's policy for you. Policy is what the kingpins want. What the others want is juvenile delinquency.

All this while, the customers had been showing up with their carts but, you know, sheep, seeing a scene, they had all bunched up on Stokesie, who shook open a paper bag as gently as peeling a peach, not wanting to miss a word. I could feel in the silence everybody getting nervous, most of all Lengel, who asks me, "Sammy, have you rung up this purchase?"

I thought and said "No" but it wasn't about that I was thinking. I go through the punches, 4, 9, groc, tot—it's more complicated than you think, and after you do it often enough, it begins to make a little song, that you hear words to, in my case "Hello (*bing*) there, you (*gung*) hap-py *pee*-pul (*splat*)!"—the *splat* being the drawer flying out. I uncrease the bill, tenderly as you may imagine, it just having come from between the two smoothest scoops of vanilla I had ever known were there, and pass a half and a penny into her narrow pink palm, and nestle the herrings in a bag and twist its neck and hand it over, all the time thinking.

The girls, and who'd blame them, are in a hurry to get out, so I say "I quit" to Lengel quick enough for them to hear, hoping they'll stop and watch me, their unsuspected hero. They keep right on going, into the electric eye; the door flies open and they flicker across the lot to their car, Queenie and Plaid and Big Tall Goony-Goony (not that as raw material she was so bad), leaving me with Lengel and a kink in his eyebrow.

"Did you say something, Sammy?"

"I said I quit."

"I thought you did."

"You didn't have to embarrass them."

"It was they who were embarrassing us."

I started to say something that came out "Fiddle-de-doo." It's a saying of my grandmother's, and I know she would have been pleased.

"I don't think you know what you're saying," Lengel said.

"I know you don't," I said. "But I do." I pull the bow at the back of my apron and start shrugging it off my shoulders. A couple customers that had been heading for my slot begin to knock against each other, like scared pigs in a chute.

Lengel sighs and begins to look very patient and old and gray. He's been a friend of my parents for years. "Sammy, you don't want to do this to your Mom and Dad," he tells me. It's true, I don't. But it seems to me that once you begin a gesture it's fatal not to go through with it. I fold the apron, "Sammy" stitched in red on the pocket, and put it on the counter, and drop the bow tie on top of it. The bow tie is theirs, if you've ever wondered. "You'll feel this for the rest of your life," Lengel says, and I know that's true, too, but remembering how he made that pretty girl blush makes me so scrunchy inside I punch the No Sale tab and the machine whirs "pee-pul" and the drawer splats out. One advantage to this scene taking place in summer, I can follow this up with a clean exit, there's no fumbling around getting your coat and galoshes, I just saunter into the electric eye in my white shirt that my mother ironed the night before, and the door heaves itself open, and outside the sunshine is skating around on the asphalt.

I look around for my girls, but they're gone, of course. There wasn't anybody but some young married screaming with her children about some candy they didn't get by the door of a powder-blue Falcon station wagon. Looking back in the big windows, over the bags of peat moss and aluminum lawn furniture stacked on the pavement, I could see Lengel in my place in the slot, checking the sheep through. His face was dark gray and his back stiff, as if he'd just had an injection of iron, and my stomach kind of fell as I felt how hard the world was going to be to me hereafter.

(1961)

Use the following questions about "A & P" as a way of reviewing the three aspects of reading fiction we have discussed: experience, interpretation, and evaluation.

QUESTIONS FOR CRITICAL THINKING AND WRITING

Experience

1. Describe your experience in reading "A & P." Did the story surprise you, entertain you, annoy you? Why? Did the story engage you and hold your interest? Why or why not?

2. Consider the attitude expressed toward the girls by both Sammy and Lengel. Whose attitude do you find more appealing? Why? Do you object to Sammy's (and perhaps Updike's) language in describing Queenie—her name, her "white prima donna legs," her "two scoops of vanilla"?
3. Did your feelings about either Lengel or Sammy change in the course of reading? If so, explain where the shift occurred and why. Did they change later, on additional reflection?

Interpretation

4. Characterize Sammy's style of telling his story. What do you learn about him from the kind of language he uses? From the details he includes? From the comparisons he employs to describe the store, the girls, and the other shoppers?
5. Look back to the story's climactic point, in which Sammy says, "I quit." Are there other passages of description, dialogue, or action that you see as closely related to this one?
6. How do you interpret Sammy's own response to his action? What does he mean by saying that he "felt how hard the world was going to be" for him afterward?

Evaluation

7. Whose values does the story seem to endorse? Whose values are criticized? How do you know? How do you see Sammy's decisive action? As heroic? As silly? Something else? Why?
8. Do you find the story meaningful? To what extent can you relate it in any significant way to your own life?
9. Do you think it is a good story, a successful example of realistic fiction? Do you find anything in it to admire from the standpoint of its language or structure?
10. Compare "A & P" to another realistic short story you have read. Which is more valuable for you? Why? Which is the more artistically wrought work? Why?

Critical Thinking

11. Imagine two different alternative endings for "A & P." Consider for each what happens to Sammy, Lengel, and the girls in bathing suits.

THE ACT OF READING FICTION

Even though we may read stories line by line, sentence by sentence, page by page, this linearity belies what happens mentally as we read. Our mental action is cyclical rather than linear. We project ahead and we glance back; we remember and we predict. By doing so, we are able to follow and understand a story in the first place, and to see more in it on subsequent readings.

To exemplify the actual process of reading a short work of fiction, we provide a stop-and-go reading of Kate Chopin's "The Story of an Hour." This story is "chunked," or broken up, into seven sections. Between these sections of the story are interpolated comments that make observations and raise questions about the story's details. These interpolated comments reflect the actual process of one reader's act of reading—his thinking about the story during his reading of it. The comments do not so much interpret the story as illustrate the act of reading; they represent the kinds of observations, inferences, and judgments we make as we move toward an understanding of the story.

KATE CHOPIN

[1851–1904]

Born and raised in St. Louis, Kate Chopin spent the years after her marriage in Louisiana as a society matron and mother of six. Business setbacks and the death of her husband in 1883 led her to assume control of the family business. Subsequently devoting herself to writing, she published short stories in magazines along with a novel, The Awakening *(1899), now considered a formative work of female self-assertion. At the time, however, this work, like some of her short stories, was condemned for its highly charged eroticism and its guiltless adultery.*

The Story of an Hour

Knowing that Mrs. Mallard was afflicted with a heart trouble, great care was taken to break to her as gently as possible the news of her husband's death.

It was her sister Josephine who told her, in broken sentences, veiled hints that revealed in half concealing. Her husband's friend Richards was there, too, near her. It was he who had been in the newspaper office when intelligence of the railroad disaster was received, with Brently Mallard's name leading the list of "killed." He had only taken the time to assure himself of its truth by a second telegram, and had hastened to forestall any less careful, less tender friend in bearing the sad message.

She did not hear the story as many women have heard the same, with a paralyzed inability to accept its significance. She wept at once, with sudden, wild abandonment, in her sister's arms. When the storm of grief had spent itself she went away to her room alone. She would have no one follow her.

▲ ***Comment*** *The opening action is presented quickly and economically. We are not given Mrs. Mallard's first name. And we might wonder if there is any significance in the name "Mallard." Do we hear something odd in the description of Mrs. Mallard's ailment as a "heart trouble"? More important than these details is the announcement of her husband's death. Mrs. Mallard is contrasted with other women who sit paralyzed by such news—women who refuse, initially at least, to accept the significance of such an announcement. Is there a difference between accepting the significance of a husband's death and accepting the simple fact of his death? We notice, finally, that Mrs. Mallard weeps with "sudden wild abandonment."*

There stood, facing the open window, a comfortable, roomy armchair. Into this she sank, pressed down by a physical exhaustion that haunted her body and seemed to reach into her soul.

She could see in the open square before her house the tops of trees that were all aquiver with the new spring life. The delicious breath of rain was in the air. In the street below a peddler was crying his wares. The notes of a distant song which some one was singing reached her faintly, and countless sparrows were twittering in the eaves.

There were patches of blue sky showing here and there through the clouds that had met and piled above the other in the west facing her window.

She sat with her head thrown back upon the cushion of the chair quite motionless, except when a sob came up into her throat and shook her, as a child who has cried itself to sleep continues to sob in its dreams.

▲ **Comment** *The setting for the middle section of the story is Mrs. Mallard's room. Is the open window through which she looks of any significance? Do the details that follow—trees, birds, rain, patches of blue sky, peddler, and song—have anything in common? We notice also that Mrs. Mallard is compared to a child who sobs in its dreams and may wonder about the implications of this comparison.*

She was young, with a fair, calm face, whose lines bespoke repression and even a certain strength. But now there was a dull stare in her eyes, whose gaze was fixed away off yonder on one of those patches of blue sky. It was not a glance of reflection, but rather indicated a suspension of intelligent thought.

There was something coming to her and she was waiting for it, fearfully. What was it? She did not know; it was too subtle and elusive to name. But she felt it, creeping out of the sky, reaching toward her through the sounds, the scents, the color that filled the air.

Now her bosom rose and fell tumultuously. She was beginning to recognize this thing that was approaching to possess her, and she was striving to beat it back with her will—as powerless as her two white slender hands would have been.

▲ **Comment** *These paragraphs alter slightly the tone and pace of the story. We are not told what Mrs. Mallard is waiting for. Whatever it is, however, she feels it; she senses it coming as she looks out the window. And we see her resisting it—powerlessly. Do we perhaps also hear sexual overtones in the description of what is "approaching to possess" her? Or do we wish to assign religious or psychological significance to this imminent possession and her ambivalent feelings about it? We notice, in addition, that Mrs. Mallard is described as not conscious of what is happening to her. Chopin says that there is "a suspension of intelligent thought." She seems to feel rather than think.*

When she abandoned herself a little whispered word escaped her slightly parted lips. She said it over and over under her breath: "Free, free, free!" The vacant stare and the look of terror that had followed it went from her eyes. They stayed keen and bright. Her pulse beat fast, and the coursing blood warmed and relaxed every inch of her body.

▲ **Comment** *In the first sentence the word "abandoned" echoes the earlier description of Mrs. Mallard's "wild abandonment." But she now seems in control of herself. Her repetition of* *"free" signals her excitement and perhaps convinces her of its truth. Her emotional excitement is rendered in physical imagery: her pulse beats fast, and her blood courses through her body—both signs of reawakened feeling.*

She did not stop to ask if it were not a monstrous joy that held her. A clear and exalted perception enabled her to dismiss the suggestion as trivial.

She knew that she would weep again when she saw the kind, tender hands folded in death; the face that had never looked save with love upon her, fixed and gray and dead. But she saw beyond that bitter moment a long procession of years to come that would belong to her absolutely. And she opened and spread her arms out to them in welcome.

There would be no one to live for during those coming years; she would live for herself. There would be no powerful will bending her in that blind persistence with which men and women believe they have a right to impose a private will upon a fellow-creature. A kind intention or a cruel intention made the act seem no less a crime as she looked upon it in that brief moment of illumination.

And yet she had loved him—sometimes. Often she had not. What did it matter! What could love, the unsolved mystery, count for in face of this possession of self-assertion which she suddenly recognized as the strongest impulse of her being!

▲ ***Comment*** *We pause over the words "monstrous joy." Clearly Mrs. Mallard is overjoyed. And from one perspective her joy, however honestly felt, is monstrous. She is happy—exultantly happy—that her husband is dead. But the author makes clear that Mrs. Mallard does not think about what she is feeling.*

The first paragraph underscores Mrs. Mallard's control and clear-sightedness. Her sense of confidence, anticipated earlier, becomes explicit and strong. We wonder if her husband treated her cruelly, but the text answers that he has been kind, which makes Mrs. Mallard's open-armed welcome of the coming years indeed monstrous. In the next paragraph Chopin does not exactly condemn Mr. Mallard but does suggest that Mrs. Mallard had to bend her will to his. Kind or not, he controlled her; loving wife or not, she resented it. Chopin here seems to move beyond the case of a particularly unhappy wife to the larger issue of the bonds of marriage, using language that strongly condemns the husband's dominance. We hear it in such words and phrases as "powerful will bending hers," "blind persistence," "impose," and "crime." This language is balanced by a lyrical evocation of Mrs. Mallard, in the years to come, living for herself rather than for her husband. The moment is described as "that brief moment of illumination." This description builds on the earlier description of her eyes as "keen and bright." Mrs. Mallard is possessed by a new sense of herself and a new self-confidence as she envisions her future life. This is the turning point of her life, a moment of recognition, insight, and enlightenment that makes her previous life with her husband pale into insignificance.

The next paragraphs could end the story:

"Free! Body and soul free!" she kept whispering.

Josephine was kneeling before the closed door with her lips to the keyhole, imploring for admission. "Louise, open the door! I beg; open the door—you will make yourself ill. What are you doing, Louise? For heaven's sake open the door."

"Go away. I am not making myself ill." No; she was drinking in a very elixir of life through that open window.

Her fancy was running riot along those days ahead of her. Spring days, and summer days, and all sorts of days that would be her own. She breathed a quick prayer that life might be long. It was only yesterday she had thought with a shudder that life might be long.

She arose at length and opened the door to her sister's importunities. There was a feverish triumph in her eyes, and she carried herself unwittingly like a goddess of Victory. She clasped her sister's waist, and together they descended the stairs. Richards stood waiting for them at the bottom.

▲ ***Comment*** *The discrepancy between what Josephine thinks is Mrs. Mallard's reason for keeping herself locked in her room and our knowledge of the real reason is ironic. There is irony, also, in Mrs. Mallard's praying for a long life, as only the day before she had shuddered at the thought of a long life with Brently Mallard. The language of these paragraphs is charged with feeling—somewhat overcharged perhaps—but it is in keeping with extending and intensifying Mrs. Mallard's emotion. She drinks in the "elixir of life," has a "feverish triumph in her eyes," and comports herself like a "goddess of Victory." These paragraphs could end the story, but they don't. Instead Chopin has a surprise:*

Some one was opening the front door with a latchkey. It was Brently Mallard who entered, a little travel-stained, composedly carrying his grip-sack and umbrella. He had been far from the scene of accident, and did not even know there had been one. He stood amazed at Josephine's piercing cry; at Richards's quick motion to screen him from the view of his wife.

But Richards was too late.

When the doctors came they said she had died of heart disease—of joy that kills.

(1894)

▲ ***Comment*** *The surprise, of course, is too much for Mrs. Mallard. Does she die of shock, of despair, of joy that kills? We are left with the impression that Josephine, Richards, and the doctor do not understand that Mrs. Mallard dies not of shock at seeing her husband alive, not out of joy, but out of something like despair. Why does the narrator suggest that none of them realize the truth?*

Some interesting questions are left unresolved by this ending. Is Mrs. Mallard being punished for harboring a desire to be free of her husband? Or is Mrs. Mallard a symbol of repressed womanhood yearning to be free of male bondage? Does the story transcend the sexual identity of its protagonist? Could we imagine a man in Mrs. Mallard's position?

QUESTIONS FOR CRITICAL THINKING AND WRITING

Experience

1. Describe your experience in reading "The Story of an Hour." Did the story surprise you, annoy you, entertain you? Why? Did it hold your interest? Why or why not?
2. Consider the attitude expressed toward Brently Mallard by his wife. What was your reaction to her feelings about her husband? Why?

3. Did your response to Mrs. Mallard change at any point in the story? If so, where—and why? If not, what was your consistent response toward her? Why?

Interpretation

4. Characterize the two major actors in the story—Brently Mallard and his wife. Whom do we understand better? Why?
5. What role do the minor characters play in the story? Are any of those characters dispensable? Why or why not?
6. What is the narrator's attitude toward Mrs. Mallard? Where do you find this attitude most clearly suggested?
7. Why does Mrs. Mallard die? To what extent is her husband responsible for her death? For her unhappiness?
8. What general idea about marriage does the story convey?

Evaluation

9. What personal and social values influence your reading of the story?
10. What values animate Mrs. Mallard's behavior and feelings?
11. What values underlie her husband's treatment of her?
12. To what extent do their values reflect or depart from society's values at the time the story was written?
13. To what extent do their values reflect or depart from today's cultural values?
14. How are any or all of these values measured against your own?

Critical Thinking

15. What do you think might have made Mrs. Mallard's experience of marriage a more positive one? What could Brently Mallard have done to make her happier? To what extent do you think this might have been possible for him?

CHAPTER TWO

Types of Short Fiction

In our discussion of reading stories in Chapter One, we considered three stories—a parable and two modern realistic short stories. But short fiction comes in more than these two varieties. Other popular forms we might know include fairy tales and mystery stories, science fiction stories, and popular romance. While we need not rehearse all of short fiction's various guises, it will nonetheless be useful to describe its more common and enduring types. We begin with some ancient forms.

EARLY FORMS: PARABLE, FABLE, AND TALE

In our discussion of "The Prodigal Son" (page 27), we defined a parable as a brief story that teaches a lesson, often of a religious or spiritual nature. Another early story form is the fable, a relative of the parable.

Like parables, *fables* are brief stories that point to a moral. The difference is that the moral of the fable is stated explicitly. The two forms also differ in subject and tone. Fables often highlight human failings. They frequently include animals as characters, and their tone is satirical. As we have stated, parables are stories through which a religious or spiritual point is made. Their purpose is instructive, their tone serious. Here is a fable attributed to Aesop, whose name has become synonymous with the form.

AESOP

[c. 620–560 b.c.]

Aesop is the author of a famous and influential book of fables, though the collection that he wrote down may actually have been a compilation of fables composed by others as well as himself. Aesop, however, has become synonymous with the fable and is generally recognized as a consummate practitioner of the form.

The Wolf and the Mastiff

A Wolf, who was almost skin and bone—so well did the dogs of the neighborhood keep guard—met, one moonshiny night, a sleek Mastiff, who was, moreover, as strong as he was fat. Bidding the Dog good-night very humbly, he praised his good looks. "It would be easy for you," replied the Mastiff, "to get as fat as I am if you liked." "What shall I have to do?" asked the Wolf. "Almost nothing," answered the Dog. They trotted off together, but, as they went along, the Wolf noticed a bare spot on the Dog's neck. "What is that mark?" said he. "Oh, the merest trifle," answered the Dog; "the collar which I wear when I am tied up is the cause of it." "Tied up!" exclaimed the Wolf, with a sudden stop; "tied up? Can you not always then run where you please?" "Well, not quite always," said the Mastiff; "but what can that matter?" "It matters much to me," rejoined the Wolf, and, leaping away, he ran once more to his native forest.

Moral: Better starve free, than be a fat slave.

Another early form of fiction is the tale. A **tale** is a story that narrates strange or fabulous happenings. A tale does not necessarily point to a moral as a fable or parable does, but it is almost as generalized in its depiction of character and setting. While we may read fables and parables to understand their *meaning,* our interest in tales will generally incline more toward *what happens* and possibly the emotions we experience. The following tale, written in the first century, is from the *Satyricon* of Petronius.

PETRONIUS

[d. A.D. 66?]

Petronius is a Latin writer believed to be one Gaius Petronius who was described as an "arbiter of taste," and is thus known as Petronius Arbiter. He is generally believed to be the author of the Satyricon, *a satirical portrait in prose and verse of life among the upper class in the first century A.D.*

The Widow of Ephesus

Once upon a time there was a certain married woman in the city of Ephesus whose fidelity to her husband was so famous that the women from all the neighboring towns and villages used to troop into Ephesus merely to stare at this prodigy. It happened, however, that her husband one day died. Finding the normal custom of following the cortege with hair unbound and beating her breast in public quite inadequate to express her grief, the lady insisted on following the corpse right into the tomb, an underground vault of the Greek type, and there set herself to guard the body, weeping and wailing night and day. Although in her extremes of grief she was clearly courting death from starvation, her parents were utterly unable to persuade her to leave, and even the magistrates, after one last supreme attempt, were rebuffed and driven away.

In short, all Ephesus had gone into mourning for this extraordinary woman, all the more since the lady was now passing her fifth consecutive day without once tasting food. Beside the failing woman sat her devoted maid, sharing her mistress's grief and relighting the lamp whenever it flickered out. The whole city could speak, in fact, of nothing else: here at last, all classes alike agreed, was the one true example of conjugal fidelity and love.

In the meantime, however, the governor of the province gave orders that several thieves should be crucified in a spot close by the vault where the lady was mourning her dead husband's corpse. So, on the following night, the soldier who had been assigned to keep watch on the crosses so that nobody could remove the thieves' bodies for burial suddenly noticed a light blazing among the tombs and heard the sounds of groaning. And prompted by a natural human curiosity to know who or what was making those sounds, he descended into the vault.

But at the sight of a strikingly beautiful woman, he stopped short in terror, thinking he must be seeing some ghostly apparition out of hell. Then, observing the corpse and seeing the tears on the lady's face and the scratches her fingernails had gashed in her cheeks, he realized what it was: a widow, in inconsolable grief. Promptly fetching his little supper back down to the tomb, he implored the lady not to persist in her sorrow or break her heart with useless mourning. All men alike, he reminded her, have the same end; the same resting place awaits us all. He used, in short, all those platitudes we use to comfort the suffering and bring them back to life. His consolations, being unwelcome, only exasperated the widow more; more violently than ever she beat her breast, and tearing out her hair by the roots, scattered it over the dead man's body. Undismayed, the soldier repeated his arguments and pressed her to take some food, until the little maid, quite overcome by the smell of the wine, succumbed and stretched out her hand to her tempter. Then, restored by the food and wine, she began herself to assail her mistress's obstinate refusal.

"How will it help you," she asked the lady, "if you faint from hunger? Why should you bury yourself alive, and go down to death before the Fates have called you? What does Vergil say?—

Do you suppose the shades and ashes of the dead are by such sorrow touched?

No, begin your life afresh. Shake off these woman's scruples; enjoy the light while you can. Look at that corpse of your poor husband: doesn't it tell you more eloquently than any words that you should live?"

None of us, of course, really dislikes being told that we must eat, that life is to be lived. And the lady was no exception. Weakened by her long days of fasting, her resistance crumbled at last, and she ate the food the soldier offered her as hungrily as the little maid had eaten earlier.

Well, you know what temptations are normally aroused in a man on a full stomach. So the soldier, mustering all those blandishments by means of which he had persuaded the lady to live, now laid determined siege to her virtue. And chaste though she was, the lady found him singularly attractive and his arguments persuasive. As for the maid, she did all she could to help the soldier's cause, repeating like a refrain the appropriate line of Vergil:

If love is pleasing, lady, yield yourself to love.

To make the matter short, the lady's body soon gave up the struggle; she yielded and our happy warrior enjoyed a total triumph on both counts. That very night their marriage was consummated, and they slept together the second and the third night too, carefully shutting the door of the tomb so that any passing friend or stranger would have thought the lady of famous chastity had at last expired over her dead husband's body.

As you can perhaps imagine, our soldier was a very happy man, utterly delighted with his lady's ample beauty and that special charm that a secret love confers. Every night, as soon as the sun had set, he bought what few provisions his slender pay permitted and smuggled them down to the tomb. One night, however, the parents of one of the crucified thieves, noticing that the watch was being badly kept, took advantage of our hero's absence to remove their son's body and bury it. The next morning, of course, the soldier was horror-struck to discover one of the bodies missing from its cross, and ran to tell his mistress of the horrible punishment which awaited him for neglecting his duty. In the circumstances, he told her, he would not wait to be tried and sentenced, but would punish himself then and there with his own sword. All he asked of her was that she make room for another corpse and allow the same gloomy tomb to enclose husband and lover together.

Our lady's heart, however, was no less tender than pure. "God forbid," she cried, "that I should have to see at one and the same time the dead bodies of the only two men I have ever loved. No, better far, I say, to hang the dead than kill the living." With these words, she gave orders that her husband's body should be taken from its bier and strung up on the empty cross. The soldier followed this good advice, and the next morning the whole city wondered by what miracle the dead man had climbed up on the cross.

(1st century A.D.)

Much of the pleasure we take in "The Widow of Ephesus" resides in its series of surprises. We may be amazed at the way the lady expresses her sorrow, surprised at her capitulation to the soldier, and amused (or appalled) at where they make love. Petronius surprises us further with the lady's amazing solution to the soldier's dilemma: putting the corpse of her dead husband up on the cross.

Our admiration for the inventiveness and economy of the tale's action, however, may not eliminate our desire to look for a moral of some sort. But in such a tale, we should search cautiously. Does the story's hypothetical moral have to do with the fickleness of women? Does it suggest that life is to be lived and enjoyed? Or does it imply that people are credulous, that, rather than doubt the widow's unadulterated devotion to her dead husband, they are ready to believe in the miraculous ascent of a dead body onto the cross?

The meaning of "The Widow of Ephesus" is not as clear-cut as those of Aesop's fable or "The Prodigal Son." And in that respect this tale more closely resembles the modern short story, whose meaning is open to a variety of interpretations.

THE SHORT STORY

The *short story* became popular in the nineteenth century. During this period, fiction tended toward a detailed representation of everyday life, typically the lives and experiences familiar to middle-class individuals. Besides its realistic impulse, the modern short story differs from the ancient forms of short fiction in the ratio between summary and scene. Parables, fables, and tales tend to tell what happens in a general overview of the action. Short stories, on the other hand, typically reveal character in dramatic scenes, in moments of action, and in exchanges of dialogue. In addition, the short story has traditionally been more concerned with the revelation of character through flashes of insight and shocks of recognition than the early fictional forms.

Typical features of the modern realistic short story include the following:

1. Its plot illustrates a sequence of causally related incidents.
2. Its characters are recognizably human, and they are motivated by identifiable social and psychological forces.
3. Its time and place are clearly established, with realistic rather than fantastic settings.
4. Its elements—plot, character, setting, style, point of view, irony, symbol and theme—work toward a single effect, unifying the story.

THE NONREALISTIC STORY

In an effort to break away from the prevailing conventions of the realistic short story, some modern storytellers have mixed features of the early story forms—elements of the supernatural, for example—with realistic conventions. I. B. Singer's "Gimpel the Fool" (page 277) includes supernatural elements. Such writers as Gabriel Garcia Márquez in "A Very Old Man with Enormous Wings" (page 272) employ legendary materials in their stories. Shifting back and forth between the realistic and fantastic worlds, these modern storytellers have discovered new ways to represent human experience powerfully and incisively.

Occasionally modern writers of short fiction employ nonrealistic detail so heavily that readers are disoriented and unsettled. When we read a story like Jorge Luis Borges's "The Garden of the Forking Paths" (page 263), we may be uncertain about what exactly is happening. Part of the reason for our initial confusion is attributable to the author's use of surrealistic action or of mystery and riddle. Our confusion derives from our expectations: We expect in part the conventions of realism to operate, and when they do not we need to readjust our sense of what we are reading.

The important thing, however, about nonrealistic stories is to accept them on their own terms. In accepting their break from realistic conventions we increase our chances of responding fully to the pleasures they offer. We also enlarge our understanding of what a short story can be.

THE SHORT NOVEL

The short novel, sometimes called the *novella,* shares characteristics with both the novel and short story. Unlike the short story, which must make its mark quickly, the short novel can allow a slower unfolding of character, incident, idea. The short story's brevity demands a single snapshot of time rather than the collage or mosaic that can be created in a novel, long or short. Yet like the short story, the short novel relies on glimpses of understanding, flashes of insight, quick turns of action to solidify theme or reveal character.

What distinguishes the short novel from its longer counterpart is its greater efficiency and sharper focus. Lacking time and space to accumulate incident, develop character, and amplify theme, the short novel cannot achieve the novel's panoramic sweep. Its advantage lies in a consistency of style and focus and a concentration and compression of effect that are the hallmarks of the short novel form.

Henry James, an American master of the short novel, called it a "blessed" form. And the novelist Vladimir Nabokov suggested that "by diminishing large things and enlarging small ones," the short novel is "intrinsically artistic." One short novel worthy of such high praise is James Joyce's "The Dead"; another is Franz Kafka's "The Metamorphosis."

CHAPTER THREE

Elements of Fiction

In learning to read fiction well, we must understand something about its plot and structure, character, setting, point of view, style and language, symbol, irony, and theme. We will discuss each of these elements separately to highlight its special features. All the elements of a story, however, work together to convey feeling and embody meaning. Thus, our analysis of any one fictional element—plot or character, for example—is related to the other elements and to the work as a whole.

PLOT AND STRUCTURE

Plot is the arrangement of events that make up a story. A story's plot keeps us turning pages: We read to find out what will happen next. For a plot to be effective, it must include a sequence of incidents that bear a significant *causal* relationship to each other. Causality is an important feature of realistic fictional plots: It simply means that one thing happens as a result of something else. An example from E. M. Forster's *Aspects of the Novel* clarifies this point. Forster notes that "The king died and then the queen died" promises a story, but not a plot. Why? Because there is no causal connection between the two deaths. But if the sentence read: "The king died and then the queen died of grief," we have such a connection and hence a plot.*

Many fictional plots turn on a **conflict,** or struggle between opposing forces, that is usually resolved by the end of the story. Typical fictional plots begin with an **exposition** that provides background information we need to make sense of the action, that describes the setting, and that introduces the major characters; these plots develop a series of **complications** or intensifications of the conflict that lead to a *crisis* or

*E. M. Forster, *Aspects of the Novel* (New York: Harcourt, Brace, and World, 1927), p. 130.

moment of great tension. The conflict may reach a **climax** or turning point, a moment of greatest tension that fixes the outcome; then, the action falls off as the plot's complications are sorted out and resolved (the **resolution** or **denouement**). The plot of a typical realistic short story can be diagrammed in the following manner:

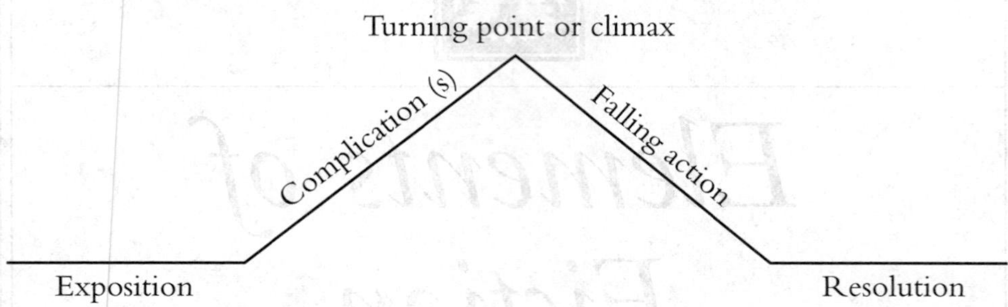

Most stories, of course, do not exhibit such strict formality of design. A story's climactic moment, for example, may occur simultaneously with its ending, with little or no formal resolution. Or its action may rise and fall repeatedly in a jagged and uneven pattern rather than according to the neat symmetry of this diagram.

The action of a realistic story is usually composed of a sequence of causally related actions or events that are not necessarily presented in chronological order. For example, flashbacks that disrupt the linear movement of the plot to present an earlier action are employed in many stories. To distill the plot from William Faulkner's "A Rose for Emily" (later in this chapter), we must untangle a set of events that shift between past and present. In doing so we can clarify our sense of what happened, how it happened, and why.

Whatever the plot of a story may be, the writer has ordered the events with a view both to the overall meaning and to the responses of readers. To appreciate fictional plot, therefore, we should be conscious of our experience in reading a story and what we think and feel at different points. This subjective dimension of our reading experience should prompt us to investigate why the writer has chosen one arrangement of incidents over another. And it should lead us to see how writers control our emotional responses, how they vary the tempo of the action, and how they prepare for reversals and surprises.

Consider the plot of Chopin's "The Story of an Hour," which you read in Chapter One, with its surprises and dramatic reversals. It begins with a reference to the accident in which Brently Mallard is purportedly killed, then shows its effect on his wife. The tempo then slows down as we watch Mrs. Mallard's reaction, particularly her behavior in her room. The plot includes an ironic twist as Mrs. Mallard's shock evolves into joyful self-assertion, and then produces a stronger and more abrupt and climactic ironic reversal with its final action: the arrival of a very much alive Brently Mallard and the collapse and death of Mrs. Mallard. Returning to the beginning of the story, we can see how Chopin set us up for these shifts, how she shaped our expectations only to surprise us.

A story's structure can be examined in relation to its plot. If plot is the sequence of unfolding action, **structure** is the *design* or form of the completed action. In examining plot, we are concerned with causality, with how one action leads into or ties in with another. In examining structure, we look for patterns, for the shape that the story as a whole possesses. Plot directs us to the story in motion, structure to the story at rest. Plot and structure together reveal aspects of the story's artistic design.

Structure is important in fiction for a number of reasons. It satisfies our need for order, for proportion, for arrangement. A story's symmetry or balance of details may please us, as may its alternation of moments of tension and relaxation. Consider the structure of "The Prodigal Son." It begins and ends with a father together with his sons, it includes repeated statements by both father and prodigal son, and it substitutes the discontent of one son for the discontent of the other. Such balances make the story's form aesthetically pleasing. But structure is important for another reason: It provides a clue to a story's meaning.

We can be alert for a story's structure even as we read it for the first time, primarily by paying attention to repeated elements and recurrent details—of action and gesture, of dialogue and description—and to shifts in direction and changes of focus. Repetition signals important connections and relationships in the story, relationships between characters, connections between ideas. Shifts in direction are often signaled by such visual or aural clues as a change of scene, a new voice, blank space in the text.

Keep these considerations about plot and structure in mind as you read Frank O'Connor's "Guests of the Nation." See how its plot, for example, both follows and deviates from the diagram on page 50. Note especially any shifts of emphasis and changes of tempo in the story's action. And once you have finished reading, look back and describe your expectations about the developing action.

FRANK O'CONNOR

[1903–1966]

Frank O'Connor was born Michael O'Donovan in Cork, Ireland. As a short-story writer and playwright, O'Connor was an important figure in the Irish Literary Revival that followed Ireland's independence from English rule in 1921. O'Connor worked initially as a librarian, while the stories he wrote were published in the Irish Statesman. *In 1935 he became codirector, with William Butler Yeats, of Dublin's Abbey Theatre. His stories contain vivid use of Irish speech and manners. His literary criticism includes* The Lonely Voice *(1966), a fine study of the short story.*

Guests of the Nation

I

At dusk the big Englishman, Belcher, would shift his long legs out of the ashes and say "Well, chums, what about it?" and Noble or me would say "All right, chum" (for we had picked up some of their curious expressions), and the little Englishman,

Hawkins, would light the lamp and bring out the cards. Sometimes Jeremiah Donovan would come up and supervise the game and get excited over Hawkins's cards, which he always played badly, and shout at him as if he was one of our own, "Ah, you divil, you, why didn't you play the tray?"

But ordinarily Jeremiah was a sober and contented poor devil like the big Englishman, Belcher, and was looked up to only because he was a fair hand at documents, though he was slow enough even with them. He wore a small cloth hat and big gaiters over his long pants, and you seldom saw him with his hands out of his pockets. He reddened when you talked to him, tilting from toe to heel and back, and looking down all the time at his big farmer's feet. Noble and me used to make fun of his broad accent, because we were from the town.

I couldn't at the time see the point of me and Noble guarding Belcher and Hawkins at all, for it was my belief that you could have planted that pair down anywhere from this to Claregalway and they'd have taken root there like a native weed. I never in my short experience seen two men to take to the country as they did.

They were handed on to us by the Second Battalion when the search for them became too hot, and Noble and myself, being young, took over with a natural feeling of responsibility, but Hawkins made us look like fools when he showed that he knew the country better than we did.

"You're the bloke they calls Bonaparte," he says to me. "Mary Brigid O'Connell told me to ask you what you done with the pair of her brother's socks you borrowed."

For it seemed, as they explained it, that the Second used to have little evenings, and some of the girls of the neighborhood turned in, and, seeing they were such decent chaps, our fellows couldn't leave the two Englishmen out of them. Hawkins learned to dance "The Walls of Limerick," "The Siege of Ennis," and "The Waves of Tory" as well as any of them, though, naturally, we couldn't return the compliment, because our lads at that time did not dance foreign dances on principle.

So whatever privileges Belcher and Hawkins had with the Second they just naturally took with us, and after the first day or two we gave up all pretense of keeping a close eye on them. Not that they could have got far, for they had accents you could cut with a knife and wore khaki tunics and overcoats with civilian pants and boots. But it's my belief that they never had any idea of escaping and were quite content to be where they were.

It was a treat to see how Belcher got off with the old woman of the house where we were staying. She was a great warrant to scold, and cranky even with us, but before ever she had a chance of giving our guests, as I may call them, a lick of her tongue, Belcher had made her his friend for life. She was breaking sticks, and Belcher, who hadn't been more than ten minutes in the house, jumped up from his seat and went over to her.

"Allow me, madam," he says, smiling his queer little smile, "please allow me"; and he takes the bloody hatchet. She was struck too paralytic to speak, and after that, Belcher would be at her heels, carrying a bucket, a basket, or a load of turf, as the case might be. As Noble said, he got into looking before she leapt, and hot water, or any little thing she wanted, Belcher would have it ready for her. For such a huge man (and though I am five foot ten myself I had to look up at him) he had an uncommon shortness—or should I say lack?—of speech. It took us some time to get used to him, walking in and out, like a ghost, without a word. Especially because Hawkins talked enough for a platoon, it was strange to hear big Belcher with his toes in the ashes come out with a solitary "Excuse me, chum," or "That's right, chum." His one and only passion was cards, and I will say for him that he was a good cardplayer. He could have fleeced myself and Noble, but whatever we lost to him Hawkins lost to us, and Hawkins played with the money Belcher gave him.

Hawkins lost to us because he had too much old gab, and we probably lost to Belcher for the same reason. Hawkins and Noble would spit at one another about religion into the early hours of the morning, and Hawkins worried the soul out of Noble, whose brother was a priest, with a string of questions that would puzzle a cardinal. To make it worse, even in treating of holy subjects, Hawkins had a deplorable tongue. I never in all my career met a man who could mix such a variety of cursing and bad language into an argument. He was a terrible man, and a fright to argue. He never did a stroke of work, and when he had no one else to talk to, he got stuck in the old woman.

He met his match in her, for one day when he tried to get her to complain profanely of the drought, she gave him a great come-down by blaming it entirely on Jupiter Pluvius (a deity neither Hawkins nor I had ever heard of, though Noble said that among the pagans it was believed that he had something to do with the rain). Another day he was swearing at the capitalists for starting the German war when the old lady laid down her iron, puckered up her little crab's mouth, and said: "Mr. Hawkins, you can say what you like about the war, and think you'll deceive me because I'm only a simple poor countrywoman, but I know what started the war. It was the Italian Count that stole the heathen divinity out of the temple in Japan. Believe me, Mr. Hawkins, nothing but sorrow and want can follow the people that disturb the hidden powers."

A queer old girl, all right.

2

We had our tea one evening, and Hawkins lit the lamp and we all sat into cards. Jeremiah Donovan came in too, and sat down and watched us for a while, and it suddenly struck me that he had no great love for the two Englishmen. It came as a great surprise to me, because I hadn't noticed anything about him before.

Late in the evening a really terrible argument blew up between Hawkins and Noble, about capitalists and priests and love of your country.

"The capitalists," says Hawkins with an angry gulp, "pays the priests to tell you about the next world so as you won't notice what the bastards are up to in this."

"Nonsense, man!" says Noble, losing his temper. "Before ever a capitalist was thought of, people believed in the next world."

Hawkins stood up as though he was preaching a sermon.

"Oh, they did, did they?" he says with a sneer. "They believed all the things you believe, isn't that what you mean? And you believe that God created Adam, and Adam created Shem, and Shem created Jehoshaphat. You believe all that silly old fairytale about Eve and Eden and the apple. Well, listen to me, chum. If you're entitled to hold a silly belief like that, I'm entitled to hold my silly belief—which is that the first thing your God created was a bleeding capitalist, with morality and Rolls-Royce complete. Am I right, chum?" he says to Belcher.

"You're right, chum," says Belcher with his amused smile, and got up from the table to stretch his long legs into the fire and stroke his moustache. So, seeing that Jeremiah Donovan was going, and that there was no knowing when the argument about religion would be over, I went out with him. We strolled down to the village together, and then he stopped and started blushing and mumbling and saying I ought to be behind, keeping guard on the prisoners. I didn't like the tone he took with me, and anyway I was bored with life in the cottage, so I replied by asking him what the hell we wanted guarding them at all for. I told him I'd talked it over with Noble, and that we'd both rather be out with a fighting column.

"What use are those fellows to us?" says I.

He looked at me in surprise and said: "I thought you knew we were keeping them as hostages."

"Hostages?" I said.

"The enemy have prisoners belonging to us," he says, "and now they're talking of shooting them. If they shoot our prisoners, we'll shoot theirs."

"Shoot them?" I said.

"What else did you think we were keeping them for?" he says.

"Wasn't it very unforeseen of you not to warn Noble and myself of that in the beginning?" I said.

"How was it?" says he. "You might have known it."

"We couldn't know it, Jeremiah Donovan," says I. "How could we when they were on our hands so long?"

"The enemy have our prisoners as long and longer," says he.

"That's not the same thing at all," says I.

"What difference is there?" says he.

I couldn't tell him, because I knew he wouldn't understand. If it was only an old dog that was going to the vet's, you'd try and not get too fond of him, but Jeremiah Donovan wasn't a man that would ever be in danger of that.

"And when is this thing going to be decided?" says I.

"We might hear tonight," he says. "Or tomorrow or the next day at latest. So if it's only hanging round here that's a trouble to you, you'll be free soon enough."

It wasn't the hanging round that was a trouble to me at all by this time. I had worse things to worry about. When I got back to the cottage the argument was still on. Hawkins was holding forth in his best style, maintaining that there was no next world, and Noble was maintaining that there was; but I could see that Hawkins had had the best of it.

"Do you know what, chum?" he was saying with a saucy smile. "I think you're just as big a bleeding unbeliever as I am. You say you believe in the next world, and you know just as much about the next world as I do, which is sweet damn-all. What's heaven? You don't know. Where's heaven? You don't know. You know sweet damn-all! I ask you again, do they wear wings?"

"Very well, then," says Noble, "they do. Is that enough for you? They do wear wings."

"Where do they get them, then? Who makes them? Have they a factory for wings? Have they a sort of store where you hands in your chit and takes your bleeding wings?"

"You're an impossible man to argue with," says Noble. "Now, listen to me—" And they were off again.

It was long after midnight when we locked up and went to bed. As I blew out the candle I told Noble what Jeremiah Donovan was after telling me. Noble took it very quietly. When we'd been in bed about an hour he asked me did I think we ought to tell the Englishmen. I didn't think we should, because it was more than likely that the English wouldn't shoot our men, and even if they did, the brigade officers, who were always up and down with the Second Battalion and knew the Englishmen well, wouldn't be likely to want them plugged. "I think so too," says Noble. "It would be great cruelty to put the wind up them now."

"It was very unforeseen of Jeremiah Donovan anyhow," says I.

It was next morning that we found it so hard to face Belcher and Hawkins. We went about the house all day scarcely saying a word. Belcher didn't seem to notice; he was stretched into the ashes as usual, with his usual look of waiting in quietness for something unforeseen to happen, but Hawkins noticed and put it down to Noble's being beaten in the argument of the night before.

"Why can't you take a discussion in the proper spirit?" he says severely. "You and your Adam and Eve! I'm a Communist, that's what I am. Communist or anarchist, it all comes to much the same thing." And for hours he went round the house, muttering when the fit took him. "Adam and Eve! Adam and Eve! Nothing better to do with their time than picking bleeding apples!"

3

I don't know how we got through that day, but I was very glad when it was over, the tea things were cleared away, and Belcher said in his peaceable way: "Well, chums, what about it?" We sat round the table and Hawkins took out the cards, and just then I heard Jeremiah Donovan's footstep on the path and a dark presentiment crossed my mind. I rose from the table and caught him before he reached the door.

"What do you want?" I asked.

"I want those two soldier friends of yours," he says, getting red.

"Is that the way, Jeremiah Donovan?" I asked.

"That's the way. There were four of our lads shot this morning, one of them a boy of sixteen."

"That's bad," I said.

At that moment Noble followed me out, and the three of us walked down the path together, talking in whispers. Feeney, the local intelligence officer, was standing by the gate.

"What are you going to do about it?" I asked Jeremiah Donovan.

"I want you and Noble to get them out; tell them they're being shifted again; that'll be the quietest way."

"Leave me out of that," says Noble under his breath.

Jeremiah Donovan looks at him hard.

"All right," he says. "You and Feeney get a few tools from the shed and dig a hole by the far end of the bog. Bonaparte and myself will be after you. Don't let anyone see you with the tools. I wouldn't like it to go beyond ourselves."

We saw Feeney and Noble go round to the shed and went in ourselves. I left Jeremiah Donovan to do the explanations. He told them that he had orders to send them back to the Second Battalion. Hawkins let out a mouthful of curses, and you could see that though Belcher didn't say anything, he was a bit upset too. The old woman was for having them stay in spite of us, and she didn't stop advising them until Jeremiah Donovan lost his temper and turned on her. He had a nasty temper, I noticed. It was pitch-dark in the cottage by this time, but no one thought of lighting the lamp, and in the darkness the two Englishmen fetched their topcoats and said good-bye to the old woman.

"Just as a man makes a home of a bleeding place, some bastard at headquarters thinks you're too cushy and shunts you off," says Hawkins, shaking her hand.

"A thousand thanks, madam," says Belcher. "A thousand thanks for everything"—as though he'd made it up.

We went round to the back of the house and down towards the bog. It was only then that Jeremiah Donovan told them. He was shaking with excitement.

"There were four of our fellows shot in Cork this morning and now you're to be shot as a reprisal."

"What are you talking about?" snaps Hawkins. "It's bad enough being mucked about as we are without having to put up with your funny jokes."

"It isn't a joke," says Donovan. "I'm sorry, Hawkins, but it's true," and begins on the usual rigmarole about duty and how unpleasant it is.

I never noticed that people who talk a lot about duty find it much of a trouble to them.

"Oh, cut it out!" says Hawkins.

"Ask Bonaparte," says Donovan, seeing that Hawkins isn't taking him seriously. "Isn't it true, Bonaparte?"

"It is," I say, and Hawkins stops.

"Ah, for Christ's sake, chum."

"I mean it, chum," I say.

"You don't sound as if you meant it."

"If he doesn't mean it, I do," says Donovan, working himself up.

"What have you against me, Jeremiah Donovan?"

"I never said I had anything against you. But why did your people take out four of our prisoners and shoot them in cold blood?"

He took Hawkins by the arm and dragged him on, but it was impossible to make him understand that we were in earnest. I had the Smith and Wesson° in my pocket and I kept fingering it and wondering what I'd do if they put up a fight for it or ran, and wishing to God they'd do one or the other. I knew if they did run for it, that I'd never fire on them. Hawkins wanted to know was Noble in it, and when we said yes, he asked us why Noble wanted to plug him. Why did any of us want to plug him? What had he done to us? Weren't we all chums? Didn't we understand him and didn't he understand us? Did we imagine for an instant that he'd shoot us for all the so-and-so officers in the so-and-so British Army?

By this time we'd reached the bog, and I was so sick I couldn't even answer him. We walked along the edge of it in the darkness, and every now and then Hawkins would call a halt and begin all over again, as if he was wound up, about our being chums, and I knew that nothing but the sight of the grave would convince him that we had to do it. And all the time I was hoping that something would happen; that they'd run for it or that Noble would take over the responsibility from me. I had the feeling that it was worse on Noble than on me.

Smith and Wesson *pistol, like the Webley later*

4

At last we saw the lantern in the distance and made towards it. Noble was carrying it, and Feeney was standing somewhere in the darkness behind him, and the picture of them so still and silent in the bogland brought it home to me that we were in earnest, and banished the last bit of hope I had.

Belcher, on recognizing Noble, said: "Hallo, chum," in his quiet way, but Hawkins flew at him at once, and the argument began all over again, only this time Noble had nothing to say for himself and stood with his head down, holding the lantern between his legs.

It was Jeremiah Donovan who did the answering. For the twentieth time, as though it was haunting his mind, Hawkins asked if anybody thought he'd shoot Noble.

"Yes, you would," says Jeremiah Donovan.

"No, I wouldn't, damn you!"

"You would, because you'd know you'd be shot for not doing it."

"I wouldn't, not if I was to be shot twenty times over. I wouldn't shoot a pal. And Belcher wouldn't—isn't that right, Belcher?"

"That's right, chum," Belcher said, but more by way of answering the question than of joining in the argument. Belcher sounded as though whatever unforeseen thing he'd always been waiting for had come at last.

"Anyway, who says Noble would be shot if I wasn't? What do you think I'd do if I was in his place, out in the middle of a blasted bog?"

"What would you do?" asks Donovan.

"I'd go with him wherever he was going, of course. Share my last bob with him and stick by him through thick and thin. No one can ever say of me that I let down a pal."

"We had enough of this," says Jeremiah Donovan, cocking his revolver. "Is there any message you want to send?"

"No, there isn't."

"Do you want to say your prayers?"

Hawkins came out with a cold-blooded remark that even shocked me and turned on Noble again.

"Listen to me, Noble," he says. "You and me are chums. You can't come over to my side, so I'll come over to your side. That show you I mean what I say? Give me a rifle and I'll go along with you and the other lads."

Nobody answered him. We knew that was no way out.

"Hear what I'm saying?" he says. "I'm through with it. I'm a deserter or anything else you like. I don't believe in your stuff, but it's no worse than mine. That satisfy you?"

Noble raised his head, but Donovan began to speak and he lowered it again without replying.

"For the last time, have you any messages to send?" says Donovan in a cold, excited sort of voice.

"Shut up, Donovan! You don't understand me, but these lads do. They're not the sort to make a pal and kill a pal. They're not the tools of any capitalist."

I alone of the crowd saw Donovan raise his Webley to the back of Hawkins's neck, and as he did so I shut my eyes and tried to pray. Hawkins had begun to say something else when Donovan fired, and as I opened my eyes at the bang, I saw Hawkins stagger at the knees and lie out flat at Noble's feet, slowly and as quiet as a kid falling asleep, with the lantern-light on his lean legs and bright farmer's boots. We all stood very still, watching him settle out in the last agony.

Then Belcher took out a handkerchief and began to tie it about his own eyes (in our excitement we'd forgotten to do the same for Hawkins), and, seeing it wasn't big enough, turned and asked for the loan of mine. I gave it to him and he knotted the two together and pointed with his foot at Hawkins.

"He's not quite dead," he says. "Better give him another."

Sure enough, Hawkins's left knee is beginning to rise. I bend down and put my gun to his head; then, recollecting myself, I get up again. Belcher understands what's in my mind.

"Give him his first," he says. "I don't mind. Poor bastard, we don't know what's happening to him now."

I knelt and fired. By this time I didn't seem to know what I was doing. Belcher, who was fumbling a bit awkwardly with the handkerchiefs, came out with a laugh as he heard the shot. It was the first time I heard him laugh and it sent a shudder down my back; it sounded so unnatural.

"Poor bugger!" he said quietly. "And last night he was so curious about it all. It's very queer, chums, I always think. Now he knows as much about it as they'll ever let him know, and last night he was all in the dark."

Donovan helped him to tie the handkerchiefs about his eyes. "Thanks, chum," he said. Donovan asked if there were any messages he wanted sent.

"No, chum," he says. "Not for me. If any of you would like to write to Hawkins's mother, you'll find a letter from her in his pocket. He and his mother were great chums. But my missus left me eight years ago. Went away with another fellow and took the kid with her. I like the feeling of a home, as you may have noticed, but I couldn't start again after that."

It was an extraordinary thing, but in those few minutes Belcher said more than in all the weeks before. It was just as if the sound of the shot had started a flood of talk in him and he could go on the whole night like that, quite happily, talking about himself. We stood round like fools now that he couldn't see us any longer. Donovan looked at Noble, and Noble shook his head. Then Donovan raised his Webley, and at that moment Belcher gives his queer laugh again. He may have thought we were talking about him, or perhaps he noticed the same thing I'd noticed and couldn't understand it.

"Excuse me, chums," he says. "I feel I'm talking the hell of a lot, and so silly, about my being so handy about a house and things like that. But this thing came on me suddenly. You'll forgive me, I'm sure."

"You don't want to say a prayer?" asked Donovan.

"No, chum," he says. "I don't think it would help. I'm ready, and you boys want to get it over."

"You understand that we're only doing our duty?" says Donovan.

Belcher's head was raised like a blind man's, so that you could only see his chin and the tip of his nose in the lantern-light.

"I never could make out what duty was myself," he said. "I think you're all good lads, if that's what you mean. I'm not complaining."

Noble, just as if he couldn't bear any more of it, raised his fist at Donovan, and in a flash Donovan raised his gun and fired. The big man went over like a sack of meal, and this time there was no need of a second shot.

I don't remember much about the burying, but that it was worse than all the rest because we had to carry them to the grave. It was all mad lonely with nothing but a patch of lantern-light between ourselves and the dark, and birds hooting and screeching all round, disturbed by the guns. Noble went through Hawkins's belongings to find the letter from his mother, and then joined his hands together. He did the same with Belcher. Then, when we'd filled in the grave, we separated from Jeremiah Donovan and Feeney and took our tools back to the shed. All the way we didn't speak a word. The kitchen was dark and cold as we'd left it, and the old woman was sitting over the hearth, saying her beads. We walked past her into the room, and Noble struck a match to light the lamp. She rose quietly and came to the doorway with all her cantankerousness gone.

"What did ye do with them?" she asked in a whisper, and Noble started so that the match went out in his hand.

"What's that?" he asked without turning round.

"I heard ye," she said.

"What did you hear?" asked Noble.

"I heard ye. Do ye think I didn't hear ye, putting the spade back in the houseen?"

Noble struck another match and this time the lamp lit for him.

"Was that what ye did to them?" she asked.

Then, by God, in the very doorway, she fell on her knees and began praying, and after looking at her for a minute or two Noble did the same by the fireplace. I pushed my way out past her and left them at it. I stood at the door, watching the stars and listening to the shrieking of the birds dying out over the bogs. It is so strange what you feel at times like that you can't describe it. Noble says he saw everything ten times the size, as though there were nothing in the whole world but that little patch of bog with the two Englishmen stiffening into it, but with me it was as if the patch of bog where the Englishmen were was a million miles away, and even Noble and the old woman, mumbling behind me, and the birds and the bloody stars were all far away, and I was somehow very small and very lost and lonely like a child astray in the snow. And anything that happened to me afterwards, I never felt the same about again.

(1931)

QUESTIONS FOR REFLECTION

1. "Guests of the Nation" is constructed in four parts. Identify the central action of each part, and explain how the parts are related.
2. Analyze the plot in terms of its exposition, complication, crisis, falling action, and denouement.

CHARACTER

As readers, we often come to care about fictional **characters,** sometimes identifying with them, sometimes judging them. Indeed, if one reason we read stories is to find out what happens (to see how the plot works out), an equally compelling reason is to follow the fortunes of the characters. Plot and character, in fact, are inseparable; we are often less concerned with "what happened" than with "what happened to him or her."

Well-wrought fictional characters come alive for us while we read. And they are real enough to live in our memories long after their stories have ended. We might say that fictional characters possess the kind of reality that dreams have, a reality no less intense for being imagined. Although fictional characters cannot step out of the pages of their stories, we grant them a kind of reality equivalent to if not identical with our own. In doing so we make an implied contract with the writer to suspend our disbelief that his or her story is "just a story," and instead take what happens as if it were real. When we grant fiction this kind of reality, we permit ourselves to be caught up in the life of the story and its characters, perhaps to the point of allowing our own lives to be affected by them.

In short, we approach fictional characters with the same concerns with which we approach people. We need to be alert for how we are to take them, for what we are to make of them, and we need to see how they may reflect our own experience. We need to observe their actions, to listen to *what* they say and *how* they say it, to notice how they relate to other characters and how other characters respond to them, especially to what they say about each other. To make inferences about characters, we look for connections, for links and clues to their function and significance in the story. In analyzing a character or characters' relationships (and fictional characters almost always exist in relation to one another) we relate one act, one speech, one physical detail to another until we understand the character.

Characters in fiction can be conveniently classified as major and minor, static and dynamic. A *major character* is an important figure at the center of the story's action or theme. Usually a character's status as major or minor is clear. On occasion, however, not one but two characters may dominate a story, their relationship being what matters most. In Margaret Atwood's "Happy Endings" (p. 289), for example, no single character dominates the story the way Emily Grierson dominates Faulkner's "A Rose for Emily" (p. 79) or the narrator dominates James Joyce's "Araby" (p. 86).

The major character is sometimes called a **protagonist** whose conflict with an **antagonist** may spark the story's conflict. Supporting the major character are one or more secondary or *minor characters* whose function is partly to illuminate the major characters. Minor characters are often *static* or unchanging: they remain the same from the beginning of a work to the end. *Dynamic characters,* on the other hand, exhibit some kind of change—of attitude, of purpose, of behavior—as the story progresses. We should be careful, however, not to automatically equate major characters with dynamic ones or minor characters with static ones. For example, Emily Grierson, the major character in "A Rose for Emily," is as static as the minor characters Richards and Brently Mallard in Kate Chopin's "The Story of an Hour."

Characterization is the means by which writers present and reveal character. Let's look at the way James Joyce characterizes Mrs. Mooney, a major character in "The Boarding House":

> Mrs. Mooney was a butcher's daughter. She was a woman who was quite able to keep things to herself: a determined woman. She had married her father's foreman and opened a butcher's shop near Spring Gardens.

The method of characterization is narrative description with explicit judgment. We are given facts (she was a butcher's daughter) and interpretive comment (she was a determined woman). From both fact and comment we derive an impression of a strong woman, one who can take care of herself. As a butcher's daughter, she does not stand high on the social ladder. This initial impression is confirmed when we later discover that after her husband had become an alcoholic, had ruined his business, and had gone after Mrs. Mooney with a meat cleaver, she left him and opened a boarding house to support herself and her two children. When the narrator informs us that "she governed the house cunningly and firmly," and when he calls her "a shrewd judge," we come to share his respect for Mrs. Mooney's abilities.

The narrator's view of Mrs. Mooney, however, is not one of unqualified admiration. We learn, for example, that "all the resident young men spoke of her as *the Madam*"—a title suggestive of authority coupled with moral disrepute. Though Mrs. Mooney does not run a house of prostitution, we can't help but connect this title with the fact that Mrs. Mooney allows her nineteen-year-old daughter, Polly, to flirt with the male residents of the boarding house.

Throughout "The Boarding House," Joyce characterizes Mrs. Mooney by coupling narrative description with explicit judgment. In introducing Polly, he varies the technique:

> Polly Mooney, the Madam's daughter, would also sing. She sang:
>
> I'm a . . . naughty girl.
> *You needn't sham.*
> You know I am.

Polly sings this seductive verse presumably with her mother's approval. The implications of the song initially serve to characterize her. Polly is further characterized by means of narrative description with *implied* judgment: "Polly was a slim girl of nineteen; she had light soft hair and a small full mouth." The crucial detail is the full mouth, which suggests sensuality. Joyce's narrator further embellishes Polly's description with the information that "her eyes . . . had a habit of glancing upwards when she spoke with anyone, which made her look like a little perverse madonna." "Madonna" sounds a bit like *madam,* but is quite different in connotation. Polly is associated with innocence and holiness while also being called "perverse," a contradiction that introduces doubts about her character.

Joyce uses two additional devices of characterization in this story: He reveals a character's state of mind through surface details (the fogging of Bob Doran's glasses and the shaking of his hand while he attempts unsuccessfully to shave); he also reveals characters by letting us enter their consciousness, telling us what they think and feel.

We can generalize from these techniques to list the following major methods of revealing character in fiction:

1. Narrative summary without judgment.
2. Narrative description with implied or explicit judgment.
3. Surface details of dress and physical appearance.
4. Characters' actions—what they do.
5. Characters' speech—what they say (and how they say it).
6. Characters' consciousness—what they think and feel.

Keep the devices of characterization in mind as you read Kay Boyle's "Astronomer's Wife." Examine the relationships among the three characters—the astronomer, his wife, and the plumber—noting especially details of speech, gesture, and behavior that reveal the nature of each. Try to account for what you think and feel about each character.

KAY BOYLE
[1902–1992]

Born in Minnesota, Kay Boyle lived in England, Austria, and France for nearly twenty years, until the onset of World War II. From 1946 to 1953 she was a correspondent for The New Yorker *magazine. The author of more than fifteen novels, seven short-story collections, books of poetry, and stories for children, Boyle has also translated books from French into English. Although some of her works depict the human spirit in conflict with oppressive forces, a number of her stories and novels explore the human need for love.*

Astronomer's Wife

There is an evil moment on awakening when all things seem to pause. But for women, they only falter and may be set in action by a single move: a lifted hand and the pendulum will swing, or the voice raised and through every room the pulse takes up its beating. The astronomer's wife felt the interval gaping and at once filled it to the brim. She fetched up her gentle voice and sent it warily down the stairs for coffee, swung her feet out upon the oval mat, and hailed the morning with her bare arms' quivering flesh drawn taut in rhythmic exercise: left, left, left my wife and fourteen children, right, right, right in the middle of the dusty road.

The day would proceed from this, beat by beat, without reflection, like every other day. The astronomer was still asleep, or feigning it, and she, once out of bed, had come into her own possession. Although scarcely ever out of sight of the impenetrable silence of his brow, she would be absent from him all the day in being clean, busy, kind. He was a man of other things, a dreamer. At times he lay still for hours, at others he sat upon the roof behind his telescope, or wandered down the pathway to the road and out across the mountains. This day, like any other, would go on from the removal of the spot left there from dinner on the astronomer's vest to the severe thrashing of the mayonnaise for lunch. That man might be each time the new arching wave, and woman the undertow that sucked him back, were things she had been told by his silence were so.

In spite of the earliness of the hour, the girl had heard her mistress's voice and was coming up the stairs. At the threshold of the bedroom she paused, and said: "Madame, the plumber is here."

The astronomer's wife put on her white and scarlet smock very quickly and buttoned it at the neck. Then she stepped carefully around the motionless spread of water in the hall.

"Tell him to come right up," she said. She laid her hands on the bannisters and stood looking down the wooden stairway. "Ah, I am Mrs. Ames," she said softly as she saw him mounting. "I am Mrs. Ames," she said softly, softly down the flight of stairs. "I am Mrs. Ames," spoken soft as a willow weeping. "The professor is still sleeping. Just step this way."

The plumber himself looked up and saw Mrs. Ames with her voice hushed, speaking to him. She was a youngish woman, but this she had forgotten. The mystery and silence of her husband's mind lay like a chiding finger on her lips. Her eyes were gray, for the light had been extinguished in them. The strange dim halo of her yellow hair was still uncombed and sideways on her head.

For all of his heavy boots, the plumber quieted the sound of his feet, and together they went down the hall, picking their way around the still lake of water that spread as far as the landing and lay docile there. The plumber was a tough, hardy man; but he took off his hat when he spoke to her and looked her fully, almost insolently in the eye.

"Does it come from the wash-basin," he said, "or from the other . . . ?"

"Oh, from the other," said Mrs. Ames without hesitation.

In this place the villas were scattered out few and primitive, and although beauty lay without there was no reflection of her face within. Here all was awkward and unfit; a sense of wrestling with uncouth forces gave everything an austere countenance. Even the plumber, dealing as does a woman with matters under hand, was grave and stately. The mountains round about seemed to have cast them into the shadow of great dignity.

Mrs. Ames began speaking of their arrival that summer in the little villa, mourning each event as it followed on the other.

"Then, just before going to bed last night," she said, "I noticed something was unusual."

The plumber cast down a folded square of sack-cloth on the brimming floor and laid his leather apron on it. Then he stepped boldly onto the heart of the island it shaped and looked long into the overflowing bowl.

"The water should be stopped from the meter in the garden," he said at last.

"Oh, I did that," said Mrs. Ames, "the very first thing last night. I turned it off at once, in my nightgown, as soon as I saw what was happening. But all this had already run in."

The plumber looked for a moment at her red kid slippers. She was standing just at the edge of the clear, pure-seeming tide.

"It's no doubt the soil lines," he said severely. "It may be that something has stopped them, but my opinion is that the water seals aren't working. That's the trouble often enough in such cases. If you had a valve you wouldn't be caught like this."

Mrs. Ames did not know how to meet this rebuke. She stood, swaying a little, looking into the plumber's blue relentless eye.

"I'm sorry—I'm sorry that my husband," she said, "is still—resting and cannot go into this with you. I'm sure it must be very interesting. . . ."

"You'll probably have to have the traps sealed," said the plumber grimly, and at the sound of this Mrs. Ames' hand flew in dismay to the side of her face. The plumber made no move, but the set of his mouth as he looked at her seemed to soften. "Anyway, I'll have a look from the garden end," he said.

"Oh, do," said the astronomer's wife in relief. Here was a man who spoke of action and object as simply as women did! But however hushed her voice had been, it carried clearly to Professor Ames who lay, dreaming and solitary, upon his bed. He heard their footsteps come down the hall, pause, and skip across the pool of overflow.

"Katherine!" said the astronomer in a ringing tone. "There's a problem worthy of your mettle!"

Mrs. Ames did not turn her head, but led the plumber swiftly down the stairs. When the sun in the garden struck her face, he saw there was a wave of color in it, but this may have been anything but shame.

"You see how it is," said the plumber, as if leading her mind away. "The drains run from these houses right down the hill, big enough for a man to stand upright in them, and clean as a whistle too." There they stood in the garden with the vegetation flowering in disorder all about. The plumber looked at the astronomer's wife. "They come out at the torrent on the other side of the forest beyond there," he said.

But the words the astronomer had spoken still sounded in her in despair. The mind of man, she knew, made steep and sprightly flights, pursued illusion, took foothold in the nameless things that cannot pass between the thumb and finger. But whenever the astronomer gave voice to the thoughts that soared within him, she returned in gratitude to the long expanses of his silence. Desert-like they stretched behind and before the articulation of his scorn.

Life, life is an open sea, she sought to explain it in sorrow, and to survive women cling to the floating debris on the tide. But the plumber had suddenly fallen upon his knees in the grass and had crooked his fingers through the ring of the drains' trap-door. When she looked down she saw that he was looking up into her face, and she saw too that his hair was as light as gold.

"Perhaps Mr. Ames," he said rather bitterly, "would like to come down with me and have a look around?"

"Down?" said Mrs. Ames in wonder.

"Into the drains," said the plumber brutally. "They're a study for a man who likes to know what's what."

"Oh, Mr. Ames," said Mrs. Ames in confusion. "He's still—still in bed, you see."

The plumber lifted his strong, weathered face and looked curiously at her. Surely it seemed to him strange for a man to linger in bed, with the sun pouring yellow as wine all over the place. The astronomer's wife saw his lean cheeks, his high, rugged bones, and the deep seams in his brow. His flesh was as firm and clean as wood, stained richly tan with the climate's rigor. His fingers were blunt, but comprehensible to her, gripped in the ring and holding the iron door wide. The backs of his hands were bound round and round with ripe blue veins of blood.

"At any rate," said the astronomer's wife, and the thought of it moved her lips to smile a little, "Mr. Ames would never go down there alive. He likes going up," she said. And she, in her turn, pointed, but impudently, towards the heavens. "On the roof. Or on the mountains. He's been up on the tops of them many times."

"It's a matter of habit," said the plumber, and suddenly he went down the trap. Mrs. Ames saw a bright little piece of his hair still shining, like a star, long after the rest of him had gone. Out of the depths, his voice, hollow and dark with foreboding, returned to her. "I think something has stopped the elbow," was what he said.

This was speech that touched her flesh and bone and made her wonder. When her husband spoke of height, having no sense of it, she could not picture it nor hear. Depth or magic passed her by unless a name were given. But madness in a daily shape, as elbow stopped, she saw clearly and well. She sat down on the grasses, bewildered that it should be a man who had spoken to her so.

She saw the weeds springing up, and she did not move to tear them up from life. She sat powerless, her senses veiled, with no action taking shape beneath her hands. In this way some men sat for hours on end, she knew, tracking a single thought back to its origin. The mind of man could balance and divide, weed out, destroy. She sat on the full, burdened grasses, seeking to think, and dimly waiting for the plumber to return.

Whereas her husband had always gone up, as the dead go, she knew now that there were others who went down, like the corporeal being of the dead. That men were then divided into two bodies now seemed clear to Mrs. Ames. This knowledge stunned her with its simplicity and took the uneasy motion from her limbs. She could not stir, but sat facing the mountains' rocky flanks, and harking in silence to lucidity. Her husband was the mind, this other man the meat, of all mankind.

After a little, the plumber emerged from the earth: first the light top of his head, then the burnt brow, and then the blue eyes fringed with whitest lash. He braced his thick hands flat on the pavings of the garden-path and swung himself completely from the pit.

"It's the soil lines," he said pleasantly. "The gases," he said as he looked down upon her lifted face, "are backing up the drains."

"What in the world are we going to do?" said the astronomer's wife softly. There was a young and strange delight in putting questions to which true answers would be given. Everything the astronomer had ever said to her was a continuous query to which there could be no response.

"Ah, come, now," said the plumber, looking down and smiling. "There's a remedy for every ill, you know. Sometimes it may be that," he said as if speaking to a child, "or sometimes the other thing. But there's always a help for everything amiss."

Things come out of herbs and make you young again, he might have been saying to her; or the first good rain will quench any drought; or time of itself will put a broken bone together.

"I'm going to follow the ground pipe out right to the torrent," the plumber was saying. "The trouble's between here and there and I'll find it on the way. There's nothing at all that can't be done over for the caring," he was saying, and his eyes were fastened on her face in insolence, or gentleness, or love.

The astronomer's wife stood up, fixed a pin in her hair, and turned around towards the kitchen. Even while she was calling the servant's name, the plumber began speaking again.

"I once had a cow that lost her cud," the plumber was saying. The girl came out on the kitchen-step and Mrs. Ames stood smiling at her in the sun.

"The trouble is very serious, very serious," she said across the garden. "When Mr. Ames gets up, please tell him I've gone down."

She pointed briefly to the open door in the pathway, and the plumber hoisted his kit on his arm and put out his hand to help her down.

"But I made her another in no time," he was saying, "out of flowers and things and what-not."

"Oh," said the astronomer's wife in wonder as she stepped into the heart of the earth. She took his arm, knowing that what he said was true.

(1936)

QUESTIONS FOR REFLECTION

1. "Astronomer's Wife" is built on two sets of character contrasts: wife versus husband; astronomer versus plumber. Explain how the characters differ. Consider physical descriptions as well as actions, words, and gestures.
2. Describe the wife's relationship with her husband.

SETTING

Writers tend to describe the world they know, its sights and sounds, its colors, textures, and accents. Stories come to life in a place, rooted in the soil of a writer's memories. This place or location of a story's action along with the time in which it occurs is its **setting.** For writers like James Joyce and William Faulkner, setting is essential to meaning. Functioning as more than a simple backdrop for action, it provides a historical and cultural context that enhances our understanding of the characters. In Joyce's "The Boarding House," for example, Bob Doran's Irish Catholicism powerfully influences his decision to marry Polly, to make "reparation" for his sexual sin. In Faulkner's "A Rose for Emily," Emily Grierson's stubborn resistance to change is a reflection of both the decay of Jefferson (a fictional town in Mississippi) and the shabby gentility of the post–Civil War South. Faulkner intensifies the idea of decline by his careful description of the Grierson house:

> It was a big, squarish frame house that had once been white, decorated with cupolas and spires and scrolled balconies in the heavily lightsome style of the seventies, set on what had once been our most select street. But garages and cotton gins had encroached and obliterated even the august names of that neighborhood; only Miss Emily's house was left, lifting its stubborn and coquettish decay above the cotton wagons and the gasoline pumps—an eyesore among eyesores.

Later we are taken inside the house, and finally inside one very unusual room. In each case, the physical details of setting are associated with the values, ideals, and attitudes of that place in different times. Setting in "A Rose for Emily" (and in fiction in general) is an important dimension of meaning since it reflects character and embodies theme.

Setting is important for an additional reason: it symbolizes the emotional state of the characters. In Kate Chopin's "The Story of an Hour" (see Chapter One), for example, Mrs. Mallard looks out the window and observes life going on—birds singing, a peddler working, trees blooming. The contrast between the enclosed space of her room and the world outside points toward Mrs. Mallard's subjugation and her desire for freedom. This contrast underscores a significant difference between the natural and the human worlds: Nature is free of social conventions and of such obligations as marriage.

Writers know that they must root stories in a reality their readers can experience imaginatively. The surest route to this end is through concreteness and particularity. Both Joyce's Dublin and Faulkner's Jefferson are realistic settings. Yet both cities transcend their particular locale to become symbolic, representative places.

One of our finest American storytellers, Eudora Welty, has spoken eloquently about the importance of one aspect of setting—place–in fiction. She suggests that "fiction depends for its life on place." Place is the "conductor of all the currents of emotion and belief and moral conviction that charge out from the story." Place, in Welty's view, both makes and keeps the characters real; it animates them, so much so that, as she observes, "every story would be another story, and unrecognizable as art, if it took up its characters and plot and happened somewhere else."*

In "Shiloh" by Bobbie Ann Mason you will read about a married couple who are trying to discover what they want from their lives. Consider what the setting contributes to our understanding of the story.

BOBBIE ANN MASON

[b. 1940]

Bobbie Ann Mason was born in Kentucky, and she draws her fictional material from the lives of rural and working-class people from that part of the United States. Shiloh and Other Stories *(1962), Mason's first book, deals with the impact of the outside world via television on people whose lives do not include knowledge and experience that most Americans take for granted. Her writing vividly conveys the regionalisms and sense of place of her native Kentucky. Before becoming a fiction writer, Mason worked as a college teacher, having earned a doctorate at the University of Connecticut.*

Shiloh

Leroy Moffitt's wife, Norma Jean, is working on her pectorals. She lifts three-pound dumbbells to warm up, then progresses to a twenty-pound barbell. Standing with her legs apart, she reminds Leroy of Wonder Woman.

"I'd give anything if I could just get these muscles to where they're real hard," says Norma Jean. "Feel this arm. It's not as hard as the other one."

"That's 'cause you're right-handed," says Leroy, dodging as she swings the barbell in an arc.

"Do you think so?"

"Sure."

Leroy is a truckdriver. He injured his leg in a highway accident four months ago, and his physical therapy, which involves weights and a pulley, prompted Norma Jean to try building herself up. Now she is attending a body-building class. Leroy has been collecting temporary disability since his tractor-trailer jackknifed in Missouri, badly twisting his left leg in its socket. He has a steel pin in his hip. He will probably not be able to drive his rig again. It sits in the backyard, like a gigantic bird that has flown

*See Eudora Welty's essay "Place in Fiction" in her book *The Eye of the Story* (New York: Random House, 1979), p. 116–33.

home to roost. Leroy has been home in Kentucky for three months, and his leg is almost healed, but the accident frightened him and he does not want to drive any more long hauls. He is not sure what to do next. In the meantime, he makes things from craft kits. He started by building a miniature log cabin from notched Popsicle sticks. He varnished it and placed it on the TV set, where it remains. It reminds him of a rustic Nativity scene. Then he tried string art (sailing ships on black velvet), a macramé owl kit, a snap-together B-17 Flying Fortress, and a lamp made out of a model truck, with a light fixture screwed in the top of the cab. At first the kits were diversions, something to kill time, but now he is thinking about building a full-scale log house from a kit. It would be considerably cheaper than building a regular house, and besides, Leroy has grown to appreciate how things are put together. He has begun to realize that in all the years he was on the road he never took time to examine anything. He was always flying past scenery.

"They won't let you build a log cabin in any of the new subdivisions," Norma Jean tells him.

"They will if I tell them it's for you," he says, teasing her. Ever since they were married, he has promised Norma Jean he would build her a new home one day. They have always rented, and the house they live in is small and nondescript. It does not even feel like a home, Leroy realizes now.

Norma Jean works at the Rexall drugstore, and she has acquired an amazing amount of information about cosmetics. When she explains to Leroy the three stages of complexion care, involving creams, toners, and moisturizers, he thinks happily of other petroleum products—axle grease, diesel fuel. This is a connection between him and Norma Jean. Since he has been home, he has felt unusually tender about his wife and guilty over his long absences. But he can't tell what she feels about him. Norma Jean has never complained about his traveling; she has never made hurt remarks, like calling his truck a "widow-maker." He is reasonably certain she has been faithful to him, but he wishes she would celebrate his permanent homecoming more happily. Norma Jean is often startled to find Leroy at home, and he thinks she seems a little disappointed about it. Perhaps he reminds her too much of the early days of their marriage, before he went on the road. They had a child who died as an infant, years ago. They never speak about their memories of Randy, which have almost faded, but now that Leroy is home all the time, they sometimes feel awkward around each other, and Leroy wonders if one of them should mention the child. He has the feeling that they are waking up out of a dream together—that they must create a new marriage, start afresh. They are lucky they are still married. Leroy has read that for most people losing a child destroys the marriage—or else he heard this on *Donahue*. He can't always remember where he learns things anymore.

At Christmas, Leroy bought an electric organ for Norma Jean. She used to play the piano when she was in high school. "It don't leave you," she told him once. "It's like riding a bicycle."

The new instrument had so many keys and buttons that she was bewildered by it at first. She touched the keys tentatively, pushed some buttons, then pecked out "Chopsticks." It came out in an amplified fox-trot rhythm, with marimba sounds.

"It's an orchestra!" she cried.

The organ had a pecan-look finish and eighteen preset chords, with optional flute, violin, trumpet, clarinet, and banjo accompaniments. Norma Jean mastered the organ almost immediately. At first she played Christmas songs. Then she bought *The Sixties Songbook* and learned every tune in it, adding variations to each with the rows of brightly colored buttons.

"I didn't like these old songs back then," she said. "But I have this crazy feeling I missed something."

"You didn't miss a thing," said Leroy.

Leroy likes to lie on the couch and smoke a joint and listen to Norma Jean play "Can't Take My Eyes Off You" and "I'll Be Back." He is back again. After fifteen years on the road, he is finally settling down with the woman he loves. She is still pretty. Her skin is flawless. Her frosted curls resemble pencil trimmings.

Now that Leroy has come home to stay, he notices how much the town has changed. Subdivisions are spreading across western Kentucky like an oil slick. The sign at the edge of town says "Pop: 11,500"—only seven hundred more than it said twenty years before. Leroy can't figure out who is living in all the new houses. The farmers who used to gather around the courthouse square on Saturday afternoons to play checkers and spit tobacco juice have gone. It has been years since Leroy has thought about the farmers, and they have disappeared without his noticing.

Leroy meets a kid named Stevie Hamilton in the parking lot at the new shopping center. While they pretend to be strangers meeting over a stalled car, Stevie tosses an ounce of marijuana under the front seat of Leroy's car. Stevie is wearing orange jogging shoes and a T-shirt that says CHATTAHOOCHEE SUPER-RAT. His father is a prominent doctor who lives in one of the expensive subdivisions in a new white-columned brick house that looks like a funeral parlor. In the phone book under his name there is a separate number, with the listing "Teenagers."

"Where do you get this stuff?" asks Leroy. "From your pappy?"

"That's for me to know and you to find out," Stevie says. He is slit-eyed and skinny.

"What else you got?"

"What you interested in?"

"Nothing special. Just wondered."

Leroy used to take speed on the road. Now he has to go slowly. He needs to be mellow. He leans back against the car and says, "I'm aiming to build me a log house, soon as I get time. My wife, though, I don't think she likes the idea."

"Well, let me know when you want me again," Stevie says. He has a cigarette in his cupped palm, as though sheltering it from the wind. He takes a long drag, then stomps it on the asphalt and slouches away.

Stevie's father was two years ahead of Leroy in high school. Leroy is thirty-four. He married Norma Jean when they were both eighteen, and their child Randy was born a few months later, but he died at the age of four months and three days. He would be about Stevie's age now. Norma Jean and Leroy were at the drive-in, watching a double feature (*Dr. Strangelove* and *Lover Come Back*), and the baby was sleeping in the back seat. When the first movie ended, the baby was dead. It was the sudden infant death syndrome. Leroy remembers handing Randy to a nurse at the emergency room, as though he were offering her a large doll as a present. A dead baby feels like a sack of flour. "It just happens sometimes," said the doctor, in what Leroy always recalls as a nonchalant tone. Leroy can hardly remember the child anymore, but he still sees vividly a scene from *Dr. Strangelove* in which the President of the United States was talking in a folksy voice on the hot line to the Soviet premier about the bomber accidentally headed toward Russia. He was in the War Room, and the world map was lit up. Leroy remembers Norma Jean standing catatonically beside him in the hospital and himself thinking: Who is this strange girl? He had forgotten who she was. Now scientists are saying that crib death is caused by a virus. Nobody knows anything, Leroy thinks. The answers are always changing.

When Leroy gets home from the shopping center, Norma Jean's mother, Mabel Beasley, is there. Until this year, Leroy has not realized how much time she spends with Norma Jean. When she visits, she inspects the closets and then the plants, informing Norma Jean when a plant is droopy or yellow. Mabel calls the plants "flowers," although there are never any blooms. She always notices if Norma Jean's laundry is piling up. Mabel is a short, overweight woman whose tight, brown-dyed curls look more like a wig than the actual wig she sometimes wears. Today she has brought Norma Jean an off-white dust ruffle she made for the bed; Mabel works in a custom-upholstery shop.

"This is the tenth one I made this year," Mabel says. "I got started and couldn't stop."

"It's real pretty," says Norma Jean.

"Now we can hide things under the bed," says Leroy, who gets along with his mother-in-law primarily by joking with her. Mabel has never really forgiven him for disgracing her by getting Norma Jean pregnant. When the baby died, she said that fate was mocking her.

"What's that thing?" Mabel says to Leroy in a loud voice, pointing to a tangle of yarn on a piece of canvas.

Leroy holds it up for Mabel to see. "It's my needlepoint," he explains. "This is a *Star Trek* pillow cover."

"That's what a woman would do," says Mabel. "Great day in the morning!"

"All the big football players on TV do it," he says.

"Why, Leroy, you're always trying to fool me. I don't believe you for one minute. You don't know what to do with yourself—that's the whole trouble. Sewing!"

"I'm aiming to build us a log house," says Leroy. "Soon as my plans come."

"Like *heck* you are," says Norma Jean. She takes Leroy's needlepoint and shoves it into a drawer. "You have to find a job first. Nobody can afford to build now anyway."

Mabel straightens her girdle and says, "I still think before you get tied down y'all ought to take a little run to Shiloh."

"One of these days, Mama," Norma Jean says impatiently.

Mabel is talking about Shiloh, Tennessee. For the past few years, she has been urging Leroy and Norma Jean to visit the Civil War battleground there. Mabel went there on her honeymoon—the only real trip she ever took. Her husband died of a perforated ulcer when Norma Jean was ten, but Mabel, who was accepted into the United Daughters of the Confederacy in 1975, is still preoccupied with going back to Shiloh.

"I've been to kingdom come and back in that truck out yonder," Leroy says to Mabel, "but we never yet set foot in that battleground. Ain't that something? How did I miss it?"

"It's not even that far," Mabel says.

After Mabel leaves, Norma Jean reads to Leroy from a list she has made. "Things you could do," she announces. "You could get a job as a guard at Union Carbide, where they'd let you set on a stool. You could get on at the lumberyard. You could do a little carpenter work, if you want to build so bad. You could—"

"I can't do something where I'd have to stand up all day."

"You ought to try standing up all day behind a cosmetics counter. It's amazing that I have strong feet, coming from two parents that never had strong feet at all." At the moment Norma Jean is holding on to the kitchen counter, raising her knees one at a time as she talks. She is wearing two-pound ankle weights.

"Don't worry," says Leroy. "I'll do something."

"You could truck calves to slaughter for somebody. You wouldn't have to drive any big old truck for that."

"I'm going to build you this house," says Leroy. "I want to make you a real home."

"I don't want to live in any log cabin."

"It's not a cabin. It's a house."

"I don't care. It looks like a cabin."

"You and me together could lift those logs. It's just like lifting weights."

Norma Jean doesn't answer. Under her breath, she is counting. Now she is marching through the kitchen. She is doing goose steps.

Before his accident, when Leroy came home he used to stay in the house with Norma Jean, watching TV in bed and playing cards. She would cook fried chicken, picnic ham, chocolate pie—all his favorites. Now he is home alone much of the time. In the mornings, Norma Jean disappears, leaving a cooling place in the bed. She eats a cereal called Body Buddies, and she leaves the bowl on the table, with the soggy tan balls floating in a milk puddle. He sees things about Norma Jean that he never realized before. When she chops onions, she stares off into a corner, as if she can't bear to look. She puts on her house slippers almost precisely at nine o'clock every evening and nudges her jogging shoes under the couch. She saves bread heels for the birds. Leroy watches the birds at the feeder. He notices the peculiar way goldfinches fly past the window. They close their wings, then fall, then spread their wings to catch and lift themselves. He wonders if they close their eyes when they fall. Norma Jean closes her eyes when they are in bed. She wants the lights turned out. Even then, he is sure she closes her eyes.

He goes for long drives around town. He tends to drive a car rather carelessly. Power steering and an automatic shift make a car feel so small and inconsequential that his body is hardly involved in the driving process. His injured leg stretches out comfortably. Once or twice he has almost hit something, but even the prospect of an accident seems minor in a car. He cruises the new subdivisions, feeling like a criminal rehearsing for a robbery. Norma Jean is probably right about a log house being inappropriate here in the new subdivisions. All the houses look grand and complicated. They depress him.

One day when Leroy comes home from a drive he finds Norma Jean in tears. She is in the kitchen making a potato and mushroom-soup casserole, with grated-cheese topping. She is crying because her mother caught her smoking.

"I didn't hear her coming. I was standing here puffing away pretty as you please," Norma Jean says, wiping her eyes.

"I knew it would happen sooner or later," says Leroy, putting his arm around her.

"She don't know the meaning of the word 'knock,'" says Norma Jean. "It's a wonder she hadn't caught me years ago."

"Think of it this way," Leroy says. "What if she caught me with a joint?"

"You better not let her!" Norma Jean shrieks. "I'm warning you, Leroy Moffitt!"

"I'm just kidding. Here, play me a tune. That'll help you relax."

Norma Jean puts the casserole in the oven and sets the timer. Then she plays a ragtime tune, with horns and banjo, as Leroy lights up a joint and lies on the couch, laughing to himself about Mabel's catching him at it. He thinks of Stevie Hamilton—a doctor's son pushing grass. Everything is funny. The whole town seems crazy and small. He is reminded of Virgil Mathis, a boastful policeman Leroy used to shoot pool with. Virgil recently led a drug bust in a back room at a bowling alley, where he seized ten thousand dollars' worth of marijuana. The newspaper had a picture of him holding up the bags of grass and grinning widely. Right now, Leroy can imagine Virgil breaking down the door and arresting him with a lungful of smoke. Virgil would probably have been alerted to the scene because of all the racket Norma Jean is making. Now she sounds like a hard-rock band. Norma Jean is terrific. When she switches to a Latin-rhythm version of "Sunshine Superman," Leroy hums along. Norma Jean's foot goes up and down, up and down.

"Well, what do you think?" Leroy says, when Norma Jean pauses to search through her music.

"What do I think about what?"

His mind has gone blank. Then he says, "I'll sell my rig and build us a house." That wasn't what he wanted to say. He wanted to know what she thought—what she *really* thought—about them.

"Don't start in on that again," says Norma Jean. She begins playing "Who'll Be the Next in Line?"

Leroy used to tell hitchhikers his whole life story—about his travels, his hometown, the baby. He would end with a question: "Well, what do you think?" It was just a rhetorical question. In time, he had the feeling that he'd been telling the same story over and over to the same hitchhikers. He quit talking to hitchhikers when he realized how his voice sounded—whining and self-pitying, like some teenage-tragedy song. Now Leroy has the sudden impulse to tell Norma Jean about himself, as if he had just met her. They have known each other so long they have forgotten a lot about each other. They could become reacquainted. But when the oven timer goes off and she runs to the kitchen, he forgets why he wants to do this.

The next day, Mabel drops by. It is Saturday and Norma Jean is cleaning. Leroy is studying the plans of his log house, which have finally come in the mail. He has them spread out on the table—big sheets of stiff blue paper, with diagrams and numbers printed in white. While Norma Jean runs the vacuum, Mabel drinks coffee. She sets her coffee cup on a blueprint.

"I'm just waiting for time to pass," she says to Leroy, drumming her fingers on the table.

As soon as Norma Jean switches off the vacuum, Mabel says in a loud voice, "Did you hear about the datsun dog that killed the baby?"

Norma Jean says, "The word is 'dachshund.' "

"They put the dog on trial. It chewed the baby's legs off. The mother was in the next room all the time." She raises her voice. "They thought it was neglect."

Norma Jean is holding her ears. Leroy manages to open the refrigerator and get some Diet Pepsi to offer Mabel. Mabel still has some coffee and she waves away the Pepsi.

"Datsuns are like that," Mabel says. "They're jealous dogs. They'll tear a place to pieces if you don't keep an eye on them."

"You better watch out what you're saying, Mabel," says Leroy.

"Well, facts is facts."

Leroy looks out the window at his rig. It is like a huge piece of furniture gathering dust in the backyard. Pretty soon it will be an antique. He hears the vacuum cleaner. Norma Jean seems to be cleaning the living room rug again.

Later, she says to Leroy, "She just said that about the baby because she caught me smoking. She's trying to pay me back."

"What are you talking about?" Leroy says, nervously shuffling blueprints.

"You know good and well," Norma Jean says. She is sitting in a kitchen chair with her feet up and her arms wrapped around her knees. She looks small and helpless. She says, "The very idea, her bringing up a subject like that! Saying it was neglect."

"She didn't mean that," Leroy says.

"She might not have *thought* she meant it. She always says things like that. You don't know how she goes on."

"But she didn't really mean it. She was just talking."

Leroy opens a king-sized bottle of beer and pours it into two glasses, dividing it carefully. He hands a glass to Norma Jean and she takes it from him mechanically. For a long time, they sit by the kitchen window watching the birds at the feeder.

Something is happening. Norma Jean is going to night school. She has graduated from her six-week body-building course and now she is taking an adult-education course in composition at Paducah Community College. She spends her evenings outlining paragraphs.

"First you have a topic sentence," she explains to Leroy. "Then you divide it up. Your secondary topic has to be connected to your primary topic."

To Leroy, this sounds intimidating. "I never was any good in English," he says.

"It makes a lot of sense."

"What are you doing this for, anyhow?"

She shrugs. "It's something to do." She stands up and lifts her dumbbells a few times.

"Driving a rig, nobody cared about my English."

"I'm not criticizing your English."

Norma Jean used to say, "If I lose ten minutes' sleep, I just drag all day." Now she stays up late, writing compositions. She got a B on her first paper—a how-to theme on soup-based casseroles. Recently Norma Jean has been cooking unusual foods—tacos, lasagna, Bombay chicken. She doesn't play the organ anymore, though her second paper was called "Why Music Is Important to Me." She sits at the kitchen table, concentrating on her outlines, while Leroy plays with his log house plans, practicing with a set of Lincoln Logs. The thought of getting a truckload of notched, numbered logs scares him, and he wants to be prepared. As he and Norma Jean work together at the kitchen table, Leroy has the hopeful thought that they are sharing something, but he knows he is a fool to think this. Norma Jean is miles away. He knows he is going to lose her. Like Mabel, he is just waiting for time to pass.

One day, Mabel is there before Norma Jean gets home from work, and Leroy finds himself confiding in her. Mabel, he realizes, must know Norma Jean better than he does.

"I don't know what's got into that girl," Mabel says. "She used to go to bed with the chickens. Now you say she's up all hours. Plus her a-smoking. I like to died."

"I want to make her this beautiful home," Leroy says, indicating the Lincoln Logs. "I don't think she even wants it. Maybe she was happier with me gone."

"She don't know what to make of you, coming home like this."

"Is that it?"

Mabel takes the roof off his Lincoln Log cabin. "You couldn't get me in a log cabin," she says. "I was raised in one. It's no picnic, let me tell you."

"They're different now," says Leroy.

"I tell you what," Mabel says, smiling oddly at Leroy.

"What?"

"Take her on down to Shiloh. Y'all need to get out together, stir a little. Her brain's all balled up over them books."

Leroy can see traces of Norma Jean's features in her mother's face. Mabel's worn face has the texture of crinkled cotton, but suddenly she looks pretty. It occurs to Leroy that Mabel has been hinting all along that she wants them to take her with them to Shiloh.

"Let's all go to Shiloh," he says. "You and me and her. Come Sunday."

Mabel throws up her hands in protest. "Oh, no, not me. Young folks want to be by theirselves."

When Norma Jean comes in with groceries, Leroy says excitedly, "Your mama here's been dying to go to Shiloh for thirty-five years. It's about time we went, don't you think?"

"I'm not going to butt in on anybody's second honeymoon," Mabel says.

"Who's going on a honeymoon, for Christ's sake?" Norma Jean says loudly.

"I never raised no daughter of mine to talk that-a-way," Mabel says.

"You ain't seen nothing yet," says Norma Jean. She starts putting away boxes and cans, slamming cabinet doors.

"There's a log cabin at Shiloh," Mabel says. "It was there during the battle. There's bullet holes in it."

"When are you going to *shut up* about Shiloh, Mama?" asks Norma Jean.

"I always thought Shiloh was the prettiest place, so full of history," Mabel goes on. "I just hoped y'all could see it once before I die, so you could tell me about it." Later, she whispers to Leroy, "You do what I said. A little change is what she needs."

"Your name means 'the king,'" Norma Jean says to Leroy that evening. He is trying to get her to go to Shiloh, and she is reading a book about another century.

"Well, I reckon I ought to be right proud."

"I guess so."

"Am I still king around here?"

Norma Jean flexes her biceps and feels them for hardness. "I'm not fooling around with anybody, if that's what you mean," she says.

"Would you tell me if you were?"

"I don't know."

"What does *your* name mean?"

"It was Marilyn Monroe's real name."

"No kidding!"

"Norma comes from the Normans. They were invaders," she says. She closes her book and looks hard at Leroy. "I'll go to Shiloh with you if you'll stop staring at me."

On Sunday, Norma Jean packs a picnic and they go to Shiloh. To Leroy's relief, Mabel says she does not want to come with them. Norma Jean drives, and Leroy, sitting beside her, feels like some boring hitchhiker she has picked up. He tries some conversation, but she answers him in monosyllables. At Shiloh, she drives aimlessly through the park, past bluffs and trails and steep ravines. Shiloh is an immense place, and Leroy cannot see it as a battleground. It is not what he expected. He thought it would look like a golf course. Monuments are everywhere, showing through the thick clusters of trees. Norma Jean passes the log cabin Mabel mentioned. It is surrounded by tourists looking for bullet holes.

"That's not the kind of log house I've got in mind," says Leroy apologetically.

"I know *that*."

"This is a pretty place. Your mama was right."

"It's O.K.," says Norma Jean. "Well, we've seen it. I hope she's satisfied."

They burst out laughing together.

At the park museum, a movie on Shiloh is shown every half hour, but they decide that they don't want to see it. They buy a souvenir Confederate flag for Mabel, and then they find a picnic spot near the cemetery. Norma Jean has brought a picnic cooler, with pimiento sandwiches, soft drinks, and Yodels. Leroy eats a sandwich and then smokes a joint, hiding it behind the picnic cooler. Norma Jean has quit smoking altogether. She is picking cake crumbs from the cellophane wrapper, like a fussy bird.

Leroy says, "So the boys in gray ended up in Corinth. The Union soldiers zapped 'em finally. April 7, 1862."

They both know that he doesn't know any history. He is just talking about some of the historical plaques they have read. He feels awkward, like a boy on a date with an older girl. They are still just making conversation.

"Corinth is where Mama eloped to," says Norma Jean.

They sit in silence and stare at the cemetery for the Union dead and, beyond, at a tall cluster of trees. Campers are parked nearby, bumper to bumper, and small children in bright clothing are cavorting and squealing. Norma Jean wads up the cake wrapper and squeezes it tightly in her hand. Without looking at Leroy, she says, "I want to leave you."

Leroy takes a bottle of Coke out of the cooler and flips off the cap. He holds the bottle poised near his mouth but cannot remember to take a drink. Finally he says, "No, you don't."

"Yes, I do."

"I won't let you."

"You can't stop me."

"Don't do me that way."

Leroy knows Norma Jean will have her own way. "Didn't I promise to be home from now on?" he says.

"In some ways, a woman prefers a man who wanders," says Norma Jean. "That sounds crazy, I know."

"You're not crazy."

Leroy remembers to drink from his Coke. Then he says, "Yes, you *are* crazy. You and me could start all over again. Right back at the beginning."

"We have started all over again," says Norma Jean. "And this is how it turned out."

"What did I do wrong?"

"Nothing."

"Is this one of those women's lib things?" Leroy asks.

"Don't be funny."

The cemetery, a green slope dotted with white markers, looks like a subdivision site. Leroy is trying to comprehend that his marriage is breaking up, but for some reason he is wondering about white slabs in a graveyard.

"Everything was fine till Mama caught me smoking," says Norma Jean, standing up. "That set something off."

"What are you talking about?"

"She won't leave me alone—*you* won't leave me alone." Norma Jean seems to be crying, but she is looking away from him. "I feel eighteen again. I can't face that all over again." She starts walking away. "No, it *wasn't* fine. I don't know what I'm saying. Forget it."

Leroy takes a lungful of smoke and closes his eyes as Norma Jean's words sink in. He tries to focus on the fact that thirty-five hundred soldiers died on the grounds around him. He can only think of that war as a board game with plastic soldiers. Leroy almost smiles, as he compares the Confederates' daring attack on the Union camps and Virgil Mathis's raid on the bowling alley. General Grant, drunk and furious, shoved the Southerners back to Corinth, where Mabel and Jet Beasley were married years later, when Mabel was still thin and good-looking. The next day, Mabel and Jet visited the battleground, and then Norma Jean was born, and then she married Leroy and they had a baby, which they lost, and now Leroy and Norma Jean are here at the same battleground. Leroy knows he is leaving out a lot. He is leaving out the insides of history. History was always just names and dates to him. It occurs to him that building a house out of logs is similarly empty—too simple. And the real inner workings of a marriage, like most of history, have escaped him. Now he sees that building a log house is the dumbest idea he could have had. It was clumsy of him to think Norma Jean would want a log house. It was a crazy idea: He'll have to think of something else, quickly. He will wad the blueprints into tight balls and fling them into the lake. Then he'll get moving again. He opens his eyes. Norma Jean has moved away and is walking through the cemetery, following a serpentine brick path.

Leroy gets up to follow his wife, but his good leg is asleep and his bad leg still hurts him. Norma Jean is far away, walking rapidly toward the bluff by the river, and he tries to hobble toward her. Some children run past him, screaming noisily. Norma Jean has reached the bluff, and she is looking out over the Tennessee River. Now she turns toward Leroy and waves her arms. Is she beckoning to him? She seems to be doing an exercise for her chest muscles. The sky is unusually pale—the color of the dust ruffle Mabel made for their bed.

(1982)

QUESTIONS FOR REFLECTION

1. What does the following information contribute to your understanding of the story? Shiloh was the location of a famous Civil War battle in which Union soldiers under the leadership of General Ulysses S. Grant soundly defeated the Confederate forces.

2. Look at the story's closing scene, which occurs at the famous battle site. How might that scene be related to what happened there during the Civil War? What other kinds of battlefields does the story describe?

POINT OF VIEW

An author's decisions about who is to tell the story and how it is to be told are among the most important he or she makes. In a story with an *objective point of view,* the writer shows what happens without directly stating more than readers can infer from its action and dialogue. The narrator, in short, does not tell us anything about what the characters think or feel. He remains a detached observer. The narrator of Kate Chopin's "The Story of an Hour" (Chapter One) does not participate in the action as a character. Chopin employs a third-person point of view, letting us know directly what Mrs. Mallard feels. We learn about the characters from an outside source; in Chopin's case, it is an authority. Imagine the story told from a detached, objective point of view in which we were not let into Mrs. Mallard's consciousness. The tone and feel of the story would be radically altered.

Although third-person point of view may take us inside a character's consciousness or remain objective, it does not assume the perspective of any character. Stories with narrators who participate in the action are presented from a *first-person point of view.* Narrators of such fictions tell their stories in their own voices with their particular limitations of knowledge and vision. The limitations of a first-person narrator offer writers the opportunity to exploit the discrepancy between the writer's vision and the narrator's. In both Edgar Allan Poe's "The Black Cat" and Ralph Ellison's "Battle Royal," for example, we encounter narrators who perceive and present themselves one way, but whom we see in different ways. Reading stories narrated in the first person, we need to question the narrator's trustworthiness and remain alert for textual signals that either ensure or undermine it.

Whether a writer uses a first- or a third-person narrator, he or she must also decide how much to let the narrator know about the characters. Narrators who know everything about all the characters are "omniscient" (all-knowing) as is the narrator of Joyce's "The Boarding House," who enters the minds of each of the characters and reveals what they think and feel. Stories with such narrators are written from an *omniscient point of view.* If, however, the narrator's knowledge is limited to only one character, major or minor, rather than to all, the narrator possesses *limited omniscience,* as in Chopin's "The Story of an Hour." James Joyce imposes no limitations on his narrator in "The Boarding House." Here is the narrator revealing the thoughts of Mrs. Mooney:

> She was sure she would win. To begin with she had all the weight of social opinion on her side: she was an outraged mother. She had allowed him to live beneath her roof, assuming that he was a man of honour, and he had simply abused her hospitality . . . youth could not be pleaded as his excuse; nor could ignorance be his excuse . . . He had simply taken advantage of Polly's youth and inexperience: that was evident. The question was: What reputation would he make?

And here is the same narrator granting us an inside view of Mr. Doran:

> He had a notion that he was being had. He could imagine his friends talking of the affair and laughing. She *was* a little vulgar; sometimes she said *I seen* and *If I had've known*. But what would grammar matter if he really loved her? He could not make up his mind whether to like her or despise her for what she had done. Of course, he had done it too. His instinct urged him to remain free, not to marry. Once you are married you are done for, it said.

Giving us an inside view of each character (Polly receives the same treatment), Joyce's omniscient narrator makes us aware of multiple perspectives. In doing so Joyce shifts our sympathies from one character to another as we come to understand their different needs and desires.

The omniscient point of view that Joyce employed in his twentieth-century story "The Boarding House" was a popular choice of eighteenth- and nineteenth-century novelists. But fashions in point of view change: The limited omniscient and first-person points of view are currently popular with contemporary writers. We have described some of the narrative points of view available to writers, but there are others. As we read stories with point of view in mind, we should remember:

1. That it is important to consider *how* point of view affects our responses to the characters.
2. That our response to a fictional narrator is influenced by the degree of a narrator's knowledge, the objectivity of a narrator's responses, and the degree of his or her participation in the action.
3. That a first-person narrator is not always a trustworthy guide; in fact, a large part of our work as readers is to determine a narrator's reliability, to estimate the truth of that narrator's disclosures.

With these considerations in mind, read William Faulkner's "A Rose for Emily." How objective is the narrator's view of Miss Emily? How does the perception we gain of her through observing her in dialogue and action with other characters compare with the narrator's view? Where and with what effect does the narrator's focus shift from presenting Miss Emily objectively to presenting her subjectively?

WILLIAM FAULKNER

[1897–1962]

William Faulkner was born into a Mississippi family whose influence and wealth had disappeared during the Civil War. Faulkner lived most of his life in the South he memorialized in his fiction, writing about the Oxford, Mississippi, of his actual life in his fictional Yoknapatawpha County. Faulkner won a Nobel price for Literature in 1949, along with a National Book Award and two Pulitzer prizes. His major novels include The Sound and the Fury, As I Lay Dying, *and* Absalom, Absalom! *"A Rose for Emily," his best-known, and perhaps best-loved, story, portrays the results of change in the post–Civil War South.*

A Rose for Emily

I

When Miss Emily Grierson died, our whole town went to her funeral: the men through a sort of respectful affection for a fallen monument, the women mostly out of curiosity to see the inside of her house, which no one save an old manservant—a combined gardener and cook—had seen in at least ten years.

It was a big, squarish frame house that had once been white, decorated with cupolas and spires and scrolled balconies in the heavily lightsome style of the seventies, set on what had once been our most select street. But garages and cotton gins had encroached and obliterated even the august names of that neighborhood; only Miss Emily's house was left, lifting its stubborn and coquettish decay above the cotton wagons and the gasoline pumps—an eyesore among eyesores. And now Miss Emily had gone to join the representatives of those august names where they lay in the cedar bemused cemetery among the ranked and anonymous graves of Union and Confederate soldiers who fell at the battle of Jefferson.

Alive, Miss Emily had been a tradition, a duty, and a care; a sort of hereditary obligation upon the town, dating from that day in 1894 when Colonel Sartoris, the mayor—he who fathered the edict that no Negro woman should appear on the streets without an apron—remitted her taxes, the dispensation dating from the death of her father on into perpetuity. Not that Miss Emily would have accepted charity. Colonel Sartoris invented an involved tale to the effect that Miss Emily's father had loaned money to the town, which the town, as a matter of business, preferred this way of repaying. Only a man of Colonel Sartoris' generation and thought could have invented it, and only a woman could have believed it.

When the next generation, with its more modern ideas, became mayors and aldermen, this arrangement created some little dissatisfaction. On the first of the year they mailed her a tax notice. February came, and there was no reply. They wrote her a formal letter, asking her to call at the sheriff's office at her convenience. A week later the mayor wrote her himself, offering to call or to send his car for her, and received in reply a note on paper of an archaic shape, in a thin, flowing calligraphy in faded ink, to the effect that she no longer went out at all. The tax notice was also enclosed, without comment.

They called a special meeting of the Board of Aldermen. A deputation waited upon her, knocked at the door through which no visitor had passed since she ceased giving china-painting lessons eight or ten years earlier. They were admitted by the old Negro into a dim hall from which a stairway mounted into still more shadow. It smelled of dust and disuse—a close, dank smell. The Negro led them into the parlor. It was furnished in heavy, leather-covered furniture. When the Negro opened the blinds of one window, they could see that the leather was cracked; and when they sat down, a faint dust rose sluggishly about their thighs, spinning with slow motes in the single sun-ray. On a tarnished gilt easel before the fireplace stood a crayon portrait of Miss Emily's father.

They rose when she entered—a small, fat woman in black, with a thin gold chain descending to her waist and vanishing into her belt, leaning on an ebony cane with a tarnished gold head. Her skeleton was small and spare; perhaps that was why what would have been merely plumpness in another was obesity in her. She looked bloated, like a body long submerged in motionless water, and of that pallid hue. Her eyes, lost in the fatty ridges of her face, looked like two small pieces of coal pressed into a lump of dough as they moved from one face to another while the visitors stated their errand.

She did not ask them to sit. She just stood in the door and listened quietly until the spokesman came to a stumbling halt. Then they could hear the invisible watch ticking at the end of the gold chain.

Her voice was dry and cold. "I have no taxes in Jefferson. Colonel Sartoris explained it to me. Perhaps one of you can gain access to the city records and satisfy yourselves."

"But we have. We are the city authorities, Miss Emily. Didn't you get a notice from the sheriff, signed by him?"

"I received a paper, yes," Miss Emily said. "Perhaps he considers himself the sheriff. . . . I have no taxes in Jefferson."

"But there is nothing on the books to show that, you see. We must go by the—"

"See Colonel Sartoris. I have no taxes in Jefferson."

"But, Miss Emily—"

"See Colonel Sartoris." (Colonel Sartoris had been dead almost ten years.) "I have no taxes in Jefferson. Tobe!" The Negro appeared. "Show these gentlemen out."

2

So she vanquished them, horse and foot, just as she had vanquished their fathers thirty years before about the smell. That was two years after her father's death and a short time after her sweetheart—the one we believed would marry her—had deserted her. After her father's death she went out very little; after her sweetheart went away, people hardly saw her at all. A few of the ladies had the temerity to call, but were not received, and the only sign of life about the place was the Negro man—a young man then—going in and out with a market basket.

"Just as if a man—any man—could keep a kitchen properly," the ladies said; so they were not surprised when the smell developed. It was another link between the gross, teeming world and the high and mighty Griersons.

A neighbor, a woman, complained to the mayor, Judge Stevens, eighty years old.

"But what will you have me do about it, madam?" he said.

"Why, send her word to stop it," the woman said. "Isn't there a law?"

"I'm sure that won't be necessary," Judge Stevens said. "It's probably just a snake or a rat that nigger of hers killed in the yard. I'll speak to him about it."

The next day he received two more complaints, one from a man who came in diffident deprecation. "We really must do something about it, Judge. I'd be the last one in the world to bother Miss Emily, but we've got to do something." That night the Board of Aldermen met—three graybeards and one younger man, a member of the rising generation.

"It's simple enough," he said. "Send her word to have her place cleaned up. Give her a certain time to do it in, and if she don't. . . ."

"Dammit, sir," Judge Stevens said, "will you accuse a lady to her face of smelling bad?"

So the next night, after midnight, four men crossed Miss Emily's lawn and slunk about the house like burglars, sniffing along the base of the brickwork and at the cellar openings while one of them performed a regular sowing motion with his hand out of a sack slung from his shoulder. They broke open the cellar door and sprinkled lime there, and in all the outbuildings. As they recrossed the lawn, a window that had been dark was lighted and Miss Emily sat in it, the light behind her, and her upright torso motionless as that of an idol. They crept quietly across the lawn and into the shadow of the locusts that lined the street. After a week or two the smell went away.

That was when people had begun to feel really sorry for her. People in our town, remembering how old lady Wyatt, her great-aunt, had gone completely crazy at last, believed that the Griersons held themselves a little too high for what they really were. None of the young men were quite good enough for Miss Emily and such. We had long thought of them as a tableau, Miss Emily a slender figure in white in the background, her father a spraddled silhouette in the foreground, his back to her and clutching a horsewhip, the two of them framed by the backflung front door. So when she got to be thirty and was still single, we were not pleased exactly, but vindicated; even with insanity in the family she wouldn't have turned down all of her chances if they had really materialized.

When her father died, it got about that the house was all that was left to her; and in a way, people were glad. At last they could pity Miss Emily. Being left alone, and a pauper, she had become humanized. Now she too would know the old thrill and the old despair of a penny more or less.

The day after his death all the ladies prepared to call at the house and offer condolence and aid, as is our custom. Miss Emily met them at the door, dressed as usual and with no trace of grief on her face. She told them that her father was not dead. She did that for three days, with the ministers calling on her, and the doctors, trying to persuade her to let them dispose of the body. Just as they were about to resort to law and force, she broke down, and they buried her father quickly.

We did not say she was crazy then. We believed she had to do that. We remembered all the young men her father had driven away, and we knew that with nothing left, she would have to cling to that which had robbed her, as people will.

3

She was sick for a long time. When we saw her again, her hair was cut short, making her look like a girl, with a vague resemblance to those angels in colored church windows—sort of tragic and serene.

The town had just let the contracts for paving the sidewalks, and in the summer after her father's death they began the work. The construction company came with niggers and mules and machinery, and a foreman named Homer Barron, a Yankee—a big, dark, ready man, with a big voice and eyes lighter than his face. The little boys would follow in groups to hear him cuss the niggers, and the niggers singing in time to the rise and fall of picks. Pretty soon he knew everybody in town. Whenever you heard a lot of laughing anywhere about the square, Homer Barron would be in the center of the group. Presently, we began to see him and Miss Emily on Sunday afternoons driving in the yellow-wheeled buggy and the matched team of bays from the livery stable.

At first we were glad that Miss Emily would have an interest, because the ladies all said, "Of course a Grierson would not think seriously of a Northerner, a day laborer." But there were still others, older people, who said that even grief could not cause a real lady to forget *noblesse oblige*—without calling it *noblesse oblige*. They just said, "Poor Emily. Her kinsfolk should come to her." She had some kin in Alabama; but years ago her father had fallen out with them over the estate of old lady Wyatt, the crazy woman, and there was no communication between the two families. They had not even been represented at the funeral.

And as soon as the old people said, "Poor Emily," the whispering began. "Do you suppose it's really so?" they said to one another. "Of course it is. What else could. . . ." This behind their hands; rustling of craned silk and satin behind jalousies closed upon the sun of Sunday afternoon as the thin, swift clop-clop-clop of the matched team passed: "Poor Emily."

She carried her head high enough—even when we believed that she was fallen. It was as if she demanded more than ever the recognition of her dignity as the last Grierson; as if it had wanted that touch of earthiness to reaffirm her imperviousness. Like when she bought the rat poison, the arsenic. That was over a year after they had begun to say "Poor Emily," and while the two female cousins were visiting her.

"I want some poison," she said to the druggist. She was over thirty then, still a slight woman, though thinner than usual, with cold, haughty black eyes in a face the flesh of which was strained across the temples and about the eyesockets as you imagine a lighthouse-keeper's face ought to look. "I want some poison," she said.

"Yes, Miss Emily. What kind? For rats and such? I'd recom—"

"I want the best you have. I don't care what kind."

The druggist named several. "They'll kill anything up to an elephant. But what you want is—"

"Arsenic," Miss Emily said. "Is that a good one?"

"Is . . . arsenic? Yes, ma'am. But what you want—"

"I want arsenic."

The druggist looked down at her. She looked back at him, erect, her face like a strained flag. "Why, of course," the druggist said. "If that's what you want. But the law requires you to tell what you are going to use it for."

Miss Emily just stared at him, her head tilted back in order to look him eye for eye, until he looked away and went and got the arsenic and wrapped it up. The Negro delivery boy brought her the package; the druggist didn't come back. When she opened the package at home there was written on the box, under the skull and bones: "For rats."

4

So the next day we all said, "She will kill herself"; and we said it would be the best thing. When she had first begun to be seen with Homer Barron, we had said, "She will marry him." Then we said, "She will persuade him yet," because Homer himself had remarked—he liked men, and it was known that he drank with the younger men in the Elks' Club—that he was not a marrying man. Later we said, "Poor Emily" behind the jalousies as they passed on Sunday afternoon in the glittering buggy, Miss Emily with her head high and Homer Barron with his hat cocked and a cigar in his teeth, reins and whip in a yellow glove.

Then some of the ladies began to say that it was a disgrace to the town and a bad example to the young people. The men did not want to interfere, but at last the ladies forced the Baptist minister—Miss Emily's people were Episcopal—to call upon her. He would never divulge what happened during that interview, but he refused to go back again. The next Sunday they again drove about the streets, and the following day the minister's wife wrote to Miss Emily's relations in Alabama.

So she had blood-kin under her roof again and we sat back to watch developments. At first nothing happened. Then we were sure that they were to be married. We learned that Miss Emily had been to the jeweler's and ordered a man's toilet set in silver, with the letters H.B. on each piece. Two days later we learned that she had bought a complete outfit of men's clothing, including a nightshirt, and we said, "They are married." We were really glad. We were glad because the two female cousins were even more Grierson than Miss Emily had ever been.

So we were not surprised when Homer Barron—the streets had been finished some time since—was gone. We were a little disappointed that there was not a public blowing-off, but we believed that he had gone on to prepare for Miss Emily's coming, or to give her a chance to get rid of the cousins. (By that time it was a cabal, and we were all Miss Emily's allies to help circumvent the cousins.) Sure enough, after another week they departed. And, as we had expected all along, within three days Homer Barron was back in town. A neighbor saw the Negro man admit him at the kitchen door at dusk one evening.

And that was the last we saw of Homer Barron. And of Miss Emily for some time. The Negro man went in and out with the market basket, but the front door remained closed. Now and then we would see her at the window for a moment, as the men did that night when they sprinkled the lime, but for almost six months she did not appear on the streets. Then we knew that this was to be expected too; as if that quality of her father which had thwarted her woman's life so many times had been too virulent and too furious to die.

When we next saw Miss Emily, she had grown fat and her hair was turning gray. During the next few years it grew grayer and grayer until it attained an even pepper-and-salt iron-gray, when it ceased turning. Up to the day of her death at seventy-four it was still that vigorous iron-gray, like the hair of an active man.

From that time on her front door remained closed, save during a period of six or seven years, when she was about forty, during which she gave lessons in china-painting. She fitted up a studio in one of the downstairs rooms, where the daughters and granddaughters of Colonel Sartoris' contemporaries were sent to her with the same regularity and in the same spirit that they were sent to church on Sundays with a twenty-five-cent piece for the collection plate. Meanwhile her taxes had been remitted.

Then the newer generation became the backbone and the spirit of the town, and the painting pupils grew up and fell away and did not send their children to her with boxes of color and tedious brushes and pictures cut from the ladies' magazines. The front door closed upon the last one and remained closed for good. When the town got free postal delivery, Miss Emily alone refused to let them fasten the metal numbers above her door and attach a mailbox to it. She would not listen to them.

Daily, monthly, yearly we watched the Negro grow grayer and more stooped, going in and out with the market basket. Each December we sent her a tax notice, which would be returned by the post office a week later, unclaimed. Now and then we would see her in one of the downstairs windows—she had evidently shut up the top floor of the house—like the carven torso of an idol in a niche, looking or not looking at us, we could never tell which. Thus she passed from generation to generation—dear, inescapable, impervious, tranquil, and perverse.

And so she died. Fell ill in the house filled with dust and shadows, with only a doddering Negro man to wait on her. We did not even know she was sick; we had long since given up trying to get any information from the Negro. He talked to no one, probably not even to her, for his voice had grown harsh and rusty, as if from disuse.

She died in one of the downstairs rooms, in a heavy walnut bed with a curtain, her gray head propped on a pillow yellow and moldy with age and lack of sunlight.

5

The Negro met the first of the ladies at the front door and let them in, with their hushed, sibilant voices and their quick, curious glances, and then he disappeared. He walked right through the house and out the back and was not seen again.

The two female cousins came at once. They held the funeral on the second day, with the town coming to look at Miss Emily beneath a mass of bought flowers, with the crayon face of her father musing profoundly above the bier and the ladies sibilant and macabre; and the very old men—some in their brushed Confederate uniforms—on the porch and the lawn, talking of Miss Emily as if she had been a contemporary of theirs, believing that they had danced with her and courted her perhaps, confusing time with its mathematical progression, as the old do, to whom all the past is not a diminishing road but, instead, a huge meadow which no winter ever quite touches, divided from them now by the narrow bottleneck of the most recent decade of years.

Already we knew that there was one room in that region above stairs which no one had seen in forty years, and which would have to be forced. They waited until Miss Emily was decently in the ground before they opened it.

The violence of breaking down the door seemed to fill this room with pervading dust. A thin, acrid pall as of the tomb seemed to lie everywhere upon this room decked and furnished as for a bridal: upon the valance curtains of faded rose color, upon the rose-shaded lights, upon the dressing table, upon the delicate array of crystal and the man's toilet things backed with tarnished silver, silver so tarnished that the monogram was obscured. Among them lay a collar and tie, as if they had just been removed, which, lifted, left upon the surface a pale crescent in the dust. Upon a chair hung the suit, carefully folded; beneath it the two mute shoes and the discarded socks.

The man himself lay in the bed.

For a long while we just stood there, looking down at the profound and fleshless grin. The body had apparently once lain in the attitude of an embrace, but now the long sleep that outlasts love, that conquers even the grimace of love, had cuckolded him. What was left of him, rotted beneath what was left of the nightshirt, had become inextricable from the bed in which he lay; and upon him and upon the pillow beside him lay that even coating of the patient and biding dust.

Then we noticed that in the second pillow was the indentation of a head. One of us lifted something from it, and leaning forward, that faint and invisible dust dry and acrid in the nostrils, we saw a long strand of iron-gray hair.

(1930)

QUESTION FOR REFLECTION

Although "A Rose for Emily" is narrated in the first person, the narrator is not "I" but "we." The narrator thus represents a communal rather than an individual point of view. How does the narrator (and the town) view Miss Emily? Find passages that represent more than one view of her and explain their significance.

LANGUAGE AND STYLE

The way a writer chooses words and arranges them determines his or her **style.** Style is the verbal identity of a writer, as unmistakable as his or her face or voice. Writers' styles convey their distinctive ways of seeing the world.

In the discussion of the language and style of fiction, we will concentrate on **diction,** the kind of word choices a writer makes; **syntax,** the order those words assume in sentences; and the presence or absence of figurative language, especially figures of comparison (**simile** and **metaphor**).*

Here is a paragraph from the beginning of William Faulkner's "A Rose for Emily."

> Alive, Miss Emily had been a tradition, a duty, and a care; a sort of hereditary obligation upon the town, dating from that day in 1894 when Colonel Sartoris, the mayor—he who fathered the edict that no Negro woman should appear on the streets without an apron—remitted her taxes, the dispensation dating from the death of her father on into perpetuity. Not that Miss Emily would have accepted charity. Colonel Sartoris invented an involved tale to the effect that Miss Emily's father had loaned money to the town, which the town, as a matter of business, preferred this way of repaying. Only a man of Colonel Sartoris' generation and thought could have invented it, and only a woman could have believed it.

In this passage, Faulkner introduces his central character, Miss Emily Grierson. He does so in a style both elegant and formal. This is equally apparent in the triple description of Miss Emily in the first sentence ("a tradition, a duty, and a care") and in the carefully balanced phrases of the final sentence ("only a man" . . . "only a woman"; and "could have invented it" . . . "could have believed it"). The sentences create an effect of eloquence, achieved partly by the balanced phrasing we have already noted, and partly by the studied formality of the long sentences, especially the first. Constructions such as "he who fathered the edict" and "the dispensation dating from" create a tone more elevated than that of everyday speech. Also contributing to this tone is the repetition of words ("had loaned money to the town, which the town") and the heavy reliance on pauses within the first and third sentences. Finally, there is the play of sound, alliteration and assonance especially, in "*da*ting from that *da*y" and "*d*ispensation *da*ting from the *d*eath."

Faulkner's prose flows in a stately progression and expansion of phrases, gathering force as each sentence unfolds. Faulkner's eloquent and exalted style seems more "written" than spoken.

*For an extensive discussion of figurative language, see Chapter 12.

The imagery and figures of comparison that Faulkner and other writers use enrich their prose and impart a personal view of the world. They are simultaneously indelible stamps of each writer's style and keys to understanding their works. The language of the following story, "Araby" by James Joyce, reveals both the narrator's conception of himself as a boy and his adult understanding of his boyhood. Note carefully the descriptions of Mangan's sister, especially their mixture of erotic and religious details. Pay close attention to the first and last paragraphs and to the religious imagery throughout.

JAMES JOYCE
[1882–1941]

James Joyce is best known as the author of Ulysses, *one of the most important literary works of the twentieth century. Joyce was born in Ireland, but left his home country to escape the stultifying influence of his country's social system, especially as reflected in institutional Catholicism.*

After a brief return to Ireland, Joyce moved permanently to Europe, living in Italy, France, and Switzerland, supporting his writing by giving language lessons. His short-story collection, Dubliners, *describes the lives of ordinary people living in the Irish capital. His novel* A Portrait of the Artist as a Young Man *exemplifies Joyce's use of stream-of-consciousness, a technique that became popular among a number of the world's writers. His masterpiece,* Ulysses *(1920), brought Joyce both international acclaim and financial freedom.*

Araby

North Richmond Street, being blind, was a quiet street except at the hour when the Christian Brothers' School set the boys free. An uninhabited house of two storeys stood at the blind end, detached from its neighbours in a square ground. The other houses of the street, conscious of decent lives within them, gazed at one another with brown imperturbable faces.

The former tenant of our house, a priest, had died in the back drawing-room. Air, musty from having been long enclosed, hung in all the rooms, and the waste room behind the kitchen was littered with old useless papers. Among these I found a few paper-covered books, the pages of which were curled and damp: *The Abbot,* by Walter Scott, *The Devout Communicant* and *The Memoirs of Vidocq.* I liked the last best because its leaves were yellow. The wild garden behind the house contained a central apple-tree and a few straggling bushes under one of which I found the late tenant's rusty bicycle-pump. He had been a very charitable priest; in his will he had left all his money to institutions and the furniture of his house to his sister.

When the short days of winter came dusk fell before we had well eaten our dinners. When we met in the street the houses had grown sombre. The space of sky above us was the colour of ever-changing violet and towards it the lamps of the street lifted their feeble lanterns. The cold air stung us and we played till our bodies glowed. Our shouts echoed in the silent street. The career of our play brought us through the dark muddy lanes behind the houses where we ran the gantlet of the rough tribes from the cottages, to the back doors of the dark dripping gardens where odours arose from the ashpits, to the dark odorous stables where a coachman smoothed and combed the horse or shook music from the buckled harness. When we returned to the street light from the kitchen windows had filled the areas. If my uncle was seen turning the corner we hid in the shadow until we had seen him safely housed. Or if Mangan's sister came out on the doorstep to call her brother in to his tea we watched her from our shadow peer up and down the street. We waited to see whether she would remain or go in and, if she remained, we left our shadow and walked up to Mangan's steps resignedly. She was waiting for us, her figure defined by the light from the half-opened door. Her brother always teased her before he obeyed and I stood by the railings looking at her. Her dress swung as she moved her body and the soft rope of her hair tossed from side to side.

Every morning I lay on the floor in the front parlour watching her door. The blind was pulled down to within an inch of the sash so that I could not be seen. When she came out on the doorstep my heart leaped. I ran to the hall, seized my books and followed her. I kept her brown figure always in my eye and, when we came near the point at which our ways diverged, I quickened my pace and passed her. This happened morning after morning. I had never spoken to her, except for a few casual words, and yet her name was like a summons to all my foolish blood.

Her image accompanied me even in places the most hostile to romance. On Saturday evenings when my aunt went marketing I had to go to carry some of the parcels. We walked through the flaring streets, jostled by drunken men and bargaining women, amid the curses of labourers, the shrill litanies of shop-boys who stood on guard by the barrels of pigs' cheeks, the nasal chanting of street-singers, who sang a *come-all-you* about O'Donovan Rossa, or a ballad about the troubles in our native land. These noises converged in a single sensation of life for me: I imagined that I bore my chalice safely through a throng of foes. Her name sprang to my lips at moments in strange prayers and praises which I myself did not understand. My eyes were often full of tears (I could not tell why) and at times a flood from my heart seemed to pour itself out into my bosom. I thought little of the future. I did not know whether I would ever speak to her or not or, if I spoke to her, how I could tell her of my confused adoration. But my body was like a harp and her words and gestures were like fingers running upon the wires.

One evening I went into the back drawing-room in which the priest had died. It was a dark rainy evening and there was no sound in the house. Through one of the broken panes I heard the rain impinge upon the earth, the fine incessant needles of water playing in the sodden beds. Some distant lamp or lighted window gleamed below me. I was thankful that I could see so little. All my senses seemed to desire to veil themselves and, feeling that I was about to slip from them, I pressed the palms of my hands together until they trembled, murmuring: *O love! O love!* many times.

At last she spoke to me. When she addressed the first words to me I was so confused that I did not know what to answer. She asked me was I going to *Araby*. I forget whether I answered yes or no. It would be a splendid bazaar, she said; she would love to go.

—And why can't you? I asked.

While she spoke she turned a silver bracelet round and round her wrist. She could not go, she said, because there would be a retreat that week in her convent. Her brother and two other boys were fighting for their caps and I was alone at the railings.

She held one of the spikes, bowing her head towards me. The light from the lamp opposite our door caught the white curve of her neck, lit up her hair that rested there and, falling, lit up the hand upon the railing. It fell over one side of her dress and caught the white border of a petticoat, just visible as she stood at ease.

—It's well for you, she said.

—If I go, I said, I will bring you something.

What innumerable follies laid waste my waking and sleeping thoughts after that evening! I wished to annihilate the tedious intervening days. I chafed against the work of school. At night in my bedroom and by day in the classroom her image came between me and the page I strove to read. The syllables of the word *Araby* were called to me through the silence in which my soul luxuriated and cast an Eastern enchantment over me. I asked for leave to go to the bazaar Saturday night. My aunt was surprised and hoped it was not some Freemason affair. I answered few questions in class. I watched my master's face pass from amiability to sternness; he hoped I was not beginning to idle. I could not call my wandering thoughts together. I had hardly any patience with the serious work of life which, now that it stood between me and my desire, seemed to me child's play, ugly monotonous child's play.

On Saturday morning I reminded my uncle that I wished to go to the bazaar in the evening. He was fussing at the hallstand, looking for the hat-brush, and answered me curtly:

—Yes, boy, I know.

As he was in the hall I could not go into the front parlour and lie at the window. I left the house in bad humour and walked slowly towards the school. The air was pitilessly raw and already my heart misgave me.

When I came home to dinner my uncle had not yet been home. Still it was early. I sat staring at the clock for some time and, when its ticking began to irritate me, I left the room. I mounted the staircase and gained the upper part of the house. The high cold empty gloomy rooms liberated me and I went from room to room singing. From the front window I saw my companions playing below in the street. Their cries reached me weakened and indistinct and, leaning my forehead against the cool glass, I looked over at the dark house where she lived. I may have stood there for an hour, seeing nothing but the brown-clad figure cast by my imagination, touched discreetly by the lamplight at the curved neck, at the hand upon the railings and at the border below the dress.

When I came downstairs again I found Mrs. Mercer sitting at the fire. She was an old garrulous woman, a pawnbroker's widow, who collected used stamps for some pious purpose. I had to endure the gossip of the tea-table. The meal was prolonged beyond an hour and still my uncle did not come. Mrs. Mercer stood up to go: she was sorry she couldn't wait any longer, but it was after eight o'clock and she did not like to be out late, as the night air was bad for her. When she had gone I began to walk up and down the room, clenching my fists. My aunt said:

—I'm afraid you may put off your bazaar for this night of Our Lord.

At nine o'clock I heard my uncle's latchkey in the halldoor. I heard him talking to himself and heard the hallstand rocking when it had received the weight of his overcoat. I could interpret these signs. When he was midway through his dinner I asked him to give me the money to go to the bazaar. He had forgotten.

—The people are in bed and after their first sleep now, he said.

I did not smile. My aunt said to him energetically:

—Can't you give him the money and let him go? You've kept him late enough as it is.

My uncle said he was very sorry he had forgotten. He said he believed in the old saying: *All work and no play makes Jack a dull boy*. He asked me where I was going and, when I had told him a second time he asked me did I know *The Arab's Farewell to his Steed*. When I left the kitchen he was about to recite the opening lines of the piece to my aunt.

I held a florin tightly in my hand as I strode down Buckingham Street towards the station. The sight of the streets thronged with buyers and glaring with gas recalled to me the purpose of my journey. I took my seat in a third-class carriage of a deserted train. After an intolerable delay the train moved out of the station slowly. It crept onward among ruinous houses and over the twinkling river. At Westland Row Station a crowd of people pressed to the carriage doors; but the porters moved them back, saying that it was a special train for the bazaar. I remained alone in the bare carriage. In a few minutes the train drew up beside an improvised wooden platform. I passed out on to the road and saw by the lighted dial of a clock that it was ten minutes to ten. In front of me was a large building which displayed the magical name.

I could not find any sixpenny entrance and, fearing that the bazaar would be closed, I passed in quickly through a turnstile, handing a shilling to a weary-looking man. I found myself in a big hall girdled at half its height by a gallery. Nearly all the stalls were closed and the greater part of the hall was in darkness. I recognised a silence like that which pervades a church after a service. I walked into the centre of the bazaar timidly. A few people were gathered about the stalls which were still open. Before a curtain, over which the words *Café Chantant* were written in coloured lamps, two men were counting money on a salver. I listened to the fall of the coins.

Remembering with difficulty why I had come I went over to one of the stalls and examined porcelain vases and flowered tea-sets. At the door of the stall a young lady was talking and laughing with two young gentlemen. I remarked their English accents and listened vaguely to their conversation.

—O, I never said such a thing!

—O, but you did!

—O, but I didn't!

—Didn't she say that?

—Yes. I heard her.

—O, there's a . . . fib!

Observing me the young lady came over and asked me did I wish to buy anything. The tone of her voice was not encouraging; she seemed to have spoken to me out of a sense of duty. I looked humbly at the great jars that stood like eastern guards at either side of the dark entrance to the stall and murmured:

—No, thank you.

The young lady changed the position of one of the vases and went back to the two young men. They began to talk of the same subject. Once or twice the young lady glanced at me over her shoulder.

I lingered before her stall, though I knew my stay was useless, to make my interest in her wares seem the more real. Then I turned away slowly and walked down the middle of the bazaar. I allowed the two pennies to fall against the sixpence in my pocket. I heard a voice call from one end of the gallery that the light was out. The upper part of the hall was now completely dark.

Gazing up into the darkness I saw myself as a creature driven and derided by vanity; and my eyes burned with anguish and anger.

(1914)

QUESTIONS FOR REFLECTION

1. Note the religious language of the fifth paragraph, especially the words "litanies," "chalice," "prayers and praises," and "confused adoration." What does this language reveal about the boy, about how he sees himself, about how he envisions what he is doing and thinking? Explain how the following sentence from this paragraph is related to the image invoked by his religious language: "But my body was like a harp and her words and gestures were like fingers running upon the wires."
2. Read the dialogue near the end of the story aloud, if possible with a friend. What do you hear? How can you characterize the conversation? What effect does it have on the boy? Why?
3. Reread the first and last paragraphs. Note repetitions and similarities in the language. Relate the use of the word "blind" for a dead-end street to the boy's situation as expressed at the end of the story. Why do the boy's "eyes" burn with "anguish" and "anger"?

THEME

In the Introduction to this book, we noted that the meaning of a literary work consists of both our experience in reading it and the ideas we may absorb from it. With that in mind, let us clarify what we mean by the theme of a story. Simply put, a story's **theme** is its idea or point (formulated as a generalization). The theme of a fable is its moral; the theme of a parable is its teaching; the theme of a short story is its implied view of life and conduct. Unlike the fable and parable, however, most fiction is not designed primarily to teach or preach. Its theme, thus, is more obliquely presented. In fact, theme in fiction is rarely *presented* at all; readers abstract it from the details of character and action that compose the story.

Theme is related to the other elements of fiction more as a consequence than as a parallel element that can be separately identified. To formulate a story's theme, we try to explain what these elements collectively suggest. Since the theme of a story derives from its details of character, plot, setting, structure, language, and point of view, any statement of theme is valid and valuable to the extent that it accounts for these details. To explain the theme of "The Prodigal Son," for example, without accounting for the father's speech to the elder son would be to distort the meaning of the story.

A statement of theme derives from the particulars of a story's language and action. In fact, the very concreteness and particularity of fiction should make us cautious in searching out theme. We should avoid thinking of theme as hidden somehow beneath the surface of the story and instead see theme as the implied significance of the story's details. It is important to remember that there are a multiplicity of ways to state a story's theme, but any such statement involves a necessary simplification of the story. In clarifying our sense of a story's idea, we also inevitably exclude some dimensions of the story and include others. We should be aware that the themes we abstract from stories are provisional understandings that never completely explain them.

With these considerations in mind, read Eudora Welty's "A Worn Path," with an eye to explaining its theme.

Photography by Curt Richter

EUDORA WELTY

[b. 1909–2001]

Eudora Welty was born in Jackson, Mississippi, and attended the Mississippi State College for Women and the University of Wisconsin. She is best known for her portraits of people and life in the deep South. During World War II she was on the staff of the New York Times Book Review, *testimony to the insatiable appetite for reading she developed as a child. She began publishing collections of stories in 1941 with Curtain of Green and won a Pulitzer prize in 1980 for* The Collected Stories, *which contains work from her numerous collections of short fiction spanning forty years. Welty has also written novels, such as* The Optimist's Daughter, *which won the Pulitzer prize in 1982, and criticism, collected in* The Eye of the Story *(1977). Her memoir,* One Writer's Beginnings, *describes her early experience with literature and her literary influences.*

A Worn Path

It was December—a bright frozen day in the early morning. Far out in the country there was an old Negro woman with her head tied in a red rag, coming along a path through the pinewoods. Her name was Phoenix Jackson. She was very old and small and she walked slowly in the dark pine shadows, moving a little from side to side in her steps, with the balanced heaviness and lightness of a pendulum in a grandfather clock. She carried a thin, small cane made from an umbrella, and with this she kept tapping the frozen earth in front of her. This made a grave and persistent noise in the still air, that seemed meditative like the chirping of a solitary little bird.

She wore a dark striped dress reaching down to her shoe tops, and an equally long apron of bleached sugar sacks, with a full pocket: all neat and tidy, but every time she took a step she might have fallen over her shoelaces, which dragged from her unlaced shoes. She looked straight ahead. Her eyes were blue with age. Her skin had a pattern all its own of numberless branching wrinkles and as though a whole little tree stood in the middle of her forehead, but a golden color ran underneath, and the two knobs of her cheeks were illumined by a yellow burning under the dark. Under the red rag her hair came down on her neck in the frailest of ringlets, still black, and with an odor like copper.

Now and then there was a quivering in the thicket. Old Phoenix said, "Out of my way, all you foxes, owls, beetles, jack rabbits, coons and wild animals! . . . Keep out from under these feet, little bob-whites. . . . Keep the big wild hogs out of my path. Don't let none of those come running my direction. I got a long way." Under her small black-freckled hand her cane, limber as a buggy whip, would switch at the brush as if to rouse up any hiding things.

On she went. The woods were deep and still. The sun made the pine needles almost too bright to look at, up where the wind rocked. The cones dropped as light as feathers. Down in the hollow was the mourning dove—it was not too late for him.

The path ran up a hill. "Seem like there is chains about my feet, time I get this far," she said, in the voice of argument old people keep to use with themselves. "Something always take a hold of me on this hill—pleads I should stay."

After she got to the top she turned and gave a full, severe look behind her where she had come. "Up through pines," she said at length. "Now down through oaks."

Her eyes opened their widest, and she started down gently. But before she got to the bottom of the hill a bush caught her dress.

Her fingers were busy and intent, but her skirts were full and long, so that before she could pull them free in one place they were caught in another. It was not possible to allow the dress to tear. "I in the thorny bush," she said. "Thorns, you doing your appointed work. Never want to let folks pass, no sir. Old eyes thought you was a pretty little *green* bush."

Finally, trembling all over, she stood free, and after a moment dared to stoop for her cane.

"Sun so high!" she cried, leaning back and looking, while the thick tears went over her eyes. "The time getting all gone here."

At the foot of this hill was a place where a log was laid across the creek.

"Now comes the trial," said Phoenix.

Putting her right foot out, she mounted the log and shut her eyes. Lifting her skirt, leveling her cane fiercely before her, like a festival figure in some parade, she began to march across. Then she opened her eyes and she was safe on the other side.

"I wasn't as old as I thought," she said.

But she sat down to rest. She spread her skirts on the bank around her and folded her hands over her knees. Up above her was a tree in a pearly cloud of mistletoe. She did not dare to close her eyes, and when a little boy brought her a plate with a slice of marble-cake on it she spoke to him. "That would be acceptable," she said. But when she went to take it there was just her own hand in the air.

So she left that tree, and had to go through a barbed-wire fence. There she had to creep and crawl, spreading her knees and stretching her fingers like a baby trying to climb the steps. But she talked loudly to herself: she could not let her dress be torn now, so late in the day, and she could not pay for having her arm or her leg sawed off if she got caught fast where she was.

At last she was safe through the fence and risen up out in the clearing. Big dead trees, like black men with one arm, were standing in the purple stalks of the withered cotton field. There sat a buzzard.

"Who you watching?"

In the furrow she made her way along.

"Glad this not the season for bulls," she said, looking sideways, "and the good Lord made his snakes to curl up and sleep in the winter. A pleasure I don't see no two-headed snake coming around that tree, where it come once. It took a while to get by him, back in the summer."

She passed through the old cotton and went into a field of dead corn. It whispered and shook and was taller than her head. "Through the maze now," she said, for there was no path.

Then there was something tall, black, and skinny there, moving before her.

At first she took it for a man. It could have been a man dancing in the field. But she stood still and listened, and it did not make a sound. It was as silent as a ghost.

"Ghost," she said sharply, "who be you the ghost of? For I have heard of nary death close by."

But there was no answer—only the ragged dancing in the wind.

She shut her eyes, reached out her hand, and touched a sleeve. She found a coat and inside that an emptiness, cold as ice.

"You scarecrow," she said. Her face lighted. "I ought to be shut up for good," she said with laughter. "My senses is gone. I too old. I the oldest people I ever know. Dance, old scarecrow," she said, "while I dancing with you."

She kicked her foot over the furrow, and with mouth drawn down, shook her head once or twice in a little strutting way. Some husks blew down and whirled in streamers about her skirts.

Then she went on, parting her way from side to side with the cane, through the whispering field. At last she came to the end, to a wagon track where the silver grass blew between the red ruts. The quail were walking around like pullets, seeming all dainty and unseen.

"Walk pretty," she said. "This the easy place. This the easy going."

She followed the track, swaying through the quiet bare fields, through the little strings of trees silver in their dead leaves, past cabins silver from weather, with the doors and windows boarded shut, all like old women under a spell sitting there. "I walking in their sleep," she said, nodding her head vigorously.

In a ravine she went where a spring was silently flowing through a hollow log. Old Phoenix bent and drank. "Sweet-gum makes the water sweet," she said, and drank more. "Nobody know who made this well, for it was here when I was born."

The track crossed a swampy part where the moss hung as white as lace from every limb. "Sleep on, alligators, and blow your bubbles." Then the track went into the road.

Deep, deep the road went down between the high green-colored banks. Overhead the live-oaks met, and it was as dark as a cave.

A black dog with a lolling tongue came up out of the weeds by the ditch. She was meditating, and not ready, and when he came at her she only hit him a little with her cane. Over she went in the ditch, like a little puff of milkweed.

Down there, her senses drifted away. A dream visited her, and she reached her hand up, but nothing reached down and gave her a pull. So she lay there and presently went to talking. "Old woman," she said to herself, "that black dog come up out of the weeds to stall you off, and now there he sitting on his fine tail, smiling at you."

A white man finally came along and found her—a hunter, a young man, with his dog on a chain.

"Well, Granny!" he laughed. "What are you doing there?"

"Lying on my back like a June-bug waiting to be turned over, mister," she said, reaching up her hand.

He lifted her up, gave her a swing in the air, and set her down. "Anything broken, Granny?"

"No, sir, them old dead weeds is springy enough," said Phoenix, when she had got her breath. "I thank you for your trouble."

"Where do you live, Granny?" he asked, while the two dogs were growling at each other.

"Away back yonder, sir, behind the ridge. You can't even see it from here."

"On your way home?"

"No sir, I going to town."

"Why, that's too far! That's as far as I walk when I come out myself, and I get something for my trouble." He patted the stuffed bag he carried, and there hung down a little closed claw. It was one of the bob-whites, with its beak hooked bitterly to show it was dead. "Now you go home, Granny!"

"I bound to go to town, mister," said Phoenix. "The time come around."

He gave another laugh, filling the whole landscape. "I know you old colored people! Wouldn't miss going to town to see Santa Claus!"

But something held old Phoenix very still. The deep lines in her face went into a fierce and different radiation. Without warning, she had seen with her own eyes a flashing nickel fall out of the man's pocket onto the ground.

"How old are you, Granny?" he was saying.

"There is no telling, mister," she said, "no telling."

Then she gave a little cry and clapped her hands and said, "Git on away from here, dog! Look! Look at that dog!" She laughed as if in admiration. "He ain't scared of nobody. He a big black dog." She whispered, "Sic him!"

"Watch me get rid of that cur," said the man. "Sic him, Pete! Sic him!"

Phoenix heard the dogs fighting, and heard the man running and throwing sticks. She even heard a gunshot. But she was slowly bending forward by that time, further and further forward, the lids stretched down over her eyes, as if she were doing this in her sleep. Her chin was lowered almost to her knees. The yellow palm of her hand came out from the fold of her apron. Her fingers slid down and along the ground under the piece of money with the grace and care they would have in lifting an egg from under a setting hen. Then she slowly straightened up, she stood erect, and the nickel was in her apron pocket. A bird flew by. Her lips moved. "God watching me the whole time. I come to stealing."

The man came back, and his own dog panted about them. "Well, I scared him off that time," he said, and then he laughed and lifted his gun and pointed it at Phoenix.

She stood straight and faced him.

"Doesn't the gun scare you?" he said, still pointing it.

"No, sir, I seen plenty go off closer by, in my day, and for less than what I done," she said, holding utterly still.

He smiled, and shouldered the gun. "Well, Granny," he said, "you must be a hundred years old, and scared of nothing. I'd give you a dime if I had any money with me. But you take my advice and stay home, and nothing will happen to you."

"I bound to go on my way, mister," said Phoenix. She inclined her head in the red rag. Then they went in different directions, but she could hear the gun shooting again and again over the hill.

She walked on. The shadows hung from the oak trees to the road like curtains. Then she smelled wood-smoke, and smelled the river, and she saw a steeple and the cabins on their steep steps. Dozens of little black children whirled around her. There ahead was Natchez shining. Bells were ringing. She walked on.

In the paved city it was Christmas time. There were red and green electric lights strung and criss-crossed everywhere, and all turned on in the daytime. Old Phoenix would have been lost if she had not distrusted her eyesight and depended on her feet to know where to take her.

She paused quietly on the sidewalk where people were passing by. A lady came along in the crowd, carrying an armful of red-, green- and silver-wrapped presents; she gave off perfume like the red roses in hot summer, and Phoenix stopped her.

"Please, missy, will you lace up my shoe?" She held up her foot.

"What do you want, Grandma?"

"See my shoe," said Phoenix. "Do all right for out in the country, but wouldn't look right to go in a big building."

"Stand still then, Grandma," said the lady. She put her packages down on the sidewalk beside her and laced and tied both shoes tightly.

"Can't lace 'em with a cane," said Phoenix. "Thank you, missy. I doesn't mind asking a nice lady to tie up my shoe, when I gets out on the street."

Moving slowly and from side to side, she went into the big building, and into a tower of steps, where she walked up and around and around until her feet knew to stop.

She entered a door, and there she saw nailed up on the wall the document that had been stamped with the gold seal and framed in the gold frame, which matched the dream that was hung up in her head.

"Here I be," she said. There was a fixed and ceremonial stiffness over her body.

"A charity case, I suppose," said an attendant who sat at the desk before her.

But Phoenix only looked above her head. There was sweat on her face, the wrinkles in her skin shone like a bright net.

"Speak up, Grandma," the woman said. "What's your name? We must have your history, you know. Have you been here before? What seems to be the trouble with you?"

Old Phoenix only gave a twitch to her face as if a fly were bothering her.

"Are you deaf?" cried the attendant.

But then the nurse came in.

"Oh, that's just old Aunt Phoenix," she said. "She doesn't come for herself—she has a little grandson. She makes these trips just as regular as clockwork. She lives away back off the Old Natchez Trace." She bent down. "Well, Aunt Phoenix, why don't you just take a seat? We won't keep you standing after your long trip." She pointed.

The old woman sat down, bolt upright in the chair.

"Now, how is the boy?" asked the nurse.

Old Phoenix did not speak.

"I said, how is the boy?"

But Phoenix only waited and stared straight ahead, her face very solemn and withdrawn into rigidity.

"Is his throat any better?" asked the nurse. "Aunt Phoenix, don't you hear me? Is your grandson's throat any better since the last time you came for the medicine?"

With her hands on her knees, the old woman waited, silent, erect and motionless, just as if she were in armor.

"You mustn't take up our time this way, Aunt Phoenix," the nurse said. "Tell us quickly about your grandson, and get it over. He isn't dead, is he?"

At last there came a flicker and then a flame of comprehension across her face, and she spoke.

"My grandson. It was my memory had left me. There I sat and forgot why I made my long trip."

"Forgot?" The nurse frowned. "After you came so far?"

Then Phoenix was like an old woman begging a dignified forgiveness for waking up frightened in the night. "I never did go to school, I was too old at the Surrender," she said in a soft voice. "I'm an old woman without an education. It was my memory fail me. My little grandson, he is just the same, and I forgot it in the coming."

"Throat never heals, does it?" said the nurse, speaking in a loud, sure voice to old Phoenix. By now she had a card with something written on it, a little list. "Yes. Swallowed lye. When was it?—January—two-three years ago—"

Phoenix spoke unasked now. "No, missy, he not dead, he just the same. Every little while his throat begin to close up again, and he not able to swallow. He not get his breath. He not able to help himself. So the time come around, and I go on another trip for the soothing medicine."

"All right. The doctor said as long as you came to get it, you could have it," said the nurse. "But it's an obstinate case."

"My little grandson, he sit up there in the house all wrapped up, waiting by himself," Phoenix went on. "We is the only two left in the world. He suffer and it don't seem to put him back at all. He got a sweet look. He going to last. He wear a little patch quilt and peep out holding his mouth open like a little bird. I remembers so plain now. I not going to forget him again, no, the whole enduring time. I could tell him from all the others in creation."

"All right." The nurse was trying to hush her now. She brought her a bottle of medicine. "Charity," she said, making a check mark in a book.

Old Phoenix held the bottle close to her eyes, and then carefully put it into her pocket.

"I thank you," she said.

"It's Christmas time, Grandma," said the attendant. "Could I give you a few pennies out of my purse?"

"Five pennies is a nickel," said Phoenix stiffly.

"Here's a nickel," said the attendant.

Phoenix rose carefully and held out her hand. She received the nickel and then fished the other nickel out of her pocket and laid it beside the new one. She stared at her palm closely, with her head on one side.

Then she gave a tap with her cane on the floor.

"This is what come to me to do," she said. "I going to the store and buy my child a little windmill they sells, made out of paper. He going to find it hard to believe there such a thing in the world. I'll march myself back where he waiting, holding it straight up in this hand."

She lifted her free hand, gave a little nod, turned around, and walked out of the doctor's office. Then her slow step began on the stairs, going down.

(1941)

QUESTIONS FOR REFLECTION

1. State in a sentence or two the idea of "A Worn Path." What point does the story seem to make?
2. Develop your understanding of the story's theme in a paragraph or a brief conversation. To support your views, cite details of plot, character, setting, and language.

IRONY AND SYMBOL

Two additional facets of fictional works are **irony** and **symbol.** While not as pervasive as elements such as plot and character, irony and symbol are tremendously important. Both allow writers to compress a great deal of meaning into a brief space. Both require our deliberation if we are to appreciate and enjoy their full range of significance. And both require us to be alert to their existence if we are to understand the works in which they occur. If we do not perceive a writer's ironic intentions, we may not just misconstrue a particular story; we may interpret it as suggesting the opposite of what it actually is intended to mean. And if we overlook a story's symbols, we may underestimate its achievement and oversimplify its significance.

Irony

Irony is not so much an element of fiction as a pervasive quality in it. It may appear in fiction (and in the other literary genres as well) in three ways: in a work's language, in its incidents, or in its point of view. But in whatever forms it emerges, *irony* always involves a contrast or discrepancy between one thing and another. The contrast may be between what is said and what is meant or between what happens and what is expected to happen.

In *verbal irony,* for example, we say the opposite of what we mean. When someone says, "That was a brilliant remark," and we know that it was anything but brilliant, we understand the speaker's ironic intention. In such relatively simple instances there is usually no problem in perceiving irony. In more complex instances, however, the designation of an action or a remark as ironic can be much more complicated. At the end of Flannery O'Connor's "Good Country People" (page 172), Mrs. Freeman says: "Some can't be that simple." "I know I never could." Should we take her literally? Or do we detect irony?

Besides verbal irony—in which we understand the opposite of what a speaker says—fiction makes use of *irony of circumstance* (sometimes called *irony of situation*). Writers sometimes create discrepancies between what seems to be and what is. In Kate Chopin's "The Story of an Hour" (p. 38), for example, Mrs. Mallard appears to be grieving over the news of her husband's death. At least that's how her action is perceived by other characters. But we soon realize that rather than grief, her tears celebrate the joy of her new-found freedom. Her tears are ironic because they indicate the opposite of what we expect them to. Another ironic situation prevails as Mrs. Mallard "prays" for long life, presumably so she can enjoy freedom from her husband: what she is praying for and why she prays for it are out of keeping with the expected reasons for prayer on such an occasion.

Irony of circumstance or situation also refers to occasions when an individual expects one thing to occur only to discover that the opposite happens. This indeed is what Mrs. Mallard experiences when she discovers her husband had not been killed in the train crash as she had thought. The final irony, of course, is that *she* dies when she sees him walk in the door.

Although verbal irony and irony of circumstance or situation are the prevalent forms irony assumes in fiction, two others deserve mention: dramatic irony and ironic vision. More typical of plays than stories, *dramatic irony* is the discrepancy between what characters know and what readers know. Writers sometimes direct our responses by letting us see things that their characters do not. At the conclusion of Flannery O'Connor's "Good Country People," for example, the reader has quite a different view of the Bible salesman's character than either Mrs. Freeman or Mrs. Hopewell has.

Some writers exploit the discrepancy between what readers and characters know to establish an ironic vision in a work. An *ironic vision* is established in a work as an overall tone that suggests how a writer views his or her characters and subject. Although characteristic of longer fictional works such as the novels *Pride and Prejudice* by Jane Austen and *The Adventures of Huckleberry Finn* by Mark Twain, we can find an ironic vision, nonetheless, in short stories such as O'Connor's "Good Country People." For the moment, however, consider how an ironic vision informs the opening of Jane Austen's *Pride and Prejudice:*

> It is a truth universally acknowledged, that a single man in possession of a good fortune, must be in want of a wife.
>
> However little known the feelings or views of such a man may be on his first entering a neighborhood, this truth is so well fixed in the minds of the surrounding families, that he is considered as the rightful property of some one or other of their daughters.

Is it a truth—that is, do we accept as fact what the opening sentence seems to assert: that a single man of means must be looking for a wife? Do we believe that this search for a wife is a phenomenon universally acknowledged, that it is recognized around the world, not merely in nineteenth-century England or twentieth-century America? It is very likely that Jane Austen's sentence presents the opposite of what we believe: that single men of means more often than not are not in search of wives. The converse is probably closer to what we have seen: That single women seek out single men of means as prospective husbands. This discrepancy between what the sentence says and what we know accounts in part for its ironic quality. We are not to take it literally; we do not accept it at face value.

We can feel more confident about the ironic quality of Austen's first sentence when we examine it in relation to the sentence that follows it. We are told there that the feelings or views of the eligible bachelor mean little. But they should mean much in such an important issue. That they do not is the opposite of what we expect and hence is ironic. An additional irony is that characteristics of marriageable eligibility are limited to bachelorhood and wealth. Nothing else is mentioned as important—not character, not intelligence, not wisdom or virtue.

Portraying characters whose view of marriage is so mercenary and limited, Austen distances herself from them and from their values. This ironic distance is enforced when Austen describes their misconceptions about single men. But there is a further irony in the fact that those misconceptions do not matter. All that matters is the final outcome: the single man's loss of his bachelorhood and his entrance into the ranks of the family. Moreover, their view represents a reversal of a traditional and familiar notion: that a wife is a man's property. This idea is given an additional twist when Austen indicates that it hardly matters which girl of which family captures the prize.

For these reasons and for others that emerge as the novel develops, Austen's tone can be described as ironic. When such an ironic tone is established strongly from the beginning of a work and when it is sustained consistently throughout, we say that it is informed by an ironic vision. The ironic vision of *Pride and Prejudice* infuses the novel: It informs the plot, it controls the dialogue, and it surfaces repeatedly in the tone of the narrator's comments.

Symbol

Symbols in fiction are simply objects, actions, or events that convey meaning. The meaning they convey extends beyond their literal significance, beyond their more obvious actual reason for being included in the story. In Kate Chopin's "The Story of an Hour," for example, the room in which Mrs. Mallard sits symbolizes her domestic, homebound life. She looks out a window into a world that has previously been closed to her. With the supposed death of her husband, she sees the outside world in a fresh and invigorating way. What she observes (the trees, for example) and how she now understands those things (in this case as emblems of life, hope, and possibility) signal, for us, that symbolism is at work in the story.

How do we know if a particular detail is symbolic? How do we decide whether we should look beyond the literal meaning of a dialogue or the literal value of an object or action? The simple answer to this question is that there is no way to be certain about the symbolic value of any particular details. But we can alert ourselves to the possible symbolic overtones of such details through the following questions.

1. How important to the story is the object, action, gesture, or dialogue that we suspect is symbolic? Does it appear more than once? Does it occur at a climactic moment? Is it described in detail?
2. Does the story seem to warrant our granting its details more significance than their immediate literal value? Why?
3. Does a symbolic interpretation make sense? Does it fit in with a literal or commonsense explanation? Or does our symbolic reading contradict or otherwise distort the literal surface of the story?
4. What objections might be raised against our symbolic interpretation?

Even if we consider such questions carefully, we may still not be sure that a particular detail is symbolic. Sometimes we will be confident that such a detail is symbolic without being able to say just what it represents. This kind of uncertainty is natural, largely because symbols by their very nature resist easy and definitive explanation.

Read the following story, D. H. Lawrence's "The Rocking-Horse Winner," with an eye to its ironies. Be alert for verbal irony, irony of situation, and dramatic irony. Consider whether the tone is sufficiently ironic to display an ironic vision. Identify and explain any symbols.

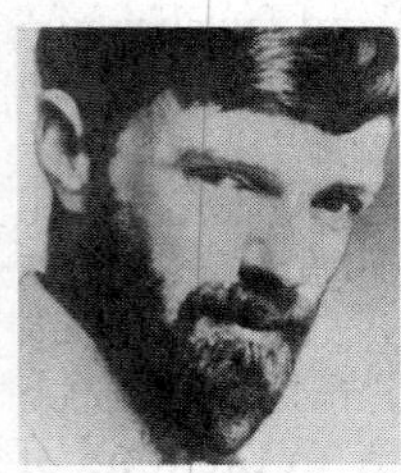

D. H. LAWRENCE

[1885–1930]

www

David Herbert Lawrence was born in Nottinghamshamshire, England, and studied at University College there. He became, for a while, a schoolteacher but left teaching to devote his full time to his writing, which flowed in abundance from his pen. Best known for his novels, such as Lady Chatterly's Lover, Women in Love, *and* Sons and Lovers, *Lawrence also published poetry, travel books, essays, and criticism. He traveled extensively and lived in Italy and Mexico as well as in England. His work is firmly anchored in the locales in which he lived and deals powerfully with natural forces, including sexuality.*

The Rocking-Horse Winner

There was a woman who was beautiful, who started with all the advantages, yet she had no luck. She married for love, and the love turned to dust. She had bonny children, yet she felt they had been thrust upon her, and she could not love them. They looked at her coldly, as if they were finding fault with her. And hurriedly she felt she must cover up some fault in herself. Yet what it was that she must cover up she never knew. Nevertheless, when her children were present, she always felt the center of her heart go hard. This troubled her, and in her manner she was all the more gentle and anxious for her children, as if she loved them very much. Only she herself knew that at the center of her heart was a hard little place that could not feel love, no, not for anybody. Everybody else said of her: "She is such a good mother. She adores her children." Only she herself, and her children themselves, knew it was not so. They read it in each other's eyes.

There were a boy and two little girls. They lived in a pleasant house, with a garden, and they had discreet servants, and felt themselves superior to anyone in the neighborhood.

Although they lived in style, they felt always an anxiety in the house. There was never enough money. The mother had a small income, and the father had a small income, but not nearly enough for the social position which they had to keep up. The father went into town to some office. But though he had good prospects, these prospects never materialized. There was always the grinding sense of the shortage of money, though the style was always kept up.

At last the mother said: "I will see if I can't make something." But she did not know where to begin. She racked her brains, and tried this thing and the other, but could not find anything successful. The failure made deep lines come into her face. Her children were growing up, they would have to go to school. There must be more money, there must be more money. The father, who was always very handsome and expensive in his tastes, seemed as if he never *would* be able to do anything worth doing. And the mother, who had a great belief in herself, did not succeed any better, and her tastes were just as expensive.

And so the house came to be haunted by the unspoken phrase: *There must be more money! There must be more money!* The children could hear it all the time though nobody said it aloud. They heard it at Christmas, when the expensive and splendid toys filled the nursery. Behind the shining modern rocking horse, behind the smart doll's house, a voice would start whispering: "There *must* be more money! There *must* be more money!" And the children would stop playing, to listen for a moment. They would look into each other's eyes, to see if they had all heard. And each one saw in the eyes of the other two that they too had heard. "There *must* be more money! There *must* be more money!"

It came whispering from the springs of the still-swaying rocking horse, and even the horse, bending his wooden, champing head, heard it. The big doll, sitting so pink and smirking in her new pram, could hear it quite plainly, and seemed to be smirking all the more self-consciously because of it. The foolish puppy, too, that took the place of the teddy bear, he was looking so extraordinarily foolish for no other reason but that he heard the secret whisper all over the house: "There *must* be more money!"

Yet nobody ever said it aloud. The whisper was everywhere, and therefore no one spoke it. Just as no one ever says: "We are breathing!" in spite of the fact that breath is coming and going all the time.

"Mother," said the boy Paul one day, "why don't we keep a car of our own? Why do we always use Uncle's, or else a taxi?"

"Because we're the poor members of the family," said the mother.

"But why are we, Mother?"

"Well—I suppose," she said slowly and bitterly, "it's because your father has no luck."

The boy was silent for some time.

"Is luck money, Mother?" he asked rather timidly.

"No, Paul. Not quite. It's what causes you to have money."

"Oh!" said Paul vaguely. "I thought when Uncle Oscar said *filthy lucker,* it meant money."

"*Filthy lucre* does mean money," said the mother. "But it's lucre, not luck."

"Oh!" said the boy. "Then what *is* luck, Mother?"

"It's what causes you to have money. If you're lucky you have money. That's why it's better to be born lucky than rich. If you're rich, you may lose your money. But if you're lucky, you will always get more money."

"Oh! Will you? And is Father not lucky?"

"Very unlucky, I should say," she said bitterly.

The boy watched her with unsure eyes.

"Why?" he asked.

"I don't know. Nobody ever knows why one person is lucky and another unlucky."

"Don't they? Nobody at all? Does *nobody* know?"

"Perhaps God. But He never tells."

"He ought to, then. And aren't you lucky either, Mother?"

"I can't be, if I married an unlucky husband."

"But by yourself, aren't you?"

"I used to think I was, before I married. Now I think I am very unlucky indeed."

"Why?"

"Well—never mind! Perhaps I'm not really," she said.

The child looked at her, to see if she meant it. But he saw, by the lines of her mouth, that she was only trying to hide something from him.

"Well, anyhow," he said stoutly, "I'm a lucky person."

"Why?" said his mother, with a sudden laugh.

He stared at her. He didn't even know why he had said it.

"God told me," he asserted, brazening it out.

"I hope He did, dear!" she said, again with a laugh, but rather bitter.

"He did, Mother!"

"Excellent!" said the mother.

The boy saw she did not believe him; or, rather, that she paid no attention to his assertion. This angered him somewhat, and made him want to compel her attention.

He went off by himself, vaguely, in a childish way, seeking for the clue to "luck." Absorbed, taking no heed of other people, he went about with a sort of stealth, seeking inwardly for luck. He wanted luck, he wanted it, he wanted it. When the two girls were playing dolls in the nursery, he would sit on his big rocking horse, charging madly into space, with a frenzy that made the little girls peer at him uneasily. Wildly the horse careered, the waving dark hair of the boy tossed, his eyes had a strange glare in them. The little girls dared not speak to him.

When he had ridden to the end of his mad little journey, he climbed down and stood in front of his rocking horse, staring fixedly into its lowered face. Its red mouth was slightly open, its big eye was wide and glassy-bright.

Now! he could silently command the snorting steed. Now, take me to where there is luck! Now take me!

And he would slash the horse on the neck with the little whip he had asked Uncle Oscar for. He *knew* the horse could take him to where there was luck, if only he forced it. So he would mount again, and start on his furious ride, hoping at last to get there. He knew he could get there.

"You'll break your horse, Paul!" said the nurse.

"He's always riding like that! I wish he'd leave off!" said his elder sister Joan.

But he only glared down on them in silence. Nurse gave him up. She could make nothing of him. Anyhow he was growing beyond her.

One day his mother and his uncle Oscar came in when he was on one of his furious rides. He did not speak to them.

"Hallo, you young jockey! Riding a winner?" said his uncle.

"Aren't you growing too big for a rocking horse? You're not a very little boy any longer, you know," said his mother.

But Paul only gave a blue glare from his big, rather close-set eyes. He would speak to nobody when he was in full tilt. His mother watched him with an anxious expression on her face.

At last he suddenly stopped forcing his horse into the mechanical gallop, and slid down.

"Well, I got there!" he announced fiercely, his blue eyes still flaring, and his sturdy long legs straddling apart.

"Where did you get to?" asked his mother.

"Where I wanted to go," he flared back at her.

"That's right, son!" said Uncle Oscar. "Don't you stop till you get there. What's the horse's name?"

"He doesn't have a name," said the boy.

"Gets on without all right?" asked the uncle.

"Well, he has different names. He was called Sansovino last week."

"Sansovino, eh? Won the Ascot. How did you know his name?"

"He always talks about horse races with Bassett," said Joan.

The uncle was delighted to find that his small nephew was posted with all the racing news. Bassett, the young gardener, who had been wounded in the left foot in the war and had got his present job through Oscar Cresswell, whose batman he had been, was a perfect blade of the "turf." He lived in the racing events, and the small boy lived with him.

Oscar Cresswell got it all from Bassett.

"Master Paul comes and asks me, so I can't do more than tell him, sir," said Bassett, his face terribly serious, as if he were speaking of religious matters.

"And does he ever put anything on a horse he fancies?"

"Well—I don't want to give him away—he's a young sport, a fine sport, sir. Would you mind asking him himself? He sort of takes a pleasure in it, and perhaps he'd feel I was giving him away, sir, if you don't mind."

Bassett was serious as a church.

The uncle went back to his nephew and took him off for a ride in the car.

"Say, Paul, old man, do you ever put anything on a horse?" the uncle asked.

The boy watched the handsome man closely.

"Why, do you think I oughtn't to?" he parried.

"Not a bit of it! I thought perhaps you might give me a tip for the Lincoln."

The car sped on into the country, going down to Uncle Oscar's place in Hampshire.

"Honor bright?" said the nephew.

"Honor bright, son!" said the uncle.

"Well, then, Daffodil."

"Daffodil! I doubt it, sonny. What about Mirza?"

"I only know the winner," said the boy. "That's Daffodil."

"Daffodil, eh?"

There was a pause. Daffodil was an obscure horse comparatively.

"Uncle!"

"Yes, son?"

"You won't let it go any further, will you? I promised Bassett."

"Bassett be damned, old man! What's he got to do with it?"

"We're partners. We've been partners from the first. Uncle, he lent me my first five shillings, which I lost. I promised him, honor bright, it was only between me and him; only you gave me that ten-shilling note I started winning with, so I thought you were lucky. You won't let it go any further, will you?"

The boy gazed at his uncle from those big, hot, blue eyes, set rather close together. The uncle stirred and laughed uneasily.

"Right you are, son! I'll keep your tip private. Daffodil, eh? How much are you putting on him?"

"All except twenty pounds," said the boy. "I keep that in reserve."

The uncle thought it a good joke.

"You keep twenty pounds in reserve, do you, you young romancer? What are you betting, then?"

"I'm betting three hundred," said the boy gravely. "But it's between you and me, Uncle Oscar! Honor bright?"

The uncle burst into a roar of laughter.

"It's between you and me all right, you young Nat Gould," he said, laughing. "But where's your three hundred?"

"Bassett keeps it for me. We're partners."

"You are, are you! And what is Bassett putting on Daffodil?"

"He won't go quite as high as I do, I expect. Perhaps he'll go a hundred and fifty."

"What, pennies?" laughed the uncle.

"Pounds," said the child, with a surprised look at his uncle. "Bassett keeps a bigger reserve than I do."

Between wonder and amusement Uncle Oscar was silent. He pursued the matter no further, but he determined to take his nephew with him to the Lincoln races.

"Now, son," he said, "I'm putting twenty on Mirza, and I'll put five for you on any horse you fancy. What's your pick?"

"Daffodil, Uncle."

"No, not the fiver on Daffodil!"

"I should if it was my own fiver," said the child.

"Good! Good! Right you are! A fiver for me and a fiver for you on Daffodil."

The child had never been to a race meeting before, and his eyes were blue fire. He pursed his mouth tight, and watched. A Frenchman just in front had put his money on Lancelot. Wild with excitement, he flailed his arms up and down, yelling "*Lancelot! Lancelot!*" in his French accent.

Daffodil came in first, Lancelot second, Mirza third. The child, flushed and with eyes blazing, was curiously serene. His uncle brought him four five-pound notes, four to one.

"What am I to do with these?" he cried, waving them before the boy's eyes.

"I suppose we'll talk to Bassett," said the boy. "I expect I have fifteen hundred now; and twenty in reserve; and this twenty."

His uncle studied him for some moments.

"Look here, son!" he said. "You're not serious about Bassett and that fifteen hundred, are you?"

"Yes, I am. But it's between you and me, Uncle. Honor bright!"

"Honor bright all right, son! But I must talk to Bassett."

"If you'd like to be a partner, Uncle, with Bassett and me, we could all be partners. Only, you'd have to promise, honor bright, Uncle, not to let it go beyond us three. Bassett and I are lucky, and you must be lucky, because it was your ten shillings I started winning with . . ."

Uncle Oscar took both Bassett and Paul into Richmond Park for an afternoon, and there they talked.

"It's like this, you see, sir," Bassett said. "Master Paul would get me talking about racing events, spinning yarns, you know, sir. And he was always keen on knowing if I'd made or if I'd lost. It's about a year since, now, that I put five shillings on Blush of Dawn for him—and we lost. Then the luck turned, with that ten shillings he had from you, that we put on Singhalese. And since then, it's been pretty steady, all things considering. What do you say, Master Paul?"

"We're all right when we're sure," said Paul. "It's when we're not quite sure that we go down."

"Oh, but we're careful then," said Bassett.

"But when are you *sure?*" Uncle Oscar smiled.

"It's Master Paul, sir," said Bassett, in a secret, religious voice. "It's as if he had it from heaven. Like Daffodil, now, for the Lincoln. That was as sure as eggs."

"Did you put anything on Daffodil?" asked Oscar Cresswell.

"Yes, sir. I made my bit."

"And my nephew?"

Bassett was obstinately silent, looking at Paul.

"I made twelve hundred, didn't I, Bassett? I told Uncle I was putting three hundred on Daffodil."

"That's right," said Bassett, nodding.

"But where's the money?" asked the uncle.

"I keep it safe locked up, sir. Master Paul he can have it any minute he likes to ask for it."

"What, fifteen hundred pounds?"

"And twenty! And forty, that is, with the twenty he made on the course."

"It's amazing!" said the uncle.

"If Master Paul offers you to be partners, sir, I would, if I were you; if you'll excuse me," said Bassett.

Oscar Cresswell thought about it.

"I'll see the money," he said.

They drove home again, and sure enough, Bassett came round to the garden house with fifteen hundred pounds in notes. The twenty pounds reserve was left with Joe Glee, in the Turf Commission deposit.

"You see, it's all right, Uncle, when I'm *sure!* Then we go strong, for all we're worth. Don't we, Bassett?"

"We do that, Master Paul."

"And when are you sure?" said the uncle, laughing.

"Oh, well, sometimes I'm *absolutely* sure, like about Daffodil," said the boy; "and sometimes I have an idea; and sometimes I haven't even an idea, have I, Bassett? Then we're careful, because we mostly go down."

"You do, do you! And when you're sure, like about Daffodil, what makes you sure, sonny?"

"Oh, well, I don't know," said the boy uneasily. "I'm sure, you know, Uncle; that's all."

"It's as if he had it from heaven, sir," Bassett reiterated.

"I should say so!" said the uncle.

But he became a partner. And when the Leger was coming on, Paul was "sure" about Lively Spark, which was a quite inconsiderable horse. The boy insisted on putting a thousand on the horse, Bassett went for five hundred, and Oscar Cresswell two hundred. Lively Spark came in first, and the betting had been ten to one against him. Paul had made ten thousand.

"You see," he said, "I was absolutely sure of him."

Even Oscar Cresswell had cleared two thousand.

"Look here, son," he said, "this sort of thing makes me nervous."

"It needn't, Uncle! Perhaps I shan't be sure again for a long time."

"But what are you going to do with your money?" asked the uncle.

"Of course," said the boy. "I started it for Mother. She said she had no luck, because Father is unlucky, so I thought if *I* was lucky, it might stop whispering."

"What might stop whispering?"

"Our house. I *hate* our house for whispering."

"What does it whisper?"

"Why—why"—the boy fidgeted—"why, I don't know. But it's always short of money, you know, Uncle."

"I know it, son, I know it."

"You know people send Mother writs, don't you, Uncle?"

"I'm afraid I do," said the uncle.

"And then the house whispers, like people laughing at you behind your back. It's awful, that is! I thought if I was lucky. . ."

"You might stop it," added the uncle.

The boy watched him with big blue eyes, that had an uncanny cold fire in them, and he said never a word.

"Well, then!" said the uncle. "What are we doing?"

"I shouldn't like Mother to know I was lucky," said the boy.

"Why not, son?"

"She'd stop me."

"I don't think she would."

"Oh!"—and the boy writhed in an odd way—"I *don't* want her to know, Uncle."

"All right, son! We'll manage it without her knowing."

They managed it very easily. Paul, at the other's suggestion, handed over five thousand pounds to his uncle, who deposited it with the family lawyer, who was then to inform Paul's mother that a relative had put five thousand pounds into his hands, which sum was to be paid out a thousand pounds at a time, on the mother's birthday, for the next five years.

"So she'll have a birthday present of a thousand pounds for five successive years," said Uncle Oscar. "I hope it won't make it all the harder for her later."

Paul's mother had her birthday in November. The house had been "whispering" worse than ever lately, and, even in spite of his luck, Paul could not bear up against it. He was very anxious to see the effect of the birthday letter, telling his mother about the thousand pounds.

When there were no visitors, Paul now took his meals with his parents, as he was beyond the nursery control. His mother went into town nearly every day. She had discovered that she had an odd knack of sketching furs and dress materials, so she worked secretly in the studio of a friend who was the chief artist for the leading drapers. She drew the figures of ladies in furs and ladies in silk and sequins for the newspaper advertisements. This young woman artist earned several thousand pounds a year, but Paul's mother only made several hundreds, and she was again dissatisfied. She so wanted to be first in something, and she did not succeed, even in making sketches for drapery advertisements.

She was down to breakfast on the morning of her birthday. Paul watched her face as she read her letters. He knew the lawyer's letter. As his mother read it, her face hardened and became more expressionless. Then a cold, determined look came on her mouth. She hid the letter under the pile of others, and said not a word about it.

"Didn't you have anything nice in the post for your birthday, Mother?" said Paul.

"Quite moderately nice," she said, her voice cold and absent.

She went away to town without saying more.

But in the afternoon Uncle Oscar appeared. He said Paul's mother had had a long interview with the lawyer, asking if the whole five thousand could not be advanced at once, as she was in debt.

"What do you think, Uncle?" said the boy.

"I leave it to you, son."

"Oh, let her have it, then! We can get some more with the other," said the boy.

"A bird in the hand is worth two in the bush, laddie!" said Uncle Oscar.

"But I'm sure to *know* for the Grand National; or the Lincolnshire; or else the Derby. I'm sure to know for one of them," said Paul.

So Uncle Oscar signed the agreement, and Paul's mother touched the whole five thousand. Then something very curious happened. The voices in the house suddenly went mad, like a chorus of frogs on a spring evening. There were certain new furnishings, and Paul had a tutor. He was *really* going to Eton, his father's school, in the following autumn. There were flowers in the winter, and a blossoming of the luxury Paul's mother had been used to. And yet the voices in the house, behind the sprays of mimosa and almond blossom, and from under the piles of iridescent cushions, simply trilled and screamed in a sort of ecstasy: "There *must* be more money! Oh-h-h; there *must* be more money. Oh, now, now-w! Now-w-w—there *must* be more money!—more than ever! More than ever!"

It frightened Paul terribly. He studied away at his Latin and Greek. But his intense hours were spent with Bassett. The Grand National had gone by; he had not "known," and had lost a hundred pounds. Summer was at hand. He was in agony for the Lincoln. But even for the Lincoln he didn't "know," and he lost fifty pounds. He became wild-eyed and strange, as if something were going to explode in him.

"Let it alone, son! Don't you bother about it!" urged Uncle Oscar. But it was as if the boy couldn't really hear what his uncle was saying.

"I've got to know for the Derby! I've got to know for the Derby!" the child reiterated, his big blue eyes blazing with a sort of madness.

His mother noticed how overwrought he was.

"You'd better go to the seaside. Wouldn't you like to go now to the seaside, instead of waiting? I think you'd better," she said, looking down at him anxiously, her heart curiously heavy because of him.

But the child lifted his uncanny blue eyes. "I couldn't possibly go before the Derby, Mother!" he said. "I couldn't possibly!"

"Why not?" she said, her voice becoming heavy when she was opposed. "Why not? You can still go from the seaside to see the Derby with your uncle Oscar, if that's what you wish. No need for you to wait here. Besides, I think you care too much about these races. It's a bad sign. My family has been a gambling family, and you won't know till you grow up how much damage it has done. But it has done damage. I shall have to send Bassett away, and ask Uncle Oscar not to talk racing to you, unless you promise to be reasonable about it; go away to the seaside and forget it. You're all nerves!"

"I'll do what you like, Mother, so long as you don't send me away till after the Derby," the boy said.

"Send you away from where? Just from this house?"

"Yes," he said, gazing at her.

"Why, you curious child, what makes you care about this house so much, suddenly? I never knew you loved it."

He gazed at her without speaking. He had a secret within a secret, something he had not divulged, even to Bassett or to his uncle Oscar.

But his mother, after standing undecided and a little bit sullen for some moments, said:

"Very well, then! Don't go to the seaside till after the Derby, if you don't wish it. But promise me you won't let your nerves go to pieces. Promise you won't think so much about horse racing and *events*, as you call them!"

"Oh, no," said the boy casually. "I won't think much about them, Mother. You needn't worry. I wouldn't worry, Mother, if I were you."

"If you were me and I were you," said his mother, "I wonder what we *should* do!"

"But you know you needn't worry, Mother, don't you?" the boy repeated.

"I should be awfully glad to know it," she said wearily.

"Oh, well you *can*, you know. I mean, you *ought* to know you needn't worry," he insisted.

"Ought I? Then I'll see about it," she said.

Paul's secret of secrets was his wooden horse, that which had no name. Since he was emancipated from a nurse and a nursery governess, he had had his rocking horse removed to his own bedroom at the top of the house.

"Surely, you're too big for a rocking horse!" his mother had remonstrated.

"Well, you see, Mother, till I can have a *real* horse, I like to have *some* sort of animal about," had been his quaint answer.

"Do you feel he keeps you company?" She laughed.

"Oh, yes! He's very good, he always keeps me company, when I'm there," said Paul. So the horse, rather shabby, stood in an arrested prance in the boy's bedroom.

The Derby was drawing near, and the boy grew more and more tense. He hardly heard what was spoken to him, he was very frail, and his eyes were really uncanny. His mother had sudden strange seizures of uneasiness about him. Sometimes, for half an hour, she would feel a sudden anxiety about him that was almost anguish. She wanted to rush to him at once, and know he was safe.

Two nights before the Derby, she was at a big party in town, when one of her rushes of anxiety about her boy, her firstborn, gripped her heart till she could hardly speak. She fought with the feeling, might and main, for she believed in common sense. But it was too strong. She had to leave the dance and go downstairs to telephone to the country. The children's nursery governess was terribly surprised and startled at being rung up in the night.

"Are the children all right, Miss Wilmot?"

"Oh, yes, they are quite all right."

"Master Paul? Is he all right?"

"He went to bed as right as a trivet. Shall I run up and look at him?"

"No," said Paul's mother reluctantly. "No! Don't trouble. It's all right. Don't sit up. We shall be home fairly soon." She did not want her son's privacy intruded upon.

"Very good," said the governess.

It was about one o'clock when Paul's mother and father drove up to their house. All was still. Paul's mother went to her room and slipped off her white fur cloak. She had told her maid not to wait up for her. She heard her husband downstairs, mixing a whisky and soda.

And then, because of the strange anxiety at her heart, she stole upstairs to her son's room. Noiselessly she went along the upper corridor. Was there a faint noise? What was it?

She stood, with arrested muscles, outside his door, listening. There was a strange, heavy, and yet not loud noise. Her heart stood still. It was a soundless noise, yet rushing and powerful. Something huge, in violent, hushed motion. What was it? What in God's name was it? She ought to know. She felt that she knew the noise. She knew what it was.

Yet she could not place it. She couldn't say what it was. And on and on it went, like a madness.

Softly, frozen with anxiety and fear, she turned the door handle.

The room was dark. Yet in the space near the window, she heard and saw something plunging to and fro. She gazed in fear and amazement.

Then suddenly she switched on the light, and saw her son, in his green pajamas, madly surging on the rocking horse. The blaze of light suddenly lit him up, as he urged the wooden horse, and lit her up, as she stood, blonde, in her dress of pale green and crystal, in the doorway.

"Paul!" she cried. "Whatever are you doing?"

"It's Malabar!" he screamed, in a powerful, strange voice. "It's Malabar!"

His eyes blazed at her for one strange and senseless second, as he ceased urging his wooden horse. Then he fell with a crash to the ground, and she, all her tormented motherhood flooding upon her, rushed to gather him up.

But he was unconscious, and unconscious he remained, with some brain fever. He talked and tossed, and his mother sat stonily by his side.

"Malabar! It's Malabar! Bassett, Bassett, I *know!* It's Malabar!"

So the child cried, trying to get up and urge the rocking horse that gave him his inspiration.

"What does he mean by Malabar?" asked the heart-frozen mother.

"I don't know," said the father stonily.

"What does he mean by Malabar?" she asked her brother Oscar.

"It's one of the horses running for the Derby," was the answer.

And, in spite of himself, Oscar Cresswell spoke to Bassett, and himself put a thousand on Malabar: at fourteen to one.

The third day of the illness was critical: they were waiting for a change. The boy, with his rather long, curly hair, was tossing ceaselessly on the pillow. He never slept nor regained consciousness, and his eyes were like blue stones. His mother sat, feeling her heart had gone, turned actually into a stone.

In the evening, Oscar Cresswell did not come, but Bassett sent a message, saying could he come up for one moment, just one moment? Paul's mother was very angry at the intrusion, but on second thought she agreed. The boy was the same. Perhaps Bassett might bring him to consciousness.

The gardener, a shortish fellow with a little brown mustache, and sharp little brown eyes, tiptoed into the room, touched his imaginary cap to Paul's mother, and stole to the bedside, staring with glittering, smallish eyes at the tossing, dying child.

"Master Paul!" he whispered. "Master Paul! Malabar came in first all right, a clean win. I did as you told me. You've made over seventy thousand pounds, you have; you've got over eighty thousand. Malabar came in all right, Master Paul."

"Malabar! Malabar! Did I say Malabar, Mother? Did I say Malabar? Do you think I'm lucky, Mother? I knew Malabar, didn't I? Over eighty thousand pounds! I call that lucky, don't you, Mother? Over eighty thousand pounds! I knew, didn't I know I knew? Malabar came in all right. If I ride my horse till I'm sure, then I tell you, Bassett, you can go as high as you like. Did you go for all you were worth, Bassett?"

"I went a thousand on it, Master Paul."

"I never told you, Mother, that if I can ride my horse, and *get there*, then I'm absolutely sure—oh, absolutely! Mother, did I ever tell you? I *am* lucky!"

"No, you never did," said the mother.

But the boy died in the night.

And even as he lay dead, his mother heard her brother's voice saying to her: "My God, Hester, you're eighty-odd thousand to the good, and a poor devil of a son to the bad. But, poor devil, poor devil, he's best gone out of a life where he rides his rocking horse to find a winner."

(1926)

QUESTIONS FOR REFLECTION

1. Identify the story's central and most important irony. Explain why it is important and how it affects our interpretation of the story and our evaluation of the narrator.
2. Consider whether the story may include other examples of irony besides that of its concluding action. Are there ironic aspects that include verbal, situational, or dramatic ironies? If so, identify a few of these and explain their significance.
3. Can the rocking horse be considered a symbol? Why or why not?
4. What is the symbolic significance of Paul's riding the rocking horse? Of the repeated statement, "There must be more money"?

CHAPTER FOUR

Writing about Fiction

REASONS FOR WRITING ABOUT FICTION

Why write about fiction? One reason is to find out—through note-taking in your journal—what you think about a story or novel. Writing about a story induces you to read it more carefully. You may write about a work of fiction because it engages you and you wish to discuss its implied ideas and values, perhaps in carrying out a course assignment.

Whatever your reasons for writing about fiction, a number of things happen when you do. First, in writing about a novel or story you tend to read it more attentively, noticing things you might overlook in a more casual reading. Second, because writing stimulates thinking, when you write about fiction you find yourself thinking more about what a particular work means and why you respond to it as you do. This focused thinking often has the effect of making a literary work more meaningful to you.

INFORMAL WAYS OF WRITING ABOUT FICTION

When you write about a novel or short story, you may write for yourself or you may write for others. Writing for yourself, writing to discover what you think, often takes casual forms such as annotation and freewriting. These informal kinds of writing are useful for helping you focus. They are helpful in studying for tests about fiction. They can serve also as preliminary forms of writing when you write more formal essays and papers about fiction.

Annotation

When you annotate a text, you make notes in the margins or at the top and bottom of pages. Annotations can also be made within the text, as underlined words, circled phrases, and bracketed sentences or paragraphs. Annotations may also assume the form of arrows, question marks, and various other marks.

Annotating a literary work offers a convenient and relatively painless way to begin writing about it. Annotating can get you started zeroing in on what you think interesting or important. You can also annotate to flag details that puzzle or disconcert you.

Your markings serve to focus your attention and clarify your understanding of a story or novel. Your annotations can save you time in rereading or studying a work. And they can also be used when you write a more formal paper.

Annotations for the following story illustrate the process.

KATHERINE ANNE PORTER

[1890–1980]

Katherine Anne Porter, short-story writer and novelist, was awarded the Pulitzer prize and National Book Award in 1966 for The Collected Stories of Katherine Anne Porter. *Born in Texas, she spent time living in Europe and Mexico, often working for newspapers. Her short-story collections include* Flowering Judas and Other Stories *(1935) and* Pale Horse, Pale Rider *(1939). Her novel,* Ship of Fools, *on which she worked for twenty years, brought her wide acclaim when it was published in 1962. Her basic concern in writing was to examine human motives and portray human experience as she had come to understand it. She received the O. Henry Award, a Guggenheim Fellowship, and numerous honorary doctorates.*

Magic

And, Madame Blanchard, believe that I am happy to be here with you and your family because it is so serene, everything, and before this I worked for a long time in a fancy house—maybe you don't know what is a fancy house? Naturally . . . everyone must have heard sometime or other. Well, Madame, I work always where there is work to be had, and so in this place I worked very hard all hours, and saw too many things, things you wouldn't believe, and I wouldn't think of telling you, only maybe it will rest you while I brush your hair. You'll excuse me too but I could not help hearing you say to the laundress maybe someone had bewitched your linens, they fall away so fast in the wash. Well, there was a girl there in

We enter into a monologue that has already begun

Does she really not want to tell Madame B. what kind of work it is?

Bewitched linens? Magic?

that house, a poor thing, thin, but well-liked by all the men who called, and you understand she could not get along with the woman who ran the house. They quarreled, the madam cheated her on her checks: you know, the girl got a check, a brass one, every time, and at the week's end she gave those back to the madam, yes, that was the way, and got her percentage, a very small little of her earnings: it is a business, you see, like any other—and the madam used to pretend the girl had given back only so many checks, you see, and really she had given many more, but after they were out of her hands, what could she do? So she would say, I will get out of this place, and curse and cry. Then the madam would hit her over the head. She always hit people over the head with bottles; it was the way she fought. My good heavens, Madame Blanchard, what confusion there would be sometimes with a girl running raving downstairs, and the madam pulling her back by the hair and smashing a bottle on her forehead.

From one kind of Madame to another

It was nearly always about the money, the girls got in debt so, and if they wished to go they could not without paying every sou marqué. The madam had full understanding with the police; the girls must come back with them or go to the jails. Well, they always came back with the policemen or with another kind of man friend of the madam: she could make men work for her too, but she paid them very well for all, let me tell you: and so the girls stayed on unless they were sick; if so, if they got too sick, she sent them away again.

What work did the men do?

Madame Blanchard said, 'You are pulling a little here,' and eased a strand of hair: 'and then what?'

Back to the present: Mme B wants to hear more.

Pardon—but this girl, there was a true hatred between her and the madam. She would say many times, I make more money than anybody else in the house, and every week were scenes. So at last she said one morning, Now I will leave this place, and she took out forty dollars from under her pillow and said, Here's your money! The madam began to shout, Where did you get all that, you—? and accused her of robbing the men who came to visit her. The girl said, Keep your hands off or I'll brain you: and at that the madam took hold of her shoulders, and began to lift her knee and kick this girl most terribly in the stomach, and even in her most secret place, Madame Blanchard, and then she beat her in the face with a bottle, and the girl fell back again into her room where I was making clean. I helped her to the bed, and she sat there holding her sides with her head hanging down, and when she got up again there was blood everywhere she had sat. So then the madam came in once more and screamed, Now you can get out, you are no good for me any more: I don't repeat all, you understand it is too much. But she took

Conflict—a fight is brewing Tension builds

all the money she could find, and at the door she gave the girl a great push in the back with her knee, so that she fell again in the street, and then got up and went away with the dress barely on her.

Climax of fight. The battle is over & the girl is literally thrown out.

After this the men who knew this girl kept saying, 'Where is Ninette?' And they kept asking this in the next days, so that the madam could not say any longer, I put her out because she is a thief. No, she began to see she was wrong to send this Ninette away, and then she said, She will be back in a few days, don't trouble yourself.

And now, Madame Blanchard, if you wish to hear, I come to the strange part, the thing recalled to me when you said your linens were bewitched. For the cook in that place was a woman, colored like myself, like myself with much French blood just the same, like myself living always among people who worked spells. But she had a very hard heart, she helped the madam in everything, she liked to watch all that happened, and she gave away tales on the girls. The madam trusted her above everything, and she said, Well, where can I find that slut? because she had gone altogether out of Basin Street before the madam began to ask the police to bring her again. Well, the cook said, I know a charm that works here in New Orleans, colored women do it to bring back their men: in seven days they come again very happy to stay and they cannot say why: even your enemy will come back to you believing you are his friend. It is a New Orleans charm for sure, for certain, they say it does not work even across the river . . . And then they did it just as the cook said. They took the chamber pot of this girl from under her bed, and in it they mixed with water and milk all the relics of her they found there: the hair from her brush, and the face powder from the puff, and even little bits of her nails they found about the edges of the carpet where she sat by habit to cut her finger- and toe-nails; and they dipped the sheets with her blood into the water, and all the time the cook said something over it in a low voice; I could not hear all, but at last she said to the madam, Now spit in it: and the madam spat, the cook said, When she comes back she will be dirt under your feet.

Magic again—this time the cook
Technique: Porter makes us curious

Vodoo? Witchcraft? More magic?

It's the madam's psychological magic that brings her back
Why does it work?

Madame Blanchard closed her perfume bottle with a thin click: 'Yes, and then?'

Then in seven nights the girl came back and she looked very sick, the same clothes and all, but happy to be there. One of the men said, Welcome home, Ninette! and when she started to speak to the madam, the madam said, Shut up and get upstairs and dress yourself. So Ninette, this girl, she said, I'll be down in just a minute. And after that she lived there quietly.

(1930)

Freewriting

Freewriting is a kind of informal writing you do for yourself. In freewriting you explore a text to find out what you think about it and how you respond to it. When you freewrite you do not know ahead of time what your idea or your response to the work will be. Instead you write about the work to see where your thinking leads you.

Freewriting leads you to explore your memories and experience as well as aspects of the text itself. You sometimes wander from the details of the story or novel you are writing about. In the process you may discover thoughts and feelings you didn't know you had or were only dimly aware of.

Here is a group of responses written after students had read Kate Chopin's "The Story of an Hour" (page 38). If you have not read the story, this will be a good time to turn back to Chapter One and do so. If you have read it, you can add your own freewriting response.

Compare your response with the student responses that follow. Then read the story again, this time paying attention to the interpolated comments. What is your reaction to your own first response? To the student responses?

Student 1 My first reaction was that Brently Mallard must have been an abusing husband. Maybe verbal or maybe physical abuse. But I noticed that Mrs. Mallard said his hands were "kind and tender" and she said his face "never looked on her save with love." Then I began to think that maybe Louise Mallard was an ungrateful wife who didn't appreciate what she had. Still, she obviously felt that she had to submit to everything he wanted. She talks about his "powerful will." So she really did feel abused in some ways and maybe that's what's important. I was confused and want to read the story again.

Student 2 Did Louise Mallard die at the end because she was shocked or because she was so upset at losing her freedom? I don't think she died of joy, even though she did have some love for her husband, so I think the doctor was wrong. She may have died of heart trouble, but maybe it was not a physical illness of the heart. Maybe what was wrong was that Louise had never had a chance to know her own heart. So when she did begin to feel some freedom and then lost it, she was sick in her spirit (what some people would call her heart). I think her death was finding a kind of freedom that she couldn't have in life. So maybe the whole incident came out for the best for Louise.

Student 3 I thought maybe Brently's friend Richards had something going with Louise. That was why he rushed right over to tell her about his death. And at the end he tries to protect her. But on the other hand, I couldn't figure out why

Louise wouldn't have some thoughts about Richards while she was imagining her freedom. If they really were having an affair. So maybe they weren't. But why would Louise be so glad to be free if she didn't have a reason?

Student 4 I liked all the metaphors and descriptions which really made you feel like you could understand how Louise's feelings changed. When she first heard the news she had a "storm of grief" but then she looks out the window and sees "patches of blue" so you get the idea that the storm is passing and that maybe Louise is not going to be so unhappy after all. When you read about her "two white slender hands" that are "powerless" they seem sort of like gentle swans, and you can imagine that Louise was sort of a household pet or a decoration for her husband. And that she did not have any way—or did not know any way—to oppose his "powerful will."

Focused freewriting is very much like making journal entries. Keeping an informal log or journal of your responses to the literary works you read is a useful and fairly easy way to prepare for class discussion of them.

FORMAL WAYS OF WRITING ABOUT FICTION

Among the more common formal ways of writing about fiction is analysis. In writing an analytical essay about a short story or a novel, your goal is to explain how one or more particular aspects or issues in the work contribute to its overall meaning. You might analyze the dialogue in Boyle's "Astronomer's Wife" (page 62), for example, in explaining what the verbal exchanges between characters contribute to the story's meaning. You might analyze the ironic qualities of Chopin's "The Story of an Hour" (page 38) or O'Connor's "Good Country People" (page 172). Or you might analyze the characters in Carver's "Cathedral" (page 313) or Lawrence's "The Rocking-Horse Winner" (page 100) to explain how the relationships between the characters reveal each story's theme.

In addition to analyzing these and other fictional elements in a single story, you might also compare two stories, perhaps by focusing on their symbolism, style, tone, setting, or point of view. Or, instead of focusing on literary elements per se, you might write to see how a particular critical perspective illumines a story. For example, you might consider the feminist implications of Updike's "A & P" (page 32) or what a psychological approach to Hawthorne's "Young Goodman Brown" (page 391) contributes to your understanding.

Each of the three student papers that follow focuses on one aspect of a story—the theme of "Guests of the Nation" the imagery of "A Good Man Is Hard to Find," the narrative structure of "A Rose for Emily."

In the first paper, Joseph E. Smith describes the impact that O'Connor's "Guests of the Nation" (page 51) had upon him. He brings his personal response to O'Connor's story into his analysis and interpretation.

Student Papers on Fiction

Joseph E. Smith
Professor Tilly
English 112
March 16, 1998

"Guests of the Nation": A Profound Story

The short story "Guests of a Nation" by Frank O'Connor deals with a tragedy of war. The author's major theme is that the greatest horror in war is the physical and mental destruction of real human beings. The reader experiences this horror vicariously in reading the story. The story appeals to me personally because I could relate to the conflict within the main character; for this reason, it made me think deeply about war and especially its effects on young men like me. Overall, my experience reading the story provides a good illustration of Robert Penn Warren's arguments in his essay on why people read fiction.

According to Robert Penn Warren, "role taking" is one important reason we read fiction (158). Warren states that children take the role of characters in fiction, which helps them to learn how other people feel in different situations. In "Guests of the Nation," we learn something about how it feels to participate in the death of someone we have come to know. Realizing that this is a common experience in wartime gives us some idea of what it is that soldiers face when they go to war.

Towards the beginning of the story, the author offers a description of the main character and of the situation. Two men, Belcher and Hawkins, are being held prisoners of war. Their guards are young men like Belcher and Hawkins, and they all seem to get along playing cards together. This is where the first conflict appears. While they do enjoy themselves, the young guards Bonaparte and Noble sense that having fun with the enemy is somehow not quite right. They feel somehow disoriented. Once, the two guards even question why they have to watch the prisoners at all.

Plenty of description is allotted to Belcher and Hawkins. Belcher is a "big Englishman" who often calls people "chum" (O'Connor 52). He gets along well with the woman who owns the house that the men occupy and helps her with her chores. He is later described as a "huge man" with "an uncommon shortness [. . .] of speech" (53). Hawkins is also described at length. He speaks more than Belcher and is fond of playing cards. He also loves to argue and is full of "old gab" (53). Through these descriptions, the men become real both to their captors and to us readers in the first pages of the story.

More important than the descriptions of their physical traits and hints of their personalities are the discussions the men have. Belcher and Hawkins often argue about God and religion. Belcher, usually passive, is content to say things like, "You're right, chum" (54). Hawkins, more aggressive, tends to make speeches: "The capitalists (sic) pays the priests to tell you about the next world so you won't notice what the bastards are up to in this" (53). After a few of these discussions, the reader knows both what Belcher and Hawkins look like and how they act. What all of this means is that we realize, along with Bonaparte, that Belcher and Hawkins are real people. Herein lies the theme.

In modern war, battles are often waged at great distances with little or no visual contact with the enemy. Killing is much harder when you see the man you kill, and even harder when you must kill him with your own hands. Spend a few days playing cards with him first, as Bonaparte has done, and killing him will tear you apart. This is the main point of the story. War is horrible; at base, all it amounts to is the slaughter of ordinary men by other ordinary men. By making the prisoners so lifelike, and then forcing us with Bonaparte to see them to their death, the author conveys the awful pain that Bonaparte felt.

At the turning point of the story, Bonaparte asks his commander, "Shoot them?" (54). It is clear that Bonaparte believes that what he is asked to do is murder, even though it is an act of war. After the deed is done, Bonaparte, Noble, and Donovan bury the bodies in a bog where it is dark and "birds are screeching" (59): Bonaparte's feeling of horror infects the atmosphere and cannot help affecting the reader. Bonaparte reports that he felt "very small and very lost and lonely" and that he "never felt the same about [anything] again"(59).

Again, according to Robert Penn Warren, the confrontation or conflict in a story helps us confront the most meaningful choices in our lives. "Guests of a Nation," like all good stories, made me re-think choices I have made and the beliefs I have held. Specifically, it made me examine my beliefs about war.

As the reader "lives" the story, he, like Bonaparte, gets to know Belcher and Hawkins as friends. Bonaparte is clearly rattled at the prospect of killing people he has come to know. After he learns that they are to be killed, he has trouble sleeping and talks it over with Noble. The next day he has trouble talking to Hawkins and Belcher, and afterwards reports, "I don't know how we got through that day, but I was very glad when it was over" (55). Bonaparte clearly has severe inner conflict at the idea of killing the "hostages," and the way that conflict is portrayed raises important questions about what's "right" and "wrong," in war and in peace.

My initial reaction to the story was simply one of sadness. At the end of the story, I could not believe that Belcher and Hawkins were so suddenly dead. I also felt sad for Bonaparte, and I think I experienced a part of the agony he must have felt as he watched the execution and then took an active role in the killing. (It is important to note that Bonaparte was the one to finish off Hawkins with a second shot.) Hawkins and Belcher are physically destroyed by the end of the story, but it seems that Bonaparte is mentally, or spiritually, destroyed.

I've always been fascinated by war. When I was younger I had a naive belief that all wars could be avoided and that all were simply senseless killing. As I grew older I realized that war is much more complicated than that. War is horrible—killing is horrible—but men fight for freedom sometimes, and I find that noble. When I read this story, I could imagine myself at war, not knowing what to do, like Bonaparte, but trying to do the right thing.

Just before his death, Belcher comments that he "never could make out what duty was [him]self" (59). I suppose I cannot either. This story forces that question on a person. Bonaparte, Noble, and Donovan killed Belcher and Hawkins because they had orders to do so, and because the other side had killed some of their boys. Should you murder in the service of a country, or to avenge the murder of others who fought with you?

This story's theme of the mental and physical destruction of men in wartime affected me most by challenging my ideas about war. I learned much about war from this account of a man torn by conflict; I also learned much about myself in terms of how I view the lives and actions of other people. Since every person is real and individual, the destruction of any one person is horrible and tragic beyond comparison. But the longer I live, and the more I experience, the more I suspect that horror and tragedy are inevitable parts of life. I don't have any answers yet, but I firmly believe in continuing to ask the questions.

Works Cited

O'Connor, Frank. "Guests of the Nation." Literature: Reading Fiction, Poetry, Drama, and the Essay. Ed. Robert DiYanni. 4th ed. New York: McGraw, 1998. 52-59.

Warren, Robert Penn. "Why Do We Read Fiction?" New and Selected Essays. New York: Random, 1989. 158-189.

Bridgid Driscoll
St. John's University
Dr. Tom Kitts
Literature in a Global Context
February 16, 2005

Religious and Natural Imagery in "A Good Man Is Hard to Find"

Flannery O'Connor, the great Southern short story writer, infuses her short stories with powerful religious and natural imagery. Several motifs, recurring from story to story, spring from this imagery and contain strong, deep implications. "A Good Man Is Hard to Find" is no exception. This story relates the tale of a family whose car accident en route to a Florida vacation leads to a deadly encounter with escaped convicts. Of course, there is much more to the tale than the murders of the family members—O'Connor compels readers to focus on the spiritual implications of the deaths, particularly the mystical revelation of the grandmother. To accomplish this, O'Connor incorporates several religious images that are especially significant, considering her Catholic upbringing and her belief in salvation. "You should be on the lookout for such things as the action of grace in the Grandmother's soul, and not for the dead bodies," writes O'Connor in *Mystery and Manners* (113).

The colors purple and red are significant motifs that O'Connor frequently employs. In the Roman Catholic Church these colors are used, respectively, to represent the seasons of Lent (the forty days before Easter, a period of repentance) and Pentecost (the "birthday of the Church," when the Holy Spirit descended on the Apostles as tongues of flame). Purple can also represent royalty, whereas red may symbolize the blood of Christ. In "A Good Man Is Hard to Find," the grandmother adorns herself with fake purple violets, although June Star remarks that her grandmother "wouldn't stay home to be queen for a day." Both colors appear on the "brilliant red clay banks slightly streaked with purple" that line the highway. This imagery prepares readers for the moment of epiphany in the story—the grandmother's salvation.

Along with color imagery, O'Connor employs an assortment of animals to illustrate her themes. She describes the mother, for instance, as wearing "a green headkerchief that had two points on the top like rabbit's ears"; she compares the grandmother's valise to a hippopotamus, and during the cloud game, one of the children notices that a cloud has a distinct cow shape. But two animals seem especially important: Pitty Sing the cat and Red Sammy's monkey. The cat is especially important to the plot. He is partly responsible for the accident which leaves the family vulnerable to the Misfit—although it is the grandmother who smuggles Pitty Sing into the car, startles him, and, therefore, is the real cause of the chain reaction that leads to the murders. The monkey tied to the chinaberry tree at Red Sammy's is a powerful and evocative image, suggesting the family's fate, which too seems to lie at the end of a very short rope. O'Connor includes animals to suggest the animality of people, especially the individuals in her stories. These animal images enable the reader to reflect on the baser parts of the grandmother, the family, the Misfit (a self-described "different breed of dog"), and his cohorts.

With natural imagery—dirt roads and "tall, dark, deep" woods—the author not only establishes setting, but also reinforces the mentality and spirituality of the characters. In fact, the woods O'Connor uses in "A Good Man Is Hard to Find" are not unlike the woods in her novel *Wise Blood*, where Jesus appears as a "wild ragged figure" moving among the trees in the back of Hazel Motes's mind (22). At one point the line of trees is described as opening behind the family, gaping like a "dark, open, mouth"—the mouth of hell, perhaps? Or is it the way to salvation? Either seems possible, given the denouement of the story.

The images of Flannery O'Connor form just one part of her carefully constructed fiction. The family is "only human," especially the grandmother; O'Connor points out that being "only human" involves some animalistic characteristics. The grandmother, for example, frantically tries to protect herself from the Misfit, much like a cornered animal. However, her salvation hinges not on her desperate attempt, but rather on her ability to disregard preserving her own life in order to recognize the criminal as "one of [her] children," and accept the grace of God—Christ works through her when she acknowledges the Misfit as her own child, the agent of her own grace. Without O'Connor's creative use of images as a code, we would not have seen the grandmother's salvation in quite the same manner. At the end of the story, we are left with the grandmother's smiling at the clearing sky with legs crossed, a martyr—and heaven welcomes her.

Works Cited

O'Connor, Flannery. *Mystery and Manners*. New York: Farrar, Straus and Giroux 1969.

——*Wise Blood*. London: Faber and Faber, 1962.

Jennie R. Mayer
Dr. Thomas M. Kitts
January 16, 2005

A Narrative Interpretation of Faulkner's "A Rose for Emily"

The narrative voice of William Faulkner's "A Rose for Emily" is a collective "we," representing the town of Jefferson, Mississippi, and the values of the Old South. This collective "we" steers through the tale of Miss Emily Grierson, revealing fragments of a life lived as a cultural monument. The narrator employs a structure, complete with a complex web of foreshadowing, that presents numerous clues until it reaches the grotesque climax and its final intention: to present truthfully but with great compassion and respect the life of Emily Grierson, a last leading symbol of the Old South. This is no easy task for the narrator, as Emily murdered her presumed fiancée and slept with his corpse for what seems to be about forty years.

The narrator begins his story with the end of Emily's life. The townspeople, many dressed in Confederate uniforms, have gathered for Emily's funeral in her house, the first of many symbols the narrator employs. Like an aging tomb, the house stands like a decrepit monument marking the town's fading connection to Old South values. More importantly, the house has come to represent Emily. Like Emily, both the exterior and interior have been in decay. Outside, its youthful white color has faded, and inside, the dusty, cracked furniture is well worn by time and neglect, and there is a dank smell. Emily, too, has decayed physically and psychologically and has not adapted well to changing conditions and passing time.

Emily has lived her entire life, living only with a servant since her father's death, a pivotal event in her life which the narrator relates, but not before offering other details. After we learn of Emily's funeral, the first event the narrator recounts is the attempt of a new generation of civic leaders to collect taxes from Emily. Emily simply refuses to pay, instead referring the men to Colonel Sartoris, the former town mayor, who generously remitted her taxes following the death of her father. The narrator admires Colonel Sartoris for not only this remittance, but also for the story he contrived to allow Emily to preserve her dignity—namely, that Mr. Grierson had lent the town money and that the waiving of taxes was the town's method of repayment. Perhaps stunned and intimidated by Emily's refusal and reference to the long-deceased former mayor, the aldermen leave, never to send her another tax notice. Significantly, Emily refers to Colonel Sartoris as a living person even though he has been dead for nearly ten years. Her reference to the colonel not only reveals her inability to assent to any authority except the old, but it also reveals her inability to accept death. Emily cannot accept death because she cannot accept the passing of time. This is signaled by the ticking gold watch that lies hidden about her waist beneath her belt. She seems unaware and undisturbed by the watch and passing time, a destructive inability brought about by her psychosis. It is this psychosis that leads her to murder her sweetheart, Homer Barron, and to sleep with and tolerate the odor of his decaying corpse. Judge Stevens, aged eighty and a member of Jefferson's old guard, further enables her illusions and psychosis to develop undetected when he refuses to allow the newer aldermen to confront her about the smell emanating from her home. Instead, the aldermen are permitted to conceal the stench with lime, thus also covering Emily's murder. It is therefore because of the old town leader's respect for Emily, and what she represents, that her psychosis is able to develop and remain untreated.

In every detail of the story the narrator presents this seemingly innocent, reclusive old woman so as to manipulate and increase the reader's sympathy for her, which serves as a kind of defense of the town as well. The narrator makes it seem as if Emily is doomed to unhappiness, as if she never had a chance to lead a normal and contented life. Because of her father's inability to find any young men acceptable, Emily is left a spinster, continuously thwarted by love. We also learn that Emily's great aunt Wyatt eventually went insane, a detail the narrator uses to foreshadow Emily's own madness. Emily's actions, therefore, cannot be faulted, she is a victim of her flawed inherited genetics.

Perhaps Emily's father was indeed overprotective of his daughter, but perhaps he also saw beginning signs of her insanity. After all, her developing psychosis demonstrates itself with his death. For three days Emily keeps her father's corpse in the house before, at the townspeople's urging, she reluctantly releases him for burial. Thereafter, the townspeople seem to take perverse pleasure in watching and gossiping about Emily as, to them, she grows more human and more needy. Her vulnerability makes the town feel necessary and perhaps superior to the once haughty and dominating Grierson family. At the same time, however, they establish Emily as a monument to old values, which they want to preserve.

The townspeople feel especially necessary when, in the summer following her father's death, Emily falls in love with Homer Barron. Homer, a northerner and the foreman of a construction company, seems to remove Emily from her isolation. But though Homer brings forth Emily's first sign of independence from the shadow of her father's legacy, some in the town are unhappy with their perceived courtship. A northerner, Homer is restructuring the town and seems on the verge of bringing Jefferson into a post-Civil War era. Not wanting to see their symbol of the Old South yield to the North, they write letters to Emily's distant relatives in hopes that they will break the romance. Their action is unnecessary, as the narrator describes Homer as a ". . . big, dark, ready man, with a big voice and eyes lighter than his face," suggesting perhaps an ethnicity not acceptable to old southerners, but more importantly, he suggests that Homer may be homosexual when he states that "it was known that he drank with the younger men in the Elks' Club—that he was not a marrying man." The narrator's purpose in selecting these details is to increase sympathy for Emily and rationalize her murder of Homer, who should not, presumably, have led her on.

The main technique by which the narrator creates sympathy for Emily is through restructuring the chronology of the major events in Emily's life following the death of her father and leading up to the final discovery of Homer's corpse. The narrative confuses time, just as Emily had, to confuse the reader and make her appear less insane, perhaps making us aware of how easy losing track of time can be. In one scene, the narrator shows Emily as she purchases the arsenic that she will use to murder Homer. When the druggist, by law, asks Emily for the required purpose of her purchase, she stares him down, refusing to submit or even respond to his request. The episode reveals her refusal to assent to any laws but the old, her Grierson old Southern pride, and the town's obsession with Emily as they gossip about the purchase, concluding that she will kill herself, an action with which they will not interfere. The narrator presents a town that would prefer to pity Emily for taking her own life, a final descent into fully human status, rather than watch her be thwarted by love yet again. However, the narrator throws us off the murder trail because he relates this episode after Emily's cousins have come to intervene, after they likely caused Homer to desert her. The reordering of the chronology thus increases sympathy for Emily and conceals her murderous intent.

In the end, the town of Jefferson sees Emily as they need and want: as a vulnerable woman representative of the traditions of the Old South. To preserve her memory, the narrator uses a structure that, like Emily's hidden gold watch, is time-fractured to deemphasize the sordidness of Emily's life and perhaps that of the Old South itself. Thus, the story preserves Emily like a dried rose between the pages of a heavy book. This is the Emily the town wants to remember, and this is the Emily those in the town honored at her funeral by dressing in Confederate uniforms, a town who has confused "time with its mathematical progression," and prefers to remember Emily nostalgically, as a gracious citizen of the past and the Old South, which they chose to see as a wide, unchanging meadow, far more gentle and graceful than the New South. Their story is the final rose thrown atop Emily's coffin.

Questions for Writing about Fiction

In writing about the elements of fiction, the following questions can help you focus your thinking and prepare yourself for writing analytical essays and papers. Use the questions as a checklist to guide you to important aspects of any story or novel you read.

Plot and Structure

1. What incidents constitute the building blocks of the story's plot?
2. How are these incidents arranged? Chronologically? With flashbacks of action? With foreshadowing?
3. To what extent is the plot unified? How are its incidents related?
4. How is the story shaped, organized, or designed?
5. What patterns can you discern in the story's action? To what extent are repetition, balance, and contrast important? Why?

Character and Characterization

6. To what extent do you identify with any of the characters? To what extent do you sympathize with them or judge them harshly? Why?
7. To what extent does your response to the characters change? If your response does change, identify where that change occurs and why.
8. Are the characters dynamic or static? In the context of the story, are their actions believable? Why or why not? Do their names convey anything about them?
9. What is the function of any minor characters in the story?
10. How does the author characterize or reveal the characters? What do the characters' speech and behavior reveal about them? What do the author's description and point of view contribute to your understanding of the characters?

Setting

11. Where and when is the action of the story set?
12. To what extent are aspects of the setting symbolic? How do you know?
13. Can you imagine the story set in another place or time? Why or why not?

Point of View

14. Who narrates the story's action? Is the point of view first person or third? Does the point of view shift during the course of the story? If so, where, why, and with what implications for meaning?
15. How much does the narrator know about the characters? Is the narrator completely omniscient? Does the narrator possess limited omniscience? Or does the narrator know only as much as the reader?
16. Is the narrator a participant in the story's action or merely an observer?
17. How trustworthy is the narrator? Is the narrator a reliable witness or commentator on the action and behavior of the story's characters? Why or why not?

Symbolism

18. Do you think any objects or events in the story are symbolic? Why or why not?
19. Are there other symbolic elements—elements of character, setting, language, for example?
20. What do the symbols contribute to the meaning of the story?

Language, Style, Tone

21. How would you characterize the style of the story? The style of the characters' dialogue? Does the style shift at any point?
22. How carefully do you have to read the text? Does the language seem particularly compelling or especially complicated at any point? If so, what makes it compelling or complicated?
23. What is the author's tone or attitude toward the story's characters and action? What aspects of language in particular—diction, imagery, syntax—create that tone?
24. Is the author's tone ironic? If so, how can you tell?

Theme

25. How would you characterize the theme of the story? Is there more than a single theme?

26. Does the author convey the theme(s) directly or indirectly? That is, can you identify a key passage in which the theme is made explicit? Or do you have to infer the theme from the story's action, dialogue, and details?
27. How does your analysis of the elements of fiction help you understand a story's theme(s)?

Critical Perspectives

28. Among the critical perspectives you might bring to bear on the story, which one(s) seem(s) particularly useful for interpreting it? Why?
29. To what extent can you base your interpretation of the story on its language and details alone? To what extent is outside information about historical and biographical context necessary or helpful in understanding it?
30. To what extent does the story mesh with your personal beliefs and values? To what extent is it antagonistic to your personal beliefs and values?

Suggestions for Writing

The Experience of Fiction

1. Write a paper in which you recount your experience of reading a particular story or series of stories by the same author. You may want to compare your initial experience with your experience when you reread the story or stories.
2. Compare the experience of reading a story with that of watching a film based on it.
3. Relate the action or situation of a story to your own experience. Explain how the story is relevant to your situation. Comment on how reading and thinking about it may have helped you view your own circumstances more clearly.

The Interpretation of Fiction

4. Describe a character who has an important decision to make. Identify the character's situation, explain the reasons for his or her decision, and speculate about the possible consequences.
5. Explicate the opening sentences or paragraph of any story. Explain the significance of the opening section in establishing the story's tone, announcing its theme, or otherwise preparing the reader for what follows.
6. Explicate the closing sentences or paragraph of any story. Explain the significance of the conclusion, commenting on its effectiveness as an ending.

7. Select two or three brief passages from a story and explain their significance. Consider how the passages may be related.
8. Analyze the plot of a story. Comment on its organization or structure. How is the plot designed to affect readers' responses? Notice whether the incidents are presented in chronological order or whether chronology is violated and, if so, for what purpose.
9. Analyze the setting of a story. Consider both the time and place of its action. Also consider small-scale aspects of setting such as whether the action takes place indoors or out. If indoors, which room does the action occur in—and why? Notice any significant changes of setting.
10. Analyze a character from a story. Evaluate the character's behavior, offering reasons and evidence for your views. Consider what the character does, says, does not say or do—and why. Identify any significant changes the character undergoes. What do other characters say about him or her, and how do they respond in action?
11. Discuss the relationship of two characters. Consider how the characters affect each other, and explain the nature and significance of their relationship.
12. Analyze the symbolism of a story. Identify its major symbols and explain their significance. Some possibilities: Faulkner's "A Rose for Emily"; Hawthorne's forest in "Young Goodman Brown"; Gilman's "The Yellow Wallpaper"; Olsen's iron in "I Stand Here Ironing"; Walker's "Everyday Use"; Poe's "Black Cat."
13. Analyze the ironic dimensions of a story. Identify examples of irony, and explain their importance in the story. Some possibilities: Poe's "Black Cat"; Joyce's "Araby" and "The Boarding House"; Ellison's "Battle Royal"; Singer's "Gimpel the Fool"; O'Connor's "Guests of the Nation."
14. Analyze the point of view of a story. How would the story be different if it were narrated from a different point of view? Consider whether the narrator is believable or is somehow limited and/or perhaps unworthy of our trust.
15. Explain the theme of any story. Identify its overriding idea. Establish the grounds for your interpretation, and explain why the idea is important.
16. Analyze the use of figurative language in any story. Identify the major types of figurative language used and explain their function, effect, and significance. What would be gained or lost without them? Some possibilities: Faulkner's "A Rose for Emily"; O'Connor's "Good Country People"; Walker's "Everyday Use."

The Evaluation of Fiction

17. Discuss the values exemplified in any story. Identify those values, relate them to your own, and comment on their significance.
18. Do a comparative evaluation of the distinctive merits of any two stories. Explain what they have in common, how they differ, and why one is more interesting, impressive, or effective than the other.

19. Evaluate a story from the standpoint of its merit or literary excellence—or lack thereof. Explain why you consider it to be a successful or unsuccessful story.

To Research or Imagine

20. Develop an alternative ending for a story, changing the outcome in whatever way you like. Be prepared to defend your revised ending. Consider why the author chose to end the story as he or she did.
21. Read some letters or essays by a fiction writer you know and enjoy. Consider how they aid your understanding or increase your pleasure in reading the writer's stories.
22. Read a full-scale biography of a fiction writer. Write a paper explaining how the writer's life is or is not reflected in the work.
23. Read a novel by a writer whose short fiction you enjoy. Write a paper explaining how the novel is related to the shorter fiction.
24. Consider a writer of fiction in his or her historical context. Read a few of the writer's stories as reflections of or denunciations of the social, moral, and cultural dispositions of his or her time.
25. Read a critical study of a fiction writer. Explain how reading the book enhanced your understanding or appreciation of the writer's fiction.

CHAPTER FIVE

Two Fiction Writers in Context

READING EDGAR ALLAN POE AND FLANNERY O'CONNOR IN DEPTH

When you read a fiction writer in even moderate depth, it is useful to look for connections among the works you read. You might read Poe's "The Black Cat," for example, in light of what he himself says in "The Imp of the Perverse" (page 164). You might also read this story in relation to others Poe has written. Although "The Black Cat" is not a horror story in the same way as "The Fall of the House of Usher," you can nonetheless find shared emphases and values reflected in both stories.

In addition to looking for shared thematic preoccupations and common values espoused by different stories, you can also be alert for artistic links. At first glance, "The Fall of the House of Usher" seems quite different from "The Black Cat" and "The Cask of Amontillado." Yet each of these stories shares stylistic traits with the others, and all three reflect characteristics of Poe's writerly temperament.

As you read for connections among a writer's works, be careful not to pour every story into the same mold. Recognize what links the stories, but remain alert for the distinctive and individual presence of each. Consider how each work manifests its individuality at the same time that it reveals shared thematic concerns and corresponding aesthetic qualities of other works by the writer.

What is said here of Poe's fiction applies with equal force to the works of Flannery O'Connor. O'Connor's fiction is often read in light of her religious faith. As a strong adherent of Roman Catholicism who has written about her faith, O'Connor seems to invite readers to bring a strong Christian perspective to their reading of her work. This invitation is strengthened by the explicit Christian references in the stories themselves. Nonetheless, when reading O'Connor's stories, readers need to maintain a balance between interpretations based on the stories' explicit use of Christian iconography and the quirky individuality of each particular fictional creation.

In reading all of the following stories, enjoy the unique pleasures each story provides while constructing a sense of each writer's fictional world. Also, while attending to what both writers have said about their fiction, attend even more to the individual fictional works themselves. "Trust the tale," as D. H. Lawrence once advised, not the teller. Or rather, trust the tale as the teller narrates it rather than as the teller describes or otherwise explains it.

You can use the following questions as a general guide for in-depth reading of fiction.

QUESTIONS FOR IN-DEPTH READING

1. What general or overall thematic connections can you make among different works?
2. What stylistic similarities do you notice between and among different works?
3. How do the works differ in emphasis, tone, and style?
4. Once you have identified a writer's major preoccupations, place each work on a spectrum or a grid that represents the range of the writer's concerns.
5. What connections and disjunctions do you find among the following literary elements as they are embodied in different stories by the same writer?
   a. plot and structure
   b. character and characterization
   c. setting and symbolism
   d. language, style, and tone
   e. theme and thought
6. To what extent are your responses to and perceptions of different works by the same writer shared by others—by critics, by classmates, and by the writers themselves?
7. What relationships and differences do you see between the work of one writer and that of another who shares similar thematic interests, stylistic proclivities, or cultural, religious, or social values?
8. Which of the critical perspectives (Chapter 30) seem most useful as analytical tools for approaching the body of work of particular writers?

EDGAR ALLAN POE IN CONTEXT

[1809–1849]

Edgar Allan Poe is certainly one of the best known and most popular of American writers. His stories are read by children, probed with the tools of psychoanalysis by critics, and transformed into films. His poems, notably "The Raven," "To Helen," and "Annabel Lee," are widely anthologized. And his critical notion that a poem (and by extension any work of verbal art) should be readable in a single sitting so as not to mute its single effect is a familiar critical principle. More importantly, Poe's poetic theories, outlined in such pieces as "The Poetic Principle," "The Rationale of Verse," and "The Philosophy of Composition," had a profound influence on the French symbolist movement.

Poe and Journalism

Before he became a famous poet and short-story writer, Poe was known as a journalist and magazine editor. He wrote numerous reviews about works now forgotten while producing his own memorable tales and poems. And though he never realized his dream of founding a literary magazine of his own, he contributed to many, including those he edited. As a writer for popular periodicals such as the *Broadway Journal* and *Graham's Lady's and Gentleman's Magazine,* and as an editor of literary periodicals such as the *Southern Literary Messenger,* Poe came to understand very well the audiences who read his work. He aimed his work, as he wrote, "not above the popular, nor below the critical, taste," turning the fictional conventions of his own time to good account.

Writers as diverse as Baudelaire and Dostoyevsky admired Poe's work. Baudelaire, who translated many of Poe's tales, in fact, acknowledged Poe's influence by writing that if Poe hadn't existed Baudelaire would have had to invent him. Dostoyevsky was unstinting in his praise of Poe's revelations of minds at war with themselves. Although Dostoyevsky's own fictional explorations of extreme states of consciousness and his dramatic depictions of behavior honed by guilt are more ambitious and monumental than Poe's sketches and tales, the Russian writer felt a kinship with Poe.

Poe's life was as tormented as were the lives and the minds of his stories' narrators. He was born to itinerant actors in Boston. His father died when he was a year old and his mother a year later. Edgar and his brother and sister were taken as foster children into the home of a Richmond tobacco merchant, John Allan. Poe was educated in England and at the University of Virginia, where he was provided with insufficient funds for food, books, and clothing by John Allan. Living among wealthy young men, Poe resorted to gambling, which further worsened his financial situation and contributed to what was an already seriously strained relationship with his foster father, who disapproved of his literary ambitions. The upshot was that Poe withdrew from the university and was left to make his own way as an author.

Virginia Clemm Poe (1822–1847)

In 1835 he married his cousin Virginia Clemm and took her mother in to live with them. By that time Poe had completed two years at the U.S. Military Academy at West Point and had served in the army. In 1837 he moved his family from Baltimore to New York, where he published his only full-length fictional work, *The Narrative of Arthur Gordon Pym.* He did hackwork before moving to Philadelphia, where he became coeditor of *Burton's Gentleman's Magazine* (1839–1840) and published his *Tales of the Grotesque and Arabesque* (1840). Poe borrowed the terms "grotesque" and "arabesque" from the Romantic poet and novelist Sir Walter Scott, and meant them to suggest the terror associated with the bizarre and the beautiful associated with the poetic. He also meant to suggest that both elements were present in many stories in his collection.

Poe and the Horror Story

Poe is perhaps most famous as a writer of horror stories, which excite the imagination of readers by creating an aura of suspense and terror. Poe's horror stories typically include narrators who have committed some horrible crime, such as murder, or who reveal some terrible secret about taboo subjects, such as incest and necrophilia. In these stories, such as "The Masque of the Red Death," "The Tell-Tale Heart," and "Ligeia," among many others, Poe attempts to thrill and shock readers through the description of frightening events and surprising twists of plot.

But there is more to his horror stories than mere frissons of horror. Poe's tales in this vein are also psychological studies of guilt, obsession, and compulsion. Like the characters in Dostoyevsky's novels, the narrators of Poe's horror stories are provocative studies in the intricacies, complexities, and contradictions of human character. Poe's narrators often perversely lead others to discover their crimes, when there appears to be every opportunity for them to escape detection. They are driven by an inner compulsion, which psychologists explain with terms such as "guilt," "self-punishment," and "masochism."

What is most horrifying about Poe's best stories is less the shocking and terrifying events they describe and more the bizarre behavior and thinking of the narrators who recount those events. This interest in the human mind and character distinguishes Poe from other writers of horror stories, whose interest is primarily if not exclusively in describing horrifying events.

"The Fall of the House of Usher" is among Poe's most famous and most accomplished tales. The house that falls is both the literal Usher habitation and the family it signifies. The house also represents the mind of Roderick Usher. In its density of detail, bizarre events, and uncanny tone, the story suggests gothic fiction. In its psychological richness and tainted family history, it reaches back to Greek tragedy.

"The Cask of Amontillado" exemplifies Poe's genius at displaying a mad narrator whose intent is to convince his listeners of his sanity. (Perhaps Poe's best-known example of this type is the narrator of "The Tell-Tale Heart.") But "The Cask of Amontillado" is an even richer story, with Poe pulling out all the stops in displaying

Movie Poster for *The Raven,* Starring Vincent Price

Illustration for "The Fall of the House of Usher." Wood engraving by Constant le Breton/The Granger Collection, New York

multiple ironies while his narrator feels compelled to tell somebody of the perfect murder he committed fifty years before. The question is why he tells this tale after so many years.

Poe and the Detective Story

Poe has also been described as the father of modern detective fiction. And though Poe himself did not refer to his crime stories as "detective stories" (he called them tales of ratiocination), they sometimes do turn on the solution to a crime. But Poe's detective stories are less tales of crime than tales of confession. He is less interested in the crime than in the motive to confess the crime. His murderers seem driven to reveal their ghastly crimes; concealing them seems too much of a torment.

Nonetheless, stories such as "The Murders in the Rue Morgue," "The Gold Bug," and "The Purloined Letter" reveal Poe's interest in the rational and analytical mind. The detective in these stories is adept at solving problems and puzzles. But he is equally adept at understanding human character and motivation, especially in placing himself in the mind of others. What makes Poe's Monsieur Dupin so successful at his work of solving crimes is his understanding of human behavior, and his ability to enter into the mind of the perpetrator.

As with his horror tales, Poe's tales of ratiocination explore the intricacies of the human mind. This interest in the workings of the mind finds expression in other Poe works, which can be classified neither as horror stories nor as detective fiction. One example is his famous poem "The Raven," which describes the death of a beautiful woman and whose speaker or narrator drives himself insane with torment over the loss of his lover, the theme of loss being one of Poe's most constant in both his stories and his poems.

In "The Purloined Letter" Poe gives way to his bent for stories of crime and punishment, this time from the outside point of view of the detective rather than from inside the criminal's mind. Rather than considering what he would have done in like circumstances, the detective, Monsieur Dupin, must try to think the way the criminal thought, which is precisely what he does en route to solving the case. The story celebrates Poe's appreciation of the rational mind and contains a number of examples of riddles and games in which Poe delighted. It also ends with an elaborate puzzle built on a complex literary allusion, which contains the key Poe uses to unlock the intricacies of the story's plot.

The Dimension of Style

Poe is a writer who sends readers to the dictionary. One element of his style is a penchant for Latinate words of multiple syllables, words such as "munificent," "appellation," "trepidation," "felicity," and "dissolution." This aspect of Poe's style is coupled with his fondness for long, convoluted sentences with multiple ramifying clauses. Together, the frequent recourse to long words and long sentences gives his style a unique, formal quality.

But what is more distinctive even than Poe's use of long sentences with polysyllabic diction is the way he employs repetition of word and phrase along with interruptions in the unfolding of sentences to create an effect of intensity, which he often uses to build up suspense and to suggest terror. His description of the house of Usher in the opening paragraph of "The Fall of the House of Usher" provides a modest example:

> I looked upon the scene before me—upon the mere house, and the simple landscape features of the domain—upon the bleak walls—upon the vacant eye-like windows—upon a few rank sedges—and upon a few white trunks of decayed trees—with an utter depression of soul which I can compare to no earthly sensation more properly than to the after-dream of the reveller upon opium—the bitter lapse into everyday life—the hideous dropping off of the veil.

In this passage, too, Poe reaches for comparisons to convey something of the mysterious feelings his narrator is experiencing. But for all the descriptive detail, the repetitions and the comparisons, the effect is one of vague trepidation, the vagueness contributing to the sense of mysterious strangeness.

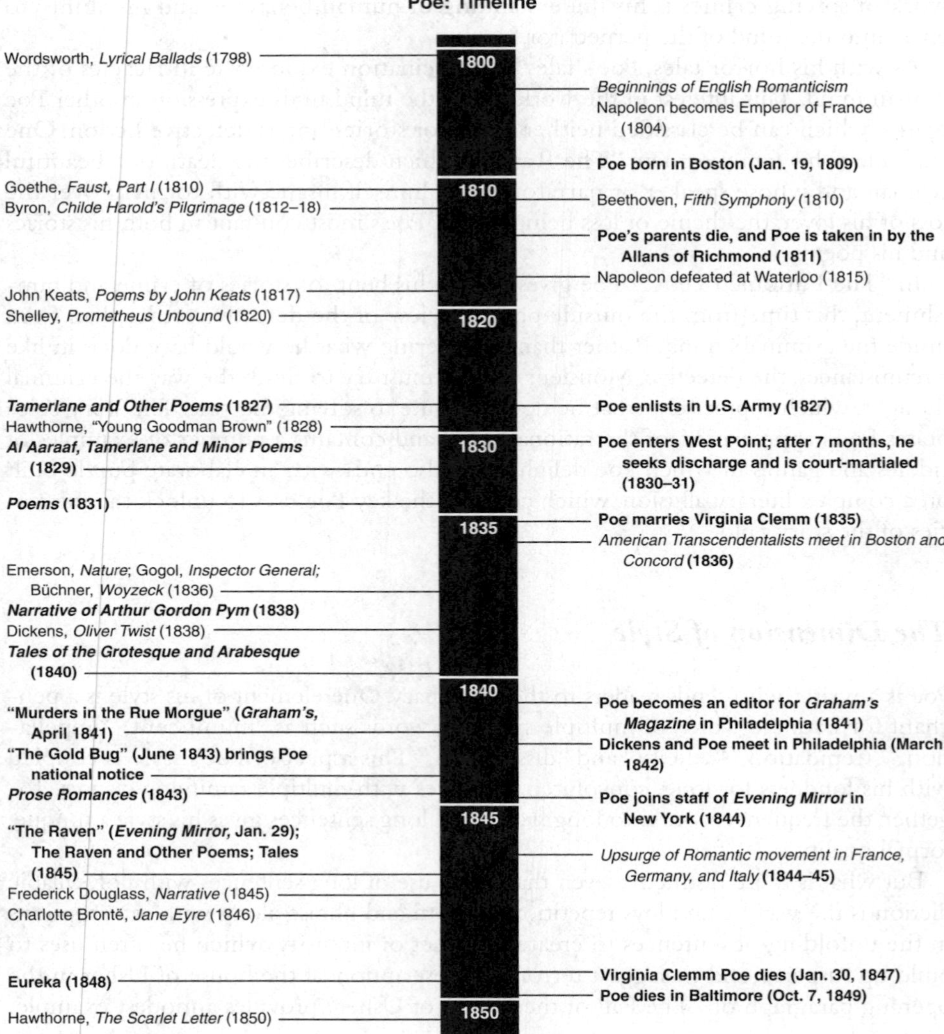
Poe: Timeline
Wordsworth, Lyrical Ballads (1798)
1800
Beginnings of English Romanticism
Napoleon becomes Emperor of France (1804)
Poe born in Boston (Jan. 19, 1809)
Goethe, Faust, Part I (1810)
Byron, Childe Harold's Pilgrimage (1812–18)
1810
Beethoven, Fifth Symphony (1810)
Poe's parents die, and Poe is taken in by the Allans of Richmond (1811)
Napoleon defeated at Waterloo (1815)
John Keats, Poems by John Keats (1817)
Shelley, Prometheus Unbound (1820)
1820
Tamerlane and Other Poems (1827)
Poe enlists in U.S. Army (1827)
Hawthorne, "Young Goodman Brown" (1828)
Al Aaraaf, Tamerlane and Minor Poems (1829)
1830
Poe enters West Point; after 7 months, he seeks discharge and is court-martialed (1830–31)
Poems (1831)
1835
Poe marries Virginia Clemm (1835)
American Transcendentalists meet in Boston and Concord (1836)
Emerson, Nature; Gogol, Inspector General; Büchner, Woyzeck (1836)
Narrative of Arthur Gordon Pym (1838)
Dickens, Oliver Twist (1838)
Tales of the Grotesque and Arabesque (1840)
1840
"Murders in the Rue Morgue" (Graham's, April 1841)
Poe becomes an editor for Graham's Magazine in Philadelphia (1841)
"The Gold Bug" (June 1843) brings Poe national notice
Dickens and Poe meet in Philadelphia (March 1842)
Prose Romances (1843)
Poe joins staff of Evening Mirror in New York (1844)
1845
"The Raven" (Evening Mirror, Jan. 29); The Raven and Other Poems; Tales (1845)
Upsurge of Romantic movement in France, Germany, and Italy (1844–45)
Frederick Douglass, Narrative (1845)
Charlotte Brontë, Jane Eyre (1846)
Eureka (1848)
Virginia Clemm Poe dies (Jan. 30, 1847)
Poe dies in Baltimore (Oct. 7, 1849)
1850
Hawthorne, The Scarlet Letter (1850)

Poe's fictional performances delighted audiences in his own time and continue to engage and intrigue readers today. Even though his style is ornate and his language far from colloquial, he remains a most readable writer, largely because he builds suspense, creates atmosphere, and probes the psychological complexities of his characters' minds and hearts. If it is the horror of his stories that first draws readers in, it is Poe's psychological richness and his control of tone that continue to bring them back for repeated readings of some unmatchable stories.

EDGAR ALLAN POE: STORIES

The Black Cat

For the most wild yet most homely narrative which I am about to pen, I neither expect nor solicit belief. Mad indeed would I be to expect it, in a case where my very senses reject their own evidence. Yet, mad am I not—and very surely do I not dream. But to-morrow I die, and to-day I would unburden my soul. My immediate purpose is to place before the world, plainly, succinctly, and without comment, a series of mere household events. In their consequences, these events have terrified—have tortured—have destroyed me. Yet I will not attempt to expound them. To me, they have presented little but horror—to many they will seem less terrible than *baroques*. Hereafter, perhaps, some intellect may be found which will reduce my phantasm to the commonplace—some intellect more calm, more logical, and far less excitable than my own, which will perceive, in the circumstances I detail with awe, nothing more than an ordinary succession of very natural causes and effects.

From my infancy I was noted for the docility and humanity of my disposition. My tenderness of heart was even so conspicuous as to make me the jest of my companions. I was especially fond of animals, and was indulged by my parents with a great variety of pets. With these I spent most of my time, and never was so happy as when feeding and caressing them. This peculiarity of character grew with my growth, and, in my manhood, I derived from it one of my principal sources of pleasure. To those who have cherished an affection for a faithful and sagacious dog, I need hardly be at the trouble of explaining the nature or the intensity of the gratification thus derivable. There is something in the unselfish and self-sacrificing love of a brute, which goes directly to the heart of him who has had frequent occasion to test the paltry friendship and gossamer fidelity of mere *Man*.

I married early, and was happy to find in my wife a disposition not uncongenial with my own. Observing my partiality for domestic pets, she lost no opportunity of procuring those of the most agreeable kind. We had birds, gold-fish, a fine dog, rabbits, a small monkey, and a *cat*.

This latter was a remarkably large and beautiful animal, entirely black, and sagacious to an astonishing degree. In speaking of his intelligence, my wife, who at heart was not a little tinctured with superstition, made frequent allusion to the ancient popular notion, which regarded all black cats as witches in disguise. Not that she was ever *serious* upon this point—and I mention the matter at all for no better reason than that it happens, just now, to be remembered.

Pluto°—this was the cat's name—was my favorite pet and playmate. I alone fed him, and he attended me wherever I went about the house. It was even with difficulty that I could prevent him from following me through the streets.

Pluto *Roman god of the dead.*

Our friendship lasted, in this manner, for several years, during which my general temperament and character—through the instrumentality of the Fiend Intemperance—had (I blush to confess it) experienced a radical alteration for the worse. I grew, day by day, more moody, more irritable, more regardless of the feelings of others. I suffered myself to use intemperate language to my wife. At length, I even offered her personal violence. My pets, of course, were made to feel the change in my disposition. I not only neglected, but ill-used them. For Pluto, however, I still retained sufficient regard to restrain me from maltreating him, as I made no scruple of maltreating the rabbits, the monkey, or even the dog, when, by accident, or through affection, they came in my way. But my disease grew upon me—for what disease is like Alcohol!—and at length even Pluto, who was now becoming old, and consequently somewhat peevish—even Pluto began to experience the effects of my ill temper.

One night, returning home, much intoxicated, from one of my haunts about town, I fancied that the cat avoided my presence. I seized him; when, in his fright at my violence, he inflicted a slight wound upon my hand with his teeth. The fury of a demon instantly possessed me. I knew myself no longer. My original soul seemed, at once, to take its flight from my body; and a more than fiendish malevolence, gin-nurtured, thrilled every fibre of my frame. I took from my waistcoat-pocket a penknife, opened it, grasped the poor beast by the throat, and deliberately cut one of its eyes from the socket! I blush, I burn, I shudder, while I pen the damnable atrocity.

When reason returned with the morning—when I had slept off the fumes of the night's debauch—I experienced a sentiment half of horror, half of remorse, for the crime of which I had been guilty; but it was, at best, a feeble and equivocal feeling, and the soul remained untouched. I again plunged into excess, and soon drowned in wine all memory of the deed.

In the meantime the cat slowly recovered. The socket of the lost eye presented, it is true, a frightful appearance, but he no longer appeared to suffer any pain. He went about the house as usual, but, as might be expected, fled in extreme terror at my approach. I had so much of my old heart left, as to be at first grieved by this evident dislike on the part of a creature which had once so loved me. But this feeling soon gave place to irritation. And then came, as if to my final and irrevocable overthrow, the spirit of Perverseness. Of this spirit philosophy takes no account. Yet I am not more sure that my soul lives, than I am that perverseness is one of the primitive impulses of the human heart—one of the indivisible primary faculties, or sentiments, which give direction to the character of Man. Who has not, a hundred times, found himself committing a vile or stupid action, for no other reason than because he knows he should *not?* Have we not a perpetual inclination, in the teeth of our best judgment, to violate that which is *Law,* merely because we understand it to be such? This spirit of perverseness, I say, came to my final overthrow. It was this unfathomable longing of the soul *to vex itself*—to offer violence to its own nature—to do wrong for the wrong's sake only—that urged me to continue and finally to consummate the injury I had inflicted upon the unoffending brute. One morning, in cold blood, I slipped a noose about its neck and hung it to the limb of a tree;—hung it with the tears streaming from my eyes, and with the bitterest remorse at my heart;—hung it *because* I knew that it had loved me, and *because* I felt it had given me no reason of offence;—hung it *because* I knew that in so doing I was committing a sin—a deadly sin that would so jeopardize my immortal soul as to place it—if such a thing were possible—even beyond the reach of the infinite mercy of the Most Merciful and Most Terrible God.

On the night of the day on which this most cruel deed was done, I was aroused from sleep by the cry of fire. The curtains of my bed were in flames. The whole house was blazing. It was with great difficulty that my wife, a servant, and myself, made our escape from the conflagration. The destruction was complete. My entire worldly wealth was swallowed up, and I resigned myself thenceforward to despair.

I am above the weakness of seeking to establish a sequence of cause and effect, between the disaster and the atrocity. But I am detailing a chain of facts—and wish not to leave even a possible link imperfect. On the day succeeding the fire, I visited the ruins. The walls, with one exception, had fallen in. This exception was found in a compartment wall, not very thick, which stood about the middle of the house, and against which had rested the head of my bed. The plastering had here, in great measure, resisted the action of the fire—a fact which I attributed to its having been recently spread. About this wall a dense crowd were collected, and many persons seemed to be examining a particular portion of it with very minute and eager attention. The words "strange!" "singular!" and other similar expressions, excited my curiosity. I approached and saw, as if graven in *bas-relief* upon the white surface, the figure of a gigantic *cat*. The impression was given with an accuracy truly marvelous. There was a rope about the animal's neck.

When I first beheld this apparition—for I could scarcely regard it as less—my wonder and my terror were extreme. But at length reflection came to my aid. The cat, I remembered, had been hung in a garden adjacent to the house. Upon the alarm of fire, this garden had been immediately filled by the crowd—by some one of whom the animal must have been cut from the tree and thrown, through an open window, into my chamber. This had probably been done with the view of arousing me from sleep. The falling of other walls had compressed the victim of my cruelty into the substance of the freshly-spread plaster, the lime of which, with the flames, and the *ammonia* from the carcass, had then accomplished the portraiture as I saw it.

Although I thus readily accounted to my reason, if not altogether to my conscience, for the startling fact just detailed, it did not the less fail to make a deep impression upon my fancy. For months I could not rid myself of the phantasm of the cat; and, during this period, there came back into my spirit a half-sentiment that seemed, but was not, remorse. I went so far as to regret the loss of the animal, and to look about me, among the vile haunts which I now habitually frequented, for another pet of the same species, and of somewhat similar appearance, with which to supply its place.

One night as I sat, half stupefied, in a den of more than infamy, my attention was suddenly drawn to some black object, reposing upon the head of one of the immense hogsheads° of gin, or of rum, which constituted the chief furniture of the apartment. I had been looking steadily at the top of this hogshead for some minutes, and what now caused me surprise was the fact that I had not sooner perceived the object thereupon. I approached it, and touched it with my hand. It was a black cat—a very large one—fully as large as Pluto, and closely resembling him in every respect but one. Pluto had not a white hair upon any portion of his body; but this cat had a large, although indefinite splotch of white, covering nearly the whole region of the breast.

hogshead *large barrels.*

Upon my touching him, he immediately arose, purred loudly, rubbed against my hand, and appeared delighted with my notice. This, then, was the very creature of which I was in search. I at once offered to purchase it of the landlord; but this person made no claim to it—knew nothing of it—had never seen it before.

I continued my caresses, and when I prepared to go home, the animal evinced a disposition to accompany me. I permitted it to do so; occasionally stooping and patting it as I proceeded. When it reached the house it domesticated itself at once, and became immediately a great favorite with my wife.

For my own part, I soon found a dislike to it arising within me. This was just the reverse of what I had anticipated; but—I know not how or why it was—its evident fondness for myself rather disgusted and annoyed me. By slow degrees these feelings of disgust and annoyance rose into the bitterness of hatred. I avoided the creature; a certain sense of shame, and the remembrance of my former deed of cruelty, preventing me from physically abusing it. I did not, for some weeks, strike, or otherwise violently ill use it; but gradually—very gradually—I came to look upon it with unutterable loathing, and to flee silently from its odious presence, as from the breath of a pestilence.

What added, no doubt, to my hatred of the beast, was the discovery on the morning after I brought it home, that like Pluto, it also had been deprived of one of its eyes. This circumstance, however, only endeared it to my wife, who, as I have already said, possessed, in a high degree, that humanity of feeling which had once been my distinguishing trait, and the source of many of my simplest and purest pleasures.

With my aversion to this cat, however, its partiality for myself seemed to increase. It followed my footsteps with a pertinacity which it would be difficult to make the reader comprehend. Whenever I sat, it would crouch beneath my chair, or spring upon my knees, covering me with its loathsome caresses. If I arose to walk it would get between my feet and thus nearly throw me down, or, fastening its long and sharp claws in my dress, clamber, in this manner, to my breast. At such times, although I longed to destroy it with a blow, I was yet withheld from so doing, partly by a memory of my former crime, but chiefly—let me confess it at once—by absolute dread of the beast.

This dread was not exactly a dread of physical evil—and yet I should be at a loss how otherwise to define it. I am almost ashamed to own—yes, even in this felon's cell, I am almost ashamed to own—that the terror and horror with which the animal inspired me, had been heightened by one of the merest chimeras it would be possible to conceive. My wife had called my attention, more than once, to the character of the mark of white hair, of which I have spoken, and which constituted the sole visible difference between the strange beast and the one I had destroyed. The reader will remember that this mark, although large, had been originally very indefinite; but, by slow degrees—degrees nearly imperceptible, and which for a long time my reason struggled to reject as fanciful—it had, at length, assumed a rigorous distinctness of outline. It was now the representation of an object that I shudder to name—and for this, above all, I loathed, and dreaded, and would have rid myself of the monster *had I dared*—it was now, I say, the image of a hideous—of a ghastly thing—of the Gallows!—oh, mournful and terrible engine of Horror and of Crime—of Agony and of Death!

And now was I indeed wretched beyond the wretchedness of mere Humanity. And *a brute beast*—whose fellow I had contemptuously destroyed—*a brute beast* to work out for *me*—for me, a man fashioned in the image of the High God—so much of insufferable woe! Alas! neither by day nor by night knew I the blessing of rest any more! During the former the creature left me no moment alone, and in the latter I started hourly from dreams of unutterable fear to find the hot breath of *the thing* upon my face, and its vast weight—an incarnate nightmare that I had not power to shake off—incumbent eternally upon my *heart!*

Beneath the pressure of torments such as these the feeble remnant of the good within me succumbed. Evil thoughts became my sole intimates—the darkest and most evil of thoughts. The moodiness of my usual temper increased to hatred of all things and of all mankind; while from the sudden, frequent, and ungovernable outbursts of a fury to which I now blindly abandoned myself, my uncomplaining wife, alas, was the most usual and the most patient of sufferers.

One day she accompanied me, upon some household errand, into the cellar of the old building which our poverty compelled us to inhabit. The cat followed me down the steep stairs, and, nearly throwing me headlong, exasperated me to madness. Uplifting an axe, and forgetting in my wrath the childish dread which had hitherto stayed my hand, I aimed a blow at the animal, which, of course, would have proved instantly fatal had it descended as I wished. But this blow was arrested by the hand of my wife. Goaded by the interference into a rage more than demoniacal, I withdrew my arm from her grasp and buried the axe in her brain. She fell dead upon the spot without a groan.

This hideous murder accomplished, I set myself forthwith, and with entire deliberation, to the task of concealing the body. I knew that I could not remove it from the house, either by day or by night, without the risk of being observed by the neighbors. Many projects entered my mind. At one period I thought of cutting the corpse into minute fragments, and destroying them by fire. At another, I resolved to dig a grave for it in the floor of the cellar. Again, I deliberated about casting it in the well in the yard—about packing it in a box, as if merchandise, with the usual arrangements, and so getting a porter to take it from the house. Finally I hit upon what I considered a far better expedient than either of these. I determined to wall it up in the cellar, as the monks of the Middle Ages are recorded to have walled up their victims.

For a purpose such as this the cellar was well adapted. Its walls were loosely constructed, and had lately been plastered throughout with a rough plaster, which the dampness of the atmosphere had prevented from hardening. Moreover, in one of the walls was a projection, caused by a false chimney, or fireplace, that had been filled up and made to resemble the rest of the cellar. I made no doubt that I could readily displace the bricks at this point, insert the corpse, and wall the whole up as before, so that no eye could detect anything suspicious.

And in this calculation I was not deceived. By means of a crowbar I easily dislodged the bricks, and, having carefully deposited the body against the inner wall, I propped it in that position, while with little trouble I relaid the whole structure as it originally stood. Having procured mortar, sand, and hair, with every possible precaution, I prepared a plaster which could not be distinguished from the old, and with this, I very carefully went over the new brick-work. When I had finished, I felt satisfied that all was right. The wall did not present the slightest appearance of having been disturbed. The rubbish on the floor was picked up with the minutest care. I looked around triumphantly, and said to myself: "Here at least, then, my labor has not been in vain."

My next step was to look for the beast which had been the cause of so much wretchedness; for I had, at length, firmly resolved to put it to death. Had I been able to meet with it at the moment, there could have been no doubt of its fate; but it appeared that the crafty animal had been alarmed at the violence of my previous anger, and forbore to present itself in my present mood. It is impossible to describe or to imagine the deep, blissful sense of relief which the absence of the detested creature occasioned in my bosom. It did not make its appearance during the night; and thus for one night, at least, since its introduction into the house, I soundly and tranquilly slept; aye, slept even with the burden of murder upon my soul.

The second and the third day passed, and still my tormentor came not. Once again I breathed as a freeman. The monster, in terror, had fled the premises for ever! I should behold it no more! My happiness was supreme! The guilt of my dark deed disturbed me but little. Some few inquiries had been made, but these had been readily answered. Even a search had been instituted—but of course nothing was to be discovered. I looked upon my future felicity as secured.

Upon the fourth day of the assassination, a party of the police came, very unexpectedly, into the house, and proceeded again to make a rigorous investigation of the premises. Secure, however, in the inscrutability of my place of concealment, I felt no embarrassment whatever. The officers bade me accompany them in their search. They left no nook or corner unexplored. At length, for the third or fourth time, they descended into the cellar. I quivered not in a muscle. My heart beat calmly as that of one who slumbers in innocence. I walked the cellar from end to end. I folded my arms upon my bosom, and roamed easily to and fro. The police were thoroughly satisfied and prepared to depart. The glee at my heart was too strong to be restrained. I burned to say if but one word, by way of triumph, and to render doubly sure their assurance of my guiltlessness.

"Gentlemen," I said at last, as the party ascended the steps, "I delight to have allayed your suspicions. I wish you all health and a little more courtesy. By the bye, gentlemen, this—this is a very well-constructed house," (in the rabid desire to say something easily, I scarcely knew what I uttered at all),—"I may say an excellently well-constructed house. These walls—are you going, gentlemen?—these walls are solidly put together"; and here, through the mere frenzy of bravado, I rapped heavily with a cane which I held in my hand, upon that very portion of the brick-work behind which stood the corpse of the wife of my bosom.

But may God shield and deliver me from the fangs of the Arch-Fiend! No sooner had the reverberation of my blows sunk into silence, than I was answered by a voice from within the tomb!—by a cry, at first muffled and broken, like the sobbing of a child, and then quickly swelling into one long, loud, and continuous scream, utterly anomalous and inhuman—a howl—a wailing shriek, half of horror and half of triumph, such as might have arisen only out of hell, conjointly from the throats of the damned in their agony and of the demons that exult in the damnation.

Of my own thoughts it is folly to speak. Swooning, I staggered to the opposite wall. For one instant the party on the stairs remained motionless, through extremity of terror and awe. In the next a dozen stout arms were toiling at the wall. It fell bodily. The corpse, already greatly decayed and clotted with gore, stood erect before the eyes of the spectators. Upon its head, with red extended mouth and solitary eye of fire, sat the hideous beast whose craft had seduced me into murder, and whose informing voice had consigned me to the hangman. I had walled the monster up within the tomb.

(1845)

QUESTIONS FOR CRITICAL THINKING AND WRITING

Experience

1. Explain your response to the various shocking revelations of the narrator throughout the story, particularly his treatment of the black cat and the murder of his wife.
2. How do you respond to the narrator's paroxysms of rage, his violent outbursts of anger? To what extent, if at all, do you sympathize with his behavior? To what extent can you understand why he behaves as he does?

Interpretation

3. Identify two ironic elements of the story and explain their significance.
4. Identify two symbolic elements of the story and explain their significance.
5. Explain why the narrator kills his wife and why he appears to have no remorse for doing so.
6. Do you accept the narrator's blaming of the cat for his actions and for his fate? Why or why not?
7. Why and how does the narrator get caught? What psychological explanation might be offered for how his actions come to light?

Evaluation

8. How well made, how successful a story is "The Black Cat" as a horror story and as a revelation of human character?

Connections

9. Explain the relationship between the narrator's remark that he hanged the cat because he knew it had loved him and because he felt that it had given him no reason for doing so—and the discussion of perverseness in Poe's "The Imp of the Perverse" (see page 164).
10. Consider "The Black Cat" in light of Poe's theory of the single effect in "The Short Story" as described on page 162.

Critical Thinking

11. To what extent can "The Black Cat" be considered a "horror" story? To what extent can it be seen as a study in human psychology? Explain.
12. Is there anything significant about the way in which the narrator treats the cat? Is there anything symbolic? Consider the context of when the story was written.

The Cask of Amontillado

The thousand injuries of Fortunato I had borne as I best could; but when he ventured upon insult, I vowed revenge. You, who so well know the nature of my soul, will not suppose, however, that I gave utterance to a threat. At length I would be avenged; this was a point definitively settled—but the very definitiveness with which it was resolved, precluded the idea of risk. I must not only punish, but punish with impunity. A wrong is unredressed when retribution overtakes its redresser. It is equally unredressed when the avenger fails to make himself felt as such to him who has done the wrong.

It must be understood, that neither by word nor deed had I given Fortunato cause to doubt my good-will. I continued, as was my wont, to smile in his face, and he did not perceive that my smile *now* was at the thought of his immolation.

He had a weak point—this Fortunato—although in other regards he was a man to be respected and even feared. He prided himself on his connoisseurship in wine. Few Italians have the true virtuoso spirit. For the most part their enthusiasm is adopted to suit the time and opportunity—to practice imposture upon the British and Austrian *millionnaires*. In painting and gemmary Fortunato, like his countrymen, was a quack—but in the matter of old wines he was sincere. In this respect I did not differ from him materially: I was skilful in the Italian vintages myself, and bought largely whenever I could.

It was about dusk, one evening during the supreme madness of the carnival season, that I encountered my friend. He accosted me with excessive warmth, for he had been drinking much. The man wore motley. He had on a tight-fitting parti-striped dress, and his head was surmounted by the conical cap and bells. I was so pleased to see him, that I thought I should never have done wringing his hand.

I said to him: "My dear Fortunato, you are luckily met. How remarkably well you are looking to-day! But I have received a pipe° of what passes for Amontillado, and I have my doubts."

"How" said he. "Amontillado? A pipe? Impossible! And in the middle of the carnival!"

"I have my doubts," I replied; "and I was silly enough to pay the full Amontillado price without consulting you in the matter. You were not to be found, and I was fearful of losing a bargain."

"Amontillado!"

"I have my doubts."

"Amontillado!"

"And I must satisfy them."

"Amontillado!"

"As you are engaged, I am on my way to Luchesi. If any one has a critical turn, it is he. He will tell me—"

"Luchesi cannot tell Amontillado from Sherry."

"And yet some fools will have it that his taste is a match for your own."

"Come, let us go."

"Whither?"

"To your vaults."

Pipe *large barrel.*

"My friend, no; I will not impose on your good nature. I perceive you have an engagement. Luchesi—"

"I have no engagement;—come."

"My friend, no. It is not the engagement, but the severe cold with which I perceive you are afflicted. The vaults are insufferably damp. They are encrusted with nitre."

"Let us go, nevertheless. The cold is merely nothing. Amontillado! You have been imposed upon. And as for Luchesi, he cannot distinguish Sherry from Amontillado."

Thus speaking, Fortunato possessed himself of my arm. Putting on a mask of black silk, and drawing a *roquelaire* closely about my person, I suffered him to hurry me to my palazzo.

There were no attendants at home; they had absconded to make merry in honor of the time. I had told them that I should not return until the morning, and had given them explicit orders not to stir from the house. These orders were sufficient, I well knew, to insure their immediate disappearance, one and all, as soon as my back was turned.

I took from their sconces two flambeaux, and giving one to Fortunato, bowed him through several suites of rooms to the archway that led into the vaults. I passed down a long and winding staircase, requesting him to be cautious as he followed. We came at length to the foot of the descent and stood together on the damp ground of the catacombs of the Montresors.

The gait of my friend was unsteady, and the bells upon his cap jingled as he strode.

"The pipe?" said he.

"It is farther on," said I; "but observe the white web-work which gleams from these cavern walls."

He turned toward me, and looked into my eyes with two filmy orbs that distilled the rheum of intoxication.

"Nitre?" he asked, at length.

"Nitre," I replied. "How long have you had that cough?"

"Ugh! ugh! ugh!—ugh! ugh! ugh!—ugh! ugh! ugh!—ugh! ugh! ugh!—ugh! ugh! ugh!"

My poor friend found it impossible to reply for many minutes.

"It is nothing," he said, at last.

"Come," I said, with decision, "we will go back; your health is precious. You are rich, respected, admired, beloved; you are happy, as once I was. You are a man to be missed. For me it is no matter. We will go back; you will be ill, and I cannot be responsible. Besides, there is Luchesi—"

"Enough," he said, "the cough is a mere nothing; it will not kill me. I shall not die of a cough."

"True—true," I replied; "and, indeed, I had no intention of alarming you unnecessarily; but you should use all proper caution. A draught of this Medoc will defend us from the damps."

Here I knocked off the neck a bottle which I drew from a long row of its fellows that lay upon the mould.

"Drink," I said, presenting him the wine.

He raised it to his lips with a leer. He paused and nodded to me familiarly, while his bells jingled.

"I drink," he said, "to the buried that repose around us."

"And I to your long life."

He again took my arm, and we proceeded.

"These vaults," he said, "are extensive."

"The Montresors," I replied, "were a great and numerous family."

"I forget your arms."

"A huge human foot d'or, in a field azure; the foot crushes a serpent rampant whose fangs are imbedded in the heel."

"And the motto?"

"Nemo me impune lacessit."°

"Good!" he said.

The wine sparkled in his eyes and the bells jingled. My own fancy grew warm with the Medoc. We had passed through walls of piled bones, with casks and puncheons intermingling, into the inmost recesses of the catacombs. I paused again, and this time I made bold to seize Fortunato by an arm above the elbow.

"The nitre!" I said; "see, it increases. It hangs like moss upon the vaults. We are below the river's bed. The drops of moisture trickle among the bones. Come, we will go back ere it is too late. Your cough—"

"It is nothing," he said; "let us go on. But first, another draught of the Medoc."

I broke and reached him a flagon of De Grâve. He emptied it at a breath. His eyes flashed with fierce light. He laughed and threw the bottle upward with a gesticulation I did not understand.

I looked at him in surprise. He repeated the movement—a grotesque one.

"You do not comprehend?" he said.

"Not I," I replied.

"Then you are not of the brotherhood."

"How?"

"You are not of the masons."

"Yes, yes," I said; "yes, yes."

"You? Impossible! A mason?"

"A mason," I replied.

"A sign," he said.

"It is this," I answered, producing a trowel from beneath the folds of my *roquelaire*.

"You jest," he exclaimed, recoiling a few paces. "But let us proceed to the Amontillado."

"Be it so," I said, replacing the tool beneath the cloak, and again offering him my arm. He leaned upon it heavily. We continued our route in search of the Amontillado. We passed through a range of low arches, descended, passed on, and descending again, arrived at a deep crypt, in which the foulness of the air caused our flambeaux rather to glow than flame.

At the most remote end of the crypt there appeared another less spacious. Its walls had been lined with human remains, piled to the vault overhead, in the fashion of the great catacombs of Paris. Three sides of this interior crypt were still ornamented in this manner. From the fourth the bones had been thrown down, and lay promiscuously upon the earth, forming at one point a mound of some size. Within the wall thus exposed by the displacing of the bones, we perceived a still interior recess, in depth about four feet, in width three, in height six or seven. It seemed to have been constructed for no especial use within itself, but formed merely the interval between

Nemo me impune lacessit *No one insults me with impunity (Latin).*

two of the colossal supports of the roof of the catacombs, and was backed by one of their circumscribing walls of solid granite.

It was in vain that Fortunato, uplifting his dull torch, endeavored to pry into the depth of the recess. Its termination the feeble light did not enable us to see.

"Proceed," I said; "herein is the Amontillado. As for Luchesi—"

"He is an ignoramus," interrupted my friend, as he stepped unsteadily forward, while I followed immediately at his heels. In an instant he had reached the extremity of the niche, and finding his progress arrested by the rock, stood stupidly bewildered. A moment more and I had fettered him to the granite. In its surface were two iron staples, distant from each other about two feet, horizontally. From one of these depended a short chain, from the other a padlock. Throwing the links about his waist, it was but the work of a few seconds to secure it. He was too much astounded to resist. Withdrawing the key I stepped back from the recess.

"Pass your hand," I said, "over the wall; you cannot help feeling the nitre. Indeed it is *very* damp. Once more let me *implore* you to return. No? Then I must positively leave you. But I must first render you all the little attentions in my power."

"The Amontillado!" ejaculated my friend, not yet recovered from his astonishment.

"True," I replied; "the Amontillado."

As I said these words I busied myself among the pile of bones of which I have before spoken. Throwing them aside, I soon uncovered a quantity of building stone and mortar. With these materials and with the aid of my trowel, I began vigorously to wall up the entrance of the niche.

I had scarcely laid the first tier of the masonry when I discovered that the intoxication of Fortunato had in a great measure worn off. The earliest indication I had of this was a low moaning cry from the depth of the recess. It was *not* the cry of a drunken man. There was then a long and obstinate silence. I laid the second tier, and the third, and the fourth; and then I heard the furious vibrations of the chain. The noise lasted for several minutes, during which, that I might hearken to it with the more satisfaction, I ceased my labors and sat down upon the bones. When at last the clanking subsided, I resumed the trowel, and finished without interruption the fifth, the sixth, and the seventh tier. The wall was now nearly upon a level with my breast. I again paused, and holding the flambeaux over the mason-work, threw a few feeble rays upon the figure within.

A succession of loud and shrill screams, bursting suddenly from the throat of the chained form, seemed to thrust me violently back. For a brief moment I hesitated—I trembled. Unsheathing my rapier, I began to grope with it about the recess; but the thought of an instant reassured me. I placed my hand upon the solid fabric of the catacombs, and felt satisfied. I reapproached the wall. I replied to the yells of him who clamored. I re-echoed—I aided—I surpassed them in volume and in strength. I did this, and the clamorer grew still.

It was now midnight, and my task was drawing to a close. I had completed the eighth, the ninth, and the tenth tier. I had finished a portion of the last and the eleventh; there remained but a single stone to be fitted and plastered in. I struggled with its weight; I placed it partially in its destined position. But now there came from out the niche a low laugh that erected the hairs upon my head. It was succeeded by a sad voice, which I had difficulty in recognizing as that of the noble Fortunato. The voice said—

"Ha! ha! ha!—he! he!—a very good joke indeed—an excellent jest. We will have many a rich laugh about it at the palazzo—he! he! he!—over our wine—he! he! he!"

"The Amontillado!" I said.

"He! he! he!—he! he! he!—yes, the Amontillado. But is it not getting late? Will not they be awaiting us at the palazzo, the Lady Fortunato and the rest? Let us be gone."

"Yes," I said, "let us be gone."

"For the love of God, Montresor!"

"Yes," I said, "for the love of God!"

But to these words I hearkened in vain for a reply. I grew impatient. I called aloud:

"Fortunato!"

No answer. I called again:

"Fortunato!"

No answer still. I thrust a torch through the remaining aperture and let it fall within. There came forth in return only a jingling of the bells. My heart grew sick—on account of the dampness of the catacombs. I hastened to make an end of my labor. I forced the last stone into its position; I plastered it up. Against the new masonry I re-erected the old rampart of bones. For the half of a century no mortal has disturbed them. *In pace requiescat!*°

(1846)

QUESTIONS FOR CRITICAL THINKING AND WRITING

Experience

1. To what extent can you sympathize with the narrator's desire for revenge? Have you ever wanted to get even with someone who insulted you? Why do we usually not act out our revenge fantasies?
2. To what extent were you surprised (or impressed) by the extent to which the narrator prepared for exacting revenge against Fortunato? Do you sympathize with Fortunato? Why or why not?

Interpretation

3. Explain the narrator's idea that he must not only punish but he must punish with impunity. What does he mean when he says that a wrong is undressed when retribution overtakes its redresser? And why must the avenger make himself known to his victim?
4. Explain the strategy used by the narrator to lure his victim to his death. How does his understanding of human nature and character help the narrator accomplish his grisly goal?
5. Identify one example each of verbal irony, dramatic irony, and irony of situation. Explain what is ironic about each example.
6. Explain what the story's setting contributes to its tone, mood, and effect.

In pace requiescat *Rest in peace (Latin).*

7. To whom is the narrator telling his tale of revenge? Why does he tell it—after half a century?

Evaluation

8. What values guide the narrator's behavior? What values does Fortunato seem to live by?
9. What do you think Poe wants us to think of his narrator? Why?

Connections

10. What connections exist between the narrators of "The Cask of Amontillado" and "The Black Cat"? What differences? Explain the significance of both.

Critical Thinking

11. Provide three possible reasons why "The Cask of Amontillado" has been one of Poe's most popular stories.

The Fall of the House of Usher

Son cœur est un luth suspendu°
Sitôt qu'on le touche il résonne.
De Béranger

During the whole of a dull, dark, and soundless day in the autumn of the year, when the clouds hung oppressively low in the heavens, I had been passing alone, on horseback, through a singularly dreary tract of country; and at length found myself, as the shades of evening drew on, within view of the melancholy House of Usher. I know not how it was—but, with the first glimpse of the building, a sense of insufferable gloom pervaded my spirit. I say insufferable; for the feeling was unrelieved by any of that half-pleasurable, because poetic, sentiment, with which the mind usually receives even the sternest natural images of the desolate or terrible. I looked upon the scene before me—upon the mere house, and the simple landscape features of the domain—upon the bleak walls—upon the vacant eye-like windows—upon a few rank sedges—and upon a few white trunks of decayed trees—with an utter depression of soul which I can compare to no earthly sensation more properly than to the after-dream of the reveller upon opium—the bitter lapse into everyday life—the hideous dropping off of the veil. There was iciness, a sinking, a sickening of the heart—an unredeemed dreariness of thought which no goading of the imagination could torture into aught of the sublime. What was it—I paused to think—what was it that so unnerved me in the

Son cœur est . . . *"Its heart is a suspended lute; as soon as it is touched, it resounds" (French), Pierre Jean de Béranger (1780–1857).*

contemplation of the House of Usher? It was a mystery all insoluble; nor could I grapple with the shadowy fancies that crowded upon me as I pondered. I was forced to fall back upon the unsatisfactory conclusion, that while, beyond doubt, there *are* combinations of very simple natural objects which have the power of thus affecting us, still the analysis of this power lies among considerations beyond our depth. It was possible, I reflected, that a mere different arrangement of the particulars of the scene, of the details of the picture, would be sufficient to modify, or perhaps to annihilate its capacity for sorrowful impression; and, acting upon this idea, I reined my horse to the precipitous brink of a black and lurid tarn° that lay in unruffled luster by the dwelling, and gazed down—but with a shudder even more thrilling than before—upon the re-modelled and inverted images of the gray sedge, and the ghastly tree-stems, and the vacant and eye-like windows.

Nevertheless, in this mansion of gloom I now proposed to myself a sojourn of some weeks. Its proprietor, Roderick Usher, had been one of my boon companions in boyhood; but many years had elapsed since our last meeting. A letter, however, had lately reached me in a distant part of the country—a letter from him—which, in its wildly importunate nature, had admitted of no other than a personal reply. The MS. gave evidence of nervous agitation. The writer spoke of acute bodily illness—of a mental disorder which oppressed him—and of an earnest desire to see me, as his best, and indeed his only personal friend, with a view of attempting, by the cheerfulness of my society, some alleviation of his malady. It was the manner in which all this, and much more, was said—it was the apparent *heart* that went with his request—which allowed me no room for hesitation; and I accordingly obeyed forthwith what I still considered a very singular summons.

Although, as boys, we had been even intimate associates, yet I really knew little of my friend. His reserve had been always excessive and habitual. I was aware, however, that his very ancient family had been noted, time out of mind, for a peculiar sensibility of temperament, displaying itself, through long ages, in many works of exalted art, and manifested, of late, in repeated deeds of munificent yet unobtrusive charity, as well as in a passionate devotion to the intricacies, perhaps even more than to the orthodox and easily recognizable beauties, of musical science. I had learned, too, the very remarkable fact, that the stem of the Usher race, all time-honored as it was, had put forth, at no period, any enduring branch; in other words, that the entire family lay in the direct line of descent, and had always, with very trifling and very temporary variation, so lain. It was this deficiency, I considered, while running over in thought the perfect keeping of the character of the premises with the accredited character of the people, and while speculating upon the possible influence which the one, in the long lapse of centuries, might have exercised upon the other—it was this deficiency, perhaps, of collateral issue, and the consequent undeviating transmission, from sire to son, of the patrimony with the name, which had, at length, so identified the two as to merge the original title of the estate in the quaint and equivocal appellation of the "House of Usher"—an appellation which seemed to include, in the minds of the peasantry who used it, both the family and the family mansion.

I have said that the sole effect of my somewhat childish experiment—that of looking down within the tarn—had been to deepen the first singular impression. There

tarn *a small lake.*

can be no doubt that the consciousness of the rapid increase of my superstition—for why should I not so term it?—served mainly to accelerate the increase itself. Such, I have long known, is the paradoxical law of all sentiments having terror as a basis. And it might have been for this reason only, that, when I again uplifted my eyes to the house itself, from its image in the pool, there grew in my mind a strange fancy—a fancy so ridiculous, indeed, that I but mention it to show the vivid force of the sensations which oppressed me. I had so worked upon my imagination as really to believe that about the whole mansion and domain there hung an atmosphere peculiar to themselves and their immediate vicinity—an atmosphere which had no affinity with the air of heaven, but which had reeked up from the decayed trees, and the gray wall, and the silent tarn—a pestilent and mystic vapor, dull, sluggish, faintly discernible, and leaden-hued.

Shaking off from my spirit what *must* have been a dream, I scanned more narrowly the real aspect of the building. Its principal feature seemed to be that of an excessive antiquity. The discoloration of ages had been great. Minute fungi overspread the whole exterior, hanging in a fine tangled web-work from the eaves. Yet all this was apart from any extraordinary dilapidation. No portion of the masonry had fallen; and there appeared to be a wild inconsistency between its still perfect adaptation of parts, and the crumbling condition of the individual stones. In this there was much that reminded me of the specious totality of old wood-work which has rotted for long years in some neglected vault, with no disturbance from the breath of the external air. Beyond this indication of extensive decay, however, the fabric gave little token of instability. Perhaps the eye of a scrutinizing observer might have discovered a barely perceptible fissure, which, extending from the roof of the building in front, made its way down the wall in a zigzag direction, until it became lost in the sullen waters of the tarn.

Noticing these things, I rode over a short causeway to the house. A servant in waiting took my horse, and I entered the Gothic archway of the hall. A valet, of stealthy step, thence conducted me, in silence, through many dark and intricate passages in my progress to the *studio* of his master. Much that I encountered on the way contributed, I know not how, to heighten the vague sentiments of which I have already spoken. While the objects around me—while the carvings of the ceilings, the somber tapestries of the walls, the ebon blackness of the floors, and the phantasmagoric armorial trophies which rattled as I strode, were but matters to which, or to such as which, I had been accustomed from my infancy—while I hesitated not to acknowledge how familiar was all this—I still wondered to find how unfamiliar were the fancies which ordinary images were stirring up. On one of the staircases, I met the physician of the family. His countenance, I thought, wore a mingled expression of low cunning and perplexity. He accosted me with trepidation and passed on. The valet now threw open a door and ushered me into the presence of his master.

The room in which I found myself was very large and lofty. The windows were long, narrow, and pointed, and at so vast a distance from the black oaken floor as to be altogether inaccessible from within. Feeble gleams of encrimsoned light made their way through the trellised panes, and served to render sufficiently distinct the more prominent objects around; the eye, however, struggled in vain to reach the remoter angles of the chamber, or the recesses of the vaulted and fretted ceiling. Dark draperies hung upon the walls. The general furniture was profuse, comfortless, antique, and tattered. Many books and musical instruments lay scattered about, but failed to give any vitality to the scene. I felt that I breathed an atmosphere of sorrow. An air of stern, deep, and irredeemable gloom hung over and pervaded all.

Upon my entrance, Usher arose from a sofa on which he had been lying at full length, and greeted me with a vivacious warmth which had much in it, I at first thought, of an overdone cordiality—of the constrained effort of the *ennuyé*° man of the world. A glance, however, at his countenance, convinced me of his perfect sincerity. We sat down; and for some moments, while he spoke not, I gazed upon him with a feeling half of pity, half of awe. Surely, a man had never before so terribly altered, in so brief a period, as had Roderick Usher! It was with difficulty that I could bring myself to admit the identity of the wan being before me with the companion of my early boyhood. Yet the character of his face had been at all times remarkable. A cadaverousness of complexion; an eye large, liquid, and luminous beyond comparison; lips somewhat thin and very pallid, but of a surpassingly beautiful curve; a nose of a delicate Hebrew model, but with a breadth of nostril unusual in similar formations; a finely moulded chin, speaking, in its want of prominence, of a want of moral energy; hair of a more than web-like softness and tenuity; these features, with an inordinate expansion above the regions of the temple, made up altogether a countenance not easily to be forgotten. And now in the mere exaggeration of the prevailing character of these features, and of the expression they were wont to convey, lay so much of change that I doubted to whom I spoke. The now ghastly pallor of the skin, and the now miraculous luster of the eye, above all things startled and even awed me. The silken hair, too, had been suffered to grow all unheeded, and as, in its wild gossamer texture, it floated rather than fell about the face, I could not, even with effort, connect its arabesque expression with any idea of simple humanity.

In the manner of my friend I was at once struck with an incoherence—an inconsistency; and I soon found this to arise from a series of feeble and futile struggles to overcome an habitual trepidancy—an excessive nervous agitation. For something of this nature I had indeed been prepared, no less by his letter, than by reminiscences of certain boyish traits, and by conclusions deduced from his peculiar physical conformation and temperament. His action was alternatively vivacious and sullen. His voice varied rapidly from a tremulous indecision (when the animal spirits seemed utterly in abeyance) to that of energetic concision—that abrupt, weighty, unhurried, and hollow-sounding enunciation—that leaden, self-balanced and perfectly modulated guttural utterance, which may be observed in the lost drunkard, or the irreclaimable eater of opium, during the periods of his most intense excitement.

It was thus that he spoke of the object of my visit, of his earnest desire to see me, and of the solace he expected me to afford him. He entered, at some length, into what he conceived to be the nature of his malady. It was, he said, a constitutional and a family evil, and one for which he despaired to find a remedy—a mere nervous affection, he immediately added, which would undoubtedly soon pass off. It displayed itself in a host of unnatural sensations. Some of these, as he detailed them, interested and bewildered me; although, perhaps, the terms, and the general manner of the narration had their weight. He suffered much from a morbid acuteness of the senses; the most insipid food was alone endurable; he could wear only garments of certain texture; the odors of all flowers were oppressive; his eyes were tortured by even a faint

ennuyé *bored (French).*

light; and there were but peculiar sounds, and these from stringed instruments, which did not inspire him with horror.

To an anomalous species of terror I found him a bounded slave. "I shall perish," said he, "I *must* perish in this deplorable folly. Thus, thus, and not otherwise, shall I be lost. I dread the events of the future, not in themselves but in their results. I shudder at the thought of any, even the most trivial, incident, which may operate upon this intolerable agitation of soul. I have, indeed, no abhorrence of danger, except in its absolute effect—in terror. In this unnerved—in this pitiable condition—I feel that the period will sooner or later arrive when I must abandon life and reason together, in some struggle with the grim phantasm, FEAR."

I learned, moreover, at intervals, and through broken and equivocal hints, another singular feature of his mental condition. He was enchained by certain superstitious impressions in regard to the dwelling which he tenanted, and whence, for many years, he had never ventured forth—in regard to an influence whose suppositious force was conveyed in terms too shadowy here to be re-stated—an influence which some peculiarities in the mere form and substance of his family mansion, had, by dint of long sufferance, he said, obtained over his spirit—an effect which the *physique* of the gray walls and turrets, and of the dim tarn into which they all looked down, had, at length, brought about upon the *morale* of his existence.

He admitted, however, although with hesitation, that much of the peculiar gloom which thus afflicted him could be traced to a more natural and far more palpable origin—to the severe and long-continued illness—indeed to the evidently approaching dissolution—of a tenderly beloved sister—his sole companion for long years—his last and only relative on earth. "Her decease," he said, with a bitterness which I can never forget, "would leave him (him the hopeless and the frail) the last of the ancient race of the Ushers." While he spoke, the lady Madeline (for so was she called) passed slowly through a remote portion of the apartment, and, without having noticed my presence, disappeared. I regarded her with an utter astonishment not unmingled with dread—and yet I found it impossible to account for such feelings. A sensation of stupor oppressed me, as my eyes followed her retreating steps. When a door, at length, closed upon her, my glance sought instinctively and eagerly the countenance of the brother—but he had buried his face in his hands, and I could only perceive that a far more than ordinary wanness had overspread the emaciated fingers through which trickled many passionate tears.

The disease of the lady Madeline had long baffled the skill of her physicians. A settled apathy, a gradual wasting away of the person, and frequent although transient affections of a partially cataleptical character, were the unusual diagnosis. Hitherto she had steadily borne up against the pressure of her malady, and had not betaken herself finally to bed; but, on the closing in of the evening of my arrival at the house, she succumbed (as her brother told me at night with inexpressible agitation) to the prostrating power of the destroyer; and I learned that the glimpse I had obtained of her person would thus probably be the last I should obtain—that the lady, at least while living, would be seen by me no more.

For several days ensuing, her name was unmentioned by either Usher or myself: and during this period I was busied in earnest endeavors to alleviate the melancholy of my friend. We painted and read together; or I listened, as if in a dream, to the wild improvisations of his speaking guitar. And thus, as a closer and still closer intimacy admitted me more unreservedly into the recesses of his spirit, the more bitterly did I perceive the futility of all attempt at cheering a mind from which darkness, as if an inherent positive quality, poured forth upon all objects of the moral and physical universe, in one unceasing radiation of gloom.

I shall ever bear about me a memory of the many solemn hours I thus spent alone with the master of the House of Usher. Yet I should fail in any attempt to convey an idea of the exact character of the studies, or of the occupations, in which he involved me, or led me the way. An excited and highly distempered ideality threw a sulphureous luster over all. His long improvised dirges will ring forever in my ears. Among other things, I hold painfully in mind a certain singular perversion and amplification of the wild air of the last waltz of Von Weber. From the paintings over which his elaborate fancy brooded, and which grew, touch by touch, into vaguenesses at which I shuddered the more thrillingly, because I shuddered knowing not why;—from these paintings (vivid as their images now are before me) I would in vain endeavor to educe more than a small portion which should lie within the compass of merely written words. By the utter simplicity, by the nakedness of his designs, he arrested and overawed attention. If ever mortal painted an idea, that mortal was Roderick Usher. For me at least—in the circumstances then surrounding me—there arose out of the pure abstractions which the hypochondriac contrived to throw upon his canvas, an intensity of intolerable awe, no shadow of which felt I ever yet in the contemplation of the certainly glowing yet too concrete reveries of Fuseli.°

One of the phantasmagoric conceptions of my friend, partaking not so rigidly of the spirit of abstraction, may be shadowed forth, although feebly, in words. A small picture presented the interior of an immensely long and rectangular vault or tunnel, with low walls, smooth, white, and without interruption or device. Certain accessory points of the design served well to convey the idea that this excavation lay at an exceeding depth below the surface of the earth. No outlet was observed in any portion of its vast extent, and no torch, or other artificial source of light was discernible; yet a flood of intense rays rolled throughout, and bathed the whole in a ghastly and inappropriate splendor.

I have just spoken of that morbid condition of the auditory nerve which rendered all music intolerable to the sufferer, with the exception of certain effects of stringed instruments. It was, perhaps, the narrow limits to which he thus confined himself upon the guitar, which gave birth, in great measure, to the fantastic character of his performances. But the fervid *facility* of his *impromptus* could not be so accounted for. They must have been, and were, in the notes, as well as in the words of his wild fantasias (for he not unfrequently accompanied himself with rhymed verbal improvisations), the result of that intense mental collectedness and concentration to which I have previously alluded as observable only in particular moments of the highest artificial excitement. The words of one of these rhapsodies I have easily remembered. I was, perhaps, the more forcibly impressed with it, as he gave it, because, in the under or mystic current of its meaning, I fancied that I perceived, and for the first time, a full consciousness on the part of Usher, of the tottering of his lofty reason upon her throne. The verses, which were entitled "The Haunted Palace," ran very nearly, if not accurately, thus:

Henry Fuseli (1741–1825) *Swiss painter with interest in the supernatural.*

I

In the greenest of our valleys,
By good angels tenanted,
Once a fair and stately palace—
Radiant palace—reared its head.
In the monarch Thought's dominion—
It stood there!
Never seraph spread a pinion
Over fabric half so fair.

II

Banners yellow, glorious, golden,
On its roof did float and flow;
(This—all this—was in the olden
Time long ago)
And every gentle air that dallied,
In that sweet day,
Along the ramparts plumed and pallid,
A winged odor went away.

III

Wanderers in that happy valley
Through two luminous windows saw
Spirits moving musically
To a lute's well-tunèd law,
Round about a throne, where sitting
(Porphyrogene!)°
In state his glory well befitting,
The ruler of the realm was seen.

IV

And all with pearl and ruby glowing
Was the fair palace door,
Through which came flowing, flowing, flowing
And sparkling evermore,
A troop of Echoes whose sweet duty
Was but to sing,
In voices of surpassing beauty,
The wit and wisdom of their king.

V

But evil things, in robes of sorrow,
Assailed the monarch's high estate;
(Ah, let us mourn, for never morrow
Shall dawn upon him, desolate!)
And, round about his home, the glory

porphyrogene *of royal birth.*

That blushed and bloomed
Is but a dim-remembered story
Of the oldtime entombed.

VI

And travellers now within that valley,
Through the red-litten windows, see
Vast forms that move fantastically
To a discordant melody;
While, like a rapid ghastly river,
Through the pale door,
A hideous throng rush out forever,
And laugh—but smile no more.

I well remember that suggestions arising from this ballad, led us into a train of thought wherein there became manifest an opinion of Usher's which I mention not so much on account of its novelty (for other men that have thought thus), as on account of the pertinacity with which he maintained it. This opinion, in its general form, was that of the sentience of all vegetable things. But, in his disordered fancy, the idea had assumed a more daring character, and trespassed, under certain conditions, upon the kingdom of inorganization. I lack words to express the full extent, of the earnest *abandon* of his persuasion. The belief, however, was connected (as I have previously hinted) with the gray stones of the home of his forefathers. The conditions of the sentience had been here, he imagined, fulfilled in the method of collocation of these stones—in the order of their arrangement, as well as in that of the many *fungi* which overspread them, and of the decayed trees which stood around—above all, in the long undisturbed endurance of this arrangement, and in its reduplication in the still waters of the tarn. Its evidence—the evidence of the sentience—was to be seen, he said (and I here started as he spoke), in the gradual yet certain condensation of an atmosphere of their own about the waters and the walls. The result was discoverable, he added, in that silent, yet importunate and terrible influence which for centuries had moulded the destinies of his family, and which made *him* what I now saw him—what he was. Such opinions need no comment, and I will make none.

Our books—the books which, for years, had formed no small portion of the mental existence of the invalid—were, as might be supposed, in strict keeping with this character of phantasm. We pored together over such works as the Vervet et Chartreuse of Gresset; the Belphegor of Machiavelli; the Heaven and Hell of Swedenborg; the Subterranean Voyage of Nicholas Klimm by Holberg; the Chiromancy of Robert Flud, of Jean D'Indaginé, and of De la Chambre; the Journey into the Blue Distance of Tieck; and the City of the Sun of Campanella. One favorite volume was a small octavo edition of the *Directorium Inquisitorum,* by the Dominican Eymeric de Gironne; and there were passages in Pomponius Mela, about the old African Satyrs and Ægipans, over which Usher would sit dreaming for hours. His chief delight, however, was found in the perusal of an exceedingly rare and curious book in quarto Gothic—the manual of a forgotten church—the *Vigilæ Mortuorum secundum Chorum Ecclesiæ Maguntinæ.*

I could not help thinking of the wild ritual of this work, and of its probable influence upon the hypochondriac, when, one evening, having informed me abruptly that the lady Madeline was no more, he stated his intention of preserving her corpse for a fortnight (previously to its final interment), in one of the numerous vaults within the main walls of the building. The worldly reason, however, assigned for this singular proceeding, was one which I did not feel at liberty to dispute. The brother had been led to his resolution (so he told me) by consideration of the unusual character of the malady of the deceased, of certain obstrusive and eager inquiries on the part of her medical men, and of the remote and exposed situation of the burial-ground of the family. I will not deny that when I called to mind the sinister countenance of the person whom I met upon the staircase, on the day of my arrival at the house, I had no desire to oppose what I regarded as at best but a harmless, and by no means an unnatural, precaution.

At the request of Usher, I personally aided him in the arrangements for the temporary entombment. The body having been encoffined, we two alone bore it to its rest. The vault in which we placed it (and which had been so long unopened that our torches, half smothered in its oppressive atmosphere, gave us little opportunity for investigation) was small, damp, and entirely without means of admission for light; lying, at great depth, immediately beneath that portion of the building in which was my own sleeping apartment. It had been used, apparently, in remote feudal times, for the worst purposes of a donjon-keep, and, in later days, as a place of deposit for powder, or some other highly combustible substance, as a portion of its floor, and the whole interior of a long archway through which we reached it, were carefully sheathed with copper. The door, of massive iron, had been, also, similarly protected. Its immense weight caused an unusually sharp grating sound, as it moved upon its hinges.

Having deposited our mournful burden upon tressels within this region of horror, we partially turned aside the yet unscrewed lid of the coffin, and looked upon the face of the tenant. A striking similitude between the brother and sister now first arrested my attention; and Usher, divining, perhaps, my thoughts, murmured out some few words from which I learned that the deceased and himself had been twins, and that sympathies of a scarcely intelligible nature had always existed between them. Our glances, however, rested not long upon the dead—for we could not regard her unawed. The disease which had thus entombed the lady in the maturity of youth, had left, as usual in all maladies of a strictly cataleptical character, the mockery of a faint blush upon the bosom and the face, and that suspiciously lingering smile upon the lip which is so terrible in death. We replaced and screwed down the lid, and, having secured the door of iron, made our way, with toil, into the scarcely less gloomy apartments of the upper portion of the house.

And now, some days of bitter grief having elapsed, an observable change came over the features of the mental disorder of my friend. His ordinary manner had vanished. His ordinary occupations were neglected or forgotten. He roamed from chamber to chamber with hurried, unequal, and objectless step. The pallor of his countenance had assumed, if possible, a more ghastly hue—but the luminousness of his eye had utterly gone out. The once occasional huskiness of his tone was heard no more; and a tremulous quaver, as if of extreme terror, habituallly characterized his utterance. There were times, indeed, when I thought his unceasingly agitated mind was laboring with some oppressive secret, to divulge which he struggled for the necessary courage. At times, again, I was obliged to resolve all into the mere inexplicable vagaries of madness, for I beheld him gazing upon vacancy for long hours, in an attitude of the profoundest attention, as if listening to some imaginary sound. It was no wonder that his condition terrified—that it infected me. I felt creeping upon me, by slow yet certain degrees, the wild influences of his own fantastic yet impressive superstitions.

It was, especially, upon retiring to bed late in the night of the seventh or eighth day after the placing of the lady Madeline within the donjon, that I experienced the full power of such feelings. Sleep came not near my couch—while the hours waned and waned away. I struggled to reason off the nervousness which had dominion over me. I endeavored to believe that much, if not all of what I felt, was due to the bewildering influence of the gloomy furniture of the room—of the dark and tattered draperies, which, tortured into motion by the breath of a rising tempest, swayed fitfully to and fro upon the walls, and rustled uneasily about the decorations of the bed. But my efforts were fruitless. An irrepressible tremor gradually pervaded my frame; and, at length, there sat upon my very heart an incubus of utterly causeless alarm. Shaking this off with a gasp and a struggle, I uplifted myself upon the pillows, and, peering earnestly within the intense darkness of the chamber, hearkened—I know not why, except that an instinctive spirit prompted me—to certain low and indefinite sounds which came, through the pauses of the storm, at long intervals, I knew not whence. Overpowered by an intense sentiment of horror, unaccountable yet unendurable, I threw my clothes on with haste (for I felt that I should sleep no more during the night), and endeavored to arouse myself from the pitiable condition into which I had fallen, by pacing rapidly to and fro through the apartment.

I had taken but few turns in this manner, when a light step on an adjoining staircase arrested my attention. I presently recognized it as that of Usher. In an instant afterward he rapped, with a gentle touch, at my door, and entered, bearing a lamp. His countenance was, as usual, cadaverously wan—but, moreover, there was a species of mad hilarity in his eyes—an evidently restrained *hysteria* in his whole demeanor. His air appalled me—but anything was preferable to the solitude which I had so long endured, and I even welcomed his presence as a relief.

"And you have not seen it?" he said abruptly, after having stared about him for some moments in silence—"you have not then seen it?—but, stay! you shall." Thus speaking, and having carefully shaded his lamp, he hurried to one of the casements, and threw it freely open to the storm.

The impetuous fury of the entering gust nearly lifted us from our feet. It was, indeed, a tempestuous yet sternly beautiful night, and one wildly singular in its terror and its beauty. A whirlwind had apparently collected its force in our vicinity; for there were frequent and violent alterations in the direction of the wind; and the exceeding density of the clouds (which hung so low as to press upon the turrets of the house) did not prevent our perceiving the lifelike velocity with which they flew careering from all points against each other, without passing away into the distance. I say that even their exceeding density did not prevent our perceiving this—yet we had no glimpse of the moon or stars—nor was there any flashing forth of the lightening. But the under surfaces of the huge masses of agitated vapor, as well as all terrestrial objects immediately around us, were glowing in the unnatural light of a faintly luminous and distinctly visible gaseous exhalation which hung about and enshrouded the mansion.

"You must not—you shall not behold this!" said I, shudderingly, to Usher, as I led him, with a gentle violence, from the window to a seat. "These appearances, which bewilder you, are merely electrical phenomena not uncommon—or it may be that they have their ghastly origin in the rank miasma of the tarn. Let us close this casement; —

the air is chilling and dangerous to your frame. Here is one of your favorite romances. I will read, and you shall listen;—and so we will pass away this terrible night together."

The antique volume which I had taken up was the "Mad Trist" of Sir Launcelot Canning; but I had called it a favorite of Usher's more in sad jest than in earnest; for, in truth, there is little in its uncouth and unimaginative prolixity which could have had interest for the lofty and spiritual ideality of my friend. It was, however, the only book immediately at hand; and I indulged a vague hope that the excitement which now agitated the hypochondriac, might find relief (for the history of mental disorder is full of similar anomalies) even in the extremeness of the folly which I should read. Could I have judged, indeed, by the wild overstrained air of vivacity with which he hearkened, or apparently hearkened, to the words of the tale, I might well have congratulated myself upon the success of my design.

I had arrived at that well-known portion of the story where Ethelred, the hero of the Trist, having sought in vain for peaceable admission into the dwelling of the hermit, proceeds to make good an entrance by force. Here, it will be remembered, the words of the narrative run thus:

"And Ethelred, who was by nature of a doughty heart, and who was now mighty withal, on account of the powerfulness of the wine which he had drunken, waited no longer to hold parley with the hermit, who, in sooth, was of an obstinate and maliceful turn, but, feeling the rain upon his shoulders, and fearing the rising of the tempest, uplifted his mace outright, and, with blows, made quickly room in the plankings of the door for his gauntleted hand; and now pulling therewith sturdily, he so cracked, and ripped, and tore all asunder, that the noise of the dry and hollow-sounding wood alarumed and reverberated throughout the forest."

At the termination of this sentence I started, and for a moment, paused; for it appeared to me (although I at once concluded that my excited fancy had deceived me)—it appeared to me that, from some very remote portion of the mansion, there came indistinctly, to my ears, what might have been, in its exact similarity of character, the echo (but a stifled and dull one certainly) of the very cracking and ripping sound which Sir Launcelot had so particularly described. It was, beyond doubt, the coincidence alone which had arrested my attention; for, amid the rattling of the sashes of the casements, and the ordinary commingled noises of the still increasing storm, the sound, in itself, had nothing, surely, which should have interested or disturbed me. I continued the story:

"But the good champion Ethelred, now entering within the door, was sore enraged and amazed to perceive no signal of the maliceful hermit; but, in the stead thereof, a dragon of a scaly and prodigious demeanor, and of a fiery tongue, which sate in guard before a palace of gold, with a floor of silver; and upon the wall there hung a shield of shining brass with this legend enwritten—

> Who entereth herein, a conqueror hath bin;
> Who slayeth the dragon, the shield he shall win;

And Ethelred uplifted his mace, and struck upon the head of the dragon, which fell before him, and gave up his pesty breath, with a shriek so horrid and harsh, and withal so piercing, that Ethelred had fain to close his ears with his hands against the dreadful noise of it, the like whereof was never before heard."

Here again, I paused abruptly, and now with a feeling of wild amazement—for there could be no doubt whatever that, in this instance, I did actually hear (although from what direction it proceeded I found it impossible to say) a low and apparently distant, but harsh, protracted, and most unusual screaming or grating sound—the exact counterpart of what my fancy had already conjured up for the dragon's unnatural shriek as described by the romancer.

Oppressed, as I certainly was, upon the occurrence of the second and most extraordinary coincidence, by a thousand conflicting sensations, in which wonder and extreme terror were predominant, I still retained sufficient presence of mind to avoid exciting, by any observation, the sensitive nervousness of my companion. I was by no means certain that he had noticed the sounds in question; although, assuredly, a strange alteration had, during the last few minutes, taken place in his demeanor. From a position fronting my own, he had gradually brought round his chair, so as to sit with his face to the door of the chamber; and thus I could but partially perceive his features, although I saw that his lips trembled as if he were murmuring inaudibly. His head had dropped upon his breast—yet I knew that he was not asleep, from the wide and rigid opening of the eye as I caught a glance of it in profile. The motion of his body, too, was at variance with this idea—for he rocked from side to side with a gentle yet constant and uniform sway. Having rapidly taken notice of all this, I resumed the narrative of Sir Launcelot, which thus proceeded:

"And now, the champion, having escaped from the terrible fury of the dragon, bethinking himself of the brazen shield, and of the breaking up of the enchantment which was upon it, removed the carcass from out of the way before him, and approached valorously over the silver pavement of the castle to where the shield was upon the wall; which in sooth tarried not for his full coming, but fell down at his feet upon the silver floor, with a mighty great and terrible ringing sound."

No sooner had these syllables passed my lips, than—as if a shield of brass had indeed, at the moment, fallen heavily upon a floor of silver—I became aware of a distinct, hollow, metallic, and clangorous, yet apparently muffled reverberation. Completely unnerved, I leaped to my feet; but the measured rocking movement of Usher was undisturbed. I rushed to the chair in which he sat. His eyes were bent fixedly before him, and throughout his whole countenance there reigned a stony rigidity. But, as I placed my hand upon his shoulder, there came a strong shudder over his whole person; a sickly smile quivered about his lips; and I saw that he spoke in a low, hurried, and gibbering murmur, as if unconscious of my presence. Bending closely over him, I at length drank in the hideous import of his words.

"Not hear it? —yes, I hear it, and *have* heard it. Long—long—long—many minutes, many hours, many days, have I heard it—yet I dared not—oh, pity me, miserable wretch that I am!—I dared not—I *dared* not speak! *We have put her living in the tomb!* Said I not that my senses were acute? I *now* tell you that I heard her first feeble movements in the hollow coffin. I heard them—many, many days ago—yet I dared not—*I dared not speak!* And now—to-night—Ethelred—ha! ha! —the breaking of the hermit's door, and the death-cry of the dragon, and the clangor of the shield! —say, rather, the rending of her coffin, and the grating of the iron hinges of her prison, and her struggles within the coppered archway of the vault! Oh whither shall I fly? Will she not be here anon? Is she not hurrying to upbraid me for my haste? Have I not heard her footstep on the stair? Do I not distinguish that heavy and horrible beating of her heart? MADMAN!" here he sprang furiously to his feet, and shrieked out his syllables, as if in the effort he were giving up his soul—"MADMAN! I TELL YOU THAT SHE NOW STANDS WITHOUT THE DOOR!"

As if in the superhuman energy of his utterance there had been found the potency of a spell—the huge antique panels to which the speaker pointed, threw slowly back, upon the instant, their ponderous and ebony jaws. It was the work of the rushing gust—but then without those doors there *did* stand the lofty and enshrouded figure of the lady Madeline of Usher. There was blood upon her white robes, and the evidence of some bitter struggle upon every portion of her emaciated frame. For a moment she remained trembling and reeling to and fro upon the threshold, then, with a low moaning cry, fell heavily inward upon the person of her brother, and in her violent and now final death-agonies, bore him to the floor a corpse, and a victim to the terrors he had anticipated.

From that chamber, and from that mansion, I fled aghast. The storm was still abroad in all its wrath as I found myself crossing the old causeway. Suddenly there shot along the path a wild light, and I turned to see whence a gleam so unusual could have issued; for the vast house and its shadows were alone behind me. The radiance was that of the full, setting, and blood-red moon which now shone vividly through that once barely-discernible fissure of which I have before spoken as extending from the roof of the building, in a zigzag direction, to the base. While I gazed, this fissure rapidly widened—there came a fierce breath of the whirlwind—the entire orb of the satellite burst at once upon my sight—my brain reeled as I saw the mighty walls rushing asunder—there was a long tumultuous shouting sound like the voice of a thousand waters—and the deep and dark tarn at my feet closed sullenly and silently over the fragments of the "HOUSE OF USHER."

(1840)

QUESTIONS FOR CRITICAL THINKING AND WRITING

Experience

1. Describe your experience of reading Poe's "The Fall of the House of Usher." To what extent did it hold your interest? Why?
2. How do you respond to Poe's extensive vocabulary? Do you enjoy the experience of being sent to the dictionary? Do the many unusual words enhance or inhibit your ability to enjoy and respond positively to Poe's story? Why?

Interpretation

3. Why does Poe go into such detail in describing the external features of the House of Usher? What symbolic implications do the details have, particularly the fissure that runs through the edifice?
4. What is the relationship between the narrator and Roderick Usher? Where is this relationship most explicitly revealed?
5. What is the relationship between Roderick Usher and his sister, the lady Madeline? What details contribute to Poe's characterization of this relationship?
6. What is the significance of Roderick Usher's poem "The Haunted Palace"? Single out one stanza for close analysis. Explain the meaning of the stanza's details in relation to the character of its author.
7. What is meant by the "fall" of the house of Usher, both literally and symbolically? Why does the "house" of Usher fall?

Evaluation

8. How does the narrator's response to what he experiences in the house of Roderick Usher convey his attitude toward Usher and toward what might be described as supra-rational or supra-natural events?
9. What attitude toward human reason, toward rational thought and logical explanation, does Poe's story suggest?

Connections

10. Compare "The Fall of the House of Usher" with "The Black Cat" in their shared concern with madness and the supernatural.

Critical Thinking

11. Why do you think "The Fall of the House of Usher" has been a favorite among academics, among scholars of Poe's work? Offer at least two explanations for why it is one of the most written about of Poe's stories.

EDGAR ALLAN POE: ESSAYS

The Short Story

FROM A REVIEW OF HAWTHORNE'S TWICE-TOLD TALES

The tale proper affords the fairest field which can be afforded by the wide domains of mere prose, for the exercise of the highest genius. Were I bidden to say how this genius could be most advantageously employed for the best display of its powers, I should answer, without hesitation, "in the composition of a rhymed poem not to exceed in length what might be perused in an hour."

Were I called upon, however, to designate that class of composition which, next to such a poem as I have suggested, should best fulfil the demands and serve the purposes of ambitious genius, should offer it the most advantageous field of exertion, and afford it the fairest opportunity of display, I should speak at once of the brief prose tale. History, philosophy, and other matters of that kind, we leave out of the question, of course. *Of course,* I say, and in spite of the gray-beards. These grave topics, to the end of time, will be best illustrated by what a discriminating world, turning up its nose at the drab pamphlets, has agreed to understand as *talent*. The ordinary novel is objectionable, from its length, for reasons analogous to those which render length objectionable in the poem. As the novel cannot be read at one sitting, it cannot avail itself of the immense benefit of *totality*. Worldly interests, intervening during the pauses of perusal, modify, counteract and annul the impressions intended. But simple cessation in reading would, of itself, be sufficient to destroy the true unity. In the brief tale, however, the author is enabled to carry out his full design without interruption. During the hour of perusal, the soul of the reader is at the writer's control.

A skilful artist has constructed a tale. He has not fashioned his thoughts to accommodate his incidents, but having deliberately conceived a certain *single effect* to be wrought, he then invents such incidents, he then combines such events, and discusses them in such tone as may best serve him in establishing this preconceived effect. If his very first sentence tend not to the outbringing of this effect, then in his very first step has he committed a blunder. In the whole composition there should be no word written of which the tendency, direct or indirect, is not to the one pre-established design. And by such means, with such care and skill, a picture is at length painted which leaves in the mind of him who contemplates it with a kindred art, a sense of the fullest satisfaction. The idea of the tale, its thesis, has been presented unblemished, because undisturbed—an end absolutely demanded, yet, in the novel, altogether unattainable.

True Poetry

FROM "THE POETIC PRINCIPLE"

I hold that a long poem does not exist. I maintain that the phrase, "a long poem," is simply a flat contradiction in terms.

I need scarcely observe that a poem deserves its title only inasmuch as it excites, by elevating the soul. The value of the poem is in the ratio of this elevating excitement. But all excitements are, through a psychal necessity, transient. That degree of excitement which would entitle a poem to be so called at all, cannot be sustained throughout a composition of any great length. After the lapse of half an hour, at the very utmost, it flags—fails—a revulsion ensues—and then the poem is, in effect, and in fact, no longer such.

There are, no doubt, many who have found difficulty in reconciling the critical dictum that the "Paradise Lost" is to be devoutly admired throughout, with the absolute impossibility of maintaining for it, during perusal, the amount of enthusiasm which that critical dictum would demand. This great work, in fact, is to be regarded as poetical, only when, losing sight of that vital requisite in all works of Art, Unity, we view it merely as a series of minor poems. If, to preserve its Unity—its totality of effect or impression—we read it (as would be necessary) at a single sitting, the result is but a constant alternation of excitement and depression. After a passage of what we feel to be true poetry, there follows, inevitably, a passage of platitude which no critical pre-judgment can force us to admire; but if, upon completing the work, we read it again; omitting the first book—that is to say, commencing with the second—we shall be surprised at now finding that admirable which we before condemned—that damnable which we had previously so much admired. It follows from all this that the ultimate, aggregate, or absolute effect of even the best epic under the sun, is a nullity:—and this is precisely the fact. . . .

On the other hand, it is clear that a poem may be improperly brief. Undue brevity degenerates into mere epigrammatism. A *very* short poem, while now and then producing a brilliant or vivid, never produces a profound or enduring effect. There must be the steady pressing down of the stamp upon the wax.

The Imp of the Perverse

FROM "THE IMP OF THE PERVERSE"

There lives no man who at some period, has not been tormented, for example, by an earnest desire to tantalize a listener by circumlocution. The speaker is aware that he displeases; he has every intention to please; he is usually curt, precise, and clear; the most laconic and luminous language is struggling for utterance upon his tongue; it is only with difficulty that he restrains himself from giving it flow; he dreads and deprecates the anger of him whom he addresses; yet, the thought strikes him, that by certain involutions and parentheses, this anger may be engendered. That single thought is enough. The impulse increases to a wish, the wish to a desire, the desire to an uncontrollable longing, and the longing (to the deep regret and mortification of the speaker, and in defiance of all consequences), is indulged.

We have a task before us which must be speedily performed. We know that it will be ruinous to make delay. The most important crisis of our life calls, trumpet-tongued, for immediate energy and action. We glow, we are consumed with eagerness to commence the work, with the anticipation of whose glorious result our whole souls are on fire. It must, it shall be undertaken to-day, and yet we put it off until to-morrow: and why? There is no answer, except that we feel perverse, using the word with no comprehension of the principle. To-morrow arrives, and with it more impatient anxiety to do our duty, but with this very increase of anxiety arrives, also, a nameless, a positively fearful, because unfathomable, craving for delay. This craving gathers strength as the moments fly. The last hour for action is at hand. We tremble with the violence of the conflict within us,—of the definite with the indefinite—of the substance with the shadow. But, if the contest have proceeded thus far, it is the shadow which prevails,—we struggle in vain. The clock strikes, and is the knell of our welfare. At the same time, it is the chanticleer-note to the ghost that has so long over-awed us. It flies—it disappears—we are free. The old energy returns. We will labor *now*. Alas, it is *too late!*

We stand upon the brink of a precipice. We peer into the abyss—we grow sick and dizzy. Our first impulse is to shrink from the danger. Unaccountably we remain. By slow degrees our sickness, and dizziness, and horror, become merged in a cloud of unnameable feeling. By gradations, still more imperceptible, this cloud assumes shape, as did the vapor from the bottle out of which arose the genius in the Arabian Nights. But out of this *our* cloud upon the precipice's edge, there grows into palpability, a shape, far more terrible than any genius, or any demon of a tale, and yet it is but a thought, although a fearful one, and one which chills the very marrow of our bones with the fierceness of the delight of its horror. It is merely the idea of what would be our sensations during the sweeping precipitancy of a fall from such a height. And this fall—this rushing annihilation—for the very reason that it involves that one most ghastly and loathsome of all the most ghastly and loathsome images of death and suffering which have ever presented themselves to our imagination—for this very cause do we now the most vividly desire it. And because our reason violently deters us from the brink, *therefore*, do we the more impetuously approach it. There is no passion in nature so demoniacally impatient, as that of him, who shuddering upon the edge of a precipice, thus meditates a plunge. To indulge for a moment, in any attempt at *thought*, is to be inevitably lost; for reflection but urges us to forbear, and *therefore* it is, I say, that we cannot. If there be no friendly arm to check us, or if we fail in a sudden effort to prostrate ourselves backward from the abyss, we plunge, and are destroyed.

Examine these and similar actions as we will, we shall find them resulting solely from the spirit of the *Perverse*. We perpetrate them merely because we feel that we should not. Beyond or behind this, there is no intelligible principle. And we might, indeed, deem this perverseness a direct instigation of the Arch-Fiend, were it not occasionally known to operate in furtherance of good.

CRITICS ON POE

CHRISTOPHER BENFEY

On "The Black Cat" and "The Tell-Tale Heart"

FROM NEW ESSAYS ON POE'S MAJOR TALES

Poe's murderers are not so much obsessive killers as obsessive talkers. Afflicted with what Poe calls in "The Black Cat" "the spirit of PERVERSENESS," their perversity lies not in their need to kill but in their need to tell. Thus, "The Imp of the Perverse" ends with the murderer's sense of safety: He's safe, he tells himself, "if I be not fool enough to make open confession." This thought is his undoing. "I well, too well understood that, to *think*, in my situation, was to be lost."

Concealment is ultimately unbearable for these killers, for whom secrets are like bodies buried alive, imprisoned souls seeking freedom. Thus, in "The Imp of the Perverse":

> For a moment, I experienced all the pangs of suffocation; I became blind, and deaf, and giddy; and then, some invisible fiend, I thought, struck me with his broad palm upon the back. The long-imprisoned secret burst forth from my soul.

Poe gives minute attention to the style of the released confession: "They say that I spoke with a distinct enunciation, but with marked emphasis and passionate hurry, as if in dread of interruption." Interruption would restore human separateness; these killers long for human transparency.

We have to consider other factors in making sense of the odd balance of crime and confession in these tales. Surely Poe had aesthetic reasons for minimizing the gore in his stories; as David Reynolds has pointed out, he wished to distance himself from popular practitioners of crime journalism, who relied on explicit horror to shock and titillate their readers. It is Poe's corresponding emphasis on the act of confession that needs explanation. "The Tell-Tale Heart," "The Black Cat," and "The Imp" all record a confession—a *perverse* confession since the crimes would otherwise have been undetected. All three tales purport to be first-person narratives; they represent confessions within confessions—confessions to the second degree. These killers need to confess to the perverse act of having confessed. The fear of the criminals is not the fear of being caught, it is the fear of being *cut off*, of being misunderstood. Thus the narrator of "The Imp of the Perverse": "Had I not been thus prolix, you might either have misunderstood me altogether, or, with the rabble, have fancied me mad." Here, as in the other two tales, the claim to sanity is a response to the fear of being cut off from other people, of being "misunderstood altogether."

LOUISE J. KAPLAN

On "The Fall of the House of Usher"

FROM NEW ESSAYS ON POE'S MAJOR TALES

Both Madeline and Roderick are dying of asceticism, of their mutual need to banish every sign of sensuality or earthly desire. Madeline's physical presence is a reminder to Roderick of his earthly passions. She is slowly wasting away, but her skin still blushes with the blood of life. In light of Roderick's conflicted feelings toward his sister, I would interpret "The Haunted Palace" as an expression of his wish to restore the spirituality of his love for Madeline. The contrasting images in this ballad represent two images of Madeline: the Madeline of childhood in her days of glorious innocence, and the bloody, lewd Madeline, the Madeline of sexual desire and the wild intoxications of the Heart.

Childhood innocence is about the life of Desire before the knowledge of female sexuality and the male-female sexual difference. It is the oedipal child, the child who must leave the world of sensate flux and free imagination and enter the symbolic order with its rules of language, reason, and morality, who resurrects the earlier uncomplicated infantile wish to merge with the mother, now as a defense against the knowledge of the irrevocable and irreversible differences between the sexes. With a full acknowledgement of these differences would come the painful acknowledgment that the life of Desire can never be pure. Once the child enters the moral order, the elevating excitements of the Soul cannot exist independently of earthly passions and the intoxications of the Heart—or the Truth of Reason.

Asceticism, the total avoidance of sensual pleasure, is an avoidance of the complex negotiations between Desire and Authority. When the effort to banish passion through asceticism fails, as eventually it must, there is either a fulfillment of a forbidden sexual desire or something worse—the madness of total emotional surrender to the other and a loss of identity.

Emotional surrender entails a total dissolution of the boundaries between the real and the not real. Thus, in ridding himself of the intoxications of the Heart, the passions of incestuous desire, Roderick is attempting a more insidious violation of the moral order. For, as Lawrence detected, latent in the undercurrent of an apparent sexual incestuous wish is the wish for a spiritual merger with the other. Roderick's deepest and most frightening wish is to merge with Madeline, to be eternally united with her in some smooth womblike utopia where the rough realities of earthly existence would no longer disturb his peace. Our most profound fears are always a reflection of our unconscious forbidden wishes. Roderick's "FEAR" of total annihilation resides in his wish to be one with Madeline, to dissolve his being in the sentience of nonliving matter.

Alongside my own interpretive version of Madeline, I am ready to acknowledge a grain of truth in previous interpretations of her as double or doppelgänger, or as representation of Roderick's darker consciousness, or unconscious desires, or as witch or vampire. They all miss the essential point of the perverse strategy employed in "The Fall of the House of Usher." This prose allegory is about the regulation of Desire through the fetishistic devices of Art. Roderick's aspiration for a Supernal Beauty, the pure excitement of the soul expressed in music and painting, is the counterpoint of his bodily asceticism. By ridding himself of all earthly passion he is attempting to repudiate his incestuous longing for Madeline. However, Roderick's sublime art only disguises and conceals his forbidden wishes and in the end the Truth is out—revealed. Roderick's effort to bury the life of Desire by de-animating his still living, breathing sister is doomed to fail. Madeline's return from her walled-off place beneath the House of Usher represents the return of Usher's repudiated desires and the granting of his forbidden wishes.

The nature of Madeline's dying gesture is ambiguous. When Madeline falls inward on Roderick is it a fulfillment of their sensual passions? Or is her apparently violent gesture an act of blanketing generosity, an affirmation of their spiritual bond, a granting of her beloved brother's wish to merge with her? Either way, Madeline's final enactment represents a destruction of the symbolic order and a violation of social morality. The civil war in the palace of the mind is over. The perverse strategy has failed.

The perverse strategy employs a symbolic structure. The perverse strategy enables illusion but also still retains a connection with the moral order and reality. The price is a split-in-the-ego, much like the barely perceptible fissure that extends down the walls of the House of Usher. On the other hand, a repudiation or total denial of earthly reality entails a breakdown of symbolic structures and always invites a return of the repudiated in its most archaic and awesome guises. Whether as witch or vampire or as the specter of incestuous desire, the terrifying, emaciated, white-shrouded, bloody Madeline returns from her tomb to grant her brother's forbidden wishes. The twins are reunited in death, merged as one for all eternity. With Madeline's substantiation of the aesthetic of pure Desire, her overthrow of moral Authority, Heaven cries out, venting its full wrath on the House of Usher, which cracks apart along its fissure, collapses like a house of cards—and is no more.

DAVID S. REYNOLDS

On "The Cask of Amontillado"

FROM NEW ESSAYS ON POE'S MAJOR TALES

There is absolutely no excess in "The Cask of Amontillado." Every sentence points inexorably to the horrifying climax. In the interest of achieving unity, Poe purposely leaves several questions unanswered. The tale is remarkable for what it leaves out. What are the "thousand injuries" Montresor has suffered at the hands of Fortunato?

In particular, what was the "insult" that has driven Montresor to the grisly extreme of murder by live burial? What personal misfortune is he referring to when he tells his foe, "you are happy, as I once was"? Like a painter who leaves a lot of suggestive white canvas, Poe sketches character and setting lightly, excluding excess material. Even so simple a detail as the location of the action is unknown. Most assume the setting is Italy, but one commentator makes a good case for France. What do we know about the main characters? As discussed, both are bibulous and proud of their connoisseurship in wines. Fortunato, besides being a Mason, is "rich, respected, admired, beloved," and there is a Lady Fortunato who will miss him. Montresor is descended from "a great and numerous family" and is wealthy enough to sustain a palazzo, servants, and extensive wine vaults.

Other than that, Poe tells very little about the two. Both exist solely to fulfill the imperatives of the plot Poe has designed. Everything Montresor does and says furthers his strategy of luring his enemy to his death. Everything Fortunato does and says reveals the fatuous extremes his vanity about wines will lead him to. Though limited, these characters are not what E. M. Forster would call flat. They swiftly come alive before our eyes because Poe describes them with acute psychological realism. Montresor is a complex Machiavellian criminal, exhibiting a full range of traits from clever ingratiation to stark sadism. Fortunato, the dupe whose pride leads to his own downfall, nevertheless exhibits enough admirable qualities that one critic has seen him as a wronged man of courtesy and good will. The drama of the story lies in the carefully orchestrated interaction between the two. Poe directs our attention away from the merely sensational and toward the psychological.

Herein lies another key difference between the tale and its precursors. In none of the popular live-burial works is the *psychology* of revenge a factor. In Headley and Lippard, the victim is unconscious and thus incognizant of the murderer's designs; similarly, in Balzac there is no communication at all between the murderer and the entombed. In Poe, the relationship between the two is, to a large degree, the story. Montresor says at the start, murder is most successful if the victim is made painfully aware of what is happening: "A wrong is unredressed. . . . when the avenger fails to make himself felt as such to him who has done the wrong." By focusing on the process of vanity falling prey to sly revenge, Poe shifts attention to psychological subtleties ignored by the other live-burial writers.

Particularly intriguing are the brilliantly cruel ploys of Montresor. An adept in what today is called reverse psychology, Montresor never once invites Fortunato to his home or his wine vaults. Instead, he cleverly plays on his victim's vanity so that it is Fortunato who is always begging to go forward into the vaults. Montresor merely says he has received a pipe of "what passes for Amontillado," that he has his doubts, and that, since Fortunato is engaged, he is on his way to consult another connoisseur, Luchesi. By arousing vanity and introducing the element of competition ("Luchesi cannot tell Amontillado from Sherry," grumbles Fortunato), Montresor never needs to push his victim toward destruction. It is the victim who does all the pushing, while the murderer repeatedly gives reasons why the journey into the cellar should be called off. This ironic role reversal begins when Fortunato, whose curiosity is piqued, demands: "Come, let us go."

> "Whither?" [askes Montresor.]
> "To your vaults."

> "My friend, no; I will not impose on your good nature. I perceive you have an engagement. Luchesi—"
>
> "I have not engagement;—come."
>
> "My friend, no. It is not the engagement, but the severe cold with which I perceive you are afflicted. The vaults are insufferably damp. They are encrusted with nitre."
>
> "Let us go, nevertheless. The cold is merely nothing."

And so, as Montresor tells us. "I suffered him to hurry me to my palazzo." Reverse psychology governs even Montresor's advance preparations for the murder: The palazzo is empty because he has told his servants they should not stir from the house since he would be away all night—an order "sufficient, I well knew, to insure their immediate disappearance, one and all, as soon as my back was turned."

FLANNERY O'CONNOR IN CONTEXT

[1925–1964]

ARIEL
WWW

Flannery O'Connor was born in Savannah, Georgia, in 1925. In 1938 she moved to Milledgeville, Georgia, the city which had been Georgia's capital before the Civil War and where she would spend most of her life. She graduated in 1945 from Women's College of Georgia, where she earned a reputation as a cartoonist, contributing weekly sketches to the campus newspaper. O'Connor then went on to earn an M.F.A. in writing from the State University of Iowa in 1947. At the age of twenty-five she was struck with a debilitating illness, disseminated lupus, which forced her to return to Milledgeville in 1950, where she lived and published her fiction until her death in 1964.

O'Connor is one of the unique literary voices to emerge from the 1950s. Her widely anthologized short stories often employ humor, irony, and paradox within a system of Christian belief in evil and redemption. And because she is a social satirist as well as a religious writer, O'Connor often highlights American cultural challenges, such as random violence, race relations, and class discrimination.

Southern Gothic

O'Connor's identity as a southerner provided her with many of the raw materials she needed to fabricate the settings and finely detailed characters of her stories. "The things we see, hear, smell, and touch," O'Connor wrote, "affect us long before we believe anything at all. The South impresses its image on the Southerner—be he Catholic or not—from the moment he is able to distinguish one sound from another."

O'Connor as editor of the college literary magazine *The Corinthian.*

O'Connor's stories are suggestive of the southern gothic tradition of storytelling in which engaging, violent, and frequently grotesque characters are often treated with colloquial humor. Other writers identified with this tradition and often considered influential on O'Connor's fiction include

Mark Twain, William Faulkner, and Katherine Anne Porter. Like O'Connor, these writers often point to the comic in calamity, while exploring moral issues in highly imaginative and symbolic ways. The novelist and critic V. S. Pritchett has suggested that the characters in O'Connor's stories are "plain human beings in whose fractured lives the writer has discovered an uncouth relationship with the lasting myths and the violent passions of human life." For O'Connor, truth was of the greatest importance—even when it revealed itself as fractured, uncouth, or violent.

The Catholic Dimension

O'Connor herself suggested that there were two strong influences on her writing: her sense of herself as a southerner and her Roman Catholic roots. Though the South served as the setting for O'Connor's fiction, Roman Catholicism allowed her to transcend the confines of regionalism to make a universal statement. "The woods are full of regional writers," she once stated, "and it is the great horror of every serious Southern writer that he will become one of them." Elsewhere, O'Connor wrote: "I see from the standpoint of Christian orthodoxy. This means that for me the meaning of life is centered in our Redemption by Christ and what I see in the world I see in its relation to that." Understanding O'Connor's religious beliefs helps to interpret her fiction, but we need not share her faith to enjoy her work. Her genius as a writer eclipsed any religious devotion. Responding to a student who once queried her as to "just what enlightenment" a student might be expected to glean from an O'Connor narrative, the author suggested that the young reader "forget about the enlightenment" and just enjoy the story.

O'Connor's Irony

The typical O'Connor story often begins with a comic protagonist who indulges in fantasies of moral or social superiority or has a false sense of the certainty of things. The protagonist then has an ironic and traumatic (if not fatal) encounter with other characters or a situation that suggests the disturbing possibility of an incomprehensible and frequently terrifying universe. In "Everything That Rises Must Converge," for example, both Julian and his mother are ironic figures convinced of their personal superiority as well as the correctness of their respective world views. Julian's mother fortifies herself against disappointing circumstances by assuming aristocratic airs. Ironically, she proclaims that "if you know who you are you can go anywhere." When she climbs into the bus, she enters the aisle "with a little smile, as if she were going into a drawing room where everyone had been waiting for her." From her perspective she and her son are the descendants of Godhighs and Chestnys, who count plantation owners and a former governor in their bloodline. Julian, on the other hand, insists that he has a truer sense of his mother's and his place in the changing world, and

> in spite of her, he had turned out so well . . . he had, on his own initiative, come out with a first-rate education; in spite of growing up dominated by a small mind, he had ended up with a large one; in spite of all her foolish views, he was free of prejudice and unafraid to face facts.

O'Connor: Timeline

Literature	Year	Events
	1925	**O'Connor born in Savannah, GA (March 25, 1925)**
Faulkner, *The Sound and the Fury* **(1929)**; *As I Lay Dying* **(1930)**	1930	Stock market crash **(1929)**; start of Great Depression
West, *Miss Lonelyhearts* **(1933)**		Nazis gain control of Germany **(1933)**
Porter, *Flowering Judas* **(1935)**	1935	
Wright, *Native Son* **(1940)**	1940	World War II **(1939–45)**; Japan bombs Pearl Harbor and U.S. enters war **(1941)**
Welty, *A Curtain of Green*; Fitzgerald, *The Last Tycoon* **(1941)**		
Williams, *The Glass Menagerie* **(1945)**	1945	**O'Connor graduates from Georgia State College**; U.S. drops atomic bomb on Japan **(1945)**
		O'Connor earns MFA at Iowa School for Writers (1947)
		O'Connor takes up residence at Yaddo (1948)
Miller, *Death of a Salesman* **(1949)**		Germany divided; Chinese Communist Party establishes People's Republic **(1949)**
O'Connor, *Wise Blood*; Ellison, *Invisible Man*; Hemingway, *The Old Man and the Sea* **(1952)**	1950	Korean War **(1950–53)**
		O'Connor diagnosed with lupus (1952)
		DNA discovered **(1953)**
A Good Man Is Hard to Find **(1955)**		Brown v. Board of Education: racial segregation in schools ruled unconstitutional; McCarthy–Army hearings **(1954)**
Hansberry, *Raisin in the Sun* **(1959)**		Cuban Revolution **(1959)**
The Violent Bear It Away **(1960)**	1960	Wave of sit-ins at segregated lunch counters in American South **(1960)**
		Berlin Wall erected **(1961)**
Albee, *Who's Afraid of Virginia Woolf?* **(1962)**		Cuban missile crisis **(1962)**
Martin Luther King Jr., *"I Have a Dream"* **(1963)**		Kennedy assassinated **(1963)**
		O'Connor dies in Milledgeville, GA (Aug. 3, 1964)
Everything That Rises Must Converge **(post., 1965)**	1965	U.S. enters Vietnam War; Malcom X assassinated **(1965)**
		Martin Luther King, Jr., assassinated **(1968)**
	1970	

The narrator, however, implies that Julian is himself an ironic figure, as affected as his mother and only slightly more subtle in his racism. Rather than insist that black people ride in the back of the bus, he tries "to strike up an acquaintance . . . with some of the better types."

The title "Everything That Rises Must Converge" is also ironic, alluding to the works of Teilhard de Chardin, a religious philosopher who explains that the future will focus on an "omega point" where everything and everyone will be joined at the end of geologic time. As the story concludes, however, the characters do not so much

Miss Flannery O'Connor Is at Home by David C. Perry.

converge as collide, and from this collision the unimagined and terrifying universe is made apparent.

Though brief and tragically curtailed by illness, Flannery O'Connor's writing career was nevertheless recognized during her lifetime. She was awarded a *Kenyon Review* fellowship in fiction in 1953; a National Institute of Arts and Letters grant in literature in 1957; an O. Henry Award in 1957; a Ford Foundation grant in 1959; an honorary doctorate of literature from St. Mary's College in 1962 and another from Smith College in 1963. She was also awarded a Henry H. Bellaman Foundation special award in 1964. In 1971, her posthumous collection, *The Complete Stories of Flannery O'Connor*, won the National Book Award. In addition to her short-story collections [*A Good Man Is Hard to Find and Other Stories* (1955); *Everything That Rises Must Converge* (1965); *The Complete Stories of Flannery O'Connor* (1971)], Flannery O'Connor published two novels, *Wise Blood* (1952) and *The Violent Bear It Away* (1960). Also significant are her essays and ideas on literature collected in *Mystery and Manners* (1969), *The Habit of Being: Selected Letters of Flannery O'Connor* (1979), and *The Correspondence of Flannery O'Connor and the Brainard Cheneys* (1986).

FLANNERY O'CONNOR: STORIES

FLANNERY O'CONNOR
[1925–1964]

Good Country People

Besides the neutral expression that she wore when she was alone, Mrs. Freeman had two others, forward and reverse, that she used for all her human dealings. Her forward expression was steady and driving like the advance of a heavy truck. Her eyes never swerved to left or right but turned as the story turned as if they followed a yellow line down the center of it. She seldom used the other expression because it was not often necessary for her to retract a statement, but when she did, her face came to a complete stop, there was an almost imperceptible movement of her black eyes, during which they seemed to be receding, and then the observer would see that Mrs. Freeman, though she might stand there as real as several grain sacks thrown on top of each other, was no longer there in spirit. As for getting anything across to her when this was the case, Mrs. Hopewell had given it up. She might talk her head off. Mrs. Freeman could never be brought to admit herself wrong on any point. She would stand there and if she could be brought to say anything, it was something like, "Well, I wouldn't of said it was and I wouldn't of said it wasn't," or letting her gaze range over the top kitchen shelf where there was an assortment of dusty bottles, she might remark, "I see you ain't ate many of them figs you put up last summer."

They carried on their most important business in the kitchen at breakfast. Every morning Mrs. Hopewell got up at seven o'clock and lit her gas heater and Joy's. Joy was her daughter, a large blonde girl who had an artificial leg. Mrs. Hopewell thought of her as a child though she was thirty-two years old and highly educated. Joy would get up while her mother was eating and lumber into the bathroom and slam the door, and before long, Mrs. Freeman would arrive at the back door. Joy would hear her mother call, "Come on in," and then they would talk for a while in low voices that were indistinguishable in the bathroom. By the time Joy came in, they had usually finished the weather report and were on one or the other of Mrs. Freeman's daughters, Glynese or Carramae. Joy called them Glycerin and Caramel. Glynese, a redhead, was eighteen and had many admirers; Carramae, a blonde, was only fifteen but already married and pregnant. She could not keep anything on her stomach. Every morning Mrs. Freeman told Mrs. Hopewell how many times she had vomited since the last report.

Mrs. Hopewell liked to tell people that Glynese and Carramae were two of the finest girls she knew and that Mrs. Freeman was a *lady* and that she was never ashamed to take her anywhere or introduce her to anybody they might meet. Then she would tell how she had happened to hire the Freemans in the first place and how they were a godsend to her and how she had had them four years. The reason for her keeping them so long was that they were not trash. They were good country people. She had telephoned the man whose name they had given as a reference and he had told her that Mr. Freeman was a good farmer but that his wife was the nosiest woman ever to walk the earth. "She's got to be into everything," the man said. "If she don't get there before the dust settles, you can bet she's dead, that's all. She'll want to know all your business. I can stand him real good," he had said, "but me nor my wife neither could have stood that woman one more minute on this place." That had put Mrs. Hopewell off for a few days.

She had hired them in the end because there were no other applicants but she had made up her mind beforehand exactly how she would handle the woman. Since she was the type who had to be into everything, then, Mrs. Hopewell had decided, she would not only let her be into everything, she would *see to it* that she was into everything—she would give her the responsibility of everything, she would put her in charge. Mrs. Hopewell had no bad qualities of her own but she was able to use other people's in such a constructive way that she never felt the lack. She had hired the Freemans and she had kept them four years.

Nothing is perfect. This was one of Mrs. Hopewell's favorite sayings. Another was: that is life! And still another, the most important, was: well, other people have their opinions too. She would make these statements, usually at the table, in a tone of gentle insistence as if no one held them but her, and the large hulking Joy, whose constant outrage had obliterated every expression from her face, would stare just a little to the side of her, her eyes icy blue, with the look of someone who has achieved blindness by an act of will and means to keep it.

When Mrs. Hopewell said to Mrs. Freeman that life was like that, Mrs. Freeman would say, "I always said so myself." Nothing had been arrived at by anyone that had not first been arrived at by her. She was quicker than Mr. Freeman. When Mrs. Hopewell said to her after they had been on the place a while, "You know, you're the wheel behind the wheel," and winked, Mrs. Freeman had said, "I know it. I've always been quick. It's some that are quicker than others."

"Everybody is different," Mrs. Hopewell said.

"Yes, most people is," Mrs. Freeman said.

"It takes all kinds to make the world."

"I always said it did myself."

The girl was used to this kind of dialogue for breakfast and more of it for dinner; sometimes they had it for supper too. When they had no guest they ate in the kitchen because that was easier. Mrs. Freeman always managed to arrive at some point during the meal and to watch them finish it. She would stand in the doorway if it were summer but in the winter she would stand with one elbow on top of the refrigerator and look down on them, or she would stand by the gas heater, lifting the back of her skirt slightly. Occasionally she would stand against the wall and roll her head from side to side. At no time was she in any hurry to leave. All this was very trying on Mrs. Hopewell but she was a woman of great patience. She realized that nothing is perfect and that in the Freemans she had good country people and that if, in this day and age, you get good country people, you had better hang onto them.

She had had plenty of experience with trash. Before the Freemans she had averaged one tenant family a year. The wives of these farmers were not the kind you would want to be around you for very long. Mrs. Hopewell, who had divorced her husband long ago, needed someone to walk over the fields with her; and when Joy had to be impressed for these services, her remarks were usually so ugly and her face so glum that Mrs. Hopewell would say, "If you can't come pleasantly, I don't want you at all," to which the girl, standing square and rigid-shouldered with her neck thrust slightly forward, would reply, "If you want me, here I am—LIKE I AM."

Mrs. Hopewell excused this attitude because of the leg (which had been shot off in a hunting accident when Joy was ten). It was hard for Mrs. Hopewell to realize that her child was thirty-two now and that for more than twenty years she had had only one leg. She thought of her still as a child because it tore her heart to think instead of the poor stout girl in her thirties who had never danced a step or had any *normal* good times. Her name was really Joy but as soon as she was twenty-one and away from home, she had had it legally changed. Mrs. Hopewell was certain that she had thought and thought until she had hit upon the ugliest name in any language. Then she had gone and had the beautiful name, Joy, changed without telling her mother until after she had done it. Her legal name was Hulga.

When Mrs. Hopewell thought the name, Hulga, she thought of the broad blank hull of a battleship. She would not use it. She continued to call her Joy, to which the girl responded but in a purely mechanical way.

Hulga had learned to tolerate Mrs. Freeman, who saved her from taking walks with her mother. Even Glynese and Carramae were useful when they occupied attention that might otherwise have been directed at her. At first she had thought she could not stand Mrs. Freeman for she had found that it was not possible to be rude to her. Mrs. Freeman would take on strange resentments and for days together she would be sullen but the source of her displeasure was always obscure; a direct attack, a positive leer, blatant ugliness to her face—these never touched her. And without warning one day, she began calling her Hulga.

She did not call her that in front of Mrs. Hopewell who would have been incensed but when she and the girl happened to be out of the house together, she would say something and add the name Hulga to the end of it, and the big spectacled Joy-Hulga would scowl and redden as if her privacy had been intruded upon. She considered the name her personal affair. She had arrived at it first purely on the basis of its ugly sound and then the full genius of its fitness had struck her. She had a vision of the name working like the ugly sweating Vulcan who stayed in the furnace and to whom, presumably, the goddess had to come when called. She saw it as the name of her highest creative act. One of her major triumphs was that her mother had not been able to turn her dust into Joy, but the greater one was that she had been able to turn it herself into Hulga. However, Mrs. Freeman's relish for using the name only irritated her. It was as if Mrs. Freeman's beady steel-pointed eyes had penetrated far enough behind her face to reach some secret fact. Something about her seemed to fascinate Mrs. Freeman and then one day Hulga realized that it was the artificial leg. Mrs. Freeman had a special fondness for the details of secret infections, hidden deformities, assaults upon children. Of diseases, she preferred the lingering or incurable. Hulga had heard Mrs. Hopewell give her the details of the hunting accident, how the leg had been literally blasted off, how she had never lost consciousness. Mrs. Freeman could listen to it any time as if it had happened an hour ago.

When Hulga stumped into the kitchen in the morning (she could walk without making the awful noise but she made it—Mrs. Hopewell was certain—because it was ugly sounding), she glanced at them and did not speak. Mrs. Hopewell would be in her red kimono with her hair tied around her head in rags. She would be sitting at the table, finishing her breakfast and Mrs. Freeman would be hanging by her elbow outward from the refrigerator, looking down at the table. Hulga always put her eggs on the stove to boil and then stood over them with her arms folded, and Mrs. Hopewell would look at her—a kind of indirect gaze divided between her and Mrs. Freeman—and would think that if she would only keep herself up a little, she wouldn't be so bad looking. There was nothing wrong with her face that a pleasant expression wouldn't help. Mrs. Hopewell said that people who looked on the bright side of things would be beautiful even if they were not.

Whenever she looked at Joy this way, she could not help but feel that it would have been better if the child had not taken the Ph.D. It had certainly not brought her out any and now that she had it, there was no more excuse for her to go to school again. Mrs. Hopewell thought it was nice for girls to go to school to have a good time but Joy had "gone through." Anyhow, she would not have been strong enough to go again. The doctors had told Mrs. Hopewell that with the best of care, Joy might see forty-five. She had a weak heart. Joy had made it plain that if it had not been for this condition, she would be far from these red hills and good country people. She would be in a university lecturing to people who knew what she was talking about. And Mrs. Hopewell could very well picture her there, looking like a scarecrow and lecturing to more of the same. Here she went about all day in a six-year-old skirt and a yellow sweat shirt with a faded cowboy on a horse embossed on it. She thought this was funny; Mrs. Hopewell thought it was idiotic and showed simply that she was still a child. She was brilliant but she didn't have a grain of sense. It seemed to Mrs. Hopewell that every year she grew less like other people and more like herself—bloated, rude, and squint-eyed. And she said such strange things! To her own mother she had said—without warning, without excuse, standing up in the middle of a meal with her face purple and her mouth half full—"Woman! do you ever look inside? Do you ever look inside and see what you are *not?* God!" she had cried sinking down again and staring at her plate, "Malebranche was right: we are not our own light. We are not our own light!" Mrs. Hopewell had no idea to this day what brought that on. She had only made the remark, hoping Joy would take it in, that a smile never hurt anyone.

The girl had taken the Ph.D. in philosophy and this left Mrs. Hopewell at a complete loss. You could say, "My daughter is a nurse," or "My daughter is a school teacher," or even, "My daughter is a chemical engineer." You could not say, "My daughter is a philosopher." That was something that had ended with the Greeks and Romans. All day Joy sat on her neck in a deep chair, reading. Sometimes she went for walks but she didn't like dogs or cats or birds or flowers or nature or nice young men. She looked at nice young men as if she could smell their stupidity.

One day Mrs. Hopewell had picked up one of the books the girl had just put down and opening it at random, she read, "Science, on the other hand, has to assert its soberness and seriousness afresh and declare that it is concerned solely with what-is. Nothing—how can it be for science anything but a horror and a phantasm? If science is right, then one thing stands firm: science wishes to know nothing of nothing. Such is after all the strictly scientific approach to Nothing. We know it by wishing to know nothing of Nothing." These words had been underlined with a blue pencil and they worked on Mrs. Hopewell like some evil incantation in gibberish. She shut the book quickly and went out of the room as if she were having a chill.

This morning when the girl came in, Mrs. Freeman was on Carramae. "She thrown up four times after supper," she said, "and was up twict in the night after three o'clock. Yesterday she didn't do nothing but ramble in the bureau drawer. All she did. Stand up there and see what she could run up on."

"She's got to eat," Mrs. Hopewell muttered, sipping her coffee, while she watched Joy's back at the stove. She was wondering what the child had said to the Bible salesman. She could not imagine what kind of a conversation she could possibly have had with him.

He was a tall gaunt hatless youth who had called yesterday to sell them a Bible. He had appeared at the door, carrying a large black suitcase that weighted him so heavily on one side that he had to brace himself against the door facing. He seemed on the point of collapse but he said in a cheerful voice, "Good morning, Mrs. Cedars!" and set the suitcase down on the mat. He was not a bad-looking young man though he had on a bright blue suit and yellow socks that were not pulled up far enough. He had prominent face bones and a streak of sticky-looking brown hair falling across his forehead.

"I'm Mrs. Hopewell," she said.

"Oh!" he said, pretending to look puzzled but with his eyes sparkling, "I saw it said 'The Cedars,' on the mailbox so I thought you was Mrs. Cedars!" and he burst out in a pleasant laugh. He picked up the satchel and under cover of a pant, he fell forward into her hall. It was rather as if the suitcase had moved first, jerking him after it. "Mrs. Hopewell!" he said and grabbed her hand. "I hope you are well!" and he laughed again and then all at once his face sobered completely. He paused and gave her a straight earnest look and said, "Lady, I've come to speak of serious things."

"Well, come in," she muttered, none too pleased because her dinner was almost ready. He came into the parlor and sat down on the edge of a straight chair and put the suitcase between his feet and glanced around the room as if he were sizing her up by it. Her silver gleamed on the two sideboards; she decided he had never been in a room as elegant as this.

"Mrs. Hopewell," he began, using her name in a way that sounded almost intimate, "I know you believe in Chrustian service."

"Well yes," she murmured.

"I know," he said and paused, looking very wise with his head cocked on one side, "that you're a good woman. Friends have told me."

Mrs. Hopewell never liked to be taken for a fool. "What are you selling?" she asked.

"Bibles," the young man said and his eye raced around the room before he added, "I see you have no family Bible in your parlor, I see that is the one lack you got!"

Mrs. Hopewell could not say, "My daughter is an atheist and won't let me keep the Bible in the parlor." She said, stiffening slightly, "I keep my Bible by my bedside." This was not the truth. It was in the attic somewhere.

"Lady," he said, "the word of God ought to be in the parlor."

"Well, I think that's a matter of taste," she began. "I think . . ."

"Lady," he said, "for a Chrustian, the word of God ought to be in every room in the house besides in his heart. I know you're a Chrustian because I can see it in every line of your face."

She stood up and said, "Well, young man, I don't want to buy a Bible and I smell my dinner burning."

He didn't get up. He began to twist his hands and looking down at them, he said softly, "Well lady, I'll tell you the truth—not many people want to buy one nowadays and besides, I know I'm real simple. I don't know how to say a thing but to say it. I'm just a country boy." He glanced up into her unfriendly face. "People like you don't like to fool with country people like me!"

"Why!" she cried, "good country people are the salt of the earth! Besides, we all have different ways of doing, it takes all kinds to make the world go 'round. That's life!"

"You said a mouthful," he said.

"Why, I think there aren't enough good country people in the world!" she said, stirred. "I think that's what's wrong with it!"

His face had brightened. "I didn't inraduce myself," he said. "I'm Manley Pointer from out in the country around Willohobie, not even from a place, just from near a place."

"You wait a minute," she said. "I have to see about my dinner." She went out to the kitchen and found Joy standing near the door where she had been listening.

"Get rid of the salt of the earth," she said, "and let's eat."

Mrs. Hopewell gave her a pained look and turned the heat down under the vegetables. "*I* can't be rude to anybody," she murmured and went back into the parlor.

He had opened the suitcase and was sitting with a Bible on each knee.

"You might as well put those up," she told him. "I don't want one."

"I appreciate your honesty," he said. "You don't see any more real honest people unless you go way out in the country."

"I know," she said, "real genuine folks!" Through the crack in the door she heard a groan.

"I guess a lot of boys come telling you they're working their way through college," he said, "but I'm not going to tell you that. Somehow," he said, "I don't want to go to college. I want to devote my life to Chrustian service. See," he said, lowering his voice, "I got this heart condition. I may not live long. When you know it's something wrong with you and you may not live long, well then, lady . . ." He paused, with his mouth open, and stared at her.

He and Joy had the same condition! She knew that her eyes were filling with tears but she collected herself quickly and murmured, "Won't you stay for dinner? We'd love to have you!" and was sorry the instant she heard herself say it.

"Yes mam," he said in an abashed voice, "I would sher love to do that!"

Joy had given him one look on being introduced to him and then throughout the meal had not glanced at him again. He had addressed several remarks to her, which she had pretended not to hear. Mrs. Hopewell could not understand deliberate rudeness, although she lived with it, and she felt she had always to overflow with hospitality to make up for Joy's lack of courtesy. She urged him to talk about himself and he did. He said he was the seventh child of twelve and that his father had been crushed under a tree when he himself was eight years old. He had been crushed very badly, in fact, almost cut in two and was practically not recognizable. His mother had got along the best she could by hard working and she had always seen that her children went to Sunday School and that they read the Bible every evening. He was now nineteen years old and he had been selling Bibles for four months. In that time he had sold seventy-seven Bibles and had the promise of two more sales. He wanted to become a missionary because he thought that was the way you could do most for people. "He who losest his life shall find it," he said simply and he was so sincere, so genuine and earnest that Mrs. Hopewell would not for the world have smiled. He prevented his peas from sliding onto the table by blocking them with a piece of bread which he later cleaned his plate with. She could see Joy observing sidewise how he handled his knife and fork and she saw too that every few minutes, the boy would dart a keen appraising glance at the girl as if he were trying to attract her attention.

After dinner Joy cleared the dishes off the table and disappeared and Mrs. Hopewell was left to talk with him. He told her again about his childhood and his father's accident and about various things that had happened to him. Every five minutes or so she would stifle a yawn. He sat for two hours until finally she told him she must go because she had an appointment in town. He packed his Bibles and thanked her and prepared to leave, but in the doorway he stopped and wrung her hand and said that not on any of his trips had he met a lady as nice as her and he asked if he could come again. She had said she would always be happy to see him.

Joy had been standing in the road, apparently looking at something in the distance, when he came down the steps toward her, bent to the side with his heavy valise. He stopped where she was standing and confronted her directly. Mrs. Hopewell could not hear what he said but she trembled to think what Joy would say to him. She could see that after a minute Joy said something and that then the boy began to speak again, making an excited gesture with his free hand. After a minute Joy said something else at which the boy began to speak once more. Then to her amazement, Mrs. Hopewell saw the two of them walk off together, toward the gate. Joy had walked all the way to the gate with him and Mrs. Hopewell could not imagine what they had said to each other, and she had not yet dared to ask.

Mrs. Freeman was insisting upon her attention. She had moved from the refrigerator to the heater so that Mrs. Hopewell had to turn and face her in order to seem to be listening. "Glynese gone out with Harvey Hill again last night," she said. "She had this sty."

"Hill," Mrs. Hopewell said absently, "is that the one who works in the garage?"

"Nome, he's the one that goes to chiropracter school," Mrs. Freeman said. "She had this sty. Been had it two days. So she says when he brought her in the other night he says, 'Lemme get rid of that sty for you,' and she says, 'How?' and he says, 'You just lay yourself down acrost the seat of that car and I'll show you.' So she done it and he popped her neck. Kept on a-popping it several times until she made him quit. This morning," Mrs. Freeman said, "she ain't got no sty. She ain't got no traces of a sty."

"I never heard of that before," Mrs. Hopewell said.

"He ast her to marry him before the Ordinary," Mrs. Freeman went on, "and she told him she wasn't going to be married in *no* office."

"Well, Glynese is a fine girl," Mrs. Hopewell said, "Glynese and Carramae are both fine girls."

"Carramae said when her and Lyman was married Lyman said it sure felt sacred to him. She said he said he wouldn't take five hundred dollars for being married by a preacher."

"How much would he take?" the girl asked from the stove.

"He said he wouldn't take five hundred dollars," Mrs. Freeman repeated.

"Well we all have work to do," Mrs. Hopewell said.

"Lyman said it just felt more sacred to him," Mrs. Freeman said. "The doctor wants Carramae to eat prunes. Says instead of medicine. Says them cramps is coming from pressure. You know where I think it is?"

"She'll be better in a few weeks," Mrs. Hopewell said.

"In the tube," Mrs. Freeman said. "Else she wouldn't be as sick as she is."

Hulga had cracked her two eggs into a saucer and was bringing them to the table along with a cup of coffee that she had filled too full. She sat down carefully and began to eat, meaning to keep Mrs. Freeman there by questions if for any reason she showed an inclination to leave. She could perceive her mother's eye on her. The first roundabout question would be about the Bible salesman and she did not wish to bring it on. "How did he pop her neck?" she asked.

Mrs. Freeman went into a description of how he had popped her neck. She said he owned a '55 Mercury but that Glynese said she would rather marry a man with only a '36 Plymouth who would be married by a preacher. The girl asked what if he had a '32 Plymouth and Mrs. Freeman said what Glynese had said was a '36 Plymouth.

Mrs. Hopewell said there were not many girls with Glynese's common sense. She said what she admired in those girls was their common sense. She said that reminded her that they had a nice visitor yesterday, a young man selling Bibles. "Lord," she said, "he bored me to death but he was so sincere and genuine I couldn't be rude to him. He was just good country people, you know," she said, "—just the salt of the earth."

"I seen him walk up," Mrs. Freeman said, "and then later—I seen him walk off," and Hulga could feel the slight shift in her voice, the slight insinuation, that he had not walked off alone, had he? Her face remained expressionless but the color rose into her neck and she seemed to swallow it down with the next spoonful of egg. Mrs. Freeman was looking at her as if they had a secret together.

"Well, it takes all kinds of people to make the world go 'round," Mrs. Hopewell said. "It's very good we aren't all alike."

"Some people are more alike than others," Mrs. Freeman said.

Hulga got up and stumped, with about twice the noise that was necessary, into her room and locked the door. She was to meet the Bible salesman at ten o'clock at the gate. She had thought about it half the night. She had started thinking of it as a great joke and then she had begun to see profound implications in it. She had lain in bed imagining dialogues for them that were insane on the surface but that reached below to depths that no Bible salesman would be aware of. Their conversation yesterday had been of this kind.

He had stopped in front of her and had simply stood there. His face was bony and sweaty and bright, with a little pointed nose in the center of it, and his look was different from what it had been at the dinner table. He was gazing at her with open curiosity, with fascination, like a child watching a new fantastic animal at the zoo, and he was breathing as if he had run a great distance to reach her. His gaze seemed somehow familiar but she could not think where she had been regarded with it before. For almost a minute he didn't say anything. Then on what seemed an insuck of breath, he whispered, "You ever ate a chicken that was two days old?"

The girl looked at him stonily. He might have just put this question up for consideration at the meeting of a philosophical association. "Yes," she presently replied as if she had considered it from all angles.

"It must have been mighty small!" he said triumphantly and shook all over with little nervous giggles, getting very red in the face, and subsiding finally into his gaze of complete admiration, while the girl's expression remained exactly the same.

"How old are you?" he asked softly.

She waited some time before she answered. Then in a flat voice she said, "Seventeen."

His smiles came in succession like waves breaking on the surface of a little lake. "I see you got a wooden leg," he said. "I think you're real brave. I think you're real sweet."

The girl stood blank and solid and silent.

"Walk to the gate with me," he said. "You're a brave sweet little thing and I liked you the minute I seen you walk in the door."

Hulga began to move forward.

"What's your name?" he asked, smiling down on the top of her head.

"Hulga," she said.

"Hulga," he murmured, "Hulga. Hulga. I never heard of anybody name Hulga before. You're shy, aren't you, Hulga?" he asked.

She nodded, watching his large red hand on the handle of the giant valise.

"I like girls that wear glasses," he said. "I think a lot. I'm not like these people that a serious thought don't ever enter their heads. It's because I may die."

"I may die too," she said suddenly and looked up at him. His eyes were very small and brown, glittering feverishly.

"Listen," he said, "don't you think some people was meant to meet on account of what all they got in common and all? Like they both think serious thoughts and all?" He shifted the valise to his other hand so that the hand nearest her was free. He caught hold of her elbow and shook it a little. "I don't work on Saturday," he said. "I like to walk in the woods and see what Mother Nature is wearing. O'er the hills and far away. Pic-nics and things. Couldn't we go on a pic-nic tomorrow? Say yes, Hulga," he said and gave her a dying look as if he felt his insides about to drop out of him. He had even seemed to sway slightly toward her.

During the night she had imagined that she seduced him. She imagined that the two of them walked on the place until they came to the storage barn beyond the two back fields and there, she imagined, that things came to such a pass that she very easily seduced him and that then, of course, she had to reckon with his remorse. True genius can get an idea across even to an inferior mind. She imagined that she took his remorse in hand and changed it into a deeper understanding of life. She took all his shame away and turned it into something useful.

She set off for the gate at exactly ten o'clock, escaping without drawing Mrs. Hopewell's attention. She didn't take anything to eat, forgetting that food is usually taken on a picnic. She wore a pair of slacks and a dirty white shirt, and as an afterthought, she had put some Vapex on the collar of it since she did not own any perfume. When she reached the gate no one was there.

She looked up and down the empty highway and had the furious feeling that she had been tricked, that he had only meant to make her walk to the gate after the idea of him. Then suddenly he stood up, very tall, from behind a bush on the opposite embankment. Smiling, he lifted his hat which was new and wide-brimmed. He had not worn it yesterday and she wondered if he had bought it for the occasion. It was toast-colored with a red and white band around it and was slightly too large for him. He stepped from behind the bush still carrying the black valise. He had on the same suit and the same yellow socks sucked down in his shoes from walking. He crossed the highway and said, "I knew you'd come!"

The girl wondered acidly how he had known this. She pointed to the valise and asked, "Why did you bring your Bibles?"

He took her elbow, smiling down on her as if he could not stop. "You can never tell when you'll need the word of God, Hulga," he said. She had a moment in which she doubted that this was actually happening and then they began to climb the embankment. They went down into the pasture toward the woods. The boy walked lightly by her side, bouncing on his toes. The valise did not seem to be heavy today; he even swung it. They crossed half the pasture without saying anything and then, putting his hand easily on the small of her back, he asked softly, "Where does your wooden leg join on?"

She turned an ugly red and glared at him and for an instant the boy looked abashed. "I didn't mean you no harm," he said. "I only meant you're so brave and all. I guess God takes care of you."

"No," she said, looking forward and walking fast, "I don't even believe in God."

At this he stopped and whistled. "No!" he exclaimed as if he were too astonished to say anything else.

She walked on and in a second he was bouncing at her side, fanning with his hat. "That's very unusual for a girl," he remarked, watching her out of the corner of his eye. When they reached the edge of the wood, he put his hand on her back again and drew her against him without a word and kissed her heavily.

The kiss, which had more pressure than feeling behind it, produced that extra surge of adrenalin in the girl that enables one to carry a packed trunk out of a burning house, but in her, the power went at once to the brain. Even before he released her, her mind, clear and detached and ironic anyway, was regarding him from a great distance, with amusement but with pity. She had never been kissed before and she was pleased to discover that it was an unexceptional experience and all a matter of the mind's control. Some people might enjoy drain water if they were told it was vodka. When the boy, looking expectant but uncertain, pushed her gently away, she turned and walked on, saying nothing as if such business, for her, were common enough.

He came along panting at her side, trying to help her when he saw a root that she might trip over. He caught and held back the long swaying blades of thorn vine until she had passed beyond them. She led the way and he came breathing heavily behind her. Then they came out on a sunlit hillside, sloping softly into another one a little smaller. Beyond, they could see the rusted top of the old barn where the extra hay was stored.

The hill was sprinkled with small pink weeds. "Then you ain't saved?" he asked suddenly, stopping.

The girl smiled. It was the first time she had smiled at him at all. "In my economy," she said, "I'm saved and you are damned but I told you I didn't believe in God."

Nothing seemed to destroy the boy's look of admiration. He gazed at her now as if the fantastic animal at the zoo had put its paw through the bars and given him a loving poke. She thought he looked as if he wanted to kiss her again and she walked on before he had the chance.

"Ain't there somewheres we can sit down sometime?" he murmured, his voice softening toward the end of the sentence.

"In that barn," she said.

They made for it rapidly as if it might slide away like a train. It was a large two-story barn, cool and dark inside. The boy pointed up the ladder that led into the loft and said, "It's too bad we can't go up there."

"Why can't we?" she asked.

"Yer leg," he said reverently.

The girl gave him a contemptuous look and putting both hands on the ladder, she climbed it while he stood below, apparently awestruck. She pulled herself expertly through the opening and then looked down at him and said, "Well, come on if you're coming," and he began to climb the ladder, awkwardly bringing the suitcase with him.

"We won't need the Bible," she observed.

"You never can tell," he said, panting. After he had got into the loft, he was a few seconds catching his breath. She had sat down in a pile of straw. A wide sheath of sunlight, filled with dust particles, slanted over her. She lay back against a bale, her face turned away, looking out the front opening of the barn where hay was thrown from a wagon into the loft. The two pink-speckled hillsides lay back against a dark ridge of woods. The sky was cloudless and cold blue. The boy dropped down by her side and put one arm under her and the other over her and began methodically kissing her face, making little noises like a fish. He did not remove his hat but it was pushed far enough back not to interfere. When her glasses got in his way, he took them off of her and slipped them into his pocket.

The girl at first did not return any of the kisses but presently she began to and after she had put several on his cheek, she reached his lips and remained there, kissing him again and again as if she were trying to draw all the breath out of him. His breath was clear and sweet like a child's and the kisses were sticky like a child's. He mumbled about loving her and about knowing when he first seen her that he loved her, but the mumbling was like the sleepy fretting of a child being put to sleep by his mother. Her mind, throughout this, never stopped or lost itself for a second to her feelings. "You ain't said you love me none," he whispered finally, pulling back from her. "You got to say that."

She looked away from him off into the hollow sky and then down at a black ridge and then down farther into what appeared to be two green swelling lakes. She didn't realize he had taken her glasses but this landscape could not seem exceptional to her for she seldom paid any close attention to her surroundings.

"You got to say it," he repeated. "You got to say you love me."

She was always careful how she committed herself. "In a sense," she began, "if you use the word loosely, you might say that. But it's not a word I use. I don't have illusions. I'm one of those people who see *through* to nothing."

The boy was frowning. "You got to say it. I said it and you got to say it," he said.

The girl looked at him almost tenderly. "You poor baby," she murmured. "It's just as well you don't understand," and she pulled him by the neck, face-down, against her. "We are all damned," she said, "but some of us have taken off our blindfolds and see that there's nothing to see. It's a kind of salvation."

The boy's astonished eyes looked blankly through the ends of her hair. "Okay," he almost whined, "but do you love me or don'tcher?"

"Yes," she said and added, "in a sense. But I must tell you something. There mustn't be anything dishonest between us." She lifted his head and looked him in the eye. "I am thirty years old," she said. "I have a number of degrees."

The boy's look was irritated but dogged. "I don't care," he said. "I don't care a thing about what all you done. I just want to know if you love me or don'tcher?" and he caught her to him and wildly planted her face with kisses until she said, "Yes, yes."

"Okay then," he said, letting her go. "Prove it."

She smiled, looking dreamily out on the shifty landscape. She had seduced him without even making up her mind to try. "How?" she asked, feeling that he should be delayed a little.

He leaned over and put his lips to her ear. "Show me where your wooden leg joins on," he whispered.

The girl uttered a sharp little cry and her face instantly drained of color. The obscenity of the suggestion was not what shocked her. As a child she had sometimes been subject to feelings of shame but education had removed the last traces of that as a good surgeon scrapes for cancer; she would no more have felt it over what he was asking than she would have believed in his Bible. But she was as sensitive about the artificial leg as a peacock about his tail. No one ever touched it but her. She took care of it as someone else would his soul, in private and almost with her own eyes turned away. "No," she said.

"I known it," he muttered, sitting up. "You're just playing me for a sucker."

"Oh no no!" she cried. "It joins on at the knee. Only at the knee. Why do you want to see it?"

The boy gave her a long penetrating look. "Because," he said, "it's what makes you different. You ain't like anybody else."

She sat staring at him. There was nothing about her face or her round freezing-blue eyes to indicate that this had moved her; but she felt as if her heart had stopped and left her mind to pump her blood. She decided that for the first time in her life she was face to face with real innocence. This boy, with an instinct that came from beyond wisdom, had touched the truth about her. When after a minute, she said in a hoarse high voice, "All right," it was like surrendering to him completely. It was like losing her own life and finding it again, miraculously, in his.

Very gently he began to roll the slack leg up. The artificial limb, in a white sock and brown flat shoe, was bound in a heavy material like canvas and ended in an ugly jointure where it was attached to the stump. The boy's face and his voice were entirely reverent as he uncovered it and said, "Now show me how to take it off and on."

She took it off for him and put it back on again and then he took it off himself, handling it as tenderly as if it were a real one. "See!" he said with a delighted child's face. "Now I can do it myself!"

"Put it back on," she said. She was thinking that she would run away with him and that every night he would take the leg off and every morning put it back on again. "Put it back on," she said.

"Not yet," he murmured, setting it on its foot out of her reach. "Leave it off for a while. You got me instead."

She gave a little cry of alarm but he pushed her down and began to kiss her again. Without the leg she felt entirely dependent on him. Her brain seemed to have stopped thinking altogether and to be about some other function that it was not very good at. Different expressions raced back and forth over her face. Every now and then the boy, his eyes like two steel spikes, would glance behind him where the leg stood. Finally she pushed him off and said, "Put it back on me now."

"Wait," he said. He leaned the other way and pulled the valise toward him and opened it. It had a pale blue spotted lining and there were only two Bibles in it. He took one of these out and opened the cover of it. It was hollow and contained a pocket flask of whiskey, a pack of cards, and a small blue box with printing on it. He laid these out in front of her one at a time in an evenly spaced row, like one presenting offerings at the shrine of a goddess. He put the blue box in her hand. THIS PRODUCT TO BE USED ONLY FOR THE PREVENTION OF DISEASE, she read, and dropped it. The boy was unscrewing the top of the flask. He stopped and pointed, with a smile, to the deck of cards. It was not an ordinary deck but one with an obscene picture on the back of each card. "Take a swig," he said, offering her the bottle first. He held it in front of her, but like one mesmerized, she did not move.

Her voice when she spoke had an almost pleading sound. "Aren't you," she murmured, "aren't you just good country people?"

The boy cocked his head. He looked as if he were just beginning to understand that she might be trying to insult him. "Yeah," he said, curling his lip slightly, "but it ain't held me back none. I'm as good as you any day in the week."

"Give me my leg," she said.

He pushed it farther away with his foot. "Come on now, let's begin to have us a good time," he said coaxingly. "We ain't got to know one another good yet."

"Give me my leg!" she screamed and tried to lunge for it but he pushed her down easily.

"What's the matter with you all of a sudden?" he asked, frowning as he screwed the top on the flask and put it quickly back inside the Bible. "You just a while ago said you didn't believe in nothing. I thought you was some girl!"

Her face was almost purple. "You're a Christian!" she hissed. "You're a fine Christian! You're just like them all—say one thing and do another. You're a perfect Christian, you're . . ."

The boy's mouth was set angrily. "I hope you don't think," he said in a lofty indignant tone, "that I believe in that crap! I may sell Bibles but I know which end is up and I wasn't born yesterday and I know where I'm going!"

"Give me my leg!" she screeched. He jumped up so quickly that she barely saw him sweep the cards and the blue box back into the Bible and throw the Bible into the valise. She saw him grab the leg and then she saw it for an instant slanted forlornly across the inside of the suitcase with a Bible at either side of its opposite ends.

He slammed the lid shut and snatched up the valise and swung it down the hole and then stepped through himself.

When all of him had passed but his head, he turned and regarded her with a look that no longer had any admiration in it. "I've gotten a lot of interesting things," he said. "One time I got a woman's glass eye this way. And you needn't to think you'll catch me because Pointer ain't really my name. I use a different name at every house I call at and don't stay nowhere long. And I'll tell you another thing, Hulga," he said, using the name as if he didn't think much of it, "you ain't so smart. I been believing in nothing ever since I was born!" and then the toast-colored hat disappeared down the hole and the girl was left, sitting on the straw in the dusty sunlight. When she turned her churning face toward the opening, she saw his blue figure struggling successfully over the green speckled lake.

Mrs. Hopewell and Mrs. Freeman, who were in the back pasture, digging up onions, saw him emerge a little later from the woods and head across the meadow toward the highway. "Why, that looks like that nice dull young man that tried to sell me a Bible yesterday," Mrs. Hopewell said, squinting. "He must have been selling them to the Negroes back in there. He was so simple," she said, "but I guess the world would be better off if we were all that simple."

Mrs. Freeman's gaze drove forward and just touched him before he disappeared under the hill. Then she returned her attention to the evil-smelling onion shoot she was lifting from the ground. "Some can't be that simple," she said. "I know I never could."

(1955)

QUESTIONS FOR CRITICAL THINKING AND WRITING

Experience

1. What was your initial response to the story's title? Did your impression of "good country people" change as you read it? Why or why not?
2. How did you respond to Hulga's loss of her artificial leg? Why?

Interpretation

3. What is the relationship between Mrs. Freeman and Mrs. Hopewell? To what extent are their names significant? What does the name change from Joy to Hulga suggest about Mrs. Hopewell's daughter?
4. What kinds of observations about life and people do Mrs. Freeman and Mrs. Hopewell make? How do the two women see themselves in relation to other people?
5. What does Hulga learn about herself and about other people through her encounter with the Bible salesman?

Evaluation

6. Which, if any, of the characters does O'Connor seem to admire, and whom does she satirize?
7. What religious values are evident in the story? What does O'Connor suggest about these values?

Connections

8. Compare O'Connor's humor in this story with her humor at the beginning of "A Good Man Is Hard to Find." Compare her use of irony in this story with that in one of her other stories.

Critical Thinking

9. What do you think of O'Connor's satire of the characters in "Good Country People"? Is her satirical treatment of these characters justified? To what extent is a writer justified in using satire as an artistic weapon?

A Good Man Is Hard to Find

The grandmother didn't want to go to Florida. She wanted to visit some of her connections in east Tennessee and she was seizing at every chance to change Bailey's mind. Bailey was the son she lived with, her only boy. He was sitting on the edge of his chair at the table, bent over the orange sports section of the *Journal*. "Now look here, Bailey," she said, "see here, read this," and she stood with one hand on her thin hip and the other rattling the newspaper at his bald head. "Here this fellow that calls himself The Misfit is aloose from the Federal Pen and headed toward Florida and you read here what it says he did to these people. Just you read it. I wouldn't take my children in any direction with a criminal like that aloose in it. I couldn't answer to my conscience if I did."

Bailey didn't look up from his reading so she wheeled around then and faced the children's mother, a young woman in slacks, whose face was as broad and innocent as a cabbage and was tied around with a green head-kerchief that had two points on the top like a rabbit's ears. She was sitting on the sofa, feeding the baby his apricots out of a jar. "The children have been to Florida before," the old lady said. "You all ought to take them somewhere else for a change so they would see different parts of the world and be broad. They never have been to east Tennessee."

The children's mother didn't seem to hear her but the eight-year-old boy, John Wesley, a stocky child with glasses, said, "If you don't want to go to Florida, why dontcha stay at home?" He and the little girl, June Star, were reading the funny papers on the floor.

"She wouldn't stay at home to be queen for a day," June Star said without raising her yellow head.

"Yes and what would you do if this fellow, The Misfit, caught you?" the grandmother asked.

"I'd smack his face," John Wesley said.

"She wouldn't stay at home for a million bucks," June Star said. "Afraid she'd miss something. She has to go everywhere we go."

"All right, Miss," the grandmother said. "Just remember that the next time you want me to curl your hair."

June Star said her hair was naturally curly.

The next morning the grandmother was the first one in the car, ready to go. She had her big black valise that looked like the head of a hippopotamus in one corner, and underneath it she was hiding a basket with Pity Sing, the cat, in it. She didn't intend for the cat to be left alone in the house for three days because he would miss her too much and she was afraid he might brush against one of the gas burners and accidentally asphyxiate himself. Her son, Bailey, didn't like to arrive at a motel with a cat.

She sat in the middle of the back seat with John Wesley and June Star on either side of her. Bailey and the children's mother and the baby sat in front and they left Atlanta at eight forty-five with the mileage on the car at 55890. The grandmother wrote this down because she thought it would be interesting to say how many miles they had been when they got back. It took them twenty minutes to reach the outskirts of the city.

The old lady settled herself comfortably, removing her white cotton gloves and putting them up with her purse on the shelf in front of the back window. The children's mother still had on slacks and still had her head tied up in a green kerchief, but the grandmother had on a navy blue straw sailor hat with a bunch of white violets on the brim and a navy blue dress with a small white dot in the print. Her collars and cuffs were white organdy trimmed with lace and at her neckline she had pinned a purple spray of cloth violets containing a sachet. In case of an accident, anyone seeing her dead on the highway would know at once that she was a lady.

She said she thought it was going to be a good day for driving, neither too hot nor too cold, and she cautioned Bailey that the speed limit was fifty-five miles an hour and that the patrolmen hid themselves behind billboards and small clumps of trees and sped out after you before you had a chance to slow down. She pointed out interesting details of the scenery: Stone Mountain; the blue granite that in some places came up to both sides of the highway; the brilliant red clay banks slightly streaked with purple; and the various crops that made rows of green lace-work on the ground. The trees were full of silver-white sunlight and the meanest of them sparkled. The children were reading comic magazines and their mother had gone back to sleep.

"Let's go through Georgia fast so we won't have to look at it much," John Wesley said.

"If I were a little boy," said the grandmother, "I wouldn't talk about my native state that way. Tennessee has the mountains and Georgia has the hills."

"Tennessee is just a hillbilly dumping ground," John Wesley said, "and Georgia is a lousy state too."

"You said it," June Star said.

"In my time," said the grandmother, folding her thin veined fingers, "children were more respectful of their native states and their parents and everything else. People did right then. Oh look at the cute little pickaninny!" she said and pointed to a Negro child standing in the door of a shack. "Wouldn't that make a picture, now?" she asked and they all turned and looked at the little Negro out of the back window. He waved.

"He didn't have any britches on," June Star said.

"He probably didn't have any," the grandmother explained. "Little niggers in the country don't have things like we do. If I could paint, I'd paint that picture," she said.

The children exchanged comic books.

The grandmother offered to hold the baby and the children's mother passed him over the front seat to her. She set him on her knee and bounced him and told him about the things they were passing. She rolled her eyes and screwed up her mouth and stuck her leathery thin face into his smooth bland one. Occasionally he gave her a faraway smile. They passed a large cotton field with five or six graves fenced in the middle of it, like a small island. "Look at the graveyard!" the grandmother said, pointing it out. "That was the old family burying ground. That belonged to the plantation."

"Where's the plantation?" John Wesley asked.

"Gone With the Wind," said the grandmother. "Ha. Ha."

When the children finished all the comic books they had brought, they opened the lunch and ate it. The grandmother ate a peanut butter sandwich and an olive and would not let the children throw the box and the paper napkins out the window. When there was nothing else to do they played a game by choosing a cloud and making the other two guess what shape it suggested. John Wesley took one of the shape of a cow and June Star guessed a cow and John Wesley said, no, an automobile, and June Star said he didn't play fair, and they began to slap each other over the grandmother.

The grandmother said she would tell them a story if they would keep quiet. When she told a story, she rolled her eyes and waved her head and was very dramatic. She said once when she was a maiden lady she had been courted by a Mr. Edgar Atkins Teagarden from Jasper, Georgia. She said he was a very good-looking man and a gentleman and that he brought her a watermelon every Saturday afternoon with his initials cut in it, E. A. T. Well, one Saturday, she said, Mr. Teagarden brought the watermelon and there was nobody at home and he left it on the front porch and returned in his buggy to Jasper, but she never got the watermelon, she said, because a nigger boy ate it when he saw the initials, E. A. T.! This story tickled John Wesley's funny bone and he giggled and giggled but June Star didn't think it was any good. She said she wouldn't marry a man that just brought her a watermelon on Saturday. The grandmother said she would have done well to marry Mr. Teagarden because he was a gentleman and had bought Coca-Cola stock when it first came out and that he had died only a few years ago, a very wealthy man.

They stopped at The Tower for barbecued sandwiches. The Tower was a part stucco and part wood filling station and dance hall set in a clearing outside of Timothy. A fat man named Red Sammy Butts ran it and there were signs stuck here and there on the building and for miles up and down the highway saying, TRY RED SAMMY'S FAMOUS BARBECUE. NONE LIKE FAMOUS RED SAMMY'S! RED SAM! THE FAT BOY WITH THE HAPPY LAUGH! A VETERAN! RED SAMMY'S YOUR MAN!

Red Sammy was lying on the bare ground outside The Tower with his head under a truck while a gray monkey about a foot high, chained to a small chinaberry tree, chattered nearby. The monkey sprang back into the tree and got on the highest limb as soon as he saw the children jump out of the car and run toward him.

Inside, The Tower was a long dark room with a counter at one end and tables at the other and dancing space in the middle. They sat down at a board table next to the nickelodeon and Red Sam's wife, a tall burnt-brown woman with hair and eyes lighter than her skin, came and took their order. The children's mother put a dime in the machine and played "The Tennessee Waltz," and the grandmother said that tune always made her want to dance. She asked Bailey if he would like to dance but he only glared at her. He didn't have a naturally sunny disposition like she did and trips made him nervous. The grandmother's brown eyes were very bright. She swayed her head from side to side and pretended she was dancing in her chair. June Star said play something she could tap to so the children's mother put in another dime and played a fast number and June Star stepped out onto the dance floor and did her tap routine.

"Ain't she cute?" Red Sam's wife said, leaning over the counter. "Would you like to come be my little girl?"

"No I certainly wouldn't," June Star said. "I wouldn't live in a broken-down place like this for a million bucks!" and she ran back to the table.

"Ain't she cute?" the woman repeated, stretching her mouth politely.

"Aren't you ashamed?" hissed the grandmother.

Red Sam came in and told his wife to quit lounging on the counter and hurry up with these people's order. His khaki trousers reached just to his hip bones and his stomach hung over them like a sack of meal swaying under his shirt. He came over and sat down at a table nearby and let out a combination sigh and yodel. "You can't win," he said. "You can't win," and he wiped his sweating red face off with a gray handkerchief. "These days you don't know who to trust," he said. "Ain't that the truth?"

"People are certainly not nice like they used to be," said the grandmother.

"Two fellers come in here last week," Red Sammy said, "driving a Chrysler. It was a old beat-up car but it was a good one and these boys looked all right to me. Said they worked at the mill and you know I let them fellers charge the gas they bought? Now why did I do that?"

"Because you're a good man!" the grandmother said at once.

"Yes'm, I suppose so," Red Sam said as if he were struck with this answer.

His wife brought the orders, carrying the five plates all at once without a tray, two in each hand and one balanced on her arm. "It isn't a soul in this green world of God's that you can trust," she said. "And I don't count nobody out of that, not nobody," she repeated, looking at Red Sammy.

"Did you read about that criminal, The Misfit, that's escaped?" asked the grandmother.

"I wouldn't be a bit surprised if he didn't attact this place right here," said the woman. "If he hears about it being here, I wouldn't be none surprised to see him. If he hears it's two cent in the cash register, I wouldn't be a tall surprised if he . . ."

"That'll do," Red Sam said. "Go bring these people their Co'-Colas," and the woman went off to get the rest of the order.

"A good man is hard to find," Red Sammy said. "Everything is getting terrible. I remember the day you could go off and leave your screen door unlatched. Not no more."

He and the grandmother discussed better times. The old lady said that in her opinion Europe was entirely to blame for the way things were now. She said the way Europe acted you would think we were made of money and Red Sam said it was no use talking about it, she was exactly right. The children ran outside into the white sunlight and looked at the monkey in the lacy chinaberry tree. He was busy catching fleas on himself and biting each one carefully between his teeth as if it were a delicacy.

They drove off again into the hot afternoon. The grandmother took cat naps and woke up every few minutes with her own snoring. Outside of Toombsboro she woke up and recalled an old plantation that she had visited in this neighborhood once when she was a young lady. She said the house had six white columns across the front and that there was an avenue of oaks leading up to it and two little wooden trellis arbors on either side in front where you sat down with your suitor after a stroll in the garden. She recalled exactly which road to turn off to get to it. She knew that Bailey would not be willing to lose any time looking at an old house, but the more she talked about it, the more she wanted to see it once again and find out if the little twin arbors were still standing. "There was a secret panel in this house," she said craftily, not telling the truth but wishing that she were, "and the story went that all the family silver was hidden in it when Sherman came through but it was never found . . ."

"Hey!" John Wesley said. "Let's go see it! We'll find it! We'll poke all the woodwork and find it! Who lives there? Where do you turn off at? Hey Pop, can't we turn off there?"

"We never have seen a house with a secret panel!" June Star shrieked. "Let's go to the house with the secret panel! Hey Pop, can't we go see the house with the secret panel!"

"It's not far from here, I know," the grandmother said. "It wouldn't take over twenty minutes."

Bailey was looking straight ahead. His jaw was as rigid as a horseshoe. "No," he said.

The children began to yell and scream that they wanted to see the house with the secret panel. John Wesley kicked the back of the front seat and June Star hung over her mother's shoulder and whined desperately into her ear that they never had any fun even on their vacation, that they could never do what THEY wanted to do. The baby began to scream and John Wesley kicked the back of the seat so hard that his father could feel the blows in his kidney.

"All right!" he shouted and drew the car to a stop at the side of the road. "Will you all shut up? Will you all just shut up for one second? If you don't shut up, we won't go anywhere."

"It would be very educational for them," the grandmother murmured.

"All right," Bailey said, "but get this: this is the only time we're going to stop for anything like this. This is the one and only time."

"The dirt road that you have to turn down is about a mile back," the grandmother directed. "I marked it when we passed."

"A dirt road," Bailey groaned.

After they had turned around and were headed toward the dirt road, the grandmother recalled other points about the house, the beautiful glass over the front doorway and the candle-lamp in the hall. John Wesley said that the secret panel was probably in the fireplace.

"You can't go inside this house," Bailey said. "You don't know who lives there."

"While you all talk to the people in front, I'll run around behind and get in a window," John Wesley suggested.

"We'll all stay in the car," his mother said.

They turned onto the dirt road and the car raced roughly along in a swirl of pink dust. The grandmother recalled the times when there were no paved roads and thirty miles was a day's journey. The dirt road was hilly and there were sudden washes in it and sharp curves on dangerous embankments. All at once they would be on a hill, looking down over the blue tops of trees for miles around, then the next minute, they would be in a red depression with the dust-coated trees looking down on them.

"This place had better turn up in a minute," Bailey said, "or I'm going to turn around."

The road looked as if no one had traveled on it in months.

"It's not much farther," the grandmother said and just as she said it, a horrible thought came to her. The thought was so embarrassing that she turned red in the face and her eyes dilated and her feet jumped up, upsetting her valise in the corner. The instant the valise moved, the newspaper top she had over the basket under it rose with a snarl and Pitty Sing, the cat, sprang onto Bailey's shoulder.

The children were thrown to the floor and their mother, clutching the baby, was thrown out the door onto the ground; the old lady was thrown into the front seat. The car turned over once and landed right-side-up in a gulch off the side of the road. Bailey remained in the driver's seat with the cat—gray-striped with a broad white face and an orange nose—clinging to his neck like a caterpillar.

As soon as the children saw they could move their arms and legs, they scrambled out of the car, shouting, "We've had an ACCIDENT!" The grandmother was curled up under the dashboard, hoping she was injured so that Bailey's wrath would not come down on her all at once. The horrible thought she had had before the accident was that the house she had remembered so vividly was not in Georgia but in Tennessee.

Bailey removed the cat from his neck with both hands and flung it out the window against the side of a pine tree. Then he got out of the car and started looking for the children's mother. She was sitting against the side of the red gutted ditch, holding the screaming baby, but she only had a cut down her face and a broken shoulder. "We've had an ACCIDENT!" the children screamed in a frenzy of delight.

"But nobody's killed," June Star said with disappointment as the grandmother limped out of the car, her hat still pinned to her head but the broken front brim standing up at a jaunty angle and the violet spray hanging off the side. They all sat down in the ditch, except the children, to recover from the shock. They were all shaking.

"Maybe a car will come along," said the children's mother hoarsely.

"I believe I have injured an organ," said the grandmother, pressing her side, but no one answered her. Bailey's teeth were clattering. He had on a yellow sport shirt with bright blue parrots designed in it and his face was as yellow as the shirt. The grandmother decided that she would not mention that the house was in Tennessee.

The road was about ten feet above and they could see only the tops of the trees on the other side of it. Behind the ditch they were sitting in there were more woods, tall and dark and deep. In a few minutes they saw a car some distance away on top of a hill, coming slowly as if the occupants were watching them. The grandmother stood up and waved both arms dramatically to attract their attention. The car continued to come on slowly, disappeared around a bend and appeared again, moving even slower, on top of the hill they had gone over. It was a big black battered hearse-like automobile. There were three men in it.

It came to a stop just over them and for some minutes, the driver looked down with a steady expressionless gaze to where they were sitting, and didn't speak. Then he turned his head and muttered something to the other two and they got out. One was a fat boy in black trousers and a red sweat shirt with a silver stallion embossed on the front of it. He moved around on the right side of them and stood staring, his mouth partly open in a kind of loose grin. The other had on khaki pants and a blue striped coat and a gray hat pulled down very low, hiding most of his face. He came around slowly on the left side. Neither spoke.

The driver got out of the car and stood by the side of it, looking down at them. He was an older man than the other two. His hair was just beginning to gray and he wore silver-rimmed spectacles that gave him a scholarly look. He had a long creased face and didn't have on any shirt or undershirt. He had on blue jeans that were too tight for him and was holding a black hat and a gun. The two boys also had guns.

"We've had an ACCIDENT!" the children screamed.

The grandmother had the peculiar feeling that the bespectacled man was someone she knew. His face was as familiar to her as if she had known him all her life but she could not recall who he was. He moved away from the car and began to come down the embankment, placing his feet carefully so that he wouldn't slip. He had on tan and white shoes and no socks, and his ankles were red and thin. "Good afternoon," he said. "I see you all had you a little spill."

"We turned over twice!" said the grandmother.

"Oncet," he corrected. "We seen it happen. Try their car and see will it run, Hiram," he said quietly to the boy with the gray hat.

"What you got that gun for?" John Wesley asked. "Whatcha gonna do with that gun?"

"Lady," the man said to the children's mother, "would you mind calling them children to sit down by you? Children make me nervous. I want all you to sit down right together there where you're at."

"What are you telling US what to do for?" June Star asked.

Behind them the line of woods gaped like a dark open mouth. "Come here," said their mother.

"Look here now," Bailey began suddenly, "we're in a predicament! We're in . . ."

The grandmother shrieked. She scrambled to her feet and stood staring. "You're The Misfit!" she said. "I recognized you at once!"

"Yes'm," the man said, smiling slightly as if he were pleased in spite of himself to be known, "but it would have been better for all of you, lady, if you hadn't of reckernized me."

Bailey turned his head sharply and said something to his mother that shocked even the children. The old lady began to cry and The Misfit reddened.

"Lady," he said, "don't you get upset. Sometimes a man says things he don't mean. I don't reckon he meant to talk to you thataway."

"You wouldn't shoot a lady, would you?" the grandmother said and removed a clean handkerchief from her cuff and began to slap at her eyes with it.

The Misfit pointed the toe of his shoe into the ground and made a little hole and then covered it up again. "I would hate to have to," he said.

"Listen," the grandmother almost screamed, "I know you're a good man. You don't look a bit like you have common blood. I know you must come from nice people!"

"Yes mam," he said, "finest people in the world." When he smiled he showed a row of strong white teeth. "God never made a finer woman than my mother and my daddy's heart was pure gold," he said. The boy with the red sweat shirt had come around behind them and was standing with his gun at his hip. The Misfit squatted down on the ground. "Watch them children, Bobby Lee," he said. "You know they make me nervous." He looked at the six of them huddled together in front of him and he seemed to be embarrassed as if he couldn't think of anything to say. "Ain't a cloud in the sky," he remarked, looking up at it. "Don't see no sun but don't see no cloud neither."

"Yes, it's a beautiful day," said the grandmother. "Listen," she said, "you shouldn't call yourself The Misfit because I know you're a good man at heart. I can just look at you and tell."

"Hush!" Bailey yelled. "Hush! Everybody shut up and let me handle this!" He was squatting in the position of a runner about to sprint forward but he didn't move.

"I pre-chate that, lady," The Misfit said and drew a little circle in the ground with the butt of his gun.

"It'll take a half a hour to fix this here car," Hiram called, looking over the raised hood of it.

"Well, first you and Bobby Lee get him and that little boy to step over yonder with you," The Misfit said, pointing to Bailey and John Wesley. "The boys want to ast you something," he said to Bailey. "Would you mind stepping back in them woods there with them?"

"Listen," Bailey began, "we're in a terrible predicament! Nobody realizes what this is," his voice cracked. His eyes were as blue and intense as the parrots in his shirt and he remained perfectly still.

The grandmother reached up to adjust her hat brim as if she were going to the woods with him but it came off in her hand. She stood staring at it and after a second she let it fall on the ground. Hiram pulled Bailey up by the arm as if he were assisting an old man. John Wesley caught hold of his father's hand and Bobby Lee followed. They went off toward the woods and just as they reached the dark edge, Bailey turned and supporting himself against a gray naked pine trunk, he shouted, "I'll be back in a minute, Mamma, wait on me!"

"Come back this instant!" his mother shrilled but they all disappeared into the woods.

"Bailey Boy!" the grandmother called in a tragic voice but she found she was looking at The Misfit squatting on the ground in front of her. "I just know you're a good man," she said desperately. "You're not a bit common!"

"Nome, I ain't a good man," The Misfit said after a second as if he had considered her statement carefully, "but I ain't the worst in the world neither. My daddy said I was a different breed of dog from my brothers and sisters. 'You know,' Daddy said, 'it's some that can live their whole life out without asking about it and it's others has to know why it is, and this boy is one of the latters. He's going to be into everything!'" He put on his black hat and looked up suddenly and then away deep into the woods as if he were embarrassed again. "I'm sorry I don't have on a shirt before you ladies," he said, hunching his shoulders slightly. "We buried our clothes that we had on when we escaped and we're just making do until we can get better. We borrowed these from some folks we met," he explained.

"That's perfectly all right," the grandmother said. "Maybe Bailey has an extra shirt in his suitcase."

"I'll look and see terrectly," The Misfit said.

"Where are they taking him?" the children's mother screamed.

"Daddy was a card himself," The Misfit said. "You couldn't put anything over on him. He never got in trouble with the Authorities though. Just had the knack of handling them."

"You could be honest too if you'd only try," said the grandmother. "Think how wonderful it would be to settle down and live a comfortable life and not have to think about somebody chasing you all the time."

The Misfit kept scratching in the ground with the butt of his gun as if he were thinking about it. "Yes'm, somebody is always after you," he murmured.

The grandmother noticed how thin his shoulder blades were just behind his hat because she was standing up looking down on him. "Do you ever pray?" she asked.

He shook his head. All she saw was the black hat wiggle between his shoulder blades. "Nome," he said.

There was a pistol shot from the woods, followed closely by another. Then silence. The old lady's head jerked around. She could hear the wind move through the tree tops like a long satisfied insuck of breath. "Bailey Boy!" she called.

"I was a gospel singer for a while," The Misfit said. "I been most everything. Been in the arm service, both land and sea, at home and abroad, been twice married, been an undertaker, been with the railroads, plowed Mother Earth, been in a tornado, seen a man burnt alive oncet," and looked up at the children's mother and the little girl who were sitting close together, their faces white and their eyes glassy; "I even seen a woman flogged," he said.

"Pray, pray," the grandmother began, "pray, pray . . ."

"I never was a bad boy that I remember of," The Misfit said in an almost dreamy voice, "but somewheres along the line I done something wrong and got sent to the penitentiary. I was buried alive," and he looked up and held her attention to him by a steady stare.

"That's when you should have started to pray," she said. "What did you do to get sent to the penitentiary that first time?"

"Turn to the right, it was a wall," The Misfit said, looking up again at the cloudless sky. "Turn to the left, it was a wall. Look up it was a ceiling, look down it was a floor. I forget what I done, lady. I set there and set there, trying to remember what it was I done and I ain't recalled it to this day. Oncet in a while, I would think it was coming to me, but it never come."

"Maybe they put you in by mistake," the old lady said vaguely.

"Nome," he said. "It wasn't no mistake. They had the papers on me."

"You must have stolen something," she said.

The Misfit sneered slightly. "Nobody had nothing I wanted," he said. "It was a headdoctor at the penitentiary said what I had done was kill my daddy but I know that for a lie. My daddy died in nineteen ought nineteen of the epidemic flu and I never had a thing to do with it. He was buried in the Mount Hopewell Baptist churchyard and you can go there and see for yourself."

"If you would pray," the old lady said, "Jesus would help you."

"That's right," The Misfit said.

"Well then, why don't you pray?" she asked trembling with delight suddenly.

"I don't want no hep," he said. "I'm doing all right by myself."

Bobby Lee and Hiram came ambling back from the woods. Bobby Lee was dragging a yellow shirt with bright blue parrots in it.

"Throw me that shirt, Bobby Lee," The Misfit said. The shirt came flying at him and landed on his shoulder and he put it on. The grandmother couldn't name what the shirt reminded her of. "No, lady," The Misfit said while he was buttoning it up, "I found out the crime don't matter. You can do one thing or you can do another, kill a man or take a tire off his car, because sooner or later you're going to forget what it was you done and just be punished for it."

The children's mother had begun to make heaving noises as if she couldn't get her breath. "Lady," he asked, "would you and that little girl like to step off yonder with Bobby Lee and Hiram and join your husband?"

"Yes, thank you," the mother said faintly. Her left arm dangled helplessly and she was holding the baby, who had gone to sleep, in the other. "Hep that lady up, Hiram," The Misfit said as she struggled to climb out of the ditch, "and Bobby Lee, you hold onto that little girl's hand."

"I don't want to hold hands with him," June Star said. "He reminds me of a pig."

The fat boy blushed and laughed and caught her by the arm and pulled her off into the woods after Hiram and her mother.

Alone with The Misfit, the grandmother found that she had lost her voice. There was not a cloud in the sky nor any sun. There was nothing around her but woods. She wanted to tell him that he must pray. She opened and closed her mouth several times before anything came out. Finally she found herself saying, "Jesus, Jesus," meaning, Jesus will help you, but the way she was saying it, it sounded as if she might be cursing.

"Yes'm," The Misfit said as if he agreed. "Jesus thrown everything off balance. It was the same case with Him as with me except He hadn't committed any crime and they could prove I had committed one because they had the papers on me. Of course," he said, "they never shown me my papers. That's why I sign myself now. I said long ago, you get you a signature and sign everything you do and keep a copy of it. Then you'll know what you done and you can hold up the crime to the punishment and see do they match and in the end you'll have something to prove you ain't been treated right. I call myself The Misfit," he said, "because I can't make what all I done wrong fit what all I gone through in punishment."

There was a piercing scream from the woods, followed closely by a pistol report. "Does it seem right to you, lady, that one is punished a heap and another ain't punished at all?"

"Jesus!" the old lady cried. "You've got good blood! I know you wouldn't shoot a lady! I know you come from nice people! Pray! Jesus, you ought not to shoot a lady. I'll give you all the money I've got!"

"Lady," The Misfit said, looking beyond her far into the woods, "there never was a body that give the undertaker a tip."

There were two more pistol reports and the grandmother raised her head like a parched old turkey hen crying for water and called, "Bailey Boy, Bailey Boy!" as if her heart would break.

"Jesus was the only One that ever raised the dead," The Misfit continued, "and He shouldn't have done it. He thrown everything off balance. If He did what He said, then it's nothing for you to do but throw away everything and follow Him, and if He didn't, then it's nothing for you to do but enjoy the few minutes you got left the best way you can—by killing somebody or burning down his house or doing some other meanness to him. No pleasure but meanness," he said and his voice had become almost a snarl.

"Maybe He didn't raise the dead," the old lady mumbled, not knowing what she was saying and feeling so dizzy that she sank down in the ditch with her legs twisted under her.

"I wasn't there so I can't say He didn't," The Misfit said. "I wisht I had of been there," he said, hitting the ground with his fist. "It ain't right I wasn't there because if I had of been there I would of known. Listen lady," he said in a high voice, "if I had of been there I would of known and I wouldn't be like I am now." His voice seemed about to crack and the grandmother's head cleared for an instant. She saw the man's face twisted close to her own as if he were going to cry and she murmured, "Why you're one of my babies. You're one of my own children!" She reached out and touched him on the shoulder. The Misfit sprang back as if a snake had bitten him and shot her three times through the chest. Then he put his gun down on the ground and took off his glasses and began to clean them.

Hiram and Bobby Lee returned from the woods and stood over the ditch, looking down at the grandmother who half sat and half lay in a puddle of blood with her legs crossed under her like a child's and her face smiling up at the cloudless sky.

Without his glasses, The Misfit's eyes were red-rimmed and pale and defenseless looking. "Take her off and throw her where you thrown the others," he said, picking up the cat that was rubbing itself against his leg.

"She was a talker, wasn't she?" Bobby Lee said, sliding down the ditch with a yodel.

"She would have been a good woman," The Misfit said, "if it had been somebody there to shoot her every minute of her life."

"Some fun!" Bobby Lee said.

"Shut up, Bobby Lee," The Misfit said. "It's no real pleasure in life."

(1955)

QUESTIONS FOR CRITICAL THINKING AND WRITING

Experience

1. Did you enjoy the opening section of the story? When did your perception of the kind of story you were reading change—if it did?
2. How did you respond to the Misfit's behavior? To his speech?

Interpretation

3. How does O'Connor characterize the grandmother? What do we learn about her from her conversation with the Misfit? What do we learn about him? What is his favorite saying, and what sense do you make of it?
4. How do you explain the story's title?

Evaluation

5. What religious qualities or elements emerge in this story? How, as the Misfit says, has Jesus "thrown everything off balance"?
6. In what sense could the grandmother have been a good woman if, as the Misfit says, there was "somebody there to shoot her every minute of her life"?

Connections

7. Compare this story's use of violence with that in Frank O'Connor's "Guests of the Nation" or in Poe's "The Black Cat."

Critical Thinking

8. Why do you think this has been one of the most frequently anthologized and most often written about of O'Connor's stories? Provide at least two explanations.

Everything That Rises Must Converge

Her doctor had told Julian's mother that she must lose twenty pounds on account of her blood pressure, so on Wednesday nights Julian had to take her downtown on the bus for a reducing class at the Y. The reducing class was designed for working girls over fifty, who weighed from 165 to 200 pounds. His mother was one of the slimmer ones, but she said ladies did not tell their age or weight. She would not ride the buses by herself at night since they had been integrated, and because the reducing class was one of her few pleasures, necessary for her health, and *free*, she said Julian could at least put himself out to take her, considering all she did for him. Julian did not like to consider all she did for him, but every Wednesday night he braced himself and took her.

She was almost ready to go, standing before the hall mirror, putting on her hat, while he, his hands behind him, appeared pinned to the door frame, waiting like Saint Sebastian for the arrows to begin piercing him. The hat was new and had cost her seven dollars and a half. She kept saying, "Maybe I shouldn't have paid that for it. No, I shouldn't have. I'll take it off and return it tomorrow. I shouldn't have bought it."

Julian raised his eyes to heaven. "Yes, you should have bought it," he said. "Put it on and let's go." It was a hideous hat. A purple velvet flap came down on one side of it and stood up on the other; the rest of it was green and looked like a cushion with the stuffing out. He decided it was less comical than jaunty and pathetic. Everything that gave her pleasure was small and depressed him.

She lifted the hat one more time and set it down slowly on top of her head. Two wings of gray hair protruded on either side of her florid face, but her eyes, sky-blue, were as innocent and untouched by experience as they must have been when she was ten. Were it not that she was a widow who had struggled fiercely to feed and clothe and put him through school and who was supporting him still, "until he got on his feet," she might have been a little girl that he had to take to town.

"It's all right, it's all right," he said. "Let's go." He opened the door himself and started down the walk to get her going. The sky was a dying violet and the houses stood out darkly against it, bulbous liver-colored monstrosities of a uniform ugliness though no two were alike. Since this had been a fashionable neighborhood forty years ago, his mother persisted in thinking they did well to have an apartment in it. Each house had a narrow collar of dirt around it in which sat, usually, a grubby child. Julian walked with his hands in his pockets, his head down and thrust forward and his eyes glazed with the determination to make himself completely numb during the time he would be sacrificed to her pleasure.

The door closed and he turned to find the dumpy figure, surmounted by the atrocious hat, coming toward him. "Well," she said, "you only live once and paying a little more for it, I at least won't meet myself coming and going."

"Some day I'll start making money," Julian said gloomily—he knew he never would—"and you can have one of those jokes whenever you take the fit." But first they would move. He visualized a place where the nearest neighbors would be three miles away on either side.

"I think you're doing fine," she said, drawing on her gloves. "You've only been out of school a year. Rome wasn't built in a day."

She was one of the few members of the Y reducing class who arrived in hat and gloves and who had a son who had been to college. "It takes time," she said, "and the world is in such a mess. This hat looked better on me than any of the others, though when she brought it out I said, 'Take that thing back. I wouldn't have it on my head,' and she said, 'Now wait till you see it on,' and when she put it on me, I said, 'we-ull,' and she said, 'If you ask me, that hat does something for you and you do something for that hat, and besides,' she said, 'with that hat, you won't meet yourself coming and going.'"

Julian thought he could have stood his lot better if she had been selfish, if she had been an old hag who drank and screamed at him. He walked along, saturated in depression, as if in the midst of his martyrdom he had lost his faith. Catching sight of his long, hopeless, irritated face, she stopped suddenly with a grief-stricken look, and pulled back on his arm. "Wait on me," she said. "I'm going back to the house and take this thing off and tomorrow I'm going to return it. I was out of my head. I can pay the gas bill with the seven-fifty."

He caught her arm in a vicious grip. "You are not going to take it back," he said. "I like it."

"Well," she said, "I don't think I ought . . ."

"Shut up and enjoy it," he muttered, more depressed than ever.

"With the world in the mess it's in," she said, "it's a wonder we can enjoy anything. I tell you, the bottom rail is on the top."

Julian sighed.

"Of course," she said, "if you know who you are, you can go anywhere." She said this every time he took her to the reducing class. "Most of them in it are not our kind of people," she said, "but I can be gracious to anybody. I know who I am."

"They don't give a damn for your graciousness," Julian said savagely. "Knowing who you are is good for one generation only. You haven't the foggiest idea where you stand now or who you are."

She stopped and allowed her eyes to flash at him. "I most certainly do know who I am," she said, "and if you don't know who you are, I'm ashamed of you."

"Oh hell," Julian said.

"Your great-grandfather was a former governor of this state," she said. "Your grandfather was a prosperous landowner. Your grandmother was a Godhigh."

"Will you look around you," he said tensely, "and see where you are now?" and he swept his arm jerkily out to indicate the neighborhood, which the growing darkness at least made less dingy.

"You remain what you are," she said. "Your great-grandfather had a plantation and two hundred slaves."

"There are no more slaves," he said irritably.

"They were better off when they were," she said. He groaned to see that she was off on that topic. She rolled onto it every few days like a train on an open track. He knew every stop, every junction, every swamp along the way, and knew the exact point at which her conclusion would roll majestically into the station: "It's ridiculous. It's simply not realistic. They should rise, yes, but on their own side of the fence."

"Let's skip it," Julian said.

"The ones I feel sorry for," she said, "are the ones that are half white. They're tragic."

"Will you skip it?"

"Suppose we were half white. We would certainly have mixed feelings."

"I have mixed feelings now," he groaned.

"Well let's talk about something pleasant," she said. "I remember going to Grandpa's when I was a little girl. Then the house had double stairways that went up to what was really the second floor—all the cooking was done on the first. I used to like to stay down in the kitchen on account of the way the walls smelled. I would sit with my nose pressed against the plaster and take deep breaths. Actually the place belonged to the Godhighs but your grandfather Chestny paid the mortgage and saved it for them. They were in reduced circumstances," she said, "but reduced or not, they never forgot who they were."

"Doubtless that decayed mansion reminded them," Julian muttered. He never spoke of it without contempt or thought of it without longing. He had seen it once when he was a child before it had been sold. The double stairways had rotted and been torn down. Negroes were living in it. But it remained in his mind as his mother had known it. It appeared in his dreams regularly. He would stand on the wide porch, listening to the rustle of oak leaves, then wander through the high-ceilinged hall into the parlor that opened onto it and gaze at the worn rugs and faded draperies. It occurred to him that it was he, not she, who could have appreciated it. He preferred its threadbare elegance to anything he could name and it was because of it that all the neighborhoods they had lived in had been a torment to him—whereas she had hardly known the difference. She called her insensitivity "being adjustable."

"And I remember the old darky who was my nurse, Caroline. There was no better person in the world. I've always had a great respect for my colored friends," she said. "I'd do anything in the world for them and they'd . . ."

"Will you for God's sake get off that subject?" Julian said. When he got on a bus by himself, he made it a point to sit down beside a Negro, in reparation as it were for his mother's sins.

"You're mighty touchy tonight," she said. "Do you feel all right?"

"Yes I feel all right," he said. "Now lay off."

She pursed her lips. "Well, you certainly are in a vile humor," she observed. "I just won't speak to you at all."

They had reached the bus stop. There was no bus in sight and Julian, his hands still jammed in his pockets and his head thrust forward, scowled down the empty street. The frustration of having to wait on the bus as well as ride on it began to creep up his neck like a hot hand. The presence of his mother was borne in upon him as she gave a pained sigh. He looked at her bleakly. She was holding herself very erect under the preposterous hat, wearing it like a banner of her imaginary dignity. There was in him an evil urge to break her spirit. He suddenly unloosened his tie and pulled it off and put it in his pocket.

She stiffened. "Why must you look like *that* when you take me to town?" she said. "Why must you deliberately embarrass me?"

"If you'll never learn where you are," he said, "you can at least learn where I am."

"You look like a—thug," she said.

"Then I must be one," he murmured.

"I'll just go home," she said. "I will not bother you. If you can't do a little thing like that for me . . ."

Rolling his eyes upward, he put his tie back on. "Restored to my class," he muttered. He thrust his face toward her and hissed, "True culture is in the mind, the *mind*," he said, and tapped his head, "the mind."

"It's in the heart," she said, "and in how you do things and how you do things is because of who you *are*."

"Nobody in the damn bus cares who you *are*."

"I care who I am," she said icily.

The lighted bus appeared on top of the next hill and as it approached, they moved out into the street to meet it. He put his hand under her elbow and hoisted her up on the creaking step. She entered with a little smile, as if she were going into a drawing room where everyone had been waiting for her. While he put in the tokens, she sat down on one of the broad front seats for three which faced the aisle. A thin woman with protruding teeth and long yellow hair was sitting on the end of it. His mother moved up beside her and left room for Julian beside herself. He sat down and looked at the floor across the aisle where a pair of thin feet in red and white canvas sandals were planted.

His mother immediately began a general conversation meant to attract anyone who felt like talking. "Can it get any hotter?" she said and removed from her purse a folding fan, black with a Japanese scene on it, which she began to flutter before her.

"I reckon it might could," the woman with the protruding teeth said, "but I know for a fact my apartment couldn't get no hotter."

"It must get the afternoon sun," his mother said. She sat forward and looked up and down the bus. It was half filled. Everybody was white. "I see we have the bus to ourselves," she said. Julian cringed.

"For a change," said the woman across the aisle, the owner of the red and white canvas sandals. "I come on one the other day and they were thick as fleas—up front and all through."

"The world is in a mess everywhere," his mother said. "I don't know how we've let it get in this fix."

"What gets my goat is all those boys from good families stealing automobile tires," the woman with the protruding teeth said. "I told my boy, I said you may not be rich but you been raised right and if I ever catch you in any such mess, they can send you on to the reformatory. Be exactly where you belong."

"Training tells," his mother said. "Is your boy in high school?"

"Ninth grade," the woman said.

"My son just finished college last year. He wants to write but he's selling typewriters until he gets started," his mother said.

The woman leaned forward and peered at Julian. He threw her such a malevolent look that she subsided against the seat. On the floor across the aisle there was an abandoned newspaper. He got up and got it and opened it out in front of him. His mother discreetly continued the conversation in a lower tone but the woman across the aisle said in a loud voice, "Well that's nice. Selling typewriters is close to writing. He can go right from one to the other."

"I tell him," his mother said, "that Rome wasn't built in a day."

Behind the newspaper Julian was withdrawing into the inner compartment of his mind where he spent most of his time. This was a kind of mental bubble in which he established himself when he could not bear to be a part of what was going on around him. From it he could see out and judge but in it he was safe from any kind of penetration from without. It was the only place where he felt free of the general idiocy of his fellows. His mother had never entered it but from it he could see her with absolute clarity.

The old lady was clever enough and he thought that if she had started from any of the right premises, more might have been expected of her. She lived according to the laws of her own fantasy world, outside of which he had never seen her set foot. The law of it was to sacrifice herself for him after she had first created the necessity to do so by making a mess of things. If he had permitted her sacrifices, it was only because her lack of foresight had made them necessary. All of her life had been a struggle to act like a Chestny without the Chestny goods, and to give him everything she thought a Chestny ought to have; but since, said she, it was fun to struggle, why complain? And when you had won, as she had won, what fun to look back on the hard times! He could not forgive her that she had enjoyed the struggle and that she thought *she* had won.

What she meant when she said she had won was that she had brought him up successfully and had sent him to college and that he had turned out so well—good looking (her teeth had gone unfilled so that his could be straightened), intelligent (he realized he was too intelligent to be a success), and with a future ahead of him (there was of course no future ahead of him). She excused his gloominess on the grounds that he was still growing up and his radical ideas on his lack of practical experience. She said he didn't yet know a thing about "life," that he hadn't even entered the real world—when already he was as disenchanted with it as a man of fifty.

The further irony of all this was that in spite of her, he had turned out so well. In spite of going to only a third-rate college, he had, on his own initiative, come out with a first-rate education; in spite of growing up dominated by a small mind, he had ended up with a large one; in spite of all her foolish views, he was free of prejudice and unafraid to face facts. Most miraculous of all, instead of being blinded by love for her as she was for him, he had cut himself emotionally free of her and could see her with complete objectivity. He was not dominated by his mother.

The bus stopped with a sudden jerk and shook him from his meditation. A woman from the back lurched forward with little steps and barely escaped falling in his newspaper as she righted herself. She got off and a large Negro got on. Julian kept his paper lowered to watch. It gave him a certain satisfaction to see injustice in daily operation. It confirmed his view that with a few exceptions there was no one worth knowing within a radius of three hundred miles. The Negro was well dressed and carried a briefcase. He looked around and then sat down on the other end of the seat where the woman with the red and white canvas sandals was sitting. He immediately unfolded a newspaper and obscured himself behind it. Julian's mother's elbow at once prodded insistently into his ribs. "Now you see why I won't ride on these buses by myself," she whispered.

The woman with the red and white canvas sandals had risen at the same time the Negro sat down and had gone further back in the bus and taken the seat of the woman who had got off. His mother leaned forward and cast her an approving look.

Julian rose, crossed the aisle, and sat down in the place of the woman with the canvas sandals. From this position, he looked serenely across at his mother. Her face had turned an angry red. He stared at her, making his eyes the eyes of a stranger. He felt his tension suddenly lift as if he had openly declared war on her.

He would have liked to get in conversation with the Negro and to talk with him about art or politics or any subject that would be above the comprehension of those around them, but the man remained entrenched behind his paper. He was either ignoring the change of seating or had never noticed it. There was no way for Julian to convey his sympathy.

His mother kept her eyes fixed reproachfully on his face. The woman with the protruding teeth was looking at him avidly as if he were a type of monster new to her.

"Do you have a light?" he asked the Negro.

Without looking away from his paper, the man reached in his pocket and handed him a packet of matches.

"Thanks," Julian said. For a moment he held the matches foolishly. A NO SMOKING sign looked down upon him from over the door. This alone would not have deterred him; he had no cigarettes. He had quit smoking some months before because he could not afford it. "Sorry," he muttered and handed back the matches. The Negro lowered the paper and gave him an annoyed look. He took the matches and raised the paper again.

His mother continued to gaze at him but she did not take advantage of his momentary discomfort. Her eyes retained their battered look. Her face seemed to be unnaturally red, as if her blood pressure had risen. Julian allowed no glimmer of sympathy to show on his face. Having got the advantage, he wanted desperately to keep it and carry it through. He would have liked to teach her a lesson that would last her a while, but there seemed no way to continue the point. The Negro refused to come out from behind his paper.

Julian folded his arms and looked stolidly before him, facing her but as if he did not see her, as if he had ceased to recognize her existence. He visualized a scene in which, the bus having reached their stop, he would remain in his seat and when she said, "Aren't you going to get off?" he would look at her as at a stranger who had rashly addressed him. The corner they got off on was usually deserted, but it was well lighted and it would not hurt her to walk by herself the four blocks to the Y. He decided to wait until the time came and then decide whether or not he would let her get off by herself. He would have to be at the Y at ten to bring her back, but he could leave her wondering if he was going to show up. There was no reason for her to think she could always depend on him.

He retired again into the high-ceilinged room sparsely settled with large pieces of antique furniture. His soul expanded momentarily but then he became aware of his mother across from him and the vision shriveled. He studied her coldly. Her feet in little pumps dangled like a child's and did not quite reach the floor. She was training on him an exaggerated look of reproach. He felt completely detached from her. At that moment he could with pleasure have slapped her as he would have slapped a particularly obnoxious child in his charge.

He began to imagine various unlikely ways by which he could teach her a lesson. He might make friends with some distinguished Negro professor or lawyer and bring him home to spend the evening. He would be entirely justified but her blood pressure would rise to 300. He could not push her to the extent of making her have a stroke, and moreover, he had never been successful at making any Negro friends. He had tried to strike up an acquaintance on the bus with some of the better types, with ones that looked like professors or ministers or lawyers. One morning he had sat down next to a distinguished-looking dark brown man who had answered his questions with a sonorous solemnity but who had turned out to be an undertaker. Another day he had sat down beside a cigar-smoking Negro with a diamond ring on his finger, but after a few stilted pleasantries, the Negro had rung the buzzer and risen, slipping two lottery tickets into Julian's hand as he climbed over him to leave.

He imagined his mother lying desperately ill and his being able to secure only a Negro doctor for her. He toyed with that idea for a few minutes and then dropped it for a momentary vision of himself participating as a sympathizer in a sit-in demonstration. This was possible but he did not linger with it. Instead, he approached the ultimate horror. He brought home a beautiful suspiciously Negroid woman. Prepare yourself, he said. There is nothing you can do about it. This is the woman I've chosen. She's intelligent, dignified, even good, and she's suffered and she hasn't thought it *fun*. Now persecute us, go ahead and persecute us. Drive her out of here, but remember, you're driving me too. His eyes were narrowed and through the indignation he had generated, he saw his mother across the aisle, purple-faced, shrunken to the dwarf-like proportions of her moral nature, sitting like a mummy beneath the ridiculous banner of her hat.

He was tilted out of his fantasy again as the bus stopped. The door opened with a sucking hiss and out of the dark a large, gaily dressed, sullen-looking colored woman got on with a little boy. The child, who might have been four, had on a short plaid suit and a Tyrolean hat with a blue feather in it. Julian hoped that he would sit down beside him and that the woman would push in beside his mother. He could think of no better arrangement.

As she waited for her tokens, the woman was surveying the seating possibilities—he hoped with the idea of sitting where she was least wanted. There was something familiar-looking about her but Julian could not place what it was. She was a giant of a woman. Her face was set not only to meet opposition but to seek it out. The downward tilt of her large lower lip was like a warning sign: DON'T TAMPER WITH ME. Her bulging figure was encased in a green crepe dress and her feet overflowed in red shoes. She had on a hideous hat. A purple velvet flap came down on one side of it and stood up on the other; the rest of it was green and looked like a cushion with the stuffing out. She carried a mammoth red pocketbook that bulged throughout as if it were stuffed with rocks.

To Julian's disappointment, the little boy climbed up on the empty seat beside his mother. His mother lumped all children, black and white, into the common category, "cute," and she thought little Negroes were on the whole cuter than little white children. She smiled at the little boy as he climbed on the seat.

Meanwhile the woman was bearing down upon the empty seat beside Julian. To his annoyance, she squeezed herself into it. He saw his mother's face change as the woman settled herself next to him and he realized with satisfaction that this was more objectionable to her than it was to him. Her face seemed almost gray and there was a look of dull recognition in her eyes, as if suddenly she had sickened at some awful confrontation. Julian saw that it was because she and the woman had, in a sense, swapped sons. Though his mother would not realize the symbolic significance of this, she would feel it. His amusement showed plainly on his face.

The woman next to him muttered something unintelligible to herself. He was conscious of a kind of bristling next to him, muted growling like that of an angry cat. He could not see anything but the red pocketbook upright on the bulging green thighs. He visualized the woman as she had stood waiting for her tokens—the ponderous figure, rising from the red shoes upward over the solid hips, the mammoth bosom, the haughty face, to the green and purple hat.

His eyes widened.

The vision of the two hats, identical, broke upon him with the radiance of a brilliant sunrise. His face was suddenly lit with joy. He could not believe that Fate had thrust upon his mother such a lesson. He gave a loud chuckle so that she would look at him and see that he saw. She turned her eyes on him slowly. The blue in them seemed to have turned a bruised purple. For a moment he had an uncomfortable sense of her innocence, but it lasted only a second before principle rescued him. Justice entitled him to laugh. His grin hardened until it said to her as plainly as if he were saying aloud: Your punishment exactly fits your pettiness. This should teach you a permanent lesson.

Her eyes shifted to the woman. She seemed unable to bear looking at him and to find the woman preferable. He became conscious again of the bristling presence at his side. The woman was rumbling like a volcano about to become active. His mother's mouth began to twitch slightly at one corner. With a sinking heart, he saw incipient signs of recovery on her face and realized that this was going to strike her suddenly as funny and was going to be no lesson at all. She kept her eyes on the woman and an amused smile came over her face as if the woman were a monkey that had stolen her hat. The little Negro was looking up at her with large fascinated eyes. He had been trying to attract her attention for some time.

"Carver!" the woman said suddenly. "Come heah!"

When he saw that the spotlight was on him at last, Carver drew his feet up and turned himself toward Julian's mother and giggled.

"Carver!" the woman said. "You heah me? Come heah!"

Carver slid down from the seat but remained squatting with his back against the base of it, his head turned slyly around toward Julian's mother, who was smiling at him. The woman reached a hand across the aisle and snatched him to her. He righted himself and hung backwards on her knees, grinning at Julian's mother. "Isn't he cute?" Julian's mother said to the woman with the protruding teeth.

"I reckon he is," the woman said without conviction.

The Negress yanked him upright but he eased out of her grip and shot across the aisle and scrambled, giggling wildly, onto the seat beside his love.

"I think he likes me," Julian's mother said, and smiled at the woman. It was the smile she used when she was being particularly gracious to an inferior. Julian saw everything lost. The lesson had rolled off her like rain on a roof.

The woman stood up and yanked the little boy off the seat as if she were snatching him from contagion. Julian could feel the rage in her at having no weapon like his mother's smile. She gave the child a sharp slap across his leg. He howled once and then thrust his head into her stomach and kicked his feet against her shins. "Behave," she said vehemently.

The bus stopped and the Negro who had been reading the newspaper got off. The woman moved over and set the little boy down with a thump between herself and Julian. She held him firmly by the knee. In a moment he put his hands in front of his face and peeped at Julian's mother through his fingers.

"I see yoooooooo!" she said and put her hand in front of her face and peeped at him.

The woman slapped his hand down. "Quit yo' foolishness," she said, "before I knock the living Jesus out of you!"

Julian was thankful that the next stop was theirs. He reached up and pulled the cord. The woman reached up and pulled it at the same time. Oh my God, he thought. He had the terrible intuition that when they got off the bus together, his mother would open her purse and give the little boy a nickel. The gesture would be as natural to her as breathing. The bus stopped and the woman got up and lunged to the front, dragging the child, who wished to stay on, after her. Julian and his mother got up and followed. As they neared the door, Julian tried to relieve her of her pocketbook.

"No," she murmured, "I want to give the little boy a nickel."

"No!" Julian hissed. "No!"

She smiled down at the child and opened her bag. The bus door opened and the woman picked him up by the arm and descended with him, hanging at her hip. Once in the street she set him down and shook him.

Julian's mother had to close her purse while she got down the bus step but as soon as her feet were on the ground, she opened it again and began to rummage inside. "I can't find but a penny," she whispered, "but it looks like a new one."

"Don't do it!" Julian said fiercely between his teeth. There was a streetlight on the corner and she hurried to get under it so that she could better see into her pocketbook. The woman was heading off rapidly down the street with the child still hanging backward on her hand.

"Oh little boy!" Julian's mother called and took a few quick steps and caught up with them just beyond the lamppost. "Here's a bright new penny for you," and she held out the coin, which shone bronze in the dim light.

The huge woman turned and for a moment stood, her shoulders lifted and her face frozen with frustrated rage, and stared at Julian's mother. Then all at once she seemed to explode like a piece of machinery that had been given one ounce of pressure too much. Julian saw the black fist swing out with the red pocketbook. He shut his eyes and cringed as he heard the woman shout, "He don't take nobody's pennies!" When he opened his eyes, the woman was disappearing down the street with the little boy staring wide-eyed over her shoulder. Julian's mother was sitting on the sidewalk.

"I told you not to do that," Julian said angrily. "I told you not to do that!"

He stood over her for a minute, gritting his teeth. Her legs were stretched out in front of her and her hat was on her lap. He squatted down and looked her in the face. It was totally expressionless. "You got exactly what you deserved," he said. "Now get up."

He picked up her pocketbook and put what had fallen out back in it. He picked the hat up off her lap. The penny caught his eye on the sidewalk and he picked that up and let it drop before her eyes into the purse. Then he stood up and leaned over and held his hands out to pull her up. She remained immobile. He sighed. Rising above them on either side were black apartment buildings, marked with irregular rectangles of light. At the end of the block a man came out of a door and walked off in the opposite direction. "All right," he said, "suppose somebody happens by and wants to know why you're sitting on the sidewalk?"

She took the hand and, breathing hard, pulled heavily up on it and then stood for a moment, swaying slightly as if the spots of light in the darkness were circling around her. Her eyes, shadowed and confused, finally settled on his face. He did not try to conceal his irritation. "I hope this teaches you a lesson," he said. She leaned forward and her eyes raked his face. She seemed trying to determine his identity. Then, as if she found nothing familiar about him, she started off with a headlong movement in the wrong direction.

"Aren't you going on to the Y?" he asked.

"Home," she muttered.

"Well, are we walking?"

For answer she kept going. Julian followed along, his hands behind him. He saw no reason to let the lesson she had had go without backing it up with an explanation of its meaning. She might as well be made to understand what had happened to her. "Don't think that was just an uppity Negro woman," he said. "That was the whole colored race which will no longer take your condescending pennies. That was your black double. She can wear the same hat as you, and to be sure," he added gratuitously (because he thought it was funny), "it looked better on her than it did on you. What all this means," he said, "is that the old world is gone. The old manners are obsolete and your graciousness is not worth a damn." He thought bitterly of the house that had been lost for him. "You aren't who you think you are," he said.

She continued to plow ahead, paying no attention to him. Her hair had come undone on one side. She dropped her pocketbook and took no notice. He stooped and picked it up and handed it to her but she did not take it.

"You needn't act as if the world had come to an end," he said, "because it hasn't. From now on you've got to live in a new world and face a few realities for a change. Buck up," he said, "it won't kill you."

She was breathing fast.

"Let's wait on the bus," he said.

"Home," she said thickly.

"I hate to see you behave like this," he said. "Just like a child. I should be able to expect more of you." He decided to stop where he was and make her stop and wait for a bus. "I'm not going any farther," he said, stopping. "We're going on the bus."

She continued to go on as if she had not heard him. He took a few steps and caught her arm and stopped her. He looked into her face and caught his breath. He was looking into a face he had never seen before. "Tell Grandpa to come get me," she said.

He stared, stricken.

"Tell Caroline to come get me," she said.

Stunned, he let her go and she lurched forward again, walking as if one leg were shorter than the other. A tide of darkness seemed to be sweeping her from him. "Mother!" he cried. "Darling, sweetheart, wait!" Crumpling, she fell to the pavement. He dashed forward and fell at her side, crying, "Mamma, Mamma!" He turned her over. Her face was fiercely distorted. One eye, large and staring, moved slightly to the left as if it had become unmoored. The other remained fixed on him, raked his face again, found nothing and closed.

"Wait here, wait here!" he cried and jumped up and began to run for help toward a cluster of lights he saw in the distance ahead of him. "Help, help!" he shouted, but his voice was thin, scarcely a thread of sound. The lights drifted farther away the faster he ran and his feet moved numbly as if they carried him nowhere. The tide of darkness seemed to sweep him back to her, postponing from moment to moment his entry into the world of guilt and sorrow.

(1950)

QUESTIONS FOR CRITICAL THINKING AND WRITING

Experience

1. What were your initial impressions of Julian and his mother? Did these impressions remain consistent or did they change?
2. To what extent does your experience with racial prejudice parallel that depicted in the story? To what extent does it differ?

Interpretation

3. What is the significance of the name Godhigh? How does Julian's attitude toward his ancestors and toward the Godhigh family home reflect the central conflict of the story?
4. What is the significance of Julian's mother's response to the black woman's hat? What is the significance of Julian's response to his mother's behavior?
5. What is the meaning of the story's concluding action and dialogue?

Evaluation

6. What principles and beliefs guide Julian? What principles and beliefs does his mother live by?
7. Whose values, if anyone's, does the story seem to endorse? What values are satirized?

Connections

8. Compare the treatment of racial prejudice in O'Connor's story with that in Ellison's "Battle Royal."

Critical Thinking

9. Offer two different explanations for the meaning of the story's title—"Everything That Rises Must Converge" Why "everything"? Why "must"? In what sense might things be said to "converge"?

FLANNERY O'CONNOR: ESSAYS AND LETTERS

On Symbol and Theme

FROM "THE NATURE AND AIM OF FICTION"

Now the word *symbol* scares a good many people off, just as the word *art* does. They seem to feel that a symbol is some mysterious thing put in arbitrarily by the writer to frighten the common reader—sort of a literary Masonic grip that is only for the initiated. They seem to think that it is a way of saying something that you aren't actually saying, and so if they can be got to read a reputedly symbolic work at all, they approach it as if it were a problem in algebra. Find x. And when they do find or think they find this abstraction, x, then they go off with an elaborate sense of satisfaction and the notion that they have "understood" the story. Many students confuse the *process* of understanding a thing with understanding it.

I think that for the fiction writer himself, symbols are something he uses simply as a matter of course. You might say that these are details that, while having their essential place in the literal level of the story, operate in depth as well as on the surface, increasing the story in every direction. . . .

People have a habit of saying, "What is the theme of your story?" and they expect you to give them a statement: "The theme of my story is the economic pressure of the machine on the middle class"—or some such absurdity. And when they've got a statement like that, they go off happy and feel it is no longer necessary to read the story.

Some people have the notion that you read the story and then climb out of it into the meaning, but for the fiction writer himself the whole story is the meaning, because it is an experience, not an abstraction. . . .

When you can state the theme of a story, when you can separate it from the story itself, then you can be sure the story is not a very good one. The meaning of a story has to be embodied in it, has to be made concrete in it. A story is a way to say something that can't be said any other way, and it takes every word in the story to say what the meaning is. You tell a story because a statement would be inadequate. When anybody asks what a story is about, the only proper thing is to tell him to read the story.

From a letter to Dr. T. R. Spivey, May 25, 1959, on "A Good Man Is Hard to Find"

Week before last I went to Wesleyan and read "A Good Man Is Hard to Find." After it I went to one of the classes where I was asked questions. There were a couple of young teachers there and one of them, an earnest type, started asking the questions. "Miss O'Connor," he said, "why was the Misfit's hat *black*?" I said most countrymen in Georgia wore black hats. He looked pretty disappointed. Then he said, "Miss

O'Connor, the Misfit represents Christ, does he not?" "He does not," I said. He looked crushed. "Well, Miss O'Connor," he said, "what is the significance of the Misfit's hat?" I said it was to cover his head; and after that he left me alone.

From a letter to a Professor of English, March 28, 1961, on "A Good Man Is Hard to Find"

There is a change of tension from the first part of the story to the second where the Misfit enters, but this is no lessening of reality. This story is, of course, not meant to be realistic in the sense that it portrays the everyday doings of people in Georgia. It is stylized and its conventions are comic even though its meaning is serious.

Bailey's only importance is as the Grandmother's boy and the driver of the car. It is the Grandmother who first recognizes the Misfit and who is most concerned with him throughout. The story is a duel of sorts between the Grandmother and her superficial beliefs and the Misfit's more profoundly felt involvement with Christ's action which set the world off balance for him.

The meaning of a story should go on expanding for the reader the more he thinks about it, but meaning cannot be captured in an interpretation. If teachers are in the habit of approaching a story as if it were a research problem for which any answer is believable so long as it is not obvious, then I think students will never learn to enjoy fiction. Too much interpretation is certainly worse than too little, and where feeling for a story is absent, theory will not supply it.

On "Good Country People"

FROM "WRITING SHORT STORIES"

In good fiction, certain of the details will tend to accumulate meaning from the action of the story itself, and when this happens they become symbolic in the way they work. I once wrote a story called "Good Country People," in which a lady Ph.D. has her wooden leg stolen by a Bible salesman whom she has tried to seduce. Now I'll admit that, paraphrased in this way, the situation is simply a low joke. The average reader is pleased to observe anybody's wooden leg being stolen. But without ceasing to appeal to him and without making any statements of high intention, this story does manage to operate at another level of experience, by letting the wooden leg accumulate meaning. Early in the story, we're presented with the fact that the Ph.D. is spiritually as well as physically crippled. She believes in nothing but her own belief in nothing, and we perceive that there is a wooden part of her soul that corresponds to her wooden leg. Now of course this is never stated. The fiction writer states as little as possible. The reader makes this connection from things he is shown. He may not even know that he makes the connection, but the connection is there nevertheless and it has its effect on him. As the story goes on, the wooden leg continues to accumulate meaning. The reader learns how the girl feels about her leg, how her mother feels about it, and how the country woman on the place feels about it; and finally, by the time the Bible salesman comes along, the leg has accumulated so much meaning that it is, as the saying goes, loaded. And when the Bible salesman steals it, the reader realizes that he has taken away part of the girl's personality and has revealed her deeper affliction to her for the first time.

If you want to say that the wooden leg is a symbol, you can say that. But it is a wooden leg first, and as a wooden leg it is absolutely necessary to the story. It has its place on the literal level of the story, but it operates in depth as well as on the surface. It increases the story in every direction, and this is essentially the way a story escapes being short.

Now a little might be said about the way in which this happens. I wouldn't want you to think that in that story I sat down and said, "I am now going to write a story about a Ph.D. with a wooden leg, using the wooden leg as a symbol for another kind of affliction." I doubt myself if many writers know what they are going to do when they start out. When I started writing that story, I didn't know there was going to be a Ph.D. with a wooden leg in it. I merely found myself one morning writing a description of two women that I knew something about, and before I realized it, I had equipped one of them with a daughter with a wooden leg. As the story progressed, I brought in the Bible salesman, but I had no idea what I was going to do with him. I didn't know he was going to steal that wooden leg until ten or twelve lines before he did it, but when I found out that this was what was going to happen, I realized that it was inevitable. This is a story that produces a shock for the reader, and I think one reason for this is that it produced a shock for the writer.

CRITICS ON O'CONNOR

FREDERICK ASALS

On "A Good Man Is Hard to Find"

FROM FLANNERY O'CONNOR: THE IMAGINATION OF EXTREMITY

"A Good Man Is Hard to Find" continues to be O'Connor's best-known work, the story most often chosen to represent her in anthologies now as during her lifetime. Yet, fine as it is, it is not self-evidently her best story: something more than quality must account for its repeated selection by textbook editors. One reason for its popularity may well be precisely that "A Good Man Is Hard to Find" writes large the representative O'Connor themes and methods—comedy, violence, theological concern—and thus makes them quickly and unmistakably available. But another, surely, is the primordial appeal of the story, for "A Good Man Is Hard to Find" captures a very old truth, that in the midst of life we are in death, in its most compelling modern form. The characteristic contemporary nightmare of the sudden onslaught of violent death, a death that chooses its victims without warning, impersonally, apparently at random, without either motivation or remorse, the victims helpless either to escape or to defend themselves—this scenario for some of our deepest, most instinctual fears is the very basis of the story and the source of its immediate hold on our imaginations.

Interestingly enough, O'Connor's own public remarks on the story dismiss this level almost entirely. Stressing its spiritual implications, she emphasizes the grandmother's final action while brushing aside everything that leads up to it, saying, "If I took out this gesture and what she says with it, I would have no story. What was left would not be worth your attention." Her advice to readers of "A Good Man Is Hard to Find" is, "You should be on the lookout for such things as the action of grace in the Grandmother's soul, and not for the dead bodies" (*Mystery and Manners*).

This is all very high-minded, but it would seem a little difficult for the unprejudiced reader of "A Good Man Is Hard to Find" to ignore the dead bodies; and while one may agree with O'Connor that the story is "something more than an account of a family murdered on the way to Florida" (*Mystery and Manners*), it surely is, most immediately, just that "account." Any full discussion of the story must deal with both the grandmother's soul and the dead bodies, and indeed with the tension between the two levels implied here, for that tension is at the very heart of the story.

KATHLEEN FEELEY

On "Good Country People"

FROM FLANNERY O'CONNOR: VOICE OF THE PEACOCK

Perhaps it was her utter truthfulness which, paradoxically, allowed her to imagine and create characters who have destroyed their own integrity to pursue a false good. In a catalog of her freaks, characters who re-create themselves according to a chosen image would mark an extreme position. They are farthest away from grace because they lack the truthful appraisal of reality which grace demands. They have set up a false god—education, or art, or economic security, or comfort—and they falsify their very being in order to pay it homage. A number of Flannery O'Connor's short stories show her imagination working on the idea of falseness in a character. Some of the protagonists in these stories look perfectly normal; others have a physical deformity which is symbolic of a spiritual one. In the course of the action, all are given an opportunity to recognize their self-deception. In the author's vision, this recognition is the first step toward truth, which is, in turn, the necessary condition of Redemption. Conversion—a change of direction—is possible only after one recognizes his perversion.

Comic perversion is a key concept in "Good Country People." Both the girl Joy-Hulga and the Bible salesman have perverted their true selves, and each is revealed in his falsity after the word of God is perverted during a seduction scene—itself a perversion of love. Even the structure of the story appears to be a perversion of a traditional short-story form. Two-thirds of the story elapses before the initial meeting of

Joy-Hulga and Manley Pointer, the Bible salesman, occurs. In the first section, Flannery O'Connor sets up a relationship between Mrs. Freeman, the hired man's wife, and Mrs. Hopewell, her employer, and between each of these women and the one-legged protagonist, Joy-Hulga. These relationships structure the story. The opening section also sketches Joy through the eyes of her mother: the hunting accident which destroyed her leg, her immersion in atheistic philosophy, and her attempt, at the age of twenty-one, to rename herself and to redirect her life. With relationships demonstrated, background sketched, and tone established, the first personal encounter of Hulga and her "saviour" takes place. From Manley Pointer's opening question ("You ever ate a chicken that was two days old?") to his final assertion ("I been believing in nothing since I was born") the story moves "like the advance of a heavy truck" to its moment of truth.

That the salesman is peddling Bibles is the central perversion of the story. Flannery O'Connor believed in the power of the word of God. The Bible was for her, as it is for Jews and for Scripture-oriented Christians, the power of God and the wisdom of God. God's scriptural word is not a dead letter; it is a living presence. Reading it does more than enlighten the intellect; it unleashes power that moves the spirit. As a perversion of Christianity has driven Joy to become Hulga, so a perversion of the meaning of Scripture jolts her into self-recognition.

DOROTHY TUCK MCFARLAND

On "Everything That Rises Must Converge"

FROM FLANNERY O'CONNOR

The stories in O'Connor's second collection reflect her concern with questions implicitly raised by the rather gnomic title "Everything That Rises Must Converge." The phrase comes from the work of Pierre Teilhard de Chardin, a Jesuit paleontologist-philosopher. Teilhard hypothesized that evolution, far from stopping with the emergence of *homo sapiens,* continues to progress toward higher levels of consciousness, and that its ultimate goal is pure consciousness, which is Being itself, or God.

Teilhard's concept of the progress of evolution, actual and predicted, can best be visualized as a globe. At the base of the globe—the beginning of the evolutionary process—lines radiate outward and upward, representing the diversification of many forms of life which are moving upward toward greater levels of biological complexity. At the mid-point of the globe the diversification stops and one species—man—comes to dominate the earth. Moving from the mid-point of the globe upward, the lines begin to converge as they approach the topmost pole, the evolutionary destination that Teilhard called the Omega point. The converging lines now represent individual human consciousnesses which, as they rise, grow closer and closer together.

One aspect of this convergence can be seen in the increased intercommunication and interdependence of men in modern mass society. The increasingly complex interaction of men, Teilhard believed, tends to generate fresh bursts of evolutionary energy that produce still higher levels of consciousness, and these increases in consciousness find material expression in new technological breakthroughs. Teilhard, however, did not equate rising in consciousness solely with social or intellectual or scientific advances; he saw these achievements as manifestations of an increase in consciousness that was primarily a growing toward the fullness of Being—God—that is the source of all life.

O'Connor certainly regarded an increase in consciousness—which in her stories is signified by an increase in vision—to be a growing toward Being. However, her characters typically resist this kind of rising and the spiritual convergence with others that accompanies it. This has led some commentators to conclude that O'Connor's use of the title "Everything That Rises Must Converge" is largely, if not completely, ironic. (According to one critic, nothing rises in the title story but Julian's mother's blood pressure.) It is true that O'Connor deliberately plays off the meaning of the title against numerous metaphors of non-convergent rising, and especially against her characters' desire to rise without convergence; for instance, the "rising" of Negroes is acceptable to Julian's mother only as long as there is no convergence: "they should rise, yes, but on their own side of the fence." The thrust of most of the stories, however, is to bring the protagonist to a vision of himself as he really is, and thus to make possible a true rising toward Being. That this rising is inevitably painful does not discredit its validity; rather, it emphasizes (as Teilhard's conception does not) the tension between the evolutionary thrust toward Being and the human warp that resists it—the warp which O'Connor would have called original sin.

CHAPTER SIX

Envisioning Narrative

VISUAL STORIES

We may not want to take literally the famous saying that a picture is worth a thousand words, but it is certainly worth noting that pictures can also tell and embellish stories. We do well to remember that just as each culture and civilization throughout history has used language as a medium for stories, so too have they used pictures. The best known examples, perhaps, are the cave paintings in Lascaux, France, and Altamira, Spain, which depict early man's hunting of animals seen on the following page.

The invention of print in the fifteenth century wedded words with visual images. Words and pictures were used together in woodcut images coupled with written quotations from the Bible. More recent works that couple words and pictures to tell stories include popular comic strips, comic books, and serious graphic novels. Comic strips, such as Peanuts by Charles Schulz, typically use humor to poke fun at human foibles and to satirize political events as well as human behavior. Comic books, which often focus on the exploits of action heroes, such as Superman, Spiderman, and the Green Lantern, spin elaborate stories in words and pictures. From this early illustrated medium have come graphic novels, an increasingly popular form of contemporary visual narrative practiced in Asia, Europe, and the United States. Unlike comics, graphic novels focus less on action heroes and more on social and political commentary, often using sophisticated irony and satire to comment on contemporary issues and problems.

As you read the following illustrated narratives, compare their tone and visual structure. Look for the influence that comics, like the *Peanuts,* have on Marjane Satrapi's autobiographical *Persepolis* and Rachel Masilamani's "Two Kinds of People." In particular, consider what each selection has in common with other examples of literature in this book. How does the tone and imagery of a *Peanuts* strip compare with a Billy Collins poem, like "The History Teacher"? As you go through this chapter, consider what makes something *literary* and whether the following illustrated narratives meet those requirements.

AN ALBUM OF VISUAL NARRATIVES

CHARLES SCHULZ

[1922–2000]

Charles M. Schulz was born in Minneapolis, Minnesota. His interest in comics was encouraged from an early age by his father, a barber, who loved them. After serving in the U.S. Army, Schulz wrote comics for Timeless Topics *and sold his cartoons to The Saturday Evening Post, a popular family magazine. His Peanuts debuted in October of 1950 and ran without interruption for fifty years, the last strip appearing the day after Schulz died on February 12, 2000. Peanuts has appeared in 2,600 newspapers in seventy-five countries. The ever-popular work has inspired a classical symphony by Ellen Zwilich and the Broadway musical* You're a Good Man Charlie Brown, *as well as art exhibitions in major U.S. museums. Peanuts has been featured on the covers of* Time *magazine and* The Saturday Review, *and Snoopy and Charlie Brown accompanied the Apollo X astronauts into outer space.*

PEANUTS © United Feature Syndicate, Inc.

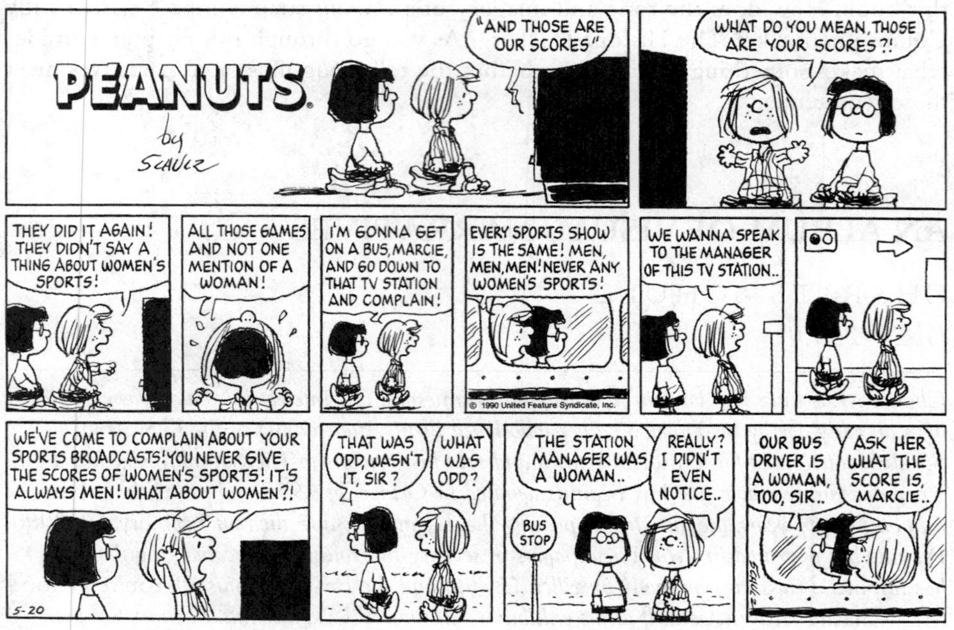

PEANUTS © United Feature Syndicate, Inc.

QUESTIONS FOR CRITICAL THINKING AND WRITING

Experience

1. To what extent were you a reader of comics growing up? Which were your favorites? Why? To what extent were you familiar with the *Peanuts* characters, and what is your response to them?

Interpretation

2. What is the point of these two different *Peanuts* comic strips? How does Schulz convey the point in each?

Evaluation

3. What social, cultural, or political value is being satirized? What human attitudes are embodied in the strips and what is Schulz's attitude toward them?

Connections

4. Compare the *Peanuts* comic strip with any other comic strip series printed in your local paper.
   How does the *Peanuts* strip compare with more politically charged strips, like Boondocks or Doonesbury? How does it compare with more general interest strips, like Garfield?

Critical Thinking

5. To what extent do you find this Peanuts strip (or other comic strips) that you know effective as social satire? As entertainment?

MARJANE SATRAPI

[b. 1969]

Marjane Satrapi was born and raised in Iran as part of a wealthy aristocratic family. Growing up in Tehran after the cultural revolution, Satrapi attended Tehran's Lycée Francais *until leaving Iran to study illustration in Germany and Austria. While living in Paris, she discovered the work of Art Speigelman, who used the graphic format to tell of his father's survival from the Nazi prison camps. Inspired by that work, she began drawing her own history of growing up in Iran after the cultural revolution that saw the Islamic clerics seize power. She has published two autobiographical graphic novels on this subject,* Persepolis 2 *(2004) and* Persepolis *(1999), from which "The Veil" has been excerpted.*

THE VEIL

THIS IS ME WHEN I WAS 10 YEARS OLD. THIS WAS IN 1980.

AND THIS IS A CLASS PHOTO. I'M SITTING ON THE FAR LEFT SO YOU DON'T SEE ME. FROM LEFT TO RIGHT: GOLNAZ, MAHSHID, NARINE, MINNA.

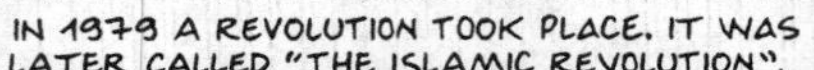

IN 1979 A REVOLUTION TOOK PLACE. IT WAS LATER CALLED "THE ISLAMIC REVOLUTION".

THEN CAME 1980: THE YEAR IT BECAME OBLIGATORY TO WEAR THE VEIL AT SCHOOL.

WEAR THIS !

WE DIDN'T REALLY LIKE TO WEAR THE VEIL, ESPECIALLY SINCE WE DIDN'T UNDERSTAND WHY WE HAD TO.
IT'S TOO HOT OUT!
EXECUTION IN THE NAME OF FREEDOM.
GIVE ME MY VEIL BACK!
YOU'LL HAVE TO LICK MY FEET!
OOH! I'M THE MONSTER OF DARKNESS.
GIDDYAP!

AND ALSO BECAUSE THE YEAR BEFORE, IN 1979, WE WERE IN A FRENCH NON-RELIGIOUS SCHOOL.

WHERE BOYS AND GIRLS WERE TOGETHER.

AND THEN SUDDENLY IN 1980...
ALL BILINGUAL SCHOOLS MUST BE CLOSED DOWN.

THEY ARE SYMBOLS OF CAPITALISM.
BRAVO!
WHAT WISDOM!

OF DECADENCE.
THIS IS CALLED A "CULTURAL REVOLUTION."

WE FOUND OURSELVES VEILED AND SEPARATED FROM OUR FRIENDS.

AND THAT WAS THAT...

QUESTIONS FOR CRITICAL THINKING AND WRITING

Experience

1. Comment on your experience reading Satrapi's "The Veil." Did the graphic story catch and sustain your interest? Explain.
2. How do you respond to the drawings?

Interpretation

3. What idea is conveyed through this graphic story?
4. What effects are achieved with the changing perspective of close-ups?

Evaluation

5. What social, cultural, or political values are central to "The Veil"? What perspective on these values does the author take? How do you know?

Connections

6. Compare "The Veil" with "Two Kinds of People." How does each author use the graphic story genre?

Critical Thinking

7. To what extent do you think Satrapi's combination of words and pictures is effective in conveying her idea? How would the story differ if told in words only?

RACHEL MASILAMANI

[b. 1977]

Rachel Masilamani graduated from Johns Hopkins University in 1999, and she is currently a cartoonist and illustrator. She is the creator of the award-winning comic series RPM Comics *from which the following was originally printed before being excepted in the* Indiana Review. *She currently lives in Las Cruces, New Mexico.*

QUESTIONS FOR CRITICAL THINKING AND WRITING

Experience

1. To what extent can you relate to the issues at stake in "Two Kinds of People"? To what extent does the picture/story transcend the specific cultural conflict it describes? Explain.

Interpretation

2. What is the central question at the heart of "Two Kinds of People"? To what extent does this question get answered in the story?

Evaluation

3. How do aspects of culture come into conflict in the story? To what extent are the cultural conflicts resolved? To what extent do you think its images are effective?

TWO KINDS OF PEOPLE

BY RACHEL MASILAMANI

IN 1968, MY DAD WENT TO GET HIS WISCONSIN DRIVER'S LICENSE. WHEN HE TOOK THE WRITTEN PART, HE HAD TO ASK THE GUY AT THE DESK A QUESTION:

RACE:
WHITE ☐
BLACK ☐

WHAT DO I CHECK?

I SWITCHED SCHOOLS IN SEVENTH GRADE. STARTED GOING TO PUBLIC SCHOOL. NITA KUMAR WAS ON MY BUS.

From Indiana Review *Vol 26.1, Summer 2004.*

IN SEVENTH GRADE, I WORE LIPSTICK EVERY DAY. I WORE POWDER.

WHAT WAS IT WITH NITA KUMAR? I NEVER RODE A SCHOOL BUS BEFORE EITHER, BUT IT WAS OBVIOUS TO ME THAT I SHOULD NOT SIT IN THE BACK.
HOW COME YOU HAVE THAT DOT?
DOESN'T IT MEAN YOU'RE MARRIED?
GROSS!

WHAT ARE YOU, HUH?
YOU KNOW YOU HAVE TO ANSWER, RIGHT?

NONE OF YOUR BUSINESS.

BITCH! I'M JUST BEING NICE!

THERE ARE OTHER WAYS TO ASK.
WHAT'S THE ORIGIN OF YOUR NAME?

WHERE ARE YOU FROM ANYWAY?

I'M FROM NEW JERSEY
HOSPITAL
287
WHERE I WAS BORN
WHERE I LIVE

I KNOW THAT, BUT WHERE ARE YOUR PARENTS FROM?

Are your parents U.S. Citizens?
Check one box (y/n).
y ☐ n ☐

NEXT QUESTION:
WHICH ONE ARE YOU?

MY MOM'S GERMAN-AMERICAN; MY DAD'S FROM INDIA.
NOT SUCH A BIG DEAL, IS IT?

BOTH.
READ
GET THE

WELL, WHICH BOX SHOULD I CHECK?
GET TH

ISN'T THERE AN 'OTHER' BOX?
OH. SO THERE IS.
FIRST TIME
GET THE FAC

MOST PEOPLE DON'T ASK THAT SECOND QUESTION.
OTHER BOX

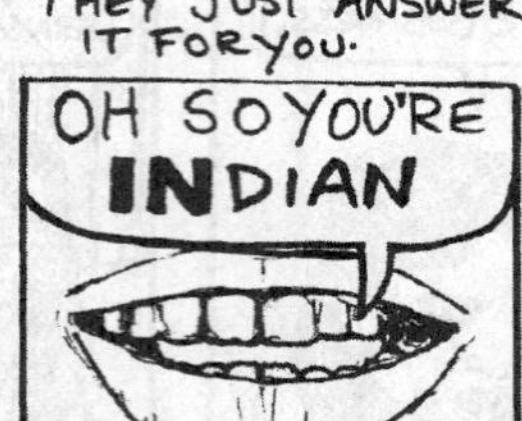
THEY JUST ANSWER IT FOR YOU.
OH SO YOU'RE INDIAN

WHAT'S IT LIKE GROWING UP INDIAN IN AMERICA?
BLOOD RELATIVE ON MOM'S SIDE

I HAVE A FILING SYSTEM TOO
I LIKE TO KEEP THINGS NEAT
I PUT EVERYTHING AWAY AS SOON AS POSSIBLE
TEACHERS
NEIGHBORS

DID YOU SEE WHAT'S HER FACE, THAT INDIAN GIRL, TOTALLY FALL ON HER ASS IN THERE?
HA! REALLY?

HEY! YOU'RE ON MY BUS. YOU KNOW HER?

KNOW WHO?

GOOD AT DODGEBALL
LOSERS
INDIAN GIRL? SKINNY?
BOYS
INDIAN GIRL

NO.

TALKS WEIRD
BLACK GIRLS
WHAT ARE YOU?
LOSERS

MAYBE THE INDIAN FILE ISN'T HOW I PICTURED IT.
YOU, YERRI, ARE VEDDY VEDDY BAD MAN!
MAYBE IT'S A FUN PLACE.
NEXT DOOR NEIGHBORS
PRETTY GIRL FROM ALGEBRA
COOL MUSICIANS
KICKASS BUFFET
BEST FRIEND FROM SIXTH GRADE
OR MAYBE IT WOULD SEEM OKAY AT FIRST.
PIONEER ANCESTORS? RECESSIVE GENE FOR BLUE EYES? HAVE YOU EVEN BEEN TO INDIA?
ONCE.
HI
I JUST THINK I'D RUN INTO PROBLEMS THERE

WHERE ARE YOU REALLY FROM?

IT WAS JUNIOR HIGH SCHOOL AND THERE WAS NOTHING TODO BUT LIE.
COLUMBIA?

IF I HAD MORE TIME, I COULDHAVE COME UP WITH THE PERFECT ANSWER:
HAWAII.
YEAH PEOPLE LIKE THAT ONE.

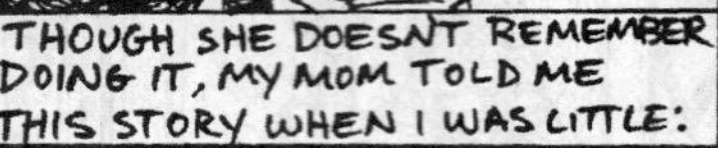

THOUGH SHE DOESN'T REMEMBER DOING IT, MY MOM TOLD ME THIS STORY WHEN I WAS LITTLE:

GOD WAS GETTING READY TO MAKE PEOPLE, SO HE SHAPED THEM AND BAKED THEM UP IN HIS OVEN.

"BUT THE FIRST BATCH CAME OUT BURNED, AND THE NEXT BATCH CAME OUT UNDERDONE..."

I'VE ALWAYS PICTURED GOD AS GEORGE WASHINGTON ON MOUNT RUSHMORE. WE NEVER WENT TO CHURCH.

BUT THE LAST BATCH CAME OUT JUST RIGHT- LIKE YOU!

I KNEW THE STORY WASN'T TRUE. IT'S THE SAME THING WITH EVERYONE. WE'RE ALL SOME SORT OF HALF-AND-HALF MIXTURE OF OUR PARENTS.

IF THERE WERE ANY REAL LINES, I WOULDN'T BE HERE.

THERE'S A CULTURE CLASH IN ALL OUR LIVING ROOMS.

NO FAMILY OF MINE SKIPS CHURCH 'CAUSE IT'S 'RAINING!'

IF YOU KEEP LETTING HIM UP THERE. HE'LL THINK HE'S ALLOWED!
HE IS.

CAN THAT PREPARE US TO MEET THE REST OF THE WORLD?

HOW COME YOUR MOM'S WHITE BUT YOUR DAD ISN'T?

WHAT ARE YOU?

MY MOM'S WHITE AND MY DAD'S FROM INDIA.

WHAT PART?

SOUTH.

OH.

WE CALLED EASTWOOD "THE HERO OF MADURAI" BUT EVERYONE LIKED ELI WALLACH BEST IN THIS ONE.
IN THIS WORLD, THERE'S TWO KINDS OF PEOPLE...
THOSE WITH LOADED GUNS, AND THOSE WHO DIG. YOU DIG.
RPM 2003

Connections

4. Compare the purposes to which Masilamani puts the genre of the graphic story with the purposes to which Satrapi puts the genre in "The Veil." What differences do you find in the way they tell and draw their stories?

Critical Thinking

5. Why do you think Masilamani may have written this piece?

CHAPTER SEVEN

A Collection of Contemporary Fiction

Fiction is not dream. Nor is it guess work. It is imagining based on facts.
MARGARET BANNING

Contemporary works of fiction speak to us in a special way because they have been created during the period in which we live. Contemporary stories bring a fresh vision and perspective about our lives now. The characters in contemporary stories seem familiar and real. They speak the way we speak, and they sound the way we overhear people speaking all the time. Yet they surprise.

Characters in contemporary fiction seem close to us because of how they act and how they think-they embody the spirit of the time and place in which their authors have created them, our time and place. Yet contemporary short stories are fun to read because, to some extent, we do not know what we are going to find in them. They are interesting precisely because they are not classics, even though some of them may become classics in the future. They are, in short, unpredictable. They speak in a voice, a tone, and an idiom that are current and often familiar; yet they may show us something new about ourselves.

SHERMAN ALEXIE

[b. 1966]

Sherman Alexie is a Spokane-Coeur d'Alene Indian raised on a reservation in the State of Washington. Alexie's work has come to be known only in the last decade with his book The Business of Fancydancing, *a collection that combines poems and stories about living on a reservation. Alexie, who now lives in Seattle, has won awards from the National Endowment for the Arts and the Lila Wallace-Reader's Digest Foundation. His work tends to irreverence and provocation. It is often playful and ironic; it can be both poignant and humorous.*

Indian Education

First Grade

My hair was too short and my U.S. Government glasses were horn-rimmed, ugly, and all that first winter in school, the other Indian boys chased me from one corner of the playground to the other. They pushed me down, buried me in the snow until I couldn't breathe, thought I'd never breathe again.

They stole my glasses and threw them over my head, around my outstretched hands, just beyond my reach, until someone tripped me and sent me falling again, facedown in the snow.

I was always falling down; my Indian name was Junior Falls Down. Sometimes it was Bloody Nose or Steal-His-Lunch. Once, it was Cries-Like-a-White-Boy, even though none of us had seen a white boy cry.

Then it was a Friday morning recess and Frenchy Sijohn threw snowballs at me while the rest of the Indian boys tortured some other *top-yogh-yaught* kid, another weakling. But Frenchy was confident enough to torment me all by himself, and most days I would have let him.

But the little warrior in me roared to life that day and knocked Frenchy to the ground, held his head against the snow and punched him so hard that my knuckles and the snow made symmetrical bruises on his face. He almost looked like he was wearing war paint.

But he wasn't the warrior. I was. And I chanted *It's a good day to die, it's a good day to die,* all the way down to the principal's office.

Second Grade

Betty Towle, missionary teacher, redheaded and so ugly that no one ever had a puppy crush on her, made me stay in for recess fourteen days straight.

"Tell me you're sorry," she said.

"Sorry for what?" I asked.

"Everything," she said and made me stand straight for fifteen minutes, eagle-armed with books in each hand. One was a math book; the other was English. But all I learned was that gravity can be painful.

For Halloween I drew a picture of her riding a broom with a scrawny cat on the back. She said that her God would never forgive me for that.

Once, she gave the class a spelling test but set me aside and gave me a test designed for junior high students. When I spelled all the words right, she crumpled up the paper and made me eat it.

"You'll learn respect," she said.

She sent a letter home with me that told my parents to either cut my braids or keep me home from class. My parents came in the next day and dragged their braids across Betty Towle's desk.

"Indians, indians, indians." She said it without capitalization. She called me "indian, indian, indian."

And I said, *Yes, I am. I am Indian. Indian, I am.*

Third Grade

My traditional Native American art career began and ended with my very first portrait: *Stick Indian Taking a Piss in My Backyard.*

As I circulated the original print around the classroom, Mrs. Schluter intercepted and confiscated my art.

Censorship, I might cry now. *Freedom of expression,* I would write in editorials to the tribal newspaper.

In third grade, though, I stood alone in the corner, faced the wall, and waited for the punishment to end.

I'm still waiting.

Fourth Grade

"You should be a doctor when you grow up," Mr. Schluter told me, even though his wife, the third grade teacher, thought I was crazy beyond my years. My eyes always looked like I had just hit-and-run someone.

"Guilty," she said. "You always look guilty."

"Why should I be a doctor?" I asked Mr. Schluter.

"So you can come back and help the tribe. So you can heal people."

That was the year my father drank a gallon of vodka a day and the same year that my mother started two hundred different quilts but never finished any. They sat in separate, dark places in our HUD house and wept savagely.

I ran home after school, heard their Indian tears, and looked in the mirror. *Doctor Victor,* I called myself, invented an education, talked to my reflection. *Doctor Victor to the emergency room.*

Fifth Grade

I picked up a basketball for the first time and made my first shot. No. I missed my first shot, missed the basket completely, and the ball landed in the dirt and sawdust, sat there like I had sat there only minutes before.

But it felt good, that ball in my hands, all those possibilities and angles. It was mathematics, geometry. It was beautiful.

At that same moment, my cousin Steven Ford sniffed rubber cement from a paper bag and leaned back on the merry-go-round. His ears rang, his mouth was dry, and everyone seemed so far away.

But it felt good, that buzz in his head, all those colors and noises. It was chemistry, biology. It was beautiful.

Oh, do you remember those sweet, almost innocent choices that the Indian boys were forced to make?

Sixth Grade

Randy, the new Indian kid from the white town of Springdale, got into a fight an hour after he first walked into the reservation school.

Stevie Flett called him out, called him a squawman, called him a pussy, and called him a punk.

Randy and Stevie, and the rest of the Indian boys, walked out into the playground.

"Throw the first punch," Stevie said as they squared off.

"No," Randy said.

"Throw the first punch," Stevie said again.

"No," Randy said again.

"Throw the first punch!" Stevie said for the third time, and Randy reared back and pitched a knuckle fastball that broke Stevie's nose.

We all stood there in silence, in awe.

That was Randy, my soon-to-be first and best friend, who taught me the most valuable lesson about living in the white world: *Always throw the first punch*.

Seventh Grade

I leaned through the basement window of the HUD house and kissed the white girl who would later be raped by her foster-parent father, who was also white. They both lived on the reservation, though, and when the headlines and stories filled the papers later, not one word was made of their color.

Just Indians being Indians, someone must have said somewhere and they were wrong.

But on the day I leaned through the basement window of the HUD house and kissed the white girl, I felt the good-byes I was saying to my entire tribe. I held my lips tight against her lips, a dry, clumsy, and ultimately stupid kiss.

But I was saying good-bye to my tribe, to all the Indian girls and women I might have loved, to all the Indian men who might have called me cousin, even brother.

I kissed that white girl and when I opened my eyes, she was gone from the reservation, and when I opened my eyes, I was gone from the reservation, living in a farm town where a beautiful white girl asked my name.

"Junior Polatkin," I said, and she laughed.

After that, no one spoke to me for another five hundred years.

Eighth Grade

At the farm town junior high, in the boys' bathroom, I could hear voices from the girls' bathroom, nervous whispers of anorexia and bulimia. I could hear the white girls' forced vomiting, a sound so familiar and natural to me after years of listening to my father's hangovers.

"Give me your lunch if you're just going to throw it up," I said to one of those girls once.

I sat back and watched them grow skinny from self-pity.

Back on the reservation, my mother stood in line to get us commodities. We carried them home, happy to have food, and opened the canned beef that even the dogs wouldn't eat.

But we ate it day after day and grew skinny from self-pity.

There is more than one way to starve.

Ninth Grade

At the farm town high school dance, after a basketball game in an overheated gym where I had scored twenty-seven points and pulled down thirteen rebounds, I passed out during a slow song.

As my white friends revived me and prepared to take me to the emergency room where doctors would later diagnose my diabetes, the Chicano teacher ran up to us.

"Hey," he said. "What's that boy been drinking? I know all about these Indian kids. They start drinking real young."

Sharing dark skin doesn't necessarily make two men brothers.

Tenth Grade

I passed the written test easily and nearly flunked the driving, but still received my Washington State driver's license on the same day that Wally Jim killed himself by driving his car into a pine tree.

No traces of alcohol in his blood, good job, wife and two kids.

"Why'd he do it?" asked a Washington State trooper.

All the Indians shrugged their shoulders, looked down at the ground.

"Don't know," we all said, but when we look in the mirror, see the history of our tribe in our eyes, taste failure in the tap water, and shake with old tears, we understand completely.

Believe me, everything looks like a noose if you stare at it long enough.

Eleventh Grade

Last night I missed two free throws which would have won the game against the best team in the state. The farm town high school I play for is nicknamed the "Indians," and I'm probably the only actual Indian ever to play for a team with such a mascot.

This morning I pick up the sports page and read the headline: INDIANS LOSE AGAIN.

Go ahead and tell me none of this is supposed to hurt me very much.

Twelfth Grade

I walk down the aisle, valedictorian of this farm town high school, and my cap doesn't fit because I've grown my hair longer than it's ever been. Later, I stand as the school board chairman recites my awards, accomplishments, and scholarships.

I try to remain stoic for the photographers as I look toward the future.

Back home on the reservation, my former classmates graduate: a few can't read, one or two are just given attendance diplomas, most look forward to the parties. The bright students are shaken, frightened, because they don't know what comes next.

They smile for the photographer as they look back toward tradition.

The tribal newspaper runs my photograph and the photograph of my former classmates side by side.

Postscript: Class Reunion

Victor said, "Why should we organize a reservation high school reunion? My graduating class has a reunion every weekend at the Powwow Tavern."

(1993)

QUESTIONS FOR CRITICAL THINKING AND WRITING

Experience

1. Consider the experience of the narrator in one of his grades. Have you experienced or observed similar incidents?

Interpretation

2. Describe the narrator. How do you think his school experiences have shaped him?
3. Consider the episodic structure of the story. How do the episodes relate to one another? How do they develop the story's theme?
4. Select one episode for a close reading. Consider the narrator at that point in his life, the tone of the episode, and its thematic implications.

Evaluation

5. Consider "Eleventh Grade." Is the narrator overly sensitive to the headline on the sports page? Why is he so hurt by the headline?
6. What values seem to clash in the story?

Connections

7. Compare the minority experience of the narrator with other fictional children such as the narrator in Ellison's "Battle Royal" and the girls in Cisneros's "Barbie Q."

Critical Thinking

8. What would be gained or lost if the Postscript were to be omitted? What does the Postscript suggest about life on the reservation? Why do you think alcohol abuse has long been a problem for Native Americans living on reservations?

© Jill Krementz

GISH JEN

[b. 1956]

Gish Jen grew up in Scarsdale, New York, and graduated from Harvard. She now lives in Massachusetts. Her work has appeared in The New Yorker, The Atlantic Monthly, *and* The Best American Short Stories of the Century. *She is the author of two novels,* Typical American *and* Mona in the Promised Land.

Who's Irish?

In China, people say mixed children are supposed to be smart, and definitely my granddaughter Sophie is smart. But Sophie is wild, Sophie is not like my daughter Natalie, or like me. I am work hard all my life, and fierce besides. My husband always used to say he is afraid of me, and in our restaurant, busboys and cooks all afraid of me too. Even the gang members come for protection money, they try to talk to my husband. When I am there, they stay away. If they come by mistake, they pretend they are come to eat. They hide behind the menu, they order a lot of food. They talk about their mothers. Oh, my mother have some arthritis, need to take herbal medicine, they say. Oh, my mother getting old, her hair all white now.

I say, Your mother's hair used to be white, but since she dye it, it become black again. Why don't you go home once in a while and take a look? I tell them, Confucius say a filial son knows what color his mother's hair is.

My daughter is fierce too, she is vice president in the bank now. Her new house is big enough for everybody to have their own room, including me. But Sophie take after Natalie's husband's family, their name is Shea. Irish. I always thought Irish people are like Chinese people, work so hard on the railroad, but now I know why the Chinese beat the Irish. Of course, not all Irish are like the Shea family, of course not. My daughter tell me I should not say Irish this, Irish that.

How do you like it when people say the Chinese this, the Chinese that, she say.

You know, the British call the Irish heathen, just like they call the Chinese, she say.

You think the Opium War was bad, how would you like to live right next door to the British, she say.

And that is that. My daughter have a funny habit when she win an argument, she take a sip of something and look away, so the other person is not embarrassed. So I am not embarrassed. I do not call anybody anything either. I just happen to mention about the Shea family, an interesting fact: four brothers in the family, and not one of them work. The mother, Bess, have a job before she got sick, she was executive secretary in a big company. She is handle everything for a big shot, you would be surprised how complicated her job is, not just type this, type that. Now she is a nice woman with a clean house. But her boys, every one of them is on welfare, or so-called severance pay, or so-called disability pay. Something. They say they cannot find work, this is not the economy of the fifties, but I say, Even the black people doing better these days, some of them live so fancy, you'd be surprised. Why the Shea family have so much trouble? They are white people, they speak English. When I come to this country, I have no money and do not speak English. But my husband and I own our restaurant before he die. Free and clear, no mortgage. Of course, I understand I am just lucky; come from a country where the food is popular all over the world. I understand it is not the Shea family's fault they come from a country where everything is boiled. Still, I say.

She's right, we should broaden our horizons, say one brother, Jim, at Thanksgiving. Forget about the car business. Think about egg rolls.

Pad thai, say another brother, Mike. I'm going to make my fortune in pad thai. It's going to be the new pizza.

I say, you people too picky about what you sell. Selling egg rolls not good enough for you, but at least my husband and I can say, We made it. What can you say? Tell me. What can you say?

Everybody chew their tough turkey.

I especially cannot understand my daughter's husband John, who has no job but cannot take care of Sophie either. Because he is a man, he say, and that's the end of the sentence.

Plain boiled food, plain boiled thinking. Even his name is plain boiled: John. Maybe because I grew up with black bean sauce and hoisin sauce and garlic sauce, I always feel something is missing when my son-in-law talk.

But, okay: so my son-in-law can be man, I am baby-sitter. Six hours a day, same as the old sitter, crazy Amy, who quit. This is not so easy, now that I am sixty-eight, Chinese age almost seventy. Still, I try. In China, daughter take care of mother. Here it is the other way around. Mother help daughter, mother ask, Anything else I can do? Otherwise daughter complain mother is not supportive. I tell daughter, We do not have this word in Chinese, supportive. But my daughter too busy to listen, she has to go to meeting, she has to write memo while her husband go to the gym to be a man. My daughter say otherwise he will be depressed. Seems like all his life he has this trouble, depression.

No one wants to hire someone who is depressed, she say. It is important for him to keep his spirits up.

Beautiful wife, beautiful daughter, beautiful house, oven can clean itself automatically. No money left over, because only one income, but lucky enough, got the baby-sitter for free. If John lived in China, he would be very happy. But he is not happy. Even at the gym things go wrong. One day, he pull a muscle. Another day, weight room too crowded. Always something.

Until finally, hooray he has a job. Then he feel pressure.

I need to concentrate, he say. I need to focus.

He is going to work for insurance company. Salesman job. A paycheck, he say, and at least he will wear clothes instead of gym shorts. My daughter buy him some special candy bars from the health-food store. They say THINK! on them, and are supposed to help John think.

John is a good-looking boy, you have to say that, especially now that he shave so you can see his face.

I am an old man in a young man's game, say John.

I will need a new suit, say John.

This time I am not going to shoot myself in the foot, say John.

Good, I say.

She means to be supportive, my daughter say. Don't start the send her back to China thing, because we can't.

Sophie is three years old American age, but already I see her nice Chinese side swallowed up by her wild Shea side. She looks like mostly Chinese. Beautiful black hair, beautiful black eyes. Nose perfect size, not so flat looks like something fell down, not so large looks like some big deal got stuck in wrong face. Everything just right, only her skin is a brown surprise to John's family. So brown, they say. Even John say it. She never goes in the sun, still she is that color, he say. Brown. They say, Nothing the matter with brown. They are just surprised. So brown. Nattie is not that brown, they say. They say, It seems like Sophie should be a color in between Nattie and John. Seems funny, a girl named Sophie Shea be brown. But she is brown, maybe her name should be Sophie Brown. She never go in the sun, still she is that color, they say. Nothing the matter with brown. They are just surprised.

The Shea family talk is like this sometimes, going around and around like a Christmas-tree train.

Maybe John is not her father, I say one day, to stop the train. And sure enough, train wreck. None of the brothers ever say the word *brown* to me again.

Instead, John's mother, Bess, say, I hope you are not offended.

She say. I did my best on those boys. But raising four boys with no father is no picnic.

You have a beautiful family, I say.

I'm getting old, she say.

You deserve a rest, I say. Too many boys make you old.

I never had a daughter, she say. You have a daughter.

I have a daughter, I say. Chinese people don't think a daughter is so great, but you're right. I have a daughter.

I was never against the marriage, you know, she say. I never thought John was marrying down. I always thought Nattie was just as good as white.

I was never against the marriage either, I say. I just wonder if they look at the whole problem.

Of course you pointed out the problem, you are a mother, she say. And now we both have a granddaughter. A little brown granddaughter, she is so precious to me.

I laugh. A little brown granddaughter, I say. To tell you the truth, I don't know how she came out so brown.

We laugh some more. These days Bess need a walker to walk. She take so many pills, she need two glasses of water to get them all down. Her favorite TV show is about bloopers, and she love her bird feeder. All day long, she can watch that bird feeder, like a cat.

I can't wait for her to grow up, Bess say. I could use some female company.

Too many boys, I say.

Boys are fine, she say. But they do surround you after a while.

You should take a break, come live with us, I say. Lots of girls at our house.

Be careful what you offer, say Bess with a wink. Where I come from, people mean for you to move in when they say a thing like that.

Nothing the matter with Sophie's outside, that's the truth. It is inside that she is like not any Chinese girl I ever see. We go to the park, and this is what she does. She stand up in the stroller. She take off all her clothes and throw them in the fountain.

Sophie! I say. Stop!

But she just laugh like a crazy person. Before I take over as baby-sitter, Sophie has that crazy-person sitter, Amy the guitar player. My daughter thought this Amy very creative—another word we do not talk about in China. In China, we talk about whether we have difficulty or no difficulty. We talk about whether life is bitter or not bitter. In America, all day long, people talk about creative. Never mind that I cannot even look at this Amy, with her shirt so short that her belly button showing. This Amy think Sophie should love her body. So when Sophie take off her diaper, Amy laugh. When Sophie run around naked, Amy say she wouldn't want to wear a diaper either. When Sophie go *shu-shu* in her lap, Amy laugh and say there are no germs in pee. When Sophie take off her shoes, Amy say bare feet is best, even the pediatrician say so. That is why Sophie now walk around with no shoes like a beggar child. Also why Sophie love to take off her clothes.

Turn around! say the boys in the park Let's see that ass!

Of course, Sophie does not understand. Sophie clap her hands, I am the only one to say, No! This is not a game.

It has nothing to do with John's family, my daughter say. Amy was too permissive, that's all.

But I think if Sophie was not wild inside, she would not take off her shoes and clothes to begin with.

You never take off your clothes when you were little, I say. All my Chinese friends had babies, I never saw one of them act wild like that.

Look, my daughter say. I have a big presentation tomorrow.

John and my daughter agree Sophie is a problem, but they don't know what to do.

You spank her, she'll stop, I say another day.

But they say, Oh no.

In America, parents not supposed to spank the child.

It gives them low self-esteem, my daughter say. And that leads to problems later, as I happen to know.

My daughter never have big presentation the next day when the subject of spanking come up.

I don't want you to touch Sophie, she say. No spanking, period.

Don't tell me what to do, I say.

I'm not telling you what to do, say my daughter. I'm telling you how I feel.

I am not your servant, I say. Don't you dare talk to me like that.

My daughter have another funny habit when she lose an argument. She spread out all her fingers and look at them, as if she like to make sure they are still there.

My daughter is fierce like me, but she and John think it is better to explain to Sophie that clothes are a good idea. This is not so hard in the cold weather. In the warm weather, it is very hard.

Use your words, my daughter say. That's what we tell Sophie. How about if you set a good example.

As if good example mean anything to Sophie. I am so fierce, the gang members who used to come to the restaurant all afraid of me, but Sophie is not afraid.

I say, Sophie, if you take off your clothes, no snack.

I say, Sophie, if you take off your clothes, no lunch.

I say, Sophie, if you take off your clothes, no park.

Pretty soon we are stay home all day, and by the end of six hours she still did not have one thing to eat. You never saw a child stubborn like that.

I'm hungry! she cry when my daughter come home.

What's the matter, doesn't your grandmother feed you? My daughter laugh.

No! Sophie say. She doesn't feed me anything!

My daughter laugh again. Here you go, she say.

She say to John, Sophie must be growing.

Growing like a weed, I say.

Still Sophie take off her clothes, until one day I spank her. Not too hard, but she cry and cry, and when I tell her if she doesn't put her clothes back on I'll spank her again, she put her clothes back on. Then I tell her she is good girl, and give her some food to eat. The next day we go to the park and, like a nice Chinese girl, she does not take off her clothes.

She stop taking off her clothes, I report. Finally!

How did you do it? my daughter ask.

After twenty-eight years experience with you, I guess I learned something, I say.

It must have been a phase, John say, and his voice is suddenly like an expert.

His voice is like an expert about everything these days, now that he carry a leather briefcase, and wear shiny shoes, and can go shopping for a new car. On the company, he say. The company will pay for it, but he will be able to drive it whenever he want. A free car, he say. How do you like that.

It's good to see you in the saddle again, my daughter say. Some of your family patterns are scary.

At least I don't drink, he say. He say, And I'm not the only one with scary family patterns.

That's for sure, say my daughter.

Everyone is happy. Even I am happy, because there is more trouble with Sophie, but now I think I can help her Chinese side fight against her wild side. I teach her to eat food with fork or spoon or chopsticks, she cannot just grab into the middle of a bowl of noodles. I teach her not to play with garbage cans. Sometimes I spank her, but not too often, and not too hard.

Still, there are problems. Sophie like to climb everything. If there is a railing, she is never next to it. Always she is on top of it. Also, Sophie like to hit the mommies of her friends. She learn this from her playground best friend, Sinbad, who is four. Sinbad wear army clothes every day and like to ambush his mommy. He is the one who dug a big hole under the play structure, a foxhole he call it, all by himself. Very hard-working. Now he wait in the foxhole with a shovel full of wet sand. When his mommy come, he throw it right at her.

Oh, it's all right, his mommy say. You can't get rid of war games, it's part of their imaginative play. All the boys go through it.

Also, he like to kick his mommy, and one day he tell Sophie to kick his mommy too. I wish this story is not true.

Kick her, kick her! Sinbad say.

Sophie kick her. A little kick, as if she just so happened was swinging her little leg and didn't realize that big mommy leg was in the way. Still I spank Sophie and make Sophie say sorry; and what does the mommy say?

Really, it's all right, she say. It didn't hurt.

After that, Sophie learn she can attack mommies in the playground, and some will say, Stop, but others will say, Oh, she didn't mean it, especially if they realize Sophie will be punished.

This is how, one day, bigger trouble come. The bigger trouble start when Sophie hide in the foxhole with that shovel full of sand. She wait, and when I come look for her, she throw it at me. All over my nice clean clothes.

Did you ever see a Chinese girl act this way?

Sophie! I say. Come out of there, say you're sorry.

But she does not come out. Instead, she laugh. Naaah, naah-na, naaa-naaa, she say. I am not exaggerate: millions of children in China, not one act like this.

Sophie! I say. Now! Come out now!

But she know she is in big trouble. She know if she come out, what will happen next. So she does not come out. I am sixty-eight, Chinese age almost seventy, how can I crawl under there to catch her? Impossible. So I yell, yell, yell, and what happen? Nothing. A Chinese mother would help, but American mothers, they look at you, they shake their head, they go home. And, of course, a Chinese child would give up, but not Sophie.

I hate you! she yell. I hate you, Meanie!

Meanie is my new name these days.

Long time this goes on, long long time. The foxhole is deep, you cannot see too much, you don't know where is the bottom. You cannot hear too much either. If she does not yell, you cannot even know she is still there or not. After a while, getting cold out, getting dark out. No one left in the playground, only us.

Sophie, I say. How did you become stubborn like this? I am go home without you now.

I try to use a stick, chase her out of there, and once or twice I hit her, but still she does not come out. So finally I leave. I go outside the gate.

Bye-bye! I say. I'm go home now.

But still she does not come out and does not come out. Now it is dinnertime, the sky is black. I think I should maybe go get help, but how can I leave a little girl by herself in the playground? A bad man could come. A rat could come. I go back in to see what is happen to Sophie. What if she have a shovel and is making a tunnel to escape?

Sophie! I say.

No answer.

Sophie!

I don't know if she is alive. I don't know if she is fall asleep down there. If she is crying, I cannot hear her.

So I take the stick and poke.

Sophie! I say. I promise I no hit you. If you come out, I give you a lollipop.

No answer. By now I worried. What to do, what to do, what to do? I poke some more, even harder, so that I am poking and poking when my daughter and John suddenly appear.

What are you doing? What is going on? say my daughter.

Put down that stick! say my daughter.

You are crazy! say my daughter.

John wiggle under the structure, into the foxhole, to rescue Sophie.

She fell asleep, say John the expert. She's okay. That is one big hole.

Now Sophie is crying and crying.

Sophia, my daughter say, hugging her. Are you okay, peanut? Are you okay?

She's just scared, say John.

Are you okay? I say too. I don't know what happen, I say.

She's okay, say John. He is not like my daughter, full of questions. He is full of answers until we get home and can see by the lamplight.

Will you look at her? he yell then. What the hell happened?

Bruises all over her brown skin and a swollen up eye.

You are crazy! say my daughter. Look at what you did! You are crazy!

I try very hard, I say.

How could you use a stick? I told you to use your words!

She is hard to handle, I say.

She's three years old! You cannot use a stick! say my daughter.

She is not like any Chinese girl I ever saw, I say.

I brush some sand off my clothes. Sophie's clothes are dirty too, but at least she has her clothes on.

Has she done this before? ask my daughter. Has she hit you before?

She hits me all the time, Sophie say, eating ice cream.

Your family, say John.

Believe me, say my daughter.

A daughter I have, a beautiful daughter. I took care of her when she could not hold her head up. I took care of her before she could argue with me, when she was a little girl with two pigtails, one of them always crooked. I took care of her when we have to escape from China, I took care of her when suddenly we live in a country with cars everywhere, if you are not careful your little girl get run over. When my husband die, I promise him I will keep the family together, even though it was just two of us, hardly a family at all.

But now my daughter take me around to look at apartments. After all, I can cook, I can clean, there's no reason I cannot live by myself, all I need is a telephone. Of course, she is sorry. Sometime she cry, I am the one to say everything will be okay. She say she have no choice, she doesn't want to end up divorced. I say divorce is terrible, I don't know who invented this terrible idea. Instead of live with a telephone, though, surprise, I come to live with Bess. Imagine that. Bess make an offer and, sure enough, where she come from, people mean for you to move in when they say things like that. A crazy idea, go to live with someone else's family, but she like to have some female company, not like my daughter, who does not believe in company. These days when my daughter visit, she does not bring Sophie. Bess say we should give Nattie time, we will see Sophie again soon. But seems like my daughter have more presentation than ever before, every time she come she have to leave.

I have a family to support, she say, and her voice is heavy, as if soaking wet. I have a young daughter and a depressed husband and no one to turn to.

When she say no one to turn to, she mean me.

These days my beautiful daughter is so tired she can just sit there in a chair and fall asleep. John lost his job again, already, but still they rather hire a baby-sitter than ask me to help, even they can't afford it. Of course, the new baby-sitter is much younger, can run around. I don't know if Sophie these days is wild or not wild. She call me Meanie, but she like to kiss me too, sometimes. I remember that every time I see a child on TV. Sophie like to grab my hair, a fistful in each hand, and then kiss me smack on the nose. I never see any other child kiss that way.

The satellite TV has so many channels, more channels than I can count, including a Chinese channel from the Mainland and a Chinese channel from Taiwan, but most of the time I watch bloopers with Bess. Also, I watch the bird feeder—so many, many kinds of birds come. The Shea sons hang around all the time, asking when will I go home, but Bess tell them, Get lost.

She's a permanent resident, say Bess. She isn't going anywhere.

Then she wink at me, and switch the channel with the remote control.

Of course, I shouldn't say Irish this, Irish that, especially now I am become honorary Irish myself, according to Bess. Me! Who's Irish? I say, and she laugh. All the same, if I could mention one thing about some of the Irish, not all of them of course, I like to mention this: Their talk just stick. I don't know how Bess Shea learn to use her words, but sometimes I hear what she say a long time later. *Permanent resident. Not going anywhere.* Over and over I hear it, the voice of Bess.

(1998)

QUESTIONS FOR CRITICAL THINKING AND WRITING

Experience

1. What is your impression of the narrator? How do you respond to her situation? Was it appropriate for her to spank her granddaughter?

Interpretation

2. Characterize the grandmother's style of telling the story. What do you learn about her from the kind of language and sentence structure she uses and from the details she includes?

3. At the end of the story, what is the significance of the narrator's reference to herself as "honorary Irish"? Consider the significance of the story's title here as well.
4. Describe the marriage of Natalie and John Shea. Is the grandmother responsible for much of its tension?

Evaluation

5. How would you characterize the cultural world from which the grandmother comes? How does it clash with American culture?

Connection

6. Compare how the grandmother in "Who's Irish?" both assimilates to mainstream American culture and preserves her own cultural roots with the way the mother in Tan's "Rules of the Game" does so.

Critical Thinking

7. What value is there in reading a story from a different cultural tradition, such as a Western college student confronting Lahiri's "Hell-Heaven"? What kinds of adjustments of expectation and judgment might it be necessary for readers from different cultural and political backgrounds to make? Why?

JHUMPA LAHIRI

[b. 1967]

Jhumpa Lahiri was born in London and grew up in Rhode Island. She received a B.A. in English literature from Barnard College and an M.A. in English, an M.A. in Creative Writing, an M.A. in Comparative Studies in Literature and the Arts, and a Ph.D. in Renaissance Studies from Boston University. Her first published collection of short stories, Interpreter of Maladies, *was a tremendous success and won the 2000 Pulitzer Prize for fiction and the PEN/Hemingway Award. Her first novel,* The Namesake, *was published in 2003. The following short story was originally published in* The New Yorker *in May 2004.*

Hell-Heaven

Pranab Chakraborty wasn't technically my father's younger brother. He was a fellow-Bengali from Calcutta who had washed up on the barren shores of my parents' social life in the early seventies, when they lived in a rented apartment in Central Square and could number their acquaintances on one hand. But I had no real uncles in America, and so I was taught to call him Pranab Kaku. Accordingly, he called my father Shyamal Da, always addressing him in the polite form, and he called my mother Boudi, which is how Bengalis are supposed to address an older brother's wife, instead of using her first name, Aparna. After Pranab Kaku was befriended by my parents, he confessed that on the day we first met him he had followed my mother and me for the better part of an afternoon around the streets of Cambridge, where she and I tended to roam after I got out of school. He had trailed behind us along Massachusetts Avenue, and in and out of the Harvard Coop, where my mother liked to look at discounted housewares. He wandered with us into Harvard Yard, where my mother often sat on the grass on pleasant days and watched the stream of students and professors filing busily along the paths, until, finally, as we were climbing the steps to Widener Library so that I could use the bathroom, he tapped my mother on the shoulder and inquired, in English, if she might be a Bengali. The answer to his question was clear, given that my mother was wearing the red and white bangles unique to Bengali married women, and a common Tangail sari, and had a thick stem of vermillion powder in the center parting of her hair, and the full round face and large dark eyes that are so typical of Bengali women. He noticed the two or three safety pins she wore fastened to the thin gold bangles that were behind the red and white ones, which she would use to replace a missing hook on a blouse or to draw a string through a petticoat at a moment's notice, a practice he associated strictly with his mother and sisters and aunts in Calcutta. Moreover, Pranab Kaku had overheard my mother speaking to me in Bengali, telling me that I couldn't buy an issue of *Archie* at the Coop. But back then, he also confessed, he was so new to America that he took nothing for granted, and doubted even the obvious.

My parents and I had lived in Central Square for three years prior to that day; before that, we had lived in Berlin, where I was born and where my father had finished his training in microbiology before accepting a position as a researcher at Mass General, and before Berlin my mother and father had lived in India, where they had been strangers to each other, and where their marriage had been arranged. Central Square is the first place I can recall living, and in my memories of our apartment, in a dark-brown shingled house on Ashburton Place, Pranab Kaku is always there. According to the story he liked to recall often, my mother invited him to accompany us back to our apartment that very afternoon, and prepared tea for the two of them; then, after learning that he had not had a proper Bengali meal in more than three months, she served him the leftover curried mackerel and rice that we had eaten for dinner the night before. He remained into the evening, for a second dinner, after my father got home, and after that he showed up for dinner almost every night, occupying the fourth chair at our square Formica kitchen table, and becoming a part of our family in practice as well as in name.

He was from a wealthy family in Calcutta and had never had to do so much as pour himself a glass of water before moving to America, to study engineering at M.I.T. Life as a graduate student in Boston was a cruel shock, and in his first month he lost nearly twenty pounds. He had arrived in January, in the middle of a snowstorm, and at the end of a week he had packed his bags and gone to Logan, prepared to abandon the opportunity he'd worked toward all his life, only to change his mind at the last minute. He was living on Trowbridge Street in the home of a divorced woman with two young children who were always screaming and crying. He rented a room in the attic and was permitted to use the kitchen only at specified times of the day, and instructed always to wipe down the stove with Windex and a sponge. My parents agreed that it was a terrible situation, and if they'd had a bedroom to spare they would have offered it to him. Instead, they welcomed him to our meals, and opened up our apartment to him at any time, and soon it was there he went between classes and on his days off, always leaving behind some vestige of himself: a nearly finished pack of cigarettes, a newspaper, a piece of mail he had not bothered to open, a sweater he had taken off and forgotten in the course of his stay.

I remember vividly the sound of his exuberant laughter and the sight of his lanky body slouched or sprawled on the dull, mismatched furniture that had come with our apartment. He had a striking face, with a high forehead and a thick mustache, and overgrown, untamed hair that my mother said made him look like the American hippies who were everywhere in those days. His long legs jiggled rapidly up and down wherever he sat, and his elegant hands trembled when he held a cigarette between his fingers, tapping the ashes into a teacup that my mother began to set aside for this exclusive purpose. Though he was a scientist by training, there was nothing rigid or predictable or orderly about him. He always seemed to be starving, walking through the door and announcing that he hadn't had lunch, and then he would eat ravenously, reaching behind my mother to steal cutlets as she was frying them, before she had a chance to set them properly on a plate with red-onion salad. In private, my parents remarked that he was a brilliant student, a star at Jadavpur who had come to M.I.T. with an impressive assistantship, but Pranab Kaku was cavalier about his classes, skipping them with frequency. "These Americans are learning equations I knew at Usha's age," he would complain. He was stunned that my second-grade teacher didn't assign any homework, and that at the age of seven I hadn't yet been taught square roots or the concept of pi.

He appeared without warning, never phoning beforehand but simply knocking on the door the way people did in Calcutta and calling out "Boudi!" as he waited for my mother to let him in. Before we met him, I would return from school and find my mother with her purse in her lap and her trenchcoat on, desperate to escape the apartment where she had spent the day alone. But now I would find her in the kitchen, rolling out dough for *luchis,* which she normally made only on Sundays for my father and me, or putting up new curtains she'd bought at Woolworth's. I did not know, back then, that Pranab Kaku's visits were what my mother looked forward to all day, that she changed into a new sari and combed her hair in anticipation of his arrival, and that she planned, days in advance, the snacks she would serve him with such nonchalance. That she lived for the moment she heard him call out "Boudi!" from the porch, and that she was in a foul humor on the days he didn't materialize.

It must have pleased her that I looked forward to his visits as well. He showed me card tricks and an optical illusion in which he appeared to be severing his own thumb with enormous struggle and strength, and taught me to memorize multiplication tables well before I had to learn them in school. His hobby was photography. He owned an expensive camera that required thought before you pressed the shutter, and I quickly became his favorite subject, round-faced, missing teeth, my thick bangs in need of a trim. They are still the pictures of myself I like best, for they convey that confidence of youth I no longer possess, especially in front of a camera. I remember having to run back and forth in Harvard Yard as he stood with the camera, trying to capture me in motion, or posing on the steps of university buildings and on the street and against the trunks of trees. There is only one photograph in which my mother appears; she is holding me as I sit straddling her lap, her head tilted toward me, her hands pressed to my ears as if to prevent me from hearing something. In that picture, Pranab Kaku's shadow, his two arms raised at angles to hold the camera to his face, hovers in the corner of the frame, his darkened, featureless shape superimposed on one side of my mother's body. It was always the three of us. I was always there when he visited. It would have been inappropriate for my mother to receive him in the apartment alone; this was something that went without saying.

They had in common all the things she and my father did not: a love of music, film, leftist politics, poetry. They were from the same neighborhood in North Calcutta, their family homes within walking distance, the façades familiar to them once the exact locations were described. They knew the same shops, the same bus and tram routes, the same holes-in-the-wall for the best *jelabis* and *moghlai parathas*. My father, on the other hand, came from a suburb twenty miles outside Calcutta, an area that my mother considered the wilderness, and even in her bleakest hours of homesickness she was grateful that my father had at least spared her a life in the stern house of her in-laws, where she would have had to keep her head covered with the end of her sari at all times and use an outhouse that was nothing but a raised platform with a hole, and where, in the rooms, there was not a single painting hanging on the walls. Within a few weeks, Pranab Kaku had brought his reel-to-reel over to our apartment, and he played for my mother medley after medley of songs from the Hindi films of their youth. They were cheerful songs of courtship, which transformed the quiet life in our apartment and transported my mother back to the world she'd left behind in order to marry my father. She and Pranab Kaku would try to recall which scene in which movie the songs were from, who the actors were and what they were wearing. My mother would describe Raj Kapoor and Nargis singing under umbrellas in the rain, or Dev Anand strumming a guitar on the beach in Goa. She and Pranab Kaku would argue passionately about these matters, raising their voices in playful combat, confronting each other in a way she and my father never did.

Because he played the part of a younger brother, she felt free to call him Pranab, whereas she never called my father by his first name. My father was thirty-seven then, nine years older than my mother. Pranab Kaku was twenty-five. My father was monkish by nature, a lover of silence and solitude. He had married my mother to placate his parents; they were willing to accept his desertion as long as he had a wife. He was wedded to his work, his research, and he existed in a shell that neither my mother nor I could penetrate. Conversation was a chore for him; it required an effort he preferred to expend at the lab. He disliked excess in anything, voiced no cravings or needs apart from the frugal elements of his daily routine: cereal and tea in the mornings, a cup of tea after he got home, and two different vegetable dishes every night with dinner. He did not eat with the reckless appetite of Pranab Kaku. My father had a survivor's mentality. From time to time, he liked to remark, in mixed company and often with no relevant provocation, that starving Russians under Stalin had resorted to eating the glue off the back of their wallpaper. One might think that he would have felt slightly jealous, or at the very least suspicious, about the regularity of Pranab Kaku's visits and the effect they had on my mother's behavior and mood. But my guess is that my father was grateful to Pranab Kaku for the companionship he provided, freed from the sense of responsibility he must have felt for forcing her to leave India, and relieved, perhaps, to see her happy for a change.

In the summer, Pranab Kaku bought a navy-blue Volkswagen Beetle, and began to take my mother and me for drives through Boston and Cambridge, and soon outside the city, flying down the highway. He would take us to India Tea and Spices in Watertown, and one time he drove us all the way to New Hampshire to look at the mountains. As the weather grew hotter, we started going, once or twice a week, to Walden Pond. My mother always prepared a picnic of hard-boiled eggs and cucumber sandwiches, and talked fondly about the winter picnics of her youth, grand expeditions with fifty of her relatives, all taking the train into the West Bengal countryside. Pranab Kaku listened to these stories with interest, absorbing the vanishing details of her past. He did not turn a deaf ear to her nostalgia, like my father, or listen uncomprehending, like me. At Walden Pond, Pranab Kaku would coax my mother through the woods, and lead her down the steep slope to the water's edge. She would unpack the picnic things and sit and watch us as we swam. His chest was matted with thick dark hair, all the way to his waist. He was an odd sight, with his pole-thin legs and a small, flaccid belly, like an otherwise svelte woman who has had a baby and not bothered to tone her abdomen. "You're making me fat, Boudi," he would complain after gorging himself on my mother's cooking. He swam noisily, clumsily, his head always above the water, he didn't know how to blow bubbles or hold his breath, as I had learned in swimming class. Wherever we went, any stranger would have naturally assumed that Pranab Kaku was my father, that my mother was his wife.

It is clear to me now that my mother was in love with him. He wooed her as no other man had, with the innocent affection of a brother-in-law. In my mind, he was just a family member, a cross between an uncle and a much older brother, for in certain respects my parents sheltered and cared for him in much the same way they cared for me. He was respectful of my father, always seeking his advice about making a life in the West, about setting up a bank account and getting a job, and deferring to his opinions about Kissinger and Watergate. Occasionally, my mother would tease him about women, asking about female Indian students at M.I.T., or showing him pictures of her younger cousins in India. "What do you think of her?" she would ask. "Isn't she pretty?" She knew that she could never have Pranab Kaku for herself, and I suppose it was her attempt to keep him in the family. But, most important, in the beginning he was totally dependent on her, needing her for those months in a way my father never did in the whole history of their marriage. He brought to my mother the first and, I suspect, the only pure happiness she ever felt. I don't think even my birth made her as happy. I was evidence of her marriage to my father, an assumed consequence of the life she had been raised to lead. But Pranab Kaku was different. He was the one totally unanticipated pleasure in her life.

In the fall of 1974, Pranab Kaku met a student at Radcliffe named Deborah, an American, and she began to accompany him to our house. I called Deborah by her first name, as my parents did, but Pranab Kaku taught her to call my father Shyamal Da and my mother Boudi, something with which Deborah gladly complied. Before they came to dinner for the first time, I asked my mother, as she was straightening up the living room, if I ought to address her as Deborah Kakima, turning her into an aunt as I had turned Pranab into an uncle. "What's the point?" my mother said, looking back at me sharply. "In a few weeks, the fun will be over and she'll leave him." And yet Deborah remained by his side, attending the weekend parties that Pranab Kaku and my parents were becoming more involved with, gatherings that were exclusively Bengali with the exception of her. Deborah was very tall, taller than both my parents and nearly as tall as Pranab Kaku. She wore her long brass-colored hair center-parted, as my mother did, but it was gathered into a low ponytail instead of a braid, or it spilled messily over her shoulders and down her back in a way that my mother considered indecent. She wore small silver spectacles and not a trace of makeup, and she studied philosophy. I found her utterly beautiful, but according to my mother she had spots on her face, and her hips were too small.

For a while, Pranab Kaku still showed up once a week for dinner on his own, mostly asking my mother what she thought of Deborah. He sought her approval, telling her that Deborah was the daughter of professors at Boston College, that her father published poetry, and that both her parents had Ph.D.s. When he wasn't around, my mother complained about Deborah's visits, about having to make the food less spicy even though Deborah said she liked spicy food, and feeling embarrassed to put a fried fish head in the dal. Pranab Kaku taught Deborah to say *khub bhalo* and *aacha* and to pick up certain foods with her fingers instead of with a fork. Sometimes they ended up feeding each other, allowing their fingers to linger in each other's mouth, causing my parents to look down at their plates and wait for the moment to pass. At larger gatherings, they kissed and held hands in front of everyone, and when they were out of earshot my mother would talk to the other Bengali women. "He used to be so different. I don't understand how a person can change so suddenly. It's just hell-heaven, the difference," she would say, always using the English words for her self-concocted, backward metaphor.

The more my mother began to resent Deborah's visits, the more I began to anticipate them. I fell in love with Deborah, the way young girls often fall in love with women who are not their mothers. I loved her serene gray eyes, the ponchos and denim wrap skirts and sandals she wore, her straight hair that she let me manipulate into all sorts of silly styles. I longed for her casual appearance; my mother insisted whenever there was a gathering that I wear one of my ankle-length, faintly Victorian dresses, which she referred to as maxis, and have party hair, which meant taking a strand from either side of my head and joining them with a barrette at the back. At parties, Deborah would, eventually, politely slip away, much to the relief of the Bengali women with whom she was expected to carry on a conversation, and she would play with me. I was older than all my parents' friends' children, but with Deborah I had a companion. She knew all about the books I read, about Pippi Longstocking and Anne of Green Gables. She gave me the sorts of gifts my parents had neither the money nor the inspiration to buy: a large book of Grimms' fairy tales with watercolor illustrations on thick, silken pages, wooden puppets with hair fashioned from yarn. She told me about her family, three older sisters and two brothers, the youngest of whom was closer to my age than to hers. Once, after visiting her parents, she brought back three Nancy Drews, her name written in a girlish hand at the top of the first page, and an old toy she'd had, a small paper theatre set with interchangeable backdrops, the exterior of a castle and a ballroom and an open field. Deborah and I spoke freely in English, a language in which, by that age, I expressed myself more easily than Bengali, which I was required to speak at home. Sometimes she asked me how to say this or that in Bengali; once, she asked me what *asobbho* meant. I hesitated, then told her it was what my mother called me if I had done something extremely naughty, and Deborah's face clouded. I felt protective of her, aware that she was unwanted, that she was resented, aware of the nasty things people said.

Outings in the Volkswagen now involved the four of us, Deborah in the front, her hand over Pranab Kaku's while it rested on the gearshift, my mother and I in the back. Soon, my mother began coming up with reasons to excuse herself, headaches and incipient colds, and so I became part of a new triangle. To my surprise, my mother allowed me to go with them, to the Museum of Fine Arts and the Public Garden and the aquarium. She was waiting for the affair to end, for Deborah to break Pranab Kaku's heart and for him to return to us, scarred and penitent. I saw no sign of their relationship foundering. Their open affection for each other, their easily expressed happiness, was a new and romantic thing to me. Having me in the back seat allowed Pranab Kaku and Deborah to practice for the future, to try on the idea of a family of their own. Countless photographs were taken of me and Deborah, of me sitting on Deborah's lap, holding her hand, kissing her on the cheek. We exchanged what I believed were secret smiles, and in those moments I felt that she understood me better than anyone else in the world. Anyone would have said that Deborah would make an excellent mother one day. But my mother refused to acknowledge such a thing. I did not know at the time that my mother allowed me to go off with Pranab Kaku and Deborah because she was pregnant for the fifth time since my birth, and was so sick and exhausted and fearful of losing another baby that she slept most of the day. After ten weeks, she miscarried once again, and was advised by her doctor to stop trying.

By summer, there was a diamond on Deborah's left hand, something my mother had never been given. Because his own family lived so far away, Pranab Kaku came to the house alone one day, to ask for my parents' blessing before giving her the ring. He showed us the box, opening it and taking out the diamond nestled inside. "I want to see how it looks on someone," he said, urging my mother to try it on, but she refused. I was the one who stuck out my hand, feeling the weight of the ring suspended at the base of my finger. Then he asked for a second thing: he wanted my parents to write to his parents, saying that they had met Deborah and that they thought highly of her. He was nervous, naturally, about telling his family that he intended to marry an American girl. He had told his parents all about us, and at one point my parents had received a letter from them, expressing appreciation for taking such good care of their son and for giving him a proper home in America. "It needn't be long," Pranab Kaku said. "Just a few lines. They'll accept it more easily if it comes from you." My father thought neither ill nor well of Deborah, never commenting or criticizing as my mother did, but he assured Pranab Kaku that a letter of endorsement would be on its way to Calcutta by the end of the week. My mother nodded her assent, but the following day I saw the teacup Pranab Kaku had used all this time as an ashtray in the kitchen garbage can, in pieces, and three Band-Aids taped to my mother's hand.

Pranab Kaku's parents were horrified by the thought of their only son marrying an American woman, and a few weeks later our telephone rang in the middle of the night: it was Mr. Chakraborty telling my father that they could not possibly bless such a marriage, that it was out of the question, that if Pranab Kaku dared to marry Deborah he would no longer acknowledge him as a son. Then his wife got on the phone, asking to speak to my mother, and attacked her as if they were intimate, blaming my mother for allowing the affair to develop. She said that they had already chosen a wife for him in Calcutta, that he'd left for America with the understanding that he'd go back after he had finished his studies, and marry this girl. They had bought the neighboring flat in their building for Pranab and his betrothed, and it was sitting empty, waiting for his return. "We thought we could trust you, and yet you have betrayed us so deeply," his mother said, taking out her anger on a stranger in a way she could not with her son. "Is this what happens to people in America?" For Pranab Kaku's sake, my mother defended the engagement, telling his mother that Deborah was a polite girl from a decent family. Pranab Kaku's parents pleaded with mine to talk him out of the engagement, but my father refused, deciding that it was not their place to get embroiled in a situation that had nothing to do with them. "We are not his parents," he told my mother. "We can tell him they don't approve but nothing more." And so my parents told Pranab Kaku nothing about how his parents had berated them, and blamed them, and threatened to disown Pranab Kaku, only that they had refused to give him their blessing. In the face of this refusal, Pranab Kaku shrugged. "I don't care. Not everyone can be as open-minded as you," he told my parents. "Your blessing is blessing enough."

After the engagement, Pranab Kaku and Deborah began drifting out of our lives. They moved in together, to an apartment in Boston, in the South End, a part of the city my parents considered unsafe. We moved as well, to a house in Natick. Though my parents had bought the house, they occupied it as if they were still tenants, touching up scuff marks with leftover paint and reluctant to put holes in the walls, and every afternoon when the sun shone through the living-room window my mother closed the blinds so that our new furniture would not fade. A few weeks before the wedding, my parents invited Pranab Kaku to the house alone, and my mother prepared a special meal to mark the end of his bachelorhood. It would be the only Bengali aspect of the wedding; the rest of it would be strictly American, with a cake and a minister and Deborah in a long white dress and veil. There is a photograph of the dinner, taken by my father, the only picture, to my knowledge, in which my mother and Pranab Kaku appear together. The picture is slightly blurry; I remember Pranab Kaku explaining to my father how to work the camera, and so he is captured looking up from the kitchen table and the elaborate array of food my mother had prepared in his honor, his mouth open, his long arm outstretched and his finger pointing, instructing my father how to read the light meter or some such thing. My mother stands beside him, one hand placed on top of his head in a gesture of blessing, the first and last time she was to touch him in her life. "She will leave him," my mother told her friends afterward. "He is throwing his life away."

The wedding was at a church in Ipswich, with a reception at a country club. It was going to be a small ceremony, which my parents took to mean one or two hundred people as opposed to three or four hundred. My mother was shocked that fewer than thirty people had been invited, and she was more perplexed than honored that, of all the Bengalis Pranab Kaku knew by then, we were the only ones on the list. At the wedding, we sat, like the other guests, first on the hard wooden pews of the church and then at a long table that had been set up for lunch. Though we were the closest thing Pranab Kaku had to a family that day, we were not included in the group photographs that were taken on the grounds of the country club, with Deborah's parents and grandparents and her many siblings, and neither my mother nor my father got up to make a toast. My mother did not appreciate the fact that Deborah had made sure that my parents, who did not eat beef, were given fish instead of filet mignon like everyone else. She kept speaking in Bengali, complaining about the formality of the proceedings, and the fact that Pranab Kaku, wearing a tuxedo, barely said a word to us because he was too busy leaning over the shoulders of his new American in-laws as he circled the table. As usual, my father said nothing in response to my mother's commentary, quietly and methodically working though his meal, his fork and knife occasionally squeaking against the surface of the china, because he was accustomed to eating with his hands. He cleared his plate and then my mother's, for she had pronounced the food inedible, and then he announced that he had overeaten and had a stomach ache. The only time my mother forced a smile was when Deborah appeared behind her chair, kissing her on the cheek and asking if we were enjoying ourselves. When the dancing started, my parents remained at the table, drinking tea, and after two or three songs they decided that it was time for us to go home, my mother shooting me looks to that effect across the room, where I was dancing in a circle with Pranab Kaku and Deborah and the other children at the wedding. I wanted to stay, and when, reluctantly, I walked over to where my parents sat Deborah followed me. "Boudi, let Usha stay. She's having such a good time," she said to my mother. "Lots of people will be heading back your way, someone can drop her off in a little while." But my mother said no, I had had plenty of fun already, and forced me to put on my coat over my long puff-sleeved dress. As we drove home from the wedding I told my mother, for the first but not the last time in my life, that I hated her.

The following year, we received a birth announcement from the Chakrabortys, a picture of twin girls, which my mother did not paste into an album or display on the refrigerator door. The girls were named Srabani and Sabitri, but were called Bonny and Sara. Apart from a thank-you card for our wedding gift, it was their only communication; we were not invited to the new house in Marblehead, bought after Pranab Kaku got a high-paying job at Stone & Webster. For a while, my parents and their friends continued to invite the Chakrabortys to gatherings, but because they never came, or left after staying only an hour, the invitations stopped. Their absences were attributed, by my parents and their circle, to Deborah, and it was universally agreed that she had stripped Pranab Kaku not only of his origins but of his independence. She was the enemy, he was her prey, and their example was invoked as a warning, and as vindication, that mixed marriages were a doomed enterprise. Occasionally, they surprised everyone, appearing at a *pujo* for a few hours with their two identical little girls who barely looked Bengali and spoke only English and were being raised so differently from me and most of the other children. They were not taken to Calcutta every summer, they did not have parents who were clinging to another way of life and exhorting their children to do the same. Because of Deborah, they were exempt from all that, and for this reason I envied them. "Usha, look at you, all grown up and so pretty," Deborah would say whenever she saw me, rekindling, if only for a minute, our bond of years before. She had cut off her beautiful long hair by then, and had a bob. "I bet you'll be old enough to babysit soon," she would say. "I'll call you—the girls would love that." But she never did.

I began to grow out of my girlhood, entering middle school and developing crushes on the American boys in my class. The crushes amounted to nothing; in spite of Deborah's compliments, I was always overlooked at that age. But my mother must have picked up on something, for she forbade me to attend the dances that were held the last Friday of every month in the school cafeteria, and it was an unspoken law that I was not allowed to date. "Don't think you'll get away with marrying an American, the way Pranab Kaku did," she would say from time to time. I was thirteen, the thought of marriage irrelevant to my life. Still, her words upset me, and I felt her grip on me tighten. She would fly into a rage when I told her I wanted to start wearing a bra, or if I wanted to go to Harvard Square with a friend. In the middle of our arguments, she often conjured Deborah as her antithesis, the sort of woman she refused to be. "If *she* were your mother, she would let you do whatever you wanted, because she wouldn't care. Is that what you want, Usha, a mother who doesn't care?" When I began menstruating, the summer before I started ninth grade, my mother gave me a speech, telling me that I was to let no boy touch me, and then she asked if I knew how a woman became pregnant. I told her what I had been taught in science, about the sperm fertilizing the egg, and then she asked if I knew how, exactly, that happened. I saw the terror in her eyes and so, though I knew that aspect of procreation as well, I lied, and told her it hadn't been explained to us.

I began keeping other secrets from her, evading her with the aid of my friends. I told her I was sleeping over at a friend's when really I went to parties, drinking beer and allowing boys to kiss me and fondle my breasts and press their erections against my hip as we lay groping on a sofa or the back seat of a car. I began to pity my mother, the older I got, the more I saw what a desolate life she led. She had never worked, and during the day she watched soap operas to pass the time. Her only job, every day, was to clean and cook for my father and me. We rarely went to restaurants, my father always pointing out, even in cheap ones, how expensive they were compared with eating at home. When my mother complained to him about how much she hated life in the suburbs and how lonely she felt, he said nothing to placate her. "If you are so unhappy, go back to Calcutta," he would offer, making it clear that their separation would not affect him one way or the other. I began to take my cues from my father in dealing with her, isolating her doubly. When she screamed at me for talking too long on the telephone, or for staying too long in my room, I learned to scream back, telling her that she was pathetic, that she knew nothing about me, and it was clear to us both that I had stopped needing her, definitively and abruptly, just as Pranab Kaku had.

Then, the year before I went off to college, my parents and I were invited to the Chakrabortys' home for Thanksgiving. We were not the only guests from my parents' old Cambridge crowd; it turned out that Pranab Kaku and Deborah wanted to have a sort of reunion of all the people they had been friendly with back then. Normally, my parents did not celebrate Thanksgiving; the ritual of a large sit-down dinner and the foods that one was supposed to eat was lost on them. They treated it as if it were Memorial Day or Veterans Day—just another holiday in the American year. But we drove out to Marblehead, to an impressive stone-faced house with a semicircular gravel driveway clogged with cars. The house was a short walk from the ocean; on our way, we had driven by the harbor overlooking the cold, glittering Atlantic, and when we stepped out of the car we were greeted by the sound of gulls and waves. Most of the living-room furniture had been moved to the basement, and extra tables joined to the main one to form a giant U. They were covered with tablecloths, set with white plates and silverware, and had centerpieces of gourds. I was struck by the toys and dolls that were everywhere, dogs that shed long yellow hairs on everything, all the photographs of Bonny and Sara and Deborah decorating the walls, still more plastering the refrigerator door. Food was being prepared when we arrived, something my mother always frowned upon, the kitchen a chaos of people and smells and enormous dirtied bowls.

Deborah's family, whom we remembered dimly from the wedding, was there, her parents and her brothers and sisters and their husbands and wives and boyfriends and babies. Her sisters were in their thirties, but, like Deborah, they could have been mistaken for college students, wearing jeans and clogs and fisherman sweaters, and her brother Matty, with whom I had danced in a circle at the wedding, was now a freshman at Amherst, with wide-set green eyes and wispy brown hair and a complexion that reddened easily. As soon as I saw Deborah's siblings, joking with one another as they chopped and stirred things in the kitchen, I was furious with my mother for making a scene before we left the house and forcing me to wear a shalwar kameez. I knew they assumed, from my clothing, that I had more in common with the other Bengalis than with them. But Deborah insisted on including me, setting me to work peeling apples with Matty, and out of my parents' sight I was given beer to drink. When the meal was ready, we were told where to sit, in an alternating boy-girl formation that made the Bengalis uncomfortable. Bottles of wine were lined up on the table. Two turkeys were brought out, one stuffed with sausage and one without. My mouth watered at the food, but I knew that afterward, on our way home, my mother would complain that it was all tasteless and bland. "Impossible," my mother said, shaking her hand over the top of her glass when someone tried to pour her a little wine.

Deborah's father, Gene, got up to say grace, and asked everyone at the table to join hands. He bowed his head and closed his eyes. "Dear Lord, we thank you today for the food we are about to receive," he began. My parents were seated next to each other, and I was stunned to see that they complied, that my father's brown fingers lightly clasped my mother's pale ones. I noticed Matty seated on the other side of the room, and saw him glancing at me as his father spoke. After the chorus of amens, Gene raised his glass and said, "Forgive me, but I never thought I'd have the opportunity to say this: Here's to Thanksgiving with the Indians." Only a few people laughed at the joke.

Then Pranab Kaku stood up and thanked everyone for coming. He was relaxed from alcohol, his once wiry body beginning to thicken. He started to talk sentimentally about his early days in Cambridge, and then suddenly he recounted the story of meeting me and my mother for the first time, telling the guests about how he had followed us that afternoon. The people who did not know us laughed, amused by the description of the encounter, and by Pranab Kaku's desperation. He walked around the room to where my mother was sitting and draped a lanky arm around her shoulder, forcing her, for a brief moment, to stand up. "This woman," he declared, pulling her close to his side, "this woman hosted my first real Thanksgiving in America. It might have been an afternoon in May, but that first meal at Boudi's table was Thanksgiving to me. If it weren't for that meal, I would have gone back to Calcutta." My mother looked away, embarrassed. She was thirty-eight, already going gray, and she looked closer to my father's age than to Pranab Kaku's; regardless of his waistline, he retained his handsome, carefree looks. Pranab Kaku went back to his place at the head of the table, next to Deborah, and concluded, "And if that had been the case I'd have never met you, my darling," and he kissed her on the mouth in front of everyone, to much applause, as if it were their wedding day all over again.

After the turkey, smaller forks were distributed and orders were taken for three different kinds of pie, written on small pads by Deborah's sisters, as if they were waitresses. After dessert, the dogs needed to go out, and Pranab Kaku volunteered to take them. "How about a walk on the beach?" he suggested, and Deborah's side of the family agreed that that was an excellent idea. None of the Bengalis wanted to go, preferring to sit with their tea and cluster together, at last, at one end of the room, speaking freely after the forced chitchat with the Americans during the meal. Matty came over and sat in the chair beside me that was now empty, encouraging me to join the walk. When I hesitated, pointing to my inappropriate clothes and shoes but also aware of my mother's silent fury at the sight of us together, he said, "I'm sure Deb can lend you something." So I went upstairs, where Deborah gave me a pair of her jeans and a thick sweater and some sneakers, so that I looked like her and her sisters.

She sat on the edge of her bed, watching me change, as if we were girlfriends, and she asked if I had a boyfriend. When I told her no, she said, "Matty thinks you're cute."

"He told you?"

"No, but I can tell."

As I walked back downstairs, emboldened by this information, in the jeans I'd had to roll up and in which I felt finally like myself, I noticed my mother lift her eyes from her teacup and stare at me, but she said nothing, and off I went, with Pranab Kaku and his dogs and his in-laws, along a road and then down some steep wooden steps to the water. Deborah and one of her sisters stayed behind, to begin the cleanup and see to the needs of those who remained. Initially, we all walked together, in a single row across the sand, but then I noticed Matty hanging back, and so the two of us trailed behind, the distance between us and the others increasing. We began flirting, talking of things I no longer remember, and eventually we wandered into a rocky inlet and Matty fished a joint out of his pocket. We turned our backs to the wind and smoked it, our cold fingers touching in the process, our lips pressed to the same damp section of the rolling paper. At first I didn't feel any effect, but then, listening to him talk about the band he was in, I was aware that his voice sounded miles away, and that I had the urge to laugh, even though what he was saying was not terribly funny. It felt as if we were apart from the group for hours, but when we wandered back to the sand we could still see them, walking out onto a rocky promontory to watch the sun set. It was dark by the time we all headed back to the house, and I dreaded seeing my parents while I was still high. But when we got there Deborah told me that my parents, feeling tired, had left, agreeing to let someone drive me home later. A fire had been lit and I was told to relax and have more pie as the leftovers were put away and the living room slowly put back in order. Of course, it was Matty who drove me home, and sitting in my parents' driveway I kissed him, at once thrilled and terrified that my mother might walk onto the lawn in her nightgown and discover us. I gave Matty my phone number, and for a few weeks I thought of him constantly, and hoped foolishly that he would call.

In the end, my mother was right, and fourteen years after that Thanksgiving, after twenty-three years of marriage, Pranab Kaku and Deborah got divorced. It was he who had strayed, falling in love with a married Bengali woman, destroying two families in the process. The other woman was someone my parents knew, though not very well. Deborah was in her forties by then, Bonny and Sara away at college. In her shock and grief, it was my mother whom Deborah turned to, calling and weeping into the phone. Somehow, through all the years, she had continued to regard us as quasi in-laws, sending flowers when my grandparents died, and giving me a compact edition of the O.E.D. as a college-graduation present. "You knew him so well. How could he do something like this?" Deborah asked my mother. And then, "Did you know anything about it?" My mother answered truthfully that she did not. Their hearts had been broken by the same man, only my mother's had long ago mended, and in an odd way, as my parents approached their old age, she and my father had grown fond of each other, out of habit if nothing else. I believe my absence from the house, once I left for college, had something to do with this, because over the years, when I visited, I noticed a warmth between my parents that had not been there before, a quiet teasing, a solidarity, a concern when one of them fell ill. My mother and I had also made peace; she had accepted the fact that I was not only her daughter but a child of America as well. Slowly, she accepted that I dated one American man, and then another, and then yet another, that I slept with them, and even that I lived with one though we were not married. She welcomed my boyfriends into our home and when things didn't work out she told me I would find someone better. After years of being idle, she decided, when she turned fifty, to get a degree in library science at a nearby university.

On the phone, Deborah admitted something that surprised my mother: that all these years she had felt hopelessly shut out of a part of Pranab Kaku's life. "I was so horribly jealous of you back then, for knowing him, understanding him in a way I never could. He turned his back on his family, on all of your really, but I still felt threatened. I could never get over that." She told my mother that she had tried, for years, to get Pranab Kaku to reconcile with his parents, and that she had also encouraged him to maintain ties with other Bengalis, but he had resisted. It had been Deborah's idea to invite us to their Thanksgiving; ironically, the other woman had been there, too. "I hope you don't blame me for taking him away from your lives, Boudi. I always worried that you did."

My mother assured Deborah that she blamed her for nothing. She confessed nothing to Deborah about her own jealousy of decades before, only that she was sorry for what had happened, that it was a sad and terrible thing for their family. She did not tell Deborah that a few weeks after Pranab Kaku's wedding, while I was at a Girl Scout meeting and my father was at work, she had gone through the house, gathering up all the safety pins that lurked in drawers and tins, and adding them to the few fastened to her bracelets. When she'd found enough, she pinned them to her sari one by one, attaching the front piece to the layer of material underneath, so that no one would be able to pull the garment off her body. Then she took a can of lighter fluid and a box of kitchen matches and stepped outside, into our chilly back yard, which was full of leaves needing to be raked. Over her sari she was wearing a knee-length lilac trenchcoat, and to any neighbor she must have looked as though she'd simply stepped out for some fresh air. She opened up the coat and removed the tip from the can of lighter fluid and doused herself, then buttoned and belted the coat. She walked over to the garbage barrel behind our house and disposed of the fluid, then returned to the middle of the yard with the box of matches in her coat pocket. For nearly an hour she stood there, looking at our house, trying to work up the courage to strike a match. It was not I who saved her, or my father, but our next-door neighbor, Mrs.

Holcomb, with whom my mother had never been particularly friendly. She came out to rake the leaves in her yard, calling out to my mother and remarking how beautiful the sunset was. "I see you've been admiring it for a while now," she said. My mother agreed, and then she went back into the house. By the time my father and I came home in the early evening, she was in the kitchen boiling rice for our dinner, as if it were any other day.

My mother told Deborah none of this. It was to me that she confessed, after my own heart was broken by a man I'd hoped to marry.

(2004)

QUESTIONS FOR CRITICAL THINKING AND WRITING

Experience

1. To what extent were you able to enter into the Bengali world of the story? How did you respond to the Bengali names, details of dress, and food?
2. How do you respond to the story's final details about the narrator's mother's near suicide? Explain.

Interpretation

3. What is the theme of the story? To what extent is the story about cultural differences—their reconcilability or irreconcilability? To what extent is the story about love, compatibility, disappointment, endurance, hope against the odds? Explain.
4. How is the narrator characterized? To what extent does she evidence signs of growth and change? Explain.
5. To what extent are details of clothing and food used symbolically or to foreshadow events? Which details of food and clothing seem symbolic? What do they represent?

Evaluation

6. What social and culture values come into conflict in the story? Which values appear to be less conflicted? Is one set of values seen as more admirable than another? Explain.
7. What judgments do the characters make about each other's choices? Whose judgments do you trust most and least? Explain.

Connection

8. Compare the marriage of the narrator's parents with the marriage described in Kay Boyle's "Astronomer's Wife."

Critical Thinking

9. Explain the significance of the story's title. Could the two words be reversed? Provide an alternative title, and explain its rationale.

CHAPTER EIGHT

A Selection of World Fiction

Fiction is like a spider's web, attached ever so slightly perhaps, but still attached to life at all four corners.

VIRGINIA WOOLF

In this section, we gather five stories from around the world. Each of these stories was either originally written in a language other than English or written by an author whose first language was not English. The stories are meant to give just a hint of the range of what is actually a vast outpouring of fiction, especially short stories, from all over the globe.

The stories collected here range from the realistic to the fantastic, from the humorous to the deadly serious, from the mundane to the mysterious. While the stories each convey a unique fictional world, their writers also convey something of the various cultural traditions from which they come.

As with the stories in other sections of *Literature,* these brief works of fiction speak to us across time and space, as well as across culture and history. As works of the imagination, they remind us of how infinitely various and unpredictable are the worlds of fiction.

CHINUA ACHEBE

[b. 1930]

Chinua Achebe was born in Nigeria in 1930. Although his native language is the African language Ibo, he writes in English, which he learned in his youth. His best-known novel in the West is Things Fall Apart *(1958) in which Achebe describes the conflict between the traditional customs embodied in African tribal culture and the encroachment of modern ways. His stories celebrate Ibo life by incorporating aspects of Ibo tribal culture, particularly its proverbs and values. He has taught in the West at the University of Connecticut and the University of Guelph in Ontario, Canada.*

Marriage Is a Private Affair

"Have you written to your dad yet?" asked Nene one afternoon as she sat with Nnaemeka in her room at 16 Kasanga Street, Lagos.

"No. I've been thinking about it. I think it's better to tell him when I get home on leave!"

"But why? Your leave is such a long way off yet—six whole weeks. He should be let into our happiness now."

Nnaemeka was silent for a while, and then began very slowly as if he groped for his words: "I wish I were sure it would be happiness to him."

"Of course it must," replied Nene, a little surprised. "Why shouldn't it?"

"You have lived in Lagos all your life, and you know very little about people in remote parts of the country."

"That's what you always say. But I don't believe anybody will be so unlike other people that they will be unhappy when their sons are engaged to marry."

"Yes. They are most unhappy if the engagement is not arranged by them. In our case it's worse—you are not even an Ibo."

This was said so seriously and so bluntly that Nene could not find speech immediately. In the cosmopolitan atmosphere of the city it had always seemed to her something of a joke that a person's tribe could determine whom he married.

At last she said, "You don't really mean that he will object to your marrying me simply on that account? I had always thought you Ibos were kindly disposed to other people."

"So we are. But when it comes to marriage, well, it's not quite so simple. And this," he added, "is not peculiar to the Ibos. If your father were alive and lived in the heart of Ibibio-land he would be exactly like my father."

"I don't know. But anyway, as your father is so fond of you, I'm sure he will forgive you soon enough. Come on then, be a good boy and send him a nice lovely letter . . ."

"It would not be wise to break the news to him by writing. A letter will bring it upon him with a shock. I'm quite sure about that."

"All right, honey, suit yourself. You know your father."

As Nnaemeka walked home that evening he turned over in his mind the different ways of overcoming his father's opposition, especially now that he had gone and found a girl for him. He had thought of showing his letter to Nene but decided on second thoughts not to, at least for the moment. He read it again when he got home and couldn't help smiling to himself. He remembered Ugoye quite well, an Amazon of a girl who used to beat up all the boys, himself included, on the way to the stream, a complete dunce at school.

> I have found a girl who will suit you admirably—Ugoye Nweke, the eldest daughter of our neighbour, Jacob Nweke. She has a proper Christian upbringing. When she stopped schooling some years ago her father (a man of sound judgment) sent her to live in the house of a pastor where she has received all the training a wife could need. Her Sunday School teacher has told me that she reads her Bible very fluently. I hope we shall begin negotiations when you come home in December.

On the second evening of his return from Lagos Nnaemeka sat with his father under a cassia tree. This was the old man's retreat where he went to read his Bible when the parching December sun had set and a fresh, reviving wind blew on the leaves.

"Father," began Nnaemeka suddenly, "I have come to ask forgiveness."

"Forgiveness? For what, my son?" he asked in amazement.

"It's about this marriage question?"

"Which marriage question."

"I can't—we must—I mean it is impossible for me to marry Nweke's daughter."

"Impossible? Why?" asked his father.

"I don't love her."

"Nobody said you did. Why should you?" he asked.

"Marriage today is different . . ."

"Look here, my son," interrupted his father, "nothing is different. What one looks for in a wife are a good character and a Christian background."

Nnaemeka saw there was no hope along the present line of argument.

"Moreover," he said, "I am engaged to marry another girl who has all of Ugoye's good qualities, and who . . ."

His father did not believe his ears. "What did you say?" he asked slowly and disconcertingly.

"She is a good Christian," his son went on, "and a teacher in a Girls' School in Lagos."

"Teacher, did you say? If you consider that a qualification for a good wife I should like to point out to you, Emeka, that no Christian woman should teach. St. Paul in his letter to the Corinthians says that women should keep silence." He rose slowly from his seat and paced forwards and backwards. This was his pet subject, and he condemned vehemently those church leaders who encouraged women to teach in their schools. After he had spent his emotion on a long homily he at last came back to his son's engagement, in a seemingly milder tone.

"Whose daughter is she, anyway?"

"She is Nene Atang."

"What!" All the mildness was gone again. "Did you say Neneataga, what does that mean?"

"Nene Atang from Calabar. She is the only girl I can marry." This was a very rash reply and Nnaemeka expected the storm to burst. But it did not. His father merely walked away into his room. This was most unexpected and perplexed Nnaemeka. His father's silence was infinitely more menacing than a flood of threatening speech. That night the old man did not eat.

When he sent for Nnaemeka a day later he applied all possible ways of dissuasion. But the young man's heart was hardened, and his father eventually gave him up as lost.

"I owe it to you, my son, as a duty to show you what is right and what is wrong. Whoever put this idea into your head might as well have cut your throat. It is Satan's work." He waved his son away.

"You will change your mind, Father, when you know Nene."

"I shall never see her," was the reply. From that night the father scarcely spoke to his son. He did not, however, cease hoping that he would realize how serious was the danger he was heading for. Day and night he put him in his prayers.

Nnaemeka, for his own part, was very deeply affected by his father's grief. But he kept hoping that it would pass away. If it had occurred to him that never in the history of his people had a man married a woman who spoke a different tongue, he might have been less optimistic. "It has never been heard," was the verdict of an old man speaking a few weeks later. In that short sentence he spoke for all of his people. This man had come with others to commiserate with Okeke when news went round about his son's behavior. By that time the son had gone back to Lagos.

"It has never been heard," said the old man again with a sad shake of his head.

"What did Our Lord say?" asked another gentleman. "Sons shall rise against their Fathers; it is there in the Holy Book."

"It is the beginning of the end," said another.

The discussion thus tending to become theological, Madubogwu, a highly practical man, brought it down once more to the ordinary level.

"Have you thought of consulting a native doctor about your son?" he asked Nnaemeka's father.

"He isn't sick," was the reply.

"What is he then? The boy's mind is diseased and only a good herbalist can bring him back to his right senses. The medicine he requires is *Amalile*, the same that women apply with success to recapture their husbands' straying affection."

"Madubogwu is right," said another gentleman. "This thing calls for medicine."

"I shall not call in a native doctor." Nnaemeka's father was known to be obstinately ahead of his more superstitious neighbors in these matters. "I will not be another Mrs. Ochuba. If my son wants to kill himself let him do it with his own hands. It is not for me to help him."

"But it was her fault," said Madubogwu. "She ought to have gone to an honest herbalist. She was a clever woman, nevertheless."

"She was a wicked murderess," said Jonathan who rarely argued with his neighbors because, he often said, they were incapable of reasoning. "The medicine was prepared for her husband, it was his name they called in its preparation and I am sure it would have been perfectly beneficial to him. It was wicked to put it into the herbalist's food, and say you were only trying it out."

Six months later, Nnaemeka was showing his young wife a short letter from his father:

> It amazes me that you could be so unfeeling as to send me your wedding picture. I would have sent it back. But on further thought I decided just to cut off your wife and send it back to

> you because I have nothing to do with her. How I wish that I had nothing to do with you either.

When Nene read through this letter and looked at the mutilated picture her eyes filled with tears, and she began to sob.

"Don't cry, my darling," said her husband. "He is essentially good-natured and will one day look more kindly on our marriage." But years passed and that one day did not come.

For eight years, Okeke would have nothing to do with his son, Nnaemeka. Only three times (when Nnaemeka asked to come home and spend his leave) did he write to him.

"I can't have you in my house," he replied on one occasion. "It can be of no interest to me where or how you spend your leave—or your life, for that matter."

The prejudice against Nnaemeka's marriage was not confined to his little village. In Lagos, especially among his people who worked there, it showed itself in a different way. Their women, when they met at their village meeting were not hostile to Nene. Rather, they paid her such excessive deference as to make her feel she was not one of them. But as time went on, Nene gradually broke through some of this prejudice and even began to make friends among them. Slowly and grudgingly they began to admit that she kept her home much better than most of them.

The story eventually got to the little village in the heart of the Ibo country that Nnaemeka and his young wife were a most happy couple. But his father was one of the few people who knew nothing about this. He always displayed so much temper whenever his son's name was mentioned that everyone avoided it in his presence. By a tremendous effort of will he had succeeded in pushing his son to the back of his mind. The strain had nearly killed him but he had persevered, and won.

Then one day he received a letter from Nene, and in spite of himself he began to glance through it perfunctorily until all of a sudden the expression on his face changed and he began to read more carefully.

> . . . Our two sons, from the day they learnt that they have a grandfather, have insisted on being taken to him. I find it impossible to tell them that you will not see them. I implore you to allow Nnaemeka to bring them home for a short time during his leave next month. I shall remain here in Lagos . . .

The old man at once felt the resolution he had built up over so many years falling in. He was telling himself that he must not give in. He tried to steel his heart against all emotional appeals. It was a reenactment of that other struggle. He leaned against a window and looked out. The sky was overcast with heavy black clouds and a high wind began to blow filling the air with dust and dry leaves. It was one of those rare occasions when even Nature takes a hand in a human fight. Very soon it began to rain, the first rain in the year. It came down in large sharp drops and was accompanied by the lightning and thunder which mark a change of season. Okeke was trying hard not to think of his two grandsons. But he knew he was now fighting a losing battle. He tried to hum a favorite hymn but the pattering of large rain drops on the roof broke up the tune. His mind immediately returned to the children. How could he shut his door against them? By a curious mental process he imagined them standing, sad and forsaken, under the harsh angry weather—shut out from his house.

That night he hardly slept, from remorse—and a vague fear that he might die without making it up to them.

(1972)

QUESTIONS FOR CRITICAL THINKING AND WRITING

Experience

1. Achebe writes about a marriage just outside his characters' immediate culture. To what extent does the experience of Nene and Nnaemeka reflect either your own experience or that of someone you know?
2. Consider Nnaemeka's relationship with his father. How similar is it to your own father–son relationship or a father–son relationship you have observed?

Interpretation

3. Describe the father. He criticizes his son for opposing cultural tradition. But does the father, either in the past or present of the story, break tribal tradition? Are he and his son more alike than he recognizes?
4. Consider the cultural tensions in the story. As part of your response, consider the father's discussion with his fellow villagers as well as the response to Nene in Lagos after her marriage.
5. Analyze the ironic dimension in the story. Consider, for instance, the "cosmopolitan atmosphere" of Lagos, the references to the Bible, and the father's having "persevered and won."

Evaluation

6. Identify the values of the father and the son. Does the author seem to endorse one set of values over the other?

Connection

7. Compare the father and the father–son relationship in "Marriage Is a Private Affair" with other fictional fathers (including father figures) and father–son relationships. You might consider those in stories and plays such as Baldwin's "Sonny's Blues" (in the next chapter) and Wilson's *Fences* (Chapter Twenty-Nine).

Critical Thinking

8. Invent two additional titles for Achebe's story. Explain the rationale for each of your alternative titles. Explain the significance of the title Achebe chose for this story.

JORGE LUIS BORGES
[1899–1986]

Borges' first language was English, though he was born in Buenos Aires, Argentina, and he wrote poetry and fiction in Spanish. Besides doing his own extensive writing, Borges anthologized Argentine literature and served as director of Argentina's National Library. His intricately plotted stories often explore philosophical themes, which frequently employ images of mirrors and mazes. Borges' poor eyesight eventuated in blindness, an occasional subject in his work. His most popular work includes the stories in his books Fictions *and* Labyrinths.

The Garden of Forking Paths

TRANSLATED BY DONALD YATES

On page 22 of Liddell Hart's *History of World War I* you will read that an attack against the Serre-Montauban line by thirteen British divisions (supported by 1,400 artillery pieces), planned for the 24th of July, 1916, had to be postponed until the morning of the 29th. The torrential rains, Captain Liddell Hart comments, caused this delay, an insignificant one, to be sure.

The following statement, dictated, reread and signed by Dr. Yu Tsun, former professor of English at the *Hochschule* at Tsingtao, throws an unsuspected light over the whole affair. The first two pages of the document are missing.

. . . and I hung up the receiver. Immediately afterwards, I recognized the voice that had answered in German. It was that of Captain Richard Madden. Madden's presence in Viktor Runeberg's apartment meant the end of our anxieties and—but this seemed, *or should have seemed,* very secondary to me—also the end of our lives. It meant that Runeberg had been arrested or murdered. Before the sun set on that day, I would encounter the same fate. Madden was implacable. Or rather, he was obliged to be so. An Irishman at the service of England, a man accused of laxity and perhaps of treason, how could he fail to seize and be thankful for such a miraculous opportunity: the discovery, capture, maybe even the death of two agents of the German Reich? I went up to my room; absurdly I locked the door and threw myself on my back on the narrow iron cot. Through the window I saw the familiar roofs and the cloud-shaded six o'clock sun. It seemed incredible to me that that day without premonitions or symbols should be the one of my inexorable death. In spite of my dead father, in spite of having been a child in a symmetrical garden of Hai Feng, was I—now—going to die?

Then I reflected that everything happens to a man precisely, precisely *now.* Centuries of centuries and only in the present do things happen; countless men in the air, on the face of the earth and the sea, and all that really is happening is happening to me . . . The almost intolerable recollection of Madden's horselike face banished these wanderings. In the midst of my hatred and terror (it means nothing to me now to speak of terror, now that I have mocked Richard Madden, now that my throat yearns for the noose) it occurred to me that the tumultuous and doubtless happy warrior did not suspect that I possessed the Secret. The name of the exact location of the new British artillery park on the River Ancre. A bird streaked across the gray sky and blindly I translated it into an airplane and that airplane into many (against the French sky) annihilating the artillery station with vertical bombs. If only my mouth, before a bullet shattered it, could cry out that secret name so it could be heard in Germany . . . My human voice was very weak. How might I make it carry to the ear of the Chief? To the ear of that sick and hateful man who knew nothing of Runeberg and me save that we were in Staffordshire and who was waiting in vain for our report in his arid office in Berlin, endlessly examining newspapers . . . I said out loud: *I must flee.* I sat up noiselessly, in a useless perfection of silence, as if Madden were already lying in wait for me. Something—perhaps the mere vain ostentation of proving my resources were nil—made me look through my pockets. I found what I knew I would find. The American watch, the nickel chain and the square coin, the key ring with the incriminating useless keys to Runeberg's apartment, the notebook, a letter which I resolved to destroy immediately (and which I did not destroy), a crown, two shillings and a few pence, the red and blue pencil, the handkerchief, the revolver with one bullet. Absurdly, I took it in my hand and weighed it in order to inspire courage within myself. Vaguely I thought that a pistol report can be heard at a great distance. In ten minutes my plan was perfected. The telephone book listed the name of the only person capable of transmitting the message; he lived in a suburb of Fenton, less than a half hour's train ride away.

I am a cowardly man. I say it now, now that I have carried to its end a plan whose perilous nature no one can deny. I know its execution was terrible. I didn't do it for Germany, no. I care nothing for a barbarous country which imposed upon me the abjection of being a spy. Besides, I know of a man from England—a modest man—who for me is no less great than Goethe. I talked with him for scarcely an hour, but during that hour he was Goethe . . . I did it because I sensed that the Chief somehow feared people of my race—for the innumerable ancestors who merge within me. I wanted to prove to him that a yellow man could save his armies. Besides, I had to flee from Captain Madden. His hands and his voice could call at my door at any moment. I dressed silently, bade farewell to myself in the mirror, went downstairs, scrutinized the peaceful street and went out. The station was not far from my home, but I judged it wise to take a cab. I argued that in this way I ran less risk of being recognized; the fact is that in the deserted street I felt myself visible and vulnerable, infinitely so. I remember that I told the cab driver to stop a short distance before the main entrance. I got out with voluntary, almost painful slowness; I was going to the village of Ashgrove but I bought a ticket for a more distant station. The train left within a very few minutes, at eight-fifty. I hurried; the next one would leave at nine-thirty. There was hardly a soul on the platform. I went through the coaches; I remember a few farmers, a woman dressed in mourning, a young boy who was reading with fervor the *Annals* of Tacitus, a wounded and happy soldier. The coaches jerked forward at last. A man whom I recognized ran in vain to the end of the platform. It was Captain Richard Madden. Shattered, trembling, I shrank into the far corner of the seat, away from the dreaded window.

From this broken state I passed into an almost abject felicity. I told myself that the duel had already begun and that I had won the first encounter by frustrating, even if for forty minutes, even if by a stroke of fate, the attack of my adversary. I argued that this slightest of victories foreshadowed a total victory. I argued (no less fallaciously) that my cowardly felicity proved that I was a man capable of carrying out the adventure successfully. From this weakness I took strength that did not abandon me. I foresee that man will resign himself each day to more atrocious undertakings; soon there will be no one but warriors and brigands; I give them this counsel: *The author of an atrocious undertaking ought to imagine that he has already accomplished it, ought to impose upon himself a future as irrevocable as the past.* Thus I proceeded as my eyes of a man already dead registered the elapsing of that day, which was perhaps the last, and the diffusion of the night. The train ran gently along, amid ash trees. It stopped, almost in the middle of the fields. No one announced the name of the station. "Ashgrove?" I asked a few lads on the platform. "Ashgrove," they replied. I got off.

A lamp enlightened the platform but the faces of the boys were in shadow. One questioned me, "Are you going to Dr. Stephen Albert's house?" Without waiting for my answer, another said, "The house is a long way from here, but you won't get lost if you take this road to the left and at every crossroads turn again to your left." I tossed them a coin (my last), descended a few stone steps and started down the solitary road. It went downhill, slowly. It was of elemental earth; overhead the branches were tangled; the low, full moon seemed to accompany me.

For an instant, I thought that Richard Madden in some way had penetrated my desperate plan. Very quickly, I understood that that was impossible. The instructions to turn always to the left reminded me that such was the common procedure for discovering the central point of certain labyrinths. I have some understanding of labyrinths: not for nothing am I the great grandson of that Ts'ui Pên who was governor of Yunnan and who renounced worldly power in order to write a novel that might be even more populous than the *Hung Lu Meng* and to construct a labyrinth in which all men would become lost. Thirteen years he dedicated to these heterogeneous tasks, but the hand of a stranger murdered him—and his novel was incoherent and no one found the labyrinth. Beneath English trees I meditated on that lost maze; I imagined it inviolate and perfect at the secret crest of a mountain; I imagined it erased by rice fields or beneath the water; I imagined it infinite, no longer composed of octagonal kiosks and returning paths, but of rivers and provinces and kingdoms . . . I thought of a labyrinth of labyrinths, of one sinuous spreading labyrinth that would encompass the past and the future and in some way involve the stars. Absorbed in these illusory images, I forgot my destiny of one pursued. I felt myself to be, for an unknown period of time, an abstract perceiver of the world. The vague, living countryside, the moon, the remains of the day worked on me, as well as the slope of the road which eliminated any possibility of weariness. The afternoon was intimate, infinite. The road descended and forked among the now confused meadows. A high-pitched, almost syllabic music approached and receded in the shifting of the wind, dimmed by leaves and distance. I thought that a man can be an enemy of other men, of the moments of other men, but not of a country: not of fireflies, woods, gardens, streams of water, sunsets. Thus I arrived before a tall, rusty gate. Between the iron bars I made out a poplar grove and a pavilion. I understood suddenly two things, the first trivial, the second almost unbelievable: the music came from the pavilion, and the music was Chinese. For precisely that reason I had openly accepted it without paying it any heed. I do not remember whether there was a bell or whether I knocked with my hand. The sparkling of the music continued.

From the rear of the house within a lantern approached: a lantern that the trees sometimes striped and sometimes eclipsed, a paper lantern that had the form of a drum and the color of the moon. A tall man bore it. I didn't see his face for the light blinded me. He opened the door and said slowly, in my own language: "I see that the pious Hsi P'êng persists in correcting my solitude. You no doubt wish to see the garden?"

I recognized the name of one of our consuls and I replied, disconcerted, "The garden?"

"The garden of forking paths."

Something stirred in my memory and I uttered with incomprehensible certainty, "The garden of my ancestor Ts'ui Pên."

"Your ancestor? Your illustrious ancestor? Come in."

The damp path zigzagged like those of my childhood. We came to a library of Eastern and Western books. I recognized bound in yellow silk several volumes of the Lost Encyclopedia, edited by the Third Emperor of the Luminous Dynasty but never printed. The record on the phonograph revolved next to a bronze phoenix. I also recall a *famille rose* vase and another, many centuries older, of that shade of blue which our craftsmen copied from the potters of Persia . . .

Stephen Albert observed me with a smile. He was, as I have said, very tall, sharp featured, with gray eyes and a gray beard. He told me that he had been a missionary in Tientsin "before aspiring to become a Sinologist."

We sat down—I on a long, low divan, he with his back to the window and a tall circular clock. I calculated that my pursuer, Richard Madden, could not arrive for at least an hour. My irrevocable determination could wait.

"An astounding fate, that of Ts'ui Pên," Stephen Albert said. "Governor of his native province, learned in astronomy, in astrology and in the tireless interpretation of the canonical books, chess player, famous poet and calligrapher—he abandoned all this in order to compose a book and a maze. He renounced the pleasures of both tyranny and justice, of his populous couch, of his banquets and even of erudition—all to close himself up for thirteen years in the Pavilion of the Limpid Solitude. When he died, his heirs found nothing save chaotic manuscripts. His family, as you may be aware, wished to condemn them to the fire; but his executor—a Taoist or Buddhist monk—insisted on their publication."

"We descendants of Ts'ui Pên," I replied, "continue to curse that monk. Their publication was senseless. The book is an indeterminate heap of contradictory drafts. I examined it once: in the third chapter the hero dies, in the fourth he is alive. As for the other undertaking of Ts'ui Pên, his labyrinth . . ."

"Here is Ts'ui Pên's labyrinth," he said, indicating a tall lacquered desk.

"An ivory labyrinth!" I exclaimed. "A minimum labyrinth."

"A labyrinth of symbols," he corrected. "An invisible labyrinth of time. To me, a barbarous Englishman, has been entrusted the revelation of this diaphanous mystery. After more than a hundred years, the details are irretrievable; but it is not hard to conjecture what happened. Ts'ui Pên must have said once: *I am withdrawing to write a book.* And another time: *I am withdrawing to construct a labyrinth.* Every one imagined two works; to no one did it occur that the book and the maze were one and the same thing. The Pavilion of the Limpid Solitude stood in the center of a garden that was perhaps intricate; that circumstance could have suggested to the heirs a physical labyrinth. Ts'ui Pên died; no one in the vast territories that were his came upon the labyrinth; the confusion of the novel suggested to me that *it* was the maze. Two circumstances gave me the correct solution of the problem. One: the curious legend that Ts'ui Pên had planned to create a labyrinth which would be strictly infinite. The other: a fragment of a letter I discovered."

Albert rose. He turned his back on me for a moment; he opened a drawer of the black and gold desk. He faced me and in his hands he held a sheet of paper that had once been crimson, but was now pink and tenuous and cross-sectioned. The fame of Ts'ui Pên as a calligrapher had been justly won. I read, uncomprehendingly and with fervor, these words written with a minute brush by a man of my blood: *I leave to the various futures (not to all) my garden of forking paths.* Wordlessly, I returned the sheet. Albert continued:

"Before unearthing this letter, I had questioned myself about the ways in which a book can be infinite. I could think of nothing other than a cyclic volume, a circular one. A book whose last page was identical with the first, a book which had the possibility of continuing indefinitely. I remembered too that night which is at the middle of the Thousand and One Nights when Scheherazade (through a magical oversight of the copyist) begins to relate word for word the story of the Thousand and One Nights, establishing the risk of coming once again to the night when she must repeat it, and thus on to infinity. I imagined as well a Platonic, hereditary work, transmitted from father to son, in which each new individual adds a chapter or corrects with pious care the pages of his elders. These conjectures diverted me; but none seemed to correspond, not even remotely, to the contradictory chapters of Ts'ui Pên. In the midst of this perplexity, I received from Oxford the manuscript you have examined. I lingered, naturally, on the sentence: *I leave to the various futures (not to all) my garden of forking paths.* Almost instantly, I understood: 'the garden of forking paths' was the chaotic novel; the phrase 'the various futures (not to all)' suggested to me the forking in time, not in space. A broad rereading of the work confirmed the theory. In all fictional works, each time a man is confronted with several alternatives, he chooses one and eliminates the others; in the fiction of Ts'ui Pên, he chooses—simultaneously—all of them. *He creates,* in this way, diverse futures, diverse times which themselves also proliferate and fork. Here, then, is the explanation of the novel's contradictions. Fang, let us say, has a secret; a stranger calls at his door; Fang resolves to kill him. Naturally, there are several possible outcomes: Fang can kill the intruder, the intruder can kill Fang, they both can escape, they both can die, and so forth. In the work of Ts'ui Pên, all possible outcomes occur; each one is the point of departure for other forkings. Sometimes, the paths of this labyrinth converge: for example, you arrive at this house, but in one of the possible pasts you are my enemy, in another, my friend. If you will resign yourself to my incurable pronunciation, we shall read a few pages."

His face, within the vivid circle of the lamplight, was unquestionably that of an old man, but with something unalterable about it, even immortal. He read with slow precision two versions of the same epic chapter. In the first, an army marches to a battle across a lonely mountain; the horror of the rocks and shadows makes the men undervalue their lives and they gain an easy victory. In the second, the same army traverses a palace where a great festival is taking place; the resplendent battle seems to them a continuation of the celebration and they win the victory. I listened with proper veneration to these ancient narratives, perhaps less admirable in themselves than the fact that they had been created by my blood and were being restored to me by a man of a remote empire, in the course of a desperate adventure, on a Western isle. I remember the last words, repeated in each version like a secret commandment: *Thus fought the heroes, tranquil their admirable hearts, violent their swords, resigned to kill and to die.*

From that moment on, I felt about me and within my dark body an invisible, intangible swarming. Not the swarming of the divergent, parallel and finally coalescent armies, but a more inaccessible, more intimate agitation that they in some manner prefigured. Stephen Albert continued:

"I don't believe that your illustrious ancestor played idly with these variations. I don't consider it credible that he would sacrifice thirteen years to the infinite execution of a rhetorical experiment. In your country, the novel is a subsidiary form of literature; in Ts'ui Pên's time it was a despicable form. Ts'ui Pên was a brilliant novelist, but he was also a man of letters who doubtless did not consider himself a mere novelist. The testimony of his contemporaries proclaims—and his life fully confirms—his metaphysical and mystical interests. Philosophic controversy usurps a good part of the novel. I know that of all problems, none disturbed him so greatly nor worked upon him so much as the abysmal problem of time. Now then, the latter is the only problem that does not figure in the pages of the *Garden*. He does not even use the word that signifies *time.* How do you explain this voluntary omission?"

I proposed several solutions—all unsatisfactory. We discussed them. Finally, Stephen Albert said to me:

"In a riddle whose answer is chess, what is the only prohibited word?"

I thought a moment and replied, "The word *chess*."

"Precisely," said Albert. "*The Garden of Forking Paths* is an enormous riddle, or parable, whose theme is time; this recondite cause prohibits its mention. To omit a word always, to resort to inept metaphors and obvious periphrases, is perhaps the most emphatic way of stressing it. That is the tortuous method preferred, in each of the meanderings of his indefatigable novel, by the oblique Ts'ui Pên. I have compared hundreds of manuscripts, I have corrected the errors that the negligence of the copyists has introduced. I have guessed the plan of this chaos, I have re-established—I believe I have re-established—the primordial organization, I have translated the entire work: it is clear to me that not once does he employ the word 'time.' The explanation is obvious: *The Garden of Forking Paths* is an incomplete, but not false, image of the universe as Ts'ui Pên conceived it. In contrast to Newton and Schopenhauer, your ancestor did not believe in a uniform, absolute time. He believed in an infinite series of times, in a growing, dizzying net of divergent, convergent and parallel times. This network of times which approached one another, forked, broke off, or were unaware of one another for centuries, embraces *all* possibilities of time. We do not exist in the majority of these times; in some you exist, and not I; in others I, and not you; in others, both of us. In the present one, which a favorable fate has granted me, you have arrived at my house; in another, while crossing the garden, you found me dead; in still another, I utter these same words, but I am a mistake, a ghost."

"In every one," I pronounced, not without a tremble to my voice, "I am grateful to you and revere you for your re-creation of the garden of Ts'ui Pên."

"Not in all," he murmured with a smile. "Time forks perpetually toward innumerable futures. In one of them I am your enemy."

Once again I felt the swarming sensation of which I have spoken. It seemed to me that the humid garden that surrounded the house was infinitely saturated with invisible persons. Those persons were Albert and I, secret, busy and multiform in other dimensions of time. I raised my eyes and the tenuous nightmare dissolved. In the yellow and black garden there was only one man; but this man was as strong as a statue . . . this man was approaching along the path and he was Captain Richard Madden.

"The future already exists," I replied, "but I am your friend. Could I see the letter again?"

Albert rose. Standing tall, he opened the drawer of the tall desk; for the moment his back was to me. I had readied the revolver. I fired with extreme caution. Albert fell uncomplainingly, immediately. I swear his death was instantaneous—a lightning stroke.

The rest is unreal, insignificant. Madden broke in, arrested me. I have been condemned to the gallows. I have won out abominably; I have communicated to Berlin the secret name of the city they must attack. They bombed it yesterday; I read it in the same papers that offered to England the mystery of the learned Sinologist Stephen Albert who was murdered by a stranger, one Yu Tsun. The Chief had deciphered this mystery. He knew my problem was to indicate (through the uproar of the war) the city called Albert, and that I had found no other means to do so than to kill a man of that name. He does not know (no one can know) my innumerable contrition and weariness.

(1941)

QUESTIONS FOR CRITICAL THINKING AND WRITING

Experience

1. Describe your experience in reading "The Garden of Forking Paths." Did the story surprise you, entertain you, annoy you? Why?
2. What motivated Yu Tsun to become a spy? Does his motivation make you more or less sympathetic to him? How do you regard his final sentence about his "innumerable contrition and weariness?"

Interpretation

3. The labyrinth is a central image in the story. How many labyrinths do you detect? What do they mean?
4. The story combines fact and fiction. For example, Liddell Hart's *History of World War I* is an actual book, but the Yu Tsun incident is not mentioned. What effect does Borges gain by combining the real with the imaginary?
5. Consider Yu Tsun's advice: "The author of an atrocious undertaking ought to imagine that he has already accomplished it, ought to impose upon himself a future as irrevocable as the past." What does this statement tell us about Yu Tsun? Does it imply any feelings of guilt?

Evaluation

6. Albert tells Yu Tsun, "In your country, the novel is a subsidiary form of literature; in Ts'ui Pên's time it was a despicable form." How is fiction regarded today? You may consider this from the point of view of family and friends as well as in a wider cultural context.
7. Do you find this story meaningful? Can you identify with any of the characters or their imperatives?

Critical Thinking

8. What is the value of reading a complex story like "The Garden of Forking Paths"? Why do you think Borges chose the detective or mystery story framework for a story with such a strong philosophical undercurrent?

© Jill Krementz

JAMAICA KINCAID
[b. 1949]

Jamaica Kincaid was born and educated on the island of Antigua. She left Antigua for the United States, where she began writing and publishing stories in magazines as diverse as Rolling Stone *and* The New Yorker, *where she later became a staff writer. Her first book,* At the Bottom of the River, *won a prize, and since then she has received widespread recognition for her unusual essays, short stories, and novels, which dispense with standard plots, characters, and dialogue. Her work is saturated in the life and culture of the British West Indies.*

Girl

Wash the white clothes on Monday and put them on the stone heap; wash the color clothes on Tuesday and put them on the clothesline to dry; don't walk barehead in the hot sun; cook pumpkin fritters in very hot sweet oil; soak your little cloths right after you take them off; when buying cotton to make yourself a nice blouse, be sure that it doesn't have gum on it, because that way it won't hold up well after a wash; soak salt fish overnight before you cook it; is it true that you sing benna in Sunday school?; always eat your food in such a way that it won't turn someone else's stomach; on Sundays try to walk like a lady and not like the slut you are so bent on becoming; don't sing benna in Sunday school; you mustn't speak to wharf-rat boys, not even to give directions; don't eat fruits on the street—flies will follow you; *but I don't sing benna on Sundays at all and never in Sunday school;* this is how to sew on a button; this is how to make a buttonhole for the button you have just sewed on; this is how to hem a dress when you see the hem coming down and so to prevent yourself from looking like the slut I know you are so bent on becoming; this is how you iron your father's khaki shirt so that it doesn't have a crease; this is how you iron your father's khaki pants so that they don't have a crease; this is how you grow okra—far from the house, because okra tree harbors red ants; when you are growing dasheen, make sure it gets plenty of water or else it makes your throat itch when you are eating it; this is how you sweep a corner; this is how you sweep a whole house; this is how you sweep a yard; this is how you smile to someone you don't like too much; this is how you smile to someone you don't like at all; this is how you smile to someone you like completely; this is how you set a table for tea; this is how you set a table for dinner; this is how you set a table for dinner with an important guest; this is how you set a table for lunch; this is how you set a table for breakfast; this is how to behave in the presence of men who don't know you very well, and this way they won't recognize immediately the slut I have warned you against becoming; be sure to wash every day, even if it is with your own spit; don't squat down to play marbles—you are not a boy, you know; don't pick people's flowers—you might catch something; don't throw stones at blackbirds, because it might not be a blackbird at all; this is how to make a bread pudding; this is how to make doukona; this is how to make pepper pot; this is how to make a good medicine for a cold; this is how to make a good medicine to throw away a child before it even becomes a child; this is how to catch a fish; this is how to throw back a fish you don't like, and that way something bad won't fall on you; this is how to bully a man; this is how a man bullies you; this is how to love a man, and if this doesn't work there are other ways, and if they don't work don't feel too bad about giving up; this is how to spit up in the air if you feel like it, and this is how to move quick so that it doesn't fall on you; this is how to make ends meet; always squeeze bread to make sure it's fresh; *but what if the baker won't let me feel the bread?*; you mean to say that after all you are really going to be the kind of woman who the baker won't let near the bread?

(1984)

QUESTIONS FOR CRITICAL THINKING AND WRITING

Experience

1. Did you find this story humorous?

Interpretation

2. How would you describe the mother–daughter relationship? Consider the mother's tone and diction as well as the implications of the title.
3. Consider the form of the story—one paragraph with the daughter's words in italics. Why do you think Kincaid presents the story this way?

Evaluation

4. Consider specific pieces of the mother's advice. What is the purpose of her advice? What does her advice imply about her culture?

Connections

5. Compare "Girl" with Olsen's "I Stand Here Ironing." Consider literary technique and the mother–daughter relationships.

Critical Thinking

6. Do you think Kincaid's "Girl" should be characterized as a story? How else might it be categorized or classified?

GABRIEL GARCIA MÁRQUEZ

[b. 1928]

Gabriel Garcia Márquez was born in Colombia and studied law in Bogota before working as a full-time journalist until 1965. He received the Nobel Prize for literature in 1982, and has won numerous international literary awards. One of the members of "El Boom," the flowering of fictional writers in South America in the 1950s and 1960s, he published his first novel, In Evil Hour *(1962), to critical acclaim.* One Hundred Years of Solitude *(1967) brought him international recognition. Through the use of "magic realism"—the embellishing of a realistic setting with surrealistic imagery and events—he created what has been described as "the greatest revolution in the Spanish language since* Don Quixote *of Cervantes."*

A Very Old Man with Enormous Wings

A Tale for Children

TRANSLATED BY GREGORY RABASSA

On the third day of rain they had killed so many crabs inside the house that Pelayo had to cross his drenched courtyard and throw them into the sea, because the newborn child had a temperature all night and they thought it was due to the stench. The world had been sad since Tuesday. Sea and sky were a single ash-gray thing and the sands of the beach, which on March nights glimmered like powdered light, had become a stew of mud and rotten shellfish. The light was so weak at noon that when Pelayo was coming back to the house after throwing away the crabs, it was hard for him to see what it was that was moving and groaning in the rear of the courtyard. He had to go very close to see that it was an old man, a very old man, lying face down in the mud, who, in spite of his tremendous efforts, couldn't get up, impeded by his enormous wings.

Frightened by that nightmare, Pelayo ran to get Elisenda, his wife, who was putting compresses on the sick child, and he took her to the rear of the courtyard. They both looked at the fallen body with mute stupor. He was dressed like a ragpicker. There were only a few faded hairs left on his bald skull and very few teeth in his mouth, and his pitiful condition of a drenched great-grandfather had taken away any sense of grandeur he might have had. His huge buzzard wings, dirty and half-plucked, were forever entangled in the mud. They looked at him so long and so closely that Pelayo and Elisenda very soon overcame their surprise and in the end found him familiar. Then they dared speak to him, and he answered in an incomprehensible dialect with a strong sailor's voice. That was how they skipped over the inconvenience of the wings and quite intelligently concluded that he was a lonely castaway from some foreign ship wrecked by the storm. And yet, they called in a neighbor woman who knew everything about life and death to see him, and all she needed was one look to show them their mistake.

"He's an angel," she told them. "He must have been coming for the child, but the poor fellow is so old that the rain knocked him down."

On the following day everyone knew that a flesh-and-blood angel was held captive in Pelayo's house. Against the judgment of the wise neighbor woman, for whom angels in those times were the fugitive survivors of a celestial conspiracy, they did not have the heart to club him to death. Pelayo watched over him all afternoon from the kitchen, armed with his bailiff's club, and before going to bed he dragged him out of the mud and locked him up with the hens in the wire chicken coop. In the middle of the night, when the rain stopped, Pelayo and Elisenda were still killing crabs. A short time afterward the child woke up without a fever and with a desire to eat. Then they felt magnanimous and decided to put the angel on a raft with fresh water and provisions for three days and leave him to his fate on the high seas. But when they went out into the courtyard with the first light of dawn, they found the whole neighborhood in front of the chicken coop having fun with the angel, without the slightest reverence, tossing him things to eat through the openings in the wire as if he weren't a supernatural creature but a circus animal.

Father Gonzaga arrived before seven o'clock, alarmed at the strange news. By that time onlookers less frivolous than those at dawn had already arrived and they were making all kinds of conjectures concerning the captive's future. The simplest among them thought that he should be named mayor of the world. Others of sterner mind felt that he should be promoted to the rank of five-star general in order to win all wars. Some visionaries hoped that he could be put to stud in order to implant on earth a race of winged wise men who could take charge of the universe. But Father Gonzaga, before becoming a priest, had been a robust woodcutter. Standing by the wire, he reviewed his catechism in an instant and asked them to open the door so that he could take a close look at that pitiful man who looked more like a huge decrepit hen among the fascinated chickens. He was lying in a corner drying his open wings in the sunlight among the fruit peels and breakfast leftovers that the early risers had thrown him. Alien to the impertinences of the world, he only lifted his antiquarian eyes and murmured something in his dialect when Father Gonzaga went into the chicken coop and said good morning to him in Latin. The parish priest had his first suspicion of an imposter when he saw that he did not understand the language of God or know how to greet His ministers. Then he noticed that seen close up he was much too human: he had an unbearable smell of the outdoors, the back side of his wings was strewn with parasites and his main feathers had been mistreated by terrestrial winds, and nothing about him measured up to the proud dignity of angels. Then he came out of the chicken coop and in a brief sermon warned the curious against the risks of being ingenuous. He reminded them that the devil had the bad habit of making use of carnival tricks in order to confuse the unwary. He argued that if wings were not the essential element in determining the difference between a hawk and an airplane, they were even less so in the recognition of angels. Nevertheless, he promised to write a letter to his bishop so that the latter would write to his primate so that the latter would write to the Supreme Pontiff in order to get the final verdict from the highest courts.

His prudence fell on sterile hearts. The news of the captive angel spread with such rapidity that after a few hours the courtyard had the bustle of a marketplace and they had to call in troops with fixed bayonets to disperse the mob that was about to knock the house down. Elisenda, her spine all twisted from sweeping up so much marketplace trash, then got the idea of fencing in the yard and charging five cents admission to see the angel.

The curious came from far away. A traveling carnival arrived with a flying acrobat who buzzed over the crowd several times, but no one paid any attention to him because his wings were not those of an angel but, rather, those of a sidereal bat. The most unfortunate invalids on earth came in search of health: a poor woman who since childhood had been counting her heartbeats and had run out of numbers; a Portuguese man who couldn't sleep because the noise of the stars disturbed him; a sleepwalker who got up at night to undo the things he had done while awake; and many others with less serious ailments. In the midst of that shipwreck disorder that made the earth tremble, Pelayo and Elisenda were happy with fatigue, for in less than a week they had crammed their rooms with money and the line of pilgrims waiting their turn to enter still reached beyond the horizon.

The angel was the only one who took no part in his own act. He spent his time trying to get comfortable in his borrowed nest, befuddled by the hellish heat of the oil lamps and sacramental candles that had been placed along the wire. At first they tried to make him eat some mothballs, which, according to the wisdom of the wise neighbor woman, were the food prescribed for angels. But he turned them down, just as he turned down the papal lunches that the penitents brought him, and they never found out whether it was because he was an angel or because he was an old man that in the end he ate nothing but eggplant mush. His only supernatural virtue seemed to be patience. Especially during the first days, when the hens pecked at him, searching for the stellar parasites that proliferated in his wings, and the cripples pulled out feathers to touch their defective parts with, and even the most merciful threw stones at him, trying to get him to rise so they could see him standing. The only time they succeeded in arousing him was when they burned his side with an iron for branding steers, for he had been motionless for so many hours that they thought he was dead. He awoke with a start, ranting in his hermetic language and with tears in his eyes, and he flapped his wings a couple of times, which brought on a whirlwind of chicken dung and lunar dust and a gale of panic that did not seem to be of this world. Although many thought that his reaction had been one not of rage but of pain, from then on they were careful not to annoy him, because the majority understood that his passivity was not that of a hero taking his ease but that of a cataclysm in repose.

Father Gonzaga held back the crowd's frivolity with formulas of maidservant inspiration while awaiting the arrival of a final judgment on the nature of the captive. But the mail from Rome showed no sense of urgency. They spent their time finding out if the prisoner had a navel, if his dialect had any connection with Aramaic, how many times he could fit on the head of a pin, or whether he wasn't just a Norwegian with wings. Those meager letters might have come and gone until the end of time if a providential event had not put an end to the priest's tribulations.

It so happened that during those days, among so many other carnival attractions, there arrived in town the traveling show of the woman who had been changed into a spider for having disobeyed her parents. The admission to see her was not only less than the admission to see the angel, but people were permitted to ask her all manner of questions about her absurd state and to examine her up and down so that no one would ever doubt the truth of her horror. She was a frightful tarantula the size of a ram and with the head of a sad maiden. What was most heart-rending, however, was not her outlandish shape but the sincere affliction with which she recounted the details of her misfortune. While still practically a child she had sneaked out of her parents' house to go to a dance, and while she was coming back through the woods after having danced all night without permission, a fearful thunderclap rent the sky in two and through the crack came the lightning bolt of brimstone that changed her into a spider. Her only nourishment came from the meatballs that charitable souls chose to toss into her mouth. A spectacle like that, full of so much human truth and with such a fearful lesson, was bound to defeat without even trying that of a haughty angel who scarcely deigned to look at mortals. Besides, the few miracles attributed to the angel showed a certain mental disorder, like the blind man who didn't recover his sight but grew three new teeth, or the paralytic who didn't get to walk but almost won the lottery, and the leper whose sores sprouted sunflowers. Those consolation miracles, which were more like mocking fun, had already ruined the angel's reputation when the woman who had been changed into a spider finally crushed him completely. That was how Father Gonzaga was cured forever of his insomnia and Pelayo's courtyard went back to being as empty as during the time it had rained for three days and crabs walked through the bedrooms.

The owners of the house had no reason to lament. With the money they saved they built a two-story mansion with balconies and gardens and high netting so that crabs wouldn't get in during the winter, and with iron bars on the windows so that angels wouldn't get in. Pelayo also set up a rabbit warren close to town and gave up his job as bailiff for good, and Elisenda bought some satin pumps with high heels and many dresses of iridescent silk, the kind worn on Sunday by the most desirable women in those times. The chicken coop was the only thing that didn't receive any attention. If they washed it down with creolin and burned tears of myrrh inside it every so often, it was not in homage to the angel but to drive away the dungheap stench that still hung everywhere like a ghost and was turning the new house into an old one. At first, when the child learned to walk, they were careful that he not get too close to the chicken coop. But then they began to lose their fears and got used to the smell, and before the child got his second teeth he'd gone inside the chicken coop to play, where the wires were falling apart. The angel was no less standoffish with him than with other mortals, but he tolerated the most ingenious infamies with the patience of a dog who had no illusions. They both came down with chicken pox at the same time. The doctor who took care of the child couldn't resist the temptation to listen to the angel's heart, and he found so much whistling in the heart and so many sounds in his kidneys that it seemed impossible for him to be alive. What surprised him most, however, was the logic of his wings. They seemed so natural on that completely human organism that he couldn't understand why other men didn't have them too.

When the child began school it had been some time since the sun and rain had caused the collapse of the chicken coop. The angel went dragging himself about here and there like a stray dying man. They would drive him out of the bedroom with a broom and a moment later find him in the kitchen. He seemed to be in so many places at the same time that they grew to think that he'd been duplicated, that he was reproducing himself all through the house, and the exasperated and unhinged Elisenda shouted that it was awful living in that hell full of angels. He could scarcely eat and his antiquarian eyes had also become so foggy that he went about bumping into posts. All he had left were the bare cannulae of his last feathers. Pelayo threw a blanket over him and extended him the charity of letting him sleep in the shed, and only then did they notice that he had a temperature at night, and was delirious with the tongue twisters of an old Norwegian. That was one of the few times they became alarmed, for they thought he was going to die and not even the wise neighbor woman had been able to tell them what to do with dead angels.

And yet he not only survived his worst winter, but seemed improved with the first sunny days. He remained motionless for several days in the farthest corner of the courtyard, where no one would see him, and at the beginning of December some large, stiff feathers began to grow on his wings, the feathers of a scarecrow, which looked more like another misfortune of decrepitude. But he must have known the reason for those changes, for he was quite careful that no one should notice them, that no one should hear the sea chanteys that he sometimes sang under the stars. One morning Elisenda was cutting some bunches of onions for lunch when a wind that seemed to come from the high seas blew into the kitchen. Then she went to the window and caught the angel in his first attempts at flight. They were so clumsy that his fingernails opened a furrow in the vegetable patch and he was on the point of knocking the shed down with the ungainly flapping that slipped on the light and couldn't get a grip on the air. But he did manage to gain altitude. Elisenda let out a sigh of relief, for herself and for him, when she saw him pass over the last houses, holding himself up in some way with the risky flapping of a senile vulture. She kept watching him even when she was through cutting the onions and she kept on watching until it was no longer possible for her to see him, because then he was no longer an annoyance in her life but an imaginary dot on the horizon of the sea.

(1955)

QUESTIONS FOR CRITICAL THINKING AND WRITING

Experience

1. Consider the attitudes expressed toward the old man. Have you heard similar attitudes expressed in your community toward foreigners or those who are different?

Interpretation

2. What is the significance of the episode of the woman who comes with the traveling show?
3. What is the Church's response to the old man? Is Márquez being satirical?

Evaluation

4. The story is subtitled "A Tale for Children." Do you think children are the primary audience for this tale? What elements in the story resemble a fairy tale? What about the subtitle suggests that Márquez is not only being intentionally misleading but also cynical?

Connection

5. Compare "A Very Old Man with Enormous Wings" to the Daedalus–Icarus myth, and its treatment in W. C. William's poem and Breughel's painting "Landscape with the Fall of Icarus."

Critical Thinking

6. Why do you think Garcia Márquez and other writers utilize fantastic and imaginative element to convey their ideas about and perspectives on human experience? Why do you think such fiction is characterized as a type of "magic realism"?

ISAAC BASHEVIS SINGER
[1904–1991]

Isaac Bashevis Singer, who won the Nobel prize in Literature in 1978, was born in Poland and lived in the United States after 1935. His short stories and novels in Yiddish deal with a society and way of life now passed out of European experience. His milieu is the world of the Eastern European shtetl, in which the characters pursue spiritual quests yet struggle with demons and other evil forces or succumb to material temptations. From a family of rabbis, Singer has drawn on that cultural background for his trilogy, which follows the course of a rabbinical family from 1800 to the Nazi takeover. His short story output was prolific, consisting of more than twelve collections, including Gimpel the Fool *(1957) and* The Spinoza of Market Street *(1961). His stories have appeared in the* Jewish Daily Forward, Commentary, Esquire, *and* The New Yorker.

Gimpel the Fool

TRANSLATED BY SAUL BELLOW

I

I am Gimpel the fool. I don't think myself a fool. On the contrary. But that's what folks call me. They gave me the name while I was still in school. I had seven names in all: imbecile, donkey, flax-head, dope, glump, ninny, and fool. The last name stuck.

What did my foolishness consist of? I was easy to take in. They said, "Gimpel, you know the rabbi's wife has been brought to childbed?" So I skipped school. Well, it turned out to be a lie. How was I supposed to know? She hadn't had a big belly. But I never looked at her belly. Was that really so foolish? The gang laughed and hee-hawed, stomped and danced and chanted a good-night prayer. And instead of the raisins they give when a woman's lying in, they stuffed my hand full of goat turds. I was no weakling. If I slapped someone he'd see all the way to Cracow. But I'm really not a slugger by nature. I think to myself: Let it pass. So they take advantage of me.

I was coming home from school and heard a dog barking. I'm not afraid of dogs, but of course I never want to start up with them. One of them may be mad, and if he bites there's not a Tartar in the world who can help you. So I made tracks. Then I looked around and saw the whole market place wild with laughter. It was no dog at all but Wolf-Leib the Thief. How was I supposed to know it was he? It sounded like a howling bitch.

When the pranksters and leg-pullers found that I was easy to fool, every one of them tried his luck with me. "Gimpel, the Czar is coming to Frampol; Gimpel, the moon fell down in Turbeen; Gimpel, little Hodel Furpiece found a treasure behind the bathhouse." And I like a golem° believed everyone. In the first place, everything is possible, as it is written in the Wisdom of the Fathers. I've forgotten just how. Second, I had to believe when the whole town came down on me! If I ever dared to say, "Ah, you're kidding!" there was trouble. People got angry. "What do you mean! You want to call everyone a liar?" What was I to do? I believed them, and I hope at least that did them some good.

I was an orphan. My grandfather who brought me up was already bent toward the grave. So they turned me over to a baker, and what a time they gave me there! Every woman or girl who came to bake a batch of noodles had to fool me at least once. "Gimpel, there's a fair in heaven; Gimpel, the rabbi gave birth to a calf in the seventh month; Gimpel, a cow flew over the roof and laid brass eggs." A student from the yeshiva came once to buy a roll, and he said, "You, Gimpel, while you stand here scraping with your baker's shovel the Messiah has come. The dead have arisen." "What do you mean?" I said. "I heard no one blowing the ram's horn!" He said, "Are you deaf?" And all began to cry, "We heard it, we heard!" Then in came Rietze the Candle-dipper and called out in her hoarse voice, "Gimpel, your father and mother have stood up from the grave. They're looking for you."

To tell the truth, I knew very well that nothing of the sort had happened, but all the same, as folks were talking, I threw on my wool vest and went out. Maybe something had happened. What did I stand to lose by looking? Well, what a cat music went up! And then I took a vow to believe nothing more. But that was no go either. They confused me so that I didn't know the big end from the small.

I went to the rabbi to get some advice. He said, "It is written, better to be a fool all your days than for one hour to be evil. You are not a fool. They are the fools. For he who causes his neighbor to feel shame loses Paradise himself." Nevertheless the rabbi's daughter took me in. As I left the rabbinical court she said, "Have you kissed the wall yet?" I said, "No; what for?" She answered, "It's the law; you've got to do it after every

golem simpleton

visit." Well, there didn't seem to be any harm in it. And she burst out laughing. It was a fine trick. She put one over on me, all right.

I wanted to go off to another town, but then everyone got busy matchmaking, and they were after me so they nearly tore my coat tails off. They talked at me and talked until I got water on the ear. She was no chaste maiden, but they told me she was virgin pure. She had a limp, and they said it was deliberate, from coyness. She had a bastard, and they told me the child was her little brother. I cried, "You're wasting your time. I'll never marry that whore." But they said indignantly, "What a way to talk! Aren't you ashamed of yourself? We can take you to the rabbi and have you fined for giving her a bad name." I saw then that I wouldn't escape them so easily and I thought: They're set on making me their butt. But when you're married the husband's the master, and if that's all right with her it's agreeable to me too. Besides, you can't pass through life unscathed, nor expect to.

I went to her clay house, which was built on the sand, and the whole gang, hollering and chorusing, came after me. They acted like bear-baiters. When we came to the well they stopped all the same. They were afraid to start anything with Elka. Her mouth would open as if it were on a hinge, and she had a fierce tongue. I entered the house. Lines were strung from wall to wall and clothes were drying. Barefoot she stood by the tub, doing the wash. She was dressed in a worn hand-me-down gown of plush. She had her hair put up in braids and pinned across her head. It took my breath away, almost, the reek of it all.

Evidently she knew who I was. She took a look at me and said, "Look who's here! He's come, the drip. Grab a seat."

I told her all; I denied nothing. "Tell me the truth," I said, "are you really a virgin, and is that mischievous Yechiel actually your little brother? Don't be deceitful with me, for I'm an orphan."

"I'm an orphan myself," she answered, "and whoever tries to twist you up, may the end of his nose take a twist. But don't let them think they can take advantage of me. I want a dowry of fifty guilders, and let them take up a collection besides. Otherwise they can kiss my you-know-what." She was very plainspoken. I said, "It's the bride and not the groom who gives a dowry." Then she said, "Don't bargain with me. Either a flat 'yes' or a flat 'no'—Go back where you came from."

I thought: No bread will ever be baked from *this* dough. But ours is not a poor town. They consented to everything and proceeded with the wedding. It so happened that there was a dysentery epidemic at the time. The ceremony was held at the cemetery gates, near the little corpse-washing hut. The fellows got drunk. While the marriage contract was being drawn up I heard the most pious high rabbi ask, "Is the bride a widow or a divorced woman?" And the sexton's wife answered for her, "Both a widow and divorced." It was a black moment for me. But what was I to do, run away from under the marriage canopy?

There was singing and dancing. An old granny danced opposite me, hugging a braided white *chalah*. The master of revels made a "God 'a mercy" in memory of the bride's parents. The schoolboys threw burrs, as on Tishe b'Av fast day. There were a lot of gifts after the sermon: a noodle board, a kneading trough, a bucket, brooms, ladles, household articles galore. Then I took a look and saw two strapping young men carrying a crib. "What do we need this for?" I asked. So they said, "Don't rack your brains about it. It's all right, it'll come in handy." I realized I was going to be rooked. Take it another way though, what did I stand to lose? I reflected: I'll see what comes of it. A whole town can't go altogether crazy.

2

At night I came where my wife lay, but she wouldn't let me in. "Say, look here, is this what they married us for?" I said. And she said, "My monthly has come." "But yesterday they took you to the ritual bath, and that's afterward, isn't it supposed to be?" "Today isn't yesterday," said she, "and yesterday's not today. You can beat it if you don't like it." In short, I waited.

Not four months later she was in childbed. The townsfolk hid their laughter with their knuckles. But what could I do? She suffered intolerable pains and clawed at the walls. "Gimpel," she cried, "I'm going. Forgive me!" The house filled with women. They were boiling pans of water. The screams rose to the welkin.°

The thing to do was to go to the House of Prayer to repeat Psalms, and that was what I did.

The townsfolk liked that, all right. I stood in a corner saying Psalms and prayers, and they shook their heads at me. "Pray, pray!" they told me. "Prayer never made any woman pregnant." One of the congregation put a straw to my mouth and said, "Hay for the cows." There was something to that too, by God!

She gave birth to a boy. Friday at the synagogue the sexton stood up before the Ark, pounded on the reading table, and announced, "The wealthy Reb Gimpel invites the congregation to a feast in honor of the birth of a son." The whole House of Prayer rang with laughter. My face was flaming. But there was nothing I could do. After all, I *was* the one responsible for the circumcision honors and rituals.

Half the town came running. You couldn't wedge another soul in. Women brought peppered chick-peas, and there was a keg of beer from the tavern. I ate and drank as much as anyone, and they all congratulated me. Then there was a circumcision, and I named the boy after my father, may he rest in peace. When all were gone and I was left with my wife alone, she thrust her head through the bed-curtain and called me to her.

"Gimpel," said she, "why are you silent? Has your ship gone and sunk?"

"What shall I say?" I answered. "A fine thing you've done to me! If my mother had known of it she'd have died a second time."

She said, "Are you crazy, or what?"

"How can you make such a fool," I said, "of one who should be the lord and master?"

"What's the matter with you?" she said. "What have you taken it into your head to imagine?"

I saw that I must speak bluntly and openly. "Do you think this is the way to use an orphan?" I said. "You have borne a bastard."

She answered, "Drive this foolishness out of your head. The child is yours."

"How can he be mine?" I argued. "He was born seventeen weeks after the wedding."

She told me then that he was premature. I said, "Isn't he a little too premature?" She said, she had had a grandmother who carried just as short a time and she resembled

welkin *the sky*

this grandmother of hers as one drop of water does another. She swore to it with such oaths that you would have believed a peasant at the fair if he had used them. To tell the plain truth, I didn't believe her; but when I talked it over next day with the schoolmaster he told me that the very same thing had happened to Adam and Eve. Two they went up to bed, and four they descended.

"There isn't a woman in the world who is not the granddaughter of Eve," he said.

That was how it was; they argued me dumb. But then, who really knows how such things are?

I began to forget my sorrow. I loved the child madly, and he loved me too. As soon as he saw me he'd wave his little hands and want me to pick him up, and when he was colicky I was the only one who could pacify him. I bought him a little bone teething ring and a little gilded cap. He was forever catching the evil eye from someone, and then I had to run to get one of those abracadabras for him that would get him out of it. I worked like an ox. You know how expenses go up when there's an infant in the house. I don't want to lie about it; I didn't dislike Elka either, for that matter. She swore at me and cursed, and I couldn't get enough of her. What strength she had! One of her looks could rob you of the power of speech. And her orations! Pitch and sulphur, that's what they were full of, and yet somehow also full of charm. I adored her every word. She gave me bloody wounds though.

In the evening I brought her a white loaf as well as a dark one, and also poppyseed rolls I baked myself. I thieved because of her and swiped everything I could lay my hands on: macaroons, raisins, almonds, cakes. I hope I may be forgiven for stealing from the Saturday pots the women left to warm in the baker's oven. I would take out scraps of meat, a chunk of pudding, a chicken leg or head, a piece of tripe, whatever I could nip quickly. She ate and became fat and handsome.

I had to sleep away from home all during the week, at the bakery. On Friday nights when I got home she always made an excuse of some sort. Either she had heartburn, or a stitch in the side, or hiccups, or headaches. You know what women's excuses are. I had a bitter time of it. It was rough. To add to it, this little brother of hers, the bastard, was growing bigger. He'd put lumps on me, and when I wanted to hit back she'd open her mouth and curse so powerfully I saw a green haze floating before my eyes. Ten times a day she threatened to divorce me. Another man in my place would have taken French leave and disappeared. But I'm the type that bears it and says nothing. What's one to do? Shoulders are from God, and burdens too.

One night there was a calamity in the bakery; the oven burst, and we almost had a fire. There was nothing to do but go home, so I went home. Let me, I thought, also taste the joy of sleeping in bed in mid-week. I didn't want to wake the sleeping mite and tiptoed into the house. Coming in, it seemed to me that I heard not the snoring of one but, as it were, a double snore, one a thin enough snore and the other like the snoring of a slaughtered ox. Oh, I didn't like that! I didn't like it at all. I went up to the bed, and things suddenly turned black. Next to Elka lay a man's form. Another in my place would have made an uproar, and enough noise to rouse the whole town, but the thought occurred to me that I might wake the child. A little thing like that—why frighten a little swallow, I thought. All right then, I went back to the bakery and stretched out on a sack of flour and till morning I never shut an eye. I shivered as if I had had malaria. "Enough of being a donkey," I said to myself. "Gimpel isn't going to be a sucker all his life. There's a limit even to the foolishness of a fool like Gimpel."

In the morning I went to the rabbi to get advice, and it made a great commotion in the town. They sent the beadle for Elka right away. She came, carrying the child. And what do you think she did? She denied it, denied everything, bone and stone! "He's out of his head," she said. "I know nothing of dreams or divinations." They yelled at her, warned her, hammered on the table, but she stuck to her guns: it was a false accusation, she said.

The butchers and the horse-traders took her part. One of the lads from the slaughterhouse came by and said to me, "We've got our eye on you, you're a marked man." Meanwhile the child started to bear down and soiled itself. In the rabbinical court there was an Ark of the Covenant, and they couldn't allow that, so they sent Elka away.

I said to the rabbi, "What shall I do?"

"You must divorce her at once," said he.

"And what if she refuses?" I asked.

He said, "You must serve the divorce. That's all you'll have to do."

I said, "Well, all right, Rabbi. Let me think about it."

"There's nothing to think about," said he. "You mustn't remain under the same roof with her."

"And if I want to see the child?" I asked.

"Let her go, the harlot," said he, "and her brood of bastards with her."

The verdict he gave was that I mustn't even cross her threshold—never again, as long as I should live.

During the day it didn't bother me so much. I thought: It was bound to happen, the abscess had to burst. But at night when I stretched out upon the sacks I felt it all very bitterly. A longing took me, for her and for the child. I wanted to be angry, but that's my misfortune exactly, I don't have it in me to be really angry. In the first place—this was how my thoughts went—there's bound to be a slip sometimes. You can't live without errors. Probably that lad who was with her led her on and gave her presents and what not, and women are often long on hair and short on sense, and so he got around her. And then since she denies it so, maybe I was only seeing things? Hallucinations do happen. You see a figure or a mannikin or something, but when you come up closer it's nothing, there's not a thing there. And if that's so, I'm doing her an injustice. And when I got so far in my thoughts I started to weep. I sobbed so that I wet the flour where I lay. In the morning I went to the rabbi and told him that I had made a mistake. The rabbi wrote on with his quill, and he said that if that were so he would have to reconsider the whole case. Until he had finished I wasn't to go near my wife, but I might send her bread and money by messenger.

3

Nine months passed before all the rabbis could come to an agreement. Letters went back and forth. I hadn't realized that there could be so much erudition about a matter like this.

Meanwhile Elka gave birth to still another child, a girl this time. On the Sabbath I went to the synagogue and invoked a blessing on her. They called me up to the Torah, and I named the child for my mother-in-law—may she rest in peace. The louts and loudmouths of the town who came into the bakery gave me a going over. All Frampol refreshed its spirits because of my trouble and grief. However, I resolved that I would always believe what I was told. What's the good of *not* believing? Today it's your wife you don't believe; tomorrow it's God Himself you won't take stock in.

By an apprentice who was her neighbor I sent her daily a corn or a wheat loaf, or a piece of pastry, rolls or bagels, or, when I got the chance, a slab of pudding, a slice of honeycake, or wedding strudel—whatever came my way. The apprentice was a good-hearted lad, and more than once he added something on his own. He had formerly annoyed me a lot, plucking my nose and digging me in the ribs, but when he started to be a visitor to my house he became kind and friendly. "Hey, you, Gimpel," he said to me, "you have a very decent little wife and two fine kids. You don't deserve them."

"But the things people say about her," I said.

"Well, they have long tongues," he said, "and nothing to do with them but babble. Ignore it as you ignore the cold of last winter."

One day the rabbi sent for me and said, "Are you certain, Gimpel, that you were wrong about your wife?"

I said, "I'm certain."

"Why, but look here! You yourself saw it."

"It must have been a shadow," I said.

"The shadow of what?"

"Just one of the beams, I think."

"You can go home then. You owe thanks to the Yanover rabbi. He found an obscure reference in Maimonides that favored you."

I seized the rabbi's hand and kissed it.

I wanted to run home immediately. It's no small thing to be separated for so long a time from wife and child. Then I reflected: I'd better go back to work now, and go home in the evening. I said nothing to anyone, although as far as my heart was concerned it was like one of the Holy Days. The women teased and twitted me as they did every day, but my thought was: Go on, with your loose talk. The truth is out, like the oil upon the water. Maimonides says it's right, and therefore it is right!

At night, when I had covered the dough to let it rise, I took my share of bread and a little sack of flour and started homeward. The moon was full and the stars were glistening, something to terrify the soul. I hurried onward, and before me darted a long shadow. It was winter, and a fresh snow had fallen. I had a mind to sing, but it was growing late and I didn't want to wake the householders. Then I felt like whistling, but I remembered that you don't whistle at night because it brings the demons out. So I was silent and walked as fast as I could.

Dogs in the Christian yards barked at me when I passed, but I thought: Bark your teeth out! What are you but mere dogs? Whereas I am a man, the husband of a fine wife, the father of promising children.

As I approached the house my heart started to pound as though it were the heart of a criminal. I felt no fear, but my heart went thump! thump! Well, no drawing back. I quietly lifted the latch and went in. Elka was asleep. I looked at the infant's cradle. The shutter was closed, but the moon forced its way through the cracks. I saw the newborn child's face and loved it as soon as I saw it—immediately—each tiny bone.

Then I came nearer to the bed. And what did I see but the apprentice lying there beside Elka. The moon went out all at once. It was utterly black, and I trembled. My teeth chattered. The bread fell from my hands, and my wife waked and said, "Who is that, ah?"

I muttered, "It's me."

"Gimpel?" she asked. "How come you're here? I thought it was forbidden."

"The rabbi said," I answered and shook as with a fever.

"Listen to me, Gimpel," she said, "go out to the shed and see if the goat's all right. It seems she's been sick." I have forgotten to say that we had a goat. When I heard she was unwell I went into the yard. The nannygoat was a good little creature. I had a nearly human feeling for her.

With hesitant steps I went up to the shed and opened the door. The goat stood there on her four feet. I felt her everywhere, drew her by the horns, examined her udders, and found nothing wrong. She had probably eaten too much bark. "Good night, little goat," I said. "Keep well." And the little beast answered with a "Maa" as though to thank me for the good will.

I went back. The apprentice had vanished.

"Where," I asked, "is the lad?"

"What lad?" my wife answered.

"What do you mean?" I said. "The apprentice. You were sleeping with him."

"The things I have dreamed this night and the night before," she said, "may they come true and lay you low, body and soul! An evil spirit has taken root in you and dazzles your sight." She screamed out, "You hateful creature! You moon calf! You spook! You uncouth man! Get out, or I'll scream all Frampol out of bed!"

Before I could move, her brother sprang out from behind the oven and struck me a blow on the back of the head. I thought he had broken my neck. I felt that something about me was deeply wrong, and I said, "Don't make a scandal. All that's needed now is that people should accuse me of raising spooks and *dybbuks*."° For that was what she had meant. "No one will touch bread of my baking."

In short, I somehow calmed her.

"Well," she said, "that's enough. Lie down, and be shattered by wheels."

Next morning I called the apprentice aside. "Listen here, brother!" I said. And so on and so forth. "What do you say?" He stared at me as though I had dropped from the roof or something.

"I swear," he said, "you'd better go to an herb doctor or some healer. I'm afraid you have a screw loose, but I'll hush it up for you." And that's how the thing stood.

To make a long story short, I lived twenty years with my wife. She bore me six children, four daughters and two sons. All kinds of things happened, but I neither saw nor heard. I believed, and that's all. The rabbi recently said to me, "Belief in itself is beneficial. It is written that a good man lives by his faith."

Suddenly my wife took sick. It began with a trifle, a little growth upon the breast. But she evidently was not destined to live long; she had no years. I spent a fortune on her. I have forgotten to say that by this time I had a bakery of my own and in Frampol was considered to be something of a rich man. Daily the healer came, and every witch doctor in the neighborhood was brought. They decided to use leeches, and after that to try cupping. They even called a doctor from Lublin, but it was too late. Before she died she called me to her bed and said, "Forgive me, Gimpel."

I said, "What is there to forgive? You have been a good and faithful wife."

dybbuks *demons or souls of the dead that enter the bodies of the living to take possession of them.*

"Woe, Gimpel!" she said. "It was ugly how I deceived you all these years. I want to go clean to my Maker, and so I have to tell you that the children are not yours."

If I had been clouted on the head with a piece of wood it couldn't have bewildered me more.

"Whose are they?" I asked.

"I don't know," she said. "There were a lot—but they're not yours." And as she spoke she tossed her head to the side, her eyes turned glassy, and it was all up with Elka. On her whitened lips there remained a smile.

I imagined that, dead as she was, she was saying, "I deceived Gimpel. That was the meaning of my brief life."

4

One night, when the period of mourning was done, as I lay dreaming on the flour sacks, there came the Spirit of Evil himself and said to me, "Gimpel, why do you sleep?"

I said, "What should I be doing? Eating *kreplach?*"

"The whole world deceives you," he said, "and you ought to deceive the world in your turn."

"How can I deceive the world?" I asked him.

He answered, "You might accumulate a bucket of urine every day and at night pour it into the dough. Let the sages of Frampol eat filth."

"What about the judgment in the world to come?" I said.

"There is no world to come," he said. "They've sold you a bill of goods and talked you into believing you carried a cat in your belly. What nonsense!"

"Well, then," I said, "and is there a God?"

He answered, "There is no God either."

"What," I said, "*is* there, then?"

"A thick mire."

He stood before my eyes with a goatish beard and horn, long-toothed, and with a tail. Hearing such words, I wanted to snatch him by the tail, but I tumbled from the flour sacks and nearly broke a rib. Then it happened that I had to answer the call of nature, and, passing, I saw the risen dough, which seemed to say to me, "Do it!" In brief, I let myself be persuaded.

At dawn the apprentice came. We kneaded the bread, scattered caraway seeds on it, and set it to bake. Then the apprentice went away, and I was left sitting in the little trench by the oven, on a pile of rags. Well, Gimpel, I thought, you've revenged yourself on them for all the shame they've put on you. Outside the frost glittered, but it was warm beside the oven. The flames heated my face. I bent my head and fell into a doze.

I saw in a dream, at once, Elka in her shroud. She called to me, "What have you done, Gimpel?"

I said to her, "It's all your fault," and started to cry.

"You fool!" she said. "You fool! Because I was false is everything false too? I never deceived anyone but myself. I'm paying for it all, Gimpel. They spare you nothing here."

I looked at her face. It was black; I was startled and waked, and remained sitting dumb. I sensed that everything hung in the balance. A false step now and I'd lose Eternal Life. But God gave me His help. I seized the long shovel and took out the loaves, carried them into the yard, and started to dig a hole in the frozen earth.

My apprentice came back as I was doing it. "What are you doing, boss?" he said, and grew pale as a corpse.

"I know what I'm doing," I said, and I buried it all before his very eyes.

Then I went home, took my hoard from its hiding place, and divided it among the children. "I saw your mother tonight," I said. "She's turning black, poor thing."

They were so astounded they couldn't speak a word.

"Be well," I said, "and forget that such a one as Gimpel ever existed." I put on my short coat, a pair of boots, took the bag that held my prayer shawl in one hand, my stock in the other, and kissed the *mezzuzah*. When people saw me in the street they were greatly surprised.

"Where are you going?" they said.

I answered, "Into the world." And so I departed from Frampol.

I wandered over the land, and good people did not neglect me. After many years I became old and white; I heard a great deal, many lies and falsehoods, but the longer I lived the more I understood that there were really no lies. Whatever doesn't really happen is dreamed at night. It happens to one if it doesn't happen to another, tomorrow if not today, or a century hence if not next year. What difference can it make? Often I heard tales of which I said, "Now this is a thing that cannot happen." But before a year had elapsed I heard that it actually had come to pass somewhere.

Going from place to place, eating at strange tables, it often happens that I spin yarns—improbable things that could never have happened—about devils, magicians, windmills, and the like. The children run after me, calling, "Grandfather, tell us a story." Sometimes they ask for particular stories, and I try to please them. A fat young boy once said to me, "Grandfather, it's the same story you told us before." The little rogue, he was right.

So it is with dreams too. It is many years since I left Frampol, but as soon as I shut my eyes I am there again. And whom do you think I see? Elka. She is standing by the washtub, as at our first encounter, but her face is shining and her eyes are as radiant as the eyes of a saint, and she speaks outlandish words to me, strange things. When I wake I have forgotten it all. But while the dream lasts I am comforted. She answers all my queries, and what comes out is that all is right. I weep and implore, "Let me be with you." And she consoles me and tells me to be patient. The time is nearer than it is far. Sometimes she strokes and kisses me and weeps upon my face. When I awaken I feel her lips and taste the salt of her tears.

No doubt the world is entirely an imaginary world, but it is only once removed from the true world. At the door of the hovel where I lie, there stands the plank on which the dead are taken away. The gravedigger Jew has his spade ready. The grave waits and the worms are hungry; the shrouds are prepared—I carry them in my beggar's sack. Another *shnorrer*° is waiting to inherit my bed of straw. When the time comes I will go joyfully. Whatever may be there, it will be real, without complication, without ridicule, without deception. God be praised: there even Gimpel cannot be deceived.

(1953)

shnorrer *a beggar; sponger*

QUESTIONS FOR CRITICAL THINKING AND WRITING

Experience

1. What are your impressions of Gimpel? Is he at least partially responsible for the town's treatment of him? Do you admire or pity him?

Interpretation

2. Why does Gimpel accept the continual abuse? How does this abuse shape him and his philosophy?
3. Consider Gimpel's relationship with the rabbi. How does the rabbi's advice affect Gimpel's approach to life?
4. Analyze the tone of the story. Is the *way* Gimpel relates the story as important as *what* he relates? Consider his rhetorical questions and his use of understatement.

Evaluation

5. Through the course of the story, Gimpel develops a philosophical approach to life. What is Gimpel's philosophy? Does the story seem to advocate his philosophy?

Connection

6. Compare Gimpel to Hawthorne's protagonist in "Young Goodman Brown." How are they alike by the end of the stories? How are they different? How do visions affect each?

Critical Thinking

7. What do you think of the ways Gimpel acts and responds? What do you think of the reasons he provides for why he acts as he does and believes what he does?

CHAPTER NINE

For Further Reading

Do not, under *any* circumstances, belittle a work of fiction by trying to turn it into a carbon copy of real life; what we search for in fiction is not so much reality but the epiphany of truth.

AZAR NAFISI

© Jill Krementz

MARGARET ATWOOD

[b. 1939]

Margaret Atwood, one of Canada's foremost writers, was born in Ottawa. She graduated from the University of Toronto and received an M.A. from Radcliffe College in 1962. The recipient of many awards and fellowships, Atwood has won international acclaim for her critical writing and fiction. One of her most widely known novels, The Handmaid's Tale, *which was made into a film, describes life in a future world where women suffer severe repression. Her numerous stories, novels, and poems are complemented by her editorial and critical work, which includes the* Oxford Book of Canadian Verse.

Happy Endings

JOHN AND MARY MEET.
WHAT HAPPENS NEXT?
IF YOU WANT A HAPPY ENDING, TRY A.

A

John and Mary fall in love and get married. They both have worthwhile and remunerative jobs which they find stimulating and challenging. They buy a charming house. Real estate values go up. Eventually, when they can afford live-in help, they have two children, to whom they are devoted. The children turn out well. John and Mary have a stimulating and challenging sex life and worthwhile friends. They go on fun vacations together. They retire. They both have hobbies which they find stimulating and challenging. Eventually they die. This is the end of the story.

B

Mary falls in love with John but John doesn't fall in love with Mary. He merely uses her body for selfish pleasure and ego gratification of a tepid kind. He comes to her apartment twice a week and she cooks him dinner, you'll notice that he doesn't even consider her worth the price of a dinner out, and after he's eaten the dinner he fucks her and after that he falls asleep, while she does the dishes so he won't think she's untidy, having all those dirty dishes lying around, and puts on fresh lipstick so she'll look good when he wakes up, but when he wakes up he doesn't even notice, he puts on his socks and his shorts and his pants and his shirt and his tie and his shoes, the reverse order from the one in which he took them off. He doesn't take off Mary's clothes, she takes them off herself, she acts as if she's dying for it every time, not because she likes sex exactly, she doesn't, but she wants John to think she does because if they do it often enough surely he'll get used to her, he'll come to depend on her and they will get married, but John goes out the door with hardly so much as a good-night and three days later he turns up at six o'clock and they do the whole thing again.

Mary gets run-down. Crying is bad for your face, everyone knows that and so does Mary but she can't stop. People at work notice. Her friends tell her John is a rat, a pig, a dog, he isn't good enough for her, but she can't believe it. Inside John, she thinks, is another John, who is much nicer. This other John will emerge like a butterfly from a cocoon, a Jack from a box, a pit from a prune, if the first John is only squeezed enough.

One evening John complains about the food. He has never complained about the food before. Mary is hurt.

Her friends tell her they've seen him in a restaurant with another woman, whose name is Madge. It's not even Madge that finally gets to Mary; it's the restaurant. John has never taken Mary to a restaurant. Mary collects all the sleeping pills and aspirins she can find, and takes them and a half a bottle of sherry. You can see what kind of a woman she is by the fact that it's not even whiskey. She leaves a note for John. She hopes he'll discover her and get her to the hospital in time and repent and then they can get married, but this fails to happen and she dies.

John marries Madge and everything continues as in A.

C

John, who is an older man, falls in love with Mary, and Mary, who is only twenty-two, feels sorry for him because he's worried about his hair falling out. She sleeps with him even though she's not in love with him. She met him at work. She's in love with someone called James, who is twenty-two also and not yet ready to settle down.

John on the contrary settled down long ago: this is what is bothering him. John has a steady, respectable job and is getting ahead in his field, but Mary isn't impressed by him, she's impressed by James, who has a motorcycle and a fabulous record collection. But James is often away on his motorcycle, being free. Freedom isn't the same for girls, so in the meantime Mary spends Thursday evenings with John. Thursdays are the only days John can get away.

John is married to a woman called Madge and they have two children, a charming house which they bought just before the real estate values went up, and hobbies which they find stimulating and challenging, when they have the time. John tells Mary how important she is to him, but of course he can't leave his wife because a commitment is a commitment. He goes on about this more than is necessary and Mary finds it boring, but older men can keep it up longer so on the whole she has a fairly good time.

One day James breezes in on his motorcycle with some top-grade California hybrid and James and Mary get higher than you'd believe possible and they climb into bed. Everything becomes very underwater, but along comes John, who has a key to Mary's apartment. He finds them stoned and entwined. He's hardly in any position to be jealous, considering Madge, but nevertheless he's overcome with despair. Finally he's middle-aged, in two years he'll be bald as an egg and he can't stand it. He purchases a handgun, saying he needs it for target practice—this is the thin part of the plot, but it can be dealt with later—and shoots the two of them and himself.

Madge, after a suitable period of mourning, marries an understanding man called Fred and everything continues as in A, but under different names.

D

Fred and Madge have no problems. They get along exceptionally well and are good at working out any little difficulties that may arise. But their charming house is by the seashore and one day a giant tidal wave approaches. Real estate values go down. The rest of the story is about what caused the tidal wave and how they escape from it. They do, though thousands drown, but Fred and Madge are virtuous and lucky. Finally on high ground they clasp each other, wet and dripping and grateful, and continue as in A.

E

Yes, but Fred has a bad heart. The rest of the story is about how kind and understanding they both are until Fred dies. Then Madge devotes herself to charity work until the end of A. If you like, it can be "Madge," "cancer," "guilty and confused," and "bird watching."

F

If you think this is all too bourgeois, make John a revolutionary and Mary a counterespionage agent and see how far that gets you. Remember, this is Canada. You'll still end up with A, though in between you may get a lustful brawling saga of passionate involvement, a chronicle of our times, sort of.

You'll have to face it, the endings are the same however you slice it. Don't be deluded by any other endings, they're all fake, either deliberately fake, with malicious intent to deceive, or just motivated by excessive optimism if not by downright sentimentality.

The only authentic ending is the one provided here:

John and Mary die. John and Mary die. John and Mary die.

So much for endings. Beginnings are always more fun. True connoisseurs, however, are known to favor the stretch in between, since it's the hardest to do anything with.

That's about all that can be said for plots, which anyway are just one thing after another, a what and a what and a what.

Now try How and Why.

(1983)

QUESTIONS FOR CRITICAL THINKING AND WRITING

Experience

1. Describe your experience in reading "Happy Endings." Did it hold your interest? Were some sections more entertaining than others?

Interpretation

2. How does the story hold together? Consider plot, characters, tone, point of view, and theme.
3. What conclusions does the story seem to reach about "happy endings"?

Evaluation

4. Do you consider "Happy Endings" a short story? Does "Happy Endings" tell us anything about the writing process?

Connection

5. Compare Atwood's authorial intrusion and obvious manipulation of plot and content with other writers such as Luke in "The Prodigal Son" and Alexie in "Indian Education."

Critical Thinking

6. Why do so many works of serious literature have unhappy endings? Why do people read literary works when they know or suspect the works end unhappily?
7. Is there a way that this story could be told with a more conventional plot? Is there a benefit to telling a story the way Atwood has chosen?

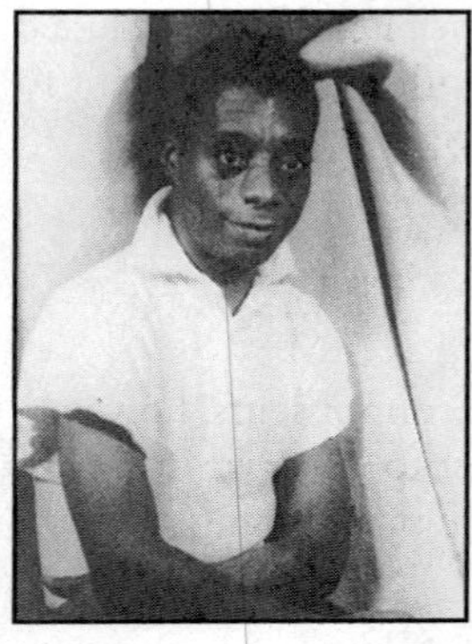

JAMES BALDWIN
[1924–1987]

James Baldwin, the son of a minister, was born in New York City. He began writing in high school and moved to Greenwich Village to pursue his career. In 1948 he moved to France to escape the daily effects of discrimination. It was there that he completed Go Tell It on the Mountain, *which describes the religious conversion of a 14-year-old black adolescent. It was published in 1953 to great critical acclaim. More books dealing with themes of racial and sexual alienation followed in rapid succession. Assuming a role as spokesman for black America, he became heavily involved in the civil rights movement in the 1960s; in 1963 his collection of essays,* The Fire Next Time, *was a best-seller. In addition to novels and essays, he wrote plays and short stories.*

Sonny's Blues

I read about it in the paper, in the subway, on my way to work. I read it, and I couldn't believe it, and I read it again. Then perhaps I just stared at it, at the newsprint spelling out his name, spelling out the story. I stared at it in the swinging lights of the subway car, and in the faces and bodies of the people, and in my own face, trapped in the darkness which roared outside.

It was not to be believed and I kept telling myself that, as I walked from the subway station to the high school. And at the same time I couldn't doubt it. I was scared, scared for Sonny. He became real to me again. A great block of ice got settled in my belly and kept melting there slowly all day long, while I taught my classes algebra. It was a special kind of ice. It kept melting, sending trickles of ice water all up and down my veins, but it never got less. Sometimes it hardened and seemed to expand until I felt my guts were going to come spilling out or that I was going to choke or scream. This would always be at a moment when I was remembering some specific thing Sonny had once said or done.

When he was about as old as the boys in my classes his face had been bright and open, there was a lot of copper in it; and he'd had wonderfully direct brown eyes, and great gentleness and privacy. I wondered what he looked like now. He had been picked up, the evening before, in a raid on an apartment downtown, for peddling and using heroin.

I couldn't believe it: but what I mean by that is that I couldn't find any room for it anywhere inside me. I had kept it outside me for a long time. I hadn't wanted to know.

I had had suspicions, but I didn't name them, I kept putting them away. I told myself that Sonny was wild, but he wasn't crazy. And he'd always been a good boy, he hadn't ever turned hard or evil or disrespectful, the way kids can, so quick, so quick, especially in Harlem. I didn't want to believe that I'd ever see my brother going down, coming to nothing, all that light in his face gone out, in the condition I'd already seen so many others. Yet it had happened and here I was, talking about algebra to a lot of boys who might, every one of them for all I knew, be popping off needles every time they went to the head. Maybe it did more for them than algebra could.

I was sure that the first time Sonny had ever had horse, he couldn't have been much older than these boys were now. These boys, now, were living as we'd been living then, they were growing up with a rush and their heads bumped abruptly against the low ceiling of their actual possibilities. They were filled with rage. All they really knew were two darknesses: the darkness of their lives, which was now closing in on them, and the darkness of the movies, which had blinded them to that other darkness, and in which they now, vindictively, dreamed, at once more together than they were at any other time, and more alone.

When the last bell rang, the last class ended, I let out my breath. It seemed I'd been holding it for all that time. My clothes were wet—I may have looked as though I'd been sitting in a steam bath, all dressed up, all afternoon. I sat alone in the classroom a long time. I listened to the boys outside, downstairs, shouting and cursing and laughing. Their laughter struck me for perhaps the first time. It was not the joyous laughter which—God knows why—one associates with children. It was mocking and insular, its intent to denigrate. It was disenchanted, and in this, also, lay the authority of their curses. Perhaps I was listening to them because I was thinking about my brother and in them I heard my brother. And myself.

One boy was whistling a tune, at once very complicated and very simple, it seemed to be pouring out of him as though he were a bird, and it sounded very cool and moving through all that harsh, bright air, only just holding its own through all those other sounds.

I stood up and walked over to the window and looked down into the courtyard. It was the beginning of the spring and the sap was rising in the boys. A teacher passed through them every now and again, quickly, as though he or she couldn't wait to get out of that courtyard, to get those boys out of their sight and off their minds. I started collecting my stuff. I thought I'd better get home and talk to Isabel.

The courtyard was almost deserted by the time I got downstairs. I saw this boy standing in the shadow of a doorway, looking just like Sonny. I almost called his name. Then I saw that it wasn't Sonny, but somebody we used to know, a boy from around our block. He'd been Sonny's friend. He'd never been mine, having been too young for me, and, anyway, I'd never liked him. And now, even though he was a grown-up man, he still hung around that block, still spent hours on the street corners, was always high and raggy. I used to run into him from time to time and he'd often work around to asking me for a quarter or fifty cents. He always had some real good excuse, too, and I always gave it to him, I don't know why.

But now, abruptly, I hated him. I couldn't stand the way he looked at me, partly like a dog, partly like a cunning child. I wanted to ask him what the hell he was doing in the school courtyard.

He sort of shuffled over to me, and he said, "I see you got the papers. So you already know about it."

"You mean about Sonny? Yes, I already know about it. How come they didn't get you?"

He grinned. It made him repulsive and it also brought to mind what he'd looked like as a kid. "I wasn't there. I stay away from them people."

"Good for you." I offered him a cigarette and I watched him through the smoke. "You come all the way down here just to tell me about Sonny?"

"That's right." He was sort of shaking his head and his eyes looked strange, as though they were about to cross. The bright sun deadened his damp dark brown skin and it made his eyes look yellow and showed up the dirt in his kinked hair. He smelled funky. I moved a little away from him and I said, "Well, thanks. But I already know about it and I got to get home."

"I'll walk you a little ways," he said. We started walking. There were a couple of kids still loitering in the courtyard and one of them said goodnight to me and looked strangely at the boy beside me.

"What're you going to do?" he asked me. "I mean, about Sonny?"

"Look. I haven't seen Sonny for over a year, I'm not sure I'm going to do anything. Anyway, what the hell *can* I do?"

"That's right," he said quickly, "ain't nothing you can do. Can't much help old Sonny no more, I guess."

It was what I was thinking and so it seemed to me he had no right to say it.

"I'm surprised at Sonny, though," he went on—he had a funny way of talking, he looked straight ahead as though he were talking to himself—"I thought Sonny was a smart boy, I thought he was too smart to get hung."

"I guess he thought so too," I said sharply, "and that's how he got hung. And now about you? You're pretty goddamn smart, I bet."

Then he looked directly at me, just for a minute. "I ain't smart," he said. "If I was smart, I'd have reached for a pistol a long time ago."

"Look. Don't tell *me* your sad story, if it was up to me, I'd give you one." Then I felt guilty—guilty, probably, for never having supposed that the poor bastard *had* a story of his own, much less a sad one, and I asked, quickly, "What's going to happen to him now?"

He didn't answer this. He was off by himself some place. "Funny thing," he said, and from his tone we might have been discussing the quickest way to get to Brooklyn, "when I saw the papers this morning, the first thing I asked myself was if I had anything to do with it. I felt sort of responsible."

I began to listen more carefully. The subway station was on the corner, just before us, and I stopped. He stopped, too. We were in front of a bar and he ducked slightly, peering in, but whoever he was looking for didn't seem to be there. The juke box was blasting away with something black and bouncy and I half watched the barmaid as she danced her way from the juke box to her place behind the bar. And I watched her face as she laughingly responded to something someone said to her, still keeping time to the music. When she smiled one saw the little girl, one sensed the doomed, still-struggling woman beneath the battered face of the semi-whore.

"I never *give* Sonny nothing," the boy said finally, "but a long time ago I come to school high and Sonny asked me how it felt." He paused, I couldn't bear to watch him, I watched the barmaid, and I listened to the music which seemed to be causing the pavement to shake. "I told him it felt great." The music stopped, the barmaid paused and watched the juke box until the music began again. "It did."

All this was carrying me some place I didn't want to go. I certainly didn't want to know how it felt. It filled everything, the people, the houses, the music, the dark, quicksilver barmaid, with menace; and this menace was their reality.

"What's going to happen to him now?" I asked again.

"They'll send him away some place and they'll try to cure him." He shook his head. "Maybe he'll even think he's kicked the habit. Then they'll let him loose"—he gestured, throwing his cigarette into the gutter. "That's all."

"What do you mean, that's *all*?"

But I knew what he meant.

"I *mean,* that's *all.*" He turned his head and looked at me, pulling down the corners of his mouth. "Don't you know what I mean?" he asked, softly.

"How the hell would I know what you mean?" I almost whispered it, I don't know why.

"That's right," he said to the air, "how would *he* know what I mean?" He turned toward me again, patient and calm, and yet I somehow felt him shaking, shaking as though he were going to fall apart. I felt that ice in my guts again, the dread I'd felt all afternoon; and again I watched the barmaid, moving about the bar, washing glasses, and singing. "Listen. They'll let him out and then it'll just start all over again. That's what I mean."

"You mean—they'll let him out. And then he'll just start working his way back in again. You mean he'll never kick the habit. Is that what you mean?"

"That's right," he said, cheerfully. "*You* see what I mean."

"Tell me," I said at last, "why does he want to die? He must want to die, he's killing himself, why does he want to die?"

He looked at me in surprise. He licked his lips. "He don't want to die. He wants to live. Don't nobody want to die, ever."

Then I wanted to ask him—too many things. He could not have answered, or if he had, I could not have borne the answers. I started walking. "Well, I guess it's none of my business."

"It's going to be rough on old Sonny," he said. We reached the subway station. "This is your station?" he asked. I nodded. I took one step down. "Damn!" he said, suddenly. I looked up at him. He grinned again. "Damn it if I didn't leave all my money home. You ain't got a dollar on you, have you? Just for a couple of days, is all."

All at once something inside gave and threatened to come pouring out of me. I didn't hate him any more. I felt that in another moment I'd start crying like a child.

"Sure," I said. "Don't sweat." I looked in my wallet and didn't have a dollar, I only had a five. "Here," I said. "That hold you?"

He didn't look at it—he didn't want to look at it. A terrible closed look came over his face, as though he were keeping the number on the bill a secret from him and me. "Thanks," he said, and now he was dying to see me go. "Don't worry about Sonny. Maybe I'll write him or something."

"Sure," I said. "You do that. So long."

"Be seeing you," he said. I went on down the steps.

And I didn't write Sonny or send him anything for a long time. When I finally did, it was just after my little girl died, he wrote me back a letter which made me feel like a bastard.

Here's what he said:

Dear brother,

You don't know how much I needed to hear from you. I wanted to write you many a time but I dug how much I must have hurt you and so I didn't write. But now I feel like a man who's been trying to climb up out of some deep, real deep and funky hole and just saw the sun up there, outside. I got to get outside.

I can't tell you much about how I got here. I mean I don't know how to tell you. I guess I was afraid of something or I was trying to escape from something and you know I have never been very strong in the head (smile). I'm glad Mama and Daddy are dead and can't see what's happened to their son and I swear if I'd known what I was doing I would never have hurt you so, you and a lot of other fine people who were nice to me and who believed in me.

I don't want you to think it had anything to do with me being a musician. It's more than that. Or maybe less than that. I can't get anything straight in my head down here and I try not to think about what's going to happen to me when I get outside again. Sometime I think I'm going to flip and *never* get outside and sometime I think I'll come straight back. I tell you one thing, though, I'd rather blow my brains out than go through this again. But that's what they all say, so they tell me. If I tell you when I'm coming to New York and if you could meet me, I sure would appreciate it. Give my love to Isabel and the kids and I was sure sorry to hear about little Gracie. I wish I could be like Mama and say the Lord's will be done, but I don't know it seems to me that trouble is the one thing that never does get stopped and I don't know what good it does to blame it on the Lord. But maybe it does some good if you believe it.

Your brother,
Sonny

Then I kept in constant touch with him and I sent him whatever I could and I went to meet him when he came back to New York. When I saw him many things I thought I had forgotten came flooding back to me. This was because I had begun, finally, to wonder about Sonny, about the life that Sonny lived inside. This life, whatever it was, had made him older and thinner and it had deepened the distant stillness in which he had always moved. He looked very unlike my baby brother. Yet, when he smiled, when we shook hands, the baby brother I'd never known looked out from the depths of his private life, like an animal waiting to be coaxed into the light.

"How you been keeping?" he asked me.

"All right. And you?"

"Just fine." He was smiling all over his face. "It's good to see you again."

"It's good to see you."

The seven years' difference in our ages lay between us like a chasm: I wondered if these years would ever operate between us as a bridge. I was remembering, and it made it hard to catch my breath, that I had been there when he was born; and I had heard the first words he had ever spoken. When he started to walk, he walked from our mother straight to me. I caught him just before he fell when he took the first steps he ever took in this world.

"How's Isabel?"

"Just fine. She's dying to see you."

"And the boys?"

"They're fine, too. They're anxious to see their uncle."

"Oh, come on. You know they don't remember me."

"Are you kidding? Of course they remember you."

He grinned again. We got into a taxi. We had a lot to say to each other, far too much to know how to begin.

As the taxi began to move, I asked, "You still want to go to India?"

He laughed. "You still remember that. Hell, no. This place is Indian enough for me."

"It used to belong to them," I said.

And he laughed again. "They damn sure knew what they were doing when they got rid of it."

Years ago, when he was around fourteen, he'd been all hipped on the idea of going to India. He read books about people sitting on rocks, naked, in all kinds of weather, but mostly bad, naturally, and walking barefoot through hot coals and arriving at wisdom. I used to say that it sounded to me as though they were getting away from wisdom as fast as they could. I think he sort of looked down on me for that.

"Do you mind," he asked, "if we have the driver drive alongside the park? On the west side—I haven't seen the city in so long."

"Of course not," I said. I was afraid that I might sound as though I were humoring him, but I hoped he wouldn't take it that way.

So we drove along, between the green of the park and the stony, lifeless elegance of hotels and apartment buildings, toward the vivid, killing streets of our childhood. These streets hadn't changed, though housing projects jutted up out of them now like rocks in the middle of a boiling sea. Most of the houses in which we had grown up had vanished, as had the stores from which we had stolen, the basements in which we had first tried sex, the rooftops from which we had hurled tin cans and bricks. But houses exactly like the houses of our past yet dominated the landscape, boys exactly like the boys we once had been found themselves smothering in these houses, came down into the streets for light and air and found themselves encircled by disaster. Some escaped the trap, most didn't. Those who got out always left something of themselves behind, as some animals amputate a leg and leave it in the trap. It might be said, perhaps, that I had escaped, after all, I was a school teacher; or that Sonny had, he hadn't lived in Harlem for years. Yet, as the cab moved uptown through streets which seemed, with a rush, to darken with dark people, and as I covertly studied Sonny's face, it came to me that what we both were seeking through our separate cab windows was that part of ourselves which had been left behind. It's always at the hour of trouble and confrontation that the missing member aches.

We hit 110th Street and started rolling up Lenox Avenue. And I'd known this avenue all my life, but it seemed to me again, as it had seemed on the day I'd first heard about Sonny's trouble, filled with a hidden menace which was its very breath of life.

"We almost there," said Sonny.

"Almost." We were both too nervous to say anything more.

We live in a housing project. It hasn't been up long. A few days after it was up it seemed uninhabitably new, now, of course, it's already rundown. It looks like a parody of the good, clean, faceless life—God knows the people who live in it do their best to make it a parody. The beat-looking grass lying around isn't enough to make their lives green, the hedges will never hold out the streets, and they know it. The big windows fool no one, they aren't big enough to make space out of no space. They don't bother with the windows, they watch the TV screen instead. The playground is most popular with the children who don't play at jacks, or skip rope, or roller skate, or swing, and they can be found in it after dark. We moved in partly because it's not too far from where I teach, and partly for the kids; but it's really just like the houses in which Sonny and I grew up. The same things happen, they'll have the same things to remember. The moment Sonny and I started into the house I had the feeling that I was simply bringing him back into the danger he had almost died trying to escape.

Sonny has never been talkative. So I don't know why I was sure he'd be dying to talk to me when supper was over the first night. Everything went fine, the oldest boy remembered him, and the youngest boy liked him, and Sonny had remembered to bring something for each of them; and Isabel, who is really much nicer than I am, more open and giving, had gone to a lot of trouble about dinner and was genuinely glad to see him. And she's always been able to tease Sonny in a way that I haven't. It was nice to see her face so vivid again and to hear her laugh and watch her make Sonny laugh. She wasn't, or, anyway, she didn't seem to be, at all uneasy or embarrassed. She chatted as though there were no subject which had to be avoided and she got Sonny past his first, faint stiffness. And thank God she was there, for I was filled with that icy dread again. Everything I did seemed awkward to me, and everything I said sounded freighted with hidden meaning. I was trying to remember everything I'd heard about dope addiction and I couldn't help watching Sonny for signs. I wasn't doing it out of malice. I was trying to find out something about my brother. I was dying to hear him tell me he was safe.

"Safe!" my father grunted, whenever Mama suggested trying to move to a neighborhood which might be safer for children. "Safe, hell! Ain't no place safe for kids, nor nobody."

He always went on like this, but he wasn't, ever, really as bad as he sounded, not even on weekends, when he got drunk. As a matter of fact, he was always on the lookout for "something a little better," but he died before he found it. He died suddenly, during a drunken weekend in the middle of the war, when Sonny was fifteen. He and Sonny hadn't ever got on too well. And this was partly because Sonny was the apple of his father's eye. It was because he loved Sonny so much and was frightened for him, that he was always fighting with him. It doesn't do any good to fight with Sonny. Sonny just moves back, inside himself, where he can't be reached. But the principal reason that they never hit it off is that they were so much alike. Daddy was big and rough and loud-talking, just the opposite of Sonny, but they both had—that same privacy.

Mama tried to tell me something about this, just after Daddy died. I was home on leave from the army.

This was the last time I ever saw my mother alive. Just the same, this picture gets all mixed up in my mind with pictures I had of her when she was younger. The way I always see her is the way she used to be on a Sunday afternoon, say, when the old folks were talking after the big Sunday dinner. I always see her wearing pale blue. She'd be sitting on the sofa. And my father would be sitting in the easy chair, not far from her. And the living room would be full of church folks and relatives. There they sit, in chairs all around the living room, and the night is creeping up outside, but nobody knows it yet. You can see the darkness growing against the windowpanes and you hear the street noises every now and again, or maybe the jangling beat of a tambourine from one of the churches close by, but it's real quiet in the room. For a moment nobody's talking, but every face looks darkening, like the sky outside. And my mother rocks a little from the waist, and my father's eyes are closed. Everyone is looking at something a child can't see. For a minute they've forgotten the children. Maybe a kid is lying on the rug, half asleep. Maybe somebody's got a kid in his lap and is absent-mindedly stroking the kid's head. Maybe there's a kid, quiet and big-eyed, curled up in a big chair in the corner. The silence, the darkness coming, and the darkness in the faces frightens the child obscurely. He hopes that the hand which strokes his forehead will never stop—will never die. He hopes that there will never come a time when the old folks won't be sitting around the living room, talking about where they've come from, and what they've seen, and what's happened to them and their kinfolk.

But something deep and watchful in the child knows that this is bound to end, is already ending. In a moment someone will get up and turn on the light. Then the old folks will remember the children and they won't talk any more that day. And when light fills the room, the child is filled with darkness. He knows that everytime this happens he's moved just a little closer to that darkness outside. The darkness outside is what the old folks have been talking about. It's what they've come from. It's what they endure. The child knows that they won't talk any more because if he knows too much about what's happened to *them,* he'll know too much too soon, about what's going to happen to him.

The last time I talked to my mother, I remember I was restless. I wanted to get out and see Isabel. We weren't married then and we had a lot to straighten out between us.

There Mama sat, in black, by the window. She was humming an old church song, *Lord, you brought me from a long ways off.* Sonny was out somewhere. Mama kept watching the streets.

"I don't know," she said, "if I'll ever see you again, after you go off from here. But I hope you'll remember the things I tried to teach you."

"Don't talk like that," I said, and smiled. "You'll be here a long time yet."

She smiled, too, but she said nothing. She was quiet for a long time. And I said, "Mama, don't you worry about nothing. I'll be writing all the time, and you be getting the checks. . . ."

"I want to talk to you about your brother," she said, suddenly. "If anything happens to me he ain't going to have nobody to look out for him."

"Mama," I said, "ain't nothing going to happen to you *or* Sonny. Sonny's all right. He's a good boy and he's got good sense."

"It ain't a question of his being a good boy," Mama said, "nor of his having good sense. It ain't only the bad ones, nor yet the dumb ones that gets sucked under." She stopped, looking at me. "Your Daddy once had a brother," she said, and she smiled in a way that made me feel she was in pain. "You didn't never know that, did you?"

"No," I said, "I never knew that," and I watched her face.

"Oh, yes," she said, "your Daddy had a brother." She looked out of the window again. "I know you never saw your Daddy cry. But *I* did—many a time, through all these years."

I asked her, "What happened to his brother? How come nobody's ever talked about him?"

This was the first time I ever saw my mother look old.

"His brother got killed," she said, "when he was just a little younger than you are now. I knew him. He was a fine boy. He was maybe a little full of the devil, but he didn't mean nobody no harm."

Then she stopped and the room was silent, exactly as it had sometimes been on those Sunday afternoons. Mama kept looking out into the streets.

"He used to have a job in the mill," she said, "and, like all young folks, he just liked to perform on Saturday nights. Saturday nights, him and your father would drift around to different places, go to dances and things like that, or just sit around with people they knew, and your father's brother would sing, he had a fine voice, and play along with himself on his guitar. Well, this particular Saturday night, him and your father was coming home from some place, and they were both a little drunk and there was a moon that night, it was bright like day. Your father's brother was feeling kind of good, and he was whistling to himself, and he had his guitar slung over his shoulder. They was coming down a hill and beneath them was a road that turned off from the highway. Well, your father's brother, being always kind of frisky, decided to run down this hill, and he did, with that guitar banging and clanging behind him, and he ran across the road, and he was making water behind a tree. And your father was sort of amused at him and he was still coming down the hill, kind of slow. Then he heard a car motor and that same minute his brother stepped from behind the tree, into the road, in the moonlight. And he started to cross the road. And your father started to run down the hill, he says he don't know why. This car was full of white men. They was all drunk, and when they seen your father's brother they let out a great whoop and holler and they aimed the car straight at him. They was having fun, they just wanted to scare him, the way they do sometimes, you know. But they was drunk. And I guess the boy, being drunk, too, and scared, kind of lost his head. By the time he jumped it was too late. Your father says he heard his brother scream when the car rolled over him, and he heard the wood of that guitar when it give, and he heard them strings go flying, and he heard them white men shouting, and the car kept on a-going and it ain't stopped till this day. And, time your father got down the hill, his brother weren't nothing but blood and pulp."

Tears were gleaming on my mother's face. There wasn't anything I could say.

"He never mentioned it," she said, "because I never let him mention it before you children. Your Daddy was like a crazy man that night and for many a night thereafter. He says he never in his life seen anything as dark as that road after the lights of that car had gone away. Weren't nothing, weren't nobody on that road, just your Daddy and his brother and that busted guitar. Oh, yes. Your Daddy never did really get right again. Till the day he died he weren't sure but that every white man he saw was the man that killed his brother."

She stopped and took out her handkerchief and dried her eyes and looked at me.

"I ain't telling you all this," she said, "to make you scared or bitter or to make you hate nobody. I'm telling you this because you got a brother. And the world ain't changed."

I guess I didn't want to believe this. I guess she saw this in my face. She turned away from me, toward the window again, searching those streets.

"But I praise my Redeemer," she said at last, "that He called your Daddy home before me. I ain't saying it to throw no flowers at myself, but, I declare, it keeps me from feeling too cast down to know I helped your father get safely through this world. Your father always acted like he was the roughest, strongest man on earth. And everybody took him to be like that. But if he hadn't had me there—to see his tears!"

She was crying again. Still, I couldn't move. I said, "Lord, Lord, Mama, I didn't know it was like that."

"Oh, honey," she said, "there's a lot that you don't know. But you are going to find it out." She stood up from the window and came over to me. "You got to hold on to your brother," she said, "and don't let him fall, no matter what it looks like is happening to him and no matter how evil you gets with him. You going to be evil with him many a time. But don't you forget what I told you, you hear?"

"I won't forget," I said. "Don't you worry, I won't forget. I won't let nothing happen to Sonny."

My mother smiled as though she were amused at something she saw in my face. Then, "You may not be able to stop nothing from happening. But you got to let him know you's *there.*"

Two days later I was married, and then I was gone. And I had a lot of things on my mind and I pretty well forgot my promise to Mama until I got shipped home on a special furlough for her funeral.

And, after the funeral, with just Sonny and me alone in the empty kitchen, I tried to find out something about him.

"What do you want to do?" I asked him.

"I'm going to be a musician," he said.

For he had graduated, in the time I had been away, from dancing to the juke box to finding out who was playing what, and what they were doing with it, and he had bought himself a set of drums.

"You mean, you want to be a drummer?" I somehow had the feeling that being a drummer might be all right for other people but not for my brother Sonny.

"I don't think," he said, looking at me very gravely, "that I'll ever be a good drummer. But I think I can play a piano."

I frowned. I'd never played the role of the older brother quite so seriously before, had scarcely ever, in fact, *asked* Sonny a damn thing. I sensed myself in the presence of something I didn't really know how to handle, didn't understand. So I made my frown a little deeper as I asked: "What kind of musician do you want to be?"

He grinned. "How many kinds do you think there are?"

"Be *serious,*" I said.

He laughed, throwing his head back, and then looked at me. "I *am* serious."

"Well, then, for Christ's sake, stop kidding around and answer a serious question. I mean, do you want to be a concert pianist, you want to play classical music and all that, or—or what?" Long before I finished he was laughing again. "For Christ's *sake,* Sonny!"

He sobered, but with difficulty. "I'm sorry. But you sound so—*scared!*" and he was off again.

"Well, you may think it's funny now, baby, but it's not going to be so funny when you have to make your living at it, let me tell you *that.*" I was furious because I knew he was laughing at me and I didn't know why.

"No," he said, very sober now, and afraid, perhaps, that he'd hurt me, "I don't want to be a classical pianist. That isn't what interests me. I mean"—he paused, looking hard at me, as though his eyes would help me to understand, and then gestured helplessly, as though perhaps his hand would help—"I mean, I'll have a lot of studying to do, and I'll have to study *everything,* but, I mean, I want to play *with*—jazz musicians." He stopped. "I want to play jazz," he said.

Well, the word had never before sounded as heavy, as real, as it sounded that afternoon in Sonny's mouth. I just looked at him and I was probably frowning a real frown by this time. I simply couldn't see why on earth he'd want to spend his time hanging around nightclubs, clowning around on bandstands, while people pushed each other around a dance floor. It seemed—beneath him, somehow. I had never thought about it before, had never been forced to, but I suppose I had always put jazz musicians in a class with what Daddy called "good-time people."

"Are you *serious?*"

"Hell, *yes,* I'm serious."

He looked more helpless than ever, and annoyed, and deeply hurt.

I suggested, helpfully: "You mean—like Louis Armstrong?"

His face closed as though I'd struck him. "No. I'm not talking about none of that old-time, down home crap."

"Well, look, Sonny, I'm sorry, don't get mad. I just don't altogether get it, that's all. Name somebody—you know, a jazz musician you admire."

"Bird."

"Who?"

"Bird! Charlie Parker! Don't they teach you nothing in the goddamn army?"

I lit a cigarette. I was surprised and then a little amused to discover that I was trembling. "I've been out of touch," I said. "You'll have to be patient with me. Now. Who's this Parker character?"

"He's just one of the greatest jazz musicians alive," said Sonny, sullenly, his hands in his pockets, his back to me. "Maybe *the* greatest," he added, bitterly, "that's probably why *you* never heard of him."

"All right," I said, "I'm ignorant. I'm sorry. I'll go out and buy all the cat's records right away, all right?"

"It don't," said Sonny, with dignity, "make any difference to me. I don't care what you listen to. Don't do me no favors."

I was beginning to realize that I'd never seen him so upset before. With another part of my mind I was thinking that this would probably turn out to be one of those things kids go through and that I shouldn't make it seem important by pushing it too hard. Still, I didn't think it would do any harm to ask: "Doesn't all this take a lot of time? Can you make a living at it?"

He turned back to me and half leaned, half sat, on the kitchen table. "Everything takes time," he said, "and—well, yes, sure, I can make a living at it. But what I don't seem to be able to make you understand is that it's the only thing I want to do."

"Well, Sonny," I said, gently, "you know people can't always do exactly what they *want* to do— "

"*No,* I don't know that," said Sonny, surprising me. "I think people *ought* to do what they want to do, what else are they alive for?"

"You getting to be a big boy," I said desperately, "it's time you started thinking about your future."

"I'm thinking about my future," said Sonny, grimly. "I think about it all the time."

I gave up. I decided, if he didn't change his mind, that we could always talk about it later. "In the meantime," I said, "you got to finish school." We had already decided that he'd have to move in with Isabel and her folks. I knew this wasn't the ideal arrangement because Isabel's folks are inclined to be dicty and they hadn't especially wanted Isabel to marry me. But I didn't know what else to do. "And we have to get you fixed up at Isabel's."

There was a long silence. He moved from the kitchen table to the window. "That's a terrible idea. You know it yourself."

"Do you have a *better* idea?"

He just walked up and down the kitchen for a minute. He was as tall as I was. He had started to shave. I suddenly had the feeling that I didn't know him at all.

He stopped at the kitchen table and picked up my cigarettes. Looking at me with a kind of mocking, amused defiance, he put one between his lips. "You mind?"

"You smoking already?"

He lit the cigarette and nodded, watching me through the smoke. "I just wanted to see if I'd have the courage to smoke in front of you." He grinned and blew a great cloud of smoke to the ceiling. "It was easy." He looked at my face. "Come on, now. I bet you was smoking at my age, tell the truth."

I didn't say anything but the truth was on my face, and he laughed. But now there was something very strained in his laugh. "Sure. And I bet that ain't all you was doing."

He was frightening me a little. "Cut the crap," I said. "We already decided that you was going to go and live at Isabel's. Now what's got into you all of a sudden?"

"*You* decided it," he pointed out. "*I* didn't decide nothing." He stopped in front of me, leaning against the stove, arms loosely folded. "Look, brother. I don't want to stay in Harlem no more, I really don't." He was very earnest. He looked at me, then over toward the kitchen window. There was something in his eyes I'd never seen before, some thoughtfulness, some worry all his own. He rubbed the muscle of one arm. "It's time I was getting out of here."

"Where do you want to *go,* Sonny?"

"I want to join the army. Or the navy, I don't care. If I say I'm old enough, they'll believe me."

Then I got mad. It was because I was so scared. "You must be crazy. You goddamn fool, what the hell do you want to go and join the *army* for?"

"I just told you. To get out of Harlem."

"Sonny, you haven't even finished *school.* And if you really want to be a musician, how do you expect to study if you're in the *army?*"

He looked at me, trapped, and in anguish. "There's ways. I might be able to work out some kind of deal. Anyway, I'll have the G.I. Bill when I come out."

"*If* you come out." We stared at each other. "Sonny, please. Be reasonable. I know the setup is far from perfect. But we got to do the best we can."

"I ain't learning nothing in school," he said. "Even when I go." He turned away from me and opened the window and threw his cigarette out into the narrow alley. I watched his back. "At least, I ain't learning nothing you'd want me to learn." He slammed the window so hard I thought the glass would fly out, and turned back to me. "And I'm sick of the stink of these garbage cans!"

"Sonny," I said, "I know how you feel. But if you don't finish school now, you're going to be sorry later that you didn't." I grabbed him by the shoulders. "And you only got another year. It ain't so bad. And I'll come back and I swear I'll help you do *whatever* you want to do. Just try to put up with it till I come back. Will you please do that? For me?"

He didn't answer and he wouldn't look at me.

"Sonny. You hear me?"

He pulled away. "I hear you. But you never hear anything *I* say."

I didn't know what to say to that. He looked out of the window and then back at me. "OK," he said, and sighed. "I'll try."

Then I said, trying to cheer him up a little, "They got a piano at Isabel's. You can practice on it."

And as a matter of fact, it did cheer him up for a minute. "That's right," he said to himself "I forgot that." His face relaxed a little. But the worry, the thoughtfulness, played on it still, the way shadows play on a face which is staring into the fire.

But I thought I'd never hear the end of that piano. At first, Isabel would write me, saying how nice it was that Sonny was so serious about his music and how, as soon as he came in from school, or wherever he had been when he was supposed to be at school, he went straight to that piano and stayed there until suppertime. And, after supper, he went back to that piano and stayed there until everybody went to bed. He was at the piano all day Saturday and all day Sunday. Then he bought a record player and started playing records. He'd play one record over and over again, all day long sometimes, and he'd improvise along with it on the piano. Or he'd play one section of the record, one chord, one change, one progression, then he'd do it on the piano. Then back to the record. Then back to the piano.

Well, I really don't know how they stood it. Isabel finally confessed that it wasn't like living with a person at all, it was like living with sound. And the sound didn't make any sense to her, didn't make any sense to any of them—naturally. They began, in a way, to be afflicted by this presence that was living in their home. It was as though Sonny were some sort of god, or monster. He moved in an atmosphere which wasn't like theirs at all. They fed him and he ate, he washed himself, he walked in and out of their door; he certainly wasn't nasty or unpleasant or rude, Sonny isn't any of those things; but it was as though he were all wrapped up in some cloud, some fire, some vision all his own; and there wasn't any way to reach him.

At the same time, he wasn't really a man yet, he was still a child, and they had to watch out for him in all kinds of ways. They certainly couldn't throw him out. Neither did they dare to make a great scene about that piano because even they dimly sensed, as I sensed, from so many thousands of miles away, that Sonny was at that piano playing for his life.

But he hadn't been going to school. One day a letter came from the school board and Isabel's mother got it—there had, apparently, been other letters but Sonny had torn them up. This day, when Sonny came in, Isabel's mother showed him the letter and asked where he'd been spending his time. And she finally got it out of him that he'd been down in Greenwich Village, with musicians and other characters, in a white girl's apartment. And this scared her and she started to scream at him and what came up, once she began—though she denies it to this day—was what sacrifices they were making to give Sonny a decent home and how little he appreciated it.

Sonny didn't play the piano that day. By evening, Isabel's mother had calmed down but then there was the old man to deal with, and Isabel herself. Isabel says she did her best to be calm but she broke down and started crying. She says she just watched Sonny's face. She could tell, by watching him, what was happening with him. And what was happening was that they penetrated his cloud, they had reached him. Even if their fingers had been a thousand times more gentle than human fingers ever are, he could hardly help feeling that they had stripped him naked and were spitting on that nakedness. For he also had to see that his presence, that music, which was life or death to him, had been torture for them and that they had endured it, not at all for his sake, but only for mine. And Sonny couldn't take that. He can take it a little better today than he could then but he's still not very good at it and, frankly, I don't know anybody who is.

The silence of the next few days must have been louder than the sound of all the music ever played since time began. One morning, before she went to work, Isabel was in his room for something and she suddenly realized that all of his records were gone. And she knew for certain that he was gone. And he was. He went as far as the navy would carry him. He finally sent me a postcard from some place in Greece and that was the first I knew that Sonny was still alive. I didn't see him any more until we were both back in New York and the war had long been over.

He was a man by then, of course, but I wasn't willing to see it. He came by the house from time to time, but we fought almost every time we met. I didn't like the way he carried himself, loose and dreamlike all the time, and I didn't like his friends, and his music seemed to be merely an excuse for the life he led. It sounded just that weird and disordered.

Then we had a fight, a pretty awful fight, and I didn't see him for months. By and by I looked him up, where he was living, in a furnished room in the Village, and I tried to make it up. But there were lots of people in the room and Sonny just lay on his bed, and he wouldn't come downstairs with me, and he treated these other people as though they were his family and I weren't. So I got mad and then he got mad, and then I told him that he might just as well be dead as live the way he was living. Then he stood up and he told me not to worry about him any more in life, that he *was* dead as far as I was concerned. Then he pushed me to the door and the other people looked on as though nothing were happening, and he slammed the door behind me. I stood in the hallway, staring at the door. I heard somebody laugh in the room and then the tears came to my eyes. I started down the steps, whistling to keep from crying, I kept whistling to myself, *You going to need me, baby, one of these cold, rainy days.*

I read about Sonny's trouble in the spring. Little Grace died in the fall. She was a beautiful little girl. But she only lived a little over two years. She died of polio and she suffered. She had a slight fever for a couple of days, but it didn't seem like anything and we just kept her in bed. And we would certainly have called the doctor, but the fever dropped, she seemed to be all right. So we thought it had just been a cold. Then, one day, she was up, playing, Isabel was in the kitchen fixing lunch for the two boys when they'd come in from school, and she heard Grace fall down in the living room. When you have a lot of children you don't always start running when one of them falls, unless they start screaming or something. And, this time, Grace was quiet. Yet, Isabel says that when she heard that *thump* and then that silence, something happened in her to make her afraid. And she ran to the living room and there was little Grace on the floor, all twisted up, and the reason she hadn't screamed was that she couldn't get her breath. And when she did scream, it was the worst sound, Isabel says, that she'd ever heard in all her life, and she still hears it sometimes in her dreams. Isabel will sometimes wake me up with a low, moaning, strangled sound and I have to be quick to awaken her and hold her to me and where Isabel is weeping against me seems a mortal wound.

I think I may have written Sonny the very day that little Grace was buried. I was sitting in the living room in the dark, by myself, and I suddenly thought of Sonny. My trouble made his real.

One Saturday afternoon, when Sonny had been living with us, or, anyway, been in our house, for nearly two weeks, I found myself wandering aimlessly about the living room, drinking from a can of beer, and trying to work up the courage to search Sonny's room. He was out, he was usually out whenever I was home, and Isabel had taken the children to see their grandparents. Suddenly I was standing still in front of the living room window, watching Seventh Avenue. The idea of searching Sonny's room made me still. I scarcely dared to admit to myself what I'd be searching for. I didn't know what I'd do if I found it. Or if I didn't.

On the sidewalk across from me, near the entrance to a barbecue joint, some people were holding an old-fashioned revival meeting. The barbecue cook, wearing a dirty white apron, his conked hair reddish and metallic in the pale sun, and a cigarette between his lips, stood in the doorway, watching them. Kids and older people paused in their errands and stood there, along with some older men and a couple of very tough-looking women who watched everything that happened on the avenue, as though they owned it, or were maybe owned by it. Well, they were watching this, too. The revival was being carried on by three sisters in black, and a brother. All they had were their voices and their Bibles and a tambourine. The brother was testifying and while he testified two of the sisters stood together, seeming to say, amen, and the third sister walked around with the tambourine outstretched and a couple of people dropped coins into it. Then the brother's testimony ended and the sister who had been taking up the collection dumped the coins into her palm and transferred them to the pocket of her long black robe. Then she raised both hands, striking the tambourine against the air, and then against one hand, and she started to sing. And the two other sisters and the brothers joined in.

It was strange, suddenly, to watch, though I had been seeing these street meetings all my life. So, of course, had everybody else down there. Yet, they paused and watched and listened and I stood still at the window. "*Tis the old ship of Zion,*" they sang, and the sister with the tambourine kept a steady, jangling beat, "*it has rescued many a thousand!*" Not a soul under the sound of their voices was hearing this song for the first time, not one of them had been rescued. Nor had they seen much in the way of rescue work being done around them. Neither did they especially believe in the holiness of the three sisters and the brother, they knew too much about them, knew where they lived, and how. The woman with the tambourine, whose voice dominated the air, whose face was bright with joy, was divided by very little from the woman who stood watching her, a cigarette between her heavy, chapped lips, her hair a cuckoo's nest, her face scarred and swollen from many beatings, and her black eyes glittering like coal. Perhaps they both knew this, which was why, when, as rarely, they addressed each other, they addressed each other as Sister. As the singing filled the air the watching, listening faces underwent a change, the eyes focusing on something within; the music seemed to soothe a poison out of them; and time seemed, nearly, to fall away from the sullen, belligerent, battered faces, as though they were fleeing back to their first condition, while dreaming of their last. The barbecue cook half shook his head and smiled, and dropped his cigarette and disappeared into his joint. A man fumbled in his pockets for change and stood holding it in his hand impatiently, as though he had just remembered a pressing appointment further up the avenue. He looked furious. Then I saw Sonny, standing on the edge of the crowd. He was carrying a wide, flat notebook with a green cover, and it made him look, from where I was standing, almost like a schoolboy. The coppery sun brought out the copper in his skin, he was very faintly smiling, standing very still. Then the singing stopped, the tambourine turned into a collection plate again. The furious man dropped in his coins and vanished, so did a couple of the women, and Sonny dropped some change in the plate, looking directly at the woman with a little smile. He started across the avenue, toward the house. He has a slow, loping walk, something like the way Harlem hipsters walk, only he's imposed on this his own half-beat. I had never really noticed it before.

I stayed at the window, both relieved and apprehensive. As Sonny disappeared from my sight, they began singing again. And they were still singing when his key turned in the lock.

"Hey," he said.

"Hey, yourself. You want some beer?"

"No. Well, maybe." But he came up to the window and stood beside me, looking out. "What a warm voice," he said.

They were singing *If I could only hear my mother pray again!*

"Yes," I said, "and she can sure beat that tambourine."

"But what a terrible song," he said, and laughed. He dropped his notebook on the sofa and disappeared into the kitchen. "Where's Isabel and the kids?"

"I think they went to see their grandparents. You hungry?"

"No." He came back into the living room with his can of beer. "You want to come some place with me tonight?"

I sensed, I don't know how, that I couldn't possibly say no. "Sure. Where?"

He sat down on the sofa and picked up his notebook and started leafing through it. "I'm going to sit in with some fellows in a joint in the Village."

"You mean, you're going to play, tonight?"

"That's right." He took a swallow of his beer and moved back to the window. He gave me a sidelong look. "If you can stand it."

"I'll try," I said.

He smiled to himself and we both watched as the meeting across the way broke up. The three sisters and the brother, heads bowed, were singing *God be with you till we meet again.* The faces around them were very quiet. Then the song ended. The small crowd dispersed. We watched the three women and the lone man walk slowly up the avenue.

"When she was singing before," said Sonny, abruptly, "her voice reminded me for a minute of what heroin feels like sometimes—when it's in your veins. It makes you feel sort of warm and cool at the same time. And distant. And—and sure." He sipped his beer, very deliberately not looking at me. I watched his face. "It makes you feel—in control. Sometimes you've got to have that feeling."

"Do you?" I sat down slowly in the easy chair.

"Sometimes." He went to the sofa and picked up his notebook again. "Some people do."

"In order," I asked, "to play?" And my voice was very ugly, full of contempt and anger.

"Well"—he looked at me with great, troubled eyes, as though, in fact, he hoped his eyes would tell me things he could never otherwise say—"they *think* so. And *if* they think so—!"

"And what do *you* think?" I asked.

He sat on the sofa and put his can of beer on the floor. "I don't know," he said, and I couldn't be sure if he were answering my question or pursuing his thoughts. His face didn't tell me. "It's not so much to *play.* It's to *stand* it, to be able to make it at all. On any level." He frowned and smiled: "In order to keep from shaking to pieces."

"But these friends of yours," I said, "they seem to shake themselves to pieces pretty goddamn fast."

"Maybe." He played with the notebook. And something told me that I should curb my tongue, that Sonny was doing his best to talk, that I should listen. "But of course you only know the ones that've gone to pieces. Some don't—or at least they haven't *yet* and that's just about all *any* of us can say." He paused. "And then there are some who just live, really, in hell, and they know it and they see what's happening and they go right on. I don't know." He sighed, dropped the notebook, folded his arms. "Some guys, you can tell from the way they play, they on something *all* the time. And you can see that, well, it makes something real for them. But of course," he picked up his beer from the floor and sipped it and put the can down again, "they *want* to, too, you've got to see that. Even some of them that say they don't—*some,* not all."

"And what about you?" I asked—I couldn't help it. "What about you? Do *you* want to?"

He stood up and walked to the window and remained silent for a long time. Then he sighed. "Me," he said. Then: "While I was downstairs before, on my way here, listening to that woman sing, it struck me all of a sudden how much suffering she must have had to go through—to sing like that. It's *repulsive* to think you have to suffer that much."

I said: "But there's no way not to suffer—is there, Sonny?"

"I believe not," he said and smiled, "but that's never stopped anyone from trying." He looked at me. "Has it?" I realized, with this mocking look, that there stood between us, forever, beyond the power of time or forgiveness, the fact that I had held silence—so long!—when he had needed human speech to help him. He turned back to the window. "No, there's no way not to suffer. But you try all kinds of ways to keep from drowning in it, to keep on top of it, and to make it seem—well, like *you*. Like you did something, all right, and now you're suffering for it. You know?" I said nothing. "Well you know," he said, impatiently, "why *do* people suffer? Maybe it's better to do something to give it a reason, *any* reason."

"But we just agreed," I said, "that there's no way not to suffer. Isn't it better, then, just to—take it?"

"But nobody just takes it," Sonny cried, "that's what I'm telling you! *Everybody* tries not to. You're just hung up on the *way* some people try—it's not *your* way!"

The hair on my face began to itch, my face felt wet. "That's not true," I said, "that's not true. I don't give a damn what other people do, I don't even care how they suffer. I just care how *you* suffer." And he looked at me. "Please believe me," I said, "I don't want to see you—die—trying not to suffer."

"I won't," he said, flatly, "die trying not to suffer. At least, not any faster than anybody else."

"But there's no need," I said, trying to laugh, "is there? in killing yourself."

I wanted to say more, but I couldn't. I wanted to talk about will power and how life could be—well, beautiful. I wanted to say that it was all within; but was it? or, rather, wasn't that exactly the trouble? And I wanted to promise that I would never fail him again. But it would all have sounded—empty words and lies.

So I made the promise to myself and prayed that I would keep it.

"It's terrible sometimes, inside," he said, "that's what's the trouble. You walk these streets, black and funky and cold, and there's not really a living ass to talk to, and there's nothing shaking, and there's no way of getting it out—that storm inside. You can't talk it and you can't make love with it, and when you finally try to get with it and play it, you realize *nobody's* listening. So *you've* got to listen. You got to find a way to listen."

And then he walked away from the window and sat on the sofa again, as though all the wind had suddenly been knocked out of him. "Sometimes you'll do *anything* to play, even cut your mother's throat." He laughed and looked at me. "Or your brother's." Then he sobered. "Or your own." Then: "Don't worry. I'm all right now and I think I'll *be* all right. But I can't forget—where I've been. I don't mean just the physical place I've been, I mean where I've *been*. And *what* I've been."

"What have you been, Sonny?" I asked.

He smiled—but sat sideways on the sofa, his elbow resting on the back, his fingers playing with his mouth and chin, not looking at me. "I've been something I didn't recognize, didn't know I could be. Didn't know anybody could be." He stopped, looking inward, looking helplessly young, looking old. "I'm not talking about it now because I feel *guilty* or anything like that—maybe it would be better if I did, I don't know. Anyway, I can't really talk about it. Not to you, not to anybody," and now he turned and faced me. "Sometimes, you know, and it was actually when I was most *out* of the world, I felt that I was in it, that I was *with* it, really, and I could play or I didn't really have to *play,* it just came out of me, it was there. And I don't know how I played, thinking about it now, but I know I did awful things, those times, sometimes, to people. Or it wasn't that I *did* anything to them—it was that they weren't real." He picked up the beer can; it was empty; he rolled it between his palms: "And other times—well, I needed a fix, I needed to find a place to lean, I needed to clear a space to *listen* —and I couldn't find it, and I—went crazy, I did terrible things to *me,* I was terrible *for* me." He began pressing the beer can between his hands, I watched the metal begin to give. It glittered, as he played with it, like a knife, and I was afraid he would cut himself, but I said nothing. "Oh well. I can never tell you. I was all by myself at the bottom of something, stinking and sweating and crying and shaking, and I smelled it, you know? *my* stink, and I thought I'd die if I couldn't get away from it and yet, all the same, I knew that everything I was doing was just locking me in with it. And I didn't know," he paused, still flattening the beer can, "I didn't know, I still *don't* know, something kept telling me that maybe it was good to smell your own stink, but I didn't think that *that* was what I'd been trying to do—and—who can stand it?" and he abruptly dropped the ruined beer can, looking at me with a small, still smile, and then rose, walking to the window as though it were the lodestone rock. I watched his face, he watched the avenue. "I couldn't tell you when Mama died—but the reason I wanted to leave Harlem so bad was to get away from drugs. And then, when I ran away, that's what I was running from—really. When I came back, nothing had changed, *I* hadn't changed, I was just—older." And he stopped, drumming with his fingers on the windowpane. The sun had vanished, soon darkness would fall. I watched his face. "It can come again," he said, almost as though speaking to himself. Then he turned to me. "It can come again," he repeated. "I just want you to know that."

"All right," I said, at last. "So it can come again, All right."

He smiled, but the smile was sorrowful. "I had to try to tell you," he said.

"Yes," I said. "I understand that."

"You're my brother," he said, looking straight at me, and not smiling at all.

"Yes," I repeated, "yes. I understand that."

He turned back to the window, looking out. "All that hatred down there," he said, "all that hatred and misery and love. It's a wonder it doesn't blow the avenue apart."

We went to the only nightclub on a short, dark street, downtown. We squeezed through the narrow, chattering, jam-packed bar to the entrance of the big room, where the bandstand was. And we stood there for a moment, for the lights were very dim in this room and we couldn't see. Then, "Hello, boy," said a voice and an enormous black man, much older than Sonny or myself, erupted out of all that atmospheric lighting and put an arm around Sonny's shoulder. "I been sitting right here," he said, "waiting for you."

He had a big voice, too, and heads in the darkness turned toward us.

Sonny grinned and pulled a little away, and said, "Creole, this is my brother. I told you about him."

Creole shook my hand. "I'm glad to meet you, son," he said, and it was clear that he was glad to meet me *there,* for Sonny's sake. And he smiled, "You got a real musician in *your* family," and he took his arm from Sonny's shoulder and slapped him, lightly, affectionately, with the back of his hand.

"Well. Now I've heard it all," said a voice behind us. This was another musician, and a friend of Sonny's, a coal-black, cheerful-looking man, built close to the ground. He immediately began confiding to me, at the top of his lungs, the most terrible things about Sonny, his teeth gleaming like a lighthouse and his laugh coming up out of him like the beginning of an earthquake. And it turned out that everyone at the bar knew Sonny, or almost everyone; some were musicians, working there, or nearby, or not working, some were simply hangers-on, and some were there to hear Sonny play. I was introduced to all of them and they were all very polite to me. Yet, it was clear that, for them, I was only Sonny's brother. Here, I was in Sonny's world. Or, rather: his kingdom. Here, it was not even a question that his veins bore royal blood.

They were going to play soon and Creole installed me, by myself, at a table in a dark corner. Then I watched them, Creole, and the little black man, and Sonny, and the others, while they horsed around, standing just below the bandstand. The light from the bandstand spilled just a little short of them and, watching them laughing and gesturing and moving about, I had the feeling that they, nevertheless, were being most careful not to step into that circle of light too suddenly: that if they moved into the light too suddenly, without thinking, they would perish in flame. Then, while I watched, one of them, the small, black man, moved into the light and crossed the bandstand and started fooling around with his drums. Then—being funny and being, also, extremely ceremonious—Creole took Sonny by the arm and led him to the piano. A woman's voice called Sonny's name and a few hands started clapping. And Sonny, also being funny and being ceremonious, and so touched, I think, that he could have cried, but neither hiding it nor showing it, riding it like a man, grinned, and put both hands to his heart and bowed from the waist.

Creole then went to the bass fiddle and a lean, very bright-skinned brown man jumped up on the bandstand and picked up his horn. So there they were, and the atmosphere on the bandstand and in the room began to change and tighten. Someone stepped up to the microphone and announced them. Then there were all kinds of murmurs. Some people at the bar shushed others. The waitress ran around, frantically getting in the last orders, guys and chicks got closer to each other, and the lights on the bandstand, on the quartet, turned to a kind of indigo. Then they all looked different there. Creole looked about him for the last time, as though he were making certain that all his chickens were in the coop, and then he—jumped and struck the fiddle. And there they were.

All I know about music is that not many people ever really hear it. And even then, on the rare occasions when something opens within, and the music enters, what we mainly hear, or hear corroborated, are personal, private, vanishing evocations. But the man who creates the music is hearing something else, is dealing with the roar rising from the void and imposing order on it as it hits the air. What is evoked in him, then, is of another order, more terrible because it has no words, and triumphant, too, for that same reason. And his triumph, when he triumphs, is ours. I just watched Sonny's face. His face was troubled, he was working hard, but he wasn't with it. And I had the feeling that, in a way, everyone on the bandstand was waiting for him, both waiting for him and pushing him along. But as I began to watch Creole, I realized that it was Creole who held them all back. He had them on a short rein. Up there, keeping the beat with his whole body, wailing on the fiddle, with his eyes half closed, he was listening to everything, but he was listening to Sonny. He was having a dialogue with Sonny. He wanted Sonny to leave the shoreline and strike out for the deep water. He was Sonny's witness that deep water and drowning were not the same thing—he had been there, and he knew. And he wanted Sonny to know. He was waiting for Sonny to do the things on the keys which would let Creole know that Sonny was in the water.

And, while Creole listened, Sonny moved, deep within, exactly like someone in torment. I had never before thought of how awful the relationship must be between the musician and his instrument. He has to fill it, this instrument, with the breath of life, his own. He has to make it do what he wants it to do. And a piano is just a piano. It's made out of so much wood and wires and little hammers and big ones, and ivory. While there's only so much you can do with it, the only way to find this out is to try; to try and make it do everything.

And Sonny hadn't been near a piano for over a year. And he wasn't on much better terms with his life, not the life that stretched before him now. He and the piano stammered, started one way, got scared, stopped; started another way, panicked, marked time, started again; then seemed to have found a direction, panicked again, got stuck. And the face I saw on Sonny I'd never seen before. Everything had been burned out of it, and, at the same time, things usually hidden were being burned in, by the fire and fury of the battle which was occurring in him up there.

Yet, watching Creole's face as they neared the end of the first set, I had the feeling that something had happened, something I hadn't heard. Then they finished, there was scattered applause, and then, without an instant's warning, Creole started into something else, it was almost sardonic, it was *Am I Blue*. And, as though he commanded, Sonny began to play. Something began to happen. And Creole let out the reins. The dry, low, black man said something awful on the drums, Creole answered, and the drums talked back. Then the horn insisted, sweet and high, slightly detached perhaps, and Creole listened, commenting now and then, dry, and driving, beautiful and calm and old. Then they all came together again, and Sonny was part of the family again. I could tell this from his face. He seemed to have found, right there beneath his fingers, a damn brand-new piano. It seemed that he couldn't get over it. Then, for awhile, just being happy with Sonny, they seemed to be agreeing with him that brand-new pianos certainly were a gas.

Then Creole stepped forward to remind them that what they were playing was the blues. He hit something in all of them, he hit something in me, myself, and the music tightened and deepened, apprehension began to beat the air. Creole began to tell us what the blues were all about. They were not about anything very new. He and his boys up there were keeping it new, at the risk of ruin, destruction, madness, and death, in order to find new ways to make us listen. For, while the tale of how we suffer, and how we are delighted, and how we may triumph is never new, it always must be heard. There isn't any other tale to tell, it's the only light we've got in all this darkness.

And this tale, according to that face, that body, those strong hands on those strings, has another aspect in every country, and a new depth in every generation. Listen, Creole seemed to be saying, listen. Now these are Sonny's blues. He made the little black man on the drums know it, and the bright, brown man on the horn. Creole wasn't trying any longer to get Sonny in the water. He was wishing him Godspeed. Then he stepped back, very slowly, filling the air with the immense suggestion that Sonny speak for himself.

Then they all gathered around Sonny and Sonny played. Every now and again one of them seemed to say, amen. Sonny's fingers filled the air with life, his life. But that life contained so many others. And Sonny went all the way back, he really began with the spare, flat statement of the opening phrase of the song. Then he began to make it his. It was very beautiful because it wasn't hurried and it was no longer a lament. I seemed to hear with what burning he had made it his, with what burning we had yet to make it ours, how we could cease lamenting. Freedom lurked around us and I understood, at last, that he could help us to be free if we would listen, that he would never be free until we did. Yet, there was no battle in his face now. I heard what he had gone through, and would continue to go through until he came to rest in earth. He had made it his: that long line, of which we knew only Mama and Daddy. And he was giving it back, as everything must be given back, so that, passing through death, it can live forever. I saw my mother's face again, and felt, for the first time, how the stones of the road she had walked on must have bruised her feet. I saw the moonlit road where my father's brother died. And it brought something else back to me, and carried me past it. I saw my little girl again and felt Isabel's tears again, and I felt my own tears begin to rise. And I was yet aware that this was only a moment, that the world waited outside, as hungry as a tiger, and that trouble stretched above us, longer than the sky.

Then it was over. Creole and Sonny let out their breath, both soaking wet, and grinning. There was a lot of applause and some of it was real. In the dark, the girl came by and I asked her to take drinks to the bandstand. There was a long pause, while they talked up there in the indigo light and after awhile I saw the girl put a Scotch and milk on top of the piano for Sonny. He didn't seem to notice it, but just before they started playing again, he sipped from it and looked toward me, and nodded. Then he put it back on top of the piano. For me, then, as they began to play again, it glowed and shook above my brother's head like the very cup of trembling.

(1957)

QUESTIONS FOR CRITICAL THINKING AND WRITING

Experience

1. To what extent does the relationship of the brothers reflect a sibling relationship of yours or one that you have observed?
2. What is the significance of music to Sonny's life? Do you or does anyone you know make music so central to life?

Interpretation

3. Describe the social milieu of the story. What seems to be the predominant response of the inhabitants to this environment?
4. Consider the women in the story. Are they very different from the men in temperament and concerns?
5. What do you think is the turning point in the narrator's relationship with his brother?

Evaluation

6. Consider the contrast in the conversations about Sonny's addiction. How does your evaluation of the narrator's character change as a result of these two specific scenes?

Connections

7. Compare the effects of environment on characters in "Sonny's Blues" with its effect on characters in stories such as Joyce's "The Boarding House" or Tan's "Rules of the Game" (both found in this chapter).
8. Compare Sonny's need to play music with the narrator's need to write in Gilman's "The Yellow Wallpaper."

Critical Thinking

9. What are Sonny's "blues"? To what extent is the music of the blues an appropriate vehicle to convey the tenor and temper of Sonny's life? Explain.

© Jill Krementz

RAYMOND CARVER

[1939–1988]

Originally from Oregon where he was raised in a working-class milieu, Raymond Carver lived in Washington and spent much of his life in California. After working at a series of low-paying odd jobs, Carver worked as an editor and as a college teacher at the University of California at Berkeley, the University of Iowa, the University of Texas at El Paso, and Syracuse University. Carver's fictional mentors include James Joyce, Ernest Hemingway, and, above all, Anton Chekhov, whose stories Carver admired above those of all other writers. His best stories are lean and spare and touch deeply on central human problems.

Cathedral

This blind man, an old friend of my wife's, he was on his way to spend the night. His wife had died. So he was visiting the dead wife's relatives in Connecticut. He called my wife from his in-laws'. Arrangements were made. He would come by train, a five-hour trip, and my wife would meet him at the station. She hadn't seen him since she worked for him one summer in Seattle ten years ago. But she and the blind man had kept in touch. They made tapes and mailed them back and forth. I wasn't enthusiastic about his visit. He was no one I knew. And his being blind bothered me. My idea of blindness came from the movies. In the movies, the blind moved slowly and never laughed. Sometimes they were led by seeing-eye dogs. A blind man in my house was not something I looked forward to.

That summer in Seattle she had needed a job. She didn't have any money. The man she was going to marry at the end of the summer was in officers' training school. He didn't have any money, either. But she was in love with the guy, and he was in love with her, etc. She'd seen something in the paper: HELP WANTED—*Reading to Blind Man,* and a telephone number. She phoned and went over, was hired on the spot. She'd worked with this blind man all summer. She read stuff to him, case studies, reports, that sort of thing. She helped him organize his little office in the county social-service department. They'd become good friends, my wife and the blind man. How do I know these things? She told me. And she told me something else. On her last day in the office, the blind man asked if he could touch her face. She agreed to this. She told me he touched his fingers to every part of her face, her nose—even her neck! She never forgot it. She even tried to write a poem about it. She was always trying to write a poem. She wrote a poem or two every year, usually after something really important had happened to her.

When we first started going out together, she showed me the poem. In the poem, she recalled his fingers and the way they had moved around over her face. In the poem, she talked about what she had felt at the time, about what went through her mind when the blind man touched her nose and lips. I can remember I didn't think much of the poem. Of course, I didn't tell her that. Maybe I just don't understand poetry. I admit it's not the first thing I reach for when I pick up something to read.

Anyway, this man who'd first enjoyed her favors, the officer-to-be, he'd been her childhood sweetheart. So okay. I'm saying that at the end of the summer she let the blind man run his hands over her face, said goodbye to him, married her childhood etc., who was now a commissioned officer, and she moved away from Seattle. But they'd kept in touch, she and the blind man. She made the first contact after a year or so. She called him up one night from an Air Force base in Alabama. She wanted to talk. They talked. He asked her to send him a tape and tell him about her life. She did this. She sent the tape. On the tape, she told the blind man about her husband and about their life together in the military. She told the blind man she loved her husband but she didn't like it where they lived and she didn't like it that he was a part of the military-industrial thing. She told the blind man she'd written a poem and he was in it. She told him that she was writing a poem about what it was like to be an Air Force officer's wife. The poem wasn't finished yet. She was still writing it. The blind man made a tape. He sent her the tape. She made a tape. This went on for years. My wife's officer was posted to one base and then another. She sent tapes from Moody AFB, McGuire, McConnell, and finally Travis, near Sacramento, where one night she got to feeling lonely and cut off from people she kept losing in that moving-around life. She got to feeling she couldn't go it another step. She went in and swallowed all the pills and capsules in the medicine chest and washed them down with a bottle of gin. Then she got into a hot bath and passed out.

But instead of dying, she got sick. She threw up. Her officer—why should he have a name? he was the childhood sweetheart, and what more does he want?—came home from somewhere, found her, and called the ambulance. In time, she put it all on a tape and sent the tape to the blind man. Over the years, she put all kinds of stuff on tapes and sent the tapes off lickety-split. Next to writing a poem every year, I think it was her chief means of recreation. On one tape, she told the blind man she'd decided to live away from her officer for a time. On another tape, she told him about her divorce. She and I began going out, and of course she told her blind man about it. She told him everything, or so it seemed to me. Once she asked me if I'd like to hear the latest tape from the blind man. This was a year ago. I was on the tape, she said. So I said okay, I'd listen to it. I got us drinks and we settled down in the living room. We made ready to listen. First she inserted the tape into the player and adjusted a couple of dials. Then she pushed a lever. The tape squeaked and someone began to talk in this loud voice. She lowered the volume. After a few minutes of harmless chitchat, I heard my own name in the mouth of this stranger, this blind man I didn't even know! And then this: "From all you've said about him, I can only conclude—" But we were interrupted, a knock at the door, something, and we didn't ever get back to the tape. Maybe it was just as well. I'd heard all I wanted to.

Now this same blind man was coming to sleep in my house.

"Maybe I could take him bowling," I said to my wife. She was at the draining board doing scalloped potatoes. She put down the knife she was using and turned around.

"If you love me," she said, "you can do this for me. If you don't love me, okay. But if you had a friend, any friend, and the friend came to visit, I'd make him feel comfortable." She wiped her hands with the dish towel.

"I don't have any blind friends," I said.

"You don't have any friends," she said. "Period. Besides," she said, "goddamn it, his wife's just died! Don't you understand that? The man's lost his wife!"

I didn't answer. She'd told me a little about the blind man's wife. Her name was Beulah. Beulah! That's a name for a colored woman.

"Was his wife a Negro?" I asked.

"Are you crazy?" my wife said. "Have you just flipped or something?" She picked up a potato. I saw it hit the floor, then roll under the stove. "What's wrong with you?" she said. "Are you drunk?"

"I'm just asking," I said.

Right then my wife filled me in with more detail than I cared to know. I made a drink and sat at the kitchen table to listen. Pieces of the story began to fall into place.

Beulah had gone to work for the blind man the summer after my wife had stopped working for him. Pretty soon Beulah and the blind man had themselves a church wedding. It was a little wedding—who'd want to go to such a wedding in the first place?—just the two of them, plus the minister and the minister's wife. But it was a church wedding just the same. It was what Beulah had wanted, he'd said. But even then Beulah must have been carrying the cancer in her glands. After they had been inseparable for eight years—my wife's word, *inseparable*—Beulah's health went into a rapid decline. She died in a Seattle hospital room, the blind man sitting beside the bed and holding on to her hand. They'd married, lived and worked together, slept together—had sex, sure—and then the blind man had to bury her. All this without his having ever seen what the goddamned woman looked like. It was beyond my understanding. Hearing this, I felt sorry for the blind man for a little bit. And then I found myself thinking what a pitiful life this woman must have led. Imagine a woman who could never see herself as she was seen in the eyes of her loved one. A woman who could go on day after day and never receive the smallest compliment from her beloved. A woman whose husband could never read the expression on her face, be it misery or something better. Someone who could wear makeup or not—what difference to him? She could, if she wanted, wear green eye-shadow around one eye, a straight pin in her nostril, yellow slacks and purple shoes, no matter. And then to slip off into death, the blind man's hand on her hand, his blind eyes streaming tears—I'm imagining now—her last thought maybe this: that he never even knew what she looked like, and she on an express to the grave. Robert was left with a small insurance policy and half of a twenty-peso Mexican coin. The other half of the coin went into the box with her. Pathetic.

So when the time rolled around, my wife went to the depot to pick him up. With nothing to do but wait—sure, I blamed him for that—I was having a drink and watching the TV when I heard the car pull into the drive. I got up from the sofa with my drink and went to the window to have a look.

I saw my wife laughing as she parked the car. I saw her get out of the car and shut the door. She was still wearing a smile. Just amazing. She went around to the other side of the car to where the blind man was already starting to get out. This blind man, feature this, he was wearing a full beard! A beard on a blind man! Too much, I say. The blind man reached into the back seat and dragged out a suitcase. My wife took his arm, shut the car door, and, talking all the way, moved him down the drive and then up the steps to the front porch. I turned off the TV. I finished my drink, rinsed the glass, dried my hands. Then I went to the door.

My wife said, "I want you to meet Robert. Robert, this is my husband. I've told you all about him." She was beaming. She had this blind man by his coat sleeve.

The blind man let go of his suitcase and up came his hand.

I took it. He squeezed hard, held my hand, and then he let it go.

"I feel like we've already met," he boomed.

"Likewise," I said. I didn't know what else to say. Then I said, "Welcome. I've heard a lot about you." We began to move then, a little group, from the porch into the living room, my wife guiding him by the arm. The blind man was carrying his suitcase in his other hand. My wife said things like, "To your left here, Robert. That's right. Now watch it, there's a chair. That's it. Sit down right here. This is the sofa. We just bought this sofa two weeks ago."

I started to say something about the old sofa. I'd liked that old sofa. But I didn't say anything. Then I wanted to say something else, small-talk, about the scenic ride along the Hudson. How going *to* New York, you should sit on the right-hand side of the train, and coming *from* New York, the left-hand side.

"Did you have a good train ride?" I said. "Which side of the train did you sit on, by the way?"

"What a question, which side!" my wife said. "What's it matter which side?" she said.

"I just asked," I said.

"Right side," the blind man said. "I hadn't been on a train in nearly forty years. Not since I was a kid. With my folks. That's been a long time. I'd nearly forgotten the sensation. I have winter in my beard now," he said. "So I've been told, anyway. Do I look distinguished, my dear?" the blind man said to my wife.

"You look distinguished, Robert," she said. "Robert," she said. "Robert, it's just so good to see you."

My wife finally took her eyes off the blind man and looked at me. I had the feeling she didn't like what she saw. I shrugged.

I've never met, or personally known, anyone who was blind. This blind man was late forties, a heavy-set, balding man with stooped shoulders, as if he carried a great weight there. He wore brown slacks, brown shoes, a light-brown shirt, a tie, a sports coat. Spiffy. He also had this full beard. But he didn't use a cane and he didn't wear dark glasses. I'd always thought dark glasses were a must for the blind. Fact was, I wished he had a pair. At first glance, his eyes looked like anyone else's eyes. But if you looked close, there was something different about them. Too much white in the iris, for one thing, and the pupils seemed to move around in the sockets without his knowing it or being able to stop it. Creepy. As I stared at his face, I saw the left pupil turn in toward his nose while the other made an effort to keep in one place. But it was only an effort, for that eye was on the roam without his knowing it or wanting it to be.

I said, "Let me get you a drink. What's your pleasure? We have a little of everything. It's one of our pastimes."

"Bub, I'm a Scotch man myself," he said fast enough in this big voice.

"Right," I said. Bub! "Sure you are. I knew it."

He let his fingers touch his suitcase, which was sitting alongside the sofa. He was taking his bearings. I didn't blame him for that.

"I'll move that up to your room," my wife said.

"No, that's fine," the blind man said loudly. "It can go up when I go up."

"A little water with the Scotch?" I said.

"Very little," he said.

"I knew it," I said.

He said, "Just a tad. The Irish actor, Barry Fitzgerald? I'm like that fellow. When I drink water, Fitzgerald said, I drink water. When I drink whiskey, I drink whiskey." My wife laughed. The blind man brought his hand up under his beard. He lifted his beard slowly and let it drop.

I did the drinks, three big glasses of Scotch with a splash of water in each. Then we made ourselves comfortable and talked about Robert's travels. First the long flight from the West Coast to Connecticut, we covered that. Then from Connecticut up here by train. We had another drink concerning that leg of the trip.

I remembered having read somewhere that the blind didn't smoke because, as speculation had it, they couldn't see the smoke they exhaled. I thought I knew that much and that much only about blind people. But this blind man smoked his cigarette down to the nubbin and then lit another one. This blind man filled his ashtray and my wife emptied it.

When we sat down at the table for dinner, we had another drink. My wife heaped Robert's plate with cube steak, scalloped potatoes, green beans. I buttered him up two slices of bread. I said, "Here's bread and butter for you." I swallowed some of my drink. "Now let us pray," I said, and the blind man lowered his head. My wife looked at me, her mouth agape. "Pray the phone won't ring and the food doesn't get cold," I said.

We dug in. We ate everything there was to eat on the table. We ate like there was no tomorrow. We didn't talk. We ate. We scarfed. We grazed that table. We were into serious eating. The blind man had right away located his foods, he knew just where everything was on his plate. I watched with admiration as he used his knife and fork on the meat. He'd cut two pieces of meat, fork the meat into his mouth, and then go all out for the scalloped potatoes, the beans next, and then he'd tear off a hunk of buttered bread and eat that. He'd follow this up with a big drink of milk. It didn't seem to bother him to use his fingers once in a while, either.

We finished everything, including half a strawberry pie. For a few moments, we sat as if stunned. Sweat beaded on our faces. Finally, we got up from the table and left the dirty plates. We didn't look back. We took ourselves into the living room and sank into our places again. Robert and my wife sat on the sofa. I took the big chair. We had us two or three more drinks while they talked about the major things that had come to pass for them in the past ten years. For the most part, I just listened. Now and then I joined in. I didn't want him to think I'd left the room, and I didn't want her to think I was feeling left out. They talked of things that had happened to them—to them!—these past ten years. I waited in vain to hear my name on my wife's sweet lips: "And then my dear husband came into my life"—something like that. But I heard nothing of the sort. More talk of Robert. Robert had done a little of everything, it seemed, a regular blind jack-of-all-trades. But most recently he and his wife had had an Amway distributorship, from which, I gathered, they'd earned their living, such as it was. The blind man was also a ham radio operator. He talked in his loud voice about conversations he'd had with fellow operators in Guam, in the Philippines, in Alaska, and even in Tahiti. He said he'd have a lot of friends there if he ever wanted to go visit those places. From time to time, he'd turn his blind face toward me, put his hand under his beard, ask me something. How long had I been in my present position? (Three years.) Did I like my work? (I didn't.) Was I going to stay with it? (What were the options?) Finally, when I thought he was beginning to run down, I got up and turned on the TV.

My wife looked at me with irritation. She was heading toward a boil. Then she looked at the blind man and said, "Robert, do you have a TV?"

The blind man said, "My dear, I have two TVs. I have a color set and a black-and-white thing, an old relic. It's funny, but if I turn the TV on, and I'm always turning it on, I turn on the color set. It's funny, don't you think?"

I didn't know what to say to that. I had absolutely nothing to say to that. No opinion. So I watched the news program and tried to listen to what the announcer was saying.

"This is a color TV," the blind man said. "Don't ask me how, but I can tell."

"We traded up a while ago," I said.

The blind man had another taste of his drink. He lifted his beard, sniffed it, and let it fall. He leaned forward on the sofa. He positioned his ashtray on the coffee table, then put the lighter to his cigarette. He leaned back on the sofa and crossed his legs at the ankles.

My wife covered her mouth, and then she yawned. She stretched. She said, "I think I'll go upstairs and put on my robe. I think I'll change into something else. Robert, you make yourself comfortable," she said.

"I'm comfortable," the blind man said.

"I want you to feel comfortable in this house," she said.

"I am comfortable," the blind man said.

After she'd left the room, he and I listened to the weather report and then to the sports roundup. By that time, she'd been gone so long I didn't know if she was going to come back. I thought she might have gone to bed. I wished she'd come back downstairs. I didn't want to be left alone with a blind man. I asked him if he wanted another drink, and he said sure. Then I asked if he wanted to smoke some dope with me. I said I'd just rolled a number. I hadn't, but I planned to do so in about two shakes.

"I'll try some with you," he said.

"Damn right," I said. "That's the stuff."

I got our drinks and sat down on the sofa with him. Then I rolled us two fat numbers. I lit one and passed it. I brought it to his fingers. He took it and inhaled.

"Hold it as long as you can," I said. I could tell he didn't know the first thing.

My wife came back downstairs wearing her pink robe and her pink slippers.

"What do I smell?" she said.

"We thought we'd have us some cannabis," I said.

My wife gave me a savage look. Then she looked at the blind man and said, "Robert, I didn't know you smoked."

He said, "I do now, my dear. There's a first time for everything. But I don't feel anything yet."

"This stuff is pretty mellow," I said. "This stuff is mild. It's dope you can reason with," I said. "It doesn't mess you up."

"Not much it doesn't, bub," he said, and laughed.

My wife sat on the sofa between the blind man and me. I passed her the number. She took it and toked and then passed it back to me. "Which way is this going?" she said. Then she said, "I shouldn't be smoking this. I can hardly keep my eyes open as it is. That dinner did me in. I shouldn't have eaten so much."

"It was the strawberry pie," the blind man said. "That's what did it," he said, and he laughed his big laugh. Then he shook his head.

"There's more strawberry pie," I said.

"Do you want some more, Robert?" my wife said.

"Maybe in a little while," he said.

We gave our attention to the TV. My wife yawned again. She said, "Your bed is made up when you feel like going to bed, Robert. I know you must have had a long day. When you're ready to go to bed, say so." She pulled his arm. "Robert?"

He came to and said, "I've had a real nice time. This beats tapes, doesn't it?"

I said, "Coming at you," and I put the number between his fingers. He inhaled, held the smoke, and then let it go. It was like he'd been doing it since he was nine years old.

"Thanks, bub," he said. "But I think this is all for me. I think I'm beginning to feel it," he said. He held the burning roach out for my wife.

"Same here," she said. "Ditto. Me, too." She took the roach and passed it to me. "I may just sit here for a while between you two guys with my eyes closed. But don't let me bother you, okay? Either one of you. If it bothers you, say so. Otherwise, I may just sit here with my eyes closed until you're ready to go to bed," she said. "Your bed's made up, Robert, when you're ready. It's right next to our room at the top of the stairs. We'll show you up when you're ready. You wake me up now, you guys, if I fall asleep." She said that and then she closed her eyes and went to sleep.

The news program ended. I got up and changed the channel. I sat back down on the sofa. I wished my wife hadn't pooped out. Her head lay across the back of the sofa, her mouth open. She'd turned so that her robe had slipped away from her legs, exposing a juicy thigh. I reached to draw her robe back over her, and it was then that I glanced at the blind man. What the hell! I flipped the robe open again.

"You say when you want some strawberry pie," I said.

"I will," he said.

I said, "Are you tired? Do you want me to take you up to your bed? Are you ready to hit the hay?"

"Not yet," he said. "No, I'll stay up with you, bub. If that's all right. I'll stay up until you're ready to turn in. We haven't had a chance to talk. Know what I mean? I feel like me and her monopolized the evening." He lifted his beard and he let it fall. He picked up his cigarettes and his lighter.

"That's all right," I said. Then I said, "I'm glad for the company."

And I guess I was. Every night I smoked dope and stayed up as long as I could before I fell asleep. My wife and I hardly ever went to bed at the same time. When I did go to sleep, I had these dreams. Sometimes I'd wake up from one of them, my heart going crazy.

Something about the church and the Middle Ages was on the TV. Not your run-of-the-mill TV fare. I wanted to watch something else. I turned to the other channels. But there was nothing on them, either. So I turned back to the first channel and apologized.

"Bub, it's all right," the blind man said. "It's fine with me. Whatever you want to watch is okay. I'm always learning something. Learning never ends. It won't hurt me to learn something tonight. I got ears," he said.

We didn't say anything for a time. He was leaning forward with his head turned at me, his right ear aimed in the direction of the set. Very disconcerting. Now and then his eyelids drooped and then they snapped open again. Now and then he put his fingers into his beard and tugged, like he was thinking about something he was hearing on the television.

On the screen, a group of men wearing cowls was being set upon and tormented by men dressed in skeleton costumes and men dressed as devils. The men dressed as devils wore devil masks, horns, and long tails. This pageant was part of a procession. The Englishman who was narrating the thing said it took place in Spain once a year. I tried to explain to the blind man what was happening.

"Skeletons," he said. "I know about skeletons," he said, and he nodded.

The TV showed this one cathedral. Then there was a long, slow look at another one. Finally, the picture switched to the famous one in Paris, with its flying buttresses and its spires reaching up to the clouds. The camera pulled away to show the whole of the cathedral rising above the skyline.

There were times when the Englishman who was telling the thing would shut up, would simply let the camera move around over the cathedrals. Or else the camera would tour the countryside, men in fields walking behind oxen. I waited as long as I could. Then I felt I had to say something. I said, "They're showing the outside of this cathedral now. Gargoyles. Little statues carved to look like monsters. Now I guess they're in Italy. Yeah, they're in Italy. There's paintings on the walls of this one church."

"Are those fresco paintings, bub?" he asked, and he sipped from his drink.

I reached for my glass. But it was empty. I tried to remember what I could remember. "You're asking me are those frescoes?" I said. "That's a good question. I don't know."

The camera moved to a cathedral outside Lisbon. The differences in the Portuguese cathedral compared with the French and Italian were not that great. But they were there. Mostly the interior stuff. Then something occurred to me, and I said, "Something has occurred to me. Do you have any idea what a cathedral is? What they look like, that is? Do you follow me? If somebody says cathedral to you, do you have any notion what they're talking about? Do you know the difference between that and a Baptist church, say?"

He let the smoke dribble from his mouth. "I know they took hundreds of workers fifty or a hundred years to build," he said. "I just heard the man say that, of course. I know generations of the same families worked on a cathedral. I heard him say that, too. The men who began their life's work on them, they never lived to see the completion of their work. In that wise, bub, they're no different from the rest of us, right?" He laughed. Then his eyelids drooped again. His head nodded. He seemed to be snoozing. Maybe he was imagining himself in Portugal. The TV was showing another cathedral now. This one was in Germany. The Englishman's voice droned on. "Cathedrals," the blind man said. He sat up and rolled his head back and forth. "If you want the truth, bub, that's about all I know. What I just said. What I heard him say. But maybe you could describe one to me? I wish you'd do it. I'd like that. If you want to know, I really don't have a good idea."

I stared hard at the shot of the cathedral on the TV. How could I even begin to describe it? But say my life depended on it. Say my life was being threatened by an insane guy who said I had to do it or else.

I stared some more at the cathedral before the picture flipped off into the countryside. There was no use. I turned to the blind man and said, "To begin with, they're very tall." I was looking around the room for clues. "They reach way up. Up and up. Toward the sky. They're so big, some of them, they have to have these supports. To help hold them up, so to speak. These supports are called buttresses. They remind me of viaducts, for some reason. But maybe you don't know viaducts, either? Sometimes the cathedrals have devils and such carved into the front. Sometimes lords and ladies. Don't ask me why this is," I said.

He was nodding. The whole upper part of his body seemed to be moving back and forth.

"I'm not doing so good, am I?" I said.

He stopped nodding and leaned forward on the edge of the sofa. As he listened to me, he was running his fingers through his beard. I wasn't getting through to him, I could see that. But he waited for me to go on just the same. He nodded, like he was trying to encourage me. I tried to think what else to say. "They're really big," I said. "They're massive. They're built of stone. Marble, too, sometimes. In those olden days, when they built cathedrals, men wanted to be close to God. In those olden days, God was an important part of everyone's life. You could tell this from their cathedral-building. I'm sorry," I said, "but it looks like that's the best I can do for you. I'm just no good at it."

"That's all right, bub," the blind man said. "Hey, listen. I hope you don't mind my asking you. Can I ask you something? Let me ask you a simple question, yes or no. I'm just curious and there's no offense. You're my host. But let me ask if you are in any way religious? You don't mind my asking?"

I shook my head. He couldn't see that, though. A wink is the same as a nod to a blind man. "I guess I don't believe in it. In anything. Sometimes it's hard. You know what I'm saying?"

"Sure, I do," he said.

"Right," I said.

The Englishman was still holding forth. My wife sighed in her sleep. She drew a long breath and went on with her sleeping.

"You'll have to forgive me," I said. "But I can't tell you what a cathedral looks like. It just isn't in me to do it. I can't do any more than I've done."

The blind man sat very still, his head down, as he listened to me.

I said, "The truth is, cathedrals don't mean anything special to me. Nothing. Cathedrals. They're something to look at on late-night TV. That's all they are."

It was then that the blind man cleared his throat. He brought something up. He took a handkerchief from his back pocket. Then he said, "I get it, bub. It's okay. It happens. Don't worry about it," he said. "Hey, listen to me. Will you do me a favor? I got an idea. Why don't you find us some heavy paper? And a pen. We'll do something. We'll draw one together. Get us a pen and some heavy paper. Go on, bub, get the stuff," he said.

So I went upstairs. My legs felt like they didn't have any strength in them. They felt like they did after I'd done some running. In my wife's room, I looked around. I found some ballpoints in a little basket on her table. And then I tried to think where to look for the kind of paper he was talking about.

Downstairs, in the kitchen, I found a shopping bag with onion skins in the bottom of the bag. I emptied the bag and shook it. I brought it into the living room and sat down with it near his legs. I moved some things, smoothed the wrinkles from the bag, spread it out on the coffee table.

The blind man got down from the sofa and sat next to me on the carpet. He ran his fingers over the paper. He went up and down the sides of the paper. The edges, even the edges. He fingered the corners.

"All right," he said. "All right, let's do her."

He found my hand, the hand with the pen. He closed his hand over my hand. "Go ahead, bub, draw," he said. "Draw. You'll see. I'll follow along with you. It'll be okay. Just begin now like I'm telling you. You'll see. Draw," the blind man said.

So I began. First I drew a box that looked like a house. It could have been the house I lived in. Then I put a roof on it. At either end of the roof, I drew spires. Crazy.

"Swell," he said. "Terrific. You're doing fine," he said. "Never thought anything like this could happen in your lifetime, did you, bub? Well, it's a strange life, we all know that. Go on now. Keep it up."

I put in windows with arches. I drew flying buttresses. I hung great doors. I couldn't stop. The TV station went off the air. I put down the pen and closed and opened my fingers. The blind man felt around over the paper. He moved the tips of his fingers over the paper, all over what I had drawn, and he nodded.

"Doing fine," the blind man said.

I took up the pen again, and he found my hand. I kept at it. I'm no artist. But I kept drawing just the same.

My wife opened up her eyes and gazed at us. She sat up on the sofa, her robe hanging open. She said, "What are you doing? Tell me, I want to know."

I didn't answer her.

The blind man said, "We're drawing a cathedral. Me and him are working on it. Press hard," he said to me. "That's right. That's good," he said. "Sure. You got it, bub. I can tell. You didn't think you could. But you can, can't you? You're cooking with gas now. You know what I'm saying? We're going to really have us something here in a minute. How's the old arm?" he said. "Put some people in there now. What's a cathedral without people?"

My wife said, "What's going on? Robert, what are you doing? What's going on?"

"It's all right," he said to her. "Close your eyes now," the blind man said to me.

I did it. I closed them just like he said.

"Are they closed?" he said. "Don't fudge."

"They're closed," I said.

"Keep them that way," he said. He said, "Don't stop now. Draw."

So we kept on with it. His fingers rode my fingers as my hand went over the paper. It was like nothing else in my life up to now.

Then he said, "I think that's it. I think you got it," he said. "Take a look. What do you think?"

But I had my eyes closed. I thought I'd keep them that way for a little longer. I thought it was something I ought to do.

"Well?" he said. "Are you looking?"

My eyes were still closed. I was in my house. I knew that. But I didn't feel like I was inside anything.

"It's really something," I said.

(1983)

QUESTIONS FOR CRITICAL THINKING AND WRITING

Experience

1. What are your impressions of the narrator? Do they change as the story progresses? Do you pity him? Why or why not?

Interpretation

2. What is the narrator's reaction to Robert's impending visit? How does Robert surprise the narrator?
3. How does Robert respond to the narrator's snide remarks and behavior? After dinner, do you think Robert determines to enlighten the narrator?
4. Chart the narrator's movement to his epiphany. What does he learn? Consider the image of the cathedral and the narrator's closing words as part of your response.

Evaluation

5. What values do you think the story endorses?

Connection

6. Compare the marriage in "Cathedral" with that of Leroy and Norma in Mason's "Shiloh" (Chapter Three).

Critical Thinking

7. Had Carver's story included a TV show about a medieval castle rather than a cathedral, would that have made a significant difference? Why or why not?

ANTON CHEKHOV

[1860–1904]

Born in southern Russia and trained to become a doctor, Anton Chekhov during his university years wrote short pieces for newspapers and magazines. By the time he received his medical degree, he was already well known as a writer, and he would eventually write hundreds of stories and half a dozen of the most important plays of the modern theater, including Uncle Vanya, The Three Sisters, The Seagull, *and* The Cherry Orchard. *The style of his stories has been considered a model by successive generations of writers.*

The Lady with the Little Dog

TRANSLATED BY RICHARD PEAVEAR AND LARISSA VOLOKHONSKY

I

The talk was that a new face had appeared on the embankment: a lady with a little dog. Dmitri Dmitrich Gurov, who had already spent two weeks in Yalta and was used to it, also began to take an interest in new faces. Sitting in a pavilion at Vernet's, he saw a young woman, not very tall, blond, in a beret, walking along the embankment; behind her ran a white spitz.

And after that he met her several times a day in the town garden or in the square. She went strolling alone, in the same beret, with the white spitz; nobody knew who she was, and they called her simply "the lady with the little dog."

"If she's here with no husband or friends," Gurov reflected, "it wouldn't be a bad idea to make her acquaintance."

He was not yet forty, but he had a twelve-year-old daughter and two sons in school. He had married young, while still a second-year student, and now his wife seemed half again his age. She was a tall woman with dark eyebrows, erect, imposing, dignified, and a thinking person, as she called herself. She read a great deal, used the new orthography, called her husband not Dmitri but Dimitri, but he secretly considered her none too bright, narrow-minded, grace less, was afraid of her, and disliked being at home. He had begun to be unfaithful to her long ago, was unfaithful often, and, probably for that reason, almost always spoke ill of women, and when they were discussed in his presence, he would say of them:

"An inferior race!"

It seemed to him that he had been taught enough by bitter experience to call them anything he liked, and yet he could not have lived without the "inferior race" even for two days. In the company of men he was bored, ill at ease, with them he was taciturn and cold, but when he was among women, he felt himself free and knew what to talk about with them and how to behave; and he was at ease even being silent with them. In his appearance, in his character, in his whole nature there was something attractive and elusive that disposed women towards him and enticed them; he knew that, and he himself was attracted to them by some force.

Repeated experience, and bitter experience indeed, had long since taught him that every intimacy, which in the beginning lends life such pleasant diversity and presents itself as a nice and light adventure, inevitably, with decent people—especially irresolute Muscovites, who are slow starters—grows into a major task, extremely complicated, and the situation finally becomes burdensome. But at every new meeting with an interesting woman, this experience somehow slipped from his memory, and he wanted to live, and everything seemed quite simple and amusing.

And so one time, towards evening, he was having dinner in the garden, and the lady in the beret came over unhurriedly to take the table next to his. Her expression, her walk, her dress, her hair told him that she belonged to decent society, was married, in Yalta for the first time, and alone, and that she was bored here . . . . In the stories about the impurity of local morals there was much untruth, he despised them and knew that these stories were mostly invented by people who would eagerly have sinned themselves had they known how; but when the lady sat down at the next table, three steps away from him, he remembered those stories of easy conquests, of trips to the mountains, and the tempting thought of a quick, fleeting liaison, a romance with an unknown woman, of whose very name you are ignorant, suddenly took possession of him.

He gently called the spitz, and when the dog came over, he shook his finger at it. The spitz growled. Gurov shook his finger again.

The lady glanced at him and immediately lowered her eyes.

"He doesn't bite," she said and blushed.

"May I give him a bone?" and, when she nodded in the affirmative, he asked affably: "Have you been in Yalta long?"

"About five days."

"And I'm already dragging through my second week here."

They were silent for a while.

"The time passes quickly, and yet it's so boring here!" she said without looking at him.

"It's merely the accepted thing to say it's boring here. The ordinary man lives somewhere in his Belevo or Zhizdra and isn't bored, then he comes here: 'Ah, how boring! Ah, how dusty!' You'd think he came from Granada."

She laughed. Then they went on eating in silence, like strangers; but after dinner they walked off together—and a light, bantering conversation began, of free, contented people, who do not care where they go or what they talk about. They strolled and talked of how strange the light was on the sea; the water was of a lilac color, so soft and warm, and over it the moon cast a golden strip. They talked of how sultry it was after the hot day. Gurov told her he was a Muscovite, a philologist by education, but worked in a bank; had once been preparing to sing in an opera company, but had dropped it, owned two houses in Moscow . . . And from her he learned that she grew up in Petersburg, but was married in S., where she had now been living for two years, that she would be staying in Yalta for about a month, and that her husband might come to fetch her, because he also wanted to get some rest. She was quite unable to explain where her husband served—in the provincial administration or the zemstvo council—and she herself found that funny. And Gurov also learned that her name was Anna Sergeevna.

Afterwards, in his hotel room, he thought about her, that tomorrow she would probably meet him again. It had to be so. Going to bed, he recalled that still quite recently she had been a schoolgirl, had studied just as his daughter was studying now, recalled how much timorousness and angularity there was in her laughter, her conversation with a stranger—it must have been the first time in her life that she was alone in such a situation, when she was followed, looked at, and spoken to with only one secret purpose, which she could not fail to guess. He recalled her slender, weak neck, her beautiful gray eyes.

"There's something pathetic in her all the same," he thought and began to fall asleep.

II

A week had passed since they became acquainted. It was Sunday. Inside it was stuffy, but outside the dust flew in whirls, hats blew off. They felt thirsty all day, and Gurov often stopped at the pavilion, offering Anna Sergeevna now a soft drink, now ice cream. There was no escape.

In the evening when it relented a little, they went to the jetty to watch the steamer come in. There were many strollers on the pier; they had come to meet people, they were holding bouquets. And here two particularities of the smartly dressed Yalta crowd distinctly struck one's eye: the elderly ladies were dressed like young ones, and there were many generals.

Owing to the roughness of the sea, the steamer arrived late, when the sun had already gone down, and it was a long time turning before it tied up. Anna Sergeevna looked at the ship and the passengers through her lorgnette, as if searching for acquaintances, and when she turned to Gurov, her eyes shone. She talked a lot, and her questions were abrupt, and she herself immediately forgot what she had asked; then she lost her lorgnette in the crowd.

The smartly dressed crowd was dispersing, the faces could no longer be seen, the wind had died down completely, and Gurov and Anna Sergeevna stood as if they were expecting someone else to get off the steamer. Anna Sergeevna was silent now and smelled the flowers, not looking at Gurov.

"The weather's improved towards evening," he said. "Where shall we go now? Shall we take a drive somewhere?"

She made no answer.

Then he looked at her intently and suddenly embraced her and kissed her on the lips, and he was showered with the fragrance and moisture of the flowers, and at once looked around timorously—had anyone seen them?

"Let's go to your place . . ." he said softly.

And they both walked quickly.

Her hotel room was stuffy and smelled of the perfumes she had bought in a Japanese shop. Gurov, looking at her now, thought: "What meetings there are in life!" From the past he had kept the memory of carefree, good-natured women, cheerful with love, grateful to him for their happiness, however brief; and of women—his wife, for example—who loved without sincerity, with superfluous talk, affectedly, with hysteria, with an expression as if it were not love, not passion, but something more significant; and of those two or three very beautiful, cold ones, in whose faces a predatory expression would suddenly flash, a stubborn wish to take, to snatch from life more than it could give, and these were women not in their first youth, capricious, unreasonable, domineering, unintelligent, and when Gurov cooled towards them, their beauty aroused hatred in him, and the lace of their underwear seemed to him like scales.

But here was all the timorousness and angularity of inexperienced youth, a feeling of awkwardness, and an impression of bewilderment, as if someone had suddenly knocked at the door. Anna Sergeevna, the "lady with the little dog," somehow took a special, very serious attitude towards what had happened, as if it were her fall—so it seemed, and that was strange and inopportune. Her features drooped and faded, and her long hair hung down sadly on both sides of her face, she sat pondering in a dejected pose, like the sinful woman in an old painting.

"It's not good," she said. "You'll be the first not to respect me now."

There was a watermelon on the table in the hotel room. Gurov cut himself a slice and unhurriedly began to eat it. At least half an hour passed in silence.

Anna Sergeevna was touching, she had about her a breath of the purity of a proper, naïve, little-experienced woman; the solitary candle burning on the table barely lit up her face, but it was clear that her heart was uneasy.

"Why should I stop respecting you?" asked Gurov. "You don't know what you're saying yourself."

"God forgive me!" she said, and her eyes filled with tears. "This is terrible."

"It's like you're justifying yourself."

"How can I justify myself? I'm a bad, low woman, I despise myself and am not even thinking of any justification. It's not my husband I've deceived, but my own self! And not only now, I've been deceiving myself for a long time. My husband may be an honest and good man, but he's lackey! I don't know what he does there, how he serves, I only know that he's a lackey. I married him when I was twenty, I was tormented by curiosity, I wanted something better. I told myself there must be a different life. I wanted to live! To live and live . . . I was burning with curiosity . . . you won't understand it, but I swear to God that I couldn't control myself any longer, something was happening to me, I couldn't restrain myself, I told my husband I was ill and came here . . . And here I go about as if in a daze, as if I'm out of my mind . . . and now I've become a trite, trashy woman, whom anyone can despise."

Gurov was bored listening, he was annoyed by the naïve tone, by this repentance, so unexpected and out of place; had it not been for the tears in her eyes, one might have thought she was joking or playing a role.

"I don't understand," he said softly, "what is it you want?"

She hid her face on his chest and pressed herself to him.

"Believe me, believe me, I beg you . . ." she said. "I love an honest, pure life, sin is vile to me, I myself don't know what I'm doing. Simple people say, 'The unclean one beguiled me.' And now I can say of myself that the unclean one has beguiled me."

"Enough, enough . . ." he muttered.

He looked into her fixed, frightened eyes, kissed her, spoke softly and tenderly, and she gradually calmed down, and her gaiety returned. They both began to laugh.

Later, when they went out, there was not a soul on the embankment, the town with its cypresses looked completely dead, but the sea still beat noisily against the shore; one barge was rocking on the waves, and the lantern on it glimmered sleepily.

They found a cab and drove to Oreanda.

"I just learned your last name downstairs in the lobby: it was written on the board—von Dideritz," said Gurov. "Is your husband German?"

"No, his grandfather was German, I think, but he himself is Orthodox."

In Oreanda they sat on a bench not far from the church, looked down on the sea, and were silent. Yalta was barely visible through the morning mist, white clouds stood motionless on the mountaintops. The leaves of the trees did not stir, cicadas called, and the monotonous, dull noise of the sea, coming from below, spoke of the peace, of the eternal sleep that awaits us. So it had sounded below when neither Yalta nor Oreanda were there, so it sounded now and would go on sounding with the same dull indifference when we are no longer here. And in this constancy, in this utter indifference to the life and death of each of us, there perhaps lies hidden the pledge of our eternal salvation, the unceasing movement of life on earth, of unceasing perfection. Sitting beside the young woman, who looked so beautiful in the dawn, appeased and enchanted by the view of this magical décor—sea, mountains, clouds, the open sky—Gurov reflected that, essentially, if you thought of it, everything was beautiful in this world, everything except for what we ourselves think and do when we forget the higher goals of being and our human dignity.

Some man came up—it must have been a watchman—looked at them, and went away. And this detail seemed such a mysterious thing, and also beautiful. The steamer from Feodosia could be seen approaching in the glow of the early dawn, its lights out.

"There's dew on the grass," said Anna Sergeevna after a silence.

"Yes. It's time to go home."

They went back to town.

After that they met on the embankment every noon, had lunch together, dined, strolled, admired the sea. She complained that she slept poorly and that her heart beat anxiously, kept asking the same questions, troubled now by jealousy, now by fear that he did not respect her enough. And often on the square or in the garden, when there was no one near them, he would suddenly draw her to him and kiss her passionately. Their complete idleness, those kisses in broad daylight, with a furtive look around and the fear that someone might see them, the heat, the smell of the sea, and the constant flashing before their eyes of idle, smartly dressed, well-fed people, seemed to transform him; he repeatedly told Anna Sergeevna how beautiful she was, and how seductive, was impatiently passionate, never left her side, while she often brooded and kept asking him to admit that he did not respect her, did not love her at all, and saw in her only a trite woman. Late almost every evening they went somewhere out of town, to Oreanda or the cascade; these outings were successful, their impressions each time were beautiful, majestic.

They were expecting her husband to arrive. But a letter came from him in which he said that his eyes hurt and begged his wife to come home quickly. Anna Sergeevna began to hurry.

"It's good that I'm leaving," she said to Gurov. "It's fate itself."

She went by carriage, and he accompanied her. They drove for a whole day. When she had taken her seat in the express train and the second bell had rung, she said:

"Let me have one more look at you . . . One more look. There."

She did not cry, but was sad, as if ill, and her face trembled.

"I'll think of you . . . remember you," she said. "God be with you. Don't think ill of me. We're saying good-bye forever, it must be so, because we should never have met. Well, God be with you."

The train left quickly, its lights soon disappeared, and a moment later the noise could no longer be heard, as if everything were conspiring on purpose to put a speedy end to this sweet oblivion, this madness. And, left alone on the platform and gazing into the dark distance, Gurov listened to the chirring of the grasshoppers and the hum of the telegraph wires with a feeling as if he had just woken up. And he thought that now there was one more affair or adventure in his life, and it, too, was now over, and all that was left was the memory . . . He was touched, saddened, and felt some slight remorse; this young woman whom he was never to see again had not been happy with him; he had been affectionate with her, and sincere, but all the same, in his treatment of her, in his tone and caresses, there had been a slight shade of mockery, the somewhat coarse arrogance of a happy man, who was, moreover, almost twice her age. She had all the while called him kind, extraordinary, lofty; obviously, he had appeared to her not as he was in reality, and therefore he had involuntarily deceived her . . .

Here at the station there was already a breath of autumn, the wind was cool.

"It's time I headed north, too," thought Gurov, leaving the platform. "High time!"

III

At home in Moscow everything was already wintry, the stoves were heated, and in the morning, when the children were getting ready for school and drinking their tea, it was dark, and the nanny would light a lamp for a short time. The frosts had already set in. When the first snow falls, on the first day of riding in sleighs, it is pleasant to see the white ground, the white roofs; one's breath feels soft and pleasant, and in those moments one remembers one's youth. The old lindens and birches, white with hoarfrost, have a good-natured look, they are nearer one's heart than cypresses and palms, and near them one no longer wants to think of mountains and the sea.

Gurov was a Muscovite. He returned to Moscow on a fine, frosty day, and when he put on his fur coat and warm gloves and strolled down Petrovka, and when on Saturday evening he heard the bells ringing, his recent trip and the places he had visited lost all their charm for him. He gradually became immersed in Moscow life, now greedily read three newspapers a day and said that he never read the Moscow newspapers on principle. He was drawn to restaurants, clubs, to dinner parties, celebrations, and felt flattered that he had famous lawyers and actors among his clients, and that at the Doctors' Club he played cards with a professor. He could eat a whole portion of selyanka from the pan . . .

A month would pass and Anna Sergeevna, as it seemed to him, would be covered by mist in his memory and would only appear to him in dreams with a touching smile, as other women did. But more than a month passed, deep winter came, and yet everything was as clear in his memory as if he had parted with Anna Sergeevna only the day before. And the memories burned brighter and brighter. Whether from the voices of his children doing their homework, which reached him in his study in the evening quiet, or from hearing a romance, or an organ in a restaurant, or the blizzard howling in the chimney, everything would suddenly rise up in his memory: what had happened on the jetty, and the early morning with mist on the mountains, and the steamer from Feodosia, and the kisses. He would pace the room for a long time, and remember, and smile, and then his memories would turn to reveries, and in his imagination the past would mingle with what was still to be. Anna Sergeevna was not a dream, she followed him everywhere like a shadow and watched him. Closing his eyes, he saw her as if alive, and she seemed younger, more beautiful, more tender than she was; and he also seemed better to himself than he had been then, in Yalta. In the evenings she gazed at him from the bookcase, the fireplace, the corner, he could hear her breathing, the gentle rustle of her skirts. In the street he followed women with his eyes, looking for one who resembled her . . .

And he was tormented now by a strong desire to tell someone his memories. But at home it was impossible to talk of his love, and away from home there was no one to talk with. Certainly not among his tenants nor at the bank. And what was there to say? Had he been in love then? Was there anything beautiful, poetic, or instructive, or merely interesting, in his relations with Anna Sergeevna? And he found himself speaking vaguely of love, of women, and no one could guess what it was about, and only his wife raised her dark eyebrows and said:

"You know, Dimitri, the role of fop doesn't suit you at all."

One night, as he was leaving the Doctors' Club together with his partner, an official, he could not help himself and said:

"If you only knew what a charming woman I met in Yalta!"

The official got into a sleigh and drove off, but suddenly turned around and called out:

"Dmitri Dmitrich!"

"What?"

"You were right earlier: the sturgeon was a bit off!"

Those words, so very ordinary, for some reason suddenly made Gurov indignant, struck him as humiliating, impure. Such savage manners, such faces! These senseless nights, and such uninteresting, unremarkable days! Frenzied card-playing, gluttony, drunkenness, constant talk about the same thing. Useless matters and conversations about the same thing took for their share the best part of one's time, the best of one's powers, and what was left in the end was some sort of curtailed, wingless life, some sort of nonsense, and it was impossible to get away or flee, as if you were sitting in a madhouse or a prison camp!

Gurov did not sleep all night and felt indignant, and as a result had a headache all the next day. And the following nights he slept poorly, sitting up in bed all the time and thinking, or pacing up and down. He was sick of the children, sick of the bank, did not want to go anywhere or talk about anything.

In December, during the holidays, he got ready to travel and told his wife he was leaving for Petersburg to solicit for a certain young man—and went to S. Why? He did not know very well himself. He wanted to see Anna Sergeevna and talk with her, to arrange a meeting, if he could.

He arrived at S. in the morning and took the best room in the hotel, where the whole floor was covered with gray army flannel and there was an inkstand on the table, gray with dust, with a horseback rider, who held his hat in his raised hand, but whose head was broken off. The hall porter gave him the necessary information: von Diderітz lives in his own house on Staro-Goncharnaya Street, not far from the hotel; he has a good life, is wealthy, keeps his own horses, everybody in town knows him. The porter pronounced it "Dridiritz."

Gurov walked unhurriedly to Staro-Goncharnaya Street, found the house. Just opposite the house stretched a fence, long, gray, with spikes.

"You could flee from such a fence," thought Gurov, looking now at the windows, now at the fence.

He reflected: today was not a workday, and the husband was probably at home. And anyhow it would be tactless to go in and cause embarrassment. If he sent a message, it might fall into the husband's hands, and that would ruin everything. It would be best to trust to chance. And he kept pacing up and down the street and near the fence and waited for his chance. He saw a beggar go in the gates and saw the dogs attack him, then, an hour later, he heard someone playing a piano, and the sounds reached him faintly, indistinctly. It must have been Anna Sergeevna playing. The front door suddenly opened and some old woman came out, the familiar white spitz running after her. Gurov wanted to call the dog, but his heart suddenly throbbed, and in his excitement he was unable to remember the spitz's name.

He paced up and down, and hated the gray fence more and more, and now he thought with vexation that Anna Sergeevna had forgotten him, and was perhaps amusing herself with another man, and that that was so natural in the situation of a young woman who had to look at this cursed fence from morning till evening. He went back to his hotel room and sat on the sofa for a long time, not knowing what to do, then had dinner, then took a long nap.

"How stupid and upsetting this all is," he thought, when he woke up and looked at the dark windows: it was already evening. "So I've had my sleep. Now what am I to do for the night?"

He sat on the bed, which was covered with a cheap, gray, hospital-like blanket, and taunted himself in vexation:

"Here's the lady with the little dog for you . . . Here's an adventure for you . . . Yes, here you sit."

That morning, at the train station, a poster with very big lettering had caught his eye: it was the opening night of *The Geisha*. He remembered it and went to the theater.

"It's very likely that she goes to opening nights," he thought.

The theater was full. And here, too, as in all provincial theaters generally, a haze hung over the chandeliers, the gallery stirred noisily; the local dandies stood in the front row before the performance started, their hands behind their backs; and here, too, in the governor's box, the governor's daughter sat in front, wearing a boa, while the governor himself modestly hid behind the portière, and only his hands could be seen; the curtain swayed, the orchestra spent a long time tuning up. All the while the public came in and took their seats, Gurov kept searching greedily with his eyes.

Anna Sergeevna came in. She sat in the third row, and when Gurov looked at her, his heart was wrung, and he realized clearly that there was now no person closer, dearer, or more important for him in the whole world; this small woman, lost in the provincial crowd, not remarkable for anything, with a vulgar lorgnette in her hand, now filled his whole life, was his grief, his joy, the only happiness he now wished for himself; and to the sounds of the bad orchestra, with its trashy local violins, he thought how beautiful she was. He thought and dreamed.

A man came in with Anna Sergeevna and sat down next to her, a young man with little side-whiskers, very tall, stooping; he nodded his head at every step, and it seemed he was perpetually bowing. This was probably her husband, whom she, in an outburst of bitter feeling that time in Yalta, had called a lackey. And indeed, in his long figure, his side-whiskers, his little bald spot, there was something of lackeyish modesty; he had a sweet smile, and the badge of some learned society gleamed in his buttonhole, like the badge of a lackey.

During the first intermission the husband went to smoke; she remained in her seat. Gurov, who was also sitting in the stalls, went up to her and said in a trembling voice and with a forced smile:

"How do you do?"

She looked at him and paled, then looked again in horror, not believing her eyes, and tightly clutched her fan and lorgnette in her hand, obviously struggling with herself to keep from fainting. Both were silent. She sat, he stood, alarmed at her confusion, not venturing to sit down next to her. The tuning-up violins and flutes sang out, it suddenly became frightening, it seemed that people were gazing at them from all the boxes. But then she got up and quickly walked to the exit, he followed her, and they both went confusedly through corridors and stairways, going up, then down, and the uniforms of the courts, the schools, and the imperial estates flashed before them, all with badges; ladies flashed by, fur coats on hangers, a drafty wind blew, drenching them with the smell of cigar stubs. And Gurov, whose heart was pounding, thought: "Oh, Lord! Why these people, this orchestra . . ."

And just then he suddenly recalled how, at the station in the evening after he had seen Anna Sergeevna off, he had said to himself that everything was over and they would never see each other again. But how far it still was from being over!

On a narrow, dark stairway with the sign "To the Amphitheater," she stopped.

"How you frightened me!" she said, breathing heavily, still pale, stunned. "Oh, how you frightened me! I'm barely alive. Why did you come? Why?"

"But understand, Anna, understand . . ." he said in a low voice, hurrying. "I beg you to understand . . ."

She looked at him with fear, with entreaty, with love, looked at him intently, the better to keep his features in her memory.

"I've been suffering so!" she went on, not listening to him. "I think only of you all the time, I've lived by my thoughts of you. And I've tried to forget, to forget, but why, why did you come?"

Further up, on the landing, two high-school boys were smoking and looking down, but Gurov did not care, he drew Anna Sergeevna to him and began kissing her face, her cheeks, her hands.

"What are you doing, what are you doing!" she repeated in horror, pushing him away from her. "We've both lost our minds. Leave today, leave at once . . . I adjure you by all that's holy, I implore you . . . Somebody's coming!"

Someone was climbing the stairs.

"You must leave . . ." Anna Sergeevna went on in a whisper. "Do you hear, Dmitri Dmitrich? I'll come to you in Moscow. I've never been happy, I'm unhappy now, and I'll never, never be happy, never! Don't make me suffer still more! I swear I'll come to Moscow. But we must part now! My dear one, my good one, my darling, we must part!"

She pressed his hand and quickly began going downstairs, turning back to look at him, and it was clear from her eyes that she was indeed not happy . . . Gurov stood for a little while, listened, then, when everything was quiet, found his coat and left the theater.

IV

And Anna Sergeevna began coming to see him in Moscow. Once every two or three months she left S., and told her husband she was going to consult a professor about her female disorder—and her husband did and did not believe her. Arriving in Moscow, she stayed at the Slavyansky Bazaar and at once sent a man in a red hat to Gurov. Gurov came to see her, and nobody in Moscow knew of it.

Once he was going to see her in that way on a winter morning (the messenger had come the previous evening but had not found him in). With him was his daughter, whom he wanted to see off to school, which was on the way. Big, wet snow was falling.

"It's now three degrees above freezing, and yet it's snowing," Gurov said to his daughter. "But it's warm only near the surface of the earth, while in the upper layers of the atmosphere the temperature is quite different."

"And why is there no thunder in winter, papa?"

He explained that, too. He spoke and thought that here he was going to a rendezvous, and not a single soul knew of it or probably would ever know. He had two lives: an apparent one, seen and known by all who needed it, filled with conventional truth and conventional deceit, which perfectly resembled the lives of his acquaintances and friends, and another that went on in secret. And by some strange coincidence, perhaps an accidental one, everything that he found important, interesting, necessary, in which he was sincere and did not deceive himself, which constituted the core of his life, occurred in secret from others, while everything that made up his life, his shell, in which he hid in order to conceal the truth—for instance, his work at the bank, his arguments at the club, his "inferior race," his attending official celebrations with his wife—all this was in full view. And he judged others by himself, did not believe what he saw, and always supposed that every man led his own real and very interesting life under the cover of secrecy, as under the cover of night. Every personal existence was upheld by a secret, and it was perhaps partly for that reason that every cultivated man took such anxious care that his personal secret should be respected.

After taking his daughter to school, Gurov went to the Slavyansky Bazaar. He took his fur coat off downstairs, went up, and knocked softly at the door. Anna Sergeevna, wearing his favorite gray dress, tired from the trip and the expectation, had been waiting for him since the previous evening; she was pale, looked at him and did not smile, and he had barely come in when she was already leaning on his chest. Their kiss was long, lingering, as if they had not seen each other for two years.

"Well, how is your life there?" he asked. "What's new?"

"Wait, I'll tell you . . . I can't."

She could not speak because she was crying. She turned away from him and pressed a handkerchief to her eyes.

"Well, let her cry a little, and meanwhile I'll sit down," he thought, and sat down in an armchair.

Then he rang and ordered tea; and then, while he drank tea, she went on standing with her face turned to the window . . . She was crying from anxiety, from a sorrowful awareness that their life had turned out so sadly; they only saw each other in secret, they hid from people like thieves! Was their life not broken?

"Well, stop now," he said.

For him it was obvious that this love of theirs would not end soon, that there was no knowing when. Anna Sergeevna's attachment to him grew ever stronger, she adored him, and it would have been unthinkable to tell her that it all really had to end at some point; and she would not have believed it.

He went up to her and took her by the shoulders to caress her, to make a joke, and at that moment he saw himself in the mirror.

His head was beginning to turn gray. And it seemed strange to him that he had aged so much in those last years, had lost so much of his good looks. The shoulders on which his hands lay were warm and trembled. He felt compassion for this life, still so warm and beautiful, but probably already near the point where it would begin to fade and wither, like his own life. Why did she love him so? Women had always taken him to be other than he was, and they had loved in him, not himself, but a man their imagination had created, whom they had greedily sought all their lives; and then, when they had noticed their mistake, they had still loved him. And not one of them had been happy with him. Time passed, he met women, became intimate, parted, but not once did he love; there was anything else, but not love.

And only now, when his head was gray, had he really fallen in love as one ought to—for the first time in his life.

He and Anna Sergeevna loved each other like very close, dear people, like husband and wife, like tender friends; it seemed to them that fate itself had destined them for each other, and they could not understand why he had a wife and she a husband; and it was as if they were two birds of passage, a male and a female, who had been caught and forced to live in separate cages. They had forgiven each other the things they were ashamed of in the past, they forgave everything in the present, and they felt that this love of theirs had changed them both.

Formerly, in sad moments, he had calmed himself with all sorts of arguments, whatever had come into his head, but now he did not care about any arguments, he felt deep compassion, he wanted to be sincere, tender . . .

"Stop, my good one," he said, "you've had your cry—and enough . . . Let's talk now, we'll think up something."

Then they had a long discussion, talked about how to rid themselves of the need for hiding, for deception, for living in different towns and not seeing each other for long periods. How could they free themselves from these unbearable bonds?

"How? How?" he asked, clutching his head. "How?"

And it seemed that, just a little more—and the solution would be found, and then a new, beautiful life would begin; and it was clear to both of them that the end was still far, far off, and that the most complicated and difficult part was just beginning.

(1899)

QUESTIONS FOR CRITICAL THINKING AND WRITING

Experience

1. To what extent did you find the two central characters engaging and interesting? Explain.
2. What is your impression of Anna and Gurov? Are you sympathetic toward either or both of them? Why or why not?

Interpretation

3. What is the significance of the story's multiple settings? What does each setting contribute to your understanding of Anna and Gurov?
4. Explain the significance of Gurov's comment about living two lives, his external everyday life and his internal "real" life.
5. What is the significance of the scene in which Gurov catches sight of himself in the mirror? Why is that scene important?
6. Why does Chekhov include the scene with Gurov and his friends talking about a dinner they shared?

Evaluation

7. What values does Anna live by? What are Gurov's values? What do you think of their values? Explain.

Connection

8. Compare the adultery in Chekhov's story with that in Chopin's "The Storm." Do you find one more understandable and more excusable than the other? Explain.

Critical Thinking

9. What is the solution to Anna's and Gurov's problem? Why haven't they resolved it? What are their options?

KATE CHOPIN

For biographical information see Chapter One, page 38.

The Storm

I

The leaves were so still that even Bibi thought it was going to rain. Bobinôt, who was accustomed to converse on terms of perfect equality with his little son, called the child's attention to certain somber clouds that were rolling with sinister intention from the west, accompanied by a sullen, threatening roar. They were at Friedheimer's store and decided to remain there till the storm had passed. They sat within the door on two empty kegs. Bibi was four years old and looked very wise.

"Mama'll be 'fraid, yes," he suggested with blinking eyes.

"She'll shut the house. Maybe she got Sylvie helpin' her this evenin'," Bobinôt responded reassuringly.

"No; she ent got Sylvie. Sylvie was helpin' her yistiday," piped Bibi.

Bobinôt arose and going across to the counter purchased a can of shrimps, of which Calixta was very fond. Then he returned to his perch on the keg and sat stolidly holding the can of shrimps while the storm burst. It shook the wooden store and seemed to be ripping great furrows in the distant field. Bibi laid his little hand on his father's knee and was not afraid.

II

Calixta, at home, felt no uneasiness for their safety. She sat at a side window sewing furiously on a sewing machine. She was greatly occupied and did not notice the approaching storm. But she felt very warm and often stopped to mop her face on which the perspiration gathered in beads. She unfastened her white sacque at the throat. It began to grow dark, and suddenly realizing the situation she got up hurriedly and went about closing windows and doors.

Out on the small front gallery she had hung Bobinôt's Sunday clothes to air and she hastened out to gather them before the rain fell. As she stepped outside, Alcée Laballière rode in at the gate. She had not seen him very often since her marriage, and never alone. She stood there with Bobinôt's coat in her hands, and the big rain drops began to fall. Alcée rode his horse under the shelter of a side projection where the chickens had huddled and there were plows and a harrow piled up in the corner.

"May I come and wait on your gallery till the storm is over, Calixta?" he asked.

"Come 'long in, M'sieur Alcée."

His voice and her own startled her as if from a trance, and she seized Bobinôt's vest. Alcée, mounting to the porch, grabbed the trousers and snatched Bibi's braided jacket that was about to be carried away by a sudden gust of wind. He expressed an intention to remain outside, but it was soon apparent that he might as well have been out in the open: the water beat in upon the boards in driving sheets, and he went inside, closing the door after him. It was even necessary to put something beneath the door to keep the water out.

"My! what a rain! It's good two years sence it rain like that," exclaimed Calixta as she rolled up a piece of bagging and Alcée helped her to thrust it beneath the crack.

She was a little fuller of figure than five years before when she married; but she had lost nothing of her vivacity. Her blue eyes still retained their melting quality; and her yellow hair, disheveled by the wind and rain, kinked more stubbornly than ever about her ears and temples.

The rain beat upon the low, shingled roof with a force and clatter that threatened to break an entrance and deluge them there. They were in the dining room—the sitting room—the general utility room. Adjoining was her bed room, with Bibi's couch along side her own. The door stood open, and the room with its white, monumental bed, its closed shutters, looked dim and mysterious.

Alcée flung himself into a rocker and Calixta nervously began to gather up from the floor the lengths of a cotton sheet which she had been sewing.

"If this keeps up, *Dieu sait*° if the levees goin' to stan' it!" she exclaimed.

"What have you got to do with the levees?"

"I got enough to do! An' there's Bobinôt with Bibi out in that storm—if he only didn' left Friedheimer's!"

"Let us hope, Calixta, that Bobinôt's got sense enough to come in out of a cyclone."

She went and stood at the window with a greatly disturbed look on her face. She wiped the frame that was clouded with moisture. It was stiflingly hot. Alcée got up and joined her at the window, looking over her shoulder. The rain was coming down in sheets obscuring the view of far-off cabins and enveloping the distant wood in a gray mist. The playing of the lightning was incessant. A bolt struck a tall chinaberry tree at the edge of the field. It filled all visible space with a blinding glare and the crash seemed to invade the very boards they stood upon.

Calixta put her hands to her eyes, and with a cry, staggered backward. Alcée's arm encircled her, and for an instant he drew her close and spasmodically to him.

"*Bonté!*"° she cried, releasing herself from his encircling arm and retreating from the window, "the house'll go next! If I only knew w'ere Bibi was!" She would not compose herself; she would not be seated. Alcée clasped her shoulders and looked into her

Dieu sait *God only knows* ***Bonté!*** *Heavens!*

face. The contact of her warm, palpitating body when he had unthinkingly drawn her into his arms, had aroused all the old-time infatuation and desire for her flesh.

"Calixta," he said, "don't be frightened. Nothing can happen. The house is too low to be struck, with so many tall trees standing about. There! aren't you going to be quiet? say, aren't you?" He pushed her hair back from her face that was warm and steaming. Her lips were as red and moist as pomegranate seed. Her white neck and a glimpse of her full, firm bosom disturbed him powerfully. As she glanced up at him the fear in her liquid blue eyes had given place to a drowsy gleam that unconsciously betrayed a sensuous desire. He looked down into her eyes and there was nothing for him to do but gather her lips in a kiss. It reminded him of Assumption.°

"Do you remember—in Assumption, Calixta?" he asked in a low voice broken by passion. Oh! she remembered; for in Assumption he had kissed her and kissed and kissed her; until his senses would well nigh fail, and to save her he would resort to a desperate flight. If she was not an immaculate dove in those days, she was still inviolate; a passionate creature whose very defenselessness had made her defense, against which his honor forbade him to prevail. Now—well, now—her lips seemed in a manner free to be tasted, as well as her round, white throat and her whiter breasts.

They did not heed the crashing torrents, and the roar of the elements made her laugh as she lay in his arms. She was a revelation in that dim, mysterious chamber; as white as the couch she lay upon. Her firm, elastic flesh that was knowing for the first time its birthright, was like a creamy lily that the sun invites to contribute its breath and perfume to the undying life of the world.

The generous abundance of her passion, without guile or trickery, was like a white flame which penetrated and found response in depths of his own sensuous nature that had never yet been reached.

When he touched her breasts they gave themselves up in quivering ecstasy, inviting his lips. Her mouth was a fountain of delight. And when he possessed her, they seemed to swoon together at the very borderland of life's mystery.

He stayed cushioned upon her, breathless, dazed, enervated, with his heart beating like a hammer upon her. With one hand she clasped his head, her lips lightly touching his forehead. The other hand stroked with a soothing rhythm his muscular shoulders.

The growl of the thunder was distant and passing away. The rain beat softly upon the shingles, inviting them to drowsiness and sleep. But they dared not yield.

The rain was over; and the sun was turning the glistening green world into a palace of gems. Calixta, on the gallery, watched Alcée ride away. He turned and smiled at her with a beaming face; and she lifted her pretty chin in the air and laughed aloud.

III

Bobinôt and Bibi, trudging home, stopped without at the cistern to make themselves presentable.

"My! Bibi, w'at will yo' mama say! You ought to be ashame'. You oughtn' put on those good pants. Look at 'em! An' that mud on yo' collar! How you got that mud on yo' collar, Bibi? I never saw such a boy!" Bibi was the picture of pathetic resignation. Bobinôt was the embodiment of serious solicitude as he strove to remove from his own person and his son's the signs of their tramp over heavy roads and through wet

Assumption *a parish west of New Orleans*

fields. He scraped the mud off Bibi's bare legs and feet with a stick and carefully removed all traces from his heavy brogans. Then, prepared for the worst—the meeting with an overscrupulous housewife, they entered cautiously at the back door.

Calixta was preparing supper. She had set the table and was dripping coffee at the hearth. She sprang up as they came in.

"Oh, Bobinôt! You back! My! but I was uneasy. W'ere you been during the rain? An' Bibi? he ain't wet? he ain't hurt?" She had clasped Bibi and was kissing him effusively. Bobinôt's explanations and apologies which he had been composing all along the way, died on his lips as Calixta felt him to see if he were dry, and seemed to express nothing but satisfaction at their safe return.

"I brought you some shrimps, Calixta," offered Bobinôt, hauling the can from his ample side pocket and laying it on the table.

"Shrimps! Oh, Bobinôt! you too good fo' anything!" and she gave him a smacking kiss on the cheek that resounded. "*J'vous réponds,*° we'll have feas' to night! umph-umph!"

Bobinôt and Bibi began to relax and enjoy themselves, and when the three seated themselves at table they laughed much and so loud that anyone might have heard them as far away as Laballière's.

IV

Alcée Laballière wrote to his wife, Clarisse, that night. It was a loving letter, full of tender solicitude. He told her not to hurry back, but if she and the babies liked it at Biloxi, to stay a month longer. He was getting on nicely; and though he missed them, he was willing to bear the separation a while longer—realizing that their health and pleasure were the first things to be considered.

V

As for Clarisse, she was charmed upon receiving her husband's letter. She and the babies were doing well. The society was agreeable; many of her old friends and acquaintances were at the bay. And the first free breath since her marriage seemed to restore the pleasant liberty of her maiden days. Devoted as she was to her husband, their intimate conjugal life was something which she was more than willing to forego for a while.

So the storm passed and everyone was happy.

(1898)

QUESTIONS FOR CRITICAL THINKING AND WRITING

Experience

1. Were you surprised at the turn of events? Why or why not?
2. What is your response to the husband, whose wife has just cheated on him?

Interpretation

3. How does Chopin use the storm as a symbol? What does it represent?

J'vous réponds *Let me tell you*

4. What do the details of the setting contribute to your understanding of the story?
5. What is the significance of the last exchange of dialogue between husband and wife?

Evaluation

6. What view of adultery is presented in the story? On what grounds is the adulterous act justified or not justified?

Connection

7. Compare the style and structure of "The Storm" with the style and structure of Chopin's "The Story of an Hour."

Critical Thinking

8. What do you predict for the future of the husband and wife? How do you see their marriage five years hence? Explain.

Photo by Diane Solis

SANDRA CISNEROS

[b. 1954]

www

Sandra Cisneros was born in Chicago to a Mexican father and a Mexican-American mother, the only daughter in a family with six sons. She began writing at the age of ten, and as a young woman studied creative writing at the Iowa Writers' Workshop, where she earned a Master of Fine Arts degree in 1978. In addition to writing both poetry and fiction, Cisneros has taught creative writing in a variety of educational contexts, including high school and college. She has taught and been a visiting writer at the University of California at Irvine and at Berkeley and at the University of Michigan. She has also worked in educational and arts administration.

Barbie-Q

For Licha

Yours is the one with the mean eyes and a ponytail. Striped swimsuit, stilettos, sunglasses, and gold hoop earrings. Mine is the one with bubble hair. Red swimsuit, stilettos, pearl earrings, and a wire stand. But that's all we can afford, besides one extra outfit apiece. Yours, "Red Flair," sophisticated A-line coatdress with a Jackie Kennedy pillbox hat, white gloves, handbag, and heels included. Mine, "Solo in the Spotlight," evening elegance in black glitter strapless gown with a puffy skirt at the bottom like a mermaid tail, formal-length gloves, pink chiffon scarf, and mike included. From so much dressing and undressing, the black glitter wears off where her titties stick out. This and a dress invented from an old sock when we cut holes here and here and here, the cuff rolled over for the glamorous, fancy-free, off-the-shoulder look.

Every time the same story. Your Barbie is roommates with my Barbie, and my Barbie's boyfriend comes over and your Barbie steals him, okay? Kiss kiss kiss. Then the two Barbies fight, You dumbbell! He's mine. Oh no he's not, you stinky! Only Ken's invisible, right? Because we don't have money for a stupid-looking boy doll when we'd both rather ask for a new Barbie outfit next Christmas. We have to make do with your mean-eyed Barbie and my bubblehead Barbie and our one outfit apiece not including the sock dress.

Until next Sunday when we are walking through the flea market on Maxwell Street and there! Lying on the street next to some tool bits, and platform shoes with the heels all squashed, and a fluorescent green wicker wastebasket, and aluminum foil, and hub-caps, and a pink shag rug, and windshield wiper blades, and dusty mason jars, and a coffee can full of rusty nails. *There!* Where? Two Mattel boxes. One with the "Career Gal" ensemble, snappy black and white business suit, three-quarter-length sleeve jacket with kick-pleat skirt, red sleeveless shell, gloves, pumps, and matching hat included. The other, "Sweet Dreams," dreamy pink-and-white plaid nightgown and matching robe, lace-trimmed slippers, hair-brush and hand mirror included. How much? Please, please, please, please, please, please, please, until they say okay.

On the outside you and me skipping and humming but inside we are doing loopity-loops and pirouetting. Until at the next vendor's stand, next to boxed pies, and bright orange toilet brushes, and rubber gloves, and wrench sets, and bouquets of feather flowers, and glass towel racks, and steel wool, and Alvin and the Chipmunks records, *there!* And *there!* And *there!* And *there!* and *there!* and *there!* and *there!* Bendable Legs Barbie with her new page-boy hairdo. Midge, Barbie's best friend. Ken, Barbie's boyfriend. Skipper, Barbie's little sister. Tutti and Todd, Barbie and Skipper's tiny twin sister and brother. Skipper's friends, Scooter and Ricky. Alan, Ken's buddy. And Francie, Barbie's MOD'ern cousin.

Everybody today selling toys, all of them damaged with water and smelling of smoke. Because a big toy warehouse on Halsted Street burned down yesterday—see there?—the smoke still rising and drifting across the Dan Ryan expressway. And now there is a big fire sale at Maxwell Street, today only.

So what if we didn't get our new Bendable Legs Barbie and Midge and Ken and Skipper and Tutti and Todd and Scooter and Ricky and Alan and Francie in nice clean boxes and had to buy them on Maxwell Street, all water-soaked and sooty. So what if our Barbies smell like smoke when you hold them up to your nose even after you wash and wash and wash them. And if the prettiest doll, Barbie's MOD'ern cousin Francie with real eyelashes, eyelash brush included, has a left foot that's melted a little—so? If you dress her in her new "Prom Pinks" outfit, satin splendor with matching coat, gold belt, clutch, and hair bow included, so long as you don't lift her dress, right?—who's to know.

(1991)

QUESTIONS FOR CRITICAL THINKING AND WRITING

Experience

1. What is your impression of the girls described in the story?
2. How do you respond to the descriptions of their Barbie dolls? Why?

Interpretation

3. What are the purpose and effect of describing the dolls' clothes and accessories in detail?
4. What is the effect of the use of repetition: the repeated use of "please," and "And there!" Of "Barbie" and "Barbie's"?
5. What is the story's theme?

Evaluation

6. With what values are the Barbie dolls associated?

Connections

7. Compare the childlike narrator of "Barbie-Q" with the narrative voice of other stories about childhood, like Lawrence's "Rocking Horse Winner," or Joyce's "Araby." Which narrator do you like best, and why?

Critical Thinking

8. Project forward for the two girls described in "Barbie-Q." What do you think they will be like in five years and in ten? Why?

RALPH ELLISON
[1914–1994]

Ralph Waldo Ellison, who was named after the nineteenth-century transcendentalist writer Ralph Waldo Emerson, was born in Oklahoma and educated at the Tuskegee Institute in Alabama, where he studied music. His short stories and his novel, Invisible Man, *for which he won the National Book Award in 1953, employ musical motifs and stylistic elements, which he describes in his essays on music, collected in* Shadow and Act. *This book also contains essays and interviews about race and race relations, the central subjects of Ellison's work.*

Battle Royal

It goes a long way back, some twenty years. All my life I had been looking for something, and everywhere I turned someone tried to tell me what it was. I accepted their answers too, though they were often in contradiction and even self-contradictory. I was naïve. I was looking for myself and asking everyone except myself questions which I, and only I, could answer. It took me a long time and much painful boomeranging of my expectations to achieve a realization everyone else appears to have been born with: That I am nobody but myself. But first I had to discover that I am an invisible man!

And yet I am no freak of nature, nor of history. It was in the cards, other things having been equal (or unequal) eighty-five years ago. I am not ashamed of my grandparents for having been slaves. I am only ashamed of myself for having at one time been ashamed. About eighty-five years ago they were told that they were free, united with others of our country in everything pertaining to the common good, and, in everything social, separate like the fingers of the hand. And they believed it. They exulted in it. They stayed in their place, worked hard, and brought up my father to do the same. But my grandfather is the one. He was an odd old guy, my grandfather, and I am told I take after him. It was he who caused the trouble. On his deathbed he called my father to him and said, "Son, after I'm gone I want you to keep up the good fight. I never told you, but our life is a war and I have been a traitor all my born days, a spy in the enemy's country ever since I give up my gun back in the Reconstruction. Live with your head in the lion's mouth. I want you to overcome 'em with yeses, undermine 'em with grins, agree 'em to death and destruction, let 'em swoller you till they vomit or bust wide open." They thought the old man had gone out of his mind. He had been the meekest of men. The younger children were rushed from the room, the shades drawn and the flame of the lamp turned so low that it sputtered on the wick like the old man's breathing. "Learn it to the younguns," he whispered fiercely; then he died.

But my folks were more alarmed over his last words than over his dying. It was as though he had not died at all, his words caused so much anxiety. I was warned emphatically to forget what he had said and, indeed, this is the first time it has been mentioned outside the family circle. It had a tremendous effect upon me, however. I could never be sure of what he meant. Grandfather had been a quiet old man who never made any trouble, yet on his deathbed he had called himself a traitor and a spy, and he had spoken of his meekness as a dangerous activity. It became a constant puzzle which lay unanswered in the back of my mind. And whenever things went well for me I remembered my grandfather and felt guilty and uncomfortable. It was as though I was carrying out his advice in spite of myself. And to make it worse, everyone loved me for it. I was praised by the most lily-white men of the town. I was considered an example of desirable conduct—just as my grandfather had been. And what puzzled me was that the old man had defined it as treachery. When I was praised for my conduct I felt a guilt that in some way I was doing something that was really against the wishes of the white folks, that if they had understood they would have desired me to act just the opposite, that I should have been sulky and mean, and that that really would have been what they wanted, even though they were fooled and thought they wanted me to act as I did. It made me afraid that some day they would look upon me as a traitor and I would be lost. Still I was more afraid to act any other way because they didn't like that at all. The old man's words were like a curse. On my graduation day I delivered an oration in which I showed that humility was the secret, indeed, the very essence of progress. (Not that I believed this—how could I, remembering my grandfather?—I only believed that it worked.) It was a great success. Everyone praised me and I was invited to give the speech at a gathering of the town's leading white citizens. It was a triumph for our whole community.

It was in the main ballroom of the leading hotel. When I got there I discovered that it was on the occasion of a smoker, and I was told that since I was to be there anyway

I might as well take part in the battle royal to be fought by some of my schoolmates as part of the entertainment. The battle royal came first.

All of the town's big shots were there in their tuxedoes, wolfing down the buffet foods, drinking beer and whiskey and smoking black cigars. It was a large room with a high ceiling. Chairs were arranged in neat rows around three sides of a portable boxing ring. The fourth side was clear, revealing a gleaming space of polished floor. I had some misgivings over the battle royal, by the way. Not from a distaste for fighting, but because I didn't care too much for the other fellows who were to take part. They were tough guys who seemed to have no grandfather's curse worrying their minds. No one could mistake their toughness. And besides, I suspected that fighting a battle royal might detract from the dignity of my speech. In those pre-invisible days I visualized myself as a potential Booker T. Washington. But the other fellows didn't care too much for me either, and there were nine of them. I felt superior to them in my way, and I didn't like the manner in which we were all crowded together into the servants' elevator. Nor did they like my being there. In fact, as the warmly lighted floors flashed past the elevator we had words over the fact that I, by taking part in the fight, had knocked one of their friends out of a night's work.

We were led out of the elevator through a rococo hall into an anteroom and told to get into our fighting togs. Each of us was issued a pair of boxing gloves and ushered out into the big mirrored hall, which we entered looking cautiously about us and whispering, lest we might accidentally be heard above the noise of the room. It was foggy with cigar smoke. And already the whiskey was taking effect. I was shocked to see some of the most important men of the town quite tipsy. They were all there—bankers, lawyers, judges, doctors, fire chiefs, teachers, merchants. Even one of the more fashionable pastors. Something we could not see was going on up front. A clarinet was vibrating sensuously and the men were standing up and moving eagerly forward. We were a small tight group, clustered together, our bare upper bodies touching and shining with anticipatory sweat; while up front the big shots were becoming increasingly excited over something we still could not see. Suddenly I heard the school superintendent, who had told me to come, yell, "Bring up the shines gentlemen! Bring up the little shines!"

We were rushed up to the front of the ballroom, where it smelled even more strongly of tobacco and whiskey. Then we were pushed into place. I almost wet my pants. A sea of faces, some hostile, some amused, ringed around us, and in the center, facing us, stood a magnificent blonde—stark naked. There was dead silence. I felt a blast of cold air chill me. I tried to back away, but they were behind me and around me. Some of the boys stood with lowered heads, trembling. I felt a wave of irrational guilt and fear. My teeth chattered, my skin turned to goose flesh, my knees knocked. Yet I was strongly attracted and looked in spite of myself. Had the price of looking been blindness, I would have looked. The hair was yellow like that of a circus kewpie doll, the face heavily powdered and rouged, as though to form an abstract mask, the eyes hollow and smeared a cool blue, the color of a baboon's butt. I felt a desire to spit upon her as my eyes brushed slowly over her body. Her breasts were firm and round as the domes of East Indian temples, and I stood so close as to see the fine skin texture and beads of pearly perspiration glistening like dew around the pink and erected buds of her nipples. I wanted at one and the same time to run from the room, to sink through the floor, or go to her and cover her from my eyes and the eyes of the others with my body; to feel the soft thighs, to caress her and destroy her, to love her and murder her, to hide from her, and yet to stroke where below the small American flag tattooed upon her belly her thighs formed a capital V. I had a notion that of all in the room she saw only me with her impersonal eyes.

And then she began to dance, a slow sensuous movement; the smoke of a hundred cigars clinging to her like the thinnest of veils. She seemed like a fair bird-girl girdled in veils calling to me from the angry surface of some gray and threatening sea. I was transported. Then I became aware of the clarinet playing and the big shots yelling at us. Some threatened us if we looked and others if we did not. On my right I saw one boy faint. And now a man grabbed a silver pitcher from a table and stepped close as he dashed ice water upon him and stood him up and forced two of us to support him as his head hung and moans issued from his thick bluish lips. Another boy began to plead to go home. He was the largest of the group, wearing dark red fighting trunks much too small to conceal the erection which projected from him as though in answer to the insinuating low-registered moaning of the clarinet. He tried to hide himself with his boxing gloves.

And all the while the blonde continued dancing, smiling faintly at the big shots who watched her with fascination, and faintly smiling at our fear. I noticed a certain merchant who followed her hungrily, his lips loose and drooling. He was a large man who wore diamond studs in a shirtfront which swelled with the ample paunch underneath, and each time the blonde swayed her undulating hips he ran his hand through the thin hair of his bald head and, with his arms upheld, his posture clumsy like that of an intoxicated panda, wound his belly in a slow and obscene grind. This creature was completely hypnotized. The music had quickened. As the dancer flung herself about with a detached expression on her face, the men began reaching out to touch her. I could see their beefy fingers sink into her soft flesh. Some of the others tried to stop them and she began to move around the floor in graceful circles, as they gave chase, slipping and sliding over the polished floor. It was mad. Chairs went crashing, drinks were spilt, as they ran laughing and howling after her. They caught her just as she reached a door, raised her from the floor, and tossed her as college boys are tossed at a hazing, and above her red, fixed-smiling lips I saw the terror and disgust in her eyes, almost like my own terror and that which I saw in some of the other boys. As I watched, they tossed her twice and her soft breasts seemed to flatten against the air and her legs flung wildly as she spun. Some of the more sober ones helped her to escape. And I started off the floor, heading for the anteroom with the rest of the boys.

Some were still crying and in hysteria. But as we tried to leave we were stopped and ordered to get into the ring. There was nothing to do but what we were told. All ten of us climbed under the ropes and allowed ourselves to be blindfolded with broad bands of white cloth. One of the men seemed to feel a bit sympathetic and tried to cheer us up as we stood with our backs against the ropes. Some of us tried to grin. "See that boy over there?" one of the men said. "I want you to run across at the bell and give it to him right in the belly. If you don't get him, I'm going to get you. I don't like his looks." Each of us was told the same. The blindfolds were put on. Yet even then I had been going over my speech. In my mind each word was as bright as flame. I felt the cloth pressed into place, and frowned so that it would be loosened when I relaxed.

But now I felt a sudden fit of blind terror. I was unused to darkness. It was as though I had suddenly found myself in a dark room filled with poisonous cottonmouths. I could hear the bleary voices yelling insistently for the battle royal to begin.

"Get going in there!"

"Let me at that big nigger!"

I strained to pick up the school superintendent's voice, as though to squeeze some security out of that slightly more familiar sound.

"Let me at those black sonsabitches!" someone yelled.

"No, Jackson, no!" another voice yelled. "Here, somebody, help me hold Jack."

"I want to get at that ginger-colored nigger. Tear him limb from limb," the first voice yelled.

I stood against the ropes trembling. For in those days I was what they called ginger-colored, and he sounded as though he might crunch me between his teeth like a crisp ginger cookie.

Quite a struggle was going on. Chairs were being kicked about and I could hear voices grunting as with a terrific effort. I wanted to see, to see more desperately than ever before. But the blindfold was as tight as a thick skin-puckering scab and when I raised my gloved hands to push the layers of white aside a voice yelled, "Oh, no you don't, black bastard! Leave that alone!"

"Ring the bell before Jackson kills him a coon!" someone boomed in the sudden silence. And I heard the bell clang and the sound of the feet scuffling forward.

A glove smacked against my head. I pivoted, striking out stiffly as someone went past, and felt the jar ripple along the length of my arm to my shoulder. Then it seemed as though all nine of the boys had turned upon me at once. Blows pounded me from all sides while I struck out as best I could. So many blows landed upon me that I wondered if I were not the only blindfolded fighter in the ring, or if the man called Jackson hadn't succeeded in getting me after all.

Blindfolded, I could no longer control my motions. I had no dignity. I stumbled about like a baby or a drunken man. The smoke had become thicker and with each new blow it seemed to sear and further restrict my lungs. My saliva became like hot bitter glue. A glove connected with my head, filling my mouth with warm blood. It was everywhere. I could not tell if the moisture I felt upon my body was sweat or blood. A blow landed hard against the nape of my neck. I felt myself going over, my head hitting the floor. Streaks of blue light filled the black world behind the blindfold. I lay prone, pretending that I was knocked out, but felt myself seized by hands and yanked to my feet. "Get going, black boy! Mix it up!" My arms were like lead, my head smarting from blows. I managed to feel my way to the ropes and held on, trying to catch my breath. A glove landed in my midsection and I went over again, feeling as though the smoke had become a knife jabbed into my guts. Pushed this way and that by the legs milling around me, I finally pulled erect and discovered that I could see the black, sweat-washed forms weaving in the smoky-blue atmosphere like drunken dancers weaving to the rapid drum-like thuds of blows.

Everyone fought hysterically. It was complete anarchy. Everybody fought everybody else. No group fought together for long. Two, three, four, fought one, then turned to fight each other, were themselves attacked. Blows landed below the belt and in the kidney, with the gloves open as well as closed, and with my eye partly opened now there was not so much terror. I moved carefully, avoiding blows, although not too many to attract attention, fighting from group to group. The boys groped about like blind, cautious crabs crouching to protect their mid-sections, their heads pulled in short against their shoulders, their arms stretched nervously before them, with their fists testing the smoke-filled air like the knobbed feelers of hypersensitive snails. In one corner I glimpsed a boy violently punching the air and heard him scream in pain as he smashed his hand against a ring post. For a second I saw him bent over holding his hand, then going down as a blow caught his unprotected head. I played one group against the other, slipping in and throwing a punch then stepping out of range while pushing the others into the melee to take the blows blindly aimed at me. The smoke was agonizing and there were no rounds, no bells at three minute intervals to relieve our exhaustion. The room spun round me, a swirl of lights, smoke, sweating bodies surrounded by tense white faces. I bled from both nose and mouth, the blood spattering upon my chest.

The men kept yelling, "Slug him, black boy! Knock his guts out!"

"Uppercut him! Kill him! Kill that big boy!"

Taking a fake fall, I saw a boy going down heavily beside me as though we were felled by a single blow, saw a sneaker-clad foot shoot into his groin as the two who had knocked him down stumbled upon him. I rolled out of range, feeling a twinge of nausea.

The harder we fought the more threatening the men became. And yet, I had begun to worry about my speech again. How would it go? Would they recognize my ability? What would they give me?

I was fighting automatically and suddenly I noticed that one after another of the boys was leaving the ring. I was surprised, filled with panic, as though I had been left alone with an unknown danger. Then I understood. The boys had arranged it among themselves. It was the custom for the two men left in the ring to slug it out for the winner's prize. I discovered this too late. When the bell sounded two men in tuxedoes leaped into the ring and removed the blindfold. I found myself facing Tatlock, the biggest of the gang. I felt sick at my stomach. Hardly had the bell stopped ringing in my ears than it clanged again and I saw him moving swiftly toward me. Thinking of nothing else to do I hit him smash on the nose. He kept coming, bringing the rank sharp violence of stale sweat. His face was a black blank of a face, only his eyes alive—with hate of me and aglow with a feverish terror from what had happened to us all. I became anxious. I wanted to deliver my speech and he came at me as though he meant to beat it out of me. I smashed him again and again, taking his blows as they came. Then on a sudden impulse I struck him lightly and as we clinched, I whispered, "Fake like I knocked you out, you can have the prize."

"I'll break your behind," he whispered hoarsely.

"For *them?*"

"For *me,* sonofabitch!"

They were yelling for us to break it up and Tatlock spun me half around with a blow, and as a joggled camera sweeps in a reeling scene, I saw the howling red faces crouching tense beneath the cloud of blue-gray smoke. For a moment the world wavered, unraveled, flowed, then my head cleared and Tatlock bounced before me. That fluttering shadow before my eyes was his jabbing left hand. Then falling forward, my head against his damp shoulder, I whispered, "I'll make it five dollars more."

"Go to hell!"

But his muscles relaxed a trifle beneath my pressure and I breathed, "Seven!"

"Give it to your ma," he said, ripping me beneath the heart.

And while I still held him I butted him and moved away. I felt myself bombarded with punches. I fought back with hopeless desperation. I wanted to deliver my speech more than anything else in the world, because I felt that only these men could judge truly my ability, and now this stupid clown was ruining my chances. I began fighting carefully now, moving in to punch him and out again with my greater speed. A lucky blow to his chin and I had him going too—until I heard a loud voice yell, "I got my money on the big boy."

Hearing this, I almost dropped my guard. I was confused: Should I try to win against the voice out there? Would not this go against my speech, and was not this a moment for humility, for nonresistance? A blow to my head as I danced about sent my right eye popping like a jack-in-the-box and settled my dilemma. The room went red as I fell. It was a dream fall, my body languid and fastidious as to where to land, until the floor became impatient and smashed up to meet me. A moment later I came to. An hypnotic voice said FIVE emphatically. And I lay there, hazily watching a dark red spot of my own blood shaping itself into a butterfly, glistening and soaking into the soiled gray world of the canvas.

When the voice drawled TEN I was lifted up and dragged to a chair. I sat dazed. My eye pained and swelled with each throb of my pounding heart and I wondered if now I would be allowed to speak. I was wringing wet, my mouth still bleeding. We were grouped along the wall now. The other boys ignored me as they congratulated Tatlock and speculated as to how much they would be paid. One boy whimpered over his smashed hand. Looking up front, I saw attendants in white jackets rolling the portable ring away and placing a small square rug in the vacant space surrounded by chairs. Perhaps, I thought, I will stand on the rug to deliver my speech.

Then the M.C. called to us, "Come on up here boys and get your money."

We ran forward to where the men laughed and talked in their chairs, waiting. Everyone seemed friendly now.

"There it is on the rug," the man said. I saw the rug covered with coins of all dimensions and a few crumpled bills. But what excited me, scattered here and there, were the gold pieces.

"Boys, it's all yours," the man said. "You get all you grab."

"That's right, Sambo," a blond man said, winking at me confidentially.

I trembled with excitement, forgetting my pain. I would get the gold and the bills, I thought. I would use both hands. I would throw my body against the boys nearest me to block them from the gold.

"Get down around the rug now," the man commanded, "and don't anyone touch it until I give the signal."

"This ought to be good," I heard.

As told, we got around the square rug on our knees. Slowly the man raised his freckled hand as we followed it upward with our eyes.

I heard, "These niggers look like they're about to pray!"

Then, "Ready," the man said. "Go!"

I lunged for a yellow coin lying on the blue design of the carpet, touching it and sending a surprised shriek to join those rising around me. I tried frantically to remove my hand but could not let go. A hot, violent force tore through my body, shaking me like a wet rat. The rug was electrified. The hair bristled up on my head as I shook myself free. My muscles jumped, my nerves jangled, writhed. But I saw that this was not stopping the other boys. Laughing in fear and embarrassment, some were holding back and scooping up the coins knocked off by the painful contortions of the others. The men roared above us as we struggled.

"Pick it up, goddamnit, pick it up!" someone called like a bass-voiced parrot. "Go on, get it!"

I crawled rapidly around the floor, picking up the coins, trying to avoid the coppers and to get greenbacks and the gold. Ignoring the shock by laughing, as I brushed the coins off quickly, I discovered that I could contain the electricity—a contradiction, but it works. Then the men began to push us onto the rug. Laughing embarrassedly, we struggled out of their hands and kept after the coins. We were all wet and slippery and hard to hold. Suddenly I saw a boy lifted into the air, glistening with sweat like a circus seal, and dropped, his wet back landing flush upon the charged rug, heard him yell and saw him literally dance upon his back, his elbows beating a frenzied tattoo upon the floor, his muscles twitching like the flesh of a horse stung by many flies. When he finally rolled off, his face was gray and no one stopped him when he ran from the floor amid booming laughter.

"Get the money," the M.C. called. "That's good hard American cash!"

And we snatched and grabbed, snatched and grabbed. I was careful not to come too close to the rug now, and when I felt the hot whiskey breath descend upon me like a cloud of foul air I reached out and grabbed the leg of a chair. It was occupied and I held on desperately.

"Leggo, nigger! Leggo!"

The huge face wavered down to mine as he tried to push me free. But my body was slippery and he was too drunk. It was Mr. Colcord, who owned a chain of movie houses and "entertainment palaces." Each time he grabbed me I slipped out of his hands. It became a real struggle. I feared the rug more than I did the drunk, so I held on, surprising myself for a moment by trying to topple *him* upon the rug. It was such an enormous idea that I found myself actually carrying it out. I tried not to be obvious, yet when I grabbed his leg, trying to tumble him out of the chair, he raised up roaring with laughter, and, looking at me with soberness dead in the eye, kicked me viciously in the chest. The chair leg flew out of my hand. I felt myself going and rolled. It was as though I had rolled through a bed of hot coals. It seemed a whole century would pass before I would roll free, a century in which I was seared through the deepest levels of my body to the fearful breath within me and the breath seared and heated to the point of explosion. It'll all be over in a flash, I thought as I rolled clear. It'll all be over in a flash.

But not yet, the men on the other side were waiting, red faces swollen as though from apoplexy as they bent forward in their chairs. Seeing their fingers coming toward me I rolled away as a fumbled football rolls off the receiver's fingertips, back into the coals. That time I luckily sent the rug sliding out of place and heard the coins ringing against the floor and the boys scuffling to pick them up and the M.C. calling, "All right, boys, that's all. Go get dressed and get your money."

I was limp as a dish rag. My back felt as though it had been beaten with wires.

When we had dressed the M.C. came in and gave us each five dollars, except Tatlock, who got ten for being last in the ring. Then he told us to leave. I was not to get a chance to deliver my speech, I thought. I was going out into the dim alley in despair when I was stopped and told to go back. I returned to the ballroom, where the men were pushing back their chairs and gathering in groups to talk.

The M.C. knocked on a table for quiet. "Gentlemen," he said, "we almost forgot an important part of the program. A most serious part, gentlemen. This boy was brought here to deliver a speech which he made at his graduation yesterday. . . ."

"Bravo!"

"I'm told that he is the smartest boy we've got out there in Greenwood. I'm told that he knows more big words than a pocket-sized dictionary."

Much applause and laughter.

"So now, gentlemen, I want you to give him your attention."

There was still laughter as I faced them, my mouth dry, my eye throbbing. I began slowly, but evidently my throat was tense, because they began shouting, "Louder! Louder!"

"We of the younger generation extol the wisdom of that great leader and educator," I shouted, "who first spoke these flaming words of wisdom: 'A ship lost at sea for many days suddenly sighted a friendly vessel. From the mast of the unfortunate vessel was seen a signal: "Water, water; we die of thirst!" The answer from the friendly vessel came back: "Cast down your bucket where you are." The captain of the distressed vessel, at last heeding the injunction, cast down his bucket, and it came up full of fresh sparkling water from the mouth of the Amazon River.' And like him I say, and in his words, 'To those of my race who depend upon bettering their condition in a foreign land, or who underestimate the importance of cultivating friendly relations with the Southern white man, who is his next-door neighbor, I would say: "Cast down your bucket where you are"—cast it down in making friends in every manly way of the people of all races by whom we are surrounded. . . .' "

I spoke automatically and with such fervor that I did not realize that the men were still talking and laughing until my dry mouth, filling up with blood from the cut, almost strangled me. I coughed, wanting to stop and go to one of the tall brass, sand filled spittoons to relieve myself, but a few of the men, especially the superintendent, were listening and I was afraid. So I gulped it down, blood, saliva and all, and continued. (What powers of endurance I had during those days! What enthusiasm! What a belief in the rightness of things!) I spoke even louder in spite of the pain. But still they talked and still they laughed, as though deaf with cotton in dirty ears. So I spoke with greater emotional emphasis. I closed my ears and swallowed blood until I was nauseated. The speech seemed a hundred times as long as before, but I could not leave out a single word. All had to be said, each memorized nuance considered, rendered. Nor was that all. Whenever I uttered a word of three or more syllables a group of voices would yell for me to repeat it. I used the phrase "social responsibility" and they yelled:

"What's the word you say, boy?"

"Social responsibility," I said.

"What?"

"Social . . ."

"Louder."

" . . . responsibility."

"More!"

"Respon—"

"Repeat!"

"—sibility."

The room filled with the uproar of laughter until, no doubt, distracted by having to gulp down my blood, I made a mistake and yelled a phrase I had often seen denounced in newspaper editorials, heard debated in private.

"Social . . ."

"What?" they yelled.

" . . . equality—"

The laughter hung smokelike in the sudden stillness. I opened my eyes, puzzled. Sounds of displeasure filled the room. The M.C. rushed forward. They shouted hostile phrases at me. But I did not understand.

A small dry mustached man in the front row blared out, "Say that slowly, son!"

"What sir?"

"What you just said!"

"Social responsibility, sir," I said.

"You weren't being smart, were you, boy?" he said, not unkindly.

"No, sir!"

"You sure that about 'equality' was a mistake?"

"Oh, yes, sir," I said. "I was swallowing blood."

"Well, you had better speak more slowly so we can understand. We mean to do right by you, but you've got to know your place at all times. All right, now, go on with your speech."

I was afraid. I wanted to leave but I wanted also to speak and I was afraid they'd snatch me down.

"Thank you, sir," I said, beginning where I had left off, and having them ignore me as before.

Yet when I finished there was a thunderous applause. I was surprised to see the superintendent come forth with a package wrapped in white tissue paper, and, gesturing for quiet, address the men.

"Gentlemen, you see that I did not overpraise this boy. He makes a good speech and some day he'll lead his people in the proper paths. And I don't have to tell you that that is important in these days and times. This is a good, smart boy, and so to encourage him in the right direction, in the name of the Board of Education I wish to present him a prize in the form of this . . ."

He paused, removing the tissue paper and revealing a gleaming calfskin brief case. " . . . in the form of this first-class article from Shad Whitmore's shop."

"Boy," he said, addressing me, "take this prize and keep it well. Consider it a badge of office. Prize it. Keep developing as you are and some day it will be filled with important papers that will help shape the destiny of your people."

I was so moved that I could hardly express my thanks. A rope of bloody saliva forming a shape like an undiscovered continent drooled upon the leather and I wiped it quickly away. I felt an importance that I had never dreamed.

"Open it and see what's inside," I was told.

My fingers a-tremble, I complied, smelling the fresh leather and finding an official-looking document inside. It was a scholarship to the state college for Negroes. My eyes filled with tears and I ran awkwardly off the floor.

I was overjoyed; I did not even mind when I discovered that the gold pieces I had scrambled for were brass pocket tokens advertising a certain make of automobile.

When I reached home everyone was excited. Next day the neighbors came to congratulate me. I even felt safe from grandfather, whose deathbed curse usually spoiled my triumphs. I stood beneath his photograph with my brief case in hand and smiled triumphantly into his stolid black peasant's face. It was a face that fascinated me. The eyes seemed to follow everywhere I went.

That night I dreamed I was at a circus with him and that he refused to laugh at the clowns no matter what they did. Then later he told me to open my brief case and read what was inside and I did, finding an official envelope stamped with the state seal; and inside the envelope I found another and another, endlessly, and I thought I would fall of weariness. "Them's years," he said. "Now open that one." And I did and in it I found an engraved document containing a short message in letters of gold. "Read it," my grandfather said. "Out loud."

"To Whom It May Concern," I intoned. "Keep This Nigger-Boy Running."

I awoke with the old man's laughter ringing in my ears.

(It was a dream I was to remember and dream again for many years after. But at the time I had no insight into its meaning. First I had to attend college.)

(1952)

QUESTIONS FOR CRITICAL THINKING AND WRITING

Experience

1. In the opening paragraph, the narrator says that he had to learn that he is invisible. What does he mean? Have you ever felt invisible over a prolonged period of time?
2. Contrast the public posture of the town leaders with their behavior during the smoker. Have you ever observed similarly contrasting behaviors in individuals?
3. How did you react when the narrator received the scholarship? Did it make you feel any differently toward the town leaders?

Interpretation

4. What does the Battle Royal represent? What is the town leaders' goal in sponsoring it?
5. What does the dancer represent? Consider the American flag tattooed on her belly. In what ways is the men's treatment of the dancer analogous to their treatment of the boys?
6. Just before the narrator is awarded a college scholarship, the superintendent says, ". . . some day he'll lead his people in the proper paths. And I don't have to tell you that that is important in these days and times." What is the superintendent implying?
7. Interpret the narrator's dream, particularly the message in the envelope.

Evaluation

8. What are the cultural values of the town? Who determines the values? How?
9. Interpret and evaluate the grandfather's advice to his children. Does it seem militant or nonagressive? Consider the historical context.

Connection

10. Compare the minority experience of the narrator in "Battle Royal" with that of the narrators in Baldwin's "Sonny's Blue" or Tan's "Rules of the Game" (found in this chapter).

Critical Thinking

11. Think of three different meanings for the term "battle royal." How many different kinds of battles the does the narrator find himself engaged in? Explain the significance of each of those battles.

WILLIAM FAULKNER

[1897–1962]

William Faulkner was born into a Mississippi family whose influence and wealth had disappeared during the Civil War. Faulkner lived most of his life in the South he memorialized in his fiction, writing about the Oxford, Mississippi, of his actual life in his fictional Yoknapatawpha County. Faulkner won a Nobel Prize for Literature in 1949, along with a National Book Award and two Pulitzer Prizes. His major novels include The Sound and the Fury, As I Lay Dying, *and* Absalom, Absalom! *"A Rose for Emily," his best-known, and perhaps best-loved, story, portrays the results of change in the post–Civil War South.*

Barn Burning

The store in which the Justice of the Peace's court was sitting smelled of cheese. The boy, crouched on his nail keg at the back of the crowded room, knew he smelled cheese, and more: from where he sat he could see the ranked shelves close-packed with the solid, squat, dynamic shapes of tin cans whose labels his stomach read, not from the lettering which meant nothing to his mind but from the scarlet devils and the silver curve of fish—this, the cheese which he knew he smelled and the hermetic meat which his intestines believed he smelled coming in intermittent gusts momentary and brief between the other constant one, the smell and sense just a little of fear because mostly of despair and grief, the old fierce pull of blood. He could not see the table where the Justice sat and before which his father and his father's enemy (*our enemy* he thought in that despair: *ourn! Mine and hisn both! He's my father!*) stood, but he could hear them, the two of them that is, because his father had said no word yet:

"But what proof have you, Mr. Harris?"

"I told you. The hog got into my corn. I caught it up and sent it back to him. He had no fence that would hold it. I told him so, warned him. The next time I put the hog in my pen. When he came to get it I gave him enough wire to patch up his pen. The next time I put the hog up and kept it. I rode down to his house and saw the wire I gave him still rolled on to the spool in his yard. I told him he could have the hog when he paid me a dollar pound fee. That evening a nigger came with the dollar and got the hog. He was a strange nigger. He said, 'He say to tell you wood and hay kin burn.' I said, 'What?' That whut he say to tell you,' the nigger said. 'Wood and hay kin burn.' That night my barn burned. I got the stock out but I lost the barn."

"Where's the nigger? Have you got him?"

"He was a strange nigger, I tell you. I don't know what became of him."

"But that's not proof. Don't you see that's not proof?"

"Get that boy up here. He knows." For a moment the boy thought too that the man meant his older brother until Harris said, "Not him. The little one. The boy," and, crouching, small for his age, small and wiry like his father, in patched and faded jeans even too small for him, with straight, uncombed, brown hair and eyes gray and wild as storm scud, he saw the men between himself and the table part and become a lane of grim faces, at the end of which he saw the justice, a shabby, collarless, graying man in spectacles, beckoning him. He felt no floor under his bare feet; he seemed to walk beneath the palpable weight of the grim turning faces. His father, still in his black Sunday coat donned not for the trial but for the moving, did not even look at him. *He aims for me to lie,* he thought, again with that frantic grief and despair. And *I will have to do hit.*

"What's your name, boy?" the Justice said.

"Colonel Sartoris Snopes," the boy whispered.

"Hey?" the Justice said. "Talk louder. Colonel Sartoris? I reckon anybody named for Colonel Sartoris in this country can't help but tell the truth, can they?" The boy said nothing, *Enemy! Enemy!* he thought; for a moment he could not even see, could not see that the Justice face was kindly nor discern that his voice was troubled when he spoke to the man named Harris: "Do you want me to question this boy?" But he could hear, and during those subsequent long seconds while there was absolutely no sound in the crowded little room save that of quiet and intent breathing it was as if he had swung outward at the end of a grape vine, over a ravine, and at the top of the swing had been caught in a prolonged instant of mesmerized gravity, weightless in time.

"No!" Harris said violently, explosively. "Damnation! Send him out of here!" Now time, the fluid world, rushed beneath him again, the voices coming to him again through the smell of cheese and sealed meat, the fear and despair and the old grief of blood:

"This case is closed. I can't find against you, Snopes, but I can give you advice. Leave this country and don't come back to it."

His father spoke for the first time, his voice cold and harsh, level, without emphasis: "I aim to. I don't figure to stay in a country among people who . . ." he said something unprintable and vile, addressed to no one.

"That'll do," the Justice said. "Take your wagon and get out of this country before dark. Case dismissed."

His father turned, and he followed the stiff black coat, the wiry figure walking a little stiffly from where a Confederate provost's man's musket ball had taken him in the heel on a stolen horse thirty years ago, followed the two backs now, since his older brother had appeared from somewhere in the crowd, no taller than the father but thicker, chewing tobacco steadily, between the two lines of grim-faced men and out of the store and across the worn gallery and down the sagging steps and among the dogs and half-grown boys in the mild May dust, where as he passed a voice hissed: "Barn burner!"

Again he could not see, whirling; there was a face in a red haze, moonlike, bigger than the full moon, the owner of it half again his size, he leaping in the red haze toward the face, feeling no blow, feeling no shock when his head struck the earth, scrabbling up and leaping again, feeling no blow this time either and tasting no blood, scrabbling up to see the other boy in full flight and himself already leaping into pursuit as his father's hand jerked him back, the harsh, cold voice speaking above him: "Go get in the wagon."

It stood in a grove of locusts and mulberries across the road. His two hulking sisters in their Sunday dresses and his mother and her sister in calico and sunbonnets were already in it, sitting on and among the sorry residue of the dozen and more movings which even the boy could remember—the battered stove, the broken beds and chairs, the clock inlaid with mother-of-pearl, which would not run, stopped at some fourteen minutes past two o'clock of a dead and forgotten day and time, which had been his mother's dowry. She was crying, though when she saw him she drew her sleeve across her face and began to descend from the wagon. "Get back," the father said.

"He's hurt. I got to get some water and wash his . . ."

"Get back in the wagon," his father said. He got in too, over the tail-gate. His father mounted to the seat where the older brother already sat and struck the gaunt mules two savage blows with the peeled willow, but without heat. It was not even sadistic; it was exactly that same quality which in later years would cause his descendants to over-run the engine before putting a motor car into motion, striking and reining back in the same movement. The wagon went on, the store with its quiet crowd of grimly watching men dropped behind; a curve in the road hid it. *Forever* he thought. *Maybe he's done satisfied now, now that he has* . . . stopping himself, not to say it aloud even to himself. His mother's hand touched his shoulder.

"Does hit hurt?" she said.

"Naw," he said. "Hit don't hurt. Lemme be."

"Can't you wipe some of the blood off before hit dries?"

"I'll wash to-night," he said. "Lemme be, I tell you."

The wagon went on. He did not know where they were going. None of them ever did or ever asked, because it was always somewhere, always a house of sorts waiting for them a day or two days or even three days away. Likely his father had already arranged to make a crop on another farm before he . . . Again he had to stop himself. He (the father) always did. There was something about his wolflike independence and even courage when the advantage was at least neutral which impressed strangers, as if they got from his latent ravening ferocity not so much a sense of dependability as a feeling that his ferocious conviction in the rightness of his own actions would be of advantage to all whose interest lay with his.

That night they camped, in a grove of oaks and beeches where a spring ran. The nights were still cool and they had a fire against it, of a rail lifted from a nearby fence and cut into lengths—a small fire, neat, niggard almost, a shrewd fire; such fires were his father's habit and custom always, even in freezing weather. Older, the boy might have remarked this and wondered why not a big one; why should not a man who had not only seen the waste and extravagance of war, but who had in his blood an inherent voracious prodigality with material not his own, have burned everything in sight? Then he might have gone a step farther and thought that that was the reason: that niggard blaze was the living fruit of nights passed during those four years in the woods hiding from all men, blue and gray, with his strings of horses (captured horses, he called them). And older still, he might have divined the true reason: that the element of fire spoke to some deep mainspring of his father's being, as the element of steel or of powder spoke to other men, as the one weapon for the preservation of integrity,

else breath were not worth the breathing, and hence to be regarded with respect and used with discretion.

But he did not think this now and he had seen those same niggard blazes all his life. He merely ate his supper beside it and was already half asleep over his iron plate when his father called him, and once more he followed the stiff back, the stiff and ruthless limp, up the slope and on to the starlit road where, turning, he could see his father against the stars but without face or depth—a shape black, flat, and bloodless as though cut from tin in the iron folds of the frockcoat which had not been made for him, the voice harsh like tin and without heat like tin:

"You were fixing to tell them. You would have told him."

He didn't answer. His father struck him with the flat of his hand on the side of the head, hard but without heat, exactly as he had struck the two mules at the store, exactly as he would strike either of them with any stick in order to kill a horse fly, his voice without heat or anger: "You're getting to be a man. You got to learn. You got to learn to stick to your own blood or you ain't going to have any blood to stick to you. Do you think either of them, any man there this morning, would? Don't you know all they wanted was a chance to get at me because they knew I had them beat? Eh?" Later, twenty years later, he was to tell himself, "If I had said they wanted only truth, justice, he would have hit me again." But now he said nothing. He was not crying. He just stood there. "Answer me," his father said.

"Yes," he whispered. His father turned.

"Get on to bed. We'll be there tomorrow."

Tomorrow they were there. In the early afternoon the wagon stopped before a paintless two-room house identical almost with the dozen others it had stopped before even in the boy's ten years, and again, as on the other dozen occasions, his mother and aunt got down and began to unload the wagon, although his two sisters and his father and brother had not moved.

"Likely hit ain't fitten for hawgs," one of the sisters said.

"Nevertheless, fit it will and you'll hog it and like it," his father said. "Get out of them chairs and help your Ma unload."

The two sisters got down, big, bovine, in a flutter of cheap ribbons; one of them drew from the jumbled wagon bed a battered lantern, the other a worn broom. His father handed the reins to the older son and began to climb stiffly over the wheel. "When they get unloaded, take the team to the barn and feed them." Then he said, and at first the boy thought he was still speaking to his brother: "Come with me."

"Me?" he said.

"Yes," his father said. "You."

"Abner," his mother said. His father paused and looked back—the harsh level stare beneath the shaggy, graying, irascible brows.

"I reckon I'll have a word with the man that aims to begin tomorrow owning me body and soul for the next eight months."

They went back up the road. A week ago—or before last night, that is—he would have asked where they were going, but not now. His father had struck him before last night but never before had he paused afterward to explain why; it was as if the blow and the following calm, outrageous voice still rang, repercussed, divulging nothing to him save the terrible handicap of being young, the light weight of his few years, just heavy enough to prevent his soaring free of the world as it seemed to be ordered but not heavy enough to keep him footed solid in it, to resist it and try to change the course of its events.

Presently he could see the grove of oaks and cedars and the other flowering trees and shrubs where the house would be, though not the house yet. They walked beside a fence massed with honeysuckle and Cherokee roses and came to a gate swinging open between two brick pillars, and now, beyond a sweep of drive, he saw the house for the first time and at that instant he forgot his father and the terror and despair both, and even when he remembered his father again (who had not stopped) the terror and despair did not return. Because, for all the twelve movings, they had sojourned until now in a poor country, a land of small farms and fields and houses, and he had never seen a house like this before. *Hit's big as a courthouse* he thought quietly, with a surge of peace and joy whose reason he could not have thought into words, being too young for that: *They are safe from him. People whose lives are a part of this peace and dignity are beyond his touch, he no more to them than a buzzing wasp: capable of stinging for a little moment but that's all; the spell of this peace and dignity rendering even the barns and stable and cribs which belong to it impervious to the puny flames he might contrive* . . . this, the peace and joy, ebbing for an instant as he looked again at the still black back, the stiff and implacable limp of the figure which was not dwarfed by the house, for the reason that it had never looked big anywhere and which now, against the serene columned backdrop, had more than ever that impervious quality of something cut ruthlessly from tin, depthless, as though, sidewise to the sun, it would cast no shadow. Watching him, the boy remarked the absolutely undeviating course which his father held and saw the stiff foot come squarely down in a pile of fresh droppings where a horse had stood in the drive and which his father could have avoided by a simple change of stride. But it ebbed only a moment, though he could not have thought this into words either, walking on in the spell of the house, which he could even want but without envy, without sorrow, certainly never with that ravening and jealous rage which unknown to him walked in the ironlike black coat before him: *Maybe he will feel it too. Maybe it will even change him now from what maybe he couldn't help but be.*

They crossed the portico. Now he could hear his father's stiff foot as it came down on the boards with clocklike finality, a sound out of all proportion to the displacement of the body it bore and which was not dwarfed either by the white door before it, as though it had attained to a sort of vicious and ravening minimum not to be dwarfed by anything—the flat, wide, black hat, the formal coat of broadcloth which had once been black but which had now that friction-glazed greenish cast of the bodies of old house flies, the lifted sleeve which was too large, the lifted hand like a curled claw. The door opened so promptly that the boy knew the Negro must have been watching them all the time, an old man with neat grizzled hair, in a linen jacket, who stood barring the door with his body, saying, "Wipe yo foots, white man, of you come in here. Major ain't home nohow."

"Get out of my way, nigger," his father said, without heat too, flinging the door back and the Negro also and entering, his hat still on his head. And now the boy saw the prints of the stiff foot on the doorjamb and saw them appear on the pale rug behind the machinelike deliberation of the foot which seemed to bear (or transmit) twice the weight which the body compassed. The Negro was shouting "Miss Lula! Miss Lula!" somewhere behind them, then the boy, deluged as though by a warm wave by a suave turn of the carpeted stair and a pendant glitter of chandeliers and a mute gleam of gold frames, heard the swift feet and saw her too, a lady—perhaps he had never seen her like before either—in a gray, smooth gown with lace at the throat and an apron tied at the waist and the sleeves turned back, wiping cake or biscuit dough from her hands with a towel as she came up the hall, looking not at his father at all but at the tracks on the blond rug with an expression of incredulous amazement.

"I tried," the Negro cried. "I tole him to . . ."

"Will you please go away?" she said in a shaking voice. "Major de Spain is not at home. Will you please go away?"

His father had not spoken again. He did not speak again. He did not even look at her. He just stood stiff in the center of the rug, in his hat, the shaggy iron-gray brows twitching slightly above the pebble-colored eyes as he appeared to examine the house with brief deliberation. Then with the same deliberation he turned; the boy watched him pivot on the good leg and saw the stiff foot drag around the arc of the turning, leaving a final long and fading smear. His father never looked at it, he never once looked down at the rug. The Negro held the door. It closed behind them, upon the hysteric and indistinguishable woman-wail. His father stopped at the top of the steps and scraped his boot clean on the edge of it. At the gate he stopped again. He stood for a moment, planted stiffly on the stiff foot, looking back at the house. "Pretty and white, ain't it?" he said. "That's sweat. Nigger sweat. Maybe it ain't white enough yet to suit him. Maybe he wants to mix some white sweat with it."

Two hours later the boy was chopping wood behind the house within which his mother and aunt and the two sisters (the mother and aunt, not the two girls, he knew that; even at this distance and muffled by walls the flat loud voices of the two girls emanated an incorrigible idle inertia) were setting up the stove to prepare a meal, when he heard the hooves and saw the linen-clad man on a fine sorrel mare, whom he recognized even before he saw the rolled rug in front of the Negro youth following on a fat bay carriage horse—a suffused, angry face vanishing, still at full gallop, beyond the corner of the house where his father and brother were sitting in the two tilted chairs; and a moment later, almost before he could have put the axe down, he heard the hooves again and watched the sorrel mare go back out of the yard, already galloping again. Then his father began to shout one of the sisters' names, who presently emerged backward from the kitchen door dragging the rolled rug along the ground by one end while the other sister walked behind it.

"If you ain't going to tote, go on and set up the wash pot," the first said.

"You, Sarty!" the second shouted. "Set up the wash pot!" His father appeared at the door, framed against that shabbiness, as he had been against that other bland perfection, impervious to either, the mother's anxious face at his shoulder.

"Go on," the father said. "Pick it up." The two sisters stooped, broad, lethargic; stooping, they presented an incredible expanse of pale cloth and a flutter of tawdry ribbons.

"If I thought enough of a rug to have to git hit all the way from France. I wouldn't keep hit where folks coming in would have to tromp on hit," the first said. They raised the rug.

"Abner," the mother said. "Let me do it."

"You go back and git dinner," his father said. "I'll tend to this."

From the woodpile through the rest of the afternoon the boy watched them, the rug spread flat in the dust beside the bubbling wash pot, the two sisters stooping over it with that profound and lethargic reluctance, while the father stood over them in turn, implacable and grim, driving them though never raising his voice again. He could smell the harsh homemade lye they were using; he saw his mother come to the door once and look toward them with an expression not anxious now but very like despair; he saw his father turn, and he fell to with the axe and saw from the corner of his eye his father raise from the ground a flattish fragment of field stone and examine it and return to the pot, and this time his mother actually spoke: "Abner. Abner. Please don't. Please, Abner."

Then he was done too. It was dusk; the whippoorwills had already begun. He could smell coffee from the room where they would presently eat the cold food remaining from the mid-afternoon meal, though when he entered the house he realized they were having coffee again probably because there was a fire on the hearth, before which the rug now lay spread over the backs of the two chairs. The tracks of his father's foot were gone. Where they had been were now long, water-cloudy scoriations resembling the sporadic course of a lilliputian mowing machine.

It still hung there while they ate the cold food and then went to bed, scattered without order or claim up and down the two rooms, his mother in one bed, where his father would later lie, the older brother in the other, himself, the aunt, and the two sisters on pallets on the floor. But his father was not in bed yet. The last thing the boy remembered was the depthless, harsh silhouette of the hat and coat bending over the rug and it seemed to him that he had not even closed his eyes when the silhouette was standing over him, the fire almost dead behind it, the stiff foot prodding him awake.

"Catch up the mule," his father said.

When he returned with the mule his father was standing in the back door, the rolled rug over his shoulder. "Ain't you going to ride?" he said.

"No. Give me your foot."

He bent his knee into his father's hand, the wiry, surprising power flowed smoothly, rising, he rising with it, on to the mule's bare back (they had owned a saddle once; the boy could remember it though not when or where) and with the same effortlessness his father swung the rug up in front of him. Now in the starlight they retraced the afternoon's path, up the dusty road rife with honeysuckle, through the gate and up the black tunnel of the drive to the lightless house, where he sat on the mule and felt the rough warp of the rug drag across his thighs and vanish.

"Don't you want me to help?" he whispered. His father did not answer and now he heard again that stiff foot striking the hollow portico with that wooden and clocklike deliberation, that outrageous overstatement of the weight it carried. The rug, hunched, not flung (the boy could tell that even in the darkness) from his father's shoulder struck the angle of wall and floor with a sound unbelievably loud, thunderous, then the foot again, unhurried and enormous; a light came on in the house and the boy sat, tense, breathing steadily and quietly and just a little fast, though the foot itself did not increase its beat at all, descending the steps now; now the boy could see him.

"Don't you want to ride now?" he whispered. "We kin both ride now," the light within the house altering now, flaring up and sinking. *He's coming down the stairs now,* he thought. He had already ridden the mule up beside the horse block; presently his father was up behind him and he doubled the reins over and slashed the mule across the neck, but before the animal could begin to trot the hard, thin arm came around him, the hard, knotted hand jerking the mule back to a walk.

In the first red rays of the sun they were in the lot, putting plow gear on the mules. This time the sorrel mare was in the lot before he heard it at all, the rider collarless and even bareheaded, trembling, speaking in a shaking voice as the woman in the house had done, his father merely looking up once before stooping again to the hame he was buckling, so that the man on the mare spoke to his stooping back:

"You must realize you have ruined that rug. Wasn't there anybody here, any of your women . . ." he ceased, shaking, the boy watching him, the older brother leaning now in the stable door, chewing, blinking slowly and steadily at nothing apparently. "It cost a hundred dollars. But you never had a hundred dollars. You never will. So I'm going to charge you twenty bushels of corn against your crop. I'll add it in your contract and when you come to the commissary you can sign it. That won't keep Mrs. de Spain quiet but maybe it will teach you to wipe your feet off before you enter her house again."

Then he was gone. The boy looked at his father, who still had not spoken or even looked up again, who was now adjusting the logger-head in the hame.

"Pap," he said. His father looked at him—the inscrutable face, the shaggy brows beneath where the gray eyes glinted coldly. Suddenly the boy went toward him, fast, stopping as suddenly. "You done the best you could!" he cried. "If he wanted hit done different why didn't he wait and tell you how? He won't git none! We'll gather hit and hide hit! I kin watch . . ."

"Did you put the cutter back in that straight stock like I told you?"

"No, sir," he said.

"Then go do it."

That was Wednesday. During the rest of that week he worked steadily, at what was within his scope and some which was beyond it, with an industry that did not need to be driven nor even commanded twice; he had this from his mother, with the difference that some at least of what he did he liked to do, such as splitting wood with the half-size axe which his mother and aunt had earned, or saved money somehow, to present him with at Christmas. In company with the two older women (and on one afternoon, even one of the sisters), he built pens for the shoat and the cow which were a part of his father's contract with the landlord, and one afternoon, his father being absent, gone somewhere on one of the mules, he went to the field.

They were running a middle buster now, his brother holding the plow straight while he handled the reins, and walking beside the straining mule, the rich black soil shearing cool and damp against his bare ankles, he thought *Maybe this is the end of it. Maybe even that twenty bushels that seems hard to have to pay for just a rug will be a cheap price for him to stop forever and always from being what he used to be;* thinking, dreaming now, so that his brother had to speak sharply to him to mind the mule: *Maybe he even won't collect the twenty bushels. Maybe it will all add up and balance and vanish—corn, rug, fire; the terror and grief; the being pulled two ways like between two teams of horses—gone, done with for ever and ever.*

Then it was Saturday; he looked up from beneath the mule he was harnessing and saw his father in the black coat and hat. "Not that," his father said. "The wagon gear." And then, two hours later, sitting in the wagon bed behind his father and brother on the seat, the wagon accomplished a final curve, and he saw the weathered paintless store with its tattered tobacco- and patent-medicine posters and the tethered wagons and saddle animals below the gallery. He mounted the gnawed steps behind his father and brother, and there again was the lane of quiet, watching faces for the three of them to walk through. He saw the man in spectacles sitting at the plank table and he did not need to be told this was a Justice of the Peace; he sent one glare of fierce, exultant, partisan defiance at the man in collar and cravat now, whom he had seen but twice before in his life, and that on a galloping horse, who now wore on his face an expression not of rage but of amazed unbelief which the boy could not have known was at the incredible circumstance of being sued by one of his own tenants, and came and stood against his father and cried at the Justice: "He ain't done it! He ain't burnt . . ."

"Go back to the wagon," his father said.

"Burnt?" the Justice said. "Do I understand this rug was burned too?"

"Does anybody here claim it was?" his father said. "Go back to the wagon."

But he did not, he merely retreated to the rear of the room, crowded as that other had been, but not to sit down this time, instead, to stand pressing among the motionless bodies, listening to the voices:

"And you claim twenty bushels of corn is too high for the damage you did to the rug?"

"He brought the rug to me and said he wanted the tracks washed out of it. I washed the tracks out and took the rug back to him."

"But you didn't carry the rug back to him in the same condition it was in before you made the tracks on it."

His father did not answer, and now for perhaps half a minute there was no sound at all save that of breathing, the faint, steady suspiration of complete and intent listening.

"You decline to answer that, Mr. Snopes?" Again his father did not answer. "I'm going to find against you, Mr. Snopes. I'm going to find that you were responsible for the injury to Major de Spain's rug and hold you liable for it. But twenty bushels of corn seems a little high for a man in your circumstances to have to pay. Major de Spain claims it cost a hundred dollars. October corn will be worth about fifty cents. I figure that if Major de Spain can stand a ninety-five dollar loss on something he paid cash for, you can stand a five-dollar loss you haven't earned yet. I hold you in damages to Major de Spain to the amount of ten bushels of corn over and above your contract with him, to be paid to him out of your crop at gathering time. Court adjourned."

It had taken no time hardly, the morning was but half begun. He thought they would return home and perhaps back to the field, since they were late, far behind all other farmers. But instead his father passed on behind the wagon, merely indicating with his hand for the older brother to follow with it, and crossed the road toward the blacksmith shop opposite, pressing on after his father, overtaking him, speaking, whispering up at the harsh, calm face beneath the weathered hat: "He won't git no ten bushels either. He won't git one. We'll . . ." until his father glanced for an instant down at him, the face absolutely calm, the grizzled eyebrows tangled above the cold eyes, the voice almost pleasant, almost gentle:

"You think so? Well, we'll wait till October anyway."

The matter of the wagon—the setting of a spoke or two and the tightening of the tires—did not take long either, the business of the tires accomplished by driving the wagon into the spring branch behind the shop and letting it stand there, the mules nuzzling into the water from time to time, and the boy on the seat with the idle reins, looking up the slope and through the sooty tunnel of the shed where the slow hammer rang and where his father sat on an upended cypress bolt, easily, either talking or listening, still sitting there when the boy brought the dripping wagon up out of the branch and halted it before the door.

"Take them on to the shade and hitch," his father said. He did so and returned. His father and the smith and a third man squatting on his heels inside the door were talking, about crops and animals; the boy, squatting too in the ammoniac dust and hoof-parings and scales of rust, heard his father tell a long and unhurried story out of the time before the birth of the older brother even when he had been a professional horsetrader. And then his father came up beside him where he stood before a tattered last year's circus poster on the other side of the store, gazing rapt and quiet at the scarlet horses, the incredible poisings and convulsions of tulle and tights and the painted leers of comedians, and said, "It's time to eat."

But not at home. Squatting beside his brother against the front wall, he watched his father emerge from the store and produce from a paper sack a segment of cheese and divide it carefully and deliberately into three with his pocket knife and produce crackers from the same sack. They all three squatted on the gallery and ate, slowly, without talking; then in the store again, they drank from a tin dipper tepid water smelling of the cedar bucket and of living beech trees. And still they did not go home. It was a horse lot this time, a tall rail fence upon and along which men stood and sat and out of which one by one horses were led, to be walked and trotted and then cantered back and forth along the road while the slow swapping and buying went on and the sun began to slant westward, they—the three of them—watching and listening, the older brother with his muddy eyes and his steady, inevitable tobacco, the father commenting now and then on certain of the animals, to no one in particular.

It was after sundown when they reached home. They ate supper by lamplight, then, sitting on the doorstep, the boy watched the night fully accomplish, listening to the whippoorwills and the frogs, when he heard his mother's voice: "Abner! No! No! Oh, God. Oh, God. Abner!" and he rose, whirled, and saw the altered light through the door where a candle stub now burned in a bottle neck on the table and his father, still in the hat and coat, at once formal and burlesque as though dressed carefully for some shabby and ceremonial violence, emptying the reservoir of the lamp back into the five-gallon kerosene can from which it had been filled, while the mother tugged at his arm until he shifted the lamp to the other hand and flung her back, not savagely or viciously, just hard, into the wall, her hands flung out against the wall for balance, her mouth open and in her face the same quality of hopeless despair as had been in her voice. Then his father saw him standing in the door.

"Go to the barn and get that can of oil we were oiling the wagon with," he said. The boy did not move. Then he could speak.

"What . . ." he cried. "What are you . . ."

"Go get that oil," his father said. "Go."

Then he was moving, running, outside the house, toward the stable: this the old habit, the old blood which he had not been permitted to choose for himself, which had been bequeathed him willy nilly and which had run for so long (and who knew where, battening on what of outrage and savagery and lust) before it came to him. *I could keep on,* he thought. *I could run on and on and never look back, never need to see his face again. Only I can't. I can't,* the rusted can in his hand now, the liquid sploshing in it as he ran back to the house and into it, into the sound of his mother's weeping in the next room, and handed the can to his father.

"Ain't you going to even send a nigger?" he cried. "At least you sent a nigger before!"

This time his father didn't strike him. The hand came even faster than the blow had, the same hand which had set the can on the table with almost excruciating care flashing from the can toward him too quick for him to follow it, gripping him by the back of his shirt and on to tiptoe before he had seen it quit the can, the face stooping at him in breathless and frozen ferocity, the cold, dead voice speaking over him to the older brother who leaned against the table, chewing with that steady, curious, sidewise motion of cows:

"Empty the can into the big one and go on. I'll catch up with you."

"Better tie him up to the bedpost," the brother said.

"Do like I told you," the father said. Then the boy was moving, his bunched shirt and the hard, bony hand between his shoulder-blades, his toes just touching the floor, across the room and into the other one, past the sisters sitting with spread heavy thighs in the two chairs over the cold hearth, and to where his mother and aunt sat side by side on the bed, the aunt's arm about his mother's shoulders.

"Hold him," the father said: The aunt made a startled movement. "Not you," the father said. "Lennie. Take hold of him. I want to see you do it." His mother took him by the wrist. "You'll hold him better than that. If he gets loose don't you know what he is going to do? He will go up yonder." He jerked his head toward the road. "Maybe I'd better tie him."

"I'll hold him," his mother whispered.

"See you do then." Then his father was gone, the stiff foot heavy and measured upon the boards, ceasing at last.

Then he began to struggle. His mother caught him in both arms, he jerking and wrenching at them. He would be stronger in the end, he knew that. But he had no time to wait for it. "Lemme go!" he cried. "I don't want to have to hit you!"

"Let him go!" the aunt said. "If he don't' go, before God, I am going up there myself!" "Don't you see I can't?" his mother cried. "Sarty! Sarty! No! No! Help me, Lizzie!"

Then he was free. His aunt grasped at him but it was too late. He whirled, running, his mother stumbled forward on to her knees behind him, crying to the nearer sister: "Catch him, Net! Catch him!" But that was too late too, the sister (the sisters were twins, born at the same time, yet either of them now gave the impression of being, encompassing as much living meat and volume and weight as any other two of the family) not yet having begun to rise from the chair, her head, face, alone merely turned, presenting to him in the flying instant an astonishing expanse of young female features untroubled by any surprise even, wearing only an expression of bovine interest. Then he was out of the room, out of the house, in the mild dust of the starlit road and the heavy rifeness of honeysuckle, the pale ribbon unspooling with terrific slowness under his running feet, reaching the gate at last and turning in, running, his heart and lungs drumming, on up the drive toward the lighted house, the lighted door. He did not knock, he burst in, sobbing for breath, incapable for the moment of speech; he saw the astonished face of the Negro in the linen jacket without knowing when the Negro had appeared.

"De Spain!" he cried, panted. "Where's . . ." then he saw the white man too emerging from a white door down the hall. "Barn!" he cried. "Barn!"

"What?" the white man said. "Barn?"

"Yes!" the boy cried. "Barn!"

"Catch him!" the white man shouted.

But it was too late this time too. The Negro grasped his shirt, but the entire sleeve, rotten with washing, carried away, and he was out that door too and in the drive again, and had actually never ceased to run even while he was screaming into the white man's face.

Behind him the white man was shouting. "My horse! Fetch my horse!" and he thought for an instant of cutting across the park and climbing the fence into the road, but he did not know the park nor how the vine-massed fence might be and he dared not risk it. So he ran on down the drive, blood and breath roaring; presently he was in the road again though he could not see it. He could not hear either: the galloping mare was almost upon him before he heard her, and even then he held his course, as if the very urgency of his wild grief and need must in a moment more find him wings, waiting until the ultimate instant to hurl himself aside and into the weed-choked roadside ditch as the horse thundered past and on, for an instant in furious silhouette against the stars, the tranquil early summer night sky which, even before the shape of the horse and rider vanished, stained abruptly and violently upward: a long, swirling roar incredible and soundless, blotting the stars, and he springing up and into the road again, running again, knowing it was too late yet still running even after he heard the shot and an instant later, two shots, pausing now without knowing he had ceased to run, crying, "Pap! Pap!", running again before he knew he had begun to run, stumbling, tripping over something and scrabbling up again without ceasing to run, looking backward over his shoulder at the glare as he got up, running on among the invisible trees, panting, sobbing, "Father! Father!"

At midnight he was sitting on the crest of a hill. He did not know it was midnight and he did not know how far he had come. But there was no glare behind him now and he sat now, his back toward what he had called home for four days anyhow, his face toward the dark woods which he would enter when breath was strong again, small, shaking steadily in the chill darkness, hugging himself into the remainder of his thin, rotten shirt, the grief and despair now no longer terror and fear but just grief and despair. *Father. My father,* he thought. "He was brave!" he cried suddenly, aloud but not loud, no more than a whisper. "He was! He was in the war! He was in Colonel Sartoris' cav'ry!" not knowing that his father had gone to that war a private in the fine old European sense, wearing no uniform, admitting the authority of and giving fidelity to no man or army or flag, going to war as Marlbrouck° himself did: for booty—it meant nothing and less than nothing to him if it were enemy booty or his own.

The slow constellations wheeled on. It would be dawn and then sun-up after a while and he would be hungry. But that would be tomorrow and now he was only cold, and walking would cure that. His breathing was easier now and he decided to get up and go on, and then he found that he had been asleep because he knew it was almost dawn, the night almost over. He could tell that from the whippoorwills. They were everywhere now among the dark trees below him, constant and inflectioned and ceaseless, so that, as the instant for giving over to the day birds drew nearer and nearer, there was no interval at all between them. He got up. He was a little stiff, but walking would cure that too as it would the cold, and soon there would be the sun. He went on down the hill, toward the dark woods within which the liquid silver

Marlbrouck *French name for John Churchill, Duke of Marlborogh who defeated the French army several times in the early 1700s.*

voices of the birds called unceasing—the rapid and urgent beating of the urgent and quiring heart of the late spring night. He did not look back.

(1939)

QUESTIONS FOR CRITICAL THINKING AND WRITING

Experience

1. How is your experience of reading Faulkner's "Barn Burning" similar to and different from your experience of reading other stories? What adjustments did you have to make in order to follow the story?
2. How do you respond to the boy? To his father? Why?

Interpretation

3. Divide the story into major parts or sections. What is the basis for your division?
4. How would you characterize Faulkner's style? Consider his diction and his sentences as well as his imagery and comparisons.
5. What details best serve to characterize the Snopes family? What overall impression of the family do those details create?
6. How would you characterize the relationship between the father and his son?
7. What is the significance of the large house Faulkner describes midway through the story?
8. How does Faulkner convey the boy's perspective on the events of the story and on the character of his father?
9. Why do you think Faulkner does not describe directly and objectively the burning of Major de Spain's barn and the shooting of the boy's father?

Evaluation

10. What values does Abner Snopes live by? What set of experiences has formed him?
11. What are the values of the world in which Snopes lives and works? What can you determine about the social, historical, and cultural context of the story?

Connection

12. Compare the style and point of view in this story with the style and point of view of Faulkner's "A Rose for Emily." What similarities and differences do you detect?

Critical Thinking

13. What do you think of the behavior of Abner Snopes—toward his children and his wife and toward his employers? Why do you think he behaves as he does toward his family and his employers? Explain.

F. SCOTT FITZGERALD
[1896–1940]

F. Scott Fitzgerald, author of the American classic The Great Gatsby *(1925), was regarded as the spokesman of the post–World War I "jazz age" generation and portrayed the extravagant world of America's fervid youth. Born and raised in Minnesota, he began to write while attending Princeton University. The publication of his first novel,* This Side of Paradise *(1920), brought him money and fame. He and his wife Zelda became exemplars of the jazz age. However, the financial demands of this lifestyle forced Fitzgerald to neglect his fiction and concentrate on writing for more popular tastes. In* The Great Gatsby, Tender Is the Night, *and his short-story collections, he dealt with the effects of such self-absorbed living on the spirit and on society. At the time of his death, his work was unread and forgotten.*

Babylon Revisited

I

"And where's Mr. Campbell?" Charlie asked.

"Gone to Switzerland. Mr. Campbell's a pretty sick man, Mr. Wales."

"I'm sorry to hear that. And George Hardt?" Charlie inquired.

"Back in America, gone to work."

"And where is the Snow Bird?"

"He was in here last week. Anyway, his friend, Mr. Schaeffer, is in Paris."

Two familiar names from the long list of a year and a half ago. Charlie scribbled an address in his notebook and tore out the page.

"If you see Mr. Schaeffer, give him this," he said. "It's my brother-in-law's address. I haven't settled on a hotel yet."

He was not really disappointed to find Paris was so empty. But the stillness in the Ritz bar was strange and portentous. It was not an American bar any more—he felt polite in it, and not as if he owned it. It had gone back into France. He felt the stillness from the moment he got out of the taxi and saw the doorman, usually in a frenzy of activity at this hour, gossiping with a *chasseur* by the servants' entrance.

Passing through the corridor, he heard only a single, bored voice in the once-clamorous women's room. When he turned into the bar he traveled the twenty feet of green carpet with his eyes fixed straight ahead by old habit; and then, with his foot firmly on the rail, he turned and surveyed the room, encountering only a single pair of eyes that fluttered up from a newspaper in the corner. Charlie asked for the head barman, Paul, who in the latter days of the bull market had come to work in his own custom-built car—disembarking, however, with due nicety at the nearest corner. But Paul was at his country house today and Alix giving him information.

"No, no more," Charlie said, "I'm going slow these days."

Alix congratulated him: "You were going pretty strong a couple of years ago."

"I'll stick to it all right," Charlie assured him. "I've stuck to it for over a year and a half now."

"How do you find conditions in America?"

"I haven't been to America for months. I'm in business in Prague, representing a couple of concerns there. They don't know about me down there."

Alix smiled.

"Remember the night of George Hardt's bachelor dinner here?" said Charlie. "By the way, what's become of Claude Fessenden?"

Alix lowered his voice confidentially: "He's in Paris, but he doesn't come here any more. Paul doesn't allow it. He ran up a bill of thirty thousand francs, charging all his drinks and his lunches, and usually his dinner, for more than a year. And when Paul finally told him he had to pay, he gave him a bad check."

Alix shook his head sadly.

"I don't understand it, such a dandy fellow. Now he's all bloated up—" He made a plump apple of his hands.

Charlie watched a group of strident queens installing themselves in a corner.

"Nothing affects them," he thought. "Stocks rise and fall, people loaf or work, but they go on forever." The place oppressed him. He called for the dice and shook with Alix for the drink.

"Here for long, Mr. Wales?"

"I'm here for four or five days to see my little girl."

"Oh-h! You have a little girl?"

Outside, the fire-red, gas-blue, ghost-green signs shone smokily through the tranquil rain. It was late afternoon and the streets were in movement; the bistros gleamed. At the corner of the Boulevard des Capucines he took a taxi. The Place de la Concorde moved by in pink majesty; they crossed the logical Seine, and Charlie felt the sudden provincial quality of the Left Bank.

Charlie directed his taxi to the Avenue de l'Opéra, which was out of his way. But he wanted to see the blue hour spread over the magnificent façade, and imagine that the cab horns, playing endlessly the first few bars of *Le Plus que Lent,* were the trumpets of the Second Empire. They were closing the iron grill in front of Brentano's Bookstore, and people were already at dinner behind the trim little bourgeois hedge of Duval's. He had never eaten at a really cheap restaurant in Paris. Five-course dinner, four francs fifty, eighteen cents, wine included. For some odd reason he wished that he had.

As they rolled on to the Left Bank, and he felt its sudden provincialism, he thought, "I spoiled this city for myself. I didn't realize it, but the days came along one after another, and then two years were gone, and everything was gone, and I was gone."

He was thirty-five, and good to look at. The Irish mobility of his face was sobered by a deep wrinkle between his eyes. As he rang his brother-in-law's bell in the Rue Palatine, the wrinkle deepened till it pulled down his brows; he felt a cramping sensation in his belly. From behind the maid who opened the door darted a lovely little girl of nine who shrieked "Daddy!" and flew up, struggling like a fish, into his arms. She pulled his head around by one ear and set her cheek against his.

"My old pie," he said.

"Oh, daddy, daddy, daddy, daddy, dads, dads, dads!"

She drew him into the salon, where the family waited, a boy and a girl his daughter's age, his sister-in-law and her husband. He greeted Marion with his voice pitched carefully to avoid either feigned enthusiasm or dislike, but her response was more frankly tepid, though she minimized her expression of unalterable distrust by directing her regard toward his child. The two men clasped hands in a friendly way and Lincoln Peters rested his for a moment on Charlie's shoulder.

The room was warm and comfortably American. The three children moved intimately about, playing through the yellow oblongs that led to other rooms; the cheer of six o'clock spoke in the eager smacks of the fire and the sounds of French activity in the kitchen. But Charlie did not relax; his heart sat up rigidly in his body and he drew confidence from his daughter, who from time to time came close to him, holding in his arms the doll he had brought.

"Really extremely well," he declared in answer to Lincoln's question. "There's a lot of business there that isn't moving at all, but we're doing even better than ever. In fact, damn well. I'm bringing my sister over from America next month to keep house for me. My income last year was bigger than it was when I had money. You see, the Czechs—"

His boasting was for a specific purpose; but after a moment, seeing a faint restiveness in Lincoln's eye, he changed the subject:

"Those are fine children of yours, well brought up, good manners."

"We think Honoria's a great little girl too."

Marion Peters came back from the kitchen. She was a tall woman with worried eyes, who had once possessed a fresh American loveliness. Charlie had never been sensitive to it and was always surprised when people spoke of how pretty she had been. From the first there had been an instinctive antipathy between them.

"Well, how do you find Honoria?" she asked.

"Wonderful. I was astonished how much she's grown in ten months. All the children are looking well."

"We haven't seen a doctor for a year. How do you like being back in Paris?"

"It seems very funny to see so few Americans around."

"I'm delighted," Marion said vehemently. "Now at least you can go into a store without their assuming you're a millionaire. We've suffered like everybody, but on the whole it's a good deal pleasanter."

"But it was nice while it lasted," Charlie said. "We were sort of royalty, almost infallible, with a sort of magic around us. In the bar this afternoon"—he stumbled, seeing his mistake—"there wasn't a man I knew."

She looked at him keenly. "I should think you'd have had enough of bars."

"I only stayed a minute. I take one drink every afternoon, and no more."

"Don't you want a cocktail before dinner?" Lincoln asked.

"I take only one drink every afternoon, and I've had that."

"I hope you keep to it," said Marion.

Her dislike was evident in the coldness with which she spoke, but Charlie only smiled; he had larger plans. Her very aggressiveness gave him an advantage, and he knew enough to wait. He wanted them to initiate the discussion of what they knew had brought him to Paris.

At dinner he couldn't decide whether Honoria was most like him or her mother. Fortunate if she didn't combine the traits of both that had brought them to disaster. A great wave of protectiveness went over him. He thought he knew what to do for her. He believed in character; he wanted to jump back a whole generation and trust in character again as the eternally valuable element. Everything else wore out.

He left soon after dinner, but not to go home. He was curious to see Paris by night with clearer and more judicious eyes than those of other days. He bought a *strapontin* for the Casino and watched Josephine Baker go through her chocolate arabesques.

After an hour he left and strolled toward Montmartre, up the Rue Pigalle into the Place Blanche. The rain had stopped and there were a few people in evening clothes disembarking from taxis in front of cabarets, and *cocottes* prowling singly or in pairs, and many Negroes. He passed a lighted door from which issued music, and stopped with the sense of familiarity; it was Bricktop's, where he had parted with so many hours and so much money. A few doors farther on he found another ancient rendezvous and incautiously put his head inside. Immediately an eager orchestra burst into sound, a pair of professional dancers leaped to their feet and a maitre d'hôtel swooped toward him, crying, "Crowd just arriving, sir!" But he withdrew quickly.

"You have to be damn drunk," he thought.

Zelli's was closed, the bleak and sinister cheap hotels surrounding it were dark; up in the Rue Blanche there was more light and a local, colloquial French crowd. The Poet's Cave had disappeared, but the two great mouths of the Café of Heaven and the Café of Hell still yawned—even devoured, as he watched, the meager contents of a tourist bus—a German, a Japanese, and an American couple who glanced at him with frightened eyes.

So much for the effort and ingenuity of Montmartre. All the catering to vice and waste was on an utterly childish scale, and he suddenly realized the meaning of the word "dissipate"—to dissipate into thin air; to make nothing out of something. In the little hours of the night every move from place to place was an enormous human jump, an increase of paying for the privilege of slower and slower motion.

He remembered thousand-franc notes given to an orchestra for playing a single number, hundred-franc notes tossed to a doorman for calling a cab.

But it hadn't been given for nothing.

It had been given, even the most wildly squandered sum, as an offering to destiny that he might not remember the things most worth remembering, the things that now he would always remember—his child taken from his control, his wife escaped to a grave in Vermont.

In the glare of a *brasserie* a woman spoke to him. He bought her some eggs and coffee, and then, eluding her encouraging stare, gave her a twenty-franc note and took a taxi to his hotel.

II

He woke upon a fine fall day—football weather. The depression of yesterday was gone and he liked the people on the streets. At noon he sat opposite Honoria at Le Grand Vatel, the only restaurant he could think of not reminiscent of champagne dinners and long luncheons that began at two and ended in a blurred and vague twilight.

"Now, how about vegetables? Oughtn't you to have some vegetables?"

"Well, yes."

"Here's *épinards* and *chou-fleur* and carrots and *haricots*."

"I'd like *chou-fleur*."

"Wouldn't you like to have two vegetables?"

"I usually only have one at lunch."

The waiter was pretending to be inordinately fond of children. "*Qu'elle est mignonne la petite! Elle parle exactement comme une française.*"

"How about dessert? Shall we wait and see?"

The waiter disappeared. Honoria looked at her father expectantly.

"What are we going to do?"

"First, we're going to that toy store in the Rue Saint-Honoré and buy you anything you like. And then we're going to the vaudeville at the Empire."

She hesitated. "I like it about the vaudeville, but not the toy store."

"Why not?"

"Well, you brought me this doll." She had it with her. "And I've got lots of things. And we're not rich any more, are we?"

"We never were. But today you are to have anything you want."

"All right," she agreed resignedly.

When there had been her mother and a French nurse he had been inclined to be strict; now he extended himself, reached out for a new tolerance; he must be both parents to her and not shut any of her out of communication.

"I want to get to know you," he said gravely. "First let me introduce myself. My name is Charles J. Wales, of Prague."

"Oh, daddy!" her voice cracked with laughter.

"And who are you, please?" he persisted, and she accepted a role immediately: "Honoria Wales, Rue Palatine, Paris."

"Married or single?"

"No, not married. Single."

He indicated the doll. "But I see you have a child, madame."

Unwilling to disinherit it, she took it to her heart and thought quickly: "Yes, I've been married, but I'm not married now. My husband is dead."

He went on quickly, "And the child's name?"

"Simone. That's after my best friend at school."

"I'm very pleased that you're doing so well at school."

"I'm third this month," she boasted. "Elsie"—that was her cousin—"is only about eighteenth, and Richard is about at the bottom."

"You like Richard and Elsie, don't you?"

"Oh yes. I like Richard quite well and I like her all right."

Cautiously and casually he asked: "And Aunt Marion and Uncle Lincoln—which do you like best?"

"Oh, Uncle Lincoln, I guess."

He was increasingly aware of her presence. As they came in, a murmur of ". . . adorable" followed them, and now the people at the next table bent all their silences upon her, staring as if she were something no more conscious than a flower.

"Why don't I live with you?" she asked suddenly. "Because mamma's dead?"

"You must stay here and learn more French. It would have been hard for daddy to take care of you so well."

"I don't really need much taking care of any more. I do everything for myself."

Going out of the restaurant, a man and a woman unexpectedly hailed him. "Well, the old Wales!"

"Hello there, Lorraine. . . . Dunc."

Sudden ghosts out of the past: Duncan Schaeffer, a friend from college. Lorraine Quarrles, a lovely, pale blonde of thirty; one of a crowd who had helped him make months into days in the lavish times of three years ago.

"My husband couldn't come this year," she said, in answer to his question. "We're poor as hell. So he gave me two hundred a month and told me I could do my worst on that. . . . This your little girl?"

"What about coming back and sitting down?" Duncan asked.

"Can't do it." He was glad for an excuse. As always, he felt Lorraine's passionate, provocative attraction, but his own rhythm was different now.

"Well, how about dinner?" she asked.

"I'm not free. Give me your address and let me call you."

"Charlie, I believe you're sober," she said judicially. "I honestly believe he's sober, Dunc. Pinch him and see if he's sober."

Charlie indicated Honoria with his head. They both laughed.

"What's your address?" said Duncan skeptically.

He hesitated, unwilling to give the name of his hotel.

"I'm not settled yet. I'd better call you. We're going to see the vaudeville at the Empire."

"There! That's what I want to do," Lorraine said. "I want to see some clowns and acrobats and jugglers. That's just what we'll do, Dunc."

"We've got to run an errand first," said Charlie. "Perhaps we'll see you there."

"All right, you snob. . . . Good-by, beautiful little girl."

"Good-by."

Honoria bobbed politely.

Somehow, an unwelcome encounter. They liked him because he was functioning, because he was serious; they wanted to see him, because he was stronger than they were now, because they wanted to draw a certain sustenance from his strength.

At the Empire, Honoria proudly refused to sit upon her father's folded coat. She was already an individual with a code of her own, and Charlie was more and more absorbed by the desire of putting a little of himself into her before she crystallized utterly. It was hopeless to try to know her in so short a time.

Between the acts they came upon Duncan and Lorraine in the lobby where the band was playing.

"Have a drink?"

"All right, but not up at the bar. We'll take a table."

"The perfect father."

Listening abstractedly to Lorraine, Charlie watched Honoria's eyes leave their table, and he followed them wistfully about the room, wondering what they saw. He met her glance and she smiled.

"I liked that lemonade," she said.

What had she said? What had he expected? Going home in a taxi afterward, he pulled her over until her head rested against his chest.

"Darling, do you ever think about your mother?"

"Yes, sometimes," she answered vaguely.

"I don't want you to forget her. Have you got a picture of her?"

"Yes, I think so. Anyhow, Aunt Marion has. Why don't you want me to forget her?"

"She loved you very much."

"I loved her too."

They were silent for a moment.

"Daddy, I want to come and live with you," she said suddenly.

His heart leaped; he had wanted it to come like this.

"Aren't you perfectly happy?"

"Yes, but I love you better than anybody. And you love me better than anybody, don't you, now that mummy's dead?"

"Of course I do. But you won't always like me best, honey. You'll grow up and meet somebody your own age and go marry him and forget you ever had a daddy."

"Yes, that's true," she agreed tranquilly.

He didn't go in. He was coming back at nine o'clock and he wanted to keep himself fresh and new for the thing he must say then.

"When you're safe inside, just show yourself in that window."

"All right. Good-by, dads, dads, dads, dads."

He waited in the dark street until she appeared, all warm and glowing, in the window above and kissed her fingers out into the night.

III

They were waiting. Marion sat behind the coffee service in a dignified black dinner dress that just faintly suggested mourning. Lincoln was walking up and down with the animation of one who had already been talking. They were as anxious as he was to get into the question. He opened it almost immediately:

"I suppose you know what I want to see you about—why I really came to Paris."

Marion played with the black stars on her necklace and frowned.

"I'm awfully anxious to have a home," he continued. "And I'm awfully anxious to have Honoria in it. I appreciate your taking in Honoria for her mother's sake, but things have changed now"—he hesitated and then continued more forcibly—"changed radically with me, and I want to ask you to reconsider the matter. It would be silly for me to deny that about three years ago I was acting badly—"

Marion looked up at him with hard eyes.

"—but all that's over. As I told you, I haven't had more than a drink a day for over a year, and I take that drink deliberately, so that the idea of alcohol won't get too big in my imagination. You see the idea?"

"No," said Marion succinctly.

"It's a sort of stunt I set myself. It keeps the matter in proportion."

"I get you," said Lincoln. "You don't want to admit it's got any attraction for you."

"Something like that. Sometimes I forget and don't take it. But I try to take it. Anyhow, I couldn't afford to drink in my position. The people I represent are more than satisfied with what I've done, and I'm bringing my sister over from Burlington to keep house for me, and I want awfully to have Honoria too. You know that even when her mother and I weren't getting along well we never let anything that happened touch Honoria. I know she's fond of me and I know I'm able to take care of her and—well, there you are. How do you feel about it?"

He knew that now he would have to take a beating. It would last an hour or two hours, and it would be difficult, but if he modulated his inevitable resentment to the chastened attitude of the reformed sinner, he might win his point in the end.

Keep your temper, he told himself. You don't want to be justified. You want Honoria.

Lincoln spoke first: "We've been talking it over ever since we got your letter last month. We're happy to have Honoria here. She's a dear little thing, and we're glad to be able to help her, but of course that isn't the question—"

Marion interrupted suddenly. "How long are you going to stay sober, Charlie?" she asked.

"Permanently, I hope."

"How can anybody count on that?"

"You know I never did drink heavily until I gave up business and came over here with nothing to do. Then Helen and I began to run around with—"

"Please leave Helen out of it. I can't bear to hear you talk about her like that."

He stared at her grimly; he had never been certain how fond of each other the sisters were in life.

"My drinking only lasted about a year and a half—from the time we came over until I—collapsed."

"It was time enough."

"It was time enough," he agreed.

"My duty is entirely to Helen," she said. "I try to think what she would have wanted me to do. Frankly, from the night you did that terrible thing you haven't really existed for me. I can't help that. She was my sister."

"Yes."

"When she was dying she asked me to look out for Honoria. If you hadn't been in a sanitarium then, it might have helped matters."

He had no answer.

"I'll never in my life be able to forget the morning when Helen knocked at my door, soaked to the skin and shivering, and said you'd locked her out."

Charlie gripped the sides of the chair. This was more difficult than he expected; he wanted to launch out into a long expostulation and explanation, but he only said: "The night I locked her out—" and she interrupted, "I don't feel up to going over that again."

After a moment's silence Lincoln said: "We're getting off the subject. You want Marion to set aside her legal guardianship and give you Honoria. I think the main point for her is whether she has confidence in you or not."

"I don't blame Marion," Charlie said slowly, "but I think she can have entire confidence in me. I had a good record up to three years ago. Of course, it's within human possibilities I might go wrong any time. But if we wait much longer I'll lose Honoria's childhood and my chance for a home." He shook his head. "I'll simply lose her, don't you see?"

"Yes, I see," said Lincoln.

"Why didn't you think of all this before?" Marion asked.

"I suppose I did, from time to time, but Helen and I were getting along badly. When I consented to the guardianship, I was flat on my back in a sanitarium and the market had cleaned me out. I knew I'd acted badly, and I thought if it would bring any peace to Helen, I'd agree to anything. But now it's different. I'm functioning, I'm behaving damn well, so far as—"

"Please don't swear at me," Marion said.

He looked at her, startled. With each remark the force of her dislike became more and more apparent. She had built up all her fear of life into one wall and faced it toward him. This trivial reproof was possibly the result of some trouble with the cook several hours before. Charlie became increasingly alarmed at leaving Honoria in this atmosphere of hostility against himself; sooner or later it would come out, in a word here, a shake of the head there, and some of that distrust would be irrevocably implanted in Honoria. But he pulled his temper down out of his face and shut it up inside him; he had won a point, for Lincoln realized the absurdity of Marion's remark and asked her lightly since when she had objected to the word "damn."

"Another thing," Charlie said: "I'm able to give her certain advantages now. I'm going to take a French governess to Prague with me. I've got a lease on a new apartment—"

He stopped, realizing that he was blundering. They couldn't be expected to accept with equanimity the fact that his income was again twice as large as their own.

"I suppose you can give her more luxuries than we can," said Marion, "When you were throwing away money we were living along watching every ten francs. . . . I suppose you'll start doing it again."

"Oh, no," he said. "I've learned. I worked hard for ten years, you know—until I got lucky in the market, like so many people. Terribly lucky. It won't happen again."

There was a long silence. All of them felt their nerves straining, and for the first time in a year Charlie wanted a drink. He was sure now that Lincoln Peters wanted him to have his child.

Marion shuddered suddenly; part of her saw that Charlie's feet were planted on the earth now, and her own maternal feeling recognized the naturalness of his desire; but she had lived for a long time with a prejudice—a prejudice founded on a curious disbelief in her sister's happiness, which, in the shock of one terrible night, had turned to hatred for him. It had all happened at a point in her life where the discouragement of ill health and adverse circumstances made it necessary for her to believe in tangible villainy and a tangible villain.

"I can't help what I think!" she cried out suddenly. "How much you were responsible for Helen's death, I don't know. It's something you'll have to square with your own conscience."

An electric current of agony surged through him; for a moment he was almost on his feet, an unuttered sound echoing in his throat. He hung on to himself for a moment, another moment.

"Hold on there," said Lincoln uncomfortably. "I never thought you were responsible for that."

"Helen died of heart trouble," Charlie said dully.

"Yes, heart trouble." Marion spoke as if the phrase had another meaning for her.

Then, in the flatness that followed her outburst, she saw him plainly and she knew he had somehow arrived at control over the situation. Glancing at her husband, she found no help from him, and as abruptly as if it were a matter of no importance, she threw up the sponge.

"Do what you like!" she cried, springing up from her chair. "She's your child. I'm not the person to stand in your way. I think if it were my child I'd rather see her—" She managed to check herself. "You two decide it. I can't stand this. I'm sick. I'm going to bed."

She hurried from the room; after a moment Lincoln said:

"This has been a hard day for her. You know how strongly she feels—" His voice was almost apologetic: "When a woman gets an idea in her head."

"Of course."

"It's going to be all right. I think she sees now that you—can provide for the child, and so we can't very well stand in your way or Honoria's way."

"Thank you, Lincoln."

"I'd better go along and see how she is."

"I'm going."

He was still trembling when he reached the street, but a walk down the Rue Bonaparte to the *quais* set him up, and as he crossed the Seine, fresh and new by the *quai* lamps, he felt exultant. But back in his room he couldn't sleep. The image of Helen haunted him. Helen whom he had loved so until they had senselessly begun to abuse each other's love, tear it into shreds. On that terrible February night that Marion remembered so vividly, a slow quarrel had gone on for hours. There was a scene at the Florida, and then he attempted to take her home, and then she kissed young Webb at a table; after that there was what she had hysterically said. When he arrived home alone he turned the key in the lock in wild anger. How could he know she would arrive an hour later alone, that there would be a snow storm in which she wandered about in slippers, too confused to find a taxi? Then the aftermath, her escaping pneumonia by a miracle, and all the attendant horror. They were "reconciled," but that was the beginning of the end, and Marion, who had seen with her own eyes and who imagined it to be one of many scenes from her sister's martyrdom, never forgot.

Going over it again brought Helen nearer, and in the white, soft light that steals upon half sleep near morning he found himself talking to her again. She said that he was perfectly right about Honoria and that she wanted Honoria to be with him. She said she was glad he was being good and doing better. She said a lot of other things—very friendly things—but she was in a swing in a white dress, and swinging faster and faster all the time, so that at the end he could not hear clearly all that she said.

IV

He woke up feeling happy. The door of the world was open again. He made plans, vistas, futures for Honoria and himself, but suddenly he grew sad, remembering all the plans he and Helen had made. She had not planned to die. The present was the thing—work to do and someone to love. But not to love too much, for he knew the injury that a father can do to a daughter or a mother to a son by attaching them too closely: afterward, out in the world, the child would seek in the marriage partner the same blind tenderness and, failing probably to find it, turn against love and life.

It was another bright, crisp day. He called Lincoln Peters at the bank where he worked and asked if he could count on taking Honoria when he left for Prague. Lincoln agreed that there was no reason for delay. One thing—the legal guardianship. Marion wanted to retain that a while longer. She was upset by the whole matter, and it would oil things if she felt that the situation was still in her control for another year. Charlie agreed, wanting only the tangible, visible child.

Then the question of a governess. Charlie sat in a gloomy agency and talked to a cross Béarnaise and to a buxom Breton peasant, neither of whom he could have endured. There were others whom he would see tomorrow.

He lunched with Lincoln Peters at Griffons, trying to keep down his exultation.

"There's nothing quite like your own child," Lincoln said. "But you understand how Marion feels too."

"She's forgotten how hard I worked for seven years there," Charlie said. "She just remembers one night."

"There's another thing." Lincoln hesitated. "While you and Helen were tearing around Europe throwing money away, we were just getting along. I didn't touch any of the prosperity because I never got ahead enough to carry anything but my insurance. I think Marion felt there was some kind of injustice in it—you not even working toward the end, and getting richer and richer."

"It went as quick as it came," said Charlie.

"Yes, a lot of it stayed in the hands of *chasseurs* and saxophone players and maitres d'hôtel—well, the big party's over now. I just said that to explain Marion's feeling about those crazy years. If you drop in about six o'clock tonight before Marion's too tired, we'll settle the details on the spot."

Back at his hotel, Charlie found a *pneumatique* that had been redirected from the Ritz bar, where Charlie had left his address for the purpose of finding a certain man.

> Dear Charlie:
>
> You were so strange when we saw you the other day that I wondered if I did something to offend you. If so, I'm not conscious of it. In fact, I have thought about you too much for the last year, and it's always been in the back of my mind that I might see you if I came over here. We *did* have such good times that crazy spring, like the night you and I stole the butcher's tricycle, and the time we tried to call on the president and you had the old derby rim and the wire cane. Everybody seems so old lately, but I don't feel old a bit. Couldn't we get together some time today for old time's sake? I've got a vile hangover for the moment, but will be feeling better this afternoon and will look for you about five in the sweatshop at the Ritz.
>
> Always devotedly,
> Lorraine

His first feeling was one of awe that he had actually, in his mature years, stolen a tricycle and pedaled Lorraine all over the Étoile between the small hours and dawn. In retrospect it was a nightmare. Locking out Helen didn't fit in with any other act of his life, but the tricycle incident did—it was one of many. How many weeks or months of dissipation to arrive at that condition of utter irresponsibility?

He tried to picture how Lorraine had appeared to him then—very attractive; Helen was unhappy about it, though she said nothing. Yesterday, in the restaurant, Lorraine had seemed trite, blurred, worn away. He emphatically did not want to see her, and he was glad Alix had not given away his hotel address. It was a relief to think, instead, of Honoria, to think of Sundays spent with her and of saying good morning to her and knowing she was there in his house at night, drawing her breath in the darkness.

At five he took a taxi and bought presents for all the Peterses—a piquant cloth doll, a box of Roman soldiers, flowers for Marion, big linen handkerchiefs for Lincoln.

He saw, when he arrived in the apartment, that Marion had accepted the inevitable. She greeted him now as though he were a recalcitrant member of the family, rather than a menacing outsider. Honoria had been told she was going; Charlie was glad to see that her tact made her conceal her excessive happiness. Only on his lap did she whisper her delight and the question "When?" before she slipped away with the other children.

He and Marion were alone for a minute in the room, and on an impulse he spoke out boldly:

"Family quarrels are bitter things. They don't go according to any rules. They're not like aches or wounds; they're more like splits in the skin that won't heal because there's not enough material. I wish you and I could be on better terms."

"Some things are hard to forget," she answered. "It's a question of confidence." There was no answer to this and presently she asked, "When do you propose to take her?"

"As soon as I can get a governess. I hoped the day after tomorrow."

"That's impossible. I've got to get her things in shape. Not before Saturday."

He yielded. Coming back into the room, Lincoln offered him a drink.

"I'll take my daily whisky," he said.

It was warm here, it was a home, people together by a fire. The children felt very safe and important; the mother and father were serious, watchful. They had things to do for the children more important than his visit here. A spoonful of medicine was, after all, more important than the strained relations between Marion and himself. They were not dull people, but they were very much in the grip of life and circumstances. He wondered if he couldn't do something to get Lincoln out of his rut at the bank.

A long peal at the doorbell; the *bonne à tout faire* passed through and went down the corridor. The door opened upon another long ring, and then voices, and the three in the salon looked up expectantly; Richard moved to bring the corridor within his range of vision, and Marion rose. Then the maid came back along the corridor, closely followed by the voices, which developed under the light into Duncan Schaeffer and Lorraine Quarrles.

They were gay, they were hilarious, they were roaring with laughter. For a moment Charlie was astounded; unable to understand how they ferreted out the Peterses' address.

"Ah-h-h!" Duncan wagged his finger roguishly at Charlie, "Ah-h-h!"

They both slid down another cascade of laughter. Anxious and at a loss, Charlie shook hands with them quickly and presented them to Lincoln and Marion. Marion nodded, scarcely speaking. She had drawn back a step toward the fire; her little girl stood beside her, and Marion put an arm about her shoulder.

With growing annoyance at the intrusion, Charlie waited for them to explain themselves. After some concentration Duncan said:

"We came to invite you out to dinner. Lorraine and I insist that all this shishi, cagy business 'bout your address got to stop."

Charlie came closer to them, as if to force them backward down the corridor.

"Sorry, but I can't. Tell me where you'll be and I'll phone you in half an hour."

This made no impression. Lorraine sat down suddenly on the side of a chair, and focusing her eyes on Richard, cried, "Oh, what a nice little boy! Come here, little boy." Richard glanced at his mother, but did not move. With a perceptible shrug of her shoulder, Lorraine turned back to Charlie:

"Come and dine. Sure your cousins won' mine. See you so sel'om. Or solemn."

"I can't," said Charlie sharply. "You two have dinner and I'll phone you."

Her voice became suddenly unpleasant. "All right, we'll go. But I remember once when you hammered on my door at four A.M. I was enough of a good sport to give you a drink. Come on, Dunc."

Still in slow motion, with blurred, angry faces, with uncertain feet, they retired along the corridor.

"Good night," Charlie said.

"Good night!" responded Lorraine emphatically.

When he went back into the salon Marion had not moved, only now her son was standing in the circle of her other arm. Lincoln was still swinging Honoria back and forth like a pendulum from side to side.

"What an outrage!" Charlie broke out. "What an absolute outrage!"

Neither of them answered. Charlie dropped into an armchair, picked up his drink, set it down again and said:

"People I haven't seen for two years having the colossal nerve—"

He broke off. Marion had made the sound "Oh!" in one swift, furious breath, turned her body from him with a jerk and left the room.

Lincoln set down Honoria carefully.

"You children go in and start your soup," he said, and when they obeyed, he said to Charlie:

"Marion's not well and she can't stand shocks. That kind of people make her really physically sick."

"I didn't tell them to come here. They wormed your name out of somebody. They deliberately—"

"Well, it's too bad. It doesn't help matters. Excuse me a minute."

Left alone, Charlie sat tense in his chair. In the next room he could hear the children eating, talking in monosyllables, already oblivious to the scene between their elders. He heard a murmur of conversation from a farther room and then the ticking bell of a telephone receiver picked up, and in a panic he moved to the other side of the room and out of earshot.

In a minute Lincoln came back. "Look here, Charlie. I think we'd better call off dinner for tonight. Marion's in bad shape."

"Is she angry with me?"

"Sort of," he said, almost roughly. "She's not strong and—"

"You mean she's changed her mind about Honoria?"

"She's pretty bitter right now. I don't know. You phone me at the bank tomorrow."

"I wish you'd explain to her I never dreamed these people would come here. I'm just as sore as you are."

"I couldn't explain anything to her now."

Charlie got up. He took his coat and hat and started down the corridor. Then he opened the door of the dining room and said in a strange voice, "Good night, children."

Honoria rose and ran around the table to hug him.

"Good night, sweetheart," he said vaguely, and then trying to make his voice more tender, trying to conciliate something. "Good night, dear children."

V

Charlie went directly to the Ritz bar with the furious idea of finding Lorraine and Duncan, but they were not there, and he realized that in any case there was nothing he could do. He had not touched his drink at the Peters, and now he ordered a whisky-and-soda. Paul came over to say hello.

"It's a great change," he said sadly. "We do about half the business we did. So many fellows I hear about back in the States lost everything, maybe not in the first crash, but then in the second. Your friend George Hardt lost every cent, I hear. Are you back in the States?"

"No, I'm in business in Prague."

"I heard that you lost a lot in the crash."

"I did," and he added grimly, "but I lost everything I wanted in the boom."

"Selling short."

"Something like that."

Again the memory of those days swept over him like a nightmare—the people they had met traveling; then people who couldn't add a row of figures or speak a coherent sentence. The little man Helen had consented to dance with at the ship's party, who had insulted her ten feet from the table; the women and girls carried screaming with drink or drugs out of public places—

The men who locked their wives out in the snow, because the snow of twenty-nine wasn't real snow. If you didn't want it to be snow, you just paid some money.

He went to the phone and called the Peterses' apartment; Lincoln answered.

"I called up because this thing is on my mind. Has Marion said anything definite?"

"Marion's sick," Lincoln answered shortly. "I know this thing isn't altogether your fault, but I can't have her go to pieces about it. I'm afraid we'll have to let it slide for six months; I can't take the chance of working her up to this state again."

"I see."

"I'm sorry, Charlie."

He went back to his table. His whisky glass was empty, but he shook his head when Alix looked at it questioningly. There wasn't much he could do now except send Honoria some things; he would send her a lot of things tomorrow. He thought rather angrily that this was just money—he had given so many people money. . . .

"No, no more," he said to another waiter. "What do I owe you?"

He would come back some day; they couldn't make him pay forever. But he wanted his child, and nothing was much good now, beside that fact. He wasn't young any more, with a lot of nice thoughts and dreams to have by himself. He was absolutely sure Helen wouldn't have wanted him to be so alone.

(1931)

QUESTIONS FOR CRITICAL THINKING AND WRITING

Experience

1. Charlie Wales is a recovering alcoholic. What do you think of his method of having one and only one drink a day?
2. How do you respond to Marion Peters? Is she genuinely concerned for Honoria and rightly suspicious of Charlie? Is she self-righteous? Does she remind you of anyone you have encountered?

Interpretation

3. Why does Charlie walk through Montmartre after having dinner with Mr. and Mrs. Peters? Explain his epiphany as he strolls those streets. Consider the title of the story in the context of your discussion.

4. Consider what might be called the "double Paris" of the story, that is Paris before and after the crash. How has life for Americans in Paris changed?

Evaluation

5. Consider the cultural values of Charlie and his wife. Have Charlie's values changed? What is the significance of his daughter's name? Compare his values to those of the other characters.

Connection

6. Compare relationship of parents, children, and money in "Babylon Revisited" and "The Rocking Horse Winner."

Critical Thinking

7. What do you think of the way Charlie is treated by the other characters? Why do they treat him as they do? Do you think they are justified in doing so? Why or why not?

CHARLOTTE PERKINS GILMAN

[1860–1935]

Charlotte Perkins Gilman was born in Hartford, Connecticut. Raised in semi-poverty, Gilman's early education was sparse, though she took up commercial art at the Rhode Island School of Design in 1878. After marriage and the birth of a daughter, Gilman experienced deep depression, the cure by rest which became the basis of her short story "The Yellow Wallpaper." Gilman became an essayist and public speaker, who espoused feminist themes. Her book Women and Economics *(1898) was one of the earliest to urge that women take a significant place in the working world. Her feminist ideas were also expressed in her Utopian novel* Herland, *which describes a world of women without men.*

The Yellow Wallpaper

It is very seldom that mere ordinary people like John and myself secure ancestral halls for the summer.

A colonial mansion, a hereditary estate, I would say a haunted house and reach the height of romantic felicity—but that would be asking too much of fate!

Still I will proudly declare that there is something queer about it.

Else, why should it be let so cheaply? And why have stood so long untenanted?

John laughs at me, of course, but one expects that.

John is practical in the extreme. He has no patience with faith, an intense horror of superstition, and he scoffs openly at any talk of things not to be felt and seen and put down in figures.

John is a physician, and *perhaps*—(I would not say it to a living soul, of course, but this is dead paper and a great relief to my mind)—*perhaps* that is one reason I do not get well faster.

You see, he does not believe I am sick! And what can one do?

If a physician of high standing, and one's own husband, assures friends and relatives that there is really nothing the matter with one but temporary nervous depression—a slight hysterical tendency—what is one to do?

My brother is also a physician, and also of high standing, and he says the same thing.

So I take phosphates or phosphites—whichever it is—and tonics, and air and exercise, and journeys, and am absolutely forbidden to "work" until I am well again.

Personally, I disagree with their ideas.

Personally, I believe that congenial work, with excitement and change, would do me good.

But what is one to do?

I did write for a while in spite of them; but it does exhaust me a good deal—having to be so sly about it, or else meet with heavy opposition.

I sometimes fancy that in my condition, if I had less opposition and more society and stimulus—but John says the very worst thing I can do is to think about my condition, and I confess it always makes me feel bad.

So I will let it alone and talk about the house.

The most beautiful place! It is quite alone, standing well back from the road, quite three miles from the village. It makes me think of English places that you read about, for there are hedges and walls and gates that lock, and lots of separate little houses for the gardeners and people.

There is a *delicious* garden! I never saw such a garden—large and shady, full of box-bordered paths, and lined with long grape-covered arbors with seats under them.

There were greenhouses, but they are all broken now.

There was some legal trouble, I believe, something about the heirs and co-heirs; anyhow, the place has been empty for years.

That spoils my ghostliness, I am afraid, but I don't care—there is something strange about the house—I can feel it.

I even said so to John one moonlight evening, but he said what I felt was a draught, and shut the window.

I get unreasonably angry with John sometimes. I'm sure I never used to be so sensitive. I think it is due to this nervous condition.

But John says if I feel so I shall neglect proper self-control; so I take pains to control myself—before him, at least, and that makes me very tired.

I don't like our room a bit. I wanted one downstairs that opened onto the piazza and had roses all over the window, and such pretty old-fashioned chintz hangings! But John would not hear of it.

He said there was only one window and not room for two beds, and no near room for him if he took another.

He is very careful and loving, and hardly lets me stir without special direction.

I have a schedule prescription for each hour in the day; he takes all care from me, and so I feel basely ungrateful not to value it more.

He said he came here solely on my account, that I was to have perfect rest and all the air I could get. "Your exercise depends on your strength, my dear," said he, "and your food somewhat on your appetite; but air you can absorb all the time." So we took the nursery at the top of the house.

It is a big, airy room, the whole floor nearly, with windows that look all ways, and air and sunshine galore. It was nursery first, and then playroom and gymnasium, I should judge, for the windows are barred for little children, and there are rings and things in the walls.

The paint and paper look as if a boys' school had used it. It is stripped off—the paper—in great patches all around the head of my bed, about as far as I can reach, and in a great place on the other side of the room low down. I never saw a worse paper in my life. One of those sprawling, flamboyant patterns committing every artistic sin.

It is dull enough to confuse the eye in following, pronounced enough constantly to irritate and provoke study, and when you follow the lame uncertain curves for a little distance they suddenly commit suicide—plunge off at outrageous angles, destroy themselves in unheard-of contradictions.

The color is repellent, almost revolting: a smouldering unclean yellow, strangely faded by the slow-turning sunlight. It is a dull yet lurid orange in some places, a sickly sulphur tint in others.

No wonder the children hated it! I should hate it myself if I had to live in this room long.

There comes John, and I must put this away—he hates to have me write a word.

We have been here two weeks, and I haven't felt like writing before, since that first day.

I am sitting by the window now, up in this atrocious nursery, and there is nothing to hinder my writing as much as I please, save lack of strength.

John is away all day, and even some nights when his cases are serious.

I am glad my case is not serious!

But these nervous troubles are dreadfully depressing.

John does not know how much I really suffer. He knows there is no reason to suffer, and that satisfies him.

Of course it is only nervousness. It does weigh on me so not to do my duty in any way!

I meant to be such a help to John, such a real rest and comfort, and here I am a comparative burden already!

Nobody would believe what an effort it is to do what little I am able—to dress and entertain, and order things.

It is fortunate Mary is so good with the baby. Such a dear baby!

And yet I *cannot* be with him, it makes me so nervous.

I suppose John never was nervous in his life. He laughs at me so about this wallpaper!

At first he meant to repaper the room, but afterward he said that I was letting it get the better of me, and that nothing was worse for a nervous patient than to give way to such fancies.

He said that after the wallpaper was changed it would be the heavy bedstead, and then the barred windows, and then that gate at the head of the stairs, and so on.

"You know the place is doing you good," he said, "and really, dear, I don't care to renovate the house just for a three months' rental."

"Then do let us go downstairs," I said. "There are such pretty rooms there."

Then he took me in his arms and called me a blessed little goose, and said he would go down cellar, if I wished, and have it whitewashed into the bargain.

But he is right enough about the beds and windows and things.

It is as airy and comfortable a room as anyone need wish, and, of course, I would not be so silly as to make him uncomfortable just for a whim.

I'm really getting quite fond of the big room, all but that horrid paper.

Out of one window I can see the garden—those mysterious deep-shaded arbors, the riotous old-fashioned flowers, and bushes and gnarly trees.

Out of another I get a lovely view of the bay and a little private wharf belonging to the estate. There is a beautiful shaded lane that runs down there from the house. I always fancy I see people walking in these numerous paths and arbors, but John has cautioned me not to give way to fancy in the least. He says that with my imaginative power and habit of story-making, a nervous weakness like mine is sure to lead to all manner of excited fancies, and that I ought to use my will and good sense to check the tendency. So I try.

I think sometimes that if I were only well enough to write a little it would relieve the press of ideas and rest me.

But I find I get pretty tired when I try.

It is so discouraging not to have any advice and companionship about my work. When I get really well, John says we will ask Cousin Henry and Julia down for a long visit; but he says he would as soon put fireworks in my pillow-case as to let me have those stimulating people about now.

I wish I could get well faster.

But I must not think about that. This paper looks to me as if it knew what a vicious influence it had!

There is a recurrent spot where the pattern lolls like a broken neck and two bulbous eyes stare at you upside down.

I get positively angry with the impertinence of it and the everlastingness. Up and down and sideways they crawl, and those absurd unblinking eyes are everywhere. There is one place where two breadths didn't match, and the eyes go all up and down the line, one a little higher than the other.

I never saw so much expression in an inanimate thing before, and we all know how much expression they have! I used to lie awake as a child and get more entertainment and terror out of blank walls and plain furniture than most children could find in a toy-store.

I remember what a kindly wink the knobs of our big old bureau used to have, and there was one chair that always seemed like a strong friend.

I used to feel that if any of the other things looked too fierce I could always hop into that chair and be safe.

The furniture in this room is no worse than inharmonious, however, for we had to bring it all from downstairs. I suppose when this was used as a playroom they had to take the nursery things out, and no wonder! I never saw such ravages as the children have made here.

The wallpaper, as I said before, is torn off in spots, and it sticketh closer than a brother—they must have had perseverance as well as hatred.

Then the floor is scratched and gouged and splintered, the plaster itself is dug out here and there, and this great heavy bed, which is all we found in the room, looks as if it had been through the wars.

But I don't mind it a bit—only the paper.

There comes John's sister. Such a dear girl as she is, and so careful of me! I must not let her find me writing.

She is a perfect and enthusiastic housekeeper, and hopes for no better profession. I verily believe she thinks it is the writing which made me sick!

But I can write when she is out, and see her a long way off from these windows.

There is one that commands the road, a lovely shaded winding road, and one that just looks off over the country. A lovely country, too, full of great elms and velvet meadows.

This wallpaper has a kind of sub-pattern in a different shade, a particularly irritating one, for you can only see it in certain lights, and not clearly then.

But in the places where it isn't faded and where the sun is just so—I can see a strange, provoking, formless sort of figure that seems to skulk about behind that silly and conspicuous front design.

There's sister on the stairs!

Well, the Fourth of July is over! The people are all gone, and I am tired out. John thought it might do me good to see a little company, so we just had Mother and Nellie and the children down for a week.

Of course I didn't do a thing. Jennie sees to everything now.

But it tired me all the same.

John says if I don't pick up faster he shall send me to Weir Mitchell° in the fall.

But I don't want to go there at all. I had a friend who was in his hands once, and she says he is just like John and my brother, only more so!

Besides, it is such an undertaking to go so far.

I don't feel as if it was worthwhile to turn my hand over for anything, and I'm getting dreadfully fretful and querulous.

I cry at nothing, and cry most of the time.

Of course I don't when John is here, or anybody else, but when I am alone.

And I am alone a good deal just now. John is kept in town very often by serious cases, and Jennie is good and lets me alone when I want her to.

So I walk a little in the garden or down that lovely lane, sit on the porch under the roses, and lie down up here a good deal.

I'm getting really fond of the room in spite of the wallpaper. Perhaps *because* of the wallpaper.

It dwells in my mind so!

I lie here on this great immovable bed—it is nailed down, I believe—and follow that pattern about by the hour. It is as good as gymnastics, I assure you. I start, we'll say, at the bottom, down in the corner over there where it has not been touched, and I determine for the thousandth time that I *will* follow that pointless pattern to some sort of a conclusion.

I know a little of the principle of design, and I know this thing was not arranged on any laws of radiation, or alternation, or repetition, or symmetry, or anything else that I ever heard of.

Weir Mitchell *Silas Weir Mitchell (1829–1914), neurologist who introduced the "rest cure" for psychoneurotics*

It is repeated, of course, by the breadths, but not otherwise.

Looked at in one way, each breadth stands alone; the bloated curves and flourishes—a kind of "debased Romanesque" with delirium tremens—go waddling up and down in isolated columns of fatuity.

But, on the other hand, they connect diagonally, and the sprawling outlines run off in great slanting waves of optic horror, like a lot of wallowing sea-weeds in full chase.

The whole thing goes horizontally, too, at least it seems so, and I exhaust myself trying to distinguish the order of its going in that direction.

They have used a horizontal breadth for a frieze, and that adds wonderfully to the confusion.

There is one end of the room where it is almost intact, and there, when the crosslights fade and the low sun shines directly upon it, I can almost fancy radiation after all—the interminable grotesque seems to form around a common center and rush off in headlong plunges of equal distraction.

It makes me tired to follow it. I will take a nap, I guess.

I don't know why I should write this.

I don't want to.

I don't feel able.

And I know John would think it absurd. But I must say what I feel and think in some way—it is such a relief!

But the effort is getting to be greater than the relief.

Half the time now I am awfully lazy, and lie down ever so much. John says I mustn't lose my strength, and has me take cod liver oil and lots of tonics and things, to say nothing of ale and wine and rare meat.

Dear John! He loves me very dearly, and hates to have me sick. I tried to have a real earnest reasonable talk with him the other day, and tell him how I wish he would let me go and make a visit to Cousin Henry and Julia.

But he said I wasn't able to go, nor able to stand it after I got there; and I did not make out a very good case for myself, for I was crying before I had finished.

It is getting to be a great effort for me to think straight. Just this nervous weakness, I suppose.

And dear John gathered me up in his arms, and just carried me upstairs and laid me on the bed, and sat by me and read to me till it tired my head.

He said I was his darling and his comfort and all he had, and that I must take care of myself for his sake, and keep well.

He says no one but myself can help me out of it, that I must use my will and self-control and not let any silly fancies run away with me.

There's one comfort—the baby is well and happy, and does not have to occupy this nursery with the horrid wallpaper.

If we had not used it, that blessed child would have! What a fortunate escape! Why, I wouldn't have a child of mine, an impressionable little thing, live in such a room for worlds.

I never thought of it before, but it is lucky that John kept me here after all; I can stand it so much easier than a baby, you see.

Of course I never mention it to them any more—I am too wise—but I keep watch for it all the same.

There are things in that wallpaper that nobody knows about but me, or ever will.

Behind that outside pattern the dim shapes get clearer every day.

It is always the same shape, only very numerous.

And it is like a woman stooping down and creeping about behind that pattern. I don't like it a bit. I wonder—I begin to think—I wish John would take me away from here!

It is so hard to talk with John about my case, because he is so wise, and because he loves me so.

But I tried it last night.

It was moonlight. The moon shines in all around just as the sun does.

I hate to see it sometimes, it creeps so slowly, and always comes in by one window or another.

John was asleep and I hated to waken him, so I kept still and watched the moonlight on that undulating wallpaper till I felt creepy.

The faint figure behind seemed to shake the pattern, just as if she wanted to get out.

I got up softly and went to feel and see if the paper *did* move, and when I came back John was awake.

"What is it, little girl?" he said. "Don't go walking about like that—you'll get cold."

I thought it was a good time to talk, so I told him that I really was not gaining here, and that I wished he would take me away.

"Why, darling!" said he. "Our lease will be up in three weeks, and I can't see how to leave before.

"The repairs are not done at home, and I cannot possibly leave town just now. Of course, if you were in any danger, I could and would, but you really are better, dear, whether you can see it or not. I am a doctor, dear, and I know. You are gaining flesh and color, your appetite is better, I feel really much easier about you."

"I don't weigh a bit more," said I, "nor as much; and my appetite may be better in the evening when you are here but it is worse in the morning when you are away!"

"Bless her little heart!" said he with a big hug. "She shall be as sick as she pleases! But now let's improve the shining hours by going to sleep, and talk about it in the morning!"

"And you won't go away?" I asked gloomily.

"Why, how can I, dear? It is only three weeks more and then we will take a nice little trip of a few days while Jennie is getting the house ready. Really, dear, you are better!"

"Better in body perhaps—" I began, and stopped short, for he sat up straight and looked at me with such a stern, reproachful look that I could not say another word.

"My darling," said he, "I beg of you, for my sake and for our child's sake, as well as for your own, that you will never for one instant let that idea enter your mind! There is nothing so dangerous, so fascinating, to a temperament like yours. It is a false and foolish fancy. Can you not trust me as a physician when I tell you so?"

So of course I said no more on that score, and we went to sleep before long. He thought I was asleep first, but I wasn't, and lay there for hours trying to decide whether that front pattern and the back pattern really did move together or separately.

On a pattern like this, by daylight, there is a lack of sequence, a defiance of law, that is a constant irritant to a normal mind.

The color is hideous enough, and unreliable enough, and infuriating enough, but the pattern is torturing.

You think you have mastered it, but just as you get well under way in following, it turns a back-somersault and there you are. It slaps you in the face, knocks you down, and tramples upon you. It is like a bad dream.

The outside pattern is a florid arabesque, reminding one of a fungus. If you can imagine a toadstool in joints, an interminable string of toadstools, budding and sprouting in endless convolutions—why, that is something like it.

That is, sometimes!

There is one marked peculiarity about this paper, a thing nobody seems to notice but myself, and that is that it changes as the light changes.

When the sun shoots in through the east window—I always watch for that first long, straight ray—it changes so quickly that I never can quite believe it.

That is why I watch it always.

By moonlight—the moon shines in all night when there is a moon—I wouldn't know it was the same paper.

At night in any kind of light, in twilight, candlelight, lamplight, and worst of all by moonlight, it becomes bars! The outside pattern, I mean, and the woman behind it is as plain as can be.

I didn't realize for a long time what the thing was that showed behind, that dim sub-pattern, but now I am quite sure it is a woman.

By daylight she is subdued, quiet. I fancy it is the pattern that keeps her so still. It is so puzzling. It keeps me quiet by the hour.

I lie down ever so much now. John says it is good for me, and to sleep all I can.

Indeed he started the habit by making me lie down for an hour after each meal.

It is a very bad habit, I am convinced, for you see, I don't sleep.

And that cultivates deceit, for I don't tell them I'm awake—oh, no!

The fact is I am getting a little afraid of John.

He seems very queer sometimes, and even Jennie has an inexplicable look.

It strikes me occasionally, just as a scientific hypothesis, that perhaps it is the paper!

I have watched John when he did not know I was looking, and come into the room suddenly on the most innocent excuses, and I've caught him several times *looking at the paper!* And Jennie too. I caught Jennie with her hand on it once.

She didn't know I was in the room, and when I asked her in a quiet, a very quiet voice, with the most restrained manner possible, what she was doing with the paper, she turned around as if she had been caught stealing, and looked quite angry—asked me why I should frighten her so!

Then she said that the paper stained everything it touched, that she had found yellow smooches on all my clothes and John's and she wished we would be more careful!

Did not that sound innocent? But I know she was studying that pattern, and I am determined that nobody shall find it out but myself!

Life is very much more exciting now than it used to be. You see, I have something more to expect, to look forward to, to watch. I really do eat better, and am more quiet than I was.

John is so pleased to see me improve! He laughed a little the other day, and said I seemed to be flourishing in spite of my wallpaper.

I turned it off with a laugh. I had no intention of telling him it was because of the wallpaper—he would make fun of me. He might even want to take me away.

I don't want to leave now until I have found it out. There is a week more, and I think that will be enough.

I'm feeling so much better!

I don't sleep much at night, for it is so interesting to watch developments; but I sleep a good deal during the daytime.

In the daytime it is tiresome and perplexing.

There are always new shoots on the fungus, and new shades of yellow all over it. I cannot keep count of them, though I have tried conscientiously.

It is the strangest yellow, that wallpaper! It makes me think of all the yellow things I ever saw—not beautiful ones like buttercups, but old, foul, bad yellow things.

But there is something else about that paper—the smell! I noticed it the moment we came into the room, but with so much air and sun it was not bad. Now we have had a week of fog and rain, and whether the windows are open or not, the smell is here.

It creeps all over the house.

I find it hovering in the dining-room, skulking in the parlor, hiding in the hall, lying in wait for me on the stairs.

It gets into my hair.

Even when I go to ride, if I turn my head suddenly and surprise it—there is that smell!

Such a peculiar odor, too! I have spent hours in trying to analyze it, to find what it smelled like.

It is not bad—at first—and very gentle, but quite the subtlest, most enduring odor I ever met.

In this damp weather it is awful. I wake up in the night and find it hanging over me.

It used to disturb me at first. I thought seriously of burning the house—to reach the smell.

But now I am used to it. The only thing I can think of that it is like is the *color* of the paper! A yellow smell.

There is a very funny mark on this wall, low down, near the mopboard. A streak that runs round the room. It goes behind every piece of furniture, except the bed, a long, straight, even *smooch,* as if it had been rubbed over and over.

I wonder how it was done and who did it, and what they did it for. Round and round and round—round and round and round—it makes me dizzy!

I really have discovered something at last.

Through watching so much at night, when it changes so, I have finally found out.

The front pattern *does* move—and no wonder! The woman behind shakes it!

Sometimes I think there are a great many women behind, and sometimes only one, and she crawls around fast, and her crawling shakes it all over.

Then in the very bright spots she keeps still, and in the very shady spots she just takes hold of the bars and shakes them hard.

And she is all the time trying to climb through. But nobody could climb through that pattern—it strangles so; I think that is why it has so many heads.

They get through and then the pattern strangles them off and turns them upside down, and makes their eyes white!

If those heads were covered or taken off it would not be half so bad.

I think that woman gets out in the daytime!

And I'll tell you why—privately—I've seen her!

I can see her out of every one of my windows!

It is the same woman, I know, for she is always creeping, and most women do not creep by daylight.

I see her in that long shaded lane, creeping up and down. I see her in those dark grape arbors, creeping all around the garden.

I see her on that long road under the trees, creeping along, and when a carriage comes she hides under the blackberry vines.

I don't blame her a bit. It must be very humiliating to be caught creeping by daylight!

I always lock the door when I creep by daylight. I can't do it at night, for I know John would suspect something at once.

And John is so queer now that I don't want to irritate him. I wish he would take another room! Besides, I don't want anybody to get that woman out at night but myself.

I often wonder if I could see her out of all the windows at once.

But, turn as fast as I can, I can only see out of one at one time.

And though I always see her, she may be able to creep faster than I can turn! I have watched her sometimes away off in the open country, creeping as fast as a cloud shadow in a wind.

If only that top pattern could be gotten off from the under one! I mean to try it, little by little.

I have found out another funny thing, but I shan't tell it this time! It does not do to trust people too much.

There are only two more days to get this paper off, and I believe John is beginning to notice. I don't like the look in his eyes.

And I heard him ask Jennie a lot of professional questions about me. She had a very good report to give.

She said I slept a good deal in the daytime.

John knows I don't sleep very well at night, for all I'm so quiet!

He asked me all sorts of questions, too, and pretended to be very loving and kind.

As if I couldn't see through him!

Still, I don't wonder he acts so, sleeping under this paper for three months.

It only interests me, but I feel sure John and Jennie are affected by it.

Hurrah! This is the last day, but it is enough. John is to stay in town over night, and won't be out until this evening.

Jennie wanted to sleep with me—the sly thing; but I told her I should undoubtedly rest better for a night all alone.

That was clever, for really I wasn't alone a bit! As soon as it was moonlight and that poor thing began to crawl and shake the pattern, I got up and ran to help her.

I pulled and she shook. I shook and she pulled, and before morning we had peeled off yards of that paper.

A strip about as high as my head and half around the room.

And then when the sun came and that awful pattern began to laugh at me, I declared I would finish it today!

We go away tomorrow, and they are moving all my furniture down again to leave things as they were before.

Jennie looked at the wall in amazement, but I told her merrily that I did it out of pure spite at the vicious thing.

She laughed and said she wouldn't mind doing it herself, but I must not get tired.

How she betrayed herself that time!

But I am here, and no person touches this paper but Me—not *alive!*

She tried to get me out of the room—it was too patent! But I said it was so quiet and empty and clean now that I believed I would lie down again and sleep all I could, and not to wake me even for dinner—I would call when I woke.

So now she is gone, and the servants are gone, and the things are gone, and there is nothing left but that great bedstead nailed down, with the canvas mattress we found on it.

We shall sleep downstairs tonight, and take the boat home tomorrow.

I quite enjoy the room, now it is bare again.

How those children did tear about here!

This bedstead is fairly gnawed!

But I must get to work.

I have locked the door and thrown the key down into the front path.

I don't want to go out, and I don't want to have anybody come in, till John comes.

I want to astonish him.

I've got a rope up here that even Jennie did not find. If that woman does get out, and tries to get away, I can tie her!

But I forgot I could not reach far without anything to stand on!

This bed will *not* move!

I tried to lift and push it until I was lame, and then I got so angry I bit off a little piece at one corner—but it hurt my teeth.

Then I peeled off all the paper I could reach standing on the floor. It sticks horribly and the pattern just enjoys it! All those strangled heads and bulbous eyes and waddling fungus growths just shriek with derision!

I am getting angry enough to do something desperate. To jump out of the window would be admirable exercise, but the bars are too strong even to try.

Besides I wouldn't do it. Of course not. I know well enough that a step like that is improper and might be misconstrued.

I don't like to *look* out of the windows even—there are so many of those creeping women, and they creep so fast.

I wonder if they all come out of that wallpaper as I did?

But I am securely fastened now by my well-hidden rope—you don't get *me* out in the road there!

I suppose I shall have to get back behind the pattern when it comes night, and that is hard!

It is so pleasant to be out in this great room and creep around as I please!

I don't want to go outside. I won't, even if Jennie asks me to.

For outside you have to creep on the ground, and everything is green instead of yellow.

But here I can creep smoothly on the floor, and my shoulder just fits in that long smooch around the wall, so I cannot lose my way.

Why, there's John at the door!

It is no use, young man, you can't open it!

How he does call and pound!

Now he's crying to Jennie for an axe.

It would be a shame to break down that beautiful door!

"John, dear!" said I in the gentlest voice. "The key is down by the front steps, under a plantain leaf!"

That silenced him for a few moments.

Then he said, very quietly indeed, "Open the door, my darling!"

"I can't," said I. "The key is down by the front door under a plantain leaf!" And then I said it again, several times, very gently and slowly, and said it so often that he had to go and see, and he got it of course, and came in. He stopped short by the door.

"What is the matter?" he cried. "For God's sake, what are you doing!"

I kept on creeping just the same, but I looked at him over my shoulder.

"I've got out at last," said I, "in spite of you and Jane. And I've pulled off most of the paper, so you can't put me back!"

Now why should that man have fainted? But he did, and right across my path by the wall, so that I had to creep over him every time!

(1892)

QUESTIONS FOR CRITICAL THINKING AND WRITING

Experience

1. Consider your attitude toward the narrator. Did it change as the story progressed? How? Why?

Interpretation

2. Is the narrator reliable? Do you trust all her statements and conclusions?
3. Is the narrator emotionally unbalanced? Chart the deterioration of her condition. Why is she obsessed with finding a pattern in the wallpaper?

Evaluation

4. Consider the marriage of the narrator and her husband. Does Gilman suggest anything about marriages at the turn of the nineteenth century? Does Gilman imply anything about the status of women?

Connections

5. Compare the narrator's need to write with Sonny's need to play music in Baldwin's "Sonny's Blues."
6. Compare the wife in "The Yellow Wallpaper" with the wives in Chopin's "Story of an Hour" and Boyle's "Astronomer's Wife."

Critical Thinking

7. Explain the importance of writing for the narrator. Explain what happens at the end of the story. Why does the narrator pull off the wallpaper, why does her husband faint when he sees her, and why does she "creep over him every time"?

NATHANIEL HAWTHORNE
[1804–1864]

Nathaniel Hawthorne lived most of his life in New England, the setting for many of his works, including his famous masterpiece, The Scarlet Letter. *During the administration of American President Franklin Pierce, Hawthorne served as American consul in Liverpool, England. He traveled in Europe, most notably in Italy, and he lived for a while in Rome, the setting for his novel* The Marble Faun. *Besides his handful of novels, Hawthorne wrote many tales and short stories that have become classics of American Literature. "Young Goodman Brown" is one of his most famous and one of his finest stories, particularly in its reflection of the Puritan frame of mind, which absorbed Hawthorne's literary imagination.*

Young Goodman Brown

Young Goodman Brown came forth at sunset, into the street of Salem village, but put his head back, after crossing the threshold, to exchange a parting kiss with his young wife. And Faith, as the wife was aptly named, thrust her own pretty head into the street, letting the wind play with the pink ribbons of her cap, while she called to Goodman Brown.

"Dearest heart," whispered she, softly and rather sadly, when her lips were close to his ear, "prithee, put off your journey until sunrise, and sleep in your own bed to-night. A lone woman is troubled with such dreams and such thoughts, that she's afeard of herself, sometimes. Pray, tarry with me this night, dear husband, of all nights in the year!"

"My love and my Faith," replied young Goodman Brown, "of all nights in the year, this one night must I tarry away from thee. My journey, as thou callest it, forth and back again, must needs be done 'twixt now and sunrise. What, my sweet, pretty wife, dost thou doubt me already, and we but three months married!"

"Then God bless you!" said Faith with the pink ribbons, "and may you find all well, when you come back."

"Amen!" cried Goodman Brown. "Say thy prayers, dear Faith, and go to bed at dusk, and no harm will come to thee."

So they parted; and the young man pursued his way, until, being about to turn the corner by the meeting-house, he looked back and saw the head of Faith still peeping after him, with a melancholy air, in spite of her pink ribbons.

"Poor little Faith!" thought he, for his heart smote him. "What a wretch am I, to leave her on such an errand! She talks of dreams, too. Methought, as she spoke, there was trouble in her face, as if a dream had warned her what work is to be done to-night. But no, no! 't would kill her to think it. Well; she's a blessed angel on earth; and after this one night, I'll cling to her skirts and follow her to Heaven."

With this excellent resolve for the future, Goodman Brown felt himself justified in making more haste on his present evil purpose. He had taken a dreary road, darkened by all the gloomiest trees of the forest, which barely stood aside to let the narrow path creep through, and closed immediately behind. It was as lonely as could be; and there is this peculiarity in such a solitude, that the traveller knows not who may be concealed by the innumerable trunks and the thick boughs overhead; so that, with lonely footsteps, he may yet be passing through an unseen multitude.

"There may be a devilish Indian behind every tree," said Goodman Brown to himself; and he glanced fearfully behind him, as he added, "What if the devil himself should be at my very elbow!"

His head being turned back, he passed a crook of the road, and looking forward again, beheld the figure of a man, in grave and decent attire, seated at the foot of an old tree. He arose at Goodman Brown's approach, and walked onward, side by side with him.

"You are late, Goodman Brown," said he. "The clock of the Old South was striking, as I came through Boston; and that is full fifteen minutes agone."

"Faith kept me back awhile," replied the young man, with a tremor in his voice, caused by the sudden appearance of his companion, though not wholly unexpected.

It was now deep dusk in the forest, and deepest in that part of it where these two were journeying. As nearly as could be discerned, the second traveller was about fifty years old, apparently in the same rank of life as Goodman Brown, and bearing a considerable resemblance to him, though perhaps more in expression than features. Still, they might have been taken for father and son. And yet, though the elder person was as simply clad as the younger, and as simple in manner too, he had an indescribable air of one who knew the world, and would not have felt abashed at the governor's dinner-table, or in King William's court, were it possible that his affairs should call him thither. But the only thing about him that could be fixed upon as remarkable, was his staff, which bore the likeness of a great black snake, so curiously wrought, that it might almost be seen to twist and wriggle itself like a living serpent. This, of course, must have been an ocular deception, assisted by the uncertain light.

"Come, Goodman Brown!" cried his fellow-traveller, "this is a dull pace for the beginning of a journey. Take my staff, if you are so soon weary."

"Friend," said the other, exchanging his slow pace for a full stop, "having kept covenant by meeting thee here, it is my purpose now to return whence I came. I have scruples, touching the matter thou wot'st of."

"Sayest thou so?" replied he of the serpent, smiling apart. "Let us walk on, nevertheless, reasoning as we go, and if I convince thee not, thou shalt turn back. We are but a little way in the forest, yet."

"Too far, too far!" exclaimed the Goodman, unconsciously resuming his walk. "My father never went into the woods on such an errand, nor his father before him. We have been a race of honest men and good Christians, since the days of the martyrs. And shall I be the first of the name of Brown that ever took this path and kept—"

"Such company, thou wouldst say," observed the elder person, interrupting his pause. "Well said, Goodman Brown! I have been as well acquainted with your family as with ever a one among the Puritans; and that's no trifle to say. I helped your grandfather, the constable, when he lashed the Quaker woman so smartly through the streets of Salem. And it was I that brought your father a pitch-pine knot, kindled at my own hearth, to set fire to an Indian village, in King Philip's war. They were my good friends, both; and many a pleasant walk have we had along this path, and returned merrily after midnight. I would fain be friends with you, for their sake."

"If it be as thou sayest," replied Goodman Brown, "I marvel they never spoke of these matters. Or, verily, I marvel not, seeing that the least rumor of the sort would have driven them from New England. We are a people of prayer and good works to boot, and abide no such wickedness."

"Wickedness or not," said the traveller with the twisted staff, "I have a very general acquaintance here in New England. The deacons of many a church have drunk the communion wine with me; the selectmen, of divers towns, make me their chairman; and a majority of the Great and General Court are firm supporters of my interest. The governor and I, too—but these are state secrets."

"Can this be so!" cried Goodman Brown, with a stare of amazement at his undisturbed companion. "Howbeit, I have nothing to do with the governor and council; they have their own ways, and are no rule for a simple husbandman like me. But, were I to go on with thee, how should I meet the eye of that good old man, our minister, at Salem village? Oh, his voice would make me tremble, both Sabbath-day and lecture-day!"

Thus far, the elder traveller had listened with due gravity, but now burst into a fit of irrepressible mirth, shaking himself so violently, that his snakelike staff actually seemed to wriggle in sympathy.

"Ha, ha, ha!" shouted he, again and again; then composing himself, "Well, go on, Goodman Brown, go on; but, prithee, don't kill me with laughing!"

"Well, then, to end the matter at once," said Goodman Brown, considerably nettled, "there is my wife, Faith. It would break her dear little heart; and I'd rather break my own!"

"Nay, if that be the case," answered the other, "e'en go thy ways, Goodman Brown. I would not, for twenty old women like the one hobbling before us, that Faith should come to any harm."

As he spoke, he pointed his staff at a female figure on the path, in whom Goodman Brown recognized a very pious and exemplary dame, who had taught him his catechism in youth, and was still his moral and spiritual adviser, jointly with the minister and Deacon Gookin.

"A marvel, truly, that Goody Cloyse should be so far in the wilderness, at nightfall!" said he. "But, with your leave, friend, I shall take a cut through the woods, until we have left this Christian woman behind. Being a stranger to you, she might ask whom I was consorting with, and whither I was going."

"Be it so," said his fellow-traveller. "Betake you to the woods, and let me keep the path."

Accordingly, the young man turned aside, but took care to watch his companion, who advanced softly along the road, until he had come within a staff's length of the old dame. She, meanwhile, was making the best of her way, with singular speed for so aged a woman, and mumbling some indistinct words, a prayer, doubtless, as she went. The traveller put forth his staff, and touched her withered neck with what seemed the serpent's tail.

"The devil!" screamed the pious old lady.

"Then Goody Cloyse knows her old friend?" observed the traveller, confronting her, and leaning on his writhing stick.

"Ah, forsooth, and is it your worship, indeed?" cried the good dame. "Yea, truly is it, and in the very image of my old gossip, Goodman Brown, the grandfather of the silly fellow that now is. But, would your worship believe it? my broomstick hath strangely disappeared, stolen, as I suspect, by that unhanged witch, Goody Cory, and that, too, when I was all anointed with the juice of smallage and cinque-foil and wolf's-bane—"

"Mingled with fine wheat and the fat of a new-born babe," said the shape of old Goodman Brown.

"Ah, your worship knows the recipe," cried the old lady, cackling aloud. "So, as I was saying, being all ready for the meeting, and no horse to ride on, I made up my mind to foot it; for they tell me there is a nice young man to be taken into communion to-night. But now your good worship will lend me your arm, and we shall be there in a twinkling."

"That can hardly be," answered her friend. "I may not spare you my arm, Goody Cloyse, but here is my staff, if you will."

So saying, he threw it down at her feet, where, perhaps, it assumed life, being one of the rods which its owner had formerly lent to the Egyptian Magi. Of this fact, however, Goodman Brown could not take cognizance. He had cast his eyes in astonishment, and looking down again, beheld neither Goody Cloyse nor the serpentine staff, but his fellow-traveller alone, who waited for him as calmly as if nothing had happened.

"That old woman taught me my catechism!" said the young man; and there was a world of meaning in this simple comment.

They continued to walk onward, while the elder traveller exhorted his companion to make good speed and persevere in the path, discoursing so aptly, that his arguments seemed rather to spring up in the bosom of his auditor, than to be suggested by himself. As they went he plucked a branch of maple, to serve for a walking-stick, and began to strip it of the twigs and little boughs, which were wet with evening dew. The moment his fingers touched them, they became strangely withered and dried up, as with a week's sunshine. Thus the pair proceeded, at a good free pace, until suddenly, in a gloomy hollow of the road, Goodman Brown sat himself down on the stump of a tree, and refused to go any farther.

"Friend," said he, stubbornly, "my mind is made up. Not another step will I budge on this errand. What if a wretched old woman do choose to go to the devil, when I thought she was going to Heaven! Is that any reason why I should quit my dear Faith, and go after her?"

"You will think better of this by and by," said his acquaintance, composedly. "Sit here and rest yourself awhile; and when you feel like moving again, there is my staff to help you along."

Without more words, he threw his companion the maple stick, and was as speedily out of sight as if he had vanished into the deepening gloom. The young man sat a few moments by the roadside, applauding himself greatly, and thinking with how clear a conscience he should meet the minister, in his morning walk, nor shrink from the eye of good old Deacon Gookin. And what calm sleep would be his, that very night, which was to have been spent so wickedly, but purely and sweetly now, in the arms of Faith! Amidst these pleasant and praiseworthy meditations, Goodman Brown heard the tramp of horses along the road, and deemed it advisable to conceal himself within the verge of the forest, conscious of the guilty purpose that had brought him thither, though now so happily turned from it.

On came the hoof-tramps and the voices of the riders, two grave old voices, conversing soberly, as they drew near. These mingled sounds appeared to pass along the road, within a few yards of the young man's hiding-place; but owing, doubtless, to the depth of the gloom, at that particular spot, neither the travellers nor their steeds were visible. Though their figures brushed the small boughs by the wayside, it could not be seen that they intercepted, even for a moment, the faint gleam from the strip of bright sky, athwart which they must have passed. Goodman Brown alternately crouched and stood on tiptoe, pulling aside the branches, and thrusting forth his head as far as he durst, without discerning so much as a shadow. It vexed him the more, because he could have sworn, were such a thing possible, that he recognized the voices of the minister and Deacon Gookin, jogging along quietly, as they were wont to do, when bound to some ordination or ecclesiastical council. While yet within hearing, one of the riders stopped to pluck a switch.

"Of the two, reverend Sir," said the voice like the deacon's, "I had rather miss an ordination dinner than to-night's meeting. They tell me that some of our community are to be here from Falmouth and beyond, and others from Connecticut and Rhode Island; besides several of the Indian powwows, who, after their fashion, know almost as much deviltry as the best of us. Moreover, there is a goodly young woman to be taken into communion."

"Mighty well, Deacon Gookin!" replied the solemn old tones of the minister. "Spur up, or we shall be late. Nothing can be done, you know, until I get on the ground."

The hoofs clattered again, and the voices, talking so strangely in the empty air, passed on through the forest, where no church had ever been gathered, nor solitary Christian prayed. Whither, then, could these holy men be journeying, so deep into the heathen wilderness? Young Goodman Brown caught hold of a tree, for support, being ready to sink down on the ground, faint and over-burthened with the heavy sickness of his heart. He looked up to the sky, doubting whether there really was a Heaven above him. Yet, there was the blue arch, and the stars brightening in it.

"With Heaven above, and Faith below, I will yet stand firm against the devil!" cried Goodman Brown.

While he still gazed upward, into the deep arch of the firmament, and had lifted his hands to pray, a cloud, though no wind was stirring, hurried across the zenith, and hid the brightening stars. The blue sky was still visible, except directly overhead, where this black mass of cloud was sweeping swiftly northward. Aloft in the air, as if from the depths of the cloud, came a confused and doubtful sound of voices. Once, the listener fancied that he could distinguish the accents of townspeople of his own, men and women, both pious and ungodly, many of whom he had met at the communion-table, and had seen others rioting at the tavern. The next moment, so indistinct were the sounds, he doubted whether he had heard aught but the murmur of the old forest, whispering without a wind. Then came a stronger swell of those familiar tones, heard daily in the sunshine, at Salem village, but never, until now, from a cloud at night. There was one voice, of a young woman, tittering lamentations, yet with an uncertain sorrow, and entreating for some favor, which, perhaps, it would grieve her to obtain. And all the unseen multitude, both saints and sinners, seemed to encourage her onward.

"Faith!" shouted Goodman Brown, in a voice of agony and desperation; and the echoes of the forest mocked him, crying—"Faith! Faith!" as if bewildered wretches were seeking her, all through the wilderness.

The cry of grief, rage, and terror was yet piercing the night, when the unhappy husband held his breath for a response. There was a scream, drowned immediately in a louder murmur of voices fading into far-off laughter, as the dark cloud swept away, leaving the clear and silent sky above Goodman Brown. But something fluttered lightly down through the air, and caught on the branch of a tree. The young man seized it and beheld a pink ribbon.

"My Faith is gone!" cried he, after one stupefied moment. "There is no good on earth, and sin is but a name. Come, devil! for to thee is this world given."

And maddened with despair, so that he laughed loud and long, did Goodman Brown grasp his staff and set forth again, at such a rate, that he seemed to fly along the forest path, rather than to walk or run. The road grew wilder and drearier, and more faintly traced, and vanished at length, leaving him in the heart of the dark wilderness, still rushing onward, with the instinct that guides mortal man to evil. The whole forest was peopled with frightful sounds: the creaking of the trees, the howling of wild beasts, and the yell of Indians; while, sometimes, the wind tolled like a distant church bell, and sometimes gave a broad roar around the traveller, as if all Nature was laughing him to scorn. But he was himself the chief horror of the scene, and shrank not from its other horrors.

"Ha! ha! ha!" roared Goodman Brown, when the wind laughed at him. "Let us hear which will laugh loudest! Think not to frighten me with your deviltry! Come witch, come wizard, come Indian powwow, come devil himself! and here comes Goodman Brown. You may as well fear him as he fear you!"

In truth, all through the haunted forest, there could be nothing more frightful than the figure of Goodman Brown. On he flew, among the black pines, brandishing his staff with frenzied gestures, now giving vent to an inspiration of horrid blasphemy, and now shouting forth such laughter, as set all the echoes of the forest laughing like demons around him. The fiend in his own shape is less hideous, than when he rages in the breast of man. Thus sped the demoniac on his course, until, quivering among the trees, he saw a red light before him, as when the felled trunks and branches of a clearing have been set on fire, and throw up their lurid blaze against the sky, at the hour of midnight. He paused, in a lull of the tempest that had driven him onward, and heard the swell of what seemed a hymn, rolling solemnly from a distance, with the weight of many voices. He knew the tune. It was a familiar one in the choir of the village meeting-house. The verse died heavily away, and was lengthened by a chorus, not of human voices, but of all the sounds of the benighted wilderness, pealing in awful harmony together. Goodman Brown cried out; and his cry was lost to his own ear, by its unison with the cry of the desert.

In the interval of silence, he stole forward, until the light glared full upon his eyes. At one extremity of an open space, hemmed in by the dark wall of the forest, arose a rock, bearing some rude, natural resemblance either to an altar or a pulpit, and surrounded by four blazing pines, their tops aflame, their stems untouched, like candles at an evening meeting. The mass of foliage, that had overgrown the summit of the rock, was all on fire, blazing high into the night, and fitfully illuminating the whole field. Each pendent twig and leafy festoon was in a blaze. As the red light arose and fell, a numerous congregation alternately shone forth, then disappeared in shadow, and again grew, as it were, out of the darkness, peopling the heart of the solitary woods at once.

"A grave and dark-clad company!" quoth Goodman Brown.

In truth, they were such. Among them, quivering to-and-fro, between gloom and splendor, appeared faces that would be seen, next day, at the council-board of the province, and others which, Sabbath after Sabbath, looked devoutly heavenward, and benignantly over the crowded pews, from the holiest pulpits in the land. Some affirm, that the lady of the governor was there. At least, there were high dames well known to her, and wives of honored husbands, and widows a great multitude, and ancient maidens, all of excellent repute, and fair young girls, who trembled lest their mothers should espy them. Either the sudden gleams of light, flashing over the obscure field, bedazzled Goodman Brown, or he recognized a score of the church members of Salem village, famous for their especial sanctity. Good old Deacon Gookin had arrived, and waited at the skirts of that venerable saint, his reverend pastor. But, irreverently consorting with these grave, reputable, and pious people, these elders of the church, these chaste dames and dewy virgins, there were men of dissolute lives and women of spotted fame, wretches given over to all mean and filthy vice, and suspected even of horrid crimes. It was strange to see, that the good shrank not from the wicked, nor were the sinners abashed by the saints. Scattered, also, among their pale-faced enemies, were the Indian priests, or powwows, who had often scared their native forest with more hideous incantations than any known to English witchcraft.

"But, where is Faith?" thought Goodman Brown; and, as hope came into his heart, he trembled.

Another verse of the hymn arose, a slow and mournful strain, such as the pious love, but joined to words which expressed all that our nature can conceive of sin, and darkly hinted at far more. Unfathomable to mere mortals is the lore of fiends. Verse after verse was sung, and still the chorus of the desert swelled between, like the deepest tone of a mighty organ. And, with the final peal of that dreadful anthem, there came a sound, as if the roaring wind, the rushing streams, the howling beasts, and every other voice of the unconverted wilderness were mingling and according with the voice of guilty man, in homage to the prince of all. The four blazing pines threw up a loftier flame, and obscurely discovered shapes and visages of horror on the smoke-wreaths, above the impious assembly. At the same moment, the fire on the rock shot redly forth, and formed a glowing arch above its base, where now appeared a figure. With reverence be it spoken, the apparition bore no slight similitude, both in garb and manner, to some grave divine of the New England churches.

"Bring forth the converts!" cried a voice, that echoed through the field and rolled into the forest.

At the word, Goodman Brown stepped forth from the shadow of the trees, and approached the congregation, with whom he felt a loathful brotherhood, by the sympathy of all that was wicked in his heart. He could have well-nigh sworn, that the shape of his own dead father beckoned him to advance, looking downward from a smoke-wreath, while a woman, with dim features of despair, threw out her hand to warn him back. Was it his mother? But he had no power to retreat one step, nor to resist, even in thought, when the minister and good old Deacon Gookin seized his arms, and led him to the blazing rock. Thither came also the slender form of a veiled female, led between Goody Cloyse, that pious teacher of the catechism, and Martha Carrier, who had received the devil's promise to be queen of hell. A rampant hag was she! And there stood the proselytes, beneath the canopy of fire.

"Welcome, my children," said the dark figure, "to the communion of your race! Ye have found, thus young, your nature and your destiny. My children, look behind you!"

They turned; and flashing forth, as it were, in a sheet of flame, the fiend-worshippers were seen; the smile of welcome gleamed darkly on every visage.

"There," resumed the sable form, "are all whom ye have reverenced from youth. Ye deemed them holier than yourselves, and shrank from your own sin, contrasting it with their lives of righteousness and prayerful aspirations heavenward. Yet, here are they all, in my worshipping assembly! This night it shall be granted you to know their secret deeds; how hoary-bearded elders of the church have whispered wanton words to the young maids of their households; how many a woman, eager for widow's weeds, has given her husband a drink at bedtime, and let him sleep his last sleep in her bosom; how beardless youths have made haste to inherit their father's wealth; and how fair damsels—blush not, sweet ones!—have dug little graves in the garden, and bidden me, the sole guest, to an infant's funeral. By the sympathy of your human hearts for sin, ye shall scent out all the places—whether in church, bed-chamber, street, field, or forest—where crime has been committed, and shall exult to behold the whole earth one stain of guilt, one mighty blood-spot. Far more than this! It shall be yours to penetrate, in every bosom, the deep mystery of sin, the fountain of all wicked arts, and which inexhaustibly supplies more evil impulses than human power—than my power, at its utmost!—can make manifest in deeds. And now, my children, look upon each other."

They did so; and, by the blaze of the hell-kindled torches, the wretched man beheld his Faith, and the wife her husband, trembling before that unhallowed altar.

"Lo! there ye stand, my children," said the figure, in a deep and solemn tone, almost sad, with its despairing awfulness, as if his once angelic nature could yet mourn for our miserable race. "Depending upon one another's hearts, ye had still hoped that virtue were not all a dream! Now are ye undeceived!—Evil is the nature of mankind. Evil must be your only happiness. Welcome, again, my children, to the communion of your race!"

"Welcome!" repeated the fiend-worshippers, in one cry of despair and triumph.

And there they stood, the only pair, as it seemed, who were yet hesitating on the verge of wickedness, in this dark world. A basin was hollowed, naturally, in the rock. Did it contain water, reddened by the lurid light? or was it blood? or, perchance, a liquid flame? Herein did the Shape of Evil dip his hand, and prepare to lay the mark of baptism upon their foreheads, that they might be partakers of the mystery of sin, more conscious of the secret guilt of others, both in deed and thought, than they could now be of their own. The husband cast one look at his pale wife, and Faith at him. What polluted wretches would the next glance show them to each other, shuddering alike at what they disclosed and what they saw!

"Faith! Faith!" cried the husband. "Look up to Heaven, and resist the Wicked One!"

Whether Faith obeyed, he knew not. Hardly had he spoken, when he found himself amid calm night and solitude, listening to a roar of the wind, which died heavily away through the forest. He staggered against the rock, and felt it chill and damp, while a hanging twig, that had been all on fire, besprinkled his cheek with the coldest dew.

The next morning, young Goodman Brown came slowly into the street of Salem village staring around him like a bewildered man. The good old minister was taking a walk along the grave-yard, to get an appetite for breakfast and meditate his sermon, and bestowed a blessing, as he passed, on Goodman Brown. He shrank from the venerable saint, as if to avoid an anathema. Old Deacon Gookin was at domestic worship, and the holy words of his prayer were heard through the open window. "What God doth the wizard pray to?" quoth Goodman Brown. Goody Cloyse, that excellent old Christian, stood in the early sunshine, at her own lattice, catechizing a little girl, who had brought her a pint of morning's milk. Goodman Brown snatched away the child, as from the grasp of the fiend himself. Turning the corner by the meeting-house, he spied the head of Faith, with the pink ribbons, gazing anxiously forth, and bursting into such joy at sight of him that she skipt along the street, and almost kissed her husband before the whole village. But Goodman Brown looked sternly and sadly into her face, and passed on without a greeting.

Had Goodman Brown fallen asleep in the forest, and only dreamed a wild dream of a witch-meeting?

Be it so, if you will. But, alas! it was a dream of evil omen for young Goodman Brown. A stern, a sad, a darkly meditative, a distrustful, if not a desperate man did he become, from the night of that fearful dream. On the Sabbath day, when the congregation were singing a holy psalm, he could not listen, because an anthem of sin rushed loudly upon his ear, and drowned all the blessed strain. When the minister spoke from the pulpit, with power and fervid eloquence, and with his hand on the open Bible, of the sacred truths of our religion, and of saint-like lives and triumphant deaths, and of future bliss or misery unutterable, then did Goodman Brown turn pale, dreading lest the roof should thunder down upon the gray blasphemer and his hearers. Often, awaking suddenly at midnight, he shrank from the bosom of Faith, and at morning or eventide, when the family knelt down at prayer, he scowled, and muttered to himself, and gazed sternly at his wife, and turned away. And when he had lived long, and was borne to his grave, a hoary corpse, followed by Faith, an aged woman, and children and grand-children, a goodly procession, besides neighbors not a few, they carved no hopeful verse upon his tombstone; for his dying hour was gloom.

(1828)

QUESTIONS FOR CRITICAL THINKING AND WRITING

Experience

1. What do you think Brown experienced in the forest? Did your conclusion change as the story progressed? What made you reconsider any initial conclusions?

Interpretation

2. Consider the story as an allegory. What evidence in the story suggests that Brown's journey into the forest represents a journey into his own heart? In this context, consider the significance of his fellow-traveler and his wife's name.
3. Analyze the point of view. How does point of view affect the descriptions of secondary characters like Brown's wife and our conclusions about those characters?

Evaluation

4. What are Brown's values at the end of the story? Did they change because of his experience in the forest? Do you admire his commitment to those values?

Connections

5. Compare "Young Goodman Brown" as an allegory with Borges's "The Garden of Forking Paths."

Critical Thinking

6. Why do you think he went on his journey into the forest? What kinds of temptations does he encounter on his journey, and how does he handle them? How are we meant to regard Young Goodman Brown? Why do you think so?

ERNEST HEMINGWAY

[1899–1961]

Born in Oak Park, Illinois, Ernest Hemingway was both a Nobel Prize and a Pulitzer Prize winner for his fiction. His career was nourished by the twentieth century's major cultural and political events, including World War I, the Spanish Civil War, and the flourishing of the arts in Paris in the 1920s. Like many American writers, Hemingway worked originally as a newspaper reporter. He also fought in Italy during World War I, was wounded, and used his war experiences in his early book of stories and sketches, In Our Time *(1925), and in his novel* A Farewell to Arms *(1929). He lived in Paris, where he met Gertrude Stein and Ezra Pound. An avid sportsman and big-game hunter, Hemingway reveled in competition and pursuits that pitted him against nature. His direct and unadorned writing style has been much imitated by subsequent writers.*

Hills Like White Elephants

The hills across the valley of the Ebro were long and white. On this side there was no shade and no trees and the station was between two lines of rails in the sun. Close against the side of the station there was the warm shadow of the building and a curtain, made of strings of bamboo beads, hung across the open door into the bar, to keep out flies. The American and the girl with him sat at a table in the shade, outside the building. It was very hot and the express from Barcelona would come in forty minutes. It stopped at this junction for two minutes and went on to Madrid.

"What should we drink?" the girl asked. She had taken off her hat and put it on the table.

"It's pretty hot," the man said.

"Let's drink beer."

"*Dos cervezas,*" the man said into the curtain.

"Big ones?" a woman asked from the doorway.

"Yes. Two big ones."

The woman brought two glasses of beer and two felt pads. She put the felt pads and the beer glasses on the table and looked at the man and the girl. The girl was looking off at the line of hills. They were white in the sun and the country was brown and dry.

"They look like white elephants," she said.

"I've never seen one," the man drank his beer.

"No, you wouldn't have."

"I might have," the man said. "Just because you say I wouldn't have doesn't prove anything."

The girl looked at the bead curtain. "They've painted something on it," she said. "What does it say?"

"Anis del Toro. It's a drink."

"Could we try it?"

The man called "Listen" through the curtain. The woman came out from the bar.

"Four *reales*."

"We want two Anis del Toro."

"With water?"

"Do you want it with water?"

"I don't know," the girl said. "Is it good with water?"

"It's all right."

"You want them with water?" asked the woman.

"Yes, with water."

"It tastes like licorice." the girl said and put the glass down.

"That's the way with everything."

"Yes," said the girl. "Everything tastes of licorice. Especially all the things you've waited so long for, like absinthe."

"Oh, cut it out."

"You started it," the girl said. "I was being amused. I was having a fine time."

"Well, let's try and have a fine time."

"All right. I was trying. I said the mountains looked like white elephants. Wasn't that bright?"

"That was bright."

"I wanted to try this new drink: That's all we do, isn't it—look at things and try new drinks?"

"I guess so."

The girl looked across at the hills.

"They're lovely hills," she said. "They don't really look like white elephants. I just meant the coloring of their skin through the trees."

"Should we have another drink?"

"All right."

The warm wind blew the bead curtain against the table.

"The beer's nice and cool," the man said.

"It's lovely," the girl said.

"It's really an awfully simple operation, Jig," the man said. "It's not really an operation at all."

The girl looked at the ground the table legs rested on.

"I know you wouldn't mind it, Jig. It's really not anything. It's just to let the air in."

The girl did not say anything.

"I'll go with you and I'll stay with you all the time. They just let the air in and then it's all perfectly natural."

"Then what will we do afterward?"

"We'll be fine afterward. Just like we were before."

"What makes you think so?"

"That's the only thing that bothers us. It's the only thing that's made us unhappy."

The girl looked at the bead curtain, put her hand out, and took hold of two of the strings of beads.

"And you think then we'll be all right and be happy."

"I know we will. You don't have to be afraid. I've known lots of people that have done it."

"So have I," said the girl. "And afterward they were all so happy."

"Well," the man said, "if you don't want to you don't have to. I wouldn't have you do it if you didn't want to. But I know it's perfectly simple."

"And you really want to?"

"I think it's the best thing to do. But I don't want you to do it if you don't really want to."

"And if I do it you'll be happy and things will be like they were and you'll love me?"

"I love you now. You know I love you."

"I know. But if I do it, then it will be nice again if I say things are like white elephants, and you'll like it?"

"I'll love it. I love it now but I just can't think about it. You know how I get when I worry."

"If I do it you won't ever worry?"

"I won't worry about that because it's perfectly simple."

"Then I'll do it. Because I don't care about me."

"What do you mean?"

"I don't care about me."

"Well, I care about you."

"Oh, yes. But I don't care about me. And I'll do it and then everything will be fine."

"I don't want you to do it if you feel that way."

The girl stood up and walked to the end of the station. Across, on the other side, were fields of grain and trees along the banks of the Ebro. Far away, beyond the river, were mountains. The shadow of a cloud moved across the field of grain and she saw the river through the trees.

"And we could have all this," she said. "And we could have everything and every day we make it more impossible."

"What did you say?"

"I said we could have everything."

"We can have everything."

"No, we can't."

"We can have the whole world."

"No, we can't."

"We can go everywhere."

"No, we can't. It isn't ours any more."

"It's ours."

"No, it isn't. And once they take it away, you never get it back."

"But they haven't taken it away."

"We'll wait and see."

"Come on back in the shade," he said. "You mustn't feel that way."

"I don't feel any way," the girl said. "I just know things."

"I don't want you to do anything that you don't want to do—"

"Nor that isn't good for me," she said. "I know. Could we have another beer?"

"All right. But you've got to realize—"

"I realize," the girl said. "Can't we maybe stop talking?"

They sat down at the table and the girl looked across at the hills on the dry side of the valley and the man looked at her and at the table.

"You've got to realize," he said, "that I don't want you to do it if you don't want to. I'm perfectly willing to go through with it if it means anything to you."

"Doesn't it mean anything to you? We could get along."

"Of course it does. But I don't want anybody but you. I don't want any one else. And I know it's perfectly simple."

"Yes, you know it's perfectly simple."

"It's all right for you to say that, but I do know it."

"Would you do something for me now?"

"I'd do anything for you."

"Would you please please please please please please please stop talking?"

He did not say anything but looked at the bags against the wall of the station. There were labels on them from all the hotels where they had spent nights.

"But I don't want you to," he said, "I don't care anything about it."

"I'll scream," the girl said.

The woman came out through the curtains with two glasses of beer and put them down on the damp felt pads. "The train comes in five minutes," she said.

"What did she say?" asked the girl.

"That the train is coming in five minutes."

The girl smiled brightly at the woman, to thank her.

"I'd better take the bags over to the other side of the station," the man said. She smiled at him.

"All right. Then come back and we'll finish the beer."

He picked up the two heavy bags and carried them around the station to the other tracks. He looked up the tracks but could not see the train. Coming back, he walked through the barroom, where people waiting for the train were drinking. He drank an Anis at the bar and looked at the people. They were all waiting reasonably for the train. He went out through the bead curtain. She was sitting at the table and smiled at him.

"Do you feel better?" he asked.

"I feel fine," she said. "There's nothing wrong with me. I feel fine."

(1927)

QUESTIONS FOR CRITICAL THINKING AND WRITING

Experience

1. How was it to read this story, mostly composed of dialogue with a few bits of descriptive detail? To what extent were you able to read between the lines and infer what the couple were really discussing?

Interpretation

2. What is the topic that the couple "discuss" without actually naming it? What details help you decide what this subject is?
3. What is your impression of the man? How is he characterized?

4. What is your impression of the "girl"? How is she characterized?
5. At what point in the story does the balance of power shift from the man to the girl?
6. What does she mean by saying "it doesn't matter" that "nothing" matters to her?
7. To what extent are the setting and the landscape symbolic? What do the hills symbolize?
8. Explain the reference to the "white elephants" in the title.
9. What do you think the girl is going to do? Do you think that she will stay with the man? Why or why not?

Evaluation

10. What values does the man live by? How do you know?
11. What is important to the girl? How do you know?

Connections

12. Compare the use of dialogue in this story with its use at the end of Joyce's "Araby."

Critical Thinking

13. Why does the girl repeat "please" seven times when asking the man to "please stop talking"?
14. Why do you think the characters never explicitly mention the topic discussed? How would the story change if they did?

ZORA NEALE HURSTON
[1891–1960]

Zora Neale Hurston was born in Notasulga, Alabama. She has written in a variety of genres, including the novel, short story, drama, and essay. She also has edited important collections of folklore. A prominent figure of the Harlem renaissance in the 1920s and 1930s, Hurston received a B.A. from Barnard College in 1928. Among her many books are the novel Their Eyes Were Watching God *and* Mules and Men, *a collection of black folklore.*

Spunk

I

A giant of a brown-skinned man sauntered up the one street of the village and out into the palmetto thickets with a small pretty woman clinging lovingly to his arm.

"Looka theah, folkses!" cried Elijah Mosley, slapping his leg gleefully. "Theah they go, big as life an' brassy as tacks."

All the loungers in the store tried to walk to the door with an air of nonchalance but with small success.

"Now pee-eople!" Walter Thomas gasped. "Will you look at 'em!"

"But that's one thing Ah likes about Spunk Banks—he ain't skeered of nothin' on God's green footstool—*nothin*'! He rides that log down at saw-mill jus' like he struts 'round wid another man's wife—jus' don't give a kitty. When Tes' Miller got cut to giblets on that circle-saw, Spunk steps right up and starts ridin'. The rest of us was skeered to go near it."

A round-shouldered figure in overalls much too large came nervously in the door and the talking ceased. The men looked at each other and winked.

"Gimme some soda-water. Sass'prilla Ah reckon," the newcomer ordered, and stood far down the counter near the open pickled pig-feet tub to drink it.

Elijah nudged Walter and turned with mock gravity to the new-comer.

"Say, Joe, how's everything up yo' way? How's yo' wife?"

Joe started and all but dropped the bottle he was holding. He swallowed several times painfully and his lips trembled.

"Aw 'Lige, you oughtn't to do nothin' like that," Walter grumbled. Elijah ignored him.

"She jus' passed heah a few minutes ago goin' thata way," with a wave of his hand in the direction of the woods.

Now Joe knew his wife had passed that way. He knew that the men lounging in the general store had seen her, moreover, he knew that the men knew *he* knew. He stood there silent for a long moment staring blankly, with his Adam's apple twitching nervously up and down his throat. One could actually *see* the pain he was suffering, his eyes, his face, his hands, and even the dejected slump of his shoulders. He set the bottle down upon the counter. He didn't bang it, just eased it out of his hand silently and fiddled with his suspender buckle.

"Well, Ah'm goin' after her to-day. Ah'm goin' an' fetch her back. Spunk's done gone too fur."

He reached deep down into his trouser pocket and drew out a hollow ground razor, large and shiny, and passed his moistened thumb back and forth over the edge.

"Talkin' like a man, Joe. 'Course that's *yo'* fambly affairs, but Ah like to see grit in anybody."

Joe Kanty laid down a nickel and stumbled out into the street.

Dusk crept in from the woods. Ike Clarke lit the swinging oil lamp that was almost immediately surrounded by candle-flies. The men laughed boisterously behind Joe's back as they watched him shamble woodward.

"You oughtn't to said whut you said to him, 'Lige—look how it worked him up," Walter chided.

"And Ah hope it did work him up. Tain't even decent for a man to take and take like he do."

"Spunk will sho' kill him."

"Aw, Ah doan know. You never kin tell. He might turn him up an' spank him fur getting' in the way, but Spunk wouldn't shoot no unarmed man. Dat razor he carried outa heah ain't gonna run Spunk down an' cut him, an' Joe ain't got the nerve to go to Spunk with it knowing he totes that Army .45. He makes that break outa heah to bluff us. He's gonna hide that razor behind the first palmetto root an' sneak back home to bed. Don't tell me nothin' 'bout that rabbit-foot colored man. Didn't he meet Spunk an' Lena face to face one day las' week an' mumbled sumthin' to Spunk 'bout lettin' his wife alone?"

"What did Spunk say?" Walter broke in. "Ah like him fine but tain't right the way he carries on wid Lena Kanty, jus' 'cause Joe's timid 'bout fightin'."

"You wrong theah, Walter. Tain't 'cause Joe's timid at all, it's 'cause Spunk wants Lena. If Joe was a passle of wile cats Spunk would tackle the job just the same. He'd go after *anything* he wanted in the same way. As Ah wuz sayin' a minute ago, he tole Joe right to his face that Lena was his. 'Call her and see if she'll come. A woman knows her boss an' she answers when he calls.' 'Lena, ain't I yo' husband?' Joe sorter whines out. Lena looked at him real disgusted but she don't answer and she don't move outa her tracks. Then Spunk reaches out an' takes hold of her arm an' says: 'Lena, youse mine. From now on Ah works for you an' fights for you an' Ah never wants you to look to nobody for a crumb of bread, a stitch of close or a shingle to go over yo' head, but *me* long as Ah live. Ah'll git the lumber foh owah house to-morrow. Go home an' git yo' things together!"

" 'Thass mah house," Lena speaks up. "Papa gimme that."

" 'Well,' says Spunk, 'doan give up whut's yours, but when youse inside doan forgit youse mine, an' let no other man git outa his place wid you!"

"Lena looked up at him with her eyes so full of love that they wuz runnin' over, an' Spunk seen it an' Joe seen it too, and his lip started to tremblin' and his Adam's apple was galloping up and down his neck like a race horse. Ah bet he's wore out half a dozen Adam's apples since Spunk's been on the job with Lena. That's all he'll do. He'll be back heah after while swallowin' an' workin' his lips like he wants to say somethin' an' can't."

"But didn't he do *nothin'* to stop 'em?"

"Nope, not a frazzlin' thing—jus' stood there. Spunk took Lena's arm and walked off jus' like nothin' ain't happened and he stood there gazin' after them till they was outa sight. Now you know a woman don't want no man like that. I'm jus' waitin' to see whut he's goin' to say when he gits back."

II

But Joe Kanty never came back, never. The men in the store heard the sharp report of a pistol somewhere in the distant palmetto thicket and soon Spunk came walking leisurely, with his big black Stetson set at the rakish angle and Lena clinging to his arm, came walking right into the general store. Lena wept in a frightened manner.

"Well," Spunk announced calmly, "Joe came out there wid a meat axe an' made me kill him."

He sent Lena home and led the men back to Joe—crumpled and limp with his right hand still clutching his razor.

"See mah back? Mah close cut clear through. He sneaked up an' tried to kill me from the back, but Ah got him, an' got him good, first shot," Spunk said.

The men glared at Elijah, accusingly.

"Take him up an' plant him in Stony Lonesome," Spunk said in a careless voice. "Ah didn't want to shoot him but he made me do it. He's a dirty coward, jumpin' on a man from behind."

Spunk turned on his heel and sauntered away to where he knew his love wept in fear for him and no man stopped him. At the general store later on, they all talked of locking him up until the sheriff should come from Orlando, but no one did anything but talk.

A clear case of self-defense, the trial was a short one, and Spunk walked out of the court house to freedom again. He could work again, ride the dangerous log-carriage that fed the singing, snarling, biting circle-saw; he could stroll the soft dark lanes with his guitar. He was free to roam the woods again; he was free to return to Lena. He did all of these things.

III

"Whut you reckon, Walt?" Elijah asked one night later. "Spunk's gittin' ready to marry Lena!"

"Naw! Why, Joe ain't had time to git cold yit. Nowhow Ah didn't figger Spunk was the marryin' kind."

"Well, he is," rejoined Elijah. "He done moved most of Lena's things—and her along wid 'em—over to the Bradley house. He's buying it. Jus' like Ah told yo' all right in heah the night Joe was kilt. Spunk's crazy 'bout Lena. He don't want folks to keep on talkin' 'bout her—thass reason he's rushin' so. Funny thing 'bout that bob-cat, wan't it?"

"What bob-cat, 'Lige? Ah ain't heered 'bout none."

"Ain't cher? Well, night befo' las' as they was goin' to bed, a big black bob-cat, black all over, you hear me, *black,* walked round and round that house and howled like forty, an' when Spunk got his gun an' when to the winder to shoot it, he says it stood right still an' looked him in the eye, an' howled right at him. The thing got Spunk so nervoused up he couldn't shoot. But Spunk says twan't no bob-cat nohow. He says it was Joe done sneaked back from Hell!"

"Humph!" sniffed Walter, "he oughter be nervous after what he done. Ah reckon Joe come back to dare him to marry Lena, or to come out an' fight. Ah bet he'll be back time and again, too. Know what Ah think? Joe wuz a braver man than Spunk."

There was a general shout of derision from the group.

"Thass a fact," went on Walter. "Lookit whut he done; took a razor an' went out to fight a man he knowed toted a gun an' wuz a crack shot, too; 'nother thing Joe wuz skeered of Spunk, skeered plumb stiff! But he went jes' the same. It took him a long time to get his nerve up. Tain't nothin' for Spunk to fight when he ain't skeered of nothin'. Now, Joe's done come back to have it out wid the man that's got all he ever had. Y'all know Joe ain't never had nothin' nor wanted nothin' besides Lena. It musta been a h'ant cause ain't nobody ever seen no black bob-cat."

"Nother thing," cut in one of the men, "Spunk was cussin' a blue streak to-day 'cause he 'lowed dat saw wuz wobblin'—almos' got 'im once. The machinist come, looked it over and said it wuz alright. Spunk must been leanin' t'wards it some. Den he claimed somebody pushed 'im but twan't nobody close to 'im. Ah wuz glad when knockin' off time came. I'm skeered of dat man when he gits hot. He'd beat you full of button holes as quick as he's look atcher."

IV

The men gathered the next evening in a different mood, no laughter. No badinage this time.

"Look, 'Lige, you goin' to set up wid Spunk?"

"Naw, Ah reckon not, Walter. Tell yuh the truth, Ah'm a li'l bit skittish. Spunk died too wicket—died cussin' he did. You know he thought he was done outa life."

"Good Lawd, who'd he think done it?"

"Joe."

"Joe Kanty? How come?"

"Walter, Ah b'leeve Ah will walk up thata way an' set. Lena would like it Ah reckon."

"But whut did he say, 'Lige?"

Elijah did not answer until they had left the lighted store and were strolling down the dark street.

"Ah wuz loadin' a wagon wid scantlin' right near the saw when Spunk fell on the carriage but 'fore Ah could git to him the saw got him in the body—awful sight. Me an' Skint Miller got him off but it was too late. Anybody could see that. The fust thing he said wuz: 'He pushed me, 'Lige—the dirty hound pushed me in the back!'—he was spittin' blood at ev'ry breath. We laid him on the sawdust pile with his face to the East so's he could die easy. He helt mah han' till the last, Walter, and said: 'It was Joe, 'Lige . . . the dirty sneak shoved me . . . he didn't dare come to mah face . . . but Ah'll git the son-of-a-wood louse soon's Ah get there an' make hell too hot for him . . . Ah felt him shove me . . . !' Thass how he died."

"If spirits kin fight, there's a powerful tussle goin' on somewhere ovah Jordan 'cause Ah b'leeve Joe's ready for Spunk an' ain't skeered any more—yas, Ah b'leeve Joe pushed 'im mahself."

They had arrived at the house. Lena's lamentations were deep and loud. She had filled the room with magnolia blossoms that gave off a heavy sweet odor. The keepers of the wake tipped about whispering in frightened tones. Everyone in the village was there, even old Jeff Kanty, Joe's father, who a few hours before would have been afraid to come within ten feet of him, stood leering triumphantly down upon the fallen giant as if his fingers had been the teeth of steel that laid him low.

The cooling board consisted of three sixteen-inch boards on saw horses, a dingy sheet was his shroud.

The women ate heartily of the funeral baked meats and wondered who would be Lena's next. The men whispered coarse conjectures between guzzles of whiskey.

(1927)

QUESTIONS FOR CRITICAL THINKING AND WRITING

Experience

1. What impressions do you have of the characters in this story, particularly Spunk, Elijah, and Joe?

Interpretation

2. The community plays an important part in this story. Consider the role of the men in the general store. What do we learn from their behavior and their comments? How do they participate in the action?

3. Consider the four-part structure of the story. What is the pivotal event in each section? How does this structure affect our response to the story?

Evaluation

4. Pleading self-defense, Spunk was found not guilty of Joe's murder. Do you find the verdict questionable? Why or why not?

Connection

5. Compare the role of the community with that of the chorus in *Oedipus Rex*.

Critical Thinking

6. Which of the critical thinking strategies described in this book's Introduction best helps you to understand the characters in "Spunk"? Why?

SHIRLEY JACKSON

(1919–1965)

Shirley Jackson was born and raised in San Francisco and moved to Rochester, New York during her high school years. She attended the University of Rochester and later Syracuse University. Married to the literary critic, Stanley Edgar Hyman, she lived her adult life in Bennington, Vermont, where she wrote stories and novels, including thrillers, such as The Haunting of Hill House *(1959) and* We Have Always Lived in the Castle *(1962). Her comic works based on the life of a homemaker raising children include* Life Among the Savages *(1953) and* Raising Demons *(1957). She published her short story "The Lottery" in 1948 in* The New Yorker, *fully intending to shock readers of that then-staid publication.*

The Lottery

The morning of June 27th was clear and sunny, with the fresh warmth of a full-summer day; the flowers were blossoming profusely and the grass was richly green. The people of the village began to gather in the square, between the post office and the bank, around ten o'clock; in some towns there were so many people that the lottery took two days and had to be started on June 26th, but in this village, where there were only about three hundred people, the whole lottery took less than two hours, so it could begin at ten o'clock in the morning and still be through in time to allow the villagers to get home for noon dinner.

The children assembled first, of course. School was recently over for the summer, and the feeling of liberty sat uneasily on most of them; they tended to gather together quietly for a while before they broke into boisterous play, and their talk was still of the classroom and the teacher, of books and reprimands. Bobby Martin had already stuffed his pockets full of stones, and the other boys soon followed his example, selecting the smoothest and roundest stones; Bobby and Harry Jones and Dickie Delacroix—the villagers pronounced this name "Dellacroy"—eventually made a great pile of stones in one corner of the square and guarded it against the raids of the other boys. The girls stood aside, talking among themselves, looking over their shoulders at the boys, and the very small children rolled in the dust or clung to the hands of their older brothers or sisters.

Soon the men began to gather, surveying their own children, speaking of planting and rain, tractors and taxes. They stood together, away from the pile of stones in the corner, and their jokes were quiet and they smiled rather than laughed. The women, wearing faded house dresses and sweaters, came shortly after their menfolk. They greeted one another and exchanged bits of gossip as they went to join their husbands. Soon the women, standing by their husbands, began to call to their children, and the children came reluctantly, having to be called four or five times. Bobby Martin ducked under his mother's grasping hand and ran, laughing, back to the pile of stones. His father spoke up sharply, and Bobby came quickly and took his place between his father and his oldest brother.

The lottery was conducted—as were the square dances, the teenage club, the Halloween program—by Mr. Summers, who had time and energy to devote to civic activities. He was a roundfaced, jovial man and he ran the coal business, and people were sorry for him, because he had no children and his wife was a scold. When he arrived in the square, carrying the black wooden box, there was a murmur of conversation among the villagers and he waved and called, "Little late today, folks." The postmaster, Mr. Graves, followed him, carrying a three-legged stool, and the stool was put in the center of the square and Mr. Summers set the black box down on it. The villagers kept their distance, leaving a space between themselves and the stool, and when Mr. Summers said, "Some of you fellows want to give me a hand?" there was a hesitation before two men, Mr. Martin and his oldest son, Baxter, came forward to hold the box steady on the stool while Mr. Summers stirred up the papers inside it.

The original paraphernalia for the lottery had been lost long ago, and the black box now resting on the stool had been put into use even before Old Man Warner, the oldest man in town, was born. Mr. Summers spoke frequently to the villagers about making a new box, but no one liked to upset even as much tradition as was represented by the black box. There was a story that the present box had been made with some pieces of the box that had preceded it, the one that had been constructed when the first people settled down to make a village here. Every year, after the lottery, Mr. Summers began talking again about a new box, but every year the subject was allowed to fade off without anything's being done. The black box grew shabbier each year; by now it was no longer completely black but splintered badly along one side to show the original wood color, and in some places faded or stained.

Mr. Martin and his oldest son, Baxter, held the black box securely on the stool until Mr. Summers had stirred the papers thoroughly with his hand. Because so much of the ritual had been forgotten or discarded, Mr. Summers had been successful in having slips of paper substituted for the chips of wood that had been used for generations. Chips of wood, Mr. Summers had argued, had been all very well when the village was tiny, but now that the population was more than three hundred and likely to keep on growing, it was necessary to use something that would fit more easily into the black box. The night before the lottery, Mr. Summers and Mr. Graves made up the slips of paper and put them in the box, and it was then taken to the safe of Mr. Summers's coal company and locked up until Mr. Summers was ready to take it to the square next morning. The rest of the year, the box was put away, sometimes one place, sometimes another; it had spent one year in Mr. Graves's barn and another year underfoot in the post office, and sometimes it was set on a shelf in the Martin grocery and left there.

There was a great deal of fussing to be done before Mr. Summers declared the lottery open. There were lists to make up—of heads of families, heads of households in each family, members of each household in each family. There was the proper swearing-in of Mr. Summers by the postmaster, as the official of the lottery; at one time, some people remembered, there had been a recital of some sort, performed by the official of the lottery, a perfunctory, tuneless chant that had been rattled off duly each year; some people believed that the official of the lottery used to stand just so when he had or sang it, others believed that he was supposed to walk among the people, but years and years ago this part of the ritual had been allowed to lapse. There had been, also, a ritual salute, which the official of the lottery had had to use in addressing each person who came up to draw from the box, but this also had changed with time, until now it was felt necessary only for the official to speak to each person approaching. Mr. Summers was very good at all this; in his clean white shirt and blue jeans, with one hand resting carelessly on the black box, he seemed very proper and important as he talked interminably to Mr. Graves and the Martins.

Just as Mr. Summers finally left off talking and turned to the assembled villagers, Mrs. Hutchinson came hurriedly along the path to the square, her sweater thrown over her shoulders, and slid into place in the back of the crowd. "Clean forgot what day it was," she said to Mrs. Delacroix, who stood next to her, and they both laughed softly. "Thought my old man was out back stacking wood," Mrs. Hutchinson went on, "and then I looked out the window and the kids were gone, and then I remembered it was the twenty-seventh and came a-running." She dried her hands on her apron, and Mrs. Delacroix said, "You're in time, though. They're still talking away up there."

Mrs. Hutchinson craned her neck to see through the crowd and found her husband and children standing near the front. She tapped Mrs. Delacroix on the arm as a farewell and began to make her way through the crowd. The people separated good-humoredly to let her through; two or three people said, in voices just loud enough to be heard across the crowd, "Here comes your Missus, Hutchinson," and "Bill, she made it after all." Mrs. Hutchinson reached her husband, and Mr. Summers, who had been waiting, said cheerfully, "Thought we were going to have to get on without you, Tessie." Mrs. Hutchinson said, grinning, "Wouldn't have me leave m'dishes in the sink, now would you, Joe?" and soft laughter ran through the crowd as the people stirred back into position after Mrs. Hutchinson's arrival.

"Well, now," Mr. Summers said soberly, "guess we better get started, get this over with, so's we can go back to work. Anybody ain't here?"

"Dunbar," several people said. "Dunbar, Dunbar."

Mr. Summers consulted his list. "Clyde Dunbar," he said. "That's right. He's broke his leg, hasn't he? Who's drawing for him?"

"Me, I guess," a woman said, and Mr. Summers turned to look at her. "Wife draws for her husband," Mr. Summers said. "Don't you have a grown boy to do it for you, Janey?" Although Mr. Summers and everyone else in the village knew the answer perfectly well, it was the business of the official of the lottery to ask such questions formally. Mr. Summers waited with an expression of polite interest while Mrs. Dunbar answered.

"Horace's not but sixteen yet," Mrs. Dunbar said regretfully. "Guess I gotta fill in for the old man this year."

"Right," Mr. Summers said. He made a note on the list he was holding. Then he asked, "Watson boy drawing this year?"

A tall boy in the crowd raised his hand. "Here," he said. "I'm drawing for m'mother and me." He blinked his eyes nervously and ducked his head as several voices in the crowd said things like "Good fellow, Jack," and "Glad to see your mother's got a man to do it."

"Well," Mr. Summers said, "guess that's everyone. Old Man Warner make it?"

"Here," a voice said, and Mr. Summers nodded.

A sudden hush fell on the crowd as Mr. Summers cleared his throat and looked at the list. "All ready?" he called. "Now, I'll read the names—heads of families first—and the men come up and take a paper out of the box. Keep the paper folded in your hand without looking at it until everyone has had a turn. Everything clear?"

The people had done it so many times that they only half listened to the directions; most of them were quiet, wetting their lips, not looking around. Then Mr. Summers raised one hand high and said, "Adams." A man disengaged himself from the crowd and came forward. "Hi, Steve," Mr. Summers said, and Mr. Adams said, "Hi, Joe." They grinned at one another humorlessly and nervously. Then Mr. Adams reached into the black box and took out a folded paper. He held it firmly by one corner as he turned and went hastily back to his place in the crowd, where he stood a little apart from his family, not looking down at his hand.

"Allen," Mr. Summers said. "Anderson. . . . Bentham."

"Seems like there's no time at all between lotteries any more," Mrs. Delacroix said to Mrs. Graves in the back row. "Seems like we got through with the last one only last week."

"Time sure goes fast," Mrs. Graves said.

"Clark. . . . Delacroix."

"There goes my old man," Mrs. Delacroix said. She held her breath while her husband went forward.

"Dunbar," Mr. Summers said, and Mrs. Dunbar went steadily to the box while one of the women said, "Go on, Janey," and another said, "There she goes."

"We're next," Mrs. Graves said. She watched while Mr. Graves came around from the side of the box, greeted Mr. Summers gravely, and selected a slip of paper from the box. By now, all through the crowd there were men holding the small folded papers in their large hands, turning them over and over nervously. Mrs. Dunbar and her two sons stood together, Mrs. Dunbar holding the slip of paper.

"Harburt. . . . Hutchinson."

"Get up there, Bill," Mrs. Hutchinson said, and the people near her laughed.

"Jones."

"They do say," Mr. Adams said to Old Man Warner, who stood next to him, "that over in the north village they're talking of giving up the lottery."

Old Man Warner snorted. "Pack of crazy fools," he said. "Listening to the young folks, nothing's good enough for *them*. Next thing you know, they'll be wanting to go back to living in caves, nobody work any more, live *that* way for a while. Used to be a saying about 'Lottery in June, corn be heavy soon.' First thing you know, we'd all be eating stewed chickweed and acorns. There's *always* been a lottery," he added petulantly. "Bad enough to see young Joe Summers up there joking with everybody."

"Some places have already quit lotteries," Mrs. Adams said.

"Nothing but trouble in *that,*" Old Man Warner said stoutly. "Pack of young fools."

"Martin." And Bobby Martin watched his father go forward. "Overdyke. . . . Percy."

"I wish they'd hurry," Mrs. Dunbar said to her older son. "I wish they'd hurry."

"They're almost through," her son said.

"You get ready to run tell Dad," Mrs. Dunbar said.

Mr. Summers called his own name and then stepped forward precisely and selected a slip from the box. Then he called, "Warner."

"Seventy-seventh year I been in the lottery," Old Man Warner said as he went through the crowd. "Seventy-seventh time."

"Watson." The tall boy came awkwardly through the crowd. Someone said, "Don't be nervous, Jack," and Mr. Summers said, "Take your time, son."

"Zanini."

After that, there was a long pause, a breathless pause, until Mr. Summers, holding his slip of paper in the air, said, "All right, fellows." For a minute, no one moved, and then all the slips of paper were opened. Suddenly, all women began to speak at once, saying, "Who is it?" "Who's got it?" "Is it the Dunbars?" "Is it the Watsons?" Then the voices began to say, "It's Hutchinson. It's Bill." "Bill Hutchinson's got it."

"Go tell your father," Mrs. Dunbar said to her older son.

People began to look around to see the Hutchinsons. Bill Hutchinson was standing quiet, staring down at the paper in his hand. Suddenly, Tessie Hutchinson shouted to Mr. Summers, "You didn't give him time enough to take any paper he wanted. I saw you. It wasn't fair!"

"Be a good sport, Tessie," Mrs. Delacroix called, and Mrs. Graves said, "All of us took the same chance."

"Shut up. Tessie," Bill Hutchinson said.

"Well, everyone," Mr. Summers said, "that was done pretty fast, and now we've got to be hurrying a little more to get done in time." He consulted his next list. "Bill," he said, "you draw for the Hutchinson family. You got any other households in the Hutchinsons?"

"There's Don and Eva," Mrs. Hutchinson yelled. "Make them take their chance!"

"Daughters draw with their husbands' families, Tessie," Mr. Summers said gently. "You know that as well as anyone else."

"It wasn't fair," Tessie said.

"I guess not, Joe," Bill Hutchinson said regretfully. "My daughter draws with her husband's family, that's only fair. And I've got no other family except the kids."

"Then, as far as drawing for families is concerned, it's you," Mr. Summers said in explanation, "and as far as drawing for households is concerned, that's you, too. Right?"

"Right," Bill Hutchinson said.

"How many kids, Bill?" Mr. Summers asked formally.

"Three," Bill Hutchinson said. "There's Bill, Jr., and Nancy, and little Dave. And Tessie and me."

"All right, then," Mr. Summers said. "Harry, you got their tickets back?"

Mr. Graves nodded and held up the slips of paper. "Put them in the box, then," Mr. Summers directed. "Take Bill's and put it in."

"I think we ought to start over," Mrs. Hutchinson said, as quietly as she could. "I tell you it wasn't *fair*. You didn't give him time enough to choose. Everybody saw that."

Mr. Graves had selected the five slips and put them in the box, and he dropped all the papers but those onto the ground, where the breeze caught them and lifted them off.

"Listen, everybody," Mrs. Hutchinson was saying to the people around her.

"Ready, Bill?" Mr. Summers asked, and Bill Hutchinson, with one quick glance around at his wife and children, nodded.

"Remember," Mr. Summers said, "take the slips and keep them folded until each person has taken one. Harry, you help little Dave." Mr. Graves took the hand of the little boy, who came willingly with him up to the box. "Take a paper out of the box, Davy," Mr. Summers said. Davy put his hand into the box and laughed. "Take just *one* paper," Mr. Summers said. "Harry, you hold it for him." Mr. Graves took the child's hand and removed the folded paper from the tight fist and held it while little Dave stood next to him and looked up at him wonderingly.

"Nancy next," Mr. Summers said. Nancy was twelve, and her school friends breathed heavily as she went forward, switching her skirt, and took a slip daintily from the box. "Bill, Jr.," Mr. Summers said, and Billy, his face red and his feet over-large, nearly knocked the box over as he got a paper out. "Tessie," Mr. Summers said. She hesitated for a minute, looking around defiantly, and then set her lips and went up to the box. She snatched a paper out and held it behind her.

"Bill," Mr. Summers said, and Bill Hutchinson reached into the box and felt around, bringing his hand out at last with the slip of paper in it.

The crowd was quiet. A girl whispered, "I hope it's not Nancy," and the sound of the whisper reached the edges of the crowd.

"It's not the way it used to be," Old Man Warner said clearly. "People ain't the way they used to be."

"All right," Mr. Summers said. "Open the papers. Harry, you open little Dave's."

Mr. Graves opened the slip of paper and there was a general sigh through the crowd as he held it up and everyone could see that it was blank. Nancy and Bill, Jr., opened theirs at the same time, and both beamed and laughed, turning around to the crowd and holding their slips of paper above their heads.

"Tessie," Mr. Summers said. There was a pause, and then Mr. Summers looked at Bill Hutchinson, and Bill unfolded his paper and showed it. It was blank.

"It's Tessie," Mr. Summers said, and his voice was hushed. "Show us her paper, Bill."

Bill Hutchinson went over to his wife and forced the slip of paper out of her hand. It had a black spot on it, the black spot Mr. Summers had made the night before with the heavy pencil in the coal-company office. Bill Hutchinson held it up, and there was a stir in the crowd.

"All right, folks," Mr. Summers said, "let's finish quickly."

Although the villagers had forgotten the ritual and lost the original black box, they still remembered to use stones. The pile of stones the boys had made earlier was ready;

there were stones on the ground with the blowing scraps of paper that had come out of the box. Mrs. Delacroix selected a stone so large she had to pick it up with both hands and turned to Mrs. Dunbar. "Come on," she said. "Hurry up."

Mrs. Dunbar had small stones in both hands, and she said, gasping for breath, "I can't run at all. You'll have to go ahead and I'll catch up with you."

The children had stones already, and someone gave little Davy Hutchinson a few pebbles.

Tessie Hutchinson was in the center of a cleared space by now, and she held her hands out desperately as the villagers moved in on her. "It isn't fair," she said. A stone hit her on the side of the head.

Old Man Warner was saying, "Come on, come on, everyone." Steve Adams was in the front of the crowd of villagers, with Mrs. Graves beside him.

"It isn't fair, it isn't right," Mrs. Hutchinson screamed, and then they were upon her.

(1948)

QUESTIONS FOR CRITICAL THINKING AND WRITING

Experience

1. What is your reaction to the climax of the story—the stoning? Consider especially the behavior of Tessie Hutchinson's husband and son.
2. When did you begin to realize that the lottery in this story was different from the lottery in which people win money and prizes?

Interpretation

3. What details of dialogue and description serve to characterize the story's central characters? Consider Tessie Hutchinson, her husband, and Old Man Warner.
4. What is the significance of Old Man Warner's statement: "Lottery in June, corn be heavy soon"?
5. How does Jackson make the black box a symbol? What does it represent?

Evaluation

6. What value does the lottery have for the community? Why is it held each year?

Connection

7. Compare the symbolism of "The Lottery" with the symbolism of Lawrence's "The Rocking Horse Winner."

Critical Thinking

8. What do you think of the reasons for the lottery? What is the value of the continuity of traditional ceremonies and rituals in an ever-changing world?

JAMES JOYCE
[1882–1941]

James Joyce is best known as the author of Ulysses, *one of the most important literary works of the twentieth century. Joyce was born in Ireland, but left his home country to escape the stultifying influence of his country's social system, especially as reflected in institutional Catholicism. After a brief return to Ireland, Joyce moved permanently to Europe, living in Italy, France, and Switzerland, supporting his writing by giving language lessons. His short-story collection* Dubliners *describes the lives of ordinary people living in the Irish capital. His novel* A Portrait of the Artist as a Young Man *exemplifies his use of stream-of-consciousness, a technique that became popular among a number of writers. Joyce's masterpiece,* Ulysses *(1920), brought him both international acclaim and financial freedom. The following story is from* Dubliners.

The Boarding House

Mrs. Mooney was a butcher's daughter. She was a woman who was quite able to keep things to herself: a determined woman. She had married her father's foreman and opened a butcher's shop near Spring Gardens. But as soon as his father-in-law was dead Mr. Mooney began to go to the devil. He drank, plundered the till, ran headlong into debt. It was no use making him take the pledge: he was sure to break out again a few days after. By fighting his wife in the presence of customers and by buying bad meat he ruined his business. One night he went for his wife with the cleaver and she had to sleep in a neighbor's house.

After that they lived apart. She went to the priest and got a separation from him with care of the children. She would give him neither money nor food nor house-room; and so he was obliged to enlist himself as a sheriff's man. He was a shabby stooped little drunkard with a white face and a white moustache and white eyebrows, pencilled above his little eyes, which were pink-veined and raw; and all day long he sat in the bailiff's room, waiting to be put on a job. Mrs. Mooney, who had taken what remained of her money out of the butcher business and set up a boarding house in Hardwicke Street, was a big imposing woman. Her house had a floating population made up of tourists from Liverpool and the Isle of Man and, occasionally, *artistes* from the music halls. Its resident population was made up of clerks from the city. She governed her house cunningly and firmly, knew when to give credit, when to be stern and when to let things pass. All the resident young men spoke of her as *The Madam.*

Mrs. Mooney's young men paid fifteen shillings a week for board and lodgings (beer or stout at dinner excluded). They shared in common tastes and occupations and for this reason they were very chummy with one another. They discussed with one another the chances of favorites and outsiders. Jack Mooney, the Madam's son, who was clerk to a commission agent in Fleet Street, had the reputation of being a hard case. He was fond of using soldiers' obscenities: usually he came home in the small hours. When he met his friends he had always a good one to tell them and he was always sure to be on to a good thing—that is to say, a likely horse or a likely *artiste*. He was also handy with the mitts and sang comic songs. On Sunday nights there would often be a reunion in Mrs. Mooney's front drawing room. The music-hall *artistes* would oblige; and Sheridan played waltzes and polkas and vamped accompaniments. Polly Mooney, the Madam's daughter, would also sing. She sang:

I'm a . . . naughty girl.
You needn't sham:
You know I am.

Polly was a slim girl of nineteen, she had light soft hair and a small full mouth. Her eyes, which were grey with a shade of green through them, had a habit of glancing upwards when she spoke with anyone, which made her look like a little perverse madonna. Mrs. Mooney had first sent her daughter to be a typist in a corn-factor's office but, as a disreputable sheriff's man used to come every other day to the office, asking to be allowed to say a word to his daughter, she had taken her daughter home again and set her to do housework. As Polly was very lively the intention was to give her the run of the young men. Besides, young men like to feel that there is a young woman not very far away. Polly, of course, flirted with the young men but Mrs. Mooney, who was a shrewd judge, knew that the young men were only passing the time away: none of them meant business. Things went on so for a long time and Mrs. Mooney began to think of sending Polly back to typewriting when she noticed that something was going on between Polly and one of the young men. She watched the pair and kept her own counsel.

Polly knew that she was being watched, but still her mother's persistent silence could not be misunderstood. There had been no open complicity between mother and daughter, no open understanding but, though people in the house began to talk of the affair, still Mrs. Mooney did not intervene. Polly began to grow a little strange in her manner and the young man was evidently perturbed. At last, when she judged it to be the right moment, Mrs. Mooney intervened. She dealt with moral problems as a cleaver deals with meat: and in this case she had made up her mind.

It was a bright Sunday morning of early summer, promising heat, but with a fresh breeze blowing. All the windows of the boarding house were open and the lace curtains ballooned gently towards the street beneath the raised sashes. The belfry of George's Church sent out constant peals and worshippers, singly or in groups, traversed the little circus before the church, revealing their purpose by their self-contained demeanor no less than by the little volumes in their gloved hands. Breakfast was over in the boarding house and the table of the breakfast-room was covered with plates on which lay yellow streaks of eggs with morsels of bacon-fat and bacon-rind. Mrs. Mooney sat in the straw arm-chair and watched the servant Mary remove the breakfast things. She made Mary collect the crusts and pieces of broken bread to help to make Tuesday's bread-pudding. When the table was cleared, the broken bread collected, the sugar and butter safe under lock and key, she began to reconstruct the interview which she had had the night before with Polly. Things were as she had suspected: she had been frank in her questions and Polly had been frank in her answers. Both had been somewhat awkward, of course. She had been made awkward by her not wishing to receive the news in too cavalier a fashion or to seem to have connived and Polly had been made awkward not merely because allusions of that kind always made her awkward but also because she did not wish it to be thought that in her wise innocence she had divined the intention behind her mother's tolerance.

Mrs. Mooney glanced instinctively at the little gilt clock on the mantelpiece as soon as she had become aware through her revery that the bells of George's Church had stopped ringing. It was seventeen minutes past eleven: she would have lots of time to have the matter out with Mr. Doran and then catch short twelve at Marlborough Street. She was sure she would win. To begin with she had all the weight of social opinion on her side: she was an outraged mother. She had allowed him to live beneath her roof, assuming that he was a man of honor, and he had simply abused her hospitality. He was thirty-four or thirty-five years of age, so that youth could not be pleaded as his excuse; nor could ignorance be his excuse since he was a man who had seen something of the world. He had simply taken advantage of Polly's youth and inexperience: that was evident. The question was: What reparation would he make?

There must be reparation made in such cases. It is all very well for the man: he can go his ways as if nothing had happened, having had his moment of pleasure, but the girl has to bear the brunt. Some mothers would be content to patch up such an affair for a sum of money; she had known cases of it. But she would not do so. For her only one reparation could make up for the loss of her daughter's honor: marriage.

She counted all her cards again before sending Mary up to Mr. Doran's room to say that she wished to speak with him. She felt sure she would win. He was a serious young man, not rakish or loud-voiced like the others. If it had been Mr. Sheridan or Mr. Meade or Bantam Lyons her task would have been much harder. She did not think he would face publicity. All the lodgers in the house knew something of the affair; details had been invented by some. Besides, he had been employed for thirteen years in a great Catholic wine-merchant's office and publicity would mean for him, perhaps, the loss of his sit. Whereas if he agreed all might be well. She knew he had a good screw for one thing and she suspected he had a bit of stuff put by.

Nearly the half-hour! She stood up and surveyed herself in the pierglass. The decisive expression of her great florid face satisfied her and she thought of some mothers she knew who could not get their daughters off their hands.

Mr. Doran was very anxious indeed this Sunday morning. He had made two attempts to shave but his hand had been so unsteady that he had been obliged to desist. Three days' reddish beard fringed his jaws and every two or three minutes a mist gathered on his glasses so that he had to take them off and polish them with his pocket-handkerchief. The recollection of his confession of the night before was a cause of acute pain to him; the priest had drawn out every ridiculous detail of the affair and in the end had so magnified his sin that he was almost thankful at being afforded a loophole of reparation. The harm was done. What could he do now but marry her or run away? He could not brazen it out. The affair would be sure to be talked of and his employer would be certain to hear of it. Dublin is such a small city: everyone knows everyone else's business. He felt his heart leap warmly in his throat as he heard in his excited imagination old Mr. Leonard calling out in his rasping voice: *Send Mr Doran here, please.*

All his long years of service gone for nothing! All his industry and diligence thrown away! As a young man he had sown his wild oats, of course; he had boasted of his free-thinking and denied the existence of God to his companions in public-houses. But that was all passed and done with . . . nearly. He still bought a copy of *Reynold's Newspaper* every week but he attended to his religious duties and for nine-tenths of the year lived a regular life. He had money enough to settle down on; it was not that. But the family would look down on her. First of all there was her disreputable father and then her mother's boarding house was beginning to get a certain fame. He had a notion that he was being had. He could imagine his friends talking of the affair and laughing. She *was* a little vulgar; sometimes she said *I seen* and *If I had've known.* But what would grammar matter if he really loved her? He could not make up his mind whether to like her or despise her for what she had done. Of course, he had done it too. His instinct urged him to remain free, not to marry. Once you are married you are done for, it said.

While he was sitting helplessly on the side of the bed in shirt and trousers she tapped lightly at his door and entered. She told him all, that she had made a clean breast of it to her mother and that her mother would speak with him that morning. She cried and threw her arms round his neck, saying:

—O, Bob! Bob! What am I to do! What am I to do at all?

She would put an end to herself, she said.

He comforted her feebly, telling her not to cry, that it would be all right, never fear. He felt against his shirt the agitation of her bosom.

It was not altogether his fault that it had happened. He remembered well, with the curious patient memory of the celibate, the first casual caresses her dress, her breath, her fingers had given him. Then late one night as he was undressing for bed she had tapped at his door, timidly. She wanted to relight her candle at his for hers had been blown out by a gust. It was her bath night. She wore a loose open combing-jacket of printed flannel. Her white instep shone in the opening of her furry slippers and the blood glowed warmly behind her perfumed skin. From her hands and wrists too as she lit and steadied her candle a faint perfume arose.

On nights when he came in very late it was she who warmed up his dinner. He scarcely knew what he was eating, feeling her beside him alone, at night, in the sleeping house. And her thoughtfulness! If the night was anyway cold or wet or windy there was sure to be a little tumbler of punch ready for him. Perhaps they could be happy together. . . .

They used to go upstairs together on tiptoe, each with a candle, and on the third landing exchange reluctant good-nights. They used to kiss. He remembered well her eyes, the touch of her hand and his delirium. . . .

But delirium passes. He echoed her phrase, applying it to himself: *What am I to do?* The instinct of the celibate warned him to hold back. But the sin was there; even his sense of honor told him that reparation must be made for such a sin.

While he was sitting with her on the side of the bed Mary came to the door and said that the missus wanted to see him in the parlor. He stood up to put on his coat and waistcoat, more helpless than ever. When he was dressed he went over to her to comfort her. It would be all right, never fear. He left her crying on the bed and moaning softly: *O my God!*

Going down the stairs his glasses became so dimmed with moisture that he had to take them off and polish them. He longed to ascend through the roof and fly away to another country where he would never hear again of his trouble, and yet a force pushed him downstairs step by step. The implacable faces of his employer and of the Madam stared upon his discomfiture. On the last flight of stairs he passed Jack Mooney who was coming up from the pantry nursing two bottles of *Bass.* They saluted coldly; and the lover's eyes rested for a second or two on a thick bulldog face and a pair of thick short arms. When he reached the foot of the staircase he glanced up and saw Jack regarding him from the door of the return room.

Suddenly he remembered the night when one of the music-hall *artistes,* a little blond Londoner, had made a rather free allusion to Polly. The reunion had been almost broken up on account of Jack's violence. Everyone tried to quiet him. The music-hall *artiste,* a little paler than usual, kept smiling and saying that there was no harm meant: but Jack kept shouting at him that if any fellow tried that sort of a game on with *his* sister he'd bloody well put his teeth down his throat, so he would.

Polly sat for a little time on the side of the bed, crying. Then she dried her eyes and went over to the looking-glass. She dipped the end of the towel in the water-jug and refreshed her eyes with the cool water. She looked at herself in profile and readjusted a hairpin above her ear. Then she went back to the bed again and sat at the foot. She regarded the pillows for a long time and the sight of them awakened in her mind secret amiable memories. She rested the nape of her neck against the cool iron bed-rail and fell into a revery. There was no longer any perturbation visible on her face.

She waited on patiently, almost cheerfully, without alarm, her memories gradually giving place to hopes and visions of the future. Her hopes and visions were so intricate that she no longer saw the white pillows on which her gaze was fixed or remembered that she was waiting for anything.

At last she heard her mother calling. She started to her feet and ran to the banisters.

—Polly! Polly!

—Yes, mamma?

Come down, dear. Mr. Doran wants to speak to you. Then she remembered what she had been waiting for.

(1914)

QUESTIONS FOR CRITICAL THINKING AND WRITING

Experience

1. As you read the story, did you find yourself sympathizing more with Polly or Doran?

Interpretation

2. Do Mrs. Mooney and Polly manipulate the engagement?
3. Consider what the following images suggest about the main characters: Mrs. Mooney "dealt with moral problems as a cleaver deals with meat"; Polly is said to

"look like a little perverse madonna"; and "every two or three minutes" Mr. Doran had to polish his constantly fogging glasses.

4. Consider the time and place of the story. What impressions does the story give you about early twentieth-century social customs in Ireland?

Evaluation

5. Polly and Doran will be married. Do they love each other? If not, why marry?

Connection

6. Compare the role of the church in the lives of the characters in "The Boarding House" and in Marquez's "A Very Old Man with Enormous Wings."

Critical Thinking

7. Imagine what is said between Mrs. Mooney and Mr. Doran in the scene just before the end of the story when they meet in the parlor. Why do you think Joyce did not describe the specifics of their conversation?

JOYCE CAROL OATES

[b. 1938]

Joyce Carol Oates, who was raised in upstate New York, is one of the most prolific contemporary writers. Author of numerous novels, story collections, plays, and books of essays and criticism, Oates is also a poet and a professor at Princeton University. Her novels, which include A Bloodsmoor Romance *(1982),* You Must Remember This *(1987),* Black Water *(1992), and* The Tattooed Girl, *among nearly 40 others, are complemented by more than two dozen collections of short stories. A National Book Award winner in 1970, Oates is also director of Ontario Review Press, a small literary publisher. Her story, "Where Are You Going, Where Have You Been?" was the basis for the 1985 film* Smooth Talk.

Where Are You Going, Where Have You Been?

For Bob Dylan

Her name was Connie. She was fifteen and she had a quick nervous giggling habit of craning her neck to glance into mirrors, or checking other people's faces to make sure her own was all right. Her mother, who noticed everything and knew everything and who hadn't much reason any longer to look at her own face, always scolded Connie about it. "Stop gawking at yourself, who are you? You think you're so pretty?" she would say. Connie would raise her eyebrows at these familiar complaints and look right through her mother, into a shadowy vision of herself as she was right at that moment: she knew she was pretty and that was everything. Her mother had been pretty once too, if you could believe those old snapshots in the album, but now her looks were gone and that was why she was always after Connie.

"Why don't you keep your room clean like your sister? How've you got your hair fixed—what the hell stinks? Hair spray? You don't see your sister using that junk."

Her sister June was twenty-four and still lived at home. She was a secretary in the high school Connie attended, and if that wasn't bad enough—with her in the same building—she was so plain and chunky and steady that Connie had to hear her praised all the time by her mother and her mother's sisters. June did this, June did that, she saved money and helped clean the house and cooked and Connie couldn't do a thing, her mind was all filled with trashy daydreams. Their father was away at work most of the time and when he came home he wanted supper and he read the newspaper at supper and after supper he went to bed. He didn't bother talking much to them, but around his bent head Connie's mother kept picking at her until Connie wished her mother was dead and she herself was dead and it was all over. "She makes me want to throw up sometimes," she complained to her friends. She had a high, breathless, amused voice which made everything she said sound a little forced, whether it was sincere or not.

There was one good thing: June went places with girl friends of hers, girls who were just as plain and steady as she, and so when Connie wanted to do that her mother had no objections. The father of Connie's best girl friend drove the girls the three miles to town and left them off at a shopping plaza, so that they could walk through the stores or go to a movie, and when he came to pick them up again at eleven he never bothered to ask what they had done.

They must have been familiar sights, walking around that shopping plaza in their shorts and flat ballerina slippers that always scuffed the sidewalk, with charm bracelets jingling on their thin wrists; they would lean together to whisper and laugh secretly if someone passed by who amused or interested them. Connie had long dark blond hair that drew anyone's eye to it, and she wore part of it pulled up on her head and puffed out and the rest of it she let fall down her back. She wore a pull-over jersey blouse that looked one way when she was at home and another way when she was away from home. Everything about her had two sides to it, one for home and one for anywhere that was not home: her walk that could be childlike and bobbing, or languid enough to make anyone think she was hearing music in her head, her mouth which was pale and smirking most of the time, but bright and pink on these evenings out, her laugh which was cynical and drawling at home—"Ha, ha, very funny"—but high-pitched and nervous anywhere else, like the jingling of the charms on her bracelet.

Sometimes they did go shopping or to a movie, but sometimes they went across the highway, ducking fast across the busy road, to a drive-in restaurant where older kids hung out. The restaurant was shaped like a big bottle, though squatter than a real bottle, and on its cap was a revolving figure of a grinning boy who held a hamburger aloft. One night in mid-summer they ran across, breathless with daring, and right away someone leaned out a car window and invited them over, but it was just a boy from high school they didn't like. It made them feel good to be able to ignore him. They went up through the maze of parked and cruising cars to the bright-lit, fly-infested restaurant, their faces pleased and expectant as if they were entering a sacred building that loomed out of the night to give them what haven and what blessing they yearned for. They sat at the counter and crossed their legs at the ankles, their thin shoulders rigid with excitement, and listened to the music that made everything so good: the music was always in the background like music at a church service, it was something to depend upon.

A boy named Eddie came in to talk with them. He sat backwards on his stool, turning himself jerkily around in semi-circles and then stopping and turning again, and after a while he asked Connie if she would like something to eat. She said she did and so she tapped her friend's arm on her way out—her friend pulled her face up into a brave droll look—and Connie said she would meet her at eleven, across the way. "I just hate to leave her like that," Connie said earnestly, but the boy said that she wouldn't be alone for long. So they went out to his car and on the way Connie couldn't help but let her eyes wander over the windshields and faces all around her, her face gleaming with a joy that had nothing to do with Eddie or even this place; it might have been the music. She drew her shoulders up and sucked in her breath with the pure pleasure of being alive, and just at that moment she happened to glance at a face just a few feet from hers. It was a boy with shaggy black hair, in a convertible jalopy painted gold. He stared at her and then his lips widened into a grin. Connie slit her eyes at him and turned away, but she couldn't help glancing back and there he was still watching her. He wagged a finger and laughed and said, "Gonna get you, baby," and Connie turned away again without Eddie noticing anything.

She spent three hours with him, at the restaurant where they ate hamburgers and drank Cokes in wax cups that were always sweating, and then down an alley a mile or so away, and when he left her off at five to eleven only the movie house was still open at the plaza. Her girl friend was there, talking with a boy. When Connie came up the two girls smiled at each other and Connie said, "How was the movie?" and the girl said, "You should know." They rode off with the girl's father, sleepy and pleased, and Connie couldn't help but look at the darkened shopping plaza with its big empty parking lot and its signs that were faded and ghostly now, and over at the drive-in restaurant where cars were still circling tirelessly. She couldn't hear the music at this distance.

Next morning June asked her how the movie was and Connie said, "So-so."

She and that girl and occasionally another girl went out several times a week that way, and the rest of the time Connie spent around the house—it was summer vacation—getting in her mother's way and thinking, dreaming, about the boys she met. But all the boys fell back and dissolved into a single face that was not even a face, but an idea, a feeling, mixed up with the urgent insistent pounding of the music and the humid night air of July. Connie's mother kept dragging her back to the daylight by finding things for her to do or saying, suddenly, "What's this about the Pettinger girl?"

And Connie would say nervously, "Oh, her. That dope." She always drew thick clear lines between herself and such girls, and her mother was simple and kindly enough to believe her. Her mother was so simple, Connie thought, that it was maybe cruel to fool her so much. Her mother went scuffling around the house in old bedroom slippers and complained over the telephone to one sister about the other, then the other called up and the two of them complained about the third one. If June's name was mentioned her mother's tone was approving, and if Connie's name was mentioned it was disapproving. This did not really mean she disliked Connie and actually Connie thought that her mother preferred her to June because she was prettier, but the two of them kept up a pretense of exasperation, a sense that they were tugging and struggling over something of little value to either of them. Sometimes, over coffee, they were almost friends, but something would come up—some vexation that was like a fly buzzing suddenly around their heads—and their faces went hard with contempt.

One Sunday Connie got up at eleven—none of them bothered with church—and washed her hair so that it could dry all day long, in the sun. Her parents and sister were going to a barbecue at an aunt's house and Connie said no, she wasn't interested, rolling her eyes to let her mother know just what she thought of it. "Stay home alone then," her mother said sharply. Connie sat out back in a lawn chair and watched them drive away, her father quiet and bald, hunched around so that he could back the car out, her mother with a look that was still angry and not at all softened through the windshield, and in the back seat poor old June all dressed up as if she didn't know what a barbecue was, with all the running yelling kids and the flies. Connie sat with her eyes closed in the sun, dreaming and dazed with the warmth about her as if this were a kind of love, the caresses of love, and her mind slipped over onto thoughts of the boy she had been with the night before and how nice he had been, how sweet it always was, not the way someone like June would suppose but sweet, gentle, the way it was in movies and promised in songs; and when she opened her eyes she hardly knew where she was, the back yard ran off into weeds and a fence-line of trees and behind it the sky was perfectly blue and still. The asbestos "ranch house" that was now three years old startled her—it looked small. She shook her head as if to get awake.

It was too hot. She went inside the house and turned on the radio to drown out the quiet. She sat on the edge of her bed, barefoot, and listened for an hour and a half to a program called XYZ Sunday Jamboree, record after record of hard, fast, shrieking songs she sang along with, interspersed by exclamations from "Bobby King": "An' look here you girls at Napoleon's—Son and Charley want you to pay real close attention to this song coming up!"

And Connie paid close attention herself, bathed in a glow of slow-pulsed joy that seemed to rise mysteriously out of the music itself and lay languidly about the airless little room, breathed in and breathed out with each gentle rise and fall of her chest.

After a while she heard a car coming up the drive. She sat up at once, startled, because it couldn't be her father so soon. The gravel kept crunching all the way in from the road—the driveway was long—and Connie ran to the window. It was a car she didn't know. It was an open jalopy, painted a bright gold that caught the sunlight opaquely. Her heart began to pound and her fingers snatched at her hair, checking it, and she whispered "Christ, Christ," wondering how bad she looked. The car came to a stop at the side door and the horn sounded four short taps as if this were a signal Connie knew.

She went into the kitchen and approached the door slowly, then hung out the screen door, her bare toes curling down off the step. There were two boys in the car and now she recognized the driver: he had shaggy, shabby black hair that looked crazy as a wig and he was grinning at her.

"I ain't late, am I?" he said.

"Who the hell do you think you are?" Connie said.

"Toldja I'd be out, didn't I?"

"I don't even know who you are."

She spoke sullenly, careful to show no interest or pleasure, and he spoke in a fast bright monotone. Connie looked past him to the other boy, taking her time. He had fair brown hair, with a lock that fell onto his forehead. His sideburns gave him a fierce, embarrassed look, but so far he hadn't even bothered to glance at her. Both boys wore sunglasses. The driver's glasses were metallic and mirrored everything in miniature.

"You wanta come for a ride?" he said.

Connie smirked and let her hair fall loose over one shoulder.

"Don'tcha like my car? New paint job," he said. "Hey."

"What?"

"You're cute."

She pretended to fidget, chasing flies away from the door.

"Don'tcha believe me, or what?" he said.

"Look, I don't even know who you are," Connie said in disgust.

"Hey, Ellie's got a radio, see. Mine's broke down." He lifted his friend's arm and showed her the little transistor the boy was holding, and now Connie began to hear the music. It was the same program that was playing inside the house.

"Bobby King?" she said.

"I listen to him all the time. I think he's great."

"He's kind of great," Connie said reluctantly.

"Listen, that guy's *great*. He knows where the action is."

Connie blushed a little, because the glasses made it impossible for her to see just what this boy was looking at. She couldn't decide if she liked him or if he was just a jerk, and so she dawdled in the doorway and wouldn't come down or go back inside. She said, "What's all that stuff painted on your car?"

"Can'tcha read it?" He opened the door very carefully, as if he was afraid it might fall off. He slid out just as carefully, planting his feet firmly on the ground, the tiny metallic world in his glasses slowing down like gelatine hardening and in the midst of it Connie's bright green blouse. "This here is my name, to begin with," he said. ARNOLD FRIEND was written in tarlike black letters on the side, with a drawing of a round grinning face that reminded Connie of a pumpkin, except it wore sunglasses. "I wanta introduce myself, I'm Arnold Friend and that's my real name and I'm gonna be your friend, honey, and inside the car's Ellie Oscar, he's kinda shy." Ellie brought his transistor radio up to his shoulder and balanced it there. "Now these numbers are a secret code, honey," Arnold Friend explained. He read off the numbers 33, 19, 17 and raised his eyebrows at her to see what she thought of that, but she didn't think much of it. The left rear fender had been smashed and around it was written, on the gleaming gold background: DONE BY CRAZY WOMAN DRIVER. Connie had to laugh at that. Arnold Friend was pleased at her laughter and looked up at her. "Around the other side's a lot more—you wanta come and see them?"

"No."

"Why not?"

"Why should I?"

"Don'tcha wanta see what's on the car? Don'tcha wanta go for a ride?"

"I don't know."

"Why not?"

"I got things to do."

"Like what?"

"Things."

He laughed as if she had said something funny. He slapped his thighs. He was standing in a strange way, leaning back against the car as if he were balancing himself. He wasn't tall, only an inch or so taller than she would be if she came down to him. Connie liked the way he was dressed, which was the way all of them dressed: tight faded jeans stuffed into black, scuffed boots, a belt that pulled his waist in and showed how lean he was, and a white pull-over shirt that was a little soiled and showed the hard small muscles of his arms and shoulders. He looked as if he probably did hard work, lifting and carrying things. Even his neck looked muscular. And his face was a familiar face, somehow: the jaw and chin and cheeks slightly darkened, because he hadn't shaved for a day or two, and the nose long and hawk-like, sniffing as if she were a treat he was going to gobble up and it was all a joke.

"Connie, you ain't telling the truth. This is your day set aside for a ride with me and you know it," he said, still laughing. The way he straightened and recovered from his fit of laughing showed that it had been all fake.

"How do you know what my name is?" she said suspiciously.

"It's Connie."

"Maybe and maybe not."

"I know my Connie," he said, wagging his finger. Now she remembered him even better, back at the restaurant, and her cheeks warmed at the thought of how she sucked in her breath just at the moment she passed him—how she must have looked to him. And he had remembered her. "Ellie and I come out here especially for you," he said. "Ellie can sit in back. How about it?"

"Where?"

"Where what?"

"Where're we going?"

He looked at her. He took off the sunglasses and she saw how pale the skin around his eyes was, like holes that were not in shadow but instead in light. His eyes were chips of broken glass that catch the light in an amiable way. He smiled. It was as if the idea of going for a ride somewhere, to some place, was a new idea to him.

"Just for a ride, Connie sweetheart."

"I never said my name was Connie," she said.

"But I know what it is. I know your name and all about you, lots of things," Arnold Friend said. He had not moved yet but stood still leaning back against the side of his jalopy. "I took a special interest in you, such a pretty girl, and found out all about you like I know your parents and sister are gone somewheres and I know where and how long they're going to be gone, and I know who you were with last night, and your best girl friend's name is Betty. Right?"

He spoke in a simple lilting voice, exactly as if he were reciting the words to a song. His smile assured her that everything was fine. In the car Ellie turned up the volume on his radio and did not bother to look around at them.

"Ellie can sit in the back seat," Arnold Friend said. He indicated his friend with a casual jerk of his chin, as if Ellie did not count and she should not bother with him.

"How'd you find out all that stuff?" Connie said.

"Listen: Betty Schultz and Tony Fitch and Jimmy Pettinger and Nancy Pettinger," he said, in a chant. "Raymond Stanley and Bob Hutter—"

"Do you know all those kids?"

"I know everybody."

"Look, you're kidding. You're not from around here."

"Sure."

"But—how come we never saw you before?"

"Sure you saw me before," he said. He looked down at his boots, as if he were a little offended. "You just don't remember."

"I guess I'd remember you," Connie said.

"Yeah?" He looked up at this, beaming. He was pleased. He began to mark time with the music from Ellie's radio, tapping his fists lightly together. Connie looked away from his smile to the car, which was painted so bright it almost hurt her eyes to look at it. She looked at that name, ARNOLD FRIEND. And up at the front fender was an expression that was familiar—MAN THE FLYING SAUCERS. It was an expression kids had used the year before, but didn't use this year. She looked at it for a while as if the words meant something to her that she did not yet know.

"What're you thinking about? Huh?" Arnold Friend demanded. "Not worried about your hair blowing around in the car, are you?"

"No."

"Think I maybe can't drive good?"

"How do I know?"

"You're a hard girl to handle. How come?" he said. "Don't you know I'm your friend? Didn't you see me put my sign in the air when you walked by?"

"What sign?"

"My sign." And he drew an X in the air, leaning out toward her. They were maybe ten feet apart. After his hand fell back to his side the X was still in the air, almost visible. Connie let the screen door close and stood perfectly still inside it, listening to the music from her radio and the boy's blend together. She stared at Arnold Friend. He stood there so stiffly relaxed, pretending to be relaxed, with one hand idly on the door handle as if he were keeping himself up that way and had no intention of ever moving again. She recognized most things about him, the tight jeans that showed his thighs and buttocks and the greasy leather boots and the tight shirt, and even that slippery friendly smile of his, that sleepy dreamy smile that all the boys used to get across ideas they didn't want to put into words. She recognized all this and also the singsong way he talked, slightly mocking, kidding, but serious and a little melancholy, and she recognized the way he tapped one fist against the other in homage to the perpetual music behind him. But all these things did not come together.

She said suddenly, "Hey, how old are you?"

His smile faded. She could see then that he wasn't a kid, he was much older—thirty, maybe more. At this knowledge her heart began to pound faster.

"That's a crazy thing to ask. Can'tcha see I'm your own age?"

"Like hell you are."

"Or maybe a coupla years older, I'm eighteen."

"Eighteen?" she said doubtfully.

He grinned to reassure her and lines appeared at the corners of his mouth. His teeth were big and white. He grinned so broadly his eyes became slits and she saw how thick the lashes were, thick and black as if painted with a black tar-like material. Then he seemed to become embarrassed, abruptly, and looked over his shoulder at Ellie. "*Him*, he's crazy," he said. "Ain't he a riot, he's a nut, a real character." Ellie was still listening to the music. His sunglasses told nothing about what he was thinking. He wore a bright orange shirt unbuttoned halfway to show his chest, which was a pale, bluish chest and not muscular like Arnold Friend's. His shirt collar was turned up all around and the very tips of the collar pointed out past his chin as if they were protecting him. He was pressing the transistor radio up against his ear and sat there in a kind of daze, right in the sun.

"He's kinda strange," Connie said.

"Hey, she says you're kinda strange! Kinda strange!" Arnold Friend cried. He pounded on the car to get Ellie's attention. Ellie turned for the first time and Connie saw with shock that he wasn't kid either—he had a fair, hairless face, cheeks reddened slightly as if the veins grew too close to the surface of his skin, the face of a forty-year-old baby. Connie felt a wave of dizziness rise in her at this sight and she stared at him as if waiting for something to change the shock of the moment, make it all right again. Ellie's lips kept shaping words, mumbling along, with the words blasting in his ear.

"Maybe you two better go away," Connie said faintly.

"What? How come?" Arnold Friend cried. "We come out here to take you for a ride. It's Sunday." He had the voice of the man on the radio now. It was the same voice, Connie thought. "Don'tcha know it's Sunday all day and honey, no matter who you were with last night today you're with Arnold Friend and don't you forget it!—Maybe you better step out here," he said, and this last was in a different voice. It was a little flatter, as if the heat was finally getting to him.

"No. I got things to do."

"Hey."

"You two better leave."

"We ain't leaving until you come with us."

"Like hell I am—"

"Connie, don't fool around with me. I mean, I mean, don't fool *around*," he said, shaking his head. He laughed incredulously. He placed his sunglasses on top of his head, carefully, as if he were indeed wearing a wig, and brought the stems down behind his ears. Connie stared at him, another wave of dizziness and fear rising in her so that for a moment he wasn't even in focus but was just a blur, standing there against his gold car, and she had the idea that he had driven up the driveway all right but had come from nowhere before that and belonged nowhere and that everything about him and even about the music that was so familiar to her was only half real.

"If my father comes and sees you—"

"He ain't coming. He's at the barbecue."

"How do you know that?"

"Aunt Tillie's. Right now they're—uh—they're drinking. Sitting around," he said vaguely, squinting as if he were staring all the way to town and over to Aunt Tillie's backyard. Then the vision seemed to get clear and he nodded energetically. "Yeah. Sitting around. There's your sister in a blue dress, huh? And high heels, the poor sad bitch—nothing like you, sweetheart! And your mother's helping some fat woman with the corn, they're cleaning the corn—husking the corn—"

"What fat woman?" Connie cried.

"How do I know what fat woman. I don't know every goddam fat woman in the world!" Arnold Friend laughed.

"Oh, that's Mrs. Hornby. . . . Who invited her?" Connie said. She felt a little lightheaded. Her breath was coming quickly.

"She's too fat. I don't like them fat. I like them the way you are, honey," he said, smiling sleepily at her. They stared at each other for a while, through the screen door. He said softly, "Now what you're going to do is this: you're going to come out that door. You're going to sit up front with me and Ellie's going to sit in the back, the hell with Ellie, right? This isn't Ellie's date. You're my date. I'm your lover, honey."

"What? You're crazy—"

"Yes, I'm your lover. You don't know what that is but you will," he said. "I know that too. I know all about you. But look: it's real nice and you couldn't ask for nobody better than me, or more polite. I always keep my word. I'll tell you how it is, I'm always nice at first, the first time. I'll hold you so tight you won't think you have to try to get away or pretend anything because you'll know you can't. And I'll come inside you where it's all secret and you'll give in to me and you'll love me—"

"Shut up! You're crazy!" Connie said. She backed away from the door. She put her hands against her ears as if she'd heard something terrible, something not meant for her. "People don't talk like that, you're crazy," she muttered. Her heart was almost too big now for her chest and its pumping made sweat break out all over her. She looked out to see Arnold Friend pause and then take a step toward the porch lurching. He almost fell. But, like a clever drunken man, he managed to catch his balance. He wobbled in his high boots and grabbed hold of one of the porch posts.

"Honey?" he said. "You still listening?"

"Get the hell out of here!"

"Be nice, honey. Listen."

"I'm going to call the police—"

He wobbled again and out of the side of his mouth came a fast spat curse, an aside not meant for her to hear. But even this "Christ!" sounded forced. Then he began to smile again. She watched this smile come, awkward as if he were smiling from inside a mask. His whole face was a mask, she thought wildly, tanned down onto his throat but then running out as if he had plastered makeup on his face but had forgotten about his throat.

"Honey—? Listen, here's how it is. I always tell the truth and I promise you this: I ain't coming in that house after you."

"You better not! I'm going to call the police if you—if you don't—"

"Honey," he said, talking right through her voice, "honey, I'm not coming in there but you are coming out here. You know why?"

She was panting. The kitchen looked like a place she had never seen before, some room she had run inside but which wasn't good enough, wasn't going to help her. The kitchen window had never had a curtain, after three years, and there were dishes in the sink for her to do—probably—and if you ran your hand across the table you'd probably feel something sticky there.

"You listening, honey? Hey?"

"—going to call the police—"

"Soon as you touch the phone I don't need to keep my promise and can come inside. You won't want that."

She rushed forward and tried to lock the door. Her fingers were shaking. "But why lock it," Arnold Friend said gently, talking right into her face. "It's just a screen door. It's just nothing." One of his boots was at a strange angle, as if his foot wasn't in it. It pointed out to the left, bent at the ankle. "I mean, anybody can break through a screen door and glass and wood and iron or anything else if he needs to, anybody at all and specially Arnold Friend. If the place got lit up with a fire honey you'd come running out into my arms, right into my arms and safe at home—like you knew I was your lover and'd stopped fooling around. I don't mind a nice shy girl but I don't like no fooling around." Part of those words were spoken with a slight rhythmic lilt, and Connie somehow recognized them—the echo of a song from last year, about a girl rushing into her boyfriend's arms and coming home again—

Connie stood barefoot on the linoleum floor, staring at him. "What do you want?" she whispered.

"I want you," he said.

"What?"

"Seen you that night and thought, that's the one, yes sir. I never needed to look any more."

"But my father's coming back. He's coming to get me. I had to wash my hair first—" She spoke in a dry, rapid voice, hardly raising it for him to hear.

"No, your daddy is not coming and yes, you had to wash your hair and you washed it for me. It's nice and shining and all for me, I thank you, sweetheart," he said, with a mock bow, but again he almost lost his balance. He had to bend and adjust his boots. Evidently his feet did not go all the way down; the boots must have been stuffed with something so that he would seem taller. Connie stared out at him and behind him Ellie in the car, who seemed to be looking off toward Connie's right, into nothing. This Ellie said, pulling the words out of the air one after another as if he were just discovering them, "You want me to pull out the phone?"

"Shut your mouth and keep it shut," Arnold Friend said, his face red from bending over or maybe from embarrassment because Connie had seen his boots. "This ain't none of your business."

"What—what are you doing? What do you want?" Connie said. "If I call the police they'll get you, they'll arrest you—"

"Promise was not to come in unless you touch that phone, and I'll keep that promise," he said. He resumed his erect position and tried to force his shoulders back. He sounded like a hero in a movie, declaring something important. He spoke too loudly and it was as if he were speaking to someone behind Connie. "I ain't made plans for coming in that house where I don't belong but just for you to come out to me, the way you should. Don't you know who I am?"

"You're crazy," she whispered. She backed away from the door but did not want to go into another part of the house, as if this would give him permission to come through the door. "What do you . . . You're crazy, you . . ."

"Huh? What're you saying, honey?"

Her eyes darted everywhere in the kitchen. She could not remember what it was, this room.

"This is how it is, honey: you come out and we'll drive away, have a nice ride. But if you don't come out we're gonna wait till your people come home and then they're all going to get it."

"You want that telephone pulled out?" Ellie said. He held the radio away from his ear and grimaced, as if without the radio the air was too much for him.

"I toldja shut up, Ellie," Arnold Friend said, "you're deaf, get a hearing aid, right? Fix yourself up. This little girl's no trouble and's gonna be nice to me, so Ellie keep to yourself, this ain't your date—right? Don't hem in on me. Don't hog. Don't crush. Don't bird dog. Don't trail me," he said in a rapid meaningless voice, as if he were running through all the expressions he'd learned but was no longer sure which one of them was in style, then rushing on to new ones, making them up with his eyes closed, "Don't crawl under my fence, don't squeeze in my chipmunk hole, don't sniff my glue, suck my popsicle, keep your own greasy fingers on yourself!" He shaded his eyes and peered in at Connie, who was backed against the kitchen table. "Don't mind him honey he's just a creep. He's a dope. Right? I'm the boy for you and like I said you come out here nice like a lady and give me your hand, and nobody else gets hurt, I mean, your nice old bald-headed daddy and your mummy and your sister in her high heels. Because listen: why bring them in this?"

"Leave me alone," Connie whispered.

"Hey, you know that old woman down the road, the one with the chickens and stuff—you know her?"

"She's dead!"

"Dead? What? You know her?" Arnold Friend said.

"She's dead—"

'Don't you like her?"

"She's dead—she's—she isn't here any more—"

"But don't you like her, I mean, you got something against her? Some grudge or something?" Then his voice dipped as if he were conscious of rudeness. He touched the sunglasses perched on top of his head as if to make sure they were still there. "Now you be a good girl."

"What are you going to do?"

"Just two things, or maybe three," Arnold Friend said. "But I promise it won't last long and you'll like me that way you get to like people you're close to. You will. It's all over for you here, so come on out. You don't want your people in any trouble, do you?"

She turned and bumped against a chair or something, hurting her leg, but she ran into the back room and picked up the telephone. Something roared in her ear, a tiny roaring, and she was so sick with fear that she could do nothing but listen to it—the telephone was clammy and very heavy and her fingers groped down to the dial but were too weak to touch it. She began to scream into the phone, into the roaring. She cried out, she cried for her mother, she felt her breath start jerking back and forth in her lungs as if it were something Arnold Friend were stabbing her with again and again with no tenderness. A noisy sorrowful wailing rose all about her and she was locked inside it the way she was locked inside the house.

After a while she could hear again. She was sitting on the floor with her wet back against the wall.

Arnold Friend was saying from the door, "That's a good girl. Put the phone back."

She kicked the phone away from her.

"No, honey. Pick it up. Put it back right."

She picked it up and put it back. The dial tone stopped.

"That's a good girl. Now come outside."

She was hollow with what had been fear, but what was now just an emptiness. All that screaming had blasted it out of her. She sat, one leg cramped under her, and deep inside her brain was something like a pinpoint of light that kept going and would not let her relax. She thought, I'm not going to see my mother again. She thought, I'm not going to sleep in my bed again. Her bright green blouse was all wet.

Arnold Friend said, in a gentle-loud voice that was like a stage voice, "The place where you came from ain't there any more, and where you had in mind to go is cancelled out. This place you are now—inside your daddy's house—is nothing but a cardboard box I can knock down any time. You know that and always did know it. You hear me?"

She thought, I have got to think. I have to know what to do.

"We'll go out to a nice field, out in the country here where it smells so nice and it's sunny," Arnold Friend said. "I'll have my arms around you so you won't need to try to get away and I'll show you what love is like, what it does. The hell with this house! It looks solid all right," he said. He ran a fingernail down the screen and the noise did not make Connie shiver, as it would have the day before. "Now put your hand on your heart, honey. Feel that? That feels solid too but we know better, be nice to me, be sweet like you can because what else is there for a girl like you but to be sweet and pretty and give in?—and get away before her people come back?"

She felt her pounding heart. Her hand seemed to enclose it. She thought for the first time in her life that it was nothing that was hers, that belonged to her, but just a pounding, living thing inside this body that wasn't really hers either.

"You don't want them to get hurt," Arnold Friend went on. "Now get up, honey. Get up all by yourself."

She stood up.

"Now turn this way. That's right. Come over here to me—Ellie, put that away, didn't I tell you? You dope. You miserable creepy dope," Arnold Friend said. His words were not angry but only part of an incantation. The incantation was kindly. "Now come out through the kitchen to me honey and let's see a smile, try it, you're a brave sweet little girl and now they're eating corn and hotdogs cooked to bursting over an outdoor fire, and they don't know one thing about you and never did and honey you're better than them because not a one of them would have done this for you."

Connie felt the linoleum under her feet; it was cool. She brushed her hair back out of her eyes. Arnold Friend let go of the post tentatively and opened his arms for her, his elbows pointing in toward each other and his wrists limp, to show that this was an embarrassed embrace and a little mocking, he didn't want to make her self-conscious.

She put out her hand against the screen. She watched herself push the door slowly open as if she were safe back somewhere in the other doorway, watching this body and this head of long hair moving out into the sunlight where Arnold Friend waited.

"My sweet little blue-eyed girl," he said, in a half-sung sigh that had nothing to do with her brown eyes but was taken up just the same by the vast sunlit reaches of the land behind him and on all sides of him, so much land that Connie had never seen before and did not recognize except to know that she was going to it.

(1970)

QUESTIONS FOR CRITICAL THINKING AND WRITING

Experience

1. To what extent did you find the story interesting, perhaps even engaging or entertaining? Explain.
2. To what extent can you relate to Connie, to June, to Arnold Friend, or to Connie's mother? Explain.

Interpretation

3. How does Oates characterize Connie? Why do you think Oates gives Connie a sister like June?
4. How does Oates help us understand Connie's thoughts and feelings?

5. How is Arnold Friend characterized? What do you make of his name?
6. How does Oates create and sustain interest in the story's action and outcome? What happens in the end? What does the story's final sentence suggest?
7. Why and how is music an important element of the story?
8. Explain the significance of the story's title.

Evaluation

9. What are Connie's values? What is important to her? How do her values compare with those of her sister and mother?
10. What values animate Arnold Friend? To what extent does Arnold represent danger, threat, or menace?

Connection

11. Compare the way Oates builds suspense in this story with the way Faulkner builds suspense in "Barn Burning." Which method is easier to follow? Why?

Critical Thinking

12. What do you think will happen to Connie? Why?

TIM O'BRIEN

[b. 1947]

Tim O'Brien was born in Austin, Minnesota, and was educated at Macalester College and Harvard University. Drafted into the army, O'Brien served as an infantryman during the Vietnam War. A memoir, If I Die in a Combat Zone *(1973), draws on his military experience, as does much of his fiction. His novel* Going After Cacciato *won the national Book Award for fiction in 1989. First published in 1986, "The Things They Carried" joined a series of other interlocking stories, including one entitled "How to Tell a True War Story." "The Things They Carried" provides ample evidence that Tim O'Brien has done exactly that.*

The Things They Carried

First Lieutenant Jimmy Cross carried letters from a girl named Martha, a junior at Mount Sebastian College in New Jersey. They were not love letters, but Lieutenant Cross was hoping, so he kept them folded in plastic at the bottom of his rucksack. In the late afternoon, after a day's march, he would dig his foxhole, wash his hands under a canteen, unwrap the letters, hold them with the tips of his fingers, and spend the last hour of light pretending. He would imagine romantic camping trips into the White Mountains in New Hampshire. He would sometimes taste the envelope flaps, knowing her tongue had been there. More than anything, he wanted Martha to love him as he loved her, but the letters were mostly chatty, elusive on the matter of love. She was a virgin, he was almost sure. She was an English major at Mount Sebastian, and she wrote beautifully about her professors and roommates and midterm exams, about her respect for Chaucer and her great affection for Virginia Woolf. She often quoted lines of poetry; she never mentioned the war, except to say, Jimmy, take care of yourself. The letters weighed ten ounces. They were signed "Love, Martha," but Lieutenant Cross understood that "Love" was only a way of signing and did not mean what he sometimes pretended it meant. At dusk, he would carefully return the letters to his rucksack. Slowly, a bit distracted, he would get up and move among his men, checking the perimeter, then at full dark he would return to his hole and watch the night and wonder if Martha was a virgin.

The things they carried were largely determined by necessity. Among the necessities or near necessities were P-38 can openers, pocket knives, heat tabs, wrist watches, dog tags, mosquito repellant, chewing gum, candy, cigarettes, salt tablets, packets of Kool-Aid, lighters, matches, sewing kits, Military Payment Certificates, C rations, and two or three canteens of water. Together, these items weighed between fifteen and twenty pounds, depending upon a man's habits or rate of metabolism. Henry Dobbins, who was a big man, carried extra rations; he was especially fond of canned peaches in heavy syrup over pound cake. Dave Jensen, who practiced field hygiene, carried a toothbrush, dental floss, and several hotel-size bars of soap he'd stolen on R&R in Sydney, Australia. Ted Lavender, who was scared, carried tranquilizers until he was shot in the head outside the village of Than Khe in mid-April. By necessity, and because it was SOP,° they all carried steel helmets that weighed five pounds including the liner and camouflage cover. They carried the standard fatigue jackets and trousers. Very few carried underwear. On their feet they carried jungle boots—2.1 pounds—and Dave Jensen carried three pairs of socks and a can of Dr. Scholl's foot powder as a precaution against trench foot. Until he was shot, Ted Lavender carried six or seven ounces of premium dope, which for him was a necessity. Mitchell Sanders, the RTO,° carried condoms. Norman Bowker carried a diary. Rat Kiley carried comic books. Kiowa, a devout Baptist, carried an illustrated New Testament that had been presented to him by his father, who taught Sunday school in Oklahoma City, Oklahoma. As a hedge against bad times, however, Kiowa also carried his grandmother's distrust of the white man, his grandfather's old hunting hatchet. Necessity dictated. Because the land was mined and booby-trapped, it was SOP for each man to carry a steel-centered, nylon-covered flak jacket, which weighed 6.7 pounds, but which on hot days seemed much heavier. Because you could die so quickly, each man carried at least one large compress bandage, usually in the helmet band for easy access. Because the nights were cold, and because the monsoons were wet, each carried a green plastic poncho that could be used as a raincoat or ground sheet or makeshift tent. With its quilted liner, the poncho weighed almost two pounds, but it was worth every ounce. In April, for instance, when Ted Lavender was shot, they used his pon-

SOP *standard operating procedure* ***RTO*** *radiotelephone operator* cho to wrap him up, then to carry him across the paddy, then to lift him into the chopper that took him away.

They were called legs or grunts.

To carry something was to "hump" it, as when Lieutenant Jimmy Cross humped his love for Martha up the hills and through the swamps. In its intransitive form, "to hump" meant "to walk," or "to march," but it implied burdens far beyond the intransitive.

Almost everyone humped photographs. In his wallet, Lieutenant Cross carried two photographs of Martha. The first was a Kodachrome snapshot signed "Love," though he knew better. She stood against a brick wall. Her eyes were gray and neutral, her lips slightly open as she stared straight-on at the camera. At night, sometimes, Lieutenant Cross wondered who had taken the picture, because he knew she had boyfriends, because he loved her so much, and because he could see the shadow of the picture taker spreading out against the brick wall. The second photograph had been clipped from the 1968 Mount Sebastian yearbook. It was an action shot—women's volleyball—and Martha was bent horizontal to the floor, reaching, the palms of her hands in sharp focus, the tongue taut, the expression frank and competitive. There was no visible sweat. She wore white gym shorts. Her legs, he thought, were almost certainly the legs of a virgin, dry and without hair, the left knee cocked and carrying her entire weight, which was just over one hundred pounds. Lieutenant Cross remembered touching that left knee. A dark theater, he remembered, and the movie was *Bonnie and Clyde,* and Martha wore a tweed skirt, and during the final scene, when he touched her knee, she turned and looked at him in a sad, sober way that made him pull his hand back, but he would always remember the feel of the tweed skirt and the knee beneath it and the sound of the gunfire that killed Bonnie and Clyde, how embarrassing it was, how slow and oppressive. He remembered kissing her good night at the dorm door. Right then, he thought, he should've done something brave. He should've carried her up the stairs to her room and tied her to the bed and touched that left knee all night long. He should've risked it. Whenever he looked at the photographs, he thought of new things he should've done.

What they carried was partly a function of rank, partly of field specialty.

As a first lieutenant and platoon leader, Jimmy Cross carried a compass, maps, code books, binoculars, and a .45-caliber pistol that weighed 2.9 pounds fully loaded. He carried a strobe light and the responsibility for the lives of his men.

As an RTO, Mitchell Sanders carried the PRC-25 radio, a killer, twenty-six pounds with its battery.

As a medic, Rat Kiley carried a canvas satchel filled with morphine and plasma and malaria tablets and surgical tape and comic books and all the things a medic must carry, including M&M's for especially bad wounds, for a total weight of nearly twenty pounds.

As a big man, therefore a machine gunner, Henry Dobbins carried the M-60, which weighed twenty-three pounds unloaded, but which was almost always loaded. In addition, Dobbins carried between ten and fifteen pounds of ammunition draped in belts across his chest and shoulders.

As PFCs or Spec 4s, most of them were common grunts and carried the standard M-16 gas-operated assault rifle. The weapon weighed 7.5 pounds unloaded, 8.2 pounds with its full twenty-round magazine. Depending on numerous factors, such as topography and psychology, the riflemen carried anywhere from twelve to twenty magazines, usually in cloth bandoliers, adding on another 8.4 pounds at minimum, fourteen pounds at maximum. When it was available, they also carried M-16 maintenance gear—rods and steel brushes and swabs and tubes of LSA oil—all of which weighed about a pound. Among the grunts, some carried the M-79 grenade launcher, 5.9 pounds unloaded, a reasonably light weapon except for the ammunition, which was heavy. A single round weighed ten ounces. The typical load was twenty-five rounds. But Ted Lavender, who was scared, carried thirty-four rounds when he was shot and killed outside Than Khe, and he went down under an exceptional burden, more than twenty pounds of ammunition, plus the flak jacket and helmet and rations and water and toilet paper and tranquilizers and all the rest, plus the unweighed fear. He was dead weight. There was no twitching or flopping. Kiowa, who saw it happen, said it was like watching a rock fall, or a big sandbag or something—just boom, then down—not like the movies where the dead guy rolls around and does fancy spins and goes ass over teakettle—not like that, Kiowa said, the poor bastard just flat-fuck fell. Boom. Down. Nothing else. It was a bright morning in mid-April. Lieutenant Cross felt the pain. He blamed himself. They stripped off Lavender's canteens and ammo, all the heavy things, and Rat Kiley said the obvious, the guy's dead, and Mitchell Sanders used his radio to report one U.S. KIA° and to request a chopper. Then they wrapped Lavender in his poncho. They carried him out to a dry paddy, established security, and sat smoking the dead man's dope until the chopper came. Lieutenant Cross kept to himself. He pictured Martha's smooth young face, thinking he loved her more than anything, more than his men, and now Ted Lavender was dead because he loved her so much and could not stop thinking about her. When the dust-off arrived, they carried Lavender aboard. Afterward they burned Than Khe. They marched until dusk, then dug their holes, and that night Kiowa kept explaining how you had to be there, how fast it was, how the poor guy just dropped like so much concrete. Boom-down, he said. Like cement.

In addition to the three standard weapons—the M-60, M-16, and M-79—they carried whatever presented itself, or whatever seemed appropriate as a means of killing or staying alive. They carried catch-as-catch-can. At various times, in various situations, they carried M-14s and CAR-15s and Swedish Ks and grease guns and captured AK-47s and Chi-Coms and RPGs and Simonov carbines and black-market Uzis and .38-caliber Smith & Wesson handguns and 66 mm LAWs and shotguns and silencers and blackjacks and bayonets and C-4 plastic explosives. Lee Strunk carried a slingshot; a weapon of last resort, he called it. Mitchell Sanders carried brass knuckles. Kiowa carried his grandfather's feathered hatchet. Every third or fourth man carried a Claymore antipersonnel mine—3.5 pounds with its firing device. They all carried fragmentation grenades—fourteen ounces each. They all carried at least one M-18 colored smoke grenade—twenty-four ounces. Some carried CS or tear-gas grenades. Some carried white-phosphorus grenades. They carried all they could bear, and then some, including a silent awe for the terrible power of the things they carried.

In the first week of April, before Lavender died, Lieutenant Jimmy Cross received a good-luck charm from Martha. It was a simple pebble, an ounce at most. Smooth to

KIA *killed in action*

the touch, it was a milky-white color with flecks of orange and violet, oval-shaped, like a miniature egg. In the accompanying letter, Martha wrote that she had found the pebble on the Jersey shoreline, precisely where the land touched water at high tide, where things came together but also separated. It was this separate-but-together quality, she wrote, that had inspired her to pick up the pebble and to carry it in her breast pocket for several days, where it seemed weightless, and then to send it through the mail, by air, as a token of her truest feelings for him. Lieutenant Cross found this romantic. But he wondered what her truest feelings were, exactly, and what she meant by separate-but-together. He wondered how the tides and waves had come into play on that afternoon along the Jersey shoreline when Martha saw the pebble and bent down to rescue it from geology. He imagined bare feet. Martha was a poet, with the poet's sensibilities, and her feet would be brown and bare, the toenails unpainted, the eyes chilly and somber like the ocean in March, and though it was painful, he wondered who had been with her that afternoon. He imagined a pair of shadows moving along the strip of sand where things came together but also separated. It was phantom jealousy, he knew, but he couldn't help himself. He loved her so much. On the march, through the hot days of early April, he carried the pebble in his mouth, turning it with his tongue, tasting sea salts and moisture. His mind wandered. He had difficulty keeping his attention on the war. On occasion he would yell at his men to spread out the column, to keep their eyes open, but then he would slip away into daydreams, just pretending, walking barefoot along the Jersey shore, with Martha, carrying nothing. He would feel himself rising. Sun and waves and gentle winds, all love and lightness.

What they carried varied by mission.

When a mission took them to the mountains, they carried mosquito netting, machetes, canvas tarps, and extra bug juice.

If a mission seemed especially hazardous, or if it involved a place they knew to be bad, they carried everything they could. In certain heavily mined AOs,° where the land was dense with Toe Poppers and Bouncing Betties, they took turns humping a twenty-eight-pound mine detector. With its headphones and big sensing plate, the equipment was a stress on the lower back and shoulders, awkward to handle, often useless because of the shrapnel in the earth, but they carried it anyway, partly for safety, partly for the illusion of safety.

On ambush, or other night missions, they carried peculiar little odds and ends. Kiowa always took along his New Testament and a pair of moccasins for silence. Dave Jensen carried night-sight vitamins high in carotin. Lee Strunk carried his slingshot; ammo, he claimed, would never be a problem. Rat Kiley carried brandy and M&M's. Until he was shot, Ted Lavender carried the starlight scope, which weighed 6.3 pounds with its aluminum carrying case. Henry Dobbins carried his girlfriend's pantyhose wrapped around his neck as a comforter. They all carried ghosts. When dark came, they would move out single file across the meadows and paddies to their ambush coordinates, where they would quietly set up the Claymores and lie down and spend the night waiting.

Other missions were more complicated and required special equipment. In mid-April, it was their mission to search out and destroy the elaborate tunnel complexes in

AOs *areas of operations*

the Than Khe area south of Chu Lai. To blow the tunnels, they carried one-pound blocks of pentrite high explosives, four blocks to a man, sixty-eight pounds in all. They carried wiring, detonators, and battery-powered clackers. Dave Jensen carried earplugs. Most often, before blowing the tunnels, they were ordered by higher command to search them, which was considered bad news, but by and large they just shrugged and carried out orders. Because he was a big man, Henry Dobbins was excused from tunnel duty. The others would draw numbers. Before Lavender died there were seventeen men in the platoon, and whoever drew the number seventeen would strip off his gear and crawl in head first with a flashlight and Lieutenant Cross's .45-caliber pistol. The rest of them would fan out as security. They would sit down or kneel, not facing the hole, listening to the ground beneath them, imagining cobwebs and ghosts, whatever was down there—the tunnel walls squeezing in—how the flashlight seemed impossibly heavy in the hand and how it was tunnel vision in the very strictest sense, compression in all ways, even time, and how you had to wiggle in—ass and elbows—a swallowed-up feeling—and how you found yourself worrying about odd things—will your flashlight go dead? Do rats carry rabies? If you screamed, how far would the sound carry? Would your buddies hear it? Would they have the courage to drag you out? In some respects, though not many, the waiting was worse than the tunnel itself. Imagination was a killer.

On April 16, when Lee Strunk drew the number seventeen, he laughed and muttered something and went down quickly. The morning was hot and very still. Not good, Kiowa said. He looked at the tunnel opening, then out across a dry paddy toward the village of Than Khe. Nothing moved. No clouds or birds or people. As they waited, the men smoked and drank Kool-Aid, not talking much, feeling sympathy for Lee Strunk but also feeling the luck of the draw. You win some, you lose some, said Mitchell Sanders, and sometimes you settle for a rain check. It was a tired line and no one laughed.

Henry Dobbins ate a tropical chocolate bar. Ted Lavender popped a tranquilizer and went off to pee.

After five minutes, Lieutenant Jimmy Cross moved to the tunnel, leaned down, and examined the darkness. Trouble, he thought—a cave-in maybe. And then suddenly, without willing it, he was thinking about Martha. The stresses and fractures, the quick collapse, the two of them buried alive under all that weight. Dense, crushing love. Kneeling, watching the hole, he tried to concentrate on Lee Strunk and the war, all the dangers, but his love was too much for him, he felt paralyzed, he wanted to sleep inside her lungs and breathe her blood and be smothered. He wanted her to be a virgin and not a virgin, all at once. He wanted to know her. Intimate secrets—why poetry? Why so sad? Why the grayness in her eyes? Why so alone? Not lonely, just alone—riding her bike across campus or sitting off by herself in the cafeteria. Even dancing, she danced alone—and it was the aloneness that filled him with love. He remembered telling her that one evening. How she nodded and looked away. And how, later, when he kissed her, she received the kiss without returning it, her eyes wide open, not afraid, not a virgin's eyes, just flat and uninvolved.

Lieutenant Cross gazed at the tunnel. But he was not there. He was buried with Martha under the white sand at the Jersey shore. They were pressed together, and the pebble in his mouth was her tongue. He was smiling. Vaguely, he was aware of how quiet the day was, the sullen paddies, yet he could not bring himself to worry about matters of security. He was beyond that. He was just a kid at war, in love. He was twenty-two years old. He couldn't help it.

A few moments later Lee Strunk crawled out of the tunnel. He came up grinning, filthy but alive. Lieutenant Cross nodded and closed his eyes while the others clapped Strunk on the back and made jokes about rising from the dead.

Worms, Rat Kiley said. Right out of the grave. Fuckin' zombie.

The men laughed. They all felt great relief.

Spook City, said Mitchell Sanders.

Lee Strunk made a funny ghost sound, a kind of moaning, yet very happy, and right then, when Strunk made that high happy moaning sound, when he went *Ahhooooo,* right then Ted Lavender was shot in the head on his way back from peeing. He lay with his mouth open. The teeth were broken. There was a swollen black bruise under his left eye. The cheekbone was gone. Oh shit, Rat Kiley said, the guy's dead. The guy's dead, he kept saying, which seemed profound—the guy's dead. I mean really.

The things they carried were determined to some extent by superstition. Lieutenant Cross carried his good-luck pebble. Dave Jensen carried a rabbit's foot. Norman Bowker, otherwise a very gentle person, carried a thumb that had been presented to him as a gift by Mitchell Sanders. The thumb was dark brown, rubbery to the touch, and weighed four ounces at most. It had been cut from a VC corpse, a boy of fifteen or sixteen. They'd found him at the bottom of an irrigation ditch, badly burned, flies in his mouth and eyes. The boy wore black shorts and sandals. At the time of his death he had been carrying a pouch of rice, a rifle, and three magazines of ammunition.

You want my opinion, Mitchell Sanders said, there's a definite moral here.

He put his hand on the dead boy's wrist. He was quiet for a time, as if counting a pulse, then he patted the stomach, almost affectionately, and used Kiowa's hunting hatchet to remove the thumb.

Henry Dobbins asked what the moral was.

Moral?

You know. *Moral.*

Sanders wrapped the thumb in toilet paper and handed it across to Norman Bowker. There was no blood. Smiling, he kicked the boy's head, watched the flies scatter, and said, It's like with that old TV show—Paladin. Have gun, will travel.

Henry Dobbins thought about it.

Yeah, well, he finally said. I don't see no moral.

There it is, man.

Fuck off.

They carried USO stationery and pencils and pens. They carried Sterno, safety pins, trip flares, signal flares, spools of wire, razor blades, chewing tobacco, liberated joss sticks and statuettes of the smiling Buddha, candles, grease pencils, *The Stars and Stripes,* fingernail clippers, Psy Ops° leaflets, bush hats, bolos, and much more. Twice a week, when the resupply choppers came in, they carried hot chow in green Mermite cans and large canvas bags filled with iced beer and soda pop. They carried plastic water containers, each with a two-gallon capacity. Mitchell Sanders carried a set of starched

Psy Ops *psychological operations*

tiger fatigues for special occasions. Henry Dobbins carried Black Flag insecticide. Dave Jensen carried empty sandbags that could be filled at night for added protection. Lee Strunk carried tanning lotion. Some things they carried in common. Taking turns, they carried the big PRC-77 scrambler radio, which weighed thirty pounds with its battery. They shared the weight of memory. They took up what others could no longer bear. Often, they carried each other, the wounded or weak. They carried infections. They carried chess sets, basketballs, Vietnamese-English dictionaries, insignia of rank, Bronze Stars and Purple Hearts, plastic cards imprinted with the Code of Conduct. They carried diseases, among them malaria and dysentery. They carried lice and ringworm and leeches and paddy algae and various rots and molds. They carried the land itself—Vietnam, the place, the soil—a powdery orange-red dust that covered their boots and fatigues and faces. They carried the sky. The whole atmosphere, they carried it, the humidity, the monsoons, the stink of fungus and decay, all of it, they carried gravity. They moved like mules. By daylight they took sniper fire, at night they were mortared, but it was not battle, it was just the endless march, village to village, without purpose, nothing won or lost. They marched for the sake of the march. They plodded along slowly, dumbly, leaning forward against the heat, unthinking, all blood and bone, simple grunts, soldiering with their legs, toiling up the hills and down into the paddies and across the rivers and up again and down, just humping, one step and then the next and then another, but no volition, no will, because it was automatic, it was anatomy, and the war was entirely a matter of posture and carriage, the hump was everything, a kind of inertia, a kind of emptiness, a dullness of desire and intellect and conscience and hope and human sensibility. Their principles were in their feet. Their calculations were biological. They had no sense of strategy or mission. They searched the villages without knowing what to look for, not caring, kicking over jars of rice, frisking children and old men, blowing tunnels, sometimes setting fires and sometimes not, then forming up and moving on to the next village, then other villages, where it would always be the same. They carried their own lives. The pressures were enormous. In the heat of early afternoon, they would remove their helmets and flak jackets, walking bare, which was dangerous but which helped ease the strain. They would often discard things along the route of march. Purely for comfort, they would throw away rations, blow their Claymores and grenades, no matter, because by nightfall the resupply choppers would arrive with more of the same, then a day or two later still more, fresh watermelons and crates of ammunition and sunglasses and woolen sweaters—the resources were stunning—sparklers for the Fourth of July, colored eggs for Easter. It was the great American war chest—the fruits of science, the smokestacks, the canneries, the arsenals at Hartford, the Minnesota forests, the machine shops, the vast fields of corn and wheat—they carried like freight trains; they carried it on their backs and shoulders—and for all the ambiguities of Vietnam, all the mysteries and unknowns, there was at least the single abiding certainty that they would never be at a loss for things to carry.

After the chopper took Lavender away, Lieutenant Jimmy Cross led his men into the village of Than Khe. They burned everything. They shot chickens and dogs, they trashed the village well, they called in artillery and watched the wreckage, then they marched for several hours through the hot afternoon, and then at dusk, while Kiowa explained how Lavender died, Lieutenant Cross found himself trembling.

He tried not to cry. With his entrenching tool, which weighed five pounds, he began digging a hole in the earth.

He felt shame. He hated himself. He had loved Martha more than his men, and as a consequence Lavender was now dead, and this was something he would have to carry like a stone in his stomach for the rest of the war.

All he could do was dig. He used his entrenching tool like an ax, slashing, feeling both love and hate, and then later, when it was full dark, he sat at the bottom of his foxhole and wept. It went on for a long while. In part, he was grieving for Ted Lavender, but mostly it was for Martha, and for himself, because she belonged to another world, which was not quite real, and because she was a junior at Mount Sebastian College in New Jersey, a poet and a virgin and uninvolved, and because he realized she did not love him and never would.

Like cement, Kiowa whispered in the dark. I swear to God—boom-down. Not a word.

I've heard this, said Norman Bowker.

A pisser, you know? Still zipping himself up. Zapped while zipping.

All right, fine. That's enough.

Yeah, but you had to see it, the guy just—

I *heard,* man. Cement. So why not shut the fuck up?

Kiowa shook his head sadly and glanced over at the hole where Lieutenant Jimmy Cross sat watching the night. The air was thick and wet. A warm, dense fog had settled over the paddies and there was the stillness that precedes rain.

After a time Kiowa sighed.

One thing for sure, he said. The Lieutenant's in some deep hurt. I mean that crying jag—the way he was carrying on—it wasn't fake or anything, it was real heavy-duty hurt. The man cares.

Sure, Norman Bowker said.

Say what you want, the man does care.

We all got problems.

Not Lavender.

No, I guess not, Bowker said. Do me a favor, though.

Shut up?

That's a smart Indian. Shut up.

Shrugging, Kiowa pulled off his boots. He wanted to say more, just to lighten up his sleep, but instead he opened his New Testament and arranged it beneath his head as a pillow. The fog made things seem hollow and unattached. He tried not to think about Ted Lavender, but then he was thinking how fast it was, no drama, down and dead, and how it was hard to feel anything except surprise. It seemed un-Christian. He wished he could find some great sadness, or even anger, but the emotion wasn't there and he couldn't make it happen. Mostly he felt pleased to be alive. He liked the smell of the New Testament under his cheek, the leather and ink and paper and glue, whatever the chemicals were. He liked hearing the sounds of night. Even his fatigue, it felt fine, the stiff muscles and the prickly awareness of his own body, a floating feeling. He enjoyed not being dead. Lying there, Kiowa admired Lieutenant Jimmy Cross's capacity for grief. He wanted to share the man's pain, he wanted to care as Jimmy Cross cared. And yet when he closed his eyes, all he could think was Boom-down, and all he could feel was the pleasure of having his boots off and the fog curling in around him and the damp soil and the Bible smells and the plush comfort of night.

After a moment Norman Bowker sat up in the dark.

What the hell, he said. You want to talk, *talk*. Tell it to me.

Forget it.

No, man, go on. One thing I hate, it's a silent Indian.

For the most part they carried themselves with poise, a kind of dignity. Now and then, however, there were times of panic, when they squealed or wanted to squeal but couldn't, when they twitched and made moaning sounds and covered their heads and said Dear Jesus and flopped around on the earth and fired their weapons blindly and cringed and sobbed and begged for the noise to stop and went wild and made stupid promises to themselves and to God and to their mothers and fathers, hoping not to die. In different ways, it happened to all of them. Afterward, when the firing ended, they would blink and peek up. They would touch their bodies, feeling shame, then quickly hiding it. They would force themselves to stand. As if in slow motion, frame by frame, the world would take on the old logic—absolute silence, then the wind, then sunlight, then voices. It was the burden of being alive. Awkwardly, the men would reassemble themselves, first in private, then in groups, becoming soldiers again. They would repair the leaks in their eyes. They would check for casualties, call in dust-offs, light cigarettes, try to smile, clear their throats and spit and begin cleaning their weapons. After a time someone would shake his head and say, No lie, I almost shit my pants, and someone else would laugh, which meant it was bad, yes, but the guy had obviously not shit his pants, it wasn't that bad, and in any case nobody would ever do such a thing and then go ahead and talk about it. They would squint into the dense, oppressive sunlight. For a few moments, perhaps, they would fall silent, lighting a joint and tracking its passage from man to man, inhaling, holding in the humiliation. Scary stuff, one of them might say. But then someone else would grin or flick his eyebrows and say, Roger-dodger, almost cut me a new asshole, *almost.*

There were numerous such poses. Some carried themselves with a sort of wistful resignation, others with pride or stiff soldierly discipline or good humor or macho zeal. They were afraid of dying but they were even more afraid to show it.

They found jokes to tell.

They used a hard vocabulary to contain the terrible softness. *Greased,* they'd say. *Offed, lit up, zapped while zipping.* It wasn't cruelty, just stage presence. They were actors and the war came at them in 3-D. When someone died, it wasn't quite dying, because in a curious way it seemed scripted, and because they had their lines mostly memorized, irony mixed with tragedy, and because they called it by other names, as if to encyst and destroy the reality of death itself. They kicked corpses. They cut off thumbs. They talked grunt lingo. They told stories about Ted Lavender's supply of tranquilizers, how the poor guy didn't feel a thing, how incredibly tranquil he was.

There's a moral here, said Mitchell Sanders.

They were waiting for Lavender's chopper, smoking the dead man's dope.

The moral's pretty obvious, Sanders said, and winked. Stay away from drugs. No joke, they'll ruin your day every time.

Cute, said Henry Dobbins.

Mind-blower, get it? Talk about wiggy—nothing left, just blood and brains.

They made themselves laugh.

There it is, they'd say, over and over, as if the repetition itself were an act of poise, a balance between crazy and almost crazy, knowing without going. There it is, which meant be cool, let it ride, because oh yeah, man, you can't change what can't be changed, there it is, there it absolutely and positively and fucking well is.

They were tough.

They carried all the emotional baggage of men who might die. Grief, terror, love, longing—these were intangibles, but the intangibles had their own mass and specific gravity, they had tangible weight. They carried shameful memories. They carried the common secret of cowardice barely restrained, the instinct to run or freeze or hide, and in many respects this was the heaviest burden of all, for it could never be put down, it required perfect balance and perfect posture. They carried their reputations. They carried the soldier's greatest fear, which was the fear of blushing. Men killed, and died, because they were embarrassed not to. It was what had brought them to the war in the first place, nothing positive, no dreams of glory or honor, just to avoid the blush of dishonor. They died so as not to die of embarrassment. They crawled into tunnels and walked point and advanced under fire. Each morning, despite the unknowns, they made their legs move. They endured. They kept humming. They did not submit to the obvious alternative, which was simply to close the eyes and fall. So easy, really. Go limp and tumble to the ground and let the muscles unwind and not speak and not budge until your buddies picked you up and lifted you into the chopper that would roar and dip its nose and carry you off to the world. A mere matter of falling, yet no one ever fell. It was not courage, exactly; the object was not valor. Rather, they were too frightened to be cowards.

By and large they carried these things inside, maintaining the masks of composure. They sneered at sick call. They spoke bitterly about guys who had found release by shooting off their own toes or fingers. Pussies, they'd say. Candyasses. It was fierce, mocking talk, with only a trace of envy or awe, but even so, the image played itself out behind their eyes.

They imagined the muzzle against flesh. They imagined the quick, sweet pain, then the evacuation to Japan, then a hospital with warm beds and cute geisha nurses.

They dreamed of freedom birds.

At night, on guard, staring into the dark, they were carried away by jumbo jets. They felt the rush of takeoff. *Gone!* they yelled. And then velocity, wings and engines, a smiling stewardess—but it was more than a plane, it was a real bird, a big sleek silver bird with feathers and talons and high screeching. They were flying. The weights fell off, there was nothing to bear. They laughed and held on tight, feeling the cold slap of wind and altitude, soaring, thinking *It's over, I'm gone!*—they were naked, they were light and free—it was all lightness, bright and fast and buoyant, light as light, a helium buzz in the brain, a giddy bubbling in the lungs as they were taken up over the clouds and the war, beyond duty, beyond gravity and mortification and global entanglements—*Sin loi!*° they yelled, *I'm sorry, motherfuckers, but I'm out of it, I'm goofed, I'm on a space cruise, I'm gone!*—and it was a restful, disencumbered sensation, just riding the light waves, sailing that big silver freedom bird over the mountains and oceans, over America, over the farms and great sleeping cities and cemeteries and highways and

Sin loi *Sorry about that*

the golden arches of McDonald's. It was flight, a kind of fleeing, a kind of falling, falling higher and higher, spinning off the edge of the earth and beyond the sun and through the vast, silent vacuum where there were no burdens and where everything weighed exactly nothing. *Gone!* they screamed, *I'm sorry but I'm gone!* And so at night, not quite dreaming, they gave themselves over to lightness, they were carried, they were purely borne.

On the morning after Ted Lavender died, First Lieutenant Jimmy Cross crouched at the bottom of his foxhole and burned Martha's letters. Then he burned the two photographs. There was a steady rain falling, which made it difficult, but he used heat tabs and Sterno to build a small fire, screening it with his body, holding the photographs over the tight blue flame with the tips of his fingers.

He realized it was only a gesture. Stupid, he thought. Sentimental, too, but mostly just stupid.

Lavender was dead. You couldn't burn the blame.

Besides, the letters were in his head. And even now, without photographs, Lieutenant Cross could see Martha playing volleyball in her white gym shorts and yellow T-shirt. He could see her moving in the rain.

When the fire died out, Lieutenant Cross pulled his poncho over his shoulders and ate breakfast from a can.

There was no great mystery, he decided.

In those burned letters Martha had never mentioned the war, except to say, Jimmy, take care of yourself. She wasn't involved. She signed the letters "Love," but it wasn't love, and all the fine lines and technicalities did not matter.

The morning came up wet and blurry. Everything seemed part of everything else, the fog and Martha and the deepening rain.

It was a war, after all.

Half smiling, Lieutenant Jimmy Cross took out his maps. He shook his head hard, as if to clear it, then bent forward and began planning the day's march. In ten minutes, or maybe twenty, he would rouse the men and they would pack up and head west, where the maps showed the country to be green and inviting. They would do what they had always done. The rain might add some weight, but otherwise it would be one more day layered upon all the other days.

He was realistic about it. There was that new hardness in his stomach.

No more fantasies, he told himself.

Henceforth, when he thought about Martha, it would be only to think that she belonged elsewhere. He would shut down the daydreams. This was not Mount Sebastian, it was another world, where there were no pretty poems or midterm exams, a place where men died because of carelessness and gross stupidity. Kiowa was right. Boom-down, and you were dead, never partly dead.

Briefly, in the rain, Lieutenant Cross saw Martha's gray eyes gazing back at him.

He understood.

It was very sad, he thought. The things men carried inside. The things men did or felt they had to do.

He almost nodded at her, but didn't.

Instead he went back to his maps. He was now determined to perform his duties firmly and without negligence. It wouldn't help Lavender, he knew that, but from this point on he would comport himself as a soldier. He would dispose of his good-luck pebble. Swallow it, maybe, or use Lee Strunk's slingshot, or just drop it along the trail. On the march he would impose strict field discipline. He would be careful to send out flank security, to prevent straggling or bunching up, to keep his troops moving at the proper pace and at the proper interval. He would insist on clean weapons. He would confiscate the remainder of Lavender's dope. Later in the day, perhaps, he would call the men together and speak to them plainly. He would accept the blame for what had happened to Ted Lavender. He would be a man about it. He would look them in the eyes, keeping his chin level, and he would issue the new SOPs in a calm, impersonal tone of voice, an officer's voice, leaving no room for argument or discussion. Commencing immediately, he'd tell them, they would no longer abandon equipment along the route of march. They would police up their acts. They would get their shit together, and keep it together, and maintain it neatly and in good working order.

He would not tolerate laxity. He would show strength, distancing himself.

Among the men there would be grumbling, of course, and maybe worse, because their days would seem longer and their loads heavier, but Lieutenant Cross reminded himself that his obligation was not to be loved but to lead. He would dispense with love; it was not now a factor. And if anyone quarreled or complained, he would simply tighten his lips and arrange his shoulders in the correct command posture. He might give a curt little nod. Or he might not. He might just shrug and say Carry on, then they would saddle up and form into a column and move out toward the villages of Than Khe.

(1986)

QUESTIONS FOR CRITICAL THINKING AND WRITING

Experience

1. What are your impressions of war after reading this story? Do you think this story is more about the physical or psychological realities of war?

Interpretation

2. In addition to the "necessities," what other tangible things do individual soldiers carry? Reread the second paragraph of the story. What do these additional "things" reveal about the soldiers who carry them?
3. What intangible things do the men carry?
4. What is the "moral" that Mitchell Sanders finds in the dead Vietcong boy in the irrigation ditch?
5. How do the soldiers keep from being overwhelmed by the threat and reality of death?

Evaluation

6. What is incongruous about "the great American war chest," which includes "sparklers of the Fourth of July [and] colored eggs for Easter"? Is there any bitterness in the narrative at this point? If so, at whom or what is it directed?

Connection

7. Consider the treatment of war in O'Connor's "Guests of the Nation." Compare and contrast it with the treatment of war in "The Things They Carried."

Critical Thinking

8. Do you think Lieutenant Cross was responsible for Lavender's death? Why does he burn Martha's letters and photographs?

TILLIE OLSEN

[b. 1912]

Tillie Olsen was born in Nebraska, where she was raised and educated in the public schools, leaving school in the eleventh grade. Her fiction has received wide recognition for its portrayal of the lives of women, especially their struggles with working-class poverty. Olsen has also often been cited for her role in guiding young writers. Her best-known works are a short-story collection, Tell Me a Riddle *(1961), from which "I Stand Here Ironing" is taken, and* Silences *(1978), which examines the forces that silence art.*

I Stand Here Ironing

I stand here ironing, and what you asked me moves tormented back and forth with the iron.

"I wish you would manage the time to come in and talk with me about your daughter. I'm sure you can help me understand her. She's a youngster who needs help and whom I'm deeply interested in helping."

"Who needs help." . . . Even if I came, what good would it do? You think because I am her mother I have a key, or that in some way you could use me as a key? She has lived for nineteen years. There is all that life that has happened outside of me, beyond me.

And when is there time to remember, to sift, to weigh, to estimate, to total? I will start and there will be an interruption and I will have to gather it all together again. Or I will become engulfed with all I did or did not do, with what should have been and what cannot be helped.

She was a beautiful baby. The first and only one of our five that was beautiful at birth. You do not guess how new and uneasy her tenancy in her now-loveliness. You did not know her all those years she was thought homely, or see her poring over her baby pictures, making me tell her over and over how beautiful she had been—and would be, I would tell her—and was now, to the seeing eye. But the seeing eyes were few or non-existent. Including mine.

I nursed her. They feel that's important nowadays. I nursed all the children, but with her, with all the fierce rigidity of first motherhood, I did like the books then said. Though her cries battered me to trembling and my breasts ached with swollenness, I waited till the clock decreed.

Why do I put that first? I do not even know if it matters, or if it explains anything.

She was a beautiful baby. She blew shining bubbles of sound. She loved motion, loved light, loved color and music and textures. She would lie on the floor in her blue overalls patting the surface so hard in ecstasy her hands and feet would blur. She was a miracle to me, but when she was eight months old I had to leave her daytimes with the woman downstairs to whom she was no miracle at all, for I worked or looked for work and for Emily's father, who "could no longer endure" (he wrote in his goodbye note) "sharing want with us."

I was nineteen. It was the pre-relief, pre-WPA world of the depression. I would start running as soon as I got off the streetcar, running up the stairs, the place smelling sour, and awake or asleep to startle awake, when she saw me she would break into a clogged weeping that could not be comforted, a weeping I can hear yet.

After a while I found a job hashing at night so I could be with her days, and it was better. But it came to where I had to bring her to his family and leave her.

It took a long time to raise the money for her fare back. Then she got chicken pox and I had to wait longer. When she finally came, I hardly knew her, walking quick and nervous like her father, looking like her father, thin, and dressed in a shoddy red that yellowed her skin and glared at the pockmarks. All the baby loveliness gone.

She was two. Old enough for nursery school they said, and I did not know then what I know now—the fatigue of the long day, and the lacerations of group life in the kinds of nurseries that are only parking places for children.

Except that it would have made no difference if I had known. It was the only place there was. It was the only way we could be together, the only way I could hold a job.

And even without knowing, I knew. I knew the teacher that was evil because all these years it has curdled into my memory, the little boy hunched in the corner, her rasp, "why aren't you outside, because Alvin hits you? that's no reason, go out, scaredy." I knew Emily hated it even if she did not clutch and implore "don't go Mommy" like the other children, mornings.

She always had a reason why we should stay home. Momma, you look sick, Momma. I feel sick. Momma, the teachers aren't there today, they're sick. Momma, we can't go, there was a fire there last night. Momma, it's a holiday today, no school, they told me.

But never a direct protest, never rebellion. I think of our others in their three-, four-year-oldness—the explosions, the tempers, the denunciations, the demands—and I feel suddenly ill. I put the iron down. What in me demanded that goodness in her? And what was the cost, the cost to her of such goodness?

The old man living in the back once said in his gentle way: "You should smile at Emily more when you look at her." What *was* in my face when I looked at her? I loved her. There were all the acts of love.

It was only with the others I remembered what he said, and it was the face of joy, and not of care or tightness or worry I turned to them—too late for Emily. She does not smile easily, let alone almost always as her brothers and sisters do. Her face is closed and somber, but when she wants, how fluid. You must have seen it in her pantomimes, you spoke of her rare gift for comedy on the stage that rouses a laughter out of the audience so dear they applaud and applaud and do not want to let her go.

Where does it come from, that comedy? There was none of it in her when she came back to me that second time, after I had had to send her away again. She had a new daddy now to learn to love, and I think perhaps it was a better time.

Except when we left her alone nights, telling ourselves she was old enough.

"Can't you go some other time, Mommy, like tomorrow?" she would ask. "Will it be just a little while you'll be gone? Do you promise?"

The time we came back, the front door open, the clock on the floor in the hall. She rigid awake. "It wasn't just a little while. I didn't cry. Three times I called you, just three times, and then I ran downstairs to open the door so you could come faster. The clock talked loud. I threw it away, it scared me what it talked."

She said the clock talked loud again that night I went to the hospital to have Susan. She was delirious with the fever that comes before red measles, but she was fully conscious all the week I was gone and the week after we were home when she could not come near the new baby or me.

She did not get well. She stayed skeleton thin, not wanting to eat, and night after night she had nightmares. She would call for me, and I would rouse from exhaustion to sleepily call back: "You're all right, darling, go to sleep, it's just a dream," and if she still called, in a sterner voice, "now go to sleep, Emily, there's nothing to hurt you." Twice, only twice, when I had to get up for Susan anyhow, I went in to sit with her.

Now when it is too late (as if she would let me hold and comfort her like I do the others) I get up and go to her at once at her moan or restless stirring. "Are you awake, Emily? Can I get you something?" And the answer is always the same: "No, I'm all right, go back to sleep, Mother."

They persuaded me at the clinic to send her away to a convalescent home in the country where "she can have the kind of food and care you can't manage for her, and you'll be free to concentrate on the new baby." They still send children to that place. I see pictures on the society page of sleek young women planning affairs to raise money for it, or dancing at the affairs, or decorating Easter eggs or filling Christmas stockings for the children.

They never have a picture of the children so I do not know if the girls still wear those gigantic red bows and the ravaged looks on the every other Sunday when parents can come to visit "unless otherwise notified"—as we were notified the first six weeks.

Oh it is a handsome place, green lawns and tall trees and fluted flower beds. High up on the balconies of each cottage the children stand, the girls in their red bows and white dresses, the boys in white suits and giant red ties. The parents stand below shrieking up to be heard and the children shriek down to be heard, and between them the invisible wall "Not To Be Contaminated by Parental Germs or Physical Affection."

There was a tiny girl who always stood hand in hand with Emily. Her parents never came. One visit she was gone. "They moved her to Rose Cottage," Emily shouted in explanation. "They don't like you to love anybody here."

She wrote once a week, the labored writing of a seven-year-old. "I am fine. How is the baby. If I write my letter nicely I will have a star. Love." There never was a star. We wrote every other day, letters she could never hold or keep but only hear read—once. "We simply do not have room for children to keep any personal possessions," they patiently explained when we pieced one Sunday's shrieking together to plead how much it would mean to Emily, who loved so to keep things, to be allowed to keep her letters and cards.

Each visit she looked frailer. "She isn't eating," they told us.

(They had runny eggs for breakfast or mush with lumps, Emily said later, I'd hold it in my mouth and not swallow. Nothing ever tasted good, just when they had chicken.)

It took us eight months to get her released home, and only the fact that she gained back so little of her seven lost pounds convinced the social worker.

I used to try to hold and love her after she came back, but her body would stay stiff, and after a while she'd push away. She ate little. Food sickened her, and I think much of life too. Oh she had physical lightness and brightness, twinkling by on skates, bouncing like a ball up and down up and down over the jump rope, skimming over the hill; but these were momentary.

She fretted about her appearance, thin and dark and foreign-looking at a time when every little girl was supposed to look or thought she should look a chubby blonde replica of Shirley Temple. The doorbell sometimes rang for her, but no one seemed to come and play in the house or be a best friend. Maybe because we moved so much.

There was a boy she loved painfully through two school semesters. Months later she told me how she had taken pennies from my purse to buy him candy. "Licorice was his favorite and I brought him some every day, but he still liked Jennifer better'n me. Why, Mommy?" The kind of question for which there is no answer.

School was a worry to her. She was not glib or quick in a world where glibness and quickness were easily confused with ability to learn. To her overworked and exasperated teachers she was an overconscientious "slow learner" who kept trying to catch up and was absent entirely too often.

I let her be absent, though sometimes the illness was imaginary. How different from my now-strictness about attendance with the others. I wasn't working. We had a new baby, I was home anyhow. Sometimes, after Susan grew old enough, I would keep her home from school, too, to have them all together.

Mostly Emily had asthma, and her breathing, harsh and labored, would fill the house with a curiously tranquil sound. I would bring the two old dresser mirrors and her boxes of collections to her bed. She would select beads and single earrings, bottle tops and shells, dried flowers and pebbles, old postcards and scraps, all sorts of oddments; then she and Susan would play Kingdom, setting up landscapes and furniture, peopling them with action.

Those were the only times of peaceful companionship between her and Susan. I have edged away from it, that poisonous feeling between them, that terrible balancing of hurts and needs I had to do between the two, and did so badly, those earlier years.

Oh there are conflicts between the others too, each one human, needing, demanding, hurting, taking—but only between Emily and Susan, no, Emily toward Susan that corroding resentment. It seems so obvious on the surface, yet it is not obvious. Susan, the second child, Susan, golden- and curly-haired and chubby, quick and articulate and assured, everything in appearance and manner Emily was not; Susan, not able to resist Emily's precious things, losing or sometimes clumsily breaking them; Susan telling jokes and riddles to company for applause while Emily sat silent (to say to me later: that was my riddle, Mother, I told it to Susan); Susan, who for all the five years' difference in age was just a year behind Emily in developing physically.

I am glad for that slow physical development that widened the difference between her and her contemporaries, though she suffered over it. She was too vulnerable for that terrible world of youthful competition, of preening and parading, of constant measuring of yourself against every other, of envy, "If I had that copper hair," "If I had that skin. . . ." She tormented herself enough about not looking like the others, there was enough of the unsureness, the having to be conscious of words before you speak, the constant caring—what are they thinking of me? without having it all magnified by the merciless physical drives.

Ronnie is calling. He is wet and I change him. It is rare there is such a cry now. That time of motherhood is almost behind me when the ear is not one's own but must always be racked and listening for the child cry, the child call. We sit for a while and I hold him, looking out over the city spread in charcoal with its soft aisles of light. "*Shoogily,*" he breathes and curls closer. I carry him back to bed, asleep. *Shoogily*. A funny word, a family word, inherited from Emily, invented by her to say: *comfort*.

In this and other ways she leaves her seal, I say aloud. And startle at my saying it. What do I mean? What did I start to gather together, to try and make coherent? I was at the terrible, growing years. War years. I do not remember them well. I was working, there were four smaller ones now, there was not time for her. She had to help be a mother, and housekeeper, and shopper. She had to set her seal. Mornings of crisis and near hysteria trying to get lunches packed, hair combed, coats and shoes found, everyone to school or Child Care on time, the baby ready for transportation. And always the paper scribbled on by a smaller one, the book looked at by Susan then mislaid, the homework not done. Running out to that huge school where she was one, she was lost, she was a drop; suffering over the unpreparedness, stammering and unsure in her classes.

There was so little time left at night after the kids were bedded down. She would struggle over books, always eating (it was in those years she developed her enormous appetite that is legendary in our family) and I would be ironing, or preparing food for the next day, or writing V-mail to Bill, or tending the baby. Sometimes, to make me laugh, or out of her despair, she would imitate happenings or types at school.

I think I said once: "Why don't you do something like this in the school amateur show?" One morning she phoned me at work, hardly understandable through the weeping: "Mother, I did it. I won, I won; they gave me first prize; they clapped and clapped and wouldn't let me go."

Now suddenly she was Somebody, and as imprisoned in her difference as she had been in anonymity.

She began to be asked to perform at other high schools, even in colleges, then at city and statewide affairs. The first one we went to, I only recognized her that first moment when thin, shy, she almost drowned herself into the curtains. Then: Was this Emily? The control, the command, the convulsing and deadly clowning, the spell, then the roaring, stamping audience, unwilling to let this rare and precious laughter out of their lives.

Afterwards: You ought to do something about her with a gift like that—but without money or knowing how, what does one do? We have left it all to her, and the gift has as often eddied inside, clogged and clotted, as been used and growing.

She is coming. She runs up the stairs two at a time with her light graceful step, and I know she is happy tonight. Whatever it was that occasioned your call did not happen today.

"Aren't you ever going to finish the ironing, Mother? Whistler painted his mother in a rocker. I'd have to paint mine standing over an ironing board." This is one of her communicative nights and she tells me everything and nothing as she fixes herself a plate of food out of the icebox.

She is so lovely. Why did you want me to come in at all? Why were you concerned? She will find her way.

She starts up the stairs to bed. "Don't get me up with the rest in the morning." "But I thought you were having midterms." "Oh, those," she comes back in, kisses me, and says lightly, "in a couple of years when we'll all be atom-dead they won't matter a bit."

She has said it before. She believes it. But because I have been dredging the past, and all that compounds a human being is so heavy and meaningful in me, I cannot endure it tonight.

I will never total it all. I will never come in to say: She was a child seldom smiled at. Her father left me before she was a year old. I had to work her first six years when there was work, or I sent her home and to his relatives. There were years she had care she hated. She was dark and thin and foreign-looking in a world where the prestige went to blondeness and curly hair and dimples, she was slow where glibness was prized. She was a child of anxious, not proud, love. We were poor and could not afford for her the soil of easy growth. I was a young mother, I was a distracted mother. There were the other children pushing up, demanding. Her younger sister seemed all that she was not. There were years she did not want me to touch her. She kept too much in herself, her life was such she had to keep too much in herself. My wisdom came too late. She has much to her and probably little will come of it. She is a child of her age, of depression, of war, of fear.

Let her be. So all that is in her will not bloom—but in how many does it? There is still enough left to live by. Only help her to know—help make it so there is cause for her to know—that she is more than this dress on the ironing board, helpless before the iron.

(1961)

QUESTIONS FOR CRITICAL THINKING AND WRITING

Experience

1. What impressions do you have of the mother–daughter relationship depicted in "I Stand Here Ironing?" Do you know of similar relationships?

Interpretation

2. The story, a meditative monologue, is as much about the mother as it is about Emily. What do we know about the mother's life since Emily's birth? Does the mother eventually come to terms with her parenting of Emily?
3. Analyze the tonal shifts in the story.
4. What does the ironing symbolize? Including the title, there are five references to ironing. Reread the references before considering your answer.

Evaluation

5. Is this a bleak story? Is there any hope for Emily or her mother?

Connection

6. Compare "I Stand Here Ironing" with Kincaid's "Girl." Consider the literary technique and the mother–daughter relationships.

Critical Thinking

7. To what extent is the mother responsible for the difficulties she encounters in parenting Emily? To what extent are mother and daughter victims of circumstances beyond their control?

KATHERINE ANNE PORTER

[1890–1960]

Katherine Anne Porter, short-story writer and novelist, was awarded the Pulitzer Prize and National Book Award in 1966 for The Collected Stories. *Born in Texas, Porter spent time living in Europe and Mexico. Her short-story collections include* Flowering Judas and Other Stories *(1935) and* Pale Horse, Pale Rider *(1939). Her novel,* Ship of Fools, *on which she worked for twenty years, brought her wide acclaim. Her basic concern in writing was to examine human motives and portray human experience as she had come to understand it.*

The Jilting of Granny Weatherall

She flicked her wrist neatly out of Doctor Harry's pudgy careful fingers and pulled the sheet up to her chin. The brat ought to be in knee breeches. Doctoring around the country with spectacles on his nose! "Get along now, take your schoolbooks and go. There's nothing wrong with me."

Doctor Harry spread a warm paw like a cushion on her forehead where the forked green vein danced and made her eyelids twitch. "Now, now, be a good girl, and we'll have you up in no time."

"That's no way to speak to a woman nearly eighty years old just because she's down. I'd have you respect your elders, young man."

"Well, Missy, excuse me." Doctor Harry patted her cheek. "But I've got to warn you, haven't I? You're a marvel, but you must be careful or you're going to be good and sorry."

"Don't tell me what I'm going to be. I'm on my feet now, morally speaking. It's Cornelia. I had to go to bed to get rid of her."

Her bones felt loose, and floated around in her skin, and Doctor Harry floated like a balloon around the foot of the bed. He floated and pulled down his waistcoat and swung his glasses on a cord. "Well, stay where you are, it certainly can't hurt you."

"Get along and doctor your sick," said Granny Weatherall. "Leave a well woman alone. I'll call for you when I want you. . . . Where were you forty years ago when I pulled through milkleg and double pneumonia? You weren't even born. Don't let Cornelia lead you on," she shouted, because Doctor Harry appeared to float up to the ceiling and out. "I pay my own bills, and I don't throw my money away on nonsense!"

She meant to wave goodby, but it was too much trouble. Her eyes closed of themselves, it was like a dark curtain drawn around the bed. The pillow rose and floated under her, pleasant as a hammock in a light wind. She listened to the leaves rustling outside the window. No, somebody was swishing newspapers: no, Cornelia and Doctor Harry were whispering together. She leaped broad awake, thinking they whispered in her ear.

"She was never like this, never like this!" "Well, what can we expect?" "Yes, eighty years old. . . . "

Well, and what if she was? She still had ears. It was like Cornelia to whisper around doors. She always kept things secret in such a public way. She was always being tactful and kind. Cornelia was dutiful; that was the trouble with her. Dutiful and good: "So good and dutiful," said Granny, "that I'd like to spank her." She saw herself spanking Cornelia and making a fine job of it.

"What'd you say, Mother?"

Granny felt her face tying up in hard knots.

"Can't a body think, I'd like to know?"

"I thought you might want something."

"I do. I want a lot of things. First off, go away and don't whisper."

She lay and drowsed, hoping in her sleep that the children would keep out and let her rest a minute. It had been a long day. Not that she was tired. It was always pleasant to snatch a minute now and then. There was always so much to be done, let me see: tomorrow.

Tomorrow was far away and there was nothing to trouble about. Things were finished somehow when the time came; thank God there was always a little margin over for peace: then a person could spread out the plan of life and tuck in the edges orderly. It was good to have everything clean and folded away, with the hair brushes and tonic bottles sitting straight on the white embroidered linen: the day started without fuss and the pantry shelves laid out with rows of jelly glasses and brown jugs and white stone-china jars with blue whirligigs and words painted on them: coffee, tea, sugar, ginger, cinnamon, allspice: and the bronze clock with the lion on top nicely dusted off. The dust that lion could collect in twenty-four hours! The box in the attic with all those letters tied up, well, she'd have to go through that tomorrow. All those letters—George's letters and John's letters and her letters to them both—lying around for the children to find afterward made her uneasy. Yes, that would be tomorrow's business. No use to let them know how silly she had been once.

While she was rummaging around she found death in her mind and it felt clammy and unfamiliar. She had spent so much time preparing for death there was no need for bringing it up again. Let it take care of itself now. When she was sixty she had felt very old, finished, and went around making farewell trips to see her children and grandchildren, with a secret in her mind: This is the very last of your mother, children! Then she made her will and came down with a long fever. That was all just a notion like a lot of other things, but it was lucky too, for she had once and for all got over the idea of dying for a long time. Now she couldn't be worried. She hoped she had better sense now. Her father had lived to be one hundred and two years old and had drunk a noggin of strong hot toddy on his last birthday. He told the reporters it was his daily habit, and he owed his long life to that. He had made quite a scandal and was very pleased about it. She believed she'd just plague Cornelia a little.

"Cornelia! Cornelia!" No footsteps, but a sudden hand on her cheek. "Bless you, where have you been?"

"Here, Mother."

"Well, Cornelia, I want a noggin of hot toddy."

"Are you cold, darling?"

"I'm chilly, Cornelia. Lying in bed stops the circulation. I must have told you that a thousand times."

Well, she could just hear Cornelia telling her husband that Mother was getting a little childish and they'd have to humor her. The thing that most annoyed her was that Cornelia thought she was deaf, dumb, and blind. Little hasty glances and tiny gestures tossed around her and over her head saying, "Don't cross her, let her have her way, she's eighty years old," and she sitting there as if she lived in a thin glass cage. Sometimes Granny almost made up her mind to pack up and move back to her own house where nobody could remind her every minute that she was old. Wait, wait, Cornelia, till your own children whisper behind your back!

In her day she had kept a better house and had got more work done. She wasn't too old yet for Lydia to be driving eighty miles for advice when one of the children jumped the track, and Jimmy still dropped in and talked things over: "Now, Mammy, you've a good business head, I want to know what you think of this? . . ." Old. Cornelia couldn't change the furniture around without asking. Little things, little things! They had been so sweet when they were little. Granny wished the old days were back again with the children young and everything to be done over. It had been a hard pull, but not too much for her. When she thought of all the food she had cooked, and all the clothes she had cut and sewed, and all the gardens she had made—well, the children showed it. There they were, made out of her, and they couldn't get away from that. Sometimes she wanted to see John again and point to them and say, Well, I didn't do so badly, did I? But that would have to wait. That was for tomorrow. She used to think of him as a man, but now all the children were older than their father, and he would be a child beside her if she saw him now. It seemed strange and there was something wrong in the idea. Why, he couldn't possibly recognize her. She had fenced in a hundred acres once, digging the postholes herself and clamping the wires with just a Negro boy to help. That changed a woman. John would be looking for a young woman with the peaked Spanish comb in her hair and the painted fan. Digging postholes changed a woman. Riding country roads in the winter when women had their babies was another thing: sitting up nights with sick horses and sick Negroes and sick children and hardly ever losing one. John, I hardly ever lost one of them! John would see that in a minute, that would be something he could understand, she wouldn't have to explain anything!

It made her feel like rolling up her sleeves and putting the whole place to rights again. No matter if Cornelia was determined to be everywhere at once, there were a great many things left undone on this place. She would start tomorrow and do them. It was good to be strong enough for everything, even if all you made melted and changed and slipped under your hands, so that by the time you finished you almost forgot what you were working for. What was it I set out to do? she asked herself intently, but she could not remember. A fog rose over the valley, she saw it marching across the creek swallowing the trees and moving up the hill like an army of ghosts. Soon it would be at the near edge of the orchard, and then it was time to go in and light the lamps. Come in, children, don't stay out in the night air.

Lighting the lamps had been beautiful. The children huddled up to her and breathed like little calves waiting at the bars in the twilight. Their eyes followed the match and watched the flame rise and settle in a blue curve, then they moved away from her. The lamp was lit, they didn't have to be scared and hang on to mother any more. Never, never, never more. God, for all my life I thank Thee. Without Thee, my God, I could never have done it. Hail, Mary, full of grace.

I want you to pick all the fruit this year and see that nothing is wasted. There's always someone who can use it. Don't let good things rot for want of using. You waste life when you waste good food. Don't let things get lost. It's bitter to lose things. Now, don't let me get to thinking, not when I am tired and taking a little nap before supper. . . .

The pillow rose about her shoulders and pressed against her heart and the memory was being squeezed out of it: oh, push down the pillow, somebody: it would smother her if she tried to hold it. Such a fresh breeze blowing and such a green day with no threats in it. But he had not come, just the same. What does a woman do when she has put on the white veil and set out the white cake for a man and he doesn't come? She tried to remember. No, I swear he never harmed me but in that. He never harmed me but in that . . . and what if he did? There was the day, the day, but a whirl of dark smoke rose and covered it, crept up and over into the bright field where everything was planted so carefully in orderly rows. That was hell, she knew hell when she saw it. For sixty years she had prayed against remembering him and against losing her soul in the deep pit of hell, and now the two things were mingled in one and the thought of him was a smoky cloud from hell that moved and crept in her head when she had just got rid of Doctor Harry and was trying to rest a minute. Wounded vanity, Ellen, said a sharp voice in the top of her mind. Don't let your wounded vanity get the upper hand of you. Plenty of girls get jilted. You were jilted, weren't you? Then stand up to it. Her eyelids wavered and let in streamers of blue-gray light like tissue paper over her eyes. She must get up and pull the shades down or she'd never sleep. She was in bed again and the shades were not down. How could that happen? Better turn over, hide from the light, sleeping in the light gave you nightmares. "Mother, how do you feel now?" and a stinging wetness on her forehead. But I don't like having my face washed in cold water!

Hapsy? George? Lydia? Jimmy? No, Cornelia, and her features were swollen and full of little puddles. "They're coming, darling, they'll all be here soon." Go wash your face, child, you look funny.

Instead of obeying, Cornelia knelt down and put her head on the pillow. She seemed to be talking but there was no sound. "Well, are you tongue-tied? Whose birthday is it? Are you going to give a party?"

Cornelia's mouth moved urgently in strange shapes. "Don't do that, you bother me, daughter."

"Oh, no, Mother. Oh, no. . . ."

Nonsense. It was strange about children. They disputed your every word. "No what, Cornelia?"

"Here's Doctor Harry."

"I won't see that boy again. He just left five minutes ago."

"That was this morning, Mother. It's night now. Here's the nurse."

"This is Doctor Harry, Mrs. Weatherall. I never saw you look so young and happy!"

"Ah, I'll never be young again—but I'd be happy if they'd let me lie in peace and get rested."

She thought she spoke up loudly, but no one answered. A warm weight on her forehead, a warm bracelet on her wrist, and a breeze went on whispering, trying to tell her something. A shuffle of leaves in the everlasting hand of God, He blew on them and they danced and rattled. "Mother, don't mind, we're going to give you a little hypodermic." "Look here, daughter, how do ants get in this bed? I saw sugar ants yesterday." Did you send for Hapsy too?

It was Hapsy she really wanted. She had to go a long way back through a great many rooms to find Hapsy standing with a baby on her arm. She seemed to herself to be Hapsy also, and the baby on Hapsy's arm was Hapsy and himself and herself, all at once, and there was no surprise in the meeting. Then Hapsy melted from within and turned flimsy as gray gauze and the baby was a gauzy shadow, and Hapsy came up close and said, "I thought you'd never come," and looked at her very searchingly and said, "You haven't changed a bit!" They leaned forward to kiss, when Cornelia began whispering from a long way off, "Oh, is there anything you want to tell me? Is there anything I can do for you?"

Yes, she had changed her mind after sixty years and she would like to see George. I want you to find George. Find him and be sure to tell him I forgot him. I want him to know I had my husband just the same and my children and my house like any other woman. A good house too and a good husband that I loved and fine children out of him. Better than I hoped for even. Tell him I was given back everything he took away and more. Oh, no, oh, God, no, there was something else besides the house and the man and the children. Oh, surely they were not all? What was it? Something not given back. . . . Her breath crowded down under her ribs and grew into a monstrous frightening shape with cutting edges; it bored up into her head, and the agony was unbelievable: Yes, John, get the Doctor now, no more talk, my time has come.

When this one was born it should be the last. The last. It should have been born first, for it was the one she had truly wanted. Everything came in good time. Nothing left out, left over. She was strong, in three days she would be as well as ever. Better. A woman needed milk in her to have her full health.

"Mother, do you hear me?"

"I've been telling you—"

"Mother, Father Connolly's here."

"I went to Holy Communion only last week. Tell him I'm not so sinful as all that."

"Father just wants to speak to you."

He could speak as much as he pleased. It was like him to drop in and inquire about her soul as if it were a teething baby, and then stay on for a cup of tea and a round of cards and gossip. He always had a funny story of some sort, usually about an Irishman who made his little mistakes and confessed them, and the point lay in some absurd thing he would blurt out in the confessional showing his struggles between native piety and original sin. Granny felt easy about her soul. Cornelia, where are your manners? Give Father Connolly a chair. She had her secret comfortable understanding with a few favorite saints who cleared a straight road to God for her. All as surely signed and sealed as the papers for the new Forty Acres. Forever . . . heirs and assigns forever. Since the day the wedding cake was not cut, but thrown out and wasted. The whole bottom dropped out of the world, and there she was blind and sweating with nothing under her feet and the walls falling away. His hand had caught her under the breast, she had not fallen, there was the freshly polished floor with the green rug on it, just as before. He had cursed like a sailor's parrot and said, "I'll kill him for you." Don't lay a hand on him, for my sake leave something to God. "Now, Ellen, you must believe what I tell you. . . ."

So there was nothing, nothing to worry about any more, except sometimes in the night one of the children screamed in a nightmare, and they both hustled out shaking and hunting for the matches and calling, "There, wait a minute, here we are!" John, get the doctor now, Hapsy's time has come. But there was Hapsy standing by the bed in a white cap. "Cornelia, tell Hapsy to take off her cap. I can't see her plain."

Her eyes opened very wide and the room stood out like a picture she had seen somewhere. Dark colors with the shadows rising toward the ceiling in long angles. The tall black dresser gleamed with nothing on it but John's picture, enlarged from a little one, with John's eyes very black when they should have been blue. You never saw him, so how do you know how he looked? But the man insisted the copy was perfect, it was very rich and handsome. For a picture, yes, but it's not my husband. The table by the bed had a linen cover and a candle and a crucifix. The light was blue from Cornelia's silk lampshades. No sort of light at all, just frippery. You had to live forty years with kerosene lamps to appreciate honest electricity. She felt very strong and she saw Doctor Harry with a rosy nimbus around him.

"You look like a saint, Doctor Harry, and I vow that's as near as you'll ever come to it."

"She's saying something."

"I heard you, Cornelia. What's all this carrying-on?"

"Father Connolly's saying—"

Cornelia's voice staggered and bumped like a cart in a bad road. It rounded corners and turned back again and arrived nowhere. Granny stepped up in the cart very lightly and reached for the reins, but a man sat beside her and she knew him by his hands, driving the cart. She did not look in his face, for she knew without seeing, but looked instead down the road where the trees leaned over and bowed to each other and a thousand birds were singing a Mass. She felt like singing too, but she put her hand in the bosom of her dress and pulled out a rosary, and Father Connolly murmured Latin in a very solemn voice and tickled her feet. My God, will you stop that nonsense? I'm a married woman. What if he did run away and leave me to face the priest by myself? I found another a whole world better. I wouldn't have exchanged my husband for anybody except St. Michael himself, and you may tell him that for me with a thank you in the bargain.

Light flashed on her closed eyelids, and a deep roaring shook her. Cornelia, is that lightning? I hear thunder. There's going to be a storm. Close all the windows. Call the children in. . . . "Mother, here we are, all of us." "Is that you, Hapsy?" "Oh, no, I'm Lydia. We drove as fast as we could." Their faces drifted above her, drifted away. The rosary fell out of her hands and Lydia put it back. Jimmy tried to help, their hands fumbled together, and Granny closed two fingers around Jimmy's thumb. Beads wouldn't do; it must be something alive. She was so amazed her thoughts ran round and round. So, my dear Lord, this is my death and I wasn't even thinking about it. My children have come to see me die. But I can't, it's not time. Oh, I always hated surprises. I wanted to give Cornelia the amethyst set—Cornelia, you're to have the amethyst set, but Hapsy's to wear it when she wants, and, Doctor Harry, do shut up. Nobody sent for you. Oh, my dear Lord, do wait a minute. I meant to do something about the Forty Acres, Jimmy doesn't need it and Lydia will later on, with that worthless husband of hers. I meant to finish the altar cloth and send six bottles of wine to Sister Borgia for her dyspepsia. I want to send six bottles of wine to Sister Borgia, Father Connolly, now don't let me forget.

Cornelia's voice made short turns and tilted over and crashed. "Oh, Mother, oh, Mother, oh, Mother. . . ."

"I'm not going, Cornelia. I'm taken by surprise. I can't go."

You'll see Hapsy again. What about her? "I thought you'd never come." Granny made a long journey outward, looking for Hapsy. What if I don't find her? What then? Her heart sank down and down, there was no bottom to death, she couldn't come to the end of it. The blue light from Cornelia's lampshade drew into a tiny point in the center of her brain, it flickered and winked like an eye, quietly it fluttered and dwindled. Granny lay curled down within herself, amazed and watchful, staring at the point of light that was herself; her body was now only a deeper mass of shadow in an endless darkness and this darkness would curl around the light and swallow it up. God, give a sign!

For the second time there was no sign. Again no bridegroom and the priest in the house. She could not remember any other sorrow because this grief wiped them all away. Oh, no, there's nothing more cruel than this—I'll never forgive it. She stretched herself with a deep breath and blew out the light.

(1930)

QUESTIONS FOR CRITICAL THINKING AND WRITING

Experience

1. Consider Cornelia's efforts on behalf of her dying mother. Does her mother fully appreciate her daughter? From your experiences and observations, would you say the mother's response is unusual?

Interpretation

2. Why is *Weatherall* a fitting name for Granny?
3. Despite her protests to the contrary, did Granny ever completely overcome her bitterness at being jilted?
4. Why is it ironic that Granny wants to see George after 60 years just to tell him that she forgot him? Is she being entirely truthful?
5. Granny felt jilted a second time at death. By whom?

Evaluation

6. Consider Porter's technique of storytelling in "The Jilting of Granny Weatherall." Why does it seem as though more than one day passes from the beginning to the end of the story?

Connection

7. Compare Granny to the protagonist in Faulkner's "A Rose for Emily." How has being jilted shaped their lives and character?

Critical Thinking

8. What do you think of Granny's desire to avenge her jilting by George? How else might Granny Weatherall have decided to respond to George's jilting?

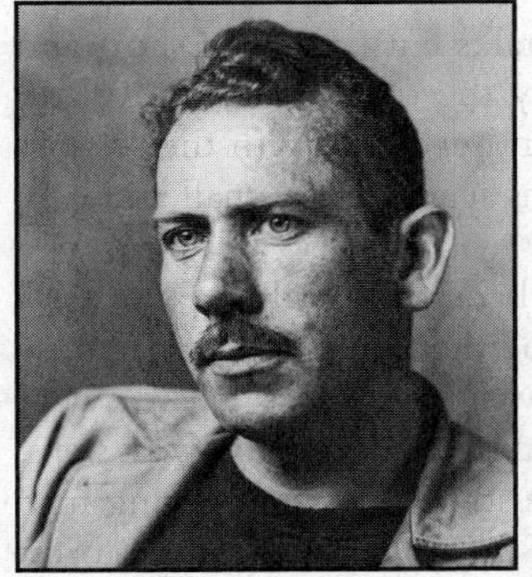

JOHN STEINBECK
[1902–1968]

John Steinbeck was born in the Salinas Valley in California, the setting of his story "The Chrysanthemums." Steinbeck attended Stanford University and worked in New York as a reporter and bricklayer. He based his fiction on the lives of poor farmers in Oklahoma and Mexico and others struggling to make a living in California. His best known work, the novel The Grapes of Wrath *(1939), is the story of a family of Oklahoma farmers migrated out of the dust bowl to California.* Of Mice and Men *(1937),* In Dubious Battle *(1936),* East of Eden, The Red Pony, *and* The Pearl, *are among his other well-known fictional works. His* Travels with Charley *(his dog) and* A Russian Journal *are among his books of nonfiction. Steinbeck won the Nobel Prize for Literature in 1962.*

The Chrysanthemums

The high grey-flannel fog of winter closed off the Salinas Valley° from the sky and from all the rest of the world. On every side it sat like a lid on the mountains and made of the great valley a closed pot. On the broad, level land floor the gang plows bit deep and left the black earth shining like metal where the shares had cut. On the foothill ranches across the Salinas River, the yellow stubble fields seemed to be bathed in pale cold sunshine, but there was no sunshine in the valley now in December. The thick willow scrub along the river flamed with sharp and positive yellow leaves.

Salinas Valley *south of San Francisco in the Coast Ranges region of California*

It was a time of quiet and of waiting. The air was cold and tender. A light wind blew up from the southwest so that the farmers were mildly hopeful of a good rain before long; but fog and rain do not go together.

Across the river, on Henry Allen's foothill ranch there was little work to be done, for the hay was cut and stored and the orchards were plowed up to receive the rain deeply when it should come. The cattle on the higher slopes were becoming shaggy and rough-coated.

Elisa Allen, working in her flower garden, looked down across the yard and saw Henry, her husband, talking to two men in business suits. The three of them stood by the tractor shed, each man with one foot on the side of the little Fordson. They smoked cigarettes and studied the machine as they talked.

Elisa watched them for a moment and then went back to her work. She was thirty-five. Her face was lean and strong and her eyes were as clear as water. Her figure looked blocked and heavy in her gardening costume, a man's black hat pulled low down over her eyes, clod-hopper shoes, a figured print dress almost completely covered by a big corduroy apron with four big pockets to hold the snips, the trowel and scratcher, the seeds and the knife she worked with. She wore heavy leather gloves to protect her hands while she worked.

She was cutting down the old year's chrysanthemum stalks with a pair of short and powerful scissors. She looked down toward the men by the tractor shed now and then. Her face was eager and mature and handsome; even her work with the scissors was over-eager, over-powerful. The chrysanthemum stems seemed too small and easy for her energy.

She brushed a cloud of hair out of her eyes with the back of her glove, and left a smudge of earth on her cheek in doing it. Behind her stood the neat white farm house with red geraniums close-banked around it as high as the windows. It was a hard-swept looking little house with hard-polished windows, and a clean mud-mat on the front steps.

Elisa cast another glance toward the tractor shed. The strangers were getting into their Ford coupe. She took off a glove and put her strong fingers down into the forest of new green chrysanthemum sprouts that were growing around the old roots. She spread the leaves and looked down among the close-growing stems. No aphids were there, no sowbugs or snails or cutworms. Her terrier fingers destroyed such pests before they could get started.

Elisa started at the sound of her husband's voice. He had come near quietly, and he leaned over the wire fence that protected her flower garden from cattle and dogs and chickens.

"At it again," he said. "You've got a strong new crop coming."

Elisa straightened her back and pulled on the gardening glove again. "Yes. They'll be strong this coming year." In her tone and on her face there was a little smugness.

"You've got a gift with things," Henry observed. "Some of those yellow chrysanthemums you had this year were ten inches across. I wish you'd work out in the orchard and raise some apples that big."

Her eyes sharpened. "Maybe I could do it, too. I've a gift with things, all right. My mother had it. She could stick anything in the ground and make it grow. She said it was having planters' hands that knew how to do it."

"Well, it sure works with flowers," he said.

"Henry, who were those men you were talking to?"

"Why, sure, that's what I came to tell you. They were from the Western Meat Company. I sold those thirty head of three-year-old steers. Got nearly my own price, too."

"Good," she said. "Good for you."

"And I thought," he continued, "I thought how it's Saturday afternoon, and we might go into Salinas for dinner at a restaurant, and then to a picture show—to celebrate, you see."

"Good," she repeated. "Oh, yes. That will be good."

Henry put on his joking tone. "There's fights tonight. How'd you like to go to the fights?"

"Oh, no," she said breathlessly. "No, I wouldn't like fights."

"Just fooling, Elisa. We'll go to a movie. Let's see. It's two now. I'm going to take Scotty and bring down those steers from the hill. It'll take us maybe two hours. We'll go in town about five and have dinner at the Cominos Hotel. Like that?"

"Of course I'll like it. It's good to eat away from home."

"All right, then. I'll go get up a couple of horses."

She said, "I'll have plenty of time to transplant some of these sets, I guess." She heard her husband calling Scotty down by the barn. And a little later she saw the two men ride up the pale yellow hillside in search of the steers.

There was a little square sandy bed kept for rooting the chrysanthemums. With her trowel she turned the soil over and over, and smoothed it and patted it firm. Then she dug ten parallel trenches to receive the sets. Back at the chrysanthemum bed she pulled out the little crisp shoots, trimmed off the leaves of each one with her scissors and laid it on a small orderly pile.

A squeak of wheels and plod of hoofs came from the road. Elisa looked up. The country road ran along the dense bank of willows and cottonwoods that bordered the river, and up this road came a curious vehicle, curiously drawn. It was an old spring-wagon, with a round canvas top on it like the cover of a prairie schooner. It was drawn by an old bay horse and a little grey-and-white burro. A big stubble-bearded man sat between the cover flaps and drove the crawling team. Underneath the wagon, between the hind wheels, a lean and rangy mongrel dog walked sedately. Words were painted on the canvas, in clumsy, crooked letters. "Pots, pans, knives, sisors, lawn mores, Fixed." Two rows of articles, and the triumphantly definitive "Fixed" below. The black paints had run down in little sharp points beneath each letter.

Elisa, squatting on the ground, watched to see the crazy, loose-jointed wagon pass by. But it didn't pass. It turned into the farm road in front of her house, crooked old wheels skirling and squeaking. The rangy dog darted from between the wheels and ran ahead. Instantly the two ranch shepherds flew out at him. Then all three stopped, and with stiff and quivering tails, with taut straight legs, with ambassadorial dignity, they slowly circled, sniffing daintily. The caravan pulled up to Elisa's wire fence and stopped. Now the newcomer dog, feeling out-numbered, lowered his tail and retired under the wagon with raised hackles and bared teeth.

The man on the wagon seat called out, "That's a bad dog in a fight when he gets started."

Elisa laughed. "I see he is. How soon does he generally get started?"

The man caught up her laughter and echoed it heartily. "Sometimes not for weeks and weeks," he said. He climbed stiffly down, over the wheel. The horse and the donkey drooped like unwatered flowers.

Elisa saw that he was a very big man. Although his hair and beard were graying, he did not look old. His worn black suit was wrinkled and spotted with grease. The laughter had disappeared from his face and eyes the moment his laughing voice ceased. His eyes were dark, and they were full of the brooding that gets in the eyes of teamsters and of sailors. The calloused hands he rested on the wire fence were cracked, and every crack was a black line. He took off his battered hat.

"I'm off my general road, ma'am," he said. "Does this dirt road cut over across the river to the Los Angeles highway?"

Elisa stood up and shoved the thick scissors in her apron pocket. "Well, yes, it does, but it winds around and then fords the river. I don't think your team could pull through the sand."

He replied with some asperity. "It might surprise you what them beasts can pull through."

"When they get started?" she asked.

He smiled for a second. "Yes. When they get started."

"Well," said Elisa, "I think you'll save time if you go back to the Salinas road and pick up the highway there."

He drew a big finger down the chicken wire and made it sing. "I ain't in any hurry, ma'am. I go from Seattle to San Diego and back every year. Takes all my time. About six months each way. I aim to follow nice weather."

Elisa took off her gloves and stuffed them in the apron pocket with the scissors. She touched the under edge of her man's hat, searching for fugitive hairs. "That sounds like a nice kind of a way to live," she said.

He leaned confidentially over the fence. "Maybe you noticed the writing on my wagon. I mend pots and sharpen knives and scissors. You got any of them things to do?"

"Oh, no," she said quickly. "Nothing like that." Her eyes hardened with resistance.

"Scissors is the worst thing," he explained. "Most people just ruin scissors trying to sharpen 'em, but I know how. I got a special tool. It's a little bobbit kind of thing, and patented. But it sure does the trick."

"No. My scissors are all sharp."

"All right, then. Take a pot," he continued earnestly, "a bent pot, or a pot with a hole. I can make it like new so you don't have to buy no new ones. That's a saving for you."

"No," she said shortly. "I tell you I have nothing like that for you to do."

His face fell to an exaggerated sadness. His voice took on a whining undertone. "I ain't had a thing to do today. Maybe I won't have no supper tonight. You see I'm off my regular road. I know folks on the highway clear from Seattle to San Diego. They save their things for me to sharpen up because they know I do it so good and save them money."

"I'm sorry," Elisa said irritably. "I haven't anything for you to do."

His eyes left her face and fell to searching the ground. They roamed about until they came to the chrysanthemum bed where she had been working. "What's them plants, ma'am?"

The irritation and resistance melted from Elisa's face. "Oh, those are chrysanthemums, giant whites and yellows. I raise them every year, bigger than anybody around here."

"Kind of a long-stemmed flower? Looks like a quick puff of colored smoke?" he asked.

"That's it. What a nice way to describe them."

"They smell kind of nasty till you get used to them," he said.

"It's a good bitter smell," she retorted, "not nasty at all."

He changed his tone quickly. "I like the smell myself."

"I had ten-inch blooms this year," she said.

The man leaned farther over the fence. "Look. I know a lady down the road a piece, has got the nicest garden you ever seen. Got nearly every kind of flower but no chrysanthemums. Last time I was mending a copper-bottom washtub for her (that's a hard job but I do it good), she said to me, 'If you ever run acrost some nice chrysanthemums I wish you'd try to get me a few seeds.' That's what she told me."

Elisa's eyes grew alert and eager. "She couldn't have known much about chrysanthemums. You *can* raise them from seed, but it's much easier to root the little sprouts you see there."

"Oh," he said. "I s'pose I can't take none to her, then."

"Why yes you can," Elisa cried. "I can put some in damp sand, and you can carry them right along with you. They'll take root in the pot if you keep them damp. And then she can transplant them."

"She'd sure like to have some, ma'am. You say they're nice ones?"

"Beautiful," she said. "Oh, beautiful." Her eyes shone. She tore off the battered hat and shook out her dark pretty hair. "I'll put them in a flower pot, and you can take them right with you. Come into the yard."

While the man came through the picket gate Elisa ran excitedly along the geranium-bordered path to the back of the house. And she returned carrying a big red flower pot. The gloves were forgotten now. She kneeled on the ground by the starting bed and dug up the sandy soil with her fingers and scooped it into the bright new flower pot. Then she picked up the little pile of shoots she had prepared. With her strong fingers she pressed them in the sand and tamped around them with her knuckles. The man stood over her. "I'll tell you what to do," she said. "You remember so you can tell the lady."

"Yes, I'll try to remember."

"Well, look. These will take root in about a month. Then she must set them out, about a foot apart in good rich earth like this, see?" She lifted a handful of dark soil for him to look at. "They'll grow fast and tall. Now remember this: In July tell her to cut them down, about eight inches from the ground."

"Before they bloom?" he asked.

"Yes, before they bloom." Her face was tight with eagerness. "They'll grow right up again. About the last of September the buds will start."

She stopped and seemed perplexed. "It's the budding that takes the most care," she said hesitantly. "I don't know how to tell you." She looked deep into his eyes, searchingly. Her mouth opened a little, and she seemed to be listening. "I'll try to tell you," she said. "Did you ever hear of planting hands?"

"Can't say I have, ma'am."

"Well, I can only tell you what it feels like. It's when you're picking off the buds you don't want. Everything goes right down into your fingertips. You watch your fingers work. They do it themselves. You can feel how it is. They pick and pick the buds. They never make a mistake. They're with the plant. Do you see? Your fingers and the plant. You can feel that, right up your arm. They know. They never make a mistake. You can feel it. When you're like that you can't do anything wrong. Do you see that? Can you understand that?"

She was kneeling on the ground looking up at him. Her breast swelled passionately.

The man's eyes narrowed. He looked away self-consciously. "Maybe I know," he said. "Sometimes in the night in the wagon there—"

Elisa's voice grew husky. She broke in on him, "I've never lived as you do, but I know what you mean. When the night is dark—why, the stars are sharp-pointed, and there's quiet. Why, you rise up and up! Every pointed star gets driven into your body. It's like that. Hot and sharp and—lovely."

Kneeling there, her hand went out toward his legs in the greasy black trousers. Her hesitant fingers almost touched the cloth. Then her hand dropped to the ground. She crouched low like a fawning dog.

He said, "It's nice, just like you say. Only when you don't have no dinner, it ain't."

She stood up then, very straight, and her face was ashamed. She held the flower pot out to him and placed it gently in his arms. "Here. Put it in your wagon, on the seat, where you can watch it. Maybe I can find something for you to do."

At the back of the house she dug in the can pile and found two old and battered aluminum saucepans. She carried them back and gave them to him. "Here, maybe you can fix these."

His manner changed. He became professional. "Good as new I can fix them." At the back of his wagon he set a little anvil, and out of an oily tool box dug a small machine hammer. Elisa came through the gate to watch him while he pounded out the dents in the kettles. His mouth grew sure and knowing. At a difficult part of the work he sucked his under-lip.

"You sleep right in the wagon?" Elisa asked.

"Right in the wagon, ma'am. Rain or shine I'm dry as a cow in there."

"It must be nice," she said. "It must be very nice. I wish women could do such things."

"It ain't the right kind of a life for a woman."

Her upper lip raised a little, showing her teeth. "How do you know? How can you tell?" she said.

"I don't know, ma'am," he protested. "Of course I don't know. Now here's your kettles, done. You don't have to buy no new ones."

"How much?"

"Oh, fifty cents'll do. I keep my prices down and my work good. That's why I have all them satisfied customers up and down the highway."

Elisa brought him a fifty-cent piece from the house and dropped it in his hand. "You might be surprised to have a rival some time. I can sharpen scissors, too. And I can beat the dents out of little pots. I could show you what a woman might do."

He put his hammer back in the oily box and shoved the little anvil out of sight. "It would be a lonely life for a woman, ma'am, and a scarey life, too, with animals creeping under the wagon all night." He climbed over the singletree, steadying himself with a hand on the burro's white rump. He settled himself in the seat, picked up the lines. "Thank you kindly, ma'am," he said. "I'll do like you told me; I'll go back and catch the Salinas road."

"Mind," she called, "if you're long in getting there, keep the sand damp."

"Sand, ma'am? . . . Sand? Oh, sure. You mean around the chrysanthemums. Sure I will." He clucked his tongue. The beasts leaned luxuriously into their collars. The mongrel dog took his place between the back wheels. The wagon turned and crawled out the entrance road and back the way it had come, along the river.

Elisa stood in front of her wire fence watching the slow progress of the caravan. Her shoulders were straight, her head thrown back, her eyes half-closed, so that the scene came vaguely into them. Her lips moved silently, forming the words "Good-bye—good-bye." Then she whispered. "That's a bright direction. There's a glowing there." The sound of her whisper startled her. She shook herself free and looked about to see whether anyone had been listening. Only the dogs had heard. They lifted their heads toward her from their sleeping in the dust, and then stretched out their chins and settled asleep again. Elisa turned and ran hurriedly into the house.

In the kitchen she reached behind the stove and felt the water tank. It was full of hot water from the noonday cooking. In the bathroom she tore off her soiled clothes and flung them into the corner. And then she scrubbed herself with a little block of pumice, legs and thighs, loins and chest and arms, until her skin was scratched and red. When she had dried herself she stood in front of a mirror in her bedroom and looked at her body. She tightened her stomach and threw out her chest. She turned and looked over her shoulder at her back.

After a while she began to dress, slowly. She put on her newest under-clothing and her nicest stockings and the dress which was the symbol of her prettiness. She worked carefully on her hair, penciled her eyebrows and rouged her lips.

Before she was finished she heard the little thunder of hoofs and the shouts of Henry and his helper as they drove the red steers into the corral. She heard the gate bang shut and set herself for Henry's arrival.

His step sounded on the porch. He entered the house calling, "Elisa, where are you?"

"In my room, dressing. I'm not ready. There's hot water for your bath. Hurry up. It's getting late."

When she heard him splashing in the tub, Elisa laid his dark suit on the bed, and shirt and socks and tie beside it. She stood his polished shoes on the floor beside the bed. Then she went to the porch and sat primly and stiffly down. She looked toward the river road where the willow-line was still yellow with frosted leaves so that under the high grey fog they seemed a thin band of sunshine. This was the only color in the grey afternoon. She sat unmoving for a long time. Her eyes blinked rarely.

Henry came banging out of the door, shoving his tie inside his vest as he came. Elisa stiffened and her face grew tight. Henry stopped short and looked at her. "Why—why, Elisa. You look so nice!"

"Nice? You think I look nice? What do you mean by 'nice'?"

Henry blundered on. "I don't know. I mean you look different, strong and happy."

"I am strong? Yes, strong. What do you mean 'strong'?"

He looked bewildered. "You're playing some kind of a game," he said helplessly. "It's a kind of a play. You look strong enough to break a calf over your knee, happy enough to eat it like a watermelon."

For a second she lost her rigidity. "Henry! Don't talk like that. You didn't know what you said." She grew complete again. "I'm strong," she boasted. "I never knew before how strong."

Henry looked down toward the tractor shed, and when he brought his eyes back to her, they were his own again. "I'll get out the car. You can put on your coat while I'm starting."

Elisa went into the house. She heard him drive to the gate and idle down his motor, and then she took a long time to put on her hat. She pulled it here and pressed it there. When Henry turned the motor off she slipped into her coat and went out.

The little roadster bounced along on the dirt road by the river, raising the birds and driving the rabbits into the brush. Two cranes flapped heavily over the willow-line and dropped into the river-bed.

Far ahead on the road Elisa saw a dark speck. She knew.

She tried not to look as they passed it, but her eyes would not obey. She whispered to herself sadly, "He might have thrown them off the road. That wouldn't have been much trouble, not very much. But he kept the pot," she explained. "He had to keep the pot. That's why he couldn't get them off the road."

The roadster turned a bend and she saw the caravan ahead. She swung full around toward her husband so she could not see the little covered wagon and the mismatched team as the car passed them.

In a moment it was over. The thing was done. She did not look back.

She said loudly, to be heard above the motor, "It will be good, tonight, a good dinner."

"Now you're changed again," Henry complained. He took one hand from the wheel and patted her knee. "I ought to take you in to dinner oftener. It would be good for both of us. We get so heavy out on the ranch."

"Henry," she asked, "could we have wine at dinner?"

"Sure we could. Say! That will be fine."

She was silent for a while; then she said, "Henry, at those prize fights, do the men hurt each other very much?"

"Sometimes a little, not often. Why?"

"Well, I've read how they break noses, and blood runs down their chests. I've read how the fighting gloves get heavy and soggy with blood."

He looked around at her. "What's the matter, Elisa? I didn't know you read things like that." He brought the car to a stop, then turned to the right over the Salinas River bridge.

"Do any women ever go to the fights?" she asked.

"Oh, sure, some. What's the matter, Elisa? Do you want to go? I don't think you'd like it, but I'll take you if you really want to go."

She relaxed limply in the seat. "Oh, no. No. I don't want to go. I'm sure I don't." Her face was turned away from him. "It will be enough if we can have wine. It will be plenty." She turned up her coat collar so he could not see that she was crying weakly—like an old woman.

(1938)

QUESTIONS FOR CRITICAL THINKING AND WRITING

Experience

1. Which parts of the story do you find most interesting and engaging? Which least? Why?
2. Which parts of the story do you find most confusing or mysterious? Why?

Interpretation

3. How does Steinbeck characterize Elisa? Which details convey the most?
4. How is her husband characterized? Which details convey most about him?
5. What can we surmise about their marriage? Which details best convey a sense of their relationship?
6. What is the significance of the traveling repair man?

7. How does Elisa behave toward him? And when does her behavior change? Why?
8. Why does he throw away the chrysanthemums? What is the significance of that act—for him and for Elisa?
9. What do the chrysanthemums symbolize?

Evaluation

10. What is important for Elisa? Why does she invest so much time and energy in her chrysanthemums? Why does she show a sudden interest in the fights at the end of the story?

Connection

11. Compare the wife in this story with the wife in Boyle's "Astronomer's Wife." Comment on the situations of each woman and the outcome of each story.

Critical Thinking

12. What kind of life do you think Elisa is best suited for? To what extent is she well suited to the life she has? Explain.

AMY TAN
[b. 1952]

Amy Tan was born in Oakland, California, three years after her parents left China during the Maoist revolution. She attended schools in California and in Switzerland and received an M.A. at the University of California at Berkeley. Before devoting herself to writing fiction and memoir, Tan worked as a writer of computer manuals. Her writing draws on her experience as a Chinese-American with a dual cultural heritage. She is best known for her novel The Joy Luck Club *(1989), which was made into a successful film, and from which the story "Rules of the Game" has been taken.*

Rules of the Game

I was six when my mother taught me the art of invisible strength. It was a strategy for winning arguments, respect from others, and eventually, though neither of us knew it at the time, chess games.

"Bite back your tongue," scolded my mother when I cried loudly, yanking her hand toward the store that sold bags of salted plums. At home, she said, "Wise guy, he not go against wind. In Chinese we say, Come from South, blow with wind—poom!—North will follow. Strongest wind cannot be seen."

The next week I bit back my tongue as we entered the store with the forbidden candies. When my mother finished her shopping, she quietly plucked a small bag of plums from the rack and put it on the counter with the rest of the items.

My mother imparted her daily truths so she could help my older brothers and me rise above our circumstances. We lived in San Francisco's Chinatown. Like most of the other Chinese children who played in the back alleys of restaurants and curio shops, I didn't think we were poor. My bowl was always full, three five-course meals every day, beginning with a soup full of mysterious things I didn't want to know the names of.

We lived on Waverly Place, in a warm, clean, two-bedroom flat that sat above a small Chinese bakery specializing in steamed pastries and dim sum. In the early morning, when the alley was still quiet, I could smell fragrant red beans as they were cooked down to a pasty sweetness. By daybreak, our flat was heavy with the odor of fried sesame balls and sweet curried chicken crescents. From my bed, I would listen as my father got ready for work, then locked the door behind him, one-two-three clicks.

At the end of our two-block alley was a small sandlot playground with swings and slides well-shined down the middle with use. The play area was bordered by wood-slat benches where old-country people sat cracking roasted watermelon seeds with their golden teeth and scattering the husks to an impatient gathering of gurgling pigeons. The best playground, however, was the dark alley itself. It was crammed with daily mysteries and adventures. My brothers and I would peer into the medicinal herb shop, watching old Li dole out onto a stiff sheet of white paper the right amount of insect shells, saffron-colored seeds, and pungent leaves for his ailing customers. It was said that he once cured a woman dying of an ancestral curse that had eluded the best of American doctors. Next to the pharmacy was a printer who specialized in gold-embossed wedding invitations and festive red banners.

Farther down the street was Ping Yuen Fish Market. The front window displayed a tank crowded with doomed fish and turtles struggling to gain footing on the slimy green-tiled sides. A hand-written sign informed tourists, "Within this store, is all for food, not for pet." Inside, the butchers with their bloodstained white smocks deftly gutted the fish while customers cried out their orders and shouted, "Give me your freshest," to which the butchers always protested, "All are freshest." On less crowded market days, we would inspect the crates of live frogs and crabs which we were warned not to poke, boxes of dried cuttlefish, and row upon row of iced prawns, squid, and slippery fish. The sanddabs made me shiver each time; their eyes lay on one flattened side and reminded me of my mother's story of a careless girl who ran into a crowded street and was crushed by a cab. "Was smash flat," reported my mother.

At the corner of the alley was Hong Sing's, a four-table café with a recessed stairwell in front that led to a door marked "Tradesmen." My brothers and I believed the bad people emerged from this door at night. Tourists never went to Hong Sing's, since the menu was printed only in Chinese. A Caucasian man with a big camera once posed me and my playmates in front of the restaurant. He had us move to the side of the picture window so the photo would capture the roasted duck with its head dangling from a juice-covered rope. After he took the picture, I told him he should go into Hong Sing's and eat dinner. When he smiled and asked me what they served, I shouted, "Guts and duck's feet and octopus gizzards!" Then I ran off with my friends, shrieking with laughter as we scampered across the alley and hid in the entryway grotto of the China Gem Company, my heart pounding with hope that he would chase us.

My mother named me after the street that we lived on: Waverly Place Jong, my official name for important American documents. But my family called me Meimei, "Little Sister." I was the youngest, the only daughter. Each morning before school, my mother would twist and yank on my thick black hair until she had formed two tightly wound pigtails. One day, as she struggled to weave a hard-toothed comb through my disobedient hair, I had a sly thought.

I asked her, "Ma, what is Chinese torture?" My mother shook her head. A bobby pin was wedged between her lips. She wetted her palm and smoothed the hair above my ear, then pushed the pin in so that it nicked sharply against my scalp.

"Who say this word?" she asked without a trace of knowing how wicked I was being. I shrugged my shoulders and said, "Some boy in my class said Chinese people do Chinese torture."

"Chinese people do many things," she said simply. "Chinese people do business, do medicine, do painting. Not lazy like American people. We do torture. Best torture."

My older brother Vincent was the one who actually got the chess set. We had gone to the annual Christmas party held at the First Chinese Baptist Church at the end of the alley. The missionary ladies had put together a Santa bag of gifts donated by members of another church. None of the gifts had names on them. There were separate sacks for boys and girls of different ages.

One of the Chinese parishioners had donned a Santa Claus costume and a stiff paper beard with cotton balls glued to it. I think the only children who thought he was the real thing were too young to know that Santa Claus was not Chinese. When my turn came up, the Santa man asked me how old I was. I thought it was a trick question; I was seven according to the American formula and eight by the Chinese calendar. I said I was born on March 17, 1951. That seemed to satisfy him. He then solemnly asked if I had been a very, very good girl this year and did I believe in Jesus Christ and obey my parents. I knew the only answer to that. I nodded back with equal solemnity.

Having watched the other children opening their gifts, I already knew that the big gifts were not necessarily the nicest ones. One girl my age got a large coloring book of biblical characters, while a less greedy girl who selected a smaller box received a glass vial of lavender toilet water. The sound of the box was also important. A ten-year-old boy had chosen a box that jangled when he shook it. It was a tin globe of the world with a slit for inserting money. He must have thought it was full of dimes and nickels, because when he saw that it had just ten pennies, his face fell with such undisguised disappointment that his mother slapped the side of his head and led him out of the church hall, apologizing to the crowd for her son who had such bad manners he couldn't appreciate such a fine gift.

As I peered into the sack, I quickly fingered the remaining presents, testing their weight, imagining what they contained. I chose a heavy, compact one that was wrapped in shiny silver foil and a red satin ribbon. It was a twelve-pack of Life Savers and I spent the rest of the party arranging and rearranging the candy tubes in the order of my favorites. My brother Winston chose wisely as well. His present turned out to be a box of intricate plastic parts; the instructions on the box proclaimed that when they were properly assembled he would have an authentic miniature replica of a World War II submarine.

Vincent got the chess set, which would have been a very decent present to get at a church Christmas party, except it was obviously used and, as we discovered later, it was missing a black pawn and a white knight. My mother graciously thanked the unknown benefactor, saying, "Too good. Cost too much." At which point, an old lady with fine white, wispy hair nodded toward our family and said with a whistling whisper, "Merry, merry Christmas."

When we got home, my mother told Vincent to throw the chess set away. "She not want it. We not want it," she said, tossing her head stiffly to the side with a tight, proud smile. My brothers had deaf ears. They were already lining up the chess pieces and reading from the dog-eared instruction book.

I watched Vincent and Winston play during Christmas week. The chessboard seemed to hold elaborate secrets waiting to be untangled. The chessmen were more powerful than old Li's magic herbs that cured ancestral curses. And my brothers wore such serious faces that I was sure something was at stake that was greater than avoiding the tradesmen's door to Hong Sing's.

"Let me! Let me!" I begged between games when one brother or the other would sit back with a deep sigh of relief and victory, the other annoyed, unable to let go of the outcome. Vincent at first refused to let me play, but when I offered my Life Savers as replacements for the buttons that filled in for the missing pieces, he relented. He chose the flavors: wild cherry for the black pawn and peppermint for the white knight. Winner could eat both.

As our mother sprinkled flour and rolled out small doughy circles for the steamed dumplings that would be our dinner that night, Vincent explained the rules, pointing to each piece. "You have sixteen pieces and so do I. One king and queen, two bishops, two knights, two castles, and eight pawns. The pawns can only move forward one step, except on the first move. Then they can move two. But they can only take men by moving crossways like this, except in the beginning, when you can move ahead and take another pawn."

"Why?" I asked as I moved my pawn. "Why can't they move more steps?"

"Because they're pawns," he said.

"But why do they go crossways to take other men? Why aren't there any women and children?"

"Why is the sky blue? Why must you always ask stupid questions?" asked Vincent. "This is a game. These are the rules. I didn't make them up. See. Here. In the book." He jabbed a page with a pawn in his hand. "Pawn. P-A-W-N. Pawn. Read it yourself."

My mother patted the flour off her hands. "Let me see book," she said quietly. She scanned the pages quickly, not reading the foreign English symbols, seeming to search deliberately for nothing in particular.

"This American rules," she concluded at last. "Every time people come out from foreign country, must know rules. You not know, judge say, Too bad, go back. They not telling you why so you can use their way go forward. They say, Don't know why, you find out yourself. But they knowing all the time. Better you take it, find out why yourself." She tossed her head back with a satisfied smile.

I found out about all the whys later. I read the rules and looked up all the big words in a dictionary. I borrowed books from the Chinatown library. I studied each chess piece, trying to absorb the power each contained.

I learned about opening moves and why it's important to control the center early on; the shortest distance between two points is straight down the middle. I learned about the middle game and why tactics between two adversaries are like clashing ideas; the one who plays better has the clearest plans for both attacking and getting out of traps. I learned why it is essential in the endgame to have foresight, a mathematical understanding of all possible moves, and patience; all weaknesses and advantages become evident to a strong adversary and are obscured to a tiring opponent. I discovered that for the whole game one must gather invisible strengths and see the endgame before the game begins.

I also found out why I should never reveal "why" to others. A little knowledge withheld is a great advantage one should store for future use. That is the power of chess. It is a game of secrets in which one must show and never tell.

I loved the secrets I found within the sixty-four black and white squares. I carefully drew a handmade chessboard and pinned it to the wall next to my bed, where at night I would stare for hours at imaginary battles. Soon I no longer lost any games or Life Savers, but I lost my adversaries. Winston and Vincent decided they were more interested in roaming the streets after school in their Hopalong Cassidy cowboy hats.

On a cold spring afternoon, while walking home from school, I detoured through the playground at the end of our alley. I saw a group of old men, two seated across a folding table playing a game of chess, others smoking pipes, eating peanuts, and watching. I ran home and grabbed Vincent's chess set, which was bound in a cardboard box with rubber bands. I also carefully selected two prized rolls of Life Savers. I came back to the park and approached a man who was observing the game.

"Want to play?" I asked him. His face widened with surprise and he grinned as he looked at the box under my arm.

"Little sister, been a long time since I play with dolls," he said, smiling benevolently. I quickly put the box down next to him on the bench and displayed my retort.

Lau Po, as he allowed me to call him, turned out to be a much better player than my brothers. I lost many games and many Life Savers. But over the weeks, with each diminishing roll of candies, I added new secrets. Lau Po gave me the names. The Double Attack from the East and West Shores. Throwing Stones on the Drowning Man. The Sudden Meeting of the Clan. The Surprise from the Sleeping Guard. The Humble Servant Who Kills the King. Sand in the Eyes of Advancing Forces. A Double Killing Without Blood.

There were also the fine points of chess etiquette. Keep captured men in neat rows, as well-tended prisoners. Never announce "Check" with vanity, lest someone with an unseen sword slit your throat. Never hurl pieces into the sandbox after you have lost a game, because then you must find them again, by yourself, after apologizing to all around you. By the end of the summer, Lau Po had taught me all he knew, and I had become a better chess player.

A small weekend crowd of Chinese people and tourists would gather as I played and defeated my opponents one by one. My mother would join the crowds during these outdoor exhibition games. She sat proudly on the bench, telling my admirers with proper Chinese humility, "Is luck."

A man who watched me play in the park suggested that my mother allow me to play in local chess tournaments. My mother smiled graciously, an answer that meant nothing. I desperately wanted to go, but I bit back my tongue. I knew she would not let me play among strangers. So as we walked home I said in a small voice that I didn't want to play in the local tournament. They would have American rules. If I lost, I would bring shame on my family.

"Is shame you fall down nobody push you," said my mother.

During my first tournament, my mother sat with me in the front row as I waited for my turn. I frequently bounced my legs to unstick them from the cold metal seat of the folding chair. When my name was called, I leapt up. My mother unwrapped something in her lap. It was her *chang,* a small tablet of red jade which held the sun's fire. "Is luck," she whispered, and tucked it into my dress pocket. I turned to my opponent, a fifteen-year-old boy from Oakland. He looked at me, wrinkling his nose.

As I began to play, the boy disappeared, the color ran out of the room, and I saw only my white pieces and his black ones waiting on the other side. A light wind began blowing past my ears. It whispered secrets only I could hear.

"Blow from the South," it murmured. "The wind leaves no trail." I saw a clear path, the traps to avoid. The crowd rustled. "Shhh! Shhh!" said the corners of the room. The wind blew stronger. "Throw sand from the East to distract him." The knight came forward ready for the sacrifice. The wind hissed, louder and louder. "Blow, blow, blow. He cannot see. He is blind now. Make him lean away from the wind so he is easier to knock down."

"Check," I said, as the wind roared with laughter. The wind died down to little puffs, my own breath.

My mother placed my first trophy next to a new plastic chess set that the neighborhood Tao society had given to me. As she wiped each piece with a soft cloth, she said, "Next time win more, lose less."

"Ma, it's not how many pieces you lose," I said. "Sometimes you need to lose pieces to get ahead."

"Better to lose less, see if you really need."

At the next tournament, I won again, but it was my mother who wore the triumphant grin.

"Lost eight piece this time. Last time was eleven. What I tell you? Better off lose less!" I was annoyed, but I couldn't say anything.

I attended more tournaments, each one farther away from home. I won all games, in all divisions. The Chinese bakery downstairs from our flat displayed my growing collection of trophies in its window, amidst the dust-covered cakes that were never picked up. The day after I won an important regional tournament, the window encased a fresh sheet cake with whipped-cream frosting and red script saying "Congratulations, Waverly Jong, Chinatown Chess Champion." Soon after that, a flower shop, headstone engraver, and funeral parlor offered to sponsor me in national tournaments.

That's when my mother decided I no longer had to do the dishes. Winston and Vincent had to do my chores.

"Why does she get to play and we do all the work," complained Vincent.

"Is new American rules," said my mother. "Meimei play, squeeze all her brains out for win chess. You play, worth squeeze towel."

By my ninth birthday, I was a national chess champion. I was still some 429 points away from grand-master status, but I was touted as the Great American Hope, a child prodigy and a girl to boot. They ran a photo of me in *Life* magazine next to a quote in which Bobby Fischer said, "There will never be a woman grand master." "Your move, Bobby," said the caption.

The day they took the magazine picture I wore neatly plaited braids clipped with plastic barrettes trimmed with rhinestones. I was playing in a large high school auditorium that echoed with phlegmy coughs and the squeaky rubber knobs of chair legs sliding across freshly waxed wooden floors. Seated across from me was an American man, about the same age as Lau Po, maybe fifty. I remember that his sweaty brow seemed to weep at my every move. He wore a dark, malodorous suit. One of his pockets was stuffed with a great white kerchief on which he wiped his palm before sweeping his hand over the chosen chess piece with great flourish.

In my crisp pink-and-white dress with scratchy lace at the neck, one of two my mother had sewn for these special occasions, I would clasp my hands under my chin, the delicate points of my elbows poised lightly on the table in the manner my mother had shown me for posing for the press. I would swing my patent leather shoes back and forth like an impatient child riding on a school bus. Then I would pause, suck in my lips, twirl my chosen piece in midair as if undecided, and then firmly plant it in its new threatening place, with a triumphant smile thrown back at my opponent for good measure.

I no longer played in the alley of Waverly Place. I never visited the playground where the pigeons and old men gathered. I went to school, then directly home to learn new chess secrets, cleverly concealed advantages, more escape routes.

But I found it difficult to concentrate at home. My mother had a habit of standing over me while I plotted out my games. I think she thought of herself as my protective ally. Her lips would be sealed tight, and after each move I made, a soft "Hmmmmph" would escape from her nose.

"Ma, I can't practice when you stand there like that," I said one day. She retreated to the kitchen and made loud noises with the pots and pans. When the crashing stopped, I could see out of the corner of my eye that she was standing in the doorway. "Hmmmmph!" Only this one came out of her tight throat.

My parents made many concessions to allow me to practice. One time I complained that the bedroom I shared was so noisy that I couldn't think. Thereafter, my brothers slept in a bed in the living room facing the street. I said I couldn't finish my rice; my head didn't work right when my stomach was too full. I left the table with half-finished bowls and nobody complained. But there was one duty I couldn't avoid. I had to accompany my mother on Saturday market days when I had no tournament to play. My mother would proudly walk with me, visiting many shops, buying very little. "This my daughter Wave-ly Jong," she said to whoever looked her way.

One day after we left a shop I said under my breath, "I wish you wouldn't do that, telling everybody I'm your daughter." My mother stopped walking. Crowds of people with heavy bags pushed past us on the sidewalk, bumping into first one shoulder, then another.

"Aiii-ya. So shame be with mother?" She grasped my hand even tighter as she glared at me.

I looked down. "It's not that, it's just so obvious. It's just so embarrassing."

"Embarrass you be my daughter?" Her voice was cracking with anger.

"That's not what I meant. That's not what I said."

"What you say?"

I knew it was a mistake to say anything more, but I heard my voice speaking, "Why do you have to use me to show off? If you want to show off, then why don't you learn to play chess."

My mother's eyes turned into dangerous black slits. She had no words for me, just sharp silence.

I felt the wind rushing around my hot ears. I jerked my hand out of my mother's tight grasp and spun around, knocking into an old woman. Her bag of groceries spilled to the ground.

"Aii-ya! Stupid girl!" my mother and the woman cried. Oranges and tin cans careened down the sidewalk. As my mother stooped to help the old woman pick up the escaping food, I took off.

I raced down the street, dashing between people, not looking back as my mother screamed shrilly, "Meimei! Meimei!" I fled down an alley, past dark curtained shops and merchants washing the grime off their windows. I sped into the sunlight, into a large street crowded with tourists examining trinkets and souvenirs. I ducked into another dark alley, down another street, up another alley. I ran until it hurt and I realized I had nowhere to go, that I was not running from anything. The alleys contained no escape routes.

My breath came out like angry smoke. It was cold. I sat down on an upturned plastic pail next to a stack of empty boxes, cupping my chin with my hands, thinking hard. I imagined my mother, first walking briskly down one street or another looking for me, then giving up and returning home to await my arrival. After two hours, I stood up on creaking legs and slowly walked home.

The alley was quiet and I could see the yellow lights shining from our flat like two tiger's eyes in the night. I climbed the sixteen steps to the door, advancing quietly up each so as not to make any warning sounds. I turned the knob; the door was locked. I heard a chair moving, quick steps, the locks turning—click! click! click!—and then the door opened.

"About time you got home," said Vincent. "Boy, are you in trouble."

He slid back to the dinner table. On a platter were the remains of a large fish, its fleshy head still connected to bones swimming upstream in vain escape. Standing there waiting for my punishment, I heard my mother speak in a dry voice.

"We not concerning this girl. This girl not have concerning for us."

Nobody looked at me. Bone chopsticks clinked against the inside of bowls being emptied into hungry mouths.

I walked into my room, closed the door, and lay down on my bed. The room was dark, the ceiling filled with shadows from the dinnertime lights of neighboring flats.

In my head, I saw a chessboard with sixty-four black and white squares. Opposite me was my opponent, two angry black slits. She wore a triumphant smile. "Strongest wind cannot be seen," she said.

Her black men advanced across the plane, slowly marching to each successive level as a single unit. My white pieces screamed as they scurried and fell off the board one by one. As her men drew closer to my edge, I felt myself growing light. I rose up into the air and flew out the window. Higher and higher, above the alley, over the tops of tiled roofs, where I was gathered up by the wind and pushed up toward the night sky until everything below me disappeared and I was alone.

I closed my eyes and pondered my next move.

(1989)

QUESTIONS FOR CRITICAL THINKING AND WRITING

Experience

1. What were your impressions of the mother? Was she fair to the narrator? What does she mean when she says the "strongest wind cannot be seen"?

Interpretation

2. What is the significance of the story's title? Could the title be applied to more than one game?
3. Does the narrator use her increasing status in her community and family for selfish reasons? Does she miss out on anything as a result?
4. When does the mother call the narrator Waverly? When does she call her Meimei? What is suggested by this distinction?
5. What does the narrator's daydream at the end of the story reveal to her and the reader?

Evaluation

6. How do American and Chinese cultural values clash in the story? Why do you think the narrator mentions food so frequently?

Connection

7. Compare the mother's immigrant experience in "Rules of the Game" with those of the mothers in Jen's "Who's Irish?" Consider their relationships with their daughters as part of your response.

Critical Thinking

8. This story is part of the longer narrative, a novel, *The Joy Luck Club*. To what extent does the story stand on its own and make coherent sense as an independent literary work?

Photography by Curt Richter

ALICE WALKER

[b. 1944]

Alice Walker, recipient of the Pulitzer Prize and National Book Award for her novel The Color Purple *(1982), was born in Georgia, one of eight children. She received a B.A. from Sarah Lawrence College and has held numerous teaching posts at American universities. In her short-story collections* In Love and Trouble *(1973) and* You Can't Keep a Good Woman Down *(1981), she focuses on black American women, whose struggles are the result of their race and their gender. Among the many honors Walker has received for her fiction and poetry are a Guggenheim Fellowship, a National Endowment for the Arts grant, and the American Academy and Institute of Arts and Letters Award.*

Everyday Use

For Your Grandmama

I will wait for her in the yard that Maggie and I made so clean and wavy yesterday afternoon. A yard like this is more comfortable than most people know. It is not just a yard. It is like an extended living room. When the hard clay is swept clean as a floor and the fine sand around the edges lined with tiny, irregular grooves anyone can come and sit and look up into the elm tree and wait for the breezes that never come inside the house.

Maggie will be nervous until after her sister goes: she will stand hopelessly in corners, homely and ashamed of the burn scars down her arms and legs, eyeing her sister with a mixture of envy and awe. She thinks her sister has held life always in the palm of one hand, that "no" is a word the world never learned to say to her.

You've no doubt seen those TV shows° where the child who has "made it" is confronted, as a surprise, by her own mother and father, tottering in weakly from backstage. (A pleasant surprise, of course: What would they do if parent and child came on the show only to curse out and insult each other?) On TV mother and child embrace and smile into each other's faces. Sometimes the mother and father weep, the child wraps them in her arms and leans across the table to tell how she would not have made it without their help. I have seen these programs.

Sometimes I dream a dream in which Dee and I are suddenly brought together on a TV program of this sort. Out of a dark and soft-seated limousine I am ushered into a

TV shows *in the early days of television, a popular show was "This Is Your Life," which the narrator describes exactly here*

bright room filled with many people. There I meet a smiling, gray, sporty man like Johnny Carson who shakes my hand and tells me what a fine girl I have. Then we are on the stage and Dee is embracing me with tears in her eyes. She pins on my dress a large orchid, even though she has told me once that she thinks orchids are tacky flowers.

In real life I am a large, big-boned woman with rough, man-working hands. In the winter I wear flannel nightgowns to bed and overalls during the day. I can kill and clean a hog as mercilessly as a man. My fat keeps me hot in zero weather. I can work outside all day, breaking ice to get water for washing; I can eat pork liver cooked over the open fire minutes after it comes steaming from the hog. One winter I knocked a bull calf straight in the brain between the eyes with a sledge hammer and had the meat hung up to chill before nightfall. But of course all this does not show on television. I am the way my daughter would want me to be: a hundred pounds lighter, my skin like an uncooked barley pancake. My hair glistens in the hot bright lights. Johnny Carson has much to do to keep up with my quick and witty tongue.

But that is a mistake. I know even before I wake up. Who ever knew a Johnson with a quick tongue? Who can even imagine me looking a strange white man in the eye? It seems to me I have talked to them always with one foot raised in flight, with my head turned in whichever way is farthest from them. Dee, though. She would always look anyone in the eye. Hesitation was no part of her nature.

"How do I look, Mama?" Maggie says, showing just enough of her thin body enveloped in pink skirt and red blouse for me to know she's there, almost hidden by the door.

"Come out into the yard," I say.

Have you ever seen a lame animal, perhaps a dog run over by some careless person rich enough to own a car, sidle up to someone who is ignorant enough to be kind to him? That is the way my Maggie walks. She has been like this, chin on chest, eyes on ground, feet in shuffle, ever since the fire that burned the other house to the ground.

Dee is lighter than Maggie, with nicer hair and a fuller figure. She's a woman now, though sometimes I forget. How long ago was it that the other house burned? Ten, twelve years? Sometimes I can still hear the flames and feel Maggie's arms sticking to me, her hair smoking and her dress falling off her in little black papery flakes. Her eyes seemed stretched open, blazed open by the flames reflected in them. And Dee. I see her standing off under the sweet gum tree she used to dig gum out of, a look of concentration on her face as she watched the last dingy gray board of the house fall in toward the red-hot brick chimney. Why don't you do a dance around the ashes? I'd wanted to ask her. She had hated the house that much.

I used to think she hated Maggie, too. But that was before we raised the money, the church and me, to send her to Augusta° to school. She used to read to us without pity; forcing words, lies, other folks' habits, whole lives upon us two, sitting trapped and ignorant underneath her voice. She washed us in a river of make-believe, burned us with a lot of knowledge we didn't necessarily need to know. Pressed us to her with the serious way she read, to shove us away at just the moment, like dimwits, we seemed about to understand.

Dee wanted nice things. A yellow organdy dress to wear to her graduation from high school; black pumps to match a green suit she'd made from an old suit somebody

Augusta *city in eastern Georgia, the location of Paine College*

gave me. She was determined to stare down any disaster in her efforts. Her eyelids would not flicker for minutes at a time. Often I fought off the temptation to shake her. At sixteen she had a style of her own: and knew what style was.

I never had an education myself. After second grade the school was closed down. Don't ask me why: in 1927 colored asked fewer questions than they do now. Sometimes Maggie reads to me. She stumbles along good-naturedly but can't see well. She knows she is not bright. Like good looks and money, quickness passed her by. She will marry John Thomas (who has mossy teeth in an earnest face) and then I'll be free to sit here and I guess just sing church songs to myself. Although I never was a good singer. Never could carry a tune. I was always better at a man's job. I used to love to milk till I was hooked in the side° in '49. Cows are soothing and slow and don't bother you, unless you try to milk them the wrong way.

I have deliberately turned my back on the house. It is three rooms, just like the one that burned, except the roof is tin; they don't make shingle roofs any more. There are no real windows, just some holes cut in the sides, like the portholes in a ship, but not round and not square, with rawhide holding the shutters up on the outside. This house is in a pasture, too, like the other one. No doubt when Dee sees it she will want to tear it down. She wrote me once that no matter where we "choose" to live, she will manage to come see us. But she will never bring her friends. Maggie and I thought about this and Maggie asked me, "Mama, when did Dee ever *have* any friends?"

She had a few. Furtive boys in pink shirts hanging about on washday after school. Nervous girls who never laughed. Impressed with her they worshiped the well-turned phrase, the cute shape, the scalding humor that erupted like bubbles in lye. She read to them.

When she was courting Jimmy T she didn't have much time to pay to us, but turned all her faultfinding power on him. He *flew* to marry a cheap city gal from a family of ignorant flashy people. She hardly had time to recompose herself.

When she comes I will meet—but there they are!

Maggie attempts to make a dash for the house, in her shuffling way, but I stay her with my hand. "Come back here," I say. And she stops and tries to dig a well in the sand with her toe.

It is hard to see them clearly through the strong sun. But even the first glimpse of leg out of the car tells me it is Dee. Her feet were always neat-looking, as if God himself had shaped them with a certain style. From the other side of the car comes a short, stocky man. Hair is all over his head a foot long and hanging from his chin like a kinky mule tail. I hear Maggie suck in her breath. "Uhnnnh," is what it sounds like. Like when you see the wriggling end of a snake just in front of your foot on the road. "Uhnnnh."

Dee next. A dress down to the ground, in this hot weather. A dress so loud it hurts my eyes. There are yellows and oranges enough to throw back the light of the sun. I feel my whole face warming from the heat waves it throws out. Earrings gold, too, and hanging down to her shoulders. Bracelets dangling and making noises when she moves her arm up to shake the folds of the dress out of her armpits. The dress is loose and flows, and as she walks closer, I like it. I hear Maggie go "Uhnnnh" again. It is her sister's hair. It stands straight up like the wool on a sheep. It is black as night and

hooked in the side *kicked by a cow*

around the edges are two long pigtails that rope about like small lizards disappearing behind her ears.

"Wa-su-zo-Tean-o!"° she says, coming on in that gliding way the dress makes her move. The short stocky fellow with the hair to his navel is all grinning and he follows up with "Asalamalakim,° my mother and sister!" He moves to hug Maggie but she falls back, right up against the back of my chair. I feel her trembling there and when I look up I see the perspiration falling off her chin.

"Don't get up," says Dee. Since I am stout it takes something of a push. You can see me trying to move a second or two before I make it. She turns, showing white heels through her sandals, and goes back to the car. Out she peeks next with a Polaroid. She stoops down quickly and lines up picture after picture of me sitting there in front of the house with Maggie cowering behind me. She never takes a shot without making sure the house is included. When a cow comes nibbling around the edge of the yard she snaps it and me and Maggie and the house. Then she puts the Polaroid in the back seat of the car, and comes up *and* kisses me on the forehead.

Meanwhile Asalamalakim is going through motions with Maggie's hand. Maggie's hand is as limp as a fish, and probably as cold, despite the sweat, and she keeps trying to pull it back. It looks like Asalamalakim wants to shake hands but wants to do it fancy. Or maybe he don't know how people shake hands. Anyhow, he soon gives up on Maggie.

"Well," I say. "Dee."

"No, Mama," she says. "Not 'Dee,' Wangero Leewanika Kemanjo!"

"What happened to 'Dee'?" I wanted to know.

"She's dead," Wangero said. "I couldn't bear it any longer being named after the people who oppress me."

"You know as well as me you was named after your aunt Dicie," I said. Dicie is my sister. She named Dee. We called her "Big Dee" after Dee was born.

"But who was she *named* after?" asked Wangero.

"I guess after Grandma Dee," I said.

"And who was she named after?" asked Wangero.

"Her mother," I said, and saw Wangero was getting tired. "That's about as far back as I can trace it," I said. Though, in fact, I probably could have carried it back beyond the Civil War through the branches.

"Well," said Asalamalakim, "there you are."

"Uhnnnh," I heard Maggie say.

"There I was not," I said, "before 'Dicie' cropped up in our family, so why should I try to trace it that far back?"

He just stood there grinning, looking down on me like somebody inspecting a Model A car.° Every once in a while he and Wangero sent eye signals over my head.

"How do you pronounce this name?" I asked.

"You don't have to call me by it if you don't want to," said Wangero.

"Why shouldn't I?" I asked. "If that's what you want us to call you, we'll call you."

"I know it might sound awkward at first," said Wangero.

Wa-su-zo-Tean-o *greeting used by black Muslims* ***Asalamalakim*** *Muslim salutation meaning "Peace be with you."* ***Model A car*** *the Ford car that replaced the Model T in the late 1920s. The Model A was proverbial for its quality and durability*

"I'll get used to it," I said. "Ream it out again."

Well, soon we got the name out of the way. Asalamalakim had a name twice as long and three times as hard. After I tripped over it two or three times he told me to just call him Hakim-a-barber. I wanted to ask him was he a barber, but I didn't really think he was, so I didn't ask.

"You must belong to those beef-cattle peoples down the road," I said. They said "Asalamalakim" when they met you, too, but they didn't shake hands. Always too busy: feeding the cattle, fixing the fences, putting up salt-lick shelters,° throwing down hay. When the white folks poisoned some of the herd the men stayed up all night with rifles in their hands. I walked a mile and a half just to see the sight.

Hakim-a-barber said, "I accept some of their doctrines, but farming and raising cattle is not my style." (They didn't tell me, and I didn't ask, whether Wangero [Dee] had really gone and married him.)

We sat down to eat and right away he said he didn't eat collards and pork was unclean. Wangero, though, went on through the chitlins and corn bread, the greens and everything else. She talked a blue streak over the sweet potatoes. Everything delighted her. Even the fact that we still used the benches her daddy made for the table when we couldn't afford to buy chairs.

"Oh, Mama!" she cried. Then turned to Hakim-a-barber. "I never knew how lovely these benches are. You can feel the rump prints," she said, running her hands underneath her and along the bench. Then she gave a sigh and her hand closed over Grandma Dee's butter dish. "That's it!" she said. "I knew there was something I wanted to ask you if I could have." She jumped up from the table and went over in the corner where the churn stood, the milk in it clabber° by now. She looked at the churn and looked at it.

"This churn top is what I need," she said. "Didn't Uncle Buddy whittle it out of a tree you all used to have?"

"Yes," I said.

"Uh huh," she said happily. "And I want the dasher, too."

"Uncle Buddy whittle that, too?" asked the barber.

Dee (Wangero) looked up at me.

"Aunt Dee's first husband whittled the dash," said Maggie so low you almost couldn't hear her. "His name was Henry, but they called him Stash."

"Maggie's brain is like an elephant's," Wangero said, laughing. "I can use the churn top as a centerpiece for the alcove table," she said, sliding a plate over the churn, "and I'll think of something artistic to do with the dasher."

When she finished wrapping the dasher the handle stuck out. I took it for a moment in my hands. You didn't even have to look close to see where hands pushing the dasher up and down to make butter had left a kind of sink in the wood. In fact, there were a lot of small sinks; you could see where thumbs and fingers had sunk into the wood. It was beautiful light yellow wood, from a tree that grew in the yard where Big Dee and Stash had lived.

After dinner Dee (Wangero) went to the trunk at the foot of my bed and started rifling through it. Maggie hung back in the kitchen over the dishpan. Out came Wangero with two quilts. They had been pieced by Grandma Dee and then Big Dee

salt-lick shelters *shelters built to prevent rain from dissolving large blocks of rock salt set up on poles for cattle*
clabber *curdled, turned sour*

and me had hung them on the quilt frames on the front porch and quilted them. One was in the Lone Star pattern. The other was Walk Around the Mountain. In both of them were scraps of dresses Grandma Dee had worn fifty and more years ago. Bits and pieces of Grandpa Jarrell's Paisley shirts. And one teeny faded blue piece, about the size of a penny matchbox, that was from Great Grandpa Ezra's uniform that he wore in the Civil War.

"Mama," Wangero said sweet as a bird. "Can I have these old quilts?"

I heard something fall in the kitchen, and a minute later the kitchen door slammed.

"Why don't you take one or two of the others?" I asked. "These old things was just done by me and Big Dee from some tops your grandma pieced before she died."

"No," said Wangero. "I don't want those. They are stitched around the borders by machine."

"That'll make them last better," I said.

"That's not the point," said Wangero. "These are all pieces of dresses Grandma used to wear. She did all this stitching by hand. Imagine!" She held the quilts securely in her arms, stroking them.

"Some of the pieces, like those lavender ones, come from old clothes her mother handed down to her," I said, moving up to touch the quilts. Dee (Wangero) moved back just enough so that I couldn't reach the quilts. They already belonged to her.

"Imagine!" she breathed again, clutching them closely to her bosom.

"The truth is," I said, "I promised to give them quilts to Maggie, for when she marries John Thomas."

She gasped like a bee had stung her.

"Maggie can't appreciate these quilts!" she said. "She'd probably be backward enough to put them to everyday use."

"I reckon she would," I said. "God knows I been saving 'em for long enough with nobody using 'em. I hope she will!" I didn't want to bring up how I had offered Dee (Wangero) a quilt when she went away to college. Then she had told me they were old-fashioned, out of style.

"But they're *priceless!*" she was saying now, furiously; for she has a temper. "Maggie would put them on the bed and in five years they'd be in rags. Less than that!"

"She can always make some more," I said. "Maggie knows how to quilt."

Dee (Wangero) looked at me with hatred. "You just will not understand. The point is these quilts, *these* quilts!"

"Well," I said, stumped. "What would *you* do with them?"

"Hang them," she said. As if that was the only thing you *could* do with quilts.

Maggie by now was standing in the door. I could almost hear the sound her feet made as they scraped over each other.

"She can have them, Mama," she said, like somebody used to never winning anything, or having anything reserved for her. "I can 'member Grandma Dee without the quilts."

I looked at her hard. She had filled her bottom lip with checkerberry snuff and it gave her face a kind of dopey, hangdog look. It was Grandma Dee and Big Dee who taught her how to quilt herself. She stood there with her scarred hands hidden in the folds of her skirt. She looked at her sister with something like fear but she wasn't mad at her. This was Maggie's portion. This was the way she knew God to work.

When I looked at her like that something hit me in the top of my head and ran down to the soles of my feet. Just like when I'm in church and the spirit of God touches me and I get happy and shout. I did something I never had done before:

hugged Maggie to me, then dragged her on into the room, snatched the quilts out of Miss Wangero's hands and dumped them into Maggie's lap. Maggie just sat there on my bed with her mouth open.

"Take one or two of the others," I said to Dee.

But she turned without a word and went out to Hakim-a-barber.

"You just don't understand," she said, as Maggie and I came out to the car.

"What don't I understand?" I wanted to know.

"Your heritage," she said. And then she turned to Maggie, kissed her, and said, "You ought to try to make something of yourself, too, Maggie. It's really a new day for us. But from the way you and Mama still live you'd never know it."

She put on some sunglasses that hid everything above the tip of her nose and her chin.

Maggie smiled; maybe at the sunglasses. But a real smile, not scared. After we watched the car dust settle I asked Maggie to bring me a dip of snuff. And then the two of us sat there just enjoying, until it was time to go in the house and go to bed.

(1973)

QUESTIONS FOR CRITICAL THINKING AND WRITING

Experience

1. Consider the relationship of the sisters. To what extent does it reflect a sibling relationship you have experienced or observed?

Interpretation

2. Compare the two sisters. What was the reaction of each girl to the house fire years before? What do their reactions reveal about their connection to the house and family tradition?
3. Why does Dee want the churn and quilts? Why does Maggie want them? Explain the significance of the story's title.
4. Reread the last paragraph. Why does Maggie smile "a real smile, not scared"? Why do mother and daughter seem so content, even triumphant?
5. The author divides the story into five sections. Define the emotional quality of each section.

Evaluation

6. Does the narrator seem to favor one character over another? Consider the descriptions of the words, actions, and gestures of characters.

Connection

7. Compare the mother in "Everyday Use" to Phoenix Jackson in "A Worn Path" (Chapter Three).
8. Compare Dee in "Everyday Use" with Joy-Hulga in O'Connor's "Good Country People" and Julian in O'Connor's "Everything That Rises Must Converge."

Critical Thinking

9. Explain, in at least two different ways, the meaning and significance of the story's title.

Photography by Curt Richter

EUDORA WELTY
[1909–2001]

Eudora Welty was born in Jackson, Mississippi, and attended the Mississippi State College for Women and the University of Wisconsin. She is best known for her portraits of people and life in the deep South. During World War II she was on the staff of the New York Times Book Review, *testimony to the insatiable appetite for reading she developed as a child. She began publishing collections of stories in 1941 with* Curtain of Green *and won a Pulitzer Prize in 1980 for* The Collected Stories, *which contains work from her numerous collections of short fiction spanning forty years. Welty has also written novels, such as* The Optimist's Daughter, *which won the Pulitzer Prize in 1982, and criticism, collected in* The Eye of the Story *(1977). Her memoir,* One Writer's Beginnings, *describes her early experience with literature and her literary influences.*

Why I Live at the P.O.

I was getting along fine with Mama, Papa-Daddy and Uncle Rondo until my sister Stella-Rondo just separated from her husband and came back home again. Mr. Whitaker! Of course I went with Mr. Whitaker first, when he first appeared here in China Grove, taking "Pose Yourself" photos, and Stella-Rondo broke us up. Told him I was one-sided. Bigger on one side than the other, which is a deliberate, calculated falsehood: I'm the same. Stella-Rondo is exactly twelve months to the day younger than I am and for that reason she's spoiled.

She's always had anything in the world she wanted and then she'd throw it away. Papa-Daddy gave her this gorgeous Add-a-Pearl necklace when she was eight years old and she threw it away playing baseball when she was nine, with only two pearls.

So as soon as she got married and moved away from home the first thing she did was separate! From Mr. Whitaker! This photographer with the popeyes she said she trusted. Came home from one of those towns up in Illinois and to our complete surprise brought this child of two.

Mama said she like to made her drop dead for a second. "Here you had this marvelous blonde child and never so much as wrote your mother a word about it," says Mama. "I'm thoroughly ashamed of you." But of course she wasn't.

Stella-Rondo just calmly takes off this *hat,* I wish you could see it. She says, "Why, Mama, Shirley-T.'s adopted, I can prove it."

"How?" says Mama, but all I says was, "H'm!" There I was over the hot stove, trying to stretch two chickens over five people and a completely unexpected child into the bargain, without one moment's notice.

"What do you mean—'H'm!'?" says Stella-Rondo, and Mama says, "I heard that, Sister."

I said that oh, I didn't mean a thing, only that whoever Shirley-T. was, she was the spit-image of Papa-Daddy if he'd cut off his beard, which of course he'd never do in the world. Papa-Daddy's Mama's papa and sulks.

Stella-Rondo got furious! She said, "Sister, I don't need to tell you you got a lot of nerve and always did have and I'll thank you to make no future reference to my adopted child whatsoever."

"Very well," I said. "Very well, very well. Of course I noticed at once she looks like Mr. Whitaker's side too. That frown. She looks like a cross between Mr. Whitaker and Papa-Daddy."

"Well, all I can say is she isn't."

"She looks exactly like Shirley Temple to me," says Mama, but Shirley-T. just ran away from her.

So the first thing Stella-Rondo did at the table was turn Papa-Daddy against me.

"Papa-Daddy," she says. He was trying to cut up his meat. "Papa-Daddy!" I was taken completely by surprise. Papa-Daddy is about a million years old and's got this long-long beard. "Papa-Daddy, Sister says she fails to understand why you don't cut off your beard."

So Papa-Daddy l-a-y-s down his knife and fork! He's real rich. Mama says he is, he says he isn't. So he says, "Have I heard correctly? You don't understand why I don't cut off my beard?"

"Why," I says, "Papa-Daddy, of course I understand, I did not say any such of a thing, the idea!"

He says, "Hussy!"

I says, "Papa-Daddy, you know I wouldn't any more want you to cut off your beard than the man in the moon. It was the farthest thing from my mind! Stella-Rondo sat there and made that up while she was eating breast of chicken."

But he says, "So the postmistress fails to understand why I don't cut off my beard. Which job I got you through my influence with the government. 'Bird's nest'—is that what you call it?"

Not that it isn't the next to smallest P.O. in the entire state of Mississippi.

I says, "Oh, Papa-Daddy," I says, "I didn't say any such of a thing, I never dreamed it was a bird's nest, I have always been grateful though this is the next to smallest P.O. in the state of Mississippi, and I do not enjoy being referred to as a hussy by my own grandfather."

But Stella-Rondo says, "Yes, you did say it too. Anybody in the world could of heard you, that had ears."

"Stop right there," says Mama, looking at *me*.

So I pulled my napkin straight back through the napkin ring and left the table.

As soon as I was out of the room Mama says, "Call her back, or she'll starve to death," but Papa-Daddy says, "This is the beard I started growing on the Coast when I was fifteen years old." He would of gone on till nightfall if Shirley-T. hadn't lost the Milky Way she ate in Cairo.

So Papa-Daddy says, "I am going out and lie in the hammock, and you can all sit here and remember my words: I'll never cut off my beard as long as I live, even one inch, and I don't appreciate it in you at all." Passed right by me in the hall and went straight out and got in the hammock.

It would be a holiday. It wasn't five minutes before Uncle Rondo suddenly appeared in the hall in one of Stella-Rondo's flesh-colored kimonos, all cut on the bias, like something Mr. Whitaker probably thought was gorgeous.

"Uncle Rondo!" I says. "I didn't know who that was! Where are you going?"

"Sister," he says, "get out of my way, I'm poisoned."

"If you're poisoned stay away from Papa-Daddy," I says. "Keep out of the hammock. Papa-Daddy will certainly beat you on the head if you come within forty miles of him. He thinks I deliberately said he ought to cut off his beard after he got me the P.O., and I've told him and told him and told him, and he acts like he just don't hear me. Papa-Daddy must of gone stone deaf."

"He picked a fine day to do it then," says Uncle Rondo, and before you could say "Jack Robinson" flew out in the yard.

What he'd really done, he'd drunk another bottle of that prescription. He does it every single Fourth of July as sure as shooting, and it's horribly expensive. Then he falls over in the hammock and snores. So he insisted on zigzagging right on out to the hammock, looking like a half-wit.

Papa-Daddy woke up with this horrible yell and right there without moving an inch he tried to turn Uncle Rondo against me. I heard every word he said. Oh, he told Uncle Rondo I didn't learn to read till I was eight years old and he didn't see how in the world I ever got the mail put up at the P.O., much less read it all, and he said if Uncle Rondo could only fathom the lengths he had gone to to get me that job! And he said on the other hand he thought Stella-Rondo had a brilliant mind and deserved credit for getting out of town. All the time he was just lying there swinging as pretty as you please and looping out his beard, and poor Uncle Rondo was *pleading* with him to slow down the hammock, it was making him as dizzy as a witch to watch it. But that's what Papa-Daddy likes about a hammock. So Uncle Rondo was too dizzy to get turned against me for the time being. He's Mama's only brother and is a good case of a one-track mind. Ask anybody. A certified pharmacist.

Just then I heard Stella-Rondo raising the upstairs window. While she was married she got this peculiar idea that it's cooler with the windows shut and locked. So she has to raise the window before she can make a soul hear her outdoors.

So she raises the window and says, "*Oh!*" You would have thought she was mortally wounded.

Uncle Rondo and Papa-Daddy didn't even look up, but kept right on with what they were doing. I had to laugh.

I flew up the stairs and threw the door open! I says, "What in the wide world's the matter, Stella-Rondo? You mortally wounded?"

"No," she says, "I am not mortally wounded but I wish you would do me the favor of looking out that window there and telling me what you see.

So I shade my eyes and look out the window.

"I see the front yard," I says.

"Don't you see any human beings?" she says.

"I see Uncle Rondo trying to run Papa-Daddy out of the hammock," I says. "Nothing more. Naturally, it's so suffocating-hot in the house, with all the windows shut and locked, everybody who cares to stay in their right mind will have to go out and get in the hammock before the Fourth of July is over."

"Don't you notice anything different about Uncle Rondo?" asks Stella-Rondo.

"Why, no, except he's got on some terrible-looking flesh-colored contraption I wouldn't be found dead in, is all I can see," I says.

"Never mind, you won't be found dead in it, because it happens to be part of my trousseau, and Mr. Whitaker took several dozen photographs of me in it," says Stella-Rondo. "What on earth could Uncle Rondo mean by wearing part of my trousseau out in the broad open daylight without saying so much as 'Kiss my foot,' knowing I only got home this morning after my separation and hung my negligee up on the bathroom door, just as nervous as I could be?"

"I'm sure I don't know, and what do you expect me to do about it?" I says. "Jump out the window?"

"No, I expect nothing of the kind. I simply declare that Uncle Rondo looks like a fool in it, that's all," she says. "It makes me sick to my stomach."

"Well, he looks as good as he can," I says. "As good as anybody in reason could." I stood up for Uncle Rondo, please remember. And I said to Stella-Rondo, "I think I would do well not to criticize so freely if I were you and came home with a two-year-old child I had never said a word about, and no explanation whatever about my separation."

"I asked you the instant I entered this house not to refer one more time to my adopted child, and you gave me your word of honor you would not," was all Stella-Rondo would say, and started pulling out every one of her eyebrows with some cheap Kress tweezers.

So I merely slammed the door behind me and went down and made some green-tomato pickle. Somebody had to do it. Of course Mama had turned both the Negroes loose; she always said no earthly power could hold one anyway on the Fourth of July, so she wouldn't even try. It turned out that Jaypan fell in the lake and came within a very narrow limit of drowning.

So Mama trots in. Lifts up the lid and says, "H'm! Not very good for your Uncle Rondo in his precarious condition, I must say. Or poor little adopted Shirley-T. Shame on you!"

That made me tired. I says, "Well, Stella-Rondo had better thank her lucky stars it was her instead of me came trotting in with that very peculiar-looking child. Now if it had been me that trotted in from Illinois and brought a peculiar-looking child of two, I shudder to think of the reception I'd of got, much less controlled the diet of an entire family."

"But you must remember, Sister, that you were never married to Mr. Whitaker in the first place and didn't go up to Illinois to live," says Mama, shaking a spoon in my face. "If you had I would of been just as overjoyed to see you and your little adopted girl as I was to see Stella-Rondo, when you wound up with your separation and came on back home."

"You would not," I says.

"Don't contradict me, I would," says Mama.

But I said she couldn't convince me though she talked till she was blue in the face. Then I said, "Besides, you know as well as I do that that child is not adopted."

"She most certainly is adopted," says Mama, stiff as a poker.

I says, "Why, Mama, Stella-Rondo had her just as sure as anything in this world, and just too stuck up to admit it."

"Why, Sister," said Mama. "Here I thought we were going to have a pleasant Fourth of July, and you start right out not believing a word your own baby sister tells you!"

"Just like Cousin Annie Flo. Went to her grave denying the facts of life," I remind Mama.

"I told you if you ever mentioned Annie Flo's name I'd slap your face," says Mama, and slaps my face.

"All right, you wait and see," I says.

"I," says Mama, "*I* prefer to take my children's word for anything when it's humanly possible." You ought to see Mama, she weighs two hundred pounds and has real tiny feet.

Just then something perfectly horrible occurred to me.

"Mama," I says, "can that child talk?" I simply had to whisper! "Mama, I wonder if that child can be—you know—in any way? Do you realize," I says, "that she hasn't spoken one single, solitary word to a human being up to this minute? This is the way she looks," I says, and I looked like this.

Well, Mama and I just stood there and stared at each other. It was horrible!

"I remember well that Joe Whitaker frequently drank like a fish," says Mama. "I believed to my soul he drank *chemicals*." And without another word she marches to the foot of the stairs and calls Stella-Rondo.

"Stella-Rondo? O-o-o-o-o! Stella-Rondo!"

"What?" says Stella-Rondo from upstairs. Not even the grace to get up off the bed.

"Can that child of yours talk?" asks Mama.

Stella-Rondo says, "Can she what?"

"Talk! Talk!" says Mama. "Burdyburdyburdyburdy!"

So Stella-Rondo yells back, "Who says she can't talk?"

"Sister says so," says Mama.

"You didn't have to tell me, I know whose word of honor don't mean a thing in this house," says Stella-Rondo.

And in a minute the loudest Yankee voice I ever heard in my life yells out, "OE'm Pop-OE the Sailor-r-r-r Ma-a-an!" and then somebody jumps up and down in the upstairs hall. In another second the house would of fallen down.

"Not only talks, she can tap-dance!" calls Stella-Rondo. "Which is more than some people I won't name can do."

"Why, the little precious darling thing!" Mama says, so surprised. "Just as smart as she can be!" Starts talking baby talk right there. Then she turns on me. "Sister, you ought to be thoroughly ashamed! Run upstairs this instant and apologize to Stella-Rondo and Shirley-T."

"Apologize for what?" I says. "I merely wondered if the child was normal, that's all. Now that she's proved she is, why, I have nothing further to say."

But Mama just turned on her heel and flew out, furious. She ran right upstairs and hugged the baby. She believed it was adopted. Stella-Rondo hadn't done a thing but turn her against me from upstairs while I stood there helpless over the hot stove. So that made Mama, Papa-Daddy and the baby all on Stella-Rondo's side.

Next, Uncle Rondo.

I must say that Uncle Rondo has been marvelous to me at various times in the past and I was completely unprepared to be made to jump out of my skin, the way it turned out. Once Stella-Rondo did something perfectly horrible to him—broke a chain letter from Flanders Field—and he took the radio back he had given her and gave it to me. Stella Rondo was furious! For six months we all had to call her Stella instead of Stella-Rondo, or she wouldn't answer. I always thought Uncle Rondo had all the brains of the entire family. Another time he sent me to Mammoth Cave, with all expenses paid.

But this would be the day he was drinking that prescription, the Fourth of July.

So at supper Stella-Rondo speaks up and says she thinks Uncle Rondo ought to try to eat a little something. So finally Uncle Rondo said he would try a little cold biscuits and ketchup, but that was all. So *she* brought it to him.

"Do you think it wise to disport with ketchup in Stella-Rondo's flesh-colored kimono?" I says. Trying to be considerate! If Stella-Rondo couldn't watch out for her trousseau, somebody had to.

"Any objections?" asks Uncle Rondo, just about to pour out all the ketchup.

"Don't mind what she says, Uncle Rondo," says Stella-Rondo. "Sister has been devoting this solid afternoon to sneering out my bedroom window at the way you look."

"What's that?" says Uncle Rondo. Uncle Rondo has got the most terrible temper in the world. Anything is liable to make him tear the house down if it comes at the wrong time.

So Stella-Rondo says, "Sister says, 'Uncle Rondo certainly does look like a fool in that pink kimono!' "

Do you remember who it was really said that?

Uncle Rondo spills out all the ketchup and jumps out of his chair and tears off the kimono and throws it down on the dirty floor and puts his foot on it. It had to be sent all the way to Jackson to the cleaners and re-pleated.

"So that's your opinion of your Uncle Rondo, is it?" he says. "I look like a fool, do I? Well, that's the last straw. A whole day in this house with nothing to do, and then to hear you come out with a remark like that behind my back!"

"I didn't say any such of a thing, Uncle Rondo," I says, "and I'm not saying who did, either. Why, I think you look all right. Just try to take care of yourself and not talk and eat at the same time," I says. "I think you better go lie down."

"Lie down my foot," says Uncle Rondo. I ought to of known by that he was fixing to do something perfectly horrible.

So he didn't do anything that night in the precarious state he was in—just played Casino with Mama and Stella-Rondo and Shirley-T. and gave Shirley-T. a nickel with a head on both sides. It tickled her nearly to death, and she called him "Papa." But at 6:30 A.M. the next morning, he threw a whole five-cent package of some unsold one-inch firecrackers from the store as hard as he could into my bedroom and they every one went off. Not one bad one in the string. Anybody else, there'd be one that wouldn't go off.

Well, I'm just terribly susceptible to noise of any kind, the doctor has always told me I was the most sensitive person he had ever seen in his whole life, and I was simply prostrated. I couldn't eat! People tell me they heard it as far as the cemetery, and old Aunt Jep Patterson, that had been holding her own so good, thought it was Judgment Day and she was going to meet her whole family. It's usually so quiet here.

And I'll tell you it didn't take me any longer than a minute to make up my mind what to do. There I was with the whole entire house on Stella-Rondo's side and turned against me. If I have anything at all I have pride.

So I just decided I'd go straight down to the P.O. There's plenty of room there in the back, I says to myself.

Well! I made no bones about letting the family catch on to what I was up to. I didn't try to conceal it.

The first thing they knew, I marched in where they were all playing Old Maid and pulled the electric oscillating fan out by the plug, and everything got real hot. Next I snatched the pillow I'd done the needle-point on right off the davenport from behind Papa-Daddy. He went "Ugh!" I beat Stella-Rondo up the stairs and finally found my charm bracelet in her bureau drawer under a picture of Nelson Eddy.

"So that's the way the land lies," says Uncle Rondo. There he was, piecing on the ham. "Well, Sister, I'll be glad to donate my army cot if you got any place to set it up, providing you'll leave right this minute and let me get some peace." Uncle Rondo was in France.

"Thank you kindly for the cot and 'peace' is hardly the word I would select if I had to resort to firecrackers at 6:30 A.M. in a young girl's bedroom," I says back to him. "And as to where I intend to go, you seem to forget my position as postmistress of China Grove, Mississippi," I says. "I've always got the P.O."

Well, that made them all sit up and take notice.

I went out front and started digging up some four-o'clocks to plant around the P.O.

"Ah-ah-ah!" says Mama, raising the window. "Those happen to be my four-o'clocks. Everything planted in that star is mine. I've never known you to make anything grow in your life."

"Very well," I says. "But I take the fern. Even you, Mama, can't stand there and deny that I'm the one watered that fern. And I happen to know where I can send in a box top and get a packet of one thousand mixed seeds, no two the same kind, free."

"Oh, where?" Mama wants to know.

But I says, "Too late. You 'tend to your house, and I'll 'tend to mine. You hear things like that all the time if you know how to listen to the radio. Perfectly marvelous offers. Get anything you want free."

So I hope to tell you I marched in and got that radio, and they could of all bit a nail in two, especially Stella-Rondo, that it used to belong to, and she well knew she couldn't get it back, I'd sue for it like a shot. And I very politely took the sewing-machine motor I helped pay the most on to give Mama for Christmas back in 1929, and a good big calendar, with the first-aid remedies on it. The thermometer and the Hawaiian ukulele certainly were rightfully mine, and I stood on the step-ladder and got all my watermelon-rind preserves and every fruit and vegetable I'd put up, every jar. Then I began to pull the tacks out of the bluebird wall vases on the archway to the dining room.

"Who told you you could have those, Miss Priss?" says Mama, fanning as hard as she could.

"I bought 'em and I'll keep track of 'em," I says. "I'll tack 'em up one on each side the post-office window, and you can see 'em when you come to ask me for your mail, if you're so dead to see 'em."

"Not I! I'll never darken the door to that post office again if I live to be a hundred," Mama says. "Ungrateful child! After all the money we spent on you at the Normal."

"Me either," says Stella-Rondo. "You can just let my mail lie there and *rot,* for all I care. I'll never come and relieve you of a single, solitary piece."

"I should worry," I says. "And who you think's going to sit down and write you all those big fat letters and postcards, by the way? Mr. Whitaker? Just because he was the only man ever dropped down in China Grove and you got him—unfairly—is he going to sit down and write you a lengthy correspondence after you come home giving no rhyme nor reason whatsoever for your separation and no explanation for the presence of that child? I may not have your brilliant mind, but I fail to see it."

So Mama says, "Sister, I've told you a thousand times that Stella-Rondo simply got homesick, and this child is far too big to be hers," and she says, "Now, why don't you all just sit down and play Casino?"

Then Shirley-T. sticks out her tongue at me in this perfectly horrible way. She has no more manners than the man in the moon. I told her she was going to cross her eyes like that some day and they'd stick.

"It's too late to stop me now," I says. "You should have tried that yesterday. I'm going to the P.O. and the only way you can possibly see me is to visit me there."

So Papa-Daddy says, "You'll never catch me setting foot in that post office, even if I should take a notion into my head to write a letter some place." He says, "I won't have you reachin' out of that little old window with a pair of shears and cuttin' off any beard of mine. I'm too smart for you!"

"We all are," says Stella-Rondo.

But I said, "If you're so smart, where's Mr. Whitaker?"

So then Uncle Rondo says, "I'll thank you from now on to stop reading all the orders I get on postcards and telling everybody in China Grove what you think is the matter with them," but I says, "I draw my own conclusions and will continue in the future to draw them." I says, "If people want to write their inmost secrets on penny postcards, there's nothing in the wide world you can do about it, Uncle Rondo."

"And if you think we'll ever *write* another postcard you're sadly mistaken," says Mama.

"Cutting off your nose to spite your face then," I says. "But if you're all determined to have no more to do with the U.S. mail, think of this: What will Stella-Rondo do now, if she wants to tell Mr. Whitaker to come after her?"

"Wah!" says Stella-Rondo. I knew she'd cry. She had a conniption fit right there in the kitchen.

"It will be interesting to see how long she holds out," I says. "And now—I am leaving."

"Good-bye," says Uncle Rondo.

"Oh, I declare," says Mama, "to think that a family of mine should quarrel on the Fourth of July, or the day after, over Stella-Rondo leaving old Mr. Whitaker and having the sweetest little adopted child! It looks like we'd all be glad!"

"Wah!" says Stella-Rondo, and has a fresh conniption fit.

"He left *her*—you mark my words," I says. "That's Mr. Whitaker. I know Mr. Whitaker. After all, I knew him first. I said from the beginning he'd up and leave her. I foretold every single thing that's happened."

"Where did he go?" asks Mama.

"Probably to the North Pole, if he knows what's good for him," I says.

But Stella-Rondo just bawled and wouldn't say another word. She flew to her room and slammed the door.

"Now look what you've gone and done, Sister," says Mama. "You go apologize."

"I haven't got time, I'm leaving," I says.

"Well, what are you waiting around for?" asks Uncle Rondo.

So I just picked up the kitchen clock and marched off, without saying "Kiss my foot" or anything, and never did tell Stella-Rondo good-bye.

There was a girl going along on a little wagon right in front.

"Girl," I says, "come help me haul these things down the hill, I'm going to live in the post office."

Took her nine trips in her express wagon. Uncle Rondo came out on the porch and threw her a nickel.

And that's the last I've laid eyes on my family or my family laid eyes on me for five solid days and nights. Stella-Rondo may be telling the most horrible tales in the world about Mr. Whitaker, but I haven't heard them. As I tell everybody, I draw my own conclusions.

But oh, I like it here. It's ideal, as I've been saying. You see, I've got everything cater-cornered, the way I like it. Hear the radio? All the war news. Radio, sewing machine, book ends, ironing board and that great big piano lamp—peace, that's what I like. Butter-bean vines planted all along the front where the strings are.

Of course, there's not much mail. My family are naturally the main people in China Grove, and if they prefer to vanish from the face of the earth, for all the mail they get or the mail they write, why, I'm not going to open my mouth. Some of the folks here in town are taking up for me and some turned against me. I know which is which. There are always people who will quit buying stamps just to get on the right side of Papa-Daddy.

But here I am, and here I'll stay. I want the world to know I'm happy.

And if Stella-Rondo should come to me this minute, on bended knees, and *attempt* to explain the incidents of her life with Mr. Whitaker, I'd simply put my fingers in both my ears and refuse to listen.

(1941)

QUESTIONS FOR CRITICAL THINKING AND WRITING

Experience

1. What are your impressions of the family? Can you compare them to any fictional or actual families you have encountered?

Interpretation

2. Explicate the opening paragraph. What do we immediately know of the narrator and her relationship with her sister? How would you characterize the tone of this paragraph?
3. Identify the *protagonist* and *antagonist* of the story. What seems to be the central conflict?
4. Is the narrator reliable? As part of your answer, consider the first paragraph again. Are there any details in the story to suggest that the narrator was not "getting along fine" with the rest of the family before Stella-Rondo's arrival?

Evaluation

5. What is commonly suggested by the phrase "family value"? Does this family exemplify any of those "family values"? What are the values of this family?

Connection

6. Compare this family with other fictional families in stories such as O'Connor's "A Good Man Is Hard to Find."

Critical Thinking

7. Do you think Sister is justified in moving out and into the Post Office? Why or why not?

PART TWO

Poetry

Poet Robert Frost reads at his home in Boston in 1939.

CHAPTER TEN

Reading Poems

In some ways reading poetry is much like reading fiction: we observe details of action and language, make connections and inferences, and draw conclusions. We also bring to poetry the same intellectual and emotional dispositions, the same general experience with life and literature that we draw on in reading fiction. And yet there is something different about reading poems. The difference, admittedly more one of degree than of kind, involves our being more attentive to the connotations of words, more receptive to the expressive qualities of sound and rhythm in line and stanza, more discerning about details of syntax and punctuation. This increased attention to linguistic detail is necessary because of the density and compression characteristic of poetry. More than fiction, poetry is an art of condensation and implication; poems concentrate meaning and distill feeling.

Learning to read poetry well and to savor its pleasures involves learning to ask questions about how we experience poems, how we interpret them, and how we evaluate them. Such questions include the following:

1. What feelings does the poem evoke? What sensations, associations, and memories does it give rise to?
2. What ideas does the poem express, either directly or indirectly?
3. What view of the world does the poet present? What do you think of the poet's view?

Our discussion is divided into three parts: the *experience* of poetry, the *interpretation* of poetry, and the *evaluation* of poetry. In the experience section we will be concerned primarily with subjective responses or personal reactions. In the interpretation section our concern will be the intellectual processes that we engage in as we develop an understanding of poetry. Here the focus will be analytical rather than impressionistic, rational rather than emotional. And in the evaluation of poetry, we will be concerned with the ways we bring our sense of who we are and what we believe into our consideration of any poem's significance, and with how to evaluate poems aesthetically.

THE EXPERIENCE OF POETRY

We begin by considering the following poem, from the standpoint of our experience.

ROBERT HAYDEN*

[1913–1980]

Those Winter Sundays

Sundays too my father got up early
and put his clothes on in the blueblack cold,
then with cracked hands that ached
from labor in the weekday weather made
banked fires blaze. No one ever thanked him.

I'd wake and hear the cold splintering, breaking.
When the rooms were warm, he'd call,
and slowly I would rise and dress,
fearing the chronic angers of that house,

Speaking indifferently to him,
who had driven out the cold
and polished my good shoes as well.
What did I know, what did I know
of love's austere and lonely offices?

[1962]

Even from a single reading we see that the speaker of "Those Winter Sundays," now an adult, is remembering how his father used to get up on cold Sunday mornings and light the fires that would warm the house for his sleeping family. We sense that he regrets how unappreciative of his father he was as a child. We may wonder what prompts these memories and feelings. Our initial reading may also call up memories of our own. This kind of reading in the context of our experience is important for our full response to the pleasures poetry offers.

Reading in Context

Here is a sampling of one reader's responses to the poem in the context of his experience. It takes the form of a set of notes that describe both memories and feelings. Notice how the responses, subjective and impressionistic as they are, nonetheless reveal the reader beginning to reflect on the poem's meaning and values.

*This asterisk and the others in Part Two indicate that this poet is featured in Chapter Twenty: Lives of Poets.

I remember how my father used to wake up at five A.M. to light the furnace so the house would be warm when the rest of the family got up. My strongest memories of this come from my early adolescence, perhaps because it was then that I began to assume this responsibility. I would never have thought to describe the cold as "blue-black" but I like how that makes me remember what the cold felt like at that merciless hour. I also remember the way my father would come and wake us up around 6:30 to get ready for school. By then the floor was warm and the radiators crackled with steam.

Like the rest of my brothers and sisters, I took my father's early morning efforts for granted. We never thought of thanking him. Perhaps we should have. He always knew that we loved him. That wasn't a problem. But as I think back, I don't remember thanking him for much of anything. I guess we were all guilty of speaking indifferently to him, or of not speaking much at all.

A couple of other things about the poem strike me. One is the shoes the father polished for his son. A nice touch, those shoes. I wonder when a boy begins to be responsible for polishing his own shoes. I can't remember when I started polishing mine—high school perhaps—but I do remember often polishing my father's as well—especially on Sundays when he would rush around to get ready for church. A more confusing item is the line about "fearing the chronic angers" of the house. How can a house be angry? Perhaps the writer is referring to the father's anger? I remember my own father becoming angry. He blew his top, as he used to say, pretty regularly, one time punching a hole in the dining room wall, another time ripping the phone off the kitchen wall. I wasn't the target of his anger often, but it was unsettling to see him lose his temper.

The last couple of lines with the repeated question, "What did I know, what did I know," hit me the hardest. I hear regret in them, regret for lost opportunities, regret for understanding too late the motive behind the attentions of the speaker's father. Perhaps there is also regret for the distance that separated father and son. I know a little about that. But I also hear in these lines how love involves sacrifice and that such quiet expressions of love don't always or even often receive the recognition they deserve. For people whose fathers are still alive there is time perhaps to compensate. For me, it's too late.

THE INTERPRETATION OF POETRY

When we interpret a poem, we concern ourselves less with how it affects us than with what it means or suggests. Interpretation relies on our intellectual comprehension and rational understanding rather than on our emotional apprehension and response.

The act of interpretation involves essentially four things: observing, connecting, inferring, and concluding. We observe details of description and action, of language and form. We look for connections among these details and begin to establish a sense of the poem's coherence (the way its details fit together in meaningful relationships). On the basis of these connections we make inferences or interpretive guesses about their significance. And finally, we come to a provisional conclusion about the poem's meaning based on our observations, connections, and inferences.

To see what Hayden's poem implies, let's give it a second look. We might notice, for example, that the first words, "Sundays too," indicate that the speaker's father performed his housewarming chores every day, including Sundays. We might notice also that the poem contrasts cold and warmth, with the cold dissipated as the warmth of the fires the father has started suffuses the house. And we might note further that the poem shifts from father to son, from "him" to "I." The first stanza, for example, describes the father's act, the second the boy's awakening to a warm house, while the third records a different kind of awakening—the speaker's realization of his earlier indifference and of his father's love. It is in this third and final stanza that we feel most strongly the contrast between the speaker's past and present, between the then and the now of the poem, between the love that the speaker neither noticed nor acknowledged and the love he later acknowledges and understands.

So far we have centered on the poem's speaker and its subject. In considering speaker and subject, we solidify our sense of what the poem implies, whether its implications concern, primarily, ideas or feelings. When the speaker notes that he feared "the chronic angers of that house," we may sense that he points toward something important. Presumably he feared his father's anger, which on occasion may have been directed at him. But by using the plural form of the word rather than the singular ("angers" rather than "anger") the speaker may be suggesting that there was discord between the father and other members of the family as well. Whatever the specific nature of his fear, the speaker intimates that his fear was the source of his own wariness and indifference toward his father.

The lines that convey the speaker's feeling most intensely, however, are those that end the poem:

> What did I know, what did I know
> of love's austere and lonely offices?

We sense the intensity of his feelings both in his repetition of the phrase "what did I know," and in the words that describe his father's actions: "love's austere and lonely offices." "Austere" suggests both the rigor and self-discipline of the father's acts and perhaps the stern severity with which he may have performed them. "Lonely" indicates that the father performed his early morning labors alone, without help from the other members of the family. It also suggests that the father was emotionally isolated from the speaker and perhaps from other members of the family.

But the word "offices" conveys other ideas as well. It implies both the duties the father fulfills and the corresponding authority he possesses. Beyond these related meanings, "offices" also refers to the daily prayers recited by clerics. Thus, the words "austere" and "offices" convey the speaker's understanding of his father's sacrifices for him. Moreover, the highly abstract language of the conclusion—so different from the concrete details of the preceding stanzas—may also indicate the speaker's inability to express affection directly (an inadequacy he intimates his father suffered from as well).

To read poetry well we need to slow down enough to observe details of language, form, and sound. By reading slowly and deliberately, we give ourselves a chance to form connections among the poem's details. Read the following poem twice, once straight through without stopping, then again with the interpolated commentary.

ROBERT FROST*
[1874–1963]

Stopping by Woods on a Snowy Evening

Whose woods these are I think I know.
His house is in the village though;
He will not see me stopping here
To watch his woods fill up with snow.

My little horse must think it queer
To stop without a farmhouse near
Between the woods and frozen lake
The darkest evening of the year.

He gives his harness bells a shake
To ask if there is some mistake.
The only other sound's the sweep
Of easy wind and downy flake.

The woods are lovely, dark and deep,
But I have promises to keep,
And miles to go before I sleep,
And miles to go before I sleep.

[1923]

Read the poem once more, this time along with the comments that follow each stanza. Attend to the way you make sense of the poem during this reading, particularly in light of the suggestions made in the commentary.

Whose woods these are I think I know.
His house is in the village though;
He will not see me stopping here
To watch his woods fill up with snow.

▲ ***Comment*** *Frost's poem opens with a speaker who seems concerned momentarily about who owns the woods. The speaker seems reassured that the owner can't see him. We might wonder why the speaker should be concerned and why he bothers to mention it. Does he feel that he is doing something wrong? The poem doesn't say; instead it paints a picture of man, of woods and snow. And it raises questions: Why does he stop? What attracts him? Again, the poem doesn't provide explicit answers.*

My little horse must think it queer
To stop without a farmhouse near
Between the woods and frozen lake
The darkest evening of the year.

▲ **Comment** *In the first stanza the speaker describes the scene and his own action. In this stanza, although he further describes this scene and action, he begins by mentioning that his horse is unaccustomed to stopping without a reason. Accustomed to stops for food and rest, the horse couldn't possibly understand the man's impractical reason for stopping. And though the horse is said to "think," we realize that the horse's thoughts are really the speaker's—that the speaker projects his thoughts onto the horse because a part of him sees the impracticality of his action.*

He gives his harness bells a shake
To ask if there is some mistake.
The only other sound's the sweep
Of easy wind and downy flake.

▲ **Comment** *The third stanza continues the emphasis of the second. The speaker interprets the horse's shaking of his harness bells as a signal to move on, as a sign that stopping there serves no useful purpose. We might notice that the poet here emphasizes the stillness of the night, the isolation and privacy of the moment, which is broken only by the sound of the horse's bell. Tension builds in the mind of the speaker: even though he seems to enjoy the stillness of the night and takes pleasure in the "easy wind" and the "downy flake," he also experiences some doubt about what he is doing.*

Stanza four:

The woods are lovely, dark and deep,
But I have promises to keep,
And miles to go before I sleep,
And miles to go before I sleep.

▲ **Comment** *It's as if the speaker here answers the question why he stopped by the woods. He stopped because he was attracted by their dark beauty. He nevertheless feels a pressure to move on, to return to his responsibilities and obligations.*

The final stanza is solemn and serious: Frost slows its pace by including pauses (indicated by punctuation) and by repeating the third line, "And miles to go before I sleep," which he uses to end the poem. In repeating this line, the poet lifts it beyond its literal meaning, inviting us to read "sleep" as the final sleep of death. Once we make this interpretive leap, we can consider "miles to go" as perhaps the time the speaker has left to live, and "promises" as the obligations and responsibilities he must fulfill before he dies. His stopping to look at the falling snow can be seen as a temporary reprieve from such responsibilities; it might also be seen as a desire to escape them. The essential point, however, seems to be the tug of war going on in the speaker's mind between the two possibilities—stopping to contemplate the beauty of nature and moving on to return to the active world of work and responsibility.

We have been reading and interpreting the poem one stanza at a time to suggest the way interpretation builds cumulatively as we move through a poem. The process, however, is not simply linear or sequential. For although we interpret later details in light of earlier ones, we also make sense of earlier ones after having interpreted later ones. The act of interpretation, like the experience of reading generally, is recursive. The process of interpretation does not end with reading the poem; it continues as we reflect on it afterward. New ideas may come to us, particularly after we have discussed the work with a teacher and classmates or after we have read other works that we can relate to it.

Reading in Context

But we can also read the poem in a larger series of contexts. First, consider the poem in the context of Frost's life. As a poet who lived in rural New England, he took pleasure in the landscape of the Northeast, a pleasure that is clearly reflected in the natural scene Frost describes. As a poet who suffered many tragedies in his family life, Frost transmutes that suffering or displaces it onto his poem's speaker, who must carry on and continue his journey to fulfill life's obligations.

Reading "Stopping by Woods" in the context of Frost's other poems, we might ask not only about how it portrays nature, but how it portrays the human figure's relationship with nature. This issue of humanity's relationship with nature is a dominant concern of Frost's poetry, surfacing again and again, in poems even as brief as "Dust of Snow," which you read in the Introduction to this text. Is there a connection between us and the natural world? Or are we cut off, alien, separated from nature? Asking such questions of Frost's poem puts it in the context of "Romanticism," the nineteenth-century European movement that took root in France, Germany, and England most forcefully, and then was responded to by American writers of the nineteenth and twentieth centuries.

Here is one final point about the interpretation of poetry (and of literature generally): interpretation never really ends. When we interpret a work, we should be concerned less with finding the single right way of understanding it than with arriving at a satisfying explanation, one that makes sense to us, and one whose logic and good sense will appeal to others. Some interpretations, nonetheless, will be more satisfying than others, largely because they take into account more of the poem's details, more of its language and form and action. Other interpretations, while perhaps not as convincing, may be valuable for the intellectual stimulation they provide and for the pleasure they afford. Because we invariably bring different experiences of life and of literature to our reading of poems, we will see different things in them and will make different kinds of sense of them. The varying interpretations we make of poems depend largely on what matters to us, what *we* consider vital. It is to this subject, evaluation, that we turn now.

THE EVALUATION OF POETRY

When we evaluate a poem, we do two different kinds of things. First, we make a judgment about how good it is and how successfully it realizes its poetic intentions. We examine its language and structure, for example, and consider how well they work together to embody meaning and convey feeling. Second, we consider how much significance the poem has for us personally, and what significance it may have for other readers—both those who are like us and those who differ in age, race, gender, culture, and ideology. Some poems "speak" to us more than others do; some poems mean more to us on some days than on other days; and some poems mean both more and less to us at different periods of our lives. In evaluating poems, we explore the how and why of such differences. In doing so, we turn inevitably to a consideration of the various cultural assumptions, moral attitudes, and political convictions that animate particular poems. We consider *context*: the circumstances of a poem's composition, the poet's life, the attitudes and beliefs he or she may have expressed in letters or other comments, the audience and occasion for which a particular poem was written, its publication history and reception by readers past and present. From even this brief list, we can see how complex literary evaluation can be.

Does this mean then that we cannot make definitive, final, and absolute evaluations of poems? Probably, since change and variety are the hallmarks of literary evaluation. The way we see and understand any poem changes as we change. We will find merit in poems whose meaning we understand and whose values are like our own. We will come to value poems whose content we have lived. And we will appreciate poems in relation to other literary works that have had an impact on our lives and our thinking.

With these considerations in mind, we can suggest a few general principles upon which to ground preliminary evaluations. First is the realization that an evaluation is essentially a judgment, a set of opinions about a literary work based on a thoughtful consideration of it. We may agree or disagree with the speaker's response to the woods in Frost's "Stopping by Woods." We may confirm or deny the models of experience illustrated in Hayden's "Those Winter Sundays." Invariably, however, we measure the sentiments of a poem against our own. We may or may not appreciate responsibility as much as Frost's speaker seems to. We may or may not cherish our memories of our fathers as Hayden's speaker seems to. And depending on these and other factors, we may arrive at very different assessments of either poem's worth.

It is important to realize that in evaluating any poem, we appraise it according to our own special combination of cultural, moral, and aesthetic values. Our moral values reflect our ethical norms—what we consider good and evil, right and wrong. They are influenced by our religious beliefs and perhaps by our political convictions as well. Our aesthetic values concern what we see as beautiful or ugly, well or poorly made.

Our response to any poem's outlook (and our opinion of it) is closely related to our interpretation of it. Evaluation depends upon interpretation, for our judgment of a poem depends on how we understand it. By bringing our intellect to bear on a work, we may discover meanings in it that were not apparent on initial reading. And while making such interpretive discoveries we may come to feel differently about a poem and derive considerable pleasure from it.

Of the kinds of evaluations we make in reading poetry, those about a poem's aesthetic merit are hardest to discuss. Aesthetic responses are difficult to describe because they involve subjective reactions about what is beautiful or not, what is pleasing or not, what is well-made or not. Our occasional unwillingness to move beyond our initial impressions, our tendency to settle into comfortable judgments and well-worn opinions, further complicates our responses. We may think that as long as we know what we like, that's enough. It's not enough if we are truly interested in developing our capacity for aesthetic appreciation.

Is Frost's "Stopping by Woods" or Hayden's "Those Winter Sundays" a beautiful poem? Does either seem to be a good example of its type—in this case, the lyric poem? What criteria will you use to make a judgment? To answer these questions, you will need to know more about poetry than you are likely to at this point. Measuring a poem's achievement requires some knowledge of how poets exploit diction, imagery, syntax, and sound; how they establish form and control tone; how they work within or against a literary tradition. We will discuss these elements in Chapter Twelve.

Admittedly, without a good deal of knowledge about poetry and without considerable practice in reading it, judgments about the aesthetic worth of particular poems need to be made with caution. But we cannot really avoid judging the poems we read any more than we avoid judging the people we meet; the process is natural. What we should strive for in evaluating poems is to understand the merits of different kinds of poems, to judge them fairly against what they were meant to be rather than something we think they should be. Our goal should be, ultimately, to develop a sense of literary *tact,* the kind of informed and balanced judgment that comes with experience in reading and living, coupled with continued thoughtful reflection on both.

We can put these ideas to the test by reading Gwendolyn Brook's "A Song in the Front Yard" from the standpoint of evaluation. The questions that follow the poem invite you to consider your experience and interpretation, as well as your evaluation of it.

Photograph © 2003 Jill Krementz

GWENDOLYN BROOKS*
[1917–2000]

A Song in the Front Yard

I've stayed in the front yard all my life.
I want to peek at the back
Where it's rough and untended and hungry weed grows.
A girl gets sick of a rose.

I want to go in the back yard now
And maybe down the alley,
To where the charity children play.
I want a good time today.

They do some wonderful things.
They have some wonderful fun.
My mother sneers, but I say it's fine
How they don't have to go in at quarter to nine.
My mother, she tells me that Johnnie Mae
Will grow up to be a bad woman.
That George'll be taken to Jail soon or late
(On account of last winter he sold our back gate).

But I say it's fine. Honest, I do.
And I'd like to be a bad woman, too.
And wear the brave stockings of night-black lace
And strut down the streets with paint on my face.

[1945]

QUESTIONS FOR CRITICAL THINKING AND WRITING

Experience

1. What feelings surfaced as you read this poem?
2. What words, phrases, and details triggered your strongest responses?
3. What associations about your own childhood do you bring to the poem?
4. Can the situation described here apply to other times of your life other than childhood. Why or why not?

Interpretation

5. What words, phrases, lines, and details may have confused or baffled you? Why?
6. What observations can you make about the poem's details?
7. What words and phrases recur? How? Where? Why?
8. What connections can you establish among the details of action and language?
9. What inferences can you draw from these connections?
10. How, for now at least, do you understand "A Song in the Front Yard"?

Evaluation

11. What values are associated with the speaker? With the speaker's mother? With the "charity children"? With Johnnie Mae and George?
12. What is the relationship among the values associated with these figures?
13. What is the speaker's attitude toward her mother and Johnnie Mae? To what extent do you think the speaker's attitudes are those of the author? On what do you base your view?
14. How do your own ideas and standards influence your experience, interpretation, and evaluation of the poem? Describe how the poem affects you as a reader. Do you like it? Comment on the poem's aesthetic accomplishment.
15. Return to this poem later in the term, after you have had the opportunity to read many more poems, or after you have discussed the poem with teacher(s) and classmates. (Perhaps you can learn something about the life and work of the poet by reading more of her poetry and prose or by reading critical studies of her work—or both.) Discuss your initial evaluation and your later evaluation, how they may have changed, and why.

THE ACT OF READING POETRY

Thus far we have read two poems, each followed by comments and questions emphasizing the experience and interpretation of poetry. Next we illustrate active reading—what we actually do when we read and reread a poem. Some of the marginal annotations record observations, others raise critical questions; all are abbreviated notes that reflect a reading that embodies both thought and feeling. In making notes about a poem in this manner, we become actively engaged in seeing and thinking.

The annotations for Theodore Roethke's "My Papa's Waltz" are not concerned with technical matters such as form, rhyme scheme, and meter, or with what such technical features contribute to meaning and feeling. Another set of annotations could be made highlighting these features. Some technical consideration of Roethke's poem in the matter of diction, or word choice, appears on page 000. We might very well make notes on this aspect of a poem. For now, however, we focus on the poem's situation and subject. Here is the poem without annotation:

THEODORE ROETHKE*

[1908–1963]

My Papa's Waltz

The whiskey on your breath
Could make a small boy dizzy;
But I hung on like death:
Such waltzing was not easy.

We romped until the pans
Slid from the kitchen shelf;
My mother's countenance
Could not unfrown itself.

The hand that held my wrist
Was battered on one knuckle;
At every step you missed
My right ear scraped a buckle.

You beat time on my head
With a palm caked hard by dirt,
Then waltzed me off to bed
Still clinging to your shirt.

[1942]

And here it is again with annotations:

My Papa's Waltz

An affectionate term for his father—"papa" (irony?)

The whiskey on your breath
Could make a small boy dizzy;
But I hung on like death:
Such waltzing was not easy.

What kind of waltzing And who instigated it?

We romped until the pans
Slid from the kitchen shelf;
My mother's countenance
Could not unfrown itself.

The hand that held my wrist
Was battered on one knuckle;
At every step you missed
My right ear scraped a buckle.

You beat time on my head
With a palm caked hard by dirt,
Then waltzed me off to bed
Still clinging to your shirt.

"Waltzed" or "danced" for "romped"?
"Face" or "expression" for "countenance"?
The mother—angry? Disapproving? mother as audience—as non-participant—
"battered" violence?
The father misses steps but he can dance—not drunk.
"scraped"
"beat time" pain
"caked hard" work?
Clinging—how? Fearfully? Joyfully? Both?

The boy's father, a manual laborer, is clearly not literally "waltzing" with his son. His "dance" is more a romp through the house with a stop in the kitchen and another at the boy's bedroom, where presumably he is unceremoniously dumped into bed. The mother watches, her frown indicating disapproval, perhaps even anger.

The dance is somewhat rough because the boy's father has been drinking. It is also rough because he scrapes the child's ear on his belt buckle as he keeps a steady rhythm by beating time on the boy's head. The boy is described as "clinging" to his father's shirt, but the language doesn't clarify whether that clinging is purely out of terror—or whether it is part of the game father and son enjoy together. Presumably this bed-time romp is a regular ritual rather than a one-time occurrence.

The tone of the poem seems nostalgic, though not sentimentally so. The boy, now a man, remembers his father as "papa," clearly an affectionate term. The high-spirited bouncing rhythm of the poem seems to counter any indication that the father's drinking or the son's fear are its central concerns.

CHAPTER ELEVEN

Types of Poetry

Poetry can be classified as *narrative* or lyric. **Narrative poems** stress story and action, and **lyric poems** stress emotion and song. Each of these types has numerous subdivisions: narrative poetry includes the epic, romance, and ballad; lyric poetry includes the elegy and epigraph, sonnet and sestina, aubade and villanelle.

NARRATIVE POETRY

The grandest of narratives is the epic. **Epics** are long narrative poems that record the adventures of a hero whose exploits are important to the history of a nation. Typically they chronicle the origins of a civilization and embody its central beliefs and values. Epics tend to be larger than life as they recount valorous deeds enacted in vast landscapes. The epic style is as grand as the action; the conventions require that the epic be formal, complex, and serious.

Among the more famous epics in Western literature are Homer's *Iliad* (about the Greek and Trojan war), Virgil's *Aeneid* (about the founding of Rome), Dante's *Divine Comedy* (a journey through hell, purgatory, and heaven), and Milton's *Paradise Lost* (about the revolt of the angels, and man's creation and fall). For a hint of the epic's subjects and language listen to these opening lines from Virgil's *Aeneid* and from Milton's *Paradise Lost*. First Virgil:

I sing of warfare and a man at war.
From the sea-coast of Troy in early days
He came to Italy by destiny,
To our Lavinian western shore,
A fugitive, this captain, buffeted
Cruelly on land as on the sea
By blows from powers of the air—behind them
Baleful Juno in her sleepless rage.
And cruel losses were his lot in war,
Till he could found a city and bring home

His gods to Latium, land of the Latin race,
The Alban lords, and the high walls of Rome.

TRANSLATED BY ROBERT FITZGERALD

And now Milton:

Of man's first disobedience, and the fruit
Of that forbidden tree whose mortal taste
Brought death into the world, and all our woe,
With loss of Eden, till one greater Man
Restore us, and regain the blissful seat,
Sing, Heavenly Muse, that, on the secret top
Of Oreb, or of Sinai, didst inspire
That shepherd who first taught the chosen seed
In the beginning how the Heavens and Earth
Rose out of Chaos: or, if Sion hill
Delight thee more, and Siloa's brook that flowed
Fast by the oracle of God, I thence
Invoke thy aid to my adventurous song,
That with no middle flight intends to soar
Above th' Aonian mount, while it pursues
Things unattempted yet in prose or rhyme.

Far less ambitious than epics, **ballads** are perhaps the most popular form of narrative poetry. Originally ballads were meant to be sung or recited. Folk ballads (or popular ballads as they are sometimes called) were passed on orally, only to be written down much later. This accounts for the different versions of many ballads such as "Barbara Allen" in Chapter Nineteen.

In addition to folk ballads of unknown authorship, there are also literary ballads (of known authorship). One example is John Keats's "La Belle Dame sans Merci" (page 815). Literary ballads imitate the folk ballad by adhering to its basic conventions—repeated lines and stanzas in a refrain, swift action with occasional surprise endings, extraordinary events evoked in direct, simple language, and scant characterization—but are more polished stylistically and more self-conscious in their use of poetic techniques.

Another type of narrative poem is the **romance**, in which adventure is a central feature. The plots of romances tend to be complex, with surprising and even magical actions common. The chief characters are human beings, though they often confront monsters, dragons, and disguised animals in a world that does not adhere consistently to the laws of nature as we know them. Romance in short deals with the marvelous—with, for example, St. George slaying a dragon in a magical forest. Popular during the Middle Ages and Renaissance, the romance as a poetic genre has fallen from favor. Nevertheless, some of its chief characteristics have found expression in popular fictional types such as the western, the adventure story, and the romantic love story.

LYRIC POETRY

Although narrative poems, especially literary ballads, combine story with song, story and action predominate. In lyric poetry, however, story is subordinated to song, and action to emotion. We can define *lyrics* as subjective poems, often brief, that express the feelings and thoughts of a single speaker (who may or may not represent the poet). The lyric is more a poetic manner than a form; it is more variable and less subject to strict convention than narrative poetry.

Lyric poetry is typically characterized by brevity, melody, and emotional intensity. The music of lyrics makes them memorable, and their brevity contributes to the intensity of their emotional expression. Originally designed to be sung to a musical accompaniment (the word *lyric* derives from the Greek *lyre*), lyrics have been the predominant type of poetry in the West for several hundred years.

Forms of lyric poetry range from the **epigram,** a brief witty poem that is often satirical, such as Alexander Pope's "On the Collar of a Dog," to the **elegy,** a lament for the dead, such as Seamus Heaney's "Mid-Term Break" (page 807). Lyric forms also include the **ode,** a long stately poem in stanzas of varied length, meter, and form; and the **aubade,** a love lyric expressing complaint that dawn means the speaker must part from his lover. An example of the ode is John Keats's "Ode to a Nightingale" (page 818); the aubade is represented by John Donne's "The Sun Rising" (page 543).

The tones, moods, and voices of lyric poems are as variable and as complexly intertwined as human feeling, thought, and imagination. Generally considered the most compressed poetic type, the lyric poem typically expresses much in little. The **sonnet,** for example, condenses into fourteen lines an expression of emotion or an articulation of idea according to one of two basic patterns: the *Italian* (or *Petrarchan*) and the *English* (or *Shakespearean*). An Italian sonnet is composed of an eight-line octave and a six-line sestet. A Shakespearean sonnet is composed of three four-line quatrains and a concluding two-line couplet. The thought and feeling expressed in each sonnet form typically follow the divisions suggested by their structural patterns. Thus an Italian sonnet may state a problem in the octave and present a solution in its sestet. A Shakespearean sonnet will usually introduce a subject in the first quatrain, expand and develop it in the second and third quatrains, and conclude something about it in its final couplet.

Although sonnets reached the height of their popularity during the Renaissance, later writers have continued to be attracted to the form. Some sonnet writers, in fact, like Gerard Manley Hopkins, William Butler Yeats, Robert Frost, and E. E. Cummings have combined the two basic patterns to suit their poetic needs. Occasionally these and other poets have modified the form itself. Robert Frost's "Acquainted with the Night" (page 685), for example, is composed of four tercets and a couplet rather than the familiar three quatrains and a couplet. Frost, moreover, has been known to write fifteen-line sonnets as well.

Less important historically than the sonnet but no less intricate and musical are two other lyric forms, sestina and villanelle, both deriving from French poetry. The **sestina** consists of six stanzas of six lines each followed by a three-line conclusion or envoy. The sestina requires a strict pattern of repetition of six key words that end the lines of the first stanza. Elizabeth Bishop's "Sestina" (page 766) is an example.

The **villanelle,** which also relies heavily on repetition, is composed of five three-line tercets and a final four-line quatrain. Its singular feature is the way its first and third lines repeat throughout the poem. The entire first line reappears as the final line of the second and fourth tercets, and again as the third line of the third and fifth tercets and as the concluding line of the poem. Dylan Thomas's "Do Not Go Gentle into That Good Night" (Chapter Nineteen), is an example.

CHAPTER TWELVE

Elements of Poetry

We can learn to interpret and appreciate poems by understanding their basic elements. The elements of a poem include a *speaker* whose voice we hear in it; its **diction** or selection of words; its **syntax** or the order of those words; its **imagery** or details of sight, sound, taste, smell, and touch; its **figurative language** or nonliteral ways of expressing one thing in terms of another, such as **symbol** and **metaphor;** its *sound effects,* especially **rhyme, assonance,** and **alliteration;** its **rhythm** and **meter** or the pattern of accents we hear in the poem's words, phrases, lines, and sentences; and its **structure** or formal pattern of organization.

VOICE: SPEAKER AND TONE

When we read or hear a poem, we hear a speaker's voice. It is this voice that conveys the poem's **tone,** its implied attitude toward its subject. Tone is an abstraction we make from the details of a poem's language: the use of meter and rhyme (or lack of them); the inclusion of certain kinds of details and exclusion of other kinds; particular choices of words and sentence pattern, of imagery and figurative language. When we listen to a poem's language and hear the voice of its speaker, we catch its tone and feeling and ultimately its meaning.

In listening to the speaker's voice, for example, in Roethke's "My Papa's Waltz" (in Chapter Ten), we hear a tone different from that of the speaker in Hayden's "Those Winter Sundays" (Chapter Ten). Roethke's speaker remembers his father fondly and addresses him ("your breath," "you missed"). He remembers and celebrates their spirited cavorting as a "romp" and a "waltz" and includes such comic details as the mother frowning while pans slide off the kitchen shelves and the father keeping time by steadily patting the boy's head. The poem's complex tone comes from its contrasted details: the boy's hanging on "like death," his ear scraping his father's belt buckle, and his "clinging" to his father's shirt.

The speaker of Hayden's "Those Winter Sundays" admires his father and perhaps feared him as a child. His attitude is suggested by the details he remembers and by the way he meticulously describes his father's attentive labors. But his tone conveys more than admiration; it conveys also a sense of regret, disappointment, and perhaps anguish at having been indifferent toward him as a child. The tone of Hayden's poem has none of the ease and playfulness of Roethke's; it is serious in its portrayal of the speaker's father and solemn in its account of the speaker's subsequent feelings.

The range of tones we find in poems is as various and complex as the range of voices and attitudes we discern in everyday experience. One of the more important and persistent is the *ironic tone* of voice. We have previously defined irony as a way of speaking that implies a discrepancy or opposition between what is said and what is meant. Stephen Crane's "War Is Kind" illustrates this ironic tone.

STEPHEN CRANE

[1871–1900]

War Is Kind

Do not weep, maiden, for war is kind.
Because your lover threw wild hands toward the sky
And the affrighted steed ran on alone,
Do not weep.
War is kind.

Hoarse, booming drums of the regiment,
Little souls who thirst for fight,
These men were born to drill and die.
The unexplained glory flies above them,
Great is the battle god, great, and his kingdom
A field where a thousand corpses lie.

Do not weep, babe, for war is kind.
Because your father tumbled in the yellow trenches,
Raged at his breast, gulped and died,
Do not weep.
War is kind.

Swift blazing flag of the regiment,
Eagle with crest of red and gold,
These men were born to drill and die.
Point for them the virtue of slaughter,
Make plain to them the excellence of killing
And a field where a thousand corpses lie.

Mother whose heart hung humble as a button
On the bright splendid shroud of your son,
Do not weep.
War is kind. [1899]

How do we know that the speaker's attitude toward war is not what his words indicate, that his words are ironic? We know because the details of death in battle are antithetical to the consoling refrain of stanzas one, three, and five: "Do not weep. War is kind." Moreover, the details of stanzas two and four also work toward the same ironic end, but in a different way. Instead of the ironic consoling voice of stanzas one, three, and five (which of course offers no real consolation given the brutality described), stanzas two and four sound more supportive of military glory: Crane uses a march-like rhythm along with words connoting military glory in a context that makes them sound hollow and false. The view that war is glorious and that death in battle is honorable is countered with images of slaughter. Compare Crane's poem to another treating the glory of dying for one's country ironically, Wilfred Owen's "Dulce et Decorum Est."

Unlike the poems we have been considering in which the speaker is alone, the next poem we will examine contains a speaker who is addressing someone present. A poem in which a speaker addresses a silent listener is called a **dramatic monologue.** As we listen to the speaker's monologue, we usually gain a vivid sense of his character and personality. The following poem, Robert Browning's "My Last Duchess," is a striking example of this form.

ROBERT BROWNING*

[1812–1889]

My Last Duchess

FERRARA

That's my last Duchess painted on the wall,
Looking as if she were alive. I call
That piece a wonder, now; Frà Pandolf's hands
Worked busily a day, and there she stands.
Will't please you sit and look at her? I said
"Frà Pandolf" by design, for never read
Strangers like you that pictured countenance,
The depth and passion of its earnest glance,
But to myself they turned (since none puts by
The curtain I have drawn for you, but I)
And seemed as they would ask me, if they durst,
How such a glance came there; so, not the first
Are you to turn and ask thus. Sir, 'twas not
Her husband's presence only, called that spot
Of joy into the Duchess' cheek; perhaps
Frà Pandolf chanced to say, "Her mantle laps
Over my lady's wrist too much," or "Paint

Must never hope to reproduce the faint
Half-flush that dies along her throat." Such stuff
Was courtesy, she thought, and cause enough
For calling up that spot of joy. She had
A heart—how shall I say?—too soon made glad,
Too easily impressed; she liked whate'er
She looked on, and her looks went everywhere.
Sir, 'twas all one! My favor at her breast,
The dropping of the daylight in the West,
The bough of cherries some officious fool
Broke in the orchard for her, the white mule
She rode with round the terrace—all and each
Would draw from her alike the approving speech,
Or blush, at least. She thanked men,—good! but thanked
Somehow—I know not how—as if she ranked
My gift of a nine-hundred-years-old name
With anybody's gift. Who'd stoop to blame
This sort of trifling? Even had you skill
In speech—which I have not—to make your will
Quite clear to such an one, and say "Just this
Or that in you disgusts me; here you miss,
Or there exceed the mark"—and if she let
Herself be lessoned so, nor plainly set
Her wits to yours, forsooth, and made excuse—
E'en then would be some stooping; and I choose
Never to stoop. Oh sir, she smiled, no doubt,
Whene'er I passed her; but who passed without
Much the same smile? This grew; I gave commands;
Then all smiles stopped together. There she stands
As if alive. Will 't please you rise? We'll meet
The company below, then. I repeat,
The Count your master's known munificence
Is ample warrant that no just pretense
Of mine for dowry will be disallowed;
Though his fair daughter's self, as I avowed
At starting, is my object. Nay, we'll go
Together down, sir. Notice Neptune, though,
Taming a sea-horse, thought a rarity,
Which Claus of Innsbruck cast in bronze for me! [1842]

The situation of the poem is this: the Duke of Ferrara, a city-state in Renaissance Italy, is addressing an ambassador who represents a count, the father of a marriageable aristocratic daughter. Although we hear only the duke's voice, we are aware of the ambassador's presence. We probably wonder how the ambassador reacts to what the duke tells him—especially to what he says in lines 45–46. But while the poet hints at the ambassador's actions (lines 12–13; 47–48, for instance) he doesn't reveal his thoughts. Instead he centers our attention on the duke, whose manner, language, gestures, and concerns all reveal the kind of man he is and how he conducted himself in his relations with his last duchess.

The duke reveals himself as a monumental egotist—proud, shrewd, arrogant, and murderous. He shows himself to be a man who will not allow his will to be thwarted or his honor ignored. Intolerant of his former duchess's joy in things other than those he provided, and unwilling to "stoop" to telling her how her behavior insulted him, the duke has had her killed: "I gave commands," he says. "Then all smiles stopped together."

But what has the duchess done to deserve her fate? She expressed joy in compliments given her; she took pleasure in simple things—riding her white mule, watching the sun set, accepting a gift of fruit. Her crime in the duke's eyes was in not recognizing the value of his aristocratic heritage: his name, rank, and pride did not mean enough to her.

Part of our shock in realizing what the duke has done comes from his certainty that he has behaved properly. What else could I do, he seems to say. And part derives perhaps also from the matter-of-fact manner in which the duke turns the conversation from his last duchess to the business at hand, the negotiations about the impending marriage and the dowry. But revealing as these things are, an even stronger index of the duke's egoistic pride is the way he refers to his last duchess as an object, as a possession that has been appropriately added to his prized collection. As a portrait on the wall, the duchess is fully and finally under the duke's control. (He even keeps her portrait behind a curtain so no one can see her without his authority.) The duke's pride in his wife's portrait is equal to his pride in his prized statue of Neptune taming a sea horse.

A few poems notable for their speakers and tones of voice follow. For each identify the speaker and situation. Describe the tone(s) of voice you hear, and consider what the speaker's tone contributes to the ideas and feelings that the poems convey.

MURIEL STUART

[b. 1889–1967]

In the Orchard

'I thought you loved me.' 'No, it was only fun.'
'When we stood there, closer than all?' 'Well, the harvest moon
Was shining and queer in your hair, and it turned my head.'
'That made you?' 'Yes.' 'Just the moon and the light it made
Under the tree?' 'Well, your mouth, too.' 'Yes, my mouth?'
'And the quiet there that sang like the drum in the booth.
You shouldn't have danced like that.' 'Like what?' 'So close,
With your head turned up, and the flower in your hair, a rose
That smelt all warm.' 'I loved you. I thought you knew
I wouldn't have danced like that with any but you.'
'I didn't know. I thought you knew it was fun.'
'I thought it was love you meant.' 'Well, it's done.' 'Yes, it's done.
I've seen boys stone a blackbird, and watched them drown
A kitten . . . it clawed at the reeds, and they pushed it down
Into the pool while it screamed. Is that fun, too?'
'Well, boys are like that . . . Your brothers . . .' 'Yes, I know.
But you, so lovely and strong! Not you! Not you!'

'They don't understand it's cruel. It's only a game.'
'And are girls fun, too?' 'No, still in a way it's the same.
It's queer and lovely to have a girl . . .' 'Go on.'
'It makes you mad for a bit to feel she's your own,
And you laugh and kiss her, and maybe you give her a ring,
But it's only in fun.' 'But I gave you everything.'
'Well, you shouldn't have done it. You know what a fellow thinks
When a girl does that.' 'Yes, he talks of her over his drinks
And calls her a—' 'Stop that now. I thought you knew.'
'But it wasn't with anyone else. It was only you.'
'How did I know? I thought you wanted it too.
I thought you were like the rest. Well, what's to be done?'
'To be done?' 'Is it all right?' 'Yes.' 'Sure?' 'Yes, but why?'
'I don't know. I thought you were going to cry.
You said you had something to tell me.' 'Yes, I know.
It wasn't anything really . . . I think I'll go.'
'Yes, it's late. There's thunder about, a drop of rain
Fell on my hand in the dark. I'll see you again
At the dance next week. You're sure that everything's right?'
'Yes,' 'Well, I'll be going.' 'Kiss me . . .' 'Good night.' . . . 'Good night.'

QUESTIONS FOR REFLECTION

1. What differences exist in the dialogue of the two speakers? How do those differences characterize the tone of each speaker's voice?
2. What do the questions, ellipses, and repeated words contribute to the poem's tone?

GERARD MANLEY HOPKINS*

[1844–1889]

[Thou art indeed just, Lord]

Justus quidem tu es, Domine, si disputem tecum: verumtamen justa loquar ad te: Quare via impiorum prosperatur? °

Thou art indeed just, Lord, if I contend
With thee; but, sir, so what I plead is just.
Why do sinners' ways prosper? and why must
Disappointment all I endeavour end?
Wert thou my enemy, O thou my friend,
How wouldst thou worse, I wonder, than thou dost
Defeat, thwart me? Oh, the sots and thralls of lust
Do in spare hours more thrive than I that spend,

"Thou art indeed just, Lord" ***Justus quidem tu es, Domine, si disputem tecum: verumtamen justa loquar ad te: Quare via impiorum prosperatur?*** *the first three lines of the poem (up to* prosper*) translate the Latin epigraph.*

Sir, life upon thy cause. See, banks and brakes
Now, leavèd how thick! lacèd they are again
With fretty chervil, look, and fresh wind shakes

Them; birds build—but not I build; no, but strain,
Time's eunuch, and not breed one work that wakes.
Mine, O thou lord of life, send my roots rain. [1889]

QUESTIONS FOR REFLECTION

1. How do the words the speaker uses to address God help establish the tone of the first four lines? What is his attitude toward God here?
2. Lines 5–7 might be paraphrased according to the familiar saying: "with friends like you, who needs enemies." What tone of voice do you hear in those lines? In lines 9–13? In the final line?

ANONYMOUS

Western Wind

Western wind, when will thou blow,
The small rain down can rain?
Christ, if my love were in my arms
And I in my bed again! [c. 1500]

QUESTIONS FOR REFLECTION

1. What tone bursts through the final couplet? What feeling does the speaker convey?
2. How does the tone of the following alteration compare with the poem's final two lines as written?

Oh God I wish I were in bed
With my lover again.

HENRY REED

[b. 1914]

Naming of Parts

Today we have naming of parts. Yesterday,
We had daily cleaning. And tomorrow morning,
We shall have what to do after firing. But today,
Today we have naming of parts. Japonica
Glistens like coral in all of the neighboring gardens,
And today we have naming of parts.

This is the lower sling swivel. And this
Is the upper sling swivel, whose use you will see,
When you are given your slings. And this is the piling swivel,
Which in your case you have not got. The branches
Hold in the gardens their silent, eloquent gestures,
  Which in our case we have not got.

This is the safety-catch, which is always released
With an easy flick of the thumb. And please do not let me
See anyone using his finger. You can do it quite easy
If you have any strength in your thumb. The blossoms
Are fragile and motionless, never letting anyone see
  Any of them using their finger.

And this you can see is the bolt. The purpose of this
Is to open the breech, as you see. We can slide it
Rapidly backwards and forwards: we call this
Easing the spring. And rapidly backwards and forwards
The early bees are assaulting and fumbling the flowers:
  They call it easing the Spring.

They call it easing the Spring: it is perfectly easy
If you have any strength in your thumb: like the bolt,
And the breech, and the cocking-piece, and the point of balance,
Which in our case we have not got; and the almond-blossom
Silent in all of the gardens and the bees going backwards and forwards,
  For today we have naming of parts.

[1946]

QUESTIONS FOR REFLECTION

1. Each stanza of "Naming of Parts" contains two distinct voices. Where does the first voice end and the second begin? Describe and characterize each voice.
2. Pinpoint the place where the two voices converge. What is the effect of their convergence?

RANDALL JARRELL

[1914–1965]

The Death of the Ball Turret Gunner

From my mother's sleep I fell into the State,
And I hunched in its belly till my wet fur froze.
Six miles from earth, loosed from its dream of life,

I woke to black flak and the nightmare fighters.
When I died they washed me out of the turret with a hose.

[1969]

QUESTION FOR REFLECTION

1. Who is the speaker, and with what tone of voice does he speak?

DICTION

At their most successful, poems include "the best words in the best order," as Samuel Taylor Coleridge has said. In reading any poem it is necessary to know what the words mean, but it is equally important to understand what the words imply or suggest. The **denotation** or dictionary meaning of *dictator,* for example, is "a person exercising absolute power, especially one who assumes absolute control without the free consent of the people." But *dictator* also carries additional **connotations** or associations both personal and public. Beyond its dictionary meaning, *dictator* may suggest repressive force and tyrannical oppression; it may call up images of bloodbaths, purges, executions; it may trigger associations that prompt us to think of Hitler, for example, or Mussolini. The same kind of associative resonance occurs with a word like *vacation,* the connotations of which far outstrip its dictionary definition: "a period of suspension of work, study, or other activity."

Because poets often hint indirectly at more than their words directly state, it is necessary to develop the habit of considering the connotations of words as well as their denotations. Often for both poets and readers the "best words" are those that do the most work; they convey feelings and indirectly imply ideas rather than state them outright. Poets choose a particular word because it suggests what they want to suggest. Its appropriateness is a function of both its denotation and its connotation. Consider, for example, the second stanza of Roethke's "My Papa's Waltz":

We romped until the pans
Slid from the kitchen shelf;
My mother's countenance
Could not unfrown itself.

"Romped" could be replaced by *danced* since the poet is describing a dance, specifically a waltz. Why "romped" then? For one thing, it means something different from *danced.* That is, its denotation provides a different meaning, indicating play or frolic of a boisterous nature. Although "romped" is not really a dance word at all, here it suggests a kind of rough, crude dancing, far less elegant and systematic than waltzing. But it also connotes the kind of vigorous roughhousing that fathers and sons occasionally engage in and from which many mothers are excluded—though here, of course, the romp is occasioned by the father's having had too much to drink. "Romped" then both describes more precisely the kind of dance and suggests the speaker's attitude toward the experience.

Perhaps the most unusual words in the stanza, however, are "countenance" and "unfrown" "Countenance" is less familiar and more surprising than face. This is also true of "unfrown," a word you won't find in the dictionary. What makes these words noticeable is not just their uncommonness but their strangeness in the context of the stanza. "Countenance," a formal word, contrasts with the informal language of the two lines before it, lines that describe the informal romp of a dance; it suggests the mother's formality as she watches the informal play of her husband and son. Although her frown indicates disapproval, perhaps annoyance that her pans are falling, the disapproval and annoyance may be put on, part of an act. It is possible that she is responding as she is expected to respond.

If we look up *countenance* in the *Random House College Dictionary,* here is what we find:

noun	1. appearance, esp. the expression of the face...
	2. the face; visage
	3. calm facial expression; composure
	4. (obsolete) bearing; behavior
trans. verb	6. to permit or tolerate
	7. to approve, support, or encourage...

Let's consider briefly the implications of these multiple denotations. The second meaning is more general than the first. It is this first meaning to which we gave priority in the discussion above. We determined our sense of the kind of expression on the mother's face from the line, "Could not unfrown itself." But in looking at definitions 3 and 4, we encounter a problem, or at least a complication. Isn't the mother's "frown" a sign of *dis*composure rather than one of the "composure" suggested by a "calm facial expression"? Or is it possible that Roethke has used *countenance* with two meanings in mind: the meaning of "facial expression" on one hand; the meanings of "tolerate and permit, approve and encourage" on the other? This double sense of *countenance* thus parallels the double sense of the experience for the child as both pleasurable and frightening.

Let us look closely at the language of the following poem.

WILLIAM WORDSWORTH*

[1770–1850]

[I wandered lonely as a cloud]

I wandered lonely as a cloud
That floats on high o'er vales and hills,
When all at once I saw a crowd,
A host, of golden daffodils;
Beside the lake, beneath the trees,
Fluttering and dancing in the breeze.

Continuous as the stars that shine
And twinkle on the milky way,
They stretched in never-ending line

Along the margin of a bay:
Ten thousand saw I at a glance,
Tossing their heads in sprightly dance.

The waves beside them danced; but they
Outdid the sparkling waves in glee:
A poet could not but be gay,
In such a jocund company:
I gazed—and gazed—but little thought
What wealth the show to me had brought:

For oft, when on my couch I lie
In vacant or in pensive mood,
They flash upon that inward eye
Which is the bliss of solitude;
And then my heart with pleasure fills,
And dances with the daffodils.

[1807]

The words of the poem are familiar; their meanings should pose no problems. We might mention that "o'er" in line 2 is an **elision,** the omission of an unstressed vowel or syllable to preserve the meter, of *over,* and that "oft" in line 19 is an abbreviated form of *often*. The language, overall, is simple, direct, and clear. We can assure ourselves of the rightness or appropriateness of the poem's diction by considering the connotations of a few words. We can take lines 3 and 4 as examples.

When all at once I saw a crowd,
A host, of golden daffodils;

Suppose they had been written this way:

When all at once I spied a bunch,
A group of yellow daffodils;

Consider the connotations of each version. "Spied" may indicate something secretive or even prying about the speaker's looking. It may also suggest that he was looking for them. In contrast, "saw" carries less intense and fewer connotations; it merely indicates that the speaker noticed the daffodils, and its tone is more matter-of-fact. The alternate version's "bunch" and "group" suggest, on the one hand, a smaller number than Wordsworth's corresponding "crowd" and, on the other, a less communal sense. "Crowd" and "host," moreover, carry connotations of a social gathering, of people congregated to share an experience or simply enjoy one another's company. This implicit humanizing or personifying of the daffodils (identifying them with human actions and feelings) brings the daffodils to life: They are described as dancing and as "tossing their heads" (line 12), and they are called a "jocund company" (line 16). "Company" underscores the sociality of the daffodils and "jocund" indicates the human quality of being joyful.

This emphasis on the happiness of the daffodils and their large number serves to point up sharply the isolation and dispiritedness of the speaker. Their vast number is emphasized in the second stanza where they are described as "continuous" and as stretching in a "never-ending line." (And, of course, in the count: "ten thousand.") But this important contrast between the isolation of the speaker and the solidarity of the daffodils, though continued into the second stanza, gives way in stanzas three and four as the speaker imagines himself among the daffodils rather than simply looking at them from a distance. More important, when he remembers them later, he thinks about being "with" them, not literally but imaginatively.

But before we look at words describing the speaker from later stanzas, we should return to the first adjective that describes the flowers: "golden" (line 4). Wordsworth uses "golden," not "yellow," or "amber," or "tawny" because "golden" suggests more than a color; it connotes light (it shines and glitters) and wealth (money and fortune). In fact the speaker uses the word "wealth" in line 18 to indicate how important the experience of seeing the daffodils has been. And in the last two stanzas, we notice that the speaker uses in succession five words denoting *joy* ("glee," "gay," "jocund," "bliss," and "pleasure") in a crescendo that suggests the intensity of the speaker's happiness.

Although Wordsworth uses various words to indicate joy, he occasionally repeats rather than varies his diction. The repetitions of the words for seeing ("saw," "gazed") inaugurate and sustain the imagery of vision that is central to the poem's meaning; the forms of the verb *to dance* ("dancing," "danced," "dance," and "dances") suggest both that the various elements of nature are in harmony with one another and that nature is also in harmony with man. The poet conveys this by bringing the elements of nature together in pairs: daffodils and wind (stanza one); daffodils and flowers, daffodils and stars (stanza two); water and wind (stanza three). Nature and man come together explicitly in stanza four when the speaker says that his heart dances with the daffodils.

A different kind of repetition appears in the movement from the loneliness of line one to the solitude of line 22. Both words denote an alone-ness, but they suggest a radical difference in the solitary person's attitude to his state of being alone. The poem moves from the sadly alienated separation felt by the speaker in the beginning to his joy in reimagining the natural scene, a movement framed by the words "loneliness" and "solitude." An analogous movement is suggested within the final stanza by the words "vacant" and "fills." The emptiness of the speaker's spirit is transformed into a fullness of feeling as he remembers the daffodils.

To gain practice in discerning and appreciating diction in poetry, read the following poems with special attention to their *words.*

EDWIN ARLINGTON ROBINSON*

[1869–1935]

Miniver Cheevy

Miniver Cheevy, child of scorn,
    Grew lean while he assailed the seasons;
He wept that he was ever born,
    And he had reasons.

Miniver loved the days of old
When swords were bright and steeds were prancing;
The vision of a warrior bold
Would set him dancing.

Miniver sighed for what was not,
And dreamed, and rested from his labors;
He dreamed of Thebes° and Camelot,°
And Priam's neighbors.°

Miniver mourned the ripe renown
That made so many a name so fragrant;
He mourned Romance, now on the town,
And Art, a vagrant.

Miniver loved the Medici,°
Albeit he had never seen one;
He would have sinned incessantly
Could he have been one.

Miniver cursed the commonplace
And eyed a khaki suit with loathing;
He missed the mediæval grace
Of iron clothing.

Miniver scorned the gold he sought,
But sore annoyed was he without it;
Miniver thought, and thought, and thought,
And thought about it.

Miniver Cheevy, born too late,
Scratched his head and kept on thinking;
Miniver coughed, and called it fate,
And kept on drinking. [1910]

QUESTIONS FOR REFLECTION

1. List the words in the poem that illustrate what is said in line 5: that "Miniver loved the days of old." List all the verbs that describe Miniver's action or inaction. What do they reveal about him?

"Miniver Cheevy" 11 ***Thebes*** *Greek city famous in history and legend.* 11 ***Camelot*** *the seat of King Arthur's court.* 12 ***Priam*** *king of Troy during the Trojan war.* 17 ***The Medici*** *family of powerful merchants and bankers, rulers of Florence in the fourteenth, fifteenth, and sixteenth centuries, who were known for their patronage of the arts.*

2. What are the connotations of "ripe" (line 13) and "fragrant" (line 14)? What does the combination of each respectively with ideas of fame and nobility suggest about these ideas? And how do the connotations of "on the town" (to describe Romance) and "a vagrant" (to characterize Art) suggest what has happened to Art and Romance?

WILLIAM WORDSWORTH*

[1770–1850]

It is a beauteous evening

It is a beauteous evening, calm and free,
The holy time is quiet as a Nun
Breathless with adoration; the broad sun
Is sinking down in its tranquility;
The gentleness of heaven broods o'er the Sea:
Listen! the mighty Being is awake,
And doth with his eternal motion make
A sound like thunder—everlastingly.
Dear Child! dear Girl! that walkest with me here,
If thou appear untouched by solemn thought,
Thy nature is not therefore less divine:
Thou liest in Abraham's bosom all the year,
And worship'st at the Temple's inner shrine,
God being with thee when we know it not. [1807]

QUESTIONS FOR REFLECTION

1. What do the following words have in common: *holy, eternal, solemn, divine, nun, adoration, heaven, God?*
2. Which words in the last four lines are congruent with these? And how does this diction reinforce the idea and feeling of the poem?

ROBERT HERRICK*

[1591–1674]

Delight in Disorder

A sweet disorder in the dress
Kindles in clothes a wantonness.
A lawn° about the shoulders thrown

"Delight in Disorder" 3 ***lawn*** *fine linen.*

Into a fine distractiön;
An erring lace, which here and there
Enthralls the crimson stomacher;°
A cuff neglectful, and thereby
Ribbons to flow confusedly;
A winning wave, deserving note,
In the tempestuous petticoat;
A careless shoestring, in whose tie
I see a wild civility;
Do more bewitch me than when art
Is too precise in every part. [1648]

QUESTIONS FOR REFLECTION

1. Examine the connotations of the words suggesting disorder: *thrown, distraction, neglectful, confusedly, careless.* Consider especially the connotations and etymology (word origin) of "erring" (line 5) and "tempestuous" (line 10).
2. Consider the words that describe the speaker's reaction to the disordered dress he describes: *sweet, kindles, wantonness, fine, wild, bewitch.* What do the connotations of these words suggest about the speaker?

IMAGERY

Poems are grounded in the concrete and the specific—in details that stimulate our senses—for it is through our senses that we perceive the world. We see daylight break and fade; we hear dogs bark and children laugh; we feel the sting of a bitterly cold wind; we smell the heavy aroma of perfume; we taste the tartness of lemon and the sweetness of chocolate. Poems include such details which trigger our memories, stimulate our feelings, and command our response.

When such specific details appear in poems they are called images. An **image** is a concrete representation of a sense impression, feeling, or idea. Images appeal to one or more of our senses. Images may be visual (something seen), aural (something heard), tactile (something felt), olfactory (something smelled), or gustatory (something tasted).

Tactile images of heat and cold inform Hayden's "Those Winter Sundays" (page 496), in which the speaker's father wakes up early "in the blueblack cold" to make "banked fires blaze." Visual and tactile images appear in Frost's "Stopping by Woods" (page 499), in which the speaker has stopped "between the woods and frozen lake" to listen to "the sweep of easy wind" and watch the fall of "downy" flakes of snow.

We sometimes use the word *imagery* to refer to a pattern of related details in a poem. Shakespeare's sonnet "That time of year thou may'st in me behold," for example (page 531), includes images of darkness and light, cold and warmth, day and night. The images cluster together to describe the passing of time. When images form pat-

[6]***stomacher*** *a garment worn under the laces of the bodice.*

terns of related details that convey an idea or feeling beyond what the images literally describe,we call them *metaphorical* or *symbolic.* Such details suggest a meaning, attitude, or idea, as for example when images of light are indicative of knowledge or of life and images of darkness are suggestive of ignorance or death.

Poetry describes specific things—daffodils, fires, and finches' wings, for example. And it describes such things in specific terms: the color of the daffodils, the glare of the fire, the beating of the finches' wings. From these and other specific details we derive both meaning and feeling.

For an indication of how images work together to convey feelings and ideas, consider the images in the following poem.

ELIZABETH BISHOP*
[1911–1979]

First Death in Nova Scotia

In the cold, cold parlor
my mother laid out Arthur
beneath the chromographs:
Edward, Prince of Wales,
with Princess Alexandra,
and King George with Queen Mary.
Below them on the table
stood a stuffed loon
shot and stuffed by Uncle
Arthur, Arthur's father.

Since Uncle Arthur fired
a bullet into him,
he hadn't said a word.
He kept his own counsel
on his white, frozen lake,
the marble-topped table.
His breast was deep and white,
cold and caressable;
his eyes were red glass,
much to be desired.

"Come," said my mother,
"Come and say good-bye
to your little cousin Arthur."
I was lifted up and given
one lily of the valley
to put in Arthur's hand.
Arthur's coffin was

a little frosted cake,
and the red-eyed loon eyed it
from his white, frozen lake.

Arthur was very small.
He was all white, like a doll
that hadn't been painted yet.
Jack Frost had started to paint him
the way he always painted
the Maple Leaf (Forever).
He had just begun on his hair,
a few red strokes, and then
Jack Frost had dropped the brush
and left him white, forever.

The gracious royal couples
were warm in red and ermine;
their feet were well wrapped up
in the ladies' ermine trains.
They invited Arthur to be
the smallest page at court.
But how could Arthur go,
clutching his tiny lily,
with his eyes shut up so tight
and the roads deep in snow?

[1965]

The poem describes a child's view of death. Through images of what the little girl sees and hears, it renders her incomprehension and confused feelings about her cousin Arthur's death. Bishop does this by filtering the child's perceptions through an adult sensibility. In a similar way, the poet presents a voice childlike in its syntactic constructions and adult in its vocabulary. Through the double perspective of the adult/child we gain a complex inner view of the speaker's impressions and understanding of her experience, vividly rendered in the poem's images.

Our first sense impression is tactile: we imagine "the cold, cold parlor." Immediately after,we see two things: a picture of the British royal family and a stuffed loon, which had been shot by the dead boy's father, also named Arthur. The second stanza describes the loon in more detail. It sits on a marble-topped table, a detail that conveys two tactile impressions, hardness and coldness. This imagery is emphasized in the description of the marble table as the loon's "white, frozen lake."

These visual images are continued in the third stanza in which the speaker sees her dead cousin in his coffin. She holds a white flower which she puts in the dead boy's hand. The images of whiteness and cold (the frozen lake, marble table top, and the dead, stuffed white loon of the previous stanzas) are continued: the speaker describes Arthur's coffin as a "frosted cake." The birthday cake image also indicates the limited extent of the speaker's comprehension of the reality and finality of death.

With the repeated details about the loon's red eyes and its frozen posture and base, the child unconsciously (and the poet consciously) associates the dead boy and the dead loon. This connection is further established by the imagery of the fourth stanza in which Arthur is described as "all white," with "a few red strokes" for his hair. Unlike the maple leaf with its complete and thorough redness, little Arthur is left "unpainted" by Jack Frost (another image of the cold) and is thus left white "forever." On the one hand, such a description clearly indicates the child's fantastic incomprehension of Arthur's death; on the other, it suggests that she intuitively senses that Arthur has been drained of color and of life. A similar combination of intuitive understanding and conscious ignorance is echoed in the speaker's comparison of Arthur with the doll. She sees how similar they look on the surface, but she does not consciously register their similar lifelessness.

The images of the final stanzas recall those of stanza one. The royal couples of the chromograph are described as dressed in red clothes with white fur trim, details that connect directly with the dead loon. Moreover, the lily of the third stanza (white and short-lived like the boy) reappears clutched in Arthur's hand. The final image is one of whiteness and coldness: deep snow covers the cold ground where Arthur will soon lie.

The poem's concrete details, mostly visual and tactile images, strongly evoke the coldness and lifelessness of the dead child. But they suggest other things as well. The portrait of the royal family and the stuffed loon suggest something of the family's social identity—especially its conservatism and propriety. More importantly, however, these details, along with the others noted above, reveal the limitation of the speaker's understanding. She sees the loon, for example, as quiet: "he hadn't said a word" and "he kept his own counsel." In addition, she fantasizes that the royal family (which she sees as very much alive in their warm furs) have invited little Arthur to serve as "the smallest page at court." Even though this may be the speaker's way of coping with death, the final two images of white lily and cold snow, and the tone in which she asks her final question all point toward her near acknowledgment of the truth.

For further practice in responding to poetic images, read the following poems.

WILLIAM BUTLER YEATS*

[1865–1939]

The Lake Isle of Innisfree

I will arise and go now, and go to Innisfree,
And a small cabin build there, of clay and
  wattles° made: interwoven twigs
Nine bean-rows will I have there, a hive for the honey-bee,
And live alone in the bee-loud glade.
And I shall have some peace there, for peace comes
  dropping slow,
Dropping from the veils of the morning to where the cricket sings;
There midnight's all a glimmer, and noon a purple glow,
And evening full of the linnet's wings.
I will arise and go now, for always night and day
I hear lake water lapping with low sounds by the shore;

While I stand on the roadway, or on the pavements gray,
I hear it in the deep heart's core. [1892]

QUESTION FOR REFLECTION

Identify the images of sound and sight, and explain what they contribute to the idea and feeling of the poem.

ROBERT BROWNING*
[1812–1889]

Meeting at Night

The gray sea and the long black land;
And the yellow half-moon large and low;
And the startled little waves that leap
In fiery ringlets from their sleep,
As I gain the cove with pushing prow,
And quench its speed i' the slushy sand.

Then a mile of warm sea-scented beach;
Three fields to cross till a farm appears;
A tap at the pane, the quick sharp scratch
And blue spurt of a lighted match,
And a voice less loud, through its joys and fears,
Than the two hearts beating each to each! [1845]

QUESTION FOR REFLECTION

In a series of images averaging one per line, the poet describes a lover traveling to meet his beloved. Identify each image, the specific sense it stimulates, and the feelings the images evoke.

H.D. (HILDA DOOLITTLE)
[1886–1961]

Heat

O wind, rend open the heat,
cut apart the heat,
rend it to tatters.
Fruit cannot drop

through this thick air—
that presses up and blunts
the points of pears
and rounds the grapes.

Cut the heat—
plow through it,
turning it on either side
of your path. [1916]

QUESTION FOR REFLECTION

By asking the wind to "rend open," "cut apart," and "plow through" the heat, the poet creates an image of it. Identify this image, and explain what stanza two contributes to it.

THOMAS HARDY
[1840–1928]

Neutral Tones

We stood by a pond that winter day,
And the sun was white, as though chidden of God,
And a few leaves lay on the starving sod;
—They had fallen from an ash, and were gray.

Your eyes on me were as eyes that rove
Over tedious riddles of years ago;
And some words played between us to and fro
On which lost the more by our love.

The smile on your mouth was the deadest thing
Alive enough to have strength to die;
And a grin of bitterness swept thereby
    Like an ominous bird a-wing. . . .

Since then, keen lessons that love deceives,
And wrings with wrong, have shaped to me
Your face, and the God-curst sun, and a tree,
    And a pond edged with grayish leaves. [1898]

QUESTIONS FOR REFLECTION

1. Examine the images of stanza one. What mood do they create? How do the images of stanzas two and three develop and expand those of the opening stanza?

2. What do you notice about the images of the final stanza in relation to those that come before?

FIGURES OF SPEECH: SIMILE AND METAPHOR

Language can be classified as either literal or figurative. When we speak literally, we mean exactly what each word conveys; when we use *figurative language* we mean something other than the actual meaning of the words. "Go jump in the lake," for example, if meant literally would be intended as a command to leave (go) and jump (not dive or wade) into a lake (not a pond or stream). In telling someone to go jump in the lake we are telling them something, to be sure, but what we mean is different from the literal meaning of the words.

Rhetoricians have catalogued more than 250 different *figures of speech,* expressions or ways of using words in a nonliteral sense. They include **hyperbole** or exaggeration ("I'll die if I miss that game"); understatement ("Being flayed alive is somewhat painful"); **synecdoche** or using a part to signify the whole ("Lend me a hand"); **metonymy** or substituting an attribute of a thing for the thing itself ("step on the gas"); **personification,** endowing inanimate objects or abstract concepts with animate characteristics or qualities ("the lettuce was lonely without tomatoes and cucumbers for company"). We will not go on to name and illustrate the others but instead will concentrate on two specially important for poetry (and for the other literary genres as well): simile and metaphor.

The heart of both these figures is comparison—the making of connections between normally unrelated things. More than 2,300 years ago Aristotle defined **metaphor** as "an intuitive perception of the similarity in dissimilars." And he suggested further that to be a "master of metaphor" is the greatest of a poet's achievements. In our century, Robert Frost has echoed Aristotle by suggesting that metaphor is central to poetry, and that, essentially, poetry is a way of "saying one thing and meaning another."

Although both figures involve comparisons between unlike things, **simile** establishes the comparison explicitly with the words *like* or *as.* Metaphor, on the other hand, employs no such explicit verbal clue. The comparison is *implied* in such a way that the figurative term is substituted for or identified with the literal one. "My daughter dances like an angel" is a simile; "my daughter is an angel" is a metaphor. In this example the difference involves more than the word *like:* The simile is more restricted in its comparative suggestion than is the metaphor. That is, the daughter's angelic attributes are more extensive in the unspecified and unrestricted metaphor. In the simile, she only dances like an angel. (There's no suggestion that she possesses other angelic qualities.)

Consider the opening line of Wordsworth's poem about the daffodils: "I wandered lonely as a cloud" (page 519). The simile suggests the speaker's isolation and his aimless wandering. But it doesn't indicate other ways in which cloud and speaker are related. Later the speaker uses another simile to compare the daffodils with stars. This simile specifically highlights one aspect of the connection between stars and flowers: number. It also contains an example of hyperbole in its suggestion that the daffodils stretch in "a never-ending line."

In these examples the poet provides explicit clues that direct us to the comparative connection. He also restricts their application, as we have noted. In a metaphor, Wordsworth writes that the daffodils "flash" upon the "inward eye" of the speaker. The "flash" (an image of light) implies that he sees the flowers in his mind's eye, the inward eye of memory. Moreover, when he "sees" the daffodils in his "inward eye," he realizes the "wealth" they have brought him. This "wealth" is also figurative—Wordsworth uses "wealth" as a metaphor for joy.

These examples of simile and metaphor from Wordsworth's poem are fairly straightforward and uncomplicated. For a more complex example, consider the use of metaphor in the following sonnet by William Shakespeare.

WILLIAM SHAKESPEARE*

[1564–1616]

That time of year thou may'st in me behold

That time of year thou may'st in me behold
When yellow leaves, or none, or few, do hang
Upon those boughs which shake against the cold,
Bare ruined choirs where late the sweet birds sang.
In me thou see'st the twilight of such day
As after sunset fadeth in the west,
Which by-and-by black night doth take away,
Death's second self that seals up all in rest.
In me thou see'st the glowing of such fire
That on the ashes of his youth doth lie,
As the deathbed whereon it must expire,
Consumed with that which it was nourished by.
　This thou perceiv'st, which makes thy love more strong,
　To love that well which thou must leave ere long. [1609]

Perhaps the first thing to mention about the poem's metaphorical language is that its images appeal to three senses: sight, hearing, and touch. The images of the first four lines include appeals to each of these senses: we *see* the yellow leaves and bare branches; we *feel* the cold that shakes the boughs; we *hear* (in memory) the singing birds of summer.

But these concrete representations of sensory experience become more than images with emotional reverberations. They become metaphors, ways of talking about one thing in terms of something else. The first image extended into a metaphor is that of autumn, "that time of year" when leaves turn yellow and branches become bare. The fourth line extends the image by describing the tree branches as a choir loft that the birds have recently vacated. Because Shakespeare's speaker says that "you" (we) can behold autumn *in him* ("In me thou see'st the twilight of such day," line 5), we know that he is speaking of more than autumn. We realize that he is talking about one thing in terms of another—about aging in terms of the seasons.

In the next four lines the metaphor of autumn gives way to another: that of twilight ending the day. The sun has set; night is coming on. The "black" night is described as taking away the sun's light (line 7); the sun's setting is seen as a dying of its light. The implied comparison of night with death is directly stated in line 8, where night is called "death's second self"; like death, night "seals up all in rest." Night's rest is, of course, temporary; death's, however, is final. The metaphor is both consoling (death is a kind of restful sleep) and frightening (death "seals up" life in a way that suggests there will be no unsealing).

So far we have noted two extended metaphors of autumn and of evening. Each comparison highlights the way death begins with a prelude: twilight precedes night; autumn precedes winter; illness or aging precedes death. The speaker knows that he is in the autumn of his life, the twilight of his time. This metaphor is continued in a third image: the dying of the fire, which represents the dying out of the speaker's life. This third image emphasizes the extinguishing of light and of heat. The speaker's youth is "ashes," which serve as the "deathbed" on which he will "expire" (line 11). Literally, the lines say that the fire will expire as it burns up the fuel that feeds it. As it does so, it glows with light and heat. The glowing fire is a metaphor for the speaker's life, which is presently still "glowing" but which is beginning to die out. We might notice that the fire will "expire," a word which means literally to "breathe out . . . to emit the last breath," an image that suggests the termination of breathing in the dying.

The final element of this image of the dying fire is given in line 12: "Consumed with that which it was nourished by." Literally the fire consumes itself by using up its fuel, burning up logs. In its very glowing it burns toward its own extinction. Analogously, the speaker's youthful vitality consumes itself in living. His very living has been and continues to be a dying.

For a few additional examples of how poets employ figurative language, read the following poems. Attend particularly to their figures of comparison and especially to how those comparisons aid your understanding.

JOHN DONNE*

[1572–1631]

Hymn to God the Father

1

Wilt thou forgive that sin where I begun,
  Which was my sin though it were done before?
Wilt thou forgive that sin through which I run,
  And do run still, though still I do deplore?
    When thou hast done, thou hast not done,
      For I have more.

2

Wilt thou forgive that sin by which I've won
  Others to sin, and made my sin their door?
Wilt thou forgive that sin which I did shun
  A year or two, but wallowed in a score?
    When thou hast done, thou hast not done,
      For I have more.

3

I have a sin of fear, that when I've spun
My last thread, I shall perish on the shore;
But swear by thyself that at my death thy son
Shall shine as he shines now, and heretofore;
And having done that, Thou hast done;
I fear no more.

[1633]

QUESTIONS FOR REFLECTION

1. Explain the images in stanza two: the door of sin and wallowing in sin. Relate these two images from stanza three: spinning the last thread and perishing on the shore.
2. The final stanza contains two puns or plays on words. Identify and explain each. What do they contribute to the meaning and tone of the poem?

ROBERT WALLACE

[b. 1932]

The Double Play

In his sea-lit
distance, the pitcher winding
like a clock about to chime comes down with

the ball, hit
sharply, under the artificial
banks of arc lights, bounds like a vanishing string

over the green
to the shortstop magically
scoops to his right whirling above his invisible

shadows
in the dust redirects
its flight to the running poised second baseman

pirouettes
leaping, above the slide, to throw
from mid-air, across the colored tightened interval,

to the leaning-
out first baseman ends the dance
drawing it disappearing into his long brown glove

stretches. What
is too swift for deception
is final, lost, among the loosened figures

jogging off the field
(the pitcher walks), casual
in the space where the poem has happened. [1965]

QUESTIONS FOR REFLECTION

1. As its title suggests the poem describes a double play in baseball—getting two offensive players out on a single play. Throughout the poem the double play is compared to a dance. Pinpoint the words and phrases that establish this metaphorical connection, and explain what precisely about the double play makes it like a dance.
2. Besides the central metaphor that controls the poem, the poet has introduced other comparisons to illuminate and describe aspects or details of the double play. Identify and explain these comparisons.
3. In what way has the double play occurred "in the space where the poem has happened" (line 24)? How has a double play occurred both on the page and in the poem?

LOUIS SIMPSON

[b. 1923]

The Battle

Helmet and rifle, pack and overcoat
Marched through a forest. Somewhere up ahead
Guns thudded. Like the circle of a throat
The night on every side was turning red.

They halted and they dug. They sank like moles
Into the clammy earth between the trees.
And soon the sentries, standing in their holes,
Felt the first snow. Their feet began to freeze.

At dawn the first shell landed with a crack.
Then shells and bullets swept the icy woods.
This lasted many days. The snow was black.
The corpses stiffened in their scarlet hoods.

Most clearly of that battle I remember
The tiredness in eyes, how hands looked thin
Around a cigarette, and the bright ember
Would pulse with all the life there was within. [1960]

QUESTIONS FOR REFLECTION

Identify and explain the figures of speech in the first two stanzas. What impression does each create? How is the mood they establish enforced by the rest of the poem?

JUDITH WRIGHT

[b. 1915]

Woman to Child

You who were darkness warmed my flesh
where out of darkness rose the seed.
Then all a world I made in me;
all the world you hear and see
hung upon my dreaming blood.

There moved the multitudinous stars,
and coloured birds and fishes moved.
There swam the sliding continents.
All time lay rolled in me, and sense,
and love that knew not its beloved.

O node and focus of the world;
I hold you deep within that well
you shall escape and not escape—
that mirrors still your sleeping shape;
that nurtures still your crescent cell.

I wither and you break from me;
yet though you dance in living light
I am the earth, I am the root,
I am the stem that fed the fruit,
the link that joins you to the night.

QUESTION FOR REFLECTION

Explain the following figurative expressions:

"All a world I made in me" (line 3)
"All time lay rolled in me" (line 9)
"I hold you deep within that well" (line 12)
"I am the earth, I am the root,"
"I am the stem that fed the fruit" (lines 18–19)

SYMBOLISM AND ALLEGORY

A **symbol** is any object or action that represents something beyond itself. A rose, for example, can represent beauty or love or transience. A tree may represent a family's roots and branches. A soaring bird might stand for freedom. Light might symbolize hope or knowledge or life. These and other familiar symbols may represent different, even opposite things, depending on how they are deployed in a particular poem. Natural symbols like light and darkness, fire and water can stand for contradictory things. Water, for example, which typically symbolizes life (rain, fertility, food, life) can also stand for death (tempests, hurricanes, floods). And fire, which often indicates destruction, can represent purgation or purification. The meaning of any symbol, whether an object, an action, or a gesture, is controlled by its context. How then do we know if a poetic detail is symbolic? How do we decide whether to leap beyond the poem's literal detail into a symbolic interpretation?

There are no simple answers to these questions. Like any interpretive connections we make in reading, the decision to view something as symbolic depends partly on our skill in reading and partly on whether the poetic context invites and rewards a symbolic reading. The following questions can guide our thinking about interpreting symbols:

1. Is the object, action, gesture, or event important to the poem? Is it described in detail? Does it occur repeatedly? Does it appear at a climactic moment in the poem?
2. Does the poem seem to warrant our granting its details more significance than their immediate literal meaning?
3. Does our symbolic reading make sense? Does it account for the literal details without either ignoring or distorting them?

Even so, there will be occasions when we are not certain that a poem is symbolic. And there will be times when, though we are fairly confident that certain details are symbolic, we are not confident about what they symbolize. Such uncertainty is due largely to the nature of interpretation, which is an art rather than a science. But these interpretive complications are also due to the differences in complexity and variability with which poets use symbols. The most complex symbols resist definitive and final explanation. We can circle around them, but we neither exhaust their significance nor define their meaning.

As an example of how literal details assume symbolic significance, observe their use in the following poem.

PETER MEINKE

[b. 1932]

Advice to My Son

The trick is, to live your days
as if each one may be your last
(for they go fast, and young men lose their lives
in strange and unimaginable ways)
but at the same time, plan long range

(for they go slow: if you survive
the shattered windshield and the bursting shell
you will arrive
at our approximation here below
of heaven or hell).

To be specific, between the peony and the rose
plant squash and spinach, turnips and tomatoes;
beauty is nectar
and nectar, in a desert, saves–
but the stomach craves stronger sustenance
than the honied vine.
Therefore, marry a pretty girl
after seeing her mother;
speak truth to one man,
work with another;
and always serve bread with your wine.

But, son,
always serve wine. [1981]

The concrete details that invite symbolic reading are these: peony and rose; squash, spinach, turnips and tomatoes; bread and wine. If we read the poem literally and assume the advice is meant that way, we learn something about the need to plant and enjoy these flowers and foods. But if we suspect that the speaker is advising his son about more than food and flowers, we will look toward their symbolic implications.

What then do the various plants and the bread and wine symbolize? How is the speaker's advice about them related to the more general advice about living? In the first stanza the general advice implies two contradictory courses of action: (1) Live each day to the fullest as if it will be the last; (2) look to the future and plan wisely so your future will not be marred by unwise decisions. By advising his son to plant peonies and roses, the speaker urges him to see the need for beauty and luxury, implying that he needs food for the spirit as well as sustenance for the body.

The symbols of bread and wine suggest a related point. The speaker urges his son to serve both bread and wine as bread is a dietary staple, something basic and common, but wine enhances the bread, making it seem more than mere common fare. Wine symbolizes something festive; it provides a touch of celebration. Thus the speaker's advice about bread and wine parallels his earlier suggestions. In each case, he urges his son to balance and blend, to fulfill both his basic and his spiritual needs. By making his advice concrete the speaker does indeed advocate literally what he says: Plant roses and peonies with your vegetables; drink wine with your bread. But by including such specific instructions in a poem that contains other more serious advice about living (live for today, live for the future) the poet invites us to see bread and wine, vegetables and flowers more than literally.

Related to symbolism, **allegory** is a form of narrative in which people, places, and happenings have hidden or symbolic meaning. Allegory differs from symbolism in establishing a strict system of correspondences between details of action and a pattern of meaning. Symbolic works that are not allegorical are less systematic and more open-ended in what their symbols mean.

The following allegorical poem describes a journey along an uphill road that ends with the traveler arriving at an inn. We can readily see that the uphill road represents a struggling journey through life, that day and night stand for a life span ending in death. The question-and-answer structure of the poem and its reassuring tone suggest that it can be read as a religious allegory, specifically a Christian one.

CHRISTINA ROSSETTI

[1830–1894]

Up-Hill

Does the road wind up-hill all the way?
  Yes, to the very end.
Will the day's journey take the whole long day?
  From morn to night, my friend.

But is there for the night a resting-place?
  A roof for when the slow dark hours begin.
May not the darkness hide it from my face?
  You cannot miss that inn.

Shall I meet other wayfarers at night?
  Those who have gone before.
Then must I knock, or call when just in sight?
  They will not keep you standing at that door.

Shall I find comfort, travel-sore and weak?
  Of labor you shall find the sum.
Will there be beds for me and all who seek?
  Yea, beds for all who come. [1862]

For more exercise in interpreting symbol and allegory, read the following poems with attention to their symbolic and allegorical details. All the poems are symbolic, but not in the same way.

www

WILLIAM BLAKE*

[1757–1827]

A Poison Tree

I was angry with my friend:
I told my wrath, my wrath did end.
I was angry with my foe:
I told it not, my wrath did grow.

And I waterd it in fears,
Night & morning with my tears;
And I sunnéd it with smiles,
And with soft deceitful wiles.

And it grew both day and night,
Till it bore an apple bright.
And my foe beheld it shine,
And he knew that it was mine,

And into my garden stole,
When the night had veild the pole;
In the morning glad I see
My foe outstretchd beneath the tree. [1794]

QUESTIONS FOR REFLECTION

1. "A Poison Tree" describes a series of events—it tells a story. Explain your understanding of the story's significance.
2. What does the apple in a garden represent? What difference would it make if it were a peach in an orchard?

ROBERT FROST*

[1874–1963]

The Road Not Taken

Two roads diverged in a yellow wood,
And sorry I could not travel both
And be one traveler, long I stood
And looked down one as far as I could
To where it bent in the undergrowth;

Then took the other, as just as fair,
And having perhaps the better claim,
Because it was grassy and wanted wear;
Though as for that, the passing there
Had worn them really about the same,

And both that morning equally lay
In leaves no step had trodden black.
Oh, I kept the first for another day!

Yet knowing how way leads on to way,
I doubted if I should ever come back.

I shall be telling this with a sigh
Somewhere ages and ages hence:
Two roads diverged in a wood, and I—
I took the one less traveled by,
And that has made all the difference.

[1916]

QUESTIONS FOR REFLECTION

1. On one level this is a poem about walking in the woods and choosing one of two paths to follow. What invites us to see the poem as something more? What is this something more?
2. Frost is careful not to specify what the two roads represent: he does not limit their possible symbolic meanings. And yet the nature of the experience he describes does pivot the poem on a central human problem: the inescapable necessity to make choices. Specify some of the choices we all must make that could be represented by the two roads of the poem.

GEORGE HERBERT*

[1593–1633]

Virtue

Sweet day, so cool, so calm, so bright,
  The bridal of the earth and sky:
The dew shall weep thy fall tonight;
  For thou must die.

Sweet rose, whose hue, angry and brave,
  Bids the rash gazer wipe his eye:
Thy root is ever in its grave,
  And thou must die.

Sweet spring, full of sweet days and roses,
  A box where sweets° compacted lie;   perfumes
My music shows ye have your closes,°   musical cadences
  And all must die.

Only a sweet and virtuous soul,
  Like seasoned timber, never gives;

But though the whole world turn to coal,
Then chiefly lives.
[1633]

QUESTIONS FOR REFLECTION

The major contrast in the poem is between things that die and the one thing that does not. Identify and comment on the aptness of Herbert's symbols for transience and mortality.

EMILY DICKINSON*

[1830–1886]

Because I could not stop for Death

Because I could not stop for Death—
He kindly stopped for me—
The Carriage held but just Ourselves—
And Immortality.

We slowly drove—He knew no haste
And I had put away
My labor and my leisure too,
For His Civility—

We passed the School, where Children strove
At Recess—in the Ring—
We passed the Fields of Gazing Grain—
We passed the Setting Sun—

Or rather—He passed Us—
The Dews drew quivering and chill—
For only Gossamer, my Gown—
My Tippet°—only Tulle— scarf or stole

We paused before a House that seemed
A Swelling of the Ground—
The Roof was scarcely visible—
The Cornice—in the Ground—

Since then—'tis Centuries—and yet
Feels shorter than the Day
I first surmised the Horses' Heads
Were toward Eternity—
[1863]

QUESTION FOR REFLECTION

Is this poem generally symbolic or is it allegorical? Explain the significance of the details in lines 9–13 and lines 17–20.

SYNTAX

We have previously defined **syntax** as the arrangement of words in a sentence, phrase, or clause. From a Greek word meaning "to arrange together," *syntax* refers to the grammatical structure of words in sentences and the deployment of sentences in longer units throughout the poem. Poets use syntax as they use imagery, diction, structure, sound, and rhythm—to express meaning and convey feeling. A poem's syntax is an important element of its tone and a guide to a speaker's state of mind. Speakers who repeat themselves or who break off abruptly in the midst of a thought, for example, reveal something about how they feel.

Let us briefly consider what syntax contributes to the meaning and feeling of a few poems discussed earlier. In "Those Winter Sundays" (page 496), Robert Hayden uses normal word order for each of the poem's four sentences, but he varies their lengths radically. In the first stanza, for example, Hayden follows a long sentence with a short one. The effect is to increase the emphasis on the short sentence: "No one ever thanked him." In the last stanza, Hayden uses a question rather than a statement for the speaker's remembrance of his father's acts of love. Both the question and the repetition of the phrase "What did I know" reveal the intensity of the speaker's regret at his belated understanding.

In "Stopping by Woods on a Snowy Evening" (page 499), Robert Frost achieves emphasis differently through *inversion* or the reversal of the standard order of words in a line or sentence. The word order of the first line of the poem is inverted:

> Whose woods these are I think I know.

Normal word order would be

> I think I know whose woods these are.

In the more conversational alternative, emphasis falls on what the speaker knows or thinks he knows. In Frost's line emphasis falls on "the woods," which are more important than what the speaker thinks he knows as he looks at them. Perhaps more important still is the difference in tone between the two versions. Frost's inverted syntax lifts the line, giving it a more even rhythm, slowing it down slightly. The alternate version lacks the rhythmic regularity of Frost's original and reads like a casual statement.

Another aspect of syntax worth noting in Frost's poem is the variations in tempo among the four stanzas. The sentences of the first and last stanzas are the most heavily stopped with punctuation and pauses. The opening stanza contains three pauses before it ends; stanza four includes three in its first line alone and five altogether. In contrast stanza three contains only one stop, halfway through. And stanza two is one long sentence without a single pause or break. Frost carefully controls the movement and speed, the pace and pause of his poem by using punctuation and grammatical form to heighten its expressiveness and to control its tone.

Unlike the inverted and varied syntax of Frost's "Stopping by Woods on a Snowy Evening," William Wordsworth's syntax in "I wandered lonely as a cloud" (page 519) is simple and direct; it does not call attention to itself. The two little syntactic twists that it does contain highlight an important dimension of the poem—visual imagery. One is an inversion: "saw I" (line 11); the other is a repetition: "I gazed—and gazed" (line 17).

Consider how syntax orders thought and highlights feeling in John Donne's "The Sun Rising."

JOHN DONNE*
[1572–1631]

The Sun Rising

Busy old fool, unruly sun,
Why dost thou thus,
Through windows, and through curtains call on us?
Must to thy motions lovers' seasons run?
Saucy pedantic wretch, go chide
Late schoolboys, and sour prentices,
Go tell court-huntsmen that the King will ride,
Call country ants to harvest offices;
Love, all alike, no season knows, nor clime,
Nor hours, days, months, which are the rags of time.

Thy beams, so reverend and strong
Why shouldst thou think?
I could eclipse and cloud them with a wink,
But that I would not lose her sight so long;
If her eyes have not blinded thine,
Look, and tomorrow late, tell me
Whether both the Indias of spice and mine
Be where thou left'st them, or lie here with me.
Ask for those kings whom thou saw'st yesterday,
And thou shalt hear, All here in one bed lay.

She's all states, and all princes, I,
Nothing else is.
Princes do but play us; compared to this,
All's honor's mimic, all wealth alchemy.
Thou, sun, art half as happy as we,
In that the world's contracted thus;
Thine age asks ease, and since thy duties be
To warm the world, that's done in warming us.
Shine here to us, and thou art everywhere;
This bed thy center is, these walls, thy sphere. [1633]

Perhaps the first thing we notice is the dislocation of syntax in the two opening questions. The first question could be rewritten so as to approximate more conventional discourse:

Unruly sun, busy old fool,
Why dost thou thus call on us
Through windows, and through curtains?

Besides an alteration of rhythm, we notice a different emphasis in Donne's lines. The alternate version puts the emphasis on "windows" and "curtains," far less important words than "us," the word Donne's lines emphasize, as the poem is about a pair of lovers.

After another inverted line ("Must to thy motions lovers' seasons run") and a short one following the longer opening line, we hear a series of tonal shifts. The speed and abruptness of Donne's second question convey the speaker's tone of impatient defiance. The two questions with their emphatic dislocations prepare the way for the series of imperatives that increase our sense of the speaker's authority. This tone gives way abruptly in the last two lines of the stanza to a more leisurely verse movement ("Love, all alike, no season knows, nor clime, / Nor hours, days, months, which are the rags of time"). The dignified and stately tone of these lines derives partly from the simple declarative sentences, partly from the monosyllabic diction, and partly from the frequent pauses marked by punctuation. The overall effect is a slower line and a more exalted tone.

In stanza two the tone shifts back to the playful exaggeration of the beginning of the poem, with similar dislocations of syntax in its opening question. The second sentence (lines 13-18), neither question, statement, nor command, is a statement of possibility. The tone remains playfully defiant ("tell me / Whether both the Indias of spice and mine / Be where thou left'st them"); the speaker continues to exaggerate. The syntax is more convoluted, the sentences more complex than in the first stanza. Again, however, as in the opening stanza, the final line of stanza two resolves into a direct authoritative assertion:

. . . All here in one bed lay.

Unlike the first two stanzas, the last begins with the declarative syntax and simple, direct assertiveness with which the other two stanzas end. The entire stanza is composed of a series of balanced statements, some parallel, some antithetical. (Not completely, however, since there is something of the complex argument of stanza two midway through this last stanza. And there is also a brief return to the imperative voice in line 29, "Shine here to us.") But from these deviations the speaker quickly returns to the authority of direct declaration, an authority enhanced by the parallel form of the final line, by its slight dislocation of the verbs, and by the tightness of its structure (eliminating a conjunction between the clauses and omitting the implied verb of the second half of the line):

This bed thy center is, these walls thy sphere.

In the poems that follow Thomas Hardy uses broken syntax in "The Man He Killed"; William Butler Yeats uses balanced syntax in "An Irish Airman Foresees His Death"; Robert Frost uses ambiguous syntax so that multiple meanings coexist and coincide in "The Silken Tent"; and E. E.Cummings uses mimetic syntax, which imitates what it describes, in "Me up at does."

THOMAS HARDY*

[1840-1928]

The Man He Killed

"Had he and I but met
By some old ancient inn,
We should have sat us down to wet
Right many a nipperkin!

"But ranged as infantry,
And staring face to face,
I shot at him as he at me,
And killed him in his place.

"I shot him dead because—
Because he was my foe,
Just so: my foe of course he was;
That's clear enough; although

"He thought he'd 'list, perhaps,
Off-hand-like—just as I—
Was out of work—had sold his traps—
No other reason why.

"Yes; quaint and curious war is!
You shoot a fellow down
You'd treat if met where any bar is,
Or help to half-a-crown."

QUESTIONS FOR REFLECTION

1. The first two stanzas are each a single sentence. Explain their logical and syntactic relationship.
2. Unlike the smooth unbroken sentences of the first two stanzas, we find breaks in the syntax (indicated by dashes) in the next two stanzas. After reading the stanzas aloud, explain what the breaks suggest about the speaker's state of mind.
3. Does the speaker's fluent syntax in the last stanza suggest that he has worked through the state of mind you found evident in stanzas three and four? Explain.

WILLIAM BUTLER YEATS*
[1865–1939]

An Irish Airman Foresees His Death

I know that I shall meet my fate
Somewhere among the clouds above;
Those that I fight I do not hate,
Those that I guard I do not love;°
My country is Kiltartan Cross
My countrymen Kiltartan's poor,
No likely end could bring them loss
Or leave them happier than before.
Nor law, nor duty bade me fight,
Nor public men, nor cheering crowds,
A lonely impulse of delight
Drove to this tumult in the clouds;
I balanced all, brought all to mind,
The years to come seemed waste of breath,
A waste of breath the years behind
In balance with this life, this death. [1939]

QUESTIONS FOR REFLECTION

1. Point out the ways the syntax of this poem is balanced and controlled. How does the poem's balanced syntax reinforce its meaning?
2. Explain the connection between its syntax and its central idea: the pilot's attitude toward his country, his enemy, his fate.

ROBERT FROST*
[1874–1963]

The Silken Tent

She is as in a field a silken tent
At midday when a sunny summer breeze
Has dried the dew and all its ropes relent,

"An Irish Airman Foresees His Death" [3–4]***Those that I fight . . . I do not love;*** *Yeats is referring to the Germans and the English respectively; the war is World War I.*

So that in guys it gently sways at ease,
And its supporting central cedar pole,
That is its pinnacle to heavenward
And signifies the sureness of the soul,
Seems to owe naught to any single cord,
But strictly held by none, is loosely bound
By countless silken ties of love and thought
To everything on earth the compass round,
And only by one's going slightly taut
In the capriciousness of summer air
Is of the slightest bondage made aware. [1942]

QUESTION FOR REFLECTION

Perhaps the most astonishing thing about this sonnet is that it is only a single sentence. Go through the poem again attending to the way the sentence develops. Account for all the conjunctions: *so* (line 4), *and* (line 5), *And* (line 7), *But* (line 9), *And* (line 12). How do those conjunctions help us follow the sentence?

www

E.E. CUMMINGS*

[1894–1962]

"Me up at does"

Me up at does
out of the floor
quietly Stare
a poisoned mouse
still who alive
is asking What
have i done that
You wouldn't have [1963]

QUESTIONS FOR REFLECTION

1. Rearrange the syntax of this poem to approximate the normal word order of an English sentence. Where do you have to make the heaviest adjustment?
2. How is Cummings's word order related to the situation the poem describes? What does Cummings gain by ordering his words as he does?

STEVIE SMITH

[1902–1971]

Mother, Among the Dustbins

Mother, among the dustbins and the manure
I feel the measure of my humanity, an allure
As of the presence of God. I am sure

In the dustbins, in the manure, in the cat at play,
Is the presence of God, in a sure way
He moves there. Mother, what do you say?

I too have felt the presence of God in the broom
I hold, in the cobwebs in the room,
But most of all in the silence of the tomb.

Ah! but that thought that informs the hope of our kind
Is but an empty thing, what lies behind?—
Naught but the vanity of a protesting mind

That would not die. This is the thought that bounces
Within a conceited head and trounces
Inquiry. Man is most frivolous when he pronounces.
Well Mother, I shall continue to think as I do,
And I think you would be wise to do so too,
Can you question the folly of man in the creation of God?
    Who are you? [1972]

QUESTION FOR REFLECTION

Examine the way the poet uses balanced phrasing, primarily repeated phrases throughout the poem. Notice the play of long sentence against short, of question against statement. What do these syntactic elements contribute to the tone and attitude of the poem?

SOUND: RHYME, ALLITERATION, ASSONANCE

The most familiar element of poetry is **rhyme,** which can be defined as the matching of final vowel or consonant sounds in two or more words. When the corresponding sounds occur at the ends of lines we have *end rhyme;* when they occur within lines we have *internal rhyme.* The opening stanza of Edgar Allan Poe's "The Raven" illustrates both:

Once upon a midnight dreary, while I pondered weak and weary,
Over many a quaint and curious volume of forgotten lore—
While I nodded nearly napping, suddenly there came a tapping,
As of some one gently rapping, rapping at my chamber door.
" 'Tis some visitor," I muttered, "tapping at my chamber door—
Only this and nothing more."

For the reader rhyme is a pleasure, for the poet a challenge. Part of its pleasure for the reader is in anticipating and hearing a poem's echoing song. Part of its challenge for the poet is in rhyming naturally, without forcing the rhythm, the syntax, or the sense. When the challenge is met successfully, the poem is a pleasure to listen to; it sounds natural to the ear, and its rhyme makes it easier to remember.

Robert Frost's "Stopping by Woods on a Snowy Evening" is one such rhyming success. Reread it once more, preferably aloud, and listen to its music.

Whose woods these are I think I know.
His house is in the village, though;
He will not see me stopping here
To watch his woods fill up with snow.

My little horse must think it queer
To stop without a farmhouse near
Between the woods and frozen lake
The darkest evening of the year.

He gives his harness bells a shake
To ask if there is some mistake.
The only other sound's the sweep
Of easy wind and downy flake.

The woods are lovely, dark and deep,
But I have promises to keep,
And miles to go before I sleep,
And miles to go before I sleep.

Notice how in each of the first three stanzas, three of the four lines rhyme (lines 1, 2, and 4), and Frost picks up the nonrhymed sound of each stanza (the third line) and links it with the rhyming sound of the stanza that follows it, until the fourth stanza when he closes with four matching rhymes. Part of our pleasure in Frost's rhyming may derive from the pattern of departure and return it voices. Part may stem also from the way the rhyme pattern supports the poem's meaning. The speaker is caught between his desire to remain still, peacefully held by the serene beauty of the woods, and his contrasting need to leave, to return to his responsibilities. In a similar way, the poem's rhyme is caught between a surge forward toward a new sound and a return to a sound repeated earlier. The pull and counterpull of the rhyme reflect the speaker's ambivalence.

The rhymes in Frost's poem are *exact* or *perfect rhymes;* that is, the rhyming words share corresponding sounds and stresses and a similar number of syllables. While Frost's poem contains perfect rhymes ("know," "though," and "snow," for example), we sometimes hear in poems a less exact, *imperfect, approximate,* or *slant rhyme.* Emily Dickinson's "Crumbling is not an instant's Act" (page 573) includes both exact rhyme ("dust"–"rust") and slant *rhyme* ("slow"–"law"). Theodore Roethke's "My Papa's Waltz" (page 505) contains a slant *rhyme* on ("dizzy"–"easy"), which also exemplifies *feminine* rhyme. In *feminine* rhyme the final syllable of a rhymed word is unstressed; in masculine rhyme the final syllable is stressed—or the words rhymed are each only one syllable.

Besides rhyme, two other forms of sound play prevail in poetry: **alliteration** or the repetition of consonant sounds, especially at the beginning of words, and **assonance** or the repetition of vowel sounds. In his witty guide to poetic technique, *Rhyme's Reason,* John Hollander describes alliteration and assonance like this:

> Assonance is the spirit of a rhyme,
> A common vowel, hovering like a sigh
> After its consonantal body dies. . . .
> . . .
> Alliteration lightly links
> Stressed syllables with common consonants.

Walt Whitman's "When I heard the learn'd astronomer" (page 000), though lacking in end rhyme, possesses a high degree of assonance. The long *i*'s in lines 1, 3, and 4 accumulate and gather force as the poem glides into its last four lines: "*I,*" "t*i*red," "r*i*sing," "gl*i*ding," "*I,*" "m*y*self," "n*i*ght," "t*i*me to t*i*me," and "s*i*lence." This assonance sweetens the sound of the second part of the poem, highlighting its radical shift of action and feeling.

Both alliteration and assonance are clearly audible in "Stopping by Woods," particularly in the third stanza:

> He gives his harness bells a shake
> To ask if there is some mistake.
> The only other sound's the sweep
> Of easy wind and downy flake.

Notice that the long *e* of "sweep" is echoed in "*ea*-sy" and "down-*y,*" and that the *ow* of "d*ow*ny" echoes the same sound in "s*ou*nd's." These repetitions of sound accentuate the images the words embody, aural images (wind-blow and snow-fall), tactile images (the soft fluff of down and the feel of the gently blowing wind), and visual images (the white flakes of snow).

The alliterative *s*'s in "*s*ome," "*s*ound," and "*s*weep" are supported by the internal and terminal *s*'s: "Give*s,*" "hi*s,*" "harne*ss* bell*s,*" and "i*s,*" and also by mid-word *s*'s: "a*s*k," "mi*s*take," and "ea*s*y." Some of these sounds are heavier than others—the two similar heavy *s*'s of "easy" and "his" contrast the lighter softer "*s*" in "harness" and "mistake."

Listen to the sound effects of rhyme, alliteration, and assonance in the following poem. Try to determine what *sound* contributes to the poem's meaning.

GERARD MANLEY HOPKINS*
[1844–1889]

In the Valley of the Elwy

I remember a house where all were good
To me, God knows, deserving no such thing:
Comforting smell breathed at very entering,

Fetched fresh, as I suppose, off some sweet wood.
That cordial air made those kind people a hood
  All over, as a bevy of eggs the mothering wing
  Will, or mild nights the new morsels of Spring:
Why, it seemed of course; seemed of right it should.

  Lovely the woods, waters, meadows, combes, vales,
All the air things wear that build this world of Wales;
  Only the inmate does not correspond:

God, lover of souls, swaying considerate scales,
Complete thy creature dear O where it fails,
  Being mighty a master, being a father and fond. [1877]

We note first that the rhyme scheme reveals a Petrarchan sonnet: *abba, abba, ccd, ccd* (see page 509). Also we might note that its rhyme pattern corresponds to its sentence structure: the octave splits into two sentences, lines 1–4 and 5–8; the sestet, though only one sentence, splits into two equal parts, lines 9–11 and 12–14. Hopkins's use of the Italian rhyme scheme keeps similar sounds repeating throughout: *good, wood, hood, should; thing, entering, wing, Spring; vales, Wales, scales, fails; correspond, fond*. (The rhyme pattern of the Shakespearean or English sonnet, by contrast, as heard in "That time of year" (page 531) contains fewer rhyming repetitions, as it uses a greater number of different sounds.)

Besides extensive rhyme, Hopkins uses alliteration and assonance—lightly in the octave and more heavily in the sestet. Lines 3-6, for example, collect short *e*'s in "sm*e*ll," "v*e*ry," "*e*ntering," "f*e*tched" and "fr*e*sh," "b*e*vy" and "*e*ggs." Lines 4–8 begin an alliterative use of *w,* which is more elaborately sounded in lines 9–10 of the sestet; in lines 4–8 we hear: "s*w*eet *w*ood," "*w*ing *W*ill," and "*w*hy." In addition, in line 7 "m*i*ld n*i*ghts" picks up the long *i* of "Wh*y*," which finds an echo in the rhyme on "r*i*ght." This seventh line also contains what we might call a reversed or crisscrossed alliteration in "*m*ild *n*ights" and "*n*ew *m*orsels."

But these sound effects are only a pale indication of what we hear in the sestet. Perhaps the most musical lines of the entire poem are the opening lines of the sestet (lines 9–10). *L*'s frame both of these lines: "*L*ovely . . . va*l*es" and "A*ll* . . . Wa*l*es." *L*'s are further sounded in "bui*l*d this wor*l*d." The *w,* which as we noted ended the octave, is carried into the sestet in "*w*oods," "*w*aters," "meado*w*s," "*w*ear," "*w*orld," and "*W*ales." The sestet also includes a variety of vowels: l*o*vely, w*oo*ds, w*a*ter, m*ea*dows, c*o*mbes, v*a*les, *a*ll, *ai*r, w*ea*r, th*a*t, b*ui*ld, th*i*s, w*o*rld, W*a*les.

Hopkins sounds a similarly varied vowel music in the last line, where he also uses alliteration and repetition to call attention to important attributes of God:

> Being mighty a master, being a father and fond.

One line, however, especially lacks music: line 11. Coming amidst such splendid sounds, it stands out even more sharply:

> Only the inmate does not correspond.

This expressive use of sound variation supports the idea that the line conveys: that in this beautiful natural world, the "inmate," the speaker in the guise of prisoner, does not fit. He feels out of place, out of harmony with his environment. In the lines that follow (12–14), he asks God to "complete" him, to make him whole, to integrate him into the world. And he prays in language that immediately picks up the sound play of assonance and alliteration that had been momentarily suspended in line 11.

The speaker's harmony and wholeness are thus restored in the poem's beauty of sound.

To further develop your ear for sound in poetry, read aloud the poems that follow:

THOMAS HARDY*

[1840–1928]

During Wind and Rain

They sing their dearest songs—
He, she, all of them—yea,
Treble and tenor and bass,
  And one to play;
With the candles mooning each face . . .
  Ah, no; the years O!
How the sick leaves reel down in throngs!

They clear the creeping moss—
Elders and juniors—aye,
Making the pathway neat
  And the garden gay;
And they build a shady seat . . .
  Ah, no; the years, the years;
See, the white stormbirds wing across!

They are blithely breakfasting all—
Men and maidens—yea,
Under the summer tree,
  With a glimpse of the bay,
While pet fowl come to the knee . . .
  Ah, no; the years O!
And the rotten rose is ripped from the wall.

They change to a high new house,
He, she, all of them—aye,
Clocks and carpets, and chairs
  On the lawn all day,
And brightest things that are theirs . . .
  Ah, no; the years, the years;
Down their carved names the rain drop ploughs. [1917]

QUESTIONS FOR REFLECTION

1. Chart the poem's rhyme scheme. Note the repetitions of lines ("Ah no: the years") and of words ("O," "aye," and "yea"). What do these repetitions contribute to the idea and feeling of the poem?
2. Identify examples of alliteration and comment on their effect.

ALEXANDER POPE*

[1688–1744]

Sound and Sense

True ease in writing comes from art, not chance,
As those move easiest who have learned to dance.
'Tis not enough no harshness gives offense,
The sound must seem an echo to the sense:
Soft is the strain when Zephyr° gently blows,
And the smooth stream in smoother numbers flows;
But when loud surges lash the sounding shore,
The hoarse, rough verse should like the torrent roar.
When Ajax° strives, some rock's vast weight to throw,
The line too labors, and the words move slow;
Not so, when swift Camilla° scours the plain,
Flies o'er th' unbending corn, and skims along the main.
Hear how Timotheus'° varied lays surprise,
And bid alternate passions fall and rise!
While, at each change, the son of Libyan Jove,
Now burns with glory, and then melts with love;
Now his fierce eyes with sparkling fury glow,
Now sighs steal out, and tears begin to flow;
Persians and Greeks like turns of nature found,
And the world's victor stood subdued by sound!
The pow'r of music all our hearts allow,
And what Timotheus was, is DRYDEN now.

[1711]

QUESTIONS FOR REFLECTION

1. How does the poet enact verbally what he asserts in line 4, that "the sound must seem an echo to the sense"?

"Sound and Sense" 5 ***Zephyr*** *the west wind.* 9 ***Ajax*** *a strong Greek warrior in the Trojan War.* 11 ***Camilla*** *an ancient Volcian queen noted for her speed and lightness of step.* 13 ***Timotheus*** *a musician in John Dryden's poem "Alexander's Feast."* 15 ***the son of Libyan Jove*** *Alexander the Great* (356–323 B.C.), *king of Macedonia and military conqueror who spread Greek culture throughout the ancient world.*

2. What contrast is described and imitated in sound effects in lines 5–6 and 7–8? Between lines 9–10 and lines 11–12?

BOB MCKENTY*
[b. 1935]

Adam's Song

Come live with me and be my love.
Come romp with me in Eden's grove
In unabated joy, not shy
But unabashed by nudity,
Where you can bare—sans shame—your breast
Until the fell Forbidden Feast.
Thereafter I shall toil and sweat
To earn whatever bread we eat
And you, in bearing children, shall
Know pain and suffering. The Fall
Will bring us sickness, death, and fear,
Embarrassment and underwear
(For which the Fig donates its leaf)
And poets who are surely deaf. [1990]

QUESTION FOR REFLECTION

Identify the sound effects at play in "Adam's Song." Consider especially the poem's rhymes.

MAY SWENSON*
[1919–1989]

The Universe

What
is it about,
the universe,
the universe about us stretching out?
We, within our brains,
within it,
think

we must unspin
the laws that spin it.
We think *why*
because we think
because.
Because we think,
we think
the universe about us.

But does it think,
the universe?
Then what about?
About us?
If not,
must there be cause
in the universe?
Must it have laws?
And what
if the universe
is not about us?
Then what?
What
is it about?
And what
about *us?*

[1963]

QUESTION FOR REFLECTION

Is this poem merely a witty game of repeating words or does it employ sound effects to sound effect? Consider especially lines 10–15 and 24–31.

HELEN CHASIN

[b. 1938]

The Word Plum

The word *plum* is delicious

pout and push, luxury of
self-love, and savoring murmur

full in the mouth and falling
like fruit

taut skin
pierced, bitten, provoked into
juice, and tart flesh

question
and reply, lip and tongue
of pleasure. [1968]

QUESTIONS FOR REFLECTION

1. How is the word *p-l-u-m* sounded and resounded in the poem? Look at and listen to lines 2–3 in particular.
2. Map out the poem's patterns of alliteration and vowel repetition.

RHYTHM AND METER

Rhythm refers to the regular recurrence of the accent or stress in poem or song. It is the pulse or beat we feel in a phrase of music or a line of poetry. We derive our sense of rhythm from everyday life and from our experience with language and music. We experience the rhythm of day and night, the seasonal rhythms of the year, the beat of our hearts, and the rise and fall of our chests as we breathe in and out. Perhaps our earliest memories of rhythm in language are associated with nursery rhymes like

JACK and JILL went UP the HILL*
to FETCH a PAIL of WAter.

Later we probably learned songs like "America," whose rhythm we might indicate like this:

MY COUN-TRY 'tis of THEE
SWEET LAND of LIberTY
Of THEE i SING.

Since then we have developed an ear for the rhythm of language in everyday speech:

I THINK I'll HIT the HAY
Did you SEE that?
Or: Did you see THAT?
or: GO and DON'T come BACK.

Poets rely heavily on rhythm to express meaning and convey feeling. In "The Sun Rising" John Donne puts words together in a pattern of stressed and unstressed syllables:

BUsy old FOOL, unRULy SUN
WHY DOST THOU THUS
Through WINdows, and through CURtains, CALL on US?

*Capitalization indicates stressed syllables, lowercase letters unstressed ones.

Donne uses four accents per line-even in the second more slowly paced short line. Later in the stanza, he retards the tempo further. Listen to the accents in the following lines:

> LOVE, all aLIKE, no SEAson knows, nor CLIME,
> Nor HOURS, DAYS, MONTHS, which ARE the RAGS of TIME.

The accents result partly from Donne's use of monosyllabic words and partly from pauses within the line (indicated by commas). Such pauses are called **caesuras** and are represented by a double slash (//). The final couplet of Donne's poem illustrates a common use of caesura—to split a line near its midpoint:

> Shine here to us, // and thou art everywhere;
> This bed thy center is, // these walls thy sphere.

Marking the accents as well,we get this:

> SHINE HERE to US, // and THOU art EVeryWHERE;
> THIS BED thy CENter IS, // THESE WALLS thy SPHERE.

Notice again how the monosyllabic diction and the balanced phrasing combine with the caesuras to slow the lines down. The stately rhythm enforces the speaker's dignified tone and serious point: "Here is everywhere; this room is a world in itself; it is all that matters to us."

In the following brief poem by Robert Frost, you can readily hear and feel the contrasting pace and rhythms of its two lines. (Capitals added to show stressed syllables.)

ROBERT FROST*

The Span of Life

> The OLD DOG BARKS BACKward withOUT GETting UP.
> I can reMEMber when HE was a PUP. [1936]

The first line is slower than the second. It is harder to pronounce and takes longer to say because Frost clusters the hard consonants, *d*, *k*, and *g* sounds in the first line, and because the first line contains seven stresses to the four accents of the second.Three of the seven stresses fall at the beginning of the line, which gets it off to a slow start, whereas the accents of the second line are evenly spaced. The contrasting rhythms of the lines reinforce their contrasting images and sound effects. More importantly, however, the differences in the sounds and rhythms in the two lines echo their contrast of youth and age.

But we cannot proceed any further in this discussion of rhythm without introducing more precise terms to refer to the patterns of accents we hear in a poem. If *rhythm* is the pulse or beat we hear in the line, then we can define **meter** as the measure or patterned count of a poetic line. Meter is a count of the stresses we feel in the poem's rhythm. By convention the unit of poetic meter in English is the **foot,** a unit of measure consisting of stressed and unstressed syllables. A poetic foot may be either *iambic* or *trochaic, anapestic* or *dactylic.* An iambic line is composed primarily of *iambs,* an **iamb** being defined as an unaccented syllable followed by an accented one as in the word "preVENT" or "conTAIN." Reversing the order of accented and unaccented syllables we get a **trochee,** which is an accented syllable followed by an unaccented one, as in "FOOTball" or "LIquor." We can represent an accented syllable by a ´ and an unaccented syllable by a ˘: thus, prĕvént(˘ ´), an iamb, and li´quŏr (´˘), a trochee. Because both iambic and trochaic feet contain two syllables per foot, they are called *duple* (or double) meters. These duple meters can be distinguished from *triple* meters (three-syllable meters) like anapestic and dactylic meters. An **anapest** (˘˘ ´) consists of two unaccented syllables followed by an accented one as in cŏmprĕHE´ND or iňtĕrVE´NE. A **dactyl** reverses the anapest, beginning with an accented syllable followed by two unaccented ones. DA´Ngĕroŭs and CHE´ERfŭllў are examples. So is the word AN´apĕst.

Three additional points must be noted about poetic meter. First, anapestic(˘˘´) and iambic (˘ ´) meters move from an unstressed syllable to a stressed one. For this reason they are called *rising* meters. (They "rise" to the stressed syllable.) Lines in anapestic or iambic meter frequently end with a stressed syllable. Trochaic (´ ˘) and dactylic (´ ˘˘) meters, on the other hand, are said to be *falling* meters because they begin with a stressed syllable and decline in pitch and emphasis. (Syllables at the ends of trochaic and dactylic lines are generally unstressed.)

Second, the regularity of a poem's meter is not inflexible. In a predominantly iambic poem (Shakespeare's sonnet "That time of year thou may'st in me behold," for example, or Frost's "Stopping by Woods"), every line will not usually conform exactly to the strict metrical pattern. Frost's poem is much more regular in its iambic meter than is Shakespeare's, but Frost avoids metrical monotony by subtly altering his rhythm. And in one important instance Frost departs from the pattern slightly. We can divide the last stanza of Frost's poem into metrical feet and mark the accents in this manner, separating the feet with slashes.

> Tȟe woo´ds / aře lo´ve / lў, da´rk / aňd de´ep. /
> Bŭt I´ / ha´ve pr´o / misĕs / tŏ ke´ep,
> Aňd mil´es / tŏ g´o /ȟefo´re / Ĭ sle´ep,
> Aňd mil´es / tŏ g´o / befo´re / Ĭ sle´ep.

If we regard the pattern of this stanza and the pattern of the poem as a whole as regularly, even insistently, iambic, then the second line of this final stanza marks a slight deviation from that norm. The second and third feet of the line can be read as two accented syllables followed by two unaccented syllables, a *spondaic* foot followed by a *pyrrhic.* Two accented syllables together is called a **spondee** (KNI´CKKNA´CK); two unaccented ones, a **pyrrhic** (ŏf tȟe). Both spondaic and pyrrhic feet serve as substitute feet for iambic and trochaic feet. Neither can serve as the metrical norm of an English poem.

Third, we give names to lines of poetry based on the number of feet they contain. You may have noticed in looking back at "Stopping by Woods on a Snowy Evening" that it consists of eight-syllable or *octosyllabic* lines. Because the meter is iambic (˘ ´) with two syllables per foot, the line contains four iambic feet and is hence called a *tetrameter* line (from the Greek word for *four*). Thus Frost's poem is written in *iambic tetrameter,* unlike Shakespeare's sonnet "That time of year thou may'st in me behold," for example, which contains ten-syllable lines, also predominantly iambic. Such five-foot lines are named *pentameters* (from the Greek "penta" for five), making the sonnet a poem in *iambic pentameter.*

Here is a chart of the various meters and poetic feet.

	Foot	**Meter**	**Example**
Rising or ascending feet	iamb anapest	iambic anapestic	prevent comprehend
Falling or descending feet	trochee dactyl	trochaic dactylic	football cheerfully
Substitute feet	spondee pyrrhic	spondaic pyrrhic	knick-knack (light) of the (world)

Duple Meters: two syllables per foot: iambic and trochaic
Triple Meters: three syllables per foot: anapestic and dactylic

Number of Feet per Line

one foot	monometer
two feet	dimeter
three feet	trimeter
four feet	tetrameter
five feet	pentameter
six feet	hexameter
seven feet	heptameter
eight feet	octameter

You should now be better able to discern the meter and rhythm of a poem. You can make an instructive comparison for yourself by taking the measure of two poems in the same meter: Shakespeare's sonnet "That time of year thou may'st in me behold" (page 531) and Hopkins's "In the Valley of the Elwy" (page 550), both written in iambic pentameter. In Hopkins's sonnet, see if you can account for the speed of the octave and the slower pace of the sestet: look to changes in the basic iambic pattern; look for caesuras; and watch for **enjambed** or run-on lines, whose sense and grammar run over and into the next line. You should be alert in both poems for how parallel sentence structure and the sound play of alliteration and assonance collaborate with rhythm and meter to support each poem's feeling and meaning. Listen carefully, especially to the last line of the octave and sestet of Hopkins's sonnet and to Shakespeare's concluding couplet.

Metrical Variation

We noted earlier that Frost's "Stopping by Woods" is written in strict iambic pentameter with only one slight variation in line 14. How then does Frost manage to avoid the monotony of fifteen lines of ta TUM / ta TUM / ta TUM / ta TUM / ?

One way is by varying the reader's focus on different details: woods, snow, and speaker (stanza one); horse and darkness (stanza two); horse and snow (stanza three); woods and darkness and speaker (stanza four). Another is to vary the syntax, as he does with the inversion of the opening line. A third is simply to use a familiar diction in a normal speaking voice. Fourth and perhaps most important is Frost's masterful control of tempo. Of the four stanzas none carry the same pattern of end stopping. Stanza one is end-stopped at the first, second, and fourth lines, with line 3 enjambed. Stanza three is the closest to the second stanza, with two end-stopped lines and two enjambed lines. Stanza four is heavily stopped with two caesuras in its initial line and with end stops at every line. (It is here that we are slowed down to feel the seductive beauty of the woods; it is here that the symbolic weight of the poem is heaviest.) But we should not overlook the contrasting second stanza, which is cast as a single flowing sentence. The iambic pattern inhabits this stanza as it beats in the others. But as a result of the variety of technical resources Frost displays in the poem,we hear the iambic beat but are not overwhelmed by it.

Frost's rhythmical variations can be compared with Whitman's expressive use of metrical variation in "When I heard the learn'd astronomer" (page 566), a poem in *free* verse, verse without a fixed metrical pattern.Whitman's poem is characteristic of much free verse in its varying line lengths and accents per line, and in its imitation of the cadences of speech.The poem's final line ("Look'd up in perfect silence at the stars"), however, differs from the others, as Paul Fussell has pointed out in his *Poetic Meter and Poetic Form.** It is written in strict iambic pentameter, a variation that carries considerable expressive power, coming after the seemingly casual metrical organization of the previous lines. Because Whitman's line must be read in the context of the whole poem for its expressive impact to be felt, you should turn to it, preferably to read it aloud. Consider whether, as some readers have suggested, the poem is not really in free verse at all, but rather in *blank verse,* unrhymed iambic pentameter.

Besides this expressive use of metrical variation, Whitman's poem exhibits additional elements of rhythmic control: in its consistency of end-stopped lines; in its flexible use of caesura (lines 2, 3, and 7); in its absence of caesura from the shorter lines (1 and 4–8).We can perhaps gain a greater appreciation of Whitman's rhythmical accomplishment by recasting his lines like this:

When I heard the learn'd astronomer,
When the proofs, the figures
Were ranged in columns before me,
When I was shown the charts and diagrams
To add, divide, and measure them,
When I sitting heard the astronomer
Where he lectured to much applause
In the lecture-room . . .

Or like this:

When I heard
The learn'd astronomer,

*Paul Fussell, *Poetic Meter and Poetic Form* (New York: Random House, 1979), p. 85.

When the proofs,
The figures were ranged
In columns
Before me,
When I was shown
The charts and diagrams
To add, divide and
Measure them . . .

Both versions destroy the poem: they eliminate the sweep of its long lines, destroying its cadences and rhythm, and ultimately inhibiting its expressiveness.

Before leaving the poem, we should note that Whitman's rhythmic effects work together with other devices of sound, structure, and diction. In the same way, for example, that the strict iambic pentameter of the last line varies the prevailing meter expressively, so too does its assonance (the long *i*'s) deviate expressively from the poem's previously established avoidance of vowel music. In addition, the meter of the final line stresses *sílĕnce* and *stárs,* both of which the speaker values. Finally, the iambic rhythm of the line has us looking ÚP and ÁT the stars, an unusual metrical effect since prepositions are almost always unstressed.

Throughout these comments on the rhythm and meter of the poems by Whitman and Frost, we have been engaged in the act of *scansion,* measuring verse, identifying its prevailing meter and rhythm, and accounting for deviations from the metrical pattern. In scanning a poem, we try to determine its dominant rhythm and meter, and to account for variations from the norm. The pattern we hear as dominant will influence how we read lines that do not conform metrically, and also how we interpret and respond to those lines. Consider, for example, the words "at a glance" abstracted from their place in a line of Wordsworth's "I wandered lonely as a cloud." Do you hear them as anapestic: ăt ă glánce? This is a likely way to hear the words outside the context of the poem. But when we return them to the poem, we may hear them another way:

Tĕn thóusănd sáw Ĭ át ă glánce.

In such a case we will probably hear both the rhythmic pattern of the normal speaking voice (ăt ă glánce) and the metrical pattern of iambic pentameter (ăt ă glánce). Our experience of rhythm thus will often involve a tension between the two patterns as we hear one superimposed on the other.

One last note about rhythm and meter. Without the turn of the poetic line, without the division of words into lines, we have no poem. For what distinguishes poetry from prose is the line; it is the line that makes verse what it is (from the Latin *versus,* to turn). And as the poet Wendell Berry has pointed out, it is the line of verse that "checks the merely impulsive flow of speech, subjects it to another pulse, to measure."* Without the measure of meter, without the turn of the line, there is no music and no poem. Meter and rhythm are not merely technical elements. All the interrelated elements of poetry *do* things to readers. We sense them and feel them and thereby understand a poem, not just with our minds, but also with our eyes and ears.

Here are a few additional poems for rhythmic and metrical consideration.

*Wendell Berry; *Standing By Words* (San Francisco: North Point Press, 1983), p. 28.

GEORGE GORDON, LORD BYRON*

[1788–1824]

The Destruction of Sennacherib°

The Assyrian came down like the wolf on the fold,
And his cohorts were gleaming in purple and gold;
And the sheen of their spears was like stars on the sea,
When the blue wave rolls nightly on deep Galilee.

Like the leaves of the forest when summer is green,
That host with their banners at sunset were seen:
Like the leaves of the forest when autumn hath blown,
That host on the morrow lay withered and strown.

For the Angel of Death spread his wings on the blast,
And breathed in the face of the foe as he passed;
And the eyes of the sleepers waxed deadly and chill,
And their hearts but once heaved—and for ever grew still!

And there lay the steed with his nostril all wide,
But through it there rolled not the breath of his pride;
And the foam of his gasping lay white on the turf,
And cold as the spray of the rock-beating surf.

And there lay the rider distorted and pale,
With the dew on his brow, and the rust on his mail;
And the tents were all silent, the banners alone,
The lances unlifted, the trumpet unblown.

And the widows of Ashur are loud in their wail,
And the idols are broke in the temple of Baal;
And the might of the Gentile, unsmote by the sword,
Hath melted like snow in the glance of the Lord!

[1814]

QUESTIONS FOR REFLECTION

1. Identify the poem's meter. What kind of movement and rhythm does the meter create?
2. How is it appropriate to the action and idea of the poem?

"The Destruction of Sennacherib" ***The Destruction of Sennacherib*** *the poem is based on the biblical account (II Kings 19:35) of the Assyrian king, Sennacherib, whose army was destroyed by the angel of the Lord in an invasion of Jerusalem.*

ANNE SEXTON*
[1928–1974]

Her Kind

I have gone out, a possessed witch,
haunting the black air, braver at night;
dreaming evil, I have done my hitch
over the plain houses, light by light:
lonely thing, twelve-fingered, out of mind.
A woman like that is not a woman, quite.
I have been her kind.

I have found the warm caves in the woods,
filled them with skillets, carvings, shelves,
closets, silks, innumerable goods;
fixed the suppers for the worms and the elves:
whining, rearranging the disaligned.
A woman like that is misunderstood.
I have been her kind.

I have ridden in your cart, driver,
waved my nude arms at villages going by,
learning the last bright routes, survivor
where your flames still bite my thigh
and my ribs crack where your wheels wind.
A woman like that is not ashamed to die.
I have been her kind. [1960]

QUESTIONS FOR REFLECTION

1. Identify the prevailing meter of the poem. How does Sexton keep the poem moving?
2. Examine her uses of caesura and enjambment, and comment on their effect on the poem's rhythm.

WILLIAM CARLOS WILLIAMS*
[1883–1963]

The Red Wheelbarrow

so much depends
upon

a red wheel
barrow

glazed with rain
water

beside the white
chickens [1923]

QUESTIONS FOR REFLECTION

1. Mark the poem's meter. Which lines match each other metrically?
2. What is the effect of the breaks between lines 3 and 4 and between lines 5 and 6?

STRUCTURE: CLOSED FORM AND OPEN FORM

When we analyze a poem's structure, we focus on its patterns of organization. *Form* exists in poems on many levels from patterns of sound and image to structures of syntax and of thought; it is as much a matter of phrase and line as of stanza and whole poem.

Among the most popular forms of poetry has been the **sonnet,** a fourteenline poem usually written in iambic pentameter. Because the form of the sonnet is strictly constrained, it is considered a **closed** or *fixed* **form.** We can recognize poems in fixed forms such as the sonnet, sestina, and villanelle by their patterns of rhyme, meter, and repetition; they reveal their structural patterns both aurally and visually. We see the shapes of their stanzas and the patterns of their line lengths; we feel their metrical beat, and we hear their play of sound.

The *Shakespearean* or *English sonnet* falls into three **quatrains** or four-line sections with the rhyme pattern *abab cdcd efef* followed by a **couplet** or pair of rhymed lines with the pattern *gg.* Let us reread Shakespeare's sonnet, "That time of year thou may'st in me behold."

That time of year thou may'st in me behold *a*
When yellow leaves, or none, or few, do hang *b*
Upon those boughs which shake against the cold, *a*
Bare ruined choirs, where late the sweet birds sang. *b*
In me thou see'st the twilight of such day *c*
As after sunset fadeth in the west; *d*
Which by-and-by black night doth take away, *c*
Death's second self that seals up all in rest. *d*
In me thou see'st the glowing of such fire *e*
That on the ashes of his youth doth lie, *f*
As the deathbed whereon it must expire, *e*
Consumed with that which it was nourished by *f*
This thou perceiv'st, which makes thy love more strong, *g*
To love that well which thou must leave ere long. *g*

Each of the three quatrains of the poem is a single sentence, as is the couplet. This organization of the poem's sentences corresponds to its rhyme and images, which are also arranged in three quatrains and a final couplet. The pattern is reinforced, moreover, by the use of repeated words in the three quatrains: "In me behold"; "In me thou see´st"; "In me thou see´st."

There is a progression in the imagery in the sonnet: daylight becomes twilight; twilight turns into night. And there is a countermovement from images of longer duration to those of shorter: from the dying of a season to the dying of a day to the dying of a fire. In addition, within each image there is a movement from optimism to pessimism. Each image begins more hopefully than it ends: the yellow leaves become "bare ruined choirs" (lines 1–4); the twilight gives way to "Death's second self" (lines 5–8); the "glowing . . . fire" becomes "ashes" on a "deathbed" (lines 9–12).

The couplet is both a logical and an emotional response to the three quatrains that precede it. In the couplet is an implied *therefore* or *because* that can be heard by reversing the word order of its first line: Since you perceive this, it makes your love more strong. The last line is both a plea and a command to "love that well which thou must leave ere long," with "which" carrying the force of *because.*

Not every sonnet Shakespeare wrote is structured as tightly as this one. Look at others of his sonnets to see how Shakespeare varies this pattern, how, for example, he uses the couplet not only to respond to the quatrains, but to summarize their point or extend their implications as well.

An alternative to the Shakespearean sonnet is the *Petrarchan* or *Italian sonnet,* which falls into two parts: an *octave* of eight lines and a *sestet* of six. The octave rhyme pattern is *abba abba* (two sets of four lines); the sestet's lines are more variable: *cde cde;* or *ced ced;* or *cd cd cd.* The following is an example of the Italian form:

JOHN KEATS*

[1795–1821]

On First Looking into Chapman's Homer°

Much have I traveled in the realms of gold *a*
  And many goodly states and kingdoms seen; *b*
  Round many western islands have I been *b*
Which bards in fealty° to Apollo° hold. *a* allegiance
Oft of one wide expanse had I been told *a*
  That deep-browed Homer ruled as his demesne;° *b* domain
  Yet never did I breathe its pure serene° *b* atmosphere
Till I heard Chapman speak out loud and bold: *a*
Then felt I like some watcher of the skies *c*
  When a new planet swims into his ken; *d*
Or like stout Cortez° when with eagle eyes *c*
  He stared at the Pacific—and all his men *d*
Looked at each other with a wild surmise— *c*
  Silent, upon a peak in Darien. *d* [1816]

"On First Looking into Chapman's Homer" ***Chapman's Homer*** *translation of Homer's* Odyssey *by George Chapman, a contemporary of Shakespeare.* [4]***Apollo*** *god of the sun and poetic inspiration.* [11–14]***Cortez . . . Darien*** *Spanish conqueror of Mexico. Balboa, not Cortez, however, was the first European to see the Pacific from Darien in Panama.*

Perhaps the most notable structural feature of the Italian sonnet is the way it turns on the ninth line. The first eight lines of Keats's sonnet describe the speaker's wide reading and compare reading with traveling. Lines 9–14 dramatically convey the speaker's feelings upon first reading Chapman's translation of Homer's great epic poems, *The Iliad* and *The Odyssey.* The speaker's excitement appears in lines 12 and 13, whose broken syntax contrasts with the smooth fluency of the first part of the sonnet. In addition, the octave and sestet differ in diction as well. The diction of the octave is elevated and formal, employing archaic words like "goodly" and "bards," and roundabout expressions like "realms of gold." Such words and phrases create an impression of the remoteness of the past, of its grandeur and dignity. In the sestet the diction is simpler and more direct. Keats's use of figures of comparison in the sestet contributes to the striking change in diction. The two major comparisons, both similes, convey the excitement of discovery. By means of descriptions of action (they "looked" and "stared") and reaction (their "wild surmise" and stunned silence) Keats conveys vividly the speaker's feeling of elation and excitement. Keats capitalizes on the structural possibilities of the Italian sonnet by reserving this elation for the sestet and by varying the diction of octave and sestet.

But not all poems are written in fixed forms. Many poets have resisted the limitations inherent in using a consistent and specific metrical pattern or in rhyming lines in a prescribed manner. As an alternative to the strictness of fixed form, they developed and discovered looser, more **open** and **free forms.** *Open* or *free form* does not imply formlessness. It suggests, instead, that poets capitalize on the freedom either to create their own forms or to use the traditional fixed forms in more flexible ways. An example of a poem in open form by Walt Whitman follows.

WALT WHITMAN*

[1819–1892]

When I heard the learn'd astronomer

When I heard the learn'd astronomer,
When the proofs, the figures, were ranged in columns before me,
When I was shown the charts and diagrams, to add, divide, and
  measure them,
When I sitting heard the astronomer where he lectured with much
  applause in the lecture-room,
How soon unaccountable I became tired and sick,
Till rising and gliding out I wander'd off by myself,
In the mystical moist night-air, and from time to time,
Look'd up in perfect silence at the stars. [1865]

Although Whitman's poem is arranged as a single sentence, it can be divided into two parts, each of four lines. The two-part division accumulates a set of contrasts: the speaker with other people and the speaker alone; the speaker sitting inside and the speaker standing outside looking at the stars; the noise inside and the silence outside;

the lecturer's activity and the speaker's passivity; the clutter of details in lines 1–4 and the spareness of details in lines 5–8.

These contrasts reflect the poem's movement from one kind of learning about nature to another: from passive listening to active observation; from indirect factual knowledge to direct mystical apprehension. Whether the poet rejects the first form of knowledge for the second, or whether he suggests that both are needed is not directly stated. The emphasis, nevertheless, is on the speaker's need to be alone and to experience nature directly. More elaborate departures from fixed form include poems such as this unusual configuration of E. E. Cummings:

E.E.CUMMINGS*

[1894–1962]

l (a

l(a

le
af
fa

ll

s)
one
l

iness [1958]

Perhaps the first things to notice are the lack of capital letters and the absence of punctuation (except for the parentheses). What we don't see is as important as what we do. We don't see any recognizable words or sentences, to say nothing of traditional stanzas or lines of poetry. The poem strikes the eye as a series of letters that stream down the page, for the most part two to a line. Rearranging the letters horizontally we find these words: *(a leaf falls) loneliness.* (The first *l* of *loneliness* appears before the parenthesis, like this: *l (a leaf falls) oneliness;* to get *loneliness* you have to move the *l* in front of *oneliness.*

A single falling leaf is a traditional symbol of loneliness; this image is not new. What is new, however, is the way Cummings has coupled the concept with the image, the way he has formed and shaped them into a nontraditional poem. But what has the poet gained by arranging his poem this way? By breaking the horizontal line of verse into a series of fragments (from the horizontal viewpoint), Cummings illustrates visually the separation that is the primary cause of loneliness. Both the word *loneliness* and the image described in *a leaf falls* are broken apart, separated in this way. In addition, by splitting the initial letter from *loneliness,* the poet has revealed the hidden *one* in the word. It's as if he is saying: loneliness is *one*-liness. This idea is further corroborated in the visual ambiguity of "l." Initially we are not sure whether this symbol "l" is a number—*one*—or the letter *l*. By shaping and arranging his poem this way, Cummings unites form and content, structure and idea. He also invites us to play the poetry game with him by remaking the poem as we put its pieces together. In doing so we step back and see in the design of the poem a leaf falling

d
o
w
n
the page. By positioning the letters as he does; Cummings pictures a leaf fall:
le
af
fa
ll
s.

If "l (a" is a poem for the eye, the following poem, also by Cummings, is arranged for voice. From the standpoint of traditional poetic form, it too exhibits peculiarities of sound and structure, line and stanza.

www

E. E. CUMMINGS*

[1894–1962]

[Buffalo Bill's]

Buffalo Bill's
defunct
who used to
ride a watersmooth-silver
stallion
and break onetwothreefourfive pigeons justlikethat
Jesus
he was a handsome man
and what i want to know is
how do you like your blueeyed boy
Mister Death [1925]

Before we listen closely to the voice of the poem, let's glance at how it hits the eye. "Buffalo Bill's," "stallion," "defunct," "Jesus," and "Mister Death" are all set on separate lines as complete lines. "Buffalo Bill's," "Mister Death," and "Jesus" are the only words capitalized. "Buffalo Bill's" and "Mister Death" frame the poem; "Jesus" is set off on its own as far to the right as the line will go. Other words also receive a visual stress. At two points in line 6, Cummings buncheswordstogetherlikethis. Both of these visual effects are translated from eye to voice to ear so that we read the poem acknowledging the stress in each case. Cummings has used typography as a formal way of laying out language on the page to direct our reading. To see and hear what he has accomplished in this respect, read aloud the following rearranged version, which deliberately flattens the special effects Cummings highlights.

> Buffalo Bill's defunct,
> Who used to ride
> a water-smooth silver stallion
> and break one, two, three, four, five
> pigeons just like that
> Jesus he was a handsome man
> And what I would like to know is
> how do you like your
> blueeyed boy, Mister Death?

Let us, finally, summarize our remarks about structure and form. By discerning a poem's structure, we gain a clue to its meaning. We can increase our ability to apprehend a poem's organization by doing the following:

1. Looking and listening for changes of diction and imagery, tone and mood, rhythm and rhyme, time and place and circumstance.
2. Watching for repeated elements: words, images, patterns of syntax, rhythm and rhyme.
3. Remembering that structure is an aspect of meaning. It is not something independent of meaning, but works with other poetic elements to embody meaning.

Test out these ideas by analyzing the form of the following poems.

WILLIAM CARLOS WILLIAMS*

[1883–1963]

The Dance

In Brueghel's° great picture, The Kermess,
the dancers go round, they go round and
around, the squeal and the blare and the
tweedle of bagpipes, a bugle and fiddles
tipping their bellies (round as the thick-
sided glasses whose wash they impound)
their hips and their bellies off balance
to turn them. Kicking and rolling about
the Fair Grounds, swinging their butts, those
shanks must be sound to bear up under such
rollicking measures, prance as they dance
in Breughel's great picture, The Kermess. [1944]

"The Dance" [1]**Brueghel** *Pieter Brueghel the Elder (1525–1569), Flemish painter of peasant life. The Kermess is a painting of a peasant wedding dance. See the color insert for a reproduction of a Breughel painting and the poem it inspired.*

QUESTIONS FOR REFLECTION

1. What kind of dance does the poem describe? What kind of action does the first long sentence imitate (lines 1–8)?
2. Comment on the relationship between the first and last lines.

DENISE LEVERTOV

[1923–1997]

O Taste and See

The world is
not with us enough.
O taste and see

the subway Bible poster said,
meaning The Lord, meaning
if anything all that lives
to the imagination's tongue,

grief, mercy, language,
tangerine, weather, to
breathe them, bite,
savor, chew, swallow, transform

into our flesh our
deaths, crossing the street, plum, quince,
living in the orchard and being

hungry, and plucking
the fruit.

[1964]

QUESTION FOR REFLECTION

Imagine this poem written as a single stanza. What is the advantage of the poet's having structured it as she has?

THEODORE ROETHKE*

[1908–1963]

The Waking

I wake to sleep, and take my waking slow.
I feel my fate in what I cannot fear.
I learn by going where I have to go.

We think by feeling. What is there to know?
I hear my being dance from ear to ear.
I wake to sleep, and take my waking slow.

Of those so close beside me, which are you?
God bless the Ground! I shall walk softly there,
And learn by going where I have to go.

Light takes the Tree; but who can tell us how?
The lowly worm climbs up a winding stair;
I wake to sleep, and take my waking slow.

Great Nature has another thing to do
To you and me; so take the lively air,
And, lovely, learn by going where to go.

This shaking keeps me steady. I should know.
What falls away is always. And is near.
I wake to sleep, and take my waking slow.
I learn by going where I have to go. [1953]

QUESTION FOR REFLECTION

Describe the patterns of repetition that prevail in the poem. Consider repeated rhyme and repeated lines. What is their effect on the poem's tone and feeling?

CHRISTINE K. MOLITO

[b. 1977]

Reflections in Black & Blue

FOR PJL

I caught you watching me
in the bathroom mirror
before cereal yesterday morning.
I looked at you, looking at me
and wondered
do you see me fading?

When you looked straight
into my blue eyes
straight through—into the part of me
only you my dear are allowed to see,
did you notice the fade to grey?

Remember you loved me first
when my black hair was long
and my blue eyes bright.
You say you love me still—love me the same
when my black falls out and my blue is grey—
This is not your choice of course
and I will always know that
my love.

[1998]

QUESTION FOR REFLECTION

Explain the logic of the poem's stanza division.

C. P. CAVAFY

[1863–1933]

The City

You said: "I'll go to another country, go to another shore,
find another city better than this one.
Whatever I try to do is fated to turn out wrong
and my heart lies buried as though it were something dead.
How long can I let my mind moulder in this place?
Wherever I turn, wherever I happen to look,
I see the black ruins of my life, here,
where I've spent so many years, wasted them, destroyed
them totally."

You won't find a new country, won't find another shore.
This city will always pursue you. You will walk
the same streets, grow old in the same neighborhoods,
will turn gray in these same houses.
You will always end up in this city. Don't hope for things
elsewhere:
there is no ship for you, there is no road.
As you've wasted your life here, in this small corner,
you've destroyed it everywhere else in the world.

Translated by Edmund Keeley and Philip Sherrard

QUESTION FOR REFLECTION

Why is the poem divided the way it is?

THEME

We have previously defined **theme** as an idea or intellectually apprehensible meaning inherent and implicit in a work (see pages 90–91). In determining a poem's theme we should be careful neither to oversimplify the poem nor to distort its meaning. To suggest that the theme of Hayden's "Those Winter Sundays," for example, is a father's loving concern for his family is to highlight only part of the poem's meaning, for it does not take into account the speaker's remorse about his indifference to his father. Analogously, if we see Roethke's "My Papa's Waltz" as a statement about a child's terror at his father's horseplay, we misrepresent the complexity of the speaker's response to his memories of his father and their bedtime ritual.

We should also recognize that poems can have multiple themes: poems can be interpreted from more than one perspective and there is more than one way to state or explain a poem's meaning. Let us briefly reconsider Frost's "Stopping by Woods on a Snowy Evening" (see page 499).

We can say, for example, that the theme of Frost's poem is the necessity to face the responsibilities inherent in adult life. We can go on to say that the poem centers on a tension in our lives between our desire for rest and peace and our need to fulfill responsibilities and meet obligations. But we shouldn't remain satisfied with this explanation. For, as we have previously stated, the speaker's "miles to go" before he "sleeps" metaphorically describes all he must accomplish before he dies. The final stanza reveals a tension between the speaker's desire to continue and an impulse to stay at rest, to ease himself into the peace of death. We might further interpret the seductiveness of death as an attractive way of escaping the pressures of circumstance and the weight of responsibility.

We can abstract yet another theme: the ability of man to appreciate beauty, particularly the beauty of nature. We might argue, for example, that Frost contrasts man's capacity for taking pleasure in watching the snow fall in a dark wood with an animal's inability to enjoy either the spectacular beauty of the scene or its serenity. Presumably, animals, unlike men, do not possess an aesthetic faculty, the ability to appreciate beauty. Consider the subject and theme of the following poem.

EMILY DICKINSON*

[1830–1886]

Crumbling is not an instant's Act

Crumbling is not an instant's Act,
A fundamental pause
Dilapidation's processes
Are organized Decays.

'Tis first a Cobweb on the Soul,
A Cuticle of Dust,
A Borer in the Axis,
An Elemental Rust—

Ruin is formal—Devil's work,
Consecutive and slow—
Fail in an instant, no man did
Slipping—is Crash's law.

[1865, 1945]

The central idea of the poem is expressed in its opening line. We might paraphrase it this way: crumbling does not happen instantaneously; it is a gradual process, occurring slowly, cumulatively over time. The gradual nature of decay is emphasized in the final stanza with the statement that no one ever failed in an "instant," that the catastrophe occurs after, and as a consequence of, a series of failures. We can thus read the poem as a statement about the process of ruin (personal, emotional, financial) as well as a description of the process of decay. And we can summarize its theme thus: failure and destruction can be traced to small-scale elements that precede and cause them in the sense of natural law ("Crash's law").

The theme is illustrated in the second stanza's four images of decay: cobweb, rust, dust, and the borer in the axis. These images are all accompanied by bits of specifying detail. The dust is a "Cuticle," an image with suggestions of something at the edges, of something on the outside and also of something human; the "Cobweb on the Soul" suggests *spiritual* deterioration ("cobwebs" suggest neglect); the "Elemental" rust puts decay at the heart of things, at the center and vital core where the "Borer" is operating. The poet applies each of these images of decay to a person, particularly to his or her soul: the dust encircling it, the cobweb netting it, the borer eating into it, and the rust corrupting it. Such an interpretation of spiritual decay seems further warranted by the first line of the third stanza: "Ruin is formal—Devil's work." *Ruin* is perhaps the word most strongly suggestive of human and spiritual collapse; "Devil's work" is a grand, "old-fashioned" image of active evil. Thus, a statement of the poem's theme must accommodate the idea of spiritual decay.

CHAPTER THIRTEEN

Writing about Poetry

REASONS FOR WRITING ABOUT POETRY

Why write about poetry? One reason is to find out what you think about a poem. Another is to induce yourself to read a poem more carefully. You may write about a work of poetry because it engages you and you wish to discuss its implied ideas and values. Still another reason is that you may simply be required to do so as a course assignment.

Whatever your reasons for writing about poetry, a number of things happen when you do. First, in writing about a poem you tend to read it more attentively, noticing things you might overlook in a more casual reading. Second, because writing stimulates thinking, when you write about poetry you find yourself thinking more about what a particular work means and why you respond to it as you do. This focused thinking often has the effect of making poetry more meaningful to you.

INFORMAL WAYS OF WRITING ABOUT POETRY

When you write about a poem, you may write for yourself or you may write for others. Writing for yourself, writing to discover what you think, often takes casual forms such as annotation and freewriting. These less formal kinds of writing are useful for helping you focus. They are helpful in studying for tests about poetry. They can also serve as preliminary forms of writing when you write more formal essays and papers about poetry.

Annotation

When you annotate a text, you make notes in the margins or at the top and bottom of pages. Annotations can also be made within the text, as underlined words, circled phrases, and bracketed sentences or paragraphs. Annotations may also assume the form of arrows, question marks, and various other marks.

Annotating a literary work offers a convenient and relatively painless way to begin writing about it. Annotating can get you started zeroing in on what you think interesting or important. You can also annotate to signal details that puzzle or disconcert you.

Your markings serve to focus your attention and clarify your understanding of a poem. Your annotations can save you time in rereading or studying a work. And they can also be used when you write a more formal paper.

Annotations for the following poem illustrate the process.

ROBERT HAYDEN

Those Winter Sundays

Sundays (too) my father got up early
and put his clothes on in the blueblack
cold,
then with cracked hands that ached
from labor in the weekday weather made
banked fires blaze. (No one) ever thanked
him.

I'd wake and hear the cold splintering,
breaking,
When the rooms were warm, he'd call,
and slowly I would rise and dress,
fearing the chronic angers of that house,

Speaking indifferently to him,
who had driven out the cold
and polished my good shoes as well.
What did I know, what did I know of
love's austere and lonely offices?

This father gets up early every day—even on Sundays.

How can cold be "blueblack"?

No one? Not other family members? Not the speaker?

Stanza one emphasizes the speaker's father; stanza two shifts emphasis to the speaker himself.

Speaker remembers his fear. Fear of what? His father's anger? Was it directed at him?

Father drives out the cold—warms the house, literally. Is the father himself a "warm" person, or "cold"?

Repeats the question. Tone? Feeling? Speaker knows now what he did not know then.

Father's loneliness/father's Love.

Freewriting

Freewriting is a kind of informal writing you do for yourself. In freewriting you explore a text to find out what you think about it and how you respond to it. When you freewrite, you do not know ahead of time what your ideas about the work will be. Freewriting leads you to explore your memories and experience as well as aspects of the text itself. You sometimes wander from the details of the poem you are writing about. In the process you may discover thoughts and feelings you didn't know you had or were only dimly aware of.

First read Robert Graves's "Symptoms of Love," then look at some sample responses written by students who had heard Graves's poem read aloud and then read it once to themselves.

ROBERT GRAVES
[1895–1985]

Symptoms of Love

Love is a universal migraine,
A bright stain on the vision
Blotting out reason.

Symptoms of true love
Are leanness, jealousy,
Laggard dawns;

Are omens and nightmares—
Listening for a knock,
Waiting for a sign:

For a touch of her fingers
In a darkened room,
For a searching look.

Take courage, lover!
Could you endure such pain
At any hand but hers?

[1925]

Student 1 This lover is really bitter. He thinks love is a headache (migraine) and sees love mainly as negative and frightening. I noticed he talked about "omens and nightmares." He could have said "promises and dreams" or something like that, but he didn't. So as far as I am concerned, this speaker is a person who does not see any hope or possibility of growing better because of love. This is all pessimistic.

Student 2 Not that I haven't seen many failed relationships, but as a "thirty-something" male, I think the speaker in this poem (who also seems to be male) is very young. He sees "true love" as something that "blots out reason" and is always jealously waiting for a sign that the lady returns his feelings. I think as most people get older, they do not spend so much time thinking about "how is she (or he, in the case of a woman) going to react to me?" Instead they are looking for someone who will not cause them pain, someone who will be on the same wavelength.

Student 3 The first thing I thought when I was listening to the poem being read was that it was a terrible way to look at love. Like a migraine headache. Then when I read it myself, it made me smile some at the end. It was a sad smile—or maybe an ironic smile is what I mean. Because at the end, the speaker advises other lovers to "Take courage," so I thought that showed that he was at least willing to try again. He seemed to be saying that, yes, love is painful but it is a pain that can be worth it if you get rewarded with that "searching look" while the two of you are "in a darkened room." What he is talking about is that "chemistry" between two people who are really attracted to each other, but maybe they aren't meant for each other because of their opposing personalities. But the physical attraction is something that you just can't always push away.

Student 4 A man wrote this poem and the character in the poem is a man, but the feelings are something I can really understand. I think more of women or girls being the ones who wait around for signs or who stay up all night or lose weight because they are in love with someone who isn't responding. I can certainly understand watching for every look and trying to figure out what it might mean and whether it might be saying that this person likes you. I've had plenty of headaches waiting for the phone to ring. Graves is right on target when he says "Love is a universal migraine."

The responses show the wide variety of reactions readers have when they encounter the same text. Note that the second reader and the fourth reader, particularly, include thoughts and feelings related to their own circumstances.

FORMAL WAYS OF WRITING ABOUT POETRY

Among the more common formal ways of writing about poetry is analysis. In writing an analytical essay about a poem, your goal is to explain how one or more particular aspects or issues in the work contribute to its overall meaning. You might analyze the dialogue in Stuart's "In the Orchard" or the voices in Reed's "Naming of Parts," for example, in explaining what the verbal exchanges between characters or the difference in voices contributes to each poem's meaning. You might analyze the imagery of H. D.'s "Heat" or Hardy's "Neutral Tones" to see what that imagery suggests about the speaker's perspective or the author's attitude. Or you might analyze the syntax of Frost's "The Silken Tent" or Cummings's "Me up at does" for what that syntax reveals about each poem's theme. (All these poems are found in Chapter Twelve.)

In addition to analyzing these and other poetic elements in a single poem, you might also write to compare two poems, perhaps by focusing on their symbolism, sound effects, rhythm and meter, structure, or figures of speech. Or, instead of focusing on literary elements per se, you might write to see how a particular critical perspective illuminates a poem. For example, you might consider the ways reader-response criticism contributes to your understanding of Sharon Old's "Rite of Passage" or new historicism contributes to your understanding of Poe's "The Raven." (Both poems are in Chapter Nineteen.)

Read Sylvia Plath's poem below. Following it, a brief analysis of Plath's "Mirror" focuses on the poem's imagery and its structure. The writer considers how Plath's language and organization convey an implied idea about women.

SYLVIA PLATH*

[1932–1963]

Mirror

I am silver and exact. I have no preconceptions.
Whatever I see I swallow immediately
Just as it is, unmisted by love or dislike.
I am not cruel, only truthful—
The eye of a little god, four-cornered.
Most of the time I meditate on the opposite wall.
It is pink, with speckles. I have looked at it so long
I think it is a part of my heart. But it flickers.
Faces and darkness separate us over and over.

Now I am a lake. A woman bends over me,
Searching my reaches for what she really is.
Then she turns to those liars, the candles or the moon.
I see her back, and reflect it faithfully.
She rewards me with tears and an agitation of hands.
I am important to her. She comes and goes.
Each morning it is her face that replaces the darkness.
In me she has drowned a young girl, and in me an old woman
Rises toward her day after day, like a terrible fish. [1961]

Student Papers on Poetry

Jennifer Stepkowski
Professor O'Leary
Introduction to Literature
March 23, 2000

Reflections on Sylvia Plath's "Mirror"

Sylvia Plath's poem, "Mirror," presents a portrayal of womanhood that is both accurate and upsetting. The mirror in Plath's poem reflects honestly both inanimate objects and the faces of those who peer into it. To convey the mirror's uncompromising accuracy in reflecting what shows in its glass surface, Plath uses such words as "exact," "truthful," "really," and "faithfully." Plath personifies her mirror and makes it the poem's speaker. "I am silver and exact," the speaker begins. "I have no preconceptions" (line 1). This exactness of the mirror's reflection of reality coupled with Plath's precise diction present a harsh reality in which women grow old inexorably. Women have old age to look forward to, an old age in which the young girls they once were have been "drowned" (17).

The image of drowning follows logically from the opening of the poem's second stanza in which the mirror is compared to a lake. It is in this lake (or mirror as lake) that a woman searches for her self, reaching, as Plath writes, "for what she really is" (11). What the woman finds, however, so disconcerts her that she responds with "an agitation of hands" (14), which calls up a vision of the woman's hands in flurried motion around her face. Yet even though she is upset by what she sees in the mirror, the woman returns repeatedly, for as the mirror says, "I am important to her" (15).

Plath is uncompromising in portraying women's need to see themselves, a need fed by a powerful concern with their appearance. She also conveys without compromise the inevitable process of aging, rendered powerfully in the simile that concludes the poem. Plath conveys a sense of the woman at three stages of life: as she is now, growing older in the poem's present; as she was once as a young girl; and as she will be as an old woman who "rises toward her day after day, like a terrible fish" (18).

The images of the second stanza—of lake and tears and agitated hands of a drowning girl and old woman rising like a fish—reflect concretely the first stanza's general statements. There Plath describes the mirror as having "no preconceptions"

(1), as "swallow[ing] immediately just as it is," whatever it sees, "unmisted by love or dislike." Soon the woman will be swallowed by the mirror as it has swallowed the young girl she once was. Only the old woman remains, coming and going from the mirror, staring into it and looking for the middle-aged woman and the young girl who will have long since vanished.

Work Cited

Plath, Sylvia. "Mirror." *Literature: Reading Fiction, Poetry, and Drama*. Robert DiYanni. Compact ed. New York: McGraw, 2000. 703.

A Paper That Compares Two Versions of a Poem

In the following paper Amanda Ackerman compares an early version of Blake's "London" with the published version (pages 595–596). The writer carefully analyzes Blake's diction and selection of detail to arrive at an interpretation of the later version. Seeing what words Blake rejected and changed helped her understand what Blake's published poem emphasizes.

Amanda Ackerman
Professor DiYanni
English 102
August 3, 1998

The Sad World of "London"

In William Blake's "London," the speaker takes a midnight walk through London's dismal streets. As the speaker travels, he remarks on the depravity, the weakness, and the sad restrictions which abound in the London society. However, because of Blake's affinity for perfection in his poetry, the speaker's footsteps are thoughtfully planned. In fact, it was necessary for Blake to make several revisions within his first draft of "London" before he was satisfied with the final version. Each change that Blake makes bears significance, whether it is as subtle as the capitalization of one letter, or as dramatic as the complete revision of an entire stanza. With each change, the poem becomes richer with connotations of restraint, with imagery far more vivid and alarming, and with an expression of a devastation ultimately more heart-felt.

The majority of the changes that Blake makes within the first three stanzas of the poem are deceptively minute, yet their impact is anything but insignificant. For example, by simply replacing three words within the first stanza of the original version, Blake allows the second version of "London" to immediately take on an altogether different feeling. In the earlier version of the poem, Blake expresses his discontent by describing the Thames and the London streets as "dirty" (lines 1-2). By sharp contrast, in the later version Blake describes the same scene as "charter'd," a word that denotes boundaries and restrictions: "I wander through each charter'd street / Near where the charter'd Thames does flow" (1-2). Instead of providing the reader with a vague and somewhat cryptic idea of London's decay, Blake instantly alerts the reader to the sad reality of London's restrictions. London is a world so devastated by repression that even the "free flowing" Thames and the city streets themselves are weakened. Nothing and no one is left untouched by London's all-consuming restrictions, for the reader "see[s] in every face [he] meet[s] / Marks of weakness, marks of woe" (3-4). This image, although disturbing, cannot compare to the deeper despair expressed in the second version, for in this version the speaker "mark[s] in every face [he] meet[s] / Marks of weakness, marks of woe" (3-4). The grief of those that the speaker sees becomes much more terrifying, for their faces are so miserable and weak that they are able to leave a permanent impression on those who see them. This is a much more powerful image than that of a person despondently "seeing" the sad faces of those around him. Also, by changing "see" to "mark," Blake creates a haunting repetition which not only enhances the fluidity of the poem, but more importantly "marks" the reader himself by echoing the dismal truth.

Again, Blake makes revisions in the second stanza which appear small, but nonetheless which add tremendously to the impact of the poem. To begin with, Blake makes what appears to be a simple grammatical change; he capitalizes words such as "Man" and "Infant" in the second version. By doing this, Blake makes those unknown people that he describes seem much more frighteningly human, for he capitalizes their names just as we would capitalize the name of an individual person. Also, the striking image of a grown man crying becomes much more devastating when that "man" becomes "Man"—a universal representation for all mankind. In addition, the capitalized letters of these words allow them to stand out, and thus magnify their impact. Blake also makes another significantly effective change within the second stanza; he changes "In every voice of every child" to "In every Infant's cry of fear" (6), a line much richer in impact and feeling. The first line gives a somewhat vague picture of the sadness in the lives of many faceless children, whereas the second line evokes a much more specific and alarming image, for it is the purest and most innocent of all human beings—the newborn baby—which even in its naivete feels the pain of repression so intensely that it "cries out."

As frightening as that image is, Blake affects the reader even more deeply by revealing the two terrifying sources of London's restricted freedom—one being the human mind. The already unnerving image of the human mind being its own means of imprisonment is made much more vivid when Blake changes the "mind forg'd links" described in the first version, to the "mind-forg'd manacles" (8) of the second. The word "manacles" is a word so rich with connotations of restraint and imprisonment that the reader is given a both alarming and sickening image of the mind itself—the only possession of man thought to be truly incapable of being barred or restricted—eating away at its own freedom. Blake also reveals the other source of London's grief and repressed freedom in a bold protest against the leadership of his time—Blake identifies the leaders themselves as the source of London's anguish. Again, by capitalizing certain words and by changing one line in the third stanza, Blake makes his attack on the leadership of his time all the more forceful and justifiable. In the second version, Blake capitalizes words such as

"Chimney-sweeper's," "Church," "Soldier's," and "Palace" in order to display his discontent much more emphatically. The reader ultimately takes much more notice of the young Chimney-sweeper's cry, and of the unfortunate Soldier whose own lifeblood "runs . . . down palace walls" (12) where the incompetent leaders reside. Blake further stresses the heartlessness of London's leaders through another significant revision; he changes the line "Blacken's o'er the church walls" to "Every black'ning Church appalls" (10). In the second version, the Church of England—thought to be a sacred place of sanctuary and of guidance—instead of providing its people with any kind of relief, is actively "appalling" or denunciating the efforts of its impoverished people, particularly the poor child-laborers who must sweep chimneys in order to survive. This is a much more horrifying image than that of the first.

However, in the last stanza Blake provides the reader with perhaps the most alarming imagery of all, as London has been reduced to a state where nothing at all is sacred. In the last stanza, Blake brings about a marked difference in the impact of the poem through several dramatic changes. The earlier version of the poem uses imagery which vaguely connotes the sadness and the depravity found in the London society. However, Blake expresses this detestable human condition much more forcefully in the final version. Instead of the "midnight harlot," "dismal street," and "curses weaving and blasting," Blake uses much more powerful words and imagery. A strong image such as "midnight streets" (13) brings a much darker and more ominous feeling to the poem. Also, in an astonishing paradox, Blake refers to the harlot as "youthful" (14). By doing this, Blake brings about a much more alarming image of the corrupted and devastated innocence of a child. Also, the "curse" (14) of the harlot appears to be much more cruel and hurtful as it "blights with plagues" (16) rather than "weave" around a marriage hearse. In this second image a youthful mother is trying to destroy her own infant's tears—no sooner has the infant experienced its first moments of life in the world, than it is feeling the sickness of repression. Nothing is sacred any longer in the dismal world of London, certainly not the bond between mother and child, and not even marriage. Blake ends the final version of his poem with the lasting impression of a "Marriage hearse" (16). This last image leaves the reader devastated, as it is marriage—probably considered the most sacred and beautiful institution of man—which itself is dead and on its way to being buried.

Although the reader encounters feelings of deep sadness, corruption, and repression within the lines of Blake's first version of "London," the walk that the reader takes through London's dreary streets in the final version of the poem provides the reader with a much more heart-felt insight into London's miserable reality. Regardless of the size of each revision, each change that Blake makes within his poem produces a more powerful understanding and a more profound idea: specifically, the idea of restriction, the idea that man himself has created a world in which he has stifled his own expression and put boundaries on his growth—in the sad world of London.

Work Cited

Blake, William. "London" (2 revisions). *Literature: Reading Fiction, Poetry, and Drama*. Ed. Robert DiYanni. Compact ed. New York: McGraw, 2000, 486-87.

Following are two more student papers of analysis, one on George Herbert's poem "Virtue" (see Chapter Twelve), and the other on Jimmy Santiago Baca's from *Meditations on the South Valley*, "XVII" (found in Chapter Nineteen).

Cadet Timothy Benedict
Major Robert Gibson
EN102: Literature
October 27, 1998

Sweetness Dies: The Timber Stands Straight

In George Herbert's "Virtue," the author uses several metaphors to contrast the temporary things of life with the eternal condition of one's soul. Herbert uses the metaphors of a "sweet day" (line 1), "sweet rose" (5) and "sweet spring" (9) to describe life. Although these metaphors convey uplifting ideas, Herbert uses the recurring curse of "thou must die" (4, 8) to contrast with these physical comparisons. After three stanzas of such metaphors, Herbert introduces a stanza with a different idea about sweetness. Ironically, when Herbert describes the only lasting simile, he uses harsh symbols that contrast with the previous metaphors. Herbert compares a virtuous soul to "seasoned timber" (14) and introduces the idea of all turning to "coal" (15); this progression shows how the moral soul lives forever while all other sweet things perish.

After reading the first two lines of Herbert's poem, the reader has a calm feeling as the poet describes the sweet day. Upon reading the third line, however, the reader finds that the night shall soon overtake the day, and the day, just like all living beings, "must die" (4). Similarly, in the second stanza, Herbert calls upon a metaphor of vibrant life: a sweet rose. The root that gives the rose its nutrients, however, betrays it. For the "root is ever in its grave / And thou must die" (7–8), showing that the life-giving dirt that the root abides in will soon become the resting-place of the dying plant. This metaphor is used to show the unimportance of superficial aspects of life. The poet believes not that external beauty is important in life, but the root of the person determines their eternal value. Finally, in the third stanza, Herbert describes the season "full of sweet days and roses" (9), a season that gives life to countless plants and animals: "sweet spring" (9). Now, Herbert foretells that "*all* [emphasis mine] must die" (12). What hope has the reader?

According to Herbert, the only thing that people can hope to live eternally is a "sweet and virtuous soul" (13). In this final stanza, Herbert not only progresses towards the eternal soul, but also breaks away from the previous three stanzas. For instance, instead of using a metaphor, Herbert uses a simile to compare a virtuous soul to seasoned timber. Why not a more uplifting simile to describe the virtuous soul? This simile implies moral straightness and uprightness, a quality more desirable than sweet days, roses, or the spring. In addition, seasoned timber indicates a soul weathered with wisdom and a strong foundation; these traits are more important to Herbert than the flower and other sweet things. Herbert also uses the idea of coal to contrast with sweetness and to give the reader a reference for time. Herbert wishes the reader to think of eternity, to look beyond the temporary sweetness of the day and spring. According to Herbert, moral integrity is more advantageous in the long run than seeking the fleeting sweet nothings in life. Even if "the whole world turn[s] to coal" (15)—old, dull, and black—the virtuous soul lives.

As Herbert's poem progresses from sweet ideas to coal, a definite change is evident between the first three stanzas and the final one. Although the day soon "dies" to the night, seasoned timber "never gives" (14). When the rose withers at the roots and its flower dies, the timber stands stiff and upright, just as the virtuous soul does throughout its life. In addition, when seasons change and give way to a world of lifeless coal, the virtuous soul lives eternally. Herbert's poem implies humans should accept temporary inconvenience by living a virtuous life, remaining pure and morally upright in order to reap the benefits of eternal life.

Work Cited

Herbert, George. "Virtue." *Literature, Reading Fiction, Poetry, Drama, and the Essay*. Ed. Robert DiYanni. 4th ed. New York: McGraw, 1998, 514.

Melissa Gerstel
Dr. DiYanni
ENG 102
November 22, 1999

Current Affairs

The wind is a powerful force of nature; it unfurls over the land, whipping victims with its icy lashes. As the wind rushes toward its prey, it leaves gusts of change in its wake: ripped tree limbs, roaring waters, clouds of dust, etc. In his poem "XVII" from *Meditations on the South Valley,* Jimmy Santiago Baca weaves violent images of the wind with the turbulent changes within a community. The fierce wind symbolizes change unleashed upon a poor, Spanish-speaking neighborhood.

The poem begins with a declaration by the narrator: "I love the wind / when it blows through my barrio" (lines 1-2). There is a trace of irony in the speaker's voice because the next four lines describe the wind's hellish destruction on the area. For example, the wind "cracks egg-shell skins / of abandoned homes" (5-6). The neglected houses, with their fragile exterior fallen into disrepair, signify the life changes of their former owners. The people who had inhabited the house suddenly moved out—perhaps even out of the barrio. The houses, once lived in, once loved even—now belong to the wind.

According to the speaker, the wind also possesses a passion for the neighborhood: "It hisses its snake love / down calles de polvo" (3-4). The wind symbolizes a predatory beast, slithering through the unpaved, dusty streets of the barrio. It "hisses" its snake-like intent—intent filled with power, deceit, and other qualities linked to snakes since the story of Adam and Eve. Its viper-like, venomous love is contradictory, much like the wind's love for the barrio and the barrio's love for the wind. However, the wind simulates an active environment for the residents.

Besides assaulting disintegrating buildings, the wind violently affects other aspects of nature. The wind's intensity strikes and causes ". . . great cottonwoods [to] rattle / like old covered wagons / stuck in stagnant waterholes" (9-11). The description of the cottonwoods' rattle evokes images of the pioneer days when horse-drawn buggies clattered along frontier trails. Like the bygone era, the cottonwoods are sealed in a certain place (surrounded by motionless water) and figuratively frozen in time.

The wind, however, shakes the trees, jolts their limbs, and rustles their leaves. Although the roots of the trees remain firmly cemented in one place, the wind hurtles through the cottonwoods, bringing change and, ultimately, action.

Actions eminently spark the life changes in people as well. The men and women of the barrio decide to transform their relationships, their situations, and themselves when the wind charges through: "full of sand and grit" (13). The "grit" the wind carries represents the strength and determination within the people as they seek to ". . . change their whole lives" (15).

Most of the destructive relationships whirl with the wind. There are ". . . divorce papers / and squalling separation" (17–18). Aggressive blasts of cold air shove objects out of the wind's path; similarly, marriages in the barrio splinter apart as the couples physically and emotionally push away from each other. The separation of husbands and wives is described as "squalling" (18), which further enhances the wind's turbulence. "Squalling" also conjures up images of harshness, ferociousness, rocky torrents, and piercing screeches. The breakups of marriages, families, and friendships cause crushing, emotionally wrenching experiences, but as they tumble, they elicit change.

As the wind wreaks its destructive force upon the neighborhood, it also bears a whispered message: ". . . The wind tells us / what others refuse to tell us, / informing men and women of a secret, / that they move away to hide from" (18–21). Perhaps the wind speaks vaguely of the hazy, uncertain future that is the result of the life changes. But it divulges the information to the people in the barrio ("us") because people outside of the neighborhood culture ("others") deprived them of it.

Furthermore, the secret hangs over people's heads like a veiled threat, and they are compelled to ". . . move away to hide from [it]" (21). The people move, scattering in all directions like pollen on the wind. The people may move out of the neighborhood, thus leaving their "abandoned homes" (6) and community behind. Or the people may remain in the barrio but "move out" of their relationships with other people.

Nonetheless, no matter what fortune or misfortune lurks in the future, one occurrence is certain—change. As the wind current lifts up the dusts of ages, it uncovers a shimmering hope, and with that hope, a new beginning.

Work Cited

Baca, Jimmy Santiago. "XVII," from *Meditations on the South Valley*. *Literature: Reading Fiction, Poetry, and Drama*. Ed. Robert DiYanni. 5th ed. New York: McGraw, 2002, 1050.

Questions for Writing about Poetry

In writing about the elements of poetry, the following questions can help you focus your thinking and prepare yourself for writing analytical essays and papers. Use the questions as a checklist to guide you to important aspects of any poem you read.

Voice: Speaker and Situation

1. Who is the speaker of the poem? How would you characterize this speaker?
2. Where does the speaker reveal his or her attitude toward the poem's subject? Do the speaker's attitude or feelings change at any point? If so, where and with what implications?
3. What is the speaker's situation? What is happening in the poem?

Diction and Imagery

4. Do you understand the denotations of all the words used in the poem? Look up any words you are not completely sure of.
5. Which words convey the richest connotations? What do these connotations contribute to your understanding of the poem?
6. What kinds of imagery does the poem include? Do you detect any patterns among the images? What do the images collectively suggest?

Figures of Speech

7. What kinds of figures of speech occur in the poem? How important are figures of comparison—simile and metaphor?
8. How do the poem's figures of speech contribute to the poem's vividness and concreteness? What do they contribute to its feeling and meaning?

Symbolism and Allegory

9. What details of language and action carry symbolic implications? How do you know?
10. Does the poem exhibit a pattern of linked allegorical details?

Syntax and Structure

11. What kinds of sentences does the poet use? What kinds of structure and pattern do the poem's sentences exhibit?

12. What does the poem's syntax reveal about the state of mind of its speaker?
13. How is the poem organized? How do its stanzas or major sections develop?
14. How are the stanzas or major sections of the poem related?

Sound, Rhythm, and Meter

15. Does the poem rhyme? Does it employ assonance, alliteration, onomatopoeia, or other forms of sound play? With what effects?
16. What kinds of rhythm and meter does the poem include? Does the rhythm change or is the meter varied at any point? With what effects?

Theme

17. How do the poetic elements create and convey the poem's meaning(s)?
18. Do you think there is more than one theme? Why or why not?
19. Is the theme of the poem explicit or implicit? Is it conveyed more clearly in one part of the poem than another?

Critical Perspectives

20. Which of the critical perspectives best helps you make sense of the poem? Why?
21. To what extent do the poem's language and details convey its meaning? To what extent do you need to go outside the poem for an understanding of its allusions, its historical or biographical implications, or other kinds of information?
22. To what extent does the poem confirm or support, confute or contradict your personal values, beliefs, attitudes, or dispositions? Why?

Suggestions for Writing

The Experience of Poetry

1. Write a paper in which you recount your experience of reading a particular poem or a series of poems by the same author. You may want to compare your initial experience of reading the poem(s) with your subsequent experience.
2. Relate the action or situation of a poem to your experience. Explain how the poem is relevant to your situation, and comment on how reading and thinking about it may have helped you view your own situation and experience more clearly.

The Interpretation of Poetry

3. Characterize the speaker of any poem. Present a sketch of the speaker's character by referring to the language of the poem. Consider not only what the speaker says but the manner in which it is said and what it reveals about the speaker.
4. Describe the narrative element in any poem. Consider how important its "story" or narrative material is, and what would be gained or lost without it. Consider also how the narrative dimension of the poem would work as a story, play, or essay.
5. Explicate the opening lines of a poem. Explain the significance of the lines in the context of the poem overall.
6. Explicate the closing lines of a poem. Consider how they can be related to earlier lines.
7. Select two or more key lines from a short poem (or groups of lines from longer ones). Explain their significance and consider their relationship to one another.
8. Read five or more poems by the same poet and discuss the features they have in common.
9. Analyze a single poem that is representative of a poet's work. Explain what makes the poem representative.
10. Analyze the diction or word choices of a poem. Consider other words the poet could have chosen. Examine the denotations and connotations of the words the poet chose. Use your analysis of the diction to develop an interpretation of the poem.
11. Analyze the imagery of a poem. List the poem's significant details (if a long poem) or all the details if it's short. Discuss what the images contribute to the poem's tone, feeling, and/or meaning.
12. Analyze the figurative language of a poem. Identify and explain each figure of speech and discuss its function in the poem overall.
13. Discuss the ironic dimensions of a poem. Identify examples of irony, and explain their significance and effect.
14. Identify the allusions in a poem and explain what they contribute to your understanding of it.
15. Analyze the structure of a poem. Consider both its overall structure and its small-scale structure—how the individual parts themselves are organized. Identify the main parts of the poem and comment on their relationship to each other.
16. Analyze the sound effects of a poem. Explain how sound contributes to its sense and spirit.
17. Analyze the rhythm and meter of a poem. Identify its prevailing metrical pattern. Acknowledge any deviations from this meter and comment on the significance of these deviations. Consider what the poem's rhythm and meter contribute to its overall meaning and feeling.

The Evaluation of Poetry

18. Discuss the values exemplified in one or more poems. Consider, that is, the cultural, moral, social, or ethical norms that either appear explicitly in the poem(s) or are implied by it. Identify those values, relate them to your own, and comment on their significance.
19. Compare two poems, evaluating their literary and linguistic merit. Explain what the two poems have in common, how they differ, and why one is superior to the other.
20. Evaluate a poem from the standpoint of its literary excellence. Explain why you consider it to be an effective or ineffective poem.

Critical Thinking and Research

21. Develop an alternative ending for a poem, changing the outcome of its action, altering its pattern of rhythm or rhyme, or making other changes. Be prepared to defend your alternative version as a reasonable possibility. Consider why the poet chose to end the poem as he or she did.
22. Read some letters or essays by a poet whose poetry you know and enjoy. Consider how your reading of the poet's prose aids your understanding or increases your enjoyment.
23. Read a full-scale biography of a poet whose work you admire. Write a paper explaining how the poet's life is or is not reflected in the poetic work.
24. Write a paper in which you examine how a particular poet worked within and/or against the prevailing social attitudes, moral beliefs, or cultural dispositions of his or her time.
25. Read a critical study of any poet you would like to learn more about. Write a paper explaining how reading the book has increased your understanding and/or appreciation of the poetry.

CHAPTER FOURTEEN

Transformations

REVISIONS

Unlike the goddess Athena, who sprang full-grown from the head of Zeus, poems rarely emerge fully formed from poets' heads. When they do, however, it is often because the poet worked on them both consciously and subconsciously before putting a word on paper. The product of labor as well as inspiration, good poems are the result of considerable care, of repeated efforts to find the right words and put them in the right order.

And yet for all the effort involved, the words and lines of a poem should seem natural, even inevitable. The great modern Irish poet William Butler Yeats put it this way:

> . . . A line will take us hours maybe;
> Yet if it does not seem a moment's thought,
> Our stitching and unstitching has been nought.

We suspect that these lines and the complete poem from which they are taken, "Adam's Curse," took more than a few moments to compose. So too did the following lines in which John Keats describes a woman preparing for bed. Keats's notebook reveals his struggle to bring them to the point where he felt satisfied with them. Here are the lines as published in his "The Eve of St. Agnes":

> . . . her vespers done,
> Of all its wreathed pearls her hair she frees
> Unclasps her warmed jewels one by one;
> Loosens her fragrant bodice; by degrees
> Her rich attire creeps rustling to her knees . . .

Other less successful renderings, however, preceded this final version of the description. Previously, for example, Keats had written "her praying done" rather than "her vespers done." And before that he had written: "her prayers said." Both of these versions are less precise and less musical than the final one. "Vespers," which means evening prayers, is more precise than "prayers"; it is also more musical, echoing the *e* of "h*e*r." For "frees" Keats had previously written "strips," a word with quite different connotations and sound. For "warmed" he had written "bosom," and for "rich," "sweet." Of her dress he had also written that it "falls light" instead of "creeps rustling" to her knees. In each case Keats worked toward phrases that possess greater sensuousness and that were richer in sound and imagistic effects. But it is in the fourth line that we can see Keats struggle hardest before he settles on "Loosens her fragrant bodice; by degrees." Here are the earlier attempts:

1. Loosens her bursting, her bodice from her
2. Loosens her bodice lace string
3. Loosens her bodice and her bosom bare
4. Loosens her fragrant bodice and doth bare / Her
5. Loosens her fragrant bodice: and down slips

We have only to consider the images and connotations of "bursting bodice" and "bosom bare" to see how different an effect is achieved with "fragrant bodice." Keats deliberately avoids the stronger sexual overtones of the earlier versions, replacing words suggesting physical sensuality with others of a sensuous rather than a sensual nature.

We can see the process of revision at work more fully in the following poem by William Blake, reprinted in two versions.

WILLIAM BLAKE*
[1757–1827]

London

I wander thro' each dirty street,
Near where the dirty Thames does flow,
And [see] mark in every face I meet
Marks of weakness, marks of woe.

In every cry of every man
In [every voice of every child] every infant's cry of fear
In every voice, in every ban
The [german] mind forg'd [links I hear] manacles I hear.

[But most] How the chimney sweeper's cry
[Blackens o'er the churches' walls]
Every black'ning church appalls,
And the hapless soldier's sigh
Runs in blood down palace walls.
[But most the midnight harlot's curse

From every dismal street I hear,
Weaves around the marriage hearse
And blasts the new born infant's tear.]

[Alternate fourth stanza]
But most [from every] thro' wintry streets I hear
How the midnight harlot's curse
Blasts the new born infant's tear,
And [hangs] smites with plagues the marriage hearse.

[1794]

London

I wander thro' each charter'd street,
Near where the charter'd Thames does flow,
And mark in every face I meet
Marks of weakness, marks of woe.

In every cry of every Man,
In every Infant's cry of fear,
In every voice, in every ban,
The mind-forg'd manacles I hear.

How the Chimney-sweeper's cry
Every black'ning Church appalls;
And the hapless Soldier's sigh
Runs in blood down Palace walls.

But most thro' midnight streets I hear
How the youthful Harlot's curse
Blasts the new born Infant's tear,
And blights with plagues the Marriage hearse.

[1794]

Let's consider the changes in "London" stanza by stanza to determine the implications of each alteration and to estimate how the accumulated changes affect the tone and meaning of the poem as Blake published it.

Stanza One In line 1 "charter'd" replaces "dirty." Although both words are trochaic, the sound of "charter'd" echoes "wander." More important than this use of assonance are the meanings of "charter'd." It denotes something for lease or hire, something established by a charter (a written certificate defining the legal conditions under which a corporate body is organized). The applicable meaning seems to be "hired out." The word's connotations include something defined, planned, laid out, bounded, limited by law, perhaps fixed or determined by decree. Both the street and the river Thames are described as "charter'd," as hired out and bound.

The second alteration in this stanza is Blake's substitution of "mark" for "see." "Mark" means "to take notice of; to give attention; to consider." But it also suggests a more emotionally moving seeing, a more intense noticing than "see." This use of *mark* as a verb in line 3 is further intensified with its appearance as a noun in the next line. Two denotations of the word there seem applicable: "something appearing distinctly on a surface, as a line, spot, scar, or dent" and "something indicative of one's condition, feelings."

Stanza Two "Man" replaces "man" and "Infant's" replaces "infant's." How important, in each case, is the difference? The early version of the second line has "voice" of a "child." Why do you think Blake changed these words to the "cry" of an infant, and a "cry of fear" at that? "German" in the fourth line means "germane," suggesting something closely related or akin. This word gives way in the later version to "mind-forg'd." "Links" is replaced by "manacles." Consider the denotations and connotations of the words of the later version. How does the meaning of "manacles" support the meanings of "charter'd" and "marks"? How can "manacles" be "mind-forg'd"? And why "forg'd" and not some other word like "made"?

Stanza Three Consider the implications of the second line in both versions. In the early version the blackening is attributed to the chimney sweeper's cry. In the revised version Blake makes "black'ning" an adjective modifying Church. How can the church's walls be blackened by the cry of a chimney sweeper? And why does Blake use the adjective "black'ning" to modify "Church"? Reflect on the connotations of "black," "blacken," and "black'ning," and consider the denotations and connotations of "appalls."

Stanza Four Here we have more than revisions of words or lines. Though many details from the early version are carried over to the later one, they are rearranged, recombined, and rethought. In addition, some details disappear and others emerge. The rhymes, though the same, are reversed, with "hear-tear" ending the early version and "curse-hearse" concluding the final one. In the later version "the midnight harlot" has become "the youthful Harlot"—the word *youthful* a detail that intensifies our emotional response. The "curse" of the second line is both the curse that the harlot passes on to her infant, blinding it at birth with the effects of venereal disease, and the curse of the harlot's own life. Her position echoes the implications of "charter'd" and "wandered" of stanza one. She wanders the streets, but she is hardly free. She is bound, fixed, a body for hire. The final line of the stanza is the most heavily altered. "Blights" and "plagues" suggest not only the ruin of the harlot and her child, but also the destruction of the social order: marriage is cursed, innocent children suffer, soldiers die senselessly, and in general the London populace exhibits signs of desperate suffering.

Blake's revisions intensify his indictment of the institutions—moral, military, and legal—responsible for the human squalor and the misery suffered by innocent people. His revisions increase the emotional intensity of the poem as they darken its view of the lives of the people of London and, by extension, the lives of other urban inhabitants.

Below you will find two versions of three different poems. For each pair examine changes in diction, imagery, syntax, structure, sound, rhythm, meter, and meaning. Explain the significance of the changes and indicate which version of each pair you prefer and why.

WILLIAM BUTLER YEATS*

[1865–1939]

A Dream of Death

I dreamed that one had died in a strange place
Near no accustomed hand,
And they had nailed the boards above her face
The peasants of that land,

And wondering planted by her solitude
A cypress and a yew.
I came and wrote upon a cross of wood—
Man had no more to do—

'She was more beautiful than thy first love,
This lady by the trees';
And gazed upon the mournful stars above,
And heard the mournful breeze.

[1893]

A Dream of Death

I dreamed that one had died in a strange place
Near no accustomed hand;
And they had nailed the boards above her face,
The peasants of that land,
Wondering to lay her in that solitude,
And raised above her mound
A cross they had made out of two bits of wood,
And planted cypress round;
And left her to the indifferent stars above
Until I carved these words:
She was more beautiful than thy first love,
But now lies under boards.

[1893]

QUESTIONS FOR CRITICAL THINKING AND WRITING

1. Compare the tone of the last four lines of each version. Consider especially the difference between "mournful stars" and "indifferent stars."
2. What details have disappeared in the second version and what has been added? To what effect?

EMILY DICKINSON*

[1830–1886]

The Wind begun to knead the Grass

The Wind begun to knead the Grass—
As Women do a Dough—
He flung a Hand full at the Plain—
A Hand full at the Sky—
The Leaves unhooked themselves from Trees—
And started all abroad—
The Dust did scoop itself like Hands—
And throw away the Road—
The Wagons quickened on the Street—
The Thunders gossiped low—
The Lightning showed a Yellow Head—
And then a livid Toe—
The Birds put up the Bars to Nests—
The Cattle flung to Barns—
Then came one drop of Giant Rain—
And then, as if the Hands
That held the Dams—had parted hold—
The Waters Wrecked the Sky—
But overlooked my Father's House—
Just Quartering a Tree—

[1864, 1955]

The Wind begun to rock the Grass

The Wind begun to rock the Grass
With threatening Tunes and low—
He threw a Menace at the Earth—
A Menace at the Sky

The Leaves unhooked themselves from Trees—
And started all abroad
The Dust did scoop itself like Hands
And threw away the Road.

The Wagons quickened on the Streets
The Thunder hurried slow—
The Lightning showed a Yellow Beak
And then a livid Claw.

The Birds put up the Bars to Nests—
The Cattle fled to Barns—
There came one drop of Giant Rain
And then as if the Hands

That held the Dams had parted hold
The Waters Wrecked the Sky,
But overlooked my Father's House—
Just quartering a Tree—

[1864, 1955]

QUESTIONS FOR CRITICAL THINKING AND WRITING

1. Comment on the change in the organization. Does the poem's appearance in stanzas make it easier or more difficult to read?
2. Compare the tone of the first four lines of each version.
3. In lines 11–12 of each version, which image is more consistent and more vivid?

D. H. LAWRENCE*

[1885–1930]

The Piano

Somewhere beneath that piano's superb sleek black
Must hide my mother's piano, little and brown, with the back
That stood close to the wall, and the front's faded silk both torn,
And the keys with little hollows, that my mother's fingers had worn.

Softly, in the shadows, a woman is singing to me
Quietly, through the years I have crept back to see
A child sitting under the piano, in the boom of the shaking strings
Pressing the little poised feet of the mother who smiles as she sings.

The full throated woman has chosen a winning, living song
And surely the heart that is in me must belong
To the old Sunday evenings, when darkness wandered outside
And hymns gleamed on our warm lips, as we watched mother's fingers glide.

Or this is my sister at home in the old front room
Singing love's first surprised gladness, alone in the gloom.
She will start when she sees me, and blushing, spread out her hands
To cover my mouth's raillery, till I'm bound in her shame's heart-spun bands.

A woman is singing me a wild Hungarian air
And her arms, and her bosom, and the whole of her soul is bare,
And the great black piano is clamouring as my mother's never could clamour
And my mother's tunes are devoured of this music's ravaging glamour.

[1923]

Piano

Softly, in the dusk, a woman is singing to me;
Taking me back down the vista of years, till I see
A child sitting under the piano, in the boom of the tingling strings
And pressing the small, poised feet of a mother who smiles as she sings.

In spite of myself, the insidious mastery of song
Betrays me back, till the heart of me weeps to belong
To the old Sunday evenings at home, with winter outside
And hymns in the cosy parlour, the tinkling piano our guide.

So now it is vain for the singer to burst into clamour
With the great black piano appassionato. The glamour
Of childish days is upon me, my manhood is cast
Down in the flood of remembrance, I weep like a child for the past.

[1923]

QUESTIONS FOR CRITICAL THINKING AND WRITING

1. Which details have been eliminated from the second version? Which have been added?
2. Discuss the difference in tone and idea between the two versions of the poem.

1st draft
May 30, 1941

BALLAD OF BOOKER T.

Old Booker T.
Was a practical man.
He said, Till the soil,
And Learn from the land.
Let down your buckets
Where you are:
In your own backyard
~~Could~~ There could
~~Might~~ be a star.
Train you ~~heart~~, head,
Your ~~head~~ heart, and your hand.
To help yourself
And your fellowman.
Thus Booker T.
Built a school.
With book-learning there
And the workman's tool.
He started out
In a simple way---
For (Yesterday
Was not today.)
Sometimes he had
Compromise in his talk---
For a man must crawl
Before he can walk.
And in Alabama in '85
A joker was lucky
To ~~stay~~ be alive.
But ~~xix~~ Booker T.
Was nobody's fool:
You may carve a dream
From an humble tool-
And the tallest tower
Can tumble down
If it is not rooted
In solid ground.
He said, Train your ~~heart~~ head,
Your head, and your hand

For smartness alone
Is hardly meet---
If you haven't got
Something to eat.

~~Train your~~
Your ~~head~~ heart, and your hand--
For Booker T.
Was a practical man.

[AC 7054]

First draft of "The Ballad of Booker T." (May 30, 1941)

LANGSTON HUGHES

[1902–1967]

Ballad of Booker T.

Booker T.
Was a practical man.
He said, Till the soil
And learn from the land.
Let down your bucket
Where you are.
Your fate is here
And not afar.
To help yourself
And your fellow man,
Train your head,
Your heart, *and your hand.*
For smartness alone's
Surely not meet—
If you haven't at the same time
Got something to eat
Thus at Tuskegee
He built a school
With book-learning there
And the workman's tool.
He started out
In a simple way—
For yesterday
Was *not* today.
Sometimes he had
Compromise in his talk—
For a man must crawl
Before he can walk—
And in Alabama in '85
A joker was lucky
To be alive.
But Booker T.
Was nobody's fool:
You may carve a dream
With an humble tool.
The tallest tower
Can tumble down
If it be not rooted
In solid ground.

So, being a far-seeing
Practical man,
He said, Train your head,
Your heart, *and your hand.*
Your fate is here
And not afar,
So let down your bucket
Where you are

[1941]

QUESTIONS FOR CRITICAL THINKING AND WRITING

1. What changes does Hughes make in the later version? What is the effect of those changes?
2. What is the speaker's attitude toward Booker T.? (He is referring to Booker T. Washington, founder of the Tuskegee Institute of Technology, a college for black students in Mississippi.)

PARODIES

A **parody** is a humorous, mocking imitation of another work. A parodic poem ridicules by distorting and exaggerating aspects of the poem it imitates. There may be distortions of the tone and purpose of the original poem or exaggerations of its stylistic mannerisms. The best parodists respect the works they parody, for to write parody well, writers must understand and appreciate what they poke fun at. Good parodies catch the special manner and flavor of the originals. In them we hear echoes of the voice of the earlier poem. By extending the original beyond its limits, a parodist can point to the virtues of the poem he or she parodies. The following parody of William Carlos Williams's "This Is Just to Say" seems to do this. First, Williams's poem.

WILLIAM CARLOS WILLIAMS*
[1883–1963]

This Is Just to Say

I have eaten
the plums
that were in
the icebox

and which
you were probably

saving
for breakfast

Forgive me
they were delicious
so sweet
and so cold

[1934]

Now Kenneth Koch's parody:

KENNETH KOCH
[1925–2001]

Variations on a Theme by William Carlos Williams

1

I chopped down the house that you had been saving to live
in next summer.
I am sorry, but it was morning, and I had nothing to do
and its wooden beams were so inviting.

2

We laughed at the hollyhocks together
And then I sprayed them with lye.
Forgive me. I simply do not know what I am doing.

3

I gave away the money that you had been saving to live on
for the next ten years.
The man who asked for it was shabby
and the firm March wind on the porch was so juicy
and cold.

4

Last evening we went dancing and I broke your leg.
Forgive me. I was clumsy, and
I wanted you here in the wards, where I am the doctor!

[1962]

QUESTIONS FOR CRITICAL THINKING AND WRITING

1. Explain Koch's title.
2. Would his parody be as effective if he cut it down to one or two stanzas? If the four stanzas were rearranged? How long, in comparison, is Williams's poem, and why do you think Koch made his parody four times as long?

3. What do the four variations have in common?
4. Does the parody seem fair to Williams? Is it a coherent and engaging poem in its own right?

In the next pair of poems you hear two very different voices. Account for the difference in tone between them. Explain how Howard Moss's poem parodies Shakespeare's sonnet. Consider, finally, the sense the later poem makes on its own, unrelated to the sonnet.

WILLIAM SHAKESPEARE*
[1564–1616]

Shall I compare thee to a summer's day

Shall I compare thee to a summer's day?
Thou art more lovely and more temperate:
Rough winds do shake the darling buds of May,
And summer's lease hath all too short a date;
Sometime too hot the eye of heaven shines,
And often is his gold complexion dimm'd;
And every fair from fair sometime declines,
By chance or nature's changing course untrimm'd:
But thy eternal summer shall not fade
Nor lose possession of that fair thou ow'st;
Nor shall Death brag thou wand'rest in his shade,
When in eternal lines to time thou grow'st;
So long as men can breathe or eyes can see,
So long lives this, and this gives life to thee.

[1609]

HOWARD MOSS
[1922–1987]

Shall I Compare Thee to a Summer's Day?

Who says you're like one of the dog days?
You're nicer. And better.
Even in May, the weather can be gray,
And a summer sub-let doesn't last forever.
Sometimes the sun's too hot;
Sometimes it is not.
Who can stay young forever?

People break their necks or just drop dead!
But you? Never!
If there's just one condensed reader left
Who can figure out the abridged alphabet
  After you're dead and gone,
  In this poem you'll live on!

[1976]

Finally, consider again the following brief poem by Robert Frost and an equally brief parody by Bob McKenty.

ROBERT FROST*

[1874–1963]

Dust of Snow

The way a crow
Shook down on me
The dust of snow
From a hemlock tree
Has given my heart
A change of mood
And saved some part
Of a day I had rued.

[1923]

BOB MCKENTY*

[b. 1935]

Snow on Frost

A wayward crow
Shook down on him
The dust of snow
From a hemlock limb.

Amused (I recall)
The poet stopped,
Delighted that's all
The black bird dropped.

[1990]

QUESTION FOR CRITICAL THINKING AND WRITING

In what ways does McKenty's parody mimic Frost's poem? In what ways does the parody depart from the original?

RESPONSES (POINT–COUNTERPOINT)

Throughout literary history poets have written poems that respond to works by earlier poets. Sometimes the later poem imitates the earlier one by adapting its poetic conventions. One famous example is Sir Walter Raleigh's reply to Christopher Marlowe's "The Passionate Shepherd to His Love." Sometimes a poet simply alludes to the title or most famous line of an earlier poem to develop a counterstatement to it. One of many such poetic counterpoints is Archibald MacLeish's "Not Marble Nor the Gilded Monuments," which offers a counterperspective to Shakespeare's sonnet of the same title. Some poets may refer specifically and by name to an earlier poet and his work as Anthony Hecht did in "The Dover Bitch," his response to Mathew Arnold's "Dover Beach."

As you read the following pairs of poems, consider how the later poet responds to the earlier. Consider what each poet seems to be saying and suggesting, and consider how the later poem modifies the view or perspective of its predecessor.

CHRISTOPHER MARLOWE
[1564–1593]

The Passionate Shepherd to His Love

Come live with me and be my love,
And we will all the pleasures prove° — try
That valleys, groves, hills, and fields,
Woods, or steepy mountain yields.

And we will sit upon the rocks,
Seeing the shepherds feed their flocks,
By shallow rivers to whose falls
Melodious birds sing madrigals.

And I will make thee beds of roses
And a thousand fragrant posies,
A cap of flowers, and a kirtle° — a long dress
Embroidered all with leaves of myrtle;

A gown made of the finest wool
Which from our pretty lambs we pull;

Fair lined slippers for the cold,
With buckles of the purest gold;

A belt of straw and ivy buds,
With coral clasps and amber studs:
And if these pleasures may thee move,
Come live with me, and be my love.

The shepherds' swains shall dance and sing
For thy delight each May morning:
If these delights thy mind may move,
Then live with me and be my love.

[1599]

SIR WALTER RALEIGH

[c. 1552–1618]

The Nymph's Reply to the Shepherd

If all the world and love were young,
And truth in every shepherd's tongue,
These pretty pleasures might me move
To live with thee and be thy love.

Time drives the flocks from field to fold
When rivers rage and rocks grow cold,
And Philomel° becometh dumb;
The rest complains of cares to come.

The flowers do fade, and wanton fields
To wayward winter reckoning yields;
A honey tongue, a heart of gall,
Is fancy's spring, but sorrow's fall.

Thy gowns, thy shoes, thy beds of roses,
Thy cap, thy kirtle,° and thy posies — long dress
Soon break, soon wither, soon forgotten—
In folly ripe, in reason rotten.

Thy belt of straw and ivy buds,
Thy coral clasps and amber studs,

7 **Philomel** *the nightingale. According to Ovid's* Metamorphoses, *Philomel's brother-in-law Tereus had her tongue cut out to prevent her from revealing that he had raped her.*

All these in me no means can move
To come to thee and be thy love.

But could youth last and love still breed,
Had joys no date° nor age no need, end
Then these delights my mind might move
To live with thee and be thy love.

[1599]

WILLIAM SHAKESPEARE*
[1564–1616]

Not marble, nor the gilded monuments

Not marble, nor the gilded monuments
Of princes, shall outlive this powerful rhyme;
But you shall shine more bright in these conténts
Than unswept stone, besmeared with sluttish time.
When wasteful war shall statues overturn,
And broils root out the work of masonry,
Nor Mars his sword nor war's quick fire shall burn
The living record of your memory.
'Gainst death and all-oblivious enmity
Shall you pace forth; your praise shall still find room.
Even in the eyes of all posterity
That wear this world out to the ending doom.° judgment day
So, till the judgment that yourself arise,
You live in this, and dwell in lovers' eyes.

[1609]

ARCHIBALD MACLEISH*
[1892–1982]

"Not Marble Nor the Gilded Monuments"

The praisers of women in their proud and beautiful poems
Naming the grave mouth and the hair and the eyes
Boasted those they loved should be forever remembered
These were lies

The words sound but the face in the Istrian sun is forgotten
The poet speaks but to her dead ears no more

The sleek throat is gone—and the breast that was troubled to listen
Shadow from door

Therefore I will not praise your knees nor your fine walking
Telling you men shall remember your name as long
As lips move or breath is spent or the iron of English
Rings from a tongue

I shall say you were young and your arms straight and your mouth scarlet
I shall say you will die and none will remember you
Your arms change and none remember the swish of your garments
Nor the click of your shoe

Not with my hand's strength not with difficult labor
Springing the obstinate words to the bones of your breast
And the stubborn line to your young stride and the breath to your breathing
And the beat to your haste
Shall I prevail on the hearts of unborn men to remember

(What is a dead girl but a shadowy ghost
Or a dead man's voice but a distant and vain affirmation
Like dream words most)

Therefore I will not speak of the undying glory of women
I will say you were young and straight and your skin fair
And you stood in the door and the sun was a shadow of leaves on your shoulders
And a leaf on your hair

I will not speak of the famous beauty of dead women
I will say the shape of a leaf lay once on your hair
Till the world ends and the eyes are out and the mouths broken
Look! It is there!

[1935]

www

WILLIAM BLAKE*

[1757–1827]

The Chimney Sweeper (Innocence)

When my mother died I was very young,
And my father sold me while yet my tongue
Could scarcely cry "'weep! 'weep! 'weep! 'weep!"
So your chimneys I sweep, and in soot I sleep.

There's little Tom Dacre, who cried when his head,
That curled like a lamb's back, was shaved: so I said
"Hush, Tom! never mind it, for when your head's bare
You know that the soot cannot spoil your white hair."

And so he was quiet, and that very night,
As Tom was a-sleeping, he had such a sight!
That thousands of sweepers, Dick, Joe, Ned, and Jack,
Were all of them locked up in coffins of black.

And by came an Angel who had a bright key,
And he opened the coffins and set them all free;
Then down a green plain leaping, laughing, they run,
And wash in a river, and shine in the sun.

Then naked and white, all their bags left behind,
They rise upon clouds and sport in the wind;
And the Angel told Tom, if he'd be a good boy,
He'd have God for his father, and never want° joy. lack

And so Tom awoke; and we rose in the dark,
And got with our bags and our brushes to work.
Though the morning was cold, Tom was happy and warm;
So if all do their duty they need not fear harm.

[1789]

The Chimney Sweeper (Experience)

A little black thing among the snow:
Crying "'weep, 'weep," in notes of woe!
"Where are thy father & mother? say?"
They are both gone up to the church to pray.

"Because I was happy upon the hearth,
And smil'd among the winters snow:
They clothed me in the clothes of death,
And taught me to sing the notes of woe.

"And because I am happy & dance & sing,
They think they have done me no injury:
And are gone to praise God & his Priest & King
Who make up a heaven of our misery."

[1794]

MATTHEW ARNOLD

[1822–1888]

Dover Beach

The sea is calm tonight.
The tide is full, the moon lies fair
Upon the straits; on the French coast the light
Gleams and is gone; the cliffs of England stand,
Glimmering and vast, out in the tranquil bay.
Come to the window, sweet is the night-air!
Only, from the long line of spray
Where the sea meets the moon-blanched land,
Listen! you hear the grating roar
Of pebbles which the waves draw back, and fling,
At their return, up the high strand,
Begin, and cease, and then again begin,
With tremulous cadence slow, and bring
The eternal note of sadness in.

Sophocles long ago
Heard it on the Aegean,° and it brought
Into his mind the turbid ebb and flow
Of human misery; we
Find also in the sound a thought,
Hearing it by this distant northern sea.

The Sea of Faith
Was once, too, at the full, and round earth's shore
Lay like the folds of a bright girdle furled.
But now I only hear
Its melancholy, long, withdrawing roar,
Retreating, to the breath
Of the night-wind, down the vast edges drear
And naked shingles of the world.

Ah, love, let us be true
To one another! for the world, which seems
To lie before us like a land of dreams,
So various, so beautiful, so new,
Hath really neither joy, nor love, nor light,
Nor certitude, nor peace, nor help for pain;
And we are here as on a darkling plain

Swept with confused alarms of struggle and flight,
Where ignorant armies clash by night.

[1867]

ANTHONY HECHT
[1923–2001]

The Dover Bitch: A Criticism of Life

FOR ANDREWS WANNING

So there stood Matthew Arnold and this girl
With the cliffs of England crumbling away behind them,
And he said to her, "Try to be true to me,
And I'll do the same for you, for things are bad
All over, etc., etc."
Well now, I knew this girl. It's true she had read
Sophocles in a fairly good translation
And caught that bitter allusion to the sea,
But all the time he was talking she had in mind
The notion of what his whiskers would feel like
On the back of her neck. She told me later on
That after a while she got to looking out
At the lights across the channel, and really felt sad,
Thinking of all the wine and enormous beds
And blandishments in French and the perfumes.
And then she got really angry. To have been brought
All the way down from London, and then be addressed
As a sort of mournful cosmic last resort
Is really tough on a girl, and she was pretty.
Anyway, she watched him pace the room
And finger his watch-chain and seem to sweat a bit,
And then she said one or two unprintable things.
But you mustn't judge her by that. What I mean to say is,
She's really all right. I still see her once in a while
And she always treats me right. We have a drink
And I give her a good time, and perhaps it's a year
Before I see her again, but there she is,
Running to fat, but dependable as they come.
And sometimes I bring her a bottle of *Nuit d'Amour*.°

[1968]

"The Dover Bitch: A Criticism of Life" [29]***Nuit d'Amour*** *brand of perfume. The French words mean "night of love."*

ADAPTATIONS (POETRY AND SONG)

Adaptations go beyond translations; they alter literary works by bringing them into a different medium. Novels and plays, for example, are frequently adapted as films; poems are often adapted as songs. For thousands of years, in fact, poetry has been closely allied with song. Below you will find a number of songs, the first three are adaptations that transform a poem into song. Examine each set and explain how the adapter (Seeger or Simon) has transformed the original (Ecclesiastes or Robinson). Consider what has been added, what deleted, and what altered. For the others, simply consider their merits as songlike poems or poemlike songs.

From Ecclesiastes: 3.1–8

To every *thing there* is a season, and a time to every
purpose under the heaven:
2 A time to be born, and a time to die; a time to plant,
and a time to pluck up *that which* is planted;
3 A time to kill, and a time to heal; a time to break
down, and a time to build up;
4 A time to weep, and a time to laugh; a time to mourn,
and a time to dance;
5 A time to cast away stones, and a time to gather stones
together; a time to embrace, and a time to refrain from
embracing;
6 A time to get, and a time to lose; a time to keep, and a
time to cast away;
7 A time to rend, and a time to sew; a time to keep
silence, and a time to speak;
8 A time to love, and a time to hate; a time of war, and a
time of peace.

PETE SEEGER

[b. 1919]

*Turn! Turn! Turn!**

To everything,
Turn, turn, turn,
There is a season,
Turn, turn, turn,
And a time to every purpose under heaven.

* *Turn! Turn! Turn! (To Everything There Is a Season).* Words from the book of *Ecclesiastes.* Adaptation and music by Pete Seeger.

A time to be born, a time to die,
A time to plant, a time to reap,
A time to kill, a time to heal,
A time to laugh, a time to weep.

To everything,
Turn, turn, turn,
There is a season,
Turn, turn, turn,
And a time to every purpose under heaven.

A time to build up, a time to break down,
A time to get, a time to want,
A time to cast away stones, a time to gather stones together.

To everything,
Turn, turn, turn,
There is a season,
Turn, turn, turn,
And a time to every purpose under heaven.

A time of love, a time of hate,
A time of war, a time of peace,
A time you may embrace, a time to refrain from embracing.

To everything,
Turn, turn, turn,
There is a season,
Turn, turn, turn,
And a time to every purpose under heaven.

A time to gain, a time to lose,
A time to rend, a time to sew,
A time for love, a time for hate,
A time for peace, I swear it's not too late.

[1962]

EDWIN ARLINGTON ROBINSON*
[1869–1935]

Richard Cory

Whenever Richard Cory went down town,
We people on the pavement looked at him:
He was a gentleman from sole to crown,
Clean favored and imperially slim.

And he was always quietly arrayed,
And he was always human when he talked;
But still he fluttered pulses when he said,
"Good-morning," and he glittered when he walked.

And he was rich—yes, richer than a king—
And admirably schooled in every grace:
In fine, we thought that he was everything
To make us wish that we were in his place.

So on we worked, and waited for the light,
And went without the meat and cursed the bread;
And Richard Cory, one calm summer night,
Went home and put a bullet through his head.

[1897]

PAUL SIMON

[b. 1942]

Richard Cory

They say that Richard Cory owns one-half of this whole town,
With political connections to spread his wealth around.
Born into society, a banker's only child,
He had everything a man could want: power, grace and style.

But I work in his factory,
And I curse the life I'm living,
And I curse my poverty
And I wish that I could be
Richard Cory.

The papers print his picture almost everywhere he goes,
Richard Cory at the opera, Richard Cory at the show,
And the rumor of his parties, and the orgies on his yacht;
Oh, he surely must be happy with everything he's got.

But I work in his factory,
And I curse the life I'm living,
And I curse my poverty
And I wish that I could be
Richard Cory.

He freely gave to charity, he had the common touch,
And they were grateful for his patronage, and they thanked him very much.
So my mind is filled with wonder, when the evening headlines read:
"Richard Cory went home last night and put a bullet through his head."

But I work in his factory,
And I curse the life I'm living,
And I curse my poverty
And I wish that I could be
Richard Cory.

[1966]

JOHN NEWTON

[1725–1807]

Amazing Grace

Amazing grace (how sweet the sound)
That saved a wretch like me!
I once was lost, but now am found,
Was blind, but now I see.

'Twas grace that taught my heart to fear,
And grace my fears relieved;
How precious did that grace appear
The hour I first believed!

Through many dangers, toils, and snares
I have already come;
'Tis grace has brought me safe thus far,
And grace will lead me home.

The Lord has promised good to me,
His word my hope secures;
He will my shield and portion be
As long as life endures.

The earth shall soon dissolve like snow,
The sun forbear to shine;
But God, who call'd me here below,
Will be forever mine.

[1779]

DON MCLEAN
[b. 1945]

Vincent

Starry, starry night*
Paint your palette blue and gray.
Look out on a summer's day
With eyes that know the darkness in my soul.

Shadows on the hills
Sketch the trees and the daffodils,
Catch the breeze and the winterchills,
In colors on the snowy linen land.

Now I understand
What you tried to say to me,
How you suffered for your sanity,
And how you tried to set them free.

They would not listen.
They did not know how.
Perhaps they'll listen now.

Starry, starry night,
Flaming flowers that brightly blaze,
Swirling clouds in violet haze
Reflect in Vincent's eyes of china blue.

Colors changing hue
Morning fields of amber gray,
Weathered faces lined in pain
Are soothed beneath the artist's loving hand.

Now I understand
What you tried to say to me,
And how you suffered for your sanity
And how you tried to set them free.

They would not listen.
They did not know how.
Perhaps they'll listen now.

*See insert that begins after page 624 for a reproduction of *The Starry Night by Vincent van Gogh*.

For they could not love you,
But still your love was true.
And when no hope was left inside
On that starry, starry night,
You took your life as lovers often do.

But I could have told you, Vincent,
This world was never meant
For one as beautiful as you.

Starry, starry night
Portraits hung in empty halls,
Frameless heads on nameless walls,
With eyes that watch the world and can't forget.

Like the strangers that you've met
The ragged men in ragged clothes,
The silver thorn and bloody rose
Lie crushed and broken on the virgin snow.

Now I think I know
What you tried to say to me,
And how you suffered for your sanity
And how you tried to set them free.

They would not listen.
They're not listening still.
Perhaps they never will.

[1971]

See Chapter Fifteen for an explanation of poetry and painting.

Vincent van Gogh, *The Starry Night*. 1889. Oil on canvas, 29" × 36-1/4". The Museum of Modern Art, New York. Acquired through the Lillie P. Bliss Bequest. Digital Image © The Museum of Modern Art/Licensed by SCALA/Art Resource, NY.

ANNE SEXTON
[1928–1974]

The Starry Night

That does not keep me from having a terrible need of—shall I say the word—religion. Then I go out at night to paint the stars.

VINCENT VAN GOGH in a letter to his brother

The town does not exist
except where one black-haired tree slips
up like a drowned woman into the hot sky.
The town is silent. The night boils with eleven stars
Oh starry starry night! This is how
I want to die.

It moves. They are all alive.
Even the moon bulges in its orange irons
to push children, like a god, from its eye.
The old unseen serpent swallows up the stars.
Oh starry starry night! This is how
I want to die:

into that rushing beast of the night,
sucked up by that great dragon, to split
from my life with no flag,
no belly,
no cry.

(1962)

Francisco de Goya, *The Third of May,* 1808: *The Execution of the Defenders of Madrid.* 1814. PRADO MUSEUM, MADRID. SCALA/ART RESOURCE

DAVID GEWANTER

[b. 1954]

Goya's "The Third of May, 1808"

I'll show you:
onto the dirt-grey
canvas he's smeared—
jam on bread—
a sticky red for blood
oozed from the broken
heads and shot-up bodies
heaped near the cowering group
agape at soldiers hunched above
their knived rifles.
The air is oil-black,
smokeless, the whole scene
painted right before the guns
report, and more killed;
see the soldiers bend
in careful aim, bent
like mothers nursing—
one geometry of care:
exact angle for Madonna,
for men aiming murder—
and yet suspended,
the crisis held up for us
to observe at leisure—
in "The Resurrection" by
Grünewald, think how Christ
has bolted from his tomb,
rising, splendid,
while blinded soldiers
hurl themselves down,
never landing—
all are trapped in place:
one can't reach heaven,
the others never fall—
and here, before the dull wedge
representing *hill,*
one of Goya's victims
raises his arms up,
waiting always—
you know him, his shirt
blank as a page—
here, hand me a butterknife
to scrape with, I'll show you how
he painted bullets
inside the painted guns.

(1997)

Pieter Brueghel the Elder, *Landscape with the Fall of Icarus.* Ca. 1558. MUSÉES ROYAUX DES BEAUX-ARTS, BRUSSELS. SCALA/ART RESOURCE, NY.

W. H. AUDEN

[1907–1973]

Musée des Beaux Arts

About suffering they were never wrong,
The old Masters: how well they understood
Its human position: how it takes place
While someone else is eating or opening a window or just walking dully along;
How, when the aged are reverently, passionately waiting
For the miraculous birth, there always must be
Children who did not specially want it to happen, skating
On a pond at the edge of the wood:
They never forgot
That even the dreadful martyrdom must run its course
Anyhow in a corner, some untidy spot
Where the dogs go on with their doggy life and the torturer's horse
Scratches its innocent behind on a tree.

In Brueghel's *Icarus,* for instance: how everything turns away
Quite leisurely from the disaster; the ploughman may
Have heard the splash, the forsaken cry,
But for him it was not an important failure; the sun shone
As it had to on the white legs disappearing into the green
Water, and the expensive delicate ship that must have seen
Something amazing, a boy falling out of the sky,
Had somewhere to get to and sailed calmly on.

(1940)

WILLIAM CARLOS WILLIAMS

[1883–1963]

Landscape with the Fall of Icarus

According to Brueghel
when Icarus fell
it was spring

a farmer was ploughing
his field
the whole pageantry

of the year was
awake tingling
near

the edge of the sea
concerned
with itself

sweating in the sun
that melted
the wings' wax

unsignificantly
off the coast
there was

a splash quite unnoticed
this was
Icarus drowning

(1963)

William Blake, *The Sick Rose of Experience.* 1794. Library of Congress, Washington, D.C./The Bridgeman Art Library.

WILLIAM BLAKE

[1757–1827]

The Sick Rose

O Rose, thou art sick!
The invisible worm
That flies in the night,
In the howling storm,

Has found out thy bed
Of crimson joy,
And his dark secret love
Does thy life destroy.

(1794)

Henri Matisse, Dance (first version, Paris). March 1909. Oil on canvas, 8' 6-1/2" × 12' 9-1/2". The Museum of Modern Art, New York, NY. Gift of Nelson A. Rockefeller in honor of Alfred H. Barr, Jr. Digital Image © The Museum of Modern Art/Licensed by SCALA/Art Resource. © 2007 Succession H. Matisse, Paris/Artists Rights Society (ARS), New York.

NATALIE SAFIR

[b. 1935]

Matisse's Dance

A break in the circle dance of naked women,
dropped stitch between the hands
of the slender figure stretching too hard
to reach her joyful sisters.

Spirals of glee sail from the arms
of the tallest woman. She pulls the circle
around with her fire. What has she found
that she doesn't keep losing,
her torso a green-burning torch?

Grass mounds curve ripely beneath
two others who dance beyond the blue.
Breasts swell and multiply and
rhythms rise to a gallop.

Hurry, frightened one, and grab on—before
the stitch is forever lost, before the dance
unravels and a black sun swirls from that space.

(1990)

Jan Vermeer, *Young Woman with a Water Jug,* c. 1662. Oil on canvas, 18" × 16". The Metropolitan Museum of Art, Gift of Henry G. Marquand, 1889, The Marquand Collection/The Bridgeman Art Library.

STEPHEN MITCHELL

[b. 1943]

Vermeer

Quia respexit humilitatem ancillae suae.°

LUKE 1:48

She stands by the table, poised
at the center of your vision,
with her left hand
just barely on
the pitcher's handle, and her right
lightly touching the windowframe.
Serene as a clear sky, luminous
in her blue dress and many-toned
white cotton wimple, she is looking
nowhere. Upon her lips
is the subtlest and most lovely
of smiles, caught
for an instant
like a snowflake in a warm hand.
How weightless her body feels
as she stands, absorbed, within this
fulfillment that has brought more
than any harbinger could.
She looks down with an infinite
tenderness in her eyes,
as though the light at the window
were a newborn child
and her arms open enough
to hold it on her breast, forever.

Quia. . . *"He has regard for the humble state of his servant."*

Marcel Duchamp, *Nude Descending a Staircase,* No. 2, 1912. Oil on Canvas, 58" × 35". Philadelphia Museum of Art/The Bridgeman Art Library. © 2007 Artists Rights Society (ARS), New York/ADAGP, Paris/Succession Marcel Duchamp.

X. J. KENNEDY

[b. 1929]

Nude Descending a Staircase

Toe upon toe, a snowing flesh,
A gold of lemon, root and rind,
She sifts in sunlight down the stairs
With nothing on. Nor on her mind.

We spy beneath the banister
A constant thresh of thigh on thigh—
Her lips imprint the swinging air
That parts to let her parts go by.

One-woman waterfall, she wears
Her slow descent like a long cape
And pausing, on the final stair
Collects her motions into shape.

Rembrandt van Rijn, *The Return of the Prodigal Son.* 1668–9. oil on canvas, 265 × 205 cm. HERMITAGE, ST. PETERSBURG, RUSSIA. PHOTO SCALA/ART RESOURCE, NY.

ELIZABETH BISHOP

[1911–1979]

The Prodigal

The brown enormous odor he lived by
was too close, with its breathing and thick hair,
for him to judge. The floor was rotten; the sty
was plastered halfway up with glass-smooth dung.
Light-lashed, self-righteous, above moving snouts,
the pigs' eyes followed him, a cheerful stare—
even to the sow that always ate her young—
till, sickening, he leaned to scratch her head.
But sometimes mornings after drinking bouts
(he hid the pints behind a two-by-four),
the sunrise glazed the barnyard mud with red;
the burning puddles seemed to reassure.
And then he thought he almost might endure
his exile yet another year or more.

But evenings the first star came to warn.
The farmer whom he worked for came at dark
to shut the cows and horses in the barn
beneath their overhanging clouds of hay,
with pitchforks, faint forked lightnings, catching light,
safe and companionable as in the Ark.
The pigs stuck out their little feet and snored.
The lantern—like the sun, going away—
laid on the mud a pacing aureole.
Carrying a bucket along a slimy board,
he felt the bats' uncertain staggering flight,
his shuddering insights, beyond his control,
touching him. But it took him a long time
finally to make his mind up to go home. (1946)

Kitagawa Utamaro, *Girl Powdering Her Neck.* Musee des Arts Asiatiques-Guimet, Paris, France. Reunion des Musees Nationaux/Art Resource.

CATHY SONG

[b. 1955]

Girl Powdering Her Neck

FROM A UKIYO-E PRINT BY UTAMARO

The light is the inside
sheen of an oyster shell,
sponged with talc and vapor,
moisture from a bath.
A pair of slippers
are placed outside
the rice-paper doors.
She kneels at a low table
in the room,
her legs folded beneath her
as she sits on a buckwheat pillow.

Her hair is black
with hints of red,
the color of seaweed
spread over rocks.

Morning begins the ritual
wheel of the body,
the application of translucent skins.
She practices pleasure:
the pressure of three fingertips
applying powder.
Fingerprints of pollen
some other hand will trace.

The peach-dyed kimono
patterned with maple leaves
drifting across the silk,
falls from right to left
in a diagonal, revealing
the nape of her neck
and the curve of a shoulder
like the slope of a hill
set deep in snow in a country
of huge white solemn birds.
Her face appears in the mirror,
a reflection in a winter pond,
rising to meet itself.

She dips a corner of her sleeve
like a brush into water
to wipe the mirror;
she is about to paint herself.
The eyes narrow
in a moment of self-scrutiny.
The mouth parts
as if desiring to disturb
the placid plum face;
break the symmetry of silence.
But the berry-stained lips,
stenciled into the mask of beauty,
do not speak.

Two chrysanthemums
touch in the middle of the lake
and drift apart.

Romare Bearden, *At Five in the Afternoon,* 1946. Oil on board, 29-1/2" × 37-1/2". Collection Fred Jones Jr. Museum of Art, The University of Oklahoma, Norman; Purchase, U.S. State Department Collection, 1948. ©Romare Bearden Foundation/Licensed by VAGA, New York, NY.

FEDERICO GARCÍA LORCA

[1898–1936]

Lament for Ignacio Sánchez Mejías

2. The Spilled Blood

I will not see it!

Tell the moon to come
for I do not want to see the blood
of Ignacio on the sand.
I will not see it!

The moon wide open.
Horse of still clouds,
and the grey bull ring of dreams
with willows in the barreras.
I will not see it!
Let my memory kindle!
Warn the jasmines
of such minute whiteness!
I will not see it!

The cow of the ancient world
passed her sad tongue
over a snout of blood
spilled on the sand,
and the bulls of Guisando,
partly death and partly stone,
bellowed like two centuries

sated with treading the earth.
No.
I do not want to see it!
I will not see it!

Ignacio goes up the tiers
with all his death on his shoulders.
He sought for the dawn
but the dawn was no more.
He seeks for his confident profile
and the dream bewilders him.
He sought for his beautiful body
and encountered his opened blood.
Do not ask me to see it!

I do not want to hear it spurt
each time with less strength:
that spurt that illuminates
the tiers of seats, and spills
over the corduroy and the leather
of a thirsty multitude.
Who shouts that I should come near!
Do not ask me to see it!

His eyes did not close
when he saw the horns near,
but the terrible mothers
lifted their heads.
And across the ranches,
an air of secret voices rose,
shouting to celestial bulls,
herdsmen of pale mist.
There was no prince in Seville
who could compare with him,
nor sword like his sword
nor heart so true.
Like a river of lions
was his marvellous strength,
and like a marble torso
his firm drawn moderation.
The air of Andalusian Rome
gilded his head
where his smile was a spikenard
of wit and intelligence.
What a great torero in the ring!
What a good peasant in the sierra!
How gentle with the sheaves!
How hard with the spurs!
How tender with the dew!
How dazzling in the fiesta!
How tremendous with the final
banderillas of darkness!

But now he sleeps without end.
Now the moss and the grass
open with sure fingers
the flower of his skull.
And now his blood comes
out singing;
singing along marshes and meadows,
sliding on frozen horns,
faltering soulless in the mist,
stumbling over a thousand hoofs
like a long, dark, sad tongue,
to form a pool of agony
close to the starry Guadalquivir.
Oh, white wall of Spain!
Oh, black bull of sorrow!
Oh, hard blood of Ignacio!
Oh, nightingale of his veins!
No.
I will not see it!
No chalice can contain it,
no swallows can drink it,
no frost of light can cool it,
nor song nor deluge of white lilies,
no glass can cover it with silver.
No.
I will not see it!

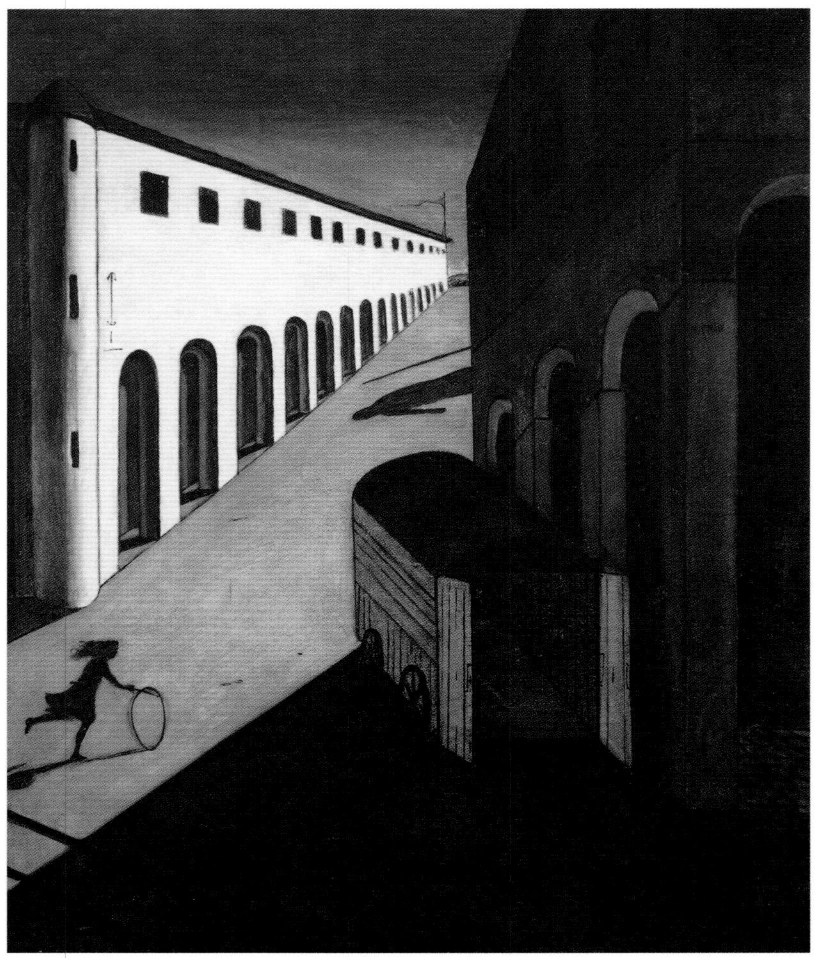

Giorgio de Chirico, *Melancholy and Mystery of a Street,* 1914. Private Collection/The Bridgeman Art Library. © 2007 Artists Rights Society (ARS), New York/SIAE, Rome.

ROY JACOBSTEIN

The Mystery and the Melancholy of the Street

Piano in Melanesian Pidgin is *big black box with teeth,*
you hit him, he cry. Must take forever to reach the end
of the sentence in Pago Pago. And why is Pago Pago
pronounced *Pango Pango,* like it rhymes with *tango?*
Where did that *n* go? If it's true the tango was invented
in Argentina over a century ago, why is their economy
such a mess today, and when will the Mothers
of the Plaza de Mayo get justice? All over the world

women are named for what blooms—*Daisy, Iris,*
Dahlia, Lily, Rose—but no man is named for a flower,
which explains a lot about human history. Lady Day
always wore a white gardenia in her hair, even though
she wasn't allowed up the elevator with white folk.
The *Infanta of Castille* may be the answer to the conundrum
of London's tube stop, *Elephant and Castle,* whose origin
otherwise—like ours—is an enigma, a vortex of mystery
that must perplex even the most jaded urban commuter.
I know it does me, these mornings when a humid breeze
bodes another scorcher in the City of Brotherly Love.
Wasn't Poor Richard lucky not to have been electrocuted,
flying his kites into those lightning storms, so later
he could have all his amorous escapades in Paris? A bad
bounce last night caromed me into the Emergency Room
with a busted clavicle. *No sweat, you'll be shooting hoops*
again in no time, the intern opined, pulling her figure-
of-eight brace taut against my chest. But who can hear
the word *hoops* without immediately seeing that little blond girl
rolling her hoop up the ochre umber burnt Sienna street
in the famous painting by Giorgio de Chirico that portends
the rise of fascism in Italy according to art historians
because the scene is a rigid geometry of arc and angle,
and her face is unseen, and though she seems carefree
in the Tuscan sun, she's rolling her big innocent hoop
into the looming shade. [2004]

Lun-Yi Tsai, *Disbelief,* 2002, OIL ON LINEN, 66 × 50 inches. Collection of the artist.

LUCILLE CLIFTON

[b. 1936]

tuesday 9/11/01

thunder and lightning and our world
is another place   no day
will ever be the same   no blood
untouched

they know this storm in otherwheres
israel   ireland   palestine
but God has blessed America
we sing

and God has blessed America
to learn that no one   is exempt
the world is one   all fear
is one   all life   all death
all one

CHAPTER FIFTEEN

Envisioning Poetry

POEMS AND PAINTINGS

In Roman times and again during the Renaissance, poems were characterized as speaking pictures and painting as silent poetry. A poem, that is, was seen as a visual image given speech, a painting as a silent visual poem. Earlier, in our discussion of structure, we noted that the shape of a poem, its arrangement on the page, is an important dimension of its effect.

Here, however, we will consider another dimension of the relationship between words and visual images. On the four-color insert following page 624 you will find poems paired with the paintings that inspired them. Breughal's "Landscape with the Fall of Icarus" is accompanied by more than one poem so you will have a chance to compare different interpretations and "translations" of a painting into a poem. As you consider each pair, spend some time looking carefully at the painting. Take an inventory of its details; observe its color and texture, its organization and perspective, its line, and its form. Think about the implications of its title; examine the action or scene it depicts. Then read the poem(s) as interpretation(s) and translation(s) of the painting. Notice what the poets include, what they omit, what they alter.

Even though you will be comparing poem with painting and poem with poem, remember that each poem is a separate and individual work. Read each the way you would read any other poem, giving careful attention to its formal elements. Consider whether the poems can stand alone without their corresponding paintings. And finally, observe how each poet has transformed the painting to create a new work, one which conveys its own feelings and bears its own implications.

QUESTIONS FOR CRITICAL THINKING AND WRITING

Vincent van Gogh, *The Starry Night*

1. Does Sexton's poem help you to see things in the painting that you had overlooked? Why or why not?
2. Does the poem seem to emphasize the painting or the painter more? Does it present a neutral description of the work? Does it imply or state a judgment about either the artist or his painting?

Francisco de Goya, *The Third of May, 1808*

1. Compare Gewanter's use of Goya with Sexton's use of Van Gogh. How does each poet convey the sense of the art he or she describes? How does each use that art for his or her own purpose?
2. Is Gewanter's poem comprehensible without the painting? Why or why not? How does the poem help you to see and understand Goya's art better?

Pieter Brueghel the Elder, *Landscape with the Fall of Icarus*

1. Where is Icarus mentioned in Auden's poem? What does Auden end with and what does that ending imply?
2. How does Auden's poem offer us a clue to its intentions from the beginning? Would it matter if Auden's stanzas were reversed? Why or why not?
3. "Musée des Beaux Arts" can be divided into two parts. What is their relationship?
4. How does the title of Auden's poem reflect its author's preoccupations with the painting?
5. Compare the form and idea of Auden's poem with the W. C. Williams poem on the same painting.

William Blake, *The Sick Rose*

1. How does Blake's art help you to understand his poem? How does it enable you to see something about the poem you may have overlooked, or to make connections you may have missed?
2. To what extent, if any, does Blake's illustration channel your reading of the poem, limiting the way you interpret it? Is it possible that the poem was written to illustrate the painting, or do you think the painting was designed to parallel the poem?

Henri Matisse, *Dance*

1. How would you characterize the mood and spirit of the painting? What elements contribute most to these?
2. What is the significance of the ring of dancers and of the space between two of them?

3. Describe the relationship between Matisse's painting and Natalie Safir's poem. To what extent do the two works share a common theme and tone?
4. Why do you think Matisse used large patches of bold simple colors against which to set his human figures? How detailed is his rendering of the human figures? What is the effect of that rendering?

Jan Vermeer, *Young Woman with a Water Jug*

1. What overall impression is conveyed by Vermeer's painting? What details does Vermeer' s light illuminate? With what effect?
2. What aspects of the painting does Stephen Mitchell emphasize in his poem?
3. What is the significance of the Latin epigraph that Mitchell includes—a verse from the gospel of Luke that translates roughly, "for he has looked upon the lowliness of his servant"?

Marcel Duchamp, *Nude Descending a Staircase*

1. How apt is the title Duchamp gave his painting? Why do you think he titled it as he did?
2. Someone once described this painting as "an explosion in a shingle factory." What aspect of the painting does that description capture?
3. To what extent does X. J. Kennedy's poem help you "see" the woman in the painting?
4. What aspects of Duchamp's painting does Kennedy highlight? With what effect?

Rembrandt van Rijn, *The Return of the Prodigal Son*

1. Bishop's poem describes the Prodigal son's experience away from his home. What aspects of his experience does she emphasize?
2. Read the story of the Prodigal Son on page 27. Then compare the details of the story with those in Bishop's poem and with the details in the painting by Rembrandt.
3. What aspect of the story does Rembrandt's painting emphasize? What idea does the painting convey?

Utamaro, *Girl Powdering Her Neck*

1. Look carefully at Utamaro's image of the girl. Describe what you see.
2. Now read Cathy Song's poem, and explain how the poem enriched your perception and understanding of the picture.

Romare Bearden, *At Five in the Afternoon*

1. Look closely at the descriptive details of Lorca's poem. What do they reveal about the bullfight?
2. What is the effect of Lorca's use of repetition?

3. Consider Romare Bearden's painting of a bullfight in conjunction with Lorca's poem. What connections can you identify between poem and painting?

Giorgio de Chirico. *The Melancholy and Mystery of a Street*

1. What significance, if any, do you ascribe to the difference in title between Jacobstein's poem and de Chirco's painting?
2. To what extent does the poem describe the painting? To what extent does it interpret the painting? Explain.

Lun-Yi Tsai, *Disbelief*

1. What is the dominant impression created by Tsai's painting? Is the title appropriate as indicating a response to the events of 9/11/01?
2. How would you describe the facial characteristics and the bodily postures of the figures depicted in *Disbelief*?
3. Like Tsai's painting, Lucille Clifton's poem, "tuesday 9/11/01," was written as a direct response to the events of 9/11. What aspects of the event does Clifton's speaker emphasize?
4. How does the pairing of Lucille Clifton's poem with Tsai's painting help you see better what the poet and the painter are saying and suggesting about the events of 9/11?

CHAPTER SIXTEEN

Three Poets in Context

READING EMILY DICKINSON, ROBERT FROST, AND LANGSTON HUGHES IN DEPTH

The primary context for reading any single poem is other poems by the same poet. Additional contexts include other poems by contemporary poets and by poets with similar thematic preoccupations or stylistic inclinations. Emily Dickinson's poems, for example, can be read in relation to those of her contemporary Walt Whitman. Dickinson's poems can also be read in relation to seventeenth-century metaphysical poetry, especially the poems of George Herbert and John Donne, with whom Dickinson shared religious interests and some stylistic traits.

Additional contexts for reading Dickinson's poetry include her letters and her life. To some extent at least, a poet's work reflects his or her life. Knowing at least the broad outlines of poets' lives can be helpful in gaining additional perspectives on their poetry.

The context of poets' lives is naturally extended by their culture and environment. Knowing something of nineteenth-century New England culture enhances a reader's understanding of Dickinson's poetry. Knowing something about the development of literary modernism and about Robert Frost's and Langston Hughes's relationship to that movement situates their poetry in the context of their time and delineates it sharply against that backdrop.

This having been said, however, it is the inner lives of these poets rather than their external lives that are of interest in their poems. Thus, primary emphasis in reading Dickinson, Frost, and Hughes should be on their artistry, on how they deploy language to create art, rather than on how their poems manifest aspects of their lives.

Still another context for reading Dickinson, Frost, and Hughes is provided by their comments on the art and craft of poetry. Dickinson discusses poetry in her letters, Frost in both letters and essays. Neither poet provides interpretations of the poems. Frost, in fact, often had fun with audiences who asked about the meanings of particular poems, frequently teasing them with irrelevant information (only occasionally accurate) about how his poems were composed. Nonetheless poets' comments on the art of poetry generally and on their particular poetic intentions can be helpful in approaching their work. Frost's interest in how a poem can convey the intonational qualities of the spoken voice is a case in point.

Dickinson, Frost, and Hughes have attracted a wide range of critical interpretation, providing still another context for their work. Samples of that criticism are included in this chapter.

QUESTIONS FOR IN-DEPTH READING

1. What general or overall thematic connections can you make between different works?
2. What stylistic similarities do you notice between and among different works?
3. How do the works differ in emphasis, tone, and style?
4. Once you have identified a writer's major preoccupations, place each work on a spectrum or a grid that represents the range of the writer's concerns.
5. What connections and disjunctions do you find among the following literary elements as they are embodied in different poems by the same writer?
   a. speaker and situation
   b. diction and imagery
   c. figures of speech
   d. symbolism and allegory
   e. syntax and structure
   f. sound and sense
   g. rhythm and meter
   h. theme and thought
6. To what extent are your responses to and perceptions of different works by the same writer shared by others—by critics, by classmates, and by the writers themselves?
7. What relationships and differences do you see between the work of one writer and that of another who shares similar thematic interests, stylistic proclivities, or cultural, religious, or social values?
8. Which of the critical perspectives (see Chapter Thirty-One) seem most useful as analytical tools for approaching the body of work of particular writers?

Amherst College Archives and Special Collections

EMILY DICKINSON IN CONTEXT

[1830–1886]

The Nineteenth-Century New England Literary Scene

The western regionalist and humorist writer Bret Harte remarked in the mid-nineteenth century that if you shot an arrow into the air in Cambridge, Massachusetts, when it came down, it would hit a writer. Around the middle of the century, Boston and its New England environs displaced Philadelphia as the center of literary and intellectual life in America. With Boston considered the Athens of America and New England as the center of the American Renaissance, the popular poets Henry Wadsworth Longfellow, James Russell Lowell, John Greenleaf Whittier, and Oliver Wendell Holmes, the Boston Brahmins, dominated New England literary culture.

Soon, however, they would be surpassed in importance if not in popularity by the Transcendentalist writers Ralph Waldo Emerson and Henry David Thoreau. Emerson wrote essays that declared America's intellectual independence from the influence of European literature. In his work he called for a new and independent spirit in American writing and eagerly awaited American writers of originality and independent thought. Thoreau's masterpiece *Walden* provided one model of literary independence and individualism, in a book that could not be readily classified, one that offered a famous challenge to readers to march to the tune of a different drummer rather than following along with the group. Herman Melville's *Moby Dick* and Nathaniel Hawthorne's *The Scarlet Letter* revealed another kind of departure from the literature being written in England. These American novels differed from their English counterparts in being less about society per se than about individuals seeking to find their way in a hostile and dangerous natural or cosmic environment. And the poetry of Walt Whitman and Emily Dickinson provided still other examples of originality and independence, with both poets breaking the formal rules of conventional poetic expectations.

Emily Dickinson's external life was remarkably circumscribed. Born in 1830 in Amherst, Massachusetts, and educated at Amherst Academy, she lived there her entire life, except for a brief stay at what was later to become Mount Holyoke College. She lived a life of seclusion, leaving Massachusetts only once and rarely leaving her father's house during the last fifteen years of her life. She died in the house where she was born.

If Dickinson's external life was unadventurous, her interior life was not. Her mind was anything but provincial. She read widely in English literature and thought deeply about what she read. She expressed a particular fondness for the poetry of John Keats and Robert Browning, the prose of John Ruskin and Sir Thomas Browne, and the novels of George Eliot and Charlotte and Emily Brontë. And although she disclaimed knowledge of Whitman's work, she treasured a book that significantly influenced both Whitman's poetry and her own: the King James translation of the Bible. She especially liked the Book of Revelation.

Photo of the Dickinson Homestead

Dickinson and Modern Poetry

Dickinson is often bracketed with Whitman as a cofounder of modern American poetry. Each brought to poetry something new, fresh, and strikingly original. But their poems, however prototypically modern, could not be more different. A mere glance at the page reveals a significant visual difference. Whitman's poems are large and expansive. The lines are long and the poems are typically ample and open. Dickinson's poems, by contrast, are highly compressed. They squeeze moments of intensely felt life and thought into tight four-line stanzas that compress feeling and condense thought.

The openness of Whitman's form is paralleled by the openness of his stance, his public outgoing manner. Dickinson's poetry is much more private, tending toward inwardness. Hers is a more meditative poetry than Whitman's, a poetry rooted partly in the metaphysical poetry of such seventeenth-century writers as John Donne and George Herbert. More directly influential on Dickinson's poetry than the metaphysical poets, however, was the tradition of Protestant hymnology. Her poems frequently employ the meter of hymns and follow their typical stanzaic pattern. Here, for example, is the opening verse of the hymn "Our God, Our Help in Ages Past," its accented syllables marked with é.

Oŭr Gód, oŭr hélp iň ágeš pást,
Oŭr hópe fŏr yeárs tŏ cóme,
Oŭr shélteř fróm thĕ stórmy̆ blást,
Aňd oúr eťérnăl hóme.

The hymn's meter and formal structure are highly regular. The first and third lines are in iambic tetrameter, the second and fourth in iambic trimeter. The lack of metrical variation results in a steady, predictable rhythm, essential for singing. Dickinson varies this standard pattern to suit her poetic purpose. Consider, for example, "I felt a Funeral, in my Brain," "I like a look of Agony," "I died for Beauty—but was scarce," and "I heard a Fly buzz—when I died."

Dickinson and Christianity

Dickinson's adaptation of hymn meter accords with her adaptation of the traditional religious doctrines of orthodox Christianity. For although her poems reflect a Calvinist heritage—particularly in their probing self-analysis—she was not an orthodox Christian. Her religious ideas, like her life and poetry, were distinctive and individual. And even when her views tend toward orthodox teaching, as in her attitude toward immortality, her literary expression of such a belief is strikingly original. In addition, Dickinson's mischievous wit contrasts sharply with the brooding solemnity characteristic of much Calvinist-inspired religious writing. Finally, her love for nature separates her from her Puritan precursors, allying her instead with such transcendentalist contemporaries as Emerson, Whitman, and Thoreau, though her vision of life is starker than theirs.

Dickinson's Style

Dickinson's poetry requires repeated and careful readings. Her diction is frequently surprising. Her elliptical syntax occasionally departs from normal patterns. Readers must consequently fill in the gaps her language creates. Her taut lines need to be loosened; her tight poems need to be opened up. Words, phrases, lines beg for the expansion of interpretive paraphrase.

We also have to extend our notion of what constitutes acceptable poetic technique—something her contemporaries found nearly impossible. Dickinson was criticized for using inexact rhymes, rough rhythms, and colloquial diction, and for taking liberties with grammar. Her odd punctuation—heavy on dashes—and her peculiar use of capitalization were also unappreciated. But Dickinson exploited these and other poetic resources to convey complex states of mind and feeling. She employed these and other poetic idiosyncrasies not for their own sake, but for emotional and psychological impact.

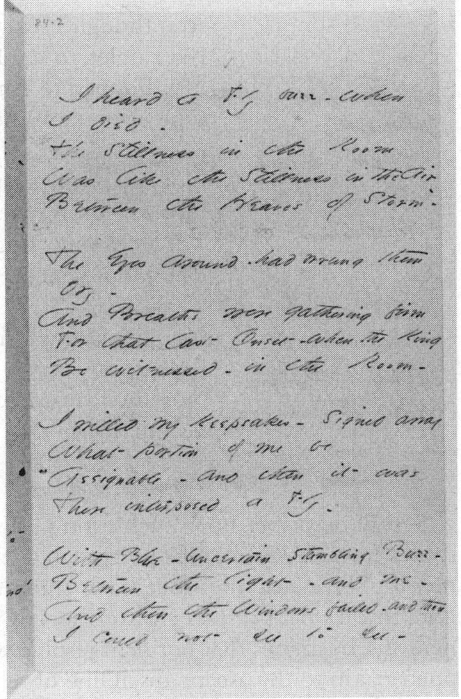

I heard a Fly buzz - when
I died -
The Stillness in the Room
Was like the Stillness in the Air
Between the Heaves of Storm -

The Eyes around - had wrung them
dry -
And Breaths were gathering firm
For that last Onset - when the King
Be witnessed - in the Room -

I willed my Keepsakes - Signed away
What portion of me be
Assignable - and then it was
There interposed a Fly -

With Blue - uncertain stumbling Buzz -
Between the light - and me -
And then the Windows failed - and then
I could not see to see -

Manuscript copy of "I heard a fly buzz—when I died"
Amherst College Archives and Special Collections

In his extensive biography of Dickinson, Richard B. Sewall describes her resolve to portray the state of her mind and being in all their unorthodox complexity. He also describes Dickinson's early and futile hopes for publication and appreciation as well as her resignation to what she termed her "barefoot rank: of anonymity." Sewall also reveals her determination to pursue truth and to make poems her way. When Thomas Wentworth Higginson, an influential contemporary critic, advised her to write a more polite poetry, less indirect and metaphoric, smoother in rhythm and rhyme, simpler in thought, and less colloquial in idiom, she replied with a poem. Her answer is that although she could have written otherwise, she chose to write as she did.

I cannot dance upon my Toes

I cannot dance upon my Toes—
No Man instructed me—
But oftentimes, among my mind,
A Glee possesseth me,

That had I Ballet knowledge—
Would put itself abroad
In Pirouette to blanch a Troupe—
Or lay a Prima, mad,

And though I had no Gown of Gauze—
No ringlet, to my Hair,
Nor hopped to Audiences—like Birds,
One claw upon the Air,

Nor tossed my shape in Eider Balls,
Nor rolled on wheels of snow
Till I was out of sight, in sound,
The House encore me so—

Nor any know I know the Art
I mention—easy—Here—
Nor any Placard boast me—
It's full as Opera

(#326)

Sewall describes how Dickinson's poems reflect her poetic vocation. He demonstrates how basic religious texts such as the Bible and Thomas à Kempis's *The Imitation of Christ* sustained her both spiritually and poetically. Though allowing that Dickinson's decision to cloister herself in her chamber could have had its roots in neurosis, he argues that her firm resolve was motivated by a commitment to the art of poetry akin to the ascetic discipline of religious devotion. In fact, he suggests that one of her more famous poems—one usually interpreted as a love poem—can be read as a dedication to the spiritual or poetic life. It can also be read as a celebration of individual choice.

The Soul selects her own Society

The Soul selects her own Society—
Then—shuts the Door—
To her divine Majority—
Present no more—

Unmoved—she notes the Chariots—pausing—
At her low Gate—
Unmoved—an Emperor be kneeling
Upon her Mat—

I've known her—from an ample nation—
Choose One—
Then—close the Valves of her attention—
Like Stone—

(#303)

Sewall's central point about the relationship between Dickinson's life and art is that although we may not be certain which interpretation to favor when considering this and many other poems, we can remain satisfied with our uncertainty because such

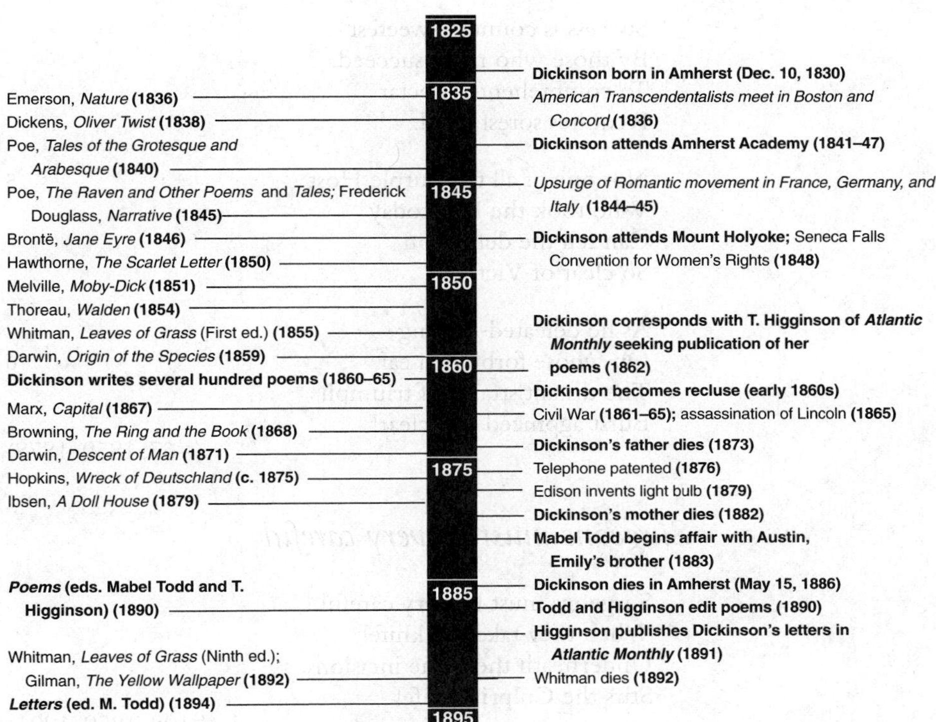

ambiguity is central to her art. She writes metaphorically, concealing as much as she reveals. As readers we share in the experience she describes—in the preceding poem, the experience of making a decisive choice involving commitment and renunciation. In doing so, however, we also supply specific details from our own lives to render the decision specific and significant. Dickinson's poetry, in other words, conveys the essence of an experience. Her poems, as Sewall aptly notes, do not tell us so much how to live as what it feels like to be alive.

Dickinson's poems do not encompass a wide range of experience; instead they probe deeply into a few of life's major experiences—love, death, doubt, and faith. In examining her experience, Dickinson makes a scrupulous effort to tell the truth, but she tells it "slant." Part of her originality and artistry includes the way she invites us to share in her search for truth. The qualified assertions we frequently find in her poems, their riddles and uncertainties, and their questioning stance demand our participation and response. In learning to share Dickinson's acute perceptions and feelings, we also come to understand our own.

EMILY DICKINSON: POEMS

EMILY DICKINSON

[1830–1886]

Success is counted sweetest

Success is counted sweetest
By those who ne'er succeed.
To comprehend a nectar
Requires sorest need.

Not one of all the purple Host
Who took the Flag today
Can tell the definition
So clear of Victory

As he defeated—dying—
On whose forbidden ear
The distant strains of triumph
Burst agonized and clear!

(#67, 1859, 1878)

Surgeons must be very careful

Surgeons must be very careful
When they take the knife!
Underneath their fine incisions
Stirs the Culprit—Life!

(#108, 1859, 1891)

These are the days when Birds come back—

These are the days when Birds come back—
A very few—a Bird or two—
To take a backward look.

These are the days when skies resume
The old—old sophistries of June—
A blue and gold mistake.

Oh fraud that cannot cheat the Bee—
Almost thy plausibility
Induces my belief.

Till ranks of seeds their witness bear—
And softly thro' the altered air
Hurries a timid leaf.

Oh Sacrament of summer days,
Oh Last Communion in the Haze—
Permit a child to join.

The sacred emblems to partake—
Thy consecrated bread to take
And thine immortal wine!

(#130, c. 1859)

Water, is taught by thirst

Water, is taught by thirst.
Land—by the Oceans passed.
Transport—by throe—
Peace—by its battles told—
Love by Memorial Mold—
Birds by the Snow.

(#135, c. 1859)

"Faith" is a fine invention

"Faith" is a fine invention
When Gentlemen can *see*—
But *Microscopes* are prudent
In an Emergency.

(#185, 1860, 1891)

QUESTIONS FOR CRITICAL THINKING AND WRITING

Experience

1. In reading poems 108 and 185, to what extent did you get Dickinson's humor? If you did not, how do you experience a reading of these two very brief poems?
2. Account for your experience of reading poems 130 and 135.

Interpretation

3. What is Dickinson's point in poem 108?
4. What does she suggest about religious faith in poem 185? And what does she mean by referring to faith as an "invention"? In that poem?
5. What is the relationship between faith and microscopes?
6. Of what significance are the religious allusions in poem 130?
7. What is "taught" and "learned" in poem 135?

Evaluation

8. What religious values are at issue in poem 185?
9. What values are at stake in poem 108?

Connection

10. What connections can you make between poem 108 and poem 185?

Critical Thinking

11. What other word choice possibilities might Dickinson have made for "careful" in poem 108 and for "prudent" in poem 185? For "timid" in poem 130 and for "throe" in poem 135?

I'm "wife"—I've finished that

I'm "wife"—I've finished that
That other state—
I'm Czar—I'm "Woman" now—
It's safer so—

How odd the Girl's life looks
Behind this soft Eclipse—
I think that Earth feels so
To folks in Heaven—now—

This being comfort—then
That other kind—was pain—

But why compare?
I'm "Wife"! Stop there!

(#199, 1860, 1890)

QUESTIONS FOR CRITICAL THINKING AND WRITING

Experience

1. On the basis of your experience of marriage either as one who is married or as one who has observed the marriages of others, how do you respond to Dickinson's portrayal of the position of a wife in poem 199?

Interpretation

2. After reading through poem 199, explain what Dickinson means by "That other state."
3. Why is it safer to be "Woman"? And what does the speaker suggest by calling herself a "Czar"?
4. Explain the analogy in stanza two.
5. Explain the contrast in the first two lines of stanza three.

Evaluation

6. What value is placed upon being a "wife" in poem 199?

Connection

7. Compare Dickinson's poem about a "wife" with May Swenson's "Women."

Critical Thinking

8. How might a feminist reading of this poem differ from a formalist one? See Chapter Thirty-One.

I taste a liquor never brewed

I taste a liquor never brewed—
From Tankards scooped in Pearl—
Not all the Vats upon the Rhine
Yield such an Alcohol!

Inebriate of Air—am I—
And Debauchee of Dew—

Reeling—thro endless summer days—
From inns of Molten Blue—

When "Landlords" turn the drunken Bee
Out of the Foxglove's door—
When Butterflies—renounce their "drams"—
I shall but drink the more!

Till Seraphs swing their snowy Hats—
And Saints—to windows run—
To see the little Tippler
Leaning against the—Sun—

(#214, 1860, 1861)

I like a look of Agony

I like a look of Agony,
Because I know it's true—
Men do not sham Convulsion,
Nor simulate, a Throe—

The Eyes glaze once—and that is Death—
Impossible to feign
The Beads upon the Forehead
By homely Anguish strung.

(#241, 1861, 1890)

Wild Nights—Wild Nights!

Wild Nights—Wild Nights!
Were I with thee
Wild Nights should be
Our luxury!

Futile—the Winds—
To a Heart in port—
Done with the Compass—
Done with the Chart!

Rowing in Eden—
Ah, the Sea!
Might I but moor—Tonight—
In Thee!

(#249, 1861, 1891)

QUESTIONS FOR CRITICAL THINKING AND WRITING

Experience

1. How do you respond to the situation in "I like a look of Agony"? How do you respond to the imagined events of "Wild Nights"?
2. Which poem did you find more difficult to comprehend? Why?

Interpretation

3. Who is the speaker and what is the situation in "Wild Nights" (Poem 249)? Who is the speaker addressing? What does the speaker long for?
4. Why does the speaker of the agony poem "like a look of Agony" (Poem 214)?
5. Why is it "impossible to feign / The Beads upon the Forehead?"

Evaluation

6. What is most valued in each poem? Why?

Connection

7. Compare either of these poems to any other poem by Dickinson. Explain the basis of your comparison.

Critical Thinking

8. Do you agree that men do not (and are not able) to fake convulsions or the throes of agonized pain? Explain.

I can wade Grief

I can wade Grief—
Whole Pools of it—
I'm used to that—
But the least push of Joy
Breaks up my feet—
And I tip—drunken—
Let no Pebble—smile—
'Twas the New Liquor—
That was all!

Power is only Pain—
Stranded, thro' Discipline,
Till Weights—will hang—
Give Balm—to Giants—

And they'll wilt, like Men—
Give Himmaleh—
They'll Carry—Him!

(#252, 1861, 1891)

There's a certain Slant of light

There's a certain Slant of light
Winter Afternoons—
That oppresses, like the Heft
Of Cathedral Tunes—

Heavenly Hurt, it gives us—
We can find no scar,
But internal difference,
Where the Meanings, are—

None may teach it—Any—
'Tis the Sea Despair—
An imperial affliction
Sent us of the Air—

When it comes, the Landscape listens—
Shadows—hold their breath—
When it goes, 'tis like the Distance
On the look of Death—

(#258, 1861, 1890)

I felt a Funeral, in my Brain

I felt a Funeral, in my Brain,
And Mourners to and fro
Kept treading—treading—till it seemed
That Sense was breaking through—

And when they all were seated,
A Service, like a Drum—
Kept beating—beating—till I thought
My Mind was going numb—

And I heard them lift a Box
And creak across my Soul
With those same Boots of Lead, again,
Then Space—began to toll,

As all the Heavens were a Bell,
And Being, but an Ear,
And I, and Silence, some strange Race
Wrecked, solitary, here—

And then a Plank in Reason, broke,
And I dropped down, and down—
And hit a World, at every plunge,
And Finished knowing—then—

(#280, 1861, 1896)

I'm Nobody! Who are you?

I'm Nobody! Who are you?
Are you—Nobody—too?
Then there's a pair of us!
Don't tell they'd banish us—you know!

How dreary—to be—Somebody!
How public—like a Frog—
To tell your name—the livelong June—
To an admiring Bog!

(#288, ca. 1861)

Some keep the Sabbath going to Church

Some keep the Sabbath going to Church—
I keep it, staying at Home—
With a Bobolink for a Chorister—
And an Orchard, for a Dome—

Some keep the Sabbath in Surplice—
I just wear my Wings—
And instead of tolling the Bell, for Church,
Our little Sexton—sings.

God preaches, a noted Clergyman—
And the sermon is never long,
So instead of getting to Heaven, at last—
I'm going, all along.

(#324, 1862, 1891)

A Bird came down the Walk

A Bird came down the Walk—
He did not know I saw—
He bit an Angleworm in halves
And ate the fellow, raw,

And then he drank a Dew
From a convenient Grass—
And then hopped sidewise to the Wall
To let a Beetle pass—

He glanced with rapid eyes
That hurried all around—
They looked like frightened Beads, I thought—
He stirred his Velvet Head

Like one in danger, Cautious,
I offered him a Crumb
And he unrolled his feathers
And rowed him softer home—

Than Oars divide the Ocean,
Too silver for a seam—
Or Butterflies, off Banks of Noon
Leap, plashless as they swim.

(#328, 1862, 1891)

QUESTIONS FOR CRITICAL THINKING AND WRITING

Experience

1. To what extent did you appreciate and enjoy the humor of poems 288, 324, and 328? Which poem do you like best? Why? Which is most accessible for you?

Interpretation

2. What point does the speaker of "I'm Nobody! Who are you?" make about fame? Do you agree with the speaker's attitude toward fame? Why or why not?
3. What contrast does the speaker establish in how the Sabbath is "kept" in "Some keep the Sabbath going to Church"?
4. What is the speaker's attitude toward the bird in "A Bird came down the Walk"? What words best convey that attitude?

Evaluation

5. What does the speaker value about the bird?

6. How is religion valued in "Some keep the Sabbath going to Church"?
7. Why is the speaker critical of fame in "I'm Nobody! Who are you"?

Connection

8. Compare any of these three poems with another poem of Dickinson's that exhibits wit and humor. Explain the wit and/or humor in each poem.

Critical Thinking

9. To what extent do you think poems that use humor can be considered serious poems—or can be taken seriously? Explain.

After great pain, a formal feeling comes

After great pain, a formal feeling comes—
The Nerves sit ceremonious, like Tombs—
The stiff Heart questions was it He, that bore,
And Yesterday, or Centuries before?

The Feet, mechanical, go round—
Of Ground, or Air, or Ought—
A Wooden way
Regardless grown,
A Quartz contentment, like a stone—

This is the Hour of Lead—
Remembered, if outlived,
As Freezing persons, recollect the Snow—
First—Chill—then Stupor—then the letting go—

(#341, 1862, 1929)

QUESTIONS FOR CRITICAL THINKING AND WRITING

Experience

1. Of poems 258 and 341, which comes closest to capturing something about despair that you have experienced or observed in the experience of others? Why?

Interpretation

2. Choose either poem 258 or 341 and do a stanza-by-stanza analysis. Try to provide a line-by-line paraphrase of each stanza, but even if you have trouble with certain lines, provide an overall sense of what each stanza is saying or suggesting.
3. Discuss briefly what your chosen poem says about despair.

Evaluation

4. What value does your chosen poem place upon suffering? What, if any, are the benefits of suffering?

Connection

5. Is there any connection between poems 258 and 341 other than their common theme of despair? Explain.

Critical Thinking

6. For poem 341 identify three possible situations that might result in "great pain."

I dreaded that first Robin, so

I dreaded that first Robin, so,
But He is mastered, now,
I'm some accustomed to Him grown,
He hurts a little, though—

I thought if I could only live
Till that first Shout got by—
Not all Pianos in the Woods
Had power to mangle me—

I dared not meet the Daffodils—
For fear their Yellow Gown
Would pierce me with a fashion
So foreign to my own—

I wished the Grass would hurry—
So—when 'twas time to see—
He'd be too tall, the tallest one
Could stretch—to look at me—

I could not bear the Bees should come,
I wished they'd stay away
In those dim countries where they go,
What word had they, for me?

They're here, though; not a creature failed—
No Blossom stayed away
In gentle deference to me—
The Queen of Calvary—

Each one salutes me, as he goes,
And I, my childish Plumes,
Lift, in bereaved acknowledgment
Of their unthinking Drums—

(#348, 1862, 1891)

We grow accustomed to the Dark

We grow accustomed to the Dark—
When Light is put away—
As when the Neighbor holds the Lamp
To witness her Goodbye—

A Moment—We uncertain step
For newness of the night—
Then—fit our Vision to the Dark—
And meet the Road—erect—

And so of larger—Darknesses—
Those Evenings of the Brain—
When not a Moon disclose a sign—
Or Star—come out—within—

The Bravest—grope a little—
And sometimes hit a Tree
Directly in the Forehead—
But as they learn to see—

Either the Darkness alters—
Or something in the sight
Adjusts itself to Midnight—
And Life steps almost straight.

(#419, 1862, 1935)

Much Madness is divinest Sense

Much Madness is divinest Sense—
To a discerning Eye—
Much Sense—the starkest Madness—
'Tis the Majority
In this, as All, prevail—
Assent—and you are sane—
Demur—you're straightway dangerous—
And handled with a Chain—

(#435, 1862, 1935)

This was a Poet—It is That

This was a Poet—It is That
Distills amazing sense
From ordinary Meanings—
And Attar so immense

From the familiar species
That perished by the Door—
We wonder it was not Ourselves
Arrested it—before—

Of Pictures, the Discloser—
The Poet—it is He—
Entitles Us—by Contrast—
To ceaseless Poverty—

Of Portion—so unconscious—
The Robbing—could not harm—
Himself—to Him—a Fortune—
Exterior—to Time—

(#448, 1862, 1929)

I died for Beauty—but was scarce

I died for Beauty—but was scarce
Adjusted in the Tomb
When One who died for Truth, was lain
In an adjoining Room—

He questioned softly "Why I failed?"
"For Beauty," I replied—
"And I—for Truth—Themself are One—
We Brethren, are," He said—

And so, as Kinsmen, met a Night—
We talked between the Rooms—
Until the Moss had reached our lips—
And covered up—our names—

(#449, 1862, 1890)

I heard a Fly buzz—when I died

I heard a Fly buzz—when I died—
The Stillness in the Room
Was like the Stillness in the Air—
Between the Heaves of Storm—

The Eyes around—had wrung them dry—
And Breaths were gathering firm
For that last Onset—when the King
Be witnessed—in the Room—

I willed my Keepsakes—Signed away
What portion of me be
Assignable—and then it was
There interposed a Fly—

With Blue—uncertain stumbling Buzz—
Between the light—and me—
And then the Windows failed—and then
I could not see to see—

(#465, 1862, 1896)

This World is not Conclusion

This World is not Conclusion.
A Species stands beyond—
Invisible, as Music—
But positive, as Sound—
It beckons, and it baffles—
Philosophy—don't know—
And through a Riddle, at the last—
Sagacity, must go—
To guess it, puzzles scholars—
To gain it, Men have borne
Contempt of Generations
And Crucifixion, shown—
Faith slips—and laughs, and rallies—
Blushes, if any see—
Plucks at a twig of Evidence—
And asks a Vane, the way—
Much Gesture, from the Pulpit—
Strong Hallelujahs roll—
Narcotics cannot still the Tooth
That nibbles at the soul—

(#501, 1862, 1896)

I'm ceded—I've stopped being Theirs

I'm ceded—I've stopped being Theirs—
The name They dropped upon my face
With water, in the country church
Is finished using, now,

And They can put it with my Dolls,
My childhood, and the string of spools,
I've finished threading—too—

Baptized, before, without the choice,
But this time, consciously, of Grace—
Unto supremest name—
Called to my Full—The Crescent dropped—
Existence's whole Arc, filled up,
With one small Diadem.

My second Rank—too small the first—
Crowned—Crowing—on my Father's breast—
A half unconscious Queen—
But this time—Adequate—Erect,
With Will to choose, or to reject,
And I choose, just a Crown—

(#508, 1862, 1890)

I reckon—when I count at all

I reckon—when I count at all—
First—Poets—Then the Sun—
Then Summer—Then the Heaven of God—
And then—the List is done—

But, looking back—the First so seems
To Comprehend the Whole—
The Others look a needless Show—
So I write—Poets—All—

Their Summer—lasts a Solid Year—
They can afford a Sun
The East—would deem extravagant—
And if the Further Heaven—

Be Beautiful as they prepare
For Those who worship Them—
It is too difficult a Grace—
To justify the Dream—

(#569, 1862, 1929)

I like to see it lap the Miles

I like to see it lap the Miles—
And lick the Valleys up—
And stop to feed itself at Tanks—
And then—prodigious step

Around a Pile of Mountains—
And supercilious peer
In Shanties—by the sides of Roads—
And then a Quarry pare

To fit its Ribs
And crawl between
Complaining all the while
In horrid—hooting stanza—
Then chase itself down Hill—

And neigh like Boanerges—
Then—punctual as a Star
Stop—docile and omnipotent
At its own stable door—

(#585, 1862, 1891)

There is a pain—so utter

There is a pain—so utter—
It swallows substance up—
Then covers the Abyss with Trance—
So Memory can step
Around—across—upon it—
As one within a Swoon—
Goes safely—where an open eye—
Would drop Him—Bone by Bone.

(#599, 1862, 1929)

The Brain—is wider than the sky

The Brain—is wider than the Sky—
For—put them side by side—
The one the other will contain
With ease—and You—beside—

The Brain is deeper than the sea—
For—hold them—Blue to Blue—
The one the other will absorb—
As Sponges—Buckets—do—

The Brain is just the weight of God—
For—Heft them—Pound for Pound—
And they will differ—if they do—
As Syllable from Sound—

(#632, 1862, 1896)

QUESTIONS FOR CRITICAL THINKING AND WRITING

Experience

1. Choose one of Dickinson's poems about religion and spirituality (poem 324, 365, 508, 512, 632) and comment on how the poem relates to your own experience.

Interpretation

2. Explain the role of each stanza in the poem. What does the stanza contribute to the poem as a whole?
3. Explain Dickinson's use of imagery and/or figurative language in the poem. How does the poem's imagery and/or figurative language help convey its meaning?
4. Analyze the sound effects of the poem, and explain what sound contributes to the poem's sense or meaning.

Evaluation

5. How do the poem's elements convey its attitude toward and perspective on spirituality and religion?

Connection

6. Consider two or more of Dickinson's poems on religion and spirituality and comment on Dickinson's attitude toward religion as expressed in the poems.

Critical Thinking

7. Based on your reading of Dickinson's religious, group of poems, how would you characterize Dickinson's attitude toward religion and the spiritual?

Pain—has an Element of Blank

Pain—has an Element of Blank—
It cannot recollect
When it begun—or if there were
A time when it was not—

It has no Future—but itself—
Its Infinite contain
Its Past—enlightened to perceive
New Periods—of Pain.

(#650, 1862, 1890)

QUESTIONS FOR CRITICAL THINKING AND WRITING

Experience

1. Choose one of Dickinson's poems about pain (poems 252, 536, 599, 650) and comment on how your experience relates to what Dickinson describes. Provide examples wherever you can.

Interpretation

2. Explain the structure of the poem you chose to analyze.
3. What are its key images?
4. Which key words resonate most? How?

Evaluation

5. What attitude toward pain is expressed or indicated by the speaker? How do you know?

Connection

6. Compare your chosen poem with one of the other poems about pain. Identify one significant basis for your comparison and explain similarities and differences that you notice.

Critical Thinking

7. In poem 536 why would dying be considered a "privilege"? Taking the five poems about pain together, what does Dickinson suggest about pain and suffering?

I dwell in Possibility

I dwell in Possibility—
A fairer House than Prose—
More numerous of Windows—
Superior—for Doors—

Of Chambers as the Cedars—
Impregnable of Eye—
And for an Everlasting Roof
The Gambrels of the Sky—

Of Visitors—the fairest—
For Occupation—This—

The spreading wide my narrow Hands
To gather Paradise— (#657, 1862, 1929)

QUESTIONS FOR CRITICAL THINKING AND WRITING

Experience

1. Choose one of Dickinson's poems about poetry—poems 448, 569, 657—for your consideration.
2. Comment on what it is like for you to read the poem—the impressions it suggests to you, along with any difficulties it may pose.

Interpretation

3. How do you understand the poem? Explain the poem's central idea.
4. How do the poem's diction and imagery help convey its meaning?

Evaluation

5. What values seem central to the poem? What perspective on the nature and importance of poetry does the poem assume?

Connection

6. Look for a connection between one of the poems about poetry and one of the poems about love—poems 249, 480, 1732.

Critical Thinking

8. Taken together, what attitudes toward poetry does this cluster of poems suggest?

"Nature" is what we see

"Nature" is what we see—
The Hill—the Afternoon—
Squirrel—Eclipse—the Bumble bee—
Nay—Nature is Heaven—
Nature is what we hear—
The Bobolink—the Sea—
Thunder—the Cricket—
Nay—Nature is Harmony—
Nature is what we know—
Yet have no art to say—
So impotent Our Wisdom is
To her Simplicity.

(#668, 1863, 1914)

My Life had stood—a Loaded Gun

My Life had stood—a Loaded Gun—
In Corners—till a Day
The Owner passed—identified—
And carried Me away—

And now We roam in Sovereign Woods—
And now We hunt the Doe—
And every time I speak for Him—
The Mountains straight reply—

And do I smile, such cordial light
Upon the Valley glow—
It is as a Vesuvian face
Had let its pleasure through—

And when at Night—Our good Day done—
I guard My Master's Head—
'Tis better than the Eider-Duck's
Deep Pillow—to have shared—

To foe of His—I'm deadly foe—
None stir the second time—
On whom I lay a Yellow Eye—
Or an emphatic Thumb—

Though I than He—may longer live
He longer must—than I—
For I have but the power to kill,
Without—the power to die—

(#754, 1863, 1929)

A narrow Fellow in the Grass

A narrow Fellow in the Grass
Occasionally rides—
You may have met Him—did you not
His notice sudden is—

The Grass divides as with a Comb—
A spotted shaft is seen—
And then it closes at your feet
And opens further on—

He likes a Boggy Acre
A floor too cool for Corn—

Yet when a Boy, and Barefoot—
I more than once at Noon
Have passed, I thought, a Whip lash
Unbraiding in the Sun
When stooping to secure it
It wrinkled, and was gone—

Several of Nature's People
I know, and they know me—
I feel for them a transport
Of cordiality—

But never met this Fellow
Attended, or alone
Without a tighter breathing
And Zero at the Bone— (#986, 1865, 1866)

QUESTIONS FOR CRITICAL THINKING AND WRITING

Experience

1. Choose one of Dickinson's poems about nature (poems 214, 328, 348, 668, 986) and comment on how your experience relates to what she describes. Provide an example from your life.

Interpretation

2. Explain how your chosen poem is organized or structured. Is it set up as a sequence of some sort, such as a narrative sequence? Is it structured as a contrast? Does it involve a set of comparisons? Or what?

Evaluation

3. What kind of value is placed upon nature in your chosen poem? What key words or images in the poem suggest this value?

Connection

4. Compare your chosen poem with one of the others in the group on whatever basis you think important or interesting. Explain the connections between the two poems.

Critical Thinking

5. How would poem 986 be different if in the last two stanzas Dickinson substituted "Creatures" for "People" and "Animal" for "Fellow?" Why do you think Dickinson chose words referring to humans in those instances even though she is writing about a snake?

The Bustle in a House

The Bustle in a House
The Morning after Death
Is solemnest of industries
Enacted upon Earth—

The Sweeping up the Heart
And putting Love away
We shall not want to use again
Until Eternity. (#1078, 1866, 1890)

QUESTIONS FOR CRITICAL THINKING AND WRITING

Experience

1. Select one of Dickinson's poems about death (poems 280, 419, 449, 465, 501, 1078). Consider the extent to which it confirms what you have seen or heard about death from your reading, your observation, or your experience.

Interpretation

2. Provide an overall interpretation of what you think the poem is saying about death.
3. How does the poem come to mean what it does? Analyze its diction, imagery, and structure to show how these poetic elements embody the poem's meaning.

Evaluation

4. What attitude toward death and dying does the poem express? Where and how is this attitude conveyed most emphatically?

Connection

5. Compare your chosen poem with one of the others in this group. Decide on a significant basis of comparison and explain the reasons for your choice. Discuss similarities and differences in the poems' language, structure, and meaning.

Critical Thinking

6. In some of Dickinson's poems about death, the speaker is identified as "I," in some as "we," and in others without using either pronoun. Identify one of the poems without "I" or "We" and indicate which pronoun might be implied and why.

Tell all the Truth but tell it slant

Tell all the Truth but tell it slant—
Success in Circuit lies
Too bright for our infirm Delight
The Truth's superb surprise

As Lightning to the Children eased
With explanation kind
The Truth must dazzle gradually
Or every man be blind— (#1129, 1868, 1945)

QUESTIONS FOR CRITICAL THINKING AND WRITING

Experience

1. Choose one of Dickinson's poems about truth—poems 67, 241, 435, 1129—for your consideration.
2. Comment on what it is like for you to read the poem—the impressions it suggests to you, along with any difficulties it may pose.

Interpretation

3. How do you understand the poem? Explain the poem's central idea.
4. How do the poem's diction and imagery help convey its meaning?

Evaluation

5. What values seem central to the poem? What perspective on the nature and importance of truth does the poem suggest?

Connection

6. Look for a connection between one of the poems about truth, and one of the poems about love—poems 249, 1732—or about pain—poems 252, 599, 650.

Critical Thinking

7. Explain the paradox of poem 435. How can "madness" make "sense"; how can what is seen as "much sense" be actually "madness"—the "starkest Madness"?

My life closed twice before its close

My life closed twice before its close—
It yet remains to see
If Immortality unveil
A third event to me

So huge, so hopeless to conceive
As these that twice befell.

Parting is all we know of heaven,
And all we need of hell.

(#1732, 1896)

QUESTIONS FOR CRITICAL THINKING AND WRITING

Experience

1. Choose one of Dickinson's poems about love (poems 249, 1732) for your consideration. Explain why the poem you chose appeals to you above the others.
2. Comment on what it is like for you to read the poem—the impressions it suggests to you, the difficulties it may pose.

Interpretation

3. How do you understand the poem? Explain the poem's central idea.
4. How do the poem's diction and imagery help convey its meaning?

Evaluation

5. What values seem central to the poem? What perspective on the nature and importance of love does the poem take?

Connection

6. Look for a connection between one of the poems about love just preceding and one of Dickinson's poems about poetry (poems 448, 569, 657). What connection do you find?

Critical Thinking

7. Taken together, what attitudes toward love does this cluster of poems convey?

QUESTIONS FOR CRITICAL THINKING AND WRITING

Experience

1. Which of Dickinson's preceding poems interested you most and why? Which did you find easiest to follow? Which hardest to read? Why?

Interpretation

2. Choose one of Dickinson's poems and provide a line-by-line paraphrase. That is, explain what is said or suggested in each line of the poem.

3. Explain the relationship of each stanza to the one before or after it.
4. Provide an overall interpretation of the poem.

Evaluation

5. For whichever poem you selected for interpretation, identify the social, cultural, religious, or other values that are of importance in the poem.
6. Explain what perspective on those values Dickinson's poem seems to take.

Connection

7. Identify one type of relationship that exists between the poem you choose—and any other of Dickinson's poems.

Critical Thinking

8. Why do you think Dickinson is considered to be a major American poet? Do you think her status as a major poet is justified? Explain.

THREE DICKINSON POEMS WITH ALTERED PUNCTUATION

After her death, Emily Dickinson's poems were published with their punctuation changed to conform to the conventional usage of the time. Compare these versions with Dickinson's originals earlier in this chapter. Which versions do you prefer—and why?

650

Pain has an element of blank;
It cannot recollect
When it began, or if there were
A day when it was not.

It has no future but itself,
Its infinite realms contain
Its past, enlightened to perceive
New periods of pain.

632

The brain is wider than the sky,
For, put them side by side,
The one the other will include
With ease, and you beside.

The brain is deeper than the sea
For, hold them, blue to blue,
The one the other will absorb,
As sponges, buckets do.

The brain is just the weight of God,
For, lift them, pound for pound,
And they will differ, if they do,
As syllable from sound.

303

The soul selects her own society,
Then shuts the door;
On her divine majority
Obtrude no more.

Unmoved, she notes the chariot's pausing
At her low gate;
Unmoved, an emperor is kneeling
Upon her mat.

I've known her from an ample nation
Choose one;
Then close the valves of her attention
Like stone.

POEMS INSPIRED BY DICKINSON

JANE HIRSHFIELD

[b. 1953]

Three Times My Life Has Opened

Three times my life has opened.
Once, into darkness and rain.
Once, into what the body carries at all times within it and starts
    to remember each time it enters the act of love.
Once, to the fire that holds all.
These three were not different.
You will recognize what I am saying or you will not.
But outside my window all day a maple has stepped from her leaves
    like a woman in love with winter, dropping the colored silks.

Neither are we different in what we know.
There is a door. It opens. Then it is closed. But a slip of light
stays, like a scrap of unreadable paper left on the floor,
or the one red leaf the snow releases in March.

(1997)

BILLY COLLINS
[b. 1941]

Taking Off Emily Dickinson's Clothes

First, her tippet made of tulle,
easily lifted off her shoulders and laid
on the back of a wooden chair.

And her bonnet,
the bow undone with a light forward pull.

Then the long white dress, a more
complicated matter with mother-of-pearl
buttons down the back,
so tiny and numerous that it takes forever
before my hands can part the fabric,
like a swimmer's dividing water,
and slip inside.

You will want to know
that she was standing
by an open window in an upstairs bedroom,
motionless, a little wide-eyed,
looking out at the orchard below,
the white dress puddled at her feet
on the wide-board, hardwood floor.

The complexity of women's undergarments
in nineteenth-century America
is not to be waved off,
and I proceeded like a polar explorer
through clips, clasps, and moorings,
catches, straps, and whalebone stays
sailing toward the iceberg of her nakedness.

Later, I wrote in a notebook
it was like riding a swan into the night,

but, of course, I cannot tell you everything—
the way she closed her eyes to the orchard,
how her hair tumbled free of its pins,
how there were sudden dashes
whenever we spoke.

What I can tell you is
it was terribly quiet in Amherst
that Sabbath afternoon,
nothing but a carriage passing the house,
a fly buzzing in a windowpane.

So I could plainly hear her inhale
when I undid the very top
hook-and-eye fastener of her corset

and I could hear her sigh when finally it was unloosed,
the way some readers sigh when they realize
that Hope has feathers,
that reason is a plank,
that life is a loaded gun
that looks right at you with a yellow eye. (1998)

FRANCIS HEANEY

[b. 1970]

Skinny Domicile

I have a skinny Domicile—
Its Door is very narrow.
'Twill keep—I hope—the Reaper out—
His Scythe—and Bones—and Marrow.

Since Death is not a portly Chap,
The Entrance must be thin—
So—when my Final Moment comes—
He cannot wriggle in.

That's why I don't go out that much—
I can't fit through that Portal.
How dumb—to waste my Social Life
On Plans to be—immortal—

(2004)

LINDA PASTAN

[b. 1932]

Emily Dickinson

We think of her hidden in a white dress
among the folded linens and sachets
of well-kept cupboards, or just out of sight
sending jellies and notes with no address
to all the wondering Amherst neighbors.
Eccentric as New England weather
the stiff wind of her mind, stinging or gentle,
blew two half-imagined lovers off.
Yet legend won't explain the shear sanity
of vision, the serious mischief
of language, the economy of pain.

(1971)

QUESTIONS FOR CRITICAL THINKING AND WRITING

Experience

1. Which of the poems inspired by Dickinson appeals to you most? Why?
2. Describe your experience of reading it.

Interpretation

3. Explain the key or central idea of the poem.
4. What poetic elements—diction, imagery, figurative language, structure, syntax, sound, rhythm and meter—contribute most forcefully to its meaning? Provide an example and an explanation.

Evaluation

5. What values in Dickinson's poetry does the poem inspired by her work that you chose suggest?

Connection

6. Identify the relationship between each of the poems and Dickinson's work. Which of Dickinson's poems does Billy Collins's poem allude to? To which aspect of Dick-

inson's poetry does Jane Hirshfield's poem allude? To what images, and the poem (of Dickinson) does Francis Heaney's poem allude? How is his poem's title "Skinny Domicile" related to Dickinson's name?

Critical Thinking

7. Why do you think each of the poets "inspired" by Dickinson wrote his or her poem? What role do you think Dickinson may have played for each of these poets?

DICKINSON ON HERSELF AND HER FIRST POEMS

Letter to Thomas Higginson

FROM A LETTER TO THOMAS WENTWORTH HIGGINSON, APRIL 25, 1862

Mr Higginson,

Your kindness claimed earlier gratitude—but I was ill—and write today, from my pillow.

Thank you for the surgery—it was not so painful as I supposed. I bring you others—as you ask—though they might not differ—

While my thought is undressed—I can make the distinction, but when I put them in the Gown—they look alike, and numb.

You asked how old I was? I made no verse—but one or two—until this winter—Sir—

I had a terror—since September—I could tell to none—and so I sing, as the Boy does by the Burying Ground—because I am afraid—You inquire my Books—For Poets—I have Keats—and Mr and Mrs Browning. For Prose—Mr Ruskin—Sir Thomas Browne—and the Revelations. I went to school—but in your manner of the phrase—had no education. When a little Girl, I had a friend, who taught me Immortality—but venturing too near, himself—he never returned—Soon after, my Tutor, died—and for several years, my Lexicon—was my only companion—Then I found one more—but he was not contented I be his scholar—so he left the Land.

You ask of my Companions Hills—Sir—and the Sundown—and a Dog—large as myself, that my Father bought me—They are better than Beings—because they know—but do not tell—and the noise in the Pool, at Noon—excels my Piano. I have a Brother and Sister—My Mother does not care for thought—and Father, too busy with his Briefs—to notice what we do—He buys me many Books—but begs me not to read them—because he fears they joggle the Mind. They are religious—except me—and address an Eclipse, every morning—whom they call their "Father." But I fear my story fatigues you—I would like to learn—Could you tell me how to grow—or is it unconveyed—like Melody—or Witchcraft?

CRITICS ON DICKINSON

ALLEN TATE

Dickinson and Knowledge

FROM "EMILY DICKINSON," IN COLLECTED ESSAYS

Dickinson pursues that knowledge wherever it is to be found, no matter how it makes her feel. She reports her pursuit, seemingly as it occurs, with such profound attention that her poems offer exhilaration, no matter how somber their topic.

To see Dickinson as an epistemological poet, a poet who advances a theory of knowledge in her work, doesn't mean that she is exclusively, or even primarily, an intellectual poet. She was brilliant, well educated, and confident in her use of conceptual, scientific, legal and linguistic terminology, but the truly remarkable quality of mind in her poetry comes from her refusal to separate this mind from the body and emotions which temper it. Dickinson writes close to the traditions of post-Romantic poetry and women's poetry in that her poetry expresses strong emotion. She stands to the side of it to the extent that the drive for knowledge dominates, and the affairs of the heart are seen as part of that knowledge, not separate. Hers is an epistemology of feeling. It is actually quite difficult to locate Dickinson's refusal to sublimate in literary-historical terms, because it is so alien to our usual structuring of dualism. Dickinson has the direct access to emotion which is thought to be—and is—a characteristic of much women's poetry. She doesn't, however, soften those emotions into acceptability or use poetry as an escape, either for herself or for her reader. Perhaps her knowledge has gone unrecognized for just this reason: she doesn't present it as a solution to human loss and pain. Rather, it is a way of experiencing fully and with utmost clarity whatever must be experienced.

Emily Dickinson's poetry runs the full emotive range from ecstatic celebration to numb despair. Huge shifts of perspective, imagery of thresholds, gems, open and closed space, stars, planets and firmaments mark Dickinson's sublime. In a few, very striking, poems she sees both human and writerly desires as capable of fulfilment. Imagery of plentitude—wine, feasting, nectar, flood and luxury—accompanies Dickinson's joyous knowledge. In these poems, her tone is often highly erotic:

> Wild Nights—Wild Nights!
> Were I with thee
> Wild Nights should be
> Our luxury!

As Dickinson would have known, the Latin word *luxus,* from which "luxury" stems, means sensual excess or debauchery. Her declaration is actually redundant, further emphasizing its ecstatic triumph by the repetition of "Wild Nights." It is as if sensuous bliss is a state in which everything means the same thing, which is itself. The second stanza of "Wild Nights—Wild Nights!" develops this oceanic emotion into a nautical metaphor as Dickinson, somewhat more conventionally, declares that

"Winds" are "futile" "To a Heart in port—." Nor will this mariner need "Compass" or "Chart" to guide herself.

The poem's last stanza takes off from this hint of exultant freedom. The sexual beat of the rower's oars gives way to sheer exclamation:

Rowing in Eden—
Ah, the Sea!
Might I but moor—Tonight—
In Thee!

The last image may look like gender reversal, with the speaker seeing herself as the active partner, but Dickinson isn't concerned with whether or not her ecstasy fits Victorian convention. The image is one of choosing to be contained by the lover. Mooring tonight is a way of remaining eternally in the oceanic paradise of Eros.

JUDITH FARR

On "Wild Nights"

FROM THE PASSION OF EMILY DICKINSON

"Wild Nights," its theatrical opening spondees worthy of turbulence and storm, justifies Dickinson's heritage as an admirer of Emily Brontë and *Wuthering Heights.* The seas that separate or unite Charlotte Brontë's heroines and their "masters" also come to mind. Here is a scene reminiscent not only of the intensity of the Brontës' world but also of hundreds of dark canvases by the Hudson River and Luminist painters. Cole's *Tornado in an American Forest* (1835), like his *Expulsion from Eden,* had made the frenzy of storm synonymous with *passio*—distress or love—while seascapes like Fitz Hugh Lane's *Ships and an Approaching Storm off Owl's Head, Maine* (1860) or Heade's *Approaching Storm: Beach Near Newport* (1860) made angry seas expressive of the sea of feeling. Furthermore, Dickinson's image of the rowboat was conceived during the 1860s, when the idea of the lone boat in contest with high seas was particularly popular. There were many studies like Church's *An Old Boat* (1850), in which failure and loss were described by an abandoned rowboat at the edge of brimming, light-filled waters. Whistler expressed *The Sea* (1865) of defeat by picturing a rowboat stranded at the edge of sullen tides. Dickinson's lyrics about the "Edifice of Ocean" with its "tumultuous Rooms" (1217) would find analogues in the vehement seascapes of Winslow Homer, for whom the ocean could also be a metaphor of grandeur and grief. As a favorite nineteenth-century sport, however, rowing on smooth water was described by Thomas Eakins' Luminist paintings: for example, the famous *Max Schmitt in a Single Scull* (1871), which has a serene if rather triste formality.

Having said all this, it is equally important to say that "Wild Nights" is among the most Dickinsonian of the lyrics: ironic, paradoxical, voluptuous, and terse all at once. At first it projects a tumultuous nocturnal seascape, the wildness Nature's. But the next three lines of the first quatrain propose this as a luxury: that is, a rare experience to be enjoyed. Thus the imagined wildness is also human, internal, joyous. The next quatrain, spoken from the vantage point of one who has felt winds, declares how futile they would be in port, at rest, where neither they nor a compass or chart—the scientific instruments of explorers—are needed. By the closing quatrain, the speaker is "Rowing in Eden," her visionary desire having triumphed over the course of a life's voyage. Dickinson may have been remembering Bowles's rowing in Eden and all those betrothed nineteenth-century lovers so often depicted rowing together as one stroke in the same boat. (Thus in chapter 41 of *Little Women,* to give a popular example, Amy and Laurie row their boat "smoothly through the water" opposite Chillon, then decide to marry.) In Eden Dickinson finds a sea of love that is pleasurable, not frightening, and a Thee in which she might safely moor or harbor. Dickinson's inclusion of a sea in Eden, a garden, reminds us that the book of Genesis provides a river in Eden that waters the garden (2:10). (Other poems, such as "My River runs to thee" [162], may be related to her imagery of primal—sexual—waters. That poem was sent in a letter to Mary Bowles in August 1861; but like most of her words to Mary, it was probably intended for her husband.) In *Expulsion from Eden* Cole included a placid lake and a gentle waterfall in his Eden. When Dickinson's first quatrain is taken together with the last in poem 249, however, the reader realizes that she means to "moor" in passion, to luxuriate in wildness. For though hers is a boat that rows rather than rides the waters, her satisfaction in "Wild Nights" comes from strong delight. Even in Eden, she hears the sea. To moor is still to be wild for this prohibited voice that prays "Might I . . ."

ALLEN TATE

On "Because I Could Not Stop for Death"

FROM "EMILY DICKINSON," IN COLLECTED ESSAYS

If the word "great" means anything in poetry, this poem is one of the greatest in the English language. The rhythm charges with movement the pattern of suspended action back of the poem. Every image is precise and, moreover, not merely beautiful, but fused with the central idea. Every image extends and intensifies every other. The third stanza especially shows Miss Dickinson's power to fuse, into a single order of perception, a heterogeneous series: the children, the grain, and the setting sun (time) have the same degree of credibility; the first subtly preparing for the last. The sharp *gazing* before *grain* instills into nature a cold vitality of which the qualitative richness has infinite depth. The content of death in the poem eludes explicit definition. He is a gentleman taking a lady out for a drive. But note the restraint that keeps the poet from carrying this so far that it becomes ludicrous and incredible; and note the subtly interfused erotic motive, which the idea of death has presented to most romantic poets, love being a symbol interchangeable with death. The terror of death is objectified through this figure of the genteel driver, who is made ironically to serve the end of Immortality. This is the heart of the poem: she has presented a typical Christian theme in its final irresolution, without making any final statements about it. There is no solution to the problem; there can be only a presentation of it in the full context of intellect and feeling. A construction of the human will, elaborated with all the abstracting powers of the mind, is put to the concrete test of experience: the idea of immortality is confronted with the fact of physical disintegration. We are not told what to think; we are told to look at the situation.

The framework of the poem is, in fact, the two abstractions, mortality and eternity, which are made to associate in equality with the images: she sees the ideas, and thinks the perceptions. She did, of course, nothing of the sort; but we must use the logical distinctions, even to the extent of paradox, if we are to form any notion of this rare quality of mind. She could not in the proper sense think at all, and unless we prefer the feeble poetry of moral ideas that flourished in New England in the eighties, we must conclude that her intellectual deficiency contributed at least negatively to her great distinction. Miss Dickinson is probably the only Anglo-American poet of her century whose work exhibits the perfect literary situation—in which is possible the fusion of sensibility and thought. Unlike her contemporaries, she never succumbed to her ideas, to easy solutions, to her private desires . . .

Neither the feeling nor the style of Miss Dickinson belongs to the seventeenth century; yet between her and Donne there are remarkable ties. Their religious ideas, their abstractions, are momently toppling from the rational plane to the level of perception. The ideas, in fact, are no longer the impersonal religious symbols created anew in the heat of emotion, that we find in poets like Herbert and Vaughan. They have become, for Donne, the terms of personality; they are mingled with the miscellany of sensation. In Miss Dickinson, as in Donne, we may detect a singularly morbid concern, not for religious truth, but for personal revelation. The modern word is self-exploitation. It is egoism grown irresponsible in religion and decadent in morals. In religion it is blasphemy; in society it means usually that culture is not self-contained and sufficient, that the spiritual community is breaking up. This is, along with some other features that do not concern us here, the perfect literary situation.

HELEN MCNEIL

Dickinson's Method

FROM EMILY DICKINSON

Many Victorian poems describe unexamined abstractions, as if society agreed about what constituted sorrow or love. These could be personified, and their attributes could be listed and elaborated metaphorically. Dickinson takes on a frightening abstraction and evolves its attributes from experience, not tradition. In poetry and philosophy, the subject—the experiencing person—may wonder about the existence of other minds. Dickinson wrote many poems on this problem. In "Pain—has an Element of Blank," she contemplates the possibility that there may be circumstances in which the perceiving consciousness also does not exist, erased by its own emotion. "The Soul has Bandaged moments—" she begins another poem; the abstract soul is a bandaged body, in a metaphor which denies dualism. Time is also represented physically, bound up by pain. As Dickinson concludes at the end of "The Soul has Bandaged moments—," such recognitions "are not brayed of Tongue—" in the public discourse of her society, or, for that matter, our society either.

Dickinson wrote about feeling, but out of feeling she constructed a theory of knowledge—not *beyond* feeling, or free from it, or in any way separate, but using it as a kind of knowing. In effect—though not in conventional terms—she is an epistemological poet, a poet who advances a theory of knowledge. Dickinson made this concern explicit. After the forms of the verb "to be," "know" is the most frequently used verb in Dickinson's poetry, appearing 230 times, more even than any noun except "day."

Dickinson's constant pressure towards knowing means that she can treat even the most tormented situations with great calm. She can begin by writing "I felt a Funeral, in my Brain," or "Pain—has an Element of Blank—" or "I felt my life with both my hands—" and then proceed to delineate that state with a commanding accuracy. In a manner more resembling the Metaphysical poets than her Victorian contemporaries, male or female, she uses emotionally heightened states as occasions for clarity.

American poetry characteristically embodies acts of process: the Dickinsonian "process" is passionate investigation. Her investigative process often implies narrative by taking speaker and reader through a sequence of rapidly changing images, even when all the action is interior. These investigations structure Dickinson's poetry; I suspect that the flexibility of her investigative movement is the major reason why Dickinson generally was contented with common meter. She may even have enjoyed the way her condensed discoveries press against the limits of a small form.

ROBERT FROST IN CONTEXT

[1874–1963]

Although Robert Frost is considered a New England farmer-poet who captures in his verse the tang of Yankee speech, he was born in San Francisco and lived there until the age of eleven, when his family moved to Lawrence, Massachusetts. He attended high school in Lawrence and was covaledictorian of his graduating class with Elinor White, whom he later married. Frost continued his education at Dartmouth College, where he remained for only one term, and later at Harvard University, where he studied for two years without taking a degree. After working at a succession of odd jobs including farming and factory work, Frost taught at Pinkerton Academy, where from 1906 to 1910 he reformed the English syllabus, directed theatrical productions, and wrote many of the poems later included in his first book, *A Boy's Will*.

In 1911, in an attempt to attract the attention of prominent and influential members in the literary world, he sold his farm in Derry, New Hampshire, and moved

Frost and son Carol in Franconia, New Hampshire, c 1916–1917

with his family to England. There he met and received the support of Ezra Pound, who helped secure publication of his first two volumes of poems, and of Edward Thomas, who reviewed them perceptively. Having launched his career, Frost returned to America in 1915 and quickly secured an American publisher—Henry Holt and Co.—for the two books published in England, *A Boy's Will* (1913) and *North of Boston* (1914), and for subsequent volumes as well. With the publication in 1916 of *Mountain Interval,* Frost's fame grew. In 1917, and periodically thereafter, he was poet in residence at Amherst College and served in a similar capacity at various other colleges and universities including Dartmouth, Wesleyan, Michigan, Harvard, and Yale. Frost received awards and prizes, among them the Bollingen Poetry Prize (1963) and four Pulitzer Prizes (1924, 1931, 1937, and 1943). In addition, many honorary degrees, including ones from Oxford and Cambridge universities, were conferred on him. Although Frost was fond of joking that he could make a blanket of the many academic hoods he had acquired, he valued them, particularly those from the British institutions. Later in his life Frost was appointed goodwill emissary to South America and the Soviet Union. At the time he was also the only American poet honored with an invitation to read his work at a presidential inauguration. In January 1961, at the inauguration of John F. Kennedy, Frost read "The Gift Outright" and another poem he had composed for the occasion.

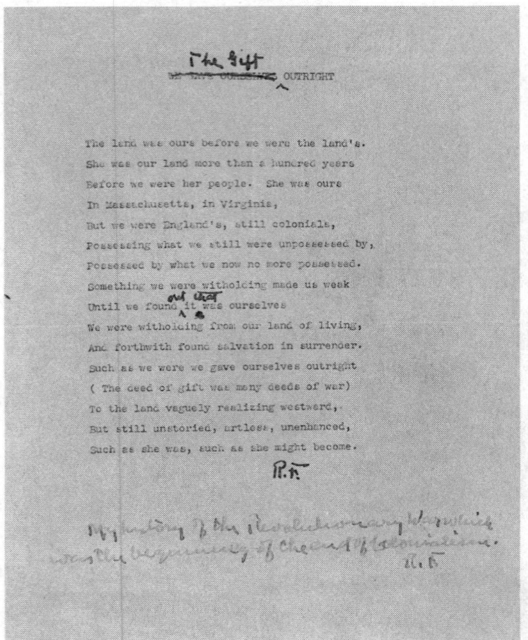

The Gift OUTRIGHT

The land was ours before we were the land's.
She was our land more than a hundred years
Before we were her people. She was ours
In Massachusetts, in Virginia,
But we were England's, still colonials,
Possessing what we still were unpossessed by,
Possessed by what we now no more possessed.
Something we were witholding made us weak
Until we found out that it was ourselves
We were witholding from our land of living,
And forthwith found salvation in surrender.
Such as we were we gave ourselves outright
(The deed of gift was many deeds of war)
To the land vaguely realizing westward,
But still unstoried, artless, unenhanced,
Such as she was, such as she might become.

R.F.

Manuscript copy of "The Gift Outright" (first published in the *Virginia Quarterly Review*, 1942)

This brief summary of Frost's career, however, oversimplifies what was in reality a more complex and arduous process. Initially an obscure writer, Frost experienced difficulty in breaking into print. He later struggled with the decline of his poetic powers. And more tragically, he suffered the deaths of his wife and three of his children, one of whom committed suicide. He also saw his sister and one of his daughters succumb to mental illness. And finally, despite his many prizes and awards, Frost was bitter that he never won a Nobel Prize. He died in 1963, two weeks short of his eighty-ninth birthday.

Frost and Popularity

Like Walt Whitman before him, Robert Frost yearned to become America's foremost poet. Aiming for both critical and popular acclaim, Frost hoped to achieve recognition as a major poet and to reach the widest possible audience. And although he did succeed in becoming a popular poet (perhaps the most popular in America's history), in the minds of some readers his very popularity diminished his critical stature. Frost himself, however, was partly responsible for this. The image he projected—folksy, lovable, homespun—undercut his reputation as a major poet. Even today, with Frost's poetic stature widely acknowledged, he is occasionally seen as a less serious, less impressive, less demanding, and hence less important poet than his contemporaries Ezra Pound, T. S. Eliot, and Wallace Stevens.

There is a measure of truth in this assessment, perhaps, but only a small measure. Frost's poems are easier to read than those of Pound, Eliot, or Stevens: his familiar vocabulary and traditional forms enhance their accessibility. But his poems are neither simple nor easy to understand. Their diction is more richly allusive and connotative than at first may appear. Their paraphrasable thought is subtler and more profound than an initial reading might suggest. Moreover, their form, though traditional, is more intricately wrought and more decisively experimental than is generally recognized. But before turning to these considerations, we should be aware of the course of Frost's poetic career, particularly of the growth of his popularity as an honored national poet, who, ironically, was first recognized abroad rather than at home.

What accounts for Frost's fame and popularity? Three things, at least: his shrewd management of his career, including the cultivation of his poetic image; his use of familiar subjects, especially the natural world and people engaged in recognizable activ-

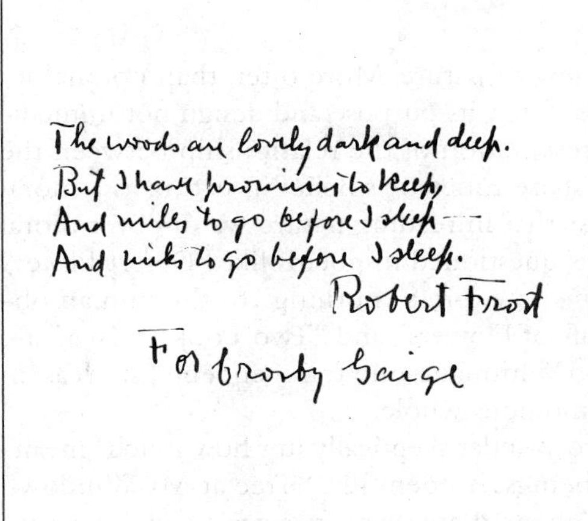

The woods are lovely dark and deep.
But I have promises to keep,
And miles to go before I sleep—
And miles to go before I sleep.
Robert Frost
For Crosby Gaige

Final four lines of "Stopping by Woods" (Frost's inscription to Crosby Gaige of a limited edition of New Hampshire)

ities; and his accessible language and apparent simplicity of thought. From the beginning, Frost skillfully managed his poetic career, going abroad to England to win the approval of the prominent poets and critics of his day. Frost, of course, did not plan every step of his rise to fame; rather he trusted to his highly developed instinct for sizing up opportunities and capitalizing on them. As William Pritchard explains in *Robert Frost: A Literary Life Reconsidered,* Frost retrospectively structured his literary life as one of adversity overcome. The most important aspect of this biographical semifictionalizing was Frost's portrayal of himself as a literary exile unappreciated in his home country. Allied with this biographical mythmaking was Frost's control over his public image. He refused, for example, to read his darker, more skeptical poems in public, preferring instead to reveal his more congenial, folksy side. And he carefully masked from public exposure his hunger for fame and an occasional nasty denigration of those poets he considered his strongest rivals.

More important to his popularity than his masterly manipulation of his public persona, however, is the readability of his poetry. Frost avoids obscure language, preferring the familiar word and the idiomatic phrase. He also shuns foreign words and shies away from all but the scantiest of references to economic, literary, and political history. And instead of the structural openness, fragmentation, and discontinuity favored by some of his contemporaries, Frost used traditional poetic forms characterized by coherence and continuity.

Yet Frost is a master of concealment, of saying one thing in terms of another, and especially of saying two or more things simultaneously. Even his most accessible poems such as "Birches," "Mending Wall," and "The Road Not Taken" contain clear invitations to consider their symbolic ramifications. To appreciate the fullness of Frost's achievement, we need to read with attention, whether we are reading the meditative blank verse of "Birches" or "Mending Wall" or the lyrical descriptions of "Desert Places" or "Stopping by Woods on a Snowy Evening."

It is also a mistake to assume, on the basis of a familiarity with a few of Frost's more famous lyrics, that his poetry lacks either drama or humor. "Departmental" reveals Frost's humorous side, while "Home Burial" shows him at work in a longer, more dramatic form. Though his poems are certainly serious, they are not solemn. This is as true of "Stopping by Woods" and "The Road Not Taken" as it is for "The Silken Tent," a witty extended comparison between a woman and a pitched tent; "Provide, Provide," a pragmatic set of admonitions about how to get on in the world; and "A Considerable Speck," a satirical jab at human limitations, particularly the performances of writers.

Frost and Nature

Complicating matters further is Frost's view of nature. More often than not, nature appears as a powerful, dangerous, and cruel force, its purpose and design not immediately apparent. Frost avoids a simple representation of the relationship between the natural and human worlds. He does not share Emerson's belief in nature as a moral teacher. He does not believe, for example, that in reading nature we discover moral and spiritual truths. That romantic view is questioned in poems like "Desert Places" and "The Most of It," where nature seems to express "nothing" to the human observer. Yet other poems, such as "The Tuft of Flowers" and "Two Look at Two," are entirely compatible with Emersonian and Whitmanesque transcendentalist ideas, in which nature and man form part of a harmonious whole.

Frost's response to nature is, essentially, to wonder skeptically just how much "meaning" in nature there really is for human beings. A poem like "Tree at My Window" explores this issue. In the first part of the poem, there seems to be a definite connection between nature (trees) and people; the human and the natural worlds intersect. But the last stanza suggests that there are radical differences between the two worlds, differences that separate them more than their similarities bind them.

It is, thus, necessary to avoid oversimplifying the way nature is characterized in Frost's poems. It is also worth noting that, when asked whether he was a "nature poet," Frost remarked that he never wrote a poem that didn't have a person in it.

Frost and the Sonnet

The complexity and richness of Frost's vision of nature are paralleled by the subtlety of his technical achievement. Though he worked in traditional forms—sonnet, heroic couplet, blank verse, four-line stanza—the effects he wrought in them are remarkable for their range and versatility. To take just one example, his sonnets include poems in both of the traditional forms, Shakespearean and Petrarchan. "Putting in the Seed" is constructed according to the Shakespearean, or English, pattern with three quatrains and a concluding couplet (though Frost alters the rhyme pattern slightly). "Design" follows the Petrarchan model: an octave of eight lines followed by a sestet of six. The octave of "Design" describes a natural scene (a white spider finding on a white flower a white moth that it kills and devours). The sestet explores the significance of the event.

Frost's sonnets often diverge in some way from the traditional sonnet and thus make something new and fresh of the form. "Mowing," for example, while composed according to the Petrarchan structure, contains a strong concluding couplet more characteristic of the Shakespearean sonnet. It also varies from the rhyme scheme of both traditional patterns. The poem displays a curious use of overlapping sound effects that Frost worked out more elaborately and systematically in other lyrics. Other sonnet variations appear in "The Silken Tent," which is constructed as a single sentence spun out over the fourteen lines in a Shakespearean pattern. Working against that rhyme scheme, however, is a logical structure more characteristic of the Petrarchan division into two major sections, with a turn at the ninth line. Such hybrid sonnets are accompanied by other sonnet experiments such as "Once by the Pacific," in seven couplets

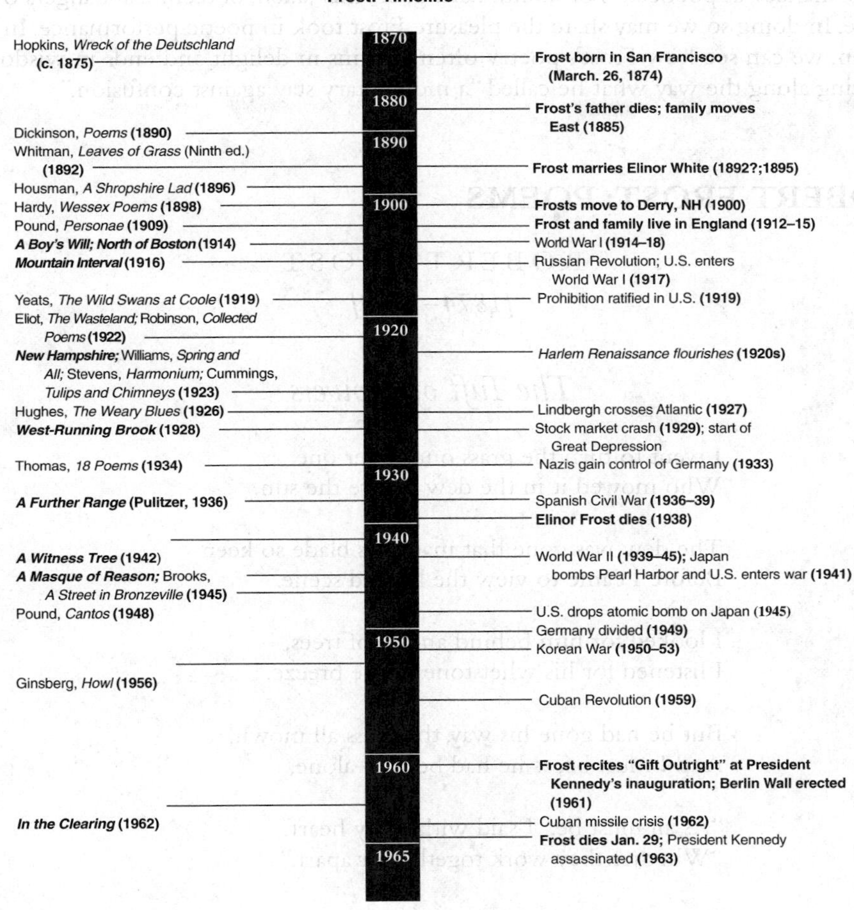

rhyming *aa bb cc dd ee ff gg,* and "Acquainted with the Night," composed in the interlocking rhymes of *terza rima: aba bcb cdc ded ee.*

Frost's Voices

Frost was a skilled wordsmith who cared about the sounds of his sentences. He noted more than once how "the sentence sound says more than the words"; how "tones of voice" can "mean more than words." In such voice tones Frost heard the sounds of sense and captured them in his verse, heightening their expressiveness by combining the inflections of ordinary speech with the measured regularity of meter. Because Frost's achievement in this regard surpasses that of most other modern American poets, we should be particularly attentive to the way he makes poetry out of the spoken word. His poems often mask the most elegant and subtle of his technical accomplishments. Perhaps the best way to read Frost's poems is to approach them as performances, as poetic acts of skillful daring, of risks taken, of technical dangers overcome. In doing so we may share the pleasure Frost took in poetic performance. In addition, we can see how Frost's poetry often "begins in delight and ends in wisdom," offering along the way what he called "a momentary stay against confusion."

ROBERT FROST: POEMS

ROBERT FROST

[1874–1963]

The Tuft of Flowers

I went to turn the grass once after one
Who mowed it in the dew before the sun.

The dew was gone that made his blade so keen
Before I came to view the leveled scene.

I looked for him behind an isle of trees;
I listened for his whetstone in the breeze.

But he had gone his way, the grass all mown,
And I must be, as he had been,—alone,

"As all must be," I said within my heart,
"Whether they work together or apart."

But as I said it, swift there passed me by
On noiseless wing a bewildered butterfly,

Seeking with memories grown dim o'er night
Some resting flower of yesterday's delight.

And once I marked his flight go round and round,
As where some flower lay withering on the ground.

And then he flew as far as eye could see,
And then on tremulous wing came back to me.

I thought of questions that have no reply,
And would have turned to toss the grass to dry;

But he turned first, and led my eye to look
At a tall tuft of flowers beside a brook,

A leaping tongue of bloom the scythe had spared
Beside a reedy brook the scythe had bared.

The mower in the dew had loved them thus,
By leaving them to flourish, not for us,

Nor yet to draw one thought of ours to him,
But from sheer morning gladness at the brim.

The butterfly and I had lit upon,
Nevertheless, a message from the dawn,

That made me hear the wakening birds around,
And hear his long scythe whispering to the ground,

And feel a spirit kindred to my own;
So that henceforth I worked no more alone;

But glad with him, I worked as with his aid,
And weary, sought at noon with him the shade;

And dreaming, as it were, held brotherly speech
With one whose thought I had not hoped to reach.

"Men work together," I told him from the heart,
"Whether they work together or apart."

(1913)

QUESTIONS FOR CRITICAL THINKING AND WRITING

Experience

1. Describe your experience of reading "The Tuft of Flowers." Where are your impressions of the experiences described strongest and clearest? Where, if any place in the poem, do you get lost or confused?

Interpretation

2. Provide an explanation of what you think "The Tuft of Flowers" says to its readers. Single out one key line of the poem and comment on its significance—its poetic elements as well as its meaning.

Evaluation

3. What values does the poem celebrate? Where are those values most clearly in evidence?

Connection

4. What connections or distinctions can you identify between "The Tuft of Flowers" and one of Dickinson's poems on nature?

Critical Thinking

5. How do you reconcile the notion that all must be alone, whether they work together or apart (lines 8–10) with the idea that "Men work together . . . Whether they work together or apart" (lines 39–40)

Mending Wall

Something there is that doesn't love a wall,
That sends the frozen-ground-swell under it,
And spills the upper boulders in the sun;
And makes gaps even two can pass abreast.
The work of hunters is another thing:
I have come after them and made repair
Where they have left not one stone on a stone,
But they would have the rabbit out of hiding,
To please the yelping dogs. The gaps I mean,
No one has seen them made or heard them made,
But at spring mending-time we find them there.
I let my neighbor know beyond the hill;
And on a day we meet to walk the line
And set the wall between us once again.
We keep the wall between us as we go.
To each the boulders that have fallen to each.
And some are loaves and some so nearly balls
We have to use a spell to make them balance:
"Stay where you are until our backs are turned!"
We wear our fingers rough with handling them.
Oh, just another kind of outdoor game,
One on a side. It comes to little more:
There where it is we do not need the wall:
He is all pine and I am apple orchard.
My apple trees will never get across
And eat the cones under his pines, I tell him.
He only says, "Good fences make good neighbors."
Spring is the mischief in me, and I wonder
If I could put a notion in his head:
"*Why* do they make good neighbors? Isn't it
Where there are cows? But here there are no cows.
Before I built a wall I'd ask to know
What I was walling in or walling out,

And to whom I was like to give offense.
Something there is that doesn't love a wall,
That wants it down." I could say "Elves" to him,
But it's not elves exactly, and I'd rather
He said it for himself. I see him there
Bringing a stone grasped firmly by the top
In each hand, like an old-stone savage armed.
He moves in darkness as it seems to me,
Not of woods only and the shade of trees.
He will not go behind his father's saying,
And he likes having thought of it so well
He says again, "Good fences make good neighbors."

(1914)

Mowing

THERE was never a sound beside the wood but one,
And that was my long scythe whispering to the ground.
What was it it whispered? I knew not well myself;
Perhaps it was something about the heat of the sun,
Something, perhaps, about the lack of sound—
And that was why it whispered and did not speak.
It was no dream of the gift of idle hours,
Or easy gold at the hand of fay or elf:
Anything more than the truth would have seemed too weak
To the earnest love that laid the swale in rows,
Not without feeble-pointed spikes of flowers
(Pale orchises), and scared a bright green snake.
The fact is the sweetest dream that labor knows.
My long scythe whispered and left the hay to make.

(1915)

Birches

When I see birches bend to left and right
Across the lines of straighter darker trees,
I like to think some boy's been swinging them.
But swinging doesn't bend them down to stay
As ice-storms do. Often you must have seen them
Loaded with ice a sunny winter morning
After a rain. They click upon themselves
As the breeze rises, and turn many-colored
As the stir cracks and crazes their enamel.
Soon the sun's warmth makes them shed crystal shells
Shattering and avalanching on the snow-crust—

Such heaps of broken glass to sweep away
You'd think the inner dome of heaven had fallen.
They are dragged to the withered bracken by the load,
And they seem not to break; though once they are bowed
So low for long, they never right themselves:
You may see their trunks arching in the woods
Years afterwards, trailing their leaves on the ground
Like girls on hands and knees that throw their hair
Before them over their heads to dry in the sun.
But I was going to say when Truth broke in
With all her matter-of-fact about the ice-storm,
I should prefer to have some boy bend them
As he went out and in to fetch the cows—
Some boy too far from town to learn baseball,

Whose only play was what he found himself,
Summer or winter, and could play alone.
One by one he subdued his father's trees
By riding them down over and over again
Until he took the stiffness out of them,
And not one but hung limp, not one was left
For him to conquer. He learned all there was
To learn about not launching out too soon
And so not carrying the tree away
Clear to the ground. He always kept his poise
To the top branches, climbing carefully
With the same pains you use to fill a cup
Up to the brim, and even above the brim.
Then he flung outward, feet first, with a swish,
Kicking his way down through the air to the ground.
So was I once myself a swinger of birches.
And so I dream of going back to be.
It's when I'm weary of considerations,
And life is too much like a pathless wood
Where your face burns and tickles with the cobwebs
Broken across it, and one eye is weeping
From a twig's having lashed across it open.
I'd like to get away from earth awhile
And then come back to it and begin over.
May no fate willfully misunderstand me
And half grant what I wish and snatch me away
Not to return. Earth's the right place for love:
I don't know where it's likely to go better.
I'd like to go by climbing a birch tree,
And climb black branches up a snow-white trunk
Toward heaven, till the tree could bear no more,
But dipped its top and set me down again.

That would be good both going and coming back.
One could do worse than be a swinger of birches.

(1916)

QUESTIONS FOR CRITICAL THINKING AND WRITING

Experience

1. In what ways might your own experience of life be reflected in what Frost describes in "Mending Wall" or "Birches"? Pick a few lines of either poem and explain how they relate to your experience.

Interpretation

2. What does the repeated line in "Mending Wall" mean? What does the final line of "Birches" mean?
3. How does Frost make the wall in "Mending Wall" a symbol—and what does it symbolize?
4. What symbolic elements does Frost introduce into "Birches"? What do they represent?

Evaluation

5. What value do each of the speakers in "Mending Wall" place upon walls?
6. What value do birch trees have for the speaker in "Birches"?

Connection

7. How are "Mending Wall" and " Birches" similar to and different from other poems by Frost that you have read?

Critical Thinking

8. Do you think that "good fences make good neighbors"? Why or why not? And what do you think Frost thinks about good fences making for good neighbors? Explain.

Home Burial

He saw her from the bottom of the stairs
Before she saw him. She was starting down,
Looking back over her shoulder at some fear.
She took a doubtful step and then undid it
To raise herself and look again. He spoke
Advancing toward her: "What is it you see
From up there always—for I want to know."

She turned and sank upon her skirts at that,
And her face changed from terrified to dull.
He said to gain time: "What is it you see"
Mounting until she cowered under him.
"I will find out now—you must tell me, dear."
She, in her place, refused him any help
With the least stiffening of her neck and silence.
She let him look, sure that he wouldn't see,
Blind creature; and awhile he didn't see.
But at last he murmured, "Oh," and again, "Oh."

"What is it—what?" she said.
"Just that I see."

"You don't," she challenged. "Tell me what it is."

"The wonder is I didn't see at once.
I never noticed it from here before.
I must be wonted to it—that's the reason.
The little graveyard where my people are!
So small the window frames the whole of it.
Not so much larger than a bedroom, is it?
There are three stones of slate and one of marble,
Broad-shouldered little slabs there in the sunlight
On the sidehill. We haven't to mind *those.*
But I understand: it is not the stones,
But the child's mound—"

"Don't, don't, don't, don't," she cried.

She withdrew shrinking from beneath his arm
That rested on the banister, and slid downstairs;
And turned on him with such a daunting look,
He said twice over before he knew himself:
"Can't a man speak of his own child he's lost?"

"Not you! Oh, where's my hat? Oh, I don't need it!
I must get out of here. I must get air.
I don't know rightly whether any man can."

"Amy! Don't go to someone else this time.
Listen to me. I won't come down the stairs."
He sat and fixed his chin between his fists.
"There's something I should like to ask you, dear."
"You don't know how to ask it."
"Help me, then."

Her fingers moved the latch for all reply.

"My words are nearly always an offense.
I don't know how to speak of anything
So as to please you. But I might be taught
I should suppose. I can't say I see how.
A man must partly give up being a man
With women-folk. We could have some arrangement
By which I'd bind myself to keep hands off
Anything special you're a-mind to name.
Though I don't like such things 'twixt those that love.
Two that don't love can't live together without them.
But two that do can't live together with them."
She moved the latch a little. "Don't—don't go.
Don't carry it to someone else this time.
Tell me about it if it's something human.
Let me into your grief. I'm not so much
Unlike other folks as your standing there
Apart would make me out. Give me my chance.
I do think, though, you overdo it a little.
What was it brought you up to think it the thing
To take your mother-loss of a first child
So inconsolably—in the face of love.
You'd think his memory might be satisfied—"

"There you go sneering now!"

"I'm not, I'm not!
You make me angry. I'll come down to you.
God, what a woman! And it's come to this,
A man can't speak of his own child that's dead."

"You can't because you don't know how to speak.
If you had any feelings, you that dug
With your own hand—how could you?—his little grave;
I saw you from that very window there,
Making the gravel leap and leap in air,
Leap up, like that, like that, and land so lightly
And roll back down the mound beside the hole.
I thought, Who is that man? I didn't know you.
And I crept down the stairs and up the stairs
To look again, and still your spade kept lifting.
Then you came in. I heard your rumbling voice
Out in the kitchen, and I don't know why,
But I went near to see with my own eyes.
You could sit there with the stains on your shoes

Of the fresh earth from your own baby's grave
And talk about your everyday concerns.
You had stood the spade up against the wall
Outside there in the entry, for I saw it."
"I shall laugh the worst laugh I ever laughed.
I'm cursed. God, if I don't believe I'm cursed."

"I can repeat the very words you were saying.
'Three foggy mornings and one rainy day
Will rot the best birch fence a man can build.'
Think of it, talk like that at such a time!
What had how long it takes a birch to rot
To do with what was in the darkened parlor?
You *couldn't* care! The nearest friends can go
With anyone to death, comes so far short
They might as well not try to go at all.
No, from the time when one is sick to death,
One is alone, and he dies more alone.
Friends make pretense of following to the grave,
But before one is in it, their minds are turned
And making the best of their way back to life
And living people, and things they understand.
But the world's evil. I won't have grief so
If I can change it. Oh, I won't, I won't!"

"There, you have said it all and you feel better.
You won't go now. You're crying. Close the door.
The heart's gone out of it: why keep it up.
Amy! There's someone coming down the road!"

"*You*—oh, you think the talk is all. I must go—
Somewhere out of this house. How can I make you—"

"If—you—do!" She was opening the door wider.
"Where do you mean to go? First tell me that.
I'll follow and bring you back by force. I *will!*—"

(1914)

QUESTIONS FOR CRITICAL THINKING AND WRITING

Experience

1. To what extent does your experience or your observation of others reflect the relationship described in "Home Burial"? Whom do you sympathize with more, the man or the woman? Why?

Interpretation

2. How does Frost characterize the man in the poem? How does he characterize the woman? What is the difference between them?
3. How does Frost capture the woman's feelings? How does he convey what the man thinks? Which lines reveal the woman's feelings and the man's thoughts most clearly?

Evaluation

4. What values underlie the man's behavior? What values are reflected in the woman's response to the death of her child?

Connection

5. What elements of drama does the poem possess? How is it like a play?

Critical Thinking

6. Which character, the man or the woman, do you most sympathize with in "Home Burial"? Why? Which do you think Frost sympathizes with most? Explain.

After Apple-Picking

My long two-pointed ladder's sticking through a tree
Toward heaven still,
And there's a barrel that I didn't fill
Beside it, and there may be two or three
Apples I didn't pick upon some bough.
But I am done with apple-picking now.
Essence of winter sleep is on the night,
The scent of apples: I am drowsing off.
I cannot rub the strangeness from my sight
I got from looking through a pane of glass
I skimmed this morning from the drinking trough
And held against the world of hoary grass.
It melted, and I let it fall and break.
But I was well
Upon my way to sleep before it fell,
And I could tell
What form my dreaming was about to take.
Magnified apples appear and disappear,
Stem end and blossom end,
And every fleck of russet showing clear.
My instep arch not only keeps the ache,
It keeps the pressure of a ladder-round.
I feel the ladder sway as the boughs bend.

And I keep hearing from the cellar bin
The rumbling sound
Of load on load of apples coming in.
For I have had too much
Of apple-picking: I am overtired
Of the great harvest I myself desired.
There were ten thousand thousand fruit to touch,
Cherish in hand, lift down, and not let fall.
For all
That struck the earth,
No matter if not bruised or spiked with stubble,
Went surely to the cider-apple heap
As of no worth.
One can see what will trouble
This sleep of mine, whatever sleep it is.
Were he not gone,
The woodchuck could say whether it's like his
Long sleep, as I describe its coming on,
Or just some human sleep.

(1916)

QUESTIONS FOR CRITICAL THINKING AND WRITING

Experience

1. Describe your experience of reading "After Apple-Picking."
2. Where does the poem's sense come most clearly into focus for you? Where is it elusive?
3. Identify a favorite line or section, and explain why it pleases you.

Interpretation

4. This poem has no stanzas. Divide the poem into sections. Explain the logic of the poem's organization. How does it develop from one section to another?
5. Identify two key images and explain their role and significance in the poem.
6. Identify the way the poem employs rhythm and/or rhyme or other forms of sound play. Explain what the play of sound and rhythm contributes to the poem.

Evaluation

7. Explain what values are central to the poem. Are these values important to the speaker? To the poet? To both?

Connection

8. Compare your selected poem to any other poem by Frost on the basis of its theme, its structure, its imagery, or its use of sound and rhythm.

Critical Thinking

9. If you had to categorize this poem as a love poem, a nature poem, or a death poem, which category would you assign it to? Why?

Fire and Ice

Some say the world will end in fire,
Some say in ice.
From what I've tasted of desire
I hold with those who favor fire.
But if it had to perish twice,
I think I know enough of hate
To say that for destruction ice
Is also great
And would suffice.

(1923)

QUESTIONS FOR CRITICAL THINKING AND WRITING

Experience

1. How do you respond to Frost's "Fire and Ice"? Does it strike you as a serious poem, a playful one, or both at the same time? Explain.

Interpretation

2. What do fire and ice represent in Frost's poem? How do you decide on the symbolic resonance of fire and of ice? What words and images are associated with fire and with ice?
3. Is this a poem about the end of the world? The end of something else?

Evaluation

4. Do you think that "Fire and Ice" is a good poem? Why or why not?

Connection

5. Compare "Fire and Ice" with another of Frost's briefer poems—with "Dust of Snow" (found in the Introduction to this book), for example. Identify similarities among "Fire and Ice" and this or another short poem.

Critical Thinking

6. Do you think "fire" or "ice" either literally or symbolically is more likely to be the cause of the way "the world will end"? Explain.

Nothing Gold Can Stay

Nature's first green is gold,
Her hardest hue to hold.
Her early leaf's a flower;
But only so an hour.
The leaf subsides to leaf.
So Eden sank to grief.
So dawn goes down to day.
Nothing gold can stay.

(1923)

QUESTIONS FOR CRITICAL THINKING AND WRITING

Experience

1. To what extent does your own experience bear out the idea that "nothing gold can stay"?
2. Which lines did you find easiest to comprehend? Which were most puzzling for you?

Interpretation

3. Why is nature's first green "gold"? Why is this golden hue hard to "hold"?
4. In what way does dawn "go down" to day? What is implied about the relationship between dawn and day?
5. What connection can you make between the dawn day relationship and the green to gold movement?
6. How is the last line related to all that comes before it?

Evaluation

7. Explain the reference to "Eden." How is the reference to the loss the humankind suffered in the garden of Eden relevant to the other images in the poem?
8. Why is gold so highly valued? Why are certain human experiences so highly valued?

Connection

9. Compare this poem to another by Frost. Explain why you chose to compare the two poems, and identify similarities and differences of significance.

Critical Thinking

10. What are some things that "gold" can stand for? To what extent do you agree that "nothing" gold can stay—that things we value do not last?

Acquainted with the Night

I have been one acquainted with the night.
I have walked out in rain—and back in rain.
I have outwalked the furthest city light.

I have looked down the saddest city lane.
I have passed by the watchman on his beat
And dropped my eyes, unwilling to explain.

I have stood still and stopped the sound of feet
When far away an interrupted cry
Came over houses from another street,

But not to call me back or say good-by;
And further still at an unearthly height
One luminary clock against the sky

Proclaimed the time was neither wrong nor right.
I have been one acquainted with the night.

(1928)

QUESTIONS FOR CRITICAL THINKING AND WRITING

Experience

1. What kind of experience does Frost describe in "Acquainted with the Night"? In what ways have you experienced what the speaker describes?

Interpretation

2. What does it mean to be "acquainted" with the night? What are the connotations of "acquainted"?
3. What effect do the repeated words and phrases have?
4. How is the poem structured? What patterns of sound and stanza do you find?

Evaluation

5. Do you think this is one of Frost's better poems or one of his worst? Why?

Connection

6. A poem similar in structure to "Acquainted with the Night" is "Provide, Provide," on page 690. Compare the two poems with respect to tone and theme.

Critical Thinking

7. Which details of the poem made the strongest impression on you? Why?

Tree at my Window

Tree at my window, window tree,
My sash is lowered when night comes on;
But let there never be curtain drawn
Between you and me.

Vague dream-head lifted out of the ground,
And thing next most diffuse to cloud,
Not all your light tongues talking aloud
Could be profound.

But, tree, I have seen you taken and tossed,
And if you have seen me when I slept,
You have seen me when I was taken and swept
And all but lost.

That day she put our heads together,
Fate had her imagination about her,
Your head so much concerned with outer,
Mine with inner, weather.

(1928)

QUESTIONS FOR CRITICAL THINKING AND WRITING

Experience

1. Do you find "Tree at my Window" an easy or a difficult poem? Why?
2. Can you relate to a speaker who talks with a tree? Why or why not?

Interpretation

3. Explain what is happening in each stanza.
4. What relationship exists between speaker and tree? How is the tree "tossed" and the speaker nearly "lost"?
5. What is meant by saying that the tree can't be "profound"?

Evaluation

6. What value is placed on the relationship between the human world and the world of nature in this poem?

Connection

7. Where does "Tree at my Window" stand in relationship to the poem "The Tuft of Flowers"?

Critical Thinking

8. Explain the last two lines of the poem. What is the "inner weather" the speaker says he is concerned with? Is this similar to or different from the tree's "outer weather"? Explain.

Departmental

An ant on the tablecloth
Ran into a dormant moth
Of many times his size.
He showed not the least surprise.
His business wasn't with such.
He gave it scarcely a touch,
And was off on his duty run.
Yet if he encountered one
Of the hive's enquiry squad
Whose work is to find out God
And the nature of time and space,
He would put him onto the case.
Ants are a curious race;
One crossing with hurried tread
The body of one of their dead
Isn't given a moment's arrest—
Seems not even impressed.
But he no doubt reports to any
With whom he crosses antennae,
And they no doubt report
To the higher up at court.
Then word goes forth in Formic:
"Death's come to Jerry McCormic,
Our selfless forager Jerry.
Will the special Janizary
Whose office it is to bury
The dead of the commissary
Go bring him home to his people.
Lay him in state on a sepal.
Wrap him for shroud in a petal.
Embalm him with ichor of nettle.
This is the word of your Queen."
And presently on the scene
Appears a solemn mortician:

And taking formal position
With feelers calmly atwiddle,
Seizes the dead by the middle,
And heaving him high in the air,
Carries him out of there.
No one stands round to stare.
It is nobody else's affair.

It couldn't be called ungentle.
But how thoroughly departmental.

(1936)

Design

I found a dimpled spider, fat and white,
On a white heal-all, holding up a moth
Like a white piece of rigid satin cloth—
Assorted characters of death and blight
Mixed ready to begin the morning right,
Like the ingredients of a witches' broth—
A snow-drop spider, a flower like a froth,
And dead wings carried like a paper kite.

What had that flower to do with being white,
The wayside blue and innocent heal-all?
What brought the kindred spider to that height,
Then steered the white moth thither in the night?
What but design of darkness to appall?—
If design govern in a thing so small.

(1936)

QUESTIONS FOR CRITICAL THINKING AND WRITING

Experience

1. Do you find "Design" or "Departmental" more accessible—easier to approach and make sense of? For the more difficult one, which words, phrases, lines do you find most challenging?

Interpretation

2. What are the possible meanings of "Design"? How is the poem designed? What kind of poem is it? How is it structured?
3. What is the relationship between the poem's two major sections?
4. Of what significance is color in the poem?
5. What is the significance of the last line?

Evaluation

6. What religious values are at stake in the poem? What perspective does the poem offer on design in and a designer of the universe?

Connection

7. Go to the library and find Frost's poem "In White." Compare it with "Design," and explain which is the better poem and why.
8. Find Walt Whitman's poem "Song of Myself." Compare what Whitman suggests about design in section 6 with what Frost's poem suggests about design.

Critical Thinking

9. Do you think there is an orderly design to the universe? If so, why? If not, why not?
10. What do you think is Frost's attitude toward the notion of "design" in the universe? Support your answer with evidence from his poems.

Desert Places

Snow falling and night falling fast, oh, fast
In a field I looked into going past,
And the ground almost covered smooth in snow,
But a few weeds and stubble showing last.

The woods around it have it—it is theirs.
All animals are smothered in their lairs.
I am too absent-spirited to count;
The loneliness includes me unawares.

And lonely as it is, that loneliness
Will be more lonely ere it will be less—
A blanker whiteness of benighted snow
With no expression, nothing to express.

They cannot scare me with their empty spaces
Between stars—on stars where no human race is.
I have it in me so much nearer home
To scare myself with my own desert places.

(1936)

QUESTIONS FOR CRITICAL THINKING AND WRITING

Experience

1. What is your impression of "Desert Places"? What is your response to its images?

Interpretation

2. Provide a stanza-by-stanza paraphrase of "Desert Places."
3. What images are of key importance in each stanza?
4. What is the meaning of the word "unawares"? What does "it" refer to in the same stanza?

Evaluation

5. Imagine that the poem ended after stanza three. What would be different about the shorter version of the poem? Would it be a better poem without stanza four? Why or why not?

Connection

6. Compare this poem with "Tree at my Window."

Critical Thinking

7. Explain the meaning of the last two lines. Why does the speaker say that he can scare himself with his "own desert places"? Are these "desert places" scarier than those "empty spaces" in the interstellar universe? Explain.

Provide, Provide

The witch that came (the withered hag)
To wash the steps with pail and rag,
Was once the beauty Abishag,

The picture pride of Hollywood.
Too many fall from great and good
For you to doubt the likelihood.

Die early and avoid the fate.
Or if predestined to die late,
Make up your mind to die in state.

Make the whole stock exchange your own!
If need be occupy a throne,
Where nobody can call *you* crone.

Some have relied on what they knew;
Others on being simply true.
What worked for them might work for you.

No memory of having starred
Atones for later disregard
Or keeps the end from being hard.

Better to go down dignified
With boughten friendship at your side
Than none at all. Provide, provide!

(1936)

QUESTIONS FOR CRITICAL THINKING AND WRITING

Experience

1. To what extent can you relate to the experiences referred to is "Provide, Provide"?

Interpretation

2. What is the central theme of the poem?
3. How would you characterize its tone? What does the rhyme pattern contribute to its tone.

Evaluation

4. What social values does the poem reflect or embody? To what extent do you share those values?

Connection

5. Compare the advice given in "Provide, Provide" with the advice offered in Meinke "Advice to My Son." (p. 536)

Critical Thinking

6. What does the speaker of "Provide, Provide" advocate? What is his advice? Do you think it is good advice? Why or why not? Explain.

POETS INSPIRED BY FROST

EDWARD THOMAS

[1878–1917]

When First

When first I came here I had hope,
Hope for I knew not what. Fast beat
My heart at sight of the tall slope
Of grass and yews, as if my feet

Only by scaling its steps of chalk
Would see something no other hill
Ever disclosed. And now I walk
Down it the last time. Never will

My heart beat so again at sight
Of any hill although as fair
And loftier. For infinite
The change, late unperceived, this year,

The twelfth, suddenly, shows me plain.
Hope now,—not health, nor cheerfulness,
Since they can come and go again,
As often one brief hour witnesses,—

Just hope has gone for ever. Perhaps
I may love other hills yet more
Than this: the future and the maps
Hide something I was waiting for.

One thing I know, that love with chance
And use and time and necessity
Will grow, and louder the heart's dance
At parting than at meeting be. (1917)

W. S. MERWIN

[b. 1927]

Unknown Bird

Out of the dry days
through the dusty leaves
far across the valley
those few notes never
heard here before

one fluted phrase
floating over its
wandering secret
all at once wells up
somewhere else

and is gone before it
goes on fallen into

its own echo leaving
a hollow through the air
that is dry as before

where it is from
hardly anyone
seems to have noticed it
so far but who now
would have been listening

it is not native here
that may be the one
thing we are sure of
it came from somewhere
else perhaps alone

so keeps on calling for
no one who is here
hoping to be heard
by another of its own
unlikely origin

trying once more the same few
notes that began the song
of an oriole last heard
years ago in another
existence there

it goes again tell
no one it is here
foreign as we are
who are filling the days
with a sound of our own

(2002)

SEAMUS HEANEY

[b. 1939]

The Forge

All I know is a door into the dark.
Outside, old axles and iron hoops rusting;
Inside, the hammered anvil's short-pitched ring,
The unpredictable fantail of sparks

Or hiss when a new shoe toughens in water.
The anvil must be somewhere in the centre,
Horned as a unicorn, at one end square,
Set there immoveable: an altar
Where he expends himself in shape and music.
Sometimes, leather-aproned, hairs in his nose,
He leans out on the jamb, recalls a clatter
Of hoofs where traffic is flashing in rows;
Then grunts and goes in, with a slam and flick
To beat real iron out, to work the bellows.

(1969)

QUESTIONS FOR CRITICAL THINKING AND WRITING

Experience

1. Which of the poems inspired by Frost appeals to you most? Why?
2. Describe your experience of reading it. How does it link up with your own experience of life?

Interpretation

3. Explain the central idea of the poem.
4. What poetic elements—diction, imagery, figurative language, structure, syntax, sound, rhythm, and meter—contribute most forcefully to its meaning? Identify two examples of how poetic elements contribute to the poem's meaning—and what they contribute.

Evaluation

5. What values in Frost's poetry does the poem inspired by his work that you chose suggest?

Connections

6. Identify the relationship between each of the poems and Frost's work. Which of Frost's poems does Edward Thomas's "When First" echo? Which poems does Merwin's "Unknown Bird" relate to? What aspects of style and theme in Heaney's "The Forge" can be related to those aspects of Frost's poetry?

Critical Thinking

7. What role do you think Frost may have played for each of the poets? Explain.

CRITICAL COMMENTS BY FROST

From "The Figure a Poem Makes"

The figure a poem makes. It begins in delight and ends in wisdom. The figure is the same as for love. No one can really hold that the ecstasy should be static and stand still in one place. It begins in delight, it inclines to the impulse, it assumes direction with the first line laid down, it runs a course of lucky events, and ends in a clarification of life—not necessarily a great clarification, such as sects and cults are founded on, but in a momentary stay against confusion. It has denouement. It has an outcome that though unforeseen was predestined from the first image of the original mood—and indeed from the very mood. It is but a trick poem and no poem at all if the best of it was thought of first and saved for the last. It finds its own name as it goes and discovers the best waiting for it in some final phrase at once wise and sad—the happy-sad blend of the drinking song.

No tears in the writer, no tears in the reader. No surprise for the writer, no surprise for the reader. For me the initial delight is in the surprise of remembering something I didn't know I knew. I am in a place, in a situation, as if I had materialized from cloud or risen out of the ground. There is a glad recognition of the long lost and the rest follows. Step by step the wonder of unexpected supply keeps growing. The impressions most useful to my purpose seem always those I was unaware of and so made no note of at the time when taken, and the conclusion is come to that like giants we are always hurling experience ahead of us to pave the future with against the day when we may want to strike a line of purpose across it for somewhere. The line will have the more charm for not being mechanically straight. We enjoy the straight crookedness of a good walking stick. Modern instruments of precision are being used to make things crooked as if by eye and hand in the old days. . . .

More than once I should have lost my soul to radicalism if it had been the originality it was mistaken for by its young converts. Originality and initiative are what I ask for my country. For myself the originality need be no more than the freshness of a poem run in the way I have described: from delight to wisdom. The figure is the same as for love. Like a piece of ice on a hot stove the poem must ride on its own melting. A poem may be worked over once it is in being, but may not be worried into being. Its most previous quality will remain its having run itself and carried away the poet with it. Read it a hundred times: it will forever keep its freshness as a metal keeps its fragrance. It can never lose its sense of a meaning that once unfolded by surprise as it went.

From "The Constant Symbol"

I give you a new definition of a sentence:

A sentence is a sound in itself on which other sounds called words may be strung. You may string words together without a sentence-sound to string them on just as you may tie clothes together by the sleeves and stretch them without a clothes line between two trees, but—it is bad for the clothes.

The number of words you may string on one sentence-sound is not fixed but there is always danger of overloading.

The sentence-sounds are very definite entities. (This is no literary mysticism I am preaching.) They are as definite as words. It is not impossible that they could be collected in a book though I don't at present see on what system they would be catalogued.

They are apprehended by the ear. They are gathered by the ear from the vernacular and brought into books. Many of them are already familiar to us in books. I think no writer invents them. The most original writer only catches them fresh from talk, where they grow spontaneously.

A man is all a writer if *all* his words are strung on definite recognizable sentence sounds. The voice of the imagination, the speaking voice must know certainly how to behave how to posture in every sentence he offers.

A man is a marked writer if his words are largely strung on the more striking sentence sounds.

A word about recognition: In literature it is our business to give people the thing that will make them say, "Oh yes I know what you mean." It is never to tell them something they don't know, but something they know and hadn't thought of saying. It must be something they recognize. . . .

The sentence as a sound in itself apart from the word sounds is no mere figure of speech. I shall show the sentence sound saying all that the sentence conveys with little or no help from the meaning of the words. I shall show the sentence sound opposing the sense of the words as in irony. And so till I establish the distinction between the grammatical sentence and the vital sentence. The grammatical sentence is merely accessory to the other and chiefly valuable as furnishing a clue to the other. You recognize the sentence sound in this: *You,* you—! It is so strong that if you hear it as I do you have to pronounce the two you's differently. Just so many sentence sounds belong to man as just so many vocal runs belong to one kind of bird. We come into the world with them and create none of them.

There are many other things I have found myself saying about poetry, but the chiefest of these is that it is metaphor, saying one thing and meaning another, saying one thing in terms of another, the pleasure of ulteriority. Poetry is simply made of metaphor. So also is philosophy—and science, too, for that matter, if it will take the soft impeachment from a friend. Every poem is a new metaphor inside or it is nothing. And there is a sense in which all poems are the same old metaphor always.

From "The Unmade Word, Or Fetching and Far-Fetching"

There are two kinds of language: the spoken language and the written language—our everyday speech which we call the vernacular; and a more literary, sophisticated, artificial, elegant language that belongs to books. We often hear it said that a man talks like a book in this second way. We object to anybody's talking in this literary, artificial English; we don't object to anybody's writing in it; we rather expect people to write in a literary, somewhat artificial style. I, myself, could get along very well without this bookish language altogether. I agree with the poet who visited this country not long ago when he said that all our literature has got to come down, sooner or later, to the talk of everyday life. William Butler Yeats says that all our words, phrases, and idioms to be effective must be in the manner of everyday speech.

We've got to come down to this speech of everyday, to begin with—the hard everyday word of the street, business, trades, work in summer—to begin with; but there is some sort of obligation laid on us, to lift the words of every day, to give them a metaphorical turn. No, you don't want to use that term—give the words a poetic touch. I'll show you what I mean by an example: take for example the word "lemon," that's a good practical word with no literary associations—a word that you use with the grocer and in the kitchen; it has no literary associations at all; "Peach" is another one; but you boys have taken these two words and given them a poetic twist.

CRITICS ON FROST

WILLIAM PRITCHARD

On "Stopping by Woods"

FROM ROBERT FROST: A LITERARY LIFE RECONSIDERED

With respect to his most anthologized poem, "Stopping by Woods . . ." which he called "my best bid for remembrance," such "feats" are seen in its rhyme scheme, with the third unrhyming line in each of the first three stanzas becoming the rhyme word of each suceeding stanza until the last one, all of whose end words rhyme and whose final couplet consists of a repeated "And miles to go before I sleep." Or they can be heard in the movement of the last two lines of stanza three:

He gives his harness bells a shake
To ask if there is some mistake.
The only other sound's the sweep
Of easy wind and downy flake.

As with "Her early leaf's a flower," the contraction effortlessly carries us along into "the sweep / Of easy wind" so that we arrive at the end almost without knowing it.

Discussion of this poem has usually concerned itself with matters of "content" or meaning (What do the woods represent? Is this a poem in which suicide is contemplated?). Frost, accordingly, as he continued to read it in public made fun of efforts to draw out or fix its meaning as something large and impressive, something to do with man's existential loneliness or other ultimate matters. Perhaps because of these efforts, and on at least one occasion—his last appearance in 1962 at the Ford Forum in Boston—he told his audience that the thing which had given him most pleasure in composing the poem was the effortless sound of that couplet about the horse and what it does when stopped by the woods: "He gives his harness bells a shake / To ask if there is some mistake." We might guess that he held these lines up for admiration because they are probably the hardest ones in the poem out of which to make anything significant: regular in their iambic rhythm and suggesting nothing more than they assert, they establish a sound against which the "other sound" of the following lines can, by contrast, make itself heard. Frost's fondness for this couplet suggests that however much he cared about the "larger" issues or questions which "Stopping by Woods . . ." raises and provokes, he wanted to direct his readers away from solemnly debating them; instead he invited them simply to be pleased with how he had put it. He was to say later about Edwin Arlington Robinson something which could more naturally have been said about himself—that his life as a poet was "a revel in the felicities of language." "Stopping by Woods . . ." can be appreciated only by removing it from its pedestal and noting how it is a miniature revel in such felicities.

RICHARD POIRIER

On "Stopping by Woods on a Snowy Evening"

FROM ROBERT FROST: THE WORK OF KNOWING

As its opening words suggest—"Whose woods these are I think I know"—["Stopping by Woods on a Snowy Evening"] is a poem concerned with ownership and also with someone who cannot be or does not choose to be very emphatic even about owning himself. He does not want or expect to be seen. And his reason, aside from being on someone else's property, is that it would apparently be out of character for him to be there, communing alone with a woods fast filling up with snow. He is, after all, a man of business who has promised his time, his future to other people. It would appear that he is not only a scheduled man but a fairly convivial one. He knows who owns which parcels of land, or thinks he does, and his language has a sort of pleasant neighborliness, as in the phrase "stopping by." It is no wonder that his little horse would think his actions "queer" or that he would let the horse, instead of himself, take responsibility for the judgment. He is in danger of losing himself; and his language by the end of the third stanza begins to carry hints of a seductive luxuriousness unlike anything preceding it—"Easy wind and downy flake . . . lovely, dark and deep." Even before the somnolent repetition of the last two lines, he is ready to drop off. His opening question about who owns the woods becomes, because of the very absence from the poem of any man "too exactly himself," a question of whether the woods are to "own" him. With the drowsy repetitiousness of rhymes in the last stanza, four in a row, it takes some optimism to be sure that (thanks mostly to his little horse, who makes the only assertive sound in the poem) he will be able to keep his promises. At issue, of course, is really whether or not he will be able to "keep" his life.

RICHARD POIRIER

On "Mending Wall"

FROM ROBERT FROST: THE WORK OF KNOWING

The limits, boundaries, or customs which define a "home," a personal property, are often taken, that is, as an occasion for freedom rather than for confinement. The real significance of the famous poem "Mending Wall" is that it suggests how much for

Frost freedom is contingent upon some degree of restriction. More specifically, it can be said that restrictions, or forms, are a precondition for expression. Without them, even nature ceases to offer itself up for a reading. Forms of any sort have been so overwhelmed in "Desert Places," for example, that the prospect is for "a blanker whiteness of benighted snow / With no expression, nothing to express," the world as a blank sheet of paper enveloped in darkness.

Natural forces in "Mending Wall," having each year to encounter the human imposition of a freshly repaired wall, tend to become expressive in a quite selective way. Whatever it is "that doesn't love a wall," "*sends* the frozen-ground-swell under it / And *spills* the upper boulders in the sun, / And *makes* gaps even two can pass abreast" (my italics). More important, this active response to human structurings prompts a counterresponse and activity from people who are committed to the making and remaking of those structures. And who are such people? The point usually missed, along with most other things importantly at work in this poem, is that it is not the neighbor, described as "an old-stone savage armed," a man who can only dully repeat, "Good fences make good neighbors"—that it is not he who initiates the fence-making. Rather it is the far more spirited, lively, and "mischievous" speaker of the poem. While admitting that they do not need the wall, it is he who each year "lets my neighbor know beyond the hill" that it is time to do the job anyway, and who will go out alone to fill the gaps made in the wall by hunters: "I have come after them and made repairs / When they have left not one stone on a stone." Though the speaker may or may not think that good neighbors are made by good fences, it is abundantly clear that he likes the yearly ritual, the yearly "outdoor game" by which fences are made. Because if fences do not "make good neighbors" the "*making*" of fences can. More is "made" in this "outdoor game" than fences. The two men also "make" talk, or at least that is what the speaker tries to do as against the reiterated assertions of his companion, which are as heavy and limited as the wall itself. So hopeless is this speaker of any response, that all his talk may be only to himself. He is looking for some acknowledgment of those forces at work which are impatient of convention and of merely repeated forms; but he is looking in vain.

YVOR WINTERS

Robert Frost: Or, the Spiritual Drifter as Poet

FROM THE FUNCTION OF CRITICISM

Frost writes of rural subjects, and the American reader of our time has an affection for rural subjects which is partly the product of the Romantic sentimentalization of "nature," but which is partly also a nostalgic looking back to the rural life which predominated in this nation a generation or two ago; the rural life is somehow regarded as the truly American life. I have no objection to the poet's employing rural settings; but we should remember that it is the poet's business to evaluate human experience, and the rural setting is no more valuable for this purpose than any other or than no particular setting, and one could argue with some plausibility that an exclusive concentration on it may be limiting.

Frost early began his endeavor to make his style approximate as closely as possible the style of conversation, and this endeavor has added to his reputation: it has helped to make him seem "natural." But poetry is not conversation, and I see no reason why poetry should be called upon to imitate conversation. Conversation is the most careless and formless of human utterance; it is spontaneous and unrevised, and its vocabulary is commonly limited. Poetry is the most difficult form of human utterance; we revise poems carefully in order to make them more nearly perfect. The two forms of expression are extremes, they are not close to each other. We do not praise a violinist for playing as if he were improvising; we praise him for playing well. And when a man plays well or writes well, his audience must have intelligence, training, and patience in order to appreciate him. We do not understand difficult matters "naturally." . . .

Frost, as far as we have examined him, then, is a poet who holds the following views: he believes that impulse is trustworthy and reason contemptible, that formative decisions should be made casually and passively, that the individual should retreat from cooperative action with his kind, should retreat not to engage in intellectual activity but in order to protect himself from the contamination of outside influence, that affairs manage themselves for the best if left alone, that ideas of good and evil need not be taken very seriously. These views are sure to be a hindrance to self-development, and they effectually cut Frost off from any really profound understanding of human experience, whether political, moral, metaphysical, or religious. The result in the didactic poems is the perversity and incoherence of thought; the result in the narrative poems is either slightness of subject or a flat and uninteresting apprehension of the subject; the result in the symbolic lyrics is a disturbing dislocation between the descriptive surface, which is frequently lovely, and the ultimate meaning, which is usually sentimental and unacceptable. The result in nearly all the poems is a measure of carelessness in the style, sometimes small and sometimes great, but usually evident: the conversational manner will naturally suit a poet who takes all experience so casually, and it is only natural that the conversational manner should often become very conversational indeed.

LANGSTON HUGHES IN CONTEXT

[1902–1967]

The Harlem Renaissance

During the 1920s, America experienced a decade of extraordinary cultural creativity, much of it centered in the section of New York City known as Harlem. The creators of this efflorescence in the arts were African-American writers and artists, musicians and dancers, who made the district of Harlem, in the words of James Weldon Johnson, "the Negro capital of the world." Among the writers central to the movement were Jean Toomer, whose *Cane* combined poetry and fiction in illuminating and affecting portraits of black life in America; Claude McKay and Countee Cullen, whose poems condemned bigotry and racial injustice often in explosive language; Zora Neale Hurston, whose studies in Black American culture and myth influenced generations of writers, including contemporary writers such as Alice Walker; and James Weldon Johnson, whose anthology of verse, *Book of American Negro Poetry,* established a framework for creating forms to express and capture "the distinctive humor and pathos of African Americans" that could also voice their "deepest and highest emotions and aspirations." One of the most prominent and influential of the Harlem Renaissance writers was Langston Hughes, whose work began to be published in the 1920s.

Hughes was a prolific writer whose published books span forty-one years (1926–1967). His output includes sixteen volumes of poems; two novels; three collections of short stories; four documentary works; three historical works; twenty dramatic pieces, including plays, musicals, and operettas; two volumes of autobiography; eight children's books; and twelve radio and television scripts. In addition, Hughes edited seven books—mostly collections of poems by black writers—and translated four others, including the poems of the renowned modern Spanish poet Federico García Lorca. Such versatility established Hughes as an important man of letters, contributing to his stature as a leading figure in the arts, especially the theater, whose audience Hughes was instrumental in enlarging.

Hughes's life was as varied as his writing. Born in Joplin, Missouri, in 1902, Hughes lived in Kansas and Ohio before studying at Columbia University in New York and later and more fully at Lincoln University in Pennsylvania. He worked as a seaman and as a newspaper correspondent and columnist for the *Chicago Defender,* the *Baltimore Afro-American,* and the *New York Post.* He also worked briefly as a cook at a fashionable restaurant in France and as a busboy in a Washington, D.C., hotel. It was there that Hughes left three of his poems beside the plate of a hotel dinner guest, the poet Vachel Lindsay, who recognized their merit and helped Hughes to secure their publication.

Hughes also founded the Harlem Suitcase Theatre (New York, 1938) and the Skyloft Players (Chicago, 1941). He traveled extensively, visiting and at various times living in Africa and Europe, especially Italy and France, as well as in Cuba, Haiti, Russia, Korea, and Japan. His life and travels are richly and engagingly chronicled in his two volumes of autobiography, *The Big Sea* (1940) and *I Wonder As I Wander* (1956).

Hughes and Music

Music was central to the flowering of culture during the Harlem Renaissance. Jazz clubs such as the Harlem Casino, the Sugar Cane Club, and the Cotton Club were frequented by both black and white patrons. Prominent jazz artists played in these clubs, including Duke Ellington, Count Basie, Bessie Smith, and Louis Armstrong. Music, in fact, is a central feature of Hughes's poetry. And the kind of music most evident in his work is the blues, an important influence in the work of many modern black writers, especially those associated with the Harlem Renaissance, the flowering of artistic activity among black artists and writers of Harlem in the 1920s. Hughes once described the blues as "sad funny songs—too sad to be funny and too funny to be sad," songs that contain "laughter and pain, hunger and heartache." The bittersweet tone and view of life reflected in Hughes's perspective on the blues is consistently

Blues 1929 by Archibald Motley Jr. (1929)

Showbill from Hughes's *Black Nativity* (Jan 21, 1961)

mirrored in his poems, which sometimes use the stanza form of the typical blues song. This stanza includes two nearly identical lines followed by a third that contrasts with the first two. "Same in Blues" exhibits this characteristic with only slight modifications. In this and other poems, Hughes succeeds in grafting the inflections of the urban black dialect onto the rhythms of the blues.

But the blues is not the only musical influence on Hughes's poetry; his work also makes use of jazz as both subject and style. Hughes's jazz poems are freer and looser in form than his blues poems. This difference reflects the improvisatory nature of jazz as well as its energy and vitality, which contrast with the more controlled idiom of the blues. The aggressive exuberance of jazz, its relaxed but vigorous informality, is evident in poems such as "Trumpet Player."

Duke Ellington and orchestra, with singer Bette Roche.

Hughes's Influences

The writers who influenced Hughes included Paul Dunbar, whose poems recreated the black vernacular, and W. E. B. DuBois, whose collection of essays on Afro-American life, *The Souls of Black Folk,* exerted a lasting influence on many writers, including novelists Richard Wright and James Baldwin. Hughes was also strongly influenced by the democratic idealism of Walt Whitman and the populism of Carl Sandburg, whom Hughes designated his "guiding star." From Sandburg, Hughes learned to write free verse. From Dunbar, he learned a method of incorporating local dialect into poems. And from DuBois, he derived what later came to be called black pride. These influences were combined and amalgamated in myriad ways, resulting in a remarkable collection of poems.

Hughes's Style

"Poetry," Langston Hughes once remarked, "should be direct, comprehensible, and the epitome of simplicity." His poems illustrate these guidelines with remarkable consistency. Avoiding the obscure and the difficult, Hughes wrote poems that could be understood by readers and listeners who had little prior experience with poetry.

Hughes's poetry offers a transcription of urban life through a portrayal of the speech, habits, attitudes, and feelings of an oppressed people. The poems do more, however,

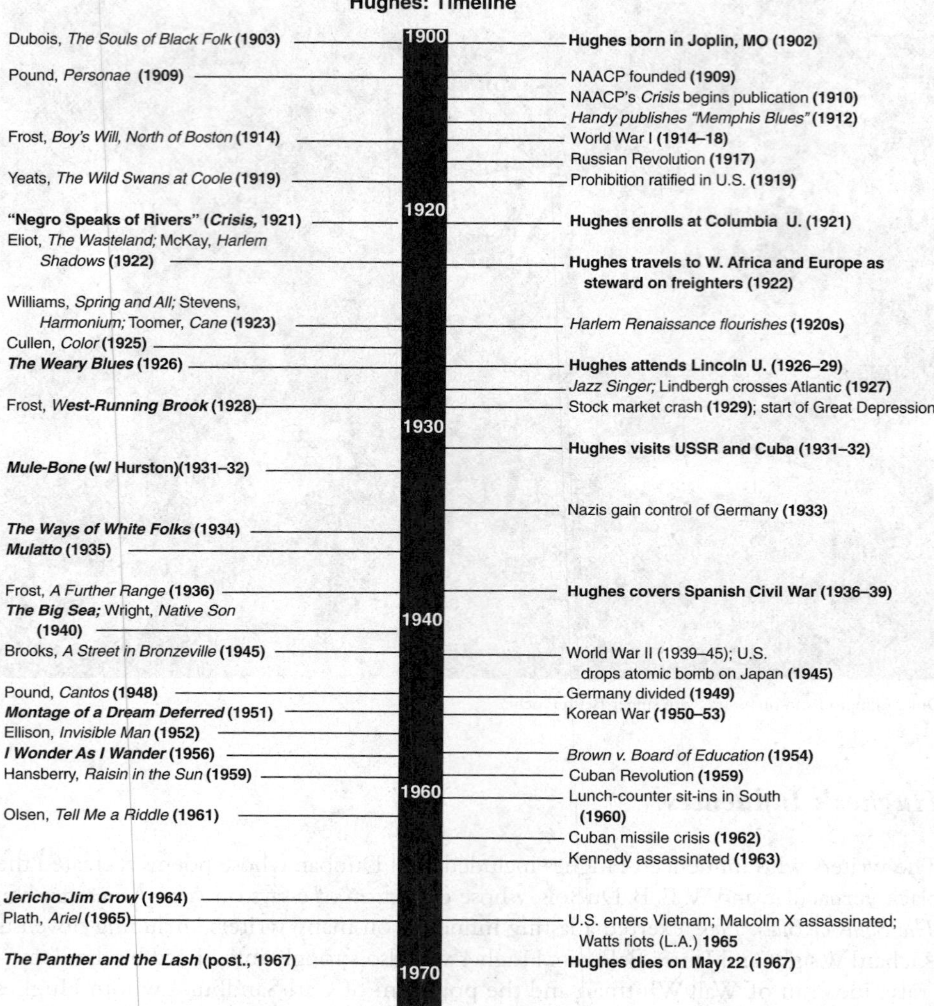

than reveal the pain of poverty. They also illustrate racial pride and dignity. Hughes's poems cling, moreover, to the spoken language. They derive from an oral tradition in which folk poetry is recited and performed, rather than published in written form. In the oral tradition poems are passed down from one generation to the next through performance and recitation. As a result Hughes's poems, more than most, need to be read aloud to be fully appreciated. Hughes himself became famous for his public readings, which were sometimes accompanied by a glee club or jazz combo.

As a writer who believed it was his vocation to "explain and illuminate the Negro condition in America," Hughes captured the experience as "the hurt of their lives, the monotony of their jobs, and the veiled weariness of their songs." He accomplished this in poems remarkable not only for their directness and simplicity but for their economy, lucidity, and wit. Whether he was writing poems of racial protest like "Dream Deferred" and "Ballad of the Landlord" or poems of racial affirmation like "Mother to Son" and "The Negro Speaks of Rivers," Hughes was able to find language and forms to express not only the pain of urban life but also its splendid vitality.

LANGSTON HUGHES: POEMS

LANGSTON HUGHES
[1902–1967]

Dream Deferred

What happens to a dream deferred?

Does it dry up
like a raisin in the sun?
Or fester like a sore—
And then run?
Does it stink like rotten meat?
Or crust and sugar over—
like a syrupy sweet?

Maybe it just sags
like a heavy load.

Or does it explode?

(1951)

QUESTIONS FOR CRITICAL THINKING AND WRITING

Experience

1. How does Hughes's "Dream Deferred" touch your experience? Have you ever had a "dream" that was put off? What effect did this have on you?

Interpretation

2. "Dream Deferred" is constructed as a series of questions. What is the effect of the accumulation of questions?
3. Explain each of the similes, which occur one per stanza, in the poem.

4. How does Hughes emphasize his final image of explosion?
5. What is this poem about?

Evaluation

6. What is the value of having dreams or hopes, whether they be personal or social, individual or communal? Explain.

Critical Thinking

7. What social and political values can be brought to bear on the poem? Consider that Hughes was an African-American poet writing in the 1930s, 1940s, 1950s, and into the 1960s.

The Negro Speaks of Rivers

I've known rivers:
I've known rivers ancient as the world and older than the flow
of human blood in human veins.
My soul has grown deep like the rivers.

I bathed in the Euphrates when dawns were young.
I built my hut near the Congo and it lulled me to sleep.
I looked upon the Nile and raised the pyramids above it.
I heard the singing of the Mississippi when Abe Lincoln
went down to New Orleans, and I've seen its muddy
bosom turn all golden in the sunset.

I've known rivers:
Ancient, dusky rivers.

My soul has grown deep like the rivers.

(1926)

Mother to Son

Well, son, I'll tell you:
Life for me ain't been no crystal stair.
It's had tacks in it,
And splinters,
And boards torn up,
And places with no carpet on the floor—
Bare.

But all the time
I'se been a-climbin' on,
And reachin' landin's,
And turnin' corners,
And sometimes goin' in the dark
Where there ain't been no light.
So boy, don't you turn back.
Don't you set down on the steps
'Cause you finds it's kinder hard.
Don't you fall now—
For I'se still goin', honey,
I'se still climbin',
And life for me ain't been no crystal stair.

(1922)

QUESTIONS FOR CRITICAL THINKING AND WRITING

Experience

1. To what extent have you had an experience like the one described in "Mother to Son"?
2. What kind of emotional response do you have to this poem? Why?

Interpretation

3. What does the poem's speaker say to her son? Why?
4. What images does Langston Hughes use to have the mother convey her message to her son? Are those images effective? Are they appropriate? Why or why not?

Evaluation

5. Do you think this is a good poem? An effective poem? Why or why not?

Connection

6. Compare Hughes's poem of advice, "Mother to Son," with Peter Meinke's "Advice to My Son."

Critical Thinking

7. Why does Hughes's have the woman speak in what might be called black urban dialect? What would be the effect of changing her language to make it more formal and grammatically correct?

I, Too

I, too, sing America.

I am the darker brother.
They send me to eat in the kitchen.
When company comes,
But I laugh,
And eat well,
And grow strong.

Tomorrow,
I'll be at the table
When company comes.
Nobody'll dare
Say to me,
"Eat in the kitchen,"
Then.

Besides,
They'll see how beautiful I am

And be ashamed—
I, too, am America.

(1923)

QUESTIONS FOR CRITICAL THINKING AND WRITING

Experience

1. How does Hughes's poem "I, Too" affect you? What is your emotional response to it? Why?

Interpretation

2. Explain the contrast that Hughes sets up in the poem.
3. What is the significance of eating in the kitchen?
4. What does the "Too" of the title mean?

Evaluation

5. How do you think readers from the minority African-American urban community would respond to this poem? Why? Explain.

Connection

6. Compare this poem with another by an African-American poet. You might consider poems by any of the following: Claude McKay; Paul Lawrence Dunbar; Rita Dove; Audre Lorde; Nikki Giovanni. You will find poems by these poets in Chapter Nineteen.

Critical Thinking

7. What social and political concerns does the poem highlight? Do you think such concerns are presented effectively? Why or why not?

My People

The night is beautiful,
So the faces of my people.

The stars are beautiful,
So the eyes of my people.

Beautiful, also, is the sun.
Beautiful, also, are the souls of my people.

(1923)

QUESTIONS FOR CRITICAL THINKING AND WRITING

Experience

1. How difficult or easy was it for you to read "My People"? Have you ever read another poem that celebrated a particular group of people?

Interpretation

2. Provide a stanza-by-stanza paraphrase of each couplet. Identify the focus of each couplet.
3. What is the relationship of each stanza to the one that follows?
4. Where does repetition occur in the poem? What is its effect?

Evaluation

5. What aspects of his people does the poet celebrate in "My People"?

Connections

6. What other poem by Hughes do you think most closely resembles "My People"? Why?

Critical Thinking

7. Should the order of the stanzas in this poem be changed? Why or why not? Explain.

Dream Variations

To fling my arms wide
In some place of the sun,
To whirl and to dance
Till the white day is done.
Then rest at cool evening
Beneath a tall tree
While night comes on gently,
Dark like me—
That is my dream.

To fling my arms wide
In the face of the sun,
Dance! Whirl! Whirl!
Till the quick day is done.
Rest at pale evening . . .
A tall, slim tree . . .
Night coming tenderly
Black like me.

(1924)

Song for a Dark Girl

Way Down South in Dixie
(Break the heart of me)
They hung my black young lover
To a cross roads tree.

Way Down South in Dixie
(Bruised body high in air)
I asked the white Lord Jesus
What was the use of prayer.

Way down South in Dixie
(Break the heart of me)

Love is a naked shadow
On a gnarled and naked tree.

(1927)

QUESTIONS FOR CRITICAL THINKING AND WRITING

Experience

1. How do you respond to "Dream Variations" and "Song for a Dark Girl"? Which poem is more emotional for you? Why?

Interpretation

2. Identify the structure of each of these poems? Explain how the structure of each poem helps accentuate its theme.
3. Who is the speaker in "Dream Variations"? In "Song for a Dark Girl"?
4. How does the poet use color images to convey meaning and feeling?

Evaluation

5. What cultural and social values are embedded in each poem? What conflicts of value do the poems include?

Connection

6. Compare either of these poems with one other poem by Hughes. Explain the reason for your choice, and identify ways the poems are similar and different.

Critical Thinking

7. Why do you think Hughes may have written these two poems? Explain.

Young Gal's Blues

I'm gonna walk to the graveyard
'Hind ma friend Miss Cora Lee.
Gonna walk to the graveyard
'Hind ma dear friend Cora Lee.
Cause when I'm dead some
Body'll have to walk behind me.

I'm goin' to the po' house
To see ma old Aunt Clew.
Goin' to the po' house
To see ma old Aunt Clew.

When I'm old an' ugly
I'll want to see somebody, too.

The po' house is lonely
An' the grave is cold.
O, the po' house is lonely,
The graveyard grave is cold.
But I'd rather be dead than
To be ugly an' old.

When love is gone what
Can a young gal do?
When love is gone, O,
What can a young gal do?
Keep on a-lovin' me, daddy,
Cause I don't want to be blue.

(1941)

The Weary Blues

Droning a drowsy syncopated tune,
Rocking back and forth to a mellow croon,
    I heard a Negro play.
Down on Lenox Avenue the other night
By the pale dull pallor of an old gas light
    He did a lazy sway. . . .
    He did a lazy sway. . . .
To the tune o' those Weary Blues.
With his ebony hands on each ivory key
He made that poor piano moan with melody.
    O Blues!
Swaying to and fro on his rickety stool
He played that sad raggy tune like a musical fool.
    Sweet Blues!
Coming from a black man's soul.
    O Blues!
In a deep song voice with a melancholy tone
I heard that Negro sing, that old piano moan—
    "Ain't got nobody in all this world,
    Ain't got nobody but ma self.
    I's gwine to quit ma frownin'
    And put ma troubles on the shelf."
Thump, thump, thump, went his foot on the floor.
He played a few chords then he sang some more—
    "I got the Weary Blues
    And I can't be satisfied.
    Got the Weary Blues
    And can't be satisfied—

I ain't happy no mo'
And I wish that I had died."
And far into the night he crooned that tune.
The stars went out and so did the moon.
The singer stopped playing and went to bed
While the Weary Blues echoed through his head
He slept like a rock or a man that's dead.

(1925)

Morning After

I was so sick last night I
Didn't hardly know my mind.
So sick last night I
Didn't know my mind.
I drunk some bad licker that
Almost made me blind.
Had a dream last night I
Thought I was in hell.
I drempt last night I
Thought I was in hell.
Woke up and looked around me—
Babe, your mouth was open like a well.
I said, Baby! Baby!
Please don't snore so loud.
Baby! Please!
Please don't snore so loud.
You jest a little bit o' woman but you
Sound like a great big crowd.

(1942)

Trumpet Player

The Negro
With the trumpet at his lips
Has dark moons of weariness
Beneath his eyes
Where the smoldering memory
Of slave ships
Blazed to the crack of whips
About his thighs.

The Negro
With the trumpet at his lips
Has a head of vibrant hair
Tamed down,
Patent-leathered now

Until it gleams
Like jet—
Were jet a crown.

The music
From the trumpet at his lips
Is honey
Mixed with liquid fire.
The rhythm
From the trumpet at his lips
Is ecstasy
Distilled from old desire—

Desire
That is longing for the moon
Where the moonlight's but a spotlight
In his eyes,
Desire
That is longing for the sea
Where the sea's a bar-glass
Sucker size.

The Negro
With the trumpet at his lips
Whose jacket
Has a *fine* one-button roll,
Does not know
Upon what riff the music slips
Its hypodermic needle
To his soul—

But softly
As the tune comes from his throat
Trouble
Mellows to a golden note.

(1947)

Dream Boogie

Good morning, daddy!
Ain't you heard
The boogie-woogie rumble
Of a dream deferred?

Listen closely:
You'll hear their feet
Beating out and beating out a—

You think
It's a happy beat?

Listen to it closely:
Ain't you heard
something underneath
like a—

What did I say?

Sure,
I'm happy!
Take it away!

Hey, pop!
Re-bop!

Mop!

Y-e-a-h!

What don't bug
them white kids
sure bugs me:
We knows everybody
ain't free!

Some of these young ones is cert'ly bad—
One batted a hard ball right through my window
and my gold fish et the glass.

What's written down
for white folks
ain't for us a-tall:
"Liberty And Justice—
Huh—For All."

Oop-pop-a-da!
Skee! Daddle-de-do!
Be-bop!

Salt'peanuts!

De-dop!

(1951)

QUESTIONS FOR CRITICAL THINKING AND WRITING

Experience

1. Which of the four musically influenced poems do you like best—"The Weary Blues," "Young Gal's Blues," "Trumpet Player," or "Dream Boogie"? Why?

Interpretation

2. Select your favorite among the musical poems and provide a commentary on how it develops.
3. Comment on its structure into stanzas or sections.
4. Comment on its images and any similes or metaphors it may contain.
5. Comment on its music—its play of sound.

Evaluation

6. Aside from music, what else does the poem seem to value, to consider important?

Connection

7. Compare the musical poem by Hughes that you chose with another from the section on Poetry and Song in Chapter Fourteen.

Critical Thinking

8. Do you think it is a good idea for poets to imitate explicit musical sounds and structures in their poems? Why or why not? Explain.

Ballad of the Landlord

Landlord, landlord,
My roof has sprung a leak.
Don't you 'member I told you about it
Way last week?

Landlord, landlord,
These steps is broken down.
When you come up yourself
It's a wonder you don't fall down.

Ten Bucks you say I owe you?
Ten Bucks you say is due?
Well, that's Ten Bucks more'n I'll pay you.
Till you fix this house up new.

What? You gonna get eviction orders?
You gonna cut off my heat?
You gonna take my furniture and
Throw it in the street?

Um-huh! You talking high and mighty.
Talk on—till you get through.
You ain't gonna be able to say a word
If I land my fist on you.

Police! Police!
Come and get this man!
He's trying to ruin the government
And overturn the land!

Copper's whistle!
Patrol bell!
Arrest.

Precinct Station.
Iron cell.
Headlines in press:

MAN THREATENS LANDLORD

TENANT HELD NO BAIL

JUDGE GIVES NEGRO 90 DAYS IN COUNTY JAIL

[1949]

Madam and the Rent Man

The rent man knocked.
He said, Howdy-do?
I said, What
Can I do for you?
He said, You know
Your rent is due.

I said, Listen,
Before I'd pay
I'd go to Hades
And rot away!

The sink is broke,
The water don't run,

And you ain't done a thing
You promised to've done.

Back window's cracked,
Kitchen floor squeaks,
There's rats in the cellar,
And the attic leaks.

He said, Madam,
It's not up to me.
I'm just the agent,
Don't you see?

I said, Naturally,
You pass the buck.
If it's money you want
You're out of luck.

He said, Madam,
I ain't pleased!
I said, Neither am I.

So we agrees!

(1943)

QUESTIONS FOR CRITICAL THINKING AND WRITING

Experience

1. Recount your experience of reading either "Ballad of the Landlord" or "Madam and the Rent Man." What is your emotional response to the poem? Why?

Interpretation

2. What point does Hughes make in the poem?
3. How does he do it?
4. What are the function and effect of dialogue or "voices" in the poem?

Evaluation

5. How does the poem raise issues of social justice? What aspects of social concerns are emphasized?

Connection

6. Compare the two poems in terms of theme, language, style, and tone.

Critical Thinking

7. Do you think poets should write poems about social justice and injustice? To what extent do you think such poems are effective catalysts for social change? Explain.

When Sue Wears Red

When Susanna Jones wears red
Her face is like an ancient cameo
Turned brown by the ages.

Come with a blast of trumpets,
    Jesus!

When Susanna Jones wears red
A queen from some time-dead Egyptian night
Walks once again.

Blow trumpets, Jesus!

And the beauty of Susanna Jones in red
Burns in my heart a love-fire sharp like pain.

Sweet silver trumpets,
    Jesus!

(1923)

Listen Here Blues

Sweet girls, sweet girls,
Listen here to me.
All you sweet girls,
Listen here to me:
Gin an' whiskey
Kin make you lose yo' 'ginity.

I used to be a good chile,
Lawd, in Sunday School.
Used to be a good chile,—
In de Sunday School,
Till these licker-headed rounders
Made me everbody's fool.

Good girls, good girls,
Listen here to me.
Oh, you good girls,

Better listen to me:
Don't you fool wid no men 'cause
They'll bring you misery.

(1926)

Consider Me

Consider me,
A colored boy,
Once sixteen,

Once five, once three,
Once nobody,
Now me.

(1951)

Theme for English B

The instructor said,

Go home and write
a page tonight.
And let that page come out of you—
Then, it will be true.

I wonder if it's that simple?

I am twenty-two, colored, born in Winston-Salem.
I went to school there, then Durham, then here
to this college on the hill above Harlem.
I am the only colored student in my class.
The steps from the hill lead down into Harlem,
through a park, then I cross St. Nicholas,
Eighth Avenue, Seventh, and I come to the Y,
the Harlem Branch Y, where I take the elevator
up to my room, sit down, and write this page:

It's not easy to know what is true for you or me
at twenty-two, my age. But I guess I'm what
I feel and see and hear. Harlem, I hear you:
hear you, hear me—we two—you, me, talk on this page.
(I hear New York, too.) Me—who?

Well, I like to eat, sleep, drink, and be in love.
I like to work, read, learn, and understand life.

I like a pipe for a Christmas present,
or records—Bessie, bop, or Bach.
I guess being colored doesn't make me *not* like
the same things other folks like who are other races.

So will my page be colored that I write?
Being me, it will not be white.
But it will be
a part of you, instructor.
You are white—
yet a part of me, as I am a part of you.

That's American.
Sometimes perhaps you don't want to be a part of me.
Nor do I often want to be a part of you.
But we are, that's true!
As I learn from you,
I guess you learn from me—
although you're older—and white—
and somewhat more free.

This is my page for English B.

(1959)

QUESTIONS FOR CRITICAL THINKING AND WRITING

Experience

1. To what extent can you relate to the situation described in "Theme for English B"? Why?
2. What is your response to the poem's speaker? Why?

Interpretation

3. What contrasts are emphasized in the poem? What similarities exist between the speaker and his teacher? What differences?
4. How does the form of the poem relate or connect to its content?
5. Where do you see the meaning of the poem emerging most clearly?

Evaluation

6. What kinds of values are centrally important in the poem? Where do you find them most clearly accentuated?

Connection

7. What connections are there among "When Sue Wears Red," "Listen Here Blues," "Consider Me," and "Theme for English B"?
8. Compare Hughes's "Theme for English B" with Frost's "Tree at my Window" in terms of the extent to which each speaker feels connected with and/or separated from, in Hughes's poem, the teacher, and in Frost's, nature.

Critical Thinking

9. To what extent do you think a middle-aged, white college instructor from the northeastern United States can be an effective teacher for a 20-year-old African-American male raised in the South? Would it be better for the student to have a teacher of his own race, and perhaps one raised in a similar social and cultural context? Explain.

Aunt Sue's Stories

Aunt Sue has a head full of stories.
Aunt Sue has a whole heart full of stories.
Summer nights on the front porch
Aunt Sue cuddles a brown-faced child to her bosom
And tells him stories.

Black slaves
Working in the hot sun,
And black slaves
Walking in the dewy night,
And black slaves
Singing sorrow songs on the banks of a mighty river
Mingle themselves softly
In the flow of old Aunt Sue's voice,
Mingle themselves softly
In the dark shadows that cross and recross
Aunt Sue's stories.

And the dark-faced child, listening,
Knows that Aunt Sue's stories are real stories.
He knows that Aunt Sue never got her stories
Out of any book at all,
But that they came
Right out of her own life.

The dark-faced child is quiet
Of a summer night
Listening to Aunt Sue's stories.

(1921)

Madrid—1937

Damaged by shells, many of the clocks on the public buildings in Madrid have stopped. At night, the streets are pitch dark.

—NEWS ITEM

Put out the lights and stop the clocks.
Let time stand still,
Again man mocks himself
And all his human will to build and grow.
    Madrid!
The fact and symbol of man's woe.
    Madrid!

Time's end and throw-back,
Birth of darkness,
Years of light reduced:
The ever minus of the brute,
The nothingness of barren land
And stone and metal,
Emptiness of gold,
The dullness of a bill of sale:
BOUGHT AND PAID FOR! SOLD!
Stupidity of hours that do not move
Because all clocks are stopped.
Blackness of nights that do not see
Because all lights are out.
    Madrid!
Beneath the bullets!
    Madrid!
Beneath the bombing planes!
    Madrid!
In the fearful dark!

Oh, mind of man!
So long to make a light
Of fire,
    of oil,
        of gas,
And now electric rays.
So long to make a clock
Of sun-dial,
    sand-dial,
    figures,
And now two hands that mark the hours.
Oh, mind of man!

So long to struggle upward out of darkness
To a measurement of time—
And now:
These guns,
These brainless killers in the Guadarrama hills
Trained on Madrid
To stop the clocks in the towers
And shatter all their faces
Into a million bits of nothingness
In the city
That will not bow its head
To darkness and to greed again:
That dares to dream a cleaner dream!
Oh, mind of man
Moulded into a metal shell—
Left-overs of the past
That rain dull hell and misery
On the world again—
Have your way
And stop the clocks!
Bomb out the lights!
And mock yourself!
Mock all the rights of those
Who live like decent folk.
Let guns alone salute
The wisdom of our age
With dusty powder marks
On yet another page of history.
Let there be no sense of time,
Nor measurement of light and dark.
In fact, no light at all!
Let mankind fall
Into the deepest pit that ignorance can dig
For us all!
Descent is quick.
To rise again is slow.
In the darkness of her broken clocks
Madrid cries NO!
In the timeless midnight of the Fascist guns,
Madrid cries NO!
To all the killers of man's dreams,
Madrid cries NO!

To break that NO apart
Will be to break the human heart.

(Madrid, September 24, 1937)

Let America Be America Again

Let America be America again.
Let it be the dream it used to be.
Let it be the pioneer on the plain
Seeking the home where he himself is free.

(America never was America to me.)

Let America be the dream the dreamers dreamed—
Let it be that great strong land of love
Where never kings connive nor tyrants scheme
That any man be crushed by one above.

(It never was America to me.)

(1936)

I'm Still Here

I've been scarred and battered.
My hopes the wind done scattered.
Snow has friz me, sun has baked me.
Looks like between 'em
They done tried to make me
Stop laughin', stop lovin', stop livin'—
But I don't care!
I'm still here!

(1957)

QUESTIONS FOR CRITICAL THINKING AND WRITING

Experience

1. Which is your favorite poem by Hughes? Why?
2. How do you like Hughes's poems in relation to another poet's who celebrates the experience of a particular racial or ethnic group? Why?
3. How does your experience of reading Langston Hughes's poems compare with reading the poems of Emily Dickinson or Robert Frost?

Interpretation

4. Select any one of the final four poems—"Aunt Sue's Stories," "Madrid—1937," "Let America Be America Again," and "I'm Still Here"—and provide an analysis and interpretation of it.

5. Comment on the poem's diction and imagery.
6. Comment on its structure.
7. Comment on its use of sound and rhythm.

Evaluation

8. What social, cultural, or political values are significant in the poem? Where do you find them most forcefully expressed or suggested?

Connection

9. What other writer that you have read—either a poet or a writer of short stories—might you compare with Hughes? Explain the basis for your comparison.

Critical Thinking

10. To what extent do Hughes's poems pose problems of interpretation? Do you think that there is very little actual interpretive work or analysis for you to do on his poems? Why or why not?

POETS INSPIRED BY HUGHES

RITA DOVE

[b. 1952]

Testimonial

Back when the earth was new
and heaven just a whisper,
back when the names of things
hadn't had time to stick;

back when the smallest breezes
melted summer into autumn,
when all the poplars quivered
sweetly in rank and file . . .

the world called, and I answered.
Each glance ignited to a gaze.
I caught my breath and called that life,
swooned between spoonfuls of lemon sorbet.

I was pirouette and flourish,
I was filigree and flame.

How could I count my blessings
when I didn't know their names?

Back when everything was still to come,
luck leaked out everywhere.
I gave my promise to the world,
and the world followed me here.

(1987)

DUDLEY RANDALL
[1914–2000]

The Ballad of Birmingham

(ON THE BOMBING OF A CHURCH IN BIRMINGHAM, ALABAMA 1963)

"Mother dear, may I go downtown
Instead of out to play,
And march the streets of Birmingham
In a Freedom March today?"
"No, baby, no, you may not go,
For the dogs are fierce and wild.
And clubs and hoses, guns and jails
Aren't good for a little child."

"But, mother, I won't be alone.
Other children will go with me,
And march the streets of Birmingham
To make our country free."

"No, baby, no, you may not go,
For I fear those guns will fire.
But you may go to church instead
And sing in the children's choir."
She has combed and brushed her night-dark hair,
And bathed rose petal sweet,
And drawn white gloves on her small brown hands,
And white shoes on her feet.

The mother smiled to know her child
Was in the sacred place,
But that smile was the last smile
To come upon her face.

For when she heard the explosion,
Her eyes grew wet and wild.

She raced through the streets of Birmingham
Calling for her child.

She clawed through bits of glass and brick,
Then lifted out a shoe.
"O, here's the shoe my baby wore,
But, baby, where are you?"

(1969)

KEVIN YOUNG
[b. 1971]

Langston Hughes

LANGSTON HUGHES
LANGSTON HUGHES
O come now
& sang
them weary blues—
Been tired here
feelin' low down
Real
tired here
since you quit town

Our ears no longer trumpets
Our mouths no more bells
FAMOUS POET©—
Busboy—Do tell
us of hell—

Mr. Shakespeare in Harlem
Mr. Theme for English B
Preach on
kind sir
of death, if it please—

We got no more promise
We only got ain't
Let us in
on how
you 'came a saint

LANGSTON
LANGSTON

LANGSTON HUGHES
Won't you send
all heaven's news

(2000)

QUESTIONS FOR CRITICAL THINKING AND WRITING

Experience

1. Which of the poems inspired by Hughes appeals to you most? Why?
2. Describe your experience of reading it. How does it link up with your own experience of life?

Interpretation

3. Explain the central idea of the poem.
4. What poetic elements—diction, imagery, figurative language, structure, syntax, sound, rhythm, and meter—contribute most forcefully to its meaning. Identify two examples of how poetic elements contribute to the poem's meaning—and what they contribute.

Evaluation

5. What values in Hughes's poetry does the poem you chose suggest?

Connections

6. Identify the relationship between each of the poems here with Hughes's work. What aspect of Hughes's poetry and world are echoed in Kevin Young's "Langston Hughes," Dudley Randall's "The Ballad of Birmingham" and in Rita Dove's "Testimonial"?

Critical Thinking

7. Do you think it's a good idea for later poets to show the influence of earlier ones? Explain.

HUGHES ON HARLEM, THE BLUES

A Toast to Harlem

Quiet can seem unduly loud at times. Since nobody at the bar was saying a word during a lull in the bright blues-blare of the Wishing Well's usually overworked juke box, I addressed my friend Simple.

"Since you told me last night you are an Indian, explain to me how it is you find yourself living in a furnished room in Harlem, my brave buck, instead of on a reservation?"

"I am a colored Indian," said Simple.

"In other words, a Negro."

"A Black Foot Indian, daddy-o, not a red one. Anyhow, Harlem is the place I always did want to be. And if it wasn't for landladies, I would be happy. That's a fact! I love Harlem."

"What is it you love about Harlem?"

"It's so full of Negroes," said Simple. "I feel like I got protection."

"From what?"

"From white folks," said Simple. "Furthermore, I like Harlem because it belongs to me."

"Harlem does not belong to you. You don't own the houses in Harlem. They belong to white folks."

"I might not own 'em," said Simple, "but I live in 'em. It would take an atom bomb to get me out."

"Or a depression," I said.

"I would not move for no depression. No, I would not go back down South, not even to Baltimore. I am in Harlem to stay! You say the houses ain't mine. Well, the sidewalk is—and don't nobody push me off. The cops don't even say, 'Move on,' hardly no more. They learned something from them Harlem riots. They used to beat your head right in public, but now they only beat it after they get you down to the stationhouse. And they don't beat it then if they think you know a colored congressman."

"Harlem has few Negro leaders," I said.

"Elected by my *own* vote," said Simple. "Here I ain't scared to vote—that's another thing I like about Harlem. I also like it because we've got subways and it does not take all day to get downtown, neither are you Crowed on the way. Why, Negroes is running some of these subway trains. This morning I rode the A Train down to 34th street. There were a Negro driving it, making ninety miles a hour. That cat *were really driving* that train! Every time he flew by one of them local stations looks like he was saying, 'Look at me! This train is mine!' That cat were gone, ole man. Which is another reason why I like Harlem! Sometimes I run into Duke Ellington on 125th Street and I say, 'What you know there, Duke?' Duke says, 'Solid, ole man.' He does not know me from Adam, but he speaks. One day I saw Lena Horne coming out of the Hotel Theresa and I said, 'Huba! Huba!' Lena smiled. Folks is friendly in Harlem. I feel like I got the world in a jug and the stopper in my hand! So drink a toast to Harlem!"

Simple lifted his glass of beer:

"Here's to Harlem!
They say Heaven is Paradise.
If Harlem ain't Heaven,
Then a mouse ain't mice!"

(1950)

I Remember the Blues

All my life I've heard the blues. In Kansas City as a child fifty years ago on a Charlotte Street corner near my uncle's barber shop, I remember a blind guitar player moaning to the long eerie sliding notes of his guitar.

I'm goin' down to de river,
Take my rockin' chair,
Yes, down to de river,
Rock in my rockin' chair,
If de blues overcome me
I'm gonna rock on away from here.

And in Chicago in my teens, all up and down State Street there were blues, indoors and out, at the Grand and the old Monogram theaters where Ma Rainey sang, in the night clubs, in the dance halls, on phonographs.

Shortly thereafter the three great Smiths—Mamie, Bessie and Clara—began to come to fame. No relation, only sisters in the blues.

It was during the summer of the great Mississippi flood of 1927, about which Bessie Smith sang her famous "Backwater Blues," that I met Bessie Smith in person.

It rained forty days
And the winds began to
blow . . .

She was staying at the same colored hotel as I was, next door to the colored theater in Macon, Georgia. I made a beeline to the theater to hear her sing, not realizing that I could sit right in my room in the hotel (which I did the rest of the week) and hear just as well her great booming voice right through the walls. She never needed a microphone in her life, and at that time, in that place, there was none.

The last time I saw Bessie was on the screen at a private showing of her film, "The St. Louis Blues," after her tragic automobile collision when she bled to death at the door of a white Southern hospital that refused to admit Negroes. To the showing of this film in New York came many of Bessie's friends and admirers. Everybody cried so during the screening that the film had to be run again so folks could see it clearly.

I hate to see
That evenin' sun go down.
Yes, I hate to see that
Evenin' sun go down.
The one I love's done
Gone and left this town.

CRITICS ON HUGHES

ARNOLD RAMPERSAD

Langston Hughes as Folk Poet

FROM LANGSTON HUGHES

Hughes was often called and sometimes called himself, a folk poet. To some people this means that his work is almost artless and thus possibly beneath criticism. The truth indeed is that Hughes published many poems that are doggerel. To reach his primary audience—the black masses—he was prepared to write "down" to them. Some of the pieces in this volume were intended for public recitation mainly; some started as song lyrics. Like many democratic poets, such as William Carlos Williams, he believed that the full range of his poetry should reach print as soon as possible; poetry is a form of social action. However, for Hughes, as for all serious poets, the writing of poetry was virtually a sacred commitment. And while he wished to write no verse that was beyond the ability of the masses of people to understand, his poetry, in common with that of other committed writers, is replete with allusions that must be respected and understood if it is to be properly appreciated. To respect Hughes's work, above all one must respect the African American people and their culture, as well as the American people in general and their national culture.

If Hughes kept at the center of his art the hopes and dreams, as well as the actual lived conditions, of African Americans, he almost always saw these factors in the context of the eternally embattled but eternally inspiring American democratic tradition, even as changes in the world order, notably the collapse of colonialism in Africa, redefined experiences of African peoples around the world. Almost always, too, Hughes attempted to preserve a sense of himself as a poet beyond race and other corrosive social pressures. By his absolute dedication to his art and to his social vision, as well as to his central audience, he fused his unique vision of himself as a poet to his production of art.

"What is poetry?" Langston Hughes was asked near his death. He answered, "It is the human soul entire, squeezed like a lemon or a lime, drop by drop, into atomic words." He wanted no definition of the poet that divorced his art from the immediacy of life. "A poet is a human being," he declared. "Each human being must live within his time, with and for his people, and within the boundaries of his country." Hughes constantly called upon himself for the courage and the endurance necessary to write according to these beliefs. "Hang yourself, poet, in your own words," he urged all those who would take up the mantle of the poet and dare to speak to the world. "Otherwise, you are dead."

ONWUCHEKWA JEMIE

Hughes and the Evolution of Consciousness in Black Poetry

FROM LANGSTON HUGHES: AN INTRODUCTION TO THE POETRY

W. E. B. DuBois's formulation of the dilemma of the black artist was one of the earliest and is still, perhaps, the most lucid. As he stated it, the black artist's problem was in deciding whether to reflect "the beauty revealed to him . . . the soul-beauty of a race which his larger audience despised," or to "articulate the message of another people." As Afro-American history is in part the history of a people caught between two conflicting worlds, and of their efforts to reconcile those worlds, to bring an end to their "double-consciousness" by merging their African and American selves into a single, undivided whole, so is Afro-American literary history in part a record of the black writer's choices between revealing the soul-beauty of his own people and articulating the message of another people; so is it the history of his efforts to bring to an end the very need for choice by somehow bringing the two things together.

The literary beauty revealed to the black writer is contained in his oral folk tradition with its vast universe of themes and images and its smooth and complex strategies of delivery. The "message of another people," on the other hand, is carried in the forms and attitudes, themes and styles and sensibilities of white American and European culture and literature. In another sense, the black writer's problem is as much one of medium as of ethos: his problem is how to actualize the oral tradition in written form, how to recreate the vital force, the sights and sounds and smells of the performance-event on dumb, flat, one-dimensional paper. This problem of *media transfer* is one which the black musician, for instance, does not have, for his art operates within the continuum of the oral medium. The black writer's problem is further complicated by the fact that he has no long written tradition of his own to emulate; and for him to abandon the effort to translate into written form that oral medium which is the full reservoir of his culture would be to annihilate his identity and become a zombie, a programmed vehicle for "the message of another people."

Hardly any black writer of any generation has found it easy, or even possible, to avoid making a choice. And as might be expected, the choices have been neither uniform nor consistent in any era. In every generation, some writers have chosen to reveal the soul-beauty of their own people, some to carry the message of another people. Sometimes the writer vacillates, yielding to the one imperative at one time or in one work, to the other in another, or attempting to answer to both imperatives at the same time and in the same works. Or the writer may undercut the self-acceptance evident in his works with actions and pronouncements indicating reservations and self-doubt.

RICHARD K. BARKSDALE

On Hughes's "Ballad of the Landlord"

FROM LANGSTON HUGHES: THE POET AND HIS CRITICS

An interesting prelude to the social, economic, and political concerns expressed in his poems about Harlem in the 1940s was Hughes's *Ballad of the Landlord,* first published in *Opportunity* (Dec. 1940) and then included as one of the poems in *Jim Crow's Last Stand* (1943) and later in *Montage of a Dream Deferred.* In 1940, the poem was a rather innocuous rendering of an imaginary dialogue between a disgruntled tenant and a tight-fisted landlord. In creating a poem about two such social archetypes, the poet was by no means taking any new steps in dramatic poetry. The literature of most capitalist and noncapitalist societies often pits the haves against the have-nots, and not infrequently the haves are wealthy men of property who "lord" it over improvident men who own nothing. So the confrontation between tenant and landlord was in 1940 just another instance of the social malevolence of a system that punished the powerless and excused the powerful. In fact, Hughes's tone of dry irony throughout the poem leads one to suspect that the poet deliberately overstated a situation and that some sardonic humor was supposed to be squeezed out of the incident. Says the Tenant in furious high dudgeon:

What? You gonna get eviction orders?
You gonna cut off my heat?
You gonna take my furniture and
Throw it in the street?

Um-huh! You talking high and mighty.
Talk on—till you get through.
You ain't gonna be able to say a word
If I land my fist on you.

The Man of Property, in fear and trembling, invokes the symbols of law and order:

Police! Police!
Come and get this man!
He's trying to ruin the government
And overturn the land!

Ironically, this poem, which in 1940 depicted a highly probable incident in American urban life and was certainly not written to incite an economic revolt or promote social unrest, became, by the mid-1960s, a verboten assignment in a literature class in a Boston high school. In his Langston Hughes headnote in *Black Voices* (1967), Abraham Chapman reported that a Boston high school English teacher named Jonathan Kozol was fired for assigning it to his students. By the mid-sixties, Boston and many other American cities had become riot-torn, racial tinderboxes, and their ghettos seethed with tenant anger and discontent. So the poem gathered new meanings reflecting the times, and the word of its tenant persona bespoke the collective anger of thousands of black have-nots. In his review of Gwendolyn Brooks's "Street in Bronzeville" in *Opportunity* (Fall 1945), Hughes praised that young poet's initial volume of poems for its incisive social and political statements and for its "picture-power." His conclusion was that "Poets often say these things better than politicians." Such a comment aptly fits "Ballad of the Landlord." At least, someone on the Boston School Committee evidently thought so.

ONWUCHEKWA JEMIE

On "The Negro Speaks of Rivers"

From Langston Hughes: An Introduction to the Poetry

"The Negro Speaks of Rivers" is perhaps the most profound of these poems of heritage and strength. Composed when Hughes was a mere 17 years old, and dedicated to W. E. B. DuBois, it is a sonorous evocation of transcendent essences so ancient as to appear timeless, predating human existence, longer than human memory. The rivers are part of God's body, and participate in his immortality. They are the earthly analogues of eternity: deep, continuous, mysterious. They are named in the order of their association with black history. The black man has drunk of their life-giving essences, and thereby borrowed their immortality. He and the rivers have become one. The magical transformation of the Mississippi from mud to gold by the sun's radiance is mirrored in the transformation of slaves into free men by Lincoln's Proclamation (and, in Hughes's poems, the transformation of shabby cabarets into gorgeous palaces, dancing girls into queens and priestesses by the spell of black music). As the rivers deepen with time, so does the black man's soul; as their waters ceaselessly flow, so will the black soul endure. The black man has seen the rise and fall of civilizations from the earliest times, seen the beauty and death-changes of the world over the thousands of years, and will survive even this America. The poem's meaning is related to Zora Neale Hurston's judgment of the mythic High John de Conquer, whom she held as a symbol of the triumphant spirit of black America: that John was of the "Be" class. "*Be* here when the ruthless man comes, and *be* here when he is gone." In a time and place where black life is held cheap and the days of black men appear to be numbered, the poem is a majestic reminder of the strength and fullness of history, of the source of that life which transcends even ceaseless labor and burning crosses.

JAMES A. EMANUEL

On "Trumpet Player"

FROM LANGSTON HUGHES

The meaning of jazz to the musician is combined with racial background in "Trumpet Player" in *Fields of Wonder.* Jazz is "honey / Mixed with liquid fire"; and the trumpet player, says the poet at the end, never knows "upon what riff the music slips / Its hypodermic needle / To his soul." Finally, to the musician, trouble "Mellows to a golden note." The first third of the poem outlines the Negro musician, tired eyes smoldering with memories of slavery, hair "tamed down." The weakest stanza shows the Negro's longing for the moon and sea as "old desire" distilled into rhythm. The quoted lines and a few others reveal the true distillation, jazz made precious by its long and sacrificial birth.

While writing "Trumpet Player," Hughes was fully abreast of the new be-bop music emerging from Minton's Playhouse in Harlem. Among the poems inspired by bebop—a rhythmically complex and experimental kind of jazz characterized by dissonance, improvisation, and unusual lyrics—the best is the leadoff "Dream Boogie" in *Montage of a Dream Deferred* (1951):

Good morning, daddy!
Ain't you heard
The boogie-woogie rumble
Of a dream deferred?

Listen closely:
You'll hear their feet
Beating out and beating out a—

You think
It's a happy beat?

Listen to it closely:
Ain't you heard
something underneath
like a—
What did I say?

Sure,
I'm happy!
Take it away!

Hey, pop!
Re-bop!
Mop!

Y-e-a-h!

Keeping up with a changing Harlem, Hughes is alert to the "hip" insider's elastic jargon as well as the generations-old truth of Negro life—the dream deferred. "Dream Boogie" perfectly fulfills its purpose, wasting no word. It has variations in mood: ease, irony, sarcasm, and terse joviality. It mixes old devices of the dramatic monologue with a contemporary boogiewoogie beat. Its rough-hewn grace adds power to its clarity.

CHAPTER SEVENTEEN

A Selection of Contemporary Poetry

Contemporary poetry is multifarious and multitudinous. It is various and variable. There is no simple way to describe, characterize, or categorize it. And that is a good thing, for sure.

Like contemporary fiction, contemporary poetry speaks to today's readers in a language that is close to what they themselves hear and use in their everyday lives. But if it is to be "poetry," it must also be written in a language that is somehow heightened, somehow surprising.

The contemporary poets included here represent a wide range of styles, voices, and perspectives. They come from all parts of the country and they display a splendid spectrum of feelings, attitudes, and views.

BILLY COLLINS

[b. 1941]

Sonnet

All we need is fourteen lines, well, thirteen now,
and after this one just a dozen
to launch a little ship on love's storm-tossed seas,

then only ten more left like rows of beans.
How easily it goes unless you get Elizabethan
and insist the iambic bongos must be played
and rhymes positioned at the ends of lines,
one for every station of the cross.
But hang on here while we make the turn
into the final six where all will be resolved,
where longing and heartache will find an end,
where Laura will tell Petrarch to put down his pen,
take off those crazy medieval tights,
blow out the lights, and come at last to bed.

(2002)

QUESTIONS FOR CRITICAL THINKING AND WRITING

Experience

1. How did you find the experience of reading Collins's sonnet? To what extent were you able to take pleasure in the way he plays with sonnet conventions?

Interpretation

2. What is the theme of Collins's sonnet? Its subject, of course, is the sonnet. But what does his sonnet "say" or suggest about the sonnet as a genre and a form?
3. What sonnet conventions does Collins's sonnet allude to, evoke, imitate, or vary?

Evaluation

4. Do you think this is a good example of its kind—a good sonnet? Why or why not?

Connections

5. Compare Collins's sonnet to a few other sonnets in this book—perhaps with one of Shakespeare's sonnets or with the sonnet by Edna St. Vincent Millay. How is Collins's sonnet related to the others?

Critical Thinking

6. Do you think sonnets can ever become as popular as there were in the past—in Shakespeare's time, for example? Why or why not?

WENDY COPE

[b. 1945]

The Ted Williams Villanelle (FOR ARI BADAINES)

Don't let anybody mess with your swing.

TED WILLIAMS, BASEBALL PLAYER

Watch the ball and do your thing.
This is the moment. Here's your chance.
Don't let anybody mess with your swing.

It's time to shine. You're in the ring.
Step forward, adopt a winning stance,
Watch the ball and do your thing,

And while that ball is taking wing,
Run, without a backward glance.
Don't let anybody mess with your swing.

Don't let envious bastards bring
You down. Ignore the sneers, the can'ts.
Watch the ball and do your thing.

Sing out, if you want to sing.
Jump up, when you long to dance.
Don't let anybody mess with your swing.

Enjoy your talents. Have your fling.
The seasons change. The years advance.
Watch the ball and do your thing,
And don't let anybody mess with your swing.

(2001)

QUESTIONS FOR CRITICAL THINKING AND WRITING

Experience

1. Have you ever read a villanelle before? If so, how does this one compare with your experience of reading those others? If not, how would you describe your experience of reading this villanelle? Did you enjoy it—or not? Explain.

Interpretation

2. How do you interpret both literally and metaphorically the line that serves as the poem's epigraph: "Don't let anybody mess with your swing."
3. What is the literal and figurative sense of the line: "Watch the ball and do your thing."
4. Identify the form of a villanelle. What makes a villanelle a villanelle?

Evaluation

5. To what extent do you find this poem meaningful and significant for your own life? Explain.

Connections

6. Compare this villanelle with another in this book—perhaps with Dylan Thomas's "Do Not Go Gentle into That Good Night." What similarities of form and what differences of theme do you notice?

Critical Thinking

7. Do you think poets should write poems about everyday subjects, popular sports such as baseball? To what extent do you think such poems can be truly meaningful? Explain.

DEBORAH GARRISON

[b. 1965]

A Working Girl Can't Win

Is this the birth of a pundit
or a slut? Is she the woman
they courted for her youthful edge
or a kiss-and-tell bimbo,
a careerist coquette?
The loyal daughter to spin doctors
losing their hair or soul sister
to feminist essayists everywhere?
Is her meteoric rise the source
of her potential demise?
Is her worldview equal parts
yuppie whine and new-age rumor?
Can we get a biopsy on her latest
breast tumor? Is she a failed

anorexic, or diet-pill faddist
who'll let it all go and get fat
in her fifties? Are her roots
rural, right-leaning? Is she Jewish,
self-hating? Past her sell-by date,
or still ovulating?
Will her husband talk?
Does he mind her success?
Does anyone know—does he see
her undressed? Has she been
photographed? Will she play
truth or dare? And more to the point,
does anyone care?
Come next year, will the masses
be reading her story? Will she be
on the cover, or well past her glory?
Either way, we'll move on, and she'll tire
before long: only her children will grieve
at the way she was wronged.

(1998)

QUESTIONS FOR CRITICAL THINKING AND WRITING

Experience

1. How do you respond to the colloquial, familiar, everyday language of this poem? How do you respond to the poem's questions?

Interpretation

2. What is the cumulative effect of the questions piled up by the poem's speaker?
3. What is the significance of the last three lines—the only lines in the poem that do not constitute a question?
4. What image of the working girl does the poem convey? How does it convey this picture?

Evaluation

5. What social and cultural values are alluded to in the poem? To what extent are these values linked with gender?
6. How does the working girl value her own self and her life? How do you know?

Connections

7. Compare this poem with another about the life of a woman.

Critical Thinking

8. How would this poem have to change to accommodate a reversal in title: A Working Girl Can Win? Or explain how the poem would have to change to accommodate a title with a gender change: A Working Guy Can't Win.

JANE KENYON
[1948–1995]

Peonies at Dusk

White peonies blooming along the porch
send out light
while the rest of the yard grows dim.

Outrageous flowers as big as human
heads! They're staggered
by their own luxuriance: I had
to prop them up with stakes and twine.

The moist air intensifies their scent,
and the moon moves around the barn
to find out what it's coming from.

In the darkening June evening
I draw a blossom near, and bending close
search it as a woman searches
a loved one's face.

(1993)

TED KOOSER
[b. 1939]

A Spiral Notebook

The bright wire rolls like a porpoise
in and out of the calm blue sea
of the cover, or perhaps like a sleeper
twisting in and out of his dreams
if you wanted to buy it for that
though it seems to be meant
for more serious work, with its

college-ruled lines and its cover
that states in emphatic white letters
5 SUBJECT NOTEBOOK. It seems
a part of growing old is no longer
to have five subjects, each
demanding an equal share of attention,
set apart by brown cardboard dividers
but instead to stand in a drugstore
and hang on to one subject
a little too long, like this notebook
you weigh in your hands, passing your fingers over its surfaces
as if it were some kind of wonder.

(2004)

QUESTIONS FOR CRITICAL THINKING AND WRITING

Experience

1. How does the poem evoke your experience of using spiral bound notebooks for your schoolwork? To what extent does it do this successfully?

Interpretation

2. Identify and explain the similes in the poem. How are the similes related thematically?
3. If you had to divide the poem into parts or stanzas, where would you break it, and why? Explain.
4. What is the symbolic significance of the notebook? How does the final word of the poem figure in that significance?

Evaluation

5. What value does the notebook have for those imagined who use it? What value does it have for the speaker?

Connection

6. Compare this poem with another about an everyday object. What similarities and differences do you notice in how the poets make the everyday, ordinary object into something symbolic?

Critical Thinking

7. What do you think about how Kooser's poem questions the simplicity and rigidity of the notebook's divisions into five equal parts—as if each subject could be "covered" in the same number of note pages, as if each were of exactly the same value?

TAYLOR MALI

[b. 1965]

Like Lilly Like Wilson

I'm writing the poem that will change the world,
and it's Lilly Wilson at my office door.
Lilly Wilson, the recovering like addict, the worst
I've ever seen.
So, like, bad the whole eighth grade started
calling her Like Lilly Like Wilson Like.
Until I declared my classroom a Like-Free Zone,
and she could not speak for days.

But when she finally did, it was to say,
Mr. Mali, this is . . . so hard.
Now I have to think before I . . . say anything.

Imagine that, Lilly.

It's for your own good.
Even if you don't like . . . it.
I'm writing the poem that will change the world,
and it's Lilly Wilson at my office door.
Lilly is writing a research paper for me about how
homosexuals shouldn't be allowed to adopt
children.
I'm writing the poem that will change the world,
and it's Like Lilly Like Wilson at my office
door.

She's having trouble finding sources, which is to
say, ones that back her up.
They all argue in favor of what I thought I was
against.

And it took four years of college, three years of
graduate school, and every incidental
teaching experience I have ever had to let out
only,

Well, that's real interesting problem, Lilly. But
what do you propose to do about it? That's
what I want to know.

And the eighth-grade mind is a beautiful thing;
Like a new-born baby's face, you can often see it
  change before your very eyes.

I can't believe I'm saying this, Mr. Mali, but I think
  I'd like to switch sides.
And I want to tell her to do more than just believe
  it, but to enjoy it!
That changing your mind is one of the best ways
  of finding out whether or not you still have
  one.
Or even that minds are like parachutes, that it
  doesn't matter what you pack them with so
  long as they open at the right time.
O God, Lilly, I want to say you make me feel like a
  teacher, and who could ask to feel more than
  that?
I want to say all this but manage only, Lilly, I am
  like so impressed with you!

So I finally taught somebody something, namely,
  how to change her mind.
And learned in the process that if I ever change
  the world it's going to be one eighth grader at
  a time.

(2004)

QUESTIONS FOR CRITICAL THINKING AND WRITING

Experience

1. How do you respond to the speaker and the voice of this poem? To what extent do you recognize the kind of student and teacher the poem portrays?

Interpretation

2. How would you characterize the speaker–teacher? How would you characterize the student portrayed in the poem?
3. What is the speaker–teacher's attitude toward the student? What does he object to and how is he trying to change the student's behavior?
4. What is the central idea—the theme of the poem? Where does it come across most strongly?
5. Explain what happens in the narrative or story the poem tells.
6. Explain the significance of the poem's title.

Evaluation

7. What does the teacher value most? Why?
8. What kind of language does the poem criticize? Why?

Connection

9. Compare this poem with another that describes a student-teacher relationship, perhaps Theodore Roethke's "Elegy for Jane." Or compare Mali's poem to another in which a person's way of speaking is a central concern—perhaps Thomas Hardy's "The Ruined Maid."

Critical Thinking

10. Do you think a teacher has the right or the obligation to try to change a student's speech habits? A student's habits of thinking? Why or why not?

CHAPTER EIGHTEEN

A Selection of World Poetry

Recognizing the importance and beauty of poetry written in languages other than English, this selection of world poetry samples modern and contemporary poems from many languages and cultures. Although the poems appear here in English translation, the richness of their imagery, the power of their feeling, and the depth of their thought are conveyed across the borders of culture and language.

CHAIRIL ANWAR (INDONESIA)

[1922–1949]

At the Mosque

TRANSLATED BY BURTON RAFFEL

I shouted at Him
Until He came

We met face to face.

Afterwards He burned in my breast.
All my strength struggles to extinguish Him

My body, which won't be driven, is soaked with sweat

This room
Is the arena where we fight

Destroying each other
One hurling insults, the other gone mad.

MATSUO BASHO* (JAPAN)

[1644–1694]

Three Haiku

TRANSLATED BY ROBERT HASS

First winter rain—
even the monkey
seems to want a raincoat.

Deep autumn-
my neighbor,
how does he live, I wonder?

Sick on a journey,
my dreams wander
the withered fields.

FAIZ AHMED FAIZ (PAKISTAN)

[1911–1984]

Before You Came

TRANSLATED BY AGHA SHAHID ALI

Before you came,
things were as they should be:
the sky was the dead-end of sight,
the road was just a road, wine merely wine.

Now everything is like my heart,
a color at the edge of blood:
the gray of your absence, the color of poison, of thorns,

the gold when we meet, the season ablaze,
the yellow of autumn, the red of flowers, of flames,
and the black when you cover the earth
with the coal of dead fires.

And the sky, the road, the glass of wine?
The sky is a shirt wet with tears,
the road a vein about to break,
and the glass of wine a mirror in which
the sky, the road, the world keep changing.

Don't leave now that you're here—
Stay. So the world may become like itself again:
so the sky may be the sky,
the road a road,
and the glass of wine not a mirror, just a glass of wine.

PABLO NERUDA (CHILE)

[1904–1973]

Ode to My Socks

TRANSLATED BY ROBERT BLY

Maru Mori brought me
a pair
of socks
which she knitted herself
with her sheepherder's hands,
two socks as soft
as rabbits.
I slipped my feet
into them
as though into
two
cases
knitted
with threads of
twilight
and goatskin.
Violet socks,
my feet were
two fish made
of wool,
two long sharks
sea-blue, shot
through
by one golden thread,
two immense blackbirds,
two cannons:

my feet
were honored
in this way
by
these
heavenly
socks.
They were
so handsome
for the first time
my feet seemed to me
unacceptable
like two decrepit
firemen, firemen
unworthy
of that woven
fire,
of those glowing
socks.
Nevertheless
I resisted
the sharp temptation
to save them somewhere
as schoolboys
keep
fireflies,
as learned men
collect
sacred texts,
I resisted
the mad impulse
to put them
into a golden
cage
and each day give them
birdseed
and pieces of pink melon.
Like explorers
in the jungle who hand
over the very rare
green deer
to the spit
and eat it
with remorse,
I stretched out
my feet
and pulled on
the magnificent

socks
and then my shoes.
The moral
of my ode is this:
beauty is twice
beauty
and what is good is doubly
good
when it is a matter of two socks
made of wool
in winter.

BORIS PASTERNAK (RUSSIA)
[1890–1960]

Hamlet

TRANSLATED BY JON STALLWORTHY AND PETER FRANCE

The buzz subsides. I have come on stage.
Leaning in an open door
I try to detect from the echo
What the future has in store.

A thousand opera-glasses level
The dark, point-blank, at me.
Abba, Father, if it be possible
Let this cup pass from me.

I love your preordained design
And am ready to play this role.
For this once let me go.
But the order of the acts is planned,
The end of the road already revealed.
Alone among the Pharisees I stand.
Life is not a stroll across a field.

OCTAVIO PAZ (MEXICO)
[1914–1998]

The Street

TRANSLATED BY MURIEL RUKEYSER

Here is a long and silent street.
I walk in blackness and I stumble and fall
and rise, and I walk blind, my feet

trampling the silent stones and the dry leaves.
Someone behind me also tramples, stones, leaves:
if I slow down, he slows;
if I run, he runs. I turn: nobody.
Everything dark and doorless,
only my steps aware of me,
I turning and turning among these corners
which lead forever to the street
where nobody waits for, nobody follows me,
where I pursue a man who stumbles
and rises and says when he sees me: nobody.

WOLE SOYINKA (NIGERIA)

[b. 1934]

Hamlet

He stilled his doubts, they rose to halt and lame
A resolution on the rack. Passion's flame
Was doused in fear of error, his mind's unease
Bred indulgence to the state's disease
Ghosts embowelled his earth; he clung to rails
In a gallery of abstractions, dissecting tales
As "told by an idiot." Passionless he set a stage
Of passion for the guilt he would engage.

Justice despaired. The turn and turn abouts
Of reason danced default to duty's counterpoint
Till treachery scratched the slate of primal clay
Then Metaphysics waived a thought's delay—
It took the salt in the wound, the "point
Envenom'd too" to steel the prince of doubts.

WISLAWA SZYMBORSKA (POLAND)

[b. 1923]

The Acrobat

TRANSLATED BY STANISLAW BARDVGAT AND CLARE CAVANAGH

From trapeze to
to trapeze, in the hush that
that follows the drum roll's sudden pause, through

through the startled air, more swiftly than
than his body's weight, which once again
again is late for its own fall.

Solo. Or even less than solo,
less, because he's crippled, missing
missing wings, missing them so much
that he can't miss the chance
to soar on shamefully unfeathered
naked vigilance alone.

Arduous ease,
watchful agility,
and calculated inspiration. Do you see
how he waits to pounce in flight; do you know
how he plots from head to toe
against his very being; do you know, do you see
how cunningly he weaves himself through his own former shape
and works to seize this swaying world
by stretching out the arms he has conceived—

beautiful beyond belief at this passing
at this very passing moment that's just passed.

DEREK WALCOTT (CARIBBEAN)

[b.1930]

House of Umbrage

OMEROS, CHAPTER XXXIII (EXCERPT)

House of umbrage, house of fear,
house of multiplying air

House of memories that grow
like shadows out of Allan Poe

House where marriages go bust,
house of telephone and lust

House of caves, behind whose door
a wave is crouching with its roar

House of toothbrush, house of sin,
of branches scratching, "Let me in!"

House whose rooms echo with rain;
of wrinkled clouds with Onan's stain

House that creaks, age fifty-seven,
wooden earth and plaster heaven

House of channelled CableVision
whose dragonned carpets sneer derision

Unlucky house that I uncurse
by rites of genuflecting verse

House I unhouse, house that can harden
as cold as stones in the lost garden

House where I look down the scorched street
but feel its ice ascend my feet

I do not live in you, I bear
my house inside me, everywhere

until your winters grow more kind
by the dancing firelight of mind

where knobs of brass do not exist,
whose doors dissolve with tenderness

House that lets in, at last, those fears
that are its guests, to sit on chairs

feasts on their human faces, and
takes pity simply by the hand

shows her her room, and feels the hum
of wood and brick becoming home.

CHAPTER NINETEEN

For Further Reading

The forms of things unknown, the poet's pen / Turns them to shapes, and gives to airy nothing / A local habitation and a name.

WILLIAM SHAKESPEARE

A good poem is a contribution to reality. The world is never the same once a good poem has been added to it.

DYLAN THOMAS

SHERMAN ALEXIE*

[b. 1966]

Indian Boy Love Song (#1)

Everyone I have lost
in the closing of a door
the click of the lock

is not forgotten, they
do not die but remain
within the soft edges
of the earth, the ash

of house fires and cancer
in sin and forgiveness
huddled under old blankets

dreaming their way into
my hands, my heart
closing tight like fists.

(1982)

Indian Boy Love Song (#2)

I never spoke
the language
of the old women

visiting my mother
in winters so cold
they could freeze
the tongue whole.

I never held my head
to their thin chests
believing in the heart.

Indian women, forgive me.
I grew up distant
and always afraid.

(1982)

ANONYMOUS

Barbara Allan

1

It was in and about the Martinmas time,°
When the green leaves were a falling,
That Sir John Graeme, in the West Country,
Fell in love with Barbara Allan.

2

He sent his man down through the town,
To the place where she was dwelling:
"O haste and come to my master dear,
Gin° ye be Barbara Allan." if

3

O hooly,° hooly rose she up, gently
To the place where he was lying,

"Barbara Allan" [1]***Martinmas*** *Mass (or feast) of St. Martin (d. 655) on November 11.*

And when she drew the curtain by:
"Young man, I think you're dying."

4

"O it's I'm sick, and very, very sick,
  And 'tis a' for Barbara Allan."
"O the better for me ye s'° never be, — shall
  Though your heart's blood were a-spilling.

5

"O dinna ye mind,° young man," said she,
  "When ye was in the tavern a drinking,
That ye made the healths gae° round and round, — go
  And slighted Barbara Allan?"

6

He turned his face unto the wall,
  And death was with him dealing:
"Adieu, adieu, my dear friends all,
  And be kind to Barbara Allan."

7

And slowly, slowly raise she up,
  And slowly, slowly left him,
And sighing said, she could not stay,
  Since death of life had reft° him. — deprived

8

She had not gane° a mile but twa,° — gone/two
  When she heard the dead-bell ringing,
And every jow° that the dead-bell geid,° — beat/gave
  It cried, "Woe to Barbara Allan!"

9

"O mother, mother, make my bed!
  O make it saft and narrow!
Since my love died for me to-day,
  I'll die for him to-morrow."

(c. 1500)

MARGARET ATWOOD*
[b. 1939]

This Is a Photograph of Me

It was taken some time ago.
At first it seems to be
a smeared

[17]***dinna ye mind*** *don't you remember.*

print: blurred lines and grey flecks
blended with the paper;

then, as you scan
it, you see in the left-hand corner
a thing that is like a branch: part of a tree
(balsam or spruce) emerging
and, to the right, halfway up
what ought to be a gentle
slope, a small frame house.

In the background there is a lake,
and beyond that, some low hills.

(The photograph was taken
the day after I drowned.

I am in the lake, in the center
of the picture, just under the surface.

It is difficult to say where
precisely, or to say
how large or small I am:
the effect of water
on light is a distortion

but if you look long enough,
eventually
you will be able to see me.)

(1966)

Spelling

My daughter plays on the floor
with plastic letters,
red, blue & hard yellow,

learning how to spell,
spelling,
how to make spells.

•

I wonder how many women
denied themselves daughters,
closed themselves in rooms,
drew the curtains
so they could mainline words.

•

A child is not a poem,
a poem is not a child.

There is no either / or.
However.

•

I return to the story
of the woman caught in the war
& in labour, her thighs tied
together by the enemy
so she could not give birth.

•

Ancestress: the burning witch,
her mouth covered by leather
to strangle words.

A word after a word
after a word is power.

•

At the point where language falls away
from the hot bones, at the point
where the rock breaks open and darkness
flows out of it like blood, at
the melting point of granite
when the bones know
they are hollow & the word
splits & doubles & speaks
the truth & the body
itself becomes a mouth.
This is a metaphor.

•

How do you learn to spell?
Blood, sky & the sun,
your own name first,
your first naming, your first name,
your first word.

(1981)

W. H. AUDEN*
[1907–1973]

The Unknown Citizen

(To Js/07/M/378 This Marble Monument Is Erected by the State)

He was found by the Bureau of Statistics to be
One against whom there was no official complaint,
And all the reports on his conduct agree

That, in the modern sense of an old-fashioned word, he was a saint,
For in everything he did he served the Greater Community.
Except for the War till the day he retired
He worked in a factory and never got fired
But satisfied his employers, Fudge Motors Inc.
Yet he wasn't a scab or odd in his views,
For his Union reports that he paid his dues,
(Our report on his Union shows it was sound)
And our Social Psychology workers found
That he was popular with his mates and liked a drink.
The Press are convinced that he bought a paper every day
And that his reactions to advertisements were normal in every way.
Policies taken out in his name prove that he was fully insured,
And his Health-card shows he was once in hospital but left it cured.
Both Producers Research and High-Grade Living declare
He was fully sensible to the advantages of the Installment Plan
And had everything necessary to the Modern Man,
A phonograph, a radio, a car and a frigidaire.
Our researchers into Public Opinion are content
That he held the proper opinions for the time of year;
When there was peace, he was for peace; when there was war, he went.
He was married and added five children to the population,
Which our Eugenist says was the right number for a parent of his
generation.
And our teachers report that he never interfered with their
education.

Was he free? Was he happy? The question is absurd:
Had anything been wrong, we should certainly have heard.

(1940)

IN MEMORY OF W. B. YEATS

[d. January 1939]

1

He disappeared in the dead of winter:
The brooks were frozen, the air-ports almost deserted,
And snow disfigured the public statues;
The mercury sank in the mouth of the dying day.
O all the instruments agree
The day of his death was a dark cold day.

Far from his illness
The wolves ran on through the evergreen forests,
The peasant river was untempted by the fashionable quays;
By mourning tongues
The death of the poet was kept from his poems.

But for him it was his last afternoon as himself,
An afternoon of nurses and rumours;
The provinces of his body revolted,
The squares of his mind were empty,
Silence invaded the suburbs,
The current of his feeling failed: he became his admirers.

Now he is scattered among a hundred cities
And wholly given over to unfamiliar affections;
To find his happiness in another kind of wood
And be punished under a foreign code of conscience.
The words of a dead man
Are modified in the guts of the living.

But in the importance and noise of to-morrow
When the brokers are roaring like beasts on the
  floor of the Bourse,° stock exchange
And the poor have the sufferings to which they are
  fairly accustomed,
And each in the cell of himself is almost convinced of his freedom;
A few thousand will think of this day
As one thinks of a day when one did something slightly unusual.

O all the instruments agree
The day of his death was a dark cold day.

2

You were silly like us: your gift survived it all;
The parish of rich women, physical decay,
Yourself; mad Ireland hurt you into poetry.
Now Ireland has her madness and her weather still,
For poetry makes nothing happen: it survives
In the valley of its saying where executives
Would never want to tamper; it flows south
From ranches of isolation and the busy griefs,
Raw towns that we believe and die in; it survives,
A way of happening, a mouth.

3

Earth, receive an honoured guest;
William Yeats is laid to rest:
Let the Irish vessel lie
Emptied of its poetry.

Time that is intolerant
Of the brave and innocent,
And indifferent in a week
To a beautiful physique,

Worships language and forgives
Everyone by whom it lives;
Pardons cowardice, conceit,
Lays its honours at their feet.

Time that with this strange excuse
Pardoned Kipling° and his views,
And will pardon Paul Claudel,°
Pardons him for writing well.

In the nightmare of the dark°
All the dogs of Europe bark,
And the living nations wait,
Each sequestered in its hate;

Intellectual disgrace
Stares from every human face,
And the seas of pity lie
Locked and frozen in each eye.

Follow, poet, follow right
To the bottom of the night,
With your unconstraining Voice
Still persuade us to rejoice;

With the farming of a verse
Make a vineyard of the curse,
Sing of human unsuccess
In a rapture of distress;

In the deserts of the heart
Let the healing fountain start,
In the prison of his days
Teach the free man how to praise.

(1940)

Funeral Blues

Stop all the clocks, cut off the telephone,
Prevent the dog from barking with a juicy bone,
Silence the pianos and with muffled drum
Bring out the coffin, let the mourners come.

"In Memory of W. B. Yeats" [55]***Kipling*** *Rudyard Kipling (1865–1936), English writer with imperialistic views.* [56]***Paul Claudel*** *French Catholic writer (1868–1955) of extreme political conservatism.* [58]***the dark*** *World War II broke out a few months after Auden wrote this poem.*

Let aeroplanes circle moaning overhead
Scribbling on the sky the message He Is Dead,
Put crepe bows round the white necks of the public doves,
Let the traffic policemen wear black cotton gloves.

"He was my North, my South, my East and West,
My working week and my Sunday rest,
My noon, my midnight, my talk, my song;
I thought that love would last for ever: I was wrong.

The stars are not wanted now: put out every one;
Pack up the moon and dismantle the sun;
Pour away the ocean and sweep up the wood;
For nothing now can ever come to any good.

(1936)

September 1, 1939

I sit in one of the dives
On Fifty-second Street
Uncertain and afraid
As the clever hopes expire
Of a low dishonest decade:
Waves of anger and fear
Circulate over the bright
And darkened lands of the earth,
Obsessing our private lives;
The unmentionable odour of death
Offends the September night.

Accurate scholarship can
Unearth the whole offence
From Luther until now
That has driven a culture mad,
Find what occurred at Linz,
What huge imago made
A psychopathic god:
I and the public know
What all schoolchildren learn,
Those to whom evil is done
Do evil in return.

Exiled Thucydides knew
All that a speech can say
About Democracy,
And what dictators do,

The elderly rubbish they talk
To an apathetic grave;
Analysed all in his book,
The enlightenment driven away,
The habit-forming pain.
Mismanagement and grief:
We must suffer them all again.

Into this neutral air
Where blind skyscrapers use
Their full height to proclaim
The strength of Collective Man,
Each language pours its vain
Competitive excuse:
But who can live for long
In an euphoric dream;
Out of the mirror they stare,
Imperialism's face
And the international wrong.

Faces along the bar
Cling to their average day:
The lights must never go out,
The music must always play,
All the conventions conspire
To make this fort assume
The furniture of home;
Lest we should see where we are,
Lost in a haunted wood,
Children afraid of the night
Who have never been happy or good.

The windiest militant trash
Important Persons shout
Is not so crude as our wish:
What mad Nijinsky wrote
About Diaghilev
Is true of the normal heart;
For the error bred in the bone
Of each woman and each man
Craves what it cannot have,
Not universal love
But to be loved alone.

From the conservative dark
Into the ethical life
The dense commuters come,

Repeating their morning vow;
"I *will* be true to the wife,
I'll concentrate more on my work,"
And helpless governors wake
To resume their compulsory game:
Who can release them now,
Who can reach the deaf,
Who can speak for the dumb?

Defenceless under the night
Our world in stupor lies;
Yet, dotted everywhere,
Ironic points of light
Flash out wherever the Just
Exchange their messages:
May I, composed like them
Or Eros and of dust,
Beleaguered by the same
Negation and despair,
Show an affirming flame.

(1939)

JIMMY SANTIAGO BACA

[b. 1952]

From Meditations on the South Valley

XVII

I love the wind
when it blows through my barrio.
It hisses its snake love
down calles de polvo,
and cracks egg-shell skins
of abandoned homes.
Stray dogs find shelter
along the river,
where great cottonwoods rattle
like old covered wagons,
stuck in stagnant waterholes.
Days when the wind blows
full of sand and grit,
men and women make decisions
that change their whole lives.
Windy days in the barrio
give birth to divorce papers

and squalling separation. The wind tells us
what others refuse to tell us,
informing men and women of a secret,
that they move away to hide from.

(1979)

© Jill Krementz

ELIZABETH BISHOP*
[1911–1979]

Sestina

September rain falls on the house.
In the failing light, the old grandmother
sits in the kitchen with the child
beside the Little Marvel Stove,
reading the jokes from the almanac,
laughing and talking to hide her tears.

She thinks that her equinoctial tears
and the rain that beats on the roof of the house
were both foretold by the almanac,
but only known to a grandmother.
The iron kettle sings on the stove.
She cuts some bread and says to the child,

It's time for tea now; but the child
is watching the teakettle's small hard tears
dance like mad on the hot black stove,
the way the rain must dance on the house.
Tidying up, the old grandmother
hangs up the clever almanac

on its string. Birdlike, the almanac
hovers half open above the child,
hovers above the old grandmother
and her teacup full of dark brown tears.
She shivers and says she thinks the house
feels chilly, and puts more wood in the stove.

It was to be, says the Marvel Stove.
I know what I know, says the almanac.
With crayons the child draws a rigid house
and a winding pathway. Then the child
puts in a man with buttons like tears
and shows it proudly to the grandmother.

But secretly, while the grandmother
busies herself about the stove,
the little moons fall down like tears
from between the pages of the almanac
into the flower bed the child
has carefully placed in the front of the house.

Time to plant tears, says the almanac.
The grandmother sings to the marvelous stove
and the child draws another inscrutable house.

(1965)

One Art

The art of losing isn't hard to master;
so many things seem filled with the intent
to be lost that their loss is no disaster.

Lose something every day. Accept the fluster
of lost door keys, the hour badly spent.
The art of losing isn't hard to master.

Then practice losing farther, losing faster:
places, and names, and where it was you meant
to travel. None of these will bring disaster.

I lost my mother's watch. And look! my last, or
next-to-last, of three loved houses went.
The art of losing isn't hard to master.

I lost two cities, lovely ones. And, vaster,
some realms I owned, two rivers, a continent.
I miss them, but it wasn't a disaster.

—Even losing you (the joking voice, a gesture
I love) I shan't have lied. It's evident
the art of losing's not too hard to master
though it may look like (*Write it!*) like disaster.

(1976)

The Fish

I caught a tremendous fish
and held him beside the boat
half out of water, with my hook

fast in a corner of his mouth.
He didn't fight.
He hadn't fought at all.
He hung a grunting weight,
battered and venerable
and homely. Here and there
his brown skin hung in strips
like ancient wall-paper,
and its pattern of darker brown
was like wall-paper:
shapes like full-blown roses
stained and lost through age.
He was speckled with barnacles,
fine rosettes of lime,
and infested
with tiny white sea-lice,
and underneath two or three
rags of green weed hung down.
While his gills were breathing in
the terrible oxygen
—the frightening gills,
fresh and crisp with blood,
that can cut so badly—
I thought of the coarse white flesh
packed in like feathers,
the big bones and the little bones,
the dramatic reds and blacks
of his shiny entrails,
and the pink swim-bladder
like a big peony.
I looked into his eyes
which were far larger than mine
but shallower, and yellowed,
the irises backed and packed
with tarnished tinfoil
seen through the lenses
of old scratched isinglass.
They shifted a little, but not
to return my stare.
—It was more like the tipping
of an object toward the light.
I admired his sullen face,
the mechanism of his jaw,
and then I saw
that from his lower lip
—if you could call it a lip—
grim, wet, and weapon-like,
hung five old pieces of fish-line,

or four and a wire leader
with the swivel still attached,
with all their five big hooks
grown firmly in his mouth.
A green line, frayed at the end
where he broke it, two heavier lines,
and a fine black thread
still crimped from the strain and snap
when it broke and he got away.
Like medals with their ribbons
frayed and wavering,
a five-haired beard of wisdom
trailing from his aching jaw.
I stared and stared
and victory filled up
the little rented boat,
from the pool of bilge
where oil had spread a rainbow
around the rusted engine
to the bailer rusted orange,
the sun-cracked thwarts,
the oarlocks on their strings,
the gunnels—until everything
was rainbow, rainbow, rainbow!
And I let the fish go.

(1946)

www

WILLIAM BLAKE*

[1757–1827]

The Clod & the Pebble

"Love seeketh not Itself to please,
Nor for itself hath any care;
But for another gives its ease,
And builds a Heaven in Hell's despair."

So sang a little Clod of Clay,
Trodden with the cattle's feet;
But a Pebble of the brook,
Warbled out these metres meet:

"Love seeketh only Self to please,
To bind another to its delight,
Joys in another's loss of ease,
And builds a Hell in Heaven's despite."

(1794)

The Lamb

Little Lamb, who made thee?
Dost thou know who made thee?
Gave thee life & bid thee feed,
By the stream & o'er the mead;
Gave thee clothing of delight,
Softest clothing wooly bright;
Gave thee such a tender voice,
Making all the vales rejoice!
Little Lamb who made thee?
Dost thou know who made thee?

Little Lamb I'll tell thee,
Little Lamb I'll tell thee!
He is calléd by thy name,
For he calls himself a Lamb:
He is meek & he is mild,
He became a little child:
I a child & thou a lamb,
We are calléd by his name.
Little Lamb God bless thee.
Little Lamb God bless thee.

(1789)

The Tyger

Tyger! Tyger! burning bright
In the forests of the night,
What immortal hand or eye
Could frame thy fearful symmetry?

In what distant deeps or skies
Burnt the fire of thine eyes?
On what wings dare he aspire?
What the hand, dare seize the fire?

And what shoulder, & what art,
Could twist the sinews of thy heart?

And when thy heart began to beat,
What dread hand? & what dread feet?

What the hammer? what the chain?
In what furnace was thy brain?
What the anvil? what dread grasp
Dare its deadly terrors clasp?

When the stars threw down their spears,
And water'd heaven with their tears,
Did he smile his work to see?
Did he who made the Lamb make thee?

Tyger! Tyger! burning bright
In the forests of the night,
What immortal hand or eye
Dare frame thy fearful symmetry?

(1794)

The Garden of Love

I went to the Garden of Love,
And saw what I never had seen:
A Chapel was built in the midst,
Where I used to play on the green.

And the gates of this Chapel were shut,
And "Thou shalt not" writ over the door;
So I turn'd to the Garden of Love,
That so many sweet flowers bore,

And I saw it was filled with graves,
And tomb-stones where flowers should be:
And Priests in black gowns were walking their rounds,
And binding with briars my joys & desires.

(1794)

EAVAN BOLAND

[b. 1944]

Anorexic

Flesh is heretic.
My body is a witch.
I am burning it.

Yes I am torching
her curves and paps and wiles.
They scorch in my self denials.

How she meshed my head
in the half-truths
of her fevers

till I renounced
milk and honey
and the taste of lunch.

I vomited
her hungers.
Now the bitch is burning.

I am starved and curveless.
I am skin and bone.
She has learned her lesson.

Thin as a rib
I turn in sleep.
My dreams probe

a claustrophobia
a sensuous enclosure.
How warm it was and wide

once by a warm drum,
once by the song of his breath
and in his sleeping side.

Only a little more,
only a few more days
sinless, foodless,

I will slip
back into him again
as if I had never been away.

Caged so
I will grow
angular and holy

past pain,
keeping his heart
such company

as will make me forget
in a small space
the fall

into forked dark,
into python needs
heaving to hips and breasts
and lips and heat
and sweat and fat and greed.

(1980)

ANNE BRADSTREET

[1612–1672]

To My Dear and Loving Husband

If ever two were one, then surely we.
If ever man were loved by wife, then thee;
If ever wife was happy in a man,
Compare with me, ye women, if you can.
I prize thy love more than whole mines of gold
Or all the riches that the East doth hold.
My love is such that rivers cannot quench,
Nor aught but love from thee give recompense.
Thy love is such I can no way repay,
The heavens reward thee manifold, I pray.
Then while we live, in love let's so perséver
That when we live no more, we may live ever.

(1678)

EDWARD KAMAU BRATHWAITE

[b. 1930]

Ogoun

FOR PAPALEGBA BOB'OB O'NEILL OF MILE AND QUARTER

My uncle made chairs. tables. balanced doors on. dug out
coffins. smoothing the white wood out

w/plane and quick sandpaper until
it shone like his short-sighted glasses

The knuckles of his hands are silver
knobs of nails hit. hurt and flattened

out w/ blast of heavy hammer. He was knock-knee'd.
flat-footed and his clip clop sandals slapped across the concrete

flooring of his little shop where canefield mulemen and a fleet
of Bedford lorry drivers dropped in to scratch themselves and talk

There was no shock of wood. no beam
of light mahogany his saw-teeth couldn't handle

When shaping squares for locks. a key hole
care tapped rat tat tat upon the handle

of his humpback'd chisel. Cold
world of wood caught fire as he whittled: rectangle

window frames. the intersecting x of folding chairs. triangle

trellises. the donkey
box-cart in its squeaking square

But he was poor and most days he was hungry
Imported cabinets w/ mirrors. formica table-

tops. spine-curving chairs made up of tubes. w/ hollow
steel-like bird-bones that sit on rubber ploughs.

thin beds. stretched not on boards. but blue high-tension cables
was what the world preferred.

And yet he had a block of wood that would have baffled them.

With knife and gimlet care he worked away at this on Sundays

explored its knotted hurts. cutting his way
along its yellow whorls until his hands could feel

how it had swell(ed) and shiver(ed). breathing air
its weathered green burning to rings of time

its contoured grain still tuned to roots and water.
And as he cut. he hear the creak of forests:

green lizard faces gulp. grey memories w/ motheyes
watch him from their shadow. soft

liquid tendrils leak among the flowers
and a black rigid thunder he had nvr hear w/ in his hammer

come stomping up the trunks. And as he work w/ in this shattered
Sunday shop. the wood take shape: dry shuttered

eye(s). slack anciently everted lips. flat
ruin face. eaten by pox. ravage by rat

and woodworm. dry cistern mouth. crack
gullet crying for the desert. the heavy black

enduring jaw. lost pain. lost iron
emerging woodwork image of his anger

(1981)

© Jill Krementz

GWENDOLYN BROOKS*
[1917–2000]

We Real Cool

THE POOL PLAYERS. SEVEN AT THE GOLDEN SHOVEL.

We real cool. We
Left school. We

Lurk late. We
Strike straight. We

Sing sin. We
Thin gin. We

Jazz June. We
Die soon.

(1950)

First fight. Then fiddle

First fight. Then fiddle. Ply the slipping string
With feathery sorcery; muzzle the note
With hurting love; the music that they wrote

Bewitch, bewilder. Qualify to sing
Threadwise. Devise no salt, no hempen thing
For the dear instrument to bear. Devote
The bow to silks and honey. Be remote
A while from malice and from murdering.
But first to arms, to armor. Carry hate
In front of you and harmony behind.
Be deaf to music and to beauty blind.
Win war. Rise bloody, maybe not too late
For having first to civilize a space
Wherein to play your violin with grace.

(1945)

ELIZABETH BARRETT BROWNING
[1806–1861]

How do I love thee? Let me count the ways

How do I love thee? Let me count the ways.
I love thee to the depth and breadth and height
My soul can reach, when feeling out of sight
For the ends of Being and ideal Grace.
I love thee to the level of everyday's
Most quiet need, by sun and candle-light.
I love thee freely, as men strive for Right;
I love thee purely, as they turn from Praise.
I love thee with the passion put to use
In my old griefs, and with my childhood's faith.
I love thee with a love I seemed to lose
With my lost saints—I love thee with the breath,
Smiles, tears, of all my life!—and, if God choose,
I shall but love thee better after death.

(1850)

ROBERT BURNS
[1759–1796]

A Red, Red Rose

O my luve's like a red, red rose,
  That's newly sprung in June;
O my luve's like the melodie
  That's sweetly played in tune.

As fair art thou, my bonnie lass,
 So deep in luve am I;
And I will luve thee still, my dear,
 Till a' the seas gang dry.

Till a' the seas gang dry, my dear,
 And the rocks melt wi' the sun:
O I will love thee still,my dear,
 While the sands o' life shall run.

And fare thee weel, my only luve,
 And fare thee weel awhile!
And I will come again, my luve,
 Though it were ten thousand mile.

(1796)

LEWIS CARROLL (CHARLES LUTWIDGE DODGSON)

[1832–1898]

Jabberwocky

'Twas brillig, and the slithy toves
 Did gyre and gimble in the wabe:
All mimsy were the borogoves,
 And the mome raths outgrabe.

"Beware the Jabberwock, my son!
 The jaws that bite, the claws that catch!
Beware the Jubjub bird, and shun
 The frumious Bandersnatch!"

He took his vorpal sword in hand:
 Long time the manxome foe he sought—
So rested he by the Tumtum tree,
 And stood awhile in thought.

And, as in uffish thought he stood,
 The Jabberwock, with eyes of flame,
Came whiffling through the tulgey wood,
 And burbled as it came!

One, two! One, two! And through and through
 The vorpal blade went snicker-snack!
He left it dead, and with its head
 He went galumphing back.

"And hast thou slain the Jabberwock?
Come to my arms, my beamish boy!
O frabjous day! Callooh! Callay!"
He chortled in his joy.

'Twas brillig, and the slithy toves
Did gyre and gimble in the wabe:
All mimsy were the borogoves,
And the mome raths outgrabe.

(1871)

RAYMOND CARVER
[1939–1988]

Photograph of My Father in His Twenty-second Year

October. Here in this dank, unfamiliar kitchen
I study my father's embarrassed young man's face.
Sheepish grin, he holds in one hand a string
of spiny yellow perch, in the other
a bottle of Carlsbad beer.

In jeans and denim shirt, he leans
against the front fender of a 1934 Ford.
He would like to pose bluff and hearty for his posterity,
wear his old hat cocked over his ear.
All his life my father wanted to be bold.

But the eyes give him away, and the hands
that limply offer the string of dead perch
and the bottle of beer. Father, I love you,
yet how can I say thank you, I who can't hold my liquor either,
and don't even know the places to fish?

(1988)

SANDRA CISNEROS*
[b. 1954]

Pumpkin Eater

I'm no trouble.
Honest to God I'm not.
I'm not

the kind of woman
who telephones in the middle of the night,
—who told you that?—
splitting the night like machete.
Before and after. After. Before.
No, no, not me.
I'm not

the she who slings words bigger than rocks,
sharper than Houdini knives,
verbal Molotovs.

The one who did that—*yo no fuí*—
that wasn't me.

I'm no hysteric,
terrorist,
emotional anarchist.

I keep inside a pumpkin shell.
There I do very well.

Shut a blind eye to where
my pumpkin-eater roams.

I keep like fruitcake.
Subsist on air.
Not a worry nor care.
Please.
I'm as free for the taking
as the eyes of Saint Lucy.
No trouble at all.

I swear, I swear, I swear . . .

(1994)

LUCILLE CLIFTON
[b. 1936]

Homage to My Hips

these hips are big hips.
they need space to
move around in.

they don't fit into little
pretty places. these hips
are free hips.
they don't like to be held back.
these hips have never been enslaved,
they go where they want to go
they do what they want to do.
these hips are mighty hips.
these hips are magic hips.
i have known them
to put a spell on a man and
spin him like a top!

(1972)

JUDITH ORTIZ COFER

[b. 1952]

The Game

The little humpbacked girl
did not go to school,
but was kept home to help her mother,
an unsmiling woman with other children
whose spines were not twisted
into the symbol of a family's shame.

At birth,
on first seeing the child
curled into a question mark,
the eternal *why*
she would have to carry home,
she gave her the name of Cruz,
for the cross Christ bore
to Calvary.

In my house,
we did not speak of her affliction,
but acted as if Cruz,
whose lovely head
sat incongruously upon a body
made of stuck-together parts—
like a child's first attempt
at cutting and pasting a paper doll—
was the same
as any of my other friends.

But when she stood at our door,
waiting for me to go out and play,
Mother fell silent, awed, perhaps,
by the sight
of one of her God's small mysteries.

Running to her backyard,
Cruz and I would enter a playhouse
she had built of palm fronds
where we'd play her favorite game: "family."
I was always cast in the role
of husband or child—perfect
in my parts—I'd praise her lavishly
for the imaginary dishes
she placed before me,
while she laughed, delighted
at my inventions, lost in the game,
until it started getting too late
to play pretend.

(1993)

SAMUEL TAYLOR COLERIDGE
[1772–1834]

Kubla Khan°

OR A VISION IN A DREAM. A FRAGMENT

In Xanadu did Kubla Khan
A stately pleasure dome decree:
Where Alph, the sacred river, ran
Through caverns measureless to man
   Down to a sunless sea.

So twice five miles of fertile ground
With walls and towers were girdled round:
And there were gardens bright with sinuous rills,
Where blossomed many an incense-bearing tree;
And here were forests ancient as the hills,
Enfolding sunny spots of greenery.

"Kubla Khan" **Kubla Khan** *the first ruler of the Mongol dynasty in thirteenth-century China. Coleridge's topography and place names are imaginary.*

But oh! that deep romantic chasm which slanted
Down the green hill athwart a cedarn cover!
A savage place! as holy and enchanted
As e'er beneath a waning moon was haunted
By woman wailing for her demon lover!
And from this chasm, with ceaseless turmoil seething,
As if this earth in fast thick pants were breathing,
A mighty fountain momently was forced:
Amid whose swift half-intermitted burst
Huge fragments vaulted like rebounding hail,
Or chaffy grain beneath the thresher's flail:
And 'mid these dancing rocks at once and ever
It flung up momently the sacred river.
Five miles meandering with a mazy motion
Through wood and dale the sacred river ran,
Then reached the caverns measureless to man,
And sank in tumult to a lifeless ocean:
And 'mid this tumult Kubla heard from far
Ancestral voices prophesying war!

The shadow of the dome of pleasure
Floated midway on the waves;
Where was heard the mingled measure
From the fountain and the caves.
It was a miracle of rare device,
A sunny pleasure dome with caves of ice!

A damsel with a dulcimer
In a vision once I saw:
It was an Abyssinian maid,
And on her dulcimer she played,
Singing of Mount Abora.
Could I revive within me
Her symphony and song,
To such a deep delight 'twould win me,
That with music loud and long,
I would build that dome in air,
That sunny dome! those caves of ice!
And all who heard should see them there,
And all should cry, Beware! Beware!
His flashing eyes, his floating hair!
Weave a circle round him thrice,
And close your eyes with holy dread,
For he on honey-dew hath fed,
And drunk the milk of Paradise.

(1798)

Photograph © 2003 by Jill Krementz

www

BILLY COLLINS*
[b. 1941]

Introduction to Poetry

I ask them to take a poem
and hold it up to the light
like a color slide

or press an ear against its hive.

I say drop a mouse into a poem
and watch him probe his way out,

or walk inside the poem's room
and feel the walls for a light switch.

I want them to water-ski
across the surface of a poem
waving at the author's name on the shore.

But all they want to do
is tie the poem to a chair with rope
and torture a confession out of it.

They begin beating it with a hose
to find out what it really means.

(1988)

The History Teacher

Trying to protect his students' innocence
he told them the Ice Age was really just
the Chilly Age, a period of a million years
when everyone had to wear sweaters.
And the Stone Age became the Gravel Age,
named after the long driveways of the time.

The Spanish Inquisition was nothing more
than an outbreak of questions such as
"How far is it from here to Madrid?"
"What do you call the matador's hat?"

The War of the Roses took place in a garden,
and the Enola Gay dropped one tiny atom
on Japan.

The children would leave his classroom
for the playground to torment the weak
and the smart,
mussing up their hair and breaking their glasses,

while he gathered up his notes and walked home
past flower beds and white picket fences,
wondering if they would believe that soldiers
in the Boer War told long, rambling stories
designed to make the enemy nod off.

(1991)

My Number

Is Death miles away from this house,
reaching for a widow in Cincinnati
or breathing down the neck of a lost hiker
in British Columbia?

Is he too busy making arrangements,
tampering with air brakes,
scattering cancer cells like seeds,
loosening the wooden beams of roller coasters

to bother with my hidden cottage
that visitors find so hard to find?

Or is he stepping from a black car
parked at the dark end of the lane,
shaking open the familiar cloak,
its hood raised like the head of a crow,
and removing the scythe from the trunk?

Did you have any trouble with the directions?
I will ask, as I start talking my way out of this.

(1988)

The Listener

I cannot see you a thousand miles from here,
but I can hear you
whenever you cough in your bedroom
or when you set down
your wineglass on a granite counter.

This afternoon
I even heard scissors moving
at the tips of your hair
and the dark snips falling
onto a marble floor.

I keep the jazz
on the radio turned off.
I walk across the floor softly,
eyes closed,
the windows in the house shut tight.

I hear a motor on the road in front,
a plane humming overhead,
someone hammering,
then there is nothing
but the white stone building of silence.

You must be asleep
for it to be this quiet,
so I will sit and wait
for the rustle of your blanket
or a noise from your dream.

Meanwhile, I will listen to the ant bearing
a dead comrade
across these floorboards—
the noble sounds
of his tread and his low keening.

(2002)

COUNTEE CULLEN
[1903–1946]

Incident

Once riding in old Baltimore,
  Heart-filled, head-filled with glee,
I saw a Baltimorean
  Keep looking straight at me.

Now I was eight and very small,
  And he was no whit bigger,
And so I smiled, but he poked out
  His tongue and called me; "Nigger."

I saw the whole of Baltimore
From May until December:
Of all the things that happened there
That's all that I remember.

(1925)

E. E. CUMMINGS*
[1894–1962]

anyone lived in a pretty how town

anyone lived in a pretty how town
(with up so floating many bells down)
spring summer autumn winter
he sang his didn't he danced his did.

Women and men (both little and small)
cared for anyone not at all
they sowed their isn't they reaped their same
sun moon stars rain

children guessed (but only a few
and down they forgot as up they grew
autumn winter spring summer)
that noone loved him more by more

when by now and tree by leaf
she laughed his joy she cried his grief
bird by snow and stir by still
anyone's any was all to her

someones married their everyones
laughed their cryings and did their dance
(sleep wake hope and then) they
said their nevers they slept their dream

stars rain sun moon
(and only the snow can begin to explain
how children are apt to forget to remember
with up so floating many bells down)

one day anyone died i guess
(and noone stooped to kiss his face)
busy folk buried them side by side
little by little and was by was
all by all and deep by deep

and more by more they dream their sleep
noone and anyone earth by april
wish by spirit and if by yes.

Women and men (both dong and ding)
summer autumn winter spring
reaped their sowing and went their came
sun moon stars rain

(1940)

i thank You God for most this amazing

i thank You God for most this amazing
day: for the leaping greenly spirits of trees
and a blue true dream of sky; and for everything
which is natural which is infinite which is yes

(i who have died am alive again today,
and this is the sun's birthday; this is the birth

day of life and of love and wings:and of the gay
great happening illimitably earth)

how should tasting touching hearing seeing
breathing any—lifted from the no
of all nothing—human merely being
doubt unimaginable You?

(now the ears of my ears awake and
now the eyes of my eyes are opened)

(1950)

Ariel
www

JOHN DONNE*

[1572–1631]

Song

Go, and catch a falling star,
    Get with child a mandrake root,°
Tell me, where all past years are,
    Or who cleft the devil's foot,

"Song" **2*mandrake root*** *Resembling a human body, the forked root of the mandrake was used as a medicine to induce conception.*

Teach me to hear mermaids singing
Or to keep off envy's stinging,
And find
What wind
Serves to advance an honest mind.

If thou beest born to strange sights,
Things invisible to see,
Ride ten thousand days and nights,
Till age snow white hairs on thee;
Thou, when thou return'st, wilt tell me
All strange wonders that befell thee,
And swear,
No where
Lives a woman true, and fair.

If thou find'st one, let me know:
Such a pilgrimage were sweet.
Yet do not, I would not go,
Though at next door we might meet:
Though she were true when you met her,
And last till you write your letter,
Yet she
Will be
False, ere I come, to two, or three.

(1633)

A Valediction: Forbidding Mourning

As virtuous men pass mildly away,
And whisper to their souls to go,
Whilst some of their sad friends do say,
"The breath goes now," and some say, "No,"

So let us melt, and make no noise,
No tear-floods, nor sigh-tempests move;
'Twere profanation of our joys
To tell the laity our love.

Moving of the earth° brings harms and fears, earthquakes
Men reckon what it did and meant;
But trepidation of the spheres,°
Though greater far, is innocent.

"A Valediction" 11 ***trepidation of the spheres*** *movement in the outermost of the heavenly spheres. In Ptolemy's astronomy these outer spheres caused others to vary from their orbits.*

Dull sublunary° lovers' love earthly
(Whose soul is sense) cannot admit
Absence, because it doth remove
Those things which elemented° it. composed

But we, by a love so much refined
That our selves know not what it is,
Inter-assured of the mind,
Care less, eyes, lips, and hands to miss.

Our two souls therefore, which are one,
Though I must go, endure not yet
A breach, but an expansion,
Like gold to airy thinness beat.

If they be two, they are two so
As stiff twin compasses° are two:
Thy soul, the fixed foot, makes no show
To move, but doth, if the other do;

And though it in the center sit,
Yet when the other far doth roam,
It leans, and hearkens after it,
And grows erect, as that comes home.

Such wilt thou be to me, who must,
Like the other foot, obliquely run;
Thy firmness makes my circle just,
And makes me end where I begun.

(1633)

The Flea

Mark but this flea, and mark in this
How little that which thou deny'st me is;
It sucked me first, and now sucks thee,
And in this flea our two bloods mingled be;

Thou know'st that this cannot be said
A sin, nor shame, nor loss of maidenhead;
Yet this enjoys before it woo,
And pampered swells with one blood made of two,
And this, alas, is more than we would do.

[26]***twin compasses*** *the two feet of a mathematical compass used for drawing circles.*

Oh stay, three lives in one flea spare,
Where we almost, yea, more than married are.
This flea is you and I, and this
Our marriage bed and marriage temple is;
Though parents grudge, and you, we are met
And cloistered in these living walls of jet.
Though use° make you apt to kill me, custom
Let not to that, self-murder added be,
And sacrilege, three sins in killing three.

Cruel and sudden, hast thou since
Purpled thy nail in blood of innocence?
Wherein could this flea guilty be,
Except in that drop which it sucked from thee?
Yet thou triumph'st and say'st that thou
Find'st not thyself, nor me the weaker now.
'Tis true. Then learn how false fears be:
Just so much honor, when thou yield'st to me,
Will waste, as this flea's death took life from thee.

(1633)

Death, be not proud

Death, be not proud, though some have calléd thee
Mighty and dreadful, for thou are not so;
For those whom thou think'st thou dost overthrow
Die not, poor Death, nor yet canst thou kill me.
From rest and sleep, which but thy pictures be,
Much pleasure; then from thee much more must flow,
And soonest our best men with thee do go,
Rest of their bones, and soul's delivery.
Thou art slave to fate, chance, kings, and desperate men,
And dost with poison, war, and sickness dwell,
And poppy or charms can make us sleep as well
And better than thy stroke; why swell'st thou then?
One short sleep past, we wake eternally
And death shall be no more; Death, thou shalt die.

(1633)

Batter my heart, three-personed God

Batter my heart, three-personed God; for You
As yet but knock, breathe, shine, and seek to mend;
That I may rise and stand, o'erthrow me, and bend
Your force to break, blow, burn, and make me new.
I, like an usurped town, to another due,

Labor to admit You, but O, to no end;
Reason, Your viceroy in me, me should defend,
But is captíved, and proves weak or untrue.
Yet dearly I love You, and would be lovéd fain,° gladly
But am betrothed unto Your enemy.
Divorce me, untie or break that knot again;
Take me to You, imprison me, for I,
Except You enthrall me, never shall be free,
Nor ever chaste, except You ravish me.

(1633)

© Jill Krementz

RITA DOVE*
[b. 1952]

Canary

FOR MICHAEL S. HARPER

Billie Holiday's burned voice
had as many shadows as lights,
a mournful candelabra against a sleek piano,
the gardenia her signature under that ruined face.

(Now you're cooking, drummer to bass,
magic spoon, magic needle.
Take all day if you have to
with your mirror and your bracelet of song.)
Fact is, the invention of women under siege
has been to sharpen love in the service of myth.

If you can't be free, be a mystery.

PAUL LAURENCE DUNBAR
[1872–1906]

We wear the mask

We wear the mask that grins and lies,
It hides our cheeks and shades our eyes—
This debt we pay to human guile;

With torn and bleeding hearts we smile,
And mouth with myriad subtleties.

Why should the world be over-wise,
In counting all our tears and sighs?
Nay, let them only see us, while
We wear the mask.

We smile, but, O great Christ, our cries
To thee from tortured souls arise.
We sing, but oh the clay is vile
Beneath our feet, and long the mile;
But let the world dream otherwise,
We wear the mask!

(1896)

T. S. ELIOT*

[1888–1965]

www

The Love Song of J. Alfred Prufrock

S'io credesse che mia risposta fosse
A persona che mai tornasse al mondo,
Questa fiamma staria senza più scosse.
Ma perciocche giammai di questo fondo
Non tornò vivo alcun, s'i'odo il vero,
Senza tema d'infamia ti rispondo.°

Let us go then, you and I,
When the evening is spread out against the sky
Like a patient etherized upon a table;
Let us go, through certain half-deserted streets,
The muttering retreats
Of restless nights in one-night cheap hotels
And sawdust restaurants with oyster-shells:
Streets that follow like a tedious argument
Of insidious intent
To lead you to an overwhelming question . . .
Oh, do not ask, "What is it?"
Let us go and make our visit.

In the room the women come and go
Talking of Michelangelo.

"The Love Song of J. Alfred Prufrock" epigraph from Dante's Inferno, *canto XXVII, 61–66. The words are spoken by Guido da Montefeltro when asked to identify himself: "If I thought my answer were given to anyone who could ever return to the world, this flame would shake no more; but since none ever did return above from this depth, if what I hear is true, without fear of infamy I answer thee."*

The yellow fog that rubs its back upon the window-panes
The yellow smoke that rubs its muzzle on the window-panes
Licked its tongue into the corners of the evening,
Lingered upon the pools that stand in drains,
Let fall upon its back the soot that falls from chimneys,
Slipped by the terrace, made a sudden leap,
And seeing that it was a soft October night,
Curled once about the house, and fell asleep.

And indeed there will be time
For the yellow smoke that slides along the street,
Rubbing its back upon the window-panes;
There will be time, there will be time
To prepare a face to meet the faces that you meet;
There will be time to murder and create,
And time for all the works and days of hands
That lift and drop a question on your plate;
Time for you and time for me,
And time yet for a hundred indecisions,
And for a hundred visions and revisions,
Before the taking of a toast and tea.

In the room the women come and go
Talking of Michelangelo.

And indeed there will be time
To wonder, "Do I dare?" and, "Do I dare?"
Time to turn back and descend the stair,
With a bald spot in the middle of my hair—
[They will say: "How his hair is growing thin!"]
My morning coat, my collar mounting firmly to the chin,
My necktie rich and modest, but asserted by a simple pin—

[They will say: "But how his arms and legs are thin!"]
Do I dare
Disturb the universe?
In a minute there is time
For decisions and revisions which a minute will reverse.

For I have known them all already, known them all:
Have known the evenings, mornings, afternoons,
I have measured out my life with coffee spoons;
I know the voices dying with a dying fall
Beneath the music from a farther room.
        So how should I presume?

And I have known the eyes already, known them all—
The eyes that fix you in a formulated phrase,

And when I am formulated, sprawling on a pin,
When I am pinned and wriggling on the wall,
Then how should I begin
To spit out all the butt-ends of my days and ways?
        And how should I presume?

And I have known the arms already, known them all—
Arms that are braceleted and white and bare
[But in the lamplight, downed with light brown hair!]
Is it perfume from a dress
That makes me so digress?
Arms that lie along a table, or wrap about a shawl.
        And should I then presume?
        And how should I begin?

Shall I say, I have gone at dusk through narrow streets
And watched the smoke that rises from the pipes
Of lonely men in shirt-sleeves, leaning out of windows? . . .

I should have been a pair of ragged claws
Scuttling across the floors of silent seas.

. . . . .

And the afternoon, the evening, sleeps so peacefully!
Smoothed by long fingers,
Asleep . . . tired . . . or it malingers,
Stretched on the floor, here beside you and me.
Should I, after tea and cakes and ices,
Have the strength to force the moment to its crisis?
But though I have wept and fasted, wept and prayed,
Though I have seen my head (grown slightly bald) brought in
    upon a platter,°
I am no prophet—and here's no great matter;
I have seen the moment of my greatness flicker,
And I have seen the eternal Footman hold my coat, and snicker,
And in short, I was afraid.

And would it have been worth it, after all,
After the cups, the marmalade, the tea,
Among the porcelain, among some talk of you and me,
Would it have been worth while,
To have bitten off the matter with a smile,
To have squeezed the universe into a ball
To roll it toward some overwhelming question,

82 ***head . . . platter*** *John the Baptist was beheaded at the order of King Herod to please his wife and daughter. See Matthew 14:1–11.*

To say: "I am Lazarus,° come from the dead,
Come back to tell you all, I shall tell you all"—
If one, settling a pillow by her head,
    Should say: "That is not what I meant at all.
    That is not it, at all."

And would it have been worth it, after all,
Would it have been worth while,
After the sunsets and the dooryards and the sprinkled streets,
After the novels, after the teacups, after the skirts that trail
  along the floor—
And this, and so much more?—
It is impossible to say just what I mean!
But as if a magic lantern threw the nerves in patterns on a screen:
Would it have been worth while
If one, settling a pillow or throwing off a shawl,
And turning toward the window, should say:
    "That is not it at all,
    That is not what I meant, at all."

. . . . .

No! I am not Prince Hamlet, nor was meant to be;
Am an attendant lord, one that will do
To swell a progress, start a scene or two,
Advise the prince; no doubt, an easy tool,
Deferential, glad to be of use,
Politic, cautious, and meticulous;
Full of high sentence,° but a bit obtuse; sententiousness
At times, indeed, almost ridiculous—
Almost, at times, the Fool.
I grow old . . . I grow old . . .
I shall wear the bottoms of my trousers rolled.

Shall I part my hair behind? Do I dare to eat a peach?

I shall wear white flannel trousers, and walk upon the beach.
I have heard the mermaids singing, each to each.

I do not think that they will sing to me.

I have seen them riding seaward on the waves
Combing the white hair of the waves blown back
When the wind blows the water white and black.
We have lingered in the chambers of the sea
By sea-girls wreathed with seaweed red and brown
Till human voices wake us, and we drown.

(1917)

94 ***Lazarus*** *Jesus raised him from the dead. See John 11:1–44.*

LOUISE ERDRICH

[b. 1954]

Indian Boarding School: The Runaways

Home's the place we head for in our sleep.
Boxcars stumbling north in dreams
don't wait for us. We catch them on the run.
The rails, old lacerations that we love,
shoot parallel across the face and break
just under Turtle Mountains. Riding scars
you can't get lost. Home is the place they cross.

The lame guard strikes a match and makes the dark
less tolerant. We watch through cracks in boards
as the land starts rolling, rolling till it hurts
to be here, cold in regulation clothes.
We know the sheriff 's waiting at midrun
to take us back. His car is dumb and warm.
The highway doesn't rock, it only hums
like a wing of long insults. The worn-down welts
of ancient punishments lead back and forth.

All runaways wear dresses, long green ones,
the color you would think shame was. We scrub
the sidewalks down because it's shameful work.
Our brushes cut the stone in watered arcs
and in the soak frail outlines shiver clear
a moment, things us kids pressed on the dark
face before it hardened, place, remembering
delicate old injuries, the spines of names and leaves.

(1984)

LAWRENCE FERLINGHETTI*

[b. 1919]

Constantly Risking Absurdity

Constantly risking absurdity
and death
whenever he performs

above the heads
of his audience

the poet like an acrobat
climbs on rime
to a high wire of his own making
and balancing on eyebeams
above a sea of faces
paces his way
to the other side of day
performing entrechats
and sleight-of-foot tricks
and other high theatrics
and all without mistaking
any thing
for what it may not be
For he's the super realist
who must perforce perceive
taut truth
before the taking of each stance or step
in his supposed advance
toward that still higher perch
where Beauty stands and waits
with gravity
to start her death-defying leap
And he
a little charleychaplin man
who may or may not catch
her fair eternal form
spreadeagled in the empty air
of existence

(1958)

CAROLYN FORCHÉ
[b. 1950]

The Memory of Elena

We spend our morning
in the flower stalls counting
the dark tongues of bells
that hang from ropes waiting
for the silence of an hour.

We find a table, ask for *paella*,
cold soup and wine, where a calm
light trembles years behind us.

In Buenos Aires only three
years ago, it was the last time his hand
slipped into her dress, with pearls
cooling her throat and bells like
these, chipping at the night—

As she talks, the hollow
clopping of a horse, the sound
of bones touched together.
The paella comes, a bed of rice
and *camarones*,° fingers and shells, shrimp
the lips of those whose lips
have been removed, mussels
the soft blue of a leg socket.

This is not *paella,* this is what
has become of those who remained
in Buenos Aires. This is the ring
of a rifle report on the stones,
her hand over her mouth,
her husband falling against her.

These are the flowers we bought
this morning, the dahlias tossed
on his grave and bells
waiting with their tongues cut out
for this particular silence.

(1981)

© Jill Krementz

NIKKI GIOVANNI*
[b. 1943]

Ego Tripping
(THERE MAY BE A REASON WHY)

I was born in the congo
I walked to the fertile crescent and built
the sphinx

I designed a pyramid so tough that a star
    that only glows every one hundred years falls
    into the center giving divine perfect light
I am bad

I sat on the throne
    drinking nectar with allah
I got hot and sent an ice age to europe
    to cool my thirst
My oldest daughter is nefertiti
    the tears from my birth pains
    created the nile
I am a beautiful woman

I gazed on the forest and burned
    out the sahara desert
    with a packet of goat's meat
    and a change of clothes
I crossed it in two hours
I am a gazelle so swift
    so swift you can't catch me

    For a birthday present when he was three
I gave my son hannibal an elephant
    He gave me rome for mother's day
My strength flows ever on
My son noah built new/ark and
I stood proudly at the helm
    as we sailed on a soft summer day
I turned myself into myself and was
    jesus
    men intone my loving name
    All praises All praises
I am the one who would save

I sowed diamonds in my back yard
My bowels deliver uranium
    the filings from my fingernails are
    semi-precious jewels
    On a trip north
I caught a cold and blew
My nose giving oil to the arab world
I am so hip even my errors are correct
I sailed west to reach east and had to round off
    the earth as I went
    The hair from my head thinned and gold was laid
    across three continents

I am so perfect so divine so ethereal so surreal
I cannot be comprehended
    except by my permission

I mean . . . I . . . can fly
    like a bird in the sky . . .

(1970)

Nikki Rosa

childhood memories are always a drag
if you're Black
you always remember things like living in Woodlawn
with no inside toilet
and if you become famous or something
they never talk about how happy you were to have
your mother
all to yourself and
how good the water felt when you got your bath
from one of those
big tubs that folk in chicago barbeque in
and somehow when you talk about home
it never gets across how much you
understood their feelings
as the whole family attended meetings about
    Hollydale
and even though you remember
your biographers never understand
your father's pain as he sells his stock
and another dream goes
And though you're poor it isn't poverty that
concerns you
and though they fought a lot
it isn't your father's drinking that makes any
    difference
but only that everybody is together and you
and your sister have happy birthdays and very good
Christmases
and I really hope no white person ever has cause
to write about me
because they'll never understand
Black love is Black wealth and they'll
probably talk about my hard childhood

and never understand that
all the while I was quite happy

(1970)

LOUISE GLÜCK

[b. 1943]

The School Children

The children go forward with their little satchels.
And all morning the mothers have labored
to gather the late apples, red and gold,
like words of another language.

And on the other shore
are those who wait behind great desks
to receive these offerings.

How orderly they are—the nails
on which the children hang
their overcoats of blue or yellow wool.

And the teachers shall instruct them in silence
and the mothers shall scour the orchards for a way out,
drawing to themselves the gray limbs of the fruit trees
bearing so little ammunition.

(1971)

GEORGE GORDON,
LORD BYRON*

[1788–1824]

She walks in beauty

1

She walks in beauty, like the night
  Of cloudless climes and starry skies;
And all that's best of dark and bright

Meet in her aspect and her eyes:
Thus mellowed to that tender light
Which heaven to gaudy day denies.

2

One shade the more, one ray the less,
Had half impaired the nameless grace
Which waves in every raven tress,
Or softly lightens o'er her face;
Where thoughts serenely sweet express
How pure, how dear their dwelling place.

3

And on that cheek, and o'er that brow,
So soft, so calm, yet eloquent,
The smiles that win, the tints that glow,
But tell of days in goodness spent,
A mind at peace with all below,
A heart whose love is innocent!

(1815)

DONALD HALL*

[b. 1928]

My son, my executioner

My son, my executioner,
I take you in my arms,
Quiet and small and just astir,
And whom my body warms.

Sweet death, small son, our instrument
Of immortality,
Your cries and hungers document
Our bodily decay.

We twenty-five and twenty-two,
Who seemed to live forever,

Observe enduring life in you
And start to die together.

(1955)

THOMAS HARDY*
[1840–1928]

The Ruined Maid

"O'Melia, my dear, this does everything crown!
Who could have supposed I should meet you in Town?
And whence such fair garments, such prosperity?"
"O didn't you know I'd been ruined?" said she.

"You left us in tatters, without shoes or socks,
Tired of digging potatoes, and spudding up docks;
And now you've gay bracelets and bright feathers three!"
"Yes: that's how we dress when we're ruined," said she.

"At home in the barton° you said 'thee' and 'thou,' — farm
And 'thik oon,' and 'theäs oon,' and 't'other'; but now
Your talking quite fits 'ee for high company!"
"Some polish is gained with one's ruin," said she.

"Your hands were like paws then, your face blue and bleak
But now I'm bewitched by your delicate cheek,
And your little gloves fit as on any lady!"
"We never do work when we're ruined," said she.

"You used to call home-life a hag-ridden dream,
And you'd sigh, and you'd sock; but at present you seem
To know not of megrims° or melancholy!" — low spirits
"True. One's pretty lively when ruined," said she.

"I wish I had feathers, a fine sweeping gown,
And a delicate face, and could strut about Town!"
"My dear—a raw country girl, such as you be,
Cannot quite expect that. You ain't ruined," said she.

(1898)

Channel Firing

That night your great guns, unawares,
Shook all our coffins as we lay,
And broke the chancel window-squares,
We thought it was the Judgment-day

And sat upright. While drearisome
Arose the howl of wakened hounds:
The mouse let fall the altar-crumb,
The worms drew back into the mounds,

The glebe° cow drooled. Till God called, "No; small field
It's gunnery practice out at sea
Just as before you went below;
The world is as it used to be:

"All nations striving strong to make
Red war yet redder. Mad as hatters
They do no more for Christés sake
Than you who are helpless in such matters.

"That this is not the judgment-hour
For some of them's a blessed thing,
For if it were they'd have to scour
Hell's floor for so much threatening. . . .

"Ha, ha. It will be warmer when
I blow the trumpet (if indeed
I ever do; for you are men,
And rest eternal sorely need)."

So down we lay again. "I wonder,
Will the world ever saner be,"
Said one, "than when He sent us under
In our indifferent century!"

And many a skeleton shook his head.
"Instead of preaching forty year,"
My neighbor Parson Thirdly said,
"I wish I had stuck to pipes and beer."

Again the guns disturbed the hour,
Roaring their readiness to avenge,
As far inland as Stourton Tower,
And Camelot, and starlit Stonehenge.°

(1914)

"Channel Firing" 36***Stonehenge*** *a circular grouping of stone monuments near Salisbury, England, dating back to the Bronze Age.*

JOY HARJO

[b. 1951]

Eagle Poem

To pray you open your whole self
To sky, to earth, to sun, to moon
To one whole voice that is you.
And know there is more
That you can't see, can't hear,
Can't know except in moments
Steadily growing, and in languages
That aren't always sound but other circles of motion.
Like eagle that Sunday morning
Over Salt River. Circled in blue sky
In wind, swept our hearts clean
With sacred wings.
We see you, see ourselves and know
That we must take the utmost care
And kindness in all things.
Breathe in, knowing we are made of All this, and breathe, knowing
We are truly blessed because we
Were born, and die soon within a
True circle of motion,
Like eagle rounding at the morning
Inside us.
We pray that it will be done
In beauty.
In beauty.

(1990)

ROBERT HAYDEN*

[1913–1980]

Frederick Douglass

When it is finally ours, this freedom, this liberty, this beautiful
and terrible thing, needful to man as air,
usable as earth; when it belongs at last to all,
when it is truly instinct, brain matter, diastole, systole,
reflex action; when it is finally won; when it is more
than the gaudy mumbo jumbo of politicians:
this man, this Douglass, this former slave, this Negro

beaten to his knees, exiled, visioning a world
where none is lonely, none hunted, alien,
this man, superb in love and logic, this man
shall be remembered. Oh, not with statues' rhetoric,
not with legends and poems and wreaths of bronze alone,
but with the lives grown out of his life, the lives
fleshing his dream of the beautiful, needful thing.

(1962)

www

SEAMUS HEANEY*

[b. 1939]

Digging

Between my finger and my thumb
The squat pen rests; snug as a gun.

Under my window, a clean rasping sound
When the spade sinks into gravelly ground:
My father, digging. I look down

Till his straining rump among the flowerbeds
Bends low, comes up twenty years away
Stooping in rhythm through potato drills
Where he was digging.

The coarse boot nestled on the lug, the shaft
Against the inside knee was levered firmly.
He rooted out tall tops, buried the bright edge deep
To scatter new potatoes that we picked
Loving their cool hardness in our hands.

By God, the old man could handle a spade.
Just like his old man.

My grandfather cut more turf in a day
Than any other man on Toner's bog.
Once I carried him milk in a bottle
Corked sloppily with paper. He straightened up
To drink it, then fell to right away

Nicking and slicing neatly, heaving sods
Over his shoulder, going down and down
For the good turf. Digging.

The cold smell of potato mould, the squelch and slap
Of soggy peat, the curt cuts of an edge
Through living roots awaken in my head.
But I've no spade to follow men like them.

Between my finger and my thumb
The squat pen rests.
I'll dig with it.

(1966)

Mid-Term Break

I sat all morning in the college sick bay
Counting bells knelling classes to a close.
At two o'clock our neighbors drove me home.

In the porch I met my father crying—
He had always taken funerals in his stride—
And Big Jim Evans saying it was a hard blow.

The baby cooed and laughed and rocked the pram
When I came in, and I was embarrassed
By old men standing up to shake my hand

And tell me they were "sorry for my trouble,"
Whispers informed strangers I was the eldest,
Away at school, as my mother held my hand

In hers and coughed out angry tearless sighs.
At ten o'clock the ambulance arrived
With the corpse, stanched and bandaged by the nurses.

Next morning I went up into the room. Snowdrops
And candles soothed the bedside; I saw him
For the first time in six weeks. Paler now,

Wearing a poppy bruise on his left temple,
He lay in the four foot box as in his cot.
No gaudy scars, the bumper knocked him clear.

A four foot box, a foot for every year.

(1966)

GEORGE HERBERT*
[1593–1633]

The Altar

A broken ALTAR, Lord, Thy servant rears,
Made of a heart and cemented with tears;
Whose parts are as Thy hand did frame;
No workman's tool hath touched the same.
A HEART alone
Is such a tone,
As nothing but
Thy power doth cut.
Wherefore each part
Of my hard heart
Meets in this frame
To praise Thy name,
That if I chance to hold my peace,
These stones to praise Thee may not cease.
Oh, let Thy blessed SACRIFICE be mine,
And sanctify this ALTAR to be Thine.

(1633)

ROBERT HERRICK*
[1591–1674]

Upon Julia's Clothes

Whenas in silks my Julia goes,
Then, then, methinks, how sweetly flows
That liquefaction of her clothes.

Next, when I cast mine eyes and see
That brave vibration each way free,
O how that glittering taketh me!

(1648)

To the Virgins, to Make Much of Time

Gather ye rosebuds while ye may:
  Old Time is still a-flying;
And this same flower that smiles today,
  Tomorrow will be dying.

The glorious lamp of heaven, the sun,
  The higher he's a-getting,
The sooner will his race be run,
  And nearer he's to setting.

That age is best which is the first,
  When youth and blood are warmer;
But being spent, the worse, and worst
  Times, still succeed the former.

Then be not coy, but use your time;
  And while ye may, go marry:
For, having lost but once your prime,
  You may for ever tarry.

(1648)

GERARD MANLEY HOPKINS*
[1844–1889]

God's Grandeur

The world is charged with the grandeur of God.
  It will flame out, like shining from shook foil;°
  It gathers to a greatness, like the ooze of oil

"God's Grandeur" 2**foil** *gold or tinsel foil*

Crushed.° Why do men then now not reck his rod?
Generations have trod, have trod, have trod;
  And all is seared with trade; bleared, smeared with toil;
  And wears man's smudge and shares man's smell: the soil
Is bare now, nor can foot feel, being shod.

And for all this, nature is never spent;
  There lives the dearest freshness deep down things;
And though the last lights off the black West went
  Oh, morning, at the brown brink eastward, springs—
Because the Holy Ghost over the bent
  World broods with warm breast and with ah! bright wings.

(1877, 1895)

The Windhover°

TO CHRIST OUR LORD

I caught this morning morning's minion,° king- — darling
  dom of daylight's dauphin,° dapple-dawn-drawn Falcon, in his riding — prince
  Of the rolling level underneath him steady air, and striding
High there, how he rung upon the rein of a wimpling° wing — rippling
In his ecstasy! then off, off forth on swing,
  As a skate's heel sweeps smooth on a bow-bend: the hurl and gliding
  Rebuffed the big wind. My heart in hiding
Stirred for a bird,—the achieve of, the mastery of the thing!
Brute beauty and valour and act, oh, air, pride, plume, here
  Buckle! AND the fire that breaks from thee then, a billion
Times told lovelier, more dangerous, O my chevalier!° — knight
  No wonder of it: shéer plód makes plough down sillion° — furrow
Shine, and blue-bleak embers, ah my dear,
  Fall, gall themselves, and gash gold-vermilion.

(1877, 1918)

Pied° *Beauty* — variegated

Glory be to God for dappled things—
  For skies of couple-colour as a brinded° cow; — brindled, streaked
    For rose-moles all in stipple upon trout that swim;

"God's Grandeur" [4]**Crushed** *as when olives are crushed for their oil.*
"The Windhover" **Windhover** *a kestrel, a kind of falcon.*

Fresh-firecoal chestnut-falls;° finches' wings;
Landscape plotted and pieced—fold, fallow, and plough;
And áll trádes, their gear and tackle and trim.° equipment
All things counter, original, spare,° strange; unusual
Whatever is fickle, freckled (who knows how?)
With swift, slow; sweet, sour; adazzle, dim;
He fathers-forth whose beauty is past change:
Praise him.

(1877, 1918)

Spring and Fall: to a Young Child

Márgarét, áre you grieving
Over Goldengrove unleaving?
Leáves, like the things of man, you
With your fresh thoughts care for, can you?
Áh! ás the heart grows older
It will come to such sights colder
By and by, nor spare a sigh
Though worlds of wanwood leafmeal lie;
And yet you *will* weep and know why.
Now no matter, child, the name:
Sórrow's springs áre the same.
Nor mouth had, no nor mind, expressed
What heart heard of, ghost guessed:
It ís the blight man was born for,
It is Márgaret you mourn for.

(1880)

A. E. HOUSMAN*
[1859–1936]

When I was one-and-twenty

When I was one-and-twenty
I heard a wise man say,
'Give crowns and pounds and guineas
But not your heart away;

"Pied Beauty" [4]**chestnut-falls** *roasted chestnuts stripped of their husks.*

Give pearls away and rubies
But keep your fancy free.'
But I was one-and-twenty,
No use to talk to me.

When I was one-and-twenty
I heard him say again,
'The heart out of the bosom
Was never given in vain;
'Tis paid with sighs a plenty
And sold for endless rue.'
And I am two-and-twenty,
And oh, 'tis true, 'tis true.

(1896)

To an Athlete Dying Young

The time you won your town the race
We chaired you through the market-place;
Man and boy stood cheering by,
And home we brought you shoulder-high.

To-day, the road all runners come,
Shoulder-high we bring you home,
And set you at your threshold down,
Townsman of a stiller town.

Smart lad, to slip betimes away
From fields where glory does not stay
And early though the laurel grows
It withers quicker than the rose.

Eyes the shady night has shut
Cannot see the record cut,
And silence sounds no worse than cheers
After earth has stopped the ears:

Now you will not swell the rout
Of lads that wore their honours out,
Runners whom renown outran
And the name died before the man.

So set, before its echoes fade,
The fleet foot on the sill of shade,
And hold to the low lintel up
The still-defended challenge-cup.

And round that early-laurelled head
Will flock to gaze the strengthless dead

And find unwithered on its curls
The garland briefer than a girl's.

(1896)

ANDREW HUDGINS

[b. 1951]

Elegy for My Father, Who Is Not Dead

One day I'll lift the telephone
and be told my father's dead. He's ready.
In the sureness of his faith, he talks
about the world beyond this world
as though his reservations have
been made. I think he wants to go,
a little bit—a new desire
to travel building up, an itch
to see fresh worlds. Or older ones.
He thinks that when I follow him
he'll wrap me in his arms and laugh,
the way he did when I arrived
on earth. I do not think he's right.
He's ready. I am not. I can't
just say good-bye as cheerfully
as if he were embarking on a trip
to make my later trip go well.
I see myself on deck, convinced
his ship's gone down, while he's convinced
I'll see him standing on the dock
and waving, shouting, *Welcome back.*

(1991)

BEN JONSON*

[1573–1637]

On My First Son

Farewell, thou child of my right hand,° and joy;
My sin was too much hope of thee, loved boy:
Seven years thou wert lent to me, and I thee pay,

"On My First Son" [1]***child of my right hand*** *the literal meaning, in Hebrew, of Benjamin, the boy's name.*

Exacted by thy fate, on the just day.°
O could I lose all father now! for why
Will man lament the state he should env´y,
To have so soon 'scaped world's and flesh's rage,
And, if no other misery, yet age?
Rest in soft peace, and asked, say, "Here doth lie
Ben Jonson his best piece of poetry."
For whose sake henceforth all his vows be such
As what he loves may never like too much. (1616)

Song: To Celia

Drink to me only with thine eyes,
And I will pledge with mine;
Or leave a kiss but in the cup,
And I'll not look for wine.
The thirst that from the soul doth rise,
Doth ask a drink divine:
But might I of Jove's nectar sup,
I would not change for thine.

I sent thee late a rosy wreath,
Not so much honoring thee,
As giving it a hope, that there
It could not withered be.
But thou thereon did'st only breathe,
And sent'st it back to me;
Since when it grows and smells, I swear,
Not of itself, but thee. (1606)

JOHN KEATS*
[1795–1821]

When I have fears that I may cease to be

When I have fears that I may cease to be
Before my pen has gleaned my teeming brain,
Before high-piléd books, in charact'ry,° — written symbols
Hold like rich garners the full-ripened grain;

"On My First Son" [4]***the just day*** *Jonson's son died on his seventh birthday.*

When I behold, upon the night's starred face,
  Huge cloudy symbols of a high romance,
And think that I may never live to trace
  Their shadows, with the magic hand of chance;
And when I feel, fair creature of an hour,
  That I shall never look upon thee more,
Never have relish in the faery° power — magical
  Of unreflecting love!—then on the shore
Of the wide world I stand alone, and think
  Till Love and Fame to nothingness do sink.

(1818, 1848)

La Belle Dame sans Merci°

O what can ail thee, Knight at arms,
  Alone and palely loitering?
The sedge has withered from the Lake
  And no birds sing!

O what can ail thee, Knight at arms,
  So haggard, and so woebegone?
The squirrel's granary is full
  And the harvest's done.

I see a lily on thy brow
  With anguish moist and fever dew,
And on thy cheeks a fading rose
  Fast withereth too.

"I met a Lady in the Meads,° — meadows
  Full beautiful, a faery's child,
Her hair was long, her foot was light
  And her eyes were wild.

"I made a Garland for her head,
  And bracelets too, and fragrant Zone;° — girdle
She looked at me as she did love
  And made sweet moan.

"I set her on my pacing steed
  And nothing else saw all day long,
For sidelong would she bend and sing
  A faery's song.

"La Belle Dame sans Merci" *the beautiful lady without mercy.*

"She found me roots of relish sweet,
And honey wild, and manna dew,
And sure in language strange she said
'I love thee true.'

"She took me to her elfin grot
And there she wept and sighed full sore,
And there I shut her wild wild eyes
With kisses four.

"And there she lulléd me asleep,
And there I dreamed, Ah Woe betide!
The latest dream I ever dreamt
On the cold hill side.

"I saw pale Kings, and Princes too,
Pale warriors, death-pale were they all;
They cried, 'La belle dame sans merci
Hath thee in thrall!'

"I saw their starved lips in the gloam
With horrid warning gapéd wide,
And I awoke, and found me here
On the cold hill's side.

"And this is why I sojourn here,
Alone and palely loitering;
Though the sedge is withered from the Lake
And no birds sing."

(1819, 1888)

Ode on a Grecian Urn

1

Thou still unravished bride of quietness,
Thou foster child of silence and slow time,
Sylvan° historian, who canst thus express — woodland
A flowery tale more sweetly than our rhyme:
What leaf-fringed legend haunts about thy shape
Of deities or mortals, or of both,
In Tempe or the dales of Arcady?°
What men or gods are these? What maidens loath?
What mad pursuit? What struggle to escape?
What pipes and timbrels? What wild ecstasy?

"Ode on a Grecian Urn" [7] ***Tempe . . . Arcady*** *in Greece, beautiful rural regions.*

2

Heard melodies are sweet, but those unheard
Are sweeter; therefore, ye soft pipes, play on;
Not to the sensual ear, but, more endeared,
Pipe to the spirit ditties of no tone:
Fair youth, beneath the trees, thou canst not leave
Thy song, nor ever can those trees be bare;
Bold Lover, never, never canst thou kiss,
Though winning near the goal—yet, do not grieve;
She cannot fade, though thou hast not thy bliss,
Forever wilt thou love, and she be fair!

3

Ah, happy, happy boughs! that cannot shed
Your leaves, nor ever bid the Spring adieu;
And, happy melodist, unweariéd,
Forever piping songs forever new;
More happy love! more happy, happy love!
Forever warm and still to be enjoyed,
Forever panting, and forever young;
All breathing human passion far above,
That leaves a heart high-sorrowful and cloyed,
A burning forehead, and a parching tongue.

4

Who are these coming to the sacrifice?
To what green altar, O mysterious priest,
Lead'st thou that heifer lowing at the skies,
And all her silken flanks with garlands dressed?
What little town by river or sea shore,
Or mountain-built with peaceful citadel,
Is emptied of this folk, this pious morn?
And, little town, thy streets forevermore
Will silent be; and not a soul to tell
Why thou art desolate, can e'er return.

5

O Attic shape! Fair attitude! with brede° — woven pattern
Of marble men and maidens overwrought,° — ornamented
With forest branches and the trodden weed;
Thou, silent form, dost tease us out of thought
As doth eternity: Cold Pastoral!
When old age shall this generation waste,
Thou shalt remain, in midst of other woe
Than ours, a friend to man, to whom thou say'st,
"Beauty is truth, truth beauty,"—that is all
Ye know on earth, and all ye need to know.

(1819, 1820)

Ode to a Nightingale

1

My heart aches, and a drowsy numbness pains
    My sense, as though of hemlock° I had drunk,
Or emptied some dull opiate to the drains°   dregs
    One minute past, and Lethe-wards° had sunk:
'Tis not through envy of thy happy lot,
    But being too happy in thine happiness—
        That thou, light-wingéd Dryad° of the trees,   tree nymph
            In some melodious plot
    Of beechen green, and shadows numberless,
        Singest of summer in full-throated ease.

2

O, for a draught of vintage! that hath been
    Cooled a long age in the deep-delvéd earth,
Tasting of Flora° and the country green,
    Dance, and Provençal song,° and sunburnt mirth!
O for a beaker full of the warm South,
    Full of the true, the blushful Hippocrene,°
        With beaded bubbles winking at the brim,
            And purple-stainéd mouth;
That I might drink, and leave the world unseen,
    And with thee fade away into the forest dim:

3

Fade far away, dissolve, and quite forget
    What thou among the leaves hast never known,
The weariness, the fever, and the fret
    Here, where men sit and hear each other groan;
Where palsy shakes a few, sad, last gray hairs,
    Where youth grows pale, and specter-thin, and dies,
        Where but to think is to be full of sorrow
            And leaden-eyed despairs,
Where Beauty cannot keep her lustrous eyes,
    Or new Love pine at them beyond tomorrow.

4

Away! away! for I will fly to thee,
    Not charioted by Bacchus and his pards,°
But on the viewless° wings of Poesy,   invisible
    Though the dull brain perplexes and retards:

"Ode to a Nightingale" [2]***hemlock*** *opiate; poisonous in large quantities.* [4]***Lethe-wards*** *toward Lethe, the river of forgetfulness.* [13]***Flora*** *goddess of the flowers.* [14]***Provençal song*** *Provence, in southern France, home of the troubadours.* [16]***true . . .*** *Hippocrene wine. A fountain on Mount Helicon in Greece, whose waters reputedly stimulated poetic imagination.* [32]***Bacchus . . . pards*** *the god of wine and revelry and the leopards who drew his chariot.*

Already with thee! tender is the night,
And haply° the Queen-Moon is on her throne, perhaps
Clustered around by all her starry Fays;° fairies
But here there is no light,
Save what from heaven is with the breezes blown
Through verdurous glooms and winding mossy ways.

5

I cannot see what flowers are at my feet,
Nor what soft incense hangs upon the boughs,
But, in embalméd° darkness, guess each sweet scented
Wherewith the seasonable month endows
The grass, the thicket, and the fruit tree wild;
White hawthorn, and the pastoral eglantine;° sweetbriar
Fast fading violets covered up in leaves;
And mid-May's eldest child,
The coming musk-rose, full of dewy wine,
The murmurous haunt of flies on summer eves.

6

Darkling° I listen; and for many a time in darkness
I have been half in love with easeful Death,
Called him soft names in many a muséd rhyme,
To take into the air my quiet breath;
Now more than ever seems it rich to die,
To cease upon the midnight with no pain,
While thou art pouring forth thy soul abroad
In such an ecstasy!
Still wouldst thou sing, and I have ears in vain—
To thy high requiem become a sod.

7

Thou wast not born for death, immortal Bird!
No hungry generations tread thee down;
The voice I hear this passing night was heard
In ancient days by emperor and clown:
Perhaps the selfsame song that found a path
Through the sad heart of Ruth, when, sick for home,
She stood in tears amid the alien corn;°
The same that oft times hath
Charmed magic casements, opening on the foam
Of perilous seas, in faery lands forlorn.

8

Forlorn! the very word is like a bell
To toll me back from thee to my sole self!

66–67 ***Ruth . . . corn*** *a Biblical heroine who worked in the harvest fields in a foreign land.*

Adieu! the fancy cannot cheat so well
As she is famed to do, deceiving elf.
Adieu! adieu! thy plaintive anthem fades
Past the near meadows, over the still stream,
Up the hill side; and now 'tis buried deep
In the next valley-glades:
Was it a vision, or a waking dream?
Fled is that music:—Do I wake or sleep?

(1819, 1820)

GALWAY KINNELL

[b. 1927]

Blackberry Eating

I love to go out in late September
among the fat, overripe, icy, black blackberries
to eat blackberries for breakfast,
the stalks very prickly, a penalty
they earn for knowing the black art
of blackberry-making; and as I stand among
them
lifting the stalks to my mouth, the ripest
berries
fall almost unbidden to my tongue,
as words sometimes do, certain peculiar words
like *strengths* or *squinched,*
many-lettered, one-syllabled lumps,
which I squeeze, squinch open, and splurge well
lift the silent, startled, icy, black language
of blackberry-eating in late September.

(1980)

YUSEF KOMUNYAKAA

[b. 1947]

Facing It

My black face fades,
hiding inside the black granite.
I said I wouldn't,
dammit: No tears.

I'm stone. I'm flesh.
My clouded reflection eyes me
like a bird of prey, the profile of night
slanted against morning. I turn
this way—the stone lets me go.
I turn that way—I'm inside
the Vietnam Veterans Memorial
again, depending on the light
to make a difference.
I go down the 58,022 names,
half-expecting to find
my own in letters like smoke.
I touch the name Andrew Johnson;
I see the booby trap's white flash.
Names shimmer on a woman's blouse
but when she walks away
the names stay on the wall.
Brushstrokes flash, a red bird's
wings cutting across my stare.
The sky. A plane in the sky.
A white vet's image floats
closer to me, then his pale eyes
look through mine. I'm a window.
He's lost his right arm
inside the stone. In the black mirror
a woman's trying to erase names:
No, she's brushing a boy's hair.

(1988)

www

D. H. LAWRENCE*
[1885–1930]

Snake

A snake came to my water-trough
On a hot, hot day, and I in pajamas for the heat,
To drink there.

In the deep, strange-scented shade of the great dark carob-tree
I came down the steps with my pitcher
And must wait, must stand and wait, for there he was at the trough before me.

He reached down from a fissure in the earth-wall in the gloom
And trailed his yellow-brown slackness soft-bellied down, over the edge of the stone trough

And rested his throat upon the stone bottom,
And where the water had dripped from the tap, in a small clearness,
He sipped with his straight mouth,
Softly drank through his straight gums, into his slack long body,
Silently.

Someone was before me at my water-trough,
And I, like a second comer, waiting.

He lifted his head from his drinking, as cattle do,
And looked at me vaguely, as drinking cattle do,
And flickered his two-forked tongue from his lips, and mused
a moment,
And stooped and drank a little more,
Being earth-brown, earth-golden from the burning bowels of the earth
On the day of Sicilian July, with Etna smoking.

The voice of my education said to me
He must be killed,
For in Sicily the black, black snakes are innocent, the gold are venomous.

And voices in me said, If you were a man
You would take a stick and break him now, and finish him off.

But must I confess how I liked him,
How glad I was he had come like a guest in quiet, to drink at my
water-trough
And depart peaceful, pacified, and thankless,
Into the burning bowels of this earth?

Was it cowardice, that I dared not kill him?
Was it perversity, that I longed to talk to him?
Was it humility, to feel so honored?
I felt so honored.

And yet those voices:
If you were not afraid, you would kill him!

And truly I was afraid, I was most afraid,
But even so, honored still more
That he should seek my hospitality
From out the dark door of the secret earth.

He drank enough
And lifted his head, dreamily, as one who has drunken,
And flickered his tongue like a forked night on the air, so black,
Seeming to lick his lips,

And looked around like a god, unseeing, into the air,
And slowly turned his head,
And slowly, very slowly, as if thrice adream,
Proceeded to draw his slow length curving round
And climb again the broken bank of my wall-face.

And as he put his head into that dreadful hole,
And as he slowly drew up, snake-easing his shoulders, and entered farther,
A sort of horror, a sort of protest against his withdrawing into that
horrid black hole,
Deliberately going into the blackness, and slowly drawing himself after,
Overcame me now his back was turned.
I looked round, I put down my pitcher,
I picked up a clumsy log
And threw it at the water-trough with a clatter.

I think it did not hit him,
But suddenly that part of him that was left behind convulsed
in undignified haste.
Writhed like lightning, and was gone
Into the black hole, the earth-lipped fissure in the wall-front,
At which, in the intense still noon, I stared with fascination.

And immediately I regretted it.
I thought how paltry, how vulgar, what a mean act!
I despised myself and the voices of my accursed human education.

And I thought of the albatross
And I wished he would come back, my snake.

For he seemed to me again like a king,
Like a king in exile, uncrowned in the underworld,
Now due to be crowned again.

And so, I missed my chance with one of the lords
Of life.
And I have something to expiate;
A pettiness.

(1923)

When I read Shakespeare

When I read Shakespeare I am struck with wonder
that such trivial people should muse and thunder
in such lovely language.

Lear, the old buffer, you wonder his daughters
didn't treat him rougher,
the old chough,° the old chuffer!° imposter

And Hamlet, how boring, how boring to live with,
so mean and self-conscious, blowing and snoring
his wonderful speeches, full of other folks' whoring!

And Macbeth and his Lady, who should have been choring,
such suburban ambition, so messily goring
old Duncan with daggers!

How boring, how small Shakespeare's people are!
Yet the language so lovely! like the dyes from gas-tar.

(1929)

AUDRE LORDE

[1934–1992]

Hanging Fire

I am fourteen
and my skin has betrayed me
the boy I cannot live without
still sucks his thumb
in secret
how come my knees are
always so ashy
what if I die
before morning
and mamma's in the bedroom
with the door closed.

I have to learn how to dance
in time for the next party
my room is too small for me
suppose I die before graduation
they will sing sad melodies
but finally
tell the truth about me
There is nothing I want to do
and too much

"When I Read Shakespeare" [6]***chough*** *a chattering jackdaw or crow.*

that has to be done
and momma's in the bedroom
with the door closed.

Nobody even stops to think
about my side of it
I should have been on Math Team
my marks were better than his
why do I have to be
the one
wearing braces
I have nothing to wear tomorrow
will I live long enough
to grow up
and momma's in the bedroom
with the door closed.

(1978)

ARCHIBALD MACLEISH*

[1892–1982]

Ars Poetica

A poem should be palpable and mute
As a globed fruit,

Dumb
As old medallions to the thumb,

Silent as the sleeve-worn stone
Of casement ledges where the moss has grown—

A poem should be wordless
As the flight of birds.

A poem should be motionless in time
As the moon climbs,

Leaving, as the moon releases
Twig by twig the night-entangled trees,

Leaving, as the moon behind the winter leaves,
Memory by memory the mind—

A poem should be motionless in time
As the moon climbs.

A poem should be equal to:
Not true.

For all the history of grief
An empty doorway and a maple leaf.

For love
The leaning grasses and two lights above the sea—

A poem should not mean
But be.

(1926)

ANDREW MARVELL
[1621–1678]

To His Coy Mistress

Had we but world enough, and time,
This coyness, lady, were no crime.
We would sit down, and think which way
To walk, and pass our long love's day.
Thou by the Indian Ganges' side
Shoudst rubies° find; I by the tide
Of Humber° would complain. I would
Love you ten years before the flood,
And you should, if you please, refuse
Till the conversion of the Jews.°
My vegetable love° should grow
Vaster than empires and more slow;
An hundred years should go to praise
Thine eyes, and on thy forehead gaze;
Two hundred to adore each breast,
But thirty thousand to the rest;
An age at least to every part,

"To His Coy Mistress" [6]***rubies*** *associated with virginity.* [7]***Humber*** *the river that runs through Marvell's native town, Hull.* [10]***the conversion of the Jews*** *supposedly to occur at the end of time.* [11]***vegetable love*** *a reference to the idea that vegetables have the power to grow but lack consciousness.*

And the last age should show your heart.
For, lady, you deserve this state,
Nor would I love at lower rate.
  But at my back I always hear
Time's wingéd chariot hurrying near;
And yonder all before us lie
Deserts of vast eternity.
Thy beauty shall no more be found;
Nor, in thy marble vault, shall sound
My echoing song; then worms shall try
That long-preserved virginity,
And your quaint° honor turn to dust, overscrupulous
And into ashes all my lust:
The grave's a fine and private place,
But none, I think, do there embrace.
  Now therefore, while the youthful hue
Sits on thy skin like morning dew
And while thy willing soul transpires° breathes forth
At every pore with instant fires,
Now let us sport us while we may,
And now, like amorous birds of prey,
Rather at once our time devour
Than languish in his slow-chapped° power. slow-jawed
Let us roll all our strength and all
Our sweetness up into one ball,
And tear our pleasures with rough strife
Through the iron gates of life:
Thus, though we cannot make our sun
Stand still, yet we will make him run.

(1681)

CLAUDE MCKAY
[1890–1948]

The Tropics in New York

Bananas ripe and green, and ginger root,
  Cocoa in pods and alligator pears,
And tangerines and mangoes and grape fruit,
  Fit for the highest prize at parish fairs,

Set in the window, bringing memories
  Of fruit-trees laden by low-singing rills,
And dewy dawns, and mystical blue skies
  In benediction over nun-like hills.

My eyes grew dim, and I could no more gaze;
A wave of longing through my body swept,
And hungry for the old familiar ways,
I turned aside and bowed my head and wept.

(1922)

EDNA ST. VINCENT MILLAY
[1892–1950]

I, Being Born a Woman and Distressed

I, being born a woman and distressed
By all the needs and notions of my kind,
Am urged by your propinquity to find
Your person fair, and feel a certain zest
To bear your body's weight upon my breast:
So subtly is the fume of life designed,
To clarify the pulse and cloud the mind,
And leave me once again undone, possessed.
Think not for this, however, the poor treason
Of my stout blood against my staggering brain,
I shall remember you with love, or season
My scorn with pity,—let me make it plain:
I find this frenzy insufficient reason
For conversation when we meet again.

(1923)

CZESLAW MILOSZ*
[1911–2004]

Encounter

TRANSLATED BY THE AUTHOR AND LILLIAN VALLEE

We were riding through frozen fields in a wagon at
dawn.
A red wing rose in the darkness.

And suddenly a hare ran across the road.
One of us pointed to it with his hand.

That was long ago. Today neither of them is alive,
Not the hare, nor the man who made the gesture.

O my love, where are they, where are they going
The flash of a hand, streak of movements, rustle of
pebbles.
I ask not out of sorrow, but in wonder.

JOHN MILTON*
[1608–1674]

When I consider how my light is spent°

When I consider how my light is spent
Ere half my days, in this dark world and wide,
And that one talent° which is death to hide
Lodged with me useless, though my soul more bent
To serve therewith my Maker, and present
My true account, lest he returning chide;
"Doth God exact day-labor, light denied?"
I fondly° ask; but Patience to prevent — foolishly
That murmur, soon replies, "God doth not need
Either man's work or his own gifts; who best
Bear his mild yoke, they serve him best. His state
Is kingly. Thousands at his bidding speed
And post o'er land and ocean without rest:
They also serve who only stand and wait."

(1673)

MARIANNE MOORE
[1887–1972]

Poetry

I, too, dislike it: there are things that are important beyond all this fiddle.
Reading it, however, with a perfect contempt for it, one discovers in
it after all, a place for the genuine.

"When I consider how my light is spent" Milton went blind in 1651. [3]***one talent*** *an allusion to Jesus's parable of the talents, in which the Servant who buried the talent given him by his master was cast into the darkness (Matthew 25:14–30).*

Hands that can grasp, eyes
that can dilate, hair that can rise
if it must, these things are important not because a

high-sounding interpretation can be put upon them but because they are
useful. When they become so derivative as to become unintelligible,
the same thing may be said for all of us, that we
do not admire what
we cannot understand: the bat
holding on upside down or in quest of something to

eat, elephants pushing, a wild horse taking a roll, a tireless wolf under
a tree, the immovable critic twitching his skin like a horse that feels
a flea, the base-
ball fan, the statistician—
nor is it valid
to discriminate against "business documents and

school-books"; all these phenomena are important. One must make
a distinction
however: when dragged into prominence by half poets, the result
is not poetry,
nor till the poets among us can be
"literalists of
the imagination"—above
insolence and triviality and can present

for inspection, "imaginary gardens with real toads in them,"
shall we have it. In the meantime, if you demand on the one hand,
the raw material of poetry in
all its rawness and
that which is on the other hand
genuine, you are interested in poetry.

(1921)

PAUL MULDOON

[b. 1951]

Hedgehog

The snail moves like a
Hovercraft held up by a
Rubber cushion of itself,
Sharing its secret

With the hedgehog. The hedgehog
Shares its secret with no one.
We say, Hedgehog, come out
Of yourself and we will love you.

We mean no harm. We want
Only to listen to what
You have to say. We want
Your answers to our questions.

The hedgehog gives nothing
Away, keeping itself to itself.
We wonder what a hedgehog
Has to hide, why it so distrusts.

We forget the god
Under this crown of thorns
We forget that never again
Will a god trust in the world.

(1973)

SHARON OLDS

[b. 1942]

Size and Sheer Will

The fine, green pajama cotton,
washed so often it is paper-thin and
iridescent, has split like a sheath
and the glossy white naked bulbs of
Gabriel's toes thrust forth like crocus
this early Spring. The boy is growing
as fast as he can, elongated
wrists dangling, lean meat
showing between the shirt and the belt.
If there were a rack to stretch himself, he would
strap his slight body to it.
If there were a machine to enter,
skip the next ten years and be
sixteen immediately, this boy would
do it. All day long he cranes his
neck, like a plant in the dark with a single
light above it, or a sailor under
tons of green water, longing
for the surface, for his rightful life.

(1975)

Rite of Passage

As the guests arrive at my son's party
they gather in the living room—
short men, men in first grade
with smooth jaws and chins.
Hands in pockets, they stand around
jostling, jockeying for place, small fights
breaking out and calming. One says to another
How old are you? Six. I'm seven. So?
They eye each other, seeing themselves
tiny in the other's pupils. They clear their
throats a lot, a room of small bankers,
they fold their arms and frown. *I could beat you
up,* a seven says to a six,
the dark cake, round and heavy as a
turret, behind them on the table. My son,
freckles like specks of nutmeg on his cheeks,
chest narrow as the balsa keel of a
model boat, long hands
cool and thin as the day they guided him
out of me, speaks up as a host
for the sake of the group.
We could easily kill a two-year-old,
he says in his clear voice. The other
men agree, they clear their throats
like Generals, they relax and get down to
playing war, celebrating my son's life.

(1975)

35/10

Brushing out my daughter's dark
silken hair before the mirror
I see the grey gleaming on my head,
the silver-haired servant behind her. Why is it
just as we begin to go
they begin to arrive, the fold in my neck
clarifying as the line bones of her
hips sharpen? As my skin shows
its dry pitting, she opens like a small
pale flower on the tip of a cactus;
as my last chances to bear a child
are falling through my body, the duds among them,
her full purse of eggs, round and

firm as hard-boiled yolks, is about
to snap its clasp. I brush her tangled
fragrant hair at bedtime. It's an old
story—the oldest we have on our planet—
the story of replacement.

(1975)

MARY OLIVER
[b. 1935]

Poem for My Father's Ghost

Now is my father
A traveler, like all the bold men
He talked of, endlessly
And with boundless admiration,
Over the supper table,
Or gazing up from his white pillow—
Book on his lap always, until
Even that grew too heavy to hold.

Now is my father free of all binding fevers.
Now is my father
Traveling where there is no road.

Finally, he could not lift a hand
To cover his eyes.
Now he climbs to the eye of the river,
He strides through the Dakotas,
He disappears into the mountains. And though he looks
Cold and hungry as any man
At the end of a questing season,

He is one of *them* now:
He cannot be stopped.

Now is my father
Walking the wind,
Sniffing the deep Pacific
That begins at the end of the world.

Vanished from us utterly,
Now is my father circling the deepest forest—
Then turning in to the last red campfire burning
In the final hills,

Where chieftains, warriors and heroes
Rise and make him welcome,
Recognizing, under the shambles of his body,
A brother who has walked his thousand miles.

(1976)

WILFRED OWEN
[1893–1918]

Dulce et Decorum Est°

Bent double, like old beggars under sacks,
Knock-kneed, coughing like hags, we cursed through sludge,
Till on the haunting flares we turned our backs
And towards our distant rest began to trudge.
Men marched asleep. Many had lost their boots
But limped on, blood-shod. All went lame; all blind;
Drunk with fatigue; deaf even to the hoots
Of tired, outstripped Five-Nines that dropped behind.

Gas! GAS! Quick, boys!—An ecstasy of fumbling,
Fitting the clumsy helmets just in time;
But someone still was yelling out and stumbling
And flound'ring like a man in fire or lime . . .
Dim, through the misty panes and thick green light,
As under a green sea, I saw him drowning.

In all my dreams, before my helpless sight,
He plunges at me, guttering, choking, drowning.
If in some smothering dreams you too could pace
Behind the wagon that we flung him in,
And watch the white eyes writhing in his face,
His hanging face, like a devil's sick of sin;
If you could hear, at every jolt, the blood
Come gargling from the froth-corrupted lungs,
Obscene as cancer, bitter as the cud
Of vile, incurable sores on innocent tongues,—
My friend, you would not tell with such high zest
To children ardent for some desperate glory,
The old Lie: *Dulce et decorum est*
Pro patria mori.

(1920)

"Dulce et Decorum Est" *"It is sweet and fitting to die for one's country." See the last two lines, which are from Horace, Odes, III, ii.13.*

LINDA PASTAN*

[b. 1932]

Ethics

In ethics class so many years ago
our teacher asked this question every fall:
if there were a fire in a museum
which would you save, a Rembrandt painting
or an old woman who hadn't many
years left anyhow? Restless on hard chairs
caring little for pictures or old age
we'd opt one year for life, the next for art
and always half-heartedly. Sometimes
the woman borrowed my grandmother's face
leaving her usual kitchen to wander
some drafty, half imagined museum.
One year, feeling clever, I replied
why not let the woman decide herself?
Linda, the teacher would report, eschews
the burdens of responsibility.
This fall in a real museum I stand
before a real Rembrandt, old woman,
or nearly so, myself. The colors
within this frame are darker than autumn,
darker even than winter—the browns of earth,
though earth's most radiant elements burn
through the canvas. I know now that woman
and painting and season are almost one
and all beyond saving by children.

(1981)

ROBERT PINSKY

[b. 1940]

Dying

Nothing to be said about it, and everything—
The change of changes, closer or further away:
The Golden Retriever next door, Gussie, is dead,

Like Sandy, the Cocker Spaniel from three doors down
Who died when I was small; and every day
Things that were in my memory fade and die.

Phrases die out: first, everyone forgets
What doornails are; then after certain decades
As a dead metaphor, *"dead as a doornail"* flickers

And fades away. But someone I know is dying—
And though one might say glibly, "everyone is,"
The different pace makes the difference absolute.

The tiny invisible spores in the air we breathe,
That settle harmlessly on our drinking water
And on our skin, happen to come together

With certain conditions on the forest floor,
Or even a shady corner of the lawn—
And overnight the fleshy, pale stalks gather,

The colorless growth without a leaf or flower;
And around the stalks, the summer grass keeps growing
With steady pressure, like the insistent whiskers

That grow between shaves on a face, the nails
Growing and dying from the toes and fingers
At their own humble pace, oblivious

As the nerveless moths, that live their night or two—
Though like a moth a bright soul keeps on beating,
Bored and impatient in the monster's mouth.

(1984)

SYLVIA PLATH*

[1932–1963]

Blackberrying

Nobody in the lane, and nothing, nothing but blackberries,
Blackberries on either side, though on the right mainly,
A blackberry alley, going down in hooks, and a sea

Somewhere at the end of it, heaving. Blackberries
Big as the ball of my thumb, and dumb as eyes
Ebon in the hedges, fat
With blue-red juices. These they squander on my fingers.
I had not asked for such a blood sisterhood; they must love me.
They accommodate themselves to my milkbottle, flattening their sides.

Overhead go the choughs in black, cacophonous flocks—
Bits of burnt paper wheeling in a blown sky.
Theirs is the only voice, protesting, protesting.
I do not think the sea will appear at all.
The high, green meadows are glowing, as if lit from within.
I come to one bush of berries so ripe it is a bush of flies,
Hanging their blue-green bellies and their wing panes in a Chinese screen.
The honey-feast of the berries has stunned them; they believe in heaven.
One more hook, and the berries and bushes end.

The only thing to come now is the sea.
From between two hills a sudden wind funnels at me,
Slapping its phantom laundry in my face.
These hills are too green and sweet to have tasted salt.
I follow the sheep path between them. A last hook brings me
To the hills' northern face, and the face is orange rock
That looks out on nothing, nothing but a great space
Of white and pewter lights, and a din like silversmiths
Beating and beating at an intractable metal.

(1971)

Metaphors

I'm a riddle in nine syllables,
An elephant, a ponderous house,
A melon strolling on two tendrils,
O red fruit, ivory, fine timbers!
This loaf 's big with its yeasty rising.
Money's new-minted in this fat purse.
I'm a means, a stage, a cow in calf.
I've eaten a bag of green apples,
Boarded the train there's no getting off.

(1959)

Morning Song

Love set you going like a fat gold watch
The midwife slapped your footsoles, and your bald cry
Took its place among the elements.

Our voices echo, magnifying your arrival. New statue.
In a drafty museum, your nakedness
Shadows our safety. We stand round blankly as walls.

I'm no more your mother
Than the cloud that distills a mirror to reflect its own slow
Effacement at the wind's hand.

All night your moth-breath
Flickers among the flat pink roses. I wake to listen:
A far sea moves in my ear.

One cry, and I stumble from bed, cow-heavy and floral
In my Victorian nightgown.
Your mouth opens clean as a cat's. The window square

Whitens and swallows its dull stars. And now you try
Your handful of notes;
The clear vowels rise like balloons.

(1961)

EDGAR ALLAN POE*
[1809–1849]

The Raven

Once upon a midnight dreary, while I pondered, weak and weary,
Over many a quaint and curious volume of forgotten lore—
While I nodded, nearly napping, suddenly there came a tapping,
As of some one gently rapping, rapping at my chamber door—
" 'Tis some visiter," I muttered, "tapping at my chamber door—
Only this and nothing more."

Ah, distinctly I remember it was in the bleak December;
And each separate dying ember wrought its ghost upon the floor.
Eagerly I wished the morrow;—vainly I had sought to borrow
From my books surcease of sorrow—sorrow for the lost Lenore—

For the rare and radiant maiden whom the angels name Lenore—
Nameless *here* for evermore.

And the silken, sad, uncertain rustling of each purple curtain
Thrilled me—filled me with fantastic terrors never felt before;
So that now, to still the beating of my heart, I stood repeating
" 'Tis some visiter entreating entrance at my chamber door—
Some late visiter entreating entrance at my chamber door;—
This it is and nothing more."

Presently my soul grew stronger; hesitating then no longer,
"Sir," said I, "or Madam, truly your forgiveness I implore;
But the fact is I was napping, and so gently you came rapping,
And so faintly you came tapping, tapping at my chamber door,
That I scarce was sure I heard you"—here I opened wide the door;—
Darkness there and nothing more.

Deep into that darkness peering, long I stood there wondering, fearing,
Doubting, dreaming dreams no mortal ever dared to dream before;
But the silence was unbroken, and the stillness gave no token,
And the only word there spoken was the whispered word, "Lenore!"
This I whispered, and an echo murmured back the word, "Lenore!"
Merely this and nothing more.

Back into the chamber turning, all my soul within me burning,
Soon again I heard a tapping somewhat louder than before.
"Surely," said I, "surely that is something at my window lattice;
Let me see, then, what thereat is, and this mystery explore—
Let my heart be still a moment and this mystery explore;—
'Tis the wind and nothing more!"

Open here I flung the shutter, when, with many a flirt and flutter,
In there stepped a stately Raven of the saintly days of yore;
Not the least obeisance made he; not a minute stopped or stayed he;
But, with mien of lord or lady, perched above my chamber door—
Perched upon a bust of Pallas° just above my chamber door—
Perched, and sat, and nothing more.

Then this ebony bird beguiling my sad fancy into smiling,
By the grave and stern decorum of the countenance it wore,
"Though thy crest be shorn and shaven, thou," I said, "art sure no craven,
Ghastly grim and ancient Raven wandering from the Nightly shore—

"The Raven" 41 ***Pallas*** *Pallas Athene, patron goddess of Athens.*

Tell me what thy lordly name is on the Night's Plutonian° shore!"
Quoth the Raven "Nevermore."

Much I marvelled this ungainly fowl to hear discourse so plainly,
Though its answer little meaning—little relevancy bore;
For we cannot help agreeing that no living human being
Ever yet was blessed with seeing bird above his chamber door—
Bird or beast upon the sculptured bust above his chamber door,
With such name as "Nevermore."

But the Raven, sitting lonely on the placid bust, spoke only
That one word, as if his soul in that one word he did outpour.
Nothing farther then he uttered—not a feather then he fluttered—
Till I scarcely more than muttered "Other friends have flown before—
On the morrow he will leave me, as my Hopes have flown before."
Then the bird said "Nevermore."

Startled at the stillness broken by reply so aptly spoken,
"Doubtless," said I, "what it utters is its only stock and store
Caught from some unhappy master whom unmerciful Disaster
Followed fast and followed faster till his songs one burden bore—
Till the dirges of his Hope that melancholy burden bore
Of 'Never—nevermore.'"

But the Raven still beguiling my sad fancy into smiling,
Straight I wheeled a cushioned seat in front of bird, and bust and door;
Then, upon the velvet sinking, I betook myself to linking
Fancy unto fancy, thinking what this ominous bird of yore—
What this grim, ungainly, ghastly, gaunt, and ominous bird of yore
Meant in croaking "Nevermore."

Thus I sat engaged in guessing, but no syllable expressing
To the fowl whose fiery eyes now burned into my bosom's core;
This and more I sat divining, with my head at ease reclining
On the cushion's velvet lining that the lamp-light gloated o'er,
But whose velvet-violet lining with the lamp-light gloating o'er,
She shall press, ah, nevermore!

Then, methought, the air grew denser, perfumed from an
unseen censer
Swung by seraphim whose foot-falls tinkled on the tufted floor.
"Wretch," I cried, "thy God hath lent thee—by these angels he
hath sent thee
Respite—respite and nepenthe from thy memories of Lenore;

"The Raven" 47 ***Plutonian*** *Pluto, god of the underworld.*

Quaff, oh quaff this kind nepenthe and forget this lost Lenore!"
    Quoth the Raven "Nevermore."

"Prophet!" said I, "thing of evil!—prophet still, if bird or devil!—
Whether Tempter sent, or whether tempest tossed thee here ashore,
Desolate yet all undaunted, on this desert land enchanted—
Oh this home by Horror haunted—tell me truly, I implore—
Is there—is there balm in Gilead?—tell me—tell me, I implore!"
    Quoth the Raven "Nevermore."

"Prophet!" said I, "thing of evil!—prophet still, if bird or devil!
By that Heaven that bends above us—by that God we both adore—
Tell this soul with sorrow laden if, within the distant Aidenn,
It shall clasp a sainted maiden whom the angels name Lenore—
Clasp a rare and radiant maiden whom the angels name Lenore."
    Quoth the Raven "Nevermore."

"Be that word our sign of parting, bird or fiend!" I shrieked, upstarting—
"Get thee back into the tempest and the Night's Plutonian shore!
Leave no black plume as a token of that lie thy soul hath spoken!
Leave my loneliness unbroken!—quit the bust above my door!
Take thy beak from out my heart, and take thy form from off my door!"
    Quoth the Raven "Nevermore."

And the Raven, never flitting, still is sitting, still is sitting
On the pallid bust of Pallas just above my chamber door;
And his eyes have all the seeming of a demon's that is dreaming,
And the lamp-light o'er him streaming throws his shadow on the floor;
And my soul from out that shadow that lies floating on the floor
    Shall be lifted—nevermore!

(1845)

ALEXANDER POPE*

[1688–1744]

from An Essay on Man

FROM EPISTLE II

I. Know then thyself, presume not God to scan;° — scrutinize
The proper study of mankind is Man.
Placed on this isthmus of a middle state,

A being darkly wise, and rudely° great; crudely
With too much knowledge for the Sceptic side,
With too much weakness for the Stoic's pride,
He hangs between; in doubt to act, or rest,
In doubt to deem himself a god, or beast;
In doubt his mind or body to prefer,
Born but to die, and reasoning but to err;
Alike in ignorance, his reason such,
Whether he thinks too little, or too much:
Chaos of thought and passion, all confused;
Still by himself abused, or disabused;
Created half to rise, and half to fall;
Great lord of all things, yet a prey to all;
Sole judge of truth, in endless error hurled:
The glory, jest, and riddle of the world!

(1711)

EZRA POUND*

[1885–1972]

In a Station of the Metro

The apparition of these faces in the crowd;
Petals on a wet, black bough.

(1913)

The River-Merchant's Wife: A Letter°

While my hair was still cut straight across my forehead
Played I about the front gate, pulling flowers.
You came by on bamboo stilts, playing horse,
You walked about my seat, playing with blue plums.
And we went on living in the village of Chōkan:
Two small people, without dislike or suspicion.

At fourteen I married My Lord you.
I never laughed, being bashful.

"The River-Merchants's Wife: A Letter" Pound translated and adapted this poem from the Chinese. Rihaku is the Japanese name for the Chinese poet Li Bai, formerly known as Li Po, who wrote the poem.

Lowering my head, I looked at the wall.
Called to, a thousand times, I never looked back.

At fifteen I stopped scowling,
I desired my dust to be mingled with yours
Forever and forever and forever.
Why should I climb the look out?

At sixteen you departed,
You went into far Ku-tō-en, by the river of swirling eddies,
And you have been gone five months.
The monkeys make sorrowful noise overhead.

You dragged your feet when you went out.
By the gate now, the moss is grown, the different mosses,
Too deep to clear them away!
The leaves fall early this autumn, in wind.
The paired butterflies are already yellow with August

Over the grass in the West garden;
They hurt me. I grow older.
If you are coming down through the narrows of the river Kiang,
Please let me know before hand,
And I will come out to meet you
As far as Chō-fū-Sa.

by Rihaku

(1916)

RAINER MARIA RILKE*

[1875–1926]

The Cadet Picture of My Father

TRANSLATED BY ROBERT LOWELL

There's absence in the eyes. The brow's in touch
with something far. Now distant boyishness
and seduction shadow his enormous lips,

the slender aristocratic uniform
with its Franz Josef braid; both the hands bulge
like gloves upon the saber's basket hilt.
The hands are quiet, they reach out toward nothing—

I hardly see them now, as if they were
the first to grasp distance and disappear,
and all the rest lies curtained in itself,
and so withdrawn, I cannot understand
my father as he bleaches on this page—

Oh quickly disappearing photograph
in my more slowly disappearing hand!

ALBERTO RIOS

[b. 1952]

A Dream of Husbands

Though we thought it, Doña Carolina did not die.
She was too old for that nonsense, and too set.
That morning she walked off just a little farther
into her favorite dream, favorite but not nice
so much, not nice and not bad, so it was not death.
She dreamed the dream of husbands
and over there she found him after all the years.
Cabrón, she called him, *animal,* very loud
so we could hear it, for us it was a loud truck
passing, or thunder, or too many cats, very loud
for having left her for so long and so far. Days now
her voice is the squeak of the rocking chair
as she complains, we hear it, it will not go
not with oils or sanding or shouts back at her.
But it becomes too the sound a spoon makes, her old
very large wooden spoon as it stirs a pot of soup.
Dinnertimes, we think of her, the good parts, of her
cooking, we like her best then, even the smell of her.
But then, *cabrones* she calls us, *animales,* irritated,
from over there, from the dream, they come, her words
they are the worst sounds of the street in the night
so that we will not get so comfortable about her,
so comfortable with her having left us

we thinking that her husband and her long dream
are so perfect, because no, they are not, not so much,
she is not so happy this way, not in this dream,
this is not heaven, don't think it. She tells us this,
sadness too is hers, a half measure, sadness at having
no time for the old things, for rice, for chairs.

(1985)

THEODORE ROETHKE*

[1908–1963]

Elegy for Jane

MY STUDENT, THROWN BY A HORSE

I remember the neckcurls, limp and damp as tendrils;
And her quick look, a sidelong pickerel smile;
And how, once startled into talk, the light syllables leaped
  for her,
And she balanced in the delight of her thought,
A wren, happy, tail into the wind,
Her song trembling the twigs and small branches.
The shade sang with her;
The leaves, their whispers turned to kissing;
And the mold sang in the bleached valleys under the rose.

Oh, when she was sad, she cast herself down into such a pure
  depth,
Even a father could not find her:
Scraping her cheek against straw;
Stirring the clearest water.

My sparrow, you are not here,
Waiting like a fern, making a spiny shadow.
The sides of wet stones cannot console me,
Nor the moss, wound with the last light.

If only I could nudge you from this sleep,
My maimed darling, my skittery pigeon.
Over this damp grave I speak the words of my love:

I, with no rights in this matter,
Neither father nor lover.

(1953)

Root Cellar

Nothing would sleep in that cellar, dank as a ditch,
Bulbs broke out of boxes hunting for chinks in the dark,
Shoots dangled and drooped,
Lolling obscenely from mildewed crates,
Hung down long yellow evil necks, like tropical snakes.
And what a congress of stinks!
Roots ripe as old bait,
Pulpy stems, rank, silo-rich,
Leaf-mold, manure, lime, piled against slippery planks.
Nothing would give up life:
Even the dirt kept breathing a small breath.

(1948)

SONIA SANCHEZ*

[b. 1934]

Towhomitmayconcern

watch out fo the full moon of sonia
shinin down on ya.
git yo/self fattened up man
you gon be doing battle with me
ima gonna stake you out
grind you down
leave greasy spots all over yo/soul
till you bone dry. man.
you gon know you done been touched by me
this time.
ima gonna tattoo me on you fo ever
leave my creases all inside yo creases
i done warned ya boy
watch out

for the full moon of Sonia
shinin down on ya.

(1999)

ANNE SEXTON*
[1928–1975]

Two Hands

From the sea came a hand,
ignorant as a penny,
troubled with the salt of its mother,
mute with the silence of the fishes,
quick with the altars of the tides,
and God reached out of His mouth
and called it man.
Up came the other hand
and God called it woman.
The hands applauded.
And this was no sin.
It was as it was meant to be.

I see them roaming the streets:
Levi complaining about his mattress,
Sarah studying a beetle,
Mandrake holding his coffee mug,
Sally playing the drum at a football game,
John closing the eyes of the dying woman,
and some who are in prison,
even the prison of their bodies,
as Christ was prisoned in His body
until the triumph came.

Unwind, hands,
you angel webs,
unwind like the coil of a jumping jack,
cup together and let yourselves fill up with sun
and applaud, world,
applaud.

(1969)

WILLIAM SHAKESPEARE*

[1564–1616]

When in disgrace with fortune and men's eyes

When, in disgrace with fortune and men's eyes,
I all alone beweep my outcast state,
And trouble deaf heaven with my bootless° cries, — useless
And look upon myself, and curse my fate,
Wishing me like to one more rich in hope,
Featured like him, like him with friends possessed,
Desiring this man's art and that man's scope,
With what I most enjoy contented least;
Yet in these thoughts myself almost despising,
Haply I think on thee—and then my state,
Like to the lark at break of day arising
From sullen earth, sings hymns at heaven's gate;
For thy sweet love remembered such wealth brings
That then I scorn to change my state with kings. (1609)

Let me not to the marriage of true minds

Let me not to the marriage of true minds
Admit impediments.° Love is not love — hindrances
Which alters when it alteration finds,
Or bends with the remover to remove:
Oh, no! it is an ever-fixéd mark,
That looks on tempests and is never shaken;
It is the star to every wandering bark,° — ship
Whose worth's unknown, although his height be taken.°
Love's not Time's fool, though rosy lips and cheeks
Within his bending sickle's compass come;
Love alters not with his brief hours and weeks,
But bears° it out even to the edge of doom.° — lasts/judgment day
If this be error and upon me proved,
I never writ, nor no man ever loved. (1609)

Th' expense of spirit in a waste of shame

Th' expense of spirit in a waste of shame
Is lust in action; and till action, lust
Is perjured, murderous, bloody, full of blame,

"Let me not to the marriage of true minds" [8]**height be taken** *its elevation be measured.*

Savage, extreme, rude, cruel, not to trust;
Enjoyed no sooner but despiséd straight:
Past reason hunted; and no sooner had,
Past reason hated, as a swallowed bait,
On purpose laid to make the taker mad:
Mad in pursuit, and in possession so;
Had, having, and in quest to have, extreme;
A bliss in proof,° and proved, a very woe; in the experience
Before, a joy proposed; behind, a dream.
All this the world well knows; yet none knows well
To shun the heaven that leads men to this hell.

(1609)

My mistress' eyes are nothing like the sun

My mistress' eyes are nothing like the sun;
Coral is far more red than her lips' red;
If snow be white, why then her breasts are dun;
If hairs be wires, black wires grow on her head.
I have seen roses damasked,° red and white, variegated
But no such roses see I in her cheeks;
And in some perfumes is there more delight
Than in the breath that from my mistress reeks.
I love to hear her speak, yet well I know
That music hath a far more pleasing sound;
I grant I never saw a goddess go;° walk
My mistress, when she walks, treads on the ground.
And yet, by heaven, I think my love as rare
As any she belied with false compare.

(1609)

PERCY BYSSHE SHELLEY*
[1792–1822]

Ozymandias°

I met a traveler from an antique land
Who said: Two vast and trunkless legs of stone
Stand in the desert . . . Near them, on the sand,

"Ozymandias" **Ozymandias** *Greek name for the Egyptian ruler Rameses II, who erected a huge statue in his own likeness, among numerous other monuments.*

Half sunk, a shattered visage lies, whose frown,
And wrinkled lip, and sneer of cold command,
Tell that its sculptor well those passions read
Which yet survive, stamped on these lifeless things,
The hand that mocked them, and the heart that fed:
And on the pedestal these words appear:
"My name is Ozymandias, king of kings:
Look on my works, ye Mighty, and despair!"
Nothing beside remains. Round the decay
Of that colossal wreck, boundless and bare
The lone and level sands stretch far away.

(1818)

GARY SOTO

[b. 1952]

Behind Grandma's House

At ten I wanted fame. I had a comb
And two Coke bottles, a tube of Bryl-creem.
I borrowed a dog, one with
Mismatched eyes and a happy tongue,
And wanted to prove I was tough
In the alley, kicking over trash cans,
A dull chime of tuna cans falling.
I hurled light bulbs like grenades
And men teachers held their heads,
Fingers of blood lengthening
On the ground. I flicked rocks at cats,
Their goofy faces spurred with foxtails.
I kicked fences. I shooed pigeons.
I broke a branch from a flowering peach
And frightened ants with a stream of spit.
I said *"Chale,"* "In your face," and "No way
Daddy-O" to an imaginary priest
Until grandma came into the alley,
Her apron flapping in a breeze,
Her hair mussed, and said, "Let me help you,"
And punched me between the eyes.

(1985)

WILLIAM STAFFORD
[1914–1993]

Traveling through the dark

Traveling through the dark I found a deer
dead on the edge of the Wilson River road.
It is usually best to roll them into the canyon:
that road is narrow; to swerve might make more dead.

By glow of the tail-light I stumbled back of the car
and stood by the heap, a doe, a recent killing;
she had stiffened already, almost cold.
I dragged her off; she was large in the belly.

My fingers touching her side brought me the reason—
her side was warm; her fawn lay there waiting,
alive, still, never to be born.
Beside that mountain road I hesitated.

The car aimed ahead its lowered parking lights;
under the hood purred the steady engine.
I stood in the glare of the warm exhaust turning red;
around our group I could hear the wilderness listen.

I thought hard for us all—my only swerving—,
then pushed her over the edge into the river.

(1957)

WALLACE STEVENS*
[1879–1955]

Thirteen Ways of Looking at a Blackbird

1

Among twenty snowy mountains,
The only moving thing
Was the eye of the blackbird.

2

I was of three minds,
Like a tree
In which there are three blackbirds.

3

The blackbird whirled in the autumn winds.
It was a small part of the pantomime.

4

A man and a woman
Are one.
A man and a woman and a blackbird
Are one.

5

I do not know which to prefer,
The beauty of inflections
Or the beauty of innuendoes,
The blackbird whistling
Or just after.

6

Icicles filled the long window
With barbaric glass.
The shadow of the blackbird
Crossed it to and fro.
The mood
Traced in the shadow
An indecipherable cause.

7

O thin men of Haddam,
Why do you imagine golden birds?
Do you not see how the blackbird
Walks around the feet
Of the women about you?

8

I know noble accents
And lucid, inescapable rhythms;
But I know, too,
That the blackbird is involved
In what I know.

9

When the blackbird flew out of sight,
It marked the edge
Of one of many circles.

10

At the sight of blackbirds
Flying in a green light,
Even the bawds of euphony
Would cry out sharply.

11

He rode over Connecticut
In a glass coach.
Once, a fear pierced him,
In that he mistook
The shadow of his equipage
For blackbirds.

12

The river is moving.
The blackbird must be flying.

13

It was evening all afternoon.
It was snowing
And it was going to snow.
The blackbird sat
In the cedar-limbs.

(1923)

Disillusionment of Ten o'clock

The houses are haunted
By white night-gowns.
None are green,
Or purple with green rings,
Or green with yellow rings,
Or yellow with blue rings.
None of them are strange,
With socks of lace
And beaded ceintures.
People are not going
To dream of baboons and periwinkles.
Only, here and there, an old sailor,
Drunk and asleep in his boots,
Catches tigers
In red weather.

(1923)

© Jill Krementz

MAY SWENSON*

[1919–1989]

Strawberrying

My hands are murder-red. Many a plump head
drops on the heap in the basket. Or, ripe
to bursting, they might be hearts, matching
the blackbird's wing-fleck. Gripped to a reed
he shrieks his ko-ka-ree in the next field.
He's left his peck in some juicy cheeks, when
at first blush and mostly white, they showed
streaks of sweetness to the marauder.

We're picking near the shore, the morning
sunny, a slight wind moving rough-veined leaves
our hands rumple among. Fingers find by feel
the ready fruit in clusters. Here and there,
their squishy wounds. . . . Flesh was perfect
yesterday. . . . June was for gorging. . . .
sweet hearts young and firm before decay.

"Take only the biggest, and not too ripe,"
a mother calls to her girl and boy, barefoot
in the furrows. "Don't step on any. Don't
change rows. Don't eat too many." Mesmerized
by the largesse, the children squat and pull
and pick handfuls of rich scarlets, half
for the baskets, half for avid mouths.
Soon, whole faces are stained.

A crop this thick begs for plunder. Ripeness
wants to be ravished, as udders of cows when hard,
the blue-veined bags distended, ache to be stripped.
Hunkered in mud between the rows, sun burning
the backs of our necks, we grope for, and rip loose
soft nippled heads. If they bleed—too soft—
let them stay. Let them rot in the heat.

When, hidden away in a damp hollow under moldy
leaves, I come upon a clump of heart-shapes
once red, now spiderspit-gray, intact but empty,
still attached to their dead stems—
families smothered as at Pompeii—I rise
and stretch. I eat one more big ripe lopped
head. Red-handed, I leave the field.

(1962)

Women

Women
should be
pedestals
moving
pedestals
moving
to the
motions
of men

Or they
should be
little horses
those wooden
sweet
oldfashioned
painted
rocking
horses

the gladdest things in the toyroom

The
pegs
of their
ears
so familiar
and dear
to the trusting
fists
To be chafed

feelingly
and then
unfeelingly
To be
joyfully
ridden
rockingly
ridden until
the restored

egos dismount and the legs stride away

Immobile
sweetlipped
sturdy
and smiling
women
should always
be waiting

willing
to be set
into motion
Women
should be
pedestals
to men

(1967)

ALFRED, LORD TENNYSON*

[1809–1892]

Ulysses°

It little profits that an idle king,
By this still hearth, among these barren crags,
Matched with an aged wife, I mete and dole
Unequal laws unto a savage race,
That hoard, and sleep, and feed, and know not me.
I cannot rest from travel; I will drink
Life to the lees. All times I have enjoyed
Greatly, have suffered greatly, both with those
That loved me, and alone; on shore, and when
Through scudding drifts the rainy Hyades°
Vext the dim sea. I am become a name;
For always roaming with a hungry heart
Much have I seen and known—cities of men
And manners,° climates, councils, governments, customs
Myself not least, but honored of them all,—
And drunk delight of battle with my peers,
Far on the ringing plains of windy Troy.
I am a part of all that I have met;
Yet all experience is an arch wherethrough
Gleams that untraveled world whose margin fades
For ever and for ever when I move.
How dull it is to pause, to make an end,
To rust unburnished, not to shine in use!
As though to breathe were life! Life piled on life
Were all too little, and of one to me
Little remains; but every hour is saved
From that eternal silence, something more,
A bringer of new things; and vile it were
For some three suns to store and hoard myself,
And this gray spirit yearning in desire
To follow knowledge like a sinking star,
Beyond the utmost bound of human thought.
  This is my son, mine own Telemachus,
To whom I leave the scepter and the isle,

"Ulysses" ***Ulysses*** *according to Dante (in The Inferno, Canto 26) Ulysses, having been away for ten years during the Trojan War, is restless upon returning to his island kingdom of Ithaca, and he persuades a band of followers to accompany him on a journey.* 10 ***Hyades*** *a constellation of stars whose rising with the sun forecasts rain.*

Well-loved of me, discerning to fulfill
This labor, by slow prudence to make mild
A rugged people, and through soft degrees
Subdue them to the useful and the good.
Most blameless is he, centered in the sphere
Of common duties, decent° not to fail — proper
In offices° of tenderness, and pay — duties
Meet° adoration to my household gods, — appropriate
When I am gone. He works his work, I mine.
  There lies the port; the vessel puffs her sail;
There gloom the dark, broad seas. My mariners,
Souls that have toiled, and wrought, and thought with me,
That ever with a frolic welcome took
The thunder and the sunshine, and opposed
Free hearts, free foreheads—you and I are old;
Old age hath yet his honor and his toil.
Death closes all; but something ere the end,
Some work of noble note, may yet be done,
Not unbecoming men that strove with gods.
The lights begin to twinkle from the rocks;
The long day wanes; the slow moon climbs; the deep
Moans round with many voices. Come, my friends,
'Tis not too late to seek a newer world.
Push off, and sitting well in order smite
The sounding furrows; for my purpose holds
To sail beyond the sunset, and the baths
Of all the western stars, until I die.
It may be that the gulfs will wash us down;
It may be we shall touch the Happy Isles,°
And see the great Achilles, whom we knew.
Though much is taken, much abides; and though
We are not now that strength which in old days
Moved earth and heaven, that which we are, we are,
One equal temper of heroic hearts,
Made weak by time and fate, but strong in will
To strive, to seek, to find, and not to yield.

(1842)

The Eagle

FRAGMENT

He clasps the crag with crooked hands;
Close to the sun in lonely lands,
Ringed with the azure world, he stands.

[63]***Happy Isles*** *the abode after death of those favored by the gods.*

The wrinkled sea beneath him crawls;
He watches from his mountain walls,
And like a thunderbolt he falls.

(1851)

DYLAN THOMAS*
[1914–1953]

Fern Hill

Now as I was young and easy under the apple boughs
About the lilting house and happy as the grass was green,
    The night above the dingle starry,
        Time let me hail and climb
    Golden in the heydays of his eyes,
And honored among wagons I was prince of the apple towns
And once below a time I lordly had the trees and leaves
        Trail with daisies and barley
    Down the rivers of the windfall light.

And as I was green and carefree, famous among the barns
About the happy yard and singing as the farm was home,
    In the sun that is young once only,
        Time let me play and be
    Golden in the mercy of his means,
And green and golden I was huntsman and herdsman, the calves
Sang to my horn, the foxes on the hills barked clear and cold,
        And the sabbath rang slowly
    In the pebbles of the holy streams.

All the sun long it was running, it was lovely, the hay
Fields high as the house, the tunes from the chimneys, it was air
    And playing, lovely and watery
        And fire green as grass.
    And nightly under the simple stars
As I rode to sleep the owls were bearing the farm away,
All the moon long I heard, blessed among stables, the night-jars
    Flying with the ricks, and the horses
        Flashing into the dark.

And then to awake, and the farm, like a wanderer white
With the dew, come back, the cock on his shoulder: it was all
Shining, it was Adam and maiden,
The sky gathered again
And the sun grew round that very day.
So it must have been after the birth of the simple light
In the first, spinning place, the spellbound horses walking warm
Out of the whinnying green stable
On to the fields of praise.

And honored among foxes and pheasants by the gay house
Under the new made clouds and happy as the heart was long,
In the sun born over and over,
I ran my heedless ways,
My wishes raced through the house high hay
And nothing I cared, at my sky blue trades, that time allows
In all his tuneful turning so few and such morning songs
Before the children green and golden
Follow him out of grace,

Nothing I cared, in the lamb white days, that time would take me
Up to the swallow thronged loft by the shadow of my hand,
In the moon that is always rising,
Nor that riding to sleep
I should hear him fly with the high fields
And wake to the farm forever fled from the childless land.
Oh as I was young and easy in the mercy of his means,
Time held me green and dying
Though I sang in my chains like the sea.

(1946)

Do not go gentle into that good night

Do not go gentle into that good night,
Old age should burn and rave at close of day;
Rage, rage against the dying of the light.

Though wise men at their end know dark is right,
Because their words had forked no lightning they
Do not go gentle into that good night.

Good men, the last wave by, crying how bright
Their frail deeds might have danced in a green bay,
Rage, rage against the dying of the light.

Wild men who caught and sang the sun in flight,
And learn, too late, they grieved it on its way,
Do not go gentle into that good night.

Grave men, near death, who see with blinding sight
Blind eyes could blaze like meteors and be gay,
Rage, rage against the dying of the light.

And you, my father, there on the sad height,
Curse, bless, me now with your fierce tears, I pray.
Do not go gentle into that good night.
Rage, rage against the dying of the light.

(1952)

JEAN TOOMER*
[1894–1967]

Song of the Son

Pour, O pour, that parting soul in song,
O pour it in the saw-dust glow of night,
Into the velvet pine-smoke air tonight,
And let the valley carry it along,
And let the valley carry it along.

O land and soil, red soil and sweet-gum tree
So scant of grass, so profligate of pines,
Now just before an epoch's sun declines
Thy son, in time, I have returned to thee,
Thy son, I have in time returned to thee.

In time, for though the sun is setting on
A song-lit race of slaves, it has not set;
Though late, O soil it is not too late yet
To catch thy plaintive soul, leaving, soon gone,
Leaving, to catch thy plaintive soul soon gone.

O Negro slaves, dark-purple ripened plums,
Squeezed, and bursting in the pine-wood air,

Passing, before they stripped the old tree bare
One plum was saved for me, one seed becomes

An everlasting song, a singing tree,
Carolling softly souls of slavery,
All that they were, and that they are to me,—
Carolling softly souls of slavery.

(1922)

Reapers

Black reapers with the sound of steel on stones
Arc sharpening scythes. I see them place the hones
In their hip-pockets as a thing that's done,
And start their silent swinging, one by one.
Black horses drive a mower through the weeds,
And there, a field rat, startled, squealing bleeds,
His belly close to ground. I see the blade,
Blood-stained, continue cutting weeds and shade.

(1923)

WALT WHITMAN*
[1819–1892]

One's Self I Sing

One's Self I sing, a simple separate person,
Yet utter the word Democratic, the word En-Masse.

Of physiology from top to toe I sing,
Not physiognomy alone nor brain alone is worthy for the Muse,
  I say the form complete is worthier far,
The Female equally with the Male I sing.

Of Life immense in passion, pulse, and power,
Cheerful, for freest action form'd under the laws divine,
The Modern Man I sing.

(1855)

A noiseless patient spider

A noiseless patient spider,
I mark'd where on a little promontory it stood isolated,
Mark'd how to explore the vacant vast surrounding,
It launch'd forth filament, filament, filament, out of itself,
Ever unreeling them, ever tirelessly speeding them.

And you O my soul where you stand,
Surrounded, detached, in measureless oceans of space,
Ceaselessly musing, venturing, throwing, seeking the spheres to
  connect them,
Till the bridge you will need be form'd, till the ductile anchor hold,
Till the gossamer thread you fling catch somewhere, O my soul.

(1881)

Crossing Brooklyn Ferry

1

Flood-tide below me! I see you face to face!
Clouds of the west—sun there half an hour high—I see you also
  face to face.
Crowds of men and women attired in the usual costumes, how curious
  you are to me!
On the ferry-boats the hundreds and hundreds that cross, returning
  home, are more
    curious to me than you suppose,
And you that shall cross from shore to shore years hence are more to
  me, and more in my meditations, than you might suppose.

2

The impalpable sustenance of me from all things at all hours of the day,
The simple, compact, well-join'd scheme, myself disintegrated, every one
  disintegrated yet part of the scheme,
The similitudes of the past and those of the future,
The glories strung like beads on my smallest sights and hearings,
  on the walk in the street and the passage over the river,
The current rushing so swiftly and swimming with me far away,
The others that are to follow me, the ties between me and them,
The certainty of others, the life, love, sight, hearing of others.
Others will enter the gates of the ferry and cross from shore to shore,
Others will watch the run of the flood-tide,
Others will see the shipping of Manhattan north and west, and the
  heights of Brooklyn to the south and east,
Others will see the islands large and small;
Fifty years hence, others will see them as they cross, the sun half an

hour high,
A hundred years hence, or ever so many hundred years hence, others will see them,
Will enjoy the sunset, the pouring-in of the flood-tide, the falling-back to the sea of the ebb-tide.

3

It avails not, time nor place—distance avails not,
I am with you, you men and women of a generation, or ever so many generations hence,
Just as you feel when you look on the river and sky, so I felt,
Just as any of you is one of a living crowd, I was one of a crowd,
Just as you are refresh'd by the gladness of the river and the bright flow, I was refresh'd,
Just as you stand and lean on the rail, yet hurry with the swift current, I stood yet was hurried,
Just as you look on the numberless masts of ships and the thick-stemm'd pipes of steamboats, I look'd.

I too many and many a time cross'd the river of old,
Watched the Twelfth-month° sea-gulls, saw them high in the air floating with motionless wings, oscillating their bodies, December
Saw how the glistening yellow lit up parts of their bodies and left the rest in strong shadow,
Saw the slow-wheeling circles and the gradual edging toward the south,
Saw the reflection of the summer sky in the water,
Had my eyes dazzled by the shimmering track of beams,
Look'd at the fine centrifugal spokes of light round the shape of my head in the sunlit water,
Look'd on the haze on the hills southward and south-westward,
Look'd on the vapor as it flew in fleeces tinged with violet,
Look'd toward the lower bay to notice the vessels arriving,
Saw their approach, saw aboard those that were near me,
Saw the white sails of schooners and sloops, saw the ships at anchor,
The sailors at work in the rigging or out astride the spars,
The round masts, the swinging motion of the hulls, the slender serpentine pennants,
The large and small steamers in motion, the pilots in their pilot-houses,
The white wake left by the passage, the quick tremulous whirl of the wheels,
The flags of all nations, the falling of them at sunset,
The scallop-edged waves in the twilight, the ladled cups, the frolicsome crests and glistening,
The stretch afar growing dimmer and dimmer, the gray walls of the granite storehouses by the docks,
On the river the shadowy group, the big steam-tug closely flank'd on each side by the barges, the hay-boat, the belated lighter,

On the neighboring shore the fires from the foundry chimneys burning
high and glaringly into the night,
Casting their flicker of black contrasted with wild red and yellow light
over the tops of houses, and down into the clefts of streets.

4

These and all else were to me the same as they are to you,
I loved well those cities, loved well the stately and rapid river,
The men and women I saw were all near to me,
Others the same—others who look back on me because I look'd
forward to them,
(The time will come, though I stop° here to-day and to-night.) stay

5

What is it then between us?
What is the count of the scores or hundreds of years between us?
Whatever it is, it avails not—distance avails not, and place avails not,
I too lived, Brooklyn of ample hills was mine,
I too walk'd the streets of Manhattan island, and bathed in the
waters around it,
I too felt the curious abrupt questionings stir within me,
In the day among crowds of people sometimes they came upon me,
In my walks home late at night or as I lay in my bed they came upon me,
I too had been struck from the float forever held in solution,
I too had receiv'd identity by my body,
That I was I knew was of my body, and what I should be I knew I
should be of my body.

6

It is not upon you alone the dark patches fall,
The dark threw its patches down upon me also,
The best I had done seem'd to me blank and suspicious,
My great thoughts as I supposed them, were they not in reality meager?
Nor is it you alone who know what it is to be evil,
I am he who knew what it was to be evil,
I too knitted the old knot of contrariety,
Blabb'd, blush'd, resented, lied, stole, grudg'd,
Had guile, anger, lust, hot wishes I dared not speak,
Was wayward, vain, greedy, shallow, sly, cowardly, malignant,
The wolf, the snake, the hog, not wanting in me,
The cheating look, the frivolous word, the adulterous wish, not wanting,
Refusals, hates, postponements, meanness, laziness, none of these wanting,
Was one with the rest, the days and haps of the rest,
Was call'd by my nighest name by clear loud voices of young men as they
saw me approaching or passing,
Felt their arms on my neck as I stood, or the negligent leaning of their
flesh against me as I sat,
Saw many I loved in the street or ferry-boat or public assembly, yet never
told them a word,

Lived the same life with the rest, the same old laughing, gnawing, sleeping,
Play'd the part that still looks back on the actor or actress,
The same old role, the role that is what we make it, as great as we like,
Or as small as we like, or both great and small.

7

Closer yet I approach you,
What thought you have of me now, I had as much of you—I laid in my
stores in advance,
I consider'd long and seriously of you before you were born.

Who was to know what should come home to me?
Who knows but I am enjoying this?
Who knows, for all the distance, but I am as good as looking at you now,
for all you cannot see me?

8

Ah, what can ever be more stately and admirable to me than
mast-hemm'd Manhattan?
River and sunset and scallop-edg'd waves of flood-tide?
The sea-gulls oscillating their bodies, the hay-boat in the twilight,
and the belated lighter?
What gods can exceed these that clasp me by the hand, and with voices
I love call me promptly and loudly by my nighest name as I approach?
What is more subtle than this which ties me to the woman or man that
looks in my face?
Which fuses me into you now, and pours my meaning into you?

We understand then do we not?
What I promis'd without mentioning it, have you not accepted?
What the study could not teach—what the preaching could not
accomplish is accomplish'd, is it not?

9

Flow on, river! flow with the flood-tide, and ebb with the ebb-tide!
Frolic on, crested and scallop-edg'd waves!
Gorgeous clouds of the sunset! drench with your splendor me, or the
men and women generations after me!
Cross from shore to shore, countless crowds of passengers!
Stand up, tall masts of Mannahatta! stand up, beautiful hills of Brooklyn!
Throb, baffled and curious brain! throw out questions and answers!
Suspend here and everywhere, eternal float of solution!
Gaze, loving and thirsting eyes, in the house or street or public assembly!
Sound out, voices of young men! loudly and musically call me by my
nighest name!
Live, old life! play the part that looks back on the actor or actress!
Play the old role, the role that is great or small according as one makes it!
Consider, you who peruse me, whether I may not in unknown ways
be looking upon you;

Be firm, rail over the river, to support those who lean idly, yet haste
  with the hasting current;
Fly on, sea birds! fly sideways, or wheel in large circles high in the air;
Receive the summer sky, you water, and faithfully hold it till all downcast
  eyes have time to take it from you!
Diverge, fine spokes of light, from the shape of my head, or any one's
  head, in the sunlit water!
Come on, ships from the lower bay! pass up or down, white-sail'd
  schooners, sloops, lighters!
Flaunt away, flags of all nations! be duly lower'd at sunset!
Burn high your fires, foundry chimneys! cast black shadows at nightfall!
  cast red and yellow light over the tops of the houses!
Appearances, now or henceforth, indicate what you are,
You necessary film, continue to envelop the soul,
About my body for me, and your body for you, be hung our divinest
  aromas,

Thrive, cities—bring your freight, bring your shows, ample and sufficient
  rivers,
Expand, being than which none else is perhaps more spiritual,
Keep your places, objects than which none else is more lasting.

You have waited, you always wait, you dumb, beautiful ministers,
We receive you with free sense at last, and are insatiate henceforward,
Not you any more shall be able to foil us, or withhold yourselves from us,
We use you, and do not cast you aside—we plant you permanently
  within us,
We fathom you not—we love you—there is perfection in you also,
You furnish your parts toward eternity,
Great or small, you furnish your parts toward the soul.

(1856)

WILLIAM CARLOS WILLIAMS*

[1883–1963]

Spring and All

By the road to the contagious hospital
under the surge of the blue
mottled clouds driven from the

northeast—a cold wind. Beyond, the
waste of broad, muddy fields
brown with dried weeds, standing and fallen
patches of standing water
the scattering of tall trees

All along the road the reddish
purplish, forked, upstanding, twiggy
stuff of bushes and small trees
with dead, brown leaves under them
leafless vines—

Lifeless in appearance, sluggish
dazed spring approaches—

They enter the new world naked,
cold, uncertain of all
save that they enter. All about them
the cold, familiar wind—

Now the grass, tomorrow
the stiff curl of wildcarrot leaf
One by one objects are defined—
It quickens: clarity, outline of leaf

But now the stark dignity of
entrance—Still, the profound change
has come upon them: rooted, they
grip down and begin to awaken

(1923)

Danse Russe

If when my wife is sleeping
and the baby and Kathleen
are sleeping
and the sun is a flame-white disc
in silken mists
above shining trees,—
if I in my north room
dance naked, grotesquely
before my mirror
waving my shirt round my head
and singing softly to myself:
"I am lonely, lonely.
I was born to be lonely,
I am best so!"

If I admire my arms, my face,
my shoulders, flanks, buttocks
against the yellow drawn shades,—

Who shall say I am not
the happy genius of my household?

(1917)

The Young Housewife

At ten A.M., the young housewife
moves about in negligee behind
the wooden walls of her husband's house.
I pass solitary in my car.

Then again she comes to the curb
to call the ice-man, fish-man, and stands
shy, uncorseted, tucking in
stray ends of hair, and I compare her
to a fallen leaf.

The noiseless wheels of my car
rush with a crackling sound over
dried leaves as I bow and pass smiling.

(1938)

WILLIAM WORDSWORTH*

[1770–1850]

The world is too much with us

The world is too much with us; late and soon,
Getting and spending, we lay waste our powers;
Little we see in Nature that is ours;
We have given our hearts away, a sordid boon!° gift
This Sea that bares her bosom to the moon,
The winds that will be howling at all hours,
And are up-gathered now like sleeping flowers,
For this, for everything, we are out of tune;

It moves us not.—Great God! I'd rather be
A Pagan suckled in a creed outworn;
So might I, standing on this pleasant lea,
Have glimpses that would make me less forlorn;
Have sight of Proteus rising from the sea;
Or hear old Triton° blow his wreathéd horn.

(1807)

The Solitary Reaper

Behold her, single in the field,
Yon solitary Highland Lass!
Reaping and singing by herself;
Stop here, or gently pass!
Alone she cuts and binds the grain,
And sings a melancholy strain;
O listen! for the Vale profound
Is overflowing with the sound.

No Nightingale did ever chaunt
More welcome notes to weary bands
Of travelers in some shady haunt,
Among Arabian sands;
A voice so thrilling ne'er was heard
In springtime from the Cuckoo bird,
Breaking the silence of the seas
Among the farthest Hebrides.

Will no one tell me what she sings?—
Perhaps the plaintive numbers flow
For old, unhappy, far-off things,
And battles long ago;
Or is it some more humble lay,
Familiar matter of today?
Some natural sorrow, loss, or pain,
That has been, and may be again?

Whate'er the theme, the Maiden sang
As if her song could have no ending;
I saw her singing at her work,
And o'er the sickle bending—
I listened, motionless and still;

"The world is too much with us" 13–14 ***Proteus . . . Triton*** *classical sea gods. Triton's conch-shell horn calmed the waves.*

And, as I mounted up the hill,
The music in my heart I bore,
Long after it was heard no more.

(1807)

Lines

Composed a Few Miles above Tintern Abbey on Revisiting the Banks of the Wye during a Tour. July 13, 1798

Five years have passed; five summers, with the length
Of five long winters! and again I hear
These waters, rolling from their mountain-springs
With a soft inland murmur. Once again
Do I behold these steep and lofty cliffs,
That on a wild secluded scene impress
Thoughts of more deep seclusion; and connect
The landscape with the quiet of the sky.
The day is come when I again repose
Here, under this dark sycamore, and view
These plots of cottage ground, these orchard tufts,
Which at this season, with their unripe fruits,
Are clad in one green hue, and lose themselves
Mid groves and copses.° Once again I see — thickets
These hedgerows, hardly hedgerows, little lines
Of sportive wood run wild; these pastoral farms,
Green to the very door; and wreaths of smoke
Sent up, in silence, from among the trees!
With some uncertain notice, as might seem
Of vagrant dwellers in the houseless woods,
Or of some Hermit's cave, where by his fire
The Hermit sits alone.
These beauteous forms,
Through a long absence, have not been to me
As is a landscape to a blind man's eye;
But oft, in lonely rooms, and 'mid the din
Of towns and cities, I have owed to them,
In hours of weariness, sensations sweet,
Felt in the blood, and felt along the heart;
And passing even into my purer mind
With tranquil restoration—feelings too
Of unremembered pleasure; such, perhaps,
As have no slight or trivial influence
On that best portion of a good man's life,
His little, nameless, unremembered, acts
Of kindness and of love. Nor less, I trust,
To them I may have owed another gift,
Of aspect more sublime; that blessed mood,

In which the burthen of the mystery,
In which the heavy and the weary weight
Of all this unintelligible world,
Is lightened—that serene and blessed mood,
In which the affections gently lead us on—
Until, the breath of this corporeal frame
And even the motion of our human blood
Almost suspended, we are laid asleep
In body, and become a living soul;
While with an eye made quiet by the power
Of harmony, and the deep power of joy,
We see into the life of things.
If this
Be but a vain belief, yet, oh! how oft—
In darkness and amid the many shapes
Of joyless daylight; when the fretful stir
Unprofitable, and the fever of the world,
Have hung upon the beatings of my heart—
How oft, in spirit, have I turned to thee,
O sylvan Wye! thou wanderer through the woods,
How often has my spirit turned to thee!

And now, with gleams of half-extinguished thought,
With many recognitions dim and faint,
And somewhat of a sad perplexity,
The picture of the mind revives again;
While here I stand, not only with the sense
Of present pleasure, but with pleasing thoughts
That in this moment there is life and food
For future years. And so I dare to hope,
Though changed, no doubt, from what I was when first
I came among these hills; when like a roe
I bounded o'er the mountains, by the sides
Of the deep rivers, and the lonely streams,
Wherever nature led—more like a man
Flying from something that he dreads than one
Who sought the thing he loved. For nature then
(The coarser pleasures of my boyish days,
And their glad animal movements all gone by)
To me was all in all.—I cannot paint
What then I was. The sounding cataract
Haunted me like a passion; the tall rock,
The mountain, and the deep and gloomy wood,
Their colors and their forms, were then to me
An appetite; a feeling and a love,
That had no need of a remoter charm,
By thought supplied, nor any interest
Unborrowed from the eye.—That time is past,

And all its aching joys are now no more,
And all its dizzy raptures. Not for this
Faint I, nor mourn nor murmur; other gifts
Have followed; for such loss, I would believe,
Abundant recompense. For I have learned
To look on nature, not as in the hour
Of thoughtless youth, but hearing oftentimes
The still, sad music of humanity,
Nor harsh nor grating, though of ample power
To chasten and subdue. And I have felt
A presence that disturbs me with the joy
Of elevated thoughts; a sense sublime
Of something far more deeply interfused,
Whose dwelling is the light of setting suns,
And the round ocean and the living air,
And the blue sky, and in the mind of man:
A motion and a spirit, that impels
All thinking things, all objects of all thought,
And rolls through all things. Therefore am I still
A lover of the meadows and the woods,
And mountains; and of all that we behold
From this green earth; of all the mighty world
Of eye, and ear—both what they half create,
And what perceive; well pleased to recognize
In nature and the language of the sense
The anchor of my purest thoughts, the nurse,
The guide, the guardian of my heart, and soul
Of all my moral being.
                                        Nor perchance,
If I were not thus taught, should I the more
Suffer my genial spirits° to decay: *powers*
For thou art with me here upon the banks
Of this fair river; thou my dearest Friend,°
My dear, dear Friend; and in thy voice I catch
The language of my former heart, and read
My former pleasures in the shooting lights
Of thy wild eyes. Oh! yet a little while
May I behold in thee what I was once,
My dear, dear Sister! and this prayer I make,
Knowing that Nature never did betray
The heart that loved her; 'tis her privilege,
Through all the years of this our life, to lead
From joy to joy: for she can so inform° *give form to*
The mind that is within us, so impress
With quietness and beauty, and so feed
With lofty thoughts, that neither evil tongues,

"Lines Composed a Few Miles above Tintern Abbey" 115 ***Friend*** *Wordsworth's sister, Dorothy.*

Rash judgments, nor the sneers of selfish men,
Nor greetings where no kindness is, nor all
The dreary intercourse of daily life,
Shall e'er prevail against us, or disturb
Our cheerful faith, that all which we behold
Is full of blessings. Therefore let the moon
Shine on thee in thy solitary walk;
And let the misty mountain winds be free
To blow against thee: and, in after years,
When these wild ecstasies shall be matured
Into a sober pleasure; when thy mind
Shall be a mansion for all lovely forms,
Thy memory be as a dwelling place
For all sweet sounds and harmonies; oh! then,
If solitude, or fear, or pain, or grief
Should be thy portion, with what healing thoughts
Of tender joy wilt thou remember me,
And these my exhortations! Nor, perchance—
If I should be where I no more can hear
Thy voice, nor catch from thy wild eyes these gleams
Of past existence—wilt thou then forget
That on the banks of this delightful stream
We stood together; and that I, so long
A worshiper of Nature, hither came
Unwearied in that service; rather say
With warmer love—oh! with far deeper zeal
Of holier love. Nor wilt thou then forget,
That after many wanderings, many years
Of absence, these steep woods and lofty cliffs,
And this green pastoral landscape, were to me
More dear, both for themselves and for thy sake!

(1798)

WILLIAM BUTLER YEATS*
[1865–1939]

The Second Coming°

Turning and turning in the widening gyre° — spiral
The falcon cannot hear the falconer;
Things fall apart; the center cannot hold;

"The Second Coming" the title alludes to the prophesied return of Jesus Christ and also to the beast of the Apocalypse. See Matthew 24 and Revelation.

Mere anarchy is loosed upon the world,
The blood-dimmed tide is loosed, and everywhere
The ceremony of innocence is drowned;
The best lack all conviction, while the worst
Are full of passionate intensity.

Surely some revelation is at hand;
Surely the Second Coming is at hand;
The Second Coming! Hardly are those words out
When a vast image out of *Spiritus Mundi*°
Troubles my sight: somewhere in sands of the desert
A shape with lion body and the head of a man,
A gaze blank and pitiless as the sun,
Is moving its slow thighs, while all about it
Reel shadows of the indignant desert birds.
The darkness drops again; but now I know
That twenty centuries of stony sleep
Were vexed to nightmare by a rocking cradle,
And what rough beast, its hour come round at last,
Slouches towards Bethlehem to be born?

(1921)

The Wild Swans at Coole

The trees are in their autumn beauty,
The woodland paths are dry,
Under the October twilight the water
Mirrors a still sky;
Upon the brimming water among the stones
Are nine-and-fifty swans.

The nineteenth autumn has come upon me
Since I first made my count;
I saw, before I had well finished,
All suddenly mount
And scatter wheeling in great broken rings
Upon their clamorous wings.

I have looked upon those brilliant creatures,
And now my heart is sore.
All's changed since I, hearing at twilight,
The first time on this shore,
The bell-beat of their wings above my head,
Trod with a lighter tread.

"The Second Coming" [12]***Spiritus Mundi*** *for Yeats, a common storehouse of images, a communal human memory.*

Unwearied still, lover by lover,
They paddle in the cold
Companionable streams or climb the air;
Their hearts have not grown old;
Passion or conquest, wander where they will,
Attend upon them still.

But now they drift on the still water,
Mysterious, beautiful;
Among what rushes will they build,
By what lake's edge or pool
Delight men's eyes when I awake some day
To find they have flown away?

(1917)

Leda and the Swan°

A sudden blow: the great wings beating still
Above the staggering girl, her thighs caressed
By the dark webs, her nape caught in his bill,
He holds her helpless breast upon his breast.

How can those terrified vague fingers push
The feathered glory from her loosening thighs?
And how can body, laid in that white rush,
But feel the strange heart beating where it lies?

A shudder in the loins engenders there
The broken wall, the burning roof and tower
And Agamemnon dead.
Being so caught up,
So mastered by the brute blood of the air,
Did she put on his knowledge with his power
Before the indifferent beak could let her drop?

(1928)

Sailing to Byzantium°

1

That is no country for old men. The young
In one another's arms, birds in the trees
—Those dying generations—at their song,

"Leda and the Swan" *Zeus, in the guise of a swan, raped Leda, Queen of Sparta. Helen, their daughter, married Menelaus, King of Sparta, but ran off with Paris, son of Priam, King of Troy. A ten-year siege of Troy by the Greeks ensued to bring Helen back.* *"Sailing to Byzantium"* *Byzantium was the capital of the eastern Roman Empire and an important center of art and architecture*

The salmon-falls, the mackerel-crowded seas,
Fish, flesh, or fowl, commend all summer long
Whatever is begotten, born, and dies.
Caught in that sensual music all neglect
Monuments of unaging intellect.

2

An aged man is but a paltry thing,
A tattered coat upon a stick, unless
Soul clap its hands and sing, and louder sing
For every tatter in its mortal dress,
Nor is there singing school but studying
Monuments of its own magnificence;
And therefore I have sailed the seas and come
To the holy city of Byzantium.

3

O sages standing in God's holy fire
As in the gold mosaic of a wall,
Come from the holy fire, perne° in a gyre,° descend/spiral
And be the singing-masters of my soul.
Consume my heart away; sick with desire
And fastened to a dying animal
It knows not what it is; and gather me
Into the artifice of eternity.

4

Once out of nature I shall never take
My bodily form from any natural thing,
But such a form as Grecian goldsmiths make
Of hammered gold and gold enameling
To keep a drowsy Emperor awake;
Or set upon a golden bough to sing
To lords and ladies of Byzantium
Of what is past, or passing, or to come.

(1927)

When you are old

When you are old and grey and full of sleep,
And nodding by the fire, take down this book,
And slowly read, and dream of the soft look
Your eyes had once, and of their shadows deep;

How many loved your moments of glad grace,
And loved your beauty with love false or true,

But one man loved the pilgrim soul in you,
And loved the sorrows of your changing face;

And bending down beside the glowing bars,
Murmur, a little sadly, how Love fled
And paced upon the mountains overhead
And hid his face amid a crowd of stars.

[1892]

Adam's Curse

We sat together at one summer's end
That beautiful mild woman your close friend
And you and I, and talked of poetry.
I said, "A line will take us hours maybe,
Yet if it does not seem a moment's thought
Our stitching and unstitching has been naught.
Better go down upon your marrow bones
And scrub a kitchen pavement, or break stones
Like an old pauper in all kinds of weather;
For to articulate sweet sounds together
Is to work harder than all these and yet
Be thought an idler by the noisy set
Of bankers, schoolmasters, and clergymen
The martyrs call the world."

That woman then
Murmured with her young voice, for whose mild sake
There's many a one shall find out all heartache
In finding that it's young and mild and low.
"There is one thing that all we women know
Although we never heard of it at school,
That we must labour to be beautiful."

I said, "It's certain there is no fine thing
Since Adam's fall but needs much labouring.
There have been lovers who thought love should be
So much compounded of high courtesy
That they would sigh and quote with learned looks
Precedents out of beautiful old books;
Yet now it seems an idle trade enough."

We sat grown quiet at the name of love.
We saw the last embers of daylight die

And in the trembling blue-green of the sky
A moon, worn as if it had been a shell
Washed by time's waters as they rose and fell
About the stars and broke in days and years.

I had a thought for no one's but your ears;
That you were beautiful and that I strove
To love you in the old high way of love;
That it had all seemed happy, and yet we'd grown
As weary hearted as that hollow moon.

[1903]

CHAPTER TWENTY

Lives of Poets

SHERMAN ALEXIE

[b. 1960]

See headnote to "Indian Education" in Chapter Seven.

MARGARET ATWOOD

[b. 1939]

See headnote to "Happy Endings" in Chapter Nine.

W. H. AUDEN

[1907–1973]

Wystan Hugh Auden was born in England but emigrated to America in 1939, becoming a U.S. citizen in 1946. As a young English poet his early work reflected Marxist and Freudian thinking as well as a droll wit. His later work revealed a more conservative political strain and a Christian sympathy. Auden was a prolific editor, anthologist, and translator as well as one of the twentieth century's most renowned poets.

MATSUO BASHŌ
[1644–1694]

The great Japanese haiku poet known simply as Basho, was born Matsuo Munefusa during the Ming dynasty, one of the great periods of artistic and literary development in Japanese cultural history. Basho grew up outside of Kyoto, the former imperial Japanese capital, then later moved to Edo, the center of political power. For a while Basho lived the life of a samurai or landed farmer, but abandoned it for a life devoted to poetry. He revitalized the spirit of haiku by combining it with the spirit of Zen Buddhism, creating poems that suggest much in a very brief compass—three lines of seventeen syllables.

His poems capture both the beauty and the sadness of life, and reflect the many losses he suffered from the loss of his father at the age of twelve, to the loss of his friend and master at age twenty-two, to the loss of his home, which burned down in 1683. But even as Basho's poetry evokes such losses, it expresses a deep reverence and appreciation for every aspect of life.

ELIZABETH BISHOP
[1911–1979]

Elizabeth Bishop was born and raised in Worcester, Massachusetts. As a consequence of her father's early death and her mother's mental illness, Bishop, at age six, went to live with her grandmother in Nova Scotia. After graduating from boarding school and Vassar College, she moved to Key West, Florida, and then to Brazil, where she lived for fifteen years. Returning to the United States, she taught at the University of Washington and at Harvard. She published her first volume of poems, *North and South,* in 1946 and later won both the Pulitzer Prize and the National Book Award. Her last collection, *Complete Poems 1927–1979,* won the National Book Critics Circle Award.

WILLIAM BLAKE
[1757–1827]

William Blake was born in London and was apprenticed to an engraver there at the age of fourteen. At age twenty-two Blake entered the Royal Academy as an engraving student, but clashes over artistic differences precipitated his return to private study of such Renaissance masters as Raphael, Durer, and Michelangelo. A revolutionary at heart, Blake moved in a circle of radical thinkers including William Godwin, Thomas Paine, and Mary Wollstonecraft. His poems, which he published himself, and for which he supplied engravings and water colors, include *Songs of Innocence* (1789), *Songs of Experience* (1794), and the prophetic *Marriage of Heaven and Hell* (1790), among others. His work is visionary and unconventional.

GWENDOLYN BROOKS
[1917–2000]

Gwendolyn Brooks was born in Topeka, Kansas, and educated at Wilson Junior College in Chicago. In the 1930s she served as publicity director for the N.A.A.C.P. Youth Council. In addition to teaching at a variety of colleges and universities, including the University of Wisconsin at Madison and the City University of New York, Brooks was also editor of *The Black Position,* a magazine focusing on African-American concerns.

Brooks published one novel, *Maud Martha,* in addition to numerous volumes of poetry, beginning with *A Street in Bronzeville* in 1945. Her work chronicles black urban life, and is by turns bitter and poignant, angry and compassionate, and always unflinchingly honest.

ROBERT BROWNING
[1812–1889]

Robert Browning was born in a London suburb and educated primarily through reading in his father's extensive library. Browning's first poems were printed in his early twenties, but he did not achieve fame as a poet until he was in his fifties. Browning was married to the poet Elizabeth Barrett, with whom he lived in Italy, returning to England after her death. The work that made him famous, *The Ring and The Book* (1868–69), which is based on a seventeenth-century Roman murder trial, represents the poetic form for which he is best known—the dramatic monologue. The form weds the character revelations of drama with the lyricism of poetry. Among Browning's most successful examples of the genre is "My Last Duchess."

BILLY COLLINS
[b. 1941]

Billy Collins is professor of English at Lehman College of the City University of New York. His poems have appeared in numerous periodicals, including *Harper's, The New Yorker, The American Poetry Review,* and *The American Scholar.* Among his five volumes of poetry are *The Art of Drowning* (1995) and *Picnic Lighting* (1998). The recipient of Guggenheim and National Endowment for the Humanities fellowships, Collins has had his poems selected for the *Pushcart Prize Anthology* and the *Best American Poetry* for 1992, 1993, and 1997. In 1992, he was selected by the New York Public Library to serve as a "Literary Lion."

E. E. CUMMINGS

[1894–1962]

Edward Estlin Cummings was born in Cambridge, Massachusetts. After attending Harvard University, he joined the Red Cross Ambulance Corps in France during World War I. Comments critical of the French army in his letters got him imprisoned, but he was released after four months. His poems, which began appearing in the 1920s, are identifiable by their unusual typography and punctuation. In addition to poetry, Cummings wrote essays and a novel, *The Enormous Room,* based on his experiences in France. He also produced graphic art, including paintings.

EMILY DICKINSON

[1830–1886]

See extended biographical essay on pages 627–632.

JOHN DONNE

[1572–1631]

John Donne was both a poet and a prelate, who made his name as a preacher at St. Paul's Cathedral in London. Before his conversion from Roman Catholicism to Anglicanism and his ordination as an Anglican priest, Donne wrote worldly love lyrics at the court of Queen Elizabeth I. His poems, which circulated in manuscript, were justly famous, and were later collected under the title *Songs and Sonnets.* Donne's poetry is justly celebrated for its striking and unusual imagery, its strong and direct language, and its probing analyses of the experiences of religious faith and doubt and of secular and sacred love.

RITA DOVE

[b. 1952]

Rita Dove was born and raised in Akron, Ohio, and educated at Miami University in Oxford, Ohio, and at the University of Iowa's Writers Workshop. She has also studied as a Fulbright scholar in Germany. A recipient of a Guggenheim fellowship and of the Pulitzer Prize for poetry in 1987, Dove has served as Poet Laureate of the United States. Her collections of poetry include *The Yellow on the Corner* and *Museum*. She teaches at Arizona State University.

T. S. ELIOT

[1888–1965]

Thomas Stearns Eliot was born in St. Louis, Missouri, but moved to England in 1914 and became a British citizen in 1927. Though he had been raised in the southwestern United States, Eliot traced his family's roots to New England, where he vacationed. He studied at the Sorbonne in Paris and at Merton College, Oxford, England. Instead of pursuing an academic life, Eliot turned to business and poetry, working as a clerk for Lloyd's Bank of London and as editor and director of the London publishing house Faber and Faber, all the while writing the poems that were to make him famous. The most explosive of these was *The Waste Land,* which burst upon the literary scene in 1922, becoming for a long time the most famous modern poem in English. Earlier, Eliot had written "The Love Song of J. Alfred Prufrock," a dramatic monologue that portrays the life of a timid, inhibited man.

LAWRENCE FERLINGHETTI

[b. 1919]

Lawrence Ferlinghetti was both a poet and a publisher who founded the City Lights bookstore in San Francisco, the country's first paperback bookstore. He also edited City Lights Books, a feature of the San Francisco poetry revival of the 1950s. Along with Allen Ginsberg, whose poem "Howl" he published, which led to his being charged with obscenity, Ferlinghetti was a central figure in the group of writers known as the "Beats." His poetry often centers on political concerns and typically reflects anti-bourgeois tendencies and attitudes. His best-known volume, however, *A Coney Island of the Mind* (1958), contains his more lyrical and freely imaginative poems.

ROBERT FROST
[1874–1963]

See extended biographical essay on pages 666–670.

NIKKI GIOVANNI
[b. 1943]

Nikki Giovanni has been called the "Princess of Black Poetry." She has received numerous awards, including honorary doctorates from several universities. She has been publishing poetry for more than thirty years, from her first volume, *Black Feeling Black Talk* in 1968 to her recent *Blues: For All the Changes* in 1999. Giovanni has also published two volumes of essays, *Gemini* (1971) and *Racism 101* (1995).

GEORGE GORDON, LORD BYRON
[1788–1824]

Byron was born in London but raised in Scotland by his mother after his father's early death. After receiving an M.A. from Trinity College, Cambridge, and after inheriting his estate and title from his great uncle in 1798, Byron took his seat in the House of Lords. Following his return to England, he published the first part of "Childe Harold's Pilgrimage." After completing this work in 1817, Byron published a steady stream of poems both lyric and dramatic. Byron shared his friend Shelley's revolutionary fervor. Following Shelley's death, Byron sailed to Greece to take part in the battle for Greek independence. He died there in 1824.

DONALD HALL
[b. 1928]

Donald Hall was born and raised in Connecticut and educated at Harvard, Oxford, and Stanford. After teaching for many years at the University of Michigan, Hall turned his attention full time to his writing. A versatile writer, he has published poetry, drama, fiction, and memoir, as well as criticism. He has also been a busy editor and anthologist, and is generally considered one of the country's foremost men of letters. *His Poems Old and New* appeared in 1990. His most recent volume, a commemoration of his wife, Jane Kenyon, who died recently, is entitled *Without*.

THOMAS HARDY

[1840–1928]

Thomas Hardy, English Victorian novelist and poet, was born in Dorsetshire, the region of England he later called Wessex in his novels. Hardy trained as an architect and began to practice in 1867, but he soon turned his attention to writing, initially poetry, then fiction, for which he became famous. His first published poetry, however, was not available until 1898, when *Wessex Poems* appeared, after he had given up his career as the novelist who had penned *Jude the Obscure* and *Tess of the D'Urbervilles.* Hardy's poetry ranges widely in style and form, as he experimented with image and idiom throughout his thirty-year career as a poet.

ROBERT E. HAYDEN

[1913–1980]

Robert Earl Hayden was born in Detroit, Michigan, in 1913. Born with extremely bad eyesight that limited his participation in outdoor activity, the young Hayden spent his time reading. In the 1930s, he attended Detroit City College (now called Wayne State University) where he researched black history for the Federal Writers' Project. Much of this early research influenced his poetry throughout his life. He published his first book of poetry in 1940 and continued with his graduate studies at the University of Michigan, where W. H. Auden taught. After he finished graduate school, he taught at Fisk University and the University of Michigan while continuing to write. During this time, his poetry gained international recognition. In 1976, he became the first African-American writer appointed as Consultant in Poetry to the Library of Congress. This is the position we now refer to as United States Poet Laureate. He died in 1980 in Ann Arbor, Michigan.

SEAMUS HEANEY

[b. 1939]

Seamus Heaney was born and raised in Northern Ireland, an area torn for decades by political, religious, and civil strife. He was educated at Queens College, Belfast, where he later taught. His first collection of poetry, *Death of a Naturalist* (1966), led a new generation of Irish poets in civil war–torn Northern Ireland. His poems, which touch on themes of nature and history as well as politics, are among the most celebrated of the century, as Heaney has been hailed as the successor to William Butler Yeats as the most important Irish poet of the later modern era.

GEORGE HERBERT

[1593–1633]

George Herbert, English poet and Anglican priest, after serving as a University of Cambridge orator, became a parson in charge of a country parish. His prose work, *The Country Parson,* was recognized as a valuable source of wise guidance for devout and useful Christian living. His poetry, collected after his death by his friend Nicholas Ferrar, was printed in 1633 as *The Temple.* Herbert's poems, while ranging widely in imagery like those of his contemporary John Donne, offer a more homely and familiar window on religious experience.

ROBERT HERRICK

[1591–1674]

Robert Herrick was an English poet best known for his pastoral and love lyrics. Herrick attended Cambridge University and became an Anglican cleric in 1627. Though a clergyman, Herrick was a lover of London's society of poets and wits, who initially regarded his work in rural England as a form of exile. Herrick was a classicist, who was influenced by his Roman predecessors. His verse is formal and refined. His best-known poem, "To the Virgins, to Make Much of Time," celebrates the theme of *carpe diem,* or seize the day.

JANE HIRSHFIELD

[b. 1953]

Jane Hirshfield is the author of five volumes of poetry, including *Lives of the Heart* (1997). She has edited an anthology of spiritual poems by women, *Women in Praise of the Sacred.* And she has also written a book of essays about poetry, *Nine Gates: Entering the Mind of Poetry.* Her work has appeared in *Antaeus, The Atlantic Monthly, The New Yorker,* and *The Paris Review,* among other periodicals. Hirshfield, who lives in northern California, has received many honors and awards, including a Guggenheim fellowship and a Pushcart Prize.

GERARD MANLEY HOPKINS

[1844–1889]

Gerard Manley Hopkins was an English poet gifted not only in his poetic resourcefulness but also in music and art. Hopkins was born in Essex, outside London. As a student at Oxford University he studied classic Greek and Roman literature. At the age of twenty-two Hopkins converted from Anglicanism to Roman Catholicism and became a Jesuit priest. He spent several years in working-class parishes until he was appointed Professor of Greek at University College in Dublin in 1877. His poetry is distinguished by an intricate form of rhythm, which he called "sprung rhythm," and by an intense musicality.

A. E. HOUSMAN

[1859–1936]

Alfred Edward Housman, British poet and scholar, was an eminent classical scholar and translator and a professor of Latin at Cambridge University from 1911 to 1936. He achieved general fame with his book *A Shropshire Lad* (1896), a collection of poems that stressed the brevity and fragility of youth and love. His lyrics, which celebrate nature, are set against the background of the English countryside and reveal the influence of English ballads and classical verse. Among his most famous poems are "When I Was One-and-Twenty" and "To an Athlete Dying Young."

LANGSTON HUGHES

[1902–1967]

See extended biographical essay on pages 700–703.

BEN JONSON

[1573–1637]

Ben Jonson was born and educated in London, where he received a strong grounding in classical Greek and Latin. He worked as a bricklayer and a soldier before becoming a playwright and poet. Jonson was famed for his wit and his ability to engage others in contests of poetry, and he was well known at The Mermaid Tavern in London for the weekly literary discussions, during which he would match wits with rival poets, including William Shakespeare. Jonson's followers called themselves the "tribe of Ben" in his honor. He was crowned as the first Poet Laureate of England in 1619.

JOHN KEATS

[1795–1821]

John Keats, who was born in London, experienced the loss of both his parents when he was still a child. After being apprenticed to a medical doctor, Keats received his own license to practice medicine, but gave up that career for poetry. At an early age

Keats was stricken with tuberculosis, and he went to Italy in the hope of regaining his health. He died in Rome at the age of twenty-five, but not before producing a small but significant body of enduring poems, including the great "Ode to a Nightingale" and "Ode on a Grecian Urn."

D. H. LAWRENCE
[1885–1930]

See headnote to "The Rocking-Horse Winner" in fiction section.

ARCHIBALD MACLEISH
[1892–1982]

Archibald MacLeish, an American poet, became an expatriate in Paris, remaining there until 1928. During this period he was influenced by the poets Ezra Pound and T. S. Eliot. His earliest published poems date from 1915 and were followed by a 1932 narrative poem, *Conquistador,* which was awarded the first of MacLeish's three Pulitzer Prizes. Although he wrote a verse drama, *J. B.,* based on the biblical book of Job, as well as a considerable amount of narrative poetry, MacLeish is best known for his lyric poems.

CZESLAW MILOSZ
[1911–2004]

The Polish poet, novelist, and critic Czeslaw Milosz was born in Lithuania in 1911 and has lived in California since 1960. Milosz grew up in Vilna, a city where many intellectual currents crossed in the early twentieth century. After graduating from law school, he went to Paris, then spent most of the Second World War in occupied Warsaw, where he was active in the underground. After the communist takeover of Poland, Milosz served for a while in the new government's diplomatic corps, defecting in Paris in 1951. He came to the United States in 1960 and joined the faculty of the University of California at Berkeley. His vast body of outstanding work as poet and translator won him the Nobel Prize for Literature in 1980.

JOHN MILTON
[1608–1674]

John Milton was born to be a poet. He was educated under private tutors at home before entering St. Paul's School and Cambridge University, where he studied Greek and Latin and mastered modern languages in his spare time. He then spent five years of independent study followed by a two-year tour of Europe all in preparation for his vocation as a poet. During the Puritan Interregnum, Milton served as a secretary to Oliver Cromwell, who ran the Commonwealth until the restoration of the English kings. Milton's poetry is vastly learned and heavily allusive, especially in his long magisterial epic poems *Paradise Lost* and *Paradise Regained*. But Milton also wrote a number of memorable poems on a smaller scale, including some of the finest sonnets in English.

LINDA PASTAN

[b. 1932]

Linda Pastan, who was born in New York City, has published ten volumes of poetry. Her *Carnival Evening* (1998) collects her latest poems along with the best of her work from 1968–1998. Pastan attended Radcliffe College and Brandeis University before settling in suburban Washington, D.C. She was the poet laureate of Maryland from 1991–1993.

SYLVIA PLATH

[1932–1963]

Sylvia Plath was born in Boston and educated at Smith College and at Harvard and Cambridge universities. Publishing her first poem at the age of eight, Plath produced two volumes of intensely introspective and vivid poetry in the 1960s—*The Colossus* (1960) and *Ariel* (1965), which was published posthumously. In addition to her confessional poetry, Plath wrote an autobiographical novel, *The Bell Jar* (1963). She was awarded a Pulitzer Prize for her *Collected Poems* (1981).

EDGAR ALLAN POE

[1809–1849]

See extended biographical essay on pages 132–136.

ALEXANDER POPE

[1688–1744]

Alexander Pope, who was educated largely at home, was born a Roman Catholic at a time when England was violently anti-Catholic. A childhood accident deformed his spine and retarded his physical growth, which led the young Alexander Pope to pursue a bookish life. He was a skillful poet early on, having written his *Pastorals* by the age of sixteen. In his mid-twenties he translated Homer's *Iliad* and *Odyssey*, edited Shakespeare's plays, and published *An Essay on Criticism,* a highly regarded work of critical thought in poetic form. Pope is best known, however, for his witty and satirical poems written in heroic couplets, *The Dunciad* and *The Rape of the Lock*.

EZRA POUND
[1885–1972]

Ezra Pound was born in Idaho, and educated at Hamilton College and the University of Pennsylvania. After a brief stint teaching at Wabash College in Indiana, he traveled in Europe and moved to London, Paris, and then Rapallo, Italy, where he remained for twenty years. Pound is considered one of the most influential of modern poets both for the originality and range of his own poetry and for the assistance he provided to other modern writers, poets and novelists alike. Pound is known as well for his support of Italian fascism during the Second World War, especially for his anti-American broadcasts for which he was arrested and imprisoned near Pisa. The list of books he wrote, edited, and translated exceeds one hundred, and includes such classics as *Personae* (1909), *The ABC of Reading* (1934), and *The Cantos* (1948), which contain some of the most complex and challenging poems ever written.

RAINER MARIA RILKE
[1875–1926]

Rainer Maria Rilke was a German poet who was born in Prague. Rilke is considered the most significant figure in twentieth-century poetry. As a young man, Rilke attended military school and trade school before attending and dropping out of the University of Prague. He was married briefly, but was divorced from his wife not long after the birth of his daughter. Rilke found married life and responsibilities incompatible with his artistic proclivities. He lived for a while in Paris, serving as secretary to the sculptor Auguste Rodin. He published his first important poetry collections *Neue Gedichte (New Poems)* in two volumes in 1907 and 1908. His best known works—and his most complex poems—are his *Duino Elegies* and *The Sonnets to Orpheus*.

E. A. ROBINSON
[1869–1935]

Edwin Arlington Robinson was raised in Gardiner, Maine, the "Tilbury Town" of such poems as "Miniver Cheevy" and "Richard Cory." He attended Harvard for two years, but had to leave because of the failure of his father's lumber business. Widely read in English and American literature, Robinson was drawn to the dark vision of novelist and poet Thomas Hardy, whose starkness of perspective can be detected in some of Robinson's ironic poems. Robinson won three Pulitzer Prizes, with special acknowledgment of the success of his dramatic monologues.

THEODORE ROETHKE

[1908–1963]

Theodore Roethke was born in Saginaw, Michigan, where his father oversaw a substantial greenhouse. After attending the University of Michigan and Harvard University, Roethke taught poetry at a number of schools before settling at the University of Washington. His influence extended to other poets, who studied with him there, including James Wright. Roethke's first book of poems, *Open House* (1941), shows his extensive knowledge of flowers and vegetation. His second volume, *The Lost Son* (1948), includes the lyric "My Papa's Waltz." He earned a Pulitzer Prize in 1953 for *The Waking.*

SONIA SANCHEZ

[b. 1935]

Sonia Sanchez, poet, scholar, and activist, is a professor of English and Women's Studies at Temple University in Philadelphia. Sanchez, who is a major figure in the Black Arts Movement, has published seven volumes of poetry, the most recent of which, *Shake Loose My Skin,* collects her new and selected poems.

ANNE SEXTON

[1928–1974]

Anne Sexton was born and raised in Massachusetts, where she later worked in the Boston literary milieu. She taught creative writing at a number of universities, and was recognized early on as a poet of considerable talent and raw power. She suffered from mental illness and depression, experiences which are reflected in her work. Before taking her own life at age forty-six, Sexton published *Live or Die* (1966), which was awarded the Pulitzer Prize for poetry.

WILLIAM SHAKESPEARE

[1564–1616]

See extended biographical essay in Chapter Twenty-Six.

PERCY BYSSHE SHELLEY

[1792–1822]

Shelley was influenced early in life by the ideals of liberty and intellectual freedom, which led him to champion rebelling against the constraints of the English politics and religion of his time. During his university years he wrote a pamphlet on atheism. Shortly thereafter he eloped and traveled the country and Ireland speaking out against political injustice. Beginning in 1812, Shelley began publishing poetry, composing many of his best known shorter works in Italy in 1819, when he wrote "The Cloud" and "Ode to the West Wind." In addition, he wrote many long philosophical poems and a verse drama, *Prometheus Unbound.*

CATHY SONG

[b. 1955]

Cathy Song was born in Honolulu, Hawaii, and was educated at Wellesley College and Boston University. A recipient of the Shelley Memorial Award and the Hawaii Award for Literature, Song has published three volumes of poetry, including *School Figures* (1994).

WALLACE STEVENS

[1879–1955]

Wallace Stevens was born in Reading, Pennsylvania, and studied at Harvard before taking a law degree from New York University. For nearly forty years Stevens was associated with the Hartford Accident and Indemnity Company, where he became a vice president. In college Stevens wrote poetry and served as president of the literary magazine and the literary society. During his years of practicing law and working as an insurance industry executive, Stevens wrote and published many poems. His first volume, *Harmonium,* was published in 1923. His *Collected Poems* (1955) won both the Pulitzer Prize and the National Book Award.

MAY SWENSON

[1919–1989]

May Swenson was born in Utah of Swedish parents, and moved to New York City after attending college. She performed editorial jobs and taught poetry while writing her own poems and winning awards for them. Her first book, *A Cage of Spines* (1958), was followed by *Half Sun Half Sleep* (1967), which includes witty descriptions of life in New York City along with translations from six Swedish poets. Swenson was a poetic experimenter who played with poetic forms, as in her shaped verse, exemplified by "Women."

ALFRED, LORD TENNYSON

[1809–1892]

Alfred, Lord Tennyson, one of the best known and liked Victorian poets, became Poet Laureate in 1850. His early poetry is influenced by the English Romantic poets, especially by John Keats. Among his more highly recognized work is the twelve-part narrative poem, *Idylls of the King,* based on King Arthur and his Round Table, which occupied Tennyson from 1859 to 1888. Tennyson, however, is justly honored as a lyric poet of exquisite musicality and deep feeling as exemplified by his long elegiac poem, In *Memoriam* (1850), inspired by the death of his friend Arthur Hallam.

DYLAN THOMAS

[1914–1953]

Dylan Thomas was born in coastal Wales, the son of an English teacher. His poetry, which centers on themes of birth and death, innocence, childhood, and sex, reflects his Welsh heritage and his rural upbringing. Thomas lacked a university education and thus, instead of supporting himself and his family by teaching, made broadcasts for BBC radio and went on extended poetry reading tours in the United States, where he was a wildly popular figure, with a reputation for being a prodigious drinker as well as a fine performer of poems. His handful of highly regarded poems is complemented by some memorable short stories and a play for voices, *Under Milk Wood* (1954).

JEAN TOOMER

[1894–1967]

An important figure in the Harlem Renaissance of the 1920s, Jean Toomer prepared for a career in law before publishing his seminal work, *Cane,* in 1923. This book, which sold only 500 copies upon publication, became an influential and inspiring point of departure for many African-American writers. *Cane* is a collection of poems, sketches, stories, and a novella, all inspired by Toomer's visit to rural Georgia. The work's title refers to the cane fields, where black descendants of African slaves worked. Toomer's writings celebrate the beauty, vitality, and courage of his people.

WALT WHITMAN

[1819–1892]

Walt Whitman was born in Huntington, New York, and was educated in the Brooklyn public schools. In his youth he worked successively as an office boy and clerk for a doctor, lawyer, and printer. After teaching school from 1836 to 1841, he began a journalistic career, which involved, at various stages, writing, typesetting, and editing the *Brooklyn Daily Eagle* and *Daily Times,* among other newspapers. During the Civil War, Whitman served as a nurse and worked briefly as a clerk in the Bureau of Indian Affairs. His wide range of experiences is reflected in his deeply democratic vision in poems remarkable for their formal freedom, their freshness of idiom, and their profound compassion.

WILLIAM CARLOS WILLIAMS

[1883–1963]

William Carlos Williams, poet, novelist, short-story writer, was born in Rutherford, New Jersey, where, after earning an M.D., he pursued a medical career as a pediatrician. In the early years of his medical practice there was little time for writing, so Williams concentrated on short forms. His poetic output, which was both innovative and prodigious, was part of a modernist literary revolution that sent poetry in new directions. His fiction is collected in *Making Light of It, The Knife of the Times,* and *The Farmer's Daughter and Other Stories,* from which "The Use of Force" is taken.

WILLIAM WORDSWORTH

[1770–1850]

William Wordsworth was born in the Lake District of northern England, which is central to many of his poems. Along with Samuel Taylor Coleridge, Wordsworth was the earliest and most influential of the English Romantic poets. With Coleridge, he published *Lyrical Ballads* (1798), which essentially launched the Romantic movement in England, calling for poetry written in a language really used by common people and about matters reflective of everyday life. Wordsworth's sister Dorothy was a constant companion and inspiration. It was from her notebook entries that he later culled the details for his poem "I Wandered Lonely as a Cloud." As with much of Wordsworth's poetry, this lyric reflects his deep love of nature, his vision of a unified world, and his celebration of the power of memory and imagination.

JAMES WRIGHT
[1927–1980]

James Wright was born in Martins Ferry, Ohio, and received his Ph.D. at the University of Washington, where he studied with Theodore Roethke. In 1966, he began teaching at Hunter College in New York, where he taught until his death. In addition to his own poetry, which first appeared in the volume *A Green Wall* (1957) and was last collected in *Above the River: The Complete Poems* (1990), Wright was also a translator of the works of Cesar Valejo, Pablo Neruda, and George Trakl.

WILLIAM BUTLER YEATS
[1865–1939]

William Butler Yeats was born in Dublin, Ireland, son of the well-known Irish painter, John Butler Yeats. W. B. Yeats himself studied painting for three years, and art would become one of the three dominant themes in his poetry, along with Irish nationalism and the occult. Yeats's interest in Irish folklore was reflected in his early poetry and in the plays he wrote based on Irish legend, especially about Cuchulain. His occult interests appear in his book *The Celtic Twilight* (1893) and *The Secret Rose* (1897). His love for things Irish is revealed throughout his work, which spans a period of nearly half a century, during which he reinvented himself as a poet numerous times, and developed a range of varying styles, voices, and perspectives. Yeats is generally considered the greatest Irish poet of the twentieth century and one of the finest poets of modern times.

PART THREE

Drama

Scene from a performance of Lorraine Hansberry's *A Raisin in the Sun*. (How is a play transformed when actors bring the written word to life? How do you think a film version of *A Raisin in the Sun* would differ from a live performance?)

CHAPTER TWENTY-ONE

Reading Plays

Drama, unlike the other literary genres, is a staged art. Plays are written to be performed by actors before an audience. But the plays we wish to see are not always performed. We might have to wait years, for example, to see a production of Sophocles' *Oedipus Rex* or Arthur Miller's *Death of a Salesman.* A reasonable alternative is to read these and other plays with attention to both their theatrical and literary dimensions.

As a literary genre, drama has affinities with fiction and poetry. Like fiction, drama possesses a narrative dimension: a play often narrates a story in the form of a plot. Like fiction, drama relies on dialogue and description, which takes the form of *stage directions,* lines describing characters, scenes, or actions with clues to production. Unlike fiction, however, in which a narrator often mediates between us and the story, there is usually no such authorial presence in drama. Instead, we hear the words of the characters directly.

Although drama is most like fiction, it shares features with poetry as well. Plays may, in fact, be written in verse: Shakespeare wrote in *blank verse* (unrhymed iambic pentameter), Molière in rhymed couplets. Plays, like lyric poems, are also overheard: we listen to characters expressing their concerns as if there were no audience present. Poems also contain dramatic elements. The dramatic lyrics and monologues of Robert Browning and some of the poems of John Donne portray characters speaking and listening to one another.

Plays may be vehicles of persuasion. Henrik Ibsen and Bernard Shaw frequently used the stage to dramatize ideas and issues. For most of his plays Shaw wrote prefaces in which he discussed the plays' dominant ideas. In drama, ideas possess more primacy than they do in poetry and fiction, something to which critics of the genre testify. Aristotle, for example, made *thought* one of his six elements of drama; Eric Bentley, a modern critic, entitled one of his books *The Playwright as Thinker.*

But if we look exclusively to the literary aspects of drama, to its poetic and fictional elements, and to its dramatization of ideas, we may fail to appreciate its uniquely theatrical idiom. To gain this appreciation we should read drama with special attention to its performance elements. We can try to hear the voices of characters, and imagine tones and inflections. We can try to see mentally how characters look, where they stand in relation to one another, how they move and gesture. We can read, in short, as armchair directors and as aspiring actors and actresses considering the physical and practical realities of performance.

When we read or view drama we are aware, if only implicitly, of its major characteristics. First is its *representational* quality. Drama is a *mimetic* art, one that imitates, or represents, human life and experience. A large part of the pleasure of drama comes from its ability to show us human life meaningfully enacted. Drama is an *active* art, in which actors portraying characters say and do things to one another. Actors are agents, doers, who make things happen through speech and bodily action. Drama is an *immediate* art, representing action that is occurring in the play's *present.* This is so even when a play's subject is historical, when its dramatic action takes place in the past. A play brings the past to life so that it seems to occur right before us. Our experience of drama is one of watching events *as* they occur. We are first-hand witnesses of present-tense actions rather than auditors who simply hear about them later from a narrator at second hand.

A critically important feature of drama derives from its mimetic, active, and immediate qualities: its *interactive* nature. Plays represent human life mainly through the interactions of the characters. The experience of a play is carried forward through *inter*-actions of the dramatic characters as they respond and relate to one another, engage one another in dialogue, actions and reactions, and visual displays. Such character interaction is the heart of drama: it is the spring of plot, the source of meaning, and the soul of dramatic experience.

Drama is interactive in still another way. Unlike fiction and poetry, which are largely verbal arts (though poetry is also allied with music or song), drama is a *composite* art—one that makes use of many of the other arts. Painting and architecture are used in the design and creation of stage sets and in the way stage and actors are lighted or kept in shadow. Music and other sound effects may be used to suggest feelings, to build tension, or to create mood and atmosphere. Sculpture and dance inform the way characters are positioned on stage and move around it. So drama is a complex art that involves a dynamic interplay of visual and aural elements. In viewing drama and in reading it we need to be as alert as possible, keeping our eyes and ears, as well as our minds, open.

Our pleasure in seeing drama arises then from the cumulative impact of a multitude of impressions. Makeup and costume, lighting and sound, speech and action, posture and gesture, movement and expression—all work together to bring plays to life, to imbue them with meaning and feeling, and most importantly to create a distinctive theatrical experience for the audience. It is this experience we attempt to capture when we *read* drama, knowing all the while that reading a play is not the same as sitting in a crowded theater watching it enacted on a stage. To compensate, we read drama *imaginatively,* as if we were watching it. We attempt to read drama *theatrically.*

But what does it mean to read a play theatrically? How do we imaginatively reconstruct a play in our minds? Essentially, we translate the script we read into a mental performance that we imagine. By attending to the performative implications of the words on the page, we see imaginatively how they might be dramatized on the stage. We learn to look not only at what a play's words mean, but also at what they suggest about characters' behavior, movements, gestures, and feelings. We learn to listen for the effect the characters' words have on one another. We try to imagine how those words might be uttered—loudly or softly, swiftly or slowly, gently or threateningly. We imagine where the characters are positioned relative to one another, how close or far apart they are. We imagine the manner of their walk, the style of their physical gestures, and the subtlest alteration of their voices and facial expressions. These details, coupled with the characters' body postures, their costumes, the play's scenery and sound effects, all contribute to the richness of our imaginative reenactment of a play. The better we can imagine these aspects of drama, the better we will absorb its atmosphere and feeling, and the more complete and theatrical will be our experience of it.

We learn to do this by reading plays patiently and deliberately. By reading with care we can train ourselves to be attentive not only to the literal meanings of dialogue but also to implications of its sound, accent, and rhythm. Reading aloud, perhaps reading with other students in small groups, and talking with others about our mental reconstructions of scenes can be helpful.

Again, in the process of learning to read plays theatrically we need to attend to the fullest expression of their literary meaning. Drama is *literature* as well as theater, for like poetry and fiction, drama is an art of language. So, while drama entertains us with its representation of life, it offers provocative ideas about the life it portrays, and it provides an imaginative extension of its possibilities.

To have said all this is to claim a great deal for drama. The true test of just how well these claims are met will be the degree to which you truly enjoy (in the broadest and deepest senses of the word) the plays included in this book. As a way of helping you toward both an understanding of the plays and an enriched experience in reading them, we include in this chapter an approach to drama that stresses three things: your *experience* of a play; your *interpretation* of its ideas; and your *evaluation* of its artistic merit and your assessment of its social, cultural, and moral values. Our discussion will thus be arranged in three parts, each devoted to a different aspect of the process of reading drama, and each based on a consideration of one of the following questions:

1. What feelings does the play evoke? Or alternatively: How am I affected by this play? How do I feel as I read it?
2. What ideas does the play express? Or alternatively: What sense do I make of it?
3. What values does the play endorse? Or alternatively: What do I think about the beliefs, attitudes, and values it displays?

THE EXPERIENCE OF DRAMA

When we read a play something happens to us. We experience the play both intellectually and emotionally. This experience involves our feelings about the play's characters and their situation, and it includes our curiosity about how its dramatic action will work out in the end. At this preliminary stage of reading a play, therefore, we are concerned with our personal and subjective involvement in the play. Instead of immediately asking ourselves what the play means, we consider what it does to us, how it affects us, and why. To examine this dimension of our experience of drama, we will read the opening section of a one-act play: Isabella Augusta Persse, Lady Gregory's *The Rising of the Moon.*

The Rising of the Moon

Scene: *Side of a quay in a seaport town. Some posts and chains. A large barrel. Enter three policemen. Moonlight.*

SERGEANT, *who is older than the others, crosses the stage to right and looks down steps. The others put down a pastepot and unroll a bundle of placards.*

POLICEMAN B: I think this would be a good place to put up a notice. (*He points to barrel.*)

POLICEMAN X: Better ask him. (Calls to SERGEANT) Will this be a good place for a placard? (*No answer.*)

POLICEMAN B: Will we put up a notice here on the barrel? (No *answer.*)

SERGEANT: There's a flight of steps here that leads to the water. This is a place that should be minded well. If he got down here, his friends might have a boat to meet him; they might send it in here from outside.

POLICEMAN B: Would the barrel be a good place to put a notice up?

SERGEANT: It might; you can put it there.

(They paste the notice up.)

SERGEANT (*reading it*): Dark hair—dark eyes, smooth face, height five feet five—there's not much to take hold of in that—It's a pity I had no chance of seeing him before he broke out of gaol.° They say he's a wonder, that it's he makes all the plans for the whole organization. There isn't another man in Ireland would have broken gaol the way he did. He must have some friends among the gaolers.

POLICEMAN B: A hundred pounds is little enough for the Government to offer for him. You may be sure any man in the force that takes him will get promotion.

SERGEANT: I'll mind this place myself. I wouldn't wonder at all if he came this way. He might come slipping along there (*points to side of quay*), and his friends might be waiting for him there (*points down steps*), and once he got away it's little chance we'd have of finding him; it's maybe under a load of kelp he'd be in a fishing boat, and not one to help a married man that wants it to the reward.

POLICEMAN X: And if we get him itself, nothing but abuse on our heads for it from the people, and maybe from our own relations.

SERGEANT: Well, we have to do our duty in the force. Haven't we the whole country depending on us to keep law and order? It's those that are down would be up and those that are up would be down, if it wasn't for us. Well, hurry on, you have plenty of other places to placard yet, and come back here then to me. You can take the lantern. Don't be too long now. It's very lonesome here with nothing but the moon.

POLICEMAN B: It's a pity we can't stop with you. The Government should have brought more police into the town, with *him* in gaol, and at assize time too. Well, good luck to your watch. (*They go out.*)

gaol *jail.*

SERGEANT *(walks up and down once or twice and looks at placard):* A hundred pounds and promotion sure. There must be a great deal of spending in a hundred pounds. It's a pity some honest man not to be the better of that.

(A ragged man appears at left and tries to slip past. SERGEANT *suddenly turns.)*

We have read too little of the play to discuss its "meaning" but enough to have our curiosity aroused by the action to follow. In thinking about our experience in reading any literary work, but plays in particular, we should attend to our moment-by-moment response to what we are given.

First we see the play's title, *The Rising of the Moon.* Almost immediately we are informed in a word that the action occurs at night under "moonlight." Before a word of dialogue is spoken we begin wondering about the importance of this detail. And we are already being affected by the way the moon's light falls on our mental stage. We must imagine the sea just beyond the steps of the quay; and we must imagine the sergeant and assisting policemen pasting up their notices, one of them being posted on the barrel.

We quickly see who is in charge by the questions and answers exchanged among the sergeant and his men. But we notice something else as well: that the sergeant seems preoccupied, more anxious and concerned than the two policemen. We notice too how none of these characters is named, how each of them is identified simply by his role. Although the stage directions don't tell us, we should also consider how the men are dressed—in uniform most likely, since they are on a duty mission.

If we read slowly and deliberately we will notice how much pointing occurs in this opening section, with policeman B pointing to the barrel and the sergeant pointing to the side of the quay and to the steps. The parenthetical stage directions that describe these actions help us to visualize the scene and the action. By clearly visualizing these specifics from the start, we will be in a better position to relate them to details of action that follow.

We will also notice how the sergeant's attitude toward the escaped criminal mixes admiration and fear with a sense of duty. His little speech after reading the placard provides us with the important fact that the sergeant has never actually seen the escapee. But it also suggests his sense of amazement at what the criminal has accomplished. From this we gain our impression of the escaped man, an impression reinforced by the large reward for his capture and by the promised promotion for whoever captures him.

In reading that the sergeant wants to take his position at the quay alone, we may think that he looks forward to the reward and possible promotion for himself. His assistants express concern that capturing the escaped man will make them unpopular with "the people" and with their own family relations. We may be surprised at this point to discover that "the people" would not want this criminal captured. And we may be further surprised by the attitude of the two policemen. In response, the sergeant simply emphasizes their duty in keeping law and order.

Very likely this opening excerpt has aroused our curiosity about the escaped man and about his anticipated arrival and confrontation with the police. We may wonder how the sergeant (and possibly his men) will respond to his appearance. In short, we want to see what will happen.

Here, now, is the entire play.

ISABELLA AUGUSTA PERSSE, LADY GREGORY

[1859–1932]

Born to a wealthy landowning family in Galway, in western Ireland, Isabella Augusta Persse, who married Sir William Gregory, a former governor of Ceylon, was a patroness of the Irish poet William Butler Yeats before she became a writer. Although she edited legendary Irish tales and translated Gaelic epics, she is best known as a writer of witty nationalistic plays such as The Rising of the Moon. *With Yeats, she founded the Irish Literary Theatre, an institution central to the rise of the Irish nationalist movement at the beginning of the twentieth century.*

The Rising of the Moon

Scene: *Side of a quay in a seaport town. Some posts and chains. A large barrel. Enter three policemen. Moonlight.*

SERGEANT *who is older than the others, crosses the stage to right and looks down steps. The others put down a pastepot and unroll a bundle of placards.*

POLICEMAN B: I think this would be a good place to put up a notice. (*He points to a barrel.*)

POLICEMAN X: Better ask him. (*Calls to* SERGEANT) Will this be a good place for a placard? (*No answer.*)

POLICEMAN B: Will we put up a notice here on the barrel? (*No answer.*)

SERGEANT: There's a flight of steps here that leads down to the water. This is a place that should be minded well. If he got down here, his friends might have a boat to meet him; they might send it in here from outside.

POLICEMAN B: Would the barrel be a good place to put a notice up?

SERGEANT: It might; you can put it there.

(*They paste the notice up.*)

SERGEANT (*reading it*): Dark hair—dark eyes, smooth face, height over five feet five—there's not much to take hold of in that—It's a pity I had no chance of seeing him before he broke out of gaol.° They say he's a wonder, that it's he makes all the plans for the whole organization. There isn't another man in Ireland would have broken gaol the way he did. He must have some friends among the gaolers.

gaol *jail.*

POLICEMAN B: A hundred pounds is little enough for the Government to offer for him. You may be sure any man in the force that takes him will get promotion.

SERGEANT: I'll mind this place myself. I wouldn't wonder at all if he came this way. He might come slipping along there (*points to side of quay*), and his friends might be waiting for him there (*points down steps*), and once he got away it's little chance we'd have of finding him; it's maybe under a load of kelp he'd be in a fishing boat, and not one to help a married man that wants it to the reward.

POLICEMAN X: And if we get him itself, nothing but abuse on our heads for it from the people, and maybe from our own relations.

SERGEANT: Well, we have to do our duty in the force. Haven't we the whole country depending on us to keep law and order? It's those that are down would be up and those that are up would be down, if it wasn't for us. Well, hurry on, you have plenty of other places to placard yet, and come back here then to me. You can take the lantern. Don't be too long now. It's very lonesome here with nothing but the moon.

POLICEMAN B: It's a pity we can't stop with you. The Government should have brought more police into the town, with *him* in gaol, and at assize time too. Well, good luck to your watch. (*They go out.*)

SERGEANT (*walks up and down once or twice and looks at placard*): A hundred pounds and promotion sure. There must be a great deal of spending in a hundred pounds. It's a pity some honest man not to be the better of that.

(A ragged man appears at left and tries to slip past. SERGEANT *suddenly turns.)*

SERGEANT: Where are you going?

MAN: I'm a poor ballad-singer, your honor. I thought to sell some of these (*holds out bundle of ballads*) to the sailors. (*He goes on.*)

SERGEANT: Stop! Didn't I tell you to stop? You can't go on there.

MAN: Oh, very well. It's a hard thing to be poor. All the world's against the poor!

SERGEANT: Who are you?

MAN: You'd be as wise as myself if I told you, but I don't mind. I'm one Jimmy Walsh, a ballad-singer.

SERGEANT: Jimmy Walsh? I don't know that name.

MAN: Ah, sure, they know it well enough in Ennis. Were you ever in Ennis, Sergeant?

SERGEANT: What brought you here?

MAN: Sure, it's to the assizes I came, thinking I might make a few shillings here or there. It's in the one train with the judges I came.

SERGEANT: Well, if you came so far, you may as well go farther, for you'll walk out of this.

MAN: I will, I will; I'll just go on where I was going. (*Goes toward steps.*)

SERGEANT: Come back from those steps; no one has leave to pass down them tonight.

MAN: I'll just sit on the top of the steps till I see will some sailor buy a ballad off me that would give me my supper. They do be late going back to the ship. It's often I saw them in Cork carried down the quay in a hand-cart.

SERGEANT: Move on, I tell you. I won't have any one lingering about the quay tonight.

MAN: Well, I'll go. It's the poor have the hard life! Maybe yourself might like one, Sergeant. Here's a good sheet now. (*Turns one over*) "Content and a pipe"—that's not much. "The Peeler and the Goat"—you wouldn't like that. "Johnny Hart"—that's a lovely song.

SERGEANT: Move on.

MAN: Ah, wait till you hear it.

(Sings.)

There was a rich farmer's daughter lived near the town of Ross;
She courted a Highland soldier, his name was Johnny Hart;
Says the mother to her daughter, "I'll go distracted mad
If you marry that Highland soldier dressed up in Highland plaid."

SERGEANT: Stop that noise.

(MAN *wraps up his ballads and shuffles toward the steps.*)

SERGEANT: Where are you going?

MAN: Sure you told me to be going, and I am going.

SERGEANT: Don't be a fool. I didn't tell you to go that way; I told you to go back to the town.

MAN: Back to the town, is it?

SERGEANT (*taking him by the shoulder and shoving him before him*): Here, I'll show you the way. Be off with you. What are you stopping for?

MAN (*who has been keeping his eye on the notice, points to it*): I think I know what you're waiting for, Sergeant.

SERGEANT: What's that to you?

MAN: And I know well the man you're waiting for—I know him well—I'll be going. (He *shuffles on.*)

SERGEANT: You know him? Come back here. What sort is he?

MAN: Come back is it, Sergeant? Do you want to have me killed?

SERGEANT: Why do you say that?

MAN: Never mind. I'm going. I wouldn't be in your shoes if the reward was ten times as much. (*Goes off stage to left*) Not if it was ten times as much.

SERGEANT (*rushing after him*): Come back here, come back. (*Drags him back*) What sort is he? Where did you see him?

MAN: I saw him in my own place, in the County Clare. I tell you you wouldn't like to be looking at him. You'd be afraid to be in the one place with him. There isn't a weapon he doesn't know the use of, and as to strength, his muscles are as hard as that board. (*Slaps barrel.*)

SERGEANT: Is he as bad as that?

MAN: He is then.

SERGEANT: Do you tell me so?

MAN: There was a poor man in our place, a sergeant from Ballyvaughan.—It was with a lump of stone he did it.

SERGEANT: I never heard of that.

MAN: And you wouldn't, Sergeant. It's not everything that happens gets into the papers. And there was a policeman in plain clothes, too . . . It is in Limerick he was. . . . It was after the time of the attack on the police barrack at Kilmallock. . . . Moonlight . . . just like this . . . waterside . . . Nothing was known for certain.

SERGEANT: Do you say so? It's a terrible county to belong to.

MAN: That's so, indeed! You might be standing there, looking out that way, thinking you saw him coming up this side of the quay (*points*) and he might be coming up this other side (*points*), and he'd be on you before you knew where you were.

SERGEANT: It's a whole troop of police they ought to put here to stop a man like that.

MAN: But if you'd like me to stop with you, I could be looking down this side. I could be sitting up here on this barrel.

SERGEANT: And you know him well, too?

MAN: I'd know him a mile off, Sergeant.

SERGEANT: But you wouldn't want to share the reward?

MAN: Is it a poor man like me, that has to be going the roads and singing in fairs, to have the name on him that he took a reward? But you don't want me. I'll be safer in the town.

SERGEANT: Well, you can stop.

MAN (*getting up on barrel*): All right, Sergeant. I wonder, now, you're not tired out, Sergeant, walking up and down the way you are.

SERGEANT: If I'm tired I'm used to it.

MAN: You might have hard work before you tonight yet. Take it easy while you can. There's plenty of room up here on the barrel, and you see farther when you're higher up

SERGEANT: Maybe so. (*Gets up beside him on barrel, facing right. They sit back to back, looking different ways*) You made me feel a bit queer with the way you talked.

MAN: Give me a match, Sergeant (*he gives it and* MAN *lights pipe*); take a draw yourself? It'll quiet you. Wait now till I give you a light, but you needn't turn round. Don't take your eye off the quay for the life of you.

SERGEANT: Never fear, I won't. (*Lights pipe. They both smoke*) Indeed it's a hard thing to be in the force, out at night and no thanks for it, for all the danger we're in. And it's little we get but abuse from the people, and no choice but to obey our orders, and never asked when a man is sent into danger, if you are a married man with a family.

MAN (*sings*):

As through the hills I walked to view the hills and shamrock plain,
I stood awhile where nature smiles to view the rocks and streams,
On a matron fair I fixed my eyes beneath a fertile vale,
As she sang her song it was on the wrong of poor old Granuaile.°

SERGEANT: Stop that; that's no song to be singing in these times.

MAN: Ah, Sergeant, I was only singing to keep my heart up. It sinks when I think of him. To think of us two sitting here, and he creeping up the quay, maybe, to get to us.

SERGEANT: Are you keeping a good lookout?

MAN: I am; and for no reward too. Amn't I the foolish man? But when I saw a man in trouble, I never could help trying to get him out of it. What's that? Did something hit me? (*Rubs his heart.*)

Granuailea *sixteenth-century woman whose struggles are an allegory of Ireland's independence against English rule.*

SERGEANT (*patting him on the shoulder*): You will get your reward in heaven.

MAN: I know that, I know that, Sergeant, but life is precious.

SERGEANT: Well, you can sing if it gives you more courage.

MAN (*sings*):

Her head was bare, her hands and feet with iron bands were bound,
Her pensive strain and plaintive wail mingles with the evening gale,
And the song she sang with mournful air, I am old Granuaile.
Her lips so sweet that monarchs kissed . . .

SERGEANT: That's not it. . . . "Her gown she wore was stained with gore." . . . That's it—you missed that.

MAN: You're right, Sergeant, so it is; I missed it. (*Repeats line*) But to think of a man like you knowing a song like that.

SERGEANT: There's many a thing a man might know and might not have any wish for.

MAN: Now, I daresay, Sergeant, in your youth, you used to be sitting up on a wall, the way you are sitting up on this barrel now, and the other lads beside you, and you singing "Granuaile"? . . .

SERGEANT: I did then.

MAN: And the "Shan Bhean Bhocht"? . . .

SERGEANT: I did then.

MAN: And the "Green on the Cape"?

SERGEANT: That was one of them.

MAN: And maybe the man you are watching for tonight used to be sitting on the wall, when he was young, and singing those same songs. . . . It's a queer world.

SERGEANT: Whisht! . . . I think I see something coming. . . . It's only a dog.

MAN: And isn't it a queer world? . . . Maybe it's one of the boys you used to be singing with that time you will be arresting today or tomorrow, and sending into the dock.

SERGEANT: That's true indeed.

MAN: And maybe one night, after you had been singing, if the other boys had told you some plan they had, some plan to free the country, you might have joined with them . . . and maybe it is you might be in trouble now.

SERGEANT: Well, who knows but I might? I had a great spirit in those days.

MAN: It's a queer world, Sergeant, and it's little any mother knows when she sees her child creeping on the floor what might happen to it before it has gone through its life, or who will be who in the end.

SERGEANT: That's a queer thought now, and a true thought. Wait now till I think it out. . . . If it wasn't for the sense I have, and for my wife and family, and for me joining the force the time I did, it might be myself now would be after breaking gaol and hiding in the dark, and it might be him that's hiding in the dark and that got out of gaol would be sitting up where I am on this barrel. . . . And it might be myself would be creeping up trying to make my escape from himself, and it might be himself would be keeping the law, and myself would be breaking it, and myself would be trying maybe to put a bullet in his head, or to take up a lump of a stone the way you said he did . . . no, that myself did. . . . Oh! (*Gasps. After a pause*) What's that? (*Grasps* MAN*'s arm.*)

MAN (*jumps off barrel and listens, looking out over water*): It's nothing, Sergeant.

SERGEANT: I thought it might be a boat. I had a notion there might be friends of his coming about the quays with a boat.

MAN: Sergeant, I am thinking it was with the people you were, and not with the law you were, when you were a young man.

SERGEANT: Well, if I was foolish then, that time's gone.

MAN: Maybe, Sergeant, it comes into your head sometimes, in spite of your belt and your tunic, that it might have been as well for you to have followed Granuaile.

SERGEANT: It's no business of yours what I think.

MAN: Maybe, Sergeant, you'll be on the side of the country yet.

SERGEANT (*gets off barrel*): Don't talk to me like that. I have my duties and I know them. (*Looks round*) That was a boat; I hear the oars. (*Goes to the steps and looks down.*)

MAN (*sings*):

O, then, tell me, Shawn O'Farrell,
Where the gathering is to be.
In the old spot by the river
Right well known to you and me!

SERGEANT: Stop that! Stop that, I tell you!

MAN (*sings louder*):

One word more, for signal token,
Whistle up the marching tune,
With your pike upon your shoulder,
At the Rising of the Moon.

SERGEANT: If you don't stop that, I'll arrest you.

(*A whistle from below answers, repeating the air.*)

SERGEANT: That's a signal. (*Stands between him and steps*) You must not pass this way. . . . Step farther back. . . . Who are you? You are no ballad-singer.

MAN : You needn't ask who I am; that placard will tell you. (*Points to placard.*)

SERGEANT: You are the man I am looking for.

MAN (*takes off hat and wig.* SERGEANT *seizes them*): I am. There's a hundred pounds on my head. There is a friend of mine below in a boat. He knows a safe place to bring me to.

SERGEANT (*looking still at hat and wig*): It's a pity! It's a pity. You deceived me. You deceived me well.

MAN: I am a friend of Granuaile. There is a hundred pounds on my head.

SERGEANT: It's a pity, it's a pity!

MAN: Will you let me pass, or must I make you let me?

SERGEANT: I am in the force. I will not let you pass.

MAN: I thought to do it with my tongue. (*Puts hand in breast*) What is that?

(*Voice of* POLICEMAN X *outside.*) Here, this is where we left him.

SERGEANT: It's my comrades coming.

MAN: You won't betray me . . . the friend of Granuaile. (*Slips behind barrel.*)

(*Voice of* POLICEMAN B.) That was the last of the placards.

POLICEMAN X (*as they come in*): If he makes his escape it won't be unknown he'll make it.

(SERGEANT *puts hat and wig behind his back.*)

POLICEMAN B: Did any one come this way?

SERGEANT (*after a pause*): No one.

POLICEMAN B: No one at all?

SERGEANT: No one at all.

POLICEMAN B: We had no orders to go back to the station; we can stop along with you.

SERGEANT: I don't want you. There is nothing for you to do here.

POLICEMAN B: You bade us to come back here and keep watch with you.

SERGEANT: I'd sooner be alone. Would any man come this way and you making all that talk? It is better the place be quiet.

POLICEMAN B: Well, we'll leave you the lantern anyhow. (*Hands it to him.*)

SERGEANT: I don't want it. Bring it with you.

POLICEMAN B: You might want it. There are clouds coming up and you have the darkness of the night before you yet. I'll leave it over here on the barrel. (*Goes to barrel.*)

SERGEANT: Bring it with you I tell you. No more talk.

POLICEMAN B: Well, I thought it might be a comfort to you. I often think when I have it in my hand and can be flashing it about into every dark corner (*doing so*) that it's the same as being beside the fire at home, and the bits of bogwood blazing up now and again. (*Flashes it about, now on the barrel, now on* SERGEANT.)

SERGEANT (*furious*): Be off the two of you, yourselves and your lantern!

(*They go out.* MAN *comes from behind barrel. He and* SERGEANT *stand looking at one another.*)

SERGEANT: What are you waiting for?

MAN: For my hat, of course, and my wig. You wouldn't wish me to get my death of cold?

(SERGEANT *gives them.*)

MAN (*going toward steps*): Well, good night, comrade, and thank you. You did me a good turn tonight, and I'm obliged to you. Maybe I'll be able to do as much for you when the small rise up and the big fall down . . . when we all change places at the Rising (*waves his hand and disappears*) of the Moon.

SERGEANT (*turning his back to audience and reading placard*): A hundred pounds reward! A hundred pounds! (*Turns toward audience*) I wonder, now, am I as great a fool as I think I am?

(1907)

QUESTIONS FOR CRITICAL THINKING AND WRITING

Experience

1. As you read *The Rising of the Moon,* at what point did you realize the sergeant's divided loyalties? How do you respond to the sergeant's predicament? To what extent do you sympathize with him? To what extent have you experienced an analogous division of loyalties? With what consequences?

Interpretation

2. What are the central issues of the play?
3. Which side do you think the playwright takes on the issues? Why?
4. What is ironic about the situations of the sergeant and the hunted man?

Evaluation

5. Lady Gregory's play turns on a conflict of values, with the sergeant caught between his sympathy for the hunted man and his desire to earn a substantial reward for turning him in. What do you think the sergeant should do? Why?

Connections

6. Compare the decision the sergeant must make with Nora Helmer's decision to forge her husband's signature in Ibsen's *A Doll House.* In each case a character goes against a law or decree. What is at stake in each case? (*A Doll's House* is found in Chapter Twenty-Seven.)

Critical Thinking

7. Imagine that Lady Gregory had written another version of *The Rising of the Moon* as a short story. What would be gained and lost in such a transformation? Which version do you think you would prefer? Why?

How do we describe our experience in reading *The Rising of the Moon?* If the play has engaged our attention, why has it done so? If not, to what do we attribute our lack of interest? Assuming that we were interested enough to become involved in the action, we can then consider our emotional reactions as we were reading. At what points did you feel the strongest pull to continue? At what points was your emotional involvement most intense? What was your reaction upon discovering that the ballad singer was the man the sergeant was seeking? How did you respond to the sergeant's moment of recognizing the criminal? To his speech about exchanging places with him? To his complicity in helping him escape? To his final question at the end of the play?

Our responses to these and other details of dialogue and action constitute our *experience* of the play. This experience may be affected by our social and political views, as well as by our gender, our age, and possibly also by our race or ethnicity. Our experience in reading *The Rising of the Moon* will also be affected by our previous experience with attending or reading other plays. And it may be further affected by our knowledge of Irish literary history and our experience with additional plays by Lady Gregory or with other literary works on similar subjects. Thus although much of our sense of the play will overlap with the experience of other readers, most readers will not experience the play in exactly the same way that we do.

We can single out only a few moments, here, for a consideration of our experience and response. Let's consider our reactions when policemen B and X return while the ballad-singer hides behind the barrel. During this climactic moment, we experience tension as we wonder whether the sergeant will turn the man in. Another highly charged moment occurs when the sergeant corrects the ballad-singer for omitting a verse of the song about Granuaile, apparently a revolutionary song about England's political domination of Ireland. Even if we know little about the history of this period, we sense that this is a revolutionary song because when the ballad-singer begins to sing it, the sergeant cuts him off sharply, saying, "Stop that; that's no song to be singing in these times." Very likely this moment gave us pause not only to reflect on the significance of the action but also to feel its emotional resonance. And although that moment certainly can be analyzed for an intellectual meaning and related to the play's meaning as a whole, it is also a wonderfully theatrical moment. Something surprising happens on stage, something we can both see and hear. It affects us emotionally before we make sense of it intellectually.

Our experience of the play, however, rests finally on our response to its ending. At the very least we should have a sense of completeness or closure, a sense that the play has ended or culminated rather than simply stopped. But we will also have a sense of satisfaction (or dissatisfaction) at the way the play's action has been resolved. Our overall experience of the play results from the accumulation of our responses to all these things, coupled with our imagining of its theatrical dimension.

THE INTERPRETATION OF DRAMA

When we interpret a play we explain it to ourselves. We make sense of it. Interpretation directs us to more objective considerations than the subjective experience in which we satisfy our personal needs as readers. When we interpret a play, we concern ourselves less with how it affects us and how it makes us feel than with what it means or suggests. Interpretation, in short, aims at understanding; it relies on our intellectual comprehension and rational understanding rather than on our emotional response.

The act of interpreting involves essentially four things: observing, connecting, inferring, and concluding. To understand a play, we first need to *observe* its details. For example, we notice the articles and decor of its stage setting; we watch the actions of its characters; we listen to dialogue and monologue; we absorb the effects of lighting, stage props, and sound effects. As we do these things, we begin formulating a sense of the play's situation, focus, and point. We arrive at this formulation, however tentative it may be, largely by making *connections* among the many details we observe. On the basis of these connections we make *inferences* or interpretive hypotheses about their significance. Finally, we come to some kind of provisional *conclusion* about the play's meaning based on our observations, connections, and inferences.

Our act of interpretation continues, moreover, as we read. We don't delay making inferences, for example, until after we have made and connected all our observations. Instead, we develop tentative conclusions *as* we read and observe, *while* we make observations and develop inferences. We may change and adjust our inferences and provisional conclusions both *during* our reading of a play and *afterward* as we think back over its details. We do not separate this intellectual process, however, from our subjective reactions and emotional responses. Although they have been separated here for convenience, the way we actually read a play combines emotional response and intellectual analysis. In the same way, the four interpretive actions of observing, connecting, inferring, and concluding occur together, sometimes simultaneously, and not in a series of neatly separated sequential stages.

Whether you were aware of it or not, you were performing this complex act of reading-interpreting when you read *The Rising of the Moon.* Our discussion of important moments of the play was based partly on an implicit interpretation. For even though we focused our discussion of our experience on the play's script, the only way to make sense of that experience is to make some sense of the action of the play. In doing so we were beginning the work of interpretation.

We will have more to say about aspects of interpretation in Chapter Twenty-Three, "Elements of Drama." But even now in this introductory overview of the interpretive process, we should apply the approach we have been discussing. Return to Lady Gregory's *The Rising of the Moon* and read it again slowly and deliberately, noticing as much as you can about its language and action. List a series of details about each, establish connections among related details, and on the basis of those connections develop a set of inferences implied by the characters' speeches and interactions. Then provide a brief and tentative interpretation or explanation of one possible meaning of the play.

One way to begin following through on this interpretive exercise would be to work first with a single scene such as the section from the entrance of the ballad-singer to the point at which the sergeant takes him by the shoulders and tells him to leave. Or look at the scene that begins at that point and ends with the sergeant reversing his order, and allowing the man instead to remain with him. The idea is to zero in on a section of the play and begin looking closely at its action and listening carefully to its language. We will illustrate by focusing on the section (or scene) beginning with the sergeant grasping the man's arm and the man's jumping off the barrel to the point at which the two policemen return.

What happens in this section? The most important event, of course, is the revelation of the man's identity. But let's consider the tissue of action and reaction, speech and gesture that surround that important moment of revelation.

We might observe first of all that, as with the policemen, the characters are identified generically rather than individually. That is, rather than being given particular, individualizing names, they are referred to as "sergeant" and "man." (The name, Jimmy Walsh, that the ballad-singer gives, is of course a fabrication.) The generic names suggest that the situation the two men find themselves in should be generalized to include not only specifically Irish social inequalities, but also problems of political and social conflict elsewhere. An even broader interpretation of the play's central characters' names can be made: the sergeant represents the law; the man represents the people the law attempts to keep in their place. Overall, the play's symbolic quality makes its situation applicable in other times and places besides those specifically indicated.

Much of the initial dialogue of this section centers on the man's attempt to persuade the sergeant that, even though he represents the law, he really sides with the people. Notice how the man's more voluble speech contrasts with the sergeant's brusqueness. When the man suggests that the sergeant may well have been a follower of Granuaile like himself, the sergeant curtly dismisses the idea. The sharpness of this and other of the sergeant's replies indicate that the sergeant probably agrees with what the man says. The sergeant's overly emphatic denial reinforces our suspicion that he sympathizes with the man. And when the sergeant says "It's a pity, it's a pity," we could interpret this to mean a number of things: (1) that it is too bad that the man must be arrested—but the sergeant has his duty to perform, and that's that; (2) that it is a pity that the sergeant is put in this difficult position; (3) that it is a shame that a man the sergeant seems to like has to be on the opposite side of the law; (4) that it is too bad that the sergeant never followed through on his youthful idealism to follow Granuaile. This line "it's a pity," in fact, has been uttered earlier in the opening scene by both the sergeant and one of the policemen. Echoing here at a climactic moment, it is endowed with a rich resonance of meanings.

Even though this scene does not bring the play to its conclusion, it does serve to point to the significant crisis at its heart. This is the decision the sergeant must make as the scene ends and his companions return. The man puts the sergeant's decision in terms of betrayal, categorically affirming (rather than questioning) that the sergeant, friend of Granuaile that he is, will not betray him. And of course, he doesn't, which leads us to ask more or less the question that the sergeant himself asks at the end of the play. Why does the sergeant act as he does? What principles motivate his action? And what does the play seem to suggest about that motivation? In pointing up and answering questions like these, we push toward an interpretation of the play overall.

In reaching an interpretation of this section of the play, of the play as a whole, or indeed of any play, we should be concerned less with finding the *right* answer than with arriving at a *satisfying* explanation. Some interpretations, nonetheless, will be more satisfying than others; they will be more convincing, largely because they take into account more of the play's details. Other interpretations, while perhaps not as convincing, may be valuable for the intellectual stimulation they provide. Still others may strain credibility to the breaking point. Because we invariably bring different experiences to our reading of plays, we will each see different things in them. Through conversation and discussion, we can debate the merits of these differing viewpoints and enrich each other's understanding and appreciation of drama.

THE EVALUATION OF DRAMA

An *evaluation* is essentially a judgment, an opinion about a text formulated as a conclusion. We may agree or disagree with the attitude toward law and order expressed by the sergeant. We may accept or reject the man's claim that the sergeant would really like to support the revolution, and that to turn the man in would be a betrayal. And we may approve or disapprove of the sergeant's decision to let the man go. However we evaluate these aspects of the play, we invariably measure them on a scale of our own values.

Evaluating is partly an unconscious process. We are not always aware, except perhaps in a vaguely general way, why we respond to something as we do. We may know that we like or dislike it without bothering much to think about why. We sometimes accept particular ideas, events, experiences, or works of art and reject others almost instinctively, even automatically. Even though part of our evaluation of a play is unconscious, we can make it more deliberate and more fully conscious. We simply need to ask ourselves how we respond to the values the work supports and why we respond as we do. By asking these questions, we should be able to consider our own values more clearly and to discuss more fairly and sensibly why we agree or disagree with the values displayed in the play.

When we evaluate a play, we appraise it according to our own unique combination of cultural, moral, and aesthetic values. Our cultural values derive from our lives as members of families and societies. Our moral values reflect our ethical norms—what we consider to be good or evil, right or wrong. Our aesthetic values concern what we see as beautiful or ugly, well made or ill made. Over time, through education and experience, our values may change. A play we once valued for what it reveals about human experience or for its moral perspective may mean little to us later. Conversely, a play that we once found uninteresting or disappointing we may later find to be powerfully engaging.

Our personal response to any play's values is closely tied to our interpretation of it. Evaluation depends upon interpretation; our judgment of a play's values (and perhaps its value as a literary work or theatrical performance as well) depends on how well we understand it. Our evaluation, moreover, may be linked to our initial experience of the play, with our first impressions and precritical, preanalytical reactions. If our reaction is unsympathetic to the play as a whole or to the values it seems to display, we may be reluctant to change both our interpretation and our evaluation, even when we discover convincing evidence to warrant a reconsideration of both.

Consider *The Rising of the Moon* from the standpoint of evaluation. What values animate the two major characters? What is the sergeant's attitude toward the men he supervises? Toward the law he enforces? Toward the people he serves? What is the man's attitude toward the law? Toward the sergeant as a representative of that law? Toward the sergeant as a man? Toward Granuaile? Asking questions such as these and considering the values—social, cultural, moral—that underlie them leads us most often to the heart of many plays.

We have already referred implicitly at least to the values and ideals that govern the behavior of the man and the sergeant. The heart of the play is the conflict between the two sets of values represented by the two men. The ballad-singer represents a revolutionary ideal that espouses the cause of Ireland's freedom from England; the sergeant represents the law and order that would prevent revolutionary upheaval in society. Alternatively, we may see the conflict occurring within the sergeant himself, one part of him siding with the social values of law and order, and another siding with the poor and the oppressed. We may wonder to what extent the sergeant resents the authority he espouses and enacts, and to what extent he resents people like the man in the play who cause him to reenact the conflict of loyalties he feels torn between. Here is where our own political attitudes, social dispositions, even moral beliefs, influence our judgment about the values the play seems to endorse.

The Rising of the Moon suggests that the sergeant is not a fool in ignoring his responsibility to uphold the law by arresting the man. Depending on our values, however, the opposite conclusion can be stated. In one sense of course the sergeant is a fool, since he wastes an opportunity to gain a promotion and to collect a sizable financial reward, to say nothing of the prestige he would have gained by such an arrest. In another sense, however, he is no fool, since he knows exactly what he is doing and why. He values the man and his cause more than his own good fortune; he values his own diminished but still living idealism more than the glory he would gain by arresting the man. Although the sergeant wonders aloud whether he has done the right thing, his wondering rests on practical rather than moral grounds. Morally, he feels vindicated. Practically, however, there is room for debate.

Your evaluation of the sergeant's decision, action, and motivation may differ from this view. If so, it is most likely linked with a different interpretation of the play's dialogue and action, as well as a contrasting set of social, political, and moral values.

Of the kinds of evaluations we make when reading drama, those about a play's aesthetic qualities are hardest to discuss. Aesthetic responses are difficult to describe because they involve our subjective personal impressions about what we find pleasing. They also involve our expectations about what we think a play should be, as well as our prior experience in reading or attending plays. Our aesthetic responses, moreover, are complicated by our tendency to react quickly and decisively to what we like and dislike, often without knowing why we respond as we do.

Admittedly, without considerable experience in reading and viewing drama, judgments about a play's values and considerations of its aesthetic merit need to be made with caution. But we must begin somewhere, since evaluation is inevitable. We cannot avoid judging the plays we read any more than we can avoid judging the people we meet. The process is natural.

How we develop our aesthetic responses to plays depends partly on letting the informed and sensitive responses of other experienced readers guide and enrich our own perceptions. These other readers may be classmates or teachers. They may be critics who have written articles and books about the plays we read and see. Their understanding of drama can deepen and enrich our own. Besides learning directly from what critics say about particular plays, we can also learn how to discuss literary and dramatic works in general. The best drama critics provide models we can emulate, while the worst can at least show us what to avoid. Our goal in reading, interpreting, and evaluating drama—and in listening to the views of critics and other readers—is to develop a sense of literary tact, the kind of balanced judgment that comes with experience in reading and living enriched by thoughtful reflection on both. There are no shortcuts or simple formulas for developing such evaluative competence and confidence. They come with practice in the attentive reading and viewing of many plays, with a patient consideration of their language and action, and a willingness to reflect on our responses to them. Understanding and appreciation are achieved by devotion, effort, and repeated acts of thoughtful attention to literary works.

CHAPTER TWENTY-TWO

Types of Drama

Some plays elicit laughter, others evoke tears. Some are comic, others tragic, still others a mixture of both. The comic view celebrates life and affirms it; it is typically joyous and festive. The tragic view highlights life's sorrows; it is typically brooding and solemn. Tragic plays end unhappily, often with the death of the hero; comedies usually end happily, often with a celebration such as a marriage. Both comedy and tragedy contain changes of fortune, with the fortunes of comic characters turning from bad to good and those of tragic characters from good to bad.

The two major dramatic modes, *tragedy* and *comedy,* have been represented traditionally by contrasting masks, one sorrowful, the other joyful. Actors once wore such masks. The masks represent more than different types of plays: they also stand for contrasting ways of looking at the world, aptly summarized in Horace Walpole's remark, "the world is a comedy to those who think and a tragedy to those who feel." That is, when you think about the contradictions in a situation it may seem funny, but when you feel them, it is sad.

TRAGEDY

In the *Poetics,* Aristotle described **tragedy** as "an imitation of an action that is serious, complete in itself, and of a certain magnitude." This definition suggests that tragedies are solemn plays concerned with grave human actions and their consequences. The action of a tragedy is complete—it possesses a beginning, a middle, and an end. Elsewhere in the *Poetics,* Aristotle notes that the incidents of a tragedy must be causally connected. The events have to be logically related, one growing naturally out of another, each leading to the inevitable catastrophe, usually the downfall of the hero.

Some readers of tragedy have suggested that, according to Aristotle, the catastrophe results from a flaw in the character of the hero. Others have contended that the hero's tragic flaw results from fate or coincidence, from circumstances beyond the hero's control. A third view proposes that tragedy results from an error of judgment committed by the hero, one that may or may not have as its source a weakness in character.

Typically, tragic protagonists make mistakes: they misjudge other characters, they misinterpret events, and they confuse appearance with reality. Shakespeare's Othello, for example, mistakes Iago for an honest, loving friend; and he mistakes his faithful wife, Desdemona, for an adultress. Sophocles' Oedipus mistakes his own identity and misconstrues his destiny. The misfortune and catastrophes of tragedy are frequently precipitated by errors of judgment; mistaken perceptions lead to misdirected actions that eventually result in catastrophe.

Tragic heroes such as Oedipus and Othello are grand, noble characters. They are men, as Aristotle says, "of high estate," who enjoy "great reputation and prosperity." Tragic heroes, in short, are privileged, exalted personages who have earned their high repute and status by heroic exploit (Othello), by intelligence (Oedipus), or by their inherent nobility (Othello and Oedipus). Their tragedy crushes not only the tragic hero but other related characters as well. Othello's tragedy includes his wife and his faithful lieutenant, Cassio. Oedipus's tragedy extends to his entire family, including his wife-mother, his two sons, his daughters, his brother-in-law, Creon, and Creon's family. Greek tragedy, typically, involves the destruction and downfall of an entire house or family, reaching across generations. The catastrophe of Shakespearean tragedy is usually not as extensive.

An essential element of the tragic hero's experience is a **recognition** of what has happened to him. Frequently this takes the form of the hero discovering something previously unknown or something he knew but misconstrued. According to Aristotle, the tragic hero's recognition (or discovery) is often allied with a reversal of his expectations. Such an ironic reversal occurs in *Oedipus Rex* when the messenger's speech unsettles rather than reassures Oedipus about who he is and what he has done. Once the reversal and discovery occur, tragic plots move swiftly to their conclusions.

We may consider why, amid such suffering and catastrophe, tragedies are not depressing. Aristotle suggested that the pity and fear aroused in the audience are purged or released and the audience experiences a cleansing of those emotions and a sense of relief that the action is over. Perhaps tragedy represents for us the ultimate downfall we will all experience in death: we watch in fascination and awe a dramatic reminder of our own inevitable mortality. Or perhaps we are exalted in witnessing the high human aspiration and the noble conception of human character embodied in tragic heroes like Oedipus and Othello, despite their all-too-human flaws.

COMEDY

Some of the same dramatic elements we find in tragedy occur in comedy as well. Discovery scenes and consequent reversals of fortune, for example, occur in both. So too do misperceptions and errors of judgment, exhibitions of human weakness and failure. But in **comedy** the reversals and errors lead not to calamity as they do in tragedy, but to prosperity and happiness. Comic heroes are usually ordinary people. Moreover, comic characters are frequently one-dimensional to the extent that many are stereotypes: the braggart, for example, or the hypocrite, the unfaithful wife, the cuckold, the ardent young lovers.

If comic characters are frequently predictable in their behavior, comic plots are not: they thrive on the surprise of the unexpected and on improbability. Cinderella stories like these are the staples of comedy: an impoverished student inherits a fortune; a beggar turns out to be a prince; a wife (or husband or child) presumed dead turns up alive and well; the war (between nations, classes, families, the sexes) ends, the two sides are reconciled, and everybody lives happily ever after. But whether the incongruities of comedy exist between a character's speech and actions, between what we expect the characters to be and what they show themselves to be, or between how they think of themselves and how we see them, things work out in the end.

The happy endings of comedies are not always happy for all the characters involved. This marks one of the significant differences between the two major types of comedy: *satiric* and *romantic* comedy. Though much of what we have said so far about comedy applies to both types, it applies more extensively to romantic than to satiric comedy, or satire. **Satire** exposes human folly, criticizes human conduct, and aims to correct it. Ridiculing the weaknesses of human nature, satiric comedy shows us the low level to which human behavior can sink. Molière's *Tartuffe* is such a satiric comedy; it exposes religious hypocrisy, castigates folly, and ultimately celebrates virtue. Although things may work out well in the end for most of the characters, the play contains some harsh moments and a bitter ending for at least one character.

Romantic comedy, on the other hand, portrays characters gently, even generously; its spirit is more tolerant and its tone more genial. Whatever adversities the heroes and heroines of romantic comedy must overcome, the tone is typically devoid of rancor and bitterness. The humor of romantic comedy is more sympathetic than corrective, and it intends more to entertain than instruct, to delight than ridicule. Shakespeare is an example of a romantic comedy.

Because of such differences, our approaches to reading satire and romance should be different. When we read satiric comedies, we should identify the object of the dramatist's criticism and determine why the behavior of certain characters is objectionable. In reading romantic comedies, we are invited simply to enjoy the raveling and unraveling of plot as the protagonists are led to the inevitable happy ending.

These distinctions, however, should serve as guidelines to prevailing tendencies rather than as rigid descriptions of dramatic types. Frequently romantic comedies may contain elements of satire and satiric comedies elements of romance.

CHAPTER TWENTY-THREE

Elements of Drama

The elements of drama include plot, character, dialogue, staging, and theme. Our discussions of each of these elements individually allow us to highlight the characteristic features of drama in a convenient way. We should remember, however, that analysis of any single element of drama (plot, for example) should not blind us to its function in conjunction with other elements (such as character). Plot is enhanced by staging and may be carried forward by dialogue; character is expressed through dialogue and staging; and so on.

PLOT

One of the reasons we read plays is to discover what happens, to see how particular consequences result from specific observable actions. We become engaged by a play's story line, and remain held by its twists and turns, until the playwright resolves things. The details of action, or incidents, in a well-organized play form a unified structure. This unified structure of a play's incidents is called its **plot.**

It is important to realize that a dramatic plot is not merely a series of haphazard occurrences. It is, rather, a carefully arranged series of *causally* related incidents. The incidents of the plot, that is, must be connected in such a way that one gives rise to another or directly results from another. And, of course, the playwright shapes and arranges the incidents of the plot to do precisely these things.

Besides being unified, a good plot will also be economical. By this we mean that all the incidents of the play contribute to its cumulative effect, its overall meaning and impression. No actions included in the play are extraneous or unnecessary. The economy of a play's plot distinguishes it from everyday life, in which a multitude of minor actions mingle indiscriminately with significantly related incidents. Dramatists, however, fit together the actions of their plays in meaningful ways.

We can describe the plots of many plays by using the following diagram:

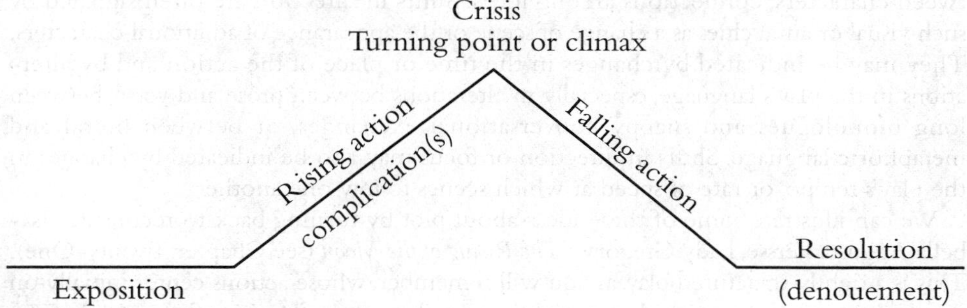

The **exposition** of a play presents background necessary for the development of the plot. The **rising action** includes the separate incidents that "complicate" the plot and build toward its most dramatic moment. These incidents often involve **conflicts** either between characters or within them, conflicts that lead to a crisis. The point of crisis toward which the play's action builds is called its **climax.** Following this high point of intensity in the play is the **falling action,** in which there is a relaxation of emotional intensity and a gradual **resolution** of the various strands of the plot in the play's **denouement** (French word that refers to the untying of a knot).

Whether playwrights use a traditional plot or vary the formula, they control our expectations about what is happening through the arrangement of incidents. Playwrights decide when to present information and when to withhold it; when to speed up a play's action and when to slow it down; when to arouse our curiosity and when to satisfy it. By the arrangement of incidents a dramatist may create suspense, evoke laughter, cause anxiety, or elicit surprise. One of our main sources of pleasure in plot is surprise, whether we are shown something we didn't expect or suddenly see *how* something will happen even when we have known *what* will happen. Surprise often follows suspense, thus fulfilling our need to find out what happens as we await the resolution of a play's action.

In considering our expectations and response to the developing action of a play, we approach the concept of plot less as a schematic diagram of a play's completed action and more as an evolving series of experiences we undergo as we read or view it. For our emotional experience in reading a play is an important aspect of the play's meaning for us. And this experience is designed by the playwright, as he or she structures the incidents of the plot, largely by keeping us guessing about something, keeping a series of temporarily unanswered questions before us as we read. We continue reading to find answers to those questions.

Another dimension of a play's structure is the way it satisfies our need for order and form. Besides considering how a play is structured to affect us emotionally, we can also consider ways it exhibits formal or artistic design. In the first instance we attend to the theatrical and psychological aspect of structure, in the second to its aesthetic dimension. Both contribute to our experience of drama and to the meaning(s) of plays.

We can be alert to a play's structure even as we read it for the first time, primarily by paying attention to (1) repeated elements and recurring details—of action and gesture, of dialogue and description—and to (2) shifts in direction and changes of focus. Repetition signals important connections and relationships in the play, relationships between characters, connections among ideas. Shifts in direction are often signaled by such visual or aural clues as a change of scene or the appearance of additional characters. They may be indicated by changes in the time or place of the action and by alterations in the play's language, especially in alterations between prose and verse, between long monologues and snappy conversational exchanges, or between literal and metaphoric language. Shifts in direction or focus may also be indicated by changes in the play's tempo, or rate of speed at which scenes follow one another.

We can illustrate some of these ideas about plot by turning back to reconsider Isabella Augusta Persse, Lady Gregory's *The Rising of the Moon* (see Chapter Twenty-One). This is a tightly structured play, as you will remember, whose actions center initially on the appearance of the wanted man and then on the sergeant's crisis of conscience. The exposition begins the play and ends with the departure of the two policemen. The first major incident occurs with the appearance of the ragged man, the ballad-singer. This incident inaugurates the play's rising action, which becomes intensified as the sergeant learns that the ballad-singer knows the wanted man and that he is dangerous. Additional incidents complicate the action, as the sergeant reveals that he is familiar with revolutionary songs. After that, the playwright slows down the tempo of the play both to provide her audience with an insight into how the positions of the two men might have been reversed and to increase suspense as we wonder what will happen. These incidents, one after another, mark the play's climax: the man reveals that he is the criminal that the sergeant seeks; the policemen return; and the sergeant chooses to hide the man's hat and wig. The falling action, though brief (consisting simply of the sergeant dismissing the two policemen) is still suspenseful since when policeman B swings around the lantern, he could catch the fugitive as well as his sergeant red-handed. The denouement is equally brief. It includes the last conversation between the man and the sergeant followed by the sergeant's final question.

Such a structured description reveals the plot's unity and economy. And it suggests as well something of its tempo, or the pace of its action (slow, then faster, faster and more intense, then slower after the climax). Additional structural details include the repetition of words and phrases, especially the sergeant's "It's a pity," and the repetition of gestures, such as the pointing of both the sergeant and the man. The repeated utterance invites consideration of its meaning. The repeated gesture indicates a connection between the sergeant and the man.

CHARACTER

If we read plays for their plots—to find out what happens—we also read them to discover the fates of their **characters.** We become interested in dramatic characters for varying, even contradictory, reasons. They may remind us in some ways of ourselves; they may appeal to us because they differ from us. They may represent alternative directions we might have taken, alternative decisions we might have made. Although fictional characters cannot be directly equated with actual people, they are usually recognizably human, and as such, subject to the changing conditions of fate and circumstance.

Characters bring plays to life. First and last we attend to characters: to how they look and what their appearance tells us about them; to what they say and what their manner of saying it expresses; to what they do and how their actions reveal who they are and what they stand for. We may come to know them and respond to them in ways we come to know and respond to actual people, all the while realizing that characters are imaginative constructions, literary imitations of human beings. Even though characters in plays are not real people, their human dimension is impossible to ignore since actors portray them, and their human qualities engage us. Nonetheless, it is helpful to remain mindful of the distinction between dramatic characters and actual people so that we do not expect them always to behave realistically, and so we do not expect playwrights to tell us more about them than we need to know.

Characters in drama can be classified as major and minor, static and dynamic, flat and round. A *major character* is an important figure at the center of the play's action and meaning. Supporting the major character are one or more secondary or *minor characters,* whose function is partly to illuminate the major characters. Minor characters are often *static* or unchanging: they remain essentially the same throughout the play. *Dynamic* characters, on the other hand, exhibit some kind of change—of attitude, of purpose, of behavior. Another way of describing static and dynamic characters is as *flat* and *round* characters. Flat characters reveal only a single dimension, and their behavior and speech are predictable; round characters are more individualized, reveal more than one aspect of their human nature, and are not predictable in behavior or speech.

The **protagonist** is the main character in a play. Generally introduced to the audience very early, this is the character that the author expects should most engage our interest and sympathies. Protagonists do not have to be especially courageous or intelligent, nor do they need to be physically attractive or admirable. However, they do have to *want* something, and they have to want it intensely. In short, the most important feature of a protagonist is a desire, or an *objective*. The objective will be clear not long after the introduction of a protagonist. For instance, in Lady Gregory's *The Rising of the Moon,* we realize almost immediately that the sergeant wants to capture the revolutionary. Although the protagonist might redefine the objective through the course of the play, or an irony might develop concerning it, as in this play, the audience, very importantly, must never be confused about a protagonist's main objective. Our interest and absorption in a play depend largely on our understanding the objective and its importance to the protagonist, and to the plot, especially, as in this play, when a new objective (*not* wanting to capture the man) finally emerges.

Clearly, the protagonist's relentless pursuit of an objective is critical to a play's success. After all, if the protagonist is not passionate about an objective, how can the audience be interested in the outcome of the play or the play itself? We watch to see if protagonists will reach their objectives, and we consider, along with them, their strategies and actions, anticipating responses from other characters. The *climax* is that point in the play when we discover whether the protagonist achieves the objective or not. Of course, secondary characters will also have objectives, but they should never obscure the protagonist's objective. The foundation of the play rests on the protagonist's objective.

The **antagonist** is the character or force against which the protagonist struggles. The antagonist may be another character, a culture and its laws or traditions, natural elements, or the protagonist divided against himself. In *The Rising of the Moon,* the sergeant's objective is to capture the wanted man. The antagonist or chief impediment to his achieving this objective is the wanted man himself, the ballad-singer. As the play develops, we realize that the sergeant is ambivalent; that is, he both wants to capture his antagonist, and he wants the antagonist to escape.

If the protagonist and his or her objective are the most important elements in the construction of a play, the antagonist follows close behind. Without an antagonist or obstacles in the protagonist's way, there would be no conflict and no drama. To create the necessary tension to sustain an audience's interest, the dramatist must be sure that the protagonist and antagonist are fairly evenly matched. If one is much stronger than the other and if the outcome is never in doubt, there will not be enough tension to sustain interest. In this way, a play is not unlike an athletic contest. Audience interest is peaked when the winner is uncertain. Also, while it is critical to a play to have just one protagonist and one objective, there can be more than one obstacle, or antagonist, impeding the protagonist's objective without threatening the unity or effect of the play.

Character is the companion of plot; the plot of a play involves the actions of its characters. Another way of defining plot is simply as characters in action (or *inter*-action). And in the same way that a play's plot must be unified, so a character must be coherent. This means that all aspects of the character—speech, dress, gesture, movement—must work together to suggest a focused and unified whole. Our sense of characters' identity and personality are derived essentially from four things: (1) their actions—what they do; (2) their words—what they say and how they say it; (3) their physical attributes—what they look like; (4) the responses of other characters to them—what others say or do to or about them. Of these, however, our sense of a character's coherence derives mainly from his or her speech and actions. From these we gain a sense of who characters are and what they are like.

Drama lives in the encounter of characters; its action is interaction, which frequently involves *conflict*. Dramatic characters come together and affect each other, making things happen by coming into conflict. Drama, in fact, is essentially the creation, development, and resolution of conflicts between and within characters. For it is in conflict that characters reveal themselves, advance the plot, and dramatize the meaning(s) of plays.

We can illustrate something of our approach to character by again looking briefly at the characters in Lady Gregory's *The Rising of the Moon.* The two policemen are clearly minor characters, necessary primarily for the plot, though they also serve to reveal the character of the sergeant. In the first scene, for example, we notice how differently the sergeant responds than his men. Policemen B and X seem more casual, less concerned about the danger of the situation and more concerned with the details of finding places to post the placards. The sergeant is shown to be more experienced at the job and more aware of what is at stake. More important, however, is the relationship—or conflict—that develops between the sergeant, the protagonist, and the wanted man, his antagonist. As it turns out, neither is what he seems to be. The sergeant does not uphold the law and arrest the man; the man does not live up to his reputation as a dangerous killer. Both have opportunities to act within their expected roles, but neither does. Each surprises the other; both surprise us and perhaps themselves as well. The conflict between them remains a potential conflict rather than an actual one.

The most significant moment of character revelation occurs as the sergeant muses about fate. He imagines his life having turned out differently, with himself as a hunted criminal and the fugitive as a policeman hunting him. The sergeant sees the connection rather than the differences between himself and the revolutionary. This perception leads him to a radically different sense of his responsibility toward the man and toward their countrymen. In a small way, the sergeant helps to bring about the wanted man's prediction that "the small [will] rise up and the big fall down," largely because a part of the sergeant believes this should occur. The sergeant is thus shown to be a more complex man than he seems initially—though his practical, orthodox side appears with his final question: "I wonder, now, am I as great a fool as I think I am?"

DIALOGUE

Our discussion of character and conflict brings us to a critical aspect of dramatic characters—their speech, or **dialogue**. Although generally we use the word *dialogue* to refer to all the speech of a play, strictly speaking, dialogue involves two speakers and **monologue** to the speech of one. An important dramatic convention of dialogue is the use of a soliloquy to express a character's state of mind. A **soliloquy** is a speech given by a character as if alone, even though other characters may be on stage. A soliloquy represents a character's thoughts so the audience can know what he or she is thinking at a given moment. Soliloquies should be distinguished from **asides,** which are comments made directly to the audience in the presence of other characters, but without those other characters hearing what is said. Unlike a soliloquy, an aside is usually a brief remark.

Dialogue is more than simply the words characters utter. It is also itself action, since characters' words have the power to affect each other as well as to affect the audience. Words in drama do things, effect change, initiate events. Through his words (and song) the wanted man in *The Rising of the Moon* convinces the sergeant not to betray him. Through his words Iago induces Othello to murder his wife, Desdemona (Chapter Twenty-Six). Dialogue, moreover, is an important index of a character's personality. This is true of what characters say about themselves and say about and to each other. It is especially true of their manner of expressing it. Lady Gregory's sergeant is forceful, authoritative, even peremptory in dialogue with his two police subordinates. And he sounds brusque and dismissive at first in dialogue with the ballad-singer. But the harshness and brusqueness evaporate in the following more meditative speech:

> . . . If it wasn't for the sense I have, and for my wife and family, and for me joining the force the time I did, it might be myself now would be after breaking gaol and hiding in the dark, and it might be him that's hiding in the dark and that got out of gaol would be sitting up where I am on this barrel. . . . And it might be myself would be creeping up trying to make my escape from himself, and it might be himself would be keeping the law, and myself would be breaking it, and myself would be trying maybe to put a bullet in his head, or to take up a lump of a stone the way you said he did . . . no, that myself did. . . .

What the sergeant says here is clear enough: he could picture himself in the other man's situation. But his manner of saying it—in a long, run-together meditative sentence strung out with numerous "ands"—is equally revealing of a more sympathetic and understanding man, one who is not as predictable and single-minded as his police subordinates. The ongoing quality of the sentence simulates the ongoing nature of his thinking. The neat balances of "him" and "I" or "myself" suggest that the sergeant acknowledges a kinship with the "other" seemingly different but ultimately similar man. The sergeant's speech and way of giving it imply that he sees that they are more alike than different.

This concern with characters' language is crucial, whether we attend plays in the theater or imagine them performed in the theaters of our minds. We need to develop our auditory imagination, our sense of how speech sounds as it is uttered, to really hear it or to imagine how it might be spoken. Ezra Pound, the modern American poet, once described drama as "persons moving about on a stage using words"—in short, people talking. Listening to their talk we hear identifiable, individual voices. In their presence we encounter persons, for dialogue inevitably brings us back to character, drama's human center. And though dialogue in plays typically has three major functions—to advance the plot, to establish setting (the time and place of the action), and to reveal character—its most important and consistent function is the revelation of character.

Consider in Act IV, Scene III of Shakespeare's *Othello* the following conversation between Desdemona (wife of the military hero Othello) and Emilia (maid to Desdemona and wife of Othello's lieutenant, Iago). They are talking about adultery. (The *Tragedy of Othello* is found in Chapter Twenty-Six.)

DESDEMONA: Dost thou in conscience think, tell me, Emilia,
That there be women do abuse their husbands
In such gross kind?
EMILIA: There be some such, no question.
DESDEMONA: Wouldst thou do such a deed for all the world?
EMILIA: Why, would not you?
DESDEMONA: No, by this heavenly light!
EMILIA: Nor I either by this heavenly light.
I might do't as well i'the dark.
DESDEMONA: Wouldst thou do such a deed for all the world?
EMILIA: The world's a huge thing; it is a great price for a small vice.
DESDEMONA: In troth, I think thou wouldst not.
EMILIA: In troth, I think I should; and undo't when I had done. Marry, I would not do such a thing for a joint-ring, nor for measures of lawn, nor gowns, petticoats, nor caps, nor any petty exhibition, but for all the whole world? Why, who would not make her husband a cuckold to make a monarch? I should venture purgatory for't.
DESDEMONA: Beshrew me if I would do such a wrong for the whole world.
EMILIA: Why, the wrong is but a wrong i' th'world; and having the world for your labor, 'tis a wrong in your own world, and you might quickly make it right.
DESDEMONA: I do not think there is any such woman.

In this dialogue we not only see and hear evidence of a radical difference of values, but we also observe a striking difference of character. Desdemona's innocence is underscored by her unwillingness to be unfaithful to her husband; her naiveté, by her inability to believe in any woman's infidelity. Emilia is willing to consider compromising her virtue. Her joking tone and bluntness also contrast with Desdemona's solemnity and inability to name directly what she is referring to: adultery.

And now listen to Iago working on Desdemona's father, Brabantio, to tell him about his daughter's elopement with Othello (Act I, Scene I):

IAGO: Zounds, sir y'are robbed! For shame. Put on your gown!
Your heart is burst, you have lost half your soul.
Even now, now, very now, an old black ram
Is tupping your white ewe. Arise, arise!
Awake the snorting citizens with the bell,
Or else the devil will make a grandsire of you.
. . .
I am one sir, that comes to tell you your daughter
And the moor are making the beast with two backs.

Iago's language reveals his coarseness; he crudely reduces sexual love to animal copulation. It also shows his ability to make things happen: he has infuriated Brabantio. The remainder of the scene shows the consequences of his speech, its power to inspire action. Iago is thus revealed as both an instigator and a man of crude sensibilities.

His language is cast in a similar mold in Act II, Scene I, when he tries to convince Roderigo, a rejected suitor of Desdemona, that Desdemona will tire of Othello and turn to someone else for sexual satisfaction. Notice how Iago's words stress the carnality of sex and reveal his violent imagination:

IAGO: . . . Her eye must be fed. And what delight
Shall she have to look on the devil? When the
Blood is made dull with the act of sport, there
Should be a game to inflame it and to give
Satiety a fresh appetite, loveliness in favor,
Sympathy in years, manners, and beauties; all
Which the moor is defective in. Now for want of
These required conveniences, her delicate tenderness will find
Itself abused, begin to heave the gorge, disrelish and
Abhor the moor. Very nature will instruct her in it
And compel her to some second choice. . . .

Othello's language later in the play reveals his decline from a courageous and confident leader to a jealous lover distracted to madness by Iago's insinuations about his wife's infidelity. The elegance and control, even the exaltation of his early speeches, give way to the crude degradation of his later remarks. Here is Othello in Act I, Scene II, responding to a search party out to find him:

OTHELLO: Hold your hands,
Both you of my inclining and the rest,
Were it my cue to fight, I should have known it
Without a prompter. Whither will you that I go
To answer this your charge?

The language of this speech is formal, stately, and controlled. It bespeaks a man in command of himself, one who assumes authority naturally and easily. His language in large part accounts for our sympathetic response to him, for our admiration, not only for his military exploits, but for his measure of control, poise, and equanimity.

By the middle of Act III, however, this view of Othello is no longer tenable. Othello is reduced by Iago to an incoherent babbler, to a man at odds with himself, one who has lost his equilibrium. In Act IV, Scene I, we see the Othello Iago has created by suggesting that Desdemona has been unchaste with Othello's lieutenant, Michael Cassio:

OTHELLO: Lie with her? Lie on her?—We say lie on her when they belie her—Lie with her! Zounds, that's fulsome. Handkerchief—confession—handkerchief—To confess, and be hanged for his labor—first to be hanged, and then to confess! I tremble at it . . . It is not words that shake me thus.—Pish! Noses, ears, and lips? Is't possible?—Confess?—Handkerchief?—O devil.

In the language of both Iago and Othello we see meaning enacted as well as expressed. The verbal dimension of their dialogue is reinforced by action, gesture, movement. We can observe in these brief excerpts and throughout the play not only how language reveals character, advances the action, and establishes the setting, but how it also makes things happen and in effect itself becomes action.

Subtext

To interpret characters and their objectives accurately, we frequently have to look beneath the surface of dialogue lines and investigate the *subtext*. Russian director and teacher Constantin Stanislavski considered the subtext "the inner essence," or the specific reason for a character's speaking any set of particular lines. Frequently in life and on stage, people and characters do not say specifically what they mean. For many reasons, they often prefer to hint or speak indirectly, hoping that the listener will grasp the meaning through implication, that is, by understanding the subtext. Of course, there is always a danger that the subtext will be missed or misunderstood. In the theater, actors help us derive the subtext through gesture, intonation, and other techniques. As Stanislavski said, "At the moment of performance the text is supplied by the playwright, and the subtext by the actor."

Consider the following lines of Lisa in Wendy Wasserstein's *Tender Offer* (which is included in Chapter Twenty-Nine):

LISA: . . . Talia Robbins told me she's much happier living without her father in the house. Her father used to come home late and go to sleep early.

PAUL: Lisa, stop it. Let's go.

LISA: I can't find my leg warmers.

PAUL: Forget your leg warmers.

LISA: Daddy.

PAUL: What is it?

LISA: I saw this show on television, I think it was WPIX Channel 11. Well, the father was crying about his daughter.

PAUL: Why was he crying? Was she sick?

LISA: No. She was at school. And he was at business. And he just missed her, so he started to cry.

PAUL: What was the name of this show?

LISA: I don't know. I came in in the middle.

What Lisa is trying to communicate to her father has little to do with the words she uses. She is angry with her father for missing her dance recital. When she mentions Talia Robbins, whose situation she cares little about at this moment, she is posing a veiled threat to her father, one she is too timid to make directly. The subtext of that line might be stated this way: "For all the attention you give me, you may as well never come home. At least I won't be so hurt and disappointed when you fail to keep a commitment to me." The father is tired and anxious to go home, and tries to ignore the subtext and his daughter's hurt feelings.

Lisa tries to delay their exit with a ploy—if we are sensitive to the subtext, we know that she has not misplaced her leg warmers. The single line of Lisa's with the one word *Daddy* can reveal great emotional depth, signaling Lisa's tenderness and love toward her father, as well as her hurt and exasperation with his inattentiveness. She wants him to know how she feels, but she is not comfortable telling him directly. Besides, she wishes he would be more attentive and figure it out for himself. She gives him hints and tries to make him feel guilty by fabricating a TV program, which she tries to authenticate by mentioning its channel. It is only through a careful consideration of the subtext of these lines that we are able to determine the depth of Lisa's emotions—her pain, frustration, desperation, and love and longing for her father.

Reading the subtext competently and confidently requires at least some understanding of a character. Early in a play we might miss or misinterpret the subtext because we are not yet sufficiently familiar with the character. However, as we move deeper into the play the subtext of the main characters becomes clearer. On second reading, we often discover an increased complexity in characters through a better understanding of the subtext. However, to grasp the implications of the subtext, we need to be active and fully attentive readers and viewers.

STAGING

By **staging** we have in mind the spectacle a play presents in performance, its visual detail. This includes such things as the positions of actors onstage (sometimes referred to as *blocking*), their nonverbal gestures and movements (also called *stage business*), the scenic background, the props and costumes, lighting, and sound effects.

Though often taken for granted, costumes can reveal the characters beneath them. In Ibsen's *A Doll House* (see Chapter Twenty-Seven), Nora changes costumes more than once. She appears by turns in ordinary clothing, in a multicolored shawl, in a dancing costume, and in a black shawl. Each costume change expresses a change in Nora's feelings.

Besides costume, any physical object that appears in a play has the potential to become an important dramatic symbol. The Christmas tree, which stands throughout Ibsen's *A Doll House,* is an ironic visual counterpart to the play's unfolding action.

More dramatic perhaps and more central to plot is the handkerchief in *Othello.* Having its own history, which we learn when Desdemona wipes Othello's brow, the handkerchief becomes a crucial dramatic object, one that offers Othello the "ocular proof" he requires to condemn Desdemona as an adulterer.

From costumes and objects, we turn to sound. Ibsen uses sound effectively in *A Doll House* when he asks for music to accompany Nora's frenzied dancing as she attempts to delay Torvald's discovery of Krogstad's letter. In this same scene Ibsen also uses sound to heighten suspense as he has Torvald open the mailbox off-stage: we hear but don't see the mailbox click open.

A playwright's stage directions will sometimes help us see and hear things such as these as we read. But with or without stage directions, we have to use our aural as well as our visual imagination. An increased imaginative alertness to the sights and sounds of a play, while no substitute for direct physical apprehension, can nonetheless help us approximate the experience of a dramatic performance. It can also enhance our appreciation of the dramatist's craftsmanship and increase our understanding of the play.

When we attend a play (and when we read one) the first thing we see is the stage set, the physical objects that suggest the world of the play. The stage set is usually indicated by the playwright, though the degree of detail and specificity of this rendering vary from one playwright to another, and from one literary period to another. Consider the stage directions for *setting* that begin *The Rising of the Moon:*

Scene: *Side of a quay in a seaport town. Some posts and chains. A large barrel. Enter three policemen. Moonlight.*

Clearly this is a simple and highly generalized set. We are given just a few basic objects and some moonlight, nothing more. Yet the objects, simple as they are, establish the elemental world of the play. It will be a play, this set suggests, and a world, in which a rich collection of "things" is not important. Far more important is a basic human conflict, seen more clearly and represented more intensely in a sparse, uncluttered setting. The sets for this play leave room for directors and stage managers to decide just how to represent the world called for. There is less room for such decisions, however, in plays with very explicit directions for stage sets.

One last point about setting. Although one-act plays typically employ a single stage set, multi-act dramas change sets, sometimes many times. (*Death of a Salesman,* found later in this book, is an example.) In longer plays such as these, it is important to notice such changes of scene and setting, and to consider what the varied sets contribute to our experience and understanding of the play.

The setting of a play is just one element of its staging, or the spectacle a play presents in performance. Staging in general, as we have said, refers to all the visual detail of a play, from the positions of actors onstage (blocking); to their postures, gestures, and even facial expressions (stage business); the scenery, props, costumes; the lighting, music, sound effects. Though some of these many details may be called for specifically in the script, decisions about staging are often left to the play's director.

We can illustrate these aspects of staging by considering briefly, once again, *The Rising of the Moon*. In this play, the first thing we might notice about the characters is their physical appearance, especially their dress. The policemen should be distinguishable from their sergeant, perhaps by an emblem or badge the superior officer wears. The greater visual distinction, of course, is that between the sergeant and the ragged man. Very likely in casting these roles, the director would make the sergeant the bigger, stronger, better fed of the two. On physical appearance alone most likely, then, our sympathy will lie with the wanted man.

The props include the placards that the two policemen are putting up. These posters are important as much for what they omit as for what they contain. They omit, for example, a picture of the man being sought; and they also omit the stories about the man's criminal exploits. Like the policemen who post them, the placards are matter-of-fact. The barrel on which they paste one of the placards is the central prop of the play. Its importance stems from the two crucial actions in which it is involved—the sergeant sits on it back-to-back with the man he seeks; and the wanted man hides behind it upon the return of the two policemen. Because of its dramatic importance, the barrel would most likely be placed center stage. Finally, and also important, are the man's hat and wig—his simple disguise—which the sergeant hides behind his back while dismissing the two policemen.

The positions of the characters onstage, as well as their postures and gestures, are not always specifically indicated in the stage directions and script. Occasionally they are, however, as when it is specified the sergeant "crosses the stage to right and looks down steps." The sergeant is also specifically directed to grasp the man's shoulder and shove him. Later, the sergeant and the ragged man echo each other's actions visually when they point to the water. Such movements and gestures are important not only because they advance the plot, but also because they direct us to the play's central concerns and imply aspects of its meaning. We noted earlier how the pointing reinforces the connection between the sergeant and the man established in the possibility of each of them being in the other's situation. And we also mentioned the irony of their sitting together in close proximity. But we should also note the related irony of the sergeant's holding in his grasp the man he waits for without being aware of whom he holds.

The lighting of the play is important as well, not only for the atmosphere it creates, but also for what it implies about the changing fortunes of the "big" and "small." The man is quite explicit about the latter of these. But the moonlit atmosphere is vaguer, less easy to pin down. Perhaps we can say simply that the quality of the lighting indicated by "moonlight" suggests literally a shadowy light from a distance. Its effect should be to increase the play's suspense and drama. Its symbolic force perhaps extends also to its being an unusual kind of light that is at its most intense only a small portion of the time (as is the sergeant's idealism and his more sympathetic nature).

Sound, too, is significant. There is the sound of the policemen's talk as they return, which is accentuated by the sparseness of the setting and by the time—late at night. There is the sound of a boat being rowed—heard by both the man and the sergeant—a sound that precipitates the play's climax. There is also the whistle signal the man's friends use as they approach the quay. And there is the sound of singing, which functions both to advance the plot and to highlight one of the central issues of the play. Notice that the songs are ballads about Irish nationalist heroes. And remember, too, how when the ballad-singer omits a verse from one ballad, the sergeant supplies it, indicating still another way in which he, the wanted man, and the common people are joined together.

A playwright's stage directions will sometimes help us see and hear things such as these as we read. But with or without stage directions, we need to use our aural as well as our visual imaginations. An increased imaginative alertness to the sights and sounds of a play, while no substitute for direct physical apprehension, can nonetheless help us approximate the experience of a dramatic performance. It can also enhance our appreciation of the dramatist's craftsmanship and increase our understanding of the play.

SYMBOLISM AND IRONY

In our discussion of the staging of *The Rising of the Moon,* and in our observations about its dialogue and conflict, we touched briefly and implicitly on two additional aspects of drama: symbolism and irony. A **symbol** can be defined simply as any object or action that means more than itself; it represents something beyond its literal self. Objects, actions, clothing, gestures, dialogue—all may have symbolic meaning. A rose, for example, might represent beauty, love, or transience (or all three at once). A tree might represent a family's roots and branches. A soaring bird might stand for freedom. Light—depending on its quality—might symbolize hope or knowledge or mystery or life. These symbolic associations, however, are not necessary or automatic, since the meaning of any symbol is controlled by its context and function in a particular dramatic scene, and is rather open-ended, too.

How, then, do we know if a particular detail is symbolic? How do we decide whether to leap beyond the literal action or dialogue into a symbolic interpretation? There is no simple rule for this. Like any interpretive connection we make in reading, the decision to view something as symbolic depends partly on our skill in reading and partly on whether the dramatic context invites and rewards a symbolic interpretation. The following questions can be used to guide your thinking about literary symbols:

1. Is the object, action, gesture, or dialogue important to the play? Is it described in detail? Does it occur more than once, or does it occur at a climactic or significant moment in the play?
2. Does the play seem to warrant our granting its details more significance than their immediate literal meaning? Why?
3. Does a symbolic interpretation make sense? Does it account for the literal details without either ignoring or distorting them? Does it add to our understanding?

There will be occasions when we are uncertain whether or not a particular object, action, or utterance is symbolic. And there will be times when, though we are fairly confident that we are dealing with a symbol, we are not confident about just what it represents. Interpretation is an art, not a science. Interpretive uncertainty reflects the complexity and variability with which dramatists use symbols and the fact that most complex symbols resist definitive explanation (as does life itself).

Consider, for example, the symbolic force of the revolutionary songs that the ballad-singer sings in *The Rising of the Moon.* At the end of the play he sings a song about "The Rising of the Moon." What does the moon's rising stand for in the context of the play? Consider also the symbolic importance of the scene in which the sergeant and the ballad-singer sit back-to-back on the barrel, looking out in opposite directions. To what extent does this action symbolize their differences or similarities of attitude, belief, and situation? And when they jump together off the barrel, can this be construed as a symbolic representation of their decision to overlook their differences?

Irony

Irony is not so much an element of a dramatic text as a pervasive quality in it. Irony may appear in plays in three basic ways: in their language, in their incidents, or in their point of view. In whatever forms it emerges, **irony** almost always arises from a contrast or discrepancy between what is said and what is meant, or between what happens and what has been expected to happen.

Simple verbal irony comes from saying the opposite of what is meant. When someone says, "That was a brilliant remark," and we know that it was anything but brilliant, we feel and understand the speaker's ironic intention. In such a relatively simple instance there is usually no problem in perceiving the irony. In more complex situations, however, the identification of an action or a remark as ironic can be much more difficult. At the end of *The Rising of the Moon,* after the sergeant has let the ballad-singer escape, he asks himself whether he was a fool for doing so. The sergeant's question is subtly ironic, since once we accept his action and understand the sympathy that motivates it, we do not expect him to express such doubts concerning it. His words seem to indicate the opposite of what they actually say, with our understanding being that he is not a fool at all.

Another type of irony is *irony of circumstance* (sometimes called *irony of situation*), in which a playwright creates a discrepancy between what characters think is the case and what actually is the case. You will find examples of irony of circumstance in many of the plays in this book, including *Othello, A Doll House,* and *Trifles.* Irony of circumstance appears forcefully in *The Rising of the Moon,* since what we expect to happen is actually not what happens at all; the opposite, in fact, is what occurs. It appears, initially, that the sergeant is out to capture the fugitive, but he abandons his opportunity to do so. It appears that the fugitive is dangerous and will act to protect himself, but instead he persuades through his speech and his song. And it appears that these two men have really nothing in common, but it turns out that they have very much in common, indeed, most importantly, their shared sense of idealism. In these and other ways, the action of the play creates ironic situations that form the heart of its dramatic action.

The final type of irony found in plays is called dramatic irony. *Dramatic irony* involves a discrepancy between what characters know and what readers or viewers know. Playwrights often let us know things that their characters do not. We know, for example, that the ballad-singer is the man the sergeant seeks even though for a while the sergeant himself does not know it. And we know that the ballad-singer is hiding behind a barrel nearby while the sergeant dismisses his two police assistants. Our ironic knowledge of these things increases our pleasure in the play's situation and action. And our awareness of our knowledge enhances our appreciation of the dramatist's skill.

When a dramatist's work is pervaded by ironies in these various forms, we may characterize such pervasiveness as an ironic point of view. The persistent use of irony we may call an ironic vision. A play like Sophocles' *Oedipus the King* is informed by an ironic vision, as is Sophocles' work overall. In such plays, the dramatist's ironic vision infuses the plot, pervades the dialogue, and surfaces repeatedly in its other dramatic elements.

THEME

From experiencing a play and examining the various elements of a play we derive a sense of its significance and meaning. We use the word **theme** to designate the main idea or point of a play stated as a generalization. Because formulating the theme of a play involves abstracting from it a generalizable idea, the notion of theme inevitably moves away from the very details of character and action that give the play its life. This is not to suggest that it is not rewarding or useful to attempt to identify a central idea or set of ideas from plays, but only that we should be aware of the limitations of our doing so.

First, we should distinguish the ideas that may appear *in* a play from the idea *of* a play. The meaning of a play—its central, governing, or animating idea—is rarely identifiable as an explicit social, political, or philosophical idea manifest in the dialogue. Rather, a play's idea or meaning is almost always implicit, bound up with and derivable from the play's whole structure, character interactions, dialogue, and staging. One of the dangers of reading plays without attending sufficiently to their theatrical dimensions is that we may overgeneralize and reduce their meaning to a single, overly simplified idea. Because the theme of a play grows out of the relationships among its concrete details, any statement of it that omits significant aspects of a play's dramatic elements will inevitably represent too severe a limitation and even a distortion of the play's meaning. Any statement of theme inevitably only approximates a play's meaning rather than fully characterizing or embodying it, so we need to be careful. And then, even when we speak of multiple themes (as we should, since plays often suggest a multiplicity of ideas), we are still concerned only with one aspect of meaning—the intellectual. As we have always suggested, a play's meaning (or the meaning of any literary work) encompasses emotional apprehension as well as intellectual comprehension.

As readers or viewers of drama, we tend to reach for theme as a way of organizing our responses to a play, of coming to terms with what it implies about how human beings live. At times we emphasize our personal responses and emotional reactions to what the play dramatizes. Or we seize on an intellectual response based on observations of its action and on inferences drawn from connections we establish from among its details. At times we look at what the play is; at times we feel what the play does. Both are important aspects of its meaning. For the meaning of any play is ultimately more than any statement of theme, any series of words and sentences that we employ to describe it. Our experience, our moment-by-moment engagement with the play on the stage or on the page constitutes its meaning for us.

Beyond this, it is not only our intellectual comprehension and emotional apprehension of the play as we read or watch it—we also remember the play after seeing or reading it. In this remembering, we remake it, reconstruct it, and often "see" aspects of it we overlooked during our moment-by-moment encounter. A play's meaning, then, is not always something readily and completely available to us as we complete our encounter with it. We can return to a play for second and subsequent encounters, and understand it differently after repeated readings or viewings. A play's meaning for us, then, is almost always provisional, tentative, temporary. Its meaning changes as we change. Its meaning includes its way of affecting us, not once and for all, but again and again in different ways.

Again, we should certainly avoid thinking of theme as somehow hidden in the dialogue for us to ferret out. And we should be aware that to reduce the play's thought to a satisfactorily inclusive statement of theme is no easy matter. At best such statements offer approximations of any play's meaning, which at best can and do clarify and illuminate our experience of drama and of life. At worst, on the other hand, statements of theme may oversimplify plays, distorting their significance and impoverishing our experience.

As far as possible, then, as we discuss the thought of a play in terms of its general significance, in terms of its implied idea(s), as we explore its central issues and speculate about its major concerns, we do so without insisting that it possesses a single, definitive, absolute message. Let us briefly consider the thought and theme of *The Rising of the Moon.*

First, it is a political play, taking as its context the political turmoil of a beleaguered Irish populace. The historical details of the political situation are not explicitly rendered, largely because they would have been familiar to Lady Gregory's audience. But they are alluded to in references to "Granuaile," who appears to be an Irish revolutionary hero. Moreover, we are meant to side with the man who fights for the cause of Granuaile, and to see the justice of that cause and the hope of its ultimate triumph over the social and political status quo. According to the wanted man (and the play overall), a social revolution is in the making. The play alludes to a spirit of optimistic idealism and a corresponding sense that injustice and inequity will not always prevail.

This political idea is closely associated with the crisis of conscience the sergeant undergoes. His decision to trust his instinctive sympathy for the man and his cause and his impulse to act in accordance with his reawakened youthful idealism rather than to capture the criminal are powerfully dramatized. Even though the play ends with a question, an answer is clearly implied. When the sergeant asks, "Am I as great a fool as I think I am?" his question directs us to consider the theme or meaning of the play not merely as an abstract intellectual idea but as a living moment of decision. Our answers to his question may vary, though one that seems endorsed by the many interrelated details and elements of the play is, "No, you're not a fool at all. In fact, you're a good man, who's trying to do what you believe is right."

As we think back to the sergeant and his crisis of conscience, to the wanted man and his ballads about Ireland, to his friends and their effort to rescue him, we begin to realize the meaning of the play. Our consideration of its personal, human, and social issues, and our memory of its effect on us, we may say constitute its theme.

CHAPTER TWENTY-FOUR

Writing about Drama

REASONS FOR WRITING ABOUT DRAMA

Why write about drama? One reason is to find out what you think about a play that interests you. You might make notes for yourself in your journal. Another reason is to induce yourself to read more carefully a play that you like. You may write about a work of drama because it engages you and you wish to discuss its implied ideas and values. Finally, you may of course be required to write about a drama as a course assignment.

Whatever your reasons for writing about drama, a number of things happen when you do. First, you read more attentively, noticing things you might overlook in a more casual reading. Second, since writing stimulates thinking, when you write about drama you find yourself thinking more about what a particular work means and why you respond to it as you do. This focused thinking often has the effect of making a play more meaningful to you.

INFORMAL WAYS OF WRITING ABOUT DRAMA

When you write about a play, you may write for yourself or you may write for others. Writing for yourself, to discover what you think, often takes casual forms such as annotation and freewriting. These less formal kinds of writing are useful for helping you focus. They are helpful in studying for tests about drama. They can also serve as preliminary forms of writing when you write more formal essays and papers.

Annotation

When you annotate a text, you make notes in the margins or at the top and bottom of pages. Annotations can also be made within the text, as underlined words, circled phrases, or bracketed sentences or paragraphs. Annotations may also assume the form of arrows, question marks, and various other marks.

Annotating a literary work offers a convenient and relatively painless way to begin writing about it. Annotating can get you started zeroing in on what you think interesting or important. You can also annotate to signal details that puzzle or disconcert you.

Your markings serve to focus your attention and clarify your understanding of a play. Your annotations can save you time in rereading or studying a work. And they can also be used when you write a more formal paper.

Annotations for the following excerpt from *The Tragedy of Othello* illustrate the process.

The following excerpt from *Othello* is Act I, Scene ii. In the previous scene, Iago, an officer in Othello's army, puts in motion a plan to enact revenge on Othello. In that scene, Iago claims to be resentful because Othello has overlooked him and chose Cassio as his lieutenant. Iago and his accomplice Roderigo wake the senator Brabantio to tell him that his daughter, Desdemona, is with Othello. Because Othello is a moor of dark complexion and because this union does not have Brabantio's acceptance, Iago hopes that this information will enrage Brabantio and that Brabantio will enact his revenge on Othello. As this scene opens, Iago has a much different attitude towards Othello because Othello is present. Thus, Iago demonstrates that he is a deceitful character, having proclaimed "I am not what I am" in the previous scene.

Scene II [A street.]

Enter OTHELLO, IAGO, ATTENDANTS *with torches.*

IAGO: Though in the trade of war I have slain men,
Yet do I hold it very stuff° o' th' conscience
To do no contrived murder. I lack iniquity
Sometime to do me service. Nine or ten times
I had thought t' have yerked° him here, under the ribs.

Ironic that Iago speaks of having a conscience.

OTHELLO: 'Tis better as it is.
IAGO: Nay, but he prated,
And spoke such scurvy and provoking terms
Against your honor, that with the little godliness I have
I did full hard forbear him. But I pray you, sir,
Are you fast married? Be assured of this,
That the magnifico° is much beloved,
And hath in his effect a voice potential
As double as the Duke's.° He will divorce you,
Or put upon you what restraint or grievance
The law, with all his might to enforce it on,
Will give him cable.°

Iago is lying. He doesn't care about Othello's honor.

Why does Iago care if he is trying to get Othello in trouble?

OTHELLO: Let him do his spite.

My services which I have done the Signiory°
Shall out-tongue his complaints. 'Tis yet to know°—
Which when I know that boasting is an honor
I shall promulgate—I fetch my life and being
From men of royal siege,° and my demerits°
May speak unbonneted to as proud a fortune
As this that I have reached.° For know, Iago,
But that I love the gentle Desdemona,
I would not my unhousèd° free condition
Put into circumscription and confine
For the seas' worth. But look, what lights come yond?

Duke, Signiory, royal siege—how much authority does Othello have?

Othello is sincere about his emotion.

Enter CASSIO, *with* [OFFICERS *and*] *torches.*

IAGO: Those are the raisèd father and his friends.
You were best go in.

Iago thinks this is Brabantio.

OTHELLO: Not I. I must be found.
My parts, my title, and my perfect soul°
Shall manifest me rightly. Is it they?
IAGO: By Janus, I think no.
OTHELLO: The servants of the Duke? And my lieutenant?
The goodness of the night upon you, friends.
What is the news?

Othello believes his reputation and soul shall serve to demonstrate him well. Compare to deceptive Iago.

CASSIO: The Duke does greet you, general;
And he requires your haste-posthaste appearance
Even on the instant.
OTHELLO: What is the matter, think you?
CASSIO: Something from Cyprus, as I may divine.
It is a business of some heat. The galleys
Have sent a dozen sequent° messengers
This very night at one another's heels,
And many of the consuls, raised and met,
Are at the Duke's already. You have been hotly called for.
When, being not at your lodging to be found,
The Senate hath sent about three several° quests
To search you out.

A war?

OTHELLO: 'Tis well I am found by you.
I will but spend a word here in the house,
And go with you. [*Exit.*]
CASSIO: Ancient, what makes he here?

Ancient? How old is Iago?

IAGO: Faith, he tonight hath boarded a land carack.°
If it prove lawful prize, he's made forever.
CASSIO: I do not understand.
IAGO: He's married.
CASSIO: To who?

Lawful prize? How cynical is Iago about Othello's relationship to Desdamona?

Iago isn't giving Cassio a straight answer.

[*Enter* OTHELLO.]

IAGO: Marry,° to—Come captain, will you go?
OTHELLO: Have with you.
CASSIO: Here comes another troop to seek for you.

Enter BRABANTIO, RODERIGO, *with* OFFICERS *and torches.*

IAGO: It is Brabantio. General, be advised. — *General—Othello's rank.*
He comes to bad intent.
OTHELLO: Holla! Stand there!
RODERIGO: Signior, it is the Moor.
BRABANTIO: Down with him, thief! — *Thief—Brabantio is upset.*
IAGO: You, Roderigo? Come, sir, I am for you.
OTHELLO: Keep up your bright swords, for the dew will rust them.
Good signior, you shall more command with years — *Othello is respectful of Brabantio's rank.*
Than with your weapons.
BRABANTIO: O thou foul thief, where hast thou stowed my daughter?
Damned as thou art, thou hast enchanted her! — *Is he accusing Othello of being a sorcerer?*
For I'll refer me to all things of sense,°
If she in chains of magic were not bound, — *How much does Brabantio know of Othello's religion?*
Whether a maid so tender, fair, and happy,
So opposite to marriage that she shunned
The wealthy, curlèd darlings of our nation,
Would ever have, t'incur a general mock,°
Run from her guardage to the sooty bosom
Of such a thing as thou—to fear, not to delight. — *A thing?! Strong words.*

[. . .]

Double-Column Notebook

Another way of writing for yourself, informally, is to use the double-column notebook. To create a double-column notebook, divide a page in half vertically (or open a notebook so that you face two blank pages side by side). On one side *take* notes, summarizing the scene's situation, action, and ideas. On the other side, the responding side, *make* notes, recording your thinking about what you summarized: ask questions; speculate; make connections.

Here is an example of a double-column notebook for the excerpt from the *Othello* excerpt that was annotated above. Notice how the entries in the double-column notebook are more detailed and written in a more formal style than the annotations.

Summary and Observations	**Responses and Reactions**
Iago is deceitful. He doesn't believe that Othello loves Desdemona, and he is duplicitous in his actions. Iago lies to Othello about how he defends Othello's honor.	Iago is evil and cynical. He flatters his superior to get ahead. Is there anything redeeming about him?
Othello is respectful towards Brabantio He also seems sincere in his love of	Othello seems righteous. He could draw swords against Brabantio, but he would

Desdemona. He knows his importance, and he relies on that to protect him from those who would impugn his character. He must be an important general if the Duke seeks his counsel.	rather talk to him. This respect is admirable.
Brabantio is accusatory and racist. He does not listen to Othello and accuses him of being a sorcerer. He does not entertain the notion that his daughter would ever really love Othello.	Brabantio is certainly misguided. Is he a protective father, a racist, or some combination? How often does Othello have to contend with attacks like this?

FORMAL WAYS OF WRITING ABOUT DRAMA

In writing an analytical essay about a play or a scene from a play, your goal is to explain how one or more elements in the work or the scene contribute to its overall meaning. You might analyze the dialogue in a scene from Ibsen's *A Doll House.* Your goal would be to explain what the verbal exchanges between characters contribute to the play's meaning and to its effect on the audience. You might analyze the imagery of Sophocles' *Oedipus the King* or Shakespeare's *Othello* to see what that imagery suggests about a character's perspective or the author's attitude toward the characters or the action.

In addition to analyzing these and other dramatic elements in a play, you might also compare two plays or scenes, perhaps by focusing on their use of stage directions, lighting, or other theatrical effects. Or, instead of focusing on literary elements per se, you might write to see how a particular critical perspective (see Chapter Thirty-One) illuminates a play. For example, you might consider the ways reader response criticism or new historicism contributes to your understanding of Hansberry's *A Raisin in the Sun.*

The following student papers analyze significant aspects of *Othello* and *Oedipus the King.* The first writer examines Iago's motives as he plots against Othello. The second and third writers analyze *Oedipus'* destiny and in the process come to opposite conclusions about this tragic hero.

Student Paper

Aaron Zook
Professor Stameshkin
English 1102
February 16, 2006

Iago: Conscious and Unconscious Motivations in Shakespeare's *Othello*

After a first reading of *Othello,* we might be tempted to characterize Iago as the ultimate villain; a master manipulator, traitor, and murderer. The man does not hesitate to stab his sidekick, his wife, or anyone who stands in his way. However, Shakespeare's antagonists are remarkable for their depth and complexity. In many cases, these "villains" have suffered real and ongoing slights and humiliations, often due to a trick of birth (such as Edmund's illegitimacy in *King Lear,* or Richard's deformity in *Richard III*), which to some extent motivates their cruel or antisocial behavior. Their accomplices may act out of simple greed, hunger for power, or violent temperament, but the most fascinating villains—Iago among them—appear to be personally and psychologically motivated. It is the extent to which Iago permits his suffering to embitter him and defeat his essential humanity that pushes him beyond our sympathy and into acts of evil.

Very early in the play, Iago attributes his hatred for Othello to jealousy and injured pride: "... it is thought that twixt my sheets/ He's done my office" (I.iii.388–39). He admits, however, that he has no evidence for this, and the supposed vengeance which he wreaks seems far too sophisticated, convoluted, and potentially dangerous to himself to have emerged from such an imagined slight. Why plot to destroy the lives of no fewer than four people (Othello, Desdemona, Cassio, and Roderigo) if the motive is revenge for cuckolding?

In the play's first scene, Iago provides a somewhat credible reason for the inclusion of Cassio in his schemes; he relates to Roderigo his resentment at having been passed over as Othello's lieutenant (I.i.9-34). As a veteran of several wars, senior among Othello's officers, he had expected, and felt he deserved, the promotion; Cassio, on the other hand, received the advancement, in Iago's view, because of his personal friendship with the general: "Preferment goes by letter and affection" (I.i.37). This is all the more galling to Iago due to Cassio's inexperience, of which he says "mere prattle without practice/Is all his soldiership" (I.i.27-28).

It is worth noting, however that this seemingly simple explanation is offered to the credulous Roderigo, to whom Iago would certainly not confide his suspicions, however baseless, of his wife's infidelity with Othello (or, possibly, Cassio: "... I fear Cassio with my nightcap too," II.i.308). Though he clearly views Roderigo with contempt, and considers him expendable, this does not account for Iago's willingness to destroy Desdemona, for whom he expresses no personal dislike throughout the play. At one point or another, he expresses admiration of all three of his active targets. Cassio is called "a proper man," (I.iii.393), and Othello receives this offhanded praise:

> The moor, howbeit that I endure him not,
> Is of a constant, loving, noble nature,
> And I dare think he'll prove to Desdemona
> A most dear husband. (II.i.289–292)

Perhaps most startlingly, in the same speech he admits of Desdemona, "I do love her too" (II.i.292), though he qualifies the statement by adding this regard is due partly to lust (II.i.293–294) and partly to her potential role in ruining her husband (II.i.295–303). In fact, the only character for whom he voices conditionless loathing is Roderigo, his supposed accomplice. Is Iago such a monster that he commits his crimes for mere sport, without any regard for human life?

As a consummate liar and trickster, Iago's every statement, even those made directly to the audience, must be viewed with skepticism. Further, he displays such enjoyment of the act of villainy– "... to plume up [his] will/in double knavery"–that a perverse pursuit of entertainment might plausibly justify all of his behavior, in the absence of any rationalization (I.iii.394–395). Thus one might conclude that he represents an essentially Satanic character in the play, whose sole function is to sow chaos and discord and to lead Othello hopelessly down a path of murder and self-destruction; indeed, once his treachery has been discovered, Othello refers to Iago, with good reason, as a "demi-devil" (V.ii.309).

Yet Iago, though utterly remorseless and cruel, is not a mere monster; his character possesses such human attributes as doubt. In Act I, he claims to know his own worth:, "I know my price; I am worth no worse a place" (I.i,12); but in Act V, he contradicts himself, expressing a very personal resentment and jealousy towards Cassio:

> ... If Cassio do remain,
> He hath a daily beauty in his life
> That makes me ugly. (V.1 II. 18–20)

As in his earlier admission of admiration for Desdemona (II.i.292), he quickly adds a selfish, practical explanation— "... the Moor/May unfold me to him," —which does not entirely persuade (V.i.20–21). Could it be that Iago, contrary to all of his admitted motives, acts not so much out of hatred for others as from self-disgust—or even a rejection of life itself?

Support for this conclusion can be drawn from a fascinating exchange between Iago and Desdemona in Act II. In the first part of their dialogue, he tells her,

> There's none so foul and foolish thereunto,
> But does foul pranks which fair and wise ones do.
> (II.i.142–143)

Later, he describes a woman of impeccable virtue, wisdom, and fidelity, only to conclude that she will merely "suckle fools and chronicle small beer" (I.i.148–158, 160). This suggests that Iago can see no difference between virtue and degradation; he reasons that, as all life leads to death, all youth leads to decrepitude, and all beauty to ugliness. By this rationale, what does it matter what a person does, since everything leads to nothingness?

This, in turn, suggests a curious explanation for his willingness—even eagerness—to destroy Desdemona. He seems genuinely to admire her; he is unable, even in seeming jest, to directly insult or criticize her, instead referring to an abstract "she." When describing the lady of virtue—who could easily be regarded as Desdemona herself—he gets carried away with the image, until interrupted—at which point, he falls back into familiar habit and sabotages the image (II.i.151–163). In this respect, Iago seems not so much a demonic figure as all-too-human sociopath; rather than watch as the world destroys beauty and happiness, he decides to take it upon himself.

Work Cited

Shakespeare, William. *Othello, the Moor of Venice. Literature: Approaches to Fiction, Poetry, and Drama.* Ed. Robert DiYanni. New York: McGraw-Hill, 2004, 1013–1098.

Two Papers on Oedipus the King

The two papers that follow were both written for a first-year humanities course. Each student writer makes a different claim about the issue of fate and freedom in Sophocles' play. Although the students' arguments differ, each of them does a very good job in making his or her case and supporting it.

Laura Zaccone
Cultural Foundations I
Y02.0101-17
Essay #2
10-31-02

Fate vs. Free Will in *Oedipus the King*

In Sophocles' play, *Oedipus the King,* the concept of fate versus free will is a pivotal theme. The main character, Oedipus, is tragically destined to kill his father and marry his mother. Although Oedipus flees to escape this fate, he runs directly into it. He has been predestined to live this curse, and fleeing it is futile. His inevitable fate ultimately catches up with him regardless of the great lengths he goes to avoid it. Nevertheless, Oedipus' actions in pursuit of the prophecy's truth are of his own volition.

When Oedipus was an infant, his parents, King Laïos and Queen Iocastê, fearing the prophecies of Apollo, ordered a shepherd to kill their son. The shepherd spared the infant's life and gave Oedipus to a Corinthian messenger, who in turn handed him over to the king and queen of Corinth. King Polybos and Queen Meropê raised Oedipus as their own son. When Oedipus hears of his fate, he leaves Corinth to escape the prophecy. While on his journey, he kills King Laïos and eventually reaches Thebes, where he marries Iocastê. In his attempt to elude his destiny, he only brings himself directly to it. The reader can only assume that Oedipus' fate has been inescapably set. Any attempts to escape that end would only be in vain.

According to Robert Fagles, "The plot of the play consists not of the actions which Oedipus was 'fated' to perform; the plot of the play consists of his discovery that he has already fulfilled the prediction. And this discovery is entirely due to his action" (Fagles 149). The play is not about Oedipus' destiny, per se. Actually, the play is based on the decisions that Oedipus makes that lead him to discover the truth. These choices are made solely by his free will.

In the beginning of the play, Oedipus sends Creon to the oracle of Apollo to find a solution to the plagues that have been afflicted on Thebes. The oracle tells Creon that the city will not be free until Laïos' murder is avenged. Learning of this decree, Oedipus embarks on a journey in search of Laïos' murderer, determined to punish the culprit. In his quest, Oedipus is pursuing a murderer who, ultimately, is none other than himself. While it is Oedipus' fate to commit Laïos' murder, thoroughly investigating it is solely his decision. In this quest, Oedipus is paving the way for his own destruction.

Oedipus is a man who takes the initiative. Although Oedipus has the choice to take action or not, he is not the type to do nothing as his city is being destroyed. He is vehemently set on discovering Laïos' murderer: "I solemnly forbid the people of this country,/ Where power and throne are mine, ever to receive that man/ Or speak to him, no matter who he is [. . .]/[. . .]/ I decree that he be driven from every house" (1.20–22, 24). Oedipus is determined to avenge Laïos' murder, regardless of the criminal's identity. He explicitly states that he will make no exceptions for those close to him. He is resolute and persistent—qualities which lead him to uncover the truth of his identity.

It is Oedipus' decision to summon Teiresias for his insight. Although Teiresias knows the truth, he is reluctant to reveal it to Oedipus, fearing the repercussions. Teiresias assures Oedipus that withholding his knowledge is for Oedipus' own good, saying, "Let me go home. Bear your own fate, and I'll/ Bear mine. It is better so: trust what I say" (1.105–106). Although Oedipus has been warned, he is adamant in his mission. Oedipus provokes Teiresias until he blurts out that Oedipus is the murderer of Laïos. Even here, Oedipus has the option of taking Teiresias' advice to leave the truth unrevealed. Oedipus is so emphatic that he continuously insults him until Teiresias angrily blurts out the truth. There is no compelling force that makes Oedipus so persistent. It is his independent decision to provoke Teiresias into revealing the mystery.

Even when Oedipus begins to suspect that he is responsible for Laïos' murder, he does not cease his pursuit. He follows through just as passionately as he had previously. When Iocastê tells Oedipus that Laïos was killed at a place "where three roads meet", Oedipus begins to come to the realization that he is the murderer. Oedipus only presses Iocastê for more information about Laïos' murderer. He disregards the probability of his guilt and is not in the least bit discouraged from uncovering the truth. Oedipus would rather learn that he is accountable for the murder than be forced to speculate about it.

When Oedipus is told that Polybos and Meropê were not his birth parents, he sends for the shepherd who gave him away as an infant. When Iocastê realizes that Oedipus is the child that she and Laïos sent away to be killed, she pleads with Oedipus to cease his search for his biological parents, attempting to shield him from the cruel truth. Oedipus, however, refuses, saying, "How can you say that,/ When the clues to my true birth are in my hands?" (3.138–139). The shepherd, like Teiresias, is unwilling to reveal his knowledge to Oedipus. Oedipus threatens to torture the shepherd if he does not disclose who gave him the infant. Intimidated by Oedipus, the shepherd affirms that Laïos gave the infant to him.

With that, Oedipus realizes the truth of the prophecy and drives pins through his eyes, blinding himself. This act is separate from the prophecies of Apollo, and the choice was made solely by Oedipus. Oedipus states, "Children, the god was Apollo/He brought my sick, sick fate upon me./ But the blinding hand was my own" (Exodos 11–3). He initially contemplates suicide, but eventually decides to take his sight rather than his life. Even if Oedipus had chosen to take his life, fate would not have deterred him as it had when he fled Corinth. Oedipus independently chooses to blind himself, although he has the freedom to react in any other way without intervention from higher authorities.

Throughout the play, several characters discourage Oedipus from his search for both Laïos' murderer and his biological parents. Teiresias and the shepherd initially withhold the truth from Oedipus for his own good. It is only when they are threatened or provoked that they tell him. Iocastê goes into a rage, pleading with Oedipus not to search for his biological parents, trying to spare him the anguish. Despite his warnings and pleas, Oedipus is unyielding. Although he could go on living happily as he is, he yearns for the truth.

In conclusion, it is not fate that leads Oedipus to uncover the truth of the prophecy. It is the inherent determination and strong will possessed by Oedipus that lead him to his discovery. His nature impels him to search harder and deeper until the truth is uncovered. Although it is the inescapable fate of Oedipus that causes him to fulfill the prophecy, it is by his own free will that he comes to the realization that he has done so.

Jon Geeting
Professor DiYanni
Cultural Foundations I
October 30, 2002

Oedipus' Destiny

A prominent question in Sophocles' *Oedipus the King* is whether or not Oedipus is to blame for fulfilling the prophesy put over his head by the oracle, and if it would have been possible for him to correct the situation. The oracle predicted that Oedipus, not yet the king of Thebes, would murder his father and marry his mother. While a reader of the famous play surely knows that this prophecy comes true, it is debatable as to whether or not Oedipus had any degree of control over his fate. Some would hold that Oedipus, having complete control over his actions, rightfully assumes full responsibility for his fate. Others would say that Oedipus knew of the prophecy and took precautions to see that it would not become realized, only to have his preventative actions injure him in the end—by no fault of his own. While it is unlikely that a definitive answer will ever arise from this debate, it is possible to gain further insight into its complexity by observing key actions taken by Oedipus throughout the play.

One major idea surrounding this topic is that Oedipus knows of the prophecy and attempts to pursue a course of action that will prevent it from being enacted. Oedipus flees Corinth, a place where he holds high status, and opts for the life of a peasant in order to avoid a horrible fate. Since he was only a baby when he was abandoned by his real parents, it would be highly impossible for him to know that Polybos and Meropê were not his biological parents. It follows that when he heard of the oracle's prediction, he would steer clear of killing Polybos and marrying Meropê. As far as Oedipus knew, these were his real parents and any events concerning the prophecy would involve them. This notion prompted him to run away. This is a strong point in favor of Oedipus' innocence, and is relatively indisputable. In this situation, however, Oedipus can be blamed for being weak-willed. His first reaction being to flee from his parents demonstrates his lack of trust in his own will-power and sends the message that had he stayed, he clearly would have been unable to prevent himself from acting out his fate. Had he been stronger-willed, he would have trusted himself to remain in Corinth with his adopted parents and would have simply resolved not to kill his father or lie with his mother for any reason whatsoever. This would certainly have been a more definitive plan than fleeing. Another case against Oedipus is that, knowing that the prophecy involved his killing of another person, he should have simply abstained from killing anyone so as not to make any mistakes. If he did not kill anyone, then he could be absolutely positive that he did not kill his father. Still, Oedipus' lack of knowledge about his own life makes a greater case for his innocence than his weak will does for his guilt.

Another concept important to deciding whether Oedipus can be fairly blamed for his fate is the level of dedication he has to the righting of the problems it caused. It can be noted that even while Oedipus had no idea that he was to blame for the natural disasters in Thebes, he still maintained a high level of dedication to finding the person who was. This is evident when Oedipus summons Teiresias and later the old shepherd to provide him with more insight into Laïos' murder. Oedipus clearly wants to find the reason why Thebes is in trouble. His thoroughness in searching absolves him of blame as it shows he did all that he could. Those who believe Oedipus is to be blamed for the tragedy could point to his fair-weather trust in experts—that he trusted Teiresias to give an accurate prophecy when he summoned him, but then lost trust in Teiresias' abilities when Teiresias gave him an undesirable prophecy. It can be noted that Oedipus was only dedicated to finding Laoïs' murderer insofar as the result did not affect him personally. Experts can be trusted when their findings suit him, and cannot be trusted when their findings do not. This tendency of Oedipus toward choosing appropriate and inappropriate versions of the truth is likely to cast him in a bad light with those who would blame him. It reveals that he might have been able to prevent later disasters by listening to Teiresias from the start and dealing with the issues he raised rationally instead of regressing, doling out childish insults, and shielding himself behind his powerful position. While it may be somewhat unfair to fully blame Oedipus for fulfilling the oracle's prophecy, it is reasonably fair to blame him for exacerbating the situation during the investigation of Laïos' murder.

These examples effectively illustrate the problems involved in determining exactly how much blame Oedipus deserves. While Oedipus could be portrayed as blameless and innocent, it is also possible to view him as weak-willed, prideful, and selfish. Therefore, it is largely impossible to derive from his actions a definitive answer to his role in determining his own destiny.

Questions for Writing about Drama

In writing about the elements of drama, the following questions can help you focus your thinking and prepare yourself for writing analytical essays and papers. Use the questions as a checklist to guide you to important aspects of any play you read.

Plot

1. How does the playwright order the incidents of the play? What is the effect of this arrangement of incidents?
2. What is the central conflict of the play? What subsidiary conflicts are related to it?
3. Where is the play's climax? How is that climax prepared for dramatically? With what effects?

Character

4. To what extent are the play's characters—its *dramatis persona*—similar to actual people? In what ways are the play's characters different from actual people?
5. Using the characters' actions and speech, how would you evaluate their behavior? How are the characters related to one another dramatically and in other ways?
6. What function does each of the minor characters serve? If there is a chorus, what are its functions?

Dialogue

7. How would you characterize the voices of the various characters? How do you imagine them sounding in each of their major soliloquies or exchanges with other characters?
8. How does the dialogue advance the plot of the play? How does the dialogue establish setting?
9. How does the dialogue reveal character and motivation? Which particular speeches or other verbal exchanges are especially important for revealing character? Why?

Staging

10. What information is explicitly provided or implicitly suggested about how the play's characters are costumed? Do they change costumes at any point?

Why? To what extent might such costume changes signal changes in attitude, behavior, or state of mind?

11. What objects or props in the play are emphasized? Which carry symbolic weight? How do you know?
12. What kinds of stage directions are provided? How do they help you understand the action? What do they contribute to your understanding of the characters?
13. How does the setting of the play contribute to its mood and theme? What do lighting and the use of sound contribute to the play's overall effects?

Theme

14. What is the central theme of the play? What subsidiary or ancillary themes support or accompany it?
15. How does your analysis of the elements of drama help you understand a play's theme?
16. Does the playwright convey the theme directly or indirectly? Can you identify one or more key passages in which the theme is made explicit? Or do you have to infer the theme from the implications of the play's dialogue and action, setting, staging, and character relationships?

Critical Perspectives

17. Among the critical perspectives you might bring to bear on the play, which one(s) seem(s) particularly useful for interpreting it? Why?
18. To what extent can you base your interpretation of the play on its language and details alone? To what extent is outside information about historical and biographical context necessary or helpful in understanding it?
19. To what extent does the play confirm or support your personal beliefs and values? To what extent is it in conflict with those beliefs and values? To what extent do your values and personal dispositions affect or influence your interpretation?
20. How do you imagine seeing the play staged would enhance your understanding, increase your emotional response, or otherwise alter your perception of the play?

Questions for In-Depth Reading

1. What general or overall thematic connections can you make between different works?
2. What stylistic similarities do you notice between and among different works?

3. How do the works differ in emphasis, tone, and style?
4. Once you have identified a writer's major preoccupations, place each work on a spectrum or a grid that represents the range of the writer's concerns.
5. What connections and disjunctions do you find among the following literary elements as they are embodied in different plays by the same writer?
   a. plot and structure
   b. character and characterization
   c. dialogue and monologue
   d. staging and setting
   e. theme and thought
6. To what extent are your responses to and perceptions of different works by the same writer shared by others—by critics, by classmates, and by the writers themselves?
7. What relationships and differences do you see between the work of one writer and that of another who shares similar thematic interests, stylistic proclivities, or cultural, religious, or social values?
8. Which of the critical perspectives (see Chapter Thirty-One) seem most useful as analytical tools for approaching the body of work of particular writers?

Suggestions for Writing

The Experience of Drama

1. Write a paper in which you recount your experience of reading a particular play or series of plays by the same author. You may want to compare your initial experience with your experience in later readings.
2. Write a paper comparing your experience reading a play with your experience witnessing a performance of it.
3. Discuss your changing perception or understanding of a particular play. Indicate how you felt about the play initially and what made you change your way of responding to it.
4. Relate the action or situation of a play to your own experience. Explain how the play is relevant to your situation, and comment on how reading and thinking about it may have helped you see your own life and experience more clearly.
5. Compare reading a play with watching a film of a performance or a film based on a play. For a filmed performance of a play, consider watching the videocassette or DVD of Arthur Miller's *Death of a Salesman,* starring Dustin Hoffman. For a film based on a play, consider viewing the movie version of Hansberry's *A Raisin in the Sun,* starring Sidney Poitier.

The Interpretation of Drama

6. Describe and characterize a single character from any play. Present a sketch of the character by referring to the language of his or her speeches and to the playwright's use of costume and stage directions.
7. Analyze a character at the moment he or she is making an important decision. Identify the situation, explain the reasons for the character's decision, and speculate about the possible consequences. Some possibilities: Nora in *A Doll House,* Othello in *Othello,* the sergeant in *The Rising of the Moon.*
8. Explicate the opening dialogue of any play. Explain the significance of the opening section in setting the tone, establishing thematic preoccupations, and preparing us for what follows.
9. Select two or three brief passages that appear to be significant in their implications. They may be descriptive passages or dialogue. Establish the connections between one passage and the others, and explain their cumulative significance.
10. Analyze the closing dialogue of any play. Explain the significance of the ending and comment on its appropriateness.
11. Analyze the imagery of a play. Consider how particular kinds of language serve to advance the play's theme(s) or to reveal its characters. Some possibilities: political and natural images in Sophocles' *Oedipus Rex;* animal imagery in *Othello;* images of dream and illusion in Arthur Miller's *Death of a Salesman.*
12. Analyze the ironic dimensions of any play. Consider how the playwright uses irony in the plot, dialogue, and/or setting. Some possibilities: *Oedipus Rex, Trifles, The Importance of Being Earnest.*
13. Explain the symbolic implications of any props used in the play. Consider the dramatic functions of the objects and their resonance as symbols. Some possibilities: the handkerchief in *Othello;* the Christmas tree in *A Doll House.*
14. Analyze the structure of any play. Consider its major parts or sections—its acts and scenes. Explain what each contributes to the whole and how the parts fit together into a unified whole.
15. Analyze the plot of a play. Comment on the way it illustrates or deviates from the classic plot structure.
16. Analyze the setting of a play. Consider both time and place. Also consider small-scale aspects of setting, such as whether the action occurs indoors or out. Notice the descriptive details about the setting, whether the setting changes, and whether the action occurs in one time or place.
17. Analyze a character from any play. Evaluate the character, offering reasons and evidence for your views. Consider what the character does, says, does not do or say—and why. Note also what other characters say about him or her, and how they respond in action. Consider whether the character changes during the course of the play and what that possible change (or lack thereof) may signify.
18. Discuss any character relationship. Consider how the characters affect each other. Explain the nature of their relationship and speculate on its probable future.

The Evaluation of Drama

19. Evaluate a play from the point of view of its merit or excellence—or lack thereof. Explain why you consider it to be a successful or unsuccessful play.
20. Do a comparative evaluation of the merit of any two plays. Explain what they share, how they differ, and why one is more impressive or effective than the other.
21. Discuss the values exemplified by the characters in any play. Identify those values, relate them to your own, and comment on their significance. You may also wish to discuss the author's point of view as you see it reflected in the play.
22. Write a review of the performance of a play. Consider the staging and lighting of the performance, the costumes, the set design, and the sound effects.
23. Write a review of a play's performance concentrating on the acting. Consider how well the actors and actresses delivered their lines, how well they worked together, and how well they communicated emotions and ideas.
24. Write a review of a film, concentrating on its theatrical characteristics and qualities.

To Research or Imagine

25. Develop an alternative ending for any play, changing the outcome in whatever way you deem appropriate. Be prepared to defend your alternative ending as a reasonable possibility. Consider why the author chose to end the play as he or she did.
26. Try your hand at writing a scene from a play. Invent a scenario, create a couple of characters, and start them talking and acting.
27. Read a few letters or essays written by a dramatist. Consider what light they shed on your reading of the play(s).
28. Read a full-scale biography of a dramatist. Write a paper explaining how the author's life is or is not reflected in his work.
29. Discuss how a particular playwright reflects or rebels against important social, political, moral, or cultural issues of his or her time.
30. Read a critical study of a writer's plays. Write a paper explaining how the book aids your understanding or enhances your enjoyment of the play(s).

CHAPTER TWENTY-FIVE

The Greek Theater: Sophocles in Context

READING SOPHOCLES IN CONTEXT

Athens in the Golden Age

The Athenian fifth century B.C. was one of the most culturally productive periods in the history of humankind. The unsurpassed Athenian achievements began with the defeat of the Persians in 479 B.C. and ended with the fall of Athens to Sparta in 404 B.C. Classical Greek civilization was crucial to the development of Western civilization. The Greeks of antiquity developed a rich and vibrant culture, reflected in preeminent works of sculpture, architecture, poetry, and drama. The classical Greeks invented democracy and passed it down as a legacy to Western Europe. Political freedom was part of Greek culture's belief in individual expression and achievement. In the arts, as in athletics, competition was encouraged, with the victor of drama competitions, for instance, crowned as a kind of hero. The annual competition of dramatists led to the creation of Sophocles' plays, including *Oedipus the King.* Against the background of warring mainland Greece in the fifth century B.C., Greek culture nevertheless flourished in a Golden Age; the Greeks still provide us a sense of unique values, balance, and harmony in not just politics and the arts, but in daily life as well.

Greek Tragedy

Greek drama developed from celebrations honoring Dionysus, the Greek god of wine and fertility. These celebrations included the dancing of a chorus as part of the religious ritual. It is possible that the leader of the **chorus** (the *choragos*) may have engaged the rest of the chorus in responsive chanting. Legend suggests that the poet Thespis introduced a speaker who, detached from the chorus, engaged in dialogue with it. At that point drama was born. A second actor was added by Aeschylus (524–456 B.C.) and a third by Sophocles (496?–406 B.C.). In Greek drama no more than three characters appeared onstage together at one time, although it was common for actors to double and triple parts, changing masks for their multiple roles.

The Acropolis today

Greek plays were performed in huge outdoor amphitheaters capable of seating upwards of fourteen thousand people. Members of the audience were seated in tiers that sloped up hillsides where the theaters were built; the hills echoed the sound of the actors' voices. The actors wore masks that amplified their voices in the manner of megaphones. The masks were large, and with the elevated shoes sometimes worn by the actors, they projected the characters as larger-than-life figures. The masks and elevated shoes restricted what the actors could do and what the dramatist could expect of them. Subtle nuances of voice, of facial expression, and of gesture were impossible. The playwright's language rather than his stage business conveyed nuances of meaning and feeling.

The plays were performed on an elevated platform. Behind the acting area was a scene building (*skene*) that functioned both as dressing room and as scenic background, and below the stage was the *orchestra* or dancing place for the chorus. Standing between the actors and the audience, the chorus represented the common or communal viewpoint.

An important function of the chorus was to mark the divisions between the scenes of a play, when the chorus would dance and chant poetry. Lyric rather than dramatic in form, these choral interludes sometimes commented on the action, sometimes generalized from it. They remained in Greek drama as vestiges of its origins in religious ritual. For modern readers these choric interludes pace the play, affording respite from the gradually intensifying action, and allowing time to ponder its implications.

The scenes of Greek plays usually consist of two, sometimes three characters with the third usually acting as an observer who occasionally comments on the debate occurring between the other two characters. Sometimes most of a scene is given over to a debate between two characters, as, for example, in Scene I of *Oedipus Rex* in which

The theater at Epidauros

Oedipus argues with Teiresias. The debates typically begin with leisurely speeches in which each character sets forth a position. The speeches are followed by rapid-fire dialogue (*stichomythia*) that brings the characters' antagonisms to a climax. This pattern is repeated throughout the play in something like a theme with variations, each scene usually developing a conflict. The accumulation of conflicts advances the action, leading to the inevitable tragic catastrophe.

Brevity is a characteristic of Greek tragedy: the plays are short with most having a playing time of roughly ninety minutes. Greek dramatists based their plays on myths that were familiar to the audience, which reduced the amount of time needed for exposition. The plays also have a musical dimension, which, combined with the dancing and chanting of the chorus, increased the emotional impact of the ancient performances.

Sophocles and His Works

The ancient Greek tragic dramatist Sophocles lived during the Athenian Golden Age, when the military power, artistic glory, and philosophical achievements of Athens were at their zenith. The most generally admired of the ancient Greek dramatists, Sophocles was also acknowledged for his musical skill and his handsome appearance.

Sophocles also held political and military positions. He served, for example, as a general with the Athenian statesman Pericles and was a commissioner of the Athenian

Sophocles: Timeline

500 B.C.

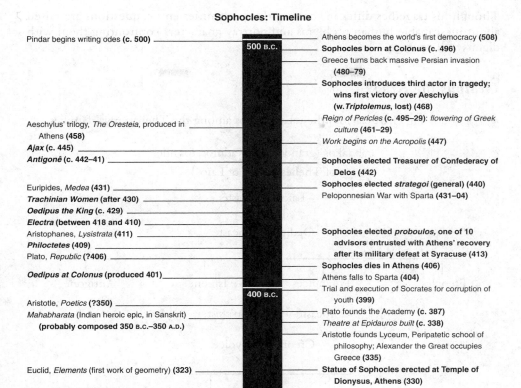

Pindar begins writing odes **(c. 500)**

Athens becomes the world's first democracy **(508)**

Sophocles born at Colonus (c. 496)

Greece turns back massive Persian invasion **(480–79)**

Sophocles introduces third actor in tragedy; wins first victory over Aeschylus (w. *Triptolemus*, lost) (468)

Reign of Pericles **(c. 495–29)**: *flowering of Greek culture* **(461–29)**

Aeschylus' trilogy, *The Oresteia,* produced in Athens **(458)**

Work begins on the Acropolis **(447)**

***Ajax* (c. 445)**

***Antigonê* (c. 442–41)**

Sophocles elected Treasurer of Confederacy of Delos (442)

Sophocles elected *strategoi* (general) (440)

Euripides, *Medea* **(431)**

Peloponnesian War with Sparta **(431–04)**

***Trachinian Women* (after 430)**

***Oedipus the King* (c. 429)**

***Electra* (between 418 and 410)**

Aristophanes, *Lysistrata* **(411)**

Sophocles elected *proboulos,* one of 10 advisors entrusted with Athens' recovery after its military defeat at Syracuse (413)

***Philoctetes* (409)**

Plato, *Republic* **(?406)**

Sophocles dies in Athens (406)

***Oedipus at Colonus* (produced 401)**

Athens falls to Sparta **(404)**

400 B.C.

Trial and execution of Socrates for corruption of youth **(399)**

Aristotle, *Poetics* **(?350)**

Mahabharata (Indian heroic epic, in Sanskrit) **(probably composed 350 B.C.–350 A.D.)**

Plato founds the Academy **(c. 387)**

Theatre at Epidauros built **(c. 338)**

Aristotle founds Lyceum, Peripatetic school of philosophy; Alexander the Great occupies Greece **(335)**

Euclid, *Elements* (first work of geometry) **(323)**

Statue of Sophocles erected at Temple of Dionysus, Athens (330)

300 B.C.

Ramayana (Indian heroic epic, in Sanskrit) **(probably composed from 300)**

empire. He was also a priest of Asclepius, the Greek god of healing and medicine. It is for his plays, however, that Sophocles is best known and most widely admired.

Sophocles wrote more than one hundred plays, only seven of which have survived. Many of his plays were entered in competition with plays by other Greek tragic dramatists, including Aeschylus and Euripides, whose work Sophocles surpassed on at least twenty occasions. More conservative than the other Greek dramatists who were his contemporaries, Sophocles emphasized the individual's uncompromising search for truth, which is evident in his play *Oedipus Rex.*

Of the three great Greek tragic dramatists, Sophocles is perhaps the most widely read today. Unlike his forebear Aeschylus, Sophocles focused his plays on human rather than religious concerns. As theater historian Peter Arnott has noted, he wrote "for a generation whose religious faith was waning."* His most famous plays center on a crisis and portray characters under duress. In *Oedipus Rex,* set against a background of the plague-stricken city of Thebes, Sophocles examines the behavior of Oedipus, who has been destined to murder his father and marry his mother.

*Peter Arnott, *The Theatre in Its Time* (Boston: Little, Brown, 1981), page 51.

Though his tragedies differ in the way their calamities ensue, questions are raised about inescapable human problems and portray characters confronting them with dignity and courage.

Oedipus the King

The following chart clarifies the relationships among the Theban royal families:

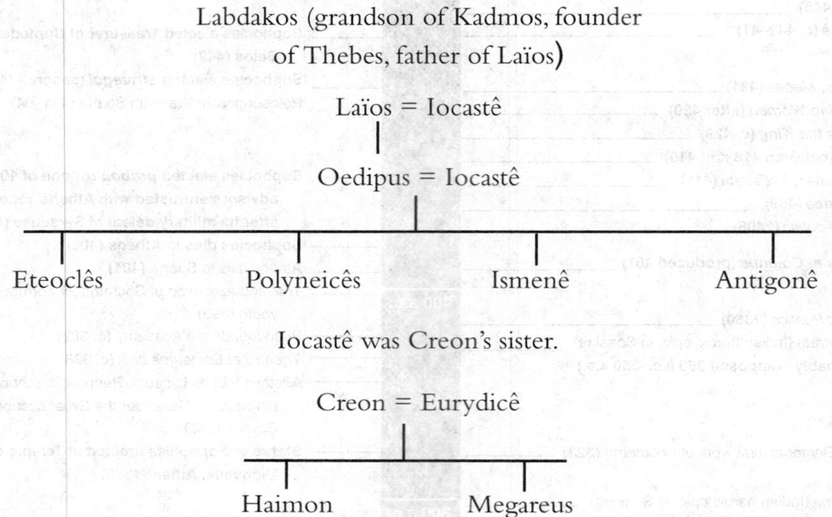

The Athenian audience that watched performances of *Oedipus Tyrannus* (the original Greek title of the play) would have been familiar with Oedipus's story from sources as early as Homer's *Odyssey.* They would have known, for example, that Oedipus was fated to kill his father and marry his mother, and that to prevent this from happening, the infant Oedipus was given up by his parents, King Laius and Queen Jocasta, and left in the wilderness to die. This plan went awry when Oedipus was taken by a shepherd to Corinth, where he was adopted by a childless couple, King Polybus and Queen Merope. The Athenian audience would also have been aware of the reason for Oedipus's clubfoot (his feet had been pinned together as an infant). They would have known too of how upon hearing the oracle pronounce his grisly fate, Oedipus had left Corinth, where he had been raised as a prince, thinking that he had to get as far away as he could from Polybus and Merope, who he assumed were his biological parents. For the Athenian audience, then, and for later audiences who know the Oedipus story, the play's power resides less in the surprising twists and turns of its plot than in its relentless tragic action.

Oedipus Rex performed by the Greek National Theater at the Colosseum, Rome, July 2000

Oedipus begins at the point when Thebes is undergoing a series of catastrophes, most important of which is a devastating plague. Prior to this series of events, Oedipus had saved Thebes from the Sphinx, a winged creature with the body of a lion and the head of a woman. The Sphinx had terrorized the city by devouring anyone who crossed its path and who was unable to answer its riddle correctly: What goes on four legs in the morning, two legs in the afternoon, and three legs in the evening? Oedipus solved the riddle by answering "Man." After he slew the Sphinx, he was given in reward the kingship of Thebes and the hand of its recently widowed queen, Jocasta. Unknown to Oedipus, but known to the Athenian audience, was the fact that Jocasta was his mother and that her recently slain husband, Laius, had been killed by Oedipus himself. All this and more Oedipus soon discovers.

SOPHOCLES: PLAY

SOPHOCLES
[c. 496–406 B.C.]

Oedipus Rex°

AN ENGLISH VERSION BY DUDLEY FITTS AND ROBERT FITZGERALD

CHARACTERS

OEDIPUS
A PRIEST
CREON
TEIRESIAS
IOCASTÊ
MESSENGER
SHEPHERD OF LAÏOS
SECOND MESSENGER
CHORUS OF THEBAN ELDERS

Scene. *Before the palace of* OEDIPUS, *King of Thebes. A central door and two lateral doors open onto a platform which runs the length of the façade. On the platform, right and left, are altars; and three steps lead down into the "orchestra," or chorus-ground. At the beginning of the action these steps are crowded by* SUPPLIANTS *who have brought branches and chaplets of olive leaves and who lie in various attitudes of despair.* OEDIPUS *enters.*

Prologue

OEDIPUS: My children, generations of the living
In the line of Kadmos,° nursed at his ancient hearth:
Why have you strewn yourselves before these altars
In supplication, with your boughs and garlands?

Rex *Latin for King.* [2]**Kadmos** *legendary founder of Thebes.*

The breath of incense rises from the city
With a sound of prayer and lamentation.
Children,
I would not have you speak through messengers,
And therefore I have come myself to hear you—
I, Oedipus, who bear the famous name.
(*To a* PRIEST.) You, there, since you are eldest in the company,
Speak for them all, tell me what preys upon you,
Whether you come in dread, or crave some blessing:
Tell me, and never doubt that I will help you
In every way I can; I should be heartless
Were I not moved to find you suppliant here.

PRIEST: O Great Oedipus, O powerful King of Thebes!
You see how all the ages of our people
Cling to your altar steps: here are boys
Who can barely stand alone, and here are priests
By weight of age, as I am a priest of God,
And young men chosen from those yet unmarried;
As for the others, all that multitude,
They wait with olive chaplets in the squares,
At the two shrines of Pallas,° and where Apollo°
Speaks in the glowing embers.
Your own eyes
Must tell you: Thebes is in her extremity
And cannot lift her head from the surge of death.
A rust consumes the buds and fruits of the earth;
The herds are sick; children die unborn,
And labor is vain. The god of plague and pyre
Raids like detestable lightning through the city,
And all the house of Kadmos is laid waste,
All emptied, and all darkened: Death alone
Battens upon the misery of Thebes.
You are not one of the immortal gods, we know;
Yet we have come to you to make our prayer
As to the man of all men best in adversity
And wisest in the ways of God. You saved us
From the Sphinx,° that flinty singer, and the tribute
We paid to her so long; yet you were never
Better informed than we, nor could we teach you:
It was some god breathed in you to set us free.

Therefore, O mighty King, we turn to you:
Find us our safety, find us a remedy,
Whether by counsel of the gods or the men.
A king of wisdom tested in the past

24 ***Pallas*** *Athena, goddess of wisdom.* 24 ***Apollo*** *god of poetry and prophecy.* 39 ***the Sphinx*** *a monster with a lion's body, birds' wings, and woman's face.*

Can act in a time of troubles, and act well.
Noblest of men, restore
Life to your city! Think how all men call you
Liberator for your triumph long ago;
Ah, when your years of kingship are remembered,
Let them not say *We rose, but later fell—*
Keep the State from going down in the storm!
Once, years ago, with happy augury,
You brought us fortune; be the same again!
No man questions your power to rule the land:
But rule over men, not over a dead city!
Ships are only hulls, citadels are nothing,
When no life moves in the empty passageways.

OEDIPUS: Poor children! You may be sure I know
All that you longed for in your coming here.
I know that you are deathly sick; and yet,
Sick as you are, not one is as sick as I.
Each of you suffers in himself alone
His anguish, not another's; but my spirit
Groans for the city, for myself, for you.

I was not sleeping, you are not waking me.
No, I have been in tears for a long while
And in my restless thought walked many ways.
In all my search, I found one helpful course,
And that I have taken: I have sent Creon,
Son of Menoikeus, brother of the Queen,
To Delphi, Apollo's place of revelation,
To learn there, if he can,
What act or pledge of mine may save the city.
I have counted the days, and now, this very day,
I am troubled, for he has overstayed his time.
What is he doing? He has been gone too long.
Yet whenever he comes back, I should do ill
To scant whatever hint the god may give.

PRIEST: It is a timely promise. At this instant
They tell me Creon is here.

OEDIPUS: O Lord Apollo!
May his news be fair as his face is radiant!

PRIEST: It could not be otherwise: he is crowned with bay,
The chaplet is thick with berries.

OEDIPUS: We shall soon know;
He is near enough to hear us now.

Enter CREON.

O Prince:
Brother: son of Menoikeus:
What answer do you bring us from the god?

CREON: It is favorable. I can tell you, great afflictions
Will turn out well, if they are taken well.
OEDIPUS: What was the oracle? These vague words
Leave me still hanging between hope and fear.
CREON: Is it your pleasure to hear me with all these
Gathered around us? I am prepared to speak,
But should we not go in?
OEDIPUS: Let them all hear it.
It is for them I suffer, more than myself.
CREON: Then I will tell you what I heard at Delphi.

In plain words
The god commands us to expel from the land of Thebes
An old defilement that it seems we shelter.
It is a deathly thing, beyond expiation.
We must not let it feed upon us longer.
OEDIPUS: What defilement? How shall we rid ourselves of it?
CREON: By exile or death, blood for blood. It was
Murder that brought the plague-wind on the city.
OEDIPUS: Murder of whom? Surely the god has named him?
CREON: My lord: long ago Laïos was our king,
Before you came to govern us.
OEDIPUS: I know;
I learned of him from others; I never saw him.
CREON: He was murdered; and Apollo commands us now
To take revenge upon whoever killed him.
OEDIPUS: Upon whom? Where are they? Where shall we find a clue
To solve that crime, after so many years?
CREON: Here in this land, he said.
If we make enquiry,
We may touch things that otherwise escape us.
OEDIPUS: Tell me: Was Laïos murdered in his house,
Or in the fields, or in some foreign country?
CREON: He said he planned to make a pilgrimage.
He did not come home again.
OEDIPUS: And was there no one,
No witness, no companion, to tell what happened?
CREON: They were all killed but one, and he got away
So frightened that he could remember one thing only.
OEDIPUS: What was that one thing? One may be the key
To everything, if we resolve to use it.
CREON: He said that a band of highwaymen attacked them,
Outnumbered them, and overwhelmed the King.
OEDIPUS: Strange, that a highwayman should be so daring—
Unless some faction here bribed him to do it.
CREON: We thought of that. But after Laïos' death
New troubles arose and we had no avenger.
OEDIPUS: What troubles could prevent your hunting down the killers?

CREON: The riddling Sphinx's song
Made us deaf to all mysteries but her own.
OEDIPUS: Then once more I must bring what is dark to light.
It is most fitting that Apollo shows,
As you do, this compunction for the dead.
You shall see how I stand by you, as I should,
To avenge the city and the city's god,
And not as though it were for some distant friend,
But for my own sake, to be rid of evil.
Whoever killed King Laïos might—who knows?—
Decide at any moment to kill me as well.
By avenging the murdered king I protect myself.
Come, then, my children: leave the altar steps,
Lift up your olive boughs!
One of you go
And summon the people of Kadmos to gather here.
I will do all that I can; you may tell them that.

(*Exit a* PAGE.)

So, with the help of God,
We shall be saved—or else indeed we are lost.
PRIEST: Let us rise, children. It was for this we came,
And now the King has promised it himself.
Phoibos° has sent us an oracle; may he descend
Himself to save us and drive out the plague.

Exeunt OEDIPUS *and* CREON *into the palace by the central door. The* PRIEST *and the* SUPPLIANTS *disperse right and left. After a short pause the* CHORUS *enters the orchestra.*

Párodos°

Strophe 1

CHORUS: What is God singing in his profound
Delphi of gold and shadow?
What oracle for Thebes, the sunwhipped city?
Fear unjoints me, the roots of my heart tremble.
Now I remember, O Healer, your power, and wonder;
Will you send doom like a sudden cloud, or weave it
Like nightfall of the past?
Speak, speak to us, issue of holy sound:
Dearest to our expectancy: be tender!

Antistrophe 1

Let me pray to Athenê, the immortal daughter of Zeus,
And to Artemis her sister

152 ***Phoibos*** *Phoebus Apollo, the sun god.* ***Párodos*** *sung as the chorus enters the stage area. Presumably they sang the strophe while dancing from right to left and the antistrophe as they reversed direction.*

Who keeps her famous throne in the market ring,
And to Apollo, bowman at the far butts of heaven—

O gods, descend! Like three streams leap against
The fires of our grief, the fires of darkness;
Be swift to bring us rest!

As in the old time from the brilliant house
Of air you stepped to save us, come again!

Strophe 2

Now our afflictions have no end,
Now all our stricken host lies down
And no man fights off death with his mind;

The noble plowland bears no grain,
And groaning mothers cannot bear—

See, how our lives like birds take wing.
Like sparks that fly when a fire soars,
To the shore of the god of evening.

Antistrophe 2

The plague burns on, it is pitiless,
Though pallid children laden with death
Lie unwept in the stony ways,
And old gray women by every path

Flock to the strand about the altars
There to strike their breasts and cry
Worship of Phoibos in wailing prayers:
Be kind, God's golden child!

Strophe 3

There are no swords in this attack by fire,
No shields, but we are ringed with cries.
Send the besieger plunging from our homes
Into the vast sea-room of the Atlantic
Or into the waves that foam eastward of Thrace—
For the day ravages what the night spares—
Destroy our enemy, lord of the thunder!
Let him be riven by lightning from heaven!

Antistrophe 3

Phoibos Apollo, stretch the sun's bowstring,
That golden cord, until it sing for us,

Flashing arrows in heaven!
Artemis,° Huntress,
Race with flaring lights upon our mountains!
O scarlet god, O golden-banded brow,
O Theban Bacchos° in a storm of Maenads,°

Enter OEDIPUS, *center.*

Whirl upon Death, that all the Undying hate!
Come with blinding cressets, come in joy!

Scene I

OEDIPUS: Is this your prayer? It may be answered. Come,
Listen to me, act as the crisis demands,
And you shall have relief from all these evils.

Until now I was a stranger to this tale,
As I had been a stranger to the crime.
Could I track down the murderer without a clue?
But now, friends,
As one who became a citizen after the murder,
I make this proclamation to all Thebans:
If any man knows by whose hand Laïos, son of Labdakos,
Met his death, I direct that man to tell me everything,
No matter what he fears for having so long withheld it.
Let it stand as promised that no further trouble
Will come to him, but he may leave the land in safety.
Moreover: If anyone knows the murderer to be foreign,
Let him not keep silent: he shall have his reward from me.
However, if he does conceal it; if any man
Fearing for his friend or for himself disobeys this edict,
Hear what I propose to do:

I solemnly forbid the people of this country,
Where power and throne are mine, ever to receive that man
Or speak to him, no matter who he is, or let him
Join in sacrifice, lustration, or in prayer.
I decree that he be driven from every house,
Being, as he is, corruption itself to us: the Delphic
Voice of Zeus has pronounced this revelation.
Thus I associate myself with the oracle
And take the side of the murdered king.

As for the criminal, I pray to God—
Whether it be a lurking thief, or one of a number—

45 ***Artemis*** *goddess of hunting and chastity.* 48 ***Bacchos . . . Maenads*** *god of wine and revelry with his attendants.*

I pray that that man's life be consumed in evil and
wretchedness.
And as for me, this curse applies no less
If it should turn out that the culprit is my guest here,
Sharing my hearth.
You have heard the penalty.
I lay it on you now to attend to this
For my sake, for Apollo's, for the sick
Sterile city that heaven has abandoned.
Suppose the oracle had given you no command:
Should this defilement go uncleansed for ever?
You should have found the murderer: your king,
A noble king, had been destroyed!
Now I,
Having the power that he held before me,
Having his bed, begetting children there
Upon his wife, as he would have, had he lived—
Their son would have been my children's brother,
If Laïos had had luck in fatherhood!
(But surely ill luck rushed upon his reign)—
I say I take the son's part, just as though
I were his son, to press the fight for him
And see it won! I'll find the hand that brought
Death to Labdakos' and Polydoros' child,
Heir of Kadmos' and Agenor's line.
And as for those who fail me,
May the gods deny them the fruit of the earth,
Fruit of the womb, and may they rot utterly!
Let them be wretched as we are wretched, and worse!
For you, for loyal Thebans, and for all
Who find my actions right, I pray the favor
Of justice, and of all the immortal gods.

CHORAGOS: Since I am under oath, my lord, I swear
I did not do the murder, I cannot name
The murderer. Might not the oracle
That has ordained the search tell where to find him?

OEDIPUS: An honest question. But no man in the world
Can make the gods do more than the gods will.

CHORAGOS: There is one last expedient—

OEDIPUS: Tell me what it is.
Though it seem slight, you must not hold it back.

CHORAGOS: A lord clairvoyant to the lord Apollo,
As we all know, is the skilled Teiresias.
One might learn much about this from him, Oedipus.

OEDIPUS: I am not wasting time:
Creon spoke of this, and I have sent for him—
Twice, in fact; it is strange that he is not here.

CHORAGOS: The other matter—that old report—seems useless.
OEDIPUS: Tell me. I am interested in all reports.
CHORAGOS: The King was said to have been killed by highwaymen.
OEDIPUS: I know. But we have no witnesses to that.
CHORAGOS: If the killer can feel a particle of dread,
  Your curse will bring him out of hiding!
OEDIPUS: No.
  The man who dared that act will fear no curse.

Enter the blind seer TEIRESIAS, *led by a* PAGE.

CHORAGOS: But there is one man who may detect the criminal.
  This is Teiresias, this is the holy prophet
  In whom, alone of all men, truth was born.
OEDIPUS: Teiresias: seer: student of mysteries,
Of all that's taught and all that no man tells,
  Secrets of Heaven and secrets of the earth:
  Blind though you are, you know the city lies
  Sick with plague; and from this plague, my lord,
  We find that you alone can guard or save us.

  Possibly you did not hear the messengers?
  Apollo, when we sent to him,
  Sent us back word that this great pestilence
  Would lift, but only if we established clearly
  The identity of those who murdered Laïos.
  They must be killed or exiled.
  Can you use
  Birdflight or any art of divination
  To purify yourself, and Thebes, and me
  From this contagion? We are in your hands.
  There is no fairer duty
  Than that of helping others in distress.
TEIRESIAS: How dreadful knowledge of the truth can be
  When there's no help in truth! I knew this well,
  But did not act on it: else I should not have come.
OEDIPUS: What is troubling you? Why are your eyes so cold?
TEIRESIAS: Let me go home. Bear your own fate, and I'll
  Bear mine. It is better so: trust what I say.
OEDIPUS: What you say is ungracious and unhelpful
  To your native country. Do not refuse to speak.
TEIRESIAS: When it comes to speech, your own is neither temperate
  Nor opportune. I wish to be more prudent.
OEDIPUS: In God's name, we all beg you—
TEIRESIAS: You are all ignorant.
  No; I will never tell you what I know.
  Now it is my misery; then, it would be yours.
OEDIPUS: What! You do know something, and will not tell us?

You would betray us all and wreck the State?
TEIRESIAS: I do not intend to torture myself, or you.
Why persist in asking? You will not persuade me.
OEDIPUS: What a wicked old man you are! You'd try a stone's
Patience! Out with it! Have you no feeling at all?
TEIRESIAS: You call me unfeeling. If you could only see
The nature of your own feelings . . .
OEDIPUS: Why,
Who would not feel as I do? Who could endure
Your arrogance toward the city?
TEIRESIAS: What does it matter!
Whether I speak or not, it is bound to come.
OEDIPUS: Then, if "it" is bound to come, you are bound
to tell me.
TEIRESIAS: No, I will not go on. Rage as you please.
OEDIPUS: Rage? Why not!
And I'll tell you what I think:
You planned it, you had it done, you all but
Killed him with your own hands: if you had eyes,
I'd say the crime was yours, and yours alone.
TEIRESIAS: So? I charge you, then,
Abide by the proclamation you have made:
From this day forth
Never speak again to these men or to me;
You yourself are the pollution of this country.
OEDIPUS: You dare say that! Can you possibly think you have
Some way of going free, after such insolence?
TEIRESIAS: I have gone free. It is the truth sustains me.
OEDIPUS: Who taught you shamelessness? It was not your craft.
TEIRESIAS: You did. You made me speak. I did not want to.
OEDIPUS: Speak what? Let me hear it again more clearly.
TEIRESIAS: Was it not clear before? Are you tempting me?
OEDIPUS: I did not understand it. Say it again.
TEIRESIAS: I say that you are the murderer whom you seek.
OEDIPUS: Now twice you have spat out infamy. You'll
pay for it!
TEIRESIAS: Would you care for more? Do you wish to be really angry?
OEDIPUS: Say what you will. Whatever you say is worthless.
TEIRESIAS: I say you live in hideous shame with those
Most dear to you. You cannot see the evil.
OEDIPUS: It seems you can go on mouthing like this for ever.
TEIRESIAS: I can, if there is power in truth.
OEDIPUS: There is:
But not for you, not for you,
You sightless, witless, senseless, mad old man!
TEIRESIAS: You are the madman. There is no one here

Who will not curse you soon, as you curse me.
OEDIPUS: You child of endless night! You cannot hurt me
Or any other man who sees the sun.
TEIRESIAS: True: it is not from me your fate will come.
That lies within Apollo's competence,
As it is his concern.
OEDIPUS: Tell me:
Are you speaking for Creon, or for yourself?
TEIRESIAS: Creon is no threat. You weave your own doom.
OEDIPUS: Wealth, power, craft of statesmanship!
Kingly position, everywhere admired!
What savage envy is stored up against these,
If Creon, whom I trusted, Creon my friend,
For this great office which the city once
Put in my hands unsought—if for this power
Creon desires in secret to destroy me!
He has brought this decrepit fortune-teller, this
Collector of dirty pennies, this prophet fraud—
Why, he is no more clairvoyant than I am!
Tell us:
Has your mystic mummery ever approached the truth?
When that hellcat the Sphinx was performing here,
What help were you to these people?
Her magic was not for the first man who came along:
It demanded a real exorcist. Your birds—
What good were they? or the gods, for the matter of that?
But I came by,
Oedipus, the simple man, who knows nothing—
I thought it out for myself, no birds helped me!
And this is the man you think you can destroy,
That you may be close to Creon when he's king!
Well, you and your friend Creon, it seems to me,
Will suffer most. If you were not an old man,
You would have paid already for your plot.
CHORAGOS: We cannot see that his words or yours
Have been spoken except in anger, Oedipus,
And of anger we have no need. How can God's will
Be accomplished best? That is what most concerns us.
TEIRESIAS: You are a king. But where argument's concerned
I am your man, as much a king as you.
I am not your servant, but Apollo's.
I have no need of Creon to speak for me.

Listen to me. You mock my blindness, do you?
But I say that you, with both your eyes, are blind:
You cannot see the wretchedness of your life,

Nor in whose house you live, no, nor with whom.
Who are your father and mother? Can you tell me?
You do not even know the blind wrongs
That you have done them, on earth and in the world below.
But the double lash of your parents' curse will whip you
Out of this land some day, with only night
Upon your precious eyes.
Your cries then—where will they not be heard?
What fastness of Kithairon will not echo them?
And that bridal-descant of yours—you'll know it then,
The song they sang when you came here to Thebes
And found your misguided berthing.
All this, and more, that you cannot guess at now,
Will bring you to yourself among your children.
Be angry, then. Curse Creon. Curse my words.
I tell you, no man that walks upon the earth
Shall be rooted out more horribly than you.

OEDIPUS: Am I to bear this from him?—Damnation
Take you! Out of this place! Out of my sight!

TEIRESIAS: I would not have come at all if you had not asked me.

OEDIPUS: Could I have told that you'd talk nonsense, that
You'd come here to make a fool of yourself, and of me?

TEIRESIAS: A fool? Your parents thought me sane enough.

OEDIPUS: My parents again!—Wait: who were my parents?

TEIRESIAS: This day will give you a father, and break your heart.

OEDIPUS: Your infantile riddles! Your damned abracadabra!

TEIRESIAS: You were a great man once at solving riddles.

OEDIPUS: Mock me with that if you like; you will find it true.

TEIRESIAS: It was true enough. It brought about your ruin.

OEDIPUS: But if it saved this town?

TEIRESIAS (*to the* PAGE): Boy, give me your hand.

OEDIPUS: Yes, boy; lead him away.
—While you are here
We can do nothing. Go; leave us in peace.

TEIRESIAS: I will go when I have said what I have to say.
How can you hurt me? And I tell you again:
The man you have been looking for all this time,
The damned man, the murderer of Laïos,
That man is in Thebes. To your mind he is foreignborn,
But it will soon be shown that he is a Theban,
A revelation that will fail to please.
A blind man,
Who has his eyes now; a penniless man, who is rich now;
And he will go tapping the strange earth with his staff;
To the children with whom he lives now he will be
Brother and father—the very same; to her

Who bore him, son and husband—the very same
Who came to his father's bed, wet with his father's blood.

Enough. Go think that over.
If later you find error in what I have said,
You may say that I have no skill in prophecy

Exit TEIRESIAS, *led by his* PAGE. OEDIPUS *goes into the palace*

Ode I°

Strophe 1

CHORUS: The Delphic stone of prophecies
Remembers ancient regicide
And a still bloody hand.
That killer's hour of flight has come.
He must be stronger than riderless
Coursers of untiring wind,
For the son of Zeus° armed with his father's thunder
Leaps in lightning after him;
And the Furies° evildoers follow him, the sad Furies.

Antistrophe 1

Holy Parnossos' peak of snow
Flashes and blinds that secret man,
That all shall hunt him down:
Though he may roam the forest shade
Like a bull gone wild from pasture
To rage through glooms of stone.
Doom comes down on him; flight will not avail him;
For the world's heart calls him desolate,
And the immortal Furies follow, for ever follow.

Strophe 2

But now a wilder thing is heard
From the old man skilled at hearing Fate in the
wingbeat of a bird.
Bewildered as a blown bird, my soul hovers and cannot find
Foothold in this debate, or any reason or rest of mind.
But no man ever brought—none can bring
Proof of strife between Thebes' royal house,
Labdakos' line,° and the son of Polybos;°
And never until now has any man brought word
Of Laïos' dark death staining Oedipus the King.

ode *a poetic song sung by the chorus.* [7]***son of Zeus*** *Apollo.* [9]***the Furies*** *three women spirits who punished* [25]***Labdakos' line*** *his descendants.* [25]***Polybos*** *King of Corinth who adopted Oedipus as an infant.*

Antistrophe 2

Divine Zeus and Apollo hold
Perfect intelligence alone of all tales ever told;
And well though this diviner works, he works in his own night;
No man can judge that rough unknown or trust in second sight,
For wisdom changes hands among the wise.
Shall I believe my great lord criminal
At a raging word that a blind old man let fall?
I saw him, when the carrion woman faced him of old,
Prove his heroic mind! These evil words are lies.

Scene II

CREON: Men of Thebes:
I am told that heavy accusations
Have been brought against me by King Oedipus.
I am not the kind of man to bear this tamely.

If in these present difficulties
He holds me accountable for any harm to him
Through anything I have said or done—why, then,
I do not value life in this dishonor.
It is not as though this rumor touched upon
Some private indiscretion. The matter is grave.
The fact is that I am being called disloyal
To the State, to my fellow citizens, to my friends.
CHORAGOS: He may have spoken in anger, not from his mind.
CREON: But did you not hear him say I was the one
Who seduced the old prophet into lying?
CHORAGOS: The thing was said; I do not know how seriously.
CREON: But you were watching him! Were his eyes steady?
Did he look like a man in his right mind?
CHORAGOS: I do not know.
I cannot judge the behavior of great men.
But here is the King himself.

Enter OEDIPUS.

OEDIPUS: So you dared come back.
Why? How brazen of you to come to my house,
You murderer!
Do you think I do not know
That you plotted to kill me, plotted to steal my throne?
Tell me, in God's name: am I coward, a fool,
That you should dream you could accomplish this?
A fool who could not see your slippery game?
A coward, not to fight back when I saw it?
You are the fool, Creon, are you not? hoping

Without support or friends to get a throne?
Thrones may be won or bought: you could do neither.
CREON: Now listen to me. You have talked; let me talk, too.
You cannot judge unless you know the facts.
OEDIPUS: You speak well: there is one fact; but I find it hard
To learn from the deadliest enemy I have.
CREON: That above all I must dispute with you.
OEDIPUS: That above all I will not hear you deny.
CREON: If you think there is anything good in being stubborn
Against all reason, then I say you are wrong.
OEDIPUS: If you think a man can sin against his own kind
And not be punished for it, I say you are mad.
CREON: I agree. But tell me: what have I done to you?
OEDIPUS: You advised me to send for that wizard, did you not?
CREON: I did. I should do it again.
OEDIPUS: Very well. Now tell me:
How long has it been since Laïos—
CREON: What of Laïos?
OEDIPUS: Since he vanished in that onset by the road?
CREON: It was long ago, a long time.
OEDIPUS: And this prophet,
Was he practicing here then?
CREON: He was; and with honor, as now.
OEDIPUS: Did he speak of me at that time?
CREON: He never did;
At least, not when I was present.
OEDIPUS: But . . . the enquiry?
I suppose you held one?
CREON: We did, but we learned nothing.
OEDIPUS: Why did the prophet not speak against me then?
CREON: I do not know; and I am the kind of man
Who holds his tongue when he has no facts to go on.
OEDIPUS: There's one fact that you know, and you could tell it.
CREON: What fact is that? If I know it, you shall have it.
OEDIPUS: If he were not involved with you, he could not say
That it was I who murdered Laïos.
CREON: If he says that, you are the one that knows it!—
But now it is my turn to question you.
OEDIPUS: Put your questions. I am no murderer.
CREON: First, then: You married my sister?
OEDIPUS: I married your sister.
CREON: And you rule the kingdom equally with her?
OEDIPUS: Everything that she wants she has from me.
CREON: And I am the third, equal to both of you?
OEDIPUS: That is why I call you a bad friend.
CREON: No. Reason it out, as I have done.
Think of this first. Would any sane man prefer

Power, with all a king's anxieties,
To that same power and the grace of sleep?
Certainly not I.
I have never longed for the king's power—only his rights.
Would any wise man differ from me in this?
As matters stand, I have my way in everything
With your consent, and no responsibilities.
If I were king, I should be a slave to policy.
How could I desire a scepter more
Than what is now mine—untroubled influence?
No, I have not gone mad; I need no honors,
Except those with the perquisites I have now.
I am welcome everywhere; every man salutes me,
And those who want your favor seek my ear,
Since I know how to manage what they ask.
Should I exchange this ease for that anxiety?
Besides, no sober mind is treasonable.
I hate anarchy
And never would deal with any man who likes it.

Test what I have said. Go to the priestess
At Delphi, ask if I quoted her correctly.
And as for this other thing: if I am found
Guilty of treason with Teiresias,
Then sentence me to death! You have my word
It is a sentence I should cast my vote for—
But not without evidence!
You do wrong
When you take good men for bad, bad men for good.
A true friend thrown aside—why, life itself
Is not more precious!
In time you will know this well:
For time, and time alone, will show the just man,
Though scoundrels are discovered in a day.
CHORAGOS: This is well said, and a prudent man would ponder it.
Judgments too quickly formed are dangerous.
OEDIPUS: But is he not quick in his duplicity?
And shall I not be quick to parry him?
Would you have me stand still, hold my peace, and let
This man win everything, through my inaction?
CREON: And you want—what is it, then? To banish me?
OEDIPUS: No, not exile. It is your death I want,
So that all the world may see what treason means.
CREON: You will persist, then? You will not believe me?
OEDIPUS: How can I believe you?
CREON: Then you are a fool.
OEDIPUS: To save myself?
CREON: In justice, think of me.

OEDIPUS: You are evil incarnate.
CREON: But suppose that you are wrong?
OEDIPUS: Still I must rule.
CREON: But not if you rule badly.
OEDIPUS: O city, city!
CREON: It is my city, too!
CHORAGOS: Now, my lords, be still. I see the Queen,
Iocastê, coming from her palace chambers;
And it is time she came, for the sake of you both.
This dreadful quarrel can be resolved through her.

Enter IOCASTÊ.

IOCASTÊ: Poor foolish men, what wicked din is this?
With Thebes sick to death, is it not shameful
That you should rake some private quarrel up?

(To OEDIPUS.*)*

Come into the house.
—And you, Creon, go now:
Let us have no more of this tumult over nothing.
CREON: Nothing? No, sister: what your husband plans for me
Is one of two great evils: exile or death.
OEDIPUS: He is right.
Why, woman, I have caught him squarely
Plotting against my life.
CREON: No! Let me die
Accurst if ever I have wished you harm!
IOCASTÊ: Ah, believe it, Oedipus!
In the name of the gods, respect this oath of his
For my sake, for the sake of these people here!

Strophe 1

CHORAGOS: Open your mind to her, my lord. Be ruled by her, I beg you!
OEDIPUS: What would you have me do?
CHORAGOS: Respect Creon's word. He has never spoken like a fool,
And now he has sworn an oath.
OEDIPUS: You know what you ask?
CHORAGOS: I do.
OEDIPUS: Speak on, then.
CHORAGOS: A friend so sworn should not be baited so,
In blind malice, and without final proof.
OEDIPUS: You are aware, I hope, that what you say
Means death for me, or exile at the least.

Strophe 2

CHORAGOS: No, I swear by Helios, first in Heaven!
May I die friendless and accurst,
The worst of deaths, if ever I meant that!

It is the withering fields
That hurt my sick heart:
Must we bear all these ills,
And now your bad blood as well?

OEDIPUS: Then let him go. And let me die, if I must,
Or be driven by him in shame from the land of Thebes.
It is your unhappiness, and not his talk,
That touches me.
As for him—
Wherever he is, I will hate him as long as I live.

CREON: Ugly in yielding, as you were ugly in rage!
Natures like yours chiefly torment themselves.

OEDIPUS: Can you not go? Can you not leave me?

CREON: I can.
You do not know me; but the city knows me,
And in its eyes I am just, if not in yours.

(Exit CREON.*)*

Antistrophe 1

CHORAGOS: Lady Iocastê, did you not ask the King
to go to his chambers?

IOCASTÊ: First tell me what has happened.

CHORAGOS: There was suspicion without evidence; yet it rankled
As even false charges will.

IOCASTÊ: On both sides?

CHORAGOS: On both.

IOCASTÊ: But what was said?

CHORAGOS: Oh let it rest, let it be done with!
Have we not suffered enough?

OEDIPUS: You see to what your decency has brought you:
You have made difficulties where my heart saw none.

Antistrophe 2

CHORAGOS: Oedipus, it is not once only I have told you—
You must know I should count myself unwise
To the point of madness, should I now forsake you—
You, under whose hand,
In the storm of another time,
Our dear land sailed out free.
But now stand fast at the helm!

IOCASTÊ: In God's name, Oedipus, inform your wife as well:
Why are you so set in this hard anger?

OEDIPUS: I will tell you, for none of these men deserves
My confidence as you do. It is Creon's work,
His treachery, his plotting against me.

IOCASTÊ: Go on, if you can make this clear to me.

OEDIPUS: He charges me with the murder of Laïos.
IOCASTÊ: Has he some knowledge? Or does he speak from hearsay?
OEDIPUS: He would not commit himself to such a charge,
But he has brought in that damnable soothsayer
To tell his story.
IOCASTÊ: Set your mind at rest.
If it is a question of soothsayers, I tell you
That you will find no man whose craft gives knowledge
Of the unknowable.
Here is my proof:

An oracle was reported to Laïos once
(I will not say from Phoibos himself, but from
His appointed ministers, at any rate)
That his doom would be death at the hands of his own son—
His son, born of his flesh and of mine!

Now, you remember the story: Laïos was killed
By marauding strangers where three highways meet;
But his child had not been three days in this world
Before the King had pierced the baby's ankles
And left him to die on a lonely mountainside.

Thus, Apollo never caused that child
To kill his father, and it was not Laïos' fate
To die at the hands of his son, as he had feared.
This is what prophets and prophecies are worth!
Have no dread of them.
It is God himself
Who can show us what he wills, in his own way.
OEDIPUS: How strange a shadowy memory crossed my mind,
Just now while you were speaking; it chilled my heart.
IOCASTÊ: What do you mean? What memory do you speak of?
OEDIPUS: If I understand you, Laïos was killed
At a place where three roads meet.
IOCASTÊ: So it was said;
We have no later story.
OEDIPUS: Where did it happen?
IOCASTÊ: Phokis, it is called: at a place where the Theban Way
Divides into the roads towards Delphi and Daulia.
OEDIPUS: When?
IOCASTÊ: We had the news not long before you came
And proved the right to your succession here.
OEDIPUS: Ah, what net has God been weaving for me?
IOCASTÊ: Oedipus! Why does this trouble you?
OEDIPUS: Do not ask me yet.
First, tell me how Laïos looked, and tell me

How old he was.
IOCASTÊ: He was tall, his hair just touched
With white; his form was not unlike your own.
OEDIPUS: I think that I myself may be accurst
By my own ignorant edict.
IOCASTÊ: You speak strangely.
It makes me tremble to look at you, my King.
OEDIPUS: I am not sure that the blind man cannot see.
But I should know better if you were to tell me—
IOCASTÊ: Anything—though I dread to hear you ask it.
OEDIPUS: Was the King lightly escorted, or did he ride
With a large company, as a ruler should?
IOCASTÊ: There were five men with him in all: one was a herald;
And a single chariot, which he was driving.
OEDIPUS: Alas, that makes it plain enough!
But who—
Who told you how it happened?
IOCASTÊ: A household servant,
The only one to escape.
OEDIPUS: And is he still
A servant of ours?
IOCASTÊ: No; for when he came back at last
And found you enthroned in the place of the dead king,
He came to me, touched my hand with his, and begged
That I would send him away to the frontier district
Where only the shepherds go—
As far away from the city as I could send him.
I granted his prayer; for although the man was a slave,
He had earned more than this favor at my hands.
OEDIPUS: Can he be called back quickly?
IOCASTÊ: Easily.
But why?
OEDIPUS: I have taken too much upon myself
Without enquiry; therefore I wish to consult him.
IOCASTÊ: Then he shall come.
But am I not one also
To whom you might confide these fears of yours!
OEDIPUS: That is your right; it will not be denied you,
Now least of all; for I have reached a pitch
Of wild foreboding. Is there anyone
To whom I should sooner speak?
Polybos of Corinth is my father.
My mother is a Dorian: Meropê.
I grew up chief among the men of Corinth
Until a strange thing happened—
Not worth my passion, it may be, but strange.

At a feast, a drunken man maundering in his cups
Cries out that I am not my father's son!
I contained myself that night, though I felt anger
And a sinking heart. The next day I visited
My father and mother, and questioned them. They stormed,
Calling it all the slanderous rant of a fool;
And this relieved me. Yet the suspicion
Remained always aching in my mind;
I knew there was talk; I could not rest;
And finally, saying nothing to my parents,
I went to the shrine at Delphi.
The god dismissed my question without reply;
He spoke of other things.
Some were clear,
Full of wretchedness, dreadful, unbearable:
As, that I should lie with my own mother, breed
Children from whom all men would turn their eyes;
And that I should be my father's murderer.

I heard all this, and fled. And from that day
Corinth to me was only in the stars
Descending in that quarter of the sky,
As I wandered farther and farther on my way
To a land where I should never see the evil
Sung by the oracle. And I came to this country
Where, so you say, King Laïos was killed.
I will tell you all that happened there, my lady.
There were three highways
Coming together at a place I passed;
And there a herald came towards me, and a chariot
Drawn by horses, with a man such as you describe
Seated in it. The groom leading the horses
Forced me off the road at his lord's command;
But as this charioteer lurched over towards me
I struck him in my rage. The old man saw me
And brought his double goad down upon my head
As I came abreast.
He was paid back, and more!
Swinging my club in this right hand I knocked him
Out of his car, and he rolled on the ground.
I killed him.

I killed them all.
Now if that stranger and Laïos were—kin,
Where is a man more miserable than I?
More hated by the gods? Citizen and alien alike

Must never shelter me or speak to me—
I must be shunned by all.
And I myself
Pronounced this malediction upon myself!

Think of it: I have touched you with these hands,
These hands that killed your husband. What defilement!

Am I all evil, then? It must be so,
Since I must flee from Thebes, yet never again
See my own countrymen, my own country,
For fear of joining my mother in marriage
And killing Polybos, my father.
Ah,
If I was created so, born to this fate,
Who could deny the savagery of God?

O holy majesty of heavenly powers!
May I never see that day! Never!
Rather let me vanish from the race of men
Than know the abomination destined me!

CHORAGOS: We too, my lord, have felt dismay at this.
But there is hope: you have yet to hear the shepherd.

OEDIPUS: Indeed, I fear no other hope is left me.

IOCASTÊ: What do you hope from him when he comes?

OEDIPUS: This much:
If his account of the murder tallies with yours,
Then I am cleared.

IOCASTÊ: What was it that I said
Of such importance?

OEDIPUS: Why, "marauders," you said,
Killed the King, according to this man's story.
If he maintains that still, if there were several,
Clearly the guilt is not mine: I was alone.
But if he says one man, singlehanded, did it,
Then the evidence all points to me.

IOCASTÊ: You may be sure that he said there were several;
And can he call back that story now? He cannot.
The whole city heard it as plainly as I.
But suppose he alters some detail of it:
He cannot ever show that Laïos' death
Fulfilled the oracle: for Apollo said
My child was doomed to kill him; and my child—
Poor baby!—it was my child that died first.

No. From now on, where oracles are concerned,
I would not waste a second thought on any.

OEDIPUS: You may be right.

But come: let someone go
For the shepherd at once. This matter must be settled.

IOCASTÊ: I will send for him.
I would not wish to cross you in anything,
And surely not in this.—Let us go in.

Exeunt into the palace.

Ode II

Strophe 1

CHORUS: Let me be reverent in the ways of right,
Lowly the paths I journey on;
Let all my words and actions keep
The laws of the pure universe
From highest Heaven handed down.
For Heaven is their bright nurse,
Those generations of the realms of light;
Ah, never of mortal kind were they begot,
Nor are they slaves of memory, lost in sleep:
Their Father is greater than Time, and ages not.

Antistrophe 1

The tyrant is a child of Pride
Who drinks from his great sickening cup
Recklessness and vanity,
Until from his high crest headlong
He plummets to the dust of hope.
That strong man is not strong.
But let no fair ambition be denied;
May God protect the wrestler for the State
In government, in comely policy,
Who will fear God, and on His ordinance wait.

Strophe 2

Haughtiness and the high hand of disdain
Tempt and outrage God's holy law;
And any mortal who dares hold
No immortal Power in awe
Will be caught up in a net of pain:
The price for which his levity is sold.
Let each man take due earnings, then,
And keep his hands from holy things,
And from blasphemy stand apart—
Else the crackling blast of heaven
Blows on his head, and on his desperate heart;

Though fools will honor impious men,
In their cities no tragic poet sings.

Antistrophe 2

Shall we lose faith in Delphi's obscurities,
We who have heard the world's core
Discredited, and the sacred wood
Of Zeus at Elis praised no more?
The deeds and the strange prophecies
Must make a pattern yet to be understood.
Zeus, if indeed you are lord of all,
Throned in light over night and day,
Mirror this in your endless mind:
Our masters call the oracle
Words on the wind, and the Delphic vision blind!
Their hearts no longer know Apollo,
And reverence for the gods has died away.

Scene III

Enter IOCASTÊ.

IOCASTÊ: Princes of Thebes, it has occurred to me
To visit the altars of the gods, bearing
These branches as a suppliant, and this incense.
Our King is not himself: his noble soul
Is overwrought with fantasies of dread,
Else he would consider
The new prophecies in the light of the old.
He will listen to any voice that speaks disaster,
And my advice goes for nothing.

She approaches the altar, right.

To you, then, Apollo,
Lycean lord, since you are nearest, I turn in prayer.
Receive these offerings, and grant us deliverance
From defilement. Our hearts are heavy with fear
When we see our leader distracted, as helpless sailors
Are terrified by the confusion of their helmsman.

Enter MESSENGER.

MESSENGER: Friends, no doubt you can direct me:
Where shall I find the house of Oedipus,
Or, better still, where is the King himself?
CHORAGOS: It is this very place, stranger; he is inside.
This is his wife and mother of his children.
MESSENGER: I wish her happiness in a happy house,
Blest in all the fulfillment of her marriage.

IOCASTÊ: I wish as much for you: your courtesy
Deserves a like good fortune. But now, tell me:
Why have you come? What have you to say to us?
MESSENGER: Good news, my lady, for your house and your husband.
IOCASTÊ: What news? Who sent you here?
MESSENGER: I am from Corinth.
The news I bring ought to mean joy for you,
Though it may be you will find some grief in it.
IOCASTÊ: What is it? How can it touch us in both ways?
MESSENGER: The people of Corinth, they say,
Intend to call Oedipus to be their king.
IOCASTÊ: But old Polybos—is he not reigning still?
MESSENGER: No. Death holds him in his sepulchre.
IOCASTÊ: What are you saying? Polybos is dead?
MESSENGER: If I am not telling the truth, may I die myself.
IOCASTÊ: (*to a* MAIDSERVANT): Go in, go quickly; tell this to your master.

O riddlers of God's will, where are you now!
This was the man whom Oedipus, long ago,
Feared so, fled so, in dread of destroying him—
But it was another fate by which he died.

Enter OEDIPUS, *center.*

OEDIPUS: Dearest Iocastê, why have you sent for me?
IOCASTÊ: Listen to what this man says, and then tell me
What has become of the solemn prophecies.
OEDIPUS: Who is this man? What is his news for me?
IOCASTÊ: He has come from Corinth to announce your father's death!
OEDIPUS: Is it true, stranger? Tell me in your own words.
MESSENGER: I cannot say it more clearly: the King is dead.
OEDIPUS: Was it by treason? Or by an attack of illness?
MESSENGER: A little thing brings old men to their rest.
OEDIPUS: It was sickness, then?
MESSENGER: Yes, and his many years.
OEDIPUS: Ah!
Why should a man respect the Pythian hearth,° or
Give heed to the birds that jangle above his head?
They prophesied that I should kill Polybos,
Kill my own father; but he is dead and buried,
And I am here—I never touched him, never,
Unless he died in grief for my departure,
And thus, in a sense, through me. No. Polybos
Has packed the oracles off with him underground.
They are empty words.
IOCASTÊ: Had I not told you so?

52***Pythian hearth*** *Delphi, also called Pytho because a large dragon, the Python, had guarded the chasm at Delphi until Apollo killed it and established his oracle on the site.*

OEDIPUS: You had; it was my faint heart that betrayed me.
IOCASTÊ: From now on never think of those things again.
OEDIPUS: And yet—must I not fear my mother's bed?
IOCASTÊ: Why should anyone in this world be afraid,
Since Fate rules us and nothing can be foreseen?
A man should live only for the present day.
Have no more fear of sleeping with your mother:
How many men, in dreams, have lain with their mothers!
No reasonable man is troubled by such things.
OEDIPUS: That is true; only—
If only my mother were not still alive!
But she is alive. I cannot help my dread.
IOCASTÊ: Yet this news of your father's death is wonderful.
OEDIPUS: Wonderful. But I fear the living woman.
MESSENGER: Tell me, who is this woman that you fear?
OEDIPUS: It is Meropê, man; the wife of King Polybos.
MESSENGER: Meropê? Why should you be afraid of her?
OEDIPUS: An oracle of the gods, a dreadful saying.
MESSENGER: Can you tell me about it or are you sworn to silence?
OEDIPUS: I can tell you, and I will.
Apollo said through his prophet that I was the man
Who should marry his own mother, shed his father's blood
With his own hands. And so, for all these years
I have kept clear of Corinth, and no harm has come—
Though it would have been sweet to see my parents again.
MESSENGER: And is this the fear that drove you out of Corinth?
OEDIPUS: Would you have me kill my father?
MESSENGER: As for that
You must be reassured by the news I gave you.
OEDIPUS: If you could reassure me, I would reward you.
MESSENGER: I had that in mind, I will confess: I thought
I could count on you when you returned to Corinth.
OEDIPUS: No: I will never go near my parents again.
MESSENGER: Ah, son, you still do not know what you are doing—
OEDIPUS: What do you mean? In the name of God tell me!
MESSENGER: —If these are your reasons for not going home.
OEDIPUS: I tell you, I fear the oracle may come true.
MESSENGER: And guilt may come upon you through your parents?
OEDIPUS: That is the dread that is always in my heart.
MESSENGER: Can you not see that all your fears are groundless?
OEDIPUS: How can you say that? They are my parents, surely?
MESSENGER: Polybos was not your father.
OEDIPUS: Not my father?
MESSENGER: No more your father than the man speaking to you.
OEDIPUS: But you are nothing to me!
MESSENGER: Neither was he.
OEDIPUS: Then why did he call me son?
MESSENGER: I will tell you:

Long ago he had you from my hands, as a gift.
OEDIPUS: Then how could he love me so, if I was not his?
MESSENGER: He had no children, and his heart turned to you.
OEDIPUS: What of you? Did you buy me? Did you find me by chance?
MESSENGER: I came upon you in the crooked pass of Kithairon.
OEDIPUS: And what were you doing there?
MESSENGER: Tending my flocks.
OEDIPUS: A wandering shepherd?
MESSENGER: But your savior, son, that day.
OEDIPUS: From what did you save me?
MESSENGER: Your ankles should tell you that.
OEDIPUS: Ah, stranger, why do you speak of that childhood pain?
MESSENGER: I cut the bonds that tied your ankles together.
OEDIPUS: I have had the mark as long as I can remember.
MESSENGER: That was why you were given the name you bear.°
OEDIPUS: God! Was it my father or my mother who did it?
Tell me!
MESSENGER: I do not know. The man who gave you to me
Can tell you better than I.
OEDIPUS: It was not you that found me, but another?
MESSENGER: It was another shepherd gave you to me.
OEDIPUS: Who was he? Can you tell me who he was?
MESSENGER: I think he was said to be one of Laïos' people.
OEDIPUS: You mean the Laïos who was king here years ago?
MESSENGER: Yes; King Laïos; and the man was one of his herdsmen.
OEDIPUS: Is he still alive? Can I see him?
MESSENGER: These men here
Know best about such things.
OEDIPUS: Does anyone here
Know this shepherd that he is talking about?
Have you seen him in the fields, or in the town?
If you have, tell me. It is time things were made plain.
CHORAGOS: I think the man he means is that same shepherd
You have already asked to see. Iocastê perhaps
Could tell you something.
OEDIPUS: Do you know anything
About him, Lady? Is he the man we have summoned?
Is that the man this shepherd means?
IOCASTÊ: Why think of him?
Forget this herdsman. Forget it all.
This talk is a waste of time.
OEDIPUS: How can you say that,
When the clues to my true birth are in my hands?
IOCASTÊ: For God's love, let us have no more questioning!
Is your life nothing to you?
My own is pain enough for me to bear.

116 ***name you bear*** *"Oedipus" means "swollen-foot."*

OEDIPUS: You need not worry. Suppose my mother a slave,
  And born of slaves: no baseness can touch you.
IOCASTÊ: Listen to me, I beg you: do not do this thing!
OEDIPUS: I will not listen; the truth must be made known.
IOCASTÊ: Everything that I say is for your own good!
OEDIPUS: My own good
  Snaps my patience, then: I want none of it.
IOCASTÊ: You are fatally wrong! May you never learn who you are!
OEDIPUS: Go, one of you, and bring the shepherd here.
  Let us leave this woman to brag of her royal name.
IOCASTÊ: Ah, miserable!
  That is the only word I have for you now.
  That is the only word I can ever have.

Exit into the palace.

CHORAGOS: Why has she left us, Oedipus? Why has she gone
  In such a passion of sorrow? I fear this silence:
  Something dreadful may come of it.
OEDIPUS: Let it come!
  However base my birth, I must know about it.
  The Queen, like a woman, is perhaps ashamed
  To think of my low origin. But I
  Am a child of luck; I cannot be dishonored.
  Luck is my mother; the passing months, my brothers,
  Have seen me rich and poor.
  If this is so,
  How could I wish that I were someone else?
  How could I not be glad to know my birth?

Ode III

Strophe

CHORUS: If ever the coming time were known
  To my heart's pondering,
  Kithairon, now by Heaven I see the torches
  At the festival of the next full moon,
  And see the dance, and hear the choir sing
  A grace to your gentle shade:
  Mountain where Oedipus was found,
  O mountain guard of a noble race!
  May the god who heals us lend his aid,
  And let that glory come to pass
  For our king's cradling-ground.

Antistrophe

  Of the nymphs that flower beyond the years,
  Who bore you, royal child,
  To Pan of the hills or the timberline Apollo,

Cold in delight where the upland clears,
Or Hermês for whom Kyllenê's heights° are piled?
Or flushed as evening cloud,
Great Dionysos, roamer of mountains,
He—was it he who found you there,
And caught you up in his own proud
Arms from the sweet god-ravisher
Who laughed by the Muses' fountains?

Scene IV

OEDIPUS: Sirs: though I do not know the man,
I think I see him coming, this shepherd we want:
He is old, like our friend here, and the men
Bringing him seem to be servants of my house.
But you can tell, if you have ever seen him.

Enter SHEPHERD *escorted by servants.*

CHORAGOS: I know him, he was Laïos' man. You can trust him.
OEDIPUS: Tell me first, you from Corinth: is this the shepherd
We were discussing?
MESSENGER: This is the very man.
OEDIPUS (*to* SHEPHERD): Come here. No, look at me. You must answer
Everything I ask.—You belonged to Laïos?
SHEPHERD: Yes: born his slave, brought up in his house.
OEDIPUS: Tell me: what kind of work did you do for him?
SHEPHERD: I was a shepherd of his, most of my life.
OEDIPUS: Where mainly did you go for pasturage?
SHEPHERD: Sometimes Kithairon, sometimes the hills near-by.
OEDIPUS: Do you remember ever seeing this man out there?
SHEPHERD: What would he be doing there? This man?
OEDIPUS: This man standing here. Have you ever seen him before?
SHEPHERD: No. At least, not to my recollection.
MESSENGER: And that is not strange, my lord. But I'll refresh
His memory: he must remember when we two
Spent three whole seasons together, March to September,
On Kithairon or thereabouts. He had two flocks;
I had one. Each autumn I'd drive mine home
And he would go back with his to Laïos' sheepfold.—
Is this not true, just as I have described it?
SHEPHERD: True, yes; but it was all so long ago.
MESSENGER: Well, then: do you remember, back in those days
That you gave me a baby boy to bring up as my own?
SHEPHERD: What if I did? What are you trying to say?
MESSENGER: King Oedipus was once that little child.
SHEPHERD: Damn you, hold your tongue!

16 ***Kyllenê's heights*** *holy mountain, birthplace of Hermes, messenger of the gods.*

OEDIPUS: No more of that!
It is your tongue needs watching, not this man's.
SHEPHERD: My King, my Master, what is it I have done wrong?
OEDIPUS: You have not answered his question about the boy.
SHEPHERD: He does not know . . . He is only making trouble . . .
OEDIPUS: Come, speak plainly, or it will go hard with you.
SHEPHERD: In God's name, do not torture an old man!
OEDIPUS: Come here, one of you; bind his arms behind him.
SHEPHERD: Unhappy king! What more do you wish to learn?
OEDIPUS: Did you give this man the child he speaks of?
SHEPHERD: I did.
And I would to God I had died that very day.
OEDIPUS: You will die now unless you speak the truth.
SHEPHERD: Yet if I speak the truth, I am worse than dead.
OEDIPUS: Very well; since you insist upon delaying—
SHEPHERD: No! I have told you already that I gave him the boy.
OEDIPUS: Where did you get him? From your house?
From somewhere else?
SHEPHERD: Not from mine, no. A man gave him to me.
OEDIPUS: Is that man here? Do you know whose slave he was?
SHEPHERD: For God's love, my King, do not ask me any more!
OEDIPUS: You are a dead man if I have to ask you again.
SHEPHERD: Then . . . Then the child was from the palace of Laïos.
OEDIPUS: A slave child? or a child of his own line?
SHEPHERD: Ah, I am on the brink of dreadful speech!
OEDIPUS: And I of dreadful hearing. Yet I must hear.
SHEPHERD: If you must be told, then . . .
They said it was Laïos' child,
But it is your wife who can tell you about that.
OEDIPUS: My wife!—Did she give it to you?
SHEPHERD: My lord, she did.
OEDIPUS: Do you know why?
SHEPHERD: I was told to get rid of it.
OEDIPUS: An unspeakable mother!
SHEPHERD: There had been prophecies . . .
OEDIPUS: Tell me.
SHEPHERD: It was said that the boy would kill his own father.
OEDIPUS: Then why did you give him over to this old man?
SHEPHERD: I pitied the baby, my King.
And I thought that this man would take him far away
To his own country.
He saved him—but for what a fate!
For if you are what this man says you are,
No man living is more wretched than Oedipus.
OEDIPUS: Ah God!
It was true!
All the prophecies!
—Now,

O Light, may I look on you for the last time!
I, Oedipus,
Oedipus, damned in his birth, in his marriage damned,
Damned in the blood he shed with his own hand!

He rushes into the palace.

Ode IV

Strophe 1

CHORUS: Alas for the seed of men.
What measure shall I give these generations
That breathe on the void and are void
And exist and do not exist?

Who bears more weight of joy
Than mass of sunlight shifting in images,
Or who shall make his thought stay on
That down time drifts away?

Your splendor is all fallen.

O naked brow of wrath and tears,
O change of Oedipus!
I who saw your days call no man blest—
Your great days like ghósts góne.

Antistrophe 1

That mind was a strong bow.
Deep, how deep you drew it then, hard archer,
At a dim fearful range,
And brought dear glory down!

You overcame the stranger—
The virgin with her hooking lion claws—
And though death sang, stood like a tower
To make pale Thebes take heart.

Fortress against our sorrow!

Divine king, giver of laws,
Majestic Oedipus!
No prince in Thebes had ever such renown,
No prince won such grace of power.

Strophe 2

And now of all men ever known
Most pitiful is this man's story:
His fortunes are most changed, his state

Fallen to a low slave's
Ground under bitter fate.

O Oedipus, most royal one!
The great door that expelled you to the light
Gave at night—ah, gave night to your glory:
As to the father, to the fathering son.

All understood too late.

How could that queen whom Laïos won,
The garden that he harrowed at his height,
Be silent when that act was done?

Antistrophe 2

But all eyes fail before time's eye,
All actions come to justice there.
Though never willed, though far down the deep past,
Your bed, your dread sirings,
Are brought to book at last.
Child by Laïos doomed to die,
Then doomed to lose that fortunate little death,
Would God you never took breath in this air
That with my wailing lips I take to cry:

For I weep the world's outcast.
I was blind, and now I can tell why:
Asleep, for you had given ease of breath
To Thebes, while the false years went by.

Exodos

Enter, from the palace, SECOND MESSENGER.

SECOND MESSENGER: Elders of Thebes, most honored in this land,
What horrors are yours to see and hear, what weight
Of sorrow to be endured, if, true to your birth,
You venerate the line of Labdakos!
I think neither Istros nor Phasis, those great rivers,
Could purify this place of the corruption
It shelters now, or soon must bring to light—
Evil not done unconsciously, but willed.

The greatest griefs are those we cause ourselves.

CHORAGOS: Surely, friend, we have grief enough already;
What new sorrow do you mean?

SECOND MESSENGER: The Queen is dead.

CHORAGOS: Iocastê? Dead? But at whose hand?

SECOND MESSENGER: Her own.
The full horror of what happened you cannot know,
For you did not see it; but I, who did, will tell you
As clearly as I can how she met her death.
When she had left us,
In passionate silence, passing through the court,
She ran to her apartment in the house,
Her hair clutched by the fingers of both hands.
She closed the doors behind her; then, by that bed
Where long ago the fatal son was conceived—
That son who should bring about his father's death—
We heard her call upon Laïos, dead so many years,
And heard her wail for the double fruit of her marriage,
A husband by her husband, children by her child.

Exactly how she died I do not know:
For Oedipus burst in moaning and would not let us
Keep vigil to the end: it was by him
As he stormed about the room that our eyes were caught.
From one to another of us he went, begging a sword,
Cursing the wife who was not his wife, the mother
Whose womb had carried his own children and himself.
I do not know: it was none of us aided him,
But surely one of the gods was in control!
For with a dreadful cry
He hurled his weight, as though wrenched out of himself,
At the twin doors: the bolts gave, and he rushed in.
And there we saw her hanging, her body swaying
From the cruel cord she had noosed about her neck.
A great sob broke from him heartbreaking to hear,
As he loosed the rope and lowered her to the ground.

I would blot out from my mind what happened next!
For the King ripped from her gown the golden brooches
That were her ornament, and raised them, and plunged them down
Straight into his own eyeballs, crying, "No more,
No more shall you look on the misery about me,
The horrors of my own doing! Too long you have known
The faces of those whom I should never have seen,
Too long been blind to those for whom I was searching!
From this hour, go in darkness!" And as he spoke,
He struck at his eyes—not once, but many times;
And the blood spattered his beard,
Bursting from his ruined sockets like red hail.

So from the unhappiness of two this evil has sprung,
A curse on the man and woman alike. The old

Happiness of the house of Labdakos
Was happiness enough: where is it today?
It is all wailing and ruin, disgrace, death—all
The misery of mankind that has a name—
And it is wholly and for ever theirs.

CHORAGOS: Is he in agony still? Is there no rest for him?

SECOND MESSENGER: He is calling for someone to lead him to the gates
So that all the children of Kadmos may look upon
His father's murderer, his mother's—no,
I cannot say it!
And then he will leave Thebes,
Self-exiled, in order that the curse
Which he himself pronounced may depart from the house.
He is weak, and there is none to lead him,
So terrible is his suffering.
But you will see:
Look, the doors are opening; in a moment
You will see a thing that would crush a heart of stone.

The central door is opened; OEDIPUS, *blinded, is led in.*

CHORAGOS: Dreadful indeed for men to see.
Never have my own eyes
Looked on a sight so full of fear.

Oedipus!
What madness came upon you, what daemon
Leaped on your life with heavier
Punishment than a mortal man can bear?
No: I cannot even
Look at you, poor ruined one.
And I would speak, question, ponder,
If I were able. No.
You make me shudder.

OEDIPUS: God. God.
Is there a sorrow greater?
Where shall I find harbor in this world?
My voice is hurled far on a dark wind.
What has God done to me?

CHORAGOS: Too terrible to think of, or to see.

Strophe 1

OEDIPUS: O cloud of night,
Never to be turned away: night coming on,
I cannot tell how: night like a shroud!
My fair winds brought me here.
Oh God. Again
The pain of the spikes where I had sight,
The flooding pain

Of memory, never to be gouged out.
CHORAGOS: This is not strange.
You suffer it all twice over, remorse in pain,
Pain in remorse.

Antistrophe 1

OEDIPUS: Ah dear friend
Are you faithful even yet, you alone?
Are you still standing near me, will you stay here,
Patient, to care for the blind?
The blind man!
Yet even blind I know who it is attends me,
By the voice's tone—
Though my new darkness hide the comforter.
CHORAGOS: Oh fearful act!
What god was it drove you to rake black
Night across your eyes?

Strophe 2

OEDIPUS: Apollo. Apollo. Dear
Children, the god was Apollo.
He brought my sick, sick fate upon me.
But the blinding hand was my own!
How could I bear to see
When all my sight was horror everywhere?
CHORAGOS: Everywhere; that is true.
OEDIPUS: And now what is left?
Images? Love? A greeting even,
Sweet to the senses? Is there anything?
Ah, no, friends: lead me away.
Lead me away from Thebes.
Lead the great wreck
And hell of Oedipus, whom the gods hate.
CHORAGOS: Your fate is clear, you are not blind to that.
Would God you had never found it out!

Antistrophe 2

OEDIPUS: Death take the man who unbound
My feet on that hillside
And delivered me from death to life! What life?
If only I had died,
This weight of monstrous doom
Could not have dragged me and my darlings down.
CHORAGOS: I would have wished the same.
OEDIPUS: Oh never to have come here
With my father's blood upon me! Never
To have been the man they call his mother's husband!
Oh accurst! Oh child of evil,

To have entered that wretched bed—
the selfsame one!
More primal than sin itself, this fell to me.
CHORAGOS: I do not know how I can answer you.
You were better dead than alive and blind.
OEDIPUS: Do not counsel me any more. This punishment
That I have laid upon myself is just.
If I had eyes,
I do not know how I could bear the sight
Of my father, when I came to the house of Death,
Or my mother: for I have sinned against them both
So vilely that I could not make my peace
By strangling my own life.
Or do you think my children,
Born as they were born, would be sweet to my eyes?
Ah never, never! Nor this town with its high walls,
Nor the holy images of the gods.
For I,
Thrice miserable—Oedipus, noblest of all the line
Of Kadmos, have condemned myself to enjoy
These things no more, by my own malediction
Expelling that man whom the gods declared
To be a defilement in the house of Laïos.
After exposing the rankness of my own guilt,
How could I look men frankly in the eyes?
No, I swear it,
If I could have stifled my hearing at its source,
I would have done it and made all this body
A tight cell of misery, blank to light and sound:
So I should have been safe in a dark agony
Beyond all recollection.
Ah Kithairon!
Why did you shelter me? When I was cast upon you,
Why did I not die? Then I should never
Have shown the world my execrable birth.

Ah Polybos! Corinth, city that I believed
The ancient seat of my ancestors: how fair
I seemed, your child! And all the while this evil
Was cancerous within me!
For I am sick
In my daily life, sick in my origin.

O three roads, dark ravine, woodland and way
Where three roads met you, drinking my father's blood,
My own blood, spilled by my own hand: can you remember
The unspeakable things I did there, and the things
I went on from there to do?

O marriage, marriage!
The act that engendered me, and again the act
Performed by the son in the same bed—
Ah, the net
Of incest, mingling fathers, brothers, sons,
With brides, wives, mothers: the last evil
That can be known by men: no tongue can say
How evil!
No. For the love of God, conceal me
Somewhere far from Thebes; or kill me; or hurl me
Into the sea, away from men's eyes for ever.
Come, lead me. You need not fear to touch me.
Of all men, I alone can bear this guilt.

Enter CREON.

CHORAGOS: We are not the ones to decide; but Creon here
May fitly judge of what you ask. He only
Is left to protect the city in your place.
OEDIPUS: Alas, how can I speak to him? What right have I
To beg his courtesy whom I have deeply wronged?
CREON: I have not come to mock you, Oedipus,
Or to reproach you, either.

(To ATTENDANTS.*)*

—You, standing there:
If you have lost all respect for man's dignity,
At least respect the flame of Lord Helios:
Do not allow this pollution to show itself
Openly here, an affront to the earth
And Heaven's rain and the light of day. No, take him
Into the house as quickly as you can.
For it is proper
That only the close kindred see his grief.
OEDIPUS: I pray you in God's name, since your courtesy
Ignores my dark expectation, visiting
With mercy this man of all men most execrable:
Give me what I ask—for your good, not for mine.
CREON: And what is it that you would have me do?
OEDIPUS: Drive me out of this country as quickly as may be
To a place where no human voice can ever greet me.
CREON: I should have done that before now—only,
God's will had not been wholly revealed to me.
OEDIPUS: But his command is plain: the parricide
Must be destroyed. I am that evil man.
CREON: That is the sense of it, yes; but as things are,
We had best discover clearly what is to be done.
OEDIPUS: You would learn more about a man like me?
CREON: You are ready now to listen to the god.

OEDIPUS: I will listen. But it is to you
That I must turn for help. I beg you, hear me.

The woman in there—
Give her whatever funeral you think proper:
She is your sister.
—But let me go, Creon!
Let me purge my father's Thebes of the pollution
Of my living here, and go out to the wild hills,
To Kithairon, that has won such fame with me,
The tomb my mother and father appointed for me,
And let me die there, as they willed I should.
And yet I know
Death will not ever come to me through sickness
Or in any natural way: I have been preserved
For some unthinkable fate. But let that be.
As for my sons, you need not care for them.
They are men, they will find some way to live.
But my poor daughters, who have shared my table,
Who never before have been parted from their father—
Take care of them, Creon; do this for me.
And will you let me touch them with my hands
A last time, and let us weep together?
Be kind, my lord,
Great prince, be kind!
Could I but touch them,
They would be mine again, as when I had my eyes.

Enter ANTIGONÊ *and* ISMENÊ, *attended.*

Ah, God!
Is it my dearest children I hear weeping?
Has Creon pitied me and sent my daughters?
CREON: Yes, Oedipus: I knew that they were dear to you
In the old days, and know you must love them still.
OEDIPUS: May God bless you for this—and be a friendlier
Guardian to you than he has been to me!

Children, where are you?
Come quickly to my hands: they are your brother's—
Hands that have brought your father's once clear eyes
To this way of seeing—
Ah dearest ones,
I had neither sight nor knowledge then, your father
By the woman who was the source of his own life!
And I weep for you—having no strength to see you—,
I weep for you when I think of the bitterness
That men will visit upon you all your lives.

What homes, what festivals can you attend
Without being forced to depart again in tears?
And when you come to marriageable age,
Where is the man, my daughters, who would dare
Risk the bane that lies on all my children?
Is there any evil wanting? Your father killed
His father; sowed the womb of her who bore him;
Engendered you at the fount of his own existence!
That is what they will say of you.
Then, whom
Can you ever marry? There are no bridegrooms for you,
And your lives must wither away in sterile dreaming.
O Creon, son of Menoikeus!
You are the only father my daughters have,
Since we, their parents, are both of us gone for ever.
They are your own blood: you will not let them
Fall into beggary and loneliness;
You will keep them from the miseries that are mine!
Take pity on them; see, they are only children,
Friendless except for you. Promise me this,
Great Prince, and give me your hand in token of it.

CREON *clasps his right hand.*

Children:
I could say much, if you could understand me,
But as it is, I have only this prayer for you:
Live where you can, be as happy as you can—
Happier, please God, than God has made your father!

CREON: Enough. You have wept enough. Now go within.
OEDIPUS: I must; but it is hard.
CREON: Time eases all things.
OEDIPUS: But you must promise—
CREON: Say what you desire.
OEDIPUS: Send me from Thebes!
CREON: God grant that I may!
OEDIPUS: But since God hates me . . .
CREON: No, he will grant your wish.
OEDIPUS: You promise?
CREON: I cannot speak beyond my knowledge.
OEDIPUS: Then lead me in.
CREON: Come now, and leave your children.
OEDIPUS: No! Do not take them from me!
CREON: Think no longer
That you are in command here, but rather think
How, when you were, you served your own destruction.

Exeunt into the house all but the CHORUS; *the* CHORAGOS *chants directly to the audience.*

CHORAGOS: Men of Thebes: look upon Oedipus.
This is the king who solved the famous riddle
And towered up, most powerful of men
No mortal eyes but looked on him with envy.
Yet in the end ruin swept over him.

Let every man in mankind's frailty
Consider his last day; and let none
Presume on his good fortune until he find
Life, at his death, a memory without pain.

(c. 430 B.C.)

QUESTIONS FOR CRITICAL THINKING AND WRITING

Experience

1. Describe your experience of reading *Oedipus Rex*. Were you surprised? Baffled? Horrified—at any point? If so, where and why?

Interpretation

2. What makes Oedipus a tragic hero? What makes his predicament fascinating rather than merely horrifying? Account for the continued appeal of the play.
3. Identify and explain the different types of irony in *Oedipus Rex*.
4. How is the imagery of light and darkness employed throughout the play? How is it related to Oedipus's blindness?
5. What roles do the chorus and choragos assume? Compare their functions in the beginning, middle, and end of the play.
6. Iocastê appears a number of times, but she has little to say. What is she like? How much do we know about her—especially her thoughts and feelings?

Evaluation

7. Evaluate Oedipus's actions. Is he to blame for what happens? Account for his change of attitude and manner by comparing his speech and behavior in the opening and closing scenes.

Connections

8. Compare Oedipus as a tragic hero with Othello.

Critical Thinking

9. Rather than dramatize on stage the shocking and horrible events in which the play culminates, Sophocles has them occur offstage, and we learn about them through a messenger's report. What are the limitations and advantages of such a method?

CRITICS ON SOPHOCLES

ARISTOTLE

[384–32 B.C.*]*

The Six Elements of Tragedy

TRANSLATED BY GERALD F. ELSE

from POETICS: TRAGEDY

At present let us deal with tragedy, recovering from what has been said so far the definition of its essential nature, as it was in development. Tragedy, then, is a process of imitating an action which has serious implications, is complete, and possesses magnitude; by means of language which has been made sensuously attractive, with each of its varieties found separately in the parts; enacted by the persons themselves and not presented through narrative; through a course of pity and fear completing the purification of tragic acts which have those emotional characteristics. By "language made sensuously attractive" I mean language that has rhythm and melody, and by "its varieties found separately" I mean the fact that certain parts of the play are carried on through spoken verses alone and others the other way around, through song.

Now first of all, since they perform the imitation through action (by acting it), the adornment of their visual appearance will perforce constitute some part of the making of tragedy; and song-composition and verbal expression also, for those are the media in which they perform the imitation. By "verbal expression" I mean the actual composition of the verses, and by "song-composition" something whose meaning is entirely clear.

Next, since it is an imitation of an action and is enacted by certain people who are performing the action, and since those people must necessarily have certain traits both of character and thought (for it is thanks to these two factors that we speak of people's actions also as having a defined character, and it is in accordance with their actions that all either succeed or fail); and since the imitation of the action is the plot, for by "plot" I mean here the structuring of the events, and by the "characters" that in accordance with which we say that the persons who are acting have a defined moral character, and by "thought" all the passages in which they attempt to prove some thesis or set forth an opinion—it follows of necessity, then, that tragedy as a whole has just six constituent elements, in relation to the essence that makes it a distinct species; and they are plot, characters, verbal expression, thought, visual adornment, and song-composition. For the elements by which they imitate are two (i.e., verbal expression and song-composition), the manner in which they imitate is one (visual adornment), the things they imitate are three (plot, characters, thought), and there is nothing more beyond these. These then are the constituent forms they use.

Simple and Complex Plots

from POETICS: TRAGEDY

Among simple plots and actions the episodic are the worst. By "episodic" plot I mean one in which there is no probability or necessity for the order in which the episodes follow one another. Such structures are composed by the bad poets because they are bad poets, but by the good poets because of the actors: in composing contest pieces for them, and stretching out the plot beyond its capacity, they are forced frequently to dislocate the sequence.

Furthermore, since the tragic imitation is not only of a complete action but also of events that are fearful and pathetic, and these come about best when they come about contrary to one's expectation yet logically, one following from the other; that way they will be more productive of wonder than if they happen merely at random, by chance—because even among chance occurrences the ones people consider most marvelous are those that seem to have come about as if on purpose: for example the way the statue of Mitys at Argos killed the man who had been the cause of Mitys's death, by falling on him while he was attending the festival; it stands to reason, people think, that such things don't happen by chance—so plots of that sort cannot fail to be artistically superior.

Some plots are simple, others are complex; indeed the actions of which the plots are imitations already fall into these two categories. By "simple" action I mean one the development of which being continuous and unified in the manner stated above, the reversal comes without peripety or recognition, and by "complex" action one in which the reversal is continuous but with recognition or peripety or both. And these developments must grow out of the very structure of the plot itself, in such a way that on the basis of what has happened previously this particular outcome follows either by necessity or in accordance with probability; for there is a great difference in whether these events happen because of those or merely after them.

"Peripety" is a shift of what is being undertaken to the opposite in the way previously stated, and that in accordance with probability or necessity as we have just been saying; as for example in the *Oedipus* the man who has come, thinking that he will reassure Oedipus, that is, relieve him of his fear with respect to his mother, by revealing who he once was, brings about the opposite; and in the *Lynceus,* as he (Lynceus) is being led away with every prospect of being executed, and Danaus pursuing him with every prospect of doing the executing, it comes about as a result of the other things that have happened in the play that *he* is executed and Lynceus is saved. And "recognition" is, as indeed the name indicates, a shift from ignorance to awareness, pointing in the direction either of close blood ties or of hostility, of people who have previously been in a clearly marked state of happiness or unhappiness.

The finest recognition is one that happens at the same time as a peripety, as is the case with the one in the *Oedipus.* Naturally, there are also other kinds of recognition: it is possible for one to take place in the prescribed manner in relation to inanimate objects and chance occurrences, and it is possible to recognize whether a person has acted or not acted. But the form that is most integrally a part of the plot, the action, is the one aforesaid; for that kind of recognition combined with peripety will excite either pity or fear (and these are the kinds of action of which tragedy is an imitation according to our definition), because both good and bad fortune will also be most likely to follow that kind of event. Since, further, the recognition is a recognition of persons, some are of one person by the other one only (when it is already known who the "other one" is), but sometimes it is necessary for both persons to go through a recognition, as for example, Iphigenia is recognized by her brother through the sending of the letter, but of him by Iphigenia another recognition is required.

These then are two elements of plot: peripety and recognition; third is the *pathos.* Of these, peripety and recognition have been discussed; a *pathos* is a destructive or painful act, such as deaths on stage, paroxysms of pain, woundings, and all that sort of thing.

SIGMUND FREUD
[1856–1939]

The Oedipus Complex

from THE INTERPRETATION OF DREAMS

The action of the play consists in nothing other than the process of revealing, with cunning delays and ever-mounting excitement—a process that can be likened to the work of a psychoanalysis—that Oedipus himself is the murderer of Laïos, but further that he is the son of the murdered man and of Iocaste. Appalled at the abomination which he has unwittingly perpetrated, Oedipus blinds himself and forsakes his home. The oracle has been fulfilled.

Oedipus Rex is what is known as a tragedy of destiny. Its tragic effect is said to lie in the contrast between the supreme will of the gods and the vain attempts of mankind to escape the evil that threatens them. The lesson which, it is said, the deeply moved spectator should learn from the tragedy is submission to the divine will and realization of his own impotence. Modern dramatists have accordingly tried to achieve a similar tragic effect by weaving the same contrast into a plot invented by themselves. But the spectators have looked on unmoved while a curse or an oracle was fulfilled in spite of all the efforts of some innocent man: later tragedies of destiny have failed in their effect.

If *Oedipus Rex* moves a modern audience no less than it did the contemporary Greek one, the explanation can only be that its effect does not lie in the contrast between destiny and human will, but is to be looked for in the particular nature of the material on which that contrast is exemplified. There must be something which makes a voice within us ready to recognize the compelling force of destiny in the *Oedipus,* while we can dismiss as merely arbitrary such dispositions as are laid down in [Grillparzer's] *Die Ahnfrau* or other modern tragedies of destiny. And a factor of this kind is in fact involved in the story of King Oedipus. His destiny moves us only because it might have been ours—because the oracle laid the same curse upon us before our birth as upon him. It is the fate of all of us, perhaps, to direct our first sexual impulse toward our mother and our first hatred and our first murderous wish against our father. Our dreams convince us that that is so. King Oedipus, who slew his father Laïos and married his mother Iocaste, merely shows us the fulfillment of our own childhood wishes. But, more fortunate than he, we have meanwhile succeeded, in so far as we have not become psychoneurotics, in detaching our sexual impulses from our mothers and in forgetting our jealousy of our fathers. Here is one in whom these primeval wishes of our childhood have been fulfilled, and we shrink back from him with the whole force of the repression by which those wishes have since that time been held down within us. While the poet, as he unravels the past, brings to light the guilt of Oedipus, he is at the same time compelling us to recognize our own inner minds, in which those same impulses, though suppressed, are still to be found. The contrast with which the closing Chorus leaves us confronted—

> . . . Fix on Oedipus your eyes,
> Who resolved the dark enigma, noblest champion and most wise.
> Like a star his envied fortune mounted beaming far and wide:
> Now he sinks in seas of anguish, whelmed beneath a raging tide . . .

—strikes as a warning at ourselves and our pride, at us who since our childhood have grown so wise and so mighty in our own eyes. Like Oedipus, we live in ignorance of these wishes, repugnant to morality, which have been forced upon us by Nature, and after their revelation we may all of us well seek to close our eyes to the scenes of our childhood.

There is an unmistakable indication in the text of Sophocles' tragedy itself that the legend of Oedipus sprang from some primeval dream material which had as its content the distressing disturbance of a child's relation to his parents owing to the first stirrings of sexuality. At a point when Oedipus, though he is not yet enlightened, has begun to feel troubled by his recollection of the oracle, Jocasta consoles him by referring to a dream which many people dream, though, as she thinks, it has no meaning:

> Many a man ere now in dreams hath lain
> With her who bare him. He hath least annoy
> Who with such omens troubleth not his mind.

Today, just as then, many men dream of having sexual relations with their mothers, and speak of the fact with indignation and astonishment. It is clearly the key to the tragedy and the complement to the dream of the dreamer's father being dead. The story of Oedipus is the reaction of the imagination to these two typical dreams. And just as these dreams, when dreamt by adults, are accompanied by feelings of repulsion, so too the legend must include horror and self-punishment. Its further modification originates once again in a misconceived secondary revision of the material, which has sought to exploit it for theological purposes. . . . The attempt to harmonize divine omnipotence with human responsibility must naturally fail in connection with this subject matter just as with any other.

BERNARD KNOX

Sophocles' Oedipus

from WORD AND ACTION

In an earlier Sophoclean play, *Antigonê,* the chorus sings a hymn to this man the conqueror. "Many are the wonders and terrors, and nothing more wonderful and terrible than man." He has conquered the sea, "this creature goes beyond the white sea pressing forward as the swell crashes about him"; and he has conquered the land, "earth, highest of the gods . . . he wears away with the turning plough." He has mastered not only the elements, sea, and land, but the birds, beasts, and fishes; "through knowledge and technique," sings the chorus, he is yoker of the horse, tamer of the bull. "And he has taught himself speech and thought swift as the wind and attitudes which enable him to live in communities and means to shelter himself from the frost and rain. Full of resources he faces the future, nothing will find him at a loss. Death, it is true, he will not avoid, yet he has thought out ways of escape from desperate diseases. His knowledge, ingenuity and technique are beyond anything that could have been foreseen." These lyrics describe the rise to power of *anthropos tyrannos;* self-taught, he seizes control of his environment, he is master of the elements, the animals, the arts and sciences of civilization. "Full of resources he faces the future"—an apt description of Oedipus at the beginning of our play.

And it is not the only phrase of this ode which is relevant; for Oedipus is connected by the terms he uses, and which are used to and about him, with the whole range of human achievement which has raised man to his present level. All the items of this triumphant catalog recur in the *Oedipus Tyrannos* [*Oedipus Rex*]*;* the images of the play define him as helmsman, conqueror of the sea, and ploughman, conqueror of the land, as hunter, master of speech and thought, inventor, legislator, physician. Oedipus is faced in the play with an intellectual problem, and as he marshals his intellectual resources to solve it, the language of the play suggests a comparison between Oedipus' methods in the play and the whole range of sciences and techniques which have brought man to mastery, made him *tyrannos* of the world.

Oedipus' problem is apparently simple: "Who is the murderer of Laïos?" But as he pursues the answer, the question changes shape. It becomes a different problem: "Who am I?" And the answer to this problem involves the gods as well as man. The answer to the question is not what he expected, it is in fact a reversal, that *peripeteia* which Aristotle speaks of in connection with this play. The state of Oedipus is reversed from "first of men" to "most accursed of men"; his attitude from the proud ἀρκτεέον, "I must rule," to the humble πειστεέον "I must obey." "Reversal," says Aristotle, "is a change of the action into the opposite," and one meaning of this much disputed phrase is that the action produces the opposite of the actor's intentions. So Oedipus curses the murderer of Laïos and it turns out that he has cursed himself. But this reversal is not confined to the action; it is also the process of all the great images of the play which identify Oedipus as the inventive, critical spirit of his century. As the images unfold, the inquirer turns into the object of inquiry, the hunter into the prey, the doctor into the patient, the investigator into the criminal, the revealer into the thing revealed, the finder into the thing found, the savior into the thing saved ("I was saved, for some dreadful destiny"), the liberator into the thing released ("I released your feet from the bonds which pierced your ankles," says the Corinthian messenger). The accuser becomes the defendant, the ruler the subject, the teacher not only the pupil but also the object lesson, the example—a change of the action into its opposite, from active to passive.

And the two opening images of the *Antigonê* ode recur with hideous effect. Oedipus the helmsman, who steers the ship of state, is seen, in Teiresias' words, as one who "steers his ship into a nameless anchorage," who, in the chorus's words, "shared the same great harbour with his father." And Oedipus the ploughman—"How," asks the chorus, "how could the furrows which your father ploughed bear you in silence for so long?"

This reversal is the movement of the play, parallel in the imagery and the action: it is the overthrow of the *tyrannos,* of man who seized power and thought himself "equated to the gods." The bold metaphor of the priest introduces another of the images which parallel in their development the reversal of the hero and suggest that Oedipus is a figure symbolic of human intelligence and achievement in general. He is not only helmsman, ploughman, inventor, legislator, liberator, revealer, doctor—he is also equator, mathematician, calculator; "equated" is a mathematical term, and it is only one of a whole complex of such terms which present Oedipus in yet a fresh aspect of man *tyrannos.* One of Oedipus' favorite words is "measure," and this is of course a significant metaphor: measure, mensuration, number, calculation—these are among the most important inventions which have brought man to power. Aeschylus' Prometheus, the mythical civilizer of human life, counts number among the foremost of his gifts to man. "And number, too, I invented, outstanding among clever devices." In the river valleys of the East, generations of mensuration and calculation had brought man to an understanding of the movements of the stars and of time: in the histories of his friend Herodotus, Sophocles had read of the calculation and mensuration which had gone into the building of the pyramids. "Measure"—it is Protagoras' word: "Man is the measure of all things." In this play man's measure is taken, his true equation found. The play is full of equations, some of them incomplete, some false; the final equation shows man equated not to the gods but to himself, as Oedipus is finally equated to himself. For there are in the play not one Oedipus but two.

One is the magnificent figure set before us in the opening scenes, *tyrannos,* the man of wealth and power, first of men, the intellect and energy which drive on the search. The other is the object of the search, a shadowy figure who has violated the most fundamental human taboos, an incestuous parricide, "most accursed of men." And even before the one Oedipus finds the other, they are connected and equated in the name which they both bear, Oedipus. Oedipus—Swollen-foot; it emphasizes the physical blemish which scars the body of the splendid *tyrannos,* a defect which he tries to forget but which reminds us of the outcast child this *tyrannos* once was and the outcast man he is soon to be. The second half of the name πουζ, "foot," recurs throughout the play, as a mocking phrase which recalls this other Oedipus. "The

Sphinx forced us to look at what was at our feet," says Creon. Teiresias invokes "the dread-footed curse of your father and mother." And the choral odes echo and re-echo with this word. "Let the murderer of Laïos set his foot in motion in flight." "The murderer is a man alone with forlorn foot." "The laws of Zeus are high-footed." "The man of pride plunges down into doom where he cannot use his foot."

These mocking repetitions of one-half the name invoke the unknown Oedipus who will be revealed: the equally emphatic repetition of the first half emphasizes the dominant attitude of the man before us.

ADRIAN POOLE

Oedipus and Athens

from TRAGEDY: SHAKESPEARE AND THE GREEK EXAMPLE

Oedipus is quick to decide and to act; he anticipates advice and suggestion. When the priest hints that he should send to Delphi for help, he has already done so; when the chorus suggests sending for Teiresias, the prophet has already been summoned and is on the way. This swiftness in action is a well-known Athenian quality, one their enemies are well aware of. "They are the only people," say the Corinthians, "who simultaneously hope for and have what they plan, because of their quick fulfillment of decisions." But this action is not rash, it is based on reflection; Oedipus reached the decision to apply to Delphi "groping, laboring over many paths of thought." This too is typically Athenian. "We are unique," says Pericles, "in our combination of the most courageous action and rational discussion of our plans." The Athenians also spoke with pride of the intelligence that informed such discussion: Pericles attributes the Athenian victories over the Persians "not to luck, but to intelligence." And this is the claim of Oedipus, too. "The flight of my own intelligence hit the mark," he says, as he recalls his solution of the riddle of the Sphinx. The riddle has sinister verbal connections with his fate (his name in Greek is *Oidipous,* and *dipous* is the Greek word for "two-footed" in the riddle, not to mention the later prophecy of Teiresias that he would leave Thebes as a blind man, "a stick tapping before him step by step"), but the answer he proposed to the riddle—"Man"—is appropriate for the optimistic picture of man's achievement and potential that the figure of Oedipus represents.

Above all, as we see from the priest's speech in the prologue and the prompt, energetic action Oedipus takes to rescue his subjects from the plague, he is a man dedicated to the interests and the needs of the city. It is this public spirit that drives him on to the discovery of the truth—to reject Creon's hint that the matter should be kept under wraps, to send for Teiresias, to pronounce the curse and sentence of banishment on the murderer of Laïos. This spirit was the great civic virtue that Pericles preached—"I would have you fix your eyes every day on the greatness of Athens until you fall in love with her"—and that the enemies of Athens knew they had to reckon with. "In the city's service," say the Corinthians, "they use their bodies as if they did not belong to them."

All this does not necessarily mean that Sophocles' audience drew a conscious parallel between Oedipus and Athens (or even that Sophocles himself did); what is important is that they could have seen in Oedipus a man endowed with the temperament and talents they prized most highly in their own democratic leaders and in their ideal vision of themselves. Oedipus the King is a dramatic embodiment of the creative vigor and intellectual daring of the fifth-century Athenian spirit.

But there is an even greater dimension to this extraordinary dramatic figure. The fifth century in Athens saw the birth of the historical spirit. The past came to be seen no longer as a golden age from which there had been a decline if not a fall, but as a steady progress from primitive barbarism to the high civilization of the city-state. . . .

The figure of Oedipus represents not only the techniques of the transition from savagery to civilization and the political achievements of the newly settled society, but also the temper and methods of the fifth-century intellectual revolution. His speeches are full of words, phrases, and attitudes that link him with the "enlightenment" of Sophocles' own Athens. "I'll bring it all to light," he says; he is like some Protagoras or Democritus dispelling the darkness of ignorance and superstition. He is a questioner, a researcher, a discoverer—the Greek words are those of the sophistic vocabulary. Above all Oedipus is presented to the audience as a symbol of two of the greatest scientific achievements of the age—mathematics and medicine. Mathematical language recurs incessantly in the imagery of the play—such terms as "measure" (*metrein*), "equate" (*isoun*), "define" (*diorizein*)—and at one climactic moment Oedipus expresses as a mathematical axiom his hope that a discrepancy in the evidence will clear him of the charge of Laïos's murder: "One can't equal many." This obsessive image, Oedipus the calculator, is one more means of investing the mythical figure with the salient characteristics of the fifth-century achievement, but it is also magnificently functional. For, in his search for truth, he is engaged in a great calculation to determine the measure of man, whom Protagoras called "the measure of all things."

CHAPTER TWENTY-SIX

The Elizabethan Theater: Shakespeare in Context

READING SHAKESPEARE IN CONTEXT

London in the Age of Elizabeth

Detail from Georg Matthaus Vischer's *Panorama of London* (1616)

London in the later sixteenth century was a thriving and turbulent city with a population of 300,000. It was a city with expanding suburbs, which made it something of a metropolis with an expansive country feeling, drawing on both worlds. At that time, with Paris and Naples, London was one of the three most important cities of the Western world. With London the political and commercial center of the country, England became, under Queen Elizabeth I, a more unified nation. London's culture was alive with ideas that would lead to a proliferation of artistic achievement in the Elizabethan Age (1558–1603). In terms of the English language, this era saw astonishing advances—during this period hundreds of new English words were coined, many by Shakespeare.

The Arts in the Age of Elizabeth

During Elizabeth's reign, England experienced a great flowering of the arts. London was the center of literary activity. During the last decade of the sixteenth century, the sonnet became the reigning literary form, its popularity unrivalled. Poets vied with one another to see who could write the most memorable, intricate, and elegant sonnets. Poets wrote extended series of linked sonnet sequences, notably Shakespeare's monumental 154 sonnets.

Drama was even more popular and virtuosic during Elizabeth's reign and for a longer period. Playwrights plied their trade writing, producing, and sometimes acting in the plays they wrote. Ben Jonson, Christopher Marlowe, Thomas Kyd, among dozens of other dramatists, vied with Shakespeare for honor on the stage.

Complementing the outpouring of poetry and drama came a stream of new musical compositions—madrigals and motets, musical works both sacred and secular, created by composers such as Thomas Weelkes and Thomas Morley. While the pens of poets, playwrights, and composers were flowing, so too were the brushes of painters. Prominent among them was the portrait painter Nicholas Hilliard, whose fame in England paralleled that of Holbein in Germany. Like Holbein, Hilliard painted aristocrats and royalty, King Henry VIII and Queen Elizabeth I, most notable, among them.

Painting and music tended to be patronized by the wealthy few, and the artists needed such patronage to survive. On the other hand, literature, especially drama, began to attract a wider audience. Supporting the rise of the drama was a growing mercantile class and broader populace hungry for entertainment both highbrow and lowbrow. One reason for Shakespeare's immense popularity in his time (and in ours) was his ability to entertain audiences from a broad range of social classes, from lower-class groundlings, who stood in the open air to view his plays, to upper-class courtiers, who, portrayed in the plays, often attended them.

Stagecraft in the Elizabethan Age

The drama of Shakespeare's time, the Elizabethan Age, shares some features with Greek drama. Like the Greek dramatists, Elizabethan playwrights wrote both comedies and tragedies, but the Elizabethans extended the possibilities of each genre. They wrote domestic tragedies, tragedies of character, and revenge tragedies; they contributed comedies of manners and comedies of humor to the earlier romantic and satiric comedies. In Greek and Elizabethan theater, props were few, scenery was simple, and dialogue often indicated changes of locale and time. Elizabethan plays were typically written in verse rather than prose.

An Elizabethan playhouse such as the Globe, where many of Shakespeare's plays were staged, had a much smaller seating capacity than the large Greek amphitheaters,

THE GLOBE THEATRE,
On the Bankside.
Bankside
As it appeared in the reign of King James I.

The Globe (ca. 1612)

which could seat thousands (15,000 at Epidaurus). The Globe could accommodate about 2,300 people, including roughly 800 groundlings who, exposed to the elements, stood around the stage. The stage itself projected from an inside wall into their midst. More prosperous spectators sat in one of the three stories that nearly encircled the stage. The vastly smaller size and seating capacity of the Elizabethan theater and the projection of its stage made for a greater intimacy between actors and audience. Though actors still had to project their voices and exaggerate their gestures, they could be heard and seen without the aid of large megaphonic masks and elevated shoes. Elizabethan actors could modulate their voices and vary their pitch, stress, and intonation in ways not suited to the Greek stage. They could also make greater and more subtle use of facial expression and of gesture to enforce their greater verbal and vocal flexibility.

In addition to greater intimacy, the Elizabethan stage also offered more versatility than its Greek counterpart. Although the Greek *skene* building could be used for scenes occurring above the ground, such as a god descending in a machine (*deus ex machina*),* the Greek stage was really a single-level acting area. Not so the Elizabethan stage, which contained a second-level balcony (from which Brabantio looks out in Act I, Scene II of *Othello*). Besides its balcony, Shakespeare's stage had doors at the back for entrances and exits, a curtained alcove (useful for scenes of intrigue), and a stage floor trapdoor. Such a stage was suitable for rapidly shifting scenes and continuous action. Thus, Elizabethan stage conventions did not include divisions between scenes as in Greek drama. The act and scene divisions that appear in *Othello* and *Hamlet* were devised by modern editors.

WILLIAM SHAKESPEARE

(1564–1616)

Shakespeare and His Works

William Shakespeare, the most famous English writer, is also among the most popular. His fame and popularity rest on his plays more than on his nondramatic

*A god who resolves the entanglements of a play by his supernatural intervention (literally, a god from the machine) or any artificial device used to resolve a plot.

poetry—though his sonnets remain perennially in fashion. What makes Shakespeare such a literary phenomenon? Why are readers so drawn to his work? Here are two simple explanations: (1) his revelation of human character, especially his exploration of complex states of mind and feeling; (2) his explosive and exuberant language, particularly the richness and variety of his metaphors. Both of these literary virtues abound in the sequence of 154 sonnets Shakespeare wrote in the 1590s. Both also consistently appear in his 37 plays, particularly in the soliloquies, those inward meditative speeches of the major characters. The richness of Shakespeare's language is also apparent in the songs he wrote for the plays, especially the songs in the comedies.

Shakespeare's plays and poems provide a repository of familiar sayings and recognizable quotations. From *Hamlet* alone we glean the following:

In my mind's eye

To the manner born

There are more things in heaven and earth

Hold the mirror up to nature

I must be cruel only to be kind.

Brevity is the soul of wit.

To be or not to be, that is the question.

Neither a borrower nor a lender be.

Something's rotten in the state of Denmark.

What a piece of work is a man.

Shakespeare, of course, is not a great writer because he is quotable; he is quotable because he is a great writer. It is his manipulation of language and his revelation of character that have made him both widely read and deeply revered.

Very little is known with certainty about Shakespeare's life. Scholars, however, have determined the following basic facts. He was born in Stratford-on-Avon in April of 1564. He attended the local grammar school, where he would have studied Latin and perhaps a little Greek. His formal education did not include attendance at the university—in his day either Oxford or Cambridge. Instead, at eighteen, he married Anne Hathaway, who bore three children in as many years, a daughter in 1583 and twins, a boy and girl, in 1585. Shakespeare wrote and acted in plays, for by 1592 he was known in London as both actor and playwright.

Many tributes have been paid to Shakespeare. One, however, stands above the rest: his contemporary Ben Jonson's judgment that "he is not for an age, but for all time."

Shakespeare: Timeline

1555

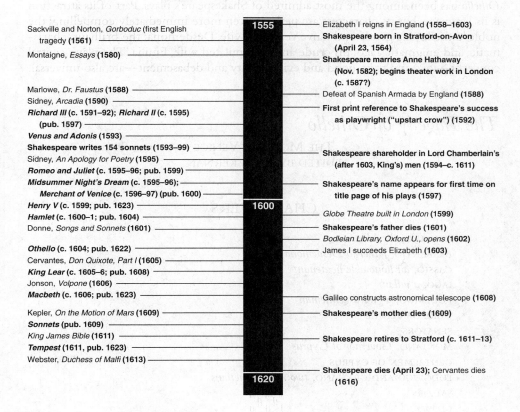

Sackville and Norton, *Gorboduc* (first English tragedy **(1561)**

Montaigne, *Essays* **(1580)**

Marlowe, *Dr. Faustus* **(1588)**

Sidney, *Arcadia* **(1590)**

***Richard III* (c. 1591–92); *Richard II* (c. 1595) (pub. 1597)**

***Venus and Adonis* (1593)**

Shakespeare writes 154 sonnets (1593–99)

Sidney, *An Apology for Poetry* **(1595)**

***Romeo and Juliet* (c. 1595–96; pub. 1599)**

***Midsummer Night's Dream* (c. 1595–96); *Merchant of Venice* (c. 1596–97) (pub. 1600)**

***Henry V* (c. 1599; pub. 1623)**

***Hamlet* (c. 1600–1; pub. 1604)**

Donne, *Songs and Sonnets* **(1601)**

***Othello* (c. 1604; pub. 1622)**

Cervantes, *Don Quixote, Part I* **(1605)**

***King Lear* (c. 1605–6; pub. 1608)**

Jonson, *Volpone* **(1606)**

***Macbeth* (c. 1606; pub. 1623)**

Kepler, *On the Motion of Mars* **(1609)**

***Sonnets* (pub. 1609)**

King James Bible **(1611)**

***Tempest* (1611, pub. 1623)**

Webster, *Duchess of Malfi* **(1613)**

Elizabeth I reigns in England **(1558–1603)**

Shakespeare born in Stratford-on-Avon (April 23, 1564)

Shakespeare marries Anne Hathaway (Nov. 1582); begins theater work in London (c. 1587?)

Defeat of Spanish Armada by England **(1588)**

First print reference to Shakespeare's success as playwright ("upstart crow") (1592)

Shakespeare shareholder in Lord Chamberlain's (after 1603, King's) men (1594–c. 1611)

Shakespeare's name appears for first time on title page of his plays (1597)

1600

Globe Theatre built in London **(1599)**

Shakespeare's father dies (1601)

Bodleian Library, Oxford U., opens **(1602)**

James I succeeds Elizabeth **(1603)**

Galileo constructs astronomical telescope **(1608)**

Shakespeare's mother dies (1609)

Shakespeare retires to Stratford (c. 1611–13)

Shakespeare dies (April 23); Cervantes dies **(1616)**

1620

SHAKESPEARE: OTHELLO

The Tragedy of Othello

Shakespeare's plays generally, and *Othello* in particular, appealed to an audience ranging from the illiterate to the educated: bawdy jokes exist alongside sublime poetry; subtle introspective moments coexist with violence and passion. *Othello* testifies to the vitality and exuberance of Shakespeare's language. Written predominantly in blank verse, *Othello* also includes prose passages (many spoken by Iago) and rhymed couplets (which punctuate the ends of some scenes). The play's language is rich in metaphor and images, puns, and other forms of wordplay.

Lawrence Fishburne and Kenneth Branagh in a film version of *Othello* (1995)

Deriving the story of *Othello* from a sixteenth-century tale by Giraldi Cinthio,

Shakespeare improved the plot, enriched the language, and deepened the characters. *Othello* has been among the most admired of Shakespeare's plays. Part of its attraction is its language, but its characters are perhaps even more immediately compelling: the noble Othello; his gentle and naive Venetian wife, Desdemona; the brilliant, charismatic, and enigmatic Iago; his crude and manipulated wife, Emilia. The play's central concerns—love and trust, good and evil, nobility and debasement—are also universal.

The Tragedy of Othello

THE MOOR OF VENICE

EDITED BY ALVIN KERNAN

CHARACTERS

OTHELLO, *the Moor*
BRABANTIO, *father to Desdemona*
CASSIO, *an honorable lieutenant*
IAGO, *a villain*
RODERIGO, *a gulled gentleman*
DUKE OF VENICE
SENATORS
MONTANO, *Governor of Cyprus*
GENTLEMEN OF CYPRUS
LODOVICO AND GRATIANO, *two noble Venetians*
SAILORS
CLOWN
DESDEMONA, *wife to Othello*
EMILIA, *wife to Iago*
BIANCA, *a courtesan*
(MESSENGER, HERALD, OFFICERS, GENTLEMEN, MUSICIANS, ATTENDANTS)

Scene. *Venice and Cyprus.*

ACT I

Scene I [Venice. A street.]

RODERIGO: Tush! Never tell me? I take it much unkindly
That thou, Iago, who hast had my purse
As if the strings were thine, shouldst know of this.
IAGO: 'Sblood,° but you'll not hear me! If ever I did dream
Of such a matter, abhor me.
RODERIGO: Thou told'st me

I.i. [4]***'Sblood*** *by God's blood.*

Thou didst hold him in thy hate.
IAGO: Despise me
If I do not. Three great ones of the city,
In personal suit to make me his lieutenant,
Off-capped° to him; and, by the faith of man,
I know my price; I am worth no worse a place.
But he, as loving his own pride and purposes,
Evades them with a bombast circumstance,°
Horribly stuffed with epithets of war;
Nonsuits° my mediators. For, "Certes," says he,
"I have already chose my officer." And what was he?
Forsooth, a great arithmetician,°
One Michael Cassio, a Florentine,
(A fellow almost damned in a fair wife)°
That never set a squadron in the field,
Nor the division of a battle knows
More than a spinster; unless the bookish theoric,
Wherein the tonguèd° consuls can propose
As masterly as he. Mere prattle without practice
Is all his soldiership. But he, sir, had th' election;
And I, of whom his eyes had seen the proof
At Rhodes, at Cyprus, and on other grounds
Christian and heathen, must be belee'd and calmed
By debitor and creditor. This counter-caster,°
He, in good time, must his lieutenant be,
And I—God bless the mark!—his Moorship's ancient.°
RODERIGO: By heaven, I rather would have been his hangman.
IAGO: Why, there's no remedy. 'Tis the curse of service:
Preferment goes by letter and affection,°
And not by old gradation,° where each second
Stood heir to th' first. Now, sir, be judge yourself,
Whether I in any just term am affined°
To love the Moor.
RODERIGO: I would not follow him then.
IAGO: O, sir, content you.
I follow him to serve my turn upon him.
We cannot all be masters, nor all masters
Cannot be truly followed. You shall mark
Many a duteous and knee-crooking° knave

[9]***Off-capped*** *doffed their caps—as a mark of respect.* [12]***bombast circumstance*** *stuffed, roundabout speech.* [14]***Nonsuits*** *rejects.* [16]***arithmetician*** *theorist (rather than practical).* [18]***(A . . . wife)*** *a much-disputed passage, probably best taken as a general sneer at Cassio as a dandy and a ladies' man. But in the story from which Shakespeare took his plot the counterpart of Cassio is married, and it may be that at the beginning of the play, Shakespeare had decided to keep him married but later changed his mind.* [22]***tonguèd*** *eloquent.* [28]***counter-caster*** *i.e., a bookkeeper who casts (reckons up) figures on a counter (abacus).* [30]***ancient*** *standard-bearer; an under-officer.* [33]***letter and affection*** *recommendations (from men of power) and personal preference.* [34]***old gradation*** *seniority.* [36]***affined*** *bound.* [42]***knee-crooking*** *bowing.*

That, doting on his own obsequious bondage,
Wears out his time, much like his master's ass,
For naught but provender; and when he's old, cashiered.
Whip me such honest knaves! Others there are
Who, trimmed in forms and visages of duty,
Keep yet their hearts attending on themselves,
And, throwing but shows of service on their lords,
Do well thrive by them, and when they have lined their coats,
Do themselves homage. These fellows have some soul;
And such a one do I profess myself. For, sir,
It is as sure as you are Roderigo,
Were I the Moor, I would not be Iago.
In following him, I follow but myself.
Heaven is my judge, not I for love and duty,
But seeming so, for my peculiar° end;
For when my outward action doth demonstrate
The native° act and figure of my heart
In complement extern,° 'tis not long after
But I will wear my heart upon my sleeve
For daws to peck at; I am not what I am.
RODERIGO: What a full fortune does the thick-lips owe°
If he can carry't thus!
IAGO: Call up her father,
Rouse him. Make after him, poison his delight,
Proclaim him in the streets, incense her kinsmen,
And though he in a fertile climate dwell,
Plague him with flies; though that his joy be joy,
Yet throw such chances of vexation on't
As it may lose some color.
RODERIGO: Here is her father's house. I'll call aloud.
IAGO: Do, with like timorous° accent and dire yell
As when, by night and negligence, the fire
Is spied in populous cities.
RODERIGO: What, ho, Brabantio! Signior Brabantio, ho!
IAGO: Awake! What, ho, Brabantio! Thieves! Thieves!
Look to your house, your daughter, and your bags!
Thieves! Thieves!

BRABANTIO *above*° [*at a window*].

BRABANTIO: What is the reason of this terrible summons?
What is the matter there?
RODERIGO: Signior, is all your family within?
IAGO: Are your doors locked?

[57]***peculiar*** *personal.* [59]***native*** *natural, innate.* [60]***complement extern*** *outward appearance.*
[63]***owe*** *own.* [72]***timorous*** *frightening.* [78]***s.d. above*** *(i.e., on the small upper stage above and to the rear of the main platform stage, which resembled the projecting upper story of an Elizabethan house).*

BRABANTIO: Why, wherefore ask you this?
IAGO: Zounds, sir, y'are robbed! For shame. Put on your gown!
Your heart is burst, you have lost half your soul.
Even now, now, very now, an old black ram
Is tupping your white ewe. Arise, arise!
Awake the snorting citizens with the bell,
Or else the devil will make a grandsire of you.
Arise, I say!
BRABANTIO: What, have you lost your wits?
RODERIGO: Most reverend signior, do you know my voice?
BRABANTIO: Not I. What are you?
RODERIGO: My name is Roderigo.
BRABANTIO: The worser welcome!
I have charged thee not to haunt about my doors.
In honest plainness thou hast heard me say
My daughter is not for thee; and now, in madness,
Being full of supper and distemp'ring draughts,°
Upon malicious knavery dost thou come
To start° my quiet.
RODERIGO: Sir, sir, sir—
BRABANTIO: But thou must needs be sure
My spirits and my place° have in their power
To make this bitter to thee.
RODERIGO: Patience, good sir.
BRABANTIO: What tell'st thou me of robbing? This is Venice,
My house is not a grange.°
RODERIGO: Most grave Brabantio,
In simple and pure soul I come to you.

IAGO: Zounds, sir, you are one of those that will not serve God if the devil bid you. Because we come to do you service and you think we are ruffians, you'll have your daughter covered with a Barbary° horse, you'll have your nephews° neigh to you, you'll have coursers for cousins,° and gennets for germans.°

BRABANTIO: What profane wretch art thou?

IAGO: I am one, sir, that comes to tell you your daughter and the Moor are making the beast with two backs.

BRABANTIO: Thou art a villain.
IAGO: You are—a senator.
BRABANTIO: This thou shalt answer. I know thee, Roderigo.
RODERIGO: Sir, I will answer anything. But I beseech you,
If't be your pleasure and most wise consent,
As partly I find it is, that your fair daughter,

[96]***distemp'ring draughts*** *unsettling drinks.* [98]***start*** *disrupt.* [100]***place*** *rank, i.e., of senator.* [103]***grange*** *isolated house.* [107]***Barbary*** *Arabian, i.e., Moorish.* [108]***nephews*** *i.e., grandsons.* [108]***cousins*** *relations.* [109]***gennets for germans*** *Spanish horses for blood relatives.*

At this odd-even° and dull watch o' th' night,
Transported, with no worse nor better guard
But with a knave of common hire, a gondolier,
To the gross clasps of a lascivious Moor—
If this be known to you, and your allowance,
We then have done you bold and saucy wrongs;
But if you know not this, my manners tell me
We have your wrong rebuke. Do not believe
That from the sense of all civility°
I thus would play and trifle with your reverence.
Your daughter, if you have not given her leave,
I say again, hath made a gross revolt,
Tying her duty, beauty, wit, and fortunes
In an extravagant° and wheeling stranger
Of here and everywhere. Straight satisfy yourself.
If she be in her chamber, or your house,
Let loose on me the justice of the state
For thus deluding you.

BRABANTIO: Strike on the tinder, ho!
Give me a taper! Call up all my people!
This accident° is not unlike my dream.
Belief of it oppresses me already.
Light, I say! Light! [*Exit above.*]

IAGO: Farewell, for I must leave you.
It seems not meet, nor wholesome to my place,
To be produced—as, if I stay, I shall—
Against the Moor. For I do know the State,
However this may gall him with some check,°
Cannot with safety cast° him; for he's embarked
With such loud reason to the Cyprus wars,
Which even now stands in act,° that for their souls
Another of his fathom° they have none
To lead their business; in which regard,
Though I do hate him as I do hell-pains,
Yet, for necessity of present life,
I must show out a flag and sign of love,
Which is indeed but sign. That you shall surely find him,
Lead to the Sagittary° that raisèd search:
And there will I be with him. So farewell. [*Exit.*]

Enter BRABANTIO [*in his nightgown*], *with* SERVANTS *and torches.*

BRABANTIO: It is too true an evil. Gone she is;

[118]***odd-even*** *between night and morning.* [126]***sense of all civility*** *feeling of what is proper.* [131]***extravagant*** *vagrant, wandering (Othello is not Venetian and thus may be considered a wandering soldier of fortune).* [137]***accident*** *happening.* [143]***check*** *restraint.* [144]***cast*** *dismiss.* [146]***stands in act*** *takes place.* [147]***fathom*** *ability.* [153]***Sagittary*** *probably the name of an inn.*

And what's to come of my despisèd time
Is naught but bitterness. Now, Roderigo,
Where didst thou see her?—O unhappy girl!—
With the Moor, say'st thou?—Who would be a father?—
How didst thou know 'twas she?—O, she deceives me
Past thought!—What said she to you? Get moe° tapers!
Raise all my kindred!—Are they married, think you?

RODERIGO: Truly I think they are.

BRABANTIO: O heaven! How got she out? O treason of the blood!
Fathers, from hence trust not your daughters' minds
By what you see them act.° Is there not charms
By which the property° of youth and maidhood
May be abused? Have you not read, Roderigo,
Of some such thing?

RODERIGO: Yes, sir, I have indeed.

BRABANTIO: Call up my brother.—O, would you had had her!—
Some one way, some another.—Do you know
Where we may apprehend her and the Moor?

RODERIGO: I think I can discover him, if you please
To get good guard and go along with me.

BRABANTIO: Pray you lead on. At every house I'll call;
I may command at most.—Get weapons, ho!
And raise some special officers of night.—
On, good Roderigo; I will deserve your pains.°

[*Exeunt.*]

Scene II [A street.]

Enter OTHELLO, IAGO, ATTENDANTS *with torches.*

IAGO: Though in the trade of war I have slain men,
Yet do I hold it very stuff° o' th' conscience
To do no contrived murder. I lack iniquity
Sometime to do me service. Nine or ten times
I had thought t' have yerked° him here, under the ribs.

OTHELLO: 'Tis better as it is.

IAGO: Nay, but he prated,
And spoke such scurvy and provoking terms
Against your honor, that with the little godliness I have
I did full hard forbear him. But I pray you, sir,
Are you fast married? Be assured of this,
That the magnifico° is much beloved,
And hath in his effect a voice potential
As double as the Duke's.° He will divorce you,

161***moe*** *more.* 166***act*** *do.* 167***property*** *true nature.* 178***deserve your pains*** *be worthy of (and reward) your efforts.* ***I.ii.*** 2***stuff*** *essence.* 5***yerked*** *stabbed.* 11***magnifico*** *nobleman.* 12–13***hath . . . Duke's*** *i.e., can be as effective as the Duke.*

Or put upon you what restraint or grievance
The law, with all his might to enforce it on,
Will give him cable.°
OTHELLO: Let him do his spite.
My services which I have done the Signiory°
Shall out-tongue his complaints. 'Tis yet to know°—
Which when I know that boasting is an honor
I shall promulgate—I fetch my life and being
From men of royal siege,° and my demerits°
May speak unbonneted to as proud a fortune
As this that I have reached.° For know, Iago,
But that I love the gentle Desdemona,
I would not my unhousèd° free condition
Put into circumscription and confine
For the seas' worth. But look, what lights come yond?

Enter CASSIO, *with* [OFFICERS *and*] *torches.*

IAGO: Those are the raisèd father and his friends.
You were best go in.
OTHELLO: Not I. I must be found.
My parts, my title, and my perfect soul°
Shall manifest me rightly. Is it they?
IAGO: By Janus, I think no.
OTHELLO: The servants of the Duke? And my lieutenant?
The goodness of the night upon you, friends.
What is the news?
CASSIO: The Duke does greet you, general;
And he requires your haste-posthaste appearance
Even on the instant.
OTHELLO: What is the matter, think you?
CASSIO: Something from Cyprus, as I may divine.
It is a business of some heat. The galleys
Have sent a dozen sequent° messengers
This very night at one another's heels,
And many of the consuls, raised and met,
Are at the Duke's already. You have been hotly called for.
When, being not at your lodging to be found,
The Senate hath sent about three several° quests
To search you out.
OTHELLO: 'Tis well I am found by you.
I will but spend a word here in the house,
And go with you. [*Exit.*]

[16]***cable*** *range, scope.* [17]***Signiory*** *the rulers of Venice.* [18]***yet to know*** *unknown as yet.* [21]***siege*** *rank.* [21]***demerits*** *deserts.* [22–23]***May . . . reached*** *i.e., are the equal of the family I have married into.* [25]***unhousèd*** *unconfined.* [30]***perfect soul*** *clear, unflawed conscience.* [40]***sequent*** *successive.* [45]***several*** *separate.*

CASSIO: Ancient, what makes he here?
IAGO: Faith, he tonight hath boarded a land carack.°
If it prove lawful prize, he's made forever.
CASSIO: I do not understand.
IAGO: He's married.
CASSIO: To who?

[*Enter* OTHELLO.]

IAGO: Marry,° to—Come captain, will you go?
OTHELLO: Have with you.
CASSIO: Here comes another troop to seek for you.

Enter BRABANTIO, RODERIGO, *with* OFFICERS *and torches.*

IAGO: It is Brabantio. General, be advised.
He comes to bad intent.
OTHELLO: Holla! Stand there!
RODERIGO: Signior, it is the Moor.
BRABANTIO: Down with him, thief! [*They draw swords.*]
IAGO: You, Roderigo? Come, sir, I am for you.
OTHELLO: Keep up your bright swords, for the dew will rust them.
Good signior, you shall more command with years
Than with your weapons.
BRABANTIO: O thou foul thief, where hast thou stowed my daughter?
Damned as thou art, thou hast enchanted her!
For I'll refer me to all things of sense,°
If she in chains of magic were not bound,
Whether a maid so tender, fair, and happy,
So opposite to marriage that she shunned
The wealthy, curlèd darlings of our nation,
Would ever have, t'incur a general mock,°
Run from her guardage to the sooty bosom
Of such a thing as thou—to fear, not to delight.
Judge me the world if 'tis not gross in sense°
That thou hast practiced° on her with foul charms,
Abused her delicate youth with drugs or minerals
That weaken motion.° I'll have't disputed on;
'Tis probable, and palpable to thinking.
I therefore apprehend and do attach° thee
For an abuser of the world, a practicer
Of arts inhibited and out of warrant.°
Lay hold upon him. If he do resist,
Subdue him at his peril.

49***carack*** *treasure ship.* 52***Marry*** *By Mary (an interjection).* 63***refer . . . sense*** *i.e., base (my argument) on all ordinary understanding of nature.* 68***general mock*** *public shame.* 71***gross in sense*** *obvious.* 72***practiced*** *used tricks.* 74***motion*** *thought, i.e., reason.* 76***attach*** *arrest.* 78***inhibited . . . warrant*** *prohibited and illegal (black magic).*

OTHELLO: Hold your hands,
Both you of my inclining and the rest.
Were it my cue to fight, I should have known it
Without a prompter. Whither will you that I go
To answer this your charge?

BRABANTIO: To prison, till fit time
Of law and course of direct session
Call thee to answer.

OTHELLO: What if I do obey?
How may the Duke be therewith satisfied,
Whose messengers are here about my side
Upon some present° business of the state
To bring me to him?

OFFICER: Tis true, most worthy signior.
The Duke's in council, and your noble self
I am sure is sent for.

BRABANTIO: How? The Duke in council?
In this time of the night? Bring him away.
Mine's not an idle cause. The Duke himself,
Or any of my brothers° of the state,
Cannot but feel this wrong as 'twere their own;
For if such actions may have passage free,
Bondslaves and pagans shall our statesmen be. *[Exeunt.]*

Scene III [A council chamber.]

Enter DUKE, SENATORS, *and* OFFICERS *[set at a table, with lights and* ATTENDANTS*]*.

DUKE: There's no composition° in this news
That gives them credit.°

FIRST SENATOR: Indeed, they are disproportioned.
My letters say a hundred and seven galleys.

DUKE: And mine a hundred forty.

SECOND SENATOR: And mine two hundred.
But though they jump° not on a just accompt°—
As in these cases where the aim° reports
'Tis oft with difference—yet do they all confirm
A Turkish fleet, and bearing up to Cyprus.

DUKE: Nay, it is possible enough to judgment.°
I do not so secure me in the error,
But the main article I do approve
In fearful sense.°

SAILOR [Within]: What, ho! What, ho! What, ho!

[89]***present*** *immediate.* [95]***brothers*** *i.e., the other senators.* ***I.iii.*** [1]***composition*** *agreement.* [2]***gives them credit*** *makes them believable.* [5]***jump*** *agree.* [5]***just accompt*** *exact counting.* [6]***aim*** *approximation.* [9]***to judgment*** *when carefully considered.* [10–12]***I do . . . sense*** *i.e., just because the numbers disagree in the reports, I do not doubt that the principal information (that the Turkish fleet is out) is fearfully true.*

Enter SAILOR.

OFFICER: A messenger from the galleys.
DUKE: Now? What's the business?
SAILOR: The Turkish preparation makes for Rhodes.
So was I bid report here to the State
By Signior Angelo.
DUKE: How say you by this change?
FIRST SENATOR: This cannot be
By no assay of reason. 'Tis a pageant°
To keep us in false gaze.° When we consider
Th' importancy of Cyprus to the Turk,
And let ourselves again but understand
That, as it more concerns the Turk than Rhodes,
So may he with more facile question° bear it,
For that it stands not in such warlike brace,°
But altogether lacks th' abilities
That Rhodes is dressed in. If we make thought of this,
We must not think the Turk is so unskillful
To leave that latest which concerns him first,
Neglecting an attempt of ease and gain
To wake and wage a danger profitless.
DUKE: Nay, in all confidence he's not for Rhodes.
OFFICER: Here is more news.

Enter a MESSENGER.

MESSENGER: The Ottomites, reverend and gracious,
Steering with due course toward the isle of Rhodes,
Have there injointed them with an after° fleet.
FIRST SENATOR: Ay, so I thought. How many, as you guess?
MESSENGER: Of thirty sail; and now they do restem
Their backward course, bearing with frank appearance
Their purposes toward Cyprus. Signior Montano,
Your trusty and most valiant servitor,
With his free duty° recommends° you thus,
And prays you to believe him.
DUKE: 'Tis certain then for Cyprus.
Marcus Luccicos, is not he in town?
FIRST SENATOR: He's now in Florence.
DUKE: Write from us to him; post-posthaste dispatch.
FIRST SENATOR: Here comes Brabantio and the valiant Moor.

Enter BRABANTIO, OTHELLO, CASSIO, IAGO, RODERIGO, *and* OFFICERS.

[18] ***pageant*** *show, pretense.* [19] ***in false gaze*** *looking the wrong way.* [23] ***facile question*** *easy struggle.* [24] ***warlike brace*** *"military posture."* [35] ***after*** *following.* [41] ***free duty*** *unlimited respect.* [41] ***recommends*** *informs.*

DUKE: Valiant Othello, we must straight° employ you
Against the general° enemy Ottoman.
[To BRABANTIO] I did not see you. Welcome, gentle signior.
We lacked your counsel and your help tonight.
BRABANTIO: So did I yours. Good your grace, pardon me.
Neither my place, nor aught I heard of business,
Hath raised me from my bed; nor doth the general care
Take hold on me; for my particular grief
Is of so floodgate and o'erbearing nature
That it engluts and swallows other sorrows,
And it is still itself.
DUKE: Why, what's the matter?
BRABANTIO: My daughter! O, my daughter!
SENATORS: Dead?
BRABANTIO: Ay, to me.
She is abused, stol'n from me, and corrupted
By spells and medicines bought of mountebanks;
For nature so prepost'rously to err,
Being not deficient, blind, or lame of sense,
Sans° witchcraft could not.
DUKE: Whoe'er he be that in this foul proceeding
Hath thus beguiled your daughter of herself,
And you of her, the bloody book of law
You shall yourself read in the bitter letter
After your own sense; yea, though our proper° son
Stood in your action.°
BRABANTIO: Humbly I thank your Grace.
Here is the man—this Moor, whom now, it seems,
Your special mandate for the state affairs
Hath hither brought.
ALL: We are very sorry for't.
DUKE [*To* OTHELLO]: What in your own part can you say to this?
BRABANTIO: Nothing, but this is so.
OTHELLO: Most potent, grave, and reverend signiors,
My very noble and approved° good masters,
That I have ta'en away this old man's daughter,
It is most true; true I have married her.
The very head and front° of my offending
Hath this extent, no more. Rude am I in my speech,
And little blessed with the soft phrase of peace.
For since these arms of mine had seven years' pith°
Till now some nine moons wasted,° they have used

[48]***straight*** *at once.* [49]***general*** *universal.* [64]***Sans*** *without.* [69]***proper*** *own.* [70]***Stood in your action*** *were the accused in your suit.* [77]***approved*** *tested, proven by past performance.* [80]***head and front*** *extreme form (front = forehead)* [83]***pith*** *strength.* [84]***wasted*** *past.*

Their dearest° action in the tented field;
And little of this great world can I speak
More than pertains to feats of broils and battle;
And therefore little shall I grace my cause
In speaking for myself. Yet, by your gracious patience,
I will a round° unvarnished tale deliver
Of my whole course of love—what drugs, what charms,
What conjuration, and what mighty magic,
For such proceeding I am charged withal,
I won his daughter—

BRABANTIO: A maiden never bold,
Of spirit so still and quiet that her motion
Blushed at herself,° and she, in spite of nature,
Of years, of country, credit, everything,
To fall in love with what she feared to look on!
It is a judgment maimed and most imperfect
That will confess perfection so could err
Against all rules of nature, and must be driven
To find out practices of cunning hell
Why this should be. I therefore vouch again
That with some mixtures pow'rful o'er the blood,
Or with some dram, conjured to this effect,
He wrought upon her.

DUKE: To vouch this is no proof,
Without more wider and more overt test
Than these thin habits° and poor likelihoods
Of modern° seeming do prefer against him.

FIRST SENATOR: But, Othello, speak.
Did you by indirect and forcèd courses
Subdue and poison this young maid's affections?
Or came it by request, and such fair question°
As soul to soul affordeth?

OTHELLO: I do beseech you,
Send for the lady to the Sagittary
And let her speak of me before her father.
If you do find me foul in her report,
The trust, the office, I do hold of you
Not only take away, but let your sentence
Even fall upon my life.

DUKE: Fetch Desdemona hither.

OTHELLO: Ancient, conduct them; you best know the place.

[*Exit* IAGO, *with two or three* ATTENDANTS.]

[85]***dearest*** *most important.* [90]***round*** *blunt.* [95–96]***her motion/Blushed at herself*** *i.e., she was so modest that she blushed at every thought (and movement).* [108]***habits*** *clothing.* [109]***modern*** *trivial.* [113]***question*** *discussion.*

And till she come, as truly as to heaven
I do confess the vices of my blood,
So justly to your grave ears I'll present
How I did thrive in this fair lady's love,
And she in mine.

DUKE: Say it, Othello.

OTHELLO: Her father loved me; oft invited me;
Still° questioned me the story of my life
From year to year, the battle, sieges, fortune
That I have passed.
I ran it through, even from my boyish days
To th' very moment that he bade me tell it.
Wherein I spoke of most disastrous chances,
Of moving accidents by flood and field,
Of hairbreadth scapes i' th' imminent° deadly breach,
Of being taken by the insolent foe
And sold to slavery, of my redemption thence
And portance° in my travel's history,
Wherein of anters° vast and deserts idle,°
Rough quarries, rocks, and hills whose heads touch heaven,
It was my hint to speak. Such was my process.
And of the Cannibals that each other eat,
The Anthropophagi,° and men whose heads
Grew beneath their shoulders. These things to hear
Would Desdemona seriously incline;
But still the house affairs would draw her thence;
Which ever as she could with haste dispatch,
She'd come again, and with a greedy ear
Devour up my discourse. Which I observing,
Took once a pliant hour, and found good means
To draw from her a prayer of earnest heart
That I would all my pilgrimage dilate,°
Whereof by parcels she had something heard,
But not intentively.° I did consent,
And often did beguile her of her tears
When I did speak of some distressful stroke
That my youth suffered. My story being done,
She gave me for my pains a world of kisses.
She swore in faith 'twas strange, 'twas passing° strange;
'Twas pitiful, 'twas wondrous pitiful.
She wished she had not heard it; yet she wished
That heaven had made her such a man. She thanked me,
And bade me, if I had a friend that loved her,

[128]***Still*** *regularly.* [135]***imminent*** *threatening.* [138]***portance*** *manner of acting.* [139]***anters*** *caves.* [139]***idle*** *empty, sterile.* [143]***Anthropophagi*** *maneaters.* [152]***dilate*** *relate in full.* [154]***intentively*** *at length and in sequence.* [159]***passing*** *surpassing.*

I should but teach him how to tell my story,
And that would woo her. Upon this hint I spake.
She loved me for the dangers I had passed,
And I loved her that she did pity them.
This only is the witchcraft I have used.
Here comes the lady. Let her witness it.

Enter DESDEMONA, IAGO, ATTENDANTS.

DUKE: I think this tale would win my daughter too.
Good Brabantio, take up this mangled matter at the best.°
Men do their broken weapons rather use
Than their bare hands.
BRABANTIO: I pray you hear her speak.
If she confess that she was half the wooer,
Destruction on my head if my bad blame
Light on the man. Come hither, gentle mistress.
Do you perceive in all this noble company
Where most you owe obedience?
DESDEMONA: My noble father,
I do perceive here a divided duty.
To you I am bound for life and education;
My life and education both do learn me
How to respect you. You are the lord of duty,
I am hitherto your daughter. But here's my husband,
And so much duty as my mother showed
To you, preferring you before her father,
So much I challenge° that I may profess
Due to the Moor my lord.
BRABANTIO: God be with you. I have done.
Please it your Grace, on to the state affairs.
I had rather to adopt a child than get° it.
Come hither, Moor.
I here do give thee that with all my heart
Which, but thou hast already, with all my heart
I would keep from thee. For your sake,° jewel,
I am glad at soul I have no other child,
For thy escape would teach me tyranny,
To hang clogs on them. I have done, my lord.
DUKE: Let me speak like yourself and lay a sentence°
Which, as a grise° or step, may help these lovers.
When remedies are past, the griefs are ended
By seeing the worst, which late on hopes depended.°
To mourn a mischief that is past and gone

[171]***take . . . best*** *i.e., make the best of this disaster.* [186]***challenge*** *claim as right.* [189]***get*** *beget.* [193]***For your sake*** *because of you.* [197]***lay a sentence*** *provide a maxim.* [198]***grise*** *step.* [200]***late on hopes depended*** *was supported by hope (of a better outcome) until lately.*

Is the next° way to draw new mischief on.
What cannot be preserved when fortune takes,
Patience her injury a mock'ry makes.
The robbed that smiles, steals something from the thief;
He robs himself that spends a bootless° grief.
BRABANTIO: So let the Turk of Cyprus us beguile:
We lose it not so long as we can smile.
He bears the sentence well that nothing bears
But the free comfort which from thence he hears;
But he bears both the sentence and the sorrow
That to pay grief must of poor patience borrow.
These sentences, to sugar, or to gall,
Being strong on both sides, are equivocal.
But words are words. I never yet did hear
That the bruisèd heart was piercèd° through the ear.
I humbly beseech you, proceed to th' affairs of state.

DUKE: The Turk with a most mighty preparation makes for Cyprus. Othello, the fortitude° of the place is best known to you; and though we have there a substitute° of most allowed sufficiency,° yet opinion, a more sovereign mistress of effects, throws a more safer voice on you.° You must therefore be content to slubber° the gloss of your new fortunes with this more stubborn and boisterous° expedition.

OTHELLO: The tyrant Custom, most grave senators,
Hath made the flinty and steel couch of war
My thrice-driven° bed of down. I do agnize°
A natural and prompt alacrity
I find in hardness and do undertake
These present wars against the Ottomites.
Most humbly, therefore, bending to your state,
I crave fit disposition for my wife,
Due reference of place, and exhibition,°
With such accommodation and besort
As levels with° her breeding.
DUKE: Why, at her father's.
BRABANTIO: I will not have it so.
OTHELLO: Nor I.
DESDEMONA: Nor would I there reside,
To put my father in impatient thoughts
By being in his eye. Most gracious Duke,

[202]***next*** *closest, surest.* [206]***bootless*** *valueless.* [216]***piercèd*** *(some editors emend to piecèd, i.e., "healed." But piercèd makes good sense: Brabantio is saying in effect that his heart cannot be further hurt [pierced] by the indignity of the useless, conventional advice the Duke offers him. Piercèd can also mean, however, "lanced" in the medical sense, and would then mean "treated").* [219]***fortitude*** *fortification.* [220]***substitute*** *viceroy.* [220]***most allowed sufficiency*** *generally acknowledged capability.* [222–223]***opinion . . . you*** *i.e., the general opinion, which finally controls affairs, is that you would be the best man in this situation.* [222]***slubber*** *besmear.* [222–223]***stubborn and boisterous*** *rough and violent.* [226]***thrice-driven*** *i.e., softest.* [226]***agnize*** *known in myself.* [232]***exhibition*** *grant of funds.* [234]***levels with*** *is suitable to.*

To my unfolding° lend your prosperous° ear,
And let me find a charter° in your voice,
T' assist my simpleness.
DUKE: What would you, Desdemona?
DESDEMONA: That I love the Moor to live with him,
My downright violence, and storm of fortunes,
May trumpet to the world. My heart's subdued
Even to the very quality of my lord.°
I saw Othello's visage in his mind,
And to his honors and his valiant parts
Did I my soul and fortunes consecrate.
So that, dear lords, if I be left behind,
A moth of peace, and he go to the war,
The rites° for why I love him are bereft me,
And I a heavy interim shall support
By his dear absence. Let me go with him.
OTHELLO: Let her have your voice.°
Vouch with me, heaven, I therefore beg it not
To please the palate of my appetite,
Nor to comply with heat°—the young affects°
In me defunct—and proper satisfaction;°
But to be free and bounteous to her mind;
And heaven defend° your good souls that you think
I will your serious and great business scant
When she is with me. No, when light-winged toys
Of feathered Cupid seel° with wanton° dullness
My speculative and officed instrument,°
That my disports corrupt and taint my business,
Let housewives make a skillet of my helm,
And all indign° and base adversities
Make head° against my estimation!°—
DUKE: Be it as you shall privately determine,
Either for her stay or going. Th' affair cries haste,
And speed must answer it.
FIRST SENATOR: You must away tonight.
OTHELLO: With all my heart.
DUKE: At nine i' th' morning here we'll meet again.
Othello, leave some officer behind,
And he shall our commission bring to you,

[239]***unfolding*** *explanation.* [239]***prosperous*** *favoring.* [240]***charter*** *permission.* [244–245]***My . . . lord*** *i.e., I have become one in nature and being with the man I married (therefore, I too would go to the wars like a soldier).* [251]***rites*** *(may refer either to the marriage rites or to the rites, formalities, of war).* [254]***voice*** *consent.* [257]***heat*** *lust.* [257]***affects*** *passions.* [258]***proper satisfaction*** *i.e., consummation of the marriage.* [260]***defend*** *forbid.* [263]***seel*** *sew up.* [263]***wanton*** *lascivious.* [264]***speculative . . . instrument*** *i.e., sight (and, by extension, the mind).* [267]***indign*** *unworthy.* [268]***Make head*** *form an army, i.e., attack.* [268]***estimation*** *reputation.*

And such things else of quality and respect
As doth import you.

OTHELLO: So please your grace, my ancient;
A man he is of honesty and trust.
To his conveyance I assign my wife,
With what else needful your good grace shall think
to be sent after me.

DUKE: Let it be so.
Good night to every one. [*To* BRABANTIO] And, noble signior,
If virtue no delighted° beauty lack,
Your son-in-law is far more fair than black.

FIRST SENATOR: Adieu, brave Moor. Use Desdemona well.

BRABANTIO: Look to her, Moor, if thou hast eyes to see:
She has deceived her father, and may thee.

[*Exeunt* DUKE, SENATORS, OFFICERS, *&c.*]

OTHELLO: My life upon her faith! Honest Iago,
My Desdemona must I leave to thee.
I prithee let thy wife attend on her,
And bring them after in the best advantage.°
Come, Desdemona. I have but an hour
Of love, of worldly matter, and direction
To spend with thee. We must obey the time.

Exit [MOOR *with* DESDEMONA].

RODERIGO: Iago?

IAGO: What say'st thou, noble heart?

RODERIGO: What will I do, think'st thou?

IAGO: Why, go to bed and sleep.

RODERIGO: I will incontinently° drown myself.

IAGO: If thou dost, I shall never love thee after. Why, thou silly gentleman?

RODERIGO: It is silliness to live when to live is torment; and then have we a prescription to die when death is our physician.

IAGO: O villainous! I have looked upon the world for four times seven years, and since I could distinguish betwixt a benefit and an injury, I never found man that knew how to love himself. Ere I would say I would drown myself for the love of a guinea hen, I would change my humanity with a baboon.

RODERIGO: What should I do? I confess it is my shame to be so fond, but it is not in my virtue° to amend it.

IAGO: Virtue? A fig! 'Tis in ourselves that we are thus, or thus. Our bodies are our gardens, to the which our wills are gardeners; so that if we will plant nettles or sow lettuce, set hyssop and weed up thyme, supply it with one gender of herbs or distract° it with many—either to have it sterile with idleness or manured with industry—why, the power and corrigible°

283 ***delighted*** *delightful.* 291 ***advantage*** *opportunity.* 299 ***incontinently*** *at once.* 309 ***virtue*** *strength (Roderigo is saying that his nature controls him).* 313 ***distract*** *vary.* 314 ***corrigible*** *corrective.*

authority of this lies in our wills. If the balance of our lives had not one scale of reason to poise another of another of sensuality, the blood and baseness of our natures would conduct us to most prepost'rous conclusions.° But we have reason to cool our raging motions, our carnal sting or unbitted° lusts, whereof I take this that you call love to be a sect or scion.°

RODERIGO: It cannot be.

IAGO: It is merely a lust of the blood and a permission of the will. Come, be a man! Drown thyself? Drown cats and blind puppies! I have professed me thy friend, and I confess me knit to thy deserving with cables of perdurable toughness. I could never better stead° thee than now. Put money in thy purse. Follow thou the wars; defeat thy favor° with an usurped° beard. I say, put money in thy purse. It cannot be long that Desdemona should continue her love to the Moor. Put money in thy purse. Nor he his to her. It was a violent commencement in her and thou shalt see an answerable° sequestration—put but money in thy purse. These Moors are changeable in their wills—fill thy purse with money. The food that to him now is as luscious as locusts° shall be to him shortly as bitter as coloquintida.° She must change for youth; when she is sated with his body, she will find the errors of her choice. Therefore, put money in thy purse. If thou wilt needs damn thyself, do it a more delicate way than drowning. Make all the money thou canst. If sanctimony° and a frail vow betwixt an erring° barbarian and supersubtle Venetian be not too hard for my wits, and all the tribe of hell, thou shalt enjoy her. Therefore, make money. A pox of drowning thyself, it is clean out of the way. Seek thou rather to be hanged in compassing° thy joy than to be drowned and go without her.

RODERIGO: Wilt thou be fast to my hopes, if I depend on the issue?

IAGO: Thou art sure of me. Go, make money. I have told thee often, and I retell thee again and again, I hate the Moor. My cause is hearted;° thine hath no less reason. Let us be conjunctive° in our revenge against him. If thou canst cuckold him, thou dost thyself a pleasure, me a sport. There are many events in the womb of time, which will be delivered. Traverse, go, provide thy money! We will have more of this tomorrow. Adieu.

RODERIGO: Where shall we meet i' th' morning?

IAGO: At my lodging.

RODERIGO: I'll be with thee betimes.

IAGO: Go to, farewell. Do you hear, Roderigo?

RODERIGO: I'll sell all my land.

[*Exit.*]

IAGO: Thus do I ever make my fool my purse;
For I mine own gained knowledge° should profane

[317]***conclusions*** *ends.* [318]***unbitted*** *i.e., uncontrolled.* [319]***sect or scion*** *off-shoot.* [324]***stead*** *serve.* [325]***defeat thy favor*** *disguise your face.* [325]***usurped*** *assumed.* [328]***answerable*** *similar.* [330]***locusts*** *(a sweet fruit).* [331]***coloquintida*** *a purgative derived from a bitter apple.* [334]***sanctimony*** *sacred bond (of marriage).* [335]***erring*** *wandering.* [338]***compassing*** *encompassing, achieving.* [341]***hearted*** *deepseated in the heart.* [342]***conjunctive*** *joined.* [352]***gained knowledge*** *i.e., practical, worldly wisdom.*

If I would time expend with such snipe
But for my sport and profit. I hate the Moor,
And it is thought abroad that 'twixt my sheets
H'as done my office. I know not if't be true,
But I, for mere suspicion in that kind,
Will do, as if for surety.° He holds me well;
The better shall my purpose work on him.
Cassio's a proper° man. Let me see now:
To get his place, and to plume up my will°
In double knavery. How? How? Let's see.
After some time, to abuse Othello's ears
That he is too familiar with his wife.
He hath a person and a smooth dispose°
To be suspected—framed° to make women false.
The Moor is of a free and open nature
That thinks men honest that but seem to be so;
And will as tenderly be led by th' nose
As asses are.
I have't! It is engendered! Hell and night
Must bring this monstrous birth to the world's light. [*Exit.*]

ACT II

Scene I [Cyprus.]

Enter MONTANO *and two* GENTLEMAN [*one above*].°

MONTANO: What from the cape can you discern at sea?
FIRST GENTLEMAN: Nothing at all, it is a high-wrought flood.
I cannot 'twixt the heaven and the main
Descry a sail.
MONTANO: Methinks the wind hath spoke aloud at land;
A fuller blast ne'er shook our battlements.
If it hath ruffianed so upon the sea,
What ribs of oak, when mountains melt on them,
Can hold the mortise? What shall we hear of this?
SECOND GENTLEMAN: A segregation° of the Turkish fleet.
For do but stand upon the foaming shore,
The chidden billow seems to pelt the clouds;
The wind-shaked surge, with high and monstrous main,°
Seems to cast water on the burning Bear

[358]***surety*** *certainty.* [360]***proper*** *handsome.* [361]***plume up my will*** *(many explanations have been offered for this crucial line, which in Q1, reads "make up my will." The general sense is something like "to make more proud and gratify my ego").* [365]***dispose*** *manner.* [366]***framed*** *designed.* ***II.i. s.d. above*** *(the Folio arrangement of this scene requires that the First Gentleman stand above—on the upper stage—and act as a lookout reporting sights which cannot be seen by Montano standing below on the main stage).* [10]***segregation*** *separation.* [13]***main*** *(both "ocean" and "strength").*

And quench the guards of th' ever-fixèd pole.°
I never did like molestation view
On the enchafèd flood.

MONTANO: If that the Turkish fleet
Be not ensheltered and embayed, they are drowned;
It is impossible to bear it out.

Enter a [*third*] GENTLEMAN.

THIRD GENTLEMAN: News, lads! Our wars are done.
The desperate tempest hath so banged the Turks
That their designment halts. A noble ship of Venice
Hath seen a grievous wrack and sufferance°
On most part of their fleet.

MONTANO: How? Is this true?

THIRD GENTLEMAN: The ship is here put in,
A Veronesa; Michael Cassio,
Lieutenant to the warlike Moor Othello,
Is come on shore; the Moor himself at sea,
And is in full commission here for Cyprus.

MONTANO: I am glad on't. 'Tis a worthy governor.

THIRD GENTLEMAN: But this same Cassio, though he speak of comfort
Touching the Turkish loss, yet he looks sadly
And prays the Moor be safe, for they were parted
With foul and violent tempest.

MONTANO: Pray heavens he be;
For I have served him, and the man commands
Like a full soldier. Let's to the seaside, ho!
As well to see the vessel that's come in
As to throw out our eyes for brave Othello,
Even till we make the main and th' aerial blue
An indistinct regard.°

THIRD GENTLEMAN: Come, let's do so;
For every minute is expectancy
Of more arrivancie.°

Enter CASSIO.

CASSIO: Thanks, you the valiant of the warlike isle,
That so approve° the Moor. O, let the heavens
Give him defense against the elements,
For I have lost him on a dangerous sea.

MONTANO: Is he well shipped?

CASSIO: His bark is stoutly timbered, and his pilot

[14–15]***Seems . . . pole*** *(the constellation Ursa Minor contains two stars which are the guards, or companions, of the pole, or North Star).* [23]***sufferance*** *damage.* [39–40]***the main . . . regard*** *i.e., the sea and sky become indistinguishable.* [42]***arrivancie*** *arrivals.* [44]***approve*** *("honor" or, perhaps, "are as warlike and valiant as your governor").*

Of very expert and approved allowance;°
Therefore my hopes, not surfeited to death,°
Stand in bold cure.° (*Within:* A sail, a sail, a sail!)
CASSIO: What noise?
FIRST GENTLEMAN: The town is empty; on the brow o' th' sea
Stand ranks of people, and they cry, "A sail!"
CASSIO: My hopes do shape him for the governor. [*A shot.*]
SECOND GENTLEMAN: They do discharge their shot of courtesy:
Our friends at least.
CASSIO: I pray you, sir, go forth
And give us truth who 'tis that is arrived.
SECOND GENTLEMAN: I shall. [*Exit.*]
MONTANO: But, good lieutenant, is your general wived?
CASSIO: Most fortunately. He hath achieved a maid
That paragons° description and wild fame;°
One that excels the quirks of blazoning pens,°
And in th' essential vesture of creation°
Does tire the ingener.°

Enter [*Second*] GENTLEMAN.

How now? Who has put in?
SECOND GENTLEMAN: 'Tis one Iago, ancient to the general.
CASSIO: H'as had most favorable and happy speed:
Tempests themselves, high seas, and howling winds,
The guttered° rocks and congregated° sands,
Traitors ensteeped° to enclog the guiltless keel,
As having sense° of beauty, do omit
Their mortal° natures, letting go safely by
The divine Desdemona.
MONTANO: What is she?
CASSIO: She that I spake of, our great captain's captain,
Left in the conduct of the bold Iago,
Whose footing° here anticipates our thoughts
A se'nnight's° speed. Great Jove, Othello guard,
And swell his sail with thine own pow'rful breath,
That he may bless this bay with his tall° ship,
Make love's quick pants in Desdemona's arms,
Give renewed fire to our extincted spirits,
And bring all Cyprus comfort!

[49]***approved allowance*** *known and tested.* [50]***not surfeited to death*** *i.e., not so great as to be in danger.* [51]***Stand in bold cure*** *i.e., are likely to be restored.* [62]***paragons*** *exceeds.* [62]***wild fame*** *extravagant report.* [63]***quirks of blazoning pens*** *ingenuities of praising pens.* [64]***essential vesture of creation*** *essential human nature as given by the Creator.* [65]***tire the ingener*** *a difficult line that probably means something like "outdo the human ability to imagine and picture."* [69]***guttered*** *jagged.* [69]***congregated*** *gathered.* [70]***ensteeped*** *submerged.* [71]***sense*** *awareness.* [72]***mortal*** *deadly.* [76]***footing*** *landing.* [77]***se'nnight's*** *week's.* [79]***tall*** *brave.*

Enter DESDEMONA, IAGO, RODERIGO, *and* EMILIA.

O, behold! The riches of the ship is come on shore!
You men of Cyprus, let her have your knees. [*Kneeling.*]
Hail to thee, lady! and the grace of heaven,
Before, behind thee, and on every hand,
Enwheel thee round.

DESDEMONA: I thank you, valiant Cassio.
What tidings can you tell of my lord?

CASSIO: He is not yet arrived, nor know I aught
But that he's well and will be shortly here.

DESDEMONA: O but I fear. How lost you company?

CASSIO: The great contention of sea and skies
Parted our fellowship. (*Within:* A sail, a sail!) [*A shot.*]
But hark. A sail!

SECOND GENTLEMAN: They give this greeting to the citadel;
This likewise is a friend.

CASSIO: See for the news. [*Exit* GENTLEMAN.]
Good ancient, you are welcome. [*To* EMILIA] Welcome, mistress.
Let it not gall your patience, good Iago,
That I extend° my manners. 'Tis my breeding°
That gives me this bold show of courtesy. [*Kisses* EMILIA.]

IAGO: Sir, would she give you so much of her lips
As of her tongue she oft bestows on me,
You would have enough.

DESDEMONA: Alas, she has no speech.

IAGO: In faith, too much.
I find it still when I have leave to sleep.°
Marry, before your ladyship,° I grant,
She puts her tongue a little in her heart
And chides with thinking.

EMILIA: You have little cause to say so.

IAGO: Come on, come on! You are pictures° out of door,
Bells in your parlors, wildcats in your kitchens,
Saints in your injuries,° devils being offended,
Players in your housewifery,° and housewives in your beds.

DESDEMONA: O, fie upon thee, slanderer!

IAGO: Nay, it is true, or else I am a Turk:
You rise to play, and go to bed to work.

EMILIA: You shall not write my praise.

IAGO: No, let me not.

98***extend*** *stretch.* 98***breeding*** *careful training in manners (Cassio is considerably more the polished gentleman than Iago, and aware of it).* 104***still . . . sleep*** *i.e., even when she allows me to sleep she continues to scold.* 105***before your ladyship*** *in your presence.* 108***pictures*** *models (of virtue).* 110***in your injuries*** *when you injure others.* 111***housewifery*** *this word can mean "careful, economical household management," and Iago would then be accusing women of only pretending to be good housekeepers, while in bed they are either [1] economical of their favors, or more likely [2] serious and dedicated workers.*

DESDEMONA: What wouldst write of me, if thou shouldst praise me?
IAGO: O gentle lady, do not put me to't.
For I am nothing if not critical.
DESDEMONA: Come on, assay. There's one gone to the harbor?
IAGO: Ay, madam.
DESDEMONA [*Aside*]: I am not merry; but I do beguile
The thing I am by seeming otherwise.—
Come, how wouldst thou praise me?
IAGO: I am about it; but indeed my invention
Comes from my pate as birdlime° does from frieze°—
It plucks out brains and all. But my Muse labors,
And thus she is delivered:
If she be fair° and wise: fairness and wit,
The one's for use, the other useth it.
DESDEMONA: Well praised. How if she be black° and witty?
IAGO: If she be black, and thereto have a wit,
She'll find a white that shall her blackness fit.
DESDEMONA: Worse and worse!
EMILIA: How if fair and foolish?
IAGO: She never yet was foolish that was fair,
For even her folly helped her to an heir.
DESDEMONA: Those are old fond° paradoxes to make fools laugh i' th' alehouse. What miserable praise hast thou for her that's foul and foolish?
IAGO: There's none so foul, and foolish thereunto,
But does foul pranks which fair and wise ones do.
DESDEMONA: O heavy ignorance. Thou praisest the worst best. But what praise couldst thou bestow on a deserving woman indeed—one that in the authority of her merit did justly put on the vouch of very malice itself?°
IAGO: She that was ever fair, and never proud;
Had tongue at will, and yet was never loud;
Never lacked gold, and yet went never gay;
Fled from her wish, and yet said "Now I may";
She that being angered, her revenge being nigh,
Bade her wrong stay, and her displeasure fly;
She that in wisdom never was so frail
To change the cod's head for the salmon's tail;°
She that could think, and nev'r disclose her mind;
See suitors following, and not look behind:
She was a wight° (if ever such wights were)—
DESDEMONA: To do what?

124***birdlime*** *a sticky substance put on branches to catch birds.* 124***frieze*** *rough cloth.* 127***fair*** *light-complexioned.* 129***black*** *brunette.* 136***fond*** *foolish.* 141–143***one . . . itself*** *i.e., a woman so honest and deserving that even malice would be forced to approve of her.* 151***To . . . tail*** *i.e., to exchange something valuable for something useless.* 154***wight*** *person.*

IAGO: To suckle fools and chronicle small beer.°

DESDEMONA: O most lame and impotent conclusion. Do not learn of him, Emilia, though he be thy husband. How say you, Cassio? Is he not a most profane and liberal° counselor?

CASSIO: He speaks home,° madam. You may relish him more in° the soldier than in the scholar. [Takes DESDEMONA's hand.]

IAGO [*Aside*]: He takes her by the palm. Ay, well said, whisper! With as little a web as this will I ensnare as great a fly as Cassio. Ay, smile upon her, do! I will gyve° thee in thine own courtship.—You say true; 'tis so, indeed!—If such tricks as these strip you out of your lieutenantry, it had been better you had not kissed your three fingers so oft—which now again you are most apt to play the sir° in. Very good! Well kissed! An excellent curtsy!° 'Tis so, indeed. Yet again your fingers to your lips? Would they were clyster pipes° for your sake! [*Trumpets within.*] The Moor! I know his trumpet.°

CASSIO: 'Tis truly so.

DESDEMONA: Let's meet him and receive him.

CASSIO: Lo, where he comes.

Enter OTHELLO *and* ATTENDANTS.

OTHELLO: O my fair warrior!

DESDEMONA: My dear Othello.

OTHELLO: It gives me wonder great as my content
To see you here before me. O my soul's joy!
If after every tempest come such calms,
May the winds blow till they have wakened death.
And let the laboring bark climb hills of seas
Olympus-high, and duck again as low
As hell's from heaven. If it were now to die,
'Twere now to be most happy; for I fear
My soul hath her content so absolute
That not another comfort like to this
Succeeds in unknown fate.

DESDEMONA: The heavens forbid
But that our loves and comforts should increase
Even as our days do grow.

OTHELLO: Amen to that, sweet powers!
I cannot speak enough of this content:
It stops me here [*touches his heart*]; it is too much of joy.
And this, and this, the greatest discords be [*They kiss.*]
That e'er our hearts shall make!

IAGO [*Aside*]: O, you are well tuned now!

[156]***chronicle small beer*** *i.e., keep household accounts (the most trivial of occupations in Iago's opinion).* [159]***liberal*** *licentious.* [160]***speaks home*** *thrusts deeply with his speech.* [160]***relish him more in*** *enjoy him more as.* [164]***gyve*** *bind.* [167]***the sir*** *the fashionable gentleman.* [168]***curtsy*** *courtesy, i.e., bow.* [169]***clyster pipes*** *enema tubes.* [170]***his trumpet*** *(great men had their own distinctive calls).*

But I'll set down the pegs° that make this music,
As honest as I am.

OTHELLO: Come, let us to the castle.
News, friends! Our wars are done; the Turks are drowned.
How does my old acquaintance of this isle?
Honey, you shall be well desired in Cyprus;
I have found great love amongst them. O my sweet,
I prattle out of fashion, and I dote
In mine own comforts. I prithee, good Iago,
Go to the bay and disembark my coffers.
Bring thou the master to the citadel;
He is a good one and his worthiness
Does challenge° much respect. Come, Desdemona,
Once more well met at Cyprus.

Exit OTHELLO *and* DESDEMONA [*and all but* IAGO *and* RODERIGO].

IAGO [*To an* ATTENDANT]: Do thou meet me presently at the harbor.
[*To* RODERIGO]
Come hither. If thou be'st valiant (as they say base men being in love have then a nobility in their natures more than is native to them), list me. The lieutenant tonight watches on the court of guard.° First, I must tell thee this: Desdemona is directly in love with him.

RODERIGO: With him? Why, 'tis not possible.

IAGO: Lay thy finger thus [*puts his finger to his lips*], and let thy soul be instructed. Mark me with what violence she first loved the Moor but for bragging and telling her fantastical lies. To love him still for prating? Let not thy discreet heart think it. Her eye must be fed. And what delight shall she have to look on the devil? When the blood is made dull with the act of sport, there should be a game° to inflame it and to give satiety a fresh appetite, loveliness in favor,° sympathy in years,° manners, and beauties; all which the Moor is defective in. Now for want of these required conveniences,° her delicate tenderness will find itself abused, begin to heave the gorge,° disrelish and abhor the Moor. Very nature will instruct her in it and compel her to some second choice. Now sir, this granted—as it is a most pregnant° and unforced position—who stands so eminent in the degree of this fortune as Cassio does? A knave very voluble; no further conscionable° than in putting on the mere form of civil and humane° seeming for the better compass of his salt° and most hidden loose° affection. Why, none! Why, none! A slipper° and subtle knave, a finder of occasion, that has an eye can stamp and counterfeit advantages, though true advantage never present itself. A devilish knave. Besides, the knave is handsome, young, and hath all those requisites in him that folly and green minds

[192]***set down the pegs*** *loosen the strings (to produce discord).* [203]***challenge*** *require, exact.* [208]***court of guard*** *guardhouse.* [216]***game*** *sport (with the added sense of "gamey," "rank").* [216]***favor*** *countenance, appearance.* [217]***sympathy in years*** *sameness of age.* [218]***conveniences*** *advantages.* [219]***heave the gorge*** *vomit.* [221]***pregnant*** *likely.* [222–223]***no further conscionable*** *having no more conscience.* [223]***humane*** *polite.* [224]***salt*** *lecherous.* [224]***loose*** *immoral.* [225]***slipper*** *slippery.*

look after. A pestilent complete knave, and the woman hath found him already.

RODERIGO: I cannot believe that in her; she's full of most blessed condition.

IAGO: Blessed fig's-end! The wine she drinks is made of grapes. If she had been blessed, she would never have loved the Moor. Blessed pudding! Didst thou not see her paddle with the palm of his hand? Didst not mark that?

RODERIGO: Yes, that I did; but that was but courtesy.

IAGO: Lechery, by this hand! [Extends his index finger.] An index° and obscure prologue to the history of lust and foul thoughts. They met so near with their lips that their breaths embraced together. Villainous thoughts, Roderigo. When these mutualities so marshal the way, hard at hand comes the master and main exercise, th' incorporate° conclusion: Pish! But, sir, be you ruled by me. I have brought you from Venice. Watch you tonight; for the command, I'll lay't upon you. Cassio knows you not. I'll not be far from you. Do you find some occasion to anger Cassio, either by speaking too loud, or tainting° his discipline, or from what other course you please which the time shall more favorably minister.

RODERIGO: Well.

IAGO: Sir, he's rash and very sudden in choler,° and haply may strike at you. Provoke him that he may; for even out of that will I cause these of Cyprus to mutiny, whose qualification shall come into no true taste° again but by the displanting of Cassio. So shall you have a shorter journey to your desires by the means I shall then have to prefer them; and the impediment most profitably removed without the which there were no expectation of our prosperity.

RODERIGO: I will do this if you can bring it to any opportunity.

IAGO: I warrant thee. Meet me by and by at the citadel. I must fetch his necessaries ashore. Farewell.

RODERIGO: Adieu. [*Exit.*]

IAGO: That Cassio loves her, I do well believe't;
That she loves him, 'tis apt and of great credit.
The Moor, howbeit that I endure him not,
Is of a constant, loving, noble nature,
And I dare think he'll prove to Desdemona
A most dear° husband. Now I do love her too;
Not out of absolute° lust, though peradventure°
I stand accountant for as great a sin,
But partly led to diet° my revenge,
For that I do suspect the lusty Moor
Hath leaped into my seat; the thought whereof
Doth, like a poisonous mineral, gnaw my inwards;
And nothing can or shall content my soul

[237]***index*** *pointer.* [241]***incorporate*** *carnal.* [244]***tainting*** *discrediting.* [248]***choler*** *anger.*
[250]***qualification . . . taste*** *i.e., appeasement will not be brought about (wine was "qualified" by adding water).*
[264]***dear*** *expensive* [265]***out of absolute*** *absolutely out of.* [265]***peradventure*** *perchance.* [267]***diet*** *feed.*

Till I am evened with him, wife for wife.
Or failing so, yet that I put the Moor
At least into a jealousy so strong
That judgment cannot cure. Which thing to do,
If this poor trash of Venice, whom I trace°
For his quick hunting, stand the putting on,
I'll have our Michael Cassio on the hip,
Abuse him to the Moor in the right garb°
(For I fear Cassio with my nightcap too),
Make the Moor thank me, love me, and reward me
For making him egregiously an ass
And practicing upon° his peace and quiet,
Even to madness. 'Tis here, but yet confused:
Knavery's plain face is never seen till used. [*Exit.*]

Scene II [A street.]

Enter OTHELLO'S HERALD, *with a proclamation.*

HERALD: It is Othello's pleasure, our noble and valiant general, that upon certain tidings now arrived importing the mere perdition° of the Turkish fleet, every man put himself into triumph. Some to dance, some to make bonfires, each man to what sport and revels his addition° leads him. For, besides these beneficial news, it is the celebration of his nuptial. So much was his pleasure should be proclaimed. All offices° are open, and there is full liberty of feasting from this present hour of five till the bell have told eleven. Bless the isle of Cyprus and our noble general Othello! [*Exit.*]

Scene III [The citadel of Cyprus.]

Enter OTHELLO, DESDEMONA, CASSIO, *and* ATTENDANTS.

OTHELLO: Good Michael, look you to the guard tonight.
Let's teach ourselves that honorable stop,
Not to outsport discretion.
CASSIO: Iago hath direction what to do;
But notwithstanding, with my personal eye
Will I look to't.
OTHELLO: Iago is most honest.
Michael, good night. Tomorrow with your earliest
Let me have speech with you. [*To* DESDEMONA] Come, my dear love,
The purchase made, the fruits are to ensue.
That profit's yet to come 'tween me and you.
Good night. *Exit* [OTHELLO *with* DESDEMONA *and* ATTENDANTS].

[276]***trace*** *(most editors emend to "trash," meaning to hang weights on a dog to slow his hunting: but "trace" clearly means something like "put on the trace" or "set on the track").* [279]***right garb*** *i.e., "proper fashion."* [283]***practicing upon*** *scheming to destroy.* ***II.ii.*** [2]***mere perdition*** *absolute destruction.* [4]***addition*** *rank.* [6]***offices*** *kitchens and storerooms of food.*

Enter IAGO.

CASSIO: Welcome, Iago. We must to the watch.

IAGO: Not this hour, lieutenant; 'tis not yet ten o' th' clock. Our general cast° us thus early for the love of his Desdemona; who let us not therefore blame. He hath not yet made wanton the night with her, and she is sport for Jove.

CASSIO: She's a most exquisite lady.

IAGO: And, I'll warrant her, full of game.

CASSIO: Indeed, she's a most fresh and delicate creature.

IAGO: What an eye she has! Methinks it sounds a parley to provocation.

CASSIO: An inviting eye; and yet methinks right modest.

IAGO: And when she speaks, is it not an alarum° to love?

CASSIO: She is indeed perfection.

IAGO: Well, happiness to their sheets! Come, lieutenant, I have a stoup° of wine, and here without are a brace of Cyprus gallants that would fain have a measure to the health of black Othello.

CASSIO: Not tonight, good Iago. I have very poor and unhappy brains for drinking; I could well wish courtesy would invent some other custom of entertainment.

IAGO: O, they are our friends. But one cup! I'll drink for you.

CASSIO: I have drunk but one tonight, and that was craftily qualified° too; and behold what innovation it makes here. I am unfortunate in the infirmity and dare not task my weakness with any more.

IAGO: What, man! 'Tis a night of revels, the gallants desire it.

CASSIO: Where are they?

IAGO: Here, at the door. I pray you call them in.

CASSIO: I'll do't, but it dislikes me. [*Exit.*]

IAGO: If I can fasten but one cup upon him
With that which he hath drunk tonight already,
He'll be as full of quarrel and offense
As my young mistress' dog. Now, my sick fool Roderigo,
Whom love hath turned almost the wrong side out,
To Desdemona hath tonight caroused
Potations pottle-deep;° and he's to watch.
Three else° of Cyprus, noble swelling spirits,
That hold their honors in a wary distance,°
The very elements of this warlike isle,
Have I tonight flustered with flowing cups,
And they watch too. Now, 'mongst this flock of drunkards
Am I to put our Cassio in some action
That may offend the isle. But here they come.

Enter CASSIO, MONTANO, *and* GENTLEMEN.

II.iii. [13]***cast*** *dismissed.* [22]***alarum*** *the call to action, "general quarters."* [24]***stoup*** *two-quart tankard.* [31]***qualified*** *diluted.* [44]***pottle-deep*** *to the bottom of the cup.* [45]***else*** *others.* [46]***hold . . . distance*** *are scrupulous in maintaining their honor.*

If consequence do but approve my dream,
My boat sails freely, both with wind and stream.

CASSIO: 'Fore God, they have given me a rouse° already.

MONTANO: Good faith, a little one; not past a pint, as I am a soldier.

IAGO: Some wine, ho!
[Sings] And let me the canakin clink, clink;
And let me the canakin clink.
A soldier's a man;
O man's life's but a span.
Why then, let a soldier drink.
Some wine, boys!

CASSIO: 'Fore God, an excellent song!

IAGO: I learned it in England, where indeed they are most potent in potting. Your Dane, your German, and your swag-bellied° Hollander—Drink, ho!—are nothing to your English.

CASSIO: Is your Englishman so exquisite° in his drinking?

IAGO: Why, he drinks you with facility your Dane dead drunk; he sweats not to overthrow your Almain; he gives your Hollander a vomit ere the next pottle can be filled.

CASSIO: To the health of our general!

MONTANO: I am for it, lieutenant, and I'll do you justice.

IAGO: O sweet England!
[Sings] King Stephen was and a worthy peer;
His breeches cost him but a crown;
He held them sixpence all too dear,
With that he called the tailor lown.°
He was a wight of high renown,
And thou art but of low degree:
'Tis pride that pulls the country down;
And take thine auld cloak about thee.
Some wine, ho!

CASSIO: 'Fore God, this is a more exquisite song than the other.

IAGO: Will you hear't again?

CASSIO: No, for I hold him to be unworthy of his place that does those things. Well, God's above all; and there be souls must be saved, and there be souls must not be saved.

IAGO: It's true, good lieutenant.

CASSIO: For mine own part—no offense to the general, nor any man of quality—I hope to be saved.

IAGO: And so do I too, lieutenant.

CASSIO: Ay, but, by your leave, not before me. The lieutenant is to be saved before the ancient. Let's have no more of this; let's to our affairs.—God forgive us our sins!—Gentlemen, let's look to our business. Do not think, gentlemen, I am drunk. This is my ancient; this is my right hand, and this is my left. I am not drunk now. I can stand well enough, and I speak well enough.

54 ***rouse*** *drink.* 65 ***swag-bellied*** *pendulous-bellied.* 67 ***exquisite*** *superb.* 77 ***lown*** *lout.*

GENTLEMEN: Excellent well!
CASSIO: Why, very well then. You must not think then that I am drunk. [*Exit.*]
MONTANO: To th' platform, masters. Come, let's set the watch.
IAGO: You see this fellow that is gone before.
He's a soldier fit to stand by Caesar
And give direction; and do but see his vice.
'Tis to his virtue a just equinox,°
The one as long as th' other. 'Tis pity of him.
I fear the trust Othello puts him in,
On some odd time of his infirmity,
Will shake this island.
MONTANO: But is he often thus?
IAGO: 'Tis evermore his prologue to his sleep:
He'll watch the horologe a double set°
If drink rock not his cradle.
MONTANO: It were well
The general were put in mind of it.
Perhaps he sees it not, or his good nature
Prizes the virtue that appears in Cassio
And looks not on his evils. Is not this true?

Enter RODERIGO.

IAGO [*Aside*]: How now, Roderigo?
I pray you after the lieutenant, go! [*Exit* RODERIGO.]
MONTANO: And 'tis great pity that the noble Moor
Should hazard such a place as his own second
With one of an ingraft° infirmity.
It were an honest action to say so
To the Moor.
IAGO: Not I, for this fair island!
I do love Cassio well and would do much
To cure him of this evil. (Help! Help! *Within.*)
But hark! What noise?

Enter CASSIO, *pursuing* RODERIGO.

CASSIO: Zounds, you rogue! You rascal!
MONTANO: What's the matter, lieutenant?
CASSIO: A knave teach me my duty? I'll beat the knave into a twiggen° bottle.
RODERIGO: Beat me?
CASSIO: Dost thou prate, rogue? [*Strikes him.*]
MONTANO: Nay, good lieutenant! I pray you, sir, hold your hand.

[*Stays him.*]

104 ***just equinox*** *exact balance (of dark and light).* 110 ***watch . . . set*** *stay awake twice around the clock.*
120 ***ingraft*** *ingrained.* 128 ***twiggen*** *wicker-covered.*

CASSIO: Let me go, sir, or I'll knock you o'er the mazzard.°
MONTANO: Come, come, you're drunk!
CASSIO: Drunk? [*They fight.*]
IAGO [Aside to RODERIGO]: Away, I say! Go out and cry a mutiny!
[*Exit* RODERIGO.]
Nay, good lieutenant. God's will, gentlemen!
Help, ho! Lieutenant. Sir. Montano.
Help, masters! Here's a goodly watch indeed! [*A bell rung.*]
Who's that which rings the bell? Diablo, ho!
The two will rise. God's will, lieutenant,
You'll be ashamed forever.

Enter OTHELLO *and* ATTENDANTS.

OTHELLO: What is the matter here?
MONTANO: Zounds, I bleed still. I am hurt to the death.
He dies. [*He and* CASSIO *fight again.*]
OTHELLO: Hold for your lives!
IAGO: Hold, ho! Lieutenant. Sir. Montano. Gentlemen!
Have you forgot all place of sense and duty?
Hold! The general speaks to you. Hold, for shame!
OTHELLO: Why, how now, ho? From whence ariseth this?
Are we turned Turks, and to ourselves do that
Which heaven hath forbid the Ottomites?°
For Christian shame put by this barbarous brawl!
He that stirs next to carve for his own rage
Holds his soul light;° he dies upon his motion.
Silence that dreadful bell! It frights the isle
From her propriety.° What is the matter, masters?
Honest Iago, that looks dead with grieving,
Speak. Who began this? On thy love, I charge thee.
IAGO: I do not know. Friends all, but now, even now,
In quarter° and in terms like bride and groom
Devesting them for bed; and then, but now—
As if some planet had unwitted men—
Swords out, and tilting one at other's breasts
In opposition bloody. I cannot speak
Any beginning to this peevish odds,°
And would in action glorious I had lost
Those legs that brought me to a part of it!
OTHELLO: How comes it, Michael, you are thus forgot?
CASSIO: I pray you pardon me; I cannot speak.
OTHELLO: Worthy Montano, you were wont to be civil;
Thy gravity and stillness of your youth

133 ***mazzard*** *head.* 151 ***heaven . . . Ottomites*** *i.e., by sending the storm which dispersed the Turks.*
154 ***Holds his soul light*** *values his soul lightly.* 156 ***propriety*** *proper order.* 160 ***In quarter*** *on duty.*
165 ***odds*** *quarrel.*

The world hath noted, and your name is great
In mouths of wisest censure.° What's the matter
That you unlace° your reputation thus
And spend your rich opinion° for the name
Of a night-brawler? Give me answer to it.

MONTANO: Worthy Othello, I am hurt to danger.
Your officer, Iago, can inform you.
While I spare speech, which something now offends° me,
Of all that I do know; nor know I aught
By me that's said or done amiss this night,
Unless self-charity be sometimes a vice,
And to defend ourselves it be a sin
When violence assails us.

OTHELLO: Now, by heaven,
My blood begins my safer guides to rule,
And passion, having my best judgment collied,°
Assays to lead the way. If I once stir
Or do but lift this arm, the best of you
Shall sink in my rebuke. Give me to know
How this foul rout began, who set it on;
And he that is approved in this offense,
Though he had twinned with me, both at a birth,
Shall lose me. What? In a town of war
Yet wild, the people's hearts brimful of fear,
To manage° private and domestic quarrel?
In night, and on the court and guard of safety?
'Tis monstrous. Iago, who began't?

MONTANO: If partially affined, or leagued in office,°
Thou dost deliver more or less than truth,
Thou art no soldier.

IAGO: Touch me not so near.
I had rather have this tongue cut from my mouth
Than it should do offense to Michael Cassio.
Yet I persuade myself to speak the truth
Shall nothing wrong him. This it is, general.
Montano and myself being in speech,
There comes a fellow crying out for help,
And Cassio following him with determined sword
To execute upon him. Sir, this gentleman
Steps in to Cassio and entreats his pause.
Myself the crying fellow did pursue,
Lest by his clamor—as it so fell out—
The town might fall in fright. He, swift of foot,

[173]***censure*** *judgment.* [174]***unlace*** *undo (the term refers specifically to the dressing of a wild boar killed in the hunt).* [175]***opinion*** *reputation.* [179]***offends*** *harms, hurts.* [186]***collied*** *darkened.* [195]***manage*** *conduct.* [198]***If . . . office*** *if you are partial because you are related ("affined") or the brother officer (of Cassio).*

Outran my purpose; and I returned then rather
For that I heard the clink and fall of swords,
And Cassio high in oath; which till tonight
I ne'er might say before. When I came back—
For this was brief—I found them close together
At blow and thrust, even as again they were
When you yourself did part them.
More of this matter cannot I report;
But men are men; the best sometimes forget.
Though Cassio did some little wrong to him,
As men in rage strike those that wish them best,
Yet surely Cassio I believe received
From him that fled some strange indignity,
Which patience could not pass.°

OTHELLO: I know, Iago,
Thy honesty and love doth mince° this matter,
Making it light to Cassio. Cassio, I love thee;
But never more be officer of mine.

Enter DESDEMONA, *attended.*

Look if my gentle love be not raised up.
I'll make thee an example.

DESDEMONA: What is the matter, dear?

OTHELLO: All's well, sweeting; come away to bed.
[*To* MONTANO] Sir, for your hurts, myself will be your surgeon.
Lead him off. [MONTANO *led off.*]
Iago, look with care about the town
And silence those whom this vile brawl distracted.
Come, Desdemona 'tis the soldiers' life
To have their balmy slumbers waked with strife.

Exit [*with all but* IAGO *and* CASSIO].

IAGO: What, are you hurt, lieutenant?

CASSIO: Ay, past all surgery.

IAGO: Marry, God forbid!

CASSIO: Reputation, reputation, reputation! O, I have lost my reputation! I have lost the immortal part of myself, and what remains is bestial. My reputation, Iago, my reputation.

IAGO: As I am an honest man, I had thought you had received some bodily wound. There is more sense° in that than in reputation. Reputation is an idle and most false imposition,° oft got without merit and lost without deserving. You have lost no reputation at all unless you repute yourself such a loser. What, man, there are more ways to recover the general again. You are but now cast in

226 ***pass*** *allow to pass.* 227 ***mince*** *cut up (i.e., tell only part of).* 246 ***sense*** *physical feeling.* 247 ***imposition*** *external thing.*

his mood°—a punishment more in policy° than in malice—even so as one would beat his offenseless dog to affright an imperious lion. Sue to him again, and he's yours.

CASSIO: I will rather sue to be despised than to deceive so good a commander with so slight, so drunken, and so indiscreet an officer. Drunk! And speak parrot!° And squabble! Swagger! Swear! and discourse fustian° with one's own shadow! O thou invisible spirit of wine, if thou hast no name to be known by, let us call thee devil!

IAGO: What was he that you followed with your sword? What had he done to you?

CASSIO: I know not.

IAGO: Is't possible?

CASSIO: I remember a mass of things, but nothing distinctly: a quarrel, but nothing wherefore. O God, that men should put an enemy in their mouths to steal away their brains! that we should with joy, pleasance, revel, and applause transform ourselves into beasts!

IAGO: Why, but you are now well enough. How came you thus recovered?

CASSIO: It hath pleased the devil drunkenness to give place to the devil wrath. One unperfectness shows me another, to make me frankly despise myself.

IAGO: Come, you are too severe a moraler. As the time, the place, and the condition of this country stands, I could heartily wish this had not befall'n; but since it is as it is, mend it for your own good.

CASSIO: I will ask him for my place again: he shall tell me I am a drunkard. Had I as many mouths as Hydra, such an answer would stop them all. To be now a sensible man, by and by a fool, and presently a beast! O strange! Every inordinate cup is unblest, and the ingredient is a devil.

IAGO: Come, come, good wine is a good familiar creature if it be well used. Exclaim no more against it. And, good lieutenant, I think you think I love you.

CASSIO: I have well approved it, sir. I drunk?

IAGO: You or any man living may be drunk at a time, man. I tell you what you shall do. Our general's wife is now the general. I may say so in this respect, for all he hath devoted and given up himself to the contemplation, mark, and devotement of her parts° and graces. Confess yourself freely to her; importune her help to put you in your place again. She is of so free, so kind, so apt, so blessed a disposition she holds it a vice in her goodness not to do more than she is requested. This broken joint between you and her husband entreat her to splinter;° and my fortunes against any lay° worth naming, this crack of your love shall grow stronger than it was before.

CASSIO: You advise me well.

IAGO: I protest, in the sincerity of love and honest kindness.

CASSIO: I think it freely; and betimes in the morning I will beseech the virtuous

250 ***cast in his mood*** *dismissed because of his anger.* 249–250 ***in policy*** *politically necessary.* 254 ***speak parrot*** *gabble without sense.* 255 ***discourse fustian*** *speak nonsense ("fustian" was a coarse cotton cloth used for stuffing).* 283 ***devotement of her parts*** *devotion to her qualities.* 287 ***splinter*** *splint.* 287 ***lay*** *wager.*

Desdemona to undertake for me. I am desperate of my fortunes if they check° me

IAGO: You are in the right. Good night, lieutenant; I must to the watch.

CASSIO: Good night, honest Iago. [*Exit* CASSIO.]

IAGO: And what's he then that says I play the villain,
When this advice is free° I give, and honest,
Probal to° thinking, and indeed the course
To win the Moor again? For 'tis most easy
Th' inclining° Desdemona to subdue
In any honest suit; she's framed as fruitful°
As the free elements.° And then for her
To win the Moor—were't to renounce his baptism,
All seals and symbols of redeemèd sin—
His soul is so enfettered to her love
That she may make, unmake, do what she list,
Even as her appetite° shall play the god
With his weak function.° How am I then a villain
To counsel Cassio to this parallel course,
Directly to his good? Divinity of hell!
When devils will the blackest sins put on,°
They do suggest at first with heavenly shows,°
As I do now. For whiles this honest fool
Plies Desdemona to repair his fortune,
And she for him pleads strongly to the Moor,
I'll pour this pestilence into his ear:
That she repeals him° for her body's lust;
And by how much she strives to do him good,
She shall undo her credit with the Moor.
So will I turn her virtue into pitch,
And out of her own goodness make the net
That shall enmesh them all. How now, Roderigo?

Enter RODERIGO.

RODERIGO: I do not follow here in the chase, not like a hound that hunts, but one that fills up the cry.° My money is almost spent; I have been tonight exceedingly well cudgeled; and I think the issue will be, I shall have so much experience for my pains; and so, with no money at all, and a little more wit, return again to Venice.

IAGO: How poor are they that have not patience!
What wound did ever heal but by degrees?
Thou know'st we work by wit, and not by witchcraft;

292 ***check*** *repulse.* 297 ***free*** *generous and open.* 298 ***Probal to*** *provable by.* 300 ***inclining*** *inclined (to be helpful).* 301 ***framed as fruitful*** *made as generous.* 302 ***elements*** *i.e., basic nature.* 307 ***appetite*** *liking.* 308 ***function*** *thought.* 311 ***put on*** *advance, further.* 312 ***shows*** *appearances.* 317 ***repeals him*** *asks for (Cassio's reinstatement).* 324 ***fills up the cry*** *makes up one of the hunting pack, adding to the noise but not actually tracking.*

And wit depends on dilatory time.
Does't not go well? Cassio hath beaten thee,
And thou by that small hurt hath cashiered Cassio.
Though other things grow fair against the sun,
Yet fruits that blossom first will first be ripe.
Content thyself awhile. By the mass, 'tis morning!
Pleasure and action make the hours seem short.
Retire thee, go where thou art billeted.
Away, I say! Thou shalt know more hereafter.
Nay, get thee gone! [*Exit* RODERIGO.]
Two things are to be done:
My wife must move° for Cassio to her mistress;
I'll set her on;
Myself awhile° to draw the Moor apart
And bring him jump° when he may Cassio find
Soliciting his wife. Ay, that's the way!
Dull not device by coldness and delay. [*Exit.*]

ACT III

Scene I [A street.]

Enter CASSIO [*and*] MUSICIANS.

CASSIO: Masters, play here. I will content your pains.°
Something that's brief; and bid "Good morrow, general." [They play.]

[*Enter* CLOWN.°]

CLOWN: Why, masters, have your instruments been in Naples° that they speak i' th' nose thus?

MUSICIAN: How, sir, how?

CLOWN: Are these, I pray you, wind instruments?

MUSICIAN: Ay, marry, are they, sir.

CLOWN: O, thereby hangs a tale.

MUSICIAN: Whereby hangs a tale, sir?

CLOWN: Marry, sir, by many a wind instrument that I know. But, masters, here's money for you; and the general so likes your music that he desires you, for love's sake, to make no more noise with it.

MUSICIAN: Well, sir, we will not.

CLOWN: If you have any music that may not be heard, to't again. But, as they say, to hear music the general does not greatly care.

MUSICIAN: We have none such, sir.

341 ***move*** *petition.* 343 ***awhile*** *at the same time.* 344 ***jump*** *at the precise moment and place.* ***III.i.*** 1 ***content your pains*** *reward your efforts.* ***s.d. Clown*** *fool.* 3 ***Naples*** *this may refer either to the Neapolitan nasal tone, or to syphilis—rife in Naples—which breaks down the nose.*

CLOWN: Then put up your pipes in your bag, for I'll away. Go, vanish into air, away! [*Exit* MUSICIANS.]

CASSIO: Dost thou hear me, mine honest friend?

CLOWN: No. I hear not your honest friend. I hear you.

CASSIO: Prithee keep up thy quillets.° There's a poor piece of gold for thee. If the gentlewoman that attends the general's wife be stirring, tell her there's one Cassio entreats her a little favor of speech. Wilt thou do this?

CLOWN: She is stirring, sir. If she will stir hither, I shall seem to notify unto her.°

[*Exit* CLOWN.]

Enter IAGO.

CASSIO: In happy time, Iago.

IAGO: You have not been abed then?

CASSIO: Why no, the day had broke
Before we parted. I have made bold, Iago,
To send in to your wife; My suit to her
Is that she will to virtuous Desdemona
Procure me some access.

IAGO: I'll send her to you presently,
And I'll devise a mean to draw the Moor
Out of the way, that your converse and business
May be more free.

CASSIO: I humbly thank you for't. [*Exit* IAGO.]
I never knew
A Florentine° more kind and honest.

Enter EMILIA.

EMILIA: Good morrow, good lieutenant. I am sorry
For your displeasure;° but all will sure be well.
The general and his wife are talking of it,
And she speaks for you stoutly. The Moor replies
That he you hurt is of great fame in Cyprus
And great affinity,° and that in wholesome wisdom
He might not but refuse you. But he protests he loves you.
And needs no other suitor but his likings
To bring you in again.

CASSIO: Yet I beseech you,
If you think fit, or that it may be done,
Give me advantage of some brief discourse
With Desdemona alone.

EMILIA: Pray you come in.

21***quillets*** *puns.* 24–25***seem . . . her*** *(the Clown is mocking Cassio's overly elegant manner of speaking).* 37***Florentine*** *i.e., Iago is as kind as if he were from Cassio's home town, Florence.* 39***displeasure*** *discomforting.* 43***affinity*** *family.*

I will bestow you where you shall have time
To speak your bosom° freely.

CASSIO: I am much bound to you. *[Exeunt.]*

Scene II [The citadel.]

Enter OTHELLO, IAGO, *and* GENTLEMEN.

OTHELLO: These letters give, Iago, to the pilot
And by him do my duties to the Senate.
That done, I will be walking on the works;
Repair° there to me.

IAGO: Well, my good lord, I'll do't.

OTHELLO: This fortification, gentlemen, shall we see't?

GENTLEMEN: We'll wait upon your lordship. *[Exeunt.]*

Scene III [The citadel.]

Enter DESDEMONA, CASSIO, *and* EMILIA.

DESDEMONA: Be thou assured, good Cassio, I will do
All my abilities in thy behalf.

EMILIA: Good madam, do. I warrant it grieves my husband
As if the cause were his.

DESDEMONA: O, that's an honest fellow. Do not doubt, Cassio,
But I will have my lord and you again
As friendly as you were.

CASSIO: Bounteous madam,
Whatever shall become of Michael Cassio,
He's never anything but your true servant.

DESDEMONA: I know't; I thank you. You do love my lord.
You have known him long, and be you well assured
He shall in strangeness stand no farther off
Than in a politic distance.°

CASSIO: Ay, but, lady,
That policy may either last so long,
Or feed upon such nice° and waterish diet,
Or breed itself so out of circumstances,°
That, I being absent, and my place supplied,°
My general will forget my love and service.

DESDEMONA: Do not doubt° that; before Emilia here
I give thee warrant of thy place. Assure thee,
If I do vow a friendship, I'll perform it
To the last article. My lord shall never rest;
I'll watch him tame° and talk him out of patience;

51 ***bosom*** *inmost thoughts.* ***III.ii.*** 4 ***Repair*** *go.* ***III.iii.*** 12–13 ***He . . . distance*** *i.e., he shall act no more distant to you than is necessary for political reasons.* 15 ***nice*** *trivial.* 16 ***Or . . . circumstances*** *i.e., or grow so on the basis of accidental happenings and political needs.* 17 ***supplied*** *filled.* 19 ***doubt*** *imagine.* 23 ***watch him tame*** *(animals were tamed by being kept awake).*

His bed shall seem a school, his board a shrift;°
I'll intermingle everything he does
With Cassio's suit. Therefore be merry, Cassio,
For thy solicitor shall rather die
Than give thy cause away.

Enter OTHELLO *and* IAGO [*at a distance*].

EMILIA: Madam, here comes my lord.
CASSIO: Madam, I'll take my leave.
DESDEMONA: Why, stay, and hear me speak.
CASSIO: Madam, not now. I am very ill at ease,
Unfit for mine own purposes.
DESDEMONA: Well, do your discretion. [*Exit* CASSIO.]
IAGO: Ha! I like not that.
OTHELLO: What dost thou say?
IAGO: Nothing, my lord; or if—I know not what.
OTHELLO: Was not that Cassio parted from my wife?
IAGO: Cassio, my lord? No, sure, I cannot think it
That he would steal away so guilty-like,
Seeing you coming.
OTHELLO: I do believe 'twas he.
DESDEMONA [*Coming to them*]: How now, my lord?
I have been talking with a suitor here,
A man that languishes in your displeasure.
OTHELLO: Who is't you mean?
DESDEMONA: Why, your lieutenant, Cassio. Good my lord,
If I have any grace or power to move you,
His present° reconciliation take.
For if he be not one that truly loves you,
That errs in ignorance, and not in cunning,
I have no judgment in an honest face.
I prithee call him back.
OTHELLO: Went he hence now?
DESDEMONA: I' sooth so humbled
That he hath left part of his grief with me
To suffer with him. Good love, call him back.
OTHELLO: Not now, sweet Desdemon; some other time.
DESDEMONA: But shall't be shortly?
OTHELLO: The sooner, sweet, for you.
DESDEMONA: Shall't be tonight at supper?
OTHELLO: No, not tonight.
DESDEMONA: Tomorrow dinner then?
OTHELLO: I shall not dine at home;
I meet the captains at the citadel.
DESDEMONA: Why then, tomorrow night, on Tuesday morn,

[24]***board a shrift*** *table (seem) a confessional.* [47]***present*** *immediate.*

On Tuesday noon, or night, on Wednesday morn.
I prithee name the time, but let it not
Exceed three days. In faith, he's penitent;
And yet his trespass, in our common reason
(Save that, they say, the wars must make example
Out of her best), is not almost a fault
T' incur a private check.° When shall he come?
Tell me, Othello. I wonder in my soul
What you would ask me that I should deny
Or stand so mamm'ring° on. What? Michael Cassio,
That came awooing with you, and so many a time,
When I have spoke of you dispraisingly,
Hath ta'en your part—to have so much to do
To bring him in? By'r Lady, I could do much—

OTHELLO: Prithee no more. Let him come when he will!
I will deny thee nothing.

DESDEMONA: Why, this is not a boon;
'Tis as I should entreat you wear your gloves,
Or feed on nourishing dishes, or keep you warm,
Or sue to you to do a peculiar profit°
To your own person. Nay, when I have a suit
Wherein I mean to touch your love indeed,
It shall be full of poise° and difficult weight,
And fearful to be granted.

OTHELLO: I will deny thee nothing!
Whereon I do beseech thee grant me this,
To leave me but a little to myself.

DESDEMONA: Shall I deny you? No. Farewell, my lord.

OTHELLO: Farewell, my Desdemona: I'll come to thee straight.°

DESDEMONA: Emilia, come. Be as your fancies teach you;
Whate'er you be, I am obedient. *Exit* [*with* EMILIA].

OTHELLO: Excellent wretch! Perdition catch my soul
But I do love thee! And when I love thee not,
Chaos is come again.

IAGO: My noble lord—

OTHELLO: What dost thou say, Iago?

IAGO: Did Michael Cassio, when you wooed my lady,
Know of your love?

OTHELLO: He did, from first to last. Why dost thou ask?

IAGO: But for a satisfaction of my thought,
No further harm.

OTHELLO: Why of thy thought, Iago?

IAGO: I did not think he had been acquainted with her.

66–67 ***is . . . check*** *is almost not serious enough for a private rebuke (let alone a public disgrace).* *70* ***mamm'ring*** *hesitating.* *79* ***peculiar profit*** *particularly personal good.* *82* ***poise*** *weight.* *87* ***straight*** *at once.*

OTHELLO: O, yes, and went between us° very oft.
IAGO: Indeed?
OTHELLO: Indeed? Ay, indeed! Discern'st thou aught in that?
Is he not honest?
IAGO: Honest, my lord?
OTHELLO: Honest? Ay, honest.
IAGO: My lord, for aught I know.
OTHELLO: What dost thou think?
IAGO: Think, my lord?
OTHELLO: Think, my lord?
By heaven, thou echoest me,
As if there were some monster in thy thought
Too hideous to be shown. Thou dost mean something.
I heard thee say even now, thou lik'st not that,
When Cassio left my wife. What didst not like?
And when I told thee he was of my counsel°
Of my whole course of wooing, thou cried'st "Indeed?"
And didst contract and purse thy brow together,
As if thou then hadst shut up in thy brain
Some horrible conceit.° If thou dost love me,
Show me thy thought.
IAGO: My lord, you know I love you.
OTHELLO: I think thou dost;
And, for I know thou'rt full of love and honesty
And weigh'st thy words before thou giv'st them breath,
Therefore these stops° of thine fright me the more;
For such things in a false disloyal knave
Are tricks of custom;° but in a man that's just
They're close dilations,° working from the heart
That passion cannot rule.
IAGO: For Michael Cassio,
I dare be sworn, I think that he is honest.
OTHELLO: I think so too.
IAGO: Men should be what they seem;
Or those that be not, would they might seem none!
OTHELLO: Certain, men should be what they seem.
IAGO: Why then, I think Cassio's an honest man.
OTHELLO: Nay, yet there's more in this?
I prithee speak to me as to thy thinkings,
As thou dost ruminate, and give thy worst of thoughts
The worst of words.
IAGO: Good my lord, pardon me:
Though I am bound to every act of duty,
I am not bound to that all slaves are free to.

100 ***between us*** *i.e., as messenger.* 111 ***of my counsel*** *in my confidence.* 115 ***conceit*** *thought.*
120 ***stops*** *interruptions.* 122 ***of custom*** *customary.* 123 ***close dilations*** *expressions of hidden thoughts.*

Utter my thoughts? Why, say they are vile and false,
As where's that palace whereinto foul things
Sometimes intrude not? Who has that breast so pure
But some uncleanly apprehensions
Keep leets and law days,° and in sessions sit
With meditations lawful?

OTHELLO: Thou dost conspire against thy friend, Iago,
If thou but think'st him wronged, and mak'st his ear
A stranger to thy thoughts.

IAGO: I do beseech you—
Though I perchance am vicious in my guess
(As I confess it is my nature's plague
To spy into abuses, and of my jealousy
Shape faults that are not), that your wisdom
From one that so imperfectly conceits
Would take no notice, nor build yourself a trouble
Out of his scattering and unsure observance.
It were not for your quiet nor your good,
Nor for my manhood, honesty, and wisdom,
To let you know my thoughts.

OTHELLO: What dost thou mean?

IAGO: Good name in man and woman, dear my lord,
Is the immediate jewel of their souls.
Who steals my purse steals trash; 'tis something, nothing;
'Twas mine, 'tis his, and has been slave to thousands;
But he that filches from me my good name
Robs me of that which not enriches him
And makes me poor indeed.

OTHELLO: By heaven, I'll know thy thoughts!

IAGO: You cannot, if my heart were in your hand;
Nor shall not whilst 'tis in my custody.

OTHELLO: Ha!

IAGO: O, beware, my lord, of jealousy!
It is the green-eyed monster, which doth mock
The meat it feeds on. That cuckold lives in bliss
Who, certain of his fate, loves not his wronger;
But O, what damnèd minutes tells° he o'er
Who dotes, yet doubts—suspects, yet fondly° loves!

OTHELLO: O misery.

IAGO: Poor and content is rich, and rich enough;
But riches fineless° is as poor as winter
To him that ever fears he shall be poor.
Good God the souls of all my tribe defend
From jealousy!

140 ***leets and law days*** *meetings of local courts.* 169 ***tells*** *counts.* 170 ***fondly*** *foolishly.* 173 ***fineless*** *infinite.*

OTHELLO: Why? Why is this?
Think'st thou I'd make a life of jealousy,
To follow still° the changes of the moon
With fresh suspicions? No! To be once in doubt
Is to be resolved. Exchange me for a goat
When I shall turn the business of my soul
To such exsufflicate and blown° surmises,
Matching thy inference. 'Tis not to make me jealous
To say my wife is fair, feeds well, loves company,
Is free of speech, sings, plays, and dances;
Where virtue is, these are more virtuous.
Nor from mine own weak merits will I draw
The smallest fear or doubt of her revolt,
For she had eyes, and chose me. No, Iago;
I'll see before I doubt; when I doubt, prove;
And on the proof there is no more but this:
Away at once with love or jealousy!
IAGO: I am glad of this; for now I shall have reason
To show the love and duty that I bear you
With franker spirit. Therefore, as I am bound,
Receive it from me. I speak not yet of proof.
Look to your wife; observe her well with Cassio;
Wear your eyes thus: not jealous nor secure.
I would not have your free and noble nature
Out of self-bounty° be abused. Look to't.
I know our country disposition well:
In Venice they do let heaven see the pranks
They dare not show their husbands; their best conscience
Is not to leave't undone, but kept unknown.°
OTHELLO: Dost thou say so?
IAGO: She did deceive her father, marrying you;
And when she seemed to shake and fear your looks,
She loved them most.
OTHELLO: And so she did.
IAGO: Why, go to then!
She that so young could give out such a seeming
To seel° her father's eyes up close as oak°—
He thought 'twas witchcraft. But I am much to blame.
I humbly do beseech you of your pardon
For too much loving you.
OTHELLO: I am bound to thee forever.
IAGO: I see this hath a little dashed your spirits.

[178]***To follow still*** *to change always (as the phase of the moon).* [182]***exsufflicate and blown*** *inflated and flyblown.* [200]***self-bounty*** *innate kindness (which attributes his own motives to others).* [203–4]***their . . . unknown*** *i.e., their morality does not forbid adultery, but it does forbid being found out.* [210]***seel*** *hoodwink.* [210]***oak*** *(a close-grained wood).*

OTHELLO: Not a jot, not a jot.
IAGO: Trust me, I fear it has.
I hope you will consider what is spoke
Comes from my love. But I do see y' are moved.
I am to pray you not to strain° my speech
To grosser issues nor to larger reach°
Than to suspicion.
OTHELLO: I will not.
IAGO: Should you do so, my lord,
My speech should fall into such vile success
Which my thoughts aimed not. Cassio's my worthy friend—
My lord, I see y' are moved.
OTHELLO: No, not much moved.
I do not think but Desdemona's honest.
IAGO: Long live she so. And long live you to think so.
OTHELLO: And yet, how nature erring from itself—
IAGO: Ay, there's the point, as (to be bold with you)
Not to affect many proposèd matches
Of her own clime, complexion, and degree,°
Whereto we see in all things nature tends°—
Foh! one may smell in such a will most rank,
Foul disproportions, thoughts unnatural.
But, pardon me, I do not in position°
Distinctly° speak of her; though I may fear
Her will, recoiling to her better judgment,
May fall to match° you with her country forms,°
And happily° repent.
OTHELLO: Farewell, farewell!
If more thou dost perceive, let me know more.
Set on thy wife to observe. Leave me, Iago.
IAGO: My lord, I take my leave. [*Going.*]
OTHELLO: Why did I marry? This honest creature doubtless
Sees and knows more, much more, than he unfolds.
IAGO [*Returns*]: My lord, I would I might entreat your honor
To scan this thing no farther. Leave it to time.
Although 'tis fit that Cassio have his place,
For sure he fills it up with great ability,
Yet, if you please to hold him off awhile,
You shall by that perceive him and his means.
Note if your lady strains his entertainment°
With any strong or vehement importunity;
Much will be seen in that. In the meantime

[218]***strain*** *enlarge the meaning.* [219]***reach*** *meaning.* [230]***degree*** *social station.* [231]***in . . . tends*** *i.e., all things in nature seek out their own kind.* [234]***position*** *general argument.* [235]***Distinctly*** *specifically* [237]***fall to match*** *happen to compare.* [237]***country forms*** *i.e., the familiar appearance of her countrymen.* [238]***happily*** *by chance.* [250]***strains his entertainment*** *urge strongly that he be reinstated.*

Let me be thought too busy in my fears
(As worthy cause I have to fear I am)
And hold her free, I do beseech your honor.
OTHELLO: Fear not my government.°
IAGO: I once more take my leave. [*Exit.*]
OTHELLO: This fellow's of exceeding honesty,
And knows all qualities,° with a learnèd spirit
Of human dealings. If I do prove her haggard,°
Though that her jesses° were my dear heartstrings,
I'd whistle her off and let her down the wind°
To prey at fortune. Haply for° I am black
And have not those soft parts° of conversation
That chamberers° have, or for I am declined
Into the vale of years—yet that's not much—
She's gone. I am abused, and my relief
Must be to loathe her. O curse of marriage,
That we can call these delicate creatures ours,
And not their appetites! I had rather be a toad
And live upon the vapor of a dungeon
Than keep a corner in the thing I love
For others' uses. Yet 'tis the plague to great ones;
Prerogatived are they less than the base.
'Tis destiny unshunnable, like death.
Even then this forkèd° plague is fated to us
When we do quicken.° Look where she comes.

Enter DESDEMONA *and* EMILIA.

If she be false, heaven mocked itself!
I'll not believe't.
DESDEMONA: How now, my dear Othello?
Your dinner, and the generous islanders
By you invited, do attend your presence.
OTHELLO: I am to blame.
DESDEMONA: Why do you speak so faintly?
Are you not well?
OTHELLO: I have a pain upon my forehead, here.°
DESDEMONA: Why, that's with watching; 'twill away again,
Let me but bind it hard, within this hour
It will be well.
OTHELLO: Your napkin° is too little;

[256]***government*** *self-control.* [258]***qualities*** *natures, types of people.* [259]***haggard*** *a partly trained hawk which has gone wild again.* [260]***jesses*** *straps which held the hawk's legs to the trainer's wrist.* [261]***I'd . . . wind*** *I would release her (like an untamable hawk) and let her fly free.* [262]***Haply for*** *it may be because.* [263]***soft parts*** *gentle qualities and manners.* [264]***chamberers*** *courtiers—or, perhaps, accomplished seducers.* [275]***forkèd*** *horned (the sign of the cuckold was horns).* [276]***do quicken*** *are born.* [283]***here*** *(he points to his imaginary horns).* [286]***napkin*** *elaborately worked handkerchief.*

[He pushes the handkerchief away, and it falls.]

Let it° alone. Come, I'll go in with you.
DESDEMONA: I am very sorry that you are not well. *Exit [with* OTHELLO].
EMILIA: I am glad I have found this napkin;
This was her first remembrance from the Moor.
My wayward husband hath a hundred times
Wooed me to steal it; but she so loves the token
(For he conjured her she should ever keep it)
That she reserves it evermore about her
To kiss and talk to. I'll have the work ta'en out°
And give't Iago. What he will do with it,
Heaven knows, not I; I nothing° but to please his fantasy.°

Enter IAGO.

IAGO: How now? What do you here alone?
EMILIA: Do not you chide; I have a thing for you.
IAGO: You have a thing for me? It is a common thing—
EMILIA: Ha?
IAGO: To have a foolish wife.
EMILIA: O, is that all? What will you give me now
For that same handkerchief?
IAGO: What handkerchief?
EMILIA: What handkerchief!
Why, that the Moor first gave to Desdemona,
That which so often you did bid me steal.
IAGO: Hast stol'n it from her?
EMILIA: No, but she let it drop by negligence,
And to th' advantage,° I, being here, took't up.
Look, here 't is.
IAGO: A good wench. Give it me.
EMILIA: What will you do with't, that you have been so earnest
To have me filch it?
IAGO: Why, what is that to you? *[Takes it.]*
EMILIA: If it be not for some purpose of import,°
Give't me again. Poor lady, she'll run mad
When she shall lack° it.
IAGO: Be not acknown on't.°
I have use for it. Go, leave me. *[Exit* EMILIA.]
I will in Cassio's lodging lose this napkin
And let him find it. Trifles light as air
Are to the jealous confirmations strong
As proofs of Holy Writ. This may do something.

[287]***it*** *(it makes a considerable difference in the interpretation of later events whether this "it" refers to Othello's forehead or to the handkerchief; nothing in the text makes the reference clear).* [295]***work ta'en out*** *needlework copied.* [297]***I nothing*** *I wish nothing.* [297]***fantasy*** *fancy, whim.* [310]***to th' advantage*** *being lucky.* [314]***import*** *importance.* [316]***lack*** *miss.* [316]***Be not acknown on't.*** *forget you ever saw it.*

The Moor already changes with my poison:
Dangerous conceits are in their natures poisons,
Which at the first are scarce found to distaste,°
But with a little,° act upon the blood,
Burn like the mines of sulfur. I did say so.

Enter OTHELLO.

Look where he comes! Not poppy nor mandragora,°
Nor all the drowsy syrups of the world,
Shall ever medicine thee to that sweet sleep
Which thou owedst° yesterday.

OTHELLO: Ha! ha! False to me?

IAGO: Why, how now, general? No more of that.

OTHELLO: Avaunt! be gone! Thou hast set me on the rack.
I swear 'tis better to be much abused
Than but to know't a little.

IAGO: How now, my lord?

OTHELLO: What sense had I of her stol'n hours of lust?
I saw't not, thought it not, it harmed not me;
I slept the next night well, fed well, was free and merry;
I found not Cassio's kisses on her lips.
He that is robbed, not wanting° what is stol'n,
Let him not know't, and he's not robbed at all.

IAGO: I am sorry to hear this.

OTHELLO: I had been happy if the general camp,
Pioners° and all, had tasted her sweet body,
So I had nothing known. O now, forever
Farewell the tranquil mind! Farewell content!
Farewell the plumèd troops, and the big wars
That make ambition virtue! O, farewell!
Farewell the neighing steed and the shrill trump,
The spirit-stirring drum, th' ear-piercing fife,
The royal banner, and all quality,
Pride, pomp, and circumstance° of glorious war!
And O you mortal engines° whose rude throats
Th' immortal Jove's dread clamors° counterfeit,
Farewell! Othello's occupation's gone!

IAGO: Is't possible, my lord?

OTHELLO: Villain, be sure thou prove my love a whore!
Be sure of it; give me the ocular proof;
Or, by the worth of mine eternal soul,
Thou hadst been better have been born a dog

[324]***are scarce found to distaste*** *scarcely can be tasted.* [325]***with a little*** *in a short time.* [327]***poppy nor mandragora*** *soporifics.* [330]***owedst*** *possessed.* [339]***wanting*** *missing.* [343]***Pioners*** *the basest manual laborers in the army, who dug trenches and mines.* [351]***circumstance*** *pageantry.* [352]***mortal engines*** *lethal weapons, i.e., cannon.* [353]***clamors*** *i.e., thunder.*

Than answer my waked wrath!
IAGO: Is't come to this?
OTHELLO: Make me to see't; or at the least so prove it
That the probation° bear no hinge nor loop
To hang a doubt on—or woe upon thy life!
IAGO: My noble lord—
OTHELLO: If thou dost slander her and torture me,
Never pray more; abandon all remorse;
On horror's head horrors accumulate;
Do deeds to make heaven weep, all earth amazed;
For nothing canst thou to damnation add
Greater than that.
IAGO: O grace! O heaven forgive me!
Are you a man? Have you a soul or sense?
God b' wi' you! Take mine office. O wretched fool,
That lov'st to make thine honesty a vice!
O monstrous world! Take note, take note, O world,
To be direct and honest is not safe.
I thank you for this profit, and from hence
I'll love no friend, sith° love breeds such offense.
OTHELLO: Nay, stay. Thou shouldst be honest.
IAGO: I should be wise; for honesty's a fool
And loses that it works for.
OTHELLO: By the world,
I think my wife be honest, and think she is not;
I think that thou art just, and think thou are not.
I'll have some proof. My name, that was as fresh
As Dian's° visage, is now begrimed and black
As mine own face. If there be cords, or knives,
Poison, or fire, or suffocating streams,
I'll not endure it. Would I were satisfied!
IAGO: I see you are eaten up with passion.
I do repent me that I put it to you.
You would be satisfied?
OTHELLO: Would? Nay, and I will.
IAGO: And may; but how? How satisfied, my lord?
Would you, the supervisor,° grossly gape on?
Behold her topped?
OTHELLO: Death and damnation! O!
IAGO: It were a tedious° difficulty, I think,
To bring them to that prospect.° Damn them then,
If ever mortal eyes do see them bolster°
More than their own! What then? How then?

362 ***probation*** *proof.* 377 ***sith*** *since.* 384 ***Dian's*** *Diana's (goddess of the moon and of chastity).* 392 ***supervisor*** *onlooker.* 394 ***tedious*** *hard to arrange.* 395 ***prospect*** *sight (where they can be seen).* 396 ***bolster*** *go to bed with.*

What shall I say? Where's satisfaction?
It is impossible you should see this,
Were they as prime° as goats, as hot as monkeys,
As salt as wolves in pride,° and fools as gross
As ignorance made drunk. But yet, I say,
If imputation and strong circumstances
Which lead directly to the door of truth
Will give you satisfaction, you might hav't.

OTHELLO: Give me a living reason she's disloyal.

IAGO: I do not like the office.°
But sith I am entered in this cause so far,
Pricked° to't by foolish honesty and love,
I will go on. I lay with Cassio lately,
And being troubled with a raging tooth,
I could not sleep.
There are a kind of men so loose of soul
That in their sleeps will mutter their affairs.
One of this kind is Cassio.
In sleep I heard him say, "Sweet Desdemona,
Let us be wary, let us hide our loves!"
And then, sir, would he gripe° and wring my hand,
Cry "O sweet creature!" Then kiss me hard,
As if he plucked up kisses by the roots
That grew upon my lips; laid his leg o'er my thigh,
And sigh, and kiss, and then cry, "Cursèd fate
That gave thee to the Moor!"

OTHELLO: O monstrous! monstrous!

IAGO: Nay, this was but his dream.

OTHELLO: But this denoted a foregone conclusion,°
'Tis a shrewd doubt,° though it be but a dream.

IAGO: And this may help to thicken other proofs
That do demonstrate° thinly.

OTHELLO: I'll tear her all to pieces!

IAGO: Nay, yet be wise. Yet we see nothing done;
She may be honest yet. Tell me but this:
Have you not sometimes seen a handkerchief
Spotted with strawberries in your wife's hand?

OTHELLO: I gave her such a one; 'twas my first gift.

IAGO: I know not that; but such a handkerchief—
I am sure it was your wife's—did I today
See Cassio wipe his beard with.

OTHELLO: If it be that—

IAGO: If it be that or any that was hers,

400–01 ***prime, salt*** *lustful.* 401 ***pride*** *heat.* 407 ***office*** *duty.* 409 ***Pricked*** *spurred.* 418 ***gripe*** *seize.* 425 ***foregone conclusion*** *consummated fact.* 426 ***shrewd doubt*** *penetrating guess.* 428 ***demonstrate*** *show, appear.*

It speaks against her with the other proofs.
OTHELLO: O, that the slave had forty thousand lives!
One is too poor, too weak for my revenge.
Now do I see 'tis true. Look here, Iago:
All my fond love thus do I blow to heaven.
'Tis gone.
Arise, black vengeance, from the hollow hell!
Yield up, O love, thy crown and hearted° throne
To tyrannous hate! Swell, bosom, with thy fraught,°
For 'tis of aspics'° tongues.
IAGO: Yet be content.°
OTHELLO: O, blood, blood, blood!
IAGO: Patience, I say. Your mind may change.
OTHELLO: Never, Iago. Like to the Pontic Sea,°
Whose icy current and compulsive course
Nev'r keeps retiring ebb, but keeps due on
To the Propontic and the Hellespont,
Even so my bloody thoughts, with violent pace,
Shall nev'r look back, nev'r ebb to humble love,
Till that a capable and wide° revenge
Swallow them up. [*He kneels.*] Now, by yond marble heaven,
In the due reverence of a sacred vow
I here engage my words.
IAGO: Do not rise yet. [IAGO *kneels.*]
Witness, you ever-burning lights above,
You elements that clip° us round about,
Witness that here Iago doth give up
The execution° of his wit, hands, heart
To wronged Othello's service! Let him command,
And to obey shall be in me remorse,°
What bloody business ever.° [*They rise.*]
OTHELLO: I greet thy love,
Not with vain thanks but with acceptance bounteous,°
And will upon the instant put thee to 't°
Within these three days let me hear thee say
That Cassio's not alive.
IAGO: My friend is dead. 'Tis done at your request.
But let her live.
OTHELLO: Damn her, lewd minx! O, damn her! Damn her!
Come, go with me apart. I will withdraw
To furnish me with some swift means of death

[445]***hearted*** *seated in the heart.* [446]***fraught*** *burden.* [447]***aspics'*** *asps'.* [447]***content*** *patient, quiet.* [450]***Pontic Sea*** *the Black Sea (famous for the strong and constant current with which it flows through the Bosporus into the Mediterranean, where the water level is lower).* [456]***capable and wide*** *sufficient and far-reaching.* [461]***clip*** *enfold.* [463]***execution*** *workings, action.* [465]***remorse*** *pity.* [466]***ever*** *soever.* [467]***bounteous*** *absolute.* [468]***to't*** *i.e., to the work you have said you are prepared to do.*

For the fair devil. Now art thou my lieutenant.
IAGO: I am your own forever. [*Exeunt.*]

Scene IV [A STREET.]

Enter DESDEMONA, EMILIA, *and* CLOWN.

DESDEMONA: Do you know, sirrah, where Lieutenant Cassio lies?°
CLOWN: I dare not say he lies anywhere.
DESDEMONA: Why, man?
CLOWN: He's a soldier, and for me to say a soldier lies, 'tis stabbing.
DESDEMONA: Go to. Where lodges he?
CLOWN: To tell you where he lodges is to tell you where I lie.
DESDEMONA: Can anything be made of this?
CLOWN: I know not where he lodges, and for me to devise a lodging, and say he lies here or he lies there, were to lie in mine own throat.°
DESDEMONA: Can you enquire him out, and be edified° by report?
CLOWN: I will catechize the world for him; that is, make questions, and by them answer.
DESDEMONA: Seek him, bid him come hither. Tell him I have moved° my lord on his behalf and hope all will be well.
CLOWN: To do this is within the compass° of man's wit, and therefore I will attempt the doing it. [*Exit* CLOWN.]
DESDEMONA: Where should° I lose the handkerchief, Emilia?
EMILIA: I know not, madam.
DESDEMONA: Believe me, I had rather have lost my purse
Full of crusadoes.° And but my noble Moor
Is true of mind, and made of no such baseness
As jealous creatures are, it were enough
To put him to ill thinking.
EMILIA: Is he not jealous?
DESDEMONA: Who? He? I think the sun where he was born
Drew all such humors° from him.
EMILIA: Look where he comes.

Enter OTHELLO.

DESDEMONA: I will not leave him now till Cassio
Be called to him. How is't with you, my lord?
OTHELLO: Well, my good lady. [*Aside*] O, hardness to dissemble!°—
How do you, Desdemona?
DESDEMONA: Well, my good lord.
OTHELLO: Give me your hand. This hand is moist,° my lady.

III.iv. [1]***lies*** *lodges.* [9]***lie in mine own throat*** *(to lie in the throat is to lie absolutely and completely).* [10]***edified*** *enlightened (Desdemona mocks the Clown's overly elaborate diction).* [13]***moved*** *pleaded with.* [15]***compass*** *reach.* [17]***should*** *might.* [20]***crusadoes*** *Portuguese gold coins.* [25]***humors*** *characteristics.* [28]***hardness to dissemble*** *(Othello may refer here either to the difficulty he has in maintaining his appearance of composure, or to what he believes to be Desdemona's hardened hypocrisy).* [30]***moist*** *(a moist, hot hand was taken as a sign of a lustful nature)*

DESDEMONA: It hath felt no age nor known no sorrow.
OTHELLO: This argues° fruitfulness and liberal° heart.
Hot, hot, and moist. This hand of yours requires
A sequester° from liberty; fasting and prayer;
Much castigation; exercise devout;
For here's a young and sweating devil here
That commonly rebels. 'Tis a good hand,
A frank one.
DESDEMONA: You may, indeed, say so;
For 'twas that hand that gave away my heart.
OTHELLO: A liberal hand! The hearts of old gave hands,
But our new heraldry° is hands, not hearts.
DESDEMONA: I cannot speak of this. Come now, your promise!
OTHELLO: What promise, chuck?
DESDEMONA: I have sent to bid Cassio come speak with you.
OTHELLO: I have a salt and sorry rheum° offends me.
Lend me thy handkerchief.
DESDEMONA: Here, my lord.
OTHELLO: That which I gave you.
DESDEMONA: I have it not about me.
OTHELLO: Not?
DESDEMONA: No, indeed, my lord.
OTHELLO: That's a fault.
That handkerchief
Did an Egyptian to my mother give.
She was a charmer,° and could almost read
The thoughts of people. She told her, while she kept it
'Twould make her amiable° and subdue my father
Entirely to her love; but if she lost it
Or made a gift of it, my father's eye
Should hold her loathèd, and his spirits should hunt
After new fancies. She, dying, gave it me,
And bid me, when my fate would have me wived,
To give it her. I did so; and take heed on't;
Make it a darling like your precious eye.
To lose't or give't away were such perdition
As nothing else could match.
DESDEMONA: Is't possible?
OTHELLO: 'Tis true. There's magic in the web° of it.
A sibyl that had numbered in the world
The sun to course two hundred compasses,

[32]***argues*** *suggests.* [32]***liberal*** *free, open (but also with a suggestion of "licentious"; from here on in this scene Othello's words bear a double meaning, seeming to be normal but accusing Desdemona of being unfaithful).* [34]***sequester*** *separation.* [41]***heraldry*** *heraldic symbolism.* [45]***a salt and sorry rheum*** *a heavy, running head cold.* [52]***charmer*** *magician.* [54]***amiable*** *desirable.* [64]***web*** *weaving.*

In her prophetic fury[°] sewed the work;
The worms were hallowed that did breed the silk,
And it was dyed in mummy[°] which the skillful
Conserved of maidens' hearts.
DESDEMONA: Indeed? Is't true?
OTHELLO: Most veritable. Therefore look to't well.
DESDEMONA: Then would to God that I had never seen't!
OTHELLO: Ha! Wherefore?
DESDEMONA: Why do you speak so startingly and rash?
OTHELLO: Is't lost? Is't gone? Speak, is it out o' th' way?
DESDEMONA: Heaven bless us!
OTHELLO: Say you?
DESDEMONA: It is not lost. But what an if it were?
OTHELLO: How?
DESDEMONA: I say it is not lost.
OTHELLO: Fetch't, let me see't!
DESDEMONA: Why, so I can; but I will not now.
This is a trick to put me from my suit:
Pray you let Cassio be received again.
OTHELLO: Fetch me the handkerchief! My mind misgives.
DESDEMONA: Come, come!
You'll never meet a more sufficient[°] man—
OTHELLO: The handkerchief!
DESDEMONA: A man that all his time
Hath founded his good fortunes on your love,
Shared dangers with you—
OTHELLO: The handkerchief!
DESDEMONA: I'faith, you are to blame.
OTHELLO: Away! *Exit* [OTHELLO.]
EMILIA: Is not this man jealous?
DESDEMONA: I nev'r saw this before.
Sure there's some wonder in this handkerchief;
I am most unhappy in the loss of it.
EMILIA: 'Tis not a year or two shows us a man.
They are all but stomachs, and we all but food;
They eat us hungerly, and when they are full,
They belch us.

Enter IAGO *and* CASSIO.

Look you, Cassio and my husband.
IAGO: There is no other way; 'tis she must do't.
And lo the happiness! Go and importune her.
DESDEMONA: How now, good Cassio? What's the news with you?
CASSIO: Madam, my former suit. I do beseech you

[67]***prophetic fury*** *seized by the spirit and able to prophesy.* [69]***mummy*** *liquid drained from embalmed bodies.*
[87]***sufficient*** *complete, with all proper qualities.*

That by your virtuous means I may again
Exist, and be a member of his love
Whom I with all the office° of my heart
Entirely honor. I would not be delayed.
If my offense be of such mortal kind
That nor my service past, nor present sorrows,
Nor purposed merit in futurity,
Can ransom me into his love again,
But to know so must be my benefit.°
So shall I clothe me in a forced content,
And shut myself up in some other course
To fortune's alms.

DESDEMONA: Alas, thrice-gentle Cassio,
My advocation° is not now in tune.
My lord is not my lord; nor should I know him
Were he in favor° as in humor altered.
So help me every spirit sanctified
As I have spoken for you all my best
And stood within the blank° of his displeasure
For my free speech. You must awhile be patient.
What I can do I will; and more I will
Than for myself I dare. Let that suffice you.

IAGO: Is my lord angry?

EMILIA: He went hence but now,
And certainly in strange unquietness.

IAGO: Can he be angry? I have seen the cannon
When it hath blown his ranks into the air
And, like the devil, from his very arm
Puffed his own brother. And is he angry?
Something of moment° then. I will go meet him.
There's matter in't indeed if he be angry.

DESDEMONA: I prithee do so. *Exit* [IAGO.]
Something sure of state,°
Either from Venice or some unhatched practice°
Made demonstrable here in Cyprus to him,
Hath puddled° his clear spirit; and in such cases
Men's natures wrangle with inferior things,
Though great ones are their object. 'Tis even so.
For let our finger ache, and it endues°
Our other, healthful members even to a sense
Of pain. Nay, we must think men are not gods,
Nor of them look for such observancy
As fits the bridal. Beshrew me much, Emilia,

[108]***office*** *duty.* [114]***benefit*** *good.* [118]***advocation*** *advocacy.* [120]***favor*** *countenance.* [123]***blank*** *bull's-eye of a target.* [133]***moment*** *importance.* [135]***of state*** *state affairs.* [136]***unhatched practice*** *undisclosed plot.* [138]***puddled*** *muddied.* [141]***endues*** *leads.*

I was, unhandsome warrior as I am,
Arraigning his unkindness with my soul;
But now I find I had suborned the witness,
And he's indicted falsely.

EMILIA: Pray heaven it be
State matters, as you think, and no conception
Nor no jealous toy° concerning you.

DESDEMONA: Alas the day! I never gave him cause.

EMILIA: But jealous souls will not be answered so;
They are not ever jealous for the cause,
But jealous for they're jealous. It is a monster
Begot upon itself, born on itself.

DESDEMONA: Heaven keep the monster from Othello's mind!

EMILIA: Lady, amen.

DESDEMONA: I will go seek him. Cassio, walk here about.
If I do find him fit,° I'll move your suit
And seek to effect it to my uttermost.

CASSIO: I humbly thank your ladyship. *Exit* [DESDEMONA *with* EMILIA].

Enter BIANCA.

BIANCA: Save you, friend Cassio!

CASSIO: What make you from home?
How is't with you, my most fair Bianca?
I' faith, sweet love, I was coming to your house.

BIANCA: And I was going to your lodging, Cassio.
What, keep a week away? Seven days and nights?
Eightscore eight hours? And lovers' absent hours
More tedious than the dial eightscore times?
O weary reck'ning.°

CASSIO: Pardon me, Bianca.
I have this while with leaden thoughts been pressed,
But I shall in a more continuate° time
Strike off this score° of absence. Sweet Bianca,

[*Gives her* DESDEMONA'S *handkerchief.*]

Take me this work out.

BIANCA: O Cassio, whence came this?
This is some token from a newer friend.
To the felt absence now I feel a cause.
Is't come to this? Well, well.

CASSIO: Go to, woman!
Throw your vile guesses in the devil's teeth,
From whence you have them. You are jealous now
That this is from some mistress, some remembrance.

[151] ***toy*** *trifle.* [160] ***fit*** *receptive.* [170] ***reck'ning*** *addition.* [172] ***continuate*** *uninterrupted.*
[173] ***Strike off this score*** *i.e., pay this bill (the score being the account of drinks kept in a tavern).*

No, by my faith, Bianca.
BIANCA: Why, whose is it?
CASSIO: I know not neither; I found it in my chamber.
I like the work well; ere it be demanded,°
As like enough it will, I would have it copied.
Take it and do't, and leave me for this time.
BIANCA: Leave you? Wherefore?
CASSIO: I do attend here on the general
And think it no addition, nor my wish,
To have him see me womaned.
BIANCA: Why, I pray you?
CASSIO: Not that I love you not.
BIANCA: But that you do not love me!
I pray you bring° me on the way a little,
And say if I shall see you soon at night.
CASSIO: 'Tis but a little way that I can bring you,
For I attend here; but I'll see you soon.
BIANCA: 'Tis very good. I must be circumstanced.° [*Exeunt omnes.*]

ACT IV

Scene I [A street.]

Enter OTHELLO *and* IAGO.

IAGO: Will you think so?
OTHELLO: Think so, Iago?
IAGO: What,
To kiss in private?
OTHELLO: An unauthorized° kiss?
IAGO: Or to be naked with her friend in bed
An hour or more, not meaning any harm?
OTHELLO: Naked in bed, Iago, and not mean harm?
It is hypocrisy against the devil.
They that mean virtuously, and yet do so,
The devil their virtue tempts, and they tempt heaven.
IAGO: If they do nothing, 'tis a venial slip.
But if I give my wife a handkerchief—
OTHELLO: What then?
IAGO: Why, then 'tis hers, my lord; and being hers,
She may, I think, bestow't on any man.
OTHELLO: She is protectress of her honor too.
May she give that?
IAGO: Her honor is an essence that's not seen;

[183] ***demanded*** *asked for (by the person who lost it).* [191] ***bring*** *accompany.* [195] ***be circumstanced*** *accept things as they are.* ***IV.i.*** [2] ***unauthorized*** *illicit.*

They have it very oft that have it not.
But for the handkerchief—

OTHELLO: By heaven, I would most gladly have forgot it!
Thou said'st—O, it comes o'er my memory
As doth the raven° o'er the infected house,
Boding to all—he had my handkerchief.

IAGO: Ay, what of that?

OTHELLO: That's not so good now.

IAGO: What if I had said I had seen him do you wrong?
Or heard him say—as knaves be such abroad°
Who having, by their own importunate suit,
Or voluntary dotage° of some mistress,
Convincèd or supplied° them, cannot choose
But they must blab—

OTHELLO: Hath he said anything?

IAGO: He hath, my lord; but be you well assured,
No more than he'll unswear.

OTHELLO: What hath he said?

IAGO: Why, that he did—I know not what he did.

OTHELLO: What? what?

IAGO: Lie—

OTHELLO: With her?

IAGO: With her, on her; what you will

OTHELLO: Lie with her? Lie on her?—We say lie on her when they belie her.—Lie with her! Zounds, that's fulsome.°—Handkerchief—confessions—handkerchief!—To confess, and be hanged for his labor—first to be hanged, and then to confess! I tremble at it. Nature would not invest herself in such shadowing passion without some instruction.° It is not words that shakes me thus.—Pish! Noses, ears, and lips? Is't possible?—Confess?—Handkerchief?—O devil! *[Falls in a trance.]*

IAGO: Work on.
My med'cine works! Thus credulous fools are caught,
And many worthy and chaste dames even thus,
All guiltless, meet reproach.° What, ho! My lord!
My lord, I say! Othello!

Enter CASSIO.

How now, Cassio?

CASSIO: What's the matter?

IAGO: My lord is fall'n into an epilepsy.
This is his second fit; he had one yesterday.

21 ***raven*** *(a harbinger of death).* 25 ***abroad*** *i.e., in the world.* 27 ***voluntary dotage*** *weakness of the will.* 28 ***Convincèd or supplied*** *persuaded or gratified (the mistress).* 37 ***fulsome*** *foul, repulsive.* 39–40 ***Nature . . . instruction*** *i.e., my mind would not become so darkened (with anger) unless there were something in this (accusation); (it should be remembered that Othello believes in the workings of magic and supernatural forces).* 46 ***reproach*** *shame.*

CASSIO: Rub him about the temples.
IAGO: The lethargy° must have his quiet course.
If not, he foams at mouth, and by and by
Breaks out to savage madness. Look, he stirs.
Do you withdraw yourself a little while.
He will recover straight. When he is gone,
I would on great occasion° speak with you. [*Exit* CASSIO.]
How is it, general? Have you not hurt your head?
OTHELLO: Dost thou mock° me?
IAGO: I mock you not, by heaven.
Would you would bear your fortune like a man.
OTHELLO: A hornèd man's a monster and a beast.
IAGO: There's many a beast then in a populous city,
And many a civil° monster.
OTHELLO: Did he confess it?
IAGO: Good, sir, be a man.
Think every bearded fellow that's but yoked
May draw° with you. There's millions now alive
That nightly lie in those unproper° beds
Which they dare swear peculiar.° Your case is better.
O, 'tis the spite of hell, the fiend's arch-mock,
To lip a wanton in a secure couch,
And to suppose her chaste. No, let me know;
And knowing what I am, I know what she shall be.
OTHELLO: O, thou art wise! 'Tis certain.
IAGO: Stand you awhile apart;
Confine yourself but in a patient list.°
Whilst you were here, o'erwhelmèd with your grief—
A passion most unsuiting such a man—
Cassio came hither. I shifted him away°
And laid good 'scuses upon your ecstasy,°
Bade him anon return, and here speak with me;
The which he promised. Do but encave° yourself
And mark the fleers,° the gibes, and notable° scorns
That dwell in every region of his face.
For I will make him tell the tale anew:
Where, how, how oft, how long ago, and when
He hath, and is again to cope your wife.
I say, but mark his gesture. Marry patience,
Or I shall say you're all in all in spleen,°

52 ***lethargy*** *coma.* *57* ***great occasion*** *very important matter.* *59* ***mock*** *(Othello takes Iago's comment as a reference to his horns—which it is).* *63* ***civil*** *city-dwelling.* *66* ***draw*** *i.e., like the horned ox.* *67* ***unproper*** *i.e., not exclusively the husband's.* *68* ***peculiar*** *their own alone.* *74* ***a patient list*** *the bounds of patience.* *77* ***shifted him away*** *got rid of him by a strategem.* *78* ***ecstasy*** *trance (the literal meaning, "outside oneself," bears on the meaning of the change Othello is undergoing).* *80* ***encave*** *hide.* *81* ***fleers*** *mocking looks or speeches.* *81* ***notable*** *obvious.* *87* ***spleen*** *passion, particularly anger.*

And nothing of a man.
OTHELLO: Dost thou hear, Iago?
I will be found most cunning in my patience;
But—dost thou hear?—most bloody.
IAGO: That's not amiss;
But yet keep time in all. Will you withdraw?

[OTHELLO *moves to one side, where his remarks are not audible to* CASSIO *and* IAGO.]

Now will I question Cassio of Bianca,
A huswife° that by selling her desires
Buys herself bread and cloth. It is a creature
That dotes on Cassio, as 'tis the strumpet's plague
To beguile many and be beguiled by one.
He, when he hears of her, cannot restrain
From the excess of laughter. Here he comes.

Enter CASSIO.

As he shall smile, Othello shall go mad:
And his unbookish° jealousy must conster°
Poor Cassio's smiles, gestures, and light behaviors
Quite in the wrong. How do you, lieutenant?
CASSIO: The worser that you give me the addition°
Whose want even kills me.
IAGO: Ply Desdemona well, and you are sure on't.
Now, if this suit lay in Bianca's power,
How quickly should you speed!
CASSIO: Alas, poor caitiff!°
OTHELLO: Look how he laughs already!
IAGO: I never knew woman love man so.
CASSIO: Alas, poor rogue! I think, i' faith, she loves me.
OTHELLO: Now he denies it faintly, and laughs it out.
IAGO: Do you hear, Cassio?
OTHELLO: Now he importunes him
To tell it o'er. Go to! Well said, well said!
IAGO: She gives it out that you shall marry her.
Do you intend it?
CASSIO: Ha, ha, ha!
OTHELLO: Do ye triumph, Roman? Do you triumph?
CASSIO: I marry? What, a customer?° Prithee bear some charity to my wit; do not think it so unwholesome. Ha, ha, ha!
OTHELLO: So, so, so, so. They laugh that win.
IAGO: Why, the cry goes that you marry her.

[93]***huswife*** *housewife (but with the special meaning here of "prostitute").* [100]***unbookish*** *ignorant.* [100]***conster*** *construe.* [103]***addition*** *title.* [107]***caitiff*** *wretch.* [118]***customer*** *one who sells, a merchant (here, a prostitute).*

CASSIO: Prithee, say true.
IAGO: I am a very villain else.
OTHELLO: Have you scored° me? Well.
CASSIO: This is the monkey's own giving out. She is persuaded I will marry her out of her own love and flattery, not out of my promise.
OTHELLO: Iago beckons me; now he begins the story.

[OTHELLO *moves close enough to hear.*]

CASSIO: She was here even now; she haunts me in every place. I was the other day talking on the sea bank with certain Venetians, and thither comes the bauble,° and falls me thus about my neck—
OTHELLO: Crying "O dear Cassio!" as it were. His gesture imports it.
CASSIO: So hangs, and lolls, and weeps upon me; so shakes and pulls me! Ha, ha, ha!
OTHELLO: Now he tells how she plucked him to my chamber. O, I see that nose of yours, but not that dog I shall throw it to.
CASSIO: Well, I must leave her company.
IAGO: Before me!° Look where she comes.

Enter BIANCA.

CASSIO: 'Tis such another fitchew!° Marry a perfumed one? What do you mean by this haunting of me?
BIANCA: Let the devil and his dam haunt you! What did you mean by that same handkerchief you gave me even now? I was a fine fool to take it. I must take out the work? A likely piece of work that you should find it in your chamber and know not who left it there! This is some minx's token, and I must take out the work? There! [*She throws down the handkerchief.*] Give it your hobbyhorse.° Wheresoever you had it, I'll take out no work on't.
CASSIO: How now, my sweet Bianca? How now? how now?
OTHELLO: By heaven, that should be my handkerchief!
BIANCA: If you'll come to supper tonight, you may; if you will not, come when you are next prepared for.° [*Exit.*]
IAGO: After her, after her!
CASSIO: Faith, I must; she'll rail in the streets else.
IAGO: Will you sup there?
CASSIO: Yes, I intend so.
IAGO: Well, I may chance to see you, for I would very fain speak with you.
CASSIO: Prithee come. Will you?
IAGO: Go to, say no more [*Exit* CASSIO.]
OTHELLO [*Comes forward*]: How shall I murder him, Iago?
IAGO: Did you perceive how he laughed at his vice?
OTHELLO: O Iago!
IAGO: And did you see the handkerchief?

124***scored*** *marked, defaced.* 129***bauble*** *plaything.* 136***Before me!*** *(an exclamation of surprise).* 137***fitchew*** *polecat, i.e., strong-smelling creature.* 143***hobbyhorse*** *prostitute.* 148***next prepared for*** *next expected—i.e., never.*

OTHELLO: Was that mine?

IAGO: Yours, by this hand! And to see how he prizes the foolish woman your wife! She gave it him, and he hath giv'n it his whore.

OTHELLO: I would have him nine years a-killing!—A fine woman, a fair woman, a sweet woman?

IAGO: Nay, you must forget that.

OTHELLO: Ay, let her rot, and perish, and be damned tonight; for she shall not live. No, my heart is turned to stone; I strike it, and it hurts my hand. O, the world hath not a sweeter creature! She might lie by an emperor's side and command him tasks.

IAGO: Nay, that's not your way.°

OTHELLO: Hang her! I do but say what she is. So delicate with her needle. An admirable musician. O, she will sing the savageness out of a bear! Of so high and plenteous wit and invention°

IAGO: She's the worse for all this.

OTHELLO: O, a thousand, a thousand times. And then, of so gentle a condition?°

IAGO: Ay, too gentle.

OTHELLO: Nay, that's certain. But yet the pity of it, Iago. O Iago, the pity of it, Iago.

IAGO: If you are so fond over her iniquity, give her patent to offend; for if it touch° not you, it comes near nobody.

OTHELLO: I will chop her into messes!° Cuckold me!

IAGO: O, 'tis foul in her.

OTHELLO: With mine officer!

IAGO: That's fouler.

OTHELLO: Get me some poison, Iago, this night. I'll not expostulate with her, lest her body and beauty unprovide my mind° again. This night, Iago!

IAGO: Do it not with poison. Strangle her in her bed, even the bed she hath contaminated.

OTHELLO: Good, good! The justice of it pleases. Very good!

IAGO: And for Cassio, let me be his undertaker.° You shall hear more by midnight.

OTHELLO: Excellent good! [*A trumpet.*]
What trumpet is that same?

IAGO: I warrant something from Venice.

Enter LODOVICO, DESDEMONA, *and* ATTENDANTS.

'Tis Lodovico.
This comes from the Duke. See, your wife's with him.

LODOVICO: God save you, worthy general.

OTHELLO: With° all my heart, sir.

LODOVICO: The Duke and the senators of Venice greet you.

[*Gives him a letter.*]

[170]***way*** *proper course.* [173]***invention*** *imagination.* [175]***gentle a condition*** *(1) well born (2) of a gentle nature.* [179]***touch*** *affects.* [181]***messes*** *bits.* [186]***unprovide my mind*** *undo my resolution.* [190]***undertaker*** *(not "burier" but "one who undertakes to do something").* [194]***With*** *i.e., I greet you with.*

OTHELLO: I kiss the instrument of their pleasures.

[*Opens the letter and reads.*]

DESDEMONA: And what's the news, good cousin Lodovico?
IAGO: I am very glad to see you, signior.
Welcome to Cyprus.
LODOVICO: I thank you. How does Lieutenant Cassio?
IAGO: Lives, sir.
DESDEMONA: Cousin, there's fall'n between him and my lord
An unkind breach; but you shall make all well.
OTHELLO: Are you sure of that?
DESDEMONA: My lord?
Othello [*Reads*]: "This fail you not to do, as you will—"
LODOVICO: He did not call; he's busy in the paper.
Is there division 'twixt my lord and Cassio?
DESDEMONA: A most unhappy one. I would do much
T' atone them, for the love I bear to Cassio.
OTHELLO: Fire and brimstone!
DESDEMONA: My lord?
OTHELLO: Are you wise?
DESDEMONA: What, is he angry?
LODOVICO: May be th' letter moved him;
For, as I think, they do command him home,
Deputing Cassio in his government.
DESDEMONA: Trust me, I am glad on't.
OTHELLO: Indeed?
DESDEMONA: My lord?
OTHELLO: I am glad to see you mad.
DESDEMONA: Why, sweet Othello—
OTHELLO: Devil! [*Strikes her.*]
DESDEMONA: I have not deserved this.
LODOVICO: My lord, this would not be believed in Venice,
Though I should swear I saw't. 'Tis very much.
Make her amends; she weeps.
OTHELLO: O devil, devil!
If that the earth could teem with woman's tears,
Each drop she falls would prove a crocodile.
Out of my sight!
DESDEMONA: I will not stay to offend you. [*Going.*]
LODOVICO: Truly, an obedient lady.
I do beseech your lordship call her back.
OTHELLO: Mistress!
DESDEMONA: My lord?
OTHELLO: What would you with her, sir?

202 ***unkind*** *unnatural.* 209 ***atone*** *reconcile.* 213 ***government*** *office.* 221 ***teem*** *conceive.* 222 ***falls*** *drops.* 222 ***crocodile*** *(the crocodile was supposed to shed false tears to lure its victims).*

LODOVICO: Who? I, my lord?
OTHELLO: Ay! You did wish that I would make her turn.
Sir, she can turn, and turn, and yet go on
And turn again; and she can weep, sir, weep;
And she's obedient; as you say, obedient.
Very obedient. Proceed you in your tears.
Concerning this, sir—O well-painted passion!
I am commanded home.—Get you away;
I'll send for you anon.—Sir, I obey the mandate
And will return to Venice.—Hence, avaunt! [*Exit* DESDEMONA.]
Cassio shall have my place. And, sir, tonight
I do entreat that we may sup together.
You are welcome, sir, to Cyprus.—Goats and monkeys! [*Exit.*]
LODOVICO: Is this the noble Moor whom our full Senate
Call all in all sufficient? Is this the nature
Whom passion could not shake? whose solid virtue
The shot of accident nor dart of chance
Could neither graze nor pierce?
IAGO: He is much changed.
LODOVICO: Are his wits safe? Is he not light of brain?
IAGO: He's that he is; I may not breathe my censure.
What he might be (if, what he might, he is not)
I would to heaven he were!
LODOVICO: What, strike his wife?
IAGO: Faith, that was not so well; yet would I knew
That stroke would prove the worst.
LODOVICO: Is it his use?°
Or did the letters work upon his blood°
And new-create his fault?
IAGO: Alas, alas!
It is not honesty in me to speak
What I have seen and known. You shall observe him,
And his own courses° will denote him so
That I may save my speech. Do but go after
And mark how he continues.
LODOVICO: I am sorry that I am deceived in him. [*Exeunt.*]

Scene II [The citadel.]

Enter OTHELLO *and* EMILIA.

OTHELLO: You have seen nothing then?
EMILIA: Nor ever heard, nor ever did suspect.
OTHELLO: Yes, you have seen Cassio and she together.
EMILIA: But then I saw no harm, and then I heard
Each syllable that breath made up° between them.

250***use*** *habit* 251***blood*** *passion.* 255***courses*** *actions.* ***IV.ii.*** 5***that breath made up*** *spoken.*

OTHELLO: What, did they never whisper?
EMILIA: Never, my lord.
OTHELLO: Nor send you out o' th' way?
EMILIA: Never.
OTHELLO: To fetch her fan, her gloves, her mask, nor nothing?
EMILIA: Never, my lord.
OTHELLO: That's strange.
EMILIA: I durst, my lord, to wager she is honest,
Lay down my soul at stake.° If you think other,
Remove your thought. It doth abuse your bosom.
If any wretch have put this in your head,
Let heaven requite it with the serpent's curse,°
For if she be not honest,° chaste, and true,
There's no man happy. The purest of their wives
Is foul as slander.
OTHELLO: Bid her come hither. Go. [*Exit* EMILIA.]
She says enough; yet she's a simple bawd°
That cannot say as much. This is a subtle whore,
A closet lock and key of villainous secrets,
And yet she'll kneel and pray; I have seen her do't.

Enter DESDEMONA *and* EMILIA.

DESDEMONA: My lord, what is your will?
OTHELLO: Pray you, chuck, come hither.
DESDEMONA: What is your pleasure?
OTHELLO: Let me see your eyes.
Look in my face.
DESDEMONA: What horrible fancy's this?
OTHELLO [*To* EMILIA]: Some of your function,° mistress:
Leave procreants alone and shut the door;
Cough or cry hem if anybody come.
Your mystery,° your mystery! Nay, dispatch! [*Exit* EMILIA.]
DESDEMONA: Upon my knee, what doth your speech import?
I understand a fury in your words.°
OTHELLO: Why, what art thou?
DESDEMONA: Your wife, my lord; your true
And loyal wife.
OTHELLO: Come, swear it, damn thyself;
Lest, being like one of heaven, the devils themselves
Should fear to seize thee. Therefore be doubledamned:
Swear thou art honest.
DESDEMONA: Heaven doth truly know it.
OTHELLO: Heaven truly knows that thou art false as hell.

13 ***at stake*** *as the wager.* 16 ***serpent's curse*** *(God's curse on the serpent after the fall of Eden).* 17 ***honest*** *chaste.* 20 ***bawd*** *procuress.* 27 ***Some of your function*** *do your proper work (as the operator of a brothel).* 30 ***mystery*** *trade.* 32 ***words*** *words (Q1 adds to this line, "But not the words").*

DESDEMONA: To whom, my lord? With whom? How am I false?
OTHELLO: Ah, Desdemon! Away! Away! Away!
DESDEMONA: Alas the heavy day! Why do you weep?
Am I the motive° of these tears, my lord?
If haply° you my father do suspect
An instrument of this your calling back,
Lay not your blame on me. If you have lost him,
I have lost him too.
OTHELLO: Had it pleased heaven
To try me with affliction, had they rained
All kinds of sores and shames on my bare head,
Steeped° me in poverty to the very lips,
Given to captivity me and my utmost hopes,
I should have found in some place of my soul
A drop of patience. But alas, to make me
The fixèd figure for the time of scorn°
To point his slow and moving finger at.
Yet could I bear that too, well, very well.
But there where I have garnered up my heart,
Where either I must live or bear no life,
The fountain from the which my current runs
Or else dries up—to be discarded thence,
Or keep it as a cistern for foul toads
To knot and gender° in—turn thy complexion there,
Patience, thou young and rose-lipped cherubin!
I here look grim as hell!°
DESDEMONA: I hope my noble lord esteems me honest.
OTHELLO: O, ay, as summer flies are in the shambles,°
That quicken even with blowing.° O thou weed,
Who art so lovely fair, and smell'st so sweet,
That the sense aches at thee, would thou hadst never been born!
DESDEMONA: Alas, what ignorant° sin have I committed?
OTHELLO: Was this fair paper, this most goodly book,
Made to write "whore" upon? What committed?
Committed? O thou public commoner,°
I should make very forges of my cheeks
That would to cinders burn up modesty,
Did I but speak thy deeds. What committed?
Heaven stops the nose at it, and the moon winks;°

[42]***motive*** *cause.* [43]***haply*** *by chance.* [49]***Steeped*** *submerged.* [53]***The . . . scorn*** *the very image of scorn in our time.* [61]***knot and gender*** *twist in bunches and procreate.* [61–63]***turn . . . hell*** *(the rough sense would seem to be "even Patience would grow pale, turn complexion, at Desdemona's perfidy, but that Othello looks grimly on).* [65]***shambles*** *abattoirs.* [66]***quicken even with blowing*** *become impregnated as soon as they lay their eggs.* [69]***ignorant*** *unknowing.* [72]***commonor*** *prostitute.* [76]***winks*** *closes its eyes (the moon was the symbol of chastity).*

The bawdy wind that kisses all it meets
Is hushed within the hollow mine of earth
And will not hear't. What committed?
DESDEMONA: By heaven, you do me wrong!
OTHELLO: Are not you a strumpet?
DESDEMONA: No, as I am a Christian!
If to preserve this vessel for my lord
From any other foul unlawful touch
Be not to be a strumpet, I am none.
OTHELLO: What, not a whore?
DESDEMONA: No, as I shall be saved!
OTHELLO: Is't possible?
DESDEMONA: O, heaven forgive us!
OTHELLO: I cry you mercy° then.
I took you for that cunning whore of Venice
That married with Othello. [*Calling*] You, mistress,

Enter EMILIA.

That have the office opposite to Saint Peter
And keep the gate of hell! You, you, ay, you!
We have done our course; there's money for your pains.

[*Throws her some coins.*]

I pray you turn the key and keep our counsel. [*Exit.*]
EMILIA: Alas, what does this gentleman conceive?
How do you, madam? How do you, my good lady?
DESDEMONA: Faith, half asleep.
EMILIA: Good madam, what's the matter with my lord?
DESDEMONA: With who?
EMILIA: Why, with my lord, madam.
DESDEMONA: Who is thy lord?
EMILIA He that is yours, sweet lady.
DESDEMONA: I have none. Do not talk to me, Emilia.
I cannot weep, nor answers have I none
But what should go by water.° Prithee tonight
Lay on my bed my wedding sheets, remember;
And call thy husband hither.
EMILIA: Here's a change indeed! [*Exit.*]
DESDEMONA: 'Tis meet I should be used so, very meet.
How have I been behaved, that he might stick
The small'st opinion on my least misuse?°

Enter IAGO *and* EMILIA.

IAGO: What is your pleasure, madam? How is't with you?

87 ***cry you mercy*** *ask your pardon.* 103 ***water*** *tears.* 107–8 ***stick . . . misuse*** *base any doubt on my smallest fault.*

DESDEMONA: I cannot tell. Those that do teach young babes
Do it with gentle means and easy tasks.
He might have chid me so; for, in good faith,
I am a child to chiding.
IAGO: What is the matter, lady?
EMILIA: Alas, Iago, my lord hath so bewhored her,
Thrown such despite° and heavy terms upon her
That true hearts cannot bear it.
DESDEMONA: Am I that name, Iago?
IAGO: What name, fair lady?
DESDEMONA: Such as she said my lord did say I was.
EMILIA: He called her whore. A beggar in his drink
Could not have laid such terms upon his callet.°
IAGO: Why did he so?
DESDEMONA: I do not know; I am sure I am none such.
IAGO: Do not weep, do not weep. Alas the day.
EMILIA: Hath she forsook so many noble matches,
Her father and her country, and her friends,
To be called whore? Would it not make one weep?
DESDEMONA: It is my wretched fortune.
IAGO: Beshrew° him for't!
How comes this trick upon him?
DESDEMONA: Nay, heaven doth know.
EMILIA: I will be hanged if some eternal villain,
Some busy and insinuating rogue,
Some cogging,° cozening slave, to get some office,
Have not devised this slander. I will be hanged else.
IAGO: Fie, there is no such man! It is impossible.
DESDEMONA: If any such there be, heaven pardon him.
EMILIA: A halter pardon him! And hell gnaw his bones!
Why should he call her whore? Who keeps her company?
What place? What time? What form? What likelihood?
The Moor's abused by some most villainous knave,
Some base notorious knave, some scurvy fellow.
O heavens, that such companions° thou'dst unfold,°
And put in every honest hand a whip
To lash the rascals naked through the world
Even from the east to th' west!
IAGO: Speak within door.°
EMILIA: O, fie upon them! Some such squire° he was
That turned your wit the seamy side without
And made you to suspect me with the Moor.
IAGO: You are a fool. Go to.

115***despite*** *abuse.* 120***callet*** *slut.* 127***Beshrew*** *curse.* 131***cogging*** *cheating.* 140***companions*** *fellows, rogues.* 140***unfold*** *disclose.* 143***within door*** *more quietly and moderately.* 144***squire*** *(a term of contempt).*

DESDEMONA: Alas, Iago,
What shall I do to win my lord again?
Good friend, go to him, for, by this light of heaven,
I know not how I lost him. Here I kneel:
If e'er my will did trespass 'gainst his love
Either in discourse of thought° or actual deed,
Or that mine eyes, mine ears, or any sense
Delighted them in any other form;
Or that I do not yet, and ever did,
And ever will (though he do shake me off
To beggarly divorcement) love him dearly,
Comfort forswear me. Unkindness may do much,
And his unkindness may defeat° my life,
But never taint my love. I cannot say "whore."
It does abhor me now I speak the word;
To do the act that might the addition earn
Not the world's mass of vanity could make me.
IAGO: I pray you be content. 'Tis but his humor.°
The business of the state does him offense.
DESDEMONA: If 'twere no other.
IAGO: It is but so, I warrant. [*Trumpets within.*]
Hark how these instruments summon to supper.
The messengers of Venice stay the meat.°
Go in, and weep not. All things shall be well.

[*Exeunt* DESDEMONA *and* EMILIA. *Enter* RODERIGO.]

How now, Roderigo?
RODERIGO: I do not find that thou deal'st justly with me.
IAGO: What in the contrary?
RODERIGO: Every day thou daff'st° me with some device,° Iago, and rather, as it seems to me now, keep'st from me all conveniency° than suppliest me with the least advantage of hope. I will indeed no longer endure it; nor am I yet persuaded to put up° in peace what already I have foolishly suffered.
IAGO: Will you hear me, Roderigo?
RODERIGO: I have heard too much, and your words and performances are no kin together.
IAGO: You charge me most unjustly.
RODERIGO: With naught but truth. I have wasted myself out of my means. The jewels you have had from me to deliver Desdemona would half have corrupted a votarist.° You have told me she hath received them, and returned me expectations and comforts of sudden respect° and acquaintance; but I find none.
IAGO: Well, go to; very well.

[152] ***discourse of thought*** *thinking.* [159] ***defeat*** *destroy.* [164] ***humor*** *mood.* [168] ***stay the meat*** *await the meal.* [173] ***daff'st*** *put off.* [173] ***device*** *scheme.* [174] ***conveniency*** *what is needful.* [176] ***put up*** *accept.* [183] ***votarist*** *nun.* [184] ***sudden respect*** *immediate consideration.*

RODERIGO: Very well? Go to? I cannot go to, man; nor 'tis not very well. Nay, I think it is scurvy, and begin to find myself fopped° in it.

IAGO: Very well.

RODERIGO: I tell you 'tis not very well. I will make myself known to Desdemona. If she will return me my jewels, I will give over my suit and repent my unlawful solicitation. If not, assure yourself I will seek satisfaction of you.

IAGO: You have said now?

RODERIGO: Ay, and said nothing but what I protest° intendment of doing.

IAGO: Why, now I see there's mettle° in thee, and even from this instant do build on thee a better opinion than ever before. Give me thy hand, Roderigo. Thou hast taken against me a most just exception,° but yet I protest I have dealt most directly° in thy affair.

RODERIGO: It hath not appeared.

IAGO: I grant indeed it hath not appeared, and your suspicion is not without wit and judgment. But, Roderigo, if thou hast that in thee indeed which I have greater reason to believe now than ever—I mean purpose, courage, and valor—this night show it. If thou the next night following enjoy not Desdemona, take me from this world with treachery and devise engines for° my life.

RODERIGO: Well, what is it? Is it within reason and compass?°

IAGO: Sir, there is especial commission come from Venice to depute Cassio in Othello's place.

RODERIGO: Is that true? Why, then Othello and Desdemona return again to Venice.

IAGO: O, no; he goes into Mauritania and taketh away with him the fair Desdemona, unless his abode be lingered here by some accident; wherein none can be so determinate° as the removing of Cassio.

RODERIGO: How do you mean, removing him?

IAGO: Why, by making him uncapable of Othello's place—knocking out his brains.

RODERIGO: And that you would have me to do?

IAGO: Ay, if you dare do yourself a profit and a right. He sups tonight with a harlotry,° and thither will I go to him. He knows not yet of his honorable fortune. If you will watch his going thence, which I will fashion to fall out° between twelve and one, you may take him at your pleasure. I will be near to second° your attempt, and he shall fall between us. Come, stand not amazed at it, but go along with me. I will show you such a necessity in his death that you shall think yourself bound to put it on him. It is now high supper time, and the night grows to waste. About it.

RODERIGO: I will hear further reason for this.

IAGO: And you shall be satisfied. *[Exeunt.]*

Scene III [The citadel.]

Enter OTHELLO, LODOVICO, DESDEMONA, EMILIA, *and* ATTENDANTS.

LODOVICO: I do beseech you, sir, trouble yourself no further.

OTHELLO: O, pardon me; 'twill do me good to walk.

187***fopped*** *duped.* 193***protest*** *aver.* 194***mettle*** *spirit.* 196***exception*** *objection.* 197***directly*** *straight-forwardly.* 203***engines for*** *schemes against.* 204***compass*** *possibility.* 211***determinate*** *effective.* 217***harlotry*** *female.* 218–219***fall out*** *occur.* 220***second*** *support.*

LODOVICO: Madam, good night. I humbly thank your ladyship.
DESDEMONA: Your honor is most welcome.
OTHELLO: Will you walk, sir? O, Desdemona.
DESDEMONA: My lord?
OTHELLO: Get you to bed on th' instant; I will be returned forthwith. Dismiss your attendant there. Look't be done.
DESDEMONA: I will, my lord. *Exit* [OTHELLO, *with* LODOVICO *and* ATTENDANTS].
EMILIA: How goes it now? He looks gentler than he did.
DESDEMONA: He says he will return incontinent,°
And hath commanded me to go to bed.
And bade me to dismiss you.
EMILIA: Dismiss me?
DESDEMONA: It was his bidding; therefore, good Emilia,
Give me my nightly wearing, and adieu.
We must not now displease him.
EMILIA: I would you had never seen him!
DESDEMONA: So would not I. My love doth so approve him
That even his stubbornness, his checks,° his frowns—
Prithee unpin me—have grace and favor.
EMILIA: I have laid these sheets you bade me on the bed.
DESDEMONA: All's one.° Good Father, how foolish are our minds!
If I do die before, prithee shroud me
In one of these same sheets.
EMILIA: Come, come! You talk.
DESDEMONA: My mother had a maid called Barbary.
She was in love; and he she loved proved mad
And did forsake her. She had a song of "Willow";
An old thing 'twas, but it expressed her fortune,
And she died singing it. That song tonight
Will not go from my mind; I have much to do
But to go hang my head all at one side
And sing it like poor Barbary. Prithee dispatch.
EMILIA: Shall I go fetch your nightgown?
DESDEMONA: No, unpin me here.
This Lodovico is a proper man.
EMILIA: A very handsome man.
DESDEMONA: He speaks well.
EMILIA: I know a lady in Venice would have walked barefoot to Palestine for a touch of his nether lip.
DESDEMONA [*Sings*]:
"The poor soul sat singing by a sycamore tree,
Sing all a green willow;
Her hand on her bosom, her head on her knee,
Sing willow, willow, willow.
The fresh streams ran by her and murmured her moans;
Sing willow, willow, willow;

IV.iii. [11]***incontinent*** *at once.* [19]***checks*** *rebukes.* [22]***All's one*** *no matter.*

Her salt tears fell from her, and soft'ned the stones—
Sing willow, willow, willow—"
Lay by these. [*Gives* EMILIA *her clothes.*]
"Willow, Willow"—
Prithee hie° thee; he'll come anon.°
"Sing all a green willow must be my garland
Let nobody blame him; his scorn I approve"—
Nay, that's not next. Hark! Who is't that knocks?

EMILIA: It is the wind.

DESDEMONA [*Sings*]:
"I called my love false love; but what said he then?
Sing willow, willow, willow:
If I court moe° women, you'll couch with moe men."
So, get thee gone; good night. Mine eyes do itch.
Doth that bode weeping?

EMILIA: 'Tis neither here nor there.

DESDEMONA: I have heard it said so. O, these men, these men.
Dost thou in conscience think, tell me, Emilia,
That there be women do abuse their husbands
In such gross kind?

EMILIA: There be some such, no question.

DESDEMONA: Wouldst thou do such a deed for all the world?

EMILIA: Why, would not you?

DESDEMONA: No, by this heavenly light!

EMILIA: Nor I neither by this heavenly light.
I might do't as well i' th' dark.

DESDEMONA: Wouldst thou do such a deed for all the world?

EMILIA: The world's a huge thing; it is a great price for a small vice.

DESDEMONA: In troth, I think thou wouldst not.

EMILIA: In troth, I think I should; and undo't when I had done. Marry, I would not do such a thing for a joint-ring,° nor for measures of lawn,° nor for gowns, petticoats, nor caps, nor any petty exhibition,° but for all the whole world? Why, who would not make her husband a cuckold to make him a monarch? I should venture purgatory for't.

DESDEMONA: Beshrew me if I would do such a wrong for the whole world.

EMILIA: Why, the wrong is but a wrong i' th' world; and having the world for your labor, 'tis a wrong in your own world, and you might quickly make it right.

DESDEMONA: I do not think there is any such woman.

EMILIA: Yes, a dozen; and as many to th' vantage as would store° the world they played for.
But I do think it is their husbands' faults
If wives do fall. Say that they slack their duties

50 ***hie*** *hurry.* 50 ***anon*** *at once.* 57 ***moe*** *more.* 72 ***joint-ring*** *(a ring with two interlocking halves).* 72 ***lawn*** *fine linen.* 73 ***exhibition*** *payment.* 80 ***to . . . store*** *in addition as would fill.*

And pour our treasures into foreign° laps;
Or else break out in peevish jealousies,
Throwing restraint upon us; or say they strike us,
Or scant our former having in despite°
Why, we have galls; and though we have some grace,
Yet have we some revenge. Let husbands know
Their wives have sense like them. They see, and smell,
And have their palates both for sweet and sour,
As husbands have. What is it that they do
When they change° us for others? Is it sport?
I think it is. And doth affection° breed it?
I think it doth. Is't frailty that thus errs?
It is so too. And have not we affections?
Desires for sport? and frailty? as men have?
Then let them use us well; else let them know,
The ills we do, their ills instruct us so.°

DESDEMONA: Good night, good night. Heaven me such uses° send,
Not to pick bad from bad, but by bad mend. [*Exeunt.*]

ACT V

Scene I [A street.]

Enter IAGO *and* RODERIGO.

IAGO: Here, stand behind this bulk;° straight will he come.
Wear thy good rapier bare, and put it home.
Quick, quick! Fear nothing; I'll be at thy elbow.
It makes us, or it mars us, think on that,
And fix most firm thy resolution.

RODERIGO: Be near at hand; I may miscarry in't.

IAGO: Here, at thy hand. Be bold, and take thy stand.

[*Moves to one side.*]

RODERIGO: I have no great devotion to the deed,
And yet he hath given me satisfying reasons.
'Tis but a man gone. Forth my sword! He dies!

IAGO: I have rubbed this young quat° almost to the sense,°
And he grows angry. Now, whether he kill Cassio,
Or Cassio him, or each do kill the other,
Every way makes my gain. Live Roderigo,
He calls me to a restitution large

[84]***foreign*** *alien, i.e., other than the wife.* [87]***scant . . . despite*** *reduce, in spite, our household allowance (?).* [93]***change*** *exchange.* [94]***affection*** *strong feeling, desire.* [99]***instruct us so*** *teach us to do likewise.* [100]***uses*** *practices.* ***v.i.*** [1]***bulk*** *projecting stall of a shop.* [11]***quat*** *pimple.* [11]***to the sense*** *raw.*

Of gold and jewels that I bobbed° from him
As gifts to Desdemona.
It must not be. If Cassio do remain,
He hath a daily beauty in his life
That makes me ugly; and besides, the Moor
May unfold me to him; there stand I in much peril.
No, he must die. But so, I hear him coming.

Enter CASSIO.

RODERIGO: I know his gait. 'Tis he. Villain, thou diest! [*Thrusts at* CASSIO.]
CASSIO: That thrust had been mine enemy indeed
But that my coat° is better than thou know'st.
I will make proof of thine. [*Fights with* RODERIGO.]
RODERIGO: O, I am slain!°
CASSIO: I am maimed forever. Help, ho! Murder! Murder!

Enter OTHELLO [*to one side*].

OTHELLO: The voice of Cassio. Iago keeps his word.
RODERIGO: O, villain that I am!
OTHELLO: It is even so.
CASSIO: O help, ho! Light! A surgeon!
OTHELLO: 'Tis he. O brave Iago, honest and just,
That hast such noble sense of thy friend's wrong!
Thou teachest me. Minion,° your dear lies dead,
And your unblest° fate hies.° Strumpet, I come.
Forth of my heart those charms, thine eyes, are blotted.
Thy bed, lust-stained, shall with lust's blood be spotted.

Exit OTHELLO. *Enter* LODOVICO *and* GRATIANO.

CASSIO: What, ho? No watch? No passage?° Murder! Murder!
GRATIANO: 'Tis some mischance. The voice is very direful.
CASSIO: O, help!
LODOVICO: Hark!
RODERIGO: O wretched villain!
LODOVICO: Two or three groan. 'Tis heavy night.
These may be counterfeits. Let's think't unsafe
To come into the cry without more help.
RODERIGO: Nobody come? Then shall I bleed to death.
LODOVICO: Hark!

Enter IAGO [*with a light*].

16***bobbed*** *swindled.* 25***coat*** *i.e., a mail shirt or bullet-proof vest.* 26***slain*** *most editors add here a stage direction that has Iago wounding Cassio in the leg from behind, but remaining unseen. However, nothing in the text requires this, and Cassio's wound can be given him in the fight with Roderigo, for presumably when Cassio attacks Roderigo the latter would not simply accept the thrust but would parry. Since Iago enters again at line 46, he must exit at some point after line 22.* 33***Minion*** *hussy, i.e., Desdemona.* 34***unblest*** *unsanctified.* 34***hies*** *approaches swiftly.* 37***passage*** *passers-by.*

GRATIANO: Here's one comes in his shirt, with light and weapons.
IAGO: Who's there? Whose noise is this that cries on murder?
LODOVICO: We do not know.
IAGO: Do not you hear a cry?
CASSIO: Here, here! For heaven's sake, help me!
IAGO: What's the matter?
GRATIANO: This is Othello's ancient, as I take it.
LODOVICO: The same indeed, a very valiant fellow.
IAGO: What are you here that cry so grievously?
CASSIO: Iago? O, I am spoiled, undone by villains.
Give me some help.
IAGO: O me, lieutenant! What villains have done this?
CASSIO: I think that one of them is hereabout
And cannot make away.
IAGO: O treacherous villains!
[*To* LODOVICO *and* GRATIANO] What are you there?
Come in, and give some help.
RODERIGO: O, help me here!
CASSIO: That's one of them.
IAGO: O murd'rous slave! O villain! [*Stabs* RODERIGO.]
RODERIGO: O damned Iago! O inhuman dog!
IAGO: Kill men i' th' dark?—Where be these bloody thieves?—
How silent is this town!—Ho! Murder! Murder!—
What may you be? Are you of good or evil?
LODOVICO: As you shall prove us, praise us.
IAGO: Signior Lodovico?
LODOVICO: He, sir.
IAGO: I cry you mercy. Here's Cassio hurt by villains.
GRATIANO: Cassio?
IAGO: How is't, brother?
CASSIO: My leg is cut in two.
IAGO: Marry, heaven forbid!
Light, gentlemen. I'll bind it with my shirt.

Enter BIANCA.

BIANCA: What is the matter, ho? Who is't that cried?
IAGO: Who is't that cried?
BIANCA: O my dear Cassio! My sweet Cassio!
O Cassio, Cassio, Cassio!
IAGO: O notable strumpet!—Cassio, may you suspect
Who they should be that have thus mangled you?
CASSIO: No.
GRATIANO: I am sorry to find you thus. I have been to seek you.
IAGO: Lend me a garter. So. O for a chair
To bear him easily hence.
BIANCA: Alas, he faints! O Cassio, Cassio, Cassio!
IAGO: Gentlemen all, I do suspect this trash

To be a party in this injury.—
Patience awhile, good Cassio.—Come, come.
Lend me a light. Know we this face or no?
Alas, my friend and my dear countryman
Roderigo? No.—Yes, sure.—Yes, 'tis Roderigo!
GRATIANO: What, of Venice?
IAGO: Even he, sir. Did you know him?
GRATIANO: Know him? Ay.
IAGO: Signior Gratiano? I cry your gentle pardon.
These bloody accidents must excuse my manners
That so neglected you.
GRATIANO: I am glad to see you.
IAGO: How do you, Cassio?—O, a chair, a chair!
GRATIANO: Roderigo?
IAGO: He, he, 'tis he! [*A chair brought in.*] O, that's well said;° the chair.
Some good man bear him carefully from hence.
I'll fetch the general's surgeon. [*To* BIANCA] For you, mistress,
Save you your labor. [*To* CASSIO] He that lies slain here, Cassio,
Was my dear friend. What malice was between you?
CASSIO: None in the world; nor do I know the man.
IAGO: What, look you pale?—O, bear him out o' th' air.

[CASSIO *is carried off.*]

Stay you, good gentlemen.—Look you pale, mistress?
Do you perceive the gastness° of her eye?
Nay, if you stare, we shall hear more anon.
Behold her well; I pray you look upon her.
Do you see, gentlemen? Nay, guiltiness will speak,
Though tongues were out of use.°

[*Enter* EMILIA.]

EMILIA: Alas, what is the matter? What is the matter, husband?
IAGO: Cassio hath here been set on in the dark
By Roderigo and fellows that are scaped.
He's almost slain, and Roderigo quite dead.
EMILIA: Alas, good gentleman! Alas, good Cassio!
IAGO: This is the fruits of whoring. Prithee, Emilia,
Go know of Cassio where he supped tonight.
[*To* BIANCA] What, do you shake at that?
BIANCA: He supped at my house; but I therefore shake not.
IAGO: O, did he so? I charge° you go with me.
EMILIA: Oh fie upon thee, strumpet!
BIANCA: I am no strumpet, but of life as honest
As you that thus abuse me.

99 ***well said*** *well done.* 107 ***gastness*** *terror.* 111 ***tongues out of use*** *men no longer spoke.*
121 ***charge*** *command.*

EMILIA: As I? Fie upon thee!
IAGO: Kind gentlemen, let's go see poor Cassio dressed.°
[*To* BIANCA] Come, mistress, you must tell's another tale.
Emilia, run you to the citadel
And tell my lord and lady what hath happed [*Exit* EMILIA.]
Will you go on afore? *Exeunt* [*all but* IAGO.]
This is the night
That either makes me or fordoes me quite.°
[*Exit.*]

Scene II. [DESDEMONA*'s chamber.*]

Enter OTHELLO [*with a light*]; *and* DESDEMONA *in her bed.*

OTHELLO: It is the cause, it is the cause, my soul.
Let me not name it to you, you chaste stars.
It is the cause. Yet I'll not shed her blood,
Nor scar that whiter skin of hers than snow
And smooth as monumental alabaster.
Yet she must die, else she'll betray more men.
Put out the light, and then put out the light.
If I quench thee, thou flaming minister,°
I can again thy former light restore,
Should I repent me; but once put out thy light,
Thou cunning'st° pattern of excelling nature,
I know not where is that Promethean heat°
That can thy light relume.° When I have plucked the rose,
I cannot give it vital° growth again;
It needs must wither. I'll smell thee on the tree.
[*He kisses her.*]
O balmy breath, that dost almost persuade
Justice to break her sword. One more, one more!
Be thus when thou art dead, and I will kill thee,
And love thee after. One more, and that's the last!
So sweet was ne'er so fatal. I must weep,
But they are cruel tears. This sorrow's heavenly;
It strikes where it doth love. She wakes.
DESDEMONA: Who's there? Othello?
OTHELLO: Ay, Desdemona.
DESDEMONA: Will you come to bed, my lord?
OTHELLO: Have you prayed tonight, Desdemon?
DESDEMONA: Ay, my lord.
OTHELLO: If you bethink yourself of any crime

125 ***dressed*** *bandaged.* 130 ***fordoes me quite*** *completely ruins me.* ***V.ii.*** 8 ***minister*** *worker, servant.* 11 ***cunning'st*** *most intricate and skilfully wrought (by nature excelling itself).* 12 ***Promethean heat*** *divine fire (Prometheus is the Titan who stole fire from heaven and gave it to man).* 13 ***relume*** *relight.* 14 ***vital*** *living.*

Unreconciled as yet to heaven and grace,
Solicit for it straight.
DESDEMONA: Alack, my lord, what may you mean by that?
OTHELLO: Well, do it, and be brief; I will walk by.°
I would not kill thy unpreparèd spirit.
No, heavens forfend! I would not kill thy soul.
DESDEMONA: Talk you of killing?
OTHELLO: Ay, I do.
DESDEMONA: Then heaven
Have mercy on me!
OTHELLO: Amen, with all my heart.
DESDEMONA: If you say so, I hope you will not kill me.
OTHELLO: Humh.
DESDEMONA: And yet I fear you; for you're fatal then
When your eyes roll so. Why I should fear I know not,
Since guiltiness I know not; but yet I feel I fear.
OTHELLO: Think on thy sins.
DESDEMONA: They are loves I bear to you.
OTHELLO: Ay, and for that thou diest.
DESDEMONA: That death's unnatural that kills for loving.
Alas, why gnaw you so your nether lip?
Some bloody passion shakes your very frame.
These are portents; but yet I hope, I hope,
They do not point on me.
OTHELLO: Peace and be still.
DESDEMONA: I will so. What's the matter?
OTHELLO: That handkerchief which I so loved and gave thee,
Thou gav'st to Cassio.
DESDEMONA: No, by my life and soul!
Send for the man and ask him.
OTHELLO: Sweet soul, take heed,
Take heed of perjury; thou art on thy deathbed.
DESDEMONA: Ay, but not yet to die.
OTHELLO: Presently.°
Therefore confess thee freely of thy sin,
For to deny each article° with oath
Cannot remove nor choke the strong conception
That I do groan withal. Thou art to die.
DESDEMONA: Then Lord have mercy on me.
OTHELLO: I say, amen.
DESDEMONA: And have you mercy too. I never did
Offend you in my life; never loved Cassio
But with such general warranty° of heaven
As I might love. I never gave him token.

30 ***by*** *nearby.* 52 ***Presently*** *immediately.* 54 ***article*** *item (of the charge of adultery. Othello makes heavy use of legal terms in this scene).* 60 ***warranty*** *allowance.*

OTHELLO: By heaven, I saw my handkerchief in's hand!
O perjured woman! thou dost stone° my heart,
And mak'st me call what I intend to do
A murder, which I thought a sacrifice.
I saw the handkerchief.
DESDEMONA: He found it then.
I never gave it him. Send for him hither.
Let him confess a truth.
OTHELLO: He hath confessed.
DESDEMONA: What, my lord?
OTHELLO: That he hath used thee.
DESDEMONA: How? Unlawfully?
OTHELLO: Ay.
DESDEMONA: He will not say so.
OTHELLO: No, his mouth is stopped.
Honest Iago hath ta'en order for't.°
DESDEMONA: O, my fear interprets. What, is he dead?
OTHELLO: Had all his hairs been lives, my great revenge
Had stomach° for them all.
DESDEMONA: Alas, he is betrayed, and I undone!
OTHELLO: Out, strumpet! Weep'st thou for him to my face?
DESDEMONA: O, banish me, my lord, but kill me not!
OTHELLO: Down, strumpet!
DESDEMONA: Kill me tomorrow; let me live tonight!
OTHELLO: Nay, if you strive—
DESDEMONA: But half an hour!
OTHELLO: Being done, there is no pause.
DESDEMONA: But while I say one prayer!
OTHELLO: It is too late.
[*Smothers her.*]

EMILIA *at the door.*

EMILIA [*Calls within*]: My lord, my lord! What, ho, my lord, my lord!
OTHELLO: What noise is this? Not dead? Not yet quite dead?
I that am cruel am yet merciful;
I would not have thee linger in thy pain.
EMILIA [*Within*]: What, ho! My lord, my lord!
OTHELLO: So, so. Who's there?
EMILIA [*Within*]: O, good my lord, I would speak a word with you.
OTHELLO: Yes, 'tis Emilia.—By and by.—She's dead.—
'Tis like she comes to speak of Cassio's death.
The noise was high.° Ha! No more moving?
Still as the grave.—Shall she come in? Were't good?—
I think she stirs again. No.—What's best to do?

[63]***stone*** *turn to stone.* [72]***ta'en order for't*** *made sure of it.* [75]***stomach*** *appetite.* [92]***high*** *loud (Q1 reads "here").*

If she come in, she'll sure speak to my wife.
My wife! My wife! What wife? I have no wife.
O, insupportable! O heavy hour!
Methinks° it should be now a huge eclipse
Of sun and moon, and that th' affrighted globe
Should yawn° at alteration.
EMILIA [*Within*]: I do beseech you
That I may speak with you, O good my lord!
OTHELLO: I had forgot thee. O, come in, Emilia.
Soft, by and by.—Let me the curtains draw.—

[*Draws the bed hangings and then opens the door.*]

Where art thou?

Enter EMILIA.

What's the matter with thee now?
EMILIA: O my good lord, yonder's foul murders done!
OTHELLO: What? Now?
EMILIA: But now, my lord.
OTHELLO: It is the very error° of the moon.
She comes more nearer earth than she was wont
And makes men mad.
EMILIA: Cassio, my lord, hath killed a young Venetian
Called Roderigo.
OTHELLO: Roderigo killed?
And Cassio killed?
EMILIA: No, Cassio is not killed.
OTHELLO: Not Cassio killed? Then murder's out of tune,
And sweet revenge grows harsh.
DESDEMONA: O, falsely, falsely murdered!
EMILIA: O Lord! What cry is that?
OTHELLO: That? What?
EMILIA: Out and alas! that was my lady's voice.
Help! Help, ho! Help! O lady, speak again!
Sweet Desdemona! O sweet mistress, speak!
DESDEMONA: A guiltless death I die.
EMILIA: O, who hath done this deed?
DESDEMONA: Nobody—I myself. Farewell.
Commend me to my kind lord. O, farewell! [*She dies.*]
OTHELLO: Why, how should she be murd'red?
EMILIA: Alas, who knows?
OTHELLO: You heard her say herself, it was not I.
EMILIA: She said so. I must needs report the truth.

98–100 ***Methinks . . . alteration*** *(the Elizabethans believed that great changes in human affairs were reflected by disorders in nature).* 100 ***yawn*** *gape open (as in an earthquake).* 108 ***error*** *wandering out of regular course (disorders in the heavens were believed by some to cause disorders on earth, as well as vice versa).*

OTHELLO: She's like a liar gone to burning hell!
'Twas I that killed her.
EMILIA: O, the more angel she,
And you the blacker devil!
OTHELLO: She turned to folly, and she was a whore.
EMILIA: Thou dost belie her, and thou art a devil.
OTHELLO: She was false as water.
EMILIA: Thou art rash as fire to say
That she was false. O, she was heavenly true!
OTHELLO: Cassio did top her. Ask thy husband else.
O, I were damned beneath all depth in hell
But that I did proceed upon just grounds
To this extremity. Thy husband knew it all.
EMILIA: My husband?
OTHELLO: Thy husband.
EMILIA: That she was false to wedlock?
OTHELLO: Ay, with Cassio. Had she been true,
If heaven would make me such another world
Of one entire and perfect chrysolite,°
I'd not have sold her for it.
EMILIA: My husband?
OTHELLO: Ay, 'twas he that told me on her first.
An honest man he is, and hates the slime
That sticks on filthy deeds.
EMILIA: My husband?
OTHELLO: What needs this iterance? Woman, I say thy husband.
EMILIA: O mistress, villainy hath made mocks with love!
My husband say she was false?
OTHELLO: He, woman.
I say, thy husband. Dost understand the word?
My friend, thy husband; honest, honest Iago.
EMILIA: If he say so, may his pernicious soul
Rot half a grain a day! He lies to th' heart.
She was too fond of her most filthy bargain.
OTHELLO: Hah?
EMILIA: Do thy worst.
This deed of thine is no more worthy heaven
Than thou wast worthy her.
OTHELLO: Peace, you were best.°
EMILIA: Thou hast not half that pow'r to do me harm
As I have to be hurt. O gull! O dolt!
As ignorant as dirt! Thou hast done a deed—

[OTHELLO *moves to draw his sword.*]

[142]***chrysolite*** *topaz.* [158]***Peace, you were best*** *i.e., you had better be silent.*

I care not for thy sword; I'll make thee known,
Though I lost twenty lives. Help! Help! Ho! Help!
The Moor hath killed my mistress! Murder! murder!

Enter MONTANO, GRATIANO, *and* IAGO [*and Others*].

MONTANO: What is the matter? How now, general?
EMILIA: O, are you come, Iago? You have done well,
That men must lay their murders on your neck.
GRATIANO: What is the matter?
EMILIA: Disprove this villain, if thou be'st a man.
He says thou told'st him that his wife was false.
I know thou didst not; thou'rt not such a villain.
Speak, for my heart is full.
IAGO: I told him what I thought, and told no more
Than what he found himself was apt and true.
EMILIA: But did you ever tell him she was false?
IAGO: I did.
EMILIA: You told a lie, an odious damnèd lie!
Upon my soul, a lie! A wicked lie!
She false with Cassio? Did you say with Cassio?
IAGO: With Cassio, mistress. Go to, charm° your tongue.
EMILIA: I will not charm my tongue; I am bound to speak:
My mistress here lies murdered in her bed.
ALL: O heavens forfend!
EMILIA: And your reports have set the murder on.
OTHELLO: Nay, stare not, masters. It is true indeed.
GRATIANO: 'Tis a strange truth.
MONTANO: O monstrous act!
EMILIA: Villainy, villainy, villainy!
I think upon't—I think I smell't!—O villainy!
I thought so then.—I'll kill myself for grief.—
O villainy, villainy!
IAGO: What, are you mad? I charge you get you home.
EMILIA: Good gentlemen, let me have leave to speak.
'Tis proper I obey him, but not now.
Perchance, Iago, I will ne'er go home.
OTHELLO: O! O! O! [*Falls on the bed.*]
EMILIA: Nay, lay thee down and roar,
For thou hast killed the sweetest innocent
That e'er did lift up eye.
OTHELLO: O, she was foul!
[*Rises.*]
I scarce did know you, uncle. There lies your niece,
Whose breath, indeed, these hands have newly stopped.
I know this act shows horrible and grim.
GRATIANO: Poor Desdemona! I am glad thy father's dead.

180 ***charm*** *control.*

Thy match was mortal to him, and pure grief
Shore his old thread in twain. Did he live now,
This sight would make him do a desperate turn;
Yea, curse his better angel from his side,
And fall to reprobation.°

OTHELLO: 'Tis pitiful; but yet Iago knows
That she with Cassio hath the act of shame
A thousand times committed. Cassio confessed it;
And she did gratify his amorous works
With that recognizance and pledge of love,
Which I first gave her. I saw it in his hand.
It was a handkerchief, an antique token
My father gave my mother.

EMILIA: O God! O heavenly God!

IAGO: Zounds, hold your peace!

EMILIA: 'Twill out, 'twill out! I peace?
No, I will speak as liberal as the north.°
Let heaven and men and devils, let them all,
All, all, cry shame against me, yet I'll speak.

IAGO: Be wise, and get you home.

EMILIA: I will not.

[IAGO *draws and threatens* EMILIA.]

GRATIANO: Fie! Your sword upon a woman?

EMILIA: O thou dull Moor, that handkerchief thou speak'st of
I found by fortune, and did give my husband;
For often with a solemn earnestness—
More than indeed belonged to such a trifle—
He begged of me to steal't.

IAGO: Villainous whore!

EMILIA: She give it Cassio? No, alas, I found it,
And I did give't my husband.

IAGO: Filth, thou liest!

EMILIA: By heaven, I do not, I do not, gentlemen.
O murd'rous coxcomb! What should such a fool
Do with so good a wife?

OTHELLO: Are there no stones° in heaven
But what serves for the thunder? Precious villain!

[*The* MOOR *runs at* IAGO, *but is disarmed by* MONTANO. IAGO *kills his wife.*]

GRATIANO: The woman falls. Sure he hath killed his wife.

EMILIA: Ay, ay. O, lay me by my mistress' side. [*Exit* IAGO.]

GRATIANO: He's gone, but his wife's killed.

MONTANO: 'Tis a notorious° villain. Take you this weapon,
Which I have recovered from the Moor.

reprobation *damnation.* [217]***liberal as the north*** *freely (and bitingly) as the north wind blows.* [231]***stones*** *thunderbolts.* [236]***notorious*** *out-and-out.*

Come, guard the door without. Let him not pass,
But kill him rather. I'll after that same villain,
For 'tis a damnèd slave. *Exit* [*with all but* OTHELLO *and* EMILIA].

OTHELLO: I am not valiant neither;
But every puny whipster° gets my sword.
But why should honor outlive honesty?
Let it go all.

EMILIA: What did thy song bode, lady?
Hark, canst thou hear me? I will play the swan,
And die in music. [*Sings*] "Willow, willow, willow."
Moor, she was chaste. She loved thee, cruel Moor,
So come my soul to bliss as I speak true.
So speaking as I think, alas, I die. [*She dies.*]

OTHELLO: I have another weapon in this chamber;
It was a sword of Spain, the ice-brook's temper.
O, here it is.—Uncle, I must come forth.

GRATIANO [*Within*]: If thou attempt it, it will cost thee dear.
Thou hast no weapon, and perforce must suffer.

OTHELLO: Look in upon me then and speak with me,
Or, naked as I am, I will assault thee.

[*Enter* GRATIANO.]

GRATIANO: What is the matter?

OTHELLO: Behold, I have a weapon;
A better never did itself sustain
Upon a soldier's thigh. I have seen the day
That with this little arm and this good sword
I have made my way through more impediments
Than twenty times your stop. But O vain boast!
Who can control his fate? 'Tis not so now.
Be not afraid, though you do see me weaponed.
Here is my journey's end, here is my butt,°
And very seamark of my utmost sail.°
Do you go back dismayed? 'Tis a lost fear.
Man but a rush° against Othello's breast.
And he retires. Where should Othello go?
Now, how dost thou look now? O ill-starred wench!
Pale as thy smock! When we shall meet at compt,°
This look of thine will hurl my soul from heaven,
And fiends will snatch at it. Cold, cold, my girl?
Even like thy chastity.
O cursèd, cursèd slave! Whip me, ye devils,
From the possession of° this heavenly sight!
Blow me about in winds! roast me in sulfur!

241 ***puny whipster*** *small top-whipping boy (?).* 264 ***butt*** *target, stopping place.* 265 ***seamark of my utmost sail*** *maker of my furthest journey.* 267 ***Man but a rush*** *attack with only a reed.* 270 ***compt*** *Judgment Day.* 275 ***the possession of*** *being possessed by.*

Wash me in steep-down gulfs of liquid fire!
O Desdemon! Dead Desdemon; dead. O! O!

Enter LODOVICO, CASSIO, MONTANO, *and* IAGO [*as prisoner,*] *with* OFFICERS.

LODOVICO: Where is this rash and most unfortunate man?
OTHELLO: That's he that was Othello? Here I am.
LODOVICO: Where is that viper? Bring the villain forth.
OTHELLO: I look down towards his feet°—but that's a fable.
If that thou be'st a devil, I cannot kill thee.

[*Wounds* IAGO.]

LODOVICO: Wrench his sword from him.

[OTHELLO *is disarmed.*]

IAGO: I bleed, sir, but not killed.
OTHELLO: I am not sorry neither. I'd have thee live;
For in my sense, 'tis happiness to die.
LODOVICO: O thou Othello that was once so good,
Fall'n in the practice° of a cursèd slave,
What shall be said to thee?
OTHELLO: Why, anything:
An honorable murderer, if you will;
For naught I did in hate, but all in honor.
LODOVICO: This wretch hath part confessed his villainy.
Did you and he consent in Cassio's death?
OTHELLO: Ay.
CASSIO: Dear general, I never gave you cause.
OTHELLO: I do believe it, and I ask your pardon.
Will you, I pray, demand that demi-devil
Why he hath thus ensnared my soul and body?
IAGO: Demand me nothing. What you know, you know.
From this time forth I never will speak word.
LODOVICO: What, not to pray?
GRATIANO: Torments will ope your lips.
OTHELLO: Well, thou dost best.
LODOVICO: Sir, you shall understand what hath befall'n,
Which, as I think, you know not. Here is a letter
Found in the pocket of the slain Roderigo;
And here another. The one of them imports
The death of Cassio to be undertook
By Roderigo.
OTHELLO: O villain!
CASSIO: Most heathenish and most gross!
LODOVICO: Now here's another discontented paper
Found in his pocket too; and this, it seems,
Roderigo meant t' have sent this damnèd villain;

282 ***towards his feet*** *i.e., for his cloven hoofs.* 288 ***practice*** *plotting.*

But that, belike, Iago in the interim
Came in and satisfied him.

OTHELLO: O thou pernicious caitiff!
How came you, Cassio, by that handkerchief
That was my wife's?

CASSIO: I found it in my chamber;
And he himself confessed it but even now
That there he dropped it for a special purpose
Which wrought to his desire.

OTHELLO: O fool! Fool! Fool!

CASSIO: There is besides in Roderigo's letter,
How he upbraids Iago that he made him
Brave me upon the watch; whereon it came
That I was cast; and even but now he spake,
After long seeming dead—Iago hurt him,
Iago set him on.

LODOVICO: You must forsake this room and go with us.
Your power and your command is taken off,
And Cassio rules in Cyprus. For this slave,
If there be any cunning cruelty
That can torment him much and hold him long,
It shall be his. You shall close prisoner rest
Till that the nature of your fault be known
To the Venetian state. Come, bring away.

OTHELLO: Soft you, a word or two before you go.
I have done the state some service and they know't.
No more of that. I pray you, in your letters,
When you shall these unlucky deeds relate,
Speak of me as I am. Nothing extenuate,
Nor set down aught in malice. Then must you speak
Of one that loved not wisely, but too well;
Of one not easily jealous, but, being wrought,
Perplexed in the extreme; of one whose hand,
Like the base Judean,° threw a pearl away
Richer than all his tribe; of one whose subdued eyes,
Albeit unusèd to the melting mood,
Drops tears as fast as the Arabian trees
Their med'cinable gum. Set you down this.
And say besides that in Aleppo once,
Where a malignant and a turbaned Turk
Beat a Venetian and traduced the state,
I took by th' throat the circumcisèd dog
And smote him—thus.

[*He stabs himself.*]

343 ***Judean*** *(most editors use the Q1 reading, "Indian," here, but F is clear: both readings point toward the infidel, the unbeliever).*

LODOVICO: O bloody period!°
GRATIANO: All that is spoke is marred.
OTHELLO: I kissed thee ere I killed thee. No way but this,
Killing myself, to die upon a kiss.

[*He falls over* DESDEMONA *and dies.*]

CASSIO: This did I fear, but thought he had no weapon;
For he was great of heart.
LODOVICO [*To* IAGO]: O Spartan dog,
More fell° than anguish, hunger, or the sea!
Look on the tragic loading of this bed.
This is thy work. The object poisons sight;
Let it be hid. [*Bed curtains drawn.*]
Gratiano, keep° the house,
And seize upon the fortunes of the Moor,
For they succeed on you. To you, lord governor,
Remains the censure of this hellish villain,
The time, the place, the torture. O, enforce it!
Myself will straight aboard, and to the state
This heavy act with heavy heart relate. [*Exeunt.*]

QUESTIONS FOR CRITICAL THINKING AND WRITING

Experience

1. Describe your experience of reading *Othello.* To what extent can you identify with any one of the play's characters? Which one(s)? Why?

Interpretation

2. What makes Othello a tragic figure? Is his tragedy self-inflicted or is it beyond his control? What is his tragic flaw?
3. Compare Othello's speeches from the beginning, middle, and end of the play (Acts I, III, and V). Explain the significance of their differences in style and tone.
4. Iago is a resourceful and clever character who knows how to manipulate people. Explain how he manipulates Roderigo, Cassio, and Othello.
5. What reason does Iago give for seeking Othello's destruction? Does this seem an adequate or a credible motive?
6. How does Emilia's role help us to better understand Iago? In what ways is she a *foil* (a contrasting character) to Desdemona? What other characters serve to balance each other?
7. Of what significance is Bianca's role in the play? Brabantio's?
8. *Othello* has a dual setting—Venice and Cyprus. With what values and ideas is each place associated, and how are these related to the action and themes of the play?

353 ***period*** *end.* 358 ***fell*** *cruel.* 361 ***keep*** *remain in.*

9. What ideas about love are expressed by Othello and Desdemona? What images of the sexual bond emerge in the speech and actions of Roderigo, Iago, and Emilia?
10. How does Shakespeare use Desdemona's handkerchief dramatically and symbolically? In which scenes is it most important? With what is it associated?
11. Examine the scene in which Othello kills Desdemona (Act V, Scene II). Read his speech beginning, "It is the cause" (lines 1–22). Explain how Othello sees himself at this point, and describe his state of mind.
12. Examine the scene in which Othello secretly watches Cassio talking to Bianca (Act IV, Scene I). Explain how Iago controls Othello's perception, leading him to misinterpret what he sees. In what other scenes does Iago direct other characters to misinterpret one another's actions and speech?
13. Any staging of Othello requires careful attention to lighting. Single out two scenes in which lighting is especially important, and explain how you would stage them.
14. Look carefully at the beginning and ending of any two acts. Consider how Shakespeare guides the audience's responses at these points. Consider also the effectiveness of each beginning and ending in relation to the development of the plot.
15. Locate two scenes in which characters' speeches shift between prose and verse. Explain the significance of these shifts.

Evaluation

16. What judgment does Shakespeare's *Othello* make about jealousy? About the power of evil over goodness?
17. How effectively do you think Shakespeare dramatizes Iago's power over others?

Connections

18. Compare Iago as a villain with Krogstad in *A Doll House.*

Critical Thinking

19. At the end of the play, Iago says that he will never speak again. Offer at least two explanations for this refusal.

CRITICS ON SHAKESPEARE

A. D. NUTTAL

Othello

from A NEW MIMESIS

Othello's tragedy indeed is strangely—and formally—introverted; it consists in the fact that he left the arena proper to tragedy, the battlefield, and entered a subtragic world for which he was not fitted. *Othello* is the story of a hero who went into a house.

Long ago A. C. Bradley observed that, if the heroes of *Hamlet* and *Othello* change places, each play ends very quickly. Hamlet would see through Iago in the first five minutes and be parodying him in the next. Othello, receiving clear instructions like "Kill that usurper" from a ghost, would simply have gone to work. Thus, as the classic problem of *Hamlet* is the hero's delay, so the classic problem of *Othello* is the hero's gullibility. The stronger our sense of Othello's incongruity in the domestic world, the less puzzling this becomes. Certainly, *Othello* is about a man who, having come from a strange and remote place, found his feet in the world of Venetian professional soldiership—and then exchanged that spacious world for a little, dim world of unimaginable horror. "War is no strife / To the dark house and the detested wife" comes not from Othello but from a comedy, but it will serve here. Its note of peculiarly masculine pain and hatred can still score the nerves. It is therefore not surprising that Shakespeare avails himself of the metaphor of the caged hawk. Desdemona says, "I'll watch him tame," at III. iii. 23. The real process of taming a hawk by keeping it awake and so breaking its spirit is described at length in T. H. White's *The Goshawk* [1953]. Othello turns the image round when he says of Desdemona,

> If I do prove her haggard,
> Though that her jesses were my dear heart-strings,
> I'd whistle her off and let her down the wind
> To prey at fortune. (III. iii. 259–262)

He speaks formally of Desdemona, but it is hard not to feel that in the last words it is his own dream of liberty which speaks.

Othello is also about insiders and outsiders. The exotic Moor finds when he leaves the public, martial sphere that he is not accepted, is not understood and cannot understand. The Venetian color bar is sexual, not professional. Iago plays on this with his "old black ram . . . tupping your white ewe" (I. i. 85–86) and the same note is struck by Roderigo with his "gross clasps of a lascivious Moor" (I. i. 121). Othello's gullibility is not really so very strange. Coal-black among the glittering Venetians, he is visibly the outsider, and in his bewilderment he naturally looks for the man who is visibly the insider, the man who knows the ropes, the sort of man who is always around in the bar, the "good chap" or (as they said then) the "honest" man. And he finds him.

There are two schools of thought on the sort of actor who should play Iago.
School A chooses a dark, waspish fellow. School B chooses a bluff, straw-haired, pink-faced sort of man, solid-looking with no nonsense about him. In production School B triumphs, for the role, cast in this way, becomes both credible and terrifying. Although Iago is everywhere spoken of as a "good chap," he has no friends, no loves, no positive desires. He, and not Othello, proves to be the true outsider of the play, for he is foreign to humanity itself. Othello comes from a remote clime, but Iago, in his simpler darkness, comes from the far side of chaos—hence the pathos of Shakespeare's best departure from his source. In Cinthio's *novella* the Ensign (that is, the Iago-figure) with a cunning affectation of reluctance, suggests that Desdemona is false and then seeing his chance, adds, "Your blackness already displeases her." In Shakespeare's play we have instead a note of bar-room masculine intimacy, in assumed complicity of sentiment. Iago says, in effect "Well, she went with black man, so what is one to think?" (III. iii. 228–233). Othello's need to be accepted and guided makes him an easy victim of this style. The hero is set for his sexual humiliation.

MAURICE CHARNEY

Shakespeare's Villains

from HOW TO READ SHAKESPEARE

The malevolence of Shakespeare's villains is difficult to account for either by their past history or by their present grievances. Shakespeare wants to avoid giving them a believable background that would justify or explain their evil. The villains are generally not motivated at all—at least not by detective-story standards—but are presented to us already securely entrenched in their moral condition. Their evil is a positive and active force, and its unquestioned energy makes the villains seem diabolic. We need to accept them as they appear without probing the origins of their conduct. This requires forbearance from the audience, whose love of scandalous explanation is deliberately frustrated.

What are we to make of the reasons Iago offers for his savage revenge on Othello? Is he acting from thwarted ambition, because Cassio has the promotion Iago thinks he himself deserves? Or are the reasons more subtle and more personal? As Iago tells us,

> I hate the Moor;
> And it is thought abroad that 'twixt my sheets
> 'Has done my office. I know not if't be true;
> Yet I, for mere suspicion in that kind,
> Will do as if for surety. (1.3.354–358)

There is a cynical coldness in "I know not if't be true," and Iago never troubles himself to find out. Personal honor means nothing to him, since in his view all women are whores and all human activity is base, coarse, gross, and disgusting. What is important is that Iago hates the Moor. That is enough, and reasons are alleged merely to satisfy public opinion.

In a much-quoted phrase, Coleridge spoke of this aspect of Iago's morality as the "motive-hunting of motiveless malignity." In other words, there are no motives and there is no cause that can account for Iago's evil. Othello never understands this, because even at the very end of the play he still wants to learn from that "demi-devil" "Why he hath thus ensnar'd my soul and body" (5.2.298). But Iago refuses any final comforts for Othello's tragic rationalism: "Demand me nothing. What you know, you know. / From this time forth I never will speak word" (299–300). Ultimately, there can be no answer to Othello's question. We have only a hint of explanation when Iago justifies the murder of Cassio: "He hath a daily beauty in his life/ That makes me ugly" (5.1.19–20). This judgment has the true satanic ring. Like Lucifer, Iago is irresistibly attracted to the beauty from which he has been excluded for all eternity, and this sense of damnation makes his revenge so monomaniacal.

Iago is Shakespeare's most brilliant villain, who dominates his play in a way no other villain can (except perhaps Macbeth, a villain-hero). He forces us to consider one of the most difficult paradoxes of tragedy: Why is the villain usually so much more intelligent, insightful, sensitive, and imaginative than his victim? The villain seems to be the surrogate for the diabolic-creative powers of the dramatist. Iago is wonderfully complex in his manipulation of the dramatic action; his plots and Shakespeare's seem to come together, so that one could speak of the stagecraft of villainy and its aesthetics. But in his moral nature Iago is wonderfully simple, if not actually simplified. The presence of both Iago and Desdemona in a single play assumes that good and evil exist as warring postulates. This is the morality play aspect of Shakespearean tragedy.

CHAPTER TWENTY-SEVEN

The Modern Realistic Theater: Ibsen in Context

READING IBSEN IN CONTEXT

Realism

Realism can be defined as the representation of everyday life in literature. Concerned with the average, the commonplace, the ordinary, realism employs theatrical conventions to create the illusion of everyday life. With realistic drama came the depiction of subjects close to the lives of middle-class people: work, marriage, and family life. From this standpoint, Arthur Miller's *Death of a Salesman* and Henrik Ibsen's *A Doll House* are more realistic than Shakespeare's *Othello,* which in turn is more realistic than Sophocles' *Oedipus Rex.* Although each of these plays possesses a true-to-life quality, each operates according to different theatrical conventions. Royal personages, gods, military heroes, and exalted language are absent from Miller's and Ibsen's plays, as modern dramatists turned to an approximation of the daily life of the lower and middle classes.

One means by which realistic drama creates the illusion of everyday life is through setting. Whereas settings consist primarily of painted backdrops in Molière's plays and are often established by dialogue in Shakespeare's plays, the settings of modern realistic plays are designed to look authentic. Moreover, setting in plays such as Ibsen's *A Doll House* often functions symbolically. In *Elements of Literature 3,* Robert Scholes has noted that the elaborately detailed setting of *A Doll House* symbolizes both "the impact of the Helmers' environment on their marriage" and the "very nature of their marriage"; it also embodies "the profound pressures placed on Helmer and Nora by the material and social conditions of their world."*

Other conventions designed to create and sustain the illusion that the audience was watching a slice of domestic life include the following: the use of a three-walled room with an open fourth wall into which the audience peers to view and overhear the action; dialogue that approximates the idiom of everyday discourse, polished to be sure, but designed especially to sound like speech rather than poetry; plots that, though highly contrived, seem to turn on a series of causally related actions; subjects not from mythology or history, but from the concerns of ordinary life.

A Note on the Theater of the Absurd

One of the most noteworthy developments in theater following the rise of realism was the emergence of the theater of the absurd in the second half of the twentieth century. *Absurdist drama* is nonrealistic, even antirealistic. Absurdist playwrights reject the conventions of realism, substituting well-contrived plots with storyless action; they replace believable characters of psychological complexity with barely recognizable figures; and for witty repartee and grand speeches they offer incoherent ramblings and disconnected dialogue.

Why such a theatrical about-face? Why such a rejection of realistic theatrical conventions? Primarily because ways of perceiving reality in the twentieth century had changed so radically that realistic dramatic conventions were considered to be inadequate to the task of representing reality as dramatists of the absurd envisioned it. Absurdist dramatists reject the implications that lie behind realistic conventions; they object, for example, to the idea that characters can be understood or that plot should be rationally ordered. For them, people are not understandable, and life is disorderly and chaotic. Absurdist writers attempt to dramatize these and other conceptions in plays that depict experience as meaningless and existence as purposeless; they portray human beings as irrational, pathetic figures, helpless against life's chaos. For the absurdist, humans are uprooted, cut off from their historical context, dispossessed of religious certainty, alienated from their social and physical environment, and unable to communicate with others.

Martin Esslin, a leading drama critic and expert on absurdist drama, has noted that the word *absurd* when used with reference to the theater of the absurd does not mean "ridiculous," but "out of harmony."‡ Modern individuals, according to the absurdist dramatists, are out of tune with nature, with other human beings, and with themselves. This sense of being at odds with life thwarts their hopes, deprives them of happiness, and robs their lives of meaning.

Esslin has also recognized that dramatists of the absurd, such as Samuel Beckett and Eugene Ionesco, have moved beyond arguing about the absurdity of the human condition to present that condition in concrete dramatic terms of the theater. When drama-

*Robert Scholes et al., *Elements of Literature 3* (New York: Oxford University Press, 1982), p. 966.

‡ Martin Esslin, *The Theatre of the Absurd* (New York: Doubleday, 1969).

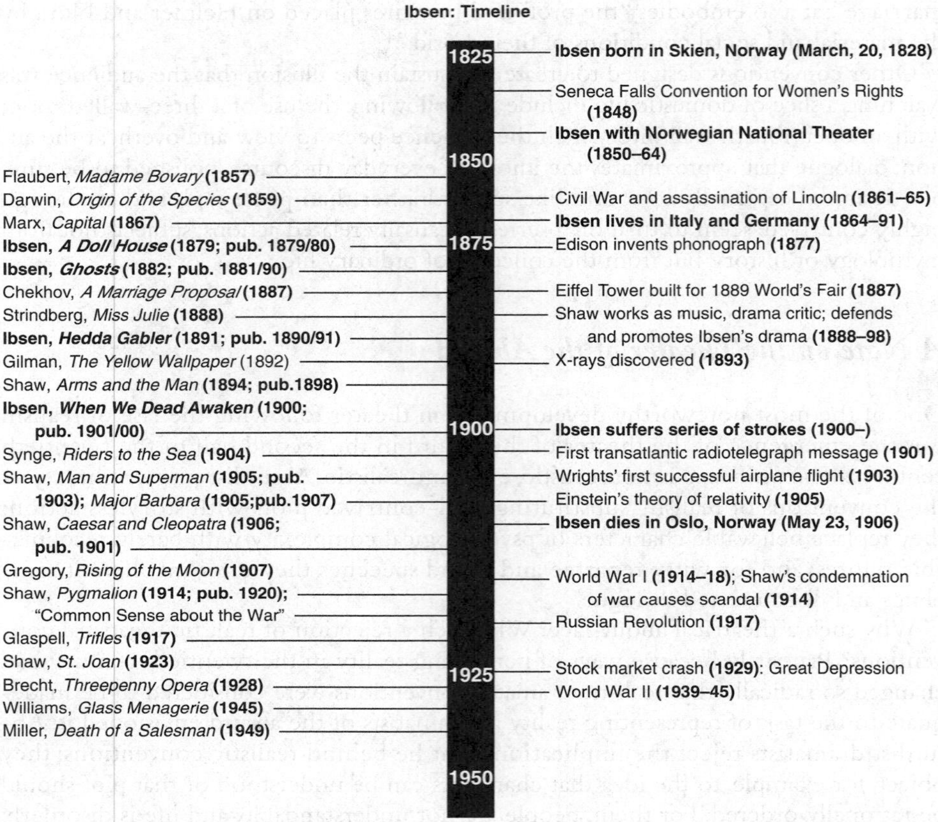

Ibsen: Timeline

1825 — 1850 — 1875 — 1900 — 1925 — 1950

Flaubert, *Madame Bovary* **(1857)**
Darwin, *Origin of the Species* **(1859)**
Marx, *Capital* (1867)
Ibsen, *A Doll House* (1879; pub. 1879/80)
Ibsen, *Ghosts* (1882; pub. 1881/90)
Chekhov, *A Marriage Proposal* **(1887)**
Strindberg, *Miss Julie* **(1888)**
Ibsen, *Hedda Gabler* (1891; pub. 1890/91)
Gilman, *The Yellow Wallpaper* (1892)
Shaw, *Arms and the Man* **(1894; pub.1898)**
Ibsen, *When We Dead Awaken* (1900; pub. 1901/00)
Synge, *Riders to the Sea* **(1904)**
Shaw, *Man and Superman* **(1905; pub. 1903)**; *Major Barbara* **(1905;pub.1907)**
Shaw, *Caesar and Cleopatra* **(1906; pub. 1901)**
Gregory, *Rising of the Moon* **(1907)**
Shaw, *Pygmalion* **(1914; pub. 1920)**; "Common Sense about the War"
Glaspell, *Trifles* **(1917)**
Shaw, *St. Joan* **(1923)**
Brecht, *Threepenny Opera* **(1928)**
Williams, *Glass Menagerie* **(1945)**
Miller, *Death of a Salesman* **(1949)**

Ibsen born in Skien, Norway (March, 20, 1828)
Seneca Falls Convention for Women's Rights **(1848)**
Ibsen with Norwegian National Theater (1850–64)
Civil War and assassination of Lincoln **(1861–65)**
Ibsen lives in Italy and Germany (1864–91)
Edison invents phonograph **(1877)**
Eiffel Tower built for 1889 World's Fair **(1887)**
Shaw works as music, drama critic; defends and promotes Ibsen's drama **(1888–98)**
X-rays discovered **(1893)**
Ibsen suffers series of strokes (1900–)
First transatlantic radiotelegraph message **(1901)**
Wrights' first successful airplane flight **(1903)**
Einstein's theory of relativity **(1905)**
Ibsen dies in Oslo, Norway (May 23, 1906)
World War I **(1914–18)**; Shaw's condemnation of war causes scandal **(1914)**
Russian Revolution **(1917)**
Stock market crash **(1929)**: Great Depression
World War II **(1939–45)**

tists of the absurd, thus, violate the rules of conventional drama, they do so because they see that strategy as the most effective way to illustrate the conditions of modern human experience as they understand them.

HENRIK IBSEN
[1828–1906]

IBSEN, EXILE, AND CHANGE

Henrik Ibsen once told a friend that for him to be understood, one had to understand the spectacular, severe northern Norwegian landscape, in which people in the nineteenth century were isolated and consequently inclined to an inward reflectiveness and even a brooding seriousness of temper. Ibsen came to associate his country with artistic exile, in which

Henri Ibsen at the Grand Café by Edvard Munch, 1898. Oil on canvas. A great admirer of Ibsen, Munch also designed stage sets

a writer was cut off from others by virtue of the divisions along the country's terrain, with people of different fjords speaking barely comprehensible, different dialects. The spirit of exile that Ibsen felt while living in Norway persisted until he left in his mid-thirties for a more literal form of exile. And though he wrote in Norwegian and returned to Norway as an acclaimed world dramatist, he was not really fully accepted and appreciated as a Norwegian writer. The tragic plays that would make him famous internationally were condemned by conservative critics at home, partly for their boldness of thought, partly for their revolt against received and conventional ideas. Ibsen was nothing if not a revolutionary thinker and artist, one who, through a determined and insistent realism, ushered in a new theatrical era.

Besides accommodating himself to the conventions of realism in *A Doll House,* Ibsen also made the play a *cause célèbre* by raising questions in it about the rights of women, a subject that was beginning to receive attention in the late nineteenth century. *A Doll House,* written in 1879, performed in London (1889) and Paris (1894), attracted attention wherever it played. Nonetheless, Ibsen insisted that the play was less about the rights of women than about human rights generally, less about the particular social conditions responsible for the position of women in nineteenth-century Norway than about the need for individuals of both sexes to treat each other with mutual respect.

A Doll House

TRANSLATED BY ROLF FJELDE

CHARACTERS

TORVALD HELMER, *a lawyer*
NORA, *his wife*
DR. RANK
MRS. LINDE
NILS KROGSTAD, *a bank clerk*
THE HELMERS' THREE SMALL CHILDREN
ANNE-MARIE, *their nurse*
HELENE, *a maid*
A DELIVERY BOY

The action takes place in HELMER'S *residence.*

Act I

A comfortable room, tastefully but not expensively furnished. A door to the right in the back wall leads to the entryway, another to the left leads to HELMER*'s study. Between these doors, a piano. Midway in the left-hand wall a door, and further back a window. Near the window a round table with an armchair and a small sofa. In the right-hand wall, toward the rear a door, and nearer the foreground a porcelain stove with two armchairs and a rocking chair beside it. Between the stove and the side door, a small table. Engravings on the walls. An etagére with china figures and other small art objects; a small bookcase with richly bound books; the floor carpeted; a fire burning in the stove. It is a winter day.*

A bell rings in the entryway; shortly after we hear the door being unlocked. NORA *comes into the room, humming happily to herself; she is wearing street clothes and carries an armload of packages, which she puts down on the table to the right. She has left the hall door open; and through it a* DELIVERY BOY *is seen, holding a Christmas tree and a basket which he gives to the* MAID *who let them in.*

NORA: Hide the tree well, Helene. The children mustn't get a glimpse of it till this evening, after it's trimmed. (*To the* DELIVERY BOY, *taking out her purse*) How much?

DELIVERY BOY: Fifty, ma'am.

NORA: There's a crown. No, keep the change. (*The* BOY *thanks her and leaves.* NORA *shuts the door. She laughs softly to herself while taking off her street things. Drawing a bag of macaroons from her pocket, she eats a couple, then steals over and listens at her husband's study door.*) Yes, he's home. (*Hums again as she moves to the table, right.*)

HELMER (*from the study*): Is that my little lark twittering out there?

NORA (*busy opening some packages*): Yes, it is.

HELMER: Is that my squirrel rummaging around?

NORA: Yes!

HELMER: When did my squirrel get in?

NORA: Just now. (*Putting the macaroon bag in her pocket and wiping her mouth*) Do come in, Torvald, and see what I've bought.

HELMER: Can't be disturbed. (*After a moment he opens the door and peers in, pen in hand.*) Bought, you say? All that there? Has the little spendthrift been out throwing money around again?

NORA: Oh, but Torvald, this year we really should let ourselves go a bit. It's the first Christmas we haven't had to economize.

HELMER: But you know we can't go squandering.

NORA: Oh yes, Torvald, we can squander a little now. Can't we? Just a tiny, wee bit. Now that you've got a big salary and are going to make piles and piles of money.

HELMER: Yes—starting New Year's. But then it's a full three months till the raise comes through.

NORA: Pooh! We can borrow that long.

HELMER: Nora! (*Goes over and playfully takes her by the ear*) Are your scatterbrains off again? What if today I borrowed a thousand crowns, and you squandered them over Christmas week, and then on New Year's Eve a roof tile fell on my head, and I lay there—

NORA (*putting her hand on his mouth*): Oh! Don't say such things!

HELMER: Yes, but what if it happened—then what?

NORA: If anything so awful happened, then it just wouldn't matter if I had debts or not.

HELMER: Well, but the people I'd borrowed from?

NORA: Them? Who cares about them! They're strangers.

HELMER: Nora, Nora, how like a woman! No, but seriously, Nora, you know what I think about that. No debts! Never borrow! Something of freedom's lost—and something of beauty, too—from a home that's founded on borrowing and debt. We've made a brave stand up to now, the two of us; and we'll go right on like that the little while we have to.

NORA (*going toward the stove*): Yes, whatever you say, Torvald.

HELMER (*following her*): Now, now, the little lark's wings mustn't droop. Come on, don't be a sulky squirrel. (*Taking out his wallet*) Nora, guess what I have here.

NORA (*turning quickly*): Money!

HELMER: There, see. (*Hands her some notes*) Good grief, I know how costs go up in a house at Christmastime.

NORA: Ten—twenty—thirty—forty. Oh, thank you. Torvald; I can manage no end on this.

HELMER: You really will have to.

NORA: Oh yes, I promise I will! But come here so I can show you everything I bought. And so cheap! Look, new clothes for Ivar here—and a sword. Here a horse and a trumpet for Bob. And a doll and a doll's bed here for Emmy; they're nothing much, but she'll tear them to bits in no time anyway. And here I have dress material and handkerchiefs for the maids. Old Anne-Marie really deserves something more.

HELMER: And what's in that package there?

NORA (*with a cry*): Torvald, no! You can't see that till tonight!

HELMER: I see. But tell me now, you little prodigal, what have you thought of for yourself?

NORA: For myself? Oh, I don't want anything at all.

HELMER: Of course you do. Tell me just what—within reason—you'd most like to have.

NORA: I honestly don't know. Oh, listen, Torvald—

HELMER: Well?

NORA (*fumbling at his coat buttons, without looking at him*): If you want to give me something, then maybe you could—you could—

HELMER: Come on, out with it.

NORA (*hurriedly*): You could give me money, Torvald. No more than you think you can spare, then one of these days I'll buy something with it.

HELMER: But Nora—

NORA: Oh, please, Torvald darling, do that! I beg you, please. Then I could hang the bills in pretty gilt paper on the Christmas tree. Wouldn't that be fun?

HELMER: What are those little birds called that always fly through their fortunes?

NORA: Oh yes, spendthrifts; I know all that. But let's do as I say, Torvald; then I'll have time to decide what I really need most. That's very sensible, isn't it?

HELMER (*smiling*): Yes, very—that is, if you actually hung onto the money I give you, and you actually used it to buy yourself something. But it goes for the house and for all sorts of foolish things, and then I only have to lay out some more.

NORA: Oh, but Torvald—

HELMER: Don't deny it, my dear little Nora. (*Putting his arm around her waist*) Spendthrifts are sweet, but they use up a frightful amount of money. It's incredible what it costs a man to feed such birds.

NORA: Oh, how can you say that! Really, I save everything I can.

HELMER (*laughing*): Yes, that's the truth. Everything you can. But that's nothing at all.

NORA (*humming, with a smile of quiet satisfaction*): Hm, if you only knew what expenses we larks and squirrels have, Torvald.

HELMER: You're an odd little one. Exactly the way your father was. You're never at a loss for scaring up money; but the moment you have it, it runs right out through your fingers; you never know what you've done with it. Well, one takes you as you are. It's deep in your blood. Yes, these things are hereditary, Nora.

NORA: Ah, I could wish I'd inherited many of Papa's qualities.

HELMER: And I couldn't wish you anything but just what you are, my sweet little lark. But wait; it seems to me you have a very—what should I call it?—a very suspicious look today—

NORA: I do?

HELMER: You certainly do. Look me straight in the eye.

NORA (*looking at him*): Well?

HELMER (*shaking an admonitory finger*): Surely my sweet tooth hasn't been running riot in town today, has she?

NORA: No. Why do you imagine that?

HELMER: My sweet tooth really didn't make a little detour through the confectioner's?

NORA: No, I assure you, Torvald—

HELMER: Hasn't nibbled some pastry?

NORA: No, not at all.

HELMER: Nor even munched a macaroon or two?

NORA: No, Torvald, I assure you, really—

HELMER: There, there now. Of course I'm only joking.

NORA (*going to the table, right*): You know I could never think of going against you.

HELMER: No, I understand that; and you *have* given me your word. (*Going over to her.*) Well, you keep your little Christmas secrets to yourself, Nora darling. I expect they'll come to light this evening, when the tree is lit.

NORA: Did you remember to ask Dr. Rank?

HELMER: No. But there's no need for that; it's assumed he'll be dining with us. All the same, I'll ask him when he stops by here this morning. I've ordered some fine wine. Nora, you can't imagine how I'm looking forward to this evening.

NORA: So am I. And what fun for the children, Torvald!

HELMER: Ah, it's so gratifying to know that one's gotten a safe, secure job, and with a comfortable salary. It's a great satisfaction, isn't it?

NORA: Oh, it's wonderful!

HELMER: Remember last Christmas? Three whole weeks before, you shut yourself in every evening till long after midnight, making flowers for the Christmas tree, and all the other decorations to surprise us. Ugh, that was the dullest time I've ever lived through.

NORA: It wasn't at all dull for me.

HELMER (*smiling*): But the outcome *was* pretty sorry, Nora.

NORA: Oh, don't tease me with that again. How could I help it that the cat came in and tore everything to shreds.

HELMER: No, poor thing, you certainly couldn't. You wanted so much to please us all, and that's what counts. But it's just as well that the hard times are past.

NORA: Yes, it's really wonderful.

HELMER: Now I don't have to sit here alone, boring myself, and you don't have to tire your precious eyes and your fair little delicate hands—

NORA (*clapping her hands*): No, is it really true, Torvald, I don't have to? Oh, how wonderfully lovely to hear! (*Taking his arm.*) Now I'll tell you just how I've thought we should plan things. Right after Christmas—(*The doorbell rings.*) Oh, the bell. (*Straightening the room up a bit.*) Somebody would have to come. What a bore!

HELMER: I'm not at home to visitors, don't forget.

MAID (*from the hall doorway*): Ma'am, a lady to see you—

NORA: All right, let her come in.

MAID (*to* HELMER): And the doctor's just come too.

HELMER: Did he go right to my study?

MAID: Yes, he did.

HELMER *goes into his room. The* MAID *shows in* MRS. LINDE, *dressed in traveling clothes, and shuts the door after her.*

MRS. LINDE (*in a dispirited and somewhat hesitant voice*): Hello, Nora.

NORA (*uncertain*): Hello—

MRS. LINDE: You don't recognize me.

NORA: No, I don't know—but wait, I think—(*Exclaiming.*) What! Kristine! Is it really you?

MRS. LINDE: Yes, it's me.

NORA: Kristine! To think I didn't recognize you. But then, how could I? (*More quietly.*) How you've changed, Kristine!

MRS. LINDE: Yes, no doubt I have. In nine—ten long years.

NORA: Is it so long since we met! Yes, it's all of that. Oh, these last eight years have been a happy time, believe me. And so now you've come in to town, too. Made the long trip in the winter. That took courage.

MRS. LINDE: I just got here by ship this morning.

NORA: To enjoy yourself over Christmas, of course. Oh, how lovely! Yes, enjoy ourselves, we'll do that. But take your coat off. You're not still cold? (*Helping her.*) There now, let's get cozy here by the stove. No, the easy chair there! I'll take the rocker here. (*Seizing her hands.*) Yes, now you have your old look again; it was only in that first moment. You're a bit more pale, Kristine—and maybe a bit thinner.

MRS. LINDE: And much, much older, Nora.

NORA: Yes, perhaps, a bit older; a tiny, tiny bit; not much at all. (*Stopping short; suddenly serious*) Oh, but thoughtless me, to sit here, chattering away. Sweet, good Kristine, can you forgive me?

MRS. LINDE: What do you mean, Nora?

NORA (*softly*): Poor Kristine, you've become a widow.

MRS. LINDE: Yes, three years ago.

NORA: Oh, I knew it, of course; I read it in the papers. Oh Kristine, you must believe me; I often thought of writing you then, but I kept postponing it, and something always interfered.

MRS. LINDE: Nora dear, I understand completely.

NORA: No, it was awful of me, Kristine. You poor thing, how much you must have gone through. And he left you nothing?

MRS. LINDE: No.

NORA: And no children?

MRS. LINDE: No.

NORA: Nothing at all, then?

MRS. LINDE: Not even a sense of loss to feed on.

NORA (*looking incredulously at her*): But Kristine, how could that be?

MRS. LINDE (*smiling wearily and smoothing her hair*): Oh, sometimes it happens, Nora.

NORA: So completely alone. How terribly hard that must be for you. I have three lovely children. You can't see them now; they're out with the maid. But now you must tell me everything—

MRS. LINDE: No, no, no, tell me about yourself.

NORA: No, you begin. Today I don't want to be selfish. I want to think only of you today. But there *is* something I must tell you. Did you hear of the wonderful luck we had recently?

MRS. LINDE: No, what's that?

NORA: My husband's been made manager in the bank, just think!

MRS. LINDE: Your husband? How marvelous!

NORA: Isn't it? Being a lawyer is such an uncertain living, you know, especially if one won't touch any cases that aren't clean and decent. And of course Torvald would never do that, and I'm with him completely there. Oh, we're simply delighted, believe me! He'll join the bank right after New Year's and start getting a huge salary and lots of commissions. From now on we can live quite differently—just as we want. Oh, Kristine, I feel so light and happy! Won't it be lovely to have stacks of money and not a care in the world?

MRS. LINDE: Well, anyway, it would be lovely to have enough for necessities.

NORA: No, not just for necessities, but stacks and stacks of money!

MRS. LINDE (*smiling*): Nora, Nora, aren't you sensible yet? Back in school you were such a free spender.

NORA (*with a quiet laugh*): Yes, that's what Torvald still says. (*Shaking her finger*) But "Nora, Nora" isn't as silly as you all think. Really, we've been in no position for me to go squandering. We've had to work, both of us.

MRS. LINDE: You too?

NORA: Yes, at odd jobs—needlework, crocheting, embroidery, and such—(*casually*) and other things too. You remember that Torvald left the department when we were married? There was no chance of promotion in his office, and of course he needed to earn more money. But that first year he drove himself terribly. He took on all kinds of extra work that kept him going morning and night. It wore him down, and then he fell deathly ill. The doctors said it was essential for him to travel south.

MRS. LINDE: Yes, didn't you spend a whole year in Italy?

NORA: That's right. It wasn't easy to get away, you know. Ivar had just been born. But of course we had to go. Oh, that was a beautiful trip, and it saved Torvald's life. But it cost a frightful sum, Kristine.

MRS. LINDE: I can well imagine.

NORA: Four thousand, eight hundred crowns it cost. That's really a lot of money.

MRS. LINDE: But it's lucky you had it when you needed it.

NORA: Well, as it was, we got it from Papa.

MRS. LINDE: I see. It was just about the time your father died.

NORA: Yes, just about then. And, you know, I couldn't make the trip out to nurse him. I had to stay here, expecting Ivar any moment, and with my poor sick Torvald to care for. Dearest Papa, I never saw him again, Kristine. Oh, that was the worst time I've known in all my marriage.

MRS. LINDE: I know how you loved him. And then you went off to Italy?

NORA: Yes. We had the means now, and the doctors urged us. So we left a month after.

MRS. LINDE: And your husband came back completely cured?

NORA: Sound as a drum!

MRS. LINDE: But—the doctor?

NORA: Who?

MRS. LINDE: I thought the maid said he was a doctor, the man who came in with me.

NORA: Yes, that was Dr. Rank—but he's not making a sick call. He's our closest friend, and he stops by at least once a day. No, Torvald hasn't had a sick moment since, and the children are fit and strong, and I am, too. (*Jumping up and clapping her hands*) Oh, dear God, Kristine, what a lovely thing to live and be happy! But how disgusting of me—I'm talking of nothing but my own affairs. (*Sits on a stool close by* KRISTINE, *arms resting across her knees*) Oh, don't be angry with me! Tell me, is it really true that you weren't in love with your husband? Why did you marry him, then?

MRS. LINDE: My mother was still alive, but bedridden and helpless—and I had two younger brothers to look after. In all conscience, I didn't think I could turn him down.

NORA: No, you were right there. But was he rich at the time?

MRS. LINDE: He was very well off, I'd say. But the business was shaky, Nora. When he died, it all fell apart, and nothing was left.

NORA: And then—?

MRS. LINDE: Yes, so I had to scrape up a living with a little shop and a little teaching and whatever else I could find. The last three years have been like one endless workday without a rest for me. Now it's over, Nora. My poor mother doesn't need me, for she's passed on. Nor the boys, either; they're working now and can take care of themselves.

NORA: How free you must feel—

MRS. LINDE: No—only unspeakably empty. Nothing to live for now. (*Standing up anxiously*) That's why I couldn't take it any longer out in that desolate hole. Maybe here it'll be easier to find something to do and keep my mind occupied. If I could only be lucky enough to get a steady job, some office work—

NORA: Oh, but Kristine, that's so dreadfully tiring, and you already look so tired. It would be much better for you if you could go off to a bathing resort.

MRS. LINDE (*going toward the window*): I have no father to give me travel money, Nora.

NORA (*rising*): Oh, don't be angry with me.

MRS. LINDE (*going to her*): Nora dear, don't you be angry with me. The worst of my kind of situation is all the bitterness that's stored away. No one to work for, and yet you're always having to snap up your opportunities. You have to live; and so you grow selfish. When you told me the happy change in your lot, do you know I was delighted less for your sakes than for mine?

NORA: How so? Oh, I see. You think maybe Torvald could do something for you.

MRS. LINDE: Yes, that's what I thought.

NORA: And he will, Kristine! Just leave it to me; I'll bring it up so delicately—find something attractive to humor him with. Oh, I'm so eager to help you.

MRS. LINDE: How very kind of you, Nora, to be so concerned over me—doubly kind, considering you really know so little of life's burdens yourself.

NORA: I—? I know so little—?

MRS. LINDE (*smiling*): Well, my heavens—a little needlework and such—Nora, you're just a child.

NORA: (*tossing her head and pacing the floor*): You don't have to act so superior.

MRS. LINDE: Oh?

NORA: You're just like the others. You all think I'm incapable of anything serious—

MRS. LINDE: Come now—

NORA: That I've never had to face the raw world.

MRS. LINDE: Nora dear, you've just been telling me all your troubles.

NORA: Hm! Trivia! (*Quietly*) I haven't told you the big thing.

MRS. LINDE: Big thing? What do you mean?

NORA: You look down on me so, Kristine, but you shouldn't. You're proud that you worked so long and hard for your mother.

MRS. LINDE: I don't look down on a soul. But it is true; I'm proud—and happy, too—to think it was given to me to make my mother's last days almost free of care.

NORA: And you're also proud thinking of what you've done for your brothers.

MRS. LINDE: I feel I've a right to be.

NORA: I agree. But listen to this, Kristine—I've also got something to be proud and happy for.

MRS. LINDE: I don't doubt it. But whatever do you mean?

NORA: Not so loud. What if Torvald heard! He mustn't, not for anything in the world. Nobody must know, Kristine. No one but you.

MRS. LINDE: But what is it, then?

NORA: Come here. (*Drawing her down beside her on the sofa*) It's true—I've also got something to be proud and happy for. I'm the one who saved Torvald's life.

MRS. LINDE: Saved—? Saved how?

NORA: I told you about the trip to Italy. Torvald never would have lived if he hadn't gone south—

MRS. LINDE: Of course, your father gave you the means—

NORA (*smiling*): That's what Torvald and all the rest think, but—

MRS. LINDE: But—?

NORA: Papa didn't give us a pin. I was the one who raised the money.

MRS. LINDE: You? The whole amount?

NORA: Four thousand, eight hundred crowns. What do you say to that?

MRS. LINDE: But Nora, how was it possible? Did you win the lottery?

NORA (*disdainfully*): The lottery? Pooh! No art to that.

MRS. LINDE: But where did you get it from then?

NORA (*humming, with a mysterious smile*): Hmm, tra-la-la-la.

MRS. LINDE: Because you couldn't have borrowed it.

NORA: No? Why not?

MRS. LINDE: A wife can't borrow without her husband's consent.

NORA (*tossing her head*): Oh, but a wife with a little business sense, a wife who knows how to manage—

MRS. LINDE: Nora, I simply don't understand—

NORA: You don't have to. Whoever said I *borrowed* the money? I could have gotten it other ways. (*Throwing herself back on the sofa*) I could have gotten it from some admirer or other. After all, a girl with my ravishing appeal—

MRS. LINDE: You lunatic.

NORA: I'll bet you're eaten up with curiosity, Kristine.

MRS. LINDE: Now listen here, Nora—you haven't done something indiscreet?

NORA (*sitting up again*): Is it indiscreet to save your husband's life?

MRS. LINDE: I think it's indiscreet that without his knowledge you—

NORA: But that's the point: he mustn't know! My Lord, can't you understand? He mustn't ever know the close call he had. It was to *me* the doctors came to say his life was in danger—that nothing could save him but a stay in the south. Didn't I try strategy then! I began talking about how lovely it would be for me to travel abroad like other young wives; I begged and I cried; I told him please to remember my condition, to be kind and indulge me; and then I dropped a hint that he could easily take out a loan. But at that, Kristine, he nearly exploded. He said I was frivolous, and it was his duty as man of the house not to indulge me in whims and fancies—as I think he called them. Aha, I thought, now you'll just have to be saved—and that's when I saw my chance.

MRS. LINDE: And your father never told Torvald the money wasn't from him?

NORA: No, never. Papa died right about then. I'd considered bringing him into my secret and begging him never to tell. But he was too sick at the time—and then, sadly, it didn't matter.

MRS. LINDE: And you've never confided in your husband since?

NORA: For heaven's sake, no! Are you serious? He's so strict on that subject. Besides—Torvald, with all his masculine pride—how painfully humiliating for him if he ever found out he was in debt to me. That would just ruin our relationship. Our beautiful happy home would never be the same.

MRS. LINDE: Won't you ever tell him?

NORA (*thoughtfully, half smiling*): Yes—maybe sometime, years from now, when I'm no longer so attractive. Don't laugh! I only mean when Torvald loves me less than now, when he stops enjoying my dancing and dressing up and reciting for him. Then it might be wise to have something in reserve—(*Breaking off*) How ridiculous! That'll never happen—Well, Kristine, what do you think of my big secret? I'm capable of something too, hm? You can imagine, of course, how this thing hangs over me. It really hasn't been easy meeting the payments on time. In the business world there's what they call quarterly interest and what they call amortization, and these are always so terribly hard to manage. I've had to skimp a little here and there, wherever I could, you know. I could hardly spare anything from my house allowance, because Torvald has to live well. I couldn't let the children go poorly dressed; whatever I got for them, I felt I had to use up completely—the darlings!

MRS. LINDE: Poor Nora, so it had to come out of your own budget, then?

NORA: Yes, of course. But I was the one most responsible, too. Every time Torvald gave me money for new clothes and such, I never used more than half; always bought the simplest, cheapest outfits. It was a godsend that everything looks so well on me that Torvald never noticed. But it did weigh me down at times, Kristine. It *is* such a joy to wear fine things. You understand.

MRS. LINDE: Oh, of course.

NORA: And then I found other ways of making money. Last winter I was lucky enough to get a lot of copying to do. I locked myself in and sat writing every evening till late in the night. Ah, I was tired so often, dead tired. But still it was wonderful fun, sitting and working like that, earning money. It was almost like being a man.

MRS. LINDE: But how much have you paid off this way so far?

NORA: That's hard to say, exactly. These accounts, you know, aren't easy to figure. I only know that I've paid out all I could scrape together. Time and again I haven't known where to turn. (*Smiling*) Then I'd sit here dreaming of a rich old gentleman who had fallen in love with me—

MRS. LINDE: What! Who is he?

NORA: Oh, really! And that he'd died, and when his will was opened, there in big letters it said, "All my fortune shall be paid over in cash, immediately, to that enchanting Mrs. Nora Helmer."

MRS. LINDE: But Nora dear—who *was* this gentleman?

NORA: Good grief, can't you understand? The old man never existed; that was only something I'd dream up time and again whenever I was at my wits' end for money. But it makes no difference now; the old fossil can go where he pleases for all I care; I don't need him or his will—because now I'm free. (*Jumping up*) Oh, how lovely to think of that, Kristine! Carefree! To know you're carefree, utterly carefree, to be able to romp and play with the children, and to keep up a beautiful, charming home—everything just the way Torvald likes it! And think, spring is coming, with big blue skies. Maybe we can travel a little then. Maybe I'll see the ocean again. Oh yes, it *is* so marvelous to live and be happy!

(*The front doorbell rings.*)

MRS. LINDE (*rising*): There's the bell. It's probably best that I go.

NORA: No, stay. No one's expected. It must be for Torvald.

MAID (*from the hall doorway*): Excuse me, ma'am—there's a gentleman here to see Mr. Helmer, but I didn't know—since the doctor's with him—

NORA: Who is the gentleman?

KROGSTAD (*from the doorway*): It's me, Mrs. Helmer.

(MRS. LINDE *starts and turns away toward the window.*)

NORA (*stepping toward him, tense, her voice a whisper*): You? What is it? Why do you want to speak to my husband?

KROGSTAD: Bank business—after a fashion. I have a small job in the investment bank, and I hear now your husband is going to be our chief—

NORA: In other words, it's—

KROGSTAD: Just dry business, Mrs. Helmer. Nothing but that.

NORA: Yes, then please be good enough to step into the study. (*She nods indifferently, as she sees him out by the hall door, then returns and begins stirring up the stove.*)

MRS. LINDE: Nora—who was that man?

NORA: That was a Mr. Krogstad—a lawyer.

MRS. LINDE: Then it really was him.

NORA: Do you know that person?

MRS. LINDE: I did once—many years ago. For a time he was a law clerk in our town.

NORA: Yes, he's been that.

MRS. LINDE: How he's changed.

NORA: I understand he had a very unhappy marriage.

MRS. LINDE: He's a widower now.

NORA: With a number of children. There now, it's burning. (*She closes the stove door and moves the rocker a bit to one side.*)

MRS. LINDE: They say he has a hand in all kinds of business.

NORA: Oh? That may be true; I wouldn't know. But let's not think about business. It's so dull.

(DR. RANK *enters from* HELMER*'s study.*)

RANK (*still in the doorway*): No, no, really—I don't want to intrude, I'd just as soon talk a little while with your wife. (*Shuts the door, then notices* MRS. LINDE) Oh, beg pardon, I'm intruding here too.

NORA: No, not at all. (*Introducing him*) Dr. Rank, Mrs. Linde.

RANK: Well now, that's a name much heard in this house. I believe I passed the lady on the stairs as I came.

MRS. LINDE: Yes, I take the stairs very slowly. They're rather hard on me.

RANK: Uh-hm, some touch of internal weakness?

MRS. LINDE: More overexertion, I'd say.

RANK: Nothing else? Then you're probably here in town to rest up in a round of parties?

MRS. LINDE: I'm here to look for work.

RANK: Is that the best cure for overexertion?

MRS. LINDE: One has to live, Doctor.

RANK: Yes, there's a common prejudice to that effect.

NORA: Oh, come on, Dr. Rank—you really do want to live yourself.

RANK: Yes, I really do. Wretched as I am, I'll gladly prolong my torment indefinitely. All my patients feel like that. And it's quite the same, too, with the morally sick. Right at this moment there's one of those moral invalids in there with Helmer—

MRS. LINDE (*softly*): Ah!

NORA: Who do you mean?

RANK: Oh, it's a lawyer, Krogstad, a type you wouldn't know. His character is rotten to the root—but even he began chattering all-importantly about how he had to *live.*

NORA: Oh? What did he want to talk to Torvald about?

RANK: I really don't know. I only heard something about the bank.

NORA: I didn't know that Krog—that this man Krogstad had anything to do with the bank.

RANK: Yes, he's gotten some kind of berth down there. (*To* MRS. LINDE) I don't know if you also have, in your neck of the woods, a type of person who scuttles about breathlessly, sniffing out hints of moral corruption, and then maneuvers his victim into some sort of key position where he can keep an eye on him. It's the healthy these days that are out in the cold.

MRS. LINDE: All the same, it's the sick who most need to be taken in.

RANK (*with a shrug*): Yes, there we have it. That's the concept that's turning society into a sanatorium.

(NORA, *lost in her thoughts, breaks out into quiet laughter and claps her hands.*)

RANK: Why do you laugh at that? Do you have any real idea of what society is?

NORA: What do I care about dreary old society? I was laughing at something quite different—something terribly funny. Tell me, Doctor—is everyone who works in the bank dependent now on Torvald?

RANK: Is that what you find so terribly funny?

NORA (*smiling and humming*): Never mind, never mind! (*Pacing the floor*) Yes, that's really immensely amusing: that we—that Torvald has so much power now over all those people. (*Taking the bag out of her pocket*) Dr. Rank, a little macaroon on that?

RANK: See here, macaroons! I thought they were contraband here.

NORA: Yes, but these are some that Kristine gave me.

MRS. LINDE: What? I—?

NORA: Now, now, don't be afraid. You couldn't possibly know that Torvald had forbidden them. You see, he's worried they'll ruin my teeth. But hmp! Just this once! Isn't that so, Dr. Rank? Help yourself! (*Puts a macaroon in his mouth*) And you too, Kristine. And I'll also have one, only a little one—or two, at the most. (*Walking about again*) Now I'm really tremendously happy. Now there's just one last thing in the world that I have an enormous desire to do.

RANK: Well! And what's that?

NORA: It's something I have such a consuming desire to say so Torvald could hear.

RANK: And why can't you say it?

NORA: I don't dare. It's quite shocking.

MRS. LINDE: Shocking?

RANK: Well, then it isn't advisable. But in front of us you certainly can. What do you have such a desire to say so Torvald could hear?

NORA: I have such a huge desire to say—to hell and be damned!

RANK: Are you crazy?

MRS. LINDE: My goodness, Nora!

RANK: Go on, say it. Here he is.

NORA (*hiding the macaroon bag*): Shh, shh, shh!

(HELMER *comes in from his study, hat in hand, overcoat over his arm.*)

NORA (*going toward him*): Well, Torvald dear, are you through with him?

HELMER: Yes, he just left.

NORA: Let me introduce you—this is Kristine, who's arrived here in town.

HELMER: Kristine—? I'm sorry, but I don't know—

NORA: Mrs. Linde, Torvald dear. Mrs. Kristine Linde.

HELMER: Of course. A childhood friend of my wife's, no doubt?

MRS. LINDE: Yes, we knew each other in those days.

NORA: And just think, she made the long trip down here in order to talk with you.

HELMER: What's this?

MRS. LINDE: Well, not exactly—

NORA: You see, Kristine is remarkably clever in office work, and so she's terribly eager to come under a capable man's supervision and add more to what she already knows—

HELMER: Very wise, Mrs. Linde.

NORA: And then when she heard that you'd become a bank manager—the story was wired out to the papers—then she came in as fast as she could and—Really, Torvald, for my sake you can do a little something for Kristine, can't you?

HELMER: Yes, it's not at all impossible. Mrs. Linde, I suppose you're a widow?

MRS. LINDE: Yes.

HELMER: Any experience in office work?

MRS. LINDE: Yes, a good deal.

HELMER: Well, it's quite likely that I can make an opening for you—

NORA (*clapping her hands*): You see, you see!

HELMER: You've come at a lucky moment, Mrs. Linde.

MRS. LINDE: Oh, how can I thank you?

HELMER: Not necessary. (*Putting his overcoat on*) But today you'll have to excuse me—

RANK: Wait, I'll go with you. (*He fetches his coat from the hall and warms it at the stove.*)

NORA: Don't stay out long, dear.

HELMER: An hour; no more.

NORA: Are you going too, Kristine?

MRS. LINDE (*putting on her winter garments*): Yes, I have to see about a room now.

HELMER: Then perhaps we can all walk together.

NORA (*helping her*): What a shame we're so cramped here, but it's quite impossible for us to—

MRS. LINDE: Oh, don't even think of it! Good-bye, Nora dear, and thanks for everything.

NORA: Good-bye for now. Of course you'll be back again this evening. And you too, Dr. Rank. What? If you're well enough? Oh, you've got to be! Wrap up tight now.

(*In a ripple of small talk the company moves out into the hall; children's voices are heard outside on the steps.*)

NORA: There they are! There they are! (*She runs to open the door. The children come in with their nurse,* ANNE-MARIE.) Come in, come in! (Bends down and kisses them) Oh, you darlings—! Look at them, Kristine. Aren't they lovely!

RANK: No loitering in the draft here.

HELMER: Come, Mrs. Linde—this place is unbearable now for anyone but mothers.

(DR. RANK, HELMER, *and* MRS. LINDE *go down the stairs.* ANNE-MARIE *goes into the living room with the children.* NORA *follows, after closing the hall door.*)

NORA: How fresh and strong you look. Oh, such red cheeks you have! Like apples and roses. (*The children interrupt her throughout the following.*) And it was so much fun? That's wonderful. Really? You pulled both Emmy and Bob on the sled? Imagine, all together! Yes, you're a clever boy, Ivar. Oh, let me hold her a bit, Anne-Marie. My sweet little doll baby! (*Takes the smallest from the nurse and dances with her*) Yes, yes, Mama will dance with Bob as well. What? Did you throw snowballs? Oh, if I'd only been there! No, don't bother, Anne-Marie—I'll undress them myself. Oh yes, let me.

It's such fun. Go in and rest; you look half frozen. There's hot coffee waiting for you on the stove. (*The nurse goes into the room to the left.* NORA *takes the children's winter things off, throwing them about, while the children talk to her all at once.*) Is that so? A big dog chased you? But it didn't bite? No, dogs never bite little, lovely doll babies. Don't peek in the packages, Ivar! What is it? Yes, wouldn't you like to know. No, no, it's an ugly something. Well? Shall we play? What shall we play? Hide-and-seek? Yes, let's play hide-and-seek. Bob must hide first. I must? Yes, let me hide first. (*Laughing and shouting, she and the children play in and out of the living room and the adjoining room to the right. At last* NORA *hides under the table. The children come storming in, search, but cannot find her, then hear her muffled laughter, dash over to the table, lift the cloth and find her. Wild shouting. She creeps forward as if to scare them. More shouts. Meanwhile, a knock at the hall door; no one has noticed it. Now the door half opens, and* KROGSTAD *appears. He waits a moment; the game goes on.*)

KROGSTAD: Beg pardon, Mrs. Helmer—

NORA (*with a strangled cry, turning and scrambling to her knees*): Oh! what do you want?

KROGSTAD: Excuse me. The outer door was ajar; it must be someone forgot to shut it—

NORA (*rising*): My husband isn't home, Mr. Krogstad.

KROGSTAD: I know that.

NORA: Yes—then what do you want here?

KROGSTAD: A word with you.

NORA: With—? (*To the children, quietly*) Go in to Anne-Marie. What? No, the strange man won't hurt Mama. When he's gone, we'll play some more. (*She leads the children into the room to the left and shuts the door after them. Then, tense and nervous*) You want to speak to me?

KROGSTAD: Yes, I want to.

NORA: Today? But it's not yet the first of the month—

KROGSTAD: No, it's Christmas Eve. It's going to be up to you how merry a Christmas you have.

NORA: What is it you want? Today I absolutely can't—

KROGSTAD: We won't talk about that till later. This is something else. You do have a moment to spare, I suppose?

NORA: Oh yes, of course—I do, except—

KROGSTAD: Good. I was sitting over at Olsen's Restaurant when I saw your husband go down the street—

NORA: Yes?

KROGSTAD: With a lady.

NORA: Yes. So?

KROGSTAD: If you'll pardon my asking: wasn't that lady a Mrs. Linde?

NORA: Yes.

KROGSTAD: Just now come into town?

NORA: Yes, today.

KROGSTAD: She's a good friend of yours?

NORA: Yes, she is. But I don't see—

KROGSTAD: I also knew her once.

NORA: I'm aware of that.

KROGSTAD: Oh? You know all about it. I thought so. Well, then let me ask you short and sweet: is Mrs. Linde getting a job in the bank?

NORA: What makes you think you can cross-examine me, Mr. Krogstad—you, one of my husband's employees? But since you ask, you might as well know—yes, Mrs. Linde's going to be taken on at the bank. And I'm the one who spoke for her, Mr. Krogstad. Now you know.

KROGSTAD: So I guessed right.

NORA (*pacing up and down*): Oh, one does have a tiny bit of influence, I should hope. Just because I am a woman, don't think it means that—When one has a subordinate position, Mr. Krogstad, one really ought to be careful about pushing somebody who—hm—

KROGSTAD: Who has influence?

NORA: That's right.

KROGSTAD (*in a different tone*): Mrs. Helmer, would you be good enough to use your influence on my behalf?

NORA: What? What do you mean?

KROGSTAD: Would you please make sure that I keep my subordinate position in the bank?

NORA: What does that mean? Who's thinking of taking away your position?

KROGSTAD: Oh, don't play the innocent with me. I'm quite aware that your friend would hardly relish the chance of running into me again; and I'm also aware now whom I can thank for being turned out.

NORA: But I promise you—

KROGSTAD: Yes, yes, yes, to the point: there's still time, and I'm advising you to use your influence to prevent it.

NORA: But Mr. Krogstad, I have absolutely no influence.

KROGSTAD: You haven't? I thought you were just saying—

NORA: You shouldn't take me so literally. I! How can you believe that I have any such influence over my husband?

KROGSTAD: Oh, I've known your husband from our student days. I don't think the great bank manager's more steadfast than any other married man.

NORA: You speak insolently about my husband, and I'll show you the door.

KROGSTAD: The lady has spirit.

NORA: I'm not afraid of you any longer. After New Year's, I'll soon be done with the whole business.

KROGSTAD (*restraining himself*): Now listen to me, Mrs. Helmer. If necessary, I'll fight for my little job in the bank as if it were life itself.

NORA: Yes, so it seems.

KROGSTAD: It's not just a matter of income; that's the least of it. It's something else—All right, out with it! Look, this is the thing. You know, just like all the others, of course, that once, a good many years ago, I did something rather rash.

NORA: I've heard rumors to that effect.

KROGSTAD: The case never got into court; but all the same, every door was closed in my face from then on. So I took up those various activities you know about. I had to grab hold somewhere; and I dare say I haven't been among the worst. But now I want to drop all that. My boys are growing up. For their sakes, I'll have to win back as much respect as possible here in town. That job in the bank was like the first rung in my ladder. And now your husband wants to kick me right back down in the mud again.

NORA: But for heaven's sake, Mr. Krogstad, it's simply not in my power to help you.

KROGSTAD: That's because you haven't the will to—but I have the means to make you.

NORA: You certainly won't tell my husband that I owe you money?

KROGSTAD: Hm—what if I told him that?

NORA: That would be shameful of you. (*Nearly in tears*) This secret—my joy and my pride—that he should learn it in such a crude and disgusting way—learn it from you. You'd expose me to the most horrible unpleasantness—

KROGSTAD: Only unpleasantness?

NORA (*vehemently*): But go on and try. It'll turn out the worst for you, because then my husband will really see what a crook you are, and then you'll *never* be able to hold your job.

KROGSTAD: I asked if it was just domestic unpleasantness you were afraid of?

NORA: If my husband finds out, then of course he'll pay what I owe at once, and then we'd be through with you for good.

KROGSTAD (*a step closer*): Listen, Mrs. Helmer—you've either got a very bad memory, or else no head at all for business. I'd better put you a little more in touch with the facts.

NORA: What do you mean?

KROGSTAD: When your husband was sick, you came to me for a loan of four thousand, eight hundred crowns.

NORA: Where else could I go?

KROGSTAD: I promised to get you that sum—

NORA: And you got it.

KROGSTAD: I promised to get you that sum, on certain conditions. You were so involved in your husband's illness, and so eager to finance your trip, that I guess you didn't think out all the details. It might just be a good idea to remind you. I promised you the money on the strength of a note I drew up.

NORA: Yes, and that I signed.

KROGSTAD: Right. But at the bottom I added some lines for your father to guarantee the loan. He was supposed to sign down there.

NORA: Supposed to? He did sign.

KROGSTAD: I left the date blank. In other words, your father would have dated his signature himself. Do you remember that?

NORA: Yes, I think—

KROGSTAD: Then I gave you the note for you to mail to your father. Isn't that so?

NORA: Yes.

KROGSTAD: And naturally you sent it at once—because only some five, six days later you brought me the note, properly signed. And with that, the money was yours.

NORA: Well, then; I've made my payments regularly, haven't I?

KROGSTAD: More or less. But—getting back to the point—those were hard times for you then, Mrs. Helmer.

NORA: Yes, they were.

KROGSTAD: Your father was very ill, I believe.

NORA: He was near the end.

KROGSTAD: He died soon after?

NORA: Yes.

KROGSTAD: Tell me, Mrs. Helmer, do you happen to recall the date of your father's death? The day of the month, I mean.

NORA: Papa died the twenty-ninth of September.

KROGSTAD: That's quite correct; I've already looked into that. And now we come to a curious thing—(*Taking out a paper*) which I simply cannot comprehend.

NORA: Curious thing? I don't know—

KROGSTAD: This is the curious thing: that your father co-signed the note for your loan three days after his death.

NORA: How—? I don't understand.

KROGSTAD: Your father died the twenty-ninth of September. But look. Here your father dated his signature October second. Isn't that curious, Mrs. Helmer? (NORA *is silent.*) Can you explain it to me? (NORA *remains silent.*) It's also remarkable that the words "October second" and the year aren't written in your father's hand, but rather in one that I think I know. Well, it's easy to understand. Your father forgot perhaps to date his signature, and then someone or other added it, a bit sloppily, before anyone knew of his death. There's nothing wrong in that. It all comes down to the signature. And there's no question about *that,* Mrs. Helmer. It really *was* your father who signed his own name here, wasn't it?

NORA (*after a short silence, throwing her head back and looking squarely at him*): No, it wasn't. I signed Papa's name.

KROGSTAD: Wait, now—are you fully aware that this is a dangerous confession?

NORA: Why? You'll soon get your money.

KROGSTAD: Let me ask you a question—why didn't you send the paper to your father?

NORA: That was impossible. Papa was so sick. If I'd asked him for his signature, I also would have had to tell him what the money was for. But I couldn't tell him, sick as he was, that my husband's life was in danger. That was just impossible.

KROGSTAD: Then it would have been better if you'd given up the trip abroad.

NORA: I couldn't possibly. The trip was to save my husband's life. I couldn't give that up.

KROGSTAD: But didn't you ever consider that this was a fraud against me?

NORA: I couldn't let myself be bothered by that. You weren't any concern of mine. I couldn't stand you, with all those cold complications you made, even though you knew how badly off my husband was.

KROGSTAD: Mrs. Helmer, obviously you haven't the vaguest idea of what you've involved yourself in. But I can tell you this: it was nothing more and nothing worse than I once did—and it wrecked my whole reputation.

NORA: You? Do you expect me to believe that you ever acted bravely to save your wife's life?

KROGSTAD: Laws don't inquire into motives.

NORA: Then they must be very poor laws.

KROGSTAD: Poor or not—if I introduce this paper in court, you'll be judged according to law.

NORA: This I refuse to believe. A daughter hasn't a right to protect her dying father from anxiety and care? A wife hasn't a right to save her husband's life? I don't know much about laws, but I'm sure that somewhere in the books these things are allowed. And you don't know anything about it—you who practice the law? You must be an awful lawyer, Mr. Krogstad.

KROGSTAD: Could be. But business—the kind of business we two are mixed up in—don't you think I know about that? All right. Do what you want now. But I'm telling you *this:* if I get shoved down a second time, you're going to keep me company.

(*He bows and goes out through the hall.*)

NORA (*pensive for a moment, then tossing her head*): Oh, really! Trying to frighten me! I'm not so silly as all that. (*Begins gathering up the children's clothes, but soon stops*) But—? No, but that's impossible! I did it out of love.

THE CHILDREN (*in the doorway, left*): Mama, that strange man's gone out the door.

NORA: Yes, yes, I know it. But don't tell anyone about the strange man. Do you hear. Not even Papa!

THE CHILDREN: No, Mama. But now will you play again?

NORA: No, not now.

THE CHILDREN: Oh, but Mama, you promised.

NORA: Yes, but I can't now. Go inside; I have too much to do. Go in, go in, my sweet darlings. (*She herds them gently back in the room and shuts the door after them. Settling on the sofa, she takes up a piece of embroidery and makes some stitches, but soon stops abruptly.*) No! (*Throws the work aside, rises, goes to the hall door and calls out*) Helene! Let me have the tree in here. (*Goes to the table, left, opens the table drawer, and stops again*) No, but that's utterly impossible!

MAID (*with the Christmas tree*): Where should I put it, Ma'am?

NORA: There. The middle of the floor.

MAID: Should I bring anything else?

NORA: No, thanks. I have what I need.

(*The* MAID, *who has set the tree down, goes out.*)

NORA (*absorbed in trimming the tree*): Candles here—and flowers here. That terrible creature! Talk, talk, talk! There's nothing to it at all. The tree's going to be lovely. I'll do anything to please you, Torvald. I'll sing for you, dance for you—

(HELMER *comes in from the hall, with a sheaf of papers under his arm.*)

NORA: Oh! You're back so soon?

HELMER: Yes. Has anyone been here?

NORA: Here? No.

HELMER: That's odd. I saw Krogstad leaving the front door.

NORA: So? Oh yes, that's true. Krogstad was here a moment.

HELMER: Nora, I can see by your face that he's been here, begging you to put in a good word for him.

NORA: Yes.

HELMER: And it was supposed to seem like your own idea? You were to hide it from me that he'd been here. He asked you that, too, didn't he?

NORA: Yes, Torvald, but—

HELMER: Nora, Nora, and you could fall for that? Talk with that sort of person and promise him anything? And then in the bargain, tell me an untruth.

NORA: An untruth—?

HELMER: Didn't you say that no one had been here? (*Wagging his finger*) My little songbird must never do that again. A songbird needs a clean beak to warble with. No false notes. (*Putting his arm about her waist*) That's the way it should be, isn't it? Yes, I'm sure of it. (*Releasing her*) And so, enough of that. (*Sitting by the stove*) Ah, how snug and cozy it is here. (*Leafing among his papers*)

NORA (*busy with the tree, after a short pause*): Torvald!

HELMER: Yes.

NORA: I'm so much looking forward to the Stenborgs' costume party, day after tomorrow.

HELMER: And I can't wait to see what you'll surprise me with.

NORA: Oh, that stupid business.

HELMER: What?

NORA: I can't find anything that's right. Everything seems so ridiculous, so inane.

HELMER: So my little Nora's come to *that* recognition?

NORA (*going behind his chair, her arms resting on its back*): Are you very busy, Torvald?

HELMER: Oh—

NORA: What papers are those?

HELMER: Bank matters.

NORA: Already?

HELMER: I've gotten full authority from the retiring management to make all necessary changes in personnel and procedure. I'll need Christmas week for that. I want to have everything in order by New Year's.

NORA: So that was the reason this poor Krogstad—

HELMER: Hm.

NORA (*still leaning on the chair and slowly stroking the nape of his neck*): If you weren't so very busy, I would have asked you an enormous favor, Torvald.

HELMER: Let's hear. What is it?

NORA: You know, there isn't anyone who has your good taste—and I want so much to look well at the costume party. Torvald, couldn't you take over and decide what I should be and plan my costume?

HELMER: Ah, is my stubborn little creature calling for a lifeguard?

NORA: Yes, Torvald, I can't get anywhere without your help.

HELMER: All right—I'll think it over. We'll hit on something.

NORA: Oh, how sweet of you. (*Goes to the tree again. Pause.*) Aren't the red flowers pretty—? But tell me, was it really such a crime that this Krogstad committed?

HELMER: Forgery. Do you have any idea what that means?

NORA: Couldn't he have done it out of need?

HELMER: Yes, or thoughtlessness, like so many others. I'm not so heartless that I'd condemn a man categorically for just one mistake.

NORA: No, of course not, Torvald!

HELMER: Plenty of men have redeemed themselves by openly confessing their crimes and taking their punishments.

NORA: Punishment—?

HELMER: But now Krogstad didn't go that way. He got himself out by sharp practices, and that's the real cause of his moral breakdown.

NORA: Do you really think that would—?

HELMER: Just imagine how a man with that sort of guilt in him has to lie and cheat and deceive on all sides, has to wear a mask even with the nearest and dearest he has, even with his own wife and children. And with the children, Nora—that's where it's most horrible.

NORA: Why?

HELMER: Because that kind of atmosphere of lies infects the whole life of a home. Every breath the children take in is filled with the terms of something degenerate.

NORA (*coming closer behind him*): Are you sure of that?

HELMER: Oh, I've seen it often enough as a lawyer. Almost everyone who goes bad early in life has a mother who's a chronic liar.

NORA: Why just—the mother?

HELMER: It's usually the mother's influence that's dominant, but the father's works in the same way, of course. Every lawyer is quite familiar with it. And still this Krogstad's been going home year in, year out, poisoning his own children with lies and pretense; that's why I call him morally lost. (*Reaching his hands out toward her*) So my sweet little Nora must promise me never to plead his cause. Your hand on it. Come, come, what's this? Give me your hand. There, now. All settled. I can tell you it'd be impossible for me to work alongside of him. I literally feel physically revolted when I'm anywhere near such a person.

NORA (*withdraws her hand and goes to the other side of the Christmas tree*): How hot it is here! And I've got so much to do.

HELMER (*getting up and gathering his papers*): Yes, and I have to think about getting some of these read through before dinner. I'll think about your costume, too. And something to hang on the tree in gilt paper, I may even see about that. (*Putting his hand on her head*) Oh you, my darling little songbird.

(*He goes into his study and closes the door after him.*)

NORA (*softly, after a silence*): Oh, really! It isn't so. It's impossible. It must be impossible.

ANNE-MARIE (*in the doorway, left*): The children are begging so hard to come in to Mama.

NORA: No, no, no, don't let them in to me! You stay with them, Anne-Marie.

ANNE-MARIE: Of course, Ma'am. (*Closes the door*)

NORA (*pale with terror*): Hurt my children—! Poison my home? (*A moment's pause; then she tosses her head.*) That's not true. Never. Never in all the world.

Act II

Same room. Beside the piano the Christmas tree now stands stripped of ornament, burned-down candle stubs on its ragged branches. NORA'S *street clothes lie on the sofa.* NORA, *alone in the room, moves restlessly about; at last she stops at the sofa and picks up her coat.*

NORA (*dropping the coat again*): Someone's coming! (*Goes toward the door, listens*) No—there's no one. Of course—nobody's coming today, Christmas Day—or tomorrow, either. But maybe—(*Opens the door and looks out*) No, nothing in the mailbox. Quite empty. (*Coming forward*) What nonsense! He won't do anything serious. Nothing terrible could happen. It's impossible. Why, I have three small children.

(ANNE-MARIE, *with a large carton, comes in from the room to the left.*)

ANNE-MARIE: Well, at last I found the box with the masquerade clothes.

NORA: Thanks. Put it on the table.

ANNE-MARIE (*does so*): But they're all pretty much of a mess.

NORA: Ahh! I'd love to rip them in a million pieces!

ANNE-MARIE: Oh, mercy, they can be fixed right up. Just a little patience.

NORA: Yes, I'll go get Mrs. Linde to help me.

ANNE-MARIE: Out again now? In this nasty weather? Miss Nora will catch cold—get sick.

NORA: Oh, worse things could happen—How are the children?

ANNE-MARIE: The poor mites are playing with their Christmas presents, but—

NORA: Do they ask for me much?

ANNE-MARIE: They're so used to having Mama around, you know.

NORA: Yes, but Anne-Marie, I *can't* be together with them as much as I was.

ANNE-MARIE: Well, small children get used to anything.

NORA: You think so? Do you think they'd forget their mother if she was gone for good?

ANNE-MARIE: Oh, mercy—gone for good!

NORA: Wait, tell me, Anne-Marie—I've wondered so often—how could you ever have the heart to give your child over to strangers?

ANNE-MARIE: But I had to, you know, to become little Nora's nurse.

NORA: Yes, but how could you *do* it?

ANNE-MARIE: When I could get such a good place? A girl who's poor and who's gotten in trouble is glad enough for that. Because that slippery fish, he didn't do a thing for me, you know.

NORA: But your daughter's surely forgotten you.

ANNE-MARIE: Oh, she certainly has not. She's written to me, both when she was confirmed and when she was married.

NORA (*clasping her about the neck*): You old Anne-Marie, you were a good mother for me when I was little.

ANNE-MARIE: Poor little Nora, with no other mother but me.

NORA: And if the babies didn't have one, then I know that you'd—What silly talk! (*Opening the carton*) Go in to them. Now I'll have to—Tomorrow you can see how lovely I'll look.

ANNE-MARIE: Oh, there won't be anyone at the party as lovely as Miss Nora.

(*She goes off into the room, left.*)

NORA (*begins unpacking the box, but soon throws it aside*): Oh, if I dared to go out. If only nobody would come. If only nothing would happen here while I'm out. What craziness—nobody's coming. Just don't think. This muff—needs a brushing. Beautiful gloves, beautiful gloves. Let it go. Let it go! One, two, three, four, five, six—(*With a cry*) Oh, there they are! (*Poises to move toward the door, but remains irresolutely standing.* MRS. LINDE *enters from the hall, where she has removed her street clothes.*)

NORA: Oh, it's you, Kristine. There's no one else out there? How good that you've come.

MRS. LINDE: I hear you were up asking for me.

NORA: Yes, I just stopped by. There's something you really can help me with. Let's get settled on the sofa. Look, there's going to be a costume party tomorrow evening at the Stenborgs' right above us, and now Torvald wants me to go as a Neapolitan peasant girl and dance the tarantella that I learned in Capri.

MRS. LINDE: Really, you are giving a whole performance?

NORA: Torvald says yes, I should. See, here's the dress. Torvald had it made for me down there; but now it's all so tattered that I just don't know—

MRS. LINDE: Oh, we'll fix that up in no time. It's nothing more than the trimmings—they're a bit loose here and there. Needle and thread? Good, now we have what we need.

NORA: Oh, how sweet of you!

MRS. LINDE (*sewing*): So you'll be in disguise tomorrow, Nora. You know what? I'll stop by then for a moment and have a look at you all dressed up. But listen, I've absolutely forgotten to thank you for that pleasant evening yesterday.

NORA (*getting up and walking about*): I don't think it was as pleasant as usual yesterday. You should have come to town a bit sooner, Kristine—Yes, Torvald really knows how to give a home elegance and charm.

MRS. LINDE: And you do, too, if you ask me. You're not your father's daughter for nothing. But tell me, is Dr. Rank always so down in the mouth as yesterday?

NORA: No, that was quite an exception. But he goes around critically ill all the time—tuberculosis of the spine, poor man. You know, his father was a disgusting thing who kept mistresses and so on—and that's why the son's been sickly from birth.

MRS. LINDE (*lets her sewing fall to her lap*): But my dearest Nora, how do you know about such things?

NORA (*walking more jauntily*): Hmp! When you've had three children, then you've had a few visits from—women who know something of medicine, and they tell you this and that.

MRS. LINDE (*resumes sewing; a short pause*): Does Dr. Rank come here every day?

NORA: Every blessed day. He's Torvald's best friend from childhood, and *my* good friend, too. Dr. Rank almost belongs to this house.

MRS. LINDE: But tell me—is he quite sincere? I mean, doesn't he rather enjoy flattering people?

NORA: Just the opposite. Why do you think that?

MRS. LINDE: When you introduced us yesterday, he was proclaiming that he'd often heard my name in this house; but later I noticed that your husband hadn't the slightest idea who I really was. So how could Dr. Rank—?

NORA: But it's all true, Kristine. You see, Torvald loves me beyond words, and, as he puts it, he'd like to keep me all to himself. For a long time he'd almost be jealous if I even mentioned any of my old friends back home. So of course I dropped that. But with Dr. Rank I talk a lot about such things, because he likes hearing about them.

MRS. LINDE: Now listen, Nora; in many ways you're still like a child. I'm a good deal older than you, with a little more experience. I'll tell you something; you ought to put an end to all this with Dr. Rank.

NORA: What should I put an end to?

MRS. LINDE: Both parts of it, I think. Yesterday you said something about a rich admirer who'd provide you with money—

NORA: Yes, one who doesn't exist—worse luck. So?

MRS. LINDE: Is Dr. Rank well off?

NORA: Yes, he is.

MRS. LINDE: With no dependents?

NORA: No, no one. But—

MRS. LINDE: And he's over here every day?

NORA: Yes, I told you that.

MRS. LINDE: How can a man of such refinement be so grasping?

NORA: I don't follow you at all.

MRS. LINDE: Now don't try to hide it, Nora. You think I can't guess who loaned you the forty-eight hundred crowns?

NORA: Are you out of your mind? How could you think of such a thing! A friend of ours, who comes here every single day. What an intolerable situation that would have been!

MRS. LINDE: Then it really wasn't him.

NORA: No, absolutely not. It never even crossed my mind for a moment—And he had nothing to lend in those days; his inheritance came later.

MRS. LINDE: Well, I think that was a stroke of luck for you, Nora dear.

NORA: No, it never would have occurred to me to ask Dr. Rank—Still, I'm quite sure that if I had asked him—

MRS. LINDE: Which you won't, of course.

NORA: No, of course not. I can't see that I'd ever need to. But I'm quite positive that if I talked to Dr. Rank—

MRS. LINDE: Behind your husband's back?

NORA: I've got to clear up this other thing; *that's* also behind his back. I've *got* to clear it all up.

MRS. LINDE: Yes, I was saying that yesterday, but—

NORA (*pacing up and down*): A man handles these problems so much better than a woman—

MRS. LINDE: One's husband does, yes.

NORA: Nonsense. (*Stopping*) When you pay everything you owe, then you get your note back, right?

MRS. LINDE: Yes, naturally.

NORA: And can rip it into a million pieces and burn it up—that filthy scrap of paper!

MRS. LINDE (*looking hard at her, laying her sewing aside, and rising slowly*): Nora, you're hiding something from me.

NORA: You can see it in my face?

MRS. LINDE: Something's happened to you since yesterday morning. Nora, what is it?

NORA (*hurrying toward her*): Kristine! (*Listening*) Shh! Torvald's home. Look, go in with the children a while. Torvald can't bear all this snipping and stitching. Let Anne-Marie help you.

MRS. LINDE (*gathering up some of the things*): All right, but I'm not leaving here until we've talked this out. (*She disappears into the room, left, as* TORVALD *enters from the hall.*)

NORA: Oh, how I've been waiting for you, Torvald dear.

HELMER: Was that the dressmaker?

NORA: No, that was Kristine. She's helping me fix up my costume. You know, it's going to be quite attractive.

HELMER: Yes, wasn't that a bright idea I had?

NORA: Brilliant! But then wasn't I good as well to give in to you?

HELMER: Good—because you give in to your husband's judgment? All right, you little goose, I know you didn't mean it like that. But I won't disturb you. You'll want to have a fitting, I suppose.

NORA: And you'll be working?

HELMER: Yes. (*Indicating a bundle of papers*) See. I've been down to the bank. (*Starts toward his study.*)

NORA: Torvald.

HELMER (*stops*): Yes.

NORA: If your little squirrel begged you, with all her heart and soul, for something—?

HELMER: What's that?

NORA: Then would you do it?

HELMER: First, naturally, I'd have to know what it was.

NORA: Your squirrel would scamper about and do tricks, if you'd only be sweet and give in.

HELMER: Out with it.

NORA: Your lark would be singing high and low in every room—

HELMER: Come on, she does that anyway.

NORA: I'd be a wood nymph and dance for you in the moonlight.

HELMER: Nora—don't tell me it's that same business from this morning?

NORA (*coming closer*): Yes, Torvald, I beg you, please!

HELMER: And you actually have the nerve to drag that up again?

NORA: Yes, yes, you've got to give in to me; you have to let Krogstad keep his job in the bank.

HELMER: My dear Nora, I've slated his job for Mrs. Linde.

NORA: That's awfully kind of you. But you could just fire another clerk instead of Krogstad.

HELMER: This is the most incredible stubbornness! Because you go and give an impulsive promise to speak up for him, I'm expected to—

NORA: That's not the reason, Torvald. It's for your own sake. That man does writing for the worst papers; you said it yourself. He could do you any amount of harm. I'm scared to death of him—

HELMER: Ah, I understand. It's the old memories haunting you.

NORA: What do you mean by that?

HELMER: Of course, you're thinking about your father.

NORA: Yes, all right. Just remember how those nasty gossips wrote in the papers about Papa and slandered him so cruelly. I think they'd have had him dismissed if the department hadn't sent you up to investigate, and if you hadn't been so kind and open-minded toward him.

HELMER: My dear Nora, there's a notable difference between your father and me. Your father's official career was hardly above reproach. But mine is; and I hope it'll stay that way as long as I hold my position.

NORA: Oh, who can ever tell what vicious minds can invent? We could be so snug and happy now in our quiet, carefree home—you and I and the children, Torvald! That's why I'm pleading with you so—

HELMER: And just by pleading for him you make it impossible for me to keep him on. It's already known at the bank that I'm firing Krogstad. What if it's rumored around now that the new bank manager was vetoed by his wife—

NORA: Yes, what then—?

HELMER: Oh yes—as long as your little bundle of stubbornness gets her way—! I should go and make myself ridiculous in front of the whole office—whole office—give people the idea I can be swayed by all kinds of outside pressure. Oh, you can bet I'd feel the effects of that soon enough! Besides—there's something that rules Krogstad right out at the bank as long as I'm the manager.

NORA: What's that?

HELMER: His moral failings I could maybe overlook if I had to—

NORA: Yes, Torvald, why not?

HELMER: And I hear he's quite efficient on the job. But he was a crony of mine back in my teens—one of those rash friendships that crop up again and again to embarrass you later in life. Well, I might as well say it straight out: we're on a first-name basis. And that tactless fool makes no effort at all to hide it in front of others. Quite the contrary—he thinks that entitles him to take a familiar air around me, and so every other second he comes booming out with his "Yes, Torvald!" and "Sure thing, Torvald!" I tell you, it's been excruciating for me. He's out to make my place in the bank unbearable.

NORA: Torvald, you can't be serious about all this.

HELMER: Oh no? Why not?

NORA: Because these are such petty considerations.

HELMER: What are you saying? Petty? You think I'm petty!

NORA: No, just the opposite, Torvald dear. That's exactly why—

HELMER: Never mind. You call my motives petty; then I might as well be just that. Petty! All right! We'll put a stop to this for good. (*Goes to the hall door and calls*) Helene!

NORA: What do you want?

HELMER (*searching among his papers*): A decision. (*The* MAID *comes in.*) Look here; take this letter; go out with it at once. Get hold of a messenger and have him deliver it. Quick now. It's already addressed. Wait, here's some money.

MAID: Yes, sir. (*She leaves with the letter.*)

HELMER (*straightening his papers*): There, now, little Miss Willful.

NORA (*breathlessly*): Torvald, what was that letter?

HELMER: Krogstad's notice.

NORA: Call it back, Torvald! There's still time. Oh, Torvald, call it back! Do it for my sake—for your sake, for the children's sake! Do you hear, Torvald; do it! You don't know how this can harm us.

HELMER: Too late.

NORA: Yes, too late.

HELMER: Nora dear, I can forgive you this panic, even though basically you're insulting me. Yes, you are! Or isn't it an insult to think that I should be afraid of a courtroom hack's revenge? But I forgive you anyway, because this shows so beautifully how much you love me. (*Takes her in his arms*) This is the way it should be, my darling Nora. Whatever comes, you'll see: when it really counts, I have strength and courage enough as a man to take on the whole weight myself.

NORA (*terrified*): What do you mean by that?

HELMER: The whole weight, I said.

NORA (*resolutely*): No, never in all the world.

HELMER: Good. So we'll share it, Nora, as man and wife. That's as it should be. (*Fondling her*) Are you happy now? There, there, there—not these frightened dove's eyes. It's nothing at all but empty fantasies—Now you should run through your tarantella and practice your tambourine. I'll go to the inner office and shut both doors, so I won't hear a thing; you can make all the noise you like. (*Turning in the doorway*) And when Rank comes, just tell him where he can find me. (*He nods to her and goes with his papers into the study, closing the door.*)

NORA (*standing as though rooted, dazed with fright, in a whisper*): He really could do it. He will do it. He'll do it in spite of everything. No, not that, never, never! Anything but that! Escape! A way out—(*The doorbell rings.*) Dr. Rank! Anything but that! Anything, whatever it is! (*Her hands pass over her face, smoothing it; she pulls herself together, goes over and opens the hall door.* DR. RANK *stands outside, hanging his fur coat up. During the following scene, it begins getting dark.*)

NORA: Hello, Dr. Rank. I recognized your ring. But you mustn't go in to Torvald yet; I believe he's working.

RANK: And you?

NORA: For you, I always have an hour to spare—you know that. (*He has entered, and she shuts the door after him.*)

RANK: Many thanks. I'll make use of these hours while I can.

NORA: What do you mean by that? While you can?

RANK: Does that disturb you?

NORA: Well, it's such an odd phrase. Is anything going to happen?

RANK: What's going to happen is what I've been expecting so long—but I honestly didn't think it would come so soon.

NORA (*gripping his arm*): What is it you've found out? Dr. Rank, you have to tell me!

RANK (*sitting by the stove*): It's all over with me. There's nothing to be done about it.

NORA (*breathing easier*): Is it you—then—?

RANK: Who else? There's no point in lying to one's self. I'm the most miserable of all my patients, Mrs. Helmer. These past few days I've been auditing my internal accounts. Bankrupt! Within a month I'll probably be laid out and rotting in the churchyard.

NORA: Oh, what a horrible thing to say.

RANK: The thing itself is horrible. But the worst of it is all the other horror before it's over. There's only one final examination left; when I'm finished with that, I'll know about when my disintegration will begin. There's something I want to say. Helmer with his sensitivity has such a sharp distaste for anything ugly. I don't want him near my sickroom.

NORA: Oh, but Dr. Rank—

RANK: I won't have him in there. Under no condition. I'll lock my door to him—As soon as I'm completely sure of the worst, I'll send you my calling card marked with a black cross, and you'll know then the wreck has started to come apart.

NORA: No, today you're completely unreasonable. And I wanted you so much to be in a really good humor.

RANK: With death up my sleeve? And then to suffer this way for somebody else's sins. Is there any justice in that? And in every single family, in some way or another, this inevitable retribution of nature goes on—

NORA (*her hands pressed over her ears*): Oh, stuff! Cheer up! Please—be gay!

RANK: Yes, I'd just as soon laugh at it all. My poor, innocent spine, serving time for my father's gay army days.

NORA (*by the table, left*): He was so infatuated with asparagus tips and *pâté de foie gras,* wasn't that it?

RANK: Yes—and with truffles.

NORA: Truffles, yes. And then with oysters, I suppose?

RANK: Yes, tons of oysters, naturally.

NORA: And then the port and champagne to go with it. It's so sad that all these delectable things have to strike at our bones.

RANK: Especially when they strike at the unhappy bones that never shared in the fun.

NORA: Ah, that's the saddest of all.

RANK (*looks searchingly at her*): Hm.

NORA (*after a moment*): Why did you smile?

RANK: No, it was you who laughed.

NORA: No, it was you who smiled, Dr. Rank!

RANK (*getting up*): You're even a bigger tease than I'd thought.

NORA: I'm full of wild ideas today.

RANK: That's obvious.

NORA (*putting both hands on his shoulders*): Dear, dear Dr. Rank, you'll never die for Torvald and me.

RANK: Oh, that loss you'll easily get over. Those who go away are soon forgotten.

NORA (*looks fearfully at him*): You believe that?

RANK: One makes new connections, and then—

NORA: Who makes new connections?

RANK: Both you and Torvald will when I'm gone. I'd say you're well under way already. What was that Mrs. Linde doing here last evening?

NORA: Oh, come—you can't be jealous of poor Kristine?

RANK: Oh yes, I am. She'll be my successor here in the house. When I'm down under, that woman will probably—

NORA: Shh! Not so loud. She's right in there.

RANK: Today as well. So you see.

NORA: Only to sew on my dress. Good gracious, how unreasonable you are. (*Sitting on the sofa*) Be nice now, Dr. Rank. Tomorrow you'll see how beautifully I'll dance, and you can imagine then that I'm dancing only for you—yes, and of course for Torvald, too—that's understood. (*Takes various items out of the carton*) Dr. Rank, sit over here and I'll show you something.

RANK (*sitting*): What's that?

NORA: Look here. Look.

RANK: Silk stockings.

NORA: Flesh-colored. Aren't they lovely? Now it's so dark here, but tomorrow—No, no, no, just look at the feet. Oh well, you might as well look at the rest.

RANK: Hm—

NORA: Why do you look so critical? Don't you believe they'll fit?

RANK: I've never had any chance to form an opinion on that.

NORA (*glancing at him a moment*): Shame on you. (*Hits him lightly on the ear with the stockings*) That's for you. (*Puts them away again*)

RANK: And what other splendors am I going to see now?

NORA: Not the least bit more, because you've been naughty. (*She hums a little and rummages among her things.*)

RANK (*after a short silence*): When I sit here together with you like this, completely easy and open, then I don't know—I simply can't imagine—whatever would have become of me if I'd never come into this house.

NORA (*smiling*): Yes, I really think you feel completely at ease with us.

RANK (*more quietly, staring straight ahead*): And then to have to go away from it all—

NORA: Nonsense, you're not going away.

RANK (*his voice unchanged*): —and not even be able to leave some poor show of gratitude behind, scarcely a fleeting regret—no more than a vacant place that anyone can fill.

NORA: And if I asked you now for—? No—

RANK: For what?

NORA: For a great proof of your friendship—

RANK: Yes, yes?

NORA: No, I mean—for an exceptionally big favor—

RANK: Would you really, for once, make me so happy?

NORA: Oh, you haven't the vaguest idea what it is.

RANK: All right, then tell me.

NORA: No, but I can't, Dr. Rank—it's all out of reason. It's advice and help, too—and a favor—

RANK: So much the better. I can't fathom what you're hinting at. Just speak out. Don't you trust me?

NORA: Of course. More than anyone else. You're my best and truest friend, I'm sure. That's why I want to talk to you. All right, then, Dr. Rank: there's something you can help me prevent. You know how deeply, how inexpressibly dearly Torvald loves me; he'd never hesitate a second to give up his life for me.

RANK (*leaning close to her*): Nora—do you think he's the only one—

NORA (*with a slight start*): Who—?

RANK: Who'd gladly give up his life for you.

NORA (*heavily*): I see.

RANK: I swore to myself you should know this before I'm gone. I'll never find a better chance. Yes, Nora, now you know. And also you know now that you can trust me beyond anyone else.

NORA (*rising, natural and calm*): Let me by.

RANK (*making room for her, but still sitting*): Nora—

NORA (*in the hall doorway*): Helene, bring the lamp in. (*Goes over to the stove*) Ah, dear Dr. Rank, that was really mean of you.

RANK (*getting up*): That I've loved you just as deeply as somebody else? Was *that* mean?

NORA: No, but that you came out and told me. That was quite unnecessary—

RANK: What do you mean? Have you known—?

(*The* MAID *comes in with the lamp, sets it on the table, and goes out again.*)

RANK: Nora—Mrs. Helmer—I'm asking you: have you known about it?

NORA: Oh, how can I tell what I know or don't know? Really, I don't know what to say.—Why did you have to be so clumsy, Dr. Rank! Everything was so good.

RANK: Well, in any case, you now have the knowledge that my body and soul are at your command. So won't you speak out?

NORA (*Looking at him*): After that?

RANK: Please, just let me know what it is.

NORA: You can't know anything now.

RANK: I have to. You mustn't punish me like this. Give me the chance to do whatever is humanly possible for you.

NORA: Now there's nothing you can do for me. Besides, actually, I don't need any help. You'll see—it's only my fantasies. That's what it is. Of course! (*Sits in the rocker, looks at him, and smiles*) What a nice one you are, Dr. Rank. Aren't you a little bit ashamed, now that the lamp is here?

RANK: No, not exactly. But perhaps I'd better go—for good?

NORA: No, you certainly can't do that. You must come here just as you always have. You know Torvald can't do without you.

RANK: Yes, but *you*?

NORA: You know how much I enjoy it when you're here.

RANK: That's precisely what threw me off. You're a mystery to me. So many times I've felt you'd almost rather be with me than with Helmer.

NORA: Yes—you see, there are some people that one loves most and other people that one would almost prefer being with.

RANK: Yes, there's something to that.

NORA: When I was back home, of course I loved Papa most. But I always thought it was so much fun when I could sneak down to the maids' quarters, because they never tried to improve me, and it was always so amusing, the way they talked to each other.

RANK: Aha, so it's *their* place that I've filled.

NORA (*jumping up and going to him*): Oh, dear sweet Dr. Rank, that's not what I meant at all. But you can understand that with Torvald it's just the same as with Papa—

(*The* MAID *enters from the hall.*)

MAID: Ma'am—please! (*She whispers to* NORA *and hands her a calling card.*)

NORA (*glancing at the card*): Ah! (*Slips it into her pocket*)

RANK: Anything wrong?

NORA: No, no, not at all. It's only some—it's my new dress—

RANK: Really? But—there's your dress.

NORA: Oh, that. But this is another one—I ordered it—Torvald mustn't know—

RANK: Ah, now we have the big secret.

NORA: That's right. Just go in with him—he's back in the inner study. Keep him there as long as—

RANK: Don't worry. He won't get away.

(*Goes into the study.*)

NORA (*to the* MAID): And he's standing waiting in the kitchen.

MAID: Yes, he came up by the back stairs.

NORA: But didn't you tell him somebody was here?

MAID: Yes, but that didn't do any good.

NORA: He won't leave?

MAID: No, he won't go till he's talked with you, ma'am.

NORA: Let him come in, then—but quietly. Helene, don't breathe a word about this. It's a surprise for my husband.

MAID: Yes, yes, I understand—

(*Goes out.*)

NORA: This horror—it's going to happen. No, no, no, it can't happen, it mustn't. (*She goes and bolts* HELMER*'s door. The* MAID *opens the hall door for* KROGSTAD *and shuts it behind him. He is dressed for travel in a fur coat, boots and a fur cap.*)

NORA (*going toward him*): Talk softly. My husband's home.

KROGSTAD: Well, good for him.

NORA: What do you want?

KROGSTAD: Some information.

NORA: Hurry up, then. What is it?

KROGSTAD: You know, of course, that I got my notice.

NORA: I couldn't prevent it, Mr. Krogstad. I fought for you to the bitter end, but nothing worked.

KROGSTAD: Does your husband's love for you run so thin? He knows everything I can expose you too, and all the same he dares to—

NORA: How can you imagine he knows anything about this?

KROGSTAD: Ah, no—I can't imagine it either, now. It's not at all like my fine Torvald Helmer to have so much guts—

NORA: Mr. Krogstad, I demand respect for my husband!

KROGSTAD: Why, of course—all due respect. But since the lady's keeping it so carefully hidden, may I presume to ask if you're also a bit better informed than yesterday about what you've actually done?

NORA: More than you ever could teach me.

KROGSTAD: Yes, I *am* such an awful lawyer.

NORA: What is it you want from me?

KROGSTAD: Just a glimpse of how you are, Mrs. Helmer. I've been thinking about you all day long. A cashier, a night-court scribbler, a—well, a type like me also has a little of what they call a heart, you know.

NORA: Then show it. Think of my children.

KROGSTAD: Did you or your husband ever think of mine? But never mind. I simply wanted to tell you that you don't need to take this thing too seriously. For the present, I'm not proceeding with any action.

NORA: Oh no, really! Well—I knew that.

KROGSTAD: Everything can be settled in a friendly spirit. It doesn't have to get around town at all; it can stay just among us three.

NORA: My husband may never know anything of this.

KROGSTAD: How can you manage that? Perhaps you can pay me the balance?

NORA: No, not right now.

KROGSTAD: Or you know some way of raising the money in a day or two?

NORA: No way that I'm willing to use.

KROGSTAD: Well, it wouldn't have done you any good, anyway. If you stood in front of me with a fistful of bills, you still couldn't buy your signature back.

NORA: Then tell me what you're going to do with it.

KROGSTAD: I'll just hold onto it—keep it on file. There's no outsider who'll even get wind of it. So if you've been thinking of taking some desperate step—

NORA: I have.

KROGSTAD: Been thinking of running away from home—

NORA: I have!

KROGSTAD: Or even of something worse—

NORA: How could you guess that?

KROGSTAD: You can drop those thoughts.

NORA: How could you guess I was thinking of *that*?

KROGSTAD: Most of us think about *that* at first. I thought about it too, but I discovered I hadn't the courage—

NORA (*lifelessly*): I don't either.

KROGSTAD (*relieved*): That's true, you haven't the courage? You too?

NORA: I don't have it—I don't have it.

KROGSTAD: It would be terribly stupid, anyway. After that first storm at home blows out, why, then—I have here in my pocket a letter for your husband—

NORA: Telling everything?

KROGSTAD: As charitably as possible.

NORA (*quickly*): He mustn't ever get that letter. Tear it up. I'll find some way to get money.

KROGSTAD: Beg pardon, Mrs. Helmer, but I think I just told you—

NORA: Oh, I don't mean the money I owe you. Let me know how much you want from my husband, and I'll manage it.

KROGSTAD: I don't want any money from your husband.

NORA: What do you want, then?

KROGSTAD: I'll tell you what. I want to recoup, Mrs. Helmer; I want to get on in the world—and there's where your husband can help me. For a year and a half I've kept myself clean of anything disreputable—all that time struggling with the worst conditions; but I was satisfied, working my way up step by step. Now I've been written right off, and I'm just not in the mood to come crawling back. I tell you, I want to move on. I want to get back in the bank—in a better position. Your husband can set up a job for me—

NORA: He'll never do that!

KROGSTAD: He'll do it. I know him. He won't dare breathe a word of protest. And once I'm in there together with him, you just wait and see! Inside of a year, I'll be the manager's right-hand man. It'll be Nils Krogstad, not Torvald Helmer, who runs the bank.

NORA: You'll never see the day!

KROGSTAD: Maybe you think you can—

NORA: I have the courage now—for *that.*

KROGSTAD: Oh, you don't scare me. A smart, spoiled lady like you—

NORA: You'll see; you'll see!

KROGSTAD: Under the ice, maybe? Down in the freezing, coal-black water? There, till you float up in the spring, ugly, unrecognizable, with your hair falling out—

NORA: You don't frighten me.

KROGSTAD: Nor do you frighten me. One doesn't do these things, Mrs. Helmer. Besides, what good would it be? I'd still have him safe in my pocket.

NORA: Afterwards? When I'm no longer—?

KROGSTAD: Are you forgetting that *I'll* be in control then over your final reputation? (NORA *stands speechless, staring at him.*) Good; now I've warned you. Don't do anything stupid. When Helmer's read my letter, I'll be waiting for his reply. And bear in mind that it's your husband himself who's forced me back to my old ways. I'll never forgive him for that. Good-bye, Mrs. Helmer.

(*He goes out through the hall.*)

NORA (*goes to the hall door, opens it a crack, and listens*): He's gone. Didn't leave the letter. Oh no, no, that's impossible too! (*Opening the door more and more*) What's that? He's standing outside—not going downstairs. He's thinking it over? Maybe he'll—? (*A letter falls in the mailbox; then* KROGSTAD*'s footsteps are heard, dying away down a flight of stairs.* NORA *gives a muffled cry and runs over toward the sofa table. A short pause.*) In the mailbox. (*Slips warily over to the hall door*) It's lying there. Torvald, Torvald—now we're lost!

MRS. LINDE (*entering with the costume from the room, left*): There now, I can't see anything else to mend. Perhaps you'd like to try—

NORA (*in a hoarse whisper*): Kristine, come here.

MRS. LINDE (*tossing the dress on the sofa*): What's wrong? You look upset.

NORA: Come here. See that letter? *There!* Look—through the glass in the mailbox.

MRS. LINDE: Yes, yes, I see it.

NORA: That letter's from Krogstad—

MRS. LINDE: Nora—it's Krogstad who loaned you the money!

NORA: Yes, and now Torvald will find out everything.

MRS. LINDE: Believe me, Nora, it's best for both of you.

NORA: There's more you don't know. I forged a name.

MRS. LINDE: But for heaven's sake—?

NORA: I only want to tell you that, Kristine, so that you can be my witness.

MRS. LINDE: Witness? Why should I—?

NORA: If I should go out of my mind—it could easily happen—

MRS. LINDE: Nora!

NORA: Or anything else occurred—so I couldn't be present here—

MRS. LINDE: Nora, Nora, you aren't yourself at all!

NORA: And someone should try to take on the whole weight, all of the guilt, you follow me—

MRS. LINDE: Yes, of course, but why do you think—?

NORA: Then you're the witness that it isn't true, Kristine. I'm very much myself; my mind right now is perfectly clear; and I'm telling you: nobody else has known about this; I alone did everything. Remember that.

MRS. LINDE: I will. But I don't understand all this.

NORA: Oh, how could you ever understand it? It's the miracle now that's going to take place.

MRS. LINDE: The miracle?

NORA: Yes, the miracle. But it's so awful, Kristine. It mustn't take place, not for anything in the world.

MRS. LINDE: I'm going right over and talk with Krogstad.

NORA: Don't go near him; he'll do you some terrible harm!

MRS. LINDE: There was a time once when he'd gladly have done anything for me.

NORA: He?

MRS. LINDE: Where does he live?

NORA: Oh, how do I know? Yes. (*Searches in her pocket*) Here's his card. But the letter, the letter—!

HELMER (*from the study, knocking on the door*): Nora!

NORA (*with a cry of fear*): Oh! What is it? What do you want?

HELMER: Now, now, don't be so frightened. We're not coming in. You locked the door—are you trying on the dress?

NORA: Yes, I'm trying it. I'll look just beautiful, Torvald.

MRS. LINDE (*who has read the card*): He's living right around the corner.

NORA: Yes, but what's the use? We're lost. The letter's in the box.

MRS. LINDE: And your husband has the key?

NORA: Yes, always.

MRS. LINDE: Krogstad can ask for his letter back unread; he can find some excuse—

NORA: But it's just this time that Torvald usually—

MRS. LINDE: Stall him. Keep him in there. I'll be back as quick as I can. (*She hurries out through the hall entrance.*)

NORA (*goes to* HELMER*'s door, opens it, and peers in*): Torvald!

HELMER (*from the inner study*): Well—does one dare set foot in one's own living room at last? Come on, Rank, now we'll get a look—(*In the doorway*) But what's this?

NORA: What, Torvald dear?

HELMER: Rank had me expecting some grand masquerade.

RANK (*in the doorway*): That was my impression, but I must have been wrong.

NORA: No one can admire me in my splendor—not until tomorrow.

HELMER: But Nora dear, you look so exhausted. Have you practiced too hard?

NORA: No, I haven't practiced at all yet.

HELMER: You know, it's necessary—

NORA: Oh, it's absolutely necessary, Torvald. But I can't get anywhere without your help. I've forgotten the whole thing completely.

HELMER: Ah, we'll soon take care of that.

NORA: Yes, take care of me, Torvald, please! Promise me that? Oh, I'm so nervous. That big party—You must give up everything this evening for me. No business—don't even touch your pen. Yes? Dear Torvald, promise?

HELMER: It's a promise. Tonight I'm totally at your service—you little helpless thing. Hm—but first there's one thing I want to—(*Goes toward the hall door*)

NORA: What are you looking for?

HELMER: Just to see if there's any mail.

NORA: No, no, don't do that, Torvald!

HELMER: Now what?

NORA: Torvald, please. There isn't any.

HELMER: Let me look, though. (*Starts out.* NORA, *at the piano, strikes the first notes of the tarantella.* HELMER, *at the door, stops.*) Aha!

NORA: I can't dance tomorrow if I don't practice with you.

HELMER (*going over to her*): Nora dear, are you really so frightened?

NORA: Yes, so terribly frightened. Let me practice right now; there's still time before dinner. Oh, sit down and play for me, Torvald. Direct me. Teach me, the way you always have.

HELMER: Gladly, if it's what you want. (*Sits at the piano*)

NORA (*snatches the tambourine up from the box, then a long, varicolored shawl, which she throws around herself, whereupon she springs forward and cries out*): Play for me now! Now I'll dance!

(HELMER *plays and* NORA *dances.* RANK *stands behind* HELMER *at the piano and looks on.*)

HELMER (*as he plays*): Slower. Slow down.

NORA: Can't change it.

HELMER: Not so violent, Nora!

NORA: Has to be just like this.

HELMER (*stopping*): No, no, that won't do at all.

NORA (*laughing and swinging her tambourine*): Isn't that what I told you?

RANK: Let me play for her.

HELMER (*getting up*): Yes, go on. I can teach her more easily then.

(RANK *sits at the piano and plays;* NORA *dances more and more wildly.* HELMER *has stationed himself by the stove and repeatedly gives her directions; she seems not to hear them; her hair loosens and falls over her shoulders; she does not notice, but goes on dancing.* MRS. LINDE *enters.*)

MRS. LINDE (*standing dumbfounded at the door*): Ah—!

NORA (*still dancing*): See what fun, Kristine!

HELMER: But Nora darling, you dance as if your life were at stake.

NORA: And it is.

HELMER: Rank, stop! This is pure madness. Stop it, I say!

(RANK *breaks off playing, and* NORA *halts abruptly.*)

HELMER (*going over to her*): I never would have believed it. You've forgotten everything I taught you.

NORA (*throwing away the tambourine*): You see for yourself.

HELMER: Well, there's certainly room for instruction here.

NORA: Yes, you see how important it is. You've got to teach me to the very last minute. Promise me that, Torvald?

HELMER: You can bet on it.

NORA: You mustn't, either today or tomorrow, think about anything else but me; you mustn't open any letters—or the mailbox—

HELMER: Ah, it's still the fear of that man—

NORA: Oh yes, yes, that too.

HELMER: Nora, it's written all over you—there's already a letter from him out there.

NORA: I don't know. I guess so. But you mustn't read such things now; there mustn't be anything ugly between us before it's all over.

RANK (*quietly to* HELMER): You shouldn't deny her.

HELMER (*putting his arm around her*): The child can have her way. But tomorrow night, after you've danced—

NORA: Then you'll be free.

MAID (*in the doorway, right*): Ma'am, dinner is served.

NORA: We'll be wanting champagne, Helene.

MAID: Very good, ma'am.

(*Goes out*)

HELMER: So—a regular banquet, hm?

NORA: Yes, a banquet—champagne till daybreak! (*Calling out*) And some macaroons, Helene. Heaps of them—just this once.

HELMER (*taking her hands*): Now, now, now—no hysterics. Be my own little lark again.

NORA: Oh, I will soon enough. But go on in—and you, Dr. Rank. Kristine, help me put up my hair.

RANK (*whispering, as they go*): There's nothing wrong—really wrong, is there?

HELMER: Oh, of course not. It's nothing more than this childish anxiety I was telling you about.

(*They go out, right.*)

NORA: Well?

MRS. LINDE: Left town.

NORA: I could see by your face.

MRS. LINDE: He'll be home tomorrow evening. I wrote him a note.

NORA: You shouldn't have. Don't try to stop anything now. After all, it's a wonderful joy, this waiting here for the miracle.

MRS. LINDE: What is it you're waiting for?

NORA: Oh, you can't understand that. Go in to them, I'll be along in a moment.

(MRS. LINDE *goes into the dining room.* NORA *stands a short while as if composing herself; then she looks at her watch.*)

NORA: Five. Seven hours to midnight. Twenty-four hours to the midnight after, and then the tarantella's done. Seven and twenty-four? Thirty-one hours to live.

HELMER (*in the doorway, right*): What's become of the little lark?

NORA (*going toward him with open arms*): Here's your lark!

ACT III

Same scene. The table, with chairs around it, has been moved to the center of the room. A lamp on the table is lit. The hall door stands open. Dance music drifts down from the floor above. MRS. LINDE *sits at the table, absently paging through a book, trying to read, but apparently unable to focus her thoughts. Once or twice she pauses, tensely listening for a sound at the outer entrance.*

MRS. LINDE (*glancing at her watch*): Not yet—and there's hardly any time left. If only he's not—(*Listening again*) Ah, there he is. (*She goes out in the hall and cautiously opens the outer door. Quiet footsteps are heard on the stairs. She whispers.*) Come in. Nobody's here.

KROGSTAD (*in the doorway*): I found a note from you at home. What's back of all this?

MRS. LINDE: I just *had* to talk to you.

KROGSTAD: Oh? And it just *had* to be here in this house?

MRS. LINDE: At my place it was impossible; my room hasn't a private entrance. Come in; we're all alone. The maid's asleep, and the Helmers are at the dance upstairs.

KROGSTAD (*entering the room*): Well, well, the Helmers are dancing tonight? Really?

MRS. LINDE: Yes, why not?

KROGSTAD: How true—why not?

MRS. LINDE: All right, Krogstad, let's talk.

KROGSTAD: Do we two have anything more to talk about?

MRS. LINDE: We have a great deal to talk about.

KROGSTAD: I wouldn't have thought so.

MRS. LINDE: No, because you've never understood me, really.

KROGSTAD: Was there anything more to understand—except what's all too common in life? A calculating woman throws over a man the moment a better catch comes by.

MRS. LINDE: You think I'm so thoroughly calculating? You think I broke it off lightly?

KROGSTAD: Didn't you?

MRS. LINDE: Nils—is that what you really thought?

KROGSTAD: If you cared, then why did you write me the way you did?

MRS. LINDE: What else could I do? If I had to break off with you, then it was my job as well to root out everything you felt for me.

KROGSTAD (*wringing his hands*): So that was it. And this—all this, simply for money!

MRS. LINDE: Don't forget I had a helpless mother and two small brothers. We couldn't wait for you, Nils; you had such a long road ahead of you then.

KROGSTAD: That may be; but you still hadn't the right to abandon me for somebody else's sake.

MRS. LINDE: Yes—I don't know. So many, many times I've asked myself if I did have that right.

KROGSTAD (*more softly*): When I lost you, it was as if all the solid ground dissolved from under my feet. Look at me; I'm a half-drowned man now, hanging onto a wreck.

MRS. LINDE: Help may be near.

KROGSTAD: It was near—but then you came and blocked it off.

MRS. LINDE: Without my knowing it, Nils. Today for the first time I learned that it's you I'm replacing at the bank.

KROGSTAD: All right—I believe you. But now that you know, will you step aside?

MRS. LINDE: No, because that wouldn't benefit you in the slightest.

KROGSTAD: Not "benefit" me, hm! I'd step aside anyway.

MRS. LINDE: I've learned to be realistic. Life and hard, bitter necessity have taught me that.

KROGSTAD: And life's taught me never to trust fine phrases.

MRS. LINDE: Then life's taught you a very sound thing. But you do have to trust in actions, don't you?

KROGSTAD: What does that mean?

MRS. LINDE: You said you were hanging on like a half-drowned man to a wreck.

KROGSTAD: I've good reason to say that.

MRS. LINDE: I'm also like a half-drowned woman on a wreck. No one to suffer with; no one to care for.

KROGSTAD: You made your choice.

MRS. LINDE: There wasn't any choice then.

KROGSTAD: So—what of it?

MRS. LINDE: Nils, if only we two shipwrecked people could reach across to each other.

KROGSTAD: What are you saying?

MRS. LINDE: Two on one wreck are at least better off than each on his own.

KROGSTAD: Kristine!

MRS. LINDE: Why do you think I came into town?

KROGSTAD: Did you really have some thought of me?

MRS. LINDE: I have to work to go on living. All my born days, as long as I can remember, I've worked, and it's been my best and my only joy. But now I'm completely alone in the world; it frightens me to be so empty and lost. To work for yourself—there's no joy in that. Nils, give me something—someone to work for.

KROGSTAD: I don't believe all this. It's just some hysterical feminine urge to go out and make a noble sacrifice.

MRS. LINDE: Have you ever found me to be hysterical?

KROGSTAD: Can you honestly mean this? Tell me—do you know everything about my past?

MRS. LINDE: Yes.

KROGSTAD: And you know what they think I'm worth around here.

MRS. LINDE: From what you were saying before, it would seem that with me you could have been another person.

KROGSTAD: I'm positive of that.

MRS. LINDE: Couldn't it happen still?

KROGSTAD: Kristine—you're saying this in all seriousness? Yes, you are! I can see it in you. And do you really have the courage, then—?

MRS. LINDE: I need to have someone to care for; and your children need a mother. We both need each other. Nils, I have faith that you're good at heart—I'll risk everything together with you.

KROGSTAD (*gripping her hands*): Kristine, thank you, thank you—Now I know I can win back a place in their eyes. Yes—but I forgot—

MRS. LINDE (*listening*): Shh! The tarantella. Go now! Go on!

KROGSTAD: Why? What is it?

MRS. LINDE: Hear the dance up there? When that's over, they'll be coming down.

KROGSTAD: Oh, then I'll go. But—it's all pointless. Of course, you don't know the move I made against the Helmers.

MRS. LINDE: Yes, Nils, I know.

KROGSTAD: And all the same, you have the courage to—?

MRS. LINDE: I know how far despair can drive a man like you.

KROGSTAD: Oh, if I only could take it all back.

MRS. LINDE: You easily could—your letter's still lying in the mailbox.

KROGSTAD: Are you sure of that?

MRS. LINDE: Positive. But—

KROGSTAD (*looks at her searchingly*): Is that the meaning of it, then? You'll have your friend at any price. Tell me straight out. Is that it?

MRS. LINDE: Nils—anyone who's sold herself for somebody else once isn't going to do it again.

KROGSTAD: I'll demand my letter back.

MRS. LINDE: No, no.

KROGSTAD: Yes, of course. I'll stay here till Helmer comes down; I'll tell him to give me my letter again—that it only involves my dismissal—that he shouldn't read it—

MRS. LINDE: No, Nils, don't call the letter back.

KROGSTAD: But wasn't that exactly why you wrote me to come here?

MRS. LINDE: Yes, in that first panic. But it's been a whole day and night since then, and in that time I've seen such incredible things in this house. Helmer's got to learn everything; this dreadful secret has to be aired; those two have to come to a full understanding; all these lies and evasions can't go on.

KROGSTAD: Well, then, if you want to chance it. But at least there's one thing I can do, and do right away—

MRS. LINDE (*listening*): Go now, go quick! The dance is over. We're not safe another second.

KROGSTAD: I'll wait for you downstairs.

MRS. LINDE: Yes, please do; take me home.

KROGSTAD: I can't believe it; I've never been so happy. (*He leaves by way of the outer door; the door between the room and the hall stays open.*)

MRS. LINDE (*straightening up a bit and getting together her street clothes*): How different now! How different! Someone to work for, to live for—a home to build. Well, it is worth the try! Oh, if they'd only come! (*Listening*) Ah, there they are. Bundle up. (*She picks up her hat and coat.* NORA*'s and* HELMER*'s voices can be heard outside; a key turns in the lock, and* HELMER *brings* NORA *into the hall almost by force. She is wearing the Italian costume with a large black shawl about her; he has on evening dress, with a black domino open over it.*)

NORA (*struggling in the doorway*): No, no, no, not inside! I'm going up again. I don't want to leave so soon.

HELMER: But Nora dear—

NORA: Oh, I beg you, please, Torvald. From the bottom of my heart, *please*—only an hour more!

HELMER: Not a single minute, Nora darling. You know our agreement. Come on, in we go; you'll catch cold out here. (*In spite of her resistance, he gently draws her into the room.*)

MRS. LINDE: Good evening.

NORA: Kristine!

HELMER: Why, Mrs. Linde—are you here so late?

MRS. LINDE: Yes, I'm sorry, but I did want to see Nora in costume.

NORA: Have you been sitting here, waiting for me?

MRS. LINDE: Yes. I didn't come early enough; you were all upstairs; and then I thought I really couldn't leave without seeing you.

HELMER (*removing* NORA*'s shawl*): Yes, take a good look. She's worth looking at, I can tell you that, Mrs. Linde. Isn't she lovely?

MRS. LINDE: Yes, I should say—

HELMER: A dream of loveliness, isn't she? That's what everyone thought at the party, too. But she's horribly stubborn—this sweet little thing. What's to be done with her? Can you imagine, I almost had to use force to pry her away.

NORA: Oh, Torvald, you're going to regret you didn't indulge me, even for just a half hour more.

HELMER: There, you see. She danced her tarantella and got a tumultuous hand—which was well earned, although the performance may have been a bit too naturalistic—I mean it rather overstepped the proprieties of art. But never mind—what's important is, she made a success, an overwhelming success. You think I could let her stay on after that and spoil the effect? Oh no; I took my lovely little Capri girl—my capricious little Capri girl, I should say—took her under my arm; one quick tour of the ballroom, a curtsy to every side, and then—as they say in novels—the beautiful vision disappeared. An exit should always be effective, Mrs. Linde, but that's what I can't get Nora to grasp. Phew, it's hot in here. (*Flings the domino on a chair and opens the door to his room*) Why's it dark in here? Oh yes, of course. Excuse me. (*He goes in and lights a couple of candles.*)

NORA (*in a sharp, breathless whisper*): So?

MRS. LINDE (*quietly*): I talked with him.

NORA: And—?

MRS. LINDE: Nora—you must tell your husband everything.

NORA (*dully*): I knew it.

MRS. LINDE: You've got nothing to fear from Krogstad, but you have to speak out.

NORA: I won't tell.

MRS. LINDE: Then the letter will.

NORA: Thanks, Kristine. I know now what's to be done. Shh!

HELMER (*reentering*): Well, then, Mrs. Linde—have you admired her?

MRS. LINDE: Yes, and now I'll say good night.

HELMER: Oh, come, so soon? Is this yours, this knitting?

MRS. LINDE: Yes, thanks. I nearly forgot it.

HELMER: Do you knit, then?

MRS. LINDE: Oh yes.

HELMER: You know what? You should embroider instead.

MRS. LINDE: Really? Why?

HELMER: Yes, because it's a lot prettier. See here, one holds the embroidery so, in the left hand, and then one guides the needle with the right—so—in an easy, sweeping curve—right?

MRS. LINDE: Yes, I guess that's—

HELMER: But, on the other hand, knitting—it can never be anything but ugly. Look, see here, the arms tucked in, the knitting needles going up and down—there's something Chinese about it. Ah, that was really a glorious champagne they served.

MRS. LINDE: Yes, good night, Nora, and don't be stubborn anymore.

HELMER: Well put, Mrs. Linde!

MRS. LINDE: Good night, Mr. Helmer.

HELMER (*accompanying her to the door*): Good night, good night. I hope you get home all right. I'd be very happy to—but you don't have far to go. Good night, good night. (*She leaves. He shuts the door after her and returns.*) There, now, at last we got her out the door. She's a deadly bore, that creature.

NORA: Aren't you pretty tired, Torvald?

HELMER: No, not a bit.

NORA: You're not sleepy?

HELMER: Not at all. On the contrary, I'm feeling quite exhilarated. But you? Yes, you really look tired and sleepy.

NORA: Yes, I'm very tired. Soon now I'll sleep.

HELMER: See! You see! I was right all along that we shouldn't stay longer.

NORA: Whatever you do is always right.

HELMER (*kissing her brow*): Now my little lark talks sense. Say, did you notice what a time Rank was having tonight?

NORA: Oh, was he? I didn't get to speak with him.

HELMER: I scarcely did either, but it's a long time since I've seen him in such high spirits. (*Gazes at her a moment, then comes nearer her*) Hm—it's marvelous, though, to be back home again—to be completely alone with you. Oh, you bewitchingly lovely young woman!

NORA: Torvald, don't look at me like that!

HELMER: Can't I look at my richest treasure? At all that beauty that's mine, mine alone—completely and utterly.

NORA (*moving around to the other side of the table*): You mustn't talk to me that way tonight.

HELMER (*following her*): The tarantella is still in your blood, I can see—and it makes you even more enticing. Listen. The guests are beginning to go. (*Dropping his voice*) Nora—it'll soon be quiet through this whole house.

NORA: Yes, I hope so.

HELMER: You do, don't you, my love? Do you realize—when I'm out at a party like this with you—do you know why I talk to you so little, and keep such a distance away; just send you a stolen look now and then—you know why I do it? It's because I'm imagining then that you're my secret darling, my secret young bride-to-be, and that no one suspects there's anything between us.

NORA: Yes, yes; oh, yes, I know you're always thinking of me.

HELMER: And then when we leave and I place the shawl over those fine young rounded shoulders—over that wonderful curving neck—then I pretend that you're my young bride, that we're just coming from the wedding, that for the first time I'm bringing you into my house—that for the first time I'm alone with you—completely alone with you, your trembling young beauty! All this evening I've longed for nothing but you. When I saw you turn and sway in the tarantella—my blood was pounding till I couldn't stand it—that's why I brought you down here so early—

NORA: Go away, Torvald! Leave me alone. I don't want all this.

HELMER: What do you mean? Nora, you're teasing me. You will, won't you? Aren't I your husband—?

(*A knock at the outside door*)

NORA (*startled*): What's that?

HELMER (*going toward the hall*): Who is it?

RANK (*outside*): It's me. May I come in a moment?

HELMER (*with quiet irritation*): Oh, what does he want now? (*Aloud*) Hold on. (*Goes and opens the door*) Oh, how nice that you didn't just pass us by!

RANK: I thought I heard your voice, and then I wanted so badly to have a look in. (*Lightly glancing about*) Ah, me, these old familiar haunts. You have it snug and cozy in here, you two.

HELMER: You seemed to be having it pretty cozy upstairs, too.

RANK: Absolutely. Why shouldn't I? Why not take in everything in life? As much as you can, anyway, and as long as you can. The wine was superb—

HELMER: The champagne especially.

RANK: You noticed that too? It's amazing how much I could guzzle down.

NORA: Torvald also drank a lot of champagne this evening.

RANK: Oh?

NORA: Yes, and that always makes him so entertaining.

RANK: Well, why shouldn't one have a pleasant evening after a well-spent day?

HELMER: Well spent? I'm afraid I can't claim that.

RANK (*slapping him on the back*): But I can, you see!

NORA: Dr. Rank, you must have done some scientific research today.

RANK: Quite so.

HELMER: Come now—little Nora talking about scientific research!

NORA: And can I congratulate you on the results?

RANK: Indeed you may.

NORA: Then they were good?

RANK: The best possible for both doctor and patient—certainty.

NORA (*quickly and searchingly*): Certainty?

RANK: Complete certainty. So don't I owe myself a gay evening afterwards?

NORA: Yes, you're right, Dr. Rank.

HELMER: I'm with you—just so long as you don't have to suffer for it in the morning.

RANK: Well, one never gets something for nothing in life.

NORA: Dr. Rank—are you very fond of masquerade parties?

RANK: Yes, if there's a good array of odd disguises—

NORA: Tell me, what should we two go as at the next masquerade?

HELMER: You little feather head—already thinking of the next!

RANK: We two? I'll tell you what: you must go as Charmed Life—

HELMER: Yes, but find a costume for *that!*

RANK: Your wife can appear just as she looks every day.

HELMER: That was nicely put. But don't you know what you're going to be?

RANK: Yes, Helmer, I've made up my mind.

HELMER: Well?

RANK: At the next masquerade I'm going to be invisible.

HELMER: That's a funny idea.

RANK: They say there's a hat—black, huge—have you never heard of the hat that makes you invisible? You put it on, and then no one on earth can see you.

HELMER (*suppressing a smile*): Ah, of course.

RANK: But I'm quite forgetting what I came for. Helmer, give me a cigar, one of the dark Havanas.

HELMER: With the greatest pleasure. (*Holds out his case*)

RANK: Thanks. (*Takes one and cuts off the tip*)

NORA (*striking a match*): Let me give you a light.

RANK: Thank you. (*She holds the match for him; he lights the cigar.*) And now good-bye.

HELMER: Good-bye, good-bye, old friend.

NORA: Sleep well, Doctor.

RANK: Thanks for that wish.

NORA: Wish me the same.

RANK: You? All right, if you like—Sleep well. And thanks for the light.

(*He nods to them both and leaves.*)

HELMER (*his voice subdued*): He's been drinking heavily.

NORA (*absently*): Could be. (HELMER *takes his keys from his pocket and goes out in the hall.*) Torvald—what are you after?

HELMER: Got to empty the mailbox; it's nearly full. There won't be room for the morning papers.

NORA: Are you working tonight?

HELMER: You know I'm not. Why—what's this? Someone's been at the lock.

NORA: At the lock—?

HELMER: Yes, I'm positive. What do you suppose—? I can't imagine one of the maids—? Here's a broken hairpin. Nora, it's yours—

NORA (*quickly*): Then it must be the children—

HELMER: You'd better break them of that. Hm, hm—well, opened it after all. (*Takes the contents out and calls into the kitchen*) Helene! Helene, would you put out the lamp in the hall. (*He returns to the room, shutting the hall door, then displays the handful of mail.*) Look how it's piled up. (*Sorting through them*) Now what's this?

NORA (*at the window*): The letter! Oh, Torvald, no!

HELMER: Two calling cards—from Rank.

NORA: From Dr. Rank?

HELMER (*examining them*): "Dr. Rank, Consulting Physician." They were on top. He must have dropped them in as he left.

NORA: Is there anything on them?

HELMER: There's a black cross over the name. See? That's a gruesome notion. He could almost be announcing his own death.

NORA: That's just what he's doing.

HELMER: What! You've heard something? Something he's told you?

NORA: Yes. That when those cards came, he'd be taking his leave of us. He'll shut himself in now and die.

HELMER: Ah, my poor friend! Of course I knew he wouldn't be here much longer. But so soon—And then to hide himself away like a wounded animal.

NORA: If it has to happen, then it's best it happens in silence—don't you think so, Torvald?

HELMER (*pacing up and down*): He's grown right into our lives. I simply can't imagine him gone. He with his suffering and loneliness—like a dark cloud setting off our sunlit happiness. Well, maybe it's best this way. For him, at least. (*Standing still*) And maybe for us too, Nora. Now we're thrown back on each other, completely. (*Embracing her*) Oh you, my darling wife, how can I hold you close enough? You know what, Nora—time and again I've wished you were in some terrible danger, just so I could stake my life and soul and everything, for your sake.

NORA (*tearing herself away, her voice firm and decisive*): Now you must read your mail, Torvald.

HELMER: No, no, not tonight. I want to stay with you, dearest.

NORA: With a dying friend on your mind?

HELMER: You're right. We've both had a shock. There's ugliness between us—these thoughts of death and corruption. We'll have to get free of them first. Until then—we'll stay apart.

NORA (*clinging about his neck*): Torvald—good night! Good night!

HELMER (*kissing her on the cheek*): Good night, little songbird. Sleep well, Nora. I'll be reading my mail now.

(*He takes the letters into his room and shuts the door after him.*) NORA (*with bewildered glances, groping about, seizing* HELMER*'s domino, throwing it around her, and speaking in short,* *hoarse, broken whispers*): Never see him again. Never, never. (*Putting her shawl over her head*) Never see the children either—them, too. Never, never. Oh, the freezing black water! The depths—down—Oh, I wish it were over—He has it now; he's reading it—now. Oh no, no, not yet. Torvald, good-bye, you and the children—(*She starts for the hall; as she does,* HELMER *throws open his door and stands with an open letter in his hand.*)

HELMER: Nora!

NORA (*screams*): Oh—!

HELMER: What is this? You know what's in this letter?

NORA: Yes, I know. Let me go! Let me out!

HELMER (*holding her back*): Where are you going?

NORA (*struggling to break loose*): You can't save me, Torvald!

HELMER (*slumping back*): True! Then it's true what he writes? How horrible! No, no, it's impossible—it can't be true.

NORA: It *is* true. I've loved you more than all this world.

HELMER: Ah, none of your slippery tricks.

NORA (*taking one step toward him*): Torvald—!

HELMER: What *is* this you've blundered into!

NORA: Just let me loose. You're not going to suffer for my sake. You're not going to take on my guilt.

HELMER: No more playacting. (*Locks the hall door*) You stay right here and give me a reckoning. You understand what you've done? Answer! You understand?

NORA (*looking squarely at him, her face hardening*): Yes. I'm beginning to understand everything now.

HELMER (*striding about*): Oh, what an awful awakening! In all these eight years—she who was my pride and joy—a hypocrite, a liar—worse, worse—a criminal! How infinitely disgusting it all is! The shame! (NORA *says nothing and goes on looking straight at him. He stops in front of her.*) I should have suspected something of the kind. I should have known. All your father's flimsy values—Be still! All your father's flimsy values have come out in you. No religion, no morals, no sense of duty—Oh, how I'm punished for letting him off! I did it for your sake, and you repay me like this.

NORA: Yes, like this.

HELMER: Now you've wrecked all my happiness—ruined my whole future. Oh, it's awful to think of. I'm in a cheap little grafter's hands; he can do anything he wants with me, ask for anything, play with me like a puppet—and I can't breathe a word. I'll be swept down miserably into the depths on account of a featherbrained woman.

NORA: When I'm gone from this world, you'll be free.

HELMER: Oh, quit posing. Your father had a mess of those speeches too. What good would that ever do me if you were gone from this world, as you say? Not the slightest. He can still make the whole thing known; and if he does, I could be falsely suspected as your accomplice. They might even think that I was behind it—that I put you up to it. And all that I can thank you for—you that I've coddled the whole of our marriage. Can you see now what you've done to me?

NORA (*icily calm*): Yes.

HELMER: It's so incredible, I just can't grasp it. But we'll have to patch up whatever we can. Take off the shawl. I said, take it off! I've got to appease him somehow or other. The thing has to be hushed up at any cost. And as for you and me, it's got to seem like everything between us is just as it was—to the outside world, that is. You'll go right on living in this house, of course. But you can't be allowed to bring up the children; I don't dare trust you with them.—Oh, to have to say this to someone I've loved so much! Well, that's done with. From now on happiness doesn't matter; all that matters is saving the bits and pieces, the appearance—(*The doorbell rings.* HELMER *starts.*) What's that? And so late. Maybe the worst—? You think he'd—? Hide, Nora! Say you're sick. (NORA *remains standing motionless.* HELMER *goes and opens the door.*)

MAID (*half dressed, in the hall*): A letter for Mrs. Helmer.

HELMER: I'll take it. (*Snatches the letter and shuts the door*) Yes, it's from him. You don't get it; I'm reading it myself.

NORA: Then read it.

HELMER (*by the lamp*): I hardly dare. We may be ruined, you and I. But—I've got to know. (*Rips open the letter, skims through a few lines, glances at an enclosure, then cries out joyfully*) Nora! (NORA *looks inquiringly at him.*) Nora! Wait—better check it again—Yes, yes, it's true. I'm saved. Nora, I'm saved!

NORA: And I?

HELMER: You too, of course. We're both saved, both of us. Look. He's sent back your note. He says he's sorry and ashamed—that a happy development in his life—oh, who cares what he says! Nora, we're saved! No one can hurt you. Oh, Nora, Nora—but first, this ugliness all has to go. Let me see—(*Takes a look at the note*) No, I don't want to see it; I want the whole thing to fade like a dream. (*Tears the note and both letters to pieces, throws them into the stove and watches them burn*) There—now there's nothing left.—He wrote that since Christmas Eve you—oh, they must have been three terrible days for you, Nora.

NORA: I fought a hard fight.

HELMER: And suffered pain and saw no escape but—no, we're not going to dwell on anything unpleasant. We'll just be grateful and keep on repeating; it's over now, it's over! You hear me, Nora? You don't seem to realize—it's over. What's it mean—that frozen look? Oh, poor little Nora, I understand. You can't believe I've forgiven you. But I have, Nora; I swear I have. I know that what you did, you did out of love for me.

NORA: That's true.

HELMER: You loved me the way a wife ought to love her husband. It's simply the means that you couldn't judge. But you think I love you any the less for not knowing how to handle your affairs? No, no—just lean on me: I'll guide you and teach you. I wouldn't be a man if this feminine helplessness didn't make you twice as attractive to me. You mustn't mind those sharp words I said—that was all in the first confusion of thinking my world had collapsed. I've forgiven you, Nora; I swear I've forgiven you.

NORA: My thanks for your forgiveness.

(*She goes out through the door, right.*)

HELMER: No, wait—(*Peers in*) What are you doing in there?

NORA (*inside*): Getting out of my costume.

HELMER (*by the open door*): Yes, do that. Try to calm yourself and collect your thoughts again, my frightened little songbird. You can rest easy now; I've got wide wings to shelter you with. (*Walking about close by the door*) How snug and nice our home is, Nora. You're safe here; I'll keep you like a hunted dove I've rescued out of a hawk's claws. I'll bring peace to your poor, shuddering heart. Gradually it'll happen, Nora; you'll see. Tomorrow all this will look different to you; then everything will be as it was. I won't have to go on repeating I forgive you; you'll feel it for yourself. How can you imagine I'd ever conceivably want to disown you—or even blame you in any way? Ah, you don't know a man's heart, Nora. For a man there's something indescribably sweet and satisfying in knowing he's forgiven his wife—and forgiven her out of a full and open heart. It's as if she belongs to him in two ways now: in a sense he's given her fresh into the world again, and she's become his wife and his child as well. From now on that's what you'll be to me—you little, bewildered, helpless thing. Don't be afraid of anything, Nora; just open your heart to me, and I'll be conscience and will to you both—(NORA *enters in her regular clothes.*) What's this? Not in bed? You've changed your dress?

NORA: Yes, Torvald, I've changed my dress.

HELMER: But why now, so late?

NORA: Tonight I'm not sleeping.

HELMER: But Nora dear—

NORA (*looking at her watch*): It's still not so very late. Sit down, Torvald; we have a lot to talk over. (*She sits at one side of the table.*)

HELMER: Nora—what is this? That hard expression—

NORA: Sit down. This'll take some time. I have a lot to say.

HELMER (*sitting at the table directly opposite her*): You worry me, Nora. And I don't understand you.

NORA: No, that's exactly it. You don't understand me. And I've never understood you either—until tonight. No, don't interrupt. You can just listen to what I say. We're closing our accounts, Torvald.

HELMER: How do you mean that?

NORA (*after a short pause*): Doesn't anything strike you about our sitting here like this?

HELMER: What's that?

NORA: We've been married now eight years. Doesn't it occur to you that this is the first time we two, you and I, man and wife, have ever talked seriously together?

HELMER: What do you mean—seriously?

NORA: In eight whole years—longer even—right from our first acquaintance, we've never exchanged a serious word on any serious thing.

HELMER: You mean I should constantly go and involve you in problems you couldn't possibly help me with?

NORA: I'm not talking of problems, I'm saying that we've never sat down seriously together and tried to get to the bottom of anything.

HELMER: But dearest, what good would that ever do you?

NORA: That's the point right there: you've never understood me. I've been wronged greatly, Torvald—first by Papa, and then by you.

HELMER: What! By us—the two people who've loved you more than anyone else?

NORA (*shaking her head*): You never loved me. You've thought it fun to be in love with me, that's all.

HELMER: Nora, what a thing to say!

NORA: Yes, it's true now, Torvald. When I lived at home with Papa, he told me all his opinions, so I had the same ones too; or if they were different I hid them, since he wouldn't have cared for that. He used to call me his doll-child, and he played with me the way I played with my dolls. Then I came into your house—

HELMER: How can you speak of our marriage like that?

NORA (*unperturbed*): I mean, then I went from Papa's hands into yours. You arranged everything to your own taste, and so I got the same taste as you—or I pretended to; I can't remember. I guess a little of both, first one, then the other. Now when I look back, it seems as if I'd lived here like a beggar—just from hand to mouth. I've lived by doing tricks for you, Torvald. But that's the way you wanted it. It's a great sin what you and Papa did to me. You're to blame that nothing's become of me.

HELMER: Nora, how unfair and ungrateful you are! Haven't you been happy here?

NORA: No, never. I thought so—but I never have.

HELMER: Not—not happy!

NORA: No, only lighthearted. And you've always been so kind to me. But our home's been nothing but a playpen. I've been your doll-wife here, just as at home I was Papa's doll-child. And in turn the children have been my dolls. I thought it was fun when you played with me, just as they thought it fun when I played with them. That's been our marriage, Torvald.

HELMER: There's some truth in what you're saying—under all the raving exaggeration. But it'll all be different after this. Playtime's over; now for the schooling.

NORA: Whose schooling—mine or the children's?

HELMER: Both yours and the children's, dearest.

NORA: Oh, Torvald, you're not the man to teach me to be a good wife to you.

HELMER: And you can say that?

NORA: And I—how am I equipped to bring up children?

HELMER: Nora!

NORA: Didn't you say a moment ago that that was no job to trust me with?

HELMER: In a flare of temper! Why fasten on that?

NORA: Yes, but you were so very right. I'm not up to the job. There's another job I have to do first. I have to try to educate myself. You can't help me with that. I've got to do it alone. And that's why I'm leaving you now.

HELMER (*jumping up*): What's that?

NORA: I have to stand completely alone, if I'm ever going to discover myself and the world out there. So I can't go on living with you.

HELMER: Nora, Nora!

NORA: I want to leave right away. Kristine should put me up for the night—

HELMER: You're insane! You've no right! I forbid you!

NORA: From here on, there's no use forbidding me anything. I'll take with me whatever is mine. I don't want a thing from you, either now or later.

HELMER: What kind of madness is this!

NORA: Tomorrow I'm going home—I mean, home where I came from. It'll be easier up there to find something to do.

HELMER: Oh, you blind, incompetent child!

NORA: I must learn to be competent, Torvald.

HELMER: Abandon your home, your husband, your children! And you're not even thinking what people will say.

NORA: I can't be concerned about that. I only know how essential this is.

HELMER: Oh, it's outrageous. So you'll run out like this on your most sacred vows.

NORA: What do you think are my most sacred vows?

HELMER: And I have to tell you that! Aren't they your duties to your husband and children?

NORA: I have other duties equally sacred.

HELMER: That isn't true. What duties are they?

NORA: Duties to myself.

HELMER: Before all else, you're a wife and a mother.

NORA: I don't believe in that anymore. I believe that, before all else, I'm a human being, no less than you—or anyway, I ought to try to become one. I know the majority thinks you're right, Torvald, and plenty of books agree with you, too. But I can't go on believing what the majority says, or what's written in books. I have to think over these things myself and try to understand them.

HELMER: Why can't you understand your place in your own home? On a point like that, isn't there one everlasting guide you can turn to? Where's your religion?

NORA: Oh, Torvald, I'm really not sure what religion is.

HELMER: What—?

NORA: I only know what the minister said when I was confirmed. He told me religion was this thing and that. When I get clear and away by myself, I'll go into that problem too. I'll see if what the minister said was right, or, in any case, if it's right for me.

HELMER: A young woman your age shouldn't talk like that. If religion can't move you, I can try to rouse your conscience. You do have some moral feeling? Or, tell me—has that gone too?

NORA: It's not easy to answer that, Torvald. I simply don't know. I'm all confused about these things. I just know I see them so differently from you. I find out, for one thing, that the law's not at all what I'd thought—but I can't get it through my head that the law is fair. A woman hasn't a right to protect her dying father or save her husband's life! I can't believe that.

HELMER: You talk like a child. You don't know anything of the world you live in.

NORA: No, I don't. But now I'll begin to learn for myself. I'll try to discover who's right, the world or I.

HELMER: Nora, you're sick; you've got a fever. I almost think you're out of your head.

NORA: I've never felt more clearheaded and sure in my life.

HELMER: And—clearheaded and sure—you're leaving your husband and children?

NORA: Yes.

HELMER: Then there's only one possible reason.

NORA: What?

HELMER: You no longer love me.

NORA: No. That's exactly it.

HELMER: Nora! You can't be serious!

NORA: Oh, this is so hard, Torvald—you've been so kind to me always. But I can't help it. I don't love you anymore.

HELMER (*struggling for composure*): Are you also clearheaded and sure about that?

NORA: Yes, completely. That's why I can't go on staying here.

HELMER: Can you tell me what I did to lose your love?

NORA: Yes, I can tell you. It was this evening when the miraculous thing didn't come—then I knew you weren't the man I'd imagined.

HELMER: Be more explicit; I don't follow you.

NORA: I've waited now so patiently eight long years—for, my Lord, I know miracles don't come every day. Then this crisis broke over me, and such a certainty filled me: *now* the miraculous event would occur. While Krogstad's letter was lying out there, I never for an instant dreamed that you could give in to his terms. I was so utterly sure you'd say to him: go on, tell your tale to the whole wide world. And when he'd done that—

HELMER: Yes, what then? When I'd delivered my own wife into shame and disgrace—!

NORA: When he'd done that, I was so utterly sure that you'd step forward, take the blame on yourself and say: I am the guilty one.

HELMER: Nora—!

NORA: You're thinking I'd never accept such a sacrifice from you? No, of course not. But what good would my protests be against you? That was the miracle I was waiting for, in terror and hope. And to stave that off, I would have taken my life.

HELMER: I'd gladly work for you day and night, Nora—and take on pain and deprivation. But there's no one who gives up honor for love.

NORA: Millions of women have done just that.

HELMER: Oh, you think and talk like a silly child.

NORA: Perhaps. But you neither think nor talk like the man I could join myself to. When your big fright was over—and it wasn't from any threat against me, only for what might damage you—when all the danger was past, for you it was just as if nothing had happened. I was exactly the same, your little lark, your doll, that you'd have to handle with double care now that I'd turned out so brittle and frail. (*Gets up*) Torvald—in that instant it dawned on me that for eight years I've been living here with a stranger, and that I'd even conceived three children—oh, I can't stand the thought of it! I could tear myself to bits.

HELMER (*heavily*): I see. There's a gulf that's opened between us—that's clear. Oh, but Nora, can't we bridge it somehow?

NORA: The way I am now, I'm no wife for you.

HELMER: I have the strength to make myself over.

NORA: Maybe—if your doll gets taken away.

HELMER: But to part! To part from you! No, Nora, no—I can't imagine it.

NORA (*going out, right*): All the more reason why it has to be. (*She reenters with her coat and a small overnight bag, which she puts on a chair by the table.*)

HELMER: Nora, Nora, not now! Wait till tomorrow.

NORA: I can't spend the night in a strange man's room.

HELMER: But couldn't we live here like brother and sister—

NORA: You know very well how long that would last. (*Throws her shawl about her*) Good-bye, Torvald. I won't look in on the children. I know they're in better hands than mine. The way I am now, I'm no use to them.

HELMER: But someday, Nora—someday—?

NORA: How can I tell? I haven't the least idea what'll become of me.

HELMER: But you're my wife, now and wherever you go.

NORA: Listen, Torvald—I've heard that when a wife deserts her husband's house just as I'm doing, then the law frees him from all responsibility. In any case, I'm freeing you from being responsible. Don't feel yourself bound, any more than I will. There has to be absolute freedom for us both. Here, take your ring back. Give me mine.

HELMER: That too?

NORA: That too.

HELMER: There it is.

NORA: Good. Well, now it's all over. I'm putting the keys here. The maids know all about keeping up the house—better than I do. Tomorrow, after I've left town, Kristine will stop by to pack up everything that's mine from home. I'd like those things shipped to me.

HELMER: Over! All over! Nora, won't you ever think about me?

NORA: I'm sure I'll think of you often, and about the children and the house here.

HELMER: May I write you?

NORA: No—never. You're not to do that.

HELMER: Oh, but let me send you—

NORA: Nothing. Nothing.

HELMER: Or help you if you need it.

NORA: No. I accept nothing from strangers.

HELMER: Nora—can I never be more than a stranger to you?

NORA (*picking up the overnight bag*): Ah, Torvald—it would take the greatest miracle of all—

HELMER: Tell me the greatest miracle!

NORA: You and I both would have to transform ourselves to the point that—oh, Torvald, I've stopped believing in miracles.

HELMER: But I'll believe. Tell me! Transform ourselves to the point that—?

NORA: That our living together could be a true marriage.

(*She goes out down the hall.*)

HELMER (*sinks down on a chair by the door, face buried in his hands*): Nora! Nora! (*Looking about and rising*) Empty. She's gone. (*A sudden hope leaps in him*) The greatest miracle—?

(*From below, the sound of a door slamming shut*)

(1879)

QUESTIONS FOR CRITICAL THINKING AND WRITING

Experience

1. Describe your experience of reading (or viewing) *A Doll House.* How do you respond to Torvald Helmer's treatment of his wife, Nora? How do you respond to Nora's behavior? Why?
2. Describe Torvald Helmer. What aspects of his character are most evident in the early scenes? Does he give any evidence of having changed by the end of the play? Do you think he is capable of sharing the kind of marriage Nora describes at the end of the play?

Interpretation

3. Consider the function of the following characters: Nils Krogstad, Dr. Rank, and Kristine Linde.

4. Examine the play's plot. How does Ibsen control our responses and arouse our curiosity? Point out places where the tempo or pace of the play changes. What effects do these changes have?
5. Identify two or three visual details or objects that function as symbols, and explain their significance.
6. Choose one scene important for its revelation of character and explain how you would dramatize it.

Evaluation

7. Evaluate Nora's behavior. Does she make the right decision in leaving her family? Why or why not?
8. Ibsen has remarked that *A Doll House* is more about human rights than women's rights. What kind of rights do you think he had in mind?

Connection

9. Compare Nora with Rose in *Fences* by August Wilson.

Critical Thinking

10. *A Doll House* has been performed with an alternative ending in which Nora and Torvald are reconciled, and Nora remains with her family. Is this an artistically appropriate and theatrically effective ending? Why or why not?
11. The title of Ibsen's *A Doll House* is sometimes translated as *A Doll's House*. What is suggested by each title? Which title do you prefer, and why?

CHAPTER TWENTY-EIGHT

Envisioning Drama: Williams and Miller in Performance

ENVISIONING *THE GLASS MENAGERIE*

As with most modern realistic drama, the specific stage directions for *The Glass Menagerie* are written into the text of the play. Since its first performance in 1944, every subsequent performance has to take these directions into account by either trying to breathe life into those words or interpreting their spirit. While these directions specifically guide each performance, there are always refinements and necessary adaptations made based on a number of factors, such as the director's vision, the actors' abilities, and the materials on hand. Following is an excerpt from Tennessee Williams's notes on that original production. Also included are an original sketch from set designer Jo Mielziner with photos from the 1944 production. Lastly, there are photos from a 1989 production of *The Glass Menagerie.* Compare the photos, sketch, and ideas with the play itself. How do the productions compare with the original sketch? How do they compare with each other? As you read the play, consider what decisions must be made when staging a performance of *The Glass Menagerie.*

TENNESSEE WILLIAMS
[1914–1983]

Tennessee Williams, who was born Thomas Lanier Williams in Columbia, Missouri, attended school in St. Louis, and graduated from the University of Iowa. As a young man Williams held a number of odd jobs, including working as a waiter in New York, a teletype operator in Florida, a bellhop in Louisiana. As a young man, he also wrote poetry and fiction, but was destined for drama after viewing a performance of Ibsen's Ghosts.

Williams' The Glass Menagerie *was both a popular and critical success, winning the Drama Critics Circle Award. Other Williams plays won awards as well, including* A Streetcar Named Desire *and* Cat on a Hot Tin Roof, *both of which won the Pulitzer Prize. One of his best-loved plays,* The Glass Menagerie *is a portrayal of loneliness among characters who confuse fantasy and reality.*

Production Notes to The Glass Menagerie

Being a "memory play," *The Glass Menagerie* can be presented with unusual freedom of convention. Because of its considerably delicate or tenuous material, atmospheric touches and subtleties of direction play a particularly important part. Expressionism and all other unconventional techniques in drama have only one valid aim, and that is a closer approach to truth. When a play employs unconventional techniques, it is not, or certainly should not be, trying to escape its responsibility of dealing with reality, or interpreting experience, but is actually or should be attempting to find a closer approach, a more penetrating and vivid expression of things as they are. The straight realistic play with its genuine Frigidaire and authentic ice-cubes, its characters who

Jo Mielziner's sketch of the set for the 1944 production.

speak exactly as its audience speaks, corresponds to the academic landscape and has the same virtue of a photographic likeness. Everyone should know nowadays the unimportance of the photographic in art: that truth, life, or reality is an organic thing which the poetic imagination can represent or suggest, in essence, only through transformation, through changing into other forms than those which were merely present in appearance.

These remarks are not meant as a preface only to this particular play. They have to do with a conception of a new, plastic theatre which must take the place of the exhausted theatre of realistic conventions if the theatre is to resume vitality as a part of our culture.

THE SCREEN DEVICE

There is *only one important difference between the original and the acting version of the play* and that is the *omission* in the latter of the device that I tentatively included in my *original* script. This device was the use of a screen on which were projected magic-lantern slides bearing images or titles. I do not regret the omission of this device from the original Broadway production. The extraordinary power of Miss Taylor's performance made it suitable to have the utmost simplicity in the physical production. But I think it may be interesting to some readers to see how this device was conceived. So I am putting it into the published manuscript. These images and legends, projected

Julie Haydon as Laura.

from behind, were cast on a section of wall between the front-room and dining-room areas, which should be indistinguishable from the rest when not in use.

The purpose of this will probably be apparent. It is to give accent to certain values in each scene. Each scene contains a particular point (or several) which is structurally the most important. In an episodic play, such as this, the basic structure or narrative line may be obscured from the audience; the effect may seem fragmentary rather than architectural. This may not be the fault of the play so much as a lack of attention in the audience. The legend or image upon the screen will strengthen the effect of what is merely allusion in the writing and allow the primary point to be made more simply and lightly than if the entire responsibility were on the spoken lines. Aside from this structural value, I think the screen will have a definite emotional appeal, less definable but just as important. An imaginative producer or director may invent many other uses for this device than those indicated in the present script. In fact the possibilities of the device seem much larger to me than the instance of this play can possibly utilize.

Julie Haydon as Laura (See p. 1157) and Laurette Taylor as Amanda (above) in the original 1944 performance. Note their costumes and compare them with the 1989 performance that follows.

THE MUSIC

Another extra-literary accent in this play is provided by the use of music. A single recurring tune, "The Glass Menagerie," is used to give emotional emphasis to suitable passages. This tune is like circus music, not when you are on the grounds or in the immediate vicinity of the parade, but when you are at some distance and very likely thinking of something else. It seems under those circumstances to continue almost interminably and it weaves in and out of your preoccupied consciousness; then it is the lightest, most delicate music in the world and perhaps the saddest. It expresses the surface vivacity of life with the underlying strain of immutable and inexpressible sorrow. When you look at a piece of delicately spun glass you think of two things: how

Ruby Dee as Amanda (left) and Tonia Rowe as Laura (right) in a 1989 production. Compare the costumes with the 1944 performance. Also, consider how staging an all African-American performance changes the possible interpretations of the play.

Set from the 1989 production. Compare with the original sketch.

beautiful it is and how easily it can be broken. Both of those ideas should be woven into the recurring tune, which dips in and out of the play as if it were carried on a wind that changes. It serves as a thread of connection and allusion between the narrator with his separate point in time and space and the subject of his story. Between each episode it returns as reference to the emotion, nostalgia, which is the first condition of the play. It is primarily Laura's music and therefore comes out most clearly when the play focuses upon her and the lovely fragility of glass which is her image.

THE LIGHTING

The lighting in the play is not realistic. In keeping with the atmosphere of memory, the stage is dim. Shafts of light are focused on selected areas or actors, sometimes in contradistinction to what is the apparent center. For instance, in the quarrel scene between Tom and Amanda, in which Laura has no active part, the clearest pool of light is on her figure. This is also true of the supper scene, when her silent figure on the sofa should remain the visual center. The light upon Laura should be distinct from the others, having a peculiar pristine clarity such as light used in early religious portraits of female saints or madonnas. A certain correspondence to light in religious paintings, such as El Greco's, where the figures are radiant in atmosphere that is relatively dusky, could be effectively used throughout the play. (It will also permit a more effective use of the screen.) A free, imaginative use of light can be of enormous value in giving a mobile, plastic quality to plays of a more or less static nature.

The Glass Menagerie

Scene One

The Wingfield apartment is in the rear of the building, one of those vast hive-like conglomerations of cellular living-units that flower as warty growths in overcrowded urban centers of lower middle-class population and are symptomatic of the impulse of this largest and fundamentally enslaved section of American society to avoid fluidity and differentiation and to exist and function as one interfused mass of automatism.

The apartment faces an alley and is entered by a fire escape, a structure whose name is a touch of accidental poetic truth, for all of these huge buildings are always burning with the slow and implacable fires of human desperation. The fire escape is part of what we see—that is, the landing of it and steps descending from it.

The scene is memory and is therefore nonrealistic. Memory takes a lot of poetic license. It omits some details; others are exaggerated, according to the emotional value of the articles it touches, for memory is seated predominantly in the heart. The interior is therefore rather dim and poetic.

At the rise of the curtain, the audience is faced with the dark, grim rear wall of the Wingfield tenement. This building is flanked on both sides by dark, narrow alleys which run into murky canyons of tangled clotheslines, garbage cans, and the sinister latticework of neighboring fire escapes. It is up and down these side alleys that exterior entrances and exits are made during the play. At the end of TOM*'s opening commentary, the dark tenement wall slowly becomes transparent and reveals the interior of the ground-floor Wingfield apartment.*

Nearest the audience is the living room, which also serves as a sleeping room for LAURA*, the sofa unfolding to make her bed. Just beyond, separated from the living room by a wide arch or second proscenium with transparent faded portieres (or second curtain), is the dining room. In an old-fashioned whatnot in the living room are seen scores of transparent glass animals. A blown-up photograph of the father hangs on the wall of the living room, to the left of the archway. It is the face of a very handsome young man in a doughboy's First World War cap. He is gallantly smiling, ineluctably smiling, as if to say "I will be smiling forever."*

Also hanging on the wall, near the photograph, are a typewriter keyboard chart and a Gregg shorthand diagram. An upright typewriter on a small table stands beneath the charts.

The audience hears and sees the opening scene in the dining room through both the transparent fourth wall of the building and the transparent gauze portieres of the dining-room arch. It is during this revealing scene that the fourth wall slowly ascends, out of sight. This transparent exterior wall is not brought down again until the very end of the play, during TOM*'s final speech.*

The narrator is an undisguised convention of the play. He takes whatever license with dramatic convention is convenient to his purposes.

TOM *enters, dressed as a merchant sailor, and strolls across the fire escape. There he stops and lights a cigarette. He addresses the audience.*

TOM: Yes, I have tricks in my pocket, I have things up my sleeve. But I am opposite of a stage magician. He gives you illusion that has the appearance of truth. I give you truth in the pleasant disguise of illusion.

To begin with, I turn back time. I reverse it to that quaint period, the thirties, when the huge middle class of America was matriculating in a school for the blind. Their eyes had failed them, or they had failed their eyes, and so they were having their fingers pressed forcibly down on the fiery Braille alphabet of the dissolving economy.

In Spain there was revolution. Here there was only shouting and confusion. In Spain there was Guernica. Here there were disturbances of labor, sometimes pretty violent, in otherwise peaceful cities such as Chicago, Cleveland, Saint Louis . . .

This is the social background of the play.

[*Music begins to play.*]

The play is memory. Being a memory play, it is dimly lighted, it is sentimental, it is not realistic. In memory everything seems to happen to music. That explains the fiddle in the wings.

I am the narrator of the play, and also a character in it. The other characters are my mother, Amanda, my sister, Laura, and a gentleman caller who appears in the final scenes. He is the most realistic character in the play, being an emissary from a world of reality that we were somehow set apart from. But since I have a poet's weakness for symbols, I am using this character also as a symbol; he is the long-delayed but always expected something that we live for.

There is a fifth character in the play who doesn't appear except in this larger-than-life-size photograph over the mantel. This is our father who left us a long time ago. He was a telephone man who fell in love with long distances; he gave up his job with the telephone company and skipped the light fantastic out of town . . .

The last we heard of him was a picture postcard from Mazatlan, on the Pacific coast of Mexico, containing a message of two words: "Hello—Goodbye!" and no address.

I think the rest of the play will explain itself. . . .

[AMANDA*'s voice becomes audible through the portieres.*]

[*Legend on screen: "Ou sont les neiges."*]

[TOM *divides the portieres and enters the dining room.* AMANDA *and* LAURA *are seated at a drop-leaf table. Eating is indicated by gestures without food or utensils.* AMANDA *faces the audience.* TOM *and* LAURA *are seated in profile. The interior has lit up softly and through the scrim we see* AMANDA *and* LAURA *seated at the table.*]

AMANDA [*calling*]: Tom?

TOM: Yes, Mother.

AMANDA: We can't say grace until you come to the table!

TOM: Coming, Mother. [*He bows slightly and withdraws, reappearing a few moments later in his place at the table.*]

AMANDA [*to her son*]: Honey, don't *push* with your *fingers.* If you have to push with something, the thing to push with is a crust of bread. And chew—chew! Animals have secretions in their stomachs which enable them to digest food without mastication, but human beings are supposed to chew their food before they swallow it down. Eat food leisurely, son, and really enjoy it. A well-cooked meal has lots of delicate flavors that have to be held in the mouth for appreciation. So chew your food and give your salivary glands a chance to function!

[TOM *deliberately lays his imaginary fork down and pushes his chair back from the table.*]

TOM: I haven't enjoyed one bite of this dinner because of your constant directions on how to eat it. It's you that make me rush through meals with your hawklike attention to every bite I take. Sickening—spoils my appetite—all this discussion of—animal's secretion—salivary glands—mastication!

AMANDA [*lightly*]: Temperament like a Metropolitan star!

[TOM *rises and walks toward the living room.*]

You're not excused from the table.

TOM: I'm getting a cigarette.

AMANDA: You smoke too much.

[LAURA *rises.*]

LAURA: I'll bring in the blanc mange.

[TOM *remains standing with his cigarette by the portieres.*]

AMANDA [*rising*]: No, sister, no, sister—you be the lady this time and I'll be the darky.

LAURA: I'm already up.

AMANDA: Resume your seat, little sister—I want you to stay fresh and pretty—for gentlemen callers!

LAURA [*sitting down*]: I'm not expecting any gentlemen callers.

AMANDA [*crossing out to the kitchenette, airily*]: Sometimes they come when they are least expected! Why, I remember one Sunday afternoon in Blue Mountain—

[*She enters the kitchenette.*]

TOM: I know what's coming!

LAURA: Yes. But let her tell it.

TOM: Again?

LAURA: She loves to tell it.

[AMANDA *returns with a bowl of dessert.*]

AMANDA: One Sunday afternoon in the Blue Mountain—your mother received—*seventeen!*—gentlemen callers! Why, sometimes there weren't chairs enough to accommodate them all. We had to send the nigger over to bring in folding chairs from the parish house.

TOM [*remaining at the portieres*]: How did you entertain those gentlemen callers?

AMANDA: I understood the art of conversation!

TOM: I bet you could talk.

AMANDA: Girls in those days *knew* how to talk, I can tell you.

TOM: Yes?

[*Image on screen:* AMANDA *as a girl on a porch, greeting callers.*]

AMANDA: They knew how to entertain their gentlemen callers. It wasn't enough for a girl to be possessed of a pretty face and a graceful figure—although I wasn't slighted in either respect. She also needed to have nimble wit and a tongue to meet all occasions.

TOM: What did you talk about?

AMANDA: Things of importance going on in the world! Never anything coarse or common or vulgar.

[*She addresses* TOM *as though he were seated in the vacant chair at the table though he remains by the portieres. He plays this scene as though reading from a script.*]

My callers were gentlemen—all! Among my callers were some of the most prominent young planters of the Mississippi Delta—planters and sons of planters!

[TOM *motions for music and a spot of light on* AMANDA. *Her eyes lift, her face glows, her voice becomes rich and elegiac.*]

[*Screen legend: "Ou sont les neiges d'antan?"*]

There was young Champ Laughlin who later became vice-president of the Delta Planters Bank. Hadley Stevenson who was drowned in Moon Lake and left his widow one hundred and fifty thousand in Government bonds. There were the Cutrere brothers, Wesley and Bates. Bates was one of my bright particular beaux! He got in a quarrel with that wild Wainwright boy. They shot it out on the floor of Moon Lake Casino. Bates was shot through the stomach. Dies in the ambulance on his way to Memphis. His widow was also well provided for, came into eight or ten thousand acres, that's all. She married him on the rebound—never loved her—carried my picture on him the night he died! And there was that boy that every girl in the Delta had set her cap for! That beautiful, brilliant young Fitzhugh boy from Greene County!

TOM: What did he leave his widow?

AMANDA: He never married! Gracious, you talk as though all of my admirers had turned up their toes to the daisies!

TOM: Isn't this the first you've mentioned that still survives?

AMANDA: That Fitzhugh boy went North and made a fortune—came to be known as the Wolf of Wall Street! He had the Midas touch, whatever he touched turned to gold! And I could have been Mrs. Duncan J. Fitzhugh, mind you! But—I picked your *father!*

LAURA [*rising*]: Mother, let me clear the table.

AMANDA: No, dear, you go in front and study your typewriter chart. Or practice your shorthand a little. Stay fresh and pretty!—It's almost time for our gentlemen callers to start arriving. [*She flounces girlishly toward the kitchenette*] How many do you suppose we're going to entertain this afternoon?

[TOM *throws down the paper and jumps up with a groan.*]

LAURA [*alone in the dining room*]: I don't believe we're going to receive any, Mother.

AMANDA [*reappearing, airily*]: What? No one—not one? You must be joking!

[LAURA *nervously echoes her laugh. She slips in a fugitive manner through the half-open portieres and draws them gently behind her. A shaft of very clear light is thrown on her face against the faded tapestry of the curtains. Faintly the music of "The Glass Menagerie" is heard as she continues, lightly:*]

Not one gentleman caller? It can't be true! There must be a flood, there must have been a tornado!

LAURA: It isn't a flood, it's not a tornado, Mother. I'm just not popular like you were in Blue Mountain. . . .

[TOM *utters another groan.* LAURA *glances at him with a faint, apologetic smile. Her voice catches a little:*]

Mother's afraid I'm going to be an old maid.

[*The scene dims out with the "Glass Menagerie" music.*]

Scene Two

On the dark stage the screen is lighted with the image of blue roses. Gradually LAURA*'s figure becomes apparent and the screen goes out. The music subsides.*

LAURA *is seated in the delicate ivory chair at the small claw-foot table. She wears a dress of soft violet material for a kimono—her hair is tied back from her forehead with a ribbon. She is washing and polishing her collection of glass.* AMANDA *appears on the fire escape steps. At the sound of her ascent,* LAURA *catches her breath, thrusts the bowl of ornaments away, and seats herself stiffly before the diagram of the typewriter keyboard as though it held her spellbound. Something has happened to* AMANDA. *It is written in her face as she climbs to the landing: a look that is grim and hopeless and a little absurd. She has on one of those cheap or imitation velvety-looking cloth coats with imitation fur collar. Her hat is five or six years old, one of those dreadful cloche hats that were worn in the late Twenties, and she is clutching an enormous black patent-leather pocketbook with nickel clasps and initials. This is her full-dress outfit, the one she usually wears to the D.A.R. Before entering she looks through the door. She purses her lips, opens her eyes very wide, rolls them upward and shakes her head. Then she slowly lets herself in the door. Seeing her mother's expression* LAURA *touches her lips with a nervous gesture.*

LAURA: Hello, Mother, I was— [*she makes a nervous gesture toward the chart on the wall.* AMANDA *leans against the shut door and stares at* LAURA *with a martyred look.*]

AMANDA: Deception? Deception? [*She slowly removes her hat and gloves, continuing the sweet suffering stare. She lets the hat and gloves fall on the floor—a bit of acting.*]

LAURA [*shakily*]: How was the D.A.R. meeting?

[AMANDA *slowly opens her purse and removes a dainty white handkerchief which she shakes out delicately and delicately touches to her lips and nostrils.*]

Didn't you go to the D.A.R. meeting, Mother?

AMANDA [*faintly, almost inaudibly*]: —No.—No. [*then more forcibly:*] I did not have the strength—to go to the D.A.R. In fact, I did not have the courage! I wanted to find a hole in the ground and hide myself in it forever! [*She crosses slowly to the wall and removes the diagram of the typewriter keyboard. She holds it in front of her for a second, staring at it sweetly and sorrowfully—then bites her lips and tears it in two pieces.*]

LAURA [*faintly*]: Why did you do that, Mother?

[AMANDA *repeats the same procedure with the chart of the Gregg Alphabet.*]

Why are you—

AMANDA: Why? Why? How old are you, Laura?

LAURA: Mother, you know my age.

AMANDA: I thought that you were an adult; it seems that I was mistaken. [*She crosses slowly to the sofa and sinks down and stares at* LAURA.]

LAURA: Please don't stare at me, Mother.

[AMANDA *closes her eyes and lowers her head. There is a ten-second pause.*]

AMANDA: What are we going to do, what is going to become of us, what is the future?

[*There is another pause.*]

LAURA: Has something happened, Mother?

[AMANDA *draws a long breath, takes out the handkerchief again, goes through the dabbing process.*]

Mother, has—something happened?

AMANDA: I'll be all right in a minute, I'm just bewildered—[*She hesitates.*]—by life. . . .

LAURA: Mother, I wish that you would tell me what's happened!

AMANDA: As you know, I was supposed to be inducted into my office at the D.A.R. this afternoon.

[*Screen image: A swarm of typewriters.*]

But I stopped off at Rubicam's Business College to speak to your teachers about your having a cold and ask them what progress they thought you were making down there.

LAURA: Oh. . . .

AMANDA: I went to the typing instructor and introduced myself as your mother. She didn't know who you were. "Wingfield," she said, "We don't have any such student enrolled at the school!"

I assured her she did, that you had been going to classes since early in January.

"I wonder," she said, "If you could be talking about that terribly shy little girl who dropped out of school after only a few days' attendance?"

"No," I said, "Laura, my daughter, has been going to school every day for the past six weeks!"

"Excuse me," she said. She took the attendance book out and there was your name, unmistakably printed, and all the dates you were absent until they decided that you had dropped out of school.

I still said, "No, there must have been some mistake! There must have been some mix-up in the records!"

And she said, "No—I remember her perfectly now. Her hands shook so that she couldn't hit the right keys! The first time we gave a speed test, she broke down completely—was sick at the stomach and almost had to be carried into the wash room! After that morning she never showed up any more. We phoned the house but never got any answer"—While I was working at Famour-Barr, I suppose, demonstrating those—

[*She indicates a brassiere with her hands.*]

Oh! I felt so weak I could barely keep on my feet! I had to sit down while they got me a glass of water! Fifty dollars' tuition, all of our plans—my hopes and ambitions for you—just gone up the spout, just gone up the spout like that.

[LAURA *draws a long breath and gets awkwardly to her feet. She crosses to the Victrola and winds it up.*]

What are you doing?

LAURA: Oh! [*She releases the handle and returns to her seat.*]

AMANDA: Laura, where have been going when you've gone out pretending that you were going to business college?

LAURA: I've just been going out walking.

AMANDA: That's not true.

LAURA: It is. I just went walking.

AMANDA: Walking? Walking? In winter? Deliberately courting pneumonia in that light coat? Where did you walk to, Laura?

LAURA: All sorts of places—mostly in the park.

AMANDA: Even after you'd started catching that cold?

LAURA: It was the lesser of two evils, Mother.

[*Screen image: Winter scene in a park.*]

I couldn't go back there. I—threw up—on the floor!

AMANDA: From half past seven till after five every day you mean to tell me you walked around in the park, because you wanted to make me think that you were still going to Rubicam's Business College?

LAURA: It wasn't as bad as it sounds. I went inside places to get warmed up.

AMANDA: Inside where?

LAURA: I went in the art museum and the bird houses at the Zoo. I visited the penguins every day! Sometimes I did without lunch and went to the movies. Lately I've been spending most of my afternoons in the Jewel Box, that big glass house where they raise the tropical flowers.

AMANDA: You did all this to deceive me, just for deception?

[LAURA *looks down.*]

Why?

LAURA: Mother, when you're disappointed, you get that awful suffering look on your face, like the picture of Jesus' mother in the museum!

AMANDA: Hush!

LAURA: I couldn't face it.

[*There is a pause. A whisper of strings is heard. Legend on screen: "The Crust of Humility."*]

AMANDA [*hopelessly fingering the huge pocketbook*]: So what are we going to do the rest of our lives? Stay home and watch the parades go by? Amuse ourselves with the glass menagerie, darling? Eternally play those worn-out phonograph records your father left as a painful reminder of him? We won't have a business career—we've given that up because it gave us nervous indigestion! [*She laughs wearily.*] What is there left but dependency all our lives? I know so well what becomes of unmarried women who aren't prepared to occupy a position. I've seen such pitiful cases in the South—barely tolerated spinsters living upon the grudging patronage of sister's husband or brother's wife!—stuck away in some little mousetrap of a room—encouraged by one in-law to visit another—little birdlike women without any nest—eating the crust of humility all their life!

Is that the future that we've mapped out for ourselves? I swear it's the only alternative I can think of! [*She pauses.*] It isn't a very pleasant alternative, is it? [*She pauses again.*] Of course—some girls *do marry.*

[LAURA *twists her hands nervously.*]

Haven't you ever liked some boy?

LAURA: Yes. I liked one once. [*She rises.*] I came across his picture a while ago.

AMANDA [*with some interest*]: He gave you his picture?

LAURA: No, it's in the yearbook.

AMANDA [*disappointed*]: Oh—a high school boy.

[*Screen image: Jim as the high school hero bearing a silver cup.*]

LAURA: Yes. His name was Jim. [*She lifts the heavy annual from the claw-foot table.*] Here he is in *The Pirates of Penzance.*

AMANDA [*absently*]: The what?

LAURA: The operetta the senior class put on. He had a wonderful voice and we sat across the aisle from each other Mondays, Wednesdays and Fridays in the Aud. Here he is with the silver cup for debating! See his grin?

AMANDA [*absently*]: He must have had a jolly disposition.

LAURA: He used to call me—Blue Roses.

[*Screen image: Blue roses.*]

AMANDA: Why did he call you such a name as that?

LAURA: When I had that attack of pleurosis—he asked me what was the matter when I came back. I said pleurosis—he thought that I said Blue Roses! So that's what he always called me after that. Whenever he saw me, he'd holler, "Hello, Blue Roses!" I didn't care for the girl that he went out with. Emily Meisenbach. Emily was the best-dressed girl at Soldan. She never struck me, though, as being sincere . . . It says in the Personal Section—they're engaged. That's—six years ago! They must be married by now.

AMANDA: Girls that aren't cut out for business careers usually wind up married to some nice man. [*She gets up with a spark of revival.*] Sister, that's what you'll do!

[LAURA *utters a startled, doubtful laugh. She reaches quickly for a piece of glass.*]

LAURA: But, Mother—

AMANDA: Yes? [*She goes over to the photograph.*]

LAURA [*in a tone of frightened apology*]: I'm—crippled!

AMANDA: Nonsense! Laura, I've told you never, never to use that word. Why, you're not crippled, you just have a little defect—hardly noticeable, even! When people have some slight disadvantage like that, they cultivate other things to make up for it—develop charm—and vivacity—and—*charm*! That's all you have to do! [*She turns again to the photograph.*] One thing your father had *plenty of*—was *charm*!

[*The scene fades out with music.*]

Scene Three

Legend on screen: "After the fiasco—"

TOM *speaks from the fire escape landing.*

TOM: After the fiasco at Rubicam's Business College, the idea of getting a gentleman caller for Laura began to play a more and more important part in Mother's calculations. It became an obsession. Like some archetype of the universal unconscious, the image of the gentleman caller haunted our small apartment. . . .

[*Screen image: A young man at the door of a house with flowers.*]

An evening at home rarely passed without some allusion to this image, this specter, this hope. . . . Even when he wasn't mentioned, his presence hung in Mother's preoccupied look and in my sister's frightened, apologetic manner—hung like a sentence passed upon the Wingfields!

Mother was a woman of action as well as words. She began to take logical steps in the planned direction. Late that winter and in the early spring—realizing that extra money would be needed to properly feather the nest and plume the bird—she conducted a vigorous campaign on the telephone, roping in subscribers to one of those magazines for matrons called *The Homemaker's Companion,* the type of journal that features the serialized sublimations of ladies of letters who think in terms of delicate cuplike breasts, slim, tapering waists, rich, creamy thighs, eyes like wood smoke in autumn, fingers that soothe and caress like strains of music, bodies as powerful as Etruscan sculpture.

[*Screen image: The cover of a glamor magazine.*]

[AMANDA *enters with the telephone on a long extension cord. She is spotlighted in the dim stage.*]

AMANDA: Ida Scott? This is Amanda Wingfield! We *missed* you at the D.A.R. last Monday! I said to myself: She's probably suffering with that sinus condition! How is that sinus condition?

Horrors! Heaven have mercy!—You're a Christian martyr, yes, that's what you are, a Christian martyr!

Well, I just now happened to notice that your subscription to the *Companion*'s about to expire! Yes, it expires with the next issue, honey!—just when that wonderful new serial by Bessie Mae Hopper is getting off to such an exciting start. Oh, honey, it's something that you can't miss! You remember how *Gone with the Wind* took everybody by storm? You simply couldn't go out if you hadn't read it. All everybody *talked* was Scarlett O'Hara. Well, this is a book that critics already compare to *Gone with the Wind*. It's the *Gone with the Wind* of the post–World War generation!—What?—Burning?—Oh, honey, don't let them burn, go take a look in the oven and I'll hold the wire! Heavens—I think she's hung up!

[*The scene dims out.*]

[*Legend on screen: "You think I'm in love with Continental Shoemakers?"*]

[*Before the lights come up again, the violent voices of* TOM *and* AMANDA *are heard. They are quarreling behind the portieres. In front of them stands* LAURA *with clenched hands and panicky expression. A clear pool of light is on her figure throughout this scene.*]

TOM: What in Christ's name am I—

AMANDA [*shrilly*]: Don't you use that—

TOM: —supposed to do!

AMANDA: —expression! Not in my—

TOM: Ohhh!

AMANDA: —presence! Have you gone out of your senses?

TOM: I have, that's true, *driven* out!

AMANDA: What is the matter with you, you—big—big—IDIOT!

TOM: Look!—I've got *no thing*, no single thing—

AMANDA: Lower your voice!

TOM: —in my life here that I can call my OWN! Everything is—

AMANDA: Stop that shouting!

TOM: Yesterday you confiscated my books! You had the nerve to—

AMANDA: I took that horrible novel back to the library—yes! That hideous book by that insane Mr. Lawrence.

[TOM *laughs wildly.*]

I cannot control the output of diseased minds or people who cater to them—

[TOM *laughs still more wildly.*]

BUT I WON'T ALLOW SUCH FILTH BROUGHT INTO MY HOUSE! No, no, no, no, no!

TOM: House, house! Who pays rent on it, who makes a slave of himself to—

AMANDA [*fairly screeching*]: Don't you DARE to—

TOM: No, no, *I* mustn't say things! *I've* got to just—

AMANDA: Let me tell you—

TOM: I don't want to hear any more!

[*He tears the portieres open. The dining-room area is lit with a turgid smoky red glow. Now we see* AMANDA; *her hair is in metal curlers and she is wearing a very old bathrobe, much too large for her slight figure, a relic of the faithless Mr. Wingfield. The upright typewriter now stands on the drop-leaf table, along with a wild disarray of manuscripts. The quarrel was probably precipitated by* AMANDA*'s interruption of* TOM*'s creative labor. A chair lies overthrown on the floor. Their gesticulating shadows are cast on the ceiling by the fiery glow.*]

AMANDA: You *will* hear more, you—

TOM: No, I won't hear more, I'm going out!

AMANDA: You come right back in—

TOM: Out, out, out! Because I'm—

AMANDA: Come back here, Tom Wingfield! I'm not through talking to you!

TOM: Oh, go—

LAURA [*desperately*]: —Tom!

AMANDA: You're going to listen, and no more insolence from you! I'm at the end of my patience!

[*He comes back toward her.*]

TOM: What do you think I'm at? Aren't I supposed to have any patience to reach the end of, Mother? I know, I know. It seems unimportant to you, what I'm *doing*—what I *want* to do—having a little *difference* between them! You don't think that—

AMANDA: I think you've been doing things that you're ashamed of. That's why you act like this. I don't believe that you go every night to the movies. Nobody goes to the movies night after night. Nobody in their right minds goes to the movies as often as you pretend to. People don't go to the movies at nearly midnight, and movies don't let out at two A.M. Come in stumbling. Muttering to yourself like a maniac! You get three hours' sleep and then go to work. Oh, I can picture the way you're doing down there. Moping, doping, because you're in no condition.

TOM [*wildly*]: No, I'm in no condition!

AMANDA: What right have you got to jeopardize your job? Jeopardize the security of us all? How do you think we'd manage if you were—

TOM: Listen! You think I'm crazy about the *warehouse?* [*He bends fiercely toward her slight figure.*] You think I'm in love with the Continental Shoemakers? You think I want to spend fifty-five *years* down there in that—*celotex interior!* with—*fluorescent—tubes!* Look! I'd rather somebody picked up a crowbar and battered out my brains—than go back mornings! I *go!* Every time you come in yelling that Goddamn *"Rise and Shine!" "Rise and Shine!"* I say to myself, "How *lucky dead* people are!" But I get up. I *go!* For sixty-five dollars a month I give up all that I dream of doing and being *ever!* And you say self—*self's* all I ever think of. Why, listen, if self is what I thought of, Mother, I'd be where he is—GONE! [*He points to his father's picture.*] As far as the system of transportation reaches! [*He starts past her. She grabs his arm.*] Don't grab at me, Mother!

AMANDA: Where are you going?

TOM: I'm going to the *movies!*

AMANDA: I don't believe that lie!

[TOM *crouches toward her, overtowering her tiny figure. She backs away, gasping.*]

TOM: I'm going to opium dens! Yes, Opium dens, dens of vice and criminals' hangouts, Mother. I've joined the Hogan Gang, I'm a hired assassin, I carry a tommy gun in a violin case! I run a string of cat houses in the Valley! They call me Killer, Killer Wingfield, I'm leading a double-life, a simple, honest warehouse worker by day, by night a dynamic *czar* of the *underworld, Mother.* I go to gambling casinos, I spin away fortunes on the roulette table! I wear a patch over one eye and a false mustache, sometimes I put on green whiskers. On those occasions they call me—*El Diablo!* Oh, I could tell you many things to make you sleepless! My enemies plan to dynamite this place. They're going to blow us all sky-high some night! I'll be glad, very happy, and so will you! You'll go up, up on a broomstick, over Blue Mountain with seventeen gentlemen callers! You ugly—babbling old—*witch. . . .* [*He goes through a series of violent, clumsy movements, seizing his overcoat, lunging to the door, pulling it fiercely open. The women watch him, aghast. His arm catches in the sleeve of the coat as he struggles to pull it on. For a moment he is pinioned by the bulky garment. With an outraged groan he tears the coat off again, splitting the shoulder of it, and hurls it across the room. It strikes against the shelf of* LAURA*'s glass collection, and there is a tinkle of shattering glass.* LAURA *cries out as if wounded.*]

[*Music.*]

[*Screen legend: "The Glass Menagerie."*]

LAURA [*shrilly*]: *My glass!*—menagerie. . . . [*She covers her face and turns away.*]

[*But* AMANDA *is still stunned and stupefied by the "ugly witch" so that she barely notices the occurrence. Now she recovers her speech.*]

AMANDA [*in an awful voice*]: I won't speak to you—until you apologize!

[*She crosses through the portieres and draws them together behind her.* TOM *is left with* LAURA. LAURA *clings weakly to the mantel with her face averted.* TOM *stares at her stupidly for a moment. Then he crosses to the shelf. He drops awkwardly on his knees to collect the fallen glass, glancing at* LAURA *as if he would speak but couldn't.*]

[*"The Glass Menagerie" music steals in as the scene dims out.*]

Scene Four

The interior of the apartment is dark. There is a faint light in the alley. A deep-voiced bell in a church is tolling the hour of five.

TOM *appears at the top of the alley. After each solemn boom of the bell in the tower, he shakes a little noisemaker or rattle as if to express the tiny spasm of man in contrast to the sustained power and dignity of the Almighty. This and the unsteadiness of his advance make it evident that he has been drinking. As he climbs the few steps to the fire escape landing light steals up inside.* LAURA *appears in the front room in a nightdress. She notices* TOM*'s bed is empty.* TOM *fishes in his pockets for his door key, removing a motley assortment of articles in the search, including a shower of movie ticket stubs and an empty bottle. At last he finds the key, but just as he is about to insert it, it slips from his fingers. He strikes a match and crouches below the door.*

TOM [*bitterly*]: One crack—and it falls through!

[LAURA *opens the door.*]

LAURA: Tom! Tom, what are you doing?

TOM: Looking for a door key.

LAURA: Where have you been all this time?

TOM: I have been at the movies.

LAURA: All this time at the movies?

TOM: There was a very long program. There was a Garbo picture and a Mickey Mouse and a travelogue and a newsreel and a preview of coming attractions. And there was an organ solo and a collection for the Milk Fund—simultaneously—which ended up in a terrible fight between a fat lady and an usher!

LAURA [*innocently*]: Did you have to stay through everything?

TOM: Of course! And, oh, I forgot! There was a big stage show! The headliner on this stage show was Malvolio the Magician. He performed wonderful tricks, many of them, such as pouring water back and forth between pitchers. First it turned to wine and then it turned to beer and then it turned to whisky. I know it was whisky it finally turned into because he needed somebody to come up out of the audience to help him, and I came up—both shows! It was Kentucky Straight Bourbon. A very generous fellow, he gave souvenirs. [*He pulls from his back pocket a shimmering rainbow-colored scarf.*] He gave me this. This is his magic scarf. You can have it, Laura. You wave it over a canary cage and you get a bowl of goldfish. You wave it over the goldfish bowl and they fly away canaries. . . . But the wonderfullest trick of all was the coffin trick. We nailed him into a coffin and he got out of the coffin without removing one nail. [*He has come inside.*] There is a trick that would come in handy for me—get me out of this two-by-four situation! [*He flops onto the bed and starts removing his shoes.*]

LAURA: Tom—shhh!

TOM: What're you shushing me for?

LAURA: You'll wake up Mother.

TOM: Goody, goody! Pay'er back for all those "Rise an' Shines." [*He lies down, groaning.*] You know it don't take much intelligence to get yourself into a nailed-up coffin, Laura. But who in hell ever got himself out of one without removing one nail?

[*As if in answer, the father's grinning photograph lights up. The scene dims out.*]

[*Immediately following, the church bell is heard striking six. At the sixth stroke the alarm clock goes off in* AMANDA*'s room, and after a few moments we hear her calling: Rise and Shine! Rise and Shine! Laura, go tell your brother to rise and shine!*]

TOM [*sitting up slowly*]: I'll rise—but I won't shine.

[*The light increases.*]

AMANDA: Laura, tell your brother his coffee is ready.

[LAURA *slips into the front room.*]

LAURA: Tom!—It's nearly seven. Don't make Mother nervous.

[*He stares at her stupidly.*]

LAURA [*beseechingly*]: Tom, speak to Mother this morning. Make up with her, apologize, speak to her!

TOM: She won't to me. It's her that started not speaking.

LAURA: If you just say you're sorry she'll start speaking.

TOM: Her not speaking — is that such a tragedy?

LAURA: Please—please!

AMANDA [*calling from the kitchenette*]: Laura, are you going to do what I asked you to do, or do I have to get dressed and go out myself?

LAURA: Going, going—soon as I get on my coat!

[*She pulls on a shapeless felt hat with a nervous, jerky movement, pleadingly glancing at* TOM*. She rushes awkwardly for her coat. The coat is one of* AMANDA*'s, inaccurately made-over, the sleeves too short for* LAURA*.*]

Butter and what else?

AMANDA [*entering from the kitchenette*]: Just butter. Tell them to charge it.

LAURA: Mother, they make such faces when I do that.

AMANDA: Sticks and stones can break our bones, but the expression on Mr. Garfinkel's face won't harm us! Tell your brother his coffee is getting cold.

LAURA [*at the door*]: Do what I asked you, will you, will you, Tom?

[*He looks sullenly away.*]

AMANDA: Laura, go now or just don't go at all!

LAURA [*rushing out*]: Going—going!

[*A second later she cries out.* TOM *springs up and crosses to the door.* TOM *opens the door.*]

TOM: Laura?

LAURA: I'm all right. I slipped, but I'm all right.

AMANDA [*peering anxiously after her*]: If anyone breaks a leg on those fire-escape steps, the landlord ought to be sued for every cent he possesses! [*She shuts the door. Now she remembers she isn't speaking to* TOM *and returns to the other room.*]

[*As* TOM *comes listlessly for his coffee, she turns her back to him and stands rigidly facing the window on the gloomy gray vault of the areaway. Its light on her face with its aged but childish features is cruelly sharp, satirical as a Daumier print.*]

[*The music of "Ave Maria" is heard softly.*]

[TOM *glances sheepishly but sullenly at her averted figure and slumps at the table. The coffee is scalding hot; he sips it and gasps and spits it back in the cup. At his gasp,* AMANDA *catches her breath and half turns. Then she catches herself and turns back to the window.* TOM *blows on his coffee, glancing sidewise at his mother. She clears her throat.* TOM *clears his. He starts to rise, sinks back down again, scratches his head, clears his throat again.* AMANDA *coughs.* TOM *raises his cup in both hands to blow on it, his eyes staring over the rim of it at his mother for several moments. Then he slowly sets the cup down and awkwardly and hesitantly rises from the chair.*]

TOM [*hoarsely*]: Mother, I—I apologize, Mother.

[AMANDA *draws a quick, shuddering breath. Her face works grotesquely. She breaks into childlike tears.*]

I'm sorry for what I said, for everything that I said, I didn't mean it.

AMANDA [*sobbingly*]: My devotion has made me a witch and so I make myself hateful to my children!

TOM: *No*, you *don't.*

AMANDA: I worry so much, don't sleep, it makes me nervous!

TOM [*gently*]: I understand that.

AMANDA: I've had to put up a solitary battle all these years. But you're my right-hand bower! Don't fall down, don't fail!

TOM [*gently*]: I try, Mother.

AMANDA [*with great enthusiasm*]: Try and you will *succeed!* [*The notion makes her breathless.*] Why, you — you're just *full* of natural endowments! Both of my children—they're *unusual* children! Don't you think I know it? I'm so—*proud!* Happy and—feel I've—so much to be thankful for but—promise me one thing, son!

TOM: What, Mother?

AMANDA: Promise, son, you'll—never be a drunkard!

TOM [*turns to her grinning*]: I will never be a drunkard, Mother.

AMANDA: That's what frightened me so, that you'd be drinking! Eat a bowl of Purina!

TOM: Just coffee, Mother.

AMANDA: Shredded wheat biscuit?

TOM: No. No, Mother, just coffee.

AMANDA: You can't put in a day's work on an empty stomach. You've got ten minutes—don't gulp! Drinking too-hot liquids makes cancer of the stomach. . . . Put cream in.

TOM: No, thank you.

AMANDA: To cool it.

TOM: No! No, thank you, I want it black.

AMANDA: I know, but it's not good for you. We have to do all that we can to build ourselves up. In these trying times we live in, all that we have to cling to is—each other . . . That's why it's so important to—Tom, I—I sent out your sister so I could discuss something with you. If you hadn't spoken I would have spoken to you. [*She sits down.*]

TOM [*gently*]: What is it, Mother, that you want to discuss?

AMANDA: *Laura*!

[TOM *puts his cup down slowly.*]

[*Legend on screen: "Laura." Music: "The Glass Menagerie."*]

TOM: —Oh.—Laura . . .

AMANDA [*touching his sleeve*]: You know how Laura is. So quiet but—still water runs deep! She notices things and I think she—broods about them.

[TOM *looks up*]

A few days ago I came in and she was crying.

TOM: What about?

AMANDA: You.

TOM: Me?

AMANDA: She has an idea that you're not happy here.

TOM: What gave her that idea?

AMANDA: What gives her any idea? However, you do act strangely. I—I'm not criticizing, understand *that!* I know your ambitions do not lie in the warehouse, that like everybody in the whole wide world—you've had to—make sacrifices, but—Tom—Tom—life's not easy, it calls for—Spartan endurance! There's so many things in my heart that I cannot describe to you! I've never told you but I—*loved* your father. . . .

TOM [*gently*]: I know that, Mother.

AMANDA: And you—when I see you taking after his ways! Staying out late—and—well,—you *had* been drinking the night you were in that—terrifying condition! Laura says that you hate the apartment and that you go out nights to get away from it! Is that true, Tom?

TOM: No. You say there's so much in your heart that you can't describe to me. That's true of me, too. There's so much in my heart that I can't describe to *you!* So let's respect each other's—

AMANDA: But, why—*why*, Tom—are you always so *restless?* Where do you *go* to, nights?

TOM: I—go to the movies.

AMANDA: Why do you go to the movies so much, Tom?

TOM: I go to the movies because—I like adventure. Adventure is something I don't have much of at work, so I go to the movies.

AMANDA: But, Tom, you go to the movies *entirely* too *much!*

TOM: I like a lot of adventure.

[AMANDA *looks baffled, then hurt. As the familiar inquisition resumes,* TOM *becomes hard and impatient again.* AMANDA *slips back into her querulous attitude toward him.*]

[*Image on screen: A sailing vessel with Jolly Roger.*]

AMANDA: Most young men find adventure in their careers.

TOM: Then most young men are not employed in a warehouse.

AMANDA: The world is full of young men employed in warehouses and offices and factories.

TOM: Do all of them find adventure in their careers?

AMANDA: They do or they do without it! Not everybody has a craze for adventure.

TOM: Man is by instinct a lover, a hunter, a fighter, and none of those instincts are given much play at the warehouse!

AMANDA: Man is by instinct! Don't quote instinct to me! Instinct is something that people have got away from! It belongs to animals! Christian adults don't want it!

TOM: What do Christian adults want, then, Mother?

AMANDA: Superior things! Things of the mind and the spirit! Only animals have to satisfy instincts! Surely your aims are somewhat higher than theirs! Than monkeys—pigs—

TOM: I reckon they're not.

AMANDA: You're joking. However, that isn't what I wanted to discuss.

TOM [*rising*]: I haven't much time.

AMANDA [*pushing his shoulders*]: Sit down.

TOM: You want me to punch in red at the warehouse, Mother?

AMANDA: You have five minutes. I want to talk about Laura.

[*Screen legend: "Plans and Provisions."*]

TOM: All right! What about Laura?

AMANDA: We have to be making some plans and provisions for her. She's older than you, two years, and nothing has happened. She just drifts along doing nothing. It frightens me terribly how she just drifts along.

TOM: I guess she's the type that people call home girls.

AMANDA: There's no such type, and if there is, it's a pity! That is unless the home is hers, with a husband!

TOM: What?

AMANDA: Oh, I can see the handwriting on the wall as plain as I see the nose in front of my face! It's terrifying! More and more you remind me of your father! He was out all hours without explanation!—Then *left! Goodbye!* And me with the bag to hold. I saw a letter you got from the Merchant Marine. I know what you're dreaming of. I'm not standing here blindfolded. [*She pauses*] Very well, then. Then *do* it! But not till there's somebody to take your place.

TOM: What do you mean?

AMANDA: I mean that as soon as Laura has got somebody to take care of her, married, a home of her own, independent—why, then you'll be free to go wherever you please, on land, on sea, whichever way the wind blows you! But until that time you've got to look out for your sister. I don't say me because I'm old and don't matter! I say for your sister because she's young and dependent.

I put her in business college—a dismal failure! Frightened her so it made her sick at the stomach. I took her over to the Young People's League at the church. Another fiasco. She spoke to nobody, nobody spoke to her. Now all she does is fool with those pieces of glass and play those worn-out records. What kind of life is that for a girl to lead?

TOM: What can I do about it?

AMANDA: Overcome selfishness! Self, self, self is all that you ever think of!

[TOM *springs up and crosses to get his coat. It is ugly and bulky. He pulls on a cap with earmuffs.*]

Where is your muffler? Put your wool muffler on!

[*He snatches it angrily from the closet, tosses it around his neck and pulls both ends tight.*]

Tom! I haven't said what I had in mind to ask you.

TOM: I'm too late to—

AMANDA [*catching his arm—very importunately; then shyly*]: Down at the warehouse, aren't there some—nice young men?

TOM: No!

AMANDA: There *must* be—*some* . . .

TOM: Mother—[*He gestures.*]

AMANDA: Find out one that's clean-living—doesn't drink and ask him out for sister!

TOM: What?

AMANDA: For *sister*! To *meet*! Get *acquainted*!

TOM [*stamping to the door*]: Oh, my *go-osh*!

AMANDA: Will you?

[*He opens the door. She says, imploringly*]

Will you?

[*He starts down the fire escape.*]

Will you? *Will* you, dear?

TOM [*calling back*]: *Yes!*

[AMANDA *closes the door hesitantly and with a troubled but faintly hopeful expression.*]

[*Screen image: The cover of a glamor magazine.*]

[*The spotlight picks up* AMANDA *at the phone.*]

AMANDA: Ella Cartwright? This is Amanda Wingfield! How are you, honey? How is that kidney condition?

[*There is a five-second pause.*]

Horrors!

[*There is another pause.*]

You're a Christian martyr, yes, honey, that's what you are, a Christian martyr! Well, I just now happened to notice in my little red book that your subscription to the *Companion* has just run out! I knew that you wouldn't want to miss out on the wonderful serial starting in this new issue. It's by Bessie Mae Hopper, the first thing she's written since *Honeymoon for Three.* Wasn't that a strange and interesting story? Well, this one is even lovelier, I believe. It has a sophisticated, society background. It's all about the horsey set on Long Island!

[*The light fades out.*]

Scene Five

Legend on the screen: "Annunciation."

Music is heard as the light slowly comes on.

It is early dusk of a spring evening. Supper has just been finished in the Wingfield apartment. AMANDA *and* LAURA*, in light-colored dresses, are removing dishes from the table in the dining room, which is shadowy, their movements formalized almost as a dance or ritual, their moving forms as pale and silent as moths.* TOM*, in white shirt and trousers, rises from the table and crosses toward the fire escape.*

AMANDA [*as he passes her*]: Son, will you do me a favor?

TOM: What?

AMANDA: Comb your hair! You look so pretty when your hair is combed!

[TOM *slouches on the sofa with the evening paper. Its enormous headline reads: "Franco Triumphs."*]

There is only one respect in which I would like you to emulate your father.

TOM: What respect is that?

AMANDA: The care he always took of his appearance. He never allowed himself to look untidy.

[*He throws down the paper and crosses to the fire escape.*]

Where are you going?

TOM: I'm going out to smoke.

AMANDA: You smoke too much. A pack a day at fifteen cents a pack. How much would that amount to in a month? Thirty times fifteen is how much, Tom? Figure it out and you will be astounded at what you could save. Enough to give you a night-school course in accounting at Washington U.! Just think what a wonderful thing that would be for you, son!

[TOM *is unmoved by the thought.*]

TOM: I'd rather smoke. [*He steps out on the landing, letting the screen door slam.*]

AMANDA [*sharply*]: I know! That's the tragedy of it. . . . [*Alone, she turns to look at her husband's picture.*]

[*Dance music: "The World Is Waiting for the Sunrise!"*]

TOM [*to the audience*]: Across the alley from us was the Paradise Dance Hall. On evenings in spring the windows and doors were open and the music came outdoors. Sometimes the lights were turned out except for a large glass sphere that hung from the ceiling. It would turn slowly about and filter the dusk with delicate rainbow colors. Then the orchestra played a waltz or a tango, something that had a slow and sensuous rhythm. Couples would come outside, to the relative privacy of the alley. You could see them kissing behind ash pits and telephone poles. This was the compensation for lives that passed like mine, without any change or adventure. Adventure and change were imminent in this year. They were waiting around the corner for all these kids. Suspended in the mist over Berchtesgaden, caught in the folds of Chamberlain's umbrella. In Spain there was Guernica! But here there was only hot swing music and liquor, dance halls, bars, and movies, and sex that hung in the gloom like a chandelier and flooded the world with brief, deceptive rainbows. . . . All the world was waiting for bombardments!

[AMANDA *turns from the picture and comes outside.*]

AMANDA [*sighing*]: A fire escape landing's a poor excuse for a porch. [*She spreads a newspaper on a step and sits down, gracefully and demurely as if she were settling into a swing on a Mississippi veranda.*] What are you looking at?

TOM: The moon.

AMANDA: Is there a moon this evening?

TOM: It's rising over Garfinkel's Delicatessen.

AMANDA: So it is! A little silver slipper of a moon. Have you made a wish on it yet?

TOM: Um-hum.

AMANDA: What did you wish for?

TOM: That's a secret.

AMANDA: A secret, huh? Well, I won't tell mine either. I will be just as mysterious as you.

TOM: I bet I can guess what yours is.

AMANDA: Is my head so transparent?

TOM: You're not a sphinx.

AMANDA: No, I don't have secrets. I'll tell you what I wished for on the moon. Success and happiness for my precious children! I wish for that whenever there's a moon, and when there isn't a moon, I wish for it, too.

TOM: I thought perhaps you wished for a gentleman caller.

AMANDA: Why do you say that?

TOM: Don't you remember asking me to fetch one?

AMANDA: I remember suggesting that it would be nice for your sister if you brought home some nice young man from the warehouse. I think that I've made that suggestion more than once.

TOM: Yes, you have made it repeatedly.

AMANDA: Well?

TOM: We are going to have one.

AMANDA: *What?*

TOM: A gentleman caller!

[*The annunciation is celebrated with music.*]

[AMANDA *rises.*]

[*Image on screen: A caller with a bouquet.*]

AMANDA: You mean you have asked some nice young man to come over?

TOM: Yep. I've asked him to dinner.

AMANDA: You really did?

TOM: I did!

AMANDA: You did, and did he—*accept?*

TOM: He did!

AMANDA: Well, well—well, well! That's—lovely!

TOM: I thought that you would be pleased.

AMANDA: It's definite then?

TOM: Very definite.

AMANDA: Soon?

TOM: Very soon.

AMANDA: For heaven's sake, stop putting on and tell me some things, will you?

TOM: What things do you want me to tell you?

AMANDA: *Naturally* I would like to know when he's *coming!*

TOM: He's coming tomorrow.

AMANDA: *Tomorrow?*

TOM: Yep. Tomorrow.

AMANDA: But, Tom!

TOM: Yes, Mother?

AMANDA: Tomorrow gives me no time!

TOM: Time for what?

AMANDA: Preparations! Why didn't you phone me at once, as soon as you asked him, the minute that he accepted? Then, don't you see, I could have been getting ready!

TOM: You don't have to make any fuss.

AMANDA: Oh, Tom, Tom, Tom, of course I have to make a fuss! I want things nice, not sloppy! Not thrown together. I'll certainly have to do some fast thinking, won't I?

TOM: I don't see why you have to think at all.

AMANDA: You just don't know. We can't have a gentleman caller in a pigsty! All my wedding silver has to be polished, the monogrammed table linen ought to be laundered! The windows have to be washed and fresh curtains put up. And how about clothes? We have to *wear* something, don't we?

TOM: Mother, this boy is no one to make a fuss over!

AMANDA: Do you realize he's the first young man we've introduced to your sister? It's terrible, dreadful, disgraceful that poor little sister has never received a single gentleman caller! Tom, come inside! [*She opens the screen door.*]

TOM: What for?

AMANDA: I want to ask you some things.

TOM: If you're going to make such a fuss, I'll call it off, I'll tell him not to come!

AMANDA: You certainly won't do anything of the kind. Nothing offends people worse than broken engagements. It simply means I'll have to work like a Turk! We won't be brilliant, but we will pass inspection. Come on inside.

[TOM *follows her inside, groaning.*]

Sit down.

TOM: Any particular place you would like me to sit?

AMANDA: Thank heavens I've got that new sofa! I'm also making payments on a floor lamp I'll have sent out! And put the chintz covers on, they'll brighten things up! Of course I'd hoped to have these walls re-papered. . . . What is the young man's name?

TOM: His name is O'Connor.

AMANDA: That, of course, means fish—tomorrow is Friday! I'll have that salmon loaf—with Durkee's dressing! What does he do? He works at the warehouse?

TOM: Of course! How else would I—

AMANDA: Tom, he—doesn't drink?

TOM: Why do you ask me that?

AMANDA: Your father *did!*

TOM: Don't get started on that!

AMANDA: He *does* drink, then?

TOM: Not that I know of!

AMANDA: Make sure, be certain! The last thing I want for my daughter's a boy who drinks!

TOM: Aren't you being a little bit premature? Mr. O'Connor has not yet appeared on the scene!

AMANDA: But will tomorrow. To meet your sister, and what do I know about his character? Nothing! Old maids are better off than wives of drunkards!

TOM: Oh, my God!

AMANDA: Be still!

TOM [*leaning forward to whisper*]: Lots of fellows meet girls whom they don't marry!

AMANDA: Oh, talk sensibly, Tom—and don't be sarcastic! [*She has gotten a hairbrush.*]

TOM: What are you doing?

AMANDA: I'm brushing that cowlick down! [*She attacks his hair with the brush.*] What is this young man's position at the warehouse?

TOM [*submitting grimly to the brush and the interrogation*]: This young man's position is that of a shipping clerk, Mother.

AMANDA: Sounds to me like a fairly responsible job, the sort of job *you* would be in if you just had more *get-up.* What is his salary? Have you any idea?

TOM: I would judge it to be approximately eighty-five dollars a month.

AMANDA: Well—not princely, but—

TOM: Twenty more than I make.

AMANDA: Yes, how well I know! But for a family man, eighty-five dollars a month is not much more than you can just get by on. . . .

TOM: Yes, but Mr. O'Connor is not a family man.

AMANDA: He might be, mightn't he? Some time in the future?

TOM: I see. Plans and provisions.

AMANDA: You are the only young man that I know of who ignores the fact that the future becomes the present, the present the past, and the past turns into everlasting regret if you don't plan for it!

TOM: I will think that over and see what I can make of it.

AMANDA: Don't be supercilious with your mother! Tell me some more about this—what do you call him?

TOM: James D. O'Connor. The D. is for Delaney.

AMANDA: Irish on *both* sides! *Gracious!* And doesn't drink?

TOM: Shall I call him up and ask him right this minute?

AMANDA: The only way to find out about those things is to make discreet inquiries at the proper moment. When I was a girl in Blue Mountain and it was suspected a young man drank, the girl whose attentions he had been receiving, if any girl *was,* would sometimes speak to the minister of his church, or rather her father would if her father was living, and sort of feel him out on the young man's character. That is the way such things are discreetly handled to keep a young woman from making a tragic mistake!

TOM: Then how did you happen to make a tragic mistake?

AMANDA: That innocent look of your father's had everyone fooled! He *smiled*—the world was *enchanted!* No girl can do worse than put herself at the mercy of a handsome appearance! I hope that Mr. O'Connor is not too good-looking.

TOM: No, he's not too good-looking. He's covered with freckles and hasn't much of a nose.

AMANDA: He's not right-down homely, though?

TOM: Not right-down homely. Just medium homely, I'd say.

AMANDA: Character's what to look for in a man.

TOM: That's what I've always said, Mother.

AMANDA: You've never said anything of the kind and I suspect you would never give it a thought.

TOM: Don't be so suspicious of me.

AMANDA: At least I hope he's the type that's up and coming.

TOM: I think he really goes in for self-improvement.

AMANDA: What reason have you to think so?

TOM: He goes to night school.

AMANDA [*beaming*]: Splendid! What does he do, I mean study?

TOM: Radio engineering and public speaking!

AMANDA: Then he has visions of being advanced in the world! Any young man who studies public speaking is aiming to have an executive job some day! And radio engineering? A thing for the future! Both of these facts are very illuminating. Those are the sort of things that a mother should know concerning any young man who comes to call on her daughter. Seriously or—not.

TOM: One little warning. He doesn't know about Laura. I didn't let on that we had dark ulterior motives. I just said, why don't you come over and have dinner with us? He said okay and that was the whole conversation.

AMANDA: I bet it was! You're eloquent as an oyster. However, he'll know about Laura when he gets here. When he sees how lovely and sweet and pretty she is, he'll thank his lucky stars he was asked to dinner.

TOM: Mother, you mustn't expect too much of Laura.

AMANDA: What do you mean?

TOM: Laura seems all those things to you and me because she's ours and we love her. We don't even notice she's crippled any more.

AMANDA: Don't say crippled! You know that I never allow that word to be used!

TOM: But face facts, Mother. She is and—that's not all—

AMANDA: What do you mean "not all"?

TOM: Laura is very different from other girls.

AMANDA: I think the difference is all to her advantage.

TOM: Not quite all—in the eyes of others—strangers—she's terribly shy and lives in a world of her own and those things make her seem a little peculiar to people outside the house.

AMANDA: Don't say peculiar.

TOM: Face the facts. She is.

[*The dance hall music changes to a tango that has a minor and somewhat ominous tone.*]

AMANDA: In what way is she peculiar—may I ask?

TOM [*gently*]: She lives in a world of her own—a world of little glass ornaments, Mother . . .

[*He gets up.* AMANDA *remains holding the brush, looking at him, troubled.*]

She plays old phonograph records and—that's about all—[*He glances at himself in the mirror and crosses to the door.*]

AMANDA [*sharply*]: Where are you going?

TOM: I'm going to the movies. [*He goes out the screen door.*]

AMANDA: Not to the movies, every night to the movies! [*She follows quickly to the screen door.*] I don't believe you always go to the movies!

[*He is gone.* AMANDA *looks worriedly after him for a moment. Then vitality and optimism return and she turns from the door, crossing to the portieres.*]

Laura! Laura!

[LAURA *answers from the kitchenette.*]

LAURA: Yes, Mother.

AMANDA: Let those dishes go and come in front!

[LAURA *appears with a dish towel.* AMANDA *speaks to her gaily.*]

Laura, come here and make a wish on the moon!

[*Screen image: The Moon.*]

LAURA [*entering*]: Moon—moon?

AMANDA: A little silver slipper of a moon. Look over your left shoulder, Laura, and make a wish!

[LAURA *looks faintly puzzled as if called out of sleep.* AMANDA *seizes her shoulders and turns her at an angle by the door.*]

Now! Now, darling, *wish!*

LAURA: What shall I wish for, Mother?

AMANDA [*her voice trembling and her eyes suddenly filling with tears*]: Happiness! Good fortune!

[*The sound of the violin rises and the stage dims out.*]

Scene Six

The light comes up on the fire escape landing. TOM *is leaning against the grill, smoking.*

[*Screen image: The high school hero.*]

TOM: And so the following evening I brought Jim home to dinner. I had known Jim slightly in high school. In high school Jim was a hero. He had tremendous Irish good nature and vitality with the scrubbed and polished look of white chinaware. He seemed to move in a continual spotlight. He was a star in basketball, captain of the debating club, president of the senior class and the glee club and he sang the male lead in the annual light operas. He was always running or bounding, never just walking. He seemed always at the point of defeating the law of gravity. He was shooting with such velocity through his adolescence that you would logically expect him to arrive at nothing short of the White House by the time he was thirty. But Jim apparently ran into more interference after his graduation from Soldan. His speed had definitely slowed. Six years after he left high school he was holding a job that wasn't much better than mine.

[*Screen image: The Clerk.*]

He was the only one at the warehouse with whom I was on friendly terms. I was valuable to him as someone who could remember his former glory, who had seen him win basketball games and the silver cup in debating. He knew of my secret practice of retiring to a cabinet of the washroom to work on poems when business was slack in the warehouse. He called me Shakespeare. And while the other boys in the warehouse regarded me with suspicious hostility, Jim took a humorous attitude toward me. Gradually his attitude affected the others, their hostility wore off and they also began to smile at me as people smile at an oddly fashioned dog who trots across their path at some distance.

I knew that Jim and Laura had known each other at Soldan, and I had heard Laura speak admiringly of his voice. I didn't know if Jim remembered her or not. In high school Laura had been as unobtrusive as Jim had been astonishing. If he did remember Laura, it was not as my sister, for when I asked him to dinner, he grinned and said, "You know, Shakespeare, I never thought of you as having folks!"

He was about to discover that I did. . . .

[*Legend on screen: "The accent of a coming foot."*]

[*The light dims out on* TOM *and comes up in the Wingfield living room—a delicate lemony light. It is about five on a Friday evening of late spring which comes "scattering poems in the sky."*]

[AMANDA *has worked like a Turk in preparation for the gentleman caller. The results are astonishing. The new floor lamp with its rose silk shade is in place, a colored paper lantern conceals the broken light fixture in the ceiling, new billowing white curtains are at the windows, chintz covers are on the chairs and sofa, a pair of new sofa pillows make their initial appearance. Open boxes and tissue paper are scattered on the floor.*]

[LAURA *stands in the middle of the room with lifted arms while* AMANDA *crouches before her, adjusting the hem of a new dress, devout and ritualistic. The dress is colored and designed by memory. The arrangement of* LAURA*'s hair is changed; it is softer and more becoming. A fragile, unearthly prettiness has come out in* LAURA. *She is like a piece of translucent glass touched by light, given a momentary radiance, not actual, not lasting.*]

AMANDA [*impatiently*]: Why are you trembling?
LAURA: Mother, you've made me so nervous!
AMANDA: How have I made you nervous?
LAURA: By all this fuss! You make it seem so important!
AMANDA: I don't understand you, Laura. You couldn't be satisfied with just sitting home, and yet whenever I try to arrange something for you, you seem to resist it. [*She gets up.*] Now take a look at yourself. No, wait! Wait just a moment—I have an idea!
LAURA: What is it now?

[AMANDA *produces two powder puffs which she wraps in handkerchiefs and stuffs in* LAURA*'s bosom.*]

LAURA: Mother, what are you doing?
AMANDA: They call them "Gay Deceivers"!
LAURA: I won't wear them!
AMANDA: You will!
LAURA: Why should I?
AMANDA: Because, to be painfully honest, your chest is flat.
LAURA: You make it seem like we are setting a trap.
AMANDA: All pretty girls are a trap, a pretty trap, and men expect them to be.

[*Legend on screen: "A pretty trap."*]

Now look at yourself, young lady. This is the prettiest you will ever be! [*She stands back to admire* LAURA.] I've got to fix myself now! You're going to be surprised by your mother's appearance!

[AMANDA *crosses through the portieres, humming gaily.* LAURA *moves slowly to the long mirror and stares solemnly at herself. A wind blows the white curtains inward in a slow, graceful motion and with a faint, sorrowful sighing.*]

AMANDA [*from somewhere behind the portieres*]: It isn't dark enough yet.

[LAURA *turns slowly before the mirror with a troubled look.*]

[*Legend on screen: "This is my sister: Celebrate her with strings!" Music plays.*]

AMANDA [*laughing, still not visible*]: I'm going to show you something. I'm going to make a spectacular appearance!
LAURA: What is it, Mother?
AMANDA: Possess your soul in patience—you will see! Something I've resurrected from that old trunk! Styles haven't changed so terribly much after all. . . . [*She parts the portieres.*] Now just look at your mother! [*She wears a girlish frock of yellowed voile with a*

blue silk sash. She carries a bunch of jonquils—the legend of her youth is nearly revived. Now she speaks feverishly]: This is the dress in which I led the cotillion. Won the cakewalk twice at Sunset Hill, wore one Spring to the Governor's Ball in Jackson! See how I sashayed around the ballroom, Laura? [*She raises her skirt and does a mincing step around the room.*] I wore it on Sundays for my gentlemen callers! I had it on the day I met your father. . . . I had malaria fever all that Spring. The change of climate from East Tennessee to the Delta—weakened resistance. I had a little temperature all the time—not enough to be serious—just enough to make me restless and giddy! Invitations poured in—parties all over the Delta! "Stay in bed," said Mother, "you have a fever!"—but I just wouldn't. I took quinine but kept on going, going! Evenings, dances! Afternoons, long, long rides! Picnics—lovely! So lovely, that country in May—all lacy with dogwood, literally flooded with jonquils! That was the spring I had the craze for jonquils. Jonquils became an absolute obsession. Mother said, "Honey, there's no more room for jonquils." And still I kept on bringing in more jonquils. Whenever, wherever I saw them, I'd say, "Stop! Stop! I see jonquils!" I made the young men help me gather the jonquils! It was a joke, Amanda and her jonquils. Finally there were no more vases to hold them, every available space was filled with jonquils. No vases to hold them? All right, I'll hold them myself! And then I—[*She stops in front of the picture. Music plays.*] met your father! Malaria fever and jonquils and then—this—boy. . . . [*She switches on the rose-colored lamp.*] I hope they get here before it starts to rain. [*She crosses the room and places the jonquils in a bowl on the table.*] I gave your brother a little extra change so he and Mr. O'Connor could take the service car home.

LAURA [*with an altered look*]: What did you say his name was?

AMANDA: O'Connor.

LAURA: What is his first name?

AMANDA: I don't remember. Oh, yes, I do. It was—Jim!

[LAURA *sways slightly and catches hold of a chair.*]

[*Legend on screen: "Not Jim!"*]

LAURA [*faintly*]: Not—Jim!

AMANDA: Yes, that was it, it was Jim! I've never known a Jim that wasn't nice!

[*The music becomes ominous.*]

LAURA: Are you sure his name is Jim O'Connor?

AMANDA: Yes. Why?

LAURA: Is he the one that Tom used to know in high school?

AMANDA: He didn't say so. I think he just got to know him at the warehouse.

LAURA: There was a Jim O'Connor we both knew in high school—[*then, with effort*] If that is the one that Tom is bringing to dinner—you'll have to excuse me, I won't come to the table.

AMANDA: What sort of nonsense is this?

LAURA: You asked me once if I'd ever liked a boy. Don't you remember I showed you this boy's picture?

AMANDA: You mean the boy you showed me in the yearbook?

LAURA: Yes, that boy.

AMANDA: Laura, Laura, were you in love with that boy?

LAURA: I don't know, Mother. All I know is I couldn't sit at the table if it was him!

AMANDA: It won't be him! It isn't the least bit likely. But whether it is or not, you will come to the table. You will not be excused.

LAURA: I'll have to be, Mother.

AMANDA: I don't intend to humor your silliness, Laura. I've had too much from you and your brother, both! So just sit down and compose yourself till they come. Tom has forgotten his key so you'll have to let them in, when they arrive.

LAURA [*panicky*]: Oh, Mother—*you* answer the door!

AMANDA [*lightly*]: I'll be in the kitchen—busy!

LAURA: Oh, Mother, please answer the door, don't make me do it!

AMANDA [*crossing into the kitchenette*]: I've got to fix the dressing for the salmon. Fuss, fuss—silliness!—over a gentleman caller!

[*The door swings shut.* LAURA *is left alone.*]

[*Legend on screen: "Terror!"*]

[*She utters a low moan and turns off the lamp—sits stiffly on the edge of the sofa, knotting her fingers together.*]

[*Legend on screen: "The Opening of a Door!"*]

[TOM *and* JIM *appear on the fire escape steps and climb to the landing. Hearing their approach,* LAURA *rises with a panicky gesture. She retreats to the portieres. The doorbell rings.* LAURA *catches her breath and touches her throat. Low drums sound.*]

AMANDA [*calling*]: Laura, sweetheart! The door!

[LAURA *stares at it without moving.*]

JIM: I think we just beat the rain.

TOM: Uh-huh. [*He rings again, nervously.* JIM *whistles and fishes for a cigarette.*]

AMANDA [*very, very, gaily*]: Laura, that is your brother and Mr. O'Connor! Will you let them in, darling?

[LAURA *crossed toward the kitchenette door.*]

LAURA [*breathlessly*]: Mother—you go to the door!

[AMANDA *steps out of the kitchenette and stares furiously at* LAURA. *She points imperiously at the door.*]

LAURA: Please, please!

AMANDA [*in a fierce whisper*]: What is the matter with you, you silly thing?

LAURA [*desperately*]: Please, you answer it, *please!*

AMANDA: I told you I wasn't going to humor you, Laura. Why have you chosen this moment to lose your mind?

LAURA: Please, please, please, you go!

AMANDA: You'll have to go to the door because I can't!

LAURA: [*despairingly*]: I can't either!

AMANDA: *Why?*

LAURA: I'm *sick!*

AMANDA: I'm sick, too—of your nonsense! Why can't you and your brother be normal people? Fantastic whims and behavior!

[TOM *gives a long ring.*]

Preposterous goings on! Can you give me one reason—[*She calls out lyrically.*] *Coming! Just one second!*—why you should be afraid to open a door? Now you answer it, Laura!

LAURA: Oh, oh, oh . . . [*she returns through the portieres, darts to the Victrola, winds it frantically and turns it on.*]

AMANDA: Laura Wingfield, you march right to that door!

LAURA: *Yes—yes, Mother!*

[*A faraway, scratchy rendition of "Dardanella" softens the air and gives her strength to move through it. She slips to the door and draws it cautiously open.* TOM *enters with the caller,* JIM O'CONNOR.]

TOM: Laura, this is Jim. Jim, this is my sister, Laura.

JIM [*stepping inside*]: I didn't know that Shakespeare had a sister!

LAURA [*retreating, stiff and trembling, from the door*]: How—how do you do?

JIM [*heartily, extending his hand*]: Okay!

[LAURA *touches it hesitantly with hers.*]

JIM: Your hand's *cold,* Laura!

LAURA: Yes, well—I've been playing the Victrola. . . .

JIM: Must have been playing classical music on it! You ought to play a little hot swing music to warm you up!

LAURA: Excuse me—I haven't finished playing the Victrola. . . . [*She turns awkwardly and hurries into the front room. She pauses a second by the Victrola. Then she catches her breath and darts through the portieres like a frightened deer.*]

JIM [*grinning*]: What was the matter?

TOM: Oh—with Laura? Laura is—terribly shy.

JIM: Shy, huh? It's unusual to meet a shy girl nowadays. I don't believe you ever mentioned you had a sister.

TOM: Well, now you know. I have one. Here is the *Post Dispatch*. You want a piece of it?

JIM: Uh-huh.

TOM: What piece? The comics?

JIM: Sports! [*He glances at it.*] Ole Dizzy Dean is on his bad behavior.

TOM [*uninterested*]: Yeah? [*He lights a cigarette and goes over to the fire-escape door.*]

JIM: Where are *you* going?

TOM: I'm going out on the terrace.

JIM [*going after him*]: You know, Shakespeare—I'm going to sell you a bill of goods!

TOM: What goods?

JIM: A course I'm taking.

TOM: Huh?

JIM: In public speaking! You and me, we're not the warehouse type.

TOM: Thanks—that's good news. But what has public speaking got to do with it?

JIM: It fits you for—executive positions!

TOM: Awww.

JIM: I tell you it's done a helluva lot for me.

[*Image on screen: Executive at his desk.*]

TOM: In what respect?

JIM: In every! Ask yourself what is the difference between you an' me and men in the office down front? Brains?—No!—Ability?—No! Then what? Just one little thing—

TOM: What is that one little thing?

JIM: Primarily it amounts to—social poise! Being able to square up to people and hold your own on any social level!

AMANDA [*from the kitchenette*]: Tom?

TOM: Yes, Mother.

AMANDA: Is that you and Mr. O'Connor?

TOM: Yes, Mother.

AMANDA: Well you just make yourselves comfortable in there.

TOM: Yes, mother.

AMANDA: Ask Mr. O'Connor if he would like to wash his hands.

JIM: Aw, no—no—thank you—I took care of that at the warehouse. Tom—

TOM: Yes?

JIM: Mr. Mendoza was speaking to me about you.

TOM: Favorably?

JIM: What do you think?

TOM: Well—

JIM: You're going to be out of a job if you don't wake up.

TOM: I am waking up—

JIM: You show no signs.

TOM: The signs are interior.

[*Image on screen: The sailing vessel with the Jolly Roger again.*]

TOM: I'm planning to change. [*He leans over the fire-escape rail, speaking with quiet exhilaration. The incandescent marquees and signs of the first-run movie houses light his face from across the alley. He looks like a voyager.*] I'm right at the point of committing myself to a future that doesn't include the warehouse and Mr. Mendoza or even a night-school course in public speaking.

JIM: What are you gassing about?

TOM: I'm tired of the movies.

JIM: Movies!

TOM: Yes, movies! Look at them—[*a wave toward the marvels of Grand Avenue*] All of those glamorous people—having adventures—hogging it all, gobbling the whole thing up! You know what happens? People go to the *movies* instead of *moving!* Hollywood characters are supposed to have all the adventures for everybody in America, while everybody in America sits in a dark room and watches them have them! Yes, until there's a war. That's when adventure becomes available to the masses! *Everyone's* dish, not only Gable's! Then the people in the dark room come out of the dark room to have some adventures themselves—goody, goody! It's our turn now, to go to the South Sea Island—to make a safari—to be exotic, far-off! But I'm not patient. I don't want to wait till then. I'm tired of the *movies* and I am *about to move!*

JIM [*incredulously*]: Move?

TOM: Yes.

JIM: When?

TOM: Soon!

JIM: Where? Where?

[*The music seems to answer the question, while* TOM *thinks it over. He searches in his pockets.*]

TOM: I'm starting to boil inside. I know I seem dreamy, but inside—well, I'm boiling! Whenever I pick up a shoe, I shudder a little thinking how short life is and what I am doing! Whatever that means, I know it doesn't mean shoes—except as something to wear on a traveler's feet! [*He finds what he has been searching for in his pockets and holds out a paper to* JIM.] Look—

JIM: What?

TOM: I'm a member.

JIM [*reading*]: The Union of Merchant Seamen.

TOM: I paid my dues this month, instead of the light bill.

JIM: You will regret it when they turn the lights off.

TOM: I won't be here.

JIM: How about your mother?

TOM: I'm like my father. The bastard son of a bastard! Did you notice how he's grinning in his picture in there? And he's been absent going on sixteen years!

JIM: You're just talking, you drip. How does your mother feel about it?

TOM: Shhh! Here comes Mother! Mother is not acquainted with my plans!

AMANDA [*coming through the portieres*]: Where are you all?

TOM: On the terrace, Mother.

[*They start inside. She advances to them.* TOM *is distinctly shocked at her appearance. Even* JIM *blinks a little. He is making his first contact with girlish Southern vivacity and in spite of the night-school course in public speaking is somewhat thrown off the beam by the unexpected outlay of social charm. Certain responses are attempted by* JIM *but are swept aside by* AMANDA*'s gay laughter and chatter.* TOM *is embarrassed but after the first shock* JIM *reacts very warmly. He grins and chuckles, is altogether won over.*]

[*Image on screen: Amanda as a girl.*]

AMANDA [*coyly smiling, shaking her girlish ringlets*]: Well, well, well, so this is Mr. O'Connor. Introductions entirely unnecessary. I've heard so much about you from my boy. I finally said to him, Tom—good gracious!—why don't you bring this paragon to supper? I'd like to meet this nice young man at the warehouse!—instead of just hearing him sing your praises so much! I don't know why my son is so stand-offish—that's not Southern behavior!

Let's sit down and—I think we could stand a little more air in here! Tom, leave the door open. I felt a nice fresh breeze a moment ago. Where has it gone to? Mmm, so warm already! And not quite summer, even. We're going to burn up when summer really gets started. However, we're having—we're having a very light supper. I think light things are better fo' this time of year. The same as light clothes are. Light clothes an' light food are what warm weather calls fo'. You know our blood gets so thick during th' winter—it takes a while fo' us to *adjust* ou'selves!—when the season changes . . . It's come so quick this year. I wasn't prepared. All of a sudden—heavens! Already summer! I ran to the trunk an' pulled out this light dress—terribly old! Historical almost! But feels so good—so good an' co-ol, y' know. . . .

TOM: Mother—

AMANDA: Yes, honey?

TOM: How about—supper?

AMANDA: Honey, you go ask Sister if supper is ready! You know that Sister is in full charge of supper! Tell her you hungry boys are waiting for it. [*to* JIM] Have you met Laura?

JIM: She—

AMANDA: Let you in? Oh, good, you've met already! It's rare for a girl as sweet an' pretty as Laura to be domestic! But Laura is, thank heavens, not only pretty but also very domestic. I'm not at all. I never was a bit. I never could make a thing but angel-food cake. Well, in the South we had so many servants. Gone, gone, gone. All vestige of gracious living! Gone completely! I wasn't prepared for what the future brought me. All of my gentlemen callers were sons of planters and so of course I assumed that I would be married to one and raise my family on a large piece of land with plenty of servants. But man proposes—and woman accepts the proposal! To vary that old, old saying a little bit—I married no planter! I married a man who worked for the telephone company! That gallantly smiling gentleman over there! [*She points to the picture.*] A telephone man who—fell in love with long-distance! Now he travels and I don't even know where! But what am I going on for about my—tribulations? Tell me yours—I hope you don't have any! Tom?

TOM [*returning*]: Yes, mother?

AMANDA: Is supper nearly ready?

TOM: It looks to me like supper is on the table.

AMANDA: Let me look—[*She rises prettily and looks through the portieres.*] Oh, lovely! But where is Sister?

TOM: Laura is not feeling well and she says that she thinks she'd better not come to the table.

AMANDA: What? Nonsense! Laura? Oh, Laura!

LAURA [*from the kitchenette, faintly*]: Yes, Mother.

AMANDA: You really must come to the table. We won't be seated until you come to the table! Come in, Mr. O'Connor. You sit over there, and I'll. . . . Laura? Laura Wingfield! You're keeping us waiting, honey! We can't say grace until you come to the table!

[*The kitchenette door is pushed weakly open and Laura comes in. She is obviously quite faint, her lips trembling, her eyes wide and staring. She moves unsteadily toward the table.*]

[*Screen legend: "Terror!"*]

[*Outside a summer storm is coming on abruptly. The white curtains billow inward at the windows and there is a sorrowful murmur from the deep blue dusk.*]

[LAURA *suddenly stumbles; she catches at a chair with a faint moan.*]

TOM: Laura!

AMANDA: Laura!

[*There is a clap of thunder.*]

[*Screen legend: "Ah!"*]

AMANDA [*despairingly*]: Why, Laura, you *are* ill, darling! Tom, help your sister into the living room, dear! Sit in the living room, Laura—rest on the sofa. Well! [*to* JIM *as* TOM *helps his sister to the sofa in the living room*] Standing over the hot stove made her ill! I told her that it was just too warm this evening, but—

[TOM *comes back to the table.*]

Is Laura all right now?

TOM: Yes.

AMANDA: What *is* that? Rain? A nice cool rain has come up! [*She gives* JIM *a frightened look.*] I think we may—have grace—now. . .

[TOM *looks at her stupidly.*] Tom, honey—you say grace!

TOM: Oh . . . "For these and all thy mercies—"

[*They bow their heads,* AMANDA *stealing a nervous glance at* JIM. *In the living room* LAURA, *stretched on the sofa, clenches her hand to her lips, to hold back a shuddering sob.*]

God's Holy Name be praised—

[*The scene dims out.*]

Scene Seven

It is half an hour later. Dinner is just being finished in the dining room. LAURA *is still huddled upon the sofa, her feet drawn under her, her head resting on a pale blue pillow, her eyes wide and mysteriously watchful. The new floor lamp with its shade of rose-colored silk gives a soft, becoming light to her face, bringing out the fragile, unearthly prettiness which usually escapes attention. From outside there is a steady murmur of rain, but it is slackening and soon stops; the air outside becomes pale and luminous as the moon breaks through the clouds. A moment after the curtain rises, the lights in both rooms flicker and go out.*

JIM: Hey, there, Mr. Light Bulb!

[AMANDA *laughs nervously.*]

[*Legend on screen: "Suspension of a public service."*]

AMANDA: Where was Moses when the lights went out? Ha-ha. Do you know the answer to that one, Mr. O'Connor?

JIM: No, Ma'am, what's the answer?

AMANDA: In the dark!

[JIM *laughs appreciatively.*]

Everybody sit still. I'll light the candles. Isn't it lucky we have them on the table? Where's a match? Which of you gentlemen can provide a match?

JIM: Here.

AMANDA: Thank you, Sir.

JIM: Not at all, Ma'am!

AMANDA [*as she lights the candles*]: I guess the fuse has burnt out. Mr. O'Connor, can you tell a burnt-out fuse? I know I can't and Tom is a total loss when it comes to mechanics.

[*They rise from the table and go into the kitchenette, from where their voices are heard.*]

AMANDA: Oh, be careful you don't bump into something. We don't want our gentleman caller to break his neck. Now wouldn't that be a fine howdy-do?

JIM: Ha-ha! Where is the fuse-box?

AMANDA: Right here next to the stove. Can you see anything?

JIM: Just a minute.

AMANDA: Isn't electricity a mysterious thing? Wasn't it Benjamin Franklin who tied a key to a kite? We live in such a mysterious universe, don't we? Some people say that science clears up all the mysteries for us. In my opinion it only creates more! Have you found it yet?

JIM: No, Ma'am. All these fuses look okay to me.

AMANDA: Tom!

TOM: Yes, Mother?

AMANDA: That light bill I gave you several days ago. The one I told you we got the notices about?

[*Legend on screen: "Ha!"*]

TOM: Oh—yeah.

AMANDA: You didn't neglect to pay it by any chance?

TOM: Why, I—

AMANDA: Didn't! I might have known it!

JIM: Shakespeare probably wrote a poem on that light bill, Mrs. Wingfield.

AMANDA: I might have known better than to trust him with it! There's such a high price for negligence in this world!

JIM: Maybe the poem will win a ten-dollar prize.

AMANDA: We'll just have to spend the remainder of the evening in the nineteenth century, before Mr. Edison made the Mazda lamp!

JIM: Candlelight is my favorite kind of light.

AMANDA: That shows you're romantic! But that's no excuse for Tom. Well, we got through dinner. Very considerate of them to let us get through dinner before they plunged us into everlasting darkness, wasn't it, Mr. O'Connor?

JIM: Ha-ha!

AMANDA: Tom, as a penalty for your carelessness you can help me with the dishes.

JIM: Let me give you a hand.

AMANDA: Indeed you will not!

JIM: I ought to be good for something.

AMANDA: Good for something? [*Her tone is rhapsodic.*] *You?* Why, Mr. O'Connor, nobody, *nobody's* given me this much entertainment in years—as you have!

JIM: Aw, now, Mrs. Wingfield!

AMANDA: I'm not exaggerating, not one bit! But Sister is all by her lonesome. You go keep her company in the parlor! I'll give you this lovely old candelabrum that used to be on the altar at the Church of the Heavenly Rest. It was melted a little out of shape when the church burnt down. Lightning struck it one spring. Gypsy Jones was holding a revival at the time and he intimated that the church was destroyed because the Episcopalians gave card parties.

JIM: Ha-ha.

AMANDA: And how about coaxing Sister to drink a little wine? I think it would be good for her! Can you carry both at once?

JIM: Sure, I'm Superman!

AMANDA: Now, Thomas, get into this apron!

[JIM *comes into the dining room, carrying the candelabrum, its candles lighted, in one hand and a glass of wine in the other. The door of the kitchenette swings closed on* AMANDA*'s gay laughter; the flickering light approaches the portieres.* LAURA *sits up nervously as* JIM *enters. She can hardly speak from the almost intolerable strain of being alone with a stranger.*]

[*Screen legend: "I don't suppose you remember me at all!"*]

[*At first, before* JIM*'s warmth overcomes her paralyzing shyness,* LAURA*'s voice is thin and breathless, as though she had just run up a steep flight of stairs.* JIMS*'s attitude is gently humorous. While the incident is apparently unimportant, it is to* LAURA *the climax of her secret life.*]

JIM: Hello there, Laura.

LAURA [*faintly*]: Hello.

[*She clears her throat.*]

JIM: How are you feeling now? Better?

LAURA: Yes. Yes, thank you.

JIM: This is for you. A little dandelion wine. [*He extends the glass toward her with extravagant gallantry.*]

LAURA: Thank you.

JIM: Drink it—but don't get drunk!

[*He laughs heartily.* LAURA *takes the glass uncertainly; she laughs shyly.*]

Where shall I set the candles?

LAURA: Oh—oh, anywhere . . .

JIM: How about here on the floor? Any objections?

LAURA: No.

JIM: I'll spread a newspaper under to catch the drippings. I like to sit on the floor. Mind if I do?

LAURA: Oh, no.

JIM: Give me a pillow?

LAURA: What?

JIM: A pillow!

LAURA: Oh . . . [*She hands him one quickly.*]

JIM: How about you? Don't you like to sit on the floor?

LAURA: Oh—yes.

JIM: Why don't you, then?

LAURA: I—will.

JIM: Take a pillow!

[LAURA *does. She sits on the floor on the other side of the candelabrum.* JIM *crosses his legs and smiles engagingly at her.*] I can't hardly see you sitting way over there.

LAURA: I can—see you.

JIM: I know, but that's not fair, I'm in the limelight.

[LAURA *moves her pillow closer.*]

Good! Now I can see you! Comfortable?

LAURA: Yes.

JIM: So am I. Comfortable as a cow! Will you have some gum?

LAURA: No, thank you.

JIM: I think that I will indulge, with your permission. [*He musingly unwraps a stick of gum and holds it up.*] Think of the fortune made by the guy that invented the first piece of chewing gum. Amazing, huh? The Wrigley Building is one of the sights of Chicago—I saw it when I went up to the Century of Progress. Did you take in the Century of Progress?

LAURA: No, I didn't.

JIM: Well, it was quite a wonderful exposition. What impressed me most was the Hall of Science. Gives you an idea of what the future will be in America, even more wonderful than the present time is! [*There is a pause.* JIM *smiles at her.*] Your brother tells me you're shy. Is that right, Laura?

LAURA: I—don't know.

JIM: I judge you to be an old-fashioned type of girl. Well, I think that's a pretty good type to be. Hope you don't think I'm being too personal—do you?

LAURA [*hastily, out of embarrassment*]: I believe I *will* take a piece of gum, if you—don't mind. [*clearing her throat*] Mr. O'Connor, have you—kept up with your singing?

JIM: Singing? Me?

LAURA: Yes. I remember what a beautiful voice you had.

JIM: When did you hear me sing?

[LAURA *does not answer, and in the long pause which follows a man's voice is heard singing offstage.*]

VOICE:
O blow, ye winds, heigh-ho,
A-roving I will go!
I'm off to my love
With a boxing glove—
Ten thousand miles away!

JIM: You say you've heard me sing?

LAURA: Oh, yes! Yes, very often . . . I—don't suppose—you remember me—at all?

JIM [*smiling doubtfully*]: You know I have an idea I've seen you before. I had that idea as soon as you opened the door. It seemed almost like I was about to remember your name. But the name I started to call you—wasn't a name! And so I stopped myself before I said it.

LAURA: Wasn't it—Blue Roses?

JIM [*springing up, grinning*]: Blue Roses! My gosh, yes—Blue Roses! That's what I had on my tongue when you opened the door! Isn't it funny what tricks your memory plays? I didn't connect you with high school somehow or other. But that's where it was; it was high school. I didn't even know you were Shakespeare's sister! Gosh, I'm sorry.

LAURA: I didn't expect you to. You—barely knew me!

JIM: But we did have a speaking acquaintance, huh?

LAURA: Yes, we—spoke to each other.

JIM: When did you recognize me?

LAURA: Oh, right away!

JIM: Soon as I came in the door?

LAURA: When I heard your name I thought it was probably you. I knew that Tom used to know you a little in high school. So when you came in the door—well, then I was—sure.

JIM: Why didn't you *say* something, then?

LAURA [*breathlessly*]: I didn't know what to say, I was—too surprised!

JIM: For goodness' sakes! You know, this sure is funny!

LAURA: Yes! Yes, isn't it, though . . .

JIM: Didn't we have a class in something together?

LAURA: Yes, we did.

JIM: What class was that?

LAURA: It was—singing—chorus!

JIM: Aw!

LAURA: I sat across the aisle from you in the Aud.

JIM: Aw.

LAURA: Mondays, Wednesdays, and Fridays.

JIM: Now I remember—you always came in late.

LAURA: Yes, it was so hard for me, getting upstairs. I had that brace on my leg—it clumped so loud!

JIM: I never heard any clumping.

LAURA [*wincing at the recollection*]: To me it sounded like—thunder!

JIM: Well, well, well, I never even noticed.

LAURA: And everybody was seated before I came in. I had to walk in front of all those people. My seat was in the back row. I had to go clumping all the way up the aisle with everyone watching!

JIM: You shouldn't have been self-conscious.

LAURA: I know, but I was. It was always such a relief when the singing started.

JIM: Aw, yes, I've placed you now! I used to call you Blue Roses. How was it that I got started calling you that?

LAURA: I was out of school a little with pleurosis. When I came back you asked me what was the matter. I said I had pleurosis—you thought I said *Blue Roses.* That's what you always called me after that!

JIM: I hope you didn't mind.

LAURA: Oh, no—I liked it. You see, I wasn't acquainted with many—people. . . .

JIM: As I remember you sort of stuck by yourself.

LAURA: I—I—never have had much luck at—making friends.

JIM: I don't see why you wouldn't.

LAURA: Well, I—started out badly.

JIM: You mean being—

LAURA: Yes, it sort of—stood between me—

JIM: You shouldn't have let it!

LAURA: I know, but it did, and—

JIM: You were shy with people!

LAURA: I tried not to be but never could—

JIM: Overcome it?

LAURA: No, I—I never could!

JIM: I guess being shy is something you have to work out of kind of gradually.

LAURA [*sorrowfully*]: Yes—I guess it—

JIM: Takes time!

LAURA: Yes—

JIM: People are not so dreadful when you know them. That's what you have to remember! And everybody has problems, not just you, but practically everybody has got some problems. You think of yourself as having the only problems, as being the only one who is disappointed. But just look around you and you will see lots of people as disappointed as you are. For instance, I hoped when I was going to high school that I would be further along at this time, six years later, than I am now. You remember that wonderful write-up I had in *The Torch?*

LAURA: Yes! [*She rises and crosses to the table.*]

JIM: It said I was bound to succeed in anything I went into!

[LAURA *returns with the high school yearbook.*]

Holy Jeez! *The Torch!*

[*He accepts it reverently. They smile across the book with mutual wonder.* LAURA *crouches beside him and they begin to turn the pages.* LAURA*'s shyness is dissolving in his warmth.*]

LAURA: Here you are in *The Pirates of Penzance!*

JIM [*wistfully*]: I sang the baritone lead in that operetta.

LAURA [*raptly*]: So—*beautifully!*

JIM [*protesting*]: Aw—

LAURA: Yes, yes—beautifully—beautifully!

JIM: You heard me?

LAURA: All three times!

JIM: No!

LAURA: Yes!

JIM: All three performances?

LAURA [*looking down*]: Yes.

JIM: Why?

LAURA: I—wanted to ask you to—autograph my program. [*She takes the program from the back of the yearbook and shows it to him.*]

JIM: Why didn't you ask me to?

LAURA: You were always surrounded by your own friends so much that I never had a chance to.

JIM: You should have just—

LAURA: Well, I—thought you might think I was—

JIM: Thought I might think you was—what?

LAURA: Oh—

JIM [*with reflective relish*]: I was beleaguered by females in those days.

LAURA: You were terribly popular!

JIM: Yeah—

LAURA: You had such a—friendly way—

JIM: I was spoiled in high school.

LAURA: Everybody—liked you!

JIM: Including you?

LAURA: I—yes, I—did, too—[*She gently closes the book in her lap.*]

JIM: Well, well, well! Give me that program, Laura.

[*She hands it to him. He signs it with a flourish.*]

There you are—better late than never!

LAURA: Oh, I—what a—surprise!

JIM: My signature isn't worth very much right now. But some day—maybe—it will increase in value! Being disappointed is one thing and being discouraged is something else. I am disappointed but I am not discouraged. I'm twenty-three years old. How old are you?

LAURA: I'll be twenty-four in June.

JIM: That's not old age!

LAURA: No, but—

JIM: You finished high school?

LAURA [*with difficulty*]: I didn't go back.

JIM: You mean you dropped out?

LAURA: I made bad grades in my final examinations. [*She rises and replaces the book and the program on the table. Her voice is strained.*] How is—Emily Meisenbach getting along?

JIM: Oh, that kraut-head!

LAURA: Why do you call her that?

JIM: That's what she was.

LAURA: You're not still—going with her?

JIM: I never see her.

LAURA: It said in the "Personal" section that you were—engaged!

JIM: I know, but I wasn't impressed by that—propaganda!

LAURA: It wasn't—the truth?

JIM: Only in Emily's optimistic opinion!

LAURA: Oh—

[*Legend: "What have you done since high school?"*]

[JIM *lights a cigarette and leans indolently back on his elbows smiling at* LAURA *with a warmth and charm which lights her inwardly with altar candles. She remains by the table, picks up a piece from the glass menagerie collection, and turns it in her hands to cover her tumult.*]

JIM [*after several reflective puffs on his cigarette*]: What have you done since high school?

[*She seems not to hear him.*]

Huh?

[LAURA *looks up.*]

I said what have you done since high school, Laura?

LAURA: Nothing much.

JIM: You must have been doing something these six long years.

LAURA: Yes.

JIM: Well, then, such as what?

LAURA: I took a business course at business college—

JIM: How did that work out?

LAURA: Well, not very—well—I had to drop out, it gave me—indigestion—

[JIM *laughs gently.*]

JIM: What are you doing now?

LAURA: I don't do anything—much. Oh, please don't think I sit around doing nothing! My glass collection takes up a good deal of time. Glass is something you have to take good care of.

JIM: What did you say—about glass?

LAURA: Collection I said—I have one—[*She clears her throat and turns away again, acutely shy.*]

JIM [*abruptly*]: You know what I judge to be the trouble with you? Inferiority complex! Know what that is? That's what they call it when someone low-rates himself! I understand it because I had it, too. Although my case was not so aggravated as yours seems to be. I had it until I took up public speaking, developed my voice, and learned that I had an aptitude for science. Before that time I never thought of myself as being outstanding in any way whatsoever! Now I've never made a regular study of it, but I have a friend who says I can analyze people better than doctors that make a profession of it. I don't claim that to be necessarily true, but I can sure guess a person's psychology, Laura! [*He takes out his gum.*] Excuse me, Laura. I always take it out when the flavor is gone. I'll use this scrap of paper to wrap it in. I know how it is to get it stuck on a shoe. [*He wraps the gum in paper and puts it in his pocket.*] Yep—that's what I judge to be your principal trouble. A lack of confidence in yourself as a person. You don't have the proper amount of faith in yourself. I'm basing that fact on a number of your remarks and also on certain observations I've made. For instance that clumping you thought was so awful in high school. You say that you even dreaded to walk into class. You see what you did? You dropped out of school, you gave up an education because of a clump, which as far as I know was practically non-existent! A little physical defect is what you have. Hardly noticeable even! Magnified thousands of times by imagination! You know what my strong advice to you is? Think of yourself as *superior* in some way!

LAURA: In what way would I think?

JIM: Why, man alive, Laura! Just look about you a little. What do you see? A world full of common people! All of 'em born and all of 'em going to die! Which of them has one-tenth of your good points! Or mine! Or anyone else's, as far as that goes—gosh! Everybody excels in some one thing. Some in many! [*He unconsciously glances at himself in the mirror.*] All you've got to do is discover in *what!* Take me, for instance. [*He adjusts his tie at the mirror.*] My interest happens to lie in electro-dynamics. I'm taking a course in radio engineering at night school, Laura, on top of a fairly responsible job at the warehouse. I'm taking that course and studying public speaking.

LAURA: Ohhhh.

JIM: Because I believe in the future of television! [*turning his back to her.*] I wish to be ready to go up right along with it. Therefore I'm planning to get in on the ground floor. In fact I've already made the right connections and all that remains is for the industry itself to get under way! Full steam—[*His eyes are starry.*] *Knowledge*—Zzzzzp! *Money*—Zzzzzp!—*Power!* That's the cycle democracy is built on!

[*His attitude is convincingly dynamic.* LAURA *stares at him, even her shyness eclipsed in her absolute wonder. He suddenly grins.*]

I guess you think I think a lot of myself?

LAURA: No—o-o-o, I—

JIM: Now how about you? Isn't there something you take more interest in than anything else?

LAURA: Well, I do—as I said—have my—glass collection—

[*A peal of girlish laughter rings from the kitchenette.*]

JIM: I'm not right sure I know what you're talking about. What kind of glass is it?

LAURA: Little articles of it, they're ornaments mostly! Most of them are little animals made out of glass, the tiniest little animals in the world. Mother calls them a glass menagerie! Here's an example of one, if you'd like to see it! This one is one of the oldest. It's nearly thirteen.

[*Music: "The Glass Menagerie."*]

[*He stretches out his hand.*]

Oh, be careful—if you breathe, it breaks!

JIM: I'd better not take it. I'm pretty clumsy with things.

LAURA: Go on, I trust you with him! [*She places the piece in his palm.*] There now—you're holding him gently! Hold him over the light, he loves the light! You see how the light shines through him?

JIM: It sure does shine!

LAURA: I shouldn't be partial, but he is my favorite one.

JIM: What kind of a thing is this one supposed to be?

LAURA: Haven't you noticed the single horn on his forehead?

JIM: A unicorn, huh?

LAURA: Mmmm-hmmmm!

JIM: Unicorns—aren't they extinct in the modern world?

LAURA: I know!

JIM: Poor little fellow, he must feel sort of lonesome.

LAURA [*smiling*]: Well, if he does, he doesn't complain about it. He stays on a shelf with some horses that don't have horns and all of them seem to get along nicely together.

JIM: How do you know?

LAURA [*lightly*]: I haven't heard any arguments among them!

JIM [*grinning*]: No arguments, huh? Well, that's a pretty good sign! Where shall I set him?

LAURA: Put him on the table. They all like a change of scenery once in a while!

JIM: Well, well, well, well—[*He places the glass piece on the table, then raises his arms and stretches.*] Look how big my shadow is when I stretch!

LAURA: Oh, oh, yes—it stretches across the ceiling!

JIM [*crossing to the door*]: I think it's stopped raining. [*He opens the fire-escape door and the background music changes to a dance tune.*] Where does the music come from?

LAURA: From the Paradise Dance Hall across the alley.

JIM: How about cutting the rug a little, Miss Wingfield?

LAURA: Oh, I—

JIM: Or is your program filled up? Let me have a look at it. [*He grasps an imaginary card.*] Why, every dance is taken! I'll just have to scratch some out.

[*Waltz music: "La Golondrina."*]

Ahhh, a waltz! [*He executes some sweeping turns by himself, then holds his arms toward* LAURA.]

LAURA [*breathlessly*]: I—can't dance!

JIM: There you go, that inferiority stuff!

LAURA: I've never danced in my life!

JIM: Come on, try!

LAURA: Oh, but I'd step on you!

JIM: I'm not made out of glass.

LAURA: How—how—how do we start?

JIM: Just leave it to me. You hold your arms out a little.

LAURA: Like this?

JIM [*taking her in his arms*]: A little bit higher. Right. Now don't tighten up, that's the main thing about it—relax.

LAURA [*laughing breathlessly*]: It's hard not to.

JIM: Okay.

LAURA: I'm afraid you can't budge me.

JIM: What do you bet I can't? [*He swings her into motion.*]

LAURA: Goodness, yes, you can!

JIM: Let yourself go, now, Laura, just let yourself go.

LAURA: I'm—

JIM: Come on!

LAURA: —trying!

JIM: Not so stiff—easy does it!

LAURA: I know but I'm—

JIM: Loosen th' backbone! There now, that's a lot better.

LAURA: Am I?

JIM: Lots, lots better! [*He moves her about the room in a clumsy waltz.*]

LAURA: Oh, my!

JIM: Ha-ha!

LAURA: Oh, my goodness!

JIM: Ha-ha-ha!

[*They suddenly bump into the table, and the glass piece on it falls to the floor.* JIM *stops the dance.*]

What did we hit on?

LAURA: Table.

JIM: Did something fall off it? I think—

LAURA: Yes.

JIM: I hope that it wasn't the little glass horse with the horn!

LAURA: Yes. [*She stoops to pick it up.*]

JIM: Aw, aw, aw. Is it broken?

LAURA: Now it is just like all the other horses.

JIM: It's lost its—

LAURA: Horn! It doesn't matter. Maybe it's a blessing in disguise.

JIM: You'll never forgive me. I bet that was your favorite piece of glass.

LAURA: I don't have favorites much. It's no tragedy, Freckles. Glass breaks so easily. No matter how careful you are. The traffic jars the shelves and things fall off them.

JIM: Still I'm awfully sorry that I was the cause.

LAURA [*smiling*]: I'll just imagine he had an operation. The horn was removed to make him feel less—freakish!

[*They both laugh*]

Now he will feel more at home with the other horses, the ones that don't have horns. . . .

JIM: Ha-ha, that's very funny! [*Suddenly he is serious.*] I'm glad to see that you have a sense of humor. You know—you're—well—very different! Surprisingly different from anyone else I know! [*His voice becomes soft and hesitant with a genuine feeling.*] Do you mind me telling you that?

[LAURA *is abashed beyond speech.*]

I mean it in a nice way—

[LAURA *nods shyly, looking away.*]

You make me feel sort of—I don't know how to put it! I'm usually pretty good at expressing things, but—this is something that I don't know how to say!

[LAURA *touches her throat and clears it—turns the broken unicorn in her hands. His voice becomes softer.*]

Has anyone ever told you that you were pretty?

[*There is a pause, and the music rises slightly.* LAURA *looks up slowly, with wonder, and shakes her head.*]

Well, you are! In a very different way from anyone else. And all the nicer because of the difference, too.

[*His voice becomes low and husky.* LAURA *turns away, nearly faint with the novelty of her emotions.*]

I wish that you were my sister. I'd teach you to have some confidence in yourself. The different people are not like other people, but being different is nothing to be ashamed of. Because other people are not such wonderful people. They're one hundred times one thousand. You're one times one! They walk all over the earth. You just stay here. They're common as—weeds, but—you—well, you're—*Blue Roses!*

[*Image on screen: Blue Roses.*]

[*The music changes.*]

LAURA: But blue is wrong for—roses. . . .

JIM: It's right for you! You're—pretty!

LAURA: In what respect am I pretty!

JIM: In all respects—believe me! Your eyes—your hair—are pretty! Your hands are pretty! [*He catches hold of her hand.*] You think I'm making this up because I'm invited to dinner and have to be nice. Oh, I could do that! I could put on an act for you, Laura, and say lots of things without being very sincere. But this time I am. I'm talking to you sincerely. I happened to notice you had this inferiority complex that keeps you from feeling comfortable with people. Somebody needs to build your confidence up and make you proud instead of shy and turning away and—blushing. Somebody—ought to—*kiss* you, Laura!

[*His hand slips slowly up her arm to her shoulder as the music swells tumultuously. He suddenly turns her about and kisses her on the lips. When he releases her,* LAURA *sinks on the sofa with a bright, dazed look.* JIM *backs away and fishes in his pockets for a cigarette.*]

[*Legend on screen: "A souvenir."*]

Stumblejohn!

[*He lights the cigarette, avoiding her look. There is a peal of girlish laughter from* AMANDA *in the kitchenette.* LAURA *slowly raises and opens her hand. It still contains the little broken glass animal. She looks at it with a tender, bewildered expression.*]

Stumblejohn! I shouldn't have done that—that was way off the beam. You don't smoke, do you?

[*She looks up, smiling, not hearing the question. He sits beside her rather gingerly. She looks at him speechlessly—waiting. He coughs decorously and moves a little farther aside as he considers the situation and senses her feelings, dimly, with perturbation. He speaks gently.*]

Would you—care for a—mint?

[*She doesn't seem to hear him but her look grows brighter even.*]

Peppermint? Life Saver? My pocket's a regular drugstore—wherever I go . . . [*He pops a mint in his mouth. Then he gulps and decides to make a clean breast of it. He speaks slowly and gingerly.*] Laura, you know, if I had a sister like you, I'd do the same thing as Tom. I'd bring out fellows and—introduce her to them. The right type of boys—of a type to—appreciate her. Only—well—he made a mistake about me. Maybe I've got no call to be saying this. That may not have been the idea in having me over. But what if it was? There's nothing wrong about that. The only trouble is that in my case—I'm not in a situation to—do the right thing. I can't take down your number and say I'll phone. I can't call up next week and—ask for a date. I thought I had better explain the situation in case you—misunderstood it and—I hurt your feelings. . . .

[*There is a pause. Slowly, very slowly,* LAURA*'s look changes, her eyes returning slowly from his to the glass figure in her palm.* AMANDA *utters another gay laugh in the kitchenette.*]

LAURA [*faintly*]: You—won't—call again?

JIM: No, Laura, I can't. [*He rises from the sofa.*] As I was just explaining, I've—got strings on me. Laura, I've—been going steady! I go out all the time with a girl named

Betty. She's a home-girl like you, and Catholic, and Irish, and in a great many ways we—get along fine. I met her last summer on a moonlight boat trip up the river to Alton, on the *Majestic.* Well—right away from the start it was—love!

[*Legend: Love!*]

[LAURA *sways slightly forward and grips the arm of the sofa. He fails to notice, now enrapt in his own comfortable being.*]

Being in love has made a new man of me!

[*Leaning stiffly forward, clutching the arm of the sofa,* LAURA *struggles visibly with her storm. But* JIM *is oblivious; she is a long way off.*]

The power of love is really pretty tremendous! Love is something that—changes the whole world, Laura!

[*The storm abates a little and* LAURA *leans back. He notices her again.*]

It happened that Betty's aunt took sick, she got a wire and had to go to Centralia. So Tom—when he asked me to dinner—I naturally just accepted the invitation, not knowing that you—that he—that I—[*He stops awkwardly.*] Huh—I'm a stumblejohn!

[*He flops back on the sofa. The holy candles on the altar of* LAURA*'s face have been snuffled out. There is a look of almost infinite desolation.* JIM *glances at her uneasily.*]

I wish that you would—say something.

[*She bites her lip which was trembling and then bravely smiles. She opens her hand again on the broken glass figure. Then she gently takes his hand and raises it level with her own. She carefully places the unicorn in the palm of his hand, then pushes his fingers closed upon it.*]

What are you—doing that for? You want me to have him? Laura?

[*She nods.*]

What for?

LAURA: A—souvenir . . .

[*She rises unsteadily and crouches beside the Victrola to wind it up.*]

[*Legend on screen: "Things have a way of turning out so badly!" Or image: "Gentleman caller waving goodbye—gaily."*]

[*At this moment* AMANDA *rushes brightly back into the living room. She bears a pitcher of fruit punch in an old-fashioned cut-glass pitcher, and a plate of macaroons. The plate has a gold border and poppies painted on it.*]

AMANDA: Well, well, well! Isn't the air delightful after the shower? I've made you children a little liquid refreshment. [*She turns gaily to* JIM.] Jim, do you know that song about lemonade?

"Lemonade, lemonade
Made in the shade and stirred with a spade—
Good enough for any old maid!"

JIM [*uneasily*]: Ha-ha! No—I never heard it.

AMANDA: Why, Laura! You look so serious!

JIM: We were having a serious conversation.

AMANDA: Good! Now you're better acquainted!

JIM [*uncertainly*]: Ha-ha! Yes.

AMANDA: You modern young people are much more serious-minded than my generation. I was so gay as a girl!

JIM: You haven't changed, Mrs. Wingfield.

AMANDA: Tonight I'm rejuvenated! The gaiety of the occasion, Mr. O'Connor! [*She tosses her head with a peal of laughter, spilling some lemonade.*] Oooo! I'm baptizing myself!

JIM: Here—let me—

AMANDA [*setting the pitcher down*]: There now. I discovered we had some maraschino cherries. I dumped them in, juice and all!

JIM: You shouldn't have gone to that trouble, Mrs. Wingfield.

AMANDA: Trouble, trouble? Why, it was loads of fun! Didn't you hear me cutting up in the kitchen? I bet your ears were burning! I told Tom how outdone with him I was for keeping you to himself so long a time! He should have brought you over much, much sooner! Well, now that you've found your way, I want you to be a very frequent caller! Not just occasional but all the time. Oh, we're going to have a lot of gay times together! I see them coming! Mmm, just breathe that air! So fresh, and the moon's so pretty! I'll skip back out—I know where my place is when young folks are having a—serious conversation!

JIM: Oh, don't go out, Mrs. Wingfield. The fact of the matter is I've got to be going.

AMANDA: Going, now? You're joking! Why, it's only the shank of the evening, Mr. O'Connor!

JIM: Well, you know how it is.

AMANDA: You mean you're a young workingman and have to keep workingmen's hours. We'll let you off early tonight. But only on the condition that next time you stay later. What's the best night for you? Isn't Saturday night the best night for you workingmen?

JIM: I have a couple of time-clocks to punch, Mrs. Wingfield. One at morning, another one at night!

AMANDA: My, but you *are* ambitious! You work at night, too?

JIM: No, Ma'am, not work but—Betty!

[*He crosses deliberately to pick up his hat. The band at the Paradise Dance Hall goes into a tender waltz.*]

AMANDA: Betty? Betty? Who's—Betty!

[*There is an ominous cracking sound in the sky.*]

JIM: Oh, just a girl. The girl I go steady with!

[*He smiles charmingly. The sky falls.*]

[*Legend: "The Sky Falls."*]

AMANDA [*a long-drawn exhalation*]: Ohhhh . . . Is it a serious romance, Mr. O'Connor?

JIM: We're going to be married the second Sunday in June.

AMANDA: Ohhhh—how nice! Tom didn't mention that you were engaged to be married.

JIM: The cat's not out of the bag at the warehouse yet. You know how they are. They call you Romeo and stuff like that. [*He stops at the oval mirror to put on his hat. He carefully shapes the brim and the crown to give a discreetly dashing effect.*] It's been a wonderful evening, Mrs. Wingfield. I guess this is what they mean by Southern hospitality.

AMANDA: It really wasn't anything at all.

JIM: I hope it don't seem like I'm rushing off. But I promised Betty I'd pick her up at the Wabash depot, an' by the time I get my jalopy down there her train'll be in. Some women are pretty upset if you keep 'em waiting.

AMANDA: Yes, I know—the tyranny of woman! [*She extends her hand.*] Goodbye, Mr. O'Connor. I wish you luck—and happiness—and success! All three of them, and so does Laura! Don't you, Laura?

LAURA: Yes!

JIM [*taking* LAURA*'s hand*]: Goodbye, Laura. I'm certainly going to treasure that souvenir. And don't you forget the good advice I gave you! [*He raises his voice to a cheery shout.*] So long, Shakespeare! Thanks again, ladies. Good night!

[*He grins and ducks jauntily out. Still bravely grimacing,* AMANDA *closes the door on the gentleman caller. Then she turns back to the room with a puzzled expression. She and* LAURA *don't dare to face each other.* LAURA *crouches beside the Victrola to wind it.*]

AMANDA [*faintly*]: Things have a way of turning out so badly. I don't believe that I would play the Victrola. Well, well—well! Our gentleman caller was engaged to be married! [*She raises her voice.*] Tom!

TOM [*from the kitchenette*]: Yes, Mother?

AMANDA: Come in here a minute. I want to tell you something awfully funny.

TOM [*entering with a macaroon and a glass of lemonade*]: Has the gentleman caller gotten away already?

AMANDA: The gentleman caller has made an early departure. What a wonderful joke you played on us!

TOM: How do you mean?

AMANDA: You didn't mention that he was engaged to be married.

TOM: Jim? Engaged?

AMANDA: That's what he just informed us.

TOM: I'll be jiggered! I didn't know about that.

AMANDA: That seems very peculiar.

TOM: What's peculiar about it?

AMANDA: Didn't you call him your best friend down at the warehouse?

TOM: He is, but how did I know?

AMANDA: It seems extremely peculiar that you wouldn't know your best friend is going to be married!

TOM: The warehouse is where I work, not where I know things about people!

AMANDA: You don't know things anywhere! You live in a dream; you manufacture illusions!

[*He crosses to the door.*]

Where are you going?

TOM: I'm going to the movies.

AMANDA: That's right, now that you've had us make such fools of ourselves. The effort, the preparations, all the expense! The new floor lamp, the rug, the clothes for Laura! All for what? To entertain some other girl's fiancé! Go to the movies, go! Don't think about us, a mother deserted, an unmarried sister who's crippled and has no job! Don't let anything interfere with your selfish pleasure! Just go, go, go—to the movies!

TOM: All right, I will! The more you shout about my selfishness to me the quicker I'll go, and I won't go the movies!

AMANDA: Go, then! Go to the moon—you selfish dreamer!

[TOM *smashes his glass on the floor. He plunges out on the fire escape, slamming the door.* LAURA *screams in fright. The dance-hall music becomes louder.* TOM *stands on the fire escape, gripping the rail. The moon breaks through the storm clouds, illuminating his face.*]

[*Legend on screen: "And so goodbye ..."*]

[TOM*'s closing speech is timed with what is happening inside the house. We see, as though through soundproof glass, that* AMANDA *appears to be making a comforting speech to* LAURA, *who is huddled upon the sofa. Now that we cannot hear the mother's speech, her silliness is gone and she has dignity and tragic beauty.* LAURA*'s hair hides her face until, at the end of the speech, she lifts her head to smile at her mother.* AMANDA*'s gestures are slow and graceful, almost dancelike, as she comforts her daughter. At the end of her speech she glances a moment at the father's picture—then withdraws through the portieres. At the close of* TOM*'s speech,* LAURA *blows out the candles, ending the play.*]

TOM: I didn't go to the moon, I went much further—for time is the longest distance between two places. Not long after that I was fired for writing a poem on the lid of a shoe-box. I left Saint Louis. I descended the steps of this fire escape for a last time and followed, from then on, in my father's footsteps, attempting to find in motion what was lost in space. I traveled around a great deal. The cities swept about me like dead leaves, leaves that were brightly colored but torn away from the branches. I would have stopped, but I was pursued by something. It always came upon me unawares, taking me altogether by surprise. Perhaps it was a familiar bit of music. Perhaps it was only a piece of transparent glass. Perhaps I am walking along a street at night, in some strange city, before I have found companions. I pass the lighted window of a shop where perfume is sold. The window is filled with pieces of colored glass, tiny transparent bottles in delicate colors, like bits of a shattered rainbow. Then all at once my sister touches my shoulder. I turn around and look into her eyes. O, Laura, Laura, I tried to leave you behind me, but I am more faithful than I intended to be! I reach for a cigarette, I cross the street, I run into the movies or a bar, I buy a drink, I speak to the nearest stranger—anything that can blow your candles out!

[LAURA *bends over the candles.*]

For nowadays the world is lit by lightning! Blow out your candles, Laura—and so goodbye. . . .

[*She blows the candles out.*]

(1944)

QUESTIONS FOR CRITICAL THINKING AND WRITING

Experience

1. With whom do you sympathize most in the play? Why? Do you harbor any unfavorable feelings toward any of the characters? Why or why not?
2. To what extent does your knowledge and experience of loneliness play into your response to the characters in Williams's play?

Interpretation

3. How is the play structured? Identify and comment on the major parts into which it is divided.
4. What is the narrator's role in the play? What would be gained or lost without him?
5. What is the significance to Laura (and to the play's meaning overall) of her collection of glass animals? Why is the unicorn singled out? What are its symbolic implications?
6. What other symbols does the play include? Identify two and explain their significance.
7. What is the significance of the interpolated "legends" that appear in the stage directions throughout the play? What would be gained or lost if they were to be omitted?
8. What does the play suggest about the importance and significance of dreams? Where do you find this concern expressed or suggested most effectively?
9. Who is the play's central character? Identify and explain the principal relationships of the central character with the other characters in the play.

Evaluation

10. What value is accorded memory in the play?
11. What values are brought into the play with references to the social and historical events that were occurring during the time of its action?

Connection

12. Compare *The Glass Menagerie* with Arthur Miller's *Death of a Salesman* as an expression of significant themes in modern American culture.
13. Read the play's production notes written by Williams. How do the play's production notes written by Williams enrich your understanding of *The Glass Menagerie?*

Critical Thinking

14. *The Glass Menagerie* was written and first produced more than 60 years ago. And unlike Miller's *Death of a Salesman,* William's play does not focus on a major aspect of American culture. What relevance do you think *The Glass Menagerie* has for today's readers and theatergoers? Why do think the play has retained its popularity?

ENVISIONING *DEATH OF A SALESMAN*

Since it was first performed in 1949, *Death of a Salesman* has been a classic of the American theater. Like much other realistic drama, the stage directions are fairly clear. Miller provides extensive and detailed stage directions. He also furnishes information about the lives his characters lead, giving us a sense of their past.

These realistic touches blend, however, with other dramatic elements that are less realistic and that we will call *expressionistic.* Expressionistic playwrights attempt to dramatize a subjective picture of reality as seen by an individual consciousness. They attempt to show the inner life of a character, portraying external reality as he or she sees it. *Death of a Salesman* is expressionistic in that it dramatizes Willy Loman's subjective sense of things, rather than exhibiting a concern for a strict and exact representation of external detail. The play is particularly expressionistic in its memory scenes, in which Willy recalls events from the past in such a way that he reenacts rather than merely remembers them. In these scenes different times, places, and states of mind fluctuate and merge as Miller reveals Willy's thoughts, attitudes, and beliefs, his inflated hopes and deflated dreams. The expressionistic quality of the play is enhanced by lighting and music that signal flashbacks and contribute to its mood.

As you read the play, consider the lighting, music, and stage directions and how they must affect the play in performance.

Following are Jo Mielziner's original sketches for the set of the play along with a diary entry about a particular scene change. In the diary entry, noticed how practical considerations of what the audience will see and hear factor into the decision about how to make a scene change. Following the sketches are photos from the original

Jo Mielziner's early sketch for the design of the original production. Note the two levels of the house with Willy below and Happy and Biff on top.

Broadway production and the most recent. Consider the similarities between the original sketches, the original performance, and the most recent performance. Working under such detailed directions, ask yourself how much freedom are individual directors and actors given when they stage a play? What are the benefits of detailed directions? What would the benefits of less detailed directions be? And how do the directions affect how you envision the play being performed?

JO MIELZINER

December 15, 1948

During my midweek check-up of unfinished *Salesman* chores, I realized that a large number of basic decisions still had to be made about the small scenes outside Willy Loman's house. Since rehearsals were due to start a couple of days after Christmas, I appealed to Kazan° for a good long session.

During the previous weeks I had been receiving from Arthur Miller, scene by scene, the final version of the rehearsal script. Although he had done the basic rewriting, he had made no attempt to say how the transitions from one scene to another would be made. This was a problem for the director and the designer to work out together as we studied the model, the ground plan, and the cut-out card-board symbols representing the props.

I pointed out to Kazan how difficult it would be in an office scene, for instance, to remove two desks, two chairs, and a hat rack (which the present script called for) and at the same time have an actor walk quickly across the stage and appear in "a hotel room in Boston where he meets a girl." I urged him to do even more cutting, not in

Kazan *Elia Kazan (1909–2003), director of the original production of Death of a Salesman.*

Jo Mielziner's painting of the original set. Note the added detail of the back drop that includes the "towering, angular shapes" that Miller calls for in the scene directions.

Photo of the original 1949 production with Mildred Dunnock (Linda), Lee J. Cobb (Willy), Arthur Kennedy (Biff), and Cameron Mitchell (Happy). Compare with the original sketch.

the text but in the props called for in this latest version of the script. We finally got the office pared down to one desk and one chair. Then I suggested going so far as to use the same desk for both office scenes—first in Heiser's office and then, with a change of other props, in Charley's office. As usual, Kazan's imagination rose to the suggestion. He replied, "Sure, let's cut this down to the bone—we can play on practically anything." This is effective abstraction, giving the spectator the opportunity to "fill in."

I had felt from the outset that the cemetery scene at the end of the play would be done on the forestage,° and I had actually drawn up a design for a trick trapdoor out of which would rise the small gravestone that we had thought necessary for this scene. I had shown Kazan the working drawing for the gravestone, explained how it would operate, and mentioned that because of union rules the man operating this mechanism would be doing this and nothing else, thereby adding a member to the crew for the sake of one effect. I had also mentioned that since the trap would be very close to the audience the sound of its opening might disturb the solemnity of the scene.

With some malice aforethought, I had also done a drawing showing the Salesman's widow sitting on the step leading to the forestage, with her two sons standing behind her, their heads bowed; on the floor at her feet was a small bouquet of flowers. The whole scene was bathed in a magic-lantern projection of autumn leaves. Here, again,

forestage *the front of the stage, closer to the audience.*

leaves were symbolic. With this kind of lighting I thought I could completely obliterate the house in the background and evoke a sense of sadness and finality that might enable us to eliminate the gravestone itself.

My hints were not lost. "I get your point," Kazan said, "Let's do it without the gravestone. No matter how quietly you move it into place, everybody nearby is going to be so busy thinking, 'How is that done?' that they'll miss the mood of the scene."

I felt that this extreme simplicity would be the best theatre possible, and later, in dress rehearsal, it proved to be the right answer.

ARTHUR MILLER
[1915–2005]

Death of a Salesman *is Arthur Miller's most famous and notable play. Produced and published in 1949, it had a long original Broadway run and has been frequently revived in the decades since. The play is in the tradition of social realism inaugurated by Ibsen and continued by Chekhov, Strindberg, and Shaw. The dialogue of the characters, their financial and emotional problems, and their behavior are all indicative of a typically realistic drama. Like Ibsen's* A Doll House, *Miller's* Salesman *raises questions about social values and attitudes—in this case, the pursuit of success and the American dream. Miller's tone mixes sympathy and judgment, criticism and compassion.*

One issue readers, audiences, and critics have consistently raised about Death of a Salesman *concerns its status as tragedy. The main question turns on whether Willy Loman is a tragic figure. Is he grand and noble enough to be a tragic hero? Is his failure tragic or merely pathetic? Over the years Miller has written about these and related questions in essays such as "On Social Drama" and "Tragedy and the Common Man." He has suggested that "the common man is as apt a subject for tragedy as kings"; and also that "the tragic feeling is evoked in us when we are in the presence of a character who is ready to lay down his life" to secure his dignity. How far these observations apply to Willy Loman is a matter for discussion.*

Death of a Salesman

CERTAIN PRIVATE CONVERSATIONS IN TWO ACTS AND A REQUIEM

CHARACTERS

WILLY LOMAN
LINDA
BIFF
HAPPY
BERNARD
THE WOMAN

Compare the 1999 production here with the original production. Note how similar it is to the 1949 production. What could change in the productions in the next 50 years?

CHARLEY
UNCLE BEN
HOWARD WAGNER
JENNY
STANLEY
MISS FORSYTHE
LETTA

The action takes place in WILLY LOMAN'S *house and yard and in various places he visits in the New York and Boston of today.*

Throughout the play, in the stage directions, left and right mean stage left and stage right.

ACT I

A melody is heard, played upon a flute. It is small and fine, telling of grass and trees and the horizon. The curtain rises.

Before us is the Salesman's house. We are aware of towering, angular shapes behind it, surrounding it on all sides. Only the blue light of the sky falls upon the house and forestage; the surrounding area shows an angry glow of orange. As more light appears, we see a solid vault of apartment houses around the small, fragile-seeming home. An air of the dream clings to the place, a dream rising out of reality. The kitchen at center seems actual enough, for there is a kitchen table with three chairs, and a refrigerator. But no other fixtures are seen. At the back of the kitchen there is a draped entrance, which leads to the livingroom. To the right of the kitchen, on a level raised two feet, is a bedroom furnished only with a brass bedstead and a straight chair. On a shelf over the bed a silver athletic trophy stands. A window opens onto the apartment house at the side.

Behind the kitchen, on a level raised six and a half feet, is the boys' bedroom, at present barely visible. Two beds are dimly seen, and at the back of the room a dormer window. (This bedroom is above the unseen livingroom.) At the left a stairway curves up to it from the kitchen.

The entire setting is wholly or, in some places, partially transparent. The roof-line of the house is one-dimensional; under and over it we see the apartment buildings. Before the house lies an apron, curving beyond the forestage into the orchestra. This forward area serves as the back yard as well as the locale of all WILLY'S *imaginings and of his city scenes. Whenever the action is in the present the actors observe the imaginary wall-lines, entering the house only through the door at the left. But in the scenes of the past these boundaries are broken, and characters enter or leave a room by stepping "through" a wall onto the forestage.*

From the right, WILLY LOMAN, *the Salesman, enters, carrying two large sample cases. The flute plays on. He hears but is not aware of it. He is past sixty years of age, dressed quietly. Even as he crosses the stage to the doorway of the house, his exhaustion is apparent. He unlocks the door, comes into the kitchen, and thankfully lets his burden down, feeling the soreness of his palms. A word-sigh escapes his lips—it might be "Oh, boy, oh, boy." He closes the door, then carries his cases out into the livingroom, through the draped kitchen doorway.*

LINDA, *his wife, has stirred in her bed at the right. She gets out and puts on a robe, listening. Most often jovial, she has developed an iron repression of her exceptions to* WILLY'S *behavior—she more than loves him, she admires him, as though his mercurial nature, his temper, his massive dreams and little cruelties, served her only as sharp reminders of the turbulent longings within him, longings which she shares but lacks the temperament to utter and follow to their end.*

LINDA (*hearing* WILLY *outside the bedroom, calls with some trepidation*): Willy!

WILLY: It's all right. I came back.

LINDA: Why? What happened? (*Slight pause.*) Did something happen, Willy?

WILLY: No, nothing happened.

LINDA: You didn't smash the car, did you?

WILLY (*with casual irritation*): I said nothing happened. Didn't you hear me?

LINDA: Don't you feel well?

WILLY: I am tired to the death. (*The flute has faded away. He sits on the bed beside her, a little numb.*) I couldn't make it. I just couldn't make it, Linda.

LINDA (*very carefully, delicately*): Where were you all day? You look terrible.

WILLY: I got as far as a little above Yonkers. I stopped for a cup of coffee. Maybe it was the coffee.

LINDA: What?

WILLY (*after a pause*): I suddenly couldn't drive any more. The car kept going onto the shoulder, y'know?

LINDA (*helpfully*): Oh. Maybe it was the steering again. I don't think Angelo knows the Studebaker.

WILLY: No, it's me, it's me. Suddenly I realize I'm goin' sixty miles an hour and I don't remember the last five minutes. I'm—I can't seem to—keep my mind to it.

LINDA: Maybe it's your glasses. You never went for your new glasses.

WILLY: No, I see everything. I came back ten miles an hour. It took me nearly four hours from Yonkers.

LINDA (*resigned*): Well, you'll just have to take a rest, Willy, you can't continue this way.

WILLY: I just got back from Florida.

LINDA: But you didn't rest your mind. Your mind is overactive, and the mind is what counts, dear.

WILLY: I'll start out in the morning. Maybe I'll feel better in the morning. (*She is taking off his shoes.*) These goddam arch supports are killing me.

LINDA: Take an aspirin. Should I get you an aspirin? It'll soothe you.

WILLY (*with wonder*): I was driving along, you understand? And I was fine. I was even observing the scenery. You can imagine, me looking at scenery, on the road every week of my life. But it's so beautiful up there, Linda, the trees are so thick, and the sun is warm. I opened the windshield and just let the warm air bathe over me. And then all of a sudden I'm goin' off the road! I'm tellin' ya, I absolutely forgot I was driving. If I'd've gone the other way over the white line I might've killed somebody. So I went on again—and five minutes later I'm dreamin' again, and I nearly—(*He presses two fingers against his eyes.*) I have such thoughts, I have such strange thoughts.

LINDA: Willy, dear. Talk to them again. There's no reason why you can't work in New York.

WILLY: They don't need me in New York. I'm the New England man. I'm vital in New England.

LINDA: But you're sixty years old. They can't expect you to keep traveling every week.

WILLY: I'll have to send a wire to Portland. I'm supposed to see Brown and Morrison tomorrow morning at ten o'clock to show the line. Goddammit, I could sell them! (*He starts putting on his jacket.*)

LINDA (*taking the jacket from him*): Why don't you go down to the place tomorrow and tell Howard you've simply got to work in New York? You're too accommodating, dear.

WILLY: If old man Wagner was alive I'd a been in charge of New York now! That man was a prince, he was a masterful man. But that boy of his, that Howard, he don't appreciate. When I went north the first time, the Wagner Company didn't know where New England was!

LINDA: Why don't you tell those things to Howard, dear?

WILLY (*encouraged*): I will, I definitely will. Is there any cheese?

LINDA: I'll make you a sandwich.

WILLY: No, go to sleep. I'll take some milk. I'll be up right away. The boys in?

LINDA: They're sleeping. Happy took Biff on a date tonight.

WILLY (*interested*): That so?

LINDA: It was so nice to see them shaving together, one behind the other, in the bathroom. And going out together. You notice? The whole house smells of shaving lotion.

WILLY: Figure it out. Work a lifetime to pay off a house. You finally own it, and there's nobody to live in it.

LINDA: Well, dear, life is a casting off. It's always that way.

WILLY: No, no, some people—some people accomplish something. Did Biff say anything after I went this morning?

LINDA: You shouldn't have criticized him, Willy, especially after he just got off the train. You mustn't lose your temper with him.

WILLY: When the hell did I lose my temper? I simply asked him if he was making any money. Is that a criticism?

LINDA: But, dear, how could he make any money?

WILLY (*worried and angered*): There's such an undercurrent in him. He became a moody man. Did he apologize when I left this morning?

LINDA: He was crestfallen, Willy. You know how he admires you. I think if he finds himself, then you'll both be happier and not fight any more.

WILLY: How can he find himself on a farm? Is that a life? A farmhand? In the beginning, when he was young, I thought, well, a young man, it's good for him to tramp around, take a lot of different jobs. But it's more than ten years now and he has yet to make thirty-five dollars a week!

LINDA: He's finding himself, Willy.

WILLY: Not finding yourself at the age of thirty-four is a disgrace!

LINDA: Shh!

WILLY: The trouble is he's lazy, goddammit!

LINDA: Willy, please!

WILLY: Biff is a lazy bum!

LINDA: They're sleeping. Get something to eat. Go on down.

WILLY: Why did he come home? I would like to know what brought him home.

LINDA: I don't know. I think he's still lost, Willy. I think he's very lost.

WILLY: Biff Loman is lost. In the greatest country in the world a young man with such—personal attractiveness, gets lost. And such a hard worker. There's one thing about Biff—he's not lazy.

LINDA: Never.

WILLY (*with pity and resolve*): I'll see him in the morning; I'll have a nice talk with him. I'll get him a job selling. He could be big in no time. My God! Remember how they used to follow him around in high school? When he smiled at one of them their faces lit up. When he walked down the street . . . (*He loses himself in reminiscences.*)

LINDA (*trying to bring him out of it*): Willy, dear, I got a new kind of American-type cheese today. It's whipped.

WILLY: Why do you get American when I like Swiss?

LINDA: I just thought you'd like a change—

WILLY: I don't want a change! I want Swiss cheese. Why am I always being contradicted?

LINDA (*with a covering laugh*): I thought it would be a surprise.

WILLY: Why don't you open a window in here, for God's sake?

LINDA (*with infinite patience*): They're all open, dear.

WILLY: The way they boxed us in here. Bricks and windows, windows and bricks.

LINDA: We should've bought the land next door.

WILLY: The street is lined with cars. There's not a breath of fresh air in the neighborhood. The grass don't grow any more, you can't raise a carrot in the back yard. They should've had a law against apartment houses. Remember those two beautiful elm trees out there? When I and Biff hung the swing between them?

LINDA: Yeah, like being a million miles from the city.

WILLY: They should've arrested the builder for cutting those down. They massacred the neighborhood. (*Lost.*) More and more I think of those days, Linda. This time of year it was lilac and wisteria. And then the peonies would come out, and the daffodils. What fragrance in this room!

LINDA: Well, after all, people had to move somewhere.

WILLY: No, there's more people now.

LINDA: I don't think there's more people. I think—

WILLY: There's more people! That's what's ruining this country! Population is getting out of control. The competition is maddening! Smell the stink from that apartment house! And another on the other side . . . How can they whip cheese?

On WILLY*'s last line,* BIFF *and* HAPPY *raise themselves up in their beds, listening.*

LINDA: Go down, try it. And be quiet.

WILLY (*turning to* LINDA, *guiltily*): You're not worried about me, are you, sweetheart?

BIFF: What's the matter?

HAPPY: Listen!

LINDA: You've got too much on the ball to worry about.

WILLY: You're my foundation and my support, Linda.

LINDA: Just try to relax, dear. You make mountains out of molehills.

WILLY: I won't fight with him any more. If he wants to go back to Texas, let him go.

LINDA: He'll find his way.

WILLY: Sure. Certain men just don't get started till later in life. Like Thomas Edison, I think. Or B. F. Goodrich. One of them was deaf. (*He starts for the bedroom doorway.*) I'll put my money on Biff.

LINDA: And Willy—if it's warm Sunday we'll drive in the country. And we'll open the windshield, and take lunch.

WILLY: No, the windshields don't open on the new cars.

LINDA: But you opened it today.

WILLY: Me? I didn't. (*He stops.*) Now isn't that peculiar! Isn't that a remarkable—(*He breaks off in amazement and fright as the flute is heard distantly.*)

LINDA: What, darling?

WILLY: That is the most remarkable thing.

LINDA: What, dear?

WILLY: I was thinking of the Chevvy. (*Slight pause.*) Nineteen twenty-eight . . . when I had that red Chevvy—(*Breaks off.*) That funny? I coulda sworn I was driving that Chevvy today.

LINDA: Well, that's nothing. Something must've reminded you.

WILLY: Remarkable. Ts. Remember those days? The way Biff used to simonize that car? The dealer refused to believe there was eighty thousand miles on it. (*He shakes his head.*) Heh! (*To* LINDA.) Close your eyes, I'll be right up. (*He walks out of the bedroom.*)

HAPPY (*to* BIFF): Jesus, maybe he smashed up the car again!

LINDA (*calling after* WILLY): Be careful on the stairs, dear! The cheese is on the middle shelf! (*She turns, goes over to the bed, takes his jacket, and goes out of the bedroom.*)

Light has risen on the boys' room. Unseen, WILLY *is heard talking to himself, "Eighty thousand miles," and a little laugh.* BIFF *gets out of bed, comes downstage a bit, and stands attentively.* BIFF *is two years older than his brother* HAPPY, *well built, but in these days bears a worn air and seems less self-assured. He has succeeded less, and his dreams are stronger and less acceptable than* HAPPY'S. HAPPY *is tall, powerfully made. Sexuality is like a visible color on him, or a scent that many women have discovered. He, like his brother, is lost, but in a different way, for he has never allowed himself to turn his face toward defeat and is thus more confused and hard-skinned, although seemingly more content.*

HAPPY (*getting out of bed*): He's going to get his license taken away if he keeps that up. I'm getting nervous about him, y'know, Biff?

BIFF: His eyes are going.

HAPPY: No, I've driven with him. He sees all right. He just doesn't keep his mind on it. I drove into the city with him last week. He stops at a green light and then it turns red and he goes. (*He laughs.*)

BIFF: Maybe he's color-blind.

HAPPY: Pop? Why he's got the finest eye for color in the business. You know that.

BIFF (*sitting down on his bed*): I'm going to sleep.

HAPPY: You're not still sour on Dad, are you, Biff?

BIFF: He's all right, I guess.

WILLY (*underneath them, in the livingroom*): Yes, sir, eighty thousand miles—eighty-two thousand!

BIFF: You smoking?

HAPPY (*holding out a pack of cigarettes*): Want one?

BIFF (*taking a cigarette*): I can never sleep when I smell it.

WILLY: What a simonizing job, heh!

HAPPY (*with deep sentiment*): Funny, Biff, y'know? Us sleeping in here again? The old beds. (*He pats his bed affectionately.*) All the talk that went across those two beds, huh? Our whole lives.

BIFF: Yeah. Lotta dreams and plans.

HAPPY (*with a deep and masculine laugh*): About five hundred women would like to know what was said in this room.

They share a soft laugh.

BIFF: Remember that big Betsy something—what the hell was her name—over on Bushwick Avenue?

HAPPY (*combing his hair*): With the collie dog!

BIFF: That's the one. I got you in there, remember?

HAPPY: Yeah, that was my first time—I think. Boy, there was a pig! (*They laugh, almost crudely.*) You taught me everything I know about women. Don't forget that.

BIFF: I bet you forgot how bashful you used to be. Especially with girls.

HAPPY: Oh, I still am, Biff.

BIFF: Oh, go on.

HAPPY: I just control it, that's all. I think I got less bashful and you got more so. What happened, Biff? Where's the old humor, the old confidence? (*He shakes* BIFF'*s knee.* BIFF *gets up and moves restlessly about the room.*) What's the matter?

BIFF: Why does Dad mock me all the time?

HAPPY: He's not mocking you, he—

BIFF: Everything I say there's a twist of mockery on his face. I can't get near him.

HAPPY: He just wants you to make good, that's all. I wanted to talk to you about Dad for a long time, Biff. Something's—happening to him. He—talks to himself.

BIFF: I noticed that this morning. But he always mumbled.

HAPPY: But not so noticeable. It got so embarrassing I sent him to Florida. And you know something? Most of the time he's talking to you.

BIFF: What's he say about me?

HAPPY: I can't make it out.

BIFF: What's he say about me?

HAPPY: I think the fact that you're not settled, that you're still kind of up in the air . . .

BIFF: There's one or two other things depressing him, Happy.

HAPPY: What do you mean?

BIFF: Never mind. Just don't lay it all to me.

HAPPY: But I think if you just got started—I mean—is there any future for you out there?

BIFF: I tell ya, Hap, I don't know what the future is. I don't know—what I'm supposed to want.

HAPPY: What do you mean?

BIFF: Well, I spent six or seven years after high school trying to work myself up. Shipping clerk, salesman, business of one kind or another. And it's a measly manner of existence. To get on that subway on the hot mornings in summer. To devote your whole life to keeping stock, or making phone calls, or selling or buying. To suffer fifty weeks of the year for the sake of a two-week vacation, when all you really desire is to be outdoors, with your shirt off. And always to have to get ahead of the next fella. And still—that's how you build a future.

HAPPY: Well, you really enjoy it on a farm? Are you content out there?

BIFF (*with rising agitation*): Hap, I've had twenty or thirty different kinds of jobs since I left home before the war, and it always turns out the same. I just realized it lately. In Nebraska when I herded cattle, and the Dakotas, and Arizona, and now in Texas. It's why I came home now, I guess, because I realized it. This farm I work on, it's spring there now, see? And they've got about fifteen new colts. There's nothing more inspiring or—beautiful than the sight of a mare and a new colt. And it's cool there now, see? Texas is cool now, and it's spring. And whenever spring comes to where I am, I suddenly get the feeling, my God, I'm not gettin' anywhere! What the hell am I doing, playing around with horses, twenty-eight dollars a week! I'm thirty-four years old, I oughta be makin' my future. That's when I come running home. And now, I get here, and I don't know what to do with myself. (*After a pause.*) I've always made a point of not wasting my life, and everytime I come back here I know that all I've done is to waste my life.

HAPPY: You're a poet, you know that, Biff? You're a—you're an idealist!

BIFF: No, I'm mixed up very bad. Maybe I oughta get married. Maybe I oughta get stuck into something. Maybe that's my trouble. I'm like a boy. I'm not married,

I'm not in business, I just—I'm like a boy. Are you content, Hap? You're a success, aren't you? Are you content?

HAPPY: Hell, no!

BIFF: Why? You're making money, aren't you?

HAPPY (*moving about with energy, expressiveness*): All I can do now is wait for the merchandise manager to die. And suppose I get to be merchandise manager? He's a good friend of mine, and he just built a terrific estate on Long Island. And he lived there about two months and sold it, and now he's building another one. He can't enjoy it once it's finished. And I know that's just what I would do. I don't know what the hell I'm workin' for. Sometimes I sit in my apartment—all alone. And I think of the rent I'm paying. And it's crazy. But then, it's what I always wanted. My own apartment, a car, and plenty of women. And still, goddammit, I'm lonely.

BIFF (*with enthusiasm*): Listen, why don't you come out West with me?

HAPPY: You and I, heh?

BIFF: Sure, maybe we could buy a ranch. Raise cattle, use our muscles. Men built like we are should be working out in the open.

HAPPY (*avidly*): The Loman Brothers, heh?

BIFF (*with vast affection*): Sure, we'd be known all over the counties!

HAPPY (*enthralled*): That's what I dream about, Biff. Sometimes I want to just rip my clothes off in the middle of the store and outbox that goddam merchandise manager. I mean I can outbox, outrun, and outlift anybody in that store, and I have to take orders from those common, petty, sons-of-bitches till I can't stand it any more.

BIFF: I'm tellin' you, kid, if you were with me I'd be happy out there.

HAPPY (*enthused*): See, Biff, everybody around me is so false that I'm constantly lowering my ideals . . .

BIFF: Baby, together we'd stand up for one another, we'd have someone to trust.

HAPPY: If I were around you—

BIFF: Hap, the trouble is we weren't brought up to grub for money. I don't know how to do it.

HAPPY: Neither can I!

BIFF: Then let's go!

HAPPY: The only thing is—what can you make out there?

BIFF: But look at your friend. Builds an estate and then hasn't the peace of mind to live in it.

HAPPY: Yeah, but when he walks into the store the waves part in front of him. That's fifty-two thousand dollars a year coming through the revolving door, and I got more in my pinky finger than he's got in his head.

BIFF: Yeah, but you just said—

HAPPY: I gotta show some of those pompous, self-important executives over there that Hap Loman can make the grade. I want to walk into the store the way he walks in. Then I'll go with you, Biff. We'll be together yet, I swear. But take those two we had tonight. Now weren't they gorgeous creatures?

BIFF: Yeah, yeah, most gorgeous I've had in years.

HAPPY: I get that any time I want, Biff. Whenever I feel disgusted. The only trouble is, it gets like bowling or something. I just keep knockin' them over and it doesn't mean anything. You still run around a lot?

BIFF: Naa. I'd like to find a girl—steady, somebody with substance.

HAPPY: That's what I long for.

BIFF: Go on! You'd never come home.

HAPPY: I would! Somebody with character, with resistance! Like Mom, y'know? You're gonna call me a bastard when I tell you this. That girl Charlotte I was with tonight is engaged to be married in five weeks. (*He tries on his new hat.*)

BIFF: No kiddin'!

HAPPY: Sure, the guy's in line for the vice-presidency of the store. I don't know what gets into me, maybe I just have an overdeveloped sense of competition or something, but I went and ruined her, and furthermore I can't get rid of her. And he's the third executive I've done that to. Isn't that a crummy characteristic? And to top it all, I go to their weddings! (*Indignantly, but laughing.*) Like I'm not supposed to take bribes. Manufacturers offer me a hundred-dollar bill now and then to throw an order their way. You know how honest I am, but it's like this girl, see. I hate myself for it. Because I don't want the girl, and, still, I take it and—I love it!

BIFF: Let's go to sleep.

HAPPY: I guess we didn't settle anything, heh?

BIFF: I just got one idea that I think I'm going to try.

HAPPY: What's that?

BIFF: Remember Bill Oliver?

HAPPY: Sure, Oliver is very big now. You want to work for him again?

BIFF: No, but when I quit he said something to me. He put his arm on my shoulder, and he said, "Biff, if you ever need anything, come to me."

HAPPY: I remember that. That sounds good.

BIFF: I think I'll go to see him. If I could get ten thousand or even seven or eight thousand dollars I could buy a beautiful ranch.

HAPPY: I bet he'd back you. 'Cause he thought highly of you, Biff, I mean, they all do. You're well liked, Biff. That's why I say to come back here, and we both have the apartment. And I'm tellin' you, Biff, any babe you want . . .

BIFF: No, with a ranch I could do the work I like and still be something. I just wonder though. I wonder if Oliver still thinks I stole that carton of basketballs.

HAPPY: Oh, he probably forgot that long ago. It's almost ten years. You're too sensitive. Anyway, he didn't really fire you.

BIFF: Well, I think he was going to. I think that's why I quit. I was never sure whether he knew or not. I know he thought the world of me, though. I was the only one he'd let lock up the place.

WILLY (*below*): You gonna wash the engine, Biff?

HAPPY: Shh!

BIFF looks at HAPPY, who is gazing down, listening. WILLY is mumbling in the parlor.

HAPPY: You hear that?

They listen. WILLY laughs warmly.

BIFF (*growing angry*): Doesn't he know Mom can hear that?

WILLY: Don't get your sweater dirty, Biff!

A look of pain crosses BIFF's face.

HAPPY: Isn't that terrible? Don't leave again, will you? You'll find a job here. You gotta stick around. I don't know what to do about him, it's getting embarrassing.

WILLY: What a simonizing job!

BIFF: Mom's hearing that!

WILLY: No kiddin', Biff, you got a date? Wonderful!

HAPPY: Go on to sleep. But talk to him in the morning, will you?

BIFF (*reluctantly getting into bed*): With her in the house. Brother!

HAPPY (*getting into bed*): I wish you'd have a good talk with him.

The light on their room begins to fade.

BIFF (*to himself in bed*): That selfish, stupid . . .

HAPPY: Sh . . . Sleep, Biff.

Their light is out. Well before they have finished speaking, WILLY*'s form is dimly seen below in the darkened kitchen. He opens the refrigerator, searches in there, and takes out a bottle of milk. The apartment houses are fading out, and the entire house and surroundings become covered with leaves. Music insinuates itself as the leaves appear.*

WILLY: Just wanna be careful with those girls, Biff, that's all. Don't make any promises. No promises of any kind. Because a girl, y'know, they always believe what you tell 'em, and you're very young, Biff, you're too young to be talking seriously to girls.

Light rises on the kitchen. WILLY*, talking, shuts the refrigerator door and comes downstage to the kitchen table. He pours milk into a glass. He is totally immersed in himself, smiling faintly.*

WILLY: Too young entirely, Biff. You want to watch your schooling first. Then when you're all set, there'll be plenty of girls for a boy like you. (*He smiles broadly at a kitchen chair.*) That so? The girls pay for you? (*He laughs.*) Boy, you must really be makin' a hit.

WILLY *is gradually addressing—physically—a point offstage, speaking through the wall of the kitchen, and his voice has been rising in volume to that of a normal conversation.*

WILLY: I been wondering why you polish the car so careful. Ha! Don't leave the hubcaps, boys. Get the chamois to the hubcaps. Happy, use newspaper on the windows, it's the easiest thing. Show him how to do it, Biff! You see, Happy? Pad it up, use it like a pad. That's it, that's it, good work. You're doin' all right, Hap. (*He pauses, then nods in approbation for a few seconds, then looks upward.*) Biff, first thing we gotta do when we get time is clip that big branch over the house. Afraid it's gonna fall in a storm and hit the roof. Tell you what. We get a rope and sling her around, and then we climb up there with a couple of saws and take her down. Soon as you finish the car, boys, I wanna see ya. I got a surprise for you, boys.

BIFF (*offstage*): Whatta ya got, Dad?

WILLY: No, you finish first. Never leave a job till you're finished—remember that. (*Looking toward the "big trees."*) Biff, up in Albany I saw a beautiful hammock. I think I'll buy it next trip, and we'll hang it right between those two elms. Wouldn't that be something? Just swingin' there under those branches. Boy, that would be . . .

YOUNG BIFF *and* YOUNG HAPPY *appear from the direction* WILLY *was addressing.* HAPPY *carries rags and a pail of water.* BIFF, *wearing a sweater with a block "S," carries a football.*

BIFF (*pointing in the direction of the car offstage*): How's that, Pop, professional?

WILLY: Terrific. Terrific job, boys. Good work, Biff.

HAPPY: Where's the surprise, Pop?

WILLY: In the back seat of the car.

HAPPY: Boy! (*He runs off.*)

BIFF: What is it, Dad? Tell me, what'd you buy?

WILLY (*laughing, cuffs him*): Never mind, something I want you to have.

BIFF (*turns and starts off*): What is it, Hap?

HAPPY (*offstage*): It's a punching bag!

BIFF: Oh, Pop!

WILLY: It's got Gene Tunney's signature on it!

HAPPY *runs onstage with a punching bag.*

BIFF: Gee, how'd you know we wanted a punching bag?

WILLY: Well, it's the finest thing for the timing.

HAPPY (*lies down on his back and pedals with his feet*): I'm losing weight, you notice, Pop?

WILLY (*to* HAPPY): Jumping rope is good too.

BIFF: Did you see the new football I got?

WILLY (*examining the ball*): Where'd you get a new ball?

BIFF: The coach told me to practice my passing.

WILLY: That so? And he gave you the ball, heh?

BIFF: Well, I borrowed it from the locker room. (*He laughs confidentially.*)

WILLY (*laughing with him at the theft*): I want you to return that.

HAPPY: I told you he wouldn't like it!

BIFF (*angrily*): Well, I'm bringing it back!

WILLY (*stopping the incipient argument, to* HAPPY): Sure, he's gotta practice with a regulation ball, doesn't he? (*To* BIFF.) Coach'll probably congratulate you on your initiative!

BIFF: Oh, he keeps congratulating my initiative all the time, Pop.

WILLY: That's because he likes you. If somebody else took that ball there'd be an uproar. So what's the report, boys, what's the report?

BIFF: Where'd you go this time, Dad? Gee we were lonesome for you.

WILLY (*pleased, puts an arm around each boy and they come down to the apron*): Lonesome, heh?

BIFF: Missed you every minute.

WILLY: Don't say? Tell you a secret, boys. Don't breathe it to a soul. Someday I'll have my own business, and I'll never have to leave home any more.

HAPPY: Like Uncle Charley, heh?

WILLY: Bigger than Uncle Charley! Because Charley is not—liked. He's liked, but he's not—well liked.

BIFF: Where'd you go this time, Dad?

WILLY: Well, I got on the road, and I went north to Providence. Met the Mayor.

BIFF: The Mayor of Providence!

WILLY: He was sitting in the hotel lobby.

BIFF: What'd he say?

WILLY: He said, "Morning!" And I said, "You've got a fine city here, Mayor." And then he had coffee with me. And then I went to Waterbury. Waterbury is a fine city. Big clock city, the famous Waterbury clock. Sold a nice bill there. And then Boston—Boston is the cradle of the Revolution. A fine city. And a couple of other towns in Mass., and on to Portland and Bangor and straight home!

BIFF: Gee, I'd love to go with you sometime, Dad.

WILLY: Soon as summer comes.

HAPPY: Promise?

WILLY: You and Hap and I, and I'll show you all the towns. America is full of beautiful towns and fine, upstanding people. And they know me, boys, they know me up and down New England. The finest people. And when I bring you fellas up, there'll be open sesame for all of us, 'cause one thing, boys: I have friends. I can park my car in any street in New England, and the cops protect it like their own. This summer, heh?

BIFF *and* HAPPY (*together*): Yeah! You bet!

WILLY: We'll take our bathing suits.

HAPPY: We'll carry your bags, Pop!

WILLY: Oh, won't that be something! Me comin' into the Boston stores with you boys carryin' my bags. What a sensation!

BIFF *is prancing around, practicing passing the ball.*

WILLY: You nervous, Biff, about the game?

BIFF: Not if you're gonna be there.

WILLY: What do they say about you in school, now that they made you captain?

HAPPY: There's a crowd of girls behind him everytime the classes change.

BIFF (*taking* WILLY'*s hand*): This Saturday, Pop, this Saturday—just for you, I'm going to break through for a touchdown.

HAPPY: You're supposed to pass.

BIFF: I'm takin' one play for Pop. You watch me, Pop, and when I take off my helmet, that means I'm breakin' out. Then you watch me crash through that line!

WILLY (*kisses* BIFF): Oh, wait'll I tell this in Boston!

BERNARD *enters in knickers. He is younger than* BIFF, *earnest and loyal, a worried boy.*

BERNARD: Biff, where are you? You're supposed to study with me today.

WILLY: Hey, looka Bernard. What're you lookin' so anemic about, Bernard?

BERNARD: He's gotta study, Uncle Willy. He's got Regents next week.

HAPPY (*tauntingly, spinning* BERNARD *around*): Let's box, Bernard!

BERNARD: Biff! (*He gets away from* HAPPY.) Listen, Biff, I heard Mr. Birnbaum say that if you don't start studyin' math he's gonna flunk you, and you won't graduate. I heard him!

WILLY: You better study with him, Biff. Go ahead now.

BERNARD: I heard him!

BIFF: Oh, Pop, you didn't see my sneakers! (*He holds up a foot for* WILLY *to look at.*)

WILLY: Hey, that's a beautiful job of printing!

BERNARD (*wiping his glasses*): Just because he printed University of Virginia on his sneakers doesn't mean they've got to graduate him, Uncle Willy!

WILLY (*angrily*): What're you talking about? With scholarships to three universities they're gonna flunk him?

BERNARD: But I heard Mr. Birnbaum say—

WILLY: Don't be a pest, Bernard! (*To his boys.*) What an anemic!

BERNARD: Okay, I'm waiting for you in my house, Biff.

BERNARD *goes off. The* LOMANS *laugh.*

WILLY: Bernard is not well liked, is he?

BIFF: He's liked, but he's not well liked.

HAPPY: That's right, Pop.

WILLY: That's just what I mean. Bernard can get the best marks in school, y'understand, but when he gets out in the business world, y'understand, you are going to be five times ahead of him. That's why I thank Almighty God you're both built like Adonises. Because the man who makes an appearance in the business world, the man who creates personal interest, is the man who gets ahead. Be liked and you will never want. You take me, for instance. I never have to wait in line to see a buyer. "Willy Loman is here!" That's all they have to know, and I go right through.

BIFF: Did you knock them dead, Pop?

WILLY: Knocked 'em cold in Providence, slaughtered 'em in Boston.

HAPPY (*on his back, pedaling again*): I'm losing weight, you notice, Pop?

LINDA *enters, as of old, a ribbon in her hair, carrying a basket of washing.*

LINDA (*with youthful energy*): Hello, dear!

WILLY: Sweetheart!

LINDA: How'd the Chevvy run?

WILLY: Chevrolet, Linda, is the greatest car ever built. (*To the boys.*) Since when do you let your mother carry wash up the stairs?

BIFF: Grab hold there, boy!

HAPPY: Where to, Mom?

LINDA: Hang them up on the line. And you better go down to your friends, Biff. The cellar is full of boys. They don't know what to do with themselves.

BIFF: Ah, when Pop comes home they can wait!

WILLY (*laughs appreciatively*): You better go down and tell them what to do, Biff.

BIFF: I think I'll have them sweep out the furnace room.

WILLY: Good work, Biff.

BIFF (*goes through wall-line of kitchen to doorway at back and calls down*): Fellas! Everybody sweep out the furnace room! I'll be right down!

VOICES: All right! Okay, Biff.

BIFF: George and Sam and Frank, come out back! We're hangin' up the wash! Come on, Hap, on the double! (*He and* HAPPY *carry out the basket.*)

LINDA: The way they obey him!

WILLY: Well, that's training, the training. I'm tellin' you, I was sellin' thousands and thousands, but I had to come home.

LINDA: Oh, the whole block'll be at that game. Did you sell anything?

WILLY: I did five hundred gross in Providence and seven hundred gross in Boston.

LINDA: No! Wait a minute, I've got a pencil. (*She pulls pencil and paper out of her apron pocket.*) That makes your commission . . . Two hundred—my God! Two hundred and twelve dollars!

WILLY: Well, I didn't figure it yet, but . . .

LINDA: How much did you do?

WILLY: Well, I—I did—about a hundred and eighty gross in Providence. Well, no—it came to—roughly two hundred gross on the whole trip.

LINDA (*without hesitation*): Two hundred gross. That's . . . (*She figures.*)

WILLY: The trouble was that three of the stores were half closed for inventory in Boston. Otherwise I woulda broke records.

LINDA: Well, it makes seventy dollars and some pennies. That's very good.

WILLY: What do we owe?

LINDA: Well, on the first there's sixteen dollars on the refrigerator—

WILLY: Why sixteen?

LINDA: Well, the fan belt broke, so it was a dollar eighty.

WILLY: But it's brand new.

LINDA: Well, the man said that's the way it is. Till they work themselves in, y'know.

They move through the wall-line into the kitchen.

WILLY: I hope we didn't get stuck on that machine.

LINDA: They got the biggest ads of any of them!

WILLY: I know, it's a fine machine. What else?

LINDA: Well, there's nine-sixty for the washing machine. And for the vacuum cleaner there's three and a half due on the fifteenth. Then the roof, you got twenty-one dollars remaining.

WILLY: It don't leak, does it?

LINDA: No, they did a wonderful job. Then you owe Frank for the carburetor.

WILLY: I'm not going to pay that man! That goddam Chevrolet, they ought to prohibit the manufacture of that car!

LINDA: Well, you owe him three and a half. And odds and ends, comes to around a hundred and twenty dollars by the fifteenth.

WILLY: A hundred and twenty dollars! My God, if business don't pick up I don't know what I'm gonna do!

LINDA: Well, next week you'll do better.

WILLY: Oh, I'll knock them dead next week. I'll go to Hartford. I'm very well liked in Hartford. You know, the trouble is, Linda, people don't seem to take to me.

They move onto the forestage.

LINDA: Oh, don't be foolish.

WILLY: I know it when I walk in. They seem to laugh at me.

LINDA: Why? Why would they laugh at you? Don't talk that way, Willy.

WILLY *moves to the edge of the stage.* LINDA *goes into the kitchen and starts to darn stockings.*

WILLY: I don't know the reason for it, but they just pass me by. I'm not noticed.

LINDA: But you're doing wonderful, dear. You're making seventy to a hundred dollars a week.

WILLY: But I gotta be at it ten, twelve hours a day. Other men—I don't know—they do it easier. I don't know why—I can't stop myself—I talk too much. A man oughta come in with a few words. One thing about Charley. He's a man of few words, and they respect him.

LINDA: You don't talk too much, you're just lively.

WILLY (*smiling*): Well, I figure, what the hell, life is short, a couple of jokes. (*To himself.*) I joke too much! (*The smile goes.*)

LINDA: Why? You're—

WILLY: I'm fat. I'm very—foolish to look at, Linda. I didn't tell you, but Christmas time I happened to be calling on F. H. Stewarts, and a salesman I know, as I was going in to see the buyer I heard him say something about—walrus. And I—I cracked him right across the face. I won't take that. I simply will not take that. But they do laugh at me. I know that.

LINDA: Darling . . .

WILLY: I gotta overcome it. I know I gotta overcome it. I'm not dressing to advantage, maybe.

LINDA: Willy, darling, you're the handsomest man in the world—

WILLY: Oh, no, Linda.

LINDA: To me you are. (*Slight pause.*) The handsomest.

From the darkness is heard the laughter of a woman. WILLY *doesn't turn to it, but it continues through* LINDA*'s lines.*

LINDA: And the boys, Willy. Few men are idolized by their children the way you are.

Music is heard as behind a scrim, to the left of the house, THE WOMAN, *dimly seen, is dressing.*

WILLY (*with great feeling*): You're the best there is, Linda, you're a pal, you know that? On the road—on the road I want to grab you sometimes and just kiss the life outa you.

The laughter is loud now, and he moves into a brightening area at the left, where THE WOMAN *has come from behind the scrim and is standing, putting on her hat, looking into a "mirror" and laughing.*

WILLY: 'Cause I get so lonely—especially when business is bad and there's nobody to talk to. I get the feeling that I'll never sell anything again, that I won't make a living for you, or a business, a business for the boys. (*He talks through* THE WOMAN*'s subsiding laughter;* THE WOMAN *primps at the "mirror."*) There's so much I want to make for—

THE WOMAN: Me? You didn't make me, Willy. I picked you.

WILLY (*pleased*): You picked me?

THE WOMAN (*who is quite proper-looking,* WILLY'S *age*): I did. I've been sitting at that desk watching all the salesmen go by, day in, day out. But you've got such a sense of humor, and we do have such a good time together, don't we?

WILLY: Sure, sure. (*He takes her in his arms.*) Why do you have to go now?

THE WOMAN: It's two o'clock . . .

WILLY: No, come on in! (*He pulls her.*)

THE WOMAN: . . . my sisters'll be scandalized. When'll you be back?

WILLY: Oh, two weeks about. Will you come up again?

THE WOMAN: Sure thing. You do make me laugh. It's good for me. (*She squeezes his arm, kisses him.*) And I think you're a wonderful man.

WILLY: You picked me, heh?

THE WOMAN: Sure. Because you're so sweet. And such a kidder.

WILLY: Well, I'll see you next time I'm in Boston.

THE WOMAN: I'll put you right through to the buyers.

WILLY (*slapping her bottom*): Right. Well, bottoms up!

THE WOMAN (*slaps him gently and laughs*): You just kill me, Willy. (*He suddenly grabs her and kisses her roughly.*) You kill me. And thanks for the stockings. I love a lot of stockings. Well, good night.

WILLY: Good night. And keep your pores open!

THE WOMAN: Oh, Willy!

THE WOMAN *bursts out laughing, and* LINDA*'s laughter blends in.* THE WOMAN *disappears into the dark. Now the area at the kitchen table brightens.* LINDA *is sitting where she was at the kitchen table, but now is mending a pair of silk stockings.*

LINDA: You are, Willy. The handsomest man. You've got no reason to feel that—

WILLY (*coming out of* THE WOMAN*'s dimming area and going over to* LINDA): I'll make it all up to you, Linda, I'll—

LINDA: There's nothing to make up, dear. You're doing fine, better than—

WILLY (*noticing her mending*): What's that?

LINDA: Just mending my stockings. They're so expensive—

WILLY (*angrily, taking them from her*): I won't have you mending stockings in this house! Now throw them out!

LINDA *puts the stockings in her pocket.*

BERNARD (*entering on the run*): Where is he? If he doesn't study!

WILLY (*moving to the forestage, with great agitation*): You'll give him the answers!

BERNARD: I do, but I can't on a Regents! That's a state exam! They're liable to arrest me!

WILLY: Where is he? I'll whip him, I'll whip him!

LINDA: And he'd better give back that football, Willy, it's not nice.

WILLY: Biff! Where is he? Why is he taking everything?

LINDA: He's too tough with the girls, Willy. All the mothers are afraid of him!

WILLY: I'll whip him!

BERNARD: He's driving the car without a license!

THE WOMAN*'s laugh is heard.*

WILLY: Shut up!

LINDA: All the mothers—

WILLY: Shut up!

BERNARD (*backing quietly away and out*): Mr. Birnbaum says he's stuck up.

WILLY: Get outa here!

BERNARD: If he doesn't buckle down he'll flunk math! (*He goes off.*)

LINDA: He's right, Willy, you've gotta—

WILLY (*exploding at her*): There's nothing the matter with him! You want him to be a worm like Bernard? He's got spirit, personality . . .

As he speaks, LINDA, *almost in tears, exits into the livingroom.* WILLY *is alone in the kitchen, wilting and staring. The leaves are gone. It is night again, and the apartment houses look down from behind.*

WILLY: Loaded with it. Loaded! What is he stealing? He's giving it back, isn't he? Why is he stealing? What did I tell him? I never in my life told him anything but decent things.

HAPPY *in pajamas has come down the stairs;* WILLY *suddenly becomes aware of* HAPPY'S *presence.*

HAPPY: Let's go now, come on.

WILLY (*sitting down at the kitchen table*): Huh! Why did she have to wax the floors herself? Everytime she waxes the floors she keels over. She knows that!

HAPPY: Shh! Take it easy. What brought you back tonight?

WILLY: I got an awful scare. Nearly hit a kid in Yonkers. God! Why didn't I go to Alaska with my brother Ben that time! Ben! That man was a genius, that man was success incarnate! What a mistake! He begged me to go.

HAPPY: Well, there's no use in—

WILLY: You guys! There was a man started with the clothes on his back and ended up with diamond mines!

HAPPY: Boy, someday I'd like to know how he did it.

WILLY: What's the mystery? The man knew what he wanted and went out and got it! Walked into a jungle, and comes out, the age of twenty-one, and he's rich! The world is an oyster, but you don't crack it open on a mattress!

HAPPY: Pop, I told you I'm gonna retire you for life.

WILLY: You'll retire me for life on seventy goddam dollars a week? And your women and your car and your apartment, and you'll retire me for life! Christ's sake, I couldn't get past Yonkers today! Where are you guys, where are you? The woods are burning! I can't drive a car!

CHARLEY *has appeared in the doorway. He is a large man, slow of speech, laconic, immovable. In all he says, despite what he says, there is pity, and, now, trepidation. He has a robe over his pajamas, slippers on his feet. He enters the kitchen.*

CHARLEY: Everything all right?

HAPPY: Yeah, Charley, everything's . . .

WILLY: What's the matter?

CHARLEY: I heard some noise. I thought something happened. Can't we do something about the walls? You sneeze in here, and in my house hats blow off.

HAPPY: Let's go to bed, Dad. Come on.

CHARLEY *signals to* HAPPY *to go.*

WILLY: You go ahead, I'm not tired at the moment.

HAPPY (*to* WILLY): Take it easy, huh? (*He exits.*)

WILLY: What're you doin' up?

CHARLEY (*sitting down at the kitchen table opposite* WILLY): Couldn't sleep good. I had a heartburn.

WILLY: Well, you don't know how to eat.

CHARLEY: I eat with my mouth.

WILLY: No, you're ignorant. You gotta know about vitamins and things like that.

CHARLEY: Come on, let's shoot. Tire you out a little.

WILLY (*hesitantly*): All right. You got cards?

CHARLEY (*taking a deck from his pocket*): Yeah, I got them. Someplace. What is it with those vitamins?

WILLY (*dealing*): They build up your bones. Chemistry.

CHARLEY: Yeah, but there's no bones in a heartburn.

WILLY: What are you talkin' about? Do you know the first thing about it?

CHARLEY: Don't get insulted.

WILLY: Don't talk about something you don't know anything about.

They are playing. Pause.

CHARLEY: What're you doin' home?

WILLY: A little trouble with the car.

CHARLEY: Oh. (*Pause.*) I'd like to take a trip to California.

WILLY: Don't say.

CHARLEY: You want a job?

WILLY: I got a job, I told you that. (*After a slight pause.*) What the hell are you offering me a job for?

CHARLEY: Don't get insulted.

WILLY: Don't insult me.

CHARLEY: I don't see no sense in it. You don't have to go on this way.

WILLY: I got a good job. (*Slight pause.*) What do you keep comin' in here for?

CHARLEY: You want me to go?

WILLY (*after a pause, withering*): I can't understand it. He's going back to Texas again. What the hell is that?

CHARLEY: Let him go.

WILLY: I got nothin' to give him, Charley, I'm clean, I'm clean.

CHARLEY: He won't starve. None a them starve. Forget about him.

WILLY: Then what have I got to remember?

CHARLEY: You take it too hard. To hell with it. When a deposit bottle is broken you don't get your nickel back.

WILLY: That's easy enough for you to say.

CHARLEY: That ain't easy for me to say.

WILLY: Did you see the ceiling I put up in the livingroom?

CHARLEY: Yeah, that's a piece of work. To put up a ceiling is a mystery to me. How do you do it?

WILLY: What's the difference?

CHARLEY: Well, talk about it.

WILLY: You gonna put up a ceiling?

CHARLEY: How could I put up a ceiling?

WILLY: Then what the hell are you bothering me for?

CHARLEY: You're insulted again.

WILLY: A man who can't handle tools is not a man. You're disgusting.

CHARLEY: Don't call me disgusting, Willy.

UNCLE BEN, *carrying a valise and an umbrella, enters the forestage from around the right corner of the house. He is a stolid man, in his sixties, with a mustache and an authoritative air. He is utterly certain of his destiny, and there is an aura of far places about him. He enters exactly as* WILLY *speaks.*

WILLY: I'm getting awfully tired, Ben.

BEN*'s music is heard.* BEN *looks around at everything.*

CHARLEY: Good, keep playing; you'll sleep better. Did you call me Ben?

BEN *looks at his watch.*

WILLY: That's funny. For a second there you reminded me of my brother Ben.

BEN: I have only a few minutes. (*He strolls, inspecting the place.* WILLY *and* CHARLEY *continue playing.*)

CHARLEY: You never heard from him again, heh? Since that time?

WILLY: Didn't Linda tell you? Couple of weeks ago we got a letter from his wife in Africa. He died.

CHARLEY: That so.

BEN (*chuckling*): So this is Brooklyn, eh?

CHARLEY: Maybe you're in for some of his money.

WILLY: Naa, he had seven sons. There's just one opportunity I had with that man . . .

BEN: I must make a train, William. There are several properties I'm looking at in Alaska.

WILLY: Sure, sure! If I'd gone with him to Alaska that time, everything would've been totally different.

CHARLEY: Go on, you'd froze to death up there.

WILLY: What're you talking about?

BEN: Opportunity is tremendous in Alaska, William. Surprised you're not up there.

WILLY: Sure, tremendous.

CHARLEY: Heh?

WILLY: There was the only man I ever met who knew the answers.

CHARLEY: Who?

BEN: How are you all?

WILLY (*taking a pot, smiling*): Fine, fine.

CHARLEY: Pretty sharp tonight.

BEN: Is Mother living with you?

WILLY: No, she died a long time ago.

CHARLEY: Who?

BEN: That's too bad. Fine specimen of a lady, Mother.

WILLY (*to* CHARLEY): Heh?

BEN: I'd hoped to see the old girl.

CHARLEY: Who died?

BEN: Heard anything from Father, have you?

WILLY (*unnerved*): What do you mean, who died?

CHARLEY (*taking a pot*): What're you talkin' about?

BEN (*looking at his watch*): William, it's half-past eight!

WILLY (*as though to dispel his confusion he angrily stops* CHARLEY*'s hand*): That's my build!

CHARLEY: I put the ace—

WILLY: If you don't know how to play the game I'm not gonna throw my money away on you!

CHARLEY (*rising*): It was my ace, for God's sake!

WILLY: I'm through, I'm through!

BEN: When did Mother die?

WILLY: Long ago. Since the beginning you never knew how to play cards.

CHARLEY (*picks up the cards and goes to the door*): All right! Next time I'll bring a deck with five aces.

WILLY: I don't play that kind of game!

CHARLEY (*turning to him*): You should be ashamed of yourself!

WILLY: Yeah?

CHARLEY: Yeah! (*He goes out.*)

WILLY (*slamming the door after him*): Ignoramus!

BEN (*as* WILLY *comes toward him through the wall-line of the kitchen*): So you're William.

WILLY (*shaking* BEN*'s hand*): Ben! I've been waiting for you so long! What's the answer? How did you do it?

BEN: Oh, there's a story in that.

LINDA *enters the forestage, as of old, carrying the wash basket.*

LINDA: Is this Ben?

BEN (*gallantly*): How do you do, my dear.

LINDA: Where've you been all these years? Willy's always wondered why you—

WILLY (*pulling* BEN *away from her impatiently*): Where is Dad? Didn't you follow him? How did you get started?

BEN: Well, I don't know how much you remember.

WILLY: Well, I was just a baby, of course, only three or four years old—

BEN: Three years and eleven months.

WILLY: What a memory, Ben!

BEN: I have many enterprises, William, and I have never kept books.

WILLY: I remember I was sitting under the wagon in—was it Nebraska?

BEN: It was South Dakota, and I gave you a bunch of wild flowers.

WILLY: I remember you walking away down some open road.

BEN (*laughing*): I was going to find Father in Alaska.

WILLY: Where is he?

BEN: At that age I had a very faulty view of geography, William. I discovered after a few days that I was heading due south, so instead of Alaska, I ended up in Africa.

LINDA: Africa!

WILLY: The Gold Coast!

BEN: Principally, diamond mines.

LINDA: Diamond mines!

BEN: Yes, my dear. But I've only a few minutes—

WILLY: No! Boys! Boys! (YOUNG BIFF *and* HAPPY *appear.*) Listen to this. This is your Uncle Ben, a great man! Tell my boys, Ben!

BEN: Why, boys, when I was seventeen I walked into the jungle, and when I was twenty-one I walked out. (*He laughs.*) And by God I was rich.

WILLY (*to the boys*): You see what I been talking about? The greatest things can happen!

BEN (*glancing at his watch*): I have an appointment in Ketchikan Tuesday week.

WILLY: No, Ben! Please tell about Dad. I want my boys to hear. I want them to know the kind of stock they spring from. All I remember is a man with a big beard, and I was in Mamma's lap, sitting around a fire, and some kind of high music.

BEN: His flute. He played the flute.

WILLY: Sure, the flute, that's right!

New music is heard, a high, rollicking tune.

BEN: Father was a very great and a very wild-hearted man. We would start in Boston, and he'd toss the whole family into the wagon, and then he'd drive the team right across the country; through Ohio, and Indiana, Michigan, Illinois, and all the Western states. And we'd stop in the towns and sell the flutes that he'd made on the way. Great inventor, Father. With one gadget he made more in a week than a man like you could make in a lifetime.

WILLY: That's just the way I'm bringing them up, Ben—rugged, well liked, all-around.

BEN: Yeah? (*To* BIFF.) Hit that, boy—hard as you can. (*He pounds his stomach.*)

BIFF: Oh, no, sir!

BEN (*taking boxing stance*): Come on, get to me! (*He laughs.*)

WILLY: Go to it, Biff! Go ahead, show him!

BIFF: Okay! (*He cocks his fist and starts in.*)

LINDA (*to* WILLY): Why must he fight, dear?

BEN (*sparring with* BIFF): Good boy! Good boy!

WILLY: How's that, Ben, heh?

HAPPY: Give him the left, Biff!

LINDA: Why are you fighting?

BEN: Good boy! (*Suddenly comes in, trips* BIFF, *and stands over him, the point of his umbrella poised over* BIFF*'s eye.*)

LINDA: Look out, Biff!

BIFF: Gee!

BEN (*patting* BIFF*'s knee*): Never fight fair with a stranger, boy. You'll never get out of the jungle that way. (*Taking* LINDA*'s hand and bowing.*) It was an honor and a pleasure to meet you, Linda.

LINDA (*withdrawing her hand coldly, frightened*): Have a nice—trip.

BEN (*to* WILLY): And good luck with your—what do you do?

WILLY: Selling.

BEN: Yes. Well . . . (*He raises his hand in farewell to all.*)

WILLY: No, Ben, I don't want you to think . . . (*He takes* BEN*'s arm to show him.*) It's Brooklyn, I know, but we hunt too.

BEN: Really, now.

WILLY: Oh, sure, there's snakes and rabbits and—that's why I moved out here. Why, Biff can fell any one of these trees in no time! Boys! Go right over to where they're building the apartment house and get some sand. We're gonna rebuild the entire front stoop right now! Watch this, Ben!

BIFF: Yes, sir! On the double, Hap!

HAPPY (*as he and* BIFF *run off*): I lost weight, Pop, you notice?

CHARLEY *enters in knickers, even before the boys are gone.*

CHARLEY: Listen, if they steal any more from that building the watchman'll put the cops on them!

LINDA (*to* WILLY): Don't let Biff . . .

BEN *laughs lustily.*

WILLY: You shoulda seen the lumber they brought home last week. At least a dozen six-by-tens worth all kinds a money.

CHARLEY: Listen, if that watchman—

WILLY: I gave them hell, understand. But I got a couple of fearless characters there.

CHARLEY: Willy, the jails are full of fearless characters.

BEN (*clapping* WILLY *on the back, with a laugh at* CHARLEY): And the stock exchange, friend!

WILLY (*joining in* BEN*'s laughter*): Where are the rest of your pants?

CHARLEY: My wife bought them.

WILLY: Now all you need is a golf club and you can go upstairs and go to sleep. (*To* BEN.) Great athlete! Between him and his son Bernard they can't hammer a nail!

BERNARD (*rushing in*): The watchman's chasing Biff!

WILLY (*angrily*): Shut up! He's not stealing anything!

LINDA (*alarmed, hurrying off left*): Where is he? Biff, dear! (*She exits.*)

WILLY (*moving toward the left, away from* BEN): There's nothing wrong. What's the matter with you?

BEN: Nervy boy. Good!

WILLY (*laughing*): Oh, nerves of iron, that Biff!

CHARLEY: Don't know what it is. My New England man comes back and he's bleedin', they murdered him up there.

WILLY: It's contacts, Charley, I got important contacts!

CHARLEY (*sarcastically*): Glad to hear it, Willy. Come in later, we'll shoot a little casino. I'll take some of your Portland money. (*He laughs at* WILLY *and exits.*)

WILLY (*turning to* BEN): Business is bad, it's murderous. But not for me, of course.

BEN: I'll stop by on my way back to Africa.

WILLY (*longingly*): Can't you stay a few days? You're just what I need, Ben, because I—I have a fine position here, but I—well, Dad left when I was such a baby and I never had a chance to talk to him and I still feel—kind of temporary about myself.

BEN: I'll be late for my train.

They are at opposite ends of the stage.

WILLY: Ben, my boys—can't we talk? They'd go into the jaws of hell for me, see, but I—

BEN: William, you're being first-rate with your boys. Outstanding, manly chaps!

WILLY (*hanging on to his words*): Oh, Ben, that's good to hear! Because sometimes I'm afraid that I'm not teaching them the right kind of—Ben, how should I teach them?

BEN (*giving great weight to each word, and with a certain vicious audacity*): William, when I walked into the jungle, I was seventeen. When I walked out I was twenty-one. And, by God, I was rich! (*He goes off into darkness around the right corner of the house.*)

WILLY: . . . was rich! That's just the spirit I want to imbue them with! To walk into a jungle! I was right! I was right! I was right!

BEN is gone, but WILLY is still speaking to him as LINDA, in nightgown and robe, enters the kitchen, glances around for WILLY, then goes to the door of the house, looks out and sees him. Comes down to his left. He looks at her.

LINDA: Willy, dear? Willy?

WILLY: I was right!

LINDA: Did you have some cheese? (*He can't answer.*) It's very late, darling. Come to bed, heh?

WILLY (*looking straight up*): Gotta break your neck to see a star in this yard.

LINDA: You coming in?

WILLY: What ever happened to that diamond watch fob? Remember? When Ben came from Africa that time? Didn't he give me a watch fob with a diamond in it?

LINDA: You pawned it, dear. Twelve, thirteen years ago. For Biff's radio correspondence course.

WILLY: Gee, that was a beautiful thing. I'll take a walk.

LINDA: But you're in your slippers.

WILLY (*starting to go around the house at the left*): I was right! I was! (*Half to LINDA, as he goes, shaking his head.*) What a man! There was a man worth talking to. I was right!

LINDA (*calling after WILLY*): But in your slippers, Willy!

WILLY is almost gone when BIFF, in his pajamas, comes down the stairs and enters the kitchen.

BIFF: What is he doing out there?

LINDA: Sh!

BIFF: God Almighty, Mom, how long has he been doing this?

LINDA: Don't, he'll hear you.

BIFF: What the hell is the matter with him?

LINDA: It'll pass by morning.

BIFF: Shouldn't we do anything?

LINDA: Oh, my dear, you should do a lot of things, but there's nothing to do, so go to sleep.

HAPPY comes down the stairs and sits on the steps.

HAPPY: I never heard him so loud, Mom.

LINDA: Well, come around more often; you'll hear him. (*She sits down at the table and mends the lining of WILLY's jacket.*)

BIFF: Why didn't you ever write me about this, Mom?

LINDA: How would I write to you? For over three months you had no address.

BIFF: I was on the move. But you know I thought of you all the time. You know that, don't you, pal?

LINDA: I know, dear, I know. But he likes to have a letter. Just to know that there's still a possibility for better things.

BIFF: He's not like this all the time, is he?

LINDA: It's when you come home he's always the worst.

BIFF: When I come home?

LINDA: When you write you're coming, he's all smiles, and talks about the future, and—he's just wonderful. And then the closer you seem to come, the more shaky he gets, and then, by the time you get here, he's arguing, and he seems angry at you. I think it's just that maybe he can't bring himself to—to open up to you. Why are you so hateful to each other? Why is that?

BIFF (*evasively*): I'm not hateful, Mom.

LINDA: But you no sooner come in the door than you're fighting!

BIFF: I don't know why. I mean to change. I'm tryin', Mom, you understand?

LINDA: Are you home to stay now?

BIFF: I don't know. I want to look around, see what's doin'.

LINDA: Biff, you can't look around all your life, can you?

BIFF: I just can't take hold, Mom. I can't take hold of some kind of a life.

LINDA: Biff, a man is not a bird, to come and go with the springtime.

BIFF: Your hair . . . (*He touches her hair.*) Your hair got so gray.

LINDA: Oh, it's been gray since you were in high school. I just stopped dyeing it, that's all.

BIFF: Dye it again, will ya? I don't want my pal looking old. (*He smiles.*)

LINDA: You're such a boy! You think you can go away for a year and . . . You've got to get it into your head now that one day you'll knock on this door and there'll be strange people here—

BIFF: What are you talking about? You're not even sixty, Mom.

LINDA: But what about your father?

BIFF (*lamely*): Well, I meant him too.

HAPPY: He admires Pop.

LINDA: Biff, dear, if you don't have any feeling for him, then you can't have any feeling for me.

BIFF: Sure I can, Mom.

LINDA: No. You can't just come to see me, because I love him. (*With a threat, but only a threat, of tears.*) He's the dearest man in the world to me, and I won't have anyone making him feel unwanted and low and blue. You've got to make up your mind now, darling, there's no leeway any more. Either he's your father and you pay him that respect, or else you're not to come here. I know he's not easy to get along with—nobody knows that better than me—but . . .

WILLY (*from the left, with a laugh*): Hey, hey, Biffo!

BIFF (*starting to go out after* WILLY): What the hell is the matter with him? (HAPPY *stops him.*)

LINDA: Don't—don't go near him!

BIFF: Stop making excuses for him! He always, always wiped the floor with you. Never had an ounce of respect for you.

HAPPY: He's always had respect for—

BIFF: What the hell do you know about it?

HAPPY (*surlily*): Just don't call him crazy!

BIFF: He's got no character—Charley wouldn't do this. Not in his own house—spewing out that vomit from his mind.

HAPPY: Charley never had to cope with what he's got to.

BIFF: People are worse off than Willy Loman. Believe me, I've seen them!

LINDA: Then make Charley your father, Biff. You can't do that, can you? I don't say he's a great man. Willy Loman never made a lot of money. His name was never in the paper. He's not the finest character that ever lived. But he's a human being, and a terrible thing is happening to him. So attention must be paid. He's not to be allowed to fall into his grave like an old dog. Attention, attention must be finally paid to such a person. You called him crazy—

BIFF: I didn't mean—

LINDA: No, a lot of people think he's lost his—balance. But you don't have to be very smart to know what his trouble is. The man is exhausted.

HAPPY: Sure!

LINDA: A small man can be just as exhausted as a great man. He works for a company thirty-six years this March, opens up unheard-of territories to their trademark, and now in his old age they take his salary away.

HAPPY (*indignantly*): I didn't know that, Mom.

LINDA: You never asked, my dear! Now that you get your spending money someplace else you don't trouble your mind with him.

HAPPY: But I gave you money last—

LINDA: Christmas time, fifty dollars! To fix the hot water it cost ninety-seven fifty! For five weeks he's been on straight commission, like a beginner, an unknown!

BIFF: Those ungrateful bastards!

LINDA: Are they any worse than his sons? When he brought them business, when he was young, they were glad to see him. But now his old friends, the old buyers that loved him so and always found some order to hand him in a pinch—they're all dead, retired. He used to be able to make six, seven calls a day in Boston. Now he takes his valises out of the car and puts them back and takes them out again and he's exhausted. Instead of walking he talks now. He drives seven hundred miles, and when he gets there no one knows him any more, no one welcomes him. And what goes through a man's mind, driving seven hundred miles home without having earned a cent? Why shouldn't he talk to himself? Why? When he has to go to Charley and borrow fifty dollars a week and pretend to me that it's his pay? How long can that go on? How long? You see what I'm sitting here and waiting for? And you tell me he has no character? The man who never worked a day but for your benefit? When does he get the medal for that? Is this his reward—to turn around at the age of sixty-three and find his sons, who he loved better than his life, one a philandering bum—

HAPPY: Mom!

LINDA: That's all you are, my baby! (*To* BIFF.) And you! What happened to the love you had for him? You were such pals! How you used to talk to him on the phone every night! How lonely he was till he could come home to you!

BIFF: All right, Mom. I'll live here in my room, and I'll get a job. I'll keep away from him, that's all.

LINDA: No, Biff. You can't stay here and fight all the time.

BIFF: He threw me out of this house, remember that.

LINDA: Why did he do that? I never knew why.

BIFF: Because I know he's a fake and he doesn't like anybody around who knows!

LINDA: Why a fake? In what way? What do you mean?

BIFF: Just don't lay it all at my feet. It's between me and him—that's all I have to say. I'll chip in from now on. He'll settle for half my pay check. He'll be all right. I'm going to bed. (*He starts for the stairs.*)

LINDA: He won't be all right.

BIFF (*turning on the stairs, furiously*): I hate this city and I'll stay here. Now what do you want?

LINDA: He's dying, Biff.

HAPPY *turns quickly to her, shocked.*

BIFF (*after a pause.*): Why is he dying?

LINDA: He's been trying to kill himself.

BIFF (*with great horror*): How?

LINDA: I live from day to day.

BIFF: What're you talking about?

LINDA: Remember I wrote you that he smashed up the car again? In February?

BIFF: Well?

LINDA: The insurance inspector came. He said that they have evidence. That all these accidents in the last year—weren't—weren't—accidents.

HAPPY: How can they tell that? That's a lie.

LINDA: It seems there's a woman . . . (*She takes a breath as*—)

BIFF (*sharply but contained*): What woman?

LINDA (*simultaneously*): . . . and this woman . . .

LINDA: What?

BIFF: Nothing. Go ahead.

LINDA: What did you say?

BIFF: Nothing. I just said what woman?

HAPPY: What about her?

LINDA: Well, it seems she was walking down the road and saw his car. She says that he wasn't driving fast at all, and that he didn't skid. She says he came to that little bridge, and then deliberately smashed into the railing, and it was only the shallowness of the water that saved him.

BIFF: Oh, no, he probably just fell asleep again.

LINDA: I don't think he fell asleep.

BIFF: Why not?

LINDA: Last month . . . (*With great difficulty.*) Oh, boys, it's so hard to say a thing like this! He's just a big stupid man to you, but I tell you there's more good in him than in many other people. (*She chokes, wipes her eyes.*) I was looking for a fuse. The lights blew out, and I went down the cellar. And behind the fuse box—it happened to fall out—was a length of rubber pipe—just short.

HAPPY: No kidding?

LINDA: There's a little attachment on the end of it. I knew right away. And sure enough, on the bottom of the water heater there's a new little nipple on the gas pipe.

HAPPY (*angrily*): That—jerk.

BIFF: Did you have it taken off?

LINDA: I'm—I'm ashamed to. How can I mention it to him? Every day I go down and take away that little rubber pipe. But, when he comes home, I put it back where it was. How can I insult him that way? I don't know what to do. I live from day to day, boys. I tell you, I know every thought in his mind. It sounds so old-fashioned and silly, but I tell you he put his whole life into you and you've turned your backs on him. (*She is bent over in the chair, weeping, her face in her hands.*) Biff, I swear to God! Biff, his life is in your hands!

HAPPY (*to* BIFF): How do you like that damned fool!

BIFF (*kissing her*): All right, pal, all right. It's all settled now. I've been remiss. I know that, Mom. But now I'll stay, and I swear to you, I'll apply myself. (*Kneeling in front of her, in a fever of self-reproach.*) It's just—you see, Mom, I don't fit in business. Not that I won't try. I'll try, and I'll make good.

HAPPY: Sure you will. The trouble with you in business was you never tried to please people.

BIFF: I know, I—

HAPPY: Like when you worked for Harrison's. Bob Harrison said you were tops, and then you go and do some damn fool thing like whistling whole songs in the elevator like a comedian.

BIFF (*against* HAPPY): So what? I like to whistle sometimes.

HAPPY: You don't raise a guy to a responsible job who whistles in the elevator!

LINDA: Well, don't argue about it now.

HAPPY: Like when you'd go off and swim in the middle of the day instead of taking the line around.

BIFF (*his resentment rising*): Well, don't you run off? You take off sometimes, don't you? On a nice summer day?

HAPPY: Yeah, but I cover myself!

LINDA: Boys!

HAPPY: If I'm going to take a fade the boss can call any number where I'm supposed to be and they'll swear to him that I just left. I'll tell you something that I hate to say, Biff, but in the business world some of them think you're crazy.

BIFF (*angered*): Screw the business world!

HAPPY: All right, screw it! Great, but cover yourself!

LINDA: Hap, Hap!

BIFF: I don't care what they think! They've laughed at Dad for years, and you know why? Because we don't belong in this nut-house of a city! We should be mixing cement on some open plain, or—or carpenters. A carpenter is allowed to whistle!

WILLY *walks in from the entrance of the house, at left.*

WILLY: Even your grandfather was better than a carpenter. (*Pause. They watch him.*) You never grew up. Bernard does not whistle in the elevator, I assure you.

BIFF (*as though to laugh* WILLY *out of it*): Yeah, but you do, Pop.

WILLY: I never in my life whistled in an elevator! And who in the business world thinks I'm crazy?

BIFF: I didn't mean it like that, Pop. Now don't make a whole thing out of it, will ya?

WILLY: Go back to the West! Be a carpenter, a cowboy, enjoy yourself!

LINDA: Willy, he was just saying—

WILLY: I heard what he said!

HAPPY (*trying to quiet* WILLY): Hey, Pop, come on now . . .

WILLY (*continuing over* HAPPY*'s line*): They laugh at me, heh? Go to Filene's, go to the Hub, go to Slattery's, Boston. Call out the name Willy Loman and see what happens! Big shot!

BIFF: All right, Pop.

WILLY: Big!

BIFF: All right!

WILLY: Why do you always insult me?

BIFF: I didn't say a word. (*To* LINDA.) Did I say a word?

LINDA: He didn't say anything, Willy.

WILLY (*going to the doorway of the livingroom*): All right, good night, good night.

LINDA: Willy, dear, he just decided . . .

WILLY (*to* BIFF): If you get tired hanging around tomorrow, paint the ceiling I put up in the livingroom.

BIFF: I'm leaving early tomorrow.

HAPPY: He's going to see Bill Oliver, Pop.

WILLY (*interestedly*): Oliver? For what?

BIFF (*with reserve, but trying, trying*): He always said he'd stake me. I'd like to go into business, so maybe I can take him up on it.

LINDA: Isn't that wonderful?

WILLY: Don't interrupt. What's wonderful about it? There's fifty men in the City of New York who'd stake him. (*To* BIFF.) Sporting goods?

BIFF: I guess so. I know something about it and—

WILLY: He knows something about it! You know sporting goods better than Spalding, for God's sake! How much is he giving you?

BIFF: I don't know, I didn't even see him yet, but—

WILLY: Then what're you talkin' about?

BIFF (*getting angry*): Well, all I said was I'm gonna see him, that's all!

WILLY (*turning away*): Ah, you're counting your chickens again.

BIFF (*starting left for the stairs*): Oh, Jesus, I'm going to sleep!

WILLY (*calling after him*): Don't curse in this house!

BIFF (*turning*): Since when did you get so clean!

HAPPY (*trying to stop them*): Wait a . . .

WILLY: Don't use that language to me! I won't have it!

HAPPY (*grabbing* BIFF, *shouts*): Wait a minute! I got an idea. I got a feasible idea. Come here, Biff, let's talk this over now, let's talk some sense here. When I was down in Florida last time, I thought of a great idea to sell sporting goods. It just came back to me. You and I, Biff—we have a line, the Loman Line. We train a couple of weeks, and put on a couple of exhibitions, see?

WILLY: That's an idea!

HAPPY: Wait! We form two basketball teams, see? Two water-polo teams. We play each other. It's a million dollars' worth of publicity. Two brothers, see? The Loman Brothers. Displays in the Royal Palms—all the hotels. And banners over the ring and the basketball court: "Loman Brothers." Baby, we could sell sporting goods!

WILLY: That is a one-million-dollar idea.

LINDA: Marvelous!

BIFF: I'm in great shape as far as that's concerned.

HAPPY: And the beauty of it is, Biff, it wouldn't be like a business. We'd be out playin' ball again . . .

BIFF (*enthused*): Yeah, that's . . .

WILLY: Million-dollar . . .

HAPPY: And you wouldn't get fed up with it, Biff. It'd be the family again. There'd be the old honor, and comradeship, and if you wanted to go off for a swim or somethin'—well, you'd do it! Without some smart cooky gettin' up ahead of you!

WILLY: Lick the world! You guys together could absolutely lick the civilized world.

BIFF: I'll see Oliver tomorrow. Hap, if we could work that out . . .

LINDA: Maybe things are beginning to—

WILLY (*wildly enthused, to* LINDA): Stop interrupting! (*To* BIFF.) But don't wear sport jacket and slacks when you see Oliver.

BIFF: No, I'll—

WILLY: A business suit, and talk as little as possible, and don't crack any jokes.

BIFF: He did like me. Always liked me.

LINDA: He loved you!

WILLY (*to* LINDA): Will you stop! (*To* BIFF.) Walk in very serious. You are not applying for a boy's job. Money is to pass. Be quiet, fine, and serious. Everybody likes a kidder, but nobody lends him money.

HAPPY: I'll try to get some myself, Biff. I'm sure I can.

WILLY: I can see great things for you, kids, I think your troubles are over. But remember, start big and you'll end big. Ask for fifteen. How much you gonna ask for?

BIFF: Gee, I don't know—

WILLY: And don't say "Gee." "Gee" is a boy's word. A man walking in for fifteen thousand dollars does not say "Gee!"

BIFF: Ten, I think, would be top though.

WILLY: Don't be so modest. You always started too low. Walk in with a big laugh. Don't look worried. Start off with a couple of your good stories to lighten things up. It's not what you say, it's how you say it—because personality always wins the day.

LINDA: Oliver always thought the highest of him—

WILLY: Will you let me talk?

BIFF: Don't yell at her, Pop, will ya?

WILLY (*angrily*): I was talking, wasn't I?

BIFF: I don't like you yelling at her all the time, and I'm tellin' you, that's all.

WILLY: What're you, takin' over this house?

LINDA: Willy—

WILLY (*turning on her*): Don't take his side all the time, goddammit!

BIFF (*furiously*): Stop yelling at her!

WILLY (*suddenly pulling on his cheek, beaten down, guilt ridden*): Give my best to Bill Oliver—he may remember me. (*He exits through the livingroom doorway.*)

LINDA (*her voice subdued*): What'd you have to start that for? (BIFF *turns away.*) You see how sweet he was as soon as you talked hopefully? (*She goes over to* BIFF.) Come up and say good night to him. Don't let him go to bed that way.

HAPPY: Come on, Biff, let's buck him up.

LINDA: Please, dear. Just say good night. It takes so little to make him happy. Come. (*She goes through the livingroom doorway, calling upstairs from within the livingroom.*) Your pajamas are hanging in the bathroom. Willy!

HAPPY (*looking toward where* LINDA *went out*): What a woman! They broke the mold when they made her. You know that, Biff?

BIFF: He's off salary. My God, working on commission!

HAPPY: Well, let's face it: he's no hot-shot selling man. Except that sometimes, you have to admit, he's a sweet personality.

BIFF (*deciding*): Lend me ten bucks, will ya? I want to buy some new ties.

HAPPY: I'll take you to a place I know. Beautiful stuff. Wear one of my striped shirts tomorrow.

BIFF: She got gray. Mom got awful old. Gee, I'm gonna go in to Oliver tomorrow and knock him for a—

HAPPY: Come on up. Tell that to Dad. Let's give him a whirl. Come on.

BIFF (*steamed up*): You know, with ten thousand bucks, boy!

HAPPY (*as they go into the livingroom*): That's the talk, Biff, that's the first time I've heard the old confidence out of you! (*From within the livingroom, fading off.*) You're gonna live with me, kid, and any babe you want just say the word . . . (*The last lines are hardly heard. They are mounting the stairs to their parents' bedroom.*)

LINDA (*entering her bedroom and addressing* WILLY, *who is in the bathroom. She is straightening the bed for him*): Can you do anything about the shower? It drips.

WILLY (*from the bathroom*): All of a sudden everything falls to pieces! Goddam plumbing, oughta be sued, those people. I hardly finished putting it in and the thing . . . (*His words rumble off.*)

LINDA: I'm just wondering if Oliver will remember him. You think he might?

WILLY (*coming out of the bathroom in his pajamas*): Remember him? What's the matter with you, you crazy? If he'd've stayed with Oliver he'd be on top by now! Wait'll Oliver gets a look at him. You don't know the average caliber any more. The average young man today—(*he is getting into bed*)—is got a caliber of zero. Greatest thing in the world for him was to bum around.

BIFF *and* HAPPY *enter the bedroom. Slight pause.*

WILLY (*stops short, looking at* BIFF): Glad to hear it, boy.

HAPPY: He wanted to say good night to you, sport.

WILLY (*to* BIFF): Yeah. Knock him dead, boy. What'd you want to tell me?

BIFF: Just take it easy, Pop. Good night. (*He turns to go.*)

WILLY (*unable to resist*): And if anything falls off the desk while you're talking to him—like a package or something—don't you pick it up. They have office boys for that.

LINDA: I'll make a big breakfast—

WILLY: Will you let me finish? (*To* BIFF.) Tell him you were in the business in the West. Not farm work.

BIFF: All right, Dad.

LINDA: I think everything—

WILLY (*going right through her speech*): And don't undersell yourself. No less than fifteen thousand dollars.

BIFF (*unable to bear him*): Okay. Good night, Mom. (*He starts moving.*)

WILLY: Because you got a greatness in you, Biff, remember that. You got all kinds a greatness . . . (*He lies back, exhausted.* BIFF *walks out.*)

LINDA (*calling after* BIFF): Sleep well, darling!

HAPPY: I'm gonna get married, Mom. I wanted to tell you.

LINDA: Go to sleep, dear.

HAPPY (*going*): I just wanted to tell you.

WILLY: Keep up the good work. (HAPPY *exits.*) God . . . remember that Ebbets Field game? The championship of the city?

LINDA: Just rest. Should I sing to you?

WILLY: Yeah. Sing to me. (LINDA *hums a soft lullaby.*) When that team came out—he was the tallest, remember?

LINDA: Oh, yes. And in gold.

BIFF *enters the darkened kitchen, takes a cigarette, and leaves the house. He comes downstage into a golden pool of light. He smokes, staring at the night.*

WILLY: Like a young god. Hercules—something like that. And the sun, the sun all around him. Remember how he waved to me? Right up from the field, with the representatives of three colleges standing by? And the buyers I brought, and the cheers when he came out—Loman, Loman, Loman! God Almighty, he'll be great yet. A star like that, magnificent, can never really fade away!

The light on WILLY *is fading. The gas heater begins to glow through the kitchen wall, near the stairs, a blue flame beneath red coils.*

LINDA (*timidly):* Willy, dear, what has he got against you?

WILLY: I'm so tired. Don't talk any more.

BIFF *slowly returns to the kitchen. He stops, stares toward the heater.*

LINDA: Will you ask Howard to let you work in New York?

WILLY: First thing in the morning. Everything'll be all right.

BIFF *reaches behind the heater and draws out a length of rubber tubing. He is horrified and turns his head toward* WILLY*'s room, still dimly lit, from which the strains of* LINDA*'s desperate but monotonous humming rise.*

WILLY (*staring through the window into the moonlight*): Gee, look at the moon moving between the buildings!

BIFF *wraps the tubing around his hand and quickly goes up the stairs. Curtain.*

ACT II

Music is heard, gay and bright. The curtain rises as the music fades away. WILLY*, in shirt sleeves, is sitting at the kitchen table, sipping coffee, his hat in his lap.* LINDA *is filling his cup when she can.*

WILLY: Wonderful coffee. Meal in itself.

LINDA: Can I make you some eggs?

WILLY: No. Take a breath.

LINDA: You look so rested, dear.

WILLY: I slept like a dead one. First time in months. Imagine, sleeping till ten on a Tuesday morning. Boys left nice and early, heh?

LINDA: They were out of here by eight o'clock.

WILLY: Good work!

LINDA: It was so thrilling to see them leaving together. I can't get over the shaving lotion in this house.

WILLY (*smiling*): Mmm—

LINDA: Biff was very changed this morning. His whole attitude seemed to be hopeful. He couldn't wait to get downtown to see Oliver.

WILLY: He's heading for a change. There's no question, there simply are certain men that take longer to get—solidified. How did he dress?

LINDA: His blue suit. He's so handsome in that suit. He could be a—anything in that suit!

WILLY *gets up from the table.* LINDA *holds his jacket for him.*

WILLY: There's no question, no question at all. Gee, on the way home tonight I'd like to buy some seeds.

LINDA (*laughing*): That'd be wonderful. But not enough sun gets back there. Nothing'll grow any more.

WILLY: You wait, kid, before it's all over we're gonna get a little place out in the country, and I'll raise some vegetables, a couple of chickens . . .

LINDA: You'll do it yet, dear.

WILLY *walks out of his jacket.* LINDA *follows him.*

WILLY: And they'll get married, and come for a weekend. I'd build a little guest house. 'Cause I got so many fine tools, all I'd need would be a little lumber and some peace of mind.

LINDA (*joyfully*): I sewed the lining . . .

WILLY: I could build two guest houses, so they'd both come. Did he decide how much he's going to ask Oliver for?

LINDA (*getting him into the jacket*): He didn't mention it, but I imagine ten or fifteen thousand. You going to talk to Howard today?

WILLY: Yeah. I'll put it to him straight and simple. He'll just have to take me off the road.

LINDA: And Willy, don't forget to ask for a little advance, because we've got the insurance premium. It's the grace period now.

WILLY: That's a hundred . . .?

LINDA: A hundred and eight, sixty-eight. Because we're a little short again.

WILLY: Why are we short?

LINDA: Well, you had the motor job on the car . . .

WILLY: That goddam Studebaker!

LINDA: And you got one more payment on the refrigerator . . .

WILLY: But it just broke again!

LINDA: Well, it's old, dear.

WILLY: I told you we should've bought a well-advertised machine. Charley bought a General Electric and it's twenty years old and it's still good, that son-of-a-bitch.

LINDA: But, Willy—

WILLY: Whoever heard of a Hastings refrigerator? Once in my life I would like to own something outright before it's broken! I'm always in a race with the junkyard! I just finished paying for the car and it's on its last legs. The refrigerator consumes belts like a goddam maniac. They time those things. They time them so when you finally paid for them, they're used up.

LINDA (*buttoning up his jacket as he unbuttons it*): All told, about two hundred dollars would carry us, dear. But that includes the last payment on the mortgage. After this payment, Willy, the house belongs to us.

WILLY: It's twenty-five years!

LINDA: Biff was nine years old when we bought it.

WILLY: Well, that's a great thing. To weather a twenty-five year mortgage is—

LINDA: It's an accomplishment.

WILLY: All the cement, the lumber, the reconstruction I put in this house! There ain't a crack to be found in it any more.

LINDA: Well, it served its purpose.

WILLY: What purpose? Some stranger'll come along, move in, and that's that. If only Biff would take this house, and raise a family . . . (*He starts to go.*) Good-by, I'm late.

LINDA (*suddenly remembering*): Oh, I forgot! You're supposed to meet them for dinner.

WILLY: Me?

LINDA: At Frank's Chop House on Forty-eighth near Sixth Avenue.

WILLY: Is that so! How about you?

LINDA: No, just the three of you. They're gonna blow you to a big meal!

WILLY: Don't say! Who thought of that?

LINDA: Biff came to me this morning, Willy, and he said, "Tell Dad, we want to blow him to a big meal." Be there six o'clock. You and your two boys are going to have dinner.

WILLY: Gee whiz! That's really somethin'. I'm gonna knock Howard for a loop, kid. I'll get an advance, and I'll come home with a New York job. Goddammit, now I'm gonna do it!

LINDA: Oh, that's the spirit, Willy!

WILLY: I will never get behind a wheel the rest of my life!

LINDA: It's changing, Willy, I can feel it changing!

WILLY: Beyond a question. G'by, I'm late. (*He starts to go again.*)

LINDA (*calling after him as she runs to the kitchen table for a handkerchief*): You got your glasses?

WILLY (*feels for them, then comes back in*): Yeah, yeah, got my glasses.

LINDA (*giving him the handkerchief*): And a handkerchief.

WILLY: Yeah, handkerchief.

LINDA: And your saccharine?

WILLY: Yeah, my saccharine.

LINDA: Be careful on the subway stairs.

She kisses him, and a silk stocking is seen hanging from her hand. WILLY *notices it.*

WILLY: Will you stop mending stockings? At least while I'm in the house. It gets me nervous. I can't tell you. Please.

LINDA hides the stocking in her hand as she follows WILLY across the forestage in front of the house.

LINDA: Remember, Frank's Chop House.

WILLY (*passing the apron*): Maybe beets would grow out there.

LINDA (*laughing*): But you tried so many times.

WILLY: Yeah. Well, don't work hard today. (*He disappears around the right corner of the house.*)

LINDA: Be careful!

As WILLY vanishes, LINDA waves to him. Suddenly the phone rings. She runs across the stage and into the kitchen and lifts it.

LINDA: Hello? Oh, Biff! I'm so glad you called, I just . . . Yes, sure, I just told him. Yes, he'll be there for dinner at six o'clock, I didn't forget. Listen, I was just dying to tell you. You know that little rubber pipe I told you about? That he connected to the gas heater? I finally decided to go down the cellar this morning and take it away and destroy it. But it's gone! Imagine? He took it away himself, it isn't there! (*She listens.*) When? Oh, then you took it. Oh—nothing, it's just that I'd hoped he'd taken it away himself. Oh, I'm not worried, darling, because this morning he left in such high spirits, it was like the old days! I'm not afraid any more. Did Mr. Oliver see you? . . . Well, you wait there then. And make a nice impression on him, darling. Just don't perspire too much before you see him. And have a nice time with Dad. He may have big news too! . . . That's right, a New York job. And be sweet to him tonight, dear. Be loving to him. Because he's only a little boat looking for a harbor. (*She is trembling with sorrow and joy.*) Oh, that's wonderful, Biff, you'll save his life. Thanks, darling. Just put your arm around him when he comes into the restaurant. Give him a smile. That's the boy . . . Good-by, dear. . . . You got your comb? . . . That's fine. Good-by, Biff dear.

In the middle of her speech, HOWARD WAGNER, thirty-six, wheels in a small typewriter table on which is a wire-recording machine and proceeds to plug it in. This is on the left forestage. Light slowly fades on LINDA as it rises on HOWARD. HOWARD is intent on threading the machine and only glances over his shoulder as WILLY appears.

WILLY: Pst! Pst!

HOWARD: Hello, Willy, come in.

WILLY: Like to have a little talk with you, Howard.

HOWARD: Sorry to keep you waiting. I'll be with you in a minute.

WILLY: What's that, Howard?

HOWARD: Didn't you ever see one of these? Wire recorder.

WILLY: Oh. Can we talk a minute?

HOWARD: Records things. Just got delivery yesterday. Been driving me crazy, the most terrific machine I ever saw in my life. I was up all night with it.

WILLY: What do you do with it?

HOWARD: I bought it for dictation, but you can do anything with it. Listen to this. I had it home last night. Listen to what I picked up. The first one is my daughter. Get this. (*He flicks the switch and "Roll out the Barrel" is heard being whistled.*) Listen to that kid whistle.

WILLY: That is lifelike, isn't it?

HOWARD: Seven years old. Get that tone.

WILLY: Ts, ts. Like to ask a little favor if you . . .

The whistling breaks off, and the voice of HOWARD'S DAUGHTER *is heard.*

HIS DAUGHTER: "Now you, Daddy."

HOWARD: She's crazy for me! (*Again the same song is whistled.*) That's me! Ha! (*He winks.*)

WILLY: You're very good!

The whistling breaks off again. The machine runs silent for a moment.

HOWARD: Sh! Get this now, this is my son.

HIS SON: "The capital of Alabama is Montgomery; the capital of Arizona is Phoenix; the capital of Arkansas is Little Rock; the capital of California is Sacramento . . ." (*And on, and on.*)

HOWARD (*holding up five fingers*): Five years old, Willy!

WILLY: He'll make an announcer some day!

HIS SON (*continuing*): "The capital . . ."

HOWARD: Get that—alphabetical order! (*The machine breaks off suddenly.*) Wait a minute. The maid kicked the plug out.

WILLY: It certainly is a—

HOWARD: Sh, for God's sake!

HIS SON: "It's nine o'clock, Bulova watch time. So I have to go to sleep."

WILLY: That really is—

HOWARD: Wait a minute! The next is my wife.

They wait.

HOWARD'S VOICE: "Go on, say something." (*Pause.*) "Well, you gonna talk?"

HIS WIFE: "I can't think of anything."

HOWARD'S VOICE: "Well, talk—it's turning."

HIS WIFE (*shyly, beaten*): "Hello." (*Silence.*) "Oh, Howard, I can't talk into this . . ."

HOWARD (*snapping the machine off*): That was my wife.

WILLY: That is a wonderful machine. Can we—

HOWARD: I tell you, Willy, I'm gonna take my camera, and my bandsaw, and all my hobbies, and out they go. This is the most fascinating relaxation I ever found.

WILLY: I think I'll get one myself.

HOWARD: Sure, they're only a hundred and a half. You can't do without it. Supposing you wanna hear Jack Benny, see? But you can't be at home at that hour. So you tell the maid to turn the radio on when Jack Benny comes on, and this automatically goes on with the radio . . .

WILLY: And when you come home you . . .

HOWARD: You can come home twelve o'clock, one o'clock, any time you like, and you get yourself a Coke and sit yourself down, throw the switch, and there's Jack Benny's program in the middle of the night!

WILLY: I'm definitely going to get one. Because lots of time I'm on the road, and I think to myself, what I must be missing on the radio!

HOWARD: Don't you have a radio in the car?

WILLY: Well, yeah, but who ever thinks of turning it on?

HOWARD: Say, aren't you supposed to be in Boston?

WILLY: That's what I want to talk to you about, Howard. You got a minute?

He draws a chair in from the wing.

HOWARD: What happened? What're you doing here?

WILLY: Well . . .

HOWARD: You didn't crack up again, did you?

WILLY: Oh, no. No . . .

HOWARD: Geez, you had me worried there for a minute. What's the trouble?

WILLY: Well, to tell you the truth, Howard, I've come to the decision that I'd rather not travel any more.

HOWARD: Not travel! Well, what'll you do?

WILLY: Remember, Christmas time, when you had the party here? You said you'd try to think of some spot for me here in town.

HOWARD: With us?

WILLY: Well, sure.

HOWARD: Oh, yeah, yeah. I remember. Well, I couldn't think of anything for you, Willy.

WILLY: I tell ya, Howard. The kids are all grown up, y'know. I don't need much any more. If I could take home—well, sixty-five dollars a week, I could swing it.

HOWARD: Yeah, but Willy, see I—

WILLY: I tell ya why, Howard. Speaking frankly and between the two of us, y' know—I'm just a little tired.

HOWARD: Oh, I could understand that, Willy. But you're a road man, Willy, and we do a road business. We've only got a half-dozen salesmen on the floor here.

WILLY: God knows, Howard, I never asked a favor of any man. But I was with the firm when your father used to carry you in here in his arms.

HOWARD: I know that, Willy, but—

WILLY: Your father came to me the day you were born and asked me what I thought of the name of Howard, may he rest in peace.

HOWARD: I appreciate that, Willy, but there just is no spot here for you. If I had a spot I'd slam you right in, but I just don't have a single, solitary spot.

He looks for his lighter. WILLY *has picked it up and gives it to him. Pause.*

WILLY (*with increasing anger*): Howard, all I need to set my table is fifty dollars a week.

HOWARD: But where am I going to put you, kid?

WILLY: Look, it isn't a question of whether I can sell merchandise, is it?

HOWARD: No, but it's a business, kid, and everybody's gotta pull his own weight.

WILLY (*desperately*): Just let me tell you a story, Howard—

HOWARD: 'Cause you gotta admit, business is business.

WILLY (*angrily*): Business is definitely business, but just listen for a minute. You don't understand this. When I was a boy—eighteen, nineteen—I was already on the road. And there was a question in my mind as to whether selling had a future for me. Because in those days I had a yearning to go to Alaska. See, there were three gold strikes in one month in Alaska, and I felt like going out. Just for the ride, you might say.

HOWARD (*barely interested*): Don't say.

WILLY: Oh, yeah, my father lived many years in Alaska. He was an adventurous man. We've got quite a little streak of self-reliance in our family. I thought I'd go out with my older brother and try to locate him, and maybe settle in the North with the old man. And I was almost decided to go, when I met a salesman in the Parker House. His name was Dave Singleman. And he was eighty-four years old, and he'd drummed merchandise in thirty-one states. And old Dave, he'd go up to his room, y'understand, put on his green velvet slippers—I'll never forget—and pick up his phone and call the buyers, and without ever leaving his room, at the age of eighty-four, he made his living. And when I saw that, I realized that selling was the greatest career a man could want. 'Cause what could be more satisfying than to be able to go, at the age of eighty-four, into twenty or thirty different cities, and pick up a phone, and be remembered and loved and helped by so many different people? Do you know? when he died—and by the way he died the death of a salesman, in his green velvet slippers in the smoker of the New York, New Haven and Hartford, going into Boston—when he died, hundreds of salesmen and buyers were at his funeral. Things were sad on a lotta trains for months after that. (*He stands up.* HOWARD *has not looked at him.*) In those days there was personality in it, Howard. There was respect, and comradeship, and gratitude in it. Today, it's all cut and dried, and there's no chance for bringing friendship to bear—or personality. You see what I mean? They don't know me any more.

HOWARD (*moving away, to the right*): That's just the thing, Willy.

WILLY: If I had forty dollars a week—that's all I'd need. Forty dollars, Howard.

HOWARD: Kid, I can't take blood from a stone, I—

WILLY (*desperation is on him now*): Howard, the year Al Smith was nominated, your father came to me and—

HOWARD (*starting to go off*): I've got to see some people, kid.

WILLY (*stopping him*): I'm talking about your father! There were promises made across this desk! You mustn't tell me you've got people to see—I put thirty-four years into this firm, Howard, and now I can't pay my insurance! You can't eat the orange and throw the peel away—a man is not a piece of fruit! (*After a pause.*) Now pay attention. Your father—in 1928 I had a big year. I averaged a hundred and seventy dollars a week in commissions.

HOWARD (*impatiently*): Now, Willy, you never averaged—

WILLY (*banging his hand on the desk*): I averaged a hundred and seventy dollars a week in the year of 1928! And your father came to me—or rather, I was in the office here—it was right over this desk—and he put his hand on my shoulder—

HOWARD (*getting up*): You'll have to excuse me, Willy, I gotta see some people. Pull yourself together. (*Going out.*) I'll be back in a little while.

On HOWARD*'s exit, the light on his chair grows very bright and strange.*

WILLY: Pull myself together! What the hell did I say to him? My God, I was yelling at him! How could I! (WILLY *breaks off, staring at the light, which occupies the chair, animating it. He approaches this chair, standing across the desk from it.*) Frank, Frank, don't you remember what you told me that time? How you put your hand on my shoulder, and Frank . . . (*He leans on the desk and as he speaks the dead man's name he accidentally switches on the recorder, and instantly—*)

HOWARD'S SON: ". . . of New York is Albany. The capital of Ohio is Cincinnati, the capital of Rhode Island is . . ." (*The recitation continues.*)

WILLY (*leaping away with fright, shouting*): Ha! Howard! Howard! Howard!

HOWARD (*rushing in*): What happened?

WILLY (*pointing at the machine, which continues nasally, childishly, with the capital cities*): Shut it off! Shut it off!

HOWARD (*pulling the plug out*): Look, Willy . . .

WILLY (*pressing his hands to his eyes*): I gotta get myself some coffee. I'll get some coffee . . .

WILLY *starts to walk out.* HOWARD *stops him.*

HOWARD (*rolling up the cord*): Willy, look . . .

WILLY: I'll go to Boston.

HOWARD: Willy, you can't go to Boston for us.

WILLY: Why can't I go?

HOWARD: I don't want you to represent us. I've been meaning to tell you for a long time now.

WILLY: Howard, are you firing me?

HOWARD: I think you need a good long rest, Willy.

WILLY: Howard—

HOWARD: And when you feel better, come back, and we'll see if we can work something out.

WILLY: But I gotta earn money, Howard. I'm in no position—

HOWARD: Where are your sons? Why don't your sons give you a hand?

WILLY: They're working on a very big deal.

HOWARD: This is no time for false pride, Willy. You go to your sons and tell them that you're tired. You've got two great boys, haven't you?

WILLY: Oh, no question, no question, but in the meantime . . .

HOWARD: Then that's that, heh?

WILLY: All right, I'll go to Boston tomorrow.

HOWARD: No, no.

WILLY: I can't throw myself on my sons. I'm not a cripple!

HOWARD: Look, kid, I'm busy this morning.

WILLY (*grasping* HOWARD*'s arm*): Howard, you've got to let me go to Boston!

HOWARD (*hard, keeping himself under control*): I've got a line of people to see this morning. Sit down, take five minutes, and pull yourself together, and then go home, will ya? I need the office, Willy. (*He starts to go, turns, remembering the recorder, starts to push off the table holding the recorder.*) Oh, yeah. Whenever you can this week, stop by and drop off the samples. You'll feel better, Willy, and then come back and we'll talk. Pull yourself together, kid, there's people outside.

HOWARD *exits, pushing the table off left.* WILLY *stares into space, exhausted. Now the music is heard—*BEN*'s music—first distantly, then closer, closer. As* WILLY *speaks,* BEN *enters from the right. He carries valise and umbrella.*

WILLY: Oh, Ben, how did you do it? What is the answer? Did you wind up the Alaska deal already?

BEN: Doesn't take much time if you know what you're doing. Just a short business trip. Boarding ship in an hour. Wanted to say good-by.

WILLY: Ben, I've got to talk to you.

BEN (*glancing at his watch*): Haven't the time, William.

WILLY (*crossing the apron to* BEN): Ben, nothing's working out. I don't know what to do.

BEN: Now, look here, William. I've bought timberland in Alaska and I need a man to look after things for me.

WILLY: God, timberland! Me and my boys in those grand outdoors!

BEN: You've a new continent at your doorstep, William. Get out of these cities, they're full of talk and time payments and courts of law. Screw on your fists and you can fight for a fortune up there.

WILLY: Yes, yes! Linda! Linda!

LINDA *enters as of old, with the wash.*

LINDA: Oh, you're back?

BEN: I haven't much time.

WILLY: No, wait! Linda, he's got a proposition for me in Alaska.

LINDA: But you've got—(*To* BEN.) He's got a beautiful job here.

WILLY: But in Alaska, kid, I could—

LINDA: You're doing well enough, Willy!

BEN (*to* LINDA): Enough for what, my dear?

LINDA (*frightened of* BEN *and angry at him*): Don't say those things to him! Enough to be happy right here, right now. (*To* WILLY, *while* BEN *laughs.*) Why must everybody conquer the world? You're well liked, and the boys love you, and someday—(*to* BEN)—why, old man Wagner told him just the other day that if he keeps it up he'll be a member of the firm, didn't he, Willy?

WILLY: Sure, sure. I am building something with this firm, Ben, and if a man is building something he must be on the right track, mustn't he?

BEN: What are you building? Lay your hand on it. Where is it?

WILLY (*hesitantly*): That's true, Linda, there's nothing.

LINDA: Why? (*To* BEN.) There's a man eighty-four years old—

WILLY: That's right, Ben, that's right. When I look at that man I say, what is there to worry about?

BEN: Bah!

WILLY: It's true, Ben. All he has to do is go into any city, pick up the phone, and he's making his living and you know why?

BEN (*picking up his valise*): I've got to go.

WILLY (*holding* BEN *back*): Look at this boy!

BIFF, *in his high school sweater, enters carrying suitcase.* HAPPY *carries* BIFF*'s shoulder guards, gold helmet, and football pants.*

WILLY: Without a penny to his name, three great universities are begging for him, and from there the sky's the limit, because it's not what you do, Ben. It's who you know and the smile on your face! It's contacts, Ben, contacts! The whole wealth of Alaska passes over the lunch table at the Commodore Hotel, and that's the wonder, the wonder of this country, that a man can end with diamonds here on the basis of being liked! (*He turns to* BIFF.) And that's why when you get out on that field today it's important. Because thousands of people will be rooting for you and loving you. (*To* BEN, *who has again begun to leave.*) And Ben! when he walks into a business office his name will sound out like a bell and all the doors will open to him! I've seen it, Ben, I've seen it a thousand times! You can't feel it with your hand like timber, but it's there!

BEN: Good-by, William.

WILLY: Ben, am I right? Don't you think I'm right? I value your advice.

BEN: There's a new continent at your doorstep, William. You could walk out rich. Rich. (*He is gone.*)

WILLY: We'll do it here, Ben! You hear me? We're gonna do it here!

Young BERNARD *rushes in. The gay music of the boys is heard.*

BERNARD: Oh, gee, I was afraid you left already!

WILLY: Why? What time is it?

BERNARD: It's half-past one!

WILLY: Well, come on, everybody! Ebbets Field next stop! Where's the pennants? (*He rushes through the wall-line of the kitchen and out into the livingroom.*)

LINDA (*to* BIFF): Did you pack fresh underwear?

BIFF (*who has been limbering up*): I want to go!

BERNARD: Biff, I'm carrying your helmet, ain't I?

HAPPY: No, I'm carrying the helmet.

BERNARD: Oh, Biff, you promised me.

HAPPY: I'm carrying the helmet.

BERNARD: How am I going to get in the locker room?

LINDA: Let him carry the shoulder guards. (*She puts her coat and hat on in the kitchen.*)

BERNARD: Can I, Biff? 'Cause I told everybody I'm going to be in the locker room.

HAPPY: In Ebbets Field it's the clubhouse.

BERNARD: I meant the clubhouse. Biff!

HAPPY: Biff!

BIFF (*grandly, after a slight pause*): Let him carry the shoulder guards.

HAPPY (*as he gives* BERNARD *the shoulder guards*): Stay close to us now.

WILLY *rushes in with the pennants.*

WILLY (*handing them out*): Everybody wave when Biff comes out on the field. (HAPPY *and* BERNARD *run off.*) You set now, boy?

The music has died away.

BIFF: Ready to go, Pop. Every muscle is ready.

WILLY (*at the edge of the apron*): You realize what this means?

BIFF: That's right, Pop.

WILLY (*feeling* BIFF*'s muscles*): You're comin' home this afternoon captain of the All-Scholastic Championship Team of the City of New York.

BIFF: I got it, Pop. And remember, pal, when I take off my helmet, that touchdown is for you.

WILLY: Let's go! (*He is starting out, with his arm around* BIFF, *when* CHARLEY *enters, as of old, in knickers.*) I got no room for you, Charley.

CHARLEY: Room? For what?

WILLY: In the car.

CHARLEY: You goin' for a ride? I wanted to shoot some casino.

WILLY (*furiously*): Casino! (*Incredulously*): Don't you realize what today is?

LINDA: Oh, he knows, Willy. He's just kidding you.

WILLY: That's nothing to kid about!

CHARLEY: No, Linda, what's goin' on?

LINDA: He's playing in Ebbets Field.

CHARLEY: Baseball in this weather?

WILLY: Don't talk to him. Come on, come on! (*He is pushing them out.*)

CHARLEY: Wait a minute, didn't you hear the news?

WILLY: What?

CHARLEY: Don't you listen to the radio? Ebbets Field just blew up.

WILLY: You go to hell! (CHARLEY *laughs. Pushing them out.*) Come on, come on! We're late.

CHARLEY (*as they go*): Knock a homer, Biff, knock a homer!

WILLY (*the last to leave, turning to* CHARLEY): I don't think that was funny, Charley. This is the greatest day of his life.

CHARLEY: Willy, when are you going to grow up?

WILLY: Yeah, heh? When this game is over, Charley, you'll be laughing out of the other side of your face. They'll be calling him another Red Grange. Twenty-five thousand a year.

CHARLEY (*kidding*): Is that so?

WILLY: Yeah, that's so.

CHARLEY: Well, then, I'm sorry, Willy. But tell me something.

WILLY: What?

CHARLEY: Who is Red Grange?

WILLY: Put up your hands. Goddam you, put up your hands!

CHARLEY, *chuckling, shakes his head and walks away, around the left corner of the stage.* WILLY *follows him. The music rises to a mocking frenzy.*

WILLY: Who the hell do you think you are, better than everybody else? You don't know everything, you big, ignorant, stupid . . . Put up your hands!

Light rises, on the right side of the forestage, on a small table in the reception room of CHARLEY*'s office. Traffic sounds are heard.* BERNARD, *now mature, sits whistling to himself. A pair of tennis rackets and an overnight bag are on the floor beside him.*

WILLY (*offstage*): What are you walking away for? Don't walk away! If you're going to say something say it to my face! I know you laugh at me behind my back. You'll laugh out of the other side of your goddam face after this game. Touchdown! Touchdown! Eighty thousand people! Touchdown! Right between the goal posts.

BERNARD *is a quiet, earnest, but self-assured young man.* WILLY*'s voice is coming from right upstage now.* BERNARD *lowers his feet off the table and listens.* JENNY, *his father's secretary, enters.*

JENNY (*distressed*): Say, Bernard, will you go out in the hall?

BERNARD: What is that noise? Who is it?

JENNY: Mr. Loman. He just got off the elevator.

BERNARD (*getting up*): Who's he arguing with?

JENNY: Nobody. There's nobody with him. I can't deal with him any more, and your father gets all upset everytime he comes. I've got a lot of typing to do, and your father's waiting to sign it. Will you see him?

WILLY (*entering*): Touchdown! Touch—(*He sees* JENNY.) Jenny, Jenny, good to see you. How're ya? Workin'? Or still honest?

JENNY: Fine. How've you been feeling?

WILLY: Not much any more, Jenny. Ha, ha! (*He is surprised to see the rackets.*)

BERNARD: Hello, Uncle Willy.

WILLY (*almost shocked*): Bernard! Well, look who's here! (*He comes quickly, guiltily, to* BERNARD *and warmly shakes his hand.*)

BERNARD: How are you? Good to see you.

WILLY: What are you doing here?

BERNARD: Oh, just stopped by to see Pop. Get off my feet till my train leaves. I'm going to Washington in a few minutes.

WILLY: Is he in?

BERNARD: Yes, he's in his office with the accountant. Sit down.

WILLY (*sitting down*): What're you going to do in Washington?

BERNARD: Oh, just a case I've got there, Willy.

WILLY: That so? (*indicating the rackets.*) You going to play tennis there?

BERNARD: I'm staying with a friend who's got a court.

WILLY: Don't say. His own tennis court. Must be fine people, I bet.

BERNARD: They are, very nice. Dad tells me Biff's in town.

WILLY (*with a big smile*): Yeah, Biff's in. Working on a very big deal, Bernard.

BERNARD: What's Biff doing?

WILLY: Well, he's been doing very big things in the West. But he decided to establish himself here. Very big. We're having dinner. Did I hear your wife had a boy?

BERNARD: That's right. Our second.

WILLY: Two boys! What do you know!

BERNARD: What kind of a deal has Biff got?

WILLY: Well, Bill Oliver—very big sporting-goods man—he wants Biff very badly. Called him in from the West. Long distance, carte blanche, special deliveries. Your friends have their own private tennis court?

BERNARD: You still with the old firm, Willy?

WILLY (*after a pause*): I'm—I'm overjoyed to see how you made the grade, Bernard, overjoyed. It's an encouraging thing to see a young man really—really—Looks very good for Biff—very—(*He breaks off, then.*) Bernard—(*He is so full of emotion, he breaks off again.*)

BERNARD: What is it, Willy?

WILLY (*small and alone*): What—what's the secret?

BERNARD: What secret?

WILLY: How—how did you? Why didn't he ever catch on?

BERNARD: I wouldn't know that, Willy.

WILLY (*confidentially, desperately*): You were his friend, his boyhood friend. There's something I don't understand about it. His life ended after that Ebbets Field game. From the age of seventeen nothing good ever happened to him.

BERNARD: He never trained himself for anything.

WILLY: But he did, he did. After high school he took so many correspondence courses. Radio mechanics; television; God knows what, and never made the slightest mark.

BERNARD (*taking off his glasses*): Willy, do you want to talk candidly?

WILLY (*rising, faces* BERNARD): I regard you as a very brilliant man, Bernard. I value your advice.

BERNARD: Oh, the hell with the advice, Willy. I couldn't advise you. There's just one thing I've always wanted to ask you. When he was supposed to graduate, and the math teacher flunked him—

WILLY: Oh, that son-of-a-bitch ruined his life.

BERNARD: Yeah, but, Willy, all he had to do was go to summer school and make up that subject.

WILLY: That's right, that's right.

BERNARD: Did you tell him not to go to summer school?

WILLY: Me? I begged him to go. I ordered him to go!

BERNARD: Then why wouldn't he go?

WILLY: Why? Why! Bernard, that question has been trailing me like a ghost for the last fifteen years. He flunked the subject, and laid down and died like a hammer hit him!

BERNARD: Take it easy, kid.

WILLY: Let me talk to you—I got nobody to talk to. Bernard, Bernard, was it my fault? Y'see? It keeps going around in my mind, maybe I did something to him. I got nothing to give him.

BERNARD: Don't take it so hard.

WILLY: Why did he lay down? What is the story there? You were his friend!

BERNARD: Willy, I remember, it was June, and our grades came out. And he'd flunked math.

WILLY: That son-of-a-bitch!

BERNARD: No, it wasn't right then. Biff just got very angry, I remember, and he was ready to enroll in summer school.

WILLY (*surprised*): He was?

BERNARD: He wasn't beaten by it at all. But then, Willy, he disappeared from the block for almost a month. And I got the idea that he'd gone up to New England to see you. Did he have a talk with you then?

WILLY *stares in silence.*

BERNARD: Willy?

WILLY (*with a strong edge of resentment in his voice*): Yeah, he came to Boston. What about it?

BERNARD: Well, just that when he came back—I'll never forget this, it always mystifies me. Because I'd thought so well of Biff, even though he'd always taken advantage of me. I loved him, Willy, y'know? And he came back after that month and took his sneakers—remember those sneakers with "University of Virginia" printed on them? He was so proud of those, wore them every day. And he took them down in the cellar, and burned them up in the furnace. We had a fist fight. It lasted at least half an hour. Just the two of us, punching each other down the cellar, and crying right through it. I've often thought of how strange it was that I knew he'd given up his life. What happened in Boston, Willy?

WILLY *looks at him as at an intruder.*

BERNARD: I just bring it up because you asked me.

WILLY (*angrily*): Nothing. What do you mean, "What happened?" What's that got to do with anything?

BERNARD: Well, don't get sore.

WILLY: What are you trying to do, blame it on me? If a boy lays down is that my fault?

BERNARD: Now, Willy, don't get—

WILLY: Well, don't—don't talk to me that way! What does that mean, "What happened?"

CHARLEY *enters. He is in his vest, and he carries a bottle of bourbon.*

CHARLEY: Hey, you're going to miss that train. (*He waves the bottle.*)

BERNARD: Yeah, I'm going. (*He takes the bottle.*) Thanks, Pop. (*He picks up his rackets and bag.*) Good-by, Willy, and don't worry about it. You know, "If at first you don't succeed . . ."

WILLY: Yes, I believe in that.

BERNARD: But sometimes, Willy, it's better for a man just to walk away.

WILLY: Walk away?

BERNARD: That's right.

WILLY: But if you can't walk away?

BERNARD (*after a slight pause*): I guess that's when it's tough. (*Extending his hand.*) Good-by, Willy.

WILLY (*shaking* BERNARD*'s hand*): Good-by, boy.

CHARLEY (*an arm on* BERNARD*'s shoulder*): How do you like this kid? Gonna argue a case in front of the Supreme Court.

BERNARD (*protesting*): Pop!

WILLY (*genuinely shocked, pained, and happy*): No! The Supreme Court!

BERNARD: I gotta run. 'By, Dad!

CHARLEY: Knock 'em dead, Bernard!

BERNARD *goes off.*

WILLY (*as* CHARLEY *takes out his wallet*): The Supreme Court! And he didn't even mention it!

CHARLEY (*counting out money on the desk*): He don't have to—he's gonna do it.

WILLY: And you never told him what to do, did you? You never took any interest in him.

CHARLEY: My salvation is that I never took any interest in anything. There's some money—fifty dollars. I got an accountant inside.

WILLY: Charley, look . . . (*With difficulty.*) I got my insurance to pay. If you can manage it—I need a hundred and ten dollars.

CHARLEY *doesn't reply for a moment; merely stops moving.*

WILLY: I'd draw it from my bank but Linda would know, and I . . .

CHARLEY: Sit down, Willy.

WILLY (*moving toward the chair*): I'm keeping an account of everything, remember. I'll pay every penny back. (*He sits.*)

CHARLEY: Now listen to me, Willy.

WILLY: I want you to know I appreciate . . .

CHARLEY (*sitting down on the table*): Willy, what're you doin'? What the hell is goin' on in your head?

WILLY: Why? I'm simply . . .

CHARLEY: I offered you a job. You can make fifty dollars a week. And I won't send you on the road.

WILLY: I've got a job.

CHARLEY: Without pay? What kind of a job is a job without pay? (*He rises.*) Now, look, kid, enough is enough. I'm no genius but I know when I'm being insulted.

WILLY: Insulted!

CHARLEY: Why don't you want to work for me?

WILLY: What's the matter with you? I've got a job.

CHARLEY: Then what're you walkin' in here every week for?

WILLY (*getting up*): Well, if you don't want me to walk in here—

CHARLEY: I am offering you a job.

WILLY: I don't want your goddam job!

CHARLEY: When the hell are you going to grow up?

WILLY (*furiously*): You big ignoramus, if you say that to me again I'll rap you one! I don't care how big you are! (*He's ready to fight.*)

Pause.

CHARLEY (*kindly, going to him*): How much do you need, Willy?

WILLY: Charley, I'm strapped. I'm strapped. I don't know what to do. I was just fired.

CHARLEY: Howard fired you?

WILLY: That snotnose. Imagine that? I named him. I named him Howard.

CHARLEY: Willy, when're you gonna realize that them things don't mean anything? You named him Howard, but you can't sell that. The only thing you got in this world is what you can sell. And the funny thing is that you're a salesman, and you don't know that.

WILLY: I've always tried to think otherwise, I guess. I always felt that if a man was impressive, and well liked, that nothing—

CHARLEY: Why must everybody like you? Who liked J. P. Morgan? Was he impressive? In a Turkish bath he'd look like a butcher. But with his pockets on he was very well liked. Now listen, Willy, I know you don't like me, and nobody can say I'm in love with you, but I'll give you a job because—just for the hell of it, put it that way. Now what do you say?

WILLY: I—I just can't work for you, Charley.

CHARLEY: What're you, jealous of me?

WILLY: I can't work for you, that's all, don't ask me why.

CHARLEY (*angered, takes out more bills*): You been jealous of me all your life, you damned fool! Here, pay your insurance. (*He puts the money in* WILLY*'s hand.*)

WILLY: I'm keeping strict accounts.

CHARLEY: I've got some work to do. Take care of yourself. And pay your insurance.

WILLY (*moving to the right*): Funny, y'know? After all the highways, and the trains, and the appointments, and the years, you end up worth more dead than alive.

CHARLEY: Willy, nobody's worth nothin' dead. (*After a slight pause.*) Did you hear what I said?

WILLY *stands still, dreaming.*

CHARLEY: Willy!

WILLY: Apologize to Bernard for me when you see him. I didn't mean to argue with him. He's a fine boy. They're all fine boys, and they'll end up big—all of them. Someday they'll all play tennis together. Wish me luck, Charley. He saw Bill Oliver today.

CHARLEY: Good luck.

WILLY (*on the verge of tears*): Charley, you're the only friend I got. Isn't that a remarkable thing? (*He goes out.*)

CHARLEY: Jesus!

CHARLEY *stares after him a moment and follows. All light blacks out. Suddenly raucous music is heard, and a red glow rises behind the screen at right.* STANLEY, *a young waiter, appears, carrying a table, followed by* HAPPY, *who is carrying two chairs.*

STANLEY (*putting the table down*): That's all right, Mr. Loman, I can handle it myself. (*He turns and takes the chairs from* HAPPY *and places them at the table.*)

HAPPY (*glancing around*): Oh, this is better.

STANLEY: Sure, in the front there you're in the middle of all kinds a noise. Whenever you got a party, Mr. Loman, you just tell me and I'll put you back here. Y'know, there's a lotta people they don't like it private, because when they go out they like to see a lotta action around them because they're sick and tired to stay in the house by theirself. But I know you, you ain't from Hackensack. You know what I mean?

HAPPY (*sitting down*): So how's it coming, Stanley?

STANLEY: Ah, it's a dog's life. I only wish during the war they'd a took me in the Army. I coulda been dead by now.

HAPPY: My brother's back, Stanley.

STANLEY: Oh, he come back, heh? From the Far West.

HAPPY: Yeah, big cattle man, my brother, so treat him right. And my father's coming too.

STANLEY: Oh, your father too!

HAPPY: You got a couple of nice lobsters?

STANLEY: Hundred per cent, big.

HAPPY: I want them with the claws.

STANLEY: Don't worry, I don't give you no mice. (HAPPY *laughs.*) How about some wine? It'll put a head on the meal.

HAPPY: No. You remember, Stanley, that recipe I brought you from overseas? With the champagne in it?

STANLEY: Oh, yeah, sure. I still got it tacked up yet in the kitchen. But that'll have to cost a buck apiece anyways.

HAPPY: That's all right.

STANLEY: What'd you, hit a number or somethin'?

HAPPY: No, it's a little celebration. My brother is—I think he pulled off a big deal today. I think we're going into business together.

STANLEY: Great! That's the best for you. Because a family business, you know what I mean?—that's the best.

HAPPY: That's what I think.

STANLEY: 'Cause what's the difference? Somebody steals? It's in the family. Know what I mean? (*Sotto voce.*) Like this bartender here. The boss is goin' crazy what kinda leak he's got in the cash register. You put it in but it don't come out.

HAPPY (*raising his head*): Sh!

STANLEY: What?

HAPPY: You notice I wasn't lookin' right or left, was I!

STANLEY: No.

HAPPY: And my eyes are closed.

STANLEY: So what's the—?

HAPPY: Strudel's comin'.

STANLEY (*catching on, looks around*): Ah, no, there's no—

He breaks off as a furred, lavishly dressed GIRL *enters and sits at the next table. Both follow her with their eyes.*

STANLEY: Geez, how'd ya know?

HAPPY: I got radar or something. (*Staring directly at her profile.*) Oooooooo . . . Stanley.

STANLEY: I think that's for you, Mr. Loman.

HAPPY: Look at that mouth. Oh, God. And the binoculars.

STANLEY: Geez, you got a life, Mr. Loman.

HAPPY: Wait on her.

STANLEY (*going to* THE GIRL*'s table*): Would you like a menu, ma'am?

GIRL: I'm expecting someone, but I'd like a—

HAPPY: Why don't you bring her—excuse me, miss, do you mind? I sell champagne, and I'd like you to try my brand. Bring her a champagne, Stanley.

GIRL: That's awfully nice of you.

HAPPY: Don't mention it. It's all company money. (*He laughs.*)

GIRL: That's a charming product to be selling, isn't it?

HAPPY: Oh, gets to be like everything else. Selling is selling, y'know.

GIRL: I suppose.

HAPPY: You don't happen to sell, do you?

GIRL: No, I don't sell.

HAPPY: Would you object to a compliment from a stranger? You ought to be on a magazine cover.

GIRL (*looking at him a little archly*): I have been.

STANLEY *comes in with a glass of champagne.*

HAPPY: What'd I say before, Stanley? You see? She's a cover girl.

STANLEY: Oh, I could see, I could see.

HAPPY (*to* THE GIRL): What magazine?

GIRL: Oh, a lot of them. (*She takes the drink.*) Thank you.

HAPPY: You know what they say in France, don't you? "Champagne is the drink of the complexion"—Hya, Biff!

BIFF *has entered and sits with* HAPPY.

BIFF: Hello, kid. Sorry I'm late.

HAPPY: I just got here. Uh, Miss—?

GIRL: Forsythe.

HAPPY: Miss Forsythe, this is my brother.

BIFF: Is Dad here?

HAPPY: His name is Biff. You might've heard of him. Great football player.

GIRL: Really? What team?

HAPPY: Are you familiar with football?

GIRL: No, I'm afraid I'm not.

HAPPY: Biff is quarterback with the New York Giants.

GIRL: Well, that is nice, isn't it? (*She drinks.*)

HAPPY: Good health.

GIRL: I'm happy to meet you.

HAPPY: That's my name. Hap. It's really Harold, but at West Point they called me Happy.

GIRL (*now really impressed*): Oh, I see. How do you do? (*She turns her profile.*)

BIFF: Isn't Dad coming?

HAPPY: You want her?

BIFF: Oh, I could never make that.

HAPPY: I remember the time that idea would never come into your head. Where's the old confidence, Biff?

BIFF: I just saw Oliver—

HAPPY: Wait a minute. I've got to see that old confidence again. Do you want her? She's on call.

BIFF: Oh, no. (*He turns to look at* THE GIRL.)

HAPPY: I'm telling you. Watch this. (*Turning to* THE GIRL.) Honey? (*She turns to him.*) Are you busy?

GIRL: Well, I am . . . but I could make a phone call.

HAPPY: Do that, will you, honey? And see if you can get a friend. We'll be here for a while. Biff is one of the greatest football players in the country.

GIRL (*standing up*): Well, I'm certainly happy to meet you.

HAPPY: Come back soon.

GIRL: I'll try.

HAPPY: Don't try, honey, try hard.

THE GIRL *exits.* STANLEY *follows, shaking his head in bewildered admiration.*

HAPPY: Isn't that a shame now? A beautiful girl like that? That's why I can't get married. There's not a good woman in a thousand. New York is loaded with them, kid!

BIFF: Hap, look—

HAPPY: I told you she was on call!

BIFF (*strangely unnerved*): Cut it out, will ya? I want to say something to you.

HAPPY: Did you see Oliver?

BIFF: I saw him all right. Now look, I want to tell Dad a couple of things and I want you to help me.

HAPPY: What? Is he going to back you?

BIFF: Are you crazy? You're out of your goddam head, you know that?

HAPPY: Why? What happened?

BIFF (*breathlessly*): I did a terrible thing today, Hap. It's been the strangest day I ever went through. I'm all numb, I swear.

HAPPY: You mean he wouldn't see you?

BIFF: Well, I waited six hours for him, see? All day. Kept sending my name in. Even tried to date his secretary so she'd get me to him, but no soap.

HAPPY: Because you're not showin' the old confidence, Biff. He remembered you, didn't he?

BIFF (*stopping* HAPPY *with a gesture*): Finally, about five o'clock, he comes out. Didn't remember who I was or anything. I felt like such an idiot, Hap.

HAPPY: Did you tell him my Florida idea?

BIFF: He walked away. I saw him for one minute. I got so mad I could've torn the walls down! How the hell did I ever get the idea I was a salesman there? I even believed myself that I'd been a salesman for him! And then he gave me one look and—I realized what a ridiculous lie my whole life has been! We've been talking in a dream for fifteen years. I was a shipping clerk.

HAPPY: What'd you do?

BIFF (*with great tension and wonder*): Well, he left, see. And the secretary went out. I was all alone in the waiting-room. I don't know what came over me, Hap. The next thing I know I'm in his office—paneled walls, everything. I can't explain it. I—Hap, I took his fountain pen.

HAPPY: Geez, did he catch you?

BIFF: I ran out. I ran down all eleven flights. I ran and ran and ran.

HAPPY: That was an awful dumb—what'd you do that for?

BIFF (*agonized*): I don't know, I just—wanted to take something, I don't know. You gotta help me, Hap. I'm gonna tell Pop.

HAPPY: You crazy? What for?

BIFF: Hap, he's got to understand that I'm not the man somebody lends that kind of money to. He thinks I've been spiting him all these years and it's eating him up.

HAPPY: That's just it. You tell him something nice.

BIFF: I can't.

HAPPY: Say you got a lunch date with Oliver tomorrow.

BIFF: So what do I do tomorrow?

HAPPY: You leave the house tomorrow and come back at night and say Oliver is thinking it over. And he thinks it over for a couple of weeks, and gradually it fades away and nobody's the worse.

BIFF: But it'll go on forever!

HAPPY: Dad is never so happy as when he's looking forward to something!

WILLY *enters.*

HAPPY: Hello, scout!

WILLY: Gee, I haven't been here in years!

STANLEY *has followed* WILLY *in and sets a chair for him.* STANLEY *starts off but* HAPPY *stops him.*

HAPPY: Stanley!

STANLEY *stands by, waiting for an order.*

BIFF (*going to* WILLY *with guilt, as to an invalid*): Sit down, Pop. You want a drink?

WILLY: Sure, I don't mind.

BIFF: Let's get a load on.

WILLY: You look worried.

BIFF: N-no. (*To* STANLEY.) Scotch all around. Make it doubles.

STANLEY: Doubles, right. (*He goes.*)

WILLY: You had a couple already, didn't you?

BIFF: Just a couple, yeah.

WILLY: Well, what happened, boy? (*Nodding affirmatively, with a smile.*) Everything go all right?

BIFF (*takes a breath, then reaches out and grasps* WILLY'*s hand*): Pal . . . (*He is smiling bravely, and* WILLY *is smiling too.*) I had an experience today.

HAPPY: Terrific, Pop.

WILLY: That so? What happened?

BIFF (*high, slightly alcoholic, above the earth*): I'm going to tell you everything from first to last. It's been a strange day. (*Silence. He looks around, composes himself as best he can, but his breath keeps breaking the rhythm of his voice.*) I had to wait quite a while for him, and—

WILLY: Oliver?

BIFF: Yeah, Oliver. All day, as a matter of cold fact. And a lot of—instances—facts, Pop, facts about my life came back to me. Who was it, Pop? Who ever said I was a salesman with Oliver?

WILLY: Well, you were.

BIFF: No, Dad, I was a shipping clerk.

WILLY: But you were practically—

BIFF (*with determination*): Dad, I don't know who said it first, but I was never a salesman for Bill Oliver.

WILLY: What're you talking about?

BIFF: Let's hold on to the facts tonight, Pop. We're not going to get anywhere bullin' around. I was a shipping clerk.

WILLY (*angrily*): All right, now listen to me—

BIFF: Why don't you let me finish?

WILLY: I'm not interested in stories about the past or any crap of that kind because the woods are burning, boys, you understand? There's a big blaze going on all around. I was fired today.

BIFF (*shocked*): How could you be?

WILLY: I was fired, and I'm looking for a little good news to tell your mother, because the woman has waited and the woman has suffered. The gist of it is that I haven't got a story left in my head, Biff. So don't give me a lecture about facts and aspects. I am not interested. Now what've you got to say to me?

STANLEY *enters with three drinks. They wait until he leaves.*

WILLY: Did you see Oliver?

BIFF: Jesus, Dad!

WILLY: You mean you didn't go up there?

HAPPY: Sure he went up there.

BIFF: I did. I—saw him. How could they fire you?

WILLY (*on the edge of his chair*): What kind of a welcome did he give you?

BIFF: He won't even let you work on commission?

WILLY: I'm out! (*Driving.*) So tell me, he gave you a warm welcome?

HAPPY: Sure, Pop, sure!

BIFF (*driven*): Well, it was kind of—

WILLY: I was wondering if he'd remember you. (*To* HAPPY.) Imagine, man doesn't see him for ten, twelve years and gives him that kind of a welcome!

HAPPY: Damn right!

BIFF (*trying to return to the offensive*): Pop, look—

WILLY: You know why he remembered you, don't you? Because you impressed him in those days.

BIFF: Let's talk quietly and get this down to the facts, huh?

WILLY (*as though* BIFF *had been interrupting*): Well, what happened? It's great news, Biff. Did he take you into his office or'd you talk in the waiting room?

BIFF: Well, he came in, see, and—

WILLY: (*with a big smile*): What'd he say? Betcha he threw his arm around you.

BIFF: Well, he kinda—

WILLY: He's a fine man. (*To* HAPPY.) Very hard man to see, y'know.

HAPPY (*agreeing*): Oh, I know.

WILLY (*to* BIFF): Is that where you had the drinks?

BIFF: Yeah, he gave me a couple of—no, no!

HAPPY (*cutting in*): He told him my Florida idea.

WILLY: Don't interrupt. (*To* BIFF.) How'd he react to the Florida idea?

BIFF: Dad, will you give me a minute to explain?

WILLY: I've been waiting for you to explain since I sat down here! What happened? He took you into his office and what?

BIFF: Well—I talked. And—and he listened, see.

WILLY: Famous for the way he listens, y'know. What was his answer?

BIFF: His answer was—(*He breaks off, suddenly angry.*) Dad, you're not letting me tell you what I want to tell you!

WILLY (*accusing, angered*): You didn't see him, did you?

BIFF: I did see him!

WILLY: What'd you insult him or something? You insulted him, didn't you?

BIFF: Listen, will you let me out of it, will you just let me out of it!

HAPPY: What the hell!

WILLY: Tell me what happened!

BIFF (*to* HAPPY): I can't talk to him!

A single trumpet note jars the ear. The light of green leaves stains the house, which holds the air of night and a dream. YOUNG BERNARD *enters and knocks on the door of the house.*

YOUNG BERNARD (*frantically*): Mrs. Loman, Mrs. Loman!

HAPPY: Tell him what happened!

BIFF (*to* HAPPY): Shut up and leave me alone!

WILLY: No, no! You had to go and flunk math!

BIFF: What math? What're you talking about?

YOUNG BERNARD: Mrs. Loman, Mrs. Loman!

LINDA *appears in the house, as of old.*

WILLY (*wildly*): Math, math, math!

BIFF: Take it easy, Pop!

YOUNG BERNARD: Mrs. Loman!

WILLY (*furiously*): If you hadn't flunked you'd've been set by now!

BIFF: Now, look, I'm gonna tell you what happened, and you're going to listen to me.

YOUNG BERNARD: Mrs. Loman!

BIFF: I waited six hours—

HAPPY: What the hell are you saying?

BIFF: I kept sending in my name but he wouldn't see me. So finally he . . . (*He continues unheard as light fades low on the restaurant.*)

YOUNG BERNARD: Biff flunked math!

LINDA: No!

YOUNG BERNARD: Birnbaum flunked him! They won't graduate him!

LINDA: But they have to. He's gotta go to the university. Where is he? Biff! Biff!

YOUNG BERNARD: No, he left. He went to Grand Central.

LINDA: Grand—You mean he went to Boston!

YOUNG BERNARD: Is Uncle Willy in Boston?

LINDA: Oh, maybe Willy can talk to the teacher. Oh, the poor, poor boy!

Light on house area snaps out.

BIFF (*at the table, now audible, holding up a gold fountain pen*): . . . so I'm washed up with Oliver, you understand? Are you listening to me?

WILLY (*at a loss*): Yeah, sure. If you hadn't flunked—

BIFF: Flunked what? What're you talking about?

WILLY: Don't blame everything on me! I didn't flunk math—you did! What pen?

HAPPY: That was awful dumb, Biff, a pen like that is worth—

WILLY (*seeing the pen for the first time*): You took Oliver's pen?

BIFF (*weakening*): Dad, I just explained it to you.

WILLY: You stole Bill Oliver's fountain pen!

BIFF: I didn't exactly steal it! That's just what I've been explaining to you!

HAPPY: He had it in his hand and just then Oliver walked in, so he got nervous and stuck it in his pocket!

WILLY: My God, Biff!

BIFF: I never intended to do it, Dad!

OPERATOR'S VOICE: Standish Arms, good evening!

WILLY (*shouting*): I'm not in my room!

BIFF (*frightened*): Dad, what's the matter? (*He and* HAPPY *stand up.*)

OPERATOR: Ringing Mr. Loman for you!

WILLY: I'm not there, stop it!

BIFF (*horrified, gets down on one knee before* WILLY): Dad, I'll make good, I'll make good. (WILLY *tries to get to his feet.* BIFF *holds him down.*) Sit down now.

WILLY: No, you're no good, you're no good for anything.

BIFF: I am, Dad, I'll find something else, you understand? Now don't worry about anything. (*He holds up* WILLY*'s face.*) Talk to me, Dad.

OPERATOR: Mr. Loman does not answer. Shall I page him?

WILLY (*attempting to stand, as though to rush and silence the* OPERATOR): No, no, no!

HAPPY: He'll strike something, Pop.

WILLY: No, no . . .

BIFF (*desperately, standing over* WILLY): Pop, listen! Listen to me! I'm telling you something good. Oliver talked to his partner about the Florida idea. You listening? He—he talked to his partner, and he came to me . . . I'm going to be all right, you hear? Dad, listen to me, he said it was just a question of the amount!

WILLY: Then you . . . got it?

HAPPY: He's gonna be terrific, Pop!

WILLY (*trying to stand*): Then you got it, haven't you? You got it! You got it!

BIFF (*agonized, holds* WILLY *down*): No, no. Look, Pop. I'm supposed to have lunch with them tomorrow. I'm just telling you this so you'll know that I can still make an impression, Pop. And I'll make good somewhere, but I can't go tomorrow, see?

WILLY: Why not? You simply—

BIFF: But the pen, Pop!

WILLY: You give it to him and tell him it was an oversight!

HAPPY: Sure, have lunch tomorrow!

BIFF: I can't say that—

WILLY: You were doing a crossword puzzle and accidentally used his pen!

BIFF: Listen, kid, I took those balls years ago, now I walk in with his fountain pen? That clinches it, don't you see? I can't face him like that! I'll try elsewhere.

PAGE'S VOICE: Paging Mr. Loman!

WILLY: Don't you want to be anything?

BIFF: Pop, how can I go back?

WILLY: You don't want to be anything, is that what's behind it?

BIFF (*now angry at* WILLY *for not crediting his sympathy*): Don't take it that way! You think it was easy walking into that office after what I'd done to him? A team of horses couldn't have dragged me back to Bill Oliver!

WILLY: Then why'd you go?

BIFF: Why did I go? Why did I go? Look at you! Look at what's become of you!

Off left, THE WOMAN *laughs.*

WILLY: Biff, you're going to go to that lunch tomorrow, or—

BIFF: I can't go. I've got no appointment!

HAPPY: Biff, for . . . !

WILLY: Are you spiting me?

BIFF: Don't take it that way! Goddammit!

WILLY (*strikes* BIFF *and falters away from the table*): You rotten little louse! Are you spiting me?

THE WOMAN: Someone's at the door, Willy!

BIFF: I'm no good, can't you see what I am?

HAPPY (*separating them*): Hey, you're in a restaurant! Now cut it out, both of you! (THE GIRLS *enter.*) Hello, girls, sit down.

THE WOMAN *laughs, off left.*

MISS FORSYTHE*:* I guess we might as well. This is Letta.

THE WOMAN*:* Willy, are you going to wake up?

BIFF (*ignoring* WILLY*):* How're ya, miss, sit down. What do you drink?

MISS FORSYTHE*:* Letta might not be able to stay long.

LETTA*:* I gotta get up very early tomorrow. I got jury duty. I'm so excited! Were you fellows ever on a jury?

BIFF: No, but I been in front of them! (THE GIRLS laugh.) This is my father.

LETTA*:* Isn't he cute? Sit down with us, Pop.

HAPPY: Sit him down, Biff!

BIFF (*going to him):* Come on, slugger, drink us under the table. To hell with it! Come on, sit down, pal.

On BIFF'S *last insistence,* WILLY *is about to sit.*

THE WOMAN (*now urgently*): Willy, are you going to answer the door!

THE WOMAN'S *call pulls* WILLY *back. He starts right, befuddled.*

BIFF: Hey, where are you going?
WILLY: Open the door.
BIFF: The door?
WILLY: The washroom . . . the door . . . where's the door?
BIFF (*leading* WILLY *to the left*): Just go straight down.

WILLY *moves left.*

THE WOMAN: Willy, Willy, are you going to get up, get up, get up, get up?

WILLY *exits left.*

LETTA: I think it's sweet you bring your daddy along.
MISS FORSYTHE: Oh, he isn't really your father!
BIFF (*at left, turning to her resentfully*): Miss Forsythe, you've just seen a prince walk by. A fine, troubled prince. A hard-working, unappreciated prince. A pal, you understand? A good companion. Always for his boys.
LETTA: That's so sweet.
HAPPY: Well, girls, what's the program? We're wasting time. Come on, Biff. Gather round. Where would you like to go?
BIFF: Why don't you do something for him?
HAPPY: Me!
BIFF: Don't you give a damn for him, Hap?
HAPPY: What're you talking about? I'm the one who—
BIFF: I sense it, you don't give a good goddam about him. (*He takes the rolled-up hose from his pocket and puts it on the table in front of* HAPPY.) Look what I found in the cellar, for Christ's sake. How can you bear to let it go on?
HAPPY: Me? Who goes away? Who runs off and—
BIFF: Yeah, but he doesn't mean anything to you. You could help him—I can't! Don't you understand what I'm talking about? He's going to kill himself, don't you know that?
HAPPY: Don't I know it! Me!
BIFF: Hap, help him! Jesus . . . help him . . . Help me, help me, I can't bear to look at his face! (*Ready to weep, he hurries out, up right.*)
HAPPY (*starting after him*): Where are you going?
MISS FORSYTHE: What's he so mad about?
HAPPY: Come on, girls, we'll catch up with him.
MISS FORSYTHE (*as* HAPPY *pushes her out*): Say, I don't like that temper of his!
HAPPY: He's just a little overstrung, he'll be all right!
WILLY (*off left, as* THE WOMAN *laughs*): Don't answer! Don't answer!
LETTA: Don't you want to tell your father—
HAPPY: No, that's not my father. He's just a guy. Come on, we'll catch Biff, and, honey, we're going to paint this town! Stanley, where's the check! Hey, Stanley!

They exit. STANLEY *looks toward left.*

STANLEY (*calling to* HAPPY *indignantly*): Mr. Loman! Mr. Loman!

STANLEY *picks up a chair and follows them off. Knocking is heard off left.* THE WOMAN *enters, laughing.* WILLY *follows her. She is in a black slip; he is buttoning his shirt. Raw, sensuous music accompanies their speech.*

WILLY: Will you stop laughing? Will you stop?

THE WOMAN: Aren't you going to answer the door? He'll wake the whole hotel.

WILLY: I'm not expecting anybody.

THE WOMAN: Whyn't you have another drink, honey, and stop being so damn self-centered?

WILLY: I'm so lonely.

THE WOMAN: You know you ruined me, Willy? From now on, whenever you come to the office, I'll see that you go right through to the buyers. No waiting at my desk any more, Willy. You ruined me.

WILLY: That's nice of you to say that.

THE WOMAN: Gee, you are self-centered! Why so sad? You are the saddest self-centeredest soul I ever did see-saw. (*She laughs. He kisses her.*) Come on inside, drummer boy. It's silly to be dressing in the middle of the night. (*As knocking is heard.*) Aren't you going to answer the door?

WILLY: They're knocking on the wrong door.

THE WOMAN: But I felt the knocking. And he heard us talking in here. Maybe the hotel's on fire!

WILLY (*his terror rising*): It's a mistake.

THE WOMAN: Then tell him to go away!

WILLY: There's nobody there.

THE WOMAN: It's getting on my nerves, Willy. There's somebody standing out there and it's getting on my nerves!

WILLY (*pushing her away from him*): All right, stay in the bathroom here, and don't come out. I think there's a law in Massachusetts about it, so don't come out. It may be that new room clerk. He looked very mean. So don't come out. It's a mistake, there's no fire.

The knocking is heard again. He takes a few steps away from her, and she vanishes into the wing. The light follows him, and now he is facing YOUNG BIFF, *who carries a suitcase.* BIFF *steps toward him. The music is gone.*

BIFF: Why didn't you answer?

WILLY: Biff! What are you doing in Boston?

BIFF: Why didn't you answer? I've been knocking for five minutes, I called you on the phone—

WILLY: I just heard you. I was in the bathroom and had the door shut. Did anything happen home?

BIFF: Dad—I let you down.

WILLY: What do you mean?

BIFF: Dad . . .

WILLY: Biffo, what's this about? (*Putting his arm around* BIFF.) Come on, let's go downstairs and get you a malted.

BIFF: Dad, I flunked math.

WILLY: Not for the term?

BIFF: The term. I haven't got enough credits to graduate.

WILLY: You mean to say Bernard wouldn't give you the answers?

BIFF: He did, he tried, but I only got a sixty-one.

WILLY: And they wouldn't give you four points?

BIFF: Birnbaum refused absolutely. I begged him, Pop, but he won't give me those points. You gotta talk to him before they close the school. Because if he saw the kind of man you are, and you just talked to him in your way, I'm sure he'd come through for me. The class came right before practice, see, and I didn't go enough. Would you talk to him? He'd like you, Pop. You know the way you could talk.

WILLY: You're on. We'll drive right back.

BIFF: Oh, Dad, good work! I'm sure he'll change it for you!

WILLY: Go downstairs and tell the clerk I'm checkin' out. Go right down.

BIFF: Yes, Sir! See, the reason he hates me, Pop—one day he was late for class so I got up at the blackboard and imitated him. I crossed my eyes and talked with a lithp.

WILLY (*laughing*): You did? The kids like it?

BIFF: They nearly died laughing!

WILLY: Yeah? What'd you do?

BIFF: The thquare root of thixthy twee is . . . (WILLY *bursts out laughing;* BIFF *joins him.*) And in the middle of it he walked in!

WILLY *laughs and* THE WOMAN *joins in offstage.*

WILLY (*without hesitating*): Hurry downstairs and—

BIFF: Somebody in there?

WILLY: No, that was next door.

THE WOMAN *laughs offstage.*

BIFF: Somebody got in your bathroom!

WILLY: No, it's the next room, there's a party—

THE WOMAN (*enters, laughing. She lisps this*): Can I come in? There's something in the bathtub, Willy, and it's moving!

WILLY *looks at* BIFF, *who is staring open-mouthed and horrified at* THE WOMAN.

WILLY: Ah—you better go back to your room. They must be finished painting by now. They're painting her room so I let her take a shower here. Go back, go back . . . (*He pushes her.*)

THE WOMAN (*resisting*): But I've got to get dressed, Willy, I can't—

WILLY: Get out of here! Go back, go back . . . (*Suddenly striving for the ordinary.*) This is Miss Francis, Biff, she's a buyer. They're painting her room. Go back, Miss Francis, go back . . .

THE WOMAN: But my clothes, I can't go out naked in the hall!

WILLY (*pushing her offstage*): Get outa here! Go back, go back!

BIFF *slowly sits down on his suitcase as the argument continues offstage.*

THE WOMAN: Where's my stockings? You promised me stockings, Willy!

WILLY: I have no stockings here!

THE WOMAN: You had two boxes of size nine sheers for me, and I want them!

WILLY: Here, for God's sake, will you get outa here!

THE WOMAN (*enters holding a box of stockings*): I just hope there's nobody in the hall. That's all I hope. (*To* BIFF.) Are you football or baseball?

BIFF: Football.

THE WOMAN (*angry, humiliated*): That's me too. G'night. (*She snatches her clothes from* WILLY, *and walks out.*)

WILLY (*after a pause*): Well, better get going. I want to get to the school first thing in the morning. Get my suits out of the closet. I'll get my valise. (BIFF *doesn't move.*) What's the matter? (BIFF *remains motionless, tears falling.*) She's a buyer. Buys for J. H. Simmons. She lives down the hall—they're painting. You don't imagine—(*He breaks off. After a pause.*) Now listen, pal, she's just a buyer. She sees merchandise in her room and they have to keep it looking just so . . . (*Pause. Assuming command.*) All right, get my suits. (BIFF *doesn't move.*) Now stop crying and do as I say. I gave you an order. Biff, I gave you an order! Is that what you do when I give you an order? How dare you cry! (*Putting his arm around* BIFF.) Now look, Biff, when you grow up you'll understand about these things. You mustn't—you mustn't overemphasize a thing like this. I'll see Birnbaum first thing in the morning.

BIFF: Never mind.

WILLY (*getting down beside* BIFF): Never mind! He's going to give you those points. I'll see to it.

BIFF: He wouldn't listen to you.

WILLY: He certainly will listen to me. You need those points for the U. of Virginia.

BIFF: I'm not going there.

WILLY: Heh? If I can't get him to change that mark you'll make it up in summer school. You've got all summer to—

BIFF (*his weeping breaking from him*): Dad . . .

WILLY (*infected by it*): Oh, my boy . . .

BIFF: Dad . . .

WILLY: She's nothing to me, Biff. I was lonely, I was terribly lonely.

BIFF: You—you gave her Mama's stockings! (*His tears break through and he rises to go.*)

WILLY (*grabbing for* BIFF): I gave you an order!

BIFF: Don't touch me, you—liar!

WILLY: Apologize for that!

BIFF: You fake! You phony little fake! You fake! (*Overcome, he turns quickly and weeping fully goes out with his suitcase.* WILLY *is left on the floor on his knees.*)

WILLY: I gave you an order! Biff, come back here or I'll beat you! Come back here! I'll whip you!

STANLEY *comes quickly in from the right and stands in front of* WILLY.

WILLY (*shouts at* STANLEY): I gave you an order . . .

STANLEY: Hey, let's pick it up, pick it up, Mr. Loman. (*He helps* WILLY *to his feet.*) Your boys left with the chippies. They said they'll see you home.

A second waiter watches some distance away.

WILLY: But we were supposed to have dinner together.

Music is heard, WILLY'*s theme.*

STANLEY: Can you make it?

WILLY: I'll—sure, I can make it. (*Suddenly concerned about his clothes.*) Do I—I look all right?

STANLEY: Sure, you look all right. (*He flicks a speck off* WILLY*'s lapel.*)

WILLY: Here—here's a dollar.

STANLEY: Oh, your son paid me. It's all right.

WILLY (*putting it in* STANLEY*'s hand*): No, take it. You're a good boy.

STANLEY: Oh, no, you don't have to . . .

WILLY: Here—here's some more, I don't need it any more. (*After a slight pause.*) Tell me—is there a seed store in the neighborhood?

STANLEY: Seeds? You mean like to plant?

As WILLY *turns,* STANLEY *slips the money back into his jacket pocket.*

WILLY: Yes. Carrots, peas . . .

STANLEY: Well, there's hardware stores on Sixth Avenue, but it may be too late now.

WILLY (*anxiously*): Oh, I'd better hurry. I've got to get some seeds. (*He starts off to the right.*) I've got to get some seeds, right away. Nothing's planted. I don't have a thing in the ground.

WILLY *hurries out as the light goes down.* STANLEY *moves over to the right after him, watches him off. The other waiter has been staring at* WILLY.

STANLEY (*to the waiter):* Well, whatta you looking at?

The waiter picks up the chairs and moves off right. STANLEY *takes the table and follows him. The light fades on this area. There is a long pause, the sound of the flute coming over. The light gradually rises on the kitchen, which is empty.* HAPPY *appears at the door of the house, followed by* BIFF. HAPPY *is carrying a large bunch of long-stemmed roses. He enters the kitchen, looks around for* LINDA. *Not seeing her, he turns to* BIFF, *who is just outside the house door, and makes a gesture with his hands, indicating "Not here, I guess." He looks into the livingroom and freezes. Inside,* LINDA, *unseen, is seated,* WILLY'S *coat on her lap. She rises ominously and quietly and moves toward* HAPPY, *who backs up into the kitchen, afraid.*

HAPPY: Hey, what're you doing up? (LINDA *says nothing but moves toward him implacably.*) Where's Pop? (*He keeps backing to the right, and now* LINDA *is in full view in the doorway to the livingroom.*) Is he sleeping?

LINDA: Where were you?

HAPPY (*trying to laugh it off*): We met two girls, Mom, very fine types. Here, we brought you some flowers. (*Offering them to her.*) Put them in your room, Ma.

She knocks them to the floor at BIFF'S *feet. He has now come inside and closed the door behind him. She stares at* BIFF, *silent.*

HAPPY: Now what'd you do that for? Mom, I want you to have some flowers—

LINDA (*cutting* HAPPY *off, violently to* BIFF): Don't you care whether he lives or dies?

HAPPY (*going to the stairs*): Come upstairs, Biff.

BIFF (*with a flare of disgust, to* HAPPY): Go away from me! (*To* LINDA.) What do you mean, lives or dies? Nobody's dying around here, pal.

LINDA: Get out of my sight! Get out of here!

BIFF: I wanna see the boss.

LINDA: You're not going near him!

BIFF: Where is he? (*He moves into the livingroom and* LINDA *follows.*)

LINDA (*shouting after* BIFF): You invite him for dinner. He looks forward to it all day—(BIFF *appears in his parents' bedroom, looks around, and exits*)—and then you desert him there. There's no stranger you'd do that to!

HAPPY: Why? He had a swell time with us. Listen, when I—(LINDA *comes back into the kitchen*)—desert him I hope I don't outlive the day!

LINDA: Get out of here!

HAPPY: Now look, Mom . . .

LINDA: Did you have to go to women tonight? You and your lousy rotten whores!

BIFF re-enters the kitchen.

HAPPY: Mom, all we did was follow Biff around trying to cheer him up! (*To* BIFF.) Boy, what a night you gave me!

LINDA: Get out of here, both of you, and don't come back! I don't want you tormenting him any more. Go on now, get your things together! (*To* BIFF.) You can sleep in his apartment. (*She starts to pick up the flowers and stops herself.*) Pick up this stuff, I'm not your maid any more. Pick it up, you bum, you!

HAPPY turns his back to her in refusal. BIFF slowly moves over and gets down on his knees, picking up the flowers.

LINDA: You're a pair of animals! Not one, not another living soul would have had the cruelty to walk out on that man in a restaurant!

BIFF (*not looking at her*): Is that what he said?

LINDA: He didn't have to say anything. He was so humiliated he nearly limped when he came in.

HAPPY: But, Mom, he had a great time with us—

BIFF (*cutting him off violently*): Shut up!

Without another word, HAPPY goes upstairs.

LINDA: You! You didn't even go in to see if he was all right!

BIFF (*still on the floor in front of* LINDA, *the flowers in his hand; with self-loathing*): No. Didn't. Didn't do a damned thing. How do you like that, heh? Left him babbling in a toilet.

LINDA: You louse. You . . .

BIFF: Now you hit it on the nose! (*He gets up, throws the flowers in the wastebasket.*) The scum of the earth, and you're looking at him!

LINDA: Get out of here!

BIFF: I gotta talk to the boss, Mom. Where is he?

LINDA: You're not going near him. Get out of this house!

BIFF (*with absolute assurance, determination*): No. We're gonna have an abrupt conversation, him and me.

LINDA: You're not talking to him!

Hammering is heard from outside the house, off right. BIFF turns toward the noise.

LINDA (*suddenly pleading*): Will you please leave him alone?

BIFF: What's he doing out there?

LINDA: He's planting the garden!

BIFF (*quietly*): Now? Oh, my God!

BIFF moves outside, LINDA following. The light dies down on them and comes up on the center of the apron as WILLY walks into it. He is carrying a flashlight, a hoe and a handful of seed packets. He raps the top of the hoe sharply to fix it firmly, and then moves to the left, measuring off the distance with his foot. He holds the flashlight to look at the seed packets, reading off the instructions. He is in the blue of night.

WILLY: Carrots . . . quarter-inch apart. Rows . . . one-foot rows. (*He measures it off.*) One foot. (*He puts down a package and measures off.*) Beets. (*He puts down another package and measures again.*) Lettuce. (*He reads the package, puts it down.*) One foot—(*He breaks off as BEN appears at the right and moves slowly down to him.*) What a proposition, ts, ts. Terrific, terrific. 'Cause she's suffered, Ben, the woman has suffered. You understand me? A man can't go out the way he came in, Ben, a man has got to add up to something. You can't, you can't—(BEN *moves toward him as though to interrupt.*) You gotta consider, now. Don't answer so quick. Remember, it's a guaranteed twenty-thousand-dollar proposition. Now look, Ben, I want you to go through the ins and outs of this thing with me. I've got nobody to talk to, Ben, and the woman has suffered, you hear me?

BEN (*standing still, considering*): What's the proposition?

WILLY: It's twenty thousand dollars on the barrelhead. Guaranteed, gilt-edged, you understand?

BEN: You don't want to make a fool of yourself. They might not honor the policy.

WILLY: How can they dare refuse? Didn't I work like a coolie to meet every premium on the nose? And now they don't pay off? Impossible!

BEN: It's called a cowardly thing, William.

WILLY: Why? Does it take more guts to stand here the rest of my life ringing up a zero?

BEN (*yielding*): That's a point, William. (*He moves, thinking, turns.*) And twenty thousand—that is something one can feel with the hand, it is there.

WILLY (*now assured, with rising power*): Oh, Ben, that's the whole beauty of it! I see it like a diamond, shining in the dark, hard and rough, that I can pick up and touch in my hand. Not like—like an appointment! This would not be another damned-fool appointment, Ben, and it changes all the aspects. Because he thinks I'm nothing, see, and so he spites me. But the funeral—(*Straightening up.*) Ben, that funeral will be massive! They'll come from Maine, Massachusetts, Vermont, New Hampshire! All the old-timers with the strange license plates—that boy will be thunder-struck, Ben, because he never realized—I am known! Rhode Island, New York, New Jersey—I am known, Ben, and he'll see it with his eyes once and for all. He'll see what I am, Ben! He's in for a shock, that boy!

BEN (*coming down to the edge of the garden*): He'll call you a coward.

WILLY (*suddenly fearful*): No, that would be terrible.

BEN: Yes. And a damned fool.

WILLY: No, no, he mustn't, I won't have that! (*He is broken and desperate.*)

BEN: He'll hate you, William.

The gay music of the boys is heard.

WILLY: Oh, Ben, how do we get back to all the great times? Used to be so full of light, and comradeship, the sleigh-riding in winter, and the ruddiness on his cheeks.

And always some kind of good news coming up, always something nice coming up ahead. And never even let me carry the valises in the house, and simonizing, simonizing that little red car! Why, why can't I give him something and not have him hate me?

BEN: Let me think about it. (*He glances at his watch.*) I still have a little time. Remarkable proposition, but you've got to be sure you're not making a fool of yourself.

BEN *drifts off upstage and goes out of sight.* BIFF *comes down from the left.*

WILLY (*suddenly conscious of* BIFF, *turns and looks up at him, then begins picking up the packages of seeds in confusion*): Where the hell is that seed? (*Indignantly.*) You can't see nothing out here! They boxed in the whole goddam neighborhood!

BIFF: There are people all around here. Don't you realize that?

WILLY: I'm busy. Don't bother me.

BIFF (*taking the hoe from* WILLY): I'm saying good-by to you, Pop. (WILLY *looks at him, silent, unable to move.*) I'm not coming back any more.

WILLY: You're not going to see Oliver tomorrow?

BIFF: I've got no appointment, Dad.

WILLY: He put his arm around you, and you've got no appointment?

BIFF: Pop, get this now, will you? Everytime I've left it's been a fight that sent me out of here. Today I realized something about myself and I tried to explain it to you and I—I think I'm just not smart enough to make any sense out of it for you. To hell with whose fault it is or anything like that. (*He takes* WILLY'S *arm.*) Let's just wrap it up, heh? Come on in, we'll tell Mom. (*He gently tries to pull* WILLY *to the left.*)

WILLY (*frozen, immobile, with guilt in his voice*): No, I don't want to see her.

BIFF: Come on! (*He pulls again, and* WILLY *tries to pull away.*)

WILLY (*highly nervous*): No, no, I don't want to see her.

BIFF (*tries to look into* WILLY'S *face, as if to find the answer there*): Why don't you want to see her?

WILLY (*more harshly now*): Don't bother me, will you?

BIFF: What do you mean, you don't want to see her? You don't want them calling you yellow, do you? This isn't your fault; it's me, I'm a bum. Now come inside! (WILLY *strains to get away.*) Did you hear what I said to you?

WILLY *pulls away and quickly goes by himself into the house.* BIFF *follows.*

LINDA (*to* WILLY): Did you plant, dear?

BIFF (*at the door, to* LINDA): All right, we had it out. I'm going and I'm not writing any more.

LINDA (*going to* WILLY *in the kitchen*): I think that's the best way, dear. 'Cause there's no use drawing it out, you'll just never get along.

WILLY *doesn't respond.*

BIFF: People ask where I am and what I'm doing, you don't know, and you don't care. That way it'll be off your mind and you can start brightening up again. All right? That clears it, doesn't it? (WILLY *is silent, and* BIFF *goes to him.*) You gonna wish me luck, scout? (*He extends his hand.*) What do you say?

LINDA: Shake his hand, Willy.

WILLY (*turning to her, seething with hurt*): There's no necessity to mention the pen at all, y'know.

BIFF (*gently*): I've got no appointment, Dad.

WILLY (*erupting fiercely*): He put his arm around . . .?

BIFF: Dad, you're never going to see what I am, so what's the use of arguing? If I strike oil I'll send you a check. Meantime forget I'm alive.

WILLY (*to* LINDA): Spite, see?

BIFF: Shake hands, Dad.

WILLY: Not my hand.

BIFF: I was hoping not to go this way.

WILLY: Well, this is the way you're going. Good-by.

BIFF *looks at him a moment, then turns sharply and goes to the stairs.*

WILLY (*stops him with*): May you rot in hell if you leave this house!

BIFF (*turning*): Exactly what is it that you want from me?

WILLY: I want you to know, on the train, in the mountains, in the valleys, wherever you go, that you cut down your life for spite!

BIFF: No, no.

WILLY: Spite, spite, is the word of your undoing! And when you're down and out, remember what did it. When you're rotting somewhere beside the railroad tracks, remember, and don't you dare blame it on me!

BIFF: I'm not blaming it on you!

WILLY: I won't take the rap for this, you hear?

HAPPY *comes down the stairs and stands on the bottom step, watching.*

BIFF: That's just what I'm telling you!

WILLY (*sinking into a chair at the table, with full accusation*): You're trying to put a knife in me—don't think I don't know what you're doing!

BIFF: All right, phony! Then let's lay it on the line. (*He whips the rubber tube out of his pocket and puts it on the table.*)

HAPPY: You crazy—

LINDA: Biff! (*She moves to grab the hose, but* BIFF *holds it down with his hand.*)

BIFF: Leave it there! Don't move it!

WILLY (*not looking at it*): What is that?

BIFF: You know goddam well what that is.

WILLY (*caged, wanting to escape*): I never saw that.

BIFF: You saw it. The mice didn't bring it into the cellar! What is this supposed to do, make a hero out of you? This supposed to make me sorry for you?

WILLY: Never heard of it.

BIFF: There'll be no pity for you, you hear it? No pity!

WILLY (*to* LINDA): You hear the spite!

BIFF: No, you're going to hear the truth—what you are and what I am!

LINDA: Stop it!

WILLY: Spite!

HAPPY (*coming down toward* BIFF): You cut it now!

BIFF (*to* HAPPY): The man don't know who we are! The man is gonna know! (*To* WILLY.) We never told the truth for ten minutes in this house!

HAPPY: We always told the truth!

BIFF (*turning on him*): You big blow, are you the assistant buyer? You're one of the two assistants to the assistant, aren't you?

HAPPY: Well, I'm practically—

BIFF: You're practically full of it! We all are! And I'm through with it. (*To* WILLY.) Now hear this, Willy, this is me.

WILLY: I know you!

BIFF: You know why I had no address for three months? I stole a suit in Kansas City and I was in jail. (*To* LINDA, *who is sobbing.*) Stop crying. I'm through with it.

LINDA *turns away from them, her hands covering her face.*

WILLY: I suppose that's my fault!

BIFF: I stole myself out of every good job since high school!

WILLY: And whose fault is that?

BIFF: And I never got anywhere because you blew me so full of hot air I could never stand taking orders from anybody! That's whose fault it is!

WILLY: I hear that!

LINDA: Don't, Biff!

BIFF: It's goddam time you heard that! I had to be boss big shot in two weeks, and I'm through with it!

WILLY: Then hang yourself! For spite, hang yourself!

BIFF: No! Nobody's hanging himself, Willy! I ran down eleven flights with a pen in my hand today. And suddenly I stopped, you hear me? And in the middle of that office building, do you hear this? I stopped in the middle of that building and I saw—the sky. I saw the things that I love in this world. The work and the food and time to sit and smoke. And I looked at the pen and said to myself, what the hell am I grabbing this for? Why am I trying to become what I don't want to be? What am I doing in an office, making a contemptuous, begging fool of myself, when all I want is out there, waiting for me the minute I say I know who I am! Why can't I say that, Willy? (*He tries to make* WILLY *face him, but* WILLY *pulls away and moves to the left.*)

WILLY (*with hatred, threateningly*): The door of your life is wide open!

BIFF: Pop! I'm a dime a dozen, and so are you!

WILLY (*turning on him now in an uncontrolled outburst*): I am not a dime a dozen! I am Willy Loman, and you are Biff Loman!

BIFF *starts for* WILLY, *but is blocked by* HAPPY. *In his fury,* BIFF *seems on the verge of attacking his father.*

BIFF: I am not a leader of men, Willy, and neither are you. You were never anything but a hard-working drummer who landed in the ash can like all the rest of them! I'm one dollar an hour, Willy! I tried seven states and couldn't raise it. A buck an hour! Do you gather my meaning? I'm not bringing home any prizes any more, and you're going to stop waiting for me to bring them home!

WILLY (*directly to* BIFF): You vengeful, spiteful mutt!

BIFF *breaks from* HAPPY. WILLY, *in fright, starts up the stairs.* BIFF *grabs him.*

BIFF (*at the peak of his fury*): Pop, I'm nothing! I'm nothing, Pop. Can't you understand that? There's no spite in it any more. I'm just what I am, that's all.

BIFF's fury has spent itself, and he breaks down, sobbing, holding on to WILLY, who dumbly fumbles for BIFF's face.

WILLY (*astonished*): What're you doing? What're you doing? (*To* LINDA.) Why is he crying?

BIFF (*crying, broken*): Will you let me go, for Christ's sake? Will you take that phony dream and burn it before something happens? (*Struggling to contain himself, he pulls away and moves to the stairs.*) I'll go in the morning. Put him—put him to bed. (*Exhausted,* BIFF *moves up the stairs to his room.*)

WILLY (*after a long pause, astonished, elevated*): Isn't that remarkable? Biff—he likes me!

LINDA: He loves you, Willy!

HAPPY (*deeply moved*): Always did, Pop.

WILLY: Oh, Biff! (*Staring wildly.*) He cried! Cried to me. (*He is choking with his love, and now cries out his promise.*) That boy—that boy is going to be magnificent!

BEN *appears in the light just outside the kitchen.*

BEN: Yes, outstanding, with twenty thousand behind him.

LINDA (*sensing the racing of his mind, fearfully, carefully*): Now come to bed, Willy. It's all settled now.

WILLY (*finding it difficult not to rush out of the house*): Yes, we'll sleep. Come on. Go to sleep, Hap.

BEN: And it does take a great kind of man to crack the jungle.

In accents of dread, BEN*'s idyllic music starts up.*

HAPPY (*his arm around* LINDA): I'm getting married, Pop, don't forget it. I'm changing everything. I'm gonna run that department before the year is up. You'll see, Mom. (*He kisses her.*)

BEN: The jungle is dark but full of diamonds, Willy.

WILLY *turns, moves, listening to* BEN.

LINDA: Be good. You're both good boys, just act that way, that's all.

HAPPY: 'Night, Pop. (*He goes upstairs.*)

LINDA (*to* WILLY): Come, dear.

BEN (*with greater force*): One must go in to fetch a diamond out.

WILLY (*to* LINDA, *as he moves slowly along the edge of the kitchen, toward the door*): I just want to get settled down, Linda. Let me sit alone for a little.

LINDA (*almost uttering her fear*): I want you upstairs.

WILLY (*taking her in his arms*): In a few minutes, Linda. I couldn't sleep right now. Go on, you look awful tired. (*He kisses her.*)

BEN: Not like an appointment at all. A diamond is rough and hard to the touch.

WILLY: Go on now. I'll be right up.

LINDA: I think this is the only way, Willy.

WILLY: Sure, it's the best thing.

BEN: Best thing!

WILLY: The only way. Everything is gonna be—go on, kid, get to bed. You look so tired.

LINDA: Come right up.

WILLY: Two minutes.

LINDA goes into the livingroom, then reappears in her bedroom. WILLY moves just outside the kitchen door.

WILLY: Loves me. (*Wonderingly.*) Always loved me. Isn't that a remarkable thing? Ben, he'll worship me for it!

BEN (*with promise*): It's dark there, but full of diamonds.

WILLY: Can you imagine that magnificence with twenty thousand dollars in his pocket?

LINDA (*calling from her room*): Willy! Come up!

WILLY (*calling from the kitchen*): Yes! Yes. Coming! It's very smart, you realize that, don't you, sweetheart? Even Ben sees it. I gotta go, baby. 'By! By! (*Going over to* BEN, *almost dancing.*) Imagine? When the mail comes he'll be ahead of Bernard again!

BEN: A perfect proposition all around.

WILLY: Did you see how he cried to me? Oh, if I could kiss him, Ben!

BEN: Time, William, time!

WILLY: Oh, Ben, I always knew one way or another we were gonna make it, Biff and I!

BEN (*looking at his watch*): The boat. We'll be late. (*He moves slowly off into the darkness.*)

WILLY (*elegiacally, turning to the house*): Now when you kick off, boy, I want a seventy-yard boot, and get right down the field under the ball, and when you hit, hit low and hit hard, because it's important, boy. (*He swings around and faces the audience.*) There's all kinds of important people in the stands, and the first thing you know . . . (*Suddenly realizing he is alone.*) Ben! Ben, where do I . . .? (*He makes a sudden movement of search.*) Ben, how do I . . .?

LINDA (*calling*): Willy, you coming up?

WILLY (*uttering a gasp of fear, whirling about as if to quiet her*): Sh! (*He turns around as if to find his way; sounds, faces, voices, seem to be swarming in upon him and he flicks at them, crying.*) Sh! Sh! (*Suddenly music, faint and high, stops him. It rises in intensity, almost to an unbearable scream. He goes up and down on his toes, and rushes off around the house.*) Shhh!

LINDA: Willy?

There is no answer. LINDA waits. BIFF gets up off his bed. He is still in his clothes. HAPPY sits up. BIFF stands listening.

LINDA (*with real fear*): Willy, answer me! Willy!

There is the sound of a car starting and moving away at full speed.

LINDA: No!

BIFF (*rushing down the stairs*): Pop!

As the car speeds off, the music crashes down in a frenzy of sound, which becomes the soft pulsation of a single cello string. BIFF slowly returns to his bedroom. He and HAPPY gravely don their jackets. LINDA slowly walks out of her room. The music has developed into a dead march. The leaves of day are appearing over everything. CHARLEY and BERNARD, somberly dressed, appear and knock on the kitchen door. BIFF and HAPPY slowly descend the stairs to the kitchen as CHARLEY and BERNARD enter. All stop a moment when LINDA, in clothes of mourning, bearing a little bunch of roses, comes through the draped doorway into the kitchen. She goes to CHARLEY and takes his arm. Now all move toward the audience, through the wall-line of the kitchen. At the limit of the apron, LINDA lays down the flowers, kneels, and sits back on her heels. All stare down at the grave.

REQUIEM

CHARLEY: It's getting dark, Linda.

LINDA *doesn't react. She stares at the grave.*

BIFF: How about it, Mom? Better get some rest, heh? They'll be closing the gate soon.

LINDA *makes no move. Pause.*

HAPPY (*deeply angered*): He had no right to do that! There was no necessity for it. We would've helped him.

CHARLEY (*grunting*): Hmmm.

BIFF: Come along, Mom.

LINDA: Why didn't anybody come?

CHARLEY: It was a very nice funeral.

LINDA: But where are all the people he knew? Maybe they blame him.

CHARLEY: Naa. It's a rough world, Linda. They wouldn't blame him.

LINDA: I can't understand it. At this time especially. First time in thirty-five years we were just about free and clear. He only needed a little salary. He was even finished with the dentist.

CHARLEY: No man only needs a little salary.

LINDA: I can't understand it.

BIFF: There were a lot of nice days. When he'd come home from a trip; or on Sundays, making the stoop; finishing the cellar; putting on the new porch; when he built the extra bathroom; and put up the garage. You know something, Charley, there's more of him in that front stoop than in all the sales he ever made.

CHARLEY: Yeah. He was a happy man with a batch of cement.

LINDA: He was so wonderful with his hands.

BIFF: He had the wrong dreams. All, all, wrong.

HAPPY (*almost ready to fight* BIFF): Don't say that!

BIFF: He never knew who he was.

CHARLEY (*stopping* HAPPY*'s movement and reply. To* BIFF.): Nobody dast blame this man. You don't understand: Willy was a salesman. And for a salesman, there is no rock bottom to the life. He don't put a bolt to a nut, he don't tell you the law or give you medicine. He's a man out there in the blue, riding on a smile and a shoeshine. And when they start not smiling back—that's an earthquake. And then you get yourself a couple of spots on your hat, and you're finished. Nobody dast blame this man. A salesman is got to dream, boy. It comes with the territory.

BIFF: Charley, the man didn't know who he was.

HAPPY (*infuriated*): Don't say that!

BIFF: Why don't you come with me, Happy?

HAPPY: I'm not licked that easily. I'm staying right in this city, and I'm gonna beat this racket! (*He looks at* BIFF, *his chin set.*) The Loman Brothers!

BIFF: I know who I am, kid.

HAPPY: All right, boy. I'm gonna show you and everybody else that Willy Loman did not die in vain. He had a good dream. It's the only dream you can have—to come out number-one man. He fought it out here, and this is where I'm gonna win it for him.

BIFF (*with a hopeless glance at* HAPPY, *bends toward his mother*): Let's go, Mom.

LINDA: I'll be with you in a minute. Go on, Charley. (*He hesitates.*) I want to, just for a minute. I never had a chance to say good-by.

CHARLEY *moves away, followed by* HAPPY. BIFF *remains a slight distance up and left of* LINDA. *She sits there, summoning herself. The flute begins, not far away, playing behind her speech.*

LINDA: Forgive me, dear. I can't cry. I don't know what it is, but I can't cry. I don't understand it. Why did you ever do that? Help me, Willy, I can't cry. It seems to me that you're just on another trip. I keep expecting you. Willy, dear, I can't cry. Why did you do it? I search and search and I search, and I can't understand it, Willy. I made the last payment on the house today. Today, dear. And there'll be nobody home. (*A sob rises in her throat.*) We're free and clear. (*Sobbing more fully, released.*) We're free. (BIFF *comes slowly toward her.*) We're free . . . We're free . . .

BIFF *lifts her to her feet and moves out up right with her in his arms.* LINDA *sobs quietly.* BERNARD *and* CHARLEY *come together and follow them, followed by* HAPPY. *Only the music of the flute is left on the darkening stage as over the house the hard towers of the apartment buildings rise into sharp focus, and—*

Curtain

(1949)

QUESTIONS FOR CRITICAL THINKING AND WRITING

Experience

1. Identify the places in the play, if any, where you were confused. What may have accounted for your confusion?
2. To what extent do you identify with the dreams of the play's characters? Why?

Interpretation

3. Comment on the significance of the title. What kinds of deaths might be referred to? Explain.
4. What significance do you attach to the names of the characters?
5. Describe Biff's relationship with his father and with his brother, Happy.
6. How does Miller characterize Willy? Which of his characteristics are highlighted? What kind of man is he? To what extent and by what means is he considered a failure? Does anyone consider him a success? Why or why not?
7. What roles do women have in this play? Comment on Willy's relationships with them. Consider Biff's relationship with women as well.
8. Identify two minor characters and explain their significance for the play's action and theme(s).
9. Describe Miller's staging of the play. Consider his use of lighting and music, and the way he dramatizes dreams and memories.

Evaluation

10. What is typically "American" about Miller's play? What cultural attitudes and values displayed by the characters provide it with an American tone?
11. *Death of a Salesman* has been among the most popular plays of the American theater. What accounts for the play's perennial appeal?

Connection

12. Consider the importance of memory for Willy in *Death of a Salesman* and for Tony in August Wilson's *Fences.* How is the past central to these characters' identities and how does it influence their relationships?

Critical Thinking

13. What contemporary actors would you cast in the various roles of the play. Choose at least two roles, and propose two actors for each role. Explain the rationale for your choices.

CHAPTER TWENTY-NINE

A Collection of Modern and Contemporary Drama

All the world's a stage,
And all the men and women merely players:
They have their exits and their entrances,
And one man in his time plays many parts. . . .
WILLIAM SHAKESPEARE, *AS YOU LIKE IT,* ii, vii

SUSAN GLASPELL

[1882–1948]

Susan Glaspell, an American novelist and playwright, was one of the cofounders of the Provincetown Players, an influential theatrical company. With her husband, George Cram Cook, she collaborated on a number of plays, including her one-act satire on Freudian psychoanalysis, Suppressed Desires, *published in 1916. In the same year Glaspell produced another fine one-act play,* Trifles, *which has continued to be her most frequently performed play.*

Trifles

CHARACTERS

GEORGE HENDERSON, *County Attorney*
HENRY PETERS, *Sheriff*
LEWIS HALE, *A Neighboring Farmer*
MRS. PETERS
MRS. HALE

Scene. *The kitchen in the now abandoned farmhouse of* JOHN WRIGHT, *a gloomy kitchen, and left without having been put in order—unwashed pans under the sink, a loaf of bread outside the breadbox, a dish towel on the table—other signs of incompleted work. At the rear the outer door opens and the* SHERIFF *comes in followed by the* COUNTY ATTORNEY *and* HALE. *The* SHERIFF *and* HALE *are men in middle life, the* COUNTY ATTORNEY *is a young man; all are much bundled up and go at once to the stove. They are followed by two women—the* SHERIFF*'s wife first; she is a slight wiry woman, a thin nervous face.* MRS. HALE *is larger and would ordinarily be called more comfortable looking, but she is disturbed now and looks fearfully about as she enters. The women have come in slowly, and stand close together near the door.*

COUNTY ATTORNEY [*rubbing his hands*]: This feels good. Come up to the fire, ladies.

MRS. PETERS [*after taking a step forward*]: I'm not—cold.

SHERIFF [*unbuttoning his overcoat and stepping away from the stove as if to mark the beginning of official business*]: Now, Mr. Hale, before we move things about, you explain to Mr. Henderson just what you saw when you came here yesterday morning.

COUNTY ATTORNEY: By the way, has anything been moved? Are things just as you left them yesterday?

SHERIFF [*looking about*]: It's just the same. When it dropped below zero last night I thought I'd better send Frank out this morning to make a fire for us—no use getting pneumonia with a big case on, but I told him not to touch anything except the stove—and you know Frank.

COUNTY ATTORNEY: Somebody should have been left here yesterday.

SHERIFF: Oh—yesterday. When I had to send Frank to Morris Center for that man who went crazy—I want you to know I had my hands full yesterday, I knew you could get back from Omaha by today and as long as I went over everything here myself—

COUNTY ATTORNEY: Well, Mr. Hale, tell just what happened when you came here yesterday morning.

HALE: Harry and I had started to town with a load of potatoes. We came along the road from my place and as I got here I said, "I'm going to see if I can't get John Wright to go in with me on a party telephone." I spoke to Wright about it once before and he put me off, saying folks talked too much anyway, and all he asked was peace and quiet—I guess you know about how much he talked himself; but I thought maybe if I went to the house and talked about it before his wife, though I said to Harry that I didn't know as what his wife wanted made much difference to John—

COUNTY ATTORNEY: Let's talk about that later, Mr. Hale. I do want to talk about that, but tell now just what happened when you got to the house.

HALE: I didn't hear or see anything; I knocked at the door, and still it was all quiet inside. I knew they must be up, it was past eight o'clock. So I knocked again, and I thought I heard somebody say, "Come in." I wasn't sure, I'm not sure yet, but I opened the door—this door [*Indicating the door by which the two women are still standing*] and there in that rocker—[*Pointing to it*] sat Mrs. Wright.

[*They all look at the rocker.*]

COUNTY ATTORNEY: What—was she doing?

HALE: She was rockin' back and forth. She had her apron in her hand and was kind of—pleating it.

COUNTY ATTORNEY: And how did she—look?

HALE: Well, she looked queer.

COUNTY ATTORNEY: How do you mean—queer?

HALE: Well, as if she didn't know what she was going to do next. And kind of done up.

COUNTY ATTORNEY: How did she seem to feel about your coming?

HALE: Why, I don't think she minded—one way or other. She didn't pay much attention. I said, "How do, Mrs. Wright, it's cold, ain't it?" And she said, "Is it?"—and went on kind of pleating at her apron. Well, I was surprised; she didn't ask me to come up to the stove, or to set down, but just sat there, not even looking at me, so I said, "I want to see John." And then she—laughed. I guess you would call it a laugh. I thought of Harry and the team outside, so I said a little sharp: "Can't I see John?" "No," she says, kind o' dull like. "Ain't he home?" says I. "Yes," says she, "he's home." "Then why can't I see him?" I asked her, out of patience. "'Cause he's dead," says she. *"Dead?"* says I. She just nodded her head, not getting a bit excited, but rockin' back and forth. "Why—where is he?" says I, not knowing what to say. She just pointed upstairs—like that [*Himself pointing to the room above*]. I got up, with the idea of going up there. I walked from there to here—then I says, "Why, what did he die of?" "He died of a rope round his neck," says she, and just went on pleatin' at her apron. Well, I went out and called Harry. I thought I might—need help. We went upstairs and there he was lyin'—

COUNTY ATTORNEY: I think I'd rather have you go into that upstairs, where you can point it all out. Just go on now with the rest of the story.

HALE: Well, my first thought was to get that rope off. It looked . . . [*Stops, his face twitches.*] . . . but Harry, he went up to him, and he said, "No, he's dead all right, and we'd better not touch anything." So we went back down stairs. She was still sitting that same way. "Has anybody been notified?" I asked. "No," says she, unconcerned. "Who did this, Mrs. Wright?" said Harry. He said it businesslike—and she stopped pleatin' of her apron. "I don't know," she says. "You don't *know?*" says Harry. "No," says she. "Weren't you sleepin' in the bed with him?" says Harry. "Yes," says she, "but I was on the inside." "Somebody slipped a rope round his neck and strangled him and you didn't wake up?" says Harry. "I didn't wake up," she said after him. We must 'a looked as if we didn't see how that could be, for after a minute she said, "I sleep sound." Harry was going to ask her more questions but I said maybe we ought to let her tell her story first to the coroner, or the sheriff, so Harry went fast as he could to Rivers' place, where there's a telephone.

COUNTY ATTORNEY: And what did Mrs. Wright do when she knew that you had gone for the coroner?

HALE: She moved from that chair to this one over here [*Pointing to a small chair in the corner*] and just sat there with her hands held together and looking down. I got a feeling that I ought to make some conversation, so I said I had come in to see if John wanted to put in a telephone, and at that she started to laugh, and then she stopped and looked at me—scared. [*The* COUNTY ATTORNEY, *who has had his notebook out, makes a note.*] I dunno, maybe it wasn't scared. I wouldn't like to say it was. Soon Harry got back, and then Dr. Lloyd came, and you, Mr. Peters, and so I guess that's all I know that you don't.

COUNTY ATTORNEY [*looking around*]: I guess we'll go upstairs first—and then out to the barn and around there. [*to the* SHERIFF] You're convinced that there was nothing important here—nothing that would point to any motive.

SHERIFF: Nothing here but kitchen things.

[*The county attorney, after again looking around the kitchen, opens the door of a cupboard closet. He gets up on a chair and looks on a shelf. Pulls his hand away, sticky.*]

COUNTY ATTORNEY: Here's a nice mess.

[*The women draw nearer.*]

MRS. PETERS [*to the other woman*]: Oh, her fruit; it did freeze. [*To the* COUNTY ATTORNEY] She worried about that when it turned so cold. She said the fire'd go out and her jars would break.

SHERIFF: Well, can you beat the women! Held for murder and worryin' about her preserves.

COUNTY ATTORNEY: I guess before we're through she may have something more serious than preserves to worry about.

HALE: Well, women are used to worrying over trifles.

[*The two women move a little closer together.*]

COUNTY ATTORNEY [*with the gallantry of a young politician*]: And yet, for all their worries, what would we do without the ladies? [*The women do not unbend. He goes to the sink, takes a dipperful of water from the pail and pouring it into a basin, washes his hands. Starts to wipe them on the roller towel, turns it for a cleaner place.*] Dirty towels! [*Kicks his foot against the pans under the sink.*] Not much of a housekeeper, would you say, ladies?

MRS. HALE [*stiffly*]: There's a great deal of work to be done on a farm.

COUNTY ATTORNEY: To be sure. And yet [*with a little bow to her*] I know there are some Dickson county farmhouses which do not have such roller towels.

[*He gives it a pull to expose its full length again.*]

MRS. HALE: Those towels get dirty awful quick. Men's hands aren't always as clean as they might be.

COUNTY ATTORNEY: Ah, loyal to your sex, I see. But you and Mrs. Wright were neighbors. I suppose you were friends, too.

MRS. HALE [*shaking her head*]: I've not seen much of her of late years. I've not been in this house—it's more than a year.

COUNTY ATTORNEY: And why was that? You didn't like her?

MRS. HALE: I liked her all well enough. Farmers' wives have their hands full, Mr. Henderson. And then—

COUNTY ATTORNEY: Yes—?

MRS. HALE [*looking about*]: It never seemed a very cheerful place.

COUNTY ATTORNEY: No—it's not cheerful. I shouldn't say she had the homemaking instinct.

MRS. HALE: Well, I don't know as Wright had, either.

COUNTY ATTORNEY: You mean that they didn't get on very well?

MRS. HALE: No, I don't mean anything. But I don't think a place'd be any cheerfuller for John Wright's being in it.

COUNTY ATTORNEY: I'd like to talk more of that a little later. I want to get the lay of things upstairs now.

[*He goes to the left, where three steps lead to a stair door.*]

SHERIFF: I suppose anything Mrs. Peters does'll be all right. She was to take in some clothes for her, you know, and a few little things. We left in such a hurry yesterday.

COUNTY ATTORNEY: Yes, but I would like to see what you take, Mrs. Peters, and keep an eye out for anything that might be of use to us.

MRS. PETERS: Yes, Mr. Henderson.

[*The women listen to the men's steps on the stairs, then look about the kitchen.*]

MRS. HALE: I'd hate to have men coming into my kitchen, snooping around and criticising.

[*She arranges the pans under sink which the* COUNTY ATTORNEY *had shoved out of place.*]

MRS. PETERS: Of course it's no more than their duty.

MRS. HALE: Duty's all right, but I guess that deputy sheriff that came out to make the fire might have got a little of this on. [*Gives the roller towel a pull.*] Wish I'd thought of that sooner. Seems mean to talk about her for not having things slicked up when she had to come away in such a hurry.

MRS. PETERS [*Who has gone to a small table in the left rear corner of the room, and lifted one end of a towel that covers a pan*]: She had bread set.

[*Stands still.*]

MRS. HALE [*eyes fixed on a loaf of bread beside the breadbox, which is on a low shelf at the other side of the room. Moves slowly toward it*]: She was going to put this in there. [*Picks up loaf, then abruptly drops it. In a manner of returning to familiar things.*] It's a shame about her fruit. I wonder if it's all gone. [*Gets up on the chair and looks.*] I think there's some here that's all right, Mrs. Peters. Yes—here; [*Holding it toward the window.*] this is cherries, too. [*Looking again.*] I declare I believe that's the only one. [*Gets down, bottle in her hand. Goes to the sink and wipes it off on the outside.*] She'll feel awful bad after all her hard work in the hot weather. I remember the afternoon I put up my cherries last summer.

[*She puts the bottle on the big kitchen table, center of the room. With a sigh, is about to sit down in the rocking-chair. Before she is seated realizes what chair it is; with a slow look at it, steps back. The chair which she has touched rocks back and forth.*]

MRS. PETERS: Well, I must get those things from the front room closet. [*She goes to the door at the right, but after looking into the other room, steps back.*] You coming with me, Mrs. Hale? You could help me carry them.

[*They go in the other room; reappear,* MRS. PETERS *carrying a dress and skirt,* MRS. HALE *following with a pair of shoes.*]

MRS. PETERS: My, it's cold in there.

[*She puts the clothes on the big table, and hurries to the stove.*]

MRS. HALE [*examining her skirt*]: Wright was close. I think maybe that's why she kept so much to herself. She didn't even belong to the Ladies Aid. I suppose she felt she couldn't do her part, and then you don't enjoy things when you feel shabby. She used to wear pretty clothes and be lively, when she was Minnie Foster, one of the town girls singing in the choir. But that—oh, that was thirty years ago. This all you was to take in?

MRS. PETERS: She said she wanted an apron. Funny thing to want, for there isn't much to get you dirty in jail, goodness knows. But I suppose just to make her feel more natural. She said they was in the top drawer in this cupboard. Yes, here. And then her little shawl that always hung behind the door. [*Opens stair door and looks.*] Yes, here it is.

[*Quickly shuts door leading upstairs.*]

MRS. HALE [*abruptly moving toward her*]: Mrs. Peters?

MRS. PETERS: Yes, Mrs. Hale?

MRS. HALE: Do you think she did it?

MRS. PETERS [*in a frightened voice*]: Oh, I don't know.

MRS. HALE: Well, I don't think she did. Asking for an apron and her little shawl. Worrying about her fruit.

MRS. PETERS [*starts to speak, glances up, where footsteps are heard in the room above. In a low voice*]: Mr. Peters says it looks bad for her. Mr. Henderson is awful sarcastic in a speech and he'll make fun of her sayin' she didn't wake up.

MRS. HALE: Well, I guess John Wright didn't wake when they was slipping that rope under his neck.

MRS. PETERS: No, it's strange. It must have been done awful crafty and still. They say it was such a—funny way to kill a man, rigging it all up like that.

MRS. HALE: That's just what Mr. Hale said. There was a gun in the house. He says that's what he can't understand.

MRS. PETERS: Mr. Henderson said coming out that what was needed for the case was a motive; something to show anger, or—sudden feeling.

MRS. HALE [who is standing by the table]: Well, I don't see any signs of anger around here. [*She puts her hand on the dish towel which lies on the table, stands looking down at table, one half of which is clean, the other half messy.*] It's wiped to here. [*Makes a move as if to finish work, then turns and looks at loaf of bread outside the breadbox. Drops towel. In that voice of coming back to familiar things.*] Wonder how they are finding things upstairs. I hope she had it a little more red-up up there. You know, it seems kind of *sneaking.* Locking her up in town and then coming out here and trying to get her own house to turn against her!

MRS. PETERS: But Mrs. Hale, the law is the law.

MRS. HALE: I s'pose 'tis. [*Unbuttoning her coat.*] Better loosen up your things, Mrs. Peters. You won't feel them when you go out.

[MRS. PETERS *takes off her fur tippet, goes to hang it on hook at back of room, stands looking at the under part of the small corner table.*]

MRS. PETERS: She was piecing a quilt.

[*She brings the large sewing basket and they look at the bright pieces.*]

MRS. HALE: It's log cabin pattern. Pretty, isn't it? I wonder if she was goin' to quilt it or just knot it?

[*Footsteps have been heard coming down the stairs. The* SHERIFF *enters followed by* HALE *and the* COUNTY ATTORNEY.]

SHERIFF: They wonder if she was going to quilt it or just knot it!

[*The men laugh; the women look abashed.*]

COUNTY ATTORNEY [*rubbing his hands over the stove*]: Frank's fire didn't do much up there, did it? Well, let's go out to the barn and get that cleared up.

[*The men go outside.*]

MRS. HALE [*resentfully*]: I don't know as there's anything so strange, our takin' up our time with little things while we're waiting for them to get the evidence. [*She sits down at the big table smoothing out a block with decision.*] I don't see as it's anything to laugh about.

MRS. PETERS [*apologetically*]: Of course they've got awful important things on their minds.

[*Pulls up a chair and joins* MRS. HALE *at the table.*]

MRS. HALE [*examining another block*]: Mrs. Peters, look at this one. Here, this is the one she was working on, and look at the sewing! All the rest of it has been so nice and even. And look at this! It's all over the place! Why, it looks as if she didn't know what she was about!

[*After she has said this they look at each other, then start to glance back at the door. After an instant* MRS. HALE *has pulled at a knot and ripped the sewing.*]

MRS. PETERS: Oh, what are you doing, Mrs. Hale?

MRS. HALE [*mildly*]: Just pulling out a stitch or two that's not sewed very good. [*Threading a needle.*] Bad sewing always made me fidgety.

MRS. PETERS [*nervously*]: I don't think we ought to touch things.

MRS. HALE: I'll just finish up this end. [*Suddenly stopping and leaning forward.*] Mrs. Peters?

MRS. PETERS: Yes, Mrs. Hale?

MRS. HALE: What do you suppose she was so nervous about?

MRS. PETERS: Oh—I don't know. I don't know as she was nervous. I sometimes sew awful queer when I'm just tired. [MRS. HALE *starts to say something, looks at* MRS. PETERS, *then goes on sewing.*] Well, I must get these things wrapped up. They may be through sooner than we think. [*Putting apron and other things together.*] I wonder where I can find a piece of paper, and string.

MRS. HALE: In that cupboard, maybe.

MRS. PETERS [*looking in cupboard*]: Why, here's a birdcage. [*Holds it up.*] Did she have a bird, Mrs. Hale?

MRS. HALE: Why, I don't know whether she did or not—I've not been here for so long. There was a man around last year selling canaries cheap, but I don't know as she took one; maybe she did. She used to sing real pretty herself.

MRS. PETERS [*glancing around*]: Seems funny to think of a bird here. But she must have had one, or why would she have a cage? I wonder what happened to it.

MRS. HALE: I s'pose maybe the cat got it.

MRS. PETERS: No, she didn't have a cat. She's got that feeling some people have about cats—being afraid of them. My cat got in her room and she was real upset and asked me to take it out.

MRS. HALE: My sister Bessie was like that. Queer, ain't it?

MRS. PETERS [*examining the cage*]: Why, look at this door. It's broke. One hinge is pulled apart.

MRS. HALE [*looking too*]: Looks as if someone must have been rough with it.

MRS. PETERS: Why, yes.

[*She brings the cage forward and puts it on the table.*]

MRS. HALE: I wish if they're going to find any evidence they'd be about it. I don't like this place.

MRS. PETERS: But I'm awful glad you came with me, Mrs. Hale. It would be lonesome for me sitting here alone.

MRS. HALE: It would, wouldn't it? [*Dropping her sewing.*] But I tell you what I do wish, Mrs. Peters. I wish I had come over sometimes when *she* was here. I—[*Looking around the room.*]—wish I had.

MRS. PETERS: But of course you were awful busy, Mrs. Hale—your house and your children.

MRS. HALE: I could've come. I stayed away because it weren't cheerful—and that's why I ought to have come. I—I've never liked this place. Maybe because it's down in a hollow and you don't see the road. I dunno what it is but it's a lonesome place and always was. I wish I had come over to see Minnie Foster sometimes. I can see now—

[*Shakes her head.*]

MRS. PETERS: Well, you mustn't reproach yourself, Mrs. Hale. Somehow we just don't see how it is with other folks until—something comes up.

MRS. HALE: Not having children makes less work—but it makes a quiet house, and Wright out to work all day, and no company when he did come in. Did you know John Wright, Mrs. Peters?

MRS. PETERS: Not to know him; I've seen him in town. They say he was a good man.

MRS. HALE: Yes—good; he didn't drink, and kept his word as well as most, I guess, and paid his debts. But he was a hard man, Mrs. Peters. Just to pass the time of day with him—[*Shivers.*] Like a raw wind that gets to the bone. [*Pauses, her eye falling on the cage.*] I should think she would 'a wanted a bird. But what do you suppose went with it?

MRS. PETERS: I don't know, unless it got sick and died.

[*She reaches over and swings the broken door, swings it again. Both women watch it.*]

MRS. HALE: You weren't raised round here, were you? [MRS. PETERS *shakes her head.*] You didn't know—her?

MRS. PETERS: Not till they brought her yesterday.

MRS. HALE: She—come to think of it, she was kind of like a bird herself—real sweet and pretty, but kind of timid and—fluttery. How—she—did—change. [*Silence; then as if struck by a happy thought and relieved to get back to every day things.*] Tell you what, Mrs. Peters, why don't you take the quilt in with you? It might take up her mind.

MRS. PETERS: Why, I think that's a real nice idea, Mrs. Hale. There couldn't possibly be any objection to it, could there? Now, just what would I take? I wonder if her patches are in here—and her things.

[*They look in the sewing basket.*]

MRS. HALE: Here's some red. I expect this has got sewing things in it. [*Brings out a fancy box.*] What a pretty box. Looks like something somebody would give you. Maybe her scissors are in here. [*Opens box. Suddenly puts her hand to her nose.*] Why—[MRS. PETERS *bends nearer, then turns her face away.*] There's something wrapped up in this piece of silk.

MRS. PETERS: Why, this isn't her scissors.

MRS. HALE [*lifting the silk*]:Oh, Mrs. Peters—it's—

[MRS. PETERS *bends closer.*]

MRS. PETERS: It's the bird.

MRS. HALE [*jumping up*]: But, Mrs. Peters—look at it! Its neck! Look at its neck! It's all—other side *to.*

MRS. PETERS: Somebody—wrung—its—neck.

[*Their eyes meet. A look of growing comprehension, of horror. Steps are heard outside.* MRS. HALE *slips box under quilt pieces, and sinks into her chair. Enter* SHERIFF *and* COUNTY ATTORNEY. MRS. PETERS *rises.*]

COUNTY ATTORNEY [*as one turning from serious things to little pleasantries*]: Well, ladies have you decided whether she was going to quilt it or knot it?

MRS. PETERS: We think she was going to—knot it.

COUNTY ATTORNEY: Well, that's interesting, I'm sure. [*Seeing the birdcage.*] Has the bird flown?

MRS. HALE [*putting more quilt pieces over the box*]: We think the—cat got it.

COUNTY ATTORNEY [*Preoccupied*]: Is there a cat?

[MRS. HALE *glances in a quick covert way at* MRS. PETERS.]

MRS. PETERS: Well, not *now.* They're superstitious, you know. They leave.

COUNTY ATTORNEY [*to* SHERIFF PETERS, *continuing an interrupted conversation*]: No sign at all of anyone having come from the outside. Their own rope. Now let's go up again and go over it piece by piece. [*They start upstairs.*] It would have to have been someone who knew just the—

[MRS. PETERS *sits down. The two women sit there not looking at one another, but as if peering into something and at the same time holding back. When they talk now it is in the manner of feeling their way over strange ground, as if afraid of what they are saying, but as if they can not help saying it.*]

MRS. HALE: She liked the bird. She was going to bury it in that pretty box.

MRS. PETERS [*in a whisper*]: When I was a girl—my kitten—there was a boy took a hatchet, and before my eyes—and before I could get there—[*Covers her face an instant.*] If they hadn't held me back I would have—[*Catches herself, looks upstairs where steps are heard, falters weakly.*]—hurt him.

MRS. HALE [*with a slow look around her*]: I wonder how it would seem never to have had any children around. [*Pause.*] No, Wright wouldn't like the bird—a thing that sang. She used to sing. He killed that, too.

MRS. PETERS [*moving uneasily*]: We don't know who killed the bird.

MRS. HALE: I knew John Wright.

MRS. PETERS: It was an awful thing was done in this house that night, Mrs. Hale. Killing a man while he slept, slipping a rope around his neck that choked the life out of him.

MRS. HALE: His neck. Choked the life out of him.

[*Her hand goes out and rests on the birdcage.*]

MRS. PETERS [*with rising voice*]: We don't know who killed him. We don't *know.*

MRS. HALE [*her own feeling not interrupted*]: If there'd been years and years of nothing, then a bird to sing to you, it would be awful—still, after the bird was still.

MRS. PETERS [*something within her speaking*]: I know what stillness is. When we homesteaded in Dakota, and my first baby died—after he was two years old, and me with no other then—

MRS. HALE [*moving*]: How soon do you suppose they'll be through, looking for the evidence?

MRS. PETERS: I know what stillness is. [*Pulling herself back.*] The law has got to punish crime, Mrs. Hale.

MRS. HALE [*not as if answering that*]: I wish you'd seen Minnie Foster when she wore a white dress with blue ribbons and stood up there in the choir and sang. [*A look around the room.*] Oh, I *wish* I'd come over here once in a while! That was a crime! That was a crime! Who's going to punish that?

MRS. PETERS [*looking upstairs*]: We mustn't—take on.

MRS. HALE: I might have known she needed help! I know how things can be—for women. I tell you, it's queer, Mrs. Peters. We live close together and we live far apart. We all go through the same things—it's all just a different kind of the same thing. [*Brushes her eyes; noticing the bottle of fruit, reaches out for it.*] If I was you I wouldn't tell her her fruit was gone. Tell her it *ain't.* Tell her it's all right. Take this in to prove it to her. She—she may never know whether it was broke or not.

MRS. PETERS [*takes the bottle, looks about for something to wrap it in; takes petticoat from the clothes brought from the other room, very nervously begins winding this around the bottle. In a false voice*]: My, it's a good thing the men couldn't hear us. Wouldn't they just laugh! Getting all stirred up over a little thing like a—dead canary. As if that could have anything to do with—with—wouldn't they *laugh!*

[*The men are heard coming down stairs.*]

MRS. HALE [*under her breath*]: Maybe they would—maybe they wouldn't.

COUNTY ATTORNEY: No, Peters, it's all perfectly clear except a reason for doing it. But you know juries when it comes to women. If there was some definite thing. Something to show—something to make a story about—a thing that would connect up with this strange way of doing it—

[*The women's eyes meet for an instant. Enter* HALE *from outer door.*]

HALE: Well, I've got the team around. Pretty cold out there.

COUNTY ATTORNEY: I'm going to stay here a while by myself. [*To the* SHERIFF.] You can send Frank out for me, can't you? I want to go over everything. I'm not satisfied that we can't do better.

SHERIFF: Do you want to see what Mrs. Peters is going to take in?

[*The* COUNTY ATTORNEY *goes to the table, picks up the apron, laughs.*]

COUNTY ATTORNEY: Oh, I guess they're not very dangerous things the ladies have picked out. [*Moves a few things about, disturbing the quilt pieces which cover the box. Steps back.*] No, Mrs. Peters doesn't need supervising. For that matter, a sheriff's wife is married to the law. Ever think of it that way, Mrs. Peters?

MRS. PETERS: Not—just that way.

SHERIFF [*Chuckling*]: Married to the law. [*Moves toward the other room.*] I just want you to come in here a minute, George. We ought to take a look at these windows.

COUNTY ATTORNEY [*scoffingly*]: Oh, windows!

SHERIFF: We'll be right out, Mr. Hale.

[HALE *goes outside. The* SHERIFF *follows the* COUNTY ATTORNEY *into the other room. Then* MRS. HALE *rises, hands tight together, looking intensely at* MRS. PETERS, *whose eyes make a slow turn, finally meeting* MRS. HALE'S. *A moment* MRS. HALE *holds her, then her own eyes point the way to where the box is concealed. Suddenly* MRS. PETERS *throws back quilt pieces and tries to put the box in the bag she is wearing. It is too big. She opens box, starts to take bird out, cannot touch it, goes to pieces, stands there helpless. Sound of a knob turning in the other room.* MRS. HALE *snatches the box and puts it in the pocket of her big coat. Enter* COUNTY ATTORNEY *and* SHERIFF.]

COUNTY ATTORNEY [*facetiously*]: Well, Henry, at least we found out that she was not going to quilt it. She was going to—what is it you call it, ladies?

MRS. HALE [*her hand against her pocket*]: We call it—knot it, Mr. Henderson.

Curtain

(*1916*)

QUESTIONS FOR CRITICAL THINKING AND WRITING

Experience

1. At what point in reading *Trifles* did you realize that Mrs. Wright had murdered her husband?
2. What is your response to the women's behavior? To the behavior of the men? Why?

Interpretation

3. Explain the significance of the title. Do you prefer this title or the one Glaspell gave her rewriting of the play as a short story, "A Jury of Her Peers"? Why?
4. How does Glaspell characterize the men in the play? The sheriff? The attorney? The neighboring farmer? What attitudes toward women do the men display?
5. How does Glaspell enlist our sympathy for the women? How do Mrs. Hale and Mrs. Peters get along with the men?
6. Which of the stage props are most important for the play's dramatic action? For its theme? Why?
7. Explain the significance of the final line of dialogue.

Evaluation

8. What does Glaspell's play suggest about the relative merits of men's and women's perspectives? What implications might we derive about men's and women's ways of seeing things after reading or viewing this play? Why?

Connection

9. Read Glaspell's "A Jury of Her Peers," a short story version of *Trifles.* Compare the presentation of plot and theme in story and play. Which work do you prefer and why?

Critical Thinking

10. Think of two alternative titles to *Trifles*. Explain why you chose each of the alternatives. Why do you think Glaspell chose *Trifles* for her title?

LORRAINE HANSBERRY
[1930–1965]

Lorraine Hansberry was born and raised in Chicago. She studied painting at the Chicago Art Institute and the University of Wisconsin before turning to writing following a move to New York. A Raisin in the Sun *(1959), her first Broadway play, was quickly made into a movie, starring Sidney Poitier and Claudia McNeil. Although the play reflects Hansberry's deep concern with civil rights, it transcends its racial and urban focus. Like Arthur Miller's* Death of a Salesman, A Raisin in the Sun *dramatizes the powerful attractions of the American dream of success. Like Miller's play also, Hansberry's is largely concerned with family life.*

A Raisin in the Sun

What happens to a dream deferred?
Does it dry up
Like a raisin in the sun?
Or fester like a sore—
And then run?
Does it stink like rotten meat?
Or crust and sugar over—
Like a syrupy sweet?

Maybe it just sags
Like a heavy load.

Or does it explode?

LANGSTON HUGHES

CHARACTERS

(*In order of appearance*)
RUTH YOUNGER
TRAVIS YOUNGER
WALTER LEE YOUNGER (BROTHER)
BENEATHA YOUNGER
LENA YOUNGER (MAMA)
JOSEPH ASAGAI
GEORGE MURCHISON
MRS. JOHNSON
KARL LINDNER
BOBO
MOVING MEN

The action of the play is set in Chicago's Southside, sometime between World War II and the present.

Act I
Scene One: *Friday morning.*
Scene Two: *The following morning.*
Act II
Scene One: *Later, the same day.*
Scene Two: *Friday night, a few weeks later.*
Scene Three: *Moving day, one week later.*
Act III
An hour later.

ACT I

Scene I

The YOUNGER *living room would be a comfortable and well-ordered room if it were not for a number of indestructible contradictions to this state of being. Its furnishings are typical and undistinguished and their primary feature now is that they have clearly had to accommodate the living of too many people for too many years—and they are tired. Still, we can see that at some time, a time probably no longer remembered by the family (except perhaps for* MAMA*), the furnishings of this room were actually selected with care and love and even hope—and brought to this apartment and arranged with taste and pride.*

That was a long time ago. Now the once loved pattern of the couch upholstery has to fight to show itself from under acres of crocheted doilies and couch covers which have themselves finally come to be more important than the upholstery. And here a table or a chair has been moved to disguise the worn places in the carpet; but the carpet has fought back by showing its weariness, with depressing uniformity, elsewhere on its surface.

Weariness has, in fact, won in this room. Everything has been polished, washed, sat on, used, scrubbed too often. All pretenses but living itself have long since vanished from the very atmosphere of this room.

Moreover, a section of this room, for it is not really a room unto itself, though the landlord's lease would make it seem so, slopes backward to provide a small kitchen area, where the family prepares the meals that are eaten in the living room proper, which must also serve as dining room. The single window that has been provided for these "two" rooms is located in this kitchen area. The sole natural light the family may enjoy in the course of a day is only that which fights its way through this little window.

At left, a door leads to a bedroom which is shared by MAMA *and her daughter,* BENEATHA. *At right, opposite, is a second room (which in the beginning of the life of this apartment was probably a breakfast room) which serves as a bedroom for* WALTER *and his wife,* RUTH.

Time: *Sometime between World War II and the present.*

Place: *Chicago's Southside.*

At Rise: It is morning dark in the living room. TRAVIS *is asleep on the make-down bed at center. An alarm clock sounds from within the bedroom at right, and presently* RUTH *enters from that room and closes the door behind her. She crosses sleepily toward the window. As she passes her sleeping son she reaches down and shakes him a little. At the window she raises the shade and a dusky Southside morning light comes in feebly. She fills a pot with water and puts it on to boil. She calls to the boy, between yawns, in a slightly muffled voice.*

RUTH *is about thirty. We can see that she was a pretty girl, even exceptionally so, but now it is apparent that life has been little that she expected, and disappointment has already begun to hang in her face. In a few years, before thirty-five even, she will be known among her people as a "settled woman."*

She crosses to her son and gives him a good, final, rousing shake.

RUTH: Come on now, boy, it's seven thirty! (*Her son sits up at last, in a stupor of sleepiness*) I say hurry up, Travis! You ain't the only person in the world got to use a bathroom! (*The child, a sturdy, handsome little boy of ten or eleven, drags himself out of the bed and almost blindly takes his towels and "today's clothes" from drawers and a closet and goes out to the bathroom, which is in an outside hall and which is shared by another family or families on the same floor.* RUTH *crosses to the bedroom door at right and opens it and calls in to her husband*) Walter Lee! . . . It's after seven thirty! Lemme see you do some waking up in there now! (*She waits*) You better get up from there, man! It's after seven thirty I tell you. (*She waits again*) All right, you just go ahead and lay there and next thing you know Travis be finished and Mr. Johnson'll be in there and you'll be fussing and cussing round here like a madman! And be late too! (*She waits, at the end of patience*) Walter Lee—it's time for you to GET UP!

(*She waits another second and then starts to go into the bedroom, but is apparently satisfied that her husband has begun to get up. She stops, pulls the door to, and returns to the kitchen area. She wipes her face with a moist cloth and runs her fingers through her sleep-disheveled hair in a vain effort and ties an apron around her housecoat. The bedroom door at right opens and her husband stands in the doorway in his pajamas, which are rumpled and mismated. He is a lean, intense young man in his middle thirties, inclined to quick nervous movements and erratic speech habits—and always in his voice there is a quality of indictment.*)

WALTER: Is he out yet?

RUTH: What you mean *out*? He ain't hardly got in there good yet.

WALTER (*wandering in, still more oriented to sleep than to a new day*): Well, what was you doing all that yelling for if I can't even get in there yet? (*Stopping and thinking*) Check coming today?

RUTH: They *said* Saturday and this is just Friday and I hopes to God you ain't going to get up here first thing this morning and start talking to me 'bout no money—'cause I 'bout don't want to hear it.

WALTER: Something the matter with you this morning?

RUTH: No—I'm just sleepy as the devil. What kind of eggs you want?

WALTER: Not scrambled. (RUTH *starts to scramble eggs*) Paper come? (RUTH *points impatiently to the rolled up* Tribune *on the table, and he gets it and spreads it out and vaguely reads the front page*) Set off another bomb yesterday.

RUTH (*maximum indifference*): Did they?

WALTER (*looking up*): What's the matter with you?

RUTH: Ain't nothing the matter with me. And don't keep asking me that this morning.

WALTER: Ain't nobody bothering you. (*Reading the news of the day absently again*) Say Colonel McCormick is sick.

RUTH (*affecting tea-party interest*): Is he now? Poor thing.

WALTER (*sighing and looking at his watch*): Oh, me. (*He waits*) Now what is that boy doing in that bathroom all this time? He just going to have to start getting up earlier. I can't be being late to work on account of him fooling around in there.

RUTH (*turning on him*): Oh, no he ain't going to be getting up no earlier no such thing! It ain't his fault that he can't get to bed no earlier nights 'cause he got a bunch of crazy good-for-nothing clowns sitting up running their mouths in what is supposed to be his bedroom after ten o'clock at night . . .

WALTER: That's what you mad about, ain't it? The things I want to talk about with my friends just couldn't be important in your mind, could they?

(He rises and finds a cigarette in her handbag on the table and crosses to the little window and looks out, smoking and deeply enjoying this first one)

RUTH *(almost matter of factly, a complaint too automatic to deserve emphasis)*: Why you always got to smoke before you eat in the morning?

WALTER *(at the window)*: Just look at 'em down there . . . Running and racing to work . . . *(He turns and faces his wife and watches her a moment at the stove, and then, suddenly)* You look young this morning, baby.

RUTH *(indifferently)*: Yeah?

WALTER: Just for a second—stirring them eggs. Just for a second it was—you looked real young again. *(He reaches for her; she crosses away. Then, drily)* It's gone now—you look like yourself again!

RUTH: Man, if you don't shut up and leave me alone.

WALTER *(looking out to the street again)*: First thing a man ought to learn in life is not to make love to no colored woman first thing in the morning. You all some eeeevil people at eight o'clock in the morning.

(TRAVIS appears in the hall doorway, almost fully dressed and quite wide awake now, his towels and pajamas across his shoulders. He opens the door and signals for his father to make the bathroom in a hurry)

TRAVIS *(watching the bathroom)*: Daddy, come on!

(WALTER gets his bathroom utensils and flies out to the bathroom)

RUTH: Sit down and have your breakfast, Travis.

TRAVIS: Mama, this is Friday. *(Gleefully)* Check coming tomorrow, huh?

RUTH: You get your mind off money and eat your breakfast.

TRAVIS *(eating)*: This is the morning we supposed to bring the fifty cents to school.

RUTH: Well, I ain't got no fifty cents this morning.

TRAVIS: Teacher say we have to.

RUTH: I don't care what teacher say. I ain't got it. Eat your breakfast, Travis.

TRAVIS: I *am* eating.

RUTH: Hush up now and just eat!

(The boy gives her an exasperated look for her lack of understanding, and eats grudgingly)

TRAVIS: You think Grandmama would have it?

RUTH: No! And I want you to stop asking your grandmother for money, you hear me?

TRAVIS *(outraged)*: Gaaaleee! I don't ask her, she just gimme it sometimes!

RUTH: Travis Willard Younger—I got too much on me this morning to be—

TRAVIS: Maybe Daddy—

RUTH: *Travis!*

(The boy hushes abruptly. They are both quiet and tense for several seconds)

TRAVIS *(presently)*: Could I maybe go carry some groceries in front of the supermarket for a little while after school then?

RUTH: Just hush, I said. *(TRAVIS jabs his spoon into his cereal bowl viciously, and rests his head in anger upon his fists)* If you through eating, you can get over there and make up your bed.

(*The boy obeys stiffly and crosses the room, almost mechanically, to the bed and more or less folds the bedding into a heap, then angrily gets his books and cap*)

TRAVIS (*sulking and standing apart from her unnaturally*): I'm gone.

RUTH (*looking up from the stove to inspect him automatically*): Come here. (*He crosses to her and she studies his head*) If you don't take this comb and fix this here head, you better! (TRAVIS *puts down his books with a great sigh of oppression, and crosses to the mirror. His mother mutters under her breath about his "slubbornness"*) 'Bout to march out of here with that head looking just like chickens slept in it! I just don't know where you get your slubborn ways . . . And get your jacket, too. Looks chilly out this morning.

TRAVIS (*with conspicuously brushed hair and jacket*): I'm gone.

RUTH: Get carfare and milk money—(*Waving one finger*)—and not a single penny for no caps, you hear me?

TRAVIS (*with sullen politeness*): Yes'm.

(*He turns in outrage to leave. His mother watches after him as in his frustration he approaches the door almost comically. When she speaks to him, her voice has become a very gentle tease*)

RUTH (*mocking; as she thinks he would say it*): Oh, Mama makes me so mad sometimes, I don't know what to do! (*She waits and continues to his back as he stands stock-still in front of the door*) I wouldn't kiss that woman good-bye for nothing in this world this morning! (*The boy finally turns around and rolls his eyes at her, knowing the mood has changed and he is vindicated; he does not, however, move toward her yet*) Not for nothing in this world! (*She finally laughs aloud at him and holds out her arms to him and we see that it is a way between them, very old and practiced. He crosses to her and allows her to embrace him warmly but keeps his face fixed with masculine rigidity. She holds him back from her presently and looks at him and runs her fingers over the features of his face. With utter gentleness—*) Now—whose little old angry man are you?

TRAVIS (*the masculinity and gruffness start to fade at last*): Aw gaalee—Mama . . .

RUTH (*Mimicking*): Aw—gaaaalleeeee, Mama! (*She pushes him, with rough playfulness and finality, toward the door*) Get on out of here or you going to be late.

TRAVIS (*in the face of love, new aggressiveness*): Mama, could I *please* go carry groceries?

RUTH: Honey, it's starting to get so cold evenings.

WALTER (*coming in from the bathroom and drawing a make-believe gun from a make-believe holster and shooting at his son*): What is it he wants to do?

RUTH: Go carry groceries after school at the supermarket.

WALTER: Well, let him go . . .

TRAVIS (*quickly, to the ally*): I *have* to—she won't gimme the fifty cents . . .

WALTER (*to his wife only*): Why not?

RUTH (*simply, and with flavor*): 'Cause we don't have it.

WALTER (*to* RUTH *only*): What you tell the boy things like that for? (*Reaching down into his pants with a rather important gesture*) Here, son—

(*He hands the boy the coin, but his eyes are directed to his wife's.* TRAVIS *takes the money happily*)

TRAVIS: Thanks, Daddy.

(*He starts out.* RUTH *watches both of them with murder in her eyes.* WALTER *stands and stares back at her with defiance, and suddenly reaches into his pocket again on an afterthought*)

WALTER (*without even looking at his son, still staring hard at his wife*): In fact, here's another fifty cents . . . Buy yourself some fruit today—or take a taxicab to school or something!

TRAVIS: Whoopee—

(*He leaps up and clasps his father around the middle with his legs, and they face each other in mutual appreciation; slowly* WALTER LEE *peeks around the boy to catch the violent rays from his wife's eyes and draws his head back as if shot*)

WALTER: You better get down now—and get to school, man.

TRAVIS (*at the door*): O.K. Good-bye.

(*He exits*)

WALTER (*after him, pointing with pride*): That's *my* boy. (*She looks at him in disgust and turns back to her work*) You know what I was thinking 'bout in the bathroom this morning?

RUTH: No.

WALTER: How come you always try to be so pleasant!

RUTH: What is there to be pleasant 'bout!

WALTER: You want to know what I was thinking 'bout in the bathroom or not!

RUTH: I know what you thinking 'bout.

WALTER (*ignoring her*): 'Bout what me and Willy Harris was talking about last night.

RUTH (*immediately—a refrain*): Willy Harris is a good-for-nothing loudmouth.

WALTER: Anybody who talks to me has got to be a good-for-nothing loudmouth, ain't he? And what you know about who is just a good-for-nothing loudmouth? Charlie Atkins was just a "good-for-nothing loudmouth" too, wasn't he! When he wanted me to go in the dry-cleaning business with him. And now—he's grossing a hundred thousand a year. A hundred thousand dollars a year! You still call *him* a loudmouth!

RUTH (*bitterly*): Oh, Walter Lee . . .

(*She folds her head on her arms over the table*)

WALTER (*rising and coming to her and standing over her*): You tired, ain't you? Tired of everything. Me, the boy, the way we live—this beat-up hole—everything. Ain't you? (*She doesn't look up, doesn't answer*) So tired—moaning and groaning all the time, but you wouldn't do nothing to help, would you? You couldn't be on my side that long for nothing, could you?

RUTH: Walter, please leave me alone.

WALTER: A man needs for a woman to back him up . . .

RUTH: Walter—

WALTER: Mama would listen to you. You know she listen to you more than she do me and Bennie. She think more of you. All you have to do is just sit down with her when you drinking your coffee one morning and talking 'bout things like you do and—(*He sits down beside her and demonstrates graphically what he thinks her methods and tone should be*)—you just sip your coffee, see, and say easy like that you been thinking 'bout that deal Walter Lee is so interested in, 'bout the store and all, and sip some more coffee, like what you saying ain't really that important to you—And the next thing you know, she be listening good and asking you questions and when I come home—I can tell her the details. This ain't no fly-by-night proposition, baby. I mean we figured it out, me and Willy and Bobo.

RUTH (*with a frown*): Bobo?

WALTER: Yeah. You see, this little liquor store we got in mind cost seventy-five thousand and we figured the initial investment on the place be 'bout thirty thousand, see. That be ten thousand each. Course, there's a couple of hundred you got to pay so's you don't spend your life just waiting for them clowns to let your license get approved—

RUTH: You mean graft?

WALTER (*frowning impatiently*): Don't call it that. See there, that just goes to show you what women understand about the world. Baby, don't *nothing* happen for you in this world 'less you pay *somebody* off!

RUTH: Walter, leave me alone! (*She raises her head and stares at him vigorously—then says, more quietly*) *Eat* your eggs, they gonna be cold.

WALTER (*straightening up from her and looking off*): That's it. There you are. Man say to his woman: I got me a dream. His woman say: Eat your eggs. (*Sadly, but gaining in power*) Man say: I got to take hold of this here world, baby! And a woman will say: Eat your eggs and go to work. (*Passionately now*) Man say: I got to change my life, I'm choking to death, baby! And his woman say—(*In utter anguish as he brings his fists down on his thighs*)—Your eggs is getting cold!

RUTH (*softly*): Walter, that ain't none of our money.

WALTER (*not listening at all or even looking at her*): This morning, I was lookin' in the mirror and thinking about it . . . I'm thirty-five years old; I been married eleven years and I got a boy who sleeps in the living room—(*Very, very quietly*)—and all I got to give him is stories about how rich white people live . . .

RUTH: Eat your eggs, Walter.

WALTER (*slams the table and jumps up*): —DAMN MY EGGS—DAMN ALL THE EGGS THAT EVER WAS!

RUTH: Then go to work.

WALTER (*looking up at her*): See—I'm trying to talk to you 'bout myself—(*Shaking his head with the repetition*)—and all you can say is eat them eggs and go to work.

RUTH (*wearily*): Honey, you never say nothing new. I listen to you every day, every night and every morning, and you never say nothing new. (*Shrugging*) So you would rather *be* Mr. Arnold than be his chauffeur. So—I would *rather* be living in Buckingham Palace.

WALTER: That is just what is wrong with the colored woman in this world . . . Don't understand about building their men up and making 'em feel like they somebody. Like they can do something.

RUTH (*drily, but to hurt*): There *are* colored men who do things.

WALTER: No thanks to the colored woman.

RUTH: Well, being a colored woman, I guess I can't help myself none.

(*She rises and gets the ironing board and sets it up and attacks a huge pile of rough-dried clothes, sprinkling them in preparation for the ironing and then rolling them into tight fat balls*)

WALTER (*mumbling*): We one group of men tied to a race of women with small minds!

(His sister BENEATHA *enters. She is about twenty, as slim and intense as her brother. She is not as pretty as her sister-in-law, but her lean, almost intellectual face has a handsomeness of its own. She wears a bright-red flannel nightie, and her thick hair stands wildly about her head. Her speech is a mixture of many things; it is different from the rest of the family's insofar as education has permeated her sense of English—and perhaps the Midwest rather than the South has finally—at last—won out in her inflection; but not altogether, because over all of it is a soft slurring and transformed use of vowels which is the decided influence of the Southside. She passes through the room without looking at either* RUTH *or* WALTER *and goes to the outside door and looks, a little blindly, out to the bathroom. She sees that it has been lost to the Johnsons. She closes the door with a sleepy vengeance and crosses to the table and sits down a little defeated)*

BENEATHA: I am going to start timing those people.

WALTER: You should get up earlier.

BENEATHA *(her face in her hands. She is still fighting the urge to go back to bed)*: Really—would you suggest dawn? Where's the paper?

WALTER *(pushing the paper across the table to her as he studies her almost clinically, as though he has never seen her before)*: You a horrible-looking chick at this hour.

BENEATHA *(drily)*: Good morning, everybody.

WALTER *(senselessly)*: How is school coming?

BENEATHA *(in the same spirit)*: Lovely. Lovely. And you know, biology is the greatest. *(Looking up at him)* I dissected something that looked just like you yesterday.

WALTER: I just wondered if you've made up your mind and everything.

BENEATHA *(gaining in sharpness and impatience)*: And what did I answer yesterday morning—and the day before that?

RUTH *(from the ironing board, like someone disinterested and old)*: Don't be so nasty, Bennie.

BENEATHA *(still to her brother)*: And the day before that and the day before that!

WALTER *(defensively)*: I'm interested in you. Something wrong with that? Ain't many girls who decide—

WALTER *and* BENEATHA *(in unison)*: —"to be a doctor."

(Silence)

WALTER: Have we figured out yet just exactly how much medical school is going to cost?

RUTH: Walter Lee, why don't you leave that girl alone and get out of here to work?

BENEATHA *(exits to the bathroom and bangs on the door)*: Come on out of there, please!

(She comes back into the room)

WALTER *(looking at his sister intently)*: You know the check is coming tomorrow.

BENEATHA *(turning on him with a sharpness all her own)*: That money belongs to Mama, Walter, and it's for her to decide how she wants to use it. I don't care if she wants to buy a house or a rocket ship or just nail it up somewhere and look at it. It's hers. Not ours—*hers.*

WALTER *(bitterly)*: Now ain't that fine! You just got your mother's interest at heart, ain't you, girl? You such a nice girl—but if Mama got that money she can always take a few thousand and help you through school too—can't she?

BENEATHA: I have never asked anyone around here to do anything for me!

WALTER: No! And the line between asking and just accepting when the time comes is big and wide—ain't it!

BENEATHA (*with fury*): What do you want from me, Brother—that I quit school or just drop dead, which!

WALTER: I don't want nothing but for you to stop acting holy 'round here. Me and Ruth done made some sacrifices for you—why can't you do something for the family?

RUTH: Walter, don't be dragging me in it.

WALTER: You are in it—Don't you get up and go work in somebody's kitchen for the last three years to help put clothes on her back?

RUTH: Oh, Walter—that's not fair . . .

WALTER: It ain't that nobody expects you to get on your knees and say thank you, Brother; thank you, Ruth; thank you, Mama—and thank you, Travis, for wearing the same pair of shoes for two semesters—

BENEATHA (*dropping to her knees*): Well—I *do*—all right?—thank everybody! And forgive me for ever wanting to be anything at all! (*Pursuing him on her knees across the floor*) FORGIVE ME, FORGIVE ME, FORGIVE ME!

RUTH: Please stop it! Your mama'll hear you.

WALTER: Who the hell told you you had to be a doctor? If you so crazy 'bout messing 'round with sick people—then go be a nurse like other women—or just get married and be quiet . . .

BENEATHA: Well—you finally got it said . . . It took you three years but you finally got it said. Walter, give up; leave me alone—it's Mama's money.

WALTER: *He was my father, too!*

BENEATHA: So what? He was mine, too—and Travis' grandfather—but the insurance money belongs to Mama. Picking on me is not going to make her give it to you to invest in any liquor stores—(*Underbreath, dropping into a chair*)—and I for one say, God bless Mama for that!

WALTER (*to* RUTH): See—did you hear? Did you hear!

RUTH: Honey, please go to work.

WALTER: Nobody in this house is ever going to understand me.

BENEATHA: Because you're a nut.

WALTER: Who's a nut?

BENEATHA: You—you are a nut. Thee is mad, boy.

WALTER (*looking at his wife and his sister from the door, very sadly*): The world's most backward race of people, and that's a fact.

BENEATHA (*turning slowly in her chair*): And then there are all those prophets who would lead us out of the wilderness—(WALTER *slams out of the house*)—into the swamps!

RUTH: Bennie, why you always gotta be pickin' on your brother? Can't you be a little sweeter sometimes? (*Door opens.* WALTER *walks in. He fumbles with his cap, starts to speak, clears throat, looks everywhere but at* RUTH. *Finally:*)

WALTER (*to* RUTH): I need some money for carfare.

RUTH (*looks at him, then warms; teasing, but tenderly*): Fifty cents? (*She goes to her bag and gets money*) Here—take a taxi!

(WALTER *exits.* MAMA *enters. She is a woman in her early sixties, full-bodied and strong. She is one of those women of a certain grace and beauty who wear it so unobtrusively that it takes a while to notice. Her dark-brown face is surrounded by the total whiteness of her hair, and, being a woman who has adjusted to many things in life and overcome many more, her face is full of strength. She has, we can see, wit and faith of a kind that keep her eyes lit and full of interest and expectancy. She is, in a word, a beautiful woman. Her bearing is perhaps most like the noble bearing of the women of the Hereros of Southwest Africa—rather as if she imagines that as she walks she still bears a basket or a vessel upon her head. Her speech, on the other hand, is as careless as her carriage is precise—she is inclined to slur everything—but her voice is perhaps not so much quiet as simply soft)*

MAMA: Who that 'round here slamming doors at this hour?

(*She crosses through the room, goes to the window, opens it, and brings in a feeble little plant growing doggedly in a small pot on the window sill. She feels the dirt and puts it back out*)

RUTH: That was Walter Lee. He and Bennie was at it again.

MAMA: My children and they tempers. Lord, if this little old plant don't get more sun than it's been getting it ain't never going to see spring again. (*She turns from the window*) What's the matter with you this morning, Ruth? You looks right peaked. You aiming to iron all them things? Leave some for me. I'll get to 'em this afternoon. Bennie honey, it's too drafty for you to be sitting 'round half dressed. Where's your robe?

BENEATHA: In the cleaners.

MAMA: Well, go get mine and put it on.

BENEATHA: I'm not cold, Mama, honest.

MAMA: I know—but you so thin . . .

BENEATHA (*irritably*): Mama, I'm not cold.

MAMA (*seeing the make-down bed as* TRAVIS *has left it*): Lord have mercy, look at that poor bed. Bless his heart—he tries, don't he?

(*She moves to the bed* TRAVIS *has sloppily made up*)

RUTH: No—he don't half try at all 'cause he knows you going to come along behind him and fix everything. That's just how come he don't know how to do nothing right now—you done spoiled that boy so.

MAMA (*folding bedding*): Well—he's a little boy. Ain't supposed to know 'bout housekeeping. My baby, that's what he is. What you fix for his breakfast this morning?

RUTH (*angrily*): I feed my son, Lena!

MAMA: I ain't meddling—(*Underbreath; busy-bodyish*) I just noticed all last week he had cold cereal, and when it starts getting this chilly in the fall a child ought to have some hot grits or something when he goes out in the cold—

RUTH (*furious*): I gave him hot oats—is that all right!

MAMA: I ain't meddling. (*Pause*) Put a lot of nice butter on it? (RUTH *shoots her an angry look and does not reply*) He likes lots of butter.

RUTH (*exasperated*): Lena—

MAMA (*to* BENEATHA. MAMA *is inclined to wander conversationally sometimes*): What was you and your brother fussing 'bout this morning?

BENEATHA: It's not important, Mama.

(*She gets up and goes to look out at the bathroom, which is apparently free, and she picks up her towels and rushes out*)

MAMA: What was they fighting about?

RUTH: Now you know as well as I do.

MAMA (*shaking her head*): Brother still worrying hisself sick about that money?

RUTH: You know he is.

MAMA: You had breakfast?

RUTH: Some coffee.

MAMA: Girl, you better start eating and looking after yourself better. You almost thin as Travis.

RUTH: Lena—

MAMA: Uh-hunh?

RUTH: What are you going to do with it?

MAMA: Now don't you start, child. It's too early in the morning to be talking about money. It ain't Christian.

RUTH: It's just that he got his heart set on that store—

MAMA: You mean that liquor store that Willy Harris want him to invest in?

RUTH: Yes—

MAMA: We ain't no business people, Ruth. We just plain working folks.

RUTH: Ain't nobody business people till they go into business. Walter Lee say colored people ain't never going to start getting ahead till they start gambling on some different kinds of things in the world—investments and things.

MAMA: What done got into you, girl? Walter Lee done finally sold you on investing.

RUTH: No. Mama, something is happening between Walter and me. I don't know what it is—but he needs something—something I can't give him any more. He needs this chance, Lena.

MAMA (*frowning deeply*): But liquor, honey—

RUTH: Well—like Walter say—I spec people going to always be drinking themselves some liquor.

MAMA: Well—whether they drinks it or not ain't none of my business. But whether I go into business selling it to 'em *is*, and I don't want that on my ledger this late in life. (*Stopping suddenly and studying her daughter-in-law*) Ruth Younger, what's the matter with you today? You look like you could fall over right there.

RUTH: I'm tired.

MAMA: Then you better stay home from work today.

RUTH: I can't stay home. She'd be calling up the agency and screaming at them, "My girl didn't come in today—send me somebody! My girl didn't come in!" Oh, she just have a fit . . .

MAMA: Well, let her have it. I'll just call her up and say you got the flu—

RUTH (*laughing*): Why the flu?

MAMA: 'Cause it sounds respectable to 'em. Something white people get, too. They know 'bout the flu. Otherwise they think you been cut up or something when you tell 'em you sick.

RUTH: I got to go in. We need the money.

MAMA: Somebody would of thought my children done all but starved to death the way they talk about money here late. Child, we got a great big old check coming tomorrow.

RUTH (*sincerely, but also self-righteously*): Now that's your money. It ain't got nothing to do with me. We all feel like that—Walter and Bennie and me—even Travis.

MAMA (*thoughtfully, and suddenly very far away*): Ten thousand dollars—

RUTH: Sure is wonderful.

MAMA: Ten thousand dollars.

RUTH: You know what you should do, Miss Lena? You should take yourself a trip somewhere. To Europe or South America or someplace—

MAMA (*throwing up her hands at the thought*): Oh, child!

RUTH: I'm serious. Just pack up and leave! Go on away and enjoy yourself some. Forget about the family and have yourself a ball for once in your life—

MAMA (*drily*): You sound like I'm just about ready to die. Who'd go with me? What I look like wandering 'round Europe by myself?

RUTH: Shoot—these here rich white women do it all the time. They don't think nothing of packing up they suitcases and piling on one of them big steamships and—swoosh!—they gone, child.

MAMA: Something always told me I wasn't no rich white woman.

RUTH: Well—what are you going to do with it then?

MAMA: I ain't rightly decided. (*Thinking. She speaks now with emphasis*) Some of it got to be put away for Beneatha and her schoolin'—and ain't nothing going to touch that part of it. Nothing. (*She waits several seconds, trying to make up her mind about something, and looks at* RUTH *a little tentatively before going on*) Been thinking that we maybe could meet the notes on a little old two-story somewhere, with a yard where Travis could play in the summertime, if we use part of the insurance for a down payment and everybody kind of pitch in. I could maybe take on a little day work again, few days a week—

RUTH (*studying her mother-in-law furtively and concentrating on her ironing, anxious to encourage without seeming to*): Well, Lord knows, we've put enough rent into this here rat trap to pay for four houses by now . . .

MAMA (*looking up at the words "rat trap" and then looking around and leaning back and sighing—in a suddenly reflective mood—*): "Rat trap"—yes, that's all it is. (*Smiling*) I remember just as well the day me and Big Walter moved in here. Hadn't been married but two weeks and wasn't planning on living here no more than a year. (*She shakes her head at the dissolved dream*) We was going to set away, little by little, don't you know, and buy a little place out in Morgan Park. We had even picked out the house. (*Chuckling a little*) Looks right dumpy today. But Lord, child, you should know all the dreams I had 'bout buying that house and fixing it up and making me a little garden in the back—(*She waits and stops smiling*) And didn't none of it happen.

(*Dropping her hands in a futile gesture*)

RUTH (*keeps her head down, ironing*): Yes, life can be a barrel of disappointments, sometimes.

MAMA: Honey, Big Walter would come in here some nights back then and slump down on that couch there and just look at the rug, and look at me and look at the rug and then back at me—and I'd know he was down then . . . really down. (*After a second very long and thoughtful pause; she is seeing back to times that only she can see*) And then, Lord, when I lost that baby—little Claude—I almost thought I was going to lose Big Walter too. Oh, that man grieved hisself! He was one man to love his children.

RUTH: Ain't nothin' can tear at you like losin' your baby.

MAMA: I guess that's how come that man finally worked hisself to death like he done. Like he was fighting his own war with this here world that took his baby from him.

RUTH: He sure was a fine man, all right. I always liked Mr. Younger.

MAMA: Crazy 'bout his children! God knows there was plenty wrong with Walter Younger—hard-headed, mean, kind of wild with women—plenty wrong with him. But he sure loved his children. Always wanted them to have something—be something. That's where Brother gets all these notions, I reckon. Big Walter used to say, he'd get right wet in the eyes sometimes, lean his head back with the water standing in his eyes and say, "Seem like God didn't see fit to give the black man nothing but dreams—but He did give us children to make them dreams seem worth while." (*She smiles*) He could talk like that, don't you know.

RUTH: Yes, he sure could. He was a good man, Mr. Younger.

MAMA: Yes, a fine man—just couldn't never catch up with his dreams, that's all.

(BENEATHA *comes in, brushing her hair and looking up to the ceiling, where the sound of a vacuum cleaner has started up*)

BENEATHA: What could be so dirty on that woman's rugs that she has to vacuum them every single day?

RUTH: I wish certain young women 'round here who I could name would take inspiration about certain rugs in a certain apartment I could also mention.

BENEATHA (*shrugging*): How much cleaning can a house need, for Christ's sakes.

MAMA (*not liking the Lord's name used thus*): Bennie!

RUTH: Just listen to her—just listen!

BENEATHA: Oh, God!

MAMA: If you use the Lord's name just one more time—

BENEATHA (*a bit of a whine*): Oh, Mama—

RUTH: Fresh—just fresh as salt, this girl!

BENEATHA (*drily*): Well—if the salt loses its savor—

MAMA: Now that will do. I just ain't going to have you 'round here reciting the scriptures in vain—you hear me?

BENEATHA: How did I manage to get on everybody's wrong side by just walking into a room?

RUTH: If you weren't so fresh—

BENEATHA: Ruth, I'm twenty years old.

MAMA: What time you be home from school today?

BENEATHA: Kind of late. (*With enthusiasm*) Madeline is going to start my guitar lessons today.

(MAMA *and* RUTH *look up with the same expression*)

MAMA: Your *what* kind of lessons?

BENEATHA: Guitar.

RUTH: Oh, Father!

MAMA: How come you done taken it in your mind to learn to play the guitar?

BENEATHA: I just want to, that's all.

MAMA (*smiling*): Lord, child, don't you know what to do with yourself? How long it going to be before you get tired of this now—like you got tired of that little play-acting group you joined last year? (*Looking at* RUTH) And what was it the year before that?

RUTH: The horseback-riding club for which she bought that fifty-five-dollar riding habit that's been hanging in the closet ever since!

MAMA (*to* BENEATHA): Why you got to flit so from one thing to another, baby?

BENEATHA (*sharply*): I just want to learn to play the guitar. Is there anything wrong with that?

MAMA: Ain't nobody trying to stop you. I just wonders sometimes why you has to flit so from one thing to another all the time. You ain't never done nothing with all that camera equipment you brought home—

BENEATHA: I don't flit! I—I experiment with different forms of expression—

RUTH: Like riding a horse?

BENEATHA: —People have to express themselves one way or another.

MAMA: What is it you want to express?

BENEATHA (*angrily*): Me! (MAMA *and* RUTH *look at each other and burst into raucous laughter*) Don't worry—I don't expect you to understand.

MAMA (*to change the subject*): Who you going out with tomorrow night?

BENEATHA (*with displeasure*): George Murchison again.

MAMA (*pleased*): Oh—you getting a little sweet on him?

RUTH: You ask me, this child ain't sweet on nobody but herself—(*Underbreath*) Express herself!

(*They laugh*)

BENEATHA: Oh—I like George all right, Mama. I mean I like him enough to go out with him and stuff, but—

RUTH (*for devilment*): What does *and stuff* mean?

BENEATHA: Mind your own business.

MAMA: Stop picking at her now, Ruth. (*She chuckles—then a suspicious sudden look at her daughter as she turns in her chair for emphasis*) What DOES it mean?

BENEATHA (*wearily*): Oh, I just mean I couldn't ever really be serious about George. He's—he's so shallow.

RUTH: Shallow—what do you mean he's shallow? He's *Rich!*

MAMA: Hush, Ruth.

BENEATHA: I know he's rich. He knows he's rich, too.

RUTH: Well—what other qualities a man got to have to satisfy you, little girl?

BENEATHA: You wouldn't even begin to understand. Anybody who married Walter could not possibly understand.

MAMA (*outraged*): What kind of way is that to talk about your brother?

BENEATHA: Brother is a flip—let's face it.

MAMA (*to* RUTH, *helplessly*): What's a flip?

RUTH (*glad to add kindling*): She's saying he's crazy.

BENEATHA: Not crazy. Brother isn't really crazy yet—he—he's an elaborate neurotic.

MAMA: Hush your mouth!

BENEATHA: As for George. Well. George looks good—he's got a beautiful car and he takes me to nice places and, as my sister-in-law says, he is probably the richest boy I will ever get to know and I even like him sometimes—but if the Youngers are sitting around waiting to see if their little Bennie is going to tie up the family with the Murchisons, they are wasting their time.

RUTH: You mean you wouldn't marry George Murchison if he asked you someday? That pretty, rich thing? Honey, I knew you was odd—

BENEATHA: No I would not marry him if all I felt for him was what I feel now. Besides, George's family wouldn't really like it.

MAMA: Why not?

BENEATHA: Oh, Mama—The Murchisons are honest-to-God-real-*live*-rich colored people, and the only people in the world who are more snobbish than rich white people are rich colored people. I thought everybody knew that. I've met Mrs. Murchison. She's a scene!

MAMA: You must not dislike people 'cause they well off, honey.

BENEATHA: Why not? It makes just as much sense as disliking people 'cause they are poor, and lots of people do that.

RUTH (*a wisdom-of-the-ages manner. To* MAMA): Well, she'll get over some of this—

BENEATHA: Get over it? What are you talking about, Ruth? Listen, I'm going to be a doctor. I'm not worried about who I'm going to marry yet—if I ever get married.

MAMA *and* RUTH: *If!*

MAMA: Now, Bennie—

BENEATHA: Oh, I probably will . . . but first I'm going to be a doctor, and George, for one, still thinks that's pretty funny. I couldn't be bothered with that. I am going to be a doctor and everybody around here better understand that!

MAMA (*kindly*): 'Course you going to be a doctor, honey, God willing.

BENEATHA (*drily*): God hasn't got a thing to do with it.

MAMA: Beneatha—that just wasn't necessary.

BENEATHA: Well—neither is God. I get sick of hearing about God.

MAMA: Beneatha!

BENEATHA: I mean it! I'm just tired of hearing about God all the time. What has He got to do with anything? Does he pay tuition?

MAMA: You 'bout to get your fresh little jaw slapped!

RUTH: That's just what she needs, all right!

BENEATHA: Why? Why can't I say what I want to around here, like everybody else?

MAMA: It don't sound nice for a young girl to say things like that—you wasn't brought up that way. Me and your father went to trouble to get you and Brother to church every Sunday.

BENEATHA: Mama, you don't understand. It's all a matter of ideas, and God is just one idea I don't accept. It's not important. I am not going out and be immoral or commit crimes because I don't believe in God. I don't even think about it. It's just that I get tired of Him getting credit for all the things the human race achieves through its own stubborn effort. There simply is no blasted God—there is only man and it is *he* who makes miracles!

(MAMA *absorbs this speech, studies her daughter and rises slowly and crosses to* BENEATHA *and slaps her powerfully across the face. After, there is only silence and the daughter drops her eyes from her mother's face, and* MAMA *is very tall before her*)

MAMA: Now—you say after me, in my mother's house there is still God. (*There is a long pause and* BENEATHA *stares at the floor wordlessly.* MAMA *repeats the phrase with precision and cool emotion*) In my mother's house there is still God.

BENEATHA: In my mother's house there is still God.

(*A long pause*)

MAMA (*walking away from* BENEATHA, *too disturbed for triumphant posture. Stopping and turning back to her daughter*): There are some ideas we ain't going to have in this house. Not long as I am at the head of this family.

BENEATHA: Yes, ma'am.

(MAMA *walks out of the room*)

RUTH (*almost gently, with profound understanding*): You think you a woman, Bennie—but you still a little girl. What you did was childish—so you got treated like a child.

BENEATHA: I see. (*Quietly*) I also see that everybody thinks it's all right for Mama to be a tyrant. But all the tyranny in the world will never put a God in the heavens!

(*She picks up her books and goes out. Pause*)

RUTH (*goes to* MAMA*'s door*): She said she was sorry.

MAMA (*coming out, going to her plant*): They frightens me, Ruth. My children.

RUTH: You got good children, Lena. They just a little off sometimes—but they're good.

MAMA: No—there's something come down between me and them that don't let us understand each other and I don't know what it is. One done almost lost his mind thinking 'bout money all the time and the other done commence to talk about things I can't seem to understand in no form or fashion. What is it that's changing, Ruth?

RUTH (*soothingly, older than her years*): Now . . . you taking it all too seriously. You just got strong-willed children and it takes a strong woman like you to keep 'em in hand.

MAMA (*looking at her plant and sprinkling a little water on it*): They spirited all right, my children. Got to admit they got spirit—Bennie and Walter. Like this little old plant that ain't never had enough sunshine or nothing—and look at it . . .

(*She has her back to* RUTH, *who has had to stop ironing and lean against something and put the back of her hand to her forehead*)

RUTH (*trying to keep* MAMA *from noticing*): You . . . sure . . . loves that little old thing, don't you? . . .

MAMA: Well, I always wanted me a garden like I used to see sometimes at the back of the houses down home. This plant is close as I ever got to having one. (*She looks out of the window as she replaces the plant*) Lord, ain't nothing as dreary as the view from this window on a dreary day, is there? Why ain't you singing this morning, Ruth? Sing that "No Ways Tired." That song always lifts me up so—(*She turns at last to see that* RUTH *has slipped quietly to the floor, in a state of semiconsciousness*) Ruth! Ruth honey—what's the matter with you . . . Ruth!

Curtain

Scene II

It is the following morning; a Saturday morning, and house cleaning is in progress at the YOUNGERS. *Furniture has been shoved hither and yon and* MAMA *is giving the kitchen-area walls a washing down.* BENEATHA, *in dungarees, with a handkerchief tied around her face, is spraying insecticide into the cracks in the walls. As they work, the radio is on and a Southside disk-jockey program is inappropriately filling the house with a rather exotic saxophone blues.* TRAVIS, *the sole idle one, is leaning on his arms, looking out of the window.*

TRAVIS: Grandmama, that stuff Bennie is using smells awful. Can I go downstairs, please?

MAMA: Did you get all them chores done already? I ain't seen you doing much.

TRAVIS: Yes'm—finished early. Where did Mama go this morning?

MAMA (*looking at* BENEATHA): She had to go on a little errand.

(*The phone rings.* BENEATHA *runs to answer it and reaches it before* WALTER, *who has entered from bedroom*)

TRAVIS: Where?

MAMA: To tend to her business.

BENEATHA: Haylo . . . (*Disappointed*) Yes, he is. (*She tosses the phone to* WALTER, *who barely catches it*) It's Willie Harris again.

WALTER (*as privately as possible under* MAMA*'s gaze*): Hello, Willie. Did you get the papers from the lawyer? . . . No, not yet. I told you the mailman doesn't get here till ten-thirty . . . No, I'll come there . . . Yeah! Right away. (*He hangs up and goes for his coat*)

BENEATHA: Brother, where did Ruth go?

WALTER (*as he exits*): How should I know!

TRAVIS: Aw come on, Grandma. Can I go outside?

MAMA: Oh, I guess so. You stay right in front of the house, though, and keep a good lookout for the postman.

TRAVIS: Yes'm. (*He darts into bedroom for stickball and bat, reenters, and sees* BENEATHA *on her knees spraying under sofa with behind upraised. He edges closer to the target, takes aim, and lets her have it. She screams*) Leave them poor little cockroaches alone, they ain't bothering you none! (*He runs as she swings the spray-gun at him viciously and playfully*) Grandma! Grandma!

MAMA: Look out there, girl, before you be spilling some of that stuff on that child!

TRAVIS (*safely behind the bastion of* MAMA): That's right—look out, now! (*He exits*)

BENEATHA (*drily*): I can't imagine that it would hurt him—it has never hurt the roaches.

MAMA: Well, little boys' hides ain't as tough as Southside roaches. You better get over there behind the bureau. I seen one marching out of there like Napoleon yesterday.

BENEATHA: There's really only one way to get rid of them, Mama—

MAMA: How?

BENEATHA: Set fire to this building! Mama, where did Ruth go?

MAMA (*looking at her with meaning*): To the doctor, I think.

BENEATHA: The doctor? What's the matter? (*They exchange glances*) You don't think—

MAMA (*with her sense of drama*): Now I ain't saying what I think. But I ain't never been wrong 'bout a woman neither.

(*The phone rings*)

BENEATHA (*at the phone*): Hay-lo . . . (*Pause, and a moment of recognition*) Well—when did you get back! . . . And how was it? . . . Of course I've missed you—in my way . . .

This morning? No . . . house cleaning and all that and Mama hates it if I let people come over when the house is like this . . . You *have?* Well, that's different . . . What is it—Oh, what the hell, come on over . . . Right, see you then. *Arrividerci.*

(*She hangs up*)

MAMA (*who has listened vigorously, as is her habit*): Who is that you inviting over here with this house looking like this? You ain't got the pride you was born with!

BENEATHA: Asagai doesn't care how houses look, Mama—he's an intellectual.

MAMA: *Who?*

BENEATHA: Asagai—Joseph Asagai. He's an African boy I met on campus. He's been studying in Canada all summer.

MAMA: What's his name?

BENEATHA: Asagai, Joseph. Ah-sah-guy . . . He's from Nigeria.

MAMA: Oh, that's the little country that was founded by slaves way back . . .

BENEATHA: No, Mama—that's Liberia.

MAMA: I don't think I never met no African before.

BENEATHA: Well, do me a favor and don't ask him a whole lot of ignorant questions about Africans. I mean, do they wear clothes and all that—

MAMA: Well, now, I guess if you think we so ignorant 'round here maybe you shouldn't bring your friends here—

BENEATHA: It's just that people ask such crazy things. All anyone seems to know about when it comes to Africa is Tarzan—

MAMA (*indignantly*): Why should I know anything about Africa?

BENEATHA: Why do you give money at church for the missionary work?

MAMA: Well, that's to help save people.

BENEATHA: You mean save them from *heathenism*—

MAMA (*innocently*): Yes.

BENEATHA: I'm afraid they need more salvation from the British and the French.

(RUTH *comes in forlornly and pulls off her coat with dejection. They both turn to look at her*)

RUTH (*dispiritedly*): Well, I guess from all the happy faces—everybody knows.

BENEATHA: You pregnant?

MAMA: Lord have mercy, I sure hope it's a little old girl. Travis ought to have a sister.

(BENEATHA *and* RUTH *give her a hopeless look for this grandmotherly enthusiasm*)

BENEATHA: How far along are you?

RUTH: Two months.

BENEATHA: Did you mean to? I mean did you plan it or was it an accident?

MAMA: What do you know about planning or not planning?

BENEATHA: Oh, Mama.

RUTH (*wearily*): She's twenty years old, Lena.

BENEATHA: Did you plan it, Ruth?

RUTH: Mind your own business.

BENEATHA: It is my business—where is he going to live, on the roof? (*There is silence following the remark as the three women react to the sense of it*) Gee—I didn't mean that, Ruth, honest. Gee, I don't feel like that at all. I—I think it is wonderful.

RUTH (*dully*): Wonderful.

BENEATHA: Yes—really.

MAMA (*looking at* RUTH, *worried*): Doctor say everything going to be all right?

RUTH (*far away*): Yes—she says everything is going to be fine . . .

MAMA (*immediately suspicious*): "She"—What doctor you went to?

(RUTH *folds over, she is near hysteria*)

MAMA (*worriedly hovering over* RUTH): Ruth honey—what's the matter with you—you sick?

(RUTH *has her fists clenched on her thighs and is fighting hard to suppress a scream that seems to be rising in her*)

BENEATHA: What's the matter with her, Mama?

MAMA (*working her fingers in* RUTH'*s shoulders to relax her*): She be all right. Women gets right depressed sometimes when they get her way. (*Speaking softly, expertly, rapidly*) Now you just relax. That's right . . . just lean back, don't think 'bout nothing at all . . . nothing at all—

RUTH: I'm all right . . .

(*The glassy-eyed look melts and then she collapses into a fit of heavy sobbing. The bell rings*)

BENEATHA: Oh, my God—that must be Asagai.

MAMA (*to* RUTH): Come on now, honey. You need to lie down and rest awhile . . . then have some nice hot food.

(*They exit,* RUTH'*s weight on her mother-in-law.* BENEATHA, *herself profoundly disturbed, opens the door to admit a rather dramatic-looking young man with a large package*)

ASAGAI: Hello, Alaiyo—

BENEATHA (*holding the door open and regarding him with pleasure*): Hello . . . (*Long pause*) Well—come in. And please excuse everything. My mother was very upset about my letting anyone come here with the place like this.

ASAGAI (*coming into the room*): You look disturbed too . . . Is something wrong?

BENEATHA (*still at the door, absently*): Yes . . . we've all got acute ghetto-itus. (*She smiles and comes toward him, finding a cigarette and sitting*) So—sit down! No! Wait! (*She whips the spraygun off the sofa where she had left it and puts the cushions back. At last perches on arm of sofa. He sits*) So, how was Canada?

ASAGAI (*a sophisticate*): Canadian.

BENEATHA (*looking at him*): Asagai, I'm very glad you are back.

ASAGAI (*looking back at her in turn*): Are you really?

BENEATHA: Yes—very.

ASAGAI: Why?—you were quite glad when I went away. What happened?

BENEATHA: You went away.

ASAGAI: Ahhhhhhhh.

BENEATHA: Before—you wanted to be so serious before there was time.

ASAGAI: How much time must there be before one knows what one feels?

BENEATHA (*stalling this particular conversation. Her hands pressed together, in a deliberately childish gesture*): What did you bring me?

ASAGAI (*handing her the package*): Open it and see.

BENEATHA (*eagerly opening the package and drawing out some records and the colorful robes of a Nigerian woman*): Oh, Asagai! . . . You got them for me! . . . How beautiful . . . and the records too! (*She lifts out the robes and runs to the mirror with them and holds the drapery up in front of herself*)

ASAGAI (*coming to her at the mirror*): I shall have to teach you how to drape it properly. (*He flings the material about her for the moment and stands back to look at her*) Ah—*Oh-pay-gay-day, oh-gbah-mu-shay.* (*A Yoruba exclamation for admiration*) You wear it well . . . very well . . . mutilated hair and all.

BENEATHA (*turning suddenly*): My hair—what's wrong with my hair?

ASAGAI (*shrugging*): Were you born with it like that?

BENEATHA (*reaching up to touch it*): No . . . of course not.

(*She looks back to the mirror, disturbed*)

ASAGAI (*smiling*): How then?

BENEATHA: You know perfectly well how . . . as crinkly as yours . . . that's how.

ASAGAI: And it is ugly to you that way?

BENEATHA (*quickly*): Oh, no—not ugly . . . (*More slowly, apologetically*) But it's so hard to manage when it's, well—raw.

ASAGAI: And so to accommodate that—you mutilate it every week?

BENEATHA: It's not mutilation!

ASAGAI (*laughing aloud at her seriousness*): Oh . . . please! I am only teasing you because you are so very serious about these things. (*He stands back from her and folds his arms across his chest as he watches her pulling at her hair and frowning in the mirror*) Do you remember the first time you met me at school? . . (*He laughs*) You came up to me and you said—and I thought you were the most serious little thing I had ever seen—you said: (*He imitates her*) "Mr. Asagai—I want very much to talk with you. About Africa. You see, Mr. Asagai, I am looking for my *identity!*"

(*He laughs*)

BENEATHA (*turning to him, not laughing*): Yes—

(*Her face is quizzical, profoundly disturbed*)

ASAGAI (*still teasing and reaching out and taking her face in his hands and turning her profile to him*): Well . . . it is true that this is not so much a profile of a Hollywood queen as perhaps a queen of the Nile—(*A mock dismissal of the importance of the question*) But what does it matter? Assimilationism is so popular in your country.

BENEATHA (*wheeling, passionately, sharply*): I am not an assimilationist!

ASAGAI (*the protest hangs in the room for a moment and* ASAGAI *studies her, his laughter fading*): Such a serious one. (*There is a pause*) So—you like the robes? You must take excellent care of them—they are from my sister's personal wardrobe.

BENEATHA (*with incredulity*): You—you sent all the way home—for me?

ASAGAI (*with charm*): For you—I would do much more . . . Well, that is what I came for. I must go.

BENEATHA: Will you call me Monday?

ASAGAI: Yes . . . We have a great deal to talk about. I mean about identity and time and all that.

BENEATHA: Time?

ASAGAI: Yes. About how much time one needs to know what one feels.

BENEATHA: You see! You never understood that there is more than one kind of feeling which can exist between a man and a woman—or, at least, there should be.

ASAGAI (*shaking his head negatively but gently*): No. Between a man and a woman there need be only one kind of feeling. I have that for you . . . Now even . . . right this moment . . .

BENEATHA: I know—and by itself—it won't do. I can find that anywhere.

ASAGAI: For a woman it should be enough.

BENEATHA: I know—because that's what it says in all the novels that men write. But it isn't. Go ahead and laugh—but I'm not interested in being someone's little episode in America or—(*With feminine vengeance*)—one of them! (ASAGAI *has burst into laughter again*) That's funny as hell, huh!

ASAGAI: It's just that every American girl I have known has said that to me. White—black—in this you are all the same. And the same speech, too!

BENEATHA (*angrily*): Yuk, yuk, yuk!

ASAGAI: It's how you can be sure that the world's most liberated women are not liberated at all. You all talk about it too much!

(MAMA *enters and is immediately all social charm because of the presence of a guest*)

BENEATHA: Oh—Mama—this is Mr. Asagai.

MAMA: How do you do?

ASAGAI (*total politeness to an elder*): How do you do, Mrs. Younger. Please forgive me for coming at such an outrageous hour on a Saturday.

MAMA: Well, you are quite welcome. I just hope you understand that our house don't always look like this. (*Chatterish*) You must come again. I would love to hear all about—(*Not sure of the name*)—your country. I think it's so sad the way our American Negroes don't know nothing about Africa 'cept Tarzan and all that. And all that money they pour into these churches when they ought to be helping you people over there drive out them French and Englishmen done taken away your land.

(*The mother flashes a slightly superior look at her daughter upon completion of the recitation*)

ASAGAI (*taken aback by this sudden and acutely unrelated expression of sympathy*): Yes . . . yes . . .

MAMA (*smiling at him suddenly and relaxing and looking him over*): How many miles is it from here to where you come from?

ASAGAI: Many thousands.

MAMA (*looking at him as she would* WALTER): I bet you don't half look after yourself, being away from your mama either. I spec you better come 'round here from time to time to get yourself some decent home-cooked meals . . .

ASAGAI (*moved*): Thank you. Thank you very much. (*They are all quiet, then—*) Well . . . I must go. I will call you Monday, Alaiyo.

MAMA: What's that he call you?

ASAGAI: Oh—"Alaiyo." I hope you don't mind. It is what you would call a nickname, I think. It is a Yoruba word. I am a Yoruba.

MAMA (*looking at* BENEATHA): I—I thought he was from—(*Uncertain*)

ASAGAI (*understanding*): Nigeria is my country. Yoruba is my tribal origin—

BENEATHA: You didn't tell us what Alaiyo means . . . for all I know, you might be calling me Little Idiot or something . . .

ASAGAI: Well . . . let me see . . . I do not know how just to explain it . . . The sense of a thing can be so different when it changes languages.

BENEATHA: You're evading.

ASAGAI: No—really it is difficult . . . (*Thinking*) It means . . . it means One for Whom Bread—Food—Is Not Enough. (*He looks at her*) Is that all right?

BENEATHA (*understanding, softly*): Thank you.

MAMA (*looking from one to the other and not understanding any of it*): Well . . . that's nice . . . You must come see us again—Mr.—

ASAGAI: Ah-sah-guy . . .

MAMA: Yes . . . Do come again.

ASAGAI: Good-bye.

(*He exits*)

MAMA (*after him*): Lord, that's a pretty thing just went out here! (*Insinuatingly, to her daughter*) Yes, I guess I see why we done commence to get so interested in Africa 'round here. Missionaries my aunt Jenny!

(*She exits*)

BENEATHA: Oh, Mama! . . .

(*She picks up the Nigerian dress and holds it up to her in front of the mirror again. She sets the headdress on haphazardly and then notices her hair again and clutches at it and then replaces the headdress and frowns at herself. Then she starts to wriggle in front of the mirror as she thinks a Nigerian woman might.* TRAVIS *enters and stands regarding her*)

TRAVIS: What's the matter, girl, you cracking up?

BENEATHA: Shut up.

(*She pulls the headdress off and looks at herself in the mirror and clutches at her hair again and squinches her eyes as if trying to imagine something. Then, suddenly, she gets her raincoat and kerchief and hurriedly prepares for going out*)

MAMA (*coming back into the room*): She's resting now. Travis, baby, run next door and ask Miss Johnson to please let me have a little kitchen cleanser. This here can is empty as Jacob's kettle.

TRAVIS: I just came in.

MAMA: Do as you told. (*He exits and she looks at her daughter*) Where you going?

BENEATHA (*halting at the door*): To become a queen of the Nile!

(*She exits in a breathless blaze of glory.* RUTH *appears in the bedroom doorway*)

MAMA: Who told you to get up?

RUTH: Ain't nothing wrong with me to be lying in no bed for. Where did Bennie go?

MAMA (*drumming her fingers*): Far as I could make out—to Egypt. (RUTH *just looks at her*) What time is it getting to?

RUTH: Ten twenty. And the mailman going to ring that bell this morning just like he done every morning for the last umpteen years.

(TRAVIS *comes in with the cleanser can*)

TRAVIS: She say to tell you that she don't have much.

MAMA (*angrily*): Lord, some people I could name sure is tight-fisted! (*Directing her grandson*) Mark two cans of cleanser down on the list there. If she that hard up for kitchen cleanser, I sure don't want to forget to get her none!

RUTH: Lena—maybe the woman is just short on cleanser—

MAMA (*not listening*): —Much baking powder as she done borrowed from me all these years, she could of done gone into the baking business!

(*The bell sounds suddenly and sharply and all three are stunned—serious and silent—mid-speech. In spite of all the other conversations and distractions of the morning, this is what they have been waiting for, even* TRAVIS, *who looks helplessly from his mother to his grandmother.* RUTH *is the first to come to life again*)

RUTH (*to* TRAVIS): *Get down them steps, boy!*

(TRAVIS *snaps to life and flies out to get the mail*)

MAMA (*her eyes wide, her hand to her breast*): You mean it done really come?

RUTH (*excited*): Oh, Miss Lena!

MAMA (*collecting herself*): Well . . . I don't know what we all so excited about 'round here for. We known it was coming for months.

RUTH: That's a whole lot different from having it come and being able to hold it in your hands . . . a piece of paper worth ten thousand dollars . . . (TRAVIS *bursts back into the room. He holds the envelope high above his head, like a little dancer, his face is radiant and he is breathless. He moves to his grandmother with sudden slow ceremony and puts the envelope into her hands. She accepts it, and then merely holds it and looks at it*) Come on! Open it . . . Lord have mercy, I wish Walter Lee was here!

TRAVIS: Open it, Grandmama!

MAMA (*staring at it*): Now you all be quiet. It's just a check.

RUTH: Open it . . .

MAMA (*still staring at it*): Now don't act silly . . . We ain't never been no people to act silly 'bout no money—

RUTH (*swiftly*): We ain't never had none before—OPEN IT!

(MAMA *finally makes a good strong tear and pulls out the thin blue slice of paper and inspects it closely. The boy and his mother study it raptly over* MAMA*'s shoulders*)

MAMA: *Travis!* (*She is counting off with doubt*) Is that the right number of zeros?

TRAVIS: Yes'm . . . ten thousand dollars. Gaalee, Grandmama, you rich.

MAMA (*she holds the check away from her, still looking at it. Slowly her face sobers into a mask of unhappiness*): Ten thousand dollars. (*She hands it to* RUTH) Put it away somewhere, Ruth. (*She does not look at* RUTH*; her eyes seem to be seeing something somewhere very far off*) Ten thousand dollars they give you. Ten thousand dollars.

TRAVIS (*to his mother, sincerely*): What's the matter with Grandmama—don't she want to be rich?

RUTH (*distractedly*): You go on out and play now, baby. (TRAVIS *exits.* MAMA *starts wiping dishes absently, humming intently to herself.* RUTH *turns to her, with kind exasperation*) You've gone and got yourself upset.

MAMA (*not looking at her*): I spec if it wasn't for you all . . . I would just put that money away or give it to the church or something.

RUTH: Now what kind of talk is that. Mr. Younger would just be plain mad if he could hear you talking foolish like that.

MAMA (*stopping and staring off*): Yes . . . he sure would. (*Sighing*) We got enough to do with that money, all right. (*She halts then, and turns and looks at her daughter-in-law hard;* RUTH *avoids her eyes and* MAMA *wipes her hands with finality and starts to speak firmly to* RUTH) Where did you go today, girl?

RUTH: To the doctor.

MAMA (*impatiently*): Now, Ruth . . . you know better than that. Old Doctor Jones is strange enough in his way but there ain't nothing 'bout him make somebody slip and call him "she"—like you done this morning.

RUTH: Well, that's what happened—my tongue slipped.

MAMA: You went to see that woman, didn't you?

RUTH (*defensively, giving herself away*): What woman you talking about?

MAMA (*angrily*): That woman who—

(WALTER *enters in great excitement*)

WALTER: Did it come?

MAMA (*quietly*): Can't you give people a Christian greeting before you start asking about money?

WALTER (*to* RUTH): Did it come? (RUTH *unfolds the check and lays it quietly before him, watching him intently with thoughts of her own.* WALTER *sits down and grasps it close and counts off the zeros*) Ten thousand dollars—(*He turns suddenly, frantically to his mother and draws some papers out of his breast pocket*) Mama—look. Old Willy Harris put everything on paper—

MAMA: Son—I think you ought to talk to your wife . . . I'll go on out and leave you alone if you want—

WALTER: I can talk to her later—Mama, look—

MAMA: Son—

WALTER: WILL SOMEBODY PLEASE LISTEN TO ME TODAY!

MAMA (*quietly*): I don't 'low no yellin' in this house, Walter Lee, and you know it—(WALTER *stares at them in frustration and starts to speak several times*) And there ain't going to be no investing in no liquor stores.

WALTER: But, Mama, you ain't even looked at it.

MAMA: I don't aim to have to speak on that again.

(*A long pause*)

WALTER: You ain't looked at it and you don't aim to have to speak on that again? You ain't even looked at it and *you* have decided—(*Crumpling his papers*) Well, *you* tell that to my boy tonight when you put him to sleep on the living-room couch . . . (*Turning to* MAMA *and speaking directly to her*) Yeah—and tell it to my wife, Mama, tomorrow when she has to go out of here to look after somebody else's kids. And tell it to *me,* Mama, every time we need a new pair of curtains and I have to watch *you* go out and work in somebody's kitchen. Yeah, you tell me then!

(WALTER *starts out*)

RUTH: Where you going?

WALTER: I'm going out!

RUTH: Where?

WALTER: Just out of this house somewhere—

RUTH (*getting her coat*): I'll come too.

WALTER: I don't want you to come!

RUTH: I got something to talk to you about, Walter.

WALTER: That's too bad.

MAMA (*still quietly*): Walter Lee—(*She waits and he finally turns and looks at her*) Sit down.

WALTER: I'm a grown man, Mama.

MAMA: Ain't nobody said you wasn't grown. But you still in my house and my presence. And as long as you are—you'll talk to your wife civil. Now sit down.

RUTH (*suddenly*): Oh, let him go on out and drink himself to death! He makes me sick to my stomach! (*She flings her coat against him and exits to bedroom*)

WALTER (*violently flinging the coat after her*): And you turn mine too, baby! (*The door slams behind her*) That was my biggest mistake—

MAMA (*still quietly*): Walter, what is the matter with you?

WALTER: Matter with me? Ain't nothing the matter with *me!*

MAMA: Yes there is. Something eating you up like a crazy man. Something more than me not giving you this money. The past few years I been watching it happen to you. You get all nervous acting and kind of wild in the eyes—(WALTER *jumps up impatiently at her words*) I said sit there now, I'm talking to you!

WALTER: Mama—I don't need no nagging at me today.

MAMA: Seem like you getting to a place where you always tied up in some kind of knot about something. But if anybody ask you 'bout it you just yell at 'em and bust out the house and go out and drink somewheres. Walter Lee, people can't live with that. Ruth's a good, patient girl in her way—but you getting to be too much. Boy, don't make the mistake of driving that girl away from you.

WALTER: Why—what she do for me?

MAMA: She loves you.

WALTER: Mama—I'm going out. I want to go off somewhere and be by myself for a while.

MAMA: I'm sorry 'bout your liquor store, son. It just wasn't the thing for us to do. That's what I want to tell you about—

WALTER: I got to go out, Mama—

(*He rises*)

MAMA: It's dangerous, son.

WALTER: What's dangerous?

MAMA: When a man goes outside his home to look for peace.

WALTER (*beseechingly*): Then why can't there never be no peace in this house then?

MAMA: You done found it in some other house?

WALTER: No—there ain't no woman! Why do women always think there's a woman somewhere when a man gets restless. (*Picks up the check*) Do you know what this money means to me? Do you know what this money can do for us? (*Puts it back*) Mama—Mama—I want so many things . . .

MAMA: Yes, son—

WALTER: I want so many things that they are driving me kind of crazy . . . Mama—look at me.

MAMA: I'm looking at you. You a good-looking boy. You got a job, a nice wife, a fine boy and—

WALTER: A job. (*Looks at her*) Mama, a job? I open and close car doors all day long. I drive a man around in his limousine and I say, "Yes, sir; no, sir; very good, sir; shall I take the Drive, sir?" Mama, that ain't no kind of job . . . that ain't nothing at all. (*Very quietly*) Mama, I don't know if I can make you understand.

MAMA: Understand what, baby?

WALTER (*quietly*): Sometimes it's like I can see the future stretched out in front of me—just plain as day. The future, Mama. Hanging over there at the edge of my days. Just waiting for me—a big, looming blank space—full of *nothing.* Just waiting for *me.* But it don't have to be. (*Pause. Kneeling beside her chair*) Mama—sometimes when I'm downtown and I pass them cool, quiet-looking restaurants where them white boys are sitting back and talking 'bout things . . . sitting there turning deals worth millions of dollars . . . sometimes I see guys don't look much older than me—

MAMA: Son—how come you talk so much 'bout money?

WALTER (*with immense passion*): Because it is life, Mama!

MAMA (*quietly*): Oh—(*Very quietly*) So now it's life. Money is life. Once upon a time freedom used to be life—now it's money. I guess the world really do change . . .

WALTER: No—it was always money, Mama. We just didn't know about it.

MAMA: No . . . something has changed. (*She looks at him*) You something new, boy. In my time we was worried about not being lynched and getting to the North if we could and how to stay alive and still have a pinch of dignity too . . . Now here come you and Beneatha—talking 'bout things we ain't never even thought about hardly, me and your daddy. You ain't satisfied or proud of nothing we done. I mean that you had a home; that we kept you out of trouble till you was grown; that you don't have to ride to work on the back of nobody's streetcar—You my children—but how different we done become.

WALTER (*a long beat. He pats her hand and gets up*): You just don't understand, Mama, you just don't understand.

MAMA: Son—do you know your wife is expecting another baby? (WALTER *stands, stunned, and absorbs what his mother has said*) That's what she wanted to talk to you about. (WALTER *sinks down into a chair*) This ain't for me to be telling—but you ought to know. (*She waits*) I think Ruth is thinking 'bout getting rid of that child.

WALTER (*slowly understanding*): —No—no—Ruth wouldn't do that.

MAMA: When the world gets ugly enough—a woman will do anything for her family. *The part that's already living.*

WALTER: You don't know Ruth, Mama, if you think she would do that.

(RUTH *opens the bedroom door and stands there a little limp*)

RUTH (*beaten*): Yes I would too, Walter. (*Pause*) I gave her a five-dollar down payment.

(*There is total silence as the man stares at his wife and the mother stares at her son*)

MAMA (*presently*): Well—(*Tightly*) Well—son, I'm waiting to hear you say something . . . (*She waits*) I'm waiting to hear how you be your father's son. Be the man he was . . . (*Pause. The silence shouts*) Your wife say she going to destroy your child. And I'm waiting to hear you talk like him and say we a people who give children life, not who destroys them—(*She rises*) I'm waiting to see you stand up and look like your daddy and say we done give up one baby to poverty and that we ain't going to give up nary another one . . . I'm waiting.

WALTER: Ruth—(*He can say nothing*)

MAMA: If you a son of mine, tell her! (WALTER *picks up his keys and his coat and walks out. She continues, bitterly*) You . . . you are a disgrace to your father's memory. Somebody get me my hat!

Curtain

ACT II

Scene I

Time: Later the same day.

At rise: RUTH *is ironing again. She has the radio going. Presently* BENEATHA*'s bedroom door opens and* RUTH*'s mouth falls and she puts down the iron in fascination.*

RUTH: What have we got on tonight!

BENEATHA (*emerging grandly from the doorway so that we can see her thoroughly robed in the costume Asagai brought*): You are looking at what a well-dressed Nigerian woman wears—(*She parades for* RUTH, *her hair completely hidden by the headdress; she is coquettishly fanning herself with an ornate oriental fan, mistakenly more like Butterfly than any Nigerian that ever was*) Isn't it beautiful? (*She promenades to the radio and, with an arrogant flourish, turns off the good loud blues that is playing*) Enough of this assimilationist junk! (RUTH *follows her with her eyes as she goes to the phonograph and puts on a record and turns and waits ceremoniously for the music to come up. Then, with a shout—*) OCOMOGOSIAY!

(RUTH *jumps. The music comes up, a lovely Nigerian melody.* BENEATHA *listens, enraptured, her eyes far away—"back to the past." She begins to dance.* RUTH *is dumbfounded*)

RUTH: What kind of dance is that?

BENEATHA: A folk dance.

RUTH (*Pearl Bailey*): What kind of folks do that, honey?

BENEATHA: It's from Nigeria. It's a dance of welcome.

RUTH: Who you welcoming?

BENEATHA: The men back to the village.

RUTH: Where they been?

BENEATHA: How should I know—out hunting or something. Anyway, they are coming back now . . .

RUTH: Well, that's good.

BENEATHA (*with the record*):
Alundi, alundi
Alundi alunya
Jop pu à jeepua
Ang gu soooooooooo
Ai yai yae . . .
Ayehaye—alundi . . .

(WALTER *comes in during this performance; he has obviously been drinking. He leans against the door heavily and watches his sister, at first with distaste. Then his eyes look off—"back to the past"—as he lifts both his fists to the roof, screaming*)

WALTER: YEAH . . . AND ETHIOPIA STRETCH FORTH HER HANDS AGAIN! . . .

RUTH (*drily, looking at him*): Yes—and Africa sure is claiming her own tonight. (*She gives them both up and starts ironing again*)

WALTER (*all in a drunken, dramatic shout*): Shut up! . . . I'm digging them drums . . . them drums move me! . . . (*He makes his weaving way to his wife's face and leans in close to her*) In my *heart of hearts*—(*He thumps his chest*)—I am much warrior!

RUTH (*without even looking up*): In your heart of hearts you are much drunkard.

WALTER (*coming away from her and starting to wander around the room, shouting*): Me and Jomo . . . (*Intently, in his sister's face. She has stopped dancing to watch him in this unknown mood*) That's my man, Kenyatta. (*Shouting and thumping his chest*) FLAMING SPEAR! HOT DAMN! (*He is suddenly in possession of an imaginary spear and actively spearing enemies all over the room*) *OCOMOGOSIAY . . .*

BENEATHA (*to encourage* WALTER, *thoroughly caught up with this side of him*): *OCOMOGOSIAY,* FLAMING SPEAR!

WALTER: THE LION IS WAKING . . . OWIMOWEH!

(*He pulls his shirt open and leaps up on the table and gestures with his spear*)

BENEATHA: OWIMOWEH!

WALTER (*on the table, very far gone, his eyes pure glass sheets. He sees what we cannot, that he is a leader of his people, a great chief, a descendant of Chaka, and that the hour to march has come*): Listen, my black brothers—

BENEATHA: OCOMOGOSIAY!

WALTER: —Do you hear the waters rushing against the shores of the coastlands—

BENEATHA: OCOMOGOSIAY!

WALTER: —Do you hear the screeching of the cocks in yonder hills beyond where the chiefs meet in council for the coming of the mighty war—

BENEATHA: OCOMOGOSIAY!

(*And now the lighting shifts subtly to suggest the world of* WALTER*'s imagination, and the mood shifts from pure comedy. It is the inner* WALTER *speaking: the Southside chauffeur has assumed an unexpected majesty*)

WALTER: —Do you hear the beating of the wings of the birds flying low over the mountains and the low places of our land—

BENEATHA: OCOMOGOSIAY!

WALTER: —Do you hear the singing of the women, singing the war songs of our fathers to the babies in the great houses? Singing the sweet war songs! (*The doorbell rings*) OH, DO YOU HEAR, MY BLACK BROTHERS!

BENEATHA (*completely gone*): We hear you, Flaming Spear—

(RUTH *shuts off the phonograph and opens the door.* GEORGE MURCHISON *enters*)

WALTER: Telling us to prepare for the GREATNESS OF THE TIME! (*Lights back to normal. He turns and sees* GEORGE) Black Brother!

(*He extends his hand for the fraternal clasp*)

GEORGE: Black Brother, hell!

RUTH (*having had enough, and embarrassed for the family*): Beneatha, you got company—what's the matter with you? Walter Lee Younger, get down off that table and stop acting like a fool . . .

(WALTER *comes down off the table suddenly and makes a quick exit to the bathroom*)

RUTH: He's had a little to drink . . . I don't know what her excuse is.

GEORGE (*to* BENEATHA): Look honey, we're going *to* the theatre—we're not going to be *in* it . . . so go change, huh?

(BENEATHA *looks at him and slowly, ceremoniously, lifts her hands and pulls off the headdress. Her hair is close-cropped and unstraightened.* GEORGE *freezes mid-sentence and* RUTH*'s eyes all but fall out of her head*)

GEORGE: What in the name of—

RUTH (*touching* BENEATHA*'s hair*): Girl, you done lost your natural mind!? Look at your head!

GEORGE: What have you done to your head—I mean your hair!

BENEATHA: Nothing—except cut it off.

RUTH: Now that's the truth—it's what ain't been done to it! You expect this boy to go out with you with your head all nappy like that?

BENEATHA (*looking at* GEORGE): That's up to George. If he's ashamed of his heritage—

GEORGE: Oh, don't be so proud of yourself, Bennie—just because you look eccentric.

BENEATHA: How can something that's natural be eccentric?

GEORGE: That's what being eccentric means—being natural. Get dressed.

BENEATHA: I don't like that, George.

RUTH: Why must you and your brother make an argument out of everything people say?

BENEATHA: Because I hate assimilationist Negroes!

RUTH: Will somebody please tell me what assimila-who-ever means!

GEORGE: Oh, it's just a college girl's way of calling people Uncle Toms—but that isn't what it means at all.

RUTH: Well, what does it mean?

BENEATHA (*cutting* GEORGE *off and staring at him as she replies to* RUTH): It means someone who is willing to give up his own culture and submerge himself completely in the dominant, and in this case *oppressive* culture!

GEORGE: Oh, dear, dear, dear! Here we go! A lecture on the African past! On our Great West African Heritage! In one second we will hear all about the great Ashanti empires; the great Songhay civilizations; and the great sculpture of Bénin—and then some poetry in the Bantu—and the whole monologue will end with the word *heritage!* (*Nastily*) Let's face it, baby, your heritage is nothing but a bunch of raggedy-assed spirituals and some grass huts!

BENEATHA: GRASS HUTS! (RUTH *crosses to her and forcibly pushes her toward the bedroom*) See there . . . you are standing there in your splendid ignorance talking about people who were the first to smelt iron on the face of the earth! (RUTH *is pushing her through the door*) The Ashanti were performing surgical operations when the English— (RUTH *pulls the door to, with* BENEATHA *on the other side, and smiles graciously at* GEORGE. BENEATHA *opens the door and shouts the end of the sentence defiantly at* GEORGE)—were still tatooing themselves with blue dragons! (*She goes back inside*)

RUTH: Have a seat, George (*They both sit.* RUTH *folds her hands rather primly on her lap, determined to demonstrate the civilization of the family*) Warm, ain't it? I mean for September. (*Pause*) Just like they always say about Chicago weather: If it's too hot or cold for you, just wait a minute and it'll change. (*She smiles happily at this cliché of clichés*) Everybody say it's got to do with them bombs and things they keep setting off. (*Pause*) Would you like a nice cold beer?

GEORGE: No, thank you. I don't care for beer. (*He looks at his watch*) I hope she hurries up.

RUTH: What time is the show?

GEORGE: It's an eight-thirty curtain. That's just Chicago, though. In New York standard curtain time is eight forty.

(*He is rather proud of this knowledge*)

RUTH (*properly appreciating it*): You get to New York a lot?

GEORGE (*offhand*): Few times a year.

RUTH: Oh—that's nice. I've never been to New York.

(WALTER *enters. We feel he has relieved himself, but the edge of unreality is still with him*)

WALTER: New York ain't got nothing Chicago ain't. Just a bunch of hustling people all squeezed up together—being "Eastern."

(*He turns his face into a screw of displeasure*)

GEORGE: Oh—you've been?

WALTER: *Plenty* of times.

RUTH (*shocked at the lie*): Walter Lee Younger!

WALTER (*staring her down*): Plenty! (*Pause*) What we got to drink in this house? Why don't you offer this man some refreshment. (*To* GEORGE) They don't know how to entertain people in this house, man.

GEORGE: Thank you—I don't really care for anything.

WALTER (*feeling his head; sobriety coming*): Where's Mama?

RUTH: She ain't come back yet.

WALTER (*looking* MURCHISON *over from head to toe, scrutinizing his carefully casual tweed sports jacket over cashmere V-neck sweater over soft eyelet shirt and tie, and soft slacks, finished off with white buckskin shoes*): Why all you college boys wear them faggoty-looking white shoes?

RUTH: Walter Lee!

(GEORGE MURCHISON *ignores the remark*)

WALTER (*to* RUTH): Well, they look crazy as hell—white shoes, cold as it is.

RUTH (*crushed*): You have to excuse him—

WALTER: No he don't! Excuse me for what? What you always excusing me for! I'll excuse myself when I needs to be excused! (*A pause*) They look as funny as them black knee socks Beneatha wears out of here all the time.

RUTH: It's the college *style,* Walter.

WALTER: Style, hell. She looks like she got burnt legs or something!

RUTH: Oh, Walter—

WALTER (*an irritable mimic*): Oh, Walter! Oh, Walter! (*To* MURCHISON) How's your old man making out? I understand you all going to buy that big hotel on the Drive? (*He finds a beer in the refrigerator, wanders over to* MURCHISON, *sipping and wiping his lips with the back of his hand, and straddling a chair backwards to talk to the other man*) Shrewd move. Your old man is all right, man. (*Tapping his head and half winking for emphasis*) I mean he knows how to operate. I mean he thinks *big,* you know what I mean, I mean for a *home,* you know? But I think he's kind of running out of ideas now. I'd like to talk to him. Listen, man, I got some plans that could turn this city upside down. I mean think like he does. *Big.* Invest big, gamble big, hell, lose *big* if you have to, you know what I mean. It's hard to find a man on this whole Southside who understands my kind of thinking—you dig? (*He scrutinizes* MURCHISON *again, drinks his beer, squints his eyes and leans in close, confidential, man to man*) Me and you ought to sit down and talk sometimes, man. Man, I got me some ideas . . .

MURCHISON (*with boredom*): Yeah—sometimes we'll have to do that, Walter.

WALTER (*understanding the indifference, and offended*): Yeah—well, when you get the time, man. I know you a busy little boy.

RUTH: Walter, please—

WALTER (*bitterly, hurt*): I know ain't nothing in this world as busy as you colored college boys with your fraternity pins and white shoes . . .

RUTH (*covering her face with humiliation*): Oh, Walter Lee—

WALTER: I see you all all the time—with the books tucked under your arms—going to your (*British A—a mimic*) "clahsses." And for what! What the hell you learning over there? Filling up your heads—(*Counting off on his fingers*)—with the sociology and the psychology—but they teaching you how to be a man? How to take over and run the world? They teaching you how to run a rubber plantation or a steel mill? Naw—just to talk proper and read books and wear them faggoty-looking white shoes . . .

GEORGE (*looking at him with distaste, a little above it all*): You're all wacked up with bitterness, man.

WALTER (*intently, almost quietly, between the teeth, glaring at the boy*): And you—ain't you bitter, man? Ain't you just about had it yet? Don't you see no stars gleaming that you can't reach out and grab? You happy?—You contented son-of-a-bitch—you happy? You got it made? Bitter? Man, I'm a volcano. Bitter? Here I am a giant—surrounded by ants! Ants who can't even understand what it is the giant is talking about.

RUTH (*passionately and suddenly*): Oh, Walter—ain't you with nobody!

WALTER (*violently*): No! 'Cause ain't nobody with me! Not even my own mother!

RUTH: Walter, that's a terrible thing to say!

(BENEATHA *enters, dressed for the evening in a cocktail dress and earrings, hair natural*)

GEORGE: Well—hey—(*Crosses to* BENEATHA; *thoughtful, with emphasis, since this is a reversal*) You look great!

WALTER (*seeing his sister's hair for the first time*): What's the matter with your head?

BENEATHA (*tired of the jokes now*): I cut it off, Brother.

WALTER (*coming close to inspect it and walking around her*): Well, I'll be damned. So that's what they mean by the African bush . . .

BENEATHA: Ha ha. Let's go, George.

GEORGE (*looking at her*): You know something? I like it. It's sharp. I mean it really is. (*Helps her into her wrap*)

RUTH: Yes—I think so, too. (*She goes to the mirror and starts to clutch at her hair*)

WALTER: Oh no! You leave yours alone, baby. You might turn out to have a pin-shaped head or something!

BENEATHA: See you all later.

RUTH: Have a nice time.

GEORGE: Thanks. Good night. (*Half out the door, he reopens it. To* WALTER) Good night, Prometheus!

(BENEATHA *and* GEORGE *exit*)

WALTER (*to* RUTH): Who is Prometheus?

RUTH: I don't know. Don't worry about it.

WALTER (*in fury, pointing after* GEORGE): See there—they get to a point where they can't insult you man to man—they got to go talk about something ain't nobody never heard of!

RUTH: How do you know it was an insult? (*To humor him*) Maybe Prometheus is a nice fellow.

WALTER: Prometheus! I bet there ain't even no such thing! I bet that simple-minded clown—

RUTH: Walter—

(*She stops what she is doing and looks at him*)

WALTER (*yelling*): Don't start!

RUTH: Start what?

WALTER: Your nagging! Where was I? Who was I with? How much money did I spend?

RUTH (*plaintively*): Walter Lee—why don't we just try to talk about it . . .

WALTER (*not listening*): I been out talking with people who understand me. People who care about the things I got on my mind.

RUTH (*wearily*): I guess that means people like Willy Harris.

WALTER: Yes, people like Willy Harris.

RUTH (*with a sudden flash of impatience*): Why don't you all just hurry up and go into the banking business and stop talking about it!

WALTER: Why? You want to know why? 'Cause we all tied up in a race of people that don't know how to do nothing but moan, pray and have babies!

(*The line is too bitter even for him and he looks at her and sits down*)

RUTH: Oh, Walter . . . (*Softly*) Honey, why can't you stop fighting me?

WALTER (*without thinking*): Who's fighting you? Who even cares about you?

(This line begins the retardation of his mood)

RUTH: Well—*(She waits a long time, and then with resignation starts to put away her things)* I guess I might as well go on to bed . . . *(More or less to herself)* I don't know where we lost it . . . but we have . . . *(Then, to him)* I—I'm sorry about this new baby, Walter. I guess maybe I better go on and do what I started . . . I guess I just didn't realize how bad things was with us . . . I guess I just didn't really realize—*(She starts out to the bedroom and stops)* You want some hot milk?

WALTER: Hot milk?

RUTH: Yes—hot milk.

WALTER: Why hot milk?

RUTH: 'Cause after all that liquor you come home with you ought to have something hot in your stomach.

WALTER: I don't want no milk.

RUTH: You want some coffee then?

WALTER: No, I don't want no coffee. I don't want nothing hot to drink. *(Almost plaintively)* Why you always trying to give me something to eat?

RUTH *(standing and looking at him helplessly)*: What *else* can I give you, Walter Lee Younger?

(She stands and looks at him and presently turns to go out again. He lifts his head and watches her going away from him in a new mood which began to emerge when he asked her "Who cares about you?")

WALTER: It's been rough, ain't it, baby? *(She hears and stops but does not turn around and he continues to her back)* I guess between two people there ain't never as much understood as folks generally thinks there is. I mean like between me and you—*(She turns to face him)* How we gets to the place where we scared to talk softness to each other. *(He waits, thinking hard himself)* Why you think it got to be like that? *(He is thoughtful, almost as a child would be)* Ruth, what is it gets into people ought to be close?

RUTH: I don't know, honey. I think about it a lot.

WALTER: On account of you and me, you mean? The way things are with us. The way something done come down between us.

RUTH: There ain't so much between us, Walter . . . Not when you come to me and try to talk to me. Try to be with me . . . a little even.

WALTER *(total honesty)*: Sometimes . . . sometimes . . . I don't even know how to try.

RUTH: Walter—

WALTER: Yes?

RUTH *(coming to him, gently and with misgiving, but coming to him)*: Honey . . . life don't have to be like this. I mean sometimes people can do things so that things are better . . . You remember how we used to talk when Travis was born . . . about the way we were going to live . . . the kind of house . . . *(She is stroking his head)* Well, it's all starting to slip away from us . . .

(He turns her to him and they look at each other and kiss, tenderly and hungrily. The door opens and MAMA enters—WALTER breaks away and jumps up. A beat)

WALTER: Mama, where have you been?

MAMA: My—them steps is longer than they used to be. Whew! *(She sits down and ignores him)* How you feeling this evening, Ruth?

(RUTH *shrugs, disturbed at having been interrupted and watching her husband knowingly*)

WALTER: Mama, where have you been all day?

MAMA (*still ignoring him and leaning on the table and changing to more comfortable shoes*): Where's Travis?

RUTH: I let him go out earlier and he ain't come back yet. Boy, is he going to get it!

WALTER: Mama!

MAMA (*as if she has heard him for the first time*): Yes, son?

WALTER: Where did you go this afternoon?

MAMA: I went downtown to tend to some business that I had to tend to.

WALTER: What kind of business?

MAMA: You know better than to question me like a child, Brother.

WALTER (*rising and bending over the table*): Where were you, Mama? (*Bringing his fists down and shouting*) Mama, you didn't go do something with that insurance money, something crazy?

(*The front door opens slowly, interrupting him, and* TRAVIS *peeks his head in, less than hopefully*)

TRAVIS (*to his mother*): Mama, I—

RUTH: "Mama I" nothing! You're going to get it, boy! Get on in that bedroom and get yourself ready!

TRAVIS: But I—

MAMA: Why don't you all never let the child explain hisself.

RUTH: Keep out of it now, Lena.

(MAMA *clamps her lips together, and* RUTH *advances toward her son menacingly*)

RUTH: A thousand times I have told you not to go off like that—

MAMA (*holding out her arms to her grandson*): Well—at least let me tell him something. I want him to be the first one to hear . . . Come here, Travis. (*The boy obeys, gladly*) Travis—(*She takes him by the shoulder and looks into his face*)—you know that money we got in the mail this morning?

TRAVIS: Yes'm—

MAMA: Well—what you think your grandmama gone and done with that money?

TRAVIS: I don't know, Grandmama.

MAMA (*putting her finger on his nose for emphasis*): She went out and she bought you a house! (*The explosion comes from* WALTER *at the end of the revelation and he jumps up and turns away from all of them in a fury.* MAMA *continues, to* TRAVIS) You glad about the house? It's going to be yours when you get to be a man.

TRAVIS: Yeah—I always wanted to live in a house.

MAMA: All right, gimme some sugar then—(TRAVIS *puts his arms around her neck as she watches her son over the boy's shoulder. Then, to* TRAVIS, *after the embrace*) Now when you say your prayers tonight, you thank God and your grandfather—'cause it was him who give you the house—in his way.

RUTH (*taking the boy from* MAMA *and pushing him toward the bedroom*): Now you get out of here and get ready for your beating.

TRAVIS: Aw, Mama—

RUTH: Get on in there—(*Closing the door behind him and turning radiantly to her mother-in-law*) So you went and did it!

MAMA (*quietly, looking at her son with pain*): Yes, I did.

RUTH (*raising both arms classically*): PRAISE GOD! (*Looks at* WALTER *a moment, who says nothing. She crosses rapidly to her husband*) Please, honey—let me be glad . . . you be glad too. (*She has laid her hands on his shoulders, but he shakes himself free of her roughly, without turning to face her*) Oh, Walter . . . a home . . . *a home.* (*She comes back to* MAMA) Well—where is it? How big is it? How much it going to cost?

MAMA: Well—

RUTH: When we moving?

MAMA (*smiling at her*): First of the month.

RUTH (*throwing back her head with jubilance*): *Praise God!*

MAMA (*tentatively, still looking at her son's back turned against her and* RUTH): It's—it's a nice house too . . . (*She cannot help speaking directly to him. An imploring quality in her voice, her manner, makes her almost like a girl now*) Three bedrooms—nice big one for you and Ruth . . . . Me and Beneatha still have to share our room, but Travis have one of his own—and (*With difficulty*) I figure if the—new baby—is a boy, we could get one of them double-decker outfits . . . And there's a yard with a little patch of dirt where I could maybe get to grow me a few flowers . . . And a nice big basement . . .

RUTH: Walter honey, be glad—

MAMA (*still to his back, fingering things on the table*): 'Course I don't want to make it sound fancier than it is . . . It's just a plain little old house—but it's made good and solid—and it will be *ours.* Walter Lee—it makes a difference in a man when he can walk on floors that belong to *him* . . .

RUTH: Where is it?

MAMA (*frightened at this telling*): Well—well—it's out there in Clybourne Park—

(RUTH*'s radiance fades abruptly, and* WALTER *finally turns slowly to face his mother with incredulity and hostility*)

RUTH: Where?

MAMA (*matter-of-factly*): Four o six Clybourne Street, Clybourne Park.

RUTH: Clybourne Park? Mama, there ain't no colored people living in Clybourne Park.

MAMA (*almost idiotically*): Well, I guess there's going to be some now.

WALTER (*bitterly*): So that's the peace and comfort you went out and bought for us today!

MAMA (*raising her eyes to meet his finally*): Son—I just tried to find the nicest place for the least amount of money for my family.

RUTH (*trying to recover from the shock*): Well—well—'course I ain't one never been 'fraid of no crackers, mind you—but—well, wasn't there no other houses nowhere?

MAMA: Them houses they put up for colored in them areas way out all seem to cost twice as much as other houses. I did the best I could.

RUTH (*struck senseless with the news, in its various degrees of goodness and trouble, she sits a moment, her fists propping her chin in thought, and then she starts to rise, bringing her fists down with vigor, the radiance spreading from cheek to cheek again*): Well—well!—All I can say is—if this is my time in life—*MY* TIME—to say good-bye—(*And she builds with momentum as she starts to circle the room with an exuberant, almost tearfully happy release*)—to these God-damned cracking walls!—(*She pounds the walls*)—and these marching roaches!—(*She wipes at an imaginary army of marching roaches*)—and this cramped little closet which ain't now or never was no kitchen! . . . then I say it loud and good, HALLELUJAH! AND GOOD-BYE MISERY . . . I DON'T NEVER WANT TO SEE YOUR UGLY FACE AGAIN! (*She laughs joyously, having practically destroyed the apartment, and flings her arms up and lets them come down happily, slowly, reflectively, over her abdomen, aware for the first time perhaps that the life therein pulses with happiness and not despair*) Lena?

MAMA (*moved, watching her happiness*): Yes, honey?

RUTH (*looking off*): Is there—is there a whole lot of sunlight?

MAMA (*understanding*): Yes, child, there's a whole lot of sunlight.

(*Long pause*)

RUTH (*collecting herself and going to the door of the room* TRAVIS *is in*): Well—I guess I better see 'bout Travis. (*To* MAMA) Lord, I sure don't feel like whipping nobody today!

(*She exits*)

MAMA (*the mother and son are left alone now and the mother waits a long time, considering deeply, before she speaks*): Son—you—you understand what I done, don't you? (WALTER *is silent and sullen*) I—I just seen my family falling apart today . . . just falling to pieces in front of my eyes . . . We couldn't of gone on like we was today. We was going backwards 'stead of forwards—talking 'bout killing babies and wishing each other was dead . . . When it gets like that in life—you just got to do something different, push on out and do something bigger . . . (*She waits*) I wish you say something, son . . . I wish you'd say how deep inside you you think I done the right thing—

WALTER (*crossing slowly to his bedroom door and finally turning there and speaking measuredly*): What you need me to say you done right for? *You* the head of this family. You run our lives like you want to. It was your money and you did what you wanted with it. So what you need for me to say it was all right for? (*Bitterly, to hurt her as deeply as he knows is possible*) So you butchered up a dream of mine—you—who always talking 'bout your children's dreams . . .

MAMA: Walter Lee—

(*He just closes the door behind him.* MAMA *sits alone, thinking heavily*)

Curtain

Scene II

Time: Friday night. A few weeks later.

At rise: Packing crates mark the intention of the family to move. BENEATHA *and* GEORGE *come in, presumably from an evening out again.*

GEORGE: O.K. . . . O.K., whatever you say . . . (*They both sit on the couch. He tries to kiss her. She moves away*) Look, we've had a nice evening; let's not spoil it, huh? . . .

(*He again turns her head and tries to nuzzle in and she turns away from him, not with distaste but with momentary lack of interest; in a mood to pursue what they were talking about*)

BENEATHA: I'm *trying* to talk to you.

GEORGE: We always talk.

BENEATHA: Yes—and I love to talk.

GEORGE (*exasperated; rising*): I know it and I don't mind it sometimes . . . I want you to cut it out, see—The moody stuff, I mean. I don't like it. You're a nice-looking girl . . . all over. That's all you need, honey, forget the atmosphere. Guys aren't going to go for the atmosphere—they're going to go for what they see. Be glad for that. Drop the Garbo routine. It doesn't go with you. As for myself, I want a nice—(*Groping*)—simple (*Thoughtfully*)—sophisticated girl . . . not a poet—O.K.?

(*He starts to kiss her, she rebuffs him again and he jumps up*)

BENEATHA: Why are you angry, George?

GEORGE: Because this is stupid! I don't go out with you to discuss the nature of "quiet desperation" or to hear all about your thoughts—because the world will go on thinking what it thinks regardless—

BENEATHA: Then why read books? Why go to school?

GEORGE (*with artificial patience, counting on his fingers*): It's simple. You read books—to learn facts—to get grades—to pass the course—to get a degree. That's all—it has nothing to do with thoughts.

(*A long pause*)

BENEATHA: I see. (*He starts to sit*) Good night, George.

(GEORGE *looks at her a little oddly, and starts to exit. He meets* MAMA *coming in*)

GEORGE: Oh—hello, Mrs. Younger.

MAMA: Hello, George, how you feeling?

GEORGE: Fine—fine, how are you?

MAMA: Oh, a little tired. You know them steps can get you after a day's work. You all have a nice time tonight?

GEORGE: Yes—a fine time. A fine time.

MAMA: Well, good night.

GEORGE: Good night. (*He exits.* MAMA *closes the door behind her*) Hello, honey. What you sitting like that for?

BENEATHA: I'm just sitting.

MAMA: Didn't you have a nice time?

BENEATHA: No.

MAMA: No? What's the matter?

BENEATHA: Mama, George is a fool—honest. (*She rises*)

MAMA (*hustling around unloading the packages she has entered with. She stops*): Is he, baby?

BENEATHA: Yes.

(BENEATHA *makes up* TRAVIS' *bed as she talks*)

MAMA: You sure?

BENEATHA: Yes.

MAMA: Well—I guess you better not waste your time with no fools.

(BENEATHA *looks up at her mother, watching her put groceries in the refrigerator. Finally she gathers up her things and starts into the bedroom. At the door she stops and looks back at her mother*)

BENEATHA: Mama—

MAMA: Yes, baby—

BENEATHA: Thank you.

MAMA: For what?

BENEATHA: For understanding me this time.

(*She exits quickly and the mother stands, smiling a little, looking at the place where* BENEATHA *just stood.* RUTH *enters*)

RUTH: Now don't you fool with any of this stuff, Lena—

MAMA: Oh, I just thought I'd sort a few things out. Is Brother here?

RUTH: Yes.

MAMA (*with concern*): Is he—

RUTH (*reading her eyes*): Yes.

(MAMA *is silent and someone knocks on the door.* MAMA *and* RUTH *exchange weary and knowing glances and* RUTH *opens it to admit the neighbor,* MRS. JOHNSON,* *who is a rather squeaky wide-eyed lady of no particular age, with a newspaper under her arm*)

MAMA (*changing her expression to acute delight and a ringing cheerful greeting*): Oh—hello there, Johnson.

JOHNSON (*This is a woman who decided long ago to be enthusiastic about EVERYTHING in life and she is inclined to wave her wrist vigorously at the height of her exclamatory comments*): Hello there, yourself! H'you this evening, Ruth?

RUTH (*not much of a deceptive type*): Fine, Mis' Johnson, h'you?

JOHNSON: Fine. (*Reaching out quickly, playfully, and patting* RUTH*'s stomach*) Ain't you starting to poke out none yet! (*She mugs with delight at the over-familiar remark and her eyes dart around looking at the crates and packing preparation;* MAMA*'s face is a cold sheet of endurance*) Oh, ain't we getting ready round here, though! Yessir! Lookathere! I'm telling you the Youngers is really getting ready to "move on up a little higher!"—Bless God!

MAMA (*a little drily, doubting the total sincerity of the Blesser*): Bless God.

JOHNSON: He's good, ain't He?

MAMA: Oh yes, He's good.

JOHNSON: I mean sometimes He works in mysterious ways . . . but He works, don't He!

MAMA (*the same*): Yes, he does.

JOHNSON: I'm just soooooo happy for y'all. And this here child—(*About* RUTH) looks like she could just pop open with happiness, don't she. Where's all the rest of the family?

MAMA: Bennie's gone to bed—

JOHNSON: Ain't no . . . (*The implication is pregnancy*) sickness done hit you—I hope . . .?

MAMA: No—she just tired. She was out this evening.

JOHNSON (*all is a coo, an emphatic coo*): Aw—ain't that lovely. She still going out with the little Murchison boy?

MAMA (*drily*): Ummmm huh.

JOHNSON: That's lovely. You sure got lovely children, Younger. Me and Isaiah talks all the time 'bout what fine children you was blessed with. We sure do.

*This character and the scene of her visit were cut from the original production and early editions of the play.

MAMA: Ruth, give Mis' Johnson a piece of sweet potato pie and some milk.

JOHNSON: Oh honey, I can't stay hardly a minute—I just dropped in to see if there was anything I could do. (*Accepting the food easily*) I guess y'all seen the news what's all over the colored paper this week . . .

MAMA: No—didn't get mine yet this week.

JOHNSON (*lifting her head and blinking with the spirit of catastrophe*): You mean you ain't read 'bout them colored people that was bombed out their place out there?

(RUTH *straightens with concern and takes the paper and reads it.* JOHNSON *notices her and feeds commentary*)

JOHNSON: Ain't it something how bad these here white folks is getting here in Chicago! Lord, getting so you think you right down in Mississippi! (*With a tremendous and rather insincere sense of melodrama*) 'Course I thinks it's wonderful how our folks keeps on pushing out. You hear some of these Negroes round here talking 'bout how they don't go where they ain't wanted and all that—but not me, honey! (*This is a lie*) Wilhemenia Othella Johnson goes anywhere, any time she feels like it! (*With head movement for emphasis*) Yes I do! Why if we left it up to these here crackers, the poor niggers wouldn't have nothing—(*She clasps her hand over her mouth*) Oh, I always forgets you don't 'low that word in your house.

MAMA (*quietly, looking at her*): No—I don't 'low it.

JOHNSON (*vigorously again*): Me neither! I was just telling Isaiah yesterday when he come using it in front of me—I said, "Isaiah, it's just like Mis' Younger says all the time—"

MAMA: Don't you want some more pie?

JOHNSON: No—no thank you; this was lovely. I got to get on over home and have my midnight coffee. I hear some people say it don't let them sleep but I finds I can't close my eyes right lessen I done had that laaaast cup of coffee . . . (*She waits. A beat. Undaunted*) My Goodnight coffee, I calls it!

MAMA (*with much eye-rolling and communication between herself and* RUTH): Ruth, why don't you give Mis' Johnson some coffee.

(RUTH *gives* MAMA *an unpleasant look for her kindness*)

JOHNSON (*accepting the coffee*): Where's Brother tonight?

MAMA: He's lying down.

JOHNSON: MMmmmmm, he sure gets his beauty rest, don't he? Good-looking man. Sure is a good-looking man! (*Reaching out to pat* RUTH'*s stomach again*) I guess that's how come we keep on having babies around here. (*She winks at* MAMA) One thing 'bout Brother, he always know how to have a *good* time. And soooooo ambitious! I bet it was his idea y'all moving out to Clybourne Park. Lord—I bet this time next month y'all's names will have been in the papers plenty—(*Holding up her hands to mark off each word of the headline she can see in front of her*) "NEGROES INVADE CLYBOURNE PARK—BOMBED!"

MAMA (*she and* RUTH *look at the woman in amazement*): We ain't exactly moving out there to get bombed.

JOHNSON: Oh, honey—you know I'm praying to God every day that don't nothing like that happen! But you have to think of life like it is—and these here Chicago peckerwoods is some baaaad peckerwoods.

MAMA (*wearily*): We done thought about all that Mis' Johnson.

(BENEATHA *comes out of the bedroom in her robe and passes through to the bathroom.* MRS. JOHNSON *turns*)

JOHNSON: Hello there, Bennie!

BENEATHA (*crisply*): Hello, Mrs. Johnson.

JOHNSON: How is school?

BENEATHA (*crisply*): Fine, thank you. (*She goes out.*)

JOHNSON (*insulted*): Getting so she don't have much to say to nobody.

MAMA: The child was on her way to the bathroom.

JOHNSON: I know—but sometimes she act like ain't got time to pass the time of day with nobody ain't been to college. Oh—I ain't criticizing her none. It's just—you know how some of our young people gets when they get a little education. (MAMA *and* RUTH *say nothing, just look at her*) Yes—well. Well, I guess I better get on home. (*Unmoving*) 'Course I can understand how she must be proud and everything—being the only one in the family to make something of herself. I know just being a chauffeur ain't never satisfied Brother none. He shouldn't feel like that, though. Ain't nothing wrong with being a chauffeur.

MAMA: There's plenty wrong with it.

JOHNSON: What?

MAMA: Plenty. My husband always said being any kind of a servant wasn't a fit thing for a man to have to be. He always said a man's hands was made to make things, or to turn the earth with—not to drive nobody's car for 'em—or—(*She looks at her own hands*) carry they slop jars. And my boy is just like him—he wasn't meant to wait on nobody.

JOHNSON (*rising, somewhat offended*): Mmmmmmmmmm. The Youngers is too much for me! (*She looks around*) You sure one proud-acting bunch of colored folks. Well—I always thinks like Booker T. Washington said that time—"Education has spoiled many a good plow hand"—

MAMA: Is that what old Booker T. said?

JOHNSON: He sure did.

MAMA: Well, it sounds just like him. The fool.

JOHNSON (*indignantly*): Well—he was one of our great men.

MAMA: Who said so?

JOHNSON (*nonplussed*): You know, me and you ain't never agreed about some things, Lena Younger. I guess I better be going—

RUTH (*quickly*): Good night.

JOHNSON: Good night. Oh—(*Thrusting it at her*) You can keep the paper! (*With a trill*) 'Night.

MAMA: Good night, Mis' Johnson.

(MRS. JOHNSON *exits*)

RUTH: If ignorance was gold . . .

MAMA: Shush. Don't talk about folks behind their backs.

RUTH: You do.

MAMA: I'm old and corrupted. (BENEATHA *enters*) You was rude to Mis' Johnson, Beneatha, and I don't like it at all.

BENEATHA (*at her door*): Mama, if there are two things we, as a people, have got to overcome, one is the Klu Klux Klan—and the other is Mrs. Johnson. (*She exits*)

MAMA: Smart aleck.

(*The phone rings*)

RUTH: I'll get it.

MAMA: Lord, ain't this a popular place tonight.

RUTH (*at the phone*): Hello—Just a minute. (*Goes to door*) Walter, it's Mrs. Arnold. (*Waits. Goes back to the phone. Tense*) Hello. Yes, this is his wife speaking . . . He's lying down now. Yes . . . well, he'll be in tomorrow. He's been very sick. Yes—I know we should have called, but we were so sure he'd be able to come in today. Yes—yes, I'm very sorry. Yes . . . Thank you very much. (*She hangs up.* WALTER *is standing in the doorway of the bedroom behind her*) That was Mrs. Arnold.

WALTER (*indifferently*): Was it?

RUTH: She said if you don't come in tomorrow that they are getting a new man. . . .

WALTER: Ain't that sad—ain't that crying sad.

RUTH: She said Mr. Arnold has had to take a cab for three days . . . Walter, you ain't been to work for three days! (*This is a revelation to her*) Where you been, Walter Lee Younger? (WALTER *looks at her and starts to laugh*) You're going to lose your job.

WALTER: That's right . . . (*He turns on the radio*)

RUTH: Oh, Walter, and with your mother working like a dog every day—

(*A steamy, deep blues pours into the room*)

WALTER: That's sad too—Everything is sad.

MAMA: What you been doing for these three days, son?

WALTER: Mama—you don't know all the things a man what got leisure can find to do in this city . . . What's this—Friday night? Well—Wednesday I borrowed Willy Harris' car and I went for a drive . . . just me and myself and I drove and drove . . . Way out . . . way past South Chicago, and I parked the car and I sat and looked at the steel mills all day long. I just sat in the car and looked at them big black chimneys for hours. Then I drove back and I went to the Green Hat. (*Pause*) And Thursday—Thursday I borrowed the car again and I got in it and I pointed it the other way and I drove the other way—for hours—way, way up to Wisconsin, and I looked at the farms. I just drove and looked at the farms. Then I drove back and I went to the Green Hat. (*Pause*) And today—today I didn't get the car. Today I just walked. All over the Southside. And I looked at the Negroes and they looked at me and finally I just sat down on the curb at Thirty-ninth and South Parkway and I just sat there and watched the Negroes go by. And then I went to the Green Hat. You all sad? You all depressed? And you know where I am going right now—

(RUTH *goes out quietly*)

MAMA: Oh, Big Walter, is this the harvest of our days?

WALTER: You know what I like about the Green Hat? I like this little cat they got there who blows a sax . . . He blows. He talks to me. He ain't but 'bout five feet tall and he's got a conked head and his eyes is always closed and he's all music—

MAMA (*rising and getting some papers out of her handbag*): Walter—

WALTER: And there's this other guy who plays the piano . . . and they got a sound. I mean they can work on some music . . . They got the best little combo in the world in the Green Hat . . . You can just sit there and drink and listen to them three men play and you realize that don't nothing matter worth a damn, but just being there—

MAMA: I've helped do it to you, haven't I, son? Walter, I been wrong.

WALTER: Naw—you ain't never been wrong about nothing, Mama.

MAMA: Listen to me, now. I say I been wrong, son. That I been doing to you what the rest of the world been doing to you. (*She turns off the radio*) Walter—(*She stops and he looks up slowly at her and she meets his eyes pleadingly*) What you ain't never understood is that I ain't got nothing, don't own nothing, ain't never really wanted nothing that wasn't for you. There ain't nothing as precious to me . . . There ain't nothing worth holding on to, money, dreams, nothing else—if it means—if it means it's going to destroy my boy. (*She takes an envelope out of her handbag and puts it in front of him and he watches her without speaking or moving*) I paid the man thirty-five hundred dollars down on the house. That leaves sixty-five hundred dollars. Monday morning I want you to take this money and take three thousand dollars and put it in a savings account for Beneatha's medical schooling. The rest you put in a checking account—with your name on it. And from now on any penny that come out of it or that go in it is for you to look after. For you to decide. (*She drops her hands a little helplessly*) It ain't much, but it's all I got in the world and I'm putting it in your hands. I'm telling you to be the head of this family from now on like you supposed to be.

WALTER (*stares at the money*): You trust me like that, Mama?

MAMA: I ain't never stop trusting you. Like I ain't never stop loving you.

(*She goes out, and* WALTER *sits looking at the money on the table. Finally, in a decisive gesture, he gets up, and, in mingled joy and desperation, picks up the money. At the same moment,* TRAVIS *enters for bed*)

TRAVIS: What's the matter, Daddy? You drunk?

WALTER (*sweetly, more sweetly than we have ever known him*): No, Daddy ain't drunk. Daddy ain't going to never be drunk again . . .

TRAVIS: Well, good night, Daddy.

(*The* FATHER *has come from behind the couch and leans over, embracing his son*)

WALTER: Son, I feel like talking to you tonight.

TRAVIS: About what?

WALTER: Oh, about a lot of things. About you and what kind of man you going to be when you grow up . . . . Son—son, what do you want to be when you grow up?

TRAVIS: A bus driver.

WALTER (*laughing a little*): A what? Man, that ain't nothing to want to be!

TRAVIS: Why not?

WALTER: 'Cause, man—it ain't big enough—you know what I mean.

TRAVIS: I don't know then. I can't make up my mind. Sometimes Mama asks me that too. And sometimes when I tell her I just want to be like you—she says she don't want me to be like that and sometimes she says she does . . .

WALTER (*gathering him up in his arms*): You know what, Travis? In seven years you going to be seventeen years old. And things is going to be very different with us in seven years, Travis . . . One day when you are seventeen I'll come home—home from my office downtown somewhere—

TRAVIS: You don't work in no office, Daddy.

WALTER: No—but after tonight. After what your daddy gonna do tonight, there's going to be offices—a whole lot of offices . . .

TRAVIS: What you gonna do tonight, Daddy?

WALTER: You wouldn't understand yet, son, but your daddy's gonna make a transaction . . . a business transaction that's going to change our lives . . . That's how come one day when you 'bout seventeen years old I'll come home and I'll be pretty tired, you know what I mean, after a day of conferences and secretaries getting things wrong the way they do . . . 'cause an executive's life is hell, man—(*The more he talks the farther away he gets*) And I'll pull the car up on the driveway . . . just a plain black Chrysler, I think, with white walls—no—black tires. More elegant. Rich people don't have to be flashy . . . though I'll have to get something a little sportier for Ruth—maybe a Cadillac convertible to do her shopping in . . . And I'll come up the steps to the house and the gardener will be clipping away at the hedges and he'll say, "Good evening, Mr. Younger." And I'll say, "Hello, Jefferson, how are you this evening?" And I'll go inside and Ruth will come downstairs and meet me at the door and we'll kiss each other and she'll take my arm and we'll go up to your room to see you sitting on the floor with the catalogues of all the great schools in America around you . . . All the great schools in the world! And—and I'll say, all right son—it's your seventeenth birthday, what is it you've decided? . . . Just tell me where you want to go to school and you'll go. Just tell me, what it is you want to be—and you'll be it . . . . Whatever you want to be—Yessir! (*He holds his arms open for* TRAVIS) You just name it, son . . . (TRAVIS *leaps into them*) and I hand you the world!

(WALTER*'s voice has risen in pitch and hysterical promise and on the last line he lifts* TRAVIS *high*)

(*Blackout*)

Scene III

Time: *Saturday, moving day, one week later.*

Before the curtain rises, RUTH*'s voice, a strident, dramatic church alto, cuts through the silence.*

It is, in the darkness, a triumphant surge, a penetrating statement of expectation: Oh, Lord, I don't feel no ways tired! Children, oh, glory hallelujah!

As the curtain rises we see that RUTH *is alone in the living room, finishing up the family's packing. It is moving day. She is nailing crates and tying cartons.* BENEATHA *enters, carrying a guitar case, and watches her exuberant sister-in-law.*

RUTH: Hey!

BENEATHA (*putting away the case*): Hi.

RUTH (*pointing at a package*): Honey—look in that package there and see what I found on sale this morning at the South Center. (RUTH *gets up and moves to the package and draws out some curtains*) Lookahere—hand-turned hems!

BENEATHA: How do you know the window size out there?

RUTH (*who hadn't thought of that*): Oh—Well, they bound to fit something in the whole house. Anyhow, they was too good a bargain to pass up. (RUTH *slaps her head, sud-*

denly remembering something) Oh, Bennie—I meant to put a special note on that carton over there. That's your mama's good china and she wants 'em to be very careful with it.

BENEATHA: I'll do it.

(BENEATHA *finds a piece of paper and starts to draw large letters on it*)

RUTH: You know what I'm going to do soon as I get in that new house?

BENEATHA: What?

RUTH: Honey—I'm going to run me a tub of water up to here . . . (*With her fingers practically up to her nostrils*) And I'm going to get in it—and I am going to sit . . . and sit . . . and sit in that hot water and the first person who knocks to tell *me* to hurry up and come out—

BENEATHA: Gets shot at sunrise.

RUTH (*laughing happily*): You said it, sister! (*Noticing how large* BENEATHA *is absent-mindedly making the note*) Honey, they ain't going to read that from no airplane.

BENEATHA (*laughing herself*): I guess I always think things have more emphasis if they are big, somehow.

RUTH (*looking up at her and smiling*): You and your brother seem to have that as a philosophy of life. Lord, that man—done changed so 'round here. You know—you know what we did last night? Me and Walter Lee?

BENEATHA: What?

RUTH (*smiling to herself*): We went to the movies. (*Looking at* BENEATHA *to see if she understands*) We went to the movies. You know the last time me and Walter went to the movies together?

BENEATHA: No.

RUTH: Me neither. That's how long it been. (*Smiling again*) But we went last night. The picture wasn't much good, but that didn't seem to matter. We went—and we held hands.

BENEATHA: Oh, Lord!

RUTH: We held hands—and you know what?

BENEATHA: What?

RUTH: When we come out of the show it was late and dark and all the stores and things was closed up . . . and it was kind of chilly and there wasn't many people on the streets . . . and we was still holding hands, me and Walter.

BENEATHA: You're killing me.

(WALTER *enters with a large package. His happiness is deep in him; he cannot keep still with his new-found exuberance. He is singing and wiggling and snapping his fingers. He puts his package in a corner and puts a phonograph record, which he has brought in with him, on the record player. As the music, soulful and sensuous, comes up he dances over to* RUTH *and tries to get her to dance with him. She gives in at last to his raunchiness and in a fit of giggling allows herself to be drawn into his mood. They dip and she melts into his arms in a classic, body-melding "slow drag"*)

BENEATHA (*regarding them a long time as they dance, then drawing in her breath for a deeply exaggerated comment which she does not particularly mean*): Talk about—olddddddddd-fashionedddddd—Negroes!

WALTER (*stopping momentarily*): What kind of Negroes? (*He says this in fun. He is not angry with her today, nor with anyone. He starts to dance with his wife again*)

BENEATHA: Old-fashioned.

WALTER (*as he dances with* RUTH): You know, when these *New Negroes* have their convention—(*Pointing at his sister*)—that is going to be the chairman of the Committee on Unending Agitation. (*He goes on dancing, then stops*) Race, race, race! . . . Girl, I do believe you are the first person in the history of the entire human race to successfully brainwash yourself. (BENEATHA *breaks up and he goes on dancing. He stops again, enjoying his tease*) Damn, even the N double A C P takes a holiday sometimes! (BENEATHA *and* RUTH *laugh. He dances with* RUTH *some more and starts to laugh and stops and pantomimes someone over an operating table*) I can just see that chick someday looking down at some poor cat on an operating table and before she starts to slice him, she says . . . (*Pulling his sleeves back maliciously*) "By the way, what are your views on civil rights down there? . . ."

(*He laughs at her again and starts to dance happily. The bell sounds*)

BENEATHA: Sticks and stones may break my bones but . . . words will never hurt me!

(BENEATHA *goes to the door and opens it as* WALTER *and* RUTH *go on with the clowning.* BENEATHA *is somewhat surprised to see a quiet-looking middle-aged white man in a business suit holding his hat and a briefcase in his hand and consulting a small piece of paper*)

MAN: Uh—how do you do, miss. I am looking for a Mrs.—(*He looks at the slip of paper*) Mrs. Lena Younger? (*He stops short, struck dumb at the sight of the oblivious* WALTER *and* RUTH)

BENEATHA (smoothing her hair with slight embarrassment): Oh—yes, that's my mother. Excuse me (She closes the door and turns to quiet the other two) Ruth! Brother! (Enunciating precisely but soundlessly: There's a white man at the door! They stop dancing, RUTH cuts off the phonograph, BENEATHA opens the door. The man casts a curious quick glance at all of them) Uh—come in please.

MAN (*coming in*): Thank you.

BENEATHA: My mother isn't here just now. Is it business?

MAN: Yes . . . well, of a sort.

WALTER (*freely, the Man of the House*): Have a seat. I'm Mrs. Younger's son. I look after most of her business matters.

(RUTH *and* BENEATHA *exchange amused glances*)

MAN (*regarding* WALTER, *and sitting*): Well—My name is Karl Lindner . . .

WALTER (*stretching out his hand*): Walter Younger. This is my wife—(RUTH *nods politely*)—and my sister.

LINDNER: How do you do.

WALTER (*amiably, as he sits himself easily on a chair, leaning forward on his knees with interest and looking expectantly into the newcomer's face*): What can we do for you, Mr. Lindner!

LINDNER (*some minor shuffling of the hat and briefcase on his knees*): Well—I am a representative of the Clybourne Park Improvement Association—

WALTER (*pointing*): Why don't you sit your things on the floor?

LINDNER: Oh—yes. Thank you. (*He slides the briefcase and hat under the chair*) And as I was saying—I am from the Clybourne Park Improvement Association and we have had it brought to our attention at the last meeting that you people—or at least your mother—has bought a piece of residential property at—(*He digs for the slip of paper again*)—four o six Clybourne Street . . .

WALTER: That's right. Care for something to drink? Ruth, get Mr. Lindner a beer.

LINDNER (*upset for some reason*): Oh—no, really. I mean thank you very much, but no thank you.

RUTH (*innocently*): Some coffee?

LINDNER: Thank you, nothing at all.

(BENEATHA *is watching the man carefully*)

LINDNER: Well, I don't know how much you folks know about our organization. (*He is a gentle man; thoughtful and somewhat labored in his manner*) It is one of these community organizations set up to look after—oh, you know, things like block upkeep and special projects and we also have what we call our New Neighbors Orientation Committee . . .

BENEATHA (*drily*): Yes—and what do they do?

LINDNER (*turning a little to her and then returning the main force to* WALTER): Well—it's what you might call a sort of welcoming committee, I guess. I mean they, we—I'm the chairman of the committee—go around and see the new people who move into the neighborhood and sort of give them the lowdown on the way we do things in Clybourne Park.

BENEATHA (*with appreciation of the two meanings, which escape* RUTH *and* WALTER): Un-huh.

LINDNER: And we also have the category of what the association calls—(*He looks elsewhere*)—uh—special community problems . . .

BENEATHA: Yes—and what are some of those?

WALTER: Girl, let the man talk.

LINDNER (*with understated relief*): Thank you. I would sort of like to explain this thing in my own way. I mean I want to explain to you in a certain way.

WALTER: Go ahead.

LINDNER: Yes. Well. I'm going to try to get right to the point. I'm sure we'll all appreciate that in the long run.

BENEATHA: Yes.

WALTER: Be still now!

LINDNER: Well—

RUTH (*still innocently*): Would you like another chair—you don't look comfortable.

LINDNER (*more frustrated than annoyed*): No, thank you very much. Please. Well—to get right to the point I—(*A great breath, and he is off at last*) I am sure you people must be aware of some of the incidents which have happened in various parts of the city when colored people have moved into certain areas—(BENEATHA *exhales heavily and starts tossing a piece of fruit up and down in the air*) Well—because we have what I think is going to be a unique type of organization in American community life—not only do we deplore that kind of thing—but we are trying to do something about it. (BENEATHA *stops tossing and turns with a new and quizzical interest to the man*) We feel—(*gaining confidence in his mission because of the interest in the faces of the people he is talking to*)—we feel that most of the trouble in this world, when you come right down to it—(*He hits his knee for emphasis*)—most of the trouble exists because people just don't sit down and talk to each other.

RUTH (*nodding as she might in church, pleased with the remark*): You can say that again, mister.

LINDNER (*more encouraged by such affirmation*): That we don't try hard enough in this world to understand the other fellow's problem. The other guy's point of view.

RUTH: Now that's right.

(BENEATHA *and* WALTER *merely watch and listen with genuine interest*)

LINDNER: Yes—that's the way we feel out in Clybourne Park. And that's why I was elected to come here this afternoon and talk to you people. Friendly like, you know, the way people should talk to each other and see if we couldn't find some way to work this thing out. As I say, the whole business is a matter of *caring* about the other fellow. Anybody can see that you are a nice family of folks, hard working and honest I'm sure. (BENEATHA *frowns slightly, quizzically, her head tilted regarding him*) Today everybody knows what it means to be on the outside of *something.* And of course, there is always somebody who is out to take advantage of people who don't always understand.

WALTER: What do you mean?

LINDNER: Well—you see our community is made up of people who've worked hard as the dickens for years to build up that little community. They're not rich and fancy people; just hard-working, honest people who don't really have much but those little homes and a dream of the kind of community they want to raise their children in. Now, I don't say we are perfect and there is a lot wrong in some of the things they want. But you've got to admit that a man, right or wrong, has the right to want to have the neighborhood he lives in a certain kind of way. And at the moment the overwhelming majority of our people out there feel that people get along better, take more of a common interest in the life of the community, when they share a common background. I want you to believe me when I tell you that race prejudice simply doesn't enter into it. It is a matter of the people of Clybourne Park believing, rightly or wrongly, as I say, that for the happiness of all concerned that our Negro families are happier when they live in their *own* communities.

BENEATHA (*with a grand and bitter gesture*): This, friends, is the Welcoming Committee!

WALTER (*dumbfounded, looking at* LINDNER): Is this what you came marching all the way over here to tell us?

LINDNER: Well, now we've been having a fine conversation. I hope you'll hear me all the way through.

WALTER (*tightly*): Go ahead, man.

LINDNER: You see—in the face of all the things I have said, we are prepared to make your family a very generous offer . . .

BENEATHA: Thirty pieces and not a coin less!

WALTER: Yeah?

LINDNER (*putting on his glasses and drawing a form out of the briefcase*): Our association is prepared, through the collective effort of our people, to buy the house from you at a financial gain to your family.

RUTH: Lord have mercy, ain't this the living gall!

WALTER: All right, you through?

LINDNER: Well, I want to give you the exact terms of the financial arrangement—

WALTER: We don't want to hear no exact terms of no arrangements. I want to know if you got any more to tell us 'bout getting together?

LINDNER (*taking off his glasses*): Well—I don't suppose that you feel . . .

WALTER: Never mind how I feel—you got any more to say 'bout how people ought to sit down and talk to each other? . . . Get out of my house, man.

(*He turns his back and walks to the door*)

LINDNER (*looking around at the hostile faces and reaching and assembling his hat and briefcase*): Well—I don't understand why you people are reacting this way. What do you think you are going to gain by moving into a neighborhood where you just aren't wanted and where some elements—well—people can get awful worked up when they feel that their whole way of life and everything they've ever worked for is threatened.

WALTER: Get out.

LINDNER (*at the door, holding a small card*): Well—I'm sorry it went like this.

WALTER: Get out.

LINDNER (*almost sadly regarding* WALTER): You just can't force people to change their hearts, son.

(*He turns and put his card on a table and exits.* WALTER *pushes the door to with stinging hatred, and stands looking at it.* RUTH *just sits and* BENEATHA *just stands. They say nothing.* MAMA *and* TRAVIS *enter*)

MAMA: Well—this all the packing got done since I left out of here this morning. I testify before God that my children got all the energy of the *dead!* What time the moving men due?

BENEATHA: Four o'clock. You had a caller, Mama.

(*She is smiling, teasingly*)

MAMA: Sure enough—who?

BENEATHA (*her arms folded saucily*): The Welcoming Committee.

(WALTER *and* RUTH *giggle*)

MAMA (*innocently*): Who?

BENEATHA: The Welcoming Committee. They said they're sure going to be glad to see you when you get there.

WALTER (*devilishly*): Yeah, they said they can't hardly wait to see your face.

(*Laughter*)

MAMA (*sensing their facetiousness*): What's the matter with you all?

WALTER: Ain't nothing the matter with us. We just telling you 'bout the gentleman who came to see you this afternoon. From the Clybourne Park Improvement Association.

MAMA: What he want?

RUTH (*in the same mood as* BENEATHA *and* WALTER): To welcome you, honey.

WALTER: He said they can't hardly wait. He said the one thing they don't have, that they just *dying* to have out there is a fine family of fine colored people! (*To* RUTH *and* BENEATHA) Ain't that right!

RUTH (*mockingly*): Yeah! He left his card—

BENEATHA (*handing card to* MAMA): In case.

(MAMA *reads and throws it on the floor—understanding and looking off as she draws her chair up to the table on which she has put her plant and some sticks and some cord*)

MAMA: Father, give us strength. (*Knowingly—and without fun*) Did he threaten us?

BENEATHA: Oh—Mama—they don't do it like that any more. He talked Brotherhood. He said everybody ought to learn how to sit down and hate each other with good Christian fellowship.

(*She and* WALTER *shake hands to ridicule the remark*)

MAMA (*sadly*): Lord, protect us . . .

RUTH: You should hear the money those folks raised to buy the house from us. All we paid and then some.

BENEATHA: What they think we going to do—eat 'em?

RUTH: No, honey, marry 'em.

MAMA (*shaking her head*): Lord, Lord, Lord . . .

RUTH: Well—that's the way the crackers crumble. (*A beat*) Joke.

BENEATHA (*laughingly noticing what her mother is doing*): Mama, what are you doing?

MAMA: Fixing my plant so it won't get hurt none on the way . . .

BENEATHA: Mama, you going to take *that* to the new house?

MAMA: Un-huh—

BENEATHA: That raggedy-looking old thing?

MAMA (*stopping and looking at her*): It expresses ME!

RUTH (*with delight, to* BENEATHA): So there, Miss Thing!

(WALTER *comes to* MAMA *suddenly and bends down behind her and squeezes her in his arms with all his strength. She is overwhelmed by the suddenness of it and, though delighted, her manner is like that of* RUTH *and* TRAVIS)

MAMA: Look out now, boy! You make me mess up my thing here!

WALTER (*his face lit, he slips down on his knees beside her, his arms still about her*): Mama . . . you know what it means to climb up in the chariot?

MAMA (*gruffly, very happy*): Get on away from me now . . .

RUTH (*near the gift-wrapped package, trying to catch* WALTER*'s eye*): Psst—

WALTER: What the old song say, Mama . . .

RUTH: Walter—Now?

(*She is pointing at the package*)

WALTER (*speaking the lines, sweetly, playfully, in his mother's face*):

I got wings . . . you got wings . . .
All God's Children got wings . . .

MAMA: Boy—get out of my face and do some work . . .

WALTER:

When I get to heaven gonna put on my wings,
Gonna fly all over God's heaven . . .

BENEATHA (*teasingly, from across the room*): Everybody talking 'bout heaven ain't going there!

WALTER (*to* RUTH, *who is carrying the box across to them*): I don't know, you think we ought to give her that . . . Seems to me she ain't been very appreciative around here.

MAMA (*eying the box, which is obviously a gift*): What is that?

WALTER (*taking it from* RUTH *and putting it on the table in front of* MAMA): Well—what you all think? Should we give it to her?

RUTH: Oh—she was pretty good today.

MAMA: I'll good you—

(*She turns her eyes to the box again*)

BENEATHA: Open it, Mama.

(*She stands up, looks at it, turns and looks at all of them, and then presses her hands together and does not open the package*)

WALTER (*sweetly*): Open it, Mama. It's for you. (MAMA *looks in his eyes. It is the first present in her life without its being Christmas. Slowly she opens her package and lifts out, one by one, a brand-new sparkling set of gardening tools.* WALTER *continues, prodding*) Ruth made up the note—read it . . .

MAMA (*picking up the card and adjusting her glasses*): "To our own Mrs. Miniver—Love from Brother, Ruth and Beneatha." Ain't that lovely . . .

TRAVIS (*tugging at his father's sleeve*): Daddy, can I give her mine now?

WALTER: All right, son. (TRAVIS *flies to get his gift*)

MAMA: Now I don't have to use my knives and forks no more . . .

WALTER: Travis didn't want to go in with the rest of us, Mama. He got his own. (*Somewhat amused*) We don't know what it is . . .

TRAVIS (*racing back in the room with a large hatbox and putting it in front of his grandmother*): Here!

MAMA: Lord have mercy, baby. You done gone and bought your grandmother a hat?

TRAVIS (*very proud*): Open it!

(*She does and lifts out an elaborate, but very elaborate, wide gardening hat, and all the adults break up at the sight of it*)

RUTH: Travis, honey, what is that?

TRAVIS (*who thinks it is beautiful and appropriate*): It's a gardening hat! Like the ladies always have on in the magazines when they work in their gardens.

BENEATHA (*giggling fiercely*): Travis—we were trying to make Mama Mrs. Miniver—not Scarlett O'Hara!

MAMA (*indignantly*): What's the matter with you all! This here is a beautiful hat! (*Absurdly*) I always wanted me one just like it!

(*She pops it on her head to prove it to her grandson, and the hat is ludicrous and considerably oversized*)

RUTH: Hot dog! Go, Mama!

WALTER (*doubled over with laughter*): I'm sorry, Mama—but you look like you ready to go out and chop you some cotton sure enough!

(*They all laugh except* MAMA, *out of deference to* TRAVIS' *feelings*)

MAMA (*gathering the boy up to her*): Bless your heart—this is the prettiest hat I ever owned—(WALTER, RUTH *and* BENEATHA *chime in—noisily, festively and insincerely congratulating*

TRAVIS *on his gift*) What are we all standing around here for? We ain't finished packin' yet. Bennie, you ain't packed one book.

(*The bell rings*)

BENEATHA: That couldn't be the movers . . . it's not hardly two good yet—

(BENEATHA *goes into her room.* MAMA *starts for door*)

WALTER (*turning, stiffening*): Wait—wait—I'll get it.

(*He stands and looks at the door*)

MAMA: You expecting company, son?

WALTER (*just looking at the door*): Yeah—yeah . . .

(MAMA *looks at* RUTH, *and they exchange innocent and unfrightened glances*)

MAMA (*not understanding*): Well, let them in, son.

BENEATHA (*from her room*): We need some more string.

MAMA: Travis—you run to the hardware and get me some string cord.

(MAMA *goes out and* WALTER *turns and looks at* RUTH. TRAVIS *goes to a dish for money*)

RUTH: Why don't you answer the door, man?

WALTER (*suddenly bounding across the floor to embrace her*): 'Cause sometimes it hard to let the future begin!

(*Stooping down in her face*)

I got wings! You got wings!
All God's children got wings!

(*He crosses to the door and throws it open. Standing there is a very slight little man in a not too prosperous business suit and with haunted frightened eyes and a hat pulled down tightly, brim up, around his forehead.* TRAVIS *passes between the men and exits.* WALTER *leans deep in the man's face, still in his jubilance*)

When I get to heaven gonna put on my wings,
Gonna fly all over God's heaven . . .

(*The little man just stares at him*)

Heaven—

(*Suddenly he stops and looks past the little man into the empty hallway*)

Where's Willy, man?

BOBO: He ain't with me.

WALTER (*not disturbed*): Oh—come on in. You know my wife.

BOBO (*dumbly, taking off his hat*): Yes—h'you, Miss Ruth.

RUTH (*quietly, a mood apart from her husband already, seeing* BOBO): Hello, Bobo.

WALTER: You right on time today . . . Right on time. That's the way! (*He slaps* BOBO *on his back*) Sit down . . . lemme hear.

(RUTH *stands stiffly and quietly in back of them, as though somehow she senses death, her eyes fixed on her husband*)

BOBO (*his frightened eyes on the floor, his hat in his hands*): Could I please get a drink of water, before I tell you about it, Walter Lee?

(WALTER *does not take his eyes off the man.* RUTH *goes blindly to the tap and gets a glass of water and brings it to* BOBO)

WALTER: There ain't nothing wrong, is there?

BOBO: Lemme tell you—

WALTER: Man—didn't nothing go wrong?

BOBO: Lemme tell you—Walter Lee. (*Looking at* RUTH *and talking to her more than to* WALTER) You know how it was. I got to tell you how it was. I mean first I got to tell you how it was all the way . . . I mean about the money I put in, Walter Lee . . .

WALTER (*with taut agitation now*): What about the money you put in?

BOBO: Well—it wasn't much as we told you—me and Willy—(*He stops*) I'm sorry, Walter. I got a bad feeling about it. I got a real bad feeling about it . . .

WALTER: Man, what you telling me about all this for? . . . Tell me what happened in Springfield . . .

BOBO: Springfield.

RUTH (*like a dead woman*): What was supposed to happen in Springfield?

BOBO (*to her*): This deal that me and Walter went into with Willy—Me and Willy was going to go down to Springfield and spread some money 'round so's we wouldn't have to wait so long for the liquor license . . . That's what we were going to do. Everybody said that was the way you had to do, you understand, Miss Ruth?

WALTER: Man—what happened down there?

BOBO (*a pitiful man, near tears*): I'm trying to tell you, Walter.

WALTER (*screaming at him suddenly*): THEN TELL ME, GODDAMMIT . . . WHAT'S THE MATTER WITH YOU?

BOBO: Man . . . I didn't go to no Springfield, yesterday.

WALTER (*halted, life hanging in the moment*): Why not?

BOBO (*the long way, the hard way to tell*): 'Cause I didn't have no reasons to . . .

WALTER: Man, what are you talking about!

BOBO: I'm talking about the fact that when I got to the train station yesterday morning—eight o'clock like we planned . . . Man—*Willy didn't never show up.*

WALTER: Why . . . where was he . . . where is he?

BOBO: That's what I'm trying to tell you . . . I don't know . . . I waited six hours . . . I called his house . . . and I waited . . . six hours . . . I waited in that train station six hours . . . (*Breaking into tears*) That was all the extra money I had in the world . . . (*Looking up at* WALTER *with the tears running down his face*) Man, *Willy is gone.*

WALTER: Gone, what you mean Willy is gone? Gone where? You mean he went by himself. You mean he went off to Springfield by himself—to take care of getting the license—(*Turns and looks anxiously at* RUTH) You mean maybe he didn't want too many people in on the business down there? (*Looks to* RUTH *again, as before*) You know Willy got his own ways. (*Looks back to* BOBO) Maybe you was late yesterday and he just went on down there without you. Maybe—maybe—he's been callin' you at home tryin' to tell you what happened or something. Maybe—maybe—he just got sick. He's somewhere—he's got to be somewhere. We just got to find him—me and you got to find him. (*Grabs* BOBO *senselessly by the collar and starts to shake him*) We got to!

BOBO (*in sudden angry, frightened agony*): What's the matter with you, Walter! *When a cat take off with your money he don't leave you no road maps!*

WALTER (*turning madly, as though he is looking for* WILLY *in the very room*): Willy! . . . Willy . . . don't do it . . . Please don't do it . . . Man, not with that money . . . Man, please, not with that money . . . Oh, God . . . Don't let it be true . . . (*He is wandering around, crying out for* WILLY *and looking for him or perhaps for help from God*) Man . . . I trusted you . . . Man, I put my life in your hands . . . (*He starts to crumple down on the floor as* RUTH *just covers her face in horror.* MAMA *opens the door and comes into the room, with* BENEATHA *behind her*) Man . . . (*He starts to pound the floor with his fists, sobbing wildly*) THAT MONEY IS MADE OUT OF MY FATHER'S FLESH—

BOBO (*standing over him helplessly*): I'm sorry, Walter . . . (*Only* WALTER*'s sobs reply.* BOBO *puts on his hat*) I had my life staked on this deal, too . . .

(*He exits*)

MAMA (*to* WALTER): Son—(*She goes to him, bends down to him, talks to his bent head*) Son . . . Is it gone? Son, I gave you sixty-five hundred dollars. Is it gone? All of it? Beneatha's money too?

WALTER (*lifting his head slowly*): Mama . . . I never . . . went to the bank at all . . .

MAMA (*not wanting to believe him*): You mean . . . your sister's school money . . . you used that too . . . Walter? . . .

WALTER: Yessss! All of it . . . It's all gone . . .

(*There is total silence.* RUTH *stands with her face covered with her hands;* BENEATHA *leans forlornly against a wall, fingering a piece of red ribbon from the mother's gift.* MAMA *stops and looks at her son without recognition and then, quite without thinking about it, starts to beat him senselessly in the face.* BENEATHA *goes to them and stops it*)

BENEATHA: Mama!

(MAMA *stops and looks at both of her children and rises slowly and wanders vaguely, aimlessly away from them*)

MAMA: I seen . . . him . . . night after night . . . come in . . . and look at that rug . . . and then look at me . . . the red showing in his eyes . . . the veins moving in his head . . . I seen him grow thin and old before he was forty . . . working and working and working like somebody's old horse . . . killing himself . . . and you—you give it all away in a day—(*She raises her arms to strike him again*)

BENEATHA: Mama—

MAMA: Oh, God . . . (*She looks up to Him*) Look down here—and show me the strength.

BENEATHA: Mama—

MAMA (*folding over*): Strength . . .

BENEATHA (*plaintively*): Mama . . .

MAMA: Strength!

Curtain

ACT III

An hour later.

At curtain, there is a sullen light of gloom in the living room, gray light not unlike that which began the first scene of Act One. At left we can see WALTER *within his room, alone with himself. He is stretched out on the bed, his shirt out and open, his arms under his head. He does not smoke, he does not cry out, he merely lies there, looking up at the ceiling, much as if he were alone in the world.*

In the living room BENEATHA *sits at the table, still surrounded by the now almost ominous packing crates. She sits looking off. We feel that this is a mood struck perhaps an hour before, and it lingers now, full of the empty sound of profound disappointment. We see on a line from her brother's bedroom the sameness of their attitudes. Presently the bell rings and* BENEATHA *rises without ambition or interest in answering. It is* ASAGAI, *smiling broadly, striding into the room with energy and happy expectation and conversation.*

ASAGAI: I came over . . . I had some free time. I thought I might help with the packing. Ah, I like the look of packing crates! A household in preparation for a journey! It depresses some people . . . but for me . . . it is another feeling. Something full of the flow of life, do you understand? Movement, progress . . . It makes me think of Africa.

BENEATHA: Africa!

ASAGAI: What kind of a mood is this? Have I told you how deeply you move me?

BENEATHA: He gave away the money, Asagai . . .

ASAGAI: Who gave away what money?

BENEATHA: The insurance money. My brother gave it away.

ASAGAI: Gave it away?

BENEATHA: He made an investment! With a man even Travis wouldn't have trusted with his most worn-out marbles.

ASAGAI: And it's gone?

BENEATHA: Gone!

ASAGAI: I'm very sorry . . . And you, now?

BENEATHA: Me? . . . Me? . . . Me, I'm nothing . . . Me. When I was very small . . . we used to take our sleds out in the wintertime and the only hills we had were the ice-covered stone steps of some houses down the street. And we used to fill them in with snow and make them smooth and slide down them all day . . . and it was very dangerous, you know . . . far too steep . . . and sure enough one day a kid named Rufus came down too fast and hit the sidewalk and we saw his face just split open right there in front of us . . . And I remember standing there looking at his bloody open face thinking that was the end of Rufus. But the ambulance came and they took him to the hospital and they fixed the broken bones and they sewed it all up . . . and the next time I saw Rufus he just had a little line down the middle of his face . . . I never got over that . . .

ASAGAI: What?

BENEATHA: That that was what one person could do for another, fix him up—sew up the problem, make him all right again. That was the most marvelous thing in the world . . . I wanted to do that. I always thought it was the one concrete thing in the world that a human being could do. Fix up the sick, you know—and make them whole again. This was truly being God . . .

ASAGAI: You wanted to be God?

BENEATHA: No—I wanted to cure. It used to be so important to me. I wanted to cure. It used to matter. I used to care. I mean about people and how their bodies hurt . . .

ASAGAI: And you've stopped caring?

BENEATHA: Yes—I think so.

ASAGAI: Why?

BENEATHA (*bitterly*): Because it doesn't seem deep enough, close enough to what ails mankind! It was a child's way of seeing things—or an idealist's.

ASAGAI: Children see things very well sometimes—and idealists even better.

BENEATHA: I know that's what you think. Because you are still where I left off. You with all your talk and dreams about Africa! You still think you can patch up the world. Cure the Great Sore of Colonialism—(*Loftily, mocking it*) with the Penicillin of Independence—!

ASAGAI: Yes!

BENEATHA: Independence *and then what*? What about all the crooks and thieves and just plain idiots who will come into power and steal and plunder the same as before—only now they will be black and do it in the name of the new Independence—WHAT ABOUT THEM?!

ASAGAI: That will be the problem for another time. First we must get there.

BENEATHA: And where does it end?

ASAGAI: End? Who even spoke of an end? To life? To living?

BENEATHA: An end to misery! To stupidity! Don't you see there isn't any real progress, Asagai, there is only one large circle that we march in, around and around, each of us with our own little picture in front of us—our own little mirage that we think is the future.

ASAGAI: That is the mistake.

BENEATHA: What?

ASAGAI: What you just said—about the circle. It isn't a circle—it is simply a long line—as in geometry, you know, one that reaches into infinity. And because we cannot see the end—we also cannot see how it changes. And it is very odd but those who see the changes—who dream, who will not give up—are called idealists . . . and those who see only the circle—we call *them* the "realists"!

BENEATHA: Asagai, while I was sleeping in that bed in there, people went out and took the future right out of my hands! And nobody asked me, nobody consulted me—they just went out and changed my life!

ASAGAI: Was it your money?

BENEATHA: What?

ASAGAI: Was it your money he gave away?

BENEATHA: It belonged to all of us.

ASAGAI: But did you earn it? Would you have had it at all if your father had not died?

BENEATHA: No.

ASAGAI: Then isn't there something wrong in a house—in a world—where all dreams, good or bad, must depend on the death of a man? I never thought to see *you* like this, Alaiyo. You! Your brother made a mistake and you are grateful to him so that now you can give up the ailing human race on account of it! You talk about what good is struggle, what good is anything! Where are we all going and why are we bothering!

BENEATHA: AND YOU CANNOT ANSWER IT!

ASAGAI (*shouting over her*): *I LIVE THE ANSWER!* (*Pause*) In my village at home it is the exceptional man who can even read a newspaper . . . or who ever sees a book at all. I will go home and much of what I will have to say will seem strange to the people of my village. But I will teach and work and things will happen, slowly and swiftly. At times it will seem that nothing changes at all . . . and then again the sudden dramatic events which make history leap into the future. And then quiet again. Retrogression even. Guns, murder, revolution. And I even will have moments when I wonder if the quiet was not better than all that death and hatred. But I will look about my village at the illiteracy and disease and ignorance and I will not wonder long. And perhaps . . . perhaps I will be a great man . . . I mean perhaps I will hold on to the substance of truth and find my way always with the right course . . . and perhaps for it I will be butchered in my bed some night by the servants of empire . . .

BENEATHA: *The martyr!*

ASAGAI (*he smiles*): . . . or perhaps I shall live to be a very old man, respected and esteemed in my new nation . . . And perhaps I shall hold office and this is what I'm trying to tell you, Alaiyo: Perhaps the things I believe now for my country will be wrong and outmoded, and I will not understand and do terrible things to have things my way or merely to keep my power. Don't you see that there will be young men and women—not British soldiers then, but my own black countrymen—to step out of the shadows some evening and slit my then useless throat? Don't you see they have always been there . . . that they always will be. And that such a thing as my own death will be an advance? They who might kill me even . . . actually replenish all that I was.

BENEATHA: Oh, Asagai, I know all that.

ASAGAI: Good! Then stop moaning and groaning and tell me what you plan to do.

BENEATHA: Do?

ASAGAI: I have a bit of a suggestion.

BENEATHA: What?

ASAGAI (*rather quietly for him*): That when it is all over—that you come home with me—

BENEATHA (*staring at him and crossing away with exasperation*): Oh—Asagai—at this moment you decide to be romantic!

ASAGAI (*quickly understanding the misunderstanding*): My dear, young creature of the New World—I do not mean across the city—I mean across the ocean: home—to Africa.

BENEATHA (*slowly understanding and turning to him with murmured amazement*): To Africa?

ASAGAI: Yes! . . . (*Smiling and lifting his arms playfully*) Three hundred years later the African Prince rose up out of the seas and swept the maiden back across the middle passage over which her ancestors had come—

BENEATHA (*unable to play*): To—to Nigeria?

ASAGAI: Nigeria. Home. (*Coming to her with genuine romantic flippancy*) I will show you our mountains and our stars; and give you cool drinks from gourds and teach you the old songs and the ways of our people—and, in time, we will pretend that—(*Very softly*)—you have only been away for a day. Say that you'll come—(*He swings her around and takes her full in his arms in a kiss which proceeds to passion*)

BENEATHA (*pulling away suddenly*): You're getting me all mixed up—

ASAGAI: Why?

BENEATHA: Too many things—too many things have happened today. I must sit down and think. I don't know what I feel about anything right this minute.

(*She promptly sits down and props her chin on her fist*)

ASAGAI (*charmed*): All right, I shall leave you. No—don't get up. (*Touching her, gently, sweetly*) Just sit awhile and think . . . Never be afraid to sit awhile and think. (*He goes to door and looks at her*) How often I have looked at you and said, "Ah—so this is what the New World hath finally wrought . . ."

(*He exits.* BENEATHA *sits on alone. Presently* WALTER *enters from his room and starts to rummage through things, feverishly looking for something. She looks up and turns in her seat*)

BENEATHA (*hissingly*): Yes—just look at what the New World hath wrought! . . . Just look! (*She gestures with bitter disgust*) There he is! *Monsieur le petit bourgeois noir*—himself! There he is—Symbol of a Rising Class! Entrepreneur! Titan of the system! (WALTER *ignores her completely and continues frantically and destructively looking for something and hurling things to floor and tearing things out of their place in his search.* BENEATHA *ignores the eccentricity of his actions and goes on with the monologue of insult*) Did you dream of yachts on Lake Michigan, Brother? Did you see yourself on that Great Day sitting down at the Conference Table, surrounded by all the mighty bald-headed men in America? All halted, waiting, breathless, waiting for your pronouncements on industry? Waiting for you—Chairman of the Board! (WALTER *finds what he is looking for—a small piece of white paper—and pushes it in his pocket and puts on his coat and rushes out without ever having looked at her. She shouts after him*) I look at you and I see the final triumph of stupidity in the world!

(*The door slams and she returns to just sitting again.* RUTH *comes quickly out of* MAMA*'s room*)

RUTH: Who was that?

BENEATHA: Your husband.

RUTH: Where did he go?

BENEATHA: Who knows—maybe he has an appointment at U.S. Steel.

RUTH (*anxiously, with frightened eyes*): You didn't say nothing bad to him, did you?

BENEATHA: Bad? Say anything bad to him? No—I told him he was a sweet boy and full of dreams and everything is strictly peachy keen, as the ofay kids say!

(MAMA *enters from her bedroom. She is lost, vague, trying to catch hold, to make some sense of her former command of the world, but it still eludes her. A sense of waste overwhelms her gait; a measure of apology rides on her shoulders. She goes to her plant, which has remained on the table, looks at it, picks it up and takes it to the window sill and sets it outside, and she stands and looks at it a long moment. Then she closes the window, straightens her body with effort and turns around to her children*)

MAMA: Well—ain't it a mess in here, though? (*A false cheerfulness, a beginning of something*) I guess we all better stop moping around and get some work done. All this unpacking and everything we got to do. (RUTH *raises her head slowly in response to the sense of the line; and* BENEATHA *in similar manner turns very slowly to look at her mother*) One of you all better call the moving people and tell 'em not to come.

RUTH: Tell 'em not to come?

MAMA: Of course, baby. Ain't no need in 'em coming all the way here and having to go back. They charges for that too. (*She sits down, fingers to her brow, thinking*) Lord, ever since I was a little girl, I always remembers people saying, "Lena—Lena Eggleston, you aims too high all the time. You needs to slow down and see life a little more like it is. Just slow down some." That's what they always used to say down home—"Lord, that Lena Eggleston is a high-minded thing. She'll get her due one day!"

RUTH: No, Lena . . .

MAMA: Me and Big Walter just didn't never learn right.

RUTH: Lena, no! We gotta go. Bennie—tell her . . . (*She rises and crosses to* BENEATHA *with her arms outstretched.* BENEATHA *doesn't respond*) Tell her we can still move . . . the notes ain't but a hundred and twenty-five a month. We got four grown people in this house—we can work . . .

MAMA (*to herself*): Just aimed too high all the time—

RUTH (*turning and going to* MAMA *fast—the words pouring out with urgency and desperation*): Lena—I'll work . . . I'll work twenty hours a day in all the kitchens in Chicago . . . I'll strap my baby on my back if I have to and scrub all the floors in America and wash all the sheets in America if I have to—but we got to MOVE! We got to get OUT OF HERE!!

(MAMA *reaches out absently and pats* RUTH*'s hand*)

MAMA: No—I sees things differently now. Been thinking 'bout some of the things we could do to fix this place up some. I seen a second-hand bureau over on Maxwell Street just the other day that could fit right there. (*She points to where the new furniture might go.* RUTH *wanders away from her*) Would need some new handles on it and then a little varnish and it look like something brand-new. And—we can put up them new curtains in the kitchen . . . Why this place be looking fine. Cheer us all up so that we forget trouble ever come . . . (*To* RUTH) And you could get some nice screens to put up in your room round the baby's bassinet . . . (*She looks at both of them, pleadingly*) Sometimes you just got to know when to give up some things . . . and hold on to what you got . . .

(WALTER *enters from the outside, looking spent and leaning against the door, his coat hanging from him*)

MAMA: Where you been, son?

WALTER (*breathing hard*): Made a call.

MAMA: To who, son?

WALTER: To The Man. (*He heads for his room*)

MAMA: What man, baby?

WALTER (*stops in the door*): The Man, Mama. Don't you know who The Man is?

RUTH: Walter Lee?

WALTER: *The Man*. Like the guys in the streets say—The Man. Captain Boss—Mistuh Charley . . . Old Cap'n Please Mr. Bossman . . .

BENEATHA (*suddenly*): Lindner!

WALTER: That's right! That's good. I told him to come right over.

BENEATHA (*fiercely, understanding*): For what? What do you want to see him for!

WALTER (*looking at his sister*): We going to do business with him.

MAMA: What you talking 'bout, son?

WALTER: Talking 'bout life, Mama. You all always telling me to see life like it is. Well—I laid in there on my back today . . . and I figured it out. Life just like it is. Who gets and who don't get. (*He sits down with his coat on and laughs*) Mama, you know it's all divided up. Life is. Sure enough. Between the takers and the "tooken." (*He laughs*) I've figured it out finally. (*He looks around at them*) Yeah. Some of us always getting "tooken." (*He laughs*) People like Willy Harris, they don't never get "tooken." And you know why the rest of us do? 'Cause we all mixed up. Mixed up bad. We get to looking 'round for the right and the wrong; and we worry about it and cry about it and stay up nights trying to figure out 'bout the wrong and the right of things all the time . . . And all the time, man, them takers is out there operating, just taking and taking. Willy Harris? Shoot—Willy Harris don't even count. He don't even count in the big scheme of things. But I'll say one thing for old Willy Harris . . . he's taught me something. He's taught me to keep my eye on what counts in this world. Yeah—(*Shouting out a little*) Thanks, Willy!

RUTH: What did you call that man for, Walter Lee?

WALTER: Called him to tell him to come on over to the show. Gonna put on a show for the man. Just what he wants to see. You see, Mama, the man came here today and he told us that them people out there where you want us to move—well they so upset they willing to pay us *not* to move! (*He laughs again*) And—and oh, Mama—you would of been proud of the way me and Ruth and Bennie acted. We told him to get out . . . Lord have mercy! We told the man to get out! Oh, we was some proud folks this afternoon, yeah. (*He lights a cigarette*) We were still full of that old-time stuff . . .

RUTH (*coming toward him slowly*): You talking 'bout taking them people's money to keep us from moving in that house?

WALTER: I ain't just talking 'bout it, baby—I'm telling you that's what's going to happen!

BENEATHA: Oh, God! Where is the bottom! Where is the real honest-to-God bottom so he can't go any farther!

WALTER: See—that's the old stuff. You and that boy that was here today. You all want everybody to carry a flag and a spear and sing some marching songs, huh? You wanna spend your life looking into things and trying to find the right and the wrong part, huh? Yeah. You know what's going to happen to that boy someday—he'll find himself sitting in a dungeon, locked in forever—and the takers will have the key! Forget it, baby! There ain't no causes—there ain't nothing but taking in this world, and he who takes most is smartest—and it don't make a damn bit of difference *how.*

MAMA: You making something inside me cry, son. Some awful pain inside me.

WALTER: Don't cry, Mama. Understand. That white man is going to walk in that door able to write checks for more money than we ever had. It's important to him and I'm going to help him . . . I'm going to put on the show, Mama.

MAMA: Son—I come from five generations of people who was slaves and sharecroppers—but ain't nobody in my family never let nobody pay 'em no money that was a way of telling us we wasn't fit to walk the earth. We ain't never been that poor. (*Raising her eyes and looking at him*) We ain't never been that—dead inside.

BENEATHA: Well—we are dead now. All the talk about dreams and sunlight that goes on in this house. It's all dead now.

WALTER: What's the matter with you all! I didn't make this world! It was give to me this way! Hell, yes, I want me some yachts someday! Yes, I want to hang some real pearls 'round my wife's neck. Ain't she supposed to wear no pearls? Somebody tell me—tell me, who decides which women is suppose to wear pearls in this world. I tell you I am a *man*—and I think my wife should wear some pearls in this world!

(*This last line hangs a good while and* WALTER *begins to move about the room. The word "Man" has penetrated his consciousness; he mumbles it to himself repeatedly between strange agitated pauses as he moves about*)

MAMA: Baby, how you going to feel on the inside?

WALTER: Fine! . . . Going to feel fine . . . a man . . .

MAMA: You won't have nothing left then, Walter Lee.

WALTER (*coming to her*): I'm going to feel fine, Mama. I'm going to look that son-of-a-bitch in the eyes and say—(*He falters*)—and say, "All right, Mr. Lindner—(*He falters even more*)—that's *your* neighborhood out there! You got the right to keep it like you want! You got the right to have it like you want! Just write the check and—the house is yours." And—and I am going to say—(*His voice almost breaks*) "And you—you people just put the money in my hand and you won't have to live next to this bunch of stinking niggers! . . ." (*He straightens up and moves away from his mother, walking around the room*) And maybe—maybe I'll just get down on my black knees . . . (*He does so;* RUTH *and* BENNIE *and* MAMA *watch him in frozen horror*) "Captain, Mistuh, Bossman—(*Groveling and grinning and wringing his hands in profoundly anguished imitation of the slow-witted movie stereotype*) A-hee-hee-hee! Oh, yassuh boss! Yasssssuh! Great white—(*Voice breaking, he forces himself to go on*)—Father, just gi' ussen de money, fo' God's sake, and we's—we's ain't gwine come out deh and dirty up yo' white folks neighborhood . . ." (*He breaks down completely*) And I'll feel fine! Fine! FINE! (*He gets up and goes into the bedroom*)

BENEATHA: That is not a man. That is nothing but a toothless rat.

MAMA: Yes—death done come in this here house. (*She is nodding, slowly, reflectively*) Done come walking in my house on the lips of my children. You what supposed to be my beginning again. You—what supposed to be my harvest. (*To* BENEATHA) You—you mourning your brother?

BENEATHA: He's no brother of mine.

MAMA: What you say?

BENEATHA: I said that that individual in that room is no brother of mine.

MAMA: That's what I thought you said. You feeling like you better than he is today? (BENEATHA *does not answer*) Yes? What you tell him a minute ago? That he wasn't a man? Yes? You give him up for me? You done wrote his epitaph too—like the rest of the world? Well, who give you the privilege?

BENEATHA: Be on my side for once! You saw what he just did, Mama! You saw him—down on his knees. Wasn't it you who taught me to despise any man who would do that? Do what he's going to do?

MAMA: Yes—I taught you that. Me and your daddy. But I thought I taught you something else too . . . I thought I taught you to love him.

BENEATHA: Love him? There is nothing left to love.

MAMA: There is *always* something left to love. And if you ain't learned that, you ain't learned nothing. (*Looking at her*) Have you cried for that boy today? I don't mean for yourself and for the family 'cause we lost the money. I mean for him: what he been through and what it done to him. Child, when do you think is the time to love somebody the most? When they done good and made things easy for everybody? Well then, you ain't through learning—because that ain't the time at all. It's when he's at his lowest and can't believe in hisself 'cause the world done whipped him so! When you starts measuring somebody, measure him right, child, measure him right. Make sure you done taken into account what hills and valleys he come through before he got to wherever he is.

(TRAVIS *bursts into the room at the end of the speech, leaving the door open*)

TRAVIS: Grandmama—the moving men are downstairs! The truck just pulled up.

MAMA (*turning and looking at him*): Are they, baby? They downstairs?

(*She sighs and sits.* LINDNER *appears in the doorway. He peers in and knocks lightly, to gain attention, and comes in. All turn to look at him*)

LINDNER (*hat and briefcase in hand*): Uh—hello . . .

(RUTH *crosses mechanically to the bedroom door and opens it and lets it swing open freely and slowly as the lights come up on* WALTER *within, still in his coat, sitting at the far corner of the room. He looks up and out through the room to* LINDNER)

RUTH: He's here.

(*A long minute passes and* WALTER *slowly gets up*)

LINDNER (*coming to the table with efficiency, putting his briefcase on the table and starting to unfold papers and unscrew fountain pens*): Well, I certainly was glad to hear from you people. (WALTER *has begun the trek out of the room, slowly and awkwardly, rather like a small boy, passing the back of his sleeve across his mouth from time to time*) Life can really be so much simpler than people let it be most of the time. Well—with whom do I negotiate? You, Mrs. Younger, or your son here? (MAMA *sits with her hands folded on her lap and her eyes closed as* WALTER *advances.* TRAVIS *goes closer to* LINDNER *and looks at the papers curiously*) Just some official papers, sonny.

RUTH: Travis, you go downstairs—

MAMA (*opening her eyes and looking into* WALTER*'s*): No. Travis, you stay right here. And you make him understand what you doing, Walter Lee. You teach him good. Like Willy Harris taught you. You show where our five generations done come to. (WALTER *looks from her to the boy, who grins at him innocently*) Go ahead, son—(*She folds her hands and closes her eyes*) Go ahead.

WALTER (*at last crosses to* LINDNER, *who is reviewing the contract*): Well, Mr. Lindner. (BENEATHA *turns away*) We called you—(*There is a profound, simple groping quality in his speech*)—because, well, me and my family (*He looks around and shifts from one foot to the other*) Well—we are very plain people . . .

LINDNER: Yes—

WALTER: I mean—I have worked as a chauffeur most of my life—and my wife here, she does domestic work in people's kitchens. So does my mother. I mean—we are plain people . . .

LINDNER: Yes, Mr. Younger—

WALTER (*really like a small boy, looking down at his shoes and then up at the man*): And—uh—well, my father, well, he was a laborer most of his life . . .

LINDNER (*absolutely confused*): Uh, yes—yes, I understand. (*He turns back to the contract*)

WALTER (*a beat; staring at him*): And my father—(*With sudden intensity*) My father almost *beat a man to death* once because this man called him a bad name or something, you know what I mean?

LINDNER (*looking up, frozen*): No, no, I'm afraid I don't—

WALTER (*a beat. The tension hangs; then* WALTER *steps back from it*): Yeah. Well—what I mean is that we come from people who had a lot of *pride.* I mean—we are very proud people. And that's my sister over there and she's going to be a doctor—and we are very proud—

LINDNER: Well—I am sure that is very nice, but—

WALTER: What I am telling you is that we called you over here to tell you that we are very proud and that this—(*Signaling to* TRAVIS) Travis, come here. (TRAVIS *crosses and* WALTER *draws him before him facing the man*) This is my son, and he makes the sixth generation our family in this country. And we have all thought about your offer—

LINDNER: Well, good . . . good—

WALTER: And we have decided to move into our house because my father—my father—he earned it for us brick by brick. (MAMA *has her eyes closed and is rocking back and forth as though she were in church, with her head nodding the Amen yes*) We don't want to make no trouble for nobody or fight no causes, and we will try to be good neighbors. And that's *all* we got to say about that. (*He looks the man absolutely in the eyes*) We don't want your money. (*He turns and walks away*)

LINDNER (*looking around at all of them*): I take it then—that you have decided to occupy . . .

BENEATHA: That's what the man said.

LINDNER (*to* MAMA *in her reverie*): Then I would like to appeal to you, Mrs. Younger. You are older and wiser and understand things better, I am sure . . .

MAMA: I am afraid you don't understand. My son said we was going to move and there ain't nothing left for me to say. (*Briskly*) You know how these young folks is nowadays, mister. Can't do a thing with 'em! (*As he opens his mouth, she rises*) Good-bye.

LINDNER (*folding up his materials*): Well—if you are that final about it . . . there is nothing left for me to say. (*He finishes, almost ignored by the family, who are concentrating on* WALTER LEE. *At the door* LINDNER *halts and looks around*) I sure hope you people know what you're getting into.

(*He shakes his head and exits*)

RUTH (*looking around and coming to life*): Well, for God's sake—if the moving men are here—LET'S GET THE HELL OUT OF HERE!

MAMA (*into action*): Ain't it the truth! Look at all this here mess. Ruth, put Travis' good jacket on him . . . Walter Lee, fix your tie and tuck your shirt in, you look like somebody's hoodlum! Lord have mercy, where is my plant? (*She flies to get it amid the general bustling of the family, who are deliberately trying to ignore the nobility of the past moment*) You all start on down . . . Travis child, don't go empty-handed . . . Ruth, where did I put that box with my skillets in it? I want to be in charge of it myself . . . I'm going to make us the biggest dinner we ever ate tonight . . . Beneatha, what's the matter with them stockings? Pull them things up, girl . . .

(*The family starts to file out as two moving men appear and begin to carry out the heavier pieces of furniture, bumping into the family as they move about*)

BENEATHA: Mama, Asagai asked me to marry him today and go to Africa—

MAMA (*in the middle of her getting-ready activity*): He did? You ain't old enough to marry nobody—(*Seeing the moving men lifting one of her chairs precariously*) Darling, that ain't no bale of cotton, please handle it so we can sit in it again! I had that chair twenty-five years . . .

(*The movers sigh with exasperation and go on with their work*)

BENEATHA (*girlishly and unreasonably trying to pursue the conversation*): To go to Africa, Mama—be a doctor in Africa . . .

MAMA (*distracted*): Yes, baby—

WALTER: *Africa!* What he want you to go to Africa for?

BENEATHA: To practice there . . .

WALTER: Girl, if you don't get all them silly ideas out your head! You better marry yourself a man with some loot . . .

BENEATHA (*angrily, precisely as in the first scene of the play*): What have you got to do with who I marry!

WALTER: Plenty. Now I think George Murchison—

BENEATHA: *George Murchison!* I wouldn't marry him if he was Adam and I was Eve!

(WALTER *and* BENEATHA *go out yelling at each other vigorously and the anger is loud and real till their voices diminish.* RUTH *stands at the door and turns to* MAMA *and smiles knowingly*)

MAMA (*fixing her hat at last*): Yeah—they something all right, my children . . .

RUTH: Yeah—they're something. Let's go, Lena.

MAMA (*stalling, starting to look around at the house*): Yes—I'm coming. Ruth—

RUTH: Yes?

MAMA (*quietly, woman to woman*): He finally come into his manhood today, didn't he? Kind of like a rainbow after the rain . . .

RUTH (*biting her lip lest her own pride explode in front of* MAMA): Yes, Lena.

(WALTER*'s voice calls for them raucously*)

WALTER (*off stage*): Y'all come on! These people charges by the hour, you know!

MAMA (*waving* RUTH *out vaguely*): All right, honey—go on down. I be down directly.

(RUTH *hesitates, then exits.* MAMA *stands, at last alone in the living room, her plant on the table before her as the lights start to come down. She looks around at all the walls and ceilings and suddenly, despite herself, while the children call below, a great heaving thing rises in her and she puts her fist to her mouth to stifle it, takes a final desperate look, pulls her coat about her, pats her hat and goes out. The lights dim down. The door opens and she comes back in, grabs her plant, and goes out for the last time*)

Curtain

(*1959*)

QUESTIONS FOR CRITICAL THINKING AND WRITING

Experience

1. Did you find this play engaging or interesting? Why or why not? What makes it specifically an urban play? A "minority" play?
2. To what extent can you relate to the experiences of the play's characters?

Interpretation

3. Describe the relationship of Mama (Lena) with her daughter, Beneatha, and with her son, Walter. What expectations does she have for the future of each? Why?
4. Give two explanations for the primary conflicts of the play. What precipitates the various arguments and battles the characters wage with one another?
5. Explain the roles of Joseph Asagai and George Murchison. Does either character have thematic significance? Explain.
6. Identify and discuss a major theme of the play. Support your ideas with references to specific events and speeches.
7. Identify two important stage props and comment on their role in the play. Discuss whether either or both may be symbolic, and why.
8. Select a scene you find compelling and describe how to stage it.

Evaluation

9. Some readers consider this play a modern American classic. What do you think may have led them to such an assessment?
10. How is Hansberry's play a comment on the Langston Hughes poem that she uses as her epigraph?

Connection

11. Compare Hansberry's *A Raisin in the Sun* with Wilson's *Fences* with respect to their portrayal of African-American family life.

Critical Thinking

12. Are you satisfied with the play's ending? Why or why not? How do you envision the future of the family, particularly of Ruth and Walter and of Beneatha?

DAVID HENRY HWANG
[b. 1957]

David Henry Hwang was born in Los Angeles and raised in San Gabriel, California, by his father, a banker, and his mother, a professional piano player. He studied English at Stanford University, earning a B.A. in 1979. During his college years he began writing plays, producing his first play, FOB, *before graduation. After teaching for a short time, Hwang attended the Yale School of Drama before moving to New York City, where* FOB *was produced, winning the first of Hwang's many awards. In addition to* M. Butterfly, *for which Hwang is best known and which won the Tony award for best play in 1988, he has written a play influenced by Japanese No drama* (The Sound of a Voice), *a science fiction music drama* (1000 Airplanes on the Roof), *and an opera* (The Voyage), *which was commissioned for the 500-year celebration of Columbus's arrival in America.*

Hwang's plays center on issues of culture and identity. As the son of immigrant Chinese parents, Hwang plays off his Chinese ancestry and his knowledge of Chinese cultural and theatrical traditions against the social and cultural aspects of living in contemporary urban America. Issues of race, assimilation, and other problems faced by recent immigrants are provocatively yet sensitively presented in Hwang's plays. In M. Butterfly, *such issues of cultural identity merge with complications of sexual identity as central themes.*

M. Butterfly

PLAYWRIGHT'S NOTES:

"A former French diplomat and a Chinese opera singer have been sentenced to six years in jail for spying for China after a two-day trial that traced a story of clandestine love and mistaken sexual identity. . . . Mr. Bouriscot was accused of passing information to China after he fell in love with Mr. Shi, whom he believed for twenty years to be a woman."

—THE NEW YORK TIMES, MAY 11, 1986

This play was suggested by international newspaper accounts of a recent espionage trial. For purposes of dramatization, names have been changed, characters created, and incidents devised or altered, and this play does not purport to be a factual record of real events or real people.

"I could escape this feeling
With my China girl . . ."

—DAVID BOWIE & IGGY POP

CHARACTERS

KUROGO
RENE GALLIMARD
SONG LILING
MARC/MAN #2/CONSUL SHARPLESS
RENEE/WOMAN AT PARTY/GIRL IN MAGAZINE
COMRADE CHIN/SUZUKI/SHU-FANG
HELGA
M. TOULON/MAN #1/JUDGE

Setting. *The action of the play takes place in a Paris prison in the present, and in recall, during the decade 1960 to 1970 in Beijing, and from 1966 to the present in Paris.*

ACT ONE

Scene 1

M. GALLIMARD*'s prison cell. Paris. Present.*

Lights fade up to reveal RENE GALLIMARD, *65, in a prison cell. He wears a comfortable bathrobe, and looks old and tired. The sparsely furnished cell contains a wooden crate upon which sits a hot plate with a kettle, and a portable tape recorder.* GALLIMARD *sits on the crate staring at the recorder, a sad smile on his face.*

Upstage SONG, *who appears as a beautiful woman in traditional Chinese garb, dances a traditional piece from the Peking Opera, surrounded by the percussive clatter of Chinese music.*

Then, slowly, lights and sound cross-fade; the Chinese opera music dissolves into a Western opera, the "Love Duet" from Puccini's Madame Butterfly. SONG *continues dancing, now to the Western accompaniment. Though her movements are the same, the difference in music now gives them a balletic quality.*

GALLIMARD *rises, and turns upstage toward the figure of* SONG, *who dances without acknowledging him.*

GALLIMARD: Butterfly, Butterfly . . .

He forces himself to turn away, as the image of SONG *fades out, and talks to us.*

GALLIMARD: The limits of my cell are as such: four-and-a-half meters by five. There's one window against the far wall; a door, very strong, to protect me from autograph hounds. I'm responsible for the tape recorder, the hot plate, and this charming coffee table.

When I want to eat, I'm marched off to the dining room—hot, steaming slop appears on my plate. When I want to sleep, the light bulb turns itself off—the work of fairies. It's an enchanted space I occupy. The French—we know how to run a prison.

But, to be honest, I'm not treated like an ordinary prisoner. Why? Because I'm a celebrity. You see, I make people laugh.

I never dreamed this day would arrive. I've never been considered witty or clever. In fact, as a young boy, in an informal poll among my grammar school classmates, I was voted "least likely to be invited to a party." It's a title I managed to hold onto for many years. Despite some stiff competition.

But now, how the tables turn! Look at me: the life of every social function in Paris. Paris? Why be modest? My fame has spread to Amsterdam, London, New York. Listen to them! In the world's smartest parlors. I'm the one who lifts their spirits!

With a flourish, GALLIMARD *directs our attention to another part of the stage.*

Scene 2

A party. Present.

Lights go up on a chic-looking parlor, where a well-dressed trio, two men and one woman, make conversation. GALLIMARD *also remains lit; he observes them from his cell.*

WOMAN: And what of Gallimard?

MAN 1: Gallimard?

MAN 2: Gallimard!

GALLIMARD (*to us*): You see? They're all determined to say my name, as if it were some new dance.

WOMAN: He still claims not to believe the truth.

MAN 1: What? Still? Even since the trial?

WOMAN: Yes. Isn't it mad?

MAN 2 (*laughing*): He says . . . it was dark . . . and she was very modest!

The trio break into laughter.

MAN 1: So—what? He never touched her with his hands

MAN 2: Perhaps he did, and simply misidentified the equipment. A compelling case for sex education in the schools.

WOMAN: To protect the National Security—the Church can't argue with that.

MAN 1: That's impossible! How could he not know?

MAN 2: Simple ignorance.

MAN 1: For twenty years?

MAN 2: Time flies when you're being stupid.

WOMAN: Well, I thought the French were ladies' men.

MAN 2: It seems Monsieur Gallimard was overly anxious to live up to his national reputation.

WOMAN: Well, he's not very good-looking.

MAN 1: No, he's not.

MAN 2: Certainly not.

WOMAN: Actually, I feel sorry for him.

MAN 2: A toast! To Monsieur Gallimard!

WOMAN: Yes! To Gallimard!

MAN 1: To Gallimard!

MAN 2: Vive la difference!

They toast, laughing. Lights down on them.

Scene 3

M. GALLIMARD*'s cell.*

GALLIMARD (*smiling*): You see? They toast me. I've become patron saint of the socially inept. Can they really be so foolish? Men like that—they should be scratching at my door, begging to learn my secrets! For I, Rene Gallimard, you see, I have known, and been loved by . . . the Perfect Woman.

Alone in this cell, I sit night after night, watching our story play through my head, always searching for a new ending, one which redeems my honor, where she returns at last to my arms. And I imagine you—my ideal audience—who come to understand and even, perhaps just a little, to envy me.

He turns on his tape recorder. Over the house speakers, we hear the opening phrases of Madame Butterfly.

GALLIMARD: In order for you to understand what I did and why, I must introduce you to my favorite opera: *Madame Butterfly.* By Giacomo Puccini. First produced at La Scala, Milan, in 1904, it is now beloved throughout the Western world.

As GALLIMARD *describes the opera, the tape segues in and out to sections he may be describing.*

GALLIMARD: And why not? Its heroine, Cio-Cio-San, also known as Butterfly, is a feminine ideal, beautiful and brave. And its hero, the man for whom she gives up everything, is—(*He pulls out a naval officer's cap from under his crate, pops it on his head, and struts about*)—not very good-looking, not too bright, and pretty much a wimp: Benjamin Franklin Pinkerton of the U.S. Navy. As the curtain rises, he's just closed on two great bargains: one on a house, the other on a woman—call it a package deal.

Pinkerton purchased the rights to Butterfly for one hundred yen—in modern currency, equivalent to about . . . sixty-six cents. So, he's feeling pretty pleased with himself as Sharpless, the American consul, arrives to witness the marriage.

MARC, *wearing an official cap to designate* SHARPLESS, *enters and plays the character.*

SHARPLESS/MARC: Pinkerton!

PINKERTON/GALLIMARD: Sharpless! How's it hangin'? It's a great day, just great. Between my house, my wife, and the rickshaw ride in from town, I've saved nineteen cents just this morning.

SHARPLESS: Wonderful. I can see the inscription on your tombstone already: "I saved a dollar, here I lie." (*He looks around*) Nice house.

PINKERTON: It's artistic. Artistic, don't you think? Like the way the shoji screens slide open to reveal the wet bar and disco mirror ball? Classy, huh? Great for impressing the chicks.

SHARPLESS: "Chicks"? Pinkerton, you're going to be a married man!

PINKERTON: Well, sort of.

SHARPLESS: What do you mean?

PINKERTON: This country—Sharpless, it is okay. You got all these geisha girls running around—

SHARPLESS: I know! I live here!

PINKERTON: Then, you know the marriage laws, right? I split for one month, it's annulled!

SHARPLESS: Leave it to you to read the fine print. Who's the lucky girl?

PINKERTON: Cio-Cio-San. Her friends call her Butterfly. Sharpless, she eats out of my hand!

SHARPLESS: She's probably very hungry.

PINKERTON: Not like American girls. It's true what they say about Oriental girls. They want to be treated bad!

SHARPLESS: Oh, please!

PINKERTON: It's true!

SHARPLESS: Are you serious about this girl?

PINKERTON: I'm marrying her, aren't I?

SHARPLESS: Yes—with generous trade-in terms.

PINKERTON: When I leave, she'll know what it's like to have loved a real man. And I'll even buy her a few nylons.

SHARPLESS: You aren't planning to take her with you?

PINKERTON: Huh? Where?

SHARPLESS: Home!

PINKERTON: You mean, America? Are you crazy? Can you see her trying to buy rice in St. Louis?

SHARPLESS: So, you're not serious.

Pause.

PINKERTON/GALLIMARD (*as Pinkerton*): Consul, I am a sailor in port. (*As Gallimard*) They then proceed to sing the famous duet, "The Whole World Over."

The duet plays on the speakers. GALLIMARD, *as* PINKERTON, *lip-syncs his lines from the opera.*

GALLIMARD: To give a rough translation: "The whole world over, the Yankee travels, casting his anchor wherever he wants. Life's not worth living unless he can win the hearts of the fairest maidens, then hotfoot it off the premises ASAP." (*He turns toward* MARC) In the preceding scene, I played Pinkerton, the womanizing cad, and my friend Marc from school . . . (MARC *bows grandly for our benefit*) played Sharpless, the sensitive soul of reason. In life, however, our positions were usually—no, always—reversed.

Scene 4

Ecole Nationale. Aix-en-Provence. 1947.

GALLIMARD: No, Marc, I think I'd rather stay home.

MARC: Are you crazy?! We are going to Dad's condo in Marseille! You know what happened last time?

GALLIMARD: Of course I do.

MARC: Of course you don't! You never know. . . . They stripped, Rene!

GALLIMARD: Who stripped?

MARC: The girls!

GALLIMARD: Girls? Who said anything about girls?

MARC: Rene, we're a buncha university guys goin' up to the woods. What are we gonna do—talk philosophy?

GALLIMARD: What girls? Where do you get them?

MARC: Who cares? The point is, they come. On trucks. Packed in like sardines. The back flips open, babes hop out, we're ready to roll.

GALLIMARD: You mean, they just—?

MARC: Before you know it, every last one of them—they're stripped and splashing around my pool. There's no moon out, they can't see what's going on, their boobs are flapping, right? You close your eyes, reach out—it's grab bag, get it? Doesn't matter whose ass is between whose legs, whose teeth are sinking into who. You're just in there, going at it, eyes closed, on and on for as long as you can stand. (*Pause*) Some fun, huh?

GALLIMARD: What happens in the morning?

MARC: In the morning, you're ready to talk some philosophy. (*Beat*) So how 'bout it?

GALLIMARD: Marc, I can't . . . I'm afraid they'll say no—the girls. So I never ask.

MARC: You don't have to ask! That's the beauty—don't you see? They don't have to say yes. It's perfect for a guy like you, really.

GALLIMARD: You go ahead . . . I may come later.

MARC: Hey, Rene—it doesn't matter that you're clumsy and got zits—they're not looking!

GALLIMARD: Thank you very much.

MARC: Wimp.

MARC *walks over to the other side of the stage, and starts waving and smiling at women in the audience.*

GALLIMARD (*to us*): We now return to my version of *Madame Butterfly* and the events leading to my recent conviction for treason.

GALLIMARD *notices* MARC *making lewd gestures.*

GALLIMARD: Marc, what are you doing?

MARC: Huh? (*Sotto voce*) Rene, there're a lotta great babes out there. They're probably lookin' at me and thinking, "What a dangerous guy."

GALLIMARD: Yes—how could they help but be impressed by your cool sophistication?

GALLIMARD *pops the* SHARPLESS *cap on* MARC*'s head, and points him offstage.* MARC *exits, leering.*

Scene 5

M. GALLIMARD*'s cell.*

GALLIMARD: Next, Butterfly makes her entrance. We learn her age—fifteen . . . but very mature for her years.

Lights come up on the area where we saw SONG *dancing at the top of the play. She appears there again, now dressed as Madame Butterfly, moving to the "Love Duet."* GALLIMARD *turns upstage slightly to watch, transfixed.*

GALLIMARD: But as she glides past him, beautiful, laughing softly behind her fan, don't we who are men sigh with hope? We, who are not handsome, nor brave, nor powerful, yet somehow believe, like Pinkerton, that we deserve a Butterfly. She arrives with all her possessions in the folds of her sleeves, lays them all out, for her man to do with as he pleases. Even her life itself—she bows her head as she whispers that she's not even worth the hundred yen he paid for her. He's already given too much, when we know he's really had to give nothing at all.

Music and lights on SONG *out.* GALLIMARD *sits at his crate.*

GALLIMARD: In real life, women who put their total worth at less than sixty-six cents are quite hard to find. The closest we come is in the pages of these magazines. (*He reaches into his crate, pulls out a stack of girlie magazines, and begins flipping through them*) Quite a necessity in prison. For three or four dollars, you get seven or eight women.

I first discovered these magazines at my uncle's house. One day, as a boy of twelve. The first time I saw them in his closet . . . all lined up—my body shook. Not with lust—no, with power. Here were women—a shelfful—who would do exactly as I wanted.

The "Love Duet" creeps in over the speakers. Special comes up, revealing, not SONG *this time, but a pinup girl in a sexy negligee, her back to us.* GALLIMARD *turns upstage and looks at her.*

GIRL: I know you're watching me.

GALLIMARD: My throat . . . it's dry.

GIRL: I leave my blinds open every night before I go to bed.

GALLIMARD: I can't move.

GIRL: I leave my blinds open and the lights on.

GALLIMARD: I'm shaking. My skin is hot, but my penis is soft. Why?

GIRL: I stand in front of the window.

GALLIMARD: What is she going to do?

GIRL: I toss my hair, and I let my lips part . . . barely.

GALLIMARD: I shouldn't be seeing this. It's so dirty. I'm so bad.

GIRL: Then, slowly, I lift off my nightdress.

GALLIMARD: Oh, god. I can't believe it. I can't—

GIRL: I toss it to the ground.

GALLIMARD: Now, she's going to walk away. She's going to—

GIRL: I stand there, in the light, displaying myself.

GALLIMARD: No. She's—why is she naked?

GIRL: To you.

GALLIMARD: In front of a window? This is wrong. No—

GIRL: Without shame.

GALLIMARD: No, she must . . . like it.

GIRL: I like it.

GALLIMARD: She . . . she wants me to see.

GIRL: I want you to see.

GALLIMARD: I can't believe it! She's getting excited!

GIRL: I can't see you. You can do whatever you want.

GALLIMARD: I can't do a thing. Why?

GIRL: What would you like me to do . . . next?

Lights go down on her. Music off. Silence, as GALLIMARD *puts away his magazines. Then he resumes talking to us.*

GALLIMARD: Act Two begins with Butterfly staring at the ocean. Pinkerton's been called back to the U.S., and he's given his wife a detailed schedule of his plans. In the column marked "return date," he's written "when the robins nest." This failed to ignite her suspicions. Now, three years have passed without a peep from him. Which brings a response from her faithful servant, Suzuki.

COMRADE CHIN *enters, playing* SUZUKI.

SUZUKI: Girl, he's a loser. What'd he ever give you? Nineteen cents and those ugly Day-Glo stockings? Look, it's finished! Kaput! Done! And you should be glad! I mean, the guy was a woofer! He tried before, you know—before he met you, he went down to geisha central and plunked down his spare change in front of the usual candidates—everyone else gagged! These are hungry prostitutes, and they were not interested, get the picture? Now, stop slathering when an American ship sails in, and let's make some bucks—I mean, yen! We are broke!

Now, what about Yamadori? Hey, hey—don't look away—the man is a prince—figuratively, and, what's even better, literally. He's rich, he's handsome, he says he'll die if you don't marry him—and he's even willing to overlook the little fact that you've been deflowered all over the place by a foreign devil. What do you mean, "But he's Japanese?" You're Japanese! You think you've been touched by the whitey god? He was a sailor with dirty hands!

SUZUKI *stalks offstage.*

GALLIMARD: She's also visited by Consul Sharpless, sent by Pinkerton on a minor errand.

MARC *enters, as* SHARPLESS.

SHARPLESS: I hate this job.

GALLIMARD: This Pinkerton—he doesn't show up personally to tell his wife he's abandoning her. No, he sends a government diplomat . . . at taxpayer's expense.

SHARPLESS: Butterfly? Butterfly? I have some bad—I'm going to be ill. Butterfly, I came to tell you—

GALLIMARD: Butterfly says she knows he'll return and if he doesn't she'll kill herself rather than go back to her own people. (*Beat*) This causes a lull in the conversation.

SHARPLESS: Let's put it this way . . .

GALLIMARD: Butterfly runs into the next room, and returns holding—

Sound cue: a baby crying. SHARPLESS, *"seeing" this, backs away.*

SHARPLESS: Well, good. Happy to see things going so well. I suppose I'll be going now. Ta ta. Ciao. (*He turns away. Sound cue out*) I hate this job. (*He exits*)

GALLIMARD: At that moment, Butterfly spots in the harbor an American ship—the *Abramo Lincoln!*

Music cue: "The Flower Duet." SONG, *still dressed as Butterfly, changes into a wedding kimono, moving to the music.*

GALLIMARD: This is the moment that redeems her years of waiting. With Suzuki's help, they cover the room with flowers—

CHIN, *as* SUZUKI, *trudges onstage and drops a lone flower without much enthusiasm.*

GALLIMARD: —and she changes into her wedding dress to prepare for Pinkerton's arrival.

SUZUKI *helps Butterfly change.* HELGA *enters, and helps* GALLIMARD *change into a tuxedo.*

GALLIMARD: I married a woman older than myself—Helga.

HELGA: My father was ambassador to Australia. I grew up among criminals and kangaroos.

GALLIMARD: Hearing that brought me to the altar—

HELGA *exits.*

GALLIMARD: —where I took a vow renouncing love. No fantasy woman would ever want me, so, yes, I would settle for a quick leap up the career ladder. Passion, I banish, and in its place—practicality!

But my vows had long since lost their charm by the time we arrived in China. The sad truth is that all men want a beautiful woman, and the uglier the man, the greater the want.

SUZUKI *makes final adjustments of Butterfly's costume, as does* GALLIMARD *of his tuxedo.*

GALLIMARD: I married late, at age thirty-one. I was faithful to my marriage for eight years. Until the day when, as a junior-level diplomat in puritanical Peking, in a parlor at the German ambassador's house, during the "Reign of a Hundred Flowers," I first saw her . . . singing the death scene from *Madame Butterfly.*

SUZUKI *runs offstage.*

Scene 6

German ambassador's house. Beijing. 1960.

The upstage special area now becomes a stage. Several chairs face upstage, representing seating for some twenty guests in the parlor. A few "diplomats"—RENEE, MARC, TOULON—*in formal dress enter and take seats.*

GALLIMARD *also sits down, but turns toward us and continues to talk. Orchestral accompaniment on the tape is now replaced by a simple piano.* SONG *picks up the death scene from the point where Butterfly uncovers the hara-kiri knife.*

GALLIMARD: The ending is pitiful. Pinkerton, in an act of great courage, stays home and sends his American wife to pick up Butterfly's child. The truth, long deferred, has come up to her door.

SONG, *playing Butterfly, sings the lines from the opera in her own voice—which, though not classical, should be decent.*

SONG: "Con onor muore/ chi non puo serbar/ vita con onore."
GALLIMARD (*simultaneously*): "Death with honor/ Is better than life/ Life with dishonor."

The stage is illuminated; we are now completely within an elegant diplomat's residence. SONG *proceeds to play out an abbreviated death scene. Everyone in the room applauds.* SONG, *shyly, takes her bows. Others in the room rush to congratulate her.* GALLIMARD *remains with us.*

GALLIMARD: They say in opera the voice is everything. That's probably why I'd never before enjoyed opera. Here . . . here was a Butterfly with little or no voice—but she had the grace, the delicacy . . . I believed this girl. I believed her suffering. I wanted to take her in my arms—so delicate, even I could protect her, take her home, pamper her until she smiled.

Over the course of the preceding speech, SONG *has broken from the upstage crowd and moved directly upstage of* GALLIMARD.

SONG: Excuse me. Monsieur . . . ?

GALLIMARD *turns upstage, shocked.*

GALLIMARD: Oh! Gallimard. Mademoiselle . . . ? A beautiful . . .
SONG: Song Liling.
GALLIMARD: A beautiful performance.
SONG: Oh, please.
GALLIMARD: I usually—
SONG: You make me blush. I'm no opera singer at all.
GALLIMARD: I usually don't like *Butterfly.*
SONG: I can't blame you in the least.
GALLIMARD: I mean, the story—
SONG: Ridiculous.
GALLIMARD: I like the story, but . . . what?
SONG: Oh, you like it?
GALLIMARD: I . . . what I mean is, I've always seen it played by huge women in so much bad makeup.

SONG: Bad makeup is not unique to the West.

GALLIMARD: But, who can believe them?

SONG: And you believe me?

GALLIMARD: Absolutely. You were utterly convincing. It's the first time—

SONG: Convincing? As a Japanese woman? The Japanese used hundreds of our people for medical experiments during the war, you know. But I gather such an irony is lost on you.

GALLIMARD: No! I was about to say, it's the first time I've seen the beauty of the story.

SONG: Really?

GALLIMARD: Of her death. It's a . . . a pure sacrifice. He's unworthy, but what can she do? She loves him . . . so much. It's a very beautiful story.

SONG: Well, yes, to a Westerner.

GALLIMARD: Excuse me?

SONG: It's one of your favorite fantasies, isn't it? The submissive Oriental woman and the cruel white man.

GALLIMARD: Well, I didn't quite mean . . .

SONG: Consider it this way: what would you say if a blonde homecoming queen fell in love with a short Japanese businessman? He treats her cruelly, then goes home for three years, during which time she prays to his picture and turns down marriage from a young Kennedy. Then, when she learns he has remarried, she kills herself. Now, I believe you would consider this girl to be a deranged idiot, correct? But because it's an Oriental who kills herself for a Westerner—ah!—you find it beautiful.

Silence.

GALLIMARD: Yes . . . well . . . I see your point . . .

SONG: I will never do Butterfly again, Monsieur Gallimard. If you wish to see some real theatre, come to the Peking Opera sometime. Expand your mind.

SONG *walks offstage.*

GALLIMARD (*to us*): So much for protecting her in my big Western arms.

Scene 7

M. GALLIMARD*'s apartment. Beijing. 1960.*

GALLIMARD *changes from his tux into a casual suit.* HELGA *enters.*

GALLIMARD: The Chinese are an incredibly arrogant people.

HELGA: They warned us about that in Paris, remember.

GALLIMARD: Even Parisians consider them arrogant. That's a switch.

HELGA: What is it that Madame Su says? "We are a very old civilization." I never know if she's talking about her country or herself.

GALLIMARD: I walk around here, all I hear every day, everywhere is how old this culture is. The fact that "old" may be synonymous with "senile" doesn't occur to them.

HELGA: You're not going to change them. "East is east, west is west, and . . ." whatever that guy said.

GALLIMARD: It's just that—silly. I met . . . at Ambassador Koening's tonight—you should've been there.

HELGA: Koening? Oh god, no. Did he enchant you all again with the history of Bavaria?

GALLIMARD: No. I met, I suppose, the Chinese equivalent of a diva. She's a singer in the Chinese opera.

HELGA: They have an opera, too? Do they sing in Chinese? Or maybe—in Italian?

GALLIMARD: Tonight, she did sing in Italian.

HELGA: How'd she manage that?

GALLIMARD: She must've been educated in the West before the Revolution. Her French is very good also. Anyway, she sang the death scene from *Madame Butterfly*.

HELGA: *Madame Butterfly!* Then I should have come. (*She begins humming, floating around the room as if dragging long kimono sleeves*) Did she have a nice costume? I think it's a classic piece of music.

GALLIMARD: That's what I thought, too. Don't let her hear you say that.

HELGA: What's wrong?

GALLIMARD: Evidently the Chinese hate it.

HELGA: She hated it, but she performed it anyway? Is she perverse?

GALLIMARD: They hate it because the white man gets the girl. Sour grapes if you ask me.

HELGA: Politics again? Why can't they just hear it as a piece of beautiful music? So, what's in their opera?

GALLIMARD: I don't know. But, whatever it is, I'm sure it must be *old*.

HELGA *exits.*

Scene 8

Chinese opera house and the streets of Beijing. 1960.

The sound of gongs clanging fills the stage.

GALLIMARD: My wife's innocent question kept ringing in my ears. I asked around, but no one knew anything about the Chinese opera. It took four weeks, but my curiosity overcame my cowardice. This Chinese diva—this unwilling Butterfly—what did she do to make her so proud?

The room was hot, and full of smoke. Wrinkled faces, old women, teeth missing—a man with a growth on his neck, like a human toad. All smiling, pipes falling from their mouths, cracking nuts between their teeth, a live chicken pecking at my foot—all looking, screaming, gawking . . . at her.

The upstage area is suddenly hit with a harsh white light. It has become the stage for the Chinese opera performance. Two dancers enter, along with SONG. GALLIMARD *stands apart, watching.* SONG *glides gracefully amidst the two dancers. Drums suddenly slam to a halt.* SONG *strikes a pose, looking straight at* GALLIMARD. *Dancers exit. Light change. Pause, then* SONG *walks right off the stage and straight up to* GALLIMARD.

SONG: Yes. You. White man. I'm looking straight at you.

GALLIMARD: Me?

SONG: You see any other white men? It was too easy to spot you. How often does a man in my audience come in a tie?

SONG *starts to remove her costume. Underneath, she wears simple baggy clothes. They are now backstage. The show is over.*

SONG: So, you are an adventurous imperialist?

GALLIMARD: I . . . thought it would further my education.

SONG: It took you four weeks. Why?

GALLIMARD: I've been busy.

SONG: Well, education has always been undervalued in the West, hasn't it?

GALLIMARD (*laughing*): I don't think it's true.

SONG: No, you wouldn't. You're a Westerner. How can you objectively judge your own values?

GALLIMARD: I think it's possible to achieve some distance.

SONG: Do you? (*Pause*) It stinks in here. Let's go.

GALLIMARD: These are the smells of your loyal fans.

SONG: I love them for being my fans, I hate the smell they leave behind. I too can distance myself from my people. (*She looks around, then whispers in his ear*) "Art for the masses" is a shitty excuse to keep artists poor. (*She pops a cigarette in her mouth*) Be a gentleman, will you? And light my cigarette.

GALLIMARD *fumbles for a match.*

GALLIMARD: I don't . . . smoke.

SONG (*lighting her own*): Your loss. Had you lit my cigarette, I might have blown a puff of smoke right between your eyes. Come.

They start to walk about the stage. It is a summer night on the Beijing streets. Sounds of the city play on the house speakers.

SONG: How I wish there were even a tiny cafe to sit in. With cappuccinos, and men in tuxedos and bad expatriate jazz.

GALLIMARD: If my history serves me correctly, you weren't even allowed into the clubs in Shanghai before the Revolution.

SONG: Your history serves you poorly, Monsieur Gallimard. True, there were signs reading "No dogs and Chinamen." But a woman, especially a delicate Oriental woman—we always go where we please. Could you imagine it otherwise? Clubs in China filled with pasty, big-thighed white women, while thousands of slender lotus blossoms wait just outside the door? Never. The clubs would be empty. (*Beat*) We have always held a certain fascination for you Caucasian men, have we not?

GALLIMARD: But . . . that fascination is imperialist, or so you tell me.

SONG: Do you believe everything I tell you? Yes. It is always imperialist. But sometimes . . . sometimes, it is also mutual. Oh—this is my flat.

GALLIMARD: I didn't even—

SONG: Thank you. Come another time and we will further expand your mind.

SONG *exits.* GALLIMARD *continues roaming the streets as he speaks to us.*

GALLIMARD: What was that? What did she mean, "Sometimes . . . it is mutual?" Women do not flirt with me. And I normally can't talk to them. But tonight, I held up my end of the conversation.

Scene 9

GALLIMARD*'s bedroom. Beijing. 1960.*

HELGA *enters.*

HELGA: You didn't tell me you'd be home late.

GALLIMARD: I didn't intend to. Something came up.

HELGA: Oh? Like what?

GALLIMARD: I went to the . . . to the Dutch ambassador's home.

HELGA: Again?

GALLIMARD: There was a reception for a visiting scholar. He's writing a six-volume treatise on the Chinese revolution. We all gathered that meant he'd have to live here long enough to actually write six volumes, and we all expressed our deepest sympathies.

HELGA: Well, I had a good night too. I went with the ladies to a martial arts demonstration. Some of those men—when they break those thick boards—(*She mimes fanning herself*) whoo—whoo!

HELGA *exits. Lights dim.*

GALLIMARD: I lied to my wife. Why? I've never had any reason to lie before. But what reason did I have tonight? I didn't do anything wrong. That night, I had a dream. Other people, I've been told, have dreams where angels appear. Or dragons, or Sophia Loren in a towel. In my dream, Marc from school appeared.

MARC *enters, in a nightshirt and cap.*

MARC: Rene! You met a girl!

GALLIMARD *and* MARC *stumble down the Beijing streets. Night sounds over the speakers.*

GALLIMARD: It's not that amazing, thank you.

MARC: No! It's so monumental, I heard about it halfway around the world in my sleep!

GALLIMARD: I've met girls before, you know.

MARC: Name one. I've come across time and space to congratulate you. (*He hands* GALLIMARD *a bottle of wine*)

GALLIMARD: Marc, this is expensive.

MARC: On those rare occasions when you become a formless spirit, why not steal the best?

MARC *pops open the bottle, begins to share it with* GALLIMARD.

GALLIMARD: You embarrass me. She . . . there's no reason to think she likes me.

MARC: "Sometimes, it is mutual"?

GALLIMARD: Oh.

MARC: "Mutual"? "Mutual"? What does that mean?

GALLIMARD: You heard!

MARC: It means the money is in the bank, you only have to write the check!

GALLIMARD: I am a married man!

MARC: And an excellent one too. I cheated after . . . six months. Then again and again, until now—three hundred girls in twelve years.

GALLIMARD: I don't think we should hold that up as a model.

MARC: Of course not! My life—it is disgusting! Phooey! Phooey! But, you—you are the model husband.

GALLIMARD: Anyway, it's impossible. I'm a foreigner.

MARC: Ah, yes. She cannot love you, it is taboo, but something deep inside her heart . . . She cannot help herself . . . she must surrender to you. It is her destiny.

GALLIMARD: How do you imagine all this?

MARC: The same way you do. It's an old story. It's in our blood. They fear us, Rene. Their women fear us. And their men—their men hate us. And, you know something? They are all correct.

They spot a light in a window.

MARC: There! There, Rene!

GALLIMARD: It's her window.

MARC: Late at night—it burns. The light—it burns for you.

GALLIMARD: I won't look. It's not respectful.

MARC: We don't have to be respectful. We're foreign devils.

Enter SONG, *in a sheer robe. The "One Fine Day" aria creeps in over the speakers. With her back to us,* SONG *mimes attending to her toilette. Her robe comes loose, revealing her white shoulders.*

MARC: All your life you've waited for a beautiful girl who would lay down for you. All your life you've smiled like a saint when it's happened to every other man you know. And you see them in magazines and you see them in movies. And you wonder, what's wrong with me? Will anyone beautiful ever want me? As the years pass, your hair thins and you struggle to hold onto even your hopes. Stop struggling, Rene. The wait is over. (*He exits*)

GALLIMARD: Marc? Marc?

At that moment, SONG, *her back still towards us, drops her robe. A second of her naked back, then a sound cue: a phone ringing, very loud. Blackout, followed in the next beat by a special up on the bedroom area, where a phone now sits.* GALLIMARD *stumbles across the stage and picks up the phone. Sound cue out. Over the course of his conversation, area lights fill in the vicinity of his bed. It is the following morning.*

GALLIMARD: Yes? Hello?

SONG (*offstage*): Is it very early?

GALLIMARD: Why, yes.

SONG (*offstage*): How early?

GALLIMARD: It's . . . it's 5:30. Why are you—?

SONG (*offstage*): But it's light outside. Already.

GALLIMARD: It is. The sun must be in confusion today.

Over the course of SONG*'s next speech, her upstage special comes up again. She sits in a chair, legs crossed, in a robe, telephone to her ear.*

SONG: I waited until I saw the sun. That was as much discipline as I could manage for one night. Do you forgive me?

GALLIMARD: Of course . . . for what?

SONG: Then I'll ask you quickly. Are you really interested in the opera?

GALLIMARD: Why, yes. Yes I am.

SONG: Then come again next Thursday. I am playing *The Drunken Beauty.* May I count on you?

GALLIMARD: Yes. You may.

SONG: Perfect. Well, I must be getting to bed. I'm exhausted. It's been a very long night for me.

SONG *hangs up; special on her goes off.* GALLIMARD *begins to dress for work.*

Scene 10

SONG LILING*'s apartment. Beijing. 1960.*

GALLIMARD: I returned to the opera that next week, and the week after that . . . she keeps our meetings so short—perhaps fifteen, twenty minutes at most. So I am left each week with a thirst which is intensified. In this way, fifteen weeks have gone by. I am starting to doubt the words of my friend Marc. But no, not really. In my heart, I know she has . . . an interest in me. I suspect this is her way. She is outwardly bold and outspoken, yet her heart is shy and afraid. It is the Oriental in her at war with her Western education.

SONG (*offstage*): I will be out in an instant. Ask the servant for anything you want.

GALLIMARD: Tonight, I have finally been invited to enter her apartment. Though the idea is almost beyond belief, I believe she is afraid of me.

GALLIMARD *looks around the room. He picks up a picture in a frame, studies it. Without his noticing,* SONG *enters, dressed elegantly in a black gown from the twenties. She stands in the doorway looking like Anna May Wong.*

SONG: That is my father.

GALLIMARD (*surprised*): Mademoiselle Song . . .

She glides up to him, snatches away the picture.

SONG: It is very good that he did not live to see the Revolution. They would, no doubt, have made him kneel on broken glass. Not that he didn't deserve such a punishment. But he is my father. I would've hated to see it happen.

GALLIMARD: I'm very honored that you've allowed me to visit your home.

SONG *curtsys.*

SONG: Thank you. Oh! Haven't you been poured any tea?

GALLIMARD: I'm really not—

SONG (*to her offstage servant*): Shu-Fang! Cha! Kwai-lah! (*To Gallimard*) I'm sorry. You want everything to be perfect—

GALLIMARD: Please.

SONG: —and before the evening even begins—

GALLIMARD: I'm really not thirsty.

SONG: —it's ruined.

GALLIMARD (*sharply*): Mademoiselle Song!

SONG *sits down.*

SONG: I'm sorry.

GALLIMARD: What are you apologizing for now?

Pause; SONG *starts to giggle.*

SONG: I don't know!

GALLIMARD *laughs.*

GALLIMARD: Exactly my point.

SONG: Oh, I am silly. Lightheaded. I promise not to apologize for anything else tonight, do you hear me?

GALLIMARD: That's a good girl.

SHU-FANG, *a servant girl, comes out with a tea tray and starts to pour.*

SONG (*to* SHU-FANG): No! I'll pour myself for the gentleman!

SHU-FANG, *staring at* GALLIMARD, *exits.*

SONG: No, I . . . I don't even know why I invited you up.

GALLIMARD: Well, I'm glad you did.

SONG *looks around the room.*

SONG: There is an element of danger to your presence.

GALLIMARD: Oh?

SONG: You must know.

GALLIMARD: It doesn't concern me. We both know why I'm here.

SONG: It doesn't concern me either. No . . . well perhaps . . .

GALLIMARD: What?

SONG: Perhaps I am slightly afraid of scandal.

GALLIMARD: What are we doing?

SONG: I'm entertaining you. In my parlor.

GALLIMARD: In France, that would hardly—

SONG: France. France is a country living in the modern era. Perhaps even ahead of it. China is a nation whose soul is firmly rooted two thousand years in the past. What I do, even pouring the tea for you now . . . it has . . . implications. The walls and windows say so. Even my own heart, strapped inside this Western dress . . . even it says things—things I don't care to hear.

SONG *hands* GALLIMARD *a cup of tea.* GALLIMARD *puts his hand over both the teacup and* SONG*'s hand.*

GALLIMARD: This is a beautiful dress.

SONG: Don't.

GALLIMARD: What?

SONG: I don't even know if it looks right on me.

GALLIMARD: Believe me—

SONG: You are from France. You see so many beautiful women.

GALLIMARD: France? Since when are the European women—?

SONG: Oh! What am I trying to do, anyway?!

SONG *runs to the door, composes herself, then turns towards* GALLIMARD.

SONG: Monsieur Gallimard, perhaps you should go.

GALLIMARD: But . . . why?

SONG: There's something wrong about this.

GALLIMARD: I don't see what.

SONG: I feel . . . I am not myself.

GALLIMARD: No. You're nervous.

SONG: Please. Hard as I try to be modern, to speak like a man, to hold a Western woman's strong face up to my own . . . in the end, I fail. A small, frightened heart beats too quickly and gives me away. Monsieur Gallimard, I'm a Chinese girl. I've never . . . never invited a man up to my flat before. The forwardness of my actions makes my skin burn.

GALLIMARD: What are you afraid of? Certainly not me, I hope.

SONG: I'm a modest girl.

GALLIMARD: I know. And very beautiful. (*He touches her hair*)

SONG: Please—go now. The next time you see me, I shall again be myself.

GALLIMARD: I like you the way you are right now.

SONG: You are a cad.

GALLIMARD: What do you expect? I'm a foreign devil.

GALLIMARD *walks downstage.* SONG *exits.*

GALLIMARD (*to us*): Did you hear the way she talked about Western women? Much differently than the first night. She does—she feels inferior to them—and to me.

Scene 11

The French embassy. Beijing. 1960.

GALLIMARD *moves towards a desk.*

GALLIMARD: I determined to try an experiment. In *Madame Butterfly,* Cio-Cio-San fears that the Western man who catches a butterfly will pierce its heart with a needle, then leave it to perish. I began to wonder: had I, too, caught a butterfly who would writhe on a needle?

MARC *enters, dressed as a bureaucrat, holding a stack of papers. As* GALLIMARD *speaks,* MARC *hands papers to him. He peruses, then signs, stamps or rejects them.*

GALLIMARD: Over the next five weeks, I worked like a dynamo. I stopped going to the opera, I didn't phone or write her. I knew this little flower was waiting for me to call, and, as I wickedly refused to do so, I felt for the first time that rush of power—the absolute power of a man.

MARC *continues acting as the bureaucrat, but he now speaks as himself.*

MARC: Rene! It's me!

GALLIMARD: Marc—I hear your voice everywhere now. Even in the midst of work.

MARC: That's because I'm watching you—all the time.

GALLIMARD: You were always the most popular guy in school.

MARC: Well, there's no guarantee of failure in life like happiness in high school. Somehow I knew I'd end up in the suburbs working for Renault and you'd be in the Orient picking exotic women off the trees. And they say there's no justice.

GALLIMARD: That's why you were my friend?

MARC: I gave you a little of my life, so that now you can give me some of yours. (*Pause*) Remember Isabelle?

GALLIMARD: Of course I remember! She was my first experience.

MARC: We all wanted to ball her. But she only wanted me.

GALLIMARD: I had her.

MARC: Right. You balled her.

GALLIMARD: You were the only one who ever believed me.

MARC: Well, there's a good reason for that. (*Beat*) C'mon. You must've guessed.

GALLIMARD: You told me to wait in the bushes by the cafeteria that night. The next thing I knew, she was on me. Dress up in the air.

MARC: She never wore underwear.

GALLIMARD: My arms were pinned to the dirt.

MARC: She loved the superior position. A girl ahead of her time.

GALLIMARD: I looked up, and there was this woman. . . bouncing up and down on my loins.

MARC: Screaming, right?

GALLIMARD: Screaming, and breaking off the branches all around me, and pounding my butt up and down into the dirt.

MARC: Huffing and puffing like a locomotive.

GALLIMARD: And in the middle of all this, the leaves were getting into my mouth, my legs were losing circulation, I thought, "God. So this is *it?*"

MARC: You thought that?

GALLIMARD: Well, I was worried about my legs falling off.

MARC: You didn't have a good time?

GALLIMARD: No, that's not what I—I had a great time!

MARC: You're sure?

GALLIMARD: Yeah. Really.

MARC: 'Cuz I wanted you to have a good time.

GALLIMARD: I did.

Pause.

MARC: Shit. (*Pause*) When all is said and done, she was kind of a lousy lay, wasn't she? I mean, there was a lot of energy there, but you never knew what she was doing with it. Like when she yelled "I'm coming!" —hell, it was so loud, you wanted to go "Look, it's not that big a deal."

GALLIMARD: I got scared. I thought she meant someone was actually coming. (*Pause*) But, Marc?

MARC: What?

GALLIMARD: Thanks.

MARC: Oh, don't mention it.

GALLIMARD: It was my first experience.

MARC: Yeah. You got her.

GALLIMARD: I got her.

MARC: Wait! Look at that letter again!

GALLIMARD *picks up one of the papers he's been stamping, and rereads it.*

GALLIMARD (*to us*): After six weeks, they began to arrive. The letters.

Upstage special on SONG, *as Madame Butterfly. The scene is underscored by the "Love Duet."*

SONG: Did we fight? I do not know. Is the opera no longer of interest to you? Please come—my audiences miss the white devil in their midst.

GALLIMARD *looks up from the letter, towards us.*

GALLIMARD (*to us*): A concession, but much too dignified. (*Beat; he discards the letter*) I skipped the opera again that week to complete a position paper on trade.

The bureaucrat hands him another letter.

SONG: Six weeks have passed since last we met. Is this your practice—to leave friends in the lurch? Sometimes I hate you, sometimes I hate myself, but always I miss you.

GALLIMARD (*to us*): Better, but I don't like the way she calls me "friend." When a woman calls a man her "friend," she's calling him a eunuch or a homosexual. (*Beat; he discards the letter*) I was absent from the opera for the seventh week, feeling a sudden urge to clean out my files.

Bureaucrat hands him another letter.

SONG: Your rudeness is beyond belief. I don't deserve this cruelty. Don't bother to call. I'll have you turned away at the door.

GALLIMARD (*to us*): I didn't. (*He discards the letter; bureaucrat hands him another*) And then finally, the letter that concluded my experiment.

SONG: I am out of words. I can hide behind dignity no longer. What do you want? I have already given you my shame.

GALLIMARD *gives the letter back to* MARC, *slowly. Special on* SONG *fades out.*

GALLIMARD (*to us*): Reading it, I became suddenly ashamed. Yes, my experiment had been a success. She was turning on my needle. But the victory seemed hollow.

MARC: Hollow?! Are you crazy?

GALLIMARD: Nothing, Marc. Please go away.

MARC (*exiting, with papers*): Haven't I taught you anything?

GALLIMARD: "I have already given you my shame." I had to attend a reception that evening. On the way, I felt sick. If there is a God, surely he would punish me now. I had finally gained power over a beautiful woman, only to abuse it cruelly. There must be justice in the world. I had the strange feeling that the ax would fall this very evening.

Scene 12

AMBASSADOR TOULON*'s residence. Beijing. 1960.*

Sound cue: party noises. Light change. We are now in a spacious residence. TOULON, *the French ambassador, enters and taps* GALLIMARD *on the shoulder.*

TOULON: Gallimard? Can I have a word? Over here.

GALLIMARD (*to us*): Manuel Toulon. French ambassador to China. He likes to think of us all as his children. Rather like God.

TOULON: Look, Gallimard, there's not much to say. I've liked you. From the day you walked in. You were no leader, but you were tidy and efficient.

GALLIMARD: Thank you, sir.

TOULON: Don't jump the gun. Okay, our needs in China are changing. It's embarrassing that we lost Indochina. Someone just wasn't on the ball there. I don't mean you personally, of course.

GALLIMARD: Thank you, sir.

TOULON: We're going to be doing a lot more information-gathering in the future. The nature of our work here is changing. Some people are just going to have to go. It's nothing personal.

GALLIMARD: Oh.

TOULON: Want to know a secret? Vice-Consul LeBon is being transferred.

GALLIMARD (*to us*): My immediate superior!

TOULON: And most of his department.

GALLIMARD (*to us*): Just as I feared! God has seen my evil heart—

TOULON: But not you.

GALLIMARD (*to us*): —and he's taking her away just as . . . (*To* TOULON) Excuse me, sir?

TOULON: Scare you? I think I did. Cheer up, Gallimard. I want you to replace LeBon as vice-consul.

GALLIMARD: You—? Yes, well, thank you, sir.

TOULON: Anytime.

GALLIMARD: I . . . accept with great humility.

TOULON: Humility won't be part of the job. You're going to coordinate the revamped intelligence division. Want to know a secret? A year ago, you would've been out. But the past few months, I don't know how it happened, you've become this new aggressive confident . . . thing. And they also tell me you get along with the Chinese. So I think you're a lucky man, Gallimard. Congratulations.

They shake hands. TOULON *exits. Party noises out.* GALLIMARD *stumbles across a darkened stage.*

GALLIMARD: Vice-consul? Impossible! As I stumbled out of the party, I saw it written across the sky: There is no God. Or, no—say that there is a God. But that God . . . understands. Of course! God who creates Eve to serve Adam, who blesses Solomon with his harem but ties Jezebel to a burning bed—that God is a man. And he understands! At age thirty-nine, I was suddenly initiated into the way of the world.

Scene 13

SONG LILING*'s apartment. Beijing. 1960.*

SONG *enters, in a sheer dressing gown.*

SONG: Are you crazy?

GALLIMARD: Mademoiselle Song—

SONG: To come here—at this hour? After . . . after eight weeks?

GALLIMARD: It's the most amazing—

SONG: You bang on my door? Scare my servants, scandalize the neighbors?

GALLIMARD: I've been promoted. To vice-consul.

Pause.

SONG: And what is that supposed to mean to me?

GALLIMARD: Are you my Butterfly?

SONG: What are you saying?

GALLIMARD: I've come tonight for an answer: are you my Butterfly?

SONG: Don't you know already?

GALLIMARD: I want you to say it.

SONG: I don't want to say it.

GALLIMARD: So, that is your answer?

SONG: You know how I feel about—

GALLIMARD: I do remember one thing.

SONG: What?

GALLIMARD: In the letter I received today.

SONG: Don't.

GALLIMARD: "I have already given you my shame."

SONG: It's enough that I even wrote it.

GALLIMARD: Well, then—

SONG: I shouldn't have it splashed across my face.

GALLIMARD: —if that's all true—

SONG: Stop!

GALLIMARD: Then what is one more short answer?

SONG: I don't want to!

GALLIMARD: Are you my Butterfly? (*Silence; he crosses the room and begins to touch her hair*) I want from you honesty. There should be nothing false between us. No false pride.

Pause.

SONG: Yes, I am. I am your Butterfly.

GALLIMARD: Then let me be honest with you. It is because of you that I was promoted tonight. You have changed my life forever. My little Butterfly, there should be no more secrets: I love you.

He starts to kiss her roughly. She resists slightly.

SONG: No . . . no . . . gently . . . please, I've never . . .

GALLIMARD: No?

SONG: I've tried to appear experienced, but . . . the truth is . . . no.

GALLIMARD: Are you cold?

SONG: Yes. Cold.

GALLIMARD: Then we will go very, very slowly.

He starts to caress her; her gown begins to open.

SONG: No . . . let me . . . keep my clothes . . .

GALLIMARD: But . . .

SONG: Please . . . it all frightens me. I'm a modest Chinese girl.

GALLIMARD: My poor little treasure.

SONG: I am your treasure. Though inexperienced, I am not . . . ignorant. They teach us things, our mothers, about pleasing a man.

GALLIMARD: Yes?

SONG: I'll do my best to make you happy. Turn off the lights.

GALLIMARD *gets up and heads for a lamp.* SONG, *propped up on one elbow, tosses her hair back and smiles.*

SONG: Monsieur Gallimard?
GALLIMARD: Yes, Butterfly?
SONG: "Vieni, vieni!"
GALLIMARD: "Come, darling."
SONG: "Ah! Dolce notte!"
GALLIMARD: "Beautiful night."
SONG: "Tutto estatico d'amor ride il ciel!"
GALLIMARD: "All ecstatic with love, the heavens are filled with laughter."

He turns off the lamp. Blackout.

ACT TWO

Scene 1

M. GALLIMARD*'s cell. Paris. Present.*

Lights up on GALLIMARD*. He sits in his cell, reading from a leaflet.*

GALLIMARD: This, from a contemporary critic's commentary on *Madame Butterfly:* "Pinkerton suffers from . . . being an obnoxious bounder whom every man in the audience itches to kick." Bully for us men in the audience! Then, in the same note: "Butterfly is the most irresistibly appealing of Puccini's 'Little Women.' Watching the succession of her humiliations is like watching a child under torture." (*He tosses the pamphlet over his shoulder*) I suggest that, while we men may all want to kick Pinkerton, very few of us would pass up the opportunity to *be* Pinkerton.

GALLIMARD *moves out of his cell.*

Scene 2

GALLIMARD *and Butterfly's flat. Beijing. 1960.*

We are in a simple but well-decorated parlor. GALLIMARD *moves to sit on a sofa, while* SONG*, dressed in a chong sam, enters and curls up at his feet.*

GALLIMARD (*to us*): We secured a flat on the outskirts of Peking. Butterfly, as I was calling her now, decorated our "home" with Western furniture and Chinese antiques. And there, on a few stolen afternoons or evenings each week, Butterfly commenced her education.

SONG: The Chinese men—they keep us down.
GALLIMARD: Even in the "New Society"?
SONG: In the "New Society," we are all kept ignorant equally. That's one of the exciting things about loving a Western man. I know you are not threatened by a woman's education.
GALLIMARD: I'm no saint, Butterfly.
SONG: But you come from a progressive society.

GALLIMARD: We're not always reminding each other how "old" we are, if that's what you mean.

SONG: Exactly. We Chinese—once, I suppose, it is true, we ruled the world. But so what? How much more exciting to be part of the society ruling the world today. Tell me—what's happening in Vietnam?

GALLIMARD: Oh, Butterfly—you want me to bring my work home?

SONG: I want to know what you know. To be impressed by my man. It's not the particulars so much as the fact that you're making decisions which change the shape of the world.

GALLIMARD: Not the world. At best, a small corner.

TOULON enters, and sits at a desk upstage.

Scene 3

French embassy. Beijing. 1961.

GALLIMARD moves downstage, to TOULON's desk. SONG remains upstage, watching.

TOULON: And a more troublesome corner is hard to imagine.

GALLIMARD: So, the Americans plan to begin bombing?

TOULON: This is very secret, Gallimard: yes. The Americans don't have an embassy here. They're asking us to be their eyes and ears. Say Jack Kennedy signed an order to bomb North Vietnam, Laos. How would the Chinese react?

GALLIMARD: I think the Chinese will squawk—

TOULON: Uh-huh.

GALLIMARD: —but, in their hearts, they don't even like Ho Chi Minh.

Pause.

TOULON: What a bunch of jerks. Vietnam was *our* colony. Not only didn't the Americans help us fight to keep them, but now, seven years later, they've come back to grab the territory for themselves. It's very irritating.

GALLIMARD: With all due respect, sir, why should the Americans have won our war for us back in '54 if we didn't have the will to win it ourselves?

TOULON: You're kidding, aren't you?

Pause.

GALLIMARD: The Orientals simply want to be associated with whoever shows the most strength and power. You live with the Chinese, sir. Do you think they like Communism?

TOULON: I live in China. Not with the Chinese.

GALLIMARD: Well, I—

TOULON: *You* live with the Chinese.

GALLIMARD: Excuse me?

TOULON: I can't keep a secret.

GALLIMARD: What are you saying?

TOULON: Only that I'm not immune to gossip. So, you're keeping a native mistress. Don't answer. It's none of my business. (*Pause*) I'm sure she must be gorgeous.

GALLIMARD: Well . . .

TOULON: I'm impressed. You have the stamina to go out into the streets and hunt one down. Some of us have to be content with the wives of the expatriate community.

GALLIMARD: I do feel . . . fortunate.

TOULON: So, Gallimard, you've got the inside knowledge—what *do* the Chinese think?

GALLIMARD: Deep down, they miss the old days. You know, cappuccinos, men in tuxedos—

TOULON: So what do we tell the Americans about Vietnam?

GALLIMARD: Tell them there's a natural affinity between the West and the Orient.

TOULON: And that you speak from experience?

GALLIMARD: The Orientals are people too. They want the good things we can give them. If the Americans demonstrate the will to win, the Vietnamese will welcome them into a mutually beneficial union.

TOULON: I don't see how the Vietnamese can stand up to American firepower.

GALLIMARD: Orientals will always submit to a greater force.

TOULON: I'll note your opinions in my report. The Americans always love to hear how "welcome" they'll be. (*He starts to exit*)

GALLIMARD: Sir?

TOULON: Mmmm?

GALLIMARD: This . . . rumor you've heard.

TOULON: Uh-huh?

GALLIMARD: How . . . widespread do you think it is?

TOULON: It's only widespread within this embassy. Where nobody talks because everybody is guilty. We were worried about you, Gallimard. We thought you were the only one here without a secret. Now you go and find a lotus blossom . . . and top us all. (*He exits*)

GALLIMARD (*to us*): Toulon knows! And he approves! I was learning the benefits of being a man. We form our own clubs, sit behind thick doors, smoke—and celebrate the fact that we're still boys. (*He starts to move downstage, towards* SONG) So, over the—

Suddenly COMRADE CHIN *enters.* GALLIMARD *backs away.*

GALLIMARD (*to* SONG): No! Why does she have to come in?

SONG: Rene, be sensible. How can they understand the story without her? Now, don't embarrass yourself.

GALLIMARD *moves down center.*

GALLIMARD (*to us*): Now, you will see why my story is so amusing to so many people. Why they snicker at parties in disbelief. Please—try to understand it from my point of view. We are all prisoners of our time and place. (*He exits*)

Scene 4

GALLIMARD *and Butterfly's flat. Beijing. 1961.*

SONG (*to us*): 1961. The flat Monsieur Gallimard rented for us. An evening after he has gone.

CHIN: Okay, see if you can find out when the Americans plan to start bombing Vietnam. If you can find out what cities, even better.

SONG: I'll do my best, but I don't want to arouse his suspicions.

CHIN: Yeah, sure, of course. So, what else?

SONG: The Americans will increase troops in Vietnam to 170,000 soldiers with 120,000 militia and 11,000 American advisors.

CHIN (*writing*): Wait, wait. 120,000 militia and—

SONG: —11,000 American—

CHIN: —American advisors. (*Beat*) How do you remember so much?

SONG: I'm an actor.

CHIN: Yeah. (*Beat*) Is that how come you dress like that?

SONG: Like what, Miss Chin?

CHIN: Like that dress! You're wearing a dress. And every time I come here, you're wearing a dress. Is that because you're an actor? Or what?

SONG: It's a . . . disguise, Miss Chin.

CHIN: Actors, I think they're all weirdos. My mother tells me actors are like gamblers or prostitutes or—

SONG: It helps me in my assignment.

Pause.

CHIN: You're not gathering information in any way that violates Communist Party principles, are you?

SONG: Why would I do that?

CHIN: Just checking. Remember: when working for the Great Proletarian State, you represent our Chairman Mao in every position you take.

SONG: I'll try to imagine the Chairman taking my positions.

CHIN: We all think of him this way. Good-bye, comrade. (*She starts to exit*) Comrade?

SONG: Yes?

CHIN: Don't forget: there is no homosexuality in China!

SONG: Yes, I've heard.

CHIN: Just checking. (*She exits*)

SONG (*to us*): What passes for a woman in modern China.

GALLIMARD *sticks his head out from the wings.*

GALLIMARD: Is she gone?

SONG: Yes, Rene. Please continue in your own fashion.

Scene 5

Beijing. 1961–63.

GALLIMARD *moves to the couch where* SONG *still sits. He lies down in her lap, and she strokes his forehead.*

GALLIMARD (*to us*): And so, over the years 1961, '62, '63, we settled into our routine, Butterfly and I. She would always have prepared a light snack and then, ever so delicately, and only if I agreed, she would start to pleasure me. With her hands, her mouth . . . too many ways to explain, and too sad, given my present situation. But mostly we would talk. About my life. Perhaps there is nothing more rare than to find a woman who passionately listens.

SONG *remains upstage, listening, as* HELGA *enters and plays a scene downstage with* GALLIMARD.

HELGA: Rene, I visited Dr. Bolleart this morning.

GALLIMARD: Why? Are you ill?

HELGA: No, no. You see, I wanted to ask him . . . that question we've been discussing.

GALLIMARD: And I told you, it's only a matter of time. Why did you bring a doctor into this? We just have to keep trying—like a crapshoot, actually.

HELGA: I went, I'm sorry. But listen: he says there's nothing wrong with me.

GALLIMARD: You see? Now, will you stop—?

HELGA: Rene, he says he'd like you to go in and take some tests.

GALLIMARD: Why? So he can find there's nothing wrong with both of us?

HELGA: Rene, I don't ask for much. One trip! One visit! And then, whatever you want to do about it—you decide.

GALLIMARD: You're assuming he'll find something defective!

HELGA: No! Of course not! Whatever he finds—if he finds nothing, we decide what to do about nothing! But go!

GALLIMARD: If he finds nothing, we keep trying. Just like we do now.

HELGA: But at least we'll know! (*Pause*) I'm sorry. (*She starts to exit*)

GALLIMARD: Do you really want me to see Dr. Bolleart?

HELGA: Only if you want a child, Rene. We have to face the fact that time is running out. Only if you want a child. (*She exits*)

GALLIMARD (*to* SONG): I'm a modern man, Butterfly. And yet, I don't want to go. It's the same old voodoo. I feel like God himself is laughing at me if I can't produce a child.

SONG: You men of the West—you're obsessed by your odd desire for equality. Your wife can't give you a child, and *you're* going to the doctor?

GALLIMARD: Well, you see, she's already gone.

SONG: And because this incompetent can't find the defect, you now have to subject yourself to him? It's unnatural.

GALLIMARD: Well, what is the "natural" solution?

SONG: In Imperial China, when a man found that one wife was inadequate, he turned to another—to give him his son.

GALLIMARD: What do you—? I can't . . . marry you, yet.

SONG: Please. I'm not asking you to be my husband. But I am already your wife.

GALLIMARD: Do you want to . . . have my child?

SONG: I thought you'd never ask.

GALLIMARD: But, your career . . . your—

SONG: Phooey on my career! That's your Western mind, twisting itself into strange shapes again. Of course I love my career. But what would I love most of all? To feel something inside me—day and night—something I know is yours. (*Pause*) Promise me . . . you won't go to this doctor. Who is this Western quack to set himself as judge over the man I love? I know who is a man, and who is not. (*She exits*)

GALLIMARD (*to us*): Dr. Bolleart? Of course I didn't go. What man would?

Scene 6

Beijing. 1963.

Party noises over the house speakers. RENEE *enters, wearing a revealing gown.*

GALLIMARD: 1963. A party at the Austrian embassy. None of us could remember the Austrian ambassador's name, which seemed somehow appropriate. (*To* RENEE) So, I tell the Americans, Diem must go. The U.S. wants to be respected by the Vietnamese, and yet they're propping up this nobody seminarian as her president. A man whose claim to fame is his sister-in-law imposing fanatic "moral order" campaigns? Oriental women—when they're good, they're very good, but when they're bad, they're Christians.

RENEE: Yeah.

GALLIMARD: And what do you do?

RENEE: I'm a student. My father exports a lot of useless stuff to the Third World.

GALLIMARD: How useless?

RENEE: You know. Squirt guns, confectioner's sugar, hula hoops . . .

GALLIMARD: I'm sure they appreciate the sugar.

RENEE: I'm here for two years to study Chinese.

GALLIMARD: Two years?

RENEE: That's what everybody says.

GALLIMARD: When did you arrive?

RENEE: Three weeks ago.

GALLIMARD: And?

RENEE: I like it. It's primitive, but . . . well, this is the place to learn Chinese, so here I am.

GALLIMARD: Why Chinese?

RENEE: I think it'll be important someday.

GALLIMARD: You do?

RENEE: Don't ask me when, but . . . that's what I think.

GALLIMARD: Well, I agree with you. One hundred percent. That's very farsighted.

RENEE: Yeah. Well of course, my father thinks I'm a complete weirdo.

GALLIMARD: He'll thank you someday.

RENEE: Like when the Chinese start buying hula hoops?

GALLIMARD: There're a billion bellies out there.

RENEE: And if they end up taking over the world—well, then I'll be lucky to know Chinese too, right?

Pause.

GALLIMARD: At this point, I don't see how the Chinese can possibly take—

RENEE: You know what I *don't* like about China?

GALLIMARD: Excuse me? No—what?

RENEE: Nothing to do at night.

GALLIMARD: You come to parties at embassies like everyone else.

RENEE: Yeah, but they get out at ten. And then what?

GALLIMARD: I'm afraid the Chinese idea of a dance hall is a dirt floor and a man with a flute.

RENEE: Are you married?

GALLIMARD: Yes. Why?

RENEE: You wanna . . . fool around?

Pause.

GALLIMARD: Sure.

RENEE: I'll wait for you outside. What's your name?

GALLIMARD: Gallimard. Rene.

RENEE: Weird. I'm Renee too. (*She exits*)

GALLIMARD (*to us*): And so, I embarked on my first extramarital affair. Renee was picture perfect. With a body like those girls in the magazines. If I put a tissue paper over my eyes, I wouldn't have been able to tell the difference. And it was exciting to be with someone who wasn't afraid to be seen completely naked. But is it possible for a woman to be *too* uninhibited, *too* willing, so as to seem almost too . . . masculine?

Chuck Berry blares from the house speakers, then comes down in volume as RENEE *enters, toweling her hair.*

RENEE: You have a nice weenie.

GALLIMARD: What?

RENEE: Penis. You have a nice penis.

GALLIMARD: Oh. Well, thank you. That's very . . .

RENEE: What—can't take a compliment?

GALLIMARD: No, it's very . . . reassuring.

RENEE: But most girls don't come out and say it, huh?

GALLIMARD: And also . . . what did you call it?

RENEE: Oh. Most girls don't call it a "weenie," huh?

GALLIMARD: It sounds very—

RENEE: Small, I know.

GALLIMARD: I was going to say, "young."

RENEE: Yeah. Young, small, same thing. Most guys are pretty, uh, sensitive about that. Like, you know, I had a boyfriend back home in Denmark. I got mad at him once and called him a little weeniehead. He got so mad! He said at least I should call him a great big weeniehead.

GALLIMARD: I suppose I just say "penis."

RENEE: Yeah. That's pretty clinical. There's "cock," but that sounds like a chicken. And "prick" is painful, and "dick" is like you're talking about someone who's not in the room.

GALLIMARD: Yes. It's a . . . bigger problem than I imagined.

RENEE: I—I think maybe it's because I really don't know what to do with them—that's why I call them "weenies."

GALLIMARD: Well, you did quite well with . . . mine.

RENEE: Thanks, but I mean, really *do* with them. Like, okay, have you ever looked at one? I mean, really?

GALLIMARD: No, I suppose when it's part of you, you sort of take it for granted.

RENEE: I guess. But, like, it just hangs there. This little . . . flap of flesh. And there's so much fuss that we make about it. Like, I think the reason we fight wars is because we wear clothes. Because no one knows—between the men, I mean—who has the bigger . . . weenie. So, if I'm a guy with a small one, I'm going to build a really big building or take over a really big piece of land or write a really long book so the other men don't know, right? But, see, it never really works, that's the problem. I mean, you conquer the country, or whatever, but you're still wearing clothes, so there's no way to prove absolutely whose is bigger or smaller. And that's what we call a civilized society. The whole world run by a bunch of men with pricks the size of pins. (*She exits*)

GALLIMARD (*to us*): This was simply not acceptable.

A high-pitched chime rings through the air. SONG, *dressed as Butterfly, appears in the upstage special. She is obviously distressed. Her body swoons as she attempts to clip the stems of flowers she's arranging in a vase.*

GALLIMARD: But I kept up our affair, wildly, for several months. Why? I believe because of Butterfly. She knew the secret I was trying to hide. But, unlike a Western woman, she didn't confront me, threaten, even pout. I remembered the words of Puccini's *Butterfly:*

SONG: "Noi siamo gente avvezza/ alle piccole cose/ umili e silenziose."

GALLIMARD: "I come from a people/ Who are accustomed to little/ Humble and silent." I saw Pinkerton and Butterfly, and what she would say if he were unfaithful . . . nothing. She would cry, alone, into those wildly soft sleeves, once full of possessions, now empty to collect her tears. It was her tears and her silence that excited me, every time I visited Renee.

TOULON (*offstage*): Gallimard!

TOULON *enters.* GALLIMARD *turns toward him. During the next section,* SONG, *up center, begins to dance with the flowers. It is a drunken dance, where she breaks small pieces off the stems.*

TOULON: They're killing him.

GALLIMARD: Who? I'm sorry? What?

TOULON: Bother you to come over at this late hour?

GALLIMARD: No . . . of course not.

TOULON: Not after you hear my secret. Champagne?

GALLIMARD: Um . . . thank you.

TOULON: You're surprised. There's something that you've wanted, Gallimard. No, not a promotion. Next time. Something in the world. You're not aware of this, but there's an informal gossip circle among intelligence agents. And some of ours heard from some of the Americans—

GALLIMARD: Yes?

TOULON: That the U.S. will allow the Vietnamese generals to stage a coup . . . and assassinate President Diem.

The chime rings again. TOULON *freezes.* GALLIMARD *turns upstage and looks at Butterfly, who slowly and deliberately clips a flower off its stem.* GALLIMARD *turns back towards* TOULON.

GALLIMARD: I think . . . that's a very wise move!

TOULON *unfreezes.*

TOULON: It's what you've been advocating. A toast?

GALLIMARD: Sure. I consider this a vindication.

TOULON: Not exactly. "To the test. Let's hope you pass."

They drink. The chime rings again. TOULON *freezes.* GALLIMARD *turns upstage, and* SONG *clips another flower.*

GALLIMARD (*to* TOULON): The test?

TOULON (*unfreezing*): It's a test of everything you've been saying. I personally think the generals probably will stop the Communists. And you'll be a hero. But if anything goes wrong, then your opinions won't be worth a pig's ear. I'm sure that won't happen. But sometimes it's easier when they don't listen to you.

GALLIMARD: They're your opinions too, aren't they?

TOULON: Personally, yes.

GALLIMARD: So we agree.

TOULON: But my opinions aren't on that report. Yours are. Cheers.

TOULON *turns away from* GALLIMARD *and raises his glass. At that instant* SONG *picks up the vase and hurls it to the ground. It shatters.* SONG *sinks down amidst the shards of the vase, in a calm, childlike trance. She sings softly, as if reciting a child's nursery rhyme.*

SONG (*repeat as necessary*): "The whole world over, the white man travels, setting anchor, wherever he likes. Life's not worth living, unless he finds, the finest maidens, of every land . . ."

GALLIMARD *turns downstage toward us.* SONG *continues singing.*

GALLIMARD: I shook as I left his house. That coward! That worm! To put the burden for his decisions on my shoulders!

I started for Renee's. But no, that was all I needed. A schoolgirl who would question the role of the penis in modern society. What I wanted was revenge. A vessel to contain my humiliation. Though I hadn't seen her in several weeks, I headed for Butterfly's.

GALLIMARD *enters* SONG*'s apartment.*

SONG: Oh! Rene . . . I was dreaming!

GALLIMARD: You've been drinking?

SONG: If I can't sleep, then yes, I drink. But then, it gives me these dreams which—Rene, it's been almost three weeks since you visited me last.

GALLIMARD: I know. There's been a lot going on in the world.

SONG: Fortunately I am drunk. So I can speak freely. It's not the world, it's you and me. And an old problem. Even the softest skin becomes like leather to a man who's touched it too often. I confess I don't know how to stop it. I don't know how to become another woman.

GALLIMARD: I have a request.

SONG: Is this a solution? Or are you ready to give up the flat?

GALLIMARD: It may be a solution. But I'm sure you won't like it.

SONG: Oh well, that's very important. "Like it?" Do you think I "like" lying here alone, waiting, always waiting for your return? Please—don't worry about what I may not "like."

GALLIMARD: I want to see you . . . naked.

Silence.

SONG: I thought you understood my modesty. So you want me to—what—strip? Like a big cowboy girl? Shiny pasties on my breasts? Shall I fling my kimono over my head and yell "ya-hoo" in the process? I thought you respected my shame!

GALLIMARD: I believe you gave me your shame many years ago.

SONG: Yes—and it is just like a white devil to use it against me. I can't believe it. I thought myself so repulsed by the passive Oriental and the cruel white man. Now I see—we are always most revolted by the things hidden within us.

GALLIMARD: I just mean—

SONG: Yes?

GALLIMARD: —that it will remove the only barrier left between us.

SONG: No, Rene. Don't couch your request in sweet words. Be yourself—a cad—and know that my love is enough, that I submit—submit to the worst you can give me. (*Pause*) Well, come. Strip me. Whatever happens, know that you have willed it. Our love, in your hands. I'm helpless before my man.

GALLIMARD *starts to cross the room.*

GALLIMARD: Did I not undress her because I knew, somewhere deep down, what I would find? Perhaps. Happiness is so rare that our mind can turn somersaults to protect it.

At the time, I only knew that I was seeing Pinkerton stalking toward his Butterfly, ready to reward her love with his lecherous hands. The image sickened me, pulled me to my knees, so I was crawling toward her like a worm. By the time I reached her, Pinkerton . . . had vanished from my heart. To be replaced by something new, something unnatural, that flew in the face of all I'd learned in the world—something very close to love.

He grabs her around the waist; she strokes his hair.

GALLIMARD: Butterfly, forgive me.

SONG: Rene . . .

GALLIMARD: For everything. From the start.

SONG: I'm . . .

GALLIMARD: I want to—

SONG: I'm pregnant. (*Beat*) I'm pregnant. (*Beat*) I'm pregnant.

Beat.

GALLIMARD: I want to marry you!

Scene 7

Gallimard and Butterfly's flat. Beijing. 1963.

Downstage, SONG *paces as* COMRADE CHIN *reads from her notepad. Upstage,* GALLIMARD *is still kneeling. He remains on his knees throughout the scene, watching it.*

SONG: I need a baby.

CHIN (*from pad*): He's been spotted going to a dorm.

SONG: I need a baby.

CHIN: At the Foreign Language Institute.

SONG: I need a baby.

CHIN: The room of a Danish girl . . . What do you mean, you need a baby?!

SONG: Tell Comrade Kang—last night, the entire mission, it could've ended.

CHIN: What do you mean?

SONG: Tell Kang—he told me to strip.

CHIN: *Strip?!*

SONG: Write!

CHIN: I tell you, I don't understand nothing about this case anymore. Nothing.

SONG: He told me to strip, and I took a chance. Oh, we Chinese, we know how to gamble.

CHIN (*writing*): ". . . told him to strip."

SONG: My palms were wet, I had to make a split-second decision.

CHIN: Hey! Can you slow down?!

Pause.

SONG: You write faster, I'm the artist here. Suddenly, it hit me—"All he wants is for her to submit. Once a woman submits, a man is always ready to become 'generous.'"

CHIN: You're just gonna end up with rough notes.

SONG: And it worked! He gave in! Now, if I can just present him with a baby. A Chinese baby with blond hair—he'll be mine for life!

CHIN: Kang will never agree! The trading of babies has to be a counterrevolutionary act!

SONG: Sometimes, a counterrevolutionary act is necessary to counter a counterrevolutionary act.

Pause.

CHIN: Wait.

SONG: I need one . . . in seven months. Make sure it's a boy.

CHIN: This doesn't sound like something the Chairman would do. Maybe you'd better talk to Comrade Kang yourself.

SONG: Good. I will.

CHIN *gets up to leave.*

SONG: Miss Chin? Why, in the Peking Opera, are women's roles played by men?

CHIN: I don't know. Maybe, a reactionary remnant of male—

SONG: No. (*Beat*) Because only a man knows how a woman is supposed to act.

CHIN *exits.* SONG *turns upstage, towards* GALLIMARD.

GALLIMARD (*calling after* CHIN): Good riddance! (*To* SONG) I could forget all that betrayal in an instant, you know. If you'd just come back and become Butterfly again.

SONG: Fat chance. You're here in prison, rotting in a cell. And I'm on a plane, winging my way back to China. Your President pardoned me of our treason, you know.

GALLIMARD: Yes, I read about that.

SONG: Must make you feel . . . lower than shit.

GALLIMARD: But don't you, even a little bit, wish you were here with me?

SONG: I'm an artist, Rene. You were my greatest . . . acting challenge. (*She laughs*) It doesn't matter how rotten I answer, does it? You still adore me. That's why I love you, Rene. (*She points to us*) So—you were telling your audience about the night I announced I was pregnant.

GALLIMARD puts his arms around SONG's waist. He and SONG are in the positions they were in at the end of Scene 6.

Scene 8

Same.

GALLIMARD: I'll divorce my wife. We'll live together here, and then later in France.

SONG: I feel so . . . ashamed.

GALLIMARD: Why?

SONG: I had begun to lose faith. And now, you shame me with your generosity.

GALLIMARD: Generosity? No, I'm proposing for very selfish reasons.

SONG: Your apologies only make me feel more ashamed. My outburst a moment ago!

GALLIMARD: Your outburst? What about my request?!

SONG: You've been very patient dealing with my . . . eccentricities. A Western man, used to women freer with their bodies—

GALLIMARD: It was sick! Don't make excuses for me.

SONG: I have to. You don't seem willing to make them for yourself.

Pause.

GALLIMARD: You're crazy.

SONG: I'm happy. Which often looks like crazy.

GALLIMARD: Then make me crazy. Marry me.

Pause.

SONG: No.

GALLIMARD: What?

SONG: Do I sound silly, a slave, if I say I'm not worthy?

GALLIMARD: Yes. In fact you do. No one has loved me like you.

SONG: Thank you. And no one ever will. I'll see to that.

GALLIMARD: So what is the problem?

SONG: Rene, we Chinese are realists. We understand rice, gold, and guns. You are a diplomat. Your career is skyrocketing. Now, what would happen if you divorced your wife to marry a Communist Chinese actress?

GALLIMARD: That's not being realistic. That's defeating yourself before you begin.

SONG: We must conserve our strength for the battles we can win.

GALLIMARD: That sounds like a fortune cookie!

SONG: Where do you think fortune cookies come from?

GALLIMARD: I don't care.

SONG: You do. So do I. And we should. That is why I say I'm not worthy. I'm worthy to love and even to be loved by you. But I am not worthy to end the career of one of the West's most promising diplomats.

GALLIMARD: It's not that great a career! I made it sound like more than it is!

SONG: Modesty will get you nowhere. Flatter yourself, and you flatter me. I'm flattered to decline your offer. (*She exits*)

GALLIMARD (*to us*): Butterfly and I argued all night. And, in the end, I left, knowing I would never be her husband. She went away for several months—to the countryside, like a small animal. Until the night I received her call.

A baby's cry from offstage. SONG *enters, carrying a child.*

SONG: He looks like you.

GALLIMARD: Oh! (*Beat; he approaches the baby*) Well, babies are never very attractive at birth.

SONG: Stop!

GALLIMARD: I'm sure he'll grow more beautiful with age. More like his mother.

SONG: "Chi vide mai/ a bimbo del Giappon . . ."

GALLIMARD: "What baby, I wonder, was ever born in Japan"—or China, for that matter—

SONG: ". . . occhi azzurrini?"

GALLIMARD: "With azure eyes"—they're actually sort of brown, wouldn't you say?

SONG: "E il labbro."

GALLIMARD: "And such lips!" (*He kisses* SONG) And such lips.

SONG: "E i ricciolini d'oro schietto?"

GALLIMARD: "And such a head of golden"—if slightly patchy—"curls?"

SONG: I'm going to call him "Peepee."

GALLIMARD: Darling, could you repeat that because I'm sure a rickshaw just flew by overhead.

SONG: You heard me.

GALLIMARD: "Song Peepee"? May I suggest Michael, or Stephan, or Adolph?

SONG: You may, but I won't listen.

GALLIMARD: You can't be serious. Can you imagine the time this child will have in school?

SONG: In the West, yes.

GALLIMARD: It's worse than naming him Ping Pong or Long Dong or—

SONG: But he's never going to live in the West, is he?

Pause.

GALLIMARD: That wasn't my choice.

SONG: It is mine. And this is my promise to you: I will raise him, he will be our child, but he will never burden you outside of China.

GALLIMARD: Why do you make these promises? I want to be burdened! I want a scandal to cover the papers!

SONG (*to us*): Prophetic.

GALLIMARD: I'm serious.

SONG: So am I. His name is as I registered it. And he will never live in the West.

SONG *exits with the child.*

GALLIMARD (*to us*): It is possible that her stubbornness only made me want her more. That drawing back at the moment of my capitulation was the most brilliant strategy she could have chosen. It is possible. But it is also possible that by this point she could have said, could have done . . . anything, and I would have adored her still.

Scene 9

Beijing. 1966.

A driving rhythm of Chinese percussion fills the stage.

GALLIMARD: And then, China began to change. Mao became very old, and his cult became very strong. And, like many old men, he entered his second childhood. So he handed over the reins of state to those with minds like his own. And children ruled the Middle Kingdom with complete caprice. The doctrine of the Cultural Revolution implied continuous anarchy. Contact between Chinese and foreigners became impossible. Our flat was confiscated. Her fame and my money now counted against us.

Two dancers in Mao suits and red-starred caps enter, and begin crudely mimicking revolutionary violence, in an agitprop fashion.

GALLIMARD: And somehow the American war went wrong too. Four hundred thousand dollars were being spent for every Viet Cong killed; so General Westmoreland's remark that the Oriental does not value life the way Americans do was oddly accurate. Why weren't the Vietnamese people giving in? Why were they content instead to die and die and die again?

TOULON *enters.*

TOULON: Congratulations, Gallimard.

GALLIMARD: Excuse me, sir?

TOULON: Not a promotion. That was last time. You're going home.

GALLIMARD: What?

TOULON: Don't say I didn't warn you.

GALLIMARD: I'm being transferred . . . because I was wrong about the American war?

TOULON: Of course not. We don't care about the Americans. We care about your mind. The quality of your analysis. In general, everything you've predicted here in the Orient . . . just hasn't happened.

GALLIMARD: I think that's premature.

TOULON: Don't force me to be blunt. Okay, you said China was ready to open to Western trade. The only thing they're trading out there are Western heads. And, yes, you said the Americans would succeed in Indochina. You were kidding, right?

GALLIMARD: I think the end is in sight.

TOULON: Don't be pathetic. And don't take this personally. You were wrong. It's not your fault.

GALLIMARD: But I'm going home.

TOULON: Right. Could I have the number of your mistress? (*Beat*) Joke! Joke! Eat a croissant for me.

TOULON *exits.* SONG, *wearing a Mao suit, is dragged in from the wings as part of the upstage dance. They "beat" her, then lampoon the acrobatics of the Chinese opera, as she is made to kneel onstage.*

GALLIMARD (*simultaneously*): I don't care to recall how Butterfly and I said our hurried farewell. Perhaps it was better to end our affair before it killed her.

GALLIMARD *exits.* COMRADE CHIN *walks across the stage with a banner reading: "The Actor Renounces His Decadent Profession!" She reaches the kneeling* SONG. *Percussion stops with a thud. Dancers strike poses.*

CHIN: Actor—oppressor, for years you have lived above the common people and looked down on their labor. While the farmer ate millet—

SONG: I ate pastries from France and sweetmeats from silver trays.

CHIN: And how did you come to live in such an exalted position?

SONG: I was a plaything for the imperialists!

CHIN: What did you do?

SONG: I shamed China by allowing myself to be corrupted by a foreigner . . .

CHIN: What does this mean? The People demand a full confession!

SONG: I engaged in the lowest perversions with China's enemies!

CHIN: What perversions? Be more clear!

SONG: I let him put it up my ass!

Dancers look over, disgusted.

CHIN: Aaaa—ya! How can you use such sickening language?!

SONG: My language . . . is only as foul as the crimes I committed . . .

CHIN: Yeah. That's better. So—what do you want to do now?

SONG: I want to serve the people.

Percussion starts up, with Chinese strings.

CHIN: What?

SONG: I want to serve the people!

Dancers regain their revolutionary smiles, and begin a dance of victory.

CHIN: What?!

SONG: I want to serve the people!!

Dancers unveil a banner: "The Actor Is Rehabilitated!" SONG *remains kneeling before* CHIN, *as the dancers bounce around them, then exit. Music out.*

Scene 10

A commune. Hunan Province. 1970.

CHIN: How you planning to do that?

SONG: I've already worked four years in the fields of Hunan, Comrade Chin.

CHIN: So? Farmers work all their lives. Let me see your hands.

SONG *holds them out for her inspection.*

CHIN: Goddamn! Still so smooth! How long does it take to turn you actors into good anythings? Hunh. You've just spent too many years in luxury to be any good to the Revolution.

SONG: I served the Revolution.

CHIN: Serve the Revolution? Bullshit! You wore dresses! Don't tell me—I was there. I saw you! You and your white vice-consul! Stuck up there in your flat, living off the People's Treasury! Yeah, I knew what was going on! You two . . . homos! Homos! Homos! (*Pause; she composes herself*) Ah! Well . . . you will serve the people, all right. But not with the Revolution's money. This time, you use your own money.

SONG: I have no money.

CHIN: Shut up! And you won't stink up China anymore with your pervert stuff. You'll pollute the place where pollution begins—the West.

SONG: What do you mean?

CHIN: Shut up! You're going to France. Without a cent in your pocket. You find your consul's house, you make him pay your expenses—

SONG: No.

CHIN: And you give us weekly reports! Useful information!

SONG: That's crazy. It's been four years.

CHIN: Either that, or back to rehabilitation center!

SONG: Comrade Chin, he's not going to support me! Not in France! He's a white man! I was just his plaything—

CHIN: Oh yuck! Again with the sickening language? Where's my stick?

SONG: You don't understand the mind of a man.

Pause.

CHIN: Oh no? No I don't? Then how come I'm married, huh? How come I got a man? Five, six years ago, you always tell me those kind of things, I felt very bad. But not now! Because what does the Chairman say? He tells us *I'm* now the smart one, you're now the nincompoop! *You're* the blackhead, the harebrain, the nitwit! You think you're so smart? You understand "The Mind of a Man"? Good! Then *you* go to France and be a pervert for Chairman Mao!

CHIN *and* SONG *exit in opposite directions.*

Scene 11

Paris. 1968–70.

GALLIMARD *enters.*

GALLIMARD: And what was waiting for me back in Paris? Well, better Chinese food than I'd eaten in China. Friends and relatives. A little accounting, regular schedule, keeping track of traffic violations in the suburbs. . . . And the indignity of students shouting the slogans of Chairman Mao at me—in French.

HELGA: Rene? Rene? (*She enters, soaking wet*) I've had a . . . a problem. (*She sneezes*)

GALLIMARD: You're wet.

HELGA: Yes, I . . . coming back from the grocer's. A group of students, waving red flags, they—

GALLIMARD *fetches a towel.*

HELGA: —they ran by, I was caught up along with them. Before I knew what was happening—

GALLIMARD *gives her the towel.*

HELGA: Thank you. The police started firing water cannons at us. I tried to shout, to tell them I was the wife of a diplomat, but—you know how it is . . . (*Pause*) Needless to say, I lost the groceries. Rene, what's happening to France?

GALLIMARD: What's—? Well, nothing, really.

HELGA: Nothing?! The storefronts are in flames, there's glass in the streets, buildings are toppling—and I'm wet!

GALLIMARD: Nothing! . . . that I care to think about.

HELGA: And is that why you stay in this room?

GALLIMARD: Yes, in fact.

HELGA: With the incense burning? You know something? I hate incense. It smells so sickly sweet.

GALLIMARD: Well, I hate the French. Who just smell—period!

HELGA: And the Chinese were better?

GALLIMARD: Please—don't start.

HELGA: When we left, this exact same thing, the riots—

GALLIMARD: No, no . . .

HELGA: Students screaming slogans, smashing down doors—

GALLIMARD: Helga—

HELGA: It was all going on in China, too. Don't you remember?!

GALLIMARD: Helga! Please! (*Pause*) You have never understood China, have you? You walk in here with these ridiculous ideas, that the West is falling apart, that China was spitting in our faces. You come in, dripping of the streets, and you leave water all over my floor. (*He grabs* HELGA*'s towel, begins mopping up the floor*)

HELGA: But it's the truth!

GALLIMARD: Helga, I want a divorce.

Pause; GALLIMARD *continues, mopping the floor.*

HELGA: I take it back. China is . . . beautiful. Incense, I like incense.

GALLIMARD: I've had a mistress.

HELGA: So?

GALLIMARD: For eight years.

HELGA: I knew you would. I knew you would the day I married you. And now what? You want to marry her?

GALLIMARD: I can't. She's in China.

HELGA: I see. You want to leave. For someone who's not here, is that right?

GALLIMARD: That's right.

HELGA: You can't live with her, but still you don't want to live with me.

GALLIMARD: That's right.

Pause.

HELGA: Shit. How terrible that I can figure that out. (*Pause*) I never thought I'd say it. But, in China, I was happy. I knew, in my own way, I knew that you were not everything you pretended to be. But the pretense—going on your arm to the embassy ball, visiting your office and the guards saying, "Good morning, good morning, Madame Gallimard"—the pretense . . . was very good indeed. (*Pause*) I hope everyone is mean to you for the rest of your life. (*She exits*)

GALLIMARD (*to us*): Prophetic.

MARC *enters with two drinks.*

GALLIMARD (*to* MARC): In China, I was different from all other men.

MARC: Sure. You were white. Here's your drink.

GALLIMARD: I felt . . . touched.

MARC: In the head? Rene, I don't want to hear about the Oriental love goddess. Okay? One night—can we just drink and throw up without a lot of conversation?

GALLIMARD: You still don't believe me, do you?

MARC: Sure I do. She was the most beautiful, et cetera, et cetera, blasé blasé.

Pause.

GALLIMARD: My life in the West has been such a disappointment.

MARC: Life in the West is like that. You'll get used to it. Look, you're driving me away. I'm leaving. Happy, now? (*He exits, then returns*) Look, I have a date tomorrow night. You wanna come? I can fix you up with—

GALLIMARD: Of course. I would love to come.

Pause.

MARC: Uh—on second thought, no. You'd better get ahold of yourself first.

He exits; GALLIMARD *nurses his drink.*

GALLIMARD (*to us*): This is the ultimate cruelty, isn't it? That I can talk and talk and to anyone listening, it's only air—too rich a diet to be swallowed by a mundane world. Why can't anyone understand? That in China, I once loved, and was loved by, very simply, the Perfect Woman.

SONG *enters, dressed as Butterfly in wedding dress.*

GALLIMARD (*to* SONG): Not again. My imagination is hell. Am I asleep this time? Or did I drink too much?

SONG: Rene?

GALLIMARD: God, it's too painful! That you speak?

SONG: What are you talking about? Rene—touch me.

GALLIMARD: Why?

SONG: I'm real. Take my hand.

GALLIMARD: Why? So you can disappear again and leave me clutching at the air? For the entertainment of my neighbors who—?

SONG *touches* GALLIMARD.

SONG: Rene?

GALLIMARD *takes* SONG*'s hand. Silence.*

GALLIMARD: Butterfly? I never doubted you'd return.

SONG: You hadn't . . . forgotten—?

GALLIMARD: Yes, actually, I've forgotten everything. My mind, you see—there wasn't enough room in this hard head—not for the world *and* for you. No, there was only room for one. (*Beat*) Come, look. See? Your bed has been waiting, with the Klimt poster you like, and—see? The xiang lu [incense burner] you gave me?

SONG: I . . . I don't know what to say.

GALLIMARD: There's nothing to say. Not at the end of a long trip. Can I make you some tea?

SONG: But where's your wife?

GALLIMARD: She's by my side. She's by my side at last.

GALLIMARD reaches to embrace SONG. SONG sidesteps, dodging him.

GALLIMARD: Why?!

SONG (*to us*): So I did return to Rene in Paris. Where I found—

GALLIMARD: Why do you run away? Can't we show them how we embraced that evening?

SONG: Please. I'm talking.

GALLIMARD: You have to do what I say! I'm conjuring you up in *my* mind!

SONG: Rene, I've never done what you've said. Why should it be any different in your mind? Now split—the story moves on, and I must change.

GALLIMARD: I welcomed you into my home! I didn't have to, you know! I could've left you penniless on the streets of Paris! But I took you in!

SONG: Thank you.

GALLIMARD: So . . . please . . . don't change.

SONG: You know I have to. You know I will. And anyway, what difference does it make? No matter what your eyes tell you, you can't ignore the truth. You already know too much.

GALLIMARD exits. SONG turns to us.

SONG: The change I'm going to make requires about five minutes. So I thought you might want to take this opportunity to stretch your legs, enjoy a drink, or listen to the musicians. I'll be here, when you return, right where you left me.

SONG goes to a mirror in front of which is a wash basin of water. She starts to remove her makeup as stagelights go to half and houselights come up.

ACT THREE

Scene 1

A courthouse in Paris. 1986.

As he promised, SONG has completed the bulk of his transformation, onstage by the time the houselights go down and the stagelights come up full. He removes his wig and kimono, leaving them on the door. Underneath, he wears a well-cut suit.

SONG: So I'd done my job better than I had a right to expect. Well, give him some credit, too. He's right—I was in a fix when I arrived in Paris. I walked from the airport into town, then I located, by blind groping, the Chinatown district. Let me make one thing clear: whatever else may be said about the Chinese, they are stingy! I slept in doorways three days until I could find a tailor who would make me this kimono on credit. As it turns out, maybe I didn't even need it. Maybe he would've been happy to see me in a simple shift and mascara. But . . . better safe than sorry.

That was 1970, when I arrived in Paris. For the next fifteen years, yes, I lived a very comfy life. Some relief, believe me, after four years on a fucking commune in Nowheresville, China. Rene supported the boy and me, and I did some demonstrations around the country as part of my "cultural exchange" cover. And then there was the spying.

SONG *moves upstage, to a chair.* TOULON *enters as a judge, wearing the appropriate wig and robes. He sits near* SONG. *It's 1986, and* SONG *is testifying in a courtroom.*

SONG: Not much at first. Rene had lost all his high-level contacts. Comrade Chin wasn't very interested in parking-ticket statistics. But finally, at my urging, Rene got a job as a courier, handling sensitive documents. He'd photograph them for me, and I'd pass them on to the Chinese embassy.

JUDGE: Did he understand the extent of his activity?

SONG: He didn't ask. He knew that I needed those documents, and that was enough.

JUDGE: But he must've known he was passing classified information.

SONG: I can't say.

JUDGE: He never asked what you were going to do with them?

SONG: Nope.

Pause.

JUDGE: There is one thing that the court—indeed, that all of France—would like to know.

SONG: Fire away.

JUDGE: Did Monsieur Gallimard know you were a man?

SONG: Well, he never saw me completely naked. Ever.

JUDGE: But surely, he must've . . . how can I put this?

SONG: Put it however you like. I'm not shy. He must've felt around?

JUDGE: Mmmmm.

SONG: Not really. I did all the work. He just laid back. Of course we did enjoy more . . . complete union, and I suppose he *might* have wondered why I was always on my stomach, but . . . But what you're thinking is "Of course a wrist must've brushed . . . a hand hit . . . over twenty years!" Yeah. Well, Your Honor, it was my job to make him think I was a woman. And chew on this: it wasn't all that hard. See, my mother was a prostitute along the Bundt before the Revolution. And, uh, I think it's fair to say she learned a few things about Western men. So I borrowed her knowledge. In service to my country.

JUDGE: Would you care to enlighten the court with this secret knowledge? I'm sure we're all very curious.

SONG: I'm sure you are. (*Pause*) Okay, Rule One is: Men always believe what they want to hear. So a girl can tell the most obnoxious lies and the guys will believe them every time—"This is my first time"—"That's the biggest I've ever seen"—or *both,* which, if you really think about it, is not possible in a single lifetime. You've maybe heard those phrases a few times in your own life, yes, Your Honor?

JUDGE: It's not my life, Monsieur Song, which is on trial today.

SONG: Okay, okay, just trying to lighten up the proceedings. Tough room.

JUDGE: Go on.

SONG: Rule Two: As soon as a Western man comes into contact with the East—he's already confused. The West has sort of an international rape mentality toward the East. Do you know rape mentality?

JUDGE: Give us your definition, please.

SONG: Basically, "Her mouth says no, but her eyes say yes."

The West thinks of itself as masculine—big guns, big industry, big money—so the East is feminine—weak, delicate, poor . . . but good at art, and full of inscrutable wisdom—the feminine mystique.

Her mouth says no, but her eyes say yes. The West believes the East, deep down, *wants* to be dominated—because a woman can't think for herself.

JUDGE: What does this have to do with my question?

SONG: You expect Oriental countries to submit to your guns, and you expect Oriental women to be submissive to your men. That's why you say they make the best wives.

JUDGE: But why would that make it possible for you to fool Monsieur Gallimard? Please—get to the point.

SONG: One, because when he finally met his fantasy woman, he wanted more than anything to believe that she was, in fact, a woman. And second, I am an Oriental. And being an Oriental, I could never be completely a man.

Pause.

JUDGE: Your armchair political theory is tenuous, Monsieur Song.

SONG: You think so? That's why you'll lose in all your dealings with the East.

JUDGE: Just answer my question: did he know you were a man?

Pause.

SONG: You know, Your Honor, I never asked.

Scene 2

Same.

Music from the "Death Scene" from Butterfly blares over the house speakers. It is the loudest thing we've heard in this play.

GALLIMARD *enters, crawling towards* SONG*'s wig and kimono.*

GALLIMARD: Butterfly? Butterfly?

SONG *remains a man, in the witness box, delivering a testimony we do not hear.*

GALLIMARD (*to us*): In my moment of greatest shame, here, in this courtroom—with that . . . person up there, telling the world . . . What strikes me especially is how shallow he is, how glib and obsequious . . . completely . . . without substance! The type that prowls around discos with a gold medallion stinking of garlic. So little like my Butterfly.

Yet even in this moment my mind remains agile, flip—flopping like a man on a trampoline. Even now, my picture dissolves, and I see that . . . witness . . . talking to me.

SONG *suddenly stands straight up in his witness box, and looks at* GALLIMARD.

SONG: Yes. You. White man.

SONG steps out of the witness box, and moves downstage toward GALLIMARD. Light change.

GALLIMARD (*to* SONG): Who? Me?

SONG: Do you see any other white men?

GALLIMARD: Yes. There're white men all around. This is a French courtroom.

SONG: So you are an adventurous imperialist. Tell me, why did it take you so long? To come back to this place?

GALLIMARD: What place?

SONG: This theatre in China. Where we met many years ago.

GALLIMARD (*to us*): And once again, against my will, I am transported.

Chinese opera music comes up on the speakers. SONG *begins to do opera moves, as he did the night they met.*

SONG: Do you remember? The night you gave your heart?

GALLIMARD: It was a long time ago.

SONG: Not long enough. A night that turned your world upside down.

GALLIMARD: Perhaps.

SONG: Oh, be honest with me. What's another bit of flattery when you've already given me twenty years' worth? It's a wonder my head hasn't swollen to the size of China.

GALLIMARD: Who's to say it hasn't?

SONG: Who's to say? And what's the shame? In pride? You think I could've pulled this off if I wasn't already full of pride when we met? No, not just pride. Arrogance. It takes arrogance, really—to believe you can will, with your eyes and your lips, the destiny of another. (*He dances*) C'mon. Admit it. You still want me. Even in slacks and a button-down collar.

GALLIMARD: I don't see what the point of—

SONG: You don't? Well maybe, Rene, just maybe—I want you.

GALLIMARD: You do?

SONG: Then again, maybe I'm just playing with you. How can you tell? (*Reprising his feminine character, he sidles up to* GALLIMARD) "How I wish there were even a small cafe to sit in. With men in tuxedos, and cappuccinos, and bad expatriate jazz." Now you want to kiss me, don't you?

GALLIMARD (*pulling away*): What makes you—?

SONG: —so sure? See? I take the words from your mouth. Then I wait for you to come and retrieve them. (*He reclines on the floor*)

GALLIMARD: Why?! Why do you treat me so cruelly?

SONG: Perhaps I *was* treating you cruelly. But now—I'm being nice. Come here, my little one.

GALLIMARD: I'm not your little one!

SONG: My mistake. It's I who am *your* little one, right?

GALLIMARD: Yes, I—

SONG: So come get your little one. If you like. I may even let you strip me.

GALLIMARD: I mean, you were! Before . . . but not like this!

SONG: I was? Then perhaps I still am. If you look hard enough. (*He starts to remove his clothes*)

GALLIMARD: What—what are you doing?

SONG: Helping you to see through my act.

GALLIMARD: Stop that! I don't want to! I don't—

SONG: Oh, but you asked me to strip, remember?

GALLIMARD: What? That was years ago! And I took it back!

SONG: No. You postponed it. Postponed the inevitable. Today, the inevitable has come calling.

From the speakers, cacophony: Butterfly mixed in with Chinese gongs.

GALLIMARD: No! Stop! I don't want to see!

SONG: Then look away.

GALLIMARD: You're only in my mind! All this is in my mind! I order you! To stop!

SONG: To what? To strip? That's just what I'm—

GALLIMARD: No! Stop! I want you—!

SONG: You want me?

GALLIMARD: To stop!

SONG: You know something, Rene? Your mouth says no, but your eyes say yes. Turn them away. I dare you.

GALLIMARD: I don't have to! Every night, you say you're going to strip, but then I beg you and you stop!

SONG: I guess tonight is different.

GALLIMARD: Why? Why should that be?

SONG: Maybe I've become frustrated. Maybe I'm saying "Look at me, you fool!" Or maybe I'm just feeling . . . sexy. (*He is down to his briefs*)

GALLIMARD: Please. This is unnecessary. I know what you are.

SONG: Do you? What am I?

GALLIMARD: A—a man.

SONG: You don't really believe that.

GALLIMARD: Yes I do! I knew all the time somewhere that my happiness was temporary, my love a deception. But my mind kept the knowledge at bay. To make the wait bearable.

SONG: Monsieur Gallimard—the wait is over.

SONG *drops his briefs. He is naked. Sound cue out. Slowly, we and* SONG *come to the realization that what we had thought to be* GALLIMARD*'s sobbing is actually his laughter.*

GALLIMARD: Oh god! What an idiot! Of course!

SONG: Rene—what?

GALLIMARD: Look at you! You're a man! (*He bursts into laughter again*)

SONG: I fail to see what's so funny!

GALLIMARD: "You fail to see—!" I mean, you never did have much of a sense of humor, did you? I just think it's ridiculously funny that I've wasted so much time on just a man!

SONG: Wait. I'm not "just a man."

GALLIMARD: No? Isn't that what you've been trying to convince me of?

SONG: Yes, but what I mean—

GALLIMARD: And now, I finally believe you, and you tell me it's not true? I think you must have some kind of identity problem.

SONG: Will you listen to me?

GALLIMARD: Why?! I've been listening to you for twenty years. Don't I deserve a vacation?

SONG: I'm not just any man!

GALLIMARD: Then, what exactly are you?

SONG: Rene, how can you ask—? Okay, what about this?

He picks up Butterfly's robes, starts to dance around. No music.

GALLIMARD: Yes, that's very nice. I have to admit.

SONG *holds out his arm to* GALLIMARD.

SONG: It's the same skin you've worshiped for years. Touch it.

GALLIMARD: Yes, it does feel the same.

SONG: Now—close your eyes.

SONG *covers* GALLIMARD*'s eyes with one hand. With the other,* SONG *draws* GALLIMARD*'s hand up to his face.* GALLIMARD*, like a blind man, lets his hands run over* SONG*'s face.*

GALLIMARD: This skin, I remember. The curve of her face, the softness of her cheek, her hair against the back of my hand . . .

SONG: I'm your Butterfly. Under the robes, beneath everything, it was always me. Now, open your eyes and admit it—you adore me. (*He removes his hand from* GALLIMARD*'s eyes*)

GALLIMARD: You, who knew every inch of my desires—how could you, of all people, have made such a mistake?

SONG: What?

GALLIMARD: You showed me your true self. When all I loved was the lie. A perfect lie, which you let fall to the ground—and now, it's old and soiled.

SONG: So—you never really loved me? Only when I was playing a part?

GALLIMARD: I'm a man who loved a woman created by a man. Everything else—simply falls short.

Pause.

SONG: What am I supposed to do now?

GALLIMARD: You were a fine spy, Monsieur Song, with an even finer accomplice. But now I believe you should go. Get out of my life!

SONG: Go where? Rene, you can't live without me. Not after twenty years.

GALLIMARD: I certainly can't live with you—not after twenty years of betrayal.

SONG: Don't be so stubborn! Where will you go?

GALLIMARD: I have a date . . . with my Butterfly.

SONG: So, throw away your pride. And come . . .

GALLIMARD: Get away from me! Tonight, I've finally learned to tell fantasy from reality. And, knowing the difference, I choose fantasy.

SONG: *I'm* your fantasy!

GALLIMARD: You? You're as real as hamburger. Now get out! I have a date with my Butterfly and I don't want your body polluting the room! (*He tosses* SONG*'s suit at him*) Look at these—you dress like a pimp.

SONG: Hey! These are Armani slacks and—! (*He puts on his briefs and slacks*) Let's just say . . . I'm disappointed in you, Rene. In the crush of your adoration, I thought you'd become something more. More like . . . a woman.

But no. Men. You're like the rest of them. It's all in the way we dress, and make up our faces, and bat our eyelashes. You really have so little imagination!

GALLIMARD: You, Monsieur SONG? Accuse me of too little imagination? You, if anyone, should know—I am pure imagination. And in imagination I will remain. Now get out!

GALLIMARD *bodily removes* SONG *from the stage, taking his kimono.*

SONG: Rene! I'll never put on those robes again! You'll be sorry!

GALLIMARD (*to* SONG): I'm already sorry! (*Looking at the kimono in his hands*) Exactly as sorry . . . as a Butterfly.

Scene 3

M. GALLIMARD*'s prison cell. Paris. Present.*

GALLIMARD: I've played out the events of my life night after night, always searching for a new ending to my story, one where I leave this cell and return forever to my Butterfly's arms.

Tonight I realize my search is over. That I've looked all along in the wrong place. And now, to you, I will prove that my love was not in vain—by returning to the world of fantasy where I first met her.

He picks up the kimono; dancers enter.

GALLIMARD: There is a vision of the Orient that I have. Of slender women in chong sams and kimonos who die for the love of unworthy foreign devils. Who are born and raised to be the perfect women. Who take whatever punishment we give them, and bounce back, strengthened by love, unconditionally. It is a vision that has become my life.

Dancers bring the wash basin to him and help him make up his face.

GALLIMARD: In public, I have continued to deny that Song Liling is a man. This brings me headlines, and is a source of great embarrassment to my French colleagues, who can now be sent into a coughing fit by the mere mention of Chinese food. But alone, in my cell, I have long since faced the truth.

And the truth demands a sacrifice. For mistakes made over the course of a lifetime. My mistakes were simple and absolute—the man I loved was a cad, a bounder. He deserved nothing but a kick in the behind, and instead I gave him . . . all my love.

Yes—love. Why not admit it all? That was my undoing, wasn't it? Love warped my judgment, blinded my eyes, rearranged the very lines on my face . . . until I could look in the mirror and see nothing but . . . a woman.

Dancers help him put on the Butterfly wig.

GALLIMARD: I have a vision. Of the Orient. That, deep within its almond eyes, there are still women. Women willing to sacrifice themselves for the love of a man. Even a man whose love is completely without worth.

Dancers assist GALLIMARD *in donning the kimono. They hand him a knife.*

GALLIMARD: Death with honor is better than life . . . life with dishonor. (*He sets himself center stage, in a seppuku position*) The love of a Butterfly can withstand many things—unfaithfulness, loss, even abandonment. But how can it face the one sin that implies all others? The devastating knowledge that, underneath it all, the object of her love was nothing more, nothing less than . . . a man. (*He sets the tip of the knife against his body*) It is 19——. And I have found her at last. In a prison on the outskirts of Paris. My name is Rene Gallimard—also known as Madame Butterfly.

GALLIMARD *turns upstage and plunges the knife into his body, as music from the "Love Duet" blares over the speakers. He collapses into the arms of the dancers, who lay him reverently on the floor. The image holds for several beats. Then a tight special up on* SONG, *who stands as a man, staring at the dead* GALLIMARD. *He smokes a cigarette; the smoke filters up through the lights. Two words leave his lips.*

SONG: Butterfly? Butterfly?

Smoke rises as lights fade slowly to black.

(1988)

Afterword

It all started in May of 1986, over casual dinner conversation. A friend asked, had I heard about the French diplomat who'd fallen in love with a Chinese actress, who subsequently turned out to be not only a spy, but a man? I later found a two-paragraph story in *The New York Times.* The diplomat, Bernard Bouriscot, attempting to account for the fact that he had never seen his "girlfriend" naked, was quoted as saying, "I thought she was very modest. I thought it was a Chinese custom."

Now, I am aware that this is *not* a Chinese custom, that Asian women are no more shy with their lovers than are women of the West. I am also aware, however, that Bouriscot's assumption was consistent with a certain stereotyped view of Asians as bowing, blushing flowers. I therefore concluded that the diplomat must have fallen in love, not with a person, but with a fantasy stereotype. I also inferred that, to the extent the Chinese spy encouraged these misperceptions, he must have played up to and exploited this image of the Oriental woman as demure and submissive. (In general, by the way, we prefer the term "Asian" to "Oriental," in the same way "Black" is superior to "Negro." I use the term "Oriental" specifically to denote an exotic or imperialistic view of the East.)

I suspected there was a play here. I purposely refrained from further research, for I was not interested in writing docudrama. Frankly, I didn't want the "truth" to interfere with my own speculations. I told Stuart Ostrow, a producer with whom I'd worked before, that I envisioned the story as a musical. I remember going so far as to speculate that it could be some "great *Madame Butterfly*–like tragedy." Stuart was very intrigued, and encouraged me with some early funding.

Before I can begin writing, I must "break the back of the story," and find some angle which compels me to set pen to paper. I was driving down Santa Monica Boulevard one afternoon, and asked myself, "What did Bouriscot think he was getting in this Chinese actress?" The answer came to me clearly: "He probably thought he had found Madame Butterfly."

The idea of doing a deconstructivist *Madame Butterfly* immediately appealed to me. This, despite the fact that I didn't even know the plot of the opera! I knew Butterfly only as a cultural stereotype; speaking of an Asian woman, we would sometimes say, "She's pulling a Butterfly," which meant playing the submissive Oriental number. Yet, I felt convinced that the libretto would include yet another lotus blossom pining away for a cruel Caucasian man, and dying for her love. Such a story has become too much of a cliché not to be included in the archetypal East-West romance that started it all. Sure enough, when I purchased the record, I discovered it contained a wealth of sexist and racist clichés, reaffirming my faith in Western culture.

Very soon after, I came up with the basic "arc" of my play: the Frenchman fantasizes that he is Pinkerton and his lover is Butterfly. By the end of the piece, he realizes that it is he who has been Butterfly, in that the Frenchman has been duped by love; the Chinese spy, who exploited that love, is therefore the real Pinkerton. I wrote a proposal to Stuart Ostrow, who found it very exciting. (On the night of the Tony Awards, Stuart produced my original two-page treatment, and we were gratified to see that it was, indeed, the play I eventually wrote.)

I wrote a play, rather than a musical, because, having "broken the back" of the story, I wanted to start immediately and not be hampered by the lengthy process of collaboration. I would like to think, however, that the play has retained many of its musical roots. So *Monsieur Butterfly* was completed in six weeks between September and mid-October, 1986. My wife, Ophelia, thought *Monsieur Butterfly* too obvious a title, and suggested I abbreviate it in the French fashion. Hence, *M. Butterfly,* far more mysterious and ambiguous, was the result.

I sent the play to Stuart Ostrow as a courtesy, assuming he would not be interested in producing what had become a straight play. Instead, he flew out to Los Angeles immediately for script conferences. Coming from a background in the not-for-profit theater, I suggested that we develop the work at a regional institution. Stuart, nothing if not bold, argued for bringing it directly to Broadway.

It was also Stuart who suggested John Dexter to direct. I had known Dexter's work only by its formidable reputation. Stuart sent the script to John, who called back the next day, saying it was the best play he'd read in twenty years. Naturally, this predisposed me to like him a great deal. We met in December in New York. Not long after, we persuaded Eiko Ishioka to design our sets and costumes. I had admired her work from afar ever since, as a college student, I had seen her poster for *Apocalypse Now* in Japan. By January 1987, Stuart had optioned *M. Butterfly,* Dexter was signed to direct, and the normally sloth-like pace of commercial theater had been given a considerable prod.

On January 4, 1988, we commenced rehearsals. I was very pleased that John Lithgow had agreed to play the French diplomat, whom I named Rene Gallimard. Throughout his tenure with us, Lithgow was every inch the center of our company, intelligent and professional, passionate and generous. B. D. Wong was forced to endure a five-month audition period before we selected him to play Song Liling. Watching B. D.'s growth was one of the joys of the rehearsal process, as he constantly attained higher levels of performance. It became clear that we had been fortunate enough to put together a company with not only great talent, but also wonderful camaraderie.

As for Dexter, I have never worked with a director more respectful of text and bold in the uses of theatricality. On the first day of rehearsal, the actors were given movement and speech drills. Then Dexter asked that everyone not required at rehearsal leave the room. A week later, we returned for an amazingly thorough run-through. It was not until that day that I first heard my play read, a note I direct at many regional theaters who "develop" a script to death.

We opened in Washington, D.C., at the National Theatre, where *West Side Story* and *Amadeus* had premiered. On the morning after opening night, most of the reviews were glowing, except for *The Washington Post.* Throughout our run in Washington, Stuart never pressured us to make the play more "commercial" in reaction to that review. We all simply concluded that the gentleman was possibly insecure about his own sexual orientation and therefore found the play threatening. And we continued our work.

Once we opened in New York, the play found a life of its own. I suppose the most gratifying thing for me is that we had never compromised to be more "Broadway"; we simply did the work we thought best. That our endeavor should be rewarded to the degree it has is one of those all-too-rare instances when one's own perception and that of the world are in agreement.

Many people have subsequently asked me about the "ideas" behind the play. From our first preview in Washington, I have been pleased that people leaving the theater were talking not only about the sexual, but also the political, issues raised by the work.

From my point of view, the "impossible" story of a Frenchman duped by a Chinese man masquerading as a woman always seemed perfectly explicable; given the degree of misunderstanding between men and women and also between East and West, it seemed inevitable that a mistake of this magnitude would one day take place.

Gay friends have told me of a derogatory term used in their community: "Rice Queen"—a gay Caucasian man primarily attracted to Asians. In these relationships, the Asian virtually always plays the role of the "woman"; the Rice Queen, culturally and sexually, is the "man." This pattern of relationships had become so codified that, until recently, it was considered unnatural for gay Asians to date one another. Such men would be taunted with a phrase which implied they were lesbians.

Similarly, heterosexual Asians have long been aware of "Yellow Fever"—Caucasian men with a fetish for exotic Oriental women. I have often heard it said that "Oriental women make the best wives." (Rarely is this heard from the mouths of Asian men, incidentally.) This mythology is exploited by the Oriental mail-order bride trade which has flourished over the past decade. American men can now send away for catalogues of "obedient, domesticated" Asian women looking for husbands. Anyone who believes such stereotypes are a thing of the past need look no further than Manhattan cable television, which advertises call girls from "the exotic east, where men are king; obedient girls, trained in the art of pleasure."

In these appeals, we see issues of racism and sexism intersect. The catalogues and TV spots appeal to a strain in men which desires to reject Western women for what they have become—independent, assertive, self-possessed—in favor of a more reactionary model—the pre-feminist, domesticated geisha girl.

That the Oriental woman is penultimately feminine does not of course imply that she is always "good." For every Madonna there is a whore; for every lotus blossom there is also a dragon lady. In popular culture, "good" Asian women are those who serve the White protagonist in his battle against her own people, often sleeping with him in the process. Stallone's *Rambo II,* Cimino's *Year of the Dragon,* Clavell's *Shogun,* Van Lustbader's *The Ninja* are all familiar examples.

Now our considerations of race and sex intersect the issue of imperialism. For this formula—good natives serve Whites, bad natives rebel—is consistent with the mentality of colonialism. Because they are submissive and obedient, good natives of both sexes necessarily take on "feminine" characteristics in a colonialist world. Gunga Din's unfailing devotion to his British master, for instance, is not so far removed from Butterfly's slavish faith in Pinkerton.

It is reasonable to assume that influences and attitudes so pervasively displayed in popular culture might also influence our policymakers as they consider the world. The neo-Colonialist notion that good elements of a native society, like a good woman, desire submission to the masculine West speaks precisely to the heart of our foreign policy blunders in Asia and elsewhere.

For instance, Frances Fitzgerald wrote in *Fire in the Lake,* "The idea that the United States could not master the problems of a country as small and underdeveloped as Vietnam did not occur to Johnson as a possibility." Here, as in so many other cases, by dehumanizing the enemy, we dehumanize ourselves. We become the Rice Queens of *realpolitik.*

M. Butterfly has sometimes been regarded as an anti-American play, a diatribe against the stereotyping of the East by the West, of women by men. Quite to the contrary, I consider it a plea to all sides to cut through our respective layers of cultural and sexual misperception, to deal with one another truthfully for our mutual good, from the common and equal ground we share as human beings.

For the myths of the East, the myths of the West, the myths of men, and the myths of women—these have so saturated our consciousness that truthful contact between nations and lovers can only be the result of heroic effort. Those who prefer to bypass the work involved will remain in a world of surfaces, misperceptions running rampant. This is, to me, the convenient world in which the French diplomat and the Chinese spy lived. This is why, after twenty years, he had learned nothing at all about his lover, not even the truth of his sex.

D. H. H.
New York City
September, 1988

QUESTIONS FOR CRITICAL THINKING AND WRITING

Experience

1. What was it like to read *M. Butterfly*? Where did you experience your greatest shocks or surprises? Why?
2. What are your impressions of the play's main characters? Whom do you like best and least, and why?

Interpretation

3. Explain the function of the Playwright's Notes and the epigraph printed at the beginning of the play.
4. Explain what each of the three different settings in the play contributes to its overall meaning and effect.
5. Explain the importance of stereotypical thinking for the play's plot. How do stereotypes about culture (Chinese customs, for example) and gender (particularly stereotypes about Asian women) influence the behavior of the play's central characters?

Evaluation

6. What social and cultural values does the play call into question? What social and cultural values does Hwang seem to favor? How do you know?
7. How do you evaluate the cultural and sexual values of the play's main characters? Why? How do the values of the main characters compare with your personal values?

Connection

8. Read the libretto or find a plot summary of the Puccini opera *Madame Butterfly.* Compare the Asian woman character in the opera with that in Hwang's play.
9. Read the comments by the playwright in his *Afterword* essay. Discuss how your understanding of the play is affected by the ideas and information contained in Hwang's *Afterword.*

Critical Thinking

10. What does the play suggest about understanding between men and women and between Asian and Western cultures?

MILCHA SANCHEZ-SCOTT

[b. 1955]

Milcha Sanchez-Scott was born in Bali, an island in Indonesia, of a Colombian father and a Chinese-Dutch-Indonesian mother. Milcha Sanchez-Scott learned English at a convent boarding school outside London, where she studied as a child. She spent her vacations at her family's home in Colombia, moving to California with her family when she was fourteen. After attending the University of San Diego, she worked at the city's famous zoo. She currently lives in southern California. Sanchez-Scott's first play, Latina, *was produced in 1980 and won a number of Drama-League awards. Besides* The Cuban Swimmer, *her other plays include* Evening Star *and* City of Angels.

The Cuban Swimmer

CHARACTERS

MARGARITA SUÁREZ, *the swimmer*
EDUARDO SUÁREZ, *her father, the coach*
SIMÓN SUÁREZ, *her brother*
AÍDA SUÁREZ, *the mother*
ABUELA, *her grandmother*
VOICE OF MEL MUNSON
VOICE OF MARY BETH WHITE
VOICE OF RADIO OPERATOR

Setting. The Pacific Ocean between San Pedro and Catalina Island. Time. *Summer.*

Live conga drums can be used to punctuate the action of the play.

Scene 1

Pacific Ocean. Midday. On the horizon, in perspective, a small boat enters upstage left, crosses to upstage right, and exits. Pause. Lower on the horizon, the same boat, in larger perspective, enters upstage right, crosses and exits upstage left. Blackout.

Scene 2

Pacific Ocean. Midday. The swimmer, MARGARITA SUÁREZ, *is swimming. On the boat following behind her are her father,* EDUARDO SUÁREZ, *holding a megaphone, and* SIMÓN, *her brother, sitting on top of the cabin with his shirt off, punk sunglasses on, binoculars hanging on his chest.*

EDUARDO (*leaning forward, shouting in time to* MARGARITA*'s swimming*): *Uno, dos, uno, dos. Y uno dos* . . . keep your shoulders parallel to the water.

SIMÓN: I'm gonna take these glasses off and look straight into the sun.

EDUARDO (*through megaphone*): *Muy bien, muy bien* . . . but punch those arms in, baby.

SIMÓN (*looking directly at the sun through binoculars*): Come on, come on, zap me. Show me something. (*He looks behind at the shoreline and ahead at the sea.*) Stop! Stop, *Papi!* Stop!

(AÍDA SUÁREZ *and* ABUELA, *the swimmer's mother and grandmother, enter running from the back of the boat.*)

AÍDA *and* ABUELA: *Qué? Qué es?*

AÍDA: *Es un* shark?

EDUARDO: Eh?

ABUELA: *Que es un* shark *dicen?*

(EDUARDO *blows whistle.* MARGARITA *looks up at the boat.*)

SIMÓN: No, *Papi,* no shark, no shark. We've reached the halfway mark.

ABUELA (*looking into the water*): *A dónde está ?*

AÍDA: It's not in the water.

ABUELA: Oh, no? Oh, no?

AÍDA: No! *A poco* do you think they're gonna have signs in the water to say you are halfway to Santa Catalina? No. It's done very scientific. *A ver, hijo,* explain it to your grandma.

SIMÓN: Well, you see, Abuela—(*He points behind.*) There's San Pedro. (*He points ahead.*) And there's Santa Catalina. Looks halfway to me.

(ABUELA *shakes her head and is looking back and forth, trying to make the decision, when suddenly the sound of a helicopter is heard.*)

ABUELA (*looking up*): Virgencita de la Caridad del Cobre. *Qué es eso?*

(*Sound of helicopter gets closes.* MARGARITA *looks up.*)

MARGARITA: Papi, Papi!

(*A small commotion on the boat, with everybody pointing at the helicopter above. Shadows of the helicopter fall on the boat.* SIMÓN *looks up at it through binoculars.*)

Papi—qué es? What is it?

EDUARDO (*through megaphone*): Uh . . . uh. . . uh, *un momentico . . . mi hija.* . . .Your *papi*'s got everything under control, understand? Uh . . . you just keep stroking. And stay . . . uh . . . close to the boat.

SIMÓN: Wow, *Papi!* We're on TV, man! Holy Christ, we're all over the fucking U.S.A.! It's Mel Munson and Mary Beth White!

AÍDA: *Por Dios!* Simón, don't swear. And put on your shirt.

(AÍDA *fluffs her hair, puts on her sunglasses and waves to the helicopter.* SIMÓN *leans over the side of the boat and yells to* MARGARITA.)

SIMÓN: Yo, Margo ! You're on TV, man.

EDUARDO: Leave your sister alone. Turn on the radio.

MARGARITA: *Papi! Qué está pasando?*

ABUELA: *Qué es la televisión dicen?* (*She shakes her head.*) *Porque como yo no puedo ver nada sin mis espejuelos.*

(ABUELA *rummages through the boat, looking for her glasses. Voices of* MEL MUNSON *and* MARY BETH WHITE *are heard over the boat's radio.*)

MEL'S VOICE: As we take a closer look at the gallant crew of *La Havana* . . . and there . . . yes, there she is . . . the little Cuban swimmer from Long Beach, California, nineteen-year-old Margarita Suárez. The unknown swimmer is our Cinderella entry . . . a bundle of tenacity, battling her way through the choppy, murky waters of the cold Pacific to reach the Island of Romance . . . Santa Catalina . . . where should she be the first to arrive, two thousand dollars and a gold cup will be waiting for her.

AÍDA: Doesn't even cover our expenses.

ABUELA: *Qué dice?*

EDUARDO: Shhhh!

MARY BETH'S VOICE: This is really a family effort, Mel, and—

MEL'S VOICE: Indeed it is. Her trainer, her coach, her mentor, is her father, Eduardo Suárez. Not a swimmer himself, it says here, Mr. Suárez is head usher of the

Holy Name Society and the owner-operator of Suárez Treasures of the Sea and Salvage Yard. I guess it's one of those places—

MARY BETH'S VOICE: If I might interject a fact here, Mel, assisting in this swim is Mrs. Suárez, who is a former Miss Cuba.

MEL'S VOICE: And a beautiful woman in her own right. Let's try and get a closer look.

(*Helicopter sound gets louder.* MARGARITA, *frightened, looks up again.*)

MARGARITA: *Papi!*

EDUARDO (*through megaphone*): *Mi hija,* don't get nervous . . . it's the press. I'm handling it.

AÍDA: I see how you're handling it.

EDUARDO (*through megaphone*): Do you hear? Everything is under control. Get back into your rhythm. Keep your elbows high and kick and kick and kick and kick . . .

ABUELA (*finds her glasses and puts them on*): *Ay sí, es la televisión . . .* (*She points to helicopter.*) *Qué lindo mira . . .* (*She fluffs her hair, gives a big wave.*) *Aló América! Viva mi Margarita, viva todo los Cubanos en los Estados Unidos!*

AÍDA: *Ay por Dios,* Cecilia, the man didn't come all this way in his helicopter to look at you jumping up and down, making a fool of yourself.

ABUELA: I don't care. I'm proud.

AÍDA: He can't understand you anyway.

ABUELA: *Viva . . .* (*She stops.*) *Simón, comó se dice viva?*

SIMÓN: Hurray.

ABUELA: Hurray for *mi Margarita y* for all the Cubans living *en* the United States, *y un abrazo . . . Simón, abrazo.*

SIMÓN: A big hug.

ABUELA: *Sí,* a big hug to all my friends in Miami, Long Beach, Union City, except for my son Carlos, who lives in New York in sin! He lives . . . (*She crosses herself.*) in Brooklyn with a Puerto Rican woman in sin! *No decente . . .*

SIMÓN: Decent.

ABUELA: Carlos, *no decente.* This family, *decente.*

AÍDA: Cecilia, *por Dios.*

MEL'S VOICE: Look at that enthusiasm. The whole family has turned out to cheer little Margarita on to victory! I hope they won't be too disappointed.

MARY BETH'S VOICE: She seems to be making good time, Mel.

MEL'S VOICE: Yes, it takes all kinds to make a race. And it's a testimonial to the all-encompassing fairness . . . the greatness of this, the Wrigley Invitational Women's Swim to Catalina, where among all the professionals there is still room for the amateurs . . . like these, the simple people we see below us on the ragtag *La Havana,* taking their long-shot chance to victory. *Vaya con Dios!*

(*Helicopter sound fading as family, including* MARGARITA, *watch silently. Static as* SIMÓN *turns radio off.* EDUARDO *walks to bow of boat, looks out on the horizon.*)

EDUARDO (*to himself*): Amateurs.

AÍDA: Eduardo, that person insulted us. Did you hear, Eduardo? That he called us a simple people in a ragtag boat? Did you hear . . . ?

ABUELA (*clenching her fist at departing helicopter*): *Mal—Rayo los parta!*

SIMÓN (*same gesture*): Asshole!

(AÍDA *follows* EDUARDO *as he goes to side of boat and stares at* MARGARITA.)

AÍDA: This person comes in his helicopter to insult your wife, your family, your daughter . . .

MARGARITA (*pops her head out of the water*): *Papi?*

AÍDA: Do you hear me, Eduardo? I am not simple.

ABUELA: *Sí.*

AÍDA: I am complicated.

ABUELA: *Sí, demasiada complicada.*

AÍDA: Me and my family are not so simple.

SIMÓN: Mom, the guy's an asshole.

ABUELA (*shaking her fist at helicopter*): Asshole!

AÍDA: If my daughter was simple, she would not be in that water swimming.

MARGARITA: Simple? *Papi* . . . ?

AÍDA: *Ahora,* Eduardo, this is what I want you to do. When we get to Santa Catalina, I want you to call the TV station and demand an apology.

EDUARDO: *Cállete mujer! Aquí mando yo.* I will decide what is to be done.

MARGARITA: *Papi,* tell me what's going on.

EDUARDO: Do you understand what I am saying to you, Aída?

SIMÓN (*leaning over side of boat, to* MARGARITA): Yo Margo! You know that Mel Munson guy on TV? He called you simple amateur and said you didn't have a chance.

ABUELA (*leaning directly behind* SIMÓN): *Mi hija, insultó a la familia. Desgraciado!*

AÍDA (*leaning in behind* ABUELA): He called us a peasants! And your father is not doing anything about it. He just knows how to yell at me.

EDUARDO (*through megaphone*): Shut up! All of you! Do you want to break her concentration? Is that what you are after? Eh?

(ABUELA, AÍDA *and* SIMÓN *shrink back.* EDUARDO *paces before them.*)

Swimming is rhythm and concentration. You win a race *aquí.* (*Pointing to his head.*) Now . . . (*To* SIMÓN.) you, take care of the boat, Aída y *Mama* . . . do something. Anything. Something practical.

(ABUELA *and* AÍDA *get on knees and pray in Spanish.*)

Hija, give it everything, eh? . . . *por la familia. Uno . . . dos. . . .* You must win.

(SIMÓN *goes into cabin. The prayers continue as lights change to indicate bright sunlight, later in the afternoon.*)

Scene 3

Tableau for a couple of beats. EDUARDO *on bow with timer in one hand as he counts strokes per minute.* SIMÓN *is in the cabin steering, wearing his sunglasses, baseball cap on backward.* ABUELA *and* AÍDA *are at the side of the boat, heads down, hands folded, still muttering prayers in Spanish.*

AÍDA *and* ABUELA (*crossing themselves*): *En el nombre del Padre, del Hijo y del Espíritu Santo amén.*

EDUARDO (*through megaphone*): You're stroking seventy-two!

SIMÓN (*singing*): Mama's stroking, Mama's stroking seventy-two . . .

EDUARDO (*through megaphone*): You comfortable with it?

SIMÓN (*singing*): Seventy-two, seventy-two, seventy-two for you.

AÍDA (*looking at the heavens*): *Ay,* Eduardo, *ven acá,* we should be grateful that *Nuestro Señor* gave us such a beautiful day.

ABUELA (*crosses herself*): *Sí, gracias a Dios.*

EDUARDO: She's stroking seventy-two, with no problem. (*He throws a kiss to the sky.*) It's a beautiful day to win.

AÍDA: *Qué hermoso!* So clear and bright. Not a cloud in the sky. *Mira! Mira!* Even rainbows on the water . . . a sign from God.

SIMÓN (*singing*): Rainbows on the water . . . you in my arms . . .

ABUELA *and* EDUARDO (*looking the wrong way*): *Dónde?*

AÍDA (*pointing toward* MARGARITA): There, dancing in front of Margarita, leading her on . . .

EDUARDO: Rainbows on . . . *Ay coño!* It's an oil slick! You . . . you . . . (*To* SIMÓN.) Stop the boat. (*Runs to bow, yelling.*) Margarita! Margarita!

(*On the next stroke,* MARGARITA *comes up all covered in black oil.*)

MARGARITA: *Papi! Papi . . . !*

(*Everybody goes to the side and stares at* MARGARITA, *who stares back.* EDUARDO *freezes.*)

AÍDA: *Apúrate,* Eduardo, move . . . what's wrong with you . . . *no me oíste,* get my daughter out of the water.

EDUARDO (*softly*): We can't touch her. If we touch her, she's disqualified.

AÍDA: But I'm her mother.

EDUARDO: Not even by her own mother. Especially by her own mother . . . You always want the rules to be different for you, you always want to be the exception. (*To* SIMÓN.) And you . . . you didn't see it, eh? You were playing again?

SIMÓN: *Papi,* I was watching . . .

AÍDA (*interrupting*): *Pues,* do something Eduardo. You are the big coach, the monitor.

SIMÓN: Mentor! Mentor!

EDUARDO: How can a person think around you? (*He walks off to bow, puts head in hands.*)

ABUELA (*looking over side*): *Mira como todos los* little birds are dead. (*She crosses herself.*)

AÍDA: Their little wings are glued to their sides.

SIMÓN: Christ, this is like the La Brea tar pits.

AÍDA: They can't move their little wings.

ABUELA: *Esa niña tiene que moverse.*

SIMÓN: Yeah, Margo, you gotta move, man.

(ABUELA *and* SIMÓN *gesture for* MARGARITA *to move.* AÍDA *gestures for her to swim.*)

ABUELA: *Anda niña, muévete.*

AÍDA: Swim, *hija,* swim or the *aceite* will stick to your wings.

MARGARITA: *Papi?*

ABUELA (*taking megaphone*): Your *papi* say "move it!"

(MARGARITA *with difficulty starts moving.*)

ABUELA, AÍDA *and* SIMÓN (*laboriously counting*): *Uno, dos . . . uno, dos . . . anda . . . uno, dos.*

EDUARDO (*running to take megaphone from* ABUELA): *Uno, dos . . .*

(SIMÓN *races into cabin and starts the engine.* ABUELA, AÍDA *and* EDUARDO *count together.*)

SIMÓN (*looking ahead*): *Papi,* it's over there!

EDUARDO: Eh?

SIMÓN (*pointing ahead and to the right*): It's getting clearer over there.

EDUARDO (*through megaphone*): Now pay attention to me. Go to the right.

(SIMÓN, ABUELA, AÍDA *and* EDUARDO *all lean over side. They point ahead and to the right, except* ABUELA, *who points to the left.*)

FAMILY (*shouting together*): *Para yá! Para yá!*

(*Lights go down on boat. A special light on* MARGARITA, *swimming through the oil, and on* ABUELA, *watching her.*)

ABUELA: *Sangre de mi sangre,* you will be another to save us. En Bolondron, where your great-grandmother Luz Suárez was born, they say one day it rained blood. All the people, they run into their houses. They cry, they pray, *pero* your great-grandmother Luz she had cojones like a man. She run outside. She look straight at the sky. She shake her fist. And she say to the evil one, *"Mira . . .* (*Beating her chest.*) *coño, Diablo, aquí estoy si me quieres."* And she open her mouth, and she drunk the blood.

Blackout.

Scene 4

Lights up on boat. AÍDA *and* EDUARDO *are on deck watching* MARGARITA *swim. We hear the gentle, rhythmic lap, lap, lap of the water, then the sound of inhaling and exhaling as* MARGARITA*'s breathing becomes louder. Then* MARGARITA*'s heartbeat is heard, with the lapping of the water and the breathing under it. These sounds continue beneath the dialogue to the end of the scene.*

AÍDA: *Dios mío.* Look how she moves through the water . . .

EDUARDO: You see, it's very simple. It is a matter of concentration.

AÍDA: The first time I put her in water she came to life, she grew before my eyes. She moved, she smiled, she loved it more than me. She didn't want my breast any longer. She wanted the water.

EDUARDO: And of course, the rhythm. The rhythm takes away the pain and helps the concentration.

(*Pause.* AÍDA *and* EDUARDO *watch* MARGARITA.)

AÍDA: Is that my child or a seal . . .

EDUARDO: Ah, a seal, the reason for that is that she's keeping her arms very close to her body. She cups her hands, and then she reaches and digs, reaches and digs.

AÍDA: To think that a daughter of mine . . .

EDUARDO: It's the training, the hours in the water. I used to tie weights around her little wrists and ankles.

AÍDA: A spirit, an ocean spirit, must have entered my body when I was carrying her.

EDUARDO (*to* MARGARITA): Your stroke is slowing down.

(*Pause. We hear* MARGARITA*'s heartbeat with the breathing under, faster now.*)

AÍDA: Eduardo, that night, the night on the boat . . .

EDUARDO: Ah, the night on the boat again . . . the moon was . . .

AÍDA: The moon was full. We were coming to America. . . . *Qué romantico.*

(*Heartbeat and breathing continue.*)

EDUARDO: We were cold, afraid, with no money, and on top of everything, you were hysterical, yelling at me, tearing at me with your nails. (*Opens his shirt, points to the base of his neck.*) Look, I still bear the scars . . . telling me that I didn't know what I was doing . . . saying that we were going to die. . . .

AÍDA: You took me, you stole me from my home . . . you didn't give me a chance to prepare. You just said we have to go now, now! Now, you said. You didn't let me take anything. I left everything behind. . . . I left everything behind.

EDUARDO: Saying that I wasn't good enough, that your father didn't raise you so that I could drown you in the sea.

AÍDA: You didn't let me say even a good-bye. You took me, you stole me, you tore me from my home.

EDUARDO: I took you so we could be married.

AÍDA: That was in Miami. But that night on the boat, Eduardo. . . . We were not married, that night on the boat.

EDUARDO: *No pasó nada!* Once and for all get it out of your head, it was cold, you hated me, and we were afraid. . . .

AÍDA: *Mentiroso!*

EDUARDO: A man can't do it when he is afraid.

AÍDA: Liar! You did it very well.

EDUARDO: I did?

AÍDA: *Sí.* Gentle. You were so gentle and then strong . . . my passion for you so deep. Standing next to you . . . I would ache . . . looking at your hands I would forget to breathe, you were irresistible.

EDUARDO: I was?

AÍDA: You took me into your arms, you touched my face with your fingertips . . . you kissed my eyes . . . *la esquina de la boca y . . .*

EDUARDO: *Sí, sí,* and then . . .

AÍDA: I look at your face on top of mine, and I see the lights of Havana in your eyes. That's when you seduced me.

EDUARDO: Shhh, they're gonna hear you.

(*Lights go down. Special on* AÍDA.)

AÍDA: That was the night. A woman doesn't forget those things . . . and later that night was the dream . . . the dream of a big country with fields of fertile land and big, giant things growing. And there by a green, slimy pond I found a giant pea pod and when I opened it, it was full of little, tiny baby frogs.

(AÍDA *crosses herself as she watches* MARGARITA. *We hear louder breathing and heartbeat.*)

MARGARITA: Santa Teresa. Little Flower of God, pray for me. San Martín de Porres, pray for me. Santa Rosa de Lima, *Virgencita de la Caridad del Cobre,* pray for me. . . . Mother pray for me.

Scene 5

Loud howling of wind is heard, as lights change to indicate unstable weather, fog and mist. FAMILY *on deck, braced and huddled against the wind.* SÍMON *is at the helm.*

AÍDA: *Ay Dios mío, qué viento!*

EDUARDO (*through megaphone*): Don't drift out . . . that wind is pushing you out. (*To* SIMÓN.) You! Slow down. Can't you see your sister is drifting out?

SIMÓN: It's the wind, *Papi.*

AÍDA: Baby, don't go so far. . . .

ABUELA (*to heaven*): *Ay Gran Poder de Dios, quita este maldito viento.*

SIMÓN: Margo! Margo! Stay close to the boat.

EDUARDO: Dig in. Dig in hard. . . . Reach down from your guts and dig in.

ABUELA (*to heaven*): *Ay Virgen de la Caridad del Cobre, por lo más tú quieres a pararla.*

AÍDA (*putting her hand out, reaching for* MARGARITA): Baby, don't go far.

(ABUELA *crosses herself. Action freezes. Lights get dimmer, special on* MARGARITA. *She keeps swimming, stops, starts again, stops, then, finally exhausted, stops altogether. The boat stops moving.*)

EDUARDO: What's going on here? Why are we stopping?

SIMÓN: *Papi,* she's not moving! Yo Margo!

(*The family all run to the side.*)

EDUARDO: *Hija! . . . Hijita!* You're tired, eh?

AÍDA: *Por supuesto* she's tired. I like to see you get in the water, waving your arms and legs from San Pedro to Santa Catalina. A person isn't a machine, a person has to rest.

SIMÓN: Yo, Mama! Cool out, it ain't fucking brain surgery.

EDUARDO (*to* SIMÓN): Shut up, you. (*Louder to* MARGARITA.) I guess your mother's right for once, huh? . . . I guess you had to stop, eh? . . . Give your brother, the idiot . . . a chance to catch up with you.

SIMÓN (*clowning like Mortimer Snerd*): Dum dee dum dee dum ooops, ah shucks . . .

EDUARDO: I don't think he's Cuban.

SIMÓN (*like Ricky Ricardo*): *Oye,* Lucy! I'm home! Ba ba lu!

EDUARDO (*joins in clowning, grabbing* SIMÓN *in a headlock*): What am I gonna do with this idiot, eh? I don't understand this idiot. He's not like us, Margarita. (*Laughing.*) You think if we put him into your bathing suit with a cap on his head . . . (*He laughs hysterically.*) You think anyone would know . . . huh? Do you think anyone would know? (*Laughs.*)

SIMÓN (*vamping*): *Ay, mi amor.* Anybody looking for tits would know.

(EDUARDO *slaps* SIMÓN *across the face, knocking him down.* AÍDA *runs to* SIMÓN*'s aid.* ABUELA *holds* EDUARDO *back.*)

MARGARITA: *Mía culpa! Mía culpa!*

ABUELA: *Qué dices hija?*

MARGARITA: *Papi,* it's my fault, it's all my fault. . . . I'm so cold, I can't move. . . . I put my face in the water . . . and I hear them whispering . . . laughing at me. . . .

AÍDA: Who is laughing at you?

MARGARITA: The fish are all biting me . . . they hate me . . . they whisper about me. She can't swim, they say. She can't glide. She has no grace. . . . Yellowtails, bonita, tuna, man-o'-war, snub-nose sharks, *los baracudas* . . . they all hate me . . . only the dolphins care . . . and sometimes I hear the whales crying . . . she is lost, she is dead. I'm so numb, I can't feel. *Papi! Papi!* Am I dead?

EDUARDO: *Vamos,* baby, punch those arms in. Come on . . . do you hear me?

MARGARITA: *Papi . . . Papi . . .* forgive me . . .

(*All is silent on the boat.* EDUARDO *drops his megaphone, his head bent down in dejection.* ABUELA, AÍDA, SIMÓN, *all leaning over the side of the boat.* SIMÓN *slowly walks away.*)

AÍDA: *Mi hija, qué tienes?*

SIMÓN: Oh, Christ, don't make her say it. Please don't make her say it.

ABUELA: Say what? *Qué cosa?*

SIMÓN: She wants to quit, can't you see she's had enough?

ABUELA: *Mira, para eso. Esta niña* is turning blue.

AÍDA *Oyeme, mi hija.* Do you want to come out of the water?

MARGARITA: *Papi?*

SIMÓN (*to* EDUARDO): She won't come out until *you* tell her.

AÍDA: Eduardo . . . answer your daughter.

EDUARDO: *Le dije* to concentrate . . . concentrate on your rhythm. Then the rhythm would carry her . . . ay, it's a beautiful thing, Aída. It's like yoga, like meditation, the mind over matter . . . the mind controlling the body . . . that's how the great things in the world have been done. I wish you . . . I wish my wife could understand.

MARGARITA: *Papi?*

SIMÓN (*to* MARGARITA): Forget him.

AÍDA (*imploring*): Eduardo, *por favor.*

EDUARDO (*walking in circles*): Why didn't you let her concentrate? Don't you understand, the concentration, the rhythm is everything. But no, you wouldn't listen. (*Screaming to the ocean.*) Goddamn Cubans, why, God, why do you make us go everywhere with our families? (*He goes to back of boat.*)

AÍDA (*opening her arms*): *Mi hija, ven,* come to *Mami.* (*Rocking.*) Your *mami* knows.

(ABUELA *has taken the training bottle, puts it in a net. She and* SIMÓN *lower it to* MARGARITA.)

SIMÓN: Take this. Drink it. (*As* MARGARITA *drinks,* ABUELA *crosses herself.*)

ABUELA: *Sangre de mi sangre.*

(*Music comes up softly.* MARGARITA *drinks, gives the bottle back, stretches out her arms, as if on a cross. Floats on her back. She begins a graceful backstroke. Lights fade on boat as special lights come up on* MARGARITA. *She stops. Slowly turns over and starts to swim, gradually picking up speed. Suddenly as if in pain she stops, tries again, then stops in pain again. She becomes disoriented and falls to the bottom of the sea. Special on* MARGARITA *at the bottom of the sea.*)

MARGARITA: *Ya no puedo* . . . I can't.. . .A person isn't a machine . . . *es mi culpa* . . . Father forgive me . . . *Papi! Papi!* One, two. *Uno, dos.* (*Pause.*) Papi! *A dónde estás?* (*Pause.*) One, two, one, two. *Papi! Ay, Papi!* Where are you . . . ? Don't leave me . . . Why don't you answer me? (*Pause. She starts to swim, slowly.*) *Uno, dos. uno dos.* Dig in, dig in. (*Stops swimming.*) *Por, favor, Papi!* (*Starts to swim again.*) One, two, one, two. Kick from your hip, kick from your hip. (*Stops swimming. Starts to cry.*) Oh God, please . . . (*Pause.*) Hail Mary, full of grace . . . dig in, dig in . . . the Lord is with thee. . . . (*She swims to the rhythm of her Hail Mary.*) Hail Mary, full of grace . . . dig in, dig in . . . the Lord is with thee . . . dig in, dig in . . . Blessed art thou among women. . . . *Mami,* it hurts. You let go of my hand. I'm lost. . . . And blessed is the fruit of thy womb, now and at the hour of our death. Amen. I don't want to die, I don't want to die.

(MARGARITA *is still swimming. Blackout. She is gone.*)

Scene 6

Lights up on boat, we hear radio static. There is a heavy mist. On deck we see only black outline of ABUELA *with shawl over her head. We hear the voices of* EDUARDO, AÍDA, *and* RADIO OPERATOR.

EDUARDO'S VOICE: La Havana! Coming from San Pedro. Over.

RADIO OPERATOR'S VOICE: Right, DT6-6, you say you've lost a swimmer.

AÍDA'S VOICE: Our child, our only daughter . . . listen to me. Her name is Margarita Inez Suárez, she is wearing a black one-piece bathing suit cut high in the legs with a white racing stripe down the sides, a white bathing cap with goggles and her whole body covered with a . . . with a . . .

EDUARDO'S VOICE: With lanolin and paraffin.

AÍDA'S VOICE: *Sí . . . con lanolin and paraffin.*

(*More radio static. Special on* SIMÓN, *on the edge of the boat.*)

SIMÓN: Margo! Yo Margo! (*Pause.*) Man don't do this. (*Pause.*) Come on. . . . Come on. . . . (*Pause.*) God, why does everything have to be so hard? (*Pause.*) Stupid. You know you're not supposed to die for this. Stupid. It's his dream and he can't even swim. (*Pause.*) Punch those arms in. Come home. Come home. I'm your little brother. Don't forget what Mama said. You're not supposed to leave me behind. *Vamos,* Margarita, take your little brother, hold his hand tight when you cross the street. He's so little. (*Pause.*) Oh, Christ, give us a sign.. . . I know! I know! Margo, I'll send you a message . . . like mental telepathy. I'll hold my breath, close my eyes, and I'll bring you home. (*He takes a deep breath; a few beats.*) This time I'll beep . . . I'll send out sonar signals like a dolphin. (*He imitates dolphin sounds.*)

(*The sound of real dolphins takes over from* SIMÓN, *then fades into sound of* ABUELA *saying the Hail Mary in Spanish, as full lights come up slowly.*)

Scene 7

EDUARDO *coming out of cabin, sobbing,* AÍDA *holding him.* SIMÓN *anxiously scanning the horizon.* ABUELA *looking calmly ahead.*

EDUARDO: *Es mi culpa, sí, es mi culpa.* (*He hits his chest.*)

AÍDA: *Ya, ya viejo . . .* it was my sin . . . I left my home.

EDUARDO: Forgive me, forgive me. I've lost our daughter, our sister, our granddaughter, *mi carne, mi sangre, mis ilusiones.* (*To heaven.*) *Dios mío,* take me . . . take me, I say . . . Goddammit, take me!

SIMÓN: I'm going in.

AÍDA *and* EDUARDO: No!

EDUARDO (*grabbing and holding* SIMÓN, *speaking to heaven*): God, take me, not my children. They are my dreams, my illusions . . . and not this one, this one is my mystery . . . he has my secret dreams. In him are the parts of me I cannot see.

(EDUARDO *embraces* SIMÓN. *Radio static becomes louder.*)

AÍDA: I think I see her.

SIMÓN: No, it's just a seal.

ABUELA (*looking out with binoculars*): *Mi nietacita, dónde estás?* (*She feels her heart.*) I don't feel the knife in my heart . . . my little fish is not lost.

(*Radio crackles with static. As lights dim on boat, voices of* MEL *and* MARY BETH *are heard over the radio.*)

MEL'S VOICE: Tragedy has marred the face of the Wrigley Invitational Women's Race to Catalina. The Cuban swimmer, little Margarita Suárez, has reportedly been lost at sea. Coast Guard and divers are looking for her as we speak. Yet in spite of this tragedy the race must go on because . . .

MARY BETH'S VOICE (*interrupting loudly*): Mel!

MEL'S VOICE (*startled*): What!

MARY BETH'S VOICE: Ah . . . excuse me, Mel . . . we have a winner. We've just received word from Catalina that one of the swimmers is just fifty yards from the breakers . . . it's, oh, it's . . . Margarita Suárez!

(*Special on family in cabin listening to radio.*)

MEL'S VOICE: What? I thought she died!

(*Special on* MARGARITA, *taking off bathing cap, trophy in hand, walking on the water.*)

MARY BETH'S VOICE: Ahh . . . unless . . . unless this is a tragic . . . No . . . there she is, Mel. Margarita Suárez! The only one in the race wearing a black bathing suit cut high in the legs with a racing stripe down the side.

(*Family cheering, embracing.*)

SIMÓN (*screaming*): Way to go, Margo!

MEL'S VOICE: This is indeed a miracle! It's a resurrection! Margarita Suárez, with a flotilla of boats to meet her, is now walking on the waters, through the breakers . . . onto the beach, with crowds of people cheering her on. What a jubilation! This is a miracle!

(*Sound of crowds cheering. Lights and cheering sounds fade.*)

Blackout.

(*1984*)

QUESTIONS FOR CRITICAL THINKING AND WRITING

Experience

1. What was your experience of reading *The Cuban Swimmer?* Where did you find yourself most engrossed in the play? Why?
2. To what extent does your own experience with and knowledge of athletic training, including the role of parents and coaches, affect your response to the play?

Interpretation

3. How is Margarita Suárez, the swimmer, described and characterized? What motivates her?
4. How does each of the characters respond to Margarita's temporary disappearance? What does this reveal about them?
5. What is the significance of Margarita's disappearance from and return to the sight of those watching her swim?

Evaluation

6. What social and cultural values does *The Cuban Swimmer* hold up for consideration? Whose values does the play endorse? Whose does it call into question?

Connection

7. Compare *The Cuban Swimmer* with Miller's *Death of a Salesman* on the basis of the relationships displayed between parents and children.

Critical Thinking

8. What is the effect of leaving many Spanish words untranslated? What would be gained or lost if they were to be translated into English?

© Jill Krementz

www

WENDY WASSERSTEIN
[1950–2006]

Wendy Wasserstein was born and raised in New York City. She was educated at Smith College and at Mount Holyoke College, from which she graduated with a B.A. in 1971. Two years later she earned a master's degree in playwriting from City College of New York. From 1973 until 1976 she studied at the Yale School of Drama, from which she received a master of fine arts. In 1989 she won the Pulitzer Prize and a Tony Award for Best Play for The Heidi Chronicles, *and in 1993 she won an Outer Circle Critics Award and a Tony nomination for* The Sisters Rosenzweig. *In addition to plays, she has written for public television and film.*

Tender Offer, *which was written and produced in 1977, is a one-act play that captures the relationship between a father and his teen-age daughter. The play's economy and its humor belie its underlying seriousness.*

Tender Offer

A girl of around nine is alone in a dance studio. She is dressed in traditional leotards and tights. She begins singing to herself, "Nothing Could Be Finer Than to Be in Carolina." She maps out a dance routine, including parts for the chorus. She builds to a finale. A man, PAUL, *around thirty-five, walks in. He has a sweet, though distant, demeanor. As he walks in,* LISA *notices him and stops.*

PAUL: You don't have to stop, sweetheart.

LISA: That's okay.

PAUL: Looked very good.

LISA: Thanks.

PAUL: Don't I get a kiss hello?

LISA: Sure.

PAUL [*embraces her.*]: Hi, Tiger.

LISA: Hi, Dad.

PAUL: I'm sorry I'm late.

LISA: That's okay.

PAUL: How'd it go?

LISA: Good.

PAUL: Just good?

LISA: Pretty good.

PAUL: "Pretty good." You mean you got a lot of applause or "pretty good" you could have done better.

LISA: Well, Courtney Palumbo's mother thought I was pretty good. But you know the part in the middle when everybody's supposed to freeze and the big girl comes out. Well, I think I moved a little bit.

PAUL: I thought what you were doing looked very good.

LISA: Daddy, that's not what I was doing. That was tap-dancing. I made that up.

PAUL: Oh. Well it looked good. Kind of sexy.

LISA: Yuch!

PAUL: What do you mean "yuch"?

LISA: Just yuch!

PAUL: You don't want to be sexy?

LISA: I don't care.

PAUL: Let's go, Tiger. I promised your mother I'd get you home in time for dinner.

LISA: I can't find my leg warmers.

PAUL: You can't find your what?

LISA: Leg warmers. I can't go home till I find my leg warmers.

PAUL: I don't see you looking for them.

LISA: I was waiting for you.

PAUL: Oh.

LISA: Daddy.

PAUL: What?

LISA: Nothing.

PAUL: Where do you think you left them?

LISA: Somewhere around here. I can't remember.

PAUL: Well, try to remember, Lisa. We don't have all night.

LISA: I told you. I think somewhere around here.

PAUL: I don't see them. Let's go home now. You'll call the dancing school tomorrow.

LISA: Daddy, I can't go home till I find them. Miss Judy says it's not professional to leave things.

PAUL: Who's Miss Judy?

LISA: She's my ballet teacher. She once danced the lead in *Swan Lake,* and she was a June Taylor dancer.

PAUL: Well, then, I'm sure she'll understand about the leg warmers.

LISA: Daddy, Miss Judy wanted to know why you were late today.

PAUL: Hmmmmmmmm?

LISA: Why were you late?

PAUL: I was in a meeting. Business. I'm sorry.

LISA: Why did you tell Mommy you'd come instead of her if you knew you had business?

PAUL: Honey, something just came up. I thought I'd be able to be here. I was looking forward to it.

LISA: I wish you wouldn't make appointments to see me.

PAUL: Hmmmmmmm.

LISA: You shouldn't make appointments to see me unless you know you're going to come.

PAUL: Of course I'm going to come.

LISA: No, you're not. Talia Robbins told me she's much happier living without her father in the house. Her father used to come home late and go to sleep early.

PAUL: Lisa, stop it. Let's go.

LISA: I can't find my leg warmers.

PAUL: Forget your leg warmers.

LISA: Daddy.

PAUL: What is it?

LISA: I saw this show on television, I think it was WPIX Channel 11. Well, the father was crying about his daughter.

PAUL: Why was he crying? Was she sick?

LISA: No. She was at school. And he was at business. And he just missed her, so he started to cry.

PAUL: What was the name of this show?

LISA: I don't know. I came in in the middle.

PAUL: Well, Lisa, I certainly would cry if you were sick or far away, but I know that you're well and you're home. So no reason to get maudlin.

LISA: What's maudlin?

PAUL: Sentimental, soppy. Frequently used by children who make things up to get attention.

LISA: I am sick! I am sick! I have Hodgkin's disease and a bad itch on my leg.

PAUL: What do you mean you have Hodgkin's disease? Don't say things like that.

LISA: Swoosie Kurtz, she had Hodgkin's disease on a TV movie last year, but she got better and now she's on *Love Sidney.*

PAUL: Who is Swoosie Kurtz?

LISA: She's an actress named after an airplane. I saw her on *Live at Five.*

PAUL: You watch too much television; you should do your homework. Now, put your coat on.

LISA: Daddy, I really do have a bad itch on my leg. Would you scratch it?

PAUL: Lisa, you're procrastinating.

LISA: Why do you use words I don't understand? I hate it. You're like Daria Feldman's mother. She always talks in Yiddish to her husband so Daria won't understand.

PAUL: Procrastinating is not Yiddish.

LISA: Well, I don't know what it is.

PAUL: Procrastinating means you don't want to go about your business.

LISA: I don't go to business. I go to school.

PAUL: What I mean is you want to hang around here until you and I are late for dinner and your mother's angry and it's too late for you to do your homework.

LISA: I do not.

PAUL: Well, it sure looks that way. Now put your coat on and let's go.

LISA: Daddy.

PAUL: Honey, I'm tired. Really, later.

LISA: Why don't you want to talk to me?

PAUL: I do want to talk to you. I promise when we get home we'll have a nice talk.

LISA: No, we won't. You'll read the paper and fall asleep in front of the news.

PAUL: Honey, we'll talk on the weekend, I promise. Aren't I taking you to the theater this weekend? Let me look. [*He takes out appointment book.*] Yes. Sunday. *Joseph and the Amazing Technicolor Raincoat* with Lisa. Okay, Tiger?

LISA: Sure. It's Dreamcoat.

PAUL: What?

LISA: Nothing. I think I see my leg warmers. [*She goes to pick them up, and an odd-looking trophy.*]

PAUL: What's that?

LISA: It's stupid. I was second best at the dance recital, so they gave me this thing. It's stupid.

PAUL: Lisa.

LISA: What?

PAUL: What did you want to talk about?

LISA: Nothing.

PAUL: Was it about my missing your recital? I'm really sorry, Tiger, I would have liked to have been here.

LISA: That's okay.

PAUL: Honest?

LISA: Daddy, you're prostrastinating.

PAUL: I'm procrastinating. Sit down. Let's talk. So. How's school?

LISA: Fine.

PAUL: You like it?

LISA: Yup.

PAUL: You looking forward to camp this summer?

LISA: Yup.

PAUL: Is Daria Feldman going back?

LISA: Nope.

PAUL: Why not?

LISA: I don't know. We can go home now. Honest, my foot doesn't itch anymore.

PAUL: Lisa, you know what you do in business when it seems like there's nothing left to say? That's when you really start talking. Put a bid on the table.

LISA: What's a bid?

PAUL: You tell me what you want and I'll tell you what I've got to offer. Like Monopoly. You want Boardwalk, but I'm only willing to give you the Railroads. Now, because you are my daughter I'd throw in Water Works and Electricity. Understand, Tiger?

LISA: No. I don't like board games. You know, Daddy, we could get Space Invaders for our home for thirty-five dollars. In fact, we could get an Osborne System for two thousand. Daria Feldman's parents . . .

PAUL: Daria Feldman's parents refuse to talk to Daria, so they bought a computer to keep Daria busy so they won't have to speak in Yiddish. Daria will probably grow up to be a homicidal maniac lesbian prostitute.

LISA: I know what that word prostitute means.

PAUL: Good. [*Pause.*] You still haven't told me about school. Do you still like your teacher?

LISA: She's okay.

PAUL: Lisa, if we're talking try to answer me.

LISA: I am answering you. Can we go home now, please?

PAUL: Damn it, Lisa, if you want to talk to me . . . Talk to me!

LISA: I can't wait till I'm old enough so I can make my own money and never have to see you again. Maybe I'll become a prostitute.

PAUL: Young lady, that's enough.

LISA: I hate you, Daddy! I hate you! [*She throws her trophy into the trash bin.*]

PAUL: What'd you do that for?

LISA: It's stupid.

PAUL: Maybe I wanted it.

LISA: What for?

PAUL: Maybe I wanted to put it where I keep your dinosaur and the picture you made of Mrs. Kimbel with the chicken pox.

LISA: You got mad at me when I made that picture. You told me I had to respect Mrs. Kimbel because she was my teacher.

PAUL: That's true. But she wasn't my teacher. I liked her better with the chicken pox. [*Pause.*] Lisa, I'm sorry. I was very wrong to miss your recital, and you don't have to become a prostitute. That's not the type of profession Miss Judy has in mind for you.

LISA [*mumbles*]: No.

PAUL: No. [*Pause.*] So Talia Robbins is really happy her father moved out?

LISA: Talia Robbins picks open the eighth-grade lockers during gym period. But she did that before her father moved out.

PAUL: You can't always judge someone by what they do or what they don't do. Sometimes you come home from dancing school and run upstairs and shut the door, and when I finally get to talk to you, everything is "okay" or "fine." Yup or nope?

LISA: Yup.

PAUL: Sometimes, a lot of times, I come home and fall asleep in front of the television. So you and I spend a lot of time being a little scared of each other. Maybe?

LISA: Maybe.

PAUL: Tell you what. I'll make you a tender offer.

LISA: What?

PAUL: I'll make you a tender offer. That's when one company publishes in the newspaper that they want to buy another company. And the company that publishes is called the Black Knight because they want to gobble up the poor little company. So the poor little company needs to be rescued. And then a White Knight comes along and makes a bigger and better offer so the shareholders won't have to tender shares to the Big Black Knight. You with me?

LISA: Sort of.

PAUL: I'll make you a tender offer like the White Knight. But I don't want to own you. I just want to make a much better offer. Okay?

LISA [*sort of understanding*]: Okay. [*Pause. They sit for a moment.*] Sort of, Daddy, what do you think about? I mean, like when you're quiet what do you think about?

PAUL: Oh, business usually. If I think I made a mistake or if I think I'm doing okay. Sometimes I think about what I'll be doing five years from now and if it's what I hoped it would be five years ago. Sometimes I think about what your life will be like, if Mount Saint Helen's will erupt again. What you'll become if you'll study penmanship or word processing. If you'll speak kindly of me to your psychiatrist when you are in graduate school. And how the hell I'll pay for your graduate school. And sometimes I try and think what it was I thought about when I was your age.

LISA: Do you ever look out your window at the clouds and try to see which kinds of shapes they are? Like one time, honest, I saw the head of Walter Cronkite in a flower vase. Really! Like look don't those kinda look like if you turn it upside down, two big elbows or two elephant trunks dancing?

PAUL: Actually still looks like Walter Cronkite in a flower vase to me. But look up a little. See the one that's still moving? That sorta looks like a whale on a thimble.

LISA: Where?

PAUL: Look up. To your right.

LISA: I don't see it. Where?

PAUL: The other way.

LISA: Oh, yeah! There's the head and there's the stomach. Yeah! [LISA *picks up her trophy.*] Hey, Daddy.

PAUL: Hey, Lisa.

LISA: You can have this thing if you want it. But you have to put it like this, because if you put it like that it is gross.

PAUL: You know what I'd like? So I can tell people who come into my office why I have this gross stupid thing on my shelf, I'd like it if you could show me your dance recital.

LISA: Now?

PAUL: We've got time. Mother said she won't be home till late.

LISA: Well, Daddy, during a lot of it I freeze and the big girl in front dances.

PAUL: Well, how 'bout the number you were doing when I walked in?

LISA: Well, see, I have parts for a lot of people in that one, too.

PAUL: I'll dance the other parts.

LISA: You can't dance.

PAUL: Young lady, I played Yvette Mimieux in a *Hasty Pudding Show.*

LISA: Who's Yvette Mimieux?

PAUL: Watch more television. You'll find out. [PAUL *stands up.*] So I'm ready. [*He begins singing.*] "Nothing could be finer than to be in Carolina."

LISA: Now I go. In the morning. And now you go. Dum-da.

PAUL [*obviously not a tap dancer*]: Da-da-dum.

LISA [*whines*]: Daddy!

PAUL [*mimics her*]: Lisa! Nothing could be finer . . .

LISA: That looks dumb.

PAUL: Oh, yeah? You think they do this better in *The Amazing Minkcoat?* No way! Now you go-da da da dum.

LISA: Da da da dum.

PAUL: If I had Aladdin's lamp for only a day, I'd make a wish. . . .

LISA: Daddy, that's maudlin!

PAUL: I know it's maudlin. And here's what I'd say:

LISA *and* PAUL: I'd say that "nothing could be finer than to be in Carolina in the moooooooooooornin'."

(1977)

QUESTIONS FOR CRITICAL THINKING AND WRITING

Experience

1. To what extent can you identify with the situation depicted in Wasserstein's play? Why?

Interpretation

2. How would you characterize the relationship between Lisa and Paul?
3. Examine the play's dialogue for shifts of direction. Account for the conversational logic of these shifts and explain their dramatic effects.
4. Explain the significance of Paul and Lisa's discussion of the meaning of "procrastination" and "maudlin."
5. What is the function of Paul's inaccuracy in naming the title of the Broadway play *Joseph and the Amazing Technicolor Dreamcoat?*
6. Consider how you would direct the actors in staging the play's final scene—the father/daughter dance routine.
7. What is the theme of the play?

Evaluation

8. How effectively does Wasserstein characterize a father–daughter relationship? Where is her depiction most convincing, least convincing, and why?

Connection

9. Compare Wasserstein's humor in this play with Wilde's humor in *The Importance of Being Earnest*. Identify the kinds of humor each playwright employs and its effects.

Critical Thinking

10. Explain the various meanings of the "tender offer" Paul makes Lisa.

OSCAR WILDE
[1854–1900]

Oscar Wilde was born in Ireland in 1854 and died in Paris in 1900, following a life of notoriety. Wilde began to become famous as an undergraduate at Trinity College, Dublin, and Magdalen College, Oxford. His first collection of poems appeared in 1884 and his first stories in 1888. His best known work outside of his plays is The Picture of Dorian Gray. *Two of Wilde's plays,* An Ideal Husband *and* The Importance of Being Earnest *have been made into popular films.*

The Importance of Being Earnest

A TRIVIAL COMEDY FOR SERIOUS PEOPLE

THE PERSONS OF THE PLAY

JOHN WORTHING, J.P.
ALGERNON MONCRIEFF
REV. CANON CHASUBLE, D.D.
MERRIMAN, *Butler*
LANE, *Manservant*
LADY BRACKNELL
HON. GWENDOLEN FAIRFAX
CECILY CARDEW
MISS PRISM, *Governess*

THE SCENES OF THE PLAY

ACT I: *Algernon Moncrieff's flat in Half-Moon Street, W.*
ACT II: *The garden at the Manor House, Woolton*
ACT III: *Drawing-room at the Manor House, Woolton*
TIME: *The Present*

FIRST ACT

Scene. *Morning-room in* ALGERNON*'s flat in Half-Moon Street. The room is luxuriously and artistically furnished. The sound of a piano is heard in the adjoining room.*

(LANE *is arranging afternoon tea on the table and, after the music has ceased,* ALGERNON *enters.)*

ALGERNON: Did you hear what I was playing, Lane?

LANE: I didn't think it polite to listen, sir.

ALGERNON: I'm sorry for that, for your sake. I don't play accurately—anyone can play accurately—but I play with wonderful expression. As far as the piano is concerned, sentiment is my forte. I keep science for Life.

LANE: Yes, sir.

ALGERNON: And, speaking of the science of Life, have you got the cucumber sandwiches cut for Lady Bracknell?

LANE: Yes, sir. (*Hands them on a salver.*)

ALGERNON: (*Inspects them, takes two, and sits down on the sofa.*) Oh! . . . by the way, Lane, I see from your book that on Thursday night, when Lord Shoreman and Mr. Worthing were dining with me, eight bottles of champagne are entered as having been consumed.

LANE: Yes, sir; eight bottles and a pint.

ALGERNON: Why is it that at a bachelor's establishment the servants invariably drink the champagne? I ask merely for information.

LANE: I attribute it to the superior quality of the wine, sir. I have often observed that in married households the champagne is rarely of a first-rate brand.

ALGERNON: Good heavens! Is marriage so demoralizing as that?

LANE: I believe it *is* a very pleasant state, sir. I have had very little experience of it myself up to the present. I have only been married once. That was in consequence of a misunderstanding between myself and a young person.

ALGERNON: (*Languidly.*) I don't know that I am much interested in your family life, Lane.

LANE: No, sir; it is not a very interesting subject. I never think of it myself.

ALGERNON: Very natural, I am sure. That will do, Lane, thank you.

LANE: Thank you, sir.

(LANE *goes out.*)

ALGERNON: Lane's views on marriage seem somewhat lax. Really, if the lower orders don't set us a good example, what on earth is the use of them? They seem, as a class, to have absolutely no sense of moral responsibility.

(*Enter* LANE.)

LANE: Mr. Ernest Worthing.

(*Enter* JACK. LANE *goes out*.)

ALGERNON: How are you, my dear Ernest? What brings you up to town?

JACK: Oh, pleasure, pleasure! What else should bring one anywhere? Eating as usual, I see, Algy!

ALGERNON: (*Stiffly*.) I believe it is customary in good society to take some slight refreshment at five o'clock. Where have you been since last Thursday?

JACK: (*Sitting down on the sofa*.) In the country.

ALGERNON: What on earth do you do there?

JACK: (*Pulling off his gloves*.) When one is in town one amuses oneself. When one is in the country one amuses other people. It is excessively boring.

ALGERNON: And who are the people you amuse?

JACK: (*Airily*.) Oh, neighbors, neighbors.

ALGERNON: Got nice neighbors in your part of Shropshire?

JACK: Perfectly horrid! Never speak to one of them.

ALGERNON: How immensely you must amuse them! (*Goes over and takes sandwich*.) By the way, Shropshire is your county, is it not?

JACK: Eh? Shropshire? Yes, of course. Hallo! Why all these cups? Why cucumber sandwiches? Why such reckless extravagance in one so young? Who is coming to tea?

ALGERNON: Oh! merely Aunt Augusta and Gwendolen.

JACK: How perfectly delightful!

ALGERNON: Yes, that is all very well; but I am afraid Aunt Augusta won't quite approve of your being here.

JACK: May I ask why?

ALGERNON: My dear fellow, the way you flirt with Gwendolen is perfectly disgraceful. It is almost as bad as the way Gwendolen flirts with you.

JACK: I am in love with Gwendolen. I have come up to town expressly to propose to her.

ALGERNON: I thought you had come up for pleasure? . . . I call that business.

JACK: How utterly unromantic you are!

ALGERNON: I really don't see anything romantic in proposing. It is very romantic to be in love. But there is nothing romantic about a definite proposal. Why, one may be accepted. One usually is, I believe. Then the excitement is all over. The very essence of romance is uncertainty. If ever I get married, I'll certainly try to forget the fact.

JACK: I have no doubt about that, dear Algy. The Divorce Court was specially invented for people whose memories are so curiously constituted.

ALGERNON: Oh, there is no use speculating on that subject. Divorces are made in Heaven—(JACK *puts out his hand to take a sandwich*. ALGERNON *at once interferes*.) Please don't touch the cucumber sandwiches. They are ordered specially for Aunt Augusta. (*Takes one and eats it*.)

JACK: Well, you have been eating them all the time.

ALGERNON: That is quite a different matter. She is my aunt. (*Takes plate from below.*) Have some bread and butter. The bread and butter is for Gwendolen. Gwendolen is devoted to bread and butter.

JACK: (*Advancing to table and helping himself.*) And very good bread and butter it is too.

ALGERNON: Well, my dear fellow, you need not eat as if you were going to eat it all. You behave as if you were married to her already. You are not married to her already, and I don't think you ever will be.

JACK: Why on earth do you say that?

ALGERNON: Well, in the first place, girls never marry the men they flirt with. Girls don't think it right.

JACK: Oh, that is nonsense!

ALGERNON: It isn't. It is a great truth. It accounts for the extraordinary number of bachelors that one sees all over the place. In the second place, I don't give my consent.

JACK: Your consent!

ALGERNON: My dear fellow, Gwendolen is my first cousin. And before I allow you to marry her, you will have to clear up the whole question of Cecily. (*Rings bell.*)

JACK: Cecily! What on earth do you mean? What do you mean, Algy, by Cecily! I don't know any one of the name of Cecily.

(*Enter* LANE.)

ALGERNON: Bring me that cigarette case Mr. Worthing left in the smoking-room the last time he dined here.

LANE: Yes, sir.

(LANE *goes out.*)

JACK: Do you mean to say you have had my cigarette case all this time? I wish to goodness you had let me know. I have been writing frantic letters to Scotland Yard about it. I was very nearly offering a large reward.

ALGERNON: Well, I wish you would offer one. I happen to be more than usually hard up.

JACK: There is no good offering a large reward now that the thing is found.

(*Enter* LANE *with the cigarette case on a salver.* ALGERNON *takes it at once.* LANE *goes out.*)

ALGERNON: I think that is rather mean of you, Ernest, I must say. (*Opens case and examines it.*) However, it makes no matter, for, now that I look at the inscription inside, I find that the thing isn't yours after all.

JACK: Of course it's mine. (*Moving to him.*) You have seen me with it a hundred times, and you have no right whatsoever to read what is written inside. It is a very ungentlemanly thing to read a private cigarette case.

ALGERNON: Oh! It is absurd to have a hard and fast rule about what one should read and what one shouldn't. More than half of modern culture depends on what one shouldn't read.

JACK: I am quite aware of the fact, and I don't propose to discuss modern culture. It isn't the sort of thing one should talk of in private. I simply want my cigarette case back.

ALGERNON: Yes; but this isn't your cigarette case. This cigarette case is a present from someone of the name of Cecily, and you said you didn't know anyone of that name.

JACK: Well, if you want to know, Cecily happens to be my aunt.

ALGERNON: Your aunt!

JACK: Yes. Charming old lady she is, too. Lives at Tunbridge Wells. Just give it back to me, Algy.

ALGERNON: (*Retreating to back of sofa.*) But why does she call herself little Cecily if she is your aunt and lives at Tunbridge Wells? (*Reading.*) "From little Cecily with her fondest love."

JACK: (*Moving to sofa and kneeling upon it.*) My dear fellow, what on earth is there in that? Some aunts are tall, some aunts are not tall. That is a matter that surely an aunt may be allowed to decide for herself. You seem to think that every aunt should be exactly like your aunt! That is absurd. For Heaven's sake give me back my cigarette case. (*Follows* ALGERNON *round the room.*)

ALGERNON: Yes. But why does your aunt call you her uncle? "From little Cecily, with her fondest love to her dear Uncle Jack." There is no objection, I admit, to an aunt being a small aunt, but why an aunt, no matter what her size may be, should call her own nephew her uncle, I can't quite make out. Besides, your name isn't Jack at all; it is Ernest.

JACK: It isn't Ernest; it's Jack.

ALGERNON: You have always told me it was Ernest. I have introduced you to every one as Ernest. You answer to the name of Ernest. You look as if your name was Ernest. You are the most earnest-looking person I ever saw in my life. It is perfectly absurd your saying that your name isn't Ernest. It's on your cards. Here is one of them. (*Taking it from case.*) 'Mr. Ernest Worthing, B.4, The Albany.' I'll keep this as a proof that your name is Ernest if ever you attempt to deny it to me, or to Gwendolen, or to anyone else. (*Puts the card in his pocket.*)

JACK: Well, my name is Ernest in town and Jack in the country, and the cigarette case was given to me in the country.

ALGERNON: Yes, but that does not account for the fact that your small Aunt Cecily, who lives at Tunbridge Wells, calls you her dear uncle. Come, old boy, you had much better have the thing out at once.

JACK: My dear Algy, you talk exactly as if you were a dentist. It is very vulgar to talk like a dentist when one isn't a dentist. It produces a false impression.

ALGERNON: Well, that is exactly what dentists always do. Now, go on! Tell me the whole thing. I may mention that I have always suspected you of being a confirmed and secret Bunburyist; and I am quite sure of it now.

JACK: Bunburyist? What on earth do you mean by a Bunburyist?

ALGERNON: I'll reveal to you the meaning of that incomparable expression as soon as you are kind enough to inform me why you are Ernest in town and Jack in the country.

JACK: Well, produce my cigarette case first.

ALGERNON: Here it is. (*Hands cigarette case.*) Now produce your explanation, and pray make it improbable. (*Sits on sofa.*)

JACK: My dear fellow, there is nothing improbable about my explanation at all. In fact it's perfectly ordinary. Old Mr. Thomas Cardew, who adopted me when I was a little boy, made me in his will guardian to his granddaughter, Miss Cecily Cardew.

Cecily, who addresses me as her uncle from motives of respect that you could not possibly appreciate, lives at my place in the country under the charge of her admirable governess, Miss Prism.

ALGERNON: Where is that place in the country, by the way?

JACK: That is nothing to you, dear boy. You are not going to be invited. . . . I may tell you candidly that the place is not in Shropshire.

ALGERNON: I suspected that, my dear fellow! I have Bunburyed all over Shropshire on two separate occasions. Now, go on. Why are you Ernest in town and Jack in the country?

JACK: My dear Algy, I don't know whether you will be able to understand my real motives. You are hardly serious enough. When one is placed in the position of guardian, one has to adopt a very high moral tone on all subjects. It's one's duty to do so. And as a high moral tone can hardly be said to conduce very much to either one's health or one's happiness, in order to get up to town I have always pretended to have a younger brother of the name of Ernest, who lives in the Albany, and gets into the most dreadful scrapes. That, my dear Algy, is the whole truth pure and simple.

ALGERNON: The truth is rarely pure and never simple. Modern life would be very tedious if it were either, and modern literature a complete impossibility!

JACK: That wouldn't be at all a bad thing.

ALGERNON: Literary criticism is not your forte, my dear fellow. Don't try it. You should leave that to people who haven't been at a University. They do it so well in the daily papers. What you really are is a Bunburyist. I was quite right in saying you were a Bunburyist. You are one of the most advanced Bunburyists I know.

JACK: What on earth do you mean?

ALGERNON: You have invented a very useful younger brother called Ernest, in order that you may be able to come up to town as often as you like. I have invented an invaluable permanent invalid called Bunbury, in order that I may be able to go down into the country whenever I choose. Bunbury is perfectly invaluable. If it wasn't for Bunbury's extraordinary bad health, for instance, I wouldn't be able to dine with you at Willis's tonight, for I have been really engaged to Aunt Augusta for more than a week.

JACK: I haven't asked you to dine with me anywhere tonight.

ALGERNON: I know. You are absurdly careless about sending out invitations. It is very foolish of you. Nothing annoys people so much as not receiving invitations.

JACK: You had much better dine with your Aunt Augusta.

ALGERNON: I haven't the smallest intention of doing anything of the kind. To begin with, I dined there on Monday, and once a week is quite enough to dine with one's own relations. In the second place, whenever I do dine there I am always treated as a member of the family, and sent down with either no woman at all, or two. In the third place, I know perfectly well whom she will place me next to, tonight. She will place me next Mary Farquhar, who always flirts with her own husband across the dinner-table. That is not very pleasant. Indeed, it is not even decent . . . and that sort of thing is enormously on the increase. The amount of women in London who flirt with their own husbands is perfectly scandalous. It looks so bad. It is simply washing one's clean linen in public. Besides, now that I know you to be a confirmed Bunburyist I naturally want to talk to you about Bunburying. I want to tell you the rules.

JACK: I'm not a Bunburyist at all. If Gwendolen accepts me, I am going to kill my brother, indeed I think I'll kill him in any case. Cecily is a little too much interested in him. It is rather a bore. So I am going to get rid of Ernest. And I strongly advise you to do the same with Mr. . . . with your invalid friend who has the absurd name.

ALGERNON: Nothing will induce me to part with Bunbury, and if you ever get married, which seems to me extremely problematic, you will be very glad to know Bunbury. A man who marries without knowing Bunbury has a very tedious time of it.

JACK: That is nonsense. If I marry a charming girl like Gwendolen, and she is the only girl I ever saw in my life that I would marry, I certainly won't want to know Bunbury.

ALGERNON: Then your wife will. You don't seem to realize, that in married life three is company and two is none.

JACK: (*Sententiously.*) That, my dear young friend, is the theory that the corrupt French Drama has been propounding for the last fifty years.

ALGERNON: Yes; and that the happy English home has proved in half the time.

JACK: For heaven's sake, don't try to be cynical. It's perfectly easy to be cynical.

ALGERNON: My dear fellow, it isn't easy to be anything nowadays. There's such a lot of beastly competition about. (*The sound of an electric bell is heard.*) Ah! that must be Aunt Augusta. Only relatives, or creditors, ever ring in that Wagnerian manner. Now, if I get her out of the way for ten minutes, so that you can have an opportunity for proposing to Gwendolen, may I dine with you tonight at Willis's?

JACK: I suppose so, if you want to.

ALGERNON: Yes, but you must be serious about it. I hate people who are not serious about meals. It is so shallow of them.

(*Enter* LANE.)

LANE: Lady Bracknell and Miss Fairfax.

(ALGERNON *goes forward to meet them. Enter* LADY BRACKNELL *and* GWENDOLEN.)

LADY BRACKNELL: Good afternoon, dear Algernon, I hope you are behaving very well.

ALGERNON: I'm feeling very well, Aunt Augusta.

LADY BRACKNELL: That's not quite the same thing. In fact the two things rarely go together. (*Sees* JACK *and bows to him with icy coldness.*)

ALGERNON: (*To* GWENDOLEN.) Dear me, you are smart!

GWENDOLEN: I am always smart! Am I not, Mr. Worthing?

JACK: You're quite perfect, Miss Fairfax.

GWENDOLEN: Oh! I hope I am not that. It would leave no room for developments, and I intend to develop in many directions. (GWENDOLEN *and* JACK *sit down together in the corner.*)

LADY BRACKNELL: I'm sorry if we are a little late, Algernon, but I was obliged to call on dear Lady Harbury. I hadn't been there since her poor husband's death. I never saw a woman so altered; she looks quite twenty years younger. And now I'll have a cup of tea, and one of those nice cucumber sandwiches you promised me.

ALGERNON: Certainly, Aunt Augusta. (*Goes over to tea-table.*)

LADY BRACKNELL: Won't you come and sit here, Gwendolen?

GWENDOLEN: Thanks, mamma, I'm quite comfortable where I am.

ALGERNON: (*Picking up empty plate in horror.*) Good heavens! Lane! Why are there no cucumber sandwiches? I ordered them specially.

LANE: (*Gravely.*) There were no cucumbers in the market this morning, sir. I went down twice.

ALGERNON: No cucumbers!

LANE: No, sir. Not even for ready money.

ALGERNON: That will do, Lane, thank you.

LANE: Thank you, sir. (*Goes out.*)

ALGERNON: I am greatly distressed, Aunt Augusta, about there being no cucumbers, not even for ready money.

LADY BRACKNELL: It really makes no matter, Algernon. I had some crumpets with Lady Harbury, who seems to me to be living entirely for pleasure now.

ALGERNON: I hear her hair has turned quite gold from grief.

LADY BRACKNELL: It certainly has changed its colour. From what cause I, of course, cannot say. (ALGERNON *crosses and hands tea.*) Thank you, I've quite a treat for you tonight, Algernon. I am going to send you down with Mary Farquhar. She is such a nice woman, and so attentive to her husband. It's delightful to watch them.

ALGERNON: I am afraid, Aunt Augusta, I shall have to give up the pleasure of dining with you tonight after all.

LADY BRACKNELL: (*Frowning.*) I hope not, Algernon. It would put my table completely out. Your uncle would have to dine upstairs. Fortunately he is accustomed to that.

ALGERNON: It is a great bore, and, I need hardly say, a terrible disappointment to me, but the fact is I have just had a telegram to say that my poor friend Bunbury is very ill again. (*Exchanges glances with* JACK.) They seem to think I should be with him.

LADY BRACKNELL: It is very strange. This Mr. Bunbury seems to suffer from curiously bad health.

ALGERNON: Yes; poor Bunbury is a dreadful invalid.

LADY BRACKNELL: Well, I must say, Algernon, that I think it is high time that Mr. Bunbury made up his mind whether he was going to live or to die. This shilly-shallying with the question is absurd. Nor do I in any way approve of the modern sympathy with invalids. I consider it morbid. Illness of any kind is hardly a thing to be encouraged in others. Health is the primary duty of life. I am always telling that to your poor uncle, but he never seems to take much notice . . . as far as any improvement in his ailment goes. I should be much obliged if you would ask Mr. Bunbury, from me, to be kind enough not to have a relapse on Saturday, for I rely on you to arrange my music for me. It is my last reception, and one wants something that will encourage conversation, particularly at the end of the season when everyone has practically said whatever they had to say, which, in most cases, was probably not much.

ALGERNON: I'll speak to Bunbury, Aunt Augusta, if he is still conscious, and I think I can promise you he'll be all right by Saturday. Of course the music is a great difficulty. You see, if one plays good music, people don't listen, and if one plays bad music people don't talk. But I'll run over the program I've drawn out, if you will kindly come into the next room for a moment.

LADY BRACKNELL: Thank you, Algernon. It is very thoughtful of you. (*Rising, and following* ALGERNON.) I'm sure the program will be delightful, after a few expurgations. French songs I cannot possibly allow. People always seem to think that they are improper, and either look shocked, which is vulgar, or laugh, which is worse. But German sounds a thoroughly respectable language, and, indeed I believe is so. Gwendolen, you will accompany me.

GWENDOLEN: Certainly, mamma.

(LADY BRACKNELL *and* ALGERNON *go into the music-room,* GWENDOLEN *remains behind.)*

JACK: Charming day it has been, Miss Fairfax.

GWENDOLEN: Pray don't talk to me about the weather, Mr. Worthing. Whenever people talk to me about the weather, I always feel quite certain that they mean something else. And that makes me so nervous.

JACK: I do mean something else.

GWENDOLEN: I thought so. In fact, I am never wrong.

JACK: And I would like to be allowed to take advantage of Lady Bracknell's temporary absence. . . .

GWENDOLEN: I would certainly advise you to do so. Mamma has a way of coming back suddenly into a room that I have often had to speak to her about.

JACK: (*Nervously.*) Miss Fairfax, ever since I met you I have admired you more than any girl . . . I have ever met since . . . I met you.

GWENDOLEN: Yes, I am quite well aware of the fact. And I often wish that in public, at any rate, you had been more demonstrative. For me you have always had an irresistible fascination. Even before I met you I was far from indifferent to you. (JACK *looks at her in amazement.*) We live, as I hope you know, Mr. Worthing, in an age of ideals. The fact is constantly mentioned in the more expensive monthly magazines, and has reached the provincial pulpits, I am told; and my ideal has always been to love someone of the name of Ernest. There is something in that name that inspires absolute confidence. The moment Algernon first mentioned to me that he had a friend called Ernest, I knew I was destined to love you.

JACK: You really love me, Gwendolen?

GWENDOLEN: Passionately!

JACK: Darling! You don't know how happy you've made me.

GWENDOLEN: My own Ernest!

JACK: But you don't really mean to say that you couldn't love me if my name wasn't Ernest?

GWENDOLEN: But your name is Ernest.

JACK: Yes, I know it is. But supposing it was something else? Do you mean to say you couldn't love me then?

GWENDOLEN: (*Glibly.*) Ah! that is clearly a metaphysical speculation, and like most metaphysical speculations has very little reference at all to the actual facts of real life, as we know them.

JACK: Personally, darling, to speak quite candidly, I don't much care about the name of Ernest. . . . I don't think the name suits me at all.

GWENDOLEN: It suits you perfectly. It is a divine name. It has music of its own. It produces vibrations.

JACK: Well, really, Gwendolen, I must say that I think there are lots of other much nicer names. I think Jack, for instance, a charming name.

GWENDOLEN: Jack? . . . No, there is very little music in the name Jack, if any at all, indeed. It does not thrill. It produces absolutely no vibrations. . . . I have known several Jacks, and they all, without exception, were more than usually plain. Besides, Jack is a notorious domesticity for John! And I pity any woman who is married to a man called John. She would probably never be allowed to know the entrancing pleasure of a single moment's solitude. The only really safe name is Ernest.

JACK: Gwendolen, I must get christened at once—I mean we must get married at once. There is no time to be lost.

GWENDOLEN: Married, Mr. Worthing?

JACK: (*Astounded.*) Well . . . surely. You know that I love you, and you led me to believe, Miss Fairfax, that you were not absolutely indifferent to me.

GWENDOLEN: I adore you. But you haven't proposed to me yet. Nothing has been said at all about marriage. The subject has not even been touched on.

JACK: Well . . . may I propose to you now?

GWENDOLEN: I think it would be an admirable opportunity. And to spare you any possible disappointment, Mr. Worthing, I think it only fair to tell you quite frankly beforehand that I am fully determined to accept you.

JACK: Gwendolen!

GWENDOLEN: Yes, Mr. Worthing, what have you got to say to me?

JACK: You know what I have got to say to you.

GWENDOLEN: Yes, but you don't say it.

JACK: Gwendolen, will you marry me? (*Goes on his knees.*)

GWENDOLEN: Of course I will, darling. How long you have been about it! I am afraid you have had very little experience in how to propose.

JACK: My own one, I have never loved any one in the world but you.

GWENDOLEN: Yes, but men often propose for practice. I know my brother Gerald does. All my girl-friends tell me so. What wonderfully blue eyes you have, Ernest! They are quite, quite blue. I hope you will always look at me just like that, especially when there are other people present.

(*Enter* LADY BRACKNELL.)

LADY BRACKNELL: Mr. Worthing! Rise, sir, from this semirecumbent posture. It is most indecorous.

GWENDOLEN: Mamma! (*He tries to rise; she restrains him.*) I must beg you to retire. This is no place for you. Besides, Mr. Worthing has not quite finished yet.

LADY BRACKNELL: Finished what, may I ask?

GWENDOLEN: I am engaged to Mr. Worthing, mamma. (*They rise together.*)

LADY BRACKNELL: Pardon me, you are not engaged to any one. When you do become engaged to some one, I, or your father, should his health permit him, will inform you of the fact. An engagement should come on a young girl as a surprise, pleasant or unpleasant, as the case may be. It is hardly a matter that she could be allowed to arrange for herself. . . . And now I have a few questions to put to you, Mr. Worthing. While I am making these inquiries, you, Gwendolen, will wait for me below in the carriage.

GWENDOLEN: (*Reproachfully.*) *Mamma!*

LADY BRACKNELL: In the carriage, Gwendolen! (GWENDOLEN *goes to the door. She and* JACK *blow kisses to each other behind* LADY BRACKNELL*'s back.* LADY BRACKNELL *looks vaguely about as if she could not understand what the noise was. Finally turns round.*) Gwendolen, the carriage!

GWENDOLEN: Yes, mamma. (*Goes out, looking back at* JACK.)

LADY BRACKNELL: (*Sitting down.*) You can take a seat, Mr. Worthing.

(*Looks in her pocket for note-book and pencil.*)

JACK: Thank you, Lady Bracknell. I prefer standing.

LADY BRACKNELL: (*Pencil and note-book in hand.*) I feel bound to tell you that you are not down on my list of eligible young men, although I have the same list as the dear Duchess of Bolton has. We work together, in fact. However, I am quite ready to enter your name, should your answers be what a really affectionate mother requires. Do you smoke?

JACK: Well, yes, I must admit I smoke.

LADY BRACKNELL: I am glad to hear it. A man should always have an occupation of some kind. There are far too many idle men in London as it is. How old are you?

JACK: Twenty-nine.

LADY BRACKNELL: A very good age to be married at. I have always been of opinion that a man who desires to get married should know either everything or nothing. Which do you know?

JACK: (*After some hesitation.*) I know nothing, Lady Bracknell.

LADY BRACKNELL: I am pleased to hear it. I do not approve of anything that tampers with natural ignorance. Ignorance is like a delicate exotic fruit; touch it and the bloom is gone. The whole theory of modern education is radically unsound. Fortunately in England, at any rate, education produces no effect whatsoever. If it did, it would prove a serious danger to the upper classes, and probably lead to acts of violence in Grosvenor Square. What is your income?

JACK: Between seven and eight thousand a year.

LADY BRACKNELL: (*Makes a note in her book.*) In land, or in investments?

JACK: In investments, chiefly.

LADY BRACKNELL: That is satisfactory. What between the duties expected of one during one's lifetime, and the duties exacted from one after one's death, land has ceased to be either a profit or a pleasure. It gives one position, and prevents one from keeping it up. That's all that can be said about land.

JACK: I have a country house with some land, of course, attached to it, about fifteen hundred acres, I believe; but I don't depend on that for my real income. In fact, as far as I can make out, the poachers are the only people who make anything out of it.

LADY BRACKNELL: A country house! How many bedrooms? Well, that point can be cleared up afterwards. You have a town house, I hope? A girl with a simple, unspoiled nature, like Gwendolen, could hardly be expected to reside in the country.

JACK: Well, I own a house in Belgrave Square, but it is let by the year to Lady Bloxham. Of course, I can get it back whenever I like, at six months' notice.

LADY BRACKNELL: Lady Bloxham? I don't know her.

JACK: Oh, she goes about very little. She is a lady considerably advanced in years.

LADY BRACKNELL: Ah, nowadays that is no guarantee of respectability of character. What number in Belgrave Square?

JACK: 149.

LADY BRACKNELL: (*Shaking her head.*) The unfashionable side. I thought there was something. However, that could easily be altered.

JACK: Do you mean the fashion, or the side?

LADY BRACKNELL: (*Sternly.*) Both, if necessary, I presume. What are your politics?

JACK: Well, I am afraid I really have none. I am a Liberal Unionist.

LADY BRACKNELL: Oh, they count as Tories. They dine with us. Or come in the evening, at any rate. Now to minor matters. Are your parents living?

JACK: I have lost both my parents.

LADY BRACKNELL: To lose one parent, Mr. Worthing, may be regarded as a misfortune; to lose both looks like carelessness. Who was your father? He was evidently a man of some wealth. Was he born in what the Radical papers call the purple of commerce, or did he rise from the ranks of the aristocracy?

JACK: I am afraid I really don't know. The fact is, Lady Bracknell, I said I had lost my parents. It would be nearer the truth to say that my parents seem to have lost me.... I don't actually know who I am by birth. I was ...well, I was found.

LADY BRACKNELL: Found!

JACK: The late Mr. Thomas Cardew, an old gentleman of a very charitable and kindly disposition, found me, and gave me the name of Worthing, because he happened to have a first-class ticket for Worthing in his pocket at the time. Worthing is a place in Sussex. It is a seaside resort.

LADY BRACKNELL: Where did the charitable gentleman who had a first-class ticket for this seaside resort find you?

JACK: (*Gravely.*) In a hand-bag.

LADY BRACKNELL: A hand-bag?

JACK: (*Very seriously.*) Yes, Lady Bracknell. I was in a hand-bag—a somewhat large, black leather hand-bag, with handles to it—an ordinary hand-bag in fact.

LADY BRACKNELL: In what locality did this Mr. James, or Thomas, Cardew come across this ordinary hand-bag?

JACK: In the cloak-room at Victoria Station. It was given to him in mistake for his own.

LADY BRACKNELL: The cloak-room at Victoria Station?

JACK: Yes. The Brighton line.

LADY BRACKNELL: The line is immaterial. Mr. Worthing, I confess I feel somewhat bewildered by what you have just told me. To be born, or at any rate bred, in a hand-bag, whether it had handles or not, seems to me to display a contempt for the ordinary decencies of family life that reminds one of the worst excesses of the French Revolution. And I presume you know what that unfortunate movement led to? As for the particular locality in which the hand-bag was found, a cloak-room at a railway station might serve to conceal a social indiscretion—has probably, indeed, been used for that purpose before now—but it could hardly be regarded as an assured basis for a recognized position in good society.

JACK: May I ask you then what you would advise me to do? I need hardly say I would do anything in the world to ensure Gwendolen's happiness.

LADY BRACKNELL: I would strongly advise you, Mr. Worthing, to try and acquire some relations as soon as possible, and to make a definite effort to produce at any rate one parent, of either sex, before the season is quite over.

JACK: Well, I don't see how I could possibly manage to do that. I can produce the hand-bag at any moment. It is in my dressing-room at home. I really think that should satisfy you, Lady Bracknell.

LADY BRACKNELL: Me, sir! What has it to do with me? You can hardly imagine that I and Lord Bracknell would dream of allowing our only daughter—a girl brought up with the utmost care—to marry into a cloak-room, and form an alliance with a parcel. Good morning, Mr. Worthing!

(LADY BRACKNELL *sweeps out in majestic indignation.*)

JACK: Good morning! (ALGERNON, *from the other room, strikes up the Wedding March.* JACK *looks perfectly furious and goes to the door.*) For goodness' sake don't play that ghastly tune, Algy! How idiotic you are!

(*The music stops and* ALGERNON *enters cheerily.*)

ALGERNON: Didn't it go off all right, old boy? You don't mean to say Gwendolen refused you? I know it is a way she has. She is always refusing people. I think it is most ill-natured of her.

JACK: Oh, Gwendolen is as right as a trivet. As far as she is concerned, we are engaged. Her mother is perfectly unbearable. Never met such a Gorgon. . . . I don't really know what a Gorgon is like, but I am quite sure that Lady Bracknell is one. In any case, she is a monster, without being a myth, which is rather unfair. . . . I beg your pardon, Algy, I suppose I shouldn't talk about your own aunt in that way before you.

ALGERNON: My dear boy, I love hearing my relations abused. It is the only thing that makes me put up with them at all. Relations are simply a tedious pack of people, who haven't got the remotest knowledge of how to live, nor the smallest instinct about when to die.

JACK: Oh, that is nonsense!

ALGERNON: It isn't!

JACK: Well, I won't argue about the matter. You always want to argue about things.

ALGERNON: That is exactly what things were originally made for.

JACK: Upon my word, if I thought that, I'd shoot myself. . . . (*A pause.*) You don't think there is any chance of Gwendolen becoming like her mother in about a hundred and fifty years, do you, Algy?

ALGERNON: All women become like their mothers. That is their tragedy. No man does. That's his.

JACK: Is that clever?

ALGERNON: It is perfectly phrased! and quite as true as any observation in civilized life should be.

JACK: I am sick to death of cleverness. Everybody is clever nowadays. You can't go anywhere without meeting clever people. The thing has become an absolute public nuisance. I wish to goodness we had a few fools left.

ALGERNON: We have.

JACK: I should extremely like to meet them. What do they talk about?

ALGERNON: The fools? Oh! about the clever people, of course.

JACK: What fools.

ALGERNON: By the way, did you tell Gwendolen the truth about your being Ernest in town, and Jack in the country?

JACK: (*In a very patronizing manner.*) My dear fellow, the truth isn't quite the sort of thing one tells to a nice, sweet, refined girl. What extraordinary ideas you have about the way to behave to a woman!

ALGERNON: The only way to behave to a woman is to make love to her, if she is pretty, and to someone else, if she is plain.

JACK: Oh, that is nonsense.

ALGERNON: What about your brother? What about the profligate Ernest?

JACK: Oh, before the end of the week I shall have got rid of him. I'll say he died in Paris of apoplexy. Lots of people die of apoplexy, quite suddenly, don't they?

ALGERNON: Yes, but it's hereditary, my dear fellow. It's a sort of thing that runs in families. You had much better say a severe chill.

JACK: You are sure a severe chill isn't hereditary, or anything of that kind?

ALGERNON: Of course it isn't!

JACK: Very well, then. My poor brother Ernest is carried off suddenly, in Paris, by a severe chill. That gets rid of him.

ALGERNON: But I thought you said that . . . Miss Cardew was a little too much interested in your poor brother Ernest? Won't she feel his loss a good deal?

JACK: Oh, that is all right. Cecily is not a silly romantic girl, I am glad to say. She has got a capital appetite, goes long walks, and pays no attention at all to her lessons.

ALGERNON: I would rather like to see Cecily.

JACK: I will take very good care you never do. She is excessively pretty, and she is only just eighteen.

ALGERNON: Have you told Gwendolen yet that you have an excessively pretty ward who is only just eighteen?

JACK: Oh! one doesn't blurt these things out to people. Cecily and Gwendolen are perfectly certain to be extremely great friends. I'll bet you anything you like that half an hour after they have met, they will be calling each other sister.

ALGERNON: Women only do that when they have called each other a lot of other things first. Now, my dear boy, if we want to get a good table at Willis's, we really must go and dress. Do you know it is nearly seven?

JACK: (*Irritably.*) Oh! it always is nearly seven.

ALGERNON: I'm hungry.

JACK: I never knew you when you weren't. . . .

ALGERNON: What shall we do after dinner? Go to a theatre?

JACK: Oh, no! I loathe listening.

ALGERNON: Well, let us go to the Club?

JACK: Oh, no! I hate talking.

ALGERNON: Well, we might trot round to the Empire at ten?

JACK: Oh, no! I can't bear looking at things. It is so silly.

ALGERNON: Well, what shall we do?

JACK: Nothing!

ALGERNON: It is awfully hard work doing nothing. However, I don't mind hard work where there is no definite object of any kind.

(*Enter* LANE.)

LANE: Miss Fairfax.

(*Enter* GWENDOLEN. LANE *goes out.*)

ALGERNON: Gwendolen, upon my word!

GWENDOLEN: Algy, kindly turn your back. I have something very particular to say to Mr. Worthing.

ALGERNON: Really, Gwendolen, I don't think I can allow this at all.

GWENDOLEN: Algy, you always adopt a strictly immoral attitude towards life. You are not quite old enough to do that. (ALGERNON *retires to the fireplace.*)

JACK: My own darling!

GWENDOLEN: Ernest, we may never be married. From the expression on mamma's face I fear we never shall. Few parents nowadays pay any regard to what their children say to them. The old-fashioned respect for the young is fast dying out. Whatever influence I ever had over mamma, I lost at the age of three. But although she may prevent us from becoming man and wife, and I may marry someone else, and marry often, nothing that she can possibly do can alter my eternal devotion to you.

JACK: Dear Gwendolen!

GWENDOLEN: The story of your romantic origin, as related to me by mamma, with unpleasing comments, has naturally stirred the deeper fibers of my nature. Your Christian name has an irresistible fascination. The simplicity of your character makes you exquisitely incomprehensible to me. Your town address at the Albany I have. What is your address in the country?

JACK: The Manor House, Woolton, Hertfordshire.

(ALGERNON, *who has been carefully listening, smiles to himself, and writes the address on his shirt-cuff. Then picks up the Railway Guide.*)

GWENDOLEN: There is a good postal service, I suppose? It may be necessary to do something desperate. That of course will require serious consideration. I will communicate with you daily.

JACK: My own one!

GWENDOLEN: How long do you remain in town?

JACK: Till Monday.

GWENDOLEN: Good! Algy, you may turn round now.

ALGERNON: Thanks, I've turned round already.

GWENDOLEN: You may also ring the bell.

JACK: You will let me see you to your carriage, my own darling?

GWENDOLEN: Certainly.

JACK: (*To* LANE, *who now enters.*) I will see Miss Fairfax out.

LANE: Yes, sir. (JACK *and* GWENDOLEN *go off.*)

(LANE *presents several letters on a salver, to* ALGERNON. *It is to be surmised that they are bills, as* ALGERNON, *after looking at the envelopes, tears them up.*)

ALGERNON: A glass of sherry, Lane.

LANE: Yes, sir.

ALGERNON: Tomorrow, Lane, I'm going Bunburying.

LANE: Yes, sir.

ALGERNON: I shall probably not be back till Monday. You can put up my dress clothes, my smoking jacket, and all the Bunbury suits . . .

LANE: Yes, sir. (*Handing sherry.*)

ALGERNON: I hope tomorrow will be a fine day, Lane.

LANE: It never is, sir.

ALGERNON: Lane, you're a perfect pessimist.

LANE: I do my best to give satisfaction, sir.

(*Enter* JACK. LANE *goes off*)

JACK: There's a sensible, intellectual girl! the only girl I ever cared for in my life. (ALGERNON *is laughing immoderately.*) What on earth are you so amused at?

ALGERNON: Oh, I'm a little anxious about poor Bunbury, that is all.

JACK: If you don't take care, your friend Bunbury will get you into a serious scrape some day.

ALGERNON: I love scrapes. They are the only things that are never serious.

JACK: Oh, that's nonsense, Algy. You never talk anything but nonsense.

ALGERNON: Nobody ever does.

(JACK *looks indignantly at him, and leaves the room.* ALGERNON *lights a cigarette, reads his shirt-cuff, and smiles.*)

Act Drop

SECOND ACT

Scene: *Garden at the Manor House. A flight of grey stone steps leads up to the house. The garden, an old-fashioned one, full of roses. Time of year, July. Basket chairs, and a table covered with books, are set under a large yew-tree.*

(MISS PRISM *discovered seated at the table.* CECILY *is at the back, watering flowers.*)

MISS PRISM: (*Calling.*) Cecily, Cecily! Surely such a utilitarian occupation as the watering of flowers is rather Moulton's duty than yours? Especially at a moment when intellectual pleasures await you. Your German grammar is on the table. Pray open it at page fifteen. We will repeat yesterday's lesson.

CECILY: (*Coming over very slowly.*) But I don't like German. It isn't at all a becoming language. I know perfectly well that I look quite plain after my German lesson.

MISS PRISM: Child, you know how anxious your guardian is that you should improve yourself in every way. He laid particular stress on your German, as he was leaving for town yesterday. Indeed, he always lays stress on your German when he is leaving for town.

CECILY: Dear Uncle Jack is so very serious! Sometimes he is so serious that I think he cannot be quite well.

MISS PRISM: (*Drawing herself up.*) Your guardian enjoys the best of health, and his gravity of demeanour is especially to be commended in one so comparatively young as he is. I know no one who has a higher sense of duty and responsibility.

CECILY: I suppose that is why he often looks a little bored when we three are together.

MISS PRISM: Cecily! I am surprised at you. Mr. Worthing has many troubles in his life. Idle merriment and triviality would be out of place in his conversation. You must remember his constant anxiety about that unfortunate young man his brother.

CECILY: I wish Uncle Jack would allow that unfortunate young man, his brother, to come down here sometimes. We might have a good influence over him, Miss Prism. I am sure you certainly would. You know German, and geology, and things of that kind influence a man very much. (CECILY *begins to write in her diary.*)

MISS PRISM: (*Shaking her head.*) I do not think that even I could produce any effect on a character that according to his own brother's admission is irretrievably weak and vacillating. Indeed I am not sure that I would desire to reclaim him. I am not in favour of this modern mania for turning bad people into good people at a moment's notice. As a man sows so let him reap. You must put away your diary, Cecily. I really don't see why you should keep a diary at all.

CECILY: I keep a diary in order to enter the wonderful secrets of my life. If I didn't write them down, I should probably forget all about them.

MISS PRISM: Memory, my dear Cecily, is the diary that we all carry about with us.

CECILY: Yes, but it usually chronicles the things that have never happened, and couldn't possibly have happened. I believe that Memory is responsible for nearly all the three-volume novels that Mudie sends us.

MISS PRISM: Do not speak slightingly of the three-volume novel, Cecily. I wrote one myself in earlier days.

CECILY: Did you really, Miss Prism? How wonderfully clever you are! I hope it did not end happily? I don't like novels that end happily. They depress me so much.

MISS PRISM: The good ended happily, and the bad unhappily. That is what Fiction means.

CECILY: I suppose so. But it seems very unfair. And was your novel ever published?

MISS PRISM: Alas! no. The manuscript unfortunately was abandoned. (CECILY *starts.*) I used the word in the sense of lost or mislaid. To your work, child, these speculations are profitless.

CECILY: (*Smiling.*) But I see dear Dr. Chasuble coming up through the garden.

MISS PRISM: (*Rising and advancing.*) Dr. Chasuble! This is indeed a pleasure.

(*Enter* CANON CHASUBLE.)

CHASUBLE: And how are we this morning? Miss Prism, you are, I trust, well?

CECILY: Miss Prism has just been complaining of a slight headache. I think it would do her so much good to have a short stroll with you in the Park, Dr. Chasuble.

MISS PRISM: Cecily, I have not mentioned anything about a headache.

CECILY: No, dear Miss Prism, I know that, but I felt instinctively that you had a headache. Indeed I was thinking about that, and not about my German lesson, when the Rector came in.

CHASUBLE: I hope, Cecily, you are not inattentive.

CECILY: Oh, I am afraid I am.

CHASUBLE: That is strange. Were I fortunate enough to be Miss Prism's pupil, I would hang upon her lips. (MISS PRISM *glares.*) I spoke metaphorically.—My metaphor was drawn from bees. Ahem! Mr. Worthing, I suppose, has not returned from town yet?

MISS PRISM: We do not expect him till Monday afternoon.

CHASUBLE: Ah yes, he usually likes to spend his Sunday in London. He is not one of those whose sole aim is enjoyment, as, by all accounts, that unfortunate young man his brother seems to be. But I must not disturb Egeria and her pupil any longer.

MISS PRISM: Egeria? My name is Laetitia, Doctor.

CHASUBLE: (*Bowing.*) A classical allusion merely, drawn from the Pagan authors. I shall see you both no doubt at Evensong?

MISS PRISM: I think, dear Doctor, I will have a stroll with you. I find I have a headache after all, and a walk might do it good.

CHASUBLE: With pleasure, Miss Prism, with pleasure. We might go as far as the schools and back.

MISS PRISM: That would be delightful. Cecily, you will read your Political Economy in my absence. The chapter on the Fall of the Rupee you may omit. It is somewhat too sensational. Even these metallic problems have their melodramatic side.

(*Goes down the garden with* DR. CHASUBLE.)

CECILY: (*Picks up books and throws them back on table.*) Horrid Political Economy! Horrid Geography! Horrid, horrid German!

(*Enter* MERRIMAN *with a card on a salver.*)

MERRIMAN: Mr. Ernest Worthing has just driven over from the station. He has brought his luggage with him.

CECILY: (*Takes the card and reads it.*) 'Mr. Ernest Worthing, B.4, The Albany, W.' Uncle Jack's brother! Did you tell him Mr. Worthing was in town?

MERRIMAN: Yes, Miss. He seemed very much disappointed. I mentioned that you and Miss Prism were in the garden. He said he was anxious to speak to you privately for a moment.

CECILY: Ask Mr. Ernest Worthing to come here. I suppose you had better talk to the housekeeper about a room for him.

MERRIMAN: Yes, Miss. (MERRIMAN *goes off.*)

CECILY: I have never met any really wicked person before. I feel rather frightened. I am so afraid he will look just like every one else.

(*Enter* ALGERNON, *very gay and debonair.*)

He does!

ALGERNON: (*Raising his hat.*) You are my little cousin Cecily, I'm sure.

CECILY: You are under some strange mistake. I am not little. In fact, I believe I am more than usually tall for my age. (ALGERNON *is rather taken aback.*) But I am your cousin Cecily. You, I see from your card, are Uncle Jack's brother, my cousin Ernest, my wicked cousin Ernest.

ALGERNON: Oh! I am not really wicked at all, Cousin Cecily. You mustn't think that I am wicked.

CECILY: If you are not, then you have certainly been deceiving us all in a very inexcusable manner. I hope you have not been leading a double life, pretending to be wicked and being really good all the time. That would be hypocrisy.

ALGERNON: (*Looks at her in amazement.*) Oh! Of course I have been rather reckless.

CECILY: I am glad to hear it.

ALGERNON: In fact, now you mention the subject, I have been very bad in my own small way.

CECILY: I don't think you should be so proud of that, though I am sure it must have been very pleasant.

ALGERNON: It is much pleasanter being here with you.

CECILY: I can't understand how you are here at all. Uncle Jack won't be back till Monday afternoon.

ALGERNON: That is a great disappointment. I am obliged to go up by the first train on Monday morning. I have a business appointment that I am anxious . . . to miss!

CECILY: Couldn't you miss it anywhere but in London?

ALGERNON: No, the appointment is in London.

CECILY: Well, I know, of course, how important it is not to keep a business engagement, if one wants to retain any sense of the beauty of life, but still I think you had better wait till Uncle Jack arrives. I know he wants to speak to you about your emigrating.

ALGERNON: About my what?

CECILY: Your emigrating. He has gone up to buy your outfit.

ALGERNON: I certainly wouldn't let Jack buy my outfit. He has no taste in neckties at all.

CECILY: I don't think you will require neckties. Uncle Jack is sending you to Australia.

ALGERNON: Australia! I'd sooner die.

CECILY: Well, he said at dinner on Wednesday night, that you would have to choose between this world, the next world, and Australia.

ALGERNON: Oh, well! The accounts I have received of Australia and the next world are not particularly encouraging. This world is good enough for me, Cousin Cecily.

CECILY: Yes, but are you good enough for it?

ALGERNON: I'm afraid I'm not that. That is why I want you to reform me. You might make that your mission, if you don't mind, Cousin Cecily.

CECILY: I'm afraid I've no time, this afternoon.

ALGERNON: Well, would you mind my reforming myself this afternoon?

CECILY: It is rather Quixotic of you. But I think you should try.

ALGERNON: I will. I feel better already.

CECILY: You are looking a little worse.

ALGERNON: That is because I am hungry.

CECILY: How thoughtless of me. I should have remembered that when one is going to lead an entirely new life, one requires regular and wholesome meals. Won't you come in?

ALGERNON: Thank you. Might I have a buttonhole first? I have never any appetite unless I have a buttonhole first.

CECILY: A Maréchal Niel? (*Picks up scissors.*)

ALGERNON: No, I'd sooner have a pink rose.

CECILY: Why? (*Cuts a flower.*)

ALGERNON: Because you are like a pink rose, Cousin Cecily.

CECILY: I don't think it can be right for you to talk to me like that. Miss Prism never says such things to me.

ALGERNON: Then Miss Prism is a short-sighted old lady. (CECILY *puts the rose in his buttonhole.*) You are the prettiest girl I ever saw.

CECILY: Miss Prism says that all good looks are a snare.

ALGERNON: They are a snare that every sensible man would like to be caught in.

CECILY: Oh, I don't think I would care to catch a sensible man. I shouldn't know what to talk to him about.

(*They pass into the house.* MISS PRISM *and* DR. CHASUBLE *return.*)

MISS PRISM: You are too much alone, dear Dr. Chasuble. You should get married. A misanthrope I can understand—a womanthrope, never!

CHASUBLE: (*With a scholar's shudder.*) Believe me, I do not deserve so neologistic a phrase. The precept as well as the practice of the Primitive Church was distinctly against matrimony.

MISS PRISM: (*Sententiously.*) That is obviously the reason why the Primitive Church has not lasted up to the present day. And you do not seem to realize, dear Doctor, that by persistently remaining single, a man converts himself into a permanent public temptation. Men should be more careful; this very celibacy leads weaker vessels astray.

CHASUBLE: But is a man not equally attractive when married?

MISS PRISM: No married man is ever attractive except to his wife.

CHASUBLE: And often, I've been told, not even to her.

MISS PRISM: That depends on the intellectual sympathies of the woman. Maturity can always be depended on. Ripeness can be trusted. Young women are green. (DR. CHASUBLE *starts.*) I spoke horticulturally. My metaphor was drawn from fruits. But where is Cecily?

CHASUBLE: Perhaps she followed us to the schools.

(*Enter* JACK *slowly from the back of the garden. He is dressed in the deepest mourning, with crepe hat-band and black gloves.*)

MISS PRISM: Mr. Worthing!

CHASUBLE: Mr. Worthing? This is indeed a surprise. We did not look for you till Monday afternoon.

JACK: (*Shakes* MISS PRISM*'s hand in a tragic manner.*) I have returned sooner than I expected. Dr. Chasuble, I hope you are well?

CHASUBLE: Dear Mr. Worthing, I trust this garb of woe does not betoken some terrible calamity?

JACK: My brother.

MISS PRISM: More shameful debts and extravagance?

CHASUBLE: Still leading his life of pleasure?

JACK: (*Shaking his head.*) Dead!

CHASUBLE: Your brother Ernest dead?

JACK: Quite dead.

MISS PRISM: What a lesson for him! I trust he will profit by it.

CHASUBLE: Mr. Worthing, I offer you my sincere condolence. You have at least the consolation of knowing that you were always the most generous and forgiving of brothers.

JACK: Poor Ernest! He had many faults, but it is a sad, sad blow.

CHASUBLE: Very sad indeed. Were you with him at the end?

JACK: No. He died abroad; in Paris, in fact. I had a telegram last night from the manager of the Grand Hotel.

CHASUBLE: Was the cause of death mentioned?

JACK: A severe chill, it seems.

MISS PRISM: As a man sows, so shall he reap.

CHASUBLE: (*Raising his hand.*) Charity, dear Miss Prism, charity! None of us are perfect. I myself am peculiarly susceptible to draughts. Will the interment take place here?

JACK: No. He seems to have expressed a desire to be buried in Paris.

CHASUBLE: In Paris! (*Shakes his head.*) I fear that hardly points to any very serious state of mind at the last. You would no doubt wish me to make some slight allusion to this tragic domestic affliction next Sunday. (JACK *presses his hand convulsively.*) My sermon on the meaning of the manna in the wilderness can be adapted to almost any occasion, joyful, or, as in the present case, distressing. (*All sigh.*) I have preached it at harvest celebrations, christenings, confirmations, on days of humiliation and festal days. The last time I delivered it was in the Cathedral, as a charity sermon on behalf of the Society for the Prevention of Discontent among the Upper Orders. The Bishop, who was present, was much struck by some of the analogies I drew.

JACK: Ah! that reminds me, you mentioned christenings I think, Dr. Chasuble? I suppose you know how to christen all right? (DR. CHASUBLE *looks astounded.*) I mean, of course, you are continually christening, aren't you?

MISS PRISM: It is, I regret to say, one of the Rector's most constant duties in this parish. I have often spoken to the poorer classes on the subject. But they don't seem to know what thrift is.

CHASUBLE: But is there any particular infant in whom you are interested, Mr. Worthing? Your brother was, I believe, unmarried, was he not?

JACK: Oh yes.

MISS PRISM: (*Bitterly.*) People who live entirely for pleasure usually are.

JACK: But it is not for any child, dear Doctor. I am very fond of children. No! the fact is, I would like to be christened myself, this afternoon, if you have nothing better to do.

CHASUBLE: But surely, Mr. Worthing, you have been christened already?

JACK: I don't remember anything about it.

CHASUBLE: But have you any grave doubts on the subject?

JACK: I certainly intend to have. Of course I don't know if the thing would bother you in any way, or if you think I am a little too old now.

CHASUBLE: Not at all. The sprinkling, and, indeed, the immersion of adults is a perfectly canonical practice.

JACK: Immersion!

CHASUBLE: You need have no apprehensions. Sprinkling is all that is necessary, or indeed I think advisable. Our weather is so changeable. At what hour would you wish the ceremony performed?

JACK: Oh, I might trot round about five if that would suit you.

CHASUBLE: Perfectly, perfectly! In fact I have two similar ceremonies to perform at that time. A case of twins that occurred recently in one of the outlying cottages on your own estate. Poor Jenkins the carter, a most hard-working man.

JACK: Oh! I don't see much fun in being christened along with other babies. It would be childish. Would half-past five do?

CHASUBLE: Admirably! Admirably! (*Takes out watch.*) And now, dear Mr. Worthing, I will not intrude any longer into a house of sorrow. I would merely beg you not to be too much bowed down by grief. What seem to us bitter trials are often blessings in disguise.

MISS PRISM: This seems to me a blessing of an extremely obvious kind.

(*Enter* CECILY *from the house.*)

CECILY: Uncle Jack! Oh, I am pleased to see you back. But what horrid clothes you have got on. Do go and change them.

MISS PRISM: Cecily!

CHASUBLE: My child! my child. (CECILY *goes toward* JACK; *he kisses her brow in a melancholy manner.*)

CECILY: What is the matter, Uncle Jack? Do look happy! You look as if you had toothache, and I have got such a surprise for you. Who do you think is in the diningroom? Your brother!

JACK: Who?

CECILY: Your brother Ernest. He arrived about half an hour ago.

JACK: What nonsense! I haven't got a brother.

CECILY: Oh, don't say that. However badly he may have behaved to you in the past he is still your brother. You couldn't be so heartless as to disown him. I'll tell him to come out. And you will shake hands with him, won't you, Uncle Jack? (*Runs back into the house.*)

CHASUBLE: These are very joyful tidings.

MISS PRISM: After we had all been resigned to his loss, his sudden return seems to me peculiarly distressing.

JACK: My brother is in the dining-room? I don't know what it all means. I think it is perfectly absurd.

(*Enter* ALGERNON *and* CECILY *hand in hand. They come slowly up to* JACK)

JACK: Good heavens! (*Motions* ALGERNON *away.*)

ALGERNON: Brother John, I have come down from town to tell you that I am very sorry for all the trouble I have given you, and that I intend to lead a better life in the future. (JACK *glares at him and does not take his hand.*)

CECILY: Uncle Jack, you are not going to refuse your own brother's hand?

JACK: Nothing will induce me to take his hand. I think his coming down here disgraceful. He knows perfectly well why.

CECILY: Uncle Jack, do be nice. There is some good in everyone. Ernest has just been telling me about his poor invalid friend Mr. Bunbury whom he goes to visit so often. And surely there must be much good in one who is kind to an invalid, and leaves the pleasures of London to sit by a bed of pain.

JACK: Oh! he has been talking about Bunbury, has he?

CECILY: Yes, he has told me all about poor Mr. Bunbury, and his terrible state of health.

JACK: Bunbury! Well, I won't have him talk to you about Bunbury or about anything else. It is enough to drive one perfectly frantic.

ALGERNON: Of course I admit that the faults were all on my side. But I must say that I think that Brother John's coldness to me is peculiarly painful. I expected a more enthusiastic welcome especially considering it is the first time I have come here.

CECILY: Uncle Jack, if you don't shake hands with Ernest, I will never forgive you.

JACK: Never forgive me?

CECILY: Never, never, never!

JACK: Well, this is the last time I shall ever do it. (*Shakes hands with* ALGERNON *and glares.*)

CHASUBLE: It's pleasant, is it not, to see so perfect a reconciliation? I think we might leave the two brothers together.

MISS PRISM: Cecily, you will come with us.

CECILY: Certainly, Miss Prism. My little task of reconciliation is over.

CHASUBLE: You have done a beautiful action today, dear child.

MISS PRISM: We must not be premature in our judgments.

CECILY: I feel very happy. (*They all go off except* JACK *and* ALGERNON.)

JACK: You young scoundrel, Algy, you must get out of this place as soon as possible. I don't allow any Bunburying here.

(*Enter* MERRIMAN.)

MERRIMAN: I have put Mr. Ernest's things in the room next to yours, sir. I suppose that is all right?

JACK: What?

MERRIMAN: Mr. Ernest's luggage, sir. I have unpacked it and put it in the room next to your own.

JACK: His luggage?

MERRIMAN: Yes, sir. Three portmanteaus, a dressing-case, two hatboxes, and a large luncheon-basket.

ALGERNON: I am afraid I can't stay more than a week this time.

JACK: Merriman, order the dog-cart at once. Mr. Ernest has been suddenly called back to town.

MERRIMAN: Yes, sir. (*Goes back into the house.*)

ALGERNON: What a fearful liar you are, Jack. I have not been called back to town at all.

JACK: Yes, you have.

ALGERNON: I haven't heard any one call me.

JACK: Your duty as a gentleman calls you back.

ALGERNON: My duty as a gentleman has never interfered with my pleasures in the smallest degree.

JACK: I can quite understand that.

ALGERNON: Well, Cecily is a darling.

JACK: You are not to talk of Miss Cardew like that. I don't like it.

ALGERNON: Well, I don't like your clothes. You look perfectly ridiculous in them. Why on earth don't you go up and change? It is perfectly childish to be in deep mourning for a man who is actually staying for a whole week with you in your house as a guest. I call it grotesque.

JACK: You are certainly not staying with me for a whole week as a guest or anything else. You have got to leave . . . by the four-five train.

ALGERNON: I certainly won't leave you so long as you are in mourning. It would be most unfriendly. If I were in mourning you would stay with me, I suppose. I should think it very unkind if you didn't.

JACK: Well, will you go if I change my clothes?

ALGERNON: Yes, if you are not too long. I never saw anybody take so long to dress, and with such little result.

JACK: Well, at any rate, that is better than being always over-dressed as you are.

ALGERNON: If I am occasionally a little over-dressed, I make up for it by being always immensely over-educated.

JACK: Your vanity is ridiculous, your conduct an outrage, and your presence in my garden utterly absurd. However, you have got to catch the four-five, and I hope you will have a pleasant journey back to town. This Bunburying, as you call it, has not been a great success for you.

(*Goes into the house.*)

ALGERNON: I think it has been a great success. I'm in love with Cecily, and that is everything.

(*Enter* CECILY *at the back of the garden. She picks up the can and begins to water the flowers.*)

But I must see her before I go, and make arrangements for another Bunbury. Ah, there she is.

CECILY: Oh, I merely came back to water the roses. I thought you were with Uncle Jack.

ALGERNON: He's gone to order the dog-cart for me.

CECILY: Oh, is he going to take you for a nice drive?

ALGERNON: He's going to send me away.

CECILY: Then have we got to part?

ALGERNON: I am afraid so. It's a very painful parting.

CECILY: It is always painful to part from people whom one has known for a very brief space of time. The absence of old friends one can endure with equanimity. But even a momentary separation from any one to whom one has just been introduced is almost unbearable.

ALGERNON: Thank you.

(*Enter* MERRIMAN.)

MERRIMAN: The dog-cart is at the door, sir.

(ALGERNON *looks appealingly at* CECILY.)

CECILY: It can wait, Merriman . . . for . . . five minutes.

MERRIMAN: Yes, Miss.

(*Exit* MERRIMAN.)

ALGERNON: I hope, Cecily, I shall not offend you if I state quite frankly and openly that you seem to me to be in every way the visible personification of absolute perfection.

CECILY: I think your frankness does you great credit, Ernest. If you will allow me, I will copy your remarks into my diary. (*Goes over to table and begins writing in diary.*)

ALGERNON: Do you really keep a diary? I'd give anything to look at it. May I?

CECILY: Oh no. (*Puts her hand over it.*) You see, it is simply a very young girl's record of her own thoughts and impressions, and consequently meant for publication. When it appears in volume form I hope you will order a copy. But pray, Ernest, don't stop. I delight in taking down from dictation. I have reached "absolute perfection." You can go on. I am quite ready for more.

ALGERNON: (*Somewhat taken aback.*) Ahem! Ahem!

CECILY: Oh, don't cough, Ernest. When one is dictating one should speak fluently and not cough. Besides, I don't know how to spell a cough. (*Writes as* ALGERNON *speaks.*)

ALGERNON: (*Speaking very rapidly.*) Cecily, ever since I first looked upon your wonderful and incomparable beauty, I have dared to love you wildly, passionately, devotedly, hopelessly.

CECILY: I don't think that you should tell me that you love me wildly, passionately, devotedly, hopelessly. Hopelessly doesn't seem to make much sense, does it?

ALGERNON: Cecily.

(*Enter* MERRIMAN.)

MERRIMAN: The dog-cart is waiting, sir.

ALGERNON: Tell it to come round next week, at the same hour.

MERRIMAN: (*Looks at* CECILY, *who makes no sign.*) Yes, sir.

(MERRIMAN *retires.*)

CECILY: Uncle Jack would be very much annoyed if he knew you were staying on till next week, at the same hour.

ALGERNON: Oh, I don't care about Jack. I don't care for anybody in the whole world but you. I love you, Cecily. You will marry me, won't you?

CECILY: You silly boy! Of course. Why, we have been engaged for the last three months.

ALGERNON: For the last three months?

CECILY: Yes, it will be exactly three months on Thursday.

ALGERNON: But how did we become engaged?

CECILY: Well, ever since dear Uncle Jack first confessed to us that he had a younger brother who was very wicked and bad, you of course have formed the chief topic of conversation between myself and Miss Prism. And of course a man who is much talked about is always very attractive. One feels there must be something in him, after all. I daresay it was foolish of me, but I fell in love with you, Ernest.

ALGERNON: Darling. And when was the engagement actually settled?

CECILY: On the 14th of February last. Worn out by your entire ignorance of my existence, I determined to end the matter one way or the other, and after a long struggle with myself I accepted you under this dear old tree here. The next day I bought this little ring in your name, and this is the little bangle with the true lover's knot I promised you always to wear.

ALGERNON: Did I give you this? It's very pretty, isn't it?

CECILY: Yes, you've wonderfully good taste, Ernest. It's the excuse I've always given for your leading such a bad life. And this is the box in which I keep all your dear letters. (*Kneels at table, opens box, and produces letters tied up with blue ribbon.*)

ALGERNON: My letters! But, my own sweet Cecily, I have never written you any letters.

CECILY: You need hardly remind me of that, Ernest. I remember only too well that I was forced to write your letters for you. I wrote always three times a week, and sometimes oftener.

ALGERNON: Oh, do let me read them, Cecily?

CECILY: Oh, I couldn't possibly. They would make you far too conceited. (*Replaces box.*) The three you wrote me after I had broken off the engagement are so beautiful, and so badly spelled, that even now I can hardly read them without crying a little.

ALGERNON: But was our engagement ever broken off?

CECILY: Of course it was. On the 22nd of last March. You can see the entry if you like. (*Shows diary.*) 'Today I broke off my engagement with Ernest. I feel it is better to do so. The weather still continues charming.'

ALGERNON: But why on earth did you break it off? What had I done? I had done nothing at all. Cecily, I am very much hurt indeed to hear you broke it off. Particularly when the weather was so charming.

CECILY: It would hardly have been a really serious engagement if it hadn't been broken off at least once. But I forgave you before the week was out.

ALGERNON: (*Crossing to her, and kneeling.*) What a perfect angel you are, Cecily.

CECILY: You dear romantic boy. (*He kisses her, she puts her fingers through his hair.*) I hope your hair curls naturally, does it?

ALGERNON: Yes, darling, with a little help from others.

CECILY: I am so glad.

ALGERNON: You'll never break off our engagement again, Cecily?

CECILY: I don't think I could break it off now that I have actually met you. Besides, of course, there is the question of your name.

ALGERNON: Yes, of course. (*Nervously.*)

CECILY: You must not laugh at me, darling, but it had always been a girlish dream of mine to love some one whose name was Ernest. (ALGERNON *rises,* CECILY *also.*) There is something in that name that seems to inspire absolute confidence. I pity any poor married woman whose husband is not called Ernest.

ALGERNON: But, my dear child, do you mean to say you could not love me if I had some other name?

CECILY: But what name?

ALGERNON: Oh, any name you like—Algernon—for instance . . .

CECILY: But I don't like the name of Algernon.

ALGERNON: Well, my own dear, sweet, loving little darling, I really can't see why you should object to the name of Algernon. It is not at all a bad name. In fact, it is rather an aristocratic name. Half of the chaps who get into the Bankruptcy Court are called Algernon. But seriously, Cecily . . . (*Moving to her.*) if my name was Algy, couldn't you love me?

CECILY: (*Rising.*) I might respect you, Ernest, I might admire your character, but I fear that I should not be able to give you my undivided attention.

ALGERNON: Ahem! Cecily! (*Picking up hat.*) Your Rector here is, I suppose, thoroughly experienced in the practice of all the rites and ceremonials of the Church?

CECILY: Oh, yes. Dr. Chasuble is a most learned man. He has never written a single book, so you can imagine how much he knows.

ALGERNON: I must see him at once on a most important christening—I mean on most important business.

CECILY: Oh!

ALGERNON: I shan't be away more than half an hour.

CECILY: Considering that we have been engaged since February the 14th, and that I only met you to-day for the first time, I think it is rather hard that you should leave me for so long a period as half an hour. Couldn't you make it twenty minutes?

ALGERNON: I'll be back in no time. (*Kisses her and rushes down the garden.*)

CECILY: What an impetuous boy he is! I like his hair so much. I must enter his proposal in my diary.

(*Enter* MERRIMAN.)

MERRIMAN: A Miss Fairfax has just called to see Mr. Worthing. On very important business, Miss Fairfax states.

CECILY: Isn't Mr. Worthing in his library?

MERRIMAN: Mr. Worthing went over in the direction of the Rectory some time ago.

CECILY: Pray ask the lady to come out here; Mr. Worthing is sure to be back soon. And you can bring tea.

MERRIMAN: Yes, Miss.

(*Goes out.*)

CECILY: Miss Fairfax! I suppose one of the many good elderly women who are associated with Uncle Jack in some of his philanthropic work in London. I don't quite like women who are interested in philanthropic work. I think it is so forward of them.

(*Enter* MERRIMAN.)

MERRIMAN: Miss Fairfax.

(*Enter* GWENDOLEN. *Exit* MERRIMAN.)

CECILY: (*Advancing to meet her.*) Pray let me introduce myself to you. My name is Cecily Cardew.

GWENDOLEN: Cecily Cardew? (*Moving to her and shaking hands.*) What a very sweet name! Something tells me that we are going to be great friends. I like you already more than I can say. My first impressions of people are never wrong.

CECILY: How nice of you to like me so much after we have known each other such a comparatively short time. Pray sit down.

GWENDOLEN: (*Still standing up.*) I may call you Cecily, may I not?

CECILY: With pleasure!

GWENDOLEN: And you will always call me Gwendolen, won't you?

CECILY: If you wish.

GWENDOLEN: Then that is all quite settled, is it not?

CECILY: I hope so. (*A pause. They both sit down together.*)

GWENDOLEN: Perhaps this might be a favourable opportunity for my mentioning who I am. My father is Lord Bracknell. You have never heard of papa, I suppose?

CECILY: I don't think so.

GWENDOLEN: Outside the family circle, papa, I am glad to say, is entirely unknown. I think that is quite as it should be. The home seems to me to be the proper sphere for the man. And certainly once a man begins to neglect his domestic duties he becomes painfully effeminate, does he not? And I don't like that. It makes men so very attractive. Cecily, mamma, whose views on education are remarkably strict, has brought me up to be extremely short-sighted; it is part of her system; so do you mind my looking at you through my glasses?

CECILY: Oh! not at all, Gwendolen. I am very fond of being looked at.

GWENDOLEN: (*After examining* CECILY *carefully through a lorgnette.*) You are here on a short visit, I suppose.

CECILY: Oh no! I live here.

GWENDOLEN: (*Severely.*) Really? Your mother, no doubt, or some female relative of advanced years, resides here also?

CECILY: Oh no! I have no mother, nor, in fact, any relations.

GWENDOLEN: Indeed?

CECILY: My dear guardian, with the assistance of Miss Prism, has the arduous task of looking after me.

GWENDOLEN: Your guardian?

CECILY: Yes, I am Mr. Worthing's ward.

GWENDOLEN: Oh! It is strange he never mentioned to me that he had a ward. How secretive of him! He grows more interesting hourly. I am not sure, however, that the news inspires me with feelings of unmixed delight. (*Rising and going to her.*) I am very fond of you, Cecily; I have liked you ever since I met you! But I am bound to state that now that I know that you are Mr. Worthing's ward, I cannot help expressing a wish you were—well, just a little older than you seem to be—and not quite so very alluring in appearance. In fact, if I may speak candidly—

CECILY: Pray do! I think that whenever one has anything unpleasant to say, one should always be quite candid.

GWENDOLEN: Well, to speak with perfect candour, Cecily, I wish that you were fully forty-two, and more than usually plain for your age. Ernest has a strong upright nature. He is the very soul of truth and honor. Disloyalty would be as impossible to him as deception. But even men of the noblest possible moral character are extremely susceptible to the influence of the physical charms of others. Modern, no less than Ancient History, supplies us with many most painful examples of what I refer to. If it were not so, indeed, History would be quite unreadable.

CECILY: I beg your pardon, Gwendolen, did you say Ernest?

GWENDOLEN: Yes.

CECILY: Oh, but it is not Mr. Ernest Worthing who is my guardian. It is his brother—his elder brother.

GWENDOLEN: (*Sitting down again.*) Ernest never mentioned to me that he had a brother.

CECILY: Sorry to say they have not been on good terms for a long time.

GWENDOLEN: Ah! that accounts for it. And now that I think of it I have never heard any man mention his brother. The subject seems distasteful to most men. Cecily, you have lifted a load from my mind. I was growing almost anxious. It would have been terrible if any cloud had come across a friendship like ours, would it not? Of course you are quite, quite sure that it is not Mr. Ernest Worthing who is your guardian?

CECILY: Quite sure. (*A pause.*) In fact, I am going to be his.

GWENDOLEN: (*Inquiringly.*) I beg your pardon?

CECILY: (*Rather shy and confidingly.*) Dearest Gwendolen, there is no reason why I should make a secret of it to you. Our little county newspaper is sure to chronicle the fact next week. Mr. Ernest Worthing and I are engaged to be married.

GWENDOLEN: (*Quite politely, rising.*) My darling Cecily, I think there must be some slight error. Mr. Ernest Worthing is engaged to me. The announcement will appear in the *Morning Post* on Saturday at the latest.

CECILY: (*Very politely, rising.*) I am afraid you must be under some misconception. Ernest proposed to me exactly ten minutes ago. (*Shows diary.*)

GWENDOLEN: (*Examines through her lorgnette carefully.*) It is very curious, for he asked me to be his wife yesterday afternoon at 5:30. If you would care to verify the incident, pray do so. (*Produces diary of her own.*) I never travel without my diary. One should always have something sensational to read in the train. I am so sorry, dear Cecily, if it is any disappointment to you, but I am afraid I have the prior claim.

CECILY: It would distress me more than I can tell you, dear Gwendolen, if it caused you any mental or physical anguish, but I feel bound to point out that since Ernest proposed to you he clearly has changed his mind.

GWENDOLEN: (*Meditatively.*) If the poor fellow has been entrapped into any foolish promise, I shall consider it my duty to rescue him at once, and with a firm hand.

CECILY: (*Thoughtfully and sadly.*) Whatever unfortunate entanglement my dear boy may have got into, I will never reproach him with it after we are married.

GWENDOLEN: Do you allude to me, Miss Cardew, as an entanglement? You are presumptuous. On an occasion of this kind it becomes more than a moral duty to speak one's mind. It becomes a pleasure.

CECILY: Do you suggest, Miss Fairfax, that I entrapped Ernest into an engagement? How dare you? This is no time for wearing the shallow mask of manners. When I see a spade I call it a spade.

GWENDOLEN: (*Satirically.*) I am glad to say that I have never seen a spade. It is obvious that our social spheres have been widely different.

(*Enter* MERRIMAN, *followed by the footman. He carries a salver, table cloth, and plate stand.* CECILY *is about to retort. The presence of the servants exercises a restraining influence under which both girls chafe.*)

MERRIMAN: Shall I lay tea here as usual, Miss?

CECILY: (*Sternly, in a calm voice.*) Yes, as usual. (MERRIMAN *begins to clear table and lay cloth. A long pause.* CECILY *and* GWENDOLEN *glare at each other.*)

GWENDOLEN: Are there many interesting walks in the vicinity, Miss Cardew?

CECILY: Oh! yes! a great many. From the top of one of the hills quite close one can see five counties.

GWENDOLEN: Five counties! I don't think I should like that; I hate crowds.

CECILY: (*Sweetly.*) I suppose that is why you live in town? (GWENDOLEN *bites her lip, and beats her foot nervously with her parasol.*)

GWENDOLEN: (*Looking around.*) Quite a well-kept garden this is, Miss Cardew.

CECILY: So glad you like it, Miss Fairfax.

GWENDOLEN: I had no idea there were any flowers in the country.

CECILY: Oh, flowers are as common here, Miss Fairfax, as people are in London.

GWENDOLEN: Personally I cannot understand how anybody manages to exist in the country, if anybody who is anybody does. The country always bores me to death.

CECILY: Ah! This is what the newspapers call agricultural depression, is it not? I believe the aristocracy are suffering very much from it just at present. It is almost an epidemic amongst them, I have been told. May I offer you some tea, Miss Fairfax?

GWENDOLEN: (*With elaborate politeness.*) Thank you. (*Aside.*) Detestable girl! But I require tea!

CECILY: (*Sweetly.*) Sugar?

GWENDOLEN: (*Superciliously.*) No, thank you. Sugar is not fashionable any more. (CECILY *looks angrily at her, takes up the tongs and puts four lumps of sugar into the cup.*)

CECILY: (*Severely.*) Cake or bread and butter?

GWENDOLEN: (*In a bored manner.*) Bread and butter, please. Cake is rarely seen at the best houses nowadays.

CECILY: (*Cuts a very large slice of cake and puts it on the tray.*) Hand that to Miss Fairfax.

(MERRIMAN *does so, and goes out with footman.* GWENDOLEN *drinks the tea and makes a grimace. Puts down cup at once, reaches out her hand to the bread and butter, looks at it, and finds it is cake. Rises in indignation.*)

GWENDOLEN: You have filled my tea with lumps of sugar, and though I asked most distinctly for bread and butter, you have given me cake. I am known for the gentleness of my disposition, and the extraordinary sweetness of my nature, but I warn you, Miss Cardew, you may go too far.

CECILY: (*Rising.*) To save my poor, innocent, trusting boy from the machinations of any other girl there are no lengths to which I would not go.

GWENDOLEN: From the moment I saw you I distrusted you. I felt that you were false and deceitful. I am never deceived in such matters. My first impressions of people are invariably right.

CECILY: It seems to me, Miss Fairfax, that I am trespassing on your valuable time. No doubt you have many other calls of a similar character to make in the neighborhood.

(*Enter* JACK.)

GWENDOLEN: (*Catching sight of him.*) Ernest! My own Ernest!

JACK: Gwendolen! Darling! (*Offers to kiss her.*)

GWENDOLEN: (*Drawing back.*) A moment! May I ask if you are engaged to be married to this young lady? (*Points to* CECILY.)

JACK: (*Laughing.*) To dear little Cecily! Of course not! What could have put such an idea into your pretty little head?

GWENDOLEN: Thank you. You may! (*Offers her cheek.*)

CECILY: (*Very sweetly.*) I knew there must be some misunderstanding, Miss Fairfax. The gentleman whose arm is at present round your waist is my guardian, Mr. John Worthing.

GWENDOLEN: I beg your pardon?

CECILY: This is Uncle Jack.

GWENDOLEN: (*Receding.*) Jack! Oh!

(*Enter* ALGERNON.)

CECILY: Here is Ernest.

ALGERNON: (*Goes straight over to* CECILY *without noticing anyone else.*) My own love! (*Offers to kiss her.*)

CECILY: (*Drawing back.*) A moment, Ernest! May I ask you—are you engaged to be married to this young lady?

ALGERNON: (*Looking round.*) To what young lady? Good heavens! Gwendolen!

CECILY: Yes: to good heavens,Gwendolen, I mean to Gwendolen.

ALGERNON: (*Laughing.*) Of course not! What could have put such an idea into your pretty little head?

CECILY: Thank you. (*Presenting her cheek to be kissed.*) You may. (ALGERNON *kisses her.*)

GWENDOLEN: I felt there was some slight error, Miss Cardew. The gentleman who is now embracing you is my cousin, Mr. Algernon Moncrieff.

CECILY: (*Breaking away from* ALGERNON.) Algernon Moncrieff! Oh! (*The two girls move toward each other and put their arms round each other's waists as if for protection.*)

CECILY: Are you called Algernon?

ALGERNON: I cannot deny it.

CECILY: Oh!

GWENDOLEN: Is your name really John?

JACK: (*Standing rather proudly.*) I could deny it if I liked. I could deny anything if I liked. But my name certainly is John. It has been John for years.

CECILY: (*To* GWENDOLEN.) A gross deception has been practiced on both of us.

GWENDOLEN: My poor wounded Cecily!

CECILY: My sweet wronged Gwendolen!

GWENDOLEN: (*Slowly and seriously.*) You will call me sister, will you not? (*They embrace.* JACK *and* ALGERNON *groan and walk up and down.*)

CECILY: (*Rather brightly.*) There is just one question I would like to be allowed to ask my guardian.

GWENDOLEN: An admirable idea! Mr. Worthing, there is just one question I would like to be permitted to put to you. Where is your brother Ernest? We are both engaged to be married to your brother Ernest, so it is a matter of some importance to us to know where your brother Ernest is at present.

JACK: (*Slowly and hesitatingly.*) Gwendolen—Cecily—it is very painful for me to be forced to speak the truth. It is the first time in my life that I have ever been reduced to such a painful position, and I am really quite inexperienced in doing anything of the kind. However, I will tell you quite frankly that I have no brother Ernest. I have no brother at all. I never had a brother in my life, and I certainly have not the smallest intention of ever having one in the future.

CECILY: (*Surprised.*) No brother at all?

JACK: (*Cheerily.*) None!

GWENDOLEN: (*Severely.*) Had you never a brother of any kind?

JACK: (*Pleasantly.*) Never. Not even of any kind.

GWENDOLEN: I am afraid it is quite clear, Cecily, that neither of us is engaged to be married to anyone.

CECILY: It is not a very pleasant position for a young girl suddenly to find herself in. Is it?

GWENDOLEN: Let us go into the house. They will hardly venture to come after us there.

CECILY: No, men are so cowardly, aren't they?

(*They retire into the house with scornful looks.*)

JACK: This ghastly state of things is what you call Bunburying I suppose?

ALGERNON: Yes, and a perfectly wonderful Bunbury it is. The most wonderful Bunbury I have ever had in my life.

JACK: Well, you've no right whatsoever to Bunbury here.

ALGERNON: That is absurd. One has a right to Bunbury anywhere one chooses. Every serious Bunburyist knows that.

JACK: Serious Bunburyist? Good heavens!

ALGERNON: Well, one must be serious about something, if one wants to have any amusement in life. I happen to be serious about Bunburying. What on earth you are serious about I haven't got the remotest idea. About everything, I should fancy. You have such an absolutely trivial nature.

JACK: Well, the only small satisfaction I have in the whole of this wretched business is that your friend Bunbury is quite exploded. You won't be able to run down to the country quite so often as you used to do, dear Algy. And a very good thing too.

ALGERNON: Your brother is a little off color, isn't he, dear Jack? You won't be able to disappear to London quite so frequently as your wicked custom was. And not a bad thing either.

JACK: As for your conduct toward Miss Cardew, I must say that your taking in a sweet, simple, innocent girl like that is quite inexcusable. To say nothing of the fact that she is my ward.

ALGERNON: I can see no possible defence at all for your deceiving a brilliant, clever, thoroughly experienced young lady like Miss Fairfax. To say nothing of the fact that she is my cousin.

JACK: I wanted to be engaged to Gwendolen, that is all, I love her.

ALGERNON: Well, I simply wanted to be engaged to Cecily. I adore her.

JACK: There is certainly no chance of your marrying Miss Cardew.

ALGERNON: I don't think there is much likelihood, Jack, of you and Miss Fairfax being united.

JACK: Well, that is no business of yours.

ALGERNON: If it was my business, I wouldn't talk about it. (*Begins to eat muffins.*) It is very vulgar to talk about one's business. Only people like stockbrokers do that, and then merely at dinner parties.

JACK: How you can sit there, calmly eating muffins when we are in this horrible trouble, I can't make out. You seem to me to be perfectly heartless.

ALGERNON: Well, I can't eat muffins in an agitated manner. The butter would probably get on my cuffs. One should always eat muffins quite calmly. It is the only way to eat them.

JACK: I say it's perfectly heartless your eating muffins at all, under the circumstances.

ALGERNON: When I am in trouble, eating is the only thing that consoles me. Indeed, when I am in really great trouble, as any one who knows me intimately will tell you, I refuse everything except food and drink. At the present moment I am eating muffins because I am unhappy. Besides, I am particularly fond of muffins. (*Rising.*)

JACK: (*Rising.*) Well, there is no reason why you should eat them all in that greedy way. (*Takes muffins from* ALGERNON.)

ALGERNON: (*Offering tea-cake.*) I wish you would have tea-cake instead. I don't like tea-cake.

JACK: Good heavens! I suppose a man may eat his own muffins in his own garden.

ALGERNON: But you have just said it was perfectly heartless to eat muffins.

JACK: I said it was perfectly heartless of you, under the circumstances. That is a very different thing.

ALGERNON: That may be. But the muffins are the same. (*He seizes the muffin-dish from* JACK.)

JACK: Algy, I wish to goodness you would go.

ALGERNON: You can't possibly ask me to go without having some dinner. It's absurd. I never go without my dinner. No one ever does, except vegetarians and people like that. Besides I have just made arrangements with Dr. Chasuble to be christened at a quarter to six under the name of Ernest.

JACK: My dear fellow, the sooner you give up that nonsense the better. I made arrangements this morning with Dr. Chasuble to be christened myself at 5:30, and I naturally will take the name of Ernest. Gwendolen would wish it. We can't both be christened Ernest. It's absurd. Besides, I have a perfect right to be christened if I like. There is no evidence at all that I have ever been christened by anybody. I should think it extremely probable I never was, and so does Dr. Chasuble. It is entirely different in your case. You have been christened already.

ALGERNON: Yes, but I have not been christened for years.

JACK: Yes, but you have been christened. That is the important thing.

ALGERNON: Quite so. So I know my constitution can stand it. If you are not quite sure about your ever having been christened, I must say I think it rather dangerous your venturing on it now. It might make you very unwell. You can hardly have forgotten that someone very closely connected with you was very nearly carried off this week in Paris by a severe chill.

JACK: Yes, but you said yourself that a severe chill was not hereditary.

ALGERNON: It usen't to be, I know—but I daresay it is now. Science is always making wonderful improvements in things.

JACK: (*Picking up the muffin-dish.*) Oh, that is nonsense; you are always talking nonsense.

ALGERNON: Jack, you are at the muffins again! I wish you wouldn't. There are only two left. (*Takes them.*) I told you I was particularly fond of muffins.

JACK: But I hate tea-cake.

ALGERNON: Why on earth then do you allow tea-cake to be served up for your guests? What ideas you have of hospitality!

JACK: Algernon! I have already told you to go. I don't want you here. Why don't you go!

ALGERNON: I haven't quite finished my tea yet! and there is still one muffin left. (JACK *groans, and sinks into a chair.* ALGERNON *continues eating.*)

Act Drop

THIRD ACT

Scene: *Drawing-room at the Manor House*

(GWENDOLEN *and* CECILY *are at the window, looking out into the garden.*)

GWENDOLEN: The fact that they did not follow us at once into the house, as anyone else would have done, seems to me to show that they have some sense of shame left.

CECILY: They have been eating muffins. That looks like repentance.

GWENDOLEN: (*After a pause.*) They don't seem to notice us at all. Couldn't you cough?

CECILY: But I haven't got a cough.

GWENDOLEN: They're looking at us. What effrontery!

CECILY: They're approaching. That's very forward of them.

GWENDOLEN: Let us preserve a dignified silence.

CECILY: Certainly. It's the only thing to do now.

(*Enter* JACK *followed by* ALGERNON. *They whistle some dreadful popular air from a British Opera.*)

GWENDOLEN: This dignified silence seems to produce an unpleasant effect.

CECILY: A most distasteful one.

GWENDOLEN: But we will not be the first to speak.

CECILY: Certainly not.

GWENDOLEN: Mr. Worthing, I have something very particular to ask you. Much depends on your reply.

CECILY: Gwendolen, your common sense is invaluable. Mr. Moncrieff, kindly answer me the following question. Why did you pretend to be my guardian's brother?

ALGERNON: In order that I might have an opportunity of meeting you.

CECILY: (*To* GWENDOLEN.) That certainly seems a satisfactory explanation, does it not?

GWENDOLEN: Yes, dear, if you can believe him.

CECILY: I don't. But that does not affect the wonderful beauty of his answer.

GWENDOLEN: True. In matters of grave importance, style, not sincerity, is the vital thing. Mr. Worthing, what explanation can you offer to me for pretending to have a brother? Was it in order that you might have an opportunity of coming up to town to see me as often as possible?

JACK: Can you doubt it, Miss Fairfax?

GWENDOLEN: I have the gravest doubts upon the subject. But I intend to crush them. This is not the moment for German scepticism. (*Moving to* CECILY.) Their explanations appear to be quite satisfactory, especially Mr. Worthing's. That seems to me to have the stamp of truth upon it.

CECILY: I am more than content with what Mr. Moncrieff said. His voice alone inspires one with absolute credulity.

GWENDOLEN: Then you think we should forgive them?

CECILY: Yes. I mean no.

GWENDOLEN: True! I had forgotten. There are principles at stake that one cannot surrender. Which of us should tell them? The task is not a pleasant one.

CECILY: Could we not both speak at the same time?

GWENDOLEN: An excellent idea! I nearly always speak at the same time as other people. Will you take the time from me?

CECILY: Certainly. (GWENDOLEN *beats time with uplifted finger.*)

GWENDOLEN and CECILY: (*Speaking together.*) Your Christian names are still an insuperable barrier. That is all!

JACK and ALGERNON: (*Speaking together.*) Our Christian names! Is that all? But we are going to be christened this afternoon.

GWENDOLEN: (*To* JACK.) For my sake you are prepared to do this terrible thing?

JACK: I am.

CECILY: (*To* ALGERNON.) To please me you are ready to face this fearful ordeal?

ALGERNON: I am!

GWENDOLEN: How absurd to talk of the equality of the sexes! Where questions of self-sacrifice are concerned, men are infinitely beyond us.

JACK: We are. (*Clasps hands with* ALGERNON.)

CECILY: They have moments of physical courage of which we women know absolutely nothing.

GWENDOLEN: (*To* JACK.) Darling!

ALGERNON: (*To* CECILY.) Darling! (*They fall into each other's arms.*)

(*Enter* MERRIMAN. *When he enters he coughs loudly, seeing the situation.*)

MERRIMAN: Ahem! Ahem! Lady Bracknell.

JACK: Good heavens!

(*Enter* LADY BRACKNELL. *The couples separate in alarm. Exit* MERRIMAN.)

LADY BRACKNELL: Gwendolen! What does this mean?

GWENDOLEN: Merely that I am engaged to be married to Mr. Worthing, mamma.

LADY BRACKNELL: Come here. Sit down. Sit down immediately. Hesitation of any kind is a sign of mental decay in the young, of physical weakness in the old. (*Turns to* JACK.) Apprised, sir, of my daughter's sudden flight by her trusty maid, whose confidence I purchased by means of a small coin, I followed her at once by a luggage train. Her unhappy father is, I am glad to say, under the impression that she is attending a more than usually lengthy lecture by the University Extension Scheme on the Influence of a Permanent Income on Thought. I do not propose to undeceive him. Indeed I have never undeceived him on any question. I would consider it wrong. But of course, you will clearly understand that all communication between yourself and my daughter must cease immediately from this moment. On this point, as indeed on all points, I am firm.

JACK: I am engaged to be married to Gwendolen, Lady Bracknell!

LADY BRACKNELL: You are nothing of the kind, sir. And now as regards Algernon! . . . Algernon!

ALGERNON: Yes, Aunt Augusta.

LADY BRACKNELL: May I ask if it is in this house that your invalid friend Mr. Bunbury resides?

ALGERNON: (*Stammering.*) Oh! No! Bunbury doesn't live here. Bunbury is somewhere else at present. In fact, Bunbury is dead.

LADY BRACKNELL: Dead! When did Mr. Bunbury die? His death must have been extremely sudden.

ALGERNON: (*Airily.*) Oh! I killed Bunbury this afternoon. I mean poor Bunbury died this afternoon.

LADY BRACKNELL: What did he die of?

ALGERNON: Bunbury? Oh, he was quite exploded.

LADY BRACKNELL: Exploded! Was he the victim of a revolutionary outrage? I was not aware that Mr. Bunbury was interested in social legislation. If so, he is well punished for his morbidity.

ALGERNON: My dear Aunt Augusta, I mean he was found out! The doctors found out that Bunbury could not live, that is what I mean—so Bunbury died.

LADY BRACKNELL: He seems to have had great confidence in the opinion of his physicians. I am glad, however, that he made up his mind at the last to some definite course of action, and acted under proper medical advice. And now that we have finally got rid of this Mr. Bunbury, may I ask, Mr. Worthing, who is that young person whose hand my nephew Algernon is now holding in what seems to me a peculiarly unnecessary manner?

JACK: That lady is Miss Cecily Cardew, my ward. (LADY BRACKNELL *bows coldly to* CECILY.)

ALGERNON: I am engaged to be married to Cecily, Aunt Augusta.

LADY BRACKNELL: I beg your pardon?

CECILY: Mr. Moncrieff and I are engaged to be married, Lady Bracknell.

LADY BRACKNELL: (*With a shiver, crossing to the sofa and sitting down.*) I do not know whether there is anything peculiarly exciting in the air of this particular part of Hertfordshire, but the number of engagements that go on seems to me considerably above the proper average that statistics have laid down for our guidance. I think some preliminary inquiry on my part would not be out of place. Mr. Worthing, is Miss Cardew at all connected with any of the larger railway stations in London? I merely desire information. Until yesterday I had no idea that there were any families or persons whose origin was a Terminus. (JACK *looks perfectly furious, but restrains himself.*)

JACK: (*In a cold, clear voice.*) Miss Cardew is the granddaughter of the late Mr. Thomas Cardew of 149 Belgrave Square, S.W.; Gervase Park, Dorking, Surrey; and the Sporran, Fifeshire, N.B.

LADY BRACKNELL: That sounds not unsatisfactory. Three addresses always inspire confidence, even in tradesmen. But what proof have I of their authenticity?

JACK: I have carefully preserved the Court Guides of the period. They are open to your inspection, Lady Bracknell.

LADY BRACKNELL: (*Grimly.*) I have known strange errors in that publication.

JACK: Miss Cardew's family solicitors are Messrs. Markby, Markby, and Markby.

LADY BRACKNELL: Markby, Markby, and Markby? A firm of the very highest position in their profession. Indeed I am told that one of the Mr. Markby's is occasionally to be seen at dinner parties. So far I am satisfied.

JACK: (*Very irritably.*) How extremely kind of you, Lady Bracknell! I have also in my possession, you will be pleased to hear, certificates of Miss Cardew's birth, baptism, whooping cough, registration, vaccination, confirmation, and the measles; both the German and the English variety.

LADY BRACKNELL: Ah! A life crowded with incident, I see; though perhaps somewhat too exciting for a young girl. I am not myself in favor of premature experiences. (*Rises. Looks at her watch.*) Gwendolen! the time approaches for our departure. We have not a moment to lose. As a matter of form, Mr. Worthing, I had better ask you if Miss Cardew has any little fortune?

JACK: Oh! about a hundred and thirty thousand pounds in the Funds. That is all. Good-bye, Lady Bracknell. So pleased to have seen you.

LADY BRACKNELL: (*Sitting down again.*) A moment, Mr. Worthing. A hundred and thirty thousand pounds! And in the Funds! Miss Cardew seems to me a most attractive young lady, now that I look at her. Few girls of the present day have any really solid qualities, any of the qualities that last, and improve with time. We live, I regret to say, in an age of surfaces. (*To* CECILY.) Come over here, dear. (CECILY *goes across.*) Pretty child! your dress is sadly simple, and your hair seems almost as Nature might have left it. But we can soon alter all that. A thoroughly experienced French maid produces a really marvellous result in a very brief space of time. I remember recommending one to young Lady Lancing, and after three months her own husband did not know her.

JACK: And after six months nobody knew her.

LADY BRACKNELL: (*Glares at* JACK *for a few moments. Then bends, with a practised smile to* CECILY.) Kindly turn round, sweet child. (CECILY *turns completely round.*) No, the side view is what I want. (CECILY *presents her profile.*) Yes, quite as I expected. There are distinct social possibilities in your profile. The two weak points in our age are its want of principle and its want of profile. The chin a little higher, dear. Style largely depends on the way the chin is worn. They are worn very high, just at present, Algernon!

ALGERNON: Yes, Aunt Augusta!

LADY BRACKNELL: There are distinct social possibilities in Miss Cardew's profile.

ALGERNON: Cecily is the sweetest, dearest, prettiest girl in the whole world. And I don't care twopence about social possibilities.

LADY BRACKNELL: Never speak disrespectfully of Society, Algernon. Only people who can't get into it do that. (*To* CECILY.) Dear child, of course you know that Algernon has nothing but his debts to depend upon. But I do not approve of mercenary marriages. When I married Lord Bracknell I had no fortune of any kind. But I never dreamed for a moment of allowing that to stand in my way. Well, I suppose I must give my consent.

ALGERNON: Thank you, Aunt Augusta.

LADY BRACKNELL: Cecily, you may kiss me!

CECILY: (*Kisses her.*) Thank you, Lady Bracknell.

LADY BRACKNELL: You may also address me as Aunt Augusta for the future.

CECILY: Thank you, Aunt Augusta.

LADY BRACKNELL: The marriage, I think, had better take place quite soon.

ALGERNON: Thank you, Aunt Augusta.

CECILY: Thank you, Aunt Augusta.

LADY BRACKNELL: To speak frankly, I am not in favor of long engagements. They give people the opportunity of finding out each other's character before marriage, which I think is never advisable.

JACK: I beg your pardon for interrupting you, Lady Bracknell, but this engagement is quite out of the question. I am Miss Cardew's guardian, and she cannot marry without my consent until she comes of age. That consent I absolutely decline to give.

LADY BRACKNELL: Upon what grounds, may I ask? Algernon is an extremely, I may almost say an ostentatiously, eligible young man. He has nothing, but he looks everything. What more can one desire?

JACK: It pains me very much to have to speak frankly to you, Lady Bracknell, about your nephew, but the fact is that I do not approve at all of his moral character. I suspect him of being untruthful. (ALGERNON *and* CECILY *look at him in indignant amazement.*)

LADY BRACKNELL: Untruthful! My nephew Algernon? Impossible! He is an Oxonian.

JACK: I fear there can be no possible doubt about the matter. This afternoon during my temporary absence in London on an important question of romance, he obtained admission to my house by means of the false pretence of being my brother. Under an assumed name he drank, I've just been informed by my butler, an entire pint bottle of my Perrier-Jouet, Brut, '89; wine I was specially reserving for myself. Continuing his disgraceful deception, he succeeded in the course of the afternoon in alienating the affections of my only ward. He subsequently stayed to tea, and devoured every single muffin. And what makes his conduct all the more heartless is, that he was perfectly well aware from the first that I have no brother, that I never had a brother, and that I don't intend to have a brother, not even of any kind. I distinctly told him so myself yesterday afternoon.

LADY BRACKNELL: Ahem! Mr. Worthing, after careful consideration I have decided entirely to overlook my nephew's conduct to you.

JACK: That is very generous of you, Lady Bracknell. My own decision, however, is unalterable. I decline to give my consent.

LADY BRACKNELL: (*To* CECILY.) Come here, sweet child. (CECILY *goes over.*) How old are you, dear?

CECILY: Well, I am really only eighteen, but I always admit to twenty when I go to evening parties.

LADY BRACKNELL: You are perfectly right in making some slight alteration. Indeed, no woman should ever be quite accurate about her age. It looks so calculating. . . . (*In a meditative manner.*) Eighteen, but admitting to twenty at evening parties. Well, it will not be very long before you are of age and free from the restraints of tutelage. So I don't think your guardian's consent is, after all, a matter of any importance.

JACK: Pray excuse me, Lady Bracknell, for interrupting you again, but it is only fair to tell you that according to the terms of her grandfather's will Miss Cardew does not come legally of age till she is thirty-five.

LADY BRACKNELL: That does not seem to me to be a grave objection. Thirty-five is a very attractive age. London society is full of women of the very highest birth who have, of their own free choice, remained thirty-five for years. Lady Dumbleton is an instance in point. To my own knowledge she has been thirty-five ever since she arrived at the age of forty, which was many years ago now. I see no reason why our dear Cecily should not be even still more attractive at the age you mention than she is at present. There will be a large accumulation of property.

CECILY: Algy, could you wait for me till I was thirty-five?

ALGERNON: Of course I could, Cecily. You know I could.

CECILY: Yes, I felt it instinctively, but I couldn't wait all that time. I hate waiting even five minutes for anybody. It always makes me rather cross. I am not punctual myself, I know, but I do like punctuality in others, and waiting, even to be married, is quite out of the question.

ALGERNON: Then what is to be done, Cecily?

CECILY: I don't know, Mr. Moncrieff.

LADY BRACKNELL: My dear Mr. Worthing, as Miss Cardew states positively that she cannot wait till she is thirty-five—a remark which I am bound to say seems to me to show a somewhat impatient nature—I would beg of you to reconsider your decision.

JACK: But my dear Lady Bracknell, the matter is entirely in your own hands. The moment you consent to my marriage with Gwendolen, I will most gladly allow your nephew to form an alliance with my ward.

LADY BRACKNELL: (*Rising and drawing herself up.*) You must be quite aware that what you propose is out of the question.

JACK: Then a passionate celibacy is all that any of us can look forward to.

LADY BRACKNELL: That is not the destiny I propose for Gwendolen. Algernon, of course, can choose for himself. (*Pulls out her watch.*) Come, dear (GWENDOLEN *rises.*), we have already missed five, if not six, trains. To miss any more might expose us to comment on the platform.

(*Enter* DR. CHASUBLE.)

CHASUBLE: Everything is quite ready for the christenings.

LADY BRACKNELL: The christenings, sir! Is not that somewhat premature?

CHASUBLE: (*Looking rather puzzled, and pointing to* JACK *and* ALGERNON.) Both these gentlemen have expressed a desire for immediate baptism.

LADY BRACKNELL: At their age? The idea is grotesque and irreligious! Algernon, I forbid you to be baptized. I will not hear of such excesses. Lord Bracknell would be highly displeased if he learned that that was the way in which you wasted your time and money.

CHASUBLE: Am I to understand then that there are to be no christenings at all this afternoon?

JACK: I don't think that, as things are now, it would be of much practical value to either of us, Dr. Chasuble.

CHASUBLE: I am grieved to hear such sentiments from you, Mr. Worthing. They savor of the heretical views of the Anabaptists, views that I have completely refuted in four of my unpublished sermons. However, as your present mood seems to be one peculiarly secular, I will return to the church at once. Indeed, I have just been informed by the pew-opener that for the last hour and a half Miss Prism has been waiting for me in the vestry.

LADY BRACKNELL: (*Starting.*) Miss Prism! Did I hear you mention a Miss Prism?

CHASUBLE: Yes, Lady Bracknell. I am on my way to join her.

LADY BRACKNELL: Pray allow me to detain you for a moment. This matter may prove to be one of vital importance to Lord Bracknell and myself. Is this Miss Prism a female of repellent aspect, remotely connected with education?

CHASUBLE: (*Somewhat indignantly.*) She is the most cultivated of ladies, and the very picture of respectability.

LADY BRACKNELL: It is obviously the same person. May I ask what position she holds in your household?

CHASUBLE: (*Severely.*) I am a celibate, madam.

JACK: (*Interposing.*) Miss Prism, Lady Bracknell, has been for the last three years Miss Cardew's esteemed governess and valued companion.

LADY BRACKNELL: In spite of what I hear of her, I must see her at once. Let her be sent for.

CHASUBLE: (*Looking off.*) She approaches; she is nigh.

(*Enter* MISS PRISM *hurriedly.*)

MISS PRISM: I was told you expected me in the vestry, dear Canon. I have been waiting for you there for an hour and three-quarters. (*Catches sight of* LADY BRACKNELL, *who has fixed her with a stony glare.* MISS PRISM *grows pale and quails. She looks anxiously round as if desirous to escape.*)

LADY BRACKNELL: (*In a severe, judicial voice.*) Prism! (MISS PRISM *bows her head in shame.*) Come here, Prism! (MISS PRISM *approaches in a humble manner.*) Prism! Where is that baby? (*General consternation. The Canon starts back in horror.* ALGERNON *and* JACK *pretend to be anxious to shield* CECILY *and* GWENDOLEN *from hearing the details of a terrible public scandal.*) Twenty-eight years ago, Prism, you left Lord Bracknell's house, Number 104, Upper Grosvenor Street, in charge of a perambulator that contained a baby of the male sex. You never returned. A few weeks later, through the elaborate investigations of the Metropolitan police, the perambulator was discovered at midnight standing by itself in a remote corner of Bayswater. It contained the manuscript of a three-volume novel of more than usually revolting sentimentality. (MISS PRISM *starts in involuntary indignation.*) But the baby was not there. (*Everyone looks at* MISS PRISM.) Prism! Where is that baby? (*A pause.*)

MISS PRISM: Lady Bracknell, I admit with shame that I do not know. I only wish I did. The plain facts of the case are these. On the morning of the day you mention, a day that is for ever branded on my memory, I prepared as usual to take the baby out in its perambulator. I had also with me a somewhat old, but capacious hand-bag in which I had intended to place the manuscript of a work of fiction that I had written during my few unoccupied hours. In a moment of mental abstraction, for which I can never forgive myself, I deposited the manuscript in the bassinette and placed the baby in the hand-bag.

JACK: (*Who has been listening attentively.*) But where did you deposit the hand-bag?

MISS PRISM: Do not ask me, Mr. Worthing.

JACK: Miss Prism, this is a matter of no small importance to me. I insist on knowing where you deposited the hand-bag that contained that infant.

MISS PRISM: I left it in the cloak-room of one of the larger railway stations in London.

JACK: What railway station?

MISS PRISM: (*Quite crushed.*) Victoria. The Brighton line. (*Sinks into a chair.*)

JACK: I must retire to my room for a moment. Gwendolen, wait here for me.

GWENDOLEN: If you are not too long, I will wait here for you all my life. (*Exit* JACK *in great excitement.*)

CHASUBLE: What do you think this means, Lady Bracknell?

LADY BRACKNELL: I dare not even suspect, Dr. Chasuble. I need hardly tell you that in families of high position strange coincidences are not supposed to occur. They are hardly considered the thing.

(*Noises heard overhead as if some one was throwing trunks about. Every one looks up.*)

CECILY: Uncle Jack seems strangely agitated.

CHASUBLE: Your guardian has a very emotional nature.

LADY BRACKNELL: This noise is extremely unpleasant. It sounds as if he was having an argument. I dislike arguments of any kind. They are always vulgar, and often convincing.

CHASUBLE: (*Looking up.*) It has stopped now. (*The noise is redoubled.*)

LADY BRACKNELL: I wish he would arrive at some conclusion.

GWENDOLEN: This suspense is terrible. I hope it will last.

(*Enter* JACK *with a hand-bag of black leather in his hand.*)

JACK: (*Rushing over to* MISS PRISM.) Is this the hand-bag, Miss Prism? Examine it carefully before you speak. The happiness of more than one life depends on your answer.

MISS PRISM: (*Calmly.*) It seems to be mine. Yes, here is the injury it received through the upsetting of a Gower Street omnibus in younger and happier days. Here is the stain on the lining caused by the explosion of a temperance beverage, an incident that occurred at Leamington. And here, on the lock, are my initials. I had forgotten that in an extravagant mood I had had them placed there. The bag is undoubtedly mine. I am delighted to have it so unexpectedly restored to me. It has been a great inconvenience being without it all these years.

JACK: (*In a pathetic voice.*) Miss Prism, more is restored to you than this hand-bag. I was the baby you placed in it.

MISS PRISM: (*Amazed.*) You?

JACK: (*Embracing her.*) Yes . . . mother!

MISS PRISM: (*Recoiling in indignant astonishment.*) Mr. Worthing. I am unmarried!

JACK: Unmarried! I do not deny that is a serious blow. But after all, who has the right to cast a stone against one who has suffered? Cannot repentance wipe out an act of folly? Why should there be one law for men, and another for women? Mother, I forgive you. (*Tries to embrace her again.*)

MISS PRISM: (*Still more indignant.*) Mr. Worthing, there is some error. (*Pointing to* LADY BRACKNELL.) There is the lady who can tell you who you really are.

JACK: (*After a pause.*) Lady Bracknell, I hate to seem inquisitive, but would you kindly inform me who I am?

LADY BRACKNELL: I am afraid that the news I have to give you will not altogether please you. You are the son of my poor sister, Mrs. Moncrieff, and consequently Algernon's elder brother.

JACK: Algy's elder brother! Then I have a brother after all. I knew I had a brother! I always said I had a brother! Cecily—how could you have ever doubted that I had a brother? (*Seizes hold of* ALGERNON.) Dr. Chasuble, my unfortunate brother. Miss Prism, my unfortunate brother. Gwendolen, my unfortunate brother. Algy, you young scoundrel, you will have to treat me with more respect in the future. You have never behaved to me like a brother in all your life.

ALGERNON: Well, not till to-day, old boy, I admit. I did my best, however, though I was out of practice.

(*Shakes hands.*)

GWENDOLEN: (*To* JACK.) My own! But what own are you? What is your Christian name, now that you have become some one else?

JACK: Good heavens! . . . I had quite forgotten that point. Your decision on the subject of my name is irrevocable, I suppose?

GWENDOLEN: I never change, except in my affections.

CECILY: What a noble nature you have, Gwendolen!

JACK: Then the question had better be cleared up at once. Aunt Augusta, a moment. At the time when Miss Prism left me in the hand-bag, had I been christened already?

LADY BRACKNELL: Every luxury that money could buy, including christening, had been lavished on you by your fond and doting parents.

JACK: Then I was christened! That is settled. Now, what name was I given? Let me know the worst.

LADY BRACKNELL: Being the eldest son you were naturally christened after your father.

JACK: (*Irritably.*) Yes, but what was my father's Christian name?

LADY BRACKNELL: (*Meditatively.*) I cannot at the present moment recall what the General's Christian name was. But I have no doubt he had one. He was eccentric, I admit. But only in later years. And that was the result of the Indian climate, and marriage, and indigestion, and other things of that kind.

JACK: Algy! Can't you recollect what our father's Christian name was?

ALGERNON: My dear boy, we were never even on speaking terms. He died before I was a year old.

JACK: His name would appear in the Army Lists of the period, I suppose, Aunt Augusta?

LADY BRACKNELL: The General was essentially a man of peace, except in his domestic life. But I have no doubt his name would appear in any military directory.

JACK: The Army Lists of the last forty years are here. These delightful records should have been my constant study. (*Rushes to bookcase and tears the books out.*) M. Generals . . . Mallam, Maxbohm, Magley—what ghastly names they have—Markby, Migsby, Mobbs, Moncrieff! Lieutenant 1840, Captain, Lieutenant-Colonel, Colonel, General 1869, Christian names, Ernest John. (*Puts book very quietly down and speaks quite calmly.*) I always told you, Gwendolen,my name was Ernest, didn't I? Well, it is Ernest after all. I mean it naturally is Ernest.

LADY BRACKNELL: Yes, I remember now that the General was called Ernest. I knew I had some particular reason for disliking the name.

GWENDOLEN: Ernest! My own Ernest! I felt from the first that you could have no other name!

JACK: Gwendolen, it is a terrible thing for a man to find out suddenly that all his life he has been speaking nothing but the truth. Can you forgive me?

GWENDOLEN: I can. For I feel that you are sure to change.

JACK: My own one!

CHASUBLE: (*To* MISS PRISM.) Laetitia! (*Embraces her.*)

MISS PRISM: (*Enthusiastically.*) Frederick! At last!

ALGERNON: Cecily! (*Embraces her.*) At last!

JACK: Gwendolen! (*Embraces her.*) At last!

LADY BRACKNELL: My nephew, you seem to be displaying signs of triviality.

JACK: On the contrary, Aunt Augusta, I've now realized for the first time in my life the vital Importance of Being Earnest.

Tableau

Curtain

(*1896*)

QUESTIONS FOR CRITICAL THINKING AND WRITING

Experience

1. How did you find the experience of reading Wilde's play? Did you find it amusing, or not? Why?
2. Which character did you enjoy most and which least? Why?

Interpretation

3. What do the many epigrammatic lines add to the play? How is wit a central ingredient of the play?
4. How are Lady Bracknell and Cecily characterized?
5. How does the setting of each of the play's acts reflect its dialogue and action?
6. What kind of plot has Wilde constructed for his play? What details are central to the twists and turns of the plot?

7. Select one scene and explain how you think it should be staged.
8. How does Wilde portray betrothal and marriage?

Evaluation

9. What codes of values does Algernon live by?
10. What aspects of marriage does Wilde satirize in the play?

Connections

11. Compare the comedy in this play with that in Wasserstein's *Tender Offer.*

Critical Thinking

12. *The Importance of Being Earnest* is considered Wilde's masterpiece. What qualities of the play do you think have contributed to this judgment? Explain.

AUGUST WILSON
[1945–2005]

August Wilson was born and raised in Pittsburgh, Pennsylvania. He quit school at sixteen and worked at various odd jobs until moving to Minneapolis–St. Paul, where he founded the Black Horizons Theatre Company. Having dropped out of school, Wilson educated himself at the public library, discovering there the work of Ralph Ellison, Richard Wright, and Langston Hughes, three modern African-American writers whose work inspired him. Wilson is the author of Ma Rainey's Black Bottom, Fences, Joe Turner's Come and Gone, The Piano Lesson, *and* Two Trains Running, *all notable for their depiction of the urban lives of African-Americans. The recipient of many awards, including two Pulitzer Prizes, a New York Drama Critics Circle Award, and a Tony Award, Wilson has provided a window on the lives of Americans struggling for success, equality, and survival.*

Fences

CHARACTERS

TROY MAXSON
JIM BONO, TROY*'s friend*
ROSE, TROY*'s wife*
LYONS, TROY*'s oldest son by previous marriage*
GABRIEL, TROY*'s brother*
CORY, TROY *and* ROSE*'s son*
RAYNELL, TROY*'s daughter*

Setting. *The setting is the yard which fronts the only entrance to the Maxson household, an ancient two-story brick house set back off a small alley in a big-city neighborhood. The entrance to the house is gained by two or three steps leading to a wooden porch badly in need of paint.*

A relatively recent addition to the house and running its full width, the porch lacks congruence. It is a sturdy porch with a flat roof. One or two chairs of dubious value sit at one end where the kitchen window opens onto the porch. An old-fashioned icebox stands silent guard at the opposite end.

The yard is a small dirt yard, partially fenced, except for the last scene, with a wooden sawhorse, a pile of lumber, and other fence-building equipment set off to the side. Opposite is a tree from which hangs a ball made of rags. A baseball bat leans against the tree. Two oil drums serve as garbage receptacles and sit near the house at right to complete the setting.

The Play. *Near the turn of the century, the destitute of Europe sprang on the city with tenacious claws and an honest and solid dream. The city devoured them. They swelled its belly until it burst into a thousand furnaces and sewing machines, a thousand butcher shops and bakers' ovens, a thousand churches and hospitals and funeral parlors and money-lenders. The city grew. It nourished itself and offered each man a partnership limited only by his talent, his guile, and his willingness and capacity for hard work. For the immigrants of Europe, a dream dared and won true.*

The descendants of African slaves were offered no such welcome or participation. They came from places called the Carolinas and the Virginias, Georgia, Alabama, Mississippi, and Tennessee. They came strong, eager, searching. The city rejected them and they fled and settled along the riverbanks and under bridges in shallow, ramshackle houses made of sticks and tarpaper. They collected rags and wood. They sold the use of their muscles and their bodies. They cleaned houses and washed clothes, they shined shoes, and in quiet desperation and vengeful pride, they stole, and lived in pursuit of their own dream. That they could breathe free, finally, and stand to meet life with the force of dignity and whatever eloquence the heart could call upon.

By 1957, the hard-won victories of the European immigrants had solidified the industrial might of America. War had been confronted and won with new energies that used loyalty and patriotism as its fuel. Life was rich, full, and flourishing. The Milwaukee Braves won the World Series, and the hot winds of change that would make the sixties a turbulent, racing, dangerous, and provocative decade had not yet begun to blow full.

ACT I

Scene 1

It is 1957. TROY *and* BONO *enter the yard, engaged in conversation.* TROY *is fifty-three years old, a large man with thick, heavy hands; it is this largeness that he strives to fill out and make an accommodation with. Together with his blackness, his largeness informs his sensibilities and the choices he has made in his life.*

Of the two men, BONO *is obviously the follower. His commitment to their friendship of thirty-odd years is rooted in his admiration of* TROY*'s honesty, capacity for hard work, and his strength, which* BONO *seeks to emulate.*

It is Friday night, payday, and the one night of the week the two men engage in a ritual of talk and drink. TROY *is usually the most talkative and at times he can be crude and almost vulgar, though he is capable of rising to profound heights of expression. The men carry lunch buckets and wear or carry burlap aprons and are dressed in clothes suitable to their jobs as garbage collectors.*

BONO: Troy, you ought to stop that lying!

TROY: I ain't lying! The nigger had a watermelon this big.

He indicates with his hands.

Talking about . . . "What watermelon, Mr. Rand?" I liked to fell out! "What watermelon, Mr. Rand?" . . . and it sitting there big as life.

BONO: What did Mr. Rand say?

TROY: Ain't said nothing. Figure if the nigger too dumb to know he carrying a watermelon, he wasn't gonna get much sense out of him. Trying to hide that great big old watermelon under his coat. Afraid to let the white man see him carrying it home.

BONO: I'm like you . . . I ain't got no time for them kind of people.

TROY: Now what he looks like getting mad cause he see the man from the union talking to Mr. Rand?

BONO: He come to me talking about . . . "Maxson gonna get us fired." I told him to get away from me with that. He walked away from me calling you a troublemaker. What Mr. Rand say?

TROY: Ain't said nothing. He told me to go down the Commissioner's office next Friday. They called me down there to see them.

BONO: Well, as long as you got your complaint filed, they can't fire you. That's what one of them white fellows tell me.

TROY: I ain't worried about them firing me. They gonna fire me cause I asked a question? That's all I did. I went to Mr. Rand and asked him, "Why? Why you got the white men driving and the colored lifting?" Told him, "What's the matter, don't I count? You think only white fellows got sense enough to drive a truck. That ain't no paper job! Hell, anybody can drive a truck. How come you got all whites driving and the colored lifting?" He told me "take it to the union." Well, hell, that's what I done! Now they wanna come up with this pack of lies.

BONO: I told Brownie if the man come and ask him any questions . . . just tell the truth! It ain't nothing but something they done trumped up on you cause you filed a complaint on them.

TROY: Brownie don't understand nothing. All I want them to do is change the job description. Give everybody a chance to drive the truck. Brownie can't see that. He ain't got that much sense.

BONO: How you figure he be making out with that gal be up at Taylors' all the time . . . that Alberta gal?

TROY: Same as you and me. Getting just as much as we is. Which is to say nothing.

BONO: It is, huh? I figure you doing a little better than me . . . and I ain't saying what I'm doing.

TROY: Aw, nigger, look here . . . I know you. If you had got anywhere near that gal, twenty minutes later you be looking to tell somebody. And the first one you gonna tell . . . that you gonna want to brag to . . . is gonna be me.

BONO: I ain't saying that. I see where you be eyeing her.

TROY: I eye all the women. I don't miss nothing. Don't never let nobody tell you Troy Maxson don't eye the women.

BONO: You been doing more than eyeing her. You done bought her a drink or two.

TROY: Hell yeah, I bought her a drink! What that mean? I bought you one, too. What that mean cause I buy her a drink? I'm just being polite.

BONO: It's all right to buy her one drink. That's what you call being polite. But when you wanna be buying two or three . . . that's what you call eyeing her.

TROY: Look here, as long as you known me . . . you ever known me to chase after women?

BONO: Hell yeah! Long as I done known you. You forgetting I knew you when.

TROY: Naw, I'm talking about since I been married to Rose?

BONO: Oh, not since you been married to Rose. Now, that's the truth, there. I can say that.

TROY: All right then! Case closed.

BONO: I see you be walking up around Alberta's house. You supposed to be at Taylor's and you be walking up around there.

TROY: What are you watching where I'm walking for? I ain't watching after you.

BONO: I see you walking around there more than once.

TROY: Hell, you liable to see me walking anywhere! That don't mean nothing cause you see me walking around there.

BONO: Where she come from anyway? She just kinda showed up one day.

TROY: Tallahassee. You can look at her and tell she one of them Florida gals. They got some big healthy women down there. Grow them right up out the ground. Got a little bit of Indian in her. Most of them niggers down in Florida got some Indian in them.

BONO: I don't know about that Indian part. But she damn sure big and healthy. Woman wear some big stockings. Got them great big old legs and hips as wide as the Mississippi River.

TROY: Legs don't mean nothing. You don't do nothing but push them out of the way. But them hips cushion the ride!

BONO: Troy, you ain't got no sense.

TROY: It's the truth! Like you riding on Goodyears!

ROSE *enters from the house. She is ten years younger than* TROY. *Her devotion to him stems from her recognition of the possibilities of her life without him: a succession of abusive men and their babies, a life of partying and running the streets, the Church, or aloneness with its attendant pain and frustration. She recognizes* TROY'*s spirit as a fine and illuminating one and she either ignores or forgives his faults, only some of which she recognizes. Though she doesn't drink, her presence is an integral part of the Friday night rituals. She alternates between the porch and the kitchen, where supper preparations are under way.*

ROSE: What you all out here getting into?

TROY: What you worried about what we getting into for? This is men talk, woman.

ROSE: What I care what you all talking about? Bono, you gonna stay for supper?

BONO: No, I thank you, Rose. But Lucille say she cooking up a pot of pigfeet.

TROY: Pigfeet! Hell, I'm going home with you! Might even stay the night if you got some pigfeet. You got something in there to top them pigfeet, Rose?

ROSE: I'm cooking up some chicken. I got some chicken and collard greens.

TROY: Well, go on back in the house and let me and Bono finish what we was talking about. This is men talk. I got some talk for you later. You know what kind of talk I mean. You go on and powder it up.

ROSE: Troy Maxson, don't you start that now!

TROY [*puts his arm around her*]: Aw, woman . . . come here. Look here, Bono . . . when I met this woman . . . I got out that place, say, "Hitch up my pony, saddle up my mare . . . there's a woman out there for me somewhere. I looked here. Looked there. Saw Rose and latched on to her." I latched on to her and told her—I'm gonna tell you the truth—I told her, "Baby, I don't wanna marry, I just wanna be your man." Rose told me . . . tell him what you told me, Rose.

ROSE: I told him if he wasn't the marrying kind, then move out the way so the marrying kind could find me.

TROY: That's what she told me. "Nigger, you in my way. You blocking the view! Move out the way so I can find me a husband." I thought it over two or three days. Come back—

ROSE: Ain't no two or three days nothing. You was back the same night.

TROY: Come back, told her . . . "Okay, baby . . . but I'm gonna buy me a banty rooster and put him out there in the backyard . . . and when he see a stranger come, he'll flap his wings and crow . . ." Look here, Bono, I could watch the front door by myself . . . it was that back door I was worried about.

ROSE: Troy, you ought not talk like that. Troy ain't doing nothing but telling a lie.

TROY: Only thing is . . . when we first got married . . . forget the rooster . . . we ain't had no yard!

BONO: I hear you tell it. Me and Lucille was staying down there on Logan Street. Had two rooms with the outhouse in the back. I ain't mind the outhouse none. But when that goddamn wind blow through there in the winter . . . that's what I'm talking about! To this day I wonder why in the hell I ever stayed down there for six long years. But see, I didn't know I could do no better. I thought only white folks had inside toilets and things.

ROSE: There's a lot of people don't know they can do no better than they doing now. That's just something you got to learn. A lot of folks still shop at Bella's.

TROY: Ain't nothing wrong with shopping at Bella's. She got fresh food.

ROSE: I ain't said nothing about if she got fresh food. I'm talking about what she charge. She charge ten cents more than the A&P.

TROY: The A&P ain't never done nothing for me. I spends my money where I'm treated right. I go down to Bella, say, "I need a loaf of bread, I'll pay you Friday." She give it to me. What sense that make when I got money to go and spend it somewhere else and ignore the person who done right by me? That ain't in the Bible.

ROSE: We ain't talking about what's in the Bible. What sense it made to shop there when she overcharge?

TROY: You shop where you want to. I'll do my shopping where the people been good to me.

ROSE: Well, I don't think it's right for her to overcharge. That's all I was saying.

BONO: Look here . . . I got to get on. Lucille going be raising all kind of hell.

TROY: Where you going, nigger? We ain't finished this pint. Come here, finish this pint.

BONO: Well, hell, I am . . . if you ever turn the bottle loose.

TROY [*hands him the bottle*]: The only thing I say about the A&P is I'm glad Cory got that job down there. Help him take care of his school clothes and things. Gabe done moved out and things getting tight around here. He got that job. . . . He can start to look out for himself.

ROSE: Cory done went and got recruited by a college football team.

TROY: I told that boy about that football stuff. The white man ain't gonna let him get nowhere with that football. I told him when he first come to me with it. Now you come telling me he done went and got more tied up in it. He ought to go and get recruited in how to fix cars or something where he can make a living.

ROSE: He ain't talking about making no living playing football. It's just something the boys in school do. They gonna send a recruiter by to talk to you. He'll tell you he ain't talking about making no living playing football. It's a honor to be recruited.

TROY: It ain't gonna get him nowhere. Bono'll tell you that.

BONO: If he be like you in the sports . . . he's gonna be all right. Ain't but two men ever played baseball as good as you. That's Babe Ruth and Josh Gibson.° Them's the only two men ever hit more home runs than you.

TROY: What it ever get me? Ain't got a pot to piss in or a window to throw it out of.

ROSE: Times have changed since you was playing baseball, Troy. That was before the war. Times have changed a lot since then.

TROY: How in hell they done changed?

ROSE: They got lots of colored boys playing ball now. Baseball and football.

BONO: You right about that, Rose. Times have changed, Troy. You just come along too early.

TROY: There ought not never have been no time called too early! Now you take that fellow . . . what's that fellow they had playing right field for the Yankees back then? You know who I'm talking about, Bono. Used to play right field for the Yankees.

ROSE: Selkirk?

TROY: Selkirk! That's it! Man batting .269, understand? .269. What kind of sense that make? I was hitting .432 with thirty-seven home runs! Man batting .269 and playing right field for the Yankees! I saw Josh Gibson's daughter yesterday. She walking around with raggedy shoes on her feet. Now I bet you Selkirk's daughter ain't walking around with raggedy shoes on her feet! I bet you that!

ROSE: They got a lot of colored baseball players now. Jackie Robinson was the first. Folks had to wait for Jackie Robinson.

TROY: I done seen a hundred niggers play baseball better than Jackie Robinson. Hell, I know some teams Jackie Robinson couldn't even make! What you talking about Jackie Robinson. Jackie Robinson wasn't nobody. I'm talking about if you could play ball then they ought to have let you play. Don't care what color you were. Come telling me I come along too early. If you could play . . . then they ought to have let you play.

TROY *takes a long drink from the bottle.*

ROSE: You gonna drink yourself to death. You don't need to be drinking like that.

Josh Gibson *(1911–1947) powerful, black baseball player known in the 1930s as the Babe Ruth of the Negro leagues.*

TROY: Death ain't nothing. I done seen him. Done wrassled with him. You can't tell me nothing about death. Death ain't nothing but a fastball on the outside corner. And you know what I'll do to that! Lookee here, Bono . . . am I lying? You get one of them fastballs, about waist high, over the outside corner of the plate where you can get the meat of the bat on it . . . and good god! You can kiss it goodbye. Now, am I lying?

BONO: Naw, you telling the truth there. I seen you do it.

TROY: If I'm lying . . . that 450 feet worth of lying!

Pause.

That's all death is to me. A fastball on the outside corner.

ROSE: I don't know why you want to get on talking about death.

TROY: Ain't nothing wrong with talking about death. That's part of life. Everybody gonna die. You gonna die, I'm gonna die. Bono's gonna die. Hell, we all gonna die.

ROSE: But you ain't got to talk about it. I don't like to talk about it.

TROY: You the one brought it up. Me and Bono was talking about baseball . . . you tell me I'm gonna drink myself to death. Ain't that right, Bono? You know I don't drink this but one night out of the week. That's Friday night. I'm gonna drink just enough to where I can handle it. Then I cuts it loose. I leave it alone. So don't you worry about me drinking myself to death. 'Cause I ain't worried about Death. I done seen him. I done wrestled with him.

Look here, Bono . . . I looked up one day and Death was marching straight at me. Like Soldiers on Parade! The Army of Death was marching straight at me. The middle of July, 1941. It got real cold just like it be winter. It seem like Death himself reached out and touched me on the shoulder. He touch me just like I touch you. I got cold as ice and Death standing there grinning at me.

ROSE: Troy, why don't you hush that talk.

TROY: I say . . . What you want, Mr. Death? You be wanting me? You done brought your army to be getting me? I looked him dead in the eye. I wasn't fearing nothing. I was ready to tangle. Just like I'm ready to tangle now. The Bible say be ever vigilant. That's why I don't get but so drunk. I got to keep watch.

ROSE: Troy was right down there in Mercy Hospital. You remember he had pneumonia? Laying there with a fever talking plumb out of his head.

TROY: Death standing there staring at me . . . carrying that sickle in his hand. Finally he say, "You want bound over for another year?" See, just like that . . . "You want bound over for another year?" I told him, "Bound over hell! Let's settle this now!"

It seem like he kinda fell back when I said that, and all the cold went out of me. I reached down and grabbed that sickle and threw it just as far as I could throw it . . . and me and him commenced to wrestling.

We wrestled for three days and three nights. I can't say where I found the strength from. Every time it seemed like he was gonna get the best of me, I'd reach way down deep inside myself and find the strength to do him one better.

ROSE: Every time Troy tell that story he find different ways to tell it. Different things to make up about it.

TROY: I ain't making up nothing. I'm telling you the facts of what happened. I wrestled with Death for three days and three nights and I'm standing here to tell you about it.

Pause.

All right. At the end of the third night we done weakened each other to where we can't hardly move. Death stood up, throwed on his robe . . . had him a white robe with a hood on it. He throwed on that robe and went off to look for his sickle. Say, "I'll be back." Just like that. "I'll be back." I told him, say, "Yeah, but . . . you gonna have to find me!" I wasn't no fool. I wasn't going looking for him. Death ain't nothing to play with. And I know he's gonna get me. I know I got to join his army . . . his camp followers. But as long as I keep my strength and see him coming . . . as long as I keep up my vigilance . . . he's gonna have to fight to get me. I ain't going easy.

BONO: Well, look here, since you got to keep up your vigilance . . . let me have the bottle.

TROY: Aw hell, I shouldn't have told you that part. I should have left out that part.

ROSE: Troy be talking that stuff and half the time don't even know what he be talking about.

TROY: Bono know me better than that.

BONO: That's right. I know you. I know you got some Uncle Remus° in your blood. You got more stories than the devil got sinners.

TROY: Aw hell, I done seen him too! Done talked with the devil.

ROSE: Troy, don't nobody wanna be hearing all that stuff.

LYONS enters the yard from the street. Thirty-four years old, TROY's son by a previous marriage, he sports a neatly trimmed goatee, sport coat, white shirt, tieless and buttoned at the collar. Though he fancies himself a musician, he is more caught up in the rituals and "idea" of being a musician than in the actual practice of the music. He has come to borrow money from TROY, and while he knows he will be successful, he is uncertain as to what extent his lifestyle will be held up to scrutiny and ridicule.

LYONS: Hey, Pop.

TROY: What you come "Hey, Popping" me for?

LYONS: How you doing, Rose?

He kisses her.

Mr. Bono. How you doing?

BONO: Hey, Lyons . . . how you been?

TROY: He must have been doing all right. I ain't seen him around here last week.

ROSE: Troy, leave your boy alone. He come by to see you and you wanna start all that nonsense.

TROY: I ain't bothering Lyons.

Offers him the bottle.

Here . . . get you a drink. We got an understanding. I know why he come by to see me and he know I know.

LYONS: Come on, Pop . . . I just stopped by to say hi . . . see how you was doing.

TROY: You ain't stopped by yesterday.

ROSE: You gonna stay for supper, Lyons? I got some chicken cooking in the oven.

Uncle Remus *Black storyteller who recounts traditional black tales in the book by Joel Chandler Harris.*

LYONS: No, Rose . . . thanks. I was just in the neighborhood and thought I'd stop by for a minute.

TROY: You was in the neighborhood all right, nigger. You telling the truth there. You was in the neighborhood cause it's my payday.

LYONS: Well, hell, since you mentioned it . . . let me have ten dollars.

TROY: I'll be damned! I'll die and go to hell and play blackjack with the devil before I give you ten dollars.

BONO: That's what I wanna know about . . . that devil you done seen.

LYONS: What . . . Pop done seen the devil? You too much, Pops.

TROY: Yeah, I done seen him. Talked to him too!

ROSE: You ain't seen no devil. I done told you that man ain't had nothing to do with the devil. Anything you can't understand, you want to call it the devil.

TROY: Look here, Bono . . . I went down to see Hertzberger about some furniture. Got three rooms for two-ninety-eight. That what it say on the radio. "Three rooms . . . two-ninety-eight." Even made up a little song about it. Go down there . . . man tell me I can't get no credit. I'm working every day and can't get no credit. What to do? I got an empty house with some raggedy furniture in it. Cory ain't got no bed. He's sleeping on a pile of rags on the floor. Working every day and can't get no credit. Come back here—Rose'll tell you—madder than hell. Sit down . . . try to figure what I'm gonna do. Come a knock on the door. Ain't been living here but three days. Who know I'm here? Open the door . . . devil standing there bigger than life. White fellow . . . got on good clothes and everything. Standing there with a clipboard in his hand. I ain't had to say nothing. First words come out of his mouth was . . . "I understand you need some furniture and can't get no credit." I liked to fell over. He say, "I'll give you all the credit you want, but you got to pay the interest on it." I told him, "Give me three rooms worth and charge whatever you want." Next day a truck pulled up here and two men unloaded them three rooms. Man that drove the truck give me a book. Say send ten dollars, first of every month to the address in the book and everything will be all right. Say if I miss a payment the devil was coming back and it'll be hell to pay. That was fifteen years ago. To this day . . . the first of the month I send my ten dollars, Rose'll tell you.

ROSE: Troy lying.

TROY: I ain't never seen that man since. Now you tell me who else that could have been but the devil? I ain't sold my soul or nothing like that, you understand. Naw, I wouldn't have truck with the devil about nothing like that. I got my furniture and pays my ten dollars the first of the month just like clockwork.

BONO: How long you say you been paying this ten dollars a month?

TROY: Fifteen years!

BONO: Hell, ain't you finished paying for it yet? How much the man done charged you?

TROY: Ah hell, I done paid for it. I done paid for it ten times over! The fact is I'm scared to stop paying it.

ROSE: Troy lying. We got that furniture from Mr. Glickman. He ain't paying no ten dollars a month to nobody.

TROY: Aw hell, woman. Bono know I ain't that big a fool.

LYONS: I was just getting ready to say . . . I know where there's a bridge for sale.

TROY: Look here, I'll tell you this . . . it don't matter to me if he was the devil. It don't matter if the devil give credit. Somebody has got to give it.

ROSE: It ought to matter. You going around talking about having truck with the devil . . . God's the one you gonna have to answer to. He's the one gonna be at the Judgment.

LYONS: Yeah, well, look here, Pop . . . let me have that ten dollars. I'll give it back to you. Bonnie got a job working at the hospital.

TROY: What I tell you, Bono? The only time I see this nigger is when he wants something. That's the only time I see him.

LYONS: Come on, Pop, Mr. Bono don't want to hear all that. Let me have the ten dollars. I told you Bonnie working.

TROY: What that mean to me? "Bonnie working." I don't care if she working. Go ask her for the ten dollars if she working. Talking about "Bonnie working." Why ain't you working?

LYONS: Aw, Pop, you know I can't find no decent job. Where am I gonna get a job at? You know I can't get no job.

TROY: I told you I know some people down there. I can get you on the rubbish if you want to work. I told you that the last time you came by here asking me for something.

LYONS: Naw, Pop . . . thanks. That ain't for me. I don't wanna be carrying nobody's rubbish. I don't wanna be punching nobody's time clock.

TROY: What's the matter, you too good to carry people's rubbish? Where you think that ten dollars you talking about come from? I'm just supposed to haul people's rubbish and give my money to you cause you too lazy to work. You too lazy to work and wanna know why you ain't got what I got.

ROSE: What hospital Bonnie working at? Mercy?

LYONS: She's down at Passavant working in the laundry.

TROY: I ain't got nothing as it is. I give you that ten dollars and I got to eat beans the rest of the week. Naw . . . you ain't getting no ten dollars here.

LYONS: You ain't got to be eating no beans. I don't know why you wanna say that.

TROY: I ain't got no extra money. Gabe done moved over to Miss Pearl's paying her the rent and things done got tight around here. I can't afford to be giving you every payday.

LYONS: I ain't asked you to give me nothing. I asked you to loan me ten dollars. I know you got ten dollars.

TROY: Yeah, I got it. You know why I got it? Cause I don't throw my money away out there in the streets. You living the fast life . . . wanna be a musician . . . running around in them clubs and things . . . then, you learn to take care of yourself. You ain't gonna find me going and asking nobody for nothing. I done spent too many years without.

LYONS: You and me is two different people, Pop.

TROY: I done learned my mistake and learned to do what's right by it. You still trying to get something for nothing. Life don't owe you nothing. You owe it to yourself. Ask Bono. He'll tell you I'm right.

LYONS: You got your way of dealing with the world . . . I got mine. The only thing that matters to me is the music.

TROY: Yeah, I can see that! It don't matter how you gonna eat . . . where your next dollar is coming from. You telling the truth there.

LYONS: I know I got to eat. But I got to live too. I need something that gonna help me to get out of the bed in the morning. Make me feel like I belong in the world. I don't bother nobody. I just stay with my music cause that's the only way I can find to live in the world. Otherwise there ain't no telling what I might do. Now I don't come criticizing you and how you live. I just come by to ask you for ten dollars. I don't wanna hear all that about how I live.

TROY: Boy, your mamma did a hell of a job raising you.

LYONS: You can't change me, Pop. I'm thirty-four years old. If you wanted to change me, you should have been there when I was growing up. I come by to see you . . . ask for ten dollars and you want to talk about how I was raised. You don't know nothing about how I was raised.

ROSE: Let the boy have ten dollars, Troy.

TROY [*to* LYONS]: What the hell you looking at me for? I ain't got no ten dollars. You know what I do with my money.

To ROSE.

Give him ten dollars if you want him to have it.

ROSE: I will. Just as soon as you turn it loose.

TROY [*handing* ROSE *the money*]: There it is. Seventy-six dollars and forty-two cents. You see this, Bono? Now, I ain't gonna get but six of that back.

ROSE: You ought to stop telling that lie. Here, Lyons. [*She hands him the money.*]

LYONS: Thanks, Rose. Look . . . I got to run . . . I'll see you later.

TROY: Wait a minute. You gonna say, "thanks, Rose" and ain't gonna look to see where she got that ten dollars from? See how they do me, Bono?

LYONS: I know she got it from you, Pop. Thanks. I'll give it back to you.

TROY: There he go telling another lie. Time I see that ten dollars . . . he'll be owing me thirty more.

LYONS: See you, Mr. Bono.

BONO: Take care, Lyons!

LYONS: Thanks, Pop. I'll see you again.

LYONS *exits the yard.*

TROY: I don't know why he don't go and get him a decent job and take care of that woman he got.

BONO: He'll be all right, Troy. The boy is still young.

TROY: The *boy* is thirty-four years old.

ROSE: Let's not get off into all that.

BONO: Look here . . . I got to be going. I got to be getting on. Lucille gonna be waiting.

TROY [*puts his arm around* ROSE]: See this woman, Bono? I love this woman. I love this woman so much it hurts. I love her so much . . . I done run out of ways of loving her. So I got to go back to basics. Don't you come by my house Monday morning talking about time to go to work . . . 'cause I'm still gonna be stroking!

ROSE: Troy! Stop it now!

BONO: I ain't paying him no mind, Rose. That ain't nothing but gin-talk. Go on, Troy. I'll see you Monday.

TROY: Don't you come by my house, nigger! I done told you what I'm gonna be doing.

The lights go down to black.

Scene 2

The lights come up on ROSE *hanging up clothes. She hums and sings softly to herself. It is the following morning.*

ROSE [*Sings*]: Jesus, be a fence all around me every day
Jesus, I want you to protect me as I travel on my way.
Jesus, be a fence all around me every day.

TROY *enters from the house.*

Jesus, I want you to protect me
As I travel on my way.

[*To* TROY] 'Morning. You ready for breakfast? I can fix it soon as I finish hanging up these clothes?

TROY: I got the coffee on. That'll be all right. I'll just drink some of that this morning.

ROSE: That 651 hit yesterday. That's the second time this month. Miss Pearl hit for a dollar . . . seem like those that need the least always get lucky. Poor folks can't get nothing.

TROY: Them numbers don't know anybody. I don't know why you fool with them. You and Lyons both.

ROSE: It's something to do.

TROY: You ain't doing nothing but throwing your money away.

ROSE: Troy, you know I don't play foolishly. I just play a nickel here and a nickel there.

TROY: That's two nickels you done thrown away.

ROSE: Now I hit sometimes . . . that makes up for it. It always comes in handy when I do hit. I don't hear you complaining then.

TROY: I ain't complaining now. I just say it's foolish. Trying to guess out of six hundred ways which way the number gonna come. If I had all the money niggers, these Negroes, throw away on numbers for one week—just one week—I'd be a rich man.

ROSE: Well, you wishing and calling it foolish ain't gonna stop folks from playing numbers. That's one thing for sure. Besides . . . some good things come from playing numbers. Look where Pope done bought him that restaurant off of numbers.

TROY: I can't stand niggers like that. Man ain't had two dimes to rub together. He walking around with his shoes all run over bumming money for cigarettes. All right. Got lucky there and hit the numbers . . .

ROSE: Troy, I know all about it.

TROY: Had good sense, I'll say that for him. He ain't throwed his money away. I seen niggers hit the numbers and go through two thousand dollars in four days. Man bought him that restaurant down there . . . fixed it up real nice . . . and then didn't want nobody to come in it! A Negro go in there and can't get no kind of service. I seen a white fellow come in there and order a bowl of stew. Pope picked all the meat out the pot for him. Man ain't had nothing but a bowl of meat! Negro come behind him and ain't got nothing but the potatoes and carrots. Talking about what numbers do for people, you picked a wrong example. Ain't done nothing but make a worser fool out of him than he was before.

ROSE: Troy, you ought to stop worrying about what happened at work yesterday.

TROY: I ain't worried. Just told me to be down there at the Commissioner's office on Friday. Everybody think they gonna fire me. I ain't worried about them firing me. You ain't got to worry about that.

Pause.

Where's Cory? Cory in the house? [*Calls*] Cory?

ROSE: He gone out.

TROY: Out, huh? He gone out 'cause he know I want him to help me with this fence. I know how he is. That boy scared of work.

GABRIEL *enters. He comes halfway down the alley and, hearing* TROY*'s voice, stops.*

TROY [*continues*]: He ain't done a lick of work in his life.

ROSE: He had to go to football practice. Coach wanted them to get in a little extra practice before the season start.

TROY: I got his practice . . . running out of here before he gets his chores done.

ROSE: Troy, what is wrong with you this morning? Don't nothing set right with you. Go on back in there and go to bed . . . get up on the other side.

TROY: Why something got to be wrong with me? I ain't said nothing wrong with me.

ROSE: You got something to say about everything. First it's the numbers . . . then it's the way the man runs his restaurant . . . then you done got on Cory. What's it gonna be next? Take a look up there and see if the weather suits you . . . or is it gonna be how you gonna put up the fence with the clothes hanging in the yard.

TROY: You hit the nail on the head then.

ROSE: I know you like I know the back of my hand. Go on in there and get you some coffee . . . see if that straighten you up. 'Cause you ain't right this morning.

TROY *starts into the house and sees* GABRIEL. GABRIEL *starts singing.* TROY*'s brother, he is seven years younger than* TROY. *Injured in World War II, he has a metal plate in his head. He carries an old trumpet tied around his waist and believes with every fiber of his being that he is the Archangel Gabriel. He carries a chipped basket with an assortment of discarded fruits and vegetables he has picked up in the strip district and which he attempts to sell.*

GABRIEL [*Singing*]: Yes, ma'am, I got plums
You ask me how I sell them
Oh ten cents apiece
Three for a quarter
Come and buy now
'Cause I'm here today
And tomorrow I'll be gone

GABRIEL *enters.*

Hey, Rose!

ROSE: How you doing, Gabe?

GABRIEL: There's Troy . . . Hey, Troy!

TROY: Hey, Gabe.

Exit into kitchen.

ROSE [*to* GABRIEL]: What you got there?

GABRIEL: You know what I got, Rose. I got fruits and vegetables.

ROSE [*looking in basket*]: Where's all these plums you talking about?

GABRIEL: I ain't got no plums today, Rose. I was just singing that. Have some tomorrow. Put me in a big order for plums. Have enough plums tomorrow for St. Peter and everybody.

TROY *enters from kitchen, crosses to steps.*

[*To* ROSE] Troy's mad at me.

TROY: I ain't mad at you. What I got to be mad at you about? You ain't done nothing to me.

GABRIEL: I just moved over to Miss Pearl's to keep out from in your way. I ain't mean no harm by it.

TROY: Who said anything about that? I ain't said anything about that.

GABRIEL: You ain't mad at me, is you?

TROY: Naw . . . I ain't mad at you, Gabe. If I was mad at you I'd tell you about it.

GABRIEL: Got me two rooms. In the basement. Got my own door too. Wanna see my key?

He holds up a key.

That's my own key! Ain't nobody else got a key like that. That's my key! My two rooms!

TROY: Well, that's good, Gabe. You got your own key . . . that's good.

ROSE: You hungry, Gabe? I was just fixing to cook Troy his breakfast.

GABRIEL: I'll take some biscuits. You got some biscuits? Did you know when I was in heaven . . . every morning me and St. Peter would sit down by the gate and eat some big fat biscuits? Oh, yeah! We had us a good time. We'd sit there and eat us them biscuits and then St. Peter would go off to sleep and tell me to wake him up when it's time to open the gates for the judgment.

ROSE: Well, come on . . . I'll make up a batch of biscuits.

ROSE *exits into the house.*

GABRIEL: Troy . . . St. Peter got your name in the book. I seen it. It say . . . Troy Maxson, I say . . . I know him! He got the same name like what I got. That's my brother!

TROY: How many times you gonna tell me that, Gabe?

GABRIEL: Ain't got my name in the book. Don't have to have my name. I done died and went to heaven. He got your name though. One morning St. Peter was looking at his book . . . marking it up for the judgment . . . and he let me see your name. Got it in there under M. Got Rose's name . . . I ain't seen it like I seen yours . . . but I know it's in there. He got a great big book. Got everybody's name what was ever been born. That's what he told me. But I seen your name. Seen it with my own eyes.

TROY: Go on in the house there. Rose going to fix you something to eat.

GABRIEL: Oh, I ain't hungry. I done had breakfast with Aunt Jemimah. She come by and cooked me up a whole mess of flapjacks. Remember how we used to eat them flapjacks?

TROY: Go on in the house and get you something to eat now.

GABRIEL: I got to go sell my plums. I done sold some tomatoes. Got me two quarters. Wanna see?

He shows TROY *his quarters.*

I'm gonna save them and buy me a new horn so St. Peter can hear me when it's time to open the gates.

GABRIEL *stops suddenly. Listens.*

Hear that? That's the hellhounds. I got to chase them out of here. Go on get out of here! Get out!

GABRIEL *exits singing.*

Better get ready for the judgment
Better get ready for the judgment
My Lord is coming down

ROSE *enters from the house.*

TROY: He gone off somewhere.

GABRIEL [*offstage*]: Better get ready for the judgment
Better get ready for the judgment morning
Better get ready for the judgment
My God is coming down

ROSE: He ain't eating right. Miss Pearl say she can't get him to eat nothing.

TROY: What you want me to do about it, Rose? I done did everything I can for the man. I can't make him get well. Man got half his head blown away . . . what you expect?

ROSE: Seem like something ought to be done to help him.

TROY: Man don't bother nobody. He just mixed up from that metal plate he got in his head. Ain't no sense for him to go back into the hospital.

ROSE: Least he be eating right. They can help him take care of himself.

TROY: Don't nobody wanna be locked up, Rose. What you wanna lock him up for? Man go over there and fight the war . . . messin' around with them Japs, get half his head blown off . . . and they give him a lousy three thousand dollars. And I had to swoop down on that.

ROSE: Is you fixing to go into that again?

TROY: That's the only way I got a roof over my head . . . cause of that metal plate.

ROSE: Ain't no sense you blaming yourself for nothing. Gabe wasn't in no condition to manage that money. You done what was right by him. Can't nobody say you ain't done what was right by him. Look how long you took care of him . . . till he wanted to have his own place and moved over there with Miss Pearl.

TROY: That ain't what I'm saying, woman! I'm just stating the facts. If my brother didn't have that metal plate in his head . . . I wouldn't have a pot to piss in or a window to throw it out of. And I'm fifty-three years old. Now see if you can understand that!

TROY *gets up from the porch and starts to exit the yard.*

ROSE: Where you going off to? You been running out of here every Saturday for weeks. I thought you was gonna work on this fence?

TROY: I'm gonna walk down to Taylors'. Listen to the ball game. I'll be back in a bit. I'll work on it when I get back.

He exits the yard. The lights go to black.

Scene 3

The lights come up on the yard. It is four hours later. ROSE *is taking down the clothes from the line.* CORY *enters carrying his football equipment.*

ROSE: Your daddy like to had a fit with you running out of here this morning without doing your chores.

CORY: I told you I had to go to practice.

ROSE: He say you were supposed to help him with this fence.

CORY: He been saying that the last four or five Saturdays, and then he don't never do nothing, but go down to Taylors'. Did you tell him about the recruiter?

ROSE: Yeah, I told him.

CORY: What he say?

ROSE: He ain't said nothing too much. You get in there and get started on your chores before he gets back. Go on and scrub down them steps before he gets back here hollering and carrying on.

CORY: I'm hungry. What you got to eat, Mama?

ROSE: Go on and get started on your chores. I got some meat loaf in there. Go on and make you a sandwich . . . and don't leave no mess in there.

CORY *exits into the house.* ROSE *continues to take down the clothes.* TROY *enters the yard and sneaks up and grabs her from behind.*

Troy! Go on, now. You liked to scared me to death. What was the score of the game? Lucille had me on the phone and I couldn't keep up with it.

TROY: What I care about the game? Come here, woman. [*He tries to kiss her.*]

ROSE: I thought you went down Taylors' to listen to the game. Go on, Troy! You supposed to be putting up this fence.

TROY [*attempting to kiss her again*]: I'll put it up when I finish with what is at hand.

ROSE: Go on, Troy. I ain't studying you.

TROY [*chasing after her*]: I'm studying you . . . fixing to do my homework!

ROSE: Troy, you better leave me alone.

TROY: Where's Cory? That boy brought his butt home yet?

ROSE: He's in the house doing his chores.

TROY [*calling*]: Cory! Get your butt out here, boy!

ROSE *exits into the house with the laundry.* TROY *goes over to the pile of wood, picks up a board, and starts sawing.* CORY *enters from the house.*

TROY: You just now coming in here from leaving this morning?

CORY: Yeah, I had to go to football practice.

TROY: Yeah, what?

CORY: Yessir.

TROY: I ain't but two seconds off you noway. The garbage sitting in there overflowing . . . you ain't done none of your chores . . . and you come in here talking about "Yeah."

CORY: I was just getting ready to do my chores, now, Pop . . .

TROY: Your first chore is to help me with this fence on Saturday. Everything else come after that. Now get that saw and cut them boards.

CORY *takes the saw and begins cutting the boards.* TROY *continues working. There is a long pause.*

CORY: Hey, Pop . . . why don't you buy a TV?

TROY: What I want with a TV? What I want one of them for?

CORY: Everybody got one. Earl, Ba Bra . . . Jesse!

TROY: I ain't asked you who had one. I say what I want with one?

CORY: So you can watch it. They got lots of things on TV. Baseball games and everything. We could watch the World Series.

TROY: Two hundred dollars, huh?

CORY: That ain't that much, Pop.

TROY: Naw, it's just two hundred dollars. See that roof you got over your head at night? Let me tell you something about that roof. It's been over ten years since that roof was last tarred. See now . . . the snow come this winter and sit up there on that roof like it is . . . and it's gonna seep inside. It's just gonna be a little bit . . . ain't gonna hardly notice it. Then the next thing you know, it's gonna be leaking all over the house. Then the wood rot from all that water and you gonna need a whole new roof. Now, how much you think it cost to get that roof tarred?

CORY: I don't know.

TROY: Two hundred and sixty-four dollars . . . cash money. While you thinking about a TV, I got to be thinking about the roof . . . and whatever else go wrong around here. Now if you had two hundred dollars, what would you do . . . fix the roof or buy a TV?

CORY: I'd buy a TV. Then when the roof started to leak . . . when it needed fixing . . . I'd fix it.

TROY: Where you gonna get the money from? You done spent it for a TV. You gonna sit up and watch the water run all over your brand new TV.

CORY: Aw, Pop. You got money, I know you do.

TROY: Where I got it at, huh?

CORY: You got it in the bank.

TROY: You wanna see my bankbook? You wanna see that seventy-three dollars and twenty-two cents I got sitting up in there.

CORY: You ain't got to pay for it all at one time. You can put a down payment on it and carry it on home with you.

TROY: Not me. I ain't gonna owe nobody nothing if I can help it. Miss a payment and they come and snatch it right out your house. Then what you got? Now, soon as I get two hundred dollars clear, then I'll buy a TV. Right now, as soon as I get two hundred and sixty-four dollars, I'm gonna have this roof tarred.

CORY: Aw . . . Pop!

TROY: You go on and get you two hundred dollars and buy one if ya want it. I got better things to do with my money.

CORY: I can't get no two hundred dollars. I ain't never seen two hundred dollars.

TROY: I'll tell you what . . . you get you a hundred dollars and I'll put the other hundred with it.

CORY: All right, I'm gonna show you.

TROY: You gonna show me how you can cut them boards right now.

CORY *begins to cut the boards. There is a long pause.*

CORY: The Pirates won today. That makes five in a row.

TROY: I ain't thinking about the Pirates. Got an all-white team. Got that boy . . . that Puerto Rican boy . . . Clemente. Don't even half-play him. That boy could be something if they give him a chance. Play him one day and sit him on the bench the next.

CORY: He gets a lot of chances to play.

TROY: I'm talking about playing regular. Playing every day so you can get your timing. That's what I'm talking about.

CORY: They got some white guys on the team that don't play every day. You can't play everybody at the same time.

TROY: If they got a white fellow sitting on the bench . . . you can bet your last dollar he can't play! The colored guy got to be twice as good before he get on the team. That's why I don't want you to get all tied up in them sports. Man on the team and what it get him? They got colored on the team and don't use them. Same as not having them. All them teams the same.

CORY: The Braves got Hank Aaron and Wes Covington. Hank Aaron hit two home runs today. That makes forty-three.

TROY: Hank Aaron ain't nobody. That's what you supposed to do. That's how you supposed to play the game. Ain't nothing to it. It's just a matter of timing . . . getting the right follow-through. Hell, I can hit forty-three home runs right now!

CORY: Not off no major-league pitching, you couldn't.

TROY: We had better pitching in the Negro leagues. I hit seven home runs off of Satchel Paige.° You can't get no better than that!

CORY: Sandy Koufax. He's leading the league in strikeouts.

TROY: I ain't thinking of no Sandy Koufax.

CORY: You got Warren Spahn and Lew Burdette. I bet you couldn't hit no home runs off of Warren Spahn.

TROY: I'm through with it now. You go on and cut them boards.

Pause.

Your mama tell me you done got recruited by a college football team? Is that right?

CORY: Yeah. Coach Zellman say the recruiter gonna be coming by to talk to you. Get you to sign the permission papers.

TROY: I thought you supposed to be working down there at the A&P. Ain't you suppose to be working down there after school?

CORY: Mr. Stawicki say he gonna hold my job for me until after the football season. Say starting next week I can work weekends.

TROY: I thought we had an understanding about this football stuff? You suppose to keep up with your chores and hold that job down at the A&P. Ain't been around here all day on a Saturday. Ain't none of your chores done . . . and now you telling me you done quit your job.

CORY: I'm gonna be working weekends.

Satchel Paige *Legendary black pitcher in the Negro leagues.*

TROY: You damn right you are! And ain't no need for nobody coming around here to talk to me about signing nothing.

CORY: Hey, Pop . . . you can't do that. He's coming all the way from North Carolina.

TROY: I don't care where he coming from. The white man ain't gonna let you get nowhere with that football noway. You go on and get your booklearning so you can work yourself up in that A&P or learn how to fix cars or build houses or something, get you a trade. That way you have something can't nobody take away from you. You go on and learn how to put your hands to some good use. Besides hauling people's garbage.

CORY: I get good grades, Pop. That's why the recruiter wants to talk with you. You got to keep your grades to get recruited. This way I'll be going to college. I'll get a chance . . .

TROY: First you gonna get your butt down there to the A&P and get your job back.

CORY: Mr. Stawicki done already hired somebody else 'cause I told him I was playing football.

TROY: You a bigger fool than I thought . . . to let somebody take away your job so you can play some football. Where you gonna get your money to take out your girlfriend and whatnot? What kind of foolishness is that to let somebody take away your job?

CORY: I'm still gonna be working weekends.

TROY: Naw . . . naw. You getting your butt out of here and finding you another job.

CORY: Come on, Pop! I got to practice. I can't work after school and play football too. The team needs me. That's what Coach Zellman say . . .

TROY: I don't care what nobody else say. I'm the boss . . . you understand? I'm the boss around here. I do the only saying what counts.

CORY: Come on, Pop!

TROY: I asked you . . . did you understand?

CORY: Yeah . . .

TROY: What?!

CORY: Yessir.

TROY: You go on down there to that A&P and see if you can get your job back. If you can't do both . . . then you quit the football team. You've got to take the crookeds with the straights.

CORY: Yessir.

Pause.

Can I ask you a question?

TROY: What the hell you wanna ask me? Mr. Stawicki the one you got the questions for.

CORY: How come you ain't never liked me?

TROY: Liked you? Who the hell say I got to like you? What law is there say I got to like you? Wanna stand up in my face and ask a damn-fool-ass question like that. Talking about liking somebody. Come here, boy, when I talk to you.

CORY *comes over to where* TROY *is working. He stands slouched over and* TROY *shoves him on his shoulder.*

Straighten up, goddammit! I asked you a question . . . what law is there say I got to like you?

CORY: None.

TROY: Well, all right then! Don't you eat every day?

Pause.

Answer me when I talk to you! Don't you eat every day?

CORY: Yeah.

TROY: Nigger, as long as you in my house, you put that sir on the end of it when you talk to me!

CORY: Yes . . . sir.

TROY: You eat every day.

CORY: Yessir!

TROY: Got a roof over your head.

CORY: Yessir!

TROY: Got clothes on your back.

CORY: Yessir.

TROY: Why you think that is?

CORY: Cause of you.

TROY: Ah, hell I know it's 'cause of me . . . but why do you think that is?

CORY [*hesitant*]: Cause you like me.

TROY: Like you? I go out of here every morning . . . bust my butt . . . putting up with them crackers° every day . . . cause I like you? You about the biggest fool I ever saw.

Pause.

It's my job. It's my responsibility! You understand that? A man got to take care of his family. You live in my house . . . sleep you behind on my bedclothes . . . fill your belly up with my food . . . cause you my son. You my flesh and blood. Not 'cause I like you! Cause it's my duty to take care of you. I owe a responsibility to you! Let's get this straight right here . . . before it go along any further . . . I ain't got to like you. Mr. Rand don't give me my money come payday cause he likes me. He gives me cause he owe me. I gave you your life! Me and your mamma worked that out between us. And liking your black ass wasn't part of the bargain. Don't you try and go through life worrying about if somebody like you or not. You best be making sure they doing right by you. You understand what I'm saying, boy?

CORY: Yessir.

TROY: Then get the hell out of my face, and get on down to that A&P.

ROSE *has been standing behind the screen door for much of the scene. She enters as* CORY *exits.*

ROSE: Why don't you let the boy go ahead and play football, Troy? Ain't no harm in that. He's just trying to be like you with the sports.

TROY: I don't want him to be like me! I want him to move as far away from my life as he can get. You the only decent thing that ever happened to me. I wish him that. But I don't wish him a thing else from my life. I decided seventeen years ago that boy wasn't getting involved in no sports. Not after what they did to me in the sports.

ROSE: Troy, why don't you admit you was too old to play in the major leagues? For once . . . why don't you admit that?

crackers *white people, often used to refer disparagingly to poor whites.*

TROY: What do you mean too old? Don't come telling me I was too old. I just wasn't the right color. Hell, I'm fifty-three years old and can do better than Selkirk's .269 right now!

ROSE: How's was you gonna play ball when you were over forty? Sometimes I can't get no sense out of you.

TROY: I got good sense, woman. I got sense enough not to let my boy get hurt over playing no sports. You been mothering that boy too much. Worried about if people like him.

ROSE: Everything that boy do . . . he do for you. He wants you to say "Good job, son." That's all.

TROY: Rose, I ain't got time for that. He's alive. He's healthy. He's got to make his own way. I made mine. Ain't nobody gonna hold his hand when he get out there in that world.

ROSE: Times have changed from when you was young, Troy. People change. The world's changing around you and you can't even see it.

TROY [*slow, methodical*]: Woman . . . I do the best I can do. I come in here every Friday. I carry a sack of potatoes and a bucket of lard. You all line up at the door with your hands out. I give you the lint from my pockets. I give you my sweat and my blood. I ain't got no tears, I done spent them. We go upstairs in that room at night . . . and I fall down on you and try to blast a hole into forever. I get up Monday morning . . . find my lunch on the table. I go out. Make my way. Find my strength to carry me through to the next Friday.

Pause.

That's all I got, Rose. That's all I got to give. I can't give nothing else.

TROY *exits into the house. The lights go down to black.*

Scene 4

It is Friday. Two weeks later. CORY *starts out of the house with his football equipment. The phone rings.*

CORY [*calling*]: I got it!

He answers the phone and stands in the screen door talking.

Hello? Hey, Jesse. Naw . . . I was just getting ready to leave now.

ROSE [*calling*]: Cory!

CORY: I told you, man, them spikes is all tore up. You can use them if you want, but they ain't no good. Earl got some spikes.

ROSE [*calling*]: Cory!

CORY [*calling to* ROSE]: Mam? I'm talking to Jesse.

Into phone.

When she say that? [*Pause.*] Aw, you lying, man. I'm gonna tell her you said that.

ROSE [*calling*]: Cory, don't you go nowhere!

CORY: I got to go to the game, Ma!

Into the phone.

Yeah, hey, look, I'll talk to you later. Yeah, I'll meet you over Earl's house. Later. Bye, Ma.

CORY *exits the house and starts out the yard.*

ROSE: Cory, where you going off to? You got that stuff all pulled out and thrown all over your room.

CORY [*in the yard*]: I was looking for my spikes. Jesse wanted to borrow my spikes.

ROSE: Get up there and get that cleaned up before your daddy get back in here.

CORY: I got to go to the game! I'll clean it up *when I get back.*

CORY *exits.*

ROSE: That's all he need to do is see that room all messed up.

ROSE *exits into the house.* TROY *and* BONO *enter the yard.* TROY *is dressed in clothes other than his work clothes.*

BONO: He told them the same thing he told you. Take it to the union.

TROY: Brownie ain't got that much sense. Man wasn't thinking about nothing. He wait until I confront them on it . . . then he wanna come crying seniority.

Calls.

Hey, Rose!

BONO: I wish I could have seen Mr. Rand's face when he told you.

TROY: He couldn't get it out of his mouth! Liked to bit his tongue! When they called me down there to the Commissioner's office . . . he thought they was gonna fire me. Like everybody else.

BONO: I didn't think they was gonna fire you. I thought they was gonna put you on the warning paper.

TROY: Hey, Rose!

To BONO.

Yeah, Mr. Rand like to bit his tongue.

TROY *breaks the seal on the bottle, takes a drink, and hands it to* BONO.

BONO: I see you run right down to Taylors' and told that Alberta gal.

TROY [*calling*]: Hey Rose! [*To* BONO] I told everybody. Hey, Rose! I went down there to cash my check.

ROSE [*entering from the house*]: Hush all that hollering, man! I know you out here. What they say down there at the Commissioner's office?

TROY: You supposed to come when I call you, woman. Bono'll tell you that.

To BONO.

Don't Lucille come when you call her?

ROSE: Man, hush your mouth. I ain't no dog . . . talk about "come when you call me."

TROY [*puts his arm around* ROSE]: You hear this, Bono? I had me an old dog used to get uppity like that. You say, "C'mere, Blue!" . . . and he just lay there and look at you. End up getting a stick and chasing him away trying to make him come.

ROSE: I ain't studying you and your dog. I remember you used to sing that old song.

TROY [*he sings*]: Hear it ring! Hear it ring! I had a dog his name was Blue.

ROSE: Don't nobody wanna hear you sing that old song.

TROY [*sings*]: You know Blue was mighty true.

ROSE: Used to have Cory running around here singing that song.

BONO: Hell, I remember that song myself.

TROY [*sings*]: You know Blue was a good old dog.
Blue treed a possum in a hollow log.
That was my daddy's song. My daddy made up that song.

ROSE: I don't care who made it up. Don't nobody wanna hear you sing it.

TROY [*makes a song like calling a dog*]: Come here, woman.

ROSE: You come in here carrying on, I reckon they ain't fired you. What they say down there at the Commissioner's office?

TROY: Look here, Rose . . . Mr. Rand called me into his office today when I got back from talking to them people down there . . . it come from up top . . . he called me in and told me they was making me a driver.

ROSE: Troy, you kidding!

TROY: No I ain't. Ask Bono.

ROSE: Well, that's great, Troy. Now you don't have to hassle them people no more.

LYONS *enters from the street.*

TROY: Aw hell, I wasn't looking to see you today. I thought you was in jail. Got it all over the front page of the *Courier* about them raiding Sefus' place . . . where you be hanging out with all them thugs.

LYONS: Hey, Pop . . . that ain't got nothing to do with me. I don't go down there gambling. I go down there to sit in with the band. I ain't got nothing to do with the gambling part. They got some good music down there.

TROY: They got some rogues . . . is what they got.

LYONS: How you been, Mr. Bono? Hi, Rose.

BONO: I see where you playing down at the Crawford Grill tonight.

ROSE: How come you ain't brought Bonnie like I told you. You should have brought Bonnie with you, she ain't been over in a month of Sundays.

LYONS: I was just in the neighborhood . . . thought I'd stop by.

TROY: Here he come . . .

BONO: Your daddy got a promotion on the rubbish. He's gonna be the first colored driver. Ain't got to do nothing but sit up there and read the paper like them white fellows.

LYONS: Hey, Pop . . . if you knew how to read you'd be all right.

BONO: Naw . . . naw . . . you mean if the nigger knew how to *drive* he'd be all right. Been fighting with them people about driving and ain't even got a license. Mr. Rand know you ain't got no driver's license?

TROY: Driving ain't nothing. All you do is point the truck where you want it to go. Driving ain't nothing.

BONO: Do Mr. Rand know you ain't got no driver's license? That's what I'm talking about. I ain't asked if driving was easy. I asked if Mr. Rand know you ain't got no driver's license.

TROY: He ain't got to know. The man ain't got to know my business. Time he find out, I have two or three driver's licenses.

LYONS [*going into his pocket*]: Say, look here, Pop . . .

TROY: I knew it was coming. Didn't I tell you, Bono? I know what kind of "Look here, Pop" that was. The nigger fixing to ask me for some money. It's Friday night. It's my payday. All them rogues down there on the avenue . . . the ones that ain't in jail . . . and Lyons is hopping in his shoes to get down there with them.

LYONS: See, Pop . . . if you give somebody else a chance to talk sometime, you'd see that I was fixing to pay you back your ten dollars like I told you. Here . . . I told you I'd pay you when Bonnie got paid.

TROY: Naw . . . you go ahead and keep that ten dollars. Put in the bank. The next time you feel like you wanna come by here and ask me for something . . . you go on down there and get that.

LYONS: Here's your ten dollars, Pop. I told you I don't want you to give me nothing. I just wanted to borrow ten dollars.

TROY: Naw . . . you go on and keep that for the next time you want to ask me.

LYONS: Come on, Pop . . . here go your ten dollars.

ROSE: Why don't you go on and let the boy pay you back, Troy?

LYONS: Here you go, Rose. If you don't take it I'm gonna have to hear about it for the next six months.

He hands her the money.

ROSE: You can hand yours over here too, Troy.

TROY: You see this, Bono. You see how they do me.

BONO: Yeah, Lucille do me the same way.

GABRIEL *is heard singing offstage. He enters.*

GABRIEL: Better get ready for the Judgment! Better get ready for . . . Hey! . . . Hey! . . . There's Troy's boy!

LYONS: How are you doing, Uncle Gabe?

GABRIEL: Lyons . . . The King of the Jungle! Rose . . . hey, Rose. Got a flower for you.

He takes a rose from his pocket.

Picked it myself. That's the same rose like you is!

ROSE: That's right nice of you, Gabe.

LYONS: What you been doing, Uncle Gabe?

GABRIEL: Oh, I been chasing hellhounds and waiting on the time to tell St. Peter to open the gates.

LYONS: You been chasing hellhounds, huh? Well . . . you doing the right thing, Uncle Gabe. Somebody got to chase them.

GABRIEL: Oh, yeah . . . I know it. The devil's strong. The devil ain't no pushover. Hellhounds snipping at everybody's heels. But I got my trumpet waiting on the judgment time.

LYONS: Waiting on the Battle of Armageddon, huh?

GABRIEL: Ain't gonna be too much of a battle when God get to waving that Judgment sword. But the people's gonna have a hell of a time trying to get into heaven if them gates ain't open.

LYONS [*putting his arm around* GABRIEL]: You hear this, Pop. Uncle Gabe, you all right!

GABRIEL [*laughing with* LYONS]: Lyons! King of the Jungle.

ROSE: You gonna stay for supper, Gabe. Want me to fix you a plate?

GABRIEL: I'll take a sandwich, Rose. Don't want no plate. Just wanna eat with my hands. I'll take a sandwich.

ROSE: How about you, Lyons? You staying? Got some short ribs cooking.

LYONS: Naw, I won't eat nothing till after we finished playing.

Pause.

You ought to come down and listen to me play, Pop.

TROY: I don't like that Chinese music. All that noise.

ROSE: Go on in the house and wash up, Gabe . . . I'll fix you a sandwich.

GABRIEL [*to* LYONS, *as he exits*]: Troy's mad at me.

LYONS: What you mad at Uncle Gabe for, Pop.

ROSE: He thinks Troy's mad at him cause he moved over to Miss Pearl's.

TROY: I ain't mad at the man. He can live where he want to live at.

LYONS: What he move over there for? Miss Pearl don't like nobody.

ROSE: She don't mind him none. She treats him real nice. She just don't allow all that singing.

TROY: She don't mind that rent he be paying . . . that's what she don't mind.

ROSE: Troy, I ain't going through that with you no more. He's over there cause he want to have his own place. He can come and go as he please.

TROY: Hell, he could come and go as he please here. I wasn't stopping him. I ain't put no rules on him.

ROSE: It ain't the same thing, Troy. And you know it.

GABRIEL *comes to the door.*

Now, that's the last I wanna hear about that. I don't wanna hear nothing else about Gabe and Miss Pearl. And next week . . .

GABRIEL: I'm ready for my sandwich, Rose.

ROSE: And next week . . . when that recruiter come from that school . . . I want you to sign that paper and go on and let Cory play football. Then that'll be the last I have to hear about that.

TROY [*to* ROSE *as she exits into the house*]: I ain't thinking about Cory nothing.

LYONS: What . . . Cory got recruited? What school he going to?

TROY: That boy walking around here smelling his piss . . . thinking he's grown. Thinking he's gonna do what he want, irrespective of what I say. Look here, Bono . . . I left the Commissioner's office and went down to the A&P . . . that boy ain't working down there. He lying to me. Telling me he got his job back . . . telling me he working weekends . . . telling me he working after school . . . Mr. Stawicki tell me he ain't working down there at all!

LYONS: Cory just growing up. He's just busting at the seams trying to fill out your shoes.

TROY: I don't care what he's doing. When he get to the point where he wanna disobey me . . . then it's time for him to move on. Bono'll tell you that. I bet he ain't never disobeyed his daddy without paying the consequences.

BONO: I ain't never had a chance. My daddy came on through . . . but I ain't never knew him to see him . . . or what he had on his mind or where he went. Just moving on through. Searching out the New Land. That's what the old folks used to call it. See a fellow moving around from place to place . . . woman to woman . . . called it searching out the New Land. I can't say if he ever found it. I come along, didn't want no kids. Didn't know if I was gonna be in one place long enough to fix on them right as their daddy. I figured I was going searching too. As it turned out I been hooked up with Lucille near about as long as your daddy been with Rose. Going on sixteen years.

TROY: Sometimes I wish I hadn't known my daddy. He ain't cared nothing about no kids. A kid to him wasn't nothing. All he wanted was for you to learn how to walk so he could start you to working. When it come time for eating . . . he ate first. If there was anything left over, that's what you got. Man would sit down and eat two chickens and give you the wing.

LYONS: You ought to stop that, Pop. Everybody feed their kids. No matter how hard times is . . . everybody care about their kids. Make sure they have something to eat.

TROY: The only thing my daddy cared about was getting them bales of cotton in to Mr. Lubin. That's the only thing that mattered to him. Sometimes I used to wonder why he was living. Wonder why the devil hadn't come and got him. "Get them bales of cotton in to Mr. Lubin" and find out he owe him money . . .

LYONS: He should have just went on and left when he saw he couldn't get nowhere. That's what I would have done.

TROY: How he gonna leave with eleven kids? And where he gonna go? He ain't knew how to do nothing but farm. No, he was trapped and I think he knew it. But I'll say this for him . . . he felt a responsibility toward us. Maybe he ain't treated us the way I felt he should have . . . but without that responsibility he could have walked off and left us . . . made his own way.

BONO: A lot of them did. Back in those days what you talking about . . . they walk out their front door and just take on down one road or another and keep on walking.

LYONS: There you go! That's what I'm talking about.

BONO: Just keep on walking till you come to something else. Ain't you never heard of nobody having the walking blues? Well, that's what you call it when you just take off like that.

TROY: My daddy ain't had them walking blues! What you talking about? He stayed right there with his family. But he was just as evil as he could be. My mama couldn't stand him. Couldn't stand that evilness. She run off when I was about eight. She sneaked off one night after he had gone to sleep. Told me she was coming back for me. I ain't never seen her no more. All his women run off and left him. He wasn't good for nobody.

When my turn come to head out, I was fourteen and got to sniffing around Joe Canewell's daughter. Had us an old mule we called Greyboy. My daddy sent me out to do some plowing and I tied up Greyboy and went to fooling around with Joe Canewell's daughter. We done found us a nice little spot, got real cozy with each other. She about thirteen and we done figures we was grown anyway . . . so we down there enjoying ourselves . . . ain't thinking about nothing. We didn't know Greyboy had got loose and wandered back to the house and my daddy was looking for me. We down there by the creek enjoying ourselves when my daddy come up on us. Surprised us. He had them leather straps off the mule and commenced to whupping me like there was no tomorrow. I jumped up, mad and embarrassed. I was scared of my daddy. When he commenced to whupping on me . . . quite naturally I run to get out of the way.

Pause.

Now I thought he was mad cause I ain't done my work. But I see where he was chasing me off so he could have the gal for himself. When I see what the matter of it was, I lost all fear of my daddy. Right there is where I become a man . . . at fourteen years of age.

Pause.

Now it was my turn to run him off. I picked up them same reins that he had used on me. I picked up them reins and commenced to whupping on him. The gal jumped up and run off . . . and when my daddy turned to face me, I could see why the devil had never come to get him . . . cause he was the devil himself. I don't know what happened. When I woke up, I was laying right there by the creek, and Blue . . . this old dog we had . . . was licking my face. I thought I was blind. I couldn't see nothing. Both my eyes were swollen shut. I layed there and cried. I didn't know what I was gonna do. The only thing I knew was the time had come for me to leave my daddy's house. And right there the world suddenly got big. And it was a long time before I could cut it down to where I could handle it.

Part of that cutting down was when I got to the place where I could feel him kicking in my blood and knew that the only thing that separated us was the matter of a few years.

GABRIEL *enters from the house with a sandwich.*

LYONS: What you got there, Uncle Gabe?

GABRIEL: Got me a ham sandwich. Rose gave me a ham sandwich.

TROY: I don't know what happened to him. I done lost touch with everybody except Gabriel. But I hope he's dead. I hope he found some peace.

LYONS: That's a heavy story, Pop. I didn't know you left home when you was fourteen.

TROY: And didn't know nothing. The only part of the world I knew was the forty-two acres of Mr. Lubin's land. That's all I knew about life.

LYONS: Fourteen's kinda young to be out on your own. [*Phone rings.*] I don't even think I was ready to be out on my own at fourteen. I don't know what I would have done.

TROY: I got up from the creek and walked on down to Mobile. I was through with farming. Figured I could do better in the city. So I walked the two hundred miles to Mobile.

LYONS: Wait a minute . . . you ain't walked no two hundred miles, Pop. Ain't nobody gonna walk no two hundred miles. You talking about some walking there.

BONO: That's the only way you got anywhere back in them days.

LYONS: Shhh. Damn if I wouldn't have hitched a ride with somebody!

TROY: Who you gonna hitch it with? They ain't had no cars and things like they got now. We talking about 1918.

ROSE [*entering*]: What you all out here getting into?

TROY [*to* ROSE]: I'm telling Lyons how good he got it. He don't know nothing about this I'm talking.

ROSE: Lyons, that was Bonnie on the phone. She say you supposed to pick her up.

LYONS: Yeah, okay, Rose.

TROY: I walked on down to Mobile and hitched up with some of them fellows that was heading this way. Got up here and found out . . . not only couldn't you get a job . . . you couldn't find no place to live. I thought I was in freedom. Shhh. Colored folks living down there on the riverbanks in whatever kind of shelter they could find for themselves. Right down there under the Brady Street Bridge. Living in shacks made of sticks and tarpaper. Messed around there and went from bad to worse. Started stealing. First it was food. Then I figured, hell, if I steal money I can buy me some food. Buy me some shoes too! One thing led to another. Met your mama. I was young and anxious to be a man. Met your mama and had you. What I do that for? Now I got to worry about feeding you and her. Got to steal three times as much. Went out one day looking for somebody to rob . . . that's what I was, a robber. I'll tell you the truth. I'm ashamed of it today. But it's the truth. Went to rob this fellow . . . pulled out my knife . . . and he pulled out a gun. Shot me in the chest. It felt just like somebody had taken a hot branding iron and laid it on me. When he shot me I jumped at him with my knife. They told me I killed him and they put me in the penitentiary and locked me up for fifteen years. That's where I met Bono. That's where I learned how to play baseball. Got out that place and your mama had taken you and went on to make life without me. Fifteen years was a long time for her to wait. But that fifteen years cured me of that robbing stuff. Rose'll tell you. She asked me when I met her if I had gotten all that foolishness out of my system. And I told her, "Baby, it's you and baseball all what count with me." You hear me, Bono? I meant it too. She say, "Which one comes first?" I told her, "Baby, ain't no doubt it's baseball . . . but you stick and get old with me and we'll both outlive this baseball." Am I right, Rose? And it's true.

ROSE: Man, hush your mouth. You ain't said no such thing. Talking about, "Baby, you know you'll always be number one with me." That's what you was talking.

TROY: You hear that, Bono. That's why I love her.

BONO: Rose'll keep you straight. You get off the track, she'll straighten you up.

ROSE: Lyons, you better get on up and get Bonnie. She waiting on you.

LYONS [*gets up to go*]: Hey, Pop, why don't you come on down to the Grill and hear me play?

TROY: I ain't going down there. I'm too old to be sitting around in them clubs.

BONO: You got to be good to play down at the Grill.

LYONS: Come on, Pop . . .

TROY: I got to get up in the morning.

LYONS: You ain't got to stay long.

TROY: Naw, I'm gonna get my supper and go on to bed.

LYONS: Well, I got to go. I'll see you again.

TROY: Don't you come around my house on my payday.

ROSE: Pick up the phone and let somebody know you coming. And bring Bonnie with you. You know I'm always glad to see her.

LYONS: Yeah, I'll do that, Rose. You take care now. See you, Pop. See you, Mr. Bono. See you, Uncle Gabe.

GABRIEL: Lyons! King of the Jungle!

LYONS *exits.*

TROY: Is supper ready, woman? Me and you got some business to take care of. I'm gonna tear it up too.

ROSE: Troy, I done told you now!

TROY [*puts his arm around* BONO]: Aw hell, woman . . . this is Bono. Bono like family. I done known this nigger since . . . how long I done know you?

BONO: It's been a long time.

TROY: I done known this nigger since Skippy was a pup. Me and him done been through some times.

BONO: You sure right about that.

TROY: Hell, I done know him longer than I known you. And we still standing shoulder to shoulder. Hey, look here, Bono . . . a man can't ask for no more than that.

Drinks to him.

I love you, nigger.

BONO: Hell, I love you too . . . but I got to get home see my woman. You got yours in hand. I got to go get mine.

BONO *starts to exit as* CORY *enters the yard, dressed in his football uniform. He gives* TROY *a hard, uncompromising look.*

CORY: What you do that for, Pop?

He throws his helmet down in the direction of TROY.

ROSE: What's the matter? Cory . . . what's the matter?

CORY: Papa done went up to the school and told Coach Zellman I can't play football no more. Wouldn't even let me play the game. Told him to tell the recruiter not to come.

ROSE: Troy . . .

TROY: What you Troying me for. Yeah, I did it. And the boy know why I did it.

CORY: Why you wanna do that to me? That was the one chance I had.

ROSE: Ain't nothing wrong with Cory playing football, Troy.

TROY: The boy lied to me. I told the nigger if he wanna play football . . . to keep up his chores and hold down that job at the A&P. That was the conditions. Stopped down there to see Mr. Stawicki . . .

CORY: I can't work after school during the football season, Pop! I tried to tell you that Mr. Stawicki's holding my job for me. You don't never want to listen to nobody. And then you wanna go and do this to me!

TROY: I ain't done nothing to you. You done it to yourself.

CORY: Just cause you didn't have a chance! You just scared I'm gonna be better than you, that's all.

TROY: Come here.

ROSE: Troy . . .

CORY *reluctantly crosses over to* TROY.

TROY: All right! See. You done made a mistake.

CORY: I didn't even do nothing!

TROY: I'm gonna tell you what your mistake was. See . . . you swung at the ball and didn't hit it. That's strike one. See, you in the batter's box now. You swung and you missed. That's strike one. Don't you strike out!

Lights fade to black.

ACT II

Scene 1

The following morning. CORY *is at the tree hitting the ball with the bat. He tries to mimic* TROY, *but his swing is awkward, less sure.* ROSE *enters from the house.*

ROSE: Cory, I want you to help me with this cupboard.

CORY: I ain't quitting the team. I don't care what Poppa say.

ROSE: I'll talk to him when he gets back. He had to go see about your Uncle Gabe. The police done arrested him. Say he was disturbing the peace. He'll be back directly. Come on in here and help me clean out the top of this cupboard.

CORY *exits into the house.* ROSE *sees* TROY *and* BONO *coming down the alley.*

Troy . . . what they say down there?

TROY: Ain't said nothing. I give them fifty dollars and they let him go. I'll talk to you about it. Where's Cory?

ROSE: He's in there helping me clean out these cupboards.

TROY: Tell him to get his butt out here.

TROY *and* BONO *go over to the pile of wood.* BONO *picks up the saw and begins sawing.*

TROY [*to* BONO]: All they want is the money. That makes six or seven times I done went down there and got him. See me coming they stick out their *hands.*

BONO: Yeah. I know what you mean. That's all they care about . . . that money. They don't care about what's right.

Pause.

Nigger, why you got to go and get some hard wood? You ain't doing nothing but building a little old fence. Get you some soft pine wood. That's all you need.

TROY: I know what I'm doing. This is outside wood. You put pine wood inside the house. Pine wood is inside wood. This here is outside wood. Now you tell me where the fence is gonna be?

BONO: You don't need this wood. You can put it up with pine wood and it'll stand as long as you gonna be here looking at it.

TROY: How you know how long I'm gonna be here, nigger? Hell, I might just live forever. Live longer than old man Horsely.

BONO: That's what Magee used to say.

TROY: Magee's a damn fool. Now you tell me who you ever heard of gonna pull their own teeth with a pair of rusty pliers.

BONO: The old folks . . . my granddaddy used to pull his teeth with pliers. They ain't had no dentists for the colored folks back then.

TROY: Get clean pliers! You understand? Clean pliers! Sterilize them! Besides we ain't living back then. All Magee had to do was walk over to Doc Goldblum's.

BONO: I see where you and that Tallahassee gal . . . that Alberta . . . I see where you all done got tight.

TROY: What you mean "got tight"?

BONO: I see where you be laughing and joking with her all the time.

TROY: I laughs and jokes with all of them, Bono. You know me.

BONO: That ain't the kind of laughing and joking I'm talking about.

CORY *enters from the house.*

CORY: How you doing, Mr. Bono?

TROY: Cory? Get that saw from Bono and cut some wood. He talking about the wood's too hard to cut. Stand back there, Jim, and let that young boy show you how it's done.

BONO: He's sure welcome to it.

CORY *takes the saw and begins to cut the wood.*

Whew-e-e! Look at that. Big old strong boy. Look like Joe Louis. Hell, must be getting old the way I'm watching that boy whip through that wood.

CORY: I don't see why Mama want a fence around the yard noways.

TROY: Damn if I know either. What the hell she keeping out with it? She ain't got nothing nobody want.

BONO: Some people build fences to keep people out . . . and other people build fences to keep people in. Rose wants to hold on to you all. She loves you.

TROY: Hell, nigger, I don't need nobody to tell me my wife loves me. Cory . . . go on in the house and see if you can find that other saw.

CORY: Where's it at?

TROY: I said find it! Look for it till you find it!

CORY *exits into the house.*

What's that supposed to mean? Wanna keep us in?

BONO: Troy . . . I done known you seem like damn near my whole life. You and Rose both. I done know both of you all for a long time. I remember when you met Rose. When you was hitting them baseball out the park. A lot of them old gals was after you then. You had the pick of the litter. When you picked Rose, I was happy for you. That was the first time I knew you had any sense. I said . . . My man Troy knows what he's doing . . . I'm gonna follow this nigger . . . he might take me somewhere. I been following you too. I done learned a whole heap of things about life watching you. I done learned how to tell where the shit lies. How to tell it from the alfalfa. You done learned me a lot of things. You showed me how to not make the same mistakes . . . to take life as it comes along and keep putting one foot in front of the other.

Pause.

Rose a good woman, Troy.

TROY: Hell, nigger, I know she a good woman. I been married to her for eighteen years. What you got on your mind, Bono?

BONO: I just say she a good woman. Just like I say anything. I ain't got to have nothing on my mind.

TROY: You just gonna say she a good woman and leave it hanging out there like that? Why you telling me she a good woman?

BONO: She loves you, Troy. Rose loves you.

TROY: You saying I don't measure up. That's what you trying to say. I don't measure up cause I'm seeing this other gal. I know what you trying to say.

BONO: I know what Rose means to you, Troy. I'm just trying to say I don't want to see you mess up.

TROY: Yeah, I appreciate that, Bono. If you was messing around on Lucille I'd be telling you the same thing.

BONO: Well, that's all I got to say. I just say that because I love you both.

TROY: Hell, you know me . . . I wasn't out there looking for nothing. You can't find a better woman than Rose. I know that. But seems like this woman just stuck onto me where I can't shake her loose. I done wrestled with it, tried to throw her off me . . . but she just stuck on tighter. Now she's stuck on for good.

BONO: You's in control . . . that's what you tell me all the time. You responsible for what you do.

TROY: I ain't ducking the responsibility of it. As long as it sets right in my heart . . . then I'm okay. Cause that's all I listen to. It'll tell me right from wrong every time. And I ain't talking about doing Rose no bad turn. I love Rose. She done carried me a long ways and I love and respect her for that.

BONO: I know you do. That's why I don't want to see you hurt her. But what you gonna do when she find out? What you got then? If you try and juggle both of them . . . sooner or later you gonna drop one of them. That's common sense.

TROY: Yeah, I hear what you saying, Bono. I been trying to figure a way to work it out.

BONO: Work it out right, Troy. I don't want to be getting all up between you and Rose's business . . . but work it so it come out right.

TROY: Ah hell, I get all up between you and Lucille's business. When you gonna get that woman that refrigerator she been wanting? Don't tell me you ain't got no money now. I know who your banker is. Mellon don't need that money bad as Lucille want that refrigerator. I'll tell you that.

BONO: Tell you what I'll do . . . when you finish building this fence for Rose . . . I'll buy Lucille that refrigerator.

TROY: You done stuck your foot in your mouth now!

TROY *grabs up a board and begins to saw.* BONO *starts to walk out the yard.*

Hey, nigger . . . where you going?

BONO: I'm going home. I know you don't expect me to help you now. I'm protecting my money. I wanna see you put that fence up by yourself. That's what I want to see. You'll be here another six months without me.

TROY: Nigger, you ain't right.

BONO: When it comes to my money . . . I'm right as fireworks on the Fourth of July.

TROY: All right, we gonna see now. You better get out your bankbook.

BONO *exits, and* TROY *continues to work.* ROSE *enters from the house.*

ROSE: What they say down there? What's happening with Gabe?

TROY: I went down there and got him out. Cost me fifty dollars. Say he was disturbing the peace. Judge set up a hearing for him in three weeks. Say to show cause why he shouldn't be recommitted.

ROSE: What was he doing that cause them to arrest him?

TROY: Some kids was teasing him and he run them off home. Say he was howling and carrying on. Some folks seen him and called the police. That's all it was.

ROSE: Well, what's you say? What'd you tell the judge?

TROY: Told him I'd look after him. It didn't make no sense to recommit the man. He stuck out his big greasy palm and told me to give him fifty dollars and take him on home.

ROSE: Where's he at now? Where'd he go off to?

TROY: He's gone on about his business. He don't need nobody to hold his hand.

ROSE: Well, I don't know. Seem like that would be the best place for him if they did put him into the hospital. I know what you're gonna say. But that's what I think would be best.

TROY: The man done had his life ruined fighting for what? And they wanna take and lock him up. Let him be free. He don't bother nobody.

ROSE: Well, everybody got their own way of looking at it I guess. Come on and get your lunch. I got a bowl of lima beans and some cornbread in the oven. Come on get something to eat. Ain't no sense you fretting over Gabe.

ROSE *turns to go into the house.*

TROY: Rose . . . got something to tell you.

ROSE: Well, come on . . . wait till I get this food on the table.

TROY: Rose!

She stops and turns around.

I don't know how to say this.

Pause.

I can't explain it none. It just sort of grows on you till it gets out of hand. It starts out like a little bush . . . and the next thing you know it's a whole forest.

ROSE: Troy . . . what is you talking about?

TROY: I'm talking, woman, let me talk. I'm trying to find a way to tell you . . . I'm gonna be a daddy. I'm gonna be somebody's daddy.

ROSE: Troy . . . you're not telling me this? You're gonna be . . . what?

TROY: Rose . . . now . . . see . . .

ROSE: You telling me you gonna be somebody's daddy? You telling your *wife* this?

GABRIEL *enters from the street. He carries a rose in his hand.*

GABRIEL: Hey, Troy! Hey, Rose!

ROSE: I have to wait eighteen years to hear something like this.

GABRIEL: Hey, Rose . . . I got a flower for you.

He hands it to her.

That's a rose. Same rose like you is.

ROSE: Thanks, Gabe.

GABRIEL: Troy, you ain't mad at me is you? Them bad mens come and put me away. You ain't mad at me is you?

TROY: Naw, Gabe, I ain't mad at you.

ROSE: Eighteen years and you wanna come with this.

GABRIEL [*takes a quarter out of his pocket*]: See what I got? Got a brand new quarter.

TROY: Rose . . . it's just . . .

ROSE: Ain't nothing you can say, Troy. Ain't no way of explaining that.

GABRIEL: Fellow that give me this quarter had a whole mess of them. I'm gonna keep this quarter till it stop shining.

ROSE: Gabe, go on in the house there. I got some watermelon in the frigidaire. Go on and get you a piece.

GABRIEL: Say, Rose . . . you know I was chasing hellhounds and them bad mens come and get me and take me away. Troy helped me. He come down there and told them they better let me go before he beat them up. Yeah, he did!

ROSE: You go on and get you a piece of watermelon, Gabe. Them bad mens is gone now.

GABRIEL: Okay, Rose . . . gonna get me some watermelon. The kind with the stripes on it.

GABRIEL *exits into the house.*

ROSE: Why, Troy? Why? After all these years to come dragging this in to me now. It don't make no sense at your age. I could have expected this ten or fifteen years ago, but not now.

TROY: Age ain't got nothing to do with it, Rose.

ROSE: I done tried to be everything a wife should be. Everything a wife could be. Been married eighteen years and I got to live to see the day you tell me you been seeing another woman and done fathered a child by her. And you know I ain't never wanted no half nothing in my family. My whole family is half. Everybody got different fathers and mothers . . . my two sisters and my brother. Can't hardly tell who's who. Can't never sit down and talk about Papa and Mama. It's your papa and your mama and my papa and my mama . . .

TROY: Rose . . . stop it now.

ROSE: I ain't never wanted that for none of my children. And now you wanna drag your behind in here and tell me something like this.

TROY: You ought to know. It's time for you to know.

ROSE: Well, I don't want to know, goddamn it!

TROY: I can't just make it go away. It's done now. I can't wish the circumstance of the thing away.

ROSE: And you don't want to either. Maybe you want to wish me and my boy away. Maybe that's what you want? Well, you can't wish us away. I've got eighteen years of my life invested in you. You ought to have stayed upstairs in my bed where you belong.

TROY: Rose . . . now listen to me . . . we can get a handle on this thing. We can talk this out . . . come to an understanding.

ROSE: All of a sudden it's "we." Where was "we" at when you was down there rolling around with some godforsaken woman? "We" should have come to an understanding before you started making a damn fool of yourself. You're a day late and dollar short when it comes to an understanding with me.

TROY: It's just . . . She gives me a different idea . . . a different understanding about myself. I can step out of this house and get away from the pressures and problems . . . be a different man. I ain't got to wonder how I'm gonna pay the bills or get the roof fixed. I can just be a part of myself that I ain't never been.

ROSE: What I want to know . . . is do you plan to continue seeing her. That's all you can say to me.

TROY: I can sit up in her house and laugh. Do you understand what I'm saying. I can laugh out loud . . . and it feels good. It reaches all the way down to the bottom of my shoes.

Pause.

Rose, I can't give that up.

ROSE: Maybe you ought to go on and stay down there with her . . . if she's a better woman than me.

TROY: It ain't about nobody being a better woman or nothing. Rose, you ain't the blame. A man couldn't ask for no woman to be a better wife than you've been. I'm responsible for it. I done locked myself into a pattern trying to take care of you all that I forgot about myself.

ROSE: What the hell was I there for? That was my job, not somebody else's.

TROY: Rose, I done tried all my life to live decent . . . to live a clean . . . hard . . . useful life. I tried to be a good husband to you. In every way I knew how. Maybe I come into the world backwards, I don't know. But . . . you born with two strikes on you before you come to the plate. You got to guard it closely . . . always looking for the curve ball on the inside corner. You can't afford to let none get past you. You can't afford a call strike. If you going down . . . you going down swinging. Everything lined up against you. What you gonna do. I fooled them, Rose. I bunted. When I found you and Cory and a halfway decent job . . . I was safe. Couldn't nothing touch me. I wasn't going back to the penitentiary. I wasn't gonna lay in the streets with a bottle of wine. I was safe. I had me a family. A job. I wasn't gonna get that last strike. I was on first looking for one of them boys to knock me in. To get me home.

ROSE: You should have stayed in my bed, Troy.

TROY: Then when I saw that gal . . . she firmed up my backbone. And I got to thinking that if I tried . . . I just might be able to steal second. Do you understand after eighteen years I wanted to steal second.

ROSE: You should have held me tight. You should have grabbed me and held on.

TROY: I stood on first base for eighteen years and I thought . . . well, goddamn it . . . go on for it!

ROSE: We're not talking about baseball! We're talking about you going off to lay in bed with another woman . . . and then bring it home to me. That's what we're talking about. We ain't talking about no baseball.

TROY: Rose, you're not listening to me. I'm trying the best I can to explain it to you. It's not easy for me to admit that I been standing in the same place for eighteen years.

ROSE: I been standing with you! I been right here with you, Troy. I got a life too. I gave eighteen years of my life to stand in the same spot with you. Don't you think I ever wanted other things? Don't you think I had dreams and hopes? What about my life? What about me. Don't you think it ever crossed my mind to want to know other men? That I wanted to lay up somewhere and forget about my responsibilities? That I wanted someone to make me laugh so I could feel good? You not the only one who's got wants and needs. But I held on to you, Troy. I took all my feelings, my wants and needs, my dreams . . . and I buried them inside you. I planted a seed and watched and prayed over it. I planted myself inside you and waited to bloom. And it didn't take me no eighteen years to find out the soil was hard and rocky and it wasn't never gonna bloom.

But I held on to you, Troy. I held you tighter. You was my husband. I owed you everything I had. Every part of me I could find to give you. And upstairs in that room . . . with the darkness falling in on me . . . I gave everything I had to try and erase the doubt that you wasn't the finest man in the world. And wherever you was going . . . I wanted to be there with you. Cause you was my husband. Cause that's the only way I was gonna survive as your wife. You always talking about what you give . . . and what you don't have to give. But you take too. You take . . . and don't even know nobody's giving!

ROSE *turns to exit into the house.* TROY *grabs her arm.*

TROY: You say I take and don't give!

ROSE: Troy! You're hurting me!

TROY: You say I take and don't give.

ROSE: Troy . . . you're hurting my arm! Let go!

TROY: I done give you everything I got. Don't you tell that lie on me.

ROSE: Troy!

TROY: Don't you tell that lie on me!

CORY *enters from the house.*

CORY: Mama!

ROSE: Troy. You're hurting me.

TROY: Don't you tell me about no taking and giving.

CORY *comes up behind* TROY *and grabs him.* TROY, *surprised, is thrown off balance just as* CORY *throws a glancing blow that catches him in the chest and knocks him down.* TROY *is stunned, as is* CORY.

ROSE: Troy. Troy. No!

TROY *gets to his feet and starts at* CORY.

Troy . . . no. Please! Troy!

ROSE *pulls on* TROY *to hold him back.* TROY *stops himself.*

TROY [*to* CORY]: All right. That's strike two. You stay away from around me, boy. Don't you strike out. You living with a full count. Don't you strike out.

TROY *exits out the yard as the lights go down.*

Scene 2

It is six months later, early afternoon. TROY *enters from the house and starts to exit the yard.* ROSE *enters from the house.*

ROSE: Troy, I want to talk to you.

TROY: All of a sudden, after all this time, you want to talk to me, huh? You ain't wanted to talk to me for months. You ain't wanted to talk to me last night. You ain't wanted no part of me then. What you wanna talk to me about now?

ROSE: Tomorrow's Friday.

TROY: I know what day tomorrow is. You think I don't know tomorrow's Friday? My whole life I ain't done nothing but look to see Friday coming and you got to tell me it's Friday.

ROSE: I want to know if you're coming home.

TROY: I always come home, Rose. You know that. There ain't never been a night I ain't come home.

ROSE: That ain't what I mean . . . and you know it. I want to know if you're coming straight home after work.

TROY: I figure I'd cash my check . . . hang out at Taylors' with the boys . . . maybe play a game of checkers . . .

ROSE: Troy, I can't live like this. I won't live like this. You livin' on borrowed time with me. It's been going on six months now you ain't been coming home.

TROY: I be here every night. Every night of the year. That's 365 days.

ROSE: I want you to come home tomorrow after work.

TROY: Rose . . . I don't mess up my pay. You know that now. I take my pay and I give it to you. I don't have no money but what you give me back. I just want to have a little time to myself . . . a little time to enjoy life.

ROSE: What about me? When's my time to enjoy life?

TROY: I don't know what to tell you, Rose. I'm doing the best I can.

ROSE: You ain't been home from work but time enough to change your clothes and run out . . . and you wanna call that the best you can do?

TROY: I'm going over to the hospital to see Alberta. She went into the hospital this afternoon. Look like she might have the baby early. I won't be gone long.

ROSE: Well, you ought to know. They went over to Miss Pearl's and got Gabe today. She said you told them to go ahead and lock him up.

TROY: I ain't said no such thing. Whoever told you that is telling a lie. Pearl ain't doing nothing but telling a big fat lie.

ROSE: She ain't had to tell me. I read it on the papers.

TROY: I ain't told them nothing of the kind.

ROSE: I saw it right there on the papers.

TROY: What it say, huh?

ROSE: It said you told them to take him.

TROY: Then they screwed that up, just the way they screw up everything. I ain't worried about what they got on the paper.

ROSE: Say the government send part of his check to the hospital and the other part to you.

TROY: I ain't got nothing to do with that if that's the way it works. I ain't made up the rules about how it work.

ROSE: You did Gabe just like you did Cory. You wouldn't sign the paper for Cory . . . but you signed for Gabe. You signed that paper.

The telephone is heard ringing inside the house.

TROY: I told you I ain't signed nothing, woman! The only thing I signed was the release form. Hell, I can't read, I don't know what they had on that paper! I ain't signed nothing about sending Gabe away.

ROSE: I said send him to the hospital . . . you said let him be free . . . now you done went down there and signed him to the hospital for half his money. You went back on yourself, Troy. You gonna have to answer for that.

TROY: See now . . . you been over there talking to Miss Pearl. She done got mad cause she ain't getting Gabe's rent money. That's all it is. She's liable to say anything.

ROSE: Troy, I seen where you signed the paper.

TROY: You ain't seen nothing I signed. What she doing got papers on my brother anyway? Miss Pearl telling a big fat lie. And I'm gonna tell her about it too! You ain't seen nothing I signed. Say . . . you ain't seen nothing I signed.

ROSE *exits into the house to answer the telephone. Presently she returns.*

ROSE: Troy . . . that was the hospital. Alberta had the baby.

TROY: What she have? What is it?

ROSE: It's a girl.

TROY: I better get on down to the hospital to see her.

ROSE: Troy . . .

TROY: Rose . . . I got to go see her now. That's only right . . . what's the matter . . . the baby's all right, ain't it?

ROSE: Alberta died having the baby.

TROY: Died . . . you say she's dead? Alberta's dead?

ROSE: They said they done all they could. They couldn't do nothing for her.

TROY: The baby? How's the baby?

ROSE: They say it's healthy. I wonder who's gonna bury her.

TROY: She had family, Rose. She wasn't living in the world by herself.

ROSE: I know she wasn't living in the world by herself.

TROY: Next thing you gonna want to know if she had any insurance.

ROSE: Troy, you ain't got to talk like that.

TROY: That's the first thing that jumped out your mouth. "Who's gonna bury her?" Like I'm fixing to take on that task for myself.

ROSE: I am your wife. Don't push me away.

TROY: I ain't pushing nobody away. Just give me some space. That's all. Just give me some room to breathe.

ROSE *exits into the house.* TROY *walks about the yard.*

TROY [*with a quiet rage that threatens to consume him*]: All right . . . Mr. Death. See now . . . I'm gonna tell you what I'm gonna do. I'm gonna take and build me a fence around this yard. See? I'm gonna build me a fence around what belongs to me. And then I want you to stay on the other side. See? You stay over there until you're ready for me. Then you come on. Bring your army. Bring your sickle. Bring your wrestling clothes. I ain't gonna fall down on my vigilance this time. You ain't gonna sneak up on me no more. When you ready for me . . . when the top of your list say Troy Maxson . . . that's when you come around here. You come up and knock on the front door. Ain't nobody else got nothing to do with this. This is between you and me. Man to man. You stay on the other side of that fence until you ready for me. Then you come up and knock on the front door. Anytime you want. I'll be ready for you.

The lights go down to black.

Scene 3

The lights come up on the porch. It is late evening three days later. ROSE *sits listening to the ball game waiting for* TROY. *The final out of the game is made and* ROSE *switches off the radio.* TROY *enters the yard carrying an infant wrapped in blankets. He stands back from the house and calls.*

ROSE *enters and stands on the porch. There is a long, awkward silence, the weight of which grows heavier with each passing second.*

TROY: Rose . . . I'm standing here with my daughter in my arms. She ain't but a wee bittie little old thing. She don't know nothing about grown-ups' business. She innocent . . . and she ain't got no mama.

ROSE: What you telling me for, Troy?

She turns and exits into the house.

TROY: Well . . . I guess we'll just sit out here on the porch.

He sits down on the porch. There is an awkward indelicateness about the way he handles the baby. His largeness engulfs and seems to swallow it. He speaks loud enough for ROSE *to hear.*

A man's got to do what's right for him. I ain't sorry for nothing I done. It felt right in my heart.

To the baby.

What you smiling at? Your daddy's a big man. Got these great big old hands. But sometimes he's scared. And right now your daddy's scared cause we sitting out here and ain't got no home. Oh, I been homeless before. I ain't had no little baby with me. But I been homeless. You just be out on the road by your lonesome and you see one of them trains coming and you just kinda go like this . . .

He sings as a lullaby.

Please, Mr. Engineer let a man ride the line
Please, Mr. Engineer let a man ride the line
I ain't got no ticket please let me ride the blinds

ROSE *enters from the house.* TROY *hearing her steps behind him, stands and faces her.*

She's my daughter, Rose. My own flesh and blood. I can't deny her no more than I can deny them boys.

Pause.

You and them boys is my family. You and them boys and this child is all I got in the world. So I guess what I'm saying is . . . I'd appreciate it if you'd help me take care of her.

ROSE: Okay, Troy . . . you're right. I'll take care of your baby for you . . . cause . . . like you say . . . she's innocent . . . and you can't visit the sins of the father upon the child. A motherless child has got a hard time.

She takes the baby from him.

From right now . . . this child got a mother. But you a womanless man.

ROSE *turns and exits into the house with the baby. Lights go down to black.*

Scene 4

It is two months later. LYONS *enters from the street. He knocks on the door and calls.*

LYONS: Hey, Rose! [*Pause.*] Rose!

ROSE [*from inside the house*]: Stop that yelling. You gonna wake up Raynell. I just got her to sleep.

LYONS: I just stopped by to pay Papa this twenty dollars I owe him. Where's Papa at?

ROSE: He should be here in a minute. I'm getting ready to go down to the church. Sit down and wait on him.

LYONS: I got to go pick up Bonnie over her mother's house.

ROSE: Well, sit it down there on the table. He'll get it.

LYONS [*enters the house and sets the money on the table*]: Tell Papa I said thanks. I'll see you again.

ROSE: All right, Lyons. We'll see you.

LYONS *starts to exit as* CORY *enters.*

CORY: Hey, Lyons.

LYONS: What's happening, Cory. Say man, I'm sorry I missed your graduation. You know I had a gig and couldn't get away. Otherwise, I would have been there, man. So what you doing?

CORY: I'm trying to find a job.

LYONS: Yeah I know how that go, man. It's rough out here. Jobs are scarce.

CORY: Yeah, I know.

LYONS: Look here, I got to run. Talk to Papa . . . he know some people. He'll be able to help get you a job. Talk to him . . . see what he say.

CORY: Yeah . . . all right, Lyons.

LYONS: You take care. I'll talk to you soon. We'll find some time to talk.

LYONS *exits the yard.* CORY *wanders over to the tree, picks up the bat, and assumes a batting stance. He studies an imaginary pitcher and swings. Dissatisfied with the result, he tries again.* TROY *enters. They eye each other for a beat.* CORY *puts the bat down and exits the yard.* TROY *starts into the house as* ROSE *exits with* RAYNELL. *She is carrying a cake.*

TROY: I'm coming in and everybody's going out.

ROSE: I'm taking the cake down to the church for the bake sale. Lyons was by to see you. He stopped by to pay you your twenty dollars. It's laying in there on the table.

TROY [*going into his pocket*]: Well . . . here go this money.

ROSE: Put it in there on the table, Troy. I'll get it.

TROY: What time you coming back?

ROSE: Ain't no use in you studying me. It don't matter what time I come back.

TROY: I just asked you a question, woman. What's the matter . . . can't I ask you a question?

ROSE: Troy, I don't want to go into it. Your dinner's in there on the stove. All you got to do is heat it up. And don't you be eating the rest of them cakes in there. I'm coming back for them. We having a bake sale at the church tomorrow.

ROSE *exits the yard.* TROY *sits down on the steps, takes a pint bottle from his pocket, opens it, and drinks. He begins to sing.*

TROY: Hear it ring! Hear it ring!
Had an old dog his name was Blue
You know Blue was a mighty true
You know Blue was a good old dog
Blue trees a possum in a hollow log
You know from that he was a good old dog

BONO *enters the yard.*

BONO: Hey, Troy.

TROY: Hey, what's happening, Bono?

BONO: I just thought I'd stop by to see you.

TROY: What you stop by and see me for? You ain't stopped by in a month of Sundays. Hell, I must owe you money or something.

BONO: Since you got your promotion I can't keep up with you. Used to see you every day. Now I don't even know what route you working.

TROY: They keep switching me around. Got me out in Greentree now . . . hauling white folks' garbage.

BONO: Greentree, huh? You lucky, at least you ain't got to be lifting them barrels. Damn if they ain't getting heavier. I'm gonna put in my two years and call it quits.

TROY: I'm thinking about retiring myself.

BONO: You got it easy. You can *drive* for another five years.

TROY: It ain't the same, Bono. It ain't like working the back of the truck. Ain't got nobody to talk to . . . feel like you working by yourself. Naw, I'm thinking about retiring. How's Lucille?

BONO: She all right. Her arthritis get to acting up on her sometime. Saw Rose on my way in. She going down to the church, huh?

TROY: Yeah, she took up going down there. All them preachers looking for somebody to fatten their pockets.

Pause.

Got some gin here.

BONO: Naw, thanks. I just stopped by to say hello.

TROY: Hell, nigger . . . you can take a drink. I ain't never known you to say no to a drink. You ain't got to work tomorrow.

BONO: I just stopped by. I'm fixing to go over to Skinner's. We got us a domino game going over his house every Friday.

TROY: Nigger, you can't play no dominoes. I used to whup you four games out of five.

BONO: Well, that learned me. I'm getting better.

TROY: Yeah? Well, that's all right.

BONO: Look here . . . I got to be getting on. Stop by sometime, huh?

TROY: Yeah, I'll do that, Bono. Lucille told Rose you bought her a new refrigerator.

BONO: Yeah, Rose told Lucille you had finally built your fence . . . so I figured we'd call it even.

TROY: I knew you would.

BONO: Yeah . . . okay. I'll be talking to you.

TROY: Yeah, take care, Bono. Good to see you. I'm gonna stop over.

BONO: Yeah. Okay, Troy.

BONO *exits.* TROY *drinks from the bottle.*

TROY: Old Blue died and I dig his grave
Let him down with a golden chain
Every night when I hear old Blue bark
I know Blue treed a possum in Noah's Ark.
Hear it ring! Hear it ring!

CORY *enters the* YARD. *They eye each other for a beat.* TROY *is sitting in the middle of the steps.* CORY *walks over.*

CORY: I got to get by.

TROY: Say what? What's you say?

CORY: You in my way. I got to get by.

TROY: You got to get by where? This is my house. Bought and paid for. In full. Took me fifteen years. And if you wanna go in my house and I'm sitting on the steps . . . you say excuse me. Like your mama taught you.

CORY: Come on, Pop . . . I got to get by.

CORY *starts to maneuver his way past* TROY. TROY *grabs his leg and shoves him back.*

TROY: You just gonna walk over top of me?

CORY: I live here, too!

TROY [*advancing toward him*]: You just gonna walk over top of me in my own house?

CORY: I ain't scared of you.

TROY: I ain't asked if you was scared of me. I asked you if you was fixing to walk over top of me in my own house? That's the question. You ain't gonna say excuse me? You just gonna walk over top of me?

CORY: If you wanna put it like that.

TROY: How else am I gonna put it?

CORY: I was walking by you to go into the house cause you sitting on the steps drunk, singing to yourself. You can put it like that.

TROY: Without saying excuse me???

CORY *doesn't respond.*

I asked you a question. Without saying excuse me???

CORY: I ain't got to say excuse me to you. You don't count around here no more.

TROY: Oh, I see . . . I don't count around here no more. You ain't got to say excuse me to your daddy. All of a sudden you done got so grown that your daddy don't count around here no more . . . Around here in his own house and yard that he done paid for with the sweat of his brow. You done got so grown to where you gonna take over. You gonna take over my house. Is that right? You gonna wear my pants. You gonna go in there and stretch out on my bed. You ain't got to say excuse me cause I don't count around here no more. Is that right?

CORY: That's right. You always talking this dumb stuff. Now, why don't you just get out my way.

TROY: I guess you got someplace to sleep and something to put in your belly. You got that, huh? You got that? That's what you need. You got that, huh?

CORY: You don't know what I got. You ain't got to worry about what I got.

TROY: You right! You one hundred percent right! I done spent the last seventeen years worrying about what you got. Now it's your turn, see? I'll tell you what to do. You grown . . . we done established that. You a man. Now, let's see you act like one. Turn your behind around and walk out this yard. And when you get out there in the alley . . . you can forget about this house. See? 'Cause this is my house. You go on and be a man and get your own house. You can forget about this. 'Cause this is mine. You go on and get yours 'cause I'm through with doing for you.

CORY: You talking about what you did for me . . . what'd you ever give me?

TROY: Them feet and bones! That pumping heart, nigger! I give you more than anybody else is ever gonna give you.

CORY: You ain't never gave me nothing! You ain't never done anything but hold me back. Afraid I was gonna be better than you. All you ever did was try and make me scared of you. I used to tremble every time you called my name. Every time I heard your footsteps in the house. Wondering all the time . . . what's Papa gonna say if I do this? . . . What's he gonna say if I do that? . . . What's Papa gonna say if I turn on the radio? And Mama, too . . . she tries . . . but she's scared of you.

TROY: You leave your mama out of this. She ain't got nothing to do with this.

CORY: I don't know how she stand you . . . after what you did to her.

TROY: I told you to leave your mama out of this!

He advances toward CORY.

CORY: What you gonna do . . . give me a whupping? You can't whip me no more. You're too old. You just an old man.

TROY [*shoves him on his shoulder*]: Nigger! That's what you are. You just another nigger on the street to me!

CORY: You crazy! You know that?

TROY: Go on now! You got the devil in you. Get on away from me!

CORY: You just a crazy old man . . . talking about I got the devil in me.

TROY: Yeah, I'm crazy! If you don't get on the other side of that yard . . . I'm gonna show you how crazy I am! Go on . . . get the hell out of my yard.

CORY: It ain't your yard! You took Uncle Gabe's money he got from the army to buy this house and then you put him out.

TROY [TROY *advances on* CORY]: Get your black ass out of my yard!

TROY*'s advance backs* CORY *up against the tree.* CORY *grabs up the bat.*

CORY: I ain't going nowhere! Come on . . . put me out! I ain't scared of you.

TROY: That's my bat!

CORY: Come on!

TROY: Put my bat down!

CORY: Come on, put me out.

CORY *swings at* TROY, *who backs across the yard.*

What's the matter? You so bad . . . put me out!

TROY *advances toward* CORY.

CORY [*backing up*]: Come on! Come on!

TROY: You're gonna have to use it! You wanna draw that bat back on me . . . you're gonna have to use it.

CORY: Come on! . . . Come on!

CORY swings the bat at TROY a second time. He misses. TROY continues to advance toward him.

TROY: You're gonna have to kill me! You wanna draw that bat back on me. You're gonna have to kill me.

CORY, backed up against the tree, can go no further. TROY taunts him. He sticks out his head and offers him a target.

Come on! Come on!

CORY is unable to swing the bat. TROY grabs it.

TROY: Then I'll show you.

CORY and TROY struggle over the bat. The struggle is fierce and fully engaged. TROY ultimately is the stronger and takes the bat from CORY and stands over him ready to swing. He stops himself.

Go on and get away from around my house.

CORY, stung by his defeat, picks himself up, walks slowly out of the yard and up the alley.

CORY: Tell Mama I'll be back for my things.

TROY: They'll be on the other side of that fence.

CORY exits.

TROY: I can't taste nothing. Helluljah! I can't taste nothing no more. [TROY *assumes a batting posture and begins to taunt Death, the fastball on the outside corner.*] Come on! It's between you and me now! Come on! Anytime you want! Come on! I be ready for you . . . but I ain't gonna be easy.

The lights go down on the scene.

Scene 5

The time is 1965. The lights come up in the yard. It is the morning of TROY's funeral. A funeral plaque with a light hangs beside the door. There is a small garden plot off to the side. There is noise and activity in the house as ROSE, GABRIEL, and BONO have gathered. The door opens and RAYNELL, seven years old, enters dressed in a flannel nightgown. She crosses to the garden and pokes around with a stick. ROSE calls from the house.

ROSE: Raynell!

RAYNELL: Mam?

ROSE: What you doing out there?

RAYNELL: Nothing.

ROSE comes to the door.

ROSE: Girl, get in here and get dressed. What you doing?

RAYNELL: Seeing if my garden growed.

ROSE: I told you it ain't gonna grow overnight. You got to wait.

RAYNELL: It don't look like it never gonna grow. Dag!

ROSE: I told you a watched pot never boils. Get in here and get dressed.

RAYNELL: This ain't even no pot, Mama.

ROSE: You just have to give it a chance. It'll grow. Now you come on and do what I told you. We got to be getting ready. This ain't no morning to be playing around. You hear me?

RAYNELL: Yes, mam.

ROSE *exits into the house.* RAYNELL *continues to poke at her garden with a stick.* CORY *enters. He is dressed in a Marine corporal's uniform, and carries a duffel bag. His posture is that of a military man, and his speech has a clipped sternness.*

CORY [*to* RAYNELL]: Hi.

Pause.

I bet your name is Raynell.

RAYNELL: Uh huh.

CORY: Is your mama home?

RAYNELL *runs up on the porch and calls through the screendoor.*

RAYNELL: Mama . . . there's some man out here. Mama?

ROSE *comes to the door.*

ROSE: Cory? Lord have mercy! Look here, you all!

ROSE *and* CORY *embrace in a tearful reunion as* BONO *and* LYONS *enter from the house dressed in funeral clothes.*

BONO: Aw, looka here . . .

ROSE: Done got all grown up!

CORY: Don't cry, Mama. What you crying about?

ROSE: I'm just so glad you made it.

CORY: Hey Lyons. How you doing, Mr. Bono.

LYONS *goes to embrace* CORY.

LYONS: Look at you, man. Look at you. Don't he look good, Rose. Got them Corporal stripes.

ROSE: What took you so long.

CORY: You know how the Marines are, Mama. They got to get all their paperwork straight before they let you do anything.

ROSE: Well, I'm sure glad you made it. They let Lyons come. Your Uncle Gabe's still in the hospital. They don't know if they gonna let him out or not. I just talked to them a little while ago.

LYONS: A Corporal in the United States Marines.

BONO: Your daddy knew you had it in you. He used to tell me all the time.

LYONS: Don't he look good, Mr. Bono?

BONO: Yeah, he remind me of Troy when I first met him.

Pause.

Say, Rose, Lucille's down at the church with the choir. I'm gonna go down and get the pallbearers lined up. I'll be back to get you all.

ROSE: Thanks, Jim.

CORY: See you, Mr. Bono.

LYONS [*with his arm around* RAYNELL]: Cory . . . look at Raynell. Ain't she precious? She gonna break a whole lot of hearts.

ROSE: Raynell, come and say hello to your brother. This is your brother, Cory. You remember Cory.

RAYNELL: No, Mam.

CORY: She don't remember me, Mama.

ROSE: Well, we talk about you. She heard us talk about you. [*To* RAYNELL.] This is your brother, Cory. Come on and say hello.

RAYNELL: Hi.

CORY: Hi. So you're Raynell. Mama told me a lot about you.

ROSE: You all come on into the house and let me fix you some breakfast. Keep up your strength.

CORY: I ain't hungry, Mama.

LYONS: You can fix me something, Rose. I'll be in there in a minute.

ROSE: Cory, you sure you don't want nothing. I know they ain't feeding you right.

CORY: No, Mama . . . thanks. I don't feel like eating. I'll get something later.

ROSE: Raynell . . . get on upstairs and get that dress on like I told you.

ROSE *and* RAYNELL *exit into the house.*

LYONS: So . . . I hear you thinking about getting married.

CORY: Yeah, I done found the right one, Lyons. It's about time.

LYONS: Me and Bonnie been split up about four years now. About the time Papa retired. I guess she just got tired of all them changes I was putting her through.

Pause.

I always knew you was gonna make something out yourself. Your head was always in the right direction. So . . . you gonna stay in . . . make it a career . . . put in your twenty years?

CORY: I don't know. I got six already, I think that's enough.

LYONS: Stick with Uncle Sam and retire early. Ain't nothing out here. I guess Rose told you what happened with me. They got me down the workhouse. I thought I was being slick cashing other people's checks.

CORY: How much time you doing?

LYONS: They give me three years. I got that beat now. I ain't got but nine more months. It ain't so bad. You learn to deal with it like anything else. You got to take the crookeds with the straights. That's what Papa used to say. He used to say that when he struck out. I seen him strike out three times in a row . . . and the next time up he hit the ball over the grandstand. Right out there in Homestead Field. He wasn't satisfied hitting in the seats . . . he want to hit it over everything! After the game he had two hundred people standing around waiting to shake his hand. You got to take the crookeds with the straights. Yeah, Papa was something else.

CORY: You still playing?

LYONS: Cory . . . you know I'm gonna do that. There's some fellows down there we got us a band . . . we gonna try and stay together when we get out . . . but yeah, I'm still playing. It still helps me to get out of bed in the morning. As long as it do that I'm gonna be right there playing and trying to make some sense out of it.

ROSE [*calling*]: Lyons, I got these eggs in the pan.

LYONS: Let me go on and get these eggs, man. Get ready to go bury Papa.

Pause.

How you doing? You doing all right?

CORY *nods.* LYONS *touches him on the shoulder and they share a moment of silent grief.* LYONS *exits into the house.* CORY *wanders about the yard.* RAYNELL *enters.*

RAYNELL: Hi.

CORY: Hi.

RAYNELL: Did you used to sleep in my room?

CORY: Yeah . . . that used to be my room.

RAYNELL: That's what Papa call it. "Cory's room." It got your football in the closet.

ROSE *comes to the door.*

ROSE: Raynell, get in there and get them good shoes on.

RAYNELL: Mama, can't I wear these? Them other one hurt my feet.

ROSE: Well, they just gonna have to hurt your feet for a while. You ain't said they hurt your feet when you went down to the store and got them.

RAYNELL: They didn't hurt then. My feet done got bigger.

ROSE: Don't you give me no backtalk now. You get in there and get them shoes on.

RAYNELL *exits into the house.*

Ain't too much changed. He still got that piece of rag tied to that tree. He was out here swinging that bat. I was just ready to go back in the house. He swung that bat and then he just fell over. Seem like he swung it and stood there with this grin on his face . . . and then he just fell over. They carried him on down to the hospital, but I knew there wasn't no need . . . why don't you come on in the house?

CORY: Mama . . . I got something to tell you. I don't know how to tell you this . . . but I've got to tell you . . . I'm not going to Papa's funeral.

ROSE: Boy, hush your mouth. That's your daddy you talking about. I don't want to hear that kind of talk this morning. I done raised you to come to this? You standing there all healthy and grown talking about you ain't going to your daddy's funeral?

CORY: Mama . . . listen . . .

ROSE: I don't want to hear it, Cory. You just get that thought out of your head.

CORY: I can't drag Papa with me everywhere I go. I've got to say no to him. One time in my life I've got to say no.

ROSE: Don't nobody have to listen to nothing like that. I know you and your daddy ain't seen eye to eye, but I ain't got to listen to that kind of talk this morning. Whatever was between you and your daddy . . . the time has come to put it aside. Just take it and set it over there on the shelf and forget about it. Disrespecting your daddy ain't gonna make you a man, Cory. You got to find a way to come to that on your own. Not going to your daddy's funeral ain't gonna make you a man.

CORY: The whole time I was growing up . . . living in his house . . . Papa was like a shadow that followed you everywhere. It weighed on you and sunk into your flesh. It would wrap around you and lay there until you couldn't tell which one was you anymore. That shadow digging in your flesh. Trying to crawl in. Trying to live through you. Everywhere I looked, Troy Maxson was staring back at me . . . hiding under the bed . . . in the closet. I'm just saying I've got to find a way to get rid of that shadow, Mama.

ROSE: You just like him. You got him in you good.

CORY: Don't tell me that, Mama.

ROSE: You Troy Maxson all over again.

CORY: I don't want to be Troy Maxson. I want to be me.

ROSE: You can't be nobody but who you are, Cory. That shadow wasn't nothing but you growing into yourself. You either got to grow into it or cut it down to fit you. But that's all you got to make life with. That's all you got to measure yourself against that world out there. Your daddy wanted you to be everything he wasn't . . . and at the same time he tried to make you into everything he was. I don't know if he was right or wrong . . . but I do know he meant to do more good than he meant to do harm. He wasn't always right. Sometimes when he touched he bruised. And sometimes when he took me in his arms he cut.

When I first met your daddy I thought . . . Here is a man I can lay down with and make a baby. That's the first thing I thought when I seen him. I was thirty years old and had done seen my share of men. But when he walked up to me and said, "I can dance a waltz that'll make you dizzy," I thought, Rose Lee, here is a man that you can open yourself up to and be filled to bursting. Here is a man that can fill all them empty spaces you been tipping around the edges of. One of them empty spaces was being somebody's mother.

I married your daddy and settled down to cooking his supper and keeping clean sheets on the bed. When your daddy walked through the house he was so big he filled it up. That was my first mistake. Not to make him leave some room for me. For my part in the matter. But at that time I wanted that. I wanted a house that I could sing in. And that's what your daddy gave me. I didn't know to keep up his strength I had to give up little pieces of mine. I did that. I took on his life as mine and mixed up the pieces so that you couldn't hardly tell which was which anymore. It was my choice. It was my life and I didn't have to live it like that. But that's what life offered me in the way of being a woman and I took it. I grabbed hold of it with both hands.

By the time Raynell came into the house, me and your daddy had done lost touch with one another. I didn't want to make my blessing off of nobody's misfortune . . . but I took on to Raynell like she was all them babies I had wanted and never had.

The phone rings.

Like I'd been blessed to relive a part of my life. And if the Lord see fit to keep up my strength . . . I'm gonna do her just like your daddy did you . . . I'm gonna give her the best of what's in me.

RAYNELL [*entering, still with her old shoes*]: Mama . . . Reverend Tollivier on the phone.

ROSE *exits into the house.*

RAYNELL: Hi.

CORY: Hi.

RAYNELL: You in the Army or the Marines?

CORY: Marines.

RAYNELL: Papa said it was the Army. Did you know Blue?

CORY: Blue? Who's Blue?

RAYNELL: Papa's dog what he sing about all the time.

CORY [*singing*]: Hear it ring! Hear it ring!
I had a dog his name was Blue
You know Blue was mighty true
You know Blue was a good old dog
Blue treed a possum in a hollow log
You know from that he was a good old dog.
Hear it ring! Hear it ring!

RAYNELL *joins in singing.*

CORY *and* RAYNELL: Blue treed a possum out on a limb
Blue looked at me and I looked at him
Grabbed that possum and put him in a sack
Blue stayed there till I came back
Old Blue's feets was big and round
Never allowed a possum to touch the ground.
Old Blue died and I dug his grave
I dug his grave with a silver spade
Let him down with a golden chain
And every night I call his name
Go on Blue, you good dog you
Go on Blue, you good dog you

RAYNELL: Blue laid down and died like a man
Blue laid down and died . . .

BOTH: Blue laid down and died like a man
Now he's treeing possums in the Promised Land
I'm gonna tell you this to let you know
Blue's gone where the good dogs go
When I hear old Blue bark
When I hear old Blue bark
Blue treed a possum in Noah's Ark,
Blue treed a possum in Noah's Ark.

ROSE *comes to the screen door.*

ROSE: Cory, we gonna be ready to go in a minute.

CORY [*to* RAYNELL]: You go on in the house and change them shoes like Mama told you so we can go to Papa's funeral.

RAYNELL: Okay, I'll be back.

RAYNELL *exits into the house.* CORY *gets up and crosses over to the tree.* ROSE *stands in the screen door watching him.* GABRIEL *enters from the alley.*

GABRIEL [*calling*]: Hey, Rose!
ROSE: Gabe?
GABRIEL: I'm here, Rose. Hey Rose, I'm here!

ROSE *enters from the house.*

ROSE: Lord . . . Look here, Lyons!
LYONS: See, I told you, Rose . . . I told you they'd let him come.
CORY: How you doing, Uncle Gabe?
LYONS: How you doing, Uncle Gabe?
GABRIEL: Hey, Rose. It's time. It's time to tell St. Peter to open the gates. Troy, you ready? You ready, Troy. I'm gonna tell St. Peter to open the gates. You get ready now.

GABRIEL, *with great fanfare, braces himself to blow. The trumpet is without a mouthpiece. He puts the end of it into his mouth and blows with great force, like a man who has been waiting some twenty-odd years for this single moment. No sound comes out of the trumpet. He braces himself and blows again with the same result. A third time he blows. There is a weight of impossible description that falls away and leaves him bare and exposed to a frightful realization. It is a trauma that a sane and normal mind would be unable to withstand. He begins to dance. A slow, strange dance, eerie and life-giving. A dance of atavistic signature and ritual.* LYONS *attempts to embrace him.* GABRIEL *pushes* LYONS *away. He begins to howl in what is an attempt at song, or perhaps a song turning back into itself in an attempt at speech. He finishes his dance and the gates of heaven stand open as wide as God's closet.*

That's the way that go!

(*1986*)

QUESTIONS FOR CRITICAL THINKING AND WRITING

Experience

1. To what extent can you relate to the situations of Wilson's characters? Why or why not?

Interpretation

2. How does Wilson establish the world of his play? What kinds of details help readers and viewers orient themselves?
3. Identify the play's most important references to religion, and explain their function.
4. How does Wilson make his characters believable? Which of them do you understand best? Why?
5. What metaphors do Troy and Rose use to make sense of their lives? How does the playwright use these metaphors for expressive purposes?

6. Identify the various kinds of "fences" the play includes. Explain the significance of the title.
7. Select one longer speech or one important exchange of dialogue, and explain its significance to the play's theme.
8. Select one scene or part of a scene, and explain how you would stage it.

Evaluation

9. Identify the values each of the characters lives by. Whose values does the play seem to endorse? Explain.

Connection

10. Compare Wilson's portrayal of the mother of a black American family with Hansberry's portrayal of the mother in *A Raisin in the Sun*.

Critical Thinking

11. Provide two alternative titles to the play. Explain why you chose each title. Explain, also, why you think Wilson chose the title *Fences* for the play.

PART FOUR

Research and Critical Perspectives

CHAPTER THIRTY

Writing with Sources

WHY DO RESEARCH ABOUT LITERATURE?

One reason to do research about the literary works you read and study is to understand them better. Another is to see how they have been interpreted over the years, perhaps even centuries, since they were written. Moreover, scholars who have devoted their lives to the study of particular authors, periods, and genres can provide insights that can enrich your understanding and deepen your appreciation of literature.

Reading and studying literature in an academic environment often requires research. You may be required to read books and articles about an author or a work, using your research in an essay on a literary topic. This is a fairly standard requirement in both general introductory literature courses and in more specialized courses for literature majors.

Even if research on the literature you read is not a requirement, you may find that what others who have read the same works have to say provides a stimulus for your own ideas. For example, you can use *The Humanities Index,* the *MLA Bibliography,* or your library's computerized catalog (see "Using Computerized Databases" in this chapter) to find articles about many of the selections in this book. You can also use *The New York Times Index* and *Book Review Digest* to find reviews of collections of short stories, essays, poems, or plays.

Locate several articles or reviews on a work you have read and, as you read them, notice when you have a particularly strong reaction. You may disagree with what you read, you may be surprised by a new point of view, or you may find your own opinions reinforced in a way you had not expected. You may find that one or more of the works consulted provides the spark for a fully developed essay of your own.

Research materials consist of two general kinds: primary sources and secondary sources. *Primary sources* are firsthand accounts, such as historical documents, diaries, journals, letters, and original literary works, including novels, stories, poems, plays, and essays. Primary sources constitute raw evidence you can use for your research paper. *Secondary sources* are materials written about primary sources. Secondary sources include critical writing that expresses opinions, draws conclusions, or explains an issue. Secondary sources include books, articles, pamphlets, and reviews.

CLARIFYING THE ASSIGNMENT

It is critical that you understand thoroughly the requirements of the assignment. Does your instructor expect you to write a three-page paper or a twenty-page paper—or, as is more likely, something in between? Are you expected to type your paper double-spaced? Are you required to use primary sources, secondary sources, or both? How many words, how many pages, and how many sources are required?

Are you expected to focus on a single work using only one or two sources, on a single work using multiple sources, on multiple works by an author—or something else? Are you expected to document your sources and to provide a list of works you cite in the paper? Be sure that you clarify the specific requirements of the assignment.

SELECTING A TOPIC

Instructors sometimes provide topics, either by assigning everyone the same topic (or some variation of it) or by giving individual students assigned topics. If that is your situation, you can skip down to the next section on finding and using sources. Most often, however, you will need to choose your own topic for a paper utilizing literary research.

You can do a number of things to simplify the task of finding a topic. First, ask your instructor for suggestions. Second, look over your class notes and your reading notes for key points of emphasis, recurrent concerns, and interesting questions and ideas. Third, talk with other students, both with your classmates and with students who have already written papers for the course you are taking. Fourth, you can consult other sources with information about the author and work (or works) you will be writing about. Any or all of these can provide guidance and suggestions about viable topics for your paper.

A *viable topic* is one you can manage in the allotted number of pages required for the assignment. It should also be a topic you can say something about in detail and with specificity. Once you have settled on a topic, it's a good idea to clear it with your instructor. Once your instructor sees what you're interested in, he or she can help you shape the topic, perhaps by narrowing or broadening it in ways that might make it more manageable or potentially more interesting, or both.

You can also get ideas for topics by consulting the ideas for writing suggestions in Chapters Four, Thirteen, and Twenty-Four. In those chapters on writing about fiction, poetry, and drama, you will find additional guidelines useful for your writing about literary works. As a general guideline for all literary papers, however, try to turn your topic into a question that your research paper answers. This question need not be explicit in your topic, but it should emerge in the opening paragraphs of your paper, either explicitly or implicitly, as you present your thesis. When you read the student papers later in this chapter, notice how the focused topics lead naturally into a manageable thesis, allowing for specific observations to be developed into a cogent argument.

FINDING AND USING SOURCES

Researchers have a number of tools available for finding secondary sources—critical studies of authors, analyses of their works, and relevant biographical, social, and historical background material. Your school library's computer databases of books and articles provide comprehensive listings of such sources. But even before tapping into those databases you can consult books in the library reference room as a preliminary step. General reference works about literature can give you an overview of an author's life and work, an introduction to a genre, such as tragedy or epic, or an understanding of a critical approach, such as new historicism, or provide some other kind of generalized prelude to the more focused search you will undertake once you have refined your topic and decided how to proceed with your research.

Works you may find helpful as preliminary guides to literary research include the following:

Columbia Literary History of the United States. Ed. Emory Elliot et al. New York: Columbia University Press, 1988.

An Encyclopedia of Continental Women Writers. Ed. Katharina Wilson. 2 vols. New York: Garland, 1991.

Encyclopedia of World Literature in the Twentieth Century. Ed. Steven Serafin. 4 vols. 3rd ed. New York: St. James, 1999.

MLA International Bibliography. Available in print, online, and on CD-ROM. New York: MLA, 1921–.

The New Cambridge Bibliography of English Literature. Cambridge: Cambridge UP, 1988.

The New Guide to Modern World Literature. Ed. Martin Seymour-Smith. 4 vols. New York: Peter Bedrick Books, 1985.

The New Princeton Encyclopedia of Poetry and Poetics. Ed. Alex Preminger and T.V. F. Brogan. 3rd ed. Princeton: Princeton UP, 1993.

The Oxford History of English Literature. 13 vols. Oxford: Oxford UP, 1945–.

A Research Guide for Undergraduate Students: English and American Literature. Eds. Nancy L. Baker, and Nancy Huling. 5th ed. New York: MLA, 2001.

Research Guide to Biography and Criticism: Literature. Ed. Walton Beacham. 2 vols. Osprey, FL: Beacham, 1985.

You can find some or all of these sources in the reference sections of many college libraries.

USING COMPUTERIZED DATABASES

A database is any collection of information that is systematically organized: a filing cabinet is a database (though an old-fashioned one). A *computerized* database is one that is organized in such a way that a computer program can quickly find desired pieces of information.

Many libraries have converted their card catalogs into computerized databases. Computerized *research databases* that are commonly used in undergraduate courses include the *MLA Bibliography* (a database of journal articles on literary topics); *ProQuest, InfoTrac,* and *EbscoHost* (databases cataloging newspapers, general interest periodicals, business and medical journals, and more); *FirstSearch* (a comprehensive collection of research databases that also offers access to the World Wide Web, full-text articles, image banks, library catalogs, and interlibrary loan); and *ERIC* (a database of education-related materials). Some of these databases simply index articles (that is, they tell you what exists and where to find it); others actually offer the full text of articles. One computerized database of particular interest to those researching literary topics is the Gale Group's *Literature Resource Center,* a nearly exhaustive collection of biographical, historical, and critical information searchable by author, title, genre, literary period, and literary theme.

Until recently, most computerized databases were stored on CD-ROMs, which school libraries typically bought for use at a designated machine. Now most computerized databases are available online, which means that the database resources can be accessed by authorized users from virtually any computer with Internet access.

You may have access to your university library with a link from your room, your home, your residence hall, or your school's computer center. You may also be able to access the library's holdings through computer terminals located in the library proper. One of the first things you should do is learn what's available to you online. Then you need to determine how to use it. If you're unsure how to proceed, you can get assistance from the library staff. Your school may even provide formal instructions in use of their online services.

All online databases are organized in a similar way. The information that is retrieved and displayed on the computer screen depends on how you make your request. Most databases offer at least three search options: author, title, and subject. For example, suppose you know that you want to write about Ernest Hemingway. You don't have a precise topic in mind and want to consult some books *about* Ernest Hemingway. To find out what is available in your school's library, you would search for "Hemingway, Ernest," as subject. (The program will give you on-screen instructions on how to start the search.) Following is what one university library's online catalog lists for Hemingway as subject:

1. Hemingway, Ernest 1898		1 entry
2. Hemingway, Ernest 1899–1961		52 entries
3. Hemingway, Ernest 1899–1961	Appreciation	1 entry
4. Hemingway, Ernest 1899–1961	Appreciation—Germany	1 entry
5. Hemingway, Ernest 1899–1961	Bibliography	10 entries
6. Hemingway, Ernest 1899–1961	Biography	12 entries
7. Hemingway, Ernest 1899–1961	Juvenile letters	1 entry
8. Hemingway, Ernest 1899–1961	Biography—Marriage	4 entries

Notice that category 2 includes fifty-two items. Since the category has no heading, to determine the kinds of books included within it, you would type 2 and scan the listings. If you type 8, "Biography—Marriage," four listings appear:

1. Along with Youth	Griffin, Peter
2. Hadley	Diliberto, Gioia
3. The Hemingway Women	Kert, Bernice
4. How It Was	Hemingway, Mary Welsh

If you want more data on one of these books, type the appropriate number. You will be provided with information about the length and size of the book, its publication date, and location. Most systems also provide information about the book's availability.

In browsing in one of these books about Hemingway's personal life, you might get an idea for a research paper that focuses on the home life depicted in "Hills Like White Elephants." Reading that story in the context of secondary biographical sources would be one way to gain added insight into the story. Another would be to consult critical secondary sources that are less biographical than analytical and interpretive. Here you might return to that large category of 52 items and begin scanning for titles that appeared promising. One such title is Paul Smith's *A Reader's Guide to the Short Stories of Ernest Hemingway* (Boston: G. K. Hall, 1989). Or you might turn to a computerized research database such as the *MLA Bibliography.* Typing in "Hills Elephants" in a "Words Anywhere" (keyword) search yields a list of recent articles on the story. This description looks interesting to you:

TITLE
"Hills Like White Elephants": The Jilting of Jig
AUTHOR(S)
Hashmi-Nilofer
SOURCE (BIBLIOGRAPHIC CITATION)
The Hemingway-Review, Moscow, ID (HN). 2003 Fall, 23:1, 72–83.
INTERNATIONAL STANDARD SERIAL NUMBER
0276–3362
LANGUAGE
English
PUBLICATION TYPE
journal-article

Your first step would be to check whether your library carries *The Hemingway Review.* If so, find the article and skim it. (If not, consult with your reference librarian about your other options.) Remember to check the article's Works Cited section: Even if the article turns out not to be useful itself, it might lead you to other articles that will be of more help.

After locating a few such sources, you are ready to read and take notes as you work toward refining your topic and developing a thesis for your paper. To do that you should use the techniques of note taking described earlier—especially annotation and the double-entry notebook—to develop a critical perspective.

USING THE INTERNET FOR RESEARCH

Through the Internet you can connect to the World Wide Web (WWW), a system of linked electronic documents. The Web is a tremendous tool for researchers. The wealth of information available on virtually any topic, however, can be intimidating to a beginner. The information that follows is designed to help you understand how to find appropriate Web sites for your research.

Searching Tips

Begin your search by going to a good search engine, like Google (www.google.com). Depending on the nature of your assignment, you might want to limit yourself to a scholarly search by using Google Scholar (scholar.google.com). Once you have settled on the type of material you are searching for and the search engine, you can begin your keyword search.

To perform a keyword search, enter the word or words that describe your subject. For example, if you are searching for information about *Internet censorship* and you enter those two words, *Google* will find Web pages that contain either of the words anywhere—together or separately. The engine returns the most popular results at the top of the list.

To narrow the search further, search for a phrase rather than words by placing the words in quotes: "Internet censorship." Then *Google* will return only those pages containing both words in a single phrase.

Most search engines function by similar rules. For specifics, check out the instructions on the engine's home page. Be sure to check out the advanced search options for any search engine you use. These advance search options can help guide your search and get you results that better meet your research requirements.

Evaluating Internet Sources

One problem you may confront in your searches is a large number of hits or potential sources. Deciding which of these are of most value requires careful analysis. Anyone can put up a Web site and place any information on that site, so you cannot be certain that the site's information is accurate, current, or unbiased.

Therefore, you must evaluate Internet sources for their reliability. You can use the following guidelines to do so.

- **Consider the source of the electronic information you discover.** Consider the credentials of the source provider. Is the source maintained by a reputable and presumably unbiased provider, such as a university? Sources can be determined in many cases by a look at the URL—"Uniform Resource Locator," also referred to as the "Web address." The first term in the URL will indicate what server hosts the material; the extension (the three letters that follow the "dot") can give you some idea what to expect from the site:

Extension	Type of Site
.edu	Educational institution. For research purposes, these sites are often the most reliable. Remember, though, that students are often given space on their schools' servers for their own Web pages, and these are not necessarily reliable for research. Exercise caution.
.org	Nonprofit organization. These often provide useful information for the researcher. Beware, though, of the potential for institutional bias.
.com	Commercial site. You will encounter these frequently. As far as research goes, they range from the legitimate (well-researched sites run by scholars and other professionals not affiliated with an institution, or by those at institutions with unreliable servers) to the questionable (ads, rants, scams, and so on). These must be evaluated carefully.
.gov	Government site. Various branches of the government provide much solid information. Though it tends to be factual/objective, beware here (as in the case of .org sites) of institutional bias.
.mil	Military site. Publicly accessible sites contain information about military institutions. See .gov and .org entries.
.net	Large computer networks. The distinction between .net and .com sites is rapidly disappearing, as competition for desirable URLs has increased. Same rules as .com apply; sites should be evaluated with care.

  The brief descriptions of the site provided by your search engine should contribute to your decision about whether the site deserves a closer look. Once you decide to visit the site, of course, the same rules you apply to print sources apply: consider authorship, the sponsoring institution, date, presumed audience/purpose, and so on.
- **Compare your electronic sources with print sources you have judged reliable.** Evaluate your electronic sources for range and depth as well as accuracy and currency of information.
- After all of these considerations, ask yourself whether you are sufficiently confident of the source's reliability to cite it in your research paper. When you're sure a site is worth using for your research, be sure you document it properly.

A Note on Plagiarism and the Internet

With the Internet come new temptations to plagiarize. Many sources *seem* almost anonymous or so hard to cite you wish they were; in addition, Web sites have sprung up offering for sale completed essays on any topic. The catch? Plagiarism is wrong. Apart from cheating yourself out of an education, you're taking credit where credit is *not* due. And, too, you're running a huge risk: Those sites are just as accessible to your instructor as they are to you.

A Sampling of Internet Resources for Literature

Electronic Texts

Alex: A Catalogue of Electronic Texts on the Internet. This site, hosted at Oxford University, provides links to many full-text works of literature.

Bartleby.com (*Project Bartleby Archive*). A project developed out of Columbia University, this site offers many complete texts of public domain literature, history, and reference works.

Project Gutenberg Online. This ever-expanding archive offers access to thousands of classic and public domain texts.

The English Server (*EServer*). A collection of over eighteen thousand online humanities texts based at the University of Washington.

Reference

The Voice of the Shuttle. This site offers an outstanding collection of online resources for the humanities "woven" by Alan Liu of the University of California, Santa Barbara. *The English Literature* main page includes a vast number of resources for the study of literature written in English. It includes breakdowns by genre, literary period, cultural context, region, ethnicity, and nationality.

Literary Resources on the Net offers a wealth of online resources for most specialties. Maintained by Jack Lynch of Rutgers University.

For guidance in documenting electronic sources, see pages 1535–1537.

DEVELOPING A CRITICAL PERSPECTIVE

How can you use outside critical sources to develop a critical perspective? Let us say, for example, that you are required to write a five- or six-page paper analyzing and interpreting a particular literary work. Let us speculate further that you are required to read and cite in your paper two or three outside sources. And let us also imagine that you have been asked to select critical sources that provide different interpretive perspectives on the work you will be writing about. What will you do? How will you go about writing this paper?

Here is where annotation and the double-entry notebook are particularly helpful. Let's assume that you have found the relevant articles or sections of books you need. If you can photocopy the appropriate pages, do that. Then annotate those pages the same way you annotated the literary work itself. (Before you actually read any criticism, however, do some preliminary writing—annotating, listing, journal keeping.) In your journal or notebook summarize in a few sentences the thesis or main idea of each source. Opposite your summaries, jot down a set of responses. When you record your summaries of the articles and your responses leave plenty of room, as you will want to add other things that you notice on rereading them.

Still another technique useful for writing critical papers is quoting key passages and commenting on their significance or validity. In writing a paper about Hemingway's "Hills Like White Elephants," for example, you could (and perhaps should) quote a bit of the story directly. Of more importance than your apt selection of such passages, however, is the way you relate them in your comments by explaining their significance. The place to get a start on this crucial process is in your reading journal or double-entry notebook, where you can record the relevant passages verbatim and practice commenting on their significance. These comments will provide the seeds from which your paper will grow.

In using outside critical sources you will find yourself usually doing one of two things. Either you will agree with the critic and use his or her comments to bolster your interpretation, or you will disagree and take exception to the critic's ideas by arguing against them in your paper. Both are acceptable ways to proceed. In fact, given a requirement to include more than two sources, it is highly unlikely that you will agree entirely with the positions taken in all of them. Thus even if you agree in part, you will need to make distinctions and to express qualified approval as you modify their viewpoints and express the reservations necessary to make them congruent with your own ideas.

DEVELOPING A THESIS

You should be able to state your thesis in a single direct sentence. Your thesis concentrates in a nutshell what you wish to emphasize—your central idea, the point you wish to make about your topic. Your essay overall elaborates your thesis, providing evidence in the form of textual support.

In general, when you develop your thesis, try to make it as specific as you can. At the same time, try to avoid oversimplifying your idea by setting up mutually exclusive "black and white" categories. Introduce qualifying terms as necessary. Words such as "although," "however," "but," and "rather" suggest an approach that reflects thoughtful consideration of the issues.

Consider the thesis of the student papers included later in this chapter. In one paper, Lucienne Retelle analyzes Alice Walker's story "Everyday Use" in the context of a critical article she read about the work. Here is her thesis:

> In relating the story ["Everyday Use"] to the Biblical Prodigal Son, Patricia Kane shows thoughtfulness and insight; however, in her eagerness to expose what she sees as differences in male/female values, she demonstrates a superficial understanding of the Gospel parable and misses the central message: one of repentance and forgiveness.

Notice how Ms. Retelle takes issue with the critical perspective offered by Patricia Kane. She uses the critic's view as a springboard from which to launch her own analysis of the story as one whose central concerns are the prodigal son's repentance and his father's forgiveness. Her thesis is clear, direct, and specific. We know what she thinks. It remains for her to flesh out her interpretation and to refute Patricia Kane's argument.

DRAFTING AND REVISING

In writing your research paper, follow the guidelines for drafting and revising your paper just as you would for an interpretive paper in which you do not use secondary sources. Set aside sufficient time to work out the basic argument of your research paper. This will involve the extra time necessary for tracking down sources, taking notes, and reflecting on their significance for your overall argument.

In your preliminary draft you should try to articulate your argument without your sources. Get your ideas down as clearly as you can. Provide the textual support you need as evidence from the work(s) you are analyzing or otherwise discussing. Then write a second draft in which you incorporate the relevant sources either to support your idea or as representing antithetical views that you attempt to refute.

Leave time for a third draft in which you further refine your thinking, taking into consideration additional evidence you find in the text or in the secondary sources. Use this third draft also to provide precise documentation for your sources—accurate parenthetical citations and precise page references.

In general, approach the drafting of a research essay or paper as you would any other essay or assignment. Make sure you get your own ideas into the initial draft before you begin relying on your secondary sources. This is critical if you want to avoid letting your sources take over the voice and content of your research essay.

CONVENTIONS

In writing about literary works you need to observe a number of conventions, including those regarding quotations, verb tenses, manuscript form, and the strict avoidance of plagiarism.

Using Quotations

In writing about literature you will need to quote lines from poems, dialogue from plays and stories, and descriptive and explanatory passages from prose fiction and nonfiction. For quoted prose passages that exceed four typed lines in your paper, begin a new line and indent ten spaces from the left margin for each line of the quotation. This format, called block quotation, does not require quotation marks because the blocked passage is set off visually from the rest of your text.

When quoting poetry, separate the lines of poetry with slashes. Include a space before and after each slash.

> Lorraine Hansberry derived the title of her best-known play, *A Raisin in the Sun,* from a poem by Langston Hughes. In "Dream Deferred," the speaker asks, "What happens to a dream deferred? / Does it dry up / like a raisin in the sun?"

Chapter Thirteen contains examples of student writers quoting from the poems they write about. For additional examples of students introducing quotations from literature into their analytical essays, see Chapters Four (on fiction) and Twenty-Four (on drama).

Verb Tense Conventions in Literary Papers

In writing about literature, you will often need to describe a story, novel, poem, or play. In doing so you will use present tense, past tense, or both. In most instances, it is conventional to use present tense when describing what happens in a literary work. Consider the following examples:

> In Robert Hayden's "Those Winter Sundays," the speaker reflects on his father and realizes how much his father loved the family.

The present tense is used to describe the speaker's actions of reflecting and realizing. The past tense is used to describe the father's action, which occurred in the past, well before the speaker's present acts of reflecting and realizing.

> Ibsen's *A Doll House* portrays a conventional middle-class environment and a conventional middle-class family. In displaying a strong concern for money and for authority, Ibsen's characters reveal their middle-class values. Ibsen often portrayed characters with everyday problems of the middle class.

The verbs describing what the play does are in the present tense. Those describing what the dramatist did are in past tense.

Manuscript Form

In preparing your paper for submission, observe the following guidelines:

1. Type your essay double-spaced on 8½-inch by 11-inch paper.
2. Leave 1-inch margins at the top and bottom, and on both sides.
3. Beginning in the upper-left corner 1 inch below the top and 1 inch from the left side, type the following on separate lines:
   a. your name
   b. your instructor's name
   c. course title, number, and section
   d. date
4. Double-space below the date and center your title. It is not necessary to put quotation marks around your title or to underline or italicize it. It is necessary to underline (or italicize) titles of books and plays used in your title. And it is necessary to put quotation marks around the titles of short stories, poems, and essays.
5. Be sure your printer's ink supply is adequate for clear, readable copy.
6. If your printer feeds connected sheets of paper, be sure to separate them before submitting your essay.

7. Number each page consecutively beginning with the second page, one-half inch from the upper-right corner.
8. Clip or staple the paper, making sure the pages are right side up and in the correct numerical order.

Plagiarism

Plagiarism is the act of using someone else's words, ideas, or organizational patterns without crediting the source. Plagiarism may be the result of careless note taking, or may be deliberate. To avoid plagiarism, it is necessary to clearly indicate what you have borrowed so your reader can distinguish your own language and ideas from those of your sources.

Research essays and papers written with little original thought and containing many long passages of quoted and summarized material strung together carelessly may inadvertently include plagiarized words and ideas. Be sure to credit each source you use at the point of borrowing, even in the midst of a paragraph or the middle of a sentence. Be sure not only to acknowledge using the source but also, if you have used exact language from the source, to put quotation marks around the borrowed words and phrases—even if you have separated some of the borrowed material and interspersed your own language.

Plagiarism is a serious offense. A form of academic *theft,* plagiarism is not tolerated in colleges and universities. Some have stringent policies, including failure for the course in which the plagiarism occurs and even expulsion from school.

To avoid plagiarism observe the following guidelines in writing your research essays and papers.

- Develop your own ideas about the works you read. Keep notes of your ideas separate from the notes you take from sources.
- Jot the title, author, and page number of a source on the page or notecard you use for your notes pertaining to material from that source.
- Put quotation marks around quoted material you copy from sources into your notes.
- When you summarize and paraphrase a source, be sure to use your own words. Avoid having the source open before you when you summarize and paraphrase.
- If you introduce any quotations from a source into your summaries and paraphrases of them, put quotation marks around the quoted words and phrases.
- Make sure that your own ideas and your own voice are the controlling centers in your research essays and papers. Use your sources to support, illustrate, and amplify your own thinking presented in your own words.
- Observe the conventions for documentation provided in the following section of this book, in your college handbook, and in *The MLA Handbook for Writers of Research Papers,* 6th ed. (2003).

DOCUMENTING SOURCES

If you incorporate the work of others into your paper, it will be necessary to credit your sources through documentation. You should always provide source credit when quoting directly, paraphrasing (rewriting a passage in your own words), borrowing ideas, or picking up facts that aren't general knowledge.

By crediting your sources, you are participating honestly and correctly in shared intellectual activity. You are showing your reader that your knowledge of a text includes some insights into what others have thought and said about it. And you are assisting your reader, who may want to consult the sources that you found valuable.

Established conventions for documenting sources vary from one academic discipline to another. For research essays and papers in literature and language the preferred style is that of the Modern Language Association (MLA). MLA documentation style has established conventions for citing sources within the text of research essays, papers, and articles. It also has established conventions for the list of works you use in preparing your research writing—usually called "List of Works Cited" or "Works Cited."

In the current MLA style, parenthetical citations within the text indicate that a source has been used. These citations refer the reader to a reference list, which should start on a new page at the end of the paper. In the "alternate" or "old" MLA style, references are marked by raised numbers in the text that correspond to numbered notes either at the foot of the page (footnotes) or the end of the paper (endnotes). Both the reference list and the endnotes and footnotes contain bibliographic information about the sources; however, the arrangement, punctuation, and capitalization of the sources differs between the two reference styles.

MLA Style: Parenthetical Citations Paired with a List of Works Cited

When you refer to a specific section of a work in the body of your paper, provide your reader with the author and page numbers of your source. Place the page numbers in parentheses, and add the author's name if it isn't contained in your sentence.

> Lawrence Lipking argues that a poet's life involves much more than his or her literal biography (30–39).

> A recent critic argues that a poet's life involves much more than his or her literal biography (Lipking 30–39).

If your paper includes two or more works by the same author, add the title of the work before the page number(s). The following are examples of other kinds of citations commonly found in literature papers.

A Work in an Anthology

> Bacon's "Of Revenge" affords us a glimpse at his view of human nature: "There is no man doth a wrong for the wrong's sake, but thereby to purchase himself profit, or pleasure, or honor, or the like" (1753).

The author and title of the anthologized selection, along with the page numbers on which it appears, should be listed in the *Works Cited* entry for the anthology. (See "The Works Cited List" below.)

A Classic Verse Play or Poem

> "She loved me for the dangers I had passed," recounts Othello, "And I loved her that she did pity them" (I.iii.166–67).

Act, scene, and line numbers are used instead of page numbers. (Arabic numbers may also be used for the act and scene.) Here's another example:

> Tennyson's Ulysses compares a dull existence to a dull sword when he says: "How dull it is to pause, to make an end, / To rust unburnished, not to shine in use!" (22–23).

Note the use of a slash [/] to indicate the end of a line in then original poem.

The Works Cited List

The items in a works cited list should be *alphabetically arranged.* The following are typical kinds of entries for a literature paper using MLA format. MLA advises underlining titles that are generally italicized in print. If you want to use italics, check with your instructor first.

A Book by a Single Author

> Lipking, Lawrence. The Life of the Poet: Beginning and Ending Poetic Careers. Chicago: U of Chicago P, 1981.

Note that second and subsequent lines are indented five spaces.

An Article in a Book

> Williams, Sherley Anne. "The Black Musician: The Black Hero as Light Bearer." James Baldwin: A Collection of Critical Essays. Ed. Kenneth Kinnamon. Englewood Cliffs, NJ: Prentice-Hall, 1974. 147–54.

The page numbers "147–54" refer to the entire article. References to specific pages would appear in parenthetical citations.

A Journal Article

> Walker, Janet. "Hardy's Somber Lyrics." Poetry 17 (1976): 25–39.

The article appeared in issue 17 of the journal Poetry. The page numbers refer to the entire article.

A Work in an Anthology

> Shakespeare, William. Hamlet: Prince of Denmark. Literature: Reading Fiction, Poetry, Drama. 5th ed. Ed. Robert DiYanni. New York: McGraw, 2002. 1395–1496.

The page numbers refer to the entire work. If you are using more than one selection from an anthology, the selections can be cited with a cross-reference to the anthology title.

> DiYanni, Robert, ed. Literature: Reading Fiction, Poetry, and Drama. 4th ed. New York: McGraw, 2002.
>
> Tennyson, Alfred, Lord. "Ulysses." DiYanni. 986–87.

A Multivolume Work; A Second Edition

> Daiches, David. A Critical History of English Literature. 2nd ed. 2 vols. New York: Ronald, 1970.

A Translation

> Auerbach, Erich. *Mimesis:* The Representation of Reality in Western Literature. Trans. Willard Trask. Princeton: Princeton UP, 1953.

DOCUMENTING ELECTRONIC SOURCES

The MLA Handbook for Writers of Research Papers, 6th ed., distinguishes electronic citation forms according to whether the material is available on a CD-ROM or whether it is available online. Because electronic media are continually changing, the details of citations may evolve even as the basic needs for citing references remain the same.

Source on CD-ROM

Citations for electronic sources are distinguished according to whether the material was published once, like a book, or whether it is published in regularly updated periodical form.

CD-ROM Produced as a One-Time Publication

Author or editor name and title followed by publication medium; edition, release, or version if relevant; place of publication; name of publisher; date of publication.

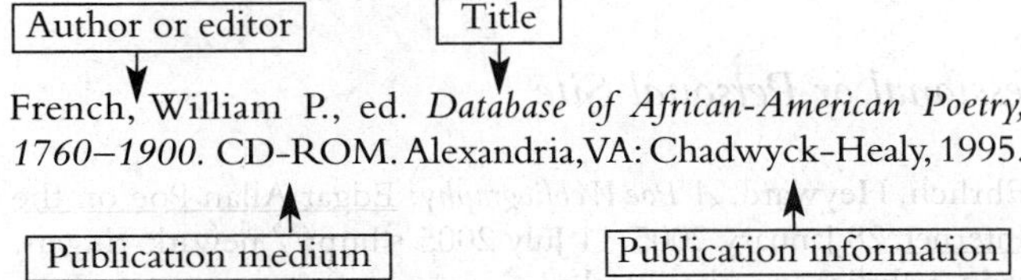

If you are not provided with an author, begin your citation with the title. If you wish to cite part of a work, place quotation marks around the part or section you cite.

"Modernism." The Oxford English Dictionary. 2nd ed. CD-ROM. Oxford: Oxford UP, 1992.

CD-ROM Updated Periodically

These are typically periodicals and reference works published both in print and on CD-ROM. To cite such a work, begin with the publication data for the printed source. Then provide all available CD-ROM-specific information (medium, title, place of publication, vendor name, date of publication).

Smith, Dinitia. "Hollywood Adopts the Canon." *New York Times* 10 Nov. 1996: D4. *New York Times Ondisc.* CD-ROM. UMI–Proquest. Dec. 1996.

If the CD-ROM is a multidisc publication, include the total number of discs if you use them all, or the disc number(s) for the one(s) you wish to cite.

Patrologia Latina Database. CD-ROM. 5 discs. Alexandria, VA: Chadwyck-Healey, 1995.

Online Sources

Citing Internet sources requires a few unique elements:

- The Internet address or URL (uniform resource locator) in angle brackets.
- If the URL is unavailable on unusable, provide the home page or search page.
- The date you accessed the site.

Otherwise the pattern is similar to that used for print publications. Not all information will be available for all sites. Provide what you can find.

Online Scholarly Project or Reference Database

African American Women Writers of the Nineteenth Century. 1999. Digital Schomburg, New York Public Library. 11 July 2005 <http://digital.nypl.org/schomburg/writers_aa19/toc.html>

This entry begins with the title of the project ("African American Women Writers of the Nineteenth Century"), followed by the date of publication and institutional information. The entry ends with the access date and URL for the site. There is no cited author or editor.

Online Professional or Personal Site

Ehrlich, Heyward. *A Poe Webliography:* Edgar Allan Poe on the Internet. 28 January 2005. 11 July 2005 <http:// newark. rutgers. edu/~ehrlich/poesites.html>

This entry begins with the author name, followed by the title, most recent publication date for the site, and access information. If this was a person's personal Web site, the phrase "Home page" can substitute for the title.

Online Book

> Whitman, Walt. Leaves of Grass. Philadelphia: David McKay, 1900. 11 July 2005 < http://www.bartleby.com/142/index1.html>

For an online book, give the publication information for the original book followed by the access information. This online version of Whitman's *Leaves of Grass* was published in Philadelphia in 1900 by publisher David McKay.

Online Periodical Article

Scholarly journal:

> Peel, Robin. "The Ideological Apprenticeship of Sylvia Plath." Journal of Modern Literature 27.4 (Summer 2004): 59–72. 11 July 2005 <http://muse.jhu.edu/journals/journal_of_modern_literature/v027/27.4peel.html>.

For an online article that first appeared in print, give the full print publication entry before the online access information.

Magazine:

> Amidon, Stephen. "Reading Jane Eyre." Salon 19 June 2005. 11 July 2005 < http://www.salon.com/books/review/2005/06/19/bronte/>

For an article that only appears online, document the publication information as you would a print source followed with the information about when and where you accessed the article.

ALTERNATE DOCUMENTATION STYLE: ENDNOTES AND FOOTNOTES

Using Endnotes and Footnotes

Raised note numbers, in consecutive order, follow the quotation or information being cited. They belong *after* all punctuation, except a dash.

> "She loved me for the dangers I had passed," recounts Othello,
> "And I loved her that she did pity them."[1]

Each raised note number corresponds to either a footnote or endnote, depending on which you are using. The only difference between footnotes and endnotes is their placement in the paper. Footnotes appear at the bottom of the page on which the reference occurs; endnotes are grouped together on a separate page immediately following the last page of text.

Endnotes List

If you use *endnotes,* your list of works cited is obviously not in alphabetical order, but in the sequence of your citations. The following endnotes contain the same sources given above in the sample works cited entries, but now in endnote form. Note that specific page references are given for each entry; these page references would have been contained in parentheses in the body of your paper in new MLA style.

[1]Lawrence Lipking, The Life of the Poet: Beginning and Ending Poetic Careers (Chicago: U of Chicago P, 1981) 30–39.

[2]Sherley Anne Williams, "The Black Musician: The Black Hero as Light Bearer," in James Baldwin: A Collection of Critical Essays, Ed. Kenneth Kinnamon (Englewood Cliffs, NJ: Prentice-Hall, 1974) 147.

[3]Janet Walker, "Hardy's Somber Lyrics," Poetry 17 (1976): 35.

[4]Francis Bacon, "Of Revenge," Literature: Reading Fiction, Poetry, Drama, and the Essay, 4th ed., Ed. Robert DiYanni (New York: McGraw, 1998) 1753.

[5]David Daiches, A Critical History of English Literature, 2d ed., 2 vols. (New York: Ronald, 1970) 2: 530.

[6]Erich Auerbach, Mimesis: The Representation of Reality in Western Literature, trans. Willard Trask (Princeton, NJ: Princeton UP, 1953) 77.

Noting Subsequent References

It is usually enough simply to list the author's name and the appropriate page(s) in subsequent references to a source.

[7]Lipking 98.

A STUDENT ESSAY USING ONE SOURCE AS A STIMULUS

The following essay by Patricia Kane, "The Prodigal Daughter in Alice Walker's 'Everyday Use,'" was discovered by Lucienne Retelle, a student who wanted to read what others had to say about Walker's story. When Lucienne found this essay, she remembered reading "The Prodigal Son" in Chapter One of this text and became intrigued with the idea of relationships between "Everyday Use" and the Biblical parable. This gave her an idea for her own essay for a class assignment. You may want to reread Walker's story (page 470) as well as "The Prodigal Son" (page 27). Then read Patricia Kane's essay and finally Lucienne Retelle's evaluation of it. How convincing do you find Kane's argument? Retelle's responding argument? How do you think Kane might answer Retelle? Note how sources are documented in these essays. Because Kane cites only one book in her works cited list and her discussion makes it clear which book is referred to as well, she includes only page numbers in parentheses in her citations.

In citing references to the Biblical story "The Prodigal Son," the student writer cites the name of the Biblical book in which the story occurs, followed by chapter and verse.

PATRICIA KANE

The Prodigal Daughter in Alice Walker's "Everyday Use"

"Everyday Use," Alice Walker's variation on the archetypal prodigal child story not only amuses with its deft humor, it also pleases by ending with the equivalent of the fatted calf remaining with the stay-at-home. Walker's tale, one of those collected in *In Love and Trouble,* displays a world in which a mother comes to see both the humbug in the returning daughter's new appreciation of the mother's realm and the everyday worth of her younger daughter. The reversals and variations from the Biblical prodigal son story suggest that when women make the choices, the tale expresses different values.

The story, narrated by the mother, begins as she awaits a visit from her older daughter, Dee. Immediately her tone establishes the values of her realm as she declares that the swept yard in which she sits is "more comfortable than most people know" (47). As she sits comfortably in her yard, she muses on her daughters. Dee, older, better looking, and brighter than Maggie, scorned the everyday world of rural blacks and went away to school. Maggie, scarred in a fire Dee may have set to destroy a house she hated, will marry a local man and remain in the familiar life. When the mother describes her life and work, including killing hogs and calves, she pictures a realm in which any special meals to mark reconciliation will be more personal than those provided through the orders of the Biblical father.

Prodigal children value what they once rejected, and the returned Dee now finds her scorned past to be fashionable. Her mother, though bemused by her exclaiming over chitlins and other familiar food, agrees to let her take the butter churn to use for a centerpiece. She humors her wish to be known as Wangero although she reminds Dee that she was named for her aunt and grandmother, not any oppressor. The elements of the familiar story seem to be in place. Although chitlins have replaced the calf at the meal, the butter churn evokes calves, and Dee/Wangero seems to now appreciate her mother's world. The matter of the name, however, which shows the mother confident of who she is while Wangero/Dee takes her sense of style from others, provides a variation in the theme and foreshadows the central scene.

Wangero/Dee claims two quilts handmade by her grandmother and earmarked for Maggie on her marriage. Wangero/Dee, who refused a quilt when she went away to college because they were out of style, proclaims these to be priceless. She will value them, she says, by hanging them whereas Maggie would "be backward enough to put them to everyday use" (57). Maggie, although this was "her portion," responds by agreeing to let her sister have the quilts because such "was the way she knew God to work" (58).

God, however, in the person of the mother, suddenly feels something like she does when the spirit of God touches her in church. She hugs Maggie for the first time and returns her portion to her. Realizing not only the worth of her daughter of everyday use, but also that even if her use of the quilts will wear them out, their value lies in use not display, she bestows the riches of her domestic kingdom not on the prodigal but on the familiar daughter. Maggie is the now-embraced lost child of this tale.

After the prodigal child leaves, the mother and Maggie sit in the yard "just enjoying" (59) in the realm of everyday use.

Student Papers

Lucienne Retelle
Prof. Judith Stanford
Introduction to Fiction
April 23, 1998

Has the Prodigal Daughter Really Returned?

Patricia Kane, in her response to Alice Walker's "Everyday Use," states that this story is a variation on the theme of the Biblical story, "The Prodigal Son." She proposes that the mother in Alice Walker's story is the feminine equivalent to the father of the Prodigal Son, and as such, they both represent God. Kane suggests, however, that the male and female express different values, and that when God is represented as female, he/she makes different choices. Kane concludes that Walker exemplifies this through Mama who ultimately "bestows the riches of her domestic kingdom not on the prodigal but on the familiar daughter (7)," and Maggie becomes the embraced lost child.

In relating the story to the Biblical Prodigal Son, Patricia Kane shows thoughtfulness and insight; however, in her eagerness to expose what she sees as differences in male/female values, she demonstrates a superficial understanding of the Gospel parable and misses the central message: one of repentance and forgiveness.

At first glance Kane's thesis is appealing and perhaps convincing; but when you compare the two stories carefully, the actions and responses of both parents have basic similarities. In both stories, the mother and father freely give their children their "portion" as they need and/or request it. The Biblical father gives his younger son his portion of property which enables him to go off to a distant place to live as he wishes (Luke 15:12). Mama in "Everyday Use" works hard to raise money from her church which enables her daughter Dee to go away to school; and she offers her a quilt as well. The father is rich and the mother is poor, but the portions they give are relatively equal based upon their means.

The Prodigal Son rejects his inheritance, just as Dee rejects part of her portion, the quilt, because at the time it held no value for her. Both the Prodigal Son and Dee, the prodigal daughter, repudiate the values of their parents, and they leave home to pursue their own way of life.

The mother's and father's responses to their children when they come back are different in character: the father is fully open and receiving, while the mother is somewhat reticent. This is *not,* as Kane suggests, because they have different values, but because the children come back for different reasons and under different circumstances. The prodigal son has not been successful in his worldly life, and comes back weary and destitute, longing for the comforts of his father's home. In contrast, Dee comes back flaunting her success and new worldly values. She is elaborately dressed while the son is probably in rags. He comes back humbly, hoping to be received; she comes back confidently, intending to take.

While their actual responses may be different in character, Mama and Biblical father both demonstrate similar parental desires and feelings for their "lost" children. The father waits for his son, sees him a long way off and is deeply moved at his return. They greet warmly and the father has no words of reproach. He immediately orders the cooking of a fatted calf by way of celebration (Luke 15:20). Similarly, Mama also "waits." She has a recurring dream in which she and Dee publicly reunite with arms around each other, Dee with tears in her eyes, grateful to her mother saying she couldn't have done anything without her mother's help. But their reunion doesn't happen as it does in Mama's dream. Dee arrives with haughty airs, gives her mother a perfunctory greeting, and immediately busies herself with her camera. Nevertheless, Mama has prepared to celebrate. She has made her yard clean and wavy and prepares the "fatted calf" represented by pork, collards, chitlins, and corn bread.

Kane observes that because the Biblical father "orders" others to do the cooking while Mama prepares her own, the mother's feast is more personal, suggesting that a woman's mark of reconciliation is "better" or has a higher value than the male's (7). This judgment is irrelevant to the message: both parents demonstrate acceptance and desire for reconciliation through their welcome and through offering the celebration meal. Their different styles of doing so, whether due to male/femaleness, lifestyles, or personal habits, do not alter the quality of the reconciliation. Their messages are the same; the setting and cultures are different.

A secondary theme of the Prodigal Son parable is the attitude of the older brother who stayed at home with his father. Kane does not address this theme, nor does she make a comparison between this brother and Maggie, which is critical if we are to understand more fully Mama's behavior.

In the Biblical story, the older brother is angry and resentful at his father's lavish display of welcome for his returning brother. The father pleads with him to join in the celebration and reassures his son by saying the older son is always with him and everything the father has is also the son's (Luke 15:28–32).

In contrast, Maggie is shy and cowers in the presence of her returning sister. No anger or resentfulness is implied on her part. In her own way she is present and participates in the celebration. Moreover, she does *not* show resentfulness, and when Dee demands the quilts, Maggie tells her she can have them. The quality of Maggie's generosity is great, considering her comparative lack of life's gifts. She is neither as intelligent, nor as attractive, nor as well educated as Dee.

Just as the Biblical father reassured his older son, Mama has a protective attitude toward Maggie; she takes back the quilts from Dee, and hugs Maggie to her. Mama has already given Dee the butter churner, which in its own way is just as important and symbolic a portion. It too has intrinsic, sentimental and "everyday use" value.

Both parents demonstrate love for their "lost" children, both waited for their return, and both celebrated. The fact that Mama gives Maggie the quilts does not take away from Dee: Dee long ago rejected this portion, so it became Maggie's.

Finally, to approach the two stories as an in toto variation on the theme of the Biblical story, based on differences in male/female values as Kane has done, is inappropriate, for two reasons: first, as previously described, the stay-at-home children are very different from one another, and Mama's attitude is clearly related to the kind of person Maggie is. Second, and more significant, Dee has not truly "returned" as the prodigal son has, and therefore a direct comparison cannot be made. Dee does not come back seeking forgiveness and does not indicate she has anything to repent. She is still "out there" in the world, breaking away, and the story ends with her leaving again.

I suggest, however, that if Alice Walker had written her story differently—according to Mama's dream—Mama's attitude and response assuredly would have been akin to the Biblical father's. She would have been tearfully and overwhelmingly joyful at Dee's return. In addition, she would have had no need to protect Maggie from her sister's demand for her "portion"—because, most likely, Dee wouldn't have demanded it in the first place.

Works Cited

Kane, Patricia. "The Prodigal Daughter in Alice Walker's 'Everyday Use.'" Notes on Contemporary Literature 15.2 (1985): 7.

The New American Bible. Gen. ed. Jean Marie Hiesberger. New York: Oxford UP, 1995.

A RESEARCH PAPER ON A SINGLE WORK USING MULTIPLE SOURCES

The following paper was prepared for a writing and literature course in which students were given a choice of works to research and write about. They were asked to focus on an issue in the work or an aspect of it and to develop a research essay that explained their idea, using at least three secondary sources in addition to the text of the work itself.

Student Papers

Marie Bertino
Prof. Hassenger
Eng 1101
May 31, 2006

Building to the Omega Point in O'Connor and Carver

Flannery O'Connor's story "Everything that Rises Must Converge" borrows its name from Pierre Teilhard de Chardin's definition of an Omega point. Pierre Teilhard de Chardin was a Jesuit priest who wrote that an Omega point is when human beings will reach their fullest consciousness by growing closer together (McFarland, 238). Given O'Connor's background with religion, her use of the Omega point, an idea with religious significance, is not surprising. What is interesting, however, is how Raymond Carver's story "Cathedral" builds to its own Omega point: a surprising epiphany for a seemingly unredeemable main character. Both stories share similar form and similar religious-themed epiphanies; however, the conclusions of those epiphanies are significantly different.

Both stories begin on similar paths. Both have secondary characters judged harshly in the biased viewpoint of the main character. In the case of "Everything that Rises Must Converge," Julian sees his mother as an old fashioned racist, more likely to worry about a fancy hat than to notice the world changing around her. As they take a bus ride to a reducing class at the Y, details about the mother are slowly revealed in Julian's head. In "Cathedral," the narrator begrudgingly makes ready for a houseguest named Robert, a blind man who has recently lost his wife. He is naturally suspicious of blind men, reasoning "My idea of blindness came from the movies. In the movies, the blind moved slowly and never laughed. Sometimes, they were led by seeing-eye dogs. A blind man in my house was not something I was looking forward to" (274). In both stories, we are led to negative views of Julian's mother and the blind man, respectively. By the end of each story, the reader's view will have changed or, at least, been blurred by the main character's epiphany, a religious-like Omega point.

In "Everything that Rises," Julian reveals details that will lead to his Omega point. We begin to learn things about his mother that are not so unlikable. While he detests his job selling typewriters, she brags about it. "'I tell him' his other said, 'that Rome wasn't built in a day'" (209). While his mother is proud of him, Julian is ashamed that his college education has not brought him further in the world. In this way, Julian's resentment could color his opinion of his mother. Perhaps he is not a reliable narrator. His behavior becomes even more peculiar as he jockeys for position in the bus, trying to sit next to black people so as to horrify his mother. "He would have liked to get into conversation with The Negro and to talk with him about art or politics or any subject that would be above the comprehension of those around them, but the man remained entrenched behind his paper. He was either ignoring the change of seating or had never noticed it. There was no way for Julian to convey his sympathy" (213). When we later learn that Julian has tried to make "Negro friends" to no avail, this man's refusal to be engaged in conversation illuminates Julian's fickle, manipulative persona. As horrified as he is by his mother's vow that she would do anything for any of her colored friends, she at least does not try to use them as ploys to hurt other people. Julian is offended when the people on the bus will not act as chess pieces.

Early in "Cathedral," the blind man's influence and promise, and the future Omega point are foreshadowed. The narrator recalls a story his wife has told him about the blind man. "On her last day in the office, the blind man asked if he could touch her face. She agreed to this. She told me he touched his fingers to every part of her face, her nose—even her neck! She never forgot it. She even tried to write a poem about it" (274). The blind man has already deeply affected the narrator's wife so it stands to reason he could affect the narrator. Also, there is the question of naming things. The narrator says of his wife's ex-boyfriend "Her officer—why would he have a name? He was the childhood sweetheart, and what more does he want?" (275). In the logic of a story whose narrator does not name insignificant people, what does it say that the blind man is the only character who gets a title, Robert, while the narrator and his wife go nameless? The blind man has already assumed a place of honor within five minutes of being in the house.

While Carver leads his characters to the dinner table, O'Connor keeps hers on the same stuffy bus. It is only when she allows them to disembark that Julian reaches his moment of consciousness, albeit too late. To Julian's horror, his mother offers a young black child a nickel, and is struck in the face by the child's mother. Initially the reader believes that the story will end with a racial awakening for his mother, however it is for Julian that the harshest blow is dealt. As his mother sputters and sways, he chastises her aggressively for her condescension, the release of his story long baiting and goading. But her face changes, and he realizes that she has had a stroke. At this point, his language becomes that of a little boy, signaling that his moment of catharsis must involve a reversion back to childhood, a point from which he has debatably ever progressed. "'Mother!' he cried. 'Darling, sweetheart, wait!' Crumpling, she fell to the pavement. He dashed forward and fell at her side, crying "Mama, Mama!'" (218). It is the only time in the story he is at a loss for something cruel to say, as we and he realize that his mother is dying. It is then too late for him to repent, as he nears "his entry into the world of guilt and sorrow" (218).

The Omega point in "Cathedral" comes as the narrator and Robert watch a documentary. Robert asks the narrator to describe the cathedral to him and the narrator, earnestly, with much thought and care, does. Feeling his efforts are not as effective as he would like, they move to a pad and pencil. Robert clasps his hand over the narrator's as the latter attempts to draw a cathedral. In his introduction to the story in <u>You've Got to Read This</u>, Tobias Wolff writes "And then something else happens. The narrator begins to enjoy Robert's company. He even allows himself to say so. The two men come together to build a cathedral of their own, a space of perfect fellowship and freedom, wherein each is granted a miracle of sight by taking on the vision of the other" (137). The narrator's Omega point is when he realizes that the blind man is teaching him how to rise out of his own sheltered life and dependencies, to see in a different way, much like he has done years ago for the wife.

It is clear that the blind man is an agent for positive change, and the narrator has undergone a change for the better. In "Raymond Carver and Postmodern Humanism," Arthur A. Brown writes that "the narrator and the blind man come to communicate: even more, they become aware not merely of their physical but of their spiritual being. The narrator shows the blind man a cathedral, and the blind man shows the narrator how to see. He shows him what a cathedral means" (136). That's significant idea: The epiphany for the narrator of "Cathedral" is a moment of understanding and consciousness, specifically of understanding the meaning behind a religious structure.

While Julian's epiphany is mixed with anguish and pain, it is also painted with religious symbols. While writing about "Everything that Rises Must Converge," W.R. Martin notes that Julian's name echoes that of Roman Emperor Julian, who is known as the Apostate because he abandoned early Christianity. Drawing a connection between the two, Martin writes "Julian [the O'Connor character] is an apostate not explicitly from the Christian faith, though his attitude is of course markedly un-Christian, but from something like natural loyalty, gratitude, and affection" (114). The historic Julian gained consciousness while dying on the battlefield. Thus, according to Martin, "both Julians attain tragic recognition." Although Martin does not prove conclusively that O'Connor used the story of Emperor Julian the Apostate as a source, the fact that O'Connor titled the story after the words used by de Chardin suggests that she knew there is a religious theme to Julian's epiphany. If we assume that Julian is named after the Apostate, we can assume that his Omega point is his conscious realization that he is his mother's son, that he has treated her poorly, and that her loss will forever change him.

In this way, both stories push towards an epiphany using similar methods. In both stories, a secondary character is disparaged at first but later is the vehicle for a religious-inspired epiphany, an Omega point. And while one realization is bitter, the other is positive. Taken together, both stories display a religious-themed epiphany that brings the main character to a greater consciousness, their own personal Omega point.

Works Cited

Brown, Arthur A. "Raymond Carver and Postmodern Humanism." Critique. 32.2 (1990): 125–136.

Carver, Raymond. "Cathedral." Literature: Approaches to Fiction, Poetry, and Drama. Ed. Robert DiYanni. New York: McGraw, 2004, 274–283.

Martin, W.R. "The Apostate in Flannery O'Connor's 'Everything that Rises Must Converge.'" American Notes and Queries. 23,7/8 (1985): 113–114.

McFarland, Dorothy Tuck. "On 'Everything that Rises Must Converge.'" Literature: Approaches to Fiction, Poetry, and Drama. Ed. Robert DiYanni. New York: McGraw, 2004, 238–239.

O'Connor, Flannery. "Everything that Rises Must Converge." Literature: Approaches to Fiction, Poetry, and Drama. Ed. Robert DiYanni. New York: McGraw, 2004, 209–218.

Wolff, Tobias. Introduction. You've Got to Read This: Contemporary American Writers Introduce Stories that Held Them in Awe. New York: Harper Collins, 1994.

Christina A. Drew
Dr. Tom Kitts
St. John's University

Death of a Salesman: Death of a Tragic Hero

"Funny, y'know? After all the highways and the rains, and the appointments, and the years, you end up worth more dead than alive." Willy Loman, the main character in Arthur Miller's *Death of a Salesman,* greatly valued being worth something. He lived his life in an effort to be accepted and well liked. He was an ordinary salesman, "a dime a dozen." Much debate has occurred over whether or not Willy can be considered a tragic hero despite his lack of grand rank. In his essay, "Tragedy and the Common Man," Miller explains that Willy can, in fact, be a tragic hero: "I believe that the common man is as apt a subject for tragedy in its highest sense as kings were."

Other than a high position in society, Willy holds all other qualities of a traditional tragic hero. Although the concept of rank as a prerequisite for a tragic hero stems from Aristotle, Socrates, and Shakespeare (Foster 103), rank is not an essential prerequisite to evoke feelings of sorrow and pity for the hero. The audience feels great pity and sympathy for Willy because we relate to his need for acceptance. Understanding this, Miller defends the possibility of a common man as a tragic hero: "On the face of it this ought to be obvious in the light of modern psychiatry, which bases its analysis upon classic formulations, such as Oedipus and Orestes complexes, for instance, which were enacted by royal beings, but which apply to everyone in similar emotional situations."

Like most tragic heroes, as well as most common individuals, Willy has a tragic flaw that leads to his downfall. His need to be accepted, especially by men, is his tragic flaw. Drama critic Jordan Miller believes that there are no outside circumstances that lead to Willy's downfall; therefore Willy cannot be a tragic hero (qtd. In Foster 108). Jordan Miller neglects to see the importance of Willy's abandonment by his father. When he was only a little child Willy's father left his wife and young son. This created in Willy a strong insecurity: "Dad left when I was such a baby and I never had the chance to talk to him and I still feel—kind of temporary about myself." This underlying need to find validation through others shaped the events of Willy's life and set the stage for his eventual demise.

Willy's career choice is an example of Willy's struggle to be well liked. Although Willy was good with his hands and could have been more successful and perhaps happier if he chose a career in construction or carpentry, he decided to be a salesman. The reason for this decision was not the result of a great love for the art of selling; instead, it stemmed from respect and validation he saw another salesman, Dave Singleman, achieve. Singleman was so well known that in-person sales calls were not necessary; he made his living over the telephone. When he died, hundreds of people from all over mourned at his funeral. Witnessing this convinced Willy that the life of a salesman would give him the validation, respect, and acceptance he craved. Unfortunately, Willy's intense need for approval led him down a path of personal and professional shortcomings. He wanted to joke and talk with the buyer, to sell himself not the product; however, these clients viewed him as a nuisance which decreased, instead of increased, his sales. Inevitably, Willy is left jobless and without the validation he sought.

When studying Willy's life we need to consider his tense relationship with his older son Biff. Until the summer of Biff's expected graduation from high school, Biff and Willy appear to have a close relationship. A flashback of Willy's reveals that at this time Biff unexpectedly visited Willy on a business trip in Boston and discovered his father in an extramarital affair. From that point forward, Biff lost all respect for his father. He blames Willy for all of his troubles and, as a result, he lives a life of spite and, consciously and unconsciously, fails in all of his endeavors (Griffin 39). Willy could not handle knowing he was partially to blame for Biff's rage and failure, so he pushed Biff away. Willy cannot find a way to deal with the tension between him and his son, so many of their conversations often turn into fights.

The torment of the strained relationship with Biff coupled with his realization of failure takes a toll on Willy's mental health. Willy begins to drift between reality and the preferred pleasantness of his past. He tells his brother Ben that he wants to return to "all the great times," yet the present continues to imprison him. As the play progresses, Willy becomes more aware that his flaw, the need for acceptance by others, has led him to failure. By emphasizing the importance of popularity, Willy neglects to stress the importance of education for his sons. Willy even defends Biff's concentration on sports over academics because through sports Biff is well liked and highly acclaimed, especially by men. Charley's relationship with his son Bernard and their concentration on education, not popularity, contrasts with Willy's relationship with Biff as well as Willy's philosophy on education.

Once Willy realizes that his way of life has brought his family to shame and uncertainty, he decides to take action. As a tragic hero must, Willy takes responsibility for the situation he created. He decides that the only way to fix the problem is to commit suicide. He believes that the $20,000 from his life insurance policy will solve his family's financial problems. In his final hours Willy clings to the illusion that he has reached his goal. He believes that his death and funeral will prove to his family that he was well liked and worth something. He sacrifices his life for the betterment of his family, especially Biff, expecting that the insurance will provide Biff with financial backing for his business.

After a final confrontation with his family Willy drives off and commits suicide. No one attends his funeral except his immediate family, Charley, and Bernard. Despite his willingness to finally make everything right, Willy never received what he wanted most: the respect and acceptance of men. The audience feels an undeniable sense of pity for this man who wanted so desperately to be liked; especially because the audience understands the effects on Willy of his abandonment by, first, his father and then his surrogate father Ben. These conditions outside of Willy's control add to the sense of tragedy.

Willy Loman is indeed a tragic hero. Despite his lower middle-class position, Willy inspires pity in the audience in the same manner as a noble and fallen king does in a Greek or Shakespearean tragedy. Perhaps the reader pities Willy even more because it is easier to relate to a common man and the everyday hardships he experiences.

Works Cited

Foster, Richard J. "Death of a Salesman as Tragedy." Readings on Arthur Miller. Ed. Thomas Siebold. San Diego: Greenhaven Press, 1997. 102–09.

Griffin, Alice. Understanding Arthur Miller. Columbia, SC: U of South Carolina P, 1996.

Miller, Arthur. Death of a Salesman. Literature: Approaches to Fiction, Poetry, and Drama. Ed. Robert DiYanni. New York: McGraw, 2004, 1352–1420.

---. "Tragedy and the Common Man." 1949. The Literary Link. Ed. Janice Pattern. 10 May 2006. <http://theliterarylink.com/miller1.html>.

CHAPTER THIRTY-ONE

Critical Theory: Approaches to the Analysis and Interpretation of Literature

READINGS FOR ANALYSIS

This chapter will introduce you to various schools or perspectives of literary theory. In the discussion of those various perspectives, we will see how the following passage by William Carlos Williams and poem by Emily Dickinson can be interpreted in different ways.

WILLIAM CARLOS WILLIAMS
[1883–1963]

The Use of Force

They were new patients to me, all I had was the name, Olson. Please come down as soon as you can, my daughter is very sick.

When I arrived I was met by the mother, a big startled looking woman, very clean and apologetic who merely said, Is this the doctor? and let me in. In the back, she added. You must excuse us, doctor, we have her in the kitchen where it is warm. It is very damp here sometimes.

The child was fully dressed and sitting on her father's lap near the kitchen table. He tried to get up, but I motioned for him not to bother, took off my overcoat and started to look things over. I could see that they were all very nervous, eyeing me up and down distrustfully. As often, in such cases, they weren't telling me more than they had to, it was up to me to tell them; that's why they were spending three dollars on me.

The child was fairly eating me up with her cold, steady eyes, and no expression to her face whatever. She did not move and seemed, inwardly, quiet; an unusually attractive little thing, and as strong as a heifer in appearance. But her face was flushed, she was breathing rapidly, and I realized that she had a high fever. She had magnificent blonde hair, in profusion. One of those picture children often reproduced in advertising leaflets and the photogravure sections of the Sunday papers.

She's had a fever for three days, began the father, and we don't know what it comes from. My wife has given her things, you know, like people do, but it don't do no good. And there's been a lot of sickness around. So we tho't you'd better look her over and tell us what is the matter.

As doctors often do I took a trial shot at it as a point of departure. Has she had a sore throat?

Both parents answered me together, No . . . No, she says her throat don't hurt her.

Does your throat hurt you? added the mother to the child. But the little girl's expression didn't change, nor did she move her eyes from my face.

Have you looked?

I tried to, said the mother, but I couldn't see.

As it happens, we had been having a number of cases of diphtheria in the school to which this child went during that month and we were all, quite apparently, thinking of that, though no one had as yet spoken of the thing.

Well, I said, suppose we take a look at the throat first. I smiled in my best professional manner and asking for the child's first name I said, come on, Mathilda, open your, mouth and let's take a look at your throat.

Nothing doing.

Aw, come on, I coaxed, just open your mouth wide and let me take a look. Look, I said opening both hands wide. I haven't anything in my hands. Just open up and let me see.

Such a nice man, put in the mother. Look how kind he is to you. Come on, do what he tells you to. He won't hurt you.

At that I ground my teeth in disgust. If only they wouldn't use the word "hurt" I might be able to get somewhere. But I did not allow myself to be hurried or disturbed, but speaking quietly and slowly I approached the child again.

As I moved my chair a little nearer, suddenly with one catlike movement both her hands clawed instinctively for my eyes and she almost reached them too. In fact she knocked my glasses flying and they fell, though unbroken, several feet away from me on the kitchen floor.

Both the mother and father almost turned themselves inside out in embarrassment and apology. You bad girl, said the mother, taking her and shaking her by one arm. Look what you've done. The nice man. . . .

For heaven's sake, I broke in. Don't call me a nice man to her. I'm here to look at her throat on the chance that she might have diphtheria and possibly die of it. But that's nothing to her. Look here, I said to the child, we're going to look at your throat. You're old enough to understand what I'm saying. Will you open it now by yourself or shall we have to open it for you?

Not a move. Even her expression hadn't changed. Her breaths however were coming faster and faster. Then the battle began. I had to do it. I had to have a throat culture for her own protection. But first I told the parents that it was entirely up to them. I explained the danger but said that I would not insist on a throat examination so long as they would take the responsibility.

If you don't do what the doctor says you'll have to go to the hospital, the mother admonished her severely.

Oh yeah? I had to smile to myself. After all, I had already fallen in love with the savage brat, the parents were contemptible to me. In the ensuing struggle they grew more and more abject, crushed, exhausted while she surely rose to magnificent heights of insane fury of effort bred of her terror of me.

The father tried his best, and he was a big man but the fact that she was his daughter, his shame at her behavior and his dread of hurting her made him release her just at the critical moment several times when I had almost achieved success, till I wanted to kill him. But his dread also that she might have diphtheria made him tell me to go on, go on though he himself was almost fainting, while the mother moved back and forth behind us raising and lowering her hands in an agony of apprehension.

Put her in front of you on your lap, I ordered, and hold both her wrists.

But as soon as he did the child let out a scream. Don't, you're hurting me. Let go of my hands. Let them go I tell you. Then she shrieked terrifyingly, hysterically. Stop it! Stop it! You're killing me!

Do you think she can stand it, doctor! said the mother.

You get out, said the husband to his wife. Do you want her to die of diphtheria?

Come on now, hold her, I said.

Then I grasped the child's head with my left hand and tried to get the wooden tongue depressor between her teeth. She fought, with clenched teeth, desperately! But now I also had grown furious—at a child. I tried to hold myself down but I couldn't. I know how to expose a throat for inspection. And I did my best. When finally I got the wooden spatula behind the last teeth and just the point of it into the mouth cavity, she opened up for an instant but before I could see anything she came down again and gripping the wooden blade between her molars she reduced it to splinters before I could get it out again.

Aren't you ashamed, the mother yelled at her. Aren't you ashamed to act like that in front of the doctor?

Get me a smooth-handled spoon of some sort, I told the mother. We're going through with this. The child's mouth was already bleeding. Her tongue was cut and she was screaming in wild hysterical shrieks. Perhaps I should have desisted and come back in an hour or more. No doubt it would have been better. But I have seen at least two children lying dead in bed of neglect in such cases, and feeling that I must get a diagnosis now or never I went at it again. But the worst of it was that I too had got beyond reason. I could have torn the child apart in my own fury and enjoyed it. It was a pleasure to attack her. My face was burning with it.

The damned little brat must be protected against her own idiocy, one says to one's self at such times. Others must be protected against her. It is social necessity. And all these things are true. But a blind fury, a feeling of adult shame, bred of a longing for muscular release are the operatives. One goes to the end.

In a final unreasoning assault I overpowered the child's neck and jaws. I forced the heavy silver spoon back of her teeth and down her throat till she gagged. And there it was—both tonsils covered with membrane. She had fought valiantly to keep me from knowing her secret. She had been hiding that sore throat for three days at least and lying to her parents in order to escape just such an outcome as this.

Now truly she was furious. She had been on the defensive before but now she attacked. Tried to get off her father's lap and fly at me while tears of defeat blinded her eyes.

EMILY DICKINSON

[1830–1886]

I'm "wife"—I've finished that—
That other state—
I'm Czar—I'm "Woman" now—
It's safer so—

How odd the Girl's life looks
Behind this soft Eclipse—
I think that Earth feels so
To folks in Heaven—now—

This being comfort—then
That other kind—was pain—
But why compare?
I'm "Wife"! Stop there!

THE CANON AND THE CURRICULUM

Interpreting literature is an art and a skill that readers develop with experience and practice. Regular reading of stories, poems, plays, and essays will give you opportunities to become a skillful interpreter. Simply reading the literary works, however, is not enough, not if you wish to participate in the invigorating critical conversations teachers and other experienced readers bring to their discussion of literature. To develop a sense of the interpretive possibilities of literary works, you will need to know something of the various critical perspectives that literary critics use to analyze and interpret literature. This chapter introduces you to a number of major critical perspectives, including historical, biographical, psychological, and sociological approaches (among others), each of which approaches the study of literature a different way.

This discussion of critical perspectives aims to provide you with a set of ideas about how literature can be analyzed and interpreted. It is not designed to explain the history of literary criticism. Nor is its goal to convert you to a particular critical approach. Neither has any attempt been made to present the intricacies and variations in interpretive analysis developed by proponents of the various critical perspectives. And although you will find in this chapter discussions of ten critical perspectives, still other approaches to literary interpretation are available, both older ones that have currently declined in use and newer approaches that are still emerging.

Before considering the first of our critical perspectives, that of formalist criticism, we should review some basic questions being debated, sometimes heatedly, throughout the educational establishment. You may have already heard about the controversy surrounding the literary "canon," or list of works considered suitable for study in a university curriculum. There is now considerable disagreement about just what books should be read in college courses, why they should be read, and how they should be read. As a way of putting the ten critical perspectives in context, we will take up each of these questions in a brief overview of the current debate about the university literature curriculum.

What We Read

The notion of a literary canon or collection of accepted books derives from the idea of a biblical canon—those books accepted as official scriptures. A scriptural canon contains those works deemed to represent the moral standards and religious beliefs of a particular group, for example, Jews, Muslims, Hindus, or Christians. A canon of accepted works also contains, by implication, its obverse or flip side—that some works are excluded from the canon. Just as certain works, such as the Book of Maccabees, were not accepted into the Hebrew Scriptures and the Gospel of Thomas was denied entry into the Christian New Testament, not every book or literary work written can become part of an officially sanctioned literary canon or a university curriculum. Certain works inevitably will be omitted while others just as necessarily are selected for inclusion. The central question revolves around which works should be included in the canon, and why.

As you may know, certain "classics" for a long time have dominated the canon of literature for study in university courses—epic poems by Homer and Dante, for example, plays by Ibsen and Shakespeare, poems by writers from many countries, but especially those from Europe and America, novels such as Charles Dickens's *Great Expectations,* Jane Austen's *Pride and Prejudice,* Mark Twain's *The Adventures of Huckleberry Finn,* Emily Bronte's *Wuthering Heights,* and many others.

In the last two decades, however, there has been a movement to alter the canon of classical works, most of which have been written by white males of European ancestry, in the more or less distant past. Some of the changes in what we read have come from adding works by writers long omitted, such as those by minority writers—African Americans, Native Americans, Asian Americans, and other writers from around the world beyond Europe, those from Australia, India, and Africa, for example. The works added by minority writers have been largely, though not exclusively, modern and contemporary ones. Still other changes in the literary canon have come from the rediscovery or recovery of older works, many from the Renaissance and the nineteenth century, especially works by women, which had for a long time been considered unworthy of serious study or of inclusion in college literature curricula.

Various objections have been raised to these changes and additions, especially that such works were considered not to have withstood "the test of time," lasting decades or centuries, as have the classics. What needs to be remembered, however, is that individuals, not time, make the choices about which books are to be taught in schools and universities, and therefore decide which books will become "classics." People today are debating not only what works should be part of the canon of literature but whether the very idea of a canon is viable at all. In other words, what is a canon for? Is a literary canon inevitable? Is it even necessary?

Why We Read

These changes in what we read are related to a debate about why we read. Classic novels and plays, stories and poems have long been read because the lessons they are presumed to teach are considered valuable. The meanings of certain American canonical works, for example, have been viewed as educationally and morally good for readers to assimilate, largely because the works are believed to reflect values central to the American way of life. They reflect values relating to the importance of friendship, responsible behavior, and hard work, for example, or values relating to decency, justice, and fair play. Of course, other works accepted into the literary canon taught in American colleges and universities do not reflect such views, both works written by American writers and works by writers of other nationalities and literary traditions, many of which are included in this book.

Canonical literary works of many traditions and genres—Henrik Ibsen's *A Doll House,* for example, or Emily Dickinson's lyric poems—disrupt and run counter to many traditional literary, social, religious, and cultural values. And works such as Shakespeare's tragedies and Keats' and Wordsworth's poetry harbor ideas and attitudes about which common readers and professional critics have long disagreed, a disagreement that derives partly from varying critical perspectives used to interpret the works and partly from their richness and complexity, which makes it impossible to say once and for all just what those enticing and intellectually provocative works mean.

Another reason for the continuity of the traditional canon is that it is easier to preserve the status quo than to initiate change. Change is neither welcomed nor embraced, even when it is inevitable. Moreover, later generations read the books of former ones because earlier generations want their descendants to read and value what they read and valued. Those earlier generations have the power to enforce such a decision since they hold the positions of authority in schools and on councils that design curricula and create reading lists for school programs and university courses.

Today, however, many of these assumptions have been reevaluated by teachers and critics from a wide range of political persuasions. With the demographic changes that have been occurring in educational institutions in the past quarter century have come additional reasons for reading. Minority groups that now form a significant population in university classrooms, minority teachers, younger faculty raised in a much altered political environment, large numbers of women faculty—all insist on the need for multiple perspectives, varying voices, different visions of experience. They argue that literary works should be read to challenge conventional ways of behaving and orthodox ways of thinking. (Some educators say that there is nothing new in this, and that, in fact, traditional canonical works have long been read this way.) For some of these other readers, however, literature exists less for moral instruction or cultural education than to help inaugurate political and social change, a view that is less widely endorsed than the view that literary works should invite critical scrutiny and stimulate questioning and debate.

How We Read

That brings us to the important question of how we read. Just how do we read? Do we simply "just read"? And if we do, then what do we mean by "just reading"? Most often just reading means something on the order of reading for pleasure, without worrying about analysis and interpretation. From the standpoint of more analytical reading, "just reading" refers to interpreting the words on the page, making sense of them in a way that seems reasonable.

But a number of assumptions lie behind this notion. One such assumption is that the meaning of a literary work is available to anyone willing to read it carefully. Another is that literary works contain layers or levels of meaning, that they have to be analyzed to understand their complex meanings. Still another is that although different readers all bring their unique experience as members of particular genders, races, religions, and nationalities to their interpretation of literary works, they finally understand the meaning of those works in the same way. In this view, literary works such as *Hamlet* or *The Scarlet Letter* mean the same thing to every reader.

Each of these assumptions, however, has been challenged by literary theorists in the past two decades, to such an extent that many serious readers find them untenable. It doesn't take long, for example, to realize that though we share some understanding of Shakespeare's play or Hawthorne's novel, we invariably see different things in them and see them differently. The differences we make of literary works and the different ways we understand them are related to the varying assumptions about literature and life that we bring to our reading. The different ways these assumptions have been modified and the different emphases and focuses serious readers and literary critics bring to bear on literary works can be categorized according to various approaches or critical perspectives. Ten critical perspectives are here presented, though others could be added.

These ten, however, reflect critical positions that many academic readers find useful, whether they are reading works new to the canon or older established ones.

For each critical perspective you will find an overview that introduces the critical approach, an application of the critical perspective to the Williams short story and the Dickinson poem reprinted at the beginning of this chapter, and a list of questions you can use to apply the critical perspective to other literary works. A set of selected readings concludes each section.

Think of these ten critical perspectives as a kind of critical smorgasbord, a set of intellectual dishes you can sample and taste. Those you find most appealing you may wish to partake of more heartily, partly by applying them in your own analytical writing, partly by reading from the list of selected books. Or your instructor may encourage you to work with ones he or she believes are especially valuable. The important thing to realize, however, is that you always interpret a literary work from a theoretical standpoint, however hidden or implicit this standpoint may be. Understanding the assumptions and procedures of the various theoretical perspectives is crucial for understanding what you are doing when you interpret literature, how you do it, and why you do it that way.

In his lively book introducing college students to literary theory, *Falling into Theory* (1994), David H. Richter of Queens College CUNY summarizes the important issues concerning literary studies today in a series of provocative questions. Richter organizes his questions according to the categories I have borrowed from him for this introductory overview: *why we read, what we read, how we read.* Keep Richter's guiding questions in mind as you read the discussion of the various critical perspectives.

Why we read. What is the place of the humanities and literary studies in society? Why should we study literature? Why do we read?

What we read. What is literature and who determines what counts as literature? Is there a core of "great books" that every student should read? What is the relationship of literature by women and minority groups to the canon? Are criteria of quality universal, or are literary values essentially political?

How we read. How do we and how should we read texts? Does meaning reside in the author, the text, or the reader? To what degree is the meaning of a text fixed? What ethical concerns do we bring to texts as readers, and how do these concerns reshape the texts we read? What do we owe the text and what does it owe us? How do the politics of race and gender shape our reading of texts? Do political approaches to literature betray or shed light on them?

Canon and Curriculum: Selected Readings

To learn more about the controversy surrounding the literary canon and the college English curriculum, the following books provide a variety of perspectives on the issues.

Alter, Robert. *The Pleasures of Reading in an Ideological Age.* 1989.

Atlas, James. *The Battle of the Books.* 1990.

D'Souza, Dinesh. *Illiberal Education: The Politics of Sex and Race on Campus.* 1991.

Eagleton, Terry. *Literary Theory: An Introduction.* 1983.

Graff, Gerald. *Beyond the Culture Wars.* 1992.

Greenblatt, Stephen, and Giles Gunn. *Redrawing the Boundaries: The Transformation of English and American Literary Studies.* 1992.

Kimball, Roger. *Tenured Radicals: How Politics Has Corrupted Higher Education.* 1990.

Lauter, Paul. *Canons and Contexts.* 1991.

Lentricchia, Frank. *Criticism and Social Change.* 1983.

Levine, George et al. *Speaking for the Humanities.* 1989.

Richter, David. *Falling into Theory.* 1994.

Scholes, Robert. *Textual Power.* 1985.

Scholes, Robert. *Protocols of Reading.* 1989.

Scholes, Robert. *The Rise and Fall of English.* 1998.

Scholes, Robert. *The Crafty Reader.* 2001.

FORMALIST PERSPECTIVES

An Overview of Formalist Criticism

Formalists emphasize the form of a literary work to determine its meaning, focusing on literary elements such as plot, character, setting, diction, imagery, structure, and point of view. Approaching literary works as independent systems with interdependent parts, formalists typically subordinate biographical information or historical data in their interpretations.

According to the formalist view, the proper concern of literary criticism is with the work itself rather than with literary history, the life of the author, or a work's social and historical contexts. For a formalist, the central meaning of a literary work is discovered through a detailed analysis of the work's formal elements rather than by going outside the work to consider other issues, whether biographical, historical, psychological, social, political, or ideological. What matters most to the formalist critic is how the work comes to mean what it does—how its resources of language are deployed by the writer to convey meaning. Implicit in the formalist perspective, moreover, is that readers can indeed determine the meanings of literary works—that literature can be understood and its meanings clarified.

Two other tenets of formalist criticism deserve mention: (1) that a literary work exists independent of any particular reader—that is, that a literary work exists outside of any reader's re-creation of it in the act of reading; (2) that the greatest literary works are "universal," their wholeness and aesthetic harmony transcending the specific particularities they describe.

The primary method of formalism is a close reading of the literary text, with an emphasis, for example, on a work's use of metaphor or symbol, its deployment of irony, its patterns of image or action. Lyric poetry lends itself especially well to the kinds of close reading favored by formalist critics because its language tends to be more compressed and metaphorical than the language of prose—at least as a general rule. Nonetheless, formal analysis of novels and plays can also focus on close reading of key passages (the opening and closing chapters of a novel, for example, or the first and last scenes of a play, or a climactic moment in the action of drama, poetry, or fiction). In addition, formalist critics analyze the large-scale structures of longer works, looking for patterns and relationships among scenes, actions, and characters.

One consistent feature of formalist criticism is an emphasis on tension and ambiguity. *Tension* refers to the way elements of a text's language reflect conflict and opposition. *Ambiguity* refers to the ways texts remain open to more than a single, unified, definitive interpretation. Both tension and ambiguity as elements of formalist critical approaches were picked up and elaborated to serve different interpretive arguments by critics employing the methodologies of *structuralism* and *deconstruction*.

The previous chapters of *Literature* you have read titled "Elements," in particular, illustrate and apply techniques of formal analysis. In Chapter Three of this text, "Elements of Fiction," in the section "Setting," for example, a paragraph from William Faulkner's short story "A Rose for Emily," is analyzed to show how one literary element—setting—functions in the story as a whole. In the same section of that chapter, the setting of Kate Chopin's "The Story of an Hour" is described in symbolic terms. Analogously, for poetry, in Chapter Twelve, "Elements of Poetry," in the section "Diction," the connotation of Wordsworth's diction in "I wandered lonely as a cloud" is analyzed to show how Wordsworth's language relates to the image patterns he creates and how diction and imagery contribute to the poem's meaning.

Throughout *Literature* you will find numerous examples of formal analysis. You can use the many focused brief analyses in particular, to model your own close readings of works in each of the three literary genres in terms of formalist criticism.

Thinking from a Formalist Perspective

A formalist critic reading William Carlos Williams's "The Use of Force" might consider how the story begins and ends, contrasting its opening matter-of-fact objective description with its concluding shift of perspective and heightening of language. A formalist perspective would typically include observations about the relations among the characters, particularly with the doctor, who is clearly an outsider, invited in among them only because of the sick daughter. Character relations are of paramount interest in Williams' story since a conflict occurs between the doctor and his patient, one that is resolved only through the use of force. The relations between the doctor and the parents are equally interesting, since their surface behavior contrasts with their feelings about each other.

Other aspects of the story of interest from a formalist perspective would include the writer's use of first-person narration, especially the way the narrator's thoughts are made known to readers (less through dialogue than through a kind of interior monologue that readers "overhear"). A formalist critic might ask what difference it would make if the story were told in the third person, or if the narrator's ideas were to be voiced in direct dialogue. At a key moment—a climactic one, in fact—the story shifts from internal report of the doctor's thoughts to direct dialogue. A formalist would be interested in the effects of this shift, especially in its artistic effectiveness.

A formalist critic reading Emily Dickinson's "I'm 'wife'" would note its neat division into three stanzas and consider the focus of each. A formalist perspective would consider why, in fact, the poem is cast in three stanzas and not one or two, four, or six. A consideration of the relationship between form and meaning might help readers notice how the poem's rhyme scheme and its sentence patterns reinforce or subvert its stanza organization.

Other considerations formalist critics would be likely to raise about the poem might include the connotations of "Czar" for the speaker. Of particular importance in this regard would be the language used to describe the "Girl's life" in the second stanza, especially how it is described as existing behind a "soft Eclipse." Readers following a formalist agenda might also question how the slant rhymes of the poem contribute to its idea and its effect.

Such questions, however, are only a starting point toward a formal analysis of Williams' story and Dickinson's poem.

A CHECKLIST OF FORMALIST CRITICAL QUESTIONS

1. How is the work structured or organized? How does it begin? Where does it go next? How does it end? What is the work's plot? How is its plot related to its structure?
2. What is the relationship of each part of the work to the work as a whole? How are the parts related to one another?
3. Who is narrating or telling what happens in the work? How is the narrator, speaker, or character revealed to readers? How do we come to know and understand this figure?
4. Who are the major and minor characters, what do they represent, and how do they relate to one another?
5. What are the time and place of the work—its setting? How is the setting related to what we know of the characters and their actions? To what extent is the setting symbolic?
6. What kind of language does the author use to describe, narrate, explain, or otherwise create the world of the literary work? More specifically, what images, similes, metaphors, symbols appear in the work? What is their function? What meanings do they convey?

Formalist Criticism: Selected Readings

Brooks, Cleanth. *The Well Wrought Urn: Studies in the Structure of Poetry.* 1947.

Burke, Kenneth. *Counterstatement.* 1930.

Eliot, T. S. *Selected Essays.* 1932.

Empson, William. *Seven Types of Ambiguity.* 1930.

Ransom, John Crowe. *The New Criticism*. 1941.

Wellek, Rene, and Austin Warren. *Theory of Literature*. 1949, 1973.

Wimsatt, W. K. *The Verbal Icon*. 1954.

BIOGRAPHICAL PERSPECTIVES

An Overview of Biographical Criticism

To what extent a writer's life should be brought to bear on an interpretation of his or her work has long been a matter of controversy. Some critics insist that *biographical* information at best distracts from and at worst distorts the process of analyzing, appreciating, and understanding literary works. These critics believe that literary works must stand on their own, stripped of the facts of their writers' lives.

Against this view, however, can be placed one that values the information readers gain from knowing about writers' lives. Biographical critics argue that there are essentially three kinds of benefits readers acquire from using biographical evidence for literary interpretation: (1) readers understand literary works better since the facts about authors' experiences can help readers decide how to interpret those works (2) readers can better appreciate a literary work for knowing the writer's struggles or difficulties in creating it, and (3) readers can better assess writers' preoccupations by studying the ways they modify and adjust their actual experience in their literary works.

Knowing, for example, that Shakespeare was an actor who performed in the plays he wrote provides an added dimension to our appreciation of his genius. It also might invite us to look at his plays from the practical standpoint of a performer rather than merely from the perspective of an armchair reader, a classroom student, or a theatergoer. Or to realize that Ernest Hemingway's stories derive from experiences he had in Africa hunting big game or in World War I or in his numerous marriages may lead readers to see just how the life and works are related, especially to see how Hemingway selected from and shaped his actual experience to create his short stories. Again our knowledge of the more circumscribed life led by Emily Dickinson may bear on our reading of her work. Considering biographical information and using it to analyze the finished literary work can be illuminating rather than distracting or distorting. Thinking about the different alternative titles a writer may have considered can also lead readers to focus on different aspects of a work, especially to emphasize different incidents and to value the viewpoints of different characters. As with any critical approach, however, a biographical perspective should be used judiciously, keeping the focus on the literary work and using the biographical information to clarify understanding and to develop an interpretation.

A biographical critic can focus on a writer's works not only to enhance understanding of them individually but also to enrich a reader's understanding of the artist. In an essay on the relations between literature and biography, Leon Edel, author of an outstanding biography of Henry James, suggests that what the literary biographer seeks to discover about the subject are his or her characteristic ways of thinking, perceiving, and feeling that may be revealed more honestly and thoroughly in the writer's work than in his or her conscious nonliterary statements. In addition, what we learn about writers from a judicious study of their work can also be linked with an understanding of the writer's world, and thus serve as a bridge to an appreciation of the social and cultural contexts in which the writer lived.

Thinking from a Biographical Perspective

Whether we focus on formalist questions to analyze "The Use of Force" or on other issues such as the doctor's psychological impulses or the power struggles among doctor, patient, and parents, biographical information can add to a reader's appreciation of the story. In addition to being a writer, William Carlos Williams was a doctor, a pediatrician with a practice in Rutherford, New Jersey. Williams never gave up medicine for literature, as some other writers did. Instead he continued to treat patients all his life. In fact, he acquired some of the raw material for his poetry, fiction, and essays directly from his practice of medicine.

Another biographical fact of interest is that Williams did some of his writing between seeing patients. He would typically jot notes, write lines of poems, sketch outlines for stories, record dialogue, and otherwise fill the gaps in his time with his writing. Some have suggested that Williams' many short sketches, brief stories, and short poems result directly from this method of composing. Of course, Williams did not do all of his writing in the short bursts of time between seeing his patients. He also wrote during vacations and more extended blocks of time. And Williams did, in fact, write one of the longest American poems of the century, *Paterson,* a book-length poem in five long sections, written and published over a period of more than twenty years.

Of biographical interest regarding Dickinson's "I'm 'wife'" is the fact that Dickinson never married. A critic with a biographical bent might see in this early poem themes and concerns that became important preoccupations for the poet, issues of gender and power, concerns about the relationship between men and women in marriage, both a marriage she may have wanted for herself and the marriage of her brother, a marriage that some biographers argue was a disappointment to her, though one she initially encouraged. Biographical questions of interest would focus on whether Dickinson's poem was based on her own experience, perhaps on frustrated hopes, or whether it was simply a metaphor she played with poetically to deflect the circumstances of everyday reality.

A CHECKLIST OF BIOGRAPHICAL CRITICAL QUESTIONS

1. What influences—persons, ideas, movements, events—evident in the writer's life does the work reflect?
2. To what extent are the events described in the work a direct transfer of what happened in the writer's actual life?
3. What modifications of the actual events has the writer made in the literary work? For what possible purposes?
4. Why might the writer have altered his or her actual experience in the literary work?

5. What are the effects of the differences between actual events and their literary transformation in the poem, story, play, or essay?
6. What has the author revealed in the work about his or her characteristic modes of thought, perception, or emotion? What place does this work have in the artist's literary development and career?

Biographical Criticism: Selected Readings

Edel, Leon. *Henry James,* 5 vols. 1953–1972.

Farr, Judith. *The Passion of Emily Dickinson.* 1992.

Mariani, Paul. *William Carlos Williams: A New World Naked.* 1981.

Sewall, Richard B. *The Life of Emily Dickinson,* 2 vols. 1974.

Williams, William Carlos. *Autobiography.* 1951, 1967.

Wolff, Cynthia Griffin. *Emily Dickinson.* 1986.

HISTORICAL PERSPECTIVES

An Overview of Historical Criticism

Historical critics approach literature in two ways: (1) they provide a context of background information necessary for understanding how literary works were perceived in their time; (2) they show how literary works reflect ideas and attitudes of the time in which they were written. These two general approaches to *historical* criticism represent methods and approaches that might be termed "old historicism" and "new historicism" respectively.

The older form of historical criticism, still in use today, insists that a literary work be read with a sense of the time and place of its creation. This is necessary, insist historical critics, because every literary work is a product of its time and its world. Understanding the social background and the intellectual currents of that time and that world illuminate literary works for later generations of readers.

Knowing something about the London of William Blake's time, for example, helps readers better appreciate and understand the power of Blake's protest against horrific social conditions and the institutions of church and state Blake held responsible for permitting such conditions to exist. In his poem "London," Blake refers to chimney sweepers, who were usually young children small enough to fit inside a chimney, and whose parents sent them to a kind of work that drastically curtailed not only their childhood but also their lives. Or, to take another example, understanding something about the role and position of women in late nineteenth-century America helps readers of the early twenty-first century better understand the protagonist of Kate Chopin's "The Story of an Hour." Readers might appreciate why, for example, Mrs. Mallard feels the need to escape from her marriage and why her feelings are described by turns as exhilarating and "monstrous."

Thinking from a New Historicist Perspective

Like earlier historical approaches, a more contemporary approach identified as "new historicism" considers historical contexts of literary works essential for understanding them. A significant difference, however, between earlier historical criticism and new historicism is the newer variety's emphasis on analyzing historical documents with the same intensity and scrutiny given foregrounded passages in the literary works to be interpreted. In reading Williams's "The Use of Force," for example, a new historicist might pay as much attention to Williams's and other doctors' medical records of the 1920s and 1930s as to the details of incident and language in the story itself. Similarly, in interpreting Dickinson's "I'm 'wife'" new historicist critics would concern themselves with diaries of women written during the early 1860s, when the poem was written. In both instances the records and diaries would be read to ascertain prevailing cultural attitudes about doctor-patient relationships and middle-class marriage, respectively. One common strategy of new historicist critics is to compare and contrast the language of contemporaneous documents and literary works to reveal hidden assumptions, biases, and cultural attitudes that relate the two kinds of texts, literary and documentary, usually to demonstrate how the literary work shares the cultural assumptions of the document.

An important feature of new historicist criticism is its concern with examining the power relations of rulers and subjects. A guiding assumption among many new historicist critics is that texts, not only literary works but also documents, diaries, records, even institutions such as hospitals and prisons, are ideological products culturally constructed from the prevailing power structures that dominate particular societies. Reading a literary work from a new historicist perspective thus becomes an exercise in uncovering the conflicting and subversive perspectives of the marginalized and suppressed, as, for example, the perspective and voice of the young patient in "The Use of Force," and the vision and values of the speaker in Dickinson's "I'm 'wife,'" whose perspectives tend to be undervalued because they are females.

While appropriating some of the methods of formalist and deconstructive critics, new historicists differ from them in a number of important ways. Most importantly, unlike critics who limit their analysis of a literary work to its language and structure, new historicists spend time analyzing nonliterary texts from the same time in which the literary work was written. New historicists, however, do apply the close reading strategies of formalist and deconstructive perspectives, but their goal is not, like the formalists, to show how the literary work manifests universal values or how it is unified. Nor is the new historicist goal to show how the text undermines and contradicts itself, an emphasis of deconstructive perspectives. Instead, new historicists analyze the cultural context embedded in the literary work and explain its relationship with the network of the assumptions and beliefs that inform social institutions and cultural practices prevalent in the historical period when the literary work was written. Finally, it is important to note that for new historicist critics, history does not provide mere "background" against which to study literary works, but is, rather, an equally important "text," one that is ultimately inseparable from the literary work, which inevitably reveals the conflicting power relations that underlie all human interaction, from the small-scale interactions with families to the large-scale interactions of social institutions.

One potential danger of applying historical perspectives to literature is that historical information and documents may be foregrounded and emphasized so heavily that readers lose sight of the literary work the historical approach is designed to illuminate. When the prism of history is used to clarify and explain elements of the literary work, however, whether in examining intellectual currents, describing social conditions, or presenting cultural attitudes, readers' understanding of literary works can be immeasurably enriched. The challenge for historical understanding, whether one uses the tools of the older historicist tradition or the methods of the new historicism, is to ascertain what the past was truly like, how its values are inscribed in its cultural artifacts, including its literature. Equally challenging is an exploration of the question, What was it possible to think or do at a particular moment of the past, including possibilities that may no longer be available to those living today?

A CHECKLIST OF HISTORICAL AND NEW HISTORICIST CRITICAL QUESTIONS

1. When was the work written? When was it published? How was it received by the critics and the public? Why?
2. What does the work's reception reveal about the standards of taste and value during the time it was published and reviewed?
3. What social attitudes and cultural practices related to the action of the work were prevalent during the time the work was written and published?
4. What kinds of power relations does the work describe, reflect, or embody?
5. How do the power relations reflected in the literary work manifest themselves in the cultural practices and social institutions prevalent during the time the work was written and published?
6. What other types of historical documents, cultural artifacts, or social institutions might be analyzed in conjunction with particular literary works? How might a close reading of such a nonliterary "text" illuminate those literary works?
7. To what extent can we understand the past as it is reflected in the literary work? To what extent does the work reflect differences from the ideas and values of its time?

Historical and New Historicist Criticism: Selected Readings

Armstrong, Nancy. *Desire and Domestic Fiction.* 1987.

Dollmore, Jonathan, and Alan Sinfield. *Political Shakespeare.* 1985.

Geertz, Clifford. *The Interpretation of Cultures.* 1973.

Greenblatt, Stephen. *Learning to Curse: Essays in Early Modern Culture.* 1990.

Greenblatt, Stephen. *Marvellous Possessions.* 1991.

Kenner, Hugh. *The Pound Era.* 1971.

Levinson, Marjorie, et al. *Rethinking Historicism.* 1989.

Lindenberger, Herbert. *Historical Drama.* 1975.

Veeser, H. Aram. *The New Historicism.* 1989.

Veeser, H. Aram. *The New Historicism: A Reader.* 1994.

PSYCHOLOGICAL PERSPECTIVES

An Overview of Psychological Criticism

Psychological criticism approaches a work of literature as the revelation of its author's mind and personality. Psychological critics see literary works as intimately linked with their authors' mental and emotional characteristics. Critics who employ a psychological perspective do so to explain how a literary work reflects its writer's consciousness and mental world, and they use what they know of writers' lives to explain features of their work. Some psychological critics are more interested in the creative processes of writers than in their literary works; these critics look into literary works for clues to a writer's creative imagination. Other psychological critics wish to study not so much a writer's creative process as his or her motivations and behavior; these critics may study a writer's works along with letters and diaries to better understand not just what a writer has done in life but why the writer behaved in a particular manner. Still other critics employ methods of Freudian psychoanalysis to understand not only the writers themselves, such as Shakespeare or Kafka, but the literary characters they create, Iago, for example, or Gregor Samsa.

Psychoanalytic criticism derives from Freud's revolutionary psychology in which he developed the notion of the "unconscious" along with the psychological mechanisms of "displacement," "condensation," "fixation," and "manifest and latent" dream content. Freud posited an unconscious element of the mind below consciousness, just beneath awareness. According to Freud, the unconscious harbors forbidden wishes and desires, often sexual, that are in conflict with an individual's or society's moral standards. Freud explains that although the individual represses or "censors" these unconscious fantasies and desires, they become "displaced" or distorted in dreams and other forms of fantasy, which serve to disguise their real meaning.

The disguised versions that appear in a person's conscious life are considered to be the "manifest" content of the unconscious wishes that are their "latent" content, which psychoanalytic critics attempt to discover and explain. Psychoanalytic critics rely heavily on symbolism to identify and explain the meaning of repressed desires, interpreting ordinary objects such as clocks and towers and natural elements such as fire and water in ways that reveal aspects of a literary character's sexuality. These critics also make use of other psychoanalytic concepts and terms such as "fixation," or "obsessive compulsion," attaching to feelings, behaviors, and fantasies that individuals presumably outgrow yet retain in the form of unconscious attractions.

Among the most important of the categories derived from Freud that psychoanalytic critics employ are those Freud used to describe mental structures and dynamics. Freud recognized three types of mental functions, which he designated the "id," the "ego," and the "superego." Freud saw the id as the storehouse of desires, primarily libidinal or sexual, but also aggressive and possessive. He saw the superego as the representative of societal and parental standards of ethics and morality. And he saw the ego as the negotiator between the desires and demands of the id and the controlling and constraining force of the superego, all influenced further by an individual's relationship with other people in the contexts of actual life. These few but important psychoanalytic concepts have been put to varied uses by critics with a wide range of psychological approaches. Freud himself analyzed Sophocles' tragic drama *Oedipus Rex* to explain how Oedipus harbored an unconscious desire to kill his father and marry his mother, events the play accounts for. Other critics have used Freud's insights—which, by the way, Freud himself says he derived from studying literary masters such as Sophocles, Shakespeare, and Kafka—to analyze the hidden motivations of literary characters. One of the most famous of all literary characters, Hamlet, has stimulated psychological critics of all persuasions to explain why he delays killing King Claudius. In his book *Hamlet and Oedipus,* Ernest Jones uses Freud's theory of the "Oedipus complex" to explain Hamlet's delay, which Jones sees, essentially, as Hamlet's inability to punish Claudius for what he, Hamlet, unconsciously wanted to do himself. (See the Critics on Sophocles and the Critics on Shakespeare sections of Chapters Twenty-Five and Twenty-Six in this text.)

Thinking from a Psychoanalytic Perspective

We can use a psychoanalytic perspective to make a few observations about the behavior of the characters in Williams's "The Use of Force" and the marital situation described in Dickinson's "I'm 'wife.' "

The doctor in "The Use of Force" can be seen as repressing his real desire to humiliate his young female patient under the guise of inspecting her throat for signs of illness. The girl's refusal can be seen as an unwillingness to expose herself to this strange overbearing man, who is forcing himself upon her. Her mouth can be interpreted as a displacement for her vagina, and the doctor's attempt to open it by force as a kind of rape. Even the parents' actions might be explained in psychoanalytic terms in that they act as voyeurs, alternately frightened and sexually excited by what they are witnessing. You might or might not find such an interpretation far-fetched.

Dickinson's speaker experiences no such overt violation. Her subjugation is more acceptable because she seems to fulfill a socially sanctioned role as "wife." What is interesting from a psychoanalytic standpoint, however, is the way she subverts that role by comparing herself to a "Czar," a powerful emperor, which seems to conflict with her role as "wife" and "Woman." Moreover, the speaker's comparison between the "Girl's life" and the wife's, which is elaborated with the analogy of differences experienced between those on Earth and in Heaven, can be seen as a displacement of her poetic ambition onto the image of a wife, which the speaker endows with spiritual and temporal powers.

A CHECKLIST OF PSYCHOLOGICAL CRITICAL QUESTIONS

1. What connections can you make between your knowledge of an author's life and the behavior and motivations of characters in his or her work?

2. How does your understanding of the characters, their relationships, their actions, and their motivations in a literary work help you better understand the mental world and imaginative life, or the actions and motivations, of the author?
3. How does a particular literary work—its images, metaphors, and other linguistic elements—reveal the psychological motivations of its characters or the psychological mindset of its author?
4. To what extent can you employ the concepts of Freudian psychoanalysis to understand the motivations of literary characters?
5. What kinds of literary works and what types of literary characters seem best suited to a critical approach that employs a psychological or psychoanalytical perspective? Why?
6. How can a psychological or psychoanalytic approach to a particular work be combined with an approach from another critical perspective—for example, that of biographical or formalist criticism, or that of feminist or deconstructionist criticism?

Psychological and Psychoanalytic Criticism: Selected Readings

Bloom, Harold. *The Anxiety of Influence.* 1973.

Chodorow, Nancy. *Feminism and Psychoanalytic Theory.* 1990.

Crews, Frederick. *The Sins of the Fathers: Hawthorne's Psychological Themes.* 1966.

Crews, Frederick. *Skeptical Engagements.* 1986.

Felman, Soshana. *Jacques Lacan and the Adventure of Insight.* 1987.

Freud, Sigmund. *The Interpretation of Dreams.* 1900.

Freud, Sigmund. *Introductory Lectures on Psychoanalysis.* 1917–1918.

Freud, Sigmund. *New Introductory Lectures on Psychoanalysis.* 1933.

Hoffman, Frederick J. *Freudianism and the Literary Mind.* 1957.

Holland, Norman. *The Dynamics of Literary Response.* 1968.

Jones, Ernest. *Hamlet and Oedipus.* 1949.

Manheim, Leonard, and Eleanor Manheim, eds. *Hidden Patterns: Studies in Psychoanalytic Literary Criticism.* 1966.

Mitchell, Juliet. *Psychoanalysis and Feminism.* 1975.

Nelson, Benjamin, ed. *Sigmund Freud on Creativity and the Unconscious.* 1958.

Skura, Meredith. *The Literary Use of the Psychoanalytic Process.* 1981.

Trilling, Lionel. *The Opposing Self.* 1955.

Wilson, Edmund. *The Wound and the Bow.* 1941.

Wright, Elizabeth, ed. *Psychoanalytic Criticism.* 1984.

SOCIOLOGICAL PERSPECTIVES

An Overview of Sociological Criticism

Like historical and biographical critics, *sociological* critics argue that literary works should not be isolated from the social contexts in which they are embedded. And also like historical critics, especially those who espouse new historicist perspectives, sociological critics emphasize the ways power relations are played out by varying social forces and institutions. Sociological critics focus on the values of a society and how those values are reflected in literary works. At one end of the sociological critical spectrum, literary works are treated simply as documents that either embody social conditions or are a product of those conditions. Critics employing a sociological perspective study the economic, political, and cultural issues expressed in literary works as those issues are reflected in the societies in which the works were produced.

A sociological approach to the study of Shakespeare's *Othello* could focus on the political organization of the Venetian state as depicted in the play and its relation to the play's depiction of authority, perhaps considering as well the breakdown of authority in the scenes set in Cyprus. Another sociological perspective might focus on the play's economic aspects, particularly how money and influence are used to manipulate others. Still other sociological issues that could be addressed include the role of women in the play and the issue of Othello's race. How, for example, does Shakespeare portray the power relations between Othello and Desdemona, Iago and Emilia, Cassio and Bianca? To what extent is each of these women's relationship with men considered from an economic standpoint? Or to what extent is Othello's blackness a factor in his demise, or is his race a defining characteristic in other characters' perceptions of him?

Two significant trends in sociological criticism have had a decisive impact on critical theory: Marxist criticism and feminist criticism. Proponents of each of these critical perspectives have used some of the tools of other critical approaches such as the close reading of the formalists and deconstructionists and the symbolic analysis of the psychoanalytic critics to espouse their respective ideologies in interpreting literature.

Marxist Critical Perspectives

In the same way that many psychoanalytic critics base their approach to literature on the theoretical works of Sigmund Freud, *Marxist* critics are indebted to the political theory of Karl Marx and Friedrich Engels. Marxist critics examine literature for its reflection of how dominant elites exploit subordinate groups, how peoples become "alienated" from each other, and how middle-class/bourgeois values lead to the control and suppression of the working classes. Marxist critics see literature's value in promoting social and economic revolution, with works that espouse Marxist ideology serving to prompt the kinds of economic and political changes that conform to Marxist principles. Such changes would include the overthrow of the dominant capitalist ideology and the loss of power by those with money and privilege. Marxist criticism is concerned both with understanding the role of politics, money, and power in literary works, and with redefining and reforming the way society distributes its resources among the classes. Fundamentally, the Marxist ideology looks toward a vision of a world not so much where class conflict has been minimized but one in which classes have disappeared altogether.

Marxist critics generally approach literary works as products of their era, especially as influenced, even determined by the economic and political ideologies that prevail at the time of their composition. The literary work is considered a "product" in relation to the actual economic and social conditions that exist at either the time of the work's composition or the time and place of the action it describes.

Marxist analyses of novels focus on the relations among classes. In British and European novels of the nineteenth century, for example, class is a significant factor in the rise and fall of the characters' fortunes. Novels such as Charles Dickens's *Little Dorritt, Dombey and Son,* and *Oliver Twist,* George Eliot's *Middlemarch,* Anthony Trollope's *The Eustace Diamonds,* and William Makepiece Thackery's *Vanity Fair* portray a panoramic vision of society with characters pressing to move up in social rank and status. These and numerous other novels from the eighteenth through the twentieth century provide abundant territory for Marxist perspectives to investigate the ways political and economic forces conspire to keep some social, ethnic, and racial groups in power and others out. The Marxist critical perspective has been brought to bear most often on the novel, next most often on drama, and least often on poetry, where issues of power, money, and political influence are not nearly as pervasive.

Thinking from a Marxist Perspective

In applying a Marxist critical perspective to a work like Williams's "The Use of Force," we would consider the ways in which power relations are played out in the story. It seems clear that the doctor is a privileged individual who wields power over both the girl and her family. The narrator's thought process shows his contempt for the parents, which may or may not be justified. Since he can refuse to treat the girl, insist on being paid more for his services, or berate the parents for their ineptitude (though he actually does none of these things), the parents are cowed by his presence. The girl, though defiant, is at his mercy since he is a "professional" and psychologically more powerful than she is. In addition to such observations, a Marxist critic might consider the story's action from an economic standpoint, in which the doctor performs a service for a fee, with the entire situation viewed strictly as an economic transaction, albeit a socially useful one. The parents are apparently poor, and we could surmise that they and their daughter might not receive the quality of medical service or the courteous delivery of medical care they would get were they more economically prosperous.

A CHECKLIST OF MARXIST CRITICAL QUESTIONS

1. What social forces and institutions are represented in the work? How are these forces portrayed? What is the author's attitude toward them?
2. What political economic elements appear in the work? How important are they in determining or influencing the lives of the characters?
3. What economic issues appear in the course of the work? How important are economic facts in influencing the motivation and behavior of the characters?

4. To what extent are the lives of the characters influenced or determined by social, political, and economic forces? To what extent are the characters aware of these forces?

Marxist Criticism: Selected Readings

Baxandall, Lee, and Stefan Morawski, eds. *Marx and Engels on Literature and Art.* 1973.

Benjamin, Walter. *Illuminations.* 1968.

Eagleton, Terry. *Marxism and Literary Criticism.* 1976.

Jameson, Fredric. *Marxism and Form.* 1971.

Lukacs, George. *Realism in Our Time.* 1972.

Trotsky, Leon. *Literature and the Revolution.* 1924.

Williams, Raymond. *Marxism and Literature.* 1977.

Feminist Critical Perspectives

Feminist criticism, like Marxist and new historicist criticism, examines the social, economic, and cultural aspects of literary works, but especially for what those works reveal about the role, position, and influence of women. Feminist critics also typically see literature as an arena in which to contest for power and control, since as sociological critics, feminist critics also see literature as an agent for social transformation.

Moreover, feminist critics seek to redress the imbalance of literary study in which all important books are written by men or the only characters of real interest are male protagonists. Feminist critics have thus begun to study women writers whose works have been previously neglected. They have begun to look at the way feminine consciousness has been portrayed in literature written by both women and men. And they have begun to change the nature of the questions asked about literature that reflect predominantly male experience. In these and other ways feminist critical perspectives have begun to undermine the patriarchal or masculinist assumptions that have dominated critical approaches to literature until relatively recently. For although feminist critics can trace their origins back to nineteenth-century politics and cite as formative influences the works of Margaret Fuller, Mary Wollstonecraft Godwin, John Stuart Mill, and Elizabeth Cady Stanton, feminist perspectives began to be broached in literary circles only with Virginia Woolf's *A Room of One's Own* (1929), which describes the difficult conditions under which women writers of the past had to work, and with Simone de Beauvoir's *The Second Sex* (1949), which analyzes the biology, psychology, and sociology of women and their place, role, and influence in Western culture. It is only in the late 1960s and early 1970s that feminist criticism per se began to emerge with the publication of Mary Ellman's *Thinking About Women* (1968), Kate Millet's *Sexual Politics* (1970), and a host of other works that have followed for more than a quarter century and show no signs of abating.

In his influential and widely used *Glossary of Literary Terms,* M. H. Abrams identifies four central tenets of much feminist criticism, summarized in the following list.

1. Western civilization is pervasively patriarchal (ruled by the father)—that is, it is male-centered and controlled, and is organized and conducted in such a way as to subordinate women to men in all cultural domains: familial, religious, political, economic, social, legal, and artistic.
2. The prevailing concepts of gender—of the traits that constitute what is masculine and what is feminine—are largely, if not entirely, cultural constructs that were generated by the omnipresent patriarchal biases of our civilization.
3. This patriarchal (or "masculinist," or "androcentric") ideology pervades those writings which have been considered great literature, and which until recently have been written almost entirely by men for men.
4. The traditional aesthetic categories and criteria for analyzing and appraising literary works . . . are in fact infused with masculine assumptions, interests, and ways of reasoning, so that the standard rankings, and also the critical treatments, of literary works have in fact been tacitly but thoroughly gender-biased.*

It should be noted, however, that Abrams' list, though helpful, tends to blur distinctions among the many different varieties of feminist criticism as currently practiced. Thus the ways these assumptions are reflected in feminist criticism vary enormously from the reader-response approaches used by feminist critics such as Judith Fetterley and Elizabeth Flynn, to the cultural studies approaches used by Jane Tompkins and Eve Kosovsky Sedgwick, to the Lacanian psychoanalytic approaches employed by Helene Cixous and Julia Kristeva. It would be better to think of feminist criticism in the plural as the criticism of feminists rather than to envision it as a singular monolithic entity.

Thinking from a Feminist Perspective

In applying the perspective of feminist criticism to "I'm 'wife,'" we might consider the way the roles of woman and wife are suggested in the poem. A feminist reading would be alert for other signs of power contestation in the poem, why for example the speaker compares herself to a "Czar," and what that means in terms of her ability to exert her will and control her destiny. Feminist readers would also ask what the masculine term "Czar" signifies in the poem, and whether there is a feminine counterpart.

Feminist readers might also interrogate the poem to ask why the state of wifehood brings "comfort" and why "That other" state—of girlhood—"was pain." They would probe beyond the text of the poem to consider the extent to which such differences in experience and feeling obtained in marriages during Dickinson's lifetime, thus sharing an interest with new historicist critics. Moreover, they might also wonder whether the poem's abrupt ending "I'm 'Wife'! Stop there!" with its insistent tone might not mask an undercurrent of fear or powerlessness.

A CHECKLIST OF FEMINIST CRITICAL QUESTIONS

1. To what extent does the representation of women (and men) in the work reflect the place and time in which the work was written?

*M. H. Abrams. *A Glossary of Literary Terms,* 6th ed. (1993), pp. 234–35.

2. How are the relations between men and women, or those between members of the same sex, presented in the work? What roles do men and women assume and perform and with what consequences?
3. Does the author present the work from within a predominantly male or female sensibility? Why might this have been done, and with what effects?
4. How do the facts of the author's life relate to the presentation of men and women in the work? To their relative degrees of power?
5. How do other works by the author correspond to this one in their depiction of the power relationships between men and women?

Feminist Criticism: Selected Readings

Baym, Nina. *Woman's Fiction.* 1978.

Buck, Claire. *The Bloomsbury Guide to Women's Literature.* 1992.

Cixous, Helene. *The Laugh of the Medusa.* 1976.

Fetterley, Judith. *The Resisting Reader.* 1978.

Gallop, Jane. *The Daughter's Seduction: Feminism and Psychoanalysis.* 1982.

Gates, Henry L., Jr. *Reading Black, Reading Feminist.* 1990.

Gilbert, Sandra, and Susan Gubar. *The Madwoman in the Attic.* 1979.

Heilbrun, Carolyn. *Toward a Recognition of Androgyny.* 1973.

Moers, Ellen. *Literary Women.* 1976.

Rich, Adrienne. *On Lies, Secrets, and Silence.* 1980.

Ruthven, K. K. *Feminist Literary Studies: An Introduction.* 1984.

Schweickart, Patricinio, and Elizabeth Flynn. *Gender and Reading.* 1986.

Showalter, Elaine. *A Literature of Their Own.* 1977.

Showalter, Elaine. *The New Feminist Criticism.* 1986.

Smith, Barbara. *Toward a Black Feminist Criticism.* 1977.

READER-RESPONSE PERSPECTIVES

An Overview of Reader-Response Criticism

Reader-response criticism raises the question of where literary meaning resides—in the literary text, in the reader, or in the interactive space between text and reader. Reader-response critics differ in the varying degrees of subjectivity they allow into their theories of interpretation. Some, such as David Bleich, see the literary text as a kind of mirror in which readers see themselves. In making sense of literature, readers re-create themselves. Other reader-response critics, such as Wolfgang Iser, focus on the text rather than on the feelings and reactions of the reader. Text-centered reader-response critics emphasize the temporal aspect of reading, suggesting that readers make sense of texts over time, moving through a text sentence by sentence, line by line, word by word, filling in gaps and making inferences about what is being implied by textual details as they read.

Still other reader-response critics, Norman Holland, for example, focus on the psychological dynamics of reading. Holland argues that every reader creates a specific identity theme unique to himself or herself in reading any literary work. He suggests that to make sense of a literary work readers must find in it, or create through the process of reading it, their identity themes.

One of the earliest and most influential reader-response critics, Louise Rosenblatt, argues against placing too much emphasis on the reader's imagination, identity, or feelings in literary interpretation. Like Iser, Rosenblatt keeps the focus on the text, though she is more concerned than is Iser with the dynamic relationship between reader and text, since it is in that interrelationship that Rosenblatt believes literary meanings are made.

For Rosenblatt, as for other reader-response critics, the meaning of a literary work cannot exist until it is "performed" by the reader. Until then literary meaning is only potential. It becomes actual when readers realize its potential through their acts of reading, responding, and interpreting.

As you might expect, reader-response critics respect not only the intellectual acts of analysis and comprehension that readers perform but also their subjective responses and their emotional apprehension of literary works. This distinction between intellectual comprehension and emotional apprehension of literature is explored earlier in this book for each of the three literary genres—fiction, poetry, and drama.

One benefit of using reader-response perspectives to interpret literary works is that you begin with what is primary and basic—your initial reactions, your primary responses. Of course, as you read, you may change your mind about your reaction to a work. You may experience opposite or different feelings. Or you may make sense of the work differently because of discoveries you make later in the process of reading. What you read in the last chapter of a novel, for example, may change your understanding of what you read in the first chapter or in a middle chapter, which you had interpreted one way until you reached the end. What's important for reader-response critics is just this kind of active reading dynamic, in which a reader's changing ideas and feelings are foregrounded. These critics describe the recursiveness of the reading process, the way in which our minds anticipate what is coming in the text based on what we have already read and, simultaneously, the way we loop back retrospectively to reconsider earlier passages in light of later ones that we read. The literary text does not disappear for reader-response critics. Instead it becomes part of readers' experience as they make their way through it.

Reader-response criticism thus emphasizes process rather than product, an experience rather than an object, a shifting subjectivity rather than a static and objective text and meaning. For reader-response critics the text is not a "thing"; it does not stand still, for it lives only in its readers' imaginations. For these critics, then, literary works do not have an independent objective meaning that is true once and for all and that is identical for all readers. Instead, they argue that readers *make* meaning through their encounters with literary texts. And the meanings they make may be as varied as the individuals who read them.

Reader-response critics emphasize two additional points about the range and variety of readers' interpretations. First, an individual reader's interpretation of a work may change, in fact, probably will change over time. Reading Shakespeare's *Julius Caesar* in high school can be a very different experience from reading it in college or later as an adult. Second, historically, readers from different generations and different centuries interpret books differently. The works say different things to readers of different historical eras because of their particular needs, concerns, and historical circumstances. In both the individual cases and the larger historical occasions, changes occur, changes that affect how individuals perceive, absorb, and understand what they read at different times of their lives.

The crucial thing for readers is to acknowledge their own subjectivity in the act of reading and to be aware that they come to literary works with a set of beliefs, ideas, attitudes, values—with all that makes them who and what they are. Being aware of our predispositions when we read can prevent our biases and prejudices from skewing our interpretations of literary works. At the same time, we need to pay attention to the details of the text. We cannot make words and sentences mean anything at all. There are limits and boundaries to what is acceptable, limits and boundaries that are subject to negotiation and debate. For most reader-response theorists, interpretation has both latitude and limits. Negotiating between them in a delicate balancing act allows readers to exercise their subjectivity while recognizing the significance of the words on the page.

Perhaps an analogy will clarify the double-sided nature of literary interpretation from a reader-response perspective, one that recognizes both the reader's freedom and the text's limits. You might think of a text as a musical score, one that is brought to life in performance. Readers make the potential meanings of a text come to life in much the same way that a musician brings a piece of music to life in performance. When musicians play a score or readers read a literary work, they cannot change the notes of the score or the words of the text. Both readers and musicians are limited by what is on the page. Yet there is room for differing interpretations and varied responses. Two interpretations of a literary work, like two musical performances, are likely to differ, sometimes in significant ways. The varying interpretations will be valid insofar as they respect the words or notes on the page, and insofar as they represent a reasonable and logically defensible approach to the work.

Thinking from a Reader-Response Perspective

In reading "The Use of Force," reader-response critics would consider a reader's emotional reactions to the story's action. They might ask how a reader responds to the doctor, how he or she reacts to the doctor's acknowledgment of his feelings about the parents and the child, how readers respond to the way he opens the girl's mouth. Like feminist critics, they would consider the extent to which female readers might respond differently from males, though the important thing for a reader-response perspective would be the intensity and nature of a particular reader's response.

Some reader-response critics would also examine the reader's responses at different points in the text, focusing on particular words and phrases that might signal a shift in the story's tone and hence a change in the reader's response. The doctor's response to the parents calling him a "nice man" is to grind his teeth in disgust. His remark to the girl after she knocks his glasses off is "Will you open it now by yourself or shall we have to open it for you?" And his reference to his contempt for the parents and to the child as a "little brat" are places for readers to consider their responses.

In reading Dickinson's "I'm 'wife,'" reader-response critics might point to the way the poem's language associates "wife" with "Woman" and with "Czar" and invite readers to consider the extent to which these terms reflect their experience or understanding of marriage. They might ask whether the idea of marriage reflected in the poem reminds you of your own relatives' marriages, of the marriage of your parents. If so, why, a reader-response critic might ask, and, if not, why not?

Reader-response critics would also ask about readers' responses to the men who are implied but not explicitly named in the poem, and to the analogy made in the second stanza, which uses the contrast between Earth and Heaven to suggest a difference between the speaker's life before and after marriage. These critics might ask readers to explore their feelings about such an analogy and invite them to consider ways in which their own lives involve a difference such as that describing the speaker's before and after states. The emphases of reader-response critics essentially, then, would be two: (1) the reader's direct experience of the language and details of the poem in the process of reading it; (2) the reader's actual experience outside the poem which he or she brings to the reading and which is used to interpret it. Where formalist critics would play down this experiential connection to the poem and encourage readers to focus solely on the words on the page, reader-response critics want to extend the readers' perceptions about the poem and deepen their response to it by deliberately evoking actual experiences of readers that they can bring to bear on both their apprehension and their comprehension of the poem.

A CHECKLIST OF READER-RESPONSE CRITICAL QUESTIONS

1. What is your initial emotional response to the work? How did you feel upon first reading it?
2. Did you find yourself responding to it or reacting differently at any point? If so, why? If not, why not?
3. At what places in the text did you have to make inferences, fill in gaps, make interpretive decisions? On what bases did you make these inferential guesses?
4. How do you respond to the characters, the speaker, or the narrator? How do you feel about them? Why?
5. What places in the text caused you to do the most serious thinking? How did you put the pieces, sections, parts of the work together to make sense of it?
6. If you have read a work more than once, how have your second and subsequent readings differed from earlier ones? How do you account for those differences, or for the fact that there are no differences in either your thoughts or your feelings about the work?

Reader-Response Criticism: Selected Readings

Bleich, David. *Readings and Feelings.* 1975.

Bleich, David. *Subjective Criticism.* 1968.

Clifford, John, ed. *The Experience of Reading.* 1991.

Eco, Umberto. *The Open Work.* 1989.

Fish, Stanley. *Is There a Text in This Class?* 1980.

Freund, Elizabeth. *The Return of the Reader.* 1987.

Holland, Norman. *The Dynamics of Literary Response.* 1968.

Holland, Norman. *Poems in Persons.* 1973.

Iser, Wolfgang. *The Act of Reading.* 1978.

Mailloux, Steven. *Interpretive Conventions.* 1982.

Rabinowitz, Peter. *Before Reading.* 1987.

Rosenblatt, Louise. *Literature as Exploration.* 1939, 1975.

Rosenblatt, Louise. *The Reader, The Text, The Poem: A Transactional Theory of the Literary Work.* 1978.

Steig, Michael. *Stories of Reading.* 1989.

Suleiman, Susan R., and Inge Crosman, eds. *The Reader in the Text.* 1980.

Tompkins, Jane, ed. *Reader-Response Criticism.* 1980.

Wimmers, Inge Crosman. *Poetics of Reading.* 1988.

MYTHOLOGICAL PERSPECTIVES

An Overview of Mythological Criticism

In general terms a "myth" is a story that explains how something came to be. Every culture creates stories to explain what it considers important, valuable, and true. Thus the Greek myth of Persephone, who was kidnapped by Pluto, the god of the underworld, and allowed to return to her mother Demeter every year, explains the changes of the seasons. Or the Biblical story of Eve's temptation by the serpent in the book of Genesis, which concludes with God's curse of the serpent, explains, among other things, why snakes crawl on their bellies.

Mythological criticism, however, is not concerned with stories that explain origins so much as those that provide universal story patterns that recur with regularity among many cultures and in many different times and places. The patterns myth critics typically identify and analyze are those that represent common, familiar, even universal human experiences, such as being born and dying, growing up and crossing the threshold into adulthood, going on a journey, engaging in sexual activity. These familiar patterns of human action and experience, however, are of interest to myth critics not primarily in and of themselves, but rather for how they represent religious beliefs, social customs, and cultural attitudes.

Birth, for example, is of interest as a symbolic beginning and death as a symbolic ending. A journey is a symbolic venturing out into the world to explore and experience what it has in store for the traveler. Sleeping and dreaming are not simply states of ordinary experience but symbolic modes of entrance into another realm and an envisioning of unusual and perhaps strange possibilities unimagined in waking life. So too with physical contests, sexual encounters, and other forms of experience, which many times are occasions for individuals to be tested, challenged, and perhaps initiated into an advanced or superior state of being—becoming a warrior, for example, a mother, a prophet, or a king.

Myth critics discover in literature of all times and places stories with basic patterns that can be explained in terms of *archetypes,* or universal symbols, which some mythological critics believe are part of every person's unconscious mind, a kind of a collective unconscious that each of us inherits by virtue of our common humanity. Besides those embodying the fundamental facts of human existence, other archetypes include typical literary characters such as the Don Juan or womanizer, the *femme fatale* or dangerous female, the trickster or con artist, the damsel in distress, the rebel, the tyrant, the hero, the betrayer. Creatures real and imaginary can also be archetypal symbols. The lion, for example, can represent strength, the eagle independence, the fox cunning, the unicorn innocence, the dragon destruction, the centaur the union of matter and spirit, animality and humanity, or even humanity and divinity.

It is on plot or the sequence of causally related incidents and actions that myth criticism focuses most heavily. The archetypal images, creatures, and characters exist within stories that themselves exhibit patterns of recurrence. So, for example, there are stories of the arduous quest fraught with perils which a protagonist must survive, perhaps to rescue an innocent victim, perhaps to prove superior courage or morality, perhaps to save others from destruction. There are stories of vengeance, of death and rebirth, of resurrection, of transformation from one state of being into another, stories of enlightenment, of devastation, of lost paradises. Many such stories can be found in the religious literature of cultures around the world. The Bible contains stories of creation (Adam and Eve), fraternal rivalry and murder (Cain and Abel), destruction (Noah) and forgiveness (the ark and the covenant), wandering and enslavement (the exodus), death and resurrection (Jesus' life and ministry)—and so on. This list can be multiplied by consulting, for example, the Taoist and Confucian religious traditions of China, the Hindu traditions of India, the Buddhist traditions of Japan, and the Islamic traditions of the Middle East.

Myth critics approach the study of literary works and the study of a culture's myths in many ways. The Canadian critic Northrop Frye, for example, explains the traditional literary genres, including the novel, the drama, and epic, with reference to the recurrence in them of mythic patterns such as death and rebirth, departure and return, ignorance and insight. Frye associates the genres of comedy, romance, tragedy, and irony or satire with the cycle of the seasons, each genre representing the natural events associated with a particular season (comedy with the fertility of spring, tragedy with the decline of the year in autumn). The French critic Claude Lévi-Strauss, who employs the strategies of structuralist and semiotic analysis, treats cultural myths as signs whose meanings are not understood by the cultures that create those myths. His work is grounded in structural anthropology and owes much to the linguistic theory of Ferdinand de Saussure, who had a profound effect on the development of French and American structuralist perspectives on literary analysis and interpretation. And the American critic of popular culture, John Cawelti, to cite still another approach, analyzes the mythic impulse and mythic elements in forms of popular literature such as the "western."

Thinking from a Mythological Perspective

What a mythological critic does with archetypal characters, stories, creatures, and even natural elements such as sun and moon, darkness and light, fire and water, is to link them up with one another, to see one literary work in relation to others of a similar type. As an example, the story of the prodigal son could be linked with other stories of sons wasting their inheritance, of fathers forgiving their children, or of one brother envying another.

In examining Williams's "The Use of Force" from a mythological perspective, a myth critic might consider the doctor an intruder who comes to menace a helpless and innocent family, or a hero who battles against the odds to save the life of a helpless victim, or an enigmatic combination of the two. A myth critic might consider the role of Dickinson's "wife" and her rank as "Czar" in the poem "I'm 'wife'" in relation to prominent female characters from myth and legend, human or divine. Myth critics would probably take note too of the references to Heaven and Earth in developing an explanation of the transformation undergone by the speaker of the poem.

A CHECKLIST OF MYTHOLOGICAL CRITICAL QUESTIONS

1. What incidents in the work seem common or familiar enough as actions that they might be considered symbolic or archetypal? Are there any journeys, battles, falls, reversals of fortune?
2. What kinds of character types appear in the work? How might they be classified?
3. What creatures, elements of nature, or man-made objects playing a role in the work might be considered symbolic?
4. What changes do the characters undergo? How can those changes be characterized or named? To what might they be related or compared?
5. What religious or quasi-religious traditions might the work's story, characters, elements, or objects be compared to or affiliated with? Why?

Mythological Criticism: Selected Readings

Bodkin, Maud, *Archetypal Patterns in Poetry.* 1934.

Campbell, Joseph. *The Hero with a Thousand Faces.* 1949.

Cawelti, John. *Adventure, Mystery, Romance.* 1976.

Chase, Richard. *Quest for Myth.* 1949.

Fiedler, Leslie. *Love and Death in the American Novel.* 1964.

Frazer, James G. *The Golden Bough,* rev. 1911.

Frye, Northrop. *Anatomy of Criticism.* 1957.

Graves, Robert. *The White Goddess.* 1948.

Jung, Carl Gustav. *Modern Man in Search of a Soul.* 1933.

Lévi-Strauss, Claude. *Structural Anthropology.* 1968.

Vickery, John B., ed. *Myth and Literature.* 1966.

STRUCTURALIST PERSPECTIVES

An Overview of Structuralist Criticism

It is important to distinguish the general meaning of "structure" as used by critics of varying persuasions from its use by adherents of structuralist criticism. In the traditional and most general sense, the word "structure" refers to the organization of a literary work—to its arrangement of incident and action (plot); its division into sections, chapters, parts, stanzas, and other literary units; its employment of repetition and contrast; its patterns of imagery (light and dark images, for example) and sound (its patterns of rhythm and rhyme).

For *structuralist* critics, however, the notion of "structure" has another meaning, one which derives from linguistics and anthropology and which refers to the systems of signs that designate meaning. To understand the structuralist perspective one needs to understand what structuralists mean by "signs" and how language is an arbitrary system of such signs. We can illustrate with a familiar example—the word "dog," which represents the four-legged animal many of us have as a pet. Why do the letters D-O-G, when put together, signify the creature who barks at the mail carrier and wags its tail while running off with our sneakers? The answer, of course, is because of a particular set of linguistic conventions that operate on the basis of common usage and agreement. Such use and agreement, such convention, however, is arbitrary. That is, it could have been otherwise. In fact, in languages such as French and Italian, the word "dog" means nothing. In those languages the furry four-footed barker is, respectively, *chien* (pronounced sheYEN) and *cane* (pronounced CAHnay), a word that looks like the English "cane," or walking stick, but which is a sign, in Italian, for what we call a dog.

But there is one additional linguistic element of importance—that of difference. We have just seen how the English word "cane" differs from the Italian *cane* and the French *chien* and how the two languages designate the faithful canine companion, perhaps named "Fido," in different ways. In both languages (as in all languages) words are differentiated from one another by sound and by spelling. Thus, in English C-A-N-E refers to a walking stick, but C-O-N-E and C-A-P-E to entirely different things. The same is true in Italian, where *cane,* our equivalent of dog, differs from *cani* (CAHknee), the Italian plural, meaning "dogs." This notion of difference is critical to the way structuralism analyzes systems of signs, for it is through differences that languages, literatures, and other social systems convey meaning.

One technique structuralist critics rely on heavily in analyzing difference is "binary opposition," in which a text's contrasting elements are identified and examined. In employing binary opposition as an analytical instrument, structuralist literary critics imitate what structural anthropologists do when they analyze societies to determine which of their social habits and customs are meaningful. The founder of structuralist anthropology, Claude Lévi-Strauss, an important influence on literary structuralism, has explained how a society's most important values can be deciphered by analyzing such binary oppositions as the distinction between "the raw and the cooked," which became a title for one of his books.

Structuralist critics find all kinds of opposition in literature, from small-scale elements, such as letters and syllables; through symbols, such as light and dark; to motions or directions (up and down), times (before and after), places (inside and outside), distances (far and near); to elements of plot and character, such as changes of feeling and reversals of fortune. Such differences are significant structural elements requiring interpretation, whether the differences are explicit or implicit, described or only hinted at.

Semiotics

Semiotics is the study of signs and sign systems; it is, more importantly, the study of codes, or the systems we use to understand the meaning of events and entities, including institutions and cultural happenings as well as verbal and visual texts—from poems to songs to advertisements, and more. Situated on the border between the humanities and the social and behavioral sciences, semiotics is concerned with how the workings of sign systems in various disciplines such as literature and psychology enable us to understand the richly textured significations of all kinds of cultural texts, from action films and television game shows and situation comedies to professional football games to parades and fourth of July celebrations; from religious rituals such as bar mitzvahs and marriage ceremonies to social occasions such as annual company picnics and New Year's parties.

Although semiotic perspectives derive from the theoretical foundations of structuralist and poststructuralist thought, semiotics does not limit itself to the goals and methods of those critical approaches. And though semiotic analysis is sometimes presented in logical symbols and mathematical terminology, it is not restricted to those forms of language. In fact, one of the strengths of a semiotic perspective is its ability to analyze the ways various discourses convey meaning, whether these discourses employ words or communicate, as does fashion, for example, by means of other signs and symbols.

Thinking from a Structuralist Perspective

We can analyze virtually anything from a structuralist perspective—a baseball or football game, an aerobics class, a restaurant menu or a three-course dinner, fashion shows, movies, MTV videos, newspaper cartoons. The possibilities are endless, and, in fact, one critic, Roland Barthes in his book *Mythologies,* has provided a series of brilliant structuralist analyses of foods, fashions, and sports, including wrestling.

Fairy tales and folktales have been a popular source of interpretations for structuralist critics, for such basic stories contain plots and character elements that lend themselves well to binary analysis, and they often reveal much about the values of the cultures that created them. Think of Cinderella, for example, and how she exists in opposition to her stepsisters (she is beautiful while they are ugly; she is poor while they are rich; she is a servant, they her masters). Remember how she loses one slipper while retaining the other, how her coach turns into a pumpkin and her footmen into mice (or is it the other way around)? Difference functions throughout the story on many levels, including the all-important one of the reversal of her fortune with that of her stepsisters and of a prince replacing her nasty stepmother as her future companion. You may also wish to consider books and movies that make use of the "Cinderella plot," where a metaphorical Prince Charming rescues a poor common girl from an oppressive and unhappy life. The films *Maid in Manhattan* and *Pretty Woman* provide two examples.

Structuralist analysis is used at a number of places in *Literature,* the textbook you are reading. Look again, for example, in Chapter Three at the discussion of setting in Kate Chopin's "The Story of an Hour" and William Faulkner's "A Rose for Emily." Chopin's story is seen as having a number of meaningful oppositions, including that between the enclosed inner space of Mrs. Mallard's bedroom and the open free space outside her home, an opposition that reflects the tension between her present marital subjugation and her yearning to be "free," as well as a difference between the natural world of birds and trees and her human world bound by ties of obligation. Faulkner's story, on the other hand, posits an opposition between the story's past and present, a time before the significant changes brought by twentieth-century modern ways, when Miss Emily Grierson could live according to a different code of values represented by an earlier time.

A structuralist perspective on "The Use of Force" would consider the difference between the doctor's initial thoughts as he enters the house and his later feelings as the parents call him a "nice" man—including the fact that he sees himself as different from their view of him. It would attend to the difference between the doctor's inner thoughts and his spoken dialogue, as well as to differences between how the doctor had hoped to attend to his patient and what he actually does to get her to open her mouth. It would also analyze the binary oppositions that exist in the story, including doctor/patient, adult/child, sickness/health, helping/hurting, and so on.

Dickinson's "I'm 'wife'" invites structuralist analysis as well. Not only do the poem's first and last lines begin with the words "I'm 'wife,'" which gives the poem something of a circular movement, but the term "Girl's life" is contrasted with the words "wife" and "Woman," and the state of being "wife" is set off against "That other state," which is unnamed but implied. In addition there is a contrast between "comfort" and "pain" and another posited between "Earth" and "Heaven." All these oppositions would be viewed by structuralist critics as key elements of signification.

A CHECKLIST OF STRUCTURALIST CRITICAL QUESTIONS

1. What are the elements of the work—words, stanzas, chapters, parts, for example—and how can these be seen as revealing "difference"?
2. How do the characters, narrators, speakers, or other voices heard in the work reveal difference?
3. How do the elements of the work's plot or overall action suggest a meaningful pattern? What changes, adjustments, transformations, shifts of tone, attitude, behavior, or feeling do you find?
4. How are the work's primary images and events related to one another? What elements of differentiation exist, and what do they signify?
5. What system of relationships governs the work as a whole?
6. What system of relations could be used to link this work with others of its kind? With different kinds of things with which it shares some similarities?

Structuralist Criticism: Selected Readings

Barthes, Roland. *Elements of Semiology.* 1967.

Culler, Jonathan. *Structuralist Poetics.* 1975.

Genette, Gerard. *Figures.* 1966.

Hawkes, Terence. *Structuralism and Semiotics.* 1977.

Lévi-Strauss, Claude. *The Raw and the Cooked.* 1966.

Macksey, Richard, and Eugenio Donato, eds. *The Structuralist Controversy.* 1970.

Scholes, Robert. *Semiotics and Interpretation.* 1982.

Scholes, Robert. *Structuralism in Literature: An Introduction.* 1974.

Smith, Barbara Herrnstein. *On the Margins of Discourse.* 1978.

Todorov, Tzvetan. *The Poetics of Prose,* trans. 1977.

DECONSTRUCTIVE PERSPECTIVES

An Overview of Deconstructive Criticism

Deconstruction arose as a further development of structuralism. Like structuralist critics, deconstructive critics look for opposition in literary works (and in other kinds of "texts" such as films, advertisements, and social institutions, including schools and hospitals). Like structuralism, deconstruction emphasizes difference, or the structure of constituent opposition in a text or any signifying system (for example, male/female, black/white, animate/inanimate). For deconstructionist critics, any meaning is constructed as the result of an opposition, which can be read as ideologically grounded.

This is the case with the use of language itself, which creates meaning by opposition (the difference in meaning between the English words "cap" and "cup," for example, is based on a difference between their middle letters). The difference is significant as the words refer to different things.

Deconstruction differs from structuralism, however, in describing at once both a pair of equally valid conflicting oppositions, and in identifying a prevailing ideology that needs to be subverted, undermined, challenged, or otherwise called into question—an ideological view, for example, that suggests that one race or gender is superior to another, or a conviction that the poor are happy with their lot. We can distinguish the more explicitly politicized type of deconstruction, "deconstructionist criticism," from a less politically animated type, "deconstructive criticism," in which the ideological impulse is implicit rather than explicit, latent rather than overtly expressed.

Through a careful analysis of a text's language, deconstructive critics unravel the text by pointing to places where it is ambivalent, contradictory, or otherwise ambiguous. Critics who employ deconstruction as a critical method actually would say that the text deconstructs itself, and that critics do not deconstruct the text so much as show how the text contradicts itself and thereby dismantles itself. They would argue that the contradictions found in any verbal text are inherent in the nature of language, which functions as a system of opposition or differences. And since language itself is radically oppositional and thereby inherently ideological, then all discourse is, first, oppositional and hence subject to deconstruction, and, second, ideological, and indicative of power differentiation. In addition, deconstructionist critics also posit the existence of absent textual qualities or characteristics by suggesting that these absent elements have been suppressed by the dominant ideology that controls the apparent meaning of the work.

Deconstructionist critics operate on the premise that language is irretrievably self-contradictory and self-destroying. They argue that since language is unstable, it cannot be controlled by writers. As a result, literary works mean more than their authors are aware of, and their meanings are as unstable as the language of which they are constructed. The aim of deconstructive analysis is to demonstrate the instability of language in texts, thereby revealing how a text's conflicting forces inevitably destroy its apparently logical or meaningful structure and how its apparently clear meaning splits into contradictory, incompatible, and ultimately undecidable possibilities.

Deconstructionist criticism favors terms like "unmasking," "unraveling," "recovering," "suppression," and "contradiction." Unlike formalist criticism, which it resembles in its scrupulous attention to textual detail and its insistence on analyzing the text as a self-contained world, deconstructionist criticism attempts to dismantle the literary work and show that it does not mean what it appears to mean. Deconstructionist criticism includes a penchant for showing how literary texts "subvert" and "betray" themselves, an elevation of criticism to an equal stature with literary creation (so that a deconstructive critical essay on "The Use of Force," for example, is as valuable an artistic production as the original story), and its radical skepticism about the ability of language to communicate anything except contradictions.

A crucial notion for deconstructionist criticism is that of difference, or "différence," as the seminal deconstructionist philosopher and critic Jacques Derrida spells it. By différence, Derrida means to suggest both the usual meaning of difference (dissimilarity) and the additional idea of deferral, both derived from the two meanings of the French verb "différer," which means "to differ" and "to defer" or "postpone." The kind of difference meant by Derrida is, specifically, a deferral of meaning that is never completed or finished because a spoken utterance or a written text means whatever it means as a function of differences among its elements. The result is that its meaning cannot be established as single or determinate. Meaning, thus, is indefinitely postponed, endlessly deferred.

This kind of playing with language is further exemplified by Derrida's explanation of the "self-effacing trace," his notion that a network of differences of meaning is implied even though those differences are not actually present in an utterance or a text. The explicit meaning, which is present, carries with it "traces" of the absent implied meanings, which for ideological reasons are suppressed, though other implications are "there" as inescapable alternative possibilities because they can be construed or imagined.

Thinking from a Deconstructive Perspective

"The Use of Force" yields a number of oppositions that deconstructionist critics would describe to unmask a prevailing ideology in need of subversion. Primary in importance among them is the conflict between doctor and patient, in which "doctor" is the privileged term and "patient" the submissive and submerged one. The doctor is the agent who acts upon the passive patient. In this story, however, we find that the patient is neither patient nor submissive. She is impatient with her parents and with the doctor. She actively knocks his glasses off and splinters the wooden tongue depressor he puts in her mouth by crushing it with her teeth. In this and other ways, the story reflects a tissue of contradictory attitudes and impulses, including the doctor's ambivalent feelings for the girl, whom he both hates and admires, his conflicted feelings toward her parents, whom he pities yet can barely tolerate, and his ambivalence about his own actions, which he both wants and does not want to perform. Other oppositions include those between male and female, older and younger, privileged and unprivileged, all located in the same doctor/patient relationship.

A deconstructive analysis of Dickinson's "I'm 'wife'" would include consideration of the binary oppositions noted in the discussion of "Thinking from a Structuralist Perspective" above. The deconstructive strategy would be to show how the terms "wife," "Woman," "Czar," and "Girl's life" cancel each other out so that a single determinate meaning of the poem is impossible to establish. Deconstructionist critics would, in addition, attempt to show how the poem's inherent contradictions privilege one pair of terms, "wife" for example, over "Girl['s]," while undermining the apparent authority and privileged status of "wife" and the state to which it refers. They would also consider absent terms suggested but not stated directly, such as "Husband."

A CHECKLIST OF DECONSTRUCTIVE CRITICAL QUESTIONS

1. What oppositions exist in the work? Which of the two opposing terms of each pair is the privileged or more powerful term? How is this shown in the work?

2. What textual elements (descriptive details, images, incidents, passages) suggest a contradiction or alternative to the privileged or more powerful term?
3. What is the prevailing ideology or set of cultural assumptions in the work? Where are these assumptions most evident?
4. What passages of the work most reveal gaps, inconsistencies, or contradictions?
5. How stable is the text? How decidable is its meaning?

Deconstructive Criticism: Selected Readings

Attridge, Derek, ed. *Acts of Literature.* 1992.

Bloom, Harold, ed. *Deconstruction and Criticism.* 1979.

Culler, Jonathan. *On Deconstruction.* 1982.

de Man, Paul. *Allegories of Reading.* 1979.

Derrida, Jacques. *Writing and Difference.* 1978.

Johnson, Barbara. *A World of Difference.* 1987.

Miller, J. Hillis. *Fiction and Repetition.* 1982.

Norris, Christopher. *Deconstruction: Theory and Practice.* 1982.

Scholes, Robert. *Protocols of Reading.* 1989.

Taylor, Mark C., ed. *Deconstruction in Context.* 1986.

CULTURAL STUDIES PERSPECTIVES

An Overview of Cultural Studies

The term *cultural studies* indicates a wide range of critical approaches to the study of literature and society. It is a kind of umbrella term that not only includes approaches to the critical analysis of society such as Marxism, feminism, structuralism, deconstruction, and new historicism, but also refers to a wide range of interdisciplinary studies, including women's studies, African-American studies, Asian, Native American, Latino studies, and other types of area studies.

Like deconstruction, feminism, and new historicism, cultural studies perspectives are multidisciplinary. These and other forms of cultural criticism typically include the perspectives of both humanistic disciplines, such as literature and art, and the social and behavioral sciences, such as anthropology, economics, and psychology. The idea of cultural studies, however, is broader than any of the particular critical perspectives described in this chapter. Cultural studies are not restricted, for example, to structuralist or deconstructionist critical procedures, nor are they solely concerned with feminist issues or Marxist causes.

As a critical perspective, cultural studies employ a definition of culture that differs from two other common ways of considering culture. Traditionally, and especially from the perspective of anthropology, culture has been considered as the way of life of a people, including its customs, beliefs, and attitudes, all of which cohere in a unified and organic way of life. This traditional anthropological notion has coexisted with another idea, one of culture as representing the best that a civilization has produced—in its institutions, its political and philosophical thought, its art, literature, music, architecture, and other lasting achievements.

Both of these ways of viewing culture are contested by the newer forms of cultural studies, which look not at the stable coherences of a society or a civilization's history, but at its dissensions and conflicts. For the newer versions of cultural criticism, the unifying concerns and values of older forms of cultural study are suspect, largely because they avoid issues of political and social inequality. In fact, one way of viewing the current debate over the humanities described in the earlier section of this chapter "The Canon and the Curriculum" is as a conflict between the older view of cultural studies that emphasizes a kind of normative national cultural consensus, and newer versions, which challenge such norms and values and question the very idea of cultural consensus. Moreover, the different goals and procedures of these contrasting cultural studies perspectives, along with the differences among the critical perspectives described earlier, powerfully illustrate how nearly everything now associated with literate culture has become contested. These areas of contestation include not only the meaning of "culture," but the meaning of teaching, learning, reading, and writing, along with notions of text, author, meaning, criticism, discipline, and department. Cultural studies perspectives breach the traditional understanding of these terms, in the process redrawing the boundaries that formerly separated them.

The notion of boundaries is one of the more helpful metaphors for thinking about the new cultural studies. That some new emergent critical schools overlap or that critical perspectives may combine forces suggests how disciplinary borders are being crossed and their boundaries reconfigured. In addition to crossing geographical and intellectual boundaries (as well as those between high and popular culture), the new cultural studies also envision a plurality of cultures rather than seeing "Culture" with a capital "C" as singular, monolithic, or universal.

One additional cultural studies perspective that has recently gained prominence is that of *gender criticism,* more specifically gay and lesbian studies. Gender criticism and studies overlap, to some extent, with feminist critical perspectives. In addition to studying the relations between women and men, gender criticism explores such intragender issues of women as lesbian sexuality and female power relations.

One of the central problems of gender studies is the way gender is defined. To what extent, for example, does gender overlap with sex? To what extent is gender a cultural category and sex a biological one? To what extent do the language of sexuality used in the past and the current uses of both "sex" and "gender" as categories reflect biological, psychological, and socially constructed elements of sexual difference? Related to these overlapping questions are others, especially considerations of what some gender critics see as heterosocial or heterosexist bias in the very concept of gender and gender relations.

Gender critics share with adherents of other socially oriented perspectives a concern for analyzing power relations and for discerning ways in which homophobic discourse and attitudes prevail in society at large. Through analysis of various forms of historical evidence and through acts of political agency, gender critics have challenged perspectives that view homosexual acts and unions as "sinful" or "diseased." They have questioned the way AIDS has been represented in the mainstream media and have opened up discussion about what constitutes such apparently familiar notions as "family," "love," and "sexual identity."

Thinking from a Cultural Studies Perspective

In considering literary works and other kinds of canonical and noncanonical texts from the various standpoints of cultural studies, it is important to note that no single approach, method, or procedure prevails. There is, then, no single "cultural studies" perspective on Williams' "The Use of Force" or Dickinson's "I'm 'wife.'" Rather there are various ways of thinking about the cultural and social issues embedded in this work. Some of these issues have been raised in the explanations of feminist, Marxist, new historicist, structuralist, and deconstructionist critical perspectives.

A CHECKLIST OF CULTURAL STUDIES CRITICAL QUESTIONS

1. What cultural conflicts are suggested by or embodied in the work?
2. What kinds of gender identity, behavior, and attitudes are reflected in the work? Is there any overtly or covertly expressed view of homosexuality or lesbianism?
3. With what kinds of social, economic, and cultural privileges (or lack thereof) are same-sex unions or relationships depicted? With what effects and consequences?

Cultural Studies: Selected Readings

Butler, Judith. *Gender Trouble.* 1989.

Comley, Nancy, and Robert Scholes. *Hemingway's Genders.* 1994.

Giroux, Henry. *Border Crossings.* 1992.

Gunn, Giles. *The Culture of Criticism and the Criticism of Culture.* 1987.

Sedgwick, Eve Kosofsky. *Between Men: English Literature and Male Homosexual Desire.* 1985.

Sedgwick, Eve Kosofsky. *Epistemology of the Closet.* 1990.

Tompkins, Jane. *Sensational Designs: The Cultural Work of American Fiction 1790–1860.* 1985.

Torgovnick, Marianna DeMarco. *Crossing Ocean Parkway.* 1994.

USING CRITICAL PERSPECTIVES AS HEURISTICS

One of your more difficult decisions regarding critical theory will be in choosing a critical perspective that is suitable and effective in analyzing a particular literary work. You might be able to offer, for example, a Marxist, deconstructionist, or feminist reading of "Humpty Dumpty" or "Little Bo Peep," even though these nursery rhymes may not be conventionally approached from any of those critical perspectives. You will need to decide whether one of those approaches offers a richer yield than a more traditional approach, such as formalism or myth criticism. The same is true of your approach to Williams' "The Use of Force" and Dickinson's "I'm 'wife.'" Although both works have been analyzed in this chapter from ten critical perspectives, you probably found that certain critical perspectives made a better interpretive fit than others for Williams's story or Dickinson's poem.

Another thing to remember is that you can combine critical perspectives. There is no rule of interpretation that says you must limit yourself to the language and method of a single critical approach or method. You may wish, for example, to combine formalist and structural perspectives in analyzing "I'm wife,'" while also raising feminist critical questions in your interpretation. Or in interpreting "The Use of Force," you may wish to combine new historicist critical concerns with those of a biographical, psychological, or structuralist approach. In some ways, in fact, various concerns of the critical perspectives explained in this chapter overlap. Feminists raise historical questions as well as psychological and biographical ones. Reader-response critics attend to structuralist and formalist issues. And new historicist critics may employ formalist or deconstructionist methods of close reading. Cultural studies draw from a variety of disciplines, as we have mentioned.

A grave danger in using any critical approach to literature is that literary texts may be read with an eye toward making them conform to a particular critical theory rather than using that critical theory to illuminate the text. In the process, critics may distort the text of a literary work by quoting from it selectively or by ignoring aspects of it that do not fit their theoretical approach or conform to their interpretive perspective. Some critics, moreover, apply their favorite critical perspective in a mechanical way, so that every work of literature is read with the idea of proving the same ideological point, regardless of how important the issue is in one work as compared with another. Or critics may put all works of literature through an identical ideological meat grinder with every work emerging ground into the same kind of critical hamburger.

The various critical perspectives you have learned about in this chapter and which you may explore further with the Selected Readings should be used as ways to think about literary works rather than as formulas for grinding out a particular kind of interpretation. Try to see the various critical perspectives as interpretive possibilities, as intellectual vistas that open up literary works, rather than as stultifying formulas that limit what can be seen in them. Try to experience the intellectual playfulness, the imaginative energy and resourcefulness which thinking with these critical perspectives may fire up in you, perhaps taking you in some new direction.

Perhaps the best way to consider these and other critical perspectives is as *heuristics,* or methods for generating ideas, in this case, ideas about literature. A heuristic often takes the form of a set of questions. Writers and speakers use a sequence of questions to think through a topic in preparation for writing or speaking about it. Greek and Roman rhetoricians developed heuristics for generating ideas and for developing and organizing their thinking by using sets of questions that would enable them to think through a subject from a variety of perspectives. They used questions that invited comparison and contrast, definition and classification, analysis and division of a topic.

You can do the same with the critical perspectives introduced in this chapter, using the questions that accompany each of the critical perspectives. Rather than deciding at first just which critical perspective is best suited to your chosen literary work, jot down answers to the questions for each of the approaches. As you think and write, you will begin to see which critical perspectives yield the most helpful ideas, which, that is, prompt your best thinking. In the course of using the critical questions to stimulate your thinking, you will also decide whether to use one critical perspective or to combine a few. You will also decide what you wish to say about the work. And you will begin to discover why you see it as you do, what you value in it, and how you can substantiate your way of seeing and experiencing it.

Consider these critical perspectives as opportunities to engage in a play of mind. Viewing a literary work (or other cultural artifact) from a variety of critical perspectives will enable you to see more of its possibilities of signification. It will also give you a chance to think and imagine inside a variety of critical methods, to put on a number of different critical hats. Enjoy the experience!

Author		Context
Aesop (c. 620–560 B.C.E.)	800	Founding of Rome (**trad. date, 753** B.C.E.)
Sophocles (496–406 B.C.E.)	B.C.E.	Athens becomes world's first democracy (**508** B.C.E.); *Age of Pericles*
Aristotle (**384–322** B.C.E.)		(**462–429** B.C.E.) *marks zenith of Greek culture*
Catullus (**84–54** B.C.E.)		Great Wall of China built (**215** B.C.E.); Venus de Milo (**140** B.C.E.)
Horace (**65–8** B.C.E.)		Julius Caesar murdered (**44** B.C.E.)
	1	Crucifixion of Jesus (**30** C.E.); London founded (**43** C.E.)
Petronius (**c. 27–66**)		Sack of Rome by Visigoths (**410** C.E.)
	1400	*Gutenberg invents movable type* (**c. 1450**)
		Columbus lands in N. America (**1492**)
	1500	Michelangelo (**1475–1564**): *Sistine Chapel* (**1508–1512**)
		Breughel (c. 1525–1569): *Landscape w. Fall of Icarus* (c. 1558);
Sidney (1551–1586)		Reign of Elizabeth I (**1558–1603**)
Shakespeare (1564–1616)		
Donne (**1572–1631**)		
Jonson (**1573–1637**)		
Herrick (1591–1674)		
Herbert (**1593–1633**)	1600	*Globe Theatre built in London* (**1599**)
Milton (**1608–1674**)		Galileo constructs astronomical telescope (**1608**)
Matsuo Bashō (**1644–1694**)		Pilgrims sail for America (**1620**)
		Parliament closes British theaters; English Civil War (**1642–1649**)
Pope (**1688–1744**)		**Vermeer (1632-1675): *Woman with Water Jug* (1664–1665)**
		Rembrandt (**1606–1669**): ***Return of the Prodigal Son***
		(**1668–1669**)
Johnson (**1709–1784**)	1700	Newton's laws of gravity (**1687**)
Blake (**1757–1827**)		*Baroque music flourishes* (**Bach and Handel, c. 1724**)
Wordsworth (**1770–1850**)		Watt patents steam engine (**1769**)
Byron (**1788–1824**)		American Revolution (**1775–1781**)
Shelley (**1792–1822**)		French Revolution begins (**1789**)
John Keats (**1795–1821**)		
Hawthorne (**1804–1864**)	1800	
Poe (**1809–1849**); **Tennyson**		*Beginnings of English Romanticism* (**c. 1800**)
(**1809–1892**)		Napoleon becomes Emperor of France (**1804**)
R. Browning (**1812–1889**)		Beethoven, *Fifth Symphony* (**1810**)
Whitman (**1819–1892**)		**Goya** (**1746–1828**): ***The Third of May, 1808* (1814)**
Ibsen (**1828–1906**)		Napoleon defeated at Waterloo (**1815**)
Dickinson (**1839–1886**)		Queen Victoria accedes to English throne (**1837**)
Hardy (**1840–1928**)		Samuel Morse invents the telegraph (**1844**)

Author		Context
Hopkins (1844–1889)		
Chopin (1851–1904)		
Gregory (1852–1932)		
Wilde (1854–1900)		
Housman (1859–1936)		
Chekhov (1860–1904);	1850	Transatlantic cable laid **(1858)**
Gilman (1860–1935)		
Yeats (1865–1939)		U.S. Civil War **(1861–1865)**; Lincoln assassinated **(1865)**
Robinson (1869–1935)		
Crane (1871–1900)		
Frost (1874–1963)		
Stevens (1879–1955)		
Glaspell (1882–1948)		
Kafka (1883–1924);		
Williams (1883–1963)	1875	Telephone patented; Wagner's *Festspielhaus opened* **(1876)**
Joyce (1884–1941)		Edison invents phonograph **(1877)** and light bulb **(1879)**
Pound (1885–1972);		
Lawrence (1885–1930)		
Eliot (1888–1965);		Eiffel Tower built for the 1889 Paris World's Fair **(1887)**
Mansfield (1888–1923)		**Van Gogh (1853–1890): *Starry Night* (1889)**
Porter (1890–1960)		
MacLeish (1892–1982);		
Millay (1892–1950)		
Cummings (1894–1962);		X-rays and radium discovered; establishment of Fabian Society,
Toomer (1894–1967)		socialist group that included G. B. Shaw **(1893)**
Fitzgerald (1896–1940)		
Faulkner (1897–1962)		
Hemingway (1899–1961);		
Borges (1899–1986)	1900	Marconi's first transatlantic radiotelegraph message **(1901)**
K. Boyle (1902–1992);		Wright brothers make successful airplane flight **(1903)**
Steinbeck (1902–1968)		
Hurston (1903–1960); Frank		Einstein's theory of relativity **(1905)**
O'Connor (1903–1966)		**Klimt (1862–1918): *The Kiss* (1907–1908);** *Picasso, Les*
		Demoiselles d'Avignon **(1907)**
Roethke (1908–1963)		**Matisse (1869–1954): *The Dance***; NAACP founded in New York
Welty (1909–2001)		**(1909)**
Bishop (1911–1979); Milosz		Republic of China replaces Manchu dynasty **(1912);**
(1911–)		**Duchamp (1887–1968). *Node Descending a Stair case,***
Olsen (1913–)		***No. 2* (1912)**
		Stravinsky, *The Rites of Spring* **(1913)**

Author		Context
Ellison (1914–1994);		World War I **(1914–1918)**
Jarrell (1914–1965)		
Randall (1914–);		
Stafford (1914–1993);		
Thomas (1914–1953);		
Williams (1914–1983)		Easter Rebellion in Ireland **(1916)**
Miller (1915–2004)		Russian Revolution; U.S. enters World War I **(1917)**
Jackson (1916–1965)		Prohibition ratified in U. S. **(1919)**
Brooks (1917–2000)		
Swenson (1919–1989)	1925	Harlem Renaissance flourishes **(1920s)**
Baldwin (1924–1987)		Schoenberg's *Suite for Piano:* first use of twelve-tone technique
O'Connor (1925–1964)		throughout entire piece **(1924)**
J. Wright (1927–1980)		*The Jazz Singer* (1927), first sound film
Garcìa Marquez (1928–);		Lindbergh crosses Atlantic **(1927)**
Hall (1928–); Sexton		Stock market crash **(1929)** ushers in Great Depression
(1928–1974)		
Rich (1929–)		
Achebe (1930–);		
Brathwaite (1930–);		
Corso (1930–)		
Munro (1931–)		FDR's "New Deal": introduces Social Security, welfare, and
Pastan (1932–); Plath		unemployment insurance **(1932)**
(1932–1963); Updike		Nazis gain control of Germany **(1933)**
(1932–)		Owens wins 4 gold track medals at Berlin Olympics **(1935)**
MacLeod (1935–); McKenty		First television broadcast (1936); Spanish Civil War **(1936–1939)**
(1935–); Shields		Joe Lewis becomes world heavyweight champion **(1937)**
(1935–2003)		
Clifton (1936–); Dubus		
(1936–1999)		
Harper (1938–)		
Atwood (1939–);		
Bambara		
(1939–1995); Carver		World War II **(1939–1945)**
(1939–1988); Heaney		
(1939–); McNally (1939–)		
Mason (1940–)		
Collins (1941–)		Japan bombs Pearl Harbor and U.S. enters war **(1941)**
Olds (1942–)		

Author		Context
Giovanni (1943–) **Walker (1944–)** **Cope (1945–); Wilson (1945–2005)**		U.S. drops atomic bomb on Hiroshima and Nagasaki U.N. formed (**1945**)
Hood (1946–) **T. O'Brien (1947–)** **Ackerman (1948–); Kenyon (1948–); Silko (1948–); T.C. Boyle (1948–)**	1950	**Romare Bearden (1912–1988):** ***At Five in the Afternoon***; Nuremberg trials (**1946**) India achieves independence (**1947**)
Kincaid (1949–) **Alvarez (1950–); Wasserstein (1950–2005); Ives (1950–)** **Muldoon (1951–)** **Baca (1952–); Cofer (1952–); Dove (1952–); Tan (1952–)** **Doty (1953–); Hirshfield (1953–)** **Song (1955–)** **Jin (1956–)** **Hwang (1957–); Leight (1957–); Moore (1957–)**		Germany divided; People's Republic of China established (**1949**) Korean War (**1950–1953**) DNA discovered (**1953**), launching modern study of genetics Brown v. Board of Education: racial segregation ruled unconstitutional; McCarthy–Army hearings (**1954**) Rosa Parks arrested (**1955**) Russia crushes revolt in Hungary (**1956**) Cuban Revolution: Fidel Castro overthrows Batista (**1959**) Sit-ins at lunch counters in American South (**1960**) Berlin Wall erected (1961); Cuban missile crisis (**1962**)
Garrison (1965–) **Alexie (1966–); Lahiri (1967–)** **Young (1971–)** **Meloy (1973–)** **Z. Smith (1975–)**	1975	Martin Luther King, Jr., arrested in Birmingham; King delivers "I Have a Dream"; Kennedy assassinated (**1963**) U.S. enters Vietnam War; Malcolm X assassinated; Watts riots (Los Angeles) (**1965**) Mao Zedong's Cultural Revolution begins (**1966**) Martin Luther King, Jr. assassinated (**1968**) American astronauts land on the moon (**1969**) Watergate burglary (**1972**) Camp David accord reached between Israel and Egypt (**1977**) Sandinista revolution in Nicaragua; Islamic revolution in Iran (**1979**) Ronald Reagan elected president (**1980**) Chernobyl nuclear power plant disaster (**1986**) Protests in Tiananmen Square, China; Berlin Wall is demolished; Eastern Europe democratized (**1989**) Soviet Union dissolves (**1991**) Bill Clinton elected president (**1992; re-elected in 1996**) George W. Bush elected president (**2000; re-elected 2004**)

Glossary

Allegory A symbolic narrative in which the surface details imply a secondary meaning. Allegory often takes the form of a story in which the characters represent moral qualities. The most famous example in English is John Bunyan's *Pilgrim's Progress,* in which the name of the central character, Pilgrim, epitomizes the book's allegorical nature. Kay Boyle's story "Astronomer's Wife" and Christina Rossetti's poem "Up-Hill" both contain allegorical elements.

Alliteration The repetition of consonant sounds, especially at the beginning of words. Example: "Fetched fresh, as I suppose, off some sweet wood." Hopkins, "In the Valley of the Elwy."

Anapest Two unaccented syllables followed by an accented one, as in *cŏmprĕhénd* or *ĭntĕrvéne.* An anapestic meter rises to the accented beat as in Byron's lines from "The Destruction of Sennacherib": "And the sheen of their spears was like stars on the sea, / When the blue wave rolls nightly on deep Galilee."

Antagonist A character or force against which another character struggles. Tiresias is the antagonist of Oedipus in Sophocles' *Oedipus the King.*

Aside Words spoken by an actor directly to the audience which are not "heard" by the other characters on stage during a play. In Shakespeare's *Othello,* Iago voices his inner thoughts a number of times as "asides" for the play's audience.

Assonance The repetition of similar vowel sounds in a sentence or a line of poetry or prose, as in "I rose and told him of my woe." Whitman's "When I Heard the Learn'd Astronomer" contains assonantal "I's" in the following lines: "How soon unaccountable I became tired and sick, / Till rising and gliding out I wander'd off by myself."

Aubade A love lyric in which the speaker complains about the arrival of the dawn, when he must part from his lover. John Donne's "The Sun Rising" exemplifies this poetic genre.

Ballad A narrative poem written in four-line stanzas, characterized by swift action and narrated in a direct style. The anonymous medieval ballad "Barbara Allan" exemplifies the genre.

Blank verse A line of poetry or prose in unrhymed iambic pentameter. Shakespeare's sonnets, Milton's epic poem *Paradise Lost,* and Robert Frost's meditative poems such as "Birches" include many lines of blank verse. Here are the opening blank verse lines of "Birches": "When I see birches bend to the left and right / Across the lines of straighter darker trees, I like to think some boy's been swingng them."

Caesura A strong pause within a line of verse. The following stanza from Hardy's "The Man He Killed" contains caesuras in the middle of two lines:

He thought he'd 'list, perhaps,
Off-hand-like-just as I—
Was out of work—had sold his traps—
No other reason why.

Catastrophe The action at the end of a tragedy that initiates the denouement or falling action of a play.

Catharsis The purging of the feelings of pity and fear that, according to Aristotle, occurs in the audience of tragic drama. The audience experiences catharsis at the end of the play, following the catastrophe.

Character An imaginary person that inhabits a literary work. Literary characters may be major or minor, static (unchanging) or dynamic (capable of change). In Shakespeare's *Othello,* Desdemona is a major character, but one who is static, like the minor character Bianca. Othello is a major character who is dynamic, exhibiting an ability to change.

Characterization The means by which writers present and reveal character. Although techniques of characterization are complex, writers typically reveal characters through their speech, dress, manner, and actions. Readers come to understand the character Miss Emily in Faulkner's story "A Rose for Emily" through what she says, how she lives, and what she does.

Chorus A group of characters in Greek tragedy (and in later forms of drama) who comment on the action of a play without participation in it. Their leader is the *choragos.* Sophocles' *Antigonê* and *Oedipus the King* both contain an explicit chorus with a *choragos.* Tennessee Williams's *Glass Menagerie* contains a character who functions like a chorus.

Climax The turning point of the action in the plot of a play or story. The climax represents the point of greatest tension in the work. The climax of John Updike's "A&P," for example, occurs when Sammy quits his job as a cashier.

Closed form A type of form or structure in poetry characterized by regularity and consistency in such elements as rhyme, line length, and metrical pattern. Frost's "Stopping by Woods on a Snowy Evening" provides one of many examples. A single stanza illustrates some of the features of closed form:

Whose woods these are I think I know.
His house is in the village though.
He will not see me stopping here
To watch his woods fill up with snow.

Comedy A type of drama in which the characters experience reversals of fortune, usually for the better. In comedy, things work out happily in the end. Comic drama may be either romantic—characterized by a tone of tolerance and geniality-or satiric. Satiric works offer a darker vision of human nature, one that ridicules human folly. Wilde's *The Importance of Being Earnest* is a romantic comedy.

Comic relief The use of a comic scene to interrupt a succession of intensely tragic dramatic moments. The comedy of scenes offering comic relief typically parallels the tragic action that the scenes interrupt. Comic relief is lacking in Greek tragedy, but occurs regularly in Shakespeare's tragedies.

Complication An intensification of the conflict in a story or play. Complication builds up, accumulates, and develops the primary or central conflict in a literary work. Frank O'Connor's story "Guests of the Nation" provides a striking example, as does Ralph Ellison's "Battle Royal."

Conflict A struggle between opposing forces in a story or play, usually resolved by the end of the work. The conflict may occur within a character as well as between characters.

Connotation The associations called up by a word that go beyond its dictionary meaning. Poets, especially, tend to use words rich in connotation. Dylan Thomas's "Do not go gentle into that good night" includes intensely connotative language, as in these lines: "Good men, the last wave by, crying how bright / Their frail deeds might have danced in a green bay, / Rage, rage against the dying of the light."

Convention A customary feature of a literary work, such as the use of a chorus in Greek tragedy, the inclusion of an explicit moral in a fable, or the use of a particular rhyme scheme in a villanelle. Literary conventions are defining features of particular literary genres, such as novel, short story, ballad, sonnet, and play.

Couplet A pair of rhymed lines that may or may not constitute a separate stanza in a poem. Shakespeare's sonnets end in rhymed couplets, as in "For thy sweet love remembered such wealth brings / That then I scorn to change my state with kings."

Dactyl A stressed syllable followed by two unstressed ones, as in *flút-tĕr-iňg* or *blúe-bĕr-řy.* The following playful lines illustrate double dactyls, two dactyls per line:

Higgledy piggledy,
Gibbering, jabbering.

Denotation The dictionary meaning of a word. Writers typically play off a word's denotative meaning against its connotations, or suggested and implied associational implications. In the following lines from Peter Meinke's "Advice to My Son," the references to flowers and fruit, bread and wine denote specific things, but also suggest something beyond the literal, dictionary meanings of the words:

To be specific, between the peony and rose
Plant squash and spinach, turnips and tomatoes;
Beauty is nectar and nectar, in a desert, saves—
. . .
and always serve bread with your wine.
But, son,
always serve wine.

Denouement The resolution of the plot of a literary work. The denouement of *Hamlet* takes place after the catastrophe, with the stage littered with corpses. During the denouement Fortinbras makes an entrance and a speech, and Horatio speaks his sweet lines in praise of Hamlet.

Deus ex machina A god who resolves the entanglements of a play by supernatural intervention. The Latin phrase means, literally, "a god from the machine." The phrase refers to the use of artificial means to resolve the plot of a play.

Dialogue The conversation of characters in a literary work. In fiction and poetry dialogue is typically enclosed within quotation marks. See Frost's "Home Burial" for an example. In plays, characters' speech is preceded by their names.

Diction The selection of words in a literary work. A work's diction forms one of its centrally important literary elements, as writers use words to convey action, reveal character, imply attitudes, identify themes, and suggest values. We can speak of the diction particular to a character, as in Iago's and Desdemona's very different ways of speaking in *Othello.* We can also refer to a poet's diction as represented over the body of his or her work, as in Donne's or Hughes's diction.

Dramatic monologue A type of poem in which a speaker addresses a silent listener. As readers, we overhear the speaker in a dramatic monologue. Robert Browning's "My Last Duchess" represents the epitome of the genre.

Dramatis personae Latin for the characters or persons in a play. Included among the *dramatis personae* of Miller's *Death of a Salesman* are Willy Loman, the salesman, his wife Linda, and his sons Biff and Happy.

Elegy A lyric poem that laments the dead. Robert Hayden's "Those Winter Sundays" is elegiac in tone. A more explicitly identified elegy is W. H. Auden's "In Memory of William Butler Yeats" and his "Funeral Blues."

Elision The omission of an unstressed vowel or syllable to preserve the meter of a line of poetry. Pope uses elision in "Sound and Sense": "Flies o'er th' unbending corn . . ."

Enjambment A run-on line of poetry in which logical and grammatical sense carries over from one line into the next. An enjambed line differs from an end-stopped line in which the grammatical and logical sense is completed within the line. In the opening lines of Robert Browning's "My Last Duchess," for example, the first line is end-stopped and the second enjambed:

> That's my last Duchess painted on the wall,
> Looking as if she were alive. I call
> That piece a wonder, now . . .

Epic A long narrative poem that records the adventures of a hero. Epics typically chronicle the origins of a civilization and embody its central values. Examples from Western literature include Homer's *Iliad* and *Odyssey,* Virgil's *Aeneid,* and Milton's *Paradise Lost.*

Epigram A brief witty poem, often satirical. Alexander Pope's "Epigram engraved on the Collar of a Dog" exemplifies the genre:

> I am his Highness' dog at Kew;
> Pray tell me, sir, whose dog are you?

Exposition The first stage of a fictional or dramatic plot, in which necessary background information is provided. Ibsen's *A Doll House,* for instance, begins with a conversation between the two central characters, a dialogue that fills the audience in on events that occurred before the action of the play begins, but which are important in the development of its plot.

Fable A brief story with an explicit moral provided by the author. Fables typically include animals as characters. Their most famous practitioner in the West is the ancient Greek writer Aesop, whose "The Wolf and the Mastiff" is included in this book. Compare *Parable.*

Falling action In the plot of a story or play, the action following the climax of the work that moves it towards its denouement or resolution. The falling action of *Othello* begins after Othello realizes that Iago is responsible for plotting against him by spurring him on to murder his wife, Desdemona.

Falling meter Poetic meters such as trochaic and dactylic that move or fall from a stressed to an unstressed syllable. The nonsense line, "Higgledy, piggledy," is dactylic, with the accent on the first syllable and the two syllables following falling off from that accent in each word. Trochaic meter is represented by this line: "Hip-hop, be-bop, treetop—freedom."

Fiction An imagined story, whether in prose, poetry, or drama, or an imagined character—a "fiction." Ibsen's Nora is fictional, a "make-believe" character in a play, as Othello. Characters like Robert Browning's Duke and Duchess from his poem "My Last Duchess" are fictional as well, though they may be based on actual historical individuals. And, of course, characters in stories and novels are fictional, though they, too, may be based, in some way, on real people. The important thing to remember is that writers embellish and embroider and alter actual life when they use real life as the basis for their work. They fictionalize facts, deviate from real life situations as they "make things up."

Figurative language A form of language use in which writers and speakers convey something other than the literal meaning of their words. Examples include *hyperbole* or exaggeration, litotes or *understatement, simile* and *metaphor,* which employ comparison, and *synecdoche* and *metonymy,* in which a part of a thing stands for the whole.

Flashback An interruption of a work's chronology to describe or present an incident that occurred prior to the main time frame of a work's action. Writers use flashbacks to complicate the sense of chronology in the plot of their works and to convey the richness of the experience of human time. Faulkner's story "A Rose for Emily" includes flashbacks.

Foil A character who contrasts and parallels the main character in a play or story. In *Othello,* Emilia and Bianca are foils for Desdemona.

Foot A metrical unit composed of stressed and unstressed syllables. For example, an *iamb* or *iambic* foot is represented by ˘´ that is, an unaccented syllable followed by an accented one. Frost's line "Whose woods these are I think I know" contains four iambs, and is thus an iambic foot.

Foreshadowing Hints of what is to come in the action of a play or a story. Ibsen's *A Doll House* includes foreshadowing. So, too, do Poe's "Cask of Amontillado" and Chopin's "Story of an Hour."

Fourth wall The imaginary wall of the box theater setting, supposedly removed to allow the audience to see the action. The fourth wall is especially common in modern and contemporary plays, such as Hansberry's *A Raisin in the Sun,* Wasserstein's *Tender Offer,* and Wilson's *Fences.*

Free verse Poetry without a regular pattern of meter or rhyme. The verse is "free" in not being bound by earlier poetic conventions requiring poems to adhere to an explicit and identifiable meter and rhyme scheme in a form such as the sonnet or ballad. Modern and contemporary poets of the twentieth and twenty-first centuries often employ free verse. Williams's "This Is Just to Say" is one of many examples.

Gesture The physical movement of a character during a play. Gesture is used to reveal character, and may include facial expressions as well as movements of other parts of an actor's body. Sometimes a playwright will be very explicit about both bodily and facial gestures, providing detailed instructions in the play's stage directions. Shaw's *Arms and the Man* includes such stage directions. See Stage direction.

Hyperbole A figure of speech involving exaggeration. John Donne uses hyperbole in his poem "Song: Go and Catch a Falling Star."

Iamb An unstressed syllable followed by a stressed one, as in *tŏdáy.* See *Foot.*

Iambic pentameter A poetic line of five iambic feet: Whĕn ín dĭsgráce wĭth fórtuňe ánd meň's eyés.

Image A concrete representation of a sense impression, a feeling, or an idea. Imagery refers to the pattern of related details in a work. In some works one image predominates either by recurring throughout the work or by appearing at a critical point in the plot. Often writers use multiple images throughout a work to suggest states of feeling and to convey implications of thought and action. Some modern poets, such as Ezra Pound and William Carlos Williams, write poems that lack discursive explanation entirely and include only images. Among the most famous examples is Pound's poem "In a Station of the Metro":

> The apparition of these faces in the crowd;
> Petals on a wet, black bough.

Imagery The pattern of related comparative aspects of language, particularly of images, in a literary work. Imagery of light and darkness pervades James Joyce's stories "Araby," "The Boarding House." So, too, does religious imagery.

Irony A contrast or discrepancy between what is said and what is meant or between what happens and what is expected to happen in life and in literature. In verbal irony, characters say the opposite of what they mean. In irony of circumstance or situation, the opposite of what is expected occurs. In dramatic irony, a character speaks in ignorance of a situation or event known to the audience or to the other characters. Flannery O'Connor's short stories employ all these forms of irony, as does Poe's "Cask of Amontillado."

Literal language A form of language in which writers and speakers mean exactly what their words denote. See *Figurative language, Denotation,* and *Connotation.*

Lyric poem A type of poem characterized by brevity, compression, and the expression of feeling. Most of the poems in this book are lyrics. The anonymous "Western Wind" epitomizes the genre:

Western Wind, when will thou blow,
The small rain down can rain?
Christ, if my love were in my arms
And I in my bed again!

Metaphor A comparison between essentially unlike things without an explicitly comparative word such as *like* or *as.* An example is "My love is a red, red rose," from Burns's "A Red, Red Rose." Langston Hughes's "Dream Deferred" is built entirely of metaphors. Metaphor is one of the most important of literary uses of language. Shakespeare employs a wide range of metaphor in his sonnets and his plays, often in such density and profusion that readers are kept busy analyzing and interpreting and unraveling them. Compare *Simile.*

Meter The measured pattern of rhythmic accents in poems. See *Foot* and *Iamb.*

Metonymy A figure of speech in which a closely related term is substituted for an object or idea. An example: "We have always remained loyal to the crown." Compare *Synecdoche.*

Monologue A speech by a single character without another character's response. See *Dramatic monologue* and *Soliloquy.*

Narrative poem A poem that tells a story. See *Ballad.*

Narrator The voice and implied speaker of a fictional work, to be distinguished from the actual living author. For example, the narrator of Joyce's "Araby" is not James Joyce himself but a literary fictional character created expressly to tell the story. Faulkner's "A Rose for Emily" contains a communal narrator, identified only as "we." See *Point of view.*

Novella A short novel.

Octave An eight-line unit, which may constitute a stanza or a section of a poem, as in the octave of a sonnet.

Ode A long, stately poem in stanzas of varied length, meter, and form. Usually a serious poem on an exalted subject, such as Keats's "Ode on a Grecian Urn," but sometimes a more lighthearted work, such as Neruda's "Ode to My Socks."

Onomatopoeia The use of words to imitate the sounds they describe. Words such as *buzz* and *crack* are onomatopoetic. The following from Pope's "Sound and Sense" onomatopoetically imitates in sound what it describes:

When Ajax strives some rock's vast weight to throw,
The line too labors, and the words move slow.

Most often, however, onomatopoeia refers to words and groups of words, such as Tennyson's description of the "murmur of innumerable bees," which attempts to capture the sound of a swarm of bees buzzing.

Open form A type of structure or form in poetry characterized by freedom from regularity and consistency in such elements as rhyme, line length, metrical pattern, and overall poetic structure. E. E. Cummings's "Buffalo Bill's" is one example. See also *Free verse.*

Parable A brief story that teaches a lesson often ethical or spiritual. Examples include "The Prodigal Son," from the New Testament, and the Zen parable, "Learning to Be Silent." Compare *Fable.*

Parody A humorous, mocking imitation of a literary work, sometimes sarcastic, but often playful and even respectful in its playful imitation. Examples include Bob McKenty's parody of Frost's "Dust of Snow" and Kenneth Koch's parody of Williams's "This Is Just to Say."

Pathos A quality of a play's action that stimulates the audience to feel pity for a character. Pathos is always an aspect of tragedy, and may be present in comedy as well.

Personification The endowment of inanimate objects or abstract concepts with animate or living qualities. An example: "The yellow leaves flaunted their color gaily in the breeze." Wordsworth's "I wandered lonely as a cloud" exemplifies personification.

Plot The unified structure of incidents in a literary work. See *Conflict, Climax, Denouement,* and *Flashback.*

Point of view The angle of vision from which a story is narrated. A work's point of view can be first person, in which the narrator is a character or an observer; objective, in which the narrator knows or appears to know no more than the reader; omniscient, in which the narrator knows everything about the characters; and limited omniscient, which allows the narrator to know some things about the characters but not everything. See *Narrator.*

Props Articles or objects that appear on stage during a play. The Christmas tree in *A Doll House* and Laura's collection of glass animals in *The Glass Menagerie* are examples.

Protagonist The main character of a literary work—Othello in the play named after him; Paul in Lawrence's "Rocking-Horse Winner."

Pyrrhic A metrical foot with two unstressed syllables ("of the").

Quatrain A four-line stanza in a poem, the first four lines and the second four lines in a Petrarchan sonnet. A Shakespearean sonnet contains three quatrain's followed by a couplet.

Recognition The point at which a character understands his or her situation as it really is. Sophocles' Oedipus comes to this point near the end of *Oedipus the King;* Othello comes to a similar understanding of his situation in Act V of *Othello.*

Resolution The sorting out or unraveling of a plot at the end of a play, novel, or story. See *Plot* and *Denouement.*

Reversal The point at which the action of the plot turns in an unexpected direction for the protagonist. Oedipus' and Othello's recognitions are also reversals. They learn what they did not expect to learn. See *Recognition* and also *Irony.*

Rhyme The matching of final vowel or consonant sounds in two or more words. The following stanza of *Richard Cory* employs alternate rhyme, with the third line rhyming with the first and the fourth with the second:

> Whenever Richard Cory went down town,
> We people on the pavement looked at him;
> He was a gentleman from sole to crown,
> Clean favored and imperially slim.

Rhythm The recurrence of accent or stress in lines of verse. In the following lines from "Same in Blues" by Langston Hughes, the accented words and syllables are underlined:

> I <u>said</u> to my baby,
> Baby take it <u>slow</u> . . .
> Lulu said to <u>Leonard</u>,
> I <u>want</u> a diamond <u>ring</u>.

Rising action A set of conflicts and crises that constitute that part of a play's or story's plot leading up to the climax. See *Climax, Denouement,* and *Plot.*

Rising meter Poetic meters such as iambic and anapestic that move or ascend from an unstressed to a stressed syllable. See *Anapest, Iamb,* and *Falling Meter.*

Satire A literary work that criticizes human misconduct and ridicules vices, stupidities, and follies. Swift's *Gulliver's Travels* is a famous example. O'Connor's "Everything That Rises Must Converge" has strong satirical elements.

Sestet A six-line unit of verse constituting a stanza or section of a poem; the last six lines of an Italian sonnet. Example: Frost's "Design."

Sestina A poem of thirty-nine lines written in iambic pentameter. Its six-line stanzas repeat in an intricate and prescribed order the final word in each of the first six lines. After the sixth stanza, there is a three-line envoi, which uses the six repeating words, two words, two per line.

Setting The time and place of a literary work that establish its context. The stories of Sandra Cisneros are set in the American Southwest in the mid- to late twentieth century, those of James Joyce in Dublin, Ireland, in the early twentieth century.

Simile A figure of speech involving a comparison between unlike things using *like, as,* or *as though*. An example: "My love is like a red, red rose." Compare *Metaphor.*

Soliloquy A speech in a play that is meant to be heard by the audience but not by other characters on the stage. If there are no other characters present, the soliloquy represents the character thinking aloud. Compare *Aside* and *Monologue.*

Sonnet A fourteen-line poem in iambic pentameter. The *Shakespearean* or *English* sonnet is arranged as three quatrains and a final couplet, rhyming *abab cdcd efef gg.* The *Petrarchan* or *Italian* sonnet divides into two parts: an eight-line octave and a six-line sestet, rhyming *abba abba cde cde* or *abba abba cd cd cd.*

Spondee A metrical foot represented by two stressed syllables, such as *knı́ck-knáck*.

Stage direction A playwright's descriptive or interpretive comments that provide readers (and actors) with information about the dialogue, setting, and action of a play. Modern playwrights, including Ibsen, Shaw, Miller, and Williams, tend to include substantial stage directions, while earlier playwrights typically used them more sparsely, implicitly, or not at all. See *Gesture.*

Staging The spectacle a play presents in performance, including the position of actors on stage, the scenic background, the props and costumes, and the lighting and sound effects. Tennessee Williams describes these in his detailed stage directions for *The Glass Menagerie* and also in his Production Notes for the play.

Stanza A division or unit of a poem that is repeated in the same form—either with similar or identical patterns or rhyme and meter, or with variations from one stanza to another. The stanzas of Rita Dove's "Canary" are irregular.

Style The way an author chooses words, and arranges them in sentences or in lines of dialogue or verse, and develops ideas and actions with description, imagery, and other literary techniques. See also *Connotation, Denotation, Diction, Figurative language, Image, Imagery, Irony, Metaphor, Narrator, Point of view, Syntax,* and *Tone.*

Subject What a story or play is about; to be distinguished from plot and theme. Faulkner's "A Rose for Emily" is about the decline of a particular way of life endemic to the American South before the Civil War. That is its *subject.* (Its plot is how Faulkner organizes the actions of the story's characters. Its theme is the overall meaning Faulkner conveys.)

Subplot A subsidiary or subordinate or parallel plot in a play or story that coexists with the main plot.

Symbol An object or action in a literary work that means more than itself, that stands for something beyond itself. The glass unicorn in *The Glass Menagerie,* the rocking horse in "The Rocking-Horse Winner," the road in Frost's "The Road Not Taken"—all are symbols in this sense.

Synecdoche A figure of speech in which a part is substituted for the whole. An example: "Lend me a hand." Compare *Metonymy.*

Syntax The grammatical order of words in a sentence or line of verse or dialogue. The organization of words and phrases and clauses in sentences of prose, verse, and dialogue. In the following example, normal syntax (subject, verb, object order) is inverted: "Whose woods these are I think I know."

Tale A story that narrates strange happenings in a direct manner, without detailed descriptions of character. Petronius' "The Widow of Ephesus" is an example.

Tercet A three-line stanza, as exemplified by Shelley's "Ode to the West Wind." The three-line stanzas or sections that together constitute the sestet of a Petrarchan or Italian sonnet.

Terza rima A three-line stanzaic pattern with interlocking tercet rhymes: *aba bcb,* and so on, as in Frost's "Acquainted with the Night."

Theme The idea of a literary work abstracted from its details of language, character, and action, and cast in the form of a generalization. See the discussion of Dickinson's "Crumbling is not an instant's Act."

Tone The implied attitude of a writer toward the subject and characters of a work, as, for example, Flannery O'Connor's ironic tone in her "Good Country People." Compare *Irony.*

Tragedy A type of drama in which the characters experience reversals of fortune, usually for the worse. In tragedy, catastrophe and suffering await many of the characters, especially the hero. Examples include Shakespeare's *Othello;* Sophocles' *Oedipus the King;* Arthur Miller's *Death of a Salesman.* See *Tragic flaw* and *Tragic Hero.*

Tragic flaw A weakness or limitation of character, resulting in the fall of the tragic hero. Othello's jealousy is one example. See *Tragedy* and *Tragic hero.*

Tragic hero A privileged, exalted character of high repute, who, by virtue of a tragic flaw and fate, suffers a fall from glory into suffering. Sophocles' Oedipus is an example. See *Tragedy* and *Tragic flaw.*

Tragicomedy Works of drama that include and blend tragic and comic elements in fairly equal measure. Shakespeare's *Merchant of Venice* is one example.

Trochee An accented syllable followed by an unaccented one, as in *fóotbăll.*

Understatement A figure of speech in which a writer or speaker says less than what he or she means; the opposite of exaggeration. The last line of Frost's "Birches" illustrates this literary device: "One could do worse than be a swinger of birches."

Unities The idea that a play should be limited to a specific time, place, and story line. The events of the plot should occur within a twenty-four hour period, should occur within a given geographic locale, and should tell a single story. Aristotle argued that Sophocles' *Oedipus the King* was the perfect play for embodying the "unities."

Villanelle A nineteen-line lyric poem that relies heavily on repetition. The first and third lines alternate throughout the poem, which is structured in six stanzas—five tercets and a concluding quatrain. Examples include Bishop's "One Art," Roethke's "The Waking," and Thomas's "Do not go gentle into that good night."

Credits

PHOTO CREDITS

Page 25: Bettmann/Corbis; **32**: © Jill Krementz; **38**: Cammie G. Henry Research Center, Northwestern State University, LA; **51**: Elliot Erwitt/Magnum Photos; **62**: Getty Images; **67**: © Pam Spaulding; **78**: Van Vechten Collection/Library of Congress; **86**: Culver Pictures; **91**: Photography by Curt Richter; **100**: Getty Images; **112**: Library of Congress; **132**: Photo by W.S.Hartshorn, 1848/The Library of Congress; **133**: Courtesy of the Edgar Allen Poe Museum, Richmond, Virginia; **134:** (left) The Everett Collection, (right) Illustration for "The Fall of the House of Usher," wood engraving by Constant le Breton/The Granger Collection, New York; **169**: (both) Flannery O'Connor Collection, Georgia College and State University Library; **172**: "Miss Flannery O'Connor is at Home" by David C. Terry. Reproduced by permission of the artist; **215**: Art Resource; **230**: Getty Images; **235**: © Jill Krementz; **243**: Marc Brasz/Corbis; **257**: The Image Works; **263**: Bettmann/Corbis; **270**: © Jill Krementz; **272**: AFP/Getty Images; **277, 288**: © Jill Krementz; **292**: Van Vechten Collection/Library of Congress; **313**: © Jill Krementz; **324**: Getty Images; **335**: Cammie G. Henry Research Center, Northwestern State University, LA; **339**: Photo by Diana Solis; **341**: New York World-Telegram & Sun Collection/Library of Congress; **352, 365**: Van Vechten Collection/Library of Congress; **379, 391**: Library of Congress; **400**: Getty Images; **404**: Van Vechten Collection/Library of Congress; **409**: AP/Wide World Photos; **416**: Culver Pictures; **421**: Christopher Felver/Corbis; **433**: AP/Wide World Photos; **446**: © Nancy Crampton; **452**: Getty Images; **459**: Bettmann/Corbis; **467**: © Jill Krementz; **476, 483**: Photography by Curt Richter; **493**: AP/Wide World Photos; **503**: © Jill Krementz; **521**: AP/Wide World Photos; **602**: Library of Congress; **627**: Amherst College Archives and Special Collections; **628**: Courtesy of the Emily Dickinson Museum, Amherst, Massachusetts; **629**: Amherst College Archives and Special Collections. Text reprinted by permission of the publishers and the Trustees of Amherst College from THE POEMS OF EMILY DICKINSON, Thomas H. Johnson, ed., J465, Cambridge, Mass.: The Belknap Press of Harvard University Press, Copyright © 1951, 1955, 1979, 1983 by the President and Fellows of Harvard College; **666**: Library of Congress; **667, 668, 669**: Robert Frost Collection, Clifton Waller Barrett Library; **700**: Van Vechten Collection/

Library of Congress; **702:** (top) Archibald Motley Jr., Blues 1929. Collection of Archie Motley and Valerie Gerrard Browne/Chicago Historical Society, (bottom) Manuscripts, Archives and Rare Books Division, Shomburg Center for Research in Black Culture, The New York Public Library, Astor, Lenox, and Tilden Foundations; **703**: Bettmann/Corbis; **748**: The Granger Collection, New York; **759**: George Cserna, ca. 1970/Library of Congress; **766**: © Jill Krementz; **769**: Thomas Phillips/Library of Congress; **775, 783**: © Jill Krementz; **786**: Self-portrait, c. 1931/New York World-Telegram & Sun Collection/Library of Congress; **787**: Getty Images; **791**: © Jill Krementz; **792**: The Granger Collection, New York; **796, 798**: © Jill Krementz; **801**: Library of Congress; **802**: AP/Wide World Photos; **803**: Getty Images; **806**: © Jill Krementz; **808:** (top) Getty Images, (bottom) Culver Pictures; **809**, **811**, **813**, **814**: Getty Images; **825**: George Fayer, ca. 1940-1950/Library of Congress; **828**: Getty Images; **829**: Library of Congress; **835**: © Margaretta K. Mitchell; **836**: Culver Pictures; **841**: Getty Images; **842**: New York World-Telegram & Sun Collection/Library of Congress; **843**: Culver Pictures; **845**: Special Collections Division, University of Washington Libraries; **846**: Courtesy Beacon Press; **847**: New York World-Telegram & Sun Collection/Library of Congress; **849**: Getty Images; **851**: Bettmann/Corbis; **854**: © Jill Krementz; **856**: Photographed by Mrs. Cameron (d.1879), engraved by T. Johnson/Library of Congress; **858**: Library of Congress; **860**: Bettmann/Corbis; **861**: Library of Congress; **866**: New York World-Telegram & Sun Collection/Library of Congress; **868**: Getty Images; **873**: Arnold Genthe/Library of Congress; **897**: Underwood & Underwood/Corbis; **904**: George Grantham Bain Collection/Library of Congress; **955**: AP/Wide World Photos; **956:** (top) José F. Poblete/Corbis, (bottom) Time Life Pictures/Getty Images; **958**: AFP/Getty Images; **1007**: Getty Images; **1009:** (top) Engraved by B. Holl (1808-1884) from print by Houbraken (1660-p. 1719)/Library of Congress, (bottom) Getty Images; **1011**: Rolf Konow/Castle Rock/Dakota Films/The Kobal Collection; **1104**: Getty Images; **1105**: Edvard Munch, Henrik Ibsen at the Grand Café, 1898. Oil on canvas. Private Collection. © 2007 The Munch Museum/The Munch-Ellingsen Group/Artists Rights Society (ARS), NY; **1156:** (top) New York World-Telegram & Sun Collection/Library of Congress, (bottom) Courtesy of the Estate of Jo Mielziner; **1157, 1158**: Billy Rose Theater Collection, New York Public Library for the Performing Arts; **1158** (bottom), **1159:** Arena Stage Collection, Special Collections and Archives George Mason University; **1208, 1209**: Billy Rose Theater Collection, New York Public Library for the Performing Arts/Courtesy of the Estate of Jo Mielziner; **1210**: Billy Rose Theater Collection, New York Public Library for the Performing Arts; **1211**: Library of Congress; **1212**: Courtesy of The Goodman Theater, Photo by Eric Y. Exit; **1280**: Bachrach/Library of Congress; **1291**: New York World-Telegram & Sun Collection/Library of Congress; **1355**: © Jill Krementz; **1406**: Courtesy Milcha Sanchez-Scott; **1418**: © Jill Krementz; **1425**: Culver Pictures; **1467**: Getty Images

INSERT PHOTO CREDITS

i1: Vincent van Gogh, The Starry Night. 1889. Oil on canvas, 29" × 36¼". The Museum of Modern Art, New York. Acquired through the Lillie Bliss Bequest. Digital Image © The Museum of Modern Art/Licensed by SCALA/Art Resource, NY; **i2:** Francisco de Goya, The Third of May, 1808: The Execution of the Defenders of Madrid. 1814. Prado Museum, Madrid. SCALA/Art Resource; **i3:** Brueghel the Elder, Landscape with the Fall of Icarus, ca. 1558. Musée d'Art Ancien, Musées Royaux des Beaux–Arts, Brussels. SCALA/Art Resource; **i4:** William Blake, The Sick Rose of Experience. 1794. Library of Congress, Washington, D.C./The Bridgeman Art Library; **i5:** Henri Matisse, Dance (first version, Paris). March 1909. Oil on canvas, 8'6½" × 12'9½". The Museum of Modern Art, New York, NY. Gift of Nelson A. Rockefeller in honor of Alfred H. Barr, Jr. Digital Image © The Museum of Modern Art/Licensed by

SCALA/Art Resource. © 2007 Succession H. Matisse, Paris/Artists Rights Society (ARS), New York; **i6:** Jan Vermeer, Young Woman with a Water Jug, c. 1662. Oil on canvas, 18" × 16". The Metropolitan Museum of Art, Gift of Henry G. Marquand, 1889, The Marquand Collection/The Bridgeman Art Library; **i7:** Marcel Duchamp, Nude Descending a Staircase, No. 2, 1912. Oil on canvas, 58 × 35 inches. Philadelphia Museum of Art/The Bridgeman Art Library. © 2007 Artists Rights Society (ARS), New York/ADAGP, Paris/Succession Marcel Duchamp; **i8:** Rembrandt van Rijn, The Return of the Prodigal Son. 1668-1669. Oil on canvas. 265 × 205 cm. Hermitage, St. Petersburg, Russia. SCALA/Art Resource; **i9:** Kitagawa Utamaro, Girl Powdering Her Neck. Musée des Arts Asiatiques-Guimet, Paris, France. Réunion des Musées Nationaux/Art Resource; **i10:** Romare Bearden, At Five in The Afternoon, 1946. Oil on board, 29½" × 37½". Collection Fred Jones Jr. Museum of Art, The University of Oklahoma, Norman; Purchase, U.S. State Department Collection, 1948. © Romare Bearden Foundation/Licensed by VAGA, New York, NY; **i11:** Giorgio de Chirico, Melancholy and Mystery of a Street, 1914. Private Collection/The Bridgeman Art Library. © 2007 Artists Rights Society (ARS), New York/SIAE, Rome; **i12:** Lun-Yi Tsai, Disbelief, 2002, Oil on linen, 66 x 50 inches, Collection of the artist.

Acknowledgments

CHINUA ACHEBE "Marriage is a Private Affair" from *Girls At War And Other Stories.* Copyright © 1972, 1973 by Chinua Achebe. Used by permission of Doubleday, a division of Random House, Inc. and Harold Ober Associates, Inc.

SHERMAN ALEXIE "Indian Education" from *The Lone Ranger and Tonto Fistfight in Heaven.* Copyright © 1993 by Sherman Alexie. Used by permission of Grove/Atlantic, Inc.

SHERMAN ALEXIE "Indian Boy Love Song 1" and "Indian Boy Love Song 2" from *The Business Of Fancydancing.* © 1982 by Sherman Alexie. Used by permission of Hanging Loose Press.

CHAIRIL ANWAR "At the Mosque" from *The Voice of the Night: The Complete Prose & Poetry of Charil Anwar,* translated by Burton Rafael. Copyright © 1993 Ohio University Press. Used with permission.

ARISTOTLE "Six Elements of Tragedy and Simple and Complex Plots" from *Poetics* translated by Gerald F. Else. Copyright © 1967 University of Michigan. Used with permission.

FREDERICK ASALS on "A Good Man is Hard to Find" from *Flannery O'Connor: The Imagination of Extremity.* Copyright © Frederick Asals. Reprinted by permission of the University of Georgia Press.

MARGARET ATWOOD "Happy Endings" from *Good Bones and Simple Murders.* Copyright © 1983, 1992, 1994 by O.W. Toad Ltd., A Nan A. Talese book. Used by permission of Doubleday, a division of Random House, Inc. and McClelland and Stewart, the Canadian Publisher.

MARGARET ATWOOD "Spelling" from *True Stories.* Copyright © 1995 by Margaret Atwood. Originally published in Canada by Oxford University Press and in the United States by Simon and Schuster.

MARGARET ATWOOD "This is a Photograph of Me" from *Selected Poems, 1965–1975.* Copyright © 1976 by Margaret Atwood. Reprinted by permission of Houghton Mifflin Company and House of Anansi Press, Toronto. All rights reserved.

W.H. AUDEN "Musée des Beaux Arts" "The Unknown Citizen," "In Memory of W.B. Yeats," and "Funeral Blues," from *W.H. Auden: Collected Poems,* edited by Edward Mendelson. Copyright 1940 and renewed © 1968 by W.H. Auden. Used by permission of Random House, Inc.

W.H. AUDEN "September 1, 1939" from *Another Time.* Copyright 1940 and renewed © 1968 by W. H. Auden. Used by permission of Random House, Inc.

JIMMY SANTIAGO BACA "Section XVII from Meditations on the South Valley" in *Martin And Meditations On The South Valley.* Copyright © 1987 by Jimmy Santiago Baca. Reprinted by permission of New Directions Publishing Corp.

JAMES BALDWIN "Sonny's Blues" was originally published in *Partisan Review.* Copyright © 1957 by James Baldwin, copyright renewed. Collected in *Going to Meet the Man,* published by Vintage Books. Reprinted by arrangement with the James Baldwin Estate.

RICHARD BARKSDALE "On Hughes's 'Ballad of the Landlord'" from *Langston Hughes: The Poet and His Critics.* Reprinted by permission of the American Library Association.

MATSUO BASHO "Three Haiku" translated by Robert Hass from *The Essential Haiku: Versions of Bash, Buson and Issa,* edited with an introduction by Robert Hass. Introduction and selection copyright © 1994 by Robert Hass. Unless otherwise noted, all translations copyright © 1994 by Robert Hass. Reprinted by permission of HarperCollins, Inc.

CHRISTOPHER BENFREY "On 'The Black Cat' and 'The Tell-Tale Heart" from *New Essays on Poe's Major Tales,* edited by Kenneth Silverman. Copyright © 1992. Reprinted by permission of Cambridge University Press.

ELIZABETH BISHOP "Sestina," "One Art," "The Fish," "First Death in Nova Scotia," and "The Prodigal" from *The Complete Poems 1927–1979* by Elizabeth Bishop. Copyright © 1979, 1983 by Alice Helen Methfessel. Reprinted with permission of Farrar Straus & Giroux LLC.

EAVAN BOLAND "Anorexic" from *In Her Own Image.* Copyright © 1989 Eavan Boland. Reprinted with permission of the author.

JOSE LUIS BORGES "The Garden of Forking Paths" translated by Donald A. Yates from *Labyrinths.* Copyright © 1962, 1964 by New Directions Publishing Corp. Reprinted by permission.

KAY BOYLE "Astronomer's Wife" from *Life Being The Best And Other Stories.* Copyright © 1988 by Kay Boyle. Reprinted by permission of New Directions Publishing Corp.

KAMAU BRATHWAITE "Ogoun" from *Black & Blues.* Copyright © 1976, 1994, 1995 by Kamau Brathwaite. Reprinted by permission of New Directions Publishing Corp.

BERTOLT BRECHT "Brecht on Theater" from "A Short Organum for the Theatre" in *Brecht On Theatre.* Copyright © Bertolt Brecht. Reprinted by permission of Farrar, Straus & Giroux LLC.

GWENDOLYN BROOKS "We real cool," "First fight, then fiddle," "Song in the front yard" from *Blacks.* Copyright © 1987 by Gwendolyn Brooks. Reprinted by consent of Brooks Permissions.

C.P. CAVAFY "The City" from *Collected Poems, Revised Edition*. Translated by Edmund Keeley and Phillip Sherrard. © 1975, 1992 Princeton University Press. Used with permission.

RAYMOND CARVER "Photograph of My Father in His Twenty-Second Year" from *Fires: Essays, Poems and Stories.* Copyright © 1983 by Raymond Carver, renewed © 1989 by Tess Gallagher. Reprinted by permission of Tess Gallagher and International Creative Management, Inc.

RAYMOND CARVER "Cathedral" from *Cathedral.* Copyright © 1981 by Raymond Carver. Reprinted by permission of Alfred A. Knopf, a division of Random House, Inc.

MAURICE CHARNEY "Shakespeare's Villains" from *How to Read Shakespeare* by Maurice Charney. Reprinted by permission of the author.

HELEN CHASIN "The Word Plum" from *Coming Close and Other Poems* by Helen Chasin. Copyright © 1968 by Helen Chasin. Reprinted by permission of Yale University Press.

ANTON CHEKHOV "The Lady with the Little Dog" translated by Richard Pevear and Larissa Volokhonsky from *The Selected Short Stories of Anton Chekhov.* Copyright © 2000 by Richard Pevear and Larissa Volokhonsky. Used by permission of Bantam Books, a division of Random House, Inc.

SANDRA CISNEROS "Barbie Q" from *Woman Hollering Creek.* Copyright © 1991 by Sandra Cisneros. Published by Vintage Books, a division of Random House, Inc., and originally in hardcover by Random House, Inc. Reprinted by permission of Susan Bergholz Literary Services, New York. All rights reserved.

SANDRA CISNEROS "Pumpkin Eater" from *Loose Woman.* Copyright © 1994 by Sandra Cisneros. Published by Vintage Books, a division of Random House, Inc., and originally in hardcover by Alfred A. Knopf, Inc. Reprinted by permission of Susan Bergholz Literary Services, New York. All rights reserved.

LUCILLE CLIFTON "homage to my hips" first published in *two-headed woman,* copyright © 1980 by The University of Massachusetts Press. Now appears in *good woman: poems and a memoir 1969-1980.* Copyright © 1987 by Lucille Clifton, published by BOA Editions. Reprinted by permission of Curtis Brown, Ltd.

LUCILLE CLIFTON "Tuesday 9/11/01" from *September 11, 2001: American Writers Respond,* ed. William Heyen, published by Etruscan Press. Reprinted by permission of Curtis Brown, Ltd.

JUDITH ORTIZ COFER "The Game" from *The Latin Deli: Prose and Poetry.* Copyright © Judith Ortiz Cofer. Reprinted by permission of the University of Georgia Press.

BILLY COLLINS "Introduction to Poetry" and "My Number" from *The Apple that Astonished Paris.* Copyright © 1993 Billy Collins. Reprinted by permission of the University of Arkansas.

BILLY COLLINS "Taking Off Emily Dickinson's Clothes" from *Picnic Lightning.* Copyright © 1998 by Billy Collins. Reprinted by permission of the University of Pittsburgh Press.

BILLY COLLINS "Sonnet" and "The Listener" from *Sailing Alone Around The Room.* Copyright © 2001 by Billy Collins. Used by permission of Random House, Inc.

BILLY COLLINS "The History Teacher" from *Questions About Angels.* Copyright © 1991. Reprinted by permission of the University of Pittsburgh Press.

WENDY COPE "The Ted Williams Villanelle" from *If I Don't Know.* Copyright © Wendy Cope. Reprinted by permission of Faber & Faber Ltd.

COUNTEE CULLEN "Incident" from *Color.* Copyright 1925 by Harper & Brothers. Copyright held by Amistad Research Center. Administered by Thompson and Thompson, New York, NY.

E.E. CUMMINGS "Me up at does," "l(a" "Buffalo Bill's" "Anyone lived in a pretty how town" "I thank you god for most this amazing" from *The Complete Poems: 1904–1962* by E.E. Cummings, edited by George J. Firmage. Copyright 1923, 1925, 1926, 1931, 1935, 1938, 1939, 1940, 1944, 1945, 1946, 1947, 1948, 1949, 1950, 1951, 1952, 1953, 1954, © 1955, 1956, 1957, 1958, 1959, 1960, 1961, 1962, 1963, 1966, 1967, 1968, 1972, 1973, 1974, 1975, 1976, 1977, 1978, 1979, 1980, 1981, 1982, 1983, 1984, 1985, 1986, 1987, 1988, 1989, 1990, 1991 by the Trustees for the E.E. Cummings Trust. Copyright © 1973, 1976, 1978, 1979, 1981, 1983, 1985, 1991 by George James Firmage. Used by permission of Liveright Publishing Corporation.

EMILY DICKINSON "Success is counted sweetest," "Surgeons must be very careful," "These are the days when birds come back," "Water is taught by thirst," "'Faith' is a fine invention," "I'm wife—I've finished that," "I taste a liquor never brewed," "I like a look of agony," "Wild nights! Wild Nights!," "I can wade grief," "There's a certain slant of light," "I felt a funeral in my brain," "I'm nobody! Who are you?" "The soul selects her own society," "Some keep the Sabbath going to church," "I cannot dance upon my toes," "A bird came down the walk" "After great pain, a formal feeling comes," "I dreaded that first robin so," "We grow accustomed to the dark," "Much madness is divinest sense," "This was a poet it is that," "I died for beauty but was scarce," "I heard a fly buzz when I died," "This world is not conclusion," "I'm ceded I've stopped being theirs," "I reckon when I count at all," "I like to see it lap the miles," "There is a pain so utter," "The brain is wider than the sky," "Pain has an element of the blank," "I dwell in possibility," "'Nature is what we see," "Because I could not stop for death," "My life had stood a loaded gun," "The wind begun to knead the grass (and variation)," "A narrow fellow in the grass," "Crumbling is not an instant's act," "The bustle in a house," "Tell all the truth but tell it slant" and "My life closed twice before its close," reprinted by permission of the publishers and Trustees of Amherst College from *The Poems of Emily Dickinson,* Thomas H. Johnson, ed., Cambridge, Mass.: The Belknap Press of Harvard University Press. Copyright © 1951, 1955, 1979, 1983 by the President and Fellows of Harvard College.

EMILY DICKINSON Letter to Thomas Wentworth Higginson from *The Letters of Emily Dickinson,* edited by Thomas H. Johnson, L261, Cambridge, Mass.: The Belknap of Harvard University Press. Copyright © 1958, 1986, The President and Fellows of Harvard College; 1914, 1924, 1932, 1942 by Martha Dickinson Bianchi; 1952 by Alfred Leete Hampson; 1960 by Mary L. Hampson. Reprinted by permission.

H.D. (HILDA DOOLITTLE) "Heat, part II of Garden" by H.D. from *Collected Poems: 1912-1944.* Copyright © 1982 by the Estate of Hilda Doolittle. Reprinted by permission of New Directions Publishing Corp.

RITA DOVE "Canary" from *Grace Notes.* Copyright © 1989 by Rita Dove. Used by permission of the author and W.W. Norton & Company, Inc.

RITA DOVE "Testimonial" from *On The Bus With Rosa Parks.* Copyright © 1999 by Rita Dove. Used by permission of W.W. Norton & Company, Inc.

BART EDELMAN "Had You Not" from *The Last Mojito.* Copyright © 2005 by Bart Edelman. Used by permission.

T.S. ELIOT "The Love Song of J. Alfred Prufrock" from *Collected Poems 1909-1962* by T.S. Eliot. Copyright 1936 by Harcourt Inc. Copyright © 1964, 1963 by T.S. Eliot, reprinted by permission of Faber & Faber Ltd.

RALPH ELLISON "Battle Royal" from *Invisible Man.* Copyright 1948 by Ralph Ellison. Used by permission of Random House, Inc.

JAMES EMANUEL "On 'Trumpet Player'" from *Langston Hughes.* Copyright © 1967 Twayne Publishers. Reprinted by permission of The Gale Group.

LOUISE ERDRICH "Indian Boarding School: The Runaways" from *Jacklight.* Copyright © 1984 by Louise Erdrich. Reprinted with the permission of the Wylie Agency, Inc.

FAIZ AHMED FAIZ "Before You Came" translated by Agha Shahid Ali from *A Rebel's Silhouette,* © 1991 Agha Shahid Ali. Reprinted by permission of University of Massachusetts Press.

JUDITH FARR "On 'Wild Nights'" reprinted by permission of the publisher from pp. 229-230 in THE PASSION OF EMILY DICKINSON by Judith Farr. Copyright © 1992 by the President and Fellows of Harvard College.

WILLIAM FAULKNER "A Rose for Emily" from *Collected Stories Of William Faulkner.* Copyright 1930 and renewed © 1958 by William Faulkner. Used by permission of Random House, Inc.

WILLIAM FAULKNER "A Barn Burning" from *Collected Stories Of William Faulkner.* Copyright 1950 by Random House, Inc. Copyright renewed 1977 by Jill Faulkner Summers. Used by permission of Random House, Inc.

KATHLEEN FEELEY on "Good Country People" from *Flannery O'Connor: Voice of the Peacock* by Kathleen Feeley. Reprinted by permission of Kathleen Feeley, S.S.N.D.

LAWRENCE FERLINGHETTI "Constantly Risking Absurdity" from *A Coney Island of the Mind.* Copyright © 1958 by Lawrence Ferlinghetti. Reprinted by permission of New Directions Publishing Corp.

F. SCOTT FITZGERALD "Babylon Revisited" from *The Short Stories Of F. Scott Fitzgerald,* edited by Matthew J. Bruccoli. Copyright 1931 by the Curtis Publishing Company. Copyright renewed © 1959 by Frances Scott Fitzgerald Lanahan. Reprinted with permission of Scribner, a division of Simon & Schuster Adult Publishing Group. All rights reserved.

CAROLYN FORCHE "The Memory of Elena" from *The Country Between Us.* Copyright © 1981 by Carolyn Forche. Reprinted by permission of HarperCollins Publishers, Inc.

ROBERT FROST "Stopping by Woods on a Snowy Evening," "The Silken Tent," "The Span of Life," "The Road Not Taken," "Mowing," "The Tuft of Flowers," "Mending Wall," "Birches," "Acquainted with the Night," "After Apple Picking," "Home Burial," "Fire and Ice," "Nothing Gold Can Stay," "Tree at my Window," "Departmental," "Design," "Desert Places," "Provide, Provide," from *The Poetry of Robert Frost,* edited by Edward Connery Latham. Copyright 1936, 1942, 1951, © 1956 by Robert Frost. © 1964, 1970 by Lesley Frost Ballantine. Copyright 1921, 1923, 1928, © 1969 by Henry Holt and Company, L.L.C.

ROBERT FROST "Dust of Snow" from *The Poetry of Robert Frost,* edited by Edward Connery Latham. Copyright 1951 by Robert Frost. Copyright 1923 and © 1969 by Henry Holt and Company, LLC. Reprinted by permission.

ROBERT FROST excerpt from "The Figure a Poem Makes" from *Selected Prose Of Robert Frost,* edited by Hyde Cox and Edward Connery Lathem. Copyright 1939, © 1967 by Henry Holt & Co.

ROBERT FROST Critical Comments from "The Constant Symbol" and "The Unmade Word, or Fetching and Far-Fetching" from *Collected Poems, Prose And Plays* by Robert Frost. Reprinted by permission of the estate of Robert Frost.

DEBORAH GARRISON "A Working Girl Can't Win" from *A Working Girl Can't Win And Other Poems.* Copyright © 1998 by Deborah Garrison. Used by permission of Random House, Inc.

DAVID GEWANTER "Goya's *The Third of May, 1808*" from *In the Belly* by David Gewanter. Copyright © 1997 by The University of Chicago. All rights reserved. Used with permission.

NIKKI GIOVANNI "Ego Tripping" and "Nikki Rosa" from *The Selected Poems of Nikki Giovanni.* Compilation copyright © 1996 by Nikki Giovanni. Reprinted by permission of HarperCollins Publishers.

LOUISE GLUCK "The School Children" from *the House on Marshland* from *the First Four Books of Poems.* Copyright © 1968, 1971, 1972, 1973, 1974, 1975, 1976, 1977, 1978, 1979, 1980, 1985, 1995 by Louise Gluck. Reprinted by permission of HarperCollins Publishers, Inc.

ROBERT GRAVES "Symptoms of Love" from *Graves Complete Poems In One.* Copyright © Robert Graves. Used by permission of Carcanet Press Ltd.

DONALD HALL "My Son, My Executioner" from *Alligator Bride* by Donald Hall. Reprinted by permission of the author.

LORRAINE HANSBERRY *A Raisin in the Sun.* Copyright © 1959 by Robert Nemiroff as an unpublished work. Copyright © 1959, 1966, 1984 by Robert Nemiroff. Used by permission of Random House, Inc.

JOY HARJO "Eagle Poem" from *In Mad Love And War.* Copyright © 1990 by Joy Harjo. Reprinted by permission of Wesleyan University Press.

ROBERT HAYDEN "Frederick Douglass" and "Those Winter Sundays" from *The Collected Poems of Robert Hayden,* edited by Frederick Glaysher. Copyright © 1966 by Robert Hayden. Used by permission of Liveright Publishing Corporation.

FRANCIS HEANEY "Skinny Domicile" from *Holy Tango of Literature.* Copyright © 2004 by Francis Heaney. Used with permission.

SEAMUS HEANEY "Digging" "The Forge" and "Mid-term Break" from *Selected Poems 1966-1987* by Seamus Heaney. Copyright © 1990 by Seamus Heaney. Reprinted by permission of Farrar, Straus & Giroux LLC.

ANTHONY HECHT "The Dover Bitch," from *Collected Earlier Poems* by Anthony Hecht. Copyright © 1990 by Anthony Hecht. Used by permission of Alfred A. Knopf, a division of Random House, Inc.

ERNEST HEMINGWAY Chapter VII vignette from *In Our Time.* Copyright 1925 by Charles Scribner's Sons. Copyright renewed 1953 by Ernest Hemingway. Reprinted with permission of Scribner, a division of Simon & Schuster Adult Publishing Group. All rights reserved.

ERNEST HEMINGWAY "Hills Like White Elephants" from *The Short Stories Of Ernest Hemingway,* copyright 1927 by Charles Scribner's Sons. Copyright renewed © 1955 by Ernest Hemingway. Reprinted with permission of Scribner, a division of Simon & Schuster Adult Publishing Group. All rights reserved.

JANE HIRSHFIELD "Three Times My Life has Opened" from *The Lives of the Heart.* Copyright © 1997 by Jane Hirshfield. Reprinted by permission of HarperCollins Publishers.

ANDREW HUDGINS "Elegy for My Father, Who is not Dead" from *The Never Ending: New Poems* by Andrew Hudgins. Copyright © 1991 by Andrew Hudgins. Reprinted by permission of Houghton Mifflin Company. All rights reserved.

LANGSTON HUGHES "Dream Deferred ("Harlem"), "The Negro Speaks of Rivers," "Mother to Son," "I, Too," "My People," "Dream Variations," "Song for a Dark Girl," "Young Gal's Blues," "The Weary Blues," "Morning After," "Trumpet Player," "Dream Boogie," "Ballad of the Landlord," "Madam and the Rent Man," "When Sue Wears Red," "Listen Here Blues," "Consider Me," "Theme for English B," "Aunt Sue's Stories," "Madrid" "Let America be America Again," "I'm Still Here" and "Ballad of Booker T" from *The Collected Poems of Langston Hughes,* copyright 1951 by Langston Hughes. Reprinted by permission of Alfred A. Knopf, a division of Random House, Inc.

LANGSTON HUGHES "A Toast to Harlem" from *The Best of Simple,* © 1989 George Houston Bass. Reprinted by permission of Farrar, Straus & Giroux LLC.

LANGSTON HUGHES "I Remember the Blues" from *Good Morning Revolution: Uncollected Writings of Social Protest, 1951,* renewed © 1979. Reprinted by permission of Harold Ober Associates, Inc.

ZORA NEALE HURSTON "Spunk" from *the Complete Stories.* Introduction copyright © 1995 by Henry Louis Gates, Jr. and Sieglinde Lemke. Compilation copyright © 1995 by Vivan Bowden, Lois Hurston Gaston, Clifford Hurston, Lucy Ann Hurston, Winifred Hurston Clark, Zora Mack Goins, Edgar Hurston, Sr., and Barbara Hurston Lewis. Afterword and Bibliography copyright © 1995 by Henry Louis Gates. Reprinted by permission of HarperCollins Publishers.

DAVID HENRY HWANG *M. Butterfly.* Copyright © 1986, 1987, 1988 by David Henry Hwang Used by permssion of Dutton Signet, a division of Penguin Group (USA) Inc.

HENRIK IBSEN "A Doll House" from *The Complete Major Prose Plays of Henrik Ibsen* by Henrik Ibsen, translated by Rolf Fjelde. Copyright © 1965, 1970, 1978 by Rolf Fjelde. Used by permission of Dutton Signet, a division of Penguin Group (USA) Inc.

SHIRLEY JACKSON *The Lottery.* Copyright © Shirley Jackson. Reprinted by permission of Farrar, Straus & Giroux LLC.

ROY JACOBSTEIN "The Mystery and Melancholy of the Street" *Indiana Review,* Summer 2004. Copyright © 2004 Roy Jacobstein. Reprinted by permission of the author.

RANDALL JARRELL "Death of the Ball Turret Gunner" from *The Complete Poems.* Copyright © 1969, renewed 1997 by Mary von. S. Jarrell. Reprinted by permission of Farrar, Straus and Giroux, LLC.

ONWUCHEKWA JEMIE "Hughes & Evolution of Consciousness in Black Poetry" and "On 'The Negro Speaks of Rivers'" from *Langston Hughes: An Introduction to the Poetry.* Copyright © 1973 Onwuchekwa Jemie. Used by permission of the author.

GISH JEN "Who's Irish?" from *Who's Irish*? Copyright © 1998 by Gish Jen. First published in *The New Yorker.* From the collection *Who's Irish?* By Gish Jen, published by Alfred A. Knopf in 1999. Reprinted by permission of the author.

JAMES JOYCE "Araby," and "The Boarding House" from *Dubliners* by James Joyce. Copyright 1916 by B.W. Heubsch. Definitive text copyright © 1967 by the Estate of James Joyce. Used by permission of Viking Penguin, a division of Penguin Group (USA) Inc.

PATRICIA KANE "The Prodigal Daughter in Alice Walker's '*Everyday Use*'" from *Notes on Contemporary Literature,* Vol. 15, No. 2, 1985, p, 7. Copyright © 1985. Used by permission.

LOUISE J. KAPLAN "The Perverse Strategy in 'The Fall of the House of Usher'" from *New Essays On Poe's Major Tales,* edited by Kenneth Silverman. Copyright © 1992. Reprinted by permission of Cambridge University Press.

X.J. KENNEDY "Nude Descending a Staircase" from *Nude Descending a Staircase,* © 1997 X.J. Kennedy. Reprinted by permission of Curtis Brown Ltd.

JANE KENYON "Peonies at Dusk" from *Collected Poems.* Copyright © 2005 by the Estate of Jane Kenyon. Reprinted with the permission of Graywolf Press, Saint Paul, Minnesota.

ALVIN KERNAN Notes from *The Tragedy of Othello* by William Shakespeare, edited by Alvin Kernan. Copyright © 1963 by Alvin Kernan. Used by permission of Dutton Signet, a division of Penguin Group (USA) Inc.

JAMAICA KINCAID "Girl" from *At the Bottom of the River.* Copyright © 1983 by Jamaica Kincaid. Reprinted by permission

GALWAY KINNELL "Blackberry Eating" from *Mortal Acts, Mortal Words.* Copyright © 1980 by Galway Kinnell. Reprinted by permission of Houghton Mifflin Company. All rights reserved.

BERNARD KNOX "Sophocles' Oedipus" from *Word and Action: Essays on the Ancient Theater,* pp. 97-99. Copyright © 1979 Bernard Knox. Reprinted with permission of The Johns Hopkins University Press.

KENNETH KOCH "Variations on a Theme by William Carlos Williams" Copyright © 1994 by Kenneth Koch. Reprinted by permission of the author.

YUSEF KOMUNYAKAA "Facing It" from *Dien Cai Dau In Pleasure Dome: New and Collected Poems.* Copyright © 2001 by Yusef Komunyakaa. Reprinted by permission of Wesleyan University Press.

TED KOOSER "A Spiral Notebook" from *Delights and Shadows.* Copyright © 2004 by Ted Kooser. Reprinted with the permission of Copper Canyon Press, P.O. Box 271, Port Townsend, WA 98368-0271.

JHUMPA LAHIRI "Hell-Heaven" originally published in *The New Yorker.* Copyright © 2004 by Jhumpa Lahiri. Reprinted by permission of the author.

D.H. LAWRENCE "Snake" and "When I Read Shakespeare" from *The Complete Poems Of D.H. Lawrence.* Copyright © 1964, 1971 by Angelo Ravagli and C.M. Weekley, executors of the Estate of Frieda Lawrence Ravagli. Used by permission of Viking Penguin, a division of Penguin Group (USA) Inc.

D.H. LAWRENCE two variations of "Piano" Copyright © 1964, 1971 by Angelo Ravagli and C.M. Weekley, executors of the Estate of Frieda Lawrence Ravagli. Used by permission of Viking Penguin, a division of Penguin Group (USA) Inc.

D.H. LAWRENCE "The Rocking Horse Winner" from *The Complete Short Stories Of D.H. Lawrence,* copyright 1933, renewed © 1961 by Angelo Ravagli and C.M. Weekley, Executors of the Estate of Frieda Lawrence. Used by permission of Viking Penguin, a division of Penguin Group (USA) Inc.

DENISE LEVERTOV "O Taste and See" from *Poems 1960–1967.* Copyright © 1964 by Denise Levertov. Reprinted by permission of New Directions Publishing Corp.

FEDERICO GARCIA LORCA "Lament for Ignacio Sanchez Mejias, Part 2" from *The Selected Poems of Federico Garcia Lorca,* translated by Stephen Spender and J.L. Gili. Copyright © 1955 by New Directions Publishing Corp. Reprinted by permission of New Directions Publishing.

AUDRE LORDE "Hanging Fire" from *The Black Unicorn.* Copyright © 1978 by Audre Lorde. Used by permission of W.W. Norton & Company, Inc.

ARCHIBALD MACLEISH "Not Marble, Nor the Gilded Monuments" and "Ars Poetica" from *Collected Poems: 1917–1982* by Archibald MacLeish. Copyright © 1985 by The Estate of Archibald MacLeish. Reprinted by permission of Houghton Mifflin Company. All rights reserved.

TAYLOR MALI "Like Lilly, Like Wilson" from *What Learning Leaves.* Copyright © 2002 by Taylor Mali. Reprinted with permission of the author and the publisher, Hanover Press.

GABRIEL GARCIA MARQUEZ "A Very Old Man with Enormous Wings" from *Leaf Storm and Other Stories* by Gabriel Garcia Márquez and translated by Gregory Rabassa. Copyright © 1971 Gabriel Garcia Marquez. Reprinted by permission of HarperCollins, Inc.

RACHEL MASILAMANI "Two Kinds of People" *Indiana Review,* Vol. 26, no. 1, Summer 2004, pp. 167-172. Copyright © 2004 Rachel Masilamani. Reprinted with permission.

BOBBIE ANN MASON "Shiloh" from *Shiloh and Other Stories.* © 1982 Bobbie Ann Mason. Reprinted by permission of International Creative Management.

DOROTHY TUCK MCFARLAND on "Everything that Rises Must Converge," from *Flannery O'Connor* by Dorothy Tuck McFarland (Frederick Ungar, 1976). Reprinted by permission of The Continuum Publishing Company.

CLAUDE MCKAY "The Tropics in New York" from *Selected Poems Of Claude McKay.* Copyright © 1981. Courtesy of the Literary Representative for the works of Claude McKay, Schomburg Center for Research in Black Culture, The New York Public Library, Astor, Lenox and Tilden Foundations.

BOB MCKENTY "Adam's Song." Copyright © 1993 Bob McKenty. Reprinted with permission.

BOB MCKENTY "Snow on Frost." Copyright © 1993 by Bob McKenty. Reprinted by permission.

DON MCLEAN "Vincent (Starry, Starry Night)." © 1971 by Music Corporation of America, Inc., Benny Bird Company, Inc. All rights administered by Songs of Universal, Inc./BMI. Used by permission. International copyright secured. All rights reserved.

HELEN MCNEIL "Dickinson's Method" from *Emily Dickinson.* Reprinted by permission of Virago Press.

PETER MEINKE "Advice to My Son" from *Liquid Paper: New and Selected Poems.* Copyright © 1991 by Peter Meinke. Reprinted by permission of the University of Pittsburgh Press.

W.S. MERWIN "Unknown Bird" first appeared in the *Atlantic Monthly.* © 1999 by W.S. Merwin. Reprinted with the permission of the Wylie Agency, Inc.

JO MIELZINER "Diary" reprinted with the permission of Scribner, an imprint of Simon & Schuster Adult Publishing Group from *Designing For The Theater: A Memoir and a Portfolio.* Copyright © 1965 by Jo Mielziner.

EDNA ST. VINCENT MILLAY "I being born a woman and distressed" from *Collected Poems,* published by HarperCollins. Copyright 1923, 1951 by Edna St. Vincent Millay and Norma Millay Ellis. All rights reserved. Reprinted by permission of Elizabeth Barnett, literary executor.

ARTHUR MILLER *Death of a Salesman.* Copyright 1949, renewed © 1977 by Arthur Miller. Used by permission of Viking Penguin, a division of Penguin Group (USA) Inc.

CSZESLAW MILOSZ "Encounter" from *The Collected Poems, 1931–1987* translated by the author and Lillian Vallee. Copyright © 1988 by Czeslaw Milosz. Reprinted by permission of HarperCollins Publishers, Inc.

STEPHEN MITCHELL "Vermeer" from *Parables and Portraits,* © 1990 Stephen Mitchell. Reprinted by permission of HarperCollins Publishers, Inc.

CHRISTINE MOLITO "Reflections in Black & Blue." Copyright © Christine Molito. Reprinted by permission of the author.

MARIANNE MOORE "Poetry" from *The Collected Poems Of Marianne Moore.* Copyright 1935 by Marianne Moore, copyright renewed © 1963 by Marianne Moore and T.S. Eliot. Reprinted with the permission of Scribner, an imprint of Simon & Schuster Adult Publishing Group.

HOWARD MOSS "Shall I Compare Thee to a Summer's Day?" from "Modified Sonnets" in *A Swim Off the Rocks,* Atheneum Publishers. Copyright © 1976 by Howard Moss.

PAUL MULDOON "Hedgehog" from *Poems 1968–1998.* Copyright © Paul Muldoon. Reprinted by permission of Farrar, Straus & Giroux LLC.

PABLO NERUDA "Ode to My Socks" from *Neruda & Vallejo,* translated by Robert Bly. Translation copyright © 1993 by Robert Bly. Used with permission.

A.D. NUTTALL "Othello" from *A New Mimesis.* Copyright © A.D. Nuttall. Used with permission.

JOYCE CAROL OATES "Where Are You Going? Where Have You Been?" Copyright © 1970 Ontario Review. Reprinted by permission of John Hawkins & Associates, Inc.

TIM O'BRIEN "The Things They Carried" from *The Things They Carried.* Copyright © 1990 by Tim O'Brien. Reprinted by permission of Houghton Mifflin Company. All rights reserved.

FLANNERY O'CONNOR "A Good Man is Hard to Find" and "Good Country People" from *A Good Man Is Hard To Find And Other Stories* by Flannery O'Connor. Copyright 1953 by Flannery O'Connor and renewed © 1981 by Regina O'Connor. Reprinted by permission of Harcourt, Inc.

FLANNERY O'CONNOR "Everything that Rises Must Converge" from *The Complete Stories* by Flannery O'Connor. Copyright © 1971 by the Estate of Mary Flannery O'Connor. Reprinted by permission of Farrar, Straus & Giroux.

FLANNERY O'CONNOR "On Symbol and Theme" from "The Nature and Aim of Fiction" and "On 'Good Country People'" from "Writing Short Stories" taken from in *Mystery & Manners.* Copyright © 1969 by the Estate of Mary Flannery O'Connor. Reprinted by permission of Farrar, Straus & Giroux.

FLANNERY O'CONNOR letter to Dr. T.R. Spivey, on "A Good Man is Hard to Find" and from a letter to a Professor on English on "A Good Man Is Hard to Find" from *The Habit Of Being: The Letters Of Flannery O'Connor.* Copyright © 1988. Reprinted by permission of Farrar, Straus & Giroux.

FRANK O'CONNOR "My Oedipus Complex" and "Guests of the Nation" from *Collected Stories.* Copyright © 1981 by Harriet O'Donovan Sheely, executrix. Reprinted by permission of Writer's House, LLC, on behalf of the proprietors and Alfred A. Knopf, a division of Random House, Inc.

SHARON OLDS "Size and Sheer Will" and "Rite of Passage," "35/10" from *The Dead and The Living.* Copyright © 1987 by Sharon Olds. Used by permission of Alfred A. Knopf, a division of Random House, Inc.

MARY OLIVER "Poem for My Father's Ghost" from *Twelve Moons.* Copyright © 1972, 1973, 1974, 1976, 1977, 1978, 1979 by Mary Oliver. First appeared in *Prairie Schooner.* Reprinted by permission of Little, Brown and Company (Inc.).

TILLIE OLSON "I Stand Here Ironing" from *Tell Me a Riddle.* Copyright © 1956, 1957, 1960, 1961 by Tillie Olsen. Used by permission of Elaine Markson Literary Agency.

WILFRED OWEN "Dulce et Decorum Est" from *The Collected Poems of Wilfred Owen.* Copyright © 1963 by Chatto & Windus, Ltd. Reprinted by permission of New Directions Publishing Corp.

LINDA PASTAN "Ethics" and "Emily Dickinson" from *Carnival Evening: New and Selected Poems 1968-1998.* Copyright © 1998 by Linda Pastan. Used by permission of W.W. Norton & Company, Inc.

BORIS PASTERNAK "Hamlet" from *Selected Poems: Boris Pasternak,* translated by Jon Stallworthy and Peter France (Penguin Books, 1983). Copyright © Peter France, 1983. Reprinted by permission of Penguin Books Ltd.

OCTAVIO PAZ "The Street" translated by Muriel Rukeyser from *Early Poems 1935–1955.* Copyright © 1963, 1973 by Octavio Paz and Muriel Rukeyser. Reprinted by permission of New Directions Publishing Corp.

PETRONIUS "The Widow of Ephesus" from *The Satyricon* by Petronius, translated by William Arrowsmith. Translation copyright © 1959, 1987 by William Arrowsmith. Used by permission of Dutton Signet, a division of Penguin Group (USA) Inc.

ROBERT PINSKY "Dying" from *The Figured Wheel: New and Collected Poems 1966–1996.* Copyright © 1996 by Robert Pinksy. Reprinted by permission of Farrar, Straus & Giroux LLC.

SYLVIA PLATH "Blackberrying" from *Crossing the Water.* Copyright © 1962 by Ted Hughes. The poem originally appeared in *Uncollected Poems,* Turret Books, London and in the *Hudson Review.* Reprinted by permission of HarperCollins Publishers.

SYLVIA PLATH "Mirror" from *Crossing the Water.* Copyright © 1971 by Ted Hughes. Reprinted by permission of HarperCollins Publishers and Faber & Faber Ltd.

SYLVIA PLATH "Morning Song" from *Ariel.* Copyright © 1961 by Ted Hughes. Reprinted by permission of HarperCollins Publishers.

SYLVIA PLATH "Metaphors" from *Crossing the Water.* Copyright © 1960 by Ted Hughes. Reprinted by permission of HarperCollins Publishers.

RICHARD POIRIER on "Stopping by Woods" and "Mending Wall" from *Robert Frost: The Work of Knowing.* Copyright © 1977 Richard Poirier. Used by permission of Oxford University Press.

ADRIAN POOLE "Oedipus and Athens" from *Tragedy: Shakespeare and the Greek Example.* Reprinted by permission of Blackwell Publishers.

KATHERINE ANNE PORTER "The Jilting of Granny Weatherall" and "Magic" from *Flowering Judas And Other Stories.* Copyright 1930 and renewed © 1958 by Katherine Anne Porter. Reprinted by permission of Harcourt, Inc.

WILLIAM PRITCHARD on "Stopping by Woods" from *Robert Frost: A Literary Life Reconsidered.* Copyright © 1984 William Pritchard. Used by permission of Oxford University Press.

ARNOLD RAMPERSAD "Langston Hughes as Folk Poet" specified excerpt from "Introduction" by Arnold Rampersand from *The Complete Poems* by Langston Hughes. © 1994 Estate of Langston Hughes. Reprinted by permission of Alfred A. Knopf, a division of Random House, Inc.

DUDLEY RANDALL "The Ballad of Birmingham" from *Cities Burning.* © 1966 Dudley Randall. Reprinted by permission.

HENRY REED "Naming of Parts" from *Collected Poems* by Henry Reed, edited by Jon Stallworthy. Copyright © 1991. Reprinted by permission of Oxford University Press.

DAVID S. REYNOLDS excerpt from "Poe's Art of Transformation: 'The Cask of Amontillado' in Its Cultural Context" from *New Essays On Poe's Major Tales,* edited by Kenneth Silverman. Copyright © 1992. Reprinted by permission of Cambridge University Press.

RAINER MARIA RILKE "The Cadet Picture of My Father" translated by Robert Lowell from *Imitations.* Copyright © 1959 by Robert Lowell. Copyright renewed © 1987 by Harriet, Sheridan and Caroline Lowell. Reprinted by permission of Farrar, Straus & Giroux LLC.

ALBERTO RIOS "A Dream of Husbands." Copyright © 1985 by Alberto Rios. First published in *Five Industries* (Sheep Meadow). Reprinted by permission of the author.

THEODORE ROETHKE "Elegy for Jane" My Papa's Waltz," "The Waking," and "Root Cellar" from *The Collected Poems of Theodore Roethke* by Theodore Roethke. Copyright 1950 by Theodore Roethke. Used by permission of Doubleday, a division of Random House, Inc.

NATALIE SAFIR "Matisse's Dance" by Natalie Safir. Used by permission of the author.

SONIA SANCHEZ "Towhomitmayconcern" from *Shake Loose My Skin: New and Selected Poems.* Published in 1999 by Beacon Press. Originally published in *Under a Soprano Sky* by Sonya Sanchez. Copyright © 1987. Reprinted by permission of Africa World Press.

MILCHA SANCHEZ-SCOTT *The Cuban Swimmer.* Copyright © Milcha Sanchez-Scott. Reprinted by permission of William Morris Agency.

MARJANE SATRAPI "The Veil" from *Persepolis: The Story of a Childhood,* translated by Mattias Ripa & Blake Ferris. Copyright © 2003 by L'Asociation, Paris, France. Used by permission of Pantheon Books, a division of Random House, Inc.

PETE SEEGER "Turn! Turn! Turn! (To Everything There Is a Season," words from the Book of Ecclesiastes. Adaptation and music by Pete Seeger. TRO © copyright 1962 (renewed) Melody Trails, Inc., New York, NY. Reprinted by permission.

ANNE SEXTON "The Starry Night" from *All My Pretty Ones* by Anne Sexton. Copyright © 1962 by Anne Sexton, renewed 1990 by Linda G. Sexton. Reprinted by permission of Houghton Mifflin Company. All rights reserved.

ANNE SEXTON "Two Hands" from *The Awful Rowing Toward God* by Anne Sexton. Copyright © 1975 by Loring Conant, Jr., Executor of the Estate of Anne Sexton. Reprinted by permission of Houghton Mifflin Company. All rights reserved.

ANNE SEXTON "Her Kind" from *To Bedlam and Part Way Back* by Anne Sexton. Copyright © 1960 by Anne Sexton, renewed 1988 by Linda G. Sexton. Reprinted by permission of Houghton Mifflin Company. All rights reserved.

PAUL SIMON "Richard Cory." Copyright © 1966 Paul Simon. Used by permission of the publisher, Paul Simon Music.

LOUISE SIMPSON "The Battle" from *Good News of Death And Other Poems.* Reprinted by permission of Louise Simpson.

ISAAC BASHEVIS SINGER "Gimpel the Fool" translated by Saul Bellow from *A Treasury Of Yiddish Stories,* edited by Irving Howe & Eliezer Greenberg. Copyright 1953, 1954, renewed © 1981, 1982 by Viking Penguin Inc. Used by permission of Viking Penguin, a division of Penguin Group (USA) Inc.

STEVIE SMITH "Mother Among the Dustbins" from *Collected Poems Of Stevie Smith.* Copyright © 1972 by Stevie Smith. Reprinted by permission of New Directions Publishing Corp.

CATHY SONG "Girl Powdering Her Neck" from *Picture Bride.* Copyright © 1983 by Cathy Song. Reprinted by permission of Yale University Press.

SOPHOCLES *The Oedipus Rex of Sophocles: An English Version* by Dudley Fitts and Robert Fitzgerald. Copyright 1949 by Harcourt, Inc. and renewed 1977 by Cornelia Fitts and Robert Fitzgerald. Reprinted by permission of publishers. CAUTION: All rights, including professional, amateur, motion picture, recitation, lecturing, public reading, radio broadcasting, and television are strictly reserved. Inquiries on all rights should be addressed to Harcourt, Inc., Permissions Department, Orlando, FL 32887.

GARY SOTO "Behind Grandma's House" from *New And Selected Poems.* Copyright © 1995 by Gary Soto. Reprinted with permission of Chronicle Books LLC, San Francisco. Visit ChronicleBooks.com

WOLE SOYINKA "Hamlet" from *A Shuttle in the Crypt.* Copyright © 1972 Hill & Wang, a subsidiary of Farrar, Straus & Giroux. Used with permission.

WILLIAM STAFFORD "Traveling through the Dark" from *The Way It Is: New and Collected Poems.* Copyright © 1962, 1998 by the Estate of William Stafford. Reprinted with permission of Graywolf Press, Saint Paul, Minnesota.

JOHN STEINBECK "Chrysanthemums" from *The Long Valley.* Copyright 1937, renewed © 1965 by John Steinbeck. Used by permission of Viking Penguin, a division of Penguin Group (USA) Inc.

GEORGE STEINER "Principal Constants of Conflict in Antigone" from *Antigone* by George Steiner. Copyright © 1984 by George Steiner. Reprinted by permission of Georges Borchardt, Inc., for the author.

WALLACE STEVENS "Thirteen Ways of Looking at a Blackbird" and "Disillusionment of Ten O'clock" from *The Collected Poems of Wallace Stevens.* Copyright 1954 by Wallace Stevens and renewed 1982 by Holly Stevens. Used by permission of Alfred A. Knopf, a division of Random House, Inc.

MURIEL STUART "In the Orchard" from *Selected Poems* by Muriel Stuart. Reprinted by permission of the Estate of Muriel Stuart.

MAY SWENSON "Strawberrying" from *The Complete Love Poems Of May Swenson.* Copyright © 1991, 2003 by The Literary Estate of May Swenson. Reprinted by permission of Houghotn Mifflin Company. All rights reserved.

MAY SWENSON "Women." Copyright © 1968 by May Swenson. Used with the permission of The Literary Estate of May Swenson.

MAY SWENSON "The Universe" by May Swenson. Copyright © 1968 by May Swenson. Used with the permission of The Literary Estate of May Swenson.

WISLAWA SZYMBORSKA "The Acrobat" from *View With A Grain Of Sand.* Copyright © 1993 by Wislawa Szymborska, english translation by Stanislaw Baranczak and Clare Cavanagh. Copyright © 1995 by Harcourt, Inc. Reprinted by permission of the publisher.

AMY TAN "Rules of the Game" from *The Joy Luck Club.* Copyright © 1989 by Amy Tan. Used by permission of G.P. Putnam's Sons, a division of Penguin Group (USA) Inc.

ALLAN TATE "Dickinson & Knowledge" and "On 'Because I could not stop for death'" from *Emily Dickinson: Collected Essays* by Allen Tate. Copyright © 1959 Swallow Press. Reprinted by permission of Helen H. Tate for the estate of the author.

DYLAN THOMAS "Fern Hill" and "Do not go gentle into that good night" from *The Poems of Dylan Thomas.* Copyright 1945, 1952 by Dylan Thomas. Reprinted by permission of New Directions Publishing Corp.

JEAN TOOMER "Song of the Sun" and "Reapers" from *Cane.* Copyright 1923 by Boni & Liveright, renewed 1951 by Jean Toomer. Used by permission of Liveright Publishing Corporation.

JOHN UPDIKE "A & P" from *Pigeon Feathers and Other Stories.* Copyright © 1962 and renewed 1990 by John Updike. Used by permission of Alfred A. Knopf, a division of Random House, Inc.

DEREK WALCOTT "House of Umbrage," from *Omeros.* Copyright © 1990 Derek Walcott. Used with permission of Farrar, Straus & Giroux LLC.

ALICE WALKER "Everyday Use" from *In Love & Trouble: Stories of Black Women.* Copyright © 1973 by Alice Walker. Reprinted by permission of Harcourt, Inc.

ROBERT WALLACE "The Double-Play" from *Views of A Ferris Wheel* by Robert Wallace. Copyright © 1961, 1965 by Robert Wallace. Reprinted by permission of the author.

WENDY WASSERSTEIN "Tender Offer." © 1991 by Wendy Wasserstein. First published in *Antaeus,* Issue #66, "Plays in One Act." No part of this material may be reproduced in whole or part, without the express written permission of the author or her agent.

EUDORA WELTY "Why I Live at the P.O." and "A Worn Path" from *A Curtain Of Green And Other Stories,* copyright 1941 and renewed © 1969 by Eudora Welty. Reprinted by permission of Harcourt, Inc.

TENNESSEE WILLIAMS *The Glass Menagerie* and "Production Notes". Copyright 1945 by Tennessee Williams and Edwina D. Williams and renewed © 1973 by Tennessee Williams. Reprinted by permission of Random House, Inc.

WILLIAM CARLOS WILLIAMS "Spring and All," "The Young Housewife," "The Red Wheelbarrow," "This is Just to Say," from *Collected Poems: 1909–1939, Vol. 1.* Copyright 1938 by New Directions Publishing Corp. Reprinted by permission of New Directions Publishing Corp.

WILLIAM CARLOS WILLIAMS "Landscape with the Fall of Icarus," "Dance Russe" and "The Dance" from *Collected Poems: 1939–1962, Vol. Ii.* Copyright 1953 by William Carlos Williams. Reprinted by permission of New Directions Publishing Corp.

WILLIAM CARLOS WILLIAMS "The Use of Force" from *The Collected Stories of William Carlos Williams.* Copyright 1938 by William Carlos Williams. Reprinted by permission of New Directions Publishing Corp.

AUGUST WILSON *Fences.* Copyright © 1986 by August Wilson. Used by permission of Dutton Signet, a division of Penguin Group (USA) Inc.

YVOR WINTERS "Robert Frost: Or, the Spiritual Drifter as Poet" from *The Function Of Criticism.* Swallow Press 1957.

JUDITH WRIGHT "Woman to Child" from *A Human Pattern: Selected Poems* (ETT Imprint, Sydney 1996). Copyright © 1996. Used with permission.

WILLIAM BUTLER YEATS "The Lake Isle of Innisfree,' "The Second Coming," "Leda and the Swan," "Adam's Curse," "Sailing to Byzantium," from *The Collected Poems of W.B. Yeats, Volume I: The Poems, Revised,* edited by Richard J. Finneran. Copyright 1924 by The Macmillan Company. Copyright renewed 1952 by Bertha Georgie Yeats. Reprinted with the permission of Scribner, an imprint of Simon & Schuster Adult Publishing Group.

WILLIAM BUTLER YEATS "The Wild Swans at Coole" "An Irish Airman Foresees His Death," "When You Are Old," "A Dream of Death" from *The Poems of W.B. Yeats*: A New Edition by Richard Finneran, 1996. Reprinted with the permission of Scribner, an imprint of Simon & Schuster Adult Publishing Group.

KEVIN YOUNG "Langston Hughes" from *To Repel Ghosts.* Copyright © Kevin Young. Reprinted with permission of Zoland Books/Steerforth Press.

Index

Selection titles appear in italics, and first lines of poems appear in roman type. Page numbers in roman type indicate the opening page of a selection; italic numbers indicate discussion. Bold page numbers indicate biographical or contextual information. Colorplates in the insert are indicated by "c."